Handbook of
MACROECONOMICS

Handbook of
MACROECONOMICS

Volume 2B

Edited by

JOHN B. TAYLOR
Stanford University
Stanford, CA, United States

HARALD UHLIG
University of Chicago
Chicago, IL, United States

ELSEVIER

Amsterdam • Boston • Heidelberg • London • New York • Oxford
Paris • San Diego • San Francisco • Singapore • Sydney • Tokyo
North-Holland is an imprint of Elsevier

N·H

North-Holland is an imprint of Elsevier

Radarweg 29, PO Box 211, 1000 AE Amsterdam, The Netherlands
The Boulevard, Langford Lane, Kidlington, Oxford OX5 1GB, United Kingdom

British Library Cataloguing-in-Publication Data
A catalogue record for this book is available from the British Library

Library of Congress Cataloging-in-Publication Data
A catalog record for this book is available from the Library of Congress

ISBN: 978-0-444-59469-3 (Vol. 2A)
ISBN: 978-0-444-59466-2 (Vol. 2B)
Set record (2A and 2B): 978-0-444-59487-7

Publisher: Zoe Kruze
Acquisition Editor: Kirsten Shankland
Editorial Project Manager: Joslyn Chaiprasert-Paguio
Production Project Manager: Radhakrishnan Lakshmanan
Cover Designer: Greg Harris

Typeset by SPi Global, India
Printed in Great Britain
Last digit is the print number: 10 9 8 7 6

INTRODUCTION TO THE SERIES

The aim of the *Handbooks in Economics* series is to produce Handbooks for various branches of economics, each of which is a definitive source, reference, and teaching supplement for use by professional researchers and advanced graduate students. Each Handbook provides self-contained surveys of the current state of a branch of economics in the form of chapters prepared by leading specialists on various aspects of this branch of economics. These surveys summarize not only received results but also newer developments, from recent journal articles and discussion papers. Some original material is also included, but the main goal is to provide comprehensive and accessible surveys. The Handbooks are intended to provide not only useful reference volumes for professional collections but also possible supplementary readings for advanced courses for graduate students in economics.

Kenneth J. Arrow and Michael D. Intriligator

CONTENTS

Volume 2B

EDITOR'S BIOGRAPHY

John B. Taylor is the Mary and Robert Raymond Professor of Economics at Stanford University and the George P. Shultz Senior Fellow in Economics at Stanford's Hoover Institution. He is also the director of Stanford's Introductory Economics Center. His research focuses on macroeconomics, monetary economics, and international economics. He coedited Volume 1 of the Handbook of Macroeconomics and recently wrote *Getting Off Track*, one of the first books on the financial crisis, and *First Principles: Five Keys to Restoring America's Prosperity*. He served as senior economist and member of the President's Council of Economic Advisers. From 2001 to 2005, he served as undersecretary of the US Treasury for international affairs. Taylor was awarded the Hoagland Prize and the Rhodes Prize by Stanford University for excellence in undergraduate teaching. He received the Alexander Hamilton Award and the Treasury Distinguished Service Award for his policy contributions at the US Treasury. Taylor received a BA in economics summa cum laude from Princeton and a PhD in economics from Stanford.

Harald Uhlig, born 1961, is a professor at the Department of Economics of the University of Chicago since 2007 and was chairman of that department from 2009 to 2012. Previously, he held positions at Princeton, Tilburg University and the Humboldt-Universität zu Berlin. His research interests are in quantitative macroeconomics, financial markets, and Bayesian econometrics. He served as coeditor of *Econometrica* from 2006 to 2010 and as editor of the *Journal of Political Economy* since 2012 (head editor since 2013). He is a consultant of the Bundesbank, the European Central Bank, and the Federal Reserve Bank of Chicago. He is a fellow of the Econometric Society and a recipient of the Gossen Preis of the Verein für Socialpolitik, awarded annually to an economist in the German language area whose work has gained an international reputation.

CONTRIBUTORS

E. Afanasyeva
IMFS, Goethe University Frankfurt, Frankfurt, Germany

M. Aguiar
Princeton University, Princeton, NJ, United States

A. Alesina
Harvard University, Cambridge, MA, United States; IGIER, Bocconi University, Milan, Italy

G.-M. Angeletos
MIT; NBER, Cambridge, MA, United States

S. Basu
Boston College, Chestnut Hill; NBER, Cambridge, MA, United States

M.D. Bordo
Rutgers University, New Brunswick, NJ; NBER, Cambridge, MA, United States

J. Borovička
New York University, New York, NY; NBER, Cambridge, MA, United States

P. Brinca
Nova School of Business and Economics, Lisboa; Centre for Economics and Finance, University of Porto, Porto, Portugal

M.K. Brunnermeier
Princeton University, Princeton, NJ, United States

V.V. Chari
University of Minnesota; Federal Reserve Bank of Minneapolis, Minneapolis, MN, United States

S. Chatterjee
Federal Reserve Bank of Philadelphia, Philadelphia, PA, United States

H. Cole
University of Pennsylvania, Philadelphia, PA, United States

P. D'Erasmo
Federal Reserve Bank of Philadelphia, Philadelphia, PA, United States

D.W. Diamond
University of Chicago Booth School of Business, Chicago, IL; National Bureau of Economic Research, Cambridge, MA, United States

M. Doepke
Northwestern University, Evanston, IL, United States

E. Farhi
Harvard University, Cambridge, MA, United States

J. Fernández-Villaverde
University of Pennsylvania, Philadelphia, PA, United States

N. Fuchs-Schündeln
Goethe University Frankfurt, Frankfurt, Germany; CEPR, London, United Kingdom

M. Gertler
NYU, New York, NY; Princeton University, Princeton, NJ; Federal Reserve Board of Governors, Washington, DC, United States

M. Golosov
Princeton University, Princeton, NJ, United States

V. Guerrieri
University of Chicago, Chicago, IL; NBER, Cambridge, MA, United States

R.E. Hall
Hoover Institution, Stanford University, CA; National Bureau of Economic Research, Cambridge, MA, United States

J.D. Hamilton
University of California, San Diego, La Jolla, CA, United States

G.D. Hansen
UCLA, Los Angeles, CA; NBER, Cambridge, MA, United States

L.P. Hansen
University of Chicago, Chicago, IL; NBER, Cambridge, MA, United States

T.A. Hassan
CEPR, London, United Kingdom; University of Chicago, Chicago, IL; NBER, Cambridge, MA, United States

J. Hassler
Institute for International Economic Studies (IIES), Stockholm University, Stockholm; University of Gothenburg, Gothenburg, Sweden; CEPR, London, United Kingdom

C.L. House
NBER, Cambridge, MA; University of Michigan, Ann Arbor, MI, United States

E. Hurst
The University of Chicago Booth School of Business, Chicago, IL, United States

C.I. Jones
Stanford GSB, Stanford, CA; NBER, Cambridge, MA, United States

A.K. Kashyap
University of Chicago Booth School of Business, Chicago, IL; National Bureau of Economic Research, Cambridge, MA, United States

P.J. Kehoe
University of Minnesota; Federal Reserve Bank of Minneapolis, Minneapolis, MN, United States; University College London, London, United Kingdom

N. Kiyotaki
NYU, New York, NY; Princeton University, Princeton, NJ; Federal Reserve Board of Governors, Washington, DC, United States

D. Krueger
University of Pennsylvania, Philadelphia, PA, United States; CEPR, London, United Kingdom; CFS, Goethe University Frankfurt, Frankfurt, Germany; NBER, Cambridge, MA, United States; Netspar, Tilburg, The Netherlands

P. Krusell
Institute for International Economic Studies (IIES), Stockholm University, Stockholm; University of Gothenburg, Gothenburg, Sweden; CEPR, London, United Kingdom; NBER, Cambridge, MA, United States

M. Kuete
IMFS, Goethe University Frankfurt, Frankfurt, Germany

E.M. Leeper
Indiana University, IN; NBER, Cambridge, MA, United States

C. Leith
University of Glasgow, Glasgow, United Kingdom

C. Lian
MIT, Cambridge, MA, United States

J. Lindé
Sveriges Riksbank; Stockholm School of Economics, Stockholm, Sweden; CEPR, London, United Kingdom

E. McGrattan
University of Minnesota; Federal Reserve Bank of Minneapolis, Minneapolis, MN, United States

C.M. Meissner
NBER, Cambridge, MA; University of California, Davis, CA, United States

E.G. Mendoza
PIER, University of Pennsylvania, Philadelphia, PA; NBER, Cambridge, MA, United States

A. Mian
Princeton University, Princeton, NJ; NBER, Cambridge, MA, United States

K. Mitman
CEPR, London, United Kingdom; IIES, Stockholm University, Stockholm, Sweden

L.E. Ohanian
UCLA, Los Angeles; NBER, Cambridge, MA; Hoover Institution, Stanford University, Stanford, CA, United States

A. Passalacqua
Harvard University, Cambridge, MA, United States

F. Perri
CEPR, London, United Kingdom; Federal Reserve Bank of Minneapolis, Minneapolis, MN, United States

M. Piazzesi
Stanford University, Stanford, CA; NBER, Cambridge, MA, United States

E.C. Prescott
Arizona State University, Tempe, AZ; Federal Reserve Bank of Minneapolis, Minneapolis, MN, United States

A. Prestipino
NYU, New York, NY; Princeton University, Princeton, NJ; Federal Reserve Board of Governors, Washington, DC, United States

V.A. Ramey
University of California, San Diego, CA; NBER, Cambridge, MA, United States

J.F. Rubio-Ramírez
Emory University; Federal Reserve Bank of Atlanta, Atlanta, GA, United States; BBVA Research, Madrid, Madrid, Spain; Fulcrum Asset Management, London, England, United Kingdom

Y. Sannikov
Princeton University, Princeton, NJ, United States

M. Schneider
Stanford University, Stanford, CA; NBER, Cambridge, MA, United States

F. Schorfheide
University of Pennsylvania, Philadelphia, PA, United States

F. Smets
ECB, Frankfurt, Germany; KU Leuven, Leuven, Belgium; CEPR, London, United Kingdom

A.A. Smith, Jr.
NBER, Cambridge, MA; Yale University, New Haven, CT, United States

Z. Stangebye
University of Notre Dame, Notre Dame, IN, United States

J.H. Stock
Harvard University; The National Bureau of Economic Research, Cambridge, MA, United States

A. Sufi
University of Chicago Booth School of Business, Chicago, IL; NBER, Cambridge, MA, United States

J.B. Taylor
Stanford University, Stanford, CA, United States

M. Tertilt
University of Mannheim, Mannheim, Germany

A. Tsyvinski
Yale University, New Haven, CT, United States

H. Uhlig
University of Chicago, Chicago, IL; NBER, Cambridge, MA, United States; CEPR, London, United Kingdom

M.W. Watson
The Woodrow Wilson School, Princeton University, Princeton, NJ; The National Bureau of Economic Research, Cambridge, MA, United States

I. Werning
MIT, Cambridge, MA, United States

N. Werquin
Toulouse School of Economics, Toulouse, France

V. Wieland
IMFS, Goethe University Frankfurt, Frankfurt, Germany

R. Wouters
National Bank of Belgium, Brussels, Belgium; CEPR, London, United Kingdom

J. Yoo
IMFS, Goethe University Frankfurt, Frankfurt, Germany; Bank of Korea, Seoul, South Korea

J. Zhang
Federal Reserve Bank of Chicago, Chicago, IL, United States

Participants-Chicago

Left to right

Last row: Jesper Linde, John Heaton, Basu (slightly stepping forward), Zighuo He, Thorsten Drautzburg, Jonas Fischer, Andrea Prestipino, Jarda Borovicka, Mathias Trabandt

Second-from-last: Manuel Amador, Marty Eichenbaum (slightly stepping forward), Guido Lorenzoni, Luigi Boccola, Satyajit Chatterjee, Campbell Leith, Lawrence Christiano, Christopher House

Forth row: Marios Angeletos, Hal Cole, Markus Brunnermeier, Lars Hansen, Jeff Campbell

Third Row: Volker Wieland, Douglas Diamond, Anil Kashyap, Rüdiger Bachmann, Harald Uhlig, Nobu Kiyotaki

Second row: Frank Smets, Michele Tertilt, Eric Leeper, Jing Zhang, Enrique Mendoza

First row: Mathias Doepke, Veronica Guerrieri, Amir Sufi, Michael Weber, John Taylor

Not Pictured:

Authors: Ivan Werning, Christopher House, Erik Hurst, Raf Wouters, Yuliy Sannikov, Alberto Alesina, Andrea Passalacqua

Discussants: Stavros Panageas, Eric Sims, Thibaut Lamadon, Alessandra Voena, Kinda Cheryl Hachem, Casey Mulligan, Alp Simsek

Participants-Stanford

Left to right

Last row: Fabrizio Perri, Pablo Kurlat, Mikhail Golosov, Patrick Kehoe, Gary Hansen, Tarek Hassan, Pete Klenow, Christopher Meissner, Frank Schorfheide, Lee Ohanian (somewhat behind), Robert Hodrick

Middle row: Kurt Mitman, Dirk Krueger (slightly behind), Tony Smith, Harald Uhlig (slightly behind), Nicolas Werquin, Mark Watson (somewhat in front), Nicola Fuchs-Schündeln, Ellen McGrattan, Valerie Ramey (somewhat in front), Sebastian DiTella (to the right/behind Valerie Ramey), Pedro Brinca (somewhat in front), Charles Kolstad, Bob Hall, John Hassler, Carl Walsh

Front row: Chad Jones, Per Krusell, Jim Hamilton, Jim Stock, John Taylor, Steve Davis, Ed Prescott, Michael Bordo, Chari, Oscar Jorda, Serguei Maliar, Amir Kermani

Not Pictured:

Authors: Monika Piazzesi, Martin Schneider, Jesus Fernandez-Villaverde, Juan Rubio-Ramirez, Aleh Tsyvinski

Discussants: Bart Hobijn, Pierre Siklos, Arvin Krishnamurthy, Christopher Tonetti, Yuriy Gorodnichenko, John Cochrane, Michael Bauer, Cosmin Ilut

PREFACE

This *Handbook* aims to survey the state of knowledge and major advances during the past two decades in the field of macroeconomics. It covers empirical, theoretical, methodological, and policy issues, including fiscal, monetary, and regulatory policies to deal with unemployment, economic growth, and crises, taking account of research developments before, during, and after the global financial crisis of 2007–2009. It can serve as a textbook and as an introduction to frontier research.

THE STATE OF MACRO, THE FINANCIAL CRISIS, AND NEW CURRENTS

The *Handbook* displays an amazing range of new and different ideas. There are neoclassical chapters on real business cycles and there are new Keynesian chapters on monetary business cycles. There are also chapters extending well beyond traditional macro, including the macroeconomics of the family, natural experiments, environmental issues, time allocation, and the fast moving areas of the connection between financial and real factors, incomplete markets, incomplete contracts, heterogeneous agents, and recursive contracts. There are also treatments of macroprudential policies, the impact of fiscal policy at the zero lower bound on interest rates, the fiscal theory of the price level, and the political economy of bailouts and debt. And there are chapters essential for research on the latest estimation and solution techniques (in continuous and discrete time), as well as encyclopedic reviews of the key facts of economic growth and economic fluctuations both at the aggregate and individual level.

A widely debated question for macroeconomics is whether the 2007–2009 financial crisis demonstrated a failure of the field or whether there was a failure of policy to follow the advice implied by the field. The chapters in the *Handbook* written by active and experienced researchers in macroeconomics can help answer that question in ways that informal policy debates cannot, and we hope that this is an important contribution of the *Handbook*.

There is no question that the field of macroeconomics has continued to progress enormously since the advent of rational expectations, microeconomic foundations, dynamic optimization, and general equilibrium models. Using this paradigm macroeconomists—before and after the financial crisis—have been able to introduce real-world rigidities in price setting, learning, incomplete markets, and financial frictions.

Since the global financial crisis and the Great Recession, some view a lack of financial frictions in macroeconomic models as an indication of failure, and of course there is much in this new *Handbook* on financial frictions and the financial sector more generally in macro models. But the 1999 *Handbook* already included work on financial frictions as evidenced by the chapter written by Ben Bernanke, Mark Gertler, and Simon Gilchrist. And an important finding reported in the chapter in this *Handbook* by Jesper Linde, Frank Smets, and Raf Wouters is that when more financial factors are added to macro models used at central banks, they do not help that much in explaining the financial crisis.

SUMMARY

The 33 chapters of the *Handbook* are divided into five sections. Each chapter starts with a short summary written by its authors, and reading these is the best way to understand what is in the *Handbook*. This short summary of the whole book shows how the chapters are organized and fit together.

Section 1, The Facts of Economic Growth and Economic Fluctuation, starts off with examination of the fundamental facts upon which macroeconomic theories are built and with which they must be consistent. It covers both the long run—going back 100 years—and the short run—tracing how shocks impact and propagate over time and how changes in policy regimes or rules affect economic fluctuations. Emphasizing microeconomic underpinnings, the chapters in this section look at the time allocation by people and families, the impact of longer decisions take on debt or purchases houses, the way wage decisions affect the allocation of labor, and the historical impact of financial and fiscal crises.

Section 2 focuses *The Methodology of Macroeconomics*. It covers factor models, structural VARs, solution methods, estimation of DSGE models, recursive contracts, endogenously incomplete markets, heterogeneous agents, natural experiments, the use of "wedges" as accounting framework for business cycle models, incomplete information, coordination frictions, and comprehensive methods of comparing models and achieving robustness.

Section 3, Financial-Real Connections, covers bank runs, the real effects of financial crises, credit markets, booms and busts, the central role of the housing market, and quantitative models of sovereign debt crises. It also shows different ways to connect the real and the financial sector including through continuous-time methods and models of the term structure of uncertainty.

Section 4, Models of Economic Growth and Fluctuations, covers several approaches to modeling the economy, including neoclassical or real business cycle models and staggered wage and price models or other rigidities that can explain slow recoveries and long slums. It takes a macroeconomic perspective on environmental issues as well as family decisions.

Section 5, Macroeconomic Policy, contains a thorough review of models used by central banks for conducting monetary policy, the analysis of regulatory policy including liquidity requirements, the fiscal theory of the price level, fiscal multipliers, liquidity traps, currency unions, and the technical sustainability vs the political economy of government debt.

John B. Taylor
Harald Uhlig

ACKNOWLEDGMENTS

First, we would like to acknowledge the initial encouragement from Kenneth Arrow and Michael Intriligator who, as Co-Editors of the *Handbook of Economics* Series, suggested in May 2007—nearly a decade ago and before the Global Financial Crisis—the need for a new *Handbook of Macroeconomics*. We are also grateful to Scott Bentley, Elsevier Acquisition Editor, who worked closely with us to get helpful comments and reviews of our initial outline, to Michael Woodford, who succeeded Mike Intriligator as Co-Editor of the Series for his helpful suggestions on organization and coverage, and to Joslyn Chaiprasert-Paguio, Editorial Project Manager, who brought the project to completion.

We—along with all the economists and students who will benefit from this volume—owe a great deal of thanks to the 74 accomplished economists who agreed to contribute to this endeavor for the time and creativity they invested in their chapters. We thank them for attending the conferences, presenting draft chapters, and then revising the chapters under strict deadlines. We particularly thank the discussants of the draft chapters whose careful comments helped improve the chapters and the overall book itself, including Manuel Amador, Ruediger Bachmann, Bob Barsky, Michael Bauer, Luigi Bocola, Jeff Campbell, John Cochrane, Sebastian Di Tella, Thorsten Drautzberg, Jonas Fisher, Yuriy Gorodnichenko, Kinda Cheryl Hachem, Zhiguo He, John Heaton, Bart Hobijn, Robert Hodrick, Cosmin Ilut, Oscar Jorda, Amir Kermani, Peter Klenow, Charles Kolstad, Arvind Krishnamurthy, Pablo Kurlat, Thibaut Lamadon, Guido Lorenzoni, Serguei Maliar, Casey Mulligan, Stavros Panageas, Pierre Siklos, Eric Sims, Alp Simsek, Christopher Tonetti, Alessandra Voena, Carl Walsh, and Michael Weber.

The two conferences at Stanford and Chicago where authors presented draft chapters and received this critical commentary were essential to the completion of the *Handbook of Macroeconomics*. We thank the Hoover Institution at Stanford University and the Becker-Friedman Institute at the University of Chicago for the financial and logistical support that made these conferences possible. We also wish to thank Marie-Christine Slakey for managing the overall manuscript and communications with authors from the very beginning of the project.

John B. Taylor
Harald Uhlig

SECTION 3

Financial-Real Connections

CHAPTER 16

Wholesale Banking and Bank Runs in Macroeconomic Modeling of Financial Crises

M. Gertler[*,†,‡], N. Kiyotaki[*,†,‡], A. Prestipino[*,†,‡]

[*]NYU, New York, NY, United States
[†]Princeton University, Princeton, NJ, United States
[‡]Federal Reserve Board of Governors, Washington, DC, United States

Contents

Handbook of Macroeconomics, Volume 2B
ISSN 1574-0048, http://dx.doi.org/10.1016/bs.hesmac.2016.03.009

Abstract

There has been considerable progress in developing macroeconomic models of banking crises. However, most of this literature focuses on the retail sector where banks obtain deposits from households. In fact, the recent financial crisis that triggered the Great Recession featured a disruption of wholesale funding markets, where banks lend to one another. Accordingly, to understand the financial crisis as well as to draw policy implications, it is essential to capture the role of wholesale banking. The objective of this chapter is to characterize a model that can be seen as a natural extension of the existing literature, but in which the analysis is focused on wholesale funding markets. The model accounts for both the buildup and collapse of wholesale banking and also sketches out the transmission of the crises to the real sector. We also draw out the implications of possible instability in the wholesale banking sector for lender-of-last resort policy as well as for macroprudential policy.

Keywords

Financial crises, Wholesale banking, Interbank markets, Rollover risk

JEL Classification Code

E44

1. INTRODUCTION

One of the central challenges for contemporary macroeconomics is adapting the core models to account for why the recent financial crisis occurred and for why it then devolved into the worst recession of the postwar period. On the eve of the crisis, the basic workhorse quantitative models used in practice largely abstracted from financial market frictions. These models were thus largely silent on how the crisis broke out and how the vast array of unconventional policy interventions undertaken by the Federal Reserve and Treasury could have worked to mitigate the effects of the financial turmoil. Similarly, these models could not provide guidance for the regulatory adjustments needed to avoid another calamity.[a]

From the start of the crisis there has been an explosion of literature aimed at meeting this challenge. Much of the early wave of this literature builds on the financial accelerator and credit cycle framework developed in Bernanke and Gertler (1989) and Kiyotaki and Moore (1997). This approach stresses the role of balance sheets in constraining borrower spending in a setting with financial market frictions. Procyclical movement in balance sheet strength amplifies spending fluctuations and thus fluctuations in aggregate economic activity. A feedback loop emerges as conditions in the real economy affect the condition of balance sheets and vice-versa. Critical to this mechanism is the role of leverage: The exposure of balance sheets to systemic risk is increasing in the degree of borrower leverage.

[a] For a description of the causes leading to the recent financial crisis see Bernanke (2010).

The new vintage of macroeconomic models with financial frictions makes progress in two directions: First, it adapts the framework to account for the distinctive features of the current crisis. In particular, during the recent crisis, it was highly leveraged financial institutions along with highly leveraged households that were most immediately vulnerable to financial distress.[b] The conventional literature featured balance sheet constraints on nonfinancial firms. Accordingly, a number of recent macroeconomic models have introduced balance sheet constraints on banks, while others have done so for households.[c] The financial accelerator remains operative, but the classes of agents most directly affected by the financial market disruption differ from earlier work.

Another direction has involved improving the way financial crises are modeled. For example, financial crises are inherently nonlinear events, often featuring a simultaneous sudden collapse in asset prices and rise in credit spreads.[d] A sharp collapse in output typically ensues. Then recovery occurs only slowly, as it is impeded by a slow process of deleveraging. A number of papers have captured this nonlinearity by allowing for the possibility that the balance sheet constraints do not always bind.[e] Financial crises are then periods where the constraints bind, causing an abrupt contraction in economic activity. Another approach to handling the nonlinearity is to allow for bank runs.[f] Indeed, runs on the shadow banking system were a salient feature of the crisis, culminating with the collapse in September 2008 of Lehman Brothers, of some major money market funds and ultimately of the entire investment banking sector. Yet another literature captures the nonlinearity inherent in financial crises by modeling network interactions (see, eg, Garleanu et al., 2015).

One area the macroeconomics literature has yet to address adequately is the distinctive role of the wholesale banking sector in the breakdown of the financial system. Our notion of wholesale banks corresponds roughly, though not exactly, to the shadow banking sector on the eve of the 2007–09 financial crisis. Shadow banking includes all financial intermediaries that operated outside the Federal Reserve's regulatory framework. By wholesale banking, we mean the subset that (i) was highly leveraged, often with

[b] To be sure, the financial distress also directly affected the behavior of nonfinancial firms. See Giroud and Mueller (2015) for evidence of firm balance sheet effects on employment during the crisis.

[c] See Gertler and Karadi (2011), Gertler and Kiyotaki (2010), and Curdia and Woodford (2010) for papers that incorporate banking and Iacoviello (2005), Eggertsson and Krugman (2012), Guerrieri and Lorenzoni (2011), and Midrigan and Philippon (2011) for papers that included household debt.

[d] See He and Krishnamurthy (2014) for evidence in support of the nonlinearity of financial crises.

[e] See Brunnermeier and Sannikov (2014), He and Krishnamurthy (2013), He and Krishnamurthy (2014), and Mendoza (2010).

[f] For the seminal contribution on bank runs see Diamond and Dybvig (1983). Some recent examples of macroeconomic models that consider bank runs include Gertler and Kiyotaki (2015), Ferrante (2015a), Robatto (2014), Martin et al (2014), Angeloni and Faia (2013) and Ennis and Keister (2003). See Boissay, Collard, and Smets (2013) for an alternative way to model banking crises that does not involve runs per se. For other related literature see Allen and Gale (2007), Cooper and Ross (1998), Farmer (1999), Holmstrom and Tirole (2011) and the references within.

short-term debt and (ii) relied heavily on borrowing from other financial institutions in "wholesale" markets, as opposed to borrowing from households in "retail" markets for bank credit.

When the crisis hit, the epicenter featured malfunctioning of the wholesale banking sector. Indeed, retail markets remained relatively stable while wholesale funding markets experienced dry-ups and runs. By contrast, much of the macroeconomic modeling of banking features traditional retail banking. In this respect, it misses some important dimensions of both the run-up to the crisis and how exactly the crisis played out. In addition, by omitting wholesale banking, the literature may be missing some important considerations for regulatory design.

In this Handbook chapter, we present a simple canonical macroeconomic model of banking crises that (i) is representative of the existing literature and (ii) extends this literature to feature a role for wholesale banking. The model will provide some insight both into the growth of wholesale banking and into how this growth led to a build-up of financial vulnerabilities that ultimately led to a collapse. Because the model builds on existing literature, our exposition of the framework will permit us to review the progress that is made. However, by turning attention to wholesale banks and wholesale funding markets, we are able to chart a direction we believe the literature should take.

In particular, the model is an extension of the framework developed in Gertler and Kiyotaki (2011), which had a similar twofold objective: first, present a canonical framework to review progress that has been made and, second, chart a new direction. That paper characterized how existing financial accelerator models that featured firm level balance sheet constraints could be extended to banking relationships in order to capture the disruption of banking during the crisis. The model developed there considered only retail banks which funded loans mainly from household deposits. While it allowed for an interbank market for credit among retail banks, it did not feature banks that relied primarily on wholesale funding, as was the case with shadow banks.

For this Handbook chapter, we modify the Gertler and Kiyotaki framework to incorporate wholesale banking alongside retail banking, where the amount credit intermediated via wholesale funding markets arises endogenously. Another important difference is that we allow for the possibility of runs on wholesale banks. We argue that both these modifications improve the ability of macroeconomic models to capture how the crisis evolved. They also provide insight into how the financial vulnerabilities built up in the first place.

As way to motivate our emphasis on wholesale banking, Section 1 presents descriptive evidence on the growth of this sector and the collapse it experienced during the Great Recession. Section 3 presents the baseline macroeconomic model with banking, where a wholesale banking sector arises endogenously. Sector 4 conducts a set of numerical experiments. While the increased size of the wholesale banking improves the efficiency of financial intermediation, it also raises the vulnerability of this sector to runs. Section 5 considers the case where runs in the wholesale sector might be anticipated. It illustrates how the model can capture some of the key phases of the financial collapse, including the slow run period up to Lehman and the ultimate "fast run" collapse. In Section 6, we introduce a second asset in which retail banks have a comparative advantage in intermediating. We then show how a crisis in wholesale banking can spill over and affect retail banking, consistent with what happened during the crisis. Section 7 analyzes government policy to contain financial crises, including both ex-post lender of last resort activity and ex-ante macroprudential regulation. Finally, we conclude in Section 8 with some directions for future research.

2. THE GROWTH AND FRAGILITY OF WHOLESALE BANKING

In this section, we provide some background motivation for the canonical macroeconomic model with wholesale funding markets that we develop in the following section. We do so by presenting a brief description of the growth and ultimate collapse of wholesale funding markets during the Great Recession. We also describe informally how the disruption of these markets contributed to the contraction of the real economy.

Fig. 1 illustrates how we consider the different roles of retail and wholesale financial intermediaries, following the tradition of Gurley and Shaw (1960).[g] The arrows indicate

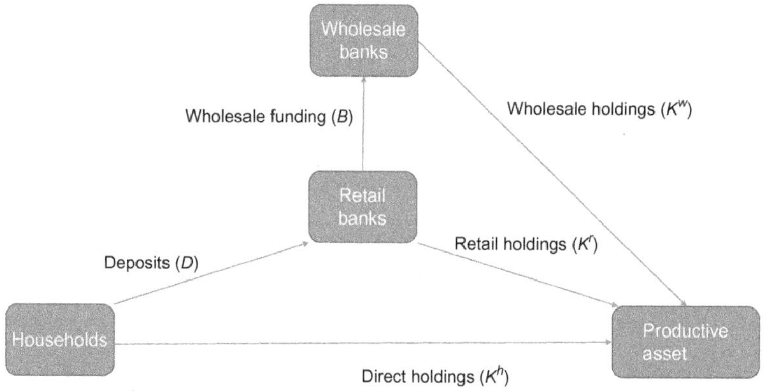

Fig. 1 Modes of financial intermediation.

[g] Gurley and Shaw (1960) consider that there are two ways to transfer funds from ultimate lenders (with surplus funds) to ultimate borrowers (who need external funds to finance expenditure): direct and indirect finance. In direct finance, ultimate borrowers sell their securities directly to ultimate lenders to raise funds. In indirect finance, financial intermediaries sell their own securities to raise funds from ultimate lenders in order to buy securities from ultimate borrowers. By doing so, financial intermediaries transform relatively risky, illiquid, and long maturity securities of ultimate borrowers into relatively safe, liquid, and short maturity securities of intermediaries. Here, we divide financial intermediaries into wholesale and retail financial intermediaries, while both involve asset transformation of risk, liquidity, and maturity. We refer to intermediaries as "banks" and to ultimate lenders as "households" for short.

the direction that credit is flowing. Funds can flow from households (ultimate lenders) to nonfinancial borrowers (ultimate borrowers) through three different paths: they can be lent directly from households to borrowers $\left(K^h\right)$; they can be intermediated by retail banks that raise deposits (D) from households and use them to make loans to nonfinancial borrowers $\left(K^r\right)$; alternatively, lenders' deposits can be further intermediated by specialized financial institutions that raise funds from retail banks in wholesale funding markets (B) and, in turn, make loans to ultimate borrowers $\left(K^w\right)$. In what follows we refer to these specialized financial institutions as wholesale banks. We think of wholesale banks as highly leveraged shadow banks that rely heavily on credit from other financial institutions, particularly short-term credit. We place in this category institutions that financed long-term assets, such as mortgaged back securities, with short-term money market instruments, including commercial paper and repurchase agreements. Examples of these kinds of financial institutions are investment banks, hedge funds, and conduits. We focus attention on institutions that relied heavily on short-term funding in wholesale markets to finance longer term assets because it was primarily these kinds of entities that experienced financial turmoil.

Our retail banking sector, in turn, includes financial institutions that rely mainly on household saving for external funding and provide a significant amount of short-term financing to the wholesale banks. Here, we have in mind commercial banks, money market funds, and mutual funds that raised funds mainly from households and on net provided financing to wholesale banks.

Fig. 1 treats wholesale banking as if it is homogenous. In order to understand how the crisis spread, it is useful to point out that there are different layers within the wholesale banking sector. While the intermediation process was rather complex, conceptually we can reduce the number of layers to three basic ones: (1) origination, (2) securitization, (3)

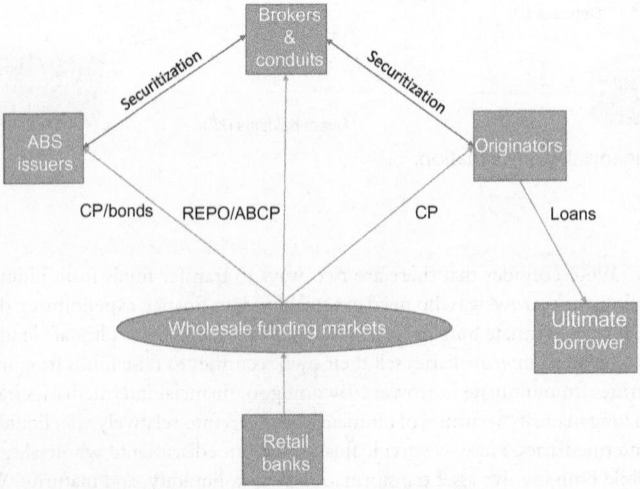

Fig. 2 Wholesale intermediation.

and funding. Fig. 2 illustrates the chain. First there are "loan originators," such as mortgage origination companies and finance companies, that made loans directly to nonfinancial borrowers. At the other end of the chain were shadow banks that held securitized pools of the loans made by originators. In between were brokers and conduits that assisted in the securitization process and provided market liquidity. Dominant in this group were the major investment banks (eg, Goldman Sachs, Morgan Stanley, and Lehman Brothers). Each of these layers relied on short-term funding, including commercial paper, asset-backed commercial paper and repurchase agreements. While there was considerable interbank lending among wholesale banks, retail banks (particularly money market funds) on net provided short-term credit in wholesale credit markets.

We next describe a set of facts about wholesale banking. We emphasize three sets of facts in particular: (1) wholesale banking grew in relative importance over the last four decades, (2) leading up to the crisis wholesale banks were highly exposed to systemic risk because they were highly leveraged and relied heavily on short-term debt, and (3) the subsequent disruption of wholesale funding markets raised credit costs and contracted credit flows, likely contributing in a major way to the Great Recession.

1. *Growth in Wholesale Banking*

We now present measures of the scale of wholesale banking relative to retail banking as well as to household's direct asset holdings. Table 1 describes how we construct measures of assets held by wholesale vs retail banks. In particular, it lists how we categorized the various types of financial intermediaries into wholesale vs retail banking.[h,i] As the table

Table 1 Wholesale and Retail sector in the Flow of Funds

Retail sector	Private depository institutions Money market mutual funds Mutual funds	
Wholesale sector	*Origination*	Finance companies Real estate investment trusts Government sponsored enterprises
	Securitization	Security brokers dealers ABS issuers
	Funding	GSE mortgage pools Funding corporations Holding companies

[h] Appendix D provides details about measurement of the time series shown in this section from Flow of Funds data.

[i] It is important to notice that the measures we report are broadly in line with analogous measures computed for shadow banking. See, eg, Adrian and Ashcraft (2012), for an alternative definition of shadow banking that yields very similar conclusions and Pozsar et al. (2013), for a detailed description of shadow banking.

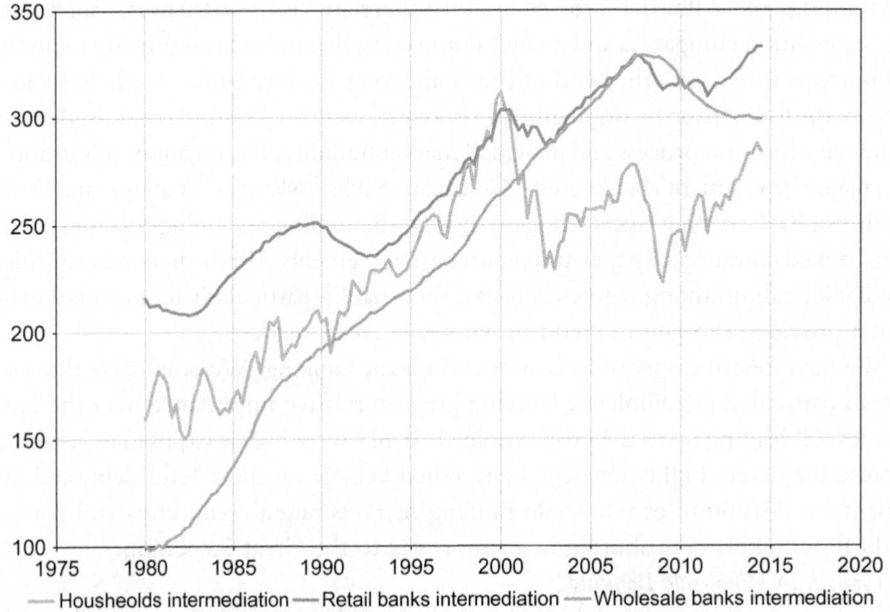

Fig. 3 Intermediation by sector. The graph shows the evolution of credit intermediated by the three different sectors. Nominal data from the Flow of Funds are deflated using the CPI and normalized so that the log of the normalized value of real wholesale intermediation in 1980 is equal to 1. The resulting time series are then multiplied by 100.

indicates, the wholesale banking sector aggregates financial institutions that originate loans, that help securitize them and that ultimately fund them. A common feature of all these institutions, though, is that they relied heavily on short-term credit in wholesale funding markets.

Fig. 3 portrays the log level of credit to nonfinancial sector provided by wholesale banks, by retail banks, and directly by households from the early 1980s until the present.[j] The figure shows the rapid increase in wholesale banking relative to the other means of credit supply to nonfinancial sector. Wholesale banks went from holding under 15% of total credit in the early 1980s to roughly 40% on the eve of the Great Recession, an amount on par with credit provided by retail banks.

Two factors were likely key to the growth of wholesale banking. The first is regulatory arbitrage. Increased capital requirements on commercial banks raised the incentive to transfer asset holding outside the commercial bank system. Second, financial innovation improved the liquidity of wholesale funding markets. The securitization process in particular improved the (perceived) safety of loans by diversifying idiosyncratic risks as

[j] The measure we present also include nonfinancial corporate equities. Excluding equities, households would become negligible but the relative size of wholesale and retail banks would evolve very similarly. See Appendix D for details on how we construct the measures reported.

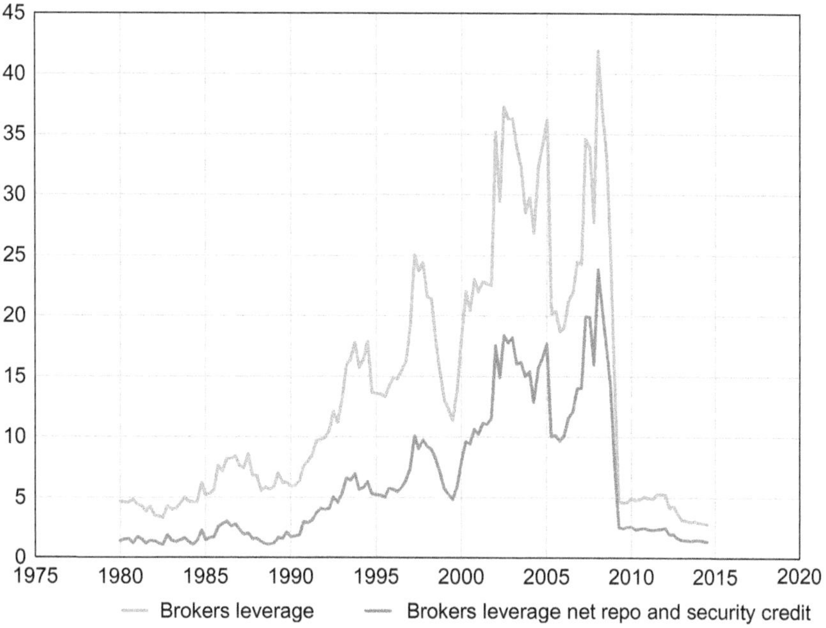

Fig. 4 Brokers leverage. Leverage is given by the ratio of total financial assets over equity. Equity is computed from the Flow of Funds by subtracting total financial liabilities from total financial assets. The net position leverage computes assets by netting out long and short positions in REPO and Security Credit. See the Appendices for details.

well as by enhancing the liquidity of secondary markets for bank assets. The net effect was to raise the borrowing capacity of the overall financial intermediary sector.

2. *Growth in Leverage and Short-Term Debt in Wholesale Banking*

Wholesale banking not only grew rapidly, it also became increasingly vulnerable to systemic disturbances. Fig. 4 presents evidence on the growth in leverage in the investment banking sector. Specifically it plots the aggregate leverage multiple for broker dealers (primarily investment banks) from 1980 to the present. We define the leverage multiple as the ratio of total assets held to equity.[k] The greater is the leverage multiple, the higher is the reliance on debt finance relative to equity. The key takeaway from Fig. 4 is that the leverage multiple grew from under five in the early 1980s to over forty at the beginning of the Great Recession, a nearly tenfold increase.

Arguably, the way securitization contributed to the overall growth of wholesale banking was by facilitating the use of leverage. By constructing assets that appeared safe and liquid, securitization permitted wholesale banks to fund these assets by issuing debt.

[k] The data is from the Flow of Funds and equity is measured by book value. We exclude nonfinancial assets from measurement as they are not reported in the Flow of Funds.

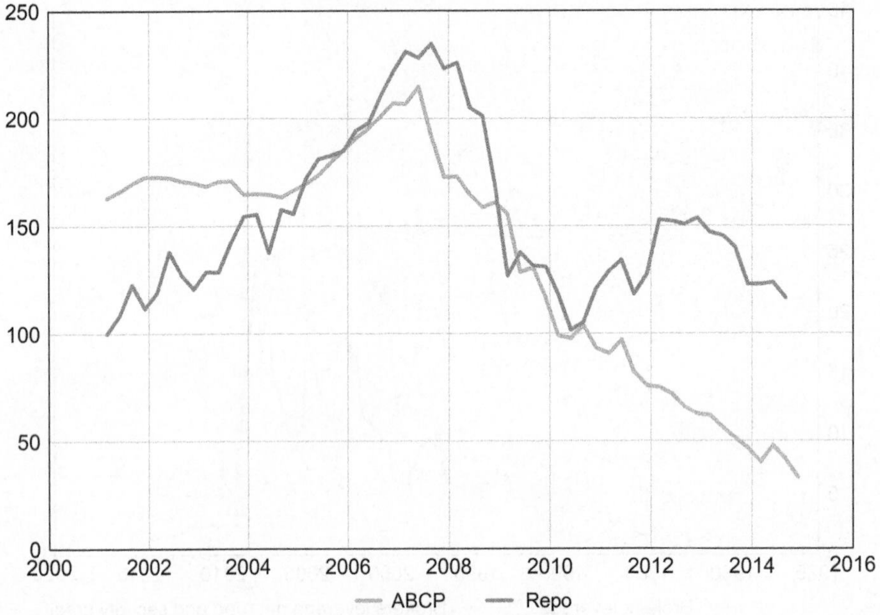

Fig. 5 Short-term wholesale funding. The graph shows the logarithm of the real value outstanding. Nominal values from Flow of Funds are deflated using the CPI.

At a minimum debt finance had the advantage of being cheaper due to the tax treatment. Debt financing was also cheaper to the extent the liabilities were liquid and thus offered a lower rate due to a liquidity premium.

Why were these assets funded in wholesale markets as opposed to retail markets? The sophistication of these assets required that creditors be highly informed to evaluate payoffs, especially given the absence of deposit insurance. The complicated asset payoff structure also suggests that having a close working relationship with borrowers is advantageous. It served to reduce the possibility of any kind of financial malfeasance. Given these considerations, it makes sense that wholesale banks obtain funding in interbank markets. In these markets lenders are sophisticated financial institutions as opposed to relatively unsophisticated households in the retail market.

Fig. 5 shows that much of the growth in leverage in wholesale banking involved short-term borrowing. The figure plots the levels of asset backed commercial paper (ABCP) and repurchase agreements (Repo). This growth reflected partly the growth in assets held by wholesale banks and partly innovation in loan securitization that made maturity transformation by wholesale banks more efficient. Also relevant, however, was a shift in retail investors demand from longer term security tranches towards short-term credit instruments as the initial fall in housing prices in 2006 raised concerns about the quality of existing securitized assets.[l,m] As we discuss next, the combination of high leverage and short-term debt is what made the wholesale banking system extremely fragile.

3. *The Crisis: The Unraveling of Wholesale Bank Funding Markets*

The losses suffered by mortgage originators due to falling housing prices in 2006 eventually created strains in wholesale funding markets. Short-term wholesale funding markets started experiencing severe turbulence in the summer of 2007. In July 2007 two Bear Sterns investment funds that had invested in subprime related products declared bankruptcy. Shortly after, BNP Paribas had to suspend withdrawals from investment funds with similar exposure. These two episodes led investors to reassess the risks associated with the collateral backing commercial paper offered by asset backed securities issuers. In August 2007 a steady contraction of Asset Backed Commercial Paper (ABCP) market began, something akin to a "slow run," in Bernanke's terminology.[n] The value of Asset Backed Commercial Paper outstanding went from a peak of 1.2 trillion dollars in July 2007 to 800 billion dollars in December of the same year and continued its descent to its current level of around 200 billion dollars.

The second significant wave of distress to hit wholesale funding markets featured the collapse of Lehman Brothers in September of 2008. Losses on short-term debt instruments issued by Lehman Brothers led the Reserve Primary Fund, a large Money Market Mutual Fund (MMMF), to "break the buck": the market value of assets fell below the value of its noncontingent liabilities. An incipient run on MMMFs was averted only by the extension of Deposit Insurance to these types of institutions. Wholesale investors,[o] however, reacted by pulling out of the Repo market, switching off the main source of funding for Security Broker Dealers. Fig. 5 shows the sharp collapse in repo financing around the time of the Lehman collapse. Indeed if the first wave of distress hitting the ABCP market had the features of a "slow run," the second, which led to the dissolution of the entire investment banking system had the features of a traditional "fast run." We emphasize that a distinctive feature of these two significant waves of financial distress is that they did not involve traditional banking institutions. In fact, the retail sector as a whole was shielded thanks to prompt government intervention that halted the run on

[l] See Brunnermeier and Oemke (2013) for a model in which investors prefer shorter maturities when release of information could lead them not to roll over debt.

[m] It is not easy to gather direct evidence on this from the aggregate composition of liabilities of wholesale banks since data from the Flow of Funds excludes the balance sheets of SIVs and CDOs from the ABS Issuers category. Our narrative is based on indirect evidence coming from ABX spreads as documented for example in Gorton (2009).

[n] Covitz et al. (2013) provide a detailed description of the run on ABCP programs in 2007. A very clear description of the role of commercial paper during the 2007–09 crisis is presented by Kacperczyk and Schnabl (2010).

[o] The poor quality of available data makes it difficult to exactly identify the identity of the investors running on Repo's. See Gorton and Metrick (2012) and Krishnamurthy et al. (2014).

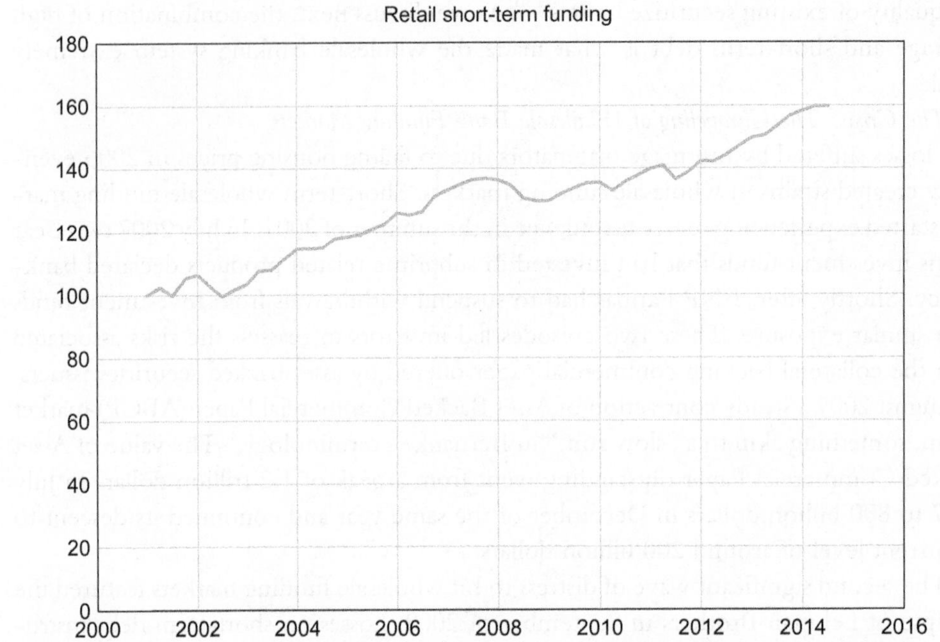

Fig. 6 Retail short-term funding. The graph shows the logarithm of the real value outstanding. Nominal values from Flow of Funds are deflated using the CPI and normalized so that the log of the normalized value of retail short-term funding in 2001 is equal to 100.

MMMFs in 2008 as well as the Troubled Asset Relief Program and other subsequent measures that supplemented the traditional safety net. In fact, total short-term liabilities of the retail sector were little affected overall (see Fig. 6). This allowed the retail banking sector to help absorb some of the intermediation previously performed by wholesale banks.

Despite the unprecedented nature and size of government intervention and the partial replacement of wholesale intermediation by retail bank lending, the distress in wholesale bank funding markets led to widespread deterioration in credit conditions. Fig. 7 plots the behavior of credit spreads and investment from 2004 to 2010. We focus on three representative credit spreads: (1) The spread between the 3 month ABCP rate and 3 month Treasury spread, (2) The financial company commercial paper spread, and (3) The Gilchrist and Zakrajsek (2012) excess bond premium. In each case, the spread is the difference between the respective rate on the private security and a similar maturity treasury security rate. The behavior of the spreads lines up with the waves of financial distress that we described. The ABCP spread jumps by 1.5% in August 2007, the beginning of the unraveling of this market. The increase in this spread implies a direct increase in credit costs for borrowing funded by ABCP including mortgages, car loans, and credit card

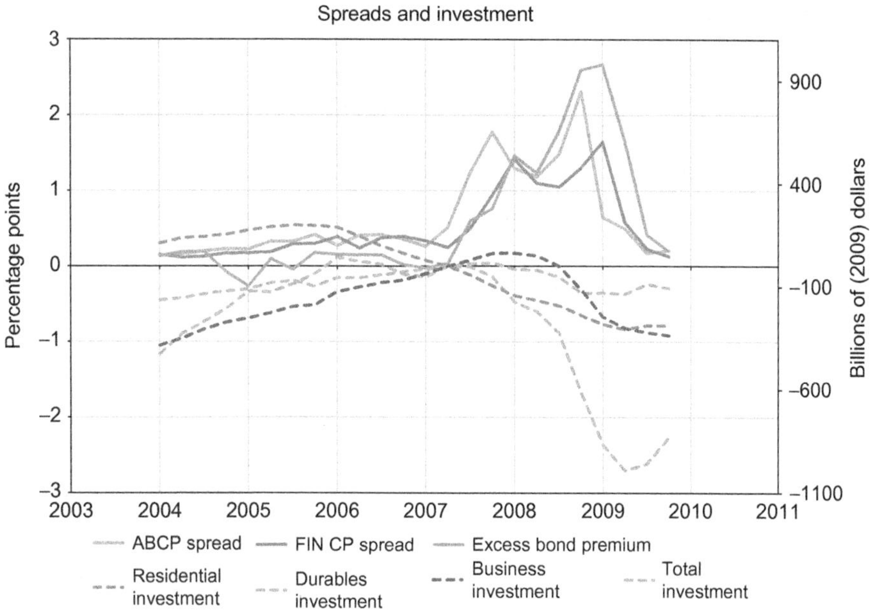

Fig. 7 Credit spreads and investment.

borrowing. As problems spread to broker dealers, the financial commercial paper spread increases reaching a peak at more than 1.5% at the time of the Lehman collapse. Increasing costs of credit for these intermediaries, in turn, helped fuel increasing borrowing costs for nonfinancial borrowers. The Gilchrist and Zakrajsek's corporate excess bond spread jumps more than 2.5% from early 2007 to the peak in late 2008.

It is reasonable to infer that the borrowing costs implied by the increased credit spreads contributed in an important way to the slowing of the economy at the onset of the recession in 2007:Q4, as well as to the sharp collapse following the Lehman failure. As shown in Fig. 7, the contraction in business investment, residential investment, durable consumption, and their sum-total investment, moves inversely with credit spreads.

In our view, there are three main conclusions to be drawn from the empirical evidence presented in this section. First, the wholesale banking sector grew into a very important component of financial intermediation by relying on securitization to reduce the risks of lending and expand the overall borrowing capacity of the financial system. Second, higher borrowing capacity came at the cost of increased fragility as high leverage made wholesale banks' net worth very sensitive to corrections in asset prices. Third, the disruptions in wholesale funding markets that took place in 2007 and 2008 seem to have played an important role in the unfolding of the Great Recession. These observations motivate our modeling approach below and our focus on interbank funding markets functioning and regulation.

3. BASIC MODEL

3.1 Key Features

Our starting point is the infinite horizon macroeconomic model with banking and bank runs developed in Gertler and Kiyotaki (2015). In order to study recent financial booms and crises, in this chapter we disaggregate banking into wholesale and retail banks. Wholesale banks make loans to the nonfinancial sector funded primarily by borrowing from retail banks. The latter use deposits from households to make loans both to the nonfinancial sector and to the wholesale financial sector. Further, the size of the wholesale banking market arises endogenously. It depends on two key factors: (1) the relative advantage wholesale banks have in managing assets over retail banks and (2) the relative advantage of retail banks over households in overcoming an agency friction that impedes lending to wholesale banks.[p]

In the previous section, we described the different layers of the wholesale sector, including origination, securitization, and funding. For tractability, in our model we consolidate these various functions into a single type of wholesale bank. Overall, our model permits capturing financial stress in wholesale funding markets which was a key feature of the recent financial crisis.

There are three classes of agents: households, retail banks, and wholesale banks. There are two goods, a nondurable good and a durable asset, "capital." Capital does not depreciate and the total supply of capital stock is fixed at $\bar{K}$. Wholesale and retail banks use borrowed funds and their own equity to finance the acquisition of capital. Households lend to banks and also hold capital directly. The sum of total holdings of capital by each type of agent equals the total supply which we normalize to unity:

$$K_t^w + K_t^r + K_t^h = \bar{K} = 1, \tag{1}$$

where K_t^w and K_t^r are the total capital held by wholesale and retail bankers and K_t^h is the amount held by households.

Agents of type j use capital and goods as inputs at t to produce output and capital at $t + 1$, as follows:

$$\begin{array}{ccc} \textit{date } t & & \textit{date } t+1 \\ \left.\begin{array}{c} K_t^j \text{ capital} \\ F^j(K_t^j) \text{ goods} \end{array}\right\} & \rightarrow & \left\{\begin{array}{c} Z_{t+1}K_t^j \text{ output} \\ K_t^j \text{ capital} \end{array}\right. \end{array} \tag{2}$$

where type $j = w$, r, and h stands for wholesale banks, retail banks, and households, respectively. Expenditure in terms of goods at date t reflects the management cost of

[p] Our setup bears some resemblance to Holmstrom and Tirole (1997), which has nonfinancial firms that face costs in raising external funds from banks that in turn face costs in raising deposits from households. In our case, it is constrained wholesale banks that raise funds from constrained retail banks.

screening and monitoring investment projects. In the case of retail banks, the management costs might also reflect various regulatory constraints. We suppose this management cost is increasing and convex in the total amount of capital, as given by the following quadratic formulation:

$$F^j(K_t^j) = \frac{\alpha^j}{2}(K_t^j)^2. \tag{3}$$

In addition, we suppose the management cost is zero for wholesale banks and highest for households (holding constant the level of capital):

$$\alpha^w = 0 < \alpha^r < \alpha^h. \qquad \text{(Assumption 1)}$$

This assumption implies that wholesale bankers have an advantage over the other agents in managing capital.[q] Retail banks in turn have a comparative advantage over households. Finally, the convex cost implies that it is increasingly costly at the margin for retail banks and households to absorb capital directly. As we will see, this cost formulation provides a simple way to limit agents with wealth but lack of expertise from purchasing assets during a firesale.

In our decentralization of the economy, a representative household provides capital management services both for itself and for retail banks. For the latter, the household charges retail banks a competitive price f_t^r per unit of capital managed, where f_t^r corresponds to the marginal cost of providing the service:

$$f_t^r = F^{r\prime}(K_t^r) = \alpha^r K_t^r. \tag{4}$$

Households obtain the profit from this activity $f_t^r K_t^r - F^r(K_t^r)$.

3.2 Households

Each household consumes and saves. Households save either by lending funds to bankers or by holding capital directly in the competitive market. They may deposit funds in either retail or wholesale banks. In addition to the returns on portfolio investments, every period each household receives an endowment of nondurable goods, $Z_t W^h$, that varies proportionately with the aggregate productivity shock Z_t.

Deposits held in a bank from t to $t+1$ are one period bonds that promise to pay the noncontingent gross rate of return $\bar{R}_{t+1}$ in the absence of a run by depositors. In the event of a deposit run, depositors only receive a fraction x_{t+1}^r of the promised return, where x_{t+1}^r

[q] In general, we have in mind that wholesale and retail banks specialize in different types of lending and, as a consequence, each has developed relative expertise in managing the type of assets they hold. We subsequently make this point clearer by introducing a second asset in which retail banks have a comparative advantage in intermediating. Also relevant are regulatory distortions, though we view this as a factor that leads to specialization in the first place.

is the total liquidation value of retail banks assets[r] per unit of promised deposit obligations. Accordingly, we can express the household's return on deposits, R_{t+1}, as follows:

$$R_{t+1} = \begin{cases} \bar{R}_{t+1} & \text{if no deposit run} \\ x_{t+1}^{r} \bar{R}_{t+1} & \text{if deposit run occurs} \end{cases} \tag{5}$$

where $0 \leq x_t^r < 1$. Note that if a deposit run occurs all depositors receive the same pro rata share of liquidated assets.

Household utility U_t is given by

$$U_t = E_t\left(\sum_{i=0}^{\infty} \beta^i \ln C_{t+i}^h\right)$$

where C_t^h is household consumption and $0 < \beta < 1$. Let Q_t be the market price of capital. The household then chooses consumption, bank deposits D_t and direct capital holdings K_t^h to maximize expected utility subject to the budget constraint

$$C_t^h + D_t + Q_t K_t^h + F^h(K_t^h) = Z_t W^h + R_t D_{t-1} + (Z_t + Q_t) K_{t-1}^h + f_t^r K_t^r - F^r(K_t^r). \tag{6}$$

Here, consumption, saving, and management costs are financed by the endowment, the returns on savings, and the profits from providing management services to retail bankers.

For pedagogical purposes, we begin with a baseline model where bank runs are completely unanticipated events. Accordingly, in this instance the household chooses consumption and saving with the expectation that the realized return on deposits, R_{t+i}, equals the promised return, $\bar{R}_{t+i}$, with certainty, and that asset prices, Q_{t+i}, are those at which capital is traded when no bank run happens. In a subsequent section, we characterize the case where agents anticipate that a bank run may occur with some likelihood.

Given that the household assigns probability zero to a bank run, the first order condition for deposits is given by

$$E_t(\Lambda_{t,t+1}) R_{t+1} = 1 \tag{7}$$

where the stochastic discount factor $\Lambda_{t,\tau}$ satisfies

$$\Lambda_{t,\tau} = \beta^{\tau - t} \frac{C_t^h}{C_\tau^h}.$$

The first order condition for direct capital holdings is given by

$$E_t\left(\Lambda_{t,t+1} R_{kt+1}^h\right) = 1 \tag{8}$$

with

$$R_{kt+1}^h = \frac{Q_{t+1} + Z_{t+1}}{Q_t + F^{h\prime}(K_t^h)}$$

where $F^{h\prime}(K_t^h) = \alpha^h K_t^h$ and R_{t+1}^h is the household's gross marginal rate of return from direct capital holdings.

[r] Under our calibration only retail banks choose to issue deposits. See later.

3.3 Banks

There are two types of bankers, retail and wholesale. Each type manages a financial intermediary. Bankers fund capital investments (which we will refer to as "nonfinancial loans") by issuing deposits to households, borrowing from other banks in an interbank market and using their own equity, or net worth. Banks can also lend in the interbank market.

As we describe later, bankers may be vulnerable to runs in the interbank market. In this case, creditor banks suddenly decide to not rollover interbank loans. In the event of an interbank run, the creditor banks receive a fraction x^w_{t+1} of the promised return on the interbank credit, where x^w_{t+1} is the total liquidation value of debtor bank assets per unit of debt obligations. Accordingly, we can express the creditor bank's return on interbank loans, R_{bt+1}, as follows:

$$R_{bt+1} = \begin{cases} \bar{R}_{bt+1} & \text{if no interbank run} \\ x^w_{t+1}\bar{R}_{bt+1} & \text{if interbank run occurs} \end{cases} \tag{9}$$

where $0 \leq x^w_t < 1$. If an interbank run occurs, all creditor banks receive the same pro rata share of liquidated assets. As in the case of deposits, we continue to restrict attention to the case where bank runs are completely unanticipated, before turning in a subsequent section to the case of anticipated runs in wholesale funding markets.

Due to financial market frictions that we specify below, bankers may be constrained in their ability to raise external funds. To the extent they may be constrained, they will attempt to save their way out of the financing constraint by accumulating retained earnings in order to move toward 100% equity financing. To limit this possibility, we assume that bankers have a finite expected lifetime: Specifically, each banker of type j (where $j = w$ and r for wholesale and retail bankers) has an i.i.d. probability σ^j of surviving until the next period and a probability $1 - \sigma^j$ of exiting. This setup provides a simple way to motivate "dividend payouts" from the banking system in order to ensure that banks use leverage in equilibrium.

Every period new bankers of type j enter with an endowment w^j that is received only in the first period of life. This initial endowment may be thought of as the start up equity for the new banker. The number of entering bankers equals the number who exit, keeping the total constant.

We assume that bankers of either type are risk neutral and enjoy utility from consumption in the period they exit. The expected utility of a continuing banker at the end of period t is given by

$$V^j_t = E_t\left[\sum_{i=1}^{\infty} \beta^i (1-\sigma^j)(\sigma^j)^{i-1} c^j_{t+i}\right],$$

where $(1 - \sigma^j)(\sigma^j)^{i-1}$ is the probability of exiting at date $t + i$, and c^j_{t+i} is terminal consumption if the banker of type j exits at $t + i$.

The aggregate shock Z_t is realized at the start of t. Conditional on this shock, the net worth of "surviving" bankers j is the gross return on nonfinancial loans net the cost of deposits and borrowing from the other banks, as follows:

$$n_t^j = (Q_t + Z_t)k_{t-1}^j - R_t d_{t-1}^j - R_{bt} b_{t-1}^j, \tag{10}$$

where d_{t-1}^j is deposit and b_{t-1}^j is interbank borrowing at $t-1$. Note that b_{t-1}^j is positive if bank j borrows and negative if j lends in the interbank market.

For new bankers at t, net worth simply equals the initial endowment:

$$n_t^j = w^j. \tag{11}$$

Meanwhile, exiting bankers no longer operate banks and simply use their net worth to consume:

$$c_t^j = n_t^j. \tag{12}$$

During each period t, a continuing bank j (either new or surviving) finances nonfinancial loans $(Q_t + f_t^j)k_t^j$ with net worth, deposit and interbank debt as follows:

$$(Q_t + f_t^j)k_t^j = n_t^j + d_t^j + b_t^j, \tag{13}$$

where f_t^r is given by (4) and $f_t^w = 0$. We assume that banks can only accumulate net worth via retained earnings. While this assumption is a reasonable approximation of reality, we do not explicitly model the agency frictions that underpin it.[s]

To derive a limit on the bank's ability to raise funds, we introduce the following moral hazard problem: After raising funds and buying assets at the beginning of t, but still during the period, the banker decides whether to operate "honestly" or to divert assets for personal use. Operating honestly means holding assets until the payoffs are realized in period $t+1$ and then meeting obligations to depositors and interbank creditors. To divert means to secretly channel funds away from investments in order to consume personally.

To motivate the use of wholesale funding markets along with retail markets, we assume that the banker's ability to divert funds depends on both the sources and uses of funds. The banker can divert the fraction θ of nonfinancial loans financed by retained earnings or funds raised from households, where $0 < \theta < 1$. On the other hand, he/she can divert only the fraction $\theta\omega$ of nonfinancial loans financed by interbank borrowing, where $0 < \omega < 1$. Here, we are capturing in a simple way that bankers lending in the wholesale market are more effective at monitoring the banks to which they lend than are households that supply deposits in the retail market. Accordingly, the total amount of funds that can be diverted by a banker who is a net borrower in the interbank market is given by

[s] See Bigio (2015) for a model that explains why banks might find it hard to raise external equity during crises in the presence of adverse selection problems.

$$\theta[(Q+f^j)k_t^j - b_t^j + \omega b_t^j]$$

where $(Q+f^j)k_t^j - b_t^j$ equals the value of funds invested in nonfinancial loans that is financed by deposits and net worth and where $b_t^j > 0$ equals the value of nonfinancial loans financed by interbank borrowing.

For bankers that lend to other banks, we suppose that it is more difficult to divert interbank loans than nonfinancial loans. Specifically, we suppose that a banker can divert only a fraction $\theta\gamma$ of its loans to other banks, where $0 < \gamma < 1$. Here, we appeal to the idea that interbank loans are much less idiosyncratic in nature than nonfinancial loans and thus easier for outside depositors to monitor. Accordingly, the total amount a bank that lends on the interbank market can divert is given by

$$\theta[(Q_t + f_t^j)k_t^j + \gamma(-b_t^j)]$$

with $b_t^j < 0$. As we will make clear shortly, key to operation of the interbank market are the parameters that govern the moral hazard problem in this market, ω and γ.

We assume that the process of diverting assets takes time: The banker cannot quickly liquidate a large amount of assets without the transaction being noticed. For this reason, the banker must decide whether to divert at t, prior to the realization of uncertainty at $t+1$. The cost to the banker of the diversion is that the creditors can force the intermediary into bankruptcy at the beginning of the next period.

The banker's decision at t boils down to comparing the franchise value of the bank V_t^j, which measures the present discounted value of future payouts from operating honestly, with the gain from diverting funds. In this regard, rational lenders will not supply funds to the banker if he has an incentive to cheat. Accordingly, any financial arrangement between the bank and its lenders must satisfy the following set of incentive constraints, which depend on whether the bank is a net borrower or lender in the interbank market:

$$\begin{aligned} V_t^j &\geq \theta[(Q+f^j)k_t^j - b_t^j + \omega b_t^j], \text{ if } b_t^j > 0 \\ V_t^j &\geq \theta[(Q_t + f_t^j)k_t^j + \gamma(-b_t^j)], \text{ if } b_t^j < 0. \end{aligned} \tag{14}$$

As will become clear shortly, each incentive constraint embeds the constraint that the net worth n_t^j must be positive for the bank to operate: This is because the franchise value V_t^j will turn out to be proportional to n_t^j.

Overall, there are two basic factors that govern the existence and relative size of the interbank market. The first is the cost advantage that wholesale banks have in managing nonfinancial loans, as described by Assumption 1. The second is the size of the parameters ω and γ which govern the comparative advantage that retail banks have over households in lending to wholesale banks. Observe that as ω and γ decline, it becomes more attractive to channel funds through wholesale bank funding markets relative to retail markets. As ω declines below unity, a bank borrowing in the wholesale market can relax its incentive constraint by substituting interbank borrowing for deposits. Similarly, as γ declines below unity, a bank lending in the wholesale market can relax its incentive constraint by shifting its composition of assets from nonfinancial loans to interbank loans.

In what follows, we restrict attention to the case in which

$$\omega + \gamma > 1. \qquad \text{(Assumption 2)}$$

In this instance, the parameters ω and γ can be sufficiently small to permit an empirically reasonable relative amount of interbank lending. However, the sum of these parameters cannot be so small as to induce a situation of pure specialization by retail banks, where these banks do not make nonfinancial loans directly but instead lend all their funds to wholesale banks.[t,u] Since in practice retail banks hold some of the same types of assets held by wholesale banks, we think it reasonable to restrict attention to this case.

We now turn to the optimization problems for both wholesale and retail bankers. Given that bankers simply consume their net worth when they exit, we can restate the bank's franchise value recursively as the expected discounted value of the sum of net worth conditional on exiting and the value conditional on continuing as:

$$\begin{aligned} V_t^j &= \beta E_t[(1-\sigma^j)n_{t+1}^j + \sigma^j V_{t+1}^j]. \\ &= E_t[\Omega_{t+1}^j n_{t+1}^j] \end{aligned} \qquad (15)$$

where

$$\Omega_{t+1}^j = \beta\left(1 - \sigma^j + \sigma^j \frac{V_{t+1}^j}{n_{t+1}^j}\right). \qquad (16)$$

The stochastic discount factor Ω_{t+1}^j, which the bankers use to value n_{t+1}^j, is a probability weighted average of the discounted marginal values of net worth to exiting and to continuing bankers at t+1. For an exiting banker at $t+1$ (which occurs with probability $1-\sigma^j$), the marginal value of an additional unit of net worth is simply unity, since he or she just consumes it. For a continuing banker (which occurs with probability σ^j), the marginal value is the franchise value per unit of net worth V_{t+1}^j/n_{t+1}^j (ie, Tobin's Q ratio). As we show shortly, V_{t+1}^j/n_{t+1}^j depends only on aggregate variables and is independent of bank-specific factors.

We can express the banker's evolution of net worth as:

$$n_{t+1}^j = R_{kt+1}^j (Q_t + f_t^j) k_t^j - R_{t+1} d_t^j - R_{bt+1} b_t^j \qquad (17)$$

[t] See Appendix A for the formal argument that shows that under Assumption 2 pure specialization of retail bankers cannot be an equilibrium.

[u] Holmstrom and Tirole (1997) make similar assumptions on the levels and sum of the agency distortions for banks and nonfinancial firms in order to explain why bank finance arises.

where R^j_{kt+1} is the rate of return on nonfinancial loans, given by

$$R^j_{kt+1} = \frac{Q_{t+1} + Z_{t+1}}{Q_t + f^j_t} \tag{18}$$

The banker's optimization problem then is to choose $\left(k^j_t, d^j_t, b^j_t\right)$ each period to maximize the franchise value (15) subject to the incentive constraint (14) and the balance sheet constraints (13) and (17).

We defer the details of the formal bank maximization problems to Appendix A. Here, we explain the decisions of wholesale and retail banks informally. Because wholesale banks have a cost advantage over retail banks in making nonfinancial loans, the rate of return on nonfinancial loans is higher for the former than for the latter (see Eq. (18)). In turn, retail banks have an advantage over households in lending to wholesale banks due to their relative advantage in recovering assets in default. Therefore, if the interbank market is active in equilibrium, wholesale banks borrow from retail banks in the interbank market to make nonfinancial loans. Indeed the only reason retail banks directly make nonfinancial loans is because wholesale banks may be constrained in the amount of this type of loan they can make.[v]

In the text, we restrict attention to the case where the interbank market is active, with wholesale banks borrowing from retail banks, and where both types of banks are constrained in raising funds externally.

3.3.1 Wholesale banks

In general, wholesale banks may raise funds either from other banks or from households. Since the kinds of financial institutions we have in mind relied exclusively on wholesale markets for funding, we focus on this kind of equilibrium. In particular, we restrict attention to model parameterization which generate an equilibrium where the conditions for the following Lemma 1 are satisfied:

Lemma 1 *$d^w_t = 0, b^w_t > 0$ and the incentive constraint is binding if and only if*

$$0 < \omega E_t\left[\Omega^w_{t+1}\left(R^w_{kt+1} - R_{t+1}\right)\right] < E_t\left[\Omega^w_{t+1}\left(R^w_{kt+1} - R_{bt+1}\right)\right] < \theta\omega$$

We first explain why $d^w_t = 0$ in this instance. The wholesale bank faces the following trade-off in using retail deposits: If the deposit interest rate is lower than the interbank

[v] We do not mean to suggest that the only reason retail banks make nonfinancial loans in practice is because wholesale banks are constrained. Rather we focus on this case for simplicity of the basic model. Later we extend the model to allow for a second type of lending, which we refer to as commercial and industrial lending, where retail banks have a comparative advantage. In this instance, spillovers emerge where problems in wholesale banking can affect the degree of intermediation of commercial and industrial loans.

interest rate so that $E_t[\Omega^w_{t+1}(R^w_{kt+1} - R_{t+1})] > E_t[\Omega^w_{t+1}(R^w_{kt+1} - R_{bt+1})]$, then the bank gains from issuing deposits to reduce interbank loans. On the other hand, because households are less efficient in monitoring wholesale bank behavior, they will apply a tighter limit on the amount they are willing to lend than will retail banks. If ω is sufficiently low so that $\omega E_t[\Omega^w_{t+1}(R^w_{kt+1} - R_{t+1})] < E_t[\Omega^w_{t+1}(R^w_{kt+1} - R_{bt+1})]$, the cost exceeds the benefit. In this instance, the wholesale bank does not use retail deposits, relying entirely on interbank borrowing for external finance. Everything else equal, by not issuing retail deposits, the wholesale bank is able to raise its overall leverage in order to make more nonfinancial loans relative to its equity base. This incentive consideration accounts for why the wholesale bank may prefer interbank borrowing to issuing deposits, even if the interbank rate lies above the deposit rate.[w]

Next we explain why the incentive constraint is binding. If $E_t[\Omega^w_{t+1}(R^w_{kt+1} - R_{bt+1})] < \theta\omega$, then at the margin the wholesale bank gains by borrowing on the interbank market and then diverting funds to its own account. Accordingly, as the incentive constraint (14) requires, rational creditor banks will restrict lending to the point where the gain from diverting equals the bank franchise value, which is what the wholesale bank would lose if it cheated.

Given Lemma 1 we can simplify the evolution of bank net worth to

$$n^w_{t+1} = [(R^w_{kt+1} - R_{bt+1})\phi^w_t + R_{bt+1}]n^w_t \tag{19}$$

where ϕ^w_t is given by

$$\phi^w_t \equiv \frac{Q_t k^w_t}{n^w_t}. \tag{20}$$

We refer to this ratio of assets to net worth as the leverage multiple.

In turn, we can simplify the wholesale banks optimization problem to choosing the leverage multiple to solve:

$$V^w_t = \max_{\phi^w_t} E_t\{\Omega^w_{t+1}[(R^w_{kt+1} - R_{bt+1})\phi^w_t + R_{bt+1}]n^w_t\} \tag{21}$$

subject to the incentive constraint

$$\theta[\omega\phi^w_t + (1-\omega)]n^w_t \le V^w_t \tag{22}$$

[w] Under our baseline parametrization, wholesale banks borrow exclusively from retail banks. We view this as the case that best corresponds to the wholesale banking system on the eve of the Great Recession. Circumstances do exist where wholesale banks will borrow from households as well as retail banks. One might interpret his situation as corresponding to the consolidation of wholesale and retail bank in the wake of the crisis, or perhaps the period before the rapid growth of wholesale banking when retail banks were performing many of the same activities as we often observe in continental Europe and Japan.

Given the incentive constraint is binding under Lemma 1, we can combine the objective with the binding incentive constraint to obtain the following solution for ϕ_t^w:

$$\phi_t^w = \frac{E_t(\Omega_{t+1}^w R_{bt+1}) - \theta(1-\omega)}{\theta\omega - E_t[\Omega_{t+1}^w (R_{kt+1}^w - R_{bt+1})]} \tag{23}$$

Note that ϕ_t^w is increasing in $E_t(\Omega_{t+1}^w R_{kt+1}^w)$ and decreasing in $E_t(\Omega_{t+1}^w R_{bt+1})$.[x] Intuitively, the franchise value V_t^w increases when returns on assets are higher and decreases when the cost of funding asset purchases rises, as Eq. (21) indicates. Increases in V_t^w, in turn, relax the incentive constraint, making lenders will to supply more credit.

Also, ϕ_t^w is a decreasing function of both θ, the diversion rate on nonfinancial loans funded by net worth, and ω, the parameter that controls the relative ease of diverting nonfinancial loans funded by interbank borrowing relative to those funded by the other means: Increases in either parameter tighten the incentive constraint, inducing lenders to cut back on the amount of credit they supply. Later we will use the inverse relationship between ϕ_t^w and ω to help account for the growth in both leverage and size of the wholesale banking sector.

Finally, from Eq. (21) we obtain an expression from the franchise value per unit of net worth

$$\frac{V_t^w}{n_t^w} = E_t\{\Omega_{t+1}^w[(R_{kt+1}^w - R_{bt+1})\phi_t^w + R_{bt+1}]\} \tag{24}$$

where ϕ_t^w is given by Eq. (23) and Ω_{t+1}^w is given by Eq. (16). It is straightforward to show that $\frac{V_t^w}{n_t^w}$ exceeds unity: ie, the shadow value of a unit of net worth is greater than one, since additional net worth permits the bank to borrow more and invest in assets earning an excess return. In addition, as we conjectured earlier, $\frac{V_t^w}{n_t^w}$ depend only on aggregate variables and not on bank-specific ones.

3.3.2 Retail banks

As with wholesale banks, we choose a parametrization where the incentive constraint binds. In addition, as discussed earlier, we restrict attention to the case where retail banks are holding both nonfinancial and interbank loans. In particular, we consider a parametrization where in equilibrium Lemma 2 is satisfied

[x] This is because $E_t(\Omega_{t+1}^w R_{kt+1}^w) > 1 > \theta$ in equilibrium as shown in Appendix.

Lemma 2 *$b_t^r < 0$, $k_t^r > 0$ and the incentive constraint is binding if and only if*

$$0 < E_t[\Omega_{t+1}^r(R_{kt+1}^r - R_{t+1})] = \frac{1}{\gamma}E_t[\Omega_{t+1}^r(R_{bt+1} - R_{t+1})] < \theta$$

For the retail bank to be indifferent between holding nonfinancial loans vs interbank loans, the rate on interbank loans R_{bt+1} must lie below the rate earned on nonfinancial loans R_{kt+1}^r in a way that satisfies the conditions for the lemma. Intuitively, the advantage for the retail bank to making an interbank loan is that households are willing to lend more to the bank per unit of net worth than for a nonfinancial loan. Thus to make the retail bank indifferent, R_{bt+1} must be less than R_{kt+1}^r.

Let ϕ_t^r be a retail bank's effective leverage multiple, namely the ratio of assets to net worth, where assets are weighted by the relative ease of diversion:

$$\phi_t^r \equiv \frac{(Q_t + f_t^r)k_t^r + \gamma(-b_t^r)}{n_t^r}. \tag{25}$$

The weight γ on $(-b_t^r)$ is the ratio of how much a retail banker can divert from interbank loans relative to nonfinancial loans.

Given the restrictions implied by Lemma 2, we can use the same procedure as in the case of wholesale bankers to express the retail banker's optimization problem as choosing ϕ_t^r to solve:

$$V_t^r = \max_{\phi_t^r} E_t\{\Omega_{t+1}^r[(R_{kt+1}^r - R_{t+1})\phi_t^r + R_{t+1}]n_t^r\} \tag{26}$$

subject to

$$\theta\phi_t^r n_t^r \leq V_t^r$$

Given Lemma 2, we can impose that incentive constraint binds, which implies

$$\phi_t^r = \frac{E_t(\Omega_{t+1}^r R_{t+1})}{\theta - E_t[\Omega_{t+1}^r(R_{kt+1}^r - R_{t+1})]}. \tag{27}$$

As with the leverage multiple for wholesale bankers, ϕ_t^r is increasing in expected asset returns on the bank's portfolio and decreasing in the diversion parameter.

Finally, from Eq. (26) we obtain an expression for the franchise value per unit of net worth

$$\frac{V_t^r}{n_t^r} = E_t\{\Omega_{t+1}^r[(R_{kt+1}^r - R_{t+1})\phi_t^r + R_{t+1}]\} \tag{28}$$

As with wholesale banks, the shadow value of a unit of net worth exceeds unity and depends only on aggregate variables.

3.4 Aggregation and Equilibrium without Bank Runs

Given that the ratio of assets and liabilities to net worth is independent of individual bank-specific factors and given a parametrization where the conditions in Lemma 1 and 2 are satisfied, we can aggregate across banks to obtain relations between total assets and net worth for both the wholesale and retail banking sectors. Let $Q_t K_t^w$ and $Q_t K_t^r$ be total nonfinancial loans held by wholesale and retail banks, D_t be retail bank deposits, B_t be total interbank debt, and N_t^w and N_t^r total net worth in each respective banking sector. Then we have:

$$Q_t K_t^w = \phi_t^w N_t^w, \tag{29}$$

$$(Q_t + f_t^r) K_t^r + \gamma B_t = \phi_t^r N_t^r, \tag{30}$$

with

$$Q_t K_t^w = N_t^w + B_t, \tag{31}$$

$$(Q_t + f_t^r) K_t^r + B_t = D_t^r + N_t^r, \tag{32}$$

and

$$E_t[\Omega_{t+1}^r (R_{kt+1}^r - R_{t+1})] = \frac{1}{\gamma} E_t[\Omega_{t+1}^r (R_{bt+1} - R_{t+1})]. \tag{33}$$

Eq. (33) ensures that the retail bank is indifferent at the margin between holding non-financial loans vs interbank loans (see Lemma 2).

Summing across both surviving and entering bankers yields the following expression for the evolution of N_t :

$$N_t^w = \sigma^w [(R_{kt}^w - R_{bt}) \phi_{t-1}^w + R_{bt}] N_{t-1}^w + W^w, \tag{34}$$

$$\begin{aligned} N_t^r = {} & \sigma^r [(R_{kt}^r - R_t) \phi_{t-1}^r + R_t] N_{t-1}^r + W^r \\ & + \sigma^r \left[R_{bt} - R_t - \gamma (R_{kt}^r - R_t) \right] B_{t-1}, \end{aligned} \tag{35}$$

where $W^j = (1 - \sigma^j) w^j$ is the total endowment of entering bankers. The first term is the accumulated net worth of bankers that operated at $t - 1$ and survived to t, which is equal to the product of the survival rate σ^j and the net earnings on bank assets.

Total consumption of bankers equals the sum of the net worth of exiting bankers in each sector:

$$C_t^b = (1 - \sigma^w) \frac{N_t^w - W^w}{\sigma^w} + (1 - \sigma^r) \frac{N_t^r - W^r}{\sigma^r} \tag{36}$$

Total gross output $\bar{Y}_t$ is the sum of output from capital, household endowment $Z_t W^h$ and bank endowment W^r and W^i :

$$\bar{Y}_t = Z_t + Z_t W^h + W^r + W^i. \tag{37}$$

Net output Y_t, which we will refer to simply as output, equals gross output minus management costs

$$Y_t = \bar{Y}_t - [F^h(K_t^h) + F^r(K_t^r)] \tag{38}$$

Eq. (38) captures in a simple way how intermediation of assets by wholesale banks improves aggregate efficiency. Finally, output is consumed by households and bankers:

$$Y_t = C_t^h + C_t^b. \tag{39}$$

The recursive competitive equilibrium without bank runs consists of aggregate quantities,

$$\left(K_t^w, K_t^r, K_t^h, B_t, D_t^r, N_t^w, N_t^r, C_t^b, C_t^h, \bar{Y}_t, Y_t\right),$$

prices

$$\left(Q_t, R_{t+1}, R_{bt+1}, f_t^r\right)$$

and bankers' variables

$$\left(\Omega_t^j, R_{kt}^j, \frac{V_t^j}{n_t^j}, \phi_t^j\right)_{j=w,r}$$

as a function of the state variables $\left(K_{t-1}^w, K_{t-1}^r, R_{bt}B_{t-1}, R_t D_{t-1}^w, R_t D_{t-1}^r, Z_t\right)$, which satisfy Eqs. (1, 4, 7, 8, 16, 18, 23, 24, and 27–39).[y]

3.5 Unanticipated Bank Runs

In this section we consider unanticipated bank runs. We defer an analysis of anticipated bank runs to Section 5. In general, three types of runs are conceivable: (i) a run on wholesale banks leaving retail banks intact, (ii) a run on just retail banks, and (iii) a run on both the wholesale and retail bank sectors. We restrict attention to (i) because it corresponds most closely to what happened in practice.

3.5.1 Conditions for a Wholesale Bank Run Equilibrium

The runs we consider are runs on the entire wholesale banking system, not on individual wholesale banks. Indeed, so long as an asset firesale by an individual wholesale bank is not large enough to affect asset prices, it is only runs on the system that will be disruptive. Given the homogeneity of wholesale banks in our model, the conditions for a run on the wholesale banking system will apply to each individual wholesale bank.

What we have in mind for a run is a spontaneous failure of the bank's creditors to roll over their short-term loans[z]. In particular, at the beginning of period t, before the

[y] In total we have a system of 23 equations. Notice that (16 and 18) have two equations. By Walras' law, the household budget constraint (6) is satisfied as long as deposit market clears as $D_t = D_t^r$.

[z] The approach follows Cole and Kehoe's (2000) model of self fulfilling debt crises.

realization of returns on bank assets, retail banks lending to a wholesale bank decide whether to roll over their loans with the bank. If they choose to "run," the wholesale bank liquidates its capital and turns the proceeds over to its retail bank creditors who then either acquire the capital or sell it to households. Importantly, both the retail banks and households cannot seamlessly acquire the capital being liquidated in the firesale by wholesale banks. The retail banks face a capital constraint which limits asset acquisition and are also less efficient at managing the capital than are wholesale banks. Households can only hold the capital directly and are even less efficient than retail banks in doing so.

Let Q_t^* be the price of capital in the event of a forced liquidation of the wholesale banking system. Then a run on the entire wholesale bank sector is possible if the liquidation value of wholesale banks assets, $(Z_t + Q_t^*)K_{t-1}^w$, is smaller than their outstanding liability to interbank creditors, $R_{bt}B_{t-1}$, so that liquidation would wipe out wholesale banks networth. In this instance, the recovery rate in the event of a wholesale bank run, x_t^w, is the ratio of $(Z_t + Q_t^*)K_{t-1}^w$ to $R_{bt}B_{t-1}$ and the condition for a bank run equilibrium to exist is that the recovery rate is less than unity, ie,

$$x_t^w = \frac{(Q_t^* + Z_t)K_{t-1}^w}{R_{bt}B_{t-1}} < 1. \tag{40}$$

Let R_{kt}^{w*} be the return on bank assets conditional on a run at t :

$$R_{kt}^{w*} \equiv \frac{Z_t + Q_t^*}{Q_{t-1}},$$

Then from (40), we can obtain a simple condition for a wholesale bank run equilibrium in terms of just two endogenous variables: (i) the ratio of R_{kt}^{w*} to the interbank borrowing rate R_{bt} and (ii) the leverage multiple ϕ_{t-1}^w :

$$x_t^w = \frac{R_{kt}^{w*}}{R_{bt}} \cdot \frac{\phi_{t-1}^w}{\phi_{t-1}^w - 1} < 1 \tag{41}$$

A bank run equilibrium exists if the realized rate of return on bank assets conditional on liquidation of assets R_{kt}^{w*} is sufficiently low relative to the gross interest rate on interbank loans, R_{bt}, and the leverage multiple is sufficiently high to satisfy condition (41). Note that the expression $\frac{\phi_{t-1}^w}{\phi_{t-1}^w - 1}$ is the ratio of bank assets $Q_{t-1}K_{t-1}^w$ to interbank borrowing B_{t-1}, which is decreasing in the leverage multiple. Also note that the condition for a run does not depend on individual bank-specific factors since R_{kt}^{w*}/R_{bt} and ϕ_{t-1}^w are the same for all in equilibrium.

Since R_{kt}^{w*}, R_{bt} and ϕ_{t-1}^w are all endogenous variables, the possibility of a bank run may vary with macroeconomic conditions. The equilibrium absent bank runs (that we described earlier) determines the behavior of R_{bt} and ϕ_{t-1}^w. The value of R_{kt}^{w*}, instead, depends on the liquidation price Q_t^*, whose determination is described in the next subsection.

3.5.2 The Liquidation Price

To determine Q_t^* we proceed as follows. A run by interbank creditors at t induces all wholesale banks that carried assets from $t-1$ to fully liquidate their asset positions and go out of business.[aa] Accordingly they sell all their assets to retail banks and households, who hold them at t. The wholesale banking system then rebuilds itself overtime as new banks enter. For the asset firesale during the panic run to be quantitatively significant, we need there to be at least a modest delay in the ability of new banks to begin operating. Accordingly, we suppose that new wholesale banks cannot begin operating until the period after the panic run.[ab]

Accordingly, when wholesale banks liquidate, they sell all their assets to retail banks and households in the wake of the run at date t, implying

$$\bar{K} = K_t^r + K_t^h. \tag{42}$$

The wholesale banking system then rebuilds its equity and assets as new banks enter at $t+1$ onwards. Given our timing assumptions and Eq. (34), bank net worth evolves in the periods after the run according to

$$N_{t+1}^w = (1+\sigma^w)W^w,$$

$$N_{t+i}^w = \sigma^w[(Z_{t+i} + Q_{t+i})K_{t+i-1}^w - R_{bt+i}B_{t+i-1}] + W^w, \text{ for all } i \geq 2.$$

Rearranging the Euler equation for the household's capital holding (8) yields the following expression for the liquidation price in terms of discounted dividends Z_{t+i} net the marginal management cost $\alpha^h K_{t+i}^h$.

$$Q_t^* = E_t\left[\sum_{i=1}^{\infty} \Lambda_{t,t+i}(Z_{t+i} - \alpha^h K_{t+i}^h)\right] - \alpha^h K_t^h. \tag{43}$$

Everything else equal, the longer it takes for the banking sector to recapitalize (measured by the time it takes K_{t+i}^h to fall back to steady state), the lower will be the liquidation price. Note also that Q_t^* will vary with cyclical conditions. In particular, a negative shock to Z_t will reduce Q_t^*, possibly moving the economy into a regime where bank runs are possible.

[aa] Our notion of the liquidation price is related to Brunnermeier and Pedersen's (2009) concept of market liquidity. See Uhlig (2010) for an alternative bank run model with endogenous liquidation prices.

[ab] Suppose for example that during the run it is not possible for retail banks to identify new wholesale banks that are financially independent of the wholesale banks being run on. New wholesale banks accordingly wait for the dust to settle and then begin raising fund in the interbank market in the subsequent period. The results are robust to alternative timing assumptions about the entry of new banks.

4. NUMERICAL EXPERIMENTS

In this section, we examine how the long run properties of the model can account for the growth of the wholesale banking sector and then turn to studying the cyclical responses to macroeconomic shocks that may or may not induce runs. Overall these numerical examples provide a description of the tradeoff between growth and stability associated with an expansion of the shadow banking sector and illustrate the real effects of bank runs in our model.

4.1 Calibration

Here, we describe our baseline calibration. This is meant to capture the state of the economy at the onset of the financial crisis in 2007.

There are 13 parameters in the model:

$$\{\theta,\omega,\gamma,\beta,\alpha^h,\alpha^r,\sigma^r,\sigma^w,W^h,W^r,W^w,Z,\rho_z\}.$$

their values are reported in Table 2, while Table 3 shows the steady state values of the equilibrium allocation.

We take the time interval in the model to be a quarter. We use conventional values for households' discount factor, $\beta = 0.99$, and the serial correlation of dividends $\rho_z = 0.9$. We normalize the steady state level of productivity Z in order for the price of loans to be unity and set W^h so that households endowment income is twice as big as their capital income.

We calibrate managerial costs of intermediating capital for households and retail bankers, α^h and α^r, in order for the spread between the deposit rate and retail bankers' returns on loans as well as the difference between wholesale bankers and retail bankers returns on loans to be 1.2% in annual in steady state.[ac]

The fraction of divertible interbank loans $\theta\gamma$ is set in order to obtain an annualized steady state spread between deposit and interbank rates of 0.8%. The fraction of divertible assets purchased by raising deposits, θ, and interbank loans, $\omega\theta$, are set in order to get leverage ratios for retail bankers and wholesale bankers of 10 and 20, respectively.

Our retail banking sector comprises of commercial banks, open end Mutual Funds and Money Market Mutual Funds (MMMF). In the case of Mutual Funds and MMMF the computation of leverage is complicated by the peculiar legal and economic details of the relationship between these institutions, their outside investors and sponsors.[ad] Hence, our choice of 10 quite closely reflects the actual leverage ratios of commercial banks,

[ac] Philippon (2015) calculates interest rate spreads charged by financial institutions to be around 200 basis points.

[ad] On the relationship between MMFs and their sponsors see, for instance, Parlatore (2015) and McCabe (2010).

Table 2 Baseline parameters

	Parameters	
Households		
β	Discount rate	0.99
α^h	Intermediation cost	0.03
W^h	Endowment	0.006
Retail banks		
σ^r	Survival probability	0.96
σ^r	Intermediation cost	0.0074
W^r	Endowment	0.0008
θ	Divertable proportion of assets	0.25
γ	Shrinkage of divertable proportion of interbank loans	0.67
Wholesale banks		
σ^w	Survival probability	0.88
σ^w	Intermediation cost	0
W^w	Endowment	0.0008
ω	Shrinkage of divertable proportion of assets	0.46
Production		
z	Steady state productivity	0.016
ρ_z	Serial correlation of productivity shocks	0.9

Table 3 Baseline steady state

	Steady state	
Q	Price of capital	1
K^r	Retail intermediation	0.4
K^w	Wholesale intermediation	0.4
R^b	Annual interbank rate	1.048
R_r^k	Annual retail return on capital	1.052
R	Annual deposit rate	1.04
R_w^k	Annual wholesale return on capital	1.064
ϕ^w	Wholesale leverage	20
ϕ^r	Retail leverage	10
Y	Output	0.0229
C^h	Consumption	0.0168
N^r	Retail banks networth	0.0781
N^w	Wholesale banks networth	0.02

which is the only sector for which a direct empirical counterpart of leverage can be easily computed.

To set our target for wholesale leverage we decided to focus on private institutions within the wholesale banking sector that relied mostly on short-term debt. A reasonable range for the leverage multiple for such institutions goes from around 10 for some ABCP issuers[ae] to values of around 40 for brokers dealers in 2007. Our choice of 20 is a conservative target within this range.

The survival rates of wholesale and retail bankers, σ^w and σ^r, are set in order for the distribution of assets across sectors to match the actual distribution in 2007. Finally, we set W^r to make new entrants net worth being equal to 1% of total retail banks net worth and W^w to ensure that wholesale bankers are perfectly specialized.

4.2 Long Run Effects of Financial Innovation

As mentioned in Section 2, the role of wholesale banks in financial intermediation has grown steadily from the 1980s to the onset of the financial crisis. This growth was largely accomplished through a series of financial innovations that enhanced the borrowing capacity of the system by relying on securitization to attract funds from institutional investors. While our model abstracts from the details of the securitization process, we capture its direct effects on wholesale banks' ability of raising funds in interbank markets with a reduction in the severity of the agency friction between retail banks and wholesale banks, which is captured by parameter ω. Hence, in this section we study the long run behavior of financial intermediation in response to a decrease in ω and compare it to the low frequency dynamics in financial intermediation documented in Section 2.

The direct effect of ameliorating the agency problem between wholesale and retail banks is a relaxation of wholesale banks' incentive constraints. The improved ability of retail banks to seize the assets of wholesale bankers in the case of cheating allows wholesale bankers to borrow more aggressively from retail bankers.

Fig. 8 shows how some key variables depend upon ω in the steady state.[af] The general equilibrium effects of a lower ω work through various channels. For an economy with a lower interbank friction ω, the leverage multiple of the wholesale banking sector is higher, with a larger capital K^w and a larger amount interbank borrowing B by wholesale banks. Conversely, capital intermediated by retail banks K^r and households K^h tends to be lower. In the absence of bank runs, the relative shift of assets to the wholesale banking sector implies a more efficient allocation of capital and consequently a higher capital price

[ae] The same caveat as in the case of MMFs applies here because it is very complicated to factor in the various lines of credit that were provided by the sponsors of these programs.

[af] Notice that as ω increases above a certain threshold, two other types of equilibria arise: one in which wholesale bankers are imperfectly specialized and raise funds in both wholesale and retail markets; and one in which the interbank market shuts down completely. See the Appendices for details.

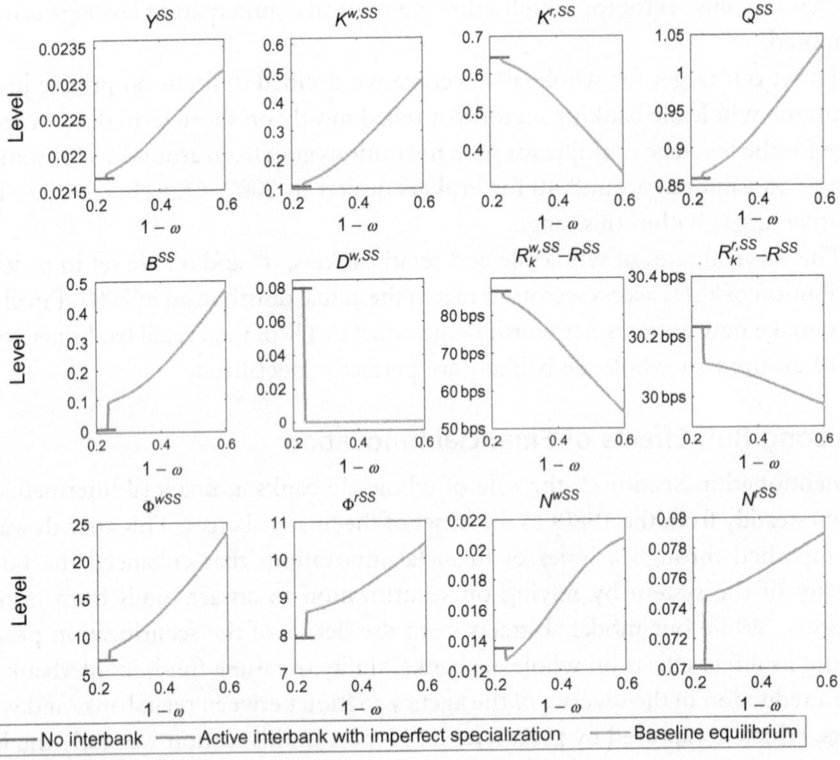

Fig. 8 Comparative statics: a reduction in ω.

Q_t. The flow of assets into wholesale banking, further, reduces the spread between the return on capital for wholesale banks and the interbank rate, as well as the spread between interbank and deposit rates. Despite lower spreads, both wholesale and retail banks enjoy higher franchise values thanks to the positive effect of higher leverage on total returns on equity. A unique aspect of financial innovation due to a lower friction in the interbank market is that the borrowing and lending among banks tends to be larger relative to the flow-of-funds from ultimate lenders (households) to ultimate nonfinancial borrowers. (See Appendix B).

Fig. 9 compares the steady state effect of financial innovations on some key measures of financial intermediation with the observed low frequency trends in their empirical counterparts. In particular, we assume that the value of ω in our baseline calibration results from a sequence of financial innovations that took place gradually from the 1980s to the financial crisis. For simplicity, we divide our sample into 2 periods of equal length and assign a value of ω to each subsample in order to match the observed percentage of intermediation of wholesale bankers over the period. In order to compute leverage of wholesale banks in Fig. 9, we compute leverage of the three sectors within the wholesale banking sector that were mainly responsible for the growth of wholesale

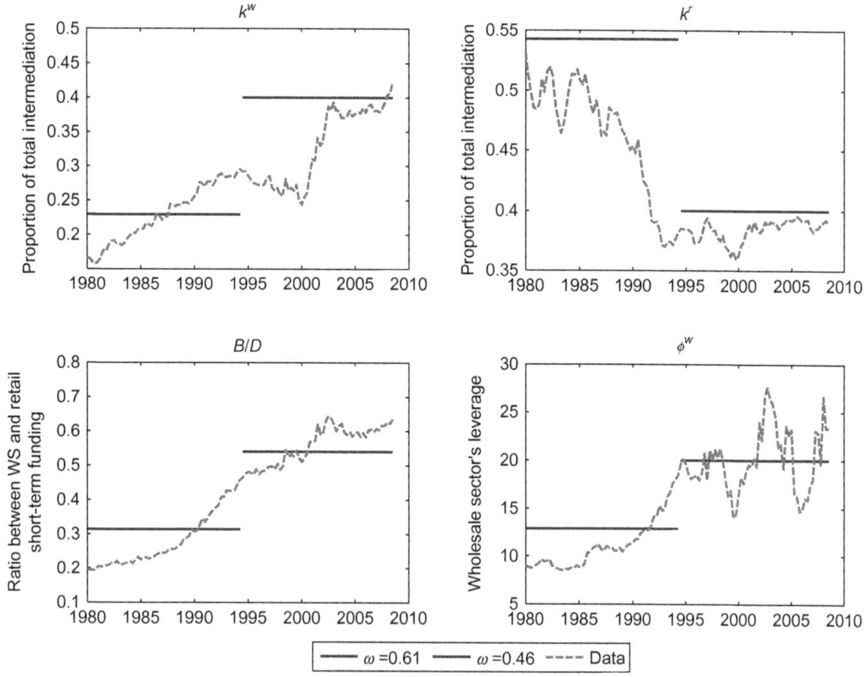

Fig. 9 Low frequency dynamics in financial intermediation.

intermediation. Overall, the steady state comparative statics capture quite well the actual low frequency dynamics in financial intermediation observed over the past few decades.[ag]

4.3 Recessions and Runs

We now turn to the cyclical behavior of our model economy. Fig. 10 shows the response of the economy to an unanticipated negative 6% shock to productivity Z_t, assuming that a run does not happen.[ah] To capture the effects of financial liberalization on the cyclical properties of the economy, we consider both our baseline parameterization and one with a higher ω which we set to be equal to the one associated with the early 1980s in Fig. 9. In both cases the presence of financial constraints activates the familiar financial accelerator mechanism of Bernanke and Gertler (1989) and Kiyotaki and Moore (1997). Leverage amplifies the effects of the drop in Z_t on bankers' net worth, inducing a tightening of

[ag] The model overstatement of the role of retail intermediation relative to household direct holding of assets can be rationalized by the lack of heterogeneity in ultimate borrowers' funding sources since, in the data, households mainly hold equities while intermediaries are responsible for most debt intermediation. Introducing a different type of asset for which intermediaries have a smaller advantage would then help to reconcile the evolution of the distribution of capital across sectors predicted by the model in response to financial innovation with the empirical one.

[ah] We choose the size of the shock to generate a fall in output similar to the one that occurred during the Great Recession.

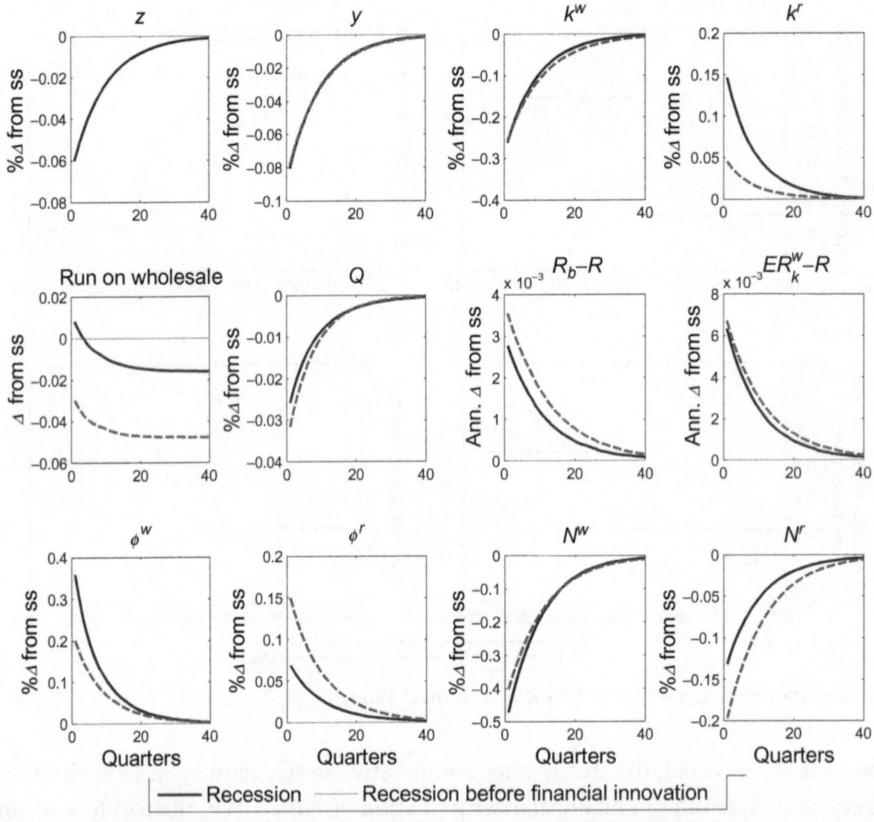

Fig. 10 A recession before and after financial innovation (NO RUN EQUILIBRIUM).

financial constraints, as reflected by an increase in credit spreads. In turn, wholesale banks sell off loans, which reduces asset prices and feeds back into lower net worth. Higher exposure to variations in Z_t and higher leverage make this effect stronger for wholesale banks that are forced into a firesale liquidation of their assets, which in turn leads them to reduce their demand for interbank loans. As a result, retail bankers increase their asset holdings and absorb, together with households, the capital flowing out of the wholesale banking sector.[ai] However, the relative inefficiency of these agents in intermediating assets makes this process costly as shown by the rise in the cost of bank credit and the amplification in the drop in output. Under our baseline calibration, spreads between gross borrowing costs for nonfinancial borrowers and the risk free rate increase by sixty basis points and output drops by 8%, which is two percentage points greater than the drop in Z_t.[aj]

[ai] The increase in households' capital holding is consistent with the shift from intermediated to unintermediated capital observed during the crisis. See, eg, Adrian et al (2012) for evidence.

[aj] Observe also that in a production economy with investment and nominal rigidities, the drop in the asset price would reduce investment and thus aggregate demand, magnifying the overall drop in output.

As we noted earlier, financial innovation makes the economy operate more efficiently in steady state. Fig. 10 shows that, absent bank runs, it also makes the economy more stable as the financial accelerator weakens. In response to the drop in Z_t, the economy with financial innovation features smaller increases in credit spreads and a smaller drop in assets prices. Intuitively, with financial innovation, retail banks provide a stronger buffer to absorb loan sales by wholesale banks, which helps stabilize asset prices. At the same time, the economy with financial innovation is more vulnerable to a bank run.

This is illustrated by the panel titled "Run on Wholesale" in Fig. 10. In this panel we plot a variable that indicates at each time t whether a run is possible at time $t+1$. To construct this variable we define

$$Run_t^w = 1 - x_t^w$$

where x_t^w is the recovery rate on wholesale debt. Hence, in order for a run to exist the run variable must be positive.

As shown by the Run^w variable, a run on wholesale banks is not possible in the steady state under both parameterization considered. With a 6% drop in Z_t, a run equilibrium remains impossible in the economy absent financial innovation, ie, the one with a high value of ω. However, for the economy with financial innovation (ie, a low ω), the same drop in Z_t is big enough to make a run on wholesale banking possible. Intuitively, in the low ω economy, wholesale bank leverage ratios are higher than would be otherwise, and asset liquidation values are lower, which raises the likelihood that the conditions for a bank run equilibrium will be satisfied.

Fig. 11 describes the effects of bank runs. In particular we assume that two periods after the unanticipated drop in Z_t, retail investors stop rolling over short-term debt issued by wholesale banks, inducing them to liquidate all of their assets and go bankrupt.

As explained in Section 3.5.1, the run on wholesale banks forces them into bankruptcy and results in K^w dropping to 0. Households and retail banks are forced to absorb all of the wholesale banks' assets, inducing asset prices to drop by about 7% in total. The intermediation costs associated with the reallocation of assets to less efficient agents leads to an additional contraction of output of around 7%, resulting in an overall drop of about 15%.

As new wholesale bankers resume operations from the period after the run, high levels of spreads for both retail and wholesale bankers allow them to increase their leverage and recapitalize financial intermediaries thanks to above average retained earnings. The reintermediation process, however, is rather lengthy and output remains depressed for a prolonged period of time.

5. ANTICIPATED RUNS

So far, we have focused on the case in which runs are completely unexpected. In this section we study how the equilibrium changes if agents anticipate that a run will occur

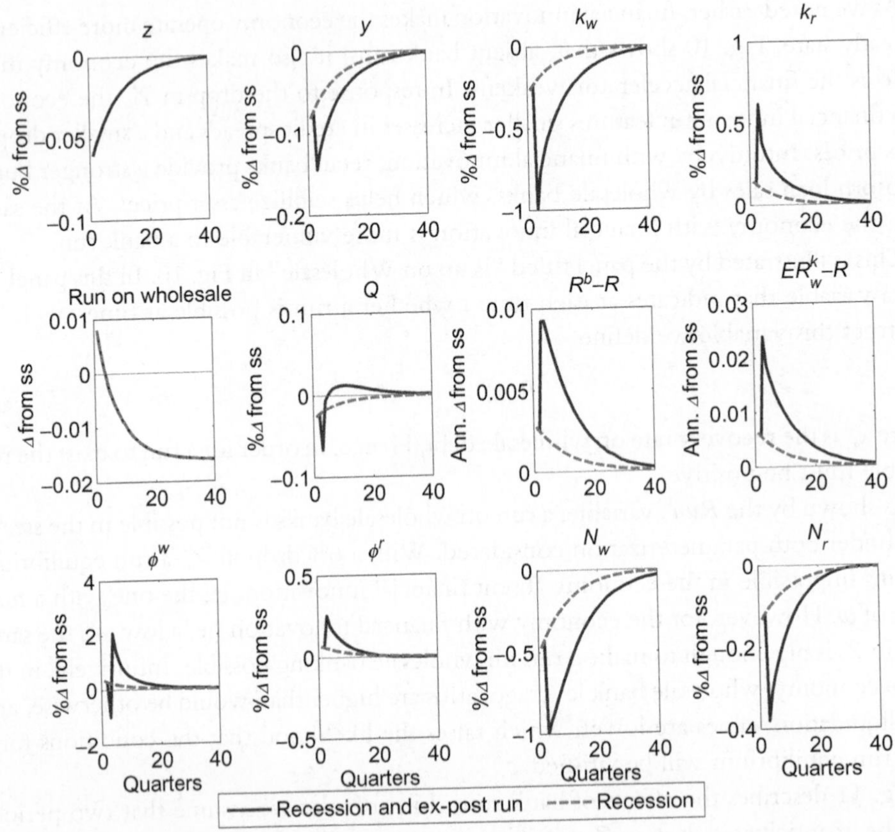

Fig. 11 A recession followed by a run on wholesale bankers.

with positive probability in the future, focusing on the more realistic case of a run on wholesale bankers only. The Appendices contains a detailed description of the equilibrium in this case.[ak] Here, we describe the key forces through which anticipation of a run in the future affects financial intermediation. To keep the analysis as simple as possible, we assume that once a negative shock to Z_t hits, Z_t obeys perfect foresight path back to steady state.

The main difference from the unanticipated case is in the market for interbank loans. In particular, once runs are anticipated, retail bankers internalize how wholesale bankers' leverage affects returns on interbank loans in case of a run and they adjust the required promised rate $\bar{R}_{bt+1}$ accordingly. We denote by p_t the time t probability that retail banks will run on wholesale banks at time $t+1$.[al] The indifference condition of the retail bank between making interbank loans and nonfinancial loans (33) becomes:

[ak] The analysis of anticipated runs draws heavily on Gertler and Kiyotaki (2015).

[al] The determination of this probability of "observing a sunspot" will be discussed later.

$$E_t[(1-p_t)\Omega^r_{t+1}(\bar{R}_{bt+1}-R_{t+1})+p_t\Omega^{r*}_{t+1}(x^w_{t+1}\bar{R}_{bt+1}-R_{t+1})] \\ =\gamma E_t[(1-p_t)\Omega^r_{t+1}(R^r_{kt+1}-R_{t+1})+p_t\Omega^{r*}_{t+1}(R^{r*}_{kt+1}-R_{t+1})], \tag{44}$$

where

$$\Omega^{r*}_{t+1}=\beta\left(1-\sigma+\sigma\frac{V^{r*}_{t+1}}{n^{r*}_{t+1}}\right)$$

is the value of the stochastic discount factor if a run occurs at $t+1$.

Using Eq. (41) to substitute for x^w_{t+1} in (44) we obtain a menu of promised rates:[am]

$$\bar{R}_{bt+1}(\phi^w_t)=(1-\gamma)R_{t+1}+\gamma\frac{E_t(\Omega^r_{t+1}R^r_{kt+1})}{E_t(\Omega^r_{t+1})}$$

$$+\frac{p_t}{(1-p_t)E_t(\Omega^r_{t+1})}E_t\left\{\Omega^{r*}_{t+1}\left[(1-\gamma)R_{t+1}+\gamma R^{r*}_{kt+1}-\frac{\phi^w}{\phi^w-1}R^{w*}_{kt+1}\right]\right\} \tag{45}$$

Notice that $\bar{R}_{bt+1}(\phi^w_t)$ is an increasing function ϕ^w_t. This is because as leverage increases, retail bankers suffer larger losses on interbank loans if a run occurs. This induces them to require higher returns in the event of no run, to compensate for the larger losses in the event of a run.

When choosing their portfolios, wholesale bankers will now have to factor in that changes in their leverage affect their cost of credit according to Eq. (45). This preserves homogeneity of the problem but the franchise value of the firm will change to reflect that with probability p_t the bank will be forced to liquidate assets at price Q^*_{t+1} in the subsequent period. This will have the effect of reducing the franchise value of wholesale banks, hence tightening their financial constraints.

In particular the franchise value of a wholesale bank will be given by[an]

$$\frac{V^w_t}{n^w_t}=(1-p_t)E_t\{\Omega^w_{t+1}[\phi^w_t(R^w_{t+1}-\bar{R}_{bt+1}(\phi^w_t))+\bar{R}_{bt+1}(\phi^w_t)]\}. \tag{46}$$

An increase in p_t reduces the franchise value through two channels: First, it decreases the likelihood that the bank will continue to operate next period. Second, it leads to an increase in the interbank loan rate each individual bank faces, $\bar{R}_{bt+1}(\phi^w_t)$, which reduces the franchise value even if the bank continues to operate.

[am] This is the relevant function for values of leverage high enough to induce bankruptcy in case of a run.

[an] Here, we are already assuming that wholesale bankers will choose a leverage high enough to result in bankruptcy when a run occurs. See the Appendices for a detailed description of the wholesale banker's problem when runs are anticipated. There, we derive the conditions that ensure that it is optimal for wholesale bankers to default in the event of a run.

In order to pin down a state dependent probability of a run, we follow Gertler and Kiyotaki (2015). In particular we assume that at each time t the probability of transitioning to a state where a run on wholesale banks occurs is given by a reduced form decreasing function of the expected recovery rate $E_t x^w_{t+1}$ as follows,

$$p_t = \left[1 - E_t(x^w_{t+1})\right]^{\delta}. \tag{47}$$

Although we don't endogenize the functional dependence of p_t on the state of the economy, the above formulation allows us to capture the idea that as wholesale balance sheet positions weaken, the likelihood of a run increases. This same qualitative conclusion would follow, for example, if the probability of a run was determined endogenously by introducing imperfect information, as in the global games approach developed by Morris and Shin (1998).[ao]

Fig. 12 demonstrates how anticipation effects work to increase financial amplification of shocks in the model. The solid line is the response of the economy to an unanticipated

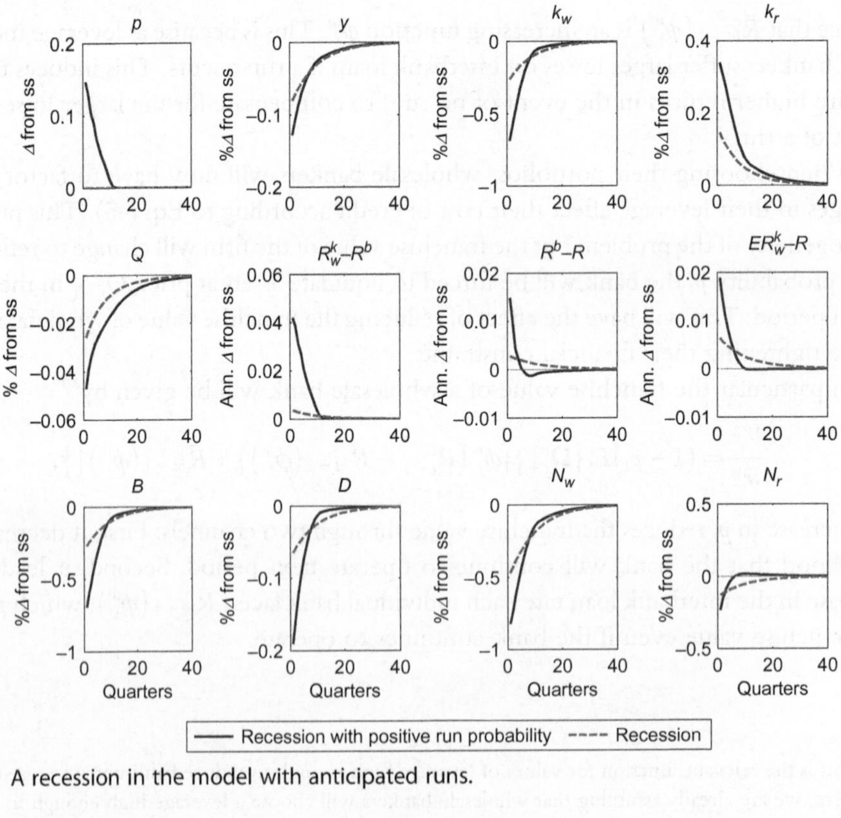

Fig. 12 A recession in the model with anticipated runs.

[ao] See Gertler et al (2016) for an alternative formulation of beliefs in a very similar setup and Goldstein and Pauzner (2005) for an application of the global games approach to bank runs.

6% shock to Z_t when agents anticipate that a run can happen at each time $t + 1$ with probability p_t as determined in Eq. (47).[ap] As we noted earlier, we assume that after the shock Z_t follows a perfect foresight path back to steady state. To isolate the effect of the anticipation of the run, we suppose in this case that the run never actually occurs ex-post. For comparison, the dotted line reports the responses of the baseline economy in which individuals assign probability zero to a bank run.

While it is still the case that in steady state a run cannot occur, the shock to Z_t leads the probability of a run to increase to 15%. As wholesale bankers' balance sheets weaken and the liquidation price decreases, retail bankers expect more losses on interbank loans in case of a run and the probability of coordinating on a run equilibrium increases as a result. The increase in p_t leads to a sharp contraction in the supply of interbank credit and a further tightening of wholesale bankers financial constraints. This, in turn, results in an overall reduction in their net worth of about 80% compared to a 50% in the baseline and to a spike in spreads between nonfinancial loan and interbank loan rates that increase by 400 basis points compared to only 30 in the baseline. As wholesale banks are forced to downsize their operations, total interbank credit falls by about 70%, more than twice the percentage drop in the baseline. These massive withdrawals of funds from wholesale markets is the model counterpart to the "slow runs" on the ABCP market in 2007. These disruptions in wholesale funding markets are then transmitted to the rest of the economy inducing a drop in asset prices of 5% and a total contraction of output of 13%.

Fig. 13 shows the case in which the run actually occurs two periods after the realization of the shock to Z_t. There are two main differences with respect to the analogous experiment performed in the case of unanticipated runs depicted in Fig. 11. First, the initial increase in the probability of a run that precedes the actual run allows the model to capture the "slow runs" followed by "fast runs" in wholesale funding markets that was a central feature of the financial crisis, as discussed in the Introduction. Second, the run induces a further increase in the probability of additional runs in the future, that goes back to about 20% the period after the run occurs. This hampers wholesale bankers ability to increase their leverage and generates higher spreads in the interbank market preventing the relatively smooth increase in asset prices that characterizes the recovery in the baseline model.

Fig. 14 shows how the model with anticipated runs can reproduce some key features of the financial disruptions that occurred in 2007 and 2008. In particular, we compare the model predicted path for interbank spreads, $\bar{R}^b_{t+1} - R_{t+1}$, and excess finance premium, $ER^w_{k,t+1} - R_{t+1}$, with their empirical counterparts over the period going from 2007Q2 to 2009Q4. For the interbank spreads we choose the ABCP spread, since the first "slow runs" in wholesale funding markets in the third quarter of 2007 took place in the ABCP market. The measure of excess borrowing costs is the Excess Bond Premium of Gilchrist

[ap] In the numerical simulations below we pick δ to be $\frac{1}{2}$.

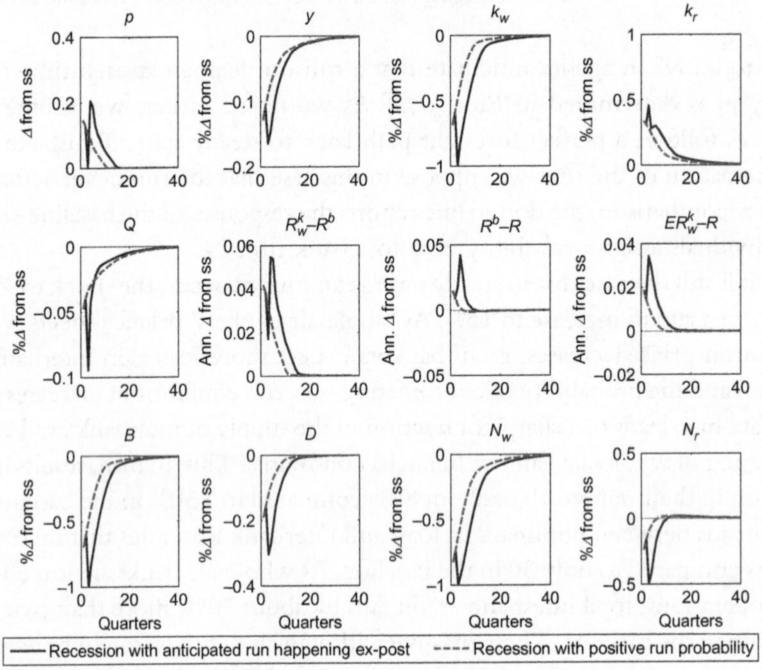

Fig. 13 A recession followed by a run in the model with anticipated runs.

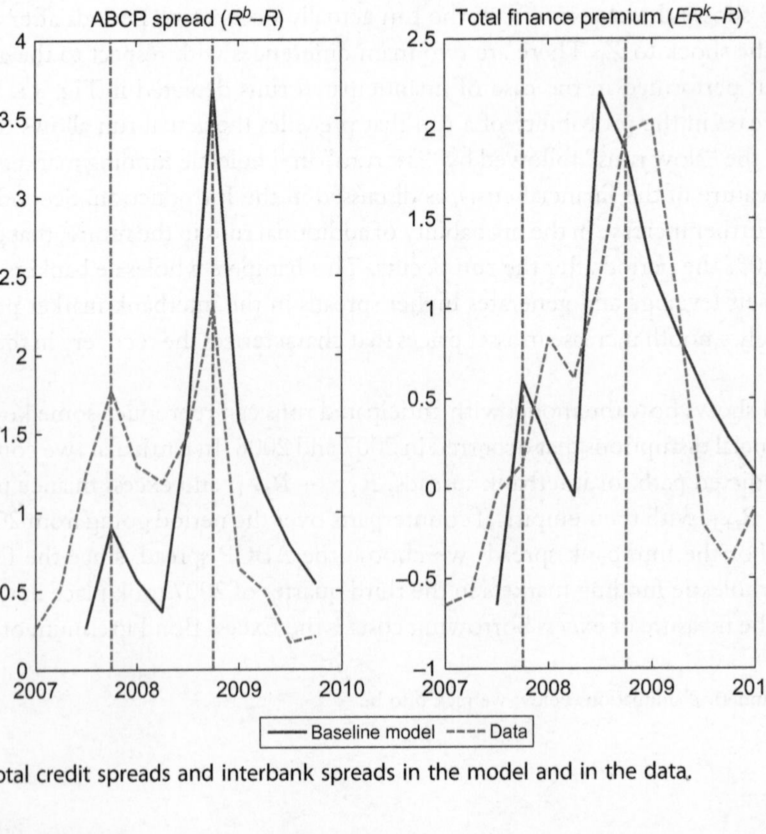

Fig. 14 Total credit spreads and interbank spreads in the model and in the data.

and Zakrajsek (2012). We assume that the economy is in steady state in 2007Q2 and the unanticipated shock hits in 2007Q3 followed by a run on wholesale banks in 2008Q3.[aq] In the data excess borrowing costs lag financial spreads, so the model predicts a stronger initial increase in $ER^{w}_{k,t+1} - R_{t+1}$ and attributes a slightly smaller proportion of the increase to interbank spreads, probably due to the behavior of the risk free rate. On the other hand, the faster decline in spreads in the data after 2009 can be attributed to the effects of government intervention in this period. Overall, the experiment can capture the credit spreads and bank equity dynamics reasonably well.

6. TWO PRODUCTIVE ASSETS AND SPILLOVER EFFECTS

In our baseline model there is only one type of capital. Wholesale banks have an efficiency advantage in holding this capital. Retail banks exist mainly because wholesale banks may be constrained by their net worth; otherwise the latter would hold all the capital. In this section we introduce a second type of capital which retail banks have an efficiency advantage in intermediating. In addition to providing a stronger motivation for the existence of retail banking, the second asset allows us to illustrate spillover effects from a crisis in wholesale banking into retail banking.

In particular, one of the salient features of the recent crisis was the strong contagion effect through which the collapse in subprime mortgage related products within the wholesale banking sector led to a deterioration in financial conditions within the commercial banking sector, ultimately affecting the flow credit through these institutions. Even though on the eve of the crisis, much of the credit provided by the retail sector had no direct reliance on shadow banks, the collapse of the latter ultimately disrupted commercial bank lending, enhancing the downturn.

As is the case with the first type of capital, we suppose the second type is fixed in supply and denote the total as $\bar{L}$. We refer to bank loans made to finance this capital as "C&I" loans (for "commercial and industrial" loans). What we have in mind are the kinds of information-intensive loans that are not easily securitized, which retail banks have historically specialized in intermediating. This contrasts with the kinds of securitized assets, involving mortgages, car loans, credit card debt, trade credit and so on, that were principally held by wholesale banks.

For simplicity, we assume that only retail banks and households fund the second type of capital. Given L^r_t and L^h_t are the amounts funded by retail banks and households, we have:

$$L^h_t + L^r_t = \bar{L} \tag{48}$$

We model retail banks' comparative advantage in making C&I loans by assuming that management costs of intermediating these loans are zero for these types of banks.

[aq] To be closer to the observed dynamics of spreads we resize the innovation to Z_t to five percentage points.

Conversely, we think of management costs for wholesale banks as being infinity. Finally, we allow households to directly fund this asset, where claims on this capital directly held by households may be thought of as corporate bonds. We suppose that households are at disadvantage to retail banks in funding the second type of capital, though at an advantage relative to wholesale banks: They must pay the management fee

$$F^L(K_t^L) = \frac{\alpha^L}{2}(K_t^L)^2$$

with $0 < \alpha^L < \infty$.

In analogy to the first type of capital, there is an exogenous dividend payout Z_t^L that obeys a stationary first order stochastic process. In addition, for simplicity we restrict attention to the case where bank runs are completely unanticipated. Accordingly, let R_{lt+1}^h be the household's rate of return from funding the second asset. Then the household's first order condition for holding the second asset is given by

$$E_t(\Lambda_{t,t+1} R_{lt+1}^h) = 1 \tag{49}$$

with

$$R_{lt+1}^h = \frac{Z_{t+1}^L + Q_{t+1}^L}{Q_t^L + \alpha_h^L L_t^h}$$

where Q_t^L is the asset price and α_h^L controls the degree of inefficiency of households in directly holding this asset.

The optimization problem of wholesale bankers is unchanged. Accordingly, we focus on retail bankers. Given retail banks now have the option of intermediating the second asset, we can rewrite the balance sheet and Flow of Funds constraints as

$$(Q_t + f_t^r)k_t^r + Q_t^L l_t^r + (-b_t^r) = n_t^r + d_t^r$$
$$n_{t+1}^r = R_{kt+1}^r (Q_t + f_t^r)k_t^r + R_{lt+1}^r Q_t^L l_t^r + R_{bt+1}(-b_t^r) - R_{t+1} d_t^r$$

where R_{lt+1}^r is the rate of return on the type L asset and is given by,

$$R_{lt+1}^r = \frac{Z_{t+1}^L + Q_{t+1}^L}{Q_t^L}.$$

Because the incentive constraint is

$$\theta[(Q_t + f_t^r)k_t^r + Q_t^L l_t^r + (-b_t^r)] \le V_t^r,$$

the effective leverage multiple for this case ϕ_t^r now includes the holdings of the second type of capital:

$$\phi_t^r \equiv \frac{(Q_t + f_t^r)k_t^r + Q_t^L l_t^r + \gamma(-b_t^r)}{n_t^r}.$$

Proceeding as earlier to solve the retail bank's maximization problem yields a solution for ϕ_t^r which is the same as in the baseline case (see Eq. (27)). In addition, at the margin the retail bank must be indifferent between holding the types of capital, which implies the following arbitrage condition:

$$E_t[\Omega_{t+1}^r (R_{lt+1}^r - R_{kt+1}^r)] = 0. \tag{50}$$

We now consider a numerical example designed to illustrate the contagion effect. The real world phenomenon that motivates the experiment is the fall in housing prices beginning in 2006 that led to the collapse of the wholesales banking sector that in turn disrupted commercial banking. In particular, we suppose that the dividend to asset L is fixed at its steady state value Z^L. Then we consider a negative shock to the dividend on the type K asset and, as in our earlier baseline experiments, allow for an unanticipated run two periods after the initial shock. Tables 4 and 5 describe the changes in the calibration for this experiment.

Table 4 Parameters in two assets model

	Parameters	
Households		
β	Discount rate	0.99
α^h	Intermediation cost	0.06
α_L^h	Intermediation cost for Cl loans	0.006
W^h	Endowment	0.016
Retail banks		
σ^r	Survival probability	0.96
α^r	Intermediation cost	0.01
α_L^r	Intermediation cost for Cl loans	0
W^r	Endowment	0.0014
θ	Divertable proportion of assets	0.27
γ	Shrinkage of divertable proportion of interbank loans	0.67
Wholesale banks		
σ^w	Survival probability	0.88
α^w	Intermediation cost	0
α_L^w	Intermediation cost for Cl loans	∞
W^w	Endowment	0.0012
ω	Shrinkage of divertable proportion of assets	0.47
Production		
Z	Steady state productivity	0.016
ρ_z	Serial correlation of productivity shocks	0.9

Table 5 Steady state in two assets model

		Steady state
Q	Price of capital	1
Q^L	Price of Cl loans	1
K^r	Retail intermediation	0.3
K^w	Wholesale intermediation	0.6
L^r	Retail holding of Cl loans	0.5
L^h	Household holding of Cl loans	0.5
R^b	Annual interbank rate	1.048
R^k_r	Annual retail return on capital	1.052
R^L_r	Annual retail return on Cl loans	1.052
R	Annual deposit rate	1.04
R^k_w	Annual wholesale return on capital	1.064
ϕ^w	Wholesale leverage	20
ϕ^r	Retail leverage	10
Y	Output	0.0466
C^h	Consumption	0.0363
N^r	Retail banks networth	0.1371
N^w	Wholesale banks networth	0.03

Fig. 15 reports the results from the experiment and demonstrates the spillover effects of shocks to Z_t on the market for L. The source of contagion in this environment is the balance sheet position of retail bankers.[ar] Losses on their capital investment and, in case of a run, on their interbank loans, result in a decrease in retail bankers' net worth and a tightening of their respective incentive constraints. As long as there are incentive costs associated with intermediating asset L, the tightening of financial constraints leads retail bankers to increase required excess returns in both markets, as shown by Eq. (50). The negative shock to returns on capital and the run on wholesale banks lead to a costly reallocation of assets to households and to an increase in spreads between returns on L_t^r and the deposit rate of about 60 basis points.

7. GOVERNMENT POLICY

In this section we study the effects of two types of policy interventions to combat banking crises: first an ex-post intervention where the central bank acts as a lender of last resort; second, an ex-ante macroprudential regulation that limits banks' risk exposure. Within the literature, these policies have largely been studied in the context of dampening negative financial accelerator effects on the economy. Here, we emphasize a somewhat

[ar] Other similar models of spillover are Bocola (2016) and Ferrante (2015b). An alternative mechanism based on market fragmentation is developed by Garleanu et al. (2015).

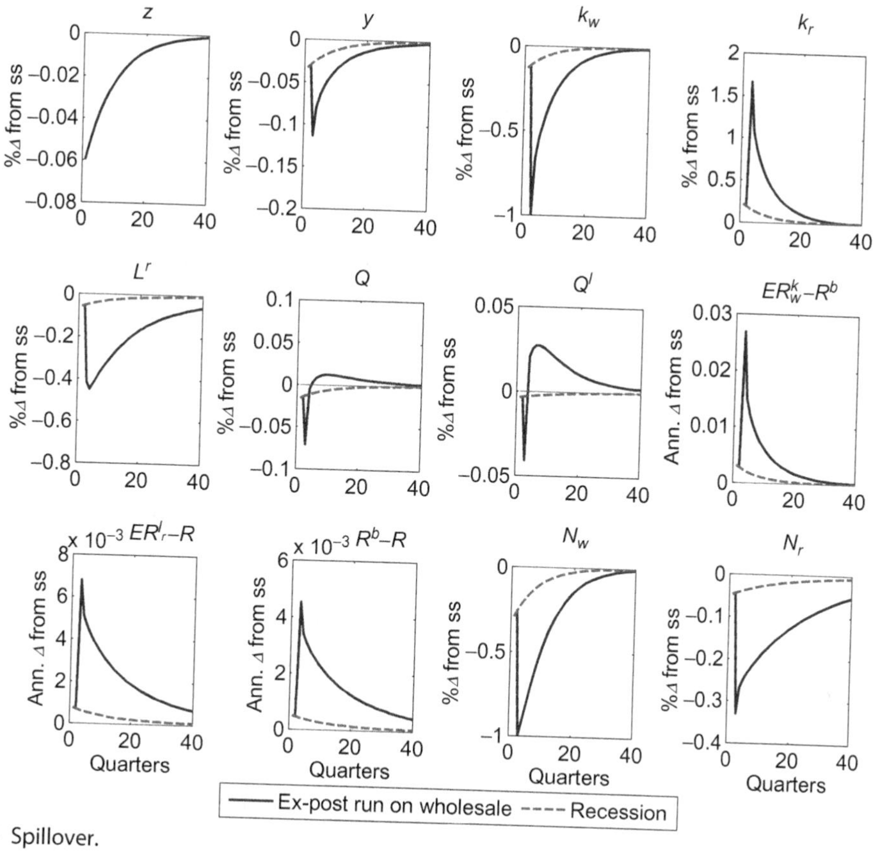

Fig. 15 Spillover.

different perspective: How these policies might be useful in reducing the likelihood of damaging bank runs? As we show, lender of last resort policy that is anticipated ex-ante in the event of an ex-post crisis reduces the likelihood of a run by raising asset liquidation prices. Macroprudential does so by reducing bank leverage.

A case for ex-ante macroprudential regulation arises because banks tend to choose an inefficiently high level of leverage in the laissez-faire economy. Roughly speaking, because individual banks ignore the consequences of their own borrowing decisions on the level of aggregate risk, they are prone to issue more debt than would be socially desirable.[as] In addition, as Farhi and Tirole (2012), Chari and Kehoe (2015), and Gertler et al. (2012) emphasize, the expectations of some type of government interventions ex-post will also encourage excessive leverage in the banking system ex-ante.

[as] See Geanakoplos and Polemarchakis (1986) for the original result of generic constrained inefficiency in a model with incomplete markets. Lorenzoni (2008) and Bianchi (2011) are recent applications to environments with financial frictions.

In this section we explore each of this kinds of policy's within our framework of Anticipated Runs of Section 5.

7.1 Ex-Post Intervention: Lender of the Last Resort

It is well known that if there are limits to arbitrage in private financial intermediation, then a central bank who plays as the lender of last resort during a financial crisis can enhance the flow of credit and in turn mitigate the economic downturn. What makes the lender of last resort effective is that the central bank can elastically obtain funds by issuing interest bearing reserves, while private financial intermediaries may be constrained in their ability to obtain funds by the condition of their balance sheets (Gertler and Karadi, 2011; Gertler and Kiyotaki, 2011).

Following the onset of the recent financial crisis, the Federal Reserve introduced a variety of lender of last resort programs. The most prominent involved large scale asset purchases (LSAPs) of high grade long-term debt, including primarily agency mortgage backed securities (AMBS), instruments that were held primarily in the shadow banking sector. The Fed announced this program in December 2008 following the collapse of the shadow banking system and began phasing it in the following March. The objective of this kind of lender of last resort intervention was to reduce the cost and thereby increase the availability of credit to the nonfinancial sector. There is evidence which suggests the Fed achieved this objective. Beyond these considerations, however, by acting as buyers in the secondary market for AMBS, the Fed raised the price and accordingly the liquidation value of these assets. As we noted, the impact of these policies on liquidation prices has important implications for banking stability. (See Eq. (40), for the condition for a bank run equilibrium.)

To model this type of intervention, we assume that the central bank can directly undertake intermediation by borrowing from retail banks and then making nonfinancial loans. The way the central bank obtains funds from retail banks is to issue interest bearing bank reserves. We assume that retail banks are unable to divert bank reserves, since they are held in an account at the Fed. Given retail banks cannot divert reserves, they are not constrained in their ability to raise deposits to fund reserves. Because there are no limits to arbitrage for banks funding reserves, the interest rate on reserves will equal the deposit rate. Therefore, when the central bank supplies interest-rate bearing reserves to retail banks, it effectively raises funds directly from households by issuing overnight government bond. What gives the central bank an advantage in intermediating assets is that, unlike retail and wholesale banks, it is not balance sheet constrained.

We also assume, following Gertler and Karadi (2011) that the central bank is less efficient than the private sector. As with retail banks and households, the government faces quadratic managerial costs $\frac{1}{2}\alpha^g (K_t^g)^2$, where K_t^g is the size of central bank's intervention and where $\alpha^h > \alpha^g > \alpha^r$. To ensure that it is desirable for the central bank to intervene only in a crisis, we also allow for inefficiency in the average performance of the government's portfolio: In particular, we assume that the return on government intermediated assets is:

$$R^g_{kt+1} = \varphi \frac{Z_{t+1} + Q_{t+1}}{Q_t + \alpha^g K^g_t} \tag{51}$$

where $\varphi \in (0,1)$ controls the relative inefficiency of central bank's intermediation for the average return on assets, independent of scale.

We assume that the central bank intervenes in credit markets whenever expected asset returns exceed its cost of borrowing. That is we posit a policy rule for central bank's intervention given by

$$\begin{aligned} K^g_t = 0, \qquad & \text{if } E_t\left(R^g_{kt+1} - R_{gt+1}\right) < 0 \\ E_t\left(R^g_{kt+1} - R_{gt+1}\right) = 0, \qquad & \text{if } K^g_t \geq 0 \end{aligned} \tag{52}$$

where R_{gt+1} is the interest paid on reserves issued to retail banks.

As we just noted, since there is no incentive problem associated with central bank intermediation, in equilibrium the interest rate on reserve R_{gt+1} must equal to the deposit rate:[at]

$$R_{gt+1} = R_{t+1}. \tag{53}$$

The key variable to which the central bank responds in determining credit market intervention is the spread between the wholesale bank's return on assets and the deposit rate, $R^w_{kt+1} - R_{t+1}$, which can be thought of as a measure of the degree of inefficiency in private financial markets. The central bank intervenes when this excess return is high.[au] In particular, the policy rule (52) prescribes that the Fed starts intermediating assets as soon as the ratio of the credit spread to the deposit rate exceeds a given threshold that varies inversely with the inefficiency parameter φ :

$$K^g_t > 0, \text{ iff } \frac{E_t(R^w_{kt+1}) - R_{t+1}}{R_{t+1}} > \frac{1-\varphi}{\varphi}.$$

[at] To see formally, first notice that, since retail bankers cannot divert reserves, their incentive constraint (14) is not affected by the amount of reserves held on their balance sheet. Hence the introduction of interest bearing reserves only affects retail bankers' optimization problem by modifying the objective function (26), which becomes

$$V^r_t = \underset{\phi^r_t, d^r_{gt}}{Max} E_t\left\{\Omega^r_{t+1}\left[\phi^r_t(R^r_{kt+1} - R_{t+1}) + R_{t+1} + d^r_{gt}(R_{gt+1} - R_{t+1})\right]n^r_t\right\}$$

where d^r_{gt} is the amount of reserves per unit of networth held by retail bankers. The optimality condition with respect to d^r_{gt} is just given by $R_{gt+1} = R_{t+1}$. Covariance terms are zero since both R_{gt+1} and R_{t+1} are known at date t.

[au] Our policy rule, which has the central bank target credit spreads, is consistent with how the central bank behaved throughout the crisis. What motivated an unconventional intervention in a given credit market was typically a sharp increase in the spread within that market.

From Eq. (52), the size of the intervention in the region where $K_t^g > 0$ is then governed by:

$$K_t^g = \frac{\varphi}{\alpha^g} Q_t \left[\frac{E_t(R_{kt+1}^w) - R_{t+1}}{R_{t+1}} - \frac{1-\varphi}{\varphi} \right].$$

We choose φ in order to ensure that the central bank only intervenes after a run happens: that is, the threshold for the credit spread to justify an intervention is reached only in the event of a run. We choose the management cost parameter α^g in order for the intervention to be around 5% of total capital.

Fig. 16 shows the response of the economy to a recession when agents anticipate that, if a run happens, the monetary authority intervenes with large scale asset purchases according to (52). Even though in this experiment the run does not happen and the central bank accordingly does not intervene, the anticipation of the intervention in the event of a run significantly dampens the downturn. It does so by reducing the probability of a run: The central bank's conditional intervention policy increases the liquidation price of

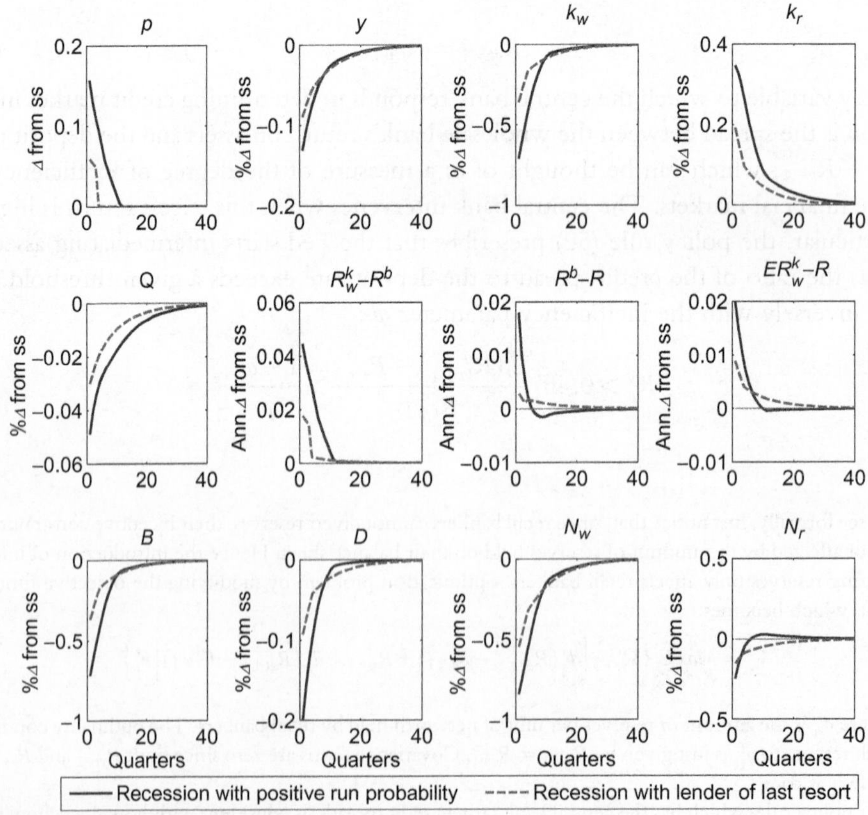

Fig. 16 Anticipation effects of government intervention.

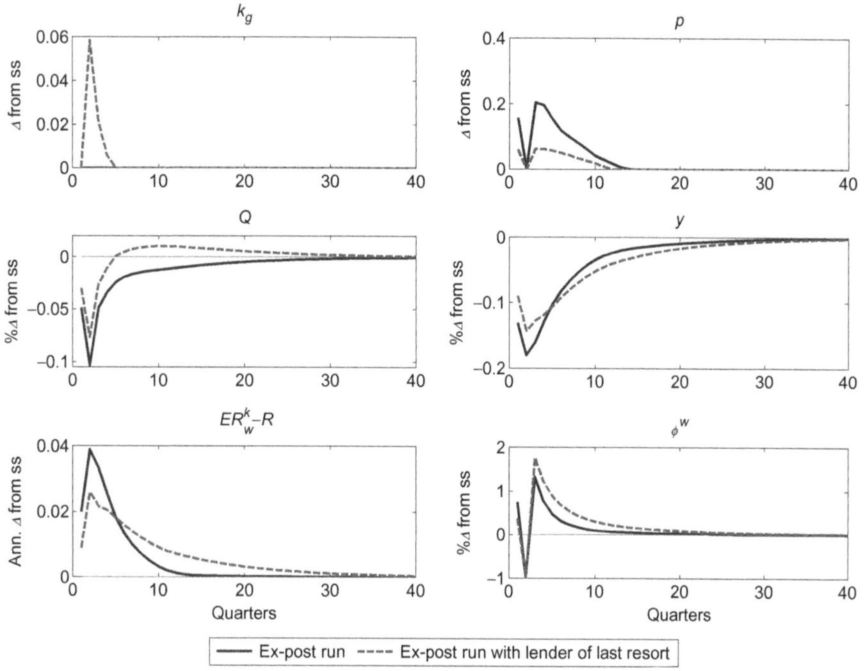

Fig. 17 Government intervention when a run happens at time 2.

wholesale banks assets. In turn, by Eq. (47), the higher recovery rate associated with higher liquidation prices decreases the probability of a run. In the experiment the probability of a run decreases by 10% in the first two periods and becomes zero thereafter. This drastic reduction in the run probability implies that, overall, anticipation of government intervention works to stimulate the economy. Notice that, even though the reduction in the run probability relaxes the incentive constraint and hence allows wholesale bankers to increase their leverage for any given level of spreads, the general equilibrium effects of asset prices on their balance sheet results in better capitalization and lower leverage in both the wholesale and retail bank sectors.

Fig. 17 illustrates the effect of the intervention when a run happens one period after the shock to Z. The intervention is around 5% of total capital and reduces the drop in asset prices and output by about 2.5 and 4%, respectively.

7.2 Ex-Ante Intervention: Macroprudential Policy

One of the most important challenges facing policy makers in the aftermath of the financial crisis is the development of financial regulations that can help prevent the recurrence of similar episodes in the future. In this respect, the most relevant innovation in the policy landscape has been the introduction of various macroprudential measures in the oversight of financial institutions, such as stress tests by central banks and the revised provisions in Basel III. These measures are aimed at ensuring that financial institutions' capital is sufficient to absorb losses during adverse economic conditions.

There is now a significant literature that analyzes the impact of capital requirements on banks for macroeconomic stability (eg, Christiano and Ikeda, 2014; Begenau, 2015; Bianchi and Mendoza, 2013; Chari and Kehoe, 2015; Gertler et al., 2012). Most of this literature analyzes how the introduction of leverage restrictions can dampen financial accelerator effects by dampening fluctuations in bank capital. The need for leverage restrictions, or equivalently capital requirements, stems from an externality that leads individual banks to fail to take into account the effect of their own borrowing on the stability of the system as a whole.[av]

Our framework offers a somewhat different perspective on the potential benefits of leverage restrictions. Not only can these restrictions dampen financial accelerator effects: Importantly, they can also make the banking system less susceptible to runs. As Eq. (41) makes clear, a bank run can only happen if the leverage ratio is high enough. Thus, by limiting the leverage ratio sufficiently, the regulatory authority can in principle eliminate the possibility of a run. The question then is what are the tradeoffs. We turn to this issue next.

We capture macroprudential policies in our model economy by introducing leverage restrictions on wholesale banks. In particular, we assume that a financial regulator can impose an upper bound on wholesale banks' leverage, $\overline{\phi}^w$. This implies that the effective limit to wholesale banks' leverage will be given by the smaller between the market imposed limit and the regulatory limit. Accordingly, constraint (22) becomes

$$\phi^w \leq \min\left\{\frac{\frac{1}{\theta}\frac{V_t^w}{n_t^w} - (1-\omega)}{\omega}, \overline{\phi}^w\right\}$$

In a fully stochastic simulation of the economy, leverage restrictions would tradeoff lower frequency of crises, resulting from reduced variation of bankers' capital, against lower average output, as the impaired ability of wholesale banks to increase their leverage would induce a costly reallocation of capital to less efficient agents. While our numerical experiments in Sections 4.2 and 4.3 provide an illustration of the tradeoff between steady state output and fragility associated to changes in the long run level of wholesale bankers'

[av] Much of the literature, following Lorenzoni (2008), features a pecuniary externality stemming from the presence of asset prices in the borrowing constraint. Farhi and Werning (2015) and Korinek and Simsek (2015) show that if aggregate demand is sensitive to aggregate leverage, a similar kind of externality can emerge.

leverage, here we focus on the conditional effects of leverage restrictions upon the occurrence of a recession that would leave the decentralized economy vulnerable to bank runs.

We focus on two possible levels for $\overline{\phi}^w$: the steady state level of wholesale banks' leverage and a level that is higher than steady state but still sufficiently low to prevent a run. Permitting a leverage ratio above the steady state allows banks to issue more debt in a recession, which has the overall effect of dampening the contraction in financial intermediation and thus dampening the downturn in real activity. Indeed, the more forgiving leverage restriction comes closer to mimicking the behavior of the leverage ratio in the decentralized economy, which moves countercylcially.

Figs. 18 and 19 compare the response of the economy with anticipated runs to a negative Z innovation, with and without macroprudential regulation. In Fig. 18 the regulator imposes the tighter leverage restriction, ie, $\overline{\phi}^w$ is set to the steady state value of wholesale leverage, while in Fig. 19 the restrictions are more lax and allow maximum regulatory leverage to exceed the steady state value by 15%. As mentioned, in both cases, the leverage restrictions are sufficient to prevent a run and hence avoid the recessionary effects associated to the endogenous increase in the probability of a run that characterizes

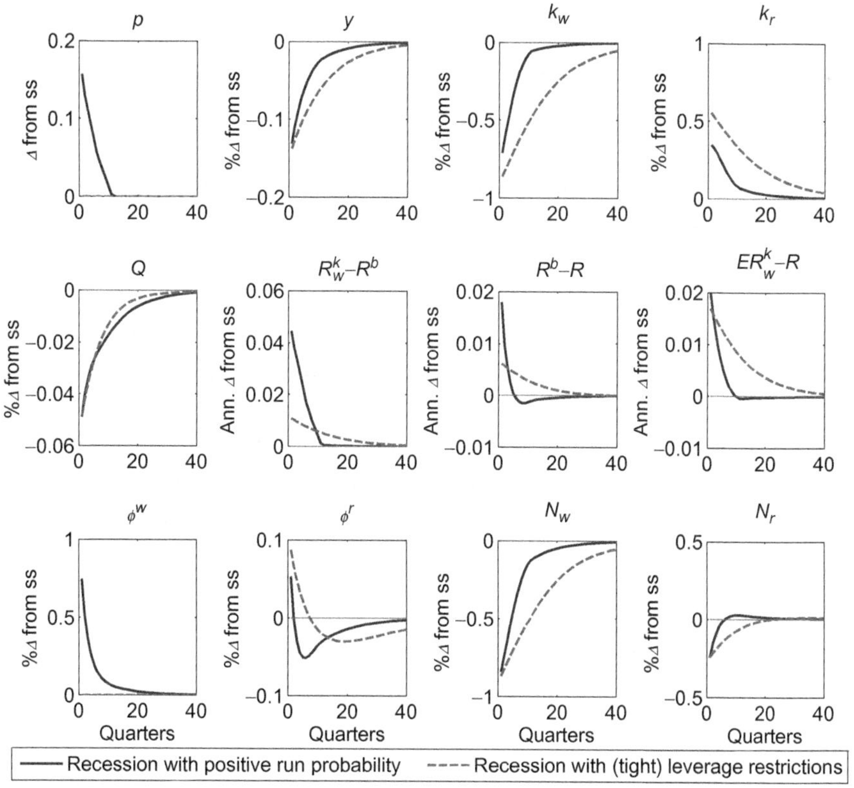

Fig. 18 Macro prudential policy: $\phi^w = \phi^{ss}$.

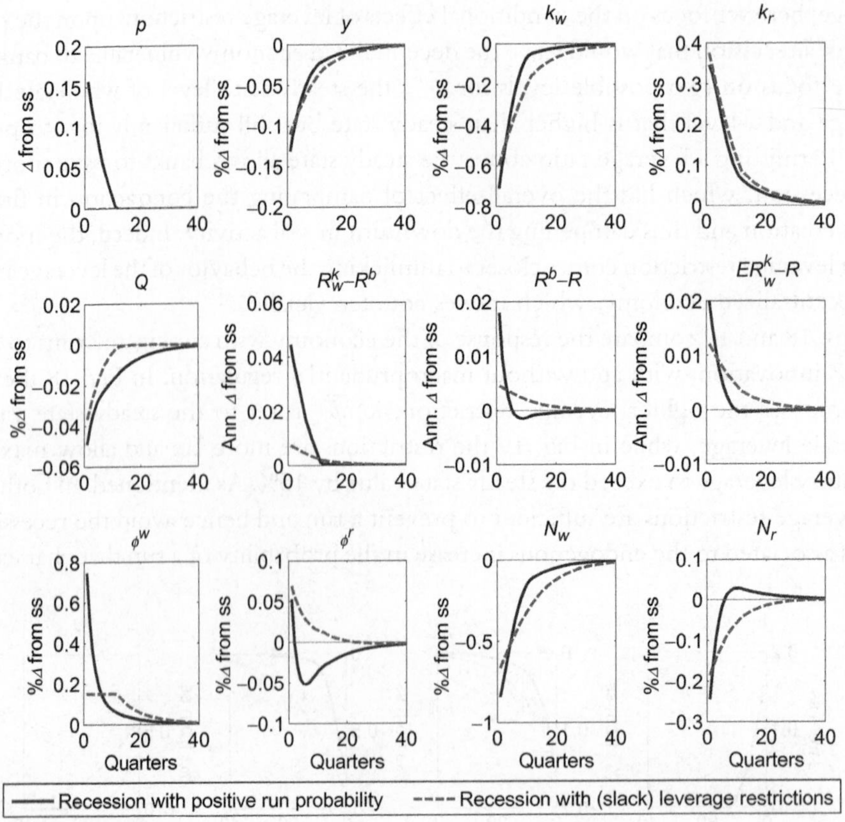

Fig. 19 Macro prudential policy: $\phi^w = 1.15\phi^{ss}$.

the unregulated economy. This results in higher asset prices in the regulated economy throughout the recession. Under the less strict requirements the stimulative effect on asset prices is significantly higher, reaching about 1.5% after the first three years of the recession. On the other hand, by constraining the ability to leverage of the most efficient intermediaries, macroprudential policies induces a costly reallocation of assets. The balance between these two contrasting forces varies overtime, in turn influencing output effects of the policy.

During the early stages of the recession, the stimulative effects of macroprudential policy are strongest because they eliminate the probability of a bank run, which in the unregulated economy is highest at this time. Under the stricter policy, the impact drop in output is very similar to the drop in the unregulated economy, while the more lax stance of policy dampens the drop in output by 2% and is stimulative throughout the first year of the recession. As time passes, the probability of a run becomes small in the unregulated economy, implying that the stimulative effects of policy decreases. On the other hand, the slower recovery of financial institutions' equity in the regulated economy that results from their impaired ability to leverage, implies a more persistent drag on output coming from financial misallocation. In both cases output costs associated with the policy peak at around 10 quarters into the recession and result in an additional drop in output of about 4% under the tighter requirements and 1.5% under the more lax stance.

8. SUMMARY AND DIRECTIONS FOR FUTURE RESEARCH

The financial crisis that triggered the Great Recession featured a disruption of wholesale funding markets, where banks lend to one another, as opposed to retail markets where banks obtain funds from depositors. It is essential to capture the roles and possible disruption of wholesale funding market to understand the financial crisis as well as to draw policy implications. Our goal in this Handbook Paper was to sketch a model based on the existing literature that provides a step toward accomplishing this objective. The model first accounts for how, through innovation in the efficiency of interbank loan markets, a wholesale banking sector emerges that intermediates loans using funds borrowed from retail banks. This wholesale sector bears a close resemblance to the shadow banking system featured in most descriptions of the crisis.

As we show, in "normal" times, the growth of the wholesale banking sector improves both efficiency and stability. Improved efficiency stems from the comparative advantage that wholesale banks having in managing certain types of loans. Improved stability arises because retail banks act as a buffer to absorb loans that wholesale banks sell off, in effect improving the liquidity of secondary loan markets. On the other hand, the growth of wholesale banking system makes the economy more vulnerable to a crisis. As occurred in practice, the high leverage of wholesale banks makes this sector susceptible to runs that can have highly disruptive effects on the economy. A contractionary disturbance that might otherwise lead to a moderate recession, can induce a run on the wholesale banking sector with devastating effects on the economy, as experienced during the Great Recession. We then describe how both lender of last resort and macroprudential policies can help reduce the likelihood of these kinds of banking crises.

Our framework also captures the buildup of safe assets prior to the crisis along with the subsequent collapse that a number of authors have emphasized (eg, Gorton and Metrick, 2015; Caballero and Farhi, 2015). The underlying mechanisms work a bit differently, in somewhat subtle ways: The "safe asset" literature points to an increased demand for safe assets as the driving force in the buildup of the shadow banking system. By making assets riskier, the crisis then reduces the ability of the shadow banking sector to create safe assets. It is this reduction in safe assets that then leads a contraction in spending, essentially for liquidity reasons. Within our framework, the increase in safe assets is a product of innovation in interbank lending markets. Indeed, this is where much of the growth in safe assets occurred. There is also a growth in households deposits as the overall banking system becomes more efficient. The crisis similarly induces a contraction in safe assets: The exact mechanism, though, is that, with an adverse shock to the net worth of banks, the probability of runs on wholesale banks becomes positive, which constrains the ability of both wholesale and retail banks to issue safe liabilities. In turn, a contraction in real activity emerges because the costs of intermediation increase, as manifested by the increase in credit spreads. In future work, it would be interesting to synthesize the role of safe assets in our framework with that in the conventional literature on this topic.

Another important area for further investigation involves the modeling of the growth of wholesale banking. Our approach was to treat this growth as the product of innovation as captured by a reduction in the agency friction in interbank lending markets. Among the factors we had in mind that motivate this reduction is technological improvements that permit less costly monitoring, such as the development of asset-backed securities and repo lending. Of course, more explicit modeling of this phenomenon would be desirable. Also important is integrating regulatory considerations. While financial innovation was important for the development of shadow banking, regulatory factors also played an important role. For example, tightening of capital requirements on commercial banks in conjunction with innovation in asset securitization induced movement of a considerable amount of mortgage lending from the retail to the wholesale banking sector. A careful integration of the roles of regulation and innovation in the development of wholesale banking would be highly desirable.

Finally, consistent with what occurred in the recent crisis, what makes the financial system within our model so vulnerable is high degree of leverage in the form of short-term debt. Here, we simply rule out a richer set of state-contingent financial contracts that would permit banks to hedge against the systemic risk implied by this liability structure. Why in practice we don't seem to observe the kind of seemingly desirable hedging is an important question for future research.[aw]

APPENDICES

Appendix A Details of the Equilibrium

From (13, 15–17), we get

$$\begin{aligned}\frac{V_t^j}{n_t^j} &= E_t\left(\Omega_{t+1}^j \cdot \frac{n_{t+1}^j}{n_t^j}\right)\\ &= E_t\left\{\Omega_{t+1}^j\left[R_{kt+1}^j + \left(R_{kt+1}^j - R_{t+1}\right)\frac{d_t^j}{n_t^j} + \left(R_{kt+1}^j - R_{bt+1}\right)\frac{b_t^j}{n_t^j}\right]\right\}\\ &= \nu_{kt}^j + \mu_{dt}^j\frac{d_t^j}{n_t^j} + \mu_{bt}^j\frac{b_t^j}{n_t^j},\end{aligned}$$

[aw] Some efforts to address this issue include Krishnamurthy (2003), Di Tella (2014), Gertler et al. (2012), and Dang et al. (2012).

where

$$\nu_{kt}^j = E_t(\Omega_{t+1}^j R_{kt+1}^j) \tag{A.1}$$

$$\mu_{dt}^j = E_t\left[\Omega_{t+1}^j \left(R_{kt+1}^j - R_{t+1}\right)\right] \tag{A.2}$$

$$\mu_{bt}^j = E_t\left[\Omega_{t+1}^j \left(R_{kt+1}^j - R_{bt+1}\right)\right]. \tag{A.3}$$

From (13), the incentive constraint (14) can be written as

$$V_t^j \geq \theta\left[n_t^j + d_t^j + \omega b_t^j \cdot I_{b_t^j>0} + (1-\gamma) b_t^j \cdot I_{b_t^j<0}\right],$$

where $I_{b_t^j>0} = 1$ if $b_t^j > 0$ and $I_{b_t^j>0} = 0$ otherwise, (and $I_{b_t^j<0} = 1$ if $b_t^j < 0$ and $I_{b_t^j<0} = 0$ otherwise).

In order to save the notations, we normalize $n_t^j = 1$ and suppress the suffix and time subscript. The generic choice of a bank is given by

$$\psi = \underset{b,d}{Max}(\nu_k + \mu_d d + \mu_b b) \tag{A.4}$$

subject to

$$\theta[1 + d + \omega b \cdot I_{b>0} + (1-\gamma) b \cdot I_{b<0}] \leq \nu_k + \mu_d d + \mu_b b, \tag{A.5}$$

$$d \geq 0,$$

$$1 + d + b \geq 0.$$

Figs. A.1 and A.2 depict the Feasible set and an Indifference Curve for Wholesale Bankers and Retail Bankers under our baseline.

Defining λ and λ_k as Lagrangian multipliers of the incentive constraint and the non-negativity constraint of capital, we have the Lagrangian as

$$\mathcal{L} = (1+\lambda)(\nu_k + \mu_d d + \mu_b b) - \lambda\theta[1 + d + \omega b \cdot I_{b>0} + (1-\gamma) b \cdot I_{b<0}] + \lambda_k(1 + d + b).$$

For the case of $b \geq 0$, we know $\lambda_k = 0$ and the first order conditions are

$$(1+\lambda)\mu_b \leq \lambda\theta\omega,$$

where $=$ holds if $b > 0$, and $<$ implies $b = 0$.

$$(1+\lambda)\mu_d \leq \lambda\theta,$$

where $=$ holds if $d > 0$, and $<$ implies $d = 0$.

In the following we restrict the attention to the case of $\mu_d > 0$, and will verify the inequality later. Thus for the case of $b > 0$, we learn

$$d > 0, \text{ if } \frac{\mu_b}{\mu_d} = \omega,$$

$$d = 0, \text{ if } \frac{\mu_b}{\mu_d} > \omega.$$

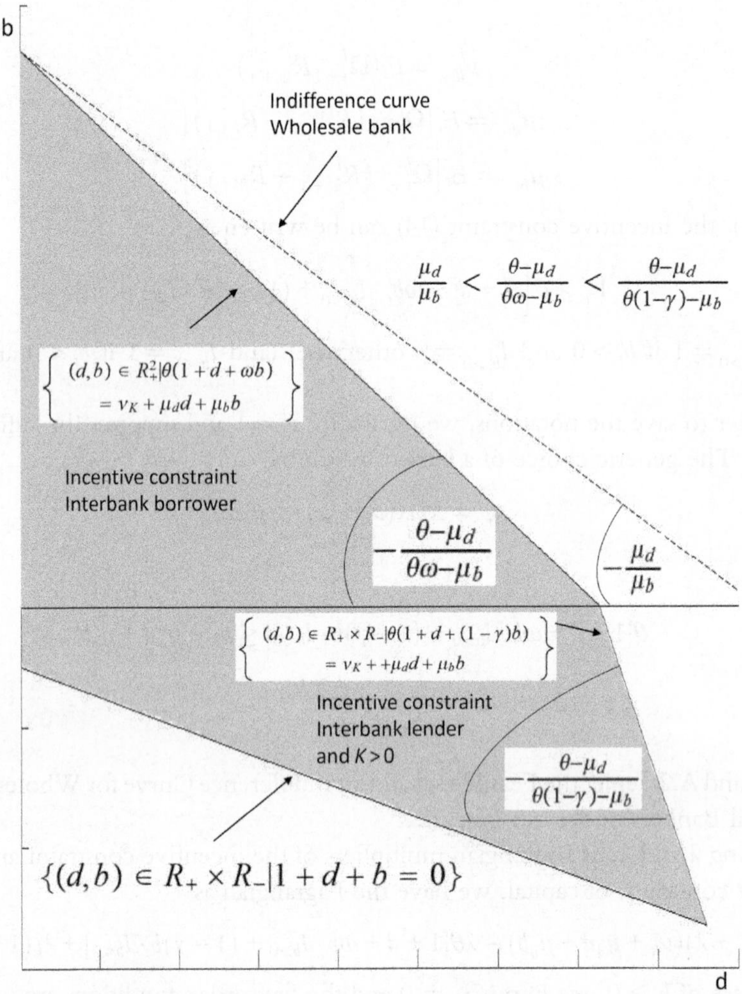

Fig. A.1 Wholesale banker's optimization.

For the case of $b \leq 0$, the first order conditions are

$$(1+\lambda)\mu_b + \lambda_k \geq \lambda\theta(1-\gamma),$$

where $=$ holds if $b<0$, and $>$ implies $b=0$.

$$(1+\lambda)\mu_d + \lambda_k \leq \lambda\theta,$$

where $=$ holds if $d>0$, and $<$ implies $d=0$.

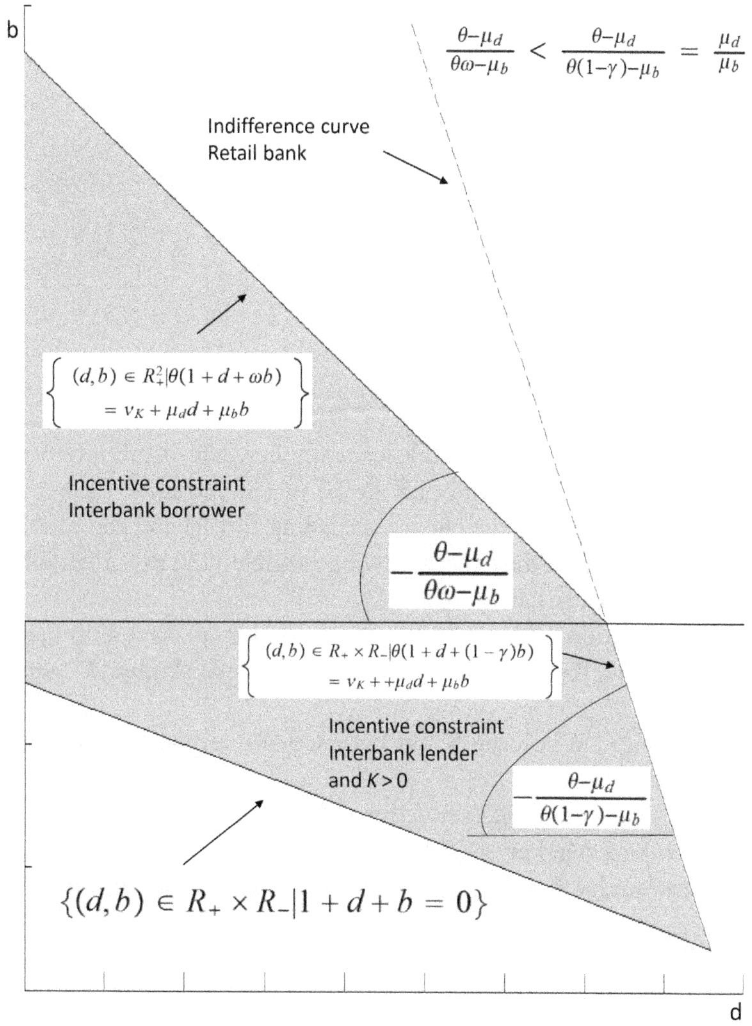

Fig. A.2 Retail banker's optimization.

Thus for the case of $b < 0$ and $d > 0$, we learn

$$k > 0, \text{ if } \frac{\mu_b}{\mu_d} = 1 - \gamma,$$

$$k = 0 \text{ and } \lambda_k > 0, \text{ if } \frac{\mu_b}{\mu_d} < 1 - \gamma.$$

Therefore, under Assumption 2: $\omega + \gamma > 1$, we can summarize the bank's choice as:

(i) $b > 0,\ d = 0,\ k > 0,$ if $\mu_b > \omega\mu_d$

(ii) $b > 0,\ d > 0,\ k > 0,$ implies $\mu_b = \omega\mu_d$

(iii) $b = 0,\ d > 0,\ k > 0$, if $(1 - \gamma)\mu_d < \mu_b < \omega\mu_d$
(iv) $b < 0,\ d > 0,\ k > 0$, implies $\mu_b = (1 - \gamma)\mu_d$
(v) $b < 0,\ d > 0,\ k = 0$, if $\mu_b < (1 - \gamma)\mu_d$.

In the steady state equilibrium, we know

$$\frac{\mu_b}{\mu_d} = \frac{R_k - R_b}{R_k - R}.$$

Because we know $R_k^w \geq R_k^r$ and $R_b \geq R$, we learn

$$\frac{\mu_b^w}{\mu_d^w} \geq \frac{\mu_b^r}{\mu_d^r}.$$

Therefore, market clearing for interbank loans implies that, if the interbank market is active wholesale bankers' choice can only be (i) or (ii) and retail banker's choice (iv) or (v). Otherwise both types must choose according to (iii) and the interbank market is inactive. That is, we have only the following possible patterns of equilibrium in the neighborhood of the steady state.

(A) Perfect Specialization with active Interbank Market: $d^w = 0, k^r = 0, b^w > 0 > b^r$
(B) Perfect Specialized Retail Banks with active Interbank Market: $d^w > 0, k^r = 0, b^w > 0 > b^r$
(C) Perfect Specialized Wholesale Banks with active Interbank Market: $d^w = 0, k^r > 0, b^w > 0 > b^r$
(D) Imperfect Specialization with active Interbank Market: $d^w > 0, k^r > 0, b^w > 0 > b^r$
(E) Inactive Interbank Market: $d^w > 0, k^r > 0, b^w = 0 = b^r$.

We can show that, under Assumption 2, there is no equilibrium of type (A) nor (B):

Proof. Equilibrium of type (A) and (B) require $\mu_b^w \geq \omega\mu_d^w$ and $(1-\gamma)\mu_d^r \geq \mu_b^r$. Thus

$$R_b \leq \omega R + (1-\omega)R_k^w,$$
$$R_b \geq (1-\gamma)R + \gamma R_k^r = (1-\gamma)R + \gamma R_k^w, \text{ as } K^r = 0 \text{ in (A)and (B)}.$$

This implies

$$\omega R + (1-\omega)R_k^w \geq (1-\gamma)R + \gamma R_k^w,$$

or

$$(\omega + \gamma - 1)R \geq (\omega + \gamma - 1)R_k^w.$$

But this is a contradiction as $\omega + \gamma > 1$ and $R_k^w > R$ (as $\mu_d^w > 0$ under our conjecture).

Equilibrium C and D: Active Interbank Market

Suppose that $0 < \mu^w_{bt} < \theta\omega$. We will verify this numerically after we characterize the equilibrium. Then the incentive constraint (A.5) holds with equality for wholesale banks. Together with Bellman equation (A.4), we have

$$\begin{aligned}\psi^w_t &= \nu^w_{kt} + \mu^w_{dt}d^w_t + \mu^w_{bt}b^w_t \\ &= \theta\left(1 + d^w_t + \omega b^w_t\right),\end{aligned}$$

or

$$b^w_t = \frac{1}{\theta\omega - \mu^w_{bt}}\left[\nu^w_{kt} - \theta - (\theta - \mu^w_{dt})d^w_t\right],$$

$$\psi^w_t = \frac{\theta}{\theta\omega - \mu^w_{bt}}\left[\omega\nu^w_{kt} - \mu^w_{bt} + (\omega\mu^w_{dt} - \mu^w_{bt})d^w_t\right].$$

Maximizing Tobin's Q, ψ^w_t, with respect to $d^w_t \geq 0$, we learn

$$d^w_t = 0, \text{ if } \mu^w_{dt} < \frac{1}{\omega}\mu^w_{bt}$$

$$d^w_t > 0 \text{ implies } \mu^w_{dt} = \frac{1}{\omega}\mu^w_{bt}.$$

This proves Lemma 1 and the argument in the text follows for wholesale banks, noting that we normalize $n^w_t = 1$ above.

Suppose also that $0 < \mu^r_{dt} < \theta$. We will verify this numerically after we characterize the equilibrium. Then the incentive constraint (A.5) holds with equality for retail banks. Together with Bellman equation (A.4), we have

$$\begin{aligned}\psi^r_t &= \nu^r_{kt} + \mu^r_{dt}d^r_t + \mu^r_{bt}b^r_t \\ &= \theta[1 + d^r_t + (1-\gamma)b^r_t].\end{aligned}$$

Then we get

$$d^r_t = \frac{1}{\theta - \mu^r_{dt}}\{\nu^r_{kt} - \theta + [\theta(1-\gamma) - \mu^r_{bt}](-b^r_t)\},$$

$$\psi^r_t = \frac{\theta}{\theta - \mu^r_{dt}}\left[\nu^r_{kt} - \mu^r_{dt} + (\mu^r_{dt} - \mu^r_{bt} - \gamma\mu^r_{dt})(-b^r_t)\right].$$

Maximizing Tobin's Q, ψ^r_t, with respect to $k^r_t \geq 0$ and $b^r_t \leq 0$, we learn

$$k^r_t > 0 \text{ and } b^r_t < 0 \text{ imply } \mu^r_{dt} - \mu^r_{bt} = \gamma\mu^r_{dt}$$

$$k^r_t = 0 \text{ and } b^r_t < 0 \text{ if } \mu^r_{dt} - \mu^r_{bt} > \gamma\mu^r_{dt}.$$

This proves Lemma 2 and the argument in the text follows for retail banks, noting that we normalize $n_t^r = 1$ above.

Therefore the argument in the text follows for the aggregate equilibrium.

Equilibrium E: No Active Interbank Market $b_t^w = b_t^r = 0$

From Bellman equation and the incentive constraint of each bank (A.4, A.5) with $\left(Q_t + f_t^j k_t^j\right) k_t^j = 1 + d_t^j$, we have

$$\psi_t^j = \theta\left(Q_t + f_t^j k_t^j\right) k_t^j = \nu_{kt}^j - \mu_{dt}^j + \mu_{dt}^j\left(Q_t + f_t^j k_t^j\right) k_t^j,$$

or

$$\left(Q_t + f_t^j k_t^j\right) k_t^j = \frac{\nu_{kt}^j - \mu_{dt}^j}{\theta - \mu_{dt}^j},$$
$$\psi_t^j = \theta \frac{\nu_{kt}^j - \mu_{dt}^j}{\theta - \mu_{dt}^j} \tag{A.6}$$

The aggregate balance sheet conditions of wholesale and retail banking sectors are

$$Q_t K_t^w = \frac{\nu_{kt}^w - \mu_{dt}^w}{\theta - \mu_{dt}^w} N_t^w = N_t^w + D_t^w \tag{A.7}$$

$$\left(Q_t + f_t^r K_t^r\right) K_t^r = \frac{\nu_{kt}^r - \mu_{dt}^r}{\theta - \mu_{dt}^r} N_t^r = N_t^r + D_t^r. \tag{A.8}$$

The recursive competitive equilibrium without bank runs consists of 24 variables-aggregate quantities $\left(K_t^w, K_t^r, K_t^h, D_t^w, D_t^r, N_t^w, N_t^r, C_t^b, C_t^h, \bar{Y}_t, Y_t\right)$, prices $\left(Q_t, R_{t+1}, f_t^r\right)$ and bankers' franchise values and leverage multiples $\left(\Omega_t^j, R_{kt}^j, \nu_{kt}^j, \mu_{dt}^j, \psi_t^j\right)_{j=w,r}$- as a function of the state variables $\left(K_{t-1}^w, K_{t-1}^r, R_t D_{t-1}^w, R_t D_{t-1}^r, Z_t\right)$, which satisfy 24 equations (1, 4, 7, 8, 16, 18, 34–39, A.1, A.2, A.6–A.8) where each of (16, 18, A.1, A.2, A.6–A.8) contain two equations.

After finding the equilibrium, we need to check the inequalities

$$\mu_{bt}^w < \omega \mu_{dt}^w,$$
$$\mu_{bt}^r > (1-\gamma)\mu_{dt}^r.$$

In the neighborhood of the steady state, it is sufficient to show

$$(1-\omega)E_t\left(\frac{Q_{t+1} + Z_{t+1}}{Q_t}\right) + \omega R_{t+1} < \gamma E_t\left(\frac{Q_{t+1} + Z_{t+1}}{Q_t + \alpha^r K_t^r}\right) + (1-\gamma)R_{t+1}. \tag{A.9}$$

Appendix B Steady State of the Economy Without Run

In order to characterize the steady state of (C,D,E), define x^j as the growth rate of the net worth of continuing bank j in the steady state:

$$x^j = \frac{n^j_{t+1}}{n^j_t} = R^j_k \frac{(Q+f^j)k^j}{n^j} - R_b \frac{b^j}{n^j} - R\frac{d^j}{n^j}$$

$$= \left(R^j_k - R_b\right)\frac{b^j}{n^j} + \left(R^j_k - R\right)\frac{d^j}{n^j} + R^j_k.$$

Then we have the aggregate net worth of bank j as

$$N^j = \sigma^j x^j N^j + W^j$$

$$= \frac{W^j}{1-\sigma^j x^j} \equiv N^j(x^j),$$

if $\sigma^j x^j < 1$, which we guess and verify later. Tobin's Q of bank j is

$$\psi^j = \beta(1-\sigma^j + \sigma^j \psi^j)x^j$$

$$= \frac{\beta(1-\sigma^j)x^j}{1-\beta\sigma^j x^j} \equiv \psi^j(x^j).$$

The ratio of bank loans to net worth is

$$\frac{Qk^w}{n^w} = \frac{\psi^w(x^w)}{\theta\omega} - \frac{1-\omega}{\omega}\left(1+\frac{d^w}{n^w}\right), \text{ if } b^w > 0,$$

$$\frac{Qk^w}{n^w} = \frac{\psi^w(x^w)}{\theta}, \text{ if } b^w = 0,$$

$$\frac{(Q+f^r)k^r}{n^r} = \frac{\psi^r(x^r)}{\theta} - \gamma\left(-\frac{b^r}{n^r}\right).$$

Case of Active Interbank Market: C and D

From the condition for the retail banks, we have

$$1-\gamma = \frac{\mu^r_b}{\mu^r_d} = \frac{R^r_k - R_b}{R^r_k - R},$$

or

$$R_b = \gamma R^r_k + (1-\gamma)R.$$

$$
\begin{aligned}
x^r - R &= (R_k^r - R_b)\frac{b^r}{n^r} + (R_k^r - R)\left(1 + \frac{d^r}{n^r}\right) \\
&= (R_k^r - R)\left[1 + \frac{d^r}{n^r} + (1-\gamma)\frac{b^r}{n^r}\right] \\
&= (R_k^r - R)\left[\frac{(Q+f^r)k^r}{n^r} + \gamma\left(-\frac{b^r}{n^r}\right)\right] \\
&= (R_k^r - R)\frac{\psi^r(x^r)}{\theta}.
\end{aligned}
$$

Thus from $R = \beta^{-1}$,

$$
\beta(R_k^r - R) = \theta\frac{\beta x^r - 1}{\psi^r(x^r)} = \theta\frac{(\beta x^r - 1)(1 - \sigma^r \beta x^r)}{(1-\sigma^r)\beta x^r} \equiv \varphi^r(\beta x^r),
$$

$$
\beta(R_b - R) = \gamma\theta\frac{\beta x^r - 1}{\psi^r(x^r)} = \gamma\varphi^r(\beta x^r).
$$

Thus R_k^r and R_b are functions of only x^r :

$$
R_k^r = R_k^r(x^r), R_b = R_b(x^r).
$$

Differentiating log of the right hand side (RHS) of the above equation with respect to x^r, we learn

$$
\begin{aligned}
\frac{d\ \ln\varphi^r(\beta x^r)}{d(\beta x^r)} &= \frac{1}{\beta x^r - 1} - \frac{\sigma^r}{1 - \beta\sigma^r x^r} - \frac{1}{\beta x^r} \\
&\propto 1 - \sigma^r(\beta x^r)^2 \\
&> 0, \text{ iff } \sigma^r(\beta x^r)^2 < 1.
\end{aligned}
$$

Thus if $\sigma^r(\beta x^r)^2 < 1$, R_k^r and R_b are increasing functions of only x^r :

$$
R_k^r = R_k^r(x^r), R_k^{r\prime}(\cdot) > 0,
$$

$$
R_b = R_b(x^r), R_b^{\prime}(\cdot) > 0.
$$

Similarly

$$\begin{aligned}
x^w - R_b &= (R_k^w - R_b)\left(1 + \frac{b^w}{n^w}\right) + (R_k^w - R)\frac{d^w}{n^w} \\
&= (R_k^w - R_b)\left(1 + \frac{b^w}{n^w}\right) + \frac{1}{\omega}(R_k^w - R_b)\frac{d^w}{n^w} \\
&= (R_k^w - R_b)\left(\frac{Qk^w}{n^w} + \frac{1-\omega}{\omega}\frac{d^w}{n^w}\right) \\
&= (R_k^w - R_b)\left(\frac{1}{\omega\theta}\psi^w - \frac{1-\omega}{\omega}\right).
\end{aligned}$$

Thus

$$R_k^w - R_b = \omega\theta\frac{x^w - R_b}{\psi^w - \theta(1-\omega)},$$

$$R_k^w - R = \frac{1}{\psi^w - \theta(1-\omega)}[\omega\theta(x^w - R) + (\psi^w - \theta)(R_b - R)].$$

Because

$$\begin{aligned}
&\frac{d}{dx^w}\ln\left[\frac{\omega\theta(x^w - R)}{\psi^w - \theta(1-\omega)}\right] \\
&\propto \frac{1}{\beta x^w - 1} - \frac{\sigma^w}{1 - \sigma^w\beta x^w} - \frac{\Delta}{\Delta\beta x^w - \theta(1-\omega)}, \text{ where } \Delta = 1 - \sigma^w + \theta(1-\omega)\sigma^w \\
&\propto (1-\sigma^w)\left[1 - \sigma^w(\beta x^w)^2\right] - \theta(1-\omega)(1 - \sigma^w\beta x^w)^2,
\end{aligned}$$

R_k^w is an increasing function of x^w and x^r

$$R_k^w = R_k^w(x^w, x^r),$$

if

$$\begin{aligned}
(1-\sigma^w)\left[1 - \sigma^w(\beta x^w)^2\right] &> \theta(1-\omega)(1 - \sigma^w\beta x^w)^2, \\
\sigma^r(\beta x^r)^2 &< 1.
\end{aligned}$$

In the following we assume these conditions to be satisfied.

In the steady state, we know the rates of returns on capital for wholesale and retail banks and households are

$$R_k^w = \frac{Z+Q}{Q}$$

$$R_k^r = \frac{Z+Q}{Q+\alpha^r K^r}$$

$$R_k^h = \frac{Z+Q}{Q+\alpha^h K^h} = R.$$

Thus we have

$$Q = \frac{Z}{R_k^w - 1},$$

$$\alpha^r K^r = \frac{Z-(R_k^r-1)Q}{R_k^r} = Z\frac{R_k^w - R_k^r}{R_k^r(R_k^w-1)},$$

$$\alpha^h K^h = \frac{Z-(R-1)Q}{R} = Z\frac{R_k^w - R}{R(R_k^w-1)},$$

and Q, K^r and K^w are functions of (x^w, x^r).

Equilibrium C: $D^w = 0$

Here, the market clearing condition of capital is given by

$$\begin{aligned} QK^w &= \frac{Qk^w}{n^w}N^w \\ &= \frac{\psi^w(x^w)-\theta(1-\omega)}{\theta\omega}N^w(x^w) \\ &= Q(x^w,x^r)\left[\bar{K} - K^r(x^w,x^r) - K^h(x^w,x^r)\right] \end{aligned} \tag{B.1}$$

The market clearing condition of interbank credit is given by

$$\begin{aligned} B &= \left(\frac{Qk^w}{n^w} - 1\right)N^w \\ &= \frac{\psi^w(x^w)-\theta}{\theta\omega}N^w(x^w) \\ &= \frac{1}{\gamma}\left\{\frac{\psi^r(x^r)}{\theta}N^r(x^r) - [Q(x^w,x^r) + \alpha^r K^r(x^w,x^r)]\cdot K^r(x^w,x^r)\right\} \end{aligned} \tag{B.2}$$

The equilibrium value of $(x^w, x^r)$is given by (x^w, x^r) which satisfies (B.1 and B.2) simultaneously.

In order to verify $\mu_d^w > 0$ and $\mu_d^r > 0$, it is sufficient to check the inequalities

$$x^w > x^r > R = \beta^{-1}.$$

For the other inequality $\mu_b^w > \omega\mu_d^w$, it is sufficient to check

$$R_k^w - R_b > \omega\left(R_k^w - R\right),$$

or

$$(1-\omega)(R_k^w - R) > R_b - R.$$

This is equivalent with

$$(1-\omega)\frac{\beta x^w - 1}{\psi^w(x^w)} > \gamma\frac{\beta x^r - 1}{\psi^r(x^r)}. \tag{B.3}$$

Equilibrium D: $D^w > 0$
For this type of equilibrium, we need $\mu_{kb}^w = \omega\mu_d^w$, or

$$R_k^w - R_b = \omega\left(R_k^w - R\right).$$

Thus

$$x^w - R = \left(R_k^w - R\right)\left(1 + \frac{d^w}{n^w} + \omega\frac{b^w}{n^w}\right)$$

$$= \left(R_k^w - R\right)\frac{\psi^w}{\theta},$$

Thus being similar to the expression for $\beta(R_k^r - R)$, we get

$$\beta(R_k^w - R) = \theta\frac{\beta x^w - 1}{\psi^w(x^w)} = \theta\frac{(\beta x^w - 1)(1 - \sigma^w\beta x^w)}{(1-\sigma^w)\beta x^w} \equiv \varphi^w(\beta x^w).$$

R_k^w is an increasing function of x^w if $\sigma^w(\beta x^w)^2 < 1$.

Also we learn

$$R_b - R = (1-\omega)\left(R_k^w - R\right) = \gamma\left(R_k^r - R\right),$$

or

$$(1-\omega)\varphi^w(\beta x^w) = \gamma\varphi^r(\beta x^r), \tag{B.4}$$

and thus x^r is an increasing function of x^w. We can solve Q and K^h as functions of x^w as

$$Q = \frac{Z}{R_k^w - 1}$$

$$= \frac{\beta Z}{\varphi^w(\beta x^w) + 1 - \beta} \equiv Q(x^w),$$

$$K^h = \frac{1}{\alpha^h}[\beta Z - (1-\beta)Q]$$
$$= \frac{1}{\alpha^h}\frac{\beta Z \varphi^w(\beta x^w)}{\varphi^w(\beta x^w) + 1 - \beta} \equiv K^h(x^w).$$

We also get

$$K^r = \frac{1}{\alpha^r}\frac{Z - (R_k^r - 1)Q}{R_k^r} = \frac{Z}{\alpha^r}\frac{R_k^w - R_k^r}{R_k^r(R_k^w - 1)}$$
$$= \frac{1}{\alpha^r}\frac{\beta Z \varphi^w(\beta x^w)}{\varphi^w(\beta x^w) + 1 - \beta}\frac{\gamma + \omega - 1}{\gamma + (1-\omega)\varphi^w(\beta x^w)}$$
$$= \frac{\gamma + \omega - 1}{\gamma + (1-\omega)\varphi^w(\beta x^w)}\frac{\alpha^h}{\alpha^r}K^h \equiv K^r(x^w)$$

The capital market equilibrium is given by

$$QK^w = \frac{1}{\theta\omega}\psi^w N^w - \frac{1-\omega}{\omega}(N^w + D^w)$$
$$= \frac{1}{\theta\omega}\psi^w N^w - \frac{1-\omega}{\omega}(QK^w - B)$$
$$= \frac{1}{\theta}\psi^w N^w + (1-\omega)B$$
$$= \frac{1}{\theta}\psi^w N^w + \frac{1-\omega}{\gamma}\left[\frac{\psi^r}{\theta}N^r - (Q + \alpha^r K^r)K^r\right]$$
$$= Q(\bar{K} - K^h - K^r).$$

Thus

$$\frac{\psi^w}{\theta}N^w + \frac{1-\omega}{\gamma}\frac{\psi^r}{\theta}N^r$$
$$= \frac{\psi^w}{\theta}\left[N^w + \frac{\beta x^r - 1}{\beta x^w - 1}N^r\right], (\because(\text{B}.4))$$
$$= Q\left[\bar{K} - K^h - K^r + \frac{1-\omega}{\gamma}\frac{Q + \alpha^r K^r}{Q}K^r\right]$$
$$= Q\left[\bar{K} - K^h - K^r + \frac{1-\omega}{\gamma}\frac{R_k^w}{R_k^r}K^r\right]$$
$$= Q\left[\bar{K} - K^h - \frac{\gamma + \omega - 1}{\gamma + (1-\omega)\varphi^w(\beta x^w)}K^r\right],$$

or

$$\begin{aligned}&\frac{\psi^w(x^w)}{\theta}\left[N^w(x^w)+\frac{\beta x^r-1}{\beta x^w-1}N^r(x^r)\right]\\&=Q(x^w)\left[\overline{K}-K^h(x^w)-\frac{\gamma+\omega-1}{\gamma+(1-\omega)\varphi^w(\beta x^w)}K^r(x^w)\right].\end{aligned} \tag{B.5}$$

The equilibrium is given by (x^r, x^w) which satisfies (B.4 and B.5).

We need to check $D^w > 0$, or

$$0<\left(\frac{\psi^w}{\theta\omega}-\frac{1-\omega}{\omega}\right)N^w-\frac{1}{\theta}\psi^w N^w-\frac{1-\omega}{\gamma}\left[\frac{\psi^r}{\theta}N^r-(Q+\alpha^r K^r)K^r\right],$$

or

$$\gamma\left[\frac{\psi^w(x^w)}{\theta}-1\right]N^w(x^w)>\omega\left[\frac{\psi^r(x^r)}{\theta}N^r(x^r)-[Q(x^w)+\alpha^r K^r(x^w)]\cdot K^r(x^w)\right].$$

Equilibrium E: No Active Interbank Market

We have for $j = w, r$ that

$$\frac{(Q+f^j)k^j}{n^j}=\frac{\psi^j(x^j)}{\theta},$$

$$x^j-R=(R_k^j-R)\frac{(Q+f^j)k^j}{n^j}=(R_k^j-R)\frac{\psi^j(x^j)}{\theta},$$

or

$$R_k^j-R=\theta\frac{x^j-R}{\psi^j(x^j)},$$

or

$$R_k^j=R_k^j(x^j),\ R_k^{j\prime}(\cdot)>0$$

if $\sigma^w(\beta x^j)^2 < 1$. Thus

$$Q=Q(x^w),Q'(\cdot)<0$$
$$K^h=K^h(x^w),K^{h\prime}(\cdot)>0.$$

The aggregate capital of retail banks satisfies

$$\begin{aligned}QK^r&=Q\frac{Z-(R_k^r-1)Q}{\alpha^r R_k^r}=Q(x^w)\frac{Z}{\alpha^r}\frac{R_k^w(x^w)-R_k^r(x^r)}{R_k^r(x^r)[R_k^w(x^w)-1]}\\&=\frac{\psi^r(x^r)}{\theta}N^r(x^r)\end{aligned} \tag{B.6}$$

The capital market clearing condition is

$$\begin{aligned} QK^w &= \frac{\psi^w(x^w)}{\theta} N^w(x^w) \\ &= Q(x^w)\left[\bar{K} - K^r(x^r, x^w) - K^h(x^w)\right] \end{aligned} \tag{B.7}$$

The equilibrium is given by (x^r, x^w) which satisfies (B.6 and B.7).

Appendix C Anticipated Bank Run Case

Here, we describe the conditions determining agents policy functions in the case of anticipated runs. As in the text, we focus on the case in which variation in Z_{t+1} is negligible. Moreover, we follow the notation by which for any given variable $\tilde{\xi}_t$

$$E_t^*\left(\tilde{\xi}_{t+1}\right) = (1-p_t)\xi_{t+1} + p_t\xi_{t+1}^*$$

where ξ_{t+1}^* is the value taken by $\tilde{\xi}_{t+1}$ when a run occurs.

Appendix C.1 Households

Households optimal choices of capital holdings and deposits are given by

$$E_t^*\left(\tilde{\Lambda}_{t,t+1}\right)R_{t+1} = 1$$

$$E_t^*\left(\tilde{\Lambda}_{t,t+1}\tilde{R}_{kt+1}^h\right) = 1$$

Appendix C.2 Retail Bankers

The conditions in Lemma 2 that guarantee that retail banks are constrained are now modified as follows:

Lemma C.1 $b_t^r < 0$, $k_t^r > 0$ *and the incentive constraint is binding off*

$$0 < E_t^*\left[\tilde{\Omega}_{t+1}^r\left(\tilde{R}_{kt+1}^r - R_{t+1}\right)\right] = \frac{1}{\gamma}E_t^*\left[\tilde{\Omega}_{t+1}^r\left(\tilde{R}_{bt+1} - R_{t+1}\right)\right] < \theta.$$

The optimal choice of leverage is

$$\phi_t^r = \frac{E_t^*\left(\tilde{\Omega}_{t+1}^r\right)R_{t+1}}{\theta - E_t^*\left[\tilde{\Omega}_{t+1}^r\left(\tilde{R}_{kt+1}^r - R_{t+1}\right)\right]}.$$

Appendix C.3 Wholesale Bankers

The optimization problem of wholesale banks when bank runs are anticipated is complicated by the fact that the banker can avoid bankruptcy by reducing its leverage in case a run materializes. Here, we derive conditions under which he does not wish to do this. For simplicity, we focus on the problem of a wholesale banker that only funds himself in the interbank market.

In this case we can derive a threshold level for leverage, ϕ_t^{wM}, under which the banker will survive a bank run, which is given by

$$\bar{R}_{bt+1} = R_{f,t+1} \equiv \frac{E_t^*\left(\widetilde{\Omega}_{t+1}^r \widetilde{R}_{\gamma,t+1}^r\right)}{E_t^*\left(\widetilde{\Omega}_{t+1}\right)} = R_{kt+1}^{w*} \frac{\phi_t^{wM}}{\phi_t^{wM} - 1}$$

where

$$\widetilde{R}_{\gamma,t+1}^r \equiv \gamma \widetilde{R}_{kt+1}^r + (1-\gamma) R_{t+1}$$

and $R_{f,t+1}$ is the risk free interbank rate that satisfies Eq. (44) with $x_{t+1}^w = 1$.

The objective function of wholesale bankers displays a kink at ϕ_t^{wM}, so that in order to derive their optimal leverage choice we need to study separately the optimal choice in the region where leverage is high enough to induce bankruptcy when a run happens, $[\phi_t^{wM}, \infty)$, and in the region where bankruptcy is avoided even if a run happens, $\left[0, \phi_t^{wM}\right]$. As long as wholesale bankers objective is strictly increasing in leverage in both of these regions, the incentive constraint holds with equality.

In the bankruptcy region, $[\phi_t^{wM}, \infty)$, (45) with deterministic Z_{t+1} is simplified to

$$\bar{R}_{bt+1}(\phi_t^w) = R_{\gamma,t+1}^r + \frac{p_t}{1-p_t} \frac{\Omega_{t+1}^{r*}}{\Omega_{t+1}^r} \left(R_{\gamma,t+1}^{r*} - \frac{\phi_t^w}{\phi_t^w - 1} R_{t+1}^{w*} \right).$$

Then the objective function of a wholesale bank with one unit of networth is given by

$$\begin{aligned}
\psi^w(\phi_t^w) &= (1-p_t)\left\{\Omega_{t+1}^w \left[\phi_t^w\left(R_{kt+1}^w - \bar{R}_{bt+1}(\phi_t^w)\right) + \bar{R}_{bt+1}(\phi_t^w)\right]\right\} \\
&= (1-p_t)\Omega_{t+1}^w \left[\phi_t^w\left(R_{t+1}^w - R_{\gamma,t+1}^r\right) + R_{\gamma,t+1}^r\right] \\
&\quad + p_t \Omega_{t+1}^w \frac{\Omega_{t+1}^{r*}}{\Omega_{t+1}^r}\left[\phi_t^w\left(R_{k,t+1}^{w*} - R_{\gamma,t+1}^{r*}\right) + R_{\gamma,t+1}^{r*}\right]
\end{aligned}$$

which is strictly increasing in ϕ_t^w if and only if

$$(1-p_t)\left(R_{kt+1}^w - R_{\gamma,t+1}^r\right) + p_t \frac{\Omega_{t+1}^{r*}}{\Omega_{t+1}^r}\left(R_{kt+1}^{w*} - R_{\gamma,t+1}^{r*}\right) > 0 \qquad \text{(C.1)}$$

Notice that condition (C.1) is implied by the condition that guarantees that retail bankers are constrained, $E_t^*\left[\tilde{\Omega}_t^r\left(\tilde{R}_{kt+1}^r - R_{t+1}\right)\right] > 0$, together with the fact that retail bankers are less efficient at intermediating capital than wholesale bankers $\alpha^r > 0$:

$$(1-p_t)\left(R_{kt+1}^w - R_{\gamma,t+1}^r\right) + p_t\frac{\Omega_{t+1}^{r*}}{\Omega_{t+1}^r}\left(R_{kt+1}^{w*} - R_{\gamma,t+1}^{r*}\right)$$

$$> (1-p_t)\left(R_{kt+1}^r - R_{\gamma,t+1}^r\right) + p_t\frac{\Omega_{t+1}^{r*}}{\Omega_{t+1}^r}\left(R_{k,t+1}^{r*} - R_{\gamma,t+1}^{r*}\right)$$

$$= \frac{(1-\gamma)}{\Omega_{t+1}^r}E_t^*\left\{\tilde{\Omega}_t^r\left(\tilde{R}_{kt+1}^r - R_{t+1}\right)\right\} > 0$$

In the region where the banker is able to avoid bankruptcy even when a run happens, $\left[0, \phi_t^{wM}\right]$, the objective is instead

$$\begin{aligned}\psi^{w,n}\left(\phi_t^w\right) &= E_t^*\left\{\tilde{\Omega}_{t+1}^w\left[\phi_t^w\left(\tilde{R}_{kt+1}^w - R_{f,t+1}\right) + R_{f,t+1}\right]\right\} \\ &= \begin{matrix}(1-p_t)\{\Omega_{t+1}^w[\phi_t^w(R_{kt+1}^w - R_{f,t+1}) + R_{f,t+1}]\} \\ +p_t\{\Omega_{t+1}^{w*}[\phi_t^w(R_{kt+1}^{w*} - R_{f,t+1}) + R_{f,t+1}]\}\end{matrix}\end{aligned}$$

and the condition that guarantees that the objective is strictly increasing in ϕ_t^w in this region is

$$E_t^*\left[\tilde{\Omega}_{t+1}^w\left(\tilde{R}_{kt+1}^w - R_{f,t+1}\right)\right] > 0. \quad \text{(C.2)}$$

Given this we can modify the conditions in Lemma 1 as follows:

Lemma C.2 *Under the conditions of Lemma C.1, the incentive constraint is binding off*

$$0 < E_t^*\left[\tilde{\Omega}_{t+1}^w\left(\tilde{R}_{kt+1}^w - R_{f,t+1}\right)\right]$$

$$\theta\omega > (1-p_t)\left(R_{kt+1}^w - R_{\gamma,t+1}^r\right) + p_t\frac{\Omega_{t+1}^{r*}}{\Omega_{t+1}^r}\left(R_{kt+1}^{w*} - R_{\gamma,t+1}^{r*}\right).$$

Appendix D Measurement

We use data from the Flow of Funds in order to construct empirical counterparts of the financial flows in the simplified intermediation process described in Fig. 1. The first step in constructing our time series is a definition of the wholesale and retail sector within the broad financial business sector.

Our classification is based on the sectors and instruments reported in the Flow of Funds. We use the liability structure of the different sectors included in the "Financial

Business" sector of the Flow of Funds in order to aggregate them into a Retail sector, a Wholesale sector, and Others. To do this, we proceed in two steps: we first classify the funding instruments in the Flow of Funds into four categories that we name Retail Funding, Wholesale Funding, Intermediated Assets, and Other Instruments; then we assign financial intermediaries to the Retail/Wholesale sector if the funding instruments they mostly rely on belong to the Retail/Wholesale category.

Table D.1 describes the four categories of funding we use. The labels in parentheses are the identifiers in the Flow of Funds.

The criterion we use to define the above categories is the composition of demand and supply for each instrument. Instruments that are supplied by financial intermediaries and demanded by households fall in the Retail category, while instruments that are mainly traded among financial intermediaries are included in Wholesale Funding. Intermediated Assets consist of all of the claims issued by domestic nonfinancial business and households. Others is a residual category.

To define our Retail and Wholesale sectors, we start by excluding some types of intermediaries from the ones that we are trying to study in our model economy. These are the intermediaries listed in the "Others" category in Table D.2. The remaining financial intermediaries appearing in the Flow of Funds are included in the Retail/Wholesale sector if they mostly rely on Retail/Wholesale funding. The resulting aggregation is described in Table D.2.

Table D.1 Classification of instruments in the flow of funds

Retail funding	Checkable deposits and currency (L.204) Time and saving deposits (L.205) Money market mutual fund shares (L.206) Mutual fund shares (L.214)	
Wholesale funding	*Short term*	Repurchase agreements (L.207) Security credit (L.224) Financial open market paper (L.208) Agency/GSE backed securities (L.210)
	Long term	Financial corporate bonds (L.212) Retail loans to wholesale (L.215)
Intermediated assets	Non-financial corporate bonds (L.212) Non-financial equity (L.213) Non-financial open market paper (L.208) Retail loans to non-financial (L.215) Mortgages (L.217) Consumer credit (L.222) Other loans (L.216)	
Other types of funding	All other instruments in the flow of funds	

Table D.2 Aggregation of financial sectors in the flow of funds

Retail sector	Private depository institutions (L.110) Money market mutual funds (L.121) Mutual funds (L.122)
Wholesale sector	Security brokers dealers (L.129) ABS issuers (L.126) GSE and GSE mortgage pools (L.124–125) Real estate investment trusts (L.128) Finance companies (L.127) Funding corporations (L.131) Holding companies (L.130)
Other intermediaries	Monetary authority (L.109) Private and public pension funds (L.117) Closed end and exchange traded funds (L.123) Insurance companies (L.115–116) Government (L.105–106) Rest of the world (L.132)
Households	L.101
Firms	L.102

Given this we construct the following measures:

1. K_t^h, K_t^r, K_t^w

The intermediation shares are constructed by computing aggregate short and long positions of Households, Retail Banks, and Wholesale banks in the markets that make up the Intermediated Assets category in Table D.1. The matrix below describes each sectors' activity in each market. If sector J has a long/short position in market X the corresponding entry is given by X_+^J / X_-^J. If sector J has both long and short positions in market X, the corresponding entry also displays its net position, $X_{net}^J(+)/X_{net}^J(-)$.

Markets	Bonds *L.212*	Equity *L.213*	Comm paper *L.208*	Loans *L.215*	Mortgages *L.208*	Consumer credit *L.222*
Sectors Retail banks	BO_+^R BO_-^R $BO_{net}^R(+)$	EQ_+^R NA ?	CP_+^R CP_-^R $CP_{net}^R(+)$	L_+^R	M_+^R	CC_+^R
Wholesale banks	BO_+^W BO_-^W $BO_{net}^W(-)$	EQ_+^W NA ?	CP_+^W CP_-^W $CP_{net}^W(-)$	L_-^W	M_+^W	CC_+^W
Other item	BO_+^O BO_-^O $BO_{net}^O(+)$	EQ_+^O NA ?	CP_+^O CP_-^O $CP_{net}^O(+)$	L_-^O	M_+^O	CC_+^O

Markets	Bonds *L*.212	Equity *L*.213	Comm paper *L*.208	Loans *L*.215	Mortgages *L*.208	Consumer credit *L*.222
Households	BO_{+}^{H}	EQ_{+}^{H}	0 0	L_{-}^{H}	M_{-}^{H}	CC_{-}^{H}
Firms	BO_{-}^{F}	EQ_{-}^{F}	CP_{+}^{F} CP_{-}^{F} $CP_{net}^{F}(-)$	L_{-}^{F}	M_{+}^{F} M_{-}^{F} $M_{net}^{F}(-)$	CC_{+}^{F}

We make several assumptions in order to conduct our measures.First, in the markets for bonds and commercial paper, some positions are potentially inconsistent with our intermediation model. This is because some sectors within the retail category are short in these markets and some in wholesale are long, $BO_{-}^{R}>0$, $CP_{-}^{R}>0$, $BO_{+}^{W}>0$ and $CP_{+}^{W}>0$. This allows for the possibility that retail banks were borrowing from wholesale in these markets. However, we rule out this possibility in constructing our measures for two reasons: given the heavy reliance on these types of instruments in financial transactions among industries within the respective categories and among financial firms within the same industry, it is reasonable to assume that the vast majority of these offsetting positions were actually arising from cross holdings among firms within the same category; moreover, the actual size of BO_{-}^{R} and CP_{-}^{R} with respect to BO_{-}^{W} and CP_{-}^{W} was very small, ie, $\frac{CP_{-}^{R}}{CP_{-}^{W}}\simeq 0.1\%$ and $\frac{CP_{-}^{R}}{CP_{-}^{W}}\simeq 3\%$ in 2007. This implies that we can safely work with the net positions for wholesalers and retailers. Given the assumptions we make in these markets we can construct model consistent measures from bonds and commercial paper data by assuming that households lend to nonfinancial firms, which is part of K^h, while retail banks (and Other intermediaries) lend to both Wholesale banks, which is part of B, and firms, which is part of K^r.[ax] We also assume that portfolio weights on nonfinancial and financial issued instruments in these markets are the same for retail banks and other intermediaries.[ay] That is, letting $F_{bo}^{i,F}$ and $F_{cp}^{i,F}$ be the proportions of lender's *i's* holdings of bonds and commercial paper that are issued by nonfinancial firms, we have

[ax] The Households' sector in the Flow of Funds is a residual category that includes Hedge Funds, private equity funds and personal trusts, which are intermediaries that our model does not directly capture. In any case, households' intermediation in bonds and commercial paper market is a small component of household intermediation so that very little would change if we instead made different assumptions about households positions in these markets.

[ay] We include long positions of nonfinancial firms in the commercial paper within intermediation performed by "Others."

$$F_{bo}^{H,F} = 1; F_{bo}^{R,F} = \left(\frac{BO_-^F - BO_+^H}{BO_-^F + BO_{net}^W - BO_+^H} \right);^{az}$$

Similarly for commercial paper: $F_{cp}^{H,F} = 0; F_{cp}^{R,F} = \frac{CP_-^F}{CP_-^F + CP_{net}^W}$ Second, for corporate equities the Flow of Funds does not report a disaggregated measure of equity issued by individual industries or the type of equity held by the various industries. Since we use this market only in measuring K^i, we simply assume that each sector holds a scaled version of the same equity portfolio consisting of the three sectors for which we have issuance data: Foreign equities, Financial Business equities, and Non-Financial Business Equities, denoted by EQ^{ROW}, EQ^{FIN}, and EQ^{NFI}, respectively. That is, in order to compute how many funds flow to nonfinancial firms from each other sector we simply scale their total equity holdings by

$$\eta = \frac{EQ^{NFI}}{EQ^{NFI} + EQ^{FIN} + EQ^{ROW}}$$

Given this we can compute

$$K_t^h = \eta EQ^H + BO_+^H$$

$$K_t^r = \eta EQ^R + F_{bo}^{R,F} BO_{net}^R + F_{cp}^{R,F} CP_{net}^R$$
$$+ L_-^F + L_-^H + M_+^R + CC_+^R$$

$$K_t^W = \eta EQ^W + M_+^W + CC_+^W$$

2. B,D

   B is simply computed as wholesale net borrowing in all of the short-term wholesale instruments: Repo, Commercial Paper, Agency Debt, and Security credit. D is given by Households and nonfinancial Business holdings of retail funding instruments.
3. Leverage multiple for broker dealers, finance companies, and GSE

   We compute financial leverage multiple for these three sectors by dividing total financial assets by financial assets minus financial liabilities plus equity investment by holding companies. We do not have a measure of nonfinancial assets in the Flow of Funds so the leverage multiple reported here overstates financial leverage multiple that would include nonfinancial assets in the computation. We compute average leverage multiple by using time varying weights corresponding to the relative sizes of these three sectors as measured by total financial assets.

[az] Notice that we attribute all household's lending in this market, BO_+^H, to "nonfinancial loans" K^h; we then allocate retail bankers supply of funds in this market to nonfinancial loans, K^r proportionally to the weight of nonfinancial firms demand for funds that is not met by households, $BO_-^F - BO_+^H$, in the total demand for funds that is not met by households, $BO_-^F + BO_{net}^W - BO_+^H$

Appendix E Computation

It is convenient for computations to introduce the ex-ante optimal values of surviving bankers at time t in the two sectors:

$$\begin{aligned}\bar{V}_t^w &= \left[1-\sigma+\sigma\theta\left(1-\omega+\omega\phi_t^w\right)\right]\frac{N_t^w-W^w}{\sigma^w} \\ &= \Omega_t^w\frac{N_t^w-W^w}{\sigma^w}\end{aligned} \tag{E.1}$$

$$\begin{aligned}\bar{V}_t^r &= \left[1-\sigma+\sigma\theta\phi_t^r\right]\frac{N_t^r-W^r}{\sigma^r} \\ &= \Omega_t^r\frac{N_t^r-W^r}{\sigma^r}\end{aligned} \tag{E.2}$$

Let the state of the economy if a run has not happened be denoted by $x=(N^w,N^r,Z)$, and the state in case a run has happened be denoted by $x^*=(0,N^r,Z)$. We use time iteration in order to approximate the functions

$$\left\{\mathbf{Q}(x),\mathbf{C}^h(x),\bar{\mathbf{V}}^r(x),\bar{\mathbf{V}}^w(x),\Gamma(x)\right\}\quad x\in\left[W^w,\bar{N}^w\right]\times\left[W^r,\bar{N}^r\right]\times\left[(0.95)Z,Z\right]$$

and

$$\left\{\mathbf{Q}^*(x),\mathbf{C}^{h*}(x^*),\bar{\mathbf{V}}^{r*}(x^*),\Gamma^*(x^*)\right\}\quad x^*\in\{0\}\times\left[W^r,\bar{N}^r\right]\times\left[(0.95)Z,Z\right]$$

where $\Gamma(x)$ and $\Gamma^*(x^*)$ are the laws determining the stochastic evolution of the state (see later).

The computational algorithm proceeds as follows:

1. Determine a functional space to use for approximating equilibrium functions. (We use piecewise linear).
2. Fix a grid of values for the state in case no run happens $G\subset\left[W^w,\bar{N}^w\right]\times\left[W^r,\bar{N}^r\right]\times[0.95,1]$ and for the state in case a run happens $G^*\subset\{0\}\times\left[W^r,\bar{N}^r\right]\times[0.95,1]$.
3. Set $j=0$ and guess initial values for

$$NRPol_{t,j}=\left\{Q_{t,j}(x),\ C_{t,j}^h(x),\ \bar{V}_{t,j}^r(x),\ \bar{V}_{t,j}^w(x),\Gamma_{t,j}(x)\right\}_{x\in G}$$

and

$$RPol_{t,j}=\left\{Q_{t,j}^*(x),\ C_{t,j}^{h*}(x^*),\ \bar{V}_{t,j}^{r*}(x^*),\Gamma_{t,j}^*(x^*)\right\}_{x^*\in G^*}.$$

The guess for $\Gamma_{t,j}(x)$ involves guessing $\left\{p_{t,j}(x),\ N_{t,j}^{r\prime}(x),\ N_{t,j}^{w\prime}(x),\ N_{t,j}^{r\prime *}(x),Z'(x)\right\}$ which implies

$$\Gamma_{t,j}(x)=\begin{cases}\left(N_{t,j}^{w\prime}(x),\ N_{t,j}^{r\prime}(x),Z'(Z)\right) & w.p.\ 1-p_{t,j}(x)\\ \left(0,\ N_{t,j}^{r\prime *}(x),Z'(Z)\right) & w.p.\ p_{t,j}(x)\end{cases}.$$

We denote by $x_{t,j}^{\prime NR}(x) = \left(N_{t,j}^{w\prime}(x), N_{t,j}^{r\prime}(x), Z'(Z)\right)$ the state evolution if there is no run in the following period and $x_{t,j}^{\prime R}(x) = \left(0, N_{t,j}^{r\prime *}(x), Z'(Z)\right)$ the evolution if a run happens in the following period.

Similarly the guess for $\Gamma_{t,j}^{*}(x^{*})$ involves guessing $\left\{\hat{N}_{t,j}^{r\prime}(x^{*}), Z'(Z)\right\}$ which implies

$$\Gamma_{t,j}^{*}(x^{*}) = \left((1+\sigma^{w})W^{w}, \hat{N}_{t,j}^{r\prime}(x^{*}), Z'(Z)\right)$$

4. Assume that $NRPol_{t,j}$ and $RPol_{t,j}$ have been found for $j \leq i < M$ where M is set to 10,000. To find $NRPol_{t,i+1}$ and $RPol_{t,i+1}$, first use $NRPol_{t,i}$ and $RPol_{t,i}$ to find functions in the approximating space that take on these values on the grid, eg, $\mathbf{Q}_i$: $[W^{w}, \bar{N}^{w}] \times [W^{r}, \bar{N}^{r}] \times [0.95, 1] \rightarrow \mathbf{R}$ is the price function that satisfies $\mathbf{Q}_i(x) = Q_{t,i}(x)$ for each $x \in G$.
5. Derive $NRPol_{t,i+1}$ and $RPol_{t,i+1}$ by assuming that from time $t+1$ onwards equilibrium outcomes are determined according to the functions associated to $NRPol_{t,i}$ and $RPol_{t,i}$ found in step 4:
   - NO RUN SYSTEM

   At any point $x_t = (N_t^{w}, N_t^{r}, Z_t) \in G$ the system determining $\{\phi_t^{w}, \phi_t^{r}, B_t, Q_t, C_t^{h}, K_t^{h}, K_t^{r}\}$ is given by

$$\theta\left[1-\omega+\omega\phi_t^{w}\right]N_t^{w} = \beta(1-\mathbf{p}_i(x_t))\bar{\mathbf{V}}_i^{w}(\mathbf{x}_i^{\prime NR}(x_t))$$

$$(\phi_t^{w}-1)N_t^{w} = B_t$$

$$\phi_t^{w}N_t^{w} = Q_t(1-K_t^{r}-K_t^{h})$$

$$\theta\phi_t^{r}N_t^{r} = \beta\left[(1-\mathbf{p}_i(x_t))\bar{\mathbf{V}}_i^{r}(\mathbf{x}_i^{\prime NR}(x)) + \mathbf{p}_i(x_t)\bar{\mathbf{V}}_i^{r*}(\mathbf{x}_i^{\prime R}(x))\right]$$

$$\phi_t^{r}N_t^{r} = (Q_t + \alpha^{r}K_t^{r})K_t^{r} + (1-\gamma)B_t$$

$$\beta E_i\left\{\frac{C_t^{h}}{\tilde{\mathbf{C}}_i^{h}(\Gamma_i(x))}\left(\mathbf{Z}'(Z_t) + \tilde{\mathbf{Q}}_i(\Gamma_i(x))\right)\right\} = Q_t + \alpha^{h}K_t^{h}$$

$$C_t^{h} + \frac{(1-\sigma_w)(N_t^{r}-W^{w})}{\sigma_w} + \frac{(1-\sigma_r)(N_t^{r}-W^{r})}{\sigma_r} + \frac{\alpha^{h}(K_t^{h})^2}{2} + \frac{\alpha^{r}(K_t^{r})^2}{2} =$$
$$Z_t(1+W^{h}) + W^{r} + W^{w} =$$

where E_i is the expectation operator associated with the stochastic realization of a run according to $\mathbf{p}_i$ and tildes denote random variables whose values depend on the realization of the sunspot. For instance,

$$\widetilde{\mathbf{C}}_i^h(\Gamma_i(x)) = \begin{cases} \mathbf{C}_i^h\left(\mathbf{N}_i^{w\prime}(x), \mathbf{N}_i^{r\prime}(x), \mathbf{Z}'(Z)\right) & w.p.\ 1-\mathbf{p}_i(x) \\ \mathbf{C}_i^{h*}\left(\mathbf{N}_i^{r\prime*}(x), \mathbf{Z}'(Z)\right) & w.p.\ \mathbf{p}_i(x) \end{cases}$$

One can then find $\left\{R_t, \bar{R}_t^b\right\}$ from

$$R_t = \frac{1}{\beta E_i\left\{\dfrac{C_t^h}{\widetilde{\mathbf{C}}_i^h(\Gamma_i(x))}\right\}}$$

$$\bar{R}_t^b = \frac{E_i\left\{\widetilde{\Omega}^r(\Gamma_i(x))\left(\gamma\dfrac{\left(\mathbf{Z}'(Z_t)+\widetilde{\mathbf{Q}}_i(\Gamma_i(x))\right)}{Q_t+\alpha^r K_t^r}+(1-\gamma)R_t\right)\right\}}{(1-\mathbf{p}_i(x_t))\boldsymbol{\Omega}^r(\mathbf{x}_i'^{NR}(x_t))} - \frac{-\mathbf{p}_i\boldsymbol{\Omega}^{r*}\left(x_i'^{R}(x_t)\right)\left(\dfrac{\left(\mathbf{Z}'(Z_t)+\widetilde{\mathbf{Q}}_i(\Gamma_i(x))\right)}{Q_t}\dfrac{\phi_t^w}{\phi_t^w-1}\right)}{(1-\mathbf{p}_i(x_t))\boldsymbol{\Omega}^r(\mathbf{x}_i'^{NR}(x_t))}$$

where

$$\widetilde{\Omega}^r(\Gamma_i(x)) = \begin{cases} \sigma^r\dfrac{\bar{\mathbf{V}}_i^r\left(\mathbf{N}_i^{w\prime}(x), \mathbf{N}_i^{r\prime}(x), \mathbf{Z}'(Z)\right)}{\mathbf{N}_i^{w\prime}(x)-W} & w.p.\ 1-\mathbf{p}_i(x) \\ \sigma^r\dfrac{\bar{\mathbf{V}}_i^{r*}\left(\mathbf{N}_i^{r\prime*}(x), \mathbf{Z}'(Z)\right)}{\mathbf{N}_i^{w\prime}(x)-W} & w.p.\ \mathbf{p}_i(x) \end{cases}$$

and finally $\left\{\bar{V}_t^r, \bar{V}_t^w, {}_t\right\}$ are given by

$$\bar{V}_t^w = \left[1-\sigma+\sigma\theta\left(1-\omega+\omega\phi_t^w\right)\right]\frac{N_t^w-W^w}{\sigma^w}$$

$$\bar{V}_t^r = \left[1-\sigma+\sigma\theta\phi_t^r\right]\frac{N_t^r-W^r}{\sigma^r}$$

$$\Gamma_t = \begin{cases} \left(N_{t+1}^w, N_{t+1}^r, Z'(Z)\right) & w.p.\ 1-p_t \\ \left(0, N_{t+1}^{r*}, Z'(Z)\right) & w.p.\ p_t \end{cases}$$

where

$$N_{t+1}^w = \sigma^w N_t^w\left[\phi_t^w\left(\frac{\mathbf{Z}'(Z_t)+\mathbf{Q}_i\left(\mathbf{x}_i'^{NR}(x)\right)}{Q_t}-\bar{R}_t^b\right)+-R_t^b\right]+W^w$$

$$N_{t+1}^r = \sigma^r\left(\left[\mathbf{Z}'(Z_t)+\mathbf{Q}_i\left(\mathbf{x}_i'^{NR}(x)\right)\right]K_t^r+B_t\bar{R}_t^b-D_tR_t\right)+W^w$$

$$N_{t+1}^{r*} = \sigma^r\left(\left[Z'(Z_t) + \mathbf{Q}_i^*\left(\mathbf{x}_i^{\prime R}(x)\right)\right]\left(K_t^r + K_t^w\right) - D_t R_t\right) + W^w$$

$$p_t = \left[1 - \frac{\dfrac{Z'(Z_t) + \mathbf{Q}_i^*\left(\mathbf{x}_i^{\prime R}(x)\right)}{Q_t}}{\bar{R}_{bt}} \cdot \frac{\phi_t^w}{\phi_t^w - 1}\right]^{\delta}$$

- RUN SYSTEM

Analogously at a point $x_t^* = \left(0, N_t^r, Z_t\right) \in G^*$ the system determining $\left\{\phi_t^{r*}, Q_t^*, C_t^{h*}, K_t^{h*}\right\}$ is given by

$$\theta\phi_t^{r*} N_t^r = \beta - \mathbf{V}_i^r\left(\Gamma_i^*\left(x_t^*\right)\right)$$

$$\phi_t^{r*} N_t^r = \left(Q_t^* + \alpha^r K_t^{r*}\right) K_t^{r*}$$

$$\beta\left\{\frac{C_t^{h*}}{\mathbf{C}_i^h\left(\Gamma_i^*\left(x_t^*\right)\right)}\left(Z'(Z_t) + \mathbf{Q}_i\left(\Gamma_i^*\left(x_t^*\right)\right)\right)\right\} = Q_t^* + \alpha^h K_t^{h*}$$

$$C_t^{h*} + \frac{(1 - \sigma_r)}{\sigma_r}\left(N_t^r - W^r\right) + \frac{\alpha^h}{2}\left(K_t^{h*}\right)^2 + \frac{\alpha^r}{2}\left(1 - K_t^{h*}\right)^2 = Z_t\left(1 + W^h\right) + W^r$$

and $\left\{R_t^*, \bar{V}_t^{r*}, \Gamma_t^*\right\}$ are given by

$$R_t^* = \frac{1}{\beta E_i\left\{\dfrac{C_t^{h*}}{\mathbf{C}_i^h\left(\Gamma_i^*\left(x_t^*\right)\right)}\right\}}$$

$$\bar{V}_t^{r*} = \left[1 - \sigma + \sigma\theta\phi_t^{r*}\right]\frac{N_t^r - W^r}{\sigma^r}$$

$$\Gamma_i^*(x^*) = \left(\left(1 + \sigma^w\right)W^w, \hat{N}_{t+1}^r, Z'(Z)\right)$$

$$\hat{N}_{t+1}^r = \sigma^r N_r^r\left[\phi_t^{r*}\left(\frac{Z'(Z_t) + \mathbf{Q}_i\left(\Gamma_i^*\left(x_t^*\right)\right)}{Q_t} - R_t^*\right) + R_t^*\right] + W^r$$

6. Compute the maximum distance between $NRPol_t = \left\{Q_t, \bar{V}_t^r, \bar{V}_t^w, C_t^h, p_t, N_{t+1}^r, N_{t+1}^w, N_{t+1}^{r*}\right\}$ and $NRPol_{t,i}$

$$dNR = \max_{x_t \in G} \max\left|NRPol_t - NRPol_{t,i}\right|$$

and similarly for $RPol_t = \left\{Q_t^*, -V_t^{r*}, C_t^{h*}, \hat{N}_{t+1}^r\right\}$ and $RPol_{t,i}$

$$dR = \max_{x_t \in G^*} \max\left|RPol_t - RPol_{t,i}\right|$$

if dNR and dR are small enough, in our case $e - 6$, set

$$NRPol_{t,i+1} = NRPol_{t,i}$$
$$RPol_{t,i+1} = RPol_{t,i}$$

Otherwise set

$$NRPol_{t,i+1} = \alpha NRPol_{t,i} + (1-\alpha)NRPol_t$$
$$RPol_{t,i+1} = \alpha RPol_{t,i} + (1-\alpha)RPol_t$$

where $\alpha \in (0,1)$.

REFERENCES

Adrian, T., Ashcraft, A., 2012. Shadow banking: a review of the literature. In: The New Palgrave Dictionary of Economics, 2012 Version, second ed. [internet]. Palgrave Macmillan, Basingstoke.
Adrian, T., Colla, P., Shin, H., 2012. Which financial frictions? Paring the evidence from financial crisis of 2007-9. In: Acemoglu, D., Parker, J., Woodford, M. (Eds.), NBER Macroeconomic Annual 2012, vol. 27, May 2013, pp. 159–214.
Allen, F., Gale, D., 2007. Understanding Financial Crises. Oxford University Press, Oxford.
Angeloni, I., Faia, E., 2013. Capital regulation and monetary policy with fragile banks. J. Monet. Policy 60, 3111–3382.
Begenau, J., 2015. Capital requirements, risk choice, and liquidity provision in a business cycle model. Harvard Business School Working Paper, no. 15-072.
Bernanke, B., 2010. Causes of the recent financial and economic crisis. Statement before the Financial Crisis Inquiry Commission, Washington, September 2.
Bernanke, B., Gertler, M., 1989. Agency costs, net worth and business fluctuations. Am. Econ. Rev. 79, 14–31.
Bianchi, J., 2011. Overborrowing and systemic externalities in the business cycle. Am. Econ. Rev. 101, 3400–3426.
Bianchi, J., Mendoza, E., 2013. Optimal time-consistent macroprudential policy. NBER Working Paper 19704.
Bigio, S., 2015. Financial risk capacity. Working Paper.
Bocola, L., 2016. The Pass-Through of Sovereign Risk. J. Polit. Econ. forthcoming.
Boissay, F., Collard, F., Smets, F., 2013. Booms and systemic banking crises. Mimeo.
Brunnermeier, M.K., Oemke, M., 2013. Maturity rat race. J. Finance 68, 483–521.
Brunnermeier, M.K., Pedersen, L., 2009. Market liquidity and funding liquidity. Rev. Financ. Stud. 22, 2201–2238.
Brunnermeier, M.K., Sannikov, Y., 2014. A macroeconomic model with a financial sector. Am. Econ. Rev. 104, 379–421.
Caballero, R., Farhi, E., 2015. The safety trap. Working Paper.
Chari, V., Kehoe, P., 2015. Bailouts, time inconsistency, and optimal regulation: a macroeconomic view. Federal Reserve Bank of Minneapolis, Research Department Staff Report 481.
Christiano, L., Ikeda, D., 2014. Leverage restrictions in a business cycle model. In: Macroeconomic and Financial Stability: Challenges for Monetary Policy.
Cole, H., Kehoe, T., 2000. Self-fulfilling debt crises. Rev. Econ. Stud. 67, 91–161.
Cooper, R., Ross, T., 1998. Bank runs: liquidity costs and investment distortions. J. Monet. Econ. 41, 27–38.
Covitz, D., Liang, N., Suarez, G., 2013. Evolution of a financial crisis: collapse of the asset-backed commercial paper market. J. Finance 68, 815.
Curdia, V., Woodford, M., 2010. Credit spreads and monetary policy. J. Money Credit Bank. 42 (6), 3–35.

Dang, T., Gorton, G., Holmstrom, B., 2012. Ignorance, debt and financial crises.
Diamond, D., Dybvig, P., 1983. Bank runs, deposit insurance, and liquidity. J. Polit. Econ. 91, 401–419.
Di Tella, S., 2014. Uncertainty shocks and balance sheet recessions. Working Paper.
Eggertsson, G., Krugman, P., 2012. Debt, Deleveraging, and Liquidity Trap: a Fisher-Minsky-Koo Approach, Q. J. Econ. 127 (3), 1469–1513.
Ennis, H., Keister, T., 2003. Economic growth, liquidity, and bank runs. J. Econ. Theory 109, 220–245.
Farhi, E., Tirole, J., 2012. Collective moral hazard, maturity mismatch and systemic bailouts. Am. Econ. Rev. 102 (1), 60–93.
Farhi, E., Werning, I., 2015. A theory of macroprudential policies in the presence of nominal rigidities. Working Paper.
Farmer, R., 1999. The Macroeconomics of Self-Fulfilling Prophecies. MIT Press.
Ferrante, F., 2015a. A model of endogenous loan quality and the collapse of the shadow banking system. Finance and Economics Discussion Series 2015-021, Federal Reserve Board.
Ferrante, F., 2015b. Risky mortgages, bank leverage and credit policy. Working Paper.
Garleanu, N., Panageas, S., Yu, J., 2015. Financial entanglement: a theory of incomplete integration, leverage, crashes and contagion. Am. Econ. Rev. 105 (7), 1979–2010.
Geanakoplos, J., Polemarchakis, H., 1986. Existence, regularity, and constrained suboptimality of competitive allocations when the asset market is incomplete. In: Uncertainty, Information, and Communication: Essays in Honor of K. J. Arrow, III. Cambridge University Press, Cambridge.
Gertler, M., Karadi, P., 2011. A model of unconventional monetary policy. J. Monet. Econ. 58 (1), 17–34.
Gertler, M., Kiyotaki, N., 2011. Financial Intermediation and Credit Policy in Business Cycle Analysis. In: Friedman, B.M., Woodford, M. (Eds.), Handbook of Monetary Economics, vol. 3A. Elsevier Science, Amsterdam, pp. 547–599.
Gertler, M., Kiyotaki, N., 2015. Banking, liquidity and bank runs in an infinite horizon economy. Am. Econ. Rev. 105 (7), 2011–2043
Gertler, M., Kiyotaki, N., Prestipino, A., 2016. Anticiapted Banking Panics. Am. Econ. Rev. Pap. Proc. 106 (5), 554–559.
Gertler, M., Kiyotaki, N., Queralto, A., 2012. Financial crises, bank risk exposure and government financial policy. J. Monet. Econ. 59, S17–S34.
Gilchrist, S., Zakrajsek, E., 2012. Credit spread and business cycle fluctuations. Am. Econ. Rev. 102, 1692–1720.
Giroud, X., Mueller, H., 2015. Firm leverage and unemployment during the great recession. Mimeo.
Goldstein, I., Pauzner, A., 2005. Demand-deposit contracts and the probability of bank runs. J. Finance 60, 1293–1327.
Gorton, G., 2009. Information, liquidity and the (ongoing) panic of 2007. Am. Econ. Rev. Pap. Proc. 99 (2), 567–572.
Gorton, G., Metrick, A., 2012. Who ran on repo? NBER Working Paper 18455.
Gorton, G., Metrick, A., 2015. The safe asset share. Am. Econ. Rev. Pap. Proc. 102 (3), 101–106.
Guerrieri, V., Lorenzoni, G., 2011. Credit crises, precautionary savings and the liquidity trap. NBER Working Paper 17583.
Gurley, J., Shaw, E., 1960. Money in Theory of Finance. Brookings Institution, Washington, DC.
He, Z., Krishnamurthy, A., 2013. Intermediary asset pricing. Am. Econ. Rev. 103 (2), 732–770.
He, Z., Krishnamurthy, A., 2014. A macroeconomic framework for quantifying systemic risk. University of Chicago and Stanford University, Working Paper.
Holmstrom, B., Tirole, J., 1997. Financial intermediation, loanable funds and the real sector. Q. J. Econ. 112 (3), 663–691.
Holmstrom, B., Tirole, J., 2011. Inside and Outside Liquidity. MIT Press, Cambridge, MA.
Iacoviello, M., 2005. House prices, borrowing constraints and monetary policy in the business cycle. Am. Econ. Rev. 95 (3), 739–764.
Kacperczyk, M., Schnabl, P., 2010. When safe proved risky: commercial paper during the financial crisis of 2007-2009. J. Econ. Perspect. 24 (1), 29–50.
Kiyotaki, N., Moore, J., 1997. Credit cycles. J. Polit. Econ. 105, 211–248.
Korinek, A., Simsek, A., 2015. Liquidity trap and excessive leverage. Working Paper.

Krishnamurthy, A., 2003. Collateral constraints and the amplification mechanism. J. Econo. Theory 111 (2), 277–292.
Krishnamurthy, A., Nagel, S., Orlov, D., 2014. Seizing up repo. J. Finance 69 (6), 2381–2417.
Lorenzoni, G., 2008. Inefficient credit boom. Rev. Econ. Stud. 75, 809–833.
Martin, A., Skeie, D., Thadden, E.V., 2014. Fragility of short-term secured funding. J. Econ. Theory 149, 15–42.
Martin, A., Skeie, D., Thadden, E.V., 2014. Repo runs. Rev. Financ. Stud. 27, 957–989.
McCabe, P., 2010. The cross section of money market fund risks and financial crises. Finance and Economics Discussion Series 2010-51, Federal Reserve Board.
Mendoza, E., 2010. Sudden stops, financial crises, and leverage. Am. Econ. Rev. 100, 1941–1966.
Midrigan, T., Philippon, T., 2011. A macroeconomic framework for quantifying systemic risk. NBER Working Paper 19885.
Morris, S., Shin, H., 1998. Unique equilibrium in a model of self-fulfilling currency attacks. Am. Econ. Rev. 88, 587–597.
Parlatore, C., 2015. Fragility in money market funds: sponsor support and regulation. Working Paper.
Philippon, T., 2015. Has the US Finance Industry Become Less Efficient? On the Theory and Measurement of Financial Intermediation. Am. Econ. Rev. 105 (4), 1408–1438.
Pozsar, Z., Adrian, T., Ashcraft, A., Boesky, H., 2013. Shadow banking. Fed. Reserv Bank. New York Econ. Policy Rev 19 (2), 1–16.
Robatto, R., 2014. Financial crises and systematic bank runs in a dynamic model of banking.
Uhlig, H., 2010. A model of a systemic bank run. J. Monet. Econ. 57, 78–96.

CHAPTER 17

Housing and Credit Markets: Booms and Busts

V. Guerrieri*,†, H. Uhlig*,†,‡
*University of Chicago, Chicago, IL, United States
†NBER, Cambridge, MA, United States
‡CEPR, London, United Kingdom

Contents

Abstract

Prompted by the recent US experience, in this chapter, we study the interaction between cycles in credit markets and cycles in housing markets. There is a large growing literature exploring two different approaches: on the one hand, a boom–bust in house prices can generate a boom–bust in credit market and, on the other hand, a boom–bust in credit markets can generate a boom–bust in house prices. We start by presenting a stark mechanical model to formalize the interaction between housing prices

Handbook of Macroeconomics, Volume 2B
ISSN 1574-0048, http://dx.doi.org/10.1016/bs.hesmac.2016.06.001

and credit markets and explore these two channels in a mechanical way. Next, we present two simple models that highlight the two approaches. First, we propose a catastrophe model, where an increase in credit availability can generate first a boom and then a bust in mortgage markets because of multiple equilibria due to adverse selection: as lending expands, the composition of borrowers worsens and at some point this can generate a crash in credit market. Second, we propose a sentiment model, where house prices increase above fundamentals because investors buy assets under the irrational belief that there is always going to be an ever more foolish buyer, willing to buy at a higher price. In the course of the chapter, we relate our simple models to the large existing literature on these topics. At the end, we also point to some empirical papers that propose related facts.

Keywords

Housing prices, Credit markets, Cycles, Leverage, Adverse selection, Bubbles, Sentiments

JEL Classification Codes:

D82, D84, E44, G21

1. INTRODUCTION

In the recent years, the United States has experienced, at the same time, a boom–bust episode in house price and a boom–bust episode in credit markets, as reflected in Figs. 1 and 2.

The purpose of this chapter is to explore the connection between financial markets and the housing market and its effects on the macroeconomic activity. There is a large and growing literature that separately explores credit cycles and house price bubbles and busts. In this chapter, we will try to connect these two streams of literature and understand the potential feedbacks between the two.

In particular, we will explore two different broad approaches to think about this connection:

1. the house price boom–bust generates the credit boom–bust;
2. the credit boom–bust generates the house price boom–bust.

Moreover, we embrace the view that, in both cases, these connected boom–bust episodes generate a boom–bust episode in aggregate activity, which, in turns, can feedback and amplify the boom and bust in the financial and housing markets. Given that the relationship between the house price boom–bust episode and the credit boom–bust episode can be itself quite rich, in this chapter we will mostly focus on that, and less on the connection with the real economy.

We start the chapter by discussing a simple mechanical baseline model in Section 2, which is meant to describe the interaction between the credit cycle and house prices, highlighted above. On purpose, it makes a number of stark assumptions to avoid several thorny issues that arise in a fully specified equilibrium model. In particular, we take as given the dynamics of both leverage and house prices. We then perform two types of

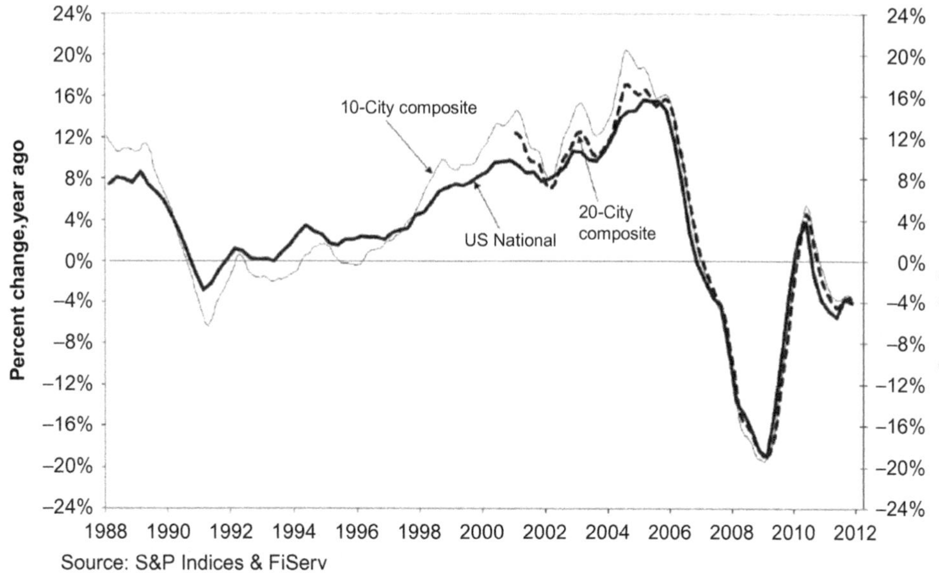

Fig. 1 The S&P/Case-Shiller home price indices. *http://www.worldpropertyjournal.com/north-america-residential-news/spcase-shiller-home-price-indices-report-fordecember-2011-case-schiller-home-price-index-median-home-prices-the-national-composite-10-city-composite-index-20-citycomposite-home-price-indices-david-m-blitzer-5351.php*

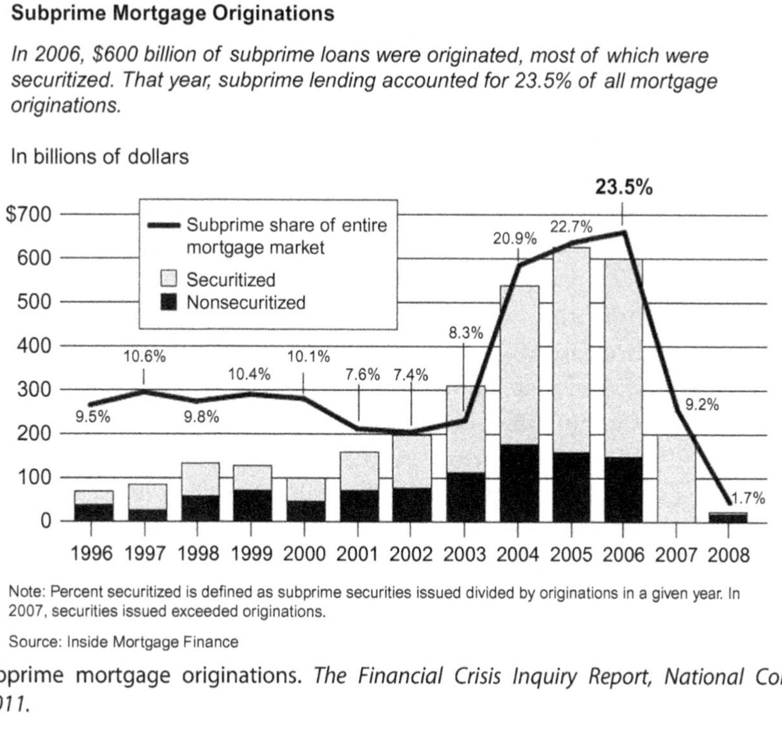

Fig. 2 Subprime mortgage originations. *The Financial Crisis Inquiry Report, National Commission, January 2011.*

exercises: first, we keep house prices constant and study the response to a boom and bust in leverage; and second, we keep the leverage constant and study the response to a boom and bust in house prices. In the rest of the chapter, we try to go deeper in understanding where these dynamics are coming from and connect these two types of exercises to the existing literature.

We next explore the idea that the boom and bust in the credit market was the fundamental shock that spilled over the housing market and the real economy. We first discuss several papers related to this idea. In Section 3, we discuss a large class of papers that explore in particular the role of leverage in the households' sector. We focus on papers that study the effects of credit constraints on house prices and, more generally, on the real economy.

In this spirit, in Section 4, we completely abstract from the housing price dynamics and focus on the boom and crash in the credit market. In particular, we propose a stylized static model of households who borrow to become homeowners and intermediaries who lack information about the quality of the borrowers. The main idea is that a simple increase in the credit availability in the economy, what we interpret as "saving glut," can endogenously generate first a boom and then a crush in lending activity because of multiple equilibria due to adverse selection issues. The basic idea that a saving glut can generate an endogenous credit cycle because of multiplicity of equilibria is inspired by Boissay et al. (2016), although the mechanism is quite different. In our model, the increase in credit availability first increases the lending activity and hence increases the "subprime market." However, as the quality of the pool of borrowers decreases, good borrowers may decide to pay a cost to separate themselves and get better credit terms. This, in turns, may make the subprime market to collapse.

Next, we move to the idea that the boom and crash in housing prices is the key element of the interaction between housing and credit markets. In particular, if house prices are expected to rise, banks are more willing to lend, although this means to lend to worse creditors, eg, subprime borrowers. Moreover, speculating households are more willing to buy as house prices appreciate. While appealing, formalizing this intuition tends to run into the "conundrum of the single equilibrium": if prices are expected to be high tomorrow, then demand for credit and thus housing demand should be high today, and that should drive up prices today, making it less likely that prices will increase. Or, put differently, as prices rise, they eventually must get to a near maximum at some date: call it "today." At that point, prices are expected to decline in the future. But if so, banks and speculating households are less likely to buy today: but then, the price should not be high today. The issue is that in a rational expectations equilibrium there should be no "fool" willing to buy at the highest price, when prices can only go down from there.

In Section 5, we discuss two strands of literature that focus on two types of bubble models. In Section 5.1, we refer to a class of bubble models, where the interest rate demanded on assets is below or at most equal to the growth rate of the economy. This can give rise to rational bubbles and stochastically bursting bubble in, essentially, dynamically inefficient (or borderline efficient) overlapping generations models, as in Carvalho et al. (2012) or Martin and Ventura (2012). These authors employ various versions of OLG models, in which, ideally, resources should be funneled from inefficient investors or savers to efficient investors or entrepreneurs. They assume that there is a lending friction: entrepreneurs cannot promise repayment. They can only issue securities, where the buyer hopes that someone else buys them: call them "bubble," "cash," or "worthless pieces of paper." Equilibria then exist, where newborn entrepreneurs create "bubble" paper. The existing bubble paper in the hands of old agents and bubble paper created by newborn entrepreneurs get sold to savers. Savers find investing in these bubbles more attractive than investing in their own inefficient technology. This technology needs to be inefficient enough so that its return is on average below the growth rate of the economy, creating the dynamic inefficiency for bubbles to arise. In that case, the "fundamental" value of any asset paying even a tiny amount per period is actually infinite. Or, put differently, the last fool to buy the bubble at the highest price is happy to do so, since the value of the bubble next period will not have gone down too much and since that fool is desperate to save.

In Section 5.2, we discuss a second class of bubble models, where the interest rate demanded on assets is above the growth rate of the economy. Here, an aggregate bubble eventually must stop growing, being bounded by the resources in the hands of "newborn" agents purchasing these assets. Rationality considerations typically rule out such bubbles, see the "conundrum" above. We therefore investigate models with irrational optimism and changing sentiments. A benchmark example in the literature, exploiting changing sentiments, is the "disease" bubble model of Burnside et al. (2013). There is some intrinsically worthless bubble component, which could be part of the price of a house. An initially pessimistic population may gradually become infected to be "optimistic" and believe that the bubble component actually has some intrinsic value: once, everyone is optimistic (forever, let's say), there is some constant price that everyone is willing to pay. However, "truth" may be revealed with some probability every period and reveals that the bubble component is worthless indeed. Then, during the pessimistically dominated population epoch, prices rise during the nonrevelation phase, since the rise in prices compensates the pessimistic investors for the risk of ending up with a worthless bubble piece, in case the truth gets revealed. The price will rise until the marginal investor is optimistic: at that point, the maximum price may be reached.

In the spirit of this stream of sentiment literature, in Section 6, we propose a simple model where prices are above fundamentals because investors buy assets under the irrational belief that there is always going to be an ever more foolish buyer, willing to buy for a higher price.

Finally, in Section 7, we juxtapose our findings to some lessons we have drawn from the existing literature regarding the empirical evidence.

We wish this chapter will trigger further research and thinking on this important connection. As shall become clear, the issues are far from resolved.

2. A STARK MODEL

In the financial crisis of 2008, the following interplay might be at work, amplifying any initial shock: (1) as house prices fell, banks became more reluctant to lend to new home buyers, and (2) as banks became more reluctant to lend to new home buyers, demand for houses and thus prices for houses fell as a consequence. In particular, banks became more reluctant to lend because the drop in house prices negatively impacted their balance sheets, hence generating a more general credit crunch, depressing real activity.

In this section, we introduce a very simple mechanical model, featuring some of that interplay, but without describing the deep reasons for some key elements. The model features a potential mismatch between the long-term assets in the form of a pool of mortgages and the short-term assets in the form of saver deposits. It allows us to study the evolution of bank balance sheets during a house price boom. The model is useful for providing some key insights regarding price crashes and leverage crashes, and their impact on the financial system. In particular, we will use it to conduct numerical experiments, illustrating the two channels emphasized in the introduction:

1. House prices are constant and there is a boom and bust in the leverage ratio.
2. The leverage ratio is constant, and there is a boom and bust in house prices.

Furthermore, the model and its analysis sets the stage for discussing the related literature and for the latter sections of the chapter.

Time is discrete and infinite, $t = \ldots, -1, 0, 1, \ldots$. There is a continuum of households, who are the borrowers. There is a competitive sector of bankers, each operating a bank. There is a group of savers who exogenously supply deposits to the banks, and a government which assumes the role of a special saver. Finally, there is a numeraire consumption good and a housing good (or simply houses).

Each period, a fraction λ of the households exit (or "die"), and they are replaced with a fraction λ of newborn households. Each period all alive households earn some exogenously fixed income y and consume a nonnegative amount of goods, while newborn households earn some initial income $\tilde{y}$ and buy a house. We allow $\tilde{y}$ to differ from y, reflecting a potential period of saving-up before purchasing the first home. Just before a household exits, it sells its house. Houses are in fixed supply and are identical to each other.

We assume that a household born at time s is willing to buy a house for any price $p_s \leq \bar{p}_s$, where the process for $\bar{p}_s \geq 0$ is exogenously given.[a] When $\tilde{y}$ is not large enough, households have to borrow in order to make that purchase. Restrictions to borrowing may then imply that the newly born households have less than $\bar{p}_s$ resources at hand.

[a] In principle, one could introduce preferences giving rise to this behavior.

We assume that the sellers get to extract all the rents, ie, we assume that the newly born households pay the lesser between the resources available and $\bar{p}_s$. Thus, only borrowing restrictions may force the market price p_s below $\bar{p}_s$.

To buy their house, households borrow from a banking sector. Consider a household born at date s who buys the house at the prevailing market price p_s. We assume that the following mortgage contract is the only type of contract offered by banks and available to households. In the initial period, households have to make a down payment of $\theta < \tilde{y}$ and borrow the remainder $l_s = \max\{p_s - \theta, 0\}$. We shall focus on parameter specifications such that in equilibrium $p_s \geq \theta$ for all s. The contract requires that households repay the principal l_s when they exit and sell their house. Failing that, they pay all resources available to them in that exiting period. In all other periods, including the period of purchase, households pay a flow interest r per unit of principal borrowed. We treat θ and r as parameters of the model. We assume that $r > 0$, while we do not necessarily restrict θ to be positive, allowing for a cash out at the time of purchase of a house when $\theta < 0$.

We will focus the analysis on equilibria with $l_s = p_s - \theta \geq 0$, where equality is the autarkic case when households do not borrow from banks. Hence, the consumption of a household born at time s in her first period of life is equal to $c_{s;s} = \tilde{y} - \theta - r(p_s - \theta)$, where the first index of $c_{s;s}$ refers to the date of consumption and the second index refers to the year of birth. As we do not allow for negative consumption, that is, $c_{s;s} \geq 0$, prices are bounded above by

$$p_s \leq p^{\max} = \frac{\tilde{y} - (1 - r)\theta}{r}. \tag{1}$$

In any subsequent period, the household will learn if she exits at the end of that period. The nonexiting households then consumes $c_{t;s} = y - r(p_s - \theta) \geq 0$, imposing another constraint on house prices:

$$p_s \leq \frac{y}{r} + \theta. \tag{2}$$

We will concentrate on parameter specifications, where (2) is tighter than (1), that is, we assume that $\tilde{y} - y > \theta$. If the household exits at time t, she sells her house at current market price p_t. If $p_t + y \geq (1 + r)(p_s - \theta)$, she can repay the interest and the principal, and before exiting can consume $c^f_{t;s} = p_t + y - (1 + r)(p_s - \theta)$, where f is meant to indicate her "final period." If $p_t + y < (1 + r)(p_s - \theta)$, the household defaults, consumes zero, and the bank receives $p_t + y$ in total, which one can split into $r(p_s - \theta)$ as the interest portion and $p_t + y - r(p_s - \theta)$ as the partial repayment of principal. One can then calculate the fraction $\phi_{t;s}$ of principal repaid by households born at date s and exiting at date t by solving for $\phi_{t;s}$ the following equation:

$$\phi_{t;s}(p_s - \theta) = \min\{p_s - \theta, p_t + y - r(p_s - \theta)\}. \tag{3}$$

The default rate is then $1 - \phi_{t;s}$.

We assume that banks discount future periods at the same rate r that they charge as interest payments on the mortgages: this is the easiest case to analyze. Consider a scenario in which households never default. Then, the date-t value $v_{t;s}$ of a contract signed at date s is independent of t, $v_{t;s} \equiv v_s$ and satisfies the recursion

$$v_s = \frac{1}{1+r}\left(r(p_s - \theta) + (1-\lambda)v_s + \lambda(p_s - \theta)\right),$$

which gives

$$v_s = p_s - \theta. \tag{4}$$

Banks only invest in mortgages. We assume that banks allow newly born households to borrow as much as they wish to borrow, provided banks have the resources to let them do that.

On the liability side, we assume that banks have deposits d_t by a group of savers as well as a deposit or loan L_t by the government. The bank pays some rate r_D per unit of deposit by savers. On the government loans, the bank pays an interest r_L, which is treated as an exogenous parameter. Additionally, banks are required to repay an exogenously given fraction μ of the principal.

To close the model, we need to specify the evolution of d_t and L_t. We choose an exogenous process for the banks' leverage ratio and set d_t to match such a process, given the endogenous value of the banks' assets. This is meant to be a simple stand-in for the view that banks finance projects by maximizing the amount of outside financing, subject to constraints on their leverage from regulatory restrictions or repayment concerns by depositors.

To calculate the value of a bank's assets, we need to take a stand on how the bank or, implicitly, some (unmodeled) regulator values the portfolio of its mortgages. We shall assume v_s to be the **book value** of a mortgage issued in period $s \leq t$ and which has not been repaid, even if the expected value or **market value** of this mortgage has been declining, due to house price decline and default considerations. Let a_t be the sum of all end-of-period book values of remaining mortgages, that is,

$$\begin{aligned} a_t &= \sum_{j=0}^{\infty} \lambda(1-\lambda)^j (p_{t-j} - \theta) \\ &= \lambda(p_t - \theta) + (1-\lambda)a_{t-1}, \end{aligned} \tag{5}$$

given that only young households, that is, a fraction λ of the population, purchase a home in each period and given Eq. (4). For example, if prices are constant forever, $p_t \equiv p^*$, then

$$a_t \equiv p^* - \theta. \tag{6}$$

Consider the balance sheet at the end of the period. We assume that the liabilities are recorded at their face value. The differences between assets and liabilities is the net worth

n_t of the bank. The (book value) net worth n_t of the bank then results from the balance sheet equation

$$a_t = d_t + L_t + n_t \tag{7}$$

We define the capital requirement or net worth requirement κ_t per

$$\kappa_t a_t = n_t + L_t, \tag{8}$$

or

$$(1 - \kappa_t) a_t = d_t, \tag{9}$$

effectively treating the government loan L_t as a perfect substitute for net worth. We choose an exogenous stochastic process for $\kappa_t \in [0, 1]$ and assume that d_t is set so as to satisfy Eq. (9). Note that $1/\kappa_t$ is the book-value leverage ratio on $n_t + L_t$.

For the evolution of L_t, we consider two alternative versions of the model. The central issue is how to treat a shortfall of funds, should it occur. For simplicity, we seek specifications of the model that avoid potential defaults on depositors, although it would be interesting to explore an extension of the model with default. In the baseline version of the model, we assume that bankers themselves inject any needed funds and hence we assume $L_t \equiv 0$. In the alternative version of the model, we shut down the channel of the injection of bank equity, and instead assume that the government provides loans, if necessary, to avoid a default on depositors and to avoid a shortfall of regulatory capital. For both versions, we need to calculate the evolution of the balance sheet.

Consider the beginning of a new period, after exiting households have sold their houses to newly born households. Let us trace out the impact of each transaction on the residual net worth. The bank receives interest payments ra_{t-1} on all outstanding mortgages, increasing net worth by that amount. A fraction λ of outstanding mortgages exits. Let us define ϕ_t the fraction of principal exiting mortgages that is repaid to the bank, so that the bank receives $\phi_t \lambda a_{t-1}$ in total. Using Eq. (3), we obtain

$$\phi_t a_{t-1} = \sum_{j=0}^{\infty} \lambda (1-\lambda)^j \min\{p_{t-1-j} - \theta, p_t + y - r(p_{t-1-j} - \theta)\} \tag{10}$$

The resulting net worth loss is $(1 - \phi_t)a_{t-1}$, as the book value a_{t-1} of the exiting mortgages is replaced by their payoff $\phi_t a_{t-1}$. In particular, if the current market price is at least as high as all past market prices, then $\phi_t = 1$ and there is no change in net worth.

The bank also receives an inflow of new deposits $d_t - d_{t-1}$, new government loans L_t, and makes new mortgage investments $\lambda(p_t - \theta)$ which do not change net worth, but just lengthen the balance sheet.

On the liability side, banks pay the market interest rate r_D per unit of deposit, so that net worth decreases by the total payments $r_D d_{t-1}$. Furthermore, the bank pays $(r_L + \mu)$ L_{t-1}, the interest and a fraction μ of the principal on the beginning-of-period government loans. After all these transactions, but excluding the new government loan position L_t, the bank has a residual cash position m_t on the asset side, expressed in units of the consumption good. This position may be negative and can be expressed as follows:

$$m_t = (r + \phi_t \lambda) a_{t-1} + d_t - (1 + r_D) d_{t-1} - (\mu + r_L) L_{t-1} - \lambda (p_t - \theta).$$

Finally, we assume that the banker consumes some amount $c_{b,t}$, reducing the net worth of its bank by that amount. It may be useful to think of this consumption as a payment to bank shareholders. In the baseline version of the model, we assume that $L_t = 0$ and that $c_{b,t} = m_t$, that is it exactly equals the cash position, so that the postbanker consumption cash position is equal to zero. Since that cash position can be negative, we must allow $c_{b,t}$ to be negative as well. One might wish to think of this as an injection of equity by the existing bank owners.

The equilibrium of the baseline model with the assumption that $L_t = 0$ can be characterized by the following equations:

$$a_t = \lambda (p_t - \theta) + (1 - \lambda) a_{t-1}, \tag{11}$$

$$d_t = (1 - \kappa_t) a_t, \tag{12}$$

$$m_t = (r + \phi_t \lambda) a_{t-1} + d_t - (1 + r_D) d_{t-1} - \lambda (p_t - \theta), \tag{13}$$

$$c_{b,t} = m_t, \tag{14}$$

$$n_t = a_t - d_t, \tag{15}$$

where ϕ_t is given by Eq. (10). Note that substituting for a_t and d_t using Eqs. (11) and (12) in (13) we obtain

$$\begin{aligned} m_t = {} & [r - r_D + r_D \kappa_{t-1} + \lambda \kappa_t + \kappa_{t-1} - \kappa_t - (1 - \phi_t) \lambda] a_{t-1} \\ & - \kappa_t \lambda (p_t - \theta) \end{aligned} \tag{16}$$

This equation has an intuitive appeal. Consider the bracket, multiplying a_{t-1}. The first term, $r - r_D$ is the interest arbitrage collected. The second term $r_D \kappa_{t-1}$ is the interest earned on the net worth portion of a_{t-1}. The third term, $\lambda \kappa_t$ concerns the repayment of principal. The difference $\kappa_{t-1} - \kappa_t$ means that cash is freed up, if the capital requirement κ_t decreases. The final term $(1 - \phi_t)\lambda$ reduces cash flow only if there are defaults, $\phi_t < 1$.

Moreover, substituting for a_t using Eq. (11) into (15), and using Eq. (15) one period backward, after some manipulation we obtain

$$n_t = n_{t-1} - \lambda a_{t-1} + \lambda (p_t - \theta) - d_t + d_{t-1}. \tag{17}$$

One can use this equation to examine the evolution of net worth. As one special case, suppose that the evolution for the exogenous process κ_t implies that deposits are constant, $d_{t-1} = d_t = d$. Then,

$$n_t = n_{t-1} - \lambda a_{t-1} + \lambda (p_t - \theta), \tag{18}$$

ie, the change in net worth is given by the book value difference between newly created and exiting mortgages. At a superficial look, it would appear that net worth is "magically" created by higher prices and that default on exiting mortgages does not matter. However, it needs to be recognized that these movements find their counterpart in the banker's consumption $c_{b,t}$, see (14): to keep d unchanged, higher prices for new houses as well as larger defaults on old mortgages reduce these shareholder payouts or even require equity injection.

Eq. (18) also reveals that net worth stays constant, if deposits are constant and prices are constant, as, according to Eq. (6), constant prices imply $a_{t-1} = p^* - \theta$. In this case, Eq. (14) implies that bankers' consumption is equal to

$$c_b^* = r(p^* - \theta) - r_D d^*. \tag{19}$$

This simply says that the interest payments on the assets, reduced by the interest payments on the liabilities, are the flow profits in this steady state situation.

Finally, the house price is easy to characterize in this baseline version of the model:

Proposition 1 *Assume that $\bar{p}_t \leq p^{\max}$, defined in Eq. (1). In the baseline version of the model, the house price is then always equal to the exogenous process, that is, $p_t = \bar{p}_t$.*

Proof This follows from the assumption that sellers extract all the rent from buying households, ie, newly born households are willing to borrow up to $\bar{p}_t - \theta$, and the assumption that banks let them do so, potentially financing the needed resources with negative banker consumption. □

For the alternative version of the model, we impose the restriction that $c_{b,t} \geq 0$, that is, the banks cannot raise equity from their owners. We assume that the government provides loans L_t, making up for any potential shortfall. The equations characterizing the equilibrium are now:

$$a_t = \lambda(p_t - \theta) + (1 - \lambda)a_{t-1}, \tag{20}$$

$$d_t = (1 - \kappa_t)a_t, \tag{21}$$

$$\begin{aligned} m_t = {} & (r + \phi_t\lambda)a_{t-1} + d_t - (1 + r_D)d_{t-1} \\ & - \lambda(p_t - \theta) - (r_L + \mu)L_{t-1}, \end{aligned} \tag{22}$$

$$c_{b,t} = \max\{0; m_t\}, \tag{23}$$

$$L_t = (1 - \mu)L_{t-1} - \min\{0, m_t\}, \tag{24}$$

$$n_t = a_t - d_t - L_t, \tag{25}$$

where again ϕ_t is given by Eq. (10). Eq. (22), compared to (13), includes the payment of the interest and of a portion μ of the principal on the outstanding government loans. Eq. (23) encodes the nonnegativity of $c_{b,t}$, compared to (14). With that, one needs to add Eq. (24) for the evolution of the government loans, which are reduced by the repayment of the principal portion, but are increased by any need of repayment for a shortfall of funds $m_t < 0$.

The alternative model is not yet complete, however. Note that larger p_t in (22) can now be compensated for by correspondingly larger loans L_t by the government. Indeed, there is potentially an interesting range of policies to consider. At the one and most generous extreme, the government may provide sufficiently large loans so as to reestablish the maximal price $p_t = \bar{p}_t$, which households are willing to pay. At the other and most stingy extreme, the government may only provide loans to assure nonnegative banker consumption, with house prices reduced all the way to $p_t = \theta$ and thus not requiring bank loans for purchases (assuming $\theta \geq 0$). In the numerical exercise for the exogenous price crash below, we shall investigate the implications of the latter extreme. Put differently, we pick the highest price p_t with $\theta < p_t \leq \bar{p}_t$, subject to the restriction that the resulting m_t in (22) is nonnegative, provided such a price exists. Note that this price will either equal $\bar{p}_t$ or result in $m_t = 0$. If no such price exists, then $p_t = \theta$, $m_t < 0$ and the newly issued loan will equal $-\min\{0, m_t\}$, as stated in Eq. (24). With that, the house price becomes endogenous, and Proposition 1 ceases to hold. In the case of a bust in the leverage ratio, we assume that the government provides a loan to the banks to make up the missing equity. A better interpretation is to view this as a partial stake in the banking system, at a required rate of return for the government. This stake is then reduced over time at the assumed required rate of the loan repayment.

2.1 Numerical Experiments: Overview

We now conduct two sets of numerical experiments to highlight the two approaches we discussed in the introduction:

1. We assume that house prices are constant and assume a boom and bust in the leverage ratio κ;
2. We assume that the leverage ratio is constant, and assume a boom and bust in house prices dynamics.

For both exercises, we consider the implications both for the baseline specification, when bankers can inject fresh equity, and the alternative specification, when they cannot and when, potentially, government loans are required to cover shortfalls of resources.

The numerical exercises are meant to be illustrative, and are not intended as careful calibrations. The parameters are picked to be broadly reasonable, but the results are quite sensitive to their choices. We shall think of a period as 1 year. An overview of the parameters is in Table 1.

Everything scales with income y, so we arbitrarily set income $y = 1$. Hence, one can read all quantities such as banker consumption, government loans or assets, as multiples of annual GDP. We assume a down payment (relative to income) of $\theta = 2$, which should be assumed to be "saved up" from prior income before agents are born and enter the

Table 1 Parameter values for the numerical experiments

y	1
p^*	5 y
κ	0.05 (precrash, experiment 1)
	0.2 (postcrash, experiment 1)
	0.1 (always, experiment 2)
θ	2 y
r	0.04
r_D	0.03
r_L	0.03
μ	0.05
λ	0.1
γ	1.13 (experiment 2)
α	19 y (experiment 2)

housing market. That is, we assume that $\tilde{y}$ is high enough, so that (2) is tighter than (1). Since $\tilde{y}$ does not play a role otherwise, we have not listed an explicit value in Table 1. The exit probability λ has been set equal to 0.1, implying a turnover of a house on average every 10 years. We assume that banks earn 4% on their assets and pay 3% on their liabilities, be they depositors or government loans. We assume that government loans have a maturity of 20 years, ie, that the fraction $\mu = 0.05$ of the outstanding bonds need to be repaid each period.

For the first set of numerical experiments, we set the maximal willingness to pay constant at $\bar{p}_t \equiv p^*$, where $p^* = 5$ y, and thus as five times (annual) income. To model the boom and subsequent bust in leverage, we assume that the required capital ratio is initially at $\kappa = 0.05$ until some date $t = -1$, implying a leverage ratio of 20, and then unexpectedly rises to $\kappa = 0.2$ at date $t = 0$, implying a leverage ratio of 5.

For the second set of numerical experiments, we keep the required capital ratio constant at $\kappa = 0.1$. To capture an initial run-up of house prices and subsequent crash, we assume that the maximal house prices $\bar{p}_t$ increase exponentially until $t = -1$ and then drop to some constant level $\bar{p}_t \equiv p^* \geq \theta$, where $p^*/y = 5$, which is also comparable to the distant past. That is, we assume that

$$\bar{p}_t = p^* + \alpha\gamma^t \tag{26}$$

for $t < 0$, and $\bar{p}_t = p^*$ for $t \geq 0$, where $\gamma \geq 1$.

2.2 An Exogenous Crash in Leverage

Let us examine the first set of numerical experiments, with a constant maximal price $\bar{p}_t = p^*$ and an exogenous crash in leverage. "Case A" is the benchmark version of the model, where we assume that bankers supply fresh equity, if needed. This is

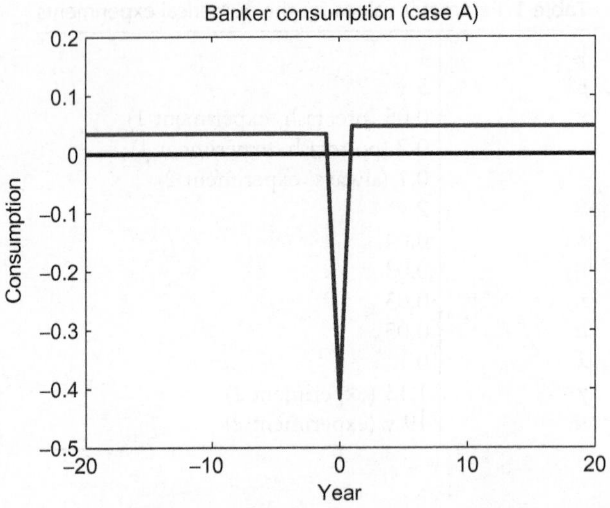

Fig. 3 An exogenous crash in leverage: Implication for banker consumption. Negative values should be interpreted as the injection of fresh bank equity.

shown in Fig. 3. There is a single period, when the leverage ratio suddenly changes, necessitating an infusion of extra cash, modeled as negative banker consumption. Once the fresh equity is injected, everything continues as before, except that banker consumption is now higher, given the new and lower leverage. The price for houses remains at $p_t = \bar{p}$.

Matters are more dramatic for "case B," the alternative specification of the model, where there is no fresh infusion of bank equity. The results are shown in Fig. 4. Prices crash endogenously, as can be seen in the top left panel. There is a fairly brief period of default, as shown in the top right panel. The government makes up the missing equity by, essentially, obtaining a partial stake in the banking system, at a required rate of return for the government. This stake is then reduced over time at the assumed required rate of the loan repayment. If the payments for interest and repayments are less than the revenue of the banking system, the consumption of the bankers are positive, as can be seen here. Finally, banks gradually rebuild their net worth to the required new ratio, as indicated by the red-dashed line in the left panel of the third row.

2.3 An Exogenous Crash in House Prices

For the second set of numerical experiments, we seek to investigate an exogenous crash in house prices, following a phase of increasing house prices, given by (26), while keeping leverage κ constant.

Consider first the run-up phase for house prices, $t < 0$. In the benchmark specification of the model, houses are always sold at the maximum price that newborn home buyers are

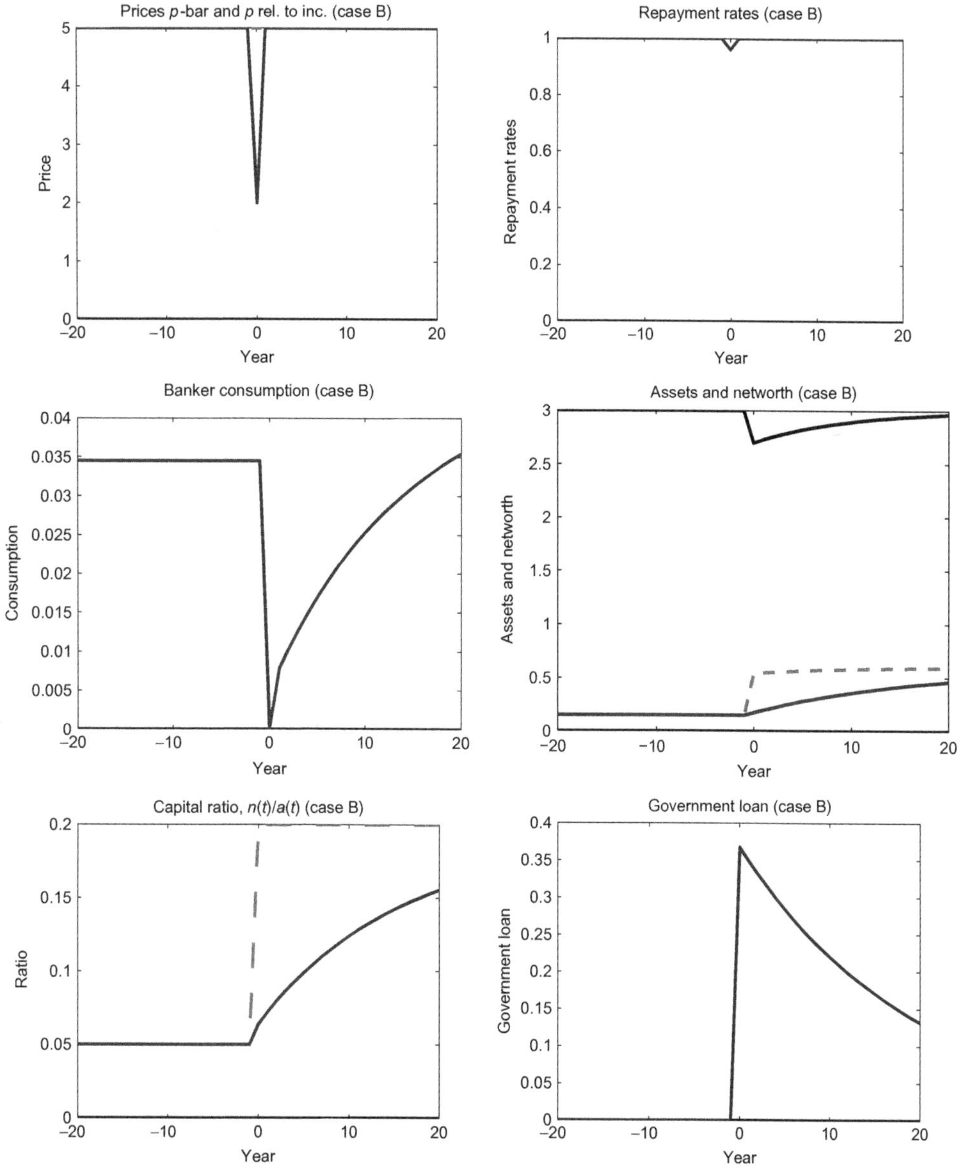

Fig. 4 An exogenous crash in leverage without infusion of bank equity. Prices crash endogenously, as can be seen in the top left panel. There is a fairly brief period of default, as shown in the top right panel. For the parameterization here, the banks gradually rebuild their net worth to the required new ratio, as indicated by the red (gray in the print version)-dashed line in the left panel of the third row.

willing to spend, ie, $p_t = \bar{p}_t$. This will also be true in the alternative specification of the model, provided that banks are able to build up net worth fast enough to finance the new loans, without necessitating the injection of further equity. This imposes some constraints on the parameters, which we shall illuminate.

Using (26) and $p_t = \bar{p}_t$ for all $t < 0$, assets a_t per Eq. (11) can be rewritten as

$$a_t = p^* - \theta + \frac{\lambda\gamma}{\gamma + \lambda - 1}(p_t - p^*)$$

for $t < 0$.

As a useful benchmark, assume $p^* = 0$ and $\theta = 0$. The asset-to-price ratio then is

$$\frac{a_t}{p_t} = \frac{\lambda\gamma}{\gamma + \lambda - 1}.$$

This relationship between current price and the stock of outstanding assets for $t < 0$ is plotted in Fig. 5. As one can see, higher house price growth makes assets look small compared to current house prices. One may interpret this as a reason, why financial institutions are less concerned about default risks during price booms. With (27) and $a_t = \gamma a_{t-1}$ for $t < 0$, Eq. (13) implies

$$\frac{m_t}{a_t} = \frac{1}{\gamma}(r - r_D(1 - \kappa) - \kappa(\gamma - 1)) \tag{27}$$

The balance sheets are growing for $t < 0$. If the banks finance this growth exactly out of earnings, so that $c_{b,t} = m_t = 0$, one obtains

$$\gamma = 1 + \frac{1}{\kappa}(r - r_D(1 - \kappa)) \tag{28}$$

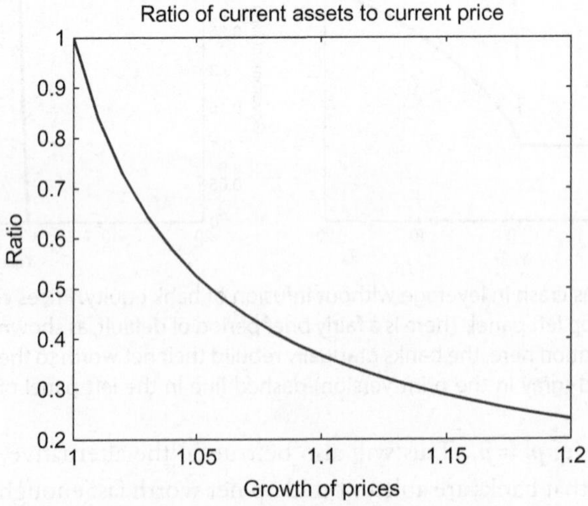

Fig. 5 Ratio of assets to prices, for various values of γ, when $\lambda = 0.05$.

which is intuitive. In particular, if $r = r_D$, then

$$\gamma = 1 + r \tag{29}$$

so that the interest paid on net worth must exactly finance its growth. Put differently, the values calculated for γ in (28) or (29) are the upper bounds for the price growth rates γ to avoid that banker consumption falls into negative territory during the price growth phase, when holding leverage constant, and when assuming that $p^* = 0$ and $\theta = 0$.

With the other parameters as listed in Table 1, Eq. (28) implies that $\gamma = 1.13$ or a 13% appreciation of maximal house prices, during the run-up phase. While the numerical experiments are intended as illustrations only, this number strikes us as perhaps a high, but not entirely unreasonable value during a house boom phase. Indeed, during the pre-2008 years, house prices grew even faster, towards the end, according to the Case-Shiller index. One may also wish to read this as a reasonable upper bound of long-time house price growth, when banks are constrained from raising new equity for financing new mortgages. Consider then the implications for banker consumption in Figs. 6 and 7. For this parameter choice, they are almost flat in the precrash phase, since the rise in higher interest payments on old mortgages is now nearly offset by the rise in resources needed for paying for new mortgages. For other choices for γ, one should not expect nearly flat banker consumption during this run-up phase.

Per Eq. (2), we must be careful in letting prices grow too large. Examining the restriction at the last precrash price $\bar{p}_{-1}$, this equation implies that

$$\alpha \leq \frac{1}{\gamma}\left(\frac{\gamma}{r} + \theta - p^*\right) \approx 19.5\,\gamma \tag{30}$$

We set $\alpha = 19\,\gamma$, so that prices crash in the last possible period. These values for γ and α are listed in Table 1. Arguably, these are pretty much at the extreme end, and chosen to provide the most dramatic numerical experiment.

Consider now the postcrash phase, $t \geq 0$. Here, numerical calculations are required. The results are in Figs. 6 and 7. Fig. 6 shows what happens in the benchmark specification "case A" of the model, when bank equity can be injected, ie, when banker consumption can become negative. House prices trade at the exogenously given levels $\bar{p}_t = p^*$. There is a temporary dip in repayments, but they recover gradually, as the top right panel shows. No government loans are necessary or provided in this case.

"Case B" is the alternative specification of the model, when no fresh injection of bank equity is available. The results are now more dramatic, and shown in Fig. 7. Now, when prices crash, they crash to the down-payment level θ and stay there, for the chosen parameter configuration. Banker consumption never recovers. There is continued

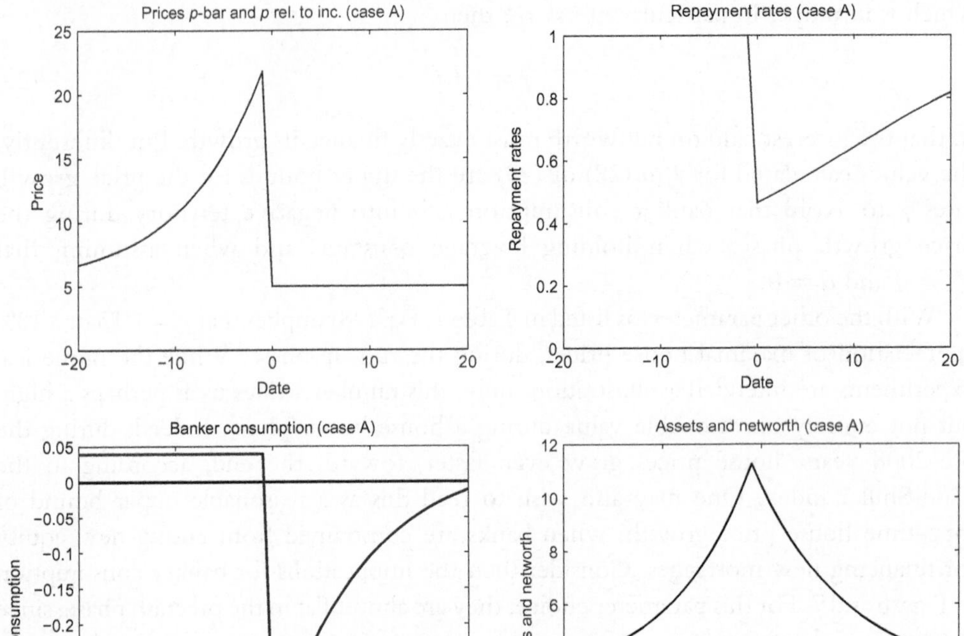

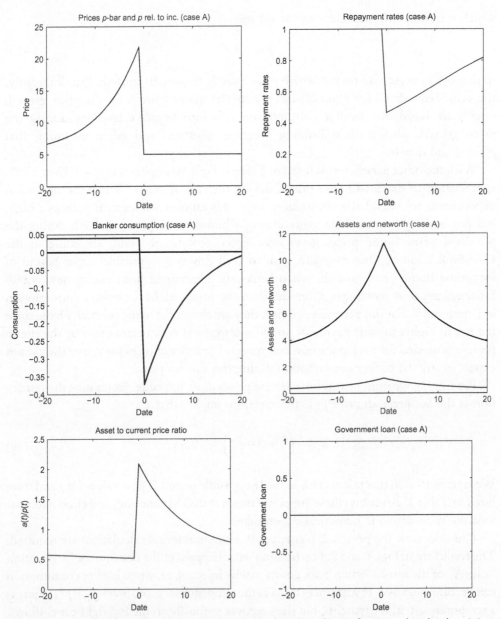

Fig. 6 House price boom and crash: Implications in the benchmark specification, when bankers inject fresh equity to cover shortfalls of funds.

default on banker assets. These are the legacy assets of precrash assets, which gradually disappear over time: households with precrash loans continue to have difficulties repaying these loans. Eventually, the government holds a bond position offset by a negative amount of net worth of bankers, without any corresponding assets.

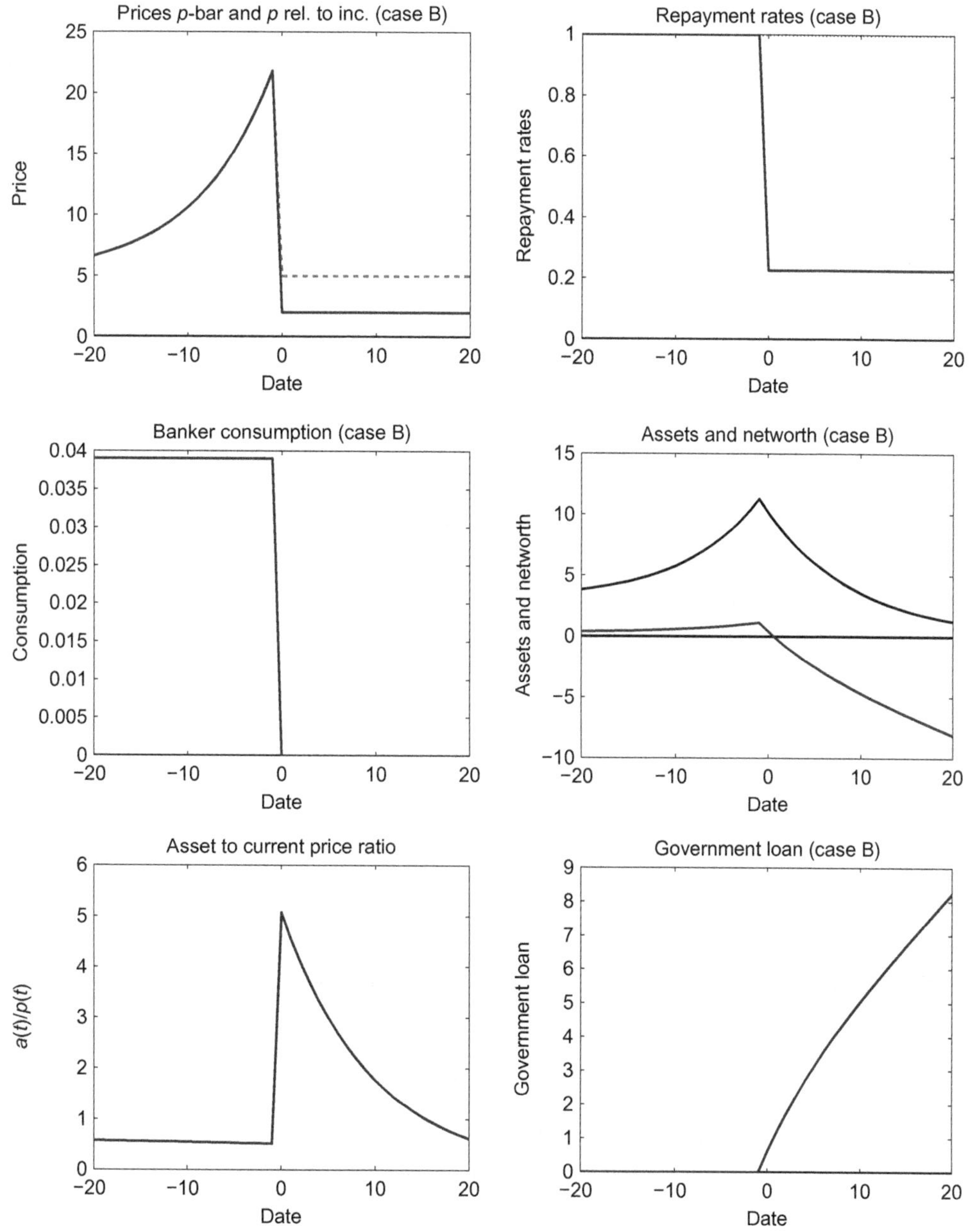

Fig. 7 House price boom and crash: Implications in the alternative specification, when bankers do not inject equity and the government provides the minimal loan to keep banks from defaulting.

2.4 Remarks

The previous numerical experiments are useful to highlight how a boom and bust in housing prices and financial markets can be qualitatively driven either by anything that affects directly house prices or by anything that affects directly banks' leverage. One important ingredient of the model that generates an interesting interaction between house prices and banks' leverage is the presence of long-term loans.

In the experiments above, a permanent decrease in leverage has more modest effects overall than an exogenous crash in house prices. However, as we repeatedly mentioned, these are only illustrative example, and the size of the exogenous crash that we imposed on leverage in the first exercise is difficult to compare to the size of the price crash that we imposed in the second exercise. It would be interesting in future work to calibrate a more realistic version of the model and try to do a horse race between the two types of shocks.

It is also interesting to highlight that in both types of numerical experiments, events unfold always more dramatically in "case B," without the fresh injection of bank equity, than in "case A." This indicates that a quick recapitalization of the banking system may be important in getting things back on track and avoiding long and persistent slumps. There is a self-feeding crisis here: without such an equity infusion, banks cannot fund new mortgages, house prices may remain low, leading to further defaults and leading to further impairments on bank balance sheets. A generous government loan program (not shown here), which supports house prices at the maximum willingness that households are willing to pay, will likewise insulate the housing markets from the drop in bank equity, but may result in keeping the government involved in the banking sector for a long time to come. Clearly, we do not model the costs of a possible government intervention, so conclusive policy recommendations are beyond the scope of this section. This is another interesting avenue for future work.

3. RELATED LITERATURE: HOUSEHOLDS' LEVERAGE

The simple model we introduced in the previous section highlights the interplay between credit cycles and boom–bust cycles in housing prices. One key ingredient in that interplay is that households borrow to become homeowners and are subject to financial constraints. Indeed one defining feature of the recent US experience is a dramatic increase in the households' gross debt to GDP ratio, which reached roughly 128% by 2008, and then sharply dropped. This drew a lot of attention on the effects of households' leveraging and deleveraging not only on housing markets, but, more generally, on aggregate activity.

3.1 Financial Frictions in Macro Models

There is a large growing literature that embeds financial frictions in macro model. Brunnermeier et al. (2011) is a comprehensive survey on this matter. We will just refer here to the seminal papers in this literature and focus next on the specific link between credit markets and house prices. One of the first papers that started a literature of macroeconomics models with financial frictions is Bernanke and Gertler (1989). They focus on long-lasting effects of temporary shocks through the feedback effect of a tightening of the financial frictions. In this model, as well as in Carlstrom and Fuerst (1997) and Bernanke et al. (1999), the key friction is the assumption of costly verification of the entrepreneur's type. Another seminal paper that had a huge impact on the macroeconomic literature is Kiyotaki and Moore (1997) who model financial frictions with a collateral constraint on borrowing rather than with a costly state verification framework. They propose a dynamic economy where durable assets play the dual role of factor of production and collateral for producers' loans. In their model, credit limits are endogenously determined and the interaction between them and asset prices generates a powerful transmission mechanism that allow temporary shocks to technology and income distribution to have large and persistent effects on asset prices and output. The mechanism is the following: after a temporary shock to productivity that reduces firms' net worth, constrained firms have to cut back their investment, hence reducing land value, and this hurts their future borrowing capacity, and reduces investment further down. This mechanism has been largely incorporated in macro models to study the real effects of financial shocks and the amplification of other types of shocks. Another influential paper on financial frictions and macro is Geanakoplos (2009) who focus on the role of leverage in boom and bust episodes. The key idea is that some investors are more optimistic than others and in good times they will lever up and drive asset prices up. However, if bad states realized, they may loose their wealth and the assets may shift in more pessimistic hands, and leverage and prices go down. This is what a leverage cycle is. Another related paper is Myerson (2012) who propose a model of credit cycles generated by moral hazard in financial intermediation.

There is a large recent literature that builds on these models to think about the role of firms' balance sheets in the macroeconomy. See for example Lorenzoni (2008), Mendoza and Quadrini (2010), Geanakoplos (2011), Brunnermeier and Sannikov (2010), He and Krishnamurthy (2013), and Bocola (2014). Gilchrist and Zakrajšek (2012) construct a new credit spread index and show that indeed a reduction in credit availability can have adverse macroeconomic consequences. However, in this chapter we focus more on the households' side and hence we tilt also the discussion of the literature in this direction.

3.2 The Effect of Credit Constraints on House Prices

There is a large strand of literature building models of the housing market where households' credit constraints play a crucial role in affecting house prices. Davis and VanNieuwerburgh (2015) also offers a nice overview of part of this literature. To the best of our knowledge, Stein (1995) is the first paper to explore the effects of down-payment requirements on house price volatility, as well as on the correlation between prices and trading volume. In particular, the paper highlights the self-reinforcing effect that runs from house prices to down payments and housing demand, back to house prices: if house prices decline, the value of households' collateral declines, depressing housing demand and hence pushing house prices further down. This multiplier effect can generate multiple equilibria and account for house price boom–bust episodes. This self-reinforcing effect is in the same spirit of the transmission mechanism in the seminal paper of Kiyotaki and Moore (1997).

In a related paper, Ortalo-Magne and Rady (2006) also explore the key role of down-payment requirements to explain house price volatility, although they focus on a different mechanism. They propose a life-cycle model of the housing market with credit constraints where there are two types of homes, "starter homes" and "trade-up homes." This allows them to focus on the key role of first-time buyers and show that income volatility of young households or relaxation of their credit constraints can explain excess volatility of house prices. Their model also delivers positive correlation between house prices and transaction volume.

More recently, Kiyotaki et al. (2011) develop a quantitative general equilibrium life-cycle model where land is a limited factor of production and is used as collateral for firms' loans. They show that, the more important is land relative to capital in the production of tangible assets, the more housing prices are sensitive to fundamental shocks as productivity growth rate or the world interest rate. Moreover, these type of shocks affect wealth and welfare of different households differently, typically making net house buyers the winners and net house sellers the losers during a housing boom. In contrast, financial innovation that relaxes collateral constraints turn out to have small effects on house prices. Similarly, Sommer et al. (2013) develop a quantitative general equilibrium model with housing and financial constraints and argue that a relaxation of financial constraints has only small effects on house prices, while movements in interest rates have large effects.

In related work, Favilukis et al. (2016) also develop a quantitative general equilibrium model with housing and collateral constraints to explore what drives fluctuations in house prices to rent ratio, but draw very different conclusions. Relative to previous quantitative papers, this model has two new features: aggregate business cycle risk and bequest heterogeneity to generate a realistic wealth distribution. In contrast to the previous literature, the authors find that a relaxation of collateral requirements can generate a large housing boom, while lower interest rates, due to an inflow of foreign capital in the domestic bond market, cannot. In particular, they show that the mechanism through which financial liberalization can generate a house price boom is by reducing the housing risk premium. In a similar spirit, Kermani (2016) propose a model to emphasize the importance of financial liberalization and its reversal to explain the housing boom and bust. He et al. (2015) also propose a model where housing collateralizes loans and house price boom and bust can be generated by financial innovation because the liquidity premium on housing is nonmonotone in the loan-to-equity ratio. In their paper, even without a change in fundamentals, house prices can be cyclical because of self-fulfilling beliefs. In a related paper, Huo and Ríos-Rull (2014) propose a model with heterogenous households, housing and credit constraints, and also show that financial shocks can generate large drops in housing prices.

In a more recent paper, Justiniano et al. (2014) ask what is the best way of formalizing the "credit easing" shock behind the recent US housing boom. Their objective is to model the shock in a way to be able to match a number of stylized facts about the housing and mortgage markets: not only the rise in house prices and households' debt, but also the fairly stable loan-to-value ratio and the decline in mortgage rates. In particular, they distinguish between a loosening of "lending constraints," ie, an increase in the availability of funds to be borrowed for the purpose of home mortgages, and a loosening of "borrowing constraints," ie, the lessening of collateral requirements. They argue that a loosening of the collateral requirements alone cannot explain the recent housing boom in the United States, but there must have been an expansion in the credit supply.

3.3 The Effect of Credit Constraints and Housing Prices on Macro

The impact of changes in credit conditions in the housing market on the overall economy and on economic policy is obviously an important question and the focus on a significant portion of the literature. Iacoviello (2005) has become a work horse model in this literature, embedding nominal households' debt and collateral constraints tied to real estate values, as in Kiyotaki and Moore (1997), into a new Keynesian model. The paper shows that demand shocks move housing and consumer prices in the same direction and hence are amplified. When demand rises due to some exogenous shock, consumer and asset prices increase. The rise in asset prices increases the borrowing capacity of the debtors, allowing them to spend and invest more. The rise in consumer prices reduces the real value of their outstanding debt obligations, positively affecting their net worth. Given that borrowers have a higher propensity to spend than lenders, the net effect on demand is positive. Thus the demand shock is amplified. Guerrieri and Iacoviello (2014) emphasize that collateral constraints drive an asymmetry in the relationship between house prices and economic activity. Brzoza-Brzezina et al. (2014) examine a DSGE model with housing and financial intermediaries. They evaluate the impact of having multiperiod vs one-period contracts on monetary and macroprudential policy, and the role of fixed-rate vs variable-rate mortgages. Garriga et al. (2016) also explore the interaction among long-term mortgages, nominal contracts and monetary policy in a similar general equilibrium model. Benes et al. (2014a) offers a richer structure yet for studying the interplay between the housing market and economic performance and its implications for macroprudential policies. Applications and extensions are in Benes et al. (2014b) and Clancy and Merola (2015).

Corbae and Quintin (2014) are interested in assessing the role of high-leverage mortgages to explain the foreclosure crisis. They propose a model with heterogenous agents who can choose between a mortgage contract with a 20% down payment and one with no down payment and can choose to default. The model show that the increase in number of high-leverage loans can explain more than 60% of the increase in foreclosure rates.

There is another strand of literature that focuses on macroeconomic models with a housing sector and collateral constraints, but takes house prices as given. Among them, Campbell and Hercowitz (2006) explores the macroeconomic consequences of the relaxation of households' collateral constraints that followed the US financial reforms in the early 1980s. They propose a general equilibrium model with heterogenous households who have access to loan contracts that require a down payment and rapid amortization. House prices are taken as given.[b] Reducing the down-payment rate or extending the term of the loans reduces macroeconomic volatility. In particular, they show that the reforms of the early 1980s can explain a large fraction of the volatility decline in hours worked, output, households debt and durables' consumption. In a similar spirit, Iacoviello and Pavan (2013) embed housing in a life-cycle general equilibrium business cycle model where households face collateral constraints. They show that higher income risk and lower down payments can explain the reduced volatility of housing investment, the procyclicality of debt and part of the reduced output volatility during the Great Moderation. They also show that looser credit conditions can make housing and debt more stable in response to small shocks but more fragile in response to large negative shock, as it happened in the Great Recession.

Since the recent boom and bust in housing prices and subsequent long recession, there has been a new wave of macro models that take households' leveraging and deleveraging as the fundamental shock affecting economic activity, even without explicitly modeling the housing market. In his 2011 Presidential Address, Hall (2011) emphasized that the "long slump" that recently hit the United States was driven by a severe decline in aggregate demand, which he attribute to the large deleveraging wave that on the onset of the 2007–08 financial crisis followed a large buildup of consumer debt at the beginning of 2000. On the empirical side, Mian and Sufi (2014) use US zip code data to argue that demand shocks were the main source of the employment decline in the recent recession. In the same spirit, there has been a growing body of work that considers a credit crunch as the fundamental shock of the economy and explores how the subsequent deleveraging affects the overall economy, and the housing market in particular. Together with

[b] In their work, house prices are constant, as in the early literature that included housing in one-sector real business cycle models in the form of capital used for home production, following the seminal papers by Benhabib et al. (1991) and Greenwood and Hercowitz (1991). More recently, Fisher (2007) extends these models by making household capital complimentary to business capital and labor in market production to reconcile the fact that household investment leads nonresidential capital over the business cycle.

Hall (2011), the first papers that develop macro models where the fundamental shock is a credit crunch type of shock (instead for example of a productivity shock) are Eggertsson and Krugman (2012) and Guerrieri and Lorenzoni (2011). Both papers propose an incomplete market model with households facing a borrowing constraint and represent a credit crunch as an unexpected tightening in the borrowing limit. In order to focus on households' gross debt positions, both papers need to introduce some form of households' heterogeneity into the model: Eggertsson and Krugman (2012) use a Keynesian model with two types of agents, borrowers and lenders, while Guerrieri and Lorenzoni (2011) use a Bewley type of model with uninsurable idiosyncratic income risk, so that households delever not only when they hit the borrowing limit, but also for precautionary reason when they are close enough to it. Both paper show that a credit crunch type of shock can have large (also persistent in Guerrieri and Lorenzoni, 2011) effects on the real economy, especially in the presence of sizeable nominal rigidities.

There has been a growing group of papers working on related incomplete market models with heterogenous households and focusing on a similar "credit tightening" shock. On a more quantitative side, Justiniano et al. (2015) and Del Negro et al. (2011) quantify the real effects of this type of shock, using different general equilibrium models and reaching different conclusions. On the one hand, Justiniano et al. (2015) builds on Iacoviello (2005) and Campbell and Hercowitz (2006) and propose a model with two types of households who can borrow using their house as collateral. They show that the leveraging and deleveraging cycle recently experienced by the United States did not have significant real effects. On the other hand, Del Negro et al. (2011) introduce liquidity frictions in an otherwise standard DSGE model and show that the effects of a liquidity shock can be large.

There are number of papers exploring the aggregate effects of a similar shock, focusing on transmission mechanisms that do not rely on nominal rigidities. Huo and Ríos-Rull (2014) study an incomplete market economy where heterogeneous households face a borrowing constraint and the fundamental shock is a tightening in the borrowing limit. The new ingredient in the model that makes the financial shock having real effects is the introduction of search frictions in some consumption markets.[c] That is, households need to engage in costly search to purchase some type of goods and hence, when the borrowing constraint tightens and households want to save more, they will also search less intensively. This will reduce demand and hence generate a recession. Moreover, there is an amplifying effect coming from the fact that consumption tilts more towards the wealthier households who are farther away from the constraint and who are the ones who exert less search effort. Another related paper is Kehoe et al. (2014) who propose a search and matching model a la Diamond–Mortensen–Pissarides with upward-sloping wage profiles

[c] The introduction of search frictions in consumption markets builds on Bai et al. Similar frictions are key in the transmission of financial shocks in Huo and Ríos-Rull (2013) who focus on a small open economy.

and risk-averse consumers who face borrowing constraints. In their model, a tightening in the borrowing limit raise workers' and firm' discount rates, hence reducing vacancy creation and employment, with a similar mechanism as in Hall (2014). This effect is amplified by the presence of on-the-job human capital accumulation and workers' debt constraints. Macera (2015) studies a model with both heterogenous households and heterogenous producers and explores the aggregate effects of a tightening in the borrowing capacity of both types of agents.

Another important related paper is Midrigan and Philippon (2011) who study a cash-in-advance economy with housing, where transactions can be conducted not only with money but also with home equity borrowing. In their economy, there is a continuum of islands that are subject to different collateral constraints. The authors parameterize the model to match the empirical evidence from Mian and Sufi (2011) at the MSA level. When house prices decline in one island, the cash-in-advance constraint tightens reducing aggregate demand in that island. This leads to a recession, thanks to nominal wage rigidities and frictions for the reallocation of labor from different sectors, which prevent households to work harder or to move to tradable sectors. The authors also consider an extension of the model with two types of households, patient and impatient, so that patient households lend to impatient households who can use housing as collateral. The authors distinguish between "liquidity shocks," ie, a tightening in the cash-in-advance constraint which affect all households, and "credit shocks," ie, a tightening the borrowing constraint which affect only impatient households, and show that liquidity shocks are very powerful. The distinction between the two types of constraints is useful to capture the empirical evidence in Johnson et al. (2006), Parker et al. (2013), and Kaplan and Violante (2014) showing that there is a large fraction of wealthy households who are liquidity constrained. In many macro models, as the ones described earlier, there is only one collateral constraint that typically captures both types of shocks.

Incomplete markets models have also been used to emphasize the effect of house prices on consumption, which is sizable according to Mian et al. (2013). There is a large empirical literature that has tried to estimate the effect of house price changes on consumption, using different data samples and different identification strategy, such as Campbell and Cocco (2007), Attanasio et al. (2009), Carroll et al. (2011), Case et al. (2013), and Ströbel and Vavra (2015) (see Iacoviello, 2012 for a more comprehensive survey on this topic). A standard permanent income hypothesis model typically delivers small consumption responses to house prices, as house prices affect households' wealth but also households' implicit rental rates. Berger et al. (2015) show that a simple incomplete market model with heterogenous agents, housing and collateral constraints, can deliver sizable consumption elasticity to house prices consistent with the empirical evidence. They show that the size of such an elasticity is determined by the correlation of marginal propensity to consume out of temporary income shocks and housing values, by deriving a simple sufficient-statistic formula for the individual elasticity. It follows that more levered economy are typically more responsive. They also analyze a boom–bust episode in the house prices similar to the one recently experience by the United States and show that a shock to expected house price appreciation can generate a large boom and bust in consumption and in residential investment at the same time. Kaplan et al. (2015) use a general equilibrium incomplete markets model with heterogeneous agents also to look at the recent boom and bust in house prices and consumption. They allow for different types of shocks: productivity shocks, taste shocks, shocks to the credit markets, and shocks to beliefs about future price appreciation. They show that this last type of shock is the most important to explain the movements in house prices, while shocks to credit conditions are important to explain homeownership, leverage and foreclosure.

Finally, there is another strand of literature that is more interested in understanding fluctuations in residential investment. Most of this literature takes house prices as exogenous. One of the seminal papers in this area is Davis and Heathcote (2005) who actually feature both endogenous housing investment and endogenous house prices. They build a neoclassical multisector stochastic growth model where one sector produces residential structures that, together with land, are used to produce houses. The model does not feature credit constraints, but already capture many facts about dynamics of residential investment. Iacoviello and Neri (2010) extend the multisector structure of Davis and Heathcote (2005) by adding, in particular, nominal rigidities and borrowing constraints. They show that demand shocks, such as housing preference shocks, are important in accounting for fluctuations in house prices. In a more recent paper, Rognlie et al. (2015) propose a model where a house price boom generates overbuilding of residential capital that would require a reallocation of resources among sectors. The authors use this model to think about the Great Recession and argue that, in the presence of a liquidity trap, this "investment hangover" can generate a recession. They show that their model is consistent with an asymmetric recovery where the residential sector has been left behind. In a related paper, Boldrin et al. (2001) use input–output tables to recover the linkages between the construction sector and the other sectors of the economy and evaluating the contribution of the construction sector to the Great Recession. This review has not included the large literature, examining the housing market in the absence of financial frictions. For example, Magnus (2011) has argued that search frictions may well be key to understanding many of the housing market phenomena such as liquidity, prices and vacancies.

4. A SIMPLE MODEL OF CATASTROPHES

In this section, we focus on the boom and bust in the credit cycle, abstracting from the dynamics of house prices. The main idea is that, if credit markets are affected by private information about the quality of the borrowers, a credit cycle can arise endogenously simply because of an increase in credit availability, which can be interpreted as a "saving glut." The idea is that when banks have easier access to credit, for example because the interest rate they face is lower, at first they will offer cheaper loans and increase their lending. However, due to the presence of adverse selection, when borrowing is cheaper worse borrowers will take loans and this can endogenously generate a crash of the credit market.

This idea is inspired by Boissay et al. (2016), but the model that we present here is quite different. The main mechanism in our model is based on adverse selection in the mortgage market, while Boissay et al. (2016) relies on a model of the interbank market affected by moral hazard. In their paper, banks are heterogeneous for their intermediation efficiency and their quality is private information. At the same time, borrowing banks can divert some of the funds to low return assets that cannot be recovered by the lending banks. This mechanism also generates endogenous credit cycles as a result of an increase in credit availability: as interest rates go down, the more efficient banks increase their activity, generating a boom of the banking sector, but as interest rates keep decreasing, worse banks have a higher incentive to divert their funds, increasing counterparty risk and possibly generating an interbank market freeze. Moreover, Boissay et al. (2016) embed their basic interbank market model in a standard DSGE model. Instead, we reduce the dynamics to 2 periods only and leave richer dynamic settings to future research.

4.1 Model

There are two periods $t = 1, 2$. The economy is populated by a continuum of three types of agents: households, lenders, and banks. Lenders and banks are homogenous, while households are heterogenous.

Households enjoy utility $u(c, h)$ in period 2, where c is consumption of a nondurable good and h is housing consumption. For simplicity, let us assume that utility is linear, that is,

$$u(c,h) = c + \gamma h.$$

Houses come in fixed size equal to $\bar{h}$, so that $h \in \{0, \bar{h}\}$, and their price is fixed to 1. Households have no endowment in period 1 but receive an income draw y in period 2. They have to decide whether to buy a house or not in period 1, so if they decide to buy a house they have to borrow the full amount.

Households are heterogenous with respect to their income process. Let $\nu \in [0, 1]$ be the household's type. Assume that ν is distributed according to some distribution function $G(\nu)$ and affects the distribution of the household's income $F_\nu(y)$. Throughout, we shall assume

Assumption 1 $F_{\nu_B}(y)$ first order stochastic dominates $F_{\nu_A}(y)$ whenever $\nu_B > \nu_A$.

Thus, higher household types have a "better" income distribution.

To buy a house in period 1, a household has to borrow 1 unit of funds from the banks at some mortgage "price" p and promise to repay $1/p$ in period 2. Let us note that the label "price" (and notation p) might be a bit confusing. It does not refer to the price of the house (which remains fixed at 1), but is period-1 price for one unit of period-2 resources.

Alternatively, one may wish to think of p as the "payment" the household receives in period $t = 1$ for each unit of promised repayment at date $t = 2$. We shall continue to refer to it as the mortgage price.

At the beginning of period 2, the household's income y is realized and then the household decides whether to repay its debt or not. If it does default on its debt it does not pay anything back to the lender, but it suffers a penalty $\delta > 0$.[d] This implies that households with higher ν are better potential borrowers, in the sense that they have a lower probability of bad income realizations. Let us denote by $\chi \in \{0, 1\}$ the repayment decision, with $\chi = 1$ denoting repayment.

The household's type ν is private information of the household. However, at the beginning of period 1, households have the option to verify their type at a utility cost $\kappa > 0$.[e] Let $v(\nu) \in \{0, 1\}$ be the decision of verifying their type ($v = 1$) or not ($v = 0$). If a household verifies its type, banks can make the lending terms type-contingent, so that the mortgage price p is going to be equal to $\tilde{p}(\nu)$. If instead a household does not verify its type, banks do not know the type of the borrower and will offer a pooling mortgage price p^P. Note that we assume that banks are restricted to offer only one mortgage price to all that have not verified. It would be interesting to extend the model allowing banks to offer more general contracts.

To sum up, households have three options: (1) do not verify their type and borrow accepting a pooling contract, that is, $h(\nu) = 1$ and $v(\nu) = 0$ and borrow at the pooling mortgage price $p = p^P$; (2) verify their type and access type-contingent contracts, that is, $h(\nu) = v(\nu) = 1$ and borrow at the type-contingent mortgage price $p = \tilde{p}(\nu)$; and (3) do not borrow at all, that is, $h(\nu) = v(\nu) = 0$.

Let us proceed backward and consider the repayment decision, conditional on borrowing in the first period, that is, on $h(\nu) = 1$. Recall that the household suffers a penalty δ, if it defaults, and that the lender does not get anything back. Then, a household with realized income y who borrows at the mortgage price p would like to repay if

$$y - 1/p + \gamma\bar{h} \geq y - \delta.$$

We assume throughout that δ is large enough so that in equilibrium any household would like to pay back its debt if it can.[f] However, it may not be able to repay because its realized

[d] The assumption that a defaulting household does not pay anything back to the lender and only suffers a penalty is stark, but simplifies the analysis. The idea is that the household could run away, at a cost which is summarized by δ. One could relax that and assume that the lender can seize only part of the income of the borrower, as it is reasonable to assume that part of it must be lost in legal fees.

[e] The household decides whether to verify its type or not before banks make their offers. Also, we assume that the verification costs is in terms of utility, because for simplicity we assume that the households start period 1 with no endowment. However, it would be easy to extend the model to make it a monetary cost.

[f] We will show below that this is a necessary condition to have a nonempty set of borrowers at the pooling mortgage price.

income is not high enough, so that $\chi(y, p) = 1$ iff $y \geq 1/p$. Let $\pi(\nu, p)$ be the ex-ante repayment probability of a household of type ν who borrows at the mortgage price p, that is,

$$\pi(\nu, p) = E[\chi(y, p) = 1|\nu, p] = 1 - F_\nu\left(\frac{1}{p}\right)$$

Then we can show the following proposition.

Proposition 2 *The repayment probability* $\pi(\nu, p)$ *is increasing in* ν *and increasing in* p.

Proof First, $\pi(\nu, p)$ is increasing in ν, since F_ν are ordered by first-order stochastic dominance. Second, $\pi(\nu, p)$ is increasing in p, since $1 - F_\nu(y)$ is decreasing in y for any ν. □

This means that a household with higher type has a higher repayment probability, for any given mortgage price p.

Let us now focus on the lending market. Let us assume that the banks can borrow from the lenders at some rate R, which is exogenously given.[g] Also, they trade the loans, which we will refer to as assets from now on, on the secondary market.[h] Each asset is characterized by the type of the associated borrower ν and has a different repayment probability $\pi(\nu, p) \in [0, 1]$. This implies that the pooling mortgage price is determined by the no-arbitrage condition

$$p^P = \frac{E\left[1 - F_\nu\left(\frac{1}{p^P}\right)|\nu \in \mathcal{S}\right]}{R}, \tag{31}$$

where $\mathcal{S} \equiv \{\nu|v(\nu) = 0\}$ is the set of households who decide not to verify their type. Likewise, the type-contingent mortgage price is determined by the no-arbitrage equation

$$\tilde{p}(\nu) = \frac{1 - F_\nu\left(\frac{1}{\tilde{p}(\nu)}\right)}{R}. \tag{32}$$

In principle, there may be none, one or several solutions to this equation. Borrowing the logic in Mankiw (1986), we assume that the highest of these prevails in equilibrium: at a lower mortgage price and thus higher promised return to all other banks, a bank could profitably deviate by offering a higher mortgage price and a better deal to the household, under mild conditions. Define ν_L as the lowest type, beyond which a type-contingent mortgage price exists for some types,

[g] The interest rate R can be interpreted as the rate at which lenders can borrow in the international market.

[h] One can potentially generalize the model to create MBS that pool different loans and a similar mechanism would go through as long as there is a constraint on the measure of types that can be pooled together.

$$\nu_L = \inf_{\nu}\{\nu \mid \text{there is a solution to Eq. (32)}\}$$

We can then show that a type-contingent mortgage price exists for all types better than ν_L.

Proposition 3 *There exist a type-contingent mortgage price* $\tilde{p}(\nu)$ *for any* $\nu > \nu_L$.

Proof Consider some ν. Let $\nu' \in [\nu_L, \nu]$ be such that there is a solution $\tilde{p}(\nu')$ to Eq. (32). Define

$$\mathcal{P}(\nu) = \{p \geq \tilde{p}(\nu') \mid p \leq \frac{1 - F_\nu\left(\frac{1}{p}\right)}{R}\}$$

Since F_ν second-order stochastically dominates $F_{\nu'}$, $\tilde{p}(\nu') \in \mathcal{P}(\nu)$ and $\mathcal{P}(\nu)$ is therefore nonempty. Let $\bar{p} = \sup\mathcal{P}(\nu)$, the supremum of $\mathcal{P}(\nu)$. Note that $\bar{p} \leq 1/R < \infty$. Consider an increasing sequence $p_j \to \bar{p}$ with $p_j \in \mathcal{P}(\nu)$. Calculate that

$$\bar{p} = \lim_{j\to\infty} p_j \leq \lim_{j\to\infty} \frac{1 - F_\nu\left(\frac{1}{p_j}\right)}{R} \leq \frac{1 - F_\nu\left(\frac{1}{\bar{p}}\right)}{R}$$

and thus $\bar{p} \in \mathcal{P}$. This shows that $\bar{p}$ is a maximum and that there is therefore at least one solution to Eq. (32). □

Obviously, households who verify their type will be able to borrow at terms that are more favourable the better their type is. That is, we can prove the following proposition.

Proposition 4 *For* $\nu > \nu_L$, *the type-contingent mortgage price* $\tilde{p}(\nu)$ *is increasing in* ν *and decreasing in* R.

Proof First, let us make a change of variable and define $\tilde{R}(\nu) \equiv 1/\tilde{p}(\nu)$. Rewrite Eq. (32) as

$$1 - \frac{R}{x} = F_\nu(x). \tag{33}$$

which we seek to solve for $\tilde{R}(\nu) = x$, for a given ν. Assume then that there is at least one solution for (32), ie, that the curves defined by the left-hand side and right-hand side of that equation cross at least once. As assumed above per the logic in Mankiw (1986), pick the lowest solution to (33) or, equivalently, the highest of the solutions for (32), if there are several. This pins down a unique $\tilde{R}(\nu)$ and unique $\tilde{p}(\nu)$ for each ν. Fix some ν and its solution $\tilde{R}(\nu) = x$. Note that the left-hand side of (33) diverges to $-\infty$, as $x \to 0$, while the right-hand side converges to a nonnegative number. Thus, at the lowest solution and as a function of x, the right-hand side of (33) approaches and then either crosses or touches the left-hand side from above, as x approaches the solution from below. Per the definition of second-order stochastic dominance, the right-hand side shifts to the right, as ν is increased. Therefore a solution continues to exist for higher ν and they are to the left of the solution fixed at the beginning of this argument. As ν is decreased, the right-hand side function shifts to the left. By the similar logic, the solution either moves to the right, when the intersection between the two sides moves locally, or will jump to a solution at a higher value, if the current intersection disappears or a solution will cease to exist altogether. In sum, if a solution $\widetilde{R}(\nu)$ exists, it is decreasing in ν. Equivalently, if a solution $p(\nu)$ exists, it is increasing in ν. Likewise, consider now an decrease in R. This shifts the left-hand side of (33) upward, a solution will continue to exist and will be lower than the previously fixed solution. If R increases, the current intersection may move locally or disappear: in either case, if a solution continues to exist, it will be higher than the previously fixed solution. This shows that $\widetilde{R}(\nu)$ is increasing and $p(\nu)$ therefore decreasing, as a function of R. □

Consider now the household's problem. Define

$$U^B(\nu,p) = \int_{\frac{1}{p}}^{\infty} \left(y - \frac{1}{p} + \gamma\bar{h}\right) dF_\nu(y) + \int_0^{\frac{1}{p}} (y - \delta)\, dF_\nu(y), \tag{34}$$

which is the expected utility of a household of type ν who decides to buy a house at the mortgage price p and does not verify its type ($h(\nu) = 1$ and $v(\nu) = 0$). For $\nu > \nu_L$, define

$$U^V(\nu) = U^B(\nu, \tilde{p}(\nu)) - \kappa, \tag{35}$$

which is the expected utility of a household who decides to borrow at mortgage price $p = \tilde{p}(\nu)$ and verify its type ($h(\nu) = v(\nu) = 1$). For $\nu < \nu_L$, no such type-contingent mortgage price exists: thus define

$$U^V(\nu) = -\infty \tag{36}$$

in that case. For $\nu = \nu_L$, use (35), if there is a solution to (32), and (36), if not. Finally, define

$$U^N(\nu) = \int y\, dF_\nu(y) = E[y \mid \nu], \tag{37}$$

which is the expected utility of a household of type ν who decides not to buy a house ($h(\nu) = v(\nu) = 0$), and equal to the expected income, given our assumption of linear utility. For a given pooling mortgage price p^P, the utility of the household of type ν and its maximization problem is now

$$\bar{U}(\nu, p^P) = \max\left\{U^B(\nu, p^P), U^V(\nu), U^N(\nu)\right\},$$

To make more progress, we need an assumption regarding the income uncertainty as expressed by F_ν.

Assumption 2 There is some $x^* \in \mathbb{R}$ so that $F_\nu(x)$ has nondecreasing slopes above x^*: for all x_1 and x_2 with $x^* \leq x_1 \leq x_2$ and all ν_A and ν_B with $\nu_L \leq \nu_A \leq \nu_B$, we have

$$F_{\nu_A}(x_2) - F_{\nu_A}(x_1) \leq F_{\nu_B}(x_2) - F_{\nu_B}(x_1) \tag{38}$$

The assumption is trivially satisfied at some x^*, where $F_1(x^*) = 1$, if such a value x^* exists, ie, if the income distribution is bounded. Obviously then, this assumption is only useful, if x^* is fairly small and smaller than some upper bound on income. Indeed, it will be particularly convenient to assume that $x^* = R$, the safe return.

The following lemma is a bit technical, and useful for an intermediate step in the proof of the next proposition.

Lemma 1

1. *Define*

$$Z(\nu,p) \equiv \left(1 - F_\nu\left(\frac{1}{p}\right)\right)\left(\gamma\bar{h} - \frac{1}{p} + \delta\right). \tag{39}$$

and suppose that $\gamma\bar{h} - (1/p) + \delta > 0$. *Then* Z($\nu$, p) *is increasing in both* ν *and* p.

2. *For* $\nu > \nu_L$, *define*

$$g(\nu,p) = Z(\nu, \tilde{p}(\nu)) - Z(\nu,p) \tag{40}$$

For $\nu < \nu_L$, *define* $g(\nu,p) = -\infty$. *For* $\nu = \nu_L$, *define* $g(\nu_L, p)$ *as in Eq. (40), if there is a solution to Eq. (32) and* $g(\nu_L,p) = -\infty$ *otherwise. Suppose that* $p \le \tilde{p}(\nu) \le 1/x^*$ *for all* $\nu > \nu_L$ *and that* $\gamma\bar{h} - (1/p) + \delta > 0$. *Impose the Assumption 2 of nondecreasing slopes. Then* g *is increasing in* ν *and decreasing in* p.

Proof It is easy to see that $Z(\nu, p)$ is increasing in both ν and p. It follows that $g(\nu, p)$ is decreasing in p. It remains to show that g is increasing in ν for $\nu \ge \nu_L$. Suppose that $\nu_A \le \nu_B$. We need to show that

$$g(\nu_A,p) \le g(\nu_B,p) \tag{41}$$

Excluding the trivial case of $\nu_B = \nu_L$ with $g(\nu_L,p) = -\infty$, calculate

$$\begin{aligned} g(\nu_B,p) - g(\nu_A,p) &= Z(\nu_B, \tilde{p}(\nu_B)) - Z(\nu_A, \tilde{p}(\nu_A)) - (Z(\nu_B,p) - Z(\nu_A,p)) \\ &\ge Z(\nu_B, \tilde{p}(\nu_A)) - Z(\nu_A, \tilde{p}(\nu_A)) - (Z(\nu_B,p) - Z(\nu_A,p)) \end{aligned}$$

where we have exploited that $\tilde{p}(\nu_A) \le \tilde{p}(\nu_B)$ per Proposition 4, and that $Z(\nu, p)$ is increasing in p. Define $x_1 = 1/\tilde{p}(\nu_A)$ and $x_2 = 1/p$ and note that $x^* \le x_1 \le x_2$. With that, rewrite the right-hand side of the last equation as

$$\begin{aligned} & g(\nu_B,p) - g(\nu_A,p) \\ & \ge (F_{\nu_A}(x_1) - F_{\nu_B}(x_1))(\gamma\bar{h} - x_1 + \delta) - (F_{\nu_A}(x_2) - F_{\nu_B}(x_2))(\gamma\bar{h} - x_2 + \delta) \\ & = ((F_{\nu_A}(x_1) - F_{\nu_B}(x_1)) - (F_{\nu_A}(x_2) - F_{\nu_B}(x_2)))(\gamma\bar{h} - x_1 + \delta) \\ & \quad + (F_{\nu_A}(x_2) - F_{\nu_B}(x_2))(x_2 - x_1) \\ & \ge 0 \end{aligned}$$

with Assumption 2. □

The following proposition shows that the households' optimal behavior can be characterized by two cutoffs values, such that, households with low types do not buy a house,

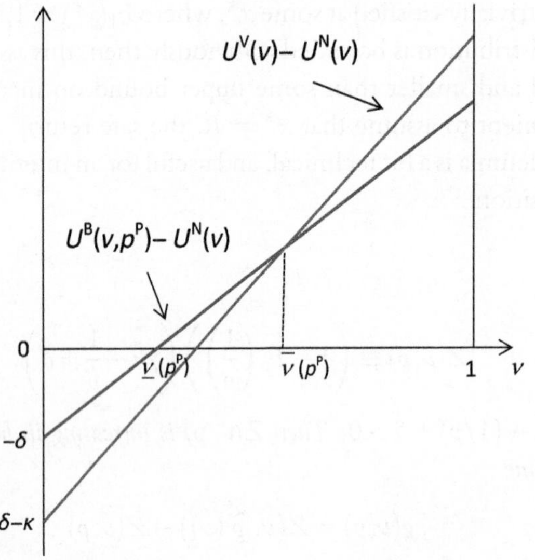

Fig. 8 Households' problem (curves are linear just for illustration).

households with high types buy a house and may verify their type, and households in the middle range, buy a house but choose to borrow at the pooling mortgage price. The logic is illustrated in Fig. 8.

Proposition 5 *Impose the Assumption 2 of nondecreasing slopes. Assume that* $x^* = R$, *the safe return. Then, there exists a value* $\underline{p}$ *so that no household buys a house at a mortgage price* $p < \underline{p}$, *whereas for all* $p^P > \underline{p}$ *there are two cutoffs* $\underline{\nu}(p^P) \leq \overline{\nu}(p^P)$ *such that*

1. $h(\nu) = 0$, *ie, no house purchase, if* $\nu < \underline{\nu}(p^P)$.
2. $h(\nu) = 1$, $v(\nu) = 0$, *ie, house purchase without verification at the pooling mortgage price* p^P, *if* $\underline{\nu}(p^P) < \nu < \overline{\nu}(p^P)$.
3. $h(\nu) = 1$, $v(\nu) = 1$, *ie, house purchase with verification at the type-contingent mortgage price* $\tilde{p}(\nu)$, *if* $\nu > \overline{\nu}(p^P)$.
4. $\mathcal{S} = [\underline{\nu}, \overline{\nu}]$ *or* $\mathcal{S} = (\underline{\nu}, \overline{\nu}]$ *or* $\mathcal{S} = [\underline{\nu}, \overline{\nu})$ *or* $\mathcal{S} = (\underline{\nu}, \overline{\nu})$, *for* $\underline{\nu} = \underline{\nu}(p^P)$ *and* $\overline{\nu} = \overline{\nu}(p^P)$.

Moreover, $\underline{\nu}(p^P)$ *and* $\overline{\nu}(p^P)$ *are respectively decreasing and increasing in* p^P.

Proof Let us rewrite

$$U^B(\nu, p) = E[y \mid \nu] + Z(\nu, p) - \delta,$$

$$U^V(\nu) = E[y \mid \nu] + Z(\nu, \tilde{p}(\nu)) - \delta - \kappa,$$

and

$$U^N(\nu) = E[y \mid \nu],$$

where $Z(\nu, p)$ is defined in Eq. (39).

Note that a type ν-household will choose to buy a house at mortgage price p without verification, iff $U^B(\nu, p) \geq U^N(\nu)$, that is, iff

$$Z(\nu, p) \geq \delta. \tag{42}$$

Let $\underline{p}$ be the infimum of all p, so that there exists a ν, satisfying Eq. (42). Therefore, no household of any type will purchase a house at a mortgage price $p < \underline{p}$ without verification and certainly not either, when paying the verification cost.

Consider now any $p > \underline{p}$. Since $Z(\nu, p) > 0$ for some ν, it follows that $\gamma \bar{h} - (1/p) - \delta > 0$. Since $Z(\bar{\nu}, p)$ is increasing in ν per Lemma 1, there is a unique cut-off $\underline{\nu}(p)$ such that such that $U^B(\nu, p) \geq U^N(\nu)$ if $\nu > \underline{\nu}(p)$. If $Z(1, p) > \delta$ and $Z(0, p) < \delta$, the cutoff $\underline{\nu}$ is implicitly defined by the infimum of all $\nu \in [0, 1]$ such that

$$Z(\nu, p) \geq \delta. \tag{43}$$

If $Z(1, p) < \delta$, then $\underline{\nu}(p) = 1$ and if $Z(0, p) > \delta$, then $\underline{\nu}(p) = 0$. Since $Z(\nu, p)$ is increasing in p, it follows that $\underline{\nu}(p)$ is decreasing (more precisely: nonincreasing) in p.

Note that a type ν-household will choose to verify and buy a house at the type-contingent mortgage price $\tilde{p}(\nu)$ rather than a mortgage pooling price p, iff $U^V(\nu) \geq U^B(\nu, p)$, that is, iff

$$Z(\nu, \tilde{p}(\nu)) - \kappa \geq Z(\nu, p) \tag{44}$$

provided a type-contingent mortgage price $\tilde{p}(\nu)$ exists, or, equivalently, iff

$$g(\nu, p) \geq \kappa \tag{45}$$

where g is defined in Eq. (40). Let $\bar{\nu}(p)$ be the infimum over all $\nu \in [0, 1]$, for which (45) holds, with the convention that $\bar{\nu}(p) = 1$, if no such ν exists. Consider some $\nu_A > \bar{\nu}(p)$ such that (45) holds. Since $Z(\nu, p)$ is increasing in p, it follows that $p \leq \tilde{p}(\nu)$. Eq. (32) implies that $\tilde{p}(\nu) \leq 1/x^*$ for all ν. Let $\nu_B > \nu_A$. Lemma 1 now implies that $g(\nu_B, p) \geq g(\nu_A, p) \geq \kappa$, ie, Eq. (45) also holds at ν_B. This proves that Eq. (45) holds for all $\nu > \bar{\nu}(p)$.

Finally, recall that $g(\nu, p)$ is decreasing in p, per Lemma 1. Therefore, if (45) holds at some ν and p, it continues to hold at some $p' < p$. It follows that $\bar{\nu}(p) \geq \bar{\nu}(p')$, ie, that $\bar{\nu}(p)$ is increasing in p. □

We have been careful to allow for discontinuities in all equations, and expressing solutions as infima or suprema for variables appearing in inequalities. In practice, it may be simpler to proceed with enough continuity and to assume that these equations hold with equality at the limiting points. Furthermore, it may be best to impose that $G(\nu)$ has no mass points. With that and in sum, an equilibrium can be represented by a separating mortgage price schedule $\tilde{p}(\nu)$ solving Eq. (32) for $\nu \geq \nu_L$, a pooling mortgage price p^P, which satisfies

$$p^P = \frac{\int_{\underline{\nu}}^{\bar{\nu}} 1 - F_\nu\left(\frac{1}{p^P}\right) G(d\nu)}{R}, \tag{46}$$

and two cutoffs $\underline{\nu}$ and $\bar{\nu}$ satisfying the two conditions

$$\left[1-F_{\underline{\nu}}\left(\frac{1}{p^P}\right)\right]\left(\gamma\bar{h}-\frac{1}{p^P}+\delta\right)=\delta, \tag{47}$$

and

$$\left[1-F_{\overline{\nu}}\left(\frac{1}{p^P}\right)\right]\left(\gamma\bar{h}-\frac{1}{p}+\delta\right)=R\widetilde{p}(\overline{\nu})(\gamma\bar{h}+\delta)-R-\kappa. \tag{48}$$

We next want to show that multiple equilibria can arise in our model performing some simple numerical exercises.

4.2 Multiple Equilibria

In our model, good households may decide to costly verify their type to signal that they are good and so not to be pooled with bad households. This feature of the model is key to generate multiple equilibria. For some parameters, we can have two equilibria: a good equilibrium where good households do not verify their type, the mortgage price is high and hence it is indeed optimal not to suffer the verification cost; and a bad equilibrium, where good households do verify their type, hence lowering the pooling mortgage price and making it indeed optimal to costly verify their type.

The possibility of multiple equilibria can generate an endogenous credit cycle, driven by a simple increase in credit availability, that is, a decrease in R. As we highlighted earlier, this can be thought as an episode of "saving glut," using Ben Bernanke language: *"I will argue that over the past decade a combination of diverse forces has created a significant increase in the global supply of saving—a global saving glut—which helps to explain both the increase in the U.S. current account deficit and the relatively low level of long-term real interest rates in the world today. The prospect of dramatic increases in the ratio of retirees to workers in a number of major industrial economies is one important reason for the high level of global saving. However, as I will discuss, a particularly interesting aspect of the global saving glut has been a remarkable reversal in the flows of credit to developing and emerging-market economies, a shift that has transformed those economies from borrowers on international capital markets to large net lenders."*

In the next section we will show a numerical example where this is the case. Let us first describe the mechanics behind such an endogenous cycle.

1. Let us imagine that we start in an equilibrium where R is relatively high so that the pool of borrowers is relatively good, that is, $\underline{\nu}$ is large, and all borrowers are pooled together, that is, $\overline{\nu}=1$.
2. Then, assume that R declines, pushing both p and $\widetilde{p}\,(\nu)$ up and hence increasing both U^B and U^V. This implies that $\underline{\nu}$ decreases and more bad households become borrowers. However, let us assume that it is still the case that $\overline{\nu}=1$. The change in the composition of the loans tends to depress mortgage prices.

However, mortgage prices have to go up on net, so the interest rate effect has to dominate.[i]

3. If R decreases further, at some point $\overline{\nu}$ will become smaller than 1 and some borrowers will decide to verify that they are good types, hence worsening the pool of households who borrow at the pooling mortgage price, p^P. There are two possibilities:
   (a) p^P increases, then both U^B and U^V shift further up and both $\underline{\nu}$ and $\overline{\nu}$ decline, dampening the increase in p^P.
   (b) p^P declines, then U^B has to shift down and $\underline{\nu}$ increases. In this case, it must be that the decline in $\overline{\nu}$ is strong enough to more than compensate the pressure upward on p^P played by the increase in R and in $\underline{\nu}$.

   Let us imagine that the second case arises.
4. If R decreases even further, the economy is now stuck in a bad equilibrium with some separation.

The shift from a good equilibrium to a bad equilibrium can be interpreted as a market crash, as mortgage prices suddenly drop or, equivalently, required interest payments on mortgages suddenly increase.

4.3 Some Numerical Examples

In this section, we show some simple numerical examples to illustrate how our model can generate an endogenous credit cycle.

For simplicity, let us assume that the income process follows a binary distribution with $y \in \{0, \bar{y}\}$, where $\bar{y} > R$ is sufficiently high that repayment is guaranteed. Let ν be the probability for the high outcome, that is, $\nu = Pr(y = \bar{y})$. The income distribution F_ν is then given by

$$F_\nu(x) = \begin{cases} 0, & \text{if } x < 0 \\ 1 - \nu, & \text{if } 0 \leq x < \bar{y} \\ 1, & \text{if } x \geq \bar{y} \end{cases}$$

Let x^* be some small, but positive real number, $0 < x^* < R$. Let $\nu_A < \nu_B$. For all x_1 and x_2 with $x^* \leq x_1 \leq x_2 < \bar{y}$ or with $\bar{y} \leq x_1 \leq x_2$, we have

$$F_{\nu_A}(x_2) - F_{\nu_A}(x_1) = 0 = F_{\nu_B}(x_2) - F_{\nu_B}(x_1) \tag{49}$$

Suppose then that $x^* \leq x_1 < \bar{y} \leq x_2$. Now,

$$F_{\nu_A}(x_2) - F_{\nu_A}(x_1) = \nu_A \leq \nu_B = F_{\nu_B}(x_2) - F_{\nu_B}(x_1) \tag{50}$$

Thus, Assumption 2 is satisfied and Proposition 5 applies.

[i] Imagine, by contradiction that p declines, then $\underline{\nu}$ has to increase, but then p has to increase, generating a contradiction.

Eq. (31) now reduces to

$$\tilde{p}(\nu) = \frac{\nu}{R}.$$

The two cut-off $\underline{\nu}$ and $\overline{\nu}$ are given by

$$\underline{\nu} = \frac{\delta}{\gamma\bar{h} + \delta - p^P - 1}, \tag{51}$$

and

$$\overline{\nu} = (R - \kappa)p^P, \tag{52}$$

where the pooling mortgage price p^P is given by condition (46), which can be rewritten as

$$p^P = \frac{E[\nu | \nu \in [\underline{\nu}, \overline{\nu}]]}{R}.$$

For all the numerical examples, we set $\gamma\bar{h} = 2$ and $\delta = 0.1$. We then experiment with different distributions H for ν.

We start by a baseline example where we assume that ν is uniformly distributed on [0, 1]. In this case, the pooling mortgage price can be solved for in closed form and is equal to

$$p^P = \left(\frac{\delta}{R - \kappa} + 1\right)\frac{1}{\gamma\bar{h} + \delta}.$$

This implies that in this simple benchmark the pooling mortgage price is monotonically decreasing in R, and hence a reduction in R is always going to increase p^P and decrease the two cutoffs $\underline{\nu}$ and $\overline{\nu}$, so there is no possibility of multiple equilibria.

Fig. 9 shows the results for this numerical case. The top panel on the left shows the equilibrium manifold for mortgage prices as a function of the exogenous interest rate R and clearly shows that in this case multiple equilibria never arise. The top panel on the right just shows the distribution for ν. The two panels in the middle illustrate that there is a unique equilibrium for any level of R, showing in particular the case of $R = 1.1$, $R = 1.4$, and $R = 1.7$. Finally the bottom panel on the left shows the two cutoffs, $\underline{\nu}$, in red, and $\overline{\nu}$, in blue, as a function of the pooling mortgage price for a specific R. Finally, the bottom right panel shows the volume of loans offered in equilibrium, again for $R = 1.1$, $R = 1.4$, and $R = 1.7$, and shows that, as expected, it is increasing both in the pooling mortgage price and in R.

We then explore the following two alternative distributions:

1. a mixture of two exponential densities,

$$h(\nu) = \omega\frac{\lambda_1 e^{-\lambda_1 \nu}}{1 - e^{-\lambda_1}} + (1 - \omega)\frac{\lambda_2 e^{-\lambda_2 \nu}}{1 - e^{-\lambda_2}};$$

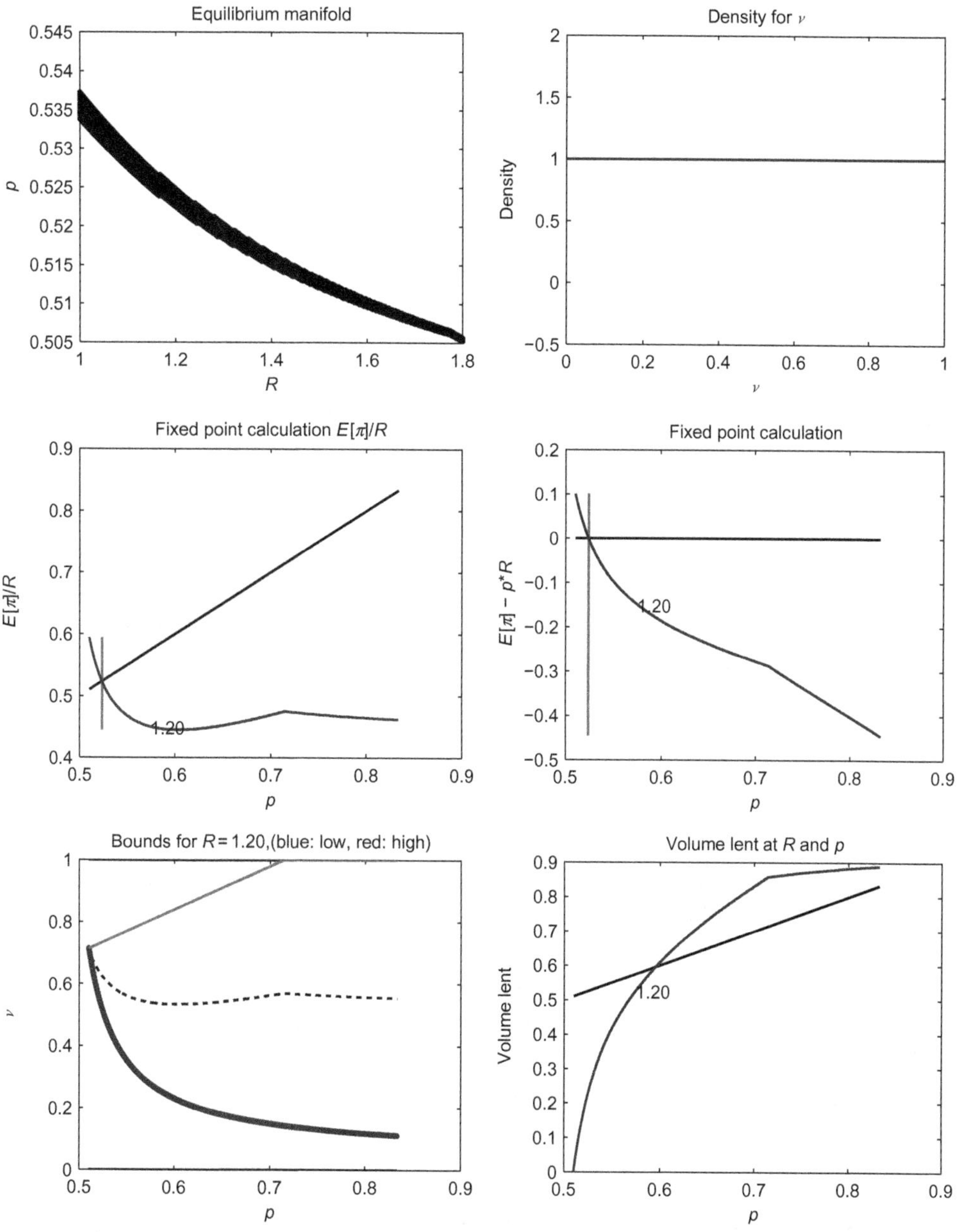

Fig. 9 Uniform distribution for ν on [0, 1]. No multiplicity.

2. a mixture of an exponential density and a truncated normal (where, in terms of the parameterization, we have not normalized the latter to integrate to unity, just the density $h(\nu)$ as a whole),

$$h(\nu) \propto \omega \frac{\lambda e^{-\lambda \nu}}{1-e^{-\lambda}} + (1-\omega) \frac{e^{-(\nu-\nu^e)^2/(2\sigma^2)}}{\sqrt{2\pi}\sigma}.$$

The first example we consider assumes that H is a mixture of an exponential density and a truncated normal, where $\kappa = 0.25$, $\lambda = -20$, $\nu^e = 0.1$, $\sigma = 0.2$, and $\omega = 0.6$. Fig. 10 shows the results for this case. The top panel on the left shows again the equilibrium manifold for mortgage prices as a function of the exogenous interest rate R and shows that for middle-range levels of R, multiple equilibria can arise. The top panel on the right just shows again the distribution for ν. The two panels in the middle show that the number of equilibrium pooling mortgage prices depends on the level of R. For example, we obtain a unique pooling equilibrium when $R = 1.5$, multiple equilibria when $R = 1.4$, and a unique separating equilibrium when $R = 1.3$.[j] In the case of multiple pooling mortgage prices, we have two stable ones and one unstable in the middle. Finally the bottom panel on the left shows again the two cutoffs, $\underline{\nu}$, in red, and $\overline{\nu}$, in blue, as a function of the pooling mortgage price, for the case $R = 1.4$. The bottom right panel shows the volume of loans offered in equilibrium as a function of the pooling mortgage price, for the three different levels of R considered above. This illustrates that if the economy starts at $R = 1.5$ and then R declines, the pooling mortgage price and the loan volume can first increase and then drop as a result of a shift from a good to a bad equilibrium.

For the second case, a mixture of two exponentials, we set the verification cost $\kappa = 0.15$, and the parameters of the H distribution to $\lambda_1 = -20$, $\lambda_2 = 5$, and $\omega = 0.8$. Fig. 11 shows the results for this numerical case. The plots are analogous to the one described earlier. In this case, we show that a unique pooling equilibrium arises when $R = 1.65$, multiple equilibria arise when $R = 1.58$ and a unique separating equilibrium arises when $R = 1.4$. This implies that, also in this case, a decline in R can generate an endogenous boom and bust in the credit markets, represented by an initial increase and a following decline in the pooling mortgage price and in the loan volume. Again, the bust is originated by a shift from a good to a bad equilibrium.

5. RELATED LITERATURE: SENTIMENTS AND BUBBLES

One story about run-ups in house prices and subsequent crashes, which appears to be popular in journalistic descriptions of financial crises, runs as follows: as prices rise,

[j] This is clearly a numerical example, not a calibration. In any case, high interest rates might be justified by the fact that mortgages are long-period contracts.

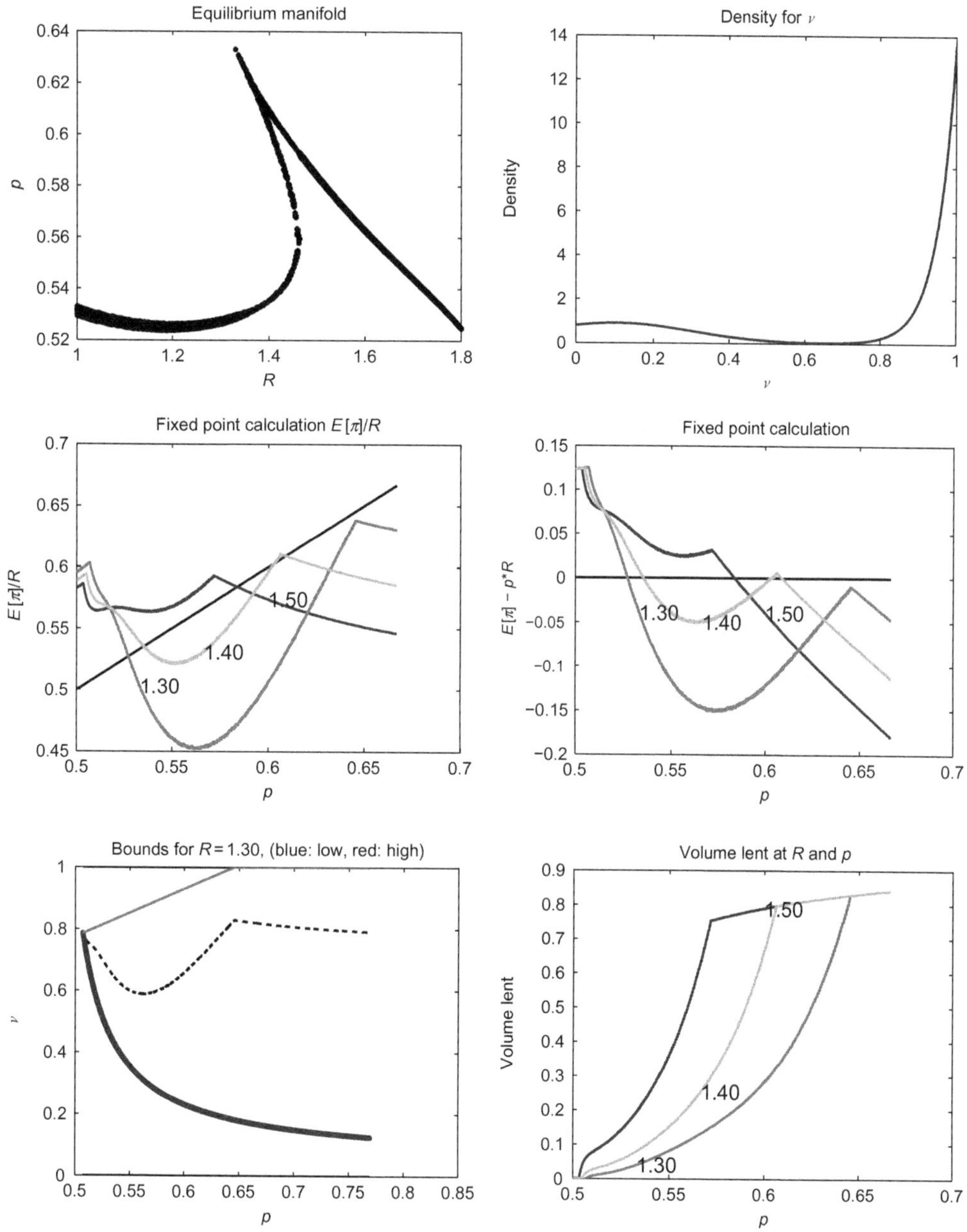

Fig. 10 For the mixture of an exponential density and a truncated normal, where $\gamma\bar{h}=2$, $\delta=0.1$, $\kappa=0.25$, $\lambda=-20$, $\nu^e=0.1$, $\sigma=0.2$, and $\omega=0.6$, we obtained a unique separating equilibrium for $R=1.3$, multiple equilibria for $R=1.4$ and a unique pooling equilibrium for $R=1.5$.

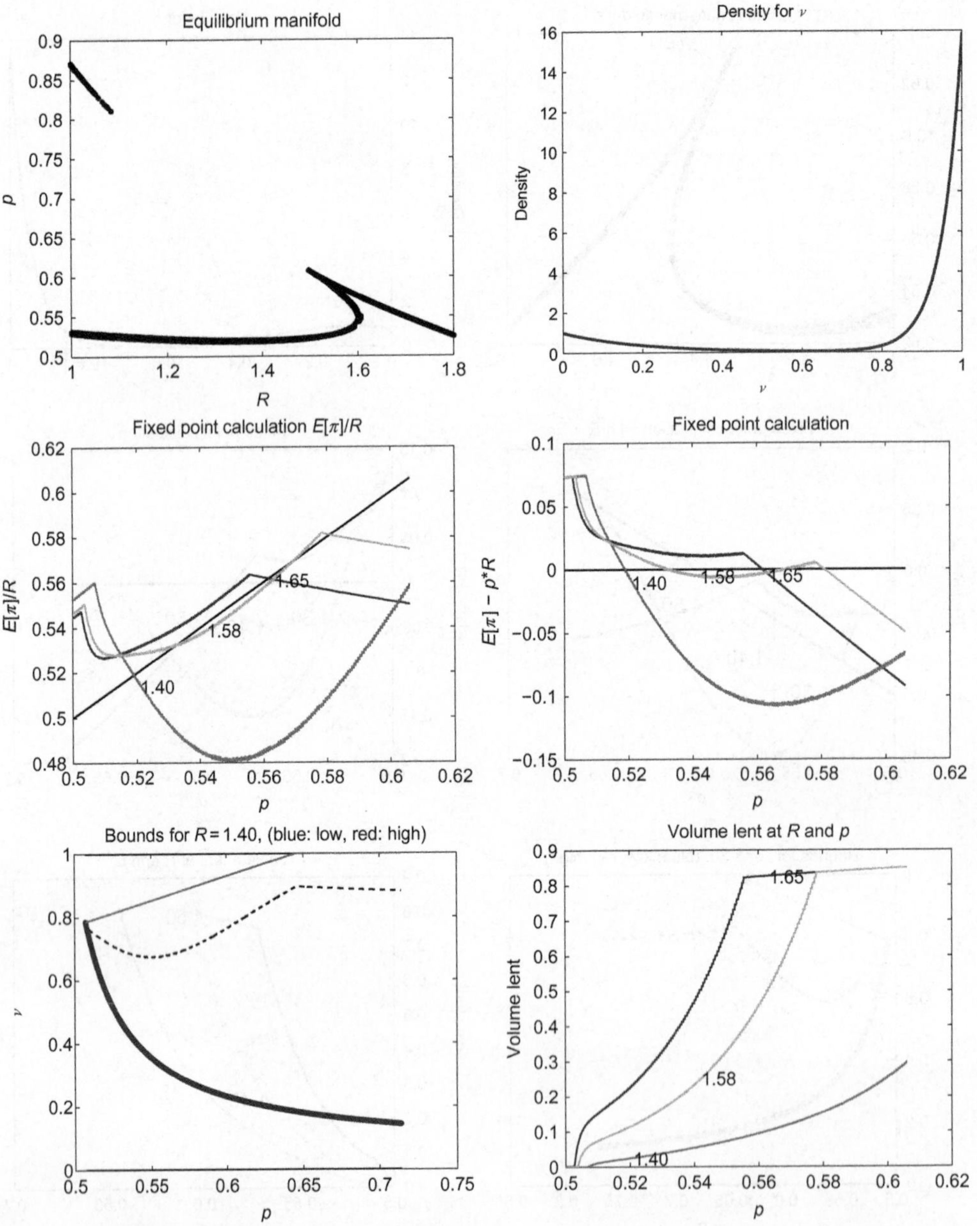

Fig. 11 For the mixture of two exponentials, where $\gamma\bar{h} = 2$, $\delta = 0.1$, $\kappa = 0.15$, $\lambda_1 = -20$, $\lambda_2 = 5$, and $\omega = 0.8$ (with κ the cost for verification), we obtained a unique separating equilibrium for $R = 1.4$, multiple equilibria for $R = 1.58$ and a unique pooling equilibrium for $R = 1.65$.

speculators are drawn to the market, hoping to sell at a higher price tomorrow. Eventually, this comes to an end, the speculators withdraw from the market and prices come crashing down. While appealing, formalizing this intuition tends to run into the obstacle that if prices are expected to be high tomorrow, then demand for credit and thus houses should be high today, and that should drive up prices today, making it less likely that prices will increase. Or, put differently, as prices rise, they eventually must get to a near maximum at some date (unless for some reason agents can buy on credit against the future resale): call that date "today." At that point, prices are expected to decline in the future. But if so, banks and speculating households are less likely to buy today and prices should not be high today to start with. These types of bubbles are typically ruled out by thinking about a "last fool" who is willing to buy at the highest price, when prices can only go down from there: such fools should not exist in rational expectations equilibria. Agents should realize that prices cannot outgrow the economy forever: using backward induction, the bubble then gets stopped dead in its tracks before it can get going at all. That is why formalizing this popular story indeed presents a challenge.

Two strands of the literature have evolved to address this challenge. One strand of the literature, that we refer to as "bubbles," keeps the expected growth rate of bubbles bounded by the growth rate of the economy, thus circumventing the backward induction logic. These models may additionally invoke irrational beliefs or differences in sentiments, but many do not. Another strand of literature, that we define "sentiments," allows agents to believe that bubbles will grow faster than the economy, but then also needs to invoke irrational beliefs for at least some portion of the agents in order to disable the backward induction logic described earlier.

Related to the literature on bubbles, there is another strand of literature that focus on generating momentum in house price changes. Among the papers in this literature, Case and Shiller (1989), Barberis et al. (1998), Hong and Stein (1999), Capozza et al. (2004), Frazzini (2006), Glaeser et al. (2014), Anenberg (2014), Head et al. (2014), Glaeser and Nathanson (2016), and Guren (2016).

5.1 Bubbles

Perhaps the most prominent and earliest example of a model with bubbles is the celebrated overlapping generations model of money by Samuelson (1958). If other means of savings do not produce a rate of return higher than the growth rate of the economy, then an intrinsically worthless asset (fiat money) can have a nonzero price in terms of goods, as it gets sold by the currently old agents to the next generation of currently young agents. Such economies need to be dynamically inefficient, satisfying the Cass criterion or Balasko–Shell criterion, see Cass (1972) and Balasko and Shell (1980). In such economies, the first welfare theorem might not hold, competitive equilibria might not be Pareto optimal. One may achieve a Pareto improvement by giving resources to the current old from the current young, who in turn receive resources, when they are old from the next young generation, ad infinitum. There are various ways to implement or interpret such a transfer scheme. Samuelson interpreted the scheme as fiat money, issued perhaps by the initially old generation. Others have interpreted it as government debt, to be rolled over forever, or as an unfunded pension system.

Another stream of literature that features rational bubbles is the search literatures with fiat money. The seminal paper in this literature is Kiyotaki and Wright (1989) that proposes a model of decentralized trade where agents meet randomly and fiat money can arise as general medium of exchange.

The literature of greatest interest to us here has interpreted this transfer scheme as a bubble, and has discussed how such bubbles might get introduced by various generations. In some of these papers, the transfer scheme is stochastic, and may end in any given period with some probability, generating a crash. For example Carvalho et al. (2012), Martin and Ventura (2010), Martin and Ventura (2012), Martin and Ventura (2014), and Martin and Ventura (2010) employ various versions of OLG models, in which, ideally, resources should be funneled from inefficient investors or savers to efficient investors or entrepreneurs. In particular, Martin and Ventura (2010) have used this framework to think about the financial crisis of 2008. There may, for example, be some lending friction, where entrepreneurs cannot promise repayment. They may be limited in how much paper they can issue against future cash flow from the project, or perhaps they need more financing than can be achieved by issuing such paper. They can additionally issue intrinsically worthless "bubble" securities, valued only because the buyer hopes that someone else buys them in the future. The issuance of such bubble paper starts another sequence of the intergenerational transfer scheme described earlier. The existing bubble paper in the hands of old agents as well as those created by newborn entrepreneurs get sold to savers. Savers find investing in these bubbles more attractive than investing in their own, inefficient technologies. This technology needs to be inefficient enough so that its return is on average below the growth rate of the economy, creating the dynamic inefficiency for bubbles to arise.

He et al. (2015) likewise focus on houses to facilitate intertemporal transactions when credit markets are imperfect, and the resulting liquidity premium for house prices. They obtain deterministic cyclic and chaotic dynamics as self-fulfilling prophecies, though their equilibria do not display an extended price run-up followed by collapse. Differences in beliefs are at the heart of trading in Scheinkman and Xiong (2003): the belief differences create a bubbly, but (on average) nongrowing component of asset prices.

Another paper that generate bubbles with fully rational agents and perfect foresight is Wright and Wong (2014). Here, bubbles arise in a model of bilateral exchange that involve chains of intermediaries in markets with search frictions and bargaining problems.

5.2 Sentiments

The other strand of literature we are going to focus in this section, is what we called "sentiment literature." In Section 6, we are going to propose a simple model that captures the "sentiment" idea that we mentioned in the introduction: asset prices may be above fundamental value because agents "irrationally" believe that there is always a "greater fool" who is going to be willing to buy at an even higher price. and discuss the related literature there. Here, we summarize a number of variants of this story formalized in different ways in the literature, where assets are trading above fundamental values due to diverse beliefs between optimists and pessimists, creating an "add-on" above the fundamental value, possibly requiring short-sale constraints on the pessimists. Static versions can be found in Geanakoplos (2002) or as in Simsek (2013). Dynamic versions are in Harrison–Kreps (1978) or in Scheinkman and Xiong (2003): in the latter paper, agents do understand, however, that the bubble will not grow faster than the economy, on average. Glaeser et al. (2014) study bubbles and their role for the housing market. They claim that rational bubbles can obtain, if there is no new construction. They do not provide a full general equilibrium formulation or description of the underlying credit market for this claim: one interpretation may be that agents can buy on credit against the future resale or have unlimited "deep pockets" to buy at any price. They rule out bubbles with elastic housing supply, and then proceed to use a model of irrational, exuberant buyers to study housing bubbles, relating the length and frequency of bubbles and their welfare consequences to the elasticity of housing supply.

Should asset price movements be taken into account in the central-bank interest rate setting? And if so, how? To answer this question, Adam and Woodford (2012) study the optimal monetary policy in a new Keynesian model with a housing sector, using near-rational equilibria, as developed in Woodford (2010) and allowing for a set of possible and internally coherent probability beliefs, that are not too different from the benchmark.

The papers incorporating diverse beliefs probably come closest to our model in Section 6. However, these models typically focus on the case where agents are either pessimistic or optimistic: by construction then, the optimists must be the "greatest fools." We instead wish to incorporate the idea that the more optimistic buyers are typically not yet the greatest fools themselves, but simply betting on even greater fools out there. At the extreme end, the "greatest fool" must be someone willing to pay for something that is intrinsically worthless (to all others), without ever being able to sell to someone at an even higher price, and there may be quite foolish people out there with overly strong optimism of being able to sell to such "greatest fools." So, at that end, the model may require substantial irrationality. The key here is, however, how this suspected strong irrationality at the upper end of the potential price distribution trickles down to the price and sales dynamic among the less foolish or even rational part of the population.

The model shares many elements with Golosov et al. (2014). There, assets are traded in a sequence of bilateral meetings between agents having different information regarding the fundamental value of the asset. By contrast here, everyone understands the asset to be intrinsically valueless: the differences arise in beliefs regarding the optimism of others. As such, our chapter is more closely related to Abreu and Brunnermeier (2003). A benchmark example for a dynamic model exploiting heterogeneous beliefs and changing sentiments, is the "disease" bubble model of Burnside et al. (2013). There is some intrinsically worthless bubble component, which could be part of the price of a house. An initially pessimistic population may gradually become infected to be "optimistic" and believe the bubble component actually has some intrinsic value: once, everyone is optimistic (forever, let's say), there is some constant price that everyone is willing to pay. However, "truth" may be revealed at some probability every period, and clarify that the bubble component is worthless indeed. Then, during the pessimistically dominated population epoch, prices rise during the nonrevelation phase, since the rise in prices there compensates the pessimistic investor for the risk of ending up with a worthless bubble piece, in case the truth gets revealed. The price will rise until the marginal investor is optimistic: at that point, the maximum price may be reached.

Another related recent paper is Bordalo et al. (2016), where credit cycles arise from "diagnostic expectations," that is, from the assumption that when they form expectations agents overweight future outcomes that seems more likely in light of the recent data. This can generate excess volatility, overreaction to news and predictable reversals.

6. A SIMPLE MODEL OF SENTIMENTS

In this section, we are going to propose a simple model to formalize and examine the following and often-told story about buyers and sellers in asset markets. We wish to use it in particular for thinking about the housing market, but it may apply more generally to the stock market or any other market in which assets get retraded.

The story we have in mind is as follows. Prices for assets sometimes bubble above their fundamental value and then come crashing down. They do so due to buyers betting on greater fools. More precisely, when a buyer buys an asset, she may realize that the price is above its fundamental value, but is betting on being able to sell the asset at a future date at an even higher price to a greater fool. What matters to the buyer is not, how foolish it is to keep the asset itself, but how foolish other participants are.

There are variants of this story formalized in various way in the literature, as we discussed in the literature review in Section 5.2. For our showcase model below and in contrast to the models of rational bubbles discussed in the literature review in Section 5.1, we do not assume that the economy is, effectively, dynamically inefficient. That is, we do not wish to assume that bubbles can be traded forever, because the return to be earned on these assets, as perceived by the agents, does not exceed the growth rate of the economy.

It may be important, however, to examine models in which the required rate of return is higher than the growth rate. It is then clear from the start that the price eventually must hit a ceiling: say, when the value of the asset exceeds all resources in the hands of the buyers. Usual backward induction arguments then rule out such bubbles in the first place, see Tirole (1985). The purpose of this section is to tweak the rationality argument per introducing a mythical "greatest fool," thwarting that backward induction. This "greatest fool" can alternatively be interpreted as a rational "collector," who just happens to value an asset at high price, while nobody else does. We will consider environments where this person is a myth indeed. Agents falsely believe, however, that this mythical collector is out there. Some particularly optimistic believers will buy the assets and hold it, in the hope of ultimately selling to the collector, but more importantly, some traders will buy the assets in the hope of selling to an agent who has an even more optimistic beliefs about the existence of a collector. This is what we mean by a sentiment-driven bubble. Note that it does not actually matter whether such collector agents are present: all that matters is the beliefs by the various agents in the presence of such agents. We allow for the belief in such collectors to suddenly disappear: if that happens, the price crashes.

It should be clear that one can construct higher-layer type theories too. For a second-layer theory, all agents may agree that there are no collectors. However, they may all believe that a certain fraction of "first-layer" agents out there does believe such collectors to be there, and the more optimistic agents may believe that fraction to be higher. Agents in such an economy will then not per se wait to sell to a collector (they know they cannot), but wait to sell to an agent who believes such collectors to be present. Furthermore, the agents that are less optimistic regarding the existence of such believers will sell to agents who are more optimistic regarding such first-layer believers. Once again, a bubble can arise, this time even if actually neither the collector nor first-layer believers are present in the economy. A third-layer theory would be about agents differing in their beliefs of meeting agents who believe that they can meet an original believer, etc. We feel that it would be fascinating to explore the ramifications and variations of the simple model below a lot further than we do. It is just meant as an inspiration and starting point.

6.1 The Model

Time is continuous, $t \geq 0$. There is initially a continuum of agents of total mass one. There is distribution of agent types $\theta \in [0, 1]$ in the economy, characterized by the distribution function $H(\theta)$. We assume that H has a density $h(\theta)$. We call agents of type $\theta = 1$ "collectors." We shall assume that $H(\theta^{\max}) = 1$ for some $\theta^{\max} < 1$, and thus, the distribution H assigns no weight to collector types.

Agents differ in their beliefs about the distribution of beliefs in the population, with θ parameterizing that belief. Specifically, we shall assume that, initially, an agent of type θ believs that other agents' type x is drawn from

$$H_\theta(x) = (1-\theta)H(x) + \theta 1_{x=1}. \tag{53}$$

In other words, agent θ uses a weighted average between the true distribution and a point mass at the collector type. Most of the analysis below carries over to a more general formulation: we leave these extensions to future research. Agents are aware of their differing beliefs, but they individually nonetheless insist on the beliefs they hold. We assume that an aggregate revelation event may arrive at the arrival rate α (or instantaneous probability αdt), at which point all agents suddenly understand that there are no collector types and their beliefs switch to the true distribution H. One might wish to assume that agents are unaware that this revelation event could occur (MIT shock), but it turns out that the mathematics is not much different if they do: so we shall assume that. In the latter case, the better interpretation is that agents believe that, with some probability αdt, the distribution of population types changes from H_θ to H, interpreting this as a taste and belief shift for other agents.

There is a single and indivisible asset (coconut), initially in the hand of an agent of type $\theta = 0$. There are random pairwise meetings between agents: due to our assumption of a single asset available for trading, it suffices to describe the meetings between the agent that currently has the asset and some other agent. If the agent currently holding the asset is of type θ and if the revelation event has not yet happened, then she will believe that she meets an agent drawn from the distribution H_θ at rate λ. The asset-holding agent (who we shall call the "seller") posts a take-it-or-leave-it price q_θ (the posted contract can be generalized, and we leave this to future research). The other agent (who we shall call the "buyer") decides to accept or reject the trade. If the trade is rejected, the seller keeps the asset and keeps on waiting for the next pairwise meeting. If the trade takes place, the buyer produces q_θ units of a consumption good or "cash," at instantaneous disutility q_θ, which the seller consumes, experiencing instantaneous utility q_θ. The future is discounted at rate ρ. The buyer receives the asset and then in turn waits for the next pairwise meeting. If the buyer turns out to be a collector, he will be willing to buy the asset at any price at or below some exogenously fixed value $v(1)$. The asset may provide some intrinsic value to the collector or the collector may simply be the "last fool," failing to understand that he can sell the asset at an even higher value in the future. In any case, the asset offers no intrinsic benefit to any agent who is not a collector. In other words, we assume that noncollector agents have preferences given by

$$U = E\left[\int_0^\infty e^{-\rho t} c_t dt\right] \tag{54}$$

where we allow c_t to be negative, and where c_t is the consumption flow resulting from these trades. We assume that the discount rate is strictly positive, $\rho > 0$.

A few brief remarks may be in order. We have not used time subscripts for q_θ, though there may be equilibria, in which these prices do depend on time. Here, we shall concentrate on time-invariant solutions, for simplicity. More importantly, it may seem odd to consider only a single asset, given that we have a whole continuum of agents at our disposal. This assumption considerably simplifies the analysis, though, as it allows us not to distinguish between meetings, where the potential buyer already owns an asset or not. Furthermore, over time, agents would need to keep track of the distribution of asset-owning types. It is plausible that these distributions shift to the right over time, ie, that it is the higher types holding assets, as time progresses. In the decision problem to be analyzed, selling agents would then need to forecast these evolutions, creating potentially intricate interactions and complications that go beyond the scope of this chapter. These would be good topics to pursue in future research.

Note that, in essence, the bubbly economies described in Section 5.1 can be understood as featuring $\rho \leq 0$ with $\alpha = 0$ (and finite lives), so that agents are willing to agree to a trade, in which they give up more today than they receive later, or at least do not insist on getting more later on. Here, we rule out this channel. Note also that the search theory models of money like Kiyotaki and Wright (1993) and their successors assume that the total sum of consumption is larger than zero, ie, that the seller benefits more from the sale than the buyer is hurt. If trades can only take place, using the intrinsically worthless asset, the asset helps in achieving a better outcome than autarky. Related modeling devices are used in Harrison–Kreps (1978) or Scheinkman and Xiong (2003). Here, by contrast, we shut down any benefits from the trade per se.

6.2 Analysis

We formulate the strategies of buyers as threshold strategies. A buyer of type θ picks some value v_θ, and purchases the asset, if the take-it-or-leave-it price is at or below that value, provided the revelation event has not yet taken place. For the collector type, $v_1 > 0$ is a parameter. A seller of type θ picks a take-it-or-leave-it price q_θ before the revelation event. After the revelation event has taken place, the asset is valued at zero by all and traded at zero price. A Nash equilibrium is then given by two functions $(v_\theta, q_\theta)_{\theta \in [0,1]}$, so that the strategies of agent θ maximize the utility function (54), given the strategies of all other agents. We shall additionally impose that v_θ is measurable. A seller can only hope to sell the asset in the future before the revelation event takes place. Put differently, we can assume that the seller discounts the future at rate $\alpha + \rho$, and that any before-revelation value of the asset to the seller in the future is discounted at that rate too. We could introduce a new symbol for $\alpha + \rho$. In slight abuse of notation (or appealing to the "MIT shock logic"), we shall continue to use ρ for that discount rate.

Consider now the before-revelation phase. We seek to characterize the Nash equilibrium or Nash equilibria. It is straightforward to see that a buyer of type θ will choose to buy at any price not bigger than v_θ, where v_θ is his continuation value of holding the asset. Consider then a seller of type θ, contemplating a sale price $0 \leq q \leq v(1)$

(obviously, it does not make sense to post a price above $v(1)$ or below zero). He assumes that his buyer's type x is drawn from the distribution H_θ, and that buyers follow their equilibrium strategy v_x and buy only if $q \leq v_x$. Hence, conditional on meeting a buyer, a seller of type θ who posts price q expects to sell with probability

$$\phi_\theta(q) = (1-\theta)\int 1_{v_x \geq q} h(x)dx + \theta \tag{55}$$

Proposition 6 *The probability of a sale $\phi_\theta(q)$ is decreasing in q and increasing in θ.*
Proof The proof is immediate, once one rewrite Eq. (55) as

$$\phi_\theta(q) = (1-\theta)\phi_0(q) + \theta. \qquad \square$$

If the trade takes place, the seller receives q. Trading possibilities arrive at rate λ, so in a time interval dt, the sale takes place with probability $\lambda\phi_\theta(q)$. Otherwise, the seller will remain owner of the asset at time $t + dt$, still valuing the asset at $V_\theta(q)$ then (provided the aggregate revelation event has not taken place: remember, that we implicitly took care of that via our discount factor ρ). Therefore, the continuation value of a seller of type θ who chooses a sale strategy q, $V_\theta(q)$, is equal to

$$V_\theta(q) = \lambda\phi_\theta(q)q\,dt + (1-\lambda\phi_\theta(q)\,dt)(1-\rho\,dt)V_\theta(q), \tag{56}$$

or, canceling higher order terms,

$$V_\theta(q) = \frac{q}{\dfrac{\rho}{\lambda\phi_\theta(q)} + 1}. \tag{57}$$

The optimal selling strategy $q = q_\theta$ is the one maximizing $V_\theta(q)$, that is,

$$q_\theta \in \operatorname{argmax} V_\theta(q) \tag{58}$$

delivering $v_\theta = V_\theta(q_\theta)$.

It is easy to construct two bounds for the optimal continuation value. On the one hand, consider the suboptimal strategy that agents will only attempt to sell to the collector, per posting the price $q = 1$. This strategy would give

$$\underline{v}_\theta = \frac{v_1}{\dfrac{\rho}{\lambda\theta} + 1}. \tag{59}$$

Clearly the optimal value function cannot be lower than $\underline{v}$, as in equilibrium there would be more trade for speculative reasons. On the other hand, consider the widely optimistic assumption, that any potential buyer is willing to purchase the asset at $q = v_1$. The value function would then be given by

$$\bar{v}_\theta = \frac{v_1}{\dfrac{\rho}{\lambda} + 1} \tag{60}$$

where the omission of θ is the difference to (60). It is straightforward to show that the equilibrium value function in between these two bounds.

Proposition 7 *Suppose that the function* $v : x \mapsto v_x$ *used for calculating* $\phi_\theta(q)$ *in Eq. (55) is measurable and satisfies* $\underline{v} \leq v_x \leq \bar{v}$. *Then* V_θ *has a maximum.*

Proof Note that $V_\theta(q)$ is bounded by $\bar{v}_\theta$. Let $q^{(j)}, j = 1, 2, \cdot$ be a sequence, so that $V_\theta(q^{(j)})$ is increasing, converging against $\sup V_\theta(q)$. Since $q^{(j)} \in [0, v(1)]$, we can find a convergent subsequence, which we can furthermore assume to be monotone. Wlog, assume that $q^{(j)} \to q^*$ for some q^* and is monotonically increasing or decreasing. If the sequence $q^{(j)}$ is monotonically increasing,

$$\bigcap_j \{x \mid v_x \geq q^{(j)}\} = \{x \mid v_x \geq q^*\}$$

Therefore $\phi_\theta(q^*) = \lim_{j\to\infty} \phi_\theta(q^{(j)})$ and hence

$$\frac{q^*}{\dfrac{\rho}{\lambda\phi_\theta(q^*)} + 1} = \lim_{j\to\infty} \frac{q^{(j)}}{\dfrac{\rho}{\lambda\phi_\theta(q^{(j)})} + 1}$$

If the sequence $q^{(j)}$ are monotonously decreasing, then

$$\bigcup_j \{x \mid v_x \geq q^{(j)}\} \subseteq \{x \mid v_x \geq q^*\}$$

and therefore $\phi_\theta(q^*) \geq \lim_{j\to\infty} \phi_\theta(q^{(j)})$. Hence

$$\frac{q^*}{\dfrac{\rho}{\lambda\phi_\theta(q^*)} + 1} \geq \lim_{j\to\infty} \frac{q^{(j)}}{\dfrac{\rho}{\lambda\phi_\theta(q^{(j)})} + 1}$$

Here, though, ">" is ruled out, since the right-hand side is the supremum of $V_\theta(q)$. We can conclude that q^* maximizes $V_\theta(q)$. □

The axiom of choice now implies that q_θ is well defined.

Proposition 8 *The value* v_Θ *of any Nash equilibrium is increasing in* θ.

Proof Let $\tilde{\theta} > \theta$. Note that $V_{\tilde{\theta}}(q) \geq V_\theta(q)$ for all q, since $\phi_{\tilde{\theta}}(q) \geq \phi_\theta(q)$. Since this is true in particular at $q = q_{\tilde{\theta}}$, the claim now follows. □

Now we can define the set of potential value functions

$$\mathcal{V} = \{v : [0,1] \to \mathbb{R} \mid v \text{ is increasing and } \underline{v} \leq v \leq \bar{v}\}.$$

Given that increasing functions are measurable, we can consider the mapping $T : \mathcal{V} \to \mathcal{V}$, defined by the following steps:

1. map $v \in \mathcal{V}$, into a function $\phi_\theta(q)$, using Eq. (55);
2. map ϕ into a function $V_\theta(q)$ using Eq. (56);
3. map $V_\theta(q)$ into the function v_θ that maximizes $V_\theta(q)$ (this maximum exists thanks to Proposition 7).

Proposition 9 *The mapping $T : \mathcal{V} \rightarrow \mathcal{V}$ is monotone and has a fixed point in $\mathcal{V}$. Therefore, a Nash equilibrium with $v \in \mathcal{V}$ exists.*

Proof For monotonicity, check that each step of the mapping is monotone. That is, if $\tilde{v} \geq v$, then $\tilde{\phi} \geq \phi$ for the first step, and so forth, where the inequalities are understood to hold pointwise for all arguments. Note that $\mathcal{V}$ is a complete lattice, with the usual order structure. Tarski's fixed point theorem now delivers the result that the set of fixed points of T forms a nonempty complete sublattice of $\mathcal{V}$. □

Next proposition shows that the equilibrium exhibits a threshold property.

Proposition 10 *For each sale price q, there is a threshold buyer type $\underline{x}(q)$ such that all buyers of type $x \geq \underline{x}(q)$ will buy the asset and all buyers of type $x < \underline{x}(q)$ will not, ie,*

$$x \geq \underline{x}(q) \quad \Leftrightarrow v_x \geq q. \tag{61}$$

The function $\underline{x}(q)$ is increasing in q. Furthermore, for $q \leq v_1$,

$$\phi_\theta(q) = (1-\theta)(1 - H(\underline{x}(q))) + \theta. \tag{62}$$

Proof The proof follows immediately from Proposition 8. □

To obtain a bit more analytic insight, consider a price q, where $\underline{x}(q)$ is differentiable.

Proposition 11 *Suppose $\underline{x}(q)$ is differentiable at $q = q_\theta$. Then, the optimal q_θ satisfies the first-order condition*

$$0 = 1 + \frac{\lambda}{\rho}\phi_\theta(q) - \eta_\theta(q) \tag{63}$$

where $\eta_\theta(q)$ is the elasticity of the sale probability,

$$\eta_\theta(q) = -\frac{\phi'_\theta(q)q}{\phi_\theta(q)} = \frac{h(\underline{x}(q))\underline{x}(q)'q}{\frac{1}{1-\theta} - H(\underline{x}(q))} \tag{64}$$

Proof Differentiate $V_\theta(q)$ with respect to q, and note that $V'_\theta(q) = 0$ at $q = q_\theta$. □

One can rewrite the sales probability elasticity a bit further. Let

$$\psi_\theta(x) = (1-\theta)(1 - H(x)) + \theta$$

be the probability of meeting a buyer of type x or better (including the collector), from the perspective of a type-θ seller. Define its elasticity

$$\eta_{\theta,\psi}(x) = \frac{\psi'_\theta(x)x}{\psi_\theta(x)} = -\frac{h(x)x}{\frac{1}{1-\theta} - H(x)}$$

Define the elasticity of the threshold buyer type,

$$\eta_{\underline{x}}(q) = \frac{\underline{x}(q)'q}{\underline{x}(q)}$$

Then

$$\eta_\theta(q) = \eta_{\theta,\psi}(\underline{x}(q))\eta_{\tilde{x}}(q).$$

This is the usual chain rule for elasticities, of course, applied to $\phi_\theta(q) = \psi_\theta(\underline{x}(q))$.

The results earlier suggest a strategy for characterizing an equilibrium. Suppose, one has some conjectured threshold buyer type function $\underline{x}(q)$, which is increasing and differentiable in q. With that, solve (63) for the optimal strategy q_θ and thereby for the value $v_\theta = V_\theta(q_\theta)$. With the value, calculate the resulting buyer threshold type function

$$\underline{x}^*(x) = \text{argmin}_x v_x \geq q$$

If $\underline{x}^*(q) = \underline{x}(q)$, one has obtained an equilibrium.

It may be possible to obtain analytical examples, for smart choices for H, exploiting this strategy. We leave this to future research to pursue. Here instead, we shall provide a numerical example.

6.3 Numerical Example

Rather than employing the first-order conditions above, we compute equilibria, using a rather brute-force grid-maximization algorithm. We create a suitable grid in q and θ. We start the iteration at the lower bound $v^{(0)} = \underline{v}$, defined over a grid in θ. We iterate on the mapping $T: \mathcal{V} \rightarrow \mathcal{V}$ described earlier. Specifically for step j, calculate $\phi_\theta^{(j)}(q)$ on the q-grid, using $\underline{x}^{(j-1)}$ on the right-hand side of Eq. (62). Now, calculate $V_\theta^{(j)}(q)$ per (57) for all grid values θ and q. For each grid value θ, find $v_\theta^{(j)}$ as the maximum of $V_\theta^{(j)}(q)$ over the grid values q. For each grid value q, find the smallest x, so that $v_x^{(j)} \geq q$, exploiting (61). This is the new $\underline{x}^{(j)}(q)$ and the next iteration step can commence. Iterate sufficiently often to obtain a reasonable degree of accuracy with the last solution.

As parameters, we chose $\lambda = 1$, $\rho = 0.1$ and let H be a uniform distribution on $[0, 0.25]$. The "collector price" was normalized at $v_1 = 1$. We used an evenly spaced grid of 500,001 points for q and 1001 points for $\theta \in [0, 1]$ or 251 points in the relevant range $[0, 0.25]$. As a starting point, we set $v^{(0)} = \underline{v}$, as defined in (60). For each grid value q, we then find the smallest $x = \underline{x}^{(0)}(q)$, so that $v_x^{(0)} \geq q$, exploiting (61).

The results are in Figs. 12 and 13. As one can see, agents with low θ pursue a strategy of seeking to sell to higher-θ agents, but beyond (approximately) $\theta = 0.1$, agents now only wait for the collector to make the sale. This can also be seen from the probability of sales. The black-dashed horizontal line shows the price chosen by the $\theta = 0$ types. This indicates that this market proceeds in two stages only, starting from the asset initially in the hands of a $\theta = 0$ agent (or an agent with a low θ). That agent will charge a price q_θ such that a sale only takes place, when meeting an agent with a fairly high $\tilde{\theta}$, who in turn hopes to sell to the collector, at $q_{\tilde{\theta}} = v_1 = 1$. It would be interesting to find examples, in

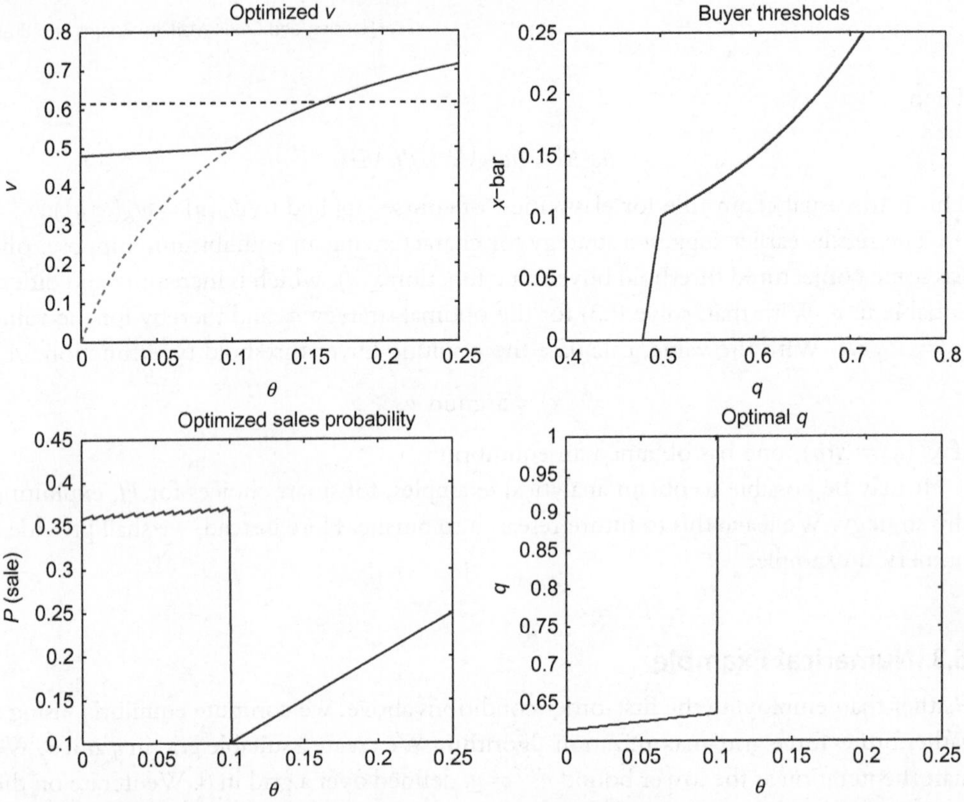

Fig. 12 Results from a numerical example. As parameters, we chose $\lambda = 1$, $\rho = 0.1$, and H to be a uniform distribution on [0, 0.25]. The "collector price" was normalized at $v_1 = 1$. In the top left panel, we compare the optimal value function to the value function $\underline{v}$ obtained per only selling to the collector. As one can see, agents with low θ pursue a strategy of seeking to sell to higher-θ agents, but beyond $\theta = 0.1$, agents now only wait for the collector to make the sale. This can also be seen from the probability of sales. The black-dashed horizontal line shows the price chosen by the $\theta = 0$ types. The top-right panel is essentially the top-left panel, flipped at the 45 degree line.

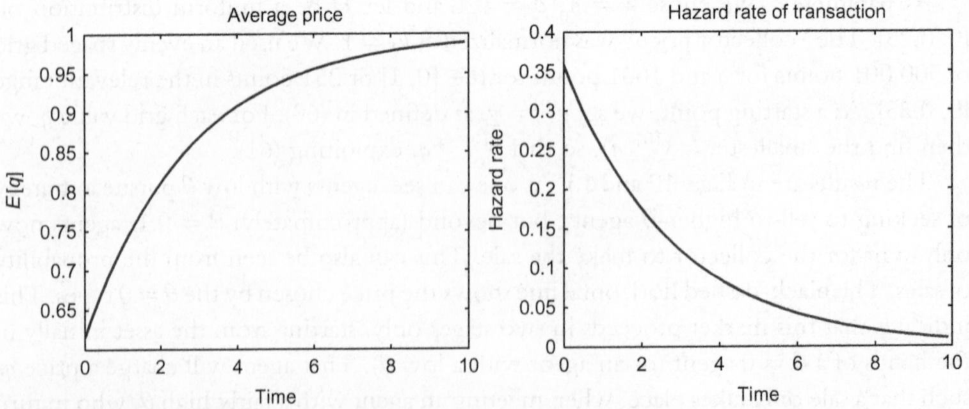

Fig. 13 Averaging over many posted price paths. The left panel shows the average price and how it is increasing over time. The right panel shows the hazard rate of a transaction and how it is decreasing over time.

which there are several stages of sale and resale to ever-more optimistic agents: we leave this to future research on this topic.

Consider now averaging across many simulations or individual markets, where the asset is initially held by the least optimistic agent $\theta = 0$. In principle, one can obtain the average price as well as the average hazard rate of a sale by simulation, using the results calculated thus far. Due to the two-stage structure of the sales process, it is easier to proceed analytically instead (and these arguments can be generalized to a multistage structure as well). If the asset is still in the hands of the initial $\theta = 0$ agent, it will be sold at the hazard rate $\xi = \phi_0(q_0)$, where we introduced the new symbol ξ for this hazard rate, to save on subsequent notation. Once the asset is sold, it will be posted at price $q_{\tilde{\theta}} = 1$ and not trade again, since there is no collector in the market. The unconditional date-t probability π_t, that the asset remains in the hands of initial $\theta = 0$ agent, solves the linear differential equation $\dot{\pi}_t = -\xi\pi_t$, with the solution given by $\pi_t = \exp(-t\xi)$. The average price is given by

$$E[q_t] = v_1 - (v_1 - q_0(q_0))\exp(-t\xi)$$

The unconditional or average hazard rate of a sale occurring is $\xi\pi_t$. Fig. 13 shows the resulting average price path and average sales hazard rate $E[\phi_\theta(q_\theta)]$. As one can see, the average posted price rises, while the average sales probability falls over time. The price path is conditional on the revelation event not occurring. Once the revelation event happens, the price crashes to zero. This captures the original story, with which this section got started.

The logic of the calculation just presented can also be used to calculate the results in Fig. 12 directly. Calculate first $v_\theta^{(0)} = \underline{v}_\theta$ for all θ per Eq. (60). Invert that function and use the distribution function H to calculate $\phi_\theta(q)$. With that, calculate $V_\theta(q)$ and find its maximum, for each q and the resulting $v_\theta^{(1)}$. The last step appears tedious, but may be solvable in closed form. This is the final result, in the situation that there are at most two stages of selling (first, sell to a more optimistic agent, second, attempt to sell to the collector), as here. One has to verify that indeed there are no further stages. Put differently, one now has to check that less optimistic agents would not now want to "change their mind" and sell to even more optimistic agents, who now value the assets higher, due to their reselling to optimistic agents. We leave the details of the calculations and the verification condition to the interested reader.

7. EVIDENCE

What caused the subprime crisis and, by extension, the financial crisis of 2008? What moved first, what moved later? What was cause and what was effect? The chapter has focused on two possible stories. One possibility is that house prices fell first for exogenous reasons, impairing bank balance sheets and leading to a financial collapse. Another possibility is that the banking system collapsed, leading to a reduction in mortgage lending and a fall in house prices. Perhaps, the fall in house prices triggered greater reluctance by banks to issue subprime loans, or perhaps and conversely, mortgage lending and, in particular, subprime borrowing, was reduced first, triggering a fall in house prices. Perhaps, subprime lending was reduced in the wake of higher delinquency rates on subprime mortgages or perhaps subprime lending was reduced, and the subsequent fall in house prices triggered delinquencies. Perhaps delinquencies rose because the pool of borrowers worsened or perhaps short-term interest rates rose, leading to higher rates for ARM mortgages and thereby higher delinquency rates. There are various ways of thinking through the interactions and tell the story. And how much did the interplay and feedback loop enhance the original shock?

Considerable research has been undertaken to seek to sort out these channels empirically: much more work still awaits to be done. We shall not attempt to give a full-fledged overview of the existing and large literature. We instead select some figures and facts from parts of the literature, and give them a somewhat impressionistic interpretation. Clearly, this is no substitute for careful empirical research on these data, but it may provide a good guide to questions and to developments to look at in the raw data. Most of the facts concern the United States. This generates a frontier of research interest and common ground for researchers to discuss, but it may miss important relationships and facts, compared to employing a world-wide perspective. We return to the latter towards the very end.

Figs. 1 and 14 show the S&P/Case-Shiller Home Price Indices. There is a run-up in house prices up to somewhere in the middle of 2006. According to the 20-city index

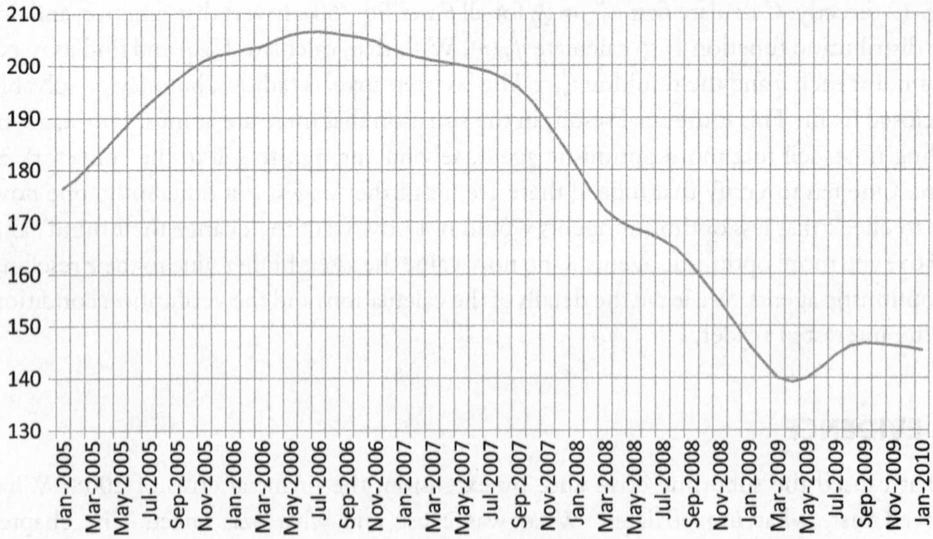

Fig. 14 The S&P/Case-Shiller home price 20 city index. *http://us.spindices.com/indices/real-estate/sp-case-shiller-20-city-composite-home-price-index.*

in Fig. 14, the peak is in July 2006. From there, prices started to drop, falling by 6.5% in October 2007, a relatively small drop. However, by October 2008, the date of the Lehman Brothers crisis and, in essence, the date of the financial collapse, house prices were at 25% below their July-2006 peak level, having fallen rather quickly and continuously from October 2007. House prices fell a bit more subsequently, reaching their bottom in April 2009, having fallen 32.6% from the original peak. From the sequence of these events, it appears plausible that house prices fell first, and the financial system collapsed subsequently.

However, the share of mortgages in the form of subprime fell quite substantially much earlier, as Fig. 2 reveals. Again, the peak subprime lending share of all mortgage originations occurred in 2006, at 23.5%, with a dramatic fall to 9.2% in 2007 and a near-zero in 2008. The peak occurred roughly at the same time as the peak of the S&P/Case-Shiller index in Figs. 1 and 14 and one might even wish to argue that the hump near the peak looks rather similar here. The decline in the peak subprime lending share from 2006 to 2007 was very sharp.

From this comparison, it appears plausible that subprime lending rose and fell together with house prices. If anything, subprime lending collapsed and decreased sharply, before house prices did. Thus, it may have been the reduction in subprime lending, causing the fall in house prices rather than vice versa.

One might wish to blame the decline in subprime lending on delinquency rates. Here, Fig. 15 is revealing. First, it shows that delinquency rates on fixed rate mortgages, be they prime or subprime, did not noticeably increase in 2006 and 2007: if anything, subprime fixed rate delinquency rates were near their all-time low of 2005.

The story is different for adjustable rate mortgages or ARMs. Here, rates did go up somewhat in 2006 and then somewhat more from their all-time low in 2004, but even there, the level in 2007 is rather comparable to the levels before 2002, both for prime adjustable rates as well as subprime adjustable rates, as Fig. 15 shows.

These movements are important for interpreting the course of events leading up to the crisis, but they are fairly small, compared to the subsequent development of delinquency rates shown in Fig. 16. Delinquencies later rose to unprecedented levels (at least for this time interval), peaking at rates somewhat above 40% for subprime adjustable rate mortgages around the end of 2009. In particular, delinquencies on subprime mortgages and prime adjustable rate mortgages had risen already considerably until October 2008, the date of the financial collapse. Overall, though, it does not seem plausible to argue that subprime lending was reduced in 2007, because delinquency rates had increased already at that point.

If anything, perhaps the delinquency rates in 2007 and the overall movement of delinquency rates on adjustable rate mortgages up to 2007 are linked to short-term interest rates. These rates are shown in Fig. 17. The Federal Reserve Bank increased the Federal Funds Rate in a sequence of small steps, starting at 1% in June 2004 to 5.25% in July 2006,

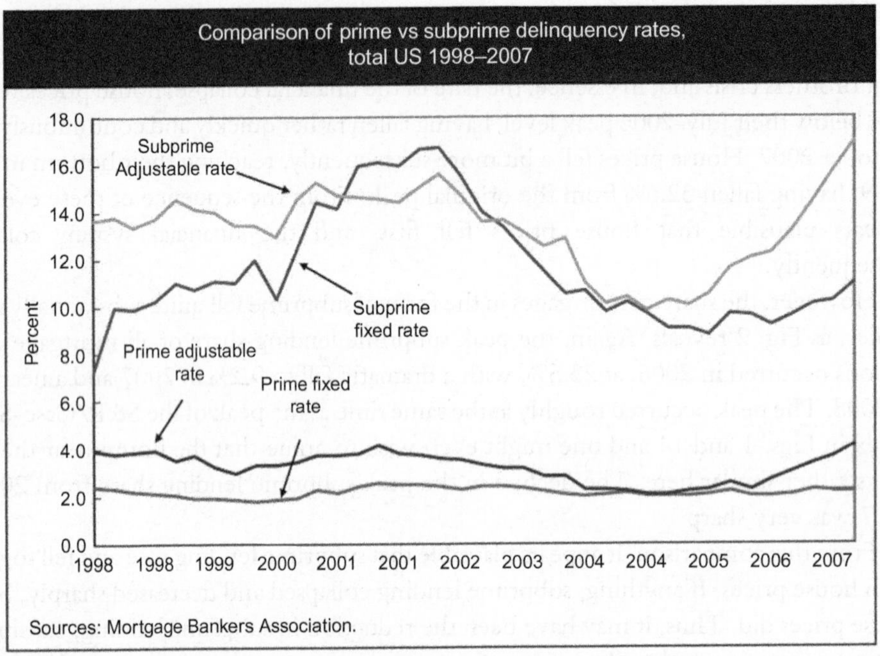

Fig. 15 Before the crisis: subprime delinquency rates 1998–2007. *Senator Schumer, Rep Maloney, Report of Joint Economic Committee, 2007.*

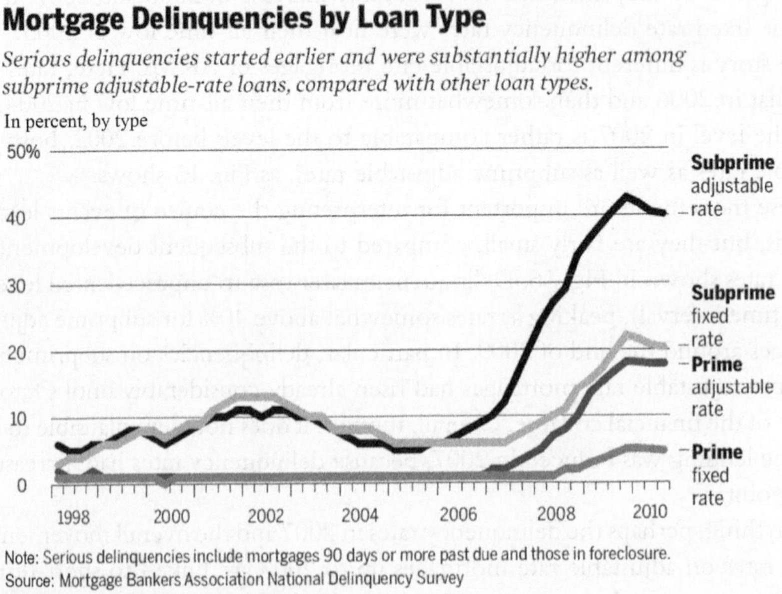

Fig. 16 Including the crisis: subprime delinquency rates 1998–2011. *The Financial Crisis Inquiry Report, National Commission, January 2011.*

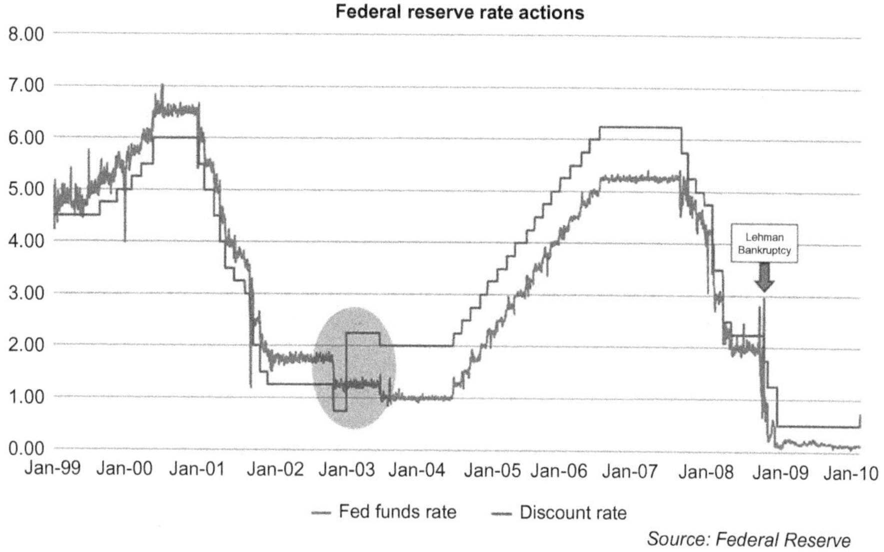

Fig. 17 Federal funds rate. *http://www.zerohedge.com/article/comparing-fed-funds-rateprimary-credit-discount-rate-over-past-decade.*

and then leveling off, before dramatically reversing course at the end of 2007. It is fairly plausible that the rise in short-term market interest rates from mid-2004 to mid-2006 resulted in the rise of delinquencies on adjustable rate mortgages from mid-2004 to mid-2006, seen in the previous figures.

Justiniano et al. (2015) have argued that house prices rose from 2000 to 2007 without an expansion of leverage, ie, at rather constant rates of mortgages to real estate, see the bottom-right panel of Fig. 18. The subsequent fall in house prices then went along with an increase in leverage and not necessarily a reduction in the volume of outstanding mortgages, see the top left panel.

These authors point to the fact that, first, there was an increase in available funds without an increase in leverage, leading to more mortgages at stable interest rates and stable leverage ratios, leading to a run-up in house prices.

For 2007 and beyond, they argue that the collateralizability of houses relative to available funds increased (or that available funds for lending decreased), leading to a rise in mortgage rates and a collapse in house prices. There certainly are some interesting comovements in Fig. 18 that deserve explanation, though not all readers may buy into the hypothesis that the collapse in house prices was caused by their relatively better collateralizability.

Most notably, Jorda, Schularick, Taylor and their coauthors have investigated the interplay between credit booms, house price booms and economic performance in a series of papers, constructing and providing new data sets along the way. Schularick

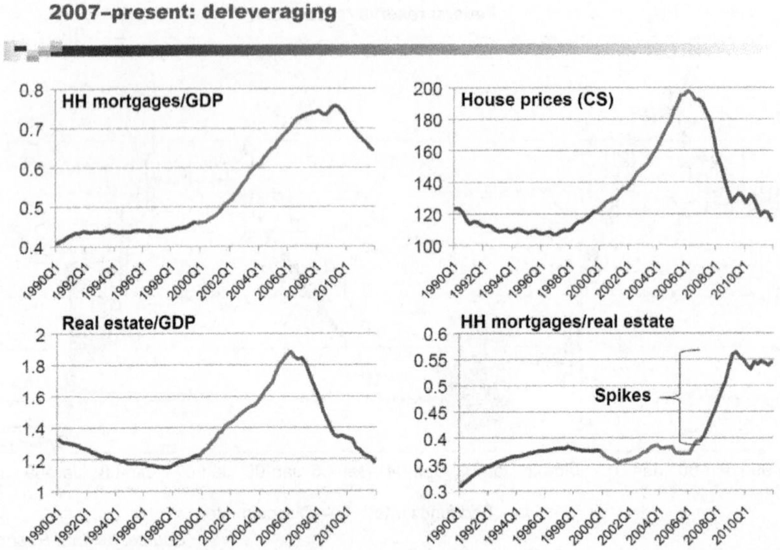

Fig. 18 The Justiniano–Primiceri–Tambalotti facts. *Justiniano, A., Primiceri, G.E., Tambalotti, A., 2015. Household leveraging and deleveraging. Rev. Econ. Dyn. 18, 3–20.*

and Taylor (2012) provide "a new long-run historical dataset for 14 developed countries over almost 140 years" and show how credit growth is a powerful predictor of financial crises. Jorda et al. (2013) subsequently argue that financial crisis recessions are costlier than typical recession. These data sets are updated and extended in Jorda et al. (2016a) for 17 advanced economies from 1870, covering disaggregated bank credit to the domestic nonfinancial private sector, with special attention to mortgage lending. They claim that "mortgage lending booms were only loosely associated with financial crisis before WWII, but …[have] become a more important predictor of impeding financial fragility" subsequently. Knoll et al. (2014) construct a house price index for 14 advanced economies from 1870 to 2012, assembling a variety of data sources. They argue that real house prices have largely followed a "hockey stick" pattern: fairly constant for a long time initially, followed a pronounced appreciation towards the end of the sample. They furthermore say that most of the price increase can be attributed to the increase in the price of land. Knoll (2016) subsequently argues that the rise in house prices coincides with a rise in the price–rent ratio. Combining data from these papers for 14 advanced economies, Jorda et al. (2015) claim that the 20th century has been an era of increasing "bets on the house." They write that "mortgage credit has risen dramatically as a share of banks' balance sheets from about one third at the beginning of the 20th century to about two thirds today." Using IV regressions, they show that "mortgage booms and house price bubbles have been closely associated with a higher likelihood of a financial crisis." Jorda et al. (2016b) provide further insights into the nature of these interactions, extending their data sets once more. They point to the fact that the build-up of leverage leads to higher tail risk. In a related paper, Mondragon et al. (2016), using a spatial IV-strategy, document empirical evidence that local credit supply shocks generate quantitatively significant boom–bust cycles in local house prices. In a similar spirit, Favara and Imbs (2015) show that an expansion in mortgage credit has significant effects on house prices, using the US branching deregulation between 1994 and 2005 as an instrument for credit. More recently, Di Maggio and Kermani (2016) show that a credit expansion can generate a boom and bust in house prices and real activity, using the change in national banks' regulation in 2004 by banning the antipredatory lending laws that a number of states adopted in 1999.

These series of papers and insights are completely in line with the fact that "a rise in household debt to GDP ratio predicts lower output growth," as shown by Mian et al. (2015).

We now show some figures taken from these papers to highlight some of these insights. Fig. 19, from Jorda et al. (2016b), show the "hockey stick" both for real house prices and mortgages.

The data can be sliced in other ways too, as Fig. 20 shows. That figure plots results both for the United States alone, their "benchmark economy," and for the sample of 17 countries investigated in Jorda et al. (2016b). House price growth and mortgage growth generally comove. In relation to real GDP, the real house price hockey stick, visible in Fig. 19, now becomes a downward trend, while the mortgage hockey stick becomes an upward trend. These figures raise intriguing, additional issues, concerning the attribution of changes in these series to their underlying causes.

Knoll et al. (2014) use Fig. 21 and additional analysis to show that house prices have risen faster than income in recent decades, while they have fallen relative to income in the first half of the 20th century and especially in the interwar period. Knoll (2016) argues that the rise in house prices coincided with a rise in the house price to rent ratio, as shown in Fig. 22. The price-to-rent ratio is similar to the often used price–dividend ratio for stocks, which has been shown to be useful for predicting stock returns. It is plausible that a similar phenomenon is at work for the housing market, as Knoll (2016) investigates.

The data sets created by these authors will be useful for further empirical investigations of the issues at hand. Luigi Bocola, in his discussion of a first draft of this chapter, combined the quarterly house price dataset from 1975 for a number of advanced countries, described by Mack and Martínez-García (2011), with the data for the 19 crisis events for advanced economies after 1975, described in Schularick and Taylor (2012). He constructed Fig. 23 to shed light on the relationship between house price growth, credit growth and GDP performance. The figure compares all crisis events (blue line) to the five events with the highest house price drop (red line) in the group: Denmark-87, Spain-08, Uk-91, Norway-88, Swe-91. This figure indicates once more the comovement of house prices and credit growth, but may suggest that the size of house price boom does not matter much for the average size of the subsequent recession.

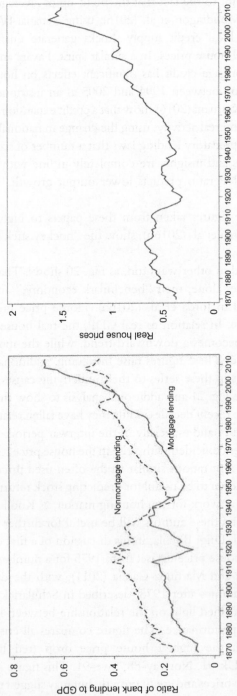

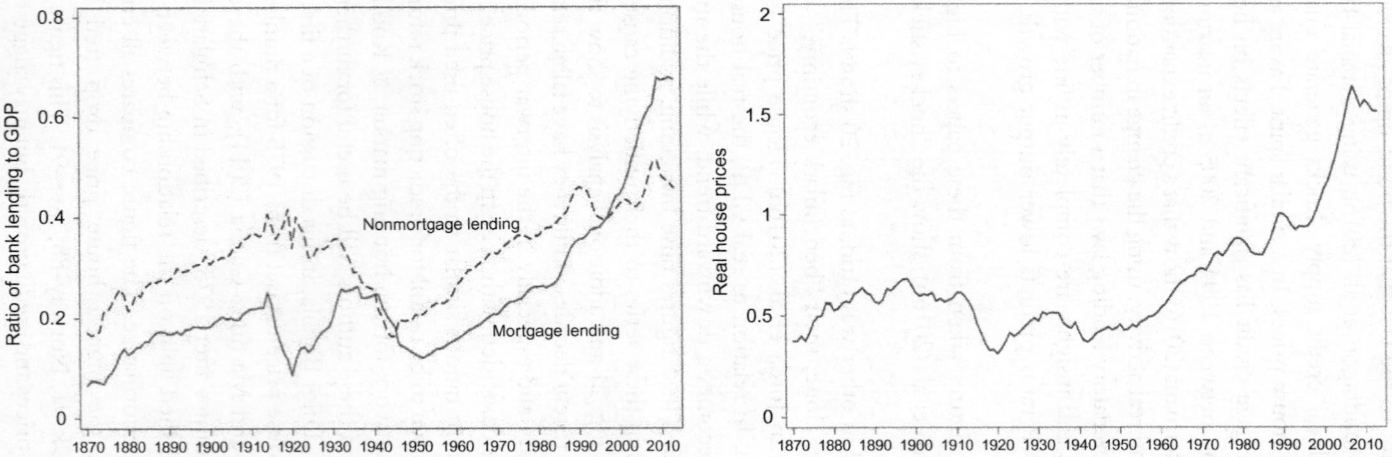

Fig. 19 Hockey sticks for real house prices and mortgages.

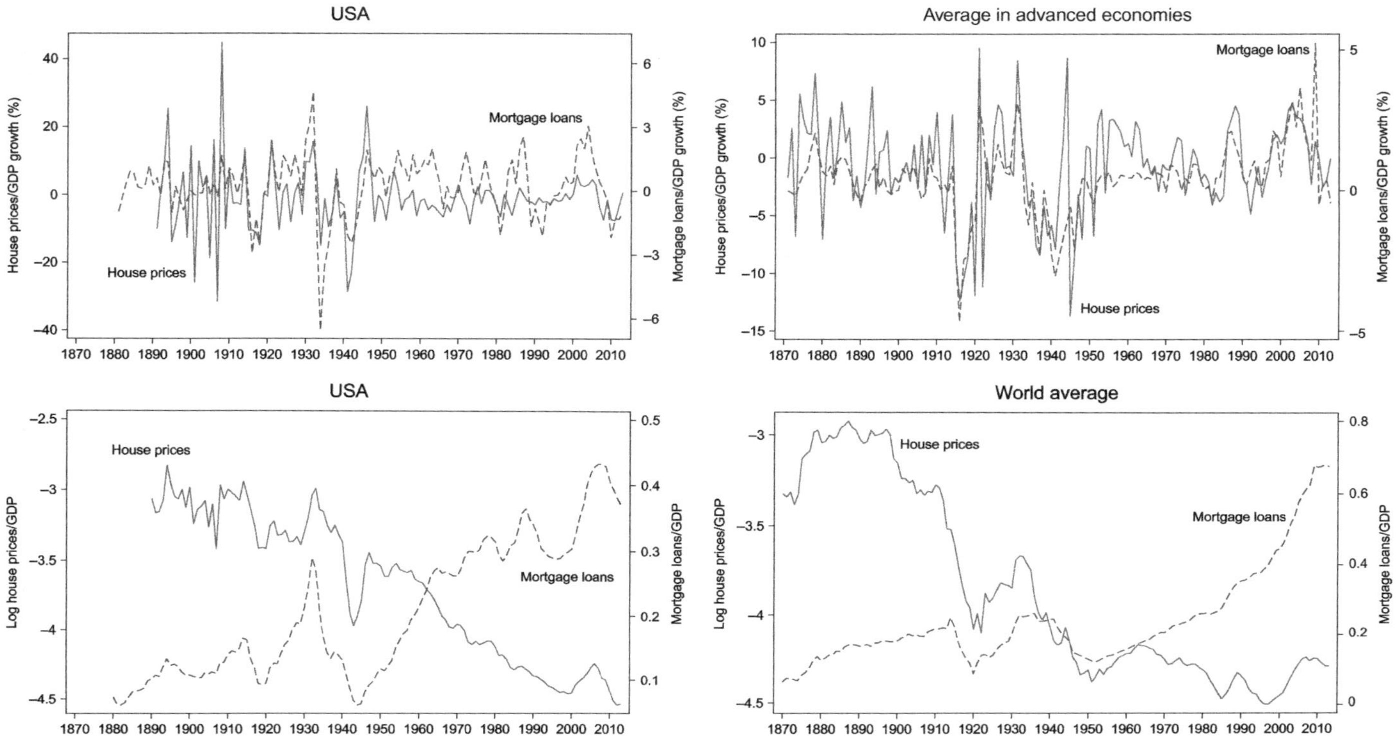

Fig. 20 Growth and trends in mortgages and house prices. *These figures have been provided by Helen Irvin and Oscar Jorda.*

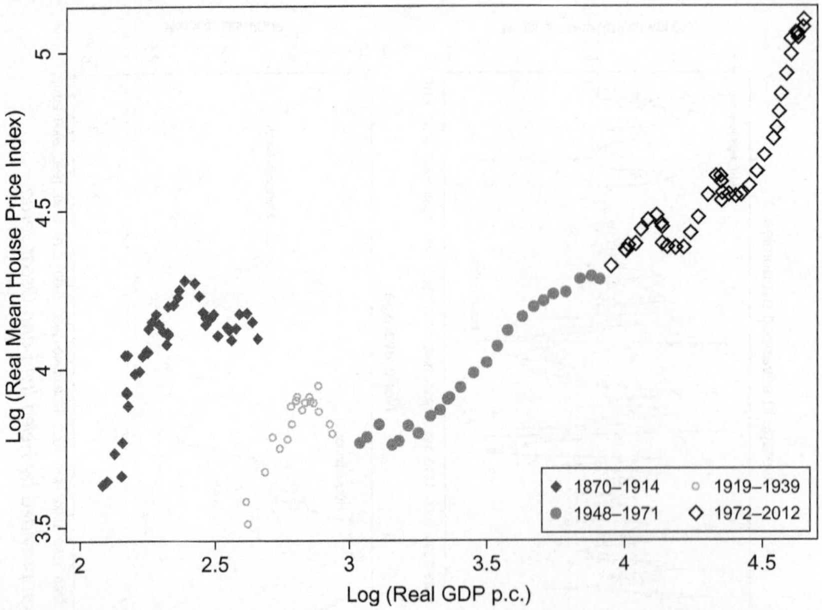

Fig. 21 House prices have risen faster than incomes in recent decades, while they have fallen relative to incomes in the first half of the 20th century and especially in the interwar period.

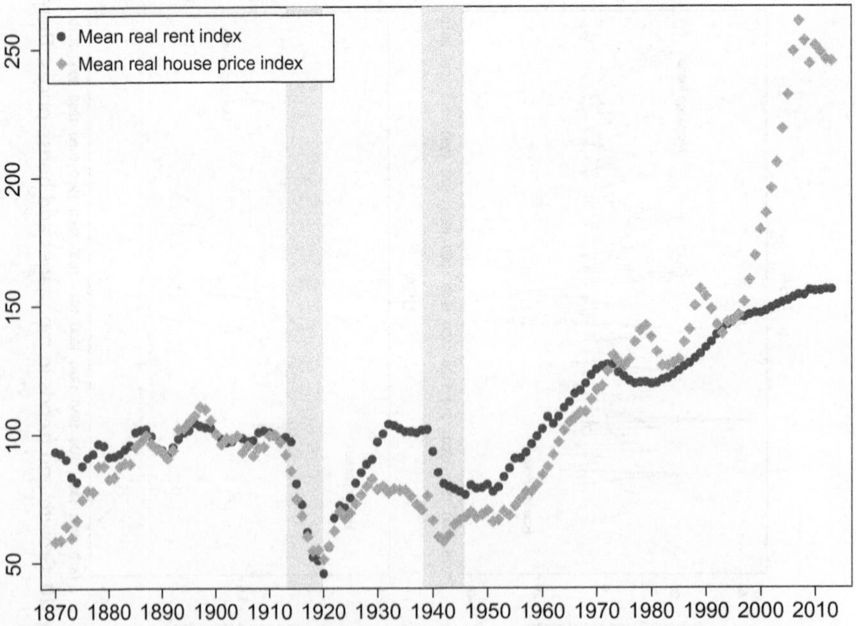

Fig. 22 The rise in house prices coincided with a rise in the house price to rent ratio.

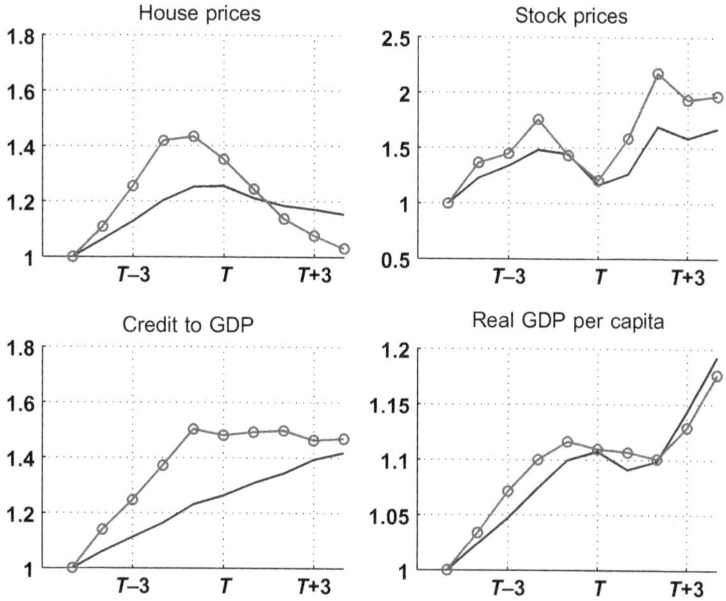

Fig. 23 Date "*T*" denotes the Schularick–Taylor crisis dates. The panels compare all crisis events (blue (dark gray in the print version) line) to the five events with the highest house price drop (red (black in the print version) line with circles) in the group: Denmark-87, Spain-08, Uk-91, Norway-88, Swe-91. The lines are cross-country averages for the four variables and normalized to equal unity at $T-5$.

Once more, we want to stress that this section is not meant to be a comprehensive review of the empirical literature on this topic. Our objective was just to report a subsample of facts and empirical papers that relate to the theoretical literature we have focused on in this chapter. These are all suggestive figures. However, the debate on whether house prices have been the main driving source of the credit cycle or financial conditions the main driving force of house price cycle is still open and hopefully future research will sheds more light on this topic.

8. CONCLUSIONS

The purpose of this chapter was to explore a key connection between boom–bust episodes in housing markets and boom–bust episodes in credit markets and to point to their effects on macroeconomic activity. To do so, we investigated several benchmark approaches and channels, and related them to the existing literature. It is already a challenge to understand the house price boom–bust together with the credit boom–bust, without analyzing the aggregate activity repercussions. We therefore mostly focused on the interaction of the first two. In particular, there are two broad possible approaches to think about this interaction:

1. The house price boom–bust generates the credit boom–bust.
2. The credit boom–bust generates the house price boom–bust.

We started the chapter by proposing a stark mechanical model to think about this interaction. On purpose, it is designed to avoid several thorny issues that arise in a fully specified equilibrium model. Next, we explored these two main approaches in more detail.

First, we proposed a simple model of catastrophes, where we focused on the credit cycle. The idea is that an increase in credit availability can generate first a boom and then a bust in mortgage markets because of adverse selection issues. In particular, in a world where banks do not know the quality of their borrowers, that is, their expected default rate, and borrowers can either pool or pay a cost to verify their type, multiple equilibria can arise. If we start from an equilibrium with pooling, an increase in credit supply translates into a decrease in the quality of the pool of active borrowers (like "subprime borrowers"). This, in turns, can generate a switch to an equilibrium where good borrowers separate themselves and the pooling market crashes.

Second, we proposed a simple model of sentiments, where we focus on the housing price cycle. The main idea is that a house price bubble can arise when speculating households believe that there is always a "bigger fool" out there that is going to be willing to buy housing at a higher price. While appealing, formalizing this intuition tends to run into the "conundrum of the single equilibrium": if prices are expected to be high tomorrow, then demand for credit and thus houses should be high today (see above), and that should drive up prices today, making it less likely that prices will increase. Or, put differently, as prices rise, they eventually must get to a near maximum at some date: call it "today." At that price, prices are expected to decline in the future. But if so, banks and speculating households are less likely to buy today: but then, the price should not be high today. That is, in rational expectations models, there should not be anybody willing to buy at the highest price when prices can only go down from there. We break the curse of the conundrum by departing from the rational expectations framework and assuming that households always believe that with some positive probability there is a bigger fool, although he does not really exists.

In the course of the chapter, we related our simple models to the large literature on these topics. At the end, we also point to some empirical papers that propose facts related to these two theoretical approaches.

We wish this chapter is going to trigger further research and thinking on this important connection. As has become clear, the issues are far from resolved.

ACKNOWLEDGMENTS

We are grateful to Chiara Fratto, Ken Kikkawa, and Chao Ying for their excellent research assistance. For helpful comments, we are grateful to Fabrice Collard, Matteo Iacoviello, Oscar Jorda, Guido Lorenzoni, Moritz Schularick, Alan M. Taylor, and, in particular, to Luigi Bocola, Zhen Huo, and Nicolas Trachter for their thoughtful discussions as well as John Taylor for his detailed and useful comments. We are also grateful to audiences at the handbook conference at the University of Chicago, the "Multiple Equilibria and Financial Crises" conference at NYU, the "Mad Money" conference at the University of Wisconsin, and the seminar audience at the University of Toronto. This research has been supported by the NSF grant SES-1227280 and by the INET grant #INO1100049, "Understanding Macroeconomic Fragility." H.U. has an ongoing consulting relationship with a Federal Reserve Bank, the Bundesbank, and the ECB. V.G. has an ongoing consulting relationship with the Chicago Federal Reserve Bank.

REFERENCES

Abreu, D., Brunnermeier, M.K., 2003. Bubbles and crashes. Econometrica 71 (1), 173–204.

Adam, K., Woodford, M., 2012. Housing prices and robustly optimal monetary policy. J. Monet. Econ. 59, 468–487.

Anenberg, E., 2014. Information frictions and housing market dynamics. Working Paper.

Attanasio, O.P., Blow, L., Hamilton, R., Leicester, A., 2009. Booms and busts: consumption, house prices and expectations. Economica 76 (301), 20–50.

Balasko, Y., Shell, K., 1980. The overlapping generations model, I: the case of pure exchange without money. J. Econ. Theory 23 (3), 281–306.

Barberis, N., Shleifer, A., Vishny, R., 1998. A model of investor sentiment. J. Financ. Econ. 49 (3), 307–343.

Benes, J., Kumhof, M., Laxton, D., 2014a. Financial crises in DSGE models: a prototype model. IMF Working Paper Series 14/57.

Benes, J., Kumhof, M., Laxton, D., 2014b. Financial crises in DSGE models: selected applications of MAPMOD. IMF Working Paper Series 14/56.

Benhabib, J., Rogerson, R., Wright, R., 1991. Homework in macroeconomics: household production and aggregate fluctuations. J. Polit. Econ. 99, 1166–1187.

Berger, D., Guerrieri, V., Lorenzoni, G., Vavra, J., 2015. House prices and consumer spending. National Bureau of Economic Research.

Bernanke, B., Gertler, M., 1989. Agency costs, net worth, and business fluctuations. Am. Econ. Rev. 79, 14–31.

Bernanke, B.S., Gertler, M., Gilchrist, S., 1999. The financial accelerator in a quantitative business cycle framework. In: Taylor, J., Woodford, M. (Eds.), Handbook of Macroeconomics, vol. 1. Elsevier, North-Holland, pp. 1341–1393.

Bocola, L., 2014. The Pass-Through of Sovereign Risk (draft). Northwestern University.

Boissay, F., Collard, F., Smets, F., 2016. Booms and banking crises. J. Polit. Econ. 124 (2), 489–538.

Boldrin, M., Christiano, L.J., Fisher, J.D.M., 2001. Habit persistence, asset returns, and the business cycle. 91 (1), 149–166.

Bordalo, P., Gennaioli, N., Shleifer, A., 2016. Diagnostic expectations and credit cycles. Working Paper.

Brunnermeier, M.K., Sannikov, Y., 2010. A Macroeconomic Model with a Financial Sector (draft). Princeton University.

Brunnermeier, M., Eisenbach, T.M., Sannikov, Y., 2011. Macroeconomics with Financial Frictions: A Survey (draft). Princeton University.

Brzoza-Brzezina, M., Gelain, P., Kolasa, M., 2014. Monetary and Macroprudential Policy with Multi-Period Loans (draft).

Burnside, C., Eichenbaum, M., Rebelo, S., 2013. Understanding booms and busts in housing markets. Working Paper, Northwestern University.

Campbell, J.Y., Cocco, J.F., 2007. How do house prices affect consumption? Evidence from micro data. J. Monet. Econ. 54 (3), 591–621.

Campbell, J.R., Hercowitz, Z., 2006. The role of collateralized household debt in macroeconomic stabilization. Working Paper.

Capozza, D.R., Hendershott, P.H., Mack, C., 2004. An anatomy of price dynamics in illiquid markets: analysis and evidence from local housing markets. Real Estate Econ. 32 (1), 1–32.

Carlstrom, C.T., Fuerst, T.S., 1997. Agency costs, net worth, and business fluctuations: a computable general equilibrium analysis. Am. Econ. Rev. 87 (5), 893–910.
Carroll, C.D., Otsuka, M., Slacalek, J., 2011. How large are housing and financial wealth effects? A new approach. J. Money Credit Bank. 43 (1), 55–79.
Carvalho, V.M., Martin, A., Ventura, J., 2012. Understanding bubbly episodes. Am. Econ. Rev. 102 (3), 95–100.
Cass, D., 1972. On capital overaccumulation in the aggregative neoclassical model of economic growth: a complete characterization. J. Econ. Theory 4 (2), 200–223.
Case, K., Shiller, R., 1989. The efficiency of the market for single-family homes. Am. Econ. Rev. 79 (1), 125–137.
Case, K.E., Quigley, J.M., Shiller, R.J., et al., 2013. Wealth effects revisited 1975–2012. Crit. Finance Rev. 2 (1), 101–128.
Clancy, D., Merola, R., 2015. Counter-cyclical capital rules for small open economies. Working Paper.
Corbae, D., Quintin, E., 2014. Leverage and the foreclosure crisis.
Davis, M.A., Heathcote, J., 2005. Housing and the business cycle. Int. Econ. Rev. 46 (3), 751–784.
Davis, M.A., VanNieuwerburgh, S., 2015. Housing, finance and the macroeconomy. In: Duranton, G., Henderson, J.V., Strange, W.C. (Eds.), Handbook of Urban and Regional Economics, vol. 5. Elsevier, pp. 753–811.
Del Negro, M., Eggertsson, G., Ferrero, A., Kiyotaki, N., 2011. The great escape? A quantitative evaluation of the Fed's liquidity facilities. Staff Report 520, Federal Reserve Bank of New York.
Di Maggio, M., Kermani, A., 2016. Credit induced boom and bust. Working Paper.
Eggertsson, G.B., Krugman, P., 2012. Debt, deleveraging, and the liquidity trap: a Fisher-Minsky-Koo approach. Q. J. Econ. 127 (3), 1469–1513.
Favara, G., Imbs, J., 2015. Credit supply and the price of housing. Am. Econ. Rev. 105, 958–992.
Favilukis, J., Ludvigson, S., Nieuwerburgh, S.V., 2016. The macroeconomic effects of housing wealth, housing finance, and limited risk-sharing in general equilibrium. J. Polit. Econ. Forthcoming.
Fisher, J.D., 2007. Why does household investment lead business investment over the business cycle? J. Polit. Econ. 115 (1), 141–168.
Frazzini, A., 2006. The disposition effect and underreaction to news. J. Finance 61 (4), 2017–2046.
Garriga, C., Kydland, F.E., Šustek, R., 2016. Mortgages and monetary policy. Working Paper.
Geanakoplos, J., 2002. Liquidity, default and crashes: endogenous contracts in general equilibrium. Discussion Paper 1316RR, Cowles Foundation for Research in Economic – Yale University.
Geanakoplos, J., 2009. The leverage cycle. Discussion Paper 1715, Cowles Foundation for Research in Economic – Yale University.
Geanakoplos, J., 2011. What's missing from macroeconomics: endogenous leverage and default. Discussion Paper 1332, Cowles Foundation for Research in Economic – Yale University.
Gilchrist, S., Zakrajšek, E., 2012. Credit spreads and business cycle fluctuations. Am. Econ. Rev. 102 (4), 1692–1720.
Glaeser, E.L., Nathanson, C.G., 2016. An extrapolative model of house price dynamics.
Glaeser, E.L., Gyourko, J., Morales, E., Nathanson, C.G., 2014. Housing dynamics: an urban approach. J. Urban Econ. 81, 45–56.
Golosov, M., Lorenzoni, G., Tsyvinski, A., 2014. Decentralized trading with private information. Econometrica 82 (3), 1055–1091.
Greenwood, J., Hercowitz, Z., 1991. The allocation of capital and time over the business cycle. J. Polit. Econ. 99 (6), 1188–1214.
Guerrieri, L., Iacoviello, M., 2014. Collateral constraints and macroeconomic asymmetries.
Guerrieri, V., Lorenzoni, G., 2011. Credit crises, precautionary savings, and the liquidity trap. NBER Working Paper Series 17583.
Guren, A.M., 2016. The causes and consequences of house price momentum.
Hall, R., 2011. The long slump. Am. Econ. Rev. 101 (2), 431–469.
Hall, R.E., 2014. High discounts and high unemployment. National Bureau of Economic Research.
Harrison, J.M., Kreps, D.M., 1978. Speculative investor behavior in a stock market with heterogeneous expectations. Q. J. Econ. 92 (2), 323–336.

He, Z., Krishnamurthy, A., 2013. Intermediary asset pricing. Am. Econ. Rev. 103 (2), 732–770.
He, C., Wright, R., Zhu, Y., 2015. Housing and liquidity. Rev. Econ. Dyn. 18 (3), 435–455.
Head, A., Lloyd-Ellis, H., Sun, H., 2014. Search, liquidity, and the dynamics of house prices and construction. Am. Econ. Rev. 104 (4), 1172–1210.
Hong, H., Stein, J.C., 1999. A unified theory of underreaction, momentum trading, and overreaction in asset markets. J. Finance 54 (6), 2143–2184.
Huo, Z., Ríos-Rull, J.V., 2013. Paradox of thrift recessions. National Bureau of Economic Research.
Huo, Z., Ríos-Rull, J.V., 2014. Financial frictions, asset prices, and the great recession.
Iacoviello, M., 2005. House prices, borrowing constraints, and monetary policy in the business cycle. Am. Econ. Rev. 95 (3), 739–764.
Iacoviello, M., 2012. Housing wealth and consumption. In: Smith, S. (Ed.), International Encyclopedia of Housing and Home. Elsevier, pp. 673–678.
Iacoviello, M., Neri, S., 2010. Housing market spillovers: evidence from an estimated DSGE model. Am. Econ. J. Macroecon. 2 (2), 125.
Iacoviello, M., Pavan, M., 2013. Housing and debt over the life cycle and over the business cycle. J. Monet. Econ. 60, 221–238.
Johnson, D.S., Parker, J.A., Souleles, N.S., 2006. Household expenditure and the income tax rebates of 2001. Am. Econ. Rev. 96 (5), 1589–1610.
Jorda, O., Schularick, M., Taylor, A.M., 2013. When credit bites back. J. Money Credit Bank. 45 (2), 3–28.
Jorda, O., Schularick, M., Taylor, A.M., 2015. Betting the house. J. Int. Econ. 96, S2–S18.
Jorda, O., Schularick, M., Taylor, A.M., 2016a. The great mortgaging: housing finance, crises and business cycles. Econ. Policy 31, 107–152.
Jorda, O., Schularick, M., Taylor, A.M., 2016b. Macrofinancial history and the new business cycle facts. In: Eichenbaum, M., Parker, J. (Eds.), NBER Macroeconomics Annual 2016. University of Chicago Press, Chicago, Il., U.S.A.
Justiniano, A., Primiceri, G.E., Tambalotti, A., 2014. Credit supply and the housing boom. Working Paper.
Justiniano, A., Primiceri, G.E., Tambalotti, A., 2015. Household leveraging and deleveraging. Rev. Econ. Dyn. 18 (1), 3–20.
Kaplan, G., Violante, G.L., 2014. A model of the consumption response to fiscal stimulus payments. Econometrica 82 (4), 1199–1239.
Kaplan, G., Mitman, K., Violante, G., 2015. Consumption and house prices in the great recession: model meets evidence. Working Paper.
Kehoe, P., Midrigan, V., Pastorino, E., 2014. Debt constraint and unemployment. Working Paper.
Kermani, A., 2016. Cheap credit, collateral and the boom-bust cycle. Working Paper.
Kiyotaki, N., Moore, J., 1997. Credit cycles. J. Polit. Econ. 105 (2), 211–248.
Kiyotaki, N., Wright, R., 1989. On money as a medium of exchange. J. Polit. Econ. 97, 927–954.
Kiyotaki, N., Wright, R., 1993. A search-theoretic approach to monetary economics. Am. Econ. Rev. 83 (1), 63–77.
Kiyotaki, N., Michaelides, A., Nikolov, K., 2011. Winners and losers in housing markets. J. Money Credit Bank. 43, 255–296.
Knoll, K., 2016. Return Predictability in International Housing Markets, 1870–2014 (Dissertation draft). University of Bonn.
Knoll, K., Schularick, M., Steger, T., 2014. No price like home: global house prices, 1870-2012. Working Paper, University of Bonn.
Lorenzoni, G., 2008. Inefficient credit booms. Rev. Econ. Stud. 75, 809–833.
Macera, M., 2015. Credit crises and private deleveraging. Working Paper.
Mack, A., Martínez-García, E., 2011. A cross-country quarterly database of real house prices: a methodological note. Working Paper 99, Federal Reserve Bank of Dallas Globalization and Monetary Policy Institute.
Magnus, G., 2011. The dynamics of prices, liquidity and vacancies in the housing market (Dissertation). University of Chicago.
Mankiw, N.G., 1986. The allocation of credit and financial collapse. Q. J. Econ. 101 (3), 455–470.

Martin, A., Ventura, J., 2010. Theoretical notes on bubbles and the current crisis. NBER Working Paper 16399, National Bureau of Economic Research.
Martin, A., Ventura, J., 2012. Economic growth with bubbles. Am. Econ. Rev. 102 (6), 3033–3058.
Martin, A., Ventura, J., 2014. Managing credit bubbles. NBER Working Paper 19960, National Bureau of Economic Research.
Mendoza, E.G., Quadrini, V., 2010. Financial globalization, financial crises and contagion. J. Monet. Econ. 57, 24–39.
Mian, A.R., Sufi, A., 2011. House prices, home equity-based borrowing, and the U.S. household leverage crisis. Am. Econ. Rev. 101 (5), 2132–2156.
Mian, A., Sufi, A., 2014. What explains the 2007–2009 drop in employment? Econometrica 82 (6), 2197–2223.
Mian, A.R., Rao, K., Sufi, A., 2013. Household Balance Sheets, Consumption, and the Economic Slump (draft). University of Chicago Booth School.
Mian, A., Sufi, A., Verner, E., 2015. Household debt and business cycles worldwide. NBER Working Papers 21581, National Bureau of Economic Research.
Midrigan, V., Philippon, T., 2011. Household leverage and the recession. NYU Working Paper.
Mondragon, J., Wieland, J., Yang, M.J., 2016. Credit supply shocks and house price boom-bust cycles. Working Paper.
Myerson, R., 2012. A model of moral-hazard credit cycles. J. Polit. Econ. 120 (5), 847–878.
Ortalo-Magne, F., Rady, S., 2006. Housing market dynamics: on the contribution of income shocks and credit constraints. Rev. Econ. Stud. 73 (2), 459–485.
Parker, J.A., Souleles, N.S., Johnson, D.S., McClelland, R., 2013. Consumer spending and the economic stimulus payments of 2008. Am. Econ. Rev. 103 (6), 2530–2553.
Rognlie, M., Shleifer, A., Simsek, A., 2015. Investment hangover and the great recession. Working Paper.
Samuelson, P.A., 1958. An exact consumption-loan model of interest with or without the social contrivance of money. J. Polit. Econ. 66 (6), 467–482.
Scheinkman, J.A., Xiong, W., 2003. Overconfidence and speculative bubbles. J. Polit. Econ. 111 (6), 1183–1220.
Schularick, M., Taylor, A., 2012. Credit booms gone bust: monetary policy. Leverage cycles, and financial crises, 1870-2008. Am. Econ. Rev. 102 (2), 1029–1061.
Simsek, A., 2013. Belief disagreements and collateral constraints. Econometrica 81, 1–53.
Sommer, K., Sullivan, P., Verbrugge, R., 2013. The equilibrium effect of fundamentals on house prices and rents. J. Monet. Econ. 60, 854–870.
Stein, J.C., 1995. Prices and trading volume in the housing market: a model with downpayment effects. Q. J. Econ. 110 (2), 379–406.
Ströbel, J., Vavra, J., 2015. House prices, local demand, and retail prices. Working Paper.
Tirole, J., 1985. Asset bubbles and overlapping generations. Econometrica 53, 1071–1100.
Woodford, M., 2010. Robustly optimal monetary policy with near-rational expectations. Am. Econ. Rev. 100, 274–303.
Wright, R., Wong, Y.Y., 2014. Buyers, sellers, and middlemen: variations on search-theoretic themes. Int. Econ. Rev. 55 (2), 375–397.

CHAPTER 18

Macro, Money, and Finance: A Continuous-Time Approach

M.K. Brunnermeier, Y. Sannikov
Princeton University, Princeton, NJ, United States

Contents

Handbook of Macroeconomics, Volume 2B
ISSN 1574-0048, http://dx.doi.org/10.1016/bs.hesmac.2016.06.002

Abstract

This chapter puts forward a manual for how to setup and solve a continuous time model that allows to analyze endogenous (1) level and risk dynamics. The latter includes (2) tail risk and crisis probability as well as (3) the Volatility Paradox. Concepts such as (4) illiquidity and liquidity mismatch, (5) endogenous leverage, (6) the Paradox of Prudence, (7) undercapitalized sectors (8) time-varying risk premia, and (9) the external funding premium are part of the analysis. Financial frictions also give rise to an endogenous (10) value of money.

Keywords

Macroeconomic modeling, Monetary Economics, (Inside) Money, Endogenous Risk Dynamics, Volatility paradox, Paradox of Prudence, Financial frictions

JEL Classification Codes:

C63, E32, E41, E44, E51, G01, G11, G20

1. INTRODUCTION

The recent financial crisis in the United States and the subsequent Euro Crisis are vivid reminders of the importance of financial frictions in understanding macroeconomic trends and cycles. While financial markets are self-stabilizing in normal times, economies become vulnerable to a crisis after a run up of (debt) imbalances and (credit) bubbles. In particular, debt, leverage, maturity and liquidity mismatch tend to rise when measured volatility is low. Vulnerability risk tends to build up in the background, and only materializes when crises erupt, a phenomenon referred to as the "Volatility Paradox."

Adverse feedback loops can make the market spiral out of balance. The dynamics of an economy with financial frictions are highly nonlinear. Small shocks lead to large economic dislocations. In situations with multiple equilibria, runs on financial institutions or sudden stops on countries can occur even absent any fundamental trigger. Empirically, these phenomena show up as fat tails in the distribution of real economic variables and asset price returns.

Our research proposes a continuous time method to capture the whole *endogenous risk dynamics* and hence goes beyond studying simply the persistence and amplification of an individual adverse shock. Instead of focusing only on levels, the first moments, the second moments, and movements of risk variables are all an integral part of the analysis, as they drive agents' consumption, (precautionary) savings and investment decisions. After a negative shock, we do not assume that the economy returns to the steady state deterministically, but rather uncertainty might be heightened making the length of the slump stochastic. As agents respond to the new situation, they affect both the risk and the risk premia.

Endogenous risk is time-varying and depends on illiquidity. Liquidity comes in three flavors. Technological illiquidity refers to the irreversibility of physical investment.

Instead of undoing the initial investment, another option is to sell off the investment. This is only reasonable when market liquidity is sufficiently high. Finally, with sufficient funding liquidity one can issue claims against the payoffs of the assets. Incentive problems dictate that these claims are typically short-term debt claims. Debt comes with the drawback that risk is concentrated in the indebted sector. In addition, short-term debt leads to liquidity risk exposure. Agents may be forced to fire-sell their assets if they cannot undo the investment, market liquidity is low and funding is restricted, eg, very short term. In short, when there is a liquidity mismatch between technological and market liquidity on the asset side and funding liquidity on the liability side of the balance sheet, the economy is vulnerable to instability.

Models with financial frictions necessarily have to encompass multiple sectors. Financial frictions prevent funds from flowing to undercapitalized sectors, create debt overhang problems, and/or preclude optimal ex-ante risk sharing. This is in contrast to a world with perfect financial markets in which only aggregate risk matters, as all agents' marginal rate of substitutions are equalized in equilibrium and consequently aggregation to a single representative agent is possible. In models with financial frictions and heterogeneous agents the wealth distribution matters.

Importantly, financial frictions also give rise to the value of money. Money is a liquid store of value and safe asset. This approach provides not only a complementary perspective to New Keynesian models, in which price and wage rigidities are the primary drivers of money value, but also enables the revival of the traditional literature on "money and banking."[a]

Ultimately, economic analysis should guide policy. It is important to go beyond partial equilibrium analysis since general equilibrium effects can be subtle and counterintuitive. A model has to be tractable enough to conduct a meaningful welfare analysis to evaluate various policy instruments. A welfare analysis lends itself to study the interaction of various policy instruments.

In sum, the goal of this chapter is to put forward a manual for how to setup and solve a continuous time macrofinance model. The tractability that continuous time offers allows us to study a host of new properties of fully solved equilibria. This includes the full characterization of endogenous (1) level and risk dynamics. The latter includes (2) tail risk and crisis probability as well as (3) the Volatility Paradox. In addition, it should help us think about (4) illiquidity and liquidity mismatch, (5) endogenous leverage, (6) Paradox of Prudence, (7) undercapitalized sectors, (8) time-varying risk premia, and (9) the external funding premium. From a welfare perspective, we would like to ask normative questions about the (10) inefficiencies of financial crises and (11) the effects of policies using various instruments.

[a] See, eg, Chandler (1948).

We start with a brief history of macro and finance research since the Great Depression in the 1930s. We then put forward arguments in favor of continuous time modeling before surveying the ongoing continuous time literature. The main part of the paper builds up a step by step outline how to solve continuous time models starting with the simplest benchmark and enriching the model by adding more building blocks.

1.1 A Brief History of Macroeconomics and Finance

Macroeconomics as a field in economics was born during the great depression in the 1930s. At that time, economists like Fisher (1933), Keynes (1936), Gurley and Shaw (1955), Minsky (1957), and Kindleberger (1978) stressed the importance of the interaction between financial instability and macroeconomic aggregates. In particular, certain sectors in the economy including the financial sector can become balance sheet impaired and can drag down parts of the economy. Patinkin (1956) and Tobin (1969) also emphasized that financial stability and price stability are intertwined and hence that macroeconomics, monetary economics and finance are closely linked.

As economics became more analytical and model based, macroeconomics and finance went into different directions. See Fig. 1. Hicks' (1937) IS-LM Keynesian macro model is both static and deterministic. Macroeconomic growth models, most prominently the Solow (1956) growth model, are dynamic and many of them are in continuous time. However, they exclude stochastic elements: risk and uncertainty play no role. In contrast, the formal finance literature starting with Markowitz (1952) portfolio theory focused exclusively on risk. These models are static models and ignore the time dimension.

In the 1970s and early 1980s macroeconomists introduced stochastic elements into their dynamic models. Early "fresh water" models that included time and stochastic elements were Brock and Mirman's (1972) stochastic growth model and real business cycle models à la Kydland and Prescott (1982). The influential graduate text book of

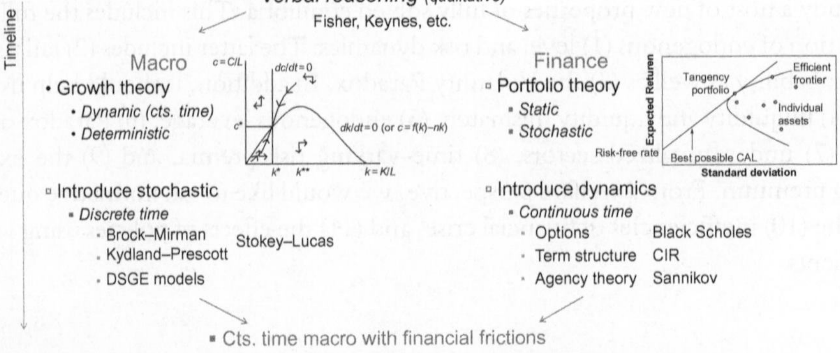

Fig. 1 Methods in macroeconomic and financial research since the great depression.

Stokey and Lucas (1989) provided the necessary toolkit for a fully microfounded dynamic and stochastic analysis. The "salt water" New Keynesian branch of macro introduced price rigidities and studied countercyclical policy in rational expectations models, Taylor (1979) and Mankiw and Romer (1991). The two branches merged and developed DSGE models which were both dynamic, the D in DSGE, and stochastic, the S in DSGE. However, unlike in many of the earlier growth models, time is discrete in real business cycle and New Keynesian DSGE models à la Woodford (2003). Most DSGE models capture only the log-linearized dynamics around the steady state. The log-linearized theoretical analysis squared nicely with its empirical counterpart, the linear Vector Autoregression Regression (VAR) estimation technique pioneered by Sims (1980).

Finance also experienced great breakthroughs in the 1970s. Stochastic Calculus (Ito calculus), which underlies the Black and Scholes (1973) option pricing model, revolutionized finance. Besides option pricing, term structure of interest rate models like Cox et al. (1985) were developed. More recently, Sannikov (2008) developed continuous time tools for financial contracting, which allow one to capture contracting frictions in a tractable way.

Our line of research is the next natural step. It essentially merges macroeconomics and finance using continuous time stochastic models. In terms of financial frictions, it builds on earlier work by Bernanke et al. (1999) (BGG), Kiyotaki and Moore (1997) (KM), Bianchi (2011), Mendoza (2010), and others. Our approach replicates two important results from the linearized versions of classic models of BGG and KM, that (1) temporary macro shocks can have a *persistent* effect on economic activity by making borrowers "undercapitalized" and (2) price movements *amplify* shocks. In KM, the leverage is limited by an always binding collateral constraint. In Bianchi (2011) and Mendoza (2010) it is occasionally binding. Our approach focuses mostly on incomplete market frictions, where the leverage of potentially undercapitalized borrowers is usually endogenous. In particular, it responds to the magnitude of fundamental (exogenous) macroeconomic shocks and the level of financial innovations that enable better risk management. Interestingly, leverage responds to a much lesser extent to the presence of endogenous tail risk. Equilibrium leverage in normal times is a key determinant of the probability of crises.

1.2 The Case for Continuous-Time Macro Models

As economists we have no hesitation in assuming a continuous action space in order to ensure nice first order optimality conditions that are free of integer problems. In the same vein, we typically assume a continuum of agents to guarantee an environment with perfect competition and (tractable) price taking behavior.

Assuming a continuous time framework has two advantages: it is often more tractable and might conceptually be a closer representation of reality. In terms of tractability, continuous time allows one to derive more analytical steps and more closed form characterizations of the equilibrium before resorting to a numerical analysis. For example, in our case one can derive explicit closed form expressions for amplification terms. The reason is that only the slope of the price function, ie, the (local) derivative w.r.t. state variables, is necessary to characterize amplification. In contrast, in discrete time settings the whole price function is needed, as the jump size may vary. Also, instantaneous returns are essentially log-normal, which makes it easy to take expectations. It is also easy to derive the portfolio choice problem and to link returns to net worth dynamics via the budget constraint. In discrete-time models, this feature can only be achieved through a (Campbell–Shiller) log-linear approximation. It is therefore not surprising that the term structure literature uses continuous time models. Admittedly, some of these features are due to the continuous nature of certain stochastic processes, like Brownian Motions and other Ito Processes. Hereby, one implicitly assumes that agents can adjust their consumption or portfolio continuously as their wealth changes. The feature that their wealth never jumps beyond a specific point, eg, the insolvency point, greatly simplifies the exposition.

Conceptually, in certain dimensions a continuous time representation might also square better with reality. People do not consume only at the end of the quarter, even though data come in quarterly. Discrete time models implicitly assume linear time aggregation within a quarter and a nonlinear one across quarters. In other words, the intertemporal elasticity of consumption within a quarter is infinite while across quarters it is given by the curvature of the utility function. Continuous time models treat every time unit the same. Similarly, it is well known that for multivariate models mixing data with different degrees of smoothness and frequency (such as consumption data and financial data) can seriously impair inference.

The biggest advantage of our continuous-time approach is that it allows a full characterization of the whole dynamical system including the risk dynamics instead of simply a log-linearized representation around the steady state. Note that impulse response functions capture only the expected path after a shock that starts at the steady state. Also, the stationary distribution can be bimodal and exhibit large swings, unlike stable normal distributions that log-linearized models imply.

1.3 The Nascent Continuous-Time Macrofinance Literature

This chapter builds on Brunnermeier and Sannikov (2014).[b] It extends this work by allowing for more general utility functions, precautionary savings and for endogenous equity issuance. Work by Basak and Cuoco (1998) and He and Krishnamurthy (2012, 2013) on intermediary asset pricing are part of the core papers in this literature.

[b] For an alternative survey on continuous time macro models, see, eg, Isohätälä et al. (2016).

Isohätälä et al. (2014) study a partial equilibrium model. DiTella (2013) introduces exogenous uncertainty shocks that can lead to balance sheet recessions even when contracting based on aggregate state variables is possible.

Phelan (2014) considers a setting in which banks issue equity and leverage can be procyclical. Adrian and Boyarchenko (2012) achieve procyclical leverage by introducing liquidity preference shocks. Adrian and Boyarchenko (2013) consider the interaction between two types of intermediaries: banks and nonbanks. Huang (2014) studies shadow banks, which circumvent regulatory constraints but are subject to an endogenous enforcement constraint. In Moreira and Savov (2016)'s macro model shadow banks issue money-like claims. In downturns they scale back their activity. This slows down the recovery and creates a scarcity in collateral. Klimenko et al. (2015) show that regulation that prohibits dividend payouts is typically superior to very tight capital requirements. In Moll (2014) capital is misallocated since productive agents are limited by collateral constraints to lever up.

Several papers also tried to calibrate continuous time macrofinance models to recent events. For example, He and Krishnamurthy (2014) do so by including housing as a second form of capital. Mittnik and Semmler (2013) employ a multi-regime vector autoregression approach to capture the nonlinearity of these models.[c]

In international economics, these methods are employed in Brunnermeier and Sannikov (2015b). In a two-good, two-country model, the overly indebted country is vulnerable to sudden stops, and hence capital controls might improve welfare. Maggiori (2013) models risk sharing across countries which are at different stages of financial development.

Models with financial frictions also open up an avenue for new models in monetary economics thereby reviving the field "money and banking." In Brunnermeier and Sannikov (2015a)'s "The I Theory of Money" money is a bubble like in Samuelson (1958) or Bewley (1977). Inside money is created endogenously by the intermediary sector, and monetary policy and macroprudential policy interact. Achdou et al. (2015) provide a solution algorithm for Bewley models with uninsurable endowment risk in a continuous time setting. In Drechsler et al. (2016) banks are less risk averse and monetary policy affects risk premia. Silva (2016) studies how unconventional monetary policy reallocates risk. Werning (2012) studies the zero lower bound problem in a tractable deterministic continuous time New Keynesian model.

Rappoport and Walsh (2012) setup a discrete-time macro model, which has similar economic results, and which converges in the continuous-time limit to the model of Brunnermeier and Sannikov (2014).

[c] Note that in the estimation of DSGE models, Fernandez-Villaverde and Rubio-Ramirez (2010) show that parameter estimates and the moments generated by the model depend quite sensitively on whether a linearized DSGE is estimated via Kalman filtering or whether the true DSGE model is estimated via particle filtering.

2. A SIMPLE REAL ECONOMY MODEL

We start first with a particularly simple model to illustrate how equilibrium conditions—utility maximization and market clearing—translate into an equilibrium characterization. This simple model trivializes most of the issues we are after, eg, the model has no price effects or endogenous risk. We do get some interesting takeaways, such as that risk premia spike in crises. After establishing the conceptual framework for what an equilibrium is, we move on to tackle more complex models.

2.1 Model Setup

This model is a variation of Basak and Cuoco (1998). The economy has a risky asset in positive net supply and a risk-free asset in zero net supply. There are two types of agents—experts and households. Only experts can hold the risky asset—households can only lend to experts at the risk-free rate r_t, determined endogenously in equilibrium. The friction is that experts can finance their holdings of the risky asset only through debt—by selling short the risk-free asset to households. That is, experts cannot issue equity. We assume that all agents are small, and behave as price-takers. That is, unlike in microstructure models with noise traders, agents have no price impact.

2.1.1 Technology

Net of investment, physical capital, k_t, generates consumption output at the rate of

$$(a - \iota_t)k_t\, dt,$$

where a is a productivity parameter and ι_t is the reinvestment rate per unit of capital. The production technology is constant returns to scale.

The productive asset (capital), k_t, evolves according to

$$\frac{dk_t}{k_t} = (\Phi(\iota_t) - \delta)\,dt + \sigma\, dZ_t, \tag{1}$$

where $\Phi(\iota_t)$ is an investment function with adjustment costs, such that $\Phi(0) = 0$, $\Phi' > 0$ and $\Phi'' \leq 0$. Thus, in the absence of investment, capital simply depreciates at rate δ. The concavity of $\Phi(\cdot)$ reflects decreasing returns to scale, and for negative values of ι_t, corresponds to *technological illiquidity*—the marginal cost of capital depends on the rate of investment/disinvestment.

The aggregate amount of capital is denoted by K_t, and q_t is the price of capital. Hence, the aggregate net worth in the economy is q_tK_t. If N_t is the aggregate net worth of experts, then the aggregate net worth of households is $q_tK_t - N_t$.

Experts' wealth share is denoted by

$$\eta_t = \frac{N_t}{q_tK_t} \in [0,1].$$

2.1.2 Preferences

For *tractability*, all agents are assumed to have logarithmic utility with discount rate ρ, of the form

$$E\left[\int_0^\infty e^{-\rho t}\log c_t dt\right],$$

where c_t is consumption at time t.

2.2 A Step-By-Step Approach

Definition An equilibrium is a map from histories of macro shocks $\{Z_s, s \leq t\}$ to the price of capital q_t, risk-free rate r_t, as well as asset holdings and consumption choices of all agents, such that

1. agents behave to maximize utility and
2. markets clear.

To find an equilibrium, we need to write down equations that the processes q_t, r_t, etc., have to satisfy, and that characterize how these processes evolve with the realizations of shocks Z. It will be convenient to express these relationships using a state variable. Here the relevant state variable, which describes the distribution of wealth, is the fraction of wealth owned by the experts, η_t. When η_t drops, experts become more balance sheet constrained.

We solve the equilibrium in three steps. First, we postulate some endogenous processes. As a second step, we use the equilibrium conditions, ie, utility maximization and market clearing, to write down restrictions q_t and r_t need to satisfy. In this simple model, we will be able to express q_t and r_t as functions of η_t in closed form. Third, we need to derive the law of motion of the state variable, the wealth share η_t.

Step 1: Postulate Equilibrium Processes. The first step is to postulate certain endogenous price processes. For example, suppose that the price per unit of capital q_t follows an Ito process

$$\frac{dq_t}{q_t} = \mu_t^q dt + \sigma_t^q \, dZ_t, \tag{2}$$

which, of course, is endogenous in equilibrium.

An investment in capital generates, in addition to the dividend rate $(a - \iota)k_t dt$, the capital gains at rate

$$\frac{d(k_t q_t)}{k_t q_t}.$$

Ito's Lemma for the product of two stochastic processes can be used to derive this process.

Ito's Formula for Product

Suppose two processes X_t and Y_t follow

$$\frac{dX_t}{X_t} = \mu_t^X dt + \sigma_t^X dZ_t \text{ and } \frac{dY_t}{Y_t} = \mu_t^Y dt + \sigma_t^Y dZ_t.$$

Then the product of two processes follows

$$\frac{d(X_t Y_t)}{X_t Y_t} = (\mu_t^X + \mu_t^Y + \sigma_t^X \sigma_t^Y)dt + (\sigma_t^X + \sigma_t^Y)dZ_t. \tag{3}$$

Using Ito's Lemma, the investment in capital generates capital gains at rate

$$\frac{d(k_t q_t)}{k_t q_t} = (\Phi(\iota_t) - \delta + \mu_t^q + \sigma\sigma_t^q)dt + (\sigma + \sigma_t^q)dZ_t.$$

Then capital earns the return of

$$dr_t^k = \underbrace{\frac{a-\iota_t}{q_t}}_{\text{dividend yield}} dt + \underbrace{(\Phi(\iota_t) - \delta + \mu_t^q + \sigma\sigma_t^q)dt + (\sigma + \sigma_t^q)dZ_t}_{\frac{d(k_t q_t)}{k_t q_t}, \text{ the capital gains rate}}. \tag{4}$$

Thus, generally a part of the risk from holding capital is fundamental, σdZ_t, and a part is endogenous, $\sigma_t^q dZ_t$.

Remarks

- For general utility functions one also has to postulate the stochastic discount factor process or equivalently a process for the marginal utility or the consumption process dc_t/c_t. For details see Section 3.1.
- Note that in monetary models like Brunnermeier and Sannikov (2015a, 2016) one also has to postulate a process p_t for the value of money which can be stochastic due to inflation risk. In Section 4 we present a simple monetary model.

Step 2: The Equilibrium Conditions.

Equilibrium conditions come in two flavors: Optimality conditions and market clearing conditions.

Optimal internal investment rate. Note that the rate of internal investment ι_t does not affect the risk of capital. The optimal investment rate that maximizes the expected return satisfies the first-order condition

$$\Phi'(\iota_t) = \frac{1}{q_t}. \tag{5}$$

Optimal consumption rate. Logarithmic utility has two convenient properties, which we derive formally for a more general case in Section 3.1. These two properties help reduce the number of equations that characterize equilibrium. First, for agents with log utility

$$\text{consumption} = \rho \cdot \text{net worth} \tag{6}$$

that is, they always consume a fixed fraction of wealth (permanent income) regardless of the risk-free rate or risky investment opportunities. The consumption Euler equation reduces to a particularly simple form.

Optimal portfolio choice. The optimal risk exposure of a log-utility agent in the optimal portfolio choice problem depends on the attractiveness of risky investment, measured by the Sharpe ratio, defined as expected excess returns divided by the standard deviation. Formally, the equilibrium condition is

$$\text{Sharpe ratio of risky investment} = \text{volatility of net worth}, \tag{7}$$

where the volatility is relative (measured as percentage change per unit of time).[d]

Goods Market clearing. We use Eqs. (6) and (7) to formalize equilibrium conditions, and characterize equilibrium. First, from condition (6), the aggregate consumption of all agents is $\rho q_t K_t$, and aggregate output is $(a - \iota(q_t))K_t$, where investment ι is an increasing function of q defined by (5). From market clearing for consumption goods, these must be equal, and so

$$\rho q_t = a - \iota(q_t). \tag{8}$$

This determines the equilibrium price of the risky capital. The aggregate consumption of experts must be $\rho N_t = \rho \eta_t q_t K_t$, and the aggregate consumption of households is $\rho(1 - \eta_t)q_t K_t$. Condition (8) alone leads to a *constant* value of the *price of capital* q. That is, $\mu_t^q = \sigma_t^q = 0$.

Example with Log Investment Function

Suppose the investment function takes the form

$$\Phi(\iota) = \frac{\log(\kappa\iota + 1)}{\kappa},$$

where κ is the adjustment cost parameter. Then $\Phi'(0) = 1$. Higher κ makes function Φ more concave, and as $\kappa \to 0, \Phi(\iota) \to \iota$, a fully elastic investment function with no adjustment costs. The optimal investment rate is $\iota = (q - 1)/\kappa$, and the market-clearing condition (8) leads to the price of

$$q = \frac{1 + \kappa a}{1 + \kappa\rho}.$$

The price converges to 1 as $\kappa \to 0$, ie, the investment technology is fully elastic. The price q converges to a/ρ as $\kappa \to \infty$.

---

[d] For example, if the annual volatility of S&P 500 is 15% and the risk premium is 3% (so that the Sharpe ratio is 3%/15% = 0.2), then a log utility agent wants to hold a portfolio with volatility 0.2 = 20%. This corresponds to a weight of 1.33 on S&P 500, and −0.33 on the risk-free asset.

Second, we can use condition (7) for experts to figure out the equilibrium *risk-free rate*. We first look at the return on risky and risk-free assets to compute the Sharpe ratio of risky investments. We then look at balance sheets of experts to compute the volatility of their wealth. Finally, we use Eq. (7) to get the risk-free rate.

Because q is constant, the risky asset earns a return of

$$dr_t^k = \underbrace{\frac{a-\iota}{q}}_{\rho,\ \text{dividend yield}} dt \quad + \underbrace{(\Phi(\iota)-\delta)dt + \sigma\, dZ_t}_{\text{capital gains rate}},$$

and the risk-free asset earns r_t. Note that the dividend yield equals ρ by the goods market clearing condition. Hence, the Sharpe ratio of risky investment is

$$\frac{\rho + \Phi(\iota) - \delta - r_t}{\sigma}.$$

Note that since the price-dividend ratio is constant any change in the risk premium must come from the variation in the risk-free rate r_t.

Because experts must hold all the risky capital in the economy, with value $q_t K_t$ (households cannot hold capital), and absorb risk through net worth N_t, the volatility of their net worth is

$$\frac{q_t K_t}{N_t}\sigma = \frac{\sigma}{\eta_t}.$$

Using (7),

$$\frac{\sigma}{\eta_t} = \frac{\rho + \Phi(\iota) - \delta - r_t}{\sigma} \quad \Rightarrow \quad r_t = \rho + \Phi(\iota) - \delta - \frac{\sigma^2}{\eta_t}. \tag{9}$$

Step 3: The Law of Motion of η_t. To finish deriving the equilibrium, we need to describe how shocks Z_t affect the state variable $\eta_t = N_t/(q_t K_t)$. First, since η_t is a ratio, the following formula will be helpful for us:

Ito's Formula for Ratio

Suppose two processes X_t and Y_t follow

$$\frac{dX_t}{X_t} = \mu_t^X dt + \sigma_t^X dZ_t \quad \text{and} \quad \frac{dY_t}{Y_t} = \mu_t^Y dt + \sigma_t^Y dZ_t.$$

Then ratio of two processes follows

$$\frac{d(X_t/Y_t)}{X_t/Y_t} = (\mu_t^X - \mu_t^Y + (\sigma_t^Y)^2 - \sigma_t^X \sigma_t^Y)dt + (\sigma_t^X - \sigma_t^Y)dZ_t. \tag{10}$$

Second, it is convenient to express the laws of motion of the numerator and denominator of η_t in terms of total risk and the Sharpe ratio given by (9). Specifically,

$$\frac{dN_t}{N_t} = r_t dt + \underbrace{\frac{\sigma}{\eta_t}}_{\text{risk}} \underbrace{\frac{\sigma}{\eta_t}}_{\text{Sharpe}} dt + \frac{\sigma}{\eta_t} dZ_t - \underbrace{\rho dt}_{\text{consumption}} \quad \text{and}$$

$$\frac{d(q_t K_t)}{q_t K_t} = r_t dt + \underbrace{\sigma}_{\text{risk}} \underbrace{\frac{\sigma}{\eta_t}}_{\text{Sharpe}} dt + \sigma dZ_t - \underbrace{\rho dt}_{\text{dividend yield}} .$$

In the latter equation, we subtract the dividend yield from the total return on capital to obtain the capital gains rate.

Using the formula for the ratio,

$$\begin{aligned} \frac{d\eta_t}{\eta_t} &= (r_t + \sigma^2/\eta_t^2 - \rho - r_t - \sigma^2/\eta_t + \rho + \sigma^2 - \sigma^2/\eta_t)dt + (\sigma/\eta_t - \sigma)dZ_t \\ &= \frac{(1-\eta_t)^2}{\eta_t^2}\sigma^2 dt + \frac{1-\eta_t}{\eta_t}\sigma dZ_t. \end{aligned} \tag{11}$$

Step 4: Expressing $q(\eta)$ as a function of η is not necessary in this simple model, since q is a constant.

2.3 Observations

Several key observations about equilibrium characteristics are worth pointing out. Variable η_t fluctuates with macro shocks—a positive shock increases the wealth share of experts. This is because experts are levered. A negative shock erodes η_t, and experts require a higher risk premium to hold risky assets. Experts must be convinced to keep holding risky assets by the increasing Sharpe ratio

$$\frac{\sigma}{\eta_t} = \frac{\rho + \Phi(\iota) - \delta - r_t}{\sigma},$$

which goes to ∞ as η_t goes to 0. Strangely, this is achieved due to the risk-free rate $r_t = \rho + \Phi(\iota) - \delta - \sigma^2/\eta_t$ going to $-\infty$, rather than due to a depressed price of the risky asset, as illustrated in the top right panel of Fig. 2.

Because q_t is constant, as illustrated in the top left panel, there is no endogenous risk, no amplification and no volatility effects. Therefore, in this model, assumptions that allow for such a simple solution also eliminate any price effects that we are so interested in. We have to work harder to get those effects.

Besides the absence of price effects, in this model it is also the case that in the long run the expert sector becomes so large that it overwhelms the whole economy. To see this,

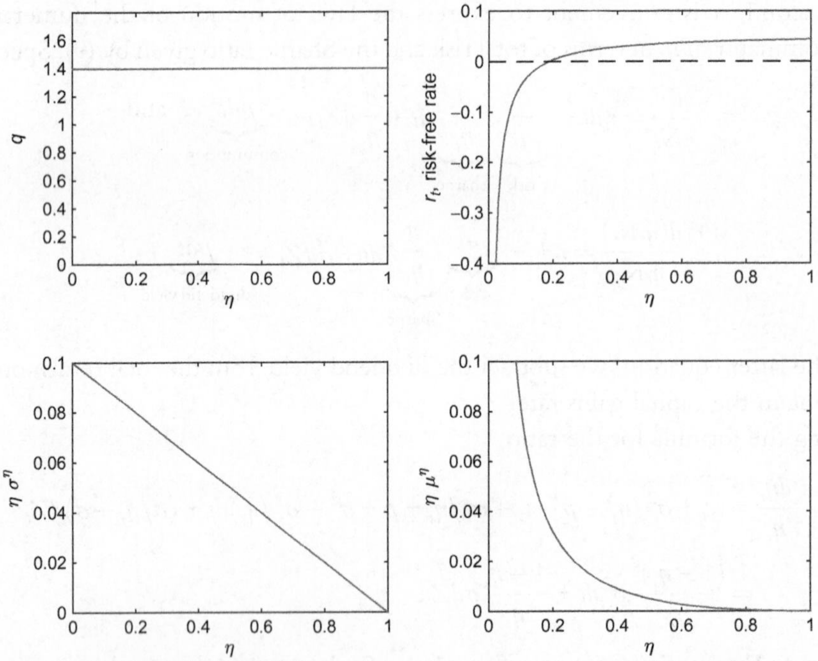

Fig. 2 Equilibrium in the simple real model, $a = 0.11$, $\rho = 5\%$, $\sigma = 0.1$, and $\Phi = \log(\kappa\iota + 1)/\kappa$ with $\kappa = 10$.

note that the drift of η_t is always positive. This feature is typical of models in which one group of agents has an advantage over another group—in this case only experts can invest in the risky asset. It is possible to prevent the expert sector from becoming too large through an additional assumption. For example, Bernanke et al. (1999) assume that experts are randomly hit by a shock that makes them households. Alternatively, if experts have a higher discount rate than households, then a greater consumption rate prevents the expert sector from becoming too large.

The main purpose of this section was to show how equilibrium conditions can be translated into formulas that describe the behavior of the economy. Next, we can consider more complicated models, in which the price of the risky asset q_t reacts to shocks. We also develop a methodology that allows for agents to have more complicated preferences and for a nontrivial distribution of assets among agents.

3. A MODEL WITH PRICE EFFECTS AND INSTABILITIES

We now illustrate how our step approach can be used to solve a more complex model, which we borrow and extend from Brunnermeier and Sannikov (2014). We will be able to get a number of important takeaways from the model:

1. Equilibrium dynamics are characterized by a relatively stable steady state, where the system spends most of the time, and a crisis regime. In the steady state, experts are adequately capitalized and risk premia fall. The experts' consumption offsets their earnings—hence the steady state is formed. Experts have the capacity to absorb most macro shocks, hence prices near the steady state are quite stable. However, an unusually long sequence of negative shocks causes experts to suffer significant losses, and pushes the equilibrium into a crisis regime. In the crisis regime, experts are undercapitalized and constrained. Shocks affect their demand for assets—market liquidity at the macro level can dry up—and thus affect prices of the assets that experts hold. This creates feedback effects, which generate fire-sales and *endogenous risk*. Volatility is endogenous and also feeds back in agents' behavior.
2. High volatility during crisis times may push the system into a very depressed region, where experts' net worth is close to 0. If that happens, it takes a long time for the economy to recover. Thus, the system spends a considerable amount of time far away from the steady state. The stationary distribution may be bimodal.
3. Endogenous risk during crises makes assets more correlated.
4. There is a "*volatility paradox*," because risk-taking is endogenous. If the aggregate risk parameter σ becomes smaller, the economy does not become more stable. The reason is that experts take on greater leverage, and pay out profits sooner, in response to lower fundamental risk. Due to greater leverage, the economy is prone to crises even when exogenous shocks are smaller. In fact, endogenous risk during crises may actually be higher when σ is lower.
5. Financial innovations, such as securitization and derivatives hedging, that allow for more efficient risk-sharing among experts, may make the system less stable in equilibrium. The reason, again, is that risk-taking is endogenous. By diversifying idiosyncratic risks, experts tend to increase leverage, amplifying systemic risks.

Before going into details of how we can extend our simple real economy model from Section 2 to display these additional features, we take a detour to discuss the classic problem of optimal consumption and portfolio choice in continuous time.

3.1 Optimal Portfolio Choice with General Utility Functions

We start with a brief description of how to extend the optimal consumption and portfolio choice conditions (such as (6) and (7)) to the case of a general utility function. The key result is that any asset, which an agent can hold, can be priced from the agent's marginal utility of wealth θ_t. The first-order condition for optimal consumption is $\theta_t = u'(c_t)$, so the marginal utility of wealth is also the marginal utility of consumption (unless the agent is "at the corner").[e]

[e] If the agent is risk-neutral, then his marginal utility of consumption is always 1, but the agent may choose to not consume if his marginal utility of wealth is greater than 1.

If the agent has discount rate ρ, then $\xi_t = e^{-\rho t}\theta_t$ is the stochastic discount factor (SDF) to price assets. We can write

$$\frac{d\xi_t}{\xi_t} = -r_t dt - \varsigma_t dZ_t, \tag{12}$$

where r_t is the (shadow) risk-free rate and ς_t is the price of risk dZ_t.

For any asset A that the agent can invest in, with return

$$dr_t^A = \mu_t^A dt + \sigma_t^A dZ_t,$$

we must have

$$\mu_t^A = r_t + \varsigma_t \sigma_t^A. \tag{13}$$

Eqs. (12) and (13) are simple, yet extremely powerful.

3.1.1 Martingale Method

To derive Eq. (13) consider a trading strategy of investing 1 dollar into asset A at time 0 and keep on reinvesting any dividends the asset might pay out. Denote the value of this strategy at time t by v_t (then $v_0 = 1$, obviously). Clearly, its capital gains rate is

$$\frac{dv_t}{v_t} = dr_t^A.$$

For an arbitrary $s \le t$ consider an investor who can only trade at s and t. That is, he faces a simple two-period portfolio problem. The Euler equation for the standard two-period portfolio problem is

$$v_s = E_s\left[\frac{\xi_t}{\xi_s} v_t\right] \Rightarrow \xi_s v_s = E_s[\xi_t v_t].$$

That is, $\xi_t v_t$ must be a martingale on the time domain $\{s, t\}$. For an investor who can trade continuously $\xi_t v_t$ must be a martingale for any t, since we picked s, t arbitrarily. Next, by Itô's formula

$$\frac{d(\xi_t v_t)}{\xi_t v_t} = (\mu_t^\xi + \mu_t^v + \sigma_t^\xi \sigma_t^v)dt + (\sigma_t^\xi + \sigma_t^v)dZ_t = (-r_t + \mu_t^A - \varsigma_t \sigma_t^A)dt + (\sigma_t^A - \varsigma_t)dZ_t.$$

This is a martingale if and only if the drift vanishes, ie, Eq. (13) holds.

3.1.2 Derivation via Stochastic Maximum Principle

One can also derive the pricing equations and consumption rule using the stochastic maximum principle. Let us consider an agent who maximizes

$$E\left[\int_0^\infty e^{-\rho t} u(c_t)\, dt\right],$$

and whose net worth follows

$$dn_t = n_t\left(r_t dt + \sum_A x_t^A((\mu_t^A - r_t)dt + \sigma_t^A dZ_t)\right) - c_t dt,$$

with initial wealth $n_0 > 0$ and where x_t^A are portfolio weights on various assets A. Investment opportunities are stochastic and exogenous, ie, they do not depend on the agent's strategy.

The stochastic maximum principle allows us to derive first-order conditions for maximization from the Hamiltonian. Introducing a multiplier ξ_t on n_t (ie, marginal utility of wealth) and denoting the volatility of ξ_t by $-\varsigma_t\xi_t$, the Hamiltonian is written as

$$H = e^{-\rho t}u(c) + \xi_t\{\underbrace{(r_t + \sum_A x^A(\mu_t^A - r_t))n_t - c}_{\text{drift of } n_t}\} - \varsigma_t\xi_t \underbrace{\sum_A x^A\sigma_t^A n_t}_{\text{volatility of } n_t}.$$

By differentiating the Hamiltonian with respect to controls, we get the first-order conditions, and by differentiating it with respect to the state n_t, we get the law of motion of the multiplier ξ_t.

The first-order condition with respect to c is

$$e^{-\rho t}u'(c_t) = \xi_t,$$

which implies that the multiplier on the agent's wealth is his discounted marginal utility of consumption. The first-order condition with respect to the portfolio weight x^A is

$$\xi_t(\mu_t^A - r_t) - \varsigma_t\xi_t\sigma_t^A = 0,$$

which implies (13).

In addition, the drift of ξ_t is

$$-H_n = -\xi_t r_t,$$

where we already used the first-order conditions with respect to x^A to perform cancellations. It follows that the law of motion of ξ_t is

$$d\xi_t = -\xi_t r_t\, dt - \varsigma_t\xi_t\, dZ_t,$$

which corresponds to (12).

3.1.3 Value Function Derivation for CRRA Utility

Macroeconomists are most familiar with this method. With CRRA utility, the agent's value function takes a power form

$$\frac{u(\omega_t n_t)}{\rho}. \tag{14}$$

This form comes from the fact that if the agent's wealth changes by a factor of x, then his optimal consumption at all future states changes by the same factor—hence ω_t is determined so that $u(\omega_t)/\rho$ is the value function at unit wealth. Marginal utility of consumption and marginal utility of wealth are equated if $c_t^{-\gamma} = \omega_t^{1-\gamma} n_t^{-\gamma}/\rho$, or

$$\frac{c_t}{n_t} = \rho^{1/\gamma}\omega_t^{1-1/\gamma}. \tag{15}$$

For log utility, $\gamma = 1$ and this equation implies that $c_t/n_t = \rho$ as we claimed in (6).

For $\gamma \neq 1$, by expressing ω_t as a function of the consumption rate c_t/n_t, we find that the agent's continuation utility is

$$\frac{c_t^{-\gamma} n_t}{1-\gamma}. \tag{16}$$

This remarkable expression shows that the agent's net worth and consumption rate are sufficient to compute the agent's welfare, and no additional information about the agent's stochastic investment opportunities is needed.

Given the agent's (postulated) consumption process of

$$\frac{dc_t}{c_t} = \mu_t^c dt + \sigma_t^c dZ_t,$$

by Ito's Lemma, marginal utility $c^{-\gamma}$ follows

$$\frac{d(c_t^{-\gamma})}{c_t^{-\gamma}} = \left(-\gamma\mu_t^c + \frac{\gamma(\gamma+1)}{2}(\sigma_t^c)^2\right)dt - \gamma\sigma_t^c dZ_t. \tag{17}$$

Substituting this into (13), we obtain the following relationship for the pricing of any risky asset relative to the risk-free asset:

$$\frac{\mu_t^A - r_t}{\sigma_t^A} = \gamma\sigma_t^c = \varsigma_t. \tag{18}$$

Recall that $\xi_t = e^{-\rho t}u'(c_t)$ and hence $\frac{d\xi_t}{\xi_t} = -\rho - \frac{d(c_t^{-\gamma})}{c_t^{-\gamma}}$. Minus the drift of the SDF is the risk-free rate, ie,

$$r_t = \rho + \gamma\mu_t^c - \frac{\gamma(\gamma+1)}{2}(\sigma_t^c)^2. \tag{19}$$

Two special cases with particularly nice analytical solutions deserve special attention.

Example with CRRA and Constant Investment Opportunities

With constant investment opportunities, then ω_t is a constant, hence (15) implies that $\sigma_t^c = \sigma_t^n$, just like in the logarithmic case. Hence, (18) implies that

$$\underbrace{\frac{\mu_t^A - r}{\sigma_t^A}}_{\varsigma} = \gamma\sigma_t^n,$$

ie, the volatility of net worth is the Sharpe ratio divided by the risk aversion coefficient γ. Note that this property also holds when ω_t is not a constant as long as it evolves deterministically.

Now, the agent's net worth follows

$$\frac{dn_t}{n_t} = rdt + \frac{\varsigma^2}{\gamma}dt + \frac{\varsigma}{\gamma}dZ_t - \frac{c_t}{n_t}dt,$$

and, since consumption is proportional to net worth, (19) implies that

$$r = \rho + \gamma\left(r + \frac{\varsigma^2}{\gamma} - \frac{c_t}{n_t}\right) - \frac{\gamma(\gamma+1)}{2}\frac{\varsigma^2}{\gamma^2} \quad \Rightarrow \quad \frac{c_t}{n_t} = \rho + \frac{\gamma-1}{\gamma}\left(r - \rho + \frac{\varsigma^2}{2\gamma}\right).$$

Hence, consumption ratio increases with better investment opportunities when $\gamma > 1$ and falls otherwise.

Example with Log Utility

We can verify that the consumption and asset-pricing relationships for logarithmic utility of equation. Note from (15) follows directly (6),

$$c_t = \rho n_t.$$

Since the SDF is $\xi_t = e^{-\rho t}/c_t = e^{-\rho t}/(\rho n_t)$ (for any ω_t) it follows that $\sigma_t^n = \sigma_t^c = \varsigma_t$ (ie, minus the volatility of ξ_t). Hence, (13) implies that

$$\frac{\mu_t^A - r_t}{\sigma_t^A} = \sigma_t^n,$$

where the left hand side is the Sharpe ratio, and the right hand side is the volatility of net worth.

3.2 Model with Heterogeneous Productivity Levels and Preferences

In order to study endogenous risk, market illiquidity, fire-sales, etc., we now assume that the household sector can also hold physical capital, but households are assumed to be less productive. Specifically, their productivity parameter $\underline{a} < a$, and hence their willingness to pay for capital, is lower than that of experts. In this generalized setting, experts now have only two ways out when they become less capitalized and want to scale back their operation: fire-sell the capital to households at a possibly large price discount (market illiquidity) or "uninvest" and suffer adjustment costs (technological illiquidity).

Less productive households earn a return of

$$dr_t^{\underline{k}} = \underbrace{\frac{\underline{a} - \iota_t}{q_t}dt}_{\text{dividend yield}} + \underbrace{(\Phi(\iota_t) - \delta + \mu_t^q + \sigma\sigma_t^q)dt + (\sigma + \sigma_t^q)dZ_t}_{\frac{d(q_t k_t)}{q_t k_t}, \text{ the capital gains rate}} \tag{20}$$

when they manage the physical capital. The households' return differs from that of experts, (4), only in the dividend yield that they earn.

We generalize the model in several other ways. (i) We enable experts to issue some (outside) equity, even though they cannot be 100% equity financed. Specifically, we suppose that experts must retain at least a fraction $\underline{\chi} \in (0, 1]$ of equity. (ii) We generalize the model by including a force that prevents experts from "saving their way out" away from the constraints. In particular, we assume that experts could have a higher discount rate ρ than that of households, $\underline{\rho}$. (iii) Equipped with the results derived in Section 3.1 we generalize experts' and households' utility functions from log to CRRA with risk aversion coefficient γ.[f]

To summarize, experts and households maximize, respectively,

$$E\left[\int_0^\infty e^{-\rho t}u(c_t)\right]dt \quad \text{and} \quad E\left[\int_0^\infty e^{-\underline{\rho} t}u(\underline{c}_t)\right]dt.$$

We denote the fraction of capital allocated to experts by $\psi_t \leq 1$ and the fraction of equity retained by experts by $\chi_t \geq \underline{\chi}$.

We want to characterize how any history of shocks $\{Z_s, s \leq t\}$ maps to equilibrium prices q_t and r_t, asset allocations ψ_t and χ_t, and consumption so that (1) all agents maximize utility through optimal consumption and portfolio choices and (2) markets clear. Agents optimize portfolios subject to constraints (no short-selling of capital and a bound on equity issuance by experts). For example, households can invest in capital, the risk-free asset, and experts' equity, and optimize over portfolio weights on these three assets (with a nonnegative weight on capital). Thus, the solution is based on a classic problem in asset pricing. Note also that because the required returns are different between households and experts, the experts' inside equity will generally earn a different return from the equity held by households—experts will earn "management fees" that households do not earn.[g]

[f] Brunnermeier and Sannikov (2014) explicitly consider the case of risk-neutral experts and households. Experts are constrained to consume nonnegative quantities, but households can consume both positive and negative amounts. This assumption leads to the simplification that the risk-free rate in the economy r_t always equals the households' discount rate $\underline{\rho}$.

[g] This is not a universal assumption in the literature. For example, He and Krishnamurthy (2013) assume that returns are equally split between experts and households, so that rationing is required to prevent households from demanding more expert equity than the total supply of expert equity.

3.3 The 4-Step Approach

We can solve for the equilibrium in four steps. First, postulate processes for prices and stochastic discount factor. Second, write down the consumption–portfolio optimization and market-clearing conditions. These conditions imply a stochastic law of motion of the price q_t, the required risk premia for experts and households ς_t and $\underline{\varsigma}_t$, together with variables ψ_t and χ_t. Third, focusing on the experts' balance sheets we write down the law of motion of expert's wealth share

$$\eta_t = \frac{N_t}{q_t K_t},$$

as a percentage of the whole wealth in the economy. As before, K_t is the total amount of capital in the economy. Fourth, we look for a Markov equilibrium, and characterize equations for q_t, ψ_t, etc., as functions of η_t. We solve these equations numerically either as a system of ordinary differential equations (using the shooting method) or as a system of partial differential equations in time, via a procedure analogous to value function iteration in discrete time.

Step 1: Postulating Equilibrium Processes. As before, we postulate the equilibrium prices process for physical capital.

$$\frac{dq_t}{q_t} = \mu_t^q dt + \sigma_t^q dZ_t.$$

Furthermore, as experts and households have different investment opportunities, we postulate two stochastic discount factor (SDF) processes, one for experts and one for households.

$$\frac{d\xi_t}{\xi_t} = -r_t dt - \varsigma_t dZ_t, \quad \text{and} \quad \frac{d\underline{\xi}_t}{\underline{\xi}_t} = -\underline{r}_t dt - \underline{\varsigma}_t dZ_t,$$

respectively.

Step 2: Equilibrium Conditions. Note that since both experts and households can trade the risk-free asset the drift of both SDF processes has to be the same, ie, $\underline{r}_t = r_t$. Moreover, (13) implies the following asset-pricing relationship for capital held by experts:

$$\frac{\frac{a-\iota_t}{q_t} + \Phi(\iota_t) - \delta + \mu_t^q + \sigma\sigma_t^q - r_t}{\sigma + \sigma_t^q} = \chi_t \varsigma_t + (1-\chi_t)\underline{\varsigma}_t, \tag{21}$$

where χ_t is the inside equity share, ie, the fraction of risk held by experts. The required return on capital held by experts depends on the equilibrium capital structure that experts use. If experts require a higher risk premium than households, then $\chi_t = \underline{\chi}$, ie, experts will issue the maximum equity they can. Thus, we have[h]

$$\chi_t = \underline{\chi} \text{ if } \varsigma_t > \underline{\varsigma}_t, \text{ otherwise } \varsigma_t = \underline{\varsigma}_t.$$

Under this condition, we can replace χ_t with $\underline{\chi}$ in (21).

An asset-pricing relationship for capital held by households is

$$\frac{\frac{\underline{a} - \iota_t}{q_t} + \Phi(\iota_t) - \delta + \mu_t^q + \sigma\sigma_t^q - r_t}{\sigma + \sigma_t^q} \leq \underline{\varsigma}_t, \tag{22}$$

with equality if $\psi_t < 1$, ie, households hold capital in positive amounts. Note that households may choose not to hold any capital, and if so, then the Sharpe ratio they would earn from capital could fall below that required by the asset-pricing relationship.

It is useful to combine (21) and (22), eliminating μ_t^q and r_t, to obtain

$$\frac{(a - \underline{a})/q_t}{\sigma + \sigma_t^q} \geq \underline{\chi}(\varsigma_t - \underline{\varsigma}_t), \tag{23}$$

with equality if $\psi_t < 1$.

The required risk premia can be tied to the agents' consumption processes via (35) in the CRRA case and to the agents' net worth processes in the special logarithmic case. Under the baseline risk-neutrality assumptions of Brunnermeier and Sannikov (2014), $\underline{\varsigma} = 0$ when households are risk-neutral and financially unconstrained—ie, they can consume negatively.

We will use these conditions to characterize q_t, ψ_t, χ_t, etc., as functions of η_t. Before we do that, though, we must derive an equation for the law of motion of $\eta_t = N_t/(q_t K_t)$.

Step 3: The Law of Motion of η_t. It is convenient to express the laws of motion of the numerator and denominator of η_t by focusing on risks and risk premia. Specifically, the experts' net worth follows

$$\frac{dN_t}{N_t} = r_t\,dt + \underbrace{\frac{\chi_t \psi_t}{\eta_t}(\sigma + \sigma_t^q)}_{\text{risk}}\,(\underbrace{\varsigma_t}_{\text{risk premium}}\,dt + dZ_t) - \frac{C_t}{N_t}dt.$$

To derive the evolution of $q_t K_t$, note that the capital gains rate is the same for both type of agents. Thus, we can just aggregate the individual laws of motion to an aggregate law of motion. After replacing the term $\Phi(\iota_t) - \delta + \mu_t^q - \sigma\sigma_t^q - r_t$ using (21), we obtain

[h] We can rule out the case that $\varsigma_t < \underline{\varsigma}_t$ and $\chi_t = 1$: experts cannot face lower risk premia than households if households hold zero risk.

$$\frac{d(q_tK_t)}{q_tK_t} = r_t dt + (\sigma + \sigma_t^q)\Big((\underline{\chi}\varsigma_t + (1-\underline{\chi})\underline{\varsigma}_t)dt + dZ_t\Big) - \frac{a - \iota_t}{q_t} dt.$$

This is the total return on capital (eg, that held by experts) minus the dividend yield.

Using the already familiar formula (10) for a ratio of two stochastic processes, we have

$$\frac{d\eta_t}{\eta_t} = \mu_t^\eta dt + \sigma_t^\eta dt = \left(\frac{a-\iota_t}{q_t} - \frac{C_t}{N_t}\right)dt + \frac{\chi_t\psi_t - \eta_t}{\eta_t}(\sigma + \sigma_t^q)\big((\varsigma_t - \sigma - \sigma_t^q)dt + dZ_t\big) + (\sigma + \sigma_t^q)(1-\underline{\chi})(\varsigma_t - \underline{\varsigma}_t)dt. \tag{24}$$

Step 4: Converting the Equilibrium Conditions and Laws of Motion (24) into Equations for $q(\eta)$, $\theta(\eta)$, $\psi(\eta)$, $\chi(\eta)$, etc. The procedure to convert the equilibrium conditions and the law of motion of η_t into numerically solvable equations for $q(\eta)$, $\psi(\eta)$, etc., depends on the underlying assumptions on the agents' preferences. (The log-utility case is the easiest to solve.) In each case, we have to use Ito's Lemma, which allows us to replace terms such as $\sigma_t^q, \sigma_t^\theta$, μ_t^q, etc., with expressions containing the derivatives of q and θ, in order to arrive at solvable differential equations for these functions in the end.

For example, using Ito's Lemma we can tie the volatility of q_t with the first derivative of $q(\eta)$ as follows

$$\sigma_t^q q(\eta) = q'(\eta)\underbrace{(\chi_t\psi_t - \eta_t)(\sigma + \sigma_t^q)}_{\eta\sigma_t^\eta}. \tag{25}$$

Rewriting Eq. (25) yields a closed form solution for the amplification mechanism.

Amplification

$$\sigma_t^\eta = \frac{\dfrac{\chi_t\psi_t}{\eta_t} - 1}{1 - \left[\dfrac{\chi_t\psi_t}{\eta_t} - 1\right]\dfrac{q'(\eta_t)}{q(\eta_t)/\eta_t}}\sigma \tag{26}$$

The numerator $\frac{\chi_t\psi_t}{\eta_t} - 1$ captures the leverage ratio of the expert sector. The amplification increases with the leverage ratio, the leverage effect. The denominator captures the "loss spiral." Mathematically, it reflects an infinite geometric series. The impact of the loss spiral increases with the product of the leverage ratio and price elasticity, $\frac{q'}{q/\eta}$. The latter measures "market illiquidity," the percentage price impact due to a percentage decline in η_t. Market illiquidity arises from the technological specialization of capital, measured here by the difference $a - \underline{a}$ between the experts' and households' productivity parameters. Market illiquidity interacts with technological illiquidity, captured by the curvature of $\Phi(\cdot)$.

There are various methods to solve the equilibrium equations. Below, we discuss two methods that have been used in practice. One method involves ordinary differential equations (ODE)—we refer to it as the "shooting method" and illustrate it using the risk-neutral preferences of Brunnermeier and Sannikov (2014). The second method involves partial differential equations, and is reminiscent of value function iteration in discrete time. A third method has been used in the literature by Drechsler et al. (2016) and Moreira and Savov (2016), namely Chebyshev collocation which is a special type of projection method, see Judd (1998), chapter 11 for details. We do not present this method here, because a global polynomial approximation is less suitable for our model whose solutions may have kinks.

3.4 Method 1: The Shooting Method

This method involves converting the equations above into a system of ODEs. Before we dive into this, in order to understand how this can be done, we review a very simple and well-known model to illustrate the gist of what we have to do. The model illustrates the pricing of a perpetual American put.

Example of Perputual American Put a la Leland (1994)

Consider the problem of pricing a perpetual option to abandon an asset for an amount K. Given a risk-free rate of r and volatility σ, if the asset pays no dividends, its value follows a geometric Brownian motion

$$\frac{dV_t}{V_t} = r\,dt + \sigma\,dZ_t \tag{27}$$

under the risk-neutral measure.

Under the risk-neutral measure, the expected return of any security must be r. Thus, if the put value P_t follows $dP_t = \mu_t^P P_t\,dt + \sigma_t^P P_t\,dZ_t$, then we must have

$$r = \mu_t^P. \tag{28}$$

Suppose we would like to calculate how the put value P_t depends on the value of the assets V_t. Then we face a problem that is completely analogous to the model with financial frictions we described in this section. We have a law of motion of the state variable V_t and a relationship (28) that the stochastic evolution of P_t has to satisfy, and we would like to characterize P_t as a function of V_t.

How can we do this? Easy. Using Ito's Lemma

$$\mu_t^P P_t = rV_t P'(V_t) + \frac{1}{2}\sigma^2 V_t^2 P''(V_t),$$

and so (28) becomes

$$r = \frac{rVP'(V) + \frac{1}{2}\sigma^2 V^2 P''(V)}{P(V)}. \tag{29}$$

If function $P(V)$ satisfies this equation, then the process $P_t = P(V_t)$ will satisfy (28). We are able to go from an equation like (28) to a differential Eq. (29) by assuming that the value of the put is a *function* of the value of the asset.

We can solve the second-order ordinary differential equation (ODE) (29) if we have two boundary conditions. We have $P(V) \to 0$ as $V \to \infty$ since the put becomes worthless if it is never exercised. We also have $P(V) - (K - V) \geq 0$, since $P(V)$ must equal the intrinsic value at the point where the put is exercised.

Our problem is similar: we have an equation for the stochastic law of motion of the state variable (24), as well as the equilibrium conditions that processes $q(\eta_t)$, $\psi(\eta_t)$, etc., must satisfy. Certainly, the equations are more complicated than those of the put-pricing problem, and the law of motion of η_t is endogenous. However, the mechanics of solving these equations is the same—we have to use Ito's Lemma.

Here, we illustrate the derivation of an appropriate set of ordinary differential equations, as well as the "shooting" method for solving them, using the risk-neutral model of Brunnermeier and Sannikov (2014). Assume that experts and households are risk neutral, and while experts must consume nonnegatively, households can have both positive and negative consumption. Then the required risk premium of households is $\underline{\varsigma}_t = 0$. The required risk premium of experts is $-\sigma_t^\theta$, where θ_t is the marginal utility of the experts' wealth that follows

$$\frac{d\theta_t}{\theta_t} = \mu_t^\theta dt + \sigma_t^\theta dZ_t.$$

We would like to construct differential equations to solve for the functions $q(\eta)$, $\theta(\eta)$ and $\psi(\eta)$. The equations will be of second order in $q(\eta)$ and $\theta(\eta)$, ie, we will design a procedure to compute $q''(\eta)$ and $\theta''(\eta)$, as well as $\psi(\eta)$, from η, $q(\eta)$, $q'(\eta)$ and $\theta(\eta)$, $\theta'(\eta)$. Note also that, since households demand no risk premium, ie, $\underline{\varsigma}_t = 0$, experts will issue the maximum allowed fraction of equity to households, so $\chi_t = \underline{\chi}$ at all times.

In this case $q(\eta)$ is an increasing function that satisfies the boundary condition

$$q(0) = \max_\iota \frac{\underline{a} - \iota}{r - \Phi(\iota) + \delta},$$

the Gordon growth formula for the value of capital when it is permanently managed by households. Any expert can get infinite utility if he can buy capital at the price of $q(0)$, so

$$\lim_{\eta \to 0} \theta(\eta) = \infty. \tag{30}$$

Function $\theta(\eta)$ is decreasing: the marginal value of the experts' net worth is declining as η rises, and investment opportunities become less valuable. Experts refrain from consumption whenever $\theta(\eta) > 1$, and consume only at point η^* where $\theta(\eta^*) = 1$, ie, the marginal value of the experts' net worth is exactly 1. That point becomes the reflecting boundary of the system. That is, the system does not go beyond the reflecting boundary and is rather thrown back. In addition, at the reflecting boundary η^* functions $q(\eta)$ and $\theta(\eta)$ must satisfy

$$q'(\eta^*) = \theta'(\eta^*) = 0.$$

Now to the differential equations. Eq. (25) implies that

$$\sigma + \sigma_t^q = \frac{\sigma}{1 - \frac{q'(\eta)}{q(\eta)}(\underline{\chi}\psi_t - \eta_t)}, \tag{31}$$

and by Ito's Lemma,

$$\sigma_t^\theta = \frac{\theta'(\eta)}{\theta(\eta)} \frac{(\underline{\chi}\psi_t - \eta_t)\sigma}{1 - \frac{q'(\eta)}{q(\eta)}(\underline{\chi}\psi_t - \eta_t)}. \tag{32}$$

Therefore, plugging these expressions into the asset-pricing Eq. (23), we obtain

$$\frac{a - \underline{a}}{q(\eta)} \geq -\underline{\chi}\frac{\theta'(\eta)}{\theta(\eta)} \frac{(\underline{\chi}\psi - \eta)\sigma^2}{\left(1 - \frac{q'(\eta)}{q(\eta)}(\underline{\chi}\psi - \eta)\right)^2}. \tag{33}$$

Assuming that $q'(\eta) > 0$ and $\theta'(\eta) < 0$, the right-hand side is increasing from 0 to ∞ as $\underline{\chi}\psi - \eta$ rises from 0 to $q(\eta)/q'(\eta)$. Thus, we have to set $\psi = 1$ whenever it is possible to do so (ie, $\underline{\chi} - \eta < q(\eta)/q'(\eta)$) and this is consistent with inequality (33). Otherwise we determine ψ by solving the quadratic Eq. (33), in which we replace the $\geq$ sign with equality.

After that, we can find σ_t^q from (31), σ_t^θ from (32), μ_t^η and σ_t^η from (24) (where we set $C_t = 0$ since experts consume only at the boundary η^*), μ_t^q from the asset-pricing condition

$$\frac{a - \iota_t}{q_t} + \Phi(\iota_t) - \delta + \mu_t^q + \sigma\sigma_t^q - r = \underline{\chi}(\sigma + \sigma_t^q)(-\sigma_t^\theta),$$

μ_t^θ from the pricing condition for the risk-free asset

$$\mu_t^\theta = \rho - r,$$

and $q''(\eta)$ as well as $\theta''(\eta)$ from Ito's formula,

$$\mu_t^q q(\eta) = \mu_t^\eta \eta q'(\eta) + \frac{1}{2}(\sigma_t^\eta)^2 \eta^2 q''(\eta) \text{ and } \mu_t^\theta \theta(\eta) = \mu_t^\eta \eta \theta'(\eta) + \frac{1}{2}(\sigma_t^\eta)^2 \eta^2 \theta''(\eta).$$

3.4.1 Solving the System of ODEs Numerically

We can use an ODE solver in Matlab, such as ode45, to solve the system of equations. We need to perform a search, since our boundary conditions are defined at two endpoints of $[0, \eta^*]$, and we also need to deal with a singularity at $\eta = 0$. The following algorithm performs an appropriate search and deals with the singularity issue, effectively, by solving the system of equations with the boundary condition $\theta(0) = M$, for a large constant M, instead of (30):[i]

Algorithm Set

$$q(0) = \max_{\iota} \frac{\underline{a} - \iota}{r - \Phi(\iota) + \underline{\delta}}, \quad \theta(0) = 1 \text{ and } \theta'(0) = -10^{10}.$$

Perform the following procedure to find an appropriate boundary condition $q'(0)$. Set $q_L = 0$ and $q_H = 10^{15}$. Repeat the following loop 50 ×. Guess $q'(0) = (q_L + q_H)/2$. Use Matlab function ode45 to solve for $q(\eta)$ and $\theta(\eta)$ on the interval [0, ?) until one of the following events is triggered, either (1) $q(\eta)$ reaches the upper bound

$$q\text{max} = \max_{\iota} \frac{a - \iota}{r - \Phi(\iota) + \delta},$$

(2) the slope $\theta'(\eta)$ reaches 0 or (3) the slope $q'(\eta)$ reaches 0. If integration has terminated for reason (3), we need to increase the initial guess of $q'(0)$ by setting $q_L = q'(0)$. Otherwise, we decrease the initial guess of $q'(0)$, by setting $q_H = q'(0)$.

At the end, $\theta'(0)$ and $q'(0)$ reach 0 at about the same point, which we denote by η^*. Divide the entire function θ by $\theta(\eta^*)$.[j] Then plot the solutions.

3.4.2 Properties of the Solution

Let us interpret the solution of the risk-neutral model. Point η^* plays the role of the steady state of our system. The drift of η_t is positive everywhere on the interval $[0, \eta^*)$, because the expert sector, which is more productive than the household sector, is growing in expectation. Thus, the system is pushed toward η^* by the drift.

It turns out that the steady state is relatively stable, because volatility is low near η^*. To see this, recall that the amount of endogenous risk in asset prices, from (25), is given by

$$\sigma_t^q = \frac{q'(\eta)}{q(\eta)} \frac{(\underline{\chi}\psi_t - \eta_t)}{1 - \frac{q'(\eta)}{q(\eta)}(\underline{\chi}\psi_t - \eta_t)} \sigma.$$

From the boundary conditions, $q'(\eta^*) = 0$, so there is no endogenous risk near η^*.

[i] Footnote j explains why it actually does not to matter what exact value one sets for $\theta(0)$.

[j] We can do this because whenever functions θ and q satisfy our system of equation, so do functions $\Theta\theta$ and q for any constant Θ. Because of that, also, it is immaterial what we set $\theta(0)$ to 1.

However, below η^*, endogenous risk increases as $q'(\eta)$ becomes larger. As prices react to shocks, fundamental risk becomes amplified. As we see from the expression for σ_t^q, this amplification effect is nonlinear, since $q'(\eta)$ enters not only the numerator, but also the denominator. This happens due to the feedback effect: an initial shock causes η_t to drop, which leads to a drop in q_t, which hurts experts who are holding capital and leads to a further decrease in η_t, and so on.

Of course, far in the depressed region the volatility of η_t, $\sigma_t^\eta \eta_t$, becomes low again in this model. This leads to a bimodal stationary distribution of η_t in equilibrium.[k]

Volatility paradox refers to the phenomenon that systemic risk can build up in quiet environments. We can illustrate this phenomenon through comparative statics on σ or the degree of the experts' equity constraint $\underline{\chi}$. One may guess that the system becomes much more stable as σ or $\underline{\chi}$ decline.

This is not the case, as illustrated in Fig. 3 for parameters $\rho = 6\%$, $r = 5\%$, $a = 11\%$, $\underline{a} = 5\%$, $\delta = 3\%$, and an investment function of the form $\Phi(\iota) = \frac{1}{\kappa}(\sqrt{1+2\kappa\iota} - 1)$, $\kappa = 10$,

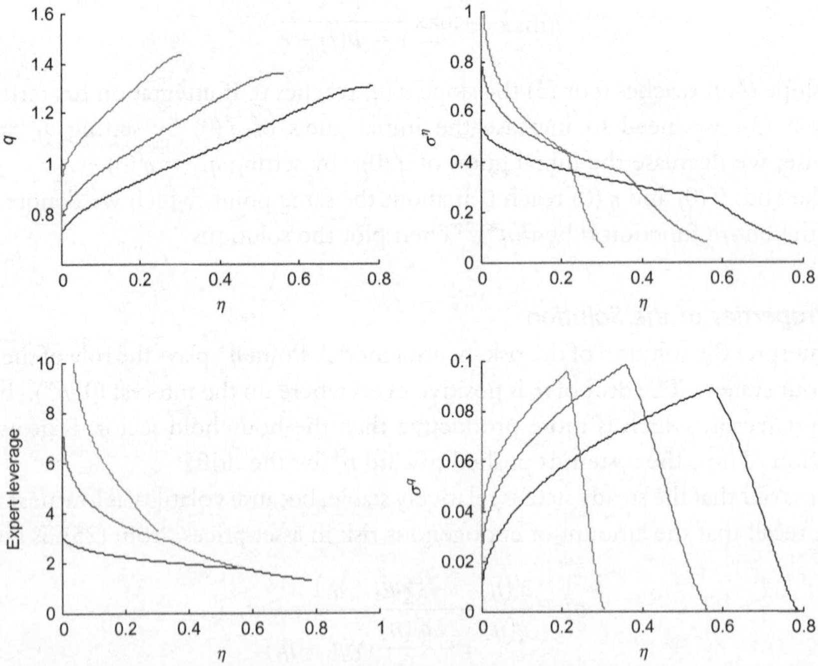

Fig. 3 Equilibrium with $\sigma = 2.5\%$ (red), 10% (blue), and 25% (black). (In the printed version red is grey and blue is dark grey.)

[k] One can prove that the stationary distribution is bimodal analytically by analyzing the asymptotic properties of the solutions near $\eta = 0$ and using the Kolmogorov forward equations that characterize the stationary density—see Brunnermeier and Sannikov (2014) for details.

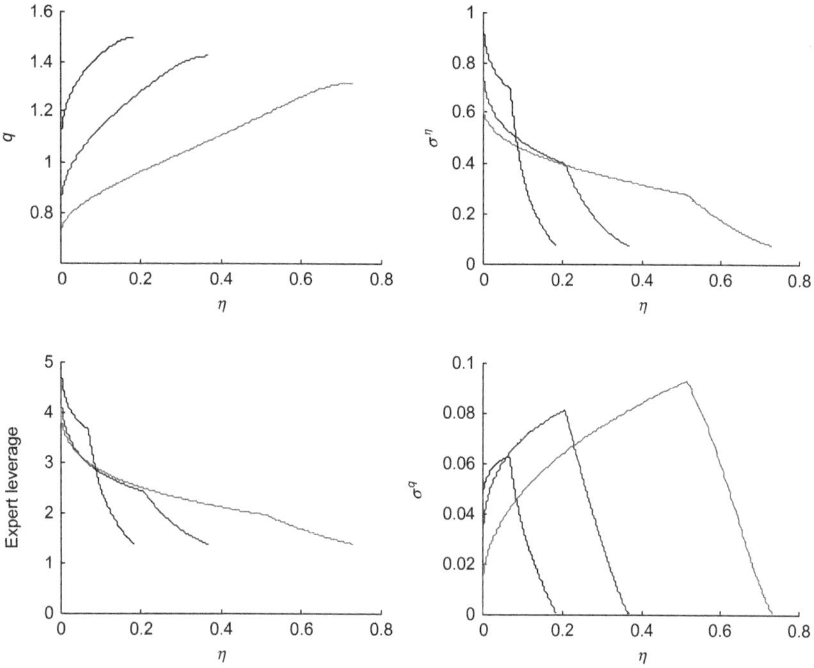

Fig. 4 Equilibrium with $\underline{\chi} = 0.25$ (black), 0.5 (blue) and 1 (red). (In the printed version blue is gray and red light gray.)

$\underline{\chi} = 1$, and various values of σ. (The investment technology in this example has quadratic adjustment costs: an investment of $\Phi + \kappa\Phi^2/2$ generates new capital at rate Φ.)

The volatility paradox shows itself in a number of metrics. As exogenous risk declines,

- maximal endogenous risk σ_t^q may increase (as σ drops from 25% to 10% in Fig. 3)
- the volatility σ_t^η near $\eta = 0$ rises (and this result can be proved analytically)
- from the steady state η^* it takes less time for volatility $\sigma + \sigma_t^q$ to double
- from the steady state, it may take less time to reach the peak of the crisis η^ψ, where experts start selling capital to households.[1]

Fig. 4 takes the same parameters and $\sigma = 20\%$, but varies $\underline{\chi}$. As $\underline{\chi}$ falls, expert net worth at the steady state η^* drops significantly, and the volatility σ_t^η in the crisis regime rises.

3.5 Method 2: The Iterative Method

Here, we describe the iterative method of finding the equilibrium, by solving a system of partial differential equations back in time away from a terminal condition. Specifically, imagine an economy that lasts for a finite time horizon $[0, T]$. Given a set of terminal conditions at time T, we would like to compute the equilibrium over the time horizon

[1] As σ declines, the system spends less time in the crisis region, so some measures of stability improve, but the amount of time spent in crisis does not converge to 0 as $\sigma \to 0$.

$[0, T]$. The iterative method is based on the premise that as we let $T \to \infty$, behavior at time 0 should converge to the equilibrium of the infinite-horizon economy. Computation uses the equilibrium conditions that express the drifts of various processes, and uses those drifts to obtain time derivatives for the corresponding functions of the state space. The iterative method is analogous to value function iteration in discrete time.

We illustrate the method here based on a model with CRRA utility

$$u(c) = \frac{c^{1-\gamma}}{1-\gamma}.$$

Equilibrium conditions (21) and (19) provide two equations that express the drift of the price q_t, as well as the drifts of aggregate consumption of experts C_t and households $\underline{C}_t$. We also have another asset-pricing condition (23), which does not contain any drift terms. In the end we have three functions but only two drift conditions. As a result, the time dimension of our computation involves only two functions—the value functions of experts and households—and the third function, the price, is found for each time point through a separate procedure.[m]

Our procedure is literally the analogue of value function iteration (but with multiple agents affecting the evolving stochastic state). It is convenient to derive directly the equations that value functions must satisfy. The value functions of experts and households can be presented in the form

$$v_t \frac{K_t^{1-\gamma}}{1-\gamma} = \frac{v_t}{(\eta_t q_t)^{1-\gamma}} \frac{N_t^{1-\gamma}}{1-\gamma} \text{ and } \underline{v}_t \frac{K_t^{1-\gamma}}{1-\gamma}.$$

Since the marginal utilities of consumption and wealth must be the same, we have

$$C_t^{-\gamma} = \frac{v_t}{(\eta_t q_t)^{1-\gamma}} N_t^{-\gamma} = \frac{v_t}{\eta_t q_t} K_t^{-\gamma} \Rightarrow C_t = N_t \frac{(\eta_t q_t)^{1/\gamma - 1}}{v_t^{1/\gamma}} = K_t \frac{(\eta_t q_t)^{1/\gamma}}{v_t^{1/\gamma}}. \tag{34}$$

Hence, the risk premia of households and experts are given by

$$\varsigma_t = \gamma \sigma_t^C = -\sigma_t^v + \sigma_t^\eta + \sigma_t^q + \gamma\sigma \text{ and } \underline{\varsigma}_t = \gamma \sigma_t^{\underline{C}} = -\sigma_t^{\underline{v}} - \frac{\eta \sigma_t^\eta}{1-\eta} + \sigma_t^q + \gamma \sigma. \tag{35}$$

Since

$$\underbrace{\int_0^t e^{-\rho s} \frac{C_s^{1-\gamma}}{1-\gamma} ds}_{\text{utility flow}} + e^{-\rho t} \underbrace{v_t \frac{K_t^{1-\gamma}}{1-\gamma}}_{\text{continuation utility}}$$

[m] If we used the shooting method to find the equilibrium with CRRA utilities, we would have a system of second-order differential equations for the value functions, and a first-order differential equation for the price.

is by standard dynamic programming arguments a martingale and

$$\frac{d(K_t^{1-\gamma})}{K_t^{1-\gamma}} = \left((1-\gamma)(\Phi(\iota_t) - \delta) - \frac{\gamma(1-\gamma)}{2}\sigma^2 \right) dt + (1-\gamma)\sigma dZ_t,$$

we have

$$\frac{C_t^{1-\gamma}}{1-\gamma} - \rho v_t \frac{K_t^{1-\gamma}}{1-\gamma} + v_t \frac{K_t^{1-\gamma}}{1-\gamma} \left(\mu_t^v + (1-\gamma)(\Phi(\iota_t) - \delta) - \frac{\gamma(1-\gamma)}{2}\sigma^2 + \sigma_t^v (1-\gamma)\sigma \right) = 0.$$

Using (34), we obtain

$$\mu_t^v = \rho - \frac{(\eta_t q_t)^{1/\gamma - 1}}{v_t^{1/\gamma}} - (1-\gamma)(\Phi(\iota_t) - \delta) + \frac{\gamma(1-\gamma)}{2}\sigma^2 - \sigma_t^v (1-\gamma)\sigma. \tag{36}$$

Likewise,

$$\mu_t^{\underline{v}} = \underline{\rho} - \frac{((1-\eta_t) q_t)^{1/\gamma - 1}}{\underline{v}_t^{1/\gamma}} - (1-\gamma)(\Phi(\iota_t) - \delta) + \frac{\gamma(1-\gamma)}{2}\sigma^2 - \sigma_t^{\underline{v}} (1-\gamma)\sigma. \tag{37}$$

Given μ_t^v and $\mu_t^{\underline{v}}$, we obtain partial differential equations for the functions $v(\eta, t)$ and $\underline{v}(\eta, t)$ using Ito's Lemma, and they are as follows:

$$\mu_t^v v(\eta, t) = \mu_t^\eta \eta v_\eta(\eta, t) + \frac{(\sigma_t^\eta \eta)^2}{2} v_{\eta\eta}(\eta, t) + v_t(\eta, t) \quad \text{and} \tag{38}$$

$$\mu_t^{\underline{v}} \underline{v}(\eta, t) = \mu_t^\eta \eta \underline{v}_\eta(\eta, t) + \frac{(\sigma_t^\eta \eta)^2}{2} \underline{v}_{\eta\eta}(\eta, t) + \underline{v}_t(\eta, t). \tag{39}$$

3.5.1 Description of the Procedure

Below we outline the procedure of how we solve for the equilibrium using Eqs. (38) and (39).[n] There are three parts.

- The terminal conditions $v(\eta, T)$ and $\underline{v}(\eta, T)$
- The static step: finding capital price $q(\eta)$, allocations $\psi(\eta)$ and $\chi(\eta)$, volatilities and drifts at a given time point t given the value functions $v(\eta, t)$ and $\underline{v}(\eta, t)$, and
- The time step: finding $v(\eta, t - \Delta t)$ and $\underline{v}(\eta, t - \Delta t)$ from prices, allocations, volatilities and drifts at time t.

[n] For more details on the finite difference method for dynamic programming problems we refer to Candler (1999). Oberman (2006) provides sufficient conditions for a numerical scheme to converge to the solution of a general class of non-linear parabolic Partial Differential Equations.

3.5.1.1 The Terminal Conditions

Our terminal conditions specify the utilities of the representative expert and household, as functions of the experts' wealth share η_t. We have not performed a detailed theoretical study of acceptable terminal conditions, but in practice any reasonable guess works well for a wide range of parameters.

For example, if we set $q_T = 1$ and $C_T/K_T = a\eta_T$, then (34) implies that

$$v_T = \eta_T(a\eta_T)^{-\gamma} \text{ and } \underline{v}_T = (1-\eta_T)(a(1-\eta_T))^{-\gamma}. \tag{40}$$

3.5.1.2 The Static Step

Suppose we know value functions through $v(\eta, t)$ and $\underline{v}(\eta, t)$. Let us describe how we can compute the price q_t and characterize equilibrium dynamics at time t.

There are three regions. When η is close enough to 0, then the experts' risk premia are so much higher than those of households that $\psi_t < 1$, ie, households hold capital, and Eq. (23) holds. In this region experts issue the maximal allowed equity share to households, so $\chi_t = \underline{\chi}$, since the households' risk premia are lower. In the middle region, $\psi_t = 1$, ie, only experts hold capital, but the experts' risk premia are still higher than those of households so $\chi_t = \underline{\chi}$. Finally, when $\eta \geq \underline{\chi}$, the capital is allocated efficiently to experts (ie, $\psi_t = 1$) and risk can be shared perfectly between households and experts by setting $\chi_t = \eta_t$. In the last region, (26) implies that $\sigma^\eta = 0$, so there is no endogenous risk, and risk premia of experts and households are both equal to $\varsigma_t = \underline{\varsigma}_t = \gamma\sigma$ by (35).

In the region where $\psi_t < 1$ we solve for $q(\eta)$, $\psi(\eta)$ and $\sigma + \sigma_t^q$ from a system of the following three equations, which ultimately gives us a first-order ODE in $q(\eta)$. We obtain the first by combining (23) and (35) together with evolution of η Eq. (24), we have

$$\frac{a-\underline{a}}{q_t} = \underline{\chi}\underbrace{\left(\frac{\underline{v}'(\eta)}{\underline{v}(\eta)} - \frac{v'(\eta)}{v(\eta)} + \frac{1}{\eta(1-\eta)}\right)(\underline{\chi}\psi_t - \eta)(\sigma+\sigma_t^q)^2}_{\left(\sigma_t^{\underline{v}} - \sigma_t^v + \frac{\sigma_t^\eta}{1-\eta}\right)(\sigma+\sigma_t^q)}. \tag{41}$$

The second we obtain from (25) and Ito's Lemma,

$$(\sigma+\sigma^q)\left(1-(\underline{\chi}\psi-\eta)\frac{q'(\eta)}{q(\eta)}\right) = \sigma. \tag{42}$$

Finally, from (34) and an analogous condition for households, the market-clearing condition for output is

$$\underbrace{\frac{(\eta_t q_t)^{1/\gamma}}{v_t^{1/\gamma}} + \frac{((1-\eta_t)q_t)^{1/\gamma}}{\underline{v}_t^{1/\gamma}}}_{(C_t+\underline{C}_t)/K_t} = a\psi + \underline{a}(1-\psi) - \iota(q(\eta)). \tag{43}$$

Once ψ_t reaches 1, condition (41) is no longer relevant. From then on, we set $\psi_t = 1$, find $q(\eta)$ from (43) and $\sigma + \sigma_t^q$ from (42). Once η_t reaches $\underline{\chi}$, we enter the last region. There we set $\psi_t = 1, \chi_t = \eta_t$, compute $q(\eta)$ from (43) and set $\sigma_t^q = 0$.

Once we know function $q(\eta)$ in all three regions, we can find the volatility of η_t from (24) and the volatilities of v_t and $\underline{v}_t$ from Ito's Lemma, ie,

$$\sigma_t^\eta = \frac{\chi_t \psi_t - \eta_t}{\eta_t}(\sigma + \sigma_t^q), \quad \sigma_t^v = \frac{v'(\eta)}{v(\eta)}\sigma_t^\eta \eta, \quad \text{and} \quad \sigma_t^{\underline{v}} = \frac{\underline{v}'(\eta)}{\underline{v}(\eta)}\sigma_t^\eta \eta. \tag{44}$$

We find the required risk premia ς_t and $\underline{\varsigma}_t$ from (35) and the drift of η_t from (24), ie,

$$\mu_t^\eta = \left(\frac{a - \iota_t}{q_t} - \frac{(\eta_t q_t)^{1/\gamma - 1}}{v_t^{1/\gamma}}\right) + \sigma_t^\eta(\varsigma_t - \sigma - \sigma_t^q) + (\sigma + \sigma_t^q)(1 - \underline{\chi})\left(\varsigma_t - \underline{\varsigma}_t\right).$$

Finally, we solve for the drifts of v_t and $\underline{v}_t$ from (36).

3.5.1.3 The Time Step

Once we have all characteristics of the equilibrium at a given time point t, we can solve for the value functions at an earlier time step $t - \Delta t$ from Eqs. (38) and (39). These are parabolic equations, which can be solved using either explicit or implicit methods.

3.5.1.4 Summary

Set terminal conditions for value functions $v(\eta, T)$ and $\underline{v}(\eta, T)$ according to (40) on a grid over η. Divide the interval $[0, T]$ into small subintervals. Going backwards in time, for each subinterval $[t - \Delta t, t]$ perform the static step and then the time step. That is, from value functions $v(\eta, t)$ and $\underline{v}(\eta, t)$ find the drift and volatility of η as well as the drifts of v and $\underline{v}$ using the following procedure (static step). Start from an initial condition near $(\eta = 0, \psi = 0)$ (perturb the condition to avoid division by 0). Solve (41), (42), and (43) (as a first-order ordinary differential equation for $q(\eta)$) until ψ reaches 1. Then set $\psi = 1$ and use (43) to find $q(\eta)$ and (42) to find σ^q. Throughout, use $\chi_t = \max(\underline{\chi}, \eta)$. With functions (of η) q, σ^q, ψ and χ obtained in this way, compute volatilities from (44), ς_t and $\underline{\varsigma}_t$ from (35), μ_t^η from (24), and the drifts of v_t and $\underline{v}_t$ from (36). Then (this is the time step) solve the partial differential Eqs. (38) and (39) for v and $\underline{v}$ backward in time over the interval $[t - \Delta t, t]$, using fixed functions $\mu_t^v, \mu_t^{\underline{v}}, \mu_t^\eta$ and σ_t^η of η computed by the static step. Continue until time 0. We get convergence when T is sufficiently large.

Remark The static step alone is sufficient to solve for the equilibrium prices, allocations and dynamics in a model with logarithmic utility (ie, $\gamma = 1$), since in this case we know that $(C_t + \underline{C}_t)/(q_t K_t) = \rho\eta + \underline{\rho}(1 - \eta)$ and expert and household risk premia are $\varsigma_t = \sigma_t^N = \chi_t \psi_t / \eta_t (\sigma + \sigma_t^q)$ and $\underline{\varsigma}_t = (1 - \chi_t \psi_t)/(1 - \eta_t)(\sigma + \sigma_t^q)$. Hence, Eqs. (41) and (43) become

$$\frac{a-\underline{a}}{q_t} = \chi \frac{\chi\psi_t - \eta}{\eta(1-\eta)}(\sigma+\sigma_t^q)^2 \quad \text{and} \quad (\rho\eta + \underline{\rho}(1-\eta))q_t = a\psi + \underline{a}(1-\psi) - \iota(q(\eta)). \tag{45}$$

Eq. (42) remains the same.

For logarithmic utility, however, we do not immediately obtain the agents' value functions. Those can be found using an extra step.

3.6 Examples of Solutions: CRRA Utility

In this section, we illustrate solutions generated by our code, using the iterative method, and what we learn from them. We use baseline parameters $\rho = 6\%, r = 5\%$, $a = 11\%, \underline{a} = 3\%, \delta = 5\%, \sigma = 10\%, \underline{\chi} = 0.5, \gamma = 2$ and an investment function of the form $\Phi(\iota) = \log(\kappa\iota + 1)/\kappa$ with $\kappa = 10$. We then study how several parameters, specifically $\underline{a}, \sigma, \underline{\chi}$ and γ affect the equilibrium.

Fig. 5 illustrates the equilibrium for the baseline set of parameters. Notice that capital price q_t has a kink—the kink separates the crisis region near $\eta = 0$ where $\psi_t < 1$, ie, households hold some capital, and the normal region where experts hold all capital in the economy.

Here, point η^* where the drift of η_t becomes 0 plays the role of a steady state of the system. In the absence of shocks, the system stays still at the steady state and in response to small shocks, drift pushes the system back to the steady state. Moving away from the crisis regime, at η^* risk premia decline sufficiently so that the experts' earnings are exactly offset by their slightly higher consumption rates.

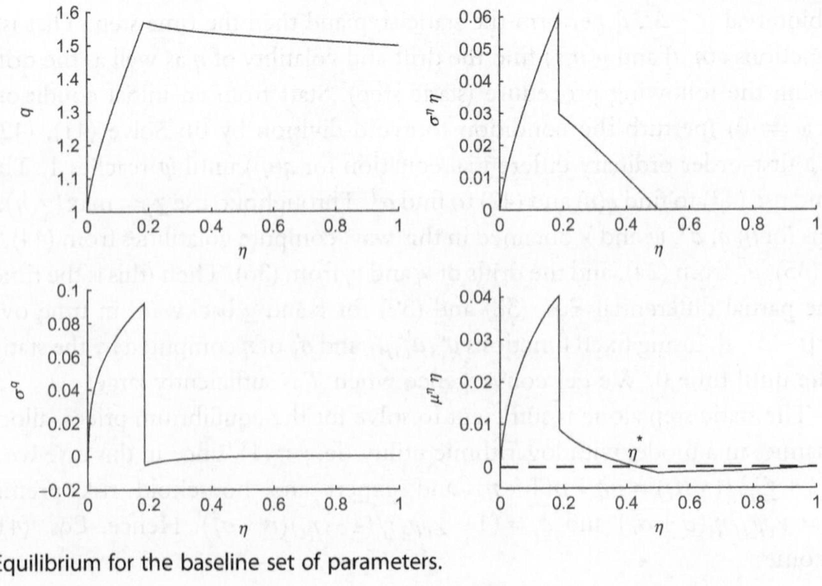

Fig. 5 Equilibrium for the baseline set of parameters.

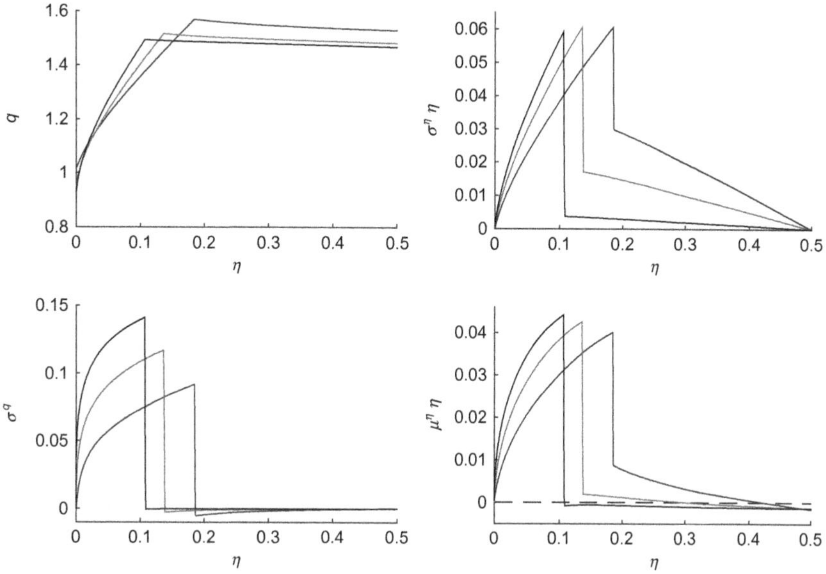

Fig. 6 Equilibrium for $\sigma = 0.01$ (black), 0.05 (red), 0.1 (blue). (In the printed version red is gray and blue is dark gray.)

Above $\eta = \underline{\chi} = 0.5$ is the region of perfect risk sharing, where the volatility of η is zero. Since the drift in that region is negative, the system never ends up there (and if the initial condition is $\eta_0 > \underline{\chi}$, then η_t drifts deterministically down to $\underline{\chi}$).

Fig. 6 shows the effect of σ on the equilibrium dynamics. We bound the horizontal axis at $\eta = \underline{\chi} = 0.5$, since the system never enters the region $\eta > \underline{\chi}$. The steady state η^* declines as σ falls, as risk premia decline in the normal regime, until η^* coincides with the boundary of the crisis region for low σ (this happens for $\sigma = 0.01$ in Fig. 6). We also observe the volatility paradox: as σ declines, endogenous risk σ_t^q does not have to fall, and may even rise.

But what happens as $\sigma \to 0$? Does endogenous risk disappear altogether, and does the solution converge to first best? The answer turns out to be no: in the limit as $\sigma \to 0$, the boundary of the crisis region η^ψ converges not to 0 but to a finite number.

Likewise, what happens if financial frictions become relaxed, and experts are able to hold capital while retaining a smaller portion of risk? It is tempting to conjecture that as financial frictions become relaxed, the system becomes more stable. Yet, as the bottom left panel of Fig. 7 demonstrates, endogenous risk σ_t^q rises sharply as $\underline{\chi}$ declines.[o]

It turns out that a crucial parameter that affects system stability is the household productivity parameter $\underline{a}$. The level of endogenous risk in crises depends strongly on the

[o] Of course, there is a discontinuity at both $\sigma = 0$ and $\underline{\chi} = 0$. As financial frictions disappear altogether, the crisis region disappears.

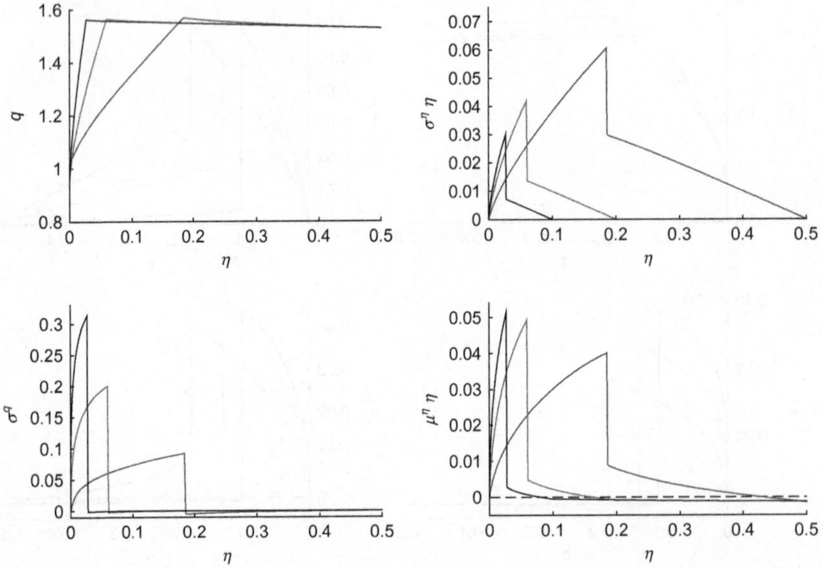

Fig. 7 Equilibrium for $\underline{\chi} = 0.1$ (black), 0.2 (red), and 0.5 (blue). (In the printed version red is gray and blue dark gray.)

market illiquidity of capital—the difference between parameter a and $\underline{a}$ that determines how much less households value capital, in the event that they have to buy it, relative to experts. Fig. 8 illustrates the equilibrium for several values of $\underline{a}$. Note that endogenous risk in crises rises sharply as $\underline{a}$ drops. However, the dynamics in the normal regime and the level of η^* have extremely low sensitivity to $\underline{a}$—only dynamics in the crisis regime are extremely sensitive. This is a surprise. While expert leverage responds endogenously to fundamental risk σ in the normal regime it does not respond strongly to endogenous tail risk. In fact, for logarithmic utility it is possible to prove analytically that the dynamics in the normal regime do not depend on $\underline{a}$ at all (but here we illustrate the dynamics for $\gamma = 2$).

Finally, let us consider risk aversion γ in Fig. 9. There are several effects. Lower risk aversion leads to a smaller crisis region (but with greater endogenous risk), and lower steady state η^* as the risk premia become lower. In this example, higher risk aversion leads to a higher price of capital, as risk creates a precautionary savings demand.

4. A SIMPLE MONETARY MODEL

So far we focused on a real model with a single risky asset, physical capital, and a risk-free asset. Now, building on Brunnermeier and Sannikov's (2015a) "I Theory of Money" we introduce instead of the (real) risk-free asset, another asset, money. In general, money has three roles: it is a unit of account, it facilitates transactions, and it serves as a store of value (safe asset). Here, we focus on its role as a store of value, which arises in our setting due to

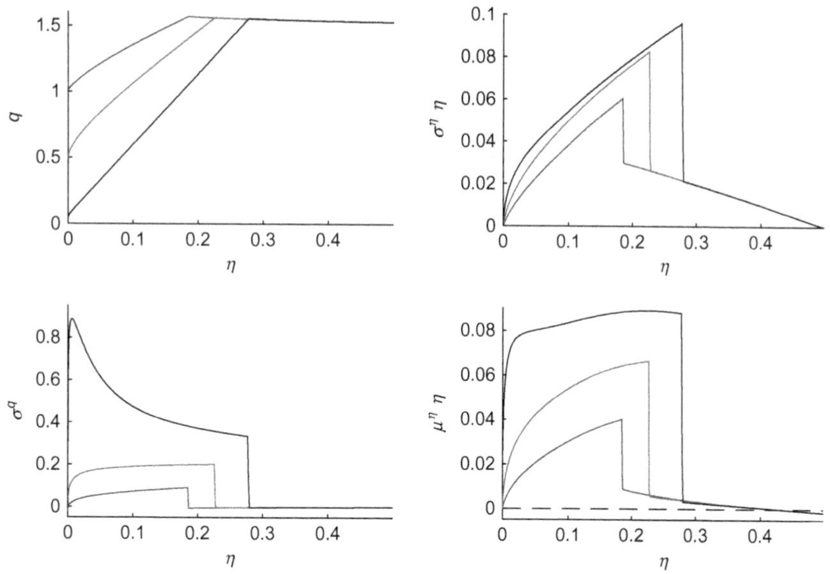

Fig. 8 Equilibrium for $\underline{a} = 0.03$ (blue), -0.03 (red), and -0.09 (black). (In the printed version blue is dark grey and red is gray.)

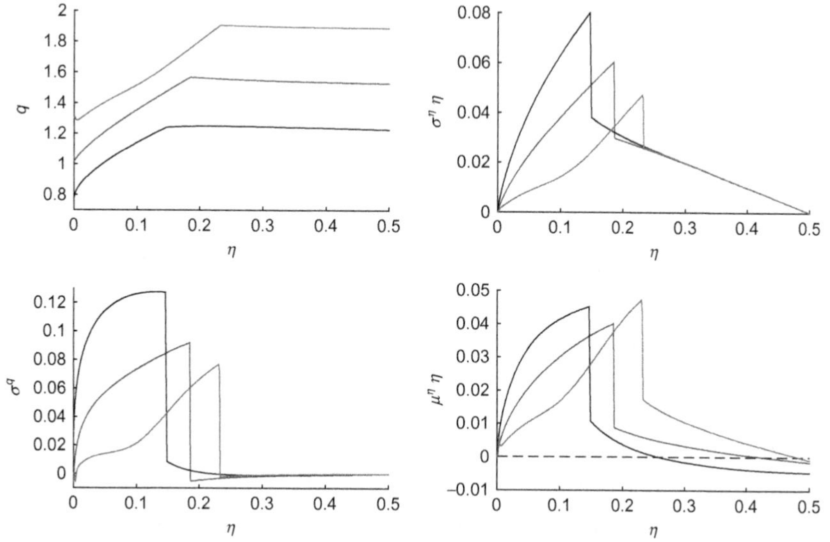

Fig. 9 Equilibrium for $\gamma = 0.5$ (black), 2 (blue), and 5 (red). (In the printed version blue is dark gray and red is gray.)

incomplete markets frictions. Unlike in New Keynesian models, which focus on the role of money as a unit of account and rely on price and wage rigidities as the key frictions, prices are fully flexible in our model.

This section focuses on the following:

1. Money can have positive value despite the fact that it never pays any dividend. That is, money is a bubble.
2. Money helps agents to share risks in an economy that is plagued by financial frictions. Hence, having a nominal store of value instead of a real short-term risk-free bond alters the equilibrium risk dynamics.
3. The "*paradox of prudence*" coined in Brunnermeier and Sannikov (2015a) arises. Experts hold money to self-insure against idiosyncratic shocks, an action which is micro-prudent but macro-*im*prudent. By selling capital to achieve a greater portfolio weight on money, experts depress aggregate investment and growth, leading to lower returns on all assets (including money). The paradox of prudence is in the risk space what Keynes' Paradox of Thrift is for the consumption-savings decision. The Paradox of Thrift describes how each person's attempt to save more paradoxically lowers overall aggregate savings.

4.1 Model with Idiosyncratic Capital Risk and Money

Let us return to the Basak–Cuoco model of Section 2 with experts holding physical capital and households who cannot, ie, $\underline{a}=-\infty$. We introduce the following two modifications: (i) Capital has in addition to aggregate risk also idiosyncratic risk. (ii) There is no risk-free asset, but there is money in fixed supply. Agents can long and short it and want to hold it to self-insure against idiosyncratic risk.

More formally, we assume as before that each expert operates a linear production technology, ak_t, with productivity a, but now they also face idiosyncratic risk $\tilde{\sigma}\, d\tilde{Z}_t$ in addition to aggregate risk σdZ_t. That is a single expert's capital k_t evolves according to

$$dk_t/k_t = (\Phi(\iota_t) - \delta)dt + \sigma dZ_t + \tilde{\sigma}\, d\tilde{Z}_t.$$

The shock dZ_t is the same for the whole economy, while the shock $d\tilde{Z}_t$ is expert-specific and orthogonal to dZ_t. Idiosyncratic shocks cancel out in the aggregate.

Since idiosyncratic risk is uninsurable due to markets incompleteness, experts also want to hold money. Money is an infinitely divisible asset in fixed supply, which can be traded without frictions. Since money does not pay off any dividends it has value in equilibrium only because agents want to self-insure against idiosyncratic shocks to their capital holdings. In other words, money is a bubble, like in Samuelson (1958) and Bewley (1980). Unlike in Bewley (1980), our idiosyncratic shocks are not endowment shocks, but investment shocks like in Angeletos (2007). We assume that idiosyncratic risk of the dividend-paying capital is large enough, $\tilde{\sigma} > \sqrt{\rho}$, so that money, which does not pay dividends, still has value in equilibrium. This is unlike Diamond (1965) who introduces physical capital in Samuelson's OLG model and Aiyagari (1994) who introduces capital in Bewley's incomplete markets setting. In those models, the presence of capital crowds out money as a store of value.[p]

Experts can invest in (outside) money and capital, while households like in Section 2 only hold money. We also assume for simplicity that all agents have logarithmic utility with time preference rate ρ.[q]

As before, let us follow our four step approach to solve the model.

4.2 The 4-Step Approach

Step 1: Postulate Price and SDF Processes. In this monetary setting we now have to postulate not only a process for the price of capital, but also for the "real price" of money. We denote (without loss of generality) the value of the total money stock in terms of the numeraire (the consumption good) by $p_t K_t$. We normalize the total value of the money stock by K_t to emphasize that, everything else being equal, the value of money should be proportional to the size of the economy.

$$\frac{dq_t}{q_t} = \mu_t^q dt + \sigma_t^q dZ_t,$$
$$\frac{dp_t}{p_t} = \mu_t^p dt + \sigma_t^p dZ_t,$$

In addition, like in Section 3 we postulate the processes for individual experts' and households' stochastic discount factors:

$$\frac{d\xi_t}{\xi_t} = -r_t dt - \varsigma_t dZ_t - \tilde{\varsigma}_t d\tilde{Z}_t \quad \text{and} \quad \frac{d\underline{\xi}_t}{\underline{\xi}_t} = -\underline{r}_t dt - \underline{\varsigma}_t dZ_t,$$

where r_t and $\underline{r}_t$ are the (real) shadow risk-free interest rates of experts and households, respectively. Note that shadow risk-free rates need not be identical, since no real risk-free asset is traded. Note also that experts require a risk premium not only for the aggregate risk ς_t but also for the idiosyncratic risk they have to bear $\tilde{\varsigma}_t$.

We will show that there exists an equilibrium in which the wealth share η_t evolves deterministically and so do the prices q_t and p_t. Hence, for simplicity we set $\sigma_t^q = \sigma_t^p = 0$. Under this conjecture the return on physical capital accruing to experts is

[p] We assume that money is intrinsically worthless, and so along with the equilibrium in which money has value, there is also an equilibrium in which money has no value. However, in a perturbation of the model, in which agents get small utility from holding money (eg, because money facilitates transactions), only the equilibrium with full value of money survives.

[q] Solving this model with CRRA models using the results on page 1511 in Section 3.1 is a worthwhile exercise.

$$dr_t^k = \frac{a - \iota_t}{q_t}dt + (\Phi(\iota_t) - \delta + \mu_t^q)dt + \sigma dZ_t + \tilde{\sigma}\, d\tilde{Z}_t$$

and world stock of money $p_t K_t$ earns the (real) return of

$$dr_t^M = \left(\Phi(\iota_t) - \delta + \mu_t^p\right)dt + \sigma dZ_t,$$

where ι_t is the investment rate in physical capital.

Step 2: Equilibrium Conditions. First, note that the optimal investment rate is determined by q_t through $\Phi'(\iota_t) = 1/q_t$. Second, the optimal consumption rate of all agents is simply ρ times their net worth, since the utility of all agents is logarithmic with time preference rate ρ. Hence, aggregate demand for the consumption good is $\rho(q_t + p_t)K_t$. Given total supply of consumption goods after investing, we have the following goods market equilibrium condition:

$$\rho(q_t + p_t)K_t = (a - \iota)K_t.$$

Next, we solve the experts' and households' portfolio problems. Notice that, given the returns dr_t^M and dr_t^k on capital and money, the only two assets traded in this economy, all agents have exposure σdZ_t to aggregate risk. At the same time, experts also have exposure $x_t \tilde{\sigma}\, d\tilde{Z}_t$ to their individual idiosyncratic shocks, where x_t is the experts' portfolio weight on capital. Hence, the required risk premia of these log-utility agents are

$$\varsigma_t = \underline{\varsigma}_t = \sigma \text{ and } \tilde{\varsigma}_t = x_t \tilde{\sigma}\,.$$

The experts' and households' asset pricing equations for money, respectively, are

$$\frac{E_t[dr_t^M]}{dt} - r_t = \frac{E_t[dr_t^M]}{dt} - \underline{r}_t = \underbrace{\sigma^2}_{=\varsigma_t\sigma = \underline{\varsigma}_t\sigma}.$$

Thus, $r_t = \underline{r}_t$: even though there is no risk-free real asset in this economy, both agent types would agree on a single real risk-free real interest rate.

The experts' asset pricing equation for physical capital is

$$\frac{E_t[dr_t^k]}{dt} - r_t = \varsigma_t\sigma + \tilde{\varsigma}_t\tilde{\sigma}\,,$$

reflecting the fact that experts are also exposed to idiosyncratic risk for which they earn an extra risk premium. Hence,

$$\frac{E_t[dr_t^k]}{dt} - \frac{E_t[dr_t^M]}{dt} = x_t\tilde{\sigma}^2. \tag{46}$$

Capital market clearing implies that

$$x_t = \frac{q_t K_t}{\eta_t (p_t + q_t) K_t} = \frac{1}{\eta_t} \frac{q_t}{p_t + q_t}, \tag{47}$$

Step 3: Evolution of η. Experts' aggregate net worth N_t evolves according to

$$\frac{dN_t}{N_t} = r_t + \sigma(\underbrace{\sigma}_{\varsigma_t} dt + dZ_t) + x_t \tilde{\sigma} \tilde{\varsigma}_t dt - \rho dt,$$

given their exposures to aggregate and idiosyncratic risk, and since idiosyncratic risk cancels out in the aggregate. The law of motion of aggregate wealth is

$$\frac{d((q_t + p_t)K_t)}{(q_t + p_t)K_t} = r_t + \sigma(\sigma dt + dZ_t) + \eta_t x_t \tilde{\sigma} \tilde{\varsigma}_t dt - \rho dt,$$

where $\eta_t = \dfrac{N_t}{(q_t + p_t)K_t}$ is the experts' net worth share and $\eta_t x_t = q_t/(p_t + q_t)$ is the exposure to idiosyncratic risk in the world portfolio. Hence,

$$\frac{d\eta_t}{\eta_t} = x_t^2 (1 - \eta_t) \tilde{\sigma}^2 dt = \left(\frac{q_t}{p_t + q_t}\right)^2 \frac{1 - \eta_t}{\eta_t^2} \tilde{\sigma}^2 dt. \tag{48}$$

Step 4: Derive ODEs for the postulated price processes q and p as a function of the state variable η. We omit this step as it is similar to the previous section.

4.3 Observations and Limit Case

The increase in experts' wealth share η_t, or equivalently the decline of households' wealth share, $1 - \eta_t$, results in part from the fact that experts earn a risk premium from taking on idiosyncratic risk. The higher the idiosyncratic risk $\tilde{\sigma}^2$, the faster experts' wealth share rises toward 100%. Interestingly, it is the fact that experts are unable to share idiosyncratic risk which makes them richer over time compared to households.

Money allows for some sharing of idiosyncratic risk, since the experts' exposure to idiosyncratic risk of $x_t \tilde{\sigma}$ is less than what it would have been without money, ie, $\tilde{\sigma}/\eta_t$, as long as $x_t < 1/\eta_t$ or $p_t > 0$.

4.3.1 Comparison with Real Model

It is instructive to contrast the settings of this section with that of Section 2, where households hold the real risk-free asset instead of money. The evolution η follows now (48) instead of (11). Note that in both settings the experts' wealth share drifts towards 100%. However, there are crucial differences. In the setting with nominal money, aggregate risk is shared fully between experts and households. Hence, both groups receive a risk premium and therefore aggregate risk does not impact the wealth share in the model with money. In contrast, in the real model experts hold all the aggregate risk and hence only they earn a risk premium, leading to a positive drift in η. More importantly, aggregate risk sharing with money makes the evolution of experts' wealth share deterministic. In contrast, in the real model that experts' wealth share is necessarily stochastic, as revealed by (11).

4.3.2 The Only Experts Case

Finally, we are able to derive a closed form solution for the absorbing state $\eta = 1$ to which the system drifts. When the state $\eta = 1$ is reached $\mu^q(1) = \mu^p(1) = 0$ and thus experts' asset pricing Eq. (46) and capital market clearing (47) can be combined and simplified as follows

$$\frac{1}{\tilde{\sigma}^2}\frac{a-\iota}{q} = \frac{E[dr^k - dr^M]/dt}{\tilde{\sigma}^2} = x_t = \frac{q}{p+q} \tag{49}$$

Combining Eq. (49) with the goods market clearing condition

$$\rho(p+q)K_t = (a-\iota)K_t \tag{50}$$

and the optimal investment rate

$$\iota = \frac{q-1}{\kappa}, \tag{51}$$

for the functional form $\Phi(\iota) = \frac{1}{\kappa}\log(\kappa\iota + 1)$ one obtains the "money equilibrium," in which money is a bubble with

$$q = \frac{1+\kappa a}{1+\kappa\sqrt{\rho}\,\tilde{\sigma}} \quad \text{and} \quad p = \frac{\tilde{\sigma} - \sqrt{\rho}}{\sqrt{\rho}}q.$$

The "money equilibrium" exists as long as $\tilde{\sigma} > \sqrt{\rho}$.

In addition, there exists a "moneyless equilibrium," obtained by setting $p = 0$ and solving (50) with (51) to obtain

$$q^0 = \frac{1+\kappa a}{1+\kappa\rho} \quad \text{and} \quad p^0 = 0.$$

Eq. (49) is no longer relevant because money is no longer an asset in which agents can put their wealth.

Note that the price of capital for the "moneyless" equilibrium is the same as in the real economy of Section 2. The growth rate of the economy in both equilibria is given by $g = \frac{1}{\kappa}\log q - \delta$. In the money equilibrium, q is lower and so is overall economic growth, but experts have to bear less risk.

4.3.3 Financial Deepening

Financial deepening or innovation that lower the amount of idiosyncratic risk households have to bear also lowers the value of money, p. However, it increases the price of capital q and with it, the investment rate, ι, and the overall economic growth rate g. Surprisingly, $q + p$ declines. That is, financial deepening lowers total wealth in the economy.

4.3.4 The Paradox of Prudence

The paradox of prudence arises when experts try to lower their risk by tilting their portfolio away from real investment and towards safe asset, money. Scaling back risky asset holding can be micro-prudent, but macro-*im*prudent. As experts try to lower their (idiosyncratic) risk exposure, the price of capital falls in Brunnermeier and Sannikov (2015a). This behavior lowers overall economic growth and with it the real return on money holdings. Since each individual expert takes prices and rates of return as given, they do not internalize this pecuniary externality. As shown in Brunnermeier and Sannikov (2015a), money holdings in this model are inefficiently high if $\tilde{\sigma}(1-\kappa\rho) > 2\sqrt{\rho}$. Our paradox of prudence is analogous to Keynes' Paradox of Thrift, but the former is about changes in portfolio choice and risk, while the latter refers to the consumption-savings decision.[r]

5. CRITICAL ASSESSMENT AND OUTLOOK

The economy with two types of agents gives rise to a number of general ideas—we describe these broader ideas in this section. We would like to make the point that continuous time has the capacity to build upon many ideas present in the literature, with fuller and less stylized models, and to drive a deeper understanding of financial frictions in the macroeconomy in new ways. We comment on how the methodology we presented above can be extended, and used fruitfully, in higher-dimensional state spaces. We also comment on the issues of uniqueness of equilibria and the characterization of the full set of equilibrium possibilities when multiple equilibria exist.

One key idea is that the wealth distribution in the economy matters. In the models we solved in Sections 2 and 3, the wealth distribution is characterized by a single state variable, the wealth share of experts η_t. When η_t is low, experts become undercapitalized. More generally, other sectors can become undercapitalized. Mian and Sufi (2009) argue that a big drag on the economy in the recent financial crisis has been the fact that many households are undercapitalized. Caballero et al. (2008) discuss how during Japan's lost

[r] Keynes' Paradox of Thrift states that an increase in the savings propensity can paradoxically lower aggregate savings. An increase in savings propensity lowers consumption demand. If the increased savings are "parked in (bubbly) money" instead of additional real investments, aggregate demand becomes depressed. This lowers aggregate income. Saving a fraction of now lower income can lower overall dollar savings.

decade it was the corporate sector that became undercapitalized. The general message here is that the wealth distribution across sectors matters for the level of economic activity—asset allocation—as well as the rates of earnings and risk exposures of various sectors. These earnings and risk exposures in turn drive the stochastic evolution of the wealth distribution.

The idea that the wealth distribution drives economic cycles is not new in the literature. Kiyotaki and Moore (1997) and Bernanke et al. (1999) consider the fluctuations of the wealth of a class of agents near the steady state. Of course, continuous-time methods facilitate a full solution of this type of a model. He and Krishnamurthy (2013) consider a model similar to the ones we presented here, but without asset misallocation and with a somewhat different assumption of the earnings of the households' holdings of expert equity.[s]

More broadly, several papers introduce the idea of intergenerational wealth distribution. This idea exists already in Bernanke and Gertler (1989), where the wealth of old entrepreneurs affects wages in the labor market, which in turn impact the accumulation of wealth by young entrepreneurs. Myerson (2012) builds a model with T generations of bankers, in which the wealth distribution evolves in cycles, causing cycles in real activities. When the wealth of old bankers is high, risk premia are low, and hence earnings of young bankers are low. Wealth distribution across sectors also matters. Brunnermeier and Sannikov (2015b) develop a rather symmetric model, in which there are two sectors that produce two essential goods, and either one of the sectors can become undercapitalized. Brunnermeier and Sannikov (2012) discuss the idea that multiple sectors can be undercapitalized, and that monetary policy can affect "bottlenecks" through its redistributive consequences. They envision an economy in which multiple assets are traded, and agents within various sectors hold specific portfolios, backed by a specific capital structure. Brunnermeier and Sannikov (2015a) provide formal backing of these ideas using a three-sector model, in which traded assets include capital, money and long-term bonds, and monetary policy can affect the prices of these assets (and hence affect the sectors that hold theses assets) in various ways.

This leads us to the obvious question about the capacity of continuous-time models to develop these complex ideas. Can continuous-time methods successfully handle models with multiple state variables, which describe, eg, the distribution of wealth across sectors together with the composition of productive capital? We believe that yes—we are highly optimistic about the potential of continuous-time models. Certainly, the curse of dimensionality still exists. However, models with as many as four state variables should be solvable through a system of partial differential equations in a matter of minutes, if not faster,

[s] In that model, households earn more than their required return, and therefore there is rationing of experts' shares. Effectively, the alternative assumption gives households some market power, which intermediaries do not have. This leads to a lower intermediary earnings rate and a slower recovery from crisis.

through the use of efficient computational methods. The authors of this chapter have some experience with computation, and on a personal level many possibilities seem feasible now which appeared out of reach 5 years ago. To gauge computational speed, DeMarzo and Sannikov (2016) solve a model with three state variables, using a system of two partial differential equations. In addition the procedure involves an integration step somewhat reminiscent of the "static step" of the procedure in Section 3.5. With $201 \times 51 \times 51$ grid points, the procedure using the explicit(!) method takes only a minute to compute the optimal contract. The implicit method of solving partial differential equations, which we use to compute the examples in Section 3.6 is significantly faster. For example, when solving a partial differential equation of the parabolic type in two dimensions (all equations for computing the value function using the iterative method are parabolic), with N grid points in space, one needs $O(N^2)$ grid points in time to ensure that the computational procedure is stable, when using the explicit method. In contrast, when using the implicit method, stability does not depend on the length of the time step, ie, the time step can be kept constant when greater resolution is required along the space dimension. Hence, we believe that by making a claim that models with four state variables are feasible to solve, we are in fact quite conservative.

We think that the iterative method, based on value function iteration for each type of agent, should prove quite fruitful. This method is based on backward induction starting from a terminal condition on the state space. At each new time interval, we start with value functions computed for the end of the interval. These value functions determine the agents' incentives through their continuation values from various portfolio choices. As a result, we can determine at each time point the allocations of assets and risk consistent of equilibrium—this is the "static step"—and hence we can compute the value function one period earlier. We see this method as fairly general and suitable for multiple dimensions.

In contrast, the shooting method aims at solving for the fixed point—equilibrium value functions and allocations in an infinite-horizon economy—up front. The straightforward extension of this method to multidimensional state spaces may be difficult to implement, as one would have to guess functions that match boundary conditions on the entire periphery of the state space, instead of just two endpoints. Nevertheless, procedures that use variations of policy iteration may lead to an efficient way of solving for a fixed point.

What makes continuous-time models particularly tractable is that transitions are local (when shocks are Brownian)—hence it is possible to determine the agents' optimal decisions and solve for their value functions by evaluating only first and second derivatives. In discrete time, with discrete transitions, the agents' decisions at any point may depend on entire value functions.

What about environments with so many dimensions that the straightforward discretization of the state space makes computation infeasible, due to the curse of dimensionality? Here, we are curious about the idea of describing state variables through certain essential moments—following the suggestions of Krusell and Smith (1998). We have not processed this possibility sufficiently to comment on it in the chapter, but generally we are very eager to know about ways to choose moments that describe the state space in a meaningful way for a given model. We should say, however, that continuous time can be helpful here as well, for describing continuation values and prices as functions of moments.

We finish this section by discussing the question of equilibrium uniqueness in the model we presented and in more complex models we envision. First, consider a finite-horizon economy that we are solving for via an iterative procedure. The procedure has two steps—the time step of value function iteration and the static step that determines prices and allocation. The time step cannot be a source of nonuniqueness—given continuation values, transition probabilities and payoff flows, the value function one period earlier is fully determined. The static step may or may not lead to nonuniqueness. In the model of Section 3 there are multiple nonstationary equilibria. For example, at any time point, the price of capital q_t can jump. If q_t jumps up by 10% then the risk-free asset must have an instantaneous return of 10% as well to ensure that the markets for capital and the risk-free asset clear. Of course, by the market-clearing condition for output (43), the price of capital q_t must correspond to the allocation of capital $\psi_t \in [0, 1]$. The allocation itself must be justified by the local volatility of capital, so that all agents have incentives to hold their portfolios. However, the possibility of jumps opens up room to many possibilities.

We compute the Markov equilibrium, in which prices and allocations are functions of η. If so, then the price of capital $q(\eta_t)$ must satisfy the differential equation that follows from (41) and (42). Notice that there are two values of $\sigma + \sigma_t^q$ consistent with the quadratic Eq. (41), positive and negative. We select the positive value, since otherwise amplification is negative, in the sense that a positive fundamental shock would result in a drop in the value of capital. Hence, the equilibrium we compute is the unique Markov equilibrium, in which the return on capital is always positively correlated with fundamental shocks to capital.

In more general models, we envision that some of the same forces are present. We also anticipate that, when there are multiple equilibria, it may be of interest to characterize the whole set of equilibria via an appropriate recursive structure. To answer this question, one may need to construct/compute a correspondence from the state space to the vector of equilibrium payoffs of all agent types. We envision that this correspondence can be found recursively by solving for the boundaries of attainable equilibrium payoff sets backwards in time, but the details of this procedure are certainly work in progress.

ACKNOWLEDGMENTS

We are grateful to comments by Zhiguo He, Lunyang Huang, Ji Huang, Falk Mazelis, Sebastian Merkel, Greg Phelan, and Christian Wolf, as well as the editors John Taylor and Harald Uhlig.

REFERENCES

Achdou, Y., Han, J., Lasry, J.M., Lions, P.L., Moll, B., 2015. Heterogeneous agent models in continuous time. Working Paper, Princeton University.

Adrian, T., Boyarchenko, N., 2012. Intermediary leverage cycles and financial stability. Working Paper, Federal Reserve Bank of New York.

Adrian, T., Boyarchenko, N., 2013. Intermediary balance sheets. FRB of New York Staff Report, Number 651.

Aiyagari, S.R., 1994. Uninsured idiosyncratic risk and aggregate saving. Q. J. Econ. 00335533. 109 (3), 659–684. http://www.jstor.org/stable/2118417.

Angeletos, G.M., 2007. Uninsured idiosyncratic investment risk and aggregate saving. Rev. Econ. Dyn. 1094-2025. 10 (1), 1–30. http://dx.doi.org/10.1016/j.red.2006.11.001. http://www.sciencedirect.com/science/article/B6WWT-4MR7DG4-1/2/321ab3b301256e6f17bf2b4003c7218d.

Basak, S., Cuoco, D., 1998. An equilibrium model with restricted stock market participation. Rev. Financ. Stud. 08939454. 11 (2), 309–341.http://www.jstor.org/stable/2646048.

Bernanke, B., Gertler, M., 1989. Agency costs, net worth, and business fluctuations. Am. Econ. Rev. 79 (1), 14–31.

Bernanke, B., Gertler, M., Gilchrist, S., 1999. The financial accelerator in a quantitative business cycle framework. In: Taylor, J.B., Woodford, M. (Eds.), Handbook of Macroeconomics. 1, Chapter 21. Elsevier, Amsterdam, The Netherlands, pp. 1341–1393.

Bewley, T.F., 1977. The permanent income hypothesis: a theoretical formulation. J. Econ. Theory 0022-0531. 16 (2), 252–292. http://dx.doi.org/10.1016/0022-0531(77)90009-6. http://www.sciencedirect.com/science/article/B6WJ3-4CYGG80-1SC/2/301c685f23755550247618450b40f612.

Bewley, T.F., 1980. The optimum quantity of money. In: Kareken, J.H., Wallace, N. (Eds.), Models of Monetary Economies. Federal Reserve Bank of Minneapolis, pp. 169–210. http://minneapolisfed.org/publications_papers/books/models/pcc169.pdf.

Bianchi, J., 2011. Overborrowing and systemic externalities in the business cycle. Am. Econ. Rev. 101 (7), 3400–3426. http://dx.doi.org/10.1257/aer.101.7.3400.

Black, F., Scholes, M., 1973. The picing of options and corporate liabilities. J. Polit. Econ. 00223808. 81 (3), 637–654. http://www.jstor.org/stable/1831029.

Brock, W., Mirman, L., 1972. Optimal economic growth and uncertainty: the discounted case. J. Econ. Theory 4 (3), 479–513.

Brunnermeier, M.K., Sannikov, Y., 2012. Redistributive monetary policy. In: Jackson Hole Symposium.1, pp. 331–384.

Brunnermeier, M.K., Sannikov, Y., 2014. A macroeconomic model with a financial sector. Am. Econ. Rev. 104 (2), 379–421.

Brunnermeier, M.K., Sannikov, Y., 2015a. The I theory of money. Working Paper, Princeton University.

Brunnermeier, M.K., Sannikov, Y., 2015b. International credit flows and pecuniary externalities. Am. Econ. J. Macroecon. 7 (1), 297–338. http://dx.doi.org/10.1257/mac.20140054.

Brunnermeier, M.K., Sannikov, Y., 2016. On the optimal inflation rate. Am. Econ. Rev. 106 (5), 484–489.

Caballero, R.J., Hoshi, T., Kashyap, A.K., 2008. Zombie lending and depressed restructuring in Japan. Am. Econ. Rev. 98 (5), 1943–1977. http://dx.doi.org/10.1257/aer.98.5.1943.

Candler, G.V., 1999. Finite-difference methods for continuous-time dynamic programming problems. In: Marimon, R., Scott, A. (Eds.), Computational Methods for the Study of Dynamic Economies. Cambridge University Press, Cambridge, England, pp. 172–194.

Chandler, L.V., 1948. The Economics of Money and Banking. Harper Brothers Publishers, New York, US.

Cox, J.C., Ingersoll, J.E., Ross, S.A., 1985. A theory of the term structure of interest rates. Econometrica 53 (2), 385–408.

DeMarzo, P., Sannikov, Y., 2016. Learning, termination and payout policy in dynamic incentive contracts. Working Paper, Princeton University.

Diamond, P.A., 1965. National debt in a neoclassical growth model. Am. Econ. Rev. 00028282. 55 (5), 1126–1150. http://www.jstor.org/stable/1809231.

DiTella, S., 2013. Uncertainty shocks and balance sheet recessions. Working paper, Stanford University.
Drechsler, I., Savov, A., Schnabl, P., 2016. A model of monetary policy and risk premia. J. Finance (forthcoming).
Fernandez-Villaverde, J., Rubio-Ramirez, J.F., 2010. Macroeconomics and volatility: data, models, and estimation. Working Paper, University of Pennsylvania.
Fisher, I., 1933. The debt-deflation theory of great depressions. Econometrica 00129682. 1 (4), 337–357. http://www.jstor.org/stable/1907327.
Gurley, J.G., Shaw, E.S., 1955. Financial aspects of economic development. Am. Econ. Rev. 00028282. 45 (4), 515–538. http://www.jstor.org/stable/1811632.
He, Z., Krishnamurthy, A., 2012. A model of capital and crises. Rev. Econ. Stud. 79 (2), 735–777.
He, Z., Krishnamurthy, A., 2013. Intermediary asset pricing. Am. Econ. Rev. 103 (2), 732–770.
He, Z., Krishnamurthy, A., 2014. A macroeconomic framework for quantifying systemic risk. Working Paper, National Bureau of Economic Research.
Hicks, J., 1937. Mr. Keynes and the 'classics': a suggested interpretation. Econometrica 3 (2), 147–159.
Huang, J., 2014. Banking and shadow banking. Working Paper, Princeton University.
Isohätälä, J., Milne, A., Roberston, D., 2014. The net worth trap: investment and output dynamics in the presence of financing constraints. Working Paper.
Isohätälä, J., Klimenko, N., Milne, A., 2016. Post-crisis macrofinancial modelling: continuous time approaches. In: Emmanuel, H., Philip, M., John, O.S.W., Sergei, F., Meryem, D. (Eds.), Handbook of Post-Crisis Financial Modelling, Chapter 10. Palgrave Macmillan, London, UK, pp. 235–282.
Judd, K.L., 1998. Numerical Methods in Economics. MIT Press, Cambridge, MA.
Keynes, J.M., 1936. The General Theory of Employment, Interest and Money. Macmillan, London, UK.
Kindleberger, C.P., 1978. Manias, Panics, and Crashes: A History of Financial Crises. Basic Books, New York, US.
Kiyotaki, N., Moore, J., 1997. Credit cycles. J. Polit. Econ. 00223808. 105 (2), 211–248. http://www.jstor.org/stable/2138839.
Klimenko, N., Pfeil, S., Rochet, J.C., 2015. Bank capital and aggregate credit. Working Paper, University of Zürich.
Krusell, P., Smith Jr., A.A., 1998. Income and wealth heterogeneity in the macroeconomy. J. Polit. Econ. 00223808. 106 (5), 867–896. http://www.jstor.org/stable/2991488.
Kydland, F.E., Prescott, E.C., 1982. Time to build and aggregate fluctuations. Econometrica 00129682. 50 (6), 1345–1370. http://www.jstor.org/stable/1913386.
Leland, H., 1994. Corporate debt value, bond covenants, and optimal capital structure. J. Finance 49 (4), 1213–1252.
Maggiori, M., 2013. Financial intermediation, international risk sharing, and reserve currencies. Working Paper, NYU.
Mankiw, G., Romer, D., 1991. New Keynesian Economics, Vol. 1: Imperfect Competition and Sticky Prices. MIT Press, Cambridge, MA.
Markowitz, H., 1952. Portfolio selection. J. Financ. 00221082. 7 (1), 77–91. http://www.jstor.org/stable/2975974.
Mendoza, E.G., 2010. Sudden stops, financial crisis, and leverage. Am. Econ. Rev. 100, 1941–1966.
Mian, A., Sufi, A., 2009. The consequences of mortgage credit expansion: evidence from the US mortgage default crisis. Q. J. Econ. 124 (4), 1449–1496.
Minsky, H.P., 1957. Central banking and money market changes. Q. J. Econ. 00335533. 71 (2), 171–187. http://www.jstor.org/stable/1883812.
Mittnik, S., Semmler, W., 2013. The real consequences of financial stress. J. Econ. Dyn. Control. 37 (8), 1479–1499.
Moll, B., 2014. Productivity losses from financial frictions: can self-financing undo capital misallocation? Am. Econ. Rev. 104 (10), 3186–3221.
Moreira, A., Savov, A., 2016. The macroeconomics of shadow banking. J. Finance (forthcoming).
Myerson, R.B., 2012. A model of moral hazard credit cycles. J. Polit. Econ. 120 (5), 847–878.
Oberman, A.M., 2006. Convergent difference schemes for degenerate elliptic and parabolic equations: Hamilton-Jacobi equations and free boundary problem. SIAM J. Numer. Anal. 44 (2), 879–889.

Patinkin, D., 1956. Money, Interest, and Prices: An Integration of Monetary and Value Theory. Row, Peterson, Evanston, IL.
Phelan, G., 2014. Financial intermediation, leverage, and macroeconomic instability. Working Paper, Williams College.
Rappoport, D., Walsh, K., 2012. A discrete-time macroeconomic model with a financial sector. Mimeo, Yale University.
Samuelson, P.A., 1958. An exact consumption-loan model of interest with or without the social contrivance of money. J. Polit. Econ. 00223808. 66 (6), 467–482. http://www.jstor.org/stable/1826989.
Sannikov, Y., 2008. A continuous-time version of the principal-agent problem. Rev. Econ. Stud. 0034652775 (3), 957–984. http://www.jstor.org/stable/20185061.
Silva, D.H., 2016. The Risk Channel of Unconventional Monetary Policy. Working Paper, MIT.
Sims, C.A., 1980. Macroeconomics and reality. Econometrica 48 (1), 1–48.
Solow, R.M., 1956. A contribution to the theory of economic growth. Q. J. Econ. 00335533. 70 (1), 65–94. http://www.jstor.org/stable/1884513.
Stokey, N., Lucas, R., 1989. Recursive Methods in Economics Dynamics. Harvard University Press, Cambridge, MA.
Taylor, J.B., 1979. Estimation and control of a macroeconomic model with rational expectations. Econometrica 00129682, 14680262. 47 (5), 1267–1286. http://www.jstor.org/stable/1911962.
Tobin, J., 1969. A general equilibrium approach to monetary theory. J. Money Credit Bank. 1 (1), 15–29.
Werning, I., 2012. Managing a liquidity trap: monetary and fiscal policy. Working Paper, MIT.
Woodford, M., 2003. Interest and Prices: Foundations of a Theory of Monetary Policy. Princeton University Press, Princeton, NJ.

CHAPTER 19

Housing and Macroeconomics

M. Piazzesi*,†, M. Schneider*,†
*Stanford University, Stanford, CA, United States
†NBER, Cambridge, MA, United States

Contents

Handbook of Macroeconomics, Volume 2B
ISSN 1574-0048, http://dx.doi.org/10.1016/bs.hesmac.2016.06.003

Abstract

This chapter surveys the literature on housing in macroeconomics. We first collect facts on house prices and quantities in both the time series and the cross section of households and housing markets. We then present a theoretical model of frictional housing markets with heterogeneous agents that nests or provides background for many studies. Finally, we describe quantitative results obtained during the last 15 years on household behavior, business cycle dynamics, and asset pricing, as well as boom bust episodes.

Keywords

Booms and busts in housing markets, land prices, market segmentation, mortgages, residential investment, expectations, collateral constraints, illiquidity, transaction costs

JEL Classification Codes

R2, R3, E2, E3, E4, G1

1. INTRODUCTION

The first volume of the *Handbook of Macroeconomics*, published in 1999, contains essentially no references to housing. This statistic accurately summarizes the state of the field at the time. Of course, housing was not entirely absent from macroeconomic studies, which typically account for all production, consumption and wealth in an economy. The lack of references instead reflected the treatment of housing as simply one component of capital, consumption or household wealth that does not deserve special attention.

At the turn of the millennium, housing was implicitly present in three loosely connected literatures. One is work on aggregate fluctuations that studies the sources of business cycles and the response of the economy to fiscal and monetary policy. In the typical 20th century model, residential structures were part of capital, or sometimes "home capital" (together with consumer durables). Housing services were part of nondurables (or home good) consumption. Models of financial frictions and the role of capital as collateral focused on borrowing by firms. Volatility of house prices played no role—in fact, any volatility of asset prices was largely a sideshow.

Second, housing was implicitly present in the large body of work on asset pricing concerned with differences in average returns and price volatility across assets. Studies in this area used to largely stay away from properties of house prices and returns. At the same time, a common modeling exercise identified a claim to all consumption with equity and tried to explain the volatility of its price with a consumption-based stochastic discount factor. Housing thus played an implicit role as part of payoffs and risk adjustment. Finally, there is work on heterogenous households that seeks to understand the role of frictions and policy for inequality as well as distributional effects of shocks. Here, housing was included as a large implicit component of household wealth as well as a share of consumption.

The first half of the 2000s saw not only the largest housing boom in postwar US history, but also new research that introduced an explicit role for housing in macroeconomics. The new research studies the interaction of house prices and collateralized household borrowing with business cycles and monetary policy. It also explores how the role of housing as a consumption good as well as a collateralizable asset affects savings, portfolio choice, and asset pricing. By the time the US housing boom turned into a spectacular bust in 2007, housing was already a prominent topic in macroeconomics. The Great Recession added important new data points and further underscored the importance and unique properties of housing. As a result, housing now routinely receives special attention in macroeconomic discussions.

While the new literature grew out of the three lines of research described earlier, the focus on housing brought out several distinctive features. First, it naturally pushed researchers toward integration of themes and tools from all three lines of research. It is difficult to describe household behavior while ignoring uncertainty about house prices, or to think about mortgage debt without heterogeneous agents. Many papers surveyed below thus employ tools from financial economics to study exposure to uncertainty, and many quantitative models are analyzed with computational techniques that allow rich heterogeneity within the household sector.

The second feature is familiar from urban economics: "the housing market" is really a collection of many markets that differ by geography as well as other attributes. Disaggregating not only the household sector but also the housing stock provides valuable insights into the transmission of shocks and alters policy conclusions. For example, shocks to financial intermediaries or policies that change the cost of mortgage credit might have stronger effects on prices in markets where the typical buyer is also a borrower. Moreover, those shocks might have larger aggregate effects if their impact cannot be shared across subpopulation of agents. Availability of new large scale micro data sets has made it possible to explicitly study the interactions of many agents in many markets, and derive the aggregate effects of those interactions.

A third, related, feature is that the literature on housing has brought to bear a lot of evidence from the cross section of markets in a single episode to complement time series evidence that is common in macroeconomics. To illustrate, one can learn a lot about the role of technology shocks for residential investment from recurrent time series patterns in postwar history. In contrast, to assess the role of recent financial innovation for house prices, such patterns are less informative. Fortunately, though, we can learn from cross-sectional patterns in financing and prices across submarkets and types of households.

The literature shows how both time series and cross-sectional patterns on housing markets lend themselves to the same style of analysis that is common elsewhere in macroeconomics. Reduced form statistical tools are used to document facts and sometimes to isolate certain properties of equilibrium relationships. Insights on the quantitative importance of different mechanisms as well as policy counterfactuals are derived from multivariate structural models. In many ways, modeling the cross-sectional comovement in a single period of, say, mortgage borrowing and wealth across households and house prices across market segments, is conceptually similar to modeling the time series comovement of, say, residential and business investment, GDP and house prices in postwar history. Both exercises require tracing out the effect of exogenous variation in some features of the environment jointly on many endogenous variables.

This chapter describes work on housing in macroeconomics in three parts. Section 2 collects the new facts that emerge once disaggregation makes housing explicit. We first document business cycle properties of housing consumption, residential investment and mortgage debt. We then look at the dynamics of house prices at the national, regional and within-city level, and compare price volatility and trading volume for housing and securities. Finally, we document the dual role of housing as a consumption good as well as an asset in household portfolios.

Section 3 describes a theoretical framework that nests or provides background for many studies in the literature. It allows for four special features of housing that are motivated by facts from Section 2: *indivisibility*, *nontradability of dividends*, *illiquidity*, and *collateralizability*. Indeed, many homeowners own only their residence, directly consume its dividend in form of housing services and bear its idiosyncratic risk. Moreover houses are relatively costly to trade and easy to pledge as collateral even for individual households. In contrast, securities such as equity and bonds are typically held in diversified portfolios, have tradable payoffs, are traded often at low cost, and are harder to use as collateral, at least for individual investors.

Section 4 summarizes quantitative results derived from versions of the general framework over the last two decades or so. While no study contains all the ingredients introduced in Section 3, each one quantifies one or more of the tradeoffs discussed there. We start by reviewing work on consumption, savings and portfolio choice. We also consider mortgage choice and the role of financial innovation for household decisions. We then move on to general equilibrium analysis of the business cycle, monetary policy and asset prices. Finally, we consider boom–bust episodes, with an emphasis on the 1970s and 2000s US housing cycles.

We interpret results from different types of quantitative exercises in light of the general framework. One approach studies structural relationships with an explicit shock structure. For example, large bodies of work assess the ability of life cycle models of consumption, savings and portfolio choice to explain cross-sectional patterns as well as the ability of DSGE models to match time series patterns. An alternative approach investigates families of Euler equations for different agents and/or markets to reconcile allocations and asset prices. A third approach tries to isolate properties of the decision rules or the equilibrium law of motion with reduced form approaches.

What have we learned so far? We highlight here two key takeaways from the new literature that underlie the quantitative successes reported in detail below. First, *frictions matter*: Quantitative modeling of household behavior now routinely relies on collateral constraints, incomplete markets and transaction costs as key ingredients. Incompleteness of markets means in particular that homeowners bear property-level price risk. A large body of reduced form evidence provides additional support for this approach. Second, *heterogeneity of households matters*: Models with heterogeneous households and frictions introduce powerful new amplification and propagation mechanisms. In particular, they provide more scope for effects of shocks to the financial sector which have become important in accounts of postwar US history, especially the recent boom–bust cycle.

We also conclude that making housing explicit improves our understanding of classic macroeconomic questions, previously studied only with models that provide an implicit role for housing. For thinking about business cycles, the comovement and relative volatility of residential and business investment provide discipline on model structure. For thinking about asset pricing, the role of housing as a consumption good as well as a collateralizable asset generate the type of slow moving state variables for model dynamics that are needed in order to understand observed low frequency changes in the risk return tradeoffs for many assets, including housing itself. Finally, financial frictions in the household sector change the transmission of both aggregate and distributional shocks and policy interventions, especially to consumption.

At the same time, many open questions remain and there is ample opportunity for future research. One issue is the tradeoff between tractability and detail faced by any macroeconomic study. There are three areas in particular where more work is needed to converge on the right level of abstraction—with possibly different outcomes depending on the question. One is aggregation across housing markets: do we gain, for example, from building more models that treat the United States as a collection of small countries identified with, say, states or metropolitan areas? Another area is choosing dimensions of household heterogeneity: since observable demographic characteristics such as age, income, and wealth explain only a small share of cross-sectional variation, how should unobservable heterogeneity be accommodated? Finally, the majority of studies reviewed below capture financial frictions by assuming short term debt and financial shocks as changes to maximum loan-to-value ratios. Given the rich and evolving contractual detail we see in the data, what are the essential elements that should enter macroeconomic models?

A major outstanding puzzle is the volatility of house prices—including but not only over the recent boom–bust episode. Rational expectations models to date cannot account for house price volatility—they inevitably run into "volatility puzzles" for housing much like for other assets. Postulating latent "housing preference shocks" helps understand how models work when prices move a lot, but is ultimately not a satisfactory foundation for policy analysis. Moreover, from model calculations as well as survey evidence, we now know that details of the expectation formation by households—and possibly lenders and developers—play a key role. A promising agenda for research is to develop models of expectation formation that can be matched to data on both market outcomes and survey expectations. A final point is that most progress we report is in making sense of household behavior. The supply side of housing as well as credit to fund housing has received relatively less attention, another interesting direction for future work.

To keep the length of chapter manageable, we have narrowed focus along some dimensions where other recent survey papers already exist. In particular, the *Handbook of Urban and Regional Economics* contains chapters on search models of housing (Han and Strange, 2015) as well as US housing policy (Olsen and Zabel, 2015).[a] Since we focus on work that is already published, we have also left out much of the important emerging literature on the housing bust and Great Recession, as well as policy at the zero lower bound for nominal interest rates. Finally, our chapter deals almost exclusively with facts and quantitative studies about the United States. This reflects the focus of the literature, which in turn has been driven in part by availability of data. Another exciting task for future research is to use the tools discussed in this chapter to study the large variation in housing market structure and housing finance across countries, surveyed for example by Badarinza et al. (2016).

2. FACTS

2.1 Quantities

Fig. 1 plots the aggregate expenditure share on housing from the National Income and Product Account (NIPA) tables. The numbers in NIPA table 2.3.5 are based on survey data. The questionnaires in these surveys (for example, the Residential Finance Survey conducted by the Census Bureau) ask renters about their actual monthly rent payments. These payments are imputed to comparable owner-occupied units (Mayerhauser and Reinsdorf, 2007). The sample consists of quarterly data from 1959:Q1 to 2013:Q4.

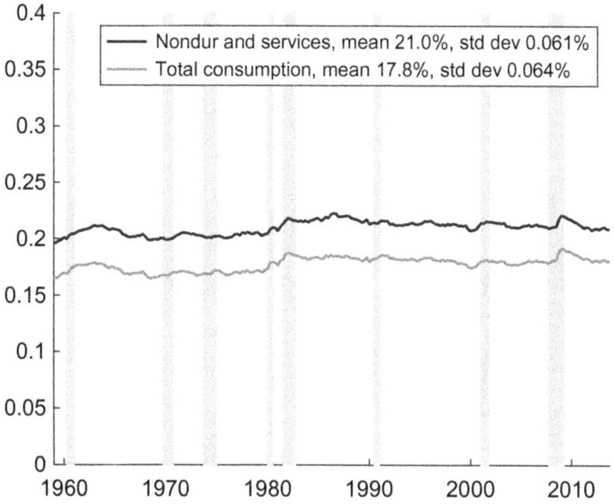

Fig. 1 Aggregate expenditure share on housing, 1959:Q1–2014:Q4.

[a] The same handbook contains a chapter on housing, finance and the macroeconomy (Davis and Van Nieuwerburgh, 2015) that also discusses some of the material covered in the present chapter.

We compute the expenditure share in two ways. The blue line shows housing expenditures as a fraction of expenditures on nondurables and services. This series has a mean of 21% and a standard deviation of 0.061%. The green line shows housing services as a fraction of total consumption (including durables). This series has a slightly lower mean of 17.8% and a bit higher standard deviation of 0.064%. The yellow bars indicate NBER recessions.

The overall impression from Fig. 1 is that the aggregate expenditure share is pretty flat over time. The expenditure share on housing is also similar across households in micro data, as shown by Piazzesi et al. (2007). Their table A.1 shows evidence from the Consumer Expenditure Survey, where the definition of housing expenditures depends on tenure choice. The CEX asks renters about their rent payments, while owner occupiers are asked about their interest payments on mortgages and other lines of credit, property taxes, insurance, ground rents, and expenses for maintenance or repairs. Davis and Ortalo-Magné (2011) use micro data on the expenditure share of renter households alone. The paper shows that individual expenditure shares based on the 1980, 1990, and 2000 Decennial Housing Surveys do not vary much within or across the top 50 US metropolitan statistical areas.

Fig. 2 plots three series: residential investment, nonresidential investment and output. The series are from NIPA table 1.1.3; they are all logged and detrended using the Hodrick–Prescott filter. The figure illustrates that both investment series are more volatile than output. Also, residential investment is twice as volatile as nonresidential investment. The volatility of residential investment is 9.7%, while nonresidential investment

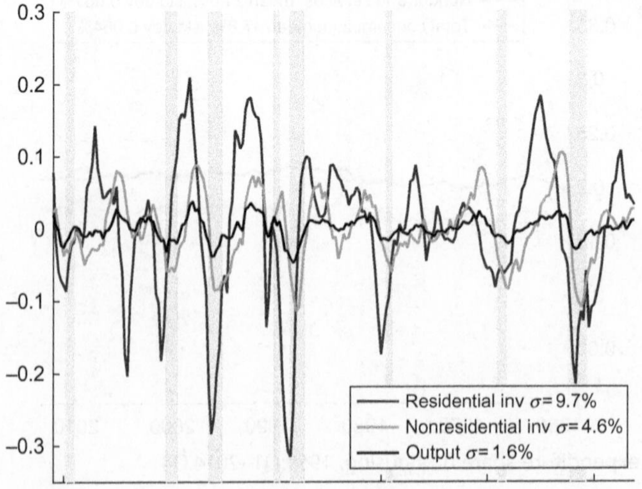

Fig. 2 Aggregate residential investment, nonresidential investment, and output; logged and detrended with Hodrick–Prescott filter.

has a volatility of 4.6% and the volatility of output is 1.6%. The figure also shows that the series for residential investment tends to increase before nonresidential investment and output, and it tends to decrease before the other two series. In other words, residential investment leads the cycle.

Once investment has created housing capital, it stays around for a long time. As reported by Fraumeni (1997), structures depreciate at rates of 1.5–3% per year. The depreciation rates for nonresidential capital are higher, between 10% and 30%. Moreover, housing combines housing capital with land, which is a fixed factor.

2.1.1 Constraints on the Supply of Housing

The degree to which new developments can increase the supply of housing varies across geographic areas. For example, developers in Indianapolis and Omaha find it easier to buy land and construct new homes than developers in San Francisco and Boston. There are two popular indices that carefully measure such housing supply constraints.

The first index is by Saiz (2010) and captures physical constraints. These geographical constraints capture two main features of land topology that make new developments difficult or impossible. The first feature is the presence of water. Saiz measures the area within 50 km from cities that is covered by oceans, lakes, rivers, and other water bodies such as wetlands. The second feature of land topology is steep slopes. Saiz computes the share of the area with a slope above 15% within a 50-km radius around an MSA.

The second measure of supply constraints captures regulatory restrictions. These are measured by the Wharton Residential Urban Land Regulation Index created by Gyourko et al. (2008). This index captures the stringency of residential growth controls in terms of zoning restrictions or project approval practices.

2.2 Prices

Fig. 3 shows the price–dividend ratio for stocks as a green line which measured on the left axis. The figure also shows the price–rent ratio for housing as a blue line with units indicated on the right axis. The figure illustrates the large volatility of the two series. The price–dividend ratio for stocks uses data from the Flow of Funds and represents the overall valuation of companies in the United States. The dividend series includes net repurchases. The price–dividend ratio fluctuates between 20 and 65, as measured on the left axis.

The numerator of the price–rent series for housing is the value of residential housing owned by partnerships, sole proprietors, and nonfinancial corporations, which are landlords for many rental units, as measured by the Flow of Funds. The denominator of the price–rent series is rents from the NIPA table 2.3.5, which includes actual rent payments as well as imputed rents for owner–occupiers (as discussed in the context of Fig. 1). The price–rent ratio fluctuates between 11 and 19, as measured on the right axis.

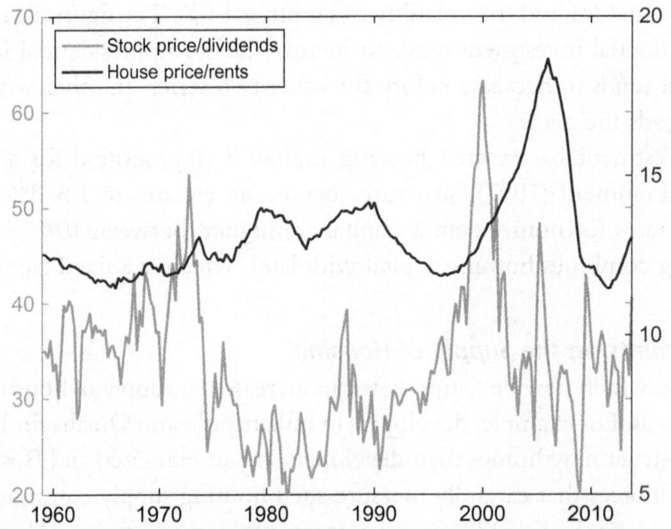

Fig. 3 Aggregate price/dividend ratio for stocks and price/rent ratio for housing.

The two valuation ratios often move inversely. For example, stocks tanked during the housing booms in the 1970s and 2000s. By contrast, stocks appreciated during the 1990s while housing did poorly. The recent boom–bust episode in housing stands out in the postwar experience.

2.2.1 Excess Volatility of Individual House Prices

House prices, like the prices of other assets, are highly volatile. The prices of individual houses are especially volatile. The volatility of various house price indices is smaller, but still a challenge for economic models—this is the excess volatility puzzle.

Most house price indices are constructed from repeat sales—average price changes in houses that sell more than once in the sample. CoreLogic constructs such city-wide indices for many metropolitan areas, various tiers of these markets, as well as the US national index. These indices are published as the S&P/Case–Shiller Home Price Indices by Standard & Poor's. The Federal Housing Finance Agency also constructs such indices from repeat sales or refinancings on the same properties (formerly called the OFHEO index). Zillow also publishes such indices for cities, states or the nation.

Case and Shiller (1989) estimate the standard deviation of annual percentage changes in individual house prices to be close to 15%. The paper concludes that individual house prices are similar to individual stock prices that are also very volatile. City-wide indices are less volatile than individual house prices. Flavin and Yamashita (2002) estimate a 14% volatility for individual house prices in their table 1A. Their table 1B reports a 4% volatility for Atlanta, 6% for Chicago, 5% for Dallas, and 7% for San Francisco. Landvoigt et al. (2015) estimate the volatility of individual house

Table 1 House price volatility

	Individual house	City	State	Aggregate
Volatility	14%	7%	5%	2–3%

Note: This table is from tables B1 and B2 in Piazzesi et al. (2007).

prices in different years. Their table 1 shows estimates that range between 8–11% during the 2000s boom and 14% during the bust.

Compared to stocks, which commove strongly with the aggregate stock market, a larger share of the volatility in individual house prices is idiosyncratic, as documented in Case and Shiller (1989). Their evidence stems from regressions of individual house price change on city-wide price changes. The regressions have low R^2s: 7% for Atlanta, 16% for Chicago, 12% for Dallas, and 27% for San Francisco.

Table 1 summarizes information from tables B1 and B2 from Piazzesi et al. (2007). The table illustrates the rule of thumb that 1/2 of the volatility in individual house prices is city-level variation, while 1/4 of the individual volatility is aggregate house price variation. This volatility decomposition illustrates the importance to understand the variation within narrow locations or individual houses. The high volatility of individual house prices together with high transaction costs lead to low Sharpe ratios (defined as average excess return on an asset, divided by its volatility) on housing. In other words, individual houses are not as attractive as an investment.

Idiosyncratic shocks to house prices are difficult to diversify. The problem with houses is that they are *indivisible*—they are sold in their entirety, not in small pieces. As a consequence, households own 100% of a specific house rather than small portions of many different houses. Moreover, the market for housing indices is not very liquid. In any given month, only a couple of futures contracts on city-wide house price indices trade on the Chicago Mercentile Exchange, if they trade at all.[b]

The ease of diversification distinguishes houses from other assets such as stocks. For example, households can save a small amount of money and invest it in a stock market index (such as the S&P 500) that tracks the value of a large stock portfolio. Alternatively, households can buy a few shares from several companies. The conventional wisdom in finance is that a small number of different stocks—such as five or six companies—are sufficient to achieve a high degree of diversification in a portfolio.

2.2.2 Momentum and Reversal

House prices have more momentum than other assets and also exhibit long-run reversal. The changes in log real prices of houses are more highly serially correlated compared to other assets. Case and Shiller (1989) provide the first evidence of such high serial

[b] The data on volume in these markets is here http://www.cmegroup.com/market-data/volume-open-interest/real-estate-volume.html

correlation. They document that a change in the log real price index in a given year and a given city tends to be followed by a change in the same direction the following year between 25% and 50% as large. Englund and Ioannides (1997) provide cross-country evidence where changes are followed by changes between 23% and 74% the next year. Glaeser et al. (2014) find changes the next year between 60% and 80%.

Cutler et al. (1991) compare the serial correlation in housing markets to that in other asset markets across many countries. For example, stocks, bonds and foreign exchange exhibit weak momentum for horizons less than a year. The monthly autocorrelation in excess stock returns is 10%, for US bonds it is 3%, 24% for foreign bonds, and 7% for foreign exchange. The excess returns on all these assets are essentially uncorrelated from year to year. In contrast, the excess returns on housing in their table 4 has an autocorrelation of 21% from year to year.

Over longer periods, house prices experience reversal. Englund and Ioannides (1997) document that changes in log real prices are followed by changes in the opposite direction after 5 years. Glaeser et al. (2014) also provide evidence of such reversal in their table 4. They estimate the autocorrelation of real house price changes over 5 years to be −0.80.

2.2.3 Predictable Excess Returns on Housing

The excess returns on many assets, including housing, are predictable. Case and Shiller (1989) show that excess returns on the city indices are predictable with excess returns in the previous year in their table 3. Case and Shiller (1990) provide further evidence of predictability for excess returns. Their table 8 runs regressions of city excess returns on rent–price ratios and construction costs divided by price. The coefficient on the rent–price ratio is positive: a high rent–price ratio predicts high excess returns over the next year.

Cochrane (2011) compares the predictability regressions for houses and stocks. Table 2 replicates his table 3. "Houses" in Table 2 refers to the aggregate stock of housing in the United States. "Stocks" refers to a value-weighted index of US stocks. The estimated slope coefficients indicate that high rents relative to prices signal high subsequent returns, not lower subsequent rents. The results for housing in the left panel look remarkably similar to those in the right panel for stocks. The returns are predictable for both, but dividend growth and rent growth are not predictable. The ratio of rents or dividends to prices is highly persistent, but stationary.

Campbell et al. (2009) decompose house price movements with the Campbell–Shiller linearization of the one-period return

$$r_{t+1} \approx \text{const.} + \rho(p_{t+1} - d_{t+1}) - (p_t - d_t) + \Delta d_{t+1},$$

where $r_{t+1} = \log R_{t+1}$ is the log housing return, $p_t = \log(P_t)$ is the log house price, $d_t = \log(D_t)$ is the log rent, $\Delta d_{t+1} = d_{t+1} - d_t$ is rent growth, and $\rho = 0.98$ is a constant in the approximation. This return identity simply says that high returns either come from higher prices (future $p - d$), lower initial prices, or higher dividends.

Table 2 House price and stock price regressions

	Houses			Stocks		
	b	***t***	R^2	***b***	***t***	R^2
r_{t+1}	0.12	(2.52)	0.15	0.13	(2.61)	0.10
Δd_{t+1}	0.03	(2.22)	0.07	0.04	(0.92)	0.02
dp_{t+1}	0.90	(16.2)	0.90	0.94	(23.8)	0.91

Note: This table is table 3 from Cochrane (2011). It reports results from regressions of the form

$$x_{t+1} = a + b \times dp_t + \varepsilon_{t+1}$$

where dp_t is either the log rent–price ratio in the left panel or the log dividend–price ratio in the right panel. In the left panel, x_{t+1} is either log annual housing returns r_{t+1}, log rent growth Δd_{t+1}, or the log rent–price ratio dp_{t+1} measured with annual data for the aggregate stock of housing in the United States, 1960–2010, from http://www.lincolninst.edu/sub centers/land-values/rent-price-ratio.asp In the right panel, x_{t+1} is either log stock returns r_{t+1}, dividend growth Δd_{t+1} , or the log dividend–price ratio dp_{t+1} measured with annual CRSP value-weighted return data, 1947–2010.

By iterating the return identity forward, we get the present value identity

$$dp_t \approx \text{const.} + \sum_{j=1}^{k} \rho^{j-1} r_{t+j} - \sum_{j=1}^{k} \rho^{j-1} \Delta d_{t+j} + \rho^k dp_{t+k}, \tag{1}$$

where $dp_t = d_t - p_t$ is the log rent–price ratio. The present value identity holds state-by-state as well as in expectation. Any movement in the rent–price ratio on houses therefore has to be associated with a movement in either the conditional expected value of future returns r_{t+j}, expected future rent growth Δd_{t+j} or a bubbly anticipation of future high prices dp_{t+k}.

Campbell et al. estimate a vector-autoregression that includes real interest rates, rent growth and excess returns on housing. The housing data are from various metropolitan regions and US aggregate data. Based on the estimated VAR, the paper evaluates the expected infinite sums of future returns and future rent growth on the right-hand side of Eq. (1) for $k \to \infty$ by imposing the no-bubble condition[c] $\lim_{k\to\infty} \rho^k dp_{t+k} = 0$. It finds that movements in price–rent ratios can be attributed to a large degree to time variation in risk premia and less so to expectations of future rent growth. The time variation in real interest rates does not explain price–rent ratio movements. Their fig. 2 also shows that the 2000s boom is hard to explain through the lense of their estimated VAR which predicts low price–rent ratios throughout the 2000s.

[c] Giglio et al. (2016) provide direct evidence on the no-bubble condition in housing markets by comparing the value of freeholds (infinite maturity ownerships of houses) with the value of leaseholds with maturities over 700 years in the United Kingdom and Singapore.

2.2.4 Value of Land vs Structures

Fig. 4 plots the value of the residential housing stock together with its two components, the value of the residential structures and the value of land. All series are from the Flow of Funds and are reported as multiples of GDP. The figure illustrates that movements in the value of the residential housing stock are mostly due to movements in the value of land. The value of structures fluctuates much less. The figure again highlights the importance of the recent boom–bust episode in the postwar housing experience.

Knoll et al. (2014) collect data on house values in many industrialized countries going back to 1870. The paper documents that real house values in most countries were largely constant from the 19th to the mid 20th century. Over the postwar period, real house prices approximately tripled. The majority of this increase in real house prices is associated with rising land prices, while real construction costs have been roughly constant.

There is also large cross-sectional variation in the share of land in the overall house value. A key component of this variation is what realtors call "location, location, location": each location is unique. There may be attractive locations with unique characteristics in fixed supply such as lake and oceanfronts, locations with strict zoning rules, outstanding amenities such as good schools or opera houses, low crime, etc. For example, table 4 in Davis and Heathcote (2007) reports that houses in San Francisco have a land share of 80.4% while houses in Oklahoma City have a land share of 12.6%. The table shows that areas with higher land shares tend to have higher house prices, higher average house price growth and more volatile house prices.

Another source of cross-sectional variation is differences in the durability and/or attractiveness of the existing structures. For example, the building material for structures in earthquake prone areas like California tends to be wood, which is cheaper and

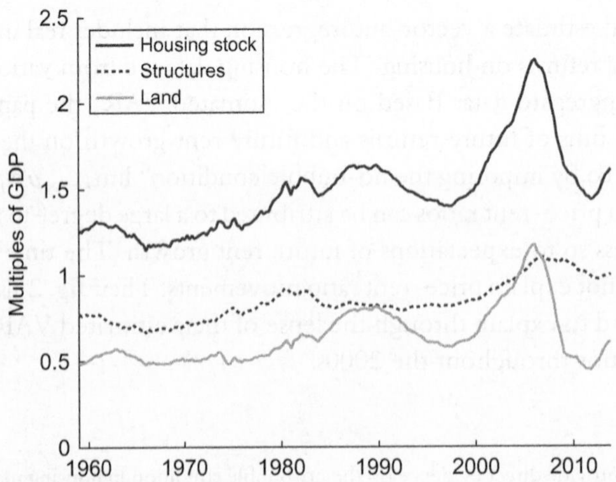

Fig. 4 The value of the residential housing stock together with its individual components, the value of residential structures, and the value of land.

deteriorates faster than brick which is used for most constructions in Pennsylvania. Architectural styles may also matter. For example, Victorian homes are valued at a premium, while 1950s postwar structures come at a discount.

2.2.5 Cross Section of House Prices

There are important cross-sectional patterns in house prices that help understand the variation across and within narrow areas. For example, during the 2000s, cheaper houses experienced a stronger boom–bust than more expensive houses. This pattern is different from previous boom–busts, where cheaper houses have experienced weaker boom–busts (such as in the 1970s.) Gentrification matters for poorer neighborhoods within a city that are in close proximity to more expensive neighborhoods. These low-price neighborhoods experience stronger booms–bust episodes than other low-price neighborhoods as well as high-price neighborhoods. Finally, the recent experience of the sand states challenges the notion that house prices in areas with an elastic housing supply should be less volatile.

Fig. 5 plots median house prices by city and tiers starting in the mid 1990s. The series are defined and constructed by Zillow Research. The top left panel shows that median house prices in the top tier of Los Angeles, California, gained 22% per year during the recent housing boom (1996–2006). The bottom tier gained *additional* 6 percentage points per year. During the housing bust (2006–11), the top tier made 4% capital losses per year, while the bottom tier dropped 5 percentage points more than the top tier.

The main stylized fact—houses in the bottom tier experienced a stronger boom–bust episode during the 2000s than houses in the upper tiers—can also be observed in other cities. In Las Vegas, houses in the bottom tier appreciated by 16% per year, while houses in the top tier only appreciated by 13%. During the bust, bottom-tier house prices fell by 14% while top-tier house prices fell only by 10% per year. In Chicago, capital gains across these tiers were the same on the way up, but there were larger losses in the lower tiers on the way down. In Omaha, the boom was not as pronounced, but still the bottom tier appreciated by 2 percentage points more than the top tier and was the only tier to experience a capital loss during the bust.

Landvoigt et al. (2015) estimate these patterns for the metro area of San Diego based on individual transaction data. The paper documents a roughly 20% difference between capital gains on the cheapest houses and most expensive houses between the years 2000 and 2005. The Zillow tiers group the cross section of houses and thereby reduce these cross-sectional differences. Kuminoff and Pope (2013) show a similar pattern for the land component of house values: cheap land appreciated more than expensive land during the 2000s boom.

Guerrieri et al. (2013) document that gentrification matters for poorer neighborhoods that are geographically close to high-price neighborhoods within a city. Their table 3

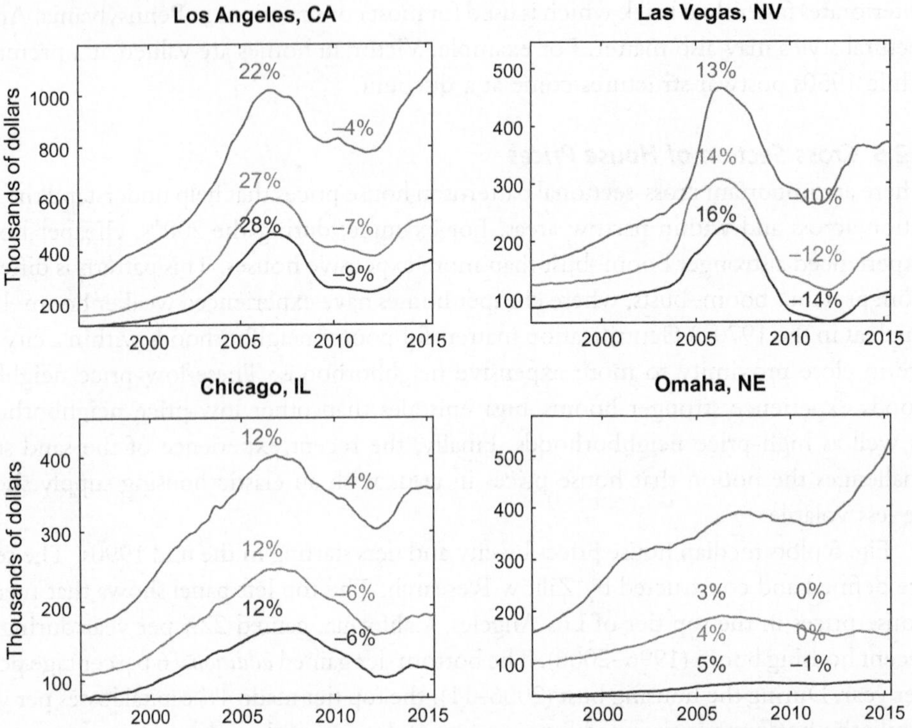

Fig. 5 Median house prices (in thousands of dollars) by city and tier: top tier (red (dark gray in the print version) line), medium tier (magenta (gray in the print version) line), and low tier (blue (black in the print version) line). The colored numbers indicate the tiered capital gains in percent per year during the housing boom (1996–2006) and during the bust (2006–11). *The data are from Zillow Research.*

shows that neighborhoods with an initially low price which were in close proximity to high-price neighborhoods appreciated more than otherwise similar initially low-price neighborhoods. For example, low-priced neighborhoods that were roughly 1 mile away from high-price neighborhoods appreciated by 12.4 percentage points more than low-priced neighborhoods that were roughly 4 miles away.

The recent experience in the "sand states"—Arizona, Florida, Nevada, and inland California—has challenged the notion that supply constraints amplify house price cycles. Fig. 1 in Davidoff (2013) shows that the magnitude of the house price cycle in the early 2000s in the sand states was larger than the cycle in coastal markets. His fig. 2 documents that the increase in the number of housing units was also larger in the sand states. Nathanson and Zwick (2015) argue that some cities, such as Las Vegas, do not have an abundance of land. Instead, these cities face long-run supply constraints in the form of tight virtual urban growth boundaries, formed by encircling federal and state lands.

2.3 Financing

Fig. 6 shows aggregate household debt from the Flow of Funds as multiple of GDP in the United States over the postwar period. The increase in the series happened in three discrete steps: right after World War II, the 1980s, and the 2000s. After the collapse of the housing market in 2006, households have been deleveraging. The red line in Fig. 6 is mortgage debt/GDP, which is roughly 3/5 of overall household debt. Most of household debt is thus collateralized. The plot shows that mortgage debt is chiefly responsible for the three discrete steps in which debt drastically increased. Household debt, especially mortgage debt, has also increased in other countries over the postwar period, as documented by Cardarelli et al. (2008). Jordà et al. (2016a) document this increase for many industrialized countries in a sample that goes back to 1870.

Jordà et al. (2016b) document that asset price boom–bust episodes that are combined with prior run-ups in leverage are associated with larger output costs during their bust. The data sample covers many industrialized countries going back to 1870. Moreover, boom–busts in housing have more severe output costs than those in equity markets.

2.3.1 Mortgage Growth During the 2000s

Mian and Sufi (2009) investigate who borrowed more during the 2000s. Did these borrowers expect higher future income growth? To address this question, Mian and Sufi use IRS data on income and mortgage debt data from the "Home Mortgage Disclosure Act" (HMDA). Their fig. 1 shows that income growth and mortgage growth are positively correlated across metro areas between 2002 and 2005 (in their top right panel). The evidence within metro areas, however, shows a *negative* correlation between income growth

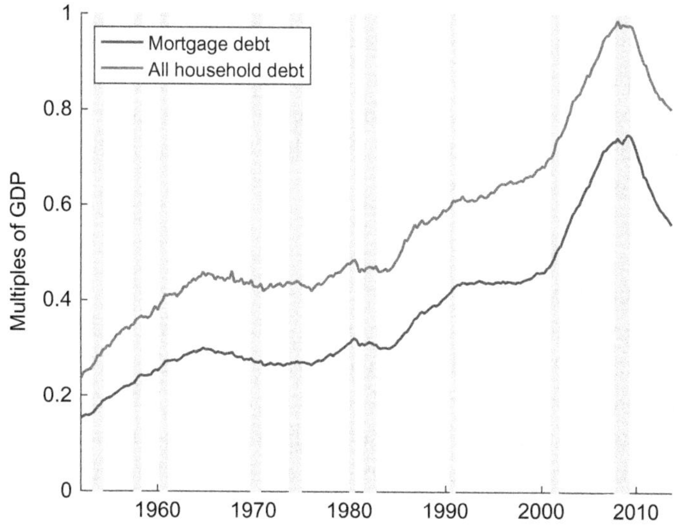

Fig. 6 Aggregate household debt and mortgage debt as fraction of GDP.

and mortgage growth across zip codes (in the lower right panel.) Moreover, they show that this negative correlation at the zip code level is unique to the 2002–05 period. These findings suggest that the 2000s were a unique episode in which mortgage debt increased in zip codes that experienced lower income growth.

Adelino et al. (2015) decompose mortgage growth into the extensive margin—the growth rate in the number of mortgages in a zip code—and the intensive margin—the growth rate in the size of individual mortgages. Their table 2 shows that the extensive margin is responsible for the negative correlation between IRS income growth and mortgage growth across zip codes. In fact, the intensive margin is *positively* correlated with IRS income at the zip code level. Moreover, Adelino et al. show that the growth rate of individual HMDA income—borrowers' income as indicated on their mortgage applications—is *positively* correlated to individual mortgage size across households. The paper argues that the negative correlation between income and mortgage growth documented by Mian and Sufi (2009) may be explained by a change in buyer composition (ie, richer buyers in poorer zip codes).

Mian and Sufi (2015) present evidence that the growth rate of HMDA income is higher than IRS reported income growth at the zip code level. They argue that the difference between the two growth rates represents mortgage fraud. Of course, the comparison of HMDA income and IRS income is tricky, because mover households who purchase a home have different characteristics than stayer households, especially during the 2000s boom. Table 2 in Landvoigt et al. (2015) compares the characteristics of home buyers and homeowners in 2000 Census data and 2005 data from the American Community Survey. They find that the median buyer in 2005 has more income and is richer than in 2000 in real terms.

Another important component of the increase in mortgage debt is existing homeowners who borrowed against the increased value of their house. Mian and Sufi (2011) document that especially homeowners in areas with stronger house price appreciation extracted equity from their houses with home equity lines of credit. Chen et al. (2013) report that a large fraction of refinancing during the 2000s were cash-outs, defined as more than 5% increases in loan amounts.

2.3.2 Mortgage Contracts

In the United States, the predominant mortgage contract is a fixed-rate mortgage with long maturity, usually 30 years. The main alternative is an adjustable-rate mortgage. In a basic adjustable-rate mortgage, the initial rate is set as a markup (or margin) on top of a benchmark, such as the 1-year Treasury rate. Adjustable rates are periodically reset to the current benchmark. During the recent housing boom, hybrid adjustable-rate mortgages became more popular. These hybrid contracts have a fixed rate for an initial period up to 10 years and adjusted periodically thereafter.

Campbell and Cocco (2003) report that fixed-rate mortgages accounted for 70% of newly issued mortgages on average during the period 1985–2001, while adjustable-rate mortgages accounted for the remaining 30%. The share of fixed-rate mortgages in new originations fluctuates over time. Fig. 2 in Campbell and Cocco (2003) shows the evolution of the share of fixed-rate mortgages, which is strongly negatively correlated with long-term interest rates.

Cardarelli et al. (2008), Andrews et al. (2011), and Badarinza et al. (2016) provide cross-country evidence on mortgage contracts. Table 4 in Andrews et al. shows that the typical mortgage maturity varies across countries between 10 years in Slovenia and Turkey to 30 years in Denmark and the United States. Table 3 in Badarinza et al. shows wide differences in the use of adjustable-rate mortgages and prepayment penalties. For example, the majority of mortgages in Australia, Finland, Portugal and Spain have an adjustable rate, while Belgium, Denmark, Germany, and the United States have mostly fixed-rate mortgages. Belgium and Germany have prepayment penalties, which make these fixed-rate mortgages highly risky. Table 3.1 in Cardarelli et al. (2008) shows that the countries with the largest fractions of securitized mortgages are the United States, Australia, Ireland, Greece, United Kingdom, and Spain.

2.3.3 Recent Financial Innovation and Lender Incentives

Leading up to the recent housing boom, the banking sector underwent a profound transformation. The traditional role of banks was to originate mortgages and hold them on their books until they are repaid. More and more, modern banks "originate-to-distribute"; banks originate mortgages, pool and tranche them, as resell them via the securitization process. In other words, mortgages are not kept on the balance sheet of the originating bank but are sold to investors. This transformation of the banking sector has changed the incentives of banks to screen mortgages. The resulting decline in lending standards has lead to a large expansion in credit.

Financial innovation also helped create new types of mortgages. Many mortgage contracts were designed to defer amortization, for example, with teaser rates or no interest rate payments during an initial period (such as "2–28 mortgages"). The share of alternative mortgages increased from below 2% until 2003 to above 30% during the peak years of the US housing boom (as documented, for example, in fig. 1 of Amromin et al., 2013). Another aspect of the deterioration of lending aspects were "no doc" loans, which did not require any documentation of income, or NINJA ("no income, no job or assets") loans.

Keys et al. (2010) provide evidence that securitization was associated with laxer screening of mortgages. The idea of the paper is to compare the performance of mortgages that are securitized with those that are not securitized. Since the 1990s, credit scoring has become the key tool to screen borrowers. The guidelines established by the government-sponsored enterprises, Fannie Mae and Freddie Mac, cautioned against lending to risky borrowers with a FICO score below 620. The 620 cutoff is also important for securitization as mortgages above the cutoff are easier to securitize. The paper studies the performance of a million mortgages over the years 2001–06. It finds that mortgages with a FICO score right above 620 performed *worse* than mortgages slightly below the 620 cutoff.

2.4 Market Structure

Housing has *broad ownership*. Roughly two thirds of US households own a house. Over the postwar period, the home ownership rate varied between 62% and 69%. It peaked at 69.2 at the end of 2004, toward the peak of the recent boom. The current ownership rate is down to 63.7%.

More households own a house than stocks. The ownership rate for stocks crucially depends on whether indirect holdings (through mutual funds and pension funds) are included or not. But even if we include indirect holdings, the ownership rate for stocks is below 50%.

Housing markets are *illiquid* relative to other asset markets. Turnover (per year) in housing markets is low relative to the stock market. The average turnover rate in the stock market is 110%, which means that every stock changes hands at least once in any given year. By contrast, the average turnover rate in the housing market is only 7%. This illiquidity is manifested in the fact that time on market—the number of days or months between listing and selling a house—is a key statistic in housing markets, while time on market plays no role in stock markets.

An important aspect of housing is that it is more *difficult to short* than other assets such as stocks. Because houses are unique and indivisible, an investor may not be able to take a short position in a particular house. The low liquidity in house price indices and their derivatives makes it either impossible or costly to take large short positions in the overall market. It is possible to short REITs, which are indexed to the value of commercial real estate. However, REITs are not perfectly correlated with the value of residential real estate. During recent housing booms, investors have used creative strategies to short housing. For example, during the recent housing boom, investors were short in mortgage-backed securities. In the ongoing Chinese boom, investors short the stock of large developers. Many of these investment strategies are costly and require sophistication, and are not perfect shorts for residential real estate.

Bachmann and Cooper (2014) document a secular decline in the turnover rate (the sum of their owner-to-owner and renter-to-owner moves) from the mid 1980s to 2000s in data from the Panel Study of Income Dynamics (PSID). Moreover, the paper documents that the turnover rate (in particular, the rate of owner-to-owner moves) is procyclical. Kathari et al. (2013) document a secular decline in moving rates of both renters and owners since the mid 1980s based on the Current Population Survey.

2.5 Household Portfolios

A sizeable literature uses various household level data sets to document cross-sectional patterns in housing consumption and the role of housing and mortgages in household portfolios. We summarize here key cross-sectional patterns that have been fairly stable over time. In particular, housing choices depend significantly on age and net worth.

It is well known that expenditure on nondurable consumption is hump-shaped over the life cycle (eg, Deaton, 1992). Fernandez-Villaverde and Krueger (2007) document a similar hump-shaped life cycle pattern for expenditure on durables. Their definition of durables includes purchases of consumer durables as well as housing expenditure by renters and owners in the CEX. Their fig. 6 shows that the hump peaks roughly at the age of 50 years, similar to the pattern for nondurables. After the peak, durables expenditure declines substantially with age. For example, durables expenditure at age 50 is twice as large as expenditure at 75.

Yang (2009) distinguishes expenditure on housing from that on other durables. For renters, housing expenditure is from CEX data. For owners, housing expenditure is from the SCF, assuming that expenditure is proportional to house value. Her fig. 4 shows that housing expenditure for owners also increases with age similar to durable expenditures. However, it peaks later in life—at age 65—rather than at age 50. Moreover, housing expenditure flattens out after age 65; unlike durable expenditure, it does not decline with age.

The homeownership rate is also hump-shaped over the life cycle. For example, table 6 in Chambers et al. (2009b) shows the homeownership rate first increases from roughly 40% for young households (aged 20–34 years) to twice that share for older households (aged 65–74 years). The homeownership rate then declines slightly for very old households.

The homeownership rate also increases with income. For example, Gyourko and Linneman (1997) study decennial census data from 1960 until 1990 to show that homeownership rates increase with income even after conditioning on age. There is also evidence that low income and minority households are less able to sustain homeownership than high income and white households. For example, Turner and Smith (2009) examine data from the PSID spanning the years 1970–2005 and document that homeowners in these groups have consistently higher exit rates from ownership.

The portfolio share on housing depends on both age and wealth. It declines monotonically with age. Young households are *house poor:* they choose highly leveraged positions in housing. As they age and accumulate wealth, they lower their portfolio weight on housing and pay down their mortgages. For example, table 2 in Flavin and Yamashita (2002) shows that young homeowners (aged 18–30) have an average portfolio weight of 3.51 on housing and −2.83 on mortgages in the PSID. Middle-aged households (aged 41–40 years) have an average weight of 1.58 on housing and −0.88 on mortgages. Older households (aged 71+) have an average weight of 0.65 on housing and −0.04 on mortgages.

The portfolio share on housing is hump-shaped in wealth. For example, table 1 of Campbell and Cocco (2003) shows that households in the bottom third of the wealth distribution are renters—they do not own a home, so their portfolio share on housing is zero. Wealthier households have a large fraction of their wealth, between 60% and 70%, invested in housing. For rich households (in the top 20% of the wealth distribution), the portfolio share on housing rapidly declines with wealth. These households shift more and more of their portfolio into stocks.

Wealth is also hump-shaped over the life cycle. Fig. 7 in Piazzesi and Schneider (2009a) uses the Survey of Consumer Finances to document the hump in wealth for middle-aged households (aged 53 years). The figure plots wealth of "rich households"—defined as the top 10% of net worth in their cohort—separately from cohort totals. These rich households own more than half of the cohort wealth—indicating a high concentration of wealth.

The hump in wealth over the life cycle multiplied by portfolio shares on housing that decline with age results in a hump-shaped pattern in housing wealth over the life cycle (third left panel in fig. 7 of Piazzesi and Schneider, 2009a). This housing wealth is somewhat concentrated—rich households own roughly a third of the housing wealth in their cohort. However, most of the overall wealth concentration can be attributed to the extremely high concentration of wealth invested in stocks: rich households own almost all of the stock wealth in their cohort.

3. THEORY

This section describes a theoretical framework that nests or provides background for many studies in the literature. At its heart is the intertemporal household decision problem with housing as both an asset and a consumption good. The papers discussed below all share a version of this problem. They differ in what other aspects of housing are included—in particular, the option to rent, collateral constraints or transaction costs—in whether equilibrium is imposed and, if yes, in how the supply side is modeled.

We thus begin with a "plain vanilla" household problem. It assumes that houses of every quality as well as other assets and consumption of the nonhousing good are all traded in competitive markets. The only friction is that consumption of housing services requires ownership of a house. Housing thus differs from other assets because of *indivisibility* and *nontradability of dividends*. Indeed, households hold either zero or one units of the housing asset and the "dividend"—that is, the value of housing services less maintenance cost—cannot be sold in a market to other households.

After introducing the plain vanilla problem, we discuss household optimization, derive asset pricing equations and define an equilibrium with a fixed aggregate supply of housing services. Here, we highlight the distinction between an exogenous distribution of house qualities and a fixed stock of housing that developers can costlessly convert into one of many distributions with the same mean. We also discuss the role of expectation formation. In later sections, we then add further key ingredients one by one: production and land, a rental market, collateral constraints and transaction costs.

3.1 Basic Setup

We work in discrete time. Studies differ in how long the economy lasts and what households' planning horizons are. To explain the basic tradeoffs, these details are not important, so we do not take a stand on them now. Instead, we focus on the period t decisions of a household who expects to also live in period $t+1$. Studies also typically assume a large number of different households who may differ in characteristics such as age, income or beliefs. We do not make such heterogeneity explicit, but instead describe a generic household problem with minimal notation.

To represent uncertainty, we fix a probability space $(\Omega, \mathcal{F}, P^0)$. The set Ω contains states of the world. Events in the σ-field $\mathcal{F}$ correspond to all exogenous events that can occur. For example, each state of the world could imply a different sequence of shocks to a household's income over his lifetime. The probability measure P^0 says how likely it is that each event $F \in \mathcal{F}$ occurs. In other words, it tells us with what probability nature draws a state of the world $\omega \in F$. In general, the "physical" probability P^0 need not coincide with the belief of a household.[d]

3.1.1 Preferences

The evolution of the households' information is summarized by a filtration $\mathcal{F}_t$ on Ω: $F \in \mathcal{F}_t$ means that the household knows in period t whether event F has occurred or not. The household's belief about states of the world is described by a probability P. In what follows, we keep these objects in the background and instead work directly with random variables and conditional moments. Our convention is that random variables dated t are contained in the household's period t information set. For example, c_t is (random) consumption of nonhousing goods and we write $E_t c_{t+1}$ for the household's expected period $t+1$ consumption given period t information.

Households derive utility from housing services s and other consumption c. Utility is state and time separable; in particular, period t utility from the two goods is given by

$$U(g(s_t, c_t)),$$

where $g: \mathbb{R}^2 \to \mathbb{R}$ is an "aggregator function" that is homogeneous of degree one and $U: \mathbb{R} \to \mathbb{R}$ is strictly increasing and concave. Decomposing utility in this way helps

[d] The physical probability is what one would use to compute or simulate the distribution of outcomes of the economy. It thus coincides with the belief of an outside observer, for example, an econometrician, who observes a large sample of data generated from the model.

distinguish substitution across goods within a period from substitution of consumption bundles $g(s_t, c_t)$ across periods.

The aggregator g describes households' willingness to substitute housing services for other consumption within a period. A common example is the CES functional form

$$g(s_t, c_t) = \left(c_t^{(\varepsilon-1)/\varepsilon} + \omega s_t^{(\varepsilon-1)/\varepsilon}\right)^{\varepsilon/(\varepsilon-1)}, \tag{2}$$

where ε is the *intra*temporal elasticity of substitution and ω is a constant. Agents are more willing to substitute within the period the higher is ε. As $\varepsilon \to \infty$, the two goods become perfect substitutes and as $\varepsilon \to 0$, they become perfect complements. The limit $\varepsilon \to 1$ represents the Cobb–Douglas case with constant expenditure shares.

The function U captures agent's willingness to substitute consumption *bundles* g over time (as well as states of nature). A common example is the power function $U(g) = g^{1-1/\sigma}/(1-1/\sigma)$ where σ is the *inter*temporal elasticity of substitution among bundles at different points in time. For $\sigma \to 0$, households want to maintain a stable bundle over time whereas for $\sigma \to \infty$ utility becomes linear in bundles. The limit $\sigma \to 1$ corresponds to logarithmic utility. With a CES aggregator, the special case $\sigma = 1/\varepsilon$ results in utility that is separable across the two goods.

While our assumptions on utility are convenient for exposition, several straightforward extensions are also common in the literature. First, some papers replace time separable utility by recursive utility, for example, the tractable functional form introduced by Epstein and Zin (1989). To deal with multiple goods, the usual recursive utility formulation is applied directly to bundles aggregated by g.[e] Second, some papers add preference shocks; in particular, a "housing preference shock" is often introduced via a random weight ω in (2). Finally, labor is often added as a third good in utility.

3.1.2 Technology

Households obtain housing services by living in exactly one house. Houses come in different qualities $h \in \mathcal{H} \subset \mathbb{R}$ where the set $\mathcal{H}$ can be either discrete or continuous. Our convention is that $\mathcal{H}$ may contain zero to accommodate households who do not live in a house. A household who lives in a house of quality h_t from t to $t+1$ obtains a flow of housing services $s_t = h_t$ that enters period t utility. In quantitative applications, the flows s_t and c_t are typically identified with the household's consumption over a time range

[e] Formally, let $W: \mathbb{R}^2 \to \mathbb{R}$ denote a function that captures substitution over time and let $v: \mathbb{R} \to \mathbb{R}$ denote a function that captures aversion to risk about utility gambles. Utility from a consumption process (c_t, g_t) is defined recursively by

$$U_t = W\left(g(c_t, s_t), v^{-1}\left(E_t[v(U_{t+1})]\right)\right).$$

Our time separable case obtains if $v = U$ and $W(x, y) = U(x) + \beta U(y)$. Epstein and Zin propose a CES aggregator for W and a power function for v.

that includes date t, and the quality of his residence h_t is an average over that time range. Our timing convention implies that the house quality h_t relevant for period t consumption is chosen based on the period t information set.[f]

The one-dimensional quality index h orders houses from low to high qualities. In general, it captures many characteristics of a house—its location, the size of the land, square footage of lot and structure, its view, amenities, etc. The underlying assumption is that households agree on the ranking of all houses within the housing market that is being studied. At the same time, households may differ in their taste for house quality relative to other consumption and hence be willing to pay different amounts for any given house.

A household who lives in a house of quality h_t from t to $t+1$ must undertake maintenance worth $I(h_t)$ units of the other (nonhousing) good. The quality of the house then evolves over time according to

$$h_{t+1} = H_{t+1}(h_t), \tag{3}$$

where the subscript $t+1$ indicates that the evolution may be random. We highlight two popular special cases. The first assumes that all depreciation is "essential maintenance" without which the house is uninhabitable. As long as essential maintenance is performed, house quality is constant, that is, $I(h_t) = \delta_h h_t$ and $H(h_t) = h_t$. A second special case is that households do not pay for maintenance but average quality deteriorates geometrically, that is, $I(h_t) = 0$ and $H(h_t) = (1-\delta_h)h_t$. In both cases, $\delta_h h_t$ is depreciation of housing. The first approach is convenient when the set of qualities $\mathcal{H}$ is finite.

3.1.3 Housing Markets

Houses are traded in competitive markets. The only friction is that consumption of housing services requires ownership of a house. Housing thus differs from other assets because of *indivisibility* and *nontradability of dividends*. Indeed, it is held in indivisible units and its "dividend"—that is, the value of housing services less maintenance cost—cannot be sold in a market. This assumption is relaxed in Section 3.6 where we introduce a market for rental housing. In line with our timing convention, utility from a house bought at date t is enjoyed at date t itself—date t house prices are thus "cum dividend."

A house of quality h_t trades in period t at the price $p_t(h_t)$, denominated in units of the nonhousing good which serves as numeraire. The price function is increasing in quality. If the set $\mathcal{H}$ consists of a finite number of house types, then house prices can be summarized by a vector. With a continuum of qualities, it often makes sense to assume that the price function is smooth—a small change in quality leads to a small change in price. For example, in some applications the price function is linear, that is, there is a number $\bar{p}_t$ such that $p_t(h) = \bar{p}_t h$ for all quality levels h.

[f] Alternative timing conventions are possible and sometimes used in the literature. For example, we might assume that quality chosen at date t yields housing services only at date $t+1$.

3.1.4 What Is a House?

The setup emphasizes indivisibility and quality differences: housing services are provided by a distribution of housing capital stocks of different qualities, one for each household. In general, pricing is nonlinear: each quality level represents a different good and relative prices depend on relative demand and supply. This approach goes back to Rosen (1974) who studied competitive equilibrium with consumers who choose one "design" of a product that is identified by a vector of characteristics.

Braid (1981, 1984) and Kaneko (1982) studied housing with a one-dimensional quality index in static models with a continuum and a finite set of qualities, respectively. Caplin and Leahy (2014) characterize comparative statics of competitive equilibria in a static setting with a finite number of agents and goods. The dynamic setup here follows the finite quality models in Ortalo-Magné and Rady (1999, 2006) and Ríos-Rull and Sánchez-Marcos (2010) as well as the continuum approach in Landvoigt et al. (2015).

At first sight, allowing for nonlinear pricing may appear unnecessary: why not assume that there is a homogenous housing capital good—akin to physical capital in many macroeconomic models—with households choosing different quantities of that good at a common per-unit price? The latter approach is a special case of the setup that obtains when some market participants can convert houses of different quality with a marginal rate of transformation of one. For example, in Section 3.4, we derive it from the presence of a developer sector who undertakes this activity.

Work on housing has more often gone beyond setups with homogeneous capital and linear pricing than work on, say, business capital. One likely reason is measurement. The difficulties with measuring house prices in national accounts have been discussed frequently. At the same time, new micro data provide evidence on price dynamics at fine levels of disaggregation by geography and type of house. The evidence in Section 2.2 suggests that linear pricing is perhaps too restrictive, since both volatility conditional on quality is high and conditional means vary systematically by quality. We return to this issue below.

While our setup nests essentially all specifications in the macro literature, it is restrictive in at least two ways. First, it may not be possible or desirable to represent the cross section of houses by a one-dimensional index. A more general approach could follow Rosen (1974) and directly model preference over many characteristics. In particular, households may rank houses differently because they disagree about the weighting of characteristics. Second, a more general approach to household capital accumulation might start from an evolution equation

$$h_{t+1} = z_{t+1} H(h_t, I_t),$$

where z_{t+1} is a depreciation shock. In this equation, initial quality h_t and improvements I_t are imperfect substitutes, so that upkeep of the house is an explicit margin for the household. This approach could generate a distribution of houses in different states of disrepair.

3.2 Household Choice

We now consider the household's decision problem when houses as well as other assets and consumption of the nonhousing good are all traded in competitive markets. The household receives an exogenous labor income stream y_t. Securities, such as equity or bonds, trade at date t at prices collected in a $J \times 1$ vector q_t and provide payoffs at date $t + 1$ summarized by a $J \times 1$ vector π_{t+1}. For long-lived securities such as equity, the payoff may contain the date $t+1$ price. We make no further assumption on market structure. Markets may be incomplete in the sense that it is not possible for households to assemble a portfolio of securities in period t with payoff equal to any given consumption plan that depends on date $t + 1$ information. With incomplete markets, households may not be able to insure against future labor income risk.

3.2.1 Recursive Household Problem

Without trading frictions, past portfolio choice—including housing choice—affects the household at date t only through its effect on wealth. We can thus formulate the problem recursively with a single endogenous state variable *cash on hand* w that comprises housing wealth, other wealth plus income from labor and securities. To start off the recursion, we define a terminal value function $V_T(w_T)$. In a finite horizon life cycle problem, this function captures utility at the end of life, perhaps including bequests. In an infinite horizon setup ($T = \infty$), existence of a value function can be derived from trading restrictions that prevent Ponzi schemes.

For a household who expects to live for an additional period, the Bellman equation is

$$V_t(w_t) = \max_{c_t, , \theta_t; h_t \in \mathcal{H}} U(g(c_t, h_t)) + \beta E_t[V_{t+1}(w_{t+1})] \tag{4}$$

$$c_t + p_t(h_t) + I(h_t) + \theta_t^\top q_t = w_t,$$

$$w_{t+1} = \theta_t^\top \pi_{t+1} + p_{t+1}(H_{t+1}(h_t)) + y_{t+1}.$$

The first condition is the current budget constraint that says how cash on hand is split into consumption, asset purchases and maintenance. The second constraint describes the evolution of cash on hand which depends on future security payoffs, house value and labor income.

The same Bellman equation works for problems with random horizon. Indeed, a common approach assumes that households survive with a probability that can depend on age. Those survival probabilities are then used in computing the conditional expectation in the Bellman equation. In the terminal period of life, households learn that this is their last period, sell all assets and either consume the proceeds or transfer wealth to children. Given our timing convention on housing services and the need for ownership, we also assume that households do not consume housing services in the terminal period of life.

3.2.2 Two Stage Solution Approach

We consider household choice in two stages. The household first decides on house quality and thus how much of cash on hand to spend on housing. In a second stage, he allocates the remaining funds to numeraire consumption and securities. The split is helpful because indivisibility and nontradability make the housing choice special. On the one hand, indivisibility means that house quality may be discrete and the pricing of house quality may be nonlinear. On the other hand, nontradability means that housing and securities are imperfect substitutes even if there is no risk—a case when all other securities become perfect substitutes.

We write the second stage problem with returns and portfolio weights, rather than asset prices and quantities. The gross return on the jth security is $R_{t+1,j} = \pi_{t+1,j}/q_{t,j}$. We assume that the Jth security is a risk-free bond and denote the gross risk-free rate by R_t^f. Moreover, the returns on securities $j = 1, \ldots, J-1$ are risky and collected in a vector R_{t+1}. The household selects a portfolio weight $\alpha_{t,j}$ for each of the risky assets j. These weights are collected in a $J-1$ vector α_t, so that $1 - \alpha_t^\top \iota$ is invested in risk-free bonds, where ι is a $J-1$ vector of ones. There are no restrictions on the sign of the portfolio position: the households can short a risky asset by choosing $\alpha_{t,j} < 0$ or borrow at the riskless rate by choosing $\alpha_t^\top \iota > 1$. The return on the portfolio is $\tilde{R}_{t+1}(\alpha_t) = \alpha_t^\top R_{t+1} + (1 - \alpha_t^\top \iota) R_t^f$.

The second stage problem is

$$\tilde{V}_t(\tilde{w}_t, h_t) = \max_{c_t, \alpha_t} U(g(c_t, h_t)) + \beta E_t[V_{t+1}(w_{t+1})]$$

$$w_{t+1} = (\tilde{w}_t - c_t)\tilde{R}_{t+1}(\alpha_t) + p_{t+1}(H_{t+1}(h_t)) + y_{t+1}. \tag{5}$$

The household starts with cash $\tilde{w}_t = w_t - p_t(h_t) - I(h_t)$ left over after housing expenditure. He then chooses numeraire consumption c_t and invests the remaining funds $\tilde{w}_t - c_t$ in securities. Cash next period consists of savings in securities multiplied by their average return plus the payoffs from housing and human capital, both of which are nontradable assets in the second stage problem.

Optimal choice depends on risk in house values, labor income and securities returns. To illustrate, we perform a second-order Taylor expansion of the future value function in (5) around expected future wealth to obtain

$$\tilde{V}_t(\tilde{w}_t, h_t) \approx U(g(c_t, h_t)) + \beta V_{t+1}(E_t w_{t+1}) + \frac{1}{2}\beta E_t V''_{t+1}(E_t w_{t+1}) var_t(w_{t+1}).$$

Without risk, the last term vanishes and the problem has a solution only if all returns are the same. Securities are then perfect substitutes and portfolio choice is indeterminate. More generally, for a risk-averse household with $V''_{t+1} < 0$, welfare declines with the volatility of future wealth. As a result, securities are imperfect substitutes. Moreover, utility declines with the volatility of future house values as well with the covariance of house values and labor income.

3.2.3 Housing Choice

The first stage problem takes as given the maximized objective $\widetilde{V}_t$ from the second stage. We assume that $\widetilde{V}_t$ is increasing in both its arguments and smooth as a function of $\widetilde{w}_t$; properties usually inherited from g, U and V_T. The first stage problem is then to choose optimal house quality to solve

$$V_t(w_t) = \max_{h_t \in \mathcal{H}} \widetilde{V}_t(w_t - p_t(h_t) - I(h_t), h_t). \tag{6}$$

The household thus trades off expenditure on a house against its indirect utility value. From (5), the latter comes from two sources: housing not only earns capital gains, but also enters utility as a consumption good—it delivers a nontradable dividend. Nontradability thus implies that housing and other assets can be imperfect substitutes even when there is no risk.

In the typical application, optimal house quality is increasing in wealth, other things equal. Indeed, the objective on the right-hand side of (6) is typically supermodular in (w, h), that is, the benefit from additional cash is increasing in house quality and vice versa. Intuitively, one key force is diminishing marginal utility of numeraire consumption and future wealth: if more is spent on housing then extra cash becomes more valuable. However, we also need that the utility value of house quality does not overturn this effect. This might happen, for example, if housing services are not a normal good in the aggregator g or if the distribution of capital gains R^h becomes much more attractive at higher qualities.

With a discrete set of house qualities, an increasing policy function is a step function in wealth: there are cutoff wealth levels at which households are indifferent between two adjacent quality levels. Households with wealth in between two cutoffs all choose the same quality level which they strictly prefer. Moreover, our setup allows for zero holdings of housing—in general, marginal utility need not increase without bound as consumption of housing services tends to zero. As a result, there can be a wealth cutoff at which households are indifferent between the lowest available house quality and not buying any house. With continuous house quality, we work with a smooth price function and also assume further that the objective $\widetilde{V}_t$ is smooth in h_t. At the optimal quality, a household is then indifferent between his optimal quality and a slightly better or worse house. Optimal choice is characterized by the first order condition

$$p_t'(h_t) + I'(h_t) = \frac{\widetilde{V}_{t,2}(w_t - p_t(h_t) - I(h_t), h_t)}{\widetilde{V}_{t,1}(w_t - p_t(h_t) - I(h_t), h_t)}, \tag{7}$$

where $\widetilde{V}_{t,i}$ are the partial derivatives of $\widetilde{V}_t$.

The marginal rate of substitution of housing for other expenditure is equated to the *slope* of the house price function at quality h. The slope appears because of indivisibility: the quantity of housing is one for all households, and indifference is across nearby quality levels. In contrast to a competitive model with divisible goods, the marginal rates of substitution of different households are not necessarily equated in equilibrium. The only exception is the case of a linear function for prices as well as linear improvements (for example, either one of the two special cases for technology highlighted above $I(h_t) = \delta_h h_t$ and $I(h_t) = 0$.). Indeed, if the slopes on the left-hand side are the same everywhere, then h_t can equivalently be interpreted as the quantity of a divisible housing capital.

3.2.4 Consumption and Savings

Consider now the second-stage problem for given house quality. The first-order conditions with respect to nonhousing consumption c_t as well as portfolio weights α_t on the $J-1$ risky securities can be arranged as

$$\begin{aligned} U'(g(c_t,h_t))g_1(c_t,h_t) &= \beta E_t\left[V'_{t+1}(w_{t+1})\right]R^f_t \\ 0 &= \beta E_t\left[V'_{t+1}(w_{t+1})\left(R_{t+1} - \iota R^f_t\right)\right]. \end{aligned} \tag{8}$$

The first equation says that households are indifferent at the margin between consumption and borrowing or lending at the risk-free rate. The second equation shows the portfolio choice margin: households are indifferent between risk-free investment and investment in any of the risky securities.

The first equation helps understand which households hold leveraged positions in housing. Indeed, suppose there are no risky securities. The first equation then determines optimal consumption, the only variable affecting future cash on hand w_{t+1} in (5) that is not predetermined given h_t, $\tilde{w}_t$ and y_{t+1}. In particular, if the household has more labor income next period, he consumes more so that his bond position $\tilde{w}_t - c_t$ declines and may become negative. We would thus expect homeowners with an upward sloping labor income profile and little initial financial wealth to leverage up. This intuition is quite general and continues to hold when labor income or security returns are risky. It allows life cycle models to successfully replicate the age profile of household portfolios in the data.

We emphasize that borrowing (that is, negative $\tilde{w}_t - c_t$) does not imply negative savings, because savings also include the positive housing position. This feature is important for matching the data where savings are rarely negative. In the model, savings can be positive because the purpose of borrowing is not necessarily to move income from the future to the present—in fact, a borrower household with positive savings moves income from the present to the future. Instead, the purpose of borrowing for such a household is to buy a large enough house to enjoy his desired flow of housing services.

3.2.5 Securities Portfolios

To get intuition on the role of housing in portfolio choice, suppose that the continuation value function V_{t+1} is known as of date t.[g] From the first order conditions for risky

[g] This is literally true only under restrictive conditions, for example, when asset returns are iid and income is deterministic. More generally, V_{t+1} is random conditional on date t because continuation values depend on state variables that forecast future asset returns and income. The optimal portfolio weights then contain an additional term that reflects "intertemporal hedging demand"—agents prefer assets that insure them against bad realizations of the state variables. We simplify here to focus on the new effects introduced by housing.

securities and using the definition of cash on hand, we can then approximate the optimal portfolio weights on risky securities by

$$\alpha_t \approx \frac{E_t w_{t+1}}{\widetilde{w}_t - c_t} var_t(R_{t+1})^{-1}\left(\rho_{t+1}^{-1}\left(E_t R_{t+1} - R_t^f\right) - cov_t\left(R_{t+1}, \frac{y_{t+1} + p_{t+1}(H_{t+1}(h_t))}{E_t w_{t+1}}\right)\right), \tag{9}$$

where $\rho_{t+1} = -E_t w_{t+1} V''_{t+1}(E_t w_{t+1}) / V'_{t+1}(E_t w_{t+1})$ reflects curvature in the value function and can be interpreted as a measure of relative risk aversion.

The optimal portfolio equation resembles textbook formulas, but makes important corrections for the presence of nontradable assets, here human capital and housing. To interpret it, consider first the scale factor $E_t w_{t+1} / \left(\widetilde{w}_t - c_t\right)$. If there are no nontradable assets, then this factor equals the expected return on the entire securities portfolio and typically has only a small effect on the optimal weights. More generally, it says that the weights should be scaled up if there a lot of nontradable assets. This is because total wealth is not only $\widetilde{w}_t - c_t$ but includes the present value of those nontradable assets.

Consider now the big bracket in (9). The first term reflects the desire to exploit premia on securities—expected returns that differ from the risk-free rate. To illustrate, suppose there is a security with payoffs that are orthogonal to any other shock including house prices and labor income. Up to the scale factor, the optimal weight on that security is simply its expected excess return divided by its variance as well as risk aversion. The household thus exploits a nonnegative premium on the security, and more so if there is less risk and he is less risk averse. The sign of the premium determines the direction of trade: the household holds the security if the premium is positive and shorts it otherwise.

The second term reflects hedging of labor income and housing risk. Consider first the role of labor income. If markets are complete, then there exists a portfolio of securities, θ_t^y say, that exactly replicates labor income, that is, $y_{t+1} = \pi_{t+1}^{\top} \theta_t^y$. Optimal portfolio choice for any risk-averse investor then involves a term that shorts the portfolio θ^y. Intuitively, the household wants to avoid risks that he is already exposed to via his nontradable human capital position. With incomplete markets, it may not be possible to short labor income. Instead, the household trades against labor income "as much as he can" with the existing set of assets. The precise meaning of "as much as he can" is given by the projection of labor income on returns $var_t(R_{t+1})^{-1} cov_t(R_{t+1}, y_{t+1})$.

Housing enters the optimal portfolio formula (9) in much the same way as labor income: it affects the demand for securities through the second "hedging demand" term. The presence of housing thus generally changes the optimal mix of securities. For example, households who work at local companies with payoffs that are correlated with their house price would optimally short the stocks of those companies. This type of interaction effect is present whether or not housing is traded in every period.

An interesting special case arises when labor income is uncorrelated with all risky securities. In this case, labor income enters (9) only because its mean increases the scale factor. The portfolio weights on all risky assets are thus scaled up along with mean labor income, regardless of labor income risk. At the same time the riskless asset position $1-\alpha_t^\top \iota$ is decreased. Households again trade away labor income, except that the portfolio best suited to do so now consists entirely of the risk-free security.

3.3 Asset Pricing

The previous section characterized households' optimal decision rules given prices. In particular, we have used household first-order conditions to interpret model implications for savings and portfolio choice that can be evaluated with data on household asset positions. As usual, the same first-order conditions imply restrictions on asset prices given consumption and payoffs. In fact, a large literature in asset pricing uses household Euler equations to test assumptions on preferences and market structure. Since Euler equations describe an equilibrium relationship between observables, they can be tested without taking a stand on other features of the economy such as asset supply.

This section considers household Euler equations for housing and contrasts them with those for securities. We thus move from the decisions of a generic household to restrictions on asset prices due to optimization by an entire population of possibly heterogeneous households. In order not to clutter notation, we mostly continue our practice of not explicitly labeling individual characteristics and choices such as income and consumption. At the same time, the discussion emphasizes that there is a large number of households whose first-order conditions hold simultaneously and whose choices and characteristics are observable.

3.3.1 Families of Euler Equations

So far, we have taken as given a household's subjective probability P and written subjective conditional expectations as E_t. When discussing asset prices, it is useful to distinguish between investor beliefs that relate prices and choices, and the "physical" probability that governs the data-generating process and is therefore relevant for describing measures of conditional moments constructed from the data. For example, an econometrician may measure expected excess returns $E_t^0 R_{t+1} - R_t^f$ by regressing excess returns on public information. From now on we assume that household beliefs and the physical probability agree on probability zero events next period and use the random variable ξ_{t+1} to indicate a change of measure: for any random variable Y, $E_t[Y] = E_t^0[\xi_{t+1} Y]$. Under rational expectations, we have $\xi_{t+1} = 1$.

Pricing Securities

We denote a generic household's intertemporal marginal rate of substitution (MRS) adjusted by the change of measure by

$$M_{t+1} = \beta \frac{U'(g(c_{t+1}, h_{t+1}))g_1(c_{t+1}, h_{t+1})}{U'(g(c_t, h_t))g_1(c_t, h_t)} \xi_{t+1}. \tag{10}$$

From (8), any household MRS serves as a stochastic discount factor: returns satisfy $E_t^0 M_{t+1} R_{t+1} = 1$ and securities prices can be written as $q_t = E_t^0 M_{t+1} \pi_{t+1}$. If markets are complete, all MRSs are equated in equilibrium and there is a unique M_{t+1} that represents the prices of contingent claims normalized by one-step-ahead conditional probabilities under P_0.

The standard pricing equation is often used (together with the definition of covariance) to decompose asset prices into expected discounted payoffs plus risk premia:

$$q_t = E_t^0 \pi_{t+1} / R_t^f + cov_t^0(M_{t+1}, \pi_{t+1}). \tag{11}$$

The risk premium required by investors is larger (and the price therefore lower) if a security pays off little when the MRS is high. A positive risk premium is equivalent to a positive expected excess return $E_t^0 R_{t+1} - R_t^f$. Measures of conditional moments $E_t^0 \pi_{t+1}$ or $E_t^0 R_{t+1}$ constructed from the data—for example, by regression on public information—imply that expected payoffs are much more stable than prices, and that expected excess returns are predictable. Similar results obtain for housing, as reviewed in Section 2.2. If investors have rational expectations and have no or mild risk aversion, this finding cannot be reconciled with (11)—the excess volatility puzzle.[h]

We say that an agent is a *marginal investor* for an asset if any small change in its price or return distribution changes his optimal position in that asset. This concept is key for understanding asset pricing in heterogeneous agent models: it tells us whose behavior changes along with asset prices. For example, shocks that mostly affect *infra*marginal agents (that is, agents who are not marginal) are unlikely to move prices. Conversely, if a shock moves the price, it must also affect the positions of marginal agents. In our setup, the first-order conditions (8) imply that all households are marginal for all assets. Asset prices thus change if and only if all households adjust their positions. This is true whether or not markets are complete.

House Prices with a Finite Number of Qualities

Indivisibility means that only few households may be marginal for houses of any given quality. Indeed, with a finite set of qualities $\mathcal{H} = \{h^1, \ldots, h^n\}$, a household who strictly prefers his optimal quality in the first stage problem (6) will not respond to a change in price. At the same time, for every quality h^k except the highest, there are marginal

[h] Eq. (11) indicates two reasons why asset prices could exhibit premia that are on average high but also volatile. First, if investors have rational expectations then the covariance of the MRS with payoffs must be negative and variable. Alternatively, investors may be more pessimistic than the econometrician (that is, ξ is high when π is low) and their relative pessimism moves over time.

investors who are indifferent at date t between h^k and the next highest quality. The indifference conditions

$$\tilde{V}_t\left(w_t - p_t\left(h^k\right) - I\left(h^k\right), h^k\right) = \tilde{V}_t\left(w_t - p_t\left(h^{k+1}\right) - I\left(h^{k+1}\right), h^{k+1}\right) \quad (12)$$

relate price steps between quality levels to the characteristics of the marginal investors. The marginal investors are thus particularly important for pricing houses.

Restrictions on house values $p_t\left(h^k\right)$ are obtained by adding up price steps implied by (12). In applications, there is typically an additional household optimality condition that serves as a boundary condition. In particular, we assume in what follows that there is always a household who is indifferent between the worst quality house or no house at all. For such a household, the indifference condition (12) holds at $h^1 = 0$ and $p_t\left(h^1\right) = 0$. Alternatively, the price of the worst quality house may be given by its value in some alternative use that leaves the house vacant.

Example 1 There are two periods, two states of nature and three house qualities 0, h^1 and h^2. The only security is risk free with a zero interest rate. There is no maintenance and future house values are h^i in state 1 and zero in state 2. There is a continuum of households with linear utility in both goods as well as future wealth. Households share the same discount rate of zero and the same wealth, but differ in their subjective probability of the high price state, say ρ. The household characteristic ρ is distributed uniformly on $[0,1]$. We consider an allocation with $1 - \rho_2$ houses of quality h^2 and $\rho_2 - \rho_1$ houses of quality h^1.[i]

The following prices and individual choices are consistent with individual optimization. There are cutoff households with subjective probabilities ρ_1 and ρ_2 who are indifferent between zero and h^1, as well as h^1 and h^2, respectively. Households with beliefs ρ_1 determine the value of a house of quality h^1 as "dividend" (housing services) plus expected resale value, $p\left(h^1\right) = h^1 + \rho_1 h^1$. Households with ρ_2 value house quality h^2 as $p\left(h^2\right) = p\left(h^1\right) + (1+\rho_2)\left(h^2 - h^1\right)$. Both expressions satisfy (12). Households with $\rho \in [\rho_2, 1]$ choose quality h^2, households with $\rho \in [\rho_1, \rho_2]$ choose h^1 and households with $\rho < h^1$ choose zero. In this example, the second stage is trivial: agents are indifferent between current and future consumption. In the first stage problem, higher-probability households buy high quality houses. Lower probability households perceive those houses as too expensive.

House Prices with Continuous Quality

With continuous house quality, every household is marginal for houses of his own optimal quality, but not necessarily for any other quality. To see this, start from the first-order

[i] One way to think of this setup is as an equilibrium model with fixed supply. More generally, it simply describes a family of households who buy a set of houses, for example, all movers in a given period.

condition (7) and substitute for the derivatives of $\widetilde{V}_t$ using (8) and the envelope theorem to obtain

$$p_t'(h_t) = \frac{g_2(c_t, h_t)}{g_1(c_t, h_t)} - I'(h_t) + E_t^0\left[M_{t+1}p_{t+1}'(H_{t+1}(h_t))H_{t+1}'(h_t)\right]. \tag{13}$$

A household who chooses h_t is indifferent between h_t and a slightly better or worse house: the slope of the equilibrium price function must equal the change in the "dividend" $g_2/g_1 - I'$ plus the change in the risk adjusted future value of the house. If now some range of houses becomes more expensive while prices around quality h_t remain unchanged, this does not affect the optimal choice of h_t. No household needs to be marginal for any quality other than his own.

The Euler equation (13) restricts the slope of the price function, much like (12) restricts price steps along a discrete quality ladder. Restrictions on house values are again derived using a boundary condition. To illustrate, we select for each quality one household who buys that quality, and denote his numeraire consumption and MRS by $\left(c_t^*(h), M_{t+1}^*(h)\right)$. We then integrate (13) starting from $p_t(0) = 0$ to write the house price at quality h as

$$p_t(h) = \int_0^h \frac{g_2(c_t^*(\widetilde{h}), \widetilde{h})}{g_1(c_t^*(\widetilde{h}), \widetilde{h})} d\widetilde{h} - I(h) + E_t^0\left[\int_0^h M_{t+1}^*(\widetilde{h})p_{t+1}'(H_{t+1}(\widetilde{h}))H_{t+1}'(\widetilde{h})d\widetilde{h}\right]. \tag{14}$$

With indivisibility, the "dividend" of a house of quality h reflects an average of intratemporal MRSs of households who purchase qualities less of equal to h. Similarly, risk adjustment reflects an average of intertemporal MRSs of those households.

A popular special case restricts price functions to be linear. Linear pricing can be derived from the assumption that developers can freely convert houses of different quality into each other, as discussed further in Section 3.4. With the same slope $p'(h_t) = \bar{p}_t$ at every quality level, the Euler equation (13) applies to the price per unit of quality $\bar{p}_t$. The value of a house of quality h is

$$\bar{p}_t h = \frac{g_2\left(c_t^*(h), h\right)}{g_1\left(c_t^*(h), h\right)} h - I'(h)h + E_t^0\left[M_{t+1}^*(h)\bar{p}_{t+1}hH_{t+1}'(h)\right]. \tag{15}$$

With linear pricing, markets for different quality housing are tied more tightly together. As a result, every household is marginal for every house, as is the case for securities. The dividend and risk adjusted payoff at quality h can then be related to the MRSs of households who buy quality h.

Example 2 To illustrate nonlinear pricing with a continuum of qualities, we adapt the simple example from above. The set of households is unchanged, but the set of qualities is now $\mathcal{H} = [0, 1 - \rho_1]$. We consider an allocation with θ_1 houses of quality zero and $1 - \theta_1$

houses of positive quality uniformly distributed along the interval. Without maintenance, the first order condition (13) simplifies to $p_t'(h) = 1 + \rho$. We again construct prices and choices that satisfy all optimality conditions. There is a cutoff household who has subjective probability ρ_1 and is indifferent between no house and an infinitesimal house. Households with $\rho < \rho_1$ buy no house, while households with $\rho > \rho_1$ buy a house of quality $h = \rho - \rho_1$. House values are $p_t(h) = h(1+\rho_1) + \frac{1}{2}h^2$.

Again higher probability households buy better houses, which lower probability households perceive to be overpriced. Let ρ_0 denote the true probability of state 1. The stochastic discount factors for securities $M_{t+1}^*(h)$ are equal to $(h + \rho_1)/\rho_0$ in state 1 and $(1-(h+\rho_1))/(1-\rho_0)$ in state 2. Since the discount rate is zero and utility is linear, they differ only by the change of measure from the subjective probability of households who buy quality h to the true probability ρ_0.[j] Every stochastic discount factor correctly prices the riskless bond, the only available security.

So far the example emphasizes heterogeneity in risk assessment through beliefs. The essential feature, however, is only that agents disagree about the future value of houses. We can thus alternatively assume that there is no risk ($\rho_0 = 1$) but ρ represents households' discount factors. For the above choices to remain optimal, we also assume that there is no risk-free security so houses are the only traded assets. Prices are then the same as above: the interpretation is that more patient households buy larger houses since they want to save more. The absence of a risk-free security is important to ensure a solution to households' problems without borrowing constraints.

3.3.2 Limits to Arbitrage

In general, there need not exist a stochastic discount factor that prices all houses. This is a key difference between houses and divisible securities with tradable payoffs. The existence of a stochastic discount factor says that all investors who choose to buy assets discount risk-free payoffs at the same rate and pay the same risk premia per unit of payoff. In a frictionless market, these properties are guaranteed by the absence of arbitrage opportunities, which in turn is necessary for the existence to a solution to the investor's optimization problem.[k]

A stochastic discount factor need not exist because indivisibility and nontradability introduce limits to arbitrage. In fact, each friction separately is sufficient to preclude discount rates or risk premia to be equated across houses. If either the quantity of assets is restricted to zero or one, or if all dividends have to be consumed, then fewer arbitrage

[j] The example relies on differences in beliefs for tractability. For the issues discussed below, it does not matter whether differences in risk attitude stem from beliefs or other household characteristics such as risk aversion or nontradable income risk.

[k] If an investor perceives two assets with same exposure but different risk premia, he expects unlimited profits from shorting the expensive portfolio and buying the cheaper one.

trades are feasible or desirable and the absence of arbitrage places weaker restrictions on prices. We consider the mechanisms in turn and then draw conclusions for matching observed prices.

Indivisibility and the Valuation of Quality Steps

Example 2 above illustrates the role of indivisibility. Suppose there was a stochastic discount factor M_{t+1} pricing all houses. With two states of nature, M_{t+1} consists of two numbers. Since houses pay off zero in state 2, the risk-adjusted future payoff from a house of quality h would have to equal h multiplied by the value of M_{t+1} in state 1. However, in Example 2 the risk adjusted payoff is $\rho_1 h + \frac{1}{2}h^2$, a contradiction. The result does not depend on a continuum of house qualities—a similar contradiction can be shown in Example 1. Moreover, it does not depend on nontradability; in fact, in the examples the housing dividend per unit of quality $g_2/g_1 - I'$ is independent of h, as it would be if dividends could be sold at a per-unit price in a rental market.

Why do optimizing households not arbitrage away differences in the valuation of house payoffs? Consider the pricing equation (13): it resembles a standard pricing equation $q_t = E_t^0 M_{t+1}\pi_{t+1}$, except that it is applied only to the quality step from h to $h + dh$.[l] The pricing of that quality step reflects the valuation of buyers of h. Buyers of lower quality houses may not share the same valuation—in fact, in the examples they perceive a lower probability of a positive payoff and would like to short the quality step at h. However, quality steps are not by themselves traded in markets: households can only trade houses, that is, portfolios of quality steps. Moreover, households cannot sell houses short. As a result, they cannot in general generate a synthetic claim that replicates the change in payoff at a quality step.[m]

If other forces equate risk-adjustment factors, a stochastic discount factor exists even with indivisibility and short sale constraints. For example, suppose that housing risk is spanned by the securities, that is, for every house there exists a portfolio of securities with the same payoff profile. Every $M_{t+1}^*(h)$ is then a valid stochastic discount factor for all houses.[n] If optimizing investors can replicate houses by trading securities, they equate

[l] Another difference is that by our timing convention house prices are always "cum dividend"—they include the current flow payoff from housing—whereas securities prices are ex dividend. This convention is not central to the discussion that follows.

[m] The effect of indivisibility is different from that of short sale constraints with divisible securities. Indeed, in models with only short sale constraints and no other constraints a stochastic discount factor does exist: for any given risk, it reflects the MRS of the investors who are most optimistic about that risk and end up as the only investors exposed to that risk in equilibrium. As a result, investors do not differ in the risk premia they pay for risks they are actually exposed to.

[n] If housing risk is spanned, the marginal rates of substitution $M_{t+1}^*(h)$ are equated on all events over which house payoffs are constant and can be pulled out of the integral in (14). Integrating over $\tilde{h}$, we obtain a standard risk-adjusted payoff.

their assessment of housing risk. For example, in the special case when markets are complete, all $M^*_{t+1}(h)$ are equal.

Nontradability and Individual Specific Returns

We refer to $g_2/g_1 - I'$ as the dividend from housing because it records the flow benefit to homeowners, as does the dividend on a security such as equity. However, nontradability implies that the housing dividend may differ across households who consume h because those households have different consumption bundles and preferences. As a result, the returns earned on the same housing position may differ across households, in contrast to the return on securities.[o] Returns on owner-occupied housing are thus more difficult to observe than those on other assets, including rental housing where the dividend to the landlord can be observed in the rental market.

Nontradability implies that a stochastic discount factor need not exist even when the pricing of houses is linear. Indeed, (15) says that with linear pricing the MRS of buyers of quality h determines the price of assets and houses of quality h. However, it is not necessarily true that the same MRS determines house prices for any other quality $h' \neq h$. Arbitrage is limited because households who disagree about the required risk-free return on assets or on the risk premium on houses may also obtain different marginal benefits from housing services, or "marginal dividends." More patient or more optimistic households thus buy larger houses, while more impatient or more pessimistic households buy smaller houses.

3.3.3 Pricing Houses vs Pricing Equity

What are the testable restrictions on the prices of houses and other assets that are implied by optimizing behavior in our framework? The large literature on the pricing of equity employs two working hypotheses. The first is that equity, or firm capital, is a divisible asset that is priced linearly, so that it suffices to focus on the properties of a single per-unit price. Second, there exists a stochastic discount factor that can be inferred from optimality conditions of some investor, for example, certain households or institutional investors. Success of a model is then measured by whether the family of stochastic discount factors implied by the model can explain how the price of equity moves relative to dividends. Moreover, one can learn about desirable features of a model up front from a reduced form approach that postulates a specific functional form for the stochastic discount factor and infers its properties from securities prices.

The previous discussion shows that models of owner-occupied housing satisfy these two working hypotheses only under restrictive assumptions. On the one hand, indivisibility implies that pricing may be nonlinear for any given observable concept of

[o] In fact, when we select households with $\left(c_t^*(h), M_t^*(h)\right)$ such that (13) holds, it is not necessarily the case that all households who buy h share those characteristics.

quality—houses of different qualities are different assets. The challenge for a model is then not to reconcile movements in one price with many household MRSs, but rather to generate the right cross-sectional links between different prices and MRSs. On the other hand, when markets are sufficiently incomplete, limits to arbitrage preclude the existence of a stochastic discount factor altogether. In this case, reduced form frictionless pricing exercises do not help infer how pricing works—a more explicit analysis of frictions is called for.

Whether or not pricing is linear or a stochastic discount factor exists, models of optimizing households imply strong testable restrictions on the joint distribution of house prices, house quality choices and household characteristics. Suppose, for example, that according to the model, wealth is the only dimension of heterogeneity among households. Optimal choice of housing implies an assignment of house qualities to wealth levels. Given that assignment, (14) predicts a cross section of prices by quality. Success of a study then depends on how well it can match the cross-sectional comovement of wealth, quality and prices when compared to micro data. The restrictions are derived from household optimization alone, much like standard Euler equation tests.

Nonlinear Pricing and the Cross Section of House Prices

With indivisibility and nontradability, the cross section of house prices is especially informative about the merits of different models. In particular, nonlinear pricing can account for richer patterns in the cross section of capital gains than linear pricing. We have seen in Section 2.2 how capital gains systematically differ across the quality spectrum over the recent US boom–bust cycle. With linear pricing, capital gains are

$$\frac{p_{t+1}(H_{t+1}(h_t))}{p_t(h_t)} = \frac{\bar{p}_{t+1}}{\bar{p}_t}\frac{H_{t+1}(h_t)}{h_t}.$$

The conditional distribution of capital gains depends on current quality h_t only via actual changes in quality between t and $t+1$. In contrast, the effects of valuation are the same for all qualities. This feature implies that models with linear pricing have trouble generating the large differences in average capital gains across quality tiers. If pricing is instead nonlinear, then changes in the characteristics of marginal investors along the quality spectrum can also affect capital gains.

Nonlinear pricing of houses can reflect various dimensions of heterogeneity. Example 2 highlights how differences in risk assessment or discount factors affect *inter*temporal MRSs. However, even if all intertemporal MRSs agree, so that a stochastic discount factor exist, the *intra*temporal MRSs (7) are not necessarily equated because of nontradability. Nonlinear payoffs and hence prices can thus obtain even in a static setting or if all intertemporal MRSs agree so that a stochastic discount factor exists.

With nonlinear pricing, individual characteristics of marginal investors at a given quality matter for the relative price of that quality. The same property arises in markets that are segmented by quality. The difference between nonlinear pricing and segmentation is that nonlinear pricing creates spillovers in pricing across qualities. For example, changes in the preferences of households who buy low quality houses affect also the values of higher quality houses.

Volatility of House Values in Heterogeneous Agent Models

Indivisibility—and to some extent also nontradability—provide extra scope for heterogeneity of agents to affect the volatility of house prices. This is promising because standard heterogeneous agent models face a challenge when it comes to generating volatility. The challenge arises because optimizing households respond to shocks by reallocating assets until all Euler equations hold jointly. If a stochastic discount factor exists, discount rates $E_t^0 M_{t+1}$ and risk premia $cov_t^0(M_{t+1}, \pi_{t+1})$ are equated across agents. Any shocks to the distribution of agent characteristics or shocks that affect a subset of agents have only a muted impact on prices because portfolio adjustments keep MRSs similar. As the simplest example, if markets are complete, pure changes in the distribution of individual income risks are offset by portfolio adjustment and prices remain unchanged.

With indivisible housing and markets sufficiently incomplete so that housing risk is not spanned, intertemporal MRSs $M_{t+1}^*(h)$ are not equated. Suppose there is a shock that affects the income or beliefs of low quality home buyers. The shock can change the MRS of low quality buyers and hence the slope of the price function at low qualities, but have no effect on the MRS of high quality buyers. Reallocation of housing risk is limited since no household buys more than one house. As a result, the shock will likely have a stronger impact on house prices in the low quality segment than the high segment, and the aggregate market will move together with the price of low quality houses.

To illustrate the implication of cross-sectional shocks on risk premia in the standard pricing equation (14), we let $D_t(h)$ denote the housing dividend and rewrite the pricing equation as

$$p_t(h) = D_t(h) + E_t^0[p_{t+1}(H_{t+1}(h))]/R_t^f + h\, cov_t^{0,U}(M_{t+1}^*(h)), p_{t+1}'(H_{t+1}(h))H_{t+1}'(h)),$$

where we have exchanged expectation and integration, and used the fact that all $M_{t+1}^*(h)$ agree on the risk-free rate. The second term on the right-hand side is the expected present value of the house discounted at the risk-free rate. The notation $cov_t^{0,U}$ indicates that the random variables vary not only across states of nature, but also across qualities, where quality is uniformly distributed on $[0, h]$ by construction—this is because we have selected one household for quality level.

For securities, MRSs are all equal and risk premia depend on variation common to all MRSs and payoffs across states of nature. Any excess volatility of prices is due to changes in this common variation. With indivisible housing, excess volatility can also be due to changes of the cross-sectional distribution of agent characteristics. In particular, changes in the environment that affect only a subset of agents that buy low quality houses can shift the distribution and affect many prices and hence the aggregate market.

When pricing is linear, nontradability implies that MRSs are still not equated across investors. However, the same per-unit price $\bar{p}_t$ appears in all Euler equations (15). Hence, the per-unit price will only change if the Euler equations of buyers at all quality levels are affected. A shock that affects only a subset of households can thus only matter for prices if it also changes the Euler equation of high quality buyers. This requires changes in either the intertemporal or the intratemporal MRS of high quality buyers. Models with linear pricing thus imply that the distribution of house choices respond more strongly, which dampens the effect on prices. Overall, the scope for price volatility is reduced.

3.4 Equilibrium

In this section we take a first look at equilibrium. We close the frictionless model presented so far by introducing an exogenous supply of securities as well as an exogenous endowment of numeraire consumption. We also assume a fixed *aggregate* supply of housing services. To emphasize the role of indivisibility, we compare two stark special cases for technology that are common in applications: a fixed distribution of house qualities, and free conversion of house qualities into each other.

We take a general approach to expectation formation that can accommodate various concepts in the literature. We first define a *temporary equilibrium* for date t as a collection of prices and allocations such that markets clear given beliefs and agents' preferences and endowments. Following Grandmont (1977), temporary equilibrium imposes market clearing and individual optimization, but does not require that each agent's belief coincide with the physical probability P^0. We then discuss further restrictions on expectations and their role in quantitative work. In particular, we compare rational expectations equilibrium and self-confirming equilibrium—a common shortcut that simplifies computations in heterogeneous agent models—as well as temporary equilibria with directly measured expectations.

3.4.1 Housing Market Clearing

We denote the mass of households that makes decisions at date t by $\mathcal{I}_t$. For each individual $i \in \mathcal{I}_t$, the solution of the individual household problem delivers decision rules for consumption, savings and portfolio choice that depend on calendar time, the endogenous state variable cash on hand and current prices. Moreover, household decisions depend on preferences and in particular beliefs about future income, prices and asset payoffs. Let P_t^i be the belief of household i at date t and $h_t^i(p_t, q_t; w_t^i, P_t^i)$ be his housing demand at date t.[p]

[p] Here, P_t^i represents a probability on infinite sequences. Beliefs at different information sets therefore do not have to be derived as conditionals from a single probability. This generality is useful to accommodate, for example, beliefs that are derived from a forecasting model estimated with data up to date t.

We assume that there are always at least as many households as houses of positive quality.[q] We thus fix the mass of houses at $\mathcal{I}_t$ and let G_t denote the date t cumulative density function of available house qualities, defined on $[0, \infty)$. If the households' choice set $\mathcal{H}$ is finite, then G_t is a step function. If $G_t(0) > 0$, then not every household will be able to buy a house of positive quality in equilibrium. The housing market clears if at every quality $h > 0$, the number of households who choose a house of quality h or better is the same as the number of houses with these qualities:

$$\Pr\left(h_t^i\left(p_t, q_t;\ w_t^i, P_t^i\right) \geq h\right) = 1 - G_t(h). \tag{16}$$

3.4.2 Fixed Supply vs Linear Conversion

If the distribution of house qualities G_t is exogenous, prices adjust so that the household sector absorbs the given distribution. The endogenous objects in this case include equilibrium house prices—one for every quality level—as well as the assignment of individual houses to individual households. In general, house prices are nonlinear in quality and reflect the distributions of qualities and household characteristics. The simple examples of Section 3.3.2 show how this can happen: if we take the set of houses used there to describe an exogenous supply, then the prices and individual choices characterize an equilibrium given that supply.

The polar opposite of a fixed quality distribution is *linear conversion*. Suppose that the total housing stock (measured as the aggregate supply of housing services) is fixed at some number H_t, but that it can be divided up every period into individual houses without cost. Since the marginal transformation across quality types is now fixed at one, pricing must be linear. There is only one price that reflects the value of a unit of housing in terms of numeraire. The distribution of qualities G_t becomes an endogenous object that is determined in equilibrium subject to a constraint on the mean

$$\int_0^1 h dG_t(h) = H_t. \tag{17}$$

A fixed distribution is interesting in applications that consider the short-term response to shocks. It is also useful for longer-term analysis if the market can be viewed as a collection of segments fixed by geography or regulation such as zoning. In contrast, linear conversion is an interesting assumption in applications that consider long-run outcomes or when studying new developments where developers design the distribution of houses from scratch. Beyond these polar opposites, it could be interesting to explore intermediate cases of costly conversion by developers. The macroeconomics literature has yet to consider this explicitly.

[q] This assumption covers most applications we discuss below. Alternatively, we would have to develop further the use of a vacant house.

To decentralize an economy with linear conversion, we assume that there is a competitive developer sector that buys existing houses and sells new houses. The endogenous distribution of houses will then satisfy our earlier assumption that the number of houses is always less or equal than the number of households. Since households have no use for more than one house, developers never create more than $\mathcal{I}_t$ houses at date t. Moreover, competition among developers and linear conversion force linear pricing: the relative price of any two qualities must equal the unitary marginal rate of transformation.

With either technology, the housing component of equilibrium includes a price function $p_t(.)$ as well as an allocation of house qualities such that the market clearing condition (16) holds. In an *equilibrium with fixed quality distribution*, (16) holds for the exogenous cdf G_t. In contrast, an *equilibrium with linear conversion*includes an equilibrium distribution of house qualities G_t that satisfies (17) and moreover features a linear price function $p_t(h) = \bar{p}_t h$.

3.4.3 Temporary Equilibrium

We assume that household $i \in \mathcal{I}_t$ enters period t endowed with a house of quality $\bar{h}_t^i$, securities $\bar{\theta}_t^i$ as well as y_t^i units of numeraire. We allow for households in their last period of life who mechanically sell any housing and securities and consume all the proceeds. To accommodate long-lived securities, we write payoffs as price plus dividend, that is, $\pi_t = \hat{\pi}(q_t) + D_t$. For example, the Jth security is a risk-free one-period bond, so $\pi_{t,J} = 1$. If the jth security is equity then $\pi_{t,j} = q_{t,j} + D_{t,j}$ where $D_{t,j}$ is the dividend.[r]

In addition to a price function, a house allocation and—with linear conversion—a distribution of house qualities, a *date ttemporary equilibrium* consists of securities and consumption allocations as well as security prices such that housing, numeraire and securities markets clear at the optimal demand, with initial wealth evaluated at the equilibrium prices. The conditions for wealth, numeraire and securities are

$$\begin{aligned} w_t^i &= y_t^i + \bar{\theta}_t^{i\top} \hat{\pi}_t(q_t) + p_t\left(\bar{h}_t^i\right); \quad i \in \mathcal{I}_t \\ \int_{\mathcal{I}_t} c_t^i\left(p_t, q_t; w_t^i, P_t^i\right) + I\left(h_t^i\left(p_t, q_t; w_t^i, P_t^i\right)\right) di &= \int_{\mathcal{I}_t} \left(y_t^i + \theta_t^{i\top} D_t\right) di \\ \int_{\mathcal{I}_t} \theta_t^i\left(p_t, q_t; w_t^i, P_t^i\right) di &= \int_{\mathcal{I}_t} \bar{\theta}_t^i di. \end{aligned} \tag{18}$$

A *sequence of temporary equilibria* is a collection of date t temporary equilibria that are connected via the updating of endowments. In particular, for any household $i \in \mathcal{I}_t$ who was already alive at date $t-1$, we impose $\bar{h}_t^i = h_{t-1}^i\left(p_{t-1}, q_{t-1}; w_{t-1}^i, P_{t-1}^i\right)$ and similar for the securities holdings. Agents who enter the economy at date t are endowed only with labor

[r] The function $\hat{\pi}$ helps accommodate debt with longer but finite maturity. For example, if the kth security is a risk-free two-period zero-coupon bond, then $\pi_{t,k} = \hat{\pi}_{t,k} = q_{t,J}$ since the two-period bond turns into a one-period bond after one period.

income y_t^i. While a sequence of temporary equilibria tracks the distribution of asset holdings over time, it still does not restrict expectations.

3.4.4 Rational Expectations Equilibrium vs Self-confirming Equilibrium

A *rational expectations equilibrium* is a sequence of temporary equilibria such that $P_t^i = P^0$ for every period t and agent i. Beliefs thus coincide with the physical probability for all events: all agents agree with the econometrician on the distribution of all exogenous and endogenous variables. Rational expectations equilibrium is common in macroeconomic studies, especially when the model has few agents and assets or when there is no aggregate risk. In such cases, it is straightforward to move from the recursive formulation of decision problems to the definition of a recursive equilibrium that expresses prices as a function of a small set of state variables.

For the simplest example, suppose there is a representative agent. Since we have assumed a fixed supply of assets, there are no endogenous state variables. Prices only depend on current variables such as consumption as well as current variables required to forecast future exogenous variables such as income and asset payoffs. With rich heterogeneity, rational expectations equilibria become more difficult to characterize. With incomplete markets as well as other frictions described below, defining a recursive equilibrium may require a large dimensional state space that contains the distribution of not only wealth but also individual asset holdings—for example, housing and long term mortgages—as well as their dependence on age.

To avoid explicitly dealing with a large state space and the resulting complicated distribution of endogenous variables, studies with heterogenous agents and aggregate risk often look for a *self-confirming equilibrium* in which agent beliefs coincide with the physical probability P^0 only on a subset of events.[s] A common approach follows Krusell and Smith (1998) and parametrizes agent beliefs about future prices with "forecast functions" that map future prices to a simple set of current predictor variables (such as the current cross-sectional mean of asset holdings) and shocks. A self-confirming equilibrium requires that the forecast functions match prices also under the physical probability.

Self-confirming equilibrium imposes different restrictions on allocations and prices than rational expectations equilibrium since the forecast functions only involve a limited set of moments of the state variables. In general, there can be other self-confirming equilibria with other forecast functions, and there is no guarantee that any particular self-confirming equilibrium is a rational expectations equilibrium.[t] Applying self-confirming

[s] The labeling here follows Sargent (1999) who in turns builds on the game theoretic concept in Fudenberg and Levine (1998). Krusell and Smith (1998) refer to "approximate equilibria."

[t] At the same time, if there exists a recursive rational expectations equilibrium, then it is also a self-confirming equilibrium for *some* forecast function (not necessarily simple). In sufficiently tractable models, one can try out different forecast functions systematically so as to establish that a self-confirming equilibrium is indeed close to a rational expectations equilibrium. This route is taken by Krusell and Smith (1998), but not in the typical application on housing reviewed below.

equilibrium with a given forecast function thus calls for justifications of assumptions on beliefs, perhaps by appealing to bounded rationality.

3.4.5 Temporary Equilibrium with Measured Expectations

An alternative approach implements temporary equilibria by directly measuring expectations about future variables that are relevant for agent decisions. The temporary equilibrium then provides a map from technology and the distribution of household characteristics *as well as expectations* into prices and allocations. To specify beliefs, one relevant source is survey data which can be informative in particular about the cross-sectional relationship between expectations and other characteristics (for example, Piazzesi and Schneider, 2009a). Alternatively, expectations about prices can be specified using a forecasting model (Landvoigt et al., 2015).

Temporary equilibrium with measured expectations also simplifies computation. It is helpful to think of the computation of equilibrium in two steps—first individual optimization given prices and then finding market clearing prices. To find temporary equilibrium prices for a given trading period means finding a solution to the nonlinear equation system (18) in as many unknowns as there are prices. This is in contrast to rational expectations equilibrium where one looks for an entire price function. Since the price finding step for temporary equilibrium is easier, the optimization step can be made more difficult: the concept lends itself well to models with a rich asset structure, for example, with many house types or many risky assets.

A conceptual difference between temporary equilibrium with measured expectations and rational expectations equilibrium is that the modeler does not a priori impose a connection between expectations at any given date and model outcomes at future dates. Of course, if the model is well specified, then this does not matter for the fit of the model: any rational expectations equilibrium gives rise to a sequence of temporary equilibria given the set of beliefs that agents hold in the rational expectation equilibrium. With a well specified model, that same set of beliefs should be apparent in expectation surveys or in a good forecasting model.

The conceptual difference is thus in how we assess the fit of a misspecified model and how we achieve identification of parameters. Rational expectations equilibrium and self-confirming equilibrium view both prices and the cross section of endowments as a function of state variables. To identify parameters that affect the coefficients in prices and decision rules requires controlled variation of the state variables. The concepts are thus most easily and most commonly applied when variables display recurrent patterns: the empirical moments of prices and other variables can then be compared to the stationary equilibrium implied by the model. In contrast, temporary equilibrium can be implemented even with data on only a single trading period. Prices are then a single set of numbers and endowments are measured directly. Identification of parameters that affect prices comes from cross-sectional variation in prices and allocations.

There is also a difference in how we deal with misspecification and counterfactuals. Rational expectations insist that expectations are "consistent with the model," so beliefs are as misspecified as the model itself. Moreover, counterfactuals—such as changes in a policy parameter—vary expectations in a way that is consistent with the model. Temporary equilibrium with measured expectations instead emphasizes that expectations are "consistent with the data" at the initial equilibrium. As a result, there is no prediction on how expectations change with parameters; any counterfactual requires a reassessment of the assumptions on expectations.[u]

There are two reasons why the use of temporary equilibrium with measured expectations is particularly attractive in models of housing. First, as we have discussed, there are payoffs from including a rich set of assets, in particular houses of many different qualities. Second, the postwar data on housing is shaped by the two boom periods—the 1970s and the 2000s—that saw several unusual shocks, as discussed in Section 4.5. Given this data situation, identification of a stationary equilibrium price function from regular patterns is less powerful. In contrast, there is much to learn from the cross section and from data on expectations for both boom episodes.

3.5 Production and Land

In this section, we describe models of housing supply that are common in the applications below. We start from a general setup that allows for land and structures as separate factors of production. We then explain when housing can nevertheless be represented by the single state variable "quality," as we have done throughout this chapter. Finally, we review additional restrictions on house prices derived from firm optimization.

Consider a general production function at the property level. When a new structure of size k^0 is paired with a lot of size l, initial house quality is $h = F^0\left(k^0, l\right)$. Once a house has been built, its lot size remains the same, whereas the structure may depreciate or improve. With a stream of investments i_t, the quality of a house of age τ is given by

$$h_{t+\tau} = z_{t+\tau} F^{\tau}\left(k_t^0, i_{t+1}, \ldots, i_{t+\tau}, l_t\right), \quad (19)$$

where $z_{t+\tau}$ is a productivity shock. The production function F^{τ} may depend on the vintage τ.

Both new structures and improvements to existing houses are produced by a construction sector from capital K_t^c and labor N_t^c. As before, the mass of houses is $\mathcal{I}_t$ and we index individual houses by $j \in [0, \mathcal{I}_t]$. We further assume that it is costless to scrap an existing house. Construction output—or residential investment—is then

[u] Predictions on expectations can be obtained by imposing more structure on expectation formation, for example, via learning rules. For a survey on learning in macroeconomics, see Evans and Honkapohja (2009).

$$\int_0^{\mathcal{I}_t} \left(k_t^0(j) + i_t(j)\right) dj = I_t^c = Z_t^c F^c\left(K_t^c, N_t^c\right), \tag{20}$$

where F^c and Z_t^c are the production function and the productivity shock for the construction sector, respectively.

We distinguish the construction sector labeled c from the rest of the business sector–labeled y—that makes numeraire from capital and labor. Capital in both sectors is made from numeraire one for one without adjustment costs and depreciates at constant rates δ^c and δ^y. The resource constraints for numeraire and the capital accumulation equations are

$$\begin{aligned} C_t + I_t^y + I_t^c &= Z_t^y F^y\left(K_t^y, N_t^y\right), \\ K_{t+1}^s &= (1-\delta^s)K_t^s + I_t^s, s = y, c. \end{aligned} \tag{21}$$

It remains to describe how costly it is to change the distribution of existing individual housing units. We distinguish different scenarios below.

In each case, the definition of equilibrium is amended by adding (*i*) construction output as a separate intermediate good that trades in a competitive market at the relative price p_t^c, (*ii*) both types of capital as securities in the households' problems that trade at a price of one and yield a net return equal to the marginal product of capital less depreciation, (*iii*) as market clearing conditions for construction output and numeraire (20) and the first equation in (21), respectively, (*iv*) labor income as labor times the competitive wage in the household budget constraint.

3.5.1 From Land and Structures to House Quality

In principle, the above technology could give rise to rich dynamics for the distribution of house types. For example, if different vintages of houses have different capital–land ratios, they may yield the same housing services, but depreciate at different rates. The macroeconomics literature has by and large sidestepped this issue with assumptions that allow housing to be summarized by one number, quality. We now discuss several special assumptions that accomplish the same outcome even when land is present. The simplest approach is to leave out land altogether, as in the literature on home production. Housing is then identified with structures only.

3.5.2 The Tree Model

Another simple approach is a "tree model" of housing that can motivate setups with a fixed or slow-moving quality distribution. Suppose that structures depreciate at rate δ, but that a house remains inhabitable (that is, yields positive housing services) only as long as structures and land are always paired in exact proportions.[v] All owners who hold

[v] In terms of the above notation, assume first that $F^0(k, l) = l$ if $k = \kappa l$ and $F^0(k, l) = 0$ otherwise, so every inhabitable house built must have a structure–land ratio of κ. Assume further that future quality F^τ is equal to l_t if $i_s = \delta k_s^0$ for all $s = t, \ldots, t + \tau$ and zero otherwise.

a house from one period to the next then make the improvement $i_t = \delta k_t^0$ every period. In other words, a house works like a tree that yields fruit equal to housing services less improvements.

The tree model implies that the state of a house can be summarized by a single variable, quality. From the perspective of households, quality is constant as long as maintenance is performed, the case of "essential maintenance" discussed in Section 3. When the distribution of lots is fixed, one can apply the definition of equilibrium with a fixed quality distribution from Section 3.4. Alternatively, we could add a technology by which lots are converted. For example, if it was possible for developers to freely redivide lots, then we would obtain an equilibrium with linear conversion.

3.5.3 A Frictionless Model

Suppose that the production of housing from land and structures has constant returns and that structures depreciate at a constant rate. Suppose further that houses are produced by a competitive developer sector who can linearly convert both land and structures. We thus have a frictionless model with two factors of production.[w] All houses built at the same point in time will share the same ratio of structures to land. From the perspective of households, the change in house quality depends on the land share together with the depreciation rate of structures. The household problem thus looks like one with geometric depreciation of quality, determined endogenously from the equilibrium land share.

The frictionless model imposes a supply-side restriction on house prices that must hold together with Euler equations from the household side discussed earlier. Indeed, from the first-order condition of a developer, we have

$$\bar{p}_t F_1^0(K_t, L) = p_t^c,$$

where K_t is aggregate structures, L is aggregate land, assumed constant, and p_t^c is the relative price of construction output. If there are many structures, then the scarcity of the fixed factor land drives up the per-unit price $\bar{p}_t$ of housing. Since aggregate structures move slowly over time, this type of model typically has trouble generating a lot of volatility in house prices relative to the price of construction output. The problem is similar to that encountered by models of the firm without adjustment costs to capital.

[w] In terms of the above notation, let

$$F^\tau(k_t^0, i_{t+1}, \ldots, i_{t+\tau}, l_t) = F^0(k_{t+\tau}, l_t),$$

where $k_{t+\tau} = (1-\delta)k_{t+\tau-1}$ is recursively defined.

3.5.4 Land as a Flow Constraint

An alternative frictionless model uses land as a constraint on the flow of new housing, as opposed to as a factor of production for all housing as above. Since the model assumes linear conversion, we write technology directly in terms of aggregate quality:

$$H_t = (1-\delta)H_{t-1} + \widetilde{F}^h\left(Z_t^c F^c\left(K_t^c, N_t^c\right), \bar{L}\right). \tag{22}$$

Here, $\widetilde{F}^h$ is a constant returns production function that transforms construction output (that is, housing investment) and a constant flow of new land into new housing. The technology is decentralized via competitive firms.

The flow constraint approach also reduces the state variables to only house quality. It does so by applying the depreciation rate directly to the bundle of land and structures. Even though different vintages of new houses will generally have different land shares, they are nevertheless assumed to depreciate at the same rate. The flow constraint also differs from the frictionless model above in the restriction on prices. Firm first-order conditions deliver

$$\bar{p}_t \widetilde{F}_1^h\left(Z_t^c F^c\left(K_t^c, N_t^c\right), \bar{L}\right) = p_t^c.$$

The ratio of house prices to the price of construction output now relates to residential investment, which is much more volatile than the level of capital.

3.6 Rental Housing

So far we have focused on owner-occupied housing, that is, we have forced households to own a house if they want to consume housing services. We now modify the model to allow for rental housing. We discuss implications for portfolio choice and discuss how additional restrictions on house prices can be derived from household as well as from landlord decisions to invest in tenant-occupied housing.

We continue to assume that households have exactly one residence that is now either owned or rented. We denote the quality of a rented residence by s_t and the rental rate at that quality by $p_t^s(s_t)$. We then modify the second-stage problem to

$$\widetilde{V}_t\left(\widetilde{w}_t, h_t\right) = \max_{c_t, \alpha_t} U\left(g\left(c_t, h_t + s_t I_{h_t=0}\right)\right) + \beta E_t\left[V_{t+1}\left(w_{t+1}\right)\right]$$

$$w_{t+1} = \left(\widetilde{w}_t - c_t - p_t^s(s_t)\right) R_{t+1}(\alpha_t) + p_{t+1}\left(H_{t+1}(h_t)\right) + y_{t+1}. \tag{23}$$

In the budget constraint, expenditure now includes rent. The indicator function in the objective ensures that only households who have not chosen to own (that is, $h_t = 0$) obtain utility from a rented residence.

To handle the landlord side of renting, we assume that tenant-occupied houses of a given quality are held in real estate investment trusts (REITs) and households can purchase shares in those trusts subject to short-sale constraints. REIT shares then enter the second stage problem much like standard securities. The dividend earned by the REIT from a house of quality h_t is given by the rent net of maintenance cost $p_t^s(h_t) - I_r(h_t)$. We allow maintenance cost to be higher when the house is tenant occupied than when it is owner occupied.

The formulation here thus introduces one advantage of ownership—lower maintenance cost—that is traded off against the disadvantage of bearing housing price risk. This approach to studying rental markets and tenure choice in an otherwise frictionless equilibrium model goes back to Henderson and Ioannides (1983). Their paper also provides microfoundations for the difference in maintenance cost using a moral hazard problem between landlord and tenant. A closely related approach assumes that homeowners receive more housing services from owned houses. In addition to the tradeoff studied here, differences in tax treatment as well as the interaction of tenure choice with collateral constraints and transaction costs are also important; they are discussed further below.

3.6.1 Optimality Conditions and Tenure Choice

Renters' first-order condition is one of intratemporal choice between the two goods, housing services and numeraire. We focus on the case of a continuum of qualities. With a smooth rent function, a household who rents a house of quality h must be indifferent between renting that house or renting a slightly better or worse house:

$$p_t^{s\prime}(h_t) = \frac{g_2(c_t, h_t)}{g_1(c_t, h_t)}. \tag{24}$$

Much like for owner occupiers, a renter of quality h_t is marginal for houses of quality h_t, but not necessarily for house of any other quality. As a result, the rent function can in general be nonlinear—a linear rent function obtains under special assumptions such as when rental houses of different qualities can be converted one for one.

The first-order conditions for REIT shares at different quality levels work like those for stocks of different companies. The intertemporal MRS of a landlord household serves as a stochastic discount factor for tenant-occupied houses. Without frictions, the typical landlord household will build a diversified portfolio that contains houses of all qualities. For tenant-occupied houses, discount rates and risk-adjustment factors are thus also equated across quality levels. This does not mean, however, that prices become linear in quality: rent and hence the dividend to the landlord is generally nonlinear due to indivisibility in the rental market.

The presence of a rental market separates the roles of housing as a consumption good and asset. While owners must commit more savings toward the housing asset and bear housing risk, renters simply pay the flow expenditure of housing services. At the same time, the difference in maintenance cost implies that the rent for a house of given quality may be higher than the dividend that a household would earn if he instead were to own the house. In the current setup with indivisibility as the only friction, we would thus expect households who perceive a higher risk-adjusted payoff from housing to become owners.

3.6.2 The User Cost of Housing

Consider a household who is indifferent between owning and renting a house of quality h. Suppose further that housing risk is spanned so that the stochastic discount factor is the intertemporal MRS of an indifferent household.[x] The indifference condition now equates the rent $p_t^s(h)$ to the "user cost of housing," that is, price less discounted payoff. Equivalently, we can write the current price as

$$p_t(h_t) = p_t^s(h_t) - I(h_t) + E_t[M_{t+1} p_{t+1}(H_{t+1}(h_t))]. \tag{25}$$

Here, the payoff from ownership includes the maintenance cost $I(h_t)$ of an owner-occupied house. We thus obtain a conventional asset pricing equation for houses at quality h.

An alternative derivation starts from the first-order condition of landlords and assumes that there is free conversion between tenant and owner-occupied houses. We can then use the landlord's MRS as a stochastic discount factor:

$$p_t(h_t) = p_t^s(h_t) - I_r(h_t) + E_t[M_{t+1} p_{t+1}(H_{t+1}(h_t))]. \tag{26}$$

For both equations to hold at the same time, we must either have no difference in maintenance cost, or the intertemporal MRSs of landlords and owners must be different. This might be, for example, because landlords are more optimistic than owners and are thus willing to incur more housing risk.

If we solve the user cost (25) forward, and impose a transversality condition on the expected weighted house price in the distant future, the price of a house of quality h can be written as the present value of future rents

$$p_t(h_t) = E_t\left[\sum_{\tau=0}^{\infty} \prod_{j=1}^{\tau} M_{t+j}(p_{t+\tau}^s(h_{t+\tau}) - I(h_t))\right]. \tag{27}$$

Since we have assumed that housing risk is spanned, we can further aggregate across quality levels and obtain pricing equations for the entire housing market.

Applied studies often take (27) as a starting point and construct a reduced-form pricing kernel. The test is analogous to testing whether a particular candidate stochastic discount factor prices equity given observable prices and dividends. As we have seen, user-cost equations hold only under special assumptions. We also emphasize that even when those assumptions are met, they represent additional restrictions on prices that hold on top of the equations already discussed above that characterize optimal quality choice conditional on owning or renting.

[x] This is true in particular if the household is a landlord and there is free conversion between tenant and owner occupancy—the household can then assemble REITs portfolios with the same payoffs as any individual house. Of course, the indifferent household may not be a landlord—in the presence of short-sale constraints not all households need to participate in the market for tenant-occupied housing.

3.7 Collateral Constraints

Much of the literature captures the role of housing as collateral by a linear constraint on the amount of short term risk-free debt, our *J*th security:

$$-q_{t,J}\theta_{t,J} \leq \phi_t p_t(h_t). \tag{28}$$

Households who take out a mortgage must make a large enough downpayment so that the loan-to-value ratio remains below ϕ_t. The maximum loan to value ratio can be random—exogenous variation in ϕ_t is a popular example of a "financial shock" that either loosens or tightens household borrowing capacity. We also shut down borrowing opportunities through risky securities by imposing short sale constraints $\theta_{t,j} \geq 0$ for $j = 1, \ldots, J-1$.

The downpayment constraint (28) goes back to theoretical work on optimal savings by Artle and Varaiya (1978). Slemrod (1982) used it in an early quantitative life cycle model. In 1990s several papers explored equilibrium effects. In static setups, Shleifer and Vishny (1992) stressed the potential for asset fire sales, while Stein (1995) considered its role in generating comovement of house prices and housing volume. Kiyotaki and Moore (1997) emphasized the amplification effects from collateral constraints in a dynamic model. Detemple and Serrat (2003) and Chien and Lustig (2009) study economies with contingent claims subject to collateral constraints. Geanakoplos (2011) endogenizes the downpayment constraint in a model that allows for default.

While the simple constraint (28) provides a tractable way to capture the benefit of housing as collateral, it leaves out several features of observed mortgages. First, while it is in principle possible for the price to drop below the face value of the mortgage over the next period, the chance of this happening is negligible in most quantitative studies. In contrast, in the data many households with long-term mortgages are "under water." Moreover, a key decision for households is whether to prepay and/or refinance mortgages in response to changes in house prices or interest rates. The simple constraint effectively assumes that refinancing is costless, so that an increase in house prices translates directly into higher borrowing capacity. While it may capture the basic tradeoffs well when the period length is relatively long, or when adjustment of mortgage terms is cheap, several applications discussed below show that details of mortgage contracts can matter significantly for quantitative results.

3.7.1 Household Optimization

The collateral constraint restricts the choice of the risk-free security in the second stage problem (5): we thus modify that problem by adding the constraints $-(\tilde{w}_t - c_t)(1-\alpha'\iota) \leq \phi_t p_t(h_t)$ and $\alpha \geq 0$. Denoting the multipliers on these constraint by ν_t and μ_t, respectively, the first order conditions (8) become

$$\begin{aligned} U'(g(c_t,h_t))g_1(c_t,h_t) &= \beta E_t[V'(w_{t+1})]R_t^f + \nu_t \\ \nu_t\iota &= \beta E_t\left[V'(w_{t+1})\left(R_{t+1} - \iota R_t^f\right)\right] + \mu_t. \end{aligned} \tag{29}$$

As long as the constraints do not bind, the conditions are unchanged. If a household runs up against his borrowing constraint, however, the marginal cost of borrowing includes not only the expected repayment, but also the shadow cost of the constraint. This affects indifference conditions at both the borrowing/lending and portfolio choice margins. In particular, if the borrowing constraint is tight (high ν_t) and the expected excess return on a risky security is low, then it may be optimal to not hold that security at all ($\mu_{t,j} > 0$).

If housing serves as collateral, its marginal benefit in (6) reflects its marginal collateral benefit, in addition to the utility benefit from housing services and the expected capital gain. To compare the three components, we focus on the case of continuous housing quality. The counterpart of (13) is

$$p_t'(h_t)\left(1-\phi_t\left(1/R_t^f - E_t^0 M_{t+1}\right)\right) = \frac{g_2(c_t,h_t)}{g_1(c_t,h_t)} - I'(h_t) + E_t^0\left[M_{t+1}p_{t+1}'(H(h_t))H_{t+1}'(h_t)\right]. \tag{30}$$

On the left hand side, the collateral benefit is expressed as a percentage discount to the pricing step p'. From (29), the discount is zero if the household is unconstrained (that is, $\nu_t = 0$ and $E_t M_{t+1} R_t^f = 1$). It is higher if the lower is the intertemporal MRS: collateral is more useful if the household has a greater need for borrowing.

3.7.2 Savings and Portfolio Choice

The constraints imply that household net worth $p_t(h_t) + q_t'\theta_t$ is nonnegative. This feature is useful for matching household portfolios in the data since negative net worth is not common. It also implies that borrowing does not move future income to the present, in contrast to a simple permanent income model. Instead borrowing is a portfolio choice decision, undertaken in order to build a large enough housing position. The forces discussed in Section 3.2 remain at work: households with a lot of future income should choose leveraged housing positions, especially if their labor income is uncorrelated with housing payoffs.

In the cross section, optimal savings depend on the relative abundance of current wealth relative to future income as well as the remaining life span. When wealth is low relative to income, households do not save at all. Young households with low wealth–income ratios save to be able to make a downpayment. As soon as they have saved enough, they build leveraged portfolios in housing and also some attractive other assets, such as stocks. Older households have higher wealth–income ratios and are thus long in all assets.

As wealth rises relative to income, households start saving until their savings rate approaches an unconstrained optimal savings rate that depends on the distribution of returns—it is constant when returns are iid. Younger households have a longer planning horizon and therefore spread their savings over more years. This effect tends to increase the savings by the young. However, middle aged households have more income, so that they can save more. The higher savings rates of young households dominate when labor income is not important, which means at high wealth–income ratios. For empirically relevant ranges of the wealth–income ratio, the higher savings of the middle aged dominate and create a hump-shaped wealth pattern, which we also see in the data.

Another implication is that constrained households are more reluctant to buy risky securities. Indeed, consider the first-order conditions (29) for households who hold securities: constrained households are indifferent between risky securities and risk-free investment only if the marginal utility weighted expected excess return is strictly positive. In contrast to housing, securities do not come with collateral benefits, and thus require higher premia in order to be held. This feature helps in applications to explain why young households with low cash relative to income do not hold equity even though the equity premium is high.

3.7.3 The Pricing of Securities

The first order conditions (29) suggest that the presence of a collateral constraint might help generate more volatile expected excess returns on risky securities, and hence help resolve the volatility puzzle. Indeed, changes in the tightness of the constraint do affect conditional risk premia. However, a problem with this effect is that it also tends to generate volatility in the risk-free interest rate. Combining the first-order conditions, we obtain

$$U'(g(c_t, h_t))g_1(c_t, h_t) = \beta E_t[V'(w_{t+1})R_{t+1}].$$

The marginal condition for the level returns of risky securities is thus the same as without a collateral constraint. In applications that generate volatility in expected excess returns, that volatility is typically due to volatility in the risk-free rate moves, as opposed to volatility in conditional risky returns as in the data.

3.7.4 House Prices

The presence of a collateral constraint also alters the pricing of houses. The most immediate effect is that if constrained households buy houses, then the collateral benefit increases house prices, holding fixed payoffs and the households' intertemporal MRS. This is a liquidity effect that occurs even with linear pricing and when dividends are tradable. Dividing (29) by the big bracket on the left hand side, we have that housing payoffs are discounted at a lower rate to price in the collateral benefit.

Whether the liquidity effect is important for price movements in a heterogeneous agent model depends on market structure and the presence of other constraints. Collateral constraints provide an important example why households can be affected differently by shocks—for example, the financial shock ϕ_t affects (30) if and only if the household is constrained. At the same time, as discussed in Section 3.3, shocks alter a family of Euler equations via both price and quantity adjustment. The effect on prices will be higher if market structure requires price adjustment because quantities do not move.

To illustrate, suppose ϕ_t increases to relax the downpayment constraint. In the typical population, some households are constrained while others are unconstrained. Suppose now the model assumes linear pricing because houses of different quality can be converted freely. In order for a housing boom to occur, the price per unit of housing will move only if the shock is strong enough to alter the valuation of payoff by unconstrained households; otherwise quantity adjustment will provide more housing for constrained households accompanied by a smaller price reaction. In contrast, with nonlinear pricing and indivisibility, the shock can strongly affect the prices of houses bought by constrained households, without a big impact on the Euler equation of the unconstrained. With limited quantity adjustment, the overall effect on prices can thus be bigger.

3.8 Transaction Costs

We now introduce a proportional transaction cost κ whenever a household sells a house. This tractable and popular specification is often motivated by the rule of thumb that about 6% of the house price are typically paid to the seller's agent in a transaction. It was first studied by Flemming (1969) in a deterministic context and by Grossman and Laroque (1990) in a stochastic model. Beyond these direct costs, it is plausible that most households face other moving costs, either pecuniary—such as changing local services—or possibly nonpecuniary, for example, disutility from leaving a familiar environment. Such costs sometimes motivate a fixed component to moving costs. In what follows we work only with proportional costs since those are sufficient to understand the key effects.

Once transaction costs are taken into account, the existing house becomes *illiquid* and its quality at the beginning of the period $\tilde{h}_t = H_t(h_{t-1})$ becomes a separate state variable in the household problem. We thus write the value function as $V_t(w_t, \tilde{h}_t)$ where w_t is total wealth at the beginning of period t as before. We introduce separate notation for $\tilde{h}_t$ since it depends not only on quality chosen in the previous period, but may also depend on random events such as depreciation. The presence of transaction costs does not affect choices in the second stage problem from Section 3.2. To keep track of the new state variable, we only need to modify the expected continuation utility in the objective to $E_t[V_{t+1}(w_{t+1}, H_{t+1}(h_t))]$.

Let $m_t \in \{0,1\}$ denote the moving choice. The first stage problem is now

$$V_t(w_t, \tilde{h}_t) = \max_{m_t, h_{t+1} \in \mathcal{H}} m_t \tilde{V}_t\left(w_t - \kappa p_t(\tilde{h}_t) - p_t(h_t), h_t\right) + (1 - m_t)\tilde{V}_t(w_t - p_t(\tilde{h}_t), \tilde{h}_t) \quad (31)$$

The first term is the utility of a mover who sells the old house, incurs the transaction cost and buys a new house. The second term is the utility of a stayer: house quality remains unchanged, and the disposable funds for consumption and securities in the second stage problem consist of *liquid wealth*, that is, wealth net of the illiquid house.

To illustrate the benefits of illiquid housing, consider the model with continuous quality. The marginal benefit of house quality at the beginning of the period consists of the effect of housing on wealth as well as the direct benefit. From the envelope theorem, the total marginal benefit is

$$V_{t,1}p'(\widetilde{h}_t) + V_{t,2} = m_t \overset{\sim\,\text{move}}{V}_{t,1} (1-\kappa)p_t'(\widetilde{h}_t) + (1-m_t)\overset{\sim\,\text{stay}}{V}_{t,2}, \tag{32}$$

where the subscripts in $\overset{\sim\,\text{move}}{V_t}$ and $\overset{\sim\,\text{stay}}{V_t}$ indicate whether $\widetilde{V}_t$ is evaluated at the first or second arguments in (31). A mover household, enjoys the marginal benefit of liquid funds conveyed by an extra unit of house quality. In contrast, a stayer household experiences no increase in liquid fund and only enjoys the continuation utility benefit of house quality.

The household problem illustrates three key new features of pricing introduced by transaction costs. First, only movers can be marginal investors in housing in any given period. Since housing has low turnover, the characteristics of only a few people matter directly for determining prices. Second, the value of housing depends less on future prices if moving is less likely. Indeed, (32) shows that the price matters more the higher is m_t. In the extreme case where households know they will never move in the future, their benefit from housing is independent of future prices. Finally, transaction costs lower marginal benefit, and this effect is capitalized into house prices. Other things equal, we thus expect lower prices in markets with higher turnover.

Transaction costs also alter portfolio choice tradeoffs described earlier. First, they make ownership more expensive than renting, and more so for households who expect to move again quickly. In a market with heterogenous agents, the price will compensate the average investor for future transaction costs. It is more likely then that frequent movers prefer renting. Second, households with rising income profiles may leverage even more so they can lock in a large housing position early and do not have to move later. Finally, collateral constraints are more likely to bind even for rich households: whether constraints bind depends on the amount of liquid resources $\widetilde{w}_t$ in the second stage problem. With transaction costs, household may let $\widetilde{w}_t$ decline even though total wealth w_t is large.[y]

4. THEORY VS DATA

We are now ready to discuss work that quantifies the framework in Section 3 and studies its implications in various applications.

4.1 Magnitudes

At the core of any quantitative work based on the framework in Section 3 is the individual household problem. For a problem in which households may choose to buy an

[y] The issue is compounded in a model with long term mortgages that are costly to adjust so that the mortgage position also becomes illiquid. The household then faces a liquidity constraint unless he either sells the house or adjusts the mortgage. As long as he does neither, a change in house prices does not alter funds available for spending.

individual house, it is important to correctly specify the risk-return trade-offs involved. As discussed in Section 2.2, the prices of individual houses are highly volatile. Moreover, a large component of this volatility is idiosyncratic. House prices may also covary with income and other asset prices. These return moments can be taken from empirical studies that estimate their means and covariances with micro data, such as individual property level data and the PSID. Below we discuss whether and how the magnitudes matter in applications.

4.1.1 Preference Parameters

Since housing expenditure shares in the data are similar over time as well as across households (as discussed in Section 2.1), a common specification of the aggregator (2) over housing consumption and nonhousing consumption is Cobb–Douglas. The preference parameter is set equal to the expenditure share on housing, which is roughly 20%.

The choice of the risk aversion parameter depends on whether the portfolio choice problem involves other assets such as stocks. As discussed in Section 2.2, high transaction costs and high volatility lower the Sharpe ratio of individual houses and thereby reduce their attractiveness. In the absence of more attractive assets, a household problem with low risk aversion around 5 will have reasonable implications for optimal portfolios. When the problem allows households to invest in more attractive assets such as stocks, low risk aversion will typically lead to extreme optimal portfolios that exploit the equity premium. To explain observed household portfolios, higher risk aversion or higher perceived risk about stock returns are needed, or high participation costs in the stock market.

4.1.2 Shocks

Exogenous moving shocks capture reasons for moving that are exogenous to the model. The probability of such shocks can be estimated from the American Housing Survey which asks households about their reasons for moving. Roughly a third of movers provide reasons that are unrelated to the economic reasons for moving captured in the models. Examples are disasters such as fires or floods, marriage, divorce, death of spouse, etc. This 1/3 probability is multiplied by the overall probability of moving which is roughly 1/10 per year, resulting in a 1/30 probability for an exogenous move per year.

Households face exogenous survival probability that depend on age. These survival probabilities can be taken from life tables published by the National Center of Health Statistics.[z]

The volatility of individual house prices has a large idiosyncratic component. As discussed in Section 2.2, the volatility of exogenous idiosyncratic shocks is around 9–15% per year. A small component of individual house prices also correlates with aggregate income and other asset prices (such as stock prices). This component can be estimated by assuming that house prices grow at the aggregate growth rate of the economy.

[z] Their website is http://www.cdc.gov/nchs/products/life_tables.htm

A common specification for individual income is

$$\log y_{it} = f(t, Z_{it}) + v_{it} + \varepsilon_{it} \tag{33}$$

where $f(t, Z_{it})$ is a deterministic function of age and a vector of other individual characteristics Z_{it}, ε_{it} is an idiosyncratic temporary shock distributed $N(0, \sigma_\varepsilon^2)$ and permanent income v_{it} is given by

$$v_{it} = v_{i,t-1} + u_{it}$$

where u_{it} is distributed as $N(0, \sigma_u^2)$ and is uncorrelated with ε_{it}.

Individual log income is the sum of the age profile, the permanent component v_{it} and a transitory shock ε_{it}. The deterministic age profile is a third-order polynomial in age, which is estimated to match the observed hump-shaped life-cycle profile of income. Carroll (1997) and Gourinchas and Parker (2002) assume that the process for the persistent component v_{it} is a random walk as in the last equation. Hubbard et al. (1995) estimate an AR(1) for v_{it} and find that the autocorrelation coefficient is indeed close to one. Cocco et al. (2005) report estimates for the standard deviation σ_u of persistent shocks around 10–13% per year in table 3, depending on education. Their estimate for the standard deviation of σ_ε of transitory shocks is around 22–31%. It is common to somewhat reduce these numbers to account for measurement error in the PSID. For example, Campbell and Cocco (2003) use 2% for σ_u and 14% for σ_ε.

The transitory shock ε_{it} is uncorrelated across households. The persistent shock u_{it} can be decomposed into an aggregate component ξ_t and an idiosyncratic component ω_{it},

$$u_{it} = \xi_t + \omega_{it}.$$

The aggregate component ξ_t helps to introduce correlation between individual labor income and aggregate variables, such as aggregate income or asset prices.

The process (33) is specified for income received in periods t before retirement τ. After retirement, income may be a fraction λ of permanent labor income in the last working year

$$\log y_{it} = \log \lambda + f(\tau, Z_{i\tau}) + v_{i\tau} \quad \text{for } t > \tau.$$

This approach is taken in Cocco, Gomes, and Maenhout (2005) , who estimate λ as the ratio between the average income for retirees in a given education group to the average labor income in the year before retirement. The estimate is between 68% and 94% in their table 2.

With this specification of the income process, households do not face any further risks after they retire. This assumption abstracts from a number of risks that older households face, especially uncertain life spans and out-of-pocket medical expenses. Recent work has made progress to quantify such risks. For example, De Nardi et al. (2010) estimate large and volatile medical expenses for retired singles. Moreover, they find that the volatility of shocks to medical expenses increases with age and permanent income. In a life cycle model, the risk of living long and requiring expensive medical care is an important reason to save for many older high-income households. More empirical work is needed that quantifies these risks for nonsingle households as well as distinguishes the savings motives in the presence of these health risks from bequest motives. In the meantime, it seems reasonable to assume the individual income process (33) for $t > \tau$ and thereby to allow for shocks during retirement.

4.1.3 Other Housing Parameters

Houses depreciate at a rate between 1.5% and 3%, as discussed in Section 2.1. With the assumption of "essential maintenance," the depreciation rate is also the fraction of the house value that is spent on maintenance. Transaction costs vary across cities and states as well as the price spectrum within cities. They are between 6% in real estate fees (for example, in California) and 10% when moving costs are included.

4.2 Consumption, Savings, and Portfolio Choice

The literature on consumption-savings problems is concerned with the facts in Section 2.5. Empirical work documents cross-sectional patterns of consumption and portfolios, and measures properties of returns and income that are relevant for optimal portfolio choice. In order to confront theory and data, a common approach is to quantify a household problem with frictions as discussed in Section 3. Some studies impose equilibrium but nevertheless emphasize cross-sectional patterns. Much of the work discussed in this section precedes the financial crisis and focuses on cross-sectional patterns that are a key feature of any quantitative study.

We divide the literature into five groups. The first considers quantitative models with housing and one other asset. The focus then is on consumption and savings in housing vs other goods or assets, respectively The second group tackles explicitly the choice of equity portfolios with return properties as in the data. This is a more challenging problem since it requires not only matching facts on housing but household behavior toward equity, a well known puzzle in its own right. Third, we consider a set of papers that looks for reduced form evidence on specific mechanisms at work in portfolio choice models, especially the role of housing as a hedge. We then discuss the effects of more complex mortgage products, as well as the effects of house prices on consumption.

Quantitative models can successfully explain wealth and portfolio patterns over the life cycle. The models predict that wealth is positive and hump shaped, as discussed in Section 9. Moreover, the models imply that young households hold highly leveraged portfolios in housing, while older and richer households have positive positions in many assets, including bonds and stocks. According to the models, the hump shape in the wealth position will translate into hump-shaped positions in other assets such as houses and stocks. These age patterns are roughly consistent with the data, especially for housing. However, the models struggle to explain the high concentration in wealth we observe in the data, especially the extreme concentration in stock wealth. The extensive margins are also hard to match for these models. It remains a puzzle why so many middle-class households choose not to participate in the stock market. It is also difficult to quantitatively match the homeownership rate along various dimensions of heterogeneity such as income and wealth.

4.2.1 Housing and Savings Over the Life Cycle

Early work on housing choice over the life cycle considered savings via multiple capital goods without price risk. Households face a two asset special case of the problem with collateral constraints in Section 3.7. Fernandez-Villaverde and Krueger (2010) consider a household with a finite horizon who accumulates capital used in production as well as a stock of durables that enters the utility function. The income process has idiosyncratic shocks and a deterministic age profile. The collateral constraint is important to explain the accumulation of durables early in life, as described in Section 3.7.

Yang (2009) narrows the definition of durables to housing consumption and focuses on the accumulation of housing. The key new feature in her setup is transaction costs for adjusting the housing stock, as in Section 3.8. Those costs are shown to be important for matching the slow downsizing of the housing stock late in life that is observed in the data. Both papers conclude that a standard life cycle model is broadly successful at explaining the hump-shaped patterns in nondurable consumption, durables, and wealth by cohort.

Focus on cohort averages omits variation along the extensive margins, that is who owns and who rents. A number of papers explore the various determinants of tenure choice discussed in Section 3.6. A new feature in these paper is uninsurable house price risk that may correlate with income risk. Li and Yao (2007) study tenure decisions in an environment where renting is expensive; rents are a higher fraction of the house value than the sum of maintenance and mortgage rates. The paper confirms the earlier findings regarding hump-shaped patterns in nonhousing consumption. A new feature in the model is a hump-shaped homeownership rate, which is the overall pattern shown in their fig. 8(a). The homeownership rate in the model shown in fig. 7(a) is a more extreme function of age than the data: all households aged 30 years and below rent, while all households aged 40–80 years own. This discrepancy illustrate the difficulty associated with quantitatively accounting for the extensive margin. The paper studies a number of counterfactuals in which older households benefit from house price increases, while younger households loose.

While Li and Yao (2007) abstract from taxes and directly assume that renting is costly, Díaz and Luengo-Prado (2008) embed the US tax system into their model. The paper carefully compares housing costs for renters and homeowners. It finds that rental equivalence approach (as used in the NIPA tables) overestimates the costs of owner-occupied housing services by roughly 11%. Reasons include the differential tax treatment of renter-occupied vs owner-occupied housing services, the tax deductability of mortgage interest rates and transaction costs in housing markets.

Chambers et al. (2009a,b) study an equilibrium model with tenure choice. with long-term mortgage contracts. The model parameters are estimated with 1994 data. Table 2 in Chambers et al. (2009b) shows that the 1994 model predictions match the homeownership rate as a function of age quite well. Its predicts, however, that all households with income in the upper 40% of the income distribution should own—again, illustrating how difficult it is to match the extensive margin along observed dimensions of heterogeneity.

Attanasio et al. (2012) match the homeownership rate by age and education in a setup with two discrete house sizes: flats and houses. The paper documents that transaction costs are crucial for both homeownership and the property ladder. Lower transaction costs increase the homeownership rate because they increase the number of young households who find it optimal to buy a flat before upgrading to a house.

Home Equity as a Buffer Stock for Consumption Smoothing

Hurst and Stafford (2004) study a life cycle problem in which homeowners may want to use the equity from their house as a buffer stock to smooth their consumption. When homeowners with low savings in liquid assets (such as checking accounts or stocks) experience an adverse income shock, they may have to drastically lower their consumption. To avoid a painful cut in consumption, these homeowners may want to refinance into a mortgage with a larger principal. While refinancing might not necessarily lower the costs of their mortgage, it helps their desire to smooth their consumption.

Hurst and Stafford provide empirical support for this mechanism with micro data from the PSID. Households who were unemployed between 1991 and 1996, and who had zero liquid assets going into 1991, were 25% more likely to refinance than otherwise similar households. They also were more likely to extract equity during the refinancing process.

The life cycle problem in Hurst and Stafford is not designed to be quantitative. For example, it has constant house prices and a fixed house that cannot be sold, the income process is iid, and mortgages are interest-only. Chen et al. (2013) introduce a choice between renting and owning, house price risk, aggregate and idiosyncratic persistent income risk, long-term mortgages, and various frictions (such as loan-to-value and loan-to-income constraints.) When the observed historical paths for house prices, aggregate income and interest rates are taken as given, the model predicts a dramatic increase in mortgage debt during the 2000s house price boom. A significant portion of the debt increase is associated with home equity extraction in the model as well as in the data.

Mian and Sufi (2011) provide new empirical evidence on the importance of this mechanism with micro data from the recent housing boom. The paper documents that existing homeowners—households who already owned their home in 1997—started to borrow significantly more during the early 2000s. The tendency to extract equity was strongest among young homeowners with low credit scores and high credit card utilization rates, while homeowners with good credit scores did not extract more equity from their house.

4.2.2 Household Portfolio Choice

Accounting for risk in household portfolios requires combining the illiquidity and collateralizability of housing with a richer menu of securities. Portfolio choice then depends on risk in multiple tradable assets, as described in Section 3.2. Houses now enable households to borrow and invest their liquid funds in assets with more attractive return properties, such as stocks. When transaction costs are high, illiquid houses act as undiversifiable background risk (similar to nontradable labor income) in portfolio choice.

Myopic Investors

Early work focused on the risk return tradeoffs in models with myopic investors. Berkovec and Fullerton (1992) study a two period general equilibrium model in which households consume housing and choose a portfolio of owner-occupied housing, housing as an investment, stocks, and bonds. Ownership is attractive because of tax subsidies, but exposes owners to undiversifiable risk. Indeed, the paper estimates the variance of house prices as the sum of national, regional and intraregional effects on house prices, resulting in a volatility of 8.2% per year.

Starting from the current US tax system, the paper runs counterfactuals to eliminate subsidies, namely that owner-occupied housing services are not taxable, nominal mortgage interest is deductable, and that there is an extra deduction for property taxes. Starting from the current US tax system, the effects are a priori ambiguous: while abolishing subsidies lowers the average return on housing, it also reduces the variance of returns—the government becomes a silent partner who shares both gains and losses on the house. The overall effect on homeownership then depends on risk attitudes and tax brackets.

Flavin and Yamashita (2002) study portfolio choice by myopic investors with an emphasis on the illiquidity of housing. The setup resembles the second stage problem from Section 3.2: the position in housing is predetermined. Households have mean variance preferences and the focus is on the asset portfolio: there is no explicit consumption margin and no labor income. The portfolio share on housing thus acts as a constraint on the problem of choosing a portfolio of financial assets, namely short and long bonds, stocks and a mortgage. Bonds and stocks cannot be sold short and there is a collateral constraint: the mortgage cannot exceed the value of the house.

Flavin and Yamashita construct the returns on an individual house from PSID data. The housing return has a high volatility as in Table 1, and a zero correlation with financial returns. The solution to the portfolio choice problem that includes housing is an efficient frontier that achieves the minimum-variance portfolio for a given expected return subject to the housing constraint. The constraint is matched to average portfolio shares on housing for various cohorts in the PSID. As discussed in Section 2, these observed portfolio shares decline in age.

For households with a high portfolio share on housing, the optimal portfolio involves the maximum possible amount of mortgage borrowing. Since leverage is risky, any remaining funds are invested in a safer financial portfolio consisting of mostly bonds, while the shorting constraint binds for the short bond. For households with a lower portfolio share on housing, the position in housing is less leveraged. These households choose more risk in their remaining portfolio by increasing their portfolio weight on stocks. Higher risk aversion lowers the risk in the optimal portfolio by reducing leverage and shifting the remaining portfolio toward bonds.

A high portfolio share on housing is typical of young households, while middle-aged households have a lower portfolio share. By connecting the magnitude of the initial housing constraint with data on age profiles, the mean-variance benchmark provides intuition for why younger households hold a lower portfolio share in stocks than older households.

Housing and Other Assets Over the Life Cycle

Cocco (2005) studies the consumption–portfolio choice problem of an owner–occupier household with finite horizon. The household receives a nontradable income process (33) with both transitory and persistent shocks. The household can choose stocks, bonds, housing and a mortgage. The returns on stocks are iid and uncorrelated with aggregate income risk, while the price of the house is perfectly correlated with aggregate income risk. The real interest rate on bonds and the (higher) mortgage rate are constant.

The consumption–portfolio problem has several important constraints. The first two of these constraints are similar to those in Flavin and Yamashita (2002). First, bonds and stocks cannot be shorted. Second, there is a downpayment constraint; the mortgage cannot exceed a fraction of the house value. A new feature in Cocco's setup is that households choose the size of their house (while the house is fixed and acts as a constraint in Flavin and Yamashita). A third constraint is that houses have a minimum size. Together with the downpayment constraint, the minimum size creates a strong motive to save for young households, especially in the absence of a rental market. There are additional frictions in the form of transaction costs for housing and a one-time fixed cost to participate in the stock market.

The model generates low rates of stock market participation among poorer households—consistent with the data—who are not willing to pay the fixed costs to participate. Households with enough wealth get a large mortgage and invest most of their portfolio in housing; they still choose not to participate in the stock market. Richer households participate in the stock market and increase their portfolio share on stocks with wealth. Over the life cycle, the model with housing is successful at predicting that young households are house poor: they take a large mortgage and buy a house, while they do not participate in the stock market. As they grow older, they pay down their mortgage and invest more in the stock market, as in the data.

Yao and Zhang (2005) study a life cycle problem in which households can choose between owning and renting a house. The possibility to rent is important for younger and poorer households who do not have enough savings to afford the downpayment.

Older, wealthier households choose to own a house. The downpayment is equity in the house, which acts as a buffer against income shocks. Once they own a house, households have riskier portfolios because of the leveraged position in housing. But homeowners still invest a larger fraction of their (nonhousing) portfolio in stocks for diversification reasons, because of the low correlation between stock and housing returns.

4.2.3 *Housing as a Hedge*

Section 3.2 emphasizes that once risk is explicitly taken into account, the attractiveness of housing depends on the covariance of housing returns with other random state variables in the future. Those state variables include, among others, (*i*) labor income, a component of future wealth (*ii*) the price of rental housing which affects continuation utility in a problem with a rental market and (*iii*) house prices in other markets if the household is subject to moving shocks or has the option to move across different markets. We now consider evidence on these effects.

Housing as a Hedge Against Income Risk

Housing is riskier for households whose incomes covary positively with house prices. For these households, housing is not as good a hedge against income risk. These households will thus tilt their portfolios away from housing toward other assets. Cocco (2005) shows that this effect is quantitatively small in his life cycle model. For example, raising the correlation coefficient between income and house prices from 0 to 0.33 lowers the portfolio share on housing by 1 percentage point. The effect is small because housing is not only an investment but also a consumption good.

Davidoff (2006) provides empirical evidence on the effect. The paper first uses time series data to estimate the covariance between income and house prices in various regions and industries. The paper then predicts the value of owner-occupied housing as well as tenure choices in the 1990 census with the estimated covariances. The results show that a one-standard deviation increase in income–price covariance is associated with a $7500 reduction in the value of the housing investment for owners. They also show that a higher income–price covariance has a negligible effect on the probability of renting.

Housing as a Hedge Against Rent Risk

A common and reasonable assumption is that every household needs to consume some housing services. In a setup with a rental market as in Section 3.6, those services can be obtained either in a rental market or by buying a housing asset that promises a stream of housing services. The rental market is a spot market, where housing services are sold at the current rental rate which fluctuates over time. By buying a house, households can lock in a known price for a stream of future housing services. They still face house price risk in case they need to sell the house later because, for example, they want to move to a new city.

Sinai and Souleles (2005) compare the two sources of risk in a simple spatial model with two locations. Households choose whether to rent or own a single housing unit to maximize their expected wealth net of the housing costs. There is a fixed number of housing units equal to the number of households. The stochastic processes for rents in the two locations are exogenous. Rents are AR(1) processes with correlated shocks. After a known number years, households move from one to the other location. The price of owner-occupied housing units is determined endogenously and clears the housing market. In the model, both the demand for homeownership and equilibrium price–rent ratios tend to increase with expected tenure, the volatility of rents and the correlation between rents across locations.

Table 1 of Sinai and Souleles documents a 2.9% volatility of real rents at the MSA level during the years 1990–98, almost half the volatility of MSA real house prices. Much of this volatility is variation across MSAs. For example, rent volatility ranges from 1.7% in Fort Lauderdale to 7.2% in Austin. Tables 2 and 3 documents that both the probability of owning estimated from a probit model and price–rent ratios are higher in areas with higher mean tenure rates and rent volatility.

Housing as a Hedge Against Future House Prices

Lu (2008) solves a life cycle problem with many locations. The problem assumes that households know that they will want to move in the future, sell their house in the current location and buy a house in the new location. Whether or not the current house can act as a hedge for the future house purchase depends on the correlation between house prices across locations. The conventional wisdom is that correlation in house prices across housing markets is low. Since house prices within MSA are more correlated than across MSAs, the hedging motive will be more important for moves within metropolitan areas. The paper documents some evidence on the importance of such within-MSA moves. It reports that among households in the PSID from 1968 to 1997, 62% of them traded up later by buying a more expensive house (in real terms). Among households who traded up, 71.3% of them moved within the same metropolitan area.

Sinai and Souleles (2013) document that the correlation of house prices across MSAs is indeed low. They estimate this correlation with annual observations on the OFHEO constant-quality MSA-level house price index over the years 1980–05. The simple unweighted median correlation in real house price growth across MSAs is 0.35. Sinai and Souleles argue that households do not move randomly across MSAs. Instead, households move between housing markets that are highly correlated. The paper computes the household's own expected correlation in house prices across MSAs by weighing each correlation with the probability that the household will move to that MSAs. The data for moving from one MSA to another MSA is from the US Department of the Treasury's County-to-County Migration Patterns. The resulting expected correlation is 0.60 for the median household.

4.2.4 Mortgage Choice and Refinancing

Mortgages are often modeled as short-term debt contracts, as we did in Section 3.7. In this case, the collateral constraints (28) can capture home equity lines of credit. Most mortgages are long-term debt contracts, however. Recent work has therefore started to incorporate longer maturities as well as other features, such as fixed vs floating mortgage rates, deferred amortization, prepayment penalties, etc. Much more work is needed in this area to understand the recent foreclosure crisis, the welfare losses associated with certain contracts more broadly, and their implications for financial regulation.

Fixed vs Adjustable Rates

Campbell and Cocco (2003) study the choice between a fixed-rate mortgage and an adjustable-rate mortgage in a life cycle model. The household receives the nontradable real labor income process (33). The growth rate in house prices experiences iid shocks. The only other asset is a short-term real bond with an interest rate that is also hit by iid shocks. Expected inflation is an AR(1), so that inflation is an ARMA(1,1). The nominal short-term interest rate is the sum of expected inflation and the real rate. Longer-term nominal interest rates are determined with the expectations hypothesis. Adjustable mortgage rates include a constant default premium, while fixed rates include a default premium as well as a compensation for prepayment risk, both are constant as well.

The household buys a house with a minimum downpayment and finances the remaining balance with either an adjustable or fixed rate mortgage. A nominal fixed-rate mortgage without prepayment option is a highly risky contract, because the real present value of its future payments is sensitive to inflation. The prepayment option insures households against a surprising fall in nominal interest rates, because they can refinance at the lower rate. The option is not free, however—it is priced into a higher fixed rate. During times of low inflation and low real rates, the fixed rate mortgage is thus an expensive form of borrowing. An adjustable-rate mortgage is safe because the real present value of its future payments is unaffected by inflation. However, it comes with real payments that vary over time with expected inflation and real rates. These high payments may coincide with adverse income shocks and low house prices, so that homeowners may not be able to borrow more to meet these payments.

The optimal choice between the two mortgage contracts compares the expected costs for the homeowner over the life of the mortgage with the risks associated with higher or lower realizations of these costs. The expected costs for the homeowner are either the expected adjusted rate over the life of the mortgage or the known fixed rate. The risks associated with higher cost realizations matter more for homeowners who are either risk averse or close to their borrowing constraints. These homeowners tend to have low savings, large houses relative to their income and volatile incomes. The horizon matters for computing the expected adjustable rate over the life of the mortgage. For homeowners who are likely to move in the near future, the current adjustable rate matters more. These homeowners will compare the current adjustable rate with the fixed rate and opt for the rate that is currently cheaper. Since fixed rates include the cost of the prepayment option and are longer maturities interest rates, the cheaper rate will on average be the adjustable 1-year rate.

More generally, the difference between the fixed rate and the expected adjustable rate over the life of the contract is determined by risk premia (as well as the cost of the prepayment option). These risk premia vary over time. Koijen et al. (2009) compute a time series these risk premia and show that they highly correlate with the actual share of adjustable-rate mortgages among newly originated mortgages. The expected adjustable rate can be computed, for example, with survey data on interest rate forecasts, VARs or some other estimated time series process, or under the assumption that beliefs are extrapolative. Badarinza, Campbell, and Ramadorai (2016) investigate the share of adjustable-rate mortgages in cross-country data. They find that low expected adjustable rates over short horizons, such as a year or a few years, relative to fixed rates are associated with a high share of adjustable rate mortgages.

Deferred Amortization Contracts

Piskorski and Tchistyi (2010) is a theoretical study of optimal mortgage design in a setup in which income by an impatient household is stochastic and unobservable by the lender. The household needs to borrow from the lender to be able to buy a house. The paper shows that the optimal contract is a combination of an interest-only mortgage and an equity line of credit—an alternative mortgage product that offers deferred amortization. The intuition behind the result is that deferred amortization helps borrowing-constrained households to smooth their consumption.

Chambers et al. (2009a,b) study mortgage choice in a quantitative general equilibrium model with tenure choice and long-term mortgage contracts. The model parameters are estimated with 1994 data. The model is recomputed with 2005 data by offering households a range of mortgage contracts with lower downpayment constraints, other forms of deferred amortization, and lower closing costs. The paper finds that these new mortgage contracts have enabled many borrowing-constrained renters to buy a house. It concludes that these mortgage innovations can explain around 70% of the large increase in the homeownership rate from 1994 to 2005.

Cocco (2013) provides empirical evidence that supports this consumption-smoothing mechanism with data from the British Household Panel Survey. The survey collects detailed housing information from a group of households over time (for example, about the type of mortgage, the year the mortgage began, the amount borrowed, monthly payments, etc.) The paper documents that, at least since 2001, households who choose alternative mortgages are better educated and have higher subsequent income growth These mortgages are used to buy expensive houses with high loan-to-value ratios. Amromin et al. (2013) document similar evidence for alternative mortgages in the United States.

Suboptimal Borrower Behavior in Mortgage Markets

Mortgages are complex products. Mortgage lenders do not have the incentives to make these contracts comparable, unless forced by regulation. Households make their mortgage choice infrequently and cannot learn much from their past mistakes. In this situation, it is not surprising that mortgage choices are not made optimally.

Woodward and Hall (2012) show that new home buyers vastly overpay for their mortgages. They use data on a sample of 30-year fixed-rate mortgages insured by the Federal Housing Administration to show that borrowers do not push brokers toward competitive pricing. Most borrowers would benefit from comparing quotes from a larger number of brokers. Borrowers would also benefit from comparing quotes of mortgages that do not involve any up-front cash payments, such as points. These findings hold especially for less educated borrowers.[aa]

A large literature on mortgage-backed securities documents that households' refinancing behavior is suboptimal. For example, Schwartz and Torous (1989) and Stanton (1995) show that many households do not refinance their fixed-rate mortgage when market rates fall below their locked-in contact rate. Other households refinance even though market rates are above their locked-in contract rate. Agarwal et al. (2013) develop a formula for the (S,s) inaction range for refinancing in the presence of fixed costs. Anderson et al. (2015) document suboptimal refinancing behavior in Denmark, especially for older, less educated and lower income households.

4.2.5 Consumption Response to Higher House Prices

House price booms are often associated with higher aggregate household consumption. What are the mechanisms that explain the consumption increase? There are two related issues. The first is to measure the marginal propensity to consume (MPC) out of housing wealth for different groups of consumers. The second is to identify what exogenous shocks might have given rise to the joint movement in house prices and consumption. For example, was the boom generated by changes in financial conditions, or rather by an increase in household income.

The household problem from Part 2 suggests potential determinants of the MPC out of housing wealth. Consider first the frictionless problem from Section 3.2. Here, an increase in the house price has three possible effects: it changes the relative price of housing services, it may change expectations of returns on housing or other assets in the future (that is, it may change the continuation utility V_{t+1}), and it changes current wealth (or cash on hand). Only the first effect is unique to housing which has a nontradable dividend—the latter two effects are shared by any other security.

[aa] Woodward and Hall (2012) also show that minority households overpay more for their mortgages. Important early work on discrimination in mortgage markets is the paper by Munnell et al. (1996). These authors show that minorities are more than twice as likely to be denied a mortgage as whites.

Berger et al. (2015) provide conditions on the problem such that only the last effect prevails. In particular, they consider permanent price changes that do not alter return expectations, and they assume Cobb–Douglas felicity so that income and substitution effects of the relative price of housing services cancel. They also point out that the result does not depend on the presence of incomplete markets, a rental market or a collateral constraint of the type (28)—indeed, the result is due to the fact that cash in hand is the only state variable that house prices affect which is true in all of these cases. The result does not hold once transaction costs for either housing or mortgages are added.

Consumption and House Prices in Life Cycle Models

Many studies have analyzed aggregate data on consumption during housing booms. For example, Muellbauer and Murphy (1990) argue that in the UK house prices in the 1980s generated a wealth effect on aggregate consumption that was enabled by financial liberalization. The liberalization allowed households to extract more wealth from the value increase in their illiquid housing investment. King (1990) and Pagano (1990) question the importance of wealth effects in accounting for the high correlation between house prices and consumption in the United Kingdom. They argue that higher income growth expectations account for the increase in consumption and also for higher house prices.

Micro evidence on household consumption helps distinguish between competing mechanism. For example, Attanasio and Weber (1994) argue that in basic life cycle models (with a single good and a single asset), wealth effects vs higher income expectations have different predictions for the consumption of younger vs older households. Older households have more wealth and have shorter horizons over which to spread an increase in their wealth. Therefore older households will increase their consumption more than younger households in response to a 1% increase in wealth. Younger households respond more to income shocks, because they have more human wealth. The paper uses micro data from the UK family expenditure survey (FES) to document that the 1980s consumption boom was driven in large part by strong consumption by young households.

In a life cycle model with housing as a collateral asset, the predictions of these mechanisms are less obvious. In this setup, higher house prices not only increase the wealth of homeowners as in the basic model, but also relax collateral constraints and thereby enable the young to consume more. Attanasio et al. (2011) solve such a life cycle problem with exogenous house price and income processes in which the collateral constraint (28) is only imposed in the period when a house is bought or the mortgage amount changes. They use the observed aggregate time series for house prices and income to extract two shock series. The paper then feeds the two shocks separately into the model and analyzes how various age cohorts adjust their consumption to a particular shock. The quantitative results show that the intuition from the basic life cycle model carries over to this model with housing: higher house prices lead to stronger consumption responses by older households, while higher income causes stronger consumption responses by young households. The paper again concludes that the evidence suggests that higher income expectations or common shocks that affect both income and house prices are more important than pure wealth effects.

Homeowners who want to consume more in response to higher house values need to adjust their portfolio position either by selling their house or by borrowing more against their house. When transaction costs are high in housing and mortgage markets, the costs of adjusting the portfolio may not make it optimal to cash out. Indeed, Berger et al. (2015) show that their theoretical result does not apply in the presence of transaction costs. They find that a model with transaction costs around 5% has approximately the same consumption elasticities than a model without transaction costs. With higher transaction costs, around 10%, the MPC × house value formula overstates consumption elasticities, especially for younger households.[ab]

Models with short-term mortgages make it easy for households to extract cash from their house and may overstate consumption elasticities. Gorea and Midrigan (2015) consider a model in which long-term mortgages are costly to refinance. When these costs are selected to match the share of mortgages that are refinanced, consumption elasticities are substantially lower.

Reduced Form Estimates and Housing Supply Elasticities as Instruments

Are consumption elasticities for individual households large enough for house price increases to generate quantitatively big effects on consumption? Reduced form estimates of the consumption elasticity vary widely across studies. Case et al. (2005) provide reduced-form evidence on the consumption elasticity to house price changes with aggregate data from many countries. Their estimate ranges from 0.02 to 0.17. Carroll et al. (2011) also use aggregate data and estimate an immediate (next quarter) consumption elasticity of 0.02, with an eventual elasticity of 0.09. Attanasio et al. (2009) use micro data from the UK family expenditure survey to estimate consumption elasticities across households. They regress the level of consumption on changes in house price and other demographic variables. The paper obtains an average elasticity of 0.15 and higher elasticities for young households. Campbell and Cocco (2007) also use the FES and obtain a much larger average elasticity of around 1.2 and higher elasticities for older homeowners than for younger renters.[ac]

Reduced form regressions should ideally have exogenous variations in house prices on their right hand side. The identification of such variation is tricky. Even if we had a good identification strategy to isolate such exogenous variation in the data, it is not possible to directly compare the observed consumption responses in the regressions with

[ab] Kaplan and Violante (2014) show that households who invest a large fraction of their wealth in an asset with high transaction costs have high MPCs.

[ac] Lustig and Van Nieuwerburgh (2010) collect data from various US metro areas to document that risk sharing between regions is reduced when the value of housing is low. More specifically, regional consumption is more sensitive to regional income when housing collateral is scarce.

those implied by a life cycle model. The response of consumption to an exogenous increase in house prices includes any general equilibrium effects of higher house prices on consumption. For example, higher house prices may encourage more residential investment and employment, and thereby increase consumption. These GE effects are typically not included in the model.

To address the identification problem, Mian et al. (2013) use IV regressions with the local housing supply elasticity index constructed by Saiz (2010) discussed in Section 2.1 as instrument. The instrument provides a source of exogenous variation in the exposure of different geographical areas to a common aggregate house price shock. Intuitively, areas with an inelastic housing supply (such as San Francisco and Boston) should experience larger house price changes than areas with a highly elastic housing supply (such as Omaha and Kansas City). The paper estimates high consumption elasticities between 0.34 and 0.38 with Mastercard data that measures credit-card spending on nondurables and house prices from Core Logic. Kaplan et al. (2016a) confirm these estimates with store-level sales from the Kilts-Nielsen Retail Scanner Dataset and Zillow house prices.

To interpret the causality of these elasticities, the housing supply elasticity instrument has to be valid. The instrument satisfies the first-stage requirement: areas with steep slopes, bodies of water and zoning restrictions tend to experience higher house price growth during booms, so that the instrument is correlated with house prices (for example, table 2 in Saiz, 2010 and table A2 in Stroebel and Vavra, 2015). A more difficult requirement to satisfy is the second stage exclusion restriction. In a standard IV approach, the supply constraints must be uncorrelated with omitted demand factors. Saiz (2010), however, documents that supply constraints are associated with high demand. For example, land-constrained areas have higher incomes, are more creative (in the sense of more patents per capita) and attract more tourists (measured by tourist visits per person.) As skilled workers sort into more attractive areas, their productivity/income growth will increase the demand for amenities and house prices. A detailed exposition of this argument is in Davidoff (2016).[ad]

4.3 Housing Over the Business Cycle

The literature on housing over the business cycle is concerned with the facts presented in Fig. 2. As for quantities, residential investment and consumption of housing services are procyclical, with residential investment being more volatile than other investment and leading the cycle. Moreover, the price of housing is procyclical and comoves positively

[ad] Various papers try to provide more direct evidence on the exclusion restriction. For example, table 5 in Mian and Sufi (2011) shows that IRS per capita wage growth is negatively correlated with supply elasticities, indicating that more constrained areas such as San Francisco experience higher wage growth. Other measures of income growth, however, appear uncorrelated with supply elasticities. Stroebel and Vavra (2015) provide additional evidence that measures of income growth are not correlated with supply constaints.

with housing investment. At the same time, the literature aims to account at least as well, or possibly better, for standard business cycle facts such as the volatility, cyclicality, autocorrelation of GDP, nonresidential investment, consumption, hours worked, as well as wages and interest rates and possibly mortgage debt.

We divide the literature into two parts. Early work focused on frictionless representative agent models; the key difference to the standard real business cycle model (RBC) is the presence of two final goods, one of which is either housing services or a "home good" with a large housing component. Papers in this line of research differ mostly in the production technology, and the bulk of the empirical work provides new evidence on technology by sector. More recent work has emphasized simple heterogeneity of agents, usually a borrower and a lender type, as well as nominal rigidities. These papers differ mostly in the asset structure and empirical work often provides new evidence on financial variables.

Models in this section are quantified using a mix of parameters from earlier literature and new estimates. Some papers work with observable shock processes—for example, sectoral TFP—which allows them to estimate the shock process in a first step before computing an equilibrium of the model. Other papers jointly estimate parameters of preferences, technology and the shock processes using GMM or maximum likelihood approaches. In all cases, model performance is assessed by comparing the empirical distribution of a set of observables to the joint distribution of those variables implied by a stationary rational expectations equilibrium of the model economy.

While much progress has been made in understanding the role of different shocks and model ingredients, the basic facts of housing over the business cycle remain puzzling. In particular, we do not yet have a joint account of the volatility and lead-lag behavior of residential investment together with the volatility of house prices. This is in part by design: most models in this section are solved by linearization around a balanced growth path and do not allow for changes in uncertainty. As a result, asset prices move only with changes in expected cash flow or interest rates which limits the scope for volatility. A promising area for future work is to place more emphasize on mechanisms for price volatility and draw tighter connections to the micro evidence on portfolios discussed in Section 4.2.

4.3.1 Home Production

Home productions models are two sector stochastic growth models. The "market" sector produces a market good using business capital and "market labor"—identified with hours as conventionally measured. The "home" sector produces a home good using home capital—identified with housing and consumer durables—together with home labor. Market output is used to make either type of capital—we can define technology as in (21) and assume that construction capital equals home capital that directly provides utility. In line with the features of housing stressed earlier, home capital is an asset with a nontradable dividend, the return of which is difficult to measure directly. Of course, nontradability and indivisibility of housing have no bite for model properties when there is only one agent.

In a frictionless two-good model, a positive TFP shock to sector A induces reallocation of labor away from sector B and hence lower output in that sector. Hours worked and output in sector B are thus more volatile than what one would expect if there were only TFP shocks to sector B itself. The home production literature exploits this mechanism to generate more volatile market hours and output than a standard RBC model. Suppose sector B is the business or market sector, then hours worked and GDP—the series usually targeted by business cycle models—correspond to hours and output in sector B. Sector A is the household sector which produces home goods using housing capital and work at home. Home good TFP shocks can then help increase the volatility of hours and output, especially if they are imperfectly correlated with business TFP.[ae]

At the same time, sectoral reallocation gives rise to a "comovement puzzle." Indeed if sectoral TFP shocks were uncorrelated, output, labor and investment would all be negatively correlated across sectors: it makes sense to move both labor and capital toward the most productive sector. The home production literature shows that this force helps make hours and GDP more volatile. However, it also makes home and business investment negatively correlated, whereas residential and nonresidential investment are both procyclical in the data. There is therefore a tension between the promise of the mechanism for labor reallocation and its implications for capital reallocation. A second puzzle follows from the input–output structure of the models. A typical assumption is that capital for both home and business use is produced by the business sector only. Consider now the response to a perfectly correlated shock to both sectors: it makes sense to shift factors to the business sector in order to build capital before increasing investment and production in the home sector. This force make home investment lag the business cycle, again contrary to the data. If the effect is strong enough, such as when the elasticity of substitution between home capital and labor is high, we can further have negative correlation of investment across sectors even with strong positive correlation of TFP.

Progress in the literature has been to compare specifications of technology that might overcome these two puzzles. Roughly, comovement obtains more easily if shocks affect sectors similarly and there are reasons not to move capital. Greenwood and Hercowitz (1991) consider highly correlated shocks together with a low elasticity of substitution between capital and labor in the home sector. In Hornstein and Praschnik (1997), all capital is produced by a durables good sector that uses nondurables as an intermediate input. Gomme et al. (2001) assume time to build in the business sector. Chang (2000) studies capital adjustment costs. The upshot of this literature is that comovement can be obtained with technologies justified by standard input–output matrices.

[ae] See Benhabib, Rogerson and Wright (1991) and Greenwood et al. (1995) for an exposition of the main mechanism.

The lead-lag pattern of residential investment has been a tougher nut to crack. Fisher (2007) proposes a model in which home capital serves as an input into business production. The idea is that workers who live in better houses are more rested and deliver higher quality work. This type of technology cannot be justified by standard NIPA input–output accounting; it is instead motivated by a regional level estimation of a production function that takes the new effect of home capital on business output into account. With that effect and appropriate elasticities, it can make sense to build home capital first in response to productivity shocks.[af]

4.3.2 Land and House Prices

Davis and Heathcote (2005) incorporate land into a two-sector stochastic growth model. Their setup is more directly geared toward housing than the typical home production model—the "home good" is explicitly identified with housing services. A simplified version of their technology is given by (21)–(22): housing services are provided by a housing asset produced by a construction sector, and while there are no adjustment costs to capital, a limited flow of new land induces an adjustment cost to housing. These assumptions on technology have been adopted by a number of later papers. The paper itself has a richer structure with input–output links between construction and other sectors via intermediate goods derived from NIPA sectoral accounts.

The model is driven by sectoral TFP shocks and produces comovement of residential and business investment, where the former is substantially more volatile, but does not lead the cycle. At the heart of the model is the construction sector, which is labor intensive and subject to particularly volatile TFP shocks. A positive construction TFP shock is amplified by hiring and generates a lot of construction output. The response of residential investment is larger than for business investment since housing is more construction intensive and depreciates more slowly. At the same time, the input–output structure ensures that comovement still obtains, but it does not allow for residential investment to lead the cycle.

The model-implied house price is procyclical but negatively correlated with residential investment. Its volatility is less than one third of that in the data. The key effect here is that a positive construction TFP shock not only increases residential investment, but also makes housing cheaper. At the same time, TFP shocks to other sectors can make the prices of all long lived assets, including the housing asset, procyclical. Put together, these results again illustrate the promise and limitations of sectoral productivity shocks as a driving force of housing. It is tricky to come up with input–output structures that generate the right quantity dynamics. Once prices are explicitly considered, further challenges arise.

[af] Recently Kydland et al. (2012) have shown that both the lead-lag behavior of residential investment and the prevalence of long term fixed rate mortgages are special features of US data. They provide a model in which residential investment leads the cycle because the cost of housing depends on forward looking long term yields in the United States, but less so in other countries.

4.3.3 Household Debt and Nominal Rigidities

A number of papers in the early 2000s extended New Keynesian models to allow for housing and collateral constraints along the lines of Section 3.7. Early work was concerned with the response to monetary policy, described further below.[ag] To illustrate the business cycle properties of such frameworks, we focus below on the results of Iacoviello and Neri (2010) (IN). On the firm side, that paper combines nominal rigidities, the technology of Davis and Heathcote, capital adjustment costs and free linear conversion of houses. There are two types of households who differ in discount factors and no rental markets so that housing dividends are nontradable. The model features many shocks and is estimated using consumption, house prices, inflation, the nominal interest rate as well as housing and nonhousing investment, hours and wages.

Heterogeneity in discount factors gives rise to a borrower-saver household sector. Impatient borrower households borrow and run into collateral constraints, whereas patient saver households are unconstrained in equilibrium. Borrowers are always constrained near the steady state, which allows for linear solutions.[ah] The assumption of linear conversion implies that there is a per-unit price of housing. Nontradability of dividends nevertheless allows for a steady state in which both types of households own housing. This makes the model different from linear two-agent models of equity pricing, in which the agent with the highest valuation of a tradable asset is typically the only owner.

Three key features distinguish New Keynesian borrower-saver models from the models discussed so far. First, a "housing preference shock" increases the felicity from housing. Together with the shock to construction productivity, it is the most important driver of house prices and residential investment. Since it increases housing demand rather than supply, it also makes those two variables move together. At the same time, it lowers comovement of business and residential investment. This tension implies that the model has trouble matching jointly the volatility and cyclicality of house prices and investment, as well as the lead-lag behavior of investment, even though it does generate volatile house prices (IN table 4).

Second, the models feature nominal rigidities which amplify "demand" shocks such as those to housing preference. In particular, with sticky wages, housing preference shocks have much larger effects on residential investment (IN fig. 2). Stickiness of prices is less

[ag] A related early borrower-saver business cycle model is Campbell and Hercowitz (2005) who study borrowing collateralized by durables with a constant price. They show that lower downpayment requirements allow borrower households to better smooth labor supply and hence lower the volatility of aggregate hours. They use this effect to relate financial innovation in the early 1980s to the Great Moderation of the US economy.

[ah] Linear solution imply symmetric business cycles. Allowing for occasionally binding constraints could alter dynamics by introducing nonlinear dynamics; for example, the response to shocks could be stronger in downturn when constraints bind, giving rises to asymmetric cycles as in the data. Guerrieri and Iacoviello (2015) develop a model to study such effects.

relevant since house prices are flexible. At the same time, however, sticky wages worsen the comovement problem: a construction productivity shock no longer increases business investment (IN fig. 4). Nominal rigidities also matter in that they allow other shocks—eg, to monetary policy and markups—to feed through to the housing sector.

The heterogeneity of households is not particularly important for the behavior of investment and house prices (IN figs. 2–4). Linear conversion of housing matters here: housing (as well as other capital) satisfies the Euler equation of the patient unconstrained investor, so investment and price dynamics look much like in a representative agent model. At the same time, the presence of collateral constrained households matters for the response of consumption to shocks. In particular, changes in housing wealth will affect aggregate consumption more. In a model with nominal rigidities, this also translates into effects on output.

4.3.4 Financial Frictions in the Business Sector

With financial frictions in the household sector, house prices can matter for output through their effects on demand. If businesses face collateral constraints, then real estate values can also affect firms' cost. For example, in Iacoviello (2005), entrepreneurs borrow using housing as collateral. Liu et al. (2013) estimate a model in which firms borrow against land as collateral. Housing or land preference shocks can then serve as a driver of the business cycle together with the price of land and the level of business debt.

In the wake of the financial crisis, it has become common to introduce shocks that directly change borrowing or intermediation costs. Some papers have studied such shocks in models with housing. For example, Dorofeenko et al. (2014) add financing constraints as well as risk shocks to the construction sector. Risk shocks then increase the volatility of house prices although this comes at the cost of overstating the volatility of residential investment. Gerali et al. (2010) estimate a model of the Euro Area. Their estimation backs out an important role for shocks to a frictional banking sector that lends to households and firms against collateral.

4.3.5 Effects of Monetary Policy

A growing literature studies the effect of monetary policy shocks in New Keynesian models with heterogenous households, following Aoki et al. (2004) and Iacoviello (2005). The goal is to match the impulse response to a change in the short term nominal interest rate obtained from structural VARs. A stylized fact is that an expansionary monetary policy shock—a decline in the short rate—increases house prices and residential investment along with output (see, for example, Calza et al. (2013) for evidence for a cross section of countries). The goal of the literature is to account for this fact as well as to show whether the presence of heterogenous agents and housing is an important force behind impulse responses for other variables.

As a benchmark, consider the response to a monetary policy shock in a New Keynesian model with a representative agent. With sticky prices, a decline in the nominal short rate generates a decline in the real short rate. From the Euler equation, the representative agent would like to substitute away from expensive future consumption and increase current consumption. Since firms are on their labor demand curve, hiring and output increase to provide extra consumption—monetary policy stimulates the economy. The Euler equation also says that the return on housing should decline—this can happen either through a drop in the dividend (an increase in the relative consumption of housing) or a drop in house prices. Finally, the return on investment declines and so does residential investment.

Suppose now instead that the short rate declines in model with heterogeneous agents and collateral constraints. Assume also that housing is priced linearly. A change in the real rate directly affects the Euler equation of unconstrained agents. Again the return on housing has to decline as well and this happens in part via an increase in housing consumption by the unconstrained—which decreases dividends—and in part through a drop in the house price. The quantity adjustment is not very large, so that the price response typically looks similar to a representative agent model. A key difference to the representative agent model is that the price change now tightens the collateral constraint and lowers consumption of constrained agents. As a result, the consumption and output responses are typically much larger than in a representative agent model, and they are driven to a much smaller extent by intertemporal substitution.

Iacoviello (2005) studies the above mechanism in a two-agent model with borrower and saver households. Aoki et al. (2004) consider savers and an entrepreneurial housing sector. Monacelli (2009) compares the implications of models with and without collateral constraints with evidence on the consumption response for durables and nondurables. Rubio (2011) introduces long term debt in a model without capital and shows that effects of monetary policy are stronger with variable rate mortgages, since real interest rate movements have larger effects. Calza et al. (2013) present SVARs evidence that monetary policy has larger effects in countries with more variable mortgages; as well as a model with capital that generates qualitatively similar effects. Garriga et al. (2013) consider a flexible price model and emphasize that variable-rate mortgages generate important nominal rigidities in their own right.

4.3.6 Rich Household Sector

Much of the literature on business cycles and monetary policy has built on traditional macro models with limited heterogeneity. In light of results on portfolio choice discussed earlier, there is considerable promise in models that allow for richer heterogeneity in both households and houses as well as for aggregate risk. Early work in this direction abstracted from house price risk. Silos (2007) studies a model with two capital stocks that also accounts for the cross section and time series properties of housing and wealth positions.

Iacoviello and Pavan (2013) allow for a rental market and emphasize the procyclicality of debt. Another interesting direction is to explicitly incorporate geography (for example, Van Nieuwerburgh and Weill (2010)).

The literature on monetary policy shocks has also been moving toward models with a richer household sector. For example, Kaplan et al. (2016b) consider a perpetual youth model with borrowing constraints and a subset of illiquid assets (including housing). Wong (2016) considers an overlapping generations model with long term mortgages and highlights the role of heterogeneity by age for the transmission mechanism. All of these papers show that the details of how the household sector is modeled matter for the strength of impulse responses.

4.4 Asset Pricing with Housing

This section summarizes work that studies regular patterns in asset prices implied by models with housing. Similarly to the business cycle analysis in the previous section, model exercises compare empirical distributions in the data to stationary equilibria implied by the model. The key difference is that explicit nonlinear solutions allow for time variation in risk implied by the role of housing as a consumption good or collateral asset. Changes in the risk return tradeoff then affect the pricing of all assets including housing.

The upshot from this literature is that the presence of housing introduces slow movement in the stochastic discount factor that lines up with observed movements in risk premia. At the same time, rational expectations versions of the models here do not generate sufficient volatility to price risky assets, unless risk aversion is large. It is an open question how much the channels described here can contribute once they are combined with less restrictive assumptions on expectations.

4.4.1 Housing as a Consumption Good

The standard consumption-based asset pricing model focuses on consumption risk: the value of an asset depends on the comovement of its return with a single factor, aggregate consumption growth. In a model with housing, households worry not only about future consumption growth, but also about the future composition of the consumption bundle (c_t, s_t). With frictionless rental markets, composition risk can be measured by the expenditure share of housing in the overall consumption bundle. Assets are then valued also for whether they provide a hedge against this second risk factor.

More formally, Piazzesi et al. (2007) assume a power utility function $U(C) = C^{1-1/\sigma}/(1-1/\sigma)$ over the CES aggregator $C = g(c, s)$, and assume a frictionless rental market. The pricing kernel (10) can then be written as

$$M_{t+1} = \beta\left(\frac{c_{t+1}}{c_t}\right)^{-1/\sigma}\left(\frac{1-x_{t+1}}{1-x_t}\right)^{\frac{\varepsilon-\sigma}{\sigma(\varepsilon-1)}}. \tag{34}$$

where x_t is the expenditure share on housing consumption. If $\sigma < 1 < \varepsilon$, then households worry both generally about recessions—low consumption growth—and in particular about "severe recessions" in which the expenditure share on housing consumption is low.

The pricing kernel (34) is observable since the housing expenditure share x_t is available in the NIPA tables. Use of expenditure shares avoids reliance on problematic measures of housing quantities s_t. Fig. 1 shows movements in x_t over the postwar period. The key feature is that the expenditure share contains a slow moving component that lines up with the low frequency component in the price dividend ratio on equity: both series are high in the 1960s, low in the 1970s and recover in the 1980s. These movements are predictable and occur at frequencies that are much lower than business cycle frequencies.

Low frequency movements in the housing share induce movements in stock prices that are in line with the data. For example, agents' concern with severe recessions increases risk premia on assets that pay off little when the expenditure share on housing drops, and more so when the housing share is already currently low. Comovement of x_t with the price dividend ratio implies that equity is such an asset. Since the expenditure share is stationary, the price-dividend ratio on stocks is persistent but mean reverting. This mean reversion explains why the price-dividend ratio forecasts excess returns on stocks. The model also implies that the housing expenditure share should predict excess stock returns, which it does in the data.

Since movements in the housing share are small, large risk premia obtain only if the exponent in (34) is sufficiently large. This can happen for two reasons. On the one hand, suppose that the intratemporal elasticity of consumption is close to one. Since household desire constant expenditure shares, the prospect of a drop in the housing share causes them large discomfort and requires high risk premia on equity even when risk aversion is low. At the same time, however, the intratemporal Euler equation (24) implies very large volatility in rents. On the other hand, high risk premia obtain without high rent volatility when risk aversion is large. In this case, the role of housing is still important in generating time variation in risk premia.

4.4.2 Adjustment Costs and Production

The same asset-pricing implications continue to hold when housing is costly to adjust (see, for example, Stokey, 2009). Adjustment costs typically alter the optimal consumption allocation—for example, consumption is constant or depreciates at a constant rate as long as there is no adjustment. At the same time, the Euler equation (8) for other securities still holds. The pricing kernel (34) continues to be observable with quantity data on housing and nonhousing consumption, or with data on nonhousing consumption and the expenditure share x_t. The argument further extends to setups with preferences over consumption and housing that deviate from expected utility. In this case, the pricing kernel has to be evaluated with continuation utility (10).

Flavin and Nakagawa (2008) measure the pricing kernel with quantity data on housing consumption. More specifically, they use square footage to measure housing consumption. An important disadvantage of this quantity-based measure is that it does not capture quality differences that would be reflected in dollar expenditures and therefore the expenditure share x_t as in (34). For example, a 2000 square foot house with a view will provide more utility than the same square footage without view. This quality difference will be reflected in a higher rent for the house with a view and an associated higher expenditure share x_t on housing.

Jaccard (2011) studies a two-sector model with production of housing. There is habit formation over the consumption bundle $g(c_t, s_t)$ and leisure. The presence of adjustment costs in housing production together with habit formation helps to generate volatile house prices. Habit formation also helps to generate a sizable equity premium as well as comovement between hours worked and output.

4.4.3 Housing as a Collateral Asset

Lustig and Van Nieuwerburgh (2005) consider the asset pricing implications of a heterogenous agents model with uninsurable idiosyncratic income risk and collateral constraints. The collateral constraint is similar to (28), except that the set of securities is a complete set of one-period-ahead contingent claims and any state contingent promise must be backed by the value of housing in the relevant state of nature next period. The presence of contingent claims allows an aggregation result that expresses the pricing kernel M_{t+1} as an aggregate consumption term as in (34) multiplied by a term that depends on the "housing collateral ratio," that is, the ratio of housing wealth relative to human wealth.

The housing collateral ratio now serves as a second state variable that describes variation in investors' required compensation for an additional risk factor. Indeed, investors perceive recessions as particularly severe when the housing collateral ratio is low and collateral constraints are more likely to bind. Moreover, if the current collateral ratio is already low, opportunities for smoothing uninsurable income shocks through collateralized borrowing are poor and required risk premia are high. Empirically, measures of the housing collateral ratio predict stock returns and also help explain the cross section of stock returns.

The paper further shows that large movements in risk premia are associated with large movements in the riskless interest rate. Indeed, if opportunities to borrow are currently low, then the supply of all contingent claims falls, which drives up the prices of all claims as well as their sum, the price of a riskless bond. This logic is not limited to models with collateral constraints on contingent claims but also applies with the constraint (28) or when default is punished by autarky. Quantitatively, it prevents rational expectations models with borrowing constraints from generating high and volatile equity premia without excessively volatile interest rates, unless risk aversion is high.

4.5 Housing Boom–Bust Cycles

A growing body of work tries to understand the mechanisms behind large house price swings and their quantitative importance. Two boom–bust episodes stand out—they were associated with high nationwide house prices both in the United States as well as many other industrialized countries. The first occurred during the Great Inflation of the 1970s, as documented in fig. 2 of Piazzesi and Schneider (2008). During the boom, houses in high quality segments of the US housing market appreciated by 11% *more* than low quality segments, as shown in table 2 of Poterba (1991). The second boom happened during the 2000s, when many countries experienced large increases in mortgage debt together with large house prices increases, as documented by Tsatsaronis and Zhu (2014). During this boom, houses in high quality segments of US housing markets appreciated *less* than low quality segments, as discussed in Section 2.2.

The typical account of a boom episode consists of one or more "shocks," that is, changes in the economic environment, together with a mechanism for how the economy responds to the shocks. Broadly, candidate shocks are changes to macroeconomic conditions that affect income and assets other than housing, changes in financial conditions that affect the ability to borrow given house prices, as well as changes in government policy and expectations about future house values. How exactly the shocks and the mechanism are modeled depends on how much of the response of the economy is endogenous in a given model exercise.

4.5.1 Overview of the Results

Studies of the 1970s housing boom show that the Great Inflation depressed user costs, especially for richer households. The lower user costs can quantitatively account for both higher overall house values as well as higher house values in high quality segments. Higher mortgage interest-rate tax deductions increased the attractiveness of homeownership. They can explain a large share of the overall increase in real house prices. The higher deductions especially benefitted households in higher tax brackets, which accounts for the higher appreciation of high quality segments. In surveys, young households reported to have higher inflation expectations and thereby lower perceived real rates than older households. This disagreement about inflation expectations and real rates across generations is consistent with the increase in credit during this episode. As a consequence, young households borrowed more at rates that they perceived as low and bought houses, pushing up prices.

User costs were again low during the 2000s boom. Credit was easy to get—with low interest rates and relaxed downpayment constraints, enabled partly by an inflow of foreign savings as well as an increase in securitization. The lower interest rates raised the present value of future housing services and thus house values across the board. The relaxation of downpayment constraints mattered mostly for poor households who were able to borrow more and buy houses, driving up house prices especially in the low quality segments of the housing market. Richer households increasingly bought low quality houses and neighborhoods gentrified, further pushing up prices in these low quality segments. All studies, however, find it difficult to quantitatively account for the entire increase in house prices. This suggests that expectations played a role during the 2000s boom. As long as households were expecting house prices to grow at trend together with income (instead of mean reverting to lower levels), it is possible to quantitatively explain the boom.

There has been much progress in our understanding of boom–bust episodes. Micro data—including on household behavior and survey expectations—have helped sort out the importance of competing mechanisms. At the same time, the nature of the shock that started the housing boom is yet not well understood. Changes in housing preferences, expectations, foreign capital inflows or downpayment constraints are essentially stand-ins for changes in various market participants' attitudes toward housing and housing credit. To understand what generates these changes requires theories of expectation formation, financial innovation as well as international capital market integration.

Another open question is the precise role of the US government during the recent boom. It is clear that many policies (for example, associated with the 1994 National Homeownership Strategy developed by the US Department of Housing and Urban Development) encouraged poor households to take out large mortgages and buy houses, especially in low quality segments. How much did these policies contribute to the boom? A related question is whether the government should promote homeownership in the first place, given that it involves a large undiversified investment and potential welfare costs in default.

4.5.2 The 1970s Boom

Poterba (1984) investigates the user cost equation with Census data from the 1970s housing boom. His findings show that high expected inflation substantially lowered the user costs of housing. High expected inflation pushes up mortgage rates and thereby increases the mortgage tax subsidy. This mechanism is able to explain a 30% increase in real house prices during the 1970s.

Poterba (1991) calculates that user costs dropped especially for households in high tax brackets. The reason is that high mortgage rates translate into a larger mortgage tax subsidy for households who earn high incomes that are taxed at higher rates. Lower user costs for richer households increase the demand for more expensive houses. Tables 3 and 4 in the paper indeed find higher capital gains for more expensive houses during the 1970s boom, while cheaper houses appreciated less percentage-wise.

Piazzesi and Schneider (2009a) study an equilibrium model with three assets—houses, stocks, and nominal bonds. Households solve life cycle consumption–portfolio choice problems with an exogenous nontradable income process (33). The paper computes temporary equilibria as described in Section 3.4 in this model. The benchmark household beliefs about future returns and income dynamics are estimated with historical data. Moreover, these dynamics feature a large idiosyncratic component in house price volatility. When the model is evaluated during the 1970s, the temporary equilibrium concept is useful for exploring the implications of higher expected inflation as well as higher inflation volatility.

When evaluated with 1990s data on income and asset endowments, the temporary equilibrium of this model is successful at matching observed asset prices as well as life cycle patterns in wealth and portfolio weights on houses, stocks and nominal bonds. In particular, the model predicts that young households borrow to buy a house and do not participate in the stock market. As they get older, households pay down their mortgage and start saving in nominal bonds and stocks.

The model is evaluated with endowment data from the Survey of Consumer Finances in the 1960s, 1970s, and 1990s. The model predicts a 25% dip in aggregate wealth during the 1970s—which is exactly the pattern we observe in the data. There are three separate mechanisms that contribute to the drop in household wealth during the Great Inflation in the model. First, the 1970s experienced a demographic shift toward more young households—the Baby Boomers—who have lower savings rates. Second, capital losses from realized inflation lowered wealth and hence savings, especially for older households. Third, lower savings were not counteracted by a large increase in interest rates, because the outside supply of bonds to the household sector also fell.

While aggregate household wealth dropped, the portfolio composition looks similar across all three periods at benchmark beliefs which do not take into account higher expected inflation rates during the 1970s. When all households believe in the high expected inflation rate from the 1970 consensus forecasts in the Michigan survey, they increase their portfolio away from stocks toward housing. This shift happens because high expected inflation generates tax effects that favor housing investments: the returns on housing are essentially untaxed, while mortgage interest rate payments are tax deductable. Disagreement about inflation expectations shifts the portfolio further toward housing. The reason is that young households expect high inflation and perceive a low real interest rate. They therefore borrow more and buy housing. The two inflation mechanisms—higher mean inflation and disagreement across cohorts—explain roughly half of the portfolio shift toward housing observed in the data.[ai] The remaining shift can be attributed to lower stock return expectations in times with high expected inflation, which lead to a large decline in price–dividend ratios for stocks while the

[ai] Relatedly, Piazzesi and Schneider (2008) study a model in which some households suffer from inflation illusion. These households confuse changes in the nominal interest rates with changes in real interest rates, while smart households understand the Fisher equation. The model predicts a nonmonotonic relationship between the price–rent ratio and nominal interest rates: house prices are high when nominal rates are either particularly high (as in the 1970s) or low (as in the 2000s).

housing market was booming. The resulting negative comovement of house and stock prices is an important step toward our understanding of the 1970s.

4.5.3 The 2000s Boom

We divide studies of the 2000s boom into three groups by the type of exercise they undertake. One set of papers evaluates versions of the user cost equation (27): it asks whether reasonable scenarios for interest rates and housing payoff expectations—as well as other parameters of the user cost equation such as taxes—are consistent with high house prices. Second, studies that employ small open economy models take securities prices—in particular interest rates—from the data and endogenously determine only house prices and allocations. Finally, papers that work with closed economy models jointly determine house prices and the prices of other assets.

As usual these three approaches are complementary. Indeed, user cost studies (as well as more generally studies of Euler equations) or small open economy models do not explain why interest rates move. At the same time, they evaluate a given model mechanism without taking a stand on the explicit shock structure as well as the details of who participates in securities markets. They thus generate conclusions that are robust to those details. While a closed economy exercise is in principle more ambitious as it makes those details explicit and takes a stand on the nature of the shocks, it is also more prone to misspecification.

User Cost Calculations

Himmelberg et al. (2005) study user costs leading up to the recent housing boom. Their approach assumes that future payoffs can be discounted at the current long-term interest rate. They conclude that the large decline in long rates during the early 2000s can explain the house price boom during that time. Glaeser et al. (2013) show that discounting all future payoffs at the low 2000s long rate is crucial for this quantitative result. In an environment in which low current rates are allowed to mean revert in the future, the magnitude of the boom is significantly reduced. They conclude that optimistic expectations played an important role in the housing boom.

House Prices in Small Open Economies

Kiyotaki et al. (2011) study a small open economy in which households solve life cycle problems, choose between renting and owning, and face collateral constraints as in Section 3.7. In the model, housing is a capital stock that is produced with land and capital. The paper compares steady states with looser collateral constraints: downpayment constraints that range from 10% to 100%. The findings in their table 3 show that varying the downpayment constraint has large quantitative effects on the homeownership rate: while only 46% of households own a home when it is not possible to borrow against housing, 90% of households own a house when the downpayment constraint is 10%.

Despite their large effects on extensive margins, Kiyotaki et al. show that lower downpayment constraints have negligible effects on house prices. The price–rent ratio is essentially constant across all steady states in table 3. This outcome is intuitive, because all homeowners in the model are marginal investors and determine the per unit price of housing. With looser collateral constraints, there is an inflow of new home buyers. However, these new buyers do not affect the per unit price of housing because the Euler equations also hold for rich households. Their table 4 studies how these results quantitatively depend on the scarcity of land for the production of housing. Kermani (2012) studies these mechanisms in a continuous-time model with a representative agent.

Sommer et al. (2013) solve a similar model but without production. Instead, the overall housing supply is fixed and there is free conversion of housing units. The paper also finds small quantitative effects of looser collateral constraints and lower interest rates, and considers higher income expectations. Chu (2014) assumes that the supply of rental housing and the supply of owner-occupied housing are fixed separately and cannot be converted into each other. As a result, looser collateral constraints have larger effects on house prices. In particular, the value of owner-occupied housing appreciates more than rental housing. The bond market in the model clears; income shocks are assumed to be more volatile in 2005 which keeps the equilibrium interest rate constant over time (instead of matching the lower interest rates observed in the data.)

Landvoigt et al. (2015) study an assignment model with indivisible and illiquid houses in a metro area. The housing demand of movers is derived from a life cycle consumption and portfolio choice problem with transaction costs and collateral constraints. As in Section 3.4, house prices are determined in a temporary equilibrium to induce households with lower demand for housing services to move into lower quality houses. The distribution of equilibrium prices thus depends on the distribution of mover characteristics as well as the distribution of house qualities. While the market for all house qualities clears, the metro area is a small open economy.

Landvoigt (2015) measure continuous distributions for movers and house qualities with micro data from San Diego County for 2 years: 2000 and 2005, the peak of the boom. The distribution of mover characteristics—age, income, and wealth—is measured with data from the American Community Survey. The 2005 distribution shows that movers were richer than in 2000. Moreover, the 2005 house-quality distribution has fatter tails than in 2000—relatively more houses traded at the low and the high end of the quality spectrum than in intermediate ranges.

To measure the distribution of house qualities, Landvoigt (2015) assume that house quality is a one-dimensional index. Therefore, house quality can be measured by price in the base year 2000. The paper documents that 2005 house prices are strictly increasing in 2000 prices. This monotonicity implies that for every 2005 quality level, there is a unique initial 2000 quality level so that the average house of that initial quality resembled the given house in 2005. The 2000 distribution of house qualities is simply the distribution of transaction prices in that year. The 2005 distribution of house qualities can be constructed from the 2005 distribution of transaction prices using the monotonicity of the map from 2000 qualities to 2005 prices.[aj]

The paper compares the predictions for equilibrium prices in both years and derives the cross section of capital gains by quality. These predictions are compared to capital gains by quality in the data. Two key mechanisms allow the model to quantitatively match the observed cross section of capital gains by quality from 2000 to 2005. The first mechanism is cheaper credit: looser collateral constraints and lower mortgage rates in 2005 allowed poorer households to borrow more and increase their demand for housing, especially at the low end of the quality spectrum. Richer households were not affected much by lower downpayment constraints. But these richer households are not marginal investors for low quality houses (as discussed in Section 3.3.1). Therefore, the higher housing demand by poor households translates into higher prices of low quality houses.

The second mechanism is that more low quality houses transacted in 2005. When the distribution of movers is assigned to the distribution of houses in 2005, the marginal buyer of a low quality house is richer compared to 2000 and pushes up low-end prices. Both mechanisms generate capital gains that monotonically decline in house quality.

Whether or not the model quantitatively matches capital gains by quality depends on expectations. An advantage of temporary equilibria is that we can find out how much expectations matter. Under the assumption that households in 2005 were expecting house prices to continue to grow at the same rate as labor income and easy credit conditions to remain, the model implies the same capital gains from 2000 to 2005 as in the data. Under the assumption that households in 2005 foresee that future house prices and credit conditions will return to their 2000 values, capital gains as a function of house quality are shifted down until expensive houses do not appreciate in value. Our conclusion is that easy credit and fatter tails in the house quality distribution predict a monotonically declining pattern in capital gains. To quantitatively explain capital gains, expectations are important. In particular, expectations in 2005 cannot be pessimistic about the future.

Closed Economy and the Determination of Interest Rates

The closed economy models considered in the literature all assume costless conversion and thus linear pricing, which by design reduces the quantitative importance of looser collateral constraints on house prices. The per-unit price of housing enters the Euler equations of all investors, which includes rich investors for whom collateral constraints do not matter. Therefore, any change in collateral constraints will have small effects on

[aj] Epple et al. (2015) also assume house quality is a one-dimensional index. They estimate house prices as well as rental values as nonlinear functions of quality with data for various metro areas using a new structural estimation approach.

per-unit house prices. A key contribution of these models is to make the point that looser collateral constraints tend to push up equilibrium interest rates, so that a major force is needed to keep rates low during the boom.

Garriga et al. (2012) study a closed economy with production in two sectors without aggregate shocks and a representative household. The production of housing involves land and irreversible investment in structures. Foreign lenders determine mortgage rates. The collateral constraint is selected to match aggregate mortgage debt to housing wealth. Under the assumption of perfect foresight about looser collateral constraints and low mortgage rates in the future, the model is able to explain roughly half of the observed increase in national house price indices. Since housing and nonhousing consumption are strong complements, higher house prices do not lead to a large consumption increase (which would be counterfactual). The paper attributes the other half of the increase to expectations.

Favilukis et al. (2016) study a closed economy with households who solve life cycle problems with uninsurable labor income shocks as well as aggregate shocks. There is no rental market, so households have to buy in order to consume housing services. The paper solves the model under the assumption that foreigners bought more bonds during the 2000s and thereby increase the mortgage supply. The paper carefully measures the size of these bond purchases and quantifies their effect on equilibrium mortgage rates. Looser collateral constraints lower risk premia and thereby increase house prices by roughly half of the observed increase in national house prices.

The asset "house" in Favilukis et al. is a claim to the national housing stock. As discussed in Section 2.2, households in the data hold individual houses instead of such diversified claims. In fact, a diversified claim has much more attractive return properties than individual houses because national house price indices are not volatile. In panel B of table 5 of Favilukis et al., the equilibrium Sharpe ratio of the national housing stock is an impressive 0.82 compared a less attractive 0.37 Sharpe ratio for stocks. To better capture the Sharpe ratios of individual houses that households face in the data, the paper considers small idiosyncratic shocks to housing depreciation. These idiosyncratic shocks increase precautionary savings and thereby depress the equilibrium risk-free rate, but they do not match the high idiosyncratic component in the variance decomposition of individual housing returns.

Justiniano et al. (2015a) consider a closed economy in which patient households lend to impatient households until their lending reaches an exogenous supply limit. There are collateral constraints, so impatient households borrow to buy houses. The paper shows that looser collateral constraints increase the demand for houses and mortgages by the impatient households. As a consequence, both house prices and mortgage rates increase in equilibrium—contrary to what we saw in the data, where mortgage rates fell. The paper then argues that an exogenous increase in the credit supply limit increases borrowing while keeping mortgage rates low in equilibrium. It is important for this argument to assume that patient household have a fixed housing demand or buy houses in a different segment from impatient households, otherwise their Euler equation would determine house prices and thereby keep house prices low. Justiniano et al. (2015b) add poorer (subprime) borrowers to the model. They show that subprime borrowers increase their mortgage borrowing more than richer borrowers in response to an increase in the credit supply.

Landvoigt (2015) endogenizes the supply of mortgages in a closed-economy model with banks and aggregate risk. Households differ in their patience as well as their risk aversion. Banks issue deposits and equity to make mortgages. Looser collateral constraints increase the demand for housing and mortgage borrowing, but increase mortgage rates—contrary to what we observed in the data. Landvoigt introduces securitization, which allows banks to sell mortgages directly to risk-tolerant savers. The boom is initiated when banks underestimate the riskiness of new borrowers during the early 2000s and collateral constraints are relaxed. As banks securitize their mortgages and sell them as MBS to savers, risk premia decline, the supply of lending increases, and the model generates a boom–bust in house prices.

Expectations

The broad conclusion from existing studies of the 2000 boom is that expectations played a quantitatively important role. This conclusion is consistent with survey expectations about future house prices. For example, table 9 in Case and Shiller (2003) reports that homebuyers in 2003 were expecting house prices to appreciate between 9% and 15% each year over the next decade. Piazzesi and Schneider (2009b) document that at the peak of the recent boom, the fraction of households who believed that house prices would continue to increase doubled.

Recent research has started to capture such house price expectations. Piazzesi and Schneider (2009b) show that since only a small fraction of houses trade every year, a few exuberant households are enough to push up equilibrium house prices in these transactions. Barlevy and Fisher (2011) assume that a stream of new households enters every period with a certain probability and the stream may stop. Burnside et al. (2011) assume infectious-disease dynamics for expectations. Adam et al. (2012) study learning dynamics that temporarily decouple house prices from fundamentals.

Landvoigt (2016) uses micro data to estimate beliefs that rationalize the consumption-portfolio decisions of households in the SCF. The estimation finds that an important feature of beliefs is higher uncertainty about future house prices which increases the option value of default and thereby leverage during the housing boom.

ACKNOWLEDGMENTS

We thank Alina Arefeva, Eran Hoffmann, Amir Kermani, Moritz Lenel, Sean Myers, Alessandra Peter, John Taylor, Harald Uhlig, and conference participants at Stanford for comments.

REFERENCES

Adam, K., Kuang, P., Marcet, A., 2012. House price booms and the current account. NBER Macroeconomics Annual, vol. 26(1), University of Chicago Press, Acemoglu and Woodford, pp. 77–122.

Adelino, M., Schoar, A., Severino, F., 2015. Loan originations and defaults in the mortgage crisis: the role of the middle class. NBER Working Paper No. 20848.

Agarwal, S., Driscoll, J., Laibson, D., 2013. Optimal mortgage refinancing: a closed form solution. J. Money Credit Bank. 45, 591–622.

Amromin, G., Huang, J., Sialm, C., Zhong, E., 2013. Complex mortgages. Working Paper, University of Texas at Austin.

Anderson, S., Campbell, J.Y., Nielsen, K.M., Ramadorai, T., 2015. Inattention and inertia in household finance: evidence from the danish mortgage market. Working Paper, Harvard.

Andrews, D., Sánchez, A.C., Johansson, Å., 2011. Housing markets and structural policies in OECD countries. OECD Economics Department Working Papers.

Aoki, K., Proudman, J., Vlieghe, G., 2004. House prices, consumption, and monetary policy: a financial accelerator approach. J. Financ. Intermed. 13, 414–435.

Artle, R., Varaiya, P., 1978. Life cycle consumption and homeownership. J. Econ. Theory 18, 38–58.

Attanasio, O.P., Weber, G., 1994. The UK consumption boom of the late 1980s: aggregate implications of microeconomic evidence. Econ. J. 104 (427), 1269–1302.

Attanasio, O.P., Blow, L., Hamilton, R., Leicester, A., 2009. Booms and busts: consumption, house prices and expectations. Economica 76, 20–50.

Attanasio, O.P., Leicester, A., Wakefield, M., 2011. Do house prices drive consumption growth? The coincident cycles of house prices and consumption in the u.k. J. Eur. Econ. Assoc. 9 (3), 399–435.

Attanasio, O.P., Bottazzi, R., Low, H.W., Nesheim, L., Wakefield, M., 2012. Modelling the demand for housing over the life cycle. Rev. Econ. Dyn. 15, 1–18.

Bachmann, R., Cooper, D., 2014. The ins and outs in the U.S. housing market. Working Paper, Notre Dame.

Badarinza, C., Campbell, J.Y., Ramadorai, T., 2016. International comparative household finance. Annu. Rev. Econ. Forthcoming.

Barlevy, G., Fisher, J.D., 2011. Mortgage choices and housing speculation. Working Paper, Federal Reserve Bank of Chicago.

Benhabib, J., Rogerson, R., Wright, R., 1991. Homework in macroeconomics: household production and aggregate fluctuations. J. Polit. Econ. 99, 1166–1187.

Berger, D., Veronica, G., Guido, L., Joseph, V., 2015. House prices and consumer spending. NBER Working Paper 21667.

Berkovec, J., Fullerton, D., 1992. A general equilibrium model of housing, taxes, and portfolio choice. J. Polit. Econ 100 (2), 390–429.

Braid, R., 1981. The short-run comparative statics of a rental housing market. J. Urban Econ. 10, 280–310.

Braid, R., 1984. The effects of government housing policies in a vintage filtering model. J. Urban Econ. 16, 272–296.

Burnside, C., Eichenbaum, M., Rebelo, S., 2011. Understanding booms and busts in housing markets. J. Polit. Econ. Forthcoming.

Calza, A., Monacelli, T., Stracca, L., 2013. Housing finance and monetary policy. J. Eur. Econ. Assoc. 11 (1), 101–122.

Campbell, J.Y., Cocco, J.F., 2003. Household risk management and optimal mortgage choice. Q. J. Econ. 118 (4), 1449–1494.

Campbell, J.R., Hercowitz, Z., 2005. The role of collateralized household debt in macroeconomic stabilization. NBER Working Paper No. 11330.

Campbell, J.Y., Cocco, J.F., 2007. How do house prices affect consumption? Evidence from micro data. J. Monet. Econ. 54 (3), 591–621.

Campbell, S., Davis, M., Gallin, J., Martin, R.F., 2009. What moves housing markets: a variance decomposition of the rent-price ratio. J. Urban Econ. 66 (2), 90–102.

Caplin, A., Leahy, J.V., 2014. A graph theoretic approach to markets for indivisible goods. J. Math. Econ. 52, 112–122.

Cardarelli, R., Igan, D., Rebucci, A., 2008. The Changing Housing Cycle and Its Implications for Monetary Policy. IMF World Economic Outlook. International Monetary Fund, Washington, DC.

Carroll, C.D., 1997. Buffer-stock saving and the life-cycle/permanet income hypothesis. Q. J. Econ. 112, 1–55.

Carroll, C.D., Otsuka, M., Slacalek, J., 2011. How large are housing and financial wealth effects? A new approach. J. Money Credit Bank. 1 (43), 55–79.

Case, K.E., Shiller, R.J., 1989. The efficiency of the market for single-family homes. Am. Econ. Rev. 79 (1), 125–137.

Case, K.E., Shiller, R.J., 1990. Forecasting prices and exess returns in the housing market. Real Estate Econ. 18 (3), 253–273.

Case, K.E., Shiller, R.J., 2003. Is there a bubble in the housing market? Brook. Pap. Econ. Act. 2, 299–362.

Case, K.E., Quigley, J., Shiller, R.J., 2005. Comparing wealth effects: the stock market versus the housing market. In: Advances in Macroeconomics, vol. 5(1), Berkeley Electronic Press, pp. 1–34. http://dx.doi.org/10.2202/1534-6013.1235.

Chambers, M.S., Garriga, C., Schlagenhauf, D.E., 2009a. The loan structure and housing tenure decisions in an equilibrium model of mortgage choice. Rev. Econ. Dyn. 12, 444–468.

Chambers, M.S., Garriga, C., Schlagenhauf, D.E., 2009b. Accounting for changes in the homeownership rate. Int. Econ. Rev. 50 (3), 677–726.

Chang, Y., 2000. Comovement, excess volatility and home production. J. Monet. Econ. 46, 385–396.

Chen, H., Michaux, M., Roussanov, N., 2013. Houses as ATMs? Mortgage refinancing and macroeconomic uncertainty. NBER Working Paper No. 19421.

Chien, Y., Lustig, H., 2009. The market price of aggregate risk and the wealth distribution. Rev. Financ. Stud. 23 (4), 1596–1650.

Chu, Y., 2014. Credit constraints, inelastic supply, and the housing boom. Rev. Econ. Dyn. 17, 52–69.

Cocco, J.F., 2005. Portfolio choice in the presence of housing. Rev. Financ. Stud. 18, 535–567.

Cocco, J.F., 2013. Evidence on the benefits of alternative mortgage products. J. Financ. 68 (4), 1663–1690.

Cocco, J.F., Gomes, F.J., Maenhout, P.J., 2005. Consumption and portfolio choice over the life cycle. Rev. Financ. Stud. 18 (2), 491–533.

Cochrane, J.H., 2011. Discount rates. J. Financ. 66 (4), 1047–1108.

Cutler, D.M., Poterba, J.M., Summers, L.H., 1991. Speculative dynamics. Rev. Econ. Stud. 58, 529–546.

Davidoff, T., 2006. Labor income, housing prices, and homeownership. J. Urban Econ. 59, 209–235.

Davidoff, T., 2013. Supply elasticity and the housing cycle of the 2000s. Real Estate Econ. 41 (4), 793–813.

Davidoff, T., 2016. Supply constraints are not valid instrumental variables for home prices because they are correlated with many demand factors. Crit. Financ. Rev. Forthcoming.

Davis, M.A., Ortalo-Magné, F., 2011. Household expenditures, wages, rents. Rev. Econ. Dyn. 14 (2), 248–261.

Davis, M.A., Heathcote, J., 2005. Housing and the business cycle. Int. Econ. Rev. 46 (3), 751–784.

Davis, M.A., Heathcote, J., 2007. The price and quantity of residential land in the united states. J. Monet. Econ. 54 (8), 2595–2620.

Davis, M.A., Van Nieuwerburgh, S., 2015. Housing, finance and the macroeconomy. In: Duranton, G., Henderson, J.V., Strange, W.C. (Eds.), Handbook of Regional and Urban Economics, vol. 5. Elsevier, Amsterdam, pp. 813–886.

De Nardi, M., French, E., Jones, J., 2010. Why do the elderly save? The role of medical expenses. J. Polit. Econ. 118, 39–75.

Deaton, A., 1992. Understanding Consumption. Oxford University Press, Oxford, UK.

Detemple, J., Serrat, A., 2003. Dynamic equilibrium with liquidity constraints. Rev. Financ. Stud. 16 (2), 597–629.

Díaz, A., Luengo-Prado, M.J., 2008. On the user cost and homeownership. Rev. Econ. Dyn. 11 (3), 584–613.

Dorofeenko, V., Lee, G.S., Salyer, K.D., 2014. Risk shocks and housing supply: a quantitative analysis. J. Econ. Dyn. Control. 45, 194–219.

Englund, P., Ioannides, Y.M., 1997. House price dynamics: an international empirical perspective. J. Hous. Econ. 6, 119–136.

Epple, D., Quintero, L., Sieg, H., 2015. A new appproach to estimating hedonic equilibrium for metropolitan housing markets. Working Paper, University of Pennsylvania.
Epstein, L.G., Zin, S.E., 1989. Substitution, Risk Aversion, and the Temporal Behavior of Consumption and Asset Returns: A Thoeretical Framework. Econometrica 57 (4), 937–969.
Evans, G.W., Honkapohja, S., 2009. Learning and macroeconomics. Annu. Rev. Econ. 1, 421–449.
Favilukis, J., Ludvigson, S.C., van Nieuwerburgh, S., 2016. The macroeconomic effects of housing wealth, housing finance and limited risk sharing in general equilibrium. J. Polit. Econ. Forthcoming.
Fernandez-Villaverde, J., Krueger, D., 2007. Consumption over the life cycle: facts from consumer expenditure survey data. Rev. Econ. Stat. 89 (3), 552–565.
Fernandez-Villaverde, J., Krueger, D., 2010. Consumption and saving over the life cycle: how important are consumer durables? Macroecon. Dyn. 15, 725–770.
Fisher, J.D., 2007. Why does household investment lead business investment over the business cycle? J. Polit. Econ. 115 (1), 141–168.
Flavin, M., Nakagawa, S., 2008. A model of housing in the presence of adjustment costs: a structural interpretation of habit persistence. Am. Econ. Rev. 98 (1), 474–495.
Flavin, M., Yamashita, T., 2002. Owner-occupied housing and the composition of the household portfolio. Am. Econ. Rev. 92 (1), 345–362.
Flemming, J.S., 1969. The utility of wealth and the utility of windfalls. Rev. Econ. Stud. 36, 55–66.
Fraumeni, B.M., 1997. The measurement of depreciation in the U.S. national income and product accounts. Surv. Curr. Bus. 77, 7–23.
Fudenberg, D., Levine, D., 1998. Learning in Games. M.I.T. Press, Cambridge, MA.
Garriga, C., Manuelli, R., Peralta-Alva, A., 2012. A model of price swings in the housing market. Working Paper, Federal Reserve Bank of St. Louis, 2012-022A.
Garriga, C., Kydland, F.E., Šustek, R., 2013. Mortgages and monetary policy. NBER Working Paper No. 19744.
Geanakoplos, J., 2011. What's missing from macroeconomics: endogenous leverage and default. In: Jarocinski, M., Smets, F., Thimann, C. (Eds.), Approaches to Monetary Policy Revisited–Lesson from the Crisis, vol. 2011, pp. 220–238.
Gerali, A., Neri, S., Sessa, L., Signoretti, F.M., 2010. Credit and banking in a DSGE model of the euro area. J. Money Credit Bank. 42 (6), 107–141.
Giglio, S., Maggiori, M., Stroebel, J., 2016. No-bubble condition: model-free tests in housing markets. Econometrica 84 (3), 1047–1091.
Glaeser, E.L., Gottlieb, J.D., Gyourko, J., 2013. Can cheap credit explain the housing boom? Housing and the Financial Crisis. National Bureau of Economic Research, Inc., pp. 301–359.
Glaeser, E.L., Gyourko, J., Morales, E., Nathanson, C.G., 2014. Housing dynamics: an urban approach. J. Urban Econ. 81, 45–56.
Gomme, P., Kyland, F.E., Rupert, P., 2001. Home production meets time to build. J. Polit. Econ. 109 (5), 1115–1131.
Gorea, D., Midrigan, V., 2015. Liquidity constraints in the U.S. housing market. Working Paper, NYU.
Gourinchas, P.O., Parker, J., 2002. Consumption over the life cycle. Econometrica 70, 47–91.
Grandmont, J.M., 1977. Temporary general equilibrium. Econometrica 45, 535–572.
Greenwood, J., Hercowitz, Z., 1991. The allocation of capital and time over the business cycle. J. Polit. Econ. 99 (6), 1188–1214.
Greenwood, J., Rogerson, R., Wright, R., 1995. Household production in real business cycle theory. In: Cooley, T.F. (Ed.), Frontiers of Business Cycle Research. Princeton University Press, Princeton, NJ, pp. 157–174.
Grossman, S.J., Laroque, G., 1990. Asset pricing and optimal portfolio choice in the presence of illiquid durable consumption goods. Econometrica 58, 22–51.
Guerrieri, L., Iacoviello, M., 2015. OccBin: a toolkit for solving dynamic models with occasionally binding constraints easily. J. Monet. Econ. 70 (C), 22–38.
Guerrieri, V., Hartley, D., Hurst, E., 2013. Endogenous gentrification and housing price dynamics. J. Public Econ. 103 (5), 1664–1696.
Gyourko, J., Linneman, P., 1997. The changing influences of education, income, family structure, and race on homeownership by age over time. J. Hous. Res. 8 (1), 1–25.

Gyourko, J., Saiz, A., Summers, A.A., 2008. A new measure of the local regulatory environment for housing markets. Urban Stud. 45 (3), 693–729.

Han, L., Strange, W., 2015. The microstructure of housing markets: search, bargaining, and brokerage. In: Duranton, G., Henderson, J.V., Strange, W.C. (Eds.), Handbook of Regional and Urban Economics, vol. 5. Elsevier, Amsterdam, pp. 813–886.

Henderson, J.V., Ioannides, Y.M., 1983. A model of housing tenure choice. Am. Econ. Rev. 73 (1), 98–113.

Himmelberg, C., Mayer, C., Sinai, T., 2005. Assessing high house prices: bubbles, fundamentals and misperceptions. J. Econ. Perspect. 19, 67–92.

Hornstein, A., Praschnik, J., 1997. Intermediate inputs and sectoral comovements in the business cycle. J. Monet. Econ. 40, 573–595.

Hubbard, R.G., Skinner, J., Zeldes, S.P., 1995. Precautionary savings and social insurance. J. Polit. Econ. 103, 360–399.

Hurst, E., Stafford, F., 2004. Home is where the equity is: mortgage refinancing and household consumption. J. Money Credit Bank. 36 (6), 985–1014.

Iacoviello, M., 2005. House prices, borrowing constraints, and monetary policy in the business cycle. Am. Econ. Rev. 95 (3), 739–764.

Iacoviello, M., Neri, S., 2010. Housing market spillovers: evidence from an estimated DSGE model. Am. Econ. Rev. 2, 125–164.

Iacoviello, M., Pavan, M., 2013. Housing and debt over the life cycle and over the business cycle. J. Monet. Econ. 60 (2), 221–238.

Jaccard, I., 2011. Asset pricing and housing supply in a production economy. J. Macroecon. 11 (1). Article 33.

Jordà, O., Schularick, M., Taylor, A.M., 2016a. The great mortgaging: housing finance, crises and business cycles. Econ. Policy 31 (85), 107–152.

Jordà, O., Schularick, M., Taylor, A.M., 2016b. Leveraged bubbles. J. Monet. Econ. Forthcoming.

Justiniano, A., Primiceri, G.E., Tambalotti, A., 2015a. Credit supply and the housing boom. Working Paper, Northwestern University.

Justiniano, A., Primiceri, G.E., Tambalotti, A., 2015b. A simple model fo subrprime borrowers and credit growth. Working Paper, Northwestern University.

Kaneko, M., 1982. The central assignment game and the assignment of markets. J. Math. Econ. 10, 205–232.

Kaplan, G., Violante, G., 2014. A model of the consumption response to fiscal stimulus. Econometrica 82 (4), 1199–1239.

Kaplan, G., Mitman, K., Violante, G., 2016a. Non-durable consumption and housing net worth in the great recession: evidence from easily accessible data. Working Paper, NYU.

Kaplan, G., Moll, B., Violante, G., 2016b. Monetary policy according to HANK. Working Paper, Princeton University.

Kathari, S., Saporta-Eksten, I., Yu, E., 2013. The (un)importance of geographical mobility in the great recession. Rev. Econ. Dyn. 16, 553–563.

Kermani, A., 2012. Cheap credit, collateral, and the boom-bust cycle. Working Paper, Berkeley.

Keys, B.J., Mukherjee, T., Seru, A., Vig, V., 2010. Did securitization lead to lax screening? Evidence from subprime loans. Q. J. Econ. 125 (1), 307–362.

King, M., 1990. Discussion. Econ. Policy 11, 383–387.

Kiyotaki, N., Moore, J., 1997. Credit Cycles. J. Polit. Econ. 105 (2), 211–248.

Kiyotaki, N., Michaelides, A., Nikolov, K., 2011. Winners and losers in housing markets. J. Money Credit Bank. 43 (2-3), 255–296.

Knoll, K., Schularick, M., Steger, T., 2014. No price like home: global house prices, 1870-2012. CEPR Working Paper No. 10166.

Koijen, R.S.J., Hemert, O., Van Nieuwerburgh, S., 2009. Mortgage timing. J. Financ. Econ. 93 (2), 292–324.

Krusell, P., Smith, T., 1998. Income and wealth heterogeneity in the macroeconomy. J. Polit. Econ. 106 (5), 867–896.

Kuminoff, N.V., Pope, J.C., 2013. The value of residential land and structures during the great housing boom and bust. Land Econ. 89 (1), 1–29.

Kydland, F.E., Rupert, P., Sustek, R., 2012. Housing dynamics over the business cycle. NBER Working Paper No. 18432.

Landvoigt, T., 2015. Financial intermediation, credit risk, and credit supply during the housing boom. Working Paper, University of Texas at Austin.

Landvoigt, T., 2016. Housing Demand During the Boom: The Role of Expectations and Credit Constraints. Forthcoming Review of Financial Studies.

Landvoigt, T., Piazzesi, M., Schneider, M., 2015. The housing market(s) of san diego. Am. Econ. Rev. 105 (4), 1371–1407.

Li, W., Yao, R., 2007. The life-cycle effects of house price changes. J. Money Credit Bank. 39 (6), 1375–1409.

Liu, Z., Wang, P., Zha, T., 2013. Land-price dynamics and macroeconomic fluctuations. Econometrica 81 (3), 1167–1184.

Lu, H., 2008. Hedging house price risk in the presence of lumpy transaction costs. J. Urban Econ. 64 (2), 270–287.

Lustig, H., Van Nieuwerburgh, S., 2005. Housing collateral, consumption insurance and risk premia: an empirical perspective. J. Financ. 60 (3), 1167–1219.

Lustig, H., Van Nieuwerburgh, S., 2010. How much does household collateral constrain regional risk sharing? Rev. Econ. Dyn. 13 (2), 265–294.

Mayerhauser, N., Reinsdorf, M., 2007. Housing services in the national economic accounts. Working Paper, Bureau of Economic Analysis.

Mian, A., Sufi, A., 2009. The consequences of mortgage credit expansion: evidence from the U.S. mortgage default crisis. Q. J. Econ. 124 (4), 1449–1496.

Mian, A., Sufi, A., 2011. House prices, home equity-based borrowing, and the U.S. household leverage crisis. Am. Econ. Rev. 101 (5), 2132–2156.

Mian, A., Sufi, A., 2015. Fraudulent income overstatement on mortgage applications during the credit expansion of 2002 to 2005. NBER Working Paper No. 20947.

Mian, A., Rao, K., Sufi, A., 2013. Household balance sheets, consumption, and the economic slump. Q. J. Econ. 128 (4), 1687–1726.

Monacelli, T., 2009. New keynesian models, durable goods, and collateral constraints. J. Monet. Econ. 56 (2), 242–254.

Muellbauer, J., Murphy, A., 1990. Is the UK balance of payments sustainable? Econ. Policy 5 (11), 347–395.

Munnell, A.H., Tootell, G.M.B., Browne, L.E., McEneaney, J., 1996. Mortgage lending in boston: interpreting HMDA data. Am. Econ. Rev. 86 (1), 25–53.

Nathanson, C.G., Zwick, E., 2015. Arrested development: theory and evidence of supply-side speculation in the housing market. Working Paper, Booth and Kellogg.

Olsen, E., Zabel, J., 2015. United States housing policies. In: Henderson, J.V., Strange, W.C. (Eds.), In: Handbook of Regional and Urban Economics, vol. 5. Elsevier, Amsterdam, pp. 887–986.

Ortalo-Magné, F., Rady, S., 1999. Boom in, bust out: young households and the housing price cycle. Eur. Econ. Rev. 43, 755–766.

Ortalo-Magné, F., Rady, S., 2006. Housing market dynamics: on the contribution of income shocks and credit constraints. Rev. Econ. Stud. 73, 459–485.

Pagano, M., 1990. Discussion. Econ. Policy 11, 387–390.

Piazzesi, M., Schneider, M., 2008. Inflation illusion, credit, and asset pricing. In: Campbell, J. (Ed.), Asset Pricing and Monetary Policy. Chicago University Press, Chicago, IL, pp. 147–181.

Piazzesi, M., Schneider, M., 2009a. Inflation and the price of real assets. Federal Reserve Bank of Minneapolis Research Department Staff Report 423.

Piazzesi, M., Schneider, M., 2009b. Momentum traders in the housing market: survey evidence and a search model. Am. Econ. Rev. 99 (2), 406–411.

Piazzesi, M., Schneider, M., Tuzel, S., 2007. Housing, consumption and asset pricing. J. Financ. Econ. 83, 531–569.

Piskorski, T., Tchistyi, A., 2010. Optimal mortgage design. Rev. Financ. Stud. 23, 3098–3140.

Poterba, J.M., 1984. Tax subsidies to owner-occupied housing: an asset-market approach. Q. J. Econ. 99, 729–752.

Poterba, J.M., 1991. House price dynamics: the role of tax policy and demography. Brook. Pap. Econ. Act. 2, 143–203.
Ríos-Rull, J.V., Sánchez-Marcos, V., 2010. An aggregate economy with different size houses. J. Eur. Econ. Assoc. 6 (2/3), 705–714.
Rosen, S., 1974. Hedonic prices and implicit markets: product differentiation in pure competition. J. Polit. Econ. 82 (1), 34–55.
Rubio, M., 2011. Fixed- and variable-rate mortgages, business cycles, and monetary policy. J. Money Credit Bank. 43 (4), 657–688.
Saiz, A., 2010. The geographic determinants of housing supply. Q. J. Econ. 125 (3), 1253–1296.
Sargent, T.J., 1999. The Conquest of American Inflation. Princeton University Press, Princeton, NJ.
Schwartz, E.S., Torous, W.N., 1989. Prepayment and the valuation of mortgage-backed securities. J. Financ. 44 (2), 375–392.
Shleifer, A., Vishny, R.W., 1992. Liquidation Values and Debt Capacity: A Market Equilibrium Approach. J. Financ. 47 (4), 1343–1366.
Silos, P., 2007. Housing, portfolio choice and the macroeconomy. J. Econ. Dyn. Control 31, 2774–2801.
Sinai, T., Souleles, N., 2005. Owner-occupied housing as a hedge against rent risk. Q. J. Econ. 120 (2), 763–789.
Sinai, T., Souleles, N., 2013. Can owning a home hedge the risk of moving? Am. Econ. J. Econ. Pol. 5 (2), 282–312.
Slemrod, J., 1982. Down-Payment Constraints: Tax Policy Effects in a Growing Economy with Rental and Owner-Occupied Housing. Public Finance Quart. 10 (2), 193–217.
Sommer, K., Sullivan, P., Verbrugge, R., 2013. The equilibrium effect of fundamentals on house prices and rents. J. Monet. Econ. 60, 854–870.
Stanton, R., 1995. Rational prepayment and the valuation of mortgage-backed securities. Rev. Financ. Stud. 8 (3), 677–708.
Stein, J., 1995. Prices and trading volume in the housing market: a model with downpayment effects. Q. J. Econ. 110 (2), 379–406.
Stokey, N., 2009. Moving costs, nondurable consumption and portfolio choice. J. Econ. Theory 144 (6), 2419–2439.
Stroebel, J., Vavra, J., 2015. House prices, local demand, and retail prices. Working Paper, NYU.
Tsatsaronis, K., Zhu, H., 2014. What drives house price dynamics: cross-country evidence. BIS Q. Rev. 65–78. March.
Turner, T.M., Smith, M.T., 2009. Exits from homeownership: the effects of race, ethnicity, and income. J. Reg. Sci. 49 (1), 1–32.
Van Nieuwerburgh, S., Weill, P.O., 2010. Why has house price dispersion gone up? Rev. Econ. Stud. 77 (4), 1567–1606.
Wong, A., 2016. Population aging and the transmission mechanism of monetary policy. Working Paper, Northwestern.
Woodward, S.E., Hall, R.E., 2012. Diagnosing consumer confusion and sub-optimal shopping effort: theory and mortgage-market evidence. Am. Econ. Rev. 102 (7), 3249–3276.
Yang, F., 2009. Consumption over the life cycle: how different is housing? Rev. Econ. Dyn. 12, 423–443.
Yao, R., Zhang, H.H., 2005. Optimal consumption and portfolio choices with risky housing and borrowing constraints. Rev. Financ. Stud. 18 (1), 197–239.

CHAPTER 20

Term Structure of Uncertainty in the Macroeconomy

J. Borovička*, L.P. Hansen†
*New York University, New York, NY; NBER, Cambridge, MA, United States
†University of Chicago, Chicago, IL; NBER, Cambridge, MA, United States

Contents

Handbook of Macroeconomics, Volume 2B
ISSN 1574-0048, http://dx.doi.org/10.1016/bs.hesmac.2016.06.005

Abstract

Dynamic economic models make predictions about impulse responses that characterize how macroeconomic processes respond to alternative shocks over different horizons. From the perspective of asset pricing, impulse responses quantify the exposure of macroeconomic processes and other cash flows to macroeconomic shocks. Financial markets provide compensations to investors who are exposed to these shocks. Adopting an asset pricing vantage point, we describe and apply methods for computing exposures to macroeconomic shocks and the implied compensations represented as elasticities over alternative payoff horizons. The outcome is a term structure of macroeconomic uncertainty.

Keywords

Asset pricing, Impulse response functions, Shock elasticities, Financing frictions, Martingales

JEL Classification Codes

C10, C32, C58, E44, G12, G32

1. INTRODUCTION

Impulse response functions quantify the impact of alternative economic shocks on future economic outcomes. In so doing, they provide a way to assess the importance of alternative sources of fluctuations. Building on the insights of Yule (1927) and Slutsky (1927),

Frisch featured an important line of research on the "impulse and propagation problem" aimed at answering the question asking what are the sources of fluctuations and how they are propagated over time. An impulse, captured formally by the realization of a random shock, has an impact on an economic time series in all of the subsequent time periods. Response functions depict the intertemporal responses. Sims (1980) showed how to apply this approach in a tractable way to multivariate time series with a vector of underlying shocks, and he exposed the underlying challenges for identification. Subsequent research developed nonlinear counterparts to impulse response functions.

Macroeconomic shocks also play an important role in asset pricing. By their very nature, macroeconomic shocks cannot be diversified and investors exposed to those shocks require compensations. The resulting market-based remunerations differ depending on how cash flows are exposed to the alternative macroeconomic shocks. We call the compensations risk prices, and there is a term structure that characterizes these prices as a function of the investment horizon. In this chapter, we study methods for depicting this term structure and illustrate its use by comparing pricing implications across models. This leads us to formalize the exposure and pricing counterpart to impulse response functions familiar to macroeconomists. We call these objects shock-exposure and shock-price elasticities. Our calculations require either an empirical-based or model-based stochastic discount factor process along with a representation of how alternative cash flows with macroeconomic components respond to shocks.

There is an alternative way to motivate the calculations that we perform. A common characterization of risk aversion looks at local certainty equivalent calculations for small variance changes in consumption. We deviate in two ways. First, when making small changes, we do not use certainty as our benchmark but rather the equilibrium consumption from the stochastic general equilibrium model. This leads us to make more refined adjustments in the exposure to uncertainty. Second, movements in consumption at future dates could be induced by any of the macroeconomic shocks with occurrences at dates between tomorrow and this future date. Thus, similar to Hansen et al. (1999) and Alvarez and Jermann (2004), we have a differential measure depending on the specific shock and the dates of the impacts.

Empirical finance often focuses on the measurement of risk premia on alternative financial assets. In our framework, these risk premia reflect the exposure to uncertainty and the compensation for that exposure. Risk premia change when exposures change, when the prices of those exposures change, or both. We use explicit economic models to help us quantify these two channels by which risk premia are determined, but a more empirically based approach could also be applied provided that the uncertainty prices for shocks could be inferred. While there are interesting challenges in identification to explore, we will abstract from those challenges in this chapter.

Our chapter:

- defines and constructs a term structure of shock-exposure and shock-price elasticities applicable to nonlinear Markov models;

- compares these constructions to impulse response functions commonly used in macroeconomics;
- describes computational approaches pertinent for discrete-time and continuous-time models;
- applies the methods to continuous-time macroeconomic models with financing frictions proposed by He and Krishnamurthy (2013) and Brunnermeier and Sannikov (2014).

2. MATHEMATICAL FRAMEWORK

We introduce a framework designed to encompass a large class of macroeconomic and asset pricing general equilibrium models. There is an underlying stationary Markov model that is used to capture the stochastic growth of a vector of time series of economic variables. The Markov model emerges as the "reduced form" of a solution to a dynamic stochastic equilibrium model of the macroeconomy. Modeling stationary growth rates allows for inclusion of shocks that have permanent effects and nontrivial long-horizon implications for risk compensations. We provide a range of illustrative applications of this framework throughout the chapter, and we devote Section 7 to a more extensive exploration of nonlinear continuous-time models with financial constraints.

We start with a probability space $(\Omega, \mathcal{F}, P)$. On this probability space, there is an n-dimensional, stationary and ergodic Markov process $X = \{X_t : t \in \mathbb{N}\}$ and a k-dimensional process W of independent and identically distributed shocks. Unless otherwise specified, we assume that each W_t is a multivariate standard normal random variable. We will have more to say about discrete states and shocks that are not normally distributed in Section 3.5.

The Markov process is initialized at X_0. Denote $\mathfrak{F} = \{\mathcal{F}_t : t \in \mathbb{N}\}$ the completed filtration generated by the histories of W and X_0. We suppose that X is a solution to a law of motion

$$\begin{aligned} X_{t+1} &= \psi(X_t, W_{t+1}) \\ Y_{t+1} - Y_t &= \phi(X_t, W_{t+1}). \end{aligned} \tag{1}$$

The state vector X_t contains both exogenously specified states and endogenous ones. We presume full information in the sense that the shock W_{t+1} can be depicted in terms of $(X_t, Y_{t+1} - Y_t)$. In more general circumstances we would incorporate a solution to a filtering problem if we are to match an information structure to (X, Y), a filtering problem that is perhaps solved by economic agents.

Consistent intertemporal pricing together with the Markov property leads us to use a class of stochastic processes called multiplicative functionals. These processes are built from the underlying Markov process and will be used to model cash flows and stochastic discount factors. Since many macroeconomic time series grow or decay over time, we use the state vector X to model the growth rate of such processes. In particular, let the dynamics of a *multiplicative functional* M be defined as[a]

$$\log M_{t+1} - \log M_t = \kappa(X_t, W_{t+1}). \tag{2}$$

The components of Y are examples of multiplicative functionals. Since X is stationary, the process $\log M$ has stationary increments. A revealing example is the conditionally linear model

$$\kappa(X_t, X_{t+1}) = \beta(X_t) + \alpha(X_t) \cdot W_{t+1}$$

where $\beta(x)$ allows for nonlinearity in the conditional mean and $\alpha(x)$ introduces stochastic volatility.

We denote G a generic cash-flow process and S the equilibrium determined stochastic discount factor process, both modeled as multiplicative functionals. While we adopt a common mathematical formulation for both, G is expected to grow and S is expected to decay over time, albeit in stochastic manners.

Equilibrium models in macroeconomics and asset pricing build on the premise of utility-maximizing investors trading in arbitrage-free markets. Arbitrage-free pricing implies the existence of a strictly positive stochastic discount factor process S that can be used to infer equilibrium asset prices. Stochastic discount factors provide a convenient way to depict the observable implications of asset pricing models.[b] In this chapter, we consider a stochastic discount factor process that compounds the one-period stochastic discount factor increments in order to value multiperiod claims.

Definition 1 A stochastic discount factor S is a positive (with probability one) stochastic process such that for any $t, j \geq 0$ and payoff G_{t+j} maturing at time $t+j$, the time-t price is given by

$$\mathcal{Q}_t\left[G_{t+j}\right] = E\left[\left(\frac{S_{t+j}}{S_t}\right) G_{t+j} \mid \mathcal{F}_t\right]. \tag{3}$$

Notice that this definition does not restrict the date zero stochastic discount factor, S_0. This initialization may be chosen in a convenient manner. If markets are complete, then this stochastic discount factor is unique up to the initialization. Equations of the type (3) arise from investors' optimality conditions in the form of Euler equations. In an equilibrium model with complete markets, the stochastic discount factor is typically equated with the marginal rate of substitution of an unconstrained investor. The identity of such a person can change over time and across states. In some models with incomplete markets, the stochastic discount factor process ceases to be unique. There are different

[a] Multiplicative functionals are often initialized at one, or equivalently $\log M_0 = 0$. We will abuse this jargon a bit by allowing ourselves other possible initiations.

[b] See Hansen and Richard (1987) for an initial discussion of stochastic discount factors.

shadow prices for nontraded risk exposures but a common pricing of the exposures with explicit compensations in financial markets. With other forms of trading frictions, the pricing equalities can be replaced by pricing inequalities, still expressed using a stochastic discount factor.

In our framework, we will suppose that equilibrium stochastic discount factors inherit the multiplicative functional structure. Market frictions, portfolio constraints, and other types of market imperfections will then introduce distortions into formula (3). We will study such distortions in models with financial constraints in Section 7.

Notice that definition (3) of the stochastic discount factor involves an expectations operator. This expectations operator in general represents investors' beliefs about the future. Here, we have imposed rational expectations by assuming that investors' beliefs are identical to the data-generating probability measure P. This measure is that implied by historical evidence or by the fully specified model. Investors' beliefs, however, may differ from P and there exists alternative approaches to modeling these deviations in interesting ways. While the modeling of investors' beliefs is an important building block of the asset pricing framework, in this chapter we abstract from these considerations and impose rational expectations throughout the text.

3. ASSET PRICING OVER ALTERNATIVE INVESTMENT HORIZONS

We price cash flows exposed to macroeconomic uncertainty and modeled as multiplicative processes. Consider a generic cash flow process G, say the dividend process or an equilibrium consumption process. We start with a baseline payoff G_t maturing in individual periods $t = 0, 1, 2, \ldots$ and parameterize stochastic perturbations of this process. In particular, we derive measures that capture the sensitivity of expected payoff to exposure to alternative macroeconomic shocks, and the sensitivity of the associated risk compensations. We follow the convention in empirical finance by depicting compensations in terms of expected returns per unit of some measure of riskiness. The compensations differ depending upon which shock we target when we construct stochastic perturbations. The method relies on a comparison of the pricing of payoff G_t relative to another payoff that is marginally more exposed to risk in a particular way.

The cash flows G arising from equilibrium models will often have the form of multiplicative processes (2). A special case of such cash flows are payoffs that are positive functions of the Markov state, $\psi(X_t)$. These payoffs will be featured prominently in our subsequent analysis.

3.1 One-Period Pricing

We are interested in the pricing of payoffs maturing at different horizons, but we start with a simple one-period conditionally lognormal environment. This environment will provide an explicit link to familiar calculations in asset valuation. Suppose that

$$\log G_1 = \beta_g(X_0) + \alpha_g(X_0) \cdot W_1$$
$$\log S_1 - \log S_0 = \beta_s(X_0) + \alpha_s(X_0) \cdot W_1$$

where G_1 is the payoff to which we assign values and S_1 is the one-period stochastic discount factor used to compute these values. The one-period return on this investment is the payoff in period one divided by the period-zero price:

$$R_1 \doteq \frac{G_1}{Q_0[G_1]} = \frac{\left(\frac{G_1}{G_0}\right)}{E\left[\left(\frac{S_1}{S_0}\right)\left(\frac{G_1}{G_0}\right) \mid X_0\right]}.$$

The logarithm of the expected return can then be calculated explicitly as:

$$\begin{aligned}\log E[R_1 \mid X_0 = x] &= \log E\left[\left(\frac{G_1}{G_0}\right) \mid X_0 = x\right] - \log E\left[\left(\frac{S_1}{S_0}\right)\left(\frac{G_1}{G_0}\right) \mid X_0 = x\right] \\ &= \underbrace{-\beta_s(x) - \frac{|\alpha_s(x)|^2}{2}}_{\text{risk-free rate}} \underbrace{-\alpha_s(x) \cdot \alpha_g(x)}_{\text{risk premium}}.\end{aligned} \tag{4}$$

This compensation is expressed in terms of expected returns as is typical in asset pricing. Notice that we are using logarithms of proportional risk premia as a starting point.

Imagine applying this calculation to a family of such payoffs parameterized in part by α_g. The vector α_g defines a vector of exposures to the components of the normally distributed shock W_1. Then $-\alpha_s$ is the vector of shock "prices" representing the compensation for exposure to these shocks.

The risk prices in this conditionally lognormal model have a familiar conditional linear structure known from one-period factor models. In these models, the so-called factor loadings α_g on the individual shocks W_1 are multiplied by factor prices $-\alpha_s$. The total compensation in terms of an expected return is thus the product of the quantity of risk (risk exposure) and the price per unit of this risk. There are analogous simplifications for continuous-time diffusion models since the local evolution in such models is conditionally normal.

In a nonlinear multiperiod environment, this calculation ceases to be straightforward. We would, however, still like to infer measures of the quantity of risk and the associated price of the risk. We therefore explore a related derivation that will yield the same results in this one-period lognormal environment but will also naturally extend to a nonlinear setup and multiple-period horizons.

3.1.1 One-Period Shock Elasticities

We parameterize a family of random variables $H_1(\mathsf{r})$ indexed by r using

$$\log H_1(\mathsf{r}) = \mathsf{r}\nu(X_0)\cdot W_1 - \frac{\mathsf{r}^2}{2}|\nu(X_0)|^2 \tag{5}$$

where r is an auxiliary scalar parameter. The vector of exposures $\alpha_h(X_0)$ is normalized to

$$E\left[|\nu(X_0)|^2\right] = 1.$$

With this normalization,

$$E[H_1(\mathsf{r})|X_0] = 1.$$

Even when shocks are not normally distributed, we shall find it convenient to construct $H_1(\mathsf{r})$ to have a unit conditional expectation.

Given the baseline payoff G_t, form a parameterized family of payoffs $G_1 H_1(\mathsf{r})$ given by

$$\log G_1 - \log G_0 + \log H_1(\mathsf{r}) = \underbrace{[\alpha_g(X_0) + \mathsf{r}\nu(X_0)]}_{\text{new shock exposure}} \cdot W_1 + \beta_g(X_0) - \frac{\mathsf{r}^2}{2}|\nu(X_0)|^2.$$

The new cash flow $G_1 H_1(\mathsf{r})$ has shock exposure $\alpha_g(X_0) + \mathsf{r}\nu(X_0)$ and is thus more exposed to the vector of shocks W_1 in the direction $\nu(X_0)$. By changing r, we alter the magnitude of the exposure in direction $\nu(X_0)$. By choosing different vectors $\nu(X_0)$, we alter the combinations of shocks whose impact we want to investigate. A typical example of an $\nu(X_0)$ would be a coordinate vector e_j with a single one in jth place. In that case, we infer the pricing implications of the jth component of the shock vector W_1. In some applications it may be convenient to make $\nu(X_0)$ explicitly depend on X_0. For instance, Borovička et al. (2011) propose scaling of ν with X_0 in models with stochastic volatility.

The payoffs $G_1 H_1(\mathsf{r})$ imply a corresponding family of logarithms of expected returns as in Eq. (4):

$$\log E[R_1(\mathsf{r}) \mid X_0 = x] = \log E\left[\left(\frac{G_1}{G_0}\right) H_1(\mathsf{r}) \mid X_0 = x\right]$$
$$- \log E\left[\left(\frac{S_1}{S_0}\right)\left(\frac{G_1}{G_0}\right) H_1(\mathsf{r}) \mid X_0 = x\right].$$

We are interested in comparing the expected return of the payoff $G_1 H_1(\mathsf{r})$ relative to $G_1 = G_1 H_1(0)$. Since our exposure direction $\nu(X_0)$ has a unit standard deviation, by differentiating with respect to r we compute an elasticity

$$\frac{d}{d\mathsf{r}} \log E[R_1(\mathsf{r}) \mid X_0 = x]\big|_{\mathsf{r}=0}$$
$$= \frac{d}{d\mathsf{r}} \log E\left[\left(\frac{G_1}{G_0}\right) H_1(\mathsf{r}) \mid X_0 = x\right]\Big|_{\mathsf{r}=0} - \frac{d}{d\mathsf{r}} \log E\left[\left(\frac{S_1}{S_0}\right)\left(\frac{G_1}{G_0}\right) H_1(\mathsf{r}) \mid X_0 = x\right]\Big|_{\mathsf{r}=0}.$$

This elasticity measures the sensitivity of the expected return on the payoff G_1 to an increase in exposure to the shock in the direction $\nu(x)$. The calculation leads us to define the counterparts of quantity and price elasticities from microeconomics:

1. The one-period *shock-exposure elasticity*

$$\varepsilon_g(x,1) = \frac{d}{d\mathsf{r}} \log E\left[\left(\frac{G_1}{G_0}\right) H_1(\mathsf{r}) \mid X_0 = x\right]\Bigg|_{\mathsf{r}=0} = \alpha_g(x)\cdot\nu(x)$$

measures the sensitivity of the expected payoff G_1 to an increase in exposure in the direction $\nu(x)$.

2. The one-period *shock-price elasticity*

$$\begin{aligned}\varepsilon_p(x,1) &= \frac{d}{d\mathsf{r}} \log E\left[\left(\frac{G_1}{G_0}\right) H_1(\mathsf{r}) \mid X_0 = x\right]\Bigg|_{\mathsf{r}=0} - \frac{d}{d\mathsf{r}} \log E\left[\left(\frac{S_1}{S_0}\right)\left(\frac{G_1}{G_0}\right) H_1(\mathsf{r}) \mid X_0 = x\right]\Bigg|_{\mathsf{r}=0} \\ &= -\alpha_s(x)\cdot\nu(x)\end{aligned}$$

measures the sensitivity of the compensation, in units of expected return, for this exposure.

Notice that the shock-exposure elasticity recovers the exposure vector $\alpha_g(x)$, and individual components of this vector can be obtained by varying the choice of the direction of the perturbation $\nu(x)$. Similarly, the shock-price elasticity recovers the vector of prices $-\alpha_s(x)$ associated with the risks embedded in the shock W_1.

In this one-period case, we replicated a straightforward decomposition of the expected return (4) into quantities and prices of risk. Now we move to the characterization of the asset pricing implications over longer horizons.

3.2 Multiperiod Investment Horizon

Consider the parameterized payoff $G_t H_1(\mathsf{r})$ with a date-zero price $E[S_t G_t H_1(\mathsf{r}) \mid X_0 = x]$. This is a payoff maturing at time t that has the same growth rate as payoff G_t except period one when the growth rate is stochastically perturbed by $H_1(\mathsf{r})$. The logarithm of the expected return (yield to maturity) is

$$\begin{aligned}\log E[R_{0,t}(\mathsf{r}) \mid X_0 = x] \doteq \log E\left[\left(\frac{G_t}{G_0}\right) H_1(\mathsf{r}) \mid X_0 = x\right] \\ -\log E\left[\left(\frac{S_t}{S_0}\right)\left(\frac{G_t}{G_0}\right) H_1(\mathsf{r}) \mid X_0 = x\right].\end{aligned}$$

Following our previous analysis, we construct two elasticities:

1. *shock-exposure elasticity*

$$\varepsilon_g(x,t) = \frac{d}{d\mathsf{r}} \log E\left[\left(\frac{G_t}{G_0}\right) H_1(\mathsf{r}) \mid X_0 = x\right]\Bigg|_{\mathsf{r}=0}$$

2. *shock-price elasticity*

$$\varepsilon_p(x,t) = \frac{d}{d\mathsf{r}} \log E\left[\left(\frac{G_t}{G_0}\right) H_1(\mathsf{r}) \mid X_0 = x\right]\Bigg|_{\mathsf{r}=0} - \frac{d}{d\mathsf{r}} \log E\left[\left(\frac{S_t}{S_0}\right)\left(\frac{G_t}{G_0}\right) H_1(\mathsf{r}) \mid X_0 = x\right]\Bigg|_{\mathsf{r}=0} \tag{6}$$

These elasticities are functions of the investment horizon t, and thus we obtain a term structure of elasticities. The dependence on the current state $X_0 = x$ incorporates possible time variation in the sensitivity of expected returns to exposure to shocks.

3.3 A Change of Measure and an Impulse Response for a Multiplicative Functional

Notice that the shock elasticities defined in the previous section have a common mathematical structure expressed using the multiplicative functionals $M = S$ and $M = SG$. Given a multiplicative functional M, we define

$$\varepsilon(x,t) = \frac{d}{d\mathsf{r}} \log E\left[\left(\frac{M_t}{M_0}\right) H_1(\mathsf{r}) \mid X_0 = x\right]\Bigg|_{\mathsf{r}=0}. \tag{7}$$

Taking the derivative in (7), we obtain

$$\varepsilon(x,t) = \nu(x) \cdot \frac{E\left[\left(\frac{M_t}{M_0}\right) W_1 \mid X_0 = x\right]}{E\left[\left(\frac{M_t}{M_0}\right) \mid X_0 = x\right]}. \tag{8}$$

Thus a major ingredient in the computation is the covariance between $\left(\frac{M_t}{M_0}\right)$ and W_1 conditioned on X_0.

The random variable $H_1(r)$ given by (5) is positive and has expectation equal to unity conditioned on X_0. Multiplication by this random variable has the interpretation of changing the probability distribution of W_1 from having mean zero to having a mean given by $\mathsf{r}\nu(X_0)$. Thus given a multiplicative process M

$$E\left[\left(\frac{M_t}{M_0}\right) H_1(\mathsf{r}) \mid X_0 = x\right] = E\left(H_1(\mathsf{r}) E\left[\left(\frac{M_t}{M_0}\right) \mid X_0, W_1\right] \mid X_0 = x\right)$$
$$= \widetilde{E}\left(E\left[\left(\frac{M_t}{M_0}\right) \mid X_0, W_1\right] \mid X_0 = x\right)$$

where $\widetilde{E}$ presumes that the random vector W_1 is distributed as a multivariate normal with mean $\mathsf{r}\nu(x)$ consistent with our multiplication by $H_1(\mathsf{r})$.

3.4 Long-Horizon Pricing

Shock elasticities depict the term structure of risk as we change the maturity of priced payoffs. To aid our understanding of the overall shape of the term structure of elasticities, we characterize the long-horizon limits of these shock elasticities. We provide a characterization for a general multiplicative process that takes the form of a factorization. A multiplicative process is a product of a geometric constant growth or decay process, a positive martingale, and a ratio of a function of the Markov state in date zero and date t. Since the factorization is applicable to any member of a general class of multiplicative processes, we apply it to both stochastic discount factor processes and positive cash flow processes.

As in Hansen and Scheinkman (2009) and Hansen (2012), we use Perron–Frobenius theory to provide a factorization of multiplicative processes. Given a multiplicative process M, solve the equation

$$E\left[\left(\frac{M_t}{M_0}\right)e(X_t)\mid X_0=x\right]=\exp(\eta t)e(x) \tag{9}$$

for an unknown function $e(x)$ that is strictly positive and an unknown number η. The solution is independent of the choice of the horizon t.

Consider the pair (e,η) that solves (9) and form

$$\frac{\widetilde{M}_t}{\widetilde{M}_0}\doteq\exp(-\eta t)\frac{e(X_t)}{e(X_0)}\left(\frac{M_t}{M_0}\right). \tag{10}$$

The stochastic process $\widetilde{M}$ is a martingale under P, since

$$\begin{aligned}E\left[\widetilde{M}_{t+1}\mid\mathcal{F}_t\right]&=\frac{\exp[-\eta(t+1)]}{e(X_0)}\frac{M_t}{M_0}\widetilde{M}_0\,E\left[\frac{M_{t+1}}{M_t}e(X_{t+1})\mid\mathcal{F}_t\right]\\&=\exp(-\eta t)\frac{e(X_t)}{e(X_0)}\frac{M_t}{M_0}\widetilde{M}_0=\widetilde{M}_t.\end{aligned}$$

Consequently, expression (10) can be reorganized as

$$\frac{M_t}{M_0}=\exp(\eta t)\frac{e(X_0)}{e(X_t)}\frac{\widetilde{M}_t}{\widetilde{M}_0}. \tag{11}$$

This formula provides a multiplicative decomposition of the multiplicative functional M into a deterministic drift $\exp(\eta t)$, a stationary function of the Markov state $e(x)$, and a martingale $\widetilde{M}$. This martingale component will be critical in characterizing long-term pricing implications.

Associated with the martingale $\widetilde{M}$ is a probability measure $\widetilde{P}$ such that for every measurable function Z of the Markov process between dates zero and t,

$$E\left(\widetilde{M}_t Z \mid X_0 = x\right) = \widetilde{E}\left(Z \mid X_0 = x\right)$$

where $\widetilde{E}(\cdot \mid X_0 = x)$ is the conditional expectation operator under the probability measure $\widetilde{P}$.[c]

In finite state spaces, Eq. (9) can be posed as a matrix problem with a solution that is an eigenvector with positive entries.

Example 3.1 In a finite-state Markov chain environment, Eq. (9) is a standard eigenvalue problem. Let realized value of the X_t be represented as alternative coordinate vectors. Suppose the ratio $\frac{M_{t+1}}{M_t}$ satisfies

$$\frac{M_{t+1}}{M_t} = (X_{t+1})' \mathbf{M} X_t$$

for some square matrix $\mathbf{M}$. In the same way, represent the one-period transition probabilities as a matrix $\mathbf{P}$. For $t = 1$, Eq. (9) becomes a vector equation

$$(\mathbf{P} * \mathbf{M})\mathbf{e} = \exp(\eta)\mathbf{e}$$

where the operator $*$ depicts elementwise multiplication, $(\mathbf{P} * \mathbf{M})_{ij} = \mathbf{P}_{ij}\mathbf{M}_{ij}$. When

$$\sum_{j=0}^{\infty} \lambda^j (\mathbf{P} * \mathbf{M})^j$$

has all strictly positive entries for some $0 < \lambda < 1$, the Perron–Frobenius theorem implies the existence of a unique normalized strictly positive eigenvector $\mathbf{e}$ associated with the largest eigenvalue $\exp(\eta)$ of the matrix $\mathbf{P} * \mathbf{M}$. Then $e(X_t)$ in formula (9) is $\mathbf{e} \cdot X_t$.

In continuous state spaces, this factorization may not yield a unique strictly positive solution $e(x)$. Hansen and Scheinkman (2009) and Borovička et al. (2015) provide selection criteria based on the stochastic stability of the probability measure implied by the martingale component to guarantee uniqueness. Stochastic stability ensures that we have a valuable way to compute limiting approximations once we change measures. Here, we will assume that we have selected such a solution.[d]

[c] In order to completely define the measure $\widetilde{P}$, we also need to specify the unconditional probability distribution. For instance, $\widetilde{M}_0$ can be initiated to make $\widetilde{P}$ stationary. Since all pricing results in this chapter utilize conditional probability distributions, we abstract from these considerations here.

[d] Our formulation presumes an underlying Markovian structure. See Qin and Linetsky (2014b) for a more general starting point and an analogous factorization.

Factorization (11) leads to a characterization of long-horizon limits for the shock elasticities. Using this factorization in expression (7), we obtain[e]

$$\varepsilon(x,t)=\nu(x)\cdot\frac{\widetilde{E}[\hat{e}(X_t)W_1 \mid X_0=x]}{\widetilde{E}\,[\hat{e}(X_t) \mid X_0=x]}$$

where $\hat{e}(x)\doteq 1/e(x)$. Under technical assumptions the long-maturity limit for the shock elasticity is given by

$$\lim_{t\to\infty}\varepsilon(x,t)=\nu(x)\cdot\widetilde{E}\,[W_1 \mid X_0=x].$$

The sensitivity of long-horizon payoffs to current shocks is therefore determined by the martingale components of the stochastic discount factor and the cash flow, and their implications for the expectations of shock W_1 as captured by the implied change in probability measures.

3.5 Non-Gaussian Frameworks

While we have made special reference to normally distributed shocks, our mathematical structure does not require this. We have featured perturbations $H_1(\mathsf{r})$ that are positive and expectations one. Risk prices in financial economics are denominated in terms of expected mean compensation per unit of risk. With normally distributed shocks, we measure risk in units of standard deviations. Provided that we adopt an interpretable way to denominate risk prices for other distributions, our methods continue to apply beyond the conditionally Gaussian framework. For instance, Zviadadze (2016) constructs shock elasticities in a stochastic environment with autoregressive gamma processes.

Another example are regime-shift models that may include both normally distributed shocks along with uncertain regimes. Exposure to macroeconomic regime-shift risk is of interest and can be characterized using shock elasticities by structuring appropriately the random variable $H_1(\mathsf{r})$. These switches can be exogenous (eg, exogenously modeled periods of low or high growth and volatility) or endogenous (eg, interest rate at the zero lower bound, financial sector in a period of binding financial constraints, or regime changes in government policies). We develop shock elasticities for regime-shift risk in Borovička et al. (2011).

For Markov chain models used to capture the regime shift dynamics of exogenous shocks see David (2008), Chen (2010), or Bianchi (2015) for some recent examples in the asset pricing literature and Liu et al. (2011) and Bianchi et al. (2013) in

[e] See Hansen and Scheinkman (2012) for a version of this result for a continuous-time diffusion model.

macroeconomic modeling. Regime switches are also utilized to model time variation in government policies, see Sims and Zha (2006), Liu et al. (2009), and Bianchi (2012) for regime switching in monetary policy rules, Davig et al. (2010, 2011) and Bianchi and Melosi (2016) for fiscal policy applications, and Chung et al. (2007) and Bianchi and Ilut (2015) for a combination of both. Farmer et al. (2011) and Foerster et al. (2014) analyze solution and estimation techniques in Markov chain models in conjunction with perturbation approximation methods. In Borovička and Hansen (2014), we introduce a tractable exponential-quadratic framework that permits semi-analytical formulas for shock elasticities and encompasses a large class of models solved using perturbation techniques.

4. RELATION TO IMPULSE RESPONSE FUNCTIONS

Impulse responses to specific structural shocks are a common way of representing the dynamic properties of macroeconomic models. As we mentioned previously, this idea goes back at least to Frisch (1933). Our elasticity computations change exposures of cash flows to shocks and explore the consequences for valuation. These constructs are closely related and in some circumstances are mathematically identical to impulse response functions. We explore these connections in this section.

To relate our elasticity calculation to an impulse response function, consider the conditional expectation

$$E\left[\left(\frac{M_t}{M_0}\right) \mid X_0, W_1 = w\right]$$

for alternative choices of w. Changing the value of w gives rise to the impulse response of M_t to a shock at date one. Instead of conditioning on alternative realized values of the shock at date one, as we have seen our computations are equivalent to changing the date zero distribution of W_1. A similarity in perspectives emerges because this distributional change could include a mean shift in the distribution for W_1. In practice, empirical macroeconomists typically study expectations of the logarithms of macroeconomic time series, often using linear models. For asset pricing it is important that we work with expectations of levels of macroeconomic quantities and cash flows, and account for nonlinearities. To compute shock *elasticities* we are lead to study the impact on the logarithm of the conditional expectation of M_t as developed in formula (7). In the remainder of this section, we consider two special cases in which the link to impulse functions is particularly close.

4.1 Lognormality

When M is a lognormal process, the impulse response functions for $\log M$ match exactly our shock elasticity as we will now see.

A linear vector-autoregression (VAR) model is a special case of the framework (1). Specifically X is a linear vector-autoregression with autoregression coefficient matrix $\overline{\mu}$ and shock-exposure matrix $\overline{\sigma}$:

$$X_{t+1} = \overline{\mu} X_t + \overline{\sigma} W_{t+1}. \tag{12}$$

We assume that the absolute values of eigenvalues of the matrix $\overline{\mu}$ are strictly less than one. Analogously, we introduce a multiplicative process M (constructed in general form in (2)) with evolution:

$$\log M_{t+1} - \log M_t = \overline{\beta} \cdot X_t + \overline{\alpha} \cdot W_{t+1}. \tag{13}$$

The shock W_{t+1} is distributed as a multivariate standard normal. With this construction of the multiplicative process M, we first study the responses of $\log M$.

4.1.1 Impulse Response Functions

Let $\nu(x) = \overline{\nu}$ where $\overline{\nu}$ is a vector with norm one. In typical applications, $\overline{\nu}$ is a coordinate vector. The impulse response function of $\log M_t$ for the linear combination of shocks chosen by the vector $\overline{\nu}$ is given by

$$E[\log M_t - \log M_0 \mid X_0 = x, W_1 = \overline{\nu}] - E[\log M_t - \log M_0 \mid X_0 = x, W_1 = 0] = \overline{\nu} \cdot \overline{\varrho}_t.$$

where the coefficients satisfy the recursions implied by (12) and (13). From (13), we have the recursion:

$$\overline{\varrho}_{t+1} - \overline{\varrho}_t = (\overline{\zeta}_t)' \overline{\beta} \tag{14}$$

with initial condition $\overline{\varrho}_1 = \overline{\alpha}$, and from (12):

$$\overline{\zeta}_{t+1} = \overline{\mu} \overline{\zeta}_t \tag{15}$$

with initial condition $\overline{\zeta}_1 = \overline{\sigma}$. Solving these recursions gives:

$$\begin{aligned} \overline{\zeta}_t &= \overline{\mu}^{t-1} \overline{\sigma} \\ \overline{\varrho}_t &= \overline{\alpha} + \left[(I - \overline{\mu})^{-1} \left(I - \overline{\mu}^{t-1} \right] \overline{\sigma} \right)' \overline{\beta}. \end{aligned} \tag{16}$$

The impulse response function in the linear model is thus a sequence of deterministic coefficients $\overline{\nu} \cdot \overline{\varrho}_t$. The first term, $\overline{\alpha} \cdot \overline{\nu}$, represents the immediate response arising from realization $\overline{\nu}$ of the current shock, while the remaining terms capture the subsequent propagation of the shock through the dynamics of state vector X as it influences $\log M$ in the future.

4.1.2 Shock Elasticities

Consider now our elasticity calculation. Write $\log M_t$ as its moving-average representation:

$$\log M_t = \sum_{j=0}^{t-1} \overline{\varrho}_j \cdot W_{t-j} + E(\log M_t \mid \mathcal{F}_0),$$

or equivalently

$$\begin{aligned}\log M_t - \log M_0 &= \sum_{j=1}^{t} \overline{\varrho}_j \cdot W_{t-j+1} + E(\log M_t - \log M_0 \mid X_0) \\ &= \sum_{j=1}^{t-1} \overline{\varrho}_j \cdot W_{t-j+1} + \overline{\varrho}_t \cdot W_1 + E(\log M_t - \log M_0 \mid X_0).\end{aligned}$$

Since the shocks W_t are independently distributed as a multivariate standard normals over time,

$$E\left[\left(\frac{M_t}{M_0}\right) \mid X_0 = x, W_1 = w\right] = \exp\left(\frac{1}{2}\sum_{j=1}^{t-1} \overline{\varrho}_j \cdot \overline{\varrho}_j\right) \exp(\overline{\varrho}_t \cdot W_1) \exp(E[\log M_t - \log M_0 \mid X_0]).$$

Using formula (8), we compute:

$$\varepsilon(x,t) = \frac{E\left[\left(\frac{M_t}{M_0}\right) W_1 \mid X_0 = x\right]}{E\left[\left(\frac{M_t}{M_0}\right) \mid X_0 = x\right]} = \frac{E[\exp(\overline{\varrho}_t \cdot W_1) W_1 \mid X_0 = x]}{E[\exp(\overline{\varrho}_t \cdot W_1)]} = \overline{\varrho}_t.$$

The second equality follows by observing that

$$\frac{\exp(\overline{\varrho}_t \cdot W_1)}{E[\exp(\overline{\varrho}_t \cdot W_1)]}$$

is strictly positive and has conditional expectation one. Multiplication by this random variable is equivalent to changing the distribution of W_1 from a multivariate standard normal to a multivariate normal with mean $\overline{\varrho}_t$. To summarize, in this lognormal case, the shock elasticities do not depend on the Markov state and they coincide with the impulse responses measured by $\overline{\nu} \cdot \overline{\varrho}_t$ for $t = 1, 2, \ldots$.

Consider in particular the shock-price elasticity (6). Notice that this shock-price elasticity consists of the difference of shock elasticities for G and SG, and thus we are lead to compute impulse response functions for $\log G$ and $\log S + \log G$. The additivity of the construction implies that the impulse response function coefficients for the latter are $\overline{\nu} \cdot \overline{\varrho}_{s,t} + \overline{\nu} \cdot \overline{\varrho}_{g,t}$, and thus the resulting shock-price elasticity corresponds to the impulse response function of $-\log S$, with coefficients $-\overline{\nu} \cdot \overline{\varrho}_{s,t}$.

4.1.3 Long-Term Pricing Revisited

In this example, as discussed in Hansen et al. (2008) there is a close link between the factorization described in Section 3.4 and the additive decompositions of linear time series. Beveridge and Nelson (1981) and Blanchard and Quah (1989) extracted a martingale component in linear models and used it to characterize the impact of permanent shocks.[f]

Consider solving

$$E\left[\left(\frac{M_1}{M_0}\right)e(X_1)\mid X_0=x\right]=\exp(\eta)e(x)$$

for the pair (e, η), where the evolution of M is given by (13). In this special case, a straightforward calculation using formulas for lognormals gives:

$$\begin{aligned}\log e(x) &= E\left(\sum_{j=0}^{\infty}\overline{\beta}\cdot X_{t+j}|X_t=x\right)\\ &= (\overline{\beta})'(I-\overline{\mu})^{-1}x,\end{aligned}$$

and[g]

$$\eta=\frac{1}{2}|\overline{\alpha}'+\overline{\beta}'(I-\overline{\mu})^{-1}\overline{\sigma}|^2.$$

Under the change of measure associated with the martingale $\widetilde{M}$ in the multiplicative factorization, W_1 has a mean equal to

$$\overline{\sigma}'(I-\overline{\mu}')^{-1}\overline{\beta}+\overline{\alpha}$$

which is independent of the state vector. Notice that this is also the limiting value of $\overline{\varrho}_t$ as given in (16). In this lognormal example

$$\log M_{t+1}-\log M_t+\log e(X_{t+1})-\log e(X_t)=\left[\overline{\beta}'(I-\overline{\mu}')^{-1}\overline{\sigma}+\overline{\alpha}'\right]W_{t+1}$$

where the right-hand side gives the permanent shock to $\log M$ as constructed in Beveridge and Nelson (1981) and Blanchard and Quah (1989). In VAR analyses, transitory shocks are typically constructed as linear combinations of W_{t+1} that are uncorrelated with this permanent shock. On the other hand $\log e(X_{t+1})$ and its innovation are typically correlated with the permanent shock.

This simple connection between permanent shocks and permanent components to pricing ceases to hold in more general nonlinear environments. Hansen (2012) has a more

[f] Hansen (2012) constructs an additive decomposition of $\log M$ in a continuous-time version of our nonlinear framework.

[g] If we were to include a constant included in the evolution of $\log M$, this would be added to η.

complete discussion of the relation between the permanent component to $\log M$ and the martingale component to M outside this lognormal specification.

4.2 Continuous-Time Diffusions

In this section, we focus on a framework with uncertainty modeled using Brownian shocks, and apply it to models with financial constraints in Section 7. While the Brownian information setup is not without loss of generality, it provides tools for a pedagogically transparent treatment and shows the close connection between shock elasticities and impulse responses. In Borovička et al. (2011) we also consider jumps in the form of regime shifts in continuous-time Markov chains and applications to consumption-based asset pricing models.

Let X be a Markov diffusion on $\mathcal{X} \subseteq \mathbb{R}^n$:

$$dX_t = \mu(X_t)dt + \sigma(X_t)dW_t$$

with initial condition $X_0 = x$. Here, $\mu(x)$ is an n-dimensional vector and $\sigma(x)$ is an $n \times k$ matrix for each vector x in $\mathbb{R}^n$. In addition W is a k-dimensional Brownian motion. We use this underlying Markov process to construct a multiplicative process M via:

$$\log M_t = \log M_0 + \int_0^t \beta(X_u)du + \int_0^t \alpha(X_u) \cdot dW_u \tag{17}$$

where $\beta(x)$ is a scalar and $\alpha(x)$ is a k-dimensional vector, or, in differential notation,

$$d\log M_t = \beta(X_t)dt + \alpha(X_t) \cdot dW_t. \tag{18}$$

Thus M_t depends on the initial conditions $(X_0, M_0) = (x, m)$ and the innovations to the Brownian motion W between dates zero and t. Let $\{\mathcal{F}_t : t \geq 0\}$ be the (completed) filtration generated by the Brownian motion between time zero and time t along with any initial information captured by $\mathcal{F}_0$.

As before, stochastic discount factors and cash flows in this environment are specific versions of a multiplicative process M. This multiplicative process is exposed to two types of risk. The first source of risk exposure is the "local," or infinitesimal, risk in term $\alpha(X_u) \cdot dW_u$ in (17). The second source of risk comes from the time variation in X_t and the state dependence of coefficients $\beta(x)$ and $\alpha(x)$, and is manifested over longer horizons.

4.2.1 Haussmann–Clark–Ocone Formula

There is a natural counterpart to a moving-average representation for diffusions. Importantly, the moving-average coefficients are, in general, state dependent. They entail computing so-called Malliavin derivatives of the date-u shock to the process $\log M_t$ for $t \geq u$, denoted $\mathcal{D}_u \log M_t$. We do not develop Malliavin differentiation as a formal mathematical construct but instead proceed heuristically.[h] This calculation of a Malliavin derivative gives the random response to a shock at date-u and is only restricted to be t-measurable where $t \geq u$. By forming the date-u conditional expectation we get the expected response as of the date of the shock. The computation is localized by making the time interval over which the shock acts on the process $\log M_t$ arbitrarily small, which allows for the formal construction of a derivative.

The calculation of $\mathcal{D}_u \log M_t$ has two uses analogous to the lognormal example we examined earlier. First, the (random) impulse response function for $\log M$

$$\varrho_t(X_0) = \nu(X_0) \cdot E(\mathcal{D}_0 \log M_t \mid F_0) = \nu(X_0) \cdot E[\mathcal{D}_0(\log M_t - \log M_0) \mid X_0]$$

for $t \geq 0$ where $\nu(X_0)$ determines which conditional linear combination of the shocks is subject to an impulse. The resulting responses depend on conditioning information captured by X_0, in contrast to lognormal models in which responses depend only on the horizon $t \geq 0$. Relatedly we obtain the Haussmann–Clark–Ocone formula for the process $\log M$ that cumulates the impact shocks at various dates as a stochastic integral:

$$\log M_t = \int_0^t E(\mathcal{D}_u \log M_t \mid F_u) \cdot dW_u + E(\log M_t \mid \mathcal{F}_0),$$

where we may think of $E(\mathcal{D}_u \log M_t \mid F_u)$ as the counterpart to a coefficient vector in a moving-average representation. These random variables satisfy recursions analogous to (14) and (15). For a more detailed construction, see Borovička et al. (2014).

We use the rules of Malliavin differentiation (analogous to more familiar forms of differentiation):

$$\mathcal{D}_u M_t = M_t \mathcal{D}_u \log M_t,$$

implying that the impulse response function for the process M is

$$\begin{aligned}\nu(X_0) \cdot E(\mathcal{D}_0 M_t | \mathcal{F}_0) &= \nu(X_0) \cdot E(M_t \mathcal{D}_0 \log M_t | \mathcal{F}_0) \\ &= M_0 \nu(X_0) \cdot E\left[\left(\frac{M_t}{M_0}\right) \mathcal{D}_0(\log M_t - \log M_0) | X_0\right)\end{aligned}$$

for $t \geq 0$.

4.2.2 Shock Elasticities for Diffusions

The construction of shock elasticities in Section 3 perturbs the cash flow by exposing it to a specified shock in the next period. In the continuous-time model, we devise a perturbation of M over a short time interval $[0, \mathrm{r}]$ and then study the implications as $\mathrm{r} \searrow 0$. The resulting construction exploits the local linearity of continuous-time models with Brownian shocks.

[h] For a textbook treatment of Malliavin calculus see Di Nunno et al. (2009) or Nualart (2006).

Specifically, we construct the process H^{r} such that

$$\log H_t^{\mathrm{r}} = \int_0^{\mathrm{r}\wedge \mathrm{t}} \nu(X_u)\cdot dW_u - \frac{1}{2}\int_0^{\mathrm{r}\wedge \mathrm{t}} |\nu(X_u)|^2 du,$$

where $\mathrm{r}\wedge\mathrm{t} = \min\{\mathrm{r},\mathrm{t}\}$. Notice that this process is exposed to the Brownian shock on the time interval $[0,\mathrm{r}]$, with exposure vector $\nu(x)$, and stays constant after r. We assume that $\nu(x)$ is restricted so that the process H^{r} is a martingale. We use H^{r} to construct the perturbed process MH^{r}:

$$\begin{aligned}\log M_t + \log H_t^{\mathrm{r}} = \log M_0 &+ \int_0^t \beta(X_u)du - \frac{1}{2}\int_0^{\mathrm{r}\wedge \mathrm{t}} |\nu(X_u)|^2 du \\ &+ \int_0^t \alpha(X_u)\cdot dW_u + \int_0^{\mathrm{r}\wedge \mathrm{t}} \nu(X_u)\cdot dW_u\end{aligned}$$

Notice that on the interval $[0,\mathrm{r}]$, the exposure of the perturbed process to the Brownian shock is

$$[\alpha(X_u)+\nu(X_u)]\cdot dW_u.$$

As $\mathrm{r}\searrow 0$, we are perturbing $\log M$ over an arbitrarily small interval.

As in Borovička et al. (2014), we define the shock elasticity for M at horizon t as

$$\varepsilon(x,t) = \lim_{\mathrm{r}\searrow 0}\frac{1}{\mathrm{r}}\log E\left[\left(\frac{M_t}{M_0}\right)H_t^{\mathrm{r}} \mid X_0 = x\right]$$

and show that this limit can be expressed as

$$\begin{aligned}\varepsilon(x,t) &= \nu(x)\cdot\frac{E\left(\mathcal{D}_0\frac{M_t}{M_0}\mid X_0 = x\right)}{E\left[\left(\frac{M_t}{M_0}\right)\mid X_0 = x\right]} \\ &= \nu(x)\cdot\frac{E\left[\left(\frac{M_t}{M_0}\right)\mathcal{D}_0\log M_t \mid X_0 = x\right)}{E\left[\left(\frac{M_t}{M_0}\right)\mid X_0 = x\right]}.\end{aligned} \tag{19}$$

The first equality in (19) is a limiting version of (8) divided by $E\left[\left(\frac{M_t}{M_0}\right)\mid X_0 = x\right]$ since the Haussmann–Clark–Ocone formula applied to $\frac{M_t}{M_0}$ has a contribution

$$E\left(\mathcal{D}_0\frac{M_t}{M_0}\mid X_0 = x\right)dW_0$$

for the date zero increment. The limiting covariance between $\frac{M_t}{M_0}$ and dW_0 is therefore $E\left(\mathcal{D}_0 \frac{M_t}{M_0} \mid X_0 = x\right)$. From the second equality in (19), these elasticities coincide with the diffusion counterpart to impulse responses $\mathcal{D}_0(\log M_t - \log M_0)$ for $\log M_t - \log M_0$ weighted by

$$\frac{\left(\frac{M_t}{M_0}\right)}{E\left[\left(\frac{M_t}{M_0}\right) \mid X_0 = x\right]}$$

when averaging over future outcomes. For the lognormal model, the weighting is inconsequential. In Borovička et al. (2011), we provide details of this derivation and some related calculations including the following alternative formula relevant for computation:

$$\varepsilon(x,t) \doteq \nu(x) \cdot \left[\sigma(x)' \left(\frac{\partial}{\partial x} \log E\left[\left(\frac{M_t}{M_0}\right) \mid X_0 = x\right]\right) + \alpha(x)\right]. \tag{20}$$

The shock-elasticity formula (20) has a natural interpretation. The sensitivity of the multiplicative process M to a shock in the next instant consists of two terms. The term $\alpha(x)$ represents the direct impact of the Brownian shock on the evolution of M in expression (18). The partial derivative with respect to x captures the sensitivity of the conditional expectation to movements in the state vector, and it is multiplied by the exposure matrix $\sigma(x)$ to express the sensitivity with respect to the shock vector W. The use of the derivative of the logarithm in (18) justifies the term shock *elasticity*. The instantaneous short-term elasticity is $\alpha(x) \cdot \nu(x)$.[i]

5. DISCRETE-TIME FORMULAS AND APPROXIMATION

In the preceding sections, we developed formulas for shock-price and shock-exposure elasticities for a wide class of models driven by a state vector with Markov dynamics (1). We now present a tractable implementation that, when applicable, makes the computations straightforward to apply. The discussion draws on methods developed in Borovička and Hansen (2014).[j] We also provide Matlab software implementing the

[i] The instantaneous shock-price elasticity is $-\alpha_s(x) \cdot \nu(x)$ which coincides with the notion of a risk price vector that represents the compensation for exposure to Brownian increments.

[j] See Nakamura et al. (2016) for another discrete-time implementation of these methods.

solution methods described in this section including a toolkit that computes shock elasticities for models solved using Dynare.[k]

We start by introducing a convenient exponential-quadratic framework that we use for modeling the state vector X and the resulting multiplicative processes. In this framework, conditional expectations of multiplicative processes and the shock elasticities are available in a convenient functional form. We then consider a special class of approximate solutions to dynamic macroeconomic models constructed using perturbation methods. We show how to approximate the equilibrium dynamics, additive and multiplicative functionals, and the resulting shock elasticities. By construction, the dynamics of these approximate solutions will be nested within the exponential-quadratic framework.

5.1 Exponential-Quadratic Framework

We study dynamic systems for which the state vector can be partitioned as $X=\left(X_1', X_2'\right)'$ where the two components follow the laws of motion:

$$\begin{aligned} X_{1,t+1} &= \Theta_{10} + \Theta_{11}X_{1,t} + \Lambda_{10}W_{t+1} \\ X_{2,t+1} &= \Theta_{20} + \Theta_{21}X_{1,t} + \Theta_{22}X_{2,t} + \Theta_{23}(X_{1,t}\otimes X_{1,t}) \\ &\quad + \Lambda_{20}W_{t+1} + \Lambda_{21}(X_{1,t}\otimes W_{t+1}) + \Lambda_{22}(W_{t+1}\otimes W_{t+1}). \end{aligned} \tag{21}$$

We restrict the matrices Θ_{11} and Θ_{22} to have stable eigenvalues. Notice that the restrictions imposed by the triangular structure imply that the process X_1 is linear, while the process X_2 is linear conditional on the evolution of X_1.

The class of multiplicative functionals M that interest us satisfies, for $Y=\log M$, the restriction

$$\begin{aligned} Y_{t+1} - Y_t &= \Gamma_0 + \Gamma_1 X_{1,t} + \Gamma_2 X_{2,t} + \Gamma_3(X_{1,t}\otimes X_{1,t}) \\ &\quad + \Psi_0 W_{t+1} + \Psi_1(X_{1,t}\otimes W_{t+1}) + \Psi_2(W_{t+1}\otimes W_{t+1}). \end{aligned} \tag{22}$$

In what follows we use a $1\times k^2$ vector Ψ to construct a $k\times k$ symmetric matrix $\mathrm{sym}[\mathrm{mat}_{k,k}(\Psi)]$ such that[l]

$$w'(\mathrm{sym}[\mathrm{mat}_{k,k}(\Psi)])w = \Psi(w\otimes w).$$

[k] Dynare is a freely available Matlab/Octave toolkit for solving and analyzing dynamic general equilibrium models (see http://www.dynare.org). Our software is available at http://borovicka.org/software.html.

[l] In this formula $\mathrm{mat}_{k,k}(\Psi)$ converts a vector into a $k\times k$ matrix and the sym operator transforms this square matrix into a symmetric matrix by averaging the matrix and its transpose. Appendix A introduces convenient notation for the algebra underlying the calculations in this and subsequent sections.

This representation will be valuable in some of the computations that follow. We use additive functionals to represent stochastic growth via a technology shock process or aggregate consumption, and to represent stochastic discounting used in representing asset values.

The system (21)–(22) is rich enough to accommodate stochastic volatility, which has been featured in the asset pricing literature and to a lesser extent in the macroeconomics literature. For instance, the state variable $X_{1,t}$ can capture a linear process for conditional volatility, and $X_{2,t}$ the conditional growth rate of cash flows. The coefficient Ψ_1 in (22) then determines the time variation in the conditional volatility of the growth rate of M, while Λ_{21} in (21) impacts the conditional volatility of the changes in the growth rate. In Section 5.2, we will map the solution obtained using perturbation approximations into this framework as well.

A virtue of parameterization (21)–(22) is that it gives quasi-analytical formulas for our dynamic elasticities. The implied model of the stochastic discount factor has been used in a variety of reduced-form asset pricing models. Later we will use an approximation to deduce this dynamical system.

We illustrate the convenience of this functional form by calculating the logarithms of conditional expectations of multiplicative functionals of the form (22). Consider a function that is linear-quadratic in $x=(x_1',x_2')'$:

$$\log f(x)=\Phi_0+\Phi_1 x_1+\Phi_2 x_2+\Phi_3(x_1\otimes x_1). \tag{23}$$

Then conditional expectations are of the form:

$$\begin{aligned}\log E\left[\left(\frac{M_{t+1}}{M_t}\right)f(X_{t+1})\mid X_t=x\right]&=\log E[\exp(Y_{t+1}-Y_t)f(X_{t+1})\mid X_t=x]\\&=\Phi_0^*+\Phi_1^*x_1+\Phi_2^*x_2+\Phi_3^*(x_1\otimes x_1)\\&=\log f^*(x)\end{aligned} \tag{24}$$

where the formulas for Φ_i^*, $i=0,\ldots,3$ are given in Appendix A. This calculation maps a function f into another function f^* with the same functional form. Our multiperiod calculations exploit this link. For instance, repeating these calculations compounds stochastic growth or discounting. Moreover, we may exploit the recursive Markov construction in (24) initiated with $f(x)=1$ to obtain:

$$\log E\left[\left(\frac{M_t}{M_0}\right)\mid X_0=x\right]=\Phi_{0,t}^*+\Phi_{1,t}^*x_1+\Phi_{2,t}^*x_2+\Phi_{3,t}^*(x_1\otimes x_1)$$

for appropriate choices of $\Phi_{i,t}^*$.

5.1.1 Shock Elasticities

To compute shock elasticities given in (8) under the convenient functional form, we construct:

$$\frac{E\left[\left(\frac{M_t}{M_0}\right)W_1 \mid X_0 = x\right]}{E\left[\left(\frac{M_t}{M_0}\right) \mid X_0 = x\right]} = \frac{E\left[\left(\frac{M_1}{M_0}\right)E\left[\left(\frac{M_t}{M_1}\right) \mid X_1\right]W_1 \mid X_0 = x\right]}{E\left[\left(\frac{M_1}{M_0}\right)E\left(\frac{M_t}{M_1} \mid X_1\right) \mid X_0 = x\right]}.$$

Notice that the random variable:

$$L_{1,t} = \frac{\left(\frac{M_1}{M_0}\right)E\left(\frac{M_t}{M_1} \mid X_1\right)}{E\left[\left(\frac{M_1}{M_0}\right)\left(\frac{M_t}{M_1} \mid X_1\right) \mid X_0 = x\right]} \tag{25}$$

has conditional expectation one. Multiplying this positive random variable by W_1 and taking expectations is equivalent to changing the conditional probability distribution and evaluating the conditional expectation of W_1 under this change of measure. Then under the transformed measure, using a complete-the-squares argument we may show that W_1 remains normally distributed with a covariance matrix that is no longer the identity and a mean conditioned on $X_0 = x$ that is affine in x_1. The formulas are given in Appendix B. Thus the shock elasticity function $\varepsilon(x,t)$ can be computed recursively using formulas that are straightforward to implement. We show in Appendix B that the resulting shock elasticity function is also affine in the state x_1.

5.2 Perturbation Methods

In macroeconomic models, the equilibrium Markov dynamics (1) is typically ex ante unknown and needs to be solved for from a set of equilibrium conditions. We now describe a solution method for dynamic general equilibrium models that yields a solution in the form of an approximate law of motion that is a special case of the exponential-quadratic functional form analyzed in Section 5.1. This solution method, based on Holmes (1995) and Lombardo and Uhlig (2014), constructs a perturbation approximation where the first- and second-order terms follow the restricted dynamics (21).

For the purposes of approximation, we consider a family of models parameterized by q and study first- and second-order approximations around this limit system in which $\mathsf{q} = 0$. For each q, we consider the system (equations

$$0 = E(g[X_{t+1}(\mathsf{q}), X_t(\mathsf{q}), X_{t-1}(\mathsf{q}), \mathsf{q}W_{t+1}, \mathsf{q}W_t, \mathsf{q}] \mid \mathcal{F}_t). \tag{26}$$

The $\mathsf{q} = 0$ equation system is one without shocks, and more generally small values q will make the shocks less consequential. There are well-known saddle-point stability conditions on the system (26) that lead to a unique equilibrium of the linear approximation (see Blanchard and Kahn, 1980 or Sims, 2002), and we assume that these are satisfied. Following Holmes (1995) and Lombardo and Uhlig (2014), we form an approximating system by deducing the dynamic evolution for the pathwise derivatives with respect to q and evaluated at $\mathsf{q} = 0$. Our derivation will be admittedly heuristic as is much of the related literature in macroeconomics.

To build a link to the parameterization in Section 5.1, we feature a second-order expansion:

$$X_t(\mathsf{q}) \approx X_{0,t} + \mathsf{q}X_{1,t} + \frac{\mathsf{q}^2}{2}X_{2,t},$$

where $X_{m,t}$ is the mth order, date t component of the stochastic process. We abstract from the dependence on initial conditions by restricting each component process to be stationary. Our approximating process will similarly be stationary.[m] The expansion leads to laws of motion for the component processes $X_{1,\cdot}$ and $X_{2,\cdot}$. The joint process $(X_{1,\cdot}, X_{2,\cdot})$ will again be Markov, although the dimension of the state vector under the approximate dynamics doubles.

5.2.1 Approximating State Vector Dynamics

While $X_t(\mathsf{q})$ serves as a state vector in the dynamic system (26), the state vector itself depends on the parameter q. Suppose that $\mathcal{F}_t$ is the σ-algebra generated by the infinite history of shocks $\{W_j : j \leq t\}$. For each dynamic system, we presume that the state vector $X_t(\mathsf{q})$ is $\mathcal{F}_t$ measurable and that in forecasting future values of the state vector conditioned on $\mathcal{F}_t$ it suffices to condition on X_t. Although $X_t(\mathsf{q})$ depends on q, the construction of $\mathcal{F}_t$ does not. We now construct the dynamics for each of the component processes. The result will be a recursive system that has the same structure as the triangular system (21).

Define $\bar{x}$ to be the solution to the equation:

$$\bar{x} = \psi(\bar{x}, 0, 0),$$

which gives the fixed point for the deterministic dynamic system. We assume that this fixed point is locally stable. That is $\psi_x(\bar{x}, 0, 0)$ is a matrix with stable eigenvalues, eigenvalues with absolute values that are strictly less than one. Then set

$$X_{0,t} = \bar{x}$$

for all t. This is the zeroth-order contribution to the solution constructed to be time invariant.

In computing pathwise derivatives, we consider the state vector process viewed as a function of the shock history. Each shock in this history is scaled by the parameter q, which results in a parameterized family of stochastic processes. We compute derivatives with respect to this parameter where the derivatives themselves are stochastic processes.

[m] As argued by Lombardo and Uhlig (2014), this approach is computationally very similar to the pruning approach described by Kim et al. (2008) or Andreasen et al. (2010).

Given the Markov representation of the family of stochastic processes, the derivative processes will also have convenient recursive representations. In what follows we derive these representations.

Using the Markov representation, we compute the derivative of the state vector process with respect to q, which we evaluate at $\mathsf{q}=0$. This derivative has the recursive representation:

$$X_{1,t+1} = \psi_q + \psi_x X_{1,t} + \psi_w W_{t+1}$$

where ψ_q, ψ_x, and ψ_w are the partial derivative matrices:

$$\psi_q \doteq \frac{\partial \psi}{\partial \mathsf{q}}(\bar{x},0,0), \quad \psi_x \doteq \frac{\partial \psi}{\partial x'}(\bar{x},0,0), \quad \psi_w \doteq \frac{\partial \psi}{\partial w'}(\bar{x},0,0).$$

In particular, the term $\psi_w W_{t+1}$ reveals the role of the shock vector in this recursive representation. Recall that we have presumed that $\bar{x}$ has been chosen so that ψ_x has stable eigenvalues. Thus the first derivative evolves as a Gaussian vector autoregression. It can be expressed as an infinite moving average of the history of shocks, which restricts the process to be stationary. The first-order approximation to the original process is:

$$X_t \approx \bar{x} + \mathsf{q} X_{1,t}.$$

In particular, the approximating process on the right-hand side has $\bar{x} + \mathsf{q}(I - \psi_x)^{-1}\psi_q$ as its unconditional mean.

We compute the pathwise second derivative with respect to q recursively by differentiating the recursion for the first derivative. As a consequence, the second derivative has the recursive representation:

$$\begin{aligned} X_{2,t+1} = {} & \psi_{qq} + 2\left(\psi_{xq} X_{1,t} + \psi_{wq} W_{t+1}\right) \\ & + \psi_x X_{2,t} + \psi_{xx}(X_{1,t} \otimes X_{1,t}) + 2\psi_{xw}(X_{1,t} \otimes W_{t+1}) + \psi_{ww}(W_{t+1} \otimes W_{t+1}) \end{aligned} \tag{27}$$

where matrices ψ_{ij} denote the second-order derivatives of ψ evaluated at $(\bar{x},0,0)$ and formed using the construction of the derivative matrices described in Appendix A.2. As noted by Schmitt-Grohé and Uribe (2004), the mixed second-order derivatives ψ_{xq} and ψ_{wq} are often zero using second-order refinements to the familiar log approximation methods.

The second-derivative process $X_{2,\cdot}$ evolves as a stable recursion that feeds back on itself and depends on the first derivative process. We have already argued that the first derivative process $X_{1,t}$ can be constructed as a linear function of the infinite history of the shocks. Since the matrix ψ_x has stable eigenvalues, $X_{2,t}$ can be expressed as a linear-quadratic function of this same shock history. Since there are no feedback effects from $X_{2,t}$ to $X_{1,t+1}$, the joint process $(X_{1,\cdot}, X_{2,\cdot})$ constructed in this manner is necessarily stationary.

The dynamic evolution for $(X_{1,\cdot}, X_{2,\cdot})$ is a special case of the triangular system (21) given in Section 5.1. When the shock vector W_t is a multivariate standard normal, we can utilize results from Section 5.1 to produce exact formulas for conditional expectations of exponentials of linear-quadratic functions in $(X_{1,t}, X_{2,t})$. We exploit this construction in the subsequent section. For details on the derivation of the approximating formulas, see Appendix A.

5.3 Approximating the Evolution of a Stationary Increment Process

Consider the approximation of a parameterized family of multiplicative processes with increments given by:

$$\log M_{t+1}(\mathsf{q}) - \log M_t(\mathsf{q}) = \kappa[X_t(\mathsf{q}), \mathsf{q} W_{t+1}, \mathsf{q}]$$

and an initial condition $\log M_0$. We use the function κ in conjunction with q to parameterize implicitly a family of additive functionals. We approximate the resulting additive functionals by

$$\log M_t \approx \log M_{0,t} + \mathsf{q} \log M_{1,t} + \frac{\mathsf{q}^2}{2} \log M_{2,t}$$

where the processes on the right-hand side have stationary increments.

Following the steps of our approximation of X, the recursive representation of the zeroth-order contribution to $\log M$ is

$$\log M_{0,t+1} - \log M_{0,t} = \kappa(\bar{x}, 0, 0) \doteq \bar{\kappa};$$

the first-order contribution is

$$\log M_{1,t+1} - \log M_{1,t} = \kappa_q + \kappa_x X_{1,t} + \kappa_w W_{t+1}$$

where κ_x and κ_w are the respective first derivatives of κ evaluated at $(\bar{x}, 0, 0)$; and the second-order contribution is

$$\begin{aligned}\log M_{2,t+1} - \log M_{2,t} = & \kappa_{qq} + 2\left(\kappa_{xq} X_{1,t} + \kappa_{wq} W_{t+1}\right) \\ & + \kappa_x X_{2,t} + \kappa_{xx}(X_{1,t} \otimes X_{1,t}) + 2\kappa_{xw}(X_{1,t} \otimes W_{t+1}) \\ & + \kappa_{ww}(W_{t+1} \otimes W_{t+1})\end{aligned}$$

where the κ_{ij}'s are the second derivative matrices constructed as in Appendix A.2. The resulting component additive functionals are special cases of the additive functional given in (22) that we introduced in Section 5.1.

5.3.1 Approximating Shock Elasticities

We could compute corresponding second-order approximations for the elasticities of multiplicative processes. Alternatively, since the approximating processes satisfy the structure given in Section 5.1, we have the formulas that we described earlier at our disposal and the supporting software. See Borovička and Hansen (2014) for further discussion.

5.4 Related Approaches

There also exist ad hoc approaches which mix orders of approximation for different components of the model or state vector. The aim of these methods is to improve the precision of the approximation along specific dimensions of interest, while retaining tractability in the computation of the derivatives of the function ψ. Justiniano and Primiceri (2008) use a first-order approximations but augment the solution with heteroskedastic innovations. Benigno et al. (2010) study second-order approximations for the endogenous state variables in which exogenous state variables follow a conditionally linear Markov process. Malkhozov and Shamloo (2011) combine a first-order perturbation with heteroskedasticity in the shocks to the exogenous process and corrections for the variance of future shocks. These solution methods are designed to produce nontrivial roles for stochastic volatility in the solution of the model and in the pricing of exposure to risk. The approach of Benigno et al. (2010) or Malkhozov and Shamloo (2011) gives alternative ways to construct the functional form used in Section 5.1.

5.5 Recursive Utility Investors

The recursive utility preference specification of Kreps and Porteus (1978) and Epstein and Zin (1989) warrants special consideration. By design, this specification of preferences avoids presuming that investors reduce intertemporal, compound consumption lotteries. Instead investors may care about the intertemporal composition of risk. It is motivated in part by an aim to allow for risk aversion to be altered without changing the elasticity of intertemporal substitution. Anderson et al. (2003), Maenhout (2004), and others extend the literature on risk-sensitive control by Jacobson (1973), Whittle (1990), and others and provide a "concern for robustness" interpretation of the utility recursion. Under this alternative interpretation the decision maker explores the potential misspecification of the transition dynamics as part of the decision-making process. This perspective yields a substantially different interpretation of the utility recursion. In establishing these connections in the control theory and economics literatures, it is sometimes advantageous to parameterize the utility recursion in a manner that depends explicitly on the parameter q. Borovička and Hansen (2013) and Bhandari et al. (2016) explore the resulting implications for approximations analogous to those studied here. Among other things, they provide a rationale for the first-order adjustments for recursive utility as suggested by Tallarini (2000), and they show novel ways in which higher-order adjustments are more impactful.

6. CONTINUOUS-TIME APPROXIMATION

Many interesting macroeconomic models specified in continuous time, including those we analyze in Section 7, require the application of numerical solution techniques. In the construction of shock elasticities, the central object of interest is the conditional expectation of M in (19). Consider the more general problem

$$\phi_t(x) \doteq E\left[\left(\frac{M_t}{M_0}\right)\phi_0(X_t) \mid X_0 = x\right] \tag{28}$$

with a given function ϕ_0. The conditional expectation of M is obtained by setting $\phi_0(x) \equiv 1$.

6.1 An Associated Partial Differential Equation

For the purposes of computation, we evaluate ϕ_t recursively. Given $\phi_{t-\Delta t}$ for small Δt, exploiting the time homogeneity of the underlying Markov process and applying the Law of Iterated Expectations gives:

$$\phi_t(x) = E\left[\left(\frac{M_{\Delta t}}{M_0}\right)\phi_{t-\Delta t}(X_{\Delta t}) \mid X_0 = x\right].$$

Itô's lemma applied to the product in the conditional expectation gives the linear, second-order partial differential equation:

$$\begin{aligned}\frac{\partial}{\partial t}\phi_t &= \left(\beta + \frac{1}{2}|\alpha|^2\right)\phi_t + \left[\frac{\partial}{\partial x}\phi_t\right]\cdot(\mu + \sigma\alpha) \\ &\quad + \frac{1}{2}\mathrm{tr}\left[\sigma'\left(\frac{\partial}{\partial x \partial x'}\phi_t\right)\sigma\right]\end{aligned} \tag{29}$$

with terminal condition ϕ_0 where tr(·) denotes the trace of the matrix argument. Eq. (29) is a generalization of the Kolmogorov backward equation for multiplicative processes of the type (17). The resulting partial differential equation can be solved using standard numerical techniques for differential equations.

6.2 Martingale Decomposition and a Change of Measure

To study the long-run implications for pricing, we proposed the extraction of a martingale component from the dynamics of the stochastic discount factors and cash flows by solving the Perron–Frobenius equation (9) for the strictly positive eigenfunction $e(x)$ and the associated eigenvalue η. In the Markov diffusion setup we localize this problem by computing

$$\lim_{t\to 0}\frac{E[M_t e(X_t)|X_0 = x] - \exp(\eta t)e(x)}{t} = 0.$$

Defining the infinitesimal operator

$$\mathbb{B}f(x) \doteq \frac{d}{dt} E[M_t f(X_t)|X_0 = x]\bigg|_{t=0}$$

we have

$$\mathbb{B}f = \left(\beta + \frac{1}{2}|\alpha|^2\right)f + (\sigma\alpha + \mu)\cdot\frac{\partial f}{\partial x} + \frac{1}{2}\mathrm{tr}\left(\sigma\sigma'\frac{\partial^2 f}{\partial x \partial x'}\right)$$

and we can write the limiting Perron–Frobenius equation as

$$\mathbb{B}e = \eta e \tag{30}$$

which is a second-order partial differential equation for the function $e(x)$ and a number η. Eq. (30) is known as the Sturm–Liouville equation. Notice that it is identical to the partial differential equation (29) when we are looking for an unknown discounted stationary function $\phi_t(x) = \exp(\eta t)e(x)$ with initial condition $\phi_0(x) = e(x)$. As before, there are typically multiple strictly positive solutions to this equation. Hansen and Scheinkman (2009) show that there is at most one such solution that preserves stochastic stability of the state vector X. We implicitly assume that we always choose such a solution.[n]

In line with the discussion from Section 3.4, we can now define the martingale $\widetilde{M}$ as[o]

$$\frac{\widetilde{M}_t}{\widetilde{M}_0} \doteq \exp(-\eta t)\frac{e(X_t)}{e(X_0)}\frac{M_t}{M_0}. \tag{31}$$

Applying Itô's lemma, we find that

$$d\log\widetilde{M}_t = \widetilde{\alpha}(X_t)\cdot dW_t - \frac{1}{2}|\widetilde{\alpha}(X_t)|dt$$

with

$$\widetilde{\alpha}(x) = \left[\sigma'(x)\frac{\partial}{\partial x}\log e(x) + \alpha(x)\right].$$

This implies that under the probability measure $\widetilde{P}$, the Brownian motion evolves as

$$dW_t = \widetilde{\alpha}(x)dt + d\widetilde{W}_t$$

where $\widetilde{W}$ is a Brownian motion under $\widetilde{P}$. It also implies that we can write the dynamics of the state vector under the change of measure as

[n] See also Borovička et al. (2015), Qin and Linetsky (2014a), Qin et al. (2016), Walden (2014), or Park (2015) for problems closely related to solving for the eigenvalue–eigenfunction pair (η, e).

[o] We note that the solution obtained using the localized version of the Perron–Frobenius problem may yield a process $\widetilde{M}$ that is only a local martingale. See Hansen and Scheinkman (2009) and Qin and Linetsky (2014b) for details and additional assumptions that assure $\widetilde{M}$ is a martingale. We will assume that such conditions are satisfied in the discussion that follows.

$$dX_t = \left[\mu(X_t) + \sigma(X_t)\,\widetilde{\alpha}(X_t)\right]dt + \sigma(X_t)\,d\widetilde{W}_t.$$

Inverting Eq. (31), we obtain the analog of the martingale decomposition in discrete time:

$$\frac{M_t}{M_0} = \exp(\eta t)\frac{e(X_0)}{e(X_t)}\frac{\widetilde{M}_t}{\widetilde{M}_0}. \tag{32}$$

To implement the factorization of the multiplicative functional M, we compute the strictly positive eigenfunction $e(x)$ and the associated eigenvalue η by solving the Perron–Frobenius problem (30). Since analytical solutions are often not available, we must rely on numerical methods. Pryce (1993) gives various numerical solution techniques for this problem. Notice that since there are typically infinitely many strictly positive solutions $e(x)$, it is necessary to determine which of these solutions is the relevant one.

An alternative approach is to utilize the time-dependent PDE (29) and exploit the fact that η is the principal eigenvalue, ie, one associated with the most durable component. In that case, one can start with an initial condition $\phi_0(x)$ that serves as a guess for the eigenfunction, and iterate on (29) to solve for $\phi_t(x)$ as $t \to \infty$. For large t, the solution should behave as

$$\phi_t(x) \approx \exp(\eta t)e(x)$$

and thus

$$\eta = \frac{\partial}{\partial t}\log\phi_t(x)\bigg|_{t\to\infty} \approx \frac{1}{\Delta t}\left[\log\phi_{t+\Delta t}(x) - \log\phi_t(x)\right]\bigg|_{t\to\infty}$$

and since the eigenfunction is only determined up to scale, we can use any proportional rescaling of ϕ_t as $e(x) \approx \exp(-\eta t)\phi_t(x)|_{t\to\infty}$.

6.3 Long-Term Pricing

We now apply the decomposition (32) in the shock elasticity formula (19) to obtain:

$$\varepsilon(x,t) \doteq \nu(x)\cdot\left[\sigma(x)'\left(\frac{\partial}{\partial x}\log e(x) + \frac{\partial}{\partial x}\log\widetilde{E}\left[\frac{1}{e(X_t)}\mid X_0 = x\right]\right) + \alpha(x)\right].$$

Taking the limit as $t \to \infty$, the conditional expectation in brackets converges to a constant provided that we select a martingale that induces a probability measure under which X is stochastically stable. See Hansen and Scheinkman (2009) and Hansen (2012) for further discussion. Therefore,

$$\lim_{t\to\infty}\varepsilon(x,t) = \nu(x)\cdot\left[\sigma(x)'\frac{\partial}{\partial x}\log e(x) + \alpha(x)\right].$$

6.4 Boundary Conditions

The construction of shock elasticity functions requires solving the conditional expectations of M, for instance, by solving the partial differential equation (29). This requires proper specification of the boundary conditions not only in terms of the terminal condition $\phi_0(x)$ but also at the boundaries of the state space for the state vector X_t. The boundary behavior of the diffusion X is a central and often economically important part of the equilibrium, as we will see in the models with financial frictions discussed in Section 7. In those models, the state variable is a univariate diffusion and there are well understood characterizations of the boundary behavior based on the classical Feller boundary classification.[p] The textbook treatment of the boundary conditions for problem (28) typically abstracts from the impact of the multiplicative process M. While a detailed discussion of the boundary characterization is beyond the scope of this chapter, we briefly discuss how the inclusion of M can alter the analysis. In what follows, we utilize the martingale decomposition introduced in Section 3.4 and draw connections to the treatment of boundaries for scalar diffusions.

We represent the conditional expectation (32) using a Kolmogorov equation under the change of measure induced by $\widetilde{M}$. Using the martingale factorization (32) we write (28) as

$$\phi_t(x) \doteq E\left[\exp(\eta t)\frac{e(X_0)}{e(X_t)}\frac{\widetilde{M}_t}{\widetilde{M}_0}\phi_0(X_t) \mid X_0 = x\right].$$

Define

$$\psi_t(x) \doteq \exp(-\eta t)\frac{\phi_t(x)}{e(x)} = \widetilde{E}\left[\frac{\phi_0(X_t)}{e(X_t)} \mid X_0 = x\right] = \widetilde{E}\left[\psi_0(X_t) \mid X_0 = x\right] \tag{33}$$

with the initial condition $\psi_0(x) = \phi_0(x)/e(x)$. This converts the boundary condition problem into a standard Kolmogorov backward equation (Eq. (28) with $M \equiv 1$), albeit under the probability measure $\widetilde{P}$. Under $\widetilde{P}$, the diffusion X satisfies the law of motion

$$dX_t = \widetilde{\mu}(X_t)dt + \sigma(X_t)d\widetilde{W}_t,$$
$$\widetilde{\mu}(x) = \mu(x) + \sigma(x)\sigma'(x)\frac{\partial}{\partial x}\log e(x) + \sigma(x)\alpha(x)$$

and the associated generator

$$\widetilde{\mathbb{B}}f = \widetilde{\mu}\cdot\frac{\partial f}{\partial x} + \frac{1}{2}\mathrm{tr}\left(\sigma\sigma'\frac{\partial^2 f}{\partial x \partial x'}\right)$$

corresponds to the generator of a diffusion with infinitesimal variance $\sigma^2(x)$ and infinitesimal mean $\widetilde{\mu}(x)$ under $\widetilde{P}$.

[p] See the seminal work by Feller (1952) and Feller (1957). Karlin and Taylor (1981), Borodin and Salminen (2002), or Linetsky (2008) offer summarizing treatments.

The boundary characterization under $\widetilde{P}$ and the associated boundary conditions for $\psi_t(x)$ follow from formulas from Section 6.4. The character of the boundary can change under $\widetilde{P}$, although a reflecting boundary remains reflecting to preserve local equivalence of measures P and $\widetilde{P}$. Observe that Eq. (33) introduces a relationship between the conditional expectation given by $\phi_t(x)$ and the eigenfunction $e(x)$. For instance, when the boundary point x_b is reflecting, the appropriate boundary condition is[q]

$$\frac{\partial}{\partial x}\psi_t(x)\bigg|_{x=x_b} = 0.$$

When both $\phi_t(x)$ and $e(x)$ are strictly positive at the boundary, this implies that

$$\frac{\partial}{\partial x}\log\phi_t(x)\bigg|_{x=x_b} = \frac{\partial}{\partial x}\log e(x)\bigg|_{x=x_b}$$

equalizing logarithmic slopes of the conditional expectation (28) and the eigenfunction $e(x)$ at the boundary.

7. MODELS WITH FINANCIAL CONSTRAINTS IN CONTINUOUS TIME

Recently, there has been renewed interest in nonlinear stochastic macroeconomic models with financing restrictions. The literature was initiated by Bernanke and Gertler (1989) and Bernanke et al. (1999), and it has been revived and extended since the advent of the financial crisis. Continuous-time models have been featured in He and Krishnamurthy (2013), Brunnermeier and Sannikov (2014), Di Tella (2015), Moreira and Savov (2016), Adrian and Boyarchenko (2012), or Klimenko et al. (2016). Differential equation methods give the equilibrium solutions, and the resulting dynamics exhibit quantitatively substantial nonlinearity. The nonlinearity emerges because of financing constraints that bind only in a specific part of the state space.[r]

To preserve tractability, models typically assume a low-dimensional specification of the state space. In this section, we analyze two such models, He and Krishnamurthy (2013) and Brunnermeier and Sannikov (2014). Both models utilize frameworks that are judiciously chosen to lead to a scalar endogenous state variable that follows the diffusion

$$dX_t = \mu(X_t)dt + \sigma(X_t)dW_t. \tag{34}$$

The endogenous state represents the allocation of wealth between households and financial experts, capturing the capitalization of the financial sector relative to the size of the

[q] This assumes that the so-called scale measure is finite at the boundary, see, eg, Borodin and Salminen (2002).

[r] See Bocola (2016) or Bianchi (2016) for discrete-time models solved using global to account for financing constraint that binds only occasionally.

economy. When the capitalization is low, the financial constraint is binding, and asset valuations are more sensitive to aggregate shocks.

Both papers also feature an exogenous process that introduces aggregate risk into their model economies. He and Krishnamurthy (2013) construct an endowment economy with a permanent shock to the aggregate dividend. On the other hand, Brunnermeier and Sannikov (2014) feature endogenous capital accumulation with a shock to the quality of the capital stock. In this section, we utilize the continuous-time tools developed in Section 6 to study the state dependence in asset pricing implications of the two models. We refer the reader to the respective papers for a detailed discussions of the underlying economic environments.

7.1 Stochastic Discount Factors

Stochastic discount factors and priced cash flows in the models we analyze can be written as special cases of multiplicative functionals introduced in Section 4.2:

$$d\log S_t = \beta(X_t)\,dt + \alpha(X_t)\cdot dW_t \tag{35}$$

with coefficients $\beta(x)$ and $\alpha(x)$ determined in equilibrium. In an arbitrage-free, complete market environment, there exists a unique stochastic discount factor that represents the prices of the traded securities.

In economies with financial market imperfections and constraints, this ceases to be true. There are two key features that are of interest to us. First, financial markets in these economies are segmented, and different investors can own specific subsets of assets. This implies the existence of alternative stochastic discount factors for individual investors that have to agree only on prices of assets traded between investors. Second, assets are valuable not only for their cash flows but also because their ownership can relax or tighten financing constraints faced by individual investors. Given the potential for these constraints to be binding, asset values include contributions from the shadow prices of these constraints.

7.2 He and Krishnamurthy (2013)

He and Krishnamurthy (2013) construct an economy populated by two types of agents, specialists and households. There are two assets in the economy, a safe asset earning an infinitesimal risk-free rate r_t and a risky asset with return R_t that is a claim on aggregate dividend

$$d\log D_t = \left(g_d - \frac{1}{2}\sigma_d^2\right)dt + \sigma_d dW_t \doteq \overline{\beta}_d dt + \overline{\alpha}_d dW_t. \tag{36}$$

7.2.1 Households and Specialists

Households have logarithmic preferences and therefore consume a constant fraction of their wealth, $C_t^h = \rho A_t^h$, where ρ is the time-preference coefficient. A fraction λ of households can only invest into the safe asset, while a fraction $1 - \lambda$ invests a share α_t^h of their wealth through an intermediary managed by the specialists who hold a portfolio with return $d\widetilde{R}_t$. Aggregate wealth of the households therefore evolves as

$$dA_t^h = \left(\ell D_t - \rho A_t^h\right)dt + A_t^h r_t dt + \alpha_t^h(1-\lambda)A_t^h\left(d\widetilde{R}_t - r_t dt\right),$$

where ℓD_t is households' income, modeled as a constant share ℓ of the dividend.

Specialists are endowed with CRRA preferences over their consumption stream C_t with risk aversion coefficient γ and trade both assets. Their stochastic discount factor is

$$\frac{S_t}{S_0} = e^{-\rho t}\left(\frac{C_t}{C_0}\right)^{-\gamma}. \tag{37}$$

This stochastic discount factor also prices all assets traded by specialists. The law of motion for their wealth is given by

$$dA_t = -C_t dt + A_t r_t dt + A_t\left(d\widetilde{R}_t - r_t dt\right).$$

The intermediary combines all wealth of the specialists A_t with the households' wealth invested through the intermediary $\alpha_t^h(1-\lambda)A_t^h$ and invests a share α_t of the combined portfolio into the risky asset. The return on the intermediary portfolio then follows

$$d\widetilde{R}_t = r_t dt + \alpha_t(dR_t - r_t dt).$$

The risky asset market clears, so that the wealth invested into the risky asset equals the market price of the asset, P_t

$$\alpha_t\left(A_t + \alpha_t^h(1-\lambda)A_t^h\right) = P_t.$$

7.2.2 Financial Friction

The critical financial friction is introduced into the portfolio choice of the household. Motivated by a moral hazard problem, the household is not willing to invest more than a fraction m of the specialists' wealth through the intermediary, which defines the *intermediation constraint*

$$\alpha_t^h(1-\lambda)A_t^h \leq mA_t. \tag{38}$$

Because of logarithmic preferences, the portfolio choice α_t^h of the household is static. The household is also not allowed to sell short any of the assets, so that it solves

$$\max_{\alpha_t^h \in [0,1]} \alpha_t^h E\left[d\widetilde{R}_t - r_t dt \mid \mathcal{F}_t\right] - \frac{1}{2}\left(\alpha_t^h\right)^2 Var\left[d\widetilde{R}_t - r_t dt \mid \mathcal{F}_t\right]$$

subject to the intermediation constraint (38).

The parameter m determines the tightness of the intermediation constraint. This constraint will be endogenously binding when the wealth of the specialists becomes sufficiently low relative to the wealth of the household. In that case, risk sharing partially breaks down and the specialists will have to absorb a large share of the risky asset in their portfolio. As an equilibrium outcome, risk premia increase and the wealth of the specialists becomes more volatile, which in turn induces larger fluctuations of the right-hand side of the constraint (38). Without the intermediation constraint, the model reduces to an endowment economy populated by agents solving a risk-sharing problem with portfolio constraints.

7.2.3 Equilibrium Dynamics

The equilibrium in this model is conveniently characterized using the wealth share of the specialists, $X_t \doteq A_t/P_t \in (0,1)$, that will play the role of the single state variable with endogenously determined dynamics (34) where the coefficients $\mu(x)$ and $\sigma(x)$ are given by the relative wealth accumulation rates of households and specialists, and the equilibrium price of the claim on the risky cash flow. He and Krishnamurthy (2013) show that both boundaries $\{0,1\}$ are entrance boundaries.

Given the homogeneity in the model, we can write the consumption of the specialists as

$$
\begin{aligned}
C_t &= D_t(1+\ell) - C_t^h = D_t\left[(1+\ell) - \frac{C_t^h}{A_t^h}\frac{A_t^h}{P_t}\frac{P_t}{D_t}\right] \\
&= D_t[(1+\ell) - \rho(1-X_t)\pi(X_t)]
\end{aligned}
$$

where $\pi(x)$ is the price-dividend ratio for the claim on the dividend stream. The price-dividend ratio is determined endogenously as part of the solution to a set of differential equations. Given a solution for the price-dividend ratio $\pi(x)$, we construct the stochastic discount factor (37).

The top row of Fig. 1 shows the drift and volatility coefficients of the state variable process X, and the associated stationary density. When the specialists' wealth share X_t is low (below $x^* = 0.091$), the intermediation constraint binds. As $X_t \to 0$, the intermediation capacity of the specialists decreases, which increases the expected return on the risky asset, thereby increasing the rate of wealth accumulation of the specialists. On the other hand, when $X_t \to 1$, the economy is unconstrained, risk premia are low, and situation reverses. The drift coefficient $\mu(x)$ in the top left panel reflects these effects.

In the moment when the constraints start binding (to the left of the point $x^* = 0.091$), volatility $\sigma(x)$ of the experts' wealth share starts rising. Ultimately, this volatility has to decline to zero as $X_t \to 0$ to prevent the experts' wealth share from hitting the zero boundary with a positive probability, but the volatility of experts' wealth *level* keeps rising as we approach the boundary.

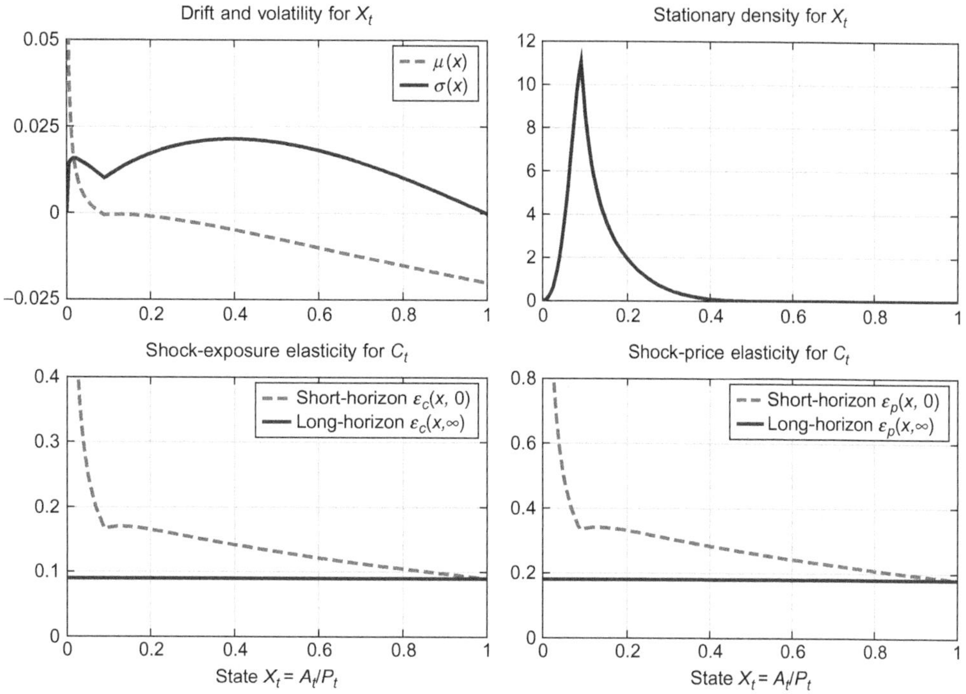

Fig. 1 Dynamics of the experts' wealth share $X_t = A_t/P_t$ (*horizontal axis*), shock-exposure and shock-price elasticities for the He and Krishnamurthy (2013) model. *Top left panel* shows the drift and volatility coefficients for the evolution of X_t, while *top right panel* the stationary density for X_t. *Panels in the bottom row* show the short- and long-horizon shock elasticity for the experts' consumption process C_t. The intermediation constraint (38) binds in the interval $X_t \in (0, 0.091)$, and $x^* = 0.091$ corresponds to the 35.3% quantile of the stationary distribution of X_t.

7.2.4 Stochastic Discount Factor and Cash Flows

Aggregate dividend D_t in (36) follows a geometric Brownian motion with drift. This directly implies a constant shock-exposure elasticity

$$\varepsilon_d(x, t) = \sigma_d.$$

Time variation in expected returns on the claim on the aggregate dividend thus must come solely from the time variation in prices of risk. In particular, the consumption process of specialists is:

$$\frac{C_t}{C_0} = \left(\frac{D_t}{D_0}\right)\left[\frac{(1+\ell) - \rho(1-X_t)\pi(X_t)}{(1+\ell) - \rho(1-X_0)\pi(X_0)}\right]. \tag{39}$$

Notice that the consumption of specialists has the same long-term stochastic growth as the aggregate dividend process. Since the dividend process D is a geometric Brownian motion, we immediately obtain the martingale factorization of C with

$$e_c(x) = [(1+\ell) - \rho(1-x)\pi(x)]^{-1}$$
$$\eta_c = g_d$$
$$\widetilde{C}_t = \exp(-\eta_c t) D_t$$

where $\widetilde{C}$ is the martingale component of C. Analogously, the stochastic discount factor of the specialists (37) is decomposed as

$$e_s(x) = [(1+\ell) - \rho(1-x)\pi(x)]^{\gamma}$$
$$\eta_s = -\rho - \gamma g_d + \frac{1}{2}\sigma_d^2 \gamma(\gamma+1)$$
$$\widetilde{S}_t = \exp[(-\eta_s - \rho)t](D_t)^{-\gamma}$$

where $\widetilde{S}$ is the martingale component.

These factorization results indicate a simple form for the long-horizon limits of the shock elasticities. The consumption and dividend processes share the same martingale component, and thus, assuming $\nu(x) = 1$, their shock-exposure elasticities imply

$$\lim_{t\to\infty} \varepsilon_c(x,t) = \lim_{t\to\infty} \varepsilon_d(x,t) = \sigma_d.$$

Similarly, the shock-price elasticities for the two cash-flow processes have the common long-horizon limit

$$\lim_{t\to\infty} \varepsilon_p(x,t) = \gamma\sigma_d.$$

As we have just verified, the intermediation constraint does not have any impact on prices of long-horizon cash flows. Long-horizon shock elasticities behave as in an economy populated only by unconstrained specialists with risk aversion γ who consume the whole dividend stream D_t. The intermediation constraint only affects the stationary part $e_s(x)$ of the stochastic discount factor.[s] As a consequence, long-term risk adjustments in this model are the same as those implied by a model with power utility function and consumption equal to dividends. The financing constraint induces deviations in short-term risk prices, which we now characterize.

7.2.5 Shock Elasticities and Term Structure of Yields

The blue solid lines in the bottom row of Fig. 1 represent the long-horizon shock-exposure and shock-price elasticities. These results are contrasted with the infinitesimal shock-exposure and shock-price elasticities, depicted with red dashed lines, that are equal to the volatility coefficients $\alpha_c(x)$ and $\alpha_s(x)$ in the differential representation (35) for the experts' consumption process (39) and stochastic discount factor process (37), respectively.

[s] Without the intermediation constraint and the debt constraint ($\lambda = 0$), the economy reduces to a complete-market risk-sharing problem between households and specialists and will converge in the long run to a homogeneous-agent economy populated only by households when $\gamma > 1$.

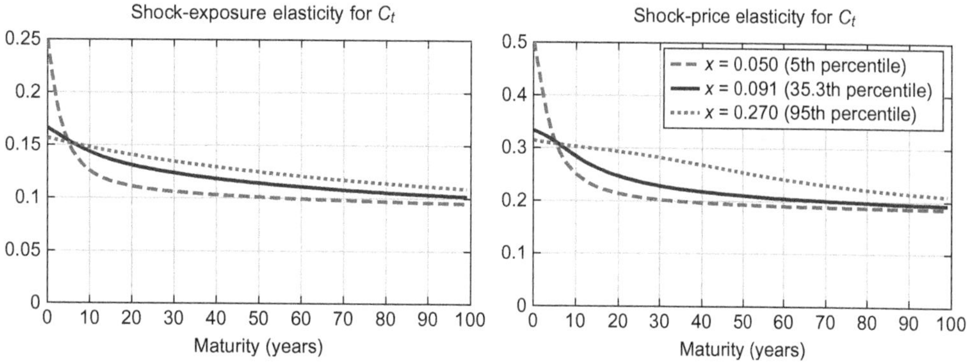

Fig. 2 Shock-exposure and shock-price elasticities for the He and Krishnamurthy (2013) model. *Individual lines* correspond to alternative choices of the current state, the experts' wealth share $X_0 = x$. The *solid line* represents the state in which the intermediation constraint (38) starts binding ($x = 0.091$), corresponding to the 35.3% quantile of the stationary distribution of X_t. The *dashed line* corresponds to the 5% quantile of the stationary distribution of X_t (intermediation constraint tightly binding), while the *dotted line* corresponds to the 95% quantile.

Fig. 2 depicts these shock elasticities evaluated at three different points in the state space. These elasticities were computed numerically.[t] A remarkable feature of the model is the following. The short-horizon consumption cash flows are more exposed to risk as revealed by a larger shock-price elasticity in the constrained region of the state space ($x = 0.05$). This finding is reversed for long-horizon cash flows, showing that the term structure of risk prices is much more strongly downward sloping for low values of the state variable. Since the state variable responds positively to shocks, low realizations of the state variable are the consequence of adverse shocks in the past.

Fig. 3 explores the implications for yields on dividends and experts' consumptions for alternative payoff horizons computed as logarithms of expected returns to the respective payoffs. While the yields on dividends and experts' consumption are initially increasing in maturity, this is all the more so when x is low. The yields are monotone over all horizons except when x is low, in which case the yields eventually decline a bit. The same effect is even more pronounced for the risk-free yield curve except the eventual decline is even slighter. Excess yields are therefore downward sloping for the experts' consumption process, and are lower for longer maturities for low values of x in contrast to high values.[u]

[t] We solved Eq. (29) for $M = C$ and $M = SC$, with $\phi_0(x) = 1$ using an implicit finite difference scheme. We used the solution for $\pi(x)$ constructed using the code from He and Krishnamurthy (2013).

[u] For empirical evidence and modeling of the downward sloping term structure of risky yields see van Binsbergen et al. (2012, 2013), Ai et al. (2013), Belo et al. (2015), Hasler and Marfè (2015), Lopez et al. (2015), or van Binsbergen and Koijen (2016).

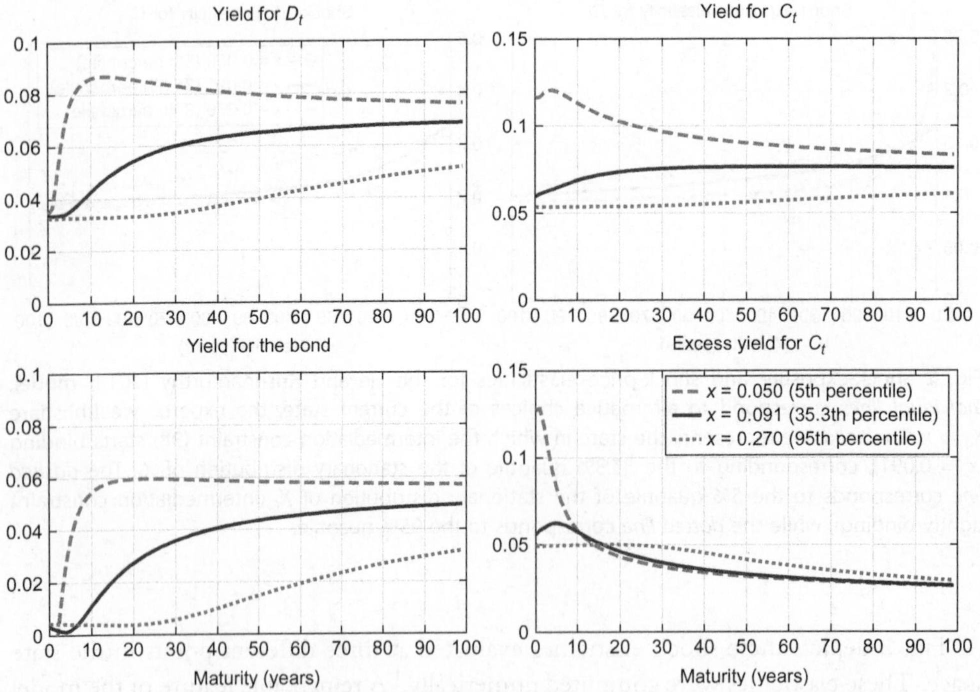

Fig. 3 Yields and excess yields for the He and Krishnamurthy (2013) model. Parameterization and description as in Fig. 2.

7.3 Brunnermeier and Sannikov (2014)

Brunnermeier and Sannikov (2014) construct a model with endogenous capital accumulation, populated by two types of agents, households and experts. The experts have access to a more productive technology for output and new capital than the households. The state variable of interest is the wealth share of experts, defined as

$$X_t = \frac{N_t}{Q_t K_t}$$

where N_t is the net worth of the experts and $Q_t K_t$ is the market value of capital. The equilibrium stock of capital evolves as

$$d\log K_t = \beta_k(X_t)dt + \overline{\alpha}_k dW_t$$

where the rate of accumulation of aggregate capital, $\beta_k(X_t)$, is determined by the wealth share of experts along with a standard local lognormal adjustment. The shock dW_t alters the quality of the capital stock.

7.3.1 Households and Experts

In the baseline model, both households and experts have linear preferences and differ in their time-preference coefficients, r and ρ, respectively, assuming that $\rho > r$. In particular, the preferences for experts are given by

$$E\left[\int_0^\infty e^{-\rho t} dC_t \mid \mathcal{F}_0\right]$$

where Cu_t is the cumulative consumption and as such is restricted to be a nondecreasing process. In contrast, the cumulative consumption of the household can have negative increments. The linearity in their preferences implies a constant equilibrium rate of interest r.

7.3.2 Financial Friction

In the model, experts are better at managing the capital stock, making it more productive. This creates a natural tendency to move the capital from the hands of the households to the hands of the experts, who in turn issue financial claims on this capital to the households. Absent any financial frictions, the experts would instantly consume the total value of their own net worth (given their higher impatience and linear utility), and accept households' capital under management by issuing equity claims.

Brunnermeier and Sannikov (2014) assume that experts cannot issue any equity and have to finance all capital purchases using risk-free borrowing. This naturally creates a leveraged portfolio on the side of the experts. When the wealth share of experts X_t decreases, they can intermediate households' capital only by increasing their leverage, and the price of capital $Q(X_t)$ has to fall in order to generate a sufficiently high expected return on capital for the experts to hold this leveraged portfolio.

7.3.3 Equilibrium Dynamics

In equilibrium, the expected return on capital has to balance the hedging demand on the side of the experts with the supply of capital from households. Experts' hedging motive (limited willingness to hold a leveraged portfolio) arises from the fact that a leveraged portfolio generates a low return after an adverse realization of the shock dW_t which, at the same time, decreases X_t and therefore increases the future expected return on capital.

On the other hand, when the wealth share of experts X_t increases, the price of capital $Q(X_t)$ increases, and the expected return falls. Define the marginal value of experts' wealth $\Theta_t = \theta(X_t)$ through

$$\Theta_t N_t = E\left[\int_t^\infty e^{-\rho(s-t)} dC_s \mid \mathcal{F}_t\right]$$

where dC is the cumulative consumption process of the experts. Linearity of preferences implies that experts' consumption is zero as long as $\Theta_t > 1$. As X_t increases, it reaches an endogenously determined threshold $\bar{x}$ for which $\theta(\bar{x}) = 1$. At this point, the marginal utility of wealth equals the marginal utility of consumption, and experts consume out of their wealth. Consequently, the equilibrium dynamics for the wealth share of experts is given by

$$dX_t = \mu(X_t)dt + \sigma(X_t)dW_t - X_t d\zeta_t,$$

where $\mu(x)$ and $\sigma(x)$ are endogenously determined coefficients that depend on relative rates of wealth accumulation of experts and households, and the consumption rate of experts $d\zeta_t \doteq dC_t/N_t > 0$ only if $X_t = \bar{x}$. Formally, the right boundary for the stochastic process X_t behaves as a reflecting boundary. See Brunnermeier and Sannikov (2014) for the construction of μ and σ.

7.3.4 Stochastic Discount Factor and Cash Flows

We now turn to the study of asset pricing implications in the model. To construct the shock elasticities, we construct the coefficients $\beta(x)$ and $\alpha(x)$ for the evolution of the stochastic discount factor and priced cash flows modeled as multiplicative functionals (35).

The marginal utility of wealth implies the following stochastic discount factor of the experts:

$$\frac{S_t}{S_0} = \exp(-\rho t)\frac{\theta(X_t)}{\theta(X_0)}.$$

The coefficients $\beta_s(x)$ and $\alpha_s(x)$ in the equation for the evolution of the stochastic discount factor functional can be constructed by applying Ito's lemma to this expression taking account of the functional dependence given by $\theta(x)$ and the evolution of X. Observe that this stochastic discount factor does not contain a martingale component. Nevertheless, since the equilibrium local risk-free interest rate is r,

$$\exp(rt)\frac{S_t}{S_0} = \exp[(r-\rho)t]\frac{\theta(X_t)}{\theta(X_0)}$$

must be a positive local martingale. As such, its expectation conditioned on date t information could decline in t implying that long-term interest rates could be higher and in fact converge to ρ. More generally, from the standpoint of valuation, the fat right tail of the process $\theta(X_t)$ could have important consequences for valuation even in the absence of a martingale component for the stochastic discount factor process.

As a priced cash flow, we consider the aggregate consumption flow process C^a given by

$$C_t^a = [a_e\psi(X_t) + a_h[1 - \psi(X_t)] - \iota(X_t)]K_t \tag{40}$$

where $\iota(x)$ is the aggregate investment rate, $\psi(x)$ is the fraction of the capital stock owned by the experts, and $a_e > a_h$ are the output productivities of the experts and households, respectively. Thus C_t^a is equal to aggregate output net of aggregate investment. Aggregate consumption is therefore given as a stationary fraction of aggregate capital. Thus aggregate consumption flow and capital stock processes share a common martingale component.[v]

7.3.5 Shock Elasticities and Term Structure of Yields

The top left panel in Fig. 4 depicts the drift and volatility coefficients for the state variable X_t. At the right boundary $\bar{x}$, the experts accumulated a sufficiently large share of capital and start consuming. Given their risk neutrality, the boundary behaves as a reflecting boundary.

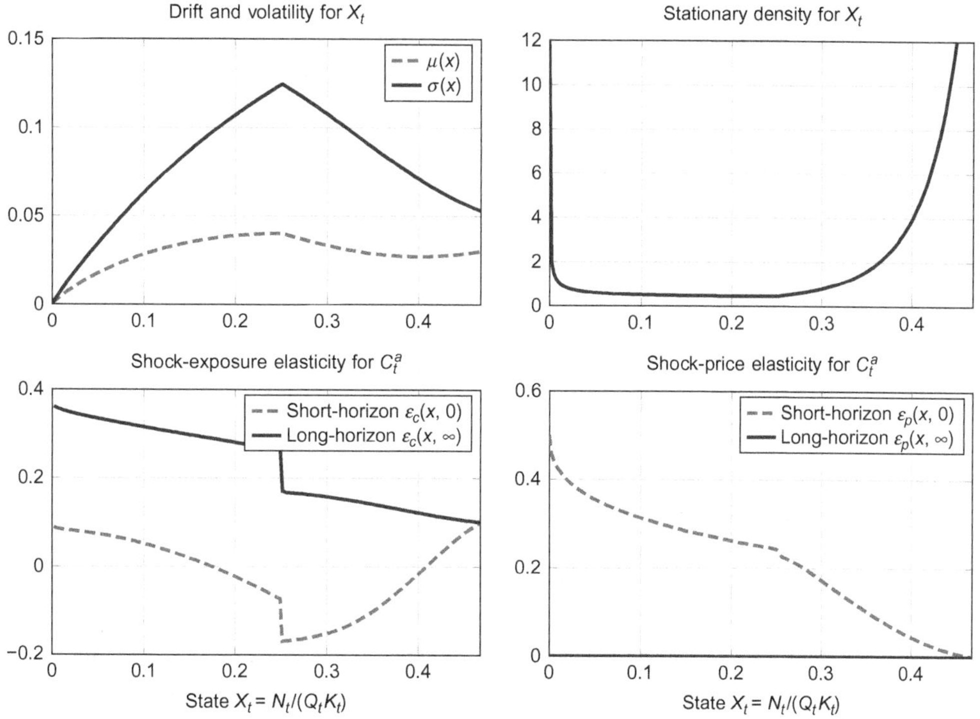

Fig. 4 Dynamics of the experts' wealth share $X_t = N_t/(Q_tK_t)$ (*horizontal axis*), shock-exposure and shock-price elasticities for the Brunnermeier and Sannikov (2014) model. *Top left panel* shows the drift and volatility coefficients for the evolution of X_t, while *top right panel* the stationary density for X_t. *Panels in the bottom row* show the short- and long-horizon shock elasticity for the aggregate consumption process C^a. The intermediation constraint binds in the interval $X_t \in (0, 0.25)$, and $x^* = 0.25$ corresponds to the 15% quantile of the stationary distribution of X.

[v] Brunnermeier and Sannikov (2014) also consider an extension where experts and households are endowed with logarithmic utilities. In that case consumption of both households and experts is given as constant fractions of their respective net worth, and the stochastic discount factor of the experts inherits the martingale component from the reciprocal of the aggregate capital process.

At the left boundary, the situation is notably different. Experts' ability to intermediate capital is limited by their own net worth, and hence their portfolio choice corresponds to an effectively risk averse agent. The left boundary is natural and nonattracting.

The existence of a stationary distribution, depicted in the second panel of Fig. 4, arises from a combination of two forces. Experts are more impatient, so whenever they accumulate a sufficient share of capital, they start consuming, which prevents them from taking over the whole economy. On the other hand, when their wealth share falls, their intermediation ability becomes scarce, the expected return on capital rises, and they use their superior investment technology to accumulate wealth at a faster rate than households.

The stationary density has peaks at each of the two boundaries. The positive drift coefficient $\mu(x)$ implies that there is a natural pull toward the right boundary, creating the peak in the density there. However, whenever a sequence of shocks brings the economy close to the left boundary, solvency constraints imply that it takes time for experts to accumulate wealth again, and the economy spends a long period time in that part of the state space. Economically, most times are "good" times when intermediation is fully operational, with rare periods of protracted "financial crises."

The bottom row of Fig. 4 plots the shock elasticities for the aggregate consumption process (40). Observe that the short-horizon exposure elasticity is negative in a part of the state space, making aggregate consumption countercyclical there. The long-horizon elasticities are noticeably higher, and particularly high when the intermediation constraint binds. The discontinuity at $X_t = x^*$ is caused by the change in consumption behavior in the moment when the intermediation constraint starts binding.

Given that the stochastic discount factor has no martingale component, the long-horizon shock-price elasticity is zero. On the other hand, the short-horizon price of risk varies strongly with the wealth share of the experts. This state dependence is also confirmed in Fig. 5 which plots the shock elasticity functions for selected points in the state space. Shock-exposure elasticities for the aggregate consumption process $\{C_t^a : t \geq 0\}$ increase with maturity, while the shock-price elasticities vanish as $t \rightarrow \infty$. Notice that there is a sign reversal in the exposure elasticities for aggregate consumption. The shock-exposure elasticities are initially negative but eventually become positive in the middle part of the state space, mirroring the bottom left panel of Fig. 4. This pattern emerges because the equilibrium investment responses over short horizons lead to more substantial longer-term consumption responses in the constrained states. Nevertheless, the shock-price elasticities are positive for all horizons and states that we consider.

Finally, Fig. 6 plots the yields on risk-free bonds and claims on horizon-specific cash flows from aggregate consumption. In line with the nonmonotonicity of the shock-exposure elasticities across states in Fig. 4, the short-maturity yields are also nonmonotonic, being lowest, and in fact lower than the risk-free rate, in the center of the distribution of the state X_t.

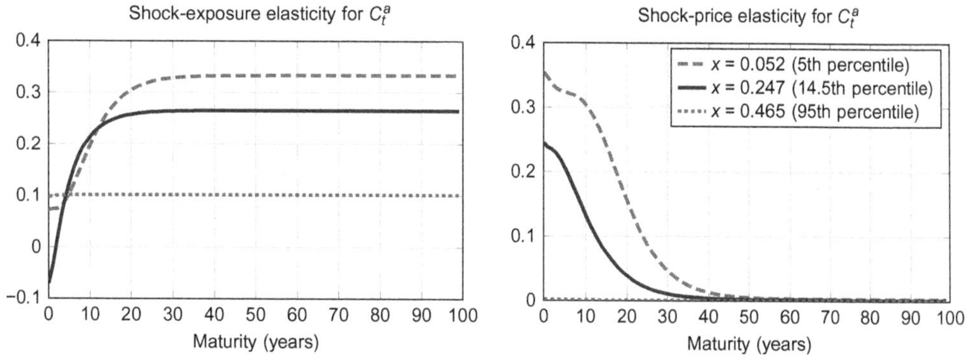

Fig. 5 Shock-exposure and shock-price elasticities for the Brunnermeier and Sannikov (2014) model. *Individual lines* correspond to alternative choices of the current state, the experts' wealth share $X_0 = x$. The *solid line* represents the state in which the intermediation constraint starts binding ($x = 0.247$), corresponding to the 14.5% quantile of the stationary distribution of X_t. The *dashed line* corresponds to the 5% quantile of the stationary distribution of X_t (intermediation constraint tightly binding), while the *dotted line* corresponds to the 95% quantile.

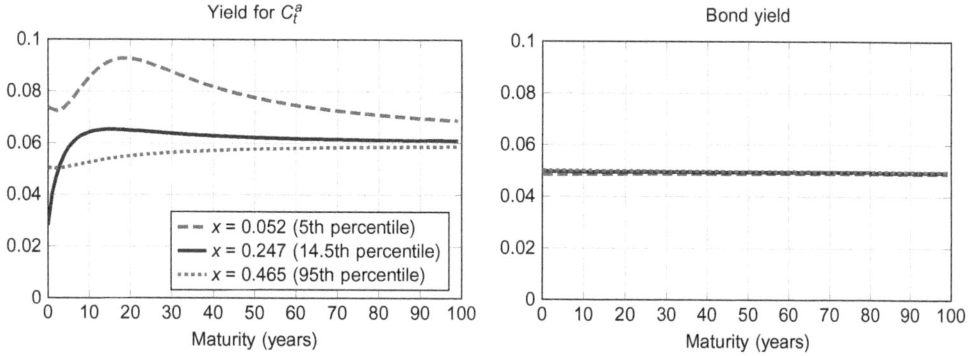

Fig. 6 Yields and excess yields for the Brunnermeier and Sannikov (2014) model. Parameterization and description as in Fig. 5.

8. DIRECTIONS FOR FURTHER RESEARCH

In this chapter, we developed dynamic value decompositions (DVDs) for the study of intertemporal asset pricing implications of dynamic equilibrium models. We constructed *shock elasticities* as building blocks for these decompositions. The DVD methods are distinct but potentially complementary to the familiar Campbell and Shiller (1988) decomposition. Campbell and Shiller use linear VAR methods to quantify the impact of (discounted) "cash flow shocks" and "expected return shocks" on price-dividend ratios. In general these shocks are correlated and are themselves combinations of shocks that are fundamental to structural models of the macroeconomy. Our aim is to explore pricing implications of models in which alternative macroeconomic shocks are identified and their impact quantified. We replaced linear approximation with local sensitivity analysis, and we characterized how cash flows are exposed to alternative macroeconomic shocks and what the corresponding price adjustments are for these exposures. We showed that shock elasticities are mathematically and economically related to impulse response functions. The shock elasticities represent sensitivities of expected cash flows to alternative macroeconomic shocks and the associated market implied compensations when looking across differing investment horizons.

We apply these DVD methods to a class of dynamic equilibrium models that feature financial frictions and segmented markets. The methods uncover the ways financial frictions contribute to pricing of alternative cash flows and to the shape of the term structure of macroeconomic risk prices.

There are two extensions of our analysis that require further investigation. First, risk prices are only well defined relative to an underlying probability distribution. In this chapter, we have not discussed the consequences for pricing when investors inside our models use different probability measures than the data-generating measure presumed by an econometrician. Typically, researchers invoke an assumption of rational expectations to connect investor perceptions with the data generation. More generally, models of investors that allow for subjective beliefs, learning, ambiguity aversion, or concerns about model misspecification alter how we interpret market-based compensations for exposure to macroeconomic fluctuations. For instance, see Hansen (2014) for further discussion. Incorporating potential belief distortions into the analysis should be a valuable extension of these methods.

Second, we left aside empirical and econometric aspects of the identification of shocks and measurement of risk premia. The empirical finance literature has made considerable progress in the characterization and measurement of the term structure of risk premia in various asset markets. The challenge for model building is to connect these empirical facts to specific sources of macroeconomic risks and financial market frictions of model economies. Our methodology suggests a way to make these connections, but further investigation is required.

Finally, we refrained from the discussion of implications for policy analysis. Financial frictions create economic externalities that can potentially be rectified by suitable policy actions. Since asset prices enter these financial constraints, understanding their behavior is an important ingredient to meaningful policy design. Forward looking asset prices provide both a source of information about private sector beliefs and an input into the regulatory challenges faced in the conduct of policy. Our methods can help to uncover asset pricing implications for alternative potential policies.

APPENDICES

Appendix A Exponential-Quadratic Framework

Let $X=(X_1', X_2')'$ be a $2n \times 1$ vector of states, $W \sim N(0, I)$ a $k \times 1$ vector of independent Gaussian shocks, and $\mathcal{F}_t$ the filtration generated by $(X_0, W_1, \ldots, W_t)$. In this appendix, we show that given the law of motion from Eq. (21)

$$\begin{aligned} X_{1,t+1} &= \Theta_{10}+\Theta_{11}X_{1,t}+\Lambda_{10}W_{t+1} \\ X_{2,t+1} &= \Theta_{20}+\Theta_{21}X_{1,t}+\Theta_{22}X_{2,t}+\Theta_{23}(X_{1,t}\otimes X_{1,t}) \\ &\quad +\Lambda_{20}W_{t+1}+\Lambda_{21}(X_{1,t}\otimes W_{t+1})+\Lambda_{22}(W_{t+1}\otimes W_{t+1}) \end{aligned} \tag{A.1}$$

and a multiplicative functional $M_t=\exp(Y_t)$ whose additive increment is given in Eq. (22):

$$\begin{aligned} Y_{t+1}-Y_t &= \Gamma_0+\Gamma_1 X_{1,t}+\Gamma_2 X_{2,t}+\Gamma_3(X_{1,t}\otimes X_{1,t}) \\ &\quad +\Psi_0 W_{t+1}+\Psi_1(X_{1,t}\otimes W_{1,t+1})+\Psi_2(W_{t+1}\otimes W_{t+1}), \end{aligned} \tag{A.2}$$

we can write the conditional expectation of M as

$$\log E[M_t \mid \mathcal{F}_0]=(\overline{\Gamma}_0)_t+(\overline{\Gamma}_1)_t X_{1,0}+(\overline{\Gamma}_2)_t X_{2,0}+(\overline{\Gamma}_3)_t(X_{1,0}\otimes X_{1,0}) \tag{A.3}$$

where $(\overline{\Gamma}_i)_t$ are constant coefficients to be determined.

The dynamics given by (A.1) and (A.2) embed the perturbation approximation constructed in Section 5.2 as a special case. The Θ and Λ matrices needed to map the perturbed model into the above structure are constructed from the first and second derivatives of the function $\psi(x, w, \mathsf{q})$ that captures the law of motion of the model, evaluated at $(\bar{x}, 0, 0)$:

$$\begin{aligned} &\Theta_{10}=\psi_q \quad \Theta_{11}=\psi_x \quad \Lambda_{10}=\psi_w \\ &\Theta_{20}=\psi_{qq} \quad \Theta_{21}=2\psi_{xq} \quad \Theta_{22}=\psi_x \quad \Theta_{23}=\psi_{xx} \\ &\Lambda_{20}=2\psi_{wq} \quad \Lambda_{21}=2\psi_{xw} \quad \Lambda_{22}=\psi_{ww} \end{aligned}$$

where the notation for the derivatives is defined in Appendix A.2.

A.1 Definitions

To simplify work with Kronecker products, we define two operators vec and $\text{mat}_{m,n}$. For an $m \times n$ matrix H, $\text{vec}(H)$ produces a column vector of length mn created by stacking the columns of H:

$$h_{(j-1)m+i}=[\text{vec}(H)]_{(j-1)m+i}=H_{ij}.$$

For a vector (column or row) h of length mn, $\text{mat}_{m,n}(h)$ produces an $m \times n$ matrix H created by "columnizing" the vector:

$$H_{ij} = [\mathrm{mat}_{m,n}(h)]_{ij} = h_{(j-1)m+i}.$$

We drop the m, n subindex if the dimensions of the resulting matrix are obvious from the context. For a square matrix A, define the sym operator as

$$\mathrm{sym}(A) = \frac{1}{2}(A + A').$$

Apart from the standard operations with Kronecker products, notice that the following is true. For a row vector $H_{1\times nk}$ and column vectors $X_{n\times 1}$ and $W_{n\times 1}$

$$H(X \otimes W) = X'[\mathrm{mat}_{k,n}(H)]' W$$

and for a matrix $A_{n\times k}$, we have

$$X'AW = (\mathrm{vec}A')'(X \otimes W). \tag{A.4}$$

Also, for $A_{n\times n}$, $X_{n\times 1}$, $K_{k\times 1}$, we have

$$(AX) \otimes K = (A \otimes K)X$$
$$K \otimes (AX) = (K \otimes A)X.$$

Finally, for column vectors $X_{n\times 1}$ and $W_{k\times 1}$,

$$(AX) \otimes (BW) = (A \otimes B)(X \otimes W)$$

and

$$(BW) \otimes (AX) = \left[B \otimes A_{\bullet j}\right]_{j=1}^{n} (X \otimes W)$$

where

$$\left[B \otimes A_{\bullet j}\right]_{j=1}^{n} = [B \otimes A_{\bullet 1} \quad B \otimes A_{\bullet 2} \quad \dots \quad B \otimes A_{\bullet n}].$$

A.2 Concise Notation for Derivatives

Consider a vector function $f(x,w)$ where x and w are column vectors of length m and n, respectively. The first-derivative matrix f_i where $i = x, w$ is constructed as follows. The kth row $[f_i]_{k\bullet}$ corresponds to the derivative of the kth component of f

$$[f_i(x,w)]_{k\bullet} = \frac{\partial f^{(k)}}{\partial i'}(x,w).$$

Similarly, the second-derivative matrix is the matrix of vectorized and stacked Hessians of individual components with kth row

$$[f_{ij}(x,w)]_{k\bullet} = \left(\mathrm{vec}\frac{\partial^2 f^{(k)}}{\partial j \partial i'}(x,w)\right)'.$$

It follows from formula (A.4) that, for example,

$$x'\left(\frac{\partial^2 f^{(k)}}{\partial x \partial w'}(x,w)\right)w=\left(\text{vec}\frac{\partial^2 f^{(k)}}{\partial w \partial x'}(x,w)\right)'(x\otimes w)=[f_{xw}(x,w)]_{k\bullet}(x\otimes w).$$

A.3 Conditional Expectations

Notice that a complete-the-squares argument implies that, for a $1\times k$ vector A, a $1\times k^2$ vector B, and a scalar function $f(w)$,

$$\begin{aligned}
&E[\exp(B(W_{t+1}\otimes W_{t+1})+AW_{t+1})f(W_{t+1})\mid \mathcal{F}_t]\\
&\quad=E\left[\exp\left(\frac{1}{2}W'_{t+1}(\text{mat}_{k,k}(2B))W_{t+1}+AW_{t+1}\right)f(W_{t+1})\mid \mathcal{F}_t\right]\\
&\quad=|I_k-\text{sym}[\text{mat}_{k,k}(2B)]|^{-1/2}\exp\left(\frac{1}{2}A(I_k-\text{sym}[\text{mat}_{k,k}(2B)])^{-1}A'\right)\widetilde{E}\left[f(W_{t+1})\mid \mathcal{F}_t\right]
\end{aligned} \tag{A.5}$$

where $\widetilde{\cdot}$ is a measure under which

$$W_{t+1}\sim N\left((I_k-\text{sym}[\text{mat}_{k,k}(2B)])^{-1}A',(I_k-\text{sym}[\text{mat}_{k,k}(2B)])^{-1}\right).$$

We start by utilizing formula (A.5) to compute

$$\begin{aligned}
\bar{Y}(X_t)=&\log E[\exp(Y_{t+1}-Y_t)\mid \mathcal{F}_t]=\Gamma_0+\Gamma_1X_{1,t}+\Gamma_2X_{2,t}+\Gamma_3(X_{1,t}\otimes X_{1,t})\\
&+\log E\left[\exp\left(\left[\Psi_0+X'_{1t}[\text{mat}_{k,n}(\Psi_1)]'\right]W_{t+1}+\frac{1}{2}W'_{t+1}[\text{mat}_{k,k}(\Psi_2)]W_{t+1}\right)\mid \mathcal{F}_t\right]\\
=&\Gamma_0+\Gamma_1X_{1,t}+\Gamma_2X_{2,t}+\Gamma_3(X_{1,t}\otimes X_{1,t})\\
&-\frac{1}{2}\log|I_k-\text{sym}[\text{mat}_{k,k}(2\Psi_2)]|+\frac{1}{2}\mu'(I_k-\text{sym}[\text{mat}_{k,k}(2\Psi_2)])^{-1}\mu
\end{aligned}$$

with μ defined as

$$\mu=\Psi'_0+[\text{mat}_{k,n}(\Psi_1)]X_{1,t}.$$

Reorganizing terms, we obtain

$$\bar{Y}(X_t)=\overline{\Gamma}_0+\overline{\Gamma}_1X_{1,t}+\overline{\Gamma}_2X_{2,t}+\overline{\Gamma}_3(X_{1,t}\otimes X_{1,t}) \tag{A.6}$$

where

$$\begin{aligned}
\overline{\Gamma}_0&=\Gamma_0-\frac{1}{2}\log|I_k-\text{sym}[\text{mat}_{k,k}(2\Psi_2)]|+\frac{1}{2}\Psi_0(I_k-\text{sym}[\text{mat}_{k,k}(2\Psi_2)])^{-1}\Psi'_0\\
\overline{\Gamma}_1&=\Gamma_1+\Psi_0(I_k-\text{sym}[\text{mat}_{k,k}(2\Psi_2)])^{-1}[\text{mat}_{k,n}(\Psi_1)]\\
\overline{\Gamma}_2&=\Gamma_2\\
\overline{\Gamma}_3&=\Gamma_3+\frac{1}{2}\text{vec}\left[[\text{mat}_{k,n}(\Psi_1)]'(I_k-\text{sym}[\text{mat}_{k,k}(2\Psi_2)])^{-1}[\text{mat}_{k,n}(\Psi_1)]\right]'.
\end{aligned} \tag{A.7}$$

For the set of parameters $\mathcal{P}=(\Gamma_0,\ldots,\Gamma_3,\Psi_0,\ldots,\Psi_2)$, Eqs. (A.7) define a mapping

$$\bar{\mathcal{P}}=\bar{\mathcal{E}}(\mathcal{P}),$$

with all $\overline{\Psi}_j=0$. We now substitute the law of motion for X_1 and X_2 to produce $\bar{Y}(X_t)=\tilde{Y}(X_{t-1},W_t)$. It is just a matter of algebraic operations to determine that

$$\begin{aligned}
\tilde{Y}(X_{t-1},W_t) &= \log E[\exp(Y_{t+1}-Y_t)\mid\mathcal{F}_t] \\
&= \tilde{\Gamma}_0+\tilde{\Gamma}_1X_{1,t-1}+\tilde{\Gamma}_2X_{2,t-1}+\tilde{\Gamma}_3(X_{1,t-1}\otimes X_{1,t-1}) \\
&\quad +\tilde{\Psi}_0W_t+\tilde{\Psi}_1(X_{1,t-1}\otimes W_t)+\tilde{\Psi}_2(W_t\otimes W_t)
\end{aligned}$$

where

$$\begin{aligned}
\tilde{\Gamma}_0 &= \overline{\Gamma}_0+\overline{\Gamma}_1\Theta_{10}+\overline{\Gamma}_2\Theta_{20}+\overline{\Gamma}_3(\Theta_{10}\otimes\Theta_{10}) \\
\tilde{\Gamma}_1 &= \overline{\Gamma}_1\Theta_{11}+\overline{\Gamma}_2\Theta_{21}+\overline{\Gamma}_3(\Theta_{10}\otimes\Theta_{11}+\Theta_{11}\otimes\Theta_{10}) \\
\tilde{\Gamma}_2 &= \overline{\Gamma}_2\Theta_{22} \\
\tilde{\Gamma}_3 &= \overline{\Gamma}_2\Theta_{23}+\overline{\Gamma}_3(\Theta_{11}\otimes\Theta_{11}) \\
\tilde{\Psi}_0 &= \overline{\Gamma}_1\Lambda_{10}+\overline{\Gamma}_2\Lambda_{20}+\overline{\Gamma}_3(\Theta_{10}\otimes\Lambda_{10}+\Lambda_{10}\otimes\Theta_{10}) \\
\tilde{\Psi}_1 &= \overline{\Gamma}_2\Lambda_{21}+\overline{\Gamma}_3\left(\Theta_{11}\otimes\Lambda_{10}+\left[\Lambda_{10}\otimes(\Theta_{11})_{\bullet j}\right]_{j=1}^{n}\right) \\
\tilde{\Psi}_2 &= \overline{\Gamma}_2\Lambda_{22}+\overline{\Gamma}_3(\Lambda_{10}\otimes\Lambda_{10}).
\end{aligned} \tag{A.8}$$

This set of equations defines the mapping

$$\tilde{\mathcal{P}}=\tilde{\mathcal{E}}(\bar{\mathcal{P}}).$$

A.4 Iterative Formulas

We can write the conditional expectation in (A.3) recursively as

$$\log E[M_t\mid\mathcal{F}_0]=\log E\left[\exp(Y_1-Y_0)E\left[\frac{M_t}{M_1}\mid\mathcal{F}_1\right]\mid\mathcal{F}_0\right].$$

Given the mappings $\bar{\mathcal{E}}$ and $\tilde{\mathcal{E}}$, we can therefore express the coefficients $\bar{\mathcal{P}}$ in (A.3) using the recursion

$$\bar{\mathcal{P}}_t=\bar{\mathcal{E}}\left(\mathcal{P}+\tilde{\mathcal{E}}(\bar{\mathcal{P}}_{t-1})\right)$$

where the addition is by coefficients and all coefficients in $\bar{\mathcal{P}}_0$ are zero matrices.

A.5 Coefficients Φ_i^*

In the above calculations, we constructed a recursion for the coefficients in the computation of the conditional expectation of the multiplicative functional M. A single iteration of this recursion can be easily adapted to compute the coefficients Φ_i^*, $i = 0, \ldots, 3,$ in the conditional expectation in Eq. (24) for an arbitrary function $\log f(x)$.

1. Associate $\log f(x_{t+1}) = \bar{Y}(x_{t+1})$ from Eq. (A.6), ie, set $\bar{\Gamma}_i$, $i = 0, \ldots, 3$, in Eq. (A.6) equal to the desired Φ_i from Eq. (23). These are the coefficients in set $\bar{\mathcal{P}}$.
2. Apply the mapping $\widetilde{\mathcal{E}}\,(\bar{\mathcal{P}})$, ie, compute $\widetilde{\Gamma}_i$, $i = 0, \ldots, 3$, and $\widetilde{\Psi}_i$, $i = 0, 1, 2$, using (A.8). This yields the function $\log \widetilde{f}\,(x_t, w_{t+1}) \equiv \log f(x_{t+1})$, with coefficient set $\widetilde{\mathcal{P}}$.
3. Add to these coefficients $\widetilde{\Gamma}_i$ and $\widetilde{\Psi}_i$ the corresponding coefficients Γ_i and Ψ_i of $Y_{t+1} - Y_t$ from Eq. (A.2), ie, form coefficient set $\mathcal{P} + \widetilde{\mathcal{E}}\,(\bar{\mathcal{P}})$.
4. Apply the mapping $\bar{\mathcal{E}}\left(\mathcal{P} + \widetilde{\mathcal{E}}(\bar{\mathcal{P}})\right)$, ie, compute (A.7) where on the right-hand side the coefficients Γ_i and Ψ_i (coefficient set $\mathcal{P}$) are replaced with coefficients computed in the previous step, ie, set $\mathcal{P} + \widetilde{\mathcal{E}}\,(\bar{\mathcal{P}})$.
5. The resulting coefficients $\bar{\Gamma}_i$, $i = 0, \ldots, 3$, are the desired coefficients Φ_i^*.

Appendix B Shock Elasticity Calculations

In this appendix, we provide details on some of the calculations underlying the derived shock elasticity formulas for the convenient functional form from Section 5.1.1. In particular we show, using a complete-the-squares argument, that under the transformed measure generated by the random variable $L_{1,t}$ from (25) the shock W_1 remains normally distributed with a covariance matrix:

$$\widetilde{\Sigma}_t = \left[I_k - 2\,\mathrm{sym}\left(\mathrm{mat}_{k,k}\left[\Psi_2 + \Phi_{2,t-1}^*\Lambda_{22} + \Phi_{3,t-1}^*(\Lambda_{10}\otimes\Lambda_{10})\right]\right)\right]^{-1},$$

where I_k is the identity matrix of dimension k.[w] We suppose that this matrix is positive definite. The conditional mean vector for W_1 under the change of measure is:

$$\widetilde{E}\,[W_1 \mid X_0 = x] = \widetilde{\Sigma}_t\left[\mu_{t,0} + \mu_{t,1}x_1\right],$$

where $\widetilde{E}$ is the expectation under the change of measure and the coefficients $\mu_{t,0}$ and $\mu_{t,1}$ are given in the following derivation.

Thus the shock elasticity is given by:

$$\begin{aligned}\varepsilon(x,t) &= \nu(x)\cdot E[L_{1,t}W_1 \mid X_0 = x] \\ &= \nu(x)'\widetilde{\Sigma}_t\left[\mu_{t,0} + \mu_{t,1}x_1\right].\end{aligned}$$

The shock elasticity function in this environment depends on the first component, x_1, of the state vector. Recall from (21) that this component has linear dynamics. The

[w] This formula uses the result that $(\Lambda_{10}W_1)\otimes(\Lambda_{10}W_1) = (\Lambda_{10}\otimes\Lambda_{10})(W_1\otimes W_1)$.

coefficient matrices for the evolution of the second component, x_2, nevertheless matter for the shock elasticities even though these elasticities do not depend on this component of the state vector.

B.1 Shock Elasticities Under the Convenient Functional Form

To calculate the shock elasticities in Section 5.1.1, utilize the formulas derived in Appendix A to deduce the one-period change of measure

$$\log L_{1,t} = \log M_1 + \log E\left(\frac{M_t}{M_1} \mid X_1\right) - \log E\left[M_1 E\left(\frac{M_t}{M_1} \mid X_1\right) \mid X_0 = x\right].$$

In particular, following the set of formulas (A.8), define

$$\mu_{0,t} = \left[\Psi_1 + \Phi^*_{1,t-1}\Lambda_{1,0} + \Phi^*_{2,t-1}\Lambda_{20} + \Phi^*_{3,t-1}(\Theta_{10}\otimes\Lambda_{10} + \Lambda_{10}\otimes\Theta_{10})\right]'$$

$$\mu_{1,t} = \mathrm{mat}_{k,n}\left[\Psi_1 + \Phi^*_{2,t-1}\Lambda_{21} + \Phi^*_{3,t-1}\left(\Theta_{11}\otimes\Lambda_{10} + \left[\Lambda_{10}\otimes(\Theta_{11})_{\bullet j}\right]_{j=1}^{n}\right)\right]$$

$$\mu_{2,t} = \mathrm{sym}\left[\mathrm{mat}_{k,k}\left(\Psi_2 + \overline{\Gamma}_2\Lambda_{22} + \overline{\Gamma}_3(\Lambda_{10}\otimes\Lambda_{10})\right)\right].$$

Then it follows that

$$\begin{aligned}\log L_{1,t} &= (\mu_{0,t} + \mu_{1,t}X_{1,0})'W_1 + (W_1)'\mu_{2,t}W_1 \\ &\quad - \frac{1}{2}\log E\left[\exp\left((\mu_{0,t} + \mu_{1,t}X_{1,0})'W_1 + (W_1)'\mu_{2,t}W_1\right) \mid \mathcal{F}_0\right].\end{aligned}$$

Expression (A.5) then implies that

$$\begin{aligned}E[L_{1,t}W_1 \mid \mathcal{F}_0] &= \widetilde{E}[W_1 \mid \mathcal{F}_0] \\ &= (I_k - 2\mu_{2,t})^{-1}(\mu_{0,t} + \mu_{1t}X_{1,0}).\end{aligned}$$

The variance of W_1 under the $\widetilde{\ }$ measure satisfies

$$\widetilde{\Sigma}_t = \left(I_k - 2\mathrm{sym}\left[\mathrm{mat}_{k,k}\left(\Psi_2 + \overline{\Gamma}_2\Lambda_{22} + \overline{\Gamma}_3(\Lambda_{10}\otimes\Lambda_{10})\right)\right]\right)^{-1}.$$

B.2 Approximation of the Shock Elasticity Function

In Section 5.3.1, we constructed the approximation of the shock elasticity function $\varepsilon(x,t)$. The first-order approximation is constructed by differentiating the elasticity function under the perturbed dynamics

$$\varepsilon_1(X_{1,0},t) = \frac{d}{d\mathsf{q}}\nu(X_0(\mathsf{q}))\cdot\left.\frac{E[M_t(\mathsf{q})W_1 \mid X_0 = x]}{E[M_t(\mathsf{q}) \mid X_0 = x]}\right|_{\mathsf{q}=0} = \nu(\bar{x})\cdot E[Y_{1,t}W_1 \mid X_0 = x].$$

The first-derivative process $Y_{1,t}$ can be expressed in terms of its increments, and we obtain a state-independent function

$$\varepsilon_1(t) = \nu(\bar{x}) \cdot E\left[\sum_{j=1}^{t-1} \kappa_x (\psi_x)^{j-1} \psi_w + \kappa_w\right]'$$

where κ_x, ψ_x, κ_w, ψ_w are derivative matrices evaluated at the steady state $(\bar{x}, 0)$.

Continuing with the second derivative, we have

$$\begin{aligned}
\varepsilon_2(X_{1,0}, X_{2,0}, t) &= \frac{d^2}{d\mathsf{q}^2} \nu(X_0(\mathsf{q})) \cdot \frac{E[M_t(\mathsf{q}) W_1 \mid X_0 = x]}{E[M_t(\mathsf{q}) \mid X_0 = x]}\bigg|_{\mathsf{q}=0} \\
&= \nu(\bar{x}) \cdot \left\{ E\left[(Y_{1,t})^2 W_1 + Y_{2,t} W_1 \mid \mathcal{F}_0\right] - 2E[Y_{1,t} W_1 \mid \mathcal{F}_0] E[Y_{1,t} \mid \mathcal{F}_0] \right\} \\
&\quad + 2\left[\frac{\partial \nu}{\partial x'}(\bar{x})\right] X_{1,0} \cdot E[Y_{1,t} W_1 \mid \mathcal{F}_0].
\end{aligned}$$

However, notice that

$$E\left[(Y_{1,t})^2 W_1 \mid \mathcal{F}_0\right] = 2\left(\sum_{j=0}^{t-1} \kappa_x (\psi_x)^j X_{1,0}\right)\left(\sum_{j=1}^{t-1} \kappa_x (\psi_x)^{j-1} \psi_w + \kappa_w\right)'$$

$$E[Y_{1,t} W_1 \mid \mathcal{F}_0] = \left(\sum_{j=1}^{t-1} \kappa_x (\psi_x)^{j-1} \psi_w + \kappa_w\right)'$$

$$E[Y_{1,t} \mid \mathcal{F}_0] = \sum_{j=0}^{t-1} \kappa_x (\psi_x)^j X_{1,0}$$

and thus

$$E\left[(Y_{1,t})^2 W_1 \mid \mathcal{F}_0\right] - 2E[Y_{1,t} W_1 \mid \mathcal{F}_0] E[Y_{1,t} \mid \mathcal{F}_0] = 0.$$

The second-order term in the approximation of the shock elasticity function thus simplifies to

$$\varepsilon_2(X_{1,0}, X_{2,0}, t) = \nu(\bar{x}) \cdot E[Y_{2,t} W_1 \mid \mathcal{F}_0] + 2\left[\frac{\partial \nu}{\partial x'}(\bar{x})\right] X_{1,0} \cdot E[Y_{1,t} W_1 \mid \mathcal{F}_0].$$

The expression for the first term on the right-hand side is

$$\begin{aligned}
E[Y_{2,t} W_1 \mid \mathcal{F}_0] &= E\left[\sum_{j=0}^{t-1} (Y_{2,j+1} - Y_{2,j}) W_1 \mid \mathcal{F}_0\right] = 2\mathrm{mat}_{k,n}(\kappa_{xw}) X_{1,0} \\
&\quad + 2\sum_{j=1}^{t-1} \left[\psi_w' (\psi_x')^{j-1} \mathrm{mat}_{n,n}(\kappa_{xx}) (\psi_x)^j + \mathrm{mat}_{k,n}\left[\kappa_x (\psi_x)^{j-1} \psi_{xw}\right]\right] X_{1,0} \\
&\quad + 2\sum_{j=1}^{t-1} \sum_{k=1}^{j-1} \left[\psi_w' (\psi_x')^{k-1} \mathrm{mat}_{n,n}\left[\kappa_x (\psi_x)^{j-k-1} \psi_{xx}\right] (\psi_x)^k\right] X_{1,0}.
\end{aligned}$$

To obtain this result, notice that repeated substitution for $Y_{1,j+1} - Y_{1,j}$ into the above formula yields a variety of terms but only those containing $X_{1,0} \otimes W_1$ have a nonzero conditional expectation when interacted with W_1.

ACKNOWLEDGMENTS

We would like to thank John Heaton and Vadim Linetsky for helpful comments. Spencer Lyon and Victor Zhorin provided excellent research assistance.

REFERENCES

Adrian, T., Boyarchenko, N., 2012. Intermediary leverage cycles and financial stability. Federal Reserve Bank of New York Staff Report No. 567.

Ai, H., Croce, M.M., Diercks, A., Li, K., 2013. Production-based term structure of equity returns.

Alvarez, F., Jermann, U.J., 2004. Using asset prices to measure the cost of business cycles. J. Polit. Econ. 112 (6), 1223–1256.

Anderson, E.W., Hansen, L.P., Sargent, T.J., 2003. A quartet of semigroups for model specification, robustness, prices of risk, and model detection. J. Eur. Econ. Assoc. 1 (1), 68–123.

Andreasen, M.M., Fernández-Villaverde, J., Rubio-Ramírez, J.F., 2010. The pruned state space system for non-linear DSGE models: Asset pricing applications to GMM and SMM. Unpublished manuscript.

Belo, F., Collin-Dufresne, P., Goldstein, R.S., 2015. Dividend dynamics and the term structure of dividend strips. J. Financ. 70 (3), 1115–1160.

Benigno, G., Benigno, P., Nisticò, S., 2010. Second-order approximation of dynamic models with time-varying risk. NBER Working Paper W16633.

Bernanke, B.S., Gertler, M., 1989. Agency costs, net worth, and business fluctuations. Am. Econ. Rev. 79 (1), 14–31.

Bernanke, B.S., Gertler, M., Gilchrist, S., 1999. The financial accelerator in a quantitative business cycle framework. In: Handbook of Macroeconomics, vol. 1, Chapter 21. Elsevier B.V., Amsterdam, Netherlands, pp. 1341–1393.

Beveridge, S., Nelson, C.R., 1981. A new approach to decomposition of economic time series into permanent and transitory components with particular attention to measurement of the 'business cycle'. J. Monet. Econ. 7, 151–174.

Bhandari, A., Borovička, J., Ho, P., 2016. Identifying ambiguity shocks in business cycle models using survey data.

Bianchi, F., 2012. Regime switches, agents' beliefs, and post-World War II U.S. macroeconomic dynamics. Rev. Econ. Stud. 67 (2), 380–405.

Bianchi, F., 2015. Rare events, financial crises, and the cross-section of asset returns.

Bianchi, J., 2016. Efficient bailouts? Am. Econ. Rev. Forthcoming.

Bianchi, F., Ilut, C., 2015. Monetary/fiscal policy mix and agents' beliefs.

Bianchi, F., Melosi, L., 2016. Modeling the evolution of expectations and uncertainty in general equilibrium. Int. Econ. Rev. 57 (2), 717–756.

Bianchi, F., Ilut, C., Schneider, M., 2013. Uncertainty shocks, asset supply and pricing over the business cycle.

Blanchard, O.J., Kahn, C.M., 1980. The solution of linear difference models under rational expectations. Econometrica 48 (5), 1305–1312.

Blanchard, O.J., Quah, D., 1989. The dynamic effects of aggregate demand and supply disturbances. Am. Econ. Rev. 79 (4), 655–673.

Bocola, L., 2016. The pass-through of sovereign risk. J. Polit. Econ. Forthcoming.

Borodin, A.N., Salminen, P., 2002. Handbook of Brownian Motion: Facts and Formulae, second edition. Birkhäuser, Basel, Boston, Berlin.

Borovička, J., Hansen, L.P., 2013. Robust preference expansions.

Borovička, J., Hansen, L.P., 2014. Examining macroeconomic models through the lens of asset pricing. J. Econom. 183 (1), 67–90.

Borovička, J., Hansen, L.P., Hendricks, M., Scheinkman, J.A., 2011. Risk-price dynamics. J. Financ. Econom. 9 (1), 3–65.
Borovička, J., Hansen, L.P., Scheinkman, J.A., 2014. Shock elasticities and impulse responses. Math. Finan. Econ. 8 (4), 333–354.
Borovička, J., Hansen, L.P., Scheinkman, J.A., 2015. Misspecified recovery. J. Financ. Forthcoming.
Brunnermeier, M.K., Sannikov, Y., 2014. A macroeconomic model with a financial sector. Am. Econ. Rev. 104 (2), 379–421.
Campbell, J.Y., Shiller, R.J., 1988. Stock prices, earnings, and expected dividends. J. Financ. 43 (3), 661–676. http://dx.doi.org/10.1111/j.1540-6261.1988.tb04598.x.
Chen, H., 2010. Macroeconomic conditions and the puzzles of credit spreads and capital structure. J. Financ. 65 (6), 2171–2212.
Chung, H., Davig, T., Leeper, E.M., 2007. Monetary and fiscal policy switching. J. Money Credit Bank. 39 (4), 809–842.
David, A., 2008. Heterogeneous beliefs, speculation, and the equity premium. J. Financ. 63 (1), 41–83.
Davig, T., Leeper, E.M., Walker, T.B., 2010. "Unfunded liabilities" and uncertain fiscal financing. J. Monet. Econ. 57 (5), 600–619.
Davig, T., Leeper, E.M., Walker, T.B., 2011. Inflation and the fiscal limit. Eur. Econ. Rev. 55 (1), 31–47.
Di Nunno, G., Øksendal, B., Proske, F., 2009. Malliavin Calculus for Lévy Processes with Applications to Finance. Springer Verlag, Berlin, Heidelberg.
Di Tella, S., 2015. Uncertainty shocks and balance sheet recessions. J. Polit. Econ. Forthcoming.
Epstein, L.G., Zin, S.E., 1989. Substitution, risk aversion, and the temporal behavior of consumption and asset returns: a theoretical framework. Econometrica 57 (4), 937–969.
Farmer, R.E., Waggoner, D.F., Zha, T., 2011. Minimal state variable solutions to Markov-switching rational expectations models. J. Econ. Dyn. Control. 35 (12), 2150–2166.
Feller, W., 1952. The parabolic differential equations and the associated semi-groups of transformations. Ann. Math. 55 (3), 468–519.
Feller, W., 1957. On boundaries and lateral conditions for the Kolmogorov differential equations. Ann. Math. 65 (3), 527–570.
Foerster, A., Rubio-Ramirez, J., Waggoner, D.F., Zha, T., 2014. Perturbation methods for Markov-switching DSGE models. NBER Working Paper W20390.
Frisch, R., 1933. Propagation problems and impulse problems in dynamic economics. In: Economic Essays in Honour of Gustav Cassel. Allen and Unwin, Oslo, pp. 171–205.
Hansen, L.P., 2012. Dynamic valuation decomposition within stochastic economies. Econometrica 80 (3), 911–967. Fisher-Schultz Lecture at the European Meetings of the Econometric Society.
Hansen, L.P., 2014. Nobel lecture: uncertainty outside and inside economic models. J. Polit. Econ. 122 (5), 945–987. https://ideas.repec.org/a/ucp/jpolec/doi10.1086-678456.html.
Hansen, L.P., Richard, S.F., 1987. The role of conditioning information in deducing testable restrictions implied by dynamic asset pricing models. Econometrica 50, 587–614.
Hansen, L.P., Scheinkman, J.A., 2009. Long term risk: an operator approach. Econometrica 77 (1), 177–234.
Hansen, L.P., Scheinkman, J.A., 2012. Pricing growth-rate risk. Finance Stochast. 16, 1–15.
Hansen, L.P., Sargent, T.J., Tallarini Jr., T.D., 1999. Robust permanent income and pricing. Rev. Econ. Stud. 66 (4), 873–907.
Hansen, L.P., Heaton, J.C., Li, N., 2008. Consumption strikes back? Measuring long-run risk. J. Polit. Econ. 116, 260–302.
Hasler, M., Marfè, R., 2015. Disaster recovery and the term structure of dividend strips.
He, Z., Krishnamurthy, A., 2013. Intermediary asset pricing. Am. Econ. Rev. 103 (2), 732–770.
Holmes, M.H., 1995. Introduction to Perturbation Methods. Springer Verlag, New York.
Jacobson, D.H., 1973. Optimal stochastic linear systems with exponential performance criteria and their relation to deterministic differential games. IEEE Trans. Autom. Control AC-18, 1124–1131.
Justiniano, A., Primiceri, G.E., 2008. The time-varying volatility of macroeconomic fluctuations. Am. Econ. Rev. 98 (3), 604–641.
Karlin, S., Taylor, H.M., 1981. A Second Course in Stochastic Processes. Academic Press, London, United Kingdom.

Kim, J., Kim, S., Schaumburg, E., Sims, C.A., 2008. Calculating and using second-order accurate solutions of discrete time dynamic equilibrium models. J. Econ. Dyn. Control 32 (11), 3397–3414.
Klimenko, N., Pfeil, S., Rochet, J.C., De Nicolò, G., 2016. Aggregate bank capital and credit dynamics.
Kreps, D.M., Porteus, E.L., 1978. Temporal resolution of uncertainty and dynamic choice theory. Econometrica 46 (1), 185–200.
Linetsky, V., 2008. Spectral methods in derivatives pricing. In: Handbooks in Operations Research and Management Science, vol. 15, Chapter 6. Elsevier B.V., Amsterdam, Netherlands, pp. 213–289.
Liu, Z., Waggoner, D.F., Zha, T., 2009. Asymmetric expectation effects of regime switches in monetary policy. Rev. Econ. Dyn. 12 (2), 284–303.
Liu, Z., Waggoner, D.F., Zha, T., 2011. Sources of macroeconomic fluctuations: a regime-switching DSGE approach. Quant. Econ. 2 (2), 251–301.
Lombardo, G., Uhlig, H., 2014. A theory of pruning. European Central Bank. https://ideas.repec.org/p/ecb/ecbwps/20141696.html. Working Paper Series 1696.
Lopez, P., Lopez-Salido, D., Vazquez-Grande, F., 2015. Nominal rigidities and the term structures of equity and bond returns.
Maenhout, P.J., 2004. Robust portfolio rules and asset pricing. Rev. Financ. Stud. 17 (4), 951–983. http://dx.doi.org/10.1093/rfs/hhh003. http://rfs.oxfordjournals.org/content/17/4/951.full.pdf+html, http://rfs.oxfordjournals.org/content/17/4/951.abstract.
Malkhozov, A., Shamloo, M., 2011. Asset prices in affine real business cycle models.
Moreira, A., Savov, A., 2016. The macroeconomics of shadow banking. J. Financ. Forthcoming.
Nakamura, E., Sergeyev, D., Steinsson, J., 2016. Growth-rate and uncertainty shocks in consumption: cross-country evidence. Columbia University. http://www.nber.org/papers/w18128.
Nualart, D., 2006. The Malliavin Calculus and Related Topics, second edition. Springer Verlag, Berlin, Heidelberg, New York.
Park, H., 2015. Ross recovery with recurrent and transient processes.
Pryce, J.D., 1993. Numerical Solution of Sturm-Liouville Problems. Oxford University Press, Oxford, United Kingdom.
Qin, L., Linetsky, V., 2014. Long term risk: a martingale approach. Mimeo, Northwestern University.
Qin, L., Linetsky, V., 2014. Positive eigenfunctions of Markovian pricing operators: Hansen-Scheinkman factorization and Ross recovery. Mimeo, Northwestern University.
Qin, L., Linetsky, V., Nie, Y., 2016. Long forward probabilities, recovery and the term structure of bond risk premiums. Mimeo, Northwestern University.
Schmitt-Grohé, S., Uribe, M., 2004. Solving dynamic general equilibrium models using a second-order approximation to the policy function. J. Econ. Dyn. Control 28 (4), 755–775.
Sims, C., 1980. Macroeconomics and reality. Econometrica 48 (1), 1–48.
Sims, C.A., 2002. Solving rational expectations models. Comput. Econ. 20 (1–2), 1–20.
Sims, C.A., Zha, T., 2006. Were there regime switches in U.S. monetary policy. Am. Econ. Rev. 96 (1), 54–81.
Slutsky, E., 1927. The summation of random causes as the source of cyclic processes. Probl. Econ. Cond. 3 (1).
Tallarini, T.D., 2000. Risk-sensitive real business cycles. J. Monet. Econ. 45 (3), 507–532. http://EconPapers.repec.org/RePEc:eee:moneco:v:45:y:2000:i:3:p:507-532.
van Binsbergen, J.H., Koijen, R.S.J., 2016. The term structure of returns: facts and theory. J. Financ. Econ. Forthcoming.
van Binsbergen, J.H., Brandt, M.W., Koijen, R.S.J., 2012. On the timing and pricing of dividends. Am. Econ. Rev. 102 (4), 1596–1618.
van Binsbergen, J., Hueskes, W., Koijen, R.S., Vrugt, E.B., 2013. Equity yields. J. Financ. Econ. 110 (3), 503–519.
Walden, J., 2014. Recovery with unbounded diffusion processes.
Whittle, P., 1990. Risk Sensitive and Optimal Control. John Wiley and Sons, West Suffix, England.
Yule, G.U., 1927. On a method of investigating periodicities in disturbed series, with special reference to Wolfer's sunspot numbers. Philos. Trans. R. Soc. 226, 267–298.
Zviadadze, I., 2016. Term structure of consumption risk premia in the cross section of currency returns. J. Financ. Forthcoming.

CHAPTER 21

Quantitative Models of Sovereign Debt Crises

M. Aguiar*, S. Chatterjee†, H. Cole‡, Z. Stangebye§
*Princeton University, Princeton, NJ, United States
†Federal Reserve Bank of Philadelphia, Philadelphia, PA, United States
‡University of Pennsylvania, Philadelphia, PA, United States
§University of Notre Dame, Notre Dame, IN, United States

Contents

Handbook of Macroeconomics, Volume 2B
ISSN 1574-0048, http://dx.doi.org/10.1016/bs.hesmac.2016.04.005

Abstract

This chapter is on quantitative models of sovereign debt crises in emerging economies. We interpret debt crises broadly to cover all of the major problems a country can experience while trying to issue new debt, including default, sharp increases in the spread and failed auctions. We examine the spreads on sovereign debt of 20 emerging market economies since 1993 and document the extent to which fluctuations in spreads are driven by country-specific fundamentals, common latent factors and observed global factors. Our findings motivate quantitative models of debt and default with the following features: (i) trend stationary or stochastic growth, (ii) risk averse competitive lenders, (iii) a strategic repayment/borrowing decision, (iv) multiperiod debt, (v) a default penalty that includes both a reputation loss and a physical output loss, and (vi) rollover defaults. For the quantitative evaluation of the model, we focus on Mexico and carefully discuss the successes and weaknesses of various versions of the model. We close with some thoughts on useful directions for future research.

Keywords

Quantitative models, Emerging markets, Stochastic trend, Capital flows, Rollover crises, Debt sustainability, Risk premia, Default risk

JEL Classification Codes:

D52, F34, E13, G15, H63

1. INTRODUCTION

This chapter is about sovereign debt crises, instances in which a government has trouble selling new debt. An important example is when a government is counting on being able to roll over its existing debt in order to service it over time. When we refer to trouble selling its debt, we include being able to sell new debt but only with a large jump in the spread on that debt over comparable risk-free debt, failed auctions, suspension of payments, creditor haircuts and outright default. So our notion of a debt crisis covers all of the major negative events that one associates with sovereign debt issuance.

We focus on debt crises in developing countries because the literature has focused on them and because these countries provide the bulk of our examples of debt crises and defaults. However, the recent debt crises in the European Union remind us that this is certainly not always the case. While the recent crises in the EU are of obvious interest, they come with a much more complicated strategic dimension, given the role played by the European Central Bank and Germany in determining the outcomes for a country like, say, Greece. For this reason we will hold to a somewhat more narrow focus. Despite this, we see our analysis as providing substantial insight into sovereign debt crises in developed countries as well.

This chapter will highlight quantitative models of the sovereign debt market. We will focus on determining where the current literature stands and where we need to go next. Hence, it will not feature an extensive literature survey, though we will of course survey the literature to some extent, including a brief overview at the end of the chapter. Instead, we will lay out a fairly cutting-edge model of sovereign debt issuance and use that model and its various permutations to gauge the successes and failures of the current literature as we see them.

The chapter will begin by considering the empirical evidence on spreads. We will examine the magnitude and volatility of spreads on sovereign debt among developing countries. We will seek to gauge the extent to which this debt features a risk premium in addition to default risk. We will also seek to characterize the extent to which the observed spread is driven by country-specific fundamentals, global financial risk and uncertainty factors, or other common drivers. To do this, we will estimate a statistical model of the spread process in our data, and this statistical model will feature several common factors that we estimate along with the statistical model. The facts that emerge from this analysis will then form the basis on which we will judge the various models that we consider in the quantitative analysis.

The chapter will then develop a quantitative model of sovereign debt that has the following key features: risk-averse competitive lenders, since it will turn out that risk premia are substantial, and a strategic sovereign who chooses how much to borrow and whether or not to repay, much as in the original Eaton and Gersovitz (1981) model. The sovereign will issue debt that has multiperiod maturity. While we will take the maturity of the debt to be parametric, being able to examine the implications of short and long maturity is an important aspect of the analysis. Default by the sovereign will feature two punishments: a period of exclusion from credit markets and a loss in output during the period of exclusion. Pure reputation effects are known to fail (Bulow and Rogoff, 1989) and even coupling them with a loss of saving as well as borrowing does not generate a sufficient incentive to repay the sorts of large debts that we see in the data. Hence, we include the direct output cost as well.

Our model will feature both fundamental defaults, in which default is taking place under the best possible terms (fixing future behavior). The model will also allow for rollover or liquidity defaults, in which default occurs when lending takes place under the worst possible terms (again, fixing future behavior) as in Cole and Kehoe (2000). We include both types of defaults since they seem to be an important component of the data. Doing so, especially with multiperiod debt maturity, will require some careful modeling of the timing of actions within the period and a careful consideration of both debt issuance and debt buybacks. In addition, the possibility of future rollover crises will affect the pricing of debt today and the incentives to default, much as in the original Calvo (1988) model.

We will consider two different growth processes for our borrowing countries. The first will feature stochastic fluctuations around a deterministic trend with constant growth. The second will feature stochastic growth shocks. We include the deterministic trend process because the literature has focused on it. However, the notion that we have roughly the same uncertainty about where the level of output of a developing country will be in 5 years and in 50 years seems sharply counterfactual, as documented by Aguiar and Gopinath (2007). Hence our preferred specification is the stochastic growth case and, so, we discuss this case as well.

There will be three shocks in the model. The first is a standard output shock that will vary depending on which growth process we assume. The second is a shock to lender wealth. The third is a belief-coordination shock that will determine whether a country gets the best or the worst possible equilibrium price schedule in a period. An important question for us will be the extent to which these shocks can generate movements in the spread that are consistent with the patterns we document in our empirical analysis of the data.

The chapter will examine two different forms of the output default cost. The first is a proportional default cost as has been assumed in the early quantitative analyses and in the theoretical literature on sovereign default. The second form is a nonlinear output cost such as was initially pioneered by Arellano (2008). In this second specification, the share of output lost in default depends positively on (predefault) output. Thus, default becomes a more effective mechanism for risk sharing compared to the proportional cost case. As noted in Chatterjee and Eyigungor (2012), adding this feature also helps to increase the volatility of sovereign spreads.

2. MOTIVATING FACTS

2.1 Data for Emerging Markets

We start with a set of facts that will guide us in developing our model of sovereign debt crises. Our sample spans the period 1993Q4–2014Q4 and includes data from 20 emerging markets: Argentina, Brazil, Bulgaria, Chile, Colombia, Hungary, India, Indonesia, Latvia, Lithuania, Malaysia, Mexico, Peru, Philippines, Poland, Romania, Russia, South Africa, Turkey, and Ukraine. For each of these economies, we have data on GDP in US dollars measured in 2005 domestic prices and exchange rates (real GDP), GDP in US dollars measured in current prices and exchange rates (nominal GDP), gross external debt in US dollars (debt), and market spreads on sovereign debt.[a]

Tables 1 and 2 report summary statistics for the sample.[b] Table 1 documents the high and volatile spreads that characterized emerging market sovereign bonds during this period. The standard deviation of the level and quarterly change in spreads 676 and

[a] Data source for GDP and debt is Haver Analytics' Emerge database. The source of the spread data is JP Morgan's Emerging Market Bond Index (EMBI).

[b] Note that Russia defaulted in 1998 and Argentina in 2001, and while secondary market spreads continued to be recorded post default, these do not shed light on the cost of new borrowing as the governments were shut out of international bond markets until they reached a settlement with creditors. Similarly, the face value of debt is carried throughout the default period for these economies.

Table 1 Sovereign spreads: Summary statistics

Country	Mean $r - r^*$	Std dev $r - r^*$	Std dev $\Delta(r - r^*)$	95th pct $\Delta(r - r^*)$	Frequency crisis
Argentina	1525	1759	610	717	0.18
Brazil	560	393	174	204	0.09
Bulgaria	524	486	129	155	0.03
Chile	146	57	34	34	0.00
Colombia	348	206	88	245	0.05
Hungary	182	154	57	88	0.02
India	225	54	47	85	0.00
Indonesia	285	137	98	73	0.02
Latvia	157	34	16	17	0.00
Lithuania	246	92	48	98	0.00
Malaysia	175	122	75	81	0.03
Mexico	345	253	134	127	0.05
Peru	343	196	84	182	0.06
Philippines	343	153	75	136	0.04
Poland	191	138	54	67	0.01
Romania	271	102	49	68	0.00
Russia	710	1096	478	175	0.06
South Africa	226	116	68	99	0.03
Turkey	395	217	95	205	0.05
Ukraine	760	607	350	577	0.11
Pooled	431	676	229	158	

229 basis points, respectively. Table 2 reports an average external debt-to-(annualized) GDP ratio of 0.46. This level is low relative to the public debt levels observed in developed economies. The fact that emerging markets generate high spreads at relatively low levels of debt-to-GDP reflects one aspect of the "debt intolerance" of these economies documented by Reinhart et al. (2003).

The final column concerns "crises," which we define as a change in spreads that lie in the top 5% of the distribution of quarterly changes. This threshold is a 158 basis-point jump in the spread. By construction, 5% of the changes are coded as crises; however, the frequency of crises is not uniform across countries. Nearly 20% of Argentina's quarter-to-quarter changes in spreads lie above the threshold, while many countries have no such changes.

While many of the countries in our sample have very high spreads, only two—Russia in 1998 and Argentina in 2001—ended up defaulting on their external debt, while a third, Ukraine, defaulted on its internal debt (in 1998). This highlights the fact that periods of high spreads are more frequent events than defaults. Nevertheless, it is noteworthy that the countries with the highest mean spreads are the ones that ended up defaulting during this period. This suggests that default risk and the spread are connected.

Table 2 Sovereign spreads: Summary statistics

Country	Mean $\frac{B}{4*Y}$	Corr $(\Delta(r-r^*),\Delta y)$	Corr $(r-r^*,\%\Delta B)$	Corr $(\Delta(r-r^*),\%\Delta B)$
Argentina	0.38	−0.35	−0.22	0.08
Brazil	0.25	−0.11	−0.18	−0.01
Bulgaria	0.77	0.09	−0.20	0.06
Chile	0.41	−0.16	−0.18	−0.11
Columbia	0.27	−0.29	−0.40	−0.07
Hungary	0.77	−0.24	−0.56	−0.05
India	0.82	−0.32	0.04	−0.65
Indonesia	0.18	−0.43	−0.03	0.07
Latvia	0.49	−0.18	−0.12	−0.16
Lithuania	1.06	−0.25	−0.17	−0.31
Malaysia	0.54	−0.56	−0.33	0.24
Mexico	0.16	−0.4	0.23	−0.13
Peru	0.48	−0.01	−0.39	−0.05
Philippines	0.47	−0.16	0.06	0.09
Poland	0.57	−0.09	−0.35	−0.38
Romania	0.61	0.5	0.42	−0.33
Russia	NA	−0.45	−0.30	0.02
South	0.26	−0.14	−0.38	−0.24
Turkey	0.38	−0.34	−0.20	0.08
Ukraine	0.64	−0.49	−0.60	−0.07
Pooled	0.46	−0.27	−0.19	0.01

2.2 Statistical Spread Model

To further evaluate the empirical behavior of emerging market government bond spreads, we fit a statistical model to our data. In this model a country's spread is allowed to depend on country-specific fundamentals as well as several mutually orthogonal common factors (common across emerging markets) that we will implicitly determine as part of the estimation. To do this, we use EMBI data at a quarterly frequency. We have data for $I=20$ countries from 1993:Q4–2015:Q2 (so $T=87$), with sporadic missing values. If we index a country by i and a quarter by t, then we observe spreads, debt-to-GDP ratios, and real GDP growth: $\{s_{it}, b_{it}, g_{it}\}_{i=1,t=1}^{I,T}$. We also suppose that there are a set of J common factors that impact all the countries (though perhaps not symmetrically): $\{\alpha_t^j\}_{j=1}^{J}$.

We specify our statistical model as follows:

$$s_{it} = \beta_i b_{it} + \gamma_i g_{it} + \sum_{j=1}^{J} \delta_i^j \alpha_t^j + \kappa_i + \epsilon_{it}, \tag{1}$$

where ϵ_{it} is a mean-zero, normally distributed shock with variance σ_i^2. Notice that we allow for the average spread and innovation volatility to vary across countries. In the estimation we impose the constraint that $\delta_i^j \geq 0$ for all i, so we are seeking common factors that cause all spreads to rise and fall together.

These common factors are permitted to evolve as follows. Let α_t be the J-dimensional vector of common factors at time t. Then

$$\alpha_t = \Gamma \alpha_{t-1} + \eta_t \tag{2}$$

where η_t is a J-dimensional vector of normally distributed i.i.d. innovations orthogonal to each other. Because we estimate separate impact coefficients for each common factor, we normalized the innovation volatilities to 0.01. We restrict Γ to be a diagonal matrix, ie, our common factors are assumed to be orthogonal and to follow AR(1) processes.

To estimate this model, we transform it into state-space form and apply MLE. We apply the (unsmoothed) Kalman Filter to compute the likelihood for a given parameterization. When the model encounters missing values, we will exclude those values from the computation of the likelihood and the updating of the Kalman Filter. Thus, missing values will count neither for nor against a given parameterization.

Table 3 reports the explanatory power of the country-specific fundamentals as well as the two global factors. Specifically, we construct a variance decomposition following the algorithm of Lindeman et al. (1980) as outlined by Gromping (2007). This procedure constructs the average marginal R^2 in the case of correlated regressors by assuming a uniform distribution over all possible permutations of the regression coefficients. We can see

Table 3 Country-specific variance decomposition average marginal R^2

Country (i)	b_{it}	g_{it}	α_t^1	α_t^2	R^2	Obs.
Argentina	0.16	0.01	0.20	0.02	0.39	39
Brazil	0.28	0.01	0.52	0.05	0.87	81
Bulgaria	0.18	0.01	0.44	0.27	0.90	59
Chile	0.05	0.13	0.38	0.21	0.77	63
Colombia	0.20	0.05	0.55	0.16	0.95	55
Hungary	0.28	0.19	0.05	0.12	0.64	63
India	0.10	0.26	0.32	0.32	1.00	8
Indonesia	0.09	0.07	0.38	0.45	0.99	43
Latvia	0.03	0.03	0.86	0.08	1.00	9
Lithuania	0.06	0.01	0.67	0.25	0.99	20
Malaysia	0.23	0.11	0.46	0.16	0.96	24
Mexico	0.01	0.23	0.59	0.17	0.99	51
Peru	0.34	0.04	0.52	0.07	0.97	71
Philippines	0.26	0.05	0.50	0.01	0.83	84
Poland	0.06	0.10	0.23	0.32	0.71	42
Romania	0.15	0.03	0.47	0.23	0.87	12
Russia	0.12	0.05	0.21	0.51	0.90	62
South Africa	0.03	0.32	0.25	0.36	0.96	48
Turkey	0.05	0.09	0.77	0.04	0.94	74
Ukraine	0.02	0.26	0.20	0.41	0.89	44

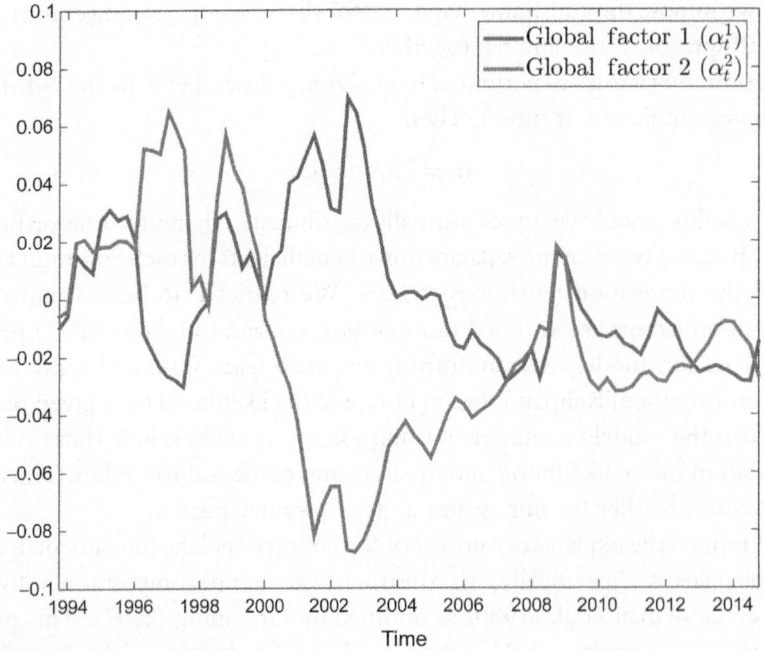

Fig. 1 Estimated common factors.

from this table first that our regressors explain much of the variation for many of the countries (as high as 99.88% for India). We can also see that country-specific fundamentals, here in the form of the debt-to-GDP ratio and the growth rate of output, explain only a modest amount of the variation in the spreads; typically less than 20%. This means that much of the movement in the spreads is explained by our two orthogonal factors.

Fig. 1 plots our two common factors.[c] Given the importance our estimation ascribes to them, we sought to uncover what is really driving their movements. To do this, we use a regression to try to construct our estimated common factors from the CBOE VIX, S&P 500 Diluted Earnings P/E ratio, and the LIBOR.[d] These regressors are standard measures of foreign financial-market uncertainty, price of risk and borrowing costs, respectively. These results are reported in table 4. The top panel reports the results from regressing the level of the factors on the level of foreign financial variables and the bottom reports the comparable regressions in first differences. We find that the foreign financial variables explain a modest amount of the variation in the level of the common factors: Each has an R^2 less than 0.3. To the extent that these objects do explain the common factors, however, it seems as if common factor 1 is driven primarily by measures of investor

[c] See Longstaff et al. (2011) for a related construction of a global risk factor.

[d] The LIBOR is almost perfectly correlated with the fed funds rate, so for precision of estimates we exclude the latter.

Table 4 Common factor regressions: Levels

Index		VIX	P/E ratio	LIBOR	R^2
Levels					
α_t^1	Coefficient	$8.32e-4$ (3.36e−4)	$2.00e-3$ (6.31e−4)	$9.75e-4$ (1.1e−3)	
	Var decomp	0.10	0.17	0.02	0.29
α_t^2	Coefficient	$6.1383e-4$ (5.0460e−4)	−0.0017 (9.4742e−4)	0.0088 (0.0017)	
	Var decomp	−4.0795e−5	−0.0058	0.2722	0.27
First differences					
α_t^1	Coefficient	0.001 (0.002)	−0.001 (0.001)	−0.001 (0.002)	
	Var decomp	0.30	0.06	0.00	0.35
α_t^2	Coefficient	0.001 (<0.001)	0.001 (0.001)	0.002 (0.003)	
	Var decomp	0.05	<0.01	0.01	0.06

uncertainty and the price of risk, while common factor 2 is driven primarily by world interest rates. In first differences, the foreign factors explain a third of the variation in the first factor but very little of the second factor.

There is an additional surprising finding about how risk pricing impacts our spreads. The coefficient on the P/E ratio for the level specification is *positive* in common factor 1, where it has a substantial impact. Since an increase in the price of risk will drive down the P/E ratio, this means that our spreads are rising when the market price of risk is falling. This is the opposite of what our intuition might suggest. This coefficient reverses sign in the first-difference specification, reflecting that the medium run and longer correlation between the P/E ratio and our first factor has the opposite sign of the quarter-to-quarter correlation. The first-difference specification is what has been studied in the literature (Longstaff et al., 2011; Borri and Verdelhan, 2011). These results show that the foreign risk premium may influence spreads differentially on impact vs in the longer run.

2.3 Excess Returns

We turn next to the relationship between spreads and defaults. One of the striking facts here is that spreads "over-predict" future defaults in that ex post returns exceed the return on risk-free assets. Hence, risk premia play an important role.

The fact that spreads are compensating lenders for more than the risk-neutral probability of default is suggested by the statistics reported in Table 1. The average spread is relatively high, and there are significant periods in which spreads are several hundred basis points. However, the sample contains only two defaults: Russia in 1998 and Argentina in 2001.

To explore this more systematically, we compute the realized returns on the EMBI+ index, which represents a value-weighted portfolio of emerging country debt constructed by JP Morgan. In Table 5, we report the return on this portfolio for the full

Table 5 Realized bond returns

Period	EMBI+	2-Year treasury	5-Year treasury
1993Q1–2014Q4	9.7	3.7	4.7
1993Q1–2003Q4	11.1	5.4	6.3
2004Q1–2014Q4	8.2	2.0	3.1

sample period the index is available, as well as two subperiods. The table also reports the returns to the portfolio of US Treasury securities of 2 years and 5 years maturity. We offer two risk-free references, as the EMBI+ does not have a fixed maturity structure and probably ranges between 2 and 5 years.

The EMBI+ index paid a return in excess of the risk-free portfolio of 5 to 6%. This excess return is roughly stable across the two subperiods as well. Whether the realized return reflects the ex ante expected return depends on whether our sample accurately reflects the population distribution of default and repayment. The assumption is that by pooling a portfolio of bonds, the EMBI+ followed over a 20 year period provides a fair indication of the expected return on a typical emerging market bond. Of course, we cannot rule out the possibility that this sample is not representative. Nevertheless, the observed returns are consistent with a fairly substantial risk premium charged to sovereign borrowers.

2.4 Deleveraging

The data from emerging markets can also shed light on debt dynamics during a crisis. Table 2 documents that periods of above-average spreads are associated with reductions in the face value of gross external debt. The pooled correlation of spreads at time t and the percentage change in debt between $t-1$ and t is -0.19. The correlation of the *change* in spread and debt is roughly zero. However, a large change in the spread (that is, a crisis period) is associated with a subsequent decline in debt. In particular, regressing the percent change in debt between t and $t+1$ on the indicator for a crisis in period t generates a coefficient of -1.6 and a t-stat of nearly 3. This relationship is robust to the inclusion of country fixed effects. This implies that a sharp spike in spreads is associated with a subsequent decline in the face value of debt.

2.5 Taking Stock

Our empirical analysis has led us to a set of criteria that we would like our model to satisfy. Specifically:

1. Crises, and particularly defaults, are low probability events;
2. Crises are not tightly connected to poor fundamentals;

3. Spreads are highly volatile;
4. Rising spreads are associated with deleveraging by the sovereign; and
5. Risk premia are an important component of sovereign spreads.

In considering which features of real-world economies are important in generating these patterns, the first thing to recognize is that sovereign debt lacks a direct enforcement mechanism: most countries default despite having the physical capacity to repay. Yet, countries seem perfectly willing to service significant amounts of debt most of the time (rescheduling of debts and outright default are relatively rare events). Without any deadweight costs of default, the level of debt that a sovereign would be willing to repay is constrained by the worst punishment lenders can inflict on the sovereign, namely, permanent exclusion from all forms of future credit. It is well known that this punishment is generally too weak, quantitatively speaking, to sustain much debt (this is spelled out in a numerical example in Aguiar and Gopinath, 2006). Thus, we need to posit substantial deadweight costs of default.

Second, defaults actually occurring in equilibrium reflect the fact that debt contracts are not fully state-contingent, and default provides an implicit form of insurance. However, with rational risk-neutral lenders who break even, on average, for every loan they make to sovereigns, the deadweight cost of default (which does not accrue to lenders) makes default an actuarially unfair form of insurance against bad states of the world for the sovereign. And, with risk-averse lenders, this insurance-through-default becomes even more actuarially unfair. Given fairly substantial deadweight costs of default and substantial risk aversion on the part of lenders, the insurance offered by the possibility of default appears to be quite costly in practice. The fact that countries carry large external debt positions despite the costs suggests that sovereigns are fairly impatient.

However, while myopia can explain in part why sovereigns borrow, it does not necessarily explain why they default. As noted already, default is a very costly form of insurance against bad states of the world. This fact—via equilibrium prices—can be expected to encourage the sovereign to stay away from debt levels for which the probability of default is significant. This has two implications. First, when crises/defaults do materialize, they come as a surprise, which is consistent with these events being low probability. Unfortunately, the other side of this coin is that getting the mean and volatility of spreads right is a challenge for quantitative models. Getting high and variable spreads means getting periods of high default risk as well as substantial variation in expected future default risk. This will be difficult to achieve when the borrower has a strong incentive to adjust his debt-to-output level to the point where the probability of future default is (uniformly) low.

3. ENVIRONMENT

Our environment is a simplified version of the one introduced in ACCS (2016). The analysis focuses on a sovereign government that makes consumption and savings/

borrowing decisions on behalf of the denizens of a small open economy facing a fluctuating endowment stream. The economy is small relative to the rest of the world in the sense that the sovereign's decisions do not affect any world prices, including the world risk-free interest rate. However, the sovereign faces a segmented credit market in that it can only borrow from a set of risk-averse potential lenders with limited wealth. In this section, we proceed by describing the economy of which the sovereign is in charge, the sovereign's decision problem and the lenders' decision problem. We then give the definition of an equilibrium and discuss issues related to equilibrium selection. We conclude the section by briefly describing how we compute the model.

3.1 The Economy

3.1.1 Endowments

Time is discrete and indexed by $t = 0, 1, 2, \ldots$. The economy receives a stochastic endowment $Y_t > 0$ each period. We assume that

$$\ln Y_t = \sum_{s=1}^{t} g_s + z_t, \tag{3}$$

where g_t and z_t follow first-order Markov processes. This specification follows Aguiar and Gopinath (2006, 2007) and nests the endowment processes that have figured in quantitative studies. In particular, setting $g_t = g$ generates a deterministic linear trend. More generally, g_t can be random, which corresponds to the case of a stochastic trend. In either case, z_t is transitory (but potentially persistent) fluctuations around trend growth. In this chapter we will study both specifications in some detail.

3.1.2 Preferences

The economy is run by an infinitely-lived sovereign government. The utility obtained by the sovereign from a sequence of aggregate consumption $\{C_t\}_{t=0}^{\infty}$ is given by:

$$\sum_{t=0}^{\infty} \beta^t u(C_t),\ 0 < \beta < 1 \tag{4}$$

and

$$u(C) = \begin{cases} C^{1-\sigma}/(1-\sigma) & \text{for } \sigma \geq 0 \text{ and } \sigma \neq 1 \\ \ln(C) & \text{for } \sigma = 1 \end{cases} \tag{5}$$

It is customary to assume that the sovereign has enough instruments to implement any feasible consumption sequence as a competitive equilibrium and, thus, abstract from the problem of individual residents of the economy. This does not mean that the government necessarily shares the preferences of its constituents, but rather that it is the relevant decision maker vis-a-vis international financial markets.[e]

3.1.3 Financial Markets and the Option to Default

The sovereign issues noncontingent bonds to a competitive pool of lenders. Bonds pay a coupon every period up to and including the period of maturity, which, without loss of generality, we normalize to r^* per unit of face value, where r^* is the (constant) international risk-free rate. With this normalization, a risk-free bond will have an equilibrium price of one. For tractability, bonds are assumed to mature randomly as in Leland (1994).[f] Specifically, the probability that a bond matures next period is a constant $\lambda \in [0,1]$. The constant hazard of maturity implies that all bonds are symmetric before the realization of maturity at the start of the period, regardless of when they were issued. The expected maturity of a bond is $1/\lambda$ periods and so $\lambda = 0$ is a consol and $\lambda = 1$ is a one-period bond. When each unit of a bond is infinitesimally small and any given unit matures independently of all other units, a fraction λ of any nondegenerate portfolio of bonds will mature with probability 1 in any period. With this setup, a portfolio of sovereign bonds of measure B gives out a payment (absent default) of $(r^* + \lambda)B$ and has a continuation face value of $(1 - \lambda)B$.

We will explore the quantitative implications of different maturities, but in any given economy, bonds with only one specific λ are traded. The stock of bonds at the start of any period—inclusive of bonds that will mature in that period—is denoted B. We do not restrict the sign of B, so the sovereign could be a creditor ($B < 0$) or a debtor ($B > 0$). If $B < 0$, the sovereign's (foreign) assets are assumed to be in risk-free bonds that mature with probability λ and pay interest (coupon) of r^* until maturity. The net issuance of bonds in any period is $B' - (1 - \lambda)B$, where B' is the stock of bonds at the end of the period. If the net issuance is negative, the government is either purchasing its outstanding debt or accumulating foreign assets; if it is positive, it is either issuing new debt or deaccumulating foreign assets.

If the sovereign is a debtor at the start of a period, it is contractually obligated to pay λB in principal and r^*B in interest (coupon) payments. The sovereign has the option to default on this obligation. The act of default immediately triggers exclusion from international financial markets (ie, no saving or borrowing is permitted) starting in the next period. Following the period of mandatory exclusion, exclusion continues with constant probability $(1 - \xi) \in (0,1)$ per period. Starting with the period of mandatory exclusion and continuing for as long as exclusion lasts, the sovereign loses a proportion $\phi(g, z)$ of

[e] In particular, one interpretation of the environment is that C_t represents public spending and Y_t the available revenue that is allocated by the government.

[f] See also Hatchondo and Martinez (2009), Chatterjee and Eyigungor (2012), and Arellano and Ramanarayanan (2012).

(nondefault state) output Y. When exclusion ends, the sovereign's debts are forgiven and it is allowed to access financial markets again.

3.1.4 Timing of Events

The timing of events within a period is depicted in Fig. 2. A sovereign in good standing observes S, the vector of current-period realizations of all exogenous shocks, and decides to auction $B' - (1 - \lambda)B$ units of debt, where B' denotes the face value of debt at the start of the next period. If the sovereign does not default at settlement, it consumes the value of its endowment plus the value of its net issuance (which could be positive or negative) and proceeds to the next period in good standing.

If the sovereign defaults at settlement, it does not receive the auction proceeds and it is excluded from international credit markets. Thus it consumes its endowment and proceeds to the next period in which it is also excluded from borrowing and lending. We assume that the amount raised via auction, if any, is disbursed to all existing bondholders in proportion to the face value of their bond positions, ie, each unit of outstanding bonds is treated equally and receives $q(S,B,B')(B' - (1 - \lambda)B)/B'$. The implication is that as long as $B > 0$ purchasers of newly issued bonds suffer an immediate loss following default. If the sovereign defaults at settlement after purchasing bonds (ie, after a buyback of existing debt), we assume that it defaults on its new payment obligations along with any remaining outstanding debt (this is a simplification relative Aguiar et al., 2016). Thus the sovereign consumes its endowments in this case as well (and moves on to the next period in a state of financial exclusion).

Our timing regarding default deviates from that of Eaton and Gersovitz (1981), which has become the standard in the quantitative literature. In the Eaton–Gersovitz timing, the bond auction occurs after that period's default decision is made. That is, the government is the Stackelberg leader in its default decision in a period. Thus newly auctioned bonds do not face any within-period default risk and, so, the price of bonds depend only on the exogenous states S and the amount of bonds the sovereign exits a period with, B'. Our timing expands the set of equilibria relative to the Eaton–Gersovitz timing, and in

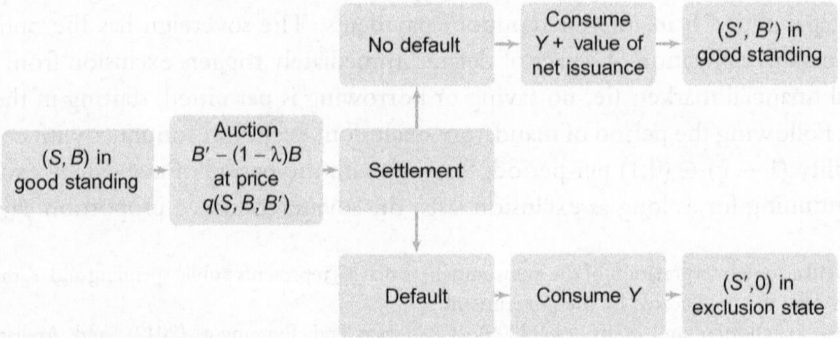

Fig. 2 Timing within a Period.

particular allows a tractable way of introducing self-fulfilling debt crises, as explained in Section 3.5.[g] It is also worth pointing out that implicit in the timing in Fig. 2 is the assumption that there is only one auction per period. While this assumption is standard, it does allow the sovereign to commit to the amount auctioned within a period.[h]

3.2 The Sovereign's Decision Problem

We will state the sovereign's decision problem in recursive form. To begin, the vector $S \in \mathscr{S}$ of exogenous state variables consists of the current endowment Y and current period realizations of the endowment shocks g and z; it also contains W, the current period wealth of the representative lender, as this will affect the supply of foreign credit; and it contains $x \in [0,1]$, a variable that indexes investor beliefs regarding the likelihood of a rollover crisis (explained more in Section 3.5). Both W and x are stochastic and assumed to follow first-order Markov processes. We assume that all conditional expectations of the form $\mathbb{E}_S f(S', \cdot)$ encountered below are well defined.

Let $V(S, B)$ denote the sovereign's optimal value conditional on S and B. Working backwards through a period, at the time of settlement the government has issued $B' - (1 - \lambda)B$ units of new debt at price $q(S,B,B')$ and owes $(r^* + \lambda)B$. If the government honors its obligations at settlement, its payoff is:

$$V^R(S,B,B') = \begin{cases} u(C) + \beta \mathbb{E}_S V(S',B') & \text{if } C \geq 0 \\ -\infty & \text{otherwise} \end{cases}. \tag{6}$$

where

$$C = Y + q(S,B,B')[B' - (1-\lambda)B] - (r^* + \lambda)B. \tag{7}$$

If the sovereign defaults at settlement, its payoff is:

$$V^D(S) = u(Y) + \beta \mathbb{E}_S V^E(S') \tag{8}$$

where

$$V^E(S) = u(Y(1 - \phi(g,z))) + \beta \mathbb{E}_S\left[\xi V(S',0) + (1-\xi) V^E(S')\right] \tag{9}$$

[g] The timing in Fig. 2 is adapted from Aguiar and Amador (2014b), which in turn is a modification of Cole and Kehoe (2000). The same timing is implicit in Chatterjee and Eyigungor's ((2012)) modeling of a Cole–Kehoe type rollover crisis. In both setups, the difference relative to Cole and Kehoe is that the sovereign is not allowed to consume the proceeds of an auction if it defaults. This simplifies the off-equilibrium analysis without materially changing the results. See Auclert and Rognlie (2014) for a discussion of how the Eaton–Gersovitz timing in some standard environments has a unique Markov equilibrium, thus ruling out self-fulfilling crises.

[h] For an exploration of an environment in which the government cannot commit to a single auction, see Lorenzoni and Werning (2014) and Hatchondo and Martinez (undated).

is the sovereign's value when it is excluded from financial markets and incurs the output costs of default. Recall that ξ is the probability of exiting the exclusion state and, when this exit occurs, the sovereign reenters financial markets with no debt. Note also that the amount of new debt implied by B' is not relevant for the default payoff as the government does not receive the auction proceeds if it defaults at settlement.

Finally, the current period value function solves:

$$V(S,B) = \max\left\langle \max_{B' \leq \theta Y} V^R(S,B,B'), V^D(S) \right\rangle, \forall\ S \text{ and } B. \tag{10}$$

The upper bound θY on the choice of B' rules out Ponzi schemes.

Let $\delta(S,B,B')$ denote the policy function for default at settlement conditional on B'. For technical reasons, we allow the sovereign to randomize over default and repayment when it is indifferent, that is, when $V^R(S,B,B') = V^D(S)$. Therefore, $\delta(S,B,B') : \mathcal{S} \times \mathbb{R} \times (-\infty, \theta Y] \rightarrow [0,1]$ is the probability the sovereign defaults at settlement, conditional on (S,B,B'). Let $A(S,B) : \mathcal{S} \times \mathbb{R} \rightarrow (-\infty, \theta Y]$ denote the policy function that solves the inner maximization problem in (10) when there is at least one B' for which C is strictly positive. The policy function of consumption is implied by those for debt and default.

3.3 Lenders

We assume financial markets are segmented and only a subset of foreign investors participates in the sovereign debt market. This assumption allows us to introduce a risk premium on sovereign bonds as well as to explore how shocks to foreign lenders' wealth influence equilibrium outcomes in the economy, all the while treating the world risk-free rate as given. For simplicity, all period t lenders participate in the sovereign bond market for one period and are replaced by a new set of lenders.

We assume there is a unit measure of identical lenders each period. Let W_i be the wealth of an individual lender in the current period (W is the *aggregate* wealth of investors and is included in the state vector S in this capacity). Each lender allocates his wealth across two assets: the risky sovereign bond and an asset that yields the world risk-free rate r^*. Lenders must hold nonnegative amounts of the sovereign bond but can have any position, positive or negative, in the risk-free asset. The lender's utility of next period (terminal) wealth, $\widetilde{W}_i$, is given by

$$k(\widetilde{W}_i) = \begin{cases} \widetilde{W}_i^{1-\gamma}/(1-\gamma) & \text{for } \gamma \geq 0 \text{ and } \gamma \neq 1 \\ \ln(\widetilde{W}_i) & \text{for } \gamma = 1 \end{cases}.$$

Note that $\widetilde{W}_i$ is distinct from the W' that appears in S' (next period's exogenous state vector) as the latter refers to the aggregate wealth of next period's new cohort of lenders.

The one-period return on sovereign bonds depends on the sovereign's default decision within the current period as well as on next period's default decision. Let $\widetilde{D}$ and $\widetilde{D}'$

denote the sovereign's realized default decisions, either 0 (no default) or 1 (default), at settlement during the current and next period, respectively. A lender who invests a fraction (or multiple) μ of his current wealth W_i has random terminal wealth $\widetilde{W}_i$ given by

$$(1-\mu)W_i(1+r^*)+\mu W_i/q(S,B,B')\,[(1-\widetilde{D})(1-\widetilde{D}')]\,[r^*+\lambda+(1-\lambda)q(S',B',B'')], \tag{11}$$

where,

$$\begin{aligned}&\widetilde{D}=1 \text{ with probability } \delta(S,B,B')\\&\widetilde{D}'=1 \text{ with probability } \delta(S',B',A(S',B'))\\&B''=A(S',B').\end{aligned} \tag{12}$$

The wealth evolution equation omits terms that are only relevant off equilibrium; namely, it omits any payments from the settlement fund after a default. These will always be zero in equilibrium.

The representative lender's decision problem is how much sovereign debt to purchase at auction. Specifically:

$$L(W_i,S,B,B')=\max_{\mu\geq 0}\mathbb{E}_S\left[k\left(\widetilde{W}_i\right)\middle|B,B'\right],$$

subject to (11) and the expressions in (12). The solution to the lender's problem implies an optimal $\mu(W_i,S,B,B')$.

The market-clearing condition for sovereign bonds is then

$$\mu(W,S,B,B')\cdot W=q(S,B,B')\cdot B' \text{ for all feasible } B'>0, \tag{13}$$

where W is the aggregate wealth of the (symmetric) lenders. The condition requires that the bond price schedule be consistent with market clearing for any potential $B'>0$ that raises positive revenue. This is a "perfection" requirement that ensures that when the sovereign chooses its policy function $A(S,B)$, its beliefs about the prices it will face for different choices of B' are consistent with the "best response" of lenders. There are no market-clearing conditions for $B'\leq 0$; the sovereign is a small player in the world capital markets and, thus, can save any amount at the world risk-free rate.

Differentiation of the objective function of the lender with respect to μ gives an FOC that implies

$$q(S,B,B')=\frac{\mathbb{E}_S[\widetilde{W}^{-\gamma}(1-\widetilde{D})(1-\widetilde{D}')(r^*+\lambda+(1-\lambda)q(S',A(S',B')))]}{(1+r^*)\mathbb{E}_S[\widetilde{W}^{-\gamma}]} \tag{14}$$

where $\widetilde{W}$ is evaluated at $\mu(W,S,B,B')$.

Eq. (14) encompasses cases that are encountered in existing quantitative studies. As noted already, in the Eaton–Gersovitz timing of events there is no possibility of default at settlement. This means $\delta(S,B,B')=0$ and the pricing of bonds at the end of the current period reflects the possibility of default in future periods only. This means $\delta(S',B',B''(S',B'))$ does not depend on B'', only on (S',B'). Thus, q depends on (S,B') only. If lenders are risk neutral and debt is short term ($\gamma=0$ and $\lambda=1$), $q(S,B,B')$ is simply the probability of repayment on the debt next period; if lenders are risk neutral but debt is long term ($\gamma=0$ and $\lambda>0$)

$$q(S,B,B')=\frac{\mathbb{E}_S(1-D(S',B'))(r^*+\lambda+(1-\lambda)q(S',A(S',B')))]}{(1+r^*)}. \tag{15}$$

3.4 Equilibrium

Definition 1 (Equilibrium) Given a first-order Markov process for S, an *equilibrium* consists of a price schedule $q:\mathscr{S}\times\mathbb{R}\times(-\infty,\theta Y]\rightarrow[0,1]$; sovereign policy functions $A:\mathscr{S}\times\mathbb{R}\rightarrow(-\infty,\theta Y]$ and $\delta:\mathscr{S}\times\mathbb{R}\times(-\infty,\theta Y]\rightarrow[0,1]$; and lender policy function $\mu:\mathbb{R}^+\times\mathscr{S}\times\mathbb{R}\times(-\infty,\theta Y]\rightarrow\mathbb{R}$; such that: (i) $A(S,B)$ and $\delta(S,B,B')$ solve the sovereign's problem from Section 3.2, conditional on $q(S,B,B')$; (ii) $\mu(W,S,B,B')$ solves the representative lender's problem from Section 3.3 conditional on $q(S,B,B')$ and the sovereign's policy functions; and (iii) market clearing: Eq. (13) holds.

3.5 Equilibrium Selection

Because the default decision is made at the time of settlement, the equilibrium of the model features defaults that occur due to lenders' refusal to roll over maturing debt. To see how this can occur, consider the decision problem of a lender who anticipates that the sovereign will default at settlement on new debt issued in the current period, ie, the lender believes $\delta(S,B,B')=1$ for all (feasible) $B'>(1-\lambda)B$. Then, the lender's optimal μ is 0 and the market-clearing condition (13) implies that $q(S,B,B')=0$ for $B'>(1-\lambda)B$. In this situation, the most debt the sovereign could exit the auction with is $(1-\lambda)B$ and consistency with lender beliefs requires that $V^D(S)\geq V^R(S,B,(1-\lambda)B)$.[i] On the other hand, for a given stock of debt and endowment, there may be a positive price schedule that can also be supported in equilibrium. That is, if $q(s,B,\tilde{B})>0$ for some $\tilde{B}>(1-\lambda)B$ (which necessarily implies that lenders do not anticipate default at settlement for $B'=\tilde{B}$) and $V^D(S)<V^R(S,B,\tilde{B})$, the sovereign would prefer issuing new bonds to help pay off maturing debt and thus find it optimal to repay at settlement. Defaults caused by lenders offering the adverse equilibrium price schedule when a more generous price schedule that induces repayment is also an equilibrium price schedule are called *rollover crises*. A default that occurs because there is no price schedule that can induce

[i] If this condition is violated, the sovereign would strictly prefer to honor its obligation even after having acquired some small amount of new debt, contrary to lender beliefs

repayment (because endowments are too low and/or debt is too high) is called a *fundamental default.*

We incorporate rollover crises via the belief shock variable x. We assume that x is uniformly distributed on the unit interval, and we denote values of $x \in [0,\pi)$ as being in the crisis zone and values of $x \in [\pi, 1]$ as being in the noncrisis zone. In the crisis zone, a rollover crisis occurs *if* one can be supported in equilibrium. That is, a crisis occurs with $q(S, B, B') = 0$ for all $B' > (1-\lambda)B$) if $V^R(S,B,(1-\lambda)B) < V^D(S)$ *and* $x(S) \in [0,\pi)$. On the other hand, if a positive price of the debt can be supported in equilibrium, conditional on the sovereign being able to roll over its debt, then this outcome is selected if $x(S) \in [\pi,1]$. If S is such that $V^R(S,B,(1-\lambda)B) \geq V^D(S)$, then no rollover crisis occurs even if $x(S) \in [0,\pi)$. We let π index the likelihood a rollover crisis, if one can be supported in equilibrium.

We end this section with a comment on the incentive to buy back debt in the event of a failed auction, defined as a situation where lenders believe that $\delta(S,B',B) = 1$ for all $B' > (1-\lambda)B$ (either because of a rollover crisis or because of a solvency default). With a failed auction and long-term debt, the government has an incentive to buy back its debt on the secondary market if the price is low enough and then avoid default at settlement. For instance, this incentive will be strong if $q(S,B,B') = 0$ for $B' < (1-\lambda)B$. In this case, the sovereign could purchase its outstanding debt at zero cost and if

$$u(Y + (r^* + \lambda)B) + \beta\mathbb{E}_S V^R(S', B, 0) > u(Y) + \beta\mathbb{E}_S V^E(S'),$$

the sovereign's incentive to default at settlement will be gone. But, then, a lender would be willing to pay the risk-free price for the last piece of debt and outbid the sovereign for it.

To square the sovereign's buyback incentives with equilibrium, we follow Aguiar and Amador (2014b) and assume that in the case of a failed auction, the price of the debt $q(S, B, B')$ for $B' \leq (1-\lambda)B$, is high enough to make the sovereign just indifferent between defaulting on the one hand and, on the other, paying off its maturing debt and buying back $(1-\lambda)B - B'$ of its outstanding debt. Given this indifference, we further assume that the sovereign randomizes between repayment and default following a buyback, with a mixing probability that is set so that current period lenders are willing to hold on to the last unit of debt in the secondary market in the event of a buyback (more details on the construction of the equilibrium price schedule are provided in the computation section).

3.6 Normalization

Since the endowment Y has a trend, the state vector S is unbounded. To make the model stationary for computation we normalize the nonstationary elements of the state vector S by the trend component of Y_t,

$$G_t = \exp\left(\sum_1^t g_s\right). \tag{16}$$

The elements of the normalized state vector s are (g, z, w, x), where w is W/G. Since Y/G is a function of z only and z already appears in S, s contains one less element than S. It will be convenient to use the same notation defined above for functions of S for functions of the normalized state vector s. Normalizing both sides of the budget constraint (7) by G and denoting C/G by c, B/G by b and B'/G by b' yields the normalized budget constraint

$$c = \exp(z) + q(s, b, b')[b' - (1-\lambda)b] - (r^* + \lambda)b. \tag{17}$$

Here we are imposing the restriction that the pricing function is homogeneous of degree 0 in the trend endowment G and, so, denote it by $q(s,b,b')$.[j]

Next, since $u(C) = G^{1-\sigma}u(c)$, we guess $V^R(S,B,B') = G^{1-\sigma}V^R(s,b,b')$ and $V(s,b) = G^{1-\sigma}V(S,B)$. This gives

$$V^R(s, b, b') = u(c) + \beta \mathbb{E}_{s'g'} g'^{1-\sigma} V(s', b'/g'). \tag{18}$$

Analogous guesses for the value functions under default and exclusion yield

$$V^D(s) = u(\exp(z)) + \beta \mathbb{E}_{s'g'} g'^{1-\sigma} V^E(s') \tag{19}$$

and

$$V^E(s) = u(\exp(z)(1 - \phi(g, z))) + \beta \mathbb{E}_{s'g'} g'^{1-\sigma}\left[\xi V(s', 0) + (1-\xi)V^E(s')\right]. \tag{20}$$

So,

$$V(s, b) = \max\left\langle \max_{b' \leq \theta \exp z} V^R(s, b, b'), V^D(s)\right\rangle, \forall \ s \text{ and } b. \tag{21}$$

We denote the sovereign's default decision rule from the stationarized model by $\delta(s,b,b')$ and we denote by $a(s,b)$ the solution to $\max_{b' \leq \theta \exp z} V^R(s, b, b'))$, provided repayment is feasible at (s,b).

Turning to the lender's problem, observe that given constant relative risk aversion, the optimal μ (the fraction devoted to the risky bond) is independent of the investor's wealth. Let $\mu(1,s,b,b')$ be the optimal μ of a lender with unit wealth. The FOC associated with the optimal choice of μ implies a normalized version of (14), namely,

[j] In particular, we are assuming that prices are functions of the ratios of debt and lenders' wealth to trend endowment but not of the level of trend endowment G itself. One could conceivably construct equilibria where this is not the case by allowing lender beliefs to vary with the level of trend endowment, conditional on these ratios. We are ruling out these sorts of equilibria.

$$q(s,b,b') = \frac{\mathbb{E}_s[\tilde{w}^{-\gamma}(1-D)(1-D')(r^* + \lambda + (1-\lambda)q(s',b',a(s',b')))]}{(1+r^*)\mathbb{E}_s[\tilde{w}^{-\gamma}]}, \tag{22}$$

where $\tilde{w}$ is the terminal wealth of the lender with unit wealth evaluated at $\mu(1,s,b,b')$ and the expectation is evaluated using the sovereign's (normalized) decision rules.

The normalized version of the key market-clearing condition is then

$$\mu(1,s,b,b') \cdot w = q(s,b,b') \cdot b' \text{ for all feasible } b' > 0. \tag{23}$$

For a given pricing function $0 \leq q(s,b,b') \leq 1$, standard Contraction Mapping arguments can be invoked to establish the existence of all value functions. For this, it is sufficient to bound b' from below by some $\underline{b} < 0$, ie, impose an upper limit on the sovereign's holdings of foreign assets (in addition to the upper limit on its issuance of debt to rule out Ponzi schemes), and assume that $\beta \mathbb{E} g'^{1-\sigma}|g < 1$ for all $g \in \mathcal{G}$.

3.7 Computation

Computing an equilibrium of this model means finding a price function $q(s,b,b')$ and associated optimal stationary decision rules $\delta(s,b,b')$, $a(s,b)$ and $\mu(1,s,b,b')$ that satisfy the stationary market-clearing condition (23). That is, it means finding a collection of functions that satisfy

$$\mu(1,s,b,b') \cdot w = \left[\frac{\mathbb{E}_s[\tilde{w}^{-\gamma}(1-\tilde{D})(1-\tilde{D}')(r + \lambda + (1-\lambda)q(s',b',a(s',b')))]}{(1+r^*)\mathbb{E}_s[\tilde{w}^{-\gamma}]}\right] b' \;\forall\, s,\, b \text{ and } b'. \tag{24}$$

If such a collection can be found, an equilibrium in the sense of Definition 1 will exist in which all the nonstationary decision rules are scaled versions of the stationary decision rules, ie, $A(S,B) = a(s,b)G$, $\delta(S,B,B') = \delta(s,b,b')$ and $\mu(W,S,B,B') = \mu(1,s,b,b')wG$.

On the face of it, this computational task seems daunting given the large state and control space. It turns out, however, that (24) can be solved by constructing the solution out of the solution of a computationally simpler model. This simpler model adheres to the Eaton–Gersovitz timing, so $\delta(s,b,b') = 0$, and thus q is a function of s and b' only. But, unlike the standard Eaton–Gersovitz model, it is modified to have rollover crises.[k] The modification is as follows: If s is such that the belief shock variable $x(s)$ is in $(\pi,1]$ (ie, it is not in the crisis zone), the sovereign is offered $q(s,b')$ where b' can be any feasible choice of debt (think of this as the price schedule in "normal times"). But if $x(s)$ is in $[0,\pi]$, the sovereign is offered a truncated *crisis* price schedule in which $q(s,b') = 0$ for all $b' > (1-\lambda)b$ provided default strictly dominates repayment under the crisis price schedule;

[k] This model is described in section E of Chatterjee and Eyigungor (2012).

if the proviso is not satisfied, the sovereign is offered the normal (nontruncated) price schedule.

To see how this construction works, let $q(s,b')$ be the equilibrium price function of this rollover-modified EG model. That is, $q(s,b')$ satisfies

$$\mu(1,s,b')\cdot w = \left[\frac{\mathbb{E}_s[\widetilde{w}^{-\gamma}(1-D(s',b'))(r+\lambda+(1-\lambda)q(s',a(s',b')))]}{(1+r)\mathbb{E}_s[\widetilde{w}^{-\gamma}]}\right]b' \tag{25}$$

where $D(s,b)$ and $a(s,b)$ are the associated equilibrium policy functions. And let $V(s,b)$ and $V^D(s)$ be the associated value functions. Next, let $G(Q;s,b,b')$ be defined as the utility gap between repayment and default at settlement when the auction price is Q:

$$u[\exp(z(s)) - (r^* + \lambda)b + Q(b' - (1-\lambda)b)] + \beta \mathbb{E}_s g'^{1-\sigma} V(s', b'/g') - V^D(s).$$

G encapsulates the incentive to default or repay at settlement in a model in which default at settlement is not permitted. The logic underlying the construction of the price schedule for the model in which default at settlement *is* permitted is this: If $G(s,b,b')$ evaluated at $Q = q(s,b')$ is nonnegative, $q(s,b,b')$ is set equal to $q(s,b')$, as there is no incentive to default at settlement; if $G(s,b,b')$ evaluated at $Q = q(s,b')$ is negative, $q(s,b,b')$ is set to 0 if the incentive to default is maintained at an auction price of zero, or it is set to some positive value between 0 and $q(s,b')$ for which the sovereign is indifferent between default and repayment.

1. For $b' \geq (1-\lambda)b$

$$q(s,b,b') = \begin{cases} 0 \text{ if } G(q(s,b');\, s,b,b') < 0 \\ q(s,b') \text{ if } G(q(s,b');\, s,b,b') \geq 0. \end{cases}$$

The top branch deals with the case where the sovereign's incentive to default at settlement is strictly positive after having issued debt at price $q(s,b')$. Since G is (weakly) increasing in Q in this case, the incentive to default at settlement is maintained at $Q = 0$ and, so, we set $q(s,b,b') = 0$. The bottom branch deals with the case where the sovereign (weakly) prefers repayment over default. In this case, the price is unchanged at $q(s,b')$.

2. For $b' < (1-\lambda)b$:

$$q(s,b,b') = \begin{cases} 0 \text{ if } G(0;\, s,b,b') < 0 \\ Q(s,b,b') \text{ if } Q \in [0, q(s,b')) \\ q(s,b') \text{ if } G(q(s,b');\, s,b,b') \geq 0. \end{cases}$$

The bottom branch offers $q(s,b')$ if $G(q(y,b');s,b,b') \geq 0$. If $G(q(y,b');s,b,b') < 0$, then two cases arise. Since G is weakly decreasing in Q, it is possible that there is a $Q \in [0, q(s,b'))$ for which the $G(Q;s,b,b') = 0$. In this case, we set $q(s,b,b') = Q$. If there is no such Q, then $G(0;s,b,b') < 0$ and we set $q(s,b,b') = 0$.

Next, we verify that given $V(s,b)$ and $V^D(s)$ (the value functions under $q(s,b)$), the optimal action under $q(s,b)$ is also an optimal action under $q(s,b,b')$. First, consider (s,b) for which the optimal action is to choose $a(s,b)$. This implies that $G(q(s,b);s,b,a(b,s)) \geq 0$. Then, by construction, $q(s,b,b') = q(s,b)$ and the payoff from choosing $a(s,b)$ is the same as under $q(s,b)$ and this payoff will (weakly) dominate the payoff from choosing any other b' for which $q(s,b,b') = q(s,b')$ (by optimality). Furthermore, the payoff from any b' for which $q(s,b,b') \neq q(s,b)$ is never better than default. It follows that $a(s,b)$ (coupled with $\delta(s,b,a(s,b)) = 0$) is an optimal choice under $q(s,b,b')$. Next, consider (s,b) for which it is optimal to default under $q(s,b)$. This implies $G(q(s,b);s,b,b') < 0$ for all feasible b'. Then, by construction, default at settlement is the best option, or one of the best for all b' under $q(s,b,b')$.

Finally, we have to verify that $q(s,b,b')$ is consistent with market clearing. For (s,b,b') such that $q(s,b,b') = q(s,b)$, market clearing is ensured because the market clears (by assumption) under $q(s,b)$. For (s,b,b') such that $q(s,b,b') = 0$, market clearing is ensured trivially. For (s,b,b') such that $q(s,b,b') \in (0,q(s,b))$, market clearing can be ensured by selecting $\delta(s,b,b')$ appropriately. For instance, if lenders are risk-neutral, $\delta(s,b,b')$ is set to satisfy $q(s,b,b') = [1 - \delta(s,b,b')]q(s,b')$. Then, with probability $\delta(s,b,b')$ the sovereign defaults and the bonds are worthless, and with probability $1 - \delta(s,b,b')$, the sovereign repays and the bonds are worth $q(s,b')$. With risk-averse lenders, $\delta(s,b,b')$ can be similarly set to make lenders willing to lend b' at $q(s,b,b')$.[1]

We conclude the description of the construction of $q(s,b,b')$ by noting how it modifies the rollover price schedule under $q(s,b')$. Under $q(s,b')$, a rollover crisis is a price schedule with (a) $x(s) \in [0,\pi]$, (b) for $b \geq ((1 - \lambda)b$, $q(s,b') = 0$, and (c) $D(s,b) = 1$. Under $q(s,b,b')$, a rollover has (a) $x(s) \in [0,\pi]$, (b) for $b' \geq (1 - \lambda)b$, $q(s,b,b') = 0$ (which, in this case, is also $q(s,b')$) and (c) for $b' < (1 - \lambda)b$, $q(s,b,b')$ is given by the construction under (ii). Thus, the only modification to the crisis price schedule is to raise the prices associated with buybacks (as discussed earlier in Section 3.5).

In the rest of this section, we describe the iterative process by which the (stationary) equilibrium of the rollover-modified EG model is computed. First, the space of feasible b' is discretized. Second, the space of x (the belief shock variable) is also discretized with "crisis" equal to a value of 1, taken with probability π, and "normal" equal to a value of 0, taken with probability $(1 - \pi)$. Suppose that $\{q^k(s,b')\}$ is the price schedule at the start of iteration k. Let $a(s,b;q^k), D(s,b;q^k)\}$ be the sovereign's decision rules conditional

[1] If $\delta(s,b,b') = 0$ lenders would be just willing to lend b' at the price $q(s,b')$ (because they are willing to do so under $q(s,b')$). If the probability of default at settlement is kept at zero and the price of the bond is lowered to $q(s,b,b')$, there will be an excess demand for bonds. This excess demand can be choked off by lowering $\delta(s,b,b')$ sufficiently.

on $q^k(s,b')$. Then, for every feasible $b' > 0$ for which $q^k(s,b')b' > 0$, the price implied by the lender's optimal choice of μ and market clearing is

$$J^k(s,b')) = \frac{\mathbb{E}_s[\widetilde{w}^{-\gamma}(1 - D(s',b';q^k))(r + \lambda + (1-\lambda)q^k(s',a(s',b';q^k)))]}{(1+r^*)\mathbb{E}_s[\widetilde{w}^{-\gamma}]}, \quad (26)$$

where, using (23), the $\mu(1,s,b';q^k)$ that appears in $\widetilde{w}$ is replaced by $[q^k(s,b) \cdot b']/w(s)$. If $|\max J^k(s,b') - q^k(s,b')|$ is less than some chosen tolerance $\epsilon > 0$, the iteration is stopped and the collection $\{q^k(s,b'),a(s,b;q^k),D(s,b;q^k),\mu(1,s,b';q^k)\}$ is accepted as an approximation of the equilibrium. If not, the price schedule is updated to

$$q^{k+1}(s,b') = \xi q^k(s,b') + (1-\xi)J^k(s,b'), \quad (27)$$

where $\xi \in (0,1)$ is a damping parameter (generally close to 1).

In a purely discrete model in which all shocks and all choices belong to discrete sets, the iterative procedure described above typically fails to converge for a wide choice of parameter values. The reason is that the equilibrium we are seeking is, in effect, a Nash equilibrium of a game between the sovereign and its lenders and we should not expect the existence of an equilibrium in *pure* strategies, necessarily. To remedy the lack of convergence, it is necessary to let the sovereign randomize appropriately between two actions that give virtually the same payoff. The purpose of the continuous i.i.d. shocks (z in the SG model and m in the DG model) is to provide this mixing. We refer the reader to Chatterjee and Eyigungor (2012) for a discussion of how continuous i.i.d. shocks allow robust computation of default models.

4. BENCHMARK MODELS

We calibrate two versions of the basic model under the assumption that rollover crises never happen. In one version, labeled DG, the endowment process of the sovereign and the wealth process of investors are modeled as independent stationary fluctuations around a common deterministic growth path. In the second version, labeled SG, the growth rates of endowments and investor wealth follow independent stationary processes with a common mean growth.

To calibrate the endowment process we use quarterly real GDP data for Mexico for the period 1980Q1–2015Q2. For the DG model, $G_t = (1+g)^t$ and log income is a stationary process plus a linear trend. The stationary component, z_t, is assumed to be composed of two parts: a persistent part e_t that follows an AR1 process and a purely transitory part m_t:

$$z_t = e_t + m_t, \quad m_t \sim N(0,\sigma_m^2) \text{ and } e_t = \rho_e e_{t-1} + v_t \quad v_t \sim N(0,\sigma_v^2) \quad (28)$$

As explained at the end of the previous section, the transitory shock m_t is required for robust computation of the equilibrium bond price function. We set $\sigma_m^2 = 0.000025$

and estimate (28) using standard state-space methods. The estimation gives $\rho_e = 0.85$ (0.045) and $\sigma_v^2 = 0.000139$ ($1.08e-05$) (standard errors in parenthesis). The slope of the trend line implies a long-run quarterly growth rate of 0.56% (or annual growth rate of 2.42%).

For the SG model, the growth rate g_t is stochastic. Now, $\ln(Y_t) = \sum_0^t g_t + z_t$ and the growth rate of the period t endowment, $\ln(Y_t) - \ln(Y_{t-1}) \equiv \Delta y = g_t + z_t - z_{t-1}$. We assume

$$g_t = \alpha + \rho_g g_{t-1} + v_t, \quad v_t \sim N(0, \sigma_v^2) \text{ and } z_t \sim N(0, \sigma_z^2) \tag{29}$$

and use the observed growth rate of real GDP to estimate (29) using state-space methods. The estimation yields $\alpha = 0.0034$ (0.0012), $\rho_g = 0.45$ (0.12), $\sigma_v^2 = 0.000119$ (0.0000281) and $\sigma_z^2 = 0.000011$ ($8.12e-06$). The estimates of α and ρ_g imply an average growth rate of 2.45% at an annual rate. These estimates are summarized in Table 6

Regarding $\phi(g,z)$, which determines the level of output under exclusion from credit markets, we assume

$$\text{for DG}: \phi(g,z) = d_0 \exp(z)^{d_1} \text{ and for SG}: \phi(g,z) = d_0 \exp(g)^{d_1}. \tag{30}$$

In either model, setting $d_1 = 0$ leads to default costs that are proportional to output. If $d_1 > 0$, then default costs rise more than proportionately with z in the DG model, and more than proportionately with g in the SG model.

We assume that g takes values in a finite set $\mathcal{G}$. In the deterministic growth case $\mathcal{G}$ is a singleton. The specification of z depends on what is being assumed for g. When g is stochastic, z is drawn from a distribution H with compact support $[-\bar{h}, \bar{h}]$ and continuous CDF. When g is deterministic, $z = e + m$, where e follows a first-order Markov process with values in a finite set $\mathcal{E}$ and m is drawn from H. In either case, z is first-order Markov in its own right (in the stochastic g case, trivially so) but it is *not* finite-state.

Aside from the parameters of the endowment process, there are 12 parameters that need to be selected. The model has 3 preference parameters, namely, β (the sovereign's discount factor), σ (the curvature parameter of the sovereign's utility function) and γ (the curvature parameter of the investors utility function). It has 2 parameters with respect to

Table 6 Parameters of endowment processes

Parameter	Description	DG	SG
–	Average annual growth rate of endowments	2.42	2.45
ρ_e	Autocorrelation of y	0.85	–
σ_v	Standard deviation of innovations to e or g	0.012	0.011
σ_m	Standard deviation of m	0.005	–
ρ_g	Autocorrelation of g	–	0.45
σ_z	Standard deviation of z	–	0.003

the bond market, namely, λ (the probability with which a bond matures), and r_f (the risk-free rate of return available to investors). It has 3 parameters with respect to the default state, namely, d_0 and d_1, the parameters of the $\phi(g,z)$ function, and ξ, the probability of reentry into credit markets from the exclusion state. Finally, there are 3 parameters governing the stochastic evolution of investor wealth w_t. For the DG version, w_t is defined as $\ln\left(W_t/\omega(1+g)^t\right)$ and for the SG version as $\ln(W_t/\omega Y_t)$, where ω controls the average wealth of investors relative to the sovereign. In either case w_t follows an AR1 process with persistence parameter ρ_w and unconditional variance σ_w^2.

Turning first to preference parameters, σ is set to 2, which is a standard value in the literature. The curvature parameter of the investor's utility function, γ, affects the compensation required by investors for default risk (risk premium). However, for any γ, the risk premium also depends on ω, as this determines the fraction of investor wealth that must reside in sovereign bonds in equilibrium. Thus, we can fix γ and vary ω to control the risk premium. With this in mind, γ was also set equal to 2.

With regard to the bond market parameters, we set the (quarterly) risk-free rate to 0.01. This value is roughly the average yield on a 3-month US Treasury bill over the period 1983–2015.[m]. The probability of a bond maturing, λ, is set to $1/8 = 0.125$ which implies that bonds mature in 2 years, on average. This is roughly consistent with the data reported in Broner et al. (2013) which show that the average maturity of bonds issued by Mexico during the Brady bonds era prior to the Tequila crisis (1993–95) was 2.5 years (postcrisis, the average maturity lengthened substantially).

The exclusion state parameters, d_0, d_1 and ξ, affect the value of the default option. The value of ξ was set to 0.125, which implies an average exclusion period of 2 years, on average. Settlements following default have generally been quick in the Brady era, so a relatively short period of exclusion seems appropriate.

Finally, we use the US P/E ratio as a proxy for investor wealth. We set the autocorrelation of the investor wealth process to 0.91, which is the autocorrelation of the P/E ratio at a quarterly frequency for the period 1993Q1–2015Q2. We assume that w takes values in a finite set $\mathcal{W}$ and its (first-order) Markov process has an unconditional mean $\omega > 0$, where ω determines the relative wealth of investors via-a-vis the sovereign.

These parameter choices are summarized in Table 7.

The remaining five parameters (β, d_0, d_1, ω, σ_w^2) are jointly determined to match moments in the data. The moments chosen are the average debt-to-GDP ratio for Mexico, the average EMBI spreads on Mexican sovereign debt, the standard deviation of the spread, the fraction of variation in Mexican spreads accounted for by the variation in investor wealth proxied by the variation in the US P/E ratio, and an annualized default frequency of 2%.[n]

[m] We use constant maturity yield computed by the Treasury and this data series begins in 1983Q3.

[n] If we date the beginning of private capital flows into emerging markets in the postwar era as the mid-1960s, Mexico has defaulted once in 50 years.

Table 7 Other parameters selected independently

Parameter	Description	Value
σ	Risk aversion of sovereign	2.000
γ	Risk aversion of investors	2.000
r_f	Risk-free rate	0.010
λ	Reciprocal of average maturity	0.125
ξ	Probability of exiting exclusion	0.125
ρ_w	Autocorrelation of wealth process	0.910

Table 8 Targets and model moments with proportional default costs

Description	Target	DG	SG
Debt-to-annual GDP	0.66	0.66	0.66
Average default freq	0.02	0.003	0.02
Average EMBI spread	0.03	0.001	0.03
R^2 of spreads on P/E	0.22	0.20	0.27

We do the moment matching exercise in two steps. First, we set the curvature parameter for default costs, d_1, to 0 so that default costs are simply proportional to output and we drop the standard deviation of spreads as a target. The results are shown in Table 8. The finding is that the SG model can be calibrated to the data quite well but the DG model could not. The DG model could get the debt-to-GDP ratio and the R^2 of the spreads on P/E regression, but the average spread and the average default frequency are an order of magnitude below their targets. These results echo those in Aguiar and Gopinath (2006).

Given the poor quantitative performance of the DG model with proportional costs, the rest of this chapter focuses on models with asymmetric default costs. We return to the proportional default cost and discuss its shortcomings in the next section after presenting our benchmark results.

5. BENCHMARK RESULTS WITH NONLINEAR DEFAULT COSTS

Table 9 reports the results of the moment matching exercise when all five parameters are chosen to match the four targets above and the standard deviation of spreads. As is evident, the performance of the DG model improves substantially and it can now deliver the target level of average spreads and default frequency.

A surprising finding is that neither model can match the observed spread volatility, which is an order of magnitude larger in the data than in the models. The finding is surprising because asymmetric default cost models have been successful in matching the volatility of spreads on Argentine sovereign bonds (the case that is most studied in the

Table 9 Targets and model moments with asymmetric default costs

Description	Target	DG	SG
Debt-to-annual GDP	0.66	0.66	0.66
Average default freq	0.02	0.02	0.02
Average EMBI spread	0.03	0.03	0.03
R^2 of spreads on P/E	0.22	0.23	0.26
SD of EMBI spread	0.03	0.005	0.002

Table 10 Parameters selected jointly

Parameter	Description	DG	SG
β	Sovereign's discount factor	0.892	0.842
d_0	Level parameter for default costs	0.075	0.068
d_1	Curvature parameter for default costs	10.0	10.0
ω	Wealth of investors relative to mean endowment	2.528	2.728
σ_w	SD of innovations to wealth	2.75	0.275

quantitative default literature). As explained later in the paper, the reason for the models' inability to match spread volatility is that neither z nor g is sufficiently volatile for Mexico (compared to Argentina) for the asymmetry in default costs to matter. Given this, the curvature parameter for default costs cannot be pinned down and we simply set it to a relatively large value and chose the remaining four parameters to match the other four targets.

The parameter values implied by this moment matching is reported in Table 10.

5.1 Equilibrium Price and Policy Functions

In this section we characterize the equilibrium bond price schedules and policy functions for debt issuance. We discuss the benchmark stochastic-growth (SG) and deterministic-growth (DG) versions of the model.

The price schedules and policy functions for our two growth cases are depicted in Fig. 3. As one can see from the first panel of the figure, the price schedules for the two different growth processes are quite similar. In both cases the price schedules are highly nonlinear, reflecting the positive feedback between the value of market access and q: the option to default lowers q for any B'/Y, which, in turn, lowers the value of market access and further increases the set of states in which default is optimal. Careful inspection will show that the DG schedule responds slightly less to an increase in debt right at the bend point.

The government's policy functions for debt issuance are depicted in the second panel of Fig. 3. These two functions exhibit an important difference. The striking fact about the

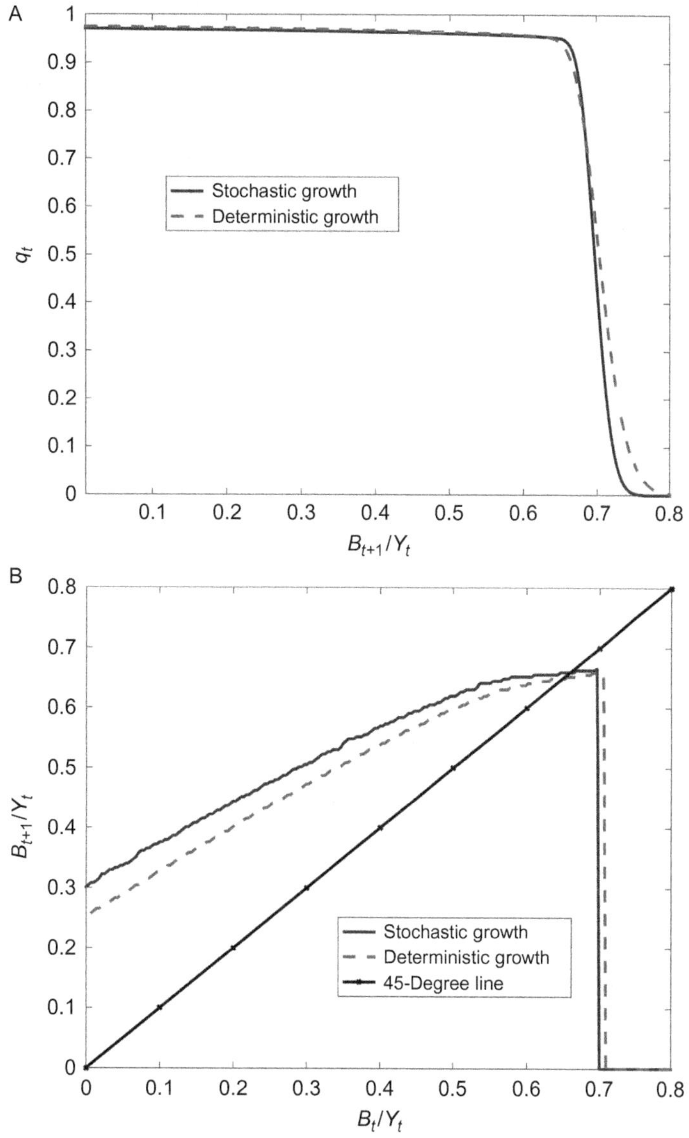

Fig. 3 Pricing schedules and policy functions. (A) Pricing schedules. (B) Policy functions.

SG debt policy functions is that it is quite flat around the 45-degree line: This implies that the optimal policy features sharp leveraging and deleveraging that offsets the impact of good and bad growth shocks, respectively, and returns B'/Y to the neighborhood of the crossing point quite rapidly. Notice also that the crossing point is not very far from the levels of debt for which default is triggered. This "distance to default," and therefore the equilibrium spreads, are essentially determined by the output costs of default.

In contrast, the policy function for debt issuance for the DG economy depicts a significantly more modest leveraging and deleveraging response to deviations in the debt-to-output ratio around the 45-degree line. As we will see below, this will lead to sharp differences in the predicted outcomes of the two versions of our model.

We turn next to trying to understand how our model will respond to shocks. To do that we examine how our bond demand schedule responds to output and wealth shocks. These are plotted in Figs. 4 and 5, respectively. With respect to output shocks, we see a

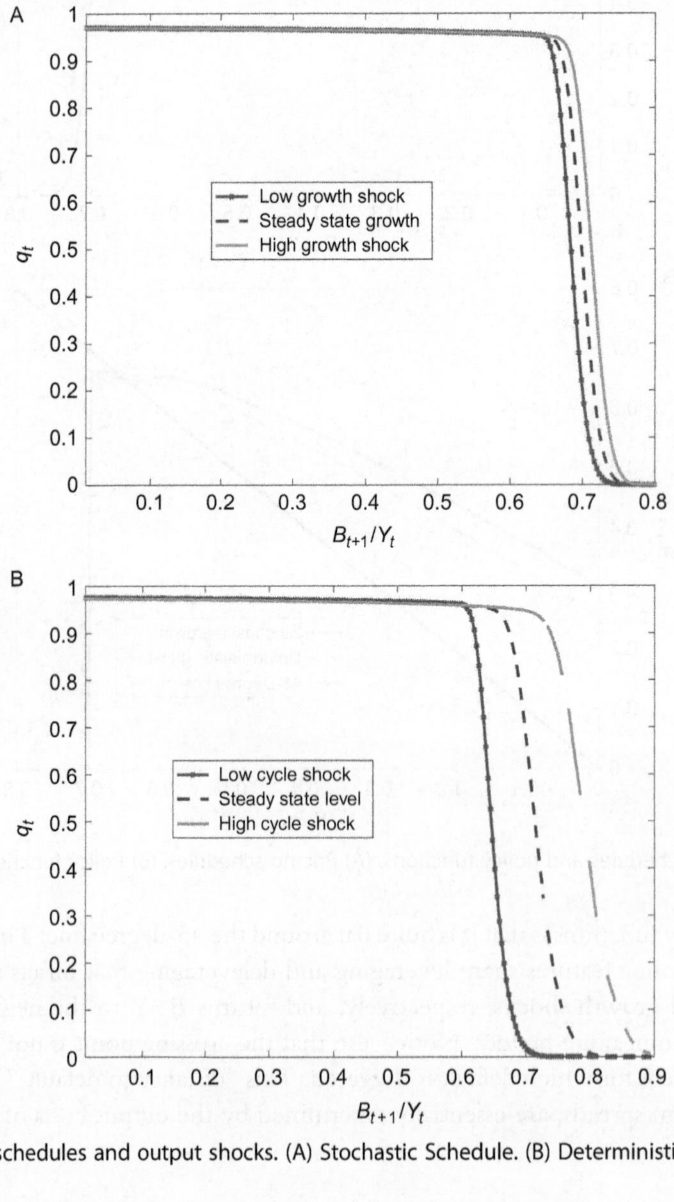

Fig. 4 Pricing schedules and output shocks. (A) Stochastic Schedule. (B) Deterministic Schedule.

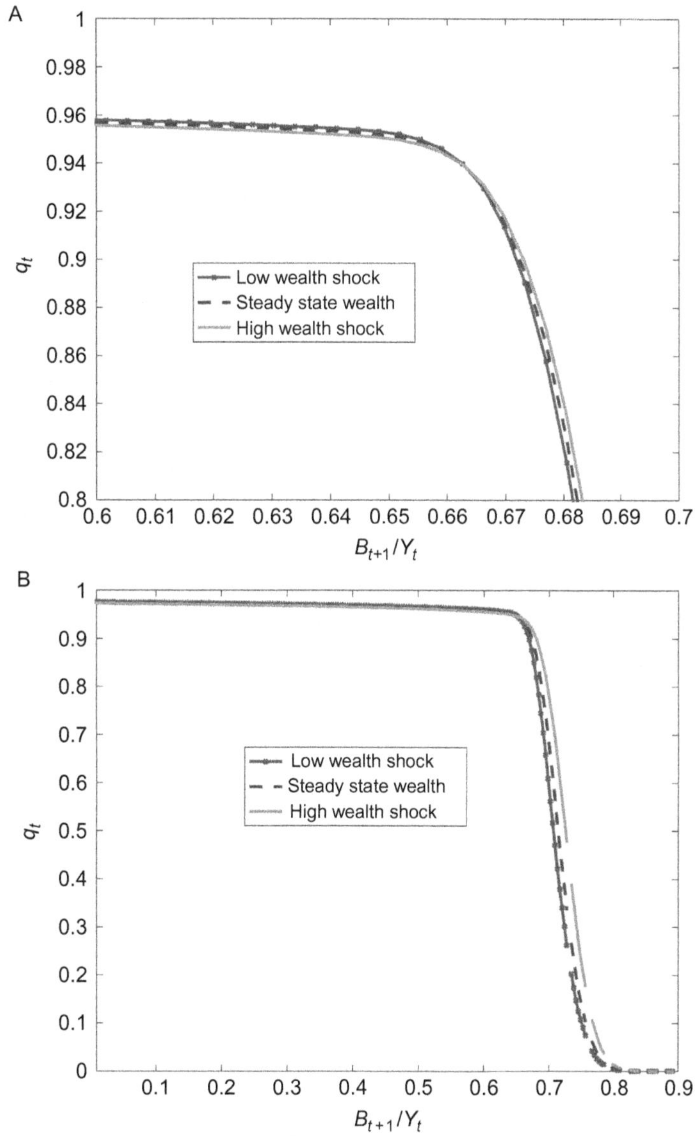

Fig. 5 Pricing schedules and wealth shocks. (A) Stochastic schedule. (B) Deterministic schedule.

fairly stark difference between our two models. Growth shocks have very little impact on the bond demand schedule in the SG model. But shocks that move output away from its deterministic trend have a fairly large effect in the DG version. This suggests that the stochastic growth version of our model will be much less responsive to output shocks than the deterministic growth version.

The reason for the difference in the response to output shocks between our two models stems from the interaction of two factors. First, when output is substantially below trend in the DG model, the agents in the economy anticipate that a recovery to trend is highly likely, making the future level of output look positive relative to the present. At the same time, our assumption of asymmetric default costs means that defaulting when output is below trend is less costly than defaulting when output has recovered to trend. Overall this creates a stronger incentive to default in the near term for given levels of B/Y and B', and this shifts in (out) the pricing schedule in response to a negative (positive) output shock. The shift in the price schedule offsets the country's desire for smoothing, but, at the same time, generates movement in the spread. Below we compare this to proportional default cost case and show that the shifts result mostly from the asymmetric default cost.

In contrast, negative growth shocks in the stochastic growth model make the expectation of future growth lower because these growth shocks are positively autocorrelated. Thus nonlinear output costs makes delaying default more attractive. In addition, the negative trajectory of output encourages the country to save, not borrow. The first effect dampens the shift in the price schedule, while the second effect dampens the incentive to borrow. Together this means that there is little or no increase in the spread today. As we will see, these differences will lead to differences in equilibrium outcomes such as the dispersion in debt-to-output levels and spreads.

Both models are quite unresponsive to wealth shocks. Interestingly, a wealth shock tends to twist the price schedule. For example, a positive wealth shock pushes out the price for high borrowing levels and but pulls it down for low borrowing levels. This last part arises from the increased incentive to dilute the current bonds in the future since the "price" of such dilution is not as high. We graphed the SG schedule on a magnified scale in order to make this twisting more apparent. This mechanism is explored in detail in Aguiar et al. (2016).

In the deterministic case, we see relatively large movements in the pricing schedule with shocks. In Fig. 6 we plot the pricing schedules for the proportional default cost case. In the DG model the price schedule does not respond to the output shock. This is because the expected positive trajectory of output makes the current debt-to-output ratio less onerous, while the proportionate default costs do not generate as strong an incentive to default today relative to the nonlinear case. Hence, the incentive to default is fairly stable and the price schedule does not shift in. At the same time, the feedback effect in the DG model with proportionate costs is so strong that the price schedule completely collapses past a certain B/Y ratio. This leads the country to stay sufficiently far inside of the collapse point that the probability of default tomorrow is virtually zero. In particular, it is very hard to generate a modest default probability and spread premium given this extreme pricing schedule. This is why this model is so hard to calibrate and why we get no volatility in the spread.

5.2 Boom-and-Bust Response

The sharp difference between our models comes from their responses to output shocks. To further understand the response of our models to growth rate shocks, we consider

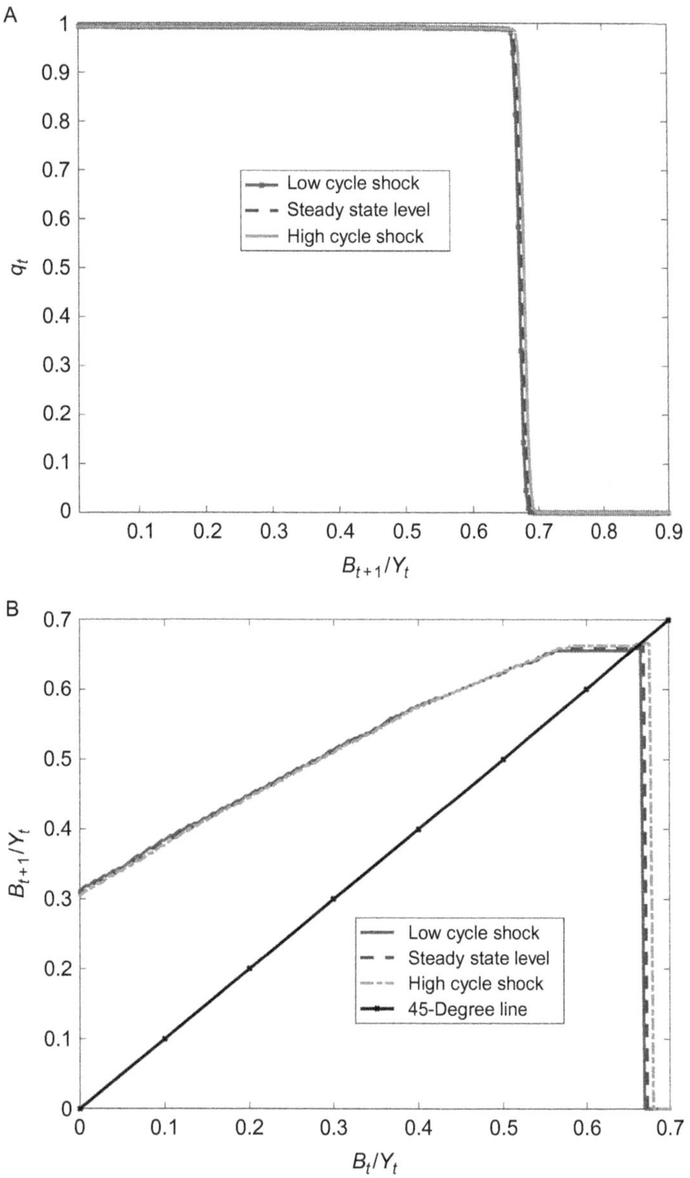

Fig. 6 DG model pricing schedule and policy function with proportionate costs. (A) Price schedule. (B) Policy function.

what happens after a sequence of positive shocks terminates in an negative shock. We refer to this as a boom-and-bust cycle.

In Fig. 7 we show the policy response to a series of positive output shocks of varying length, followed by a bad output shock. We also show the impact on the equilibrium spread. In both cases, the fairly high degree of persistence in our output shocks leads

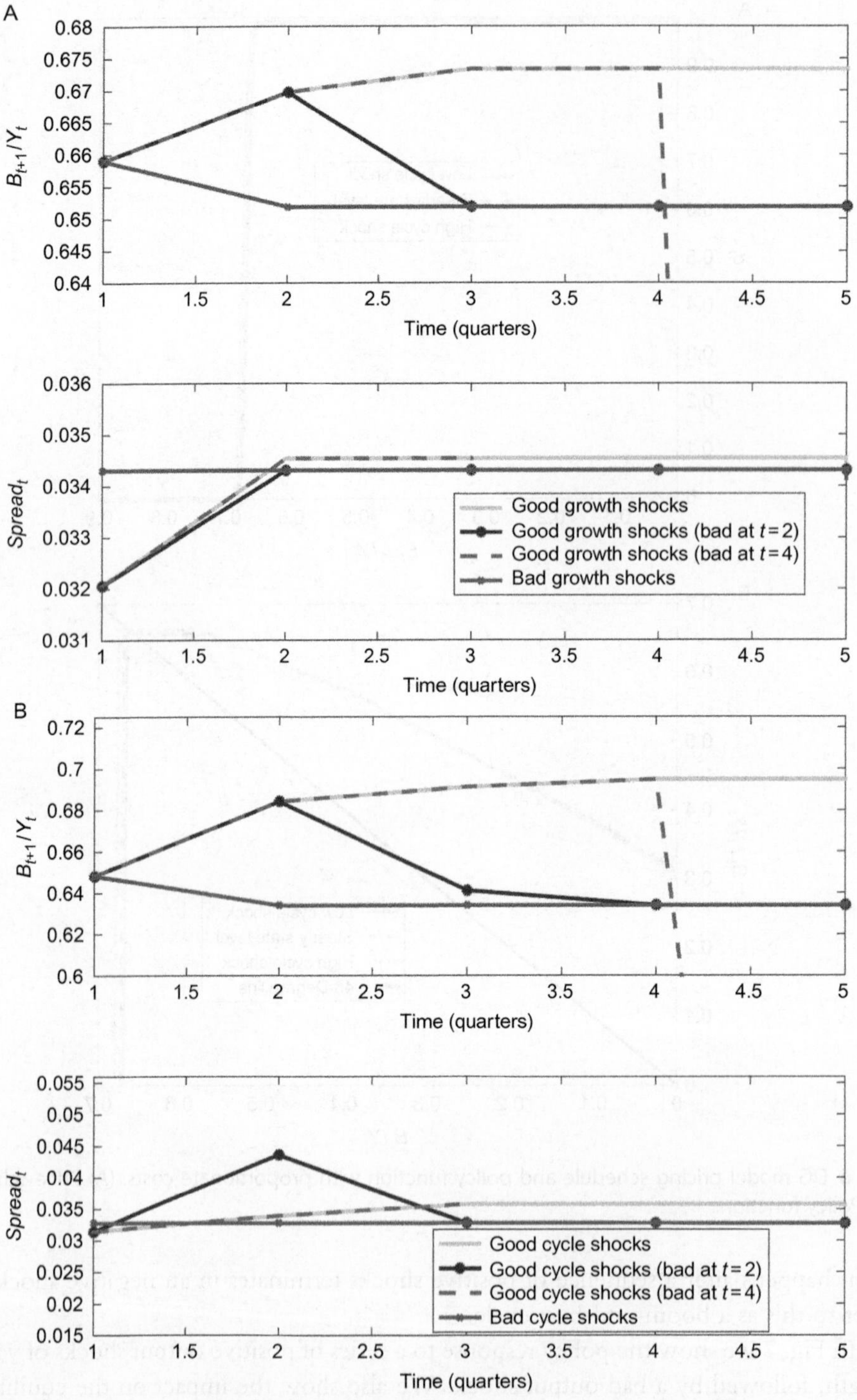

Fig. 7 Boom-and-bust cycle. (A) Stochastic. (B) Deterministic.

the government to borrow into a boom, raising the debt-to-output ratio. In the SG model, the government chooses to immediately delever in response to the negative output shock if it comes early enough in the boom; if it comes late, it defaults. The government in the DG model behaves similarly, except that it chooses to delever slightly more slowly in the case of a boom of intermediate length.

The spread behaves somewhat differently across the two versions of our model. In the SG version, the spread initially falls in respond to a positive output shock, but then it bounces back to essentially the same level as before in response to continued positive growth rate shocks because of the government's decision to lever up. More important, even in the period in which a negative growth rate shock first occurs, the government's decision to sharply delever means that the spread does not change in response to the negative shock. While the policy response of the government in the DG model is very similar to that of the SG model, the slightly slower deleveraging in response to a negative output shock leads to a sharp temporary rise in the spread.

5.3 Equilibrium Outcomes

In this section we lay out the results for both versions of our model with nonlinear output loses. Our first set of results are presented in Table 11. The first three statistics, which were targeted, match the long-run data for Mexico and are in the ball park for other emerging economies. The sixth statistic we report is the R^2 of a regression of the spread on the investor wealth shock w. This too is targeted to match the results of the regression of the spread on the US price-earnings ratio and is roughly in line with the data.

There are two nontargeted moments in Table 11. The first is the correlation of the average excess return and the growth rate of output. For the stochastic growth economy, the sign of this correlation is positive, which is surprising, since one would expect positive growth rate shocks to lower the spread. However, the magnitude of this correlation is in the ball park in that the correlation is quite weak as it is in the data. In the DG model this correlation is both of the wrong sign and also substantially higher. This reflects that

Table 11 Basic statistics: Stochastic and deterministic growth models

	Stochastic benchmark	Deterministic benchmark	Deterministic Argentina
Debt-to-GDP	0.66	0.66	0.28
Average default freq.	0.02	0.02	0.04
Average spread	0.03	0.03	0.06
SD of spreads	0.002	0.004	0.07
Corr of spreads with Δy or z	0.15	0.46	−0.76
R^2 of spreads on w	0.26	0.17	0.01

economy's greater responsiveness to output shocks, which we discussed earlier in reference to Fig. 4. Below we more closely examine the evidence on spreads and shocks using regression analysis to compare model and data results.

The other nontargeted moment is the standard deviation of the spread. This moment is too low, since it should be roughly equal to the average level of the spread. The fact that the spread's relative variation was still so low even with nonlinear default costs is surprising given that the literature has found that such costs can generate relatively realistic variation levels. However, the papers that have found this result have been calibrated to Argentina, which has a much more volatile output series.

To examine whether this might be at the root of our failure, we examined the implications of the DG model when we calibrate output to Argentina. When we calibrate our output process to Argentina, the autocorrelation coefficient for our output deviation from trend, z_t, rises from 0.853 to 0.930, thereby becoming more persistent. In addition, the standard deviation of z rises from 0.023 to 0.074, so the output deviations from trend are more volatile overall. All of the other model parameters are left unchanged. We report the results from this experiment in the last column of Table 11.

When we switch to the Argentine growth process for the deterministic model, the average debt-to-output level falls sharply, to 0.28, which is somewhat inconsistent with the fact that Argentina has a much higher value of this ratio than Mexico. In addition, the average spread rises sharply, to 0.06, and the volatility of the spread increases to 0.07. Both of these changes are consistent with the data in that Argentina has a much higher average spread and a much more volatile spread. This last finding indicates that the key to the literature's positive finding on spread volatility is the combination of nonlinear default costs and quite high output volatility. However, this story cannot explain the spread volatility in a country like Mexico with lower output volatility.

One other stark difference between the results with the Mexico and the Argentina output calibrations concerns the correlation of the spread and the percent deviation of output from trend. This has now become very negative. In Table 2 the average correlation in our sample was −0.27, and the highest value was only −0.56 for Malaysia. The correlation in Argentina was −0.35 and in Mexico it was −0.4. So a value of −0.76 with the Argentine calibration for output looks too high. Below in the regression analysis, we examine more closely the extent to which this success comes at the price of making spreads too dependent on output fluctuations.

The ergodic distributions of the debt-to-income ratio and the spread is depicted in Fig. 8. For the stochastic growth case, both the debt-to-income and the spread distributions are very tight and symmetric around their mean. The distribution of the debt-to-income ratio for the DG case is also symmetrical, but it is substantially more dispersed. For the spread distribution, the deterministic growth distribution is not completely symmetric and is again substantially more dispersed than the stochastic case. The greater dispersion in the debt-to-GDP ratio and the spread in the deterministic growth model is

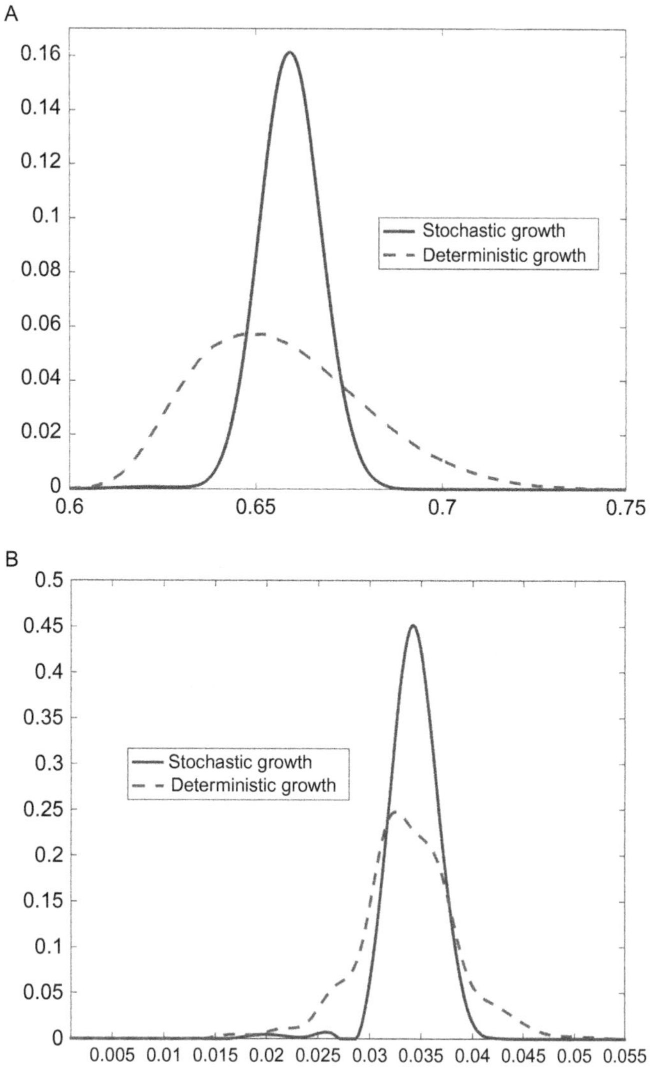

Fig. 8 Ergodic distributions. (A) Debt-to-income. (B) Spreads.

consistent with our earlier observation that the deterministic economy was more responsive to output shocks.

This spread can be decomposed into a default premium and a risk premium. Specifically, the risk premium is the standard difference between the expected implied yield on sovereign bonds and the risk-free interest rate. The default premium is the promised yield that would equate the expected return on sovereign bonds (inclusive of default) to a risk-free bond; that is, the yield that would leave a risk-neutral lender indifferent. The top panel of Fig. 9 depicts the risk premium and the bottom panel depicts the default

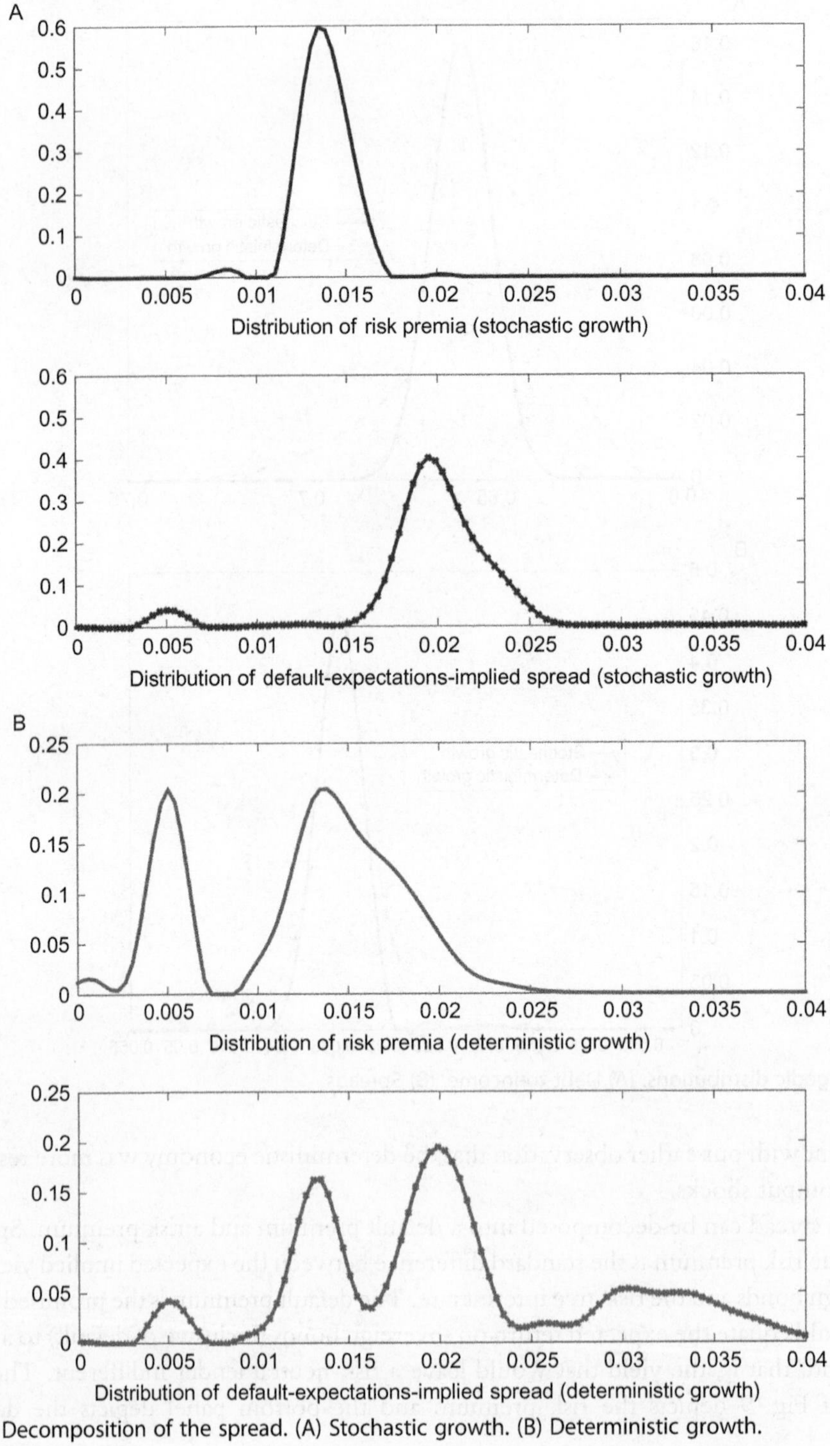

Fig. 9 Decomposition of the spread. (A) Stochastic growth. (B) Deterministic growth.

Table 12 Default and crisis statistics for the nonlinear default cost economies

	Def. share with output collapse	Def. Share with w collapse	Crisis share with output collapse	Crisis share with w collapse
Stochastic	0.80	0.02	0.31	0.01
Deterministic	0.60	0.06	0.66	0.03

premium. In both cases the risk and default spreads quite similar to each other, suggesting that the two are moving closely in parallel. On average, roughly 60% is the default premium and the rest is risk premium. This reflects our calibration target of 3% average spread and 2% default probability.

To understand the circumstances in which we are getting defaults and crises in our models, we examine the share of defaults and crises with large negative output changes and large negative investor wealth shocks. These negative changes are 1.5 standard deviations relative to the unconditional distribution. We use negative growth rate realizations for output so we are using the same metric for both models. The results are reported in Table 12. The results imply that, in the SG model, defaults are almost always associated with negative growth rate shocks and almost never with negative wealth shocks. In the deterministic growth model, the dependence of defaults on negative output shocks is a bit weaker and investor wealth shocks play essentially no role. When we turn to spread crises, we see much less dependence on growth shocks in the SG model and again essentially no dependance on wealth shocks. This is because a very negative growth shock leads to either an immediate default or rapid deleveraging. In contrast, in the DG model, the dependence of spread crises on growth shocks is even higher than it is for defaults.

5.4 Simulation Regressions

To compare the model to the data more closely, we take our model-simulated data and regress the spread on a constant and our three shocks. Besides the benchmark versions of SG and DG, we also included the results when we calibrate the output process to Argentina in the DG case. The results are in Table 13. We have already reported the results of estimating our statistical model in Table 3. However, those regressions included our two common factors. To make a closer comparison with the model regressions, we examine regressions for several of our countries with just the financial controls we considered in decomposing the common factors. We believe that including these financial controls as important in making this comparison. In our model data the output and wealth shocks are orthogonal by construction. In the actual data, an important concern is the feedback from interest rate or risk premium shocks to growth (as emphasized by Neumeyer and Perri, 2005).

Table 13 Spread regressions with wealth (simulated data)

	B_t/Y_t	g_t or z_t	w_t	R^2
SG benchmark calibration				
Coefficient	0.0286	0.0191	0.0070	
Var decomp	0.3850	0.0154	0.1660	0.5663
DG benchmark calibration				
Coefficient	0.0412	−0.0707	9.2928e−4	
Var decomp	0.3016	0.1145	0.1323	0.5484
DG argentina calibration				
Coefficient	0.307443	−0.77599	−0.00067	
Var decomp	0.030814	0.532024	0.000354	0.563191

While our two benchmark models were calibrated to Mexico, which we view as representive of countries subject to sovereign debt crises, the data series are fairly short to evaluate these somewhat rare events. Hence, it is useful to compare our model regression results to a range of countries in the data. To aid in this comparison, we also consider the DG version of our model with a growth process calibrated to Argentina.

In the SG model the output shock is the growth rate, or g_t, while in the DG model it is the deviation from trend, or z_t. To make a consistent comparison to the data-based regressions, we did them both with the growth rate of output as the shock and with the deviation of log output from a linear trend. These results are reported in Tables 14 and 15.

When we examine the results for the SG benchmark model with nonlinear default costs, one sees that the debt-to-output ratio has a positive coefficient and is explaining 38% of the movements in the spread as measured by the marginal R^2. This finding is consistent with the data regressions where this variable always has a positive coefficient and explains almost half of the spread in three of our countries and virtually nothing in two of them. The marginal R^2 for the growth rate shock is 0.01, which is very consistent with our growth rate regressions in Table 14 and the sign of that coefficient is positive. The wealth shock explains 17% of the variation according to the marginal R^2. This too is consistent with the data, since in some countries the financial variables explain very little, and in several others, particularly Mexico, they explain a great deal.

There are two major surprises in the SG model regression. First, the sign of the output shock is positive in the SG model, indicating that positive growth rate shocks raise the spread. This is contrary to the sign of this term in the data regressions. However, this result seems consistent with the results we showed for a boom-bust cycle in Fig. 7. There, only the initial response to a good output shock was negative while a sequence of good output shocks led the government to raise its debt-to-output ratio and thereby induce an

Table 14 Spread regressions (data): output shock = growth rate

Country	B_t/Y_t	g_t	VIX	P/E ratio	LIBOR	R^2
Argentina:						
Coefficients	0.0067 (9.9307e−4)	−1.0480 (0.6770)	7.8592e − 4 (0.0013)	0.0034 (0.0046)	−0.0372 (0.0072)	
Var decomp	0.4962	0.0120	0.0059	0.0085	0.0880	0.6105
Brazil:						
Coefficients	0.0026 (3.1092e−4)	−0.3134 (0.2297)	0.0013 (4.4568e−4)	1.8695e − 4 (8.1841e−4)	0.0023 (0.0014)	
Var decomp	0.4943	0.0150	0.0537	0.0093	0.0482	0.6204
Colombia:						
Coefficients	0.0018 (1.5892e−4)	−0.1535 (0.1102)	0.0011 (1.2462e−4)	7.5692e − 4 (3.0964e−4)	5.2909e − 4 (5.3118−4)	
Var decomp	0.4900	0.0236	0.2594	0.1017	0.0062	0.8809
Mexico:						
Coefficients	7.2889 − 4 (2.2988−4)	−0.1595 (0.0467)	6.2858e − 4 (6.0880e−5)	6.4423e − 4 (1.2801e−4)	1.1697e − 4 (3.5179e−4)	
Var decomp	−0.0226	0.1350	0.6598	0.1212	−0.0087	0.8847
Russia:						
Coefficients	2.5708e − 4 (8.0133−4)	−0.7400 (0.7191)	0.0025 (0.0015)	0.0117 (0.0031)	0.0058 (0.0075)	
Var decomp	0.0210	0.0109	0.0540	0.3217	0.0696	0.4771
Turkey:						
Coefficients	0.0012 (1.7406−4)	−0.2489 (0.0660)	7.3488e − 4 (1.9433e−4)	0.0028 (3.4963e−4)	4.8343e − 4 (7.1599e−4)	
Var decomp	0.1520	0.0911	0.1413	0.3847	0.0068	0.7759

Table 15 Spread regressions (data): Output shock = deviation from trend

Country	B_t/Y_t	z_t	VIX	P/E Ratio	LIBOR	R^2
Argentina						
Coefficients	0.0058 (0.0016)	−22.2293 (38.4213)	0.0014 (0.0013)	0.0011 (0.0062)	−0.0384 (0.0080)	
Var decomp	0.2463	0.1060	0.0138	0.0098	0.2080	0.5839
Brazil						
Coefficients	0.0027 (0.0004)	11.6322 (12.8857)	0.0015 (0.0004)	0.0005 (0.0009)	0.0021 (0.0014)	
Var decomp	0.3778	0.0638	0.0512	0.0657	0.0564	0.6150
Colombia						
Coefficients	0.0015 (0.0002)	−19.6663 (7.9572)	0.0011 (0.0001)	0.0009 (0.0003)	0.0013 (0.0006)	
Var decomp	0.3178	0.1130	0.2353	0.2000	0.0245	0.8903
Mexico						
Coefficients	0.0007 (0.0002)	−4.8005 (3.3338)	0.0007 ($6.0951e-5$)	0.0006 (0.0001)	0.0006 (0.0005)	
Var decomp	0.0371	0.1085	0.5613	0.1058	0.0473	0.8599
Russia						
Coefficients	$-7.0e-4$ (0.0006)	−96.9253 (17.1416)	0.0027 (0.0013)	0.0024 (0.0030)	0.0185 (0.0051)	
Var decomp	0.0705	0.2624	0.0494	0.1642	0.1072	0.6536
Turkey						
Coefficients	0.0009 (0.0002)	−18.3784 (4.1594)	0.0008 (0.0002)	0.0013 (0.0005)	0.0027 (0.0008)	
Var decomp	0.0956	0.2719	0.1433	0.2271	0.0519	0.7898

increase in the spread. Note that this response is not present in the DG model. Instead, because the government was slower to delever, a sequence of positive shocks followed by a negative one led to a temporary jump upwards in the spread.

Second, the sign of the wealth factor is positive, indicating that an increase in investor wealth, which should lower risk pricing holding everything else fixed, actually raises the spread. This result is consistent, however, with our earlier surprise finding that the sign of the P/E ratio in the data regressions is positive, indicating that a fall in the risk premium in the data also raises the spread. We will seek to better understand this finding in our quantitative exercises below.

In the simulated data regressions from the DG benchmark and DG Argentine models we also see that the debt-to-output ratio explains 30% of the variation in output and that the sign of this term is positive. However, if we compare this explanatory power to the regressions in Table 15, this is high relative to what we find when we take the output shock to be a deviation from trend. The sign on the deviation is negative, as one would expect and as we see in the data. In the DG benchmark the explanatory power of the output shock is only 11% which is consistent with the regression results. However, the explanatory power of this variable under the Argentine growth process is over 50%, which is much higher than anything we see in the data regressions. Thus it does seem like the ability of the nonlinear output cost element to increase the spread volatility when the variability of output is sufficiently high comes at the expense of tying the spread much too closely to output fluctuations. In addition, the sign of the wealth term changes when we move from the benchmark to the Argentinian output calibration. However, the positive sign in the benchmark case is consistent with the positive sign of the P/E ratio in the data regressions.

5.5 Comparative Experiments

We want to examine how the equilibrium predictions of our two benchmark models respond to changes in several key parameters. This will help us understand exactly what is driving our outcomes. In these experiments we change only the parameter in question, and we explicitly do not recalibrate the other parameters. The results are given in Table 16.

The first set of results in column 2 examines the impact of shortening the average maturity from 2 years to 1 quarter. In both the SG and the DG versions, this shortening of the maturity sharply reduces the default rate and the average spread almost to zero. This occurs because with debt that matures in a single period, future debt issuance has no effect on the value of bonds currently being issued. With longer maturity bond this is not the case and future issuances dilutes the value of current debt. Since capital loss on outstanding bonds from new issuance of debt is not borne by the sovereign, long maturity bonds induce over-borrowing and higher default risk. Put differently, with short maturity debt,

Table 16 Comparative statistics: Stochastic and deterministic growth models

	Stochastic growth				
	Benchmark	**Short maturity**	**High risk aversion**	**i.i.d. w**	**i.i.d. g**
Debt-to-GDP	0.66	0.68	0.66	0.66	0.78
Average default freq.	0.02	0.007	0.001	0.02	0.006
Average spreads	0.03	0.002	0.03	0.03	0.01
SD of spreads	0.002	0.001	0.002	0.002	0.002
Corr of spreads with Δy	0.15	0.15	0.14	0.17	−0.23
R^2 of spreads on w	0.26	0.008	0.43	0.003	0.29
	Deterministic growth				
	Benchmark	**Short maturity**	**High risk aversion**	**i.i.d. w**	**Low auto. z**
Debt-to-GDP	0.66	0.67	0.65	0.66	0.87
Average default freq.	0.02	0.002	0.01	0.02	0.003
Average spreads	0.03	0.003	0.03	0.03	0.007
SD spreads	0.004	0.001	0.005	0.004	0.001
Corr of spreads with z	0.46	0.09	0.39	0.51	−0.21
R^2 of spreads on w	0.17	0.01	0.36	0.001	0.23

the government is forced to internalize the full cost of a rise in default risk and therefore chooses to constrains its borrowing.

The second set of results concerns the impact of risk aversion on our equilibrium outcomes. In both the SG and DG cases, the frequency of default falls sharply. However, the increase in the price of risk just offsets this drop, so the average spread stays roughly unchanged. This indicates the greater discipline imposed on sovereign's borrowing behavior from a higher risk aversion on part of lenders. The greater discipline comes from the fact that the spread required per unit of default risk is higher with greater risk aversion, making default risk much more expensive for the sovereign. As a result, the sovereign optimally chooses to lower its expected future default risk. This result can also sheds light on why an increase in w raised the spread rather than lowering it. Future risk pricing can discipline future behavior. How strong that is will determine the extent to which it shows up as an increase or a decrease in the spread today. But it will increase the frequency of defaults.

The third set of results concerns the impact of making wealth shocks i.i.d. In this case, the disciplining affect of having a high future price of risk because of a low value of w today is removed. In the benchmark cases, this future discipline led to a twisting of the price schedules. When the debt-to-output is low, the future disciplinary effect dominates the static risk pricing effect and, as a result, a high w shocks lowers the price of debt. When the debt-to-output ratio is high, the static pricing effect dominates and rise in w increases the price of debt (see Fig. 5). With i.i.d. w, this twisting effect is gone and an increase in w strictly increases q where it is below the risk-free rate. In both the SG and DG models this leads to a sharp fall in the impact of wealth shocks on the spread as measured by the R^2. Consistent with this, the correlation of the wealth shock and the spread goes from 0.15 in the benchmark to 0.002 with i.i.d. w in the SG model and from 0.40 to 0.03 in the DG model.

The final set of results concerns the impact of autocorrelation of output shocks. For the SG model we reduce the correlation in the output growth rate g from 0.45 to 0, and in the DG model we reduce the correlation in the deviations from trend from 0.85 to 0.45. In both models the debt-to-output ratio goes up as the hedging motive goes up. In both models the default frequency goes down as the likelihood of a sequence of bad shocks driving a country into default goes down. In addition, in both models the incentive to borrow into a boom goes down as the likelihood of the good times continuing is reduced. As a result, the correlation of the spread and the growth rate of output is now negative in both models. At the same time spreads and default frequencies fall in both models.

5.6 Taking Stock

Our models of sovereign borrowing, default and the spread can match a number of key facts in the data. They can match the overall borrowing level, but this comes at the expense of assuming that default costs are large so that we can get the sovereign to repay, and that the sovereign is fairly myopic since borrowing and occasionally defaulting is, as we noted earlier a poor way of getting insurance.

Risk aversion on part of lenders leads to the average spread being greater than the average frequency of default, hence lenders earn a positive risk premium of about 1%.

The sovereign tends to borrow into booms, which is consistent with the boom-bust cycle we observe in many emerging economies. Also, the end of the boom is associated with a sudden shift in the price schedule for debt, which resembles the lending cutoff (sudden stops) observed in the data. This borrowing into booms depends on future optimism, which here comes through the autocorrelation in output shocks. If we make growth rates i.i.d. in the SG model or reduce the persistence of deviations from trend in the DG model, borrowing-into-booms effect largely goes away. This in turn leads to a sharp fall in the frequency of default and therefore the spread.

When we compare the spread regressions in the model simulated data with those in the data, the overall behavior is broadly consistent with that observed in the data. For both the SG and DG benchmark models, the importance of the debt-to-output ratio and the output shock is consistent with the regression results. However, the positive impact of a growth shock on the spread in the SG model is not consistent with the negative sign of the coefficient on this variable in the regression. This indicates that the reliance on a boom-bust cycle as opposed to the smoothing of consumption is excessive in this version of the model.

Global risk pricing shocks, which we model as shocks to the wealth of investors, have a surprisingly limited impact in our model. Interestingly, an increase in lenders' risk aversion that stems from a decrease in their wealth leads to a *fall* in the spread. A similar impact occurs when we increase investors' risk aversion in our comparative statics exercises. This result comes through the higher price of debt issuance, which lowers the extent to which current lenders need to worry about the dilution of the value of their claims in the future. The threat of future dilution goes away with short maturity debt. This is why we see a sharp fall in default rates and spreads when we switch to one-period debt.

The impact of persistent wealth shocks stemming from changes in borrowing discipline in the future leads to one of the surprising empirical successes of our models. In our spread regressions, a decrease in the price of risk increases the P/E ratio, but increases in the P/E ratio are associated with increases, not decreases, in the spread on emerging market sovereign bonds. This inverse relationship between the price of risk and spreads is predicted by both models. In our comparative statics exercise we saw that this correlation essentially goes away when wealth shocks become i.i.d., confirming that the inverse relationship is driven by anticipation of changes in future borrowing behavior.

The major failure of our benchmark models is with respect to the volatility of the spread. It is much too low in the model relative to the data. This indicates that the levering/delevering response to output shocks is too strong, resulting in a spread that is too smooth. This was particularly true in the initial version of our model with proportionate output costs, but is still true when we switch to nonlinear output costs of default (which improves the insurance offered by defaulting).

Increasing the variance of the output process in the DG model can substantially increase the variance of the spread, bringing it in line with the data for most countries. However, this positive result comes at a cost. First, it implies that the model cannot account for counties in our sample, such as Mexico, which have less volatile output processes. Additionally, relative to the data, higher volatility leads to too strong a dependence of spreads on output shocks.

These results suggest that what is needed is:

1. An additional shock to the pricing of debt that is not tied to country fundamentals or global risk pricing factors. This is indicated by the importance of the two common factors in the spread regressions and their lack of dependance on global asset pricing factors.
2. A reduction in the levering/delevering incentive or at least a drawing out of debt crises, which leads to high levels of the spread in response to these crises.

6. ROLLOVER CRISES

Our model was constructed to allow for rollover crises along the lines of Cole and Kehoe (2000). Here we conduct a preliminary investigation of the potential for rollover crises to add to the volatility of the spread in our models without tying this volatility too tightly to country fundamentals.

Rollover crises emerge from investors' failure to coordinate their beliefs on the good equilibrium outcome in which the government is offered a generous price schedule and therefore chooses to not default. Instead, investors adopt pessimistic beliefs about government's behavior, which leads them to offer an adverse price schedule—specifically, a zero price for new issuance of bonds—and this, in turn, induces the government to default. The government's default then validates the investors' pessimistic beliefs. What is empirically attractive about this mechanism is that while requiring that the country's fundamentals be bad enough to generate a default under the adverse price schedule, it allows relatively wide latitude in the timing of a sovereign debt crises.

In constructing a quantitative model of rollover crises, the first question is: what is a plausible process for beliefs? Beliefs, unlike, say, output, cannot be directly observed, and hence its impact and its stochastic evolution must be inferred. Aguiar et al. (2016) estimate shifts in beliefs from spreads. Another alternative is to adopt a state-space approach in which the belief process and it's realizations are estimated jointly along with other parameters of the model as in Bocola and Dovis (2015). A related alternative would be to construct belief processes that replicated the impact and time series properties of the common factors estimated in the spread regressions reported earlier. However, undertakings such as these are beyond the scope of a handbook chapter. So, instead, we follow Cole and Kehoe (2000) and its quantitative implementation in Chatterjee and Eyigungor (2012) and assume that there is a constant probability of a crisis. This limits the empirical scope of self-fulfilling rollover crises, but does allow us to partially gauge their potential impact. Also, we do not recalibrate the models so this too is a quantitative comparative statics exercise.

The results are presented in Table 17 along with our baseline results (for the nonlinear output loss from default). Here, we assume that if a country is in the crisis zone (ie, a rollover crisis can be supported in equilibrium) then a rollover crisis transpires with a 20% probability. Several results stand out. First, the possibility of rollover crises reduces

Table 17 Stochastic and deterministic growth models: Benchmark vs rollover crises

	Stochastic benchmark	**Stochastic w. RC**	**Deterministic benchmark**	**Deterministic w. RC**
Debt-to-GDP	0.66	0.63	0.66	0.65
Average default freq.	0.02	0.02	0.02	0.02
Average spread	0.03	0.04	0.03	0.04
SD of spreads	0.002	0.002	0.004	0.004
Corr of spreads with Δy or z	0.15	0.06	0.46	0.11
R^2 of spreads on w	0.26	0.18	0.17	0.09
Share of rollover defaults	0	0.70	0	0.30

the average debt-to-output ratio. This makes sense because rollover defaults are generally more costly than fundamental defaults (they can occur even when output is relatively high) and this makes the sovereign wary about borrowing too much. In contrast, the average default frequency does not change much with the addition of rollover crisis and, as a result, the impact on the average spread is fairly small (in the SG model it stays the same, while in the DG model it rises slightly). However, there is significant change in the nature of defaults since many of them are now being induced by rollover crises. This is particularly pronounced in the case of the SG model, where 70% are now rollover-induced defaults. Along with this change in the nature of the defaults comes a change in the relationship between the spread and our fundamental shocks. In both models the correlation of the spread and the output shocks falls. This is particularly pronounced in the DG model, where it falls from 0.46 to 0.11.[o] In a similar fashion, the R^2 of the regressions of our spread on our wealth shock w falls in both models. In the SG model it falls by one-third, while in the DG model it falls by one-half. At the same time, the standard deviation of the spread hardly changes with belief shocks.

The lack of increase in the spread's volatility is surprising. To understand a bit better what is going on, we plot default indifference curves for both the benchmark SG model and the SG model with rollover crises in response to belief shocks in Fig. 10. We start first with the benchmark model. The indifference condition between defaulting and not defaulting traces out combinations of the debt-to-output ratio and the current growth rate. Since growth is positively autocorrelated in this model, high growth today is good news about future output and hence reduces the incentive to default. Of course, a high debt burden encourages default. This gives us the trade-off we see in the first panel of the figure. We have also plotted the stationary debt levels (ie, the debt level where $b = a(s,b)$) as a function of the current growth rate of output. These debt levels are important because the government finds it optimal to lever/delever back to this point in response to a shock. The fact that the stationary points are positively sloped reflects the tendency to borrow into a boom discussed earlier. Defaults occur in equilibrium largely because a sufficiently low growth rate shock from a debt position close to the stationary points last period generated a current debt-to-output level that is on the wrong side of the indifference curve. In which case, the government optimally chooses to default. The fact that the gap between the indifference curve and the stationary point is increasing in g illustrates why default is closely associated with low output shocks.

In the second panel of Fig. 10, we see a similar graph for the SG model with rollover crises. Only now there are two indifference curves: one for fundamental defaults as in the

[o] Another feature of rollover defaults is that they can occur for fundamentals that are, on average, better than in the case of fundamental defaults. Thus, the correlation between defaults and fundamentals is also weakened, consistent with evidence reported in Tomz and Wright (2007). See also Yeyati and Panizza (2011) for an empirical evaluation of the timing of output losses surrounding default episodes.

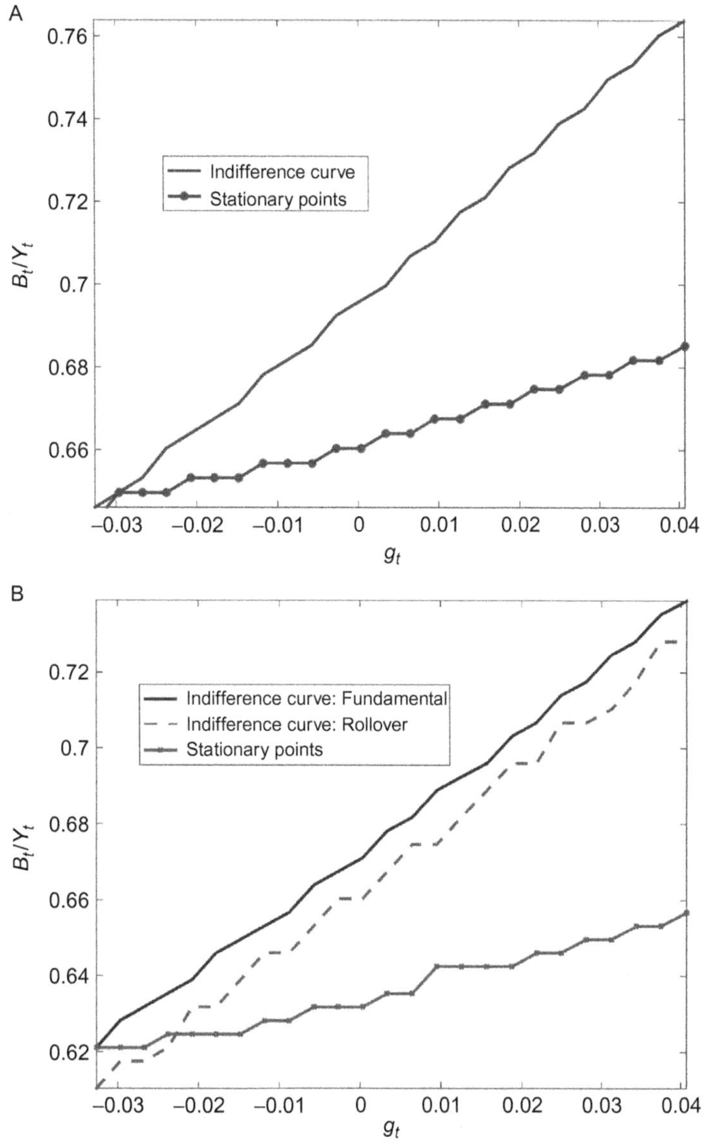

Fig. 10 Default indifference curves and stationary policy choices. (A) Benchmark. (B) w. Rollover crises.

benchmark model and one for rollover crises defaults. Since the lending terms are worse, the rollover indifference curve lies below the fundamental curve, indicating that a rollover crisis is possible for a given growth rate g_t at a strictly lower level of b_t. Note that the fundamental indifference curve is lower than in the benchmark model. This is because the future prospect of rollover crises lowers the payoff even when these crises do not occur today and this has shifted down the solvency indifference curve. As a result, defaults will occur at lower debt levels fixing g than in the benchmark model. Next, note that the stationary debt level curve has also been shifted down. This is because the increased likelihood of a default and its adverse consequences means that the optimal level of borrowing has decreased. The fact that 70% of the defaults occur under the crisis pricing schedule means that the likelihood of drawing a sufficiently bad output shock to force the government over the fundamental indifference curve has gone down substantially. In this sense the gap between the solvency indifference curve and the stationary debt levels has widened.

There is a sense in which virtually all of the defaults in the model with rollover crises are driven by beliefs. This is because, if we asked whether the states in which realized defaults are in equilibrium, very few of them are on the wrong side of the benchmark indifference schedule. It is also worth noting that if we suddenly switch from a situation in which the benchmark pricing schedule, policy function and beliefs applied, to one in which the rollover ones did, then the government would have to sharply delever in the face of a worse price schedule, even if a crisis did not formally occur in the current period. This sort of transition might be a way to generate more volatility in the spread, especially if the government could be induced to slow down the rate at which it delevered.

7. EXTENSIONS AND LITERATURE REVIEW

Beginning with Aguiar and Gopinath (2006) and Arellano (2008), there is now a substantial body of work drawing on the Eaton–Gersovitz framework. Aguiar and Amador (2014a) discuss the theoretical and conceptual issues in this area. This section provides a brief guide to the evolving quantitative literature (the reader is encouraged to consult the studies mentioned here for additional related work).

Existence and Uniqueness of Equilibrium: The existence of an equilibrium when both endowments and assets are continuous is an open question.[p] Aguiar and Amador (2014a) discuss that the operator whose fixed point characterizes the equilibrium (with permanent autarky as punishment) is monotone and note how this can be useful to compute an equilibrium. When both b and the non i.i.d. component of endowments are discrete, Chatterjee and Eyigungor (2012) establish the existence of an equilibrium for debt with arbitrary maturity and temporary or permanent autarky following default.

[p] Eaton and Gersovitz (1981) pointed out that *if* the probability of default $\mathbb{E}_s(D(s',b')$ is differentiable in b', the solution to the bond pricing equation amounts to the solution of a first-order nonlinear differential equation. However, differentiability of $\mathbb{E}_s D(s',b')$ requires everywhere differentiability of the value function, which is not true in a model with default.

The issue of uniqueness of equilibrium is more subtle. For the case where default is punished with permanent autarky, Auclert and Rognlie (2014) prove uniqueness for the Eaton–Gersovitz model with one-period debt. Passadore and Xandri (2015) study the multiplicity that arises when the state space for debt is restricted to be nonnegative (that is, no saving). Stangebye (2015a) and Aguiar and Amador (2016) discuss how multiplicity in the Eaton–Gersovitz model arises in the absence of one-period debt due to the vulnerability to dilution. More generally, one can often construct multiple equilibria with variations on the standard set up. Cole and Kehoe (2000) alter the Stackelberg nature of the government's default decision in order to generate self-fulfilling rollover crises. Chatterjee and Eyigungor (2012) exploits a similar variation to generate (investor) belief-driven rollover crises in a model that otherwise resembles the Eaton–Gersovitz setup.

The Strategic Structure of the Debt Market: In the Eaton–Gersovitz setup, the sovereign accesses the debt market at most once within a period. If the sovereign may access the market as many times within a period as it wishes, lenders at any given round of borrowing must anticipate the sovereign's future within-period borrowing decisions (Bizer and DeMarzo, 1992). As shown in Hatchondo and Martinez (undated) equilibrium implications of this is that investors will offer the sovereign a state-dependent pair of bond price and debt limit, $\{\bar{q}(y,b), \bar{x}(y,b)\}$, with the sovereign free to borrow any $b' \leq \bar{x}(y,b)$ at the price $\bar{q}(y,b)$. Interestingly, the bond *price* depends on inherited debt b (while in the standard setup the bond price *schedule* $q(y,b')$ is independent of b) and, so, borrowing history matters for the terms of credit. Lorenzoni and Werning (2014) and Ayres et al. (2015) discuss this issue in detail.

Contract Choice: In the standard setup, the structure of a unit bond is fixed and described by the pair (z,λ). At the cost of enlarging the state space, more flexible contractual structures are possible. Bai et al. (2014) define a unit bond by (T,δ), where the bond pays $(1+\delta)^{-\tau}$, $0 \leq \tau \leq T$ periods from maturity. Sanchez et al. (2015) consider the case where $\delta = 0$. Both relax the fixity of the contractual structure by letting the sovereign replace old debt each period with new debt with a different contractual structure.

Maturity Choice: Cole and Kehoe (1996) discuss the role of maturity in the presence of self-fulfilling debt crises. In the standard setup, market incompleteness is extreme in that only one type of debt contract can be issued at any time. Arellano and Ramanarayanan (2012) consider the case where the sovereign can simultaneously buy and sell bonds of different maturities and show that the average maturity shortens as fundamentals weaken. Aguiar and Amador (2014b) show that when default probabilities are high, the sovereign has an incentive to reduce its stock of one-period debt. Shorter maturity provides the sovereign the correct incentives to minimize the inefficiencies represented by default. Bocola and Dovis (2015) discuss the role of maturity choice in the presence of both fundamental and rollover crises and analyze their separate roles in the recent Eurozone debt crisis.

Exchange Rates, Default Risk, and Currency Denomination: Sovereign defaults are generally preceded by a depreciation of the country's currency, with a further sharp depreciation occurring soon after default. Asonuma (2014) documents these facts and develops a two-country model with traded and nontraded goods in which one country is the borrower and the other the lender. Negative shocks to productivity in the borrowing country can trigger a real exchange rate depreciation which, in turn, can raise the likelihood of a default on sovereign debt. Gumus (2013) examines the currency denomination of debt in a similar model with two types of debt: In one, the payoff is linked to the domestic price index (a proxy for local currency debt) and in the other to the price of the tradeable good (a proxy for foreign currency debt). Although the default risk on "local currency debt" is not uniformly lower than the default risk on "foreign currency debt," the former is found to be the better (higher welfare) arrangement.

Explicit Treatment of the Government: For some purposes, it is important to model the sovereign separately from private-sector agents. Cuadra and Sapriza (2008) analyze borrowing and default behavior when redistributive conflict and the risk of political turnover impart myopia (present-bias) *a lá* Alesina and Tabellini (1990). In their model, the sovereign discounts the future more than citizens do, which helps to partially rationalize the low discount factors often used in quantitative models. Hatchondo et al. (2009) consider two types of governments that differ in their discount factors with the goal of analyzing how political risk affects default probabilities and the volatility of spreads. Cuadra et al. (2010) model the government sector in order to give an account of the strongly procyclical nature of fiscal policy in emerging economies.[q]

Settlement Following Default: Sovereign defaults end with a settlement on the defaulted debt, wherein creditors accept a haircut and the sovereign regains (unencumbered) access to credit markets. Generally, settlement occurs after a significant amount of time has elapsed since default. In the context of one-period debt and equal treatment of all creditors in default (the so-called *pari passu* clause), Yue (2010) models settlement as the outcome of a one-shot Nash bargain between the sovereign and the representative creditor in the period of default. Following agreement, the sovereign is assumed to repay the renegotiated debt over time, with no possibility of default or access to new borrowing. This produces a theory of haircuts but not of delays. Bi (2008) assumes that defaulted debts must be settled in cash but employs the stochastic alternating-offers game developed in Merlo and Wilson (1995) to produce a theory of both haircuts and delays. Benjamin and Wright (2009) observe that settlement is typically done with new debt (rather than just cash) and allow for this possibility within the context of the stochastic

[q] Amador (2012) shows that once the equilibrium of the political game between different groups comprising the government is taken into account, it becomes possible to sustain positive levels of debt even when punishment for default is limited to exclusion from future credit (*contra*; Bulow and Rogoff, 1989)

alternating-offers game. In both models, delays arise because it is optimal for both parties to defer settlement until the sovereign's endowment is sufficiently high.[r]

Restructuring Without Default: Default and debt restructuring is a form of ex-post state contingency. Logically, and in practice, ex-post state contingency need not involve default. Hatchondo et al. (2014) point to voluntary debt exchanges as debt write-offs that occur when a sequence of bad endowment shocks places the sovereign on the wrong side of the revenue Laffer curve. Relatedly, Asonuma and Trebesch (2015) document that about a third of all restructurings in the last several decades occurred in the absence of default, termed *preemptive* restructuring. They extend the Eaton–Gersovitz model to allow for such restructurings and show that they occur when the likelihood of a future default is high. Salomao (2014) has analyzed how the presence of a credit default swap (CDS) market impacts debt renegotiation, when the outcome of the negotiation determines whether a "credit event" is triggered.

Partial Default: Default is typically modeled as a binary event on a single type of debt. In reality, sovereigns have a range of external obligations outstanding at any point in time, including trade credit, bank loans, bonds, bilateral (government-to-government) loans, loans from multilateral agencies (IMF, World Bank and other agencies) and they may choose to default on some types of loans but not on others. Thus, in the aggregate, default tends to be partial. Based on this observation, Arellano et al. (2013) develop a one-period debt model in which the sovereign can partially default on existing debt. Unpaid debts accumulate arrears and there is an output loss that is increasing in the ratio of unpaid to total debts. In their model, moderately bad output shocks trigger partial default that gets "cured" as output recovers.

Reputation: Quantitative sovereign debt models generally do not give any role to reputation in sustaining debt, although the idea that reputation matters is invoked in Eaton and Gersovitz, and, more comprehensively, in Tomz (2007). D'Erasmo (2012) extends the Eaton–Gerovitz model to the case where investors are uncertain about the sovereign's discount factor (degree of patience), which is taken to be stochastic. Investors' perception of the likelihood that the sovereign is the patient type now appears as an additional state variable in the sovereign's dynamic program. The patient type's desire to separate itself from the impatient type encourages more disciplined borrowing behavior on its part. In equilibrium, the patient type can sustain a higher level of debt on average. Generally speaking, the impatient type defaults and the patient type reaches settlement on the defaulted debt.

[r] Bai and Zhang (2012) explore the role of asymmetric information in creating delays in reaching settlement in a stylized environment. The uninformed party (the sovereign) screens creditors (who privately know their reservation value) by making successively attractive offers over time. They show that delay is shorter when the defaulted debt is traded in the secondary market because the price partially reveals the creditors' reservation value.

Sudden Stops: There is a large literature on "sudden stops" that focuses on the macroeconomic implications of a halt of capital inflows into emerging markets. This literature does not base the "sudden stop" on a rollover problem and abstracts from the possibility of sovereign default induced by the sudden stop (see, for instance, Mendoza (2010) and the references cited therein). Bianchi et al. (2014) make the connection to sovereign default by extending the Eaton–Gersovitz model to allow for an exogenous stop in capital inflows and study the role of international reserves (which cannot be grabbed by foreign investors in the event of default) as a hedge against such stops.[s]

Fiscal Rules and Default: There is a literature aimed at understanding the equilibrium implications of fiscal policy rules. Ghosh et al. (2011) analyze a model where the government adheres to some given fiscal rule as long as the deficit implied by the rule can be financed at a finite interest rate. In terms of our notation, this is a setup in which there is some function $c(y,b)$ (the fiscal policy rule) and b' is chosen each period to satisfy $q(y,b')\cdot[b'-(1-\lambda)b]=y-(r^*+\lambda)b-c(y,b)$. Because the revenue curve $q(y,b')b'$ is an inverted U, there may be no b' that satisfies this equation in which case the sovereign defaults. Furthermore, if there is one b' that satisfies the budget constraint, there will always exist another b' on the "wrong side" of the revenue Laffer curve that will also satisfy this equation. Ghosh et al. assume that the sovereign and investors avoid the wrong side of the Laffer curve and compute the highest debt level $\bar{b}$ beyond which default is certain. Lorenzoni and Werning (2014) and Stangebye (2015b) study a similar setup but the focus is on the rise in interest rates if investors temporarily coordinate on the low price (and therefore high debt) equilibrium path. These authors focus on the recent Eurozone experience.

Debt Dilution and Alternative Trading Arrangements: In quantitative models with long-term debt, "debt-dilution" is an important force leading to excessive borrowing and default. This leads to consideration of alternative trading arrangements that mitigate the adverse effects of debt dilution. Chatterjee and Eyigungor (2015) analyze how respecting seniority during (postdefault) debt renegotiations can improve incentives and the welfare of the sovereign. Hatchondo et al. (2015) analyze how adherence to a fiscal policy rule that binds future sovereigns' borrowing decisions can improve the welfare of the current sovereign.

Decentralized Borrowing and Centralized Default: A growing portion of a country's external debt is debts incurred by private borrowers. Kim and Zhang (2012) analyze an Eaton–Gersovitz model in which private agents choose how much to borrow but the sovereign chooses whether to default. Because private borrowers act as price-takers,

[s] The accumulation of foreign reserves to mitigate rollover risk has been examined from an optimal contracting perspective in Hur and Kondo (2014). They point to the drop-off in the frequency of sudden stops following reserve accumulation by emerging markets as evidence that reserves affect the likelihood of a rollover crisis.

the equilibrium resembles one in which the sovereign can access the credit market unboundedly many times within a period.

Contagion and Correlated Defaults: Lizarazo (2009) studies how the terms of credit offered to sovereigns are affected if sovereigns share a common risk-averse lender. Correlated defaults may occur because a default by one sovereign lowers the wealth of the lender and reduces the supply of credit to all sovereigns. The reduction in supply could push another sovereign into default. Arellano and Bai (2014) study a similar environment but include renegotiation on the defaulted debt and show that bargaining protocols (independent vs coordinated bargaining with sovereigns following default) differentially affect the likelihood of correlated defaults.

Inflation and Default: The bulk of the quantitative-theoretic literature on debt and default models real economies. Two exceptions are Nuno and Thomas (2015) and Du and Schreger (2015). The former compares (in a continuous-time setting) outcomes where sovereign debt is denominated in real terms (with the possibility of outright default) to one where it is nominal and the sovereign chooses monetary and fiscal policy under discretion. The latter studies default risk on sovereign debt denominated in local currency, when private borrowers issue debt denominated in foreign currency. The existence of foreign currency private debt makes inflating away local currency sovereign debt expensive and, thus, keeps default risk on local currency sovereign debt positive (as observed in the data).

News Shocks: Sovereign defaults do not occur only when fundamentals are weak. One possible explanation of this fact could be that they occur when the sovereign and investors receive bad news about the future. Durdu et al. (2013) extend the standard Eaton–Gersovitz set up to include news shocks about future TFP. In addition to default triggered by bad news, the precision of news about future TFP is shown to have quantitatively significant effects the bond pricing schedule.

Default Costs: Quantitative-theoretic models of debt and default typically take the structure of the output costs of default as given. Two exceptions to this practice are Mendoza and Yue (2012) and Perez (2015). In the former, the default costs are grounded in producers' inability to import foreign intermediate inputs when the country is in default. The key implication of this setup is asymmetric default costs: the output costs of default are proportionally higher when TFP is high because that is when the loss of foreign intermediate inputs is proportionately more costly. In the latter, the output costs of default are grounded on the loss of net worth of financial intermediaries (who hold sovereign debt) that occurs with default and the consequent fall in the level and efficiency of financial intermediation, which then depresses output.

Investment and Default: The quantitative debt and default literature has uniformly examined endowment economies. An exception is Gordon and Guerron-Quintana (2016) who extend—both substantively and computationally—the long-term debt model of Chatterjee and Eyigungor (2012) to include capital accumulation (with costly adjustment) and labor-leisure choice. Their goals are a more complete understanding of emerging market business cycles and of the impact of phyisical capital on debt sustainability.

8. CONCLUSION: WHERE WE'VE BEEN AND WHERE WE NEED TO GO?

This chapter has documented a number of important facts about sovereign default crises, including:

1. Average spreads, spread volatility and the frequency of spread crises vary quite a bit across developing countries.
2. Fundamentals explain only a limited share of spread movements.
3. Spreads have some common factors driving them. However, these factors do not seem tightly connected to standard measures of risk pricing, uncertainty or the risk-free rate.

We have also examined alternative versions of the standard model of sovereign borrowing and defaults. Some of these versions explain many of the main facts, such as the average spread, the default frequency and average debt-to-GDP ratios. However, all of these models struggle to simultaneously explain the volatility of spreads and its apparent lack of connection to country fundamentals. Specifically:

1. In our model countries engage in very limited borrowing and saving to smooth consumption. While this leveraging and deleveraging behavior is found in the data, it seems much less pronounced. As a result, the variation in the debt-to-output ratio is smaller in the model than in the data. This leads to much less variation in the models' implied spread.
2. Nonlinear default costs can increase the volatility of the spread in the DG model when the volatility of output is high. But this increase in the spread comes at the expense of tightly tying movements in the spread to country fundamentals.
3. The SG model is much less sensitive to including nonlinear default costs in part because the low current output realizations do not stimulate much borrowing as growth rates are modestly positively persistent and because the volatility in growth rates is small relative to volatility in the deviation from trend.

Both increases in the risk aversion of our lenders and negative shocks to their wealth did not lead to sharp increases in the spread as simple intuition might suggest. Instead the disciplinary effect of the increase in the price of default risk reduces the future incentive of the government to issue debt into the range that will generate a positive probability of default. This increase in future discipline lower creditors' anticipation of future dilution of their claims by the government and can actually reduces spreads. This negative relationship between the pricing of default risk and the equilibrium spread also appears to be an important factor in the data, thus, validating this surprising implication of our models.

The failure of our models to explain the volatility of spreads stems from the fact that the debt-to-output ratio is largely pinned down by a couple of key features. First, because the government is quite myopic, smoothing plays a limited role in it's optimal policy choice; instead, borrowing is driven by impatience that is ultimately held in check by lack of commitment. Second, because of the strong feedback effect of default risk and risk premia on the government's incentive to default, the debt price schedule is highly nonlinear in the relevant region. As a result, the location of the kink in the price schedule interacts with the sovereign's myopia to almost completely determine its borrowing behavior. In the end, this leads to sharp leveraging/deleveraging in response to positive and negative output shocks and very little variation in the spread. These forces are somewhat ameliorated in cases where the output shock is sufficiently volatile (so the nonlinearity in the default cost can play a role), but even in those cases the sovereign's behavior responds sharply to the contemporaneous shock realization and does not display the history dependance that expenditure-smoothing would have implied. As a result, only the current output shock matters for spreads and this ends up overloading its importance relative to the data.

Rollover crises are a promising way of generating debt crises, particularly since they don't imply an overly tight connection to country fundamentals. However, the sort of stationary rollover risk that we have considered here is not sufficient to produce the kind of variability in the spread that we see in the data. Instead, they seem to simply crowd out standard fundamental crises. What is needed is a more dynamic version of time-varying risks. At the same time, we need to rationalize a reduction in the speed with which the government chooses to undo the impact of negative shocks on the spread by borrowing less and yet not default on the debt.

ACKNOWLEDGMENTS

We thank the editors Harald Uhlig and John Taylor, our discussant Manuel Amador, and participants at the March 2015 Handbook conference in Chicago for thoughtful comments. We also thank St. Martin's "Conference on the Sand." The views expressed here are those of the authors and do not necessarily represent the views of the Federal Reserve Bank of Philadelphia or the Federal Reserve System.

REFERENCES

Aguiar, M., Amador, M., 2014a. Sovereign debt. In: Gopinath, G., Helpman, E., Rogoff, K. (Eds.), Handbook of International Economics, vol. 4. North Holland, pp. 647–687.

Aguiar, M., Amador, M., 2014b. Take the short route: how to repay and restructure sovereign debt with multiple maturities. Mimeo.

Aguiar, M., Amador, M., 2016. Maturity and multiplicity in sovereign debt models. Working Paper.

Aguiar, M., Chatterjee, S., Cole, H.L., Stangebye, Z.R., 2016. Self-fulfilling Debt Crisis, Revisited: The Art of the Desperate Deal. Mimeo.

Aguiar, M., Gopinath, G., 2006. Defaultable debt, interest rate and the current account. J. Int. Econ. 69, 64–83.

Aguiar, M., Gopinath, G., 2007. Emerging market business cycles: the cycle is the trend. J. Polit. Econ. 115, 69–102.

Alesina, A., Tabellini, G., 1990. A positive theory of fiscal deficits and government debt in a democracy. Rev. Econ. Stud. 57, 403–414.

Amador, M., 2012. Sovereign debt and the tragedy of the commons. Mimeo.

Arellano, C., 2008. Default risk and income fluctuations in emerging markets. Am. Econ. Rev. 98 (3), 690–712.

Arellano, C., Bai, Y., 2014. Linkages across sovereign debt markets. Research Department Staff Report 491, Federal Reserve Bank of Minneapolis.

Arellano, C., Mateos-Planos, X., Rios-Rull, V., 2013. Partial default. Federal Reserve Bank of Minneapolis, Mimeo, Working Paper.

Arellano, C., Ramanarayanan, A., 2012. Default and maturity structure in sovereign bonds. J. Polit. Econ. 120, 187–232.

Asonuma, T., 2014. Sovereign defaults, external debt and real exchange rate dynamics. International Monetary Fund, Mimeo.

Asonuma, T., Trebesch, C., 2015. Sovereign debt restructurings: preemptive or post-default. Discussion Paper 10950, Center for Economic Policy Research.

Auclert, A., Rognlie, M., 2014. Unique equilibrium in the Eaton-Gersovitz model of sovereign debt. Mimeo.

Ayres, J., Navarro, G., Nicolini, J.P., Teles, P., 2015. Sovereign default: the role of expectations. Federal Reserve Bank of Minneapolis Working Paper 723.

Bai, Y., Zhang, J., 2012. Duration of sovereign debt renegotiation. J. Int. Econ. 86 (2), 252–268.

Bai, Y., Kim, S.T., Mihalache, G., 2014. The maturity and payment schedule of sovereign debt. Mimeo.

Benjamin, D., Wright, M.L., 2009. Recovery before redemption: a theory of sovereign debt renegotiation. Mimeo.

Bi, R., 2008. "Beneficial delays" delays in restructuring negotiations. Working Paper WP/08/38, International Monetary Fund.

Bianchi, J., Hatchondo, J.C., Martinez, L., 2014. International reserves and rollover risk. Mimeo.

Bizer, D.S., DeMarzo, P.M., 1992. Sequential banking. J. Polit. Econ. 100, 41–61.

Bocola, L., Dovis, A., 2015. Self-fulfilling debt crisis: a quantitative analysis. Mimeo.

Borri, N., Verdelhan, A., 2011. Sovereign risk premia. Working Paper.

Broner, F., Lorenzoni, G., Schmukler, S.L., 2013. Why do emerging economies borrow short term? J. Eur. Econ. Assoc. 11 (S1), 67–100.

Bulow, J., Rogoff, K.S., 1989. Sovereign debt: is to forgive to forget? Am. Econ. Rev. 79 (1), 43–50.

Calvo, G.A., 1988. Servicing the public debt: the role of expectations. Am. Econ. Rev. 78 (4), 647–661.

Chatterjee, S., Eyigungor, B., 2012. Maturity, indebtedness and default risk. Am. Econ. Rev. 102 (6), 2674–2699.

Chatterjee, S., Eyigungor, B., 2015. A seniority arrangement for sovereign debt. Am. Econ. Rev. 105 (12), 3740–3765.

Cole, H.L., Kehoe, T., 1996. A self-fulfilling model of Mexico's 1994-1995 debt crisis. J. Int. Econ. 41, 309–330.

Cole, H.L., Kehoe, T., 2000. Self-fulfilling debt crisis. Rev. Econ. Stud. 67 (1), 91–116.

Cuadra, G., Sanchez, J.M., Sapriza, H., 2010. Fiscal policy and default risk in emerging markets. Rev. Econ. Dyn. 13, 452–469.

Cuadra, G., Sapriza, H., 2008. Sovereign defaults, interest rates and political uncertainty in emerging markets. J. Int. Econ. 76, 77–88.

D'Erasmo, P., 2012. Government reputation and debt repayment in emerging economies. Mimeo.

Du, W., Schreger, J., 2015. Sovereign risk, currency risk and corporate balance sheets. Mimeo.

Durdu, B., Nunes, R., Sapriza, H., 2013. News and default risk in small open economies. J. Int. Econ. 91 (1), 1–17.

Eaton, J., Gersovitz, M., 1981. Debt with potential repudiation: theoretical and empirical analysis. Rev. Econ. Stud. 48 (2), 289–309.

Ghosh, A.R., Kim, J.I., Mendoza, E.G., Ostry, J.D., Qureshi, M.S., 2011. Fiscal fatigue, fiscal space and debt sustainability in advanced economies. Working Paper 16782, National Bureau of Economic Research.

Gordon, G., Guerron-Quintana, P.A., 2016. Dynamics of investment, debt, and default. Mimeo.

Gromping, U., 2007. Estimators of relative importance in linear regression based on variance decomposition. Am. Stat. 61 (2), 139–147.
Gumus, I., 2013. Debt denomination and default risk in emerging markets. Macroecon. Dyn. 17, 1070–1095.
Hatchondo, J.C., Martinez, L., 2009. Long duration bonds and sovereign defaults. J. Int. Econ. 79 (1), 117–125.
Hatchondo, J.C., Martinez, L., undated. Credit risk without commitment. Mimeo.
Hatchondo, J.C., Martinez, L., Sapriza, H., 2009. Heterogeneous borrowers in quantitative models of sovereign default. Int. Econ. Rev. 50 (4), 1129–1151.
Hatchondo, J.C., Martinez, L., Sosa-Padilla, C., 2014. Voluntary debt exchanges. J. Monet. Econ. 61, 32–50.
Hatchondo, J.C., Martinez, L., Roch, F., 2015. Fiscal rules and the sovereign default premium. Mimeo.
Hur, S., Kondo, I.O., 2014. A theory of rollover risk, sudden stops, and foreign reserves. Mimeo.
Kim, Y.J., Zhang, J., 2012. Decentralized borrowing and centralized default. J. Int. Econ. 88, 121–133.
Leland, H., 1994. Bond prices, yield spreads, and optimal capital structure with default risk. IBER Finance Working Paper 240.
Lindeman, R., Merenda, P.F., Gold, R., 1980. Introduction to Bivariate and Multivariate Analysis. Scott Foresman, Glenview, IL.
Lizarazo, S.V., 2009. Contagion of financial crisis in sovereign debt markets. Munich Personal RePec Archive, Discussion paper.
Longstaff, F., Pan, J., Pedersen, L., Singleton, K., 2011. How sovereign is sovereign credit risk. Am. Econ. J.: Macroecon. 3, 75–103.
Lorenzoni, G., Werning, I., 2014. Slow moving debt crises. Mimeo.
Mendoza, E.G., 2010. Sudden stops, financial crises, and leverage. Am. Econ. Rev. 100 (5), 1941–1966.
Mendoza, E.G., Yue, V.Z., 2012. A general equilibrium model of sovereign default and business cycles. Q. J. Econ. 127 (2), 889–946.
Merlo, A., Wilson, C., 1995. A stochastic model of sequential bargaining with complete information. Econometrica 63 (2), 371–399.
Neumeyer, P.A., Perri, F., 2005. Business cycles in emerging economies: the role of interest rates. J. Monet. Econ. 52 (2), 345–380.
Nuno, G., Thomas, C., 2015. Monetary policy and sovereign debt vulnerability. Mimeo.
Passadore, J., Xandri, J.P., 2015. Robust conditional prediction in dynamic games: an application to sovereign debt. Mimeo.
Perez, D.J., 2015. Sovereign debt, domestic banks and the provision of public liquidity. Mimeo.
Reinhart, C.M., Rogoff, K.S., Savastano, M.A., 2003. Debt intolerance. Brook. Pap. Econ. Act. 34, 2003-1, 1–74.
Salomao, J., 2014. Sovereign debt renegotiations and credit default swaps. University of Minnesota, Mimeo.
Sanchez, J., Sapriza, H., Yurdagul, E., 2015. Sovereign default and choice of maturity. FRB St. Louis Working Paper 2014-031B.
Stangebye, Z.R., 2015a. Dynamic panics: theory and application to the eurozone. Working Paper.
Stangebye, Z.R., 2015b. Lifetime-laffer curves and the eurozone. University of Notre Dame, Mimeo.
Tomz, M., 2007. Reputation and International Cooperation. Princeton University Press, Princeton, NJ.
Tomz, M., Wright, M.L.J., 2007. Do countries default in "bad times"? J. Eur. Econ. Assoc. 5 (2-3), 352–360.
Yeyati, E.L., Panizza, U., 2011. The elusive costs of sovereign defaults. J. Dev. Econ. 94, 95–105.
Yue, V.Z., 2010. Sovereign default and debt renegotiation. J. Int. Econ. 80 (2), 176–187.

SECTION 4

Models of Economic Growth and Fluctuations

CHAPTER 22

RBC Methodology and the Development of Aggregate Economic Theory

E.C. Prescott
Arizona State University, Tempe, AZ, United States
Federal Reserve Bank of Minneapolis, Minneapolis, MN, United States

Contents

Handbook of Macroeconomics, Volume 2B
ISSN 1574-0048, http://dx.doi.org/10.1016/bs.hesmac.2016.03.001

Abstract

This essay reviews the development of neoclassical growth theory, a unified theory of aggregate economic phenomena that was first used to study business cycles and aggregate labor supply. Subsequently, the theory has been used to understand asset pricing, growth miracles and disasters, monetary economics, capital accounts, aggregate public finance, economic development, and foreign direct investment.

The focus of this essay is on real business cycle (RBC) methodology. Those who employ the discipline behind the methodology to address various quantitative questions come up with essentially the same answer—evidence that the theory has a life of its own, directing researchers to essentially the same conclusions when they apply its discipline. Deviations from the theory sometimes arise and remain open for a considerable period before they are resolved by better measurement and extensions of the theory. Elements of the discipline include selecting a model economy or sometimes a set of model economies. The model used to address a specific question or issue must have a consistent set of national accounts with all the accounting identities holding. In addition, the model assumptions must be consistent across applications and be consistent with micro as well as aggregate observations. Reality is complex, and any model economy used is necessarily an abstraction and therefore false. This does not mean, however, that model economies are not useful in drawing scientific inference.

The vast number of contributions made by many researchers who have used this methodology precludes reviewing them all in this essay. Instead, the contributions reviewed here are ones that illustrate methodological points or extend the applicability of neoclassical growth theory. Of particular interest will be important developments subsequent to the Cooley and Hansen (1995) volume, *Frontiers of Business Cycle Research*. The interaction between theory and measurement is emphasized because this is the way in which hard quantitative sciences progress.

Keywords

Neoclassical growth theory, Aggregate economic theory, RBC methodology, Aggregation, Business cycle fluctuations, Development, Aggregate financial economics, Prosperities, Depressions

JEL Classification Codes

B4, C10, E00, E13, E32, E60

1. INTRODUCTION

This chapter reviews the development and use of a quantitative, unified theory of aggregate variables both across time and across economies at a point in time. This theory accounts not only for traditional business cycle fluctuations but also for prosperities and depressions, as well as for the vast difference in living standards across countries. This unified quantitative dynamic general equilibrium theory accounts for the large movements in asset values relative to gross national income (GNI), the consequences of alternative monetary policies and tax systems, and the behavior of current accounts as well.

No competing quantitative theory has been developed for the study of aggregate economic behavior. This disciplined theory is unified and has been tested through successful use. The assumptions made when constructing a model economy, or in some cases a set of economies, to address a given question must be consistent with assumptions made in the previous successful applications. Deviations from this theory have arisen, which is evidence that some real theory is involved.[a] Other deviations remain to be discovered. Some of the recognized deviations or puzzles have been resolved via further development of the theory, others by better measurement. This interaction between theory and measurement is the way in which a hard quantitative science progresses.

We call this theory neoclassical growth theory. Key features of this theory are the allocation of productive time between market and household activities and the allocation of output between consumption and investment. Depending on the application, other features of reality must be included, such as sector detail, the nature of the financial system as specified by laws and regulations, and the contracting technology available. Heterogeneity of people in the model economy, with respect to age and idiosyncratic shocks, must be and has been included in models used to address issues such as the consequences of an aging population for various tax policy regimes.

The underlying theoretical framework is the theory of value, in particular the capital theory variant. This means the models used to draw scientific inference will have a recursive structure. This is a crucial feature for the model economies being used to draw scientific inference because the national account statistics can be constructed and compared with actual statistics.

To summarize, aggregate economics is now a hard quantitative science. It has been tested through successful use in all substantive fields of economics.

2. A BRIEF HISTORY OF BUSINESS CYCLES

Fluctuations in the level of business activity have long been a topic of concern. Mitchell (1913, 1927) collected many indicators of the level of economic activity. He viewed the level of economic activity as being cyclical with alternating periods of contractions and expansions. He developed the National Bureau of Economic Research (NBER) definition of recession, which is a period of contraction in the level of economic activity. This definition is still used by the NBER. He categorized his set of indicators into leading indicators, lagging indicators, and contemporaneous indicators. This was the framework he used for forecasting, and it did improve forecasting.

Mitchell called these fluctuations "business cycles." Wicksell (1918) used a rocking horse analogy to think about business cycles. Rocking horses display damped oscillations absent new shocks. This development led the profession to search for an economic structure with these properties. Frisch (1933) viewed business cycle research as the search for shocks or impulses to the economy and a damped oscillatory propagation mechanism.

[a] Trade theory is a disciplined theory. All using the discipline of trade theory come up with essentially the same findings. See Arkolakis et al. (2012).

Samuelson (1939) developed his multiplier–accelerator macroeconomic model that displayed these properties. His model had a consumption function and an investment equation. His model was also a second-order linear equation in real output with parameters that gave rise to damped oscillatory behavior.

The NBER definition of recessions is flawed along three dimensions. First, no corrections are made for trend growth or population size. With the NBER definition, the economy is in expansion 90% of the time and in recession or contraction 10% of the time. With trend-corrected real gross domestic product (GDP) per person 16 years and older, the economy is expanding approximately half of the time and contracting half of the time. Second, the NBER definition of recession is not revised subsequent to revisions in the economic time series. These revisions are sometimes large and are made years later as recent census data become available. If the revised data were used, the timing and magnitude of recessions and expansions would change. Third, the NBER definition of recession is not well defined and has a large subjective element.

The biggest problem in business cycle theory is that these so-called business cycles are not cyclical. This was established by Adelman and Adelman (1959), who found that the Klein–Goldberg model—the first econometric model to be used to forecast business cycles—displays damped nonoscillatory behavior. This finding, however, does not rule out the existence of longer cycles in the level of business activity. Kuznets's (1930) view was that there were 15- to 20-year cycles in output and prices in the United States. He labeled these fluctuations "secondary secular movements." Subsequently, they were called Kuznets cycles. Kondratieff and Stolper (1935) hypothesized even longer business fluctuations with 50- to 60-year cycles.

There are, of course, seasonal cycles, which are cycles in the true sense of the word. But they are of little interest and receive little attention in aggregate analysis. To handle them, the economic data used in aggregate analyses are seasonally adjusted.

2.1 The National Accounts: Defining Macroeconomics

A goal in the early 1930s was to come up with a measure of the performance of the business sector. Kuznets (1930) came up with one that proved to be useful. This measure is gross national product (GNP), the value of all final goods and services produced. Other researchers measured the value of the inputs to the business sector, which are the services of capital stocks. The most important category of these services is the services of different types of human capital. The aggregate value of human capital services is commonly called labor income. The services of tangible capital make up the other major category. The aggregate value of these services is called capital income. Claims against output are by definition income, and given that all businesses have a residual claimant, income equals product.

In the late 1930s, Tinbergen (1952) developed quantitative dynamic time series models and used them for forecasting. Given his background in physics, he thought in terms of empirically determined dynamic systems with instruments and targets.

On the other hand, Lawrence R. Klein, the father of macroeconometric modeling, had a theory underlying the dynamic aggregate models he developed and used for forecasting. The theory is the Hicksian IS-LM theory, later augmented with a Phillips curve. The beauty of Klein's work was that it featured a fully specified dynamic system, which had national accounts. All accounting identities held, which resulted in a consistent set of forecasts for all of the variables. Over time, these macroeconometric models grew in size as the sector detail became richer. Klein's model and other macroeconometric models in his framework came to dominate because their use dramatically improved forecasting. After World War II, for example, most economists thought the United States would experience another Great Depression. Using his model, Klein correctly forecasted that no depression would occur.

The nature of macroeconomics in the 1960s was coming up with a better equation to be included in the basic macroeconomic model. The generally held view was that the neoclassical foundations for the empirically determined aggregate dynamic system would subsequently be developed. The famous Phelps Conference at the University of Pennsylvania in 1969, entitled "Micro Foundations of Wage and Price Determination," tried to bring about the synthesis of macroeconometric models into neoclassical economics.

This neoclassical synthesis, however, was not to be. Lucas (1976a), in his paper entitled "Econometric Policy Evaluation: A Critique," found that the existence of a policy-invariant dynamic system is inconsistent with dynamic economic theory. The implication of this finding was that there was no hope for the neoclassical synthesis. The use of dynamic economic theory to evaluate policy requires that the dynamic system governing the evolution of the national accounts be an endogenous element and not a policy-invariant element, which can be empirically determined.

What happens at a point in time depends on what policy regime will be followed in the future. An implication of this fact is that economic theory cannot predict what will happen as a consequence of a possible current policy action choice. What will happen as the result of a policy action is not a well-posed question in the language of dynamic economic theory. What will happen if some policy rule or regime is followed in the future is a well-posed economic question—a point made by Lucas (1976a).

No one challenged Lucas's conclusions, and those who continued to support the use of macroeconometric models for evaluating policy took the position that a different theoretical framework was needed for the study of business cycle fluctuations. Indeed, many used the theory underlying macroeconometric models of the 1960s to confidently predict that the unemployment rate could be decreased by increasing the inflation rate. In 1969 the unemployment rate and inflation rate were both about 4%. The policy consensus based on the perceived trade-off between inflation and unemployment was that the unemployment rate should be reduced because the social gains from having a lower unemployment rate exceeded the cost of the higher inflation.

This consensus led to an attempt to exploit this trade-off in the 1970s. As Lucas and Sargent (1979) point out, this attempt failed—and failed spectacularly, as predicted by dynamic economic theory.[b] Given this failure of Keynesian macroeconomics, the question was what would replace it.

2.2 Neoclassical Growth Theory: The Theory Used in Aggregate Analysis

The development of aggregate measures of outputs and inputs to the business accounts led to the identification of a set of growth facts. Kaldor's (1957) stylized view of these facts for long-term economic growth in the United States and the United Kingdom are as follows. Roughly constant are capital and labor shares of national income, consumption and investment shares of output, the return on investment, and the capital–output ratio. Growing at the same rate over time are national income and the real wage.

Solow (1956) developed a simple, elegant model that accounted for these facts. The model has an aggregate production function with constant returns to scale, with labor and capital being paid their marginal product. All productivity change is labor augmenting. Investment is a constant share of output, and the time allocated to market production per worker is a constant. Thus, the household makes no decisions. Following Frisch (1970), I therefore refer to the model as being classical.

Around the same time, Swan (1956) developed his growth model that is also consistent with the Kaldor growth facts. The key difference between his model and Solow's model is that Swan did not require neutral technology change. Instead, he assumed a unit elasticity of substitution between the factors of production. In the Swan (1956) paper, he carries out some output accounting. The Swan model is the one that has been used for output accounting.

2.3 The Classical Growth Model and Business Cycle Fluctuations

Lucas (1976b) defined business cycles as being recurrent fluctuations of output and employment about trend and the key facts to be the nature of comovements of aggregate variables about trend. But without a definition of trend, this is not a fully specified definition of business cycle fluctuations. This led Hodrick and Prescott (1980) to develop an operational definition of trend, and they used it to represent time series as the sum of a trend component and a business cycle component. In constructing the trend, a penalty was imposed on the sum of squares of the second differences of the trend. In mathematical terms, a time series y_t is represented as the sum of a trend component g_t and a cyclical component c_t; that is,

$$y_t = g_t + c_t.$$

Given the values of the y_t, the g_t is selected to minimize

[b] Lucas (1972), in what was probably the first dynamic aggregate theory paper, developed a model that displayed an empirical Phillips curve. He predicted that if attempts were made to exploit, they would fail. This prediction was made prior to the attempts to lower the unemployment rate by increasing the inflation rate.

$$\sum_{t=1}^{T} c_t^2 + \lambda \sum_{t=-1}^{T} [(g_t - g_{t-1}) - (g_{t-1} - g_{t-2})]^2.$$

This simple operational procedure has a single smoothing parameter, $\lambda \geq 0$. This parameter is chosen to mimic the smooth curve researchers would draw through the data. The larger its value, the smoother is the trend component. For quarterly data, the first number that Hodrick and I chose and ended up using was 1600. There is no right or wrong number, and it cannot be estimated because it is part of an operational definition. What is desirable is that the same statistics are used across studies of business cycle fluctuations of this type. This uniformity permits comparisons across studies.

A feature of this procedure is that the same linear transformation of the logarithm of all the inputs and outputs to the business sector is made. Consequently, Swan's (1956) output accounting could be used for the operationally defined cyclical component of the time series.

In examining the nature of these fluctuations, researchers documented some business cycle facts for the deviations from trend for the US economy for the 1950.1 to 1979.2 period:

(i) Consumption, investment, market hours, and labor productivity all moved procyclically.
(ii) The standard deviation of fixed investment was 5.1%, and the standard deviation of consumption was only 1.3%.
(iii) Market hours and GDP per hour were roughly orthogonal, with hours having twice the variance.
(iv) The standard deviation of quarterly log output was 1.8%, and the first-order serial correlation was 0.74.
(v) Stocks of capital lagged output, with the lag increasing with the durability of the capital. Inventory stock was almost contemporaneous, producer durables stocks lagged a few quarters, and structures lagged a couple of years.

2.4 The Neoclassical Growth Model

Kydland and Prescott (1982) added an aggregate household to the classical growth model in order to endogenize two key allocation decisions. The first of these allocation decisions is the split of output between investment and consumption. The split varies cyclically. The second of these allocation decisions is how much productive time is allocated to the business sector and how much to the household sector. These allocations are endogenous elements of the neoclassical growth model and, with respect to the aggregate household, depend on both its willingness and its ability to substitute. Thus, this extension of the growth model made it neoclassical in the sense of Frisch (1970).

Kydland and I found that if there were persistent shocks to factors determining the balanced growth path *level* of the neoclassical growth model and if the aggregate household was sufficiently willing to intertemporally substitute market time, the neoclassical growth model displayed fluctuations of the business cycle variety. The aggregate utility function of the stand-in household had a high Frisch labor supply elasticity, much higher than the one labor economists estimated using a representative household construct.

If there are common homothetic convex preferences across households, the aggregated household's labor supply elasticity is the same as that of the individuals being aggregated. Empirically, however, these elasticities are not the same. Kydland and Prescott (1982) found that the aggregate labor supply elasticity must be in excess of 3 for the neoclassical growth model to predict business cycle fluctuations, whereas MaCurdy (1981), using panel data, estimated the labor supply elasticity of prime-age males working continuously to be only 0.15. The aggregate and disaggregate estimates must be consistent, and a reason for this difference is needed.

2.5 Why the Discrepancy Between Micro and Aggregate Elasticity Estimates?

Rogerson (1984) came up with the reason for the discrepancy between micro and aggregate estimates. He observed that the principal margin of adjustment in aggregate labor supply was in the number of people working in a given week and not in the hours worked per worker. Consequently, the micro estimate of the labor supply using a theoretical structure predicting just the opposite has to be dismissed as an estimate of the aggregate labor supply elasticity. The labor economist conclusion that tax rates had little consequence for aggregate labor supply was wrong. This is an important example of the failure of micro theory in drawing *aggregate* scientific inference. Aggregation matters. This was recognized by Marshall in his classic textbook first published in 1890 and by Wicksell around the same time. The aggregate production function, given that there is entry and exit of production units, is very different from the production functions of individual units.

Rogerson (1984) developed a formal theory of the aggregate utility function when there was labor indivisibility. This theory was developed in a static context. Hansen (1985) introduced it into the basic neoclassical growth model and found that the resulting model displayed business cycle fluctuations. This research resolved the puzzling discrepancy between micro and aggregate observations.

2.6 Why Is There Labor Indivisibility?

The puzzle of what could give rise to labor indivisibility was resolved by Hornstein and Prescott (1993), who found that if individuals' outputs of labor services is a function of the capital that each worker uses, the margin of adjustment is the number of people working and not the number of hours worked. The fraction working is the margin used up to the point at which all are working. This model endogenized labor indivisibility in a simple version of the optimal growth model. An important point is that it breaks the clean separation between preferences and technology in determining the aggregate elasticity of labor supply.

An alternative theory of labor indivisibility was subsequently developed by Prescott et al. (2009). The key feature of this theory is that the mapping of time allocated to the market to units of labor services supplied is not linear. The increasing mapping is initially convex. Reasons for this nonlinearity include the time needed to update information on which decisions are made and the time needed to get organized. Then the mapping becomes concave; one reason is that workers become tired and perform tasks less well or at a lower rate.

One implication of this theory is that workweeks of different lengths are different commodities. This was recognized by labor economist Rosen (1978). Hansen and Sargent (1988) have two workweek lengths in their business cycle paper: a standard workweek and an overtime workweek. The micro evidence in support of workweeks of different lengths being different commodities is strong. For example, two half-time workers on average are paid significantly less than one full-time worker with similar human capital. Additional evidence is that the normal workweek length differs across occupations. With this theory, the reason for the differences in workweek lengths across occupations is that the mapping from time allocated to the market to units of labor services produced is different across occupations. When important nonconvexities are present, the micro and aggregate elasticities are different even if all the micro units are identical.

This is true for both the household and the business sectors. At the production unit level, investment is very lumpy, yet at the aggregate level, aggregate investment is smooth. Thomas (2002) established that valuation equilibrium theory predicts that the fraction of units making discrete adjustments to production capacity will be the margin of adjustment used, as it is, and aggregate investment will be smooth.

Time series methods used to model aggregate time series use linear models. This is because there are no obvious nonlinearities in the time series. The one case in which nonlinearity was found to be significant was in the Hansen and Prescott (2005) model with a capacity utilization constraint. If capacity constraints are occasionally binding, aggregation theory leads to an aggregate production function that has a kink, which results in the labor income share falling when the capacity constraint is binding. It also implies that business cycle peaks will be flatter and smaller than troughs for the detrended data as they are. This is an improvement in theory but is of second-order importance.

2.7 A Digression on Methodology of Aggregate Analysis

Theory is a set of instructions for constructing a model economy to address a given question. The criterion for a good theory is that it is useful. Models are instruments used to draw scientific inference. What constitutes a good model depends on what question is being addressed. Reality is incredibly complex, and any model is necessarily an abstraction and therefore false.

The model economy selected in a particular application is not the one that best fits a particular set of economic statistics. It must fit along selected dimensions of reality given the question. To illustrate this idea, consider the question of how much of the higher average return on publicly traded stocks is a premium for bearing aggregate risk. The highly liquid short-term debt is called the safe asset. However, it is not a perfectly safe asset, as is the model economy's safe asset. A perfectly safe asset does not exist. Government debt is not safe because governments default fully or partially in extreme events. Therefore, the nature of the consumption process in the model economy used must not have the possibility of extreme events.

The model economy that Mehra and Prescott (1985) used to address this issue had only one type of infinitely lived households and a pure endowment process. We specified a Markov chain process on the growth rate of this endowment, which rules out extreme events. Equilibrium consumption was the output of the endowment process. The relation examined was the return on the endowment process and a security that paid one unit of consumption in the next market in the sequence with certainty in the sequence of market equilibria. Empirically, the difference in average yields on equity and short-term relatively risk-free liquid debt was over 6%. The finding was that only a small part of the difference in average yields on the two classes of securities was accounted for by a premium for bearing nondiversifiable aggregate risk.

Will a class of model economies with a richer class of processes on consumption growth rates resolve this puzzle? The answer is no because the abstraction used permits *any* stationary process on consumption growth rates. Our abstraction did rule out extreme events because truly risk-free assets do not exist.

This finding raised the question of what factors were giving rise to this big difference. McGrattan and Prescott (2005) subsequently learned that introducing taxes on distributions by corporations to owners reduced the premium by a third. Economic theory says it is after-tax distributions that should be considered in determining the return on different assets.

Another significant factor is the cost of managing assets. Pension funds have sizable costs that reduce the return on equity realized by households who are the indirect owners of the equity held by these funds. On the other hand, the cost of managing a portfolio of short-term liquid assets is small. The magnitude of the asset management and intermediation costs can be estimated using national income and product accounts. The aggregate value of the corporate equity held either directly or indirectly by the household sector can be estimated using aggregate balance sheet statistics. The annual costs are about 2% of the total value of the assets. This exercise was carried out in Mehra et al. (2011).

Most of the remainder of the difference in average yields is almost surely due to a liquidity premium for carry-out transactions. This leads to the conclusion that the equity premium puzzle is no longer a puzzle. Better measurement may identify a deviation from theory, but for the time being, theory is ahead of measurement with respect to the equity premium.

The model economy used to measure and estimate the premium for bearing nondiversifiable aggregate risk has no investment. In fact, investment is a sizable share of output. The model is not realistic along this dimension. However, this very simple model is sufficiently rich to address the question asked. The salient features of reality are incorporated into the model being used to address the given issue. The general principle is, if the question can be addressed with a simpler model, use the simpler one.

2.8 The Need for Discipline

A useful theory must have an associated discipline. Scientists, who employ the discipline and use the theory to answer a given question, reach the same conclusion as to what the theory says or does not say. Given the current state of the theory, the conclusion may state that the theory has to be extended before the question can be addressed. Or it may say that the answer depends on the magnitude of certain parameters, which have not yet been measured sufficiently accurately. The theory used in aggregate analysis is neoclassical growth theory. A crucial feature of this discipline is that when researchers extend the theory in order to resolve a deviation from theory or to expand its domain of applicability, the extended theory must be consistent with previously successful applications of the theory.

In the subsequent sections of this chapter, the development and use of neoclassical growth theory will be reviewed. This theory is applicable to virtually all substantive areas of economics including not only traditional business cycle fluctuations but also differences in per capita output levels across countries and across times. It is the theory in aggregate public finance, financial asset pricing, labor economics, monetary economics, environmental economics, and international finance.

The model economy used in an application is restricted by more disaggregated statistics. For example, the assumed time-to-build for new structures must be consistent with how long it typically takes to build a new structure. Econometricians have constructed statistical tests that rejected the Hansen (1985) model of business cycles. That model abstracted from time-to-build, because Hansen found this feature of reality to be of secondary importance in understanding business cycle fluctuations. Using data generated by the Kydland and Prescott (1982) model, which has a time-to-build technology, these statistical tests would lead to a rejection of the RBC model generating the data. It would be easy to come up with another test that would result in the rejection of the model with time-to-build. The implication is that statistical hypothesis testing is of little use in selecting a model to address some given question.

3. THE NATURE OF THE DISCIPLINE

3.1 The Back and Forth Between Theory and Measurement

The study of business cycle fluctuations led to the construction of dynamic stochastic general equilibrium models of these fluctuations. These early models had a quadratic household utility flow function and linear technology constraint. This research program did not produce models with national accounts that could be compared to the actual ones. Their use did not satisfy the Klein discipline. Examples of these early models include Sargent (1976) and Kydland and Prescott (1977). Another limitation was that using other observations in economics to restrict the choice of the model economy was difficult and, in some cases, impossible.

What turned out to be the big breakthrough was the use of growth theory to study business cycle fluctuations. A question is, why did it take so long before it was used for this purpose? The answer is that, based on micro theory reasoning, dynamic economic theory was viewed as being useless in understanding business cycle fluctuations. This view arose because, cyclically, leisure and consumption moved in opposite directions. Being that these goods are both normal goods and there is little cyclical movement in their relative price, micro reasoning leads to the conclusion that leisure should move procyclically when in fact it moves strongly countercyclically. Another fact is that labor productivity is a procyclical variable; this runs counter to the prediction of micro theory that it should be countercyclical, given the aggregate labor input to production. Micro reasoning leads to the incorrect conclusion that these aggregate observations violated the law of diminishing returns.

In order to use growth theory to study business cycle fluctuations, the investment-consumption decision and the labor-leisure decision must be endogenized. Kydland and Prescott (1982) introduced an aggregate household to accomplish this. We restricted attention to the household utility function for which the model economies had a balanced growth path, and this balanced growth path displayed the growth facts. With this extension, growth theory and business cycle theory were integrated. It turned out that the predictions of dynamic aggregate theory were consistent with the business cycle facts that ran counter to the conclusion of those using microeconomic reasoning.

That time-to-build model economy had only technology shocks, so the analysis was restricted to determining the consequences of different types of technological shock processes for the cyclical behavior of the neoclassical growth model. Kydland and Prescott (1982) found that if there are persistent technology shocks and the aggregate elasticity of labor supply is high, neoclassical growth theory can predict fluctuations of the business cycle variety. By construction, the model economy displayed the growth facts. However, the aggregate Frisch elasticity of labor supply is not tied down by the growth facts. Two questions needed to be answered before one could say that the neoclassical growth model displays business cycle fluctuations of the nature observed. The first question was whether the Frisch elasticity of the aggregate household labor supply was at least 3. The second question was whether technology shocks were highly persistent and of the right magnitude.

One criticism of Kydland's and my analysis was that empirically, cyclical labor productivity and total hours were roughly orthogonal during the period studied, whereas for the model economy, they were highly correlated. If productivity shocks were the only factor contributing to fluctuations, this would be a valid criticism, and business cycle fluctuations would be inconsistent with neoclassical growth theory. But productivity shocks were not the only factor giving rise to business cycle fluctuations during this period. To determine how much of the business cycle fluctuations were accounted for by productivity shocks, an estimate of the variance of these shocks was needed. This was provided by Prescott (1986). Given the estimate, labor productivity and aggregate hours worked should be roughly orthogonal, as they were during the period studied. The finding is that the US economy would have been 70% as volatile as it was during the period considered if productivity shocks were the only shocks.

The nature of the shock is important in the theory. If one thinks that all productivity change is due to the growth of knowledge useful in production, productivity shocks generally should be negative; in fact, however, productivity shocks are sometimes negative. One implication is that variations in the growth of the stock of useful knowledge cannot be the only reason for changes in productivity. Another factor giving rise to changes in productivity are changes in legal and regulatory constraints. Such changes can both increase and decrease productivity. The huge differences in productivity that are observed across countries provide strong evidence that the legal and regulatory systems are of great importance in determining the level of productivity.

3.2 Monopolistic Competition: Small Consequences for Business Cycle Accounting

Neoclassical growth theory assumes price taking in market transactions. Does abstracting from the fact that some businesses and groups of factor suppliers have market power and are not price takers alter the conclusions of the simple abstraction? Hornstein (1993) introduced monopolistic competition and found that for measuring the contribution of productivity shocks to business cycle fluctuations, it mattered little. He calibrated a monopolistic competitive model to the same set of statistics as those using the neoclassical growth model did. With monopolistic competition, the response to the shocks is greater, but this is offset by a smaller estimate of the variance of the underlying productivity shock. For this purpose, abstracting from market power mattered little for the estimate of the contribution of productivity shocks to business cycle fluctuations. For some other issues, this is probably not the case. This illustrates the way in which the theory progresses. A finding is successfully challenged by showing that introducing some feature of reality in a disciplined way changes the answer to the question. The results of unsuccessful challenges are of interest, for they add to the confidence in the original study.

3.3 Nonneutral Technological Change: Little Consequence in Basic Model

The relative price of the composite investment good and the composite consumption good has not been constant, as it is in the basic neoclassical growth model. Secularly, what is more or less constant is the value of investment goods produced relative to the value of all goods produced in nominal terms. A world in which the relative price of the investment good falls is one with the following aggregate production relation:

$$c_t + (1+\gamma)^{-t} x_t \leq A k_t^{\theta} h_t^{1-\theta},$$

where $\gamma > 0$. There is balanced growth with the relative price of the investment good to the consumption good falling at rate γ. Greenwood et al. (1988) show this. Another interesting finding in their paper concerns the nature of depreciation for the theory of business cycle fluctuations.

3.4 Nature of Depreciation: Matters

The standard abstraction for depreciation is the perpetual inventory assumption with a constant depreciation rate:

$$k_{t+1} = (1-\delta)k_t + x_t.$$

Greenwood et al. (1988) assume that the rate of depreciation increases with the intensity of the use of capital; that is, they assume a Taubman and Wilkinson (1970) depreciation technology. Let u_t denote the capital utilization rate. Capital services provided are $u_t k_t$. The depreciation rate is an increasing function of the utilization rate, $\delta_t = \delta(u_t)$. With this assumption, the response to productivity shocks is bigger and the aggregate elasticity of labor supply smaller for the model calibrated to the growth facts.

I am sure that this alternative theory of depreciation was considered by the national income and product accountants and found not to be important. It is true that during periods of high economic activity, some capital is utilized more intensely. However, for many capital goods, depreciation does not depend on the intensity of use. One reason is that during boom periods, machines are well maintained in order to keep them operating efficiently. Better maintenance lowers the depreciation rate. Higher occupancy rates of office buildings do not increase their depreciation rate. The national accounts stuck with the perpetual inventory method and useful life in calculating aggregate depreciation because it was consistent with the prices of used capital equipment. This is another example of micro evidence restricting the model economy being used to address an aggregate issue.

If this alternative theory of depreciation had passed the micro test, it would have introduced a number of discrepancies within the theory. Business cycle observations would imply a smaller aggregate labor supply elasticity, and this in turn would imply that the theory predictions for cross-country differences in aggregate labor supply arising from differences in the marginal tax rate on labor income would be much smaller than what they are. About the only way to resolve these discrepancies would be to assume country-specific differences in preferences that give rise to both higher marginal tax rates and lower labor supply. With this resolution, however, there would be big discrepancies between the predictions of theory for aggregate labor supply during growth miracles.

The important point is that preference and technology parameters, with the discipline reviewed here, must be consistent across applications.

3.5 Monetary Policy: Little Consequence for Business Cycle Fluctuations

The general view prior to the development of quantitative aggregate economic theory was that monetary policy had important real consequences for the behavior of real variables, in particular real output and employment. Once explicit transactions abstractions were developed that gave rise to a demand for money, it was possible to introduce them into the neoclassical growth theory and to assess their quantitative consequences for real variables. Cooley and Hansen (1995) did this and found that the real consequences were small for monetary policies that did not give rise to very high rates of inflation. This supported the empirical findings of Sargent and Sims (1977) that real movements were not the result of monetary factors in the postwar US economy.

Sticky wage and nominal staggered wage contracting arrangements were subsequently introduced into the neoclassical growth model and their quantitative consequences for real findings determined by Chari et al. (2000). The finding was that these mechanisms did not give rise to business cycle fluctuations of the nature observed.

Another bit of strong evidence for the unimportance of monetary policy is the fact that RBC models that abstract from monetary factors do not have large deviations from observations during periods with high variations in inflation rates, such as during the period 1978–82 in the United States.

3.6 Two Important Methodological Advances

In critiquing the use of neoclassical growth theory to study business cycle fluctuations, Summers (1986) asked a good question: What are these shocks? An important methodological advancement to the theory was needed before his question could be answered. The advancement was path analysis.

3.6.1 Path Analysis

Hansen and Prescott (1993) used path analysis when they addressed the question of whether technology shocks caused the 1990–91 recession. In that paper, the dynamic system for the model was used to generate time paths of the variables given the realized values of the stocks. The finding was that yes, productivity shocks did cause that recession.

That paper offered another interesting finding. A prediction of the technology-shock-only model is that the economy should have recovered in 1993–94, since productivity had returned to trend. Other factors had to be depressing the economy during this period. Subsequently, the factors were identified. They were increases in tax rates.

3.6.2 Distribution of Firms with Inventories a State Variable

A widely held view was that inventory behavior was important for understanding business cycle fluctuations given the large cyclical variability of inventory investment. The micro theory of inventory investment was developed, but introducing this feature into quantitative neoclassical growth theory was impossible given the lack of needed tools.

Fisher and Hornstein (2000) developed a way to introduce inventory investment when firms faced fixed resource costs when making an inventory investment. This made the stock of inventory a firm state variable and the distribution of firms as indexed by their inventory stock an aggregate state variable. This methodological advance was also used by Hornstein (1993) to assess the quantitative importance of monopolistic competition.

3.7 The Big Aggregate Economic Puzzle of the 1990s

A boom in output and employment in the United States began about 1994 and continued until the very end of the decade. This boom was puzzling from the perspective of what was then aggregate economic theory. In this boom, the corporate profit share of GNI was low. In other booms, this share was higher than normal. Another puzzling observation was that GDP per hour, the commonly used measure of productivity, was low in this boom. Normally, productivity accounts for about a third of the cyclical variation in GDP and market hours the other two-thirds. In this boom, the accounting was 125% due to market hours worked and negative 25% due to productivity. No changes in labor market policies or tax rates could account for these phenomena. This puzzle remained open for at least 6 years. One explanation consistent with general equilibrium theory was that Americans—as well as Europeans—experienced a contagious case of workaholism; that is, the rate at which people's willingness to substitute labor for leisure in the aggregate changed. Such explanations violate the discipline of dynamic aggregate theory reviewed in this essay.

To answer this question, two developments in quantitative aggregate theory were crucial. One was the use of an equilibrium condition for a class of economies that depend on current-period variables to account for the large differences in hours worked per working-age person across countries and across time. This equilibrium condition used was that the marginal rate of consumption and leisure is equal to the after-tax wage. A Cobb–Douglas production function was assumed, so the wage was just aggregate labor income divided by aggregate hours.[c] The elasticity of substitution between consumption and leisure for the aggregate household was the same as the one needed for the neoclassical growth model to display business cycle fluctuations.

The reason that Western Europeans now work 30% less than other advanced industrial countries is not that they are lazy or are better at making use of nonmarket productive time. It is that these countries have higher marginal tax rates on labor income and on consumption. These higher tax rates introduce a large tax wedge between the intratemporal marginal rate of substitution and the marginal rate of transformation between consumption and market time.

The second development was to use this methodology to account for the large secular movements in the value of corporations relative to GNP in the United States and the United Kingdom in the 1960–2000 period. The equilibrium relation used for the class of models considered was the following one. The market value of corporations is equal to the market value of the capital stocks owned by the firm. Given the importance of intangible capital in determining the value of corporations, this stock had to be included in the analysis. Brand names, organization capital, patents, and technology know-how embodied in the organization all contribute to the value of the business enterprise.

With these two developments, the stage was set for resolving the US hours boom of the 1990s.

4. MAJOR DEVELOPMENTS AND THEIR APPLICATIONS POST-1995

Important theoretical advancements in neoclassical growth theory have continued to occur and have expanded the theory's applicability. Also important was the development of new and better data sets that are easily accessible. These data sets are more uniform across countries, which facilitates the study of factors giving rise to international differences in economic aggregates. Increases in computing power made possible the introduction of demographics into models being used to draw scientific inference using the theory. The life cycle is crucial for understanding aggregate savings behavior as it gives rise to savings for retirement.

4.1 Clubs in the Theory and France's 35-Hour Workweek Policy

A development in valuation theory was the introduction of clubs. Clubs are arrangements that internalize externalities, whether they are positive or negative, within organizations that are small relative to the economy. One extremely important type of club is the household. In classical valuation theory, household clubs are a primitive. For each household, there is an agent that chooses an optimal point in a subset of the commodity

[c] This is the measure of wages used by Lucas and Rapping (1969) when they introduced labor supply into macroeconometric modeling.

space—that is, in that household's consumption possibility set—subject to its budget constraint. Business organizations are clubs as well. A firm is defined by its production possibility set, which is a subset of the commodity space, and the households' shares of ownership. Cole and Prescott (1997) extend valuation equilibrium theory to permit clubs.

To date, this development has been little used in quantitative aggregate analyses. To the best of my knowledge, I am aware of only one aggregate quantitative application using clubs. This application is due to Fitzgerald (1998), who uses this extension of the basic theory to predict the consequences of France's 35-hour workweek constraint. His framework has two types of households and two types of labor services: skilled and unskilled. Type 1 household can only supply unskilled labor. Type 2 household can supply either type. The important constraint is that for each firm, the work schedule of those performing the skilled and the unskilled tasks must be equal. The skilled workers' tasks include supervising, monitoring, and coordinating the unskilled workers.

The goal of the French 35-hour workweek policy was to help the unskilled and not the highly paid skilled workers. It turned out that the skilled are made better off under the 35-hour workweek and the unskilled worse off, counter to this objective. The legal constraint, which changed the technology set of a firm, had an unintended consequence. The program did have the intended consequence of increasing the employment rate of the unskilled.

4.2 Cartelization Policies and the Resolution of the US Great Depression Puzzle

Cole and Ohanian (1999) initiated a program of using the theory to study great depressions. They found a big deviation from the theory for the 1930–39 US Great Depression. This deviation was the failure of market hours per working-age person to recover to their predepression level. Throughout the 1930s, market hours per working-age person were 20–25% below their predepression level. The reasons for depressed labor supply were not financial. No financial crises occurred during the period 1934–39. The period had no deflation, and interest rates were low. This led Cole and Ohanian to rule out monetary policy as the reason for the depressed labor supply. Neither was the behavior of productivity the reason. Productivity recovered to trend in 1934 and subsequently stayed near the trend path.

These findings led Cole and Ohanian to search for an extension of the theory that would resolve this puzzling failure of the US economy to recover in the 1930s. They observed that relative wages in the cartelized industries increased relative to those in the noncartelized industries. Employment in the cartelized industries was the most depressed and did not recover. Those in the cartelized industries were the insiders and those in the competitive industries the outsiders. The problem Cole and Ohanian had to solve was to figure out how to introduce a cartelization arrangement into quantitative aggregate theory.

Eventually, Cole and Ohanian (2004) figured out a way and found that the cartelization policy was a major factor in accounting for the failure of the US economy to recover from the Great Depression subsequent to the recovery of productivity. They estimated that the cartelization policy alone accounted for over half of the depression in employment in the US Great Depression of the 1930s. It turned out that tax and wage policies can account for much of the remainder, so the Great Depression is no longer a puzzle.

McGrattan (2012) extended the theory to permit the consequences of expected future tax rate increases on the distributions from businesses to their owners. She found that they were important in accounting for the great decline in output in 1930. Businesses made large cash distributions to their owners rather than using cash to finance new investment. Fisher and Hornstein (2002) established that wage policies that set the wage above equilibrium value gave rise to the Great Depression in Germany from 1927 to 1932. The elimination of these policies late in 1932 resulted in rapid recovery from Germany's Great Depression, just as theory predicts.

4.3 Taxes and Country Labor Supply: Cross-Application Verification

The question is whether the theory used to study business cycle fluctuations accounts for the large difference in labor supply, as measured by market hours per working-age person, between Americans and Western Europeans. During the period 1993–96, Americans worked on average 40% more than did the French, Italian, and Germans. This was not always the case. In the period 1970–74, market hours per working-age person were comparable in both the United States and Western Europe and comparable to what they are now in the advanced industrial countries, with the notable exception of Western Europe.

The equilibrium relation used in Prescott (2004) to predict the difference in labor supply as a function of the effective tax rate on labor income was that the marginal rate of substitution between nonmarket productive time and consumption is equal to the after-tax real wage. A Cobb–Douglas aggregate production was assumed.

This equilibrium condition for country i can be written as

$$h_{it} = \frac{1-\theta}{1-\theta + \frac{c_{it}}{y_{it}}\frac{\alpha}{1-\tau_{it}}}.$$

Here, θ is the capital share parameter, α the value of leisure parameter, h_{it} the market hours per working-age person, τ_{it} the effective average marginal tax rate on labor income, and c_{it}/y_{it} the fraction of aggregate output consumed.

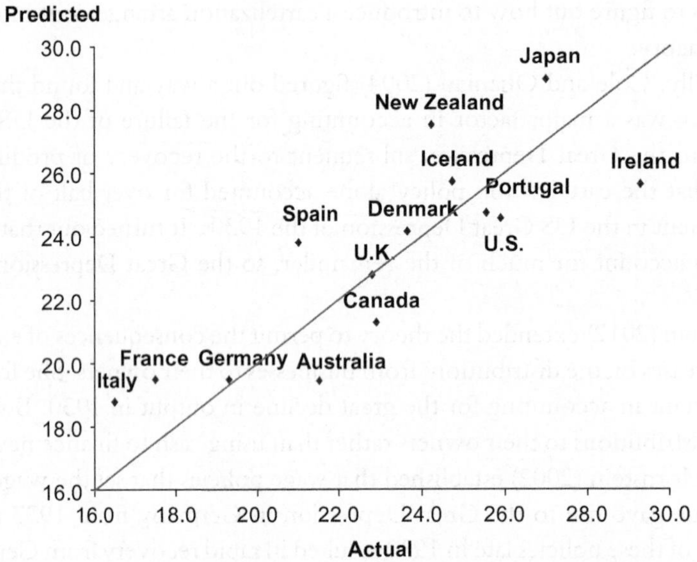

Fig. 1 Predicted and actual hours worked per working-age person, 1990–2002.

The analysis has only one free parameter, namely, the preference parameter α. This parameter is not tied down by the balanced growth facts. The capital income share parameter was nearly constant across countries and periods and was set equal to 1/3. The preference parameter α was picked so that the relation held for the United States.

The US boom in the 1990s was unlike previously studied booms and was at variance with the basic neoclassical growth model as discussed previously. Fig. 1 plots predicted and actual hours worked per working-age person for the period 1990–2002 using the model without intangible capital. It was a puzzle in the theory that remained open for 8 years. No alternative theory predicted this boom.

4.4 Use of the Overlapping Generations Abstract

For many issues, it does not matter whether the dynastic family or the overlapping generation structure is used. Before the great increase in computing capabilities, using the overlapping generation structure was not feasible. Braun et al. (2009) exploited this increase in computing capabilities and found that both the dynasty and the overlapping generation constructs are consistent with the fall in Japanese savings rates in the 1990s. However, the two constructs for aggregate households imply very different behavior for the Japanese savings rate post-2010. Because of Japan's large baby boom in the 1960s, the fraction of people who were dissaving to finance retirement would increase subsequent to 2010, and the aggregate savings rate would fall. Quantitatively, the savings rate did just what the theory with an overlapping generation structure predicted it would do.

5. INTANGIBLE CAPITAL EXPANDS THE APPLICABILITY OF THE THEORY

That intangible capital investment financed and owned by firms is big has never been in dispute. A question is why intangible capital was not incorporated into quantitative aggregate theory. The answer is that there was no disciplined way to incorporate this largely unreported component of output into the theory. The development of a consistent set of balance sheets for the household and business sectors was key to resolving this problem. Balance sheets, among other things, report the value of ownership of corporate equity.

5.1 The Value of Corporate Businesses

The price of capital good K_j is $q_j(\pi)$, where π specifies tax policy. Tax policy includes not only tax rates on corporate accounting profits but also the tax rate on distributions to owners, the nature of the capital consumption allowance, and the inflation rate. An important input to production is the services of human capital owned by the employees of the corporation. It is rivalrous and does not show up in the value of corporations. Consequently, it need not be included in the model used to determine the value of corporate businesses.

The aggregate corporate market value V, where subscript T denotes tangible capital and subscript I denotes firm-owned intangible capital, is

$$V = q_T(\pi)K_T + q_I(\pi)K_I.$$

If there were no capital income taxes, the prices of capital in units of the consumption good would be 1. But there are capital income taxes.

The price of one unit of tangible capital in terms of the consumption good, given that nearly all investment is financed through retained earnings, is

$$q_T = (1 - \tau_{\text{dist}}),$$

where τ_{dist} is the tax rate on distributions from corporations to owners. The average marginal tax rate on distributions is used. In the 1960s, virtually all distributions were in the form of dividends. The tax rate used was the average of the individual marginal tax rates weighted by the total dividends received by the group subject to that marginal tax rate. In the 1960s, this average tax rate was about 45%. Beginning in the 1980s, buybacks began to be used and permitted distributions to be deferred to when the capital gains were realized. This lowered the average tax on distributions.

Intangible capital was expensed, and as a consequence, its price to the owners of the businesses making the investment is smaller than the cost of producing it. The price of intangible capital is

$$q_I = (1 - \tau_{\text{dist}})\left(1 - \tau_{\text{corp profits}}\right).$$

In both the United States and the United Kingdom, there were large movements in V relative to annual GNI over the period studied by McGrattan and Prescott (2005) using this theory. The V/GNI number varied by a factor of 2.5 in the United States and by a factor of 3.0 in the United Kingdom during the period 1860–2000. This variation was not due to variation in the ratio of after-tax corporate income to GNI. This ratio varied little over the period. The theory found that the reason for the large secular changes was due to changes in taxes and regulations. Intangible capital was an important part of the value of corporations.

The big change in the tax system that increased the value of corporations was the deferred compensation individual savings account. These accounts permitted households to save for retirement free of capital income taxes. Insofar as the withdrawals are used to finance retirement consumption, there is no intertemporal wedge between the marginal rate of substitution between current and future consumption and the marginal rate of transformation between current and future consumption.

The added capital alone had little consequence for business cycle fluctuation accounting, so no new puzzles were created with this extension. An old puzzle that has not been resolved is the LeRoy and Porter (1981) and Shiller (1981) excess asset price volatility puzzle. Indeed, by looking at the values of the capital stocks owned by firms rather than at the present value of dividends, McGrattan and Prescott (2005) strengthened this excess volatility puzzle. These capital stocks vary smoothly, so the theory predicts their prices should as well.

In the model with intangible capital owned by business enterprises, we used an alternative aggregate production technology to the aggregate production function. There are three inputs: the services of tangible capital, the services of rival human capital, and the services of intangible capital. There are two output goods: one the composite output good less intangible capital investment and the other intangible capital investment. There were two *activities*: one producing intangible capital and one producing other final goods.

It is not a two-sector model because the services of intangible capital are not allocated between activities, as are the services of the other two inputs, but are used in both simultaneously by both activities. Otherwise, the production technology is standard. Letting Y_1 be output less intangible investment output, Y_2 intangible investment output, K_T tangible capital stock, K_I intangible capital stock, and L rival human capital services (labor), total output of the two activities is

$$\begin{aligned} Y_1 &= A_1 F_1(K_{T1}, K_I, L_1) \\ Y_2 &= A_2 F_2(K_{T2}, K_I, L_2) \\ K_T &= K_{T1} + K_{T2} \\ L &= L_1 + L_2 \end{aligned}$$

One unit of capital produces one unit of its services. All variables implicitly have a time subscript including the productivity parameters A_1 and A_2. The functions F_1 and F_2 have all the standard properties of the aggregate production function.

The important feature of the technology is that K_I has no activity subscript. A brand name can be used to produce a product sold in the market as well as in the development of a related product. The same is true of patents. The other two inputs are allocated between the activities. If productivity change is neutral in the sense that A_{1t}/A_{2t} stays constant, the implications for business cycles are the same. Thus, this technology works where the basic neoclassical growth model works. This part of the discipline is satisfied.

A problem is that most intangible capital investment made by firms and owned by firms is expensed and therefore not part of measured output. The question is how to incorporate this unobservable in a disciplined way. McGrattan developed a way (see McGrattan and Prescott, 2010b). The size of intangible capital net investment has implications for accounting profits of the corporate sector. Knowing the initial stock, the stocks can be computed from statistics reported in the national income and product accounts (NIPA).

5.2 US Hours Boom in the 1990s: A Crisis in RBC

The basic neoclassical growth theory model accurately predicted the behavior of the US economy prior to the 1990s, taking productivity taxes and demographics as exogenous. Theory was then ahead of measurement. In the 1990s it did not predict accurately. Market hours boomed while GDP per hour, the usual measure of productivity relative to trend, declined. The simple accounting was that the labor input accounted for 125% of the output and the standard measure of productivity for *minus* 25%. Typically, hours account for about two-thirds of the detrended change and productivity for the other third.

Taxes were not the answer, since the intratemporal tax wedge was, if anything, larger than before the boom. There were no major labor market reforms that improved the performance of the labor market. Economists were faced with the puzzle of why people were working so much. Fig. 2 plots the predicted and actual paths using the basic growth model without the introduction of intangible capital into the theory.

It was recognized that large investments in intangible capital were being made, and most were not reported as part of output because they were expensed. At the time, only computer software investment was reported.

Aggregate economics is not the only science with unobservable variables. A translation of a quote by Albert Einstein reads: "Not everything that counts can be counted, and not everything that can be counted counts." The key relation is the accounting profit equation. The bigger the net unmeasured intangible investment, the smaller were these problems. This finding, along with the fact that accounting profits were a small share of GDP in this hours boom period, is consistent with intangible investment being large. Other evidence is from the National Science Foundation. The NSF provides estimates of private R&D expenditures, which are an important

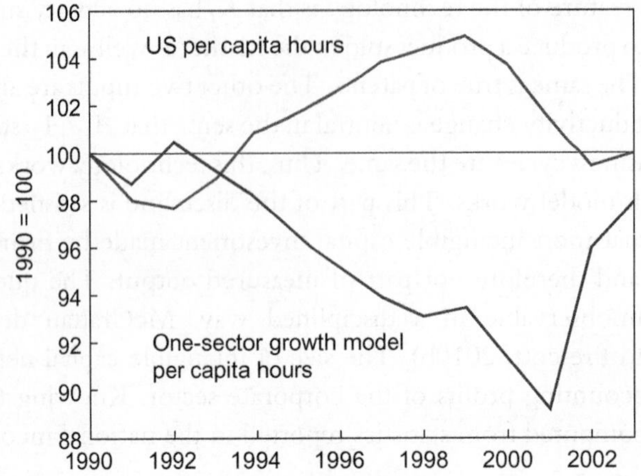

Fig. 2 Without intangible capital: big deviation from theory.

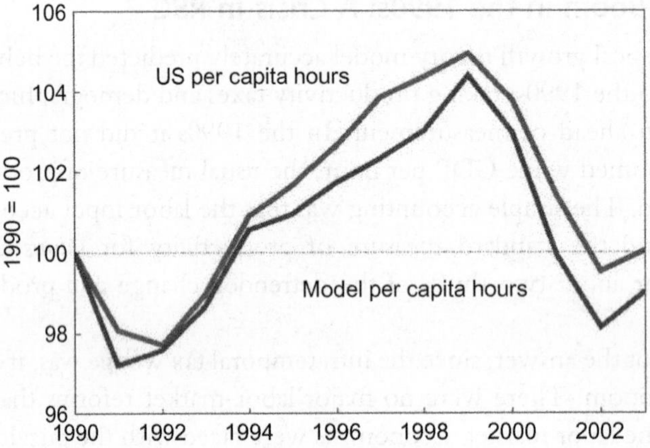

Fig. 3 With intangible capital: no deviation from theory.

component of intangible capital investment. These investment expenditures in percentage terms increased much more than measured investment expenditures during the 1990s boom.

With the introduction of intangible capital and nonneutral technology change in the production of GDP and intangible capital investment, measurement was again in conformity with theory. This is shown in Fig. 3.

The extended theory accounts for capital gains reported in the Federal Reserve System's flow of funds accounts. About half of these investments are financed by the owners of corporations subject to the corporate income tax and half by worker-owners of other businesses, which matches with micro observations.

5.3 Technology Capital

Intangible capital falls into different categories. Some are specific to the local production units and market. Some are assets with services that can be used at multiple locations. Virtually every metropolitan area in the United States has the same set of major retailers. Each of these major retailers uses the same know-how and name for all their retail outlets. The branches rely on their central headquarters for supply-side management, financial services, and advertising services. Intangible capital that can be used at multiple locations is technology capital. Investment in this type of capital is financed by location rents.

There are no increasing returns to scale, even though a closed economy with more locations will be richer than a closed economy with fewer locations, other things being equal. A production unit at a given location faces decreasing returns to scale. The production unit, being a price taker, realizes location rents. With technology capital, a reason for foreign direct investment (FDI) exists.

5.4 Use in Estimating Gains from Openness

Estimating gains from openness was originally introduced to study the role of openness in economic development (see McGrattan and Prescott, 2009). The observation was that for 50 years prior to World War II, the EU-6 GDP labor productivity was only a little more than half that of the United States, as it was in 1957 when the Treaty of Rome was signed. In the subsequent 30 years, EU-6 productivity caught up to that in the United States. This strongly suggests that openness fosters economic development. The role of trade can account for only one-ninth of the gain if the model used in the estimation is restricted to be consistent with the trade flows. Technology capital accounts for about one-third. This evidence indicates that other factors associated with openness are even more important. Two factors that have not yet been incorporated into the theory that empirically seem important are the faster diffusion of public knowledge and increasing competition reducing barriers to adopting more efficient technologies in production.

The technology extension has already permitted the theory to be used to assess China's direct foreign investment policy. Holmes et al. (2015) find that the Chinese policy of requiring access to technology capital of the foreign multinational making FDI in China in return for access to the huge Chinese market was in China's economic interest. In making these restrictions, China is violating the rules of the World Trade Organization. With the renminbi gaining reserve currency, interest in becoming more open to direct foreign investment will increase in China. This illustrates the usefulness of the theory in still another area, and, as stated earlier, usefulness is one criterion for a successful scientific theory.

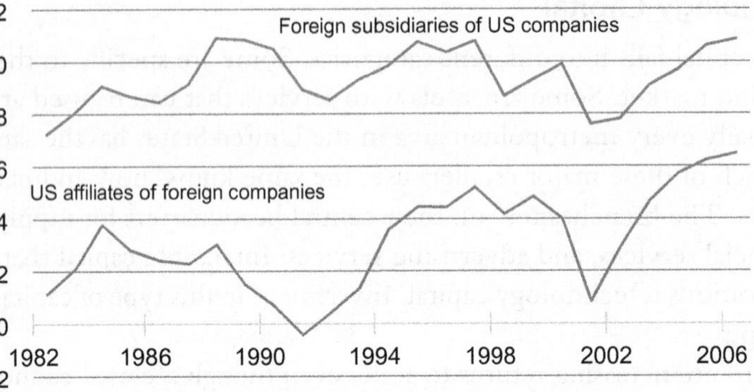

Fig. 4 BEA average FDI annual returns.

5.5 Use in Accounting for Features of US Current Accounts

A feature of US current accounts is the high reported earnings of US companies on their FDI and the low reported earnings of foreign companies' FDI in the United States. As reported by the Bureau of Economic Analysis (BEA), during the period 1982–2005, US companies earned an average return of 9.3 percentage points on their FDI, whereas foreign companies earned an average of 3.0 percentage points on their US FDI. Annual average returns for the period are plotted in Fig. 4. A question addressed by McGrattan and Prescott (2010a) naturally arises: why is the return differential so large and persistent?

The introduction of technology capital accounts for over 60% of the difference. Intangible capital investment stock is important because it increases profits but not the BEA stock of capital. It does increase the stock of capital, which lowers the economic return. US multinationals made large FDI earlier and, as a result, have relatively larger stocks of intangible capital than foreign multinationals have in their US subsidiaries. The age of the foreign subsidiaries matters because intangible investment is high and therefore BEA profits low when they are young. This micro evidence strongly supports the theory.

Using economic returns, the differential between the average return on US FDI and the average return on foreigners' FDI is reduced from 6.3 percentage points to about 2.5 percentage points. A question that naturally arises, is what accounts for the remaining 40% of the difference? Corporate tax rates differ across countries, and through transfer pricing, profits are shifted to countries where this tax rate is lower. Indeed, an important field of corporate finance is concerned with setting prices for goods and services transferred between multinationals and their foreign subsidiaries.

6. CONCLUDING COMMENTS

So much has been learned through the successful use of neoclassical growth theory and its extensions. This theory has directed the development of aggregate economics.

The availability of better data sets is fostering further development. As these better data sets become available, great progress is being made in incorporating features of the household sector,[d] which, like the business sector, is of great economic importance. In the earlier stages of the development and use of neoclassical growth theory, the household was a primitive. Now, however, its structure is becoming an endogenous element. The household sector has changed significantly over time and is not policy invariant.

In reporting household sector statistics, a household is the set of people residing at a dwelling—that is, a postal address. The size of households has changed significantly in the United States. Further, many households consist of married couples. Over time, the nature of matching has changed, as found by Greenwood et al. (2016). They find an important change is the increase in positive assortative matching. With more two-professional households, these changes have had major consequences for the distribution of household incomes.

Another important economic sector is the government sector. The question of how a group of people can set up sustainable collective government arrangements that result in outcomes preferred by the members of this group is an important one. Answering this question will require developments in pure theory.

Through the interaction of theory and measurement, the rapid development of quantitative aggregate economic theory is certain to continue. It will be interesting to see what these developments are.

REFERENCES

Adelman, I., Adelman, F., 1959. The dynamic properties of the Klein-Goldberger model. Econometrica 27 (4), 596–625.

Arkolakis, C., Costinot, C., Rodríquez-Clare, A., 2012. New trade models, same old gains? Am. Econ. Rev. 102 (1), 94–103.

Braun, R.A., Ikeda, D., Joines, D.H., 2009. The saving rate in Japan: why it has fallen and why it will remain low. Int. Econ. Rev. 50 (1), 291–321.

Chari, V.V., Kehoe, P., McGrattan, E.R., 2000. Sticky price models of the business cycle: can the contract multiplier solve the persistence problem? Econometrica 68 (5), 1151–1179.

Cole, H.L., Ohanian, L.E., 1999. The Great Depression in the United States from a neoclassical perspective. Fed. Reserve Bank Minneapolis Quart. Rev. 23 (1), 2–24.

Cole, H.L., Ohanian, L.E., 2004. New Deal policies and the persistence of the Great Depression: a general equilibrium analysis. J. Polit. Econ. 112 (4), 779–816.

Cole, H.L., Prescott, E.C., 1997. Valuation equilibrium with clubs. J. Econ. Theory 74 (1), 19–39.

Cooley, T.F., Hansen, G.D., 1995. Money and the business cycle. In: Cooley, T.F. (Ed.), Frontiers of Business Cycle Research. Princeton University Press, Princeton.

Fisher, J.D.M., Hornstein, A., 2000. (*S*,*s*) inventory policies in general equilibrium. Rev. Econ. Stud. 67 (1), 117–145.

Fisher, J.D.M., Hornstein, A., 2002. The role of real wages, productivity, and fiscal policy in Germany's Great Depression 1928–1937. Rev. Econ. Dyn. 5 (1), 100–127.

[d] McGrattan et al. (1997) introduce home production by the household into the theory. The implications for business cycles did not change.

Fitzgerald, T.J., 1998. Work schedules, wages, and employment in a general equilibrium model with team production. Rev. Econ. Dyn. 1 (4), 809–834.
Frisch, R., 1933. Propagation problems and impulse problems in dynamic economics. In: Kock, K. (Ed.), Economic Essays in Honour of Gustav Cassel. Allen & Unwin, London.
Frisch, R., 1970. From Utopian Theory to Practical Applications: The Case of Econometrics. (Lecture to the Memory of Alfred Nobel, June 17).
Greenwood, J., Hercowitz, Z., Huffman, G.W., 1988. Investment, capacity utilization, and the real business cycle. Am. Econ. Rev. 78 (3), 402–417.
Greenwood, J., Guner, N., Kocharkov, G., Santos, C., 2016. Technology and the changing family: a unified model of marriage, divorce, educational attainment and married female labor-force participation. Am. Econ. J. Macroecon. 8 (1), 1–41.
Hansen, G.D., 1985. Indivisible labor and the business cycle. J. Monet. Econ. 16 (3), 309–327.
Hansen, G.D., Prescott, E.C., 1993. Did technology shocks cause the 1990–1991 recession? Am. Econ. Rev. 83 (2), 280–286.
Hansen, G.D., Prescott, E.C., 2005. Capacity constraints, asymmetries, and the business cycle. Rev. Econ. Dyn. 8 (4), 850–865.
Hansen, G.D., Sargent, T.J., 1988. Straight time and overtime in general equilibrium. J. Monet. Econ. 21 (213), 281–304.
Hodrick, R.J., Prescott, E.C., 1980. Post-War U.S. Business Cycles: An Empirical Investigation. Northwestern University, Evanston, IL, pp. 1–28 (Discussion Paper No. 451).
Holmes, T.J., McGrattan, E.R., Prescott, E.C., 2015. Quid pro quo: technology capital transfers for market access in China. Rev. Econ. Stud. 82 (3), 1154–1193.
Hornstein, A., 1993. Monopolistic competition, increasing returns to scale, and the importance of productivity shocks. J. Monet. Econ. 31 (3), 299–316.
Hornstein, A., Prescott, E.C., 1993. The firm and the plant in general equilibrium theory. In: Becker, R., Boldrin, R., Jones, R., Thomson, W. (Eds.), General Equilibrium, Growth, and Trade II: The Legacy of Lionel McKenzie. Academic Press, San Diego, pp. 393–410.
Kaldor, N., 1957. A model of economic growth. Econ. J. 67 (268), 591–624.
Kondratieff, N.D., Stolper, W.F., 1935. The long waves in economic life. Rev. Econ. Stat. 17 (6), 105–115.
Kuznets, S., 1930. Secular movements in production and prices: their nature and their bearing upon cyclical fluctuations. Am. Econ. Rev. 20 (4), 787–789.
Kydland, F.E., Prescott, E.C., 1977. Rules rather than discretion: the inconsistency of optimal plans. J. Polit. Econ. 85 (3), 473–491.
Kydland, F.E., Prescott, E.C., 1982. Time to build and aggregate fluctuations. Econometrica 50 (6), 1345–1370.
LeRoy, S.F., Porter, R.D., 1981. The present-value relation: tests based on implied variance bounds. Econometrica 49 (3), 555–574.
Lucas Jr., R.E., 1972. Expectations and the neutrality of money. J. Econ. Theory 4 (2), 103–123.
Lucas Jr., R.E., 1976a. Econometric policy evaluation: a critique. Carnegie-Rochester Conference Series on Public Policy, vol. 1. Elsevier, Amsterdam, pp. 19–46.
Lucas Jr., R.E., 1976b. Understanding business cycles. Carnegie-Rochester Conference Series on Public Policy, vol. 5. Elsevier, Amsterdam, pp. 7–29.
Lucas Jr., R.E., Rapping, L.A., 1969. Real wages, employment and inflation. J. Polit. Econ. 77 (5), 721–754.
Lucas Jr., R.E., Sargent, T.J., 1979. After Keynesian macroeconomics. Fed. Reserve Bank Minneapolis Quart. Rev. 3 (2), 1–16.
MaCurdy, T.E., 1981. An empirical model of labor supply in a life cycle setting. J. Polit. Econ. 89 (6), 1059–1085.
McGrattan, E.R., 2012. Capital taxation during the U.S. Great Depression. Q. J. Econ. 127 (3), 1515–1550.
McGrattan, E.R., Prescott, E.C., 2005. Taxes, regulations, and the value of U.S. and U.K. corporations. Rev. Econ. Stud. 72 (3), 767–796.
McGrattan, E.R., Prescott, E.C., 2009. Openness, technology capital, and development. J. Econ. Theory 144 (6), 2454–2476.

McGrattan, E.R., Prescott, E.C., 2010a. Technology capital and the U.S. current account. Am. Econ. Rev. 100 (4), 1493–1522.
McGrattan, E.R., Prescott, E.C., 2010b. Unmeasured investment and the puzzling U.S. boom in the 1990s. Am. Econ. J. Macroecon. 2 (4), 88–123.
McGrattan, E.R., Rogerson, R., Wright, R., 1997. An equilibrium model of the business cycle with household production and fiscal policy. Int. Econ. Rev. 38 (2), 267–290.
Mehra, R., Prescott, E.C., 1985. The equity premium: a puzzle. J. Monet. Econ. 15 (2), 145–161.
Mehra, R., Piguillem, F., Prescott, E.C., 2011. Costly financial intermediation in neoclassical growth theory. Quant. Econ. 2 (1), 1–36.
Mitchell, W., 1913. Business Cycles. University of California Press, Berkeley.
Mitchell, W., 1927. Business Cycles: The Problem and Its Setting. National Bureau of Economic Research, New York.
Prescott, E.C., 1986. Theory ahead of business cycle measurement. Fed. Reserve Bank Minneapolis Quart. Rev. 10 (4), 9–22.
Prescott, E.C., 2004. Why do Americans work so much more than Europeans? Fed. Reserve Bank Minneapolis Quart. Rev. 28 (1), 2–13.
Prescott, E.C., Rogerson, R., Wallenius, J., 2009. Lifetime aggregate labor supply with endogenous workweek length. Rev. Econ. Dyn. 12 (1), 23–36.
Rogerson, R., 1984. Topics in the Theory of Labor Markets. (PhD Thesis). University of Minnesota.
Rosen, S., 1978. The supply of work schedules and employment. In: Work Time and Employment: A Conference Report. National Commission for Manpower Policy, Washington, DC.
Samuelson, P.A., 1939. A synthesis of the principle of acceleration and the multiplier. J. Polit. Econ. 47 (6), 786–797.
Sargent, T.J., 1976. A classical macroeconometric model for the United States. J. Polit. Econ. 84 (2), 207–238.
Sargent, T.J., Sims, C.A., 1977. Business cycle modeling without pretending to have too much *a priori* economic theory. In: Sims, C.A. (Ed.), New Methods in Business Cycle Research: Proceedings from a Conference. Federal Reserve Bank of Minneapolis, Minneapolis, pp. 45–110.
Shiller, R.J., 1981. Do stock prices move too much to be justified by subsequent changes in dividends? Am. Econ. Rev. 71 (3), 421–436.
Solow, R.M., 1956. A contribution to the theory of economic growth. Quant. J. Econ. 70 (1), 65–94.
Summers, L.H., 1986. Some skeptical observations on real business cycle theory. Fed. Reserve Bank Minneapolis Quart. Rev. 10 (4), 23–27.
Swan, T.W., 1956. Economic growth and capital accumulation. Econ. Rec. 32 (2), 334–361.
Taubman, P., Wilkinson, M., 1970. User cost, capital utilization and investment theory. Int. Econ. Rev. 11 (2), 209–215.
Thomas, J.K., 2002. Is lumpy investment relevant for the business cycle? J. Polit. Econ. 110 (3), 508–534.
Tinbergen, J., 1952. Business cycles in the United Kingdom, 1870–1914. Econ. J. 62 (248), 872–875.
Wicksell, K., 1918. Ett bidrag till krisernas teori. Review of Goda och daliga tider. Ekonomisk Tidskrift 20 (2), 66–75.

CHAPTER 23

Families in Macroeconomics

M. Doepke*, M. Tertilt†
*Northwestern University, Evanston, IL, United States
†University of Mannheim, Mannheim, Germany

Contents

Handbook of Macroeconomics, Volume 2B
ISSN 1574-0048, http://dx.doi.org/10.1016/bs.hesmac.2016.04.006

Abstract

Much of macroeconomics is concerned with the allocation of physical capital, human capital, and labor over time and across people. The decisions on savings, education, and labor supply that generate these variables are made within families. Yet the family (and decision making in families) is typically ignored in macroeconomic models. In this chapter, we argue that family economics should be an integral part of macroeconomics and that accounting for the family leads to new answers to classic macro questions. Our discussion is organized around three themes. We start by focusing on short- and medium-run fluctuations and argue that changes in family structure in recent decades have important repercussions for the determination of aggregate labor supply and savings. Next, we turn to economic growth and describe how accounting for families is central for understanding differences between rich and poor countries and for the determinants of long-run development. We conclude with an analysis of the role of the family as a driver of political and institutional change.

Keywords

Family economics, Macroeconomics, Business cycles, Growth, Households, Fertility, Labor supply, Human capital, Gender

JEL Classification Codes

E20, E30, J10, J20, O40

1. INTRODUCTION

First impressions suggest that family economics and macroeconomics should be the two fields within economics at the greatest distance from each other: one looks at interactions between at most a handful of members of the same family, whereas the other considers the aggregated behavior of the millions of actors in an economy as a whole. Despite this contrast between the small and the large, we argue in this chapter that family economics and macroeconomics are in fact intimately related, and that much can be learned from making the role of the family in the macroeconomy more explicit.[a]

There are two different ways in which family economics and macroeconomics intersect. One side of the coin is to focus on questions that originate in family economics, but

[a] The basic point that family economics matters for macroeconomics was made by Becker in his AEA Presidential Address (Becker, 1988). At the time, Becker placed a challenge that inspired a sizeable amount of follow-up research. However, much of the early work at the intersection family economics and macroeconomics was focused on economic growth, whereas we argue in this chapter that family economics is equally relevant for other parts of macroeconomics.

use the methodology of dynamic macroeconomics to answer the questions. For example, macroeconomic models can be adapted to answer questions about how fertility rates, marriage rates, divorce rates, or the assortativeness of mating are determined and how they evolve over time. There is an active and exciting literature that takes this approach, but it is not the focus of this chapter.[b] Rather, our interest here is in the reverse possibility, namely that incorporating family economics into macroeconomics leads to new answers for classic macroeconomic questions. These questions concern, for example, the determination of the level and volatility of employment, the factors shaping the national savings rate, the sources of macroeconomic inequality, and the origins of economic growth.

We choose this path because, so far, it has been less traveled, yet we believe that it holds great promise. This belief is founded on the observation that many of the key decision margins in macroeconomic models, such as labor supply, consumption and saving, human capital investments, and fertility decisions, are made in large part within the family. The details of families then matter for how decisions are made; for example, the organization of families (eg, prevalence of nuclear vs extended families or monogamous vs polygynous marriage) changes the incentives to supply labor, affects motives for saving and acquiring education, and determines possibilities for risk sharing. Yet typical macroeconomic models ignore the family and instead build on representative agent modeling that abstracts from the presence of multiple family members, who may have conflicting interests, who might make separate decisions, and who may split up and form new households.

One might argue that subsuming all family details into one representative household decision maker constitutes a useful abstraction. This would perhaps be the case if the structure and behavior of families were a given constant. However, the structure of the family has changed dramatically over time and is likely to continue to do so in the future. Large changes have occurred in the size and composition of households. Fertility rates have declined, divorce risk has increased (and then decreased), the fraction of single households has grown steadily, and women have entered the labor force in large numbers. Given these trends, the nature of family interactions has changed dramatically over time, and so have the implications of family economics for macroeconomics.

There is a small, but growing, literature that opens the family black box within macro models. The goal of this chapter is to survey this literature, to summarize the main results, and to point to open questions and fruitful avenues for future research. We also aim to introduce macroeconomists to the tools of family economics.

There are multiple ways in which families can be incorporated into macroeconomics. The first generation of macroeconomists who took the family more seriously added home production to business cycle models (eg, Benhabib et al., 1991; Greenwood and Hercowitz, 1991). The insight was that home production cannot be ignored if

[b] See Greenwood et al. (2016b) for an excellent recent survey of that kind of family economics.

the cyclicality of investment and labor supply is to be understood. A large part of investment happens within the household in the form of consumer durables, a large part of time is spent on home production, and both vary over the cycle. The interaction of market time and business investment with these variables that are decided within the family is therefore important for understanding business cycles. In the home production literature, the family is a place of production, but decision making is still modeled in the then-standard way using a representative household with a single utility function.

In this chapter, we take the notion of families a step further. We emphasize that families consist of multiple members and that the interaction between these multiple members is important. We look at both horizontal interactions in the family, ie, between husband and wife, and vertical interactions, ie, between parents and children. Family members may have different interests, resources, and abilities. How potential conflicts of interests within the family are resolved has repercussions for what families do, including macrorelevant decisions on variables such as savings, education, fertility, and labor supply.

This chapter has three parts. We first consider how the family matters for short- and medium-run fluctuations. Second, we turn to economic growth. Third, we consider the role of families for understanding political and institutional change.

Our discussion of short- and medium-run fluctuations uses the US economy as an example to demonstrate how changes in family structure feed back into macroeconomics. We start by documenting how US families have changed in recent decades, including a decline in fertility rates, a large increase in the labor force participation especially of married women, and changes to marriage and divorce. We then analyze how these changes affect the evolution of aggregate labor supply over the business cycle and the determination of the savings rate. With regard to labor supply, we emphasize that couples can provide each other with insurance for labor market risk. For example, a worker may decide to increase labor supply if the worker's spouse becomes unemployed, and couples may make career and occupation choices that minimize the overall labor market risk for the family. The extent to which such insurance channels operate depends on family structure (eg, the fraction of single and married households and divorce rates) and on the relative education levels and labor force participation rates of women and men. We argue that recent changes to family structure have likely changed the volatility of aggregate labor supply and contributed to the "Great Moderation" in economic fluctuations observed between the 1980s and the Great Recession. We also discuss research that suggests that changes in female labor force participation are the main reason behind the recent phenomenon of jobless recoveries. Regarding savings rates, we emphasize how changes to divorce risk affect couples' incentives to save. We conclude this part of the chapter by discussing alternative models of the family and their use within macroeconomics. We argue that there is a need for more detailed dynamic modeling of family decision making, an area where methods widely used in macroeconomics may be fruitfully applied to family economics.

The second part of the chapter focuses on the long run, ie, economic growth. Here education, human capital accumulation, and fertility are the key choices of interest. We start by documenting sharp correlations between measures of family structure and measures of economic development in cross-country data. In a series of simple growth models, we then show how different family dimensions affect the growth rate. The first dimension is the interaction between parents and children, noting that, typically, parents make education decisions for their children. We then add fertility choice and discuss government-imposed fertility restrictions such as the one-child policy in China. Next we move from one-gender to two-gender models by first adding a second person in decision making and then adding a distinction between the two in technology. We use the framework to discuss the implications of the widely observed son preference for economic growth. We conclude the section with a discussion on the importance of nonwestern family structures (such as polygyny) and endogenous marriage.

The third part examines the role of the family in the context of political economy. We argue that the family is an important driver of political and institutional change in the course of development. Throughout the development process, all of today's rich countries (except a few countries whose wealth is built on oil) went through a similar series of reforms. Democracy was introduced, public education was initiated, child labor laws were implemented, the legal position of women was improved, and welfare and social security systems were established. Two important questions are why these reforms were implemented at a particular stage of development, and why many poorer countries failed to introduce similar reforms. We emphasize that most of these reforms concern the nature of the family. Public schooling moved the responsibility of education from the family to the public sphere, and public pension did the same for old age support. Child labor laws put constraints on the power parents have over their children. The introduction of women's rights changed the nature of the interaction between husband and wife. We discuss mechanisms linking the family and political change and the possibility of a two-way feedback between economic development and political reform. We then focus on the political economy of two specific reforms, namely the expansion of women's economic rights and the introduction of child labor laws.[c]

Throughout this chapter, we point out promising directions for future research. In line with the overall theme of the chapter, most of these research directions concern using family economics to generate new answers for questions that originate from macroeconomics. However, we also see a lot of potential for intellectual arbitrage in the opposite direction, namely using tools that are widely used in macroeconomics to build improved models of the family. In particular, a striking difference between the fields is that almost all macroeconomic models are dynamic, whereas in family economics static modeling is still

[c] The political economy of women's rights is addressed in more detail by Doepke et al. (2012).

common. In reality, dynamic considerations should be just as important in family economics as in macroeconomics. For example, if a woman decides to stay at home with her children, she will usually be aware that her absence from the labor market decreases her outside option. Similarly, when a woman and a man decide on whether to have a child, how the child will affect their future interactions will be an important consideration. There is a small literature that documents the importance of dynamics for the family. In particular, Mazzocco (2008) shows empirically that Euler equations hold at the individual but not the household level, and Mazzocco (2007) and Lise and Yamada (2015) provide evidence suggesting that bargaining power within the household evolves over time. To capture such phenomena and to better understand the link between family decisions and aggregate outcomes, more dynamic family bargaining models are needed. Tools that are widely used in macroeconomics, such as dynamic contracting under limited commitment and private information constraints, should prove useful for building such models.

In the following section, we start our analysis by considering the implications of the family for macroeconomic outcomes in the short and the medium run. In Section 3, we investigate the role of the family for economic growth, and Section 4 puts the spotlight on the family as a driver of political change. Section 5 concludes by discussing yet other dimensions in which the family matters for macroeconomics and by providing thoughts on promising directions for future research. Proofs for propositions are contained in the Appendices.

2. THE FAMILY AND THE MACROECONOMY IN THE SHORT AND MEDIUM RUN

Ever since micro-founded modeling became dominant in the 1970s and the 1980s, explicit models of household decision making have been a standard ingredient in macroeconomic models. Depending on the application, the household may face a variety of decisions, such as choosing labor supply, accumulating assets, or investing in human capital. However, within macroeconomics comparatively few attempts have been made to explicitly model families. By modeling families, we mean to account for the fact that households may contain multiple members, who may have different interests, who may make separate decisions, and who may split up in divorce or join others and form new households.

In the following sections, we argue that modeling families can make a big difference in understanding aggregate household behavior in the short and the medium run. We focus on the most basic role of the household sector in macroeconomic models, namely to provide a theory of labor supply and savings.

2.1 The Point of Departure: Representative Households

Traditional macroeconomic models used for business cycle and monetary analysis are populated by an infinitely lived, representative household, who derives utility from consumption and leisure and derives income from supplying labor and accumulating savings. A prototype household problem looks like this (eg, Cooley and Prescott, 1995):

$$\max_{\{c_t, l_t\}} E\left\{\sum_{t=0}^{\infty} \beta^t U(c_t, l_t)\right\} \tag{1}$$

subject to:

$$\begin{aligned} c_t + a_{t+1} &= w_t l_t + (1 + r_t) a_t, \\ a_{t+1} &\geq -B, \\ a_0 &= 0, \\ 0 \leq l_t &\leq T. \end{aligned}$$

Here c_t is consumption, l_t is labor supply, w_t and r_t are the wage and the interest rate (taken as given by the household), β is a discount factor that satisfies $0 < \beta < 1$, and $B > 0$ defines a slack borrowing constraint that rules out running a Ponzi scheme. The first-order conditions for the household's maximization problem are:

$$-\frac{U_l(c_t, l_t)}{U_c(c_t, l_t)} = w_t, \tag{2}$$

$$U_c(c_t, l_t) = \beta E\{(1 + r_{t+1}) U_c(c_{t+1}, l_{t+1})\}. \tag{3}$$

Here (2) is the requirement that the marginal rate of substitution between labor and leisure is equal to the wage, and (3) is the intertemporal Euler equation for consumption. Condition (2) pins down average labor supply and the elasticity of labor supply as a function of the relative wage and overall wealth, and (3) determines savings as a function of wealth, interest rates, and expectations over future leisure and consumption.

A representative household based on a problem similar to (1) underlies most of the macroeconomic modeling in the real business cycle literature, the monetary DSGE literature, and many other subfields of macroeconomics. A theory of labor supply and savings that is build on a representative household has a number of limitations, including the obvious one that such a theory has nothing to say about questions that involve heterogeneity and inequality across households. Of course, there is nothing wrong with simplifying assumptions in principle; after all, models are intended to be simplified representations of reality. The limitations of the representative household become a bigger concern, however, when some of the driving forces the model abstracts from are subject to changes over time that substantially alter macroeconomic behavior.

There is already a sizeable literature that extends the representative-household framework in other key dimensions, in particular by accounting for heterogeneity in age (ie, allowing for the life cycle) and heterogeneity in wealth and income.[d] This literature has characterized some of the macroeconomic changes brought about by the changing economic environment in recent decades, such as the large rise in income inequality and returns to education since the 1970s, and the population aging in industrial societies that resulted from rising life expectancy and low fertility. There is much less work on the dimension that this chapter focuses on, namely allowing for the fact that many households have multiple members, ie, accounting for families.

In the following sections, we argue that accounting for families is just as important as the existing extensions of the representative-agent framework. The main reason for this is that families have changed substantially in recent decades; for example, there have been large changes to rates of marriage and divorce, to female labor force participation, and to fertility rates. We start by outlining the main facts of changing families in the United States (to the extent that they are relevant from a macroeconomic perspective), and we then outline channels for how these changes are relevant for determining aggregate labor supply and savings. We note that while there is a lot of existing work documenting and explaining the family trends, there are few papers that focus specifically on the implications of these changes for macroeconomics. In our view, this presents a high-return area for future research, with a lot of low-hanging fruit.

2.2 The Facts: Changing Families in the United States

Throughout the 20th century, the major industrialized countries underwent large changes in the composition and behavior of families. We illustrate this transformation with statistics from the US economy as an example. In the following sections, we explain the relevance of these trends for macroeconomics.

The first transformation concerns changes in fertility over time. Fig. 1 displays the number of children ever born to US women by birth cohort (ie, the horizontal axis is the year in which a mother is born; the corresponding births mostly take place 20–40 years later). As in all industrialized countries, the main trend associated with long-run development is declining fertility. In the case of the United States, fertility fell almost threefold from the cohorts born in the mid-19th century to those born in the late 20th century. The trend was not uniform, however. In the middle of the 20th century there was a phase of rising fertility: the US baby boom. In the course of the baby boom, fertility rose from about two to about three children per woman, and then sharply reversed course to fall back toward two again. These changes have led to large variations

[d] Much of this literature is surveyed by Heathcote et al. (2009) and in the chapter "Macroeconomics and household heterogeneity" by Krueger, Mitman, and Perri (in this volume).

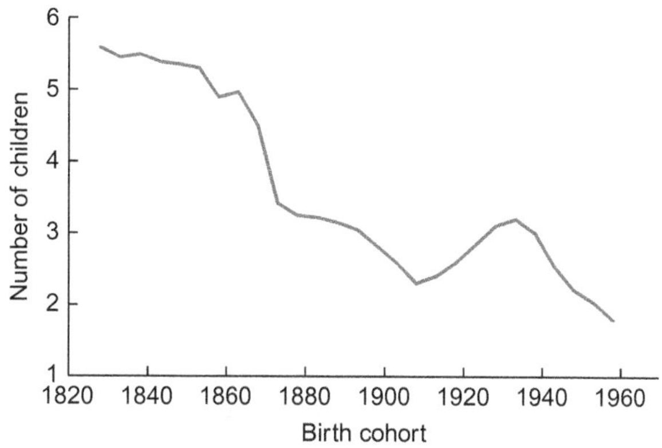

Fig. 1 Children ever born by cohort, United States (ie, average number of children for women born in a given year). *Jones, L.E., Tertilt, M., 2008. An economic history of the relationship between occupation and fertility—U.S. 1826–1960. In: Rupert, P. (Ed.), Frontiers of Family Economics, vol. 1. Emerald Group Publishing Limited, Bingley, UK (Table 1A).*

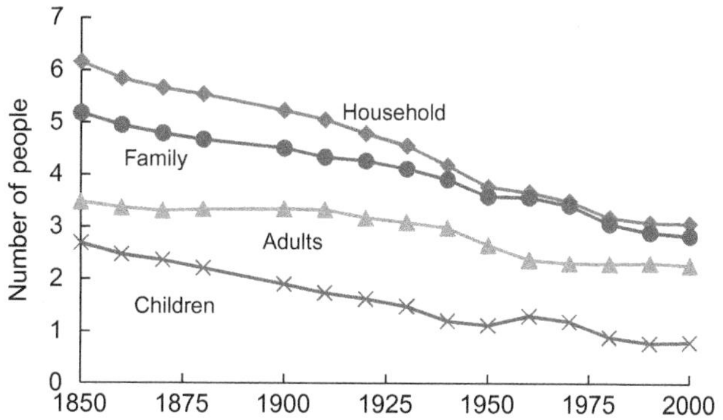

Fig. 2 Household size over time, United States. *Salcedo, A., Schoellmann, T., Tertilt, M., 2012. Families as roommates: changes in US household size from 1850 to 2000. Quant. Econ. 3 (1), 133–175 (Figure 1).*

in cohort sizes, which will affect the macroeconomy for decades to come now that the baby boom cohorts (ie, the babies, not the mothers) are reaching retirement age.

Fig. 2 displays a closely related change: a secular decline in the average size of households. Fertility decline is a main driver of this change; ie, the decline in fertility resulted in fewer children per household and thus a lower household size. However, there are additional factors because the number of adults per household also declined over time. This is in part due to fewer adults within families; ie, a smaller fraction of families include multiple generations of adults, and more families are headed by a single adult. In addition, fewer households include adults who are not related to each other.

Fig. 3 shows that there is not just a decline in the size of households but also a dramatic change in the composition of household types. As recently as 1950, most households

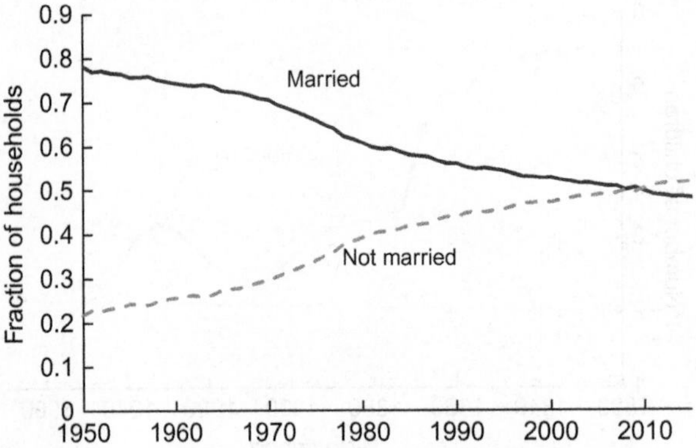

Fig. 3 Proportion of households including a married couple vs all other households over time, United States. *US Census Bureau, Historical Time Series, Current Population Survey, March and Annual Social and Economic Supplements, 2015 and earlier.*

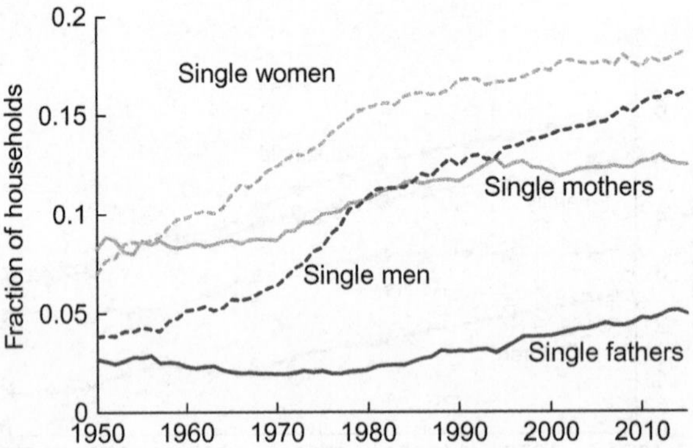

Fig. 4 Nonmarried households by type over time, United States. *US Census Bureau, Historical Time Series, Current Population Survey, March and Annual Social and Economic Supplements, 2015 and earlier.*

(about 80%) included at least one married couple. Now, married-couple households are no longer the majority. Fig. 4 breaks down the nonmarried households into further subcategories, with increases in every subcategory. The figures for single women and single men rise most, indicating primarily lower marriage rates, a higher age at first marriage, and a higher divorce rate. Single mother and single father households have also increased since the 1970s. Fig. 5 looks specifically at the role of marriage and divorce. The figure shows that the decline in the fraction of married women is due in almost equal parts to a rise in the number of never married women and a rise in the number of divorced women. Fig. 6 shows the divorce rate (defined as the number of divorces per 1000 women). Apart from the spike after World War II, the divorce rate was roughly constant from 1940 until the late 1960s and then increased sharply over the course of a decade. It has been relatively constant since the early 1980s, albeit at a much higher level.

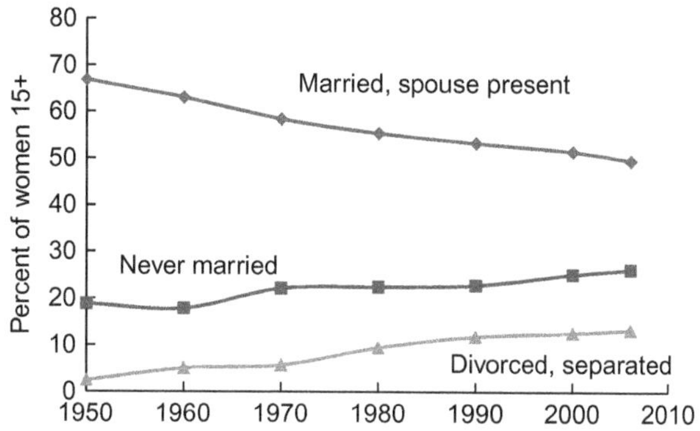

Fig. 5 Breakdown of marital status of women age 15+ over time, United States. *US Census Bureau, Families and Living Arrangements, Current Population Reports.*

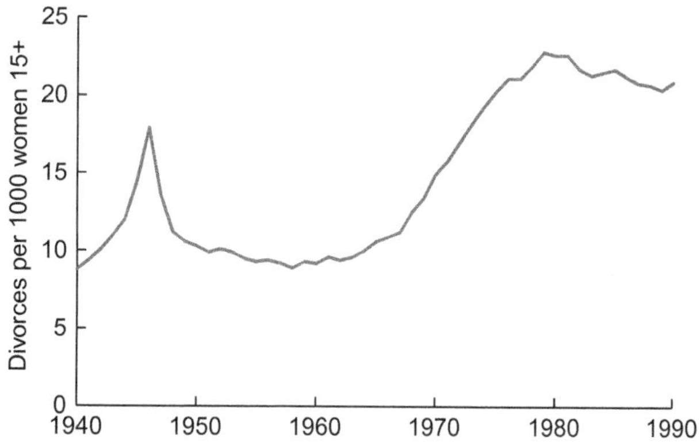

Fig. 6 Divorce rate over time, United States. *US Vital Statistics; Clarke, S.C., 1995. Advance report of final marriage statistics, 1989 and 1990. Monthly Vital Stat. Rep. 43 (12), 3–5.*

Another key trend linking family economics and macroeconomics is the rise in female labor force participation in the postwar era. From the beginning of the 20th century until the 1950s, for married households the single male breadwinner model was the norm. Since then, female labor force participation has risen steadily over a number of decades. As Fig. 7 shows, overall female participation rose from about 30% to more than 60% of the adult population between 1950 and 1990. In the late 1990s, female participation flattened out and declined a little in the current century. Female participation still falls short of male participation, but by a small margin compared to the 1950s. As we will see later (Fig. 13), the rise in female participation is predominantly due to married women. There is also a compositional effect due to the increase in the share of single women coupled with the fact that single women are more likely to work than married women are.

A trend closely related to the rise in female labor market participation is a decline in time spent on home production by women. Figs. 8 and 9 display the average hours men

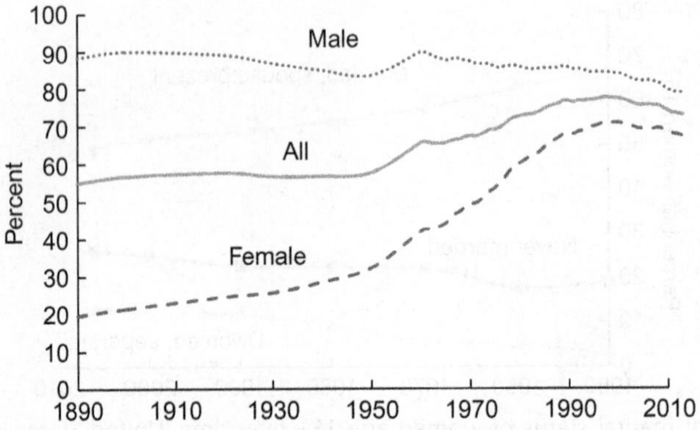

Fig. 7 Labor force participation by gender over time, all persons 16–64 years old, United States. *OECD LFS Sex and Age Indicators and US Department of Commerce, Bureau of the Census, "Historical Statistics of the United States: Colonial Times to 1970," Bicentennial Edition, Part 1, 1975, Tables A119–134 and D29–41.*

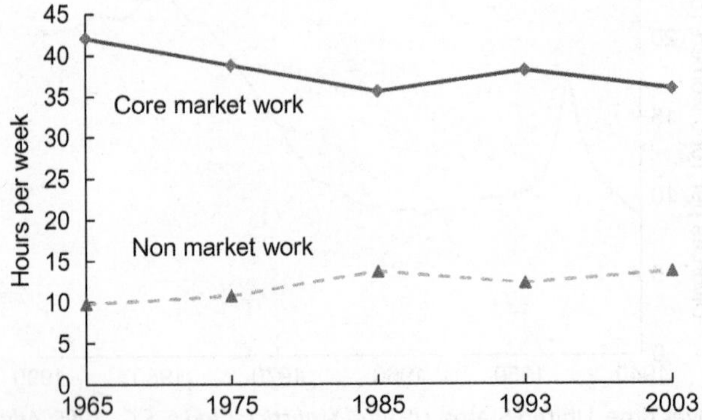

Fig. 8 Men's weekly market vs nonmarket (ie, home) work hours over time, United States. *Aguiar, M., Hurst, E., 2007. Measuring trends in leisure: the allocation of time over five decades. Q. J. Econ. 122 (3), 969–1006 (Table II).*

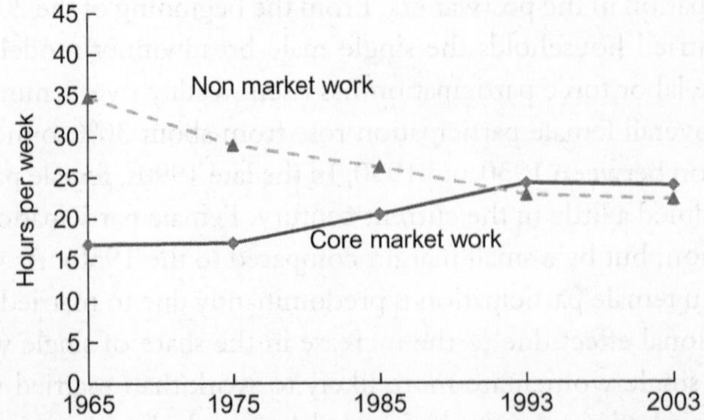

Fig. 9 Women's weekly market vs nonmarket (ie, home) work hours over time, United States. *Aguiar, M., Hurst, E., 2007. Measuring trends in leisure: the allocation of time over five decades. Q. J. Econ. 122 (3), 969–1006 (Table II).*

and women spent per week on market work vs nonmarket work, ie, home production (activities such as child care, cleaning, and preparing food). For men, there is a small decline in market work and an equally small corresponding rise in nonmarket work. For women, in contrast, since 1965 there has been a major transformation in time use: time spent on nonmarket work has dropped sharply while market work has risen, and now exceeds nonmarket time use.

Another closely related fact is the change in relative wages of men and women. Over the course of the 20th century, women have been catching up dramatically in terms of pay. Fig. 10 displays women's median earnings relative to men's earnings. In both cases only full-time, year-round workers are considered. As the figure shows, at the beginning of the 20th century, women earned less than half of what men earned. The ratio increased steadily and had reached 65% by 1955. There was a drop in the late 1960s and 1970s, but from the 1970s onward, the ratio continuously increased again. Today, female relative earnings have reached an all-time high of 80%.

While our focus here is on changes over time in the United States, an interesting pattern in cross-country data is that there is a positive correlation between the fertility rate and the female labor-force participation rate across industrialized countries (Fig. 11). That is, the OECD countries with the highest fertility rates (the United States, France, and the Scandinavian countries) all have relatively high female labor force participation rates, whereas in low fertility countries (such as Italy and Spain) fewer women work in the labor market. The pattern is important because it goes against the relationship between these variables in time-series data: within most countries, the trend through the last 100 years or so has been toward lower fertility and higher female participation. Working in the market and caring for children are alternative uses of women's time. If a single force (say, a rise in

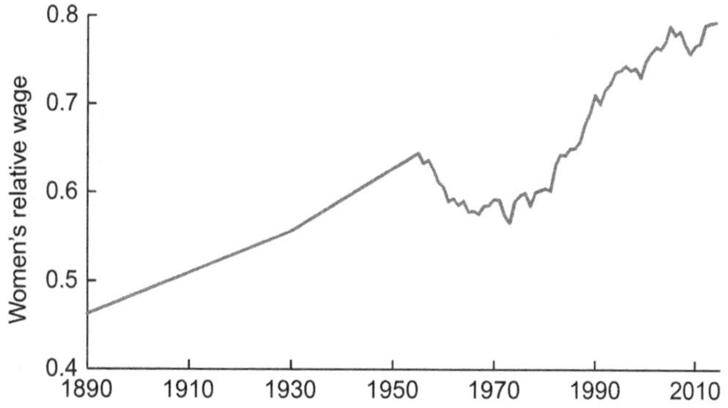

Fig. 10 Gender wage gap: median earnings of full-time, year-round, female workers 15 years and older, relative to men, United States. *US Census Bureau, Historical Income Tables. Numbers for 1890 and 1930 are from Goldin, C., 1990. Understanding the Gender Gap: An Economic History of American Women. Oxford University Press, Oxford (Table 3.2).*

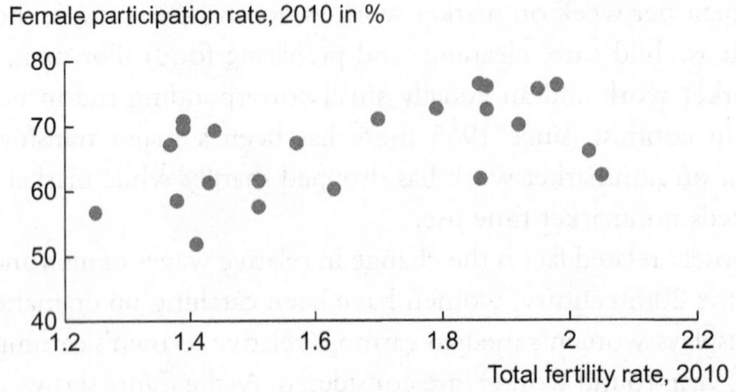

Fig. 11 Fertility vs female labor force participation across European OECD countries. *OECD LFS sex and age indicators and world development indicators.*

relative female wages) was responsible for changes to both labor force participation and fertility, we would expect these variables to always move in opposite directions. The observation in Fig. 11 that, across countries, these variables are positively correlated suggests that such a one-dimensional explanation is at odds with the data and is informative for which kind of theories can explain the family trends described here.

2.3 Explaining the Facts

There is a large literature (spanning family economics, labor economics, development economics, and macroeconomics) that provides explanations for the transformation of the family described above. We keep our discussion of this literature brief, since the goal of this chapter is not explaining these family facts but rather studying their importance for macroeconomic analysis. For a comprehensive survey of the literature on the drivers of changes in the family, we refer the reader to Greenwood et al. (2016b).

The best-known explanations for the historical fertility decline are based on the quantity–quality trade-off together with the idea that returns to education were increasing over time due to technological progress (see also Section 3.3). The more recent fertility decline that followed the baby boom is often connected to the increasing value of female time. The baby boom itself still presents a bit of a puzzle. The conventional wisdom of women catching up on their fertility after the war is clearly not the main driver, as it was young women (not of child-bearing age during the war) who had most children during the baby boom, as Fig. 1 shows. Doepke et al. (2015) suggest that the increase in labor force participation during the war was a major driver for the baby boom. The war generation of women accumulated valuable labor market experience, and after the war these women provided strong competition in the labor market for younger women who lacked that experience. Doepke, Hazan, and Maoz argue that many of these younger women were crowded out of the labor force and decided to start having children earlier instead.[e] Other papers provide a complementary explanation by attributing part of the baby boom to a decline in the cost of child bearing, for example, due to medical progress that made childbirth less risky to mothers (Albanesi and Olivetti, 2014) or improvements in household technology that lowered the time cost of children (Greenwood et al., 2005a).[f]

The causes for the secular increase in female participation have also been widely explored. Some of the explanations focus on the alternative uses of female time and argue that the time required for home production (such as child care, preparing food, or cleaning the home) fell, freeing up time for work. Greenwood et al. (2005b) attribute the reduction in time required for home production to technological progress, and in particular the introduction of time saving appliances. Even if technology had stayed as it was, home production time would have fallen because of the large reduction in the average fertility rate from the baby boom period of the 1950s to the present. Figs. 8 and 9 show that time use data indeed display a large reduction in nonmarket work (ie, home production) for women that closely mirrors the rise in market work. We also observe a small rise in home production for men, suggesting that some of the reduction in female home production arises from substitution within the household. However, the rise in male home production is quantitatively small compared to the decline in female home production. A related theory put forth by Albanesi and Olivetti (2016) is based on technological advances in health. Innovations such as infant formula made it much easier to reconcile work and motherhood and thus were an important contributor to the contemporaneous increase in fertility and female participation between 1930 and 1960.

Another factor contributing to the rise in female participation in the labor market is the decline in the gender wage gap between men and women, as shown in Fig. 10. While some of the overall rise in relative female pay is due to endogenous decisions such as education and the accumulation of work experience, other factors such as the disappearance of marriage bars can be regarded as exogenous driving forces.[g] The gender gap may also have narrowed because of technological change in the market sector that made male and female work more similar. If men have the comparative advantage in brawn and women in brain, then as knowledge becomes more important, female relative wages go up.[h] The role of the

[e] See also Goldin (1990) and Goldin and Olivetti (2013) for other perspectives on the long-run impact of World War II on the female labor market.

[f] Yet another possibility is a link between economic and demographic cycles; Jones and Schoonbroodt (2015) provide a model in which the baby boom arises due to the recovery from the Great Depression in terms of both income and fertility.

[g] Eckstein and Lifshitz (2011) decompose the effect of rising education and the decline in the gender gap conditional on education and find that rising female education accounts for a larger fraction of the increase in female participation.

[h] This idea was first formally modeled by Galor and Weil (1996). See Albanesi and Olivetti (2009) for an alternative theory of how a gender wage gap can arise from private information on work effort and specialization within the household.

declining gender gap in explaining the rise in participation is emphasized by Jones et al. (2015), who also allow for technological improvements in home production, but find them not to be quantitatively important. Attanasio et al. (2008) study the life-cycle labor supply of three cohorts of American women, born in the 1930s, 1940s, and 1950s. Their model allows for a number of potential determinants of labor supply, including changes in the gender wage gap, the number and cost of children, and changes in the returns to labor market experience. They find that for the cohorts considered, both a reduction in the costs of children and a decrease in the gender wage gap need to be allowed to explain the rise in participation. More recent contributions connect the decline in the gender wage gap explicitly with the rise of the service sector (Rendall, 2010; Ngai and Petrongolo, 2014).

Another channel that can affect relative male and female labor supply is endogenous bargaining within the household. In explicit household bargaining models (see Section 2.5), the outside options of the spouses are usually important determinants of bargaining power. Improved labor market opportunities for women (through whichever channel they occur) improve women's outside options and thus should improve women's bargaining power in marriage. Using a quantitative model, Knowles (2013) argues that an endogenous increase in female bargaining power is important in explaining the rise in female labor supply over the 1970–2000 period without implying a (counterfactual) large decline in male labor supply. Eckstein and Lifshitz (2015) estimate a labor supply model in which couples differ in how bargaining takes place (eg, cooperative vs noncooperative bargaining) and find that bargaining has a large impact on female, but not male labor supply.

The link between fertility and employment decisions is likely to have become more important throughout the last few decades. Before the 1960s, in industrialized countries most mothers were not in the labor force, so that for many the employment margin was not operative as far as decisions on additional births were concerned. Today, in the United States and other industrialized countries, most mothers are in the labor force. Hence, having children interacts with employment more directly, through margins such as deciding to work full or part time or the choice between career paths that differ in flexibility for dealing with child care needs. Recently, Adda et al. (2016) have provided a detailed study of the costs of children in terms of mother's careers based on a detailed life cycle model of female employment and fertility matched to German data. They show that the career costs of having children are substantial and that realized and expected fertility can account for a large fraction of the gender wage gap.[i] Based on the same data,

[i] See also Miller (2011) who estimates the career costs of children, using US data on biological fertility shocks as instruments. Guvenen et al. (2014) provide a recent analysis of the gender pay gap at the very top of the income distribution. They argue that a large part of the underrepresentation of women among top earners is due to the "paper floor," ie, a higher likelihood of women dropping out of the top pay percentiles, part of which may be due to fertility decisions.

Bick (2016) provides a quantitative analysis of the importance of the availability of market-based child care for fertility and female labor supply.

As discussed in Section 2.2, if a single force was responsible for both the upward trend in female labor force participation and the downward trend in fertility, we would expect these variables to always move in opposite directions. However, if we look at the cross section of industrialized countries, a positive correlation between female labor force participation and fertility emerges (see Fig. 11).[j] A number of recent studies have developed theories that are consistent with this pattern. The general intuition for these results is that many women now want to have both children and careers. In places where policies (or cultural expectations) are such that mothers can easily combine having children and careers, fertility and female labor force participation will both be high. In contrast, if there are obstacles to combing motherhood with working, many women will choose one or the other, and both fertility and participation will be lower. One of the first papers to formalize this intuition is Da Rocha and Fuster (2006), who focus on differences in labor market frictions across countries. Using a quantitative model, they find that in countries where unemployment risk is high, women both work less and are more likely to postpone births. Similarly, Erosa et al. (2010) find that more generous parental leave policies can increase both fertility and female labor force participation. Another source of variation can be cultural expectations for the roles of mothers and fathers in raising children. Doepke and Kindermann (2015) show that in European countries with exceptionally low fertility rates, women bear a disproportionately large share of the burden of caring for children. In a model of household bargaining over fertility decisions, they show that this leads to many women being opposed to having (additional) children. Hence, once again fertility will be lower, while at the same time many mothers are not able to work due to their child care duties.

The causes behind the decline in marriage, rise in divorce, and increase in single motherhood (as shown in Figs. 3–6) are likely related to the increase in female labor force participation. For a discussion of the causes behind these changes in the family structure, see Greenwood et al. (2016b).

2.4 Changing Families and Aggregate Labor Supply

We now turn to the main focus of this section, namely how changes to the family affect how labor supply and savings are determined in the aggregate. We start with aggregate labor supply, where the role of changes in female labor market behavior takes center stage.

A common thread through the studies of the rise in female participation is that the female participation decision is qualitatively different than the male participation decision. At least in part, this is due to a higher fixed cost of participation for women,

[j] A similar phenomenon has emerged recently in cross-sectional data in the United States. Hazan and Zoabi (2015a) document a U-shaped relationship between female education and fertility.

who often bear the primary responsibility for child care. The different nature of female labor supply suggests that today, aggregate labor supply is determined in a qualitatively different fashion compared to a few decades ago. We now consider a deliberately simplified model to illustrate the main channels through which the joint determination of female and male labor supply within a family affects the macroeconomic properties of labor supply.

2.4.1 Joint Labor Supply in the Family

To focus on the extensive margin, we consider a setting where an individual can either work full time or not at all.[k] The utility function of an individual of gender $g \in \{f, m\}$ is given by:

$$U_g(c_g, l_g) = \log(c_g) - \eta_g l_g,$$

where $l_g \in \{0,1\}$ is labor supply and c_g is consumption.[l] The relative weight of leisure in utility η_g varies in the population. People can live either as singles or as married (or cohabiting) couples. The budget constraint for a single individual is:

$$c_g + \psi l_g = w_g l_g + y_g,$$

where w_g is the wage for gender g, y_g is unearned income (ie, endowment or transfer income), and ψ represents the fixed cost of running a household conditional on working. The implicit assumption is that a person who does not work can replace the cost ψ through costless home production. We assume that ψ is a scalar that satisfies $0 < \psi < \min(w_f, w_m)$. The model is static, but alternatively we can interpret the decision problem as representing the labor-supply decision of a long-lived individual/household with exogenous saving in a given period, in which case y_g represents exogenous net saving/dissaving in the period.

For a married couple, the same fixed cost of running a household applies, but only if both spouses are working.[m] The joint budget constraint for a couple then is:

$$c_f + c_m + \psi \min(l_f, l_m) = w_f l_f + w_m l_m + y, \tag{4}$$

[k] We focus on the extensive margin for tractability. However, similar forces will be effective at the intensive margin as well.

[l] Here we assume that consumption is a private good. Many family models assume that consumption in the family is a public good. We consider pure public goods in Section 3. In reality, there are some private and some public elements in household consumption (see Salcedo et al., 2012 for a detailed analysis of this point).

[m] See Cho and Rogerson (1988) for an early contribution on the implications of this type of fixed cost of participation for the elasticity of labor supply.

where $y = y_f + y_m$. In this setting, the decision problem for a single person is straightforward. Comparing the utility conditional on working vs not working, an individual chooses to work if the condition,

$$\log(w_g + y_g - \psi) - \eta_g \geq \log(y_g),$$

is satisfied, or, equivalently, if the opportunity cost of working is sufficiently low:

$$\eta_g \leq \log\left(\frac{w_g + y_g - \psi}{y_g}\right).$$

For a married couple, we have to take a stand on how the inherent conflict of interest between the spouses given their different preferences is resolved. We assume cooperative bargaining, ie, the household solves a Pareto problem with welfare weights λ_f and λ_m for the wife and the husband, with $\lambda_f + \lambda_m = 1$. The problem solved by a married couple is then given by:

$$\max\{\lambda_f[\log(c_f) - \eta_f l_f] + \lambda_m[\log(c_m) - \eta_m l_m]\} \tag{5}$$

subject to the budget constraint (4). The maximization problem can be solved by using first-order conditions to characterize the consumption allocation conditional on a given pattern of labor supply, and then comparing utilities to determine optimal labor supply. To simplify notation, we focus on the case where husbands always work as long as $w_m > 0$. If the wife does not work, household income is given by $w_m + y$ and the consumption allocation is $c_f = \lambda_f(w_m + y)$, $c_m = \lambda_m(w_m + y)$. If the wife also works, household income net of the participation cost is $w_f + w_m + y - \psi$, and the consumption allocation is $c_f = \lambda_f(w_f + w_m + y - \psi)$, $c_m = \lambda_m(w_f + w_m + y - \psi)$. Denote by $V(l_f, l_m)$ the value of the objective function of the household (5) given labor supply and the optimal conditional consumption allocation. The wife will work if $V(l_f = 1, l_m = 1) \geq V(l_f = 0, l_m = 1)$, which can be written as[n]:

$$\begin{aligned} \log(w_f + w_m + y - \psi) + \lambda_f \log(\lambda_f) + \lambda_m \log(\lambda_m) - \lambda_f \eta_f - \lambda_m \eta_m \\ \geq \log(w_m + y) + \lambda_f \log(\lambda_f) + \lambda_m \log(\lambda_m) - \lambda_m \eta_m. \end{aligned}$$

Simplifying, women will work if and only if:

$$\eta_f \leq \frac{1}{\lambda_f}\log\left(\frac{w_f + w_m + y - \psi}{w_m + y}\right).$$

Hence, women are more likely to work if the participation cost ψ or male wages w_m are low, and if female wages w_f are high. A low bargaining power for women λ_f also translates into higher participation because households then place less value on the wife's leisure.

[n] For now we assume full commitment, ie, people get married before disutilities from working are realized, and they stay together even if being single would provide higher utility.

Note that the assumption of full commitment is important here. If the bargaining power of women is low, women pay the utility cost of working and consume little. Such a woman may prefer not to be a married at all. Later we endogenize the bargaining weights to ensure that participation constraints hold.

We can now consider the implications of the simple model for the variability of labor supply. Consider, first, the own-wage elasticity of labor supply. Consider the case where the only dimension of heterogeneity in the population is in leisure preference η_g, the distribution of which is described by the distribution function $F(\eta_g)$ with continuous marginal density $f(\eta_g) = F'(\eta_g)$. We assume that the density satisfies the assumptions $F(0) = 0$, $F'(\eta_g) > 0$ for $\eta_g > 0$, $\lim_{\eta_g \to 0} f(\eta_g) = 0$, and $\lim_{\eta_g \to \infty} f(\eta_g) = 0$. That is, all individuals place at least some value on leisure and the distribution thins out at each tail (one example is a log-normal distribution for η_g). For singles of gender g, the fraction working N_g^s given wage w_g is given by:

$$N_g^s = F\left(\log\left(\frac{w_g + \gamma_g - \psi}{\gamma_g}\right)\right).$$

The aggregate wage elasticity of labor supply is then given by:

$$\frac{\partial N_g^s}{\partial w_g}\frac{w_g}{N_g^s} = \frac{w_g}{w_g + \gamma_g - \psi}\frac{F'\left(\log\left(\frac{w_g + \gamma_g - \psi}{\gamma_g}\right)\right)}{F\left(\log\left(\frac{w_g + \gamma_g - \psi}{\gamma_g}\right)\right)}.$$

Note that this elasticity focuses on the extensive margin and hence is different from what is typically measured in the micro data (eg, Pistaferri, 2003 measures only the intensive margin elasticity).[o]

Consider now married couples. By assumption, we focus on the case where married men always work if they are able to. The fraction of married women working is then given by:

$$N_f^m = F\left(\frac{1}{\lambda_f}\log\left(\frac{w_f + w_m + \gamma - \psi}{w_m + \gamma}\right)\right)$$

and the elasticity of their labor supply is:

$$\frac{\partial N_f^m}{\partial w_f}\frac{w_f}{N_f^m} = \frac{w_f}{\lambda_f(w_f + w_m + \gamma - \psi)}\frac{F'\left(\frac{1}{\lambda_f}\log\left(\frac{w_f + w_m + \gamma - \psi}{w_m + \gamma}\right)\right)}{F\left(\frac{1}{\lambda_f}\log\left(\frac{w_f + w_m + \gamma - \psi}{w_m + \gamma}\right)\right)}.$$

[o] Recent contributions that explicitly consider the extensive margin include Chetty et al. (2011, 2012) and Attanasio et al. (2015).

The relative size of single and married women's labor supply elasticity cannot be unambiguously signed, because this depends on the shape of the distribution function F and the size of unearned income. However, married women's labor supply will be more elastic than the labor supply of single women if unearned income y_f is sufficiency small:

Proposition 1 (Labor Supply Elasticity of Single vs Married Women) *If unearned income* y_f *is sufficiently small, married women's labor supply elasticity is higher than that of unmarried women.*

Intuitively, if unearned income is small, singles have to work if they want to consume, whereas a married woman can rely in part on her spouse's income. This result is in line with the empirical observation that married women's labor supply is much more elastic than that of married men or single women at the microlevel (see, eg, the survey by Blundell and MaCurdy, 1999). Of course, if the labor supply of married men were endogenized, they would also have more scope for variability in supply compared to single men. In practice, as long as the gender wage gap was sizeable and social expectations were that women do more child care and home work, the assumption that men are the default earners was broadly realistic. But as gender roles have become more equalized over time, we can expect the labor supply behavior of men and women to converge also.

Ultimately we would like to assess the implications of changes in the family for the behavior of aggregate labor supply. The results so far may seem to suggest that a higher proportion of married households should make aggregate labor supply more variable. However, so far we have only considered the own wage elasticity of female labor supply. Another important dimension of the family is the possibility of insurance within the family. Specifically, if in a marriage the working husband experiences a negative shock such as a layoff, the wife may be able to offer insurance by starting to work. Hence, in the aggregate, the variable labor supply of married women may dampen fluctuations in total labor supply, by offsetting shocks experienced by men.[p]

To analyze the possibility of insurance within the family, consider an extension of the environment with unemployment shocks. With probability u, a given individual is unable to work, or equivalently, the potential wage is zero. The realization of the shock is independent across spouses. We can now consider how aggregate labor supply reacts to changes in u, where an increase in u can represent a recession.

As before, we start by considering singles. Their aggregate labor supply is:

$$N_g^s = (1-u)F\left(\log\left(\frac{w_g + y_g - \psi}{y_g}\right)\right).$$

[p] An early study of this insurance channel is provided by Attanasio et al. (2005).

For singles, the elasticity of labor supply with respect to the probability of employment $1-u$ is unity:

$$\frac{\partial N_g^s}{\partial(1-u)}\frac{1-u}{N_g^s}=1.$$

For married couples, labor supply is driven by two different thresholds for the wife's leisure preference, depending on whether the husband is working or not. Denote these thresholds by:

$$\hat{\eta}_e=\frac{1}{\lambda_f}\log\left(\frac{w_f+w_m+\gamma-\psi}{w_m+\gamma}\right),$$
$$\hat{\eta}_u=\frac{1}{\lambda_f}\log\left(\frac{w_f+\gamma}{\gamma}\right).$$

The average labor supply per married couple is then:

$$N^m=(1-u)(1+(1-u)F(\hat{\eta}_e))+u(1-u)F(\hat{\eta}_u).$$

Here the first term corresponds to employed husbands, and the second term corresponds to unemployed husbands. Wives of unemployed husbands work with a strictly higher probability than wives of employed husbands, because the cost ψ does not have to be paid (a substitution effect) and overall income is lower (an income effect working in the same direction). The derivative of labor supply with respect to $1-u$ for the married couples is:

$$\frac{\partial N^m}{\partial(1-u)}=(1+(1-u)F(\hat{\eta}_e))+(1-u)F(\hat{\eta}_e)+uF(\hat{\eta}_u)-(1-u)F(\hat{\eta}_u),$$

$$\frac{\partial N^m}{\partial(1-u)}=(1+2(1-u)F(\hat{\eta}_e))-(1-2u)F(\hat{\eta}_u).$$

The elasticity of married labor supply with respect to $1-u$ is then:

$$\frac{\partial N^m}{\partial(1-u)}\frac{1-u}{N^m}=\frac{1+2(1-u)F(\hat{\eta}_e)-(1-2u)F(\hat{\eta}_u)}{1+(1-u)F(\hat{\eta}_e)+uF(\hat{\eta}_u)}.$$

If it were the case that $F(\hat{\eta}_u)=F(\hat{\eta}_e)$, the expression once again would yield an elasticity of unity as for the singles. However, in fact we have $\hat{\eta}_u>\hat{\eta}_e$ and hence $F(\hat{\eta}_u)>F(\hat{\eta}_e)$, so that the elasticity of labor supply by married couples is strictly smaller than one. Intuitively, there is a fraction of women (given by $F(\hat{\eta}_u)-F(\hat{\eta}_e)$) who do not work if their husband is working, but choose to enter the labor force if the husband is unemployed. Hence, there is insurance in the family that dampens fluctuations in aggregate employment. Even though married female labor supply is more elastic at the microlevel, it contributes to a dampening of the volatility of aggregate labor supply due to this intra-family insurance effect.[q]

In the data, married female employment rose massively in the second half of the 20th century (see Fig. 7), and there were also large shifts in the composition of household types (see Figs. 3 and 4). The model suggests that these changes should affect the volatility of aggregate labor supply. The following proposition summarizes the main results.

Proposition 2 (Family Determinants of Volatility of Aggregate Labor Supply) *Consider a population of measure one consisting of* M *married households (with two members each) and* 1–2M *single households. We then have:*

1. *The elasticity of aggregate labor supply* N *with respect to* $1 - u$ *(the fraction of workers not affected by the unemployment shock) is equal to one if the fraction of married people is* $M = 0$ *and decreases with* M *for* $M > 0$.
2. *For a fixed* $M > 0$, *the elasticity of aggregate labor supply* N *with respect to* $1 - u$ *is strictly smaller than one, but approaches one when* w_f *converges to zero or to infinity.*

The first premise suggests that the large shifts in the composition of households in the past few decades may have had a marked effect on the response of aggregate labor supply to shocks. The second premise suggests that, in addition, the increase in female labor supply should also affect the behavior of aggregate labor supply, albeit in a nonmonotone way. Regarding the married households, what is at stake is the potential for insurance within the family. When conditions are such that women do not work even if their husbands are unemployed (captured here by the case of a female wage close to zero), there is no potential for insurance, and hence the labor supply of married households will be just as elastic as that of single households. Conversely, when conditions are such that all women work regardless of the employment status of their husbands (captured by the case of the female wages approaching infinity), there is no potential for insurance either. Insurance does play an important role when there is a sizeable group of women who do not work if their husbands are employed, but are willing to enter the market when the husband loses his job. Hence, the mechanism would predict the greatest role for insurance at a time when the rise in female employment is well underway, but still not close to being completed.

Fig. 12 displays how the elasticity of total labor supply by married households with respect to the unemployment shock depends on relative female wages in a computed example.[r] The male wage is normalized to one, and the source of variation is the relative

[q] There is an active debate in the literature on how micro- and macroestimates of labor supply elasticities can be reconciled (see Chetty et al., 2011, 2012; Keane and Rogerson, 2012 for recent contributions).

[r] Parameter values: $w_m = 1$, $\gamma = 0.1$, $\psi = 0.1$, and $\lambda_f = 0.5$. The distribution of leisure preferences is log-normal with $\mu = 0.5$ and $\sigma = 1$, and the elasticity of labor supply is evaluated at an unemployment rate of $u = 0.1$.

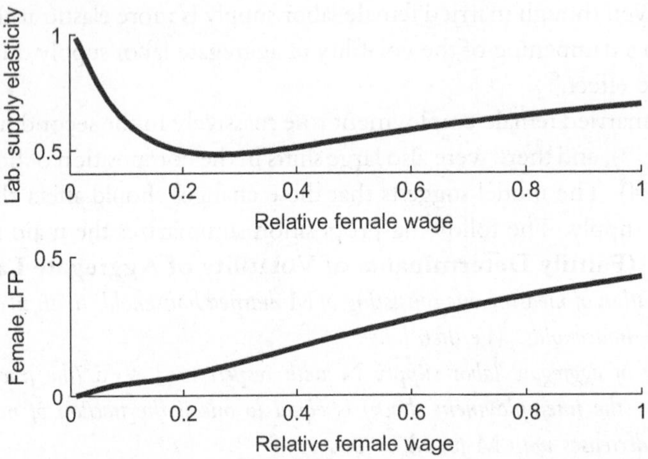

Fig. 12 Aggregate labor supply elasticity and female labor force participation (LFP) as a function of relative female wage in labor supply model.

female wage. The lower panel shows female labor supply as a function of the relative female wage. Not surprisingly, at a zero female wage, female labor supply is zero as well. However, even with very low wages some women work, namely those whose husbands are unable to work and who have a low leisure preference. The upper panel shows that this implies that the aggregate elasticity is U-shaped in relative female wages. In light of the observed decline in the gender wage gap and the increase in female labor force participation in US data (see Figs. 7 and 10), the findings suggest that the aggregate labor supply elasticity should have changed substantially in recent decades.

2.4.2 Endogenous Bargaining

The analysis of married couples' decisions has been carried out so far under the assumption of exogenous bargaining weights and full commitment. As mentioned above, if female bargaining power is low and female wages are high, women are likely to work a lot and consume little, and hence such women may prefer not to be married at all. Without full commitment, ie, if women were allowed to leave such a marriage, efficient bargaining subject to the limited commitment constraint would dictate that bargaining weights adjust to ensure that married women get at least as much utility as they would if they were single. Adjusting bargaining weights in this way is possible as long as the surplus from marriage is positive, which is guaranteed in our setting as long as $\psi > 0$ (married couples economize on the cost of running a household).[s]

[s] Other reasons for a positive marital surplus include consumption being a public good (see Section 3) and a utility benefit from being married (see Section 2.5).

Now consider how bargaining weights would adjust to changing wages w_g in this setting.[t] The utility of a single female is the maximum value between working and not working as a single:

$$U_f^s = \max\{\log(w_f + y_f - \psi) - \eta_f, \log(y_f)\}.$$

Assume that w_f is high enough (or y_f low enough) so that as a single, she always prefers to work. Comparing her utility as a single with that when married, she will prefer to be single if:

$$w_f + y_f > \frac{\lambda_f}{1-\lambda_f}(w_m + y_m) + \psi.$$

This condition will hold, for example, when her wages are high or her bargaining power is low. In such a case, the bargaining power in marriage should adjust to guarantee her at least her reservation (ie, single) utility:

$$\lambda_f = \frac{w_f + y_f - \psi}{w_m + y_m + w_f + y_f - \psi}.$$

Of course, any λ_f higher than the expression above would also guarantee that her participation constraint is satisfied.

We can use this logic to assess what would happen in a dynamic model with shocks to wages and participation cost. Suppose the couple starts out with a large marital surplus and bargaining weights such that neither participation constraint is binding. Suppose now that her wage increases unexpectedly such that, holding λ_f constant, her participation constraint would be violated. In response, her bargaining weight will increase. Similarly, a fall in the participation cost ψ may also lead to a tightening of the participation constraint and hence a shift in bargaining weights.[u] Bargaining positions will also be affected by changes in unearned income such as lottery winnings or an inheritance.

Now consider how such changes in bargaining weights affect the elasticity of labor supply. Qualitatively, the effects described in Propositions 1 and 2 rely on the possibility of insurance within the family and do not depend on the assumption of fixed bargaining weights. However, endogenous bargaining may well matter for the quantitative size of the effects. Both Knowles (2013) and Voena (2015) examine this issue, although their

[t] The model is static of course so there is no adjustment over time. Rather, one should think of bargaining weights differing across couples in an economy with heterogeneity in relative wages. However, the basic logic would carry over to a dynamic model with limited commitment where similar forces would lead to adjustments in the bargaining weights over time, see Mazzocco (2007) and Voena (2015).

[u] Since a decline in ψ affects both the male and female participation constraint, the direction of the change will depend on the details and in particular the status quo bargaining weight. Suppose her constraint is exactly binding before the shock lowering ψ is realized. Then, clearly, since he is currently reaping the entire surplus, her weight will have to go up to ensure continued participation in marriage by the female.

analyses are concerned with longer-term changes rather than with the business cycle. Nevertheless, the forces they identify should also be active at the business cycle frequency. If a higher wage increases bargaining power, it also increases the weight in the bargaining process on the leisure of the spouse who is receiving the raise. This effect lowers the response of labor supply to wage changes. Indeed, Knowles (2013) argues that the overall response of aggregate labor supply to the increase in female wages is dampened because of shifts in bargaining power. Whether such shifts in bargaining power also dampen aggregate labor volatility is less clear, as the opposite effect will apply to the other spouse. We view this as a fruitful area for future research.

2.4.3 Linking Changes in the US Labor Market to Family Labor Supply

We now relate the theoretical channels linking the family to variations in aggregate labor supply outlined above to empirical evidence on fluctuations in employment and output in the United States. We are interested in how the variability of aggregate labor supply varies between men and women and single and married individuals, and how these factors changed over time. Our analysis is based on annual data from the Current Population Survey (CPS) for the years 1962–2014. We focus on average weekly hours worked per person for the population aged 25–65.[v] Fig. 13 shows how this measure of labor supply

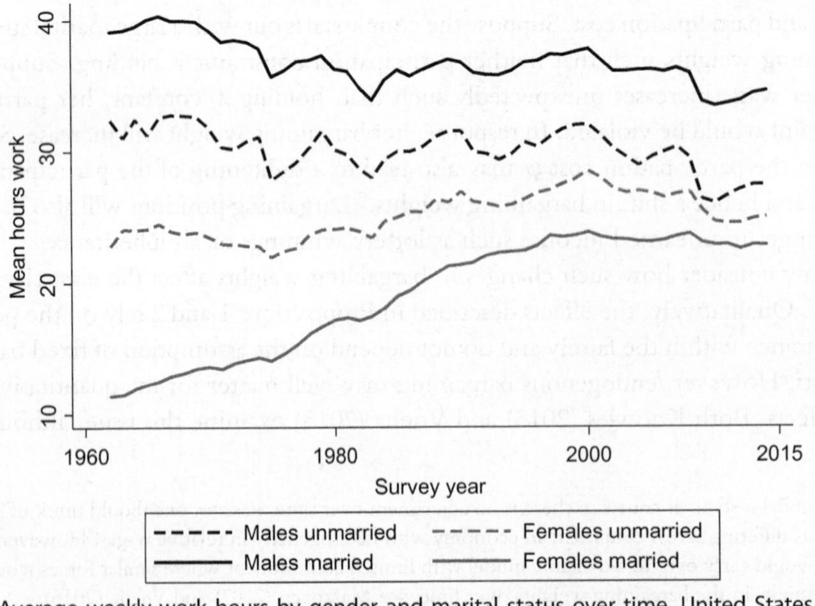

Fig. 13 Average weekly work hours by gender and marital status over time, United States. *Current Population Survey, March and Annual Social and Economic Supplements, 1962–2014.*

[v] The sample includes self-employed individuals.

evolves over time by gender and marital status. The sharp upward trend in married women's labor supply from the 1960s to the 1990s is apparent, as well as the comparatively larger drop in male labor supply since the Great Recession of 2008.

To focus on fluctuations at the business cycle frequently, we compute the cyclical component as the residual after subtracting a Hodrick–Prescott trend from the logarithm of each series (with a smoothing parameter of 6.25). The cyclical component of labor supply by gender and marital status is displayed in Fig. 14. It is immediately apparent that aggregate male labor supply is more volatile than aggregate female labor supply. Single men experience the largest fluctuations in labor supply over the cycle, whereas the smallest fluctuations are observed for married women.

The large differences in the volatility of female and male labor supply together with the large increase in female labor supply suggest that family trends may have had repercussions for the cyclical properties of aggregate labor supply over the observed period. To examine this possibility more formally, Table 1 provides detailed information on fluctuations in aggregate labor supply in the United States in relation to gender and marital status. In the table, the total volatility of a given series is the percentage standard deviation of the cyclical component of average labor supply per person in the group. Cyclical volatility is the percentage standard deviation of the predicted value from a regression of the cyclical component of employment in each group on the cyclical component of real GDP per capita (also computed using the HP filter). Cyclical volatility captures the

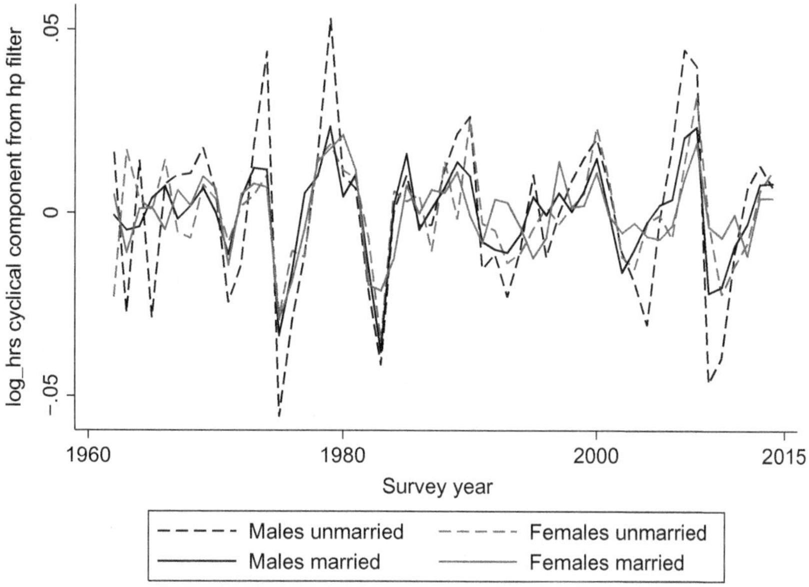

Fig. 14 Cyclical component of average weekly work hours by gender and marital status over time, United States (cyclical component is deviation from Hodrick–Prescott trend, smoothing parameter 6.25). *Current Population Survey, March and Annual Social and Economic Supplements, 1962–2014.*

Table 1 Volatility of hours worked in the United States, by gender and marital status

	All			Married		Single	
	Total	Women	Men	Women	Men	Women	Men
1962–2014							
Total volatility	1.25	1.04	1.46	1.04	1.25	1.33	2.33
Cyclical volatility	0.99	0.72	1.18	0.67	1.01	0.74	1.68
Hours share		38.09	61.91	23.90	47.71	14.19	14.20
Volatility share		27.22	72.78	16.20	48.98	10.64	24.17
1962–88							
Total volatility	1.35	1.19	1.48	1.26	1.36	1.37	2.44
Cyclical volatility	1.08	0.87	1.19	0.87	1.09	0.79	1.65
Hours share		33.71	66.29	21.99	55.29	11.72	11.00
Volatility share		27.14	72.86	18.02	56.29	8.67	17.02
1989–2014							
Total volatility	1.15	0.87	1.47	0.79	1.16	1.30	2.25
Cyclical volatility	0.91	0.51	1.23	0.38	0.95	0.70	1.82
Hours share		42.64	57.36	25.89	39.83	16.75	17.53
Volatility share		23.68	76.32	10.80	41.51	12.88	34.81

Notes: All data from Current Population Survey, March and Annual Social and Economic Supplements, 1962–2014. Total volatility is the percentage standard deviation of the Hodrick-Prescott residual of average labor supply per person in each group. Cyclical volatility is the percentage deviation of the predicted value of a regression of the HP-residual on the HP-residual of GDP per capita. Hours share is the share of each component in total hours. Volatility share is share of each group in the cyclical volatility of total hours.

component of employment volatility that is related to aggregate economic fluctuations. The hours share and volatility share break down the contribution of each component to aggregate hours and to the cyclical volatility of aggregate labor supply.[w]

The first column displays the volatility of aggregate labor supply (women and men combined), and the next two columns break down labor supply between women and men. Over the entire sample, women's labor supply is less volatile than men's labor supply. Moreover, for women cyclical volatility is a smaller fraction of total volatility compared to men; ie, less of the variation in female labor supply is related to aggregate economic fluctuations. As a consequence, even though over the entire sample women contribute close to 40% of total hours, they account for less than 30% of volatility in aggregate labor supply.

A key observation is that female labor supply is less variable than male labor supply in the aggregate, even though at the microlevel women have a much higher labor supply

[w] The computation of cyclical volatility and hours and volatility shares follows the methodology used by Jaimovich and Siu (2009) and Jaimovich et al. (2013) to characterize the contributions of the young and the old to aggregate fluctuations.

elasticity than men. These facts can be reconciled if some of the microvariability in female labor supply is due to adjustments that move in the opposite direction of aggregate changes, such as women increasing labor supply in a recession. We would expect such movements to be especially likely to arise among married households, where the spouses can provide each other with some insurance. To evaluate this possibility, in the further columns the fluctuations in labor supply are further broken down into married vs single individuals. Consistent with a role for insurance, we see that, for both women and men, fluctuations are much smaller for the married than for the single individuals.

At first sight, the lower variability of married labor supply may appear to contradict Proposition 1, which states that married women should have a higher wage elasticity of labor supply than single women. However, Table 1 captures macroeconomic fluctuations rather than microelasticities, and we would expect married women to have lower aggregate volatility precisely if their higher microelasticity arises from a fraction of married women adjusting their labor supply countercyclically in response to changes in their husbands' earnings.[x]

Some of the lower variability of female labor supply is related to the fact that a larger share of women is employed in the service sector, which is less cyclical than the manufacturing sector where men dominate. However, when we compare workers employed in manufacturing and services, we find that within each sector women experience a lower cyclical volatility than men. Moreover, the link to the sector of employment does not contradict a role for insurance within the family, because the choice of sector (and also occupation) is endogenous and may be made in part precisely to offset risk encountered by a worker's spouse.[y]

The theoretical mechanisms outlined in the previous section suggest that the aggregate elasticity of labor supply should respond to changes in female labor force participation. To explore this possibility, the remainder of Table 1 compares fluctuations during the first half of our sample (1962–88), when female labor supply was rising quickly from an initially low level, to the period 1989–2014, when female labor supply had reached a

[x] A second factor driving the higher aggregate volatility of single labor supply (which is not captured in the model) is that singles tend to be younger than married people, and the young generally have more variable labor supply for other reasons (such as a more important education margin, see Jaimovich et al., 2013). We can control for the effect of age by considering narrower age brackets. For example, among people aged 25–30, the total volatility of the labor supply of married and single women is about the same.

[y] The special role of the service sector in the rise of female employment is analyzed by Buera et al. (2013), Ngai and Petrongolo (2014), and Rendall (2015). Olivetti and Petrongolo (2016) provide an empirical study of the role of industry structure for trends in female employment, working hours, and relative wages in a cross-section of developed economies, and argue that the rise of the service sector accounts for at least half of the long-term variation in female hours. Albanesi and Şahin (2013) study the role of industry composition for male-female differences in cyclical fluctuations in employment in the United States, and show that that industry composition was not important for pre-1990 recessions, but mattered more once female participation flattened out in the 1990s.

higher plateau. The most important observation here is that whereas the volatility of male labor supply is essentially unchanged, the volatility of female labor supply has substantially decreased, and particularly so the cyclical volatility. The breakdown by marital status shows that this change is driven primarily by married women. Married women already have a low total volatility of about 0.8% in the second half of the sample, and less than half of this total volatility is accounted for by cyclical volatility. These numbers suggest, as predicted by the simple theoretical model in the previous section, that the rise in female labor force participation had a substantial dampening effect on the volatility of total labor supply. In contrast, there are no substantial changes in the cyclical volatility of the labor supply of singles, with a small decrease in volatility for single women and a small increase for single men.

The overall result of the changes is that at the same time women increased their share of total hours (from 34% to 43%), they accounted for a smaller share of total volatility (24% in 1989–2014 compared to 27% in 1962–88). As a consequence, the total volatility and cyclical volatility of aggregate labor supply fell substantially (see first column), even though the volatility of male labor supply slightly increased over the period. Hence, the rise in female participation dampened the volatility of aggregate labor supply over the cycle, in line with Proposition 2 and the declining portion of the aggregate elasticity in Fig. 12. Rising female participation may thus have been one of the driving forces of the "Great Moderation" in US aggregate fluctuations observed from the mid-1980s to the onset of the Great Recession in 2007.[z] Of course, the Great Recession appears to have brought the Great Moderation to an end, and hence one may wonder whether this dampening effect is still operative. The data suggest that female labor supply continues to partially offset aggregate fluctuations. A division of the sample into three periods shows that the most recent era displays the lowest volatility of female labor supply, with a cyclical volatility for married women of only 0.37%. The dampening role of married women's labor supply was particularly pronounced during the Great Recession itself. From 2007 to 2010, the average labor supply by married men declined by more than 8%, whereas the decrease was less than 3% for married women.

If the trend toward more gender equality continues, according to Proposition 2 the volatility of female and male labor supply should ultimately become more similar again (see also Fig. 12). In part, as married women become even more strongly attached to the labor force (eg, in the sense of more women being the main breadwinner for their family), their labor supply will become less elastic (this can already be observed at the

[z] See Galí and Gambetti (2009) for an overview of the discussion on the Great Moderation, and Jaimovich and Siu (2009) for an explanation that focuses on changes in the age composition of the labor force. Mennuni (2015) also considers the impact of demographic trends on the Great Moderation (although without considering the distinction of single and married individuals), and finds that demographics (including the rise in female participation) account for about 20% of the Great Moderation in the United States.

microlevel, eg, Heim, 2007). Conversely, men will become more able to rely on their wives' incomes, which should make their labor supply more elastic at the microlevel but also less cyclical in the aggregate. Hence, family trends will continue to play a role in shaping aggregate fluctuations.

2.4.4 Jobless Recoveries

A phenomenon that has received a lot of attention recently in business cycle research is the so-called jobless recoveries. This term refers to a recent change in the employment response to recessions in the United States. Before the 1990s, most postwar recessions were characterized by a strong rise in employment from the trough of the recession. In contrast, since the 1990s the increase in employment during the recovery has been anemic.

A variety of explanations have been proposed for the recent jobless recoveries, including structural change (Groshen and Potter, 2003), an increase in "job polarization" (the disappearance of jobs in the middle of the skill distribution in recessions; see Jaimovich and Siu, 2014), and fixed costs of labor adjustment (Bachmann, 2012). However, in recent work, Albanesi (2014) makes a strong case for jobless recoveries at least in part being due to changes within families, and more specifically to changes in female labor force participation. In a nutshell, Albanesi argues that employment differed in the aftermath of pre-1990 and post-1990 recessions because the earlier recessions took place in the context of a strong secular upward trend in female labor force participation, whereas the more recent ones did not. As Fig. 7 shows, female labor force participation in the United States followed a sharp upward trend, but participation leveled out after about 1990, and even declined somewhat in the last 15 years.

Table 2 summarizes the employment response to recent recessions and breaks them down by male vs female employment. Each entry in the table is a percentage change in the employment to population ratio (E/P) in the 4 years following the trough of the recession. The first column reproduces the basic fact of jobless recoveries. In the pre-1990 recessions, employment had fully recovered (and even increased a little) 4 years after the downturn, whereas for the post-1990 recessions the E/P ratio is on average close to 3% lower at that point of the recovery (1.35% if the Great Recession is excluded). Hence, it appears that recoveries after 1990 are qualitatively different from earlier recoveries. The next two columns break down the overall employment change into changes in the E/P ratio for women and men. The main message from these data is that, statistically, the jobless recoveries are due to changes in the behavior of female but not male employment. For men, recoveries have been "jobless" even before 1990, in the sense that the E/P ratio is down by 2.62% on average 4 years after the trough. The decline in E/P after 1990 is of a similar order of magnitude, and in fact a little smaller when the Great Recession is excluded. In contrast, we see a dramatic change for women. In the pre-1990 recessions, the female E/P ratio recovers strongly after each recession, with an average increase of

Table 2 Jobless recoveries: change in employment/population ratio in 4 years after peak in unemployment rate, in percentage points, by gender (includes three pre-1990 and tree post-1990 recessions)

	Change in E/P		
Period	**Total**	**Men**	**Women**
Pre-1990	0.65	−2.62	5.85
Post-1990	−2.78	−3.94	−1.41
Post-1990, excl. Great Recession	−1.35	−2.47	−0.07

Notes: Pre-1990 recessions include the 1969, 1973, and 1981 recessions. Post-1990 recessions include the 1990, 2001, and 2007 recessions.

close to 6% after 4 years. In contrast, in the post-1990 downturns female employment declines and now follows a pattern similar to that of male employment.

Table 2 suggests that, in a statistical sense, the change in the trend in female labor supply is responsible for jobless recoveries. Specifically, for men recoveries have always been jobless, whereas for women, before 1990 recession-related job losses were quickly made up by the secular upward trend in female participation. Of course, the empirical findings alone are not conclusive evidence in favor of such an explanation. For example, it is conceivable that if in the pre-1990s recessions female employment had risen more slowly, male employment would have suffered fewer losses. To fully evaluate the role of the changing trend in female labor supply for explaining jobless recoveries, one needs to spell out an economic model. Albanesi (2014) considers a model in which the increase in female participation is driven by gender-biased technological change, ie, tasks at which women have a comparative advantage become more important compared to those that favor men (such as those relying on physical strength). Albanesi shows that the model can reproduce both the long-run trend in female participation and the occurrence of jobless recoveries after female employment levels out.

2.4.5 Additional Notes on Related Literature

Whereas few papers explicitly consider how family trends change business cycle dynamics, there is a larger literature that incorporates at least some of the features of the family labor supply model described above into business cycle research. An early example is the literature on home production in macroeconomics (see Greenwood et al., 1995 for an early overview of this work). The first models did not explicitly distinguish between male and female labor supply, but by incorporating the possibility of working in the home (on child care, food production, and so on), the literature took implicit account of the different nature of female labor supply. Benhabib et al. (1991) is an early contribution focusing on the importance of home production for explaining business cycle facts. In their model, households derive utility from home and market consumption and supply both home and market hours. They find that the model with home production is much better at matching various volatilities and correlations over the business cycle than standard macro models. Closely related arguments are made by Greenwood and Hercowitz (1991) and Ríos-Rull (1993).

The role of family labor supply in the context of search models of the labor market has been analyzed by Guler et al. (2012). Spouses who are both in the labor force can provide each other insurance in the case of unemployment. They find that the possibility of insurance lowers the search effort of unemployed workers and also provides higher welfare compared to a setting where all workers are singles. Ortigueira and Siassi (2013) use a quantitative model to assess the importance of risk sharing within the family, and find that insurance through spousal labor supply is particularly important for wealth-poor households who lack access to other insurance mechanisms.

Family labor supply also plays a central role in a recent macroeconomic literature on the effects of tax reform. Using a quantitative life-cycle model with single and married households calibrated to US data, Guner et al. (2012a) explore the economic consequences of revenue-neutral tax reforms that adopt either a flat income tax or separate taxation of married couples (ie, separate filing). In either case, the reform generates a large increase in labor supply, which is mostly driven by married women (see also Guner et al., 2012b). Guner et al. (2014) extend this work to consider the effects of child care subsidies. They find that such subsidies have large effects on female labor supply, in particular at the bottom of the skill distribution. Bick and Fuchs-Schündeln (2014) document differences in labor supply of married couples across 18 OECD countries, and find that variation in tax systems (in particular joint vs separate taxation) can account for most of the differences.[aa]

In the labor literature, the phenomenon of a wife entering the labor market in response to her husband's unemployment that partly underlies Proposition 2 is known as the "added worker effect" (Lundberg, 1985). Empirical studies using data from the early 1980s or earlier have generally only found weak evidence in favor of the added worker effect. Using CPS data over a long time period, Juhn and Potter (2007) find evidence in support of the added worker effect but also argue that it has diminished in strength recently, in part because assortative mating has led to a higher intrahousehold correlation of the labor market shocks faced by wives and husbands.

The large differences in the cyclical volatility of the labor supply of single and married women and men documented above suggest that insurance within the family goes beyond a narrow added worker affect (which specifically concerns wives entering the labor force *after* their husbands become unemployed). Other forms of insurance include entering employment already in response to higher unemployment risk for the spouse (rather than the actual realization of unemployment, when entering the labor force quickly may be difficult), and adjustments on the intensive margin when both spouses

[aa] See also Chade and Ventura (2005) for an analysis of the welfare consequences of different tax treatments for married couples.

are in the labor force. Hyslop (2001) and Shore (2010, 2015) provide evidence in favor of a more general sharing of labor market risk in terms of the correlation of earnings within couples. Using a structural model of life cycle decisions, Blundell et al. (2016) similarly find strong evidence in favor of insurance within the family. Using CPS data, Mankart and Oikonomou (2015) document a substantial response of female labor force participation to spousal unemployment, where the response is more drawn out over time compared to early tests of the added worker effect. Moreover, Shore (2010) provides evidence that intrahousehold risk sharing is particularly strong within recessions. Our findings of a shift over time in the aggregate behavior of labor supply by gender and marital status suggest that it would be productive to expand on these findings by examining whether insurance within the family has undergone similar shifts at the microlevel.[ab]

Our analysis of family labor supply has focused on the interaction between husbands and wives. Another dimension of insurance within the family concerns the interaction between young and old family members. Quantitative studies that focus on this dimension include Jaimovich et al. (2013), who aim to explain age differences in the volatility of labor supply, and Kaplan (2012), who quantifies the role of the option of moving in and out of the parental home as an insurance mechanism for young workers. Building on this work, Dyrda et al. (2016) develop a business cycle model that allows for the option of young people moving in with their parents. They find that living arrangements matter a lot for labor supply elasticities: the elasticity is three times larger for young people who live with their parents compared to those who live alone. Accounting for household formation also implies that the aggregate labor supply elasticity is much larger than the microelasticity for stable households.

2.5 Changing Families and Aggregate Savings

In addition to providing a theory of labor supply, the representative household that populates baseline macroeconomic models also provides a theory of savings. In this section, we argue that models that go beyond representative households by explicitly modeling families have important implications for the determination of savings in the macroeconomy.

There are a few different channels through which families matter for savings; they relate to the life cycle savings motive and the precautionary savings motive. First, changes in the size of the household over time (eg, through marriage, divorce, and having children) imply that consumption needs vary over the life cycle, which is reflected in the optimal level of saving. Second, the precautionary savings motive also plays an important role in macroeconomic models (at least since Aiyagari, 1994). The strength of the precautionary motive depends on the insurance mechanisms people have access to. Similar to our analysis of labor supply above, we will argue that insurance within the family plays

[ab] Some evidence in this direction is provided by Blau and Kahn (2007), who show that married women's labor supply has become less responsive to their husbands' wages since the 1980s.

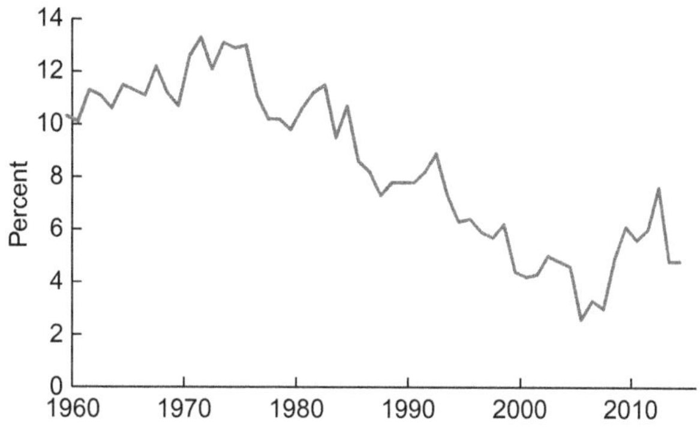

Fig. 15 Personal savings rate, United States. *Bureau of Economic Analysis, retrieved from FRED, St. Louis Fed.*

an important role in the sharing of income risk and hence in the determination of savings. Third, not only do families affect the sharing of existing sources of risk, but accounting for families also introduces new sources of risk. Getting married and having children can lead to (sometimes large) additional expenses, and to the extent that people face uncertainty over marriage and fertility, this should affect their precautionary savings. Equally important is the probability that a family dissolves: divorce is common and in many cases represents a sizeable financial risk.

The large shifts in fertility, marriage, and divorce over the last few decades suggest that the family determinants of savings may have been responsible for some of the changes in aggregate savings behavior over time. In particular, in the United States the personal savings rate has declined steadily from more than 10% in the late 1970s to less than 5% in the mid-2000s (see Fig. 15). Various explanations have been proposed for this change, although no single explanation is widely accepted (see Guidolin and Jeunesse, 2007 for an overview and discussion). In this section, we examine the possibility that changes at the family level may have played a role.

As far as the life cycle savings motive is concerned, there is a substantial literature within macroeconomics that accounts for the life cycle using a unitary model of the household, ie, without making an explicit distinction between the interests of different household members. Life cycle models were first introduced to modern business cycle research by Attanasio and Browning (1995) and Ríos-Rull (1996). In such models, the varying consumption needs due to changes in family composition over the life cycle can be incorporated through consumption equivalence scales.[ac] There is a small literature that uses life cycle models to quantify the impact of population aging on savings (Miles, 1999; Ríos-Rull, 2001). Depending on future population growth, these effects on the

[ac] See, for example, Fernández-Villaverde and Krueger (2007) and Fernández-Villaverde and Krueger (2011).

savings rate can be large, although they generally occur too slowly to explain much of the rapid decline in the savings rate in recent decades.

Given that there is already a sizeable literature on the life-cycle motive for saving, our discussion here is focused primarily on the implications of marriage and divorce for aggregate savings, a topic on which relatively few papers exist.

2.5.1 Savings and Divorce

In the models discussed in Section 2.4, we examined differences in the behavior of single and married households, while taking the existence of these different types of households as given. In reality, most adults start out as singles, marry at some point in their life, and many return to being single, eg, due to divorce. We now consider the implications for savings of the possibility of divorce. We start by taking marital bargaining power as given and by modeling divorce as an exogenous shock; endogenous bargaining and endogenous divorce will be considered below.

We consider a married couple whose life extends over two periods. The couple is married in the first period, and in the second period the union continues with probability $1-\pi$, whereas with probability π a divorce occurs. The divorce regime is that in the case of a divorce the wife retains fraction κ_f of assets, and the husbands receives $\kappa_m = 1 - \kappa_f$.

We focus on implications for savings and take as given that both spouses work in both periods.[ad] Let d' denote savings. The couple bargains cooperatively with bargaining weights given by λ_f and $\lambda_m = 1 - \lambda_f$. The couple's decision problem in the first period can be formulated as follows:

$$\max_{c_f, c_m, d'} \{\lambda_f \log(c_f) + \lambda_m \log(c_m)$$
$$+\beta[\lambda_f(\pi V_f^D(d') + (1-\pi) V_f(d')) + \lambda_m(\pi V_m^D(d') + (1-\pi) V_m(d'))]\}$$

subject to the budget constraint:

$$c_f + c_m + d' = w_f + w_m.$$

Here $V_g(d')$ is the second period value function for spouse $g \in \{f,m\}$ if the union continues, and $V_g^D(d')$ is the value function in the case of divorce.

In the case of divorce, in the second period each spouse simply consumes earnings and savings, which earn interest at rate r. We therefore have:

$$V_g^D(d') = \log(w_g' + (1+r)\kappa_g d').$$

[ad] Clearly, the possibility of divorce also affects the incentive to work, in part by altering the marginal utility of wealth, and in more complex environments also through the accumulation of individual-specific labor market experience.

In contrast, if the marriage continues, consumption shares are given by bargaining weights:

$$V_g(a') = \log(\lambda_g(w'_f + w'_m + (1+r)a')).$$

We can now consider the savings problem in the first period. The first-order condition for a' is given by:

$$\begin{aligned}\frac{1}{w_f + w_m - a'} = \beta\pi\left[\frac{\lambda_f(1+r)\kappa_f}{w'_f + (1+r)\kappa_f a'} + \frac{\lambda_m(1+r)\kappa_m}{w'_m + (1+r)\kappa_m a'}\right] \\ + \beta(1-\pi)\frac{1+r}{w'_f + w'_m + (1+r)a'}.\end{aligned} \tag{6}$$

The optimal savings in the case of no divorce risk ($\pi = 0$) are:

$$\tilde{a} = \frac{\beta(1+r)(w_f + w_m) - w'_f - w'_m}{(1+\beta)(1+r)}.$$

Now consider the case $\pi > 0$. The optimal savings will be unchanged at $\tilde{a}$ if the following condition is satisfied:

$$\frac{w'_g + (1+r)\kappa_g \tilde{a}}{\lambda_g} = w'_f + w'_m + (1+r)\tilde{a}$$

for $g \in \{f, m\}$, or:

$$\kappa_f = \tilde{\kappa f} \equiv \frac{-\lambda_m w'_f + \lambda_f w'_m + \lambda_f(1+r)\tilde{a}}{(1+r)\tilde{a}},$$

$$\kappa_m = \tilde{\kappa m} \equiv \frac{\lambda_m w'_f - \lambda_f w'_m + \lambda_m(1+r)\tilde{a}}{(1+r)\tilde{a}},$$

where we have $\tilde{\kappa}_f + \tilde{\kappa}_m = 1$ as required. Intuitively, this specific divorce regime recreates the same consumption allocation that would have been obtained had the marriage continued, and hence savings incentives are unchanged. What happens when κ_f does not equal $\tilde{\kappa}_f$ depends on relative female and male bargaining power. The derivative of the right-hand side of (6) with respect to κ_f is given by:

$$\beta\pi(1+r)\left(\frac{\lambda_f w'_f}{(w'_f + (1+r)\kappa_f a')^2} - \frac{\lambda_m w'_m}{(w'_m + (1+r)\kappa_m a')^2}\right)$$

Evaluating this expression at $a' = \tilde{a}$, $\kappa_f = \tilde{\kappa}_f$, and $\kappa_m = \tilde{\kappa}_m$ gives:

$$\frac{\beta\pi(1+r)}{\left(w'_f + w'_m + (1+r)\tilde{a}\right)^2}\left(\frac{w'_f}{\lambda_f} - \frac{w'_m}{\lambda_m}\right).$$

Hence, the derivative is positive if $w'_f/\lambda_f > w'_m/\lambda_m$, which is equivalent to $\tilde{\kappa}_f < \lambda_f$. A positive derivative, in turn, implies that when $\kappa_f > \tilde{\kappa}_f$, the optimal savings a' satisfy

$a' > \tilde{a}$, ie, the presence of divorce risk increases savings. More generally, divorce risk increases savings if for the spouse who is made worse off by divorce the asset share in divorce exceeds the relative bargaining power in marriage. Intuitively, under this condition increasing savings lowers the additional inequality across spouses brought about by divorce, which generates a precautionary demand for savings.[ae] If the couple starts out with equal bargaining power and there is an equal division divorce regime $\lambda_f = \lambda_m = \kappa_f = \kappa_m = 0.5$, the possibility of divorce always leads to precautionary savings, except in the knife edge case where the divorce regime that exactly reproduces the married allocation. The intuition is the same as for the usual motive for precautionary savings with preferences that display prudence. Under divorce, one spouse ends up with less consumption and the other one with more consumption compared to the married state. Due to the curvature in utility, the outcome of the less fortunate spouse receives higher weight when savings are determined in the first period, leading to an increase in precautionary savings.

We derived these results under the assumption that the divorce leaves the consumption possibilities of the couple unchanged. Realistically, there are also direct costs of divorce and forgone returns to scale from having a joint household. Hence, the possibility of divorce would also induce a negative income effect, which further increases desired savings.

To summarize the results, the effect of divorce risk on savings depends on the divorce regime (ie, the property division rule in divorce) and also on the relative bargaining power of the spouses. In practice, the most common divorce regimes in the data are the title-based regime and the equitable distribution regime.[af] Under the title-based regime, each spouse gets to keep the marital assets that are already in her or his name; ie, real estate goes to the owner listed in the title, bank accounts go to the account owner, and so on. Under the equitable distribution regime, judges have discretion in dividing assets in divorce. Often an equal division of marital assets is a starting point, but judges can make allowances for different needs (eg, the spouse with custody for children may receive more assets). When men are the main breadwinners and also hold title to major assets such as real estate, cars, and bank accounts, we would expect divorce under the title-based regime to lead to a precautionary demand for savings, because the wife is likely to be worse off in divorce compared to marriage. However, the precautionary demand only arises if the wife is able to save in her own name, because otherwise she would not be able to increase her outcome in divorce. Predictions are more ambiguous under the equitable distribution regime, because in this regime the wife may obtain more consumption in divorce compared to marriage. Comparing across regimes for a given divorce rate, as long as equitable distribution is more advantageous for the spouse with less power than the title-based system (as seems likely), a switch to equitable distribution (which occurred

[ae] This is a local result close to the marriage allocation.

[af] Additional possibilities include an equal division regime, and a regime where the division of assets is set through enforced prenuptial agreements.

in most US states in the 1970s) will weaken the precautionary motive and hence lead to lower savings.

What is more, individual labor earnings are likely to make up a large fraction of income in divorce. The rise in married women's earnings over time also implies that women are better able to support themselves after divorce (under either divorce regime). Hence, for a given divorce risk, the rise in married women's labor force participation and the decline in the gender pay gap are likely to have lowered the precautionary demand for savings associated with divorce over time.

2.5.2 Savings and Divorce with Endogenous Bargaining Power

The analysis so far suggests that divorce may have a substantial impact on a country's personal savings rate. Divorce is one of the largest and most common risks people face today (along with unemployment and ill health). Moreover, changes in the divorce rate, the divorce regime, and female labor force participation all affect how much precautionary saving arises from divorce risk, and thus may be in part responsible for changes in the savings rate over time.

In the preceding analysis, we introduced divorce as an exogenous shock, and the impact of divorce risk on couples' behavior was proportional to the probability with which this shock occurred. In this setting, the possibility of divorce has large effects only if the divorce rate is high. We now extend our analysis by endogenizing the divorce decision and the evolution of bargaining power within the marriage. We will see that in this extended model, the mere possibility of divorce can affect household behavior, so that large impacts on behavior can arise even if few couples divorce in equilibrium. Hence, the extension further amplifies the potential role of divorce for explaining how a country's savings rate is determined.

We consider a variant of the model above in which bargaining and divorce are endogenous. The ability of the spouses to commit to future allocations is limited by the ability to divorce, so that divorce functions as a threat point that informs bargaining during the marriage. In the first period, the couple is married and starts out with initial bargaining power λ_f and λ_m, where $\lambda_f + \lambda_m = 1$. In the second period, the couple experience marriage quality shocks ξ_f, ξ_m, which can be positive or negative. There is a unilateral divorce regime; that is, the marriage continues in the second period only if both spouses are at least as well off married compared to being divorced.

In the first period, the couple's decision problem can be written as:

$$\max\left\{\lambda_f \log(c_f) + \lambda_m \log(c_m) + \beta\left[\lambda_f E(V_f(a', \xi_f, \xi_m)) + \lambda_m E(V_m(a', \xi_f, \xi_m))\right]\right\},$$

subject to the budget constraint:

$$c_f + c_m + a' = w_f + w_m.$$

Here $V_g(d', \xi_f, \xi_m))$ is the expected utility of spouse g in the second period as a function of the state variables d', ξ_f, and ξ_m.

In the second period, the decision problem of the couple is constrained by the possibility of divorce. If a divorce takes place, existing property is divided with share κ_f for the wife and $\kappa_m = 1 - \kappa_f$ for the husband. Utilities conditional on divorce are therefore given by:

$$V_g^D(d') = \log(w_g' + (1+r)\kappa_g d').$$

The full decision problem in the second period can then be written as:

$$\max_{D \in \{0,1\}, c_f, c_m} \left\{ \lambda_f \left[(1-D)\left(\log(c_f) + \xi_f\right) + D V_f^D(d') \right] + \lambda_m \left[(1-D)(\log(c_m) + \xi_m) + D V_m^D(d') \right] \right\} \quad (7)$$

subject to:

$$c_f + c_m = w_f' + w_m' + (1+r)d', \quad (8)$$

$$(1-D)\left(\log(c_f) + \xi_f\right) + D V_f^D(d') \geq V_f^D(d'), \quad (9)$$

$$(1-D)(\log(c_m) + \xi_m) + D V_m^D(d') \geq V_m^D(d'). \quad (10)$$

Here $D \in \{0,1\}$ denotes the endogenous divorce decision and c_f, c_m is the consumption allocation conditional on staying married. Clearly, by setting $D = 1$ (divorce) the constraints (9) and (10) can always be met. However, divorcing is optimal only if there is no consumption allocation that leaves both spouses at least as well off married compared to divorced.

The decision problem in the second period can be solved by first considering a spouse who ends up just indifferent between divorce and staying married. Let $\tilde{\lambda}_g$ denote the consumption share that would make spouse g indifferent between these options, for a given ξ_g. The indifference condition is:

$$\log\left(\tilde{\lambda}_g\left(w_f' + w_m' + (1+r)d'\right)\right) + \xi_g = \log\left(w_g' + (1+r)\kappa_g d'\right),$$

which can be solved to give:

$$\tilde{\lambda}_g = \frac{w_g' + (1+r)\kappa_g d'}{\exp(\xi_g)\left(w_f' + w_m' + (1+r)d'\right)}.$$

The second period outcome can now be determined by comparing the implicit bargaining weights $\tilde{\lambda}_f$ and $\tilde{\lambda}_m$ to the actual ex ante bargaining weights λ_f and λ_m. In particular:

Proposition 3 (Divorce and Bargaining Power in Limited Commitment Model)

The outcome of the couple's decision problem in the second period can be characterized as follows:

- *If* $\tilde{\lambda}_f \leq \lambda_f$ *and* $\tilde{\lambda}_m \leq \lambda_m$*, the couple stays married* ($D = 0$)*, and consumption is:*

$$c_f = \lambda_f \left(w_f' + w_m' + (1+r)d' \right),$$
$$c_m = \lambda_m \left(w_f' + w_m' + (1+r)d' \right).$$

- *If* $\tilde{\lambda}_f > \lambda_f$ *and* $\tilde{\lambda}_f + \tilde{\lambda}_m \leq 1$*, the couple stays married* ($D = 0$)*, but the wife's consumption share is increased to satisfy her participation constraint. Consumption is:*

$$c_f = \tilde{\lambda}_f \left(w_f' + w_m' + (1+r)d' \right),$$
$$c_m = w_f' + w_m' + (1+r)d' - c_f.$$

- *If* $\tilde{\lambda}_m > \lambda_m$ *and* $\tilde{\lambda}_f + \tilde{\lambda}_m \leq 1$*, the couple stays married* ($D = 0$)*, but the husband's consumption share is increased to satisfy his participation constraint. Consumption is:*

$$c_m = \tilde{\lambda}_m \left(w_f' + w_m' + (1+r)d' \right),$$
$$c_f = w_f' + w_m' + (1+r)d' - c_m.$$

- *If* $\tilde{\lambda}_f + \tilde{\lambda}_m > 1$*, the couple divorces* ($D = 1$)*, and consumption is:*

$$c_f = w_f' + (1+r)\kappa_f d',$$
$$c_m = w_m' + (1+r)\kappa_m d'.$$

The implications of the possibility of divorce for savings are similar to those of the exogenous-divorce model above, but savings are affected already when one of the spouses' participation constraints is binding, even if the marriage continues.

Fig. 16 presents a computed example to show how the trend toward higher labor market participation of married women would affect divorce and the savings rate in the model with endogenous bargaining and divorce.[ag] Male earnings are normalized to $w_m = 1$, and the equilibrium savings rate and divorce rate are shown for female earnings varying from $w_f = 0.1$ to $w_f = 0.8$. The divorce regime is unilateral divorce with an equal division of marital assets upon divorce. Given that total earnings are constant and the interest rate equals the inverse of the discount factor, if there was no possibility of divorce, the savings rate would be equal to zero regardless of female earnings. Hence, any positive savings are due to the precautionary motive generated by the possibility of divorce.

[ag] The parameter values used are $\lambda_f = 0.4$, $\lambda_m = 0.6$, $r = 0.05$, and $\beta = 1/(1+r)$. The divorce regime features equal division of assets, $\kappa_f = \kappa_m = 0.5$, and the marriage quality shocks ξ_f and ξ_m are uniformly distributed on the interval $[-0.2, 1]$ and are independent across the spouses.

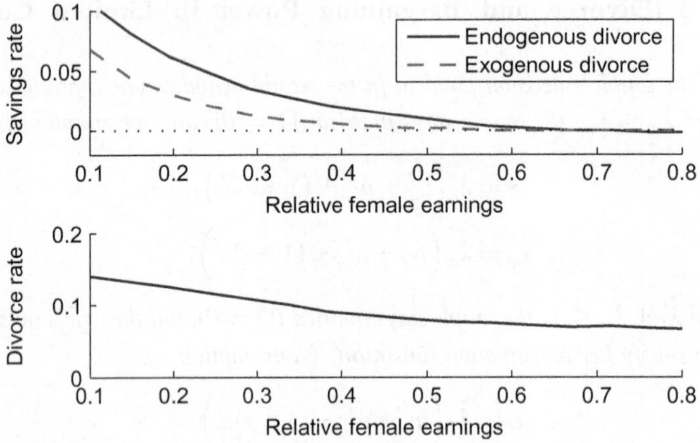

Fig. 16 Savings rate and divorce rate as a function of relative female earnings.

With endogenous bargaining and divorce, we see that the savings rate and divorce rate are both positive, and sharply decreasing in relative female earnings. Once female earnings are above 60% of male earnings, the savings rate approaches zero (the value that would be obtained without the possibility of divorce). The intuition for these findings is that for low female earnings, divorce leaves women much worse off compared to marriage. The equal division of assets only provides limited insurance, because most of the second period income of the couple is due to the husband's earnings. Thus, the possibility of divorce leads to a precautionary demand for savings primarily to insure women against the possibility of divorce. Own earnings provide an alternative route of insurance and also increase the overall share of income that women can claim in divorce. Hence, as earnings rise, precautionary savings are much reduced and ultimately disappear.

The picture also displays the savings rate in the exogenous divorce model when the equilibrium divorce rate (displayed in the lower panel) is fed as an exogenous variable into the model of the previous section (ie, the exogenous divorce rate varies together with female earnings). The exogenous divorce model generates qualitatively similar findings, but the impact on savings is much smaller in size. In the exogenous divorce model, as long as the couple stays married, bargaining power stays at the initial value. In contrast, in the endogenous divorce model, there are couples where, say, the husband is at the participation constraint (the realization of ξ_m is low), so that the wife has to offer additional compensation to the husband for the husband to stay. This need to compensate the other spouse generates an additional need for precautionary savings. Hence, the endogenous divorce model generally leads to a larger impact on the savings rate and can generate a feedback from the possibility of divorce on aggregate variables even if the realized divorce rate is low.

2.5.3 Additional Notes on Related Literature

There are only a few papers that use models of the type outlined here to address macroeconomic questions. Dynamic models of marriage under limited commitment with the possibility of divorce have been introduced by Mazzocco (2007), Mazzocco et al. (2013), and Voena (2015). In these models, the shifts in bargaining power that are necessary when one of the spouses' participation constraint is binding have persistent effects on the marital allocation. By specifically addressing how divorce law affects incentives for saving, Voena (2015) is the closest to the questions addressed here. Voena finds (using an estimated structural model) that the introduction of unilateral divorce (in states with an equal division of property) leads to higher savings and lower female employment. Intuitively, the introduction of unilateral divorce removes spouses' veto power in the divorce decision, which reduces risk sharing and increases precautionary savings. To our knowledge, there are no studies that analyze how the possibility of divorce (in a given divorce regime) affects the private savings rate (and other aggregate variables) in light of other observed changes to the family, such as the rise in female labor force participation and relative female earnings and the decline in fertility.

An early study that considers the role of divorce as an exogenous shock is Cubeddu and Ríos-Rull (2003). They assess the potential role of divorce for asset accumulation by comparing counterfactuals that differ in when (or if) people marry and divorce, and in how costly divorce is. Unlike in the model outlined above, consumption within marriage is constrained to be equal across spouses. They find that the impact of marriage and divorce can be large in their setting, but they do not directly relate this finding to observed changes in macro variables.[ah]

Love (2010) documents empirically (and analyzes in a quantitative model) how asset allocations change with marital-status transitions. As in Cubeddu and Ríos-Rull (2003) and Hong and Rios-Rull (2012), changes in marital status are modeled as exogenous shocks, and there is only public consumption in marriage. The theoretical model predicts that portfolio shares (ie, the fraction of wealth invested in stocks vs bonds) should react sharply to fertility, marriage, and divorce. Empirical results based on the Health and Retirement Study and the Panel Study on Income Dynamics are supportive of some of the predictions of the model, although not for all groups of households.

Fernández and Wong (2014a,b) use a quantitative life cycle model with exogenous divorce to study the importance of the likelihood of divorce for explaining the rise in female labor force participation from the 1960s to the 1990s. They argue that the increase in divorce risk accounts for a substantial fraction of the increase in female labor force participation. The main reason for this finding is that women (who often have lower wages

[ah] A similar framework is used by Hong and Rios-Rull (2012) in a setting that also accounts for the arrival of children, stochastic survival, and bequest motives, and uses information on life insurance holdings to infer how the utilities of different household members interact.

than their husbands and need to provide for their children) face lower consumption possibilities after a divorce, which increases desired savings. One way of increasing savings is to work more during marriage, which raises the total resources of the household and facilitates the smoothing of consumption between the married and divorced states. In Fernández and Wong (2014c) this analysis is extended to a setting with endogenous divorce.

In addition to increasing savings and increasing labor supply, another insurance mechanism that is likely to be relevant in the data is education. In Guvenen and Rendall (2015), women acquire education in part as insurance against a bad marriage. Guvenen and Rendall argue that the introduction of unilateral divorce increases this insurance motive, accounting for a sizeable fraction of the increase in female education and helping rationalize the observation that women now obtain more higher education than do men.[ai]

2.6 Private Information in the Household

Throughout Section 2, we have used a number of different approaches for modeling husband–wife interactions. We now step back from the applied questions to discuss the relative advantages of different models of the family and their uses within macroeconomics. The pioneering work of Gary Becker was largely based on the so-called unitary model of the family. A unitary model distinguishes between, say, male and female labor supply, but does so in the context of a single household utility function rather than allowing for separate preferences for each spouse. This approach is also how the family was first introduced into macroeconomics in the literature on home production and the business cycle (eg, Benhabib et al., 1991; Greenwood and Hercowitz, 1991). The limitation of the unitary approach is that since it does not distinguish individual utility functions, it does not allow for conflict of interest between spouses. This restricts the range of questions that can be addressed by the unitary model. Moreover, there is a sizeable literature in family economics that empirically tests the unitary model against richer alternatives that allow for bargaining, and finds strong evidence against the unitary model.[aj]

To go beyond the unitary model, one needs to start with women and men (characterized by separate utility functions) as primitives and then analyze how they act either together as couples or as singles. Within couples, one has to specify some form of bargaining process that determines how the couple resolves the conflict of interest between the spouses. Two broad classes of bargaining models that can be used for this purpose are

[ai] Another perspective on higher premarital investments by women is provided by Iyigun and Walsh (2007a), who focus on the impact of investments both on sorting of spouses and on bargaining power within marriage (see also Iyigun and Walsh, 2007b; Chiappori et al., 2009).

[aj] See Alderman et al. (1995) for an early summary of the evidence, and Attanasio and Lechene (2002) for an influential contribution based on Progresa data from Mexico.

noncooperative bargaining models (where the interaction between the spouses is modeled as a noncooperative game, using standard game theory tools) and cooperative bargaining models (where the spouses are able to achieve an outcome that is at least statically efficient). A common argument in favor of cooperative bargaining is that marriage is usually a sustained long-term relationship, which suggests that the spouses should be able to avoid major inefficiencies. However, while the majority of recent work in family economics uses a cooperative approach, other authors provide evidence in favor of inefficient bargaining outcomes within the family,[ak] and noncooperative models have been used by Lundberg and Pollak (1994), Konrad and Lommerud (1995), and Doepke and Tertilt (2014), among others.

Within the literature on cooperative bargaining in the family, many papers use explicit bargaining models such as Nash bargaining subject to divorce as the outside option.[al] Another popular approach, introduced by Chiappori (1988; 1992), is to only impose that the couple reaches a statically efficient outcome, but to remain agnostic about the details of the bargaining process. Empirical implementations of this approach often allow bargaining power to be a function of observables (called "distribution factors") such as the relative education or the relative age of the spouses, without specifying the mechanism through which these variables matter.[am] The advantage of this approach, labeled the "collective model," is its generality, because all (static) efficient allocations can be characterized in this way. The labor supply model employed in Section 2.4 is an example of a collective model (albeit with fixed bargaining power).

The collective approach is less suitable for dynamic contexts, because it does not provide an explicit theory for how bargaining within a couple evolves. This would perhaps not matter much if bargaining weights were constant over time, which would also imply ex-ante efficiency, ie, full insurance in the household. Yet there is plenty of empirical evidence of limited risk sharing in couples. For example, based on data from Kenya, Robinson (2012) documents that private expenditures increase in own labor income. Duflo and Udry (2004) use data from the Ivory Coast to show that the composition of household expenditure is sensitive to the gender of the recipient of a rainfall shock that affects male and female income differentially. The evidence is not exclusive to developing countries. Cesarini et al. (2015) document a larger fall in labor earnings after winning a lottery for the winners relative to their spouses in Sweden. One could rationalize such findings in a collective model where the bargaining weights move due to shifts in relative income, wages, or lottery winnings. However, this approach has the downside of

[ak] See, eg, Udry (1996), Duflo and Udry (2004), and Goldstein and Udry (2008).

[al] The classic papers are Manser and Brown (1980) and McElroy and Horney (1981). Another classic is the "separate spheres" bargaining model of Lundberg and Pollak (1993), which is an interesting hybrid between a cooperative and a noncooperative model.

[am] See, for example, Attanasio and Lechene (2014).

violating ex-ante efficiency without being explicit about the underlying bargaining friction. Moreover, the approach precludes transitions to a (presumably) noncooperative state such as divorce, which is an important limitation given that divorce is commonplace (see Fig. 6).

A more fruitful avenue in our view is to take a stand on the friction that prevents couples from achieving full insurance and model it explicitly. One obvious friction is limited commitment. Since spouses usually have the option to walk away from each other (ie, divorce or separation), at any point in time each spouse should get at least as much utility as his or her outside option. This is what we alluded to at the end of Section 2.4 and modeled more explicitly in the endogenous bargaining model of Section 2.5. A limited literature on dynamic household decisions pursues this avenue.[an] A model based on limited commitment will lead to endogenous shifts in bargaining power over time, namely whenever the commitment constraint becomes binding. When divorce is the outside option, limited commitment implies shifts in bargaining power only when a couple is close to divorce. An alternative is to consider an outside option of noncooperation within marriage as in Lundberg and Pollak (1993). Doepke and Kindermann (2015) is a recent example of a dynamic bargaining model with such an outside option. Such limited commitment models are consistent with the empirical evidence on continuously shifting bargaining power within couples provided by Lise and Yamada (2015).

An alternative friction that so far has received much less attention is private information within the household. Before showing how this friction can be modeled, let us discuss some indications that private information may indeed be relevant for bargaining between spouses. There are many things that spouses may not precisely know about each other, such as income, assets, consumption, work effort, or preferences. Contrary to the belief that love and altruism will lead to perfect information sharing between spouses, the evidence suggests otherwise. The most obvious example may be that people do not typically tell their partner when they are having an extramarital affair. Relatedly, some people do not disclose that they have HIV or other sexually transmitted diseases to their partner. Women sometimes hide from their partners that they are using birth control (or, depending on the context, that they are not using birth control).[ao] More directly related to the context of this chapter is that people do not always disclose income, spending, and savings behavior to their spouse. de Laat (2014) shows that husbands in split-migrant couples in Kenya invest significant resources into monitoring the spending behavior of their wives. When given the option, people often prefer to put money into private (and possibly secret) accounts.[ap] Hoel (2015) finds in Kenyan data that 31% of people say their spouse was not aware of any income they had received the preceding week.

[an] See in particular Mazzocco (2007) and Voena (2015).

[ao] For example, Ashraf et al. (2014) show that women in Zambia hide the use of birth control from their husbands when given the chance.

[ap] See Anderson and Baland (2002), Ashraf (2009), and Schaner (2015).

Further, evidence from lab and field experiments suggests that information treatments affect intrahousehold allocations, suggesting that information frictions are important.[aq] Most of this evidence is from developing countries and in some dimensions (such as uncertainty about a spouse's income) couples in industrialized countries with joint checking accounts and tax filings may be less affected by information frictions. However, private information about preferences and hidden effort is likely to be equally relevant all around the world.

In sum, there is ample evidence that private information plays an important role in household bargaining. Nevertheless, hardly any work has been done on this issue in terms of explicit models of the bargaining process. We believe this is an important area for future work. While most of this chapter concerns applying family economics to macroeconomics, the issue of information frictions presents an opportunity for intellectual arbitrage in the opposite direction: while in family economics static models are still common, in macroeconomics dynamic contracting models that make the underlying frictions explicit have been widespread for many years. In particular, it should be possible to apply some of the tools to analyze informational frictions currently used in theoretical macroeconomics and public finance to issues in family economics.[ar] Some work of this kind exists in development economics (eg, Townsend, 2010; Karaivanov and Townsend, 2014; Kinnan, 2014), but the question is a different one as the degree of insurance within a village—as opposed to within a couple—is analyzed.

We currently explore how to account for information frictions in household bargaining in ongoing work (Doepke and Tertilt, 2015). As a simple example for modeling such a friction, consider a variant of the model analyzed above under private information about each spouse's labor income w_g. To simplify the exposition, we assume that there is a private income realization only in the first period, whereas there is no income in the second period, $w_f' = w_m' = 0$. Bargaining is assumed to be efficient subject to the constraints imposed by private information, with initial welfare weights λ_f and λ_m. The constrained efficient allocation can be computed as a mechanism design problem. The revelation principle can be applied and implies that we can restrict attention to truth-telling mechanisms with truth-telling constraints imposed. Hence, the spouses will simultaneously report their income w_f and w_m to each other, and consumption is given by functions $c_g(w_f, w_m)$ and $c_g'(w_f, w_m)$, which depend on the reports. For simplicity, we

[aq] When income is private information in dictator games, less is transferred to the partner Hoel (2015). Migrants send home less cash to family members when their choice is not revealed to the recipients (Ambler, 2015). More is spent on goods that are hard to monitor or difficult to reverse and less on household public goods when a transfer is given privately to one spouse relative to a full information transfer (Castilla and Walker, 2013).

[ar] See Atkeson and Lucas (1992) and the follow-up literature for applications of models with information frictions in macroeconomics. For a survey of the literature incorporating information frictions into public finance, see Golosov et al. (2006).

assume that each income is drawn from a finite set $w_g \in W_g$ with independent probability distributions denoted by $p(w_g)$.

With these preliminaries, the optimization problem faced by the household can be written as follows:

$$\max E \;\{\lambda_f[\log(c_f(w_f,w_m)) + \beta \log(c_f'(w_f,w_m))].\\ + \lambda_m[\log(c_m(w_f,w_m)) + \beta \log(c_m'(w_f,w_m))]\},$$

subject to the budget constraints:

$$c_f + c_m + a' = w_f + w_m,$$
$$c_f' + c_m' = (1+r)a.$$

The maximization problem is also subject to truth-telling constraints. Consider first the wife. For each w_f and each alternative $\tilde{w}_f \in W_f$, we impose:

$$\sum_{w_m} p(w_m)[\log(c_f(w_f,w_m)) + \beta \log(c_f'(w_f,w_g))]\\ \geq \sum_{w_m} p(w_m)[\log(c_f(\tilde{w}_f,w_m) + w_f - \tilde{w}_f) + \beta \log(c_f'(\tilde{w}_f,w_m))].$$

Similarly, for the husband we have:

$$\sum_{w_f} p(w_f)\left[\log(c_m(w_f,w_m)) + \beta \log(c_m'(w_f,w_g))\right]\\ \geq \sum_{w_f} p(w_f)\left[\log(c_m(w_f,\tilde{w}_m) + w_m - \tilde{w}_m) + \beta \log(c_m'(w_m,\tilde{w}_m))\right].$$

A direct implication of this model is that consumption is more responsive to a change in own income than to a change in the spouse's income. The reason is that incentives need to be provided to tell the truth about own income shocks. Other frictions (such as unobservable effort or unobservable preference shocks) can be modeled along similar lines.

Models of bargaining with limited commitment frictions and private information frictions have distinct implications for how consumption and leisure depend on bargaining power. Consider, for example, a limited commitment model where the outside option responds to income shocks. In such a setting, a positive income shock for a given spouse increases this spouse's bargaining weight, which (all else equal) tends to increase leisure and lower labor supply. In contrast, in a hidden effort model it is costly to distort the effort of a productive spouse; hence, a more productive spouse may be provided more incentives to work and end up working more. This example shows that the underlying friction matters for how household bargaining reacts to family trends such as the increase in women's labor market attachment. We believe that further work on incorporating methods for dealing with dynamic contracting frictions into family economics will be productive for improving our understanding of these issues.

3. THE FAMILY AND ECONOMIC GROWTH

The most fundamental questions in macroeconomics concern economic growth. As Robert Lucas put it, once one starts to think about the determinants of cross-country income differences and policies that may allow poor countries to catch up with rich ones, "it is hard to think about anything else" (Lucas, 1988, p. 5).

Early theorizing on the sources of economic growth was focused on firms rather than families. The Solow model, for example, puts investment in physical capital by the business sector into the spotlight, coupled with exogenous improvements in productivity. To be sure, even in a model driven by capital accumulation families matter for growth; after all, investment has to be financed by savings, and savings are determined within the family. Both husband-wife and parent-child interactions are relevant for savings. First, as already shown in Section 2.5, a couple's savings rate responds to the possibility of divorce. More generally, if husbands and wives disagree about the consumption-savings trade-off (eg, because they differ in their degree of patience), then how spouses negotiate affects the savings rate. Second, a large part of long-run wealth accumulation is due to bequests, for which interactions between parents and children are crucial.

Family decisions have become even more central to growth theory with more recent developments that emphasize the importance of human capital accumulation and endogenous population growth. The importance of human capital accumulation for growth has been well recognized since the work of Lucas (1988). To fix ideas, consider a simple endogenous growth model based on accumulation of human capital H and physical capital K. Final output is produced using physical capital and effective units of labor as inputs. Effective units of labor depend both on time spent working u and the stock of human capital. Assuming a simple Cobb–Douglas production function, output is:

$$Y = K^{\alpha}(uH)^{1-\alpha}.$$

Human capital is accumulated by spending time studying. The higher the level of human capital and the more time spent in school $(1-u)$, the higher is tomorrow's human capital,

$$H' = B(1-u)H, \tag{11}$$

where B is a technology parameter. In the simplest model, the fraction of time spent in school is given exogenously. Then, the growth rate of output in the balanced growth path is simply $B(1-u)$. Growth thus depends not only on technology but also on the time spent in school.

So far we have taken u to be an exogenous parameter. But clearly the time spent on education is a choice. Who makes the choice? A large part of education happens during childhood and hence, leaving mandatory schooling laws aside, it is parents who make education decisions for their children. In other words, education is a family decision. Note also that the formulation of the human capital production function above assumes past human capital enters into next period's human capital. Intuitively, the initial human capital stock of a new member in society is proportional to the level already attained by older members of the family. As Lucas put it, "human capital accumulation is a social activity, involving groups of people in a way that has no counterpart in the accumulation of physical capital" (Lucas, 1988, p. 19). Much of the time, the group in which the accumulation happens is the family, where children learn from parents both by imitating them and by being actively taught.

Understanding the human capital accumulation process is an active research area. Many open questions remain, but what is understood by now is that education and skill formation are complex processes that involve many ingredients. Inputs both in forms of time (own time, teacher time, parental time) and goods (textbooks, school buildings) are important, as is the age at which specific investments take place. For example, Jim Heckman and coauthors have emphasized the importance of early childhood education for long-run outcomes (Heckman, 2008). Citing Cunha and Heckmann (2007), "The family plays a powerful role [...] through parental investments and through choice of childhood environments." Recent research captures such links in formal models of human capital investments within families (eg, Caucutt and Lochner, 2012; Aizer and Cunha, 2012). Del Boca et al. (2014) find that both paternal and maternal time input are essential inputs into child development.

So far, we have motivated the importance of families for growth based on the intuitive argument that human capital and savings decisions are made in the family. An equally compelling argument for the importance of families can be made on the basis of empirical findings. As we will document in the next section, cross-country data show strong correlations between development indicators such as GDP per capita and measures of family structure. While such findings constitute no proof of causality, they suggest a close link between family structure and development. After documenting these facts, we will show in a sequence of simple growth models how modeling increasingly complex family interactions can affect economic growth in an economy. While the most straightforward link from families to growth concerns fertility decisions, we emphasize that there are many dimensions to families, their role in producing new people being only one of them. Families typically consist of many family members (husband, wife, sons, daughters), who may differ in preferences and skills. When preferences differ, the exact nature of the decision process in the family becomes important. When skills differ, ie, when men and women are not perfect substitutes in production, then the details of how they enter differently into the human capital and goods production functions will also matter for growth. Further, families may have different attitudes toward sons and daughters, affecting human capital investment, and institutions such as polygyny may also affect incentives for investing in human and physical capital.

3.1 Cross-Country Family Facts

In this section, we report strong correlations between indicators of economic development and measures of family structure. Perhaps the most well-known example is the close link between the fertility rate and development. Fig. 17 displays a strong negative relationship between the total fertility rate and GDP per capita across countries.[as] Fertility, in turn, is strongly negatively correlated with measures of schooling (Fig. 18).

Many other measures of family structure are related to development as well. Fig. 19 displays the fraction of teenage girls (15–19 years) that has ever been married. The figure reveals a striking negative relationship between GDP per capita and early marriage. In poor countries, such as Ghana and Malawi, almost 50% of 15–19 year old girls are

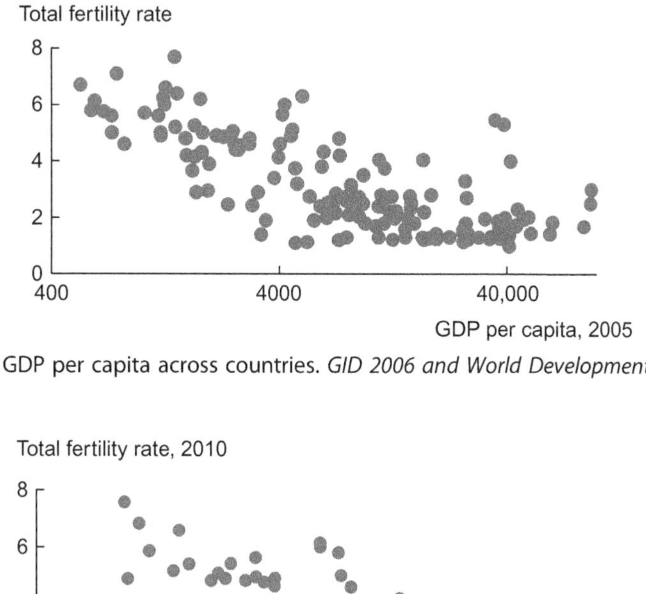

Fig. 17 TFR and GDP per capita across countries. *GID 2006 and World Development Indicators 2005.*

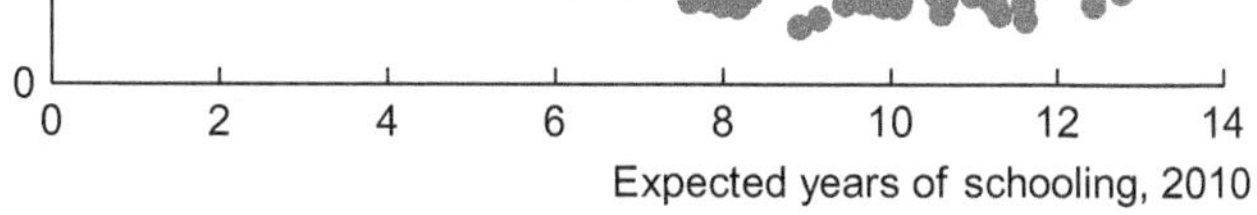

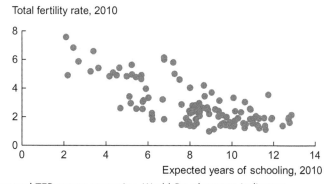

Fig. 18 Schooling and TFR across countries. *World Development Indicators.*

[as] A similar relationship can be observed over time within countries: in most cases, the demographic transition took place during times of rapid economic growth. For the United States, the decline in children ever born by birth cohort of mothers is shown in Fig. 1.

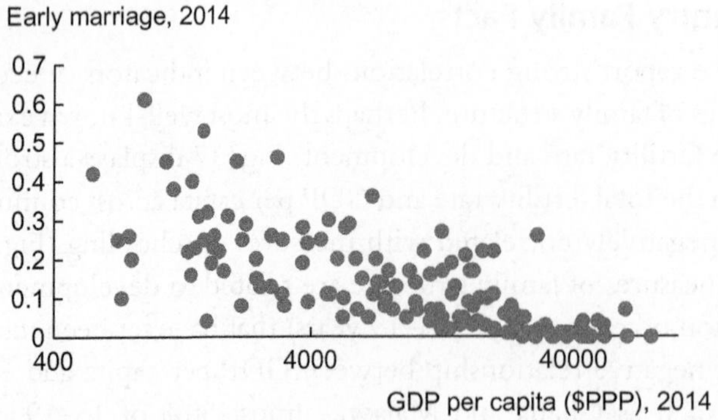

Fig. 19 Early marriage and GDP per capita across countries. *OECD Gender Statistics 2014 and World Development Indicators.*

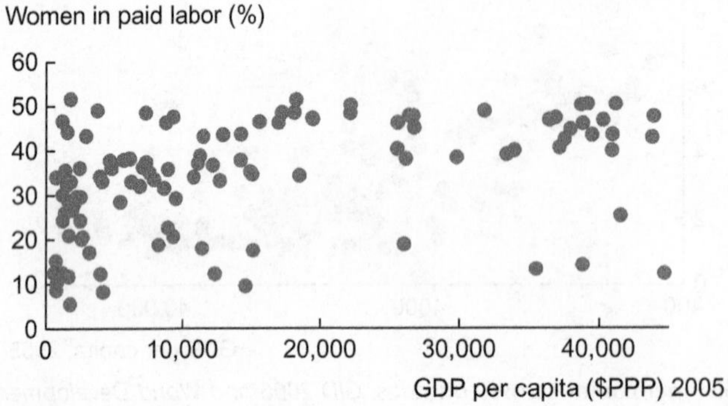

Fig. 20 Women in paid labor and GDP per capita across countries. *OECD Gender Statistics 2006 and World Development Indicators.*

married, compared to less than 5% in countries with a GDP per capita of more than $25,000 (in 2005 PPP terms). Fig. 20 plots the relationship between female labor force participation and GDP per capita. Since rates of formal employment are low for women and men alike in many poor countries, rather than plotting the absolute participation rate, Fig. 20 depicts the fraction of formal employment accounted for by women. In virtually all countries with a GDP per capita higher than $20,000, women make up 40% or more percent of the paid labor force, while in many poor countries women account for less than 20%.[at]

The figures discussed so far were chosen to highlight a few particularly interesting and pronounced relationships between family structure and development. Yet, essentially all indicators of family structure are related to development, including both measures of outcomes and measures of legal differences between men and women. Table 3 gives

[at] The few rich countries with low female labor force participation are oil-rich countries such as Saudi Arabia and the United Arab Emirates.

correlations of family variables with two measures of economic development, GDP per capita and the share of the agricultural sector in GDP (which is typically low in developed countries). The first three rows are about children: Fertility rates are high, child mortality is high, and schooling is low in poor countries. The next two rows show that a preference for sons is systematically related to development. First, people in poor countries are more likely to state that when resources are scarce, educating boys is more important than educating girls. Second, inheritance laws favor sons over daughters. The next three rows are about the education and work of women relative to men. Women are more likely to be illiterate than men in poor countries. They work less in the market and provide a larger burden of unpaid family care work, such as taking care of children and the elderly. The next set of indicators show that the legal position of women is negatively related to development. Women obtained access to politics (through representation in national parliaments) earlier in today's rich countries. They also have better access to land ownership and usage. There is also a tight relationship between the United Nations' Gender Empowerment Measure and GDP per capita. The last set of indicators show that the position specifically of married women is weaker in poor countries. Women in poor countries marry earlier than in rich countries and wife beating is more accepted. The legal position also favors men in poor countries: inheritance laws are more likely to favor

Table 3 Correlations between family variables and GDP per capita and share of agriculture across countries

Variable	GDP p.c.	Share agric.
Total fertility rate, GID 2006	−0.49	0.71
Child mortality rate, WDI 2014	−0.54	0.75
Average years of schooling, WDI 2003	0.76	−0.79
Son preference in education, GID 2014	−0.26	0.33
Inheritance discrimination against daughters, GID 2014	−0.24	0.45
Female literacy relative to male, GID 2006	0.37	−0.65
Percent females in paid labor force, GID 2006	0.32	−0.52
Unpaid care work by women, GID 2014	−0.37	0.43
Year first woman in parliament, UN 2004	−0.58	0.36
Women's access to land, GID 2014	−0.41	0.54
Gender empowerment measure, UN 2004	0.70	−0.60
Early marriage, GID 2014	−0.50	0.65
Agreement with wife beating, GID 2014	−0.42	0.57
Inheritance discrimination against widows, GID 2014	−0.21	0.42
Laws on domestic violence, GID 2014	−0.16	0.46

Notes: Data are from OECD gender, institutions, and development data base (GID 2006 and 2014), the world development indicators (WDI 2003, 2005, and 2014), and the UN Development Report 2004. Correlations are computed with GDP per capita and percentage of value-added in agriculture from the WDI in two different years: 2005 and 2014. See the Appendices for variable definitions and further details.

Table 4 Differences between polygynous countries and monogamous countries close to the equator

	Polygynous	Monogamous
Total fertility rate	6.8	4.6
Husband–wife age gap	6.4	2.8
Aggregate capital–output ratio	1.1	1.9
GDP per capita (dollars)	975	2798
Number of countries	28	58

Notes: Data are either from 1980 or an average for the 1960–85 time period. Details and sources are given in Tertilt (2005). Polygynous countries defined as countries with at least 10% of men in polygamous unions. Monogamous countries are all other countries within 20 degrees of latitude from the equator, to control for the fact that most polygynous countries are in sub-Saharan Africa.

widowers over widows, and laws against domestic violence (if they exist in the first place) are less strict compared to developed countries.

A family structure that has long been illegal in most developed countries but is still practiced in many poorer countries is polygyny, which is the practice of men being married to multiple wives. Table 4 shows that polygynous countries are among the poorest in the world, display extremely high fertility rates, invest little, and are characterized by large age gaps between husbands and wives.

3.2 Parents and Children

The strong empirical association between economic development and measures of family structure suggests that changes to the family are an integral part of the growth process. We now analyze a series of simple growth models to highlight a number of specific channels that tie development and families together.

We start with a simple view of the family. In this first version of the model, each family consists of a parent and a child. Parents care about children in a warm-glow fashion. Specifically, they derive utility from their children's full income.[au] Fertility is exogenous. In other words, we start with a single sex model where each parent has exactly one child. Since the children themselves will have children again, the model is an overlapping generations model. The difference to the standard OLG setup is that generations are explicitly linked through parent-child relationships.

Preferences are given by the utility function

$$u(c) + \delta u(y'),$$

where c is the parent's consumption and y' is the child's full income (as an adult in the next period). For simplicity, we assume consumption goods are produced at home with a

[au] Models with true altruism would yield qualitatively similar results, but are less tractable.

production function that uses effective units of time as the only input.[av] Let H denote the human capital of the parent and ℓ the units of time the parent devotes to production. Then consumption, or equivalently GDP (per adult), is given by:

$$c = A\ell H,$$

where A is a technology parameter. We define full income as the income that would be obtained if the parent was working full time:

$$y = AH.$$

Not all time will be devoted to production, because the parent will also spend some time educating the child. Let e denote this education time. Human capital of the child is given by the following production function:

$$H' = (Be)^{\theta} H,$$

where B and θ are technology parameters. Here θ is an especially important parameter as it captures the returns to education. Each parent is endowed with one unit of time. Thus, the parent faces the following time constraint: $\ell + e \leq 1$. Assuming log utility, we can write the objective function of the parent as follows:

$$\max \log(c) + \delta\theta \log(e).$$

The equilibrium is characterized by the optimal education choice $e^* = \frac{\delta\theta}{1+\delta\theta}$. The equilibrium growth rate (for both human capital and consumption) is:

$$\frac{H'}{H} = \left(B\frac{\delta\theta}{1+\delta\theta}\right)^{\theta}. \tag{12}$$

As in the simple Lucas model at the beginning of this section (Eq. 11), the human capital accumulation technology in part determines the growth rate. What is different from the Lucas model is that how much parents care about their children's well-being also enters. In contrast, in standard growth models that abstract from intergenerational links, it is the individual's discount factor that matters. There is no reason for the rate of time preference across periods for a given person to coincide with the intergenerational discount factor. A related point is that the intergenerational elasticity of substitution may differ from the intertemporal elasticity of substitution (IES). In other words, estimates of the IES in the business cycle context are not necessarily relevant for calibrating growth models based on trade-offs across generations.[aw] There is a need for empirical research in this

[av] This is isomorphic to a model with market production. The home production formulation has the advantage that we do not need notation for wages and, later, interest rates.

[aw] See Cordoba and Ripoll (2014) for a formal treatment of this point.

area, as good estimates of the intergenerational discount factor and the intergenerational elasticity of substitution are currently not available.

The model as written assumes that all families accumulate human capital independently from each other. An alternative vision of the process of human capital accumulation is that much of the increase in people's productivity over time is due to the dissemination of productive ideas, implying that exchange of knowledge between different families is crucial for growth. In a setting that makes this engine of growth explicit, de la Croix et al. (2016) examine the role of institutions that organize the exchange of knowledge for growth. They compare both family-based institutions (knowledge exchange within nuclear families or families/clans) and market-based institutions, and argue that institutions that facilitated the exchange of ideas across families were crucial for the economic ascendency of Western Europe in the centuries leading up to industrialization.

3.3 Adding Fertility Choice

Next, we enrich the model by endogenizing fertility choice. The analysis of fertility choices in explicit dynamic growth models was pioneered by Becker and Barro (1988) and Barro and Becker (1989). These papers assume an altruistic utility function (ie, the children's utility enters the parent's utility), whereas we will stick to the warm-glow motive for investing in children. This distinction makes no difference for most qualitative results and allows more closed form solutions. In contrast to Barro and Becker (1989), which features exogenous technological progress, our focus is on human capital as the engine of growth.

For simplicity (and in line with the majority of existing analyses of fertility in dynamic models), we stick with one-parent families. However, conceptually it is straightforward to consider fertility decisions in a two-parent model (see Doepke and Tertilt, 2009 for an example).[ax]

To give the parent a reason to want children, we modify the utility function as follows:

$$u(c) + \delta^n u(n) + \delta u(y'),$$

where n is the number of children chosen by the parent. It takes ϕ units of time to raise a child in addition to the e units of education time devoted to each child. Note that ϕ is a fixed cost, while e is a choice variable. The time constraint is thus

[ax] Doepke and Kindermann (2015) document empirically that spouses often disagree about whether to have another child and present a bargaining model of fertility decisions to analyze the implications of this fact.

$$\ell + (\phi + e)n \leq 1.$$

We keep everything else (ie, production and human capital accumulation) as before. Assuming log utility, the objective function can be written as

$$\max \log(c) + \delta^n \log(n) + \delta\theta \log(e).$$

To guarantee that the problem is well defined, we assume $\delta^n > \delta\theta$.

The equilibrium is characterized by the following education and fertility choices:

$$e^* = \frac{\delta\theta}{\delta^n - \delta\theta}\phi,$$

$$n^* = \frac{(\delta^n - \delta\theta)}{\phi(1 + \delta^n)}.$$

The equilibrium growth rate is:

$$\frac{H'}{H} = \left(B\frac{\delta\theta\phi}{\delta^n - \delta\theta}\right)^{\theta}. \tag{13}$$

Comparing the expression for n^* and the equilibrium growth factor given in (13), it becomes apparent that many of the same features leading to high fertility, such as a low cost of children and low returns to education, also lead to a low growth rate. The negative dependence of fertility on growth was already a feature in Barro and Becker (1989), albeit in a model of exogenous growth. The importance of human capital as an engine for growth in a model with endogenous fertility was first analyzed by Becker et al. (1990). While the exact expression is different, they also derive a growth rate that depends positively on the returns to education, the fixed cost of children, and an altruism parameter.

Comparing the growth rate given in (13) with the growth rate in the model without fertility choice (12), two points emerge. First, two types of intergenerational preference parameters appear now: δ and δ^n. In other words, how much parents care about the quality vs the quantity of children is a determinant of the growth rate. Second, the return to human capital enters positively into the optimal education choice and negatively into the optimal fertility choice.

These results may help in understanding some empirical regularities, such as the negative relationship between fertility and schooling, on the one hand, and fertility and GDP per capita, on the other hand (Figs. 17 and 18). In the model, these relationships would arise if countries differ in the return to skill θ or the cost of children ϕ. Similarly, within most countries fertility decreased, while education increased over time. The model can generate this pattern if the return to education increases gradually from generation to generation. The resulting theory interprets the demographic transition to low fertility as driven by a move from investing in child quantity to emphasizing child quality (ie, education).

There is a substantial literature aiming to account for the historical relationship between fertility and growth based on this mechanism. Before the onset of industrialization in the 18th century, living standards around the world were stagnant, and fertility rates were high. In most countries, this "Malthusian" stage was followed by a transition to growing incomes and declining fertility rates. The first theory to fully account for such a transition is Galor and Weil (2000), which is based on the quantity–quality trade-off, a Malthusian constraint due to the role of land in agriculture, and human capital as an engine for growth. The role of structural change in the transition is highlighted by Hansen and Prescott (2002), who model the endogenous transition from a stagnant land-intensive technology to a capital-intensive growth technology. Population growth changes with growing incomes in their model. However, rather than explicitly modeling fertility choice, the authors assume a particular dependence of population growth on consumption. Greenwood and Seshadri (2002) introduce explicit fertility preferences when analyzing a similar transition from an agricultural to a manufacturing society. Doepke (2004) also models fertility preferences explicitly to analyze the importance of education and child labor policies for the transition from stagnation to growth. Some authors argue that the transition was triggered by declines in mortality, which increased the incentive to educate children. Soares (2005) provides a model where gains in life expectancy lead to reductions in fertility and increases in human capital accumulation, leading to an endogenous transition from a Malthusian to a long-run growth equilibrium.[ay] However, Hazan and Zoabi (2006) show that the impact of increasing longevity on human capital investment is mitigated by the fact that higher longevity also raises the incentive to have more children, which works against human capital investment through the quantity–quality trade-off.

One could also use variants of this setup to understand cross-country fertility differences today. For example, Manuelli and Seshadri (2009) study international fertility differences using a life-cycle version of the Barro–Becker model with human and health capital. They find that differences in productivity, social security, and taxes can go a long way in explaining the observed differences.

The empirical regularities that characterize differences across countries are also visible across families. There is a sizeable empirical literature documenting that in the cross section of families in a given country, quantity and quality of children are negatively related.[az] An augmented version of the model with heterogeneity across families in δ^n (or, similarly, δ) would deliver this empirical regularity. The overall economy-wide

[ay] The importance of changes in mortality for development is also analyzed in Cervellati and Sunde (2005).

[az] See, for example, Rosenzweig and Wolpin (1980) and Bleakley and Lange (2009). Vogl (2016) argues that the negative relationship of quantity and quality may be a relatively recent phenomenon. He documents that in many developing countries there was a reversal in the education-fertility relationship from positive to negative. Baudin et al. (2015) provide an analysis that also allows for the possibility of childlessness, and argue that childlessness is U-shaped as economies develop.

growth rate would then depend on how many parents of each type exist, and also on whether such preferences are passed on from parents to children or randomly distributed in the population.[ba] de la Croix and Doepke (2003) explore the association between inequality and growth based on the differential fertility channel and argue that it explains a large part of the observed relationship between inequality and growth across countries.[bb]

3.3.1 Fertility Restrictions

The link between fertility and human capital accumulation suggests that countries may be able to speed up economic development by limiting fertility rates. Out of the many policies that can affect a country's fertility rate, the most direct is a hard limit on how many children a couple can have. Several countries have implemented such fertility restrictions, the most famous example of which is the one-child policy of China. Another examples are forced sterilization policies implemented by the Indian government in the 1980s. Other countries have used more subtle family planning policies, either through monetary incentive schemes or in the form of media campaigns, often advocating a two-child norm.

We can incorporate such policies into the model by adding a fertility limit $\bar{n}$. Whenever the constraint is binding, the optimal education decision is:

$$e^* = \frac{\delta\theta[\frac{1}{\bar{n}} - \phi]}{1 + \delta\theta}.$$

Education increases with a tighter fertility restriction. Thus, fertility restrictions do speed up economic growth in our model. Yet, they are not the panacea one might have hoped for, as fertility restrictions also come with a cost. Fig. 21 illustrates these effects in a computed example of our model.[bc] The top panels show how fertility and education change with different levels of fertility restrictions, while the bottom panels depict the growth rate and steady state utility as a function of the restrictions. The optimal (unrestricted) fertility rate in the example is 3. Thus, only restrictions below 3 are binding. Tighter restrictions lead to higher levels of education and higher growth rates, but they lower equilibrium utility. In our simple model, this negative effect on utility comes from parents being deprived of (part of) the enjoyment they

[ba] Thus, whether differential fertility increases or decreases the growth rate depends on many factors. See Vogl (2016) for an analysis of this point. The specific role of preference transmission in the context of the British Industrial Revolution is analyzed by Doepke and Zilibotti (2008).

[bb] de la Croix and Doepke (2004, 2009) analyze the importance of this mechanism in the context of education policies.

[bc] The parameters in the example are: $\delta'' = 0.8$, $\delta = 0.5$, $\phi = 0.1$, $B = 1$, $\theta = 0.5$, $A = 10$. The initial level of human capital is normalized at $H = 1$ and the fertility restriction ranges from 1 to 5.

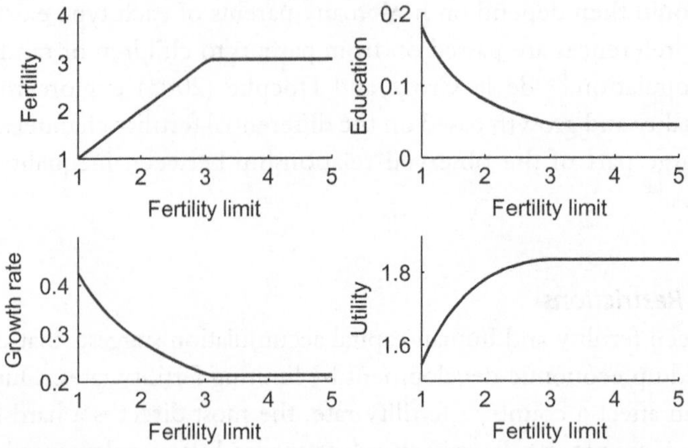

Fig. 21 Fertility restrictions.

obtain from children.[bd] In more elaborate settings, such negative effects can also arise from the differential effect of the fertility constraint on a heterogeneous population. Also, with a public social security system, lower fertility depresses future payouts, ie, the demographic dividend declines, a problem that is starting to become pressing in China right now.

These issues are analyzed in a small emerging literature. Liao (2013) analyzes how the one-child policy in China increased human capital and output. She simulates counterfactual experiments to analyze the effects of a relaxation of the policy. The main findings are that results differ across generations and skill groups. In particular, the initial old would benefit from a sudden unexpected relaxation of the policy, but future generations would be hurt. Moreover, such a policy would hurt unskilled people more than skilled people. Choukhmane et al. (2014) conduct a richer analysis using a life-cycle model and more detailed micro data. They argue that a large part of the rise in aggregate savings in China can be attributed to the one-child policy. The focus in Banerjee et al. (2014) is on the importance of general equilibrium effects when estimating how fertility restrictions (and their removal) would impact savings. These authors argue that appropriately taking general equilibrium effects into account reduces the size of such estimates. Coeurdacier et al. (2014) focus on the interaction between fertility policies and social security reform.[be] Since an expansion of social security lowers the incentives to have children (and thereby lowers the number of contributors to the system), the relaxation of the one child policy is likely to have smaller effects than typically anticipated. The authors find that this effect is quantitatively important for China.

[bd] The mechanism that lower fertility decreases utility is analyzed in Cordoba (2015), who finds that, during the 1970–2005 period, world growth in well-being was lower than the growth rate in per capita consumption precisely because fertility fell so dramatically during that period.

[be] Song et al. (2015) also analyze the consequences of low fertility for pension reform in China, albeit in a model with exogenous fertility.

3.4 Two-Parent Families: Decision Making

The vast majority of the literature on fertility and growth focuses on the interaction between parents and children in one-gender models. In other words, reproduction is asexual and differences between men and women in technology and preferences are abstracted from. We now expand our analysis by introducing two-gender families. In this version of our growth model, children have two parents: a mother and a father. For simplicity we return to exogenous fertility for now and assume that each couple has two children. Thus, families now consist of a husband, a wife, a son, and a daughter. Suppose men and women disagree about how much they care about their children's well-being.[bf] As in Section 2.4, suppose that the couple solves a Pareto problem with fixed bargaining weights, where λ_f is the bargaining weight of the woman, and λ_m is the weight of the man. Then the objective function is:

$$\lambda_f[u(c) + \delta_f u(y')] + (1 - \lambda_f)[u(c) + \delta_m u(y')].$$

To keep the rest of the model comparable to the previous section, we assume that all consumption in marriage is public and the total time endowment (of the couple) is still one. We also make no distinction between sons and daughters in the parent's objective function. We will relax these assumptions further below. Assuming log utility, the objective function can be written as:

$$\max \lambda[\log(c) + \delta_f\theta \log(e)] + (1 - \lambda)[\log(c) + \delta_m\theta \log(e)].$$

Equilibrium education now is

$$e^* = \frac{\tilde{\delta}\theta}{1 + \tilde{\delta}\theta},$$

where $\tilde{\delta} \equiv \lambda_f\delta_f + (1 - \lambda_f)\delta_m$. Thus, the equilibrium growth rate is:

$$\frac{H'}{H} = \left(B\frac{\tilde{\delta}\theta}{1 + \tilde{\delta}\theta}\right)^{\theta}. \tag{14}$$

A comparison of Eqs. (12) and (14) shows not only that gender preference gaps matter for the growth rate, but also how such preferences make their way into decisions within the family. Specifically, assuming mothers care more about children than fathers do ($\delta_f > \delta_m$), the economy grows faster, the larger the bargaining power of women. Doepke and

[bf] There could be many reasons for such a disagreement, ranging from biological/evolutionary arguments to cultural factors. See Alger and Cox (2013) for a survey.

Tertilt (2009) explore the endogenous evolution of women's rights based on such a mechanism (details will be discussed in Section 4). However, whether female empowerment enhances growth depends on the details of the bargaining process within the household. Doepke and Tertilt (2014) use a noncooperative model to show that what looks like gender differences in preferences may ultimately be due to specialization in tasks within the household. Based on this mechanism, Doepke and Tertilt (2014) show that monetary transfers to women may reduce growth, even if women are more likely to spend transfers on children. The reason is that the equilibrium is characterized by a division of labor in which women are in charge of time-intensive tasks such as education, while men provide money-intensive goods and hence are in charge of savings and physical capital accumulation. In such a world, exogenous transfers to women (financed by a tax on men) increase human capital accumulation but reduce physical capital accumulation. Depending on the production function, such a reallocation may increase or decrease growth. Specifically, when returns to physical capital relative to human capital are high, then such a policy would lower growth. To assess whether this is an issue in reality, more empirical research is needed. The current literature on the effects of transfers to women largely focuses on child expenditures, but there is little work analyzing effects on savings and investment.

3.5 Two-Parent Families: Technology

Empirical research (eg, Del Boca et al., 2014) has shown that mothers and fathers are both important factors in the human capital formation process of their children. In most families, both mothers and fathers spend a significant amount of time with children (Schoonbroodt, 2016). Further, men and women may not be perfect substitutes in market production.[bg] To address these issues, we now extend our view of the family to include fathers and mothers explicitly in the human capital formation process and also men and women as entering separately into production. To isolate the role of women in technology (vs their role as decision makers), we assume again that all consumption in families is public and that men and women have the same preferences regarding their children. In other words, we ignore here the additional complication that arises if fathers and mothers disagree (which we analyzed in Section 3.4). We also focus on the education decision (rather than fertility choice); however, it would be straightforward to include both margins in the same model.

[bg] Large and persistent gender wage differentials exist (see Blau and Kahn, 2000 for a survey). There is an extensive empirical literature trying to analyze their causes. We do not take a stand here on what the ultimate cause is, but rather explore the implications of men and women being imperfect substitutes in production. Whether the gap is due to different innate skills, different preferences, or cultural factors leading to differences in skill acquisition is largely irrelevant for our analysis.

In contrast to the previous versions of the model, men and women enter differently into technology. The consumption good is produced with a Cobb-Douglas production function using both male and female efficiency units of time as inputs,

$$c = A(\ell_f H_f)^{\alpha}(H_m)^{1-\alpha},$$

where $\alpha \in (0,1)$. For simplicity, we assume that only women raise children, while men work full time. The female time constraint is $\ell_f + e_f + e_m \leq 1$, where e_f is the time invested in educating daughters, and e_m is time devoted to the education of sons. Full income is defined as the production function evaluated at $\ell_f = 1$ and is therefore given by:

$$y = AH_f^{\alpha} H_m^{1-\alpha}.$$

Each couple has two children: a daughter and a son. Both mothers and fathers are essential for their children's human capital accumulation:

$$H_f' = (Be_f)^{\theta} H_f^{\beta} H_m^{1-\beta}, \tag{15}$$

$$H_m' = (Be_m)^{\theta} H_f^{\beta} H_m^{1-\beta}, \tag{16}$$

with $\beta \in (0,1)$. In summary, there are two gender differences in this setup: the relative importance of women vs men in transmitting own human capital to children (β) and the relative importance of women vs men in production (α).[bh]

Assuming log utility, the objective function can be written as:

$$\max \log(c) + \delta[\alpha\theta \log(e_f) + (1-\alpha)\theta \log(e_m)].$$

The equilibrium allocation is:

$$\ell_f^* = \frac{\alpha}{\alpha + (1-\alpha)\delta\theta + \alpha\delta\theta},$$

$$e_m^* = \frac{(1-\alpha)\delta\theta}{\alpha + (1-\alpha)\delta\theta + \alpha\delta\theta},$$

$$e_f^* = \frac{\alpha\delta\theta}{\alpha + (1-\alpha)\delta\theta + \alpha\delta\theta}.$$

The equilibrium ratio of female to male human capital is given by:

$$\frac{H_f}{H_m} = \left(\frac{e_f}{e_m}\right)^{\theta} = \left(\frac{\alpha}{1-\alpha}\right)^{\theta}.$$

Note that the asymmetry between mothers and fathers in the human capital production function captured by β does not appear in this expression. This is not a fundamental

[bh] A third asymmetry is that we have assumed that only women can spend time educating children. But this asymmetry is made for tractability and is not essential for the qualitative results.

result, but rather a feature of our warm-glow altruism. In an altruistic model, parents would take into account that educating their children will turn the children themselves into better parents, and hence enable them to provide grandchildren with more education. In such a formulation, the relative importance of fathers vs mothers in child development will also enter the relative human capital of men and women in equilibrium.

This model features a gender education gap and accordingly a gender wage gap.[bi] Specifically, the wage ratio per unit of time is $\frac{w_f}{w_m} = \frac{\alpha}{1-\alpha}$. The more productive women are in production (higher α), the smaller is the gender education gap. Higher female wage increase the opportunity cost of time and hence make children more costly. In a variant of the model with endogenous fertility, this logic would lead to fertility decline in response to rising female productivity. This mechanism is analyzed by Galor and Weil (1996), who explore how this channel contributed to the demographic transition.

In a fully altruistic model, parents would further take into account that their sons and daughters will be working different hours in the market (because of the child-bearing obligations of mothers) and accordingly invest less in daughters.[bj] This amplification channel is explored by Echevarria and Merlo (1999). Lagerlöf (2003) further explores the effect of the marriage market in this context and stresses the importance of multiple equilibria. If all families invest more into sons, then daughters on average expect high spousal income, which lowers the incentive for each individual family to educate daughters. However, complete gender equality is also an equilibrium in his model.

Plugging the ratio of human capital back into the human capital production function, we get the following equilibrium growth rate (for both male and female human capital, and hence also output and consumption):

$$\frac{H'}{H} = B^{\theta}(e_m)^{(1-\beta)\theta}(e_f)^{\theta\beta} = \left\{\frac{B\delta\theta}{\alpha+\delta\theta}(1-\alpha)^{1-\beta}\alpha^{\beta}\right\}^{\theta}. \tag{17}$$

Eq. (17) shows that the growth rate depends on many features of the family. As before, the more parents care about their children, the higher the growth rate. What is new is that gender differences in technology also matter for growth. This is true for both the role women play in production (as captured by α) and the relative importance of fathers and mothers in human capital transmission (captured by β). Moreover, the two dimensions of technology interact. For example, in a world where men and women enter symmetrically into production ($\alpha = 0.5$), the relative importance of mothers and fathers in human capital transmission becomes irrelevant. On the other hand, α always enters,

[bi] Strictly speaking there are no wages in our formulation with home production. However, the model can be reinterpreted as one with market production and wages given by marginal products.

[bj] Our warm-glow altruism does not capture this channel, because parents care about the full income of their children and do not take into account the time daughters will spend on child-bearing.

even in a world where mothers and fathers are equally important in human capital transmission ($\beta = 0.5$). Closer inspection of (17) shows that the growth rate is hump-shaped in α. Thus, whether an increase in α increases or decreases the growth depends on the starting point. Starting from a low role of women in production, an increase in α will lead to a reduction in the gender education gap, an increase in relative female wages, an increase in female labor force participation, and an acceleration of economic growth. This mechanism may well have been historically relevant: recall that Fig. 20 displays a strong positive relationship between GDP per capita and the role of women in paid labor. Similarly, recall that Table 3 showed a negative correlation between the gender education gap and development.

Since World War II, all developed countries went through a period of increasing female labor force participation and declining gender wage gaps. How women's role for production evolved over longer historical time periods is less clear. Humphries and Weisdorf (2015) construct measures of relative male and female wages in England dating back to 1270 and find large swings over the centuries. They also try to measure the wages of married and single women separately, using the distinction between casual work (more relevant for married women) and annual contracts (mostly used for unmarried women). Using their data and accepting their interpretation, we find that the relative wages of married vs single women over time have sometimes moved in the opposite directions (Fig. 22). There is also evidence suggesting that in the long run, the relationship between development and female market work is not always monotonic. Specifically, based on cross-country data, Goldin (1995) argues that female labor supply is U-shaped in development.[bk] A similar point is made by Costa (2000), who argues

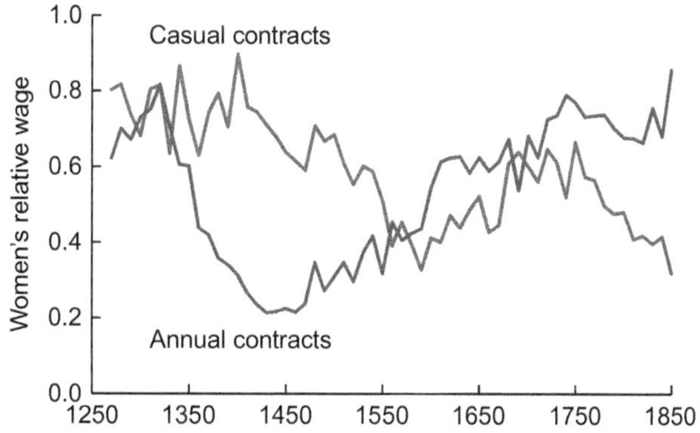

Fig. 22 Historical wage gap in England. *Humphries, J., Weisdorf, J., 2015. The wages of women in England, 1260–1850. J. Econ. Hist. 75 (2), 405–447 (Table A1).*

[bk] See also Olivetti (2014) for evidence of a U-shape in time series data of 16 developed countries (including the United States) and Mammen and Paxson (2000) for evidence from India and Thailand.

that female labor force participation is N-shaped if one goes back far enough in time. Establishing such historical facts is difficult not only due to lack of reliable data but also because of the lack of a sharp distinction between market and home production in agricultural economies.[bl]

A further complication arises when market production is made up of different tasks. If individuals differ in their ability to perform different tasks, then the allocation of talent to activities becomes important. Norms about gender roles (or other barriers) can then be an obstacle to the optimal allocation of talent to tasks. Hsieh et al. (2013) analyze the importance of this channel in the United States. They find that an improved allocation of talent across genders (and also ethnic groups) accounts for 15–20% of US growth during the 1960–2008 period. Lee (2015) explores the importance of misallocation of female talent for cross-country income differences. The paper finds that entry barriers for women in the nonagricultural sector play a large role for the observed low agricultural productivity in poor countries.

3.6 Two-Parent Families: Endogenous Bargaining

In Section 3.4, we have seen that who makes decisions in the household matters for growth. Hence, an important question is what determines bargaining power in marriage.[bm] Here we are interested in what changes bargaining weights across generations, which is distinct from the analysis of endogenous bargaining over time for a given couple (which we considered in Section 2). Initial bargaining power should be determined at time of marriage, which we do not model here. It is often assumed that relative educational attainments matter in the marriage market and hence for bargaining power. Relative education between men and women may itself be endogenous as we have seen in Section 3.5. In this section, we connect these two forces. To do so, we impose that the bargaining weight is a function of the gender education gap, which is itself chosen in the family. This assumption allows us to analyze the feedback from a gender education gap to bargaining power in the family.[bn]

We use a model that combines the setup with a gender preference gap in Section 3.4 with gender differences in technology as explored in Section 3.5. First, consider such a

[bl] For example, Goldin (1995) includes unpaid farm and family firm workers, while our Fig. 20 includes only paid workers.

[bm] There is a sizeable literature estimating models of household decision making. Key for identification is typically the existence of so-called distribution factors that affect bargaining weights but are exogenous to the bargaining process (see, for example, Blundell et al., 2005).

[bn] Basu (2006) also explores the implications of endogenous bargaining power, albeit in a different context. We are interested in how bargaining power changes across generations, while Basu (2006) analyzes the dynamic implications for a given couple. By adjusting labor supply, and thus income, spouses may affect their bargaining power in the household.

setup with exogenous bargaining power. Combining the features of the two models, the couple solves the following maximization problem:

$$\max_{c,\, e_f,\, e_m} u(c) + \tilde{\delta}\left\{\alpha\theta\log(e_f) + (1-\alpha)\theta\log(e_m)\right\}$$

subject to:

$$1 = \ell_f + e_m + e_f,$$
$$c = A(\ell_f H_f)^{\alpha} H_m^{1-\alpha},$$

where $\tilde{\delta} \equiv \lambda_f\delta_f + (1-\lambda_f)\delta_m$. As before, human capital evolves according to (15) and (16). This is the same problem as in Section 3.5, but with a modified δ. Thus, the equilibrium growth rate is:

$$1 + g^{exog} = \left\{\frac{B\tilde{\delta}\theta}{\alpha + \tilde{\delta}\theta}(1-\alpha)^{1-\beta}\alpha^{\beta}\right\}^{\theta}.$$

Now we can explore how endogenous bargaining differs from exogenous bargaining in this setup by assuming that λ is a function of relative education. A simple functional form assumption that captures this dependence and at the same time guarantees a bargaining weight between zero and one is $\lambda(e_f, e_m) = \dfrac{e_f}{e_f + e_m}$. Recall that relative education is a function of the relative importance of female labor in the market: $\dfrac{e_f}{e_f + e_m} = \alpha$. Thus, we can replace λ_f by α and write the growth rate as[bo]:

$$1 + g^{end} = \left\{\frac{B[\alpha\delta_f + (1-\alpha)\delta_m]\theta}{\alpha + [\alpha\delta_f + (1-\alpha)\delta_m]\theta}(1-\alpha)^{1-\beta}\alpha^{\beta}\right\}^{\theta}. \tag{18}$$

Proposition 4 *Assume $\delta_f > \delta_m$. If $\lambda_f < \alpha$, then the growth rate is higher in the endogenous bargaining model, while $\lambda_f > \alpha$ implies a higher growth rate in the exogenous bargaining model.*
This result relates women's role in technology to women's role in decision making. Specifically when women's power in decision making is low relative to their importance for production, then endogenizing the link from education to bargaining power increases the growth rate. The opposite is true when women have a lot of bargaining power relative to their importance in production.

[bo] Note that with our warm-glow altruism, parents do not take into account that when increasing their daughter's education, they also increase the daughter's bargaining weight. de la Croix and Vander Donckt (2010) analyze a model with altruism where parents explicitly consider the impact of education choices on their children's future bargaining power.

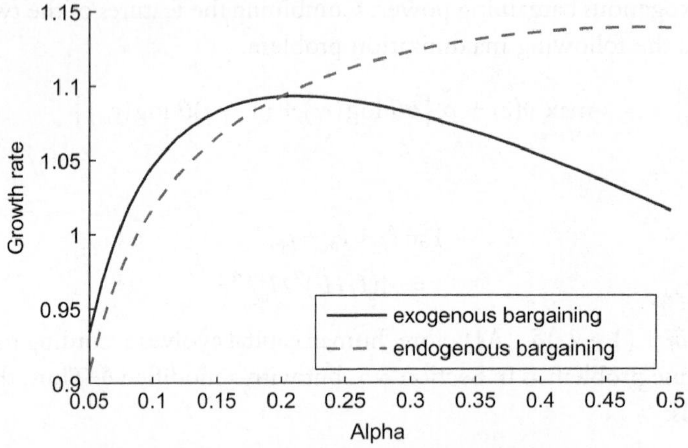

Fig. 23 Growth rate as a function of α, exogenous vs endogenous bargaining.

This result is illustrated in Fig. 23 with a numerical example.[bp] As was discussed in Section 3.5, the growth rate of the exogenous bargaining model is hump-shaped in α. This is not necessarily true in the endogenous bargaining model. In the example, growth monotonically increases in α. With fixed bargaining weights, an increase in women's role in production can lower growth because the resulting rise in female labor force participation decreases education time with children and thereby slows down human capital accumulation. This effect is mitigated in the endogenous bargaining model, where the resulting increase in bargaining power pushes toward more education (given that in the model women care more about children's education than men do). This example shows that the details of decision making in the family matter for growth and that asymmetries between men and women in decision making interact with asymmetries in technology.

3.7 Son Preferences

Many cultures are characterized by a preference for sons. This preference typically has effects on fertility behavior, where families that have only daughters are more likely to have another child (eg, Anukriti, 2014). Recently, sex-selective abortion has also been a concern (Ebenstein, 2010). Son preferences also manifest themselves in boys being treated better than girls. For example, Jayachandran and Kuziemko (2011) document gender differences in breast-feeding rates and Tarozzi and Mahajan (2007) document better nutritional status for boys in India. Further, such a preference is more pronounced in poorer countries (see Table 3).

[bp] The parameters in the example are: $\beta = 0.7, \theta = 0.5, B = 10, \delta_f = 0.5, \delta_m = 0.2, \lambda = 0.2$.

We now investigate the growth consequences of such a son preference in an extension of our model.[bq] First, consider an economy with physical capital in which parents leave bequests to sons and daughters. As before, consumption in marriage is public, fertility is exogenous, and each couple has one son and one daughter. Also as before, parents care about their children in a warm-glow fashion. In this case, parents derive utility from the bequest they give to their children. Output is produced using a linear technology in capital, ie, output is given by $y = AK$, where A is a parameter. All sons and daughters will be married. Without heterogeneity, it is irrelevant who marries whom. The capital of any given couple is made up of the sum of the bequests they each got, ie, $k = b_s + b_d$, where s denotes sons and d daughters.

Preferences are given by:

$$u(c) + \delta_s u(b_s) + \delta_d u(b_d),$$

where $\delta_s > \delta_d$ would capture a son preference. The budget constraint is $c + b_s + b_d \leq y$.

Assuming log utility, equilibrium bequests are

$$b_s = \frac{\delta_s}{1 + \delta_s + \delta_d} y,$$
$$b_d = \frac{\delta_d}{1 + \delta_s + \delta_d} y.$$

The equilibrium growth rate of income is:

$$\frac{y'}{y} = \frac{A(\delta_s + \delta_d)}{1 + \delta_s + \delta_d}.$$

The key result here is that the son preference is irrelevant for the growth rate. The only thing that matters is how much parents care on average about their children, ie, only the sum $\delta_s + \delta_d$ appears.

The finding changes if human capital accumulation is considered, as long as there are decreasing returns to educating a given person. In contrast to physical capital (where ownership does not matter for growth), it is plausible that total knowledge in an economy will be larger if knowledge is shared by more people. We now show how a son preference will interact with such decreasing returns in individual human capital.

The technologies for producing output and human capital are the same as in Section 3.5. Parents care only about their own children and hence they do not take into account that educating their daughter/son will also benefit the future son-in-law/daughter-in-law. Rather, they anticipate that their son-in-law will be endowed with the average male human capital in the economy, which we denote by $\bar{H}'_m$, and daughters-in-law are

[bq] Hazan and Zoabi (2015b) analyze endogenous son preferences in a related model with endogenous fertility.

anticipated to have human capital $\bar{H}'_f$. The optimization problem of a couple endowed with human capital (H_f, H_m) is thus given by:

$$\max_{e_f, e_m, \ell_f} u(c) + \delta_d u(y'_d) + \delta_s u(y'_s)$$

subject to:

$$c = A(\ell_f H_f)^\alpha H_m^{1-\alpha},$$
$$1 \geq \ell_f + e_f + e_m,$$
$$y'_d = A(H'_f)^\alpha (\bar{H}'_m)^{1-\alpha},$$
$$y'_s = A(\bar{H}'_f)^\alpha (H'_m)^{1-\alpha},$$
$$H'_f = (Be_f)^\theta H_f^\beta H_m^{1-\beta},$$
$$H'_m = (Be_m)^\theta H_f^\beta H_m^{1-\beta},$$

where $\bar{H}'_f$ and $\bar{H}'_m$ are taken as given.

Assuming log utility, the maximization problem reduces to

$$\max_{\ell_f, e_f, e_m} \alpha \log(\ell_f) + \delta_d \alpha\theta \log(e_f) + \delta_s (1-\alpha)\theta \log(e_m)$$

subject to:

$$\ell_f + e_f + e_m \leq 1.$$

The resulting optimal education choices are

$$e_m^* = \frac{\delta_s(1-\alpha)\theta}{\alpha + \delta_s(1-\alpha)\theta + \alpha\delta_d\theta},$$

$$e_f^* = \frac{\delta_d \alpha\theta}{\alpha + \delta_s(1-\alpha)\theta + \alpha\delta_d\theta}.$$

As before, human capital, income, and consumption all grow at the same rate on the balanced growth path. The equilibrium growth rate is:

$$\left\{ \frac{B\theta}{\alpha + [\delta_d \alpha + \delta_s(1-\alpha)]\theta} (\delta_s[1-\alpha])^{1-\beta} (\delta_d \alpha)^\beta \right\}^\theta.$$

This expression shows how the effect of a son preference on the growth rate depends on the technology for goods production and human capital accumulation. First, consider the symmetric case where men and women are equally important in production (by setting $\beta = \alpha = 0.5$). Fix the total weight parents put on children: $\delta_s + \delta_d = 1$. In this case, the growth rate is maximized at $\delta_s = \delta_d = 0.5$. In other words, a son preference lowers growth. This is in contrast to the economy with only physical capital, where a son preference is irrelevant. Hence, a son preference is only growth-reducing when knowledge is the engine of growth. But even in a knowledge economy a son preference is not always disadvantageous. If men have the comparative advantage in knowledge production ($\beta < 0.5$), the growth-maximizing weight on children will display a son preference, the strength of which depends on the extent of men's comparative advantage.

On the other hand, in a world where men have a comparative advantage in goods production ($\alpha < 0.5$), but we have $\beta = 0.5$, a slight daughter preference enhances growth. The reason is that human capital is the engine of growth, implying that educating sons and daughters equally is the growth-maximizing strategy. Parents, on the other hand, do not maximize the growth rate, but rather output in the next period, where sons have the comparative advantage in production. Thus, parents overinvest in sons (compared to growth-maximizing solution). A son preference amplifies this problem.

Empirical evidence also links son preferences to the increasingly asymmetric sex ratios in some countries. In China, for example, in 2005 over 120 boys were born for each 100 girls (Wei and Zhang, 2011). Such asymmetries may have important aggregate consequences, which are largely unexplored in the literature. A notable exception is Wei and Zhang (2011), who find that rising sex ratios are an important determinant of the high Chinese savings rate. Du and Wei (2010) take this idea a step further and show in a calibrated model that this channel explains more than 50% of the current account surplus in China.

3.8 Polygyny

The role model for the family considered in most of this chapter is the Western nuclear family. The dominance of the nuclear family consisting of a husband, a wife, and the couple's own children is a relatively recent phenomenon, and even today typical families in some parts of the world do not follow this norm. Historically, the extended family (with multiple generations living together) was more prevalent than it is today.[br] Moreover, many families today no longer include married couples, as single parents are on the rise and many individuals no longer live in families at all (see Figs. 3 and 4 in Section 2.2).

Another important type of family structure is polygamy. In many parts of Africa men marrying multiple wives (polygyny) is common to the present day.[bs] Does such a family structure matter for macroeconomic outcomes? Tertilt (2005) suggests it does. The paper builds a model of polygynous families in which men buy brides and sell daughters to future husbands. The family structure reduces output (relative to enforced monogamy) through two channels. The market for daughters turns women into a valuable asset. This has two implications. First, the revenues from selling daughters become a useful way of financing old age, which depresses savings and thus physical capital. Second, it increases fertility as men want many daughters. This results in higher population growth rates,

[br] Although, because of shorter life spans, perhaps not as prevalent as one might think. See Ruggles (1994) for an extensive historical account of changing household structures in the United States over the last 150 years.

[bs] Polyandry (women having multiple husbands) is extremely rare, but a few societies exist as well.

which depresses capital per person and thus GDP per capita. The paper uses a calibrated general equilibrium model to show that this effect is quantitatively important, and shows that the mechanism can account for a large part of the observed differences between polygynous and monogamous countries shown in Table 4.

Polygyny matters for growth through its effect on brideprices. Thus, the marriage market is essential for the mechanism. It is not the case that an individual polygynous couple would save less than a monogamous couple living in the same country. Rather, if a large fraction of households is polygynous, the equilibrium price of women is high, which changes incentives for all families. In other words, polygyny lowers output precisely because of the general equilibrium effects in the marriage market. We thus turn to the importance of marriage markets for growth in the next section.

A few papers attempt to understand why polygyny exists in some cultures and not in others. Gould et al. (2008) and Lagerlöf (2005) relate the disappearance of polygyny to economic development. Heterogeneity plays a key role in both papers. Gould, Moav, and Simhon argue that the increasing skill premium has led men to want fewer, higher quality children. To educate their children, they accordingly demand higher quality wives, but fewer of them, which naturally leads to fewer wives per men. Lagerlöf relates the disappearance of polygyny to the decline in male inequality over time. Primitive societies are arguably more unequal, which allows wealthy men to marry more wives and have more children. Over time, this dilutes their wealth, making societies more equal, which eventually leads to a more equal distribution of wives across men. In both papers, the decline in polygyny goes hand in hand with fertility decline and economic growth. Both papers explain the decline in polygyny prevalence, but are silent on the introduction of formal restrictions.

Two recent papers analyze the political economy of the introduction of monogamy. Lagerlöf (2010) proposes a theory related to inequality of wives across men. When polygyny is allowed, the elites have many wives, while poor men have none. This may lead to revolutions and thus creates an incentive for the elites to impose a formal ban on polygyny. de la Croix and Mariani (2015) provide a comprehensive political economy analysis of the switch from polygyny to monogamy and then to serial monogamy. The theory is based on the voting behavior of the entire population (including women), rather than the incentives of the elites. The transition between regimes is endogenously generated by human capital accumulation that changes the coalitions that stand to gain from a change in the marriage regime.

3.9 The Marriage Market

While there is a substantial literature on marriage choices within family economics, incorporating a marriage market into macroeconomic models is no trivial undertaking. One approach was proposed by Tertilt (2005), who models a competitive market for brides featuring an equilibrium brideprice that clears the market. However, such a formulation works only if there is no heterogeneity; if potential spouses vary in "quality," it matters who marries whom.

A number of recent contributions analyze marriage formation with heterogeneous agents within macro models. This allows the analysis of questions such as the impact of changes in the assortativeness of mating on income inequality. An early example is Fernández et al. (2005).[bt] The paper investigates the relationship between inequality, assortative mating, human capital accumulation, and per capita GDP. Mating is modeled through a search model with random matching. The model also features an intergenerational transmission mechanism, because parental income is used as collateral that children need when investing in education. One main finding is that such a model can generate multiple steady states that differ in wage inequality. Across steady states, marital sorting and wage inequality are positively related, while marital sorting and GDP per capita are negatively related.

Eika et al. (2014) document empirically the importance of assortative mating for income inequality in the United States. While assortative mating is found to be an important determinant of inequality, the study finds that changes in inequality cannot be attributed to changes in sorting patterns. Greenwood et al. (2016a) analyze such a link in a structural quantitative model.

Beyond these few contributions, the importance of marriage for growth is largely unexplored. In part, this may be due to the computational complexity of models that feature sorting with heterogeneous agents. However, with recent advances in computational power allowing increasingly complex models to be analyzed, we expect this to be an active research area in the near future.

4. THE FAMILY AND THE POLITICAL ECONOMY OF INSTITUTIONAL CHANGE

Long-run economic development is characterized not just by economic transformations but also by a set of striking regularities in terms of political change. During the development process, almost all of today's rich countries went through a series of similar policy reforms: for instance, democracy spread, public education systems were built, and public pension systems were introduced. The only exception to this pattern are countries that are rich primarily because of endowments with natural resources such as oil. Among countries who owe their wealth to the productivity of their citizens, these political transformations are a universal characteristic of the development process.

The tight link between economic and political transformations raises the question of how the causality runs between the two realms. Does economic growth trigger political

[bt] Fernández and Rogerson (2001), Choo and Siow (2006), and Greenwood et al. (2014, 2016a) also analyze the relationship between marital sorting and income inequality, but do not consider broader macroeconomic implications.

change, or is political change a precondition for growth? Can today's poor countries, many of which have implemented only a subset of the political reforms that characterize rich countries, foster faster economic development by adopting rich-country political institutions and reforms?

In this section, we argue that in answering such questions the family once again plays a central role. Many of the political reforms that go along with development are directly about the family (such as the introduction of child labor laws and the expansion of women's rights). In other cases (such as education and pension reforms), the political changes concern areas that originally were organized within families but in which, over time, the state played an increasing role. We provide a brief overview of the facts of political change during the development process. We then discuss some of the political economy literature analyzing the causes and consequences of political change, arguing that in many cases changes in family life were driving reform. We illustrate the role of the family by zooming in on two specific reforms—the expansion of women's rights and the introduction of child labor laws.

4.1 Political Economy Facts

The main political transformations that go along with the development process are the introduction of democracy, public and compulsory schooling, and child labor regulation; the gradual expansion of women's rights; and more generally the creation of large welfare states that raise a significant fraction of GDP in tax revenue to provide welfare benefits and old-age pensions. Before the onset of modern economic growth (say, in 1750), no country in the world had any of these institutions. Most poor countries today have some but not all of these features.

There is considerable variation across countries in the timing of reforms. For some countries, the first transformation was the introduction of democracy, starting with the founding of the United States in 1776 and then followed by a series of franchise extensions in Britain. Other countries adopted other reforms first and achieved democracy later. Some European countries democratized after World War I, and others had to wait until after the fall of the Iron Curtain in the early 1990s. In some countries (such as South Korea and Taiwan), democracy was introduced only after most other political reforms had been implemented and after rapid economic growth had been achieved.

Initially, democracy generally meant that men, but not women, obtained the right to vote and run for office. In the United States, the first state to give women the right to vote was Wyoming in 1869, and most other states had followed by World War I.[bu] At the federal level, universal suffrage was introduced with the Nineteenth Amendment in

[bu] See Doepke et al. (2012) for a detailed timeline of the introduction of women's rights in the United States.

1920. In many European countries women were able to vote after World War I, but once again there is a lot of variation across countries. For example, in Switzerland women received the right to vote in federal elections only in 1972, and the last canton to allow women to vote was Appenzell Innerrhoden in 1990.[bv]

Compared to the spread of political rights, the timing of education reforms is more uniform across countries. In the United States, Canada, and the industrializing Western European countries, public and compulsory education was widely introduced in the late 19th and early 20th centuries. In many cases, these reforms went along with significant restrictions of child labor.

The first country to introduce a public pension system was Germany in 1891. Mandatory health and accident insurance for workers were introduced around the same time. Most other European countries, Canada, and the United States had followed these steps before the middle of the 20th century. The first unemployment benefit scheme was introduced in the United Kingdom with the National Insurance Act 1911. In the midst of the Great Depression, the US Congress passed the Social Security Act, which contained provisions for old age insurance, welfare, and unemployment insurance. Most European countries and Canada introduced similar provisions during the first half of the 20th century.

The timing of political reforms that affected families most directly (in particular the regulation of child labor, the public provision of education, and the spread of women's rights) is closely associated with a major transformation of families themselves. As discussed in Section 3, as countries transition from a preindustrial society to modern growth, they universally undergo a demographic transition from high to low fertility. In North America and Western Europe, the main phase of fertility decline took place between the middle of the 19th century and World War I. Access to primary education became near-universal during the same period. Given that formal schooling moved children from the family home (where many had been working from a young age) to schools, the rise of mass education implied a transformation of family life on its own.

4.2 The Family as a Driver of Political Change

To understand the political economy of reforms, one needs to understand who the winners and losers of a reform are. Political reforms happen if there is a constituency that stands to gain from the reform, and if this constituency has sufficient political power to implement the desired policy. The trigger for a reform can either be a change in how a policy affects specific groups, or an increase in the political power of a group that

[bv] In fact, the last canton to voluntarily introduce the right to vote for women was Appenzell Aussenrhoden in 1989. In Appenzell Innerrhoden women's suffrage was mandated by a Supreme Court decision in 1990.

stands to gain from a reform. One might expect that democratization, which increased the political power of broad parts of the population at the expense of established elites, should be a major engine for political change. While there are examples of democratization triggering reform, the introduction of the major reforms associated with economic development described above is not closely correlated with expansions in political rights. We therefore focus on mechanisms that change who gains and who loses from reforms, and take as given that the relevant groups have sufficient political power to be heard.[bw]

We argue that for most of the major political reforms associated with economic development, the reorganization of families is a key reason for why political incentives changed. Technological and structural change affects fertility choices, education choices, and the division of labor in the family, all of which determine how people are affected by reforms. For example, reforms such as mandatory schooling laws and public pensions move responsibilities from the family to the public sphere and affect the relationship between parents and children. How people feel about such changes will depend in part on how many children they have, on whether they plan to educate their children, and on whether they anticipate living with their children in old age. Other reforms—such as the expansion of women's rights—affect the interaction between spouses. How people are affected by such reforms depend in part on the division of labor in the household and on women's labor force participation, both of which vary with development.

Consider the introduction of public schooling systems. Before public schooling, most children were working with their parents from a young age. Hence, the spread of public and compulsory education implied a major change of parent-child relations. Galor and Moav (2006) provide a theory that explains the public provision of education as a consequence of the rising importance of human capital in the economy. They consider a model economy populated by capitalists and workers. The model features heterogeneity in wealth, and initially only capitalists are accumulating capital through bequests to their children. However, the model features complementary between physical and human capital, and as the stock of physical capital rises, over time the capitalists stand to gain from higher education among the workers. Ultimately, both workers and capitalists support a tax on capitalists to support public education. The accumulation of physical and human capital within families is central to this mechanism. The public provision of schooling was often followed by mandatory schooling laws. Such laws affect the family even more directly by forcing parents to send their children to school. A closely related policy is a child labor ban, which we will analyze in Section 4.4.

In the case of schooling and child labor bans, who is a winner and who is a loser from reform depends on people's factor endowments (physical capital and human capital) and

[bw] Key contributions examining the causes of expansions of political rights include Acemoglu and Robinson (2000) and Lizzeri and Persico (2004).

also on fertility. Thus, potential conflicts arise between capitalists and skilled workers on the one hand, and unskilled workers with large families and no desire to educate their children on the other hand. For other types of reforms, gender and marital status are the dividing lines. This point is emphasized in Edlund and Pande (2002), who analyze the importance of women as voters. The paper shows that the political gender gap in the United States—women are more likely to vote Democrat than men—is a relatively recent phenomenon. Up until the mid-1960s, women voted more conservative than men on average. The paper argues that the change in political preferences (which in turn may have impacted other reforms) was due to a specific change in the family, namely the increase in divorce. A large increase in divorce rates during the 1960s and 1970s (see Fig. 6) increased the fraction of relatively poor single women. These women tend to benefit from redistribution, which is typically favored by Democrats. The paper provides evidence in support of the hypothesis by showing that marriage tends to make a woman more Republican, while divorce tends to make her more Democrat.

There are also a few papers that emphasize the importance of women as policymakers. Chattopadhyay and Duflo (2004) use gender quotas in India to empirically analyze which public projects are implemented at the village level depending on the gender of the leader. While the paper is not specifically about reforms, it shows that the gender of the leader affects the types of public goods that are provided. A related point is made by Washington (2008) and Oswald and Powdthavee (2010), who show that the gender composition of children affects the voting behavior of (male) legislators in both the United States and the United Kingdom: having more daughters makes politicians take more liberal positions.

Another important reform is the introduction of public pension systems.[bx] Social security programs transfer resources from young and middle-aged workers to the elderly. Without public systems, such transfers typically happen within the family, with altruistic children voluntarily taking care of elderly parents. Because of the dramatic fertility decline during the 19th century (see Fig. 1), more people ended up without children caring for them during old age, increasing the risk of poverty. This fact probably played an important role in the introduction of public pension systems. At the same time, the existence of such systems further decreases the incentive to have children, which leads to a two-way interaction between the structure of the family and political reforms.

Finally, a large class of reforms affected the legal position of women. These include reforms affecting ownership rights of women (such as the Married Women's Property Act of 1870 in England), reforms affecting child custody laws, the introduction of suffrage for women, and laws banning labor market discrimination and removing occupational

[bx] There is a large literature on social security systems (see, for example, Cooley and Soares, 1996; Boldrin and Montes, 2005; Caucutt et al., 2013).

restrictions (such as allowing women to become judges and soldiers). Reforming the legal position of women also impacts the position of women in the household, eg, by changing their outside options. And conversely, changes in family structure (such as the decline in fertility and the increase in female labor force participation) affected the gains from such reforms. We will discuss the political economy of women's economic rights (such as married women's property rights) in Section 4.3. Other types of women's rights, such as suffrage or labor rights, imply different political economy trade-offs. While there is some empirical work on these other rights, there is a lack of work that formally analyzes the political economy of other types of rights for women.[by] We believe that this is an important issue to be addressed by future research.

4.3 Voting for Women's Rights

Throughout the course of development, all industrialized countries implemented reforms that changed the legal position of women. Doepke and Tertilt (2009) propose a mechanism that provides a causal link between women's rights and economic growth. The mechanism is based on women's role in nurturing children. In contrast, Geddes and Lueck (2002) argue that the initial expansion of women's rights was related to women's role in the labor market. Given that the main phase of expanding women's economic rights was in the 19th century, a time when female labor force participation was low, we argue that a mechanism related to a women's role in the family is more plausible.

We now illustrate the basic mechanism of Doepke and Tertilt (2009) in a simplified framework. The setup is similar to that in Section 3.4 with a modified utility function. We now assume that consumption is a private good, which allows for a stronger conflict of interest between husbands and wives. We also introduce grandchildren and assume that people derive utility from the human capital of children and grandchildren. This assumption introduces a conflict across generations: men want their grandchildren to have as much human capital as possible, but it is the next generation that makes the decision. Since the next generation also cares about their own consumption, fathers will not invest as much in their children's education as desired by the grandfathers. We will now show how this conflict across generations may induce men to vote for female empowerment.

Let the utility function of spouse of gender g be

$$\log(c_g) + \delta_g \log(H') + \delta_g^G \log(H'),$$

where δ_g is the weight spouse g attaches to the human capital of own children, while δ_g^G is the weight on grandchildren. As in Section 3.4, we assume that $\delta_f > \delta_m$.[bz] Given the private goods assumption, the budget constraint is

[by] See Duflo (2012) and Doepke et al. (2012) for two surveys.

[bz] While it may seem natural to assume the same for grandchildren, $\delta_f^G > \delta_m^G$, this assumption is not needed for the analysis.

$$c_m + c_f = A\ell H,$$

where ℓ is total working time of the couple. Assuming that each spouse has a time endowment of 1, the family time constraint is

$$\ell + 2e \leq 2,$$

where e is education time for each of two children.

We now consider two political regimes. In the first one—*patriarchy*—only men make decisions. In the second regime—*empowerment*—men and women make decisions jointly, ie, they solve a collective bargaining problem with equal weights. To find the equilibrium allocation under patriarchy, one can solve the following maximization problem:

$$\max_{\ell, e} \log(c_g) + \delta_g \log(H') + \delta_g^G \log(H')$$

subject to:

$$\ell + 2e \leq 2,$$

$$H' = (Be)^{\theta},$$

$$c_m + c_f = A\ell H,$$

$$c_m, c_f \geq 0.$$

Note that $H'' = (Be')^{\theta}$, where e' is determined by the next generation and is taken as given by the grandparent. Given the technology, the choice of education for own children e will not affect H'', ie, there is no interdependence between the choices of different generations. Further, since a man does not derive utility from his wife's consumption, women's consumption will be zero, and hence male consumption equals production.[ca] The equilibrium allocation under patriarchy is:

$$e^P = \frac{\delta_m \theta}{1 + \delta_m \theta},$$

$$\ell^P = \frac{2}{1 + \delta_m \theta},$$

$$c_m^P = \frac{2AH}{1 + \delta_m \theta}.$$

[ca] This counterfactual result can be easily modified by introducing altruism, as we do in Doepke and Tertilt (2009).

In contrast, under empowerment, couples solve a joint maximization problem with equal bargaining weights. The objective function then is

$$\frac{1}{2}\log(c_m) + \frac{1}{2}\log(c_f) + \tilde{\delta}\,\log(H') + \tilde{\delta}^G\log(H''),$$

where $\tilde{\delta} = \frac{\delta_f + \delta_m}{2}$ and $\tilde{\delta}^G = \frac{\delta_f^G + \delta_m^G}{2}$. Given the objective function, women and men consume equal amounts, $c_f^E = c_m^E$. The optimal education and labor choices are:

$$e^E = \frac{\tilde{\delta}\theta}{1 + \tilde{\delta}\theta},$$

$$\ell^E = \frac{2}{1 + \tilde{\delta}\theta}.$$

Consumption is equalized and depends on the initial human capital:

$$c_m^E = c_f^E = \frac{AH}{1 + \tilde{\delta}\theta}.$$

We are interested in understanding under what conditions men prefer to live in a patriarchal world and when they prefer empowering women. We focus on men's preferences because women's economic rights were expanded long before women gained the right to vote. Hence, the expansion of women's right can be viewed as a voluntary sharing of power by men. To understand men's political preferences, we compare the indirect utility function of a man in both regimes starting from the same initial human capital. Denote the indirect utility functions by U^E and U^P. Plugging in the equilibrium allocations and simplifying, we see that $U^E > U^P$ if and only if:

$$(\delta_m + \delta_m^G)\theta\log\left(\frac{\tilde{\delta}}{\delta_m}\frac{1 + \delta_m\theta}{1 + \tilde{\delta}\theta}\right) > \log\left(\frac{2(1 + \tilde{\delta}\theta)}{1 + \delta_m\theta}\right). \tag{19}$$

From a man's perspective, there is a trade-off. Patriarchy implies strictly higher own consumption, since resources do not need to be shared with one's wife. On the other hand, from the grandfather's perspective, the son will underinvest in the education of the grandchild. Empowering women will lead the future daughter in law to have more bargaining power, and, given that women care more about children than men do ($\delta_f > \delta_m$), this will increase the education of the grandchildren.

We will now show how this trade-off changes with development. Assume that the human capital technology improves over time, ie, θ increases. When the returns to education are zero, ie, $\theta = 0$, men strictly prefer to live under patriarchy (this follows from

Eq. 19). The intuition is that with $\theta = 0$, there is no reason to educate children. With zero education, from a man's perspective empowering women imposes a cost in terms of lost consumption, but does not bring any benefits. However, as θ increases, the concern about the grandchildren's education becomes increasingly important. The next proposition shows that as long as the concern about grandchildren is above a threshold, when θ becomes large enough, the grandchild effect dominates and hence men gain from switching to the empowerment regime.

Proposition 5 *If the weight δ_m^G men attach to grandchildren is above a threshold (given in the proof), there is a threshold $\overline{\theta}$ such that men prefer empowerment if $\theta > \overline{\theta}$.*

Fig. 24 illustrates the result with a numerical example.[cb] The equilibrium education choice e increases with θ in both regimes. Initially, for low levels of θ, men prefer to live under patriarchy. However, as θ increases, patriarchy becomes too costly for men. By introducing women's empowerment, men gain because of the positive effect on grandchildren.

The result is in line with what was observed during the 19th century in both the United States and England. Primary education expanded rapidly at the same time when male legislators passed laws to grant property and other economic rights to married women. Fertility rates also decreased quickly and economic growth increased. These features can be incorporated by adding fertility choice and assuming that parental human capital is an input in children's human capital. In Doepke and Tertilt (2009), we analyze such an augmented model in a fully dynamic context. The main result of the model is also in line with cross-country data. Fig. 25 shows that the position

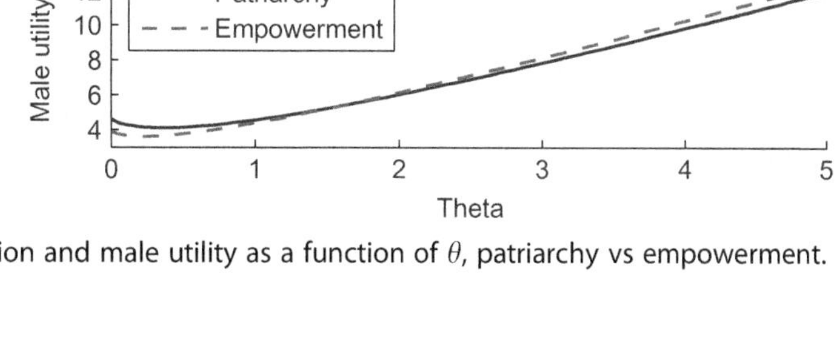

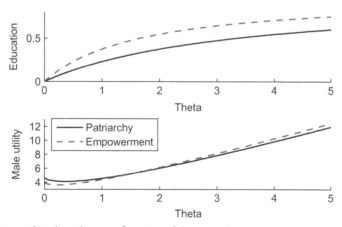

Fig. 24 Education and male utility as a function of θ, patriarchy vs empowerment.

[cb] The parameters used in the example are $\delta_m = 0.3$, $\delta_f = 0.9$, $\delta_m^G = 1.2$, $A = B = 5$. The initial level of human capital is set to $H_0 = 10$. The return to education θ varies between 0 and 5.

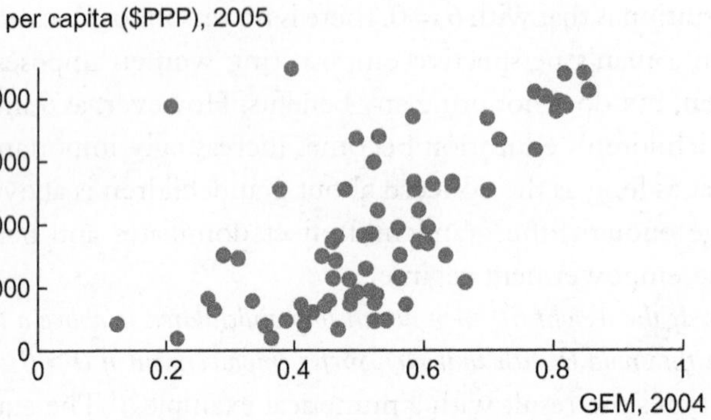

Fig. 25 Gender empowerment measure (GEM) and GDP per capita across countries. *GEM is an index constructed by the UN (Human Development Report, 2004), and GDP numbers are from the World Development Indicators.*

of women, as measured by the gender empowerment measure (GEM) constructed by the United Nations, is strongly positively correlated with GDP per capita. Assuming that returns to education differ systematically across countries, the model reproduces the same relationship.

A complementary theory is proposed by Fernández (2014). As in Doepke and Tertilt (2009), father's concern for their children is a central element. However, the key issue is not investment in education, but fathers preferring a more equal outcome between sons and daughters than what is produced under patriarchy. Economic growth widens disparities between sons and daughters in the patriarchy regime, which ultimately induces fathers to vote for empowerment. Fernández (2014) also provides empirical evidence based on the variation in extensions of women's economic rights across US states, showing that per capita wealth is positively associated with reform, whereas the association with fertility rates is negative (which is in line with the theories of both Doepke and Tertilt, 2009 and Fernández, 2014).

4.4 Voting for Children's Rights

Another near-universal policy reform associated with long-run development is the restriction of child labor. In preindustrial societies, child labor was the norm. In Western Europe and the United States, concern about child labor increased with industrialization, and ultimately industrializing countries introduced a variety of child labor restrictions such as minimum age laws and laws against working in hazardous occupations. A closely related policy reform that often coincided with child labor legislation is the introduction of compulsory schooling. This policy is usually the most effective constraint on child labor (in part because enforcement is straightforward). The close link between child labor and schooling is also part of the reason why child labor reforms matter for growth, as rising educational attainment is one engine of long-run development.

Whereas child labor bans are now in place in all industrial countries, in many developing countries child labor continues to be widespread. Child labor is especially common among poorer families who depend on the additional income. In these countries, public support for introducing restrictions is low.

What explains the passing of child labor reform in some countries, and persistent failure to do so in others? These questions are addressed in Doepke and Zilibotti (2005a), who present an analysis of the political economy of child labor legislation within a dynamic framework that endogenizes skill premia as well as fertility and education decisions.[cc] Here we use a simpler, static framework to highlight the main trade-offs. To understand the political support for and opposition to child labor laws, it is necessary to identify which groups stand to gain or lose from the introduction of regulation. Doepke and Zilibotti argue that the group that stands to gain most from banning child labor consists of unskilled adult workers. To the extent that these workers compete with children in the labor market, by banning child labor they can reduce competition and potentially raise their own wages.[cd] However, the situation is complicated by the fact that the same workers may also have working children themselves, so that the potential wage gains have to be traded off against the loss of child-labor income. A family's fertility and education choices therefore also matter.

To analyze these trade-offs more formally, consider an economy with N_S skilled and N_U unskilled workers. We start under the assumption that each worker has n children, but that only the children of the unskilled workers are working. This is consistent with the observation that child labor is generally more prevalent among poorer families, whereas richer, more highly educated families tend to send their children to school rather than to work. The production technology is:

$$Y = AX_S^{\alpha} X_U^{1-\alpha},$$

where X_S is skilled labor and X_U is unskilled labor. Each working child supplies λ units of unskilled labor, where $\lambda < 1$, reflecting that children are less productive than adult workers. If child labor is legal (the *laissez faire* policy), labor supply is given by:

$$X_S^{\text{laissez faire}} = N_S,$$

$$X_U^{\text{laissez faire}} = N_U + \lambda n N_U,$$

cc An analysis of the welfare implications of banning child labor is contained in Doepke and Krueger (2008).

cd The feedback from regulation to wages is also central to the seminal analysis of Basu and Van (1998), which focuses on the possibility of multiple equilibria.

and, under the assumption of competitive production, wages are given by:

$$w_S^{\text{laissez faire}} = A\alpha\left(\frac{(1+\lambda n)N_U}{N_S}\right)^{1-\alpha},$$

$$w_U^{\text{laissez faire}} = A(1-\alpha)\left(\frac{N_S}{(1+\lambda n)N_U}\right)^{\alpha}.$$

Workers seek to maximize their total income (ie, consumption). Adding adult and child-labor income, total family income for the two types of workers is given by:

$$I_S^{\text{laissez faire}} = w_S = A\alpha\left(\frac{(1+\lambda n)N_U}{N_S}\right)^{1-\alpha},$$

$$I_U^{\text{laissez faire}} = (1+\lambda n)w_U = (1+\lambda n)^{1-\alpha}A(1-\alpha)\left(\frac{N_S}{N_U}\right)^{\alpha}.$$

Let us now see who would gain or lose if child labor were to be banned. Under a child labor ban, no children are working, so that labor supply is simply $X_S^{\text{Ban}} = N_S$ and $X_U^{\text{Ban}} = N_U$, and wages are:

$$w_S^{\text{Ban}} = A\alpha\left(\frac{N_U}{N_S}\right)^{1-\alpha},$$

$$w_U^{\text{Ban}} = A(1-\alpha)\left(\frac{N_S}{N_U}\right)^{\alpha}.$$

The ratios of wages under the two policies are:

$$\frac{w_S^{\text{Ban}}}{w_S^{\text{laissez faire}}} = \left(\frac{1}{1+\lambda n}\right)^{1-\alpha} < 1,$$

$$\frac{w_U^{\text{Ban}}}{w_U^{\text{laissez faire}}} = (1+\lambda n)^{\alpha} > 1.$$

Thus, the skilled wage falls and the unskilled wage increases. This happens because child labor is a substitute for unskilled but a complement for skilled adult labor. The result suggests that unskilled workers may be in favor of banning child labor. However, this is no longer clear when we look at what happens to total family income:

$$I_S^{\text{Ban}} = w_S^{\text{Ban}} = A\alpha\left(\frac{N_U}{N_S}\right)^{1-\alpha},$$

$$I_U^{\text{Ban}} = w_U^{\text{Ban}} = A(1-\alpha)\left(\frac{N_S}{N_U}\right)^{\alpha}.$$

The income ratios are:

$$\frac{I_S^{\text{Ban}}}{I_S^{\text{laissez faire}}} = \left(\frac{1}{1+\lambda n}\right)^{1-\alpha} < 1,$$

$$\frac{I_U^{\text{Ban}}}{I_U^{\text{laissez faire}}} = \left(\frac{1}{1+\lambda n}\right)^{1-\alpha} < 1.$$

We see that, in fact, income falls for both groups, including the unskilled. The reason is that the unskilled workers' gain in terms of higher wages is more than offset by the loss of child labor income. Intuitively, the loss of child labor income is proportional to the total reduction in the supply of unskilled labor, whereas the increase in the unskilled wage is less than proportional to the decline in labor supply.

The analysis suggests that in a country where unskilled workers' children are working as well, public support for introducing child-labor restrictions should be low. The support for child labor restrictions should rise, however, if there is a group of unskilled workers whose children are not working (say, because they send their children to school). Assume that fraction s of unskilled workers send their children to school, while only fraction $(1 - s)$ has working children. The wages then become:

$$w_S^{\text{laissez faire}} = A\alpha\left(\frac{(1+\lambda(1-s)n)N_U}{N_S}\right)^{1-\alpha},$$

$$w_U^{\text{laissez faire}} = A(1-\alpha)\left(\frac{N_S}{(1+\lambda(1-s)n)N_U}\right)^{\alpha}$$

Income is now given by:

$$I_S^{\text{laissez faire}} = w_S = A\alpha\left(\frac{(1+\lambda(1-s)n)N_U}{N_S}\right)^{1-\alpha},$$

$$I_U^{\text{laissez faire}}(\text{working children}) = (1+\lambda n)w_U = (1+\lambda n)A(1-\alpha)\left(\frac{N_S}{(1+\lambda(1-s)n)N_U}\right)^{\alpha},$$

$$I_U^{\text{laissez faire}}(\text{children in school}) = w_U = A(1-\alpha)\left(\frac{N_S}{(1+\lambda(1-s)n)N_U}\right)^{\alpha}.$$

If child labor is now banned, incomes are:

$$I_S^{\text{Ban}} = w_S^{\text{Ban}} = A\alpha\left(\frac{N_U}{N_S}\right)^{1-\alpha},$$

$$I_U^{\text{Ban}}(\text{working children}) = I_U^{\text{Ban}}(\text{children in school}) = A(1-\alpha)\left(\frac{N_S}{N_U}\right)^{\alpha}.$$

Thus, for the unskilled workers with children in school, the introduction of a child labor ban unambiguously increases income. This result explains why child labor reform tends to happen in times when child labor is already declining for other reasons, such as an increased demand for human capital and a higher propensity among unskilled workers to send children to school. It is unskilled workers who do not depend on child labor themselves who should be the strongest advocates of reform.

Notice that the basic mechanism outlined so far is similar to our analysis of the political economy of women's rights in Section 4.3. First, technological change (not modeled explicitly here) increases the demand for human capital; next, the higher demand for human capital induces families to start educating their children; and finally, the families who now send their children to school become supporters of a child labor ban, triggering reform.

So far, we have focused on the case of a country in which child labor is initially legal. Our results show that as long as child labor is widespread among unskilled workers, support for introducing a child-labor ban will remain low. In cross-country data, we observe that differences in child-labor regulations are highly persistent over time, which suggests the existence of a status-quo bias. To examine whether such a bias can arise in our model, let us now consider the opposite situation of a country where a child labor ban is already in place. Are there any reasons why people might be more supportive of banning child labor if a child labor ban is already in place? As we will see, a status-quo bias can indeed arise in our theory, but only if fertility decisions are endogenous and depend on the current political regime.

We would like to find conditions under which the electorate would be willing to abandon an already existing child-labor ban. Consider first the case where fertility is independent of the policy, ie, every household continues to have n children as before. In this case, the trade-off that arises from abandoning an existing ban is exactly the reverse of the trade-off following from introducing a ban described above. In particular, if all unskilled households would actually send their children to work once the ban is abandoned, they would stand to gain from introducing child labor and abandoning the ban. In other words, the preferred policy is independent of the current policy, and a status-quo bias does not arise.

The situation is different, however, if the number of children depends on the current state of the law. It is a common observation that parents face a quantity–quality trade-off in their decisions on children: Parents who invest a lot in their children in terms of education tend to have fewer children than parents who send their children to work. We would therefore expect that once a child labor ban is in place (which effectively makes children more expensive), fertility would be lower. For concreteness, assume that fraction o of unskilled workers have already chosen their number of children under the assumption that the child-labor ban will stay in place, and that their fertility rate is $n^{\text{Ban}} < n$. The remaining families choose their family size later; in particular, if the ban is abandoned, they will optimally choose the larger fertility size n to maximize child labor income. What are now the relevant trade-offs? As above, in the presence of a ban, workers' incomes are $I_S^{\text{Ban}} = A\alpha(N_U/N_S)^{1-\alpha}$ and $I_U^{\text{Ban}} = A(1-\alpha)(N_S/N_U)^{\alpha}$, respectively. If the ban is now abandoned, income is:

$$I_S^{\text{laissez faire}} = A\alpha\left(\frac{(1+\lambda(on^{\text{Ban}}+(1-o)n))N_U}{N_S}\right)^{1-\alpha}$$

for the skilled,

$$I_U^{\text{laissez faire}}(\text{old}) = (1+\lambda n^{\text{Ban}})A(1-\alpha)\left(\frac{N_S}{(1+\lambda(on^{\text{Ban}}+(1-o)n))N_U}\right)^{\alpha}$$

for the "old" unskilled with small families, and:

$$I_U^{\text{laissez faire}}(\text{young}) = (1+\lambda n)A(1-\alpha)\left(\frac{N_S}{(1+\lambda(on^{\text{Ban}}+(1-o)n))N_U}\right)^{\alpha}$$

for the "young" unskilled with larger families. Comparing incomes, we can see that the old unskilled can now lose from the introduction of child labor. Their income ratio is:

$$\frac{I_U^{\text{laissez faire}}(\text{old})}{I_U^{\text{Ban}}(\text{old})} = \frac{1+\lambda n^{\text{Ban}}}{(1+\lambda(on^{\text{Ban}}+(1-o)n))^{\alpha}},$$

which is smaller than one if n^{Ban} is sufficiently small relative to n. These families made their low fertility choice under the assumption that child labor would not be an option. Given that they cannot change fertility ex-post, they have little to gain from making their own children work, but lose from the lower wages due to other families' children entering the labor force.

This mechanism induces policy persistence: Once a ban is in place, families start to make decisions that in the future increase political support for maintaining the ban. This mechanism can explain why differences in child labor and its regulations can be highly persistent across countries. In particular, the theory predicts that some countries can get locked into steady state equilibria featuring high fertility, high incidence of child labor, and little political support for the introduction of child labor regulation. In contrast, other countries with otherwise identical economic fundamentals have low fertility, no child labor, and widespread support for the ban of child labor.

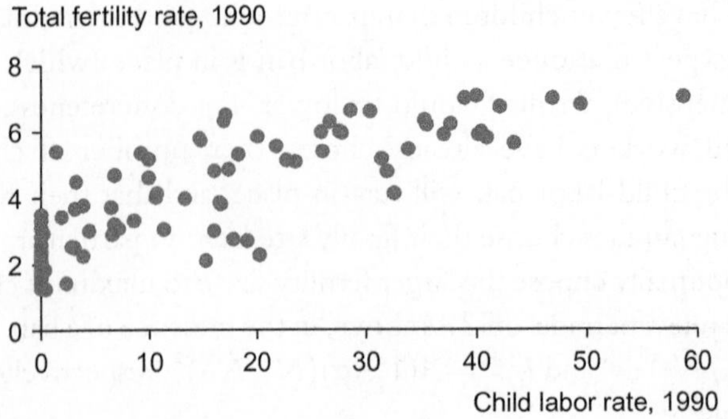

Fig. 26 The child labor rate (percentage of children aged 10–14 economically active) and total fertility rate across countries. *World Bank Development Indicators.*

Consistent with these predictions, we observe large cross-country differences in child labor rates, even among today's developing countries that are at similar levels of income per capita. The theory also predicts a positive correlation between fertility and child labor rates, even after controlling for other variables that might affect child labor or fertility. As Fig. 26 shows, there is a strong positive relationship between fertility rates and child labor rates across countries in contemporary data. Doepke and Zilibotti (2005a) examine the prediction more formally using an international panel of 125 countries from 1960 to 1990. They regress child labor rates on fertility rates, controlling for time dummies, GDP per capita, the Gini coefficient, and the share of agriculture in employment (arguably an independent factor affecting child labor) and find a positive and highly significant coefficient on the fertility rate, implying that a one standard deviation increase in fertility is associated with an increase in the child labor rate of 2.5 percentage points. The results are robust to the inclusion of country fixed effects.

The preceding analysis shows that the key feature of the political economy of child-labor regulation is that the group that most stands to gain from banning child labor (unskilled workers) is often simultaneously economically invested in child labor (because their own children are working). This observation leads to an explanation of why child labor was banned only after an increasing share of parents sent their children to school instead of work, and why differences in child labor and child-labor regulation across countries can be highly persistent over time. The analysis can also be used to help in designing policies that facilitate the passing of child labor regulations in developing countries today. Doepke and Zilibotti (2009, 2010) examine interventions such as international labor standards and trade restrictions aimed at reducing child labor from this perspective and argue that such well-intentioned policies can backfire and reduce the likelihood of comprehensive action of child labor within developing countries.

5. CONCLUSION

In this chapter, we have argued that accounting for the family should be an integral part of macroeconomics. The family is where many of the key decisions that are relevant for macroeconomics are made. Since families have been changing, with fewer marriages, more single households, lower fertility, and higher female labor supply, the answers to standard macroeconomic questions concerning, say, how labor supply and savings react to the business cycle have likely changed, too. Family structure also differs across countries. Developing countries are characterized by higher fertility, more traditional gender roles, often a son preference, and sometimes polygyny. These differences matter for the decisions that families make, and hence for the size and age structure of the population, for the accumulation of human and physical capital, and ultimately for the rate of economic growth.

The family matters not just for its role in household-level decisions but also through its effect on the evolution of institutions. Long-run economic development is characterized by a strikingly universal process of political change. Almost all of today's rich countries went through a series of similar reforms: democracy spread, public education systems were built, women and children gained rights, and public pension systems and the welfare state were introduced. We argue that many of these reforms transfer responsibility from the household to the public sphere, and that the ultimate triggers behind the reforms were often related to changes in the family.

There are additional ways in which the family matters for macroeconomics which we did not cover in this chapter. For example, the issues we discussed here are largely positive in nature. We touched only briefly on normative questions in a few places, for example, the discussion of the one child policy. We purposely did not talk about efficiency in this context, since this is not straightforward to do. The regular notion of Pareto efficiency is not defined in models where population size is endogenous, which includes all models with endogenous fertility. To evaluate policies that may affect fertility—such as education policies, child labor laws, policies banning abortion, or subsidies for single mothers—new concepts are required. Golosov et al. (2007) propose two new notions—$\mathcal{A}$- and $\mathcal{P}$-efficiency—and show how they can be used in standard fertility models. Schoonbroodt and Tertilt (2014) use the concepts to explore under what conditions fertility choice may be inefficiently low and hence pronatalist policies may be desired.

There is also a burgeoning literature on the role of the family for the transmission of preferences, cultural values, and attitudes, which can also feed back into macroeconomic outcomes. Theoretical models of the transmission of preferences and values in the family are developed by Bisin and Verdier (2001) and Doepke and Zilibotti (2005b, 2008). Empirical evidence for the intergenerational transmission of risk attitudes is provided by Dohmen et al. (2012). In Fernández et al. (2004), men's preferences for working vs stay-at-home wives are formed in childhood by the work behavior of their mothers. This leads to a dynamic process affecting female labor supply over time. Cultural transmission may also occur in society more generally. For example, in Fogli and Veldkamp (2011) and Fernández (2013), women learn from others about the costs of working. Both papers argue that a reduction in the perceived cost of working through this learning process is key to understanding the increase in female labor supply. The cultural transmission of fertility and female labor supply decisions is established empirically using data from second-generation immigrants to the United States by Fernández and Fogli (2006). Alesina and Giuliano (2010, 2014) argue that the strength of family ties varies across countries, and that these differences matter for cultural attitudes and macroeconomic outcomes. Alesina et al. (2013) take a historical perspective and trace unequal gender norms back to plough agriculture (and ultimately to soil type).[ce] Doepke and Zilibotti (2015) expand theories of preference transmission in the family to account for different parenting styles and link changes in parenting to macroeconomic trends such as increasing demand for human capital and increasing occupational differentiation in society.

Another important research area focuses on the importance of the family for understanding inequality. For example, de Nardi (2004) emphasizes the importance of bequest motives for the wealth distribution. Scholz and Seshadri (2009) build on this insight by investigating more generally the importance of children and fertility choice for the US wealth distribution. The interaction between parents and children is also analyzed for insights into the causes of intergenerational persistence of earnings.[cf] For example, parental inputs may amplify persistence if high-skill parents spend more resources and time on their children than low-skill parents. Other authors have emphasized the role of differences between women and men (and their interactions as couples) for understanding the distribution of earnings (and changes in earnings inequality over time). For example, Heathcote et al. (2010b) explicitly include male and female labor supply in their analysis of the US rising wage inequality. Other authors take this a step further and analyze how sorting and changes in sorting pattern have impacted inequality.[cg] Recent research also makes an explicit distinction between individual and household inequality.[ch] True consumption inequality may be lower than what is measured based on individual income data if the family plays a role in providing insurance (Blundell et al., 2008). Conversely, if family members do not provide full insurance

[ce] This hypothesis was first put forth by Boserup (1970), but had not been tested empirically until recently.

[cf] See, for example, Restuccia and Urrutia (2004), Lee and Seshadri (2015), and Yum (2015).

[cg] See, for example, Fernández and Rogerson (2001), Fernández et al. (2005), Choo and Siow (2006), and Greenwood et al. (2014, 2016a).

[ch] See Heathcote et al. (2010a).

to each other, true consumption inequality may be higher than what is measured based on household expenditure data (Lise and Seitz, 2011). Further, the mapping between individual and household inequality may change over time if the structure of the family is changing.

In our view, the intersection of family economics and macroeconomics offers many promising avenues for future research. Throughout this chapter, we have pointed out a number of particular questions that are in need of answers, and which could be addressed with the data, models, and methods available today. There is also a need to push out the frontier of theoretical modeling; in particular, we see a strong potential for intellectual arbitrage by applying methods of dynamic modeling that are common in macroeconomics to better understand the dynamics of household bargaining under commitment and private information frictions. Finally, there are promising applied topics that have barely been explored yet. For example, an important topic in recent macroeconomics concerns house price dynamics (see the chapter "Housing and macroeconomics" by Piazzesi and Schneider). Changes in family structure—such as the rise in single households—have a direct impact on housing demand. Further, singles are more eager to live in cities (where they can meet other singles) compared to families, who place higher value on space. Hence, changes in family formation and family structure should matter for the housing market. We hope that this and other research topics will be picked up by more researchers as family economics continues to become an integral part of macroeconomics.

APPENDICES

A Proofs for Propositions

Proof of Proposition 1 *As γ_f approaches zero, the density $f(\eta_g) = F'(\eta_g)$ approaches zero, so that the elasticity of labor supply approaches zero also. In contrast, for married women, the fact that $w_m > 0$ guarantees that the elasticity of labor supply is bounded away from zero.* □

Proof of Proposition 2 *The first part follows from the fact that aggregate labor supply elasticity for single households equals one, whereas for married households, it is strictly smaller than one.*

For the second part, for any $w_f > 0$, we have $\hat{\eta}_u > \hat{\eta}_e$, which implies that the elasticity is smaller than one. As w_f converges to zero, $\hat{\eta}_e$ and $\hat{\eta}_u$ both converge to zero. Since $F(0) = 0$ and F is continuous, we then have that $F(\hat{\eta}_e)$ and $F(\hat{\eta}_u)$ both converge to zero, which implies that the elasticity of labor supply converges to one. Conversely, as w_f converges to infinity, $\hat{\eta}_e$ and $\hat{\eta}_u$ both converge to infinity, implying that $F(\hat{\eta}_e)$ and $F(\hat{\eta}_u)$ both converge to one and once again resulting in an elasticity of one. □

Proof of Proposition 3 *If $\tilde{\lambda}_f \leq \lambda_f$ and $\tilde{\lambda}_m \leq \lambda_m$, neither participation constraint (9) and (10) is binding. Hence, it is optimal to stay married, $D = 0$, and the consumption allocation follows from maximizing (7) subject to the budget constraint (8). If $\tilde{\lambda}_f > \lambda_f$ and $\tilde{\lambda}_f + \tilde{\lambda}_m \leq 1$, the wife's* *participation constraint is binding. Staying married (D = 0) continues to be optimal, however, because it is possible to increase the wife's consumption share to make her indifferent between marriage and divorce, with the husband continuing to be better off married. The wife's consumption can then be solved from solving for* c_f *in her participation constraint (9) (imposed as an equality) while setting* $D = 0$*. The husband's consumption then follows from the budget constraint (8). The case where the husband's participation constraint is binding is parallel. Finally, when there is no allocation of ex-post bargaining power that keeps both spouses at least as well off married compared to being divorced, divorce (D = 1) is the optimal choice, and consumption follows from the individual budget constraints in the divorced state.* □

Proof of Proposition 4 *The ratio of the growth factors is*

$$\frac{1+g^{end}}{1+g^{exog}} = \left\{ \left(\frac{\alpha\delta_f + (1-\alpha)\delta_m}{\lambda_f\delta_f + (1-\lambda_f)\delta_m} \right) \left(\frac{\alpha + [\lambda_f\delta_f + (1-\lambda_f)\delta_m]\theta}{\alpha + [\alpha\delta_f + (1-\alpha)\delta_m]\theta} \right) \right\}^{\theta}.$$

Thus the result follows trivially, given the assumption $\delta_f > \delta_m$ *and* $\theta < 1$. □

Proof of Proposition 5 *Take the limit as* $\theta \to \infty$ *on both sides of Eq. (19) separately. The limit of the left-hand side can be written as:*

$$\lim_{\theta\to\infty} (\delta_m + \delta_m^G) \lim_{\theta\to\infty} \frac{\log\left(\frac{\tilde{\delta}}{\delta_m} \frac{1+\delta_m\theta}{1+\tilde{\delta}\theta} \right)}{\frac{1}{\theta}}.$$

Note that both numerator and denominator converge to zero. Applying L'Hopital's Rule, canceling terms and rearranging, the limit can be written as:

$$(\delta_m + \delta_m^G) \lim_{\theta\to\infty} \left(\frac{(\tilde{\delta} - \delta_m)}{\left(\frac{1}{\theta} + \tilde{\delta}\right)\left(\frac{1}{\theta} + \delta_m\right)} \right)$$

From this expression, we can see that the limit exits and is equal to:

$$(\delta_m + \delta_m^G) \left(\frac{\tilde{\delta} - \delta_m}{\tilde{\delta}\delta_m} \right).$$

The limit of the right hand side of (19) is $\log\left(\frac{2\tilde{\delta}}{\delta_m}\right)$. *Thus, in the limit* $U^E > U^P$ *if and only if* $(\delta_m + \delta_m^G)\left(\frac{\tilde{\delta} - \delta_m}{\tilde{\delta}\delta_m}\right) > \log\left(\frac{2\tilde{\delta}}{\delta_m}\right)$. *Using the definition of* $\tilde{\delta}$ *and rearranging, this can be expressed as:*

$$\delta_m^G > \log\left(\frac{\delta_f + \delta_m}{\delta_m}\right)\left(\frac{(\delta_f + \delta_m)\delta_m}{\delta_f - \delta_m}\right) - \delta_m.$$

Hence, as long as δ_m^G *is large enough, the equation is satisfied.* □

B Data Definitions and Sources

The data used in Table 3 are from two different editions of the OECD Gender, Institutions and Development Data Base (GID 2006 and 2014), the World Development Indicators (WDI 2003, 2005, and WDI 2014) and the United Nations Human Development Report 2004. Here we give the definition of each variable and its source.

GDP per capita: GDP data were used from two different years. The variables from GID 2014 and WDI 2014 were correlated with GDP p.c. from the WDI 2014. The variables from WDI 2003, UN 2004, and GID 2006 were correlated with GDP p.c. from the WDI 2005.

Share of agriculture: Measured as the value-added share of agriculture in GDP. Data were used from two different years. The variables from GID 2014 and WDI 2014 were correlated with percent agriculture from the WDI 2014. The variables from WDI 2003, UN 2004, and GID 2006 were correlated with percent agriculture from the WDI 2005.

Total fertility rate: Source: GID 2006.

Child mortality rate: Under-five mortality rate. Source: WDI 2014.

Average years of schooling: Source: WDI 2003.

Boy/girl sex ratio at birth: Measured as boys born per girl. Source: GID 2006.

Son preference in education: Percentage of people agreeing that university is more important for boys than for girls. GID 2014.

Inheritance discrimination against daughters: Whether daughters have the same inheritance rights as sons. Reported in three categories between 0 ("equal") and 1 ("unequal"). Source: GID 2014.

Female literacy relative to male: Female literacy as percentage of male literacy. Source: GID 2006.

Percent females in paid labor force: Percentage of women among wage and salaried workers. Source: GID 2006.

Unpaid care work by women: Female to male ratio of time devoted to unpaid care work. Source: GID 2014.

Year first woman in parliament: Source: Human Development Report 2004.

Women's access to land: Whether women and men have equal and secure access to land use, control and ownership. Categorical (three categories = 0, 0.5, 1), where 1 ("full") and 0 ("impossible"). Source: GID 2014.

Gender empowerment measure: Measures inequality between men's and women's opportunities, combining measures of inequality in political participation and decision making, in economic participation and decision making, and in power over economic resources. The level is between 1 ("full equality") and 0 ("no equality"). Source: UN 2004.

Early marriage: Share of female population between ages 15 and 19 ever married. GID 2014.

Agreement with wife beating: Percentage of women who agree that a husband/partner is justified in beating his wife/partner under certain circumstances. Source: GID 2014.

Inheritance discrimination against widows: Whether a widow has the same inheritance rights as a widower. Reported in three categories (0, 0.5, 1), where 0 means equal rights. Source: GID 2014.

Laws on domestic violence: Whether the legal framework offers women legal protection from domestic violence. Reported in five categories = 0, 0.25, 0.5, 0.75, 1, where 1 means no protection and 0 full protection. Source: GID 2014.

ACKNOWLEDGMENTS

We thank Stefania Albanesi, Raquel Fernández, Moshe Hazan, Claudia Olivetti, Víctor Ríos-Rull, John Taylor, Harald Uhlig, and Alessandra Voena for comments that helped to greatly improve the manuscript. Titan Alon, Florian Exler, Xue Zhang, Tim Hildebrand, Katarina Kuske, and Clara Schäper provided excellent research assistance. Financial support from the National Science Foundation (Grant SES-1260961) and the European Research Council (Grant SH1-313719) is gratefully acknowledged

REFERENCES

Acemoglu, D., Robinson, J.A., 2000. Why did the west extend the Franchise? Democracy, inequality and growth in historical perspective. Q. J. Econ. 115 (4), 1167–1199.

Adda, J., Dustmann, C., Stevens, K., 2016. The career costs of children. J. Polit. Econ., forthcoming.

Aguiar, M., Hurst, E., 2007. Measuring trends in leisure: the allocation of time over five decades. Q. J. Econ 122 (3), 969–1006 (Table II).

Aiyagari, S.R., 1994. Uninsured idiosyncratic risk and aggregate saving. Q. J. Econ. 109 (3), 659–684.

Aizer, A., Cunha, F., 2012. The production of child human capital: endowments, investments and fertility. NBER Working Paper No. 18429.

Albanesi, S., 2014. Jobless recoveries and gender biased technological change. Unpublished Manuscript, Federal Reserve Bank of New York.

Albanesi, S., Olivetti, C., 2009. Home production, market production, and the gender wage gap: Incentives and expectations. Rev. Econ. Dyn. 12 (1), 80–107.

Albanesi, S., Olivetti, C., 2014. Maternal health and the baby boom. Quant.Econ. 5 (2), 225–269.

Albanesi, S., Olivetti, C., 2016. Gender roles and medical progress. J. Polit. Econ. 124, 650–695.

Albanesi, S., Şahin, A., 2013. The gender unemployment gap. Federal Reserve Bank of New York Staff Report 613.

Alderman, H., Chiappori, P.A., Haddad, L., Hoddinott, J., Kanbur, R., 1995. Unitary versus collective models of the household: is it time to shift the burden of proof? World Bank Research Observer 10 (1), 1–19. ISSN 0257-3032, 1564-6971. http://www.jstor.org/stable/3986564.

Alesina, A., Giuliano, P., 2010. The power of the family. J. Econ. Growth 15 (2), 93–125.
Alesina, A., Giuliano, P., 2014. Family ties. In: Aghion, P., Durlauf, S.N. (Eds.), Handbook of Economic Growth, vol. 2A. North Holland, Amsterdam, Netherlands, pp. 177–215.
Alesina, A., Giuliano, P., Nunn, N., 2013. On the origins of gender roles: women and the plough. Q. J. Econ. 128 (2), 469–530.
Alger, I., Cox, D., 2013. The evolution of altruistic preferences: Mothers versus fathers. Rev. Econ. Household 11 (3), 421–446.
Ambler, K., 2015. Don't tell on me: experimental evidence of asymmetric information in transnational households. J. Dev. Econ. 113, 52–69.
Anderson, S., Baland, J.M., 2002. The economics of roscas and intrahousehold resource allocation. Q. J. Econ. 117 (3), 963–995. ISSN 0033-5533. http://www.jstor.org/stable/4132493.
Anukriti, S., 2014. Financial incentives and the fertility-sex ratio trade-off. Unpublished Manuscript, Boston College.
Ashraf, N., 2009. Spousal control and intra-household decision making: an experimental study in the Philippines. Am. Econ. Rev. 99 (4), 1245–1277. http://dx.doi.org/10.1257/aer.99.4.1245. http://www.ingentaconnect.com/content/aea/aer/2009/00000099/00000004/art00008.
Ashraf, N., Field, E., Lee, J., 2014. Household bargaining and excess fertility: an experimental study in Zambia. Am. Econ. Rev. 104 (7), 2210–2237.
Atkeson, A., Lucas Jr., R.E., 1992. On efficient distribution with private information. Rev. Econe Stud. 59 (3), 427–453.
Attanasio, O.P., Browning, M., 1995. Consumption over the life cycle and over the business cycle. Am. Econ. Rev. 85 (5), 1118–1137. ISSN 0002-8282. http://www.jstor.org/stable/2950978.
Attanasio, O., Lechene, V., 2002. Tests of income pooling in household decisions. Rev. Econ. Dyn. 5 (4), 720–748. http://dx.doi.org/10.1006/redy.2002.0191. http://www.sciencedirect.com/science/article/B6WWT-473VNCJ-2/2/cf9affb1fba57fc0d782dbe93c7753db. ISSN 1094-2025.
Attanasio, O., Lechene, V., 2014. Efficient responses to targeted cash transfers. J. Polit. Econ. 122 (1), 178–222.
Attanasio, O., Low, H., Sánchez-Marcos, V., 2005. Female labor supply as insurance against idiosyncratic risk. J. Eur. Econ. Assoc. 3 (2/3), 755–764. http://www.jstor.org/stable/40005017. ISSN 1542-4766.
Attanasio, O., Low, H., Sánchez-Marcos, V., 2008. Explaining changes in female labor supply in a life-cycle model. Am. Econ. Rev. 98 (4), 1517–1552.
Attanasio, O., Levell, P., Low, H., Sánchez-Marcos, V., 2015. Aggregating elasticities: intensive and extensive margins of female labour supply. NBER Working Paper No. 21315.
Bachmann, R., 2012. Understanding the jobless recoveries after 1991 and 2001. Unpublished Manuscript, University of Notre Dame.
Banerjee, A., Meng, X., Porzio, T., Qian, N., 2014. Aggregate fertility and household savings: a general equilibrium analysis with micro data. NBER Working Paper No. 20050.
Barro, R.J., Becker, G.S., 1989. Fertility choice in a model of economic growth. Econometrica 57 (2), 481–501.
Basu, K., 2006. Gender and say: a model of household behaviour with endogenously determined balance of power. Econ. J. 116 (511), 558–580.
Basu, K., Van, P.H., 1998. The economics of child labor. Am. Econ. Rev. 88 (3), 412–427.
Baudin, T., de la Croix, D., Gobbi, P.E., 2015. Fertility and childlessness in the United States. Am. Econ. Rev. 105 (6), 1852–1882. http://dx.doi.org/10.1257/aer.20120926.
Becker, G.S., 1988. Family economics and macro behavior. Am. Econ. Rev. 78 (1), 1–13.
Becker, G.S., Barro, R.J., 1988. A reformulation of the economic theory of fertility. Q. J. Econ. 103 (1), 1–25.
Becker, G.S., Murphy, K.M., Tamura, R., 1990. Human capital, fertility, and economic growth. J. Polit. Econ. 98 (5), 12–37.
Benhabib, J., Rogerson, R., Wright, R., 1991. Homework in macroeconomics: household production and aggregate fluctuations. J. Polit. Econ. 99 (6), 1166–1187.
Bick, A., 2016. The quantitative role of child care for female labor force participation and fertility. J. Eur. Econ. Assoc., 13 (3), 639–668.

Bick, A., Fuchs-Schündeln, N., 2014. Taxation and labor supply of married couples across countries: a macroeconomic analysis. Unpublished Manuscript, Arizona State University.
Bisin, A., Verdier, T., 2001. The economics of cultural transmission and the dynamics of preferences. J. Econ. Theor. 97 (2), 298–319.
Blau, F., Kahn, L., 2000. Gender differences in pay. J. Econ. Perspect. 14 (4), 75–99.
Blau, F., Kahn, L., 2007. Changes in the labor supply behavior of married women: 1980–2000. J. Labor Econ. 25 (3), 393–438.
Bleakley, H., Lange, F., 2009. Chronic disease burden and the interaction of education, fertility, and growth. Rev. Econ. Stat. 91 (1), 52–65.
Blundell, R., MaCurdy, T., 1999. Labor supply: a review of alternative approaches. In: Ashenfelter, O., Card, D. (Eds.), Chapter 27 of Handbook of Labor Economics, vol. 3. Elsevier, Amsterdam, Netherlands.
Blundell, R., Chiappori, P.A., Meghir, C., 2005. Collective labor supply with children. J. Polit. Econ. 113 (6), 1277–1306.
Blundell, R., Pistaferri, L., Preston, I., 2008. Consumption inequality and partial insurance. Am. Econ. Rev. 98 (5), 1887–1921.
Blundell, R., Pistaferri, L., Saporta-Eksten, I., 2016. Consumption inequality and family labor supply. Am. Econ. Rev. 106 (2), 387–435.
Boldrin, M., Montes, A., 2005. The intergenerational state, education and pensions. Rev. Econ. Stud. 72 (3), 651–664.
Boserup, E., 1970. Women's Role in Economic Development. George Allen and Unwin Ltd, London.
Buera, F.J., Kaboski, J.P., Zhao, M.Q., 2013. The rise of services: the role of skills, scale, and female labor supply. NBER Working Paper No. 19372. http://www.nber.org/papers/w19372.
Castilla, C., Walker, T., 2013. Is ignorance bliss? The effect of asymmetric information between spouses on intra-household allocations. Am. Econ. Rev. 103 (3), 263–268.
Caucutt, E., Lochner, L., 2012. Early and late human capital investments, borrowing constraints, and the family. Unpublished Manuscript, University of Western Ontario.
Caucutt, E., Cooley, T.F., Guner, N., 2013. The farm, the city, and the emergence of social security. J. Econ. Growth 18 (1), 1–32.
Cervellati, M., Sunde, U., 2005. Human capital formation, life expectancy, and the process of development. Am. Econ. Rev. 95 (5), 1653–1672.
Cesarini, D., Lindqvist, E., Notowidigdo, M.J., Östling, R., 2015. The effect of wealth on individual and household labor supply: evidence from Swedish lotteries. Unpublished Manuscript, Northwestern University.
Chade, H., Ventura, G., 2005. Income taxation and marital decisions. Rev. Econ. Dyn. 8 (3), 565–599. ISSN 1094-2025. http://dx.doi.org/10.1016/j.red.2005.01.008. http://www.sciencedirect.com/science/article/pii/S109420250500013X.
Chattopadhyay, R., Duflo, E., MIT, 2004. Women as policy makers: evidence from a randomized policy experiment in India. Econometrica 72 (5), 1409–1443. ISSN 0012-9682. http://search.ebscohost.com/login.aspx?direct=true&db=ecn&AN=0749671&site=ehost-live.
Chetty, R., Guren, A., Manoli, D., Weber, A., 2011. Are micro and macro labor supply elasticities consistent? A review of evidence on the intensive and extensive margins. Am. Econ. Rev. 101 (3), 471–475.
Chetty, R., Guren, A., Manoli, D., Weber, A., 2012. Does indivisible labor explain the difference between micro and macro elasticities? A meta-analysis of extensive margin elasticities. NBER Macroecon. Annu. 27, 1–56.
Chiappori, P.A., 1988. Rational household labor supply. Econometrica 56 (1), 63–90. ISSN 0012-9682. http://www.jstor.org/stable/1911842.
Chiappori, P.A., 1992. Collective labor supply and welfare. J. Polit. Econ.y 100 (3), 437–467. ISSN 0022-3808. http://www.jstor.org/stable/2138727.
Chiappori, P.A., Iyigun, M., Weiss, Y., 2009. Investment in schooling and the marriage market. Am. Econ. Rev. 99 (5), 1689–1713. http://dx.doi.org/10.1257/aer.99.5.1689.
Cho, J.O., Rogerson, R., 1988. Family labor supply and aggregate fluctuations. J. Monetary Econ. 21 (2–3), 233–245. ISSN 0304-3932. http://dx.doi.org/10.1016/0304-3932(88)90031-1.
Choo, E., Siow, A., 2006. Who marries whom and why. J. Polit. Econ. 114 (1), 175–201.

Choukhmane, T., Coeurdacier, N., Jin, K., 2014. The one child policy and household savings. Unpublished Manuscript, London School of Economics.
Clarke, S.C., 1995. Advance report of final marriage statistics, 1989 and 1990. Monthly Vital Stat. Rep. 43 (12), 3–5.
Coeurdacier, N., Guibaud, S., Jin, K., 2014. Fertility policies and social security reforms in China. IMF Econ. Rev. 62 (3), 371–408.
Cooley, T.F., Prescott, E.C., 1995. Economic growth and business cycles. In: Cooley, T.F. (Ed.), Frontiers of Business Cycle Research. Princeton University Press, Princeton.
Cooley, T.F., Soares, J., 1996. Will social security survive the baby boom? Carnegie-Rochester Conference Series Publ. Policy 45, 89–121.
Cordoba, J.C., 2015. Children, dynastic altruism and the wealth of nations. Rev. Econ. Dyn. 18 (4), 774–791.
Cordoba, J., Ripoll, M., 2014. The elasticity of intergenerational substitution, parental altruism, and fertility choice. Unpublished Manuscript, University of Pittsburgh.
Costa, D.L., 2000. From mill town to board room: the rise of women's paid labor. J. Econ. Perspect. 14 (4), 101–122.
Cubeddu, L., Ríos-Rull, J.V., 2003. Families as shocks. J. Eur. Econ. Assoc. 1 (2–3), 671–682.
Cunha, F., Heckmann, J., 2007. The technology of skill formation. Am. Econ. Rev. 97 (2), 31–47.
Da Rocha, J.M., Fuster, L., 2006. Why are fertility rates and female employment ratios positively correlated across OECD countries? Int. Econ. Rev. 47 (4), 1187–1222. ISSN 1468-2354. http://dx.doi.org/10.1111/j.1468-2354.2006.00410.x.
de la Croix, D., Doepke, M., 2003. Inequality and growth: why differential fertility matters. Am. Econ. Rev. 93 (4), 1091–1113.
de la Croix, D., Doepke, M., 2004. Public versus private education when differential fertility matters. J. Dev. Econ. 73 (2), 607–629.
de la Croix, D., Doepke, M., 2009. To segregate or to integrate: education politics and democracy. Rev. Econ. Stud. 76 (2), 597–628.
de la Croix, D., Mariani, F., 2015. From polygyny to serial monogamy: a unified theory of marriage institutions. Rev. Econ. Stud. 82 (2), 565–607.
de la Croix, D., Vander Donckt, M., 2010. Would empowering women initiate the demographic transition in least developed countries? J. Hum. Capital 4 (2), 85–129.
de la Croix, D., Doepke, M., Mokyr, J., 2016. Clans, guilds, and markets: apprenticeship institutions and growth in the pre-industrial economy. Unpublished Manuscript, Northwestern University.
de Laat, J., 2014. Household allocations and endogenous information: the case of split migrants in Kenya. J. Dev. Econ. 106, 108–117.
de Nardi, M., 2004. Wealth inequality and intergenerational links. Rev. Econ. Stud. 71 (3), 743–768.
Del Boca, D., Flinn, C., Wiswall, M., 2014. Household choices and child development. Rev. Econ. Stud. 81 (1), 137–185.
Doepke, M., 2004. Accounting for fertility decline during the transition to growth. J. Econ. Growth 9 (3), 347–383.
Doepke, M., Kindermann, F., 2015. Bargaining over babies: theory, evidence, and policy implications. Unpublished Manuscript, Northwestern University.
Doepke, M., Krueger, D., 2008. Origins and consequences of child labor restrictions: a macroeconomic perspective. In: Rupert, P. (Ed.), Frontiers of Family Economics. Emerald Press, Bingley, UK (England).
Doepke, M., Tertilt, M., 2009. Women's liberation: what's in it for men? Q. J. Econ. 124 (4), 1541–1591.
Doepke, M., Tertilt, M., 2014. Does female empowerment promote economic development? NBER Working Paper No. 19888.
Doepke, M., Tertilt, M., 2015. Asymmetric information in couples. Unpublished Manuscript, Northwestern University.
Doepke, M., Zilibotti, F., 2005a. The macroeconomics of child labor regulation. Am. Econ. Rev. 95 (5), 1492–1524.
Doepke, M., Zilibotti, F., 2005b. Social class and the spirit of capitalism. J. Eur. Econ. Assoc. 3 (2–3), 516–524.
Doepke, M., Zilibotti, F., 2008. Occupational choice and the spirit of capitalism. Q. J. Econ. 123 (2), 747–793.

Doepke, M., Zilibotti, F., 2009. International labor standards and the political economy of child labor regulation. J. Eur. Econ. Assoc. 7 (2–3), 508–518.

Doepke, M., Zilibotti, F., 2010. Do international labor standards contribute to the persistence of the child labor problem? J. Econ. Growth 15 (1), 1–31.

Doepke, M., Zilibotti, F., 2015. Parenting with style: altruism and paternalism in intergenerational preference transmission. Unpublished Manuscript, Northwestern University.

Doepke, M., Tertilt, M., Voena, A., 2012. The economics and politics of women's rights. Annu. Rev. Econ. 4, 339–372.

Doepke, M., Hazan, M., Maoz, Y.D., 2015. The Baby Boom and World War II: a macroeconomic analysis. Rev. Econ. Stud. 82 (3), 1031–1073.

Dohmen, T., Falk, A., Huffman, D., Sunde, U., 2012. The intergenerational transmission of risk and trust attitudes. Rev. Econ. Stud. 79 (2), 645–677.

Du, Q., Wei, S.-J., 2010. A sexually unbalanced model of current account imbalances. NBER Working Paper No. 10498.

Duflo, E., 2012. Women empowerment and economic development. J. Econ. Liter. 50 (4), 1051–1079.

Duflo, E., Udry, C., 2004. Intrahousehold resource allocation in Cote d'ivoire: social norms, separate accounts and consumption choices. NBER Working Paper No. 10498. http://www.nber.org/papers/w10498.

Dyrda, S., Kaplan, G., Ríos-Rull, J.V., 2016. Business cycles and household formation. Unpublished Manuscript, University of Pennsylvania.

Ebenstein, A., 2010. The 'missing girls' of China and the unintended consequences of the one child policy. J. Hum. Resour. 45 (1), 87–115.

Echevarria, C., Merlo, A., 1999. Gender differences in education in a dynamic household bargaining model. Int. Econ. Rev. 40 (2), 265–286.

Eckstein, Z., Lifshitz, O., 2011. Dynamic female labor supply. Econometrica 79 (6), 1675–1726. ISSN 0012-9682, 1468-0262. http://www.jstor.org/stable/41336534.

Eckstein, Z., Lifshitz, O., 2015. Household interaction and the labor supply of married women. Int. Econ. Rev. 56 (2), 427–455. ISSN 0012-9682, 1468-0262. http://www.jstor.org/stable/41336534.

Edlund, L., Pande, R., Columbia, U., 2002. Why have women become left-wing? the political gender gap and the decline in marriage. Q. J. Econ. 117 (3), 917–961. ISSN 0033-5533. http://search.ebscohost.com/login.aspx?direct=true&db=ecn&AN=0620220&site=ehost-live.

Eika, L., Mogstad, M., Zafar, B., 2014. Educational assortative mating and household income inequality. NBER Working Paper No. 20271.

Erosa, A., Fuster, L., Restuccia, D., 2010. A general equilibrium analysis of parental leave policies. Rev. Econ. Dyn. 13 (4), 742–758.

Fernández, R., 2013. Cultural change as learning: the evolution of female labor force participation over a century. Am. Econ. Rev. 103 (1), 472–500.

Fernández, R., 2014. Women's rights and development. J. Econ. Growth 19 (1), 37–80.

Fernández, R., Fogli, A., 2006. Fertility: the role of culture and family experience. J. Eur. Econ. Assoc. 4 (2–3), 552–561.

Fernández, R., Rogerson, R., 2001. Sorting and long-run inequality. Q. J. Econ. 116 (4), 1305–1341.

Fernández, R., Wong, J.C., 2014a. Unilateral divorce, the decreasing gender gap, and married women's labor force participation. Am. Econ. Rev. 104 (5), 342–347. http://dx.doi.org/10.1257/aer.104.5.342.

Fernández, R., Wong, J.C., 2014b. Divorce risk, wages and working wives: a quantitative life-cycle analysis of female labour force participation. Econ. J. 124 (576), 319–358. ISSN 1468-0297. http://dx.doi.org/10.1111/ecoj.12136.

Fernández, R., Wong, J.C., 2014c. Free to leave? A welfare analysis of divorce regimes. Unpublished Manuscript, NYU. doi:10.1111/ecoj.12136.

Fernández, R., Fogli, A., Olivetti, C., 2004. Mothers and sons: preference formation and female labor force dynamics. Q. J. Econ. 119 (4), 1249–1299.

Fernández, R., Guner, N., Knowles, J., 2005. Love and money: a theoretical and empirical analysis of household sorting and inequality. Q. J. Econ. 120 (1), 273–344.

Fernández-Villaverde, J., Krueger, D., 2007. Consumption over the life cycle: facts from consumer expenditure survey data. Rev. Econ. Stat. 89 (3), 552–565. ISSN 0034-6535, 1530-9142. http://www.jstor.org/stable/40043048.
Fernández-Villaverde, J., Krueger, D., 2011. Consumption and saving over the life cycle: how important are consumer durables? Macroecon. Dyn. 15, 725–770. http://dx.doi.org/10.1017/S1365100510000180. ISSN 1469-8056.
Fogli, A., Veldkamp, L., 2011. Nature or nurture? Learning and the geography of female labor force participation. Econometrica 79 (4), 1103–1138.
Galí, J., Gambetti, L., 2009. On the sources of the great moderation. Am. Econ. J. Macroecon. 1 (1), 26–57.
Galor, O., Moav, O., 2006. Das Human-Kapital: a theory of the demise of the class structure. Rev. Econ. Stud. 73 (1), 85–117.
Galor, O., Weil, D.N., 1996. The gender gap, fertility, and growth. Am. Econ. Rev. 86 (3), 374–387.
Galor, O., Weil, D.N., 2000. Population, technology, and growth: from malthusian stagnation to the demographic transition and beyond. Am. Econ. Rev. 90 (4), 806–828.
Geddes, R., Lueck, D., 2002. The gains from self-ownership and the expansion of women's rights. Am. Econ. Rev. 92 (4), 1079–1092.
Goldin, C., 1990. Understanding the Gender Gap: An Economic History of American Women. Oxford University Press, Oxford.
Goldin, C., 1995. The u-shaped female labor force function in economic development and economic history. In: Schultz, T.P. (Ed.), Investment in Women's Human Capital and Economic Development. University of Chicago Press, Chicago, IL, USA, pp. 61–90.
Goldin, C., Olivetti, C., 2013. Shocking labor supply: a reassessment of the role of world war ii on women's labor supply. Am. Econ. Rev. 103 (3), 257–262. http://dx.doi.org/10.1257/aer.103.3.257.
Goldstein, M., Udry, C., 2008. The profits of power: land rights and agricultural investment in ghana. J. Polit. Econ. 116 (6), 981–1022.
Golosov, M., Tsyvinski, A., Werning, I., 2006. New dynamic public finance: a user's guide. In: Acemoglu, D., Rogoff, K., Woodford, M. (Eds.), NBER Macroeconomic Annual, vol. 21. MIT Press, Cambridge, MA, USA, pp. 317–388.
Golosov, M., Jones, L.E., Tertilt, M., 2007. Efficiency with endogenous population growth. Econometrica 75 (4), 1039–1071.
Gould, E., Moav, O., Simhon, A., 2008. The mystery of monogamy. Am. Econ. Rev. 98 (1), 333–357.
Greenwood, J., Hercowitz, Z., 1991. The allocation of capital and time over the business cycle. J. Polit. Econ. 99 (4), 1188–1214.
Greenwood, J., Seshadri, A., 2002. The U.S. demographic transition. Am. Econ. Rev. 92 (2), 153–159.
Greenwood, J., Rogerson, R., Wright, R., 1995. Household production in real business cycle theory. In: Cooley, T.F. (Ed.), Frontiers of Real Business Cycle Theory. Princeton University Press, Princeton.
Greenwood, J., Seshadri, A., Vandenbroucke, G., 2005a. The baby boom and baby bust. Am. Econ. Rev. 95 (1), 183–207.
Greenwood, J., Seshadri, A., Yorukoglu, M., 2005b. Engines of liberation. Rev. Econ. Stud. 72 (1), 109–133.
Greenwood, J., Guner, N., Kocharkov, G., Santos, C., 2014. Marry your like: assortative mating and income inequality. Am. Econ. Rev. 104 (5), 348–353.
Greenwood, J., Guner, N., Kocharkov, G., Santos, C., 2016a. Technology and the changing family: a unified model of marriage, divorce, educational attainment and married female labor-force participation. Am. Econ. J. Macroecon. 8 (1), 1–41.
Greenwood, J., Guner, N., Vandenbroucke, G., 2016b. Family economics writ large. J. Econ. Liter., forthcoming.
Groshen, E.L., Potter, S., 2003. Has structural change contributed to a jobless recovery? Curr. Issues Econ. Finan. Fed. Reserv. Bank N. Y. 9 (8), 1–7.
Guidolin, M., Jeunesse, E.A.L., 2007. The decline in the U.S. personal saving rate: is it real or is it a puzzle? Fed. Reserv. Bank St. Louis Rev. 89 (6), 491–514.

Guler, B., Guvenen, F., Violante, G., 2012. Joint-search theory: new opportunities and new frictions. J. Monetary Econ. 59 (4), 352–369.

Guner, N., Kaygusuz, R., Ventura, G., 2012a. Taxation and household labour supply. Rev. Econ. Stud. 79, 1113–1149.

Guner, N., Kaygusuz, R., Ventura, G., 2012b. Taxing women: a macroeconomic analysis. J. Monetary Econ. 59 (1), 111–128. http://dx.doi.org/10.1016/j.jmoneco.2011.10.004. http://www.sciencedirect.com/science/article/pii/S0304393211001036ISSN 0304-3932.

Guner, N., Kaygusuz, R., Ventura, G., 2014. Childcare subsidies and household labor supply. Unpublished Manuscript, University of Arizona.

Guvenen, F., Rendall, M., 2015. Women's emancipation through education: a macroeconomic analysis. Rev. Econ. Dyn. 18 (4), 931–956.

Guvenen, F., Kaplan, G., Song, J., 2014. The glass ceiling and the paper floor: gender differences among top earners, 1981–2012. NBER Working Paper No. 20560.

Hansen, G.D., Prescott, E.C., 2002. Malthus to solow. Am. Econ. Rev. 92 (4), 1205–1217.

Hazan, M., Zoabi, H., 2015a. Do highly educated women choose smaller families? Econ. J. 125 (587), 1191–1226.

Hazan, M., Zoabi, H., 2015b. Sons or daughters? Sex preferences and the reversal of the gender educational gap. J. Demograph. Econ. 81 (2), 179–201.

Hazan, M., Zoabi, H., 2006. Does longevity cause growth? A theoretical critique. J. Econ. Growth 11 (4), 363–376. http://www.jstor.org/stable/40216110. ISSN 1381-4338, 1573-7020.

Heathcote, J., Storesletten, K., Violante, G.L., 2009. Quantitative macroeconomics with heterogeneous households. Ann. Rev. Econ. 1 (1), 319–354. http://dx.doi.org/10.1146/annurev.economics.050708.142922.

Heathcote, J., Perri, F., Violante, G.L., 2010a. Unequal we stand: an empirical analysis of economic inequality in the United States, 1967–2006. Rev. Econ. Dyn. 13 (1), 15–51.

Heathcote, J., Storesletten, K., Violante, G.L., 2010b. The macroeconomic implications of rising wage inequality in the united states. J. Polit. Econ. 118 (4), 681–722.

Heckman, J.J., 2008. Schools, skills, and synapses. Econ. Inquiry 46 (3), 289–324.

Heim, B.T., 2007. The incredible shrinking elasticities: married female labor supply, 1978–2002. J. Hum. Resour. 42 (4), 881–918. http://www.jstor.org/stable/40057333. 0022-166X.

Hoel, J.B., 2015. Heterogeneous households: a within-subject test of asymmetric information between spouses in Kenya. J. Econ. Behav. Org. 118, 123–135.

Hong, J.H., Rios-Rull, J.V., 2012. Life insurance and household consumption. Am. Econ. Rev. 102 (7), 3701–3730.

Hsieh, C.T., Hurst, E., Jones, C.I., Klenow, P.J., 2013. The allocation of talent and U.S. economic growth. Unpublished Manuscript, Stanford University.

Humphries, J., Weisdorf, J., 2015. The wages of women in England, 1260–1850. J. Econ. Hist. 75 (2), 405–447.

Hyslop, D.R., 2001. Rising U.S. earnings inequality and family labor supply: the covariance structure of intrafamily earnings. Am. Econ. Rev. 91 (4), 755–777. http://dx.doi.org/10.1257/aer.91.4.755.

Iyigun, M., Walsh, R.P., 2007a. Building the family nest: premarital investments, marriage markets, and spousal allocations. Rev. Econ. Stud. 74 (2), 507–535.

Iyigun, M., Walsh, R.P., 2007b. Endogenous gender power, household labor supply, and the quantity-quality tradeoff. J. Dev. Econ. 82 (1), 138–155.

Jaimovich, N., Siu, H.E., 2009. The young, the old, and the restless: demographic and business cycle volatility. Am. Econ. Rev. 99 (3), 804–826.

Jaimovich, N., Siu, H.E., 2014. The trend is the cycle: job polarization and jobless recoveries. Unpublished Manuscript, USC.

Jaimovich, N., Pruitt, S., Siu, H.E., 2013. The demand for youth: explaining age differences in the volatility of hours. Am. Econ. Rev. 103 (7), 3022–3044.

Jayachandran, S., Kuziemko, I., 2011. Why do mothers breastfeed girls less than boys: evidence and implications for child health in India. Q. J. Econ. 126 (3), 1485–1538.

Jones, L.E., Schoonbroodt, A., 2015. Baby busts and baby booms: the fertility response to shocks in dynastic models. Unpublished Manuscript, University of Minnesota.

Jones, L.E., Tertilt, M., 2008. An economic history of the relationship between occupation and fertility—U.S. 1826–1960. In: Rupert, P. (Ed.), Frontiers of Family Economics, vol. 1. Emerald Group Publishing Limited, Bingley, UK.

Jones, L.E., Manuelli, R.E., McGrattan, E.R., 2015. Why are married women working so much? J. Demograph. Econ. 81 (1), 75–114.

Juhn, C., Potter, S., 2007. Is there still an added-worker effect? Federal Reserve Bank of New York Staff Report 310.

Kaplan, G., 2012. Moving back home: insurance against labor market risk. J. Polit. Econ. 120 (3), 446–512.

Karaivanov, A., Townsend, R.M., 2014. Dynamic financial constraints: distinguishing mechanism design from exogenously incomplete regimes. Econometrica 82 (3), 887–959. http://dx.doi.org/10.3982/ECTA9126. ISSN 1468-0262.

Keane, M., Rogerson, R., 2012. Micro and macro labor supply elasticities: a reassessment of conventional wisdom. J. Econ. Liter. 50 (2), 464–476.

Kinnan, C., 2014, December. Distinguishing barriers to insurance in Thai villages. Unpublished Manuscript, Northwestern University.

Knowles, J.A., 2013. Why are married men working so much? An aggregate analysis of intra-household bargaining and labour supply. Rev. Econ. Stud. 80 (3), 1055–1085. http://dx.doi.org/10.1093/restud/rds043. http://restud.oxfordjournals.org/content/80/3/1055.abstract.

Konrad, K.A., Lommerud, K.E., 1995. Family policy with non-cooperative families. Scand. J. Econ. 97 (4), 581–601.

Lagerlöf, N.P., 2003. Gender equality and long-run growth. J. Econ. Growth 8 (4), 403–426.

Lagerlöf, N.P., 2005. Sex, equality, and growth. Can. J. Econ. 38 (3), 807–831.

Lagerlöf, N.P., 2010. Pacifying monogamy. J. Econ. Growth 15 (3), 235–262.

Lee, M., 2015. Allocation of female talent and cross-country productivity differences. Unpublished Manuscript, University of Chicago.

Lee, T., Seshadri, A., 2015. On the intergenerational transmission of economic status. Unpublished Manuscript, University of Mannheim.

Liao, P.J., 2013. The one-child policy: a macroeconomic analysis. J. Dev. Econ. 101, 49–62.

Lise, J., Seitz, S., 2011. Consumption inequality and intra-household allocations. Rev. Econ. Stud. 78, 328–355.

Lise, J., Yamada, K., 2015. Household sharing and commitment: evidence from panel data on individual expenditures and time use. Unpublished Manuscript, University College London.

Lizzeri, A., Persico, N., 2004. Why did the elites extend the suffrage? Democracy and the scope of government, with an application to Britain's 'age of reform'. Q. J. Econ. 119 (2), 705–763.

Love, D.A., 2010. The effects of marital status and children on savings and portfolio choice. Rev. Finan. Stud. 23 (1), 385–432.

Lucas, R.E., 1988. On the mechanics of economic development. J. Monetary Econ. 22 (1), 3–42.

Lundberg, S., 1985. The added worker effect. J. Labor Econ. 3 (1), 11–37. http://www.jstor.org/stable/2535048. ISSN 0734-306X, 1537-5307.

Lundberg, S., Pollak, R.A., 1993. Separate spheres bargaining and the marriage market. J. Polit. Econ. 101 (6), 988–1010. http://www.jstor.org/stable/2138569. ISSN 0022-3808.

Lundberg, S., Pollak, R.A., 1994. Noncooperative bargaining models of marriage. Am. Econ. Rev. 84 (2), 132–137.http://www.jstor.org/stable/2138558ISSN 0895-3309.

Mammen, K., Paxson, C., 2000. Women's work and economic development. J. Econ. Perspect. 14 (4), 141–164.

Mankart, J., Oikonomou, R., 2015. Household search and the aggregate labor market. Unpublished Manuscript, UC Louvain.

Manser, M., Brown, M., 1980. Marriage and household decision-making: a bargaining analysis. Int. Econ. Rev. 21 (1), 31–44. http://www.jstor.org/stable/2526238. ISSN 0020-6598.

Manuelli, R., Seshadri, A., 2009. Explaining international fertility differences. Q. J. Econ. 124 (2), 771–807.

Mazzocco, M., 2007. Household intertemporal behaviour: A collective characterization and a test of commitment. Rev. Econ. Stud. 74 (3), 857–895. http://search.ebscohost.com/login.aspx?direct=true&db=bth&AN=25378400&site=ehost-live. ISSN 0034-6527.

Mazzocco, M., 2008. Individual rather than household euler equations: identification and estimation of individual preferences using household data. Unpublished Manuscript, UCLA.

Mazzocco, M., Ruiz, C., Yamaguchi, S., 2013. Labor supply, wealth dynamics, and marriage decisions. Unpublished Manuscript, UCLA.

McElroy, M.B., Horney, M.J., 1981. Nash-bargained household decisions: toward a generalization of the theory of demand. Int. Econ. Rev. 22 (2), 333–349. http://www.jstor.org/stable/2526280. ISSN 0020-6598.

Mennuni, A., 2015. Labour force composition and aggregate fluctuations. Unpublished Manuscript, University of Southampton.

Miles, D., 1999. Modelling the impact of demographic change upon the economy. Econ. J. 109 (452), 1–36. http://www.jstor.org/stable/2565892. ISSN 0013-0133, 1468-0297.

Miller, A.R., 2011. The effects of motherhood timing on career path. J. Popul. Econ. 24 (3), 1071–1100.

Ngai, L.R., Petrongolo, B., 2014. Gender gaps and the rise of the service economy. IZA Discussion Paper No. 8134.

Olivetti, C., 2014. The female labor force and long-run development: the American experience in comparative perspective. In: Boustan, L.P., Frydman, C., Margo, R.A. (Eds.), Human Capital in History: The American Record. University of Chicago Press, Chicago, IL, USA.

Olivetti, C., Petrongolo, B., 2016. The evolution of gender gaps in industrialized countries. Annu. Rev. Econ., 8, forthcoming.

Ortigueira, S., Siassi, N., 2013. How important is intra-household risk sharing for savings and labor supply? J. Monetary Econ. 60 (6), 650–666.

Oswald, A.J., Powdthavee, N., 2010. Daughters and left-wing voting. Rev. Econ. Stat. 92 (2), 213–227.

Pistaferri, L., 2003. Anticipated and unanticipated wage changes, wage risk, and intertemporal labor supply. J. Labor Econ. 21 (3), 729–754.

Rendall, M., 2010. Brain versus brawn: the realization of womens comparative advantage. Unpublished Manuscript, University of Zurich.

Rendall, M., 2015. Female market work, tax regimes, and the rise of the service sector. Unpublished Manuscript, University of Zurich.

Restuccia, D., Urrutia, C., 2004. Intergenerational persistence of earnings: the role of early and college education. Am. Econ. Rev. 94 (5), 1354–1378.

Ríos-Rull, J.V., 1993. Working in the market, working at home, and the acquisition of skills: a general-equilibrium approach. Am. Econ. Rev. 83 (4), 893–907.

Ríos-Rull, J.V., 1996. Life-cycle economies and aggregate fluctuations. Rev. Econ. Stud. 63 (3), 465–489. http://dx.doi.org/10.2307/2297891.http://restud.oxfordjournals.org/content/63/3/465.abstract.

Ríos-Rull, J.V., 2001. Population changes and capital accumulation: the aging of the baby boom. B.E. J. Macroecon. Adv. Macroecon. 1 (1), Article 7. http://dx.doi.org/10.2307/2297891. http://restud.oxfordjournals.org/content/63/3/465.abstract.

Robinson, J., 2012. Limited insurance within the household: evidence from a field experiment in Kenya. Am. Econ. J. Appl. Econ. 4 (4), 140–164.

Rosenzweig, M.R., Wolpin, K.I., 1980. Testing the quantity-quality fertility model: the use of twins as a natural experiment. Econometrica 48 (1), 227–240.

Ruggles, S., 1994. The transformation of American family structure. Am. Hist. Rev. 99 (1), 103–128.

Salcedo, A., Schoellmann, T., Tertilt, M., 2012. Families as roommates: changes in U.S. household size from 1850 to 2000. Quant. Econ. 3 (1), 133–175.

Schaner, S.G., 2015. Do opposites detract? intrahousehold preference heterogeneity and inefficient strategic savings. Am. Econ. J. Appl. Econ., 7 (2), 135–174.

Scholz, J.K., Seshadri, A., 2009. Children and household wealth. Unpublished Manuscript, University of Wisconsin.

Schoonbroodt, A., 2016. Parental child care during and outside of typical work hours. Rev. Econ. Househ. forthcoming.

Schoonbroodt, A., Tertilt, M., 2014. Property rights and efficiency in OLG models with endogenous fertility. Journal of Economic Theory 150, 551–582.

Shore, S.H., 2010. For better, for worse: intrahousehold risk-sharing over the business cycle. Rev. Econ. Stat. 92 (3), 536–548.

Shore, S.H., 2015. The co-movement of couples incomes. Rev. Econ. Household 13 (3), 569–588.

Soares, R., 2005. Mortality reductions, educational attainment, and fertility choice. Am. Econ. Rev. 95 (3), 580–601.

Song, Z., Storesletten, K., Wang, Y., Zilibotti, F., 2015. Sharing high growth across generations: pensions and demographic transition in China. Am. Econ. J. Macroecon. 7 (2), 1–39.

Tarozzi, A., Mahajan, A., 2007. Child nutrition in India in the nineties. Econ. Dev. Cult. Change 55 (3), 441–486.

Tertilt, M., 2005. Polygyny, fertility, and savings. J. Polit. Econ. 113 (6), 1341–1371.

Townsend, R., 2010. Financial structure and economic welfare: applied general equilibrium development economics. Annu. Rev. Econ. 2 (1), 507–546. http://dx.doi.org/10.1146/annurev.economics.102308.124427.

Udry, C., 1996. Gender, agricultural production, and the theory of the household. J. Polit. Econ. 104 (5), 1010–1046.

Voena, A., 2015. Yours, mine, and ours: do divorce laws affect the intertemporal behavior of married couples? Am. Econ. Rev. 105 (8), 2295–2332.

Vogl, T., 2016. Differential fertility, human capital, and development. Rev. Econ. Stud. 83 (1), 365–401.

Washington, E., 2008. Female socialization: how daughters affect their legislator fathers. Am. Econ. Rev. 98 (1), 311–332.

Wei, S.J., Zhang, X., 2011. The competitive saving motive: evidence from rising sex ratios and savings rates in China. J. Polit. Econ. 119 (3), 511–564.

Yum, M., 2015. Parental time investment and intergenerational mobility. Unpublished Manuscript, University of Mannheim.

CHAPTER 24

Environmental Macroeconomics

J. Hassler[*,†,‡], P. Krusell[*,†,‡,§], A.A. Smith, Jr.[§,¶]
[*]Institute for International Economic Studies (IIES), Stockholm University, Stockholm, Sweden
[†]University of Gothenburg, Gothenburg, Sweden
[‡]CEPR, London, United Kingdom
[§]NBER, Cambridge, MA, United States
[¶]Yale University, New Haven, CT, United States

Contents

Handbook of Macroeconomics, Volume 2B
ISSN 1574-0048, http://dx.doi.org/10.1016/bs.hesmac.2016.04.007

Abstract

We discuss climate change and resource scarcity from the perspective of macroeconomic modeling and quantitative evaluation. Our focus is on climate change: we build a very simple "integrated assessment model," ie, a model that integrates the global economy and the climate in a unified framework. Such a model has three key modules: the climate, the carbon cycle, and the economy. We provide a description of how to build tractable and yet realistic modules of the climate and the carbon cycle. The baseline economic model, then, is static but has a macroeconomic structure, ie, it has the standard features of modern macroeconomic analysis. Thus, it is quantitatively specified and can be calibrated to obtain an approximate social cost of carbon. The static model is then used to illustrate a number of points that have been made in the broad literature on climate change. Our chapter begins, however, with a short discussion of resource scarcity—also from the perspective of standard macroeconomic modeling—offering a dynamic framework of analysis and stating the key challenges. Our last section combines resource scarcity and the integrated assessment setup within a fully dynamic general equilibrium model with uncertainty. That model delivers positive and normative quantitative implications and can be viewed as a platform for macroeconomic analysis of climate change and sustainability issues more broadly.

Keywords

Climate system, Climate change, Carbon cycle, Damages, Growth, Discounting, Externality, Pigou tax

JEL Classification Code

H23, O4, Q01, Q3, Q4, Q54

1. INTRODUCTION

In this chapter we discuss climate change and resource scarcity from the perspective of macroeconomic modeling and quantitative evaluation. Our focus is to build toward an "integrated assessment model," (IAM) ie, a model that integrates the global economy and the climate in a unified framework. The chapter is not meant to be a survey of the rather broad field defined by interconnections between climate and economics. Rather, it has a sharp focus on the use of microeconomics-based macroeconomic models in this area, parameterized to match historical data and used for positive and normative work. Our understanding of the literature is that this approach, which is now standard macroeconomic in analyses (rather broadly defined), has not been dominant in the literature focused on developing IAMs, let alone anywhere else in the climate literature. We consider it a very promising approach also for climate-economy work, however, having contributed to it recently; in fact, the treatment we offer here is naturally built up around some of our own models and substantive contributions. Although there is a risk that this fact will be interpreted as undue marketing of our own work, it is rather that our climate-economy work from the very beginning made an effort precisely to formulate the IAM, and all the issues that can be discussed with an IAM, in terms of a standard macroeconomic settings and in such a way that calibration and model evaluation could be conducted with standard methods. Ex-post, then, one can say that our work grew out of an effort to write something akin to a climate-economy handbook for macroeconomists, even though the kind offer to write an actual such a chapter arrived much later. At this point, with this work, we are simply hopeful that macroeconomists with modern training will find our exposition useful as a quick introduction to a host of issues and perhaps also as inspiration for doing research on climate change and sustainability. We do find the area of great importance and, at the same time, rather undeveloped in many ways.

One exception to our claim that IAMs are not microeconomics-based macroeconomic models is Nordhaus's work, which started in the late 1970s and which led to the industry standards DICE and RIce: dynamic integrated models of climate and the economy, DICE depicting a one-region world and RICE a multiregion world. However, these models remain the nearest thing to the kind of setting we have in mind, and even the DICE and RICE models are closer to pure planning problems. That is, they do not fully specify market structures and, hence, do not allow a full analysis of typical policies such as a carbon tax or a quota system. Most of the models in the literature—to the extent they are fully specified models—are simply planning problems, so a question such as "What happens if we pursue a suboptimal policy?" cannot be addressed. This came as a surprise to us when we began to study the literature. Our subsequent research and the present chapter thus simply reflect this view: some more focus on the approach used in modern macroeconomics is a useful one.

So as a means of abstract introduction, consider a growth economy inhabited by a representative agent with utility function $\sum_{t=0}^{\infty}\beta^t u(C_t, S_t)$ with a resource constraint $C_t + K_{t+1} = (1-\delta)K_t + F(K_t, E_t, S_t)$ and with a law of motion $S_{t+1} = H(S_t, E_t)$. The new variables, relative to a standard macroeconomic setting, are S and E. S, a stock, represents something that is affects utility directly and/or affects production, whereas E, a flow, represents an activity that influences the stock. To a social planner, this would be nothing but an augmented growth model, with (interrelated) Euler equations both for K and S. In fact, standard models of human capital accumulation map into this setup, with H increasing in both arguments and F increasing in S but decreasing in E.[a] However, here we are interested in issues relating to environmental management—from a macroeconomic perspective—and then the same setup can be thought of, at least in abstract, with different labels: we could identify S with, say, clean air or biodiversity, and E with an activity that raises output but lowers the stock S. Our main interest will be in the connections between the economy and the climate. Then, S_t can be thought of as the climate at t, or a key variable that influences it, namely, the stock of carbon in the atmosphere; and E_t would be emissions of carbon dioxide caused by the use of fossil fuel in production. The carbon stock S then hurts both utility (perhaps because a warmer climate makes people suffer more in various ways) and output. Thus, $u_2 < 0$, $F_2 > 0$, $F_3 < 0$, $H_1 > 0$, and $H_2 > 0$. The setting still does not appear fully adequate for looking at the climate issue, because there ought to be another stock: that of the available amounts of fossil fuel (oil, coal, and natural gas), which are depletable resources in finite supply. Indeed, many of our settings below do include such stocks, but as we will argue even the setting without an additional stock is quite useful for analyzing the climate issue.

[a] See, eg, Lucas, 1988.

Furthermore, one would also think that technology, and technological change of different sorts, must play a role, and indeed we agree. Technology can enhance the production possibilities in a neutral manner but also amount to specific forms of innovation aimed at developing nonfossil energy sources or more generally saving on fossil-based energy. We will discuss these issues in the chapter too, including endogenous technology, but the exposition covers a lot of ground and therefore only devotes limited attention to technology endogeneity.

Now so far the abstract setting just described simply describes preferences and technology. So how would markets handle the evolution of the two stocks K and S? The key approach here is that it is reasonable to assume, in the climate case, that the evolution of S is simply a byproduct of economic activity: an externality. Thus, tracing out the difference between an optimal path for K and S and a laissez-faire market path becomes important, as does thinking about what policies could be used to move the market outcome toward the optimum as well as what intermediate cases would imply. Thus, the modern macroeconomist approach would be to (i) define a dynamic competitive equilibrium with policy (say, a unit tax on E), with firms, consumers, and markets clearly spelled out, then (ii) look for insights about optimal policy both qualitatively and quantitatively (based on, say, calibration), and perhaps (iii) characterize outcomes for the future for different (optimal and suboptimal) policy scenarios. This is the overall approach we will follow here.

We proceed in three steps. In the first step, contained in Section 2, we discuss a setting with resource scarcity alone—such as an economy with a limited amount of oil. How will markets then price the resource, and how will it be used up over time? Thus, in this section we touch on the broader area of "sustainability," whereby the question is how the economy manages a set of depletable resources. It appears to be a common view in the public debate that markets do not carry this task out properly, and our view is that it really is an open question whether they do or not; indeed, we find this issue intriguing in itself, quite aside from any interest in the specific area of climate change. The basic market mechanisms we go through involve the Hotelling rule for pricing and then, coupled with a representative agent with preferences defined over time as in our abstract setting above and a specific demand for the resource (say, from its use in production), a dynamic path for resource use. As a preliminary exploration into whether our market-based analysis works, one can compare the models implications for prices and quantities and we briefly do. As a rough summary, it is far from clear that Hotelling-based pricing can explain our past data for depletable resources (like fossil fuel or metals). Similarly, it is challenging to account for the historical patterns of resource use, though here the predictions of the theory are arguably less sharp. Taken together, this suggests that it is not obvious that at least our benchmark theories of markets match the data, so it seems fruitful to at least consider alternatives. In Section 2 we also look at the case of fossil fuel in more detail and, in this context, look at (endogenous) technical change: we look at how markets could potentially react to resource scarcity by saving on the scarce resource instead of saving on other inputs. Thus, we apply the notion of "directed technical change" in this context and propose it as an interesting avenue for conducting further macroeconomic research within the area of sustainability more broadly. Finally, Section 2 should be viewed as a delivering a building block for the IAMs to be discussed later in the chapter, in particular that in Section 5.

In Section 4, we take our second step and develop a very simple, static integrated assessment model of climate change and the global economy. Despite its being simple and stylized, this baseline model does have a macroeconomic structure, ie, it makes assumptions that are standard in modern macroeconomic analysis. Many of its key parameters are therefore straightforwardly calibrated to observables and thus, with the additional calibration necessary to introduce climate into the model, it can be used to obtain an approximate social cost of carbon. The static model is then used to illustrate a number of points that have been made in broad literature on climate change. None of these applications do full justice to the literature, of course, since our main purpose is to introduce the macroeconomic analyst to it. At the same time, we do offer a setting that is quantitatively oriented and one can imagine embedding each application in a fully dynamic and calibrated model; in fact, as far as we are aware, only a (minority) subset of these applications exist as full quantitative studies in the literature.

In our last section, Section 5, which is also the third and final step of the chapter, we describe a fully dynamic, stochastic IAM setting. With it, we show how to derive a robust formula for the (optimal) marginal cost of carbon and, hence, the appropriate Pigou tax. We show how to assign parameter values and compute the size of the optimal tax. The model can also be used as a complete setting for predicting the climate in the future—along with the paths for consumption, output, etc.—for different policy paths. We conclude that although the optimal-tax formula is quite robust, the positive side of the model involves rather strong sensitivity to some parameters, such as those involving different sources for energy generation and, of course, the total sizes of the stocks of fossil fuels.

Before transiting from discussing sustainability in Section 2 to climate modeling in Section 4, we offer a rather comprehensive introduction to the natural-science aspects of climate change. Section 3 is important for explaining what we perceive as the basic and (among expert natural scientists) broadly agreed upon mechanisms behind global warming: how the climate is influenced by the carbon concentration in the atmosphere (the climate model) and how the carbon concentration evolves over time as a function of the time path for emissions (the model of the carbon cycle). This presentation thus offers two "modules" that are crucial elements in IAMs. These modules are extremely simplified versions of what actual climate models and carbon-cycle models in use look like. However, they are, we argue, decent approximations of up-to-date models. The reason why simplifications are necessary is that our economic models have forward-looking agents and it is well known that such models are much more difficult to analyze, given any complexity in the laws of motions of stocks given flows: they involve finding dynamic fixed points, unlike any natural-science model where particles behave mechanically.[b]

Finally, although it should be clear already, let us reiterate that this chapter fails to discuss many environmental issues that are of general as well as macroeconomic interest. For example, the section on sustainability does not discuss, either empirically or theoretically, the possible existence of a "pollution Kuznets curve": the notion that over the course of economic development, pollution (of some or all forms) first increases and then decreases.[c] That section also does not offer any theoretical discussion of other common-pool problems than that associated with our climate (such as overfishing or pollution). The sections on IAMs, moreover, does not contain a listing/discussion of the different such models in the literature; such a treatment would require a full survey in itself.

2. LIMITED NATURAL RESOURCES AND SUSTAINABILITY CONCERNS

Climate change is a leading example within environmental economics where global macroeconomic analysis is called for. It involves a global externality that arises from the release of carbon dioxide into the atmosphere. This release is a byproduct of our economies' burning of fossil fuel, and it increases the carbon dioxide concentration worldwide and thus causes warming not just where the emission occurs. In two ways, climate change makes contact with the broader area of *sustainability*: it involves two stocks that are important for humans and that are affected by human activity. The first stock is the carbon concentration in the atmosphere. It exerts an influence on the global climate; to the extent warming causes damages on net, it is a stock whose size negatively impacts human welfare. The second stock is that of fossil fuels, ie, coal, oil, and natural gas. These stocks are not harmful per se but thus can be to the extent they are burnt.

More generally, sustainability concerns can be thought of in terms of the existence of stocks in finite supply with two properties: (i) their size is affected by economic activity and (ii) they influence human welfare.[d] Obvious stocks are natural resources in finite supply, and these are often traded in markets. Other stocks are "commons," such as air quality, the atmosphere, oceans, ecosystems, and biodiversity. Furthermore, recently, the term "planetary boundaries" has appeared (Rockström et al., 2009). These boundaries represent other limits that may be exceeded with sufficient economic growth (and therefore, according to the authors, growth should be limited). This specific *Nature* article lists

[b] The statement about the complexity of economic models does not rely on fully rational expectations, which we do assume here, but at least on some amount of forward-looking because any forward-looking will involve a dynamic fixed-point problem.

[c] See, eg, Grossman and Krueger, 1991 and Stokey, 1998.

[d] Relatedly, but less relevant from the perspective taken in this section, there is theoretical work on sustainability, defining, based on a utility-function representation, what the term means: roughly, an allocation is sustainable if the indirect utility function of generation t is not be below that of generation $t-k$.

nine boundaries, among them climate change; the remaining items are (i) stratospheric ozone depletion, (ii) loss of biosphere integrity (biodiversity loss and extinctions), (iii) chemical pollution and the release of novel entities, (iv) ocean acidification, (v) freshwater consumption and the global hydrological cycle, (vi) land system change, (vii) nitrogen and phosphorus flows to the biosphere and oceans, and (viii) atmospheric aerosol loading. Thus, these are other examples of commons.

Aside from in the work on climate change, the macroeconomic literature has had relatively little to say on the effects and management of global stocks. The Club of Rome (that started in the late 1960s) was concerned with population growth and a lack of food and energy. The oil crisis in the 1970s prompted a discussion about the finiteness of oil (see, eg, the 1974 *Review of Economic Studies* issue on this topic), but new discoveries and a rather large fall in the oil price in the 1980s appeared to have eliminated the concern about oil among macroeconomists. Similarly, technology advances in agriculture seemed to make limited food supply less of an issue. Nordhaus (1973, 1974) discussed a limited number of metals in finite supply, along with their prices, and concluded that the available stocks were so large at that point that there was no cause for alarm in the near to medium-run future. Thus, the concerns of these decades did not have a long-lasting impact on macroeconomics. Perhaps relatedly, so-called green accounting, where the idea is to measure the relevant stocks and count their increases or decreases as part of an extended notion of national economic product, was proposed but has been implemented and used in relatively few countries.[e] Limited resources and sustainability are typically not even mentioned in introductory or intermediate undergraduate textbooks in macroeconomics, let alone in PhD texts. In PhD texts specifically on growth, there is also very little: Aghion and Howitt's (2008) growth book has a very short, theoretical chapter on the subject, Jones (2001) has a chapter in his growth book which mentions some data; Acemoglu's (2009) growth book has nothing.[f]

The purpose here is not to review the literature but to point to this broad area as one of at least potential relevance and as one where we think that more macroeconomic research could be productive. To this end, we will discuss the basic theory and its confrontation with data. This discussion will lay bare some challenges and illustrate the need for more work.

We will focus on finite resources that are traded in markets and hence abstract from commons, mainly because these have not been subject to much economic macroeconomic analysis (with the exception of the atmosphere and climate change, which we will

[e] For example, in the United States, the BEA started such an endeavor in the 1990s but it was discontinued.

[f] The area of *ecological economics* is arguably further removed from standard economic analysis and certainly from macroeconomics. It is concerned precisely with limited resources but appears, at least in some of its versions, to have close connections Marx's labor theory of value, but with "labor" replaced by "limited resources" more broadly and, in specific cases, "energy" or "fossil fuel".

discuss in detail later). Thus, our discussion begins with price formation and quantity determination in markets for finite resources and then moves on to briefly discuss endogenous technological change in the form of resource saving.

2.1 Prices and Quantities in Markets for Finite Resources

To begin with, let us consider the simplest of all cases: a resource e in finite supply R that is costless to extract and that has economic value. Let us suppose the economic value is given by an inverse demand function $p_t = D(e_t)$, which we assume is time-invariant and negatively sloped. In a macroeconomic context we can derive such a function assuming, say, that e is an input into production. Abstracting from capital formation, suppose $y_t = F(n_t, e_t) = An_t^{1-\nu}e_t^{\nu}$, with inelastic labor supply $n_t = 1$, that $c_t = y_t$, and that utility is $\sum_{t=0}^{\infty}\beta^t \log c_t$.[g] Let time be $t = 0, \ldots, T$, with T possibly infinite. Here, the demand function would be derived from the firm's input decision: $p_t = \nu A e_t^{\nu-1}$.

2.1.1 The Hotelling Result: The Price Equation in a Baseline Case

The key notion now is that the resource can be saved. We assume initially that extraction/use of the resource is costless. The decision to save is therefore a dynamic one: should the resource be sold today or in the future? For a comparison, an interest rate is needed, so let r_t denote the interest rate between $t-1$ and t. If the resource is sold in two consecutive periods, it would then have to be that on the margin, the owner of the resource is indifferent between selling at t and at $t+1$:

$$p_t = \frac{1}{1 + r_{t+1}} p_{t+1}.$$

This is the *Hotelling equation*, presented in Hotelling (1931). The price of the finite resource, thus, grows at the real rate of interest. The equation can also be turned around, using the inverse demand function, to deliver predictions for how the quantity sold will develop; for now, however, let us focus on the price. Thus, we notice that an arbitrage condition delivers a sharp prediction for the dynamics of the price that is independent of the demand. For the *price dynamics*, the demand is only relevant to the extent it may be such that the resource is not demanded at all at some point in time. For the *price level(s)*, however, demand is of course key: one needs to solve the difference equation along with the inverse demand function and the constraint on the resource to arrive at a value for p_0 (and, consequently, all its subsequent values). Here, p_t would be denoted the *Hotelling rent* accruing to the owner: as it is costless to extract it, the price is a pure rent. Thus, to the extent the demand is higher, the price/rent path will be at a higher level. Similarly, if there is more of the resource, the price/rent path will be lower, since more will be used at each point in time.

[g] In all of this section, we use logarithmic utility. More general CRRA preferences would only slightly change the analysis and all the key insights remain the same in this more general case.

2.1.2 Prices and Quantities in Equilibrium: Using a Planning Problem

Let us consider the planning problem implicit in the earlier discussion and let us for simplicity assume that $T=\infty$. Thus the planner would maximize $\nu\sum_{t=0}^{T}\beta^t \log c_t$ subject to $c_t = Ae_t^{\nu}$ for all t and $\sum_{t=0}^{T} e_t = R$.[h] This delivers the condition $\nu\beta^t/e_t=\mu$, where μ is the multiplier on the resource constraint, and hence $e_{t+1}=\beta e_t$. Inserting this into the resource constraint, one obtains $e_0(1+\beta+\ldots)=e_0/(1-\beta)=R$. Hence, $e_0=(1-\beta)R$ and the initial price of the resource in terms of consumption (which can be derived from the decentralization) will be $p_0=A\nu((1-\beta)R)^{\nu-1}$. Furthermore, $p_t=A\nu((1-\beta)R)^{\nu-1}\beta^{(\nu-1)t}$; notice that the gross interest rate here is constant over time and equal to $\beta^{\nu-1}$.[i] We see that a more abundant resource translates into a lower price/rent. In particular, as R goes to infinity, the price approaches 0: marginal cost. Similarly, higher demand (eg, through a higher A or higher weight on future consumption, β, so that the resource is demanded in more periods and will thus not experience as much diminishing returns per period), delivers a higher price/rent. Consider also the extension where the demand parameter A is time varying. Then the extraction path is not affected at all, due to income and substitution effects canceling. The consumption interest rates will change, since the relative price between consumption and the resource must change. The equation for price dynamics applies just as before, however, so price growth is affected only to the extent the interest rate changes. The price level, of course, is also affected by overall demand shifts.

2.1.3 Extraction Costs

More generally, suppose that the marginal cost of extraction of the resource is c_t in period t, and let us for simplicity assume that these marginal costs are exogenous (more generally it would depend on the amount extracted and the total remaining amount of the resource). The Hotelling formula for price dynamics becomes

$$p_t - c_t = \frac{1}{1+r_{t+1}}(p_{t+1} - c_{t+1}).$$

Put differently, the Hotelling rent, which is now the marginal profit per unit, $p-c$, grows at the real rate of interest. This is thus the more general formula that applies. It is robust in a number of ways; eg, allowing endogenous extraction costs delivers the same formula and the consideration of uncertainty reproduces the formula in expectation).[j] The discussion of determinants of prices and quantities above thus still applies, though the

[h] For $\nu=1$ this is a standard cake-eating problem.

[i] The Euler equation of the consumer delivers $1+r_{t+1}=c_{t+1}/(c_t\beta)=e_{t+1}^{\nu}/(e_t^{\nu}\beta)=\beta^{\nu}/\beta=\beta^{\nu-1}$.

[j] The case where the natural resource is owned by a monopolist produces a more complicated formula, as one has to consider marginal revenue instead of price and as the interest rate possibly becomes endogenous. However, the case of monopoly does not appear so relevant, at least not today. In the case of oil, Saudi oil production is currently only about 10% of world production.

key object now becomes the marginal profit per unit. First, the general idea that more of the resource (higher R) lowers the price survives: more of the resource moves the price toward marginal cost, thus gradually eliminating the rent. Second, regarding the effects of costs, let us consider three key cases: one where marginal costs are constant (and positive), one where they are declining, and one where they are increasing. We assume, for simplicity, that there is a constant interest rate. A constant positive marginal cost thus implies that the price is rising at a somewhat lower rate initially than when extraction is costless, since early on the price is a smaller fraction of the rent (early on, there is more left of the resource). If the marginal cost of extraction rises over time—a case that would apply in the absence of technological change if the easy-to-extract sources are exploited first—the price will rise at a higher rate; and under the assumption of a falling marginal extraction cost, typically reflecting productivity improvements in extraction, prices rise more slowly. Quantity paths change accordingly, when we use an invariant demand function. With a faster price rise, quantities fall faster, and vice versa. In particular, when the future promises lower (higher) extraction costs, extraction is postponed (slowed down) and so falls less (more) rapidly.

2.2 Confronting Theory with Data

The Hotelling predictions are, in principle, straightforwardly compared with data. The ambition here is not to review all the empirical work evaluating the Hotelling equation for finite resources but merely to mention some stylized facts and make some general points.[k] As for prices, it is well known that (real) prices of metals fall at a modest rate over the "long run," measured as one hundred years or more; see, eg, Harvey et al. (2010). The prices of fossil fuels (oil, coal, and natural gas) have been stable, with a slight net increase over the last 40 or so years. The volatilities of all these time series are high, on the order of magnitude of those for typical stock-market indices.[l] When it comes to quantities, these time series have been increasing steadily, and with lower fluctuations than displayed by the corresponding prices. Are these observations broadly consistent with Hotelling's theory?

To answer this question, note that Hotelling's theory is mainly an arbitrage-based theory of prices and that quantity predictions involve more assumptions on supply and demand, such as those invoked in our planning problem above. To evaluate Hotelling's rule, we first need to have an idea of the path for extraction costs, as they figure prominently in the more general version of the theory. The situation is somewhat complicated by the fact that extraction occurs on multiple sites. For oil at least, it is also clear that the marginal costs differ greatly between active oil wells, for example with much lower costs in Saudi Arabia than in the North Sea. This in itself appears inefficient, as the less

[k] For excellent discussions, see, eg, Krautkraemer, 1998 and Cuddington and Nülle, 2014.

[l] There are also attempts to identify long-run cycles; see, eg, Erten and Ocampo, 2012.

expensive oil ought to be extracted first in order to minimize overall present-value costs. We know of no study that has good measurements of marginal extraction costs going far back in time. Suppose, however, that productivity growth in the mining/extraction sector was commensurate with that in the rest of our economies. Then it would be reasonable to assume that the *relative* cost of extracting natural resources—and that is the relevant price given that we are referring to evidence on real prices—does not have any sharp movements upward or downward. Hence, the Hotelling formula, given a known total depletable stock of the resource, would imply an increasing price series, at a rate of a few percent per year, with a slightly lower growth rate early on, as explained earlier. This is clearly not what we see. It is, alternatively, possible that extraction costs have developed unevenly. Pindyck (1978) argues, for the case of oil, that lower and lower extraction costs explained a stable price path initially but that later extraction costs stabilized (or even increased), hence pushing prices up. In retrospect, however, although prices rose again in 1979 they did not continue increasing after that and rather fell overall; today, the oil price is back at a real price that is not terribly far from the pre-1973 level.

An proposed explanation for the lack of price growth in the data is a gradual finding of new deposits (of oil, metals, and so on). As explained earlier, the theory does predict lower prices for higher total deposits of the resource. However, it would then have to be that markets systematically underpredicted the successes of new explorations, and over very long periods of time.

Relatedly, it is possible that markets expect technological change in the form of the appearance of close substitutes to the resource in question. Consider a very simple case with a costless-to-extract raw material as in the baseline Hotelling model but where next period a perfect substitute, in infinite supply and with a constant marginal cost $\bar{p}$, appears with some probability. Then the arbitrage equation reads $p_t = \frac{1}{1+r_{t+1}}(\pi_{t+1}p_{t+1} + (1-\pi_{t+1})\bar{p})$, where π_{t+1} is the probability of the perfect substitute appearing. Clearly, such uncertainty and potential price competition will influence price dynamics and will lead to richer predictions. However, we know of no systematic study evaluating a quantitative version of this kind of hypothesis and comparing it to data.

A different view of the prices of natural resources (and commodities more generally) is the Prebisch (1962) and Singer (1950) hypothesis: that commodities have lower demand elasticities, so that when income rises, prices fall. Their hypothesis, thus, is in contrast with Hotelling's rule, since scarcity is abstracted from. Clearly, if one formulated a model with the Prebisch–Singer assumption and scarcity, as discussed earlier, the Hotelling formula would survive, and any demand effects would merely affect the level of the price path and not its dynamics.

In sum, although many authors claim that richer versions of the Hotelling model take its predictions closer to data, it seems safe to say that there is no full resolution of the contrast between the model's prediction of rising prices/profits per unit (at the rate of interest) and the data showing a stable or declining real price of the typical resource.

Some would argue that markets are not fully rational, or not forward-looking enough: the power of the scarcity argument in Hotelling's seminal work is very powerful but relies crucially on forward-looking with a long horizon, to the extent there is a relatively large amount of the resource left in ground. It seems to us that this hypothesis deserves some attention, though it is a challenge even to formulate it.[m]

To evaluate quantities, as underlined earlier, a fuller theory needs to be specified. This leads to challenges as well, as we shall see. Here, we will simply look at an application, albeit a well-known one and one that is relevant to the climate context. In the context of this application, we will also discuss technological change as a means toward saving on a scarce resource.

2.3 An Application: Fossil Energy

On a broad level, when a resource is in scarce supply, a key question is its substitutability with alternative resources. In this section, we look at fossil energy and provide an outline of how one could go about looking at one aspect of scarcity in this market: the response of energy saving, ie, one of the ways in which markets can respond to a shortage. This analysis, like the rest of this chapter (that addresses climate change), is built on a quantitatively oriented macroeconomic model. It can also be regarded as one of the building blocks in the climate-economy model; indeed, the exhaustible-resource formulation in Section 5 coincides with the core formulation entertained here.

The starting point is the extension of basic growth theory to include energy; the standard reference is Dasgupta and Heal (1974), but noteworthy other contributions include those by Solow (1974) and Stiglitz (1974). One of the main concerns here was precisely sustainability, ie, whether production functions (or various sorts) would allow future generations to be as well off as current generations. The Cobb–Douglas function was found to be an in-between case here; with more substitutability between energy and the other inputs, sustainability was possible. This line of work did not much address technical change, neither quantitatively nor theoretically. Clearly, much of the literature on scarce resources was written shortly after the oil-price hikes in the 1970s and it was not until the late 1980s that the theoretical developments allowed technological change to be endogenized in market-based environments.

We build a similar framework to that in Dasgupta and Heal's work and formulate an aggregate production function with three inputs—capital, labor, and fossil energy—and we use it to account for postwar US data. This analysis follows Hassler et al. (2015) closely. We allow technical change in this production function in the form of capital/labor saving and energy saving and we consider three broad issues: (i) what substitution elasticity (between a capital-labor composite, on the one hand, and energy, on the other) fits the data best; (ii) measurement of the series for input saving and to what extent they appear to respond to price movements (ie, does energy-saving appear to respond to the price of fossil fuel?); and (iii) the model's predictions for future input saving and fossil-fuel

[m] See, eg, Spiro (2014).

dependence. The model focuses on energy demand, as derived from an aggregate production function, and all of the discussion can be carried out without modeling supply.

So consider an aggregate production function of the nested CES form

$$y = \left[(1-\nu)\left[Ak^{\alpha}l^{1-\alpha}\right]^{\frac{\varepsilon-1}{\varepsilon}} + \left[A^{e}e\right]^{\frac{\varepsilon-1}{\varepsilon}} \right]^{\frac{\varepsilon}{\varepsilon-1}},$$

with the obvious notation.[n] Here, we see that $\varepsilon \in [0, \infty]$ expresses the substitutability between capital/labor and energy. A is the technology parameter describing capital/labor saving and A^e correspondingly describes energy saving. If there is perfect competition for inputs, firms set the marginal product of each input equal to its price, delivering—expressed in terms of shares—the equations

$$\frac{wl}{y} = (1-\alpha)(1-\gamma)\left[\frac{Ak^{\alpha}l^{1-\alpha}}{y}\right]^{\frac{\varepsilon-1}{\varepsilon}} \tag{1}$$

and

$$\frac{pe}{y} = \gamma\left[\frac{A^{e}e}{y}\right]^{\frac{\varepsilon-1}{\varepsilon}}. \tag{2}$$

2.3.1 Accounting for Input Saving Using US Data

Eqs. (1) and (2) can be rearranged and solved directly for the two technology trends A and A^E. This means that it is possible, as do Hassler et al., to use data on output and inputs and their prices to generate time paths for the input-saving technology series. This is parallel with Solow's growth-accounting exercise, only using a specific functional form. In particular, A^e can be examined over the postwar period, when the price of fossil fuel—oil in particular—has moved around significantly, as shown in Fig. 1.

The authors use this setting and these data to back out series for A^e and A, conditional on a value for ε. With the view that the A and A^e series are technology series mainly, one can then examine the extent to which the backed-out series for different ε look like technology series: are fairly smooth and mostly nondecreasing. It turns out that ε has to be close to zero for the A^e series to look like a technology series at all; if ε is higher than 0.2 or so, the implied up-and-down swings in A^e are too high to be plausible. On the other hand, for a range of ε values between 0 (implying that production is Leontief) and 0.1, the series is rather smooth and looks like it could be a technology series. Fig. 2 plots both the A and A^e series. We see that A^e grows very slowly until prices rise; then it starts

[n] This production function introduces a key elasticity, along with input-specific technology levels, in the most tightly parameterized way. Extensions beyond this functional class, eg, to the translog case, would be interesting not only for further generality but because it would introduce a number of additional technology shifters; see, eg, Berndt and Christensen, 1973.

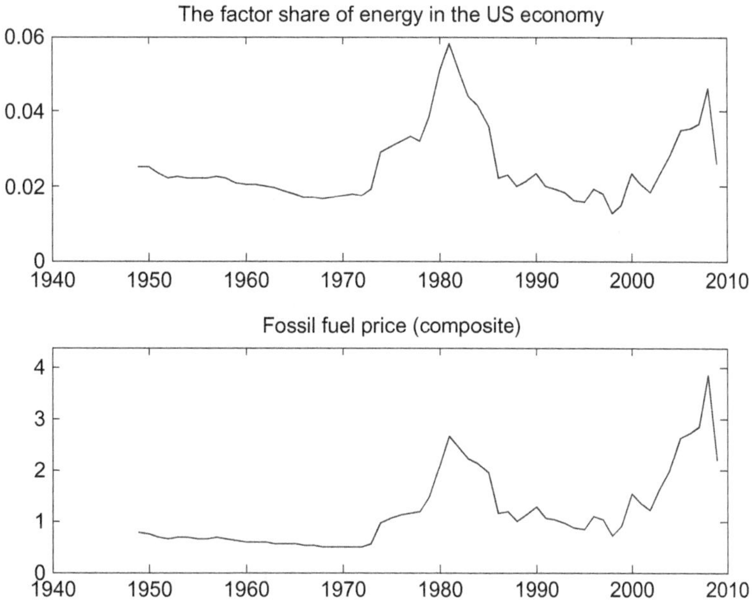

Fig. 1 Fossil energy share and its price.

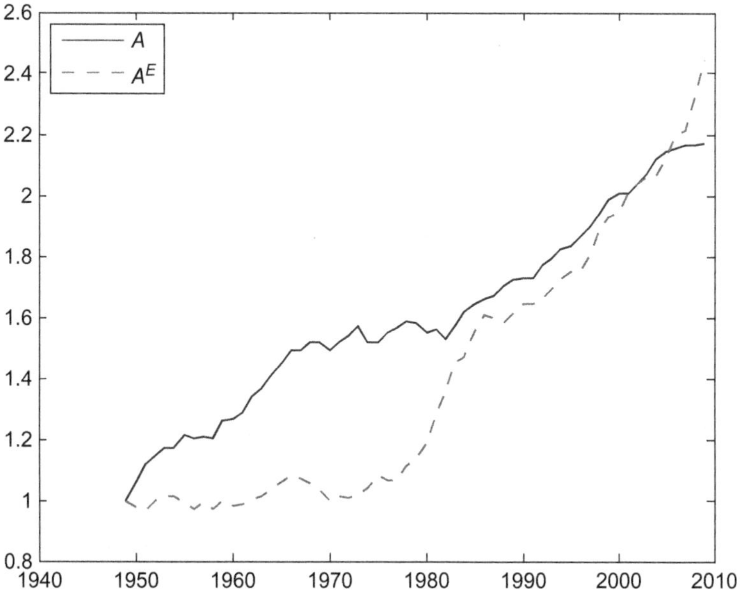

Fig. 2 Energy- and capital/labor-saving technologies compared.

growing significantly. Hence, the figure does suggest that the scarcity mechanism is operative in a quantitatively important way. It is also informative to look at how the two series compare. A it looks like TFP overall, but more importantly it does seem to covary negatively in the medium run with A^e, thus suggesting that the concept of *directed technical change* may be at play. In other words, when the oil price rose, the incentives to save on oil and improve oil efficiency went up, and to the extent these efforts compete for a scarce resource that could alternatively be used for saving on/improving the efficiency of capital and labor, as a result the latter efforts would have fallen.

Hassler et al. (2015) go on to suggest a formal model for this phenomenon and use it, with a calibration of the technology parameters in R&D based on the negative historical association between A and A^E, to also predict the future paths of technology and of energy dependence. We will briefly summarize this research later, but first it is necessary to formulate a quantitatively oriented dynamic macroeconomic model with energy demand and supply included explicitly.

2.3.2 A Positive Model of Energy Supply and Demand with a Finite Resource

Using the simple production function above and logarithmic preferences, it is straightforward to formulate a planner's problem, assuming that energy comes from a finite stock. We will first illustrate with a production function that is in the specified class and that is often used but that does not (as argued earlier) fit the macroeconomic data: the Cobb–Douglas case, where $F(Ak^\alpha, A^e e) = k^\alpha e^\nu$, where a constant labor supply (with a share $1-\alpha-\nu$) is implicit and we have normalized overall TFP including labor to 1. We also assume, to simplify matters, that (i) there is 100% depreciation of capital between periods (which fits a period of, say, 20 years or more) and that (ii) the extraction of energy is costless (which fits oil rather well, as its marginal cost is much lower than its price, at least for much of the available oil). For now, we abstract from technological change; we will revisit it later. Thus, the planner would maximize

$$\sum_{t=0}^{\infty} \log c_t$$

subject to

$$c_t + k_{t+1} = k_t^\alpha e_t^\nu$$

and $\sum_{t=0}^{\infty} e_t = R$, with R being the total available stock. It is straightforward to verify that we obtain a closed-form solution here: consumption is a constant fraction $1-\alpha\beta$ of output and $e_t = (1-\beta)\beta^t R$, ie, energy use falls at the rate of discount. As energy falls, so does capital, consumption, and output. In fact, this model asymptotically delivers balanced (negative) growth at a gross rate g satisfying (from the resource constraint) $g = g^\alpha \beta^\nu = \beta^{\frac{\nu}{1-\alpha}}$. Capital is not on the balanced path at all times, unless its initial value is in the proper relation to initial energy use.[o] This model of course also generates the Hotelling result: p_{t+1} must equal $p_t(1 + r_{t+1})$, where $1 + r$ is the marginal product of capital and $1 + r$ hence the gross real interest rate. Notice, thus, that the interest rate will be constant on the balanced growth path but that it obeys transition dynamics. Hence, even though energy use falls at a constant rate at all times, the energy price will not grow at a constant rate at all times (unless the initial capital stock is at its balanced-growth level): it will grow either faster or slower. Consumption, along with output and capital, goes to zero here along a balanced growth path, but when there is sufficient growth in technology (which is easily added in the model), there will be positive balanced growth. The striking fall in energy use over time would of course be mitigated by an assumption that marginal extraction costs are positive and decreasing over time, as discussed earlier, but it is not obvious that such an assumption is warranted.

Fig. 3, which is borrowed from Hassler et al. (2015), shows that, in the data, energy (defined as a fossil composite) rises significantly over time. In contrast, as we have just shown, the simple Cobb–Douglas model predicts falling energy use, at a rate equaling the discount rate. Suppose instead one adopts the model Hassler et al. (2015) argue fit the data better, ie, a function that is near Leontief in k^α and e. Let us first assume that the technology coefficients A and A^e are constant over time. Then, there will be transition

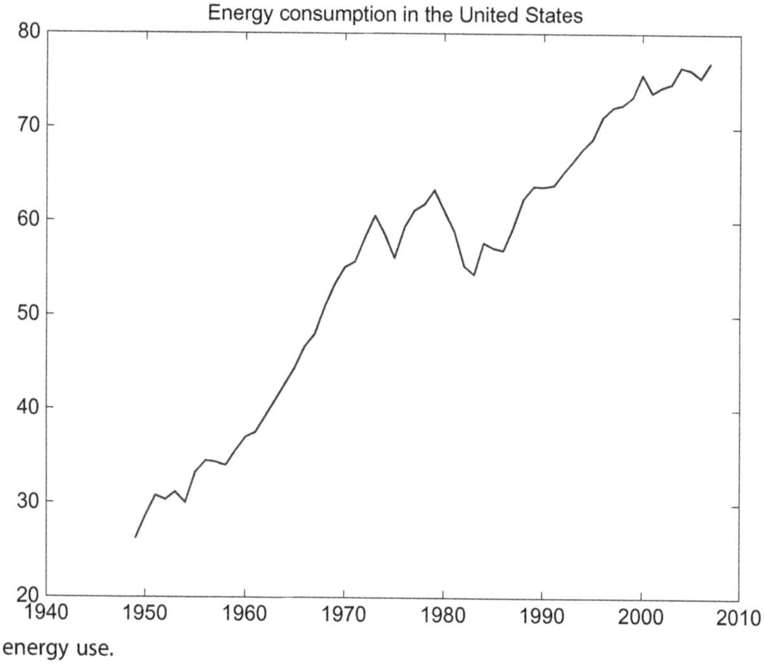

Fig. 3 US energy use.

[o] Initial capital then has to equal $(\alpha(R(1-\beta))^\nu)^{\frac{1}{1-\alpha}}\beta^{\frac{1-\alpha-\nu}{1-\alpha}}$.

dynamics in energy use, for Ak^{α} has to equal $A^e e$ at all points in time. Thus, the initial value of capital and R may not admit balanced growth in e at all times, given A and A^e. Intuitively, if Ak_0^{α} is too low, e will be held back initially and grow over time as capital catches up to its balanced path. Thus, it is possible to obtain an increasing path for energy use over a period of time. Eventually, of course, energy use has to fall. There is no exact balanced growth path in this case. Instead, the saving rate has to go to zero since any positive long-run saving rate would imply a positive capital stock.[p] Hence, the asymptotic economy will be like one without capital and in this sense behave like in a cake-eating problem: consumption and energy will fall at rate β. In sum, this model can deliver *peak oil*, ie, a path for oil use with a maximum later than at time 0. As already pointed out, increasing oil use can also be produced from other assumptions, such as a decreasing sequence of marginal extraction costs for oil; these explanations are complementary.

With exogenous technology growth in A and A^e it is possible that very different long-run extraction behavior results.[q] In particular, it appears that a balanced growth path with the property that $g_A g^{\alpha} = g_{A^e} g_e = g$ is at least feasible. Here, the first equality follows from the two arguments of the production function growing at the same rate—given that the production function F is homogeneous of degree one in the two arguments Ak^{α} and $A^e e$—and the second equality says that output and capital have to grow at that same rate. Clearly, if the planner chooses such asymptotic behavior, g_e can be solved for from the two equations to equal $g_A^{\frac{1}{1-\alpha}}/g_{A^e}$, a number that of course needs to be less than 1. Thus, in such a case, g_e will not generally equal β. A more general study of these cases is beyond the scope of the present chapter.

2.3.3 Endogenous Energy-Saving Technical Change

Given the backed-out series for A and A^e, which showed negative covariation in the medium run, let us consider the model of technology choice Hassler et al. (2015) propose. In it, there is an explicit tradeoff between raising A and raising A^e. Such a tradeoff arguably offers one of the economy's key behavioral responses to scarcity. That is, growth in A^e can be thought of as energy-saving technological change. In line with the authors' treatment, we consider a setup with directed technological change in the form of a planning problem, thus interpreting the outcome as one where the government has used policy optimally to internalize any spillovers in the research sector. It would be straightforward, along the lines of the endogenous-growth literature following Romer (1990), to consider market mechanisms based on variety expansion or quality improvements,

[p] If the saving rate asymptotically stayed above $s > 0$, then $k_{t+1} \geq s\, Ak_t^{\alpha}$. This would imply that capital would remain uniformly bounded below from zero. However, here, it does have to go to zero as its complement energy has to go to zero.

[q] An exception is the Cobb–Douglas case for which it is easy to show that the result above generalizes: e falls at rate β.

monopoly power, possibly with Schumpeterian elements, and an explicit market sector for R&D. Such an analysis would be interesting and would allow interesting policy questions to be analyzed. For example, is the market mechanism not allowing enough technical change in response to scarcity, and does the answer depend on whether there are also other market failures such as a climate externality? We leave these interesting questions for future research and merely focus here on efficient outcomes. The key mechanism we build in rests on the following simple structure: we introduce one resource, a measure one of "researchers." Researchers can direct their efforts to the advancement of A and A^e. We look at a very simple formulation:

$$A_{t+1} = A_t f(n_t) \quad \text{and} \quad A^e_{t+1} = A^e_t f_e(1 - n_t),$$

where $n_t \in [0,1]$ summarizes the R&D choice at time t and where f and f_e are both strictly increasing and strictly concave; these functions thus jointly demarcate the frontier for technologies at $t+1$ given their positions at t. Hence, at a point in time t, A_t and A^e_t are fixed. In the case of a Leontief technology, there would be absolutely no substitutability at all between capital and energy ex-post, ie, at time t when A_t and A^e_t have been chosen, but there is substitutability ex-ante, by varying n_s for $s<t$. With a less extreme production function there would be substitutability ex-post too but less so than ex-ante.[r] Relatedly, whereas the share of income in this economy that accrues to each of the inputs is endogenous and, typically, varies with the state of the economy, on a balanced growth path the share settles down. As we shall see, in fact, the share is determined in a relatively simple manner.

The analysis proceeds by adding these two equations to the above planning problem. Taking first-order conditions and focusing on a balanced-growth outcome, this model rather surprisingly delivers the result that the extraction rate must be equal to β, regardless of the values of all the other primitives.[s] This means, in turn, that two equations jointly determining the long-run growth rates of A and A_e can be derived. One captures the technology tradeoff and follows directly from the equations above stating that these growth rates, respectively, are $g_A = f(n)$ and $g_{A^e} = f^e(1-n)$. The other equation comes from the balanced-growth condition that $A_t k_t^\alpha = A^e_t e_t$, given that F is homogeneous of degree one; from this equality the growth rates of A and A^e are positively related. In fact, given that e_t falls at rate β, we obtain n from $g_A^{\frac{1}{1-\alpha}} = g_{A^e}\beta$.

[r] The Cobb–Douglas case is easy to analyze. It leads to an interior choice for n that is constant over time, regardless of initial conditions and hence looks like the case above where the two technology factors are exogenous.

[s] The proof is straightforward; for details, see Hassler et al. (2015). It is thus the endogeneity of the technology levels in the CES formulation that makes energy fall at rate β; when they grow exogenously, we saw that energy does not have to go to zero at rate β.

One can also show, quite surprisingly as well, that the long run share of energy s_e in output is determined by $(1-s_e)/s_e = -\partial \log g_A/\partial \log g_{A^e}$.[t] In steady state, this expression is a function of n only, and as we saw above it is determined straightforwardly knowing β, α, f, and f^e. How, then, can these primitives be calibrated? One way to proceed is to look at historical data to obtain information about the tradeoff relation between g_A and g_{A^e}. If this relation is approximately log-linear (ie, the net rates are related linearly), the observed slope is all that is needed, since it then gives $\partial \log g_A/\partial \log g_{A^e}$ directly. The postwar behaviors of A and A^e reported above imply a slope of -0.235 and hence a predicted long-run value of s_e of around 0.19, which is significantly above its current value, which is well below 0.1.

2.3.4 Takeaway from the Fossil-Energy Application

The fossil-energy application shows that standard macroeconomic modeling with the inclusion of an exhaustible resource can be used to derive predictions for the time paths for quantities and compare them to data. Moreover, the same kind of framework augmented with endogenous directed technical change can be used to look at optimal/market responses to scarcity. It even appears possible to use historical data reflecting past technological tradeoffs in input saving to make predictions for the future. The presentation here has been very stylized and many important real-world features have largely been abstracted from, such as the nature of extraction technologies over time and space. The focus has also been restricted to the long-run behaviors of the prices and quantities of the resources in limited supply, but there are other striking facts as well, such as the high volatilities in most of these markets. Natural resources in limited supply can become increasingly limiting for economic activity in the future and more macroeconomic research may need to be directed to these issues. Hopefully the analysis herein can give some insights into fruitful avenues for such research.

3. CLIMATE CHANGE: THE NATURAL-SCIENCE BACKGROUND

An economic model of climate change needs to describe three phenomena and their dynamic interactions. These are (i) economic activity; (ii) carbon circulation; and (iii) the climate. From a conceptual as well as a modeling point of view it is convenient to view the three phenomena as distinct sub-subsystems. We begin with a very brief description of the three subsystems and then focus this section on the two latter.

The economy consists of individuals that act as consumers, producers and perhaps as politicians. Their actions are drivers of the economy. In particular, the actions are determinants of emissions and other factors behind climate change. The actions are also

[t] The authors show that this result follows rather generally in the model: utility is allowed to be any power function and production any function with constant returns to scale.

responses to current and expected changes in the climate by adaptation. Specifically, when fossil fuel is burned, carbon dioxide (CO_2) is released and spreads very quickly in the atmosphere. The atmosphere is part of the carbon circulation subsystem where carbon is transported between different reservoirs; the atmosphere is thus one such reservoir. The biosphere (plants, and to a much smaller extent, animals including humans) and the soil are other reservoirs. The oceans constitute the largest carbon reservoir.

The climate is a system that determines the distribution of weather events over time and space and is, in particular, affected by the carbon dioxide concentration in the atmosphere. Due to its molecular structure, carbon dioxide more easily lets through short-wave radiation, like sun-light, than long-wave, infrared radiation. Relative to the energy outflow from earth, the inflow consists of more short-wave radiation. Therefore, an increase in the atmospheric CO_2 concentration affects the difference between energy inflow and outflow. This is the *greenhouse effect.*

It is straightforward to see that we need at minimum the three subsystems to construct a climate-economy model. The economy is needed to model emissions and economic effects of climate change. The carbon circulation model is needed to specify how emissions over time translate into a path of CO_2 concentration. Finally, the climate model is needed to specify the link between the atmospheric CO_2 concentration and the climate.

3.1 The Climate

3.1.1 The Energy Budget

We will now present the simplest possible climate model. As described earlier, the purpose of the climate model is to determine how the (path of) CO_2 concentration determines the (path of the) climate. A minimal description of the climate is the global mean atmospheric temperature near the surface. Thus, at minimum we need a relationship between the path of the CO_2 concentration and the global mean temperature. We start the discussion by describing the *energy budget* concept.

Suppose that the earth is in a radiative steady state where the incoming flow of short-wave radiation from the sun light is equal to the outgoing flow of largely infrared radiation.[u] The energy budget of the earth is then balanced, implying that the earth's heat content and the global mean temperature is constant.[v] Now consider a perturbation of this equilibrium that makes the net inflow positive by an amount F. Such an increase could be caused by an increase in the incoming flow and/or a reduction in the outgoing flow. Regardless of how this is achieved, the earth's energy budget is now in surplus

[u] We neglect the additional outflow due to the nuclear process in the interior of the earth, which is in the order of one to ten thousands in relative terms when compared to the incoming flux from the sun; see the Kam et al. (2011).

[v] We disregard the obvious fact that energy flows vary with latitude and over the year producing differences in temperatures over space and time. Since the outflow of energy is a nonlinear (convex) function of the temperature, the distribution of temperature affects the average outflow.

causing an accumulation of heat in the earth and thus a higher temperature. The speed at which the temperature increases is higher the larger is the difference between the inflow and outflow of energy, ie, the larger the surplus in the energy budget.

As the temperature rises, the outgoing energy flow increases since all else equal, a hotter object radiates more energy. Sometimes this simple mechanism is referred to as the 'Planck feedback'. As an approximation, let this increase be proportional to the increase in temperature over its initial value. Denoting the temperature perturbation relative to the initial steady state at time t by T_t and the proportionality factor between energy flows and temperature by κ, we can summarize these relations in the following equation:

$$\frac{dT_t}{dt} = \sigma(F - \kappa T_t). \tag{3}$$

The left-hand side of the equation is the speed of change of the temperature at time t. The term in parenthesis on the right-hand side is the net energy flow, ie, the difference in incoming and outgoing flows. The equation is labeled the energy budget and we note that it should be thought of as a flow budget with an analogy to how the difference between income and spending determines the speed of change of assets.

When the right-hand side of (3) is positive, the energy budget is in surplus, heat is accumulated, and the temperature increases. Vice versa, if the energy budget has a deficit, heat is lost, and the temperature falls. When discussing climate change, the variable F is typically called *forcing* and it is then defined as the change in the energy budget caused by human activities. The parameter σ is (inversely) related to the heat capacity of the system for which the energy budget is defined and determines how fast the temperature changes for a given imbalance of the energy budget.[w]

We can use Eq. (3) to find how much the temperature needs to rise before the system reaches a new steady state, ie, when the temperature has settled down to a constant. Such an equilibrium requires that the energy budget has become balanced, so that the term in parenthesis in (3) again has become zero. Let the steady-state temperature associated with a forcing F be denoted $T(F)$. At $T(F)$, the temperature is constant, which requires that the energy budget is balanced, ie, that $F - \kappa T(F) = 0$. Thus,

$$T(F) = \frac{F}{\kappa}. \tag{4}$$

Furthermore, the path of the temperature is given by

$$T_t = e^{-\sigma\kappa t}\left(T_0 - \frac{F}{\kappa}\right) + \frac{F}{\kappa}.$$

[w] The heat capacity of the atmosphere is much lower than that of the oceans, an issue we will return to below.

Measuring temperature in Kelvin (K), and F in Watt per square meter, the unit of κ is $\frac{W/m^2}{K}$.[x] If the earth were a blackbody without an atmosphere, we could calculate the exact value of κ from laws of physics. In fact, at the earth's current mean temperature $\frac{1}{\kappa}$ would be approximately 0.3, ie, an increase in forcing by 1 W/m^2 would lead to an increase in the global temperature of 0.3 K (an equal amount in degrees Celsius).[y] In reality, various feedback mechanisms make it difficult to assess the true value of κ. One of the important feedbacks is that a higher temperature increases the concentration of water vapor, which is also is a greenhouse gas; another is that the polar ice sheets melt, which decreases direct reflection of sun light and changes the cloud formation. We will return to this issue below but note that the value of κ is likely to be substantially smaller than the blackbody value of 0.3^{-1}, leading to a higher steady-state temperature for a given forcing.

Now consider how a given concentration of CO_2 determines F. This relationship can be well approximated by a logarithmic function. Thus, F, the change in the energy budget relative to preindustrial times, can be written as a logarithmic function of the increase in CO_2 concentration relative to the preindustrial level or, equivalently, as a logarithmic function of the amount of carbon in the atmosphere relative to the amount in preindustrial times. Let S_t and $\bar{S}$, respectively, denote the current and preindustrial amounts of carbon in the atmosphere. Then, forcing can be well approximated by the following equation.[z]

$$F_t = \frac{\eta}{\log 2} \log\left(\frac{S_t}{\bar{S}}\right). \tag{5}$$

The parameter η has a straightforward interpretation: if the amount of carbon in the atmosphere in period t has doubled relative to preindustrial times, forcing is η. If it quadruples, it is 2η, and so forth. An approximate value for η is 3.7, implying that a doubling of the amount of carbon in the atmosphere leads to a forcing of 3.7 watts per square meter on earth.[aa]

[x] Formally, a flow rate per area unit is denoted flux. However, since we deal with systems with constant areas, flows and fluxes are proportional and the terms are used interchangeably.

[y] See Schwartz et al. (2010) who report that if earth were a blackbody radiator with a temperature of $288K \approx 15°C$, an increase in the temperature of 1.1 K would increase the outflow by 3.7 W/m^2, implying $\kappa^{-1} = 1.1/3.7 \approx 0.3$.

[z] This relation was first demonstrated by the Swedish physicist and chemist and 1903 Nobel Prize winner in Chemistry, Svante Arrhenius. Therefore, the relation is often referred to as the *Arrhenius's Greenhouse Law*. See Arrhenius (1896).

[aa] See Schwartz et al. (2014). The value 3.7 is, however, not undisputed. Otto et al. (2013) use a value of 3.44 in their calculations.

We are now ready to present a relation between the long-run change in the earth's average temperature as a function of the carbon concentration in the atmosphere. Combining Eqs. (4) and (5) we obtain

$$T(F_t) = \frac{\eta}{\kappa} \frac{1}{\log 2} \log\left(\frac{S_t}{\bar{S}}\right). \tag{6}$$

As we can see, a doubling of the carbon concentration in the atmosphere leads to an increase in temperature given by $\frac{\eta}{\kappa}$. Using the Planck feedback, $\eta/\kappa \approx 1.1°C$. This is a modest sensitivity, and as already noted very likely too low an estimate of the overall sensitivity of the global climate due to the existence of positive feedbacks.

A straightforward way of including feedbacks in the energy budget is by adding a term to the energy budget. Suppose initially that feedbacks can be approximated by a linear term xT_t, where x captures the marginal impact on the energy budget due to feedbacks. The energy budget now becomes

$$\frac{dT_t}{dt} = \sigma(F + xT_t - \kappa T_t), \tag{7}$$

where we think of κ as solely determined by the Planck feedback. The steady-state temperature is now given by

$$T(F) = \frac{\eta}{\kappa - x} \frac{1}{\ln 2} \ln\left(\frac{S}{\bar{S}}\right). \tag{8}$$

Since the ratio $\eta/(\kappa - x)$ has such an important interpretation, it is often labeled the*Equilibrium Climate Sensitivity (ECS)* and we will use the notation λ for it.[ab] Some feedbacks are positive but not necessarily all of them; theoretically, we cannot rule out either $x < 0$ or $x \geq \kappa$. In the latter case, the dynamics would be explosive, which appears inconsistent with historical reactions to natural variations in the energy budget. Also $x < 0$ is difficult to reconcile with the observation that relatively small changes in forcing in the earth's history have had substantial impact on the climate. However, within these bands a large degree of uncertainty remains.

According to the IPCC, the ECS is "likely in the range 1.5–4.5°C," "extremely unlikely less than 1°C," and "very unlikely greater than 6° C."[ac] Another concept, taking some account of the shorter run dynamics, is the *Transient Climate Response (TCR)*. This is the defined as the increase in global mean temperature at the time the CO_2 concentration

[ab] Note that equilibrium here refers to the energy budget. For an economist, it might have been more natural to call λ the *steady-state climate sensitivity*.

[ac] See IPCC (2013, page 81 and Technical Summary). The report states that "likely" should be taken to mean a probability of 66–100%, "extremely unlikely" 0–5%, and "very unlikely" 0–10%.

has doubled following a 70-year period of annual increases of 1%.[ad] IPCC et al. (2013b, Box 12.1) states that the TCR is "likely in the range 1°C–2.5°C" and "extremely unlikely greater than 3°C."

3.1.2 Nonlinearities and Uncertainty

It is important to note that the fact that $\frac{1}{\kappa - x}$ is a nonlinear transformation of x has important consequences for how uncertainty about the strength of feedbacks translate into uncertainty about the equilibrium climate sensitivity.[ae] Suppose, for example, that the uncertainty about the strength in the feedback mechanism can be represented by a symmetric triangular density function with mode 2.1 and endpoints at 1.35 and 2.85. This is represented by the upper panel of Fig. 4. The mean, and most likely, value of x translates into a climate sensitivity of 3. However, the implied distribution of climate sensitivities is severely skewed to the right.[af] This is illustrated in the lower panel, where $\frac{\eta}{\kappa - x}$ is plotted with $\eta = 3.7$ and $\kappa = 0.3^{-1}$.

The models have so far assumed linearity. There are obvious arguments in favor of relaxing this linearity. Changes in the albedo due to shrinking ice sheets and abrupt weaking of the Gulf are possible examples.[ag] Such effects could simply be introduced by making x in (7) depend on temperature. This could for example, introduce dynamics with so-called *tipping points*. Suppose, for example, that

$$x = \begin{cases} 2.1 \text{ if } T < 3^{o}C \\ 2.72 \text{ else} \end{cases}$$

Using the same parameters as earlier, this leads to a discontinuity in the climate sensitivity. For CO_2, concentrations below $2 \times \bar{S}$ corresponding to a global mean temperature deviation of 3 degrees, the climate sensitivity is 3. Above that tipping point, the climate sensitivity is 6. The mapping between $\frac{S_t}{\bar{S}}$ and the global mean temperature using Eq. (6) is shown in Fig. 5.

[ad] This is about twice as fast as the current increases in the CO_2 concentration. Over the 5, 10, and 20 year-periods ending in 2014, the average increases in the CO_2 concentration have been 0.54%, 0.54%, and 0.48% per year, respectively. However, note that also other greenhouse gases, in particular methane, affect climate change. For data, see the Global Monitor Division of the Earth System Research Labroratory at the US Department of Commerce.

[ae] The presentation follows Roe and Baker (2007).

[af] The policy implications of the possibility of a very large climate sensitivity is discussed in Weitzman (2011).

[ag] Many state-of-the-art climate models feature regional tipping points; see Drijfhouta et al. (2015) for a list. Currently, there is, however, no consensus on the existence of specific global tipping points at particular threshold levels; see Lenton et al. (2008), Levitan (2013), and IPCC (2013, Technical Summary page 70).

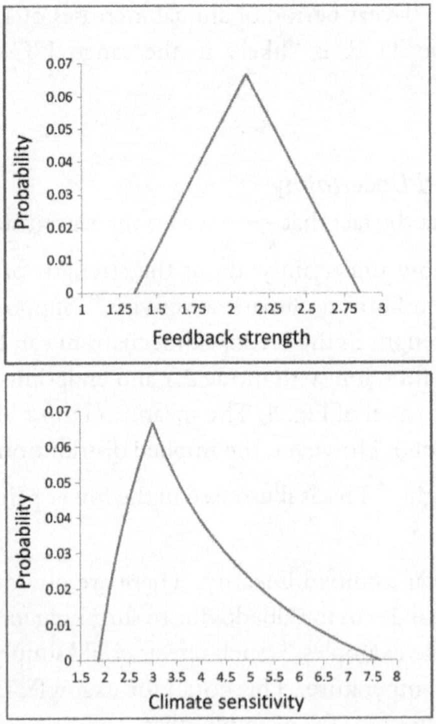

Fig. 4 Example of symmetric uncertainty of feedbacks producing right-skewed climate sensitivity.

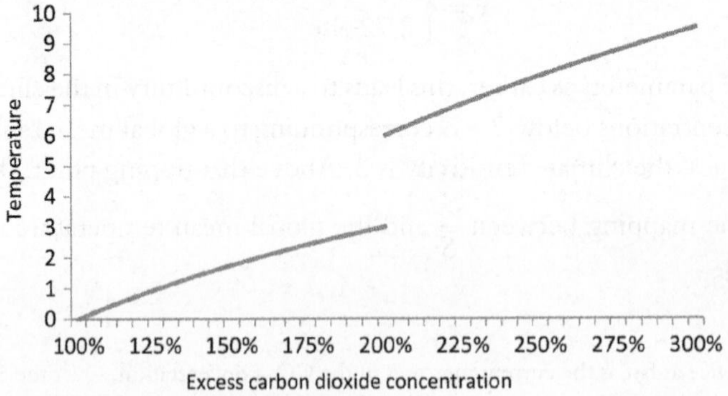

Fig. 5 Tipping point at 3 K due to stronger feedback.

It is also straightforward to introduce irreversibilities, for example by assuming that feedbacks are stronger (higher x) if a state variable like temperature or CO_2 concentration has ever been above some threshold value.

3.1.3 Ocean Drag

We have presented the simplest possible model of how the CO_2 concentration determines climate change. There are of course endless possibilities of extending this simplest framework. An example is to include another energy-budget equation. In Eqs. (3) and (7), we described *laws of motion* for the atmospheric temperature, which heats much faster than the oceans. During the adjustment to a steady state, there will be net energy flows between the ocean and the atmosphere. Let T_t and T_t^L, respectively, denote the atmospheric and ocean temperatures in period t, both measured as deviations from the initial (preindustrial) steady state. With two temperatures, we can define energy budgets separately for the atmosphere and for the oceans. Furthermore, allow for a variation in forcing over time and let F_t denote the forcing at time t. We then arrive at an extended version of Eq. (7) given by

$$\frac{dT_t}{dt} = \sigma_1\left(F_t + xT_t - \kappa T_t - \sigma_2\left(T_t - T_t^L\right)\right). \tag{9}$$

Comparing (9) to (7), we see that the term $\sigma_2\left(T_t - T_t^L\right)$ is added. This term represents a new flow in the energy budget (now defined specifically for the atmosphere), namely the net energy flow from the atmosphere to the ocean. To understand this term, note that if the ocean is cooler than the atmosphere, energy flows from the atmosphere to the ocean. This flow is captured in the energy budget by the term $-\sigma_2\left(T_t - T_t^L\right)$. If $T_t > T_t^L$, this flow has a negative impact on the atmosphere's energy budget and likewise on the rate of change in temperature in the atmosphere (the LHS). The cooler is the ocean relative to the atmosphere, the larger is the negative impact on the energy budget.

To complete this dynamic model, we need to specify how the ocean temperature evolves by using the energy budget of the ocean. If the temperature is higher in the atmosphere than in the oceans, energy will flow to the oceans, thus causing an increase in the ocean temperature. Expressing this as a linear equation delivers

$$\frac{dT_t^L}{dt} = \sigma_3\left(T_t - T_t^L\right). \tag{10}$$

Eqs. (9) and (10) together complete the specification of how the temperatures of the atmosphere and the oceans are affected by a change in forcing.

We can simulate the behavior of the system once we specify the parameters of the system (σ_1, σ_2, σ_3, and κ all positive) and feed in a sequence of forcing levels F_t. Nordhaus and Boyer (2000) use $\sigma_1 = 0.226$, $\sigma_2 = 0.44$, and $\sigma_3 = 0.02$ for a discrete-time version of (9) and (10) defined as the analogous difference equations with a 10-year step. In (6) we show the dynamic response of this model to a constant forcing of $1\,W/m^2$ for $(\kappa - x)^{-1} = 0.81$. The lower curve represents the ocean temperature T_t^L, which increases quite slowly. The middle curve is the atmospheric temperature, T_t, which increases more quickly (Fig. 6).

Clearly, the long-run increase in both temperatures is given by $\frac{1}{\kappa}$ times the increase in forcing, ie, by 0.81°C. Most of the adjustment to the long-run equilibrium is achieved after a few decades for the atmosphere but takes several hundred years for the ocean temperature. Without the dragging effect of the oceans, the temperature increases faster, as

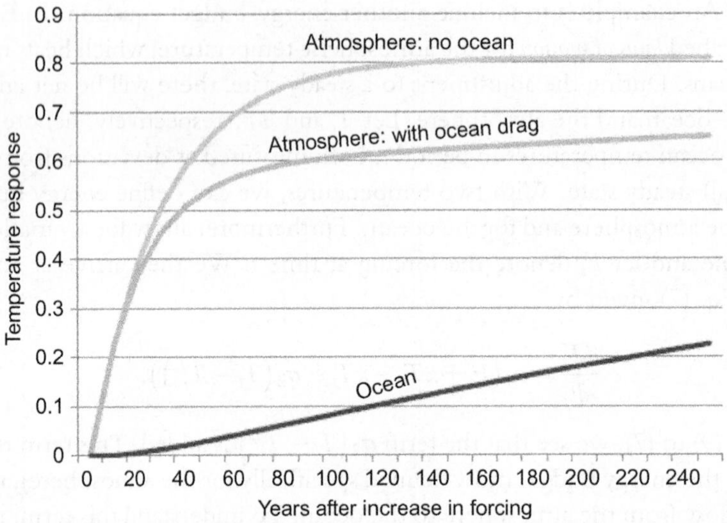

Fig. 6 Increase in atmospheric and ocean temperatures after a permanent forcing of $1 W/m^2$.

shown by the top curve where we have set $\sigma_2 = 0$, which shuts down the effect of the slower warming of the ocean. However, we see that the time until half of the adjustment is achieved is not very different in the two cases.

3.1.4 Global Circulation Models

The climate models discussed so far are extremely limited in scope from the perspective of a climate scientist. In particular, they are based on the concept of an energy budget. Such models are by construction incapable of predicting the large disparity in climates over the world. For this, substantially more complex general circulation models (GCMs) need to be used. Such models are based on the fact that the energy flow to earth is unevenly spread over the globe both over time and space. This leads to movements in air and water that are the drivers of weather events and the climate. These models exist in various degrees of complexity, often with an extremely large number of state variables.[ah]

The complexity of general circulation models make them difficult to use in economics. In contrast to systems without human agents, such models do not contain any forward-looking agents. Thus, causality runs in one time direction only and the evolution of the system does not depend on expectations about the future. Therefore, solving such a complex climate model with a very large set of state variables may pose difficulties—in practice, because they are highly nonlinear and often feature chaotic behavior—but not the kind of difficulties economists face when solving their dynamic models.

[ah] See IPCC (2013, chapter 9) for a list and discussion of GCMs.

One way of modeling a heterogeneous world climate that does not require a combination of a very large state space and forward-looking behavior builds on *statistical downscaling.*[ai] The output of large-scale dynamic circulation models or historical data is then used to derive a *statistical* relation between aggregate and disaggregated variables. This is in contrast to the actual nonlinear high-dimensional models because they do not feature randomness; the model output only looks random due to the nonlinearities. The basic idea in statistical downscaling is thus to treat a small number of state variables as sufficient statistics for a more detailed description of the climate. This works well due in part to the fact that climate change is ultimately driven by a global phenomenon: the disruption of the energy balance due to the release of green house gases, where CO_2 plays the most prominent role.

Let $T_{i,t}$ denote a particular measure of the climate, eg, the yearly average temperature, in region i in period t. We can then estimate a model like

$$\begin{aligned} T_{i,t} &= \bar{T}_i + f(l_i, \psi_1) T_t + z_{i,t} \\ z_{i,t} &= \rho z_{i,t-1} + \nu_{i,t} \\ \text{var}(\nu_{i,t}) &= g(l_i, \psi_2) \\ \text{corr}(\nu_{i,t}, \nu_{j,t}) &= h(d(l_i, l_j), \psi_3). \end{aligned}$$

This very simple system, used for illustration mainly, explains downscaling conceptually. Here, $\bar{T}_i$ is the baseline temperature in region i. f, g, and h are specified functions parameterized by ψ_1, ψ_2, and ψ_3. $z_{i,t}$ is the prediction error and it is assumed to follow an AR(1) process. l_i is some observed characteristic of the region, eg, latitude, and $d(l_i, l_j)$ is a distance measure. Krusell and Smith (2014) estimate such a model on historical data. The upper panel in Fig. 7 shows the estimated function f with l_i denoting latitude. We see that an increase in the global mean temperature T_t has an effect on regional temperature levels that depends strongly on the latitude. The effect of a 1°C increase in the global temperature ranges from 0.25°C to 3.6°C. The lower panel in the figure shows the correlation pattern of prediction errors using d to measure Euclidian distance.

Now consider a dynamic economic model (where agents are forward-looking) with a small enough number of state variables that the model can be solved numerically. With one of these state variables playing the role of global temperature in the above equation system, one can imagine adding a large amount of heterogeneity without losing tractability, so long as the heterogeneous climate outcomes (eg, the realization of the local temperature distribution) do not feed back into global temperature. This is the approach featured in Krusell and Smith (2015), whose model can be viewed as otherwise building directly on the models (static and dynamic) presented in the sections later in this chapter.[aj]

[ai] See IPCC (2013, chapter 9) for a discussion of statistical downscaling.

[aj] Krusell and Smith (2015) actually allow some feedback, through economic variables, from the temperature distribution on global temperature but develop numerical methods that nevertheless allow the model to be solved.

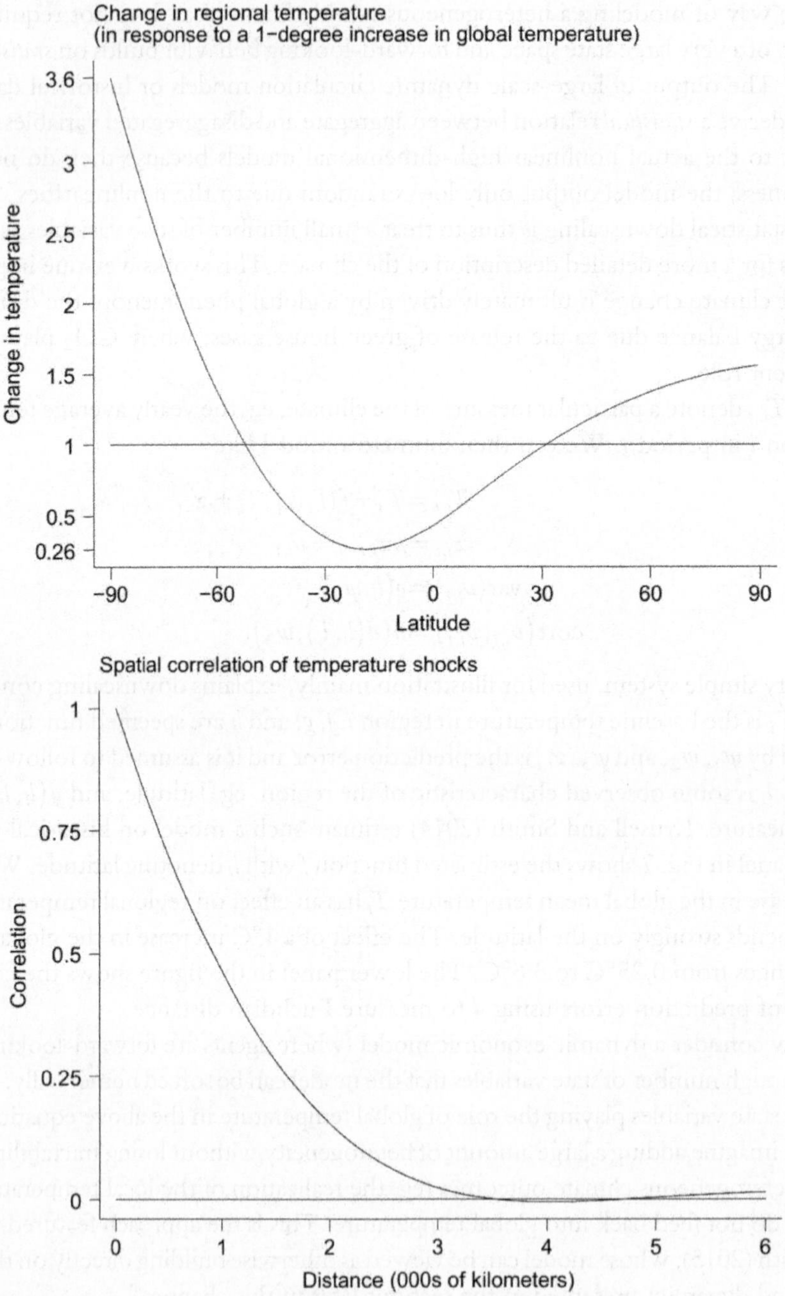

Fig. 7 Statistical downscaling: regional climate responses to global temperature.

3.2 Carbon Circulation

We now turn to carbon circulation (also called the carbon cycle). The purpose of the modeling here is to produce a mapping between emissions of CO_2 and the path of the CO_2 concentration in the atmosphere. The focus on CO_2 is due to the fact that while other gases emitted by human activities, in particular methane, are also important contributors to the greenhouse effect, CO_2 leaves the atmosphere much more slowly. The half-life of methane is on the order of 10 years, while as we will see, a sizeable share of emitted CO_2 remains in the atmosphere for thousands of years.[ak]

3.2.1 Carbon Sinks and Stores

The burning of fossil fuel leads to emissions of carbon dioxide into the atmosphere. The carbon then enters into a circulation system between different global reservoirs of carbon (carbon sinks) of which the atmosphere is one. In Fig. 8, the carbon reservoirs are represented by boxes. The number in black in each box indicates the size of the reservoir in GtC, ie, billions of tons of carbon. As we can see, the biggest reservoir by far is the intermediate/deep ocean, with more than 37,000 GtC. The vegetation and the atmosphere are of about the same size, around 600 GtC, although the uncertainty about the former is substantial. Soils represent a larger stock as does carbon embedded in the permafrost. Black arrows in the figure indicate preindustrial flows between the stocks measured in GtC per year. The flows between the atmosphere and the ocean were almost balanced, implying a constant atmospheric CO_2 concentration.

By transforming carbon dioxide into organic substances, vegetation in the earth's biosphere induces a flow of carbon from the atmosphere to the biosphere. This is the photosynthesis. The reverse process, respiration, is also taking place in plants' fungi, bacteria, and animals. This, together with oxidation, fires, and other physical processes in the soil, leads to the release of carbon in the form of CO_2 to the atmosphere. A similar process is taking place in the sea, where carbon is taken up by phytoplankton through photosynthesis and released back into the surface ocean. When phytoplankton sink into deeper layers they take carbon with them. A small fraction of the carbon that is sinking into the deep oceans is eventually buried in the sediments of the ocean floor, but most of the carbon remains in the circulation system between lower and higher ocean water. Between the atmosphere and the upper ocean, CO_2 is exchanged directly. Carbon dioxide reacts with water and forms dissolved inorganic carbon that is stored in the water. When the CO_2-rich surface water cools down in the winter, it falls to the deeper ocean and a similar exchange occurs in the other direction. From the figure, we also note that there are large flows of carbon between the upper layers of the ocean and the atmosphere via gas exchange. These flows are smaller than, but of the same order of magnitude as, the photosynthesis and respiration.

[ak] Prather et al. (2012) derive a half-life of methane of 9.1 years with a range of uncertainty of 0.9 years.

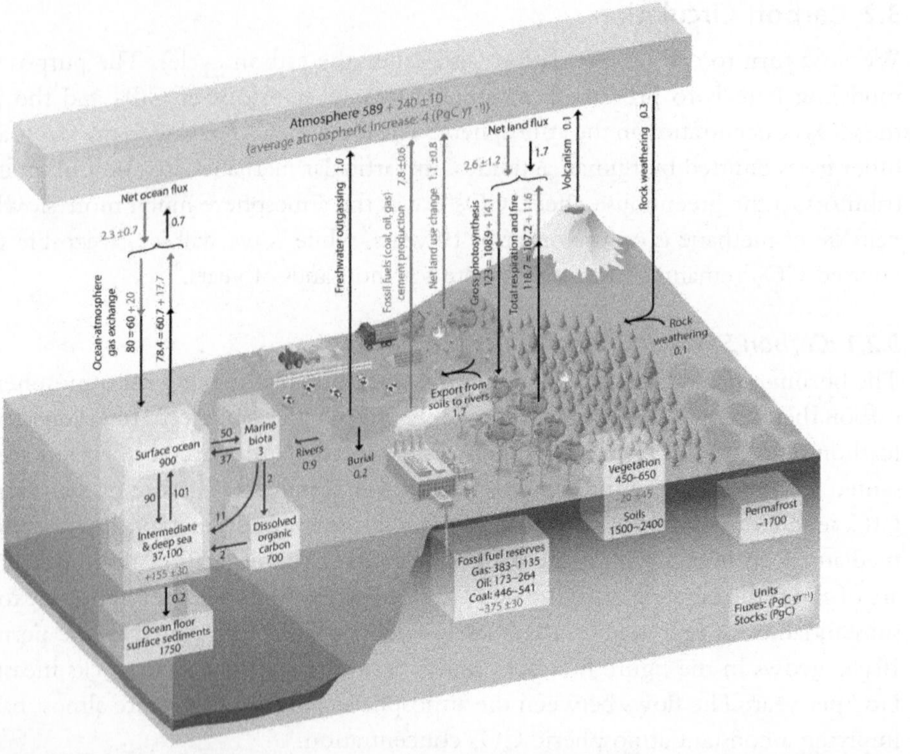

Fig. 8 Global carbon cycle. Stocks in GtC and flows GtC/year. *IPCC, Stocker, T.F., Qin, D., Plattner, G.K., Tignor, M., Allen, S.K., Boschung, J., Nauels, A., Xia, Y., Bex, V., Midgley, P.M., 2013. Climate Change 2013: the Physical Science Basis. Cambridge University Press, Cam- Q16 bridge, UK, fig. 6.1).*

3.2.2 Human Influence on Carbon Circulation

Before the industrial revolution, human influence on carbon circulation was small. However, atmospheric CO_2 concentration started to rise from the mid-18th century and onwards, mainly due to the burning of fossil fuels and deforestation but also as a result of rising cement production.

In Fig. 8, the red figures denote changes in the reservoirs and flows over and above preindustrial values. The figures for reservoirs refer to 2011 while flows are yearly averages during the period 2000–09. At the bottom of the picture, we see that the stock of fossil fuel in the ground has been depleted by 365 ± 30 GtC since the beginning of industrialization. The flow to the atmosphere due to fossil-fuel use and cement production is reported to be 7.8 ± 0.6 GtC per year. In addition, changed land use adds 1.1 ± 0.8 GtC per year to the flow of carbon to the atmosphere. In the other direction, the net flows from the atmosphere to the terrestrial biosphere and to the oceans have increased. All in all, we note that while the fossil reserves have shrunk, the amount of carbon in the atmosphere has gone from close to 600 to around 840 GtC and currently increases at a rate of 4 GtC per year. A sizeable but somewhat smaller increase has taken place in the oceans while the amount of carbon in the vegetation has remained largely constant.

We see that the gross flows of carbon are large relative to the additions due to fossil-fuel burning. Furthermore, the flows may be indirectly affected by climate change, creating feedback mechanism. For example, the ability of the biosphere to store carbon is affected by temperature and precipitation. Similarly, the ability of the oceans to store carbon is affected by the temperature. Deposits of carbon in the soil may also be affected by climate change. We will return to these mechanisms below.

3.2.3 The Reserves of Fossil Fuel

The extent to which burning of fossil fuel is a problem from the perspective of climate change obviously depends on how much fossil fuel remains to (potentially) be burnt. This amount is not known and the available estimates depends on definitions. The amount of fossil resources that eventually can be used depends on estimates of future findings as well as on forecasts about technological developments and relative prices. Often, reserves are defined in successively wider classes. For example, the US Energy Information Agency defines four classes for oil and gas. The smallest is *proved reserves*, which are reserves that geologic and engineering data demonstrate with reasonable certainty to be recoverable in future years from known reservoirs under existing economic and operating conditions. As technology and prices change, this stock normally increases over time. Successively larger ones are *economically recoverable resources*, *technically recoverable resources*, and *remaining oil and natural gas in place*.

Given different definitions and estimation procedures the estimated stocks differ and will change over time. Therefore, the numbers in this section can only be taken as indications. Furthermore, reserves of different types of fossil fuels are measured in different units, often barrels for oil, cubic meters or cubic feet for gas, and tons for coal. However, for our purpose, it is convenient to express all stocks in terms of their carbon content. Therefore nontrivial conversion must be undertaken. Given these caveats, we calculate from BP (2015) global proved reserves of oil and natural gas to be approximately 200 GtC and 100 GtC, respectively.[al] At current extraction rates, both these stocks would last approximately 50 years. Putting these numbers in perspective, we note that the

[al] BP (2015) reports proved oil reserves to 239,8 Gt. For conversion, we use IPCC (2006, table 1.2 and 1.3). From these, we calculate a carbon content of 0.846 GtC per Gt of oil. BP (2015) reports proved natural gas reserves to be 187.1 trillion m^3. The same source states an energy content of 35.7 trillion BtU per trillion m^3 equal to 35.9 trillion kJ. IPCC (2006) reports 15.3 kgC/GJ for natural gas. This means that 1 trillion m^3 natural gas contains 0.546 GtC. For coal, we use the IPCC (2006) numbers for antracite, giving 0.716 GtC per Gt of coal. For all these conversions, it should be noted that there is substantial variation in carbon content depending on the quality of the fuel and the numbers used must therefore be used with caution.

atmosphere currently contains over 800 GtC. Given the results in the previous sections, we note that burning all proved reserves of oil and natural gas would have fairly modest effects on the climate.[am] Again using BP (2015), we calculate proved reserves of coal to around 600 GtC, providing more potential dangers for the climate.

Using wider definitions of reserves, stocks are much larger. Specifically, using data from McGlade and Ekins (2015) we calculate ultimately recoverable reserves of oil, natural gas and coal to close to 600 GtC, 400 GtC and 3000 GtC.[an] Rogner (1997) estimates coal reserves to be 3500 GtC with a marginal extraction cost curve that is fairly flat. Clearly, if all these reserves are used, climate change can hardly be called modest.

3.2.4 A Linear Carbon Circulation Model

A natural starting point is a linear carbon circulation model. Let us begin with a two-stock model as in Nordhaus and Boyer (2000). We let the variables S_t and S_t^L denote the amount of carbon in the two reservoirs, respectively: S_t for the atmosphere and S_t^L for the ocean. Emissions, denoted E_t, enter into the atmosphere. Under the linearity assumption, we assume that a constant share ϕ_1 of S_t flows to S_t^L per unit of time and, conversely, a share ϕ_2 of S_t^L flows in the other direction implying

$$\begin{aligned} \frac{dS_t}{dt} &= -\phi_1 S_t + \phi_2 S_t^L + E_t, \\ \frac{dS_t^L}{dt} &= \phi_1 S_t - \phi_2 S_t^L. \end{aligned} \tag{11}$$

Eq. (11) form a linear system of differential equations, similar to Eqs. (9) and (10). However, there is a key difference: additions of carbon to this system through emissions get "trapped" in the sense that there is no outflow from the system as a whole, reflecting the fact that one of the characteristic roots of the system in (11) is zero.[ao] This implies that if E settles down to a positive constant, the sizes of the reservoirs S and S^L will not approach a steady state, but will grow forever. If emissions eventually stop and remain zero, the sizes of the reservoirs will settle down to some steady-state values, but these values will depend on the amount of emissions accumulated before that. This steady state satisfies a zero net flow as per

$$0 = -\phi_1 S + \phi_2 S^L, \tag{12}$$

[am] As we will soon see, a substantial share of burned fossil fuel quickly leaves the atmosphere.

[an] See footnote al for conversions.

[ao] If we were to also define a stock of fossil fuel in the ground from which emissions are taken, total net flows would be zero. Since it is safe to assume that flows into the stock of fossil fuel are negligible, we could simply add an equation $\frac{dR_t}{dt} = -E_t$ to the other equations, which would thus capture the depletion of fossil reserves.

implying that

$$\frac{S}{S^L} = \frac{\phi_2}{\phi_1}$$

and that the rate of convergence is determined by the nonzero root $-(\phi_1 + \phi_2)$.

As we have seen above, CO_2 is mixed very quickly into the atmosphere. CO_2 also passes quickly through the ocean surface implying that a new balance between the amount of carbon in the atmosphere and the shallow ocean water is reached quickly.[ap] The further transport of carbon to the deep oceans is much slower, motivating a third model reservoir: the deep oceans. This is the choice made in recent versions of the DICE and RICE models (Nordhaus and Sztorc, 2013), which use a three-reservoir linear system similar to (11).

3.2.5 Reduced-Form Depreciation Models

Although the stock-flow model has a great deal of theoretical and intuitive appeal, it runs the risk of simplifying complicated processes too much. For example, the ability of the terrestrial biosphere to store carbon depends on temperature and precipitation. Therefore, changes in the climate may have an effect on the flows to and from the biosphere not captured in the model described earlier. Similarly, the storage capacity of the oceans depends (negatively) on the temperature. These shortcomings could possibly be addressed by including temperature and precipitation as separate variables in the system. Furthermore, also the processes involved in the deep oceans are substantially more complicated than what is expressed in the linear model. In particular, the fact that carbon in the oceans exists in different chemical forms and that the balance between these has an important role for the dynamics of the carbon circulation is ignored but can potentially be of importance.

An important problem with the linear specification (see, Archer, 2005 and Archer et al., 2009) is due to the so-called Revelle buffer factor (Revelle and Suess, 1957). As CO_2 is accumulated in the oceans, the water is acidified. This dramatically limits its capacity to absorb more CO_2, making the effective "size" of the oceans as a carbon reservoir decrease by approximately a factor of 15 (Archer, 2005). Very slowly, the acidity decreases and the preindustrial equilibrium can be restored. This process is so slow, however, that it can be ignored in economic models. IPCC (2007, p. 25, Technical Summary), take account of the Revelle buffer factor and conclude that "About half of a CO_2 pulse to the atmosphere is removed over a time scale of 30 years; a further 30% is removed within a few centuries; and the remaining 20% will typically stay in the atmosphere for many thousands of years." The conclusion of Archer (2005) is that

[ap] This takes 1–2 years IPCC (2013).

a good approximation is that 75% of an excess atmospheric carbon concentration has a mean lifetime of 300 years and the remaining 25% remain several thousands of years.[aq]

A way of representing this is to define a depreciation model. Golosov et al. (2014) define a carbon depreciation function. Let $1-d(s)$ represent the amount of a marginal unit of emitted carbon that remains in the atmosphere after s periods. Then postulate that

$$1-d(s)=\varphi_L+(1-\varphi_L)\varphi_0(1-\varphi)^s. \tag{13}$$

The three parameters in (13) are easily calibrated to match the three facts in the earlier IPCC quote; we do this in Section 5. A similar approach is described in IPCC (2007a, table 2.14). There,

$$1-d(s)=a_0+\sum_{i=1}^{3}\left(a_i e^{-\frac{s}{\tau_i}}\right), \tag{14}$$

with $a_0=0.217$, $a_1=0.259$, $a_2=0.338$, $a_3=0.186$, $\tau_1=172.9$, $\tau_2=18.51$, and $\tau_3=1.186$, where s and the τ_is are measured in years. With this parametrization, 50% of an emitted unit of carbon has left the atmosphere after 30 years, 75% after 356 years, and 21.7% stays forever. It is important to note that this depreciation model is appropriate for a marginal emission at an initial CO_2 concentration equal to the current one (around 800 GtC). The parameters of the depreciation function should be allowed to depend on initial conditions and inframarginal future emissions. If emissions are very large, a larger share will remain in the atmosphere for a long time. To provide a measure for how sensitive the parameters are, note that of an extremely large emission pulse of 5000 GtC, which is more than $1\times$ the current accumulated emissions, around 40% remains after a thousand years, as opposed to half as much for a much smaller pulse.[ar]

3.2.6 A Linear Relation Between Emissions and Temperature

As discussed earlier, it may be too simplistic to analyze the carbon circulation in isolation. The storage capacity of the various carbon sinks depends on how the climate develops. One might think that including these interactions would make the model more complicated. However, this does not have to be the case. In fact, there is evidence that various feedbacks and nonlinearity in the climate and carbon-cycle systems tend to cancel each other out, making the combined system behave in a much simpler and, in fact, linear way.[as] In order to briefly discuss this, let us defined the variable CCR_m (Carbon-Climate Response) as the change in the global mean temperature over some specified time interval m per unit of emissions of fossil carbon into the atmosphere over that same time interval

[aq] Similar findings are reported in IPCC (2013, Box 6.1).

[ar] See IPCC (2013, Box 6.1).

[as] This subsection is based on Matthews et al. (2009).

$$CCR_m \equiv \frac{T_{t+m} - T_t}{\int_t^m E_s ds}.$$

Given our previous discussions in this and the previous sections, one would think that this variable is far from a constant: the dynamic behavior of the climate and the carbon cycle will in general make the CCR_m depend on the length of the time interval considered. For example, since it takes time to heat the oceans, the temperature response could depend on whether the time interval is a decade or a century. Similarly, since also the carbon dynamics are slow, the extra CO_2 concentration induced by a unit of emission tends to be lower the longer the time interval considered. Furthermore, the CCR_m might depend on how much emissions have already occurred; higher previous emissions can reduce the effectiveness of carbon sinks and even turn them into net contributors. The marginal effect on temperature from an increase in the CO_2 concentration also depends on the level of CO_2 concentration due to the logarithmic relation between CO_2 concentration and the greenhouse effect.

Quite surprisingly, Matthews et al. (2009) show that the dynamic and nonlinear effects tend to cancel, making it a quite good approximation to consider the CCR_m as a constant, CCR, independent of both the time interval considered and the amount of previous emissions. Of course, knowledge about the value of CCR is incomplete but Matthews et al. (2012) quantify this knowledge gap and argue that a 90% confidence interval is between 1 and 2.5°C per 1000 GtC.[at] This means that we can write the (approximate) linear relationship

$$T_{t+m} = T_t + CCR \int_t^m E_s ds.$$

To get some understanding for this surprising result, first consider the time independence. We have shown in the previous chapter that when the ocean is included in the analysis, there is a substantial delay in the temperature response of a given forcing. Thus, if the CO_2 concentration permanently jumps to a higher level, it takes many decades before even half the final change in temperature has taken place. On the other hand, if carbon is released into the atmosphere, a large share of it is removed quite slowly from the atmosphere. It happens to be the case that these dynamics cancel each other, at least if the time scale is from a decade up to a millennium. Thus, in the shorter run, the CO_2 concentration and thus forcing is higher but this is balanced by the cooling effect of the oceans.

Second, for the independence of CCR with respect to previous emissions note that the Arrhenius law discussed in the previous chapter implies a logarithmic relation

[at] IPCC (2013) defines the very similar concept, the Transient Climate Response to cumulative carbon Emissions (TCRE), and states that it is likely between 0.8 and 2.5°C per 1000 GtC for cumulative emissions below 2000 GtC.

between CO_2 concentration and the temperature. Thus, at higher CO_2 concentrations, an increase in the CO_2 concentration has a smaller effect on the temperature. On the other hand, existing carbon cycle models tend to have the property that the storage capacity of the sinks diminishes as more CO_2 is released into the atmosphere. These effects also balance—at higher levels of CO_2 concentration, an additional unit of emissions increases the CO_2 concentration more but the effect of CO_2 concentration on temperature is lower by roughly the same proportion.

Given a value of *CCR*, it is immediate to calculate how much more emissions can be allowed in order to limit global warming to a particular value. Suppose, for example, we use a value of $CCR=1.75$. Then, to limit global warming to 2°C, we cannot emit more than $(2/1.75)\times 1000=1140$ GtC, implying that only around 600 GtC can be emitted in the future. If, on the other hand, we use the upper limit of the 95% confidence interval ($CCR=2.5$) and aim to reduce global warming to 2°C, accumulated emissions cannot be more than a total of 800 GtC of which most is already emitted.

3.3 Damages

In this section, we discuss how the economy is affected by climate change. Since economic analysis of climate change tends to rely on cost-benefit calculation, it is not only a necessary cornerstone of the analysis but arguably also a key challenge for climate economics. For several reasons, this is a very complicated area, however. First, there is an almost infinite number of ways in which climate change can affect the economy. Second, carbon emissions are likely to affect the climate for a very long time: for thousands of years. This implies that the quantitative issue of what weight to attach to the welfare of future generations becomes of key importance for the valuation. Third, global climate change can potentially be much larger than experienced during the modern history of mankind. Historical relations between climate change and the economy must therefore be extrapolated significantly if they are to be used to infer the consequences of future climate change. Fourth, many potential costs are to goods and services without market prices.

The idea that the climate affect the economy is probably as old as the economy itself, or rather as old as mankind. That the distribution of weather outcomes—the climate—affects agricultural output must have been obvious for humans since the Neolithic revolution. The literature on how the climate affects agriculture is vast and not reviewed here. It is also well known that in a cross-country setting, a hotter climate is strongly associated with less income per capita. Also within countries, such a negative relation between temperature and income per capita can be found (Nordhaus, 2006). However, Nordhaus (2006) also finds a hump-shaped relation between output density, ie, output per unit of land area, and average temperature. This suggests that a method of adaptation is geographic mobility. An overview is provided in Tol (2009). A more recent economic literature using modern methods emphasizing identification is now rapidly expanding. The focus is broad and climate change is allowed to have many different effects, including a heterogeneous effect on the economic productivity of different production sectors, effects on health, mortality, social unrest, conflicts, and much more. Dell et al. (2014) provide an overview of this newer literature.

Climate change thus likely has extremely diverse effects, involving a large number of different mechanisms affecting different activities differently. The effects are spatially heterogeneous and have different dynamics. Despite this, it appears important to aggregate the effects to a level that can be handled by macroeconomic models.[au]

3.3.1 Nordhaus's Approach

Early attempts to aggregate the economic impacts of climate change were carried out in Nordhaus (1991).[av] Nordhaus (1992, 1993) constructed the path-breaking integrated assessment model named DICE, ie, a model with the three interlinked systems—the climate, the carbon cycle, and the economy.[aw] This is a global growth model with carbon circulation, and climate module, and a damage function. This very early incarnation of the damage function assumed that the economic losses from global warming were proportional to GDP and a function of the global mean temperature, measured as a deviation from the preindustrial average temperature. Nordhaus's assumption in the first version of DICE was that the fraction of output lost was

$$D(T) = 0.0133\left(\frac{T}{3}\right)^2.$$

Nordhaus underlines the very limited knowledge that supported this specification. His own study (Nordhaus, 1991) studies a number of activities in the United States and concludes that these would contribute to a loss of output of 0.25% of US GDP for a temperature deviation of 3°C. He argues that a reasonable guess is that the this estimate omits important factors and that the United States losses rather are on the order of 1% of GDP and that the global losses are somewhat larger. Nordhaus (1992) cites Cline (1992) for an estimate of the power on temperature in the damage function but chooses 2 rather than the cited 1.3.

Later work (Nordhaus and Boyer, 2000) provided more detailed sectorial estimates of the damage function. Here, the aggregation includes both damages that accrue to market activities and those that could affect goods, services, and other values that are not traded.

[au] Macroeconomic modeling with large degrees of heterogeneity is developing rapidly, however. In the context of climate economy modeling, see eg, Krusell and Smith (2015) for a model with nearly 20,000 regions.

[av] Other early examples are Cline (1992), Fankhauser (1994), and Titus (1992).

[aw] DICE stands for Dynamic Integrated Climate-Economy model.

An attempt to value the risk of catastrophic consequences of climate change is also included. Obviously, this is an almost impossible task, given the little quantitative knowledge about tail risks. Nordhaus and Boyer use a survey, where climate experts are asked to assess the probability of permanent and dramatic losses of output at different increases in the global mean temperature.

The latest version of DICE (Nordhaus and Sztorc, 2013) instead goes back to a more ad-hoc calibration of the damage function. Based on results in a survey in Tol (2009) and IPCC (2007b) depicted in Fig. 9, they postulate a damage function given by

$$D(T) = 1 - \frac{1}{1 + 0.00267T^2}. \tag{15}$$

The functional form in (15) is chosen so that damages are necessarily smaller than 1 but for the intended ranges of temperature, it may be noted that $1 - \frac{1}{1+0.00267T^2} \approx 0.023\left(\frac{T}{3}\right)^2$.[ax] Thus, the functional form remains similar to the first version of DICE but the estimated damages at three degrees have increased from 1.3% to 2.3% of global GDP.

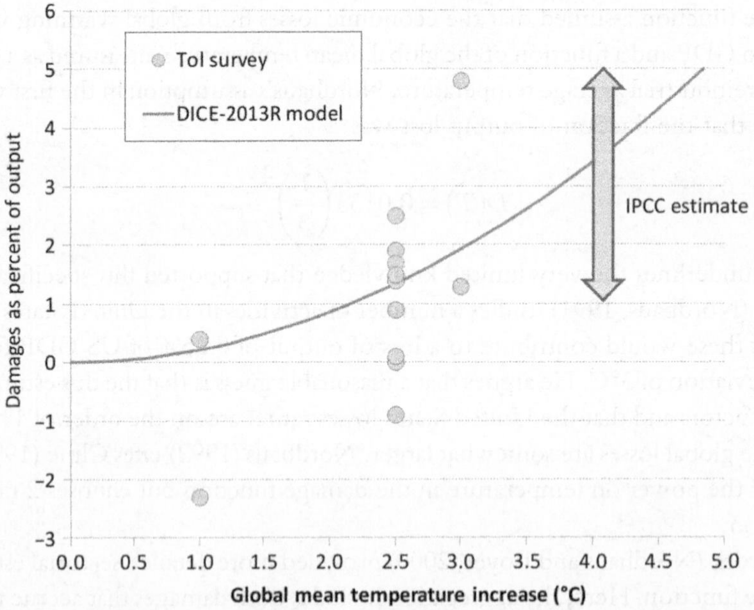

Fig. 9 Global damage estimates. Dots are from Tol (2009). The solid line is the estimate from the DICE-2013R model. The arrow is from the IPCC (2007b, page 17). *Reprinted from Nordhaus, W.D., Sztorc, P., 2013. DICE 2013R: introduction and users manual. Mimeo, Yale University.*

[ax] It is important to note that Nordhaus and Sztorc (2013) warn against using their damage function for temperature deviations over 3°C.

Nordhaus has also developed models with multiple regions, RICE (Regional Integrated Climate-Economy model). The later versions of this model have different damage functions defined for 12 regions. Here, the linear-quadratic function of the global mean temperature is appended with a threshold effect at a four-degree temperature deviation: at this level, the exponent on the temperature is increased to six. Separate account is also taken for sea-level rise, whose damages are described using a linear-quadratic function.

Similar aggregate damage functions are used in other global integrated assessment models; prominent examples are WITCH, FUND, and PAGE.[ay]. Specifically, WITCH has quadratic, region-specific damage functions for eight global regions. FUND uses eight different sectorial damage functions defined for each of 16 regions. PAGE, which was used in the highly influential Stern report (Stern, 2007), uses four separate damage functions for different types of damages in each of eight regions. A special feature of the damage functions in FUND is that the exponent on the global mean temperature is assumed to be a random variable in the interval [1.5–3].

3.3.2 Explicit Damage Aggregation

The damage functions described so far has only been derived to a limited degree from a "bottom-up approach" where explicit damages to particular regions and economic sectors are defined and aggregated. To the extent that such an approach has been used, the final results have been adjusted in an ad-hoc manner, often in the direction of postulating substantially larger damages than found in the explicit aggregation. Furthermore, the work has abstracted from general-equilibrium effects and simply added estimated damages sector by sector and region by region. Obviously this is problematic as the welfare consequences of productivity losses to a particular sector in a particular region depend on the extent to which production can move to other regions or be substituted for by other goods.

An example of a detailed high-resolution modeling of climate damages where (regional) general equilibrium effects are taken into account is the PESETA project, initiated by the European Commission.[az] Damages estimated are for coastal damages, flooding, agriculture, tourism, and health in the European Union. A reference scenario there is a 3.1°C increase in the temperature in the EU by the end of this century relative to the average over 1961–90. The resulting damages imply an EU-wide loss of 1.8% of GDP. The largest part of this loss is due to higher premature mortality in particular in south-central EU.[ba] In the northern parts of the EU, welfare gains associated mainly with lower energy expenditures are approximately balanced by negative impacts in

[ay] See Bosetti et al. (2006), Tol (1995), and Chris et al. (1993) for descriptions of WITCH, FUND, and PAGE, respectively.

[az] See Ciscar et al. (2011) for a short description.

[ba] France, Austria, Czech Republic, Slovakia, Hungary, Slovenia, and Romania.

human health and coastal area damages.[bb] Clearly, these effects are small relative to the expectations for economic growth over this period as well as compared to fears of dramatic impacts often expressed in the policy debate about climate change.

3.3.3 Top-Down Approaches

An alternative approach to the bottom-up approach is to estimate a reduced-form relation between aggregate measures like GDP, consumption, and investments and climate. The idea here is to associate natural historical variation in climate to changes in the aggregate variables of interest. Most of this work thus focuses on short-run changes in temperature as opposed to climate change. Examples of this approach are Dell et al. (2012) who examine how natural year-to-year variation in a country's temperature affects its GDP. Using data from 1950–2003, they find strong and persistent effects of a temporary deviation in temperature, with a point estimate of 1.4% of GDP per degrees Celsius—*but only in poor countries*. A similar result, but using global variation in the temperature, is reported by Bansal and Ochoa (2011). Krusell and Smith (2015), however, find that positive temperature shocks affect the level of GDP but not its rate of growth, and they do not find evidence of a difference between rich and poor countries.

Another approach is taken in Mendelsohn et al. (1994). Instead of attempting to measure a direct relation between climate and output, ie, estimating a production function with climate as an input, the focus is here on agricultural land prices. They label this a *Ricardian approach*.The advantage of this is that adaptation, for example changed crops, can be taken into account. The finding is that higher temperature, except in the fall, is associated with lower land prices. However, the strength in this relation is lower than what is suggested by estimates based on traditional production function analysis. This indicates that the latter underestimates the potential for adaptation.

Burke et al. (2015) estimate empirical relations between economic activity and climate by assuming that local damages are a function not of global temperature but of local temperature. That is, heterogeneity here is built in not in terms of differences in responses to global temperature changes but simply through how local climates are very different to start with. If a region is very cold, warming can be beneficial, and if a region is very warm, further warming will likely be particularly detrimental. In line with Nordhaus (2006), a hump-shaped relation between economic activity and average yearly temperature is then estimated, with a maximum around 12–13°C. If this relation is taken as a causal relation from climate to productivity, it can be used to measure the long-run consequences of climate change. However, the use of the relation to evaluate long-run consequences precludes a study of short- and medium-run costs. This holds in particular for the costs of geographic reallocation of people, an area where little is known. In line with Burke et al. (2015) and Krusell and Smith (2015) postulate a unique damage function of local

[bb] This area is defined by Sweden, Finland, Estonia, Lithuania, Latvia, and Denmark.

temperature for a large number of regions and impose the condition that this function generate Nordhaus's estimated aggregate damages for warming of 1°C, 2.5°C, and 5°C. They find a somewhat lower ideal temperature than do Burke et al. but that the losses from having local temperatures far from the ideal value can be very large.

3.3.4 Remarks

The section on damage measurements in this chapter is short and does not do full justice to the literature. However, even a very ambitious survey would make clear that the research area of damage measurement is at a very early stage and provides frustratingly little guidance for cost-benefit analysis. On the one hand, most of the evidence points to rather limited aggregate global damages, at last for moderate degrees of climate change. On the other hand, it is not possible to rule out large damages, at least if climate change is more than moderate. After all, if the damages from climate change cannot be measured and quantified, how can we arrive at policy recommendations? There is no quick answer; much more research on this is clearly needed. In the absence of more solid evidence there is unfortunately ample room for extreme views—on both sides of the climate debate—to make claims about damage functions that support any desired action. We therefore prefer to proceed cautiously and to base our calibrations of damage functions on the evidence that, after all, has been gathered and put together. But before moving on to a description of the approach we take here, let us make some remarks about some mechanisms we will be abstracting from and that could nevertheless prove to be important.

One aspect of damages concerns the long run: is it possible that a warmer climate hurts (or helps?) long-run economic development, and might it even affect the growth rate of output? The work by Dell et al. (2012) as well as Burke et al. (2015) suggest such effects might be present on the local level, though without providing evidence on mechanisms. For an overall growth-rate effect on world GDP, there is as far as we know no evidence. Clearly, any growth effects—by naturally adding effects over time—will lead to large total effects, and that regions at different ends of the distribution would diverge in their levels of production and welfare, and it is not clear that our growth data support this conclusion. At the same time, the large implied effects make it all the more important to dig deeper and understand whether growth effects could actually be present. To be clear, our null hypothesis is that there are no effects on long-run growth rates of climate change.

Relatedly, it is common—following Nordhaus's lead—to describe damages as essentially proportional to GDP. This formulation, which to an important extent appears to be untested, has some important implications. One is that higher GDP ceteris paribus leads to higher damages. Another is that, since lower GDP means less to consume and consumption (typically, in macroeconomic models) is assumed to be associated with diminishing marginal utility, the welfare losses from a unit of damage measured in consumption units are lower the higher is GDP. Thus, if future generations will have higher GDP than we have today, there are two opposing forces: the total damages in consumption units will be higher but each of those units will hurt future generations less. As we shall see, under reasonable assumptions on utility, those two forces cancel, or roughly cancel. However, there are various ways to depart from Nordhaus approach. One is to assume that damages occur in consumption units but are not (linearly) proportional to GDP (eg, our capital stock could be damaged). Another is to think of damages as occurring to specific consumption bundles that may not display the same degree of diminishing returns as consumption as a whole (examples include effects on leisure, health, or longevity). Damages can also occur in the form of changes in the distribution of resources and in other ways that are not easily thought of in terms of an aggregate damage function proportional to GDP.

Climate change can also lead to social conflict, as it changes the values of different activities and, more generally, "endowments." One channel occurs via migration: if a region is hit hard by a changed climate and people migrate out, history tells us that the probability of conflict in the transition/destination areas will rise (see eg, Miguel et al., 2004, Burke et al., 2009, Jia, 2014, Harari and La Ferrara, 2014, and Burke et al., 2015, for an overview). At the same time, migration is also one of the main ways humans have to adapt to a changing climate. In fact, one view is that "populations can simply move toward the poles a bit" and hence drastically limit any damages from warmer weather; see Desmet and Rossi-Hansberg (2015) for an analysis that takes the migration mechanism seriously (see also Brock et al., 2014). A related aspect is that climate change will have very diverse effects. It may be true that aggregated damages are small as a share of GDP and that those who lose a lot could be compensated by other, losing less or nothing at all. However, such global insurance schemes do not exist, at least not presently. The extent to which there are compensating transfers will likely to greatly impact any reasonable cost-benefit analysis of climate change and policies against it.

Tipping points are often mentioned in the climate-economy area and earlier we discussed some possible tipping points in the natural-science sections. Damages can also have tipping points in various ways and on some level a tipping point is simply a highly nonlinear damage function. One example leading to tipping points is the case of rising sea levels due to the melting of the ice caps. Clearly, some areas may become flooded and uninhabitable if the sea level rises enough, and the outcome is thus highly nonlinear. This argument speaks clearly in favor of using highly nonlinear damage functions on the local level, at least when it comes to some aspects of higher global temperatures. However, the sea-level rise equally clearly does not necessarily amount to a global nonlinearity in damages. Suffice it to say here that very little is known on the topic of global tipping points in damages. We will proceed with the null that a smooth convex aggregate damage function is a good starting point: we follow Nordhaus in this respect as well.

On an even broader level, let us be clear that different approaches are needed in this area. Bottom-up structural approaches like the PESETA project are very explicit and allow extrapolation, but they are limited to a certain number of factors and may miss important other mechanisms. Reduced-form micro-based approaches allow credible identification but may also miss important factors and general-equilibrium effects. Reduced-form aggregate approaches are less likely to miss mechanisms or general-equilibrium effects but necessarily involve a small number of observables and are much harder to interpret and extrapolate from. There is, we believe, no alternative at this point other than proceeding forward on all fronts in this important part of the climate-economy research area.

3.3.5 The Operational Approach: A Direct Relation

We now discuss a very convenient tool for the rest of the analysis in this chapter: a way of incorporating the existing damage estimates into our structural integrated-assessment models. In Section 3.1.1, we have noted that the relation between the CO_2 concentration and the greenhouse effect is concave (it is approximately logarithmic). The existence of feedbacks is likely to imply an amplification of the direct effect, but in the absence of known global threshold effects, the logarithmic relation is likely to survive. Above we have also noted that that modelers so far typically have chosen a convex relation between temperature and damages: at least for moderate degrees of heating, a linear-quadratic formulation is often chosen. Golosov et al. (2014) show that the combination of a concave mapping from CO_2 concentrations to temperature and a convex mapping from temperature to damages for standard parameterizations imply an approximately constant marginal effect of higher CO_2 concentration on damages as a share of GDP. Therefore, they postulate

$$D(T(S)) = 1 - e^{-\gamma(S-\bar{S})}, \tag{16}$$

where S is the amount of carbon in the atmosphere at a point in time and $\bar{S}$ is its preindustrial level. This formulation disregards the dynamic relation between CO_2 concentration and temperature. It also disregards the possibility of abrupt increases in the convexity of the damage mapping and threshold effects in the climate system. These are important considerations, in particular when large increases in temperature are considered. However, the approximation provides a very convenient benchmark by implying that the marginal damage measured as a share of GDP per marginal unit of carbon in the atmosphere is constant and given by γ.[bc] Measuring S in billions of tons of carbon (GtC), Golosov et al. (2014) show that a good approximation to the damages used to derive the damage function in DICE (Nordhaus, 2007) is given by (16) with $\gamma = 5.3 \cdot 10^{-5}$.

In Fig. 10, we show an exponential damage function with this parameter. Specifically, the figure shows the implied damage function plotted against temperature using the relationship $T(S) = 3\frac{\ln S - \ln S_0}{\ln 2}$, ie, using a climate sensitivity of 3 degrees. Comparing this damage function to the Nordhaus function as depicted in Fig. 9, we see that the former is

[bc] Output net of damages is $e^{-\gamma(S-S_0)}Y$. Marginal damages as a share of net-of-damage output then become $[d((1-e^{-\gamma(S-S_0)})Y)/dS]/e^{-\gamma(S-S_0)}Y = \gamma$.

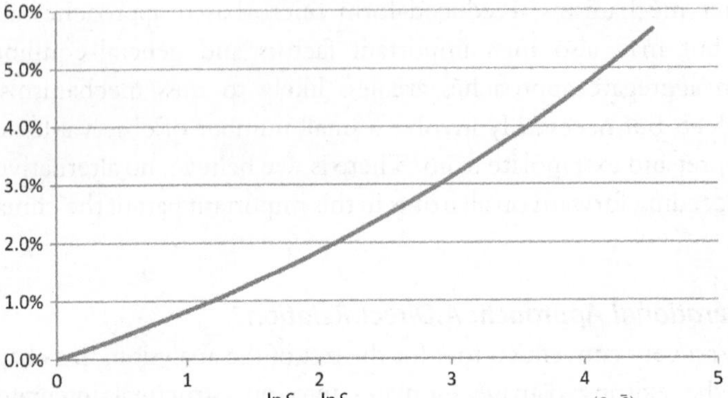

Fig. 10 Damage function using $T(S) = 3\frac{\ln S - \ln S_0}{\ln 2}$ and $D(T(S)) = 1 - e^{-\gamma(S-\bar{S})}$.

slightly less convex.[bd] While the exponential damage function implies a constant marginal loss of 0.0053% per GtC, the quadratic formulation implies increasing marginal loss up to approximately 4°C. However, in the important range 2.5–5.0°C, the marginal loss is fairly constant within the range 0.0053% and 0.0059% per GtC.

4. A STATIC GLOBAL ECONOMY-CLIMATE MODEL

Our discussion of integrated assessment models comes in two parts. The first part—in the present section—introduces an essentially static and highly stylized model, whereas the second part presents a fully dynamic and quantitatively oriented setup. The simple model in the present section can be viewed as a first step and an organizational tool: we can use it to formally discuss a large number of topics that have been studied in the literature. Moreover, for some of these topics we can actually use the model for a quantitative assessment, since it has most of the features of the macroeconomic structure in the later section. The model is thus a static version of Golosov et al. (2014) and it is also very similar to Nordhaus's DICE model.

We consider a world economy where the production of output—a consumption good—is given by

$$c = A(S)k^{\alpha}n^{1-\alpha-\nu}E^{\nu} - \zeta E.$$

Here, $A(S)$ denotes global TFP, which we take to be a function of the amount of carbon in the atmosphere, S. Moreover, we normalize so that S measures the excess carbon concentration, relative to a preindustrial average, $\bar{S}$. That is, the actual concentration is $S + \bar{S}$, whereas we will only need to use S in our modeling. The discussion in Section 3.3 allows us to use this notation and, moreover, to use a simple functional form that we argue is a

[bd] Reducing the exponent on temperature to 1.5 and increasing the constant in front of temperature to 0.0061 in (15) produces a damage function very close to the exponential one.

decent approximation to the complex system mapping the amount of carbon in the atmosphere to temperature and then mapping temperature, with its negative impacts on the economy, to TFP. We will thus use

$$A(S) = e^{-\gamma S},$$

with $\gamma > 0$. Recall from the previous discussions that the map from S to T is logarithmic, so it features decreasing marginal impacts of increased atmospheric carbon concentration on temperature. The estimated mapping from T to TFP, on the other hand, is usually convex, so that the combined mapping actually can be described with the negative exponential function. Thus, damages are $(1 - e^{-\gamma S})k^{\alpha} n^{1-\alpha-\nu} E^{\nu}$, which is increasing and concave in S. (Note that we let energy, E, be capitalized henceforth, to distinguish it from Euler's number, e, used in the exponential damage function.) Though we argue above that this form for the damage function is a good one, it is straightforward to change it in this simple model, as we will below in one of our model applications. The exponential function is also useful because it simplifies the algebra and thus helps us in our illustrations. We will occasionally refer to γ as the *damage elasticity of output*.

The inputs in production include capital and labor, which we take to be exogenously supplied in the static model. The production function is Cobb–Douglas in the three inputs. As for capital and labor entering this way, we just use the standard macroeconomic formulation. The substitution elasticity between the capital-labor composite and energy is also unitary here, which is not far from available estimates of long-run elasticities, and we think of the static model as a short-cut representation of a long-run model. The short-run elasticity is estimated to be far lower, as discussed in Section 2.3.

We also see that the generation of output involves a cost ζE of producing energy. We will discuss in detail below how energy is generated but the simple linear form here is useful because it allows us to illustrate with some main cases. One of these cases is that when energy is only produced from oil. Much of the oil (say, the Saudi oil) is very cheap to produce relative to its market price, so in fact we can think of this case as characterized by $\zeta = 0$. Oil exists in finite supply, so this case comes along with an upper bound on energy: $E \leq \bar{E}$.

A second case is that when energy comes from coal. Coal is very different because its market price is close to its marginal cost, so here we can think of ζ as a positive deep parameter representing a constant marginal cost in terms of output units (and hence the cost of producing energy in terms of capital and labor, and energy itself, has the same characteristics as does the final-output good). Coal is also only available in a finite amount but the available amount here is so large that we can think of it as infinite; in fact, if we were to use up all the coal within, say, the next 500 years, the implied global warming will be so high that most analysts would regard the outcome as disastrous, and hence the presumption in this case is that not all of the amount will be used up (and hence considering the available amount to be infinite is not restrictive). In reality, the supply of fossil fuel is of course not dichotomous: a range of fuels with intermediate extraction costs exists (see the discussion earlier in Section 3.2.3).

A third case is that with "green energy," where a constant marginal cost in terms of output is also a reasonable assumption. Finally, we can imagine a combination of these three assumptions and we will indeed discuss such possibilities below, but it is useful to consider coal and oil first separately first.

Turning to the mapping between energy use and atmospheric carbon concentration, the different energy sources correspond to different cases. In the case of oil and coal, we will simply assume that $S = \phi E + \bar{S}$, where $\bar{S}$ is the part of carbon concentration that is not of anthropogenic origin. As constants in TFP do not influence any outcomes here, we normalize $\bar{S}$ to equal zero. The equation thus states that carbon concentration is increased by the amount of emissions times ϕ. The constant ϕ represents the role of the carbon cycle over the course of a model period—which we will later calibrate to 100 years—and captures the fraction of the emissions during a period that end up in the atmosphere. A explained in Section 3.2, the depreciation structure of carbon in the atmosphere, though nontrivial in nature, can be rather well approximated linearly. Emissions, in turn, are proportional to the amount of fossil fuel used.[be]

We consider a consumer's utility function that, for now, only has consumption as an argument. Hence, so long as it is strictly increasing in consumption the model is complete.

We will discuss outcomes in a market economy of this sort where the consumer owns the capital and supplies labor under price taking, just like in standard macroeconomic models. Firms buy inputs, including energy, in competitive markets and energy is produced competitively. Formally, we can think of there being two sectors where isoquants have the same shape but where in the consumption-goods sector firms solve

$$\max_{k,l,E} e^{-\gamma S} k^{\alpha} n^{1-\alpha-\nu} E^{\nu} - wn - rk - pE,$$

where we denote wages and rental rates by w and r, respectively, and where p is the price of energy; the consumption good is the numéraire. In the energy sector the firms thus solve

$$\max_{k,l,E} p \frac{e^{-\gamma S}}{\zeta} k^{\alpha} n^{1-\alpha-\nu} E^{\nu} - wn - rk - pE.$$

It is straightforward to show, because the Cobb–Douglas share parameters are the same in the two sectors and inputs can be moved across sectors without cost, that this delivers

[be] Constants of proportion are omitted and are inconsequential in this simple model. In a more general framework one must take into account how oil and coal differ in the transformation between the basic carbon content and the resulting emissions as well as how they differ in productive use. We discuss these issues below when we consider coal and oil jointly.

$p = \zeta$ (whenever energy is nontrivially produced, so in the coal and green-energy cases, $1/\zeta$ becomes the TFP in the energy sector relative to that in the final-goods sector). Note also that GDP, y, equals the production of the consumption good, since energy here is an intermediate input.[bf]

Note that in both of the above profit maximization problems firms do not choose S, ie, they do not perceive an effect on TFP in their choice, even though $S = \phi E$ in equilibrium. This is as it should be: the climate damage from emissions are a pure, and global, externality. Markets fail to take this effect into account and optimal policy should be designed to steer markets in the right direction.

The associated planning problem thus reads

$$\max_{E} e^{-\gamma\phi E} k^{\alpha} n^{1-\alpha-\nu} E^{\nu} - \zeta E;$$

here, clearly, the externality is taken into account. In the case of oil, for which $\zeta = 0$ is assumed, there is an additional constraint for the planner, namely that $E \leq \bar{E}$.

We will now discuss the solution to this problem for the different cases, starting with the case of oil.

4.1 The Case of Oil

Here, $\zeta = 0$ and the energy-producing sector is trivial. Under laissez-faire, all of the oil is supplied to the market and its price will be given by its marginal product: $p \equiv \bar{p} = \nu e^{-\gamma\phi\bar{E}} k^{\alpha} n^{1-\alpha-\nu} \bar{E}^{\nu-1}$. To the extent $\bar{E}$ and $\gamma\phi$ are large, this will involve an allocation with large damages to welfare.

The planner, on the other hand, may not use up all the oil. It is straightforward to see that the solution to the planner's problem is a corner solution whenever $\bar{E} < \nu/(\gamma\phi)$: the planner would then, like the markets, use up all the available oil. Thus, there is a negative by-product of emissions but it is not, at its maximal use, so bad as to suggest that its use should be limited. (In fact, as we shall argue below, this is not an unreasonable conclusion for oil given a more general, calibrated structure.) If, on the other hand, $\bar{E} \geq \nu/(\gamma\phi)$, the solution is interior at an E that solves $E = \nu/(\gamma\phi)$.

4.1.1 Optimal Taxes

What are the policy implications of this model? For a range of parameter values—for $\bar{E} < \nu/(\gamma\phi)$—no policy is needed. At the same time, taxes are not necessarily harmful: if we think of a unit tax on the use of oil (the firms, whose maximization problems are displayed earlier), so that users of oil pay $p + \tau$ per unit instead of p, all tax rates on

[bf] We do not explicitly have a home sector demanding energy. We take GDP to include housing services and to the extent they can be thought of as produced according to the market production function, these energy needs are included, but other home energy needs (such as gasoline for cars) are simply abstracted from.

oil less than $\bar{p}$ will deliver the optimal outcome (recall that the price of oil is a pure rent and the tax will therefore not affect the allocation). If the unit tax is exactly equal to $\bar{p}$, the market price of oil will be zero and oil producers are indifferent between producing or not. At this level there is still an equilibrium which delivers the optimal amount of oil, namely, when all producers choose to produce; otherwise, not enough oil is used.

So suppose instead that $\bar{E} > \nu/(\gamma\phi)$. Now a tax is needed, and the tax should be set so that $p=0$; the price is zero at the socially optimal use of oil. Otherwise, no oil producer would restrict its production and the outcome would be $\bar{E}$. With a tax that is high enough that the price oil producers receive is zero, ie,

$$\tau = \nu e^{-\nu} k^{\alpha} n^{1-\alpha-\nu} \left(\frac{\nu}{\gamma\phi}\right)^{\nu-1},$$

there exists an equilibrium where precisely oil output is equal to $\nu/(\gamma\phi) < \bar{E}$.

4.1.2 Pigou and the Social Cost of Carbon: A Simple Formula

A different way of getting at optimal policy here is to directly compute the optimal tax of carbon to be that direct damage cost of a unit of emission that is not taken into account by markets. This "marginal externality damage" is referred to in the literature as the *social cost of carbon*.[bg] Moreover, the concept needs to be sharpened as the marginal externality damage can be computed at different allocations. We thus refer to the *optimal social cost of carbon* (OSCC) as the marginal externality damage of a unit of carbon emission evaluated at the optimal allocation. Let the optimal carbon amount be denoted E^*. Given Pigou's principle (Pigou, 1920), the OSCC is the way to think about optimal tax policy, so the tax to be applied is

$$\tau^* = \gamma\phi e^{-\gamma\phi E^*} k^{\alpha} n^{1-\alpha-\nu} (E^*)^{\nu},$$

since this is the derivative of the production function with respect to E where it appears as an externality, evaluated at E^*. The idea here is that this tax always allows the government to achieve the optimal outcome as a competitive equilibrium with taxes. To check that this is consistent with the brute-force analysis earlier, note first that for the case where $E^* = \bar{E}$, $\tau^* = \gamma\phi y^* < \nu y^*/\bar{E}$, where y^* is the optimal level of output. Thus, in equilibrium $p = \nu y^*/\bar{E} - \gamma\phi y^* > 0$, which is consistent with all oil being sold. For the case where $\bar{E} > \nu/(\gamma\phi)$, the optimal tax formula $\tau^* = \gamma\phi y^*$ implies, at the interior solution $E^* = \nu/(\gamma\phi)$, that $p + \tau^* = \nu y^*/E^* = \gamma\phi y^*$ so that $p=0$. In other words, oil producers are indifferent between producing or not and E^* is therefore an optimal choice.

[bg] The terminology is perhaps a little misleading since one might be led to think that the social cost is the sum of the private and the externality cost, ie, the total cost. Instead "social" just refers to the part not taken into account by the market.

More generally, it is important to understand that Pigou pricing proceeds in two steps: (i) work out the optimal allocation, by solving the planning problem; and (ii) find the OSCC at this allocation and impose that tax. The first step is straightforward in principle but can be challenging if the planning problem is not convex, eg, because the damage function is highly nonlinear; in such a case, there may in particular be multiple solutions to the planner's first-order conditions. The second step has a potential difficulty if for a given tax there are multiple market equilibria. The simple baseline model here does not admit multiple equilibria for a given tax rate but such models are not inconceivable. One important case may be where there are coordination problems in which technology a society chooses—perhaps between a fossil and a green technology. We discuss such cases later.

The OSCC formula that we derived says that the optimal unit tax on carbon is proportional to the value of GDP at the optimal allocation, with a constant of proportionality given by $\gamma\phi$. This result is an adaptation of the finding in Golosov et al. (2014) who derive the OSCC to be proportional to GDP in a much more general setting—a dynamic model that is calibrated to long-run data. The constant of proportionality in that model is also a function of other parameters relating to intertemporal preferences and the carbon cycle, both elements of which are dynamic modeling aspects. They also find this result to be very robust to a number of modeling changes. We shall review these results later but it is important to note already at this point that the core of the proportionality of the OSCC to output can be explained within the structure of the simple static model here.

4.1.3 Costs of Carbon When Taxes are not Optimally Set

Let us emphasize what the OSCC formula says and does not say. It tells us what the marginal externality cost of carbon is, provided we are in an optimal allocation. However, as there appear to be damages from global warming on net and very few countries have carbon taxes, the real world is not at an optimal allocation with respect to carbon use, and this fact suggests that there is another measure that might be relevant: what the marginal externality cost of carbon is today, in the suboptimal allocation. So let SCC, the *social cost of carbon*, be a concept that can be evaluated at any allocation, and suppose we look at the laissez-faire allocation.

One can, conceptually, define a SCC in more than one way. We will define it here as the marginal externality damage of carbon emissions *keeping constant behavior in the given allocation*. This is an important qualification, because if an additional unit of carbon is emitted into the atmosphere, equilibrium decisions will change—whether we are in an optimal allocation or not—and if the given allocation is not optimal, the induced changes in behavior will, in general, have a first-order effect on utility. Hence, an alternative definition would, somehow, take the induced changes in decisions into account. (If the allocation is optimal, these effects can be ignored based on an envelope-theorem argument.)

Let us thus compute the SCC for the case of our static model. Let us assume $\bar{E} > \nu/(\gamma\phi)$, so that there is excessive carbon use. Then the SCC, $\gamma\phi y$, is lower than the OSCC, $\gamma\phi y^*$. This is of course true since $y^* > y$ by definition: the planner's aim is precisely to maximize GDP in this simple model and laissez-faire markets fail to. Note also that the percentage difference between the two measures here is only a function of $\bar{E}$ and E^* and not of other indicators of the "size" of the economy, such as the amount of capital or labor.

Depending on the allocation we are looking at, the SCC may in general be higher or lower than the OSCC. There is also no presumption that the laissez-faire SCC have to be higher than the OSCC, which one might imagine if the marginal damages of emissions rise with the level of emissions. In the simple static model we just looked at here, however, the SCC is always be below the OSCC, because damages appear in TFP and are of a form that implies proportionality to output; the OSCC is chosen to maximize output in this setting, so the OSCC must then be higher than the SCC. In contrast, in our dynamic model in Section 5, although the SCC will be proportional to current output there too, the SCC will typically be above the OSCC. The reason there is that current output tends to be rising with higher current fossil use—it is primarily future output that will fall with current emissions, due to the incurred damages—implying that the SCC will be higher for higher levels of current emissions, and in particular the SCC will be higher than the OSCC since the latter dictates lower emissions. The comparison between the SCC and the OSCC is of practical importance: suppose we are in a laissez-faire allocation today, and that econometricians have measured SCC, ie, damages from emissions based on our current allocation. Then this SCC measure is not of direct relevance for taxation; in fact, for the calibrated dynamic model, we would conclude that the optimal tax is below the econometricians' laissez-faire SCC estimates.

Most of the integrated-assessment literature on the social cost of carbon computes the cost as is indicated above, ie, as a marginal cost at an optimal allocation and, more generally, comparisons between suboptimal and optimal allocations are rather unusual. The simple model here does allow such comparisons (as does the dynamic benchmark model described later). Thus define the *percentage consumption equivalent* as the value λ such that $u(c^*(1-\lambda)) = u(c)$, where c^* is the optimal consumption level and c any suboptimal level. Thus we can compute the laissez-faire value for λ in the simple model (i) to be 0, in the case where there is little enough carbon that all of it should be used ($\bar{E} > \nu/(\gamma\phi)$); and (ii), in the case where too much carbon is available, to satisfy

$$1-\lambda = \frac{e^{-\gamma\phi\bar{E}} k^{\alpha} n^{1-\alpha-\nu} \bar{E}^{\nu}}{e^{-\gamma\phi E^*} k^{\alpha} n^{1-\alpha-\nu} (E^*)^{\nu}} = e^{-\gamma\phi\left(\bar{E}-\frac{\nu}{\gamma\phi}\right)} \left(\frac{\gamma\phi\bar{E}}{\nu}\right)^{\nu}.$$

It is straightforward to verify that λ is increasing in $\bar{E}$ here. Note, however, that variables such as capital or labor do not enter, nor would the size of the population if it were introduced as a separate variable. So the "size" of the economy is not important for this measure.

4.2 The Case of Coal

Here, $\zeta > 0$ and we interpret E as coal. Laissez faire now always involves an interior solution for E and it is such that its (private) benefit equals its (private) cost $p = \zeta = \nu e^{-\gamma\phi E} k^{\alpha} n^{1-\alpha-\nu} E^{\nu-1}$. The planner chooses a lower amount of E: E^* is chosen so that the private benefit of coal minus its social cost equals its private cost:

$$-\gamma\phi e^{-\gamma\phi E^*} k^{\alpha} n^{1-\alpha-\nu} (E^*)^{\nu} + \nu e^{-\gamma\phi E^*} k^{\alpha} n^{1-\alpha-\nu} (E^*)^{\nu-1} = \zeta.$$

Notice here that when coal production becomes more productive (ζ falls), markets use more coal. The same is true for the planner, since the left-hand side of the above equation must be decreasing at an optimum level E^* (so that the second-order condition is satisfied): if ζ falls, the left-hand side must fall, requiring E^* to rise. Thus, technical improvements in coal production imply higher emissions.

4.2.1 *Optimal Taxes and the Optimal Social Cost of Carbon*

Recall that, in the benchmark model, we think of coal as produced at a constant marginal cost in terms of output goods. Given that GDP, y, equals consumption or $e^{-\gamma\phi E} k^{\alpha} n^{1-\alpha-\nu} (E)^{\nu} - \zeta E$, we can write the equation determining the optimal coal use as

$$-\gamma\phi(y^* + \zeta E^*) + \nu(y^* + \zeta E^*)/E^* = \zeta.$$

Hence, the optimal social cost of carbon, OSCC, is now $\gamma\phi y^*(1 + \zeta E^*/Y^*) = \gamma\phi y^*(1 + \frac{pE^*}{y^*})$. So it is not quite proportional to GDP (as it was in the case of oil) but rather to GDP plus firms' energy costs as a share of GDP. In practice, energy costs are less than 10% of GDP so a rule of thumb that sets the unit tax on coal equal to $\gamma\phi$ times GDP is still approximately correct.

4.2.2 *Costs of Carbon When Taxes are not Optimally Set*

What is the social cost of carbon at the laissez-faire allocation? It is $\gamma\phi(y + \zeta E)$, where y is laissez-faire GDP and E is laissez-faire carbon use, where we know that $y < y^*$ and $E > E^*$. Unlike in the case of oil, it is not clear whether this amount is smaller than the OSCC. The subtlety here is that the production of coal itself—an intermediate input—is hampered by a damage from climate change and thus the total externality from coal production is not just $\gamma\phi y$.

Consumption in the laissez-faire allocation is lower by a fraction λ that satisfies

$$1-\lambda=\frac{e^{-\gamma\phi E}k^{\alpha}n^{1-\alpha-\nu}E^{\nu}-\zeta E}{e^{-\gamma\phi E^*}k^{\alpha}n^{1-\alpha-\nu}(\bar{E}^*)^{\nu}-\zeta E^*}=\frac{e^{-\gamma\phi E}k^{\alpha}n^{1-\alpha-\nu}E^{\nu}}{e^{-\gamma\phi E^*}k^{\alpha}n^{1-\alpha-\nu}(\bar{E}^*)^{\nu}}\frac{1-\nu}{1-\nu+\gamma\phi E^*},$$

where for the second equality we have used the equilibrium and planner's conditions, respectively. This expression is, unlike in the oil example, not explicit in terms of primitives. In general, it depends nontrivially on the size of the economy (of course, one can derive first-order conditions determining both E and E^* as a function of primitives but, for the latter, not in closed form).

4.2.3 Coal Production Only Requires Labor: Our Benchmark Model

The case where coal is produced at a constant marginal cost in terms of output units is somewhat less tractable than the following alternative: coal production does not require capital and does not experience TFP losses from climate change. Ie, $E=\chi n_E$, where n_E is labor used in coal production and χ is a productivity parameter. This case is less realistic but given that energy production is a rather small part of firms' costs, it is convenient to use this specification for some purposes. In this case, we have output given as

$$y=e^{-\gamma\phi\chi n_E}k^{\alpha}(1-n_E)^{1-\alpha-\nu}(\chi n_E)^{\nu},$$

where total labor is now normalized: $n=1$. In a laissez-faire allocation, we obtain that $n_E=\frac{\nu}{1-\alpha}$. The planner's allocation delivers optimal n_E^* from

$$-\gamma\phi\chi+\frac{\nu}{n_E^*}=\frac{1-\alpha-\nu}{1-n_E^*}.$$

It is straightforward to check that higher productivity in producing coal will increase emissions both in the laissez-faire allocation and in the optimal one.

Here, moreover, the social cost of carbon will be exactly proportional to GDP, as in the oil case: $\gamma\phi y^*$. The reason is that no indirect externality (through the production of fossil fuel) is involved in this case. Similarly, we can solve for laissez-faire measures of the cost of carbon and the welfare gap relative to the full optimum.

In what follows, when we focus on coal production or oil production that occurs at positive marginal cost, we will use this formulation since it allows for simpler algebra without forsaking quantitatively important realism.

4.3 Calibration

We will now calibrate the static model. This is of course heroic, given that so many aspects of the climate-economy nexus feature dynamics, but the point here is merely to show that the static model can be thought of in quantitative terms. It is also possible to compare the results here to those in the calibration of the fully dynamic model in Section 5.2.

So let the heroics begin by calling our model period 100 years. The benchmark model will have coal as the only source energy; as we will argue later, the stock of oil is rather small relative to the stock of coal, and we leave out renewables for now (in the dynamic model in the later section, we calibrate the production of energy services as using three sources: oil, coal, and green). We assume that coal is produced from labor alone as in the previous section, and the model thus has five parameters: γ, ϕ, α, ν, and χ. We thus need five observations to pin these down.

Output being a flow, we can straightforwardly set α and ν based on average historic data; we select 0.3 and 0.04, respectively (see Hassler et al., 2015). For the rest of the model parameters, let us relate the model's laissez-faire equilibrium to some other observables. We thus need to relate the equilibrium outcomes for the key variables—E, S, n_E, and y—to relevant data targets. A business-as-usual scenario with continuously increasing emissions can lead to increases of the temperature of around 4°C at the end of the century.[bh] We interpret business as usual as our laissez-faire allocation. Let us use this information to find out the associated atmospheric concentration and emissions implied to generate this result, given our model. Arrhenius's formula gives

$$4 = \Delta T = \lambda \frac{\log \frac{S+\bar{S}}{\bar{S}}}{\log 2} = 3 \frac{\log \frac{S+600}{600}}{\log 2},$$

which allows us to solve for S as roughly 900 (GtC, in excess of the preindustrial level 600). What are the corresponding emissions required? The model says $S = \phi E$. To select ϕ, use the estimated linear carbon depreciation formula in Section 3.2.5 above for computing the average depreciation from emitting a constant amount per decade. This amounts to a straight average of the consecutive depreciation rates and a value for ϕ of 0.48: the atmospheric carbon concentration rises by about one half of each emitted unit.

To calibrate γ, let us take IPCC's upper estimate from Fig. 9: at a warming of 4 ○C, they report a total loss of 5% of GDP. This is a flow measure and thus easy to map into our present structure. We thus need $e^{-\gamma S}$ to equal 0.95. This delivers $\gamma = 5.7 \cdot 10^{-5}$.

It remains to calibrate the parameter χ of the coal sector: its labor productivity. We can find it as follows. To reach 900 GtC, one needs to emit 900/0.48 units given the calculation above. In the model solution, $n_E = \nu/(1-\alpha)$. This means that $900/0.48 = \chi n_E = \chi \cdot 0.04/0.7$, which delivers a χ of approximately 32,813.

4.4 A Few Quantitative Experiments with the Calibrated Model

We now illustrate the workings of the simple baseline model with coal with a few quantitative experiments. The chief purpose is to check robustness of the main results.

[bh] Scenario RCP8.5 from IPCC's 5th Assessment Report.

Similar exercises could be carried out in all of the applications that follow (dealing with uncertainty, tipping points, tax-vs-quota policy comparisons, and so on). We have left such quantitative analysis out for brevity but for each application it would be valuable to use the baseline calibration as discussed here, calibrate the new parameters relevant to the application, and then produce output in the form of tables and graphs. Indeed, such exercises appear ideal for teaching the present material.

Starting out from the calibrated benchmark, let us vary two of the parameters within reasonable ranges. We first look at the effect of the damage elasticity of output, varying it from a half of its estimated value to much higher ones. We see that a doubling of the damage elasticity a little more than doubles the GDP gap between laissez-faire and the optimum. For damages 10 × higher than the baseline estimate, the loss of GDP is almost a quarter of GDP.

Externality cost	$1-\frac{y}{y^*}$
$\gamma/2$	0.0037
γ	0.0177
2γ	0.0454
4γ	0.0983
6γ	0.1482
8γ	0.1954
10γ	0.2400

Turning to carbon depreciation, the robustness looks at a tighter range around the baseline calibration as compared to that for damages (the uncertainty about damages, after all, is much higher). Modest changes in carbon depreciation, as depicted in the table later, do nevertheless have some impact: a change of ϕ by 25 percentage point changes the output gap by about seven tenths of a percent and temperature by a little over half a degree.

1–carbon depreciation	ΔT	$1-\frac{y}{y^*}$
0.75ϕ	3.2624	0.0107
0.95ϕ	3.8340	0.0164
ϕ	3.9658	0.0177
1.05ϕ	4.0938	0.0192
1.15ϕ	4.3388	0.0219
1.25ϕ	4.5707	0.0247

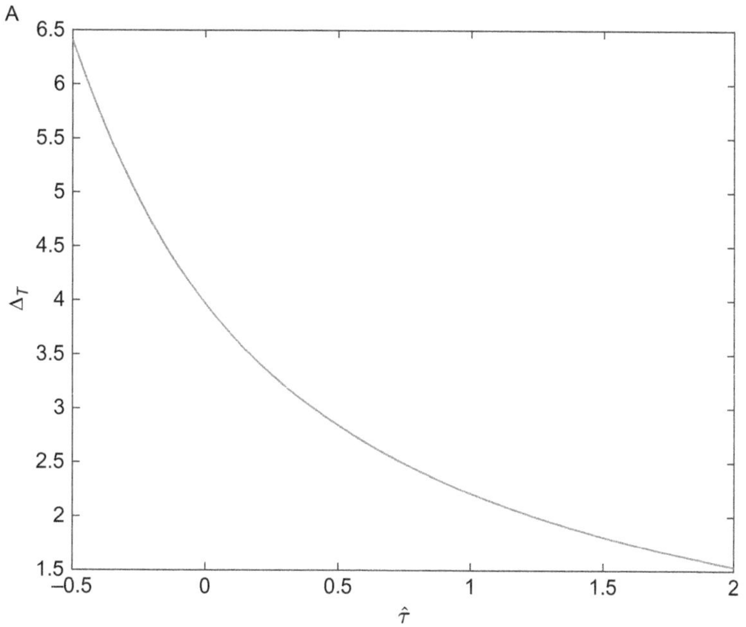

Fig. 11 Outcomes as a function of the tax-GDP rate, $\hat{\tau}$h. (A) Temperature change.

Finally, let us look at a more complete range of suboptimal taxes for the baseline calibration. The table and figures below illustrate by varying the tax, measured as a percent of GDP. Fig. 11 illustrates rather clearly that the model is more nonlinear for negative than for positive taxes: if the tax is turned into a sizeable subsidy the warming and output losses are substantial.

$(\tau/y)/(\tau^*/y^*)$	ΔT	$1-\frac{y}{y^*}$	n_E
−0.5	6.4084	0.0975	0.1294
0	3.9658	0.0177	0.0571
0.5	2.8365	0.0024	0.0353
1	2.2110	0	0.0254
2	1.5346	0.0035	0.0162

4.5 Summary: Core Model

We have built a simple static model which can be used to think about the key long-run aspects of carbon emissions and climate change. Though only a full dynamic, and much more complex, model can do the analysis of climate change full justice, our simple model does have some features that makes it quantitatively reasonable. The mapping from

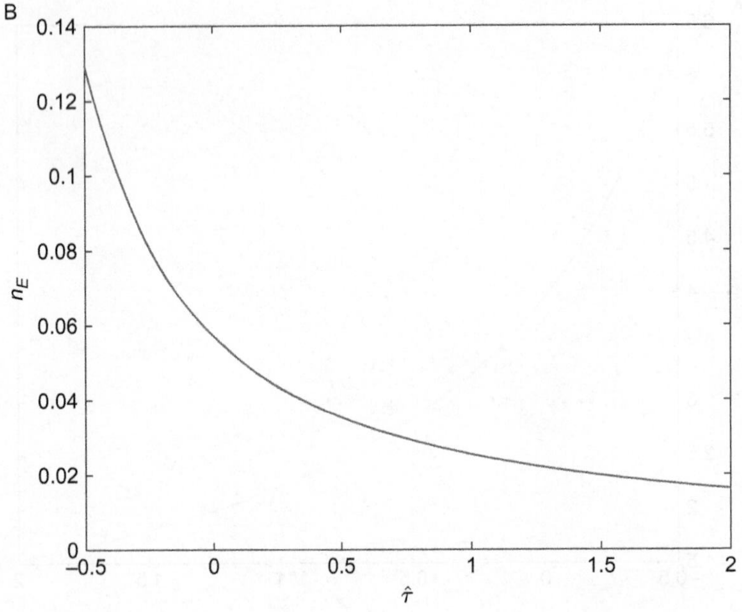

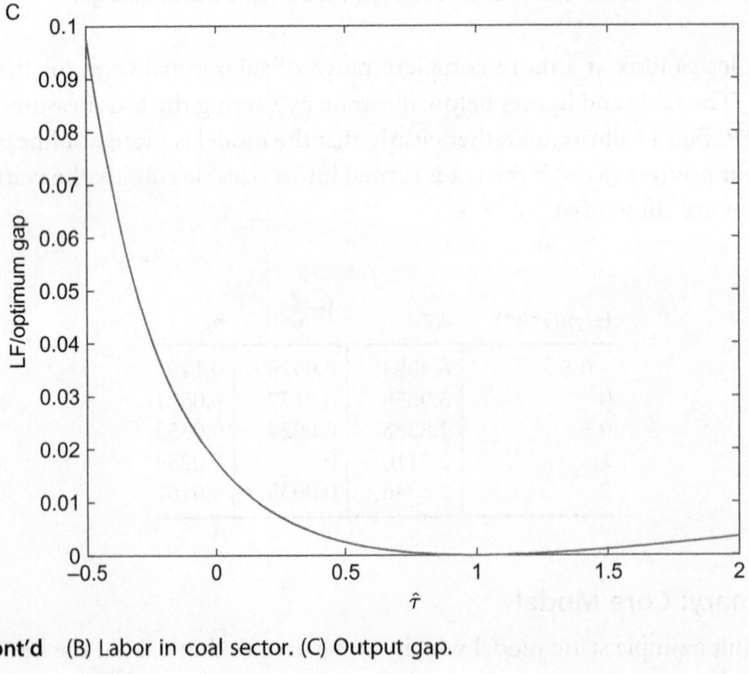

Fig. 11—cont'd (B) Labor in coal sector. (C) Output gap.

emissions to damages is described with a simple closed form but it captures the key features of this mapping in much more elaborate dynamic models, such as Nordhaus's DICE and RICE models. The role of fossil fuels in the economy is also described in a very rudimentary way but it too is the most natural starting point in dynamic quantitative models.

The simple model implies that the optimal social cost of carbon—the marginal externality damage at the optimal allocation—is proportional to GDP; this result is exactly true in some special cases of the model and approximately true otherwise. Also more generally, evaluated as a fraction of output, the (marginal) social cost of carbon (ignoring indirect effects on behavior of raising emissions) is independent of the allocation at which it is measured. This also means that the social cost of carbon is lower in the laissez-faire allocation than in the optimal allocation, because in the static model where damages appear to TFP optimal output by definition is higher than laissez-faire output. This feature will disappear in a dynamic model—where laissez-faire output tends to be higher (in the short run) than in the optimal allocation because less energy is used—and in a model where damages do not affect output, eg, by affecting utility directly. We will of course look at these kinds of extensions below. Moreover, in the simple static model we formulated here, the utility loss from not using taxes to curb carbon use, expressed in percentages of consumption, is scale-independent.

Next, we use the simple model to address some issues that have featured prominently in the literature. These include the choice of policy instruments—in particular the comparison between price and quantity regulations (taxes vs quotas)—along with extensions to consider utility damages, uncertainty, tipping points, technological change, and more.

4.6 Utility Damages

We can, instead of or in addition to the damages to TFP, imagine that higher global temperatures affect welfare directly. This could occur in a variety of ways, through effects on health, the value of leisure, or more generally perceived life quality. Ignoring TFP damages for simplicity, consider first a utility function of a specific functional form:

$$u(c, E) = \log c - \gamma S,$$

where, again, $S = \phi E$ is carbon concentration in excess of the preindustrial level. Here, thus, atmospheric carbon concentration, and hence emissions, influence utility linearly, whereas consumption has decreasing marginal utility. This means that the value of one less unit of emissions in terms of consumption increases as the economy gets richer: $u_E / u_c = \gamma \phi c$. This implies, immediately, that the social cost of carbon in this economy is identical to that above: it is proportional to output. Thus, if the utility cost has the structure just assumed, the implications for how to tax carbon remain the same as in the more common case of TFP damages. In fact, we can now interpret the formulation with TFP damages as possibly coming from two sources: direct damages to TFP and utility damages.

With the remaining parts of the economy unchanged (except that we now view TFP as unaffected by emissions), we can solve for the laissez-faire equilibrium exactly as before. For sake of illustration, let us focus on coal and on the case where energy is produced linearly from labor. The social planner's problem is to solve

$$\max_{n_E} \log\left(k^{\alpha}(n-n_E)^{1-\alpha-\nu}(\chi n_E)^{\nu}\right)-\gamma\phi\chi n_E.$$

The problem simplifies to solving

$$\max_{n_E}(1-\alpha-\nu)\log(n-n_E)+\nu\log n_E-\gamma\phi\chi n_E.$$

The first-order condition gives $\frac{\nu}{n_E}=\frac{1-\alpha-\nu}{n-n_E}+\gamma\phi\chi$, which is the exact same equation as in the corresponding model with TFP damages.

What is the optimal tax/the OSCC in this model? The consumption-good firm's first-order condition for energy (assuming a unit tax τ) is $p+\tau=\nu k^{\alpha}(n-E/\chi)^{1-\alpha-\nu}E^{\nu-1}$, whereas the energy firm's first-order condition reads $p\chi=w$, with $w=(1-\alpha-\nu)k^{\alpha}(n-E/\chi)^{-\alpha-\nu}E^{\nu}$. This delivers $\frac{1-\alpha-\nu}{\chi}k^{\alpha}(n-E/\chi)^{-\alpha-\nu}E^{\nu}+\tau=\nu k^{\alpha}(n-E/\chi)^{1-\alpha-\nu}E^{\nu-1}$, from which we see that $\tau^*=\gamma\phi y^*$ is the optimal tax here as well.

More generally, the SCC at any consumption/energy allocation here can be obtained as $-u_E(c,E)/u_c(c,E)=\gamma\phi c$, and since consumption is GDP in the static model we again have that the SCC equals $\gamma\phi y$. We can, finally, define the utility loss in the laissez-faire allocation, measured in terms of a percentage consumption loss (ie, from $u(c^*(1-\lambda), E^*)=u(c,E)$). We obtain $\log(1-\lambda)=\log\frac{c}{c^*}-\gamma\phi(E-E^*)$ and thus that $1-\lambda=e^{-\gamma\phi(E-E^*)}\frac{c}{c^*}$ which has the same form as before and, thus, is scale-independent.

4.7 Other Damage Functions

Our assessment in the section earlier on damages from climate change is that this is the subarea in the climate-economy literature with the most striking knowledge gaps. Integrated assessment models differ to some extent in how they formulate damages as a function of climate (temperature) and how they parameterize their functions but the functional form used in Nordhaus's work (the DICE and RICE models) is the most common one. One possibility is that the overall damage *levels* are very different from the most common estimates in the literature, and another is that the functional-form assumptions are wrong. For this discussion, let us use the utility-damage formulation just outlined, and where we argued that $\log c-\gamma S$ is a formulation that is quantitatively close to that used by Nordhaus, given that this function should be viewed as a composition of the mapping from emissions to atmospheric carbon concentration and the mapping from the latter to damages. Let us therefore think about the choice of damage functions in terms of the more general formulation $\log c - \Gamma(S)$, with Γ being a more nontrivial function.[bi] The function Γ, if truly described globally, should probably be increasing for positive values of S (since $S=0$ corresponds to the preindustrial concentration) and convex. For sufficiently low values of S (below 0), the function ought to be decreasing, since there is a reasonable notion of an "appropriate" climate: human beings could not survive if it is too cold either.

A concrete argument for a convex $\Gamma(S)$, rather than the linear one we use in our benchmark, is based on the arguments in Section 3.2.6: there appears to be an approximate reduced-form relationship between the global temperature and the unweighted cumulative amount of past anthropogenic emissions (since the industrial era began), which is *linear*. This was labeled the *CCR* (Carbon-Climate Response) formulation. Then take, say, Nordhaus's global damage function mapping temperature to output losses as given, and combine it with this approximate linear relationship. The resulting $\Gamma(S)$ must then be convex.[bj]

With the more general damage function $\Gamma(S)$, all the earlier analysis goes through with the only difference being that $\Gamma'(S)$ now replaces γ earlier. Obviously, Γ could be calibrated so that $\Gamma'(S)=\gamma$ (with a standard calibration for γ) for current total emission levels, so the added insights here are about how the OSCC (and optimal tax) and the SCCs evolve as GDP evolves.

The SCC in this case becomes $\Gamma'(S)y$, where y again is GDP. Thus, to the extent Γ is convex, the optimal tax (as well as the SCC more generally) would not just be proportional to output but it would also increase with emissions; how much it would increase simply depends on the degree of convexity of Γ. Moreover, imagine an exogenous improvement in TFP. Such a shock would now increase the OSCC (the optimal tax) through two channels. The first channel was present before: a direct positive effect on y (leading to a higher tax by the same percentage amount). The second channel is an indirect effect via a higher demand for E. In terms of the decentralized economy, a higher TFP would, for a given tax, make firms demand a higher E, and since $\Gamma'(S)$ is increasing, this would then call for a further increase in the optimal tax rate.[bk]

[bi] We maintain logarithmic curvature without loss of generality.

[bj] Note, however, that the approximate linearity appears to be in somewhat of a conflict with Arrhenius's insight that the temperature change is proportional to the logarithm of the atmospheric carbon concentration (thus, a concave function). The conflict is not as strong as it seems, however. Our approximation that $\Gamma(S)$ is linear relies on a description of a carbon cycle that is rather realistic (eg, has more complex dynamics) and that uses Arrhenius's formula, which still has widespread acceptance. The upshot of this really is that the just-mentioned convexity after all cannot be very strong.

[bk] This discussion is a reminder that the optimal-tax formula $\tau^* = \Gamma'(S^*)y^*$ is not a closed form, since S^* and y^* are endogenous.

Similarly, the percentage consumption equivalent loss in welfare λ from remaining at laissez-faire can be computed from

$$\log(1-\lambda) = \log\frac{c}{c^*} - (\Gamma(S) - \Gamma(S^*)).$$

To the extent Γ is convex, this expression potentially increases faster in $S - S^*$ (and, more generally, depends on both these emission levels separately).

Now consider a highly nonlinear damage function, and let us investigate whether such a case poses a difficulty for the Pigou approach to the climate problem. Consider the possibility that at a low level of emissions, so for a low S, the social cost of carbon is actually zero: $\Gamma'(S) = 0$. However, $\Gamma(S)$ is at the same time increasing rapidly for higher values of S, after which it again levels off and becomes flat: $\Gamma'(S) = 0$ also for high enough values of S. The latter amounts to a "disaster" outcome where more atmospheric carbon concentration actually does not hurt because all the horrible events that could happen have already happened given that S is so high. Here, though low emissions have a zero SCC, such low emissions are not what Pigou's formula would prescribe: they would prescribe that the SCC equal the net private benefits from emissions, and they are high for low emission levels. The net private benefits of emissions are, in particular, globally declining here (and, since damages appear in preferences and not to production in the particular case under study, always positive). So instead, it is optimal to raise emissions to a point with a S^* such that $\Gamma'(S^*)$ is positive, perhaps one where Γ is increasing rapidly. The example shows that although a rapidly rising damage function in some sense poses a threat, the Pigou approach still works rather well. A key here is that for any given tax rate, the market equilibrium is unique; in the argument earlier, this manifested itself in the statement that the net private benefits from emissions are globally declining. They may not be, ie, there may be multiple market equilibria, but such cases are unusual. We consider such examples in Section 4.14.1 in the context of coordination problems in technology choice.

In conclusion, the model is well-designed also for incorporating "more convex" damage functions, and the qualitative differences in conclusions are not major nor difficult to understand. The key conclusion remains: more research on the determination and nature of damages—including the mechanisms whereby a warmer climate imposes costs on people—is of utmost importance in this literature, and integrated assessment modeling stands ready to incorporate the latest news from any such endeavors.

4.8 Tipping Points

A tipping point typically refers to a phenomenon either in the carbon cycle or in the climate system where there is a very strong nonlinearity. Ie, if the emissions exceed a certain level, a more drastic effect on climate, and hence on damages, is realized. As discussed earlier in the natural-science part of the chapter, one can for example imagine a departure from the Arrhenius approximation of the climate model. Recall that the Arrhenius approximation was that the temperature increase relative to that in the preindustrial era is proportional to the logarithm of the atmospheric carbon concentration (as a fraction of the preindustrial concentration), where the constant of proportionality—often labeled λ—is referred to as climate sensitivity. One way to express a tipping point is that λ shoots up beyond some critical level of carbon concentration. Another is that the carbon cycle has a nonlinearity making ϕ a(n increasing) function of S, due to carbon sinks becoming less able to absorb carbon. Finally, we can imagine that damages feature a stronger convexity beyond a certain temperature point; for example, sufficiently high temperature and humidity make it impossible for humans and animals to survive outdoors.

Notice that all these examples simply amount to a different functional form for damages than that assumed earlier (whether damages appear to TFP or to utility). Thus, one can proceed as in the previous section and simply replace the total damage γS by a damage function $\Gamma(S)$, where this function has a strong nonlinearity. One could imagine many versions of nonlinearity. One involves a kink, whereby we would have a linear function $\gamma_{lo}S$ for $S \leq \underline{S}$ and $\gamma_{hi}S$ for $S > \underline{S}$, with $\gamma_{lo} << \gamma_{hi}$. A second possibility is simply a globally more convex (and smooth) function Γ. One example is Acemoglu et al. (2012), who assume that there is something labeled "environmental quality" that, at zero, leads to minus infinity utility and has infinitely positive marginal utility (without quantitative scientific references). One can also imagine that there is randomness in the carbon cycle or the climate, and this kind of randomness may allow for outcomes that are more extreme than those given by a simple (and deterministic) linear function γS. Finally, the $\Gamma(S)$ function could feature an irreversibility so that it attains a higher value if S ever has been above some threshold, thus even if S later falls below this threshold.

As discussed in the previous subsection, the formulation with a tipping point does not change the analysis of the laissez-faire equilibrium. It does, however, alter the social planner's problem. In particular, in place of γ as representing the negative externality of emissions in the planner's first-order condition we now have $\Gamma'(S)$ and this derivative may be very high. It is still possible to implement the optimum with a carbon tax, though it will no longer just be proportional to the optimal level of GDP and may respond nonlinearly to any parametric change, as discussed earlier. Suppose, for example, that γ becomes "infinite" beyond some $\underline{S}$. Then, from the perspective of a government choosing the optimal tax rate on carbon emissions, the objective function would have highly asymmetric payoffs from the tax choice: if the tax rate is chosen to be too low, the damage would be infinite, and more generally changes in the environment (such as increases in the capital stock or labor input, which would increase the demand for energy) would necessitate appropriate increases in the tax so as to avoid disaster.

Overall, in order to handle tipping points in a quantitative study based on an integrated assessment model one would need to calibrate the nonlinear damage function.

In terms of our first example, how would one estimate $\underline{S}$? As we argued in the natural-science sections 3.1.2 and 3.3.4 earlier, our interpretation of the consensus is that whereas a number of tipping points have been identified, some of which are also quantified, these are tipping points for rather local systems, or systems of limited global impact in the shorter run. To the extent there is a global (and quantitatively important) tipping point, there does not appear to be a consensus on where it would lie in S space. Therefore, at this point and in waiting for further evidence either on aggregate nonlinearities in the carbon cycle or climate system or in how climate maps into economic costs, we maintain a linear formulation (or, in the case damages appear in TFP, in the equivalent exponential form). Performing comparative statics on γ is of course very important and we return to it later.

4.9 Uncertainty

It is possible to analyze uncertainty in a small extension of the simple benchmark model. Suppose we consider a prestage of the economy when the decisions on emissions need to be made—by markets as well as by a fictitious planner. We then think of utility as of the expected-utility kind, and we begin by using a utility formulation common in dynamic macroeconomic models: $u(c) = \log c$. Thus, the objective is $E(\log(c))$. Uncertainty could appear in various forms, but let us simply consider a reduced-form representation of it by letting γ, the damage elasticity of output, be random. That is, in some states of nature emissions are very costly and in some they are not. Recall that the uncertainty can be about the economic damages given any temperature level or about how given emissions influence temperature.

For the sake of illustration, we first consider the simplest of cases: γ is either high, γ_{hi}, or low, γ_{lo}, with probabilities π and $1-\pi$, respectively. The emissions decision has to be made—either by a planner or by actors in decentralized markets—ex-ante, but there is no "prior period" in which there is consumption or any other decisions than just how high to make E. We consider the case of coal here, and with coal production requiring labor only, without associated TFP damages.

Looking at the planning problem first, we have

$$\max_E \pi \log\left(e^{-\gamma_{hi}\phi E} k^{\alpha}\left(1-\frac{E}{\chi}\right)^{1-\alpha-\nu} E^{\nu}\right) + (1-\pi)\log\left(e^{-\gamma_{lo}\phi E} k^{\alpha}\left(1-\frac{E}{\chi}\right)^{1-\alpha-\nu} E^{\nu}\right).$$

Save for a constant, this problem simplifies to

$$\max_E -(\pi\gamma_{hi} + (1-\pi)\gamma_{lo})\phi E + (1-\alpha-\nu)\log\left(1-\frac{E}{\chi}\right) + \nu \log E.$$

A key feature of this maximization problem is that the damage elasticity appears only in expected value! This means that the solution of the problem will depend on the expected value of γ but not on any higher-order properties of its distribution. This feature, which of course holds regardless of the distributional assumptions of γ, will not hold exactly if coal/oil is produced with constant marginal cost in terms of final output (as in our very first setting above), but approximately the same solution will obtain in any calibrated version of the model since the fossil-fuel costs are small as a fraction of output.

Notice that the "certainty equivalence" result obtains here even though the consumer is risk-averse. However, it obtains for logarithmic utility only. If the utility function curvature is higher than logarithmic, the planner will take into account the variance in outcomes: higher variance will reduce the choice for E.[bl] Formally, and as an example, consider the utility function $c^{1-\sigma}/(1-\sigma)$ so that the planner's objective is

$$\mathbf{E}_{\gamma}\frac{\left(e^{-\gamma E}k^{\alpha}\left(1-\frac{E}{\chi}\right)^{1-\alpha-\nu}E^{\nu}\right)^{1-\sigma}}{1-\sigma}.$$

Since E is predetermined, we can write this as

$$\frac{\left(k^{\alpha}\left(1-\frac{E}{\chi}\right)^{1-\alpha-\nu}E^{\nu}\right)^{1-\sigma}}{1-\sigma}\mathbf{E}_{\gamma}e^{-\gamma E(1-\sigma)}.$$

Assume now that γ is normally distributed with mean $\bar{\mu}$ and variance σ_{μ}^2. Then we obtain the objective

$$\frac{\left(e^{-\Gamma(E)}k^{\alpha}\left(1-\frac{E}{\chi}\right)^{1-\alpha-\nu}E^{\nu}\right)^{1-\sigma}}{1-\sigma},$$

with

$$\Gamma(E)=-\bar{\gamma}E+\frac{\sigma_{\mu}^2E^2(1-\sigma)}{2}.$$

Thus, the objective function is a monotone transformation of consumption, with consumption determined as usual in this model except for the fact that the damage expression γE is now replaced by $\Gamma(E)$, a convex function for $\sigma>1$ (higher curvature than logarithmic). To the extent that the variance σ_{μ}^2 is large and σ is significantly above 1, we thus have uncertainty play the role of a "more convex damage function," as discussed earlier. We see that the logarithmic function that is our benchmark does apply as a special case.

[bl] The asset pricing literature offers many utility functions that, jointly with random processes for consumption, can deliver large welfare costs; several of these approaches have also been pursued in the climate-economy literature, such as in Barro (2013), Gollier (2013), Crost and Traeger (2014), and Lemoine (2015).

4.9.1 The Dismal Theorem

In this context let us briefly discuss the so-called *Dismal Theorem* derived and discussed by Weitzman in a series of papers (eg, Weitzman, 2009; see also the discussion in Nordhaus, 2009). Weitzman provides conditions under which, in a rather abstract context where governmental action could eliminate climate uncertainty, expected utility is minus infinity in the absence of appropriate government action. Thus, one can (as does Weitzman) see this as an argument for (radical) government action. His result follows, very loosely speaking, if the uncertainty has fat enough tails, the risk aversion is high enough, and the government is able to entirely eliminate the tail uncertainty, but the details of the derivation depend highly on specifics. In our present context, a normal distribution for γ is clearly not fat-tailed enough and the only way for the government to shut down tail risk is to set E to zero. However, imagine that the economy has an amount of free green energy, denoted $\widetilde{E}$, ie, the production function is $e^{-\gamma E}k^{\alpha}\left(1-\frac{E}{\chi}\right)^{1-\alpha-\nu}(\widetilde{E}+E)^{\nu}$; then setting $E=0$ still allows positive output. Now imagine that γ has a distribution with fat enough tails, ie, one allowing infinitely high values for γ and slowly decreasing density there. Then expected utility will become infinite if σ is large enough.[bm]

The Dismal Theorem is not connected to data, nor applied in a quantitatively specified integrated assessment model. It relies fundamentally on a shock structure that allows infinitely negative shocks (in percentage terms), and our historical data is too limited to allow us to distinguish the shape of the left tail of this uncertainty in conjunction with the shape of marginal utility near zero; at this point, it seems hard enough to be sure of the mean of the shocks.

4.10 Taxes vs Quotas

In the discussion earlier, we have been focusing on a tax as the obvious candidate policy instrument. Indeed the damage externality is a pure externality for which the Pigou theorem applies straightforwardly. What are alternative policies? The Coase theorem applies too as well but it does not seem possible in practice to define property rights for the atmosphere (into which emissions can then be made, in exchange for a payment to the owner). What about regulating quantities? Indeed the "cap-and-trade" system, which is a quota-based mechanism, has been the main system proposed in the international negotiations to

[bm] A simpler, reduced form setting is that where consumption is given by a t distribution (which has fatter tails than the normal distribution), representing some risk which in this case would be labeled climate risk. Then with power utility, $u(c)=c^{1-\sigma}/(1-\sigma)$, and if σ is high enough, the marginal utility at zero goes to infinity fast enough that expected utility is minus infinity. This point was original made by Geweke (2001). If the government can shut down the variance, or otherwise provide a lower bound for consumption, it would then be highly desirable.

come to a global agreement on climate change. A cap-and-trade system is indeed in place in Europe since 2005.[bn] There is a debate on whether a tax or a quota system is better, and here we will only allude to the main arguments. Our main purpose here, instead, is to make a few basic theoretical points in the comparison between the two systems. These points are also relevant in practice.

Before proceeding to the analysis, let us briefly describe the "-and-trade" part, which we will not subject to theoretical analysis. If a region is subject to a quantity cap—emissions cannot exceed a certain amount—the determination of who gets to emit how much, among the users of fossil energy in the region, must still be decided on. The idea is then to allocate *emission rights* and to allow trade in these rights. The trading, in theory at least, will then ensure that emissions are made efficiently. The initial allocation of emission rights can be made in many ways, eg, through grandfathering (giving rights in proportion to historic use) or auctions. To analyze the trading system formally we would need to introduce heterogeneity among users, which would be straightforward but not yield insights beyond that just mentioned.

The first, and most basic, point in comparing quotas and taxes is that, if there is no uncertainty or if policies can be made contingent on the state of nature, both instruments can be used to attain any given allocation.[bo] If a tax is used, the tax applies to all users; if a quota is used, regardless of how the initial emission rights are used, the market price of an emission right will play the role of the tax: it will impose an extra cost per unit emission and this cost will be the same for all users, provided the market for emission rights works well.

Second, suppose there is uncertainty and the policy cannot be made state-contingent. This is a rather restrictive assumption—there is no clear theoretical reason why policies could not change as the state of nature changes—but still an interesting one since it appears that political/institutional restrictions of this sort are sometimes present. To analyze this case, let us again consider uncertainty and an ex-ante period of decisions. To capture the essence of the restriction we assume that the only decision made ex-ante is the policy decision. A policy could be either a unit tax or a quantity cap. We assume that the quantity cap is set so that it is always binding ex-post, in which case one can view the government as simply choosing the level of emissions ex-ante.

The choice between a tax and a quota when there is uncertainty (or private information on the part of "the industry") has been studied extensively in the environmental literature since Weitzman (1974) and similar analyses are available in other parts of economics (eg, Poole, 1970). One can clearly provide conditions under which one

[bn] The European Union Emission Trading System (EU ETS) was launched in 2005 covering about half the CO_2 emissions in the union (Ellerman and Buchner, 2007).

[bo] This statement requires a qualification for taxes in the (rather unusual) cases for which a Pigou rule is not sufficient, as discussed already.

policy or the other is better, along the lines of Weitzman's original paper. Weitzman considered a cost and a benefit of a pollutant, each of which depended on some random variable, and the two random variables were assumed to be independent. He then showed that what instrument would be best depended on the relative slopes of the marginal benefits and cost curves. Follow-up papers relaxed and changed assumptions in a variety of directions, but there appear to be no general theorems that apply in the climate-change application to conclude decisively in one way or the other. In fact, we know of no quantitatively parameterized dynamic model that looks at the issue so what we will do here is simply provide a straightforward example using our simple static model and then discuss a couple of separate, and we believe important, special cases.

For our example, we use one type of uncertainty only: that of the cost of producing fossil fuel, χ. With the calibrated model and a uniform distribution around the calibrated value for χ we obtained the ex-ante utility levels for a range of taxes and for a range of emissions, both committed to before the randomness is realized. Fig. 12 shows the results: a range of tax values around the optimal tax outperform the optimal quota. In this case, the precommitted tax rate is a fixed value. If it could be set as a proportion of output, which is ruled out now by assumption since the tax cannot be state-contingent

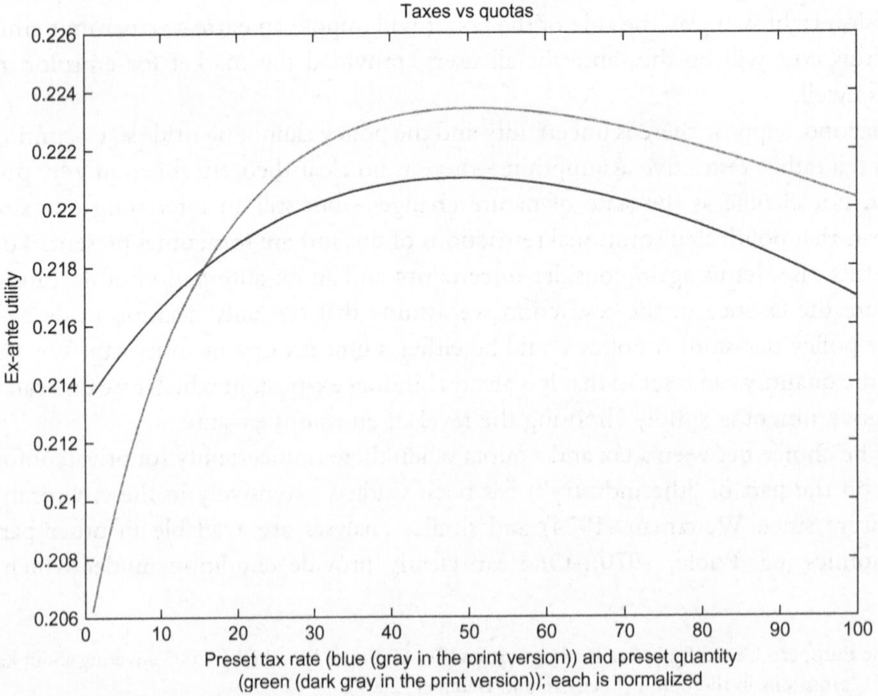

Fig. 12 Utility from precommitting to a unit tax (blue (gray in the print version), with the tax on the x-axis) or a quantity cap (green (dark gray in the print version), with the quantity cap on the x-axis).

but output will be, it would be fully optimal also ex-post, since the best tax ex-post is always a fraction $\gamma\phi$ of output. Apparently, the ex-post randomness of output is not significant enough to overturn this result. It is straightforward to look at other types of shocks. Shocks to γ deliver more similar welfare outcomes for (optimal and precommitted) taxes and quotas.

Now suppose that we consider a case of a tipping point and that the uncertainty is coming from energy demand (through, say, a separate, exogenous and random TFP factor) or from the cost of coal production (through χ). If the tipping point is known to be $\underline{E}$, and $\Gamma(E)$ is equal to zero for $E < \underline{E}$ but positive and very high otherwise, what is then the best policy from an ex-ante perspective? Clearly, a policy with an emissions cap would simply be set at $\underline{E}$, a cap that may or may not bind ex-post: if the demand for energy is low, or the cost of producing it is high, the ex-post market solution will (efficiently) be to stay below $\underline{E}$, and otherwise the cap will (efficiently) bind. A tax will not work equally well. One can set the tax so that the economy stays below the tipping point, but in case the energy demand is low, or its production costs are high, ex-post, output will be inefficiently depressed. Thus, when we are dealing with *asymmetric* payoffs of this sort (relative to the amount of emissions), a quantity cap is better.

The previous example would have emissions rights trading at a positive price sometimes and at a zero price otherwise. Thus, the system with a quantity cap leads to a random cost for firms of emitting carbon dioxide (beyond the price the firms pay the energy producers). Variations in the supply of emissions rights, decided on by regulatory action, influence the price of the trading rights as well. The experience in Europe since the cap-and-trade system illustrates these points well: carbon prices have fluctuated between over 30 euro and virtually zero since the system started. Such fluctuations are observed also in other regions with cap-and-trade systems (eg, New Zealand). Clearly, since optimal carbon pricing should reflect the social cost of carbon, such fluctuations are only efficient if the social cost of carbon experiences fluctuations. Damages from carbon emissions are likely not experiencing large fluctuations, but our assessments of how large they are of course change over time as scientific knowledge accumulates. The recent large drops in the price of emission rights can therefore be viewed as problematic from a policy perspective.

A cap-and-trade system could be augmented with a "central emission bank" that would have as its role to stabilize the price of emission rights by trading actively in this market, hence avoiding the large and inefficient swings observed in the EU system. Notice, however, that we would then be very close in spirit to a tax system: a tax system would just be a completely stable (provided the chosen tax is stable) way of implementing a stable price of emissions for firms.[bp]

[bp] This and other issues in this policy discussion are covered in Hassler et al. (2016).

4.11 Carbon Taxation in the Presence of Other Distortionary Taxes

Suppose the government needs to raise revenue and needs to do this in a distortionary manner; the most common example would involve labor taxation and it is also a form of taxation that can be studied in the baseline model here by the addition of valued leisure. How, then, will the optimal carbon tax change? For example, suppose preferences are $\log c + \psi \log l$, where l is leisure, so that the labor input in the final-goods sector would be $1 - n_E - l$ (and, as before, n_E in the coal sector). Suppose also that the government has a distortionary tax on labor income, τ_l. Taxes are used to pay for an exogenous amount G of consumption good (that does not enter agents' utility). Lump-sum taxation is ruled out (but lump-sum transfers are not), and thus the setup mimics a typical second-best situation in public finance.[bq]

Consider first a planning solution where the government is unrestricted and can just mandate quantities. Thus, it maximizes

$$\log\left(e^{-\gamma\phi\chi n_E}(1-n_E-l)^{1-\alpha-\nu}(\chi n_E)^{\nu} - G\right) + \psi \log l$$

by choice of n_E and l. This delivers two first-order conditions. One is familiar from our baseline model:

$$-\gamma\phi\chi_E - \frac{1-\alpha-\nu}{1-n_E-l} + \frac{\nu}{n_E} = 0.$$

The other is the standard macro-labor condition

$$-\frac{1}{c} \cdot \frac{(1-\alpha-\nu)y}{1-n_e-l} + \frac{\psi}{l} = 0,$$

which says that the marginal utility of consumption times the marginal product of labor has to equal the marginal utility of leisure (in the expression, of course, y denotes $e^{-\gamma\phi\chi n_E}(1-n_E-l)^{1-\alpha-\nu}(\chi n_E)^{\nu}$ and $c = y - G$). These two first-order conditions can be solved for first-best levels of n_E and l given any G.

Now consider in contrast a competitive equilibrium which is laissez-faire with regard to the taxation of carbon and which only uses labor taxes to raise revenue. Then, the two conditions above would be replaced, first, by the laissez-faire condition for coal

$$-\frac{1-\alpha-\nu}{1-n_E-l} + \frac{\nu}{n_E} = 0$$

[bq] One can also consider an alternative assumption: there is no need to raise revenue ($G=0$), there is an exogenous tax rate on labor income, $\tau > 0$, and any tax revenues are rebated back lump-sum.

and, second, a distorted macro-labor condition

$$-\frac{1}{c}\cdot\frac{(1-\alpha-\nu)y(1-\tau_l)}{1-n_E-l}+\frac{\psi}{l}=0,$$

with the additional constraint that the government budget balances: $\tau_l(1-\alpha-\nu)y/(1-n_E-l)=G$. These three conditions now determine n_E, l, and τ_l and do not deliver the first best. In particular, one can think of two "wedges" defining different departures from the first best: the externality wedge due to climate damages and the tax wedge on labor supply (these are defined as the differences between the left-hand sides of the above equations with taxes and the corresponding ones from the first-best first-order conditions).

Now suppose we increase the carbon tax marginally from 0. Then (i) the climate wedge would become smaller and (ii) because τ_l falls—the government budget now reads $\tau_l(1-\alpha-\nu)y/(1-n_E-l)+\tau\chi n_E=G$ so that $\tau>0$ allows a lower τ_l—the labor wedge would fall as well. Hence relative to a laissez-faire situation from the perspective of coal, introducing coal taxation involves a *double dividend*: it diminishes the climate externality and it reduces the labor distortion. This is an often-discussed point in the climate literature; for example Jorgenson et al. (2013b,a) argue that the double dividends are quantitatively important for the United States and China, respectively.[br] Of course, the extent to which labor taxes can be reduced depends on the size of the coal tax base.

What, then, will the best level of carbon taxation be? Will carbon taxes be higher than in the absence of distortionary labor taxation? It would be straightforward to derive an answer in the present model by maximizing consumer welfare—with the same objective as that used by the planner—subject to the macro-labor first-order condition above, $\tau\chi/y-\frac{1-\alpha-\nu}{1-n_E-l}+\frac{\nu}{n_E}=0$ for the market's marginal condition for coal, and the government's budget constraint. One can derive a marginal condition for the planner's choice of τ which involves the setting of a weighted combination of wedges to zero; this condition can be solved numerically, together with the other equations, for the endogenous variables. The final level of taxes in this second-best solution is hard to characterize in terms of primitives but some intuition can perhaps be gleaned. If the use of coal is complementary with labor (which it is in the Cobb–Douglas formulation of production), on the margin the reduction of coal will hurt labor supply because it lowers the marginal product of labor. This speaks for a second best with a coal tax that is lower than in the absence of distortionary labor taxation. If coal were instead complementary with leisure (say because people burn coal to heat their homes when not working), this effect would go in the opposite direction on the margin. However, exactly how all these effects play

[br] One can also identify a third dividend from introducing coal taxation: the reduce in local pollution from the burning of coal, a factor which appears of first-order relevance particularly in China.

out depends on the details of preferences and technology. For recent work on these issues that in addition also addresses distortions due to capital taxation, see Schmitt (2014), who pursues this approach in a dynamic model closely related to the setup here, and Barrage (2015), who looks at a closely related setting and uses a primal approach to taxation.[bs]

4.12 A More Detailed Energy Sector

We set out with a stylized description of energy production using either oil, coal, or some green alternative. In practice it is not either or; rather, these sources can all be used and are partially, but not fully, substitutable. Some integrated assessment models include very complex energy systems (eg, WITCH or MERGE; the latter is described in Manne et al., 1995). One way to incorporate multiple energy sources explicitly is to keep one kind of energy as an input into production but let this energy itself be produced from an array of sources, including fossil fuel. Thus, consider the CES technology

$$E = \left(\kappa_o E_o^\rho + \kappa_c E_c^\rho + (1-\kappa_o-\kappa_c)E_g^\rho\right)^{\frac{1}{\rho}},$$

where E_i is the energy produced from source i, with $i=o$ representing oil (and natural gas), $i=c$ representing coal, and $i=g$ representing energy generated without fossil fuel.[bt] This description is still stylized but it allows us to look into some interesting issues. The parameter $\rho \in (-\infty, 1]$ regulates the (constant) elasticity of substitution between the different energy sources.[bu] The κ_is are share parameters regarded as exogenous in all of our analysis. We continue to think about the production of oil, coal, and green energy as in the previous discussion.

It is straightforward to check that the social cost of carbon is still γy with this formulation. Thus, this extension is not interesting from the perspective of optimal policy. Its value, instead, is to deliver a much richer view of what the cost is of remaining at laissez-faire, or in any case far from the optimum, because this cost turns out to crucially depend on the elasticity of substitution between the different kinds of energy.

First, and just for illustration, let us look at the case where there is just oil and coal, ie, where there is no green energy. Clearly, then, if the degree of substitutability between oil and coal is very low, the difference between laissez-faire and the optimum is small. Consider the extreme case: a Leontief function, ie, $\rho = -\infty$. Then if the total stock of oil is small enough that the optimum involves using it all, the laissez-faire and optimal

[bs] As is typically the case, in dynamic analyses it makes a difference whether the government has commitment or not; Schmitt considers cases without commitment.

[bt] It would be natural to consider a slight extension of this formulation with a nested CES between a composite of oil and coal, on the one hand, and green energy on the other. Thus, oil and coal would form a separate CES aggregate and one could consider the quantitatively reasonable case with a high degree of substitutability between oil and coal and a lower one between the oil–coal composite and green energy.

[bu] The elasticity is $1/(1-\rho)$.

allocations are identical. With some more substitutability, the laissez-faire allocation is not optimal, because coal use should be reduced given the externality and its unlimited supply (recall its constant marginal cost in terms of labor). However, the difference is still limited. In practice, however, oil and coal are rather good substitutes, so let us instead (again, for illustration only) consider the opposite extreme case: perfect substitutability ($\rho = 1$). Then the level of coal is determined very differently: laissez faire is far from the optimum (provided γ is large). Thus, in this case there will be significant total losses from government inaction.

According to available estimates, the remaining amount of (low-cost) oil left is quite limited, in particular in comparison with the amount of remaining coal, so oil is not of key importance for climate change.[bv] What is of importance, however, is the substitutability with green energy. So, second, let us consider fossil fuel (interpreted as coal) vs green energy. In a metastudy, Stern (2012) reports a long-run elasticity of substitution of 0.95, as an average of oil–coal, oil–electricity, and coal–electricity elasticity measures. Thus, this unweighted average is close to a Cobb–Douglas specification. In this case, there can be a rather significant difference between the optimum and laissez-faire; relatedly, price incentives, or the effects of imposing a tax, are large if there is a nontaxed good that is a close substitute.[bw] However, it is conceivable that green technology in the future will be a very good substitute with fossil fuel. Considering a higher elasticity than the unitary Cobb–Douglas elasticity is therefore a relevant robustness check. In this case, the difference between the optimum and laissez-faire is rather large. For example, Golosov et al. report, using a calibrated dynamic counterpart of the model here, that an elasticity of 2 leads laissez-faire coal use 100 years from now to rise to levels that imply exhaustion of all the coal deposits and would likely have catastrophic consequences for the climate. In contrast, in the optimum, coal use in 100 years is *lower* than it is today, and the climate as a result is rather manageable.

By definition, in the case of green energy vs fossil fuel, the observation that a high elasticity of substitution leads to large welfare losses from not imposing a carbon tax (or a quota) at the same time means that there is a large potential social benefit from climate change action. A closely related implication is that there are, in such a case, strong incentives—high social payoffs—from doing research to come up with green alternatives. We turn to this issue in Section 4.14.

4.13 The Substitutability Between Energy and Other Inputs

What aspects of the earlier analysis are influenced by the nature of the production function? We have assumed a Cobb–Douglas structure in part for simplicity and part because the energy share, though having gone through large swings over shorter periods of time,

[bv] See McGlade and Ekins (2015) for supply curves of different types of fossil fuel.

[bw] The Cobb–Douglas case is very similar to the case with only coal considered above.

has remained fairly stable over the longer horizon (recall Fig. 1 in Section 2). It is nevertheless necessary to also discuss departures from unitary elasticity. In this discussion, we will maintain the assumption of a unitary elasticity between the capital and labor inputs, thus confining attention to a different elasticity between the capital-labor composite, on the one hand, and energy on the other.

Consider the aggregate production function $e^{-\gamma S}F(Ak^{\alpha}n^{1-\alpha}, A_E E)$, where F is CES and A and A_E are technology parameters, thus maintaining the assumption that damages appear as decreases in TFP. The social cost of carbon with this formulation will then obey the same structure as before, ie, the marginal externality damage of fossil fuel (through increased emissions E) is $\gamma\phi y$. What is different, however, is the difference between the laissez-faire allocation and the optimum or, expressed differently, the consumption equivalent cost of a suboptimal allocation. Consider oil, ie, a fossil fuel with zero extraction costs in a finite supply $\bar{E}$. Assume that it is not optimal to use all of the oil, and let us simply examine the two extreme cases: Leontief and perfect substitutability.

We begin with the Leontief case. Here, output is given by $e^{-\gamma\phi E}\min\left\{Ak^{\alpha}n^{1-\alpha}, A_E E\right\}$. Ie, there is no substitutability between the capital-labor composite and oil. In laissez-faire, oil use is $\bar{E}$. It is easy to show from the planner's first-order condition that $E^* = 1/(\gamma\phi)$ in this case.[bx] Recall from Section 4.1.3 that, under Cobb–Douglas, the optimal allocation is $E^* = \nu/(\gamma\phi)$ and that the ratio of optimal to laissez-faire output is $e^{\gamma\phi(\bar{E}-\nu/(\gamma\phi))}\left(\frac{\nu}{\gamma\phi\bar{E}}\right)^{\nu} > 1$. Now we obtain $e^{\gamma\phi(\bar{E}-1/(\gamma\phi))}\frac{1}{\gamma\phi\bar{E}}$. Because $-\nu + \nu\log\nu$ is decreasing we therefore conclude that in the Leontief case, the difference between the optimal and the laissez-faire allocation is smaller than under unitary elasticity. The fall in energy use is smaller, and this effect dominates the stronger impact on output of any given fall in energy.

Under perfect substitutability, we have output given by $e^{-\gamma S}\left(Ak^{\alpha}n^{1-\alpha} + A_E E\right)$ and we assume that capital and labor are in use. Now the planner's first-order condition leads to $E^* = 1/(\gamma\phi) - Ak^{\alpha}n^{1-\alpha}/A_E$, which (as for the unitary-elasticity case) is a smaller amount than in the Leontief case. It is also possible to show that the wedge between optimal and laissez-faire output in this case is smaller than in the Leontief case.

In sum, we see that the energy use can be different than in the case with unitary elasticity between energy and other inputs. With production functions with very low substitution elasticity between energy and other inputs, energy use will dictate that energy use in the optimum fall more, but there is also a corresponding gain in a higher TFP. There does not, perhaps surprisingly, therefore appear to be a very strong effect on

[bx] This holds so long as there is an interior solution, ie, if $1/(\gamma\phi) < Ak^{\alpha}n^{1-\alpha}/A^E$. Note that there is abundance of capital and labor now: on the one hand, the market uses oil to the point where $E = Ak^{\alpha}n^{1-\alpha}$, so that there is excessive oil. On the other hand, the planner may want to decrease the oil use if the just stated inequality holds, so that from the planner's perspective, there is an abundance of capital and labor instead.

the net gap between optimal output and laissez-faire output as the elasticity of substitution between inputs is varied. This is comforting given that the Cobb–Douglas formulation is much easier to handle analytically.

4.14 Green Technology and Directed Technical Change

The existence of the green technology was taken as given earlier; green technologies of various sorts—versions of water and wind power—have of course existed since before the industrial revolution. These technologies have been improved and there are also new sources of electricity production that do not involve fossil fuels, such as nuclear power and solar power.[by] A central issue of concern in the area of climate change is the further development of these technologies and research toward new ones. In the macroeconomically oriented literature on climate change, various models have been developed, with early papers by Bovenberg and Smulders and others (see, eg, Bovenberg and Smulders, 1995). More recently, Acemoglu et al. (2012) provided a setting of directed technical change and made the point that there may be *path dependence* in R&D efforts toward the development of different energy technologies. We will now use the simple model to illustrate these facts and some other points that have been made in the literature.

A static model cannot fully do justice to the much more elaborate dynamic settings where many of the arguments in this part of the literature have been developed. It does, however, allow us to make a number of basic points. One simplification in our analysis here is that we will not explicitly describe a decentralized R&D sector.[bz] We will distinguish between two different kinds of technological developments: new techniques for the efficient use of energy ("energy saving") and new techniques for the production of energy. We begin with the latter.

4.14.1 Energy Production

We will mostly abstract from the determination of the overall efforts toward technological developments, which one could model as well (say as a tradeoff between these activities and using labor directly in production), and simply assume that there is an R&D input available in fixed supply; we set the total amount to 1 without loss of generality. The use of this input can be *directed* toward either improving the productivity in producing energy from fossil sources, m_c, or from green sources, m_g, with the constraint that $m_c + m_g = 1$. Eg, we can think of this choice as one between improving the drilling/extraction technologies for North Sea oil and technological improvements in the

[by] Nuclear power is problematic from an environmental perspective too but we do not discuss this issue here.

[bz] We could have developed such a version even in our static model but it would have complicated notation without adding much of significance.

cost-efficiency of solar-based units. The most straightforward setting would maintain the production function in a two-energy-input form:

$$e^{-\gamma E_c} k^{\alpha} n^{1-\alpha-\nu} \left(\lambda_c E_c^{\rho} + (1-\lambda_c) E_g^{\rho} \right)^{\frac{\nu}{\rho}},$$

with the production of energy given by

$$E_c = \chi_c n_c \quad \text{and} \quad E_g = \chi_g n_g$$

with $n + n_c + n_g = 1$. Along the lines indicated earlier, for given values of χ_c and χ_g, this model is straightforwardly solved either for the optimum or for a laissez-faire allocation.

A very simple way of modeling research into making energy production more efficient can now be expressed as follows:

$$\chi_c = \bar{\chi} m_c \quad \text{and} \quad \chi_g = \bar{\chi} m_g,$$

with $m_c + m_g = 1$. (If $\lambda_c = 1/2$, this setting is now entirely symmetric.)

A decentralized version of this model would have no agent—either the producer or the user of fossil fuel—take into account the negative externality. However, notice that there are increasing returns to scale in producing energy: double n_c, n_g, m_c, and m_g, and E_c and E_g more than double. A decentralized equilibrium here would then have a much more elaborate structure of varieties within each energy type, either with variety expansion à la Romer or fixed variety but creative destruction Aghion and Howitt (1992), monopolistic competition with profits, and then perfectly competitive research firms producing new varieties (in the Romer case) or product improvements (in the Aghion–Howitt case). We will not spell the variety structure out, but we will make the assumption that the aggregation across varieties is identical for fossil fuel and green energy, eg, implying identical markups across these two energy sectors. Finally, there would normally (in dynamic models) also be spillovers, mostly for tractability, but they are not needed here.[ca] We will, however, discuss spillovers later because there are substantive issues surrounding them.

A decentralized model such as that just described delivers equilibrium existence despite the technological nonconvexity but we omit the description of it for brevity; see Romer (1990) for the basic variety-expansion structure and Acemoglu (2009) for a more recent description of a range of endogenous-growth models and many of their uses. Monopolistic competition would distort the allocation, in the direction of underprovision of energy, which itself would be beneficial for counterbalancing the climate externality and thus to some extent relieve the government of the pressure to tax fossil fuel. In the laissez-faire equilibrium, in the case of symmetry between fossil fuel and

[ca] The reason they improve tractability is that if the researchers' output does not give the researcher herself dynamic gains, the R&D decision becomes static.

energy, the markets will produce whatever the total energy composite is in an efficient manner.[cb] Denoting this level E, the laissez-faire allocation will minimize $n_c + n_g$ subject to

$$E_c^{\rho} + E_g^{\rho} \geq E^{\rho}, \quad E_c = n_c \overline{\chi} m_c, \quad E_g = n_g \overline{\chi} m_g, \quad \text{and} \quad m_c + m_g = 1.$$

The solution to this problem depends critically on ρ. So long as $\rho < 1/2$, ie, so long as the two sources of energy are poor enough substitutes, the solution is to set $n_g = n_e$ and $m_c = m_g = 1/2$; it is straightforward to compute the implied total labor use. If, on the other hand, $\rho > 1/2$, then the outcome is to set either $n_c = m_c = 0$ or $n_g = m_g = 0$, ie, a corner solution obtains, with another easily computed labor use. So if the energy inputs are substitutable enough, there are multiple equilibria. The multiplicity is knife-edge in this case since we assumed full symmetry. However, the essential insight here is not multiplicity but rather sensitivity to parameters, as we will now elaborate on.

Suppose now, instead, that we change the setting slightly and assume

$$\chi_c = \overline{\chi}_c m_c \quad \text{and} \quad \chi_g = \overline{\chi}_g m_g,$$

ie, we assume that there are two separate constants in the two research production functions. Then, in the case where ρ is high enough, there will be full specialization but the direction of the specialization will be given by the relative sizes of $\overline{\chi}_c$ and $\overline{\chi}_g$. If the former is higher, the energy will be produced by fossil fuel only; if the latter is higher, the energy will be produced by green energy only. If the economy experienced a small change in these parameters switching their order, we would have a complete switch in the nature of the energy supplies. Crucially, now, note that we can think of $\overline{\chi}_c$ and $\overline{\chi}_g$ as given by historical R&D activities. Then we can identify the kind of *path dependence* emphasized in Acemoglu et al. (2012). These authors argued that temporary efforts, via subsidies/taxes, to promote the research on "clean goods"—those produced using green energy—would have permanent effects on our energy supplies by managing to shift our dependence on fossil fuel over to a dependence on green energy.[cc] This can be thought of, in terms of this model, as having managed to make $\overline{\chi}_g > \overline{\chi}_c$ by past subsidies to green R&D. Acemoglu et al. used a dynamic model with details that differ from those here—among other things, they assumed much stronger convexities in damages so that a switch to green energy was necessary or else utility would be minus infinity—but this is the gist of their argument.

One can question whether the substitutability is strong enough for the path-dependence argument to apply. For example, Hart (2013) argues that there are strong

[cb] The assumption of symmetry across the two energy sectors, and hence identical markups, is an important assumption behind this result.

[cc] In their analysis, the authors use a notion of two kinds of goods, one clean and one dirty, with labels deriving from the energy source used to produce them. The setting we use here, with an energy composite relevant for the whole economy, is of course also an abstraction but we prefer it because it lends itself more easily to calibration and comparison with data.

complementarities in research across dirty and clean technologies. These complementarities could, in practice, take the form of external effects/spillovers. For example, research into improving electric cars can be helpful for improving the efficiency of cars running on gasoline or diesel, and whether these complementarities are fully paid for or not in the marketplace is not obvious. A way of expressing this formally within our simple framework is a further generalization of our framework as follows:

$$\chi_c = \bar{\chi}_c m_c^{\zeta} m_g^{1-\zeta} \text{ and } \chi_g = \bar{\chi}_g m_g^{\zeta} m_c^{1-\zeta}.$$

To the extent ζ is not too much higher than 1/2 here, there are strong complementarities in technology development and path dependence would not apply. Hart (2013) argues this is the relevant case, but it would be hard to argue that the case is settled. Aghion et al. (2014), furthermore, show that there is empirical support for persistence, though whether these effects are strong enough to generate the kind of path dependence emphasized in Acemoglu et al. (2012) is still not clear.

Turning, finally, to the planning problem in these economies, it is clear that the planner faces a tradeoff between the forces discussed here and the climate externality generated by fossil fuel. The setting is rather tractable and it is straightforward to determine the optimal mix of energy supplies. We leave out the detailed analysis for brevity.

4.14.2 Energy Saving

Research into alternative (green) energy supplies is definitely one way of decreasing our fossil-fuel use. Another is energy saving. To formalize this idea, let the energy composite be written in a somewhat more general way, again emphasizing two energy sources (c and g) only:

$$E = \left(\lambda_c (A_c E_c)^{\rho} + (1-\lambda_c)\left(A_g E_g\right)^{\rho}\right)^{\frac{1}{\rho}}.$$

The technology factors A_i here indicate the "efficiency" with which different energy sources are used. Note, parenthetically, that there is a direct parallel with how we treated energy vs a capital-labor composite in Section 2. Now the A_is introduce asymmetry between the different energy sources through another channel, and moreover we can think of them as being chosen deliberately. One interpretation of these choices is temporary decisions to save on energy, eg, by directing effort toward closing windows or making sure machines don't run unnecessarily. Another interpretation emphasizes research toward energy efficiency that are of a permanent nature. One example is the development of more fuel-efficient cars; another is to develop methods for using less jet fuels when airplanes land. In parallel with our treatment of energy production, we then add the equations

$$A_c = \bar{A}_c m_c^{\zeta} m_g^{1-\zeta} \text{ and } A_g = \bar{A}_g m_g^{\zeta} m_c^{1-\zeta},$$

again with the constraint $m_c + m_g = 1$.[cd] With this structure as well, market allocations may end up with specialization for a range of parameter configurations, as will the solution to the planning problem, and path dependence is again possible.

An important concern in the modeling of energy saving or the efficiency of producing energy is that there is a natural upper limit to efficiency. For example, light produced with LED has almost reached the efficiency limit and the same is true for electrical engines. However, this does not mean that we are close to maximal energy efficiency in the production of transportation services. For the transportation example it is less appropriate to capture efficiency through A_g; rather, improvements come about through increasing general energy efficiency (say, a coefficient in front of E in the overall production function). The limits to efficiency are normally not made explicit in economic models but arguably should be in quantitative applications.

4.14.3 Are Subsidies for Green Technology Needed?

To attain the optimal allocation, the planner will of course need to tax the use of fossil fuel. What other taxes and subsidies might be necessary? To the extent there is monopoly power, and the energy sources undersupplied, subsidies are needed. Should the green R&D sector be subsidized? Following Pigou's principle, it should be to the extent there are positive spillovers. So in the absence of technology spillovers in the green R&D sector, there would actually be no reason to subsidize. Moreover, if there are spillovers but they are identical for the two sorts of energy, it is not clear that green technology should receive stronger subsidies than should fossil-fuel technology, so long as fossil fuel is taxed at the optimal rate.

In a second-best allocation, of course, matters are quite different. Suppose no coal tax is used. Then subsidies to the production of green energy, or to the development of new green technologies, would be called for. In political debates, subsidies to the development of green technology appear to be quite popular, and our analysis is in agreement with this view insofar as an optimal (global) carbon tax is not feasible. In practical policy implementation, though less so in debates, it also appears that coal subsidies are popular, perhaps not as per-unit instruments but as support in the construction of plants. A study (Hassler and Krusell, 2014) in fact claims that the average global tax on carbon is set at about the right magnitude but with the wrong sign—owing to large subsidies for coal production across the world.

The view expressed in Acemoglu et al. (2012) appears to contrast somewhat with ours. They argue, based on their model of path dependence, that subsidies to green technology are necessary for attaining an optimum and that carbon taxes would not suffice.

[cd] One can also state these constraints using other functional forms, such as $(\bar{A}_c A_c)^\zeta + (\bar{A}_g A_g)^\zeta \leq A^\zeta$. It is an empirical matter what formulation works best, and it is probably fair to say that the literature is so far silent on this issue.

They obtain this result not only because their model features strong intertemporal spillovers to R&D but also because they make assumptions such that if the "clean good" does not take over from the "dirty good," the climate damages will be infinitely costly (thus, they have strong nonconvexities in their damage function, a tipping point of sorts). Moreover, their model has a second-best structure with spillovers and very limited patent lives. How can we understand this result from the perspective of Pigou taxation? Recall that we pointed out that Pigou taxation may not work if there are multiple market equilibria, and the kind of setting Acemoglu et al. describe has a feature of this kind. The simplest parallel in our static model is the coal-green setup we described in Section 4.14.1. There, we looked at a planning problem with a choice between two energy sources. So suppose that $\bar{\chi}_c = \bar{\chi}_g = \chi$ there, and let us imagine a market allocation where the labor productivity of coal and green energy production, χm_c and χm_g, respectively, derive from variety expansion in patent efforts (m_c and m_g) driven by monopoly profits for intermediate, specialized goods. Suppose, moreover, that there are no research spillovers in this setting: this assumption is perhaps natural in a static model (but less so in a dynamic one). In this framework, then, there would be two equilibria if ρ, the parameter guiding the key energy elasticity, is high enough. Suppose, moreover, that damages are to preferences, as in Section 4.6, and with highly nonlinear features, as discussed in Section 4.7: the marginal damages are first zero for a range of low emission levels, then high and positive, and then again zero in a "disaster zone." Suppose, moreover, that if the economy ends up using coal, emissions will end up in the disaster zone. Then the Pigou procedure would amount to finding the optimal solution—that with green technology only—and an associated tax on carbon that is zero, since the marginal damage at zero emissions is zero. So here Pigou's procedure is highly problematic, since there are now two market outcomes given a zero tax on carbon, and one of them is a disaster outcome! Thus another instrument would be needed to select among the two market outcomes, and one option would be a large enough subsidy to green technology creation to rule out an equilibrium where markets engage in the research on coal technologies.[ce]

4.14.4 Green Technology as a Commitment Mechanism

Some argue that future decision makers cannot be trusted to make good decisions and that, therefore, to the extent we can affect their decisions with irreversible decisions made today, we should. Why would future decision makers not make good decisions? One reason is based on time-inconsistent discounting, as discussed earlier: the current decision maker may have lower discount rates between any two future cohorts than that between the current and next cohort, and if this profile of decreasing discount rates is shared by future cohorts—updated by the appropriate number of cohorts—then profiles are

[ce] With monopolistic competition, one would in general also need to encourage production to prevent undersupply for those technologies that end up being patented.

time-inconsistent. In particular, from the perspective of the current cohort, future cohorts look too impatient. Since future carbon taxes cannot literally be committed to today, then, the current cohort is restricted and appears to not be able to attain its preferred outcome.[cf] Another conceptually distinct reason for disagreements is that politicians (and possibly the voters who support them) may be "myopic"; Amador (2003) shows that rationality-based dynamic voting games in fact can lead to reduced forms characterized by time-inconsistent preferences of politicians.[cg] Finally, Weitzman (1998) provides further arguments for falling discount rates based on the idea that the true future discount rate may be uncertain.

If current decision makers cannot decide directly on the future use of fossil fuels, they may be able to at least influence outcomes, for example by investing in green technology that, ex-post, will tilt the decision makers in the future in the right direction. To illustrate, consider a model where production is given by

$$e^{-\gamma\phi\chi_E n_E}(1-n_E-n_g)^{1-\alpha-\nu}(\chi_E n_E+\chi_g n_g)^{\nu}.$$

$E=\chi_E n_E$ is coal-produced energy and $E_g=\chi_g n_g$ is green energy; we make the assumption, only for obtaining simpler expressions, that these two energy sources are perfect substitutes. Now assume that there is an ex-ante period where an irreversible decision can be made: that on n_g. The cost is incurred ex-post, so only the decision is made ex-ante. Moreover, it is possible to increase n_g ex-post but not decrease it: it is not possible to literally reverse the first decision.[ch] Finally, assume that the ex-ante decision maker perceives a different damage elasticity than the ex-post decision maker (they have different γs, with the ex-ante value higher than the ex-post value): this captures, in a simple way, the intertemporal disagreement.

We make two further simplifying assumptions, for tractability. First, we take the ex-post decision maker to perceive a damage elasticity of exactly 0 and the ex-ante decision maker to use the value $\gamma>0$. Second, we assume that $\chi_E>\chi_g$, ie, that—climate effects aside—the coal technology is a more efficient one for producing energy, regardless of the level at which the two technologies are used (due to the assumption of perfect substitutability). How can we now think about outcomes without commitment?

It is clear that the ex-post decision maker sees no reason to use the green technology at all. Facing a given amount of n_g that he cannot decrease (and will not want to increase), the level of n_E will be determined by the first-order condition

[cf] Karp (2005), Gerlagh and Liski (2012), and Iverson (2014) analyze optimal taxes in the presence of time-inconsistent preferences.

[cg] See also Azzimonti (2011) for a similar derivation.

[ch] We may think of this setup as a reduced-form representation for a case when an ex-ante investment in capital or a new technology makes it profitable to use at least n_g units of labor in green energy production, even if it the emission reduction is not valued per se. In a dynamic model, the cost of this investment would at least partly arise ex-ante, but this is not of qualitative importance for the argument.

$$\frac{1-\alpha-\nu}{1-n_E-n_g}=\frac{\nu\chi_E}{\chi_E n_E+\chi_g n_g}. \tag{17}$$

This expression delivers a linear (affine) and decreasing expression for n_E as a function of n_g: $n_E=h(n_g)$, with $h'<0$ and independent of n_g.

What is the implied behavior of the ex-ante decision maker without commitment? She will want to maximize

$$e^{-\gamma\phi\chi_E h(n_g)}\left(1-h(n_g)-n_g\right)^{1-\alpha-\nu}\left(\chi_E h(n_g)+\chi_g n_g\right)^{\nu}$$

by choice of n_g, a decision that delivers a second-order polynomial equation as first-order condition, just like in the baseline case (though now with somewhat more involved coefficients in the polynomial). Does this first-order condition admit the first best outcome of the ex-ante decision maker? Such a first best would amount to the solution of the two first-order conditions

$$\gamma\phi\chi_E+\frac{1-\alpha-\nu}{1-n_E-n_g}=\frac{\nu\chi_E}{\chi_E n_E+\chi_g n_g} \tag{18}$$

and

$$\frac{1-\alpha-\nu}{1-n_E-n_g}=\frac{\nu\chi_g}{\chi_E n_E+\chi_g n_g} \tag{19}$$

which result from taking derivatives with respect to n_E and n_g, respectively. It is easy to see that these cannot deliver the same solution as the problem without commitment. For one, Eqs. (19) and (17) cannot deliver the same values for both n_E and n_g, since they differ in one place only and $\chi_E>\chi_g$. Thus, we are in a second-best world where the ex-ante decision maker uses her instrument but cannot, without an additional instrument, obtain her first-best outcome. Moreover, total energy use and/or total labor used to produce energy will be lower with the ex-ante decision on green energy than in the absence of it, comparing Eqs. (17) and (18). This model is stylized and it would appear that the specific predictions could change when moving to a more general setting. However, the second-best nature of the setting would remain.

4.14.5 The Green Paradox

The Green Paradox, a term coined by Sinn (2008), refers to the following logical chain. Decisions to subsidize green technology so as to speed up the research efforts in this direction will, if these efforts are successful, lead to better and better alternatives to fossil fuel over time. This, in turn, implies that fossil-fuel producers have an incentive to produce more in advance of these developments, given that their product is more competitive now than it will be in the future. As an extreme example, imagine that cold fusion is invented but takes one year to implement, so that one year from now we have essentially free, green energy in the entire economy. Then owners of oil wells will produce at maximum capacity today and, hence, there will be much higher carbon dioxide emissions than if cold fusion had not been invented. Hence the "paradox": green technology (appearing in the future) is good but therefore bad (in the short run).

Our static model fully cannot express the Green Paradox, of course, since the essence of the paradox has to do with how events play out over time. Consider therefore a very simple two-period version of the model that allows us to think about how the intertemporal decision for oil producers depends on the availability of green technology. We assume that consumers' preferences are linear so that the gross interest rate is given by $1/\beta$. We assume that fossil fuel is (free-to-produce) oil and that $\rho = 1$, so that oil and green energy are perfect substitutes. We also assume that there is no green technology in the first period. A simplified production function thus reads $e^{-\gamma\phi_1 E_1} k^\alpha E_1^\nu$ for period 1 and $e^{-\gamma\phi_1(E_2+\phi_2 E_1)} k^\alpha (E_2 + E_g)^\nu$ for period 2; for simplicity, we also abstract from the costs for producing green energy and set E_g to be exogenous, with $n = 1$ in both periods). Here, ϕ_1 and ϕ_2 allow us to capture a carbon depreciation process that does not occur at a geometric rate, a feature we argued is realistic. Our notation reveals that capital cannot be accumulated in this example, but we will comment on accumulable capital later.

Given this setting, the price of oil in period 1 is given by $p_1 = \nu e^{-\gamma\phi_1 E_1} k^\alpha E_1^{\nu-1}$ and in period 2 it is given by $p_2 = \nu e^{-\gamma\phi_1(E_2+\phi_2 E_1)} k^\alpha (E_2 + E_g)^{\nu-1}$. All of the available oil, $\bar{E}$, will be used up in the laissez-faire allocation and so oil use in the two periods will be given by the Hotelling condition, a condition we derived and analyzed in Section 2: $p_1 = \beta p_2$. Recall that this equation expresses the indifference between producing a marginal unit of oil in period 1 and in period 2. This condition implies that E_1 can be solved for from $e^{-\gamma\phi_1 E_1} E_1^{\nu-1} = \beta e^{-\gamma\phi_1(\bar{E}-E_1(1-\phi_2))} (\bar{E} - E_1 + E_g)^{\nu-1}$. Clearly, this equation has a unique solution and comparative statics with respect to E_g shows that more green energy in period 2 makes E_1 rise and E_2 fall. Hence the Green Paradox.

Is the move of emissions from period 2 to period 1 bad for welfare? The negative externality (SCC) of emissions in period 1 is $\gamma\phi_1(y_1 + \beta\phi_2 y_2)$ and the present value of the corresponding externality in period 2 is $\gamma\phi_1\beta y_2$. In the absence of a green technology in period 2 ($E_g = 0$) it is easy to show that $y_2 < y_1$ in the laissez-faire allocation and, hence, at least for a range of positive values of E_g, the externality damage is higher for early emissions. Intuitively, emissions in period 2 have two advantages. One is that they hurt the economy only once: emissions in period 1 will, except for the depreciated fraction $1 - \phi_2$, remain in the atmosphere—a significant factor given calibrated carbon-cycle dynamics—and hence also lower second-period TFP. The second advantage of emissions in the future is that their negative effect is discounted (to the extent we assume $\beta < 1$). Note, finally, that the possibility of accumulating physical capital would not change any of these conclusions: with more green energy in the second period, capital accumulation with rise somewhat to counteract the initial effect, and it would work toward an increase in p_2, but this mechanism would not overturn our main observation.

Can the future appearance of green technology also make overall welfare go down in the laissez-faire allocation? This is much less clear, as an additional unit of E_g (for free) has a direct positive welfare effect.[ci] However, now consider competitive production of green energy under laissez-faire, at a unit labor cost χ_g. Here, a second-best argument would suggest that there is a negative "induced externality" of green energy production: since the economy is far from the optimum, and emissions in period 1 would be detrimental, any additional unit of E_g would have a negative side-effect on welfare. Hence, a(t least a small) *tax* on green energy production would be desirable! The reason for this perhaps counterintuitive effect—aside from the Green-Paradox logic—is that the total amount of fossil fuel used will still be $\bar{E}$: green technology, in this setting, will not curb the use of fossil fuel, only change the timing of emissions (in the wrong direction).

The previous example points to counterintuitive policy implications: green technology should be discouraged. However, aside from the assumptions that make the Green Paradox relevant, this result also relies on second-best analysis. In the social optimum, green technology should not be taxed (nor subsidized): there is, simply, no externality from producing green technology in this model. If green technology is developed in an R&D activity, then support of this activity (relative to other activities) may be called for, but only if there is an R&D externality to green technology development that is, in the appropriate sense, larger than the corresponding one for fossil-fuel technology developments. Hence, the optimum (in this economy, where oil is free to produce) involves fossil-fuel taxes but no net support to green technology.

Is the Green Paradox empirically relevant? The key assumption that leads to the paradox is that the accumulated use of fossil fuel is the same under laissez-faire as in the optimal allocation. In this case, suboptimality only comes from the speed at which the fossil reserves are used. That all reserves are used also in the optimal allocation is arguably reasonable when it comes to conventional oil with low extraction costs (eg, Saudi oil). However, it is not reasonable for nonconventional reserves and coal. Here, policy, including subsidies to the development of future green energy production, can and should affect how much fossil resources are left in ground. So suppose, instead, that we focus on fossil fuel in the form of coal and that we maintain our assumption that the marginal cost of coal is constant (in terms of labor or some other unit). Then an increase in E_g would lead to a lower demand for coal and hence have an impact on coal use: it would clearly induce lower coal production in the second period. Lower coal use, in turn, has a positive externality on the economy. Moreover, coal use in period 1 is not affected. Hence, the conclusion here is the opposite one: green energy has a positive effect on the economy (beyond its direct positive effect, to the extent it comes for free).

[ci] If there are strong nonlinearities, like a threshold CO_2 concentration level above which climate damages are catastrophic, then the introduction of a green technology in the second period could make laissez-faire welfare fall.

In addition, relative to a laissez-faire allocation it would be beneficial to subsidize, not tax, green energy production. Which case appears most relevant? We take the view that the latter is more relevant. The argument has two parts. First, the intertemporal reallocation of emissions emphasized in the Green-Paradox argument, though logically coherent, is not, by our measure, quantitatively important. The main reason is that the total amount of oil is rather small and its effect on climate is limited, and a reallocation of emissions due to oil over time is of second-order importance compared to being able to control the cumulated (over time) emissions. Second, if the fossil fuel is costly to extract then there would be lower emissions, as argued earlier, and in terms of the total amount of fossil fuel available, most of it is costly to extract (most of it is coal). Coal is produced at a price much closer to marginal cost and the Hotelling part of the coal price appears small. This argument, moreover, is quantitatively important given the large amounts of coal available.

4.15 Regional Heterogeneity

Nordhaus's basic DICE model is a one-region integrated assessment model, but there are by now several calibrated models in the literature with more than one region. His own RICE (R for Regional) model was perhaps the first multiregion model and it had 7 regions, defined by geographic and economic indicators; Krusell and Smith (2015) have developed a model at the extreme end of heterogeneity, treating one region as a 1-by-1-degree square with land mass on the global map. Regional models can serve a variety of purposes and we first briefly discuss the chief purposes. We then use a multiregion version of our basic model as an illustration; in particular, we use a simple version of Hassler and Krusell (2012) and look at some extensions.

A major purpose for looking at regional heterogeneity comes from recognizing that damages are very different in different parts of the world; some regions, such as Canada and most of Russia, are even expected to gain from a warmer climate. Thus, using a multiregion IAM as a simulation device, one can trace out the heterogeneous effects of climate change under different policy scenarios. Even if there is no agreement on a social welfare function for the world, surely policymakers are very interested in this heterogeneity.

Another purpose of a multiregion IAM is to look at the effects of regionally heterogeneous policies. Suppose the Western world adopts a strict carbon tax and the rest of the world does not. How effective will then the western policies be in combatting climate change, and what will its distributional consequences be?

Relatedly, one of the key concepts in policymakers' studies of climate change is *carbon leakage*. The idea here is simply that when carbon is taxed at higher rates in some regions than in others, the decreases in carbon use in the high-tax regions will presumably be (partially, or fully) offset by increases in carbon use in other regions. *Direct carbon leakage* would for example occur if the oil shipments are simply redirected away from low-tax to high-tax regions. But there can also be *indirect carbon leakage* in that the other factors of production (capital and/or labor) can move to where carbon taxes are lower—and hence carbon will be used more there as a result. Differential policies can also affect outcomes through trade (see, eg, Gars, 2012 and Hémous, 2013). Finally, when there is R&D in the development of fossil-fuel and green technologies, differential policies in this regard come into play as well (Hémous, 2013, looks at this case as well).

Still another important aspect of a multiregion IAM is its potential for discussing *adaptation* to climate change through the migration of people (along with other production factors).[cj] Adaptation is not just important in practice but it is important to think about from a theoretical and quantitative perspective since the damages from climate change really are endogenous and depend on how costly it is to migrate. If migration were costless, significant warming would potentially be less detrimental to human welfare since there are vast areas on our continents that are too cold today but, with significant warming, inhabitable. There is very little research on this issue so far (Brock et al., 2014 and Desmet and Rossi-Hansberg, 2015 are promising exceptions) but we believe it is an important area for future research and one with much potential. Empirical research on the costs of migration is also scant, but some work does exist (Feng et al., 2010 and, for a study of conflict in this context, see Harari and La Ferrara (2014); see also the review Burke et al., 2015).

4.15.1 A Two-Region IAM with Homogeneous Policy: Oil

Our simple model is easily extendable to include another region (or more). Let us look at a series of simple cases in order to illustrate some of the main points made in the literature.[ck] Let us first look at heterogeneous damages, so assume that production in region 1 is $e^{-\gamma_1 E} k_1^{\alpha} n_1^{1-\alpha-\nu} E_1^{\nu}$ whereas production in region 2 is $e^{-\gamma_2 E} k_2^{\alpha} n_2^{1-\alpha-\nu} E_2^{\nu}$. Energy is coming from fossil fuel only, and let us first assume that it is (costless-to-produce) oil available at a total amount $\bar{E}$ in a third region of the world, which supplies the oil under perfect competition (the third region thus plays no role here other than as a mechanical supplier of oil). Let us also for simplicity start out by assuming that the two regions are homogeneous in the absence of climate damages, so that $k_1 = k_2 = k$ and $n_1 = n_2 = n$. It is easy to work out a laissez-faire equilibrium for this world and we can look at different cases, the first of which is that when neither capital nor labor can move. Thus, the only trade that occurs takes the form that the oil-producing region sends oil to the two other regions and is paid in consumption goods; regions 1 and 2 do not interact, other than by trading in the

[cj] For a recent example, see Krusell and Smith (2015), who allow for the migration of capital.

[ck] It should be noted, however, that there are very few examples of multiregion IAM that are studied in full general equilibrium. Thus the number of formal results from the literature is therefore very limited relative to the number of informal conjectures.

competitive world oil market. All of the oil will be used and the equilibrium oil distribution will now be determined by the following condition:

$$e^{-\gamma_1 \bar{E}} E_1^{\nu-1} = e^{-\gamma_2 E} E_2^{\nu-1},$$

ie, by ($E_1 + E_2 = \bar{E}$ and)

$$\frac{E_1}{E_2} = e^{\frac{\gamma_2 - \gamma_1}{1-\nu}\bar{E}}.$$

Thus, the relative use of oil is higher in the country with lower climate damages.[cl] Suppose that region 1 experiences stronger damages. Clearly, then, region 1 is worse off and the damage has a small "multiplier effect" to the extent that its energy used is curbed: more energy is used in region 2. In other words, we would see lower TFP in region 1 but lower activity there also because of reduced energy use. Consumption is a fraction $1-\nu$ of output, with the remainder sent to the third, oil-producing region.

If we also allow capital to move—but maintain that the populations cannot move—the output effect will be somewhat strengthened as capital will also move to region 2 to some extent. If half of capital is owned by each region, this makes region 1 gain, however, because its GNP will rise even though its GDP will fall. In the real world, there are moving costs and cultural and other attachments to regions, so full and costless migration is probably not an appropriate assumption even in the long run (as the static model is supposed to capture a longer-run perspective).

Suppose now that regions 1 and 2 consider a common tax τ on carbon and suppose that this tax is collected in each country and redistributed back lump-sum to the local citizens. Would such a tax be beneficial? To regions 1 and 2, yes. The analysis depends on the size of the tax but suppose the tax is low enough that firms are not sufficiently discouraged from using oil that the total amount of oil use is lowered. Then the relative energy uses in the two regions will still satisfy the equations above and the levels will not change either. The price of oil, p, will satisfy

$$p = \nu y_1 / E_1 - \tau,$$

the first term of which is independent of the tax size (for a small enough tax). Hence, country i's consumption will now be $y_i - (p+\tau)E_i + \tau E_i = (1-\nu)y_i + \tau E_i$ so that consumption is strictly increasing in τ for both regions. Thus, the two regions can use the tax to shift oil revenues from the oil-producing region to its own citizens, without affecting output at all.[cm] When the tax is high enough that p reaches zero, the level of production responds to taxation: as producers now receive nothing for their oil, they

[cl] Of course this result depends on damages occurring to TFP; if they affect utility, oil use is identical in the two regions.

[cm] This argument is of course unrelated to any climate externality; the climate is unaffected by the taxation.

are indifferent as to how much to supply. At that tax level, the total energy supply will still be given by $\bar{E}$ and the equations above, but now consider a slightly higher tax, still with a zero price of oil. Then the total amount of energy E is then lower and is determined from

$$\tau = \nu e^{-\gamma_1 E} k^{\alpha} n^{1-\alpha-\nu} E_1^{\nu-1} \quad \text{and} \quad \frac{E_1}{E - E_1} = e^{\frac{\gamma_2 - \gamma_1}{1-\nu} E}.$$

It is straightforward to show, if the γs are not too far apart, that these two equations imply a lower E and E_1 as τ is raised and that E_1/E_2 will rise. Now, for each region there would be an optimal τ and there would be a conflict between these two values. Generally, the region with a higher climate externality would favor a higher tax.

4.15.2 A Two-Region IAM with Homogeneous Policy: Coal

These discussions all refer to the case of oil, ie, a free-to-extract fossil fuel. Suppose we instead look at coal, and assume that coal is domestically produced: it costs $1/\chi_i$ units of labor per unit, as in most of our analysis earlier. We also assume that the transport costs for coal are inhibitive so that there is no trade at all. The only connection between the regions is thus the climate externality. In the absence of taxes the world equilibrium is then determined independently of the externality and according to

$$\frac{1-\alpha-\nu}{\chi_i - E_i} = \frac{\nu}{E_i}$$

for $i = 1,2$.

Now the reason to tax in order to transfer resources away from a third region and to the home country is no longer applicable; the only reason to tax is the climate externality. As in the oil case, let us assume that any tax on coal is lump-sum transferred back to domestic consumers. What is then the best outcome for each of the two regions? The two countries can, in principle, act in a coordinated fashion so as to maximize overall welfare—by maximizing world output—and then choose a point on the Pareto frontier by the use of transfers. World output is maximized by setting the tax equal to the marginal damage externality in the world, ie, $\gamma_1 y_1 + \gamma_2 y_2$. Thus, the social planner chooses E_1 and E_2 to solve

$$\gamma_1 e^{-\gamma_1(E_1+E_2)} k_1^{\alpha} \left(1 - \frac{E_1}{\chi_1}\right)^{1-\alpha-\nu} E_1^{\nu} + \gamma_2 e^{-\gamma_2(E_1+E_2)} k_2^{\alpha} \left(1 - \frac{E_2}{\chi_2}\right)^{1-\alpha-\nu} E_2^{\nu} =$$

$$e^{-\gamma_1(E_1+E_2)} k_1^{\alpha} \left(1 - \frac{E_1}{\chi_1}\right)^{1-\alpha-\nu} E_1^{\nu} \left(\frac{1-\nu-\alpha}{\chi_1 - E_1} - \frac{\nu}{E_1}\right) =$$

$$e^{-\gamma_2(E_1+E_2)} k_2^{\alpha} \left(1 - \frac{E_2}{\chi_2}\right)^{1-\alpha-\nu} E_2^{\nu} \left(\frac{1-\nu-\alpha}{\chi_2 - E_2} - \frac{\nu}{E_2}\right).$$

The first line represents the global damage externality (which is also the optimal tax on coal); it has to be set equal to the net benefit of emissions in each of the two regions (the following two lines). The allocation will have lower E_1 and E_2 amounts (provided, at least, both γs are positive) than in the laissez-faire allocation.

Suppose, however, that the regions cannot use transfers to arrive at a Pareto-optimal allocation. Then an optimal allocation would be obtained by maximizing a weighted value of the utilities of consumers in the two regions. Often, macroeconomic models adopt the utilitarian approach. Assuming, as in a benchmark case above, logarithmic utility of consumption, and a utilitarian social welfare function, we would then need to solve

$$\max_{E_1, E_2} \log\left(e^{-\gamma_1(E_1+E_2)}k_1^{\alpha}\left(1-\frac{E_1}{\chi_1}\right)^{1-\alpha-\nu}E_1^{\nu}\right)+\log\left(e^{-\gamma_2(E_1+E_2)}k_2^{\alpha}\left(1-\frac{E_2}{\chi_2}\right)^{1-\alpha-\nu}E_2^{\nu}\right).$$

This problem delivers two simple first-order conditions:

$$\gamma_1+\gamma_2=\frac{1-\nu-\alpha}{\chi_1-E_1}-\frac{\nu}{E_1}=\frac{1-\nu-\alpha}{\chi_2-E_2}-\frac{\nu}{E_2}.$$

It is easy to see from these two equations the only parameters that influence emissions in country i are parameters specific to that country plus the damage elasticity parameter of the other country. Suppose now that we try to back out what tax on coal in country i would be necessary to attain this allocation. From the firm's first-order condition we obtain

$$\tau_i=e^{-\gamma_1(E_1+E_2)}k_i^{\alpha}\left(1-\frac{E_i}{\chi_i}\right)^{1-\alpha-\nu}E_i^{\nu}\left(\frac{1-\nu-\alpha}{\chi_i-E_i}-\frac{\nu}{E_i}\right).$$

Let us now evaluate the right-hand side at the utilitarian optimum as given by the previous equations. This delivers

$$\tau_i=(\gamma_1+\gamma_2)e^{-\gamma_1(E_1+E_2)}k_i^{\alpha}\left(1-\frac{E_i}{\chi_i}\right)^{1-\alpha-\nu}E_i^{\nu}.$$

Does this imply a uniform tax across countries? The answer is no. We obtain, in particular, that

$$\frac{\tau_1}{\tau_2}=\left(\frac{k_1}{k_2}\right)^{\alpha}\left(\frac{1-\frac{E_1}{\chi_1}}{1-\frac{E_2}{\chi_2}}\right)^{1-\alpha-\nu}\left(\frac{E_1}{E_2}\right)^{\nu}=\frac{y_1}{y_2}.$$

Clearly, this expression is not 1 in general. It depends on the ratio of capital stocks (note that E_1 and E_2 do not) and the expression involving the Es and χs is also not equal to 1 in general: it is above (below) 1 if χ_1 is above χ_2. In the latter case, the richer country imposes a larger tax on carbon. Note, however, that we obtain a common tax rate, ie, a *common tax on coal per output unit.*

We have learned from the earlier analysis (i) that the Pareto optimum involves a globally uniform tax on coal (along with some chosen lump-sum transfers across regions) but (ii) the utilitarian optimum assuming no transfers across regions does not, and instead prescribes—in the benchmark case we look at—a tax that is proportional to the country's output. It is straightforward to go through a similar exercise with population sizes differing across regions; in this case, the optimal tax rate in region i is equal to the region's per-capita income times the world's population-weighted γs.

4.15.3 Policy Heterogeneity and Carbon Leakage

International agreements appear hard to reach and it is therefore of interest to analyze policy heterogeneity from a more general perspective. So suppose region 1 considers a tax on its fossil fuel but knows that region 2 will not use taxes. What are the implications for the output levels of the two regions and for the climate implied by such a scenario? We again begin the analysis by looking at the case of oil, and we start off by assuming that neither capital nor labor can move across regions.

In a decentralized equilibrium, oil use in region 1 is given by

$$p+\tau=\nu e^{-\gamma_1(E_1+E_2)}k_1^{\alpha}n_1^{1-\alpha-\nu}E_1^{\nu-1}$$

and in region 2 it is given by

$$p=\nu e^{-\gamma_2(E_1+E_2)}k_2^{\alpha}n_2^{1-\alpha-\nu}E_2^{\nu-1}.$$

Thus, we can solve for E_1 and E_2 given $E_1+E_2\leq\bar{E}$. Clearly, we must have $p>0$—otherwise, region 2 would demand an infinite amount of oil—and so we first conclude that $E_1+E_2=\bar{E}$: there is no way for one country, however large, to influence total emissions. What the tax will do is change energy use across regions: region 1 will use less and region 2 more. Moreover, in utility terms region 1 is worse off and region 2 better off from this unilateral tax policy. This example illustrates direct (and full) carbon leakage: if one region taxes oil, oil use will fall in this region but there will be an exact offset elsewhere in the world.

In the coal example, the situation is rather different. The laissez-faire allocation is now given by

$$\tau_1=e^{-\gamma_1(E_1+E_2)}k_1^{\alpha}\left(1-\frac{E_1}{\chi_1}\right)^{1-\alpha-\nu}E_1^{\nu}\left(\frac{1-\nu-\alpha}{\chi_1-E_1}-\frac{\nu}{E_1}\right)$$

and

$$0 = \frac{1-\nu-\alpha}{\chi_2 - E_2} - \frac{\nu}{E_2}.$$

We see that coal use in region 2 now is independent of the tax policy in region 1.[cn] It is easy to show that region 1's coal use will fall and that, at least if both γs are positive and locally around $\tau_1 = 0$, welfare will go up in both regions. There will be an optimal tax, from the point of view of region 1's utility, and it is given by the SCC (computed ignoring the negative externality on region 2), ie, $\gamma_1 y_1$.

If one allows capital mobility, as in Krusell and Smith (2015), there will be indirect carbon leakage. In the case of oil, a tax in region 1 would act as a multiplier and tilt the relative oil use more across regions, ie, increase the leakage. In the case of coal, whereas there is no leakage when capital cannot flow, there is now some leakage: the lower use of coal will decrease the return to capital in region 1 and some capital will then move to region 2, in turn increasing emissions there. We thus see that the extent of leakage depends on (i) how costly fossil fuel is to extract and (ii) to what extent other input factor flow across regions.[co]

It would be straightforward to apply this model, and even dynamic versions of it as they can allow closed-form analysis, for a range of qualitative and quantitative studies. A recent example is Hillebrand and Hillebrand (2016), who study tax-and-transfer schemes in a dynamic multiregion version of the model.

4.15.4 More Elaborate Regional Models

Multiregion models of the sort discussed here can be applied rather straightforwardly, and without much relying on numerical solution techniques, in a number of directions. However, some extensions require significant computational work. One example is the case where the intertemporal cross-regional trade is restricted; a specific case is that where there are shocks and these shocks cannot be perfectly insured. Krusell and Smith (2014, 2015) study such models and also compare outcomes across different assumptions regarding such trade; in their models with regional temperature shocks, the model is similar to that in Aiyagari (1994), with the Aiyagari consumers replaced by regions, and where the numerical methods borrow in part from Krusell and Smith (1998). The Krusell and Smith (2015) model has regions represent squares that are 1 by 1 degree on the map; Nordhaus's G-Econ database with population and production on that level of aggregation can then

[cn] Our particular assumptions on how coal is produced explains why there is no effect at all on coal use in region 2: the costs and the benefits of coal are both lowered by the same proportion as a result of the tax in region 1. With coal produced with a constant marginal cost in terms of output (as opposed to in terms of labor), there would be a small effect on region 2's coal use.

[co] We did not consider the case where coal is costless to trade and potentially produced in a third region but it is straightforwardly analyzed.

be used to calibrate the model. Thus, the calibration makes the initial model output distribution match that in the data, and the marginal products of capital are assumed to be equal initially—these two restrictions are made possible by choosing TFP and capital-stock levels for each region. There is also heterogeneity in two aspects of how regions respond to climate change. One is that for any given increase in global temperature, the regional responses differ quite markedly according to certain patterns, as discussed in Section 3.1.4; Krusell and Smith use the estimates implied by a number of simulations of advanced climate models to obtain region-specific parameters. These estimated "climate sensitivities" are plotted by region on the global map in left panel of Fig. 13.

A second element is differences in damages from climate change across regions. In the latest version of their work and as mentioned in Section 3.3.3, Krusell and Smith use the assumption that there is a common, U-shaped damage function for all regions defined in terms of the local temperature, ie, there ideal temperature is the same at all locations. This common damage function has three parameters which are estimated to match, when the model is solved, the aggregate (global) damages implied by Nordhaus's DICE damage function for three different warming scenarios (1, 2.5, and 5 degrees of global warming). The estimates imply that an average daily temperature of 11.1°C (taken as a 24-h average) is optimal.

The right panel of Fig. 13 displays the model's predicted laissez-faire outcomes in year 2200. We see large gains in percent of GDP in most of the northern parts of the northern hemisphere and large losses in the south. Overall, the damage heterogeneity is what is striking here: the differences across regions swamp those obtained for any comparisons over time of global average damages. The results in this figure of course rely on the assumption that the damage function is the same everywhere so that warming implies gains for those regions that are too cold initially and losses for those that are too warm. This, however, seems like a reasonable assumption to start with and, moreover, is in line with recent damage-function estimates using cross-sectional data: see Burke et al. (2015). These results at the very least suggest that the returns from further research on heterogeneity should be rather high.

We already mentioned Hémous's (2013) work on the R&D allocation across regions, emphasizing the importance of understanding the determinants and consequences of the regional distribution of R&D and of trade in goods with different carbon content.[cp] Another very promising and recent line of research that we also made reference to above is that on endogenous migration pursued in Brock et al. (2014) and Desmet and Rossi-Hansberg (2015). The latter study, which is an early adopter of the kind of damage-function assumption (for both agriculture and manufacturing) used in the later study by Krusell and Smith (2015), assumes free mobility and that there is technology heterogeneity across regions, with operative region-to-region spillovers. The model

[cp] See also Acemoglu et al. (2014).

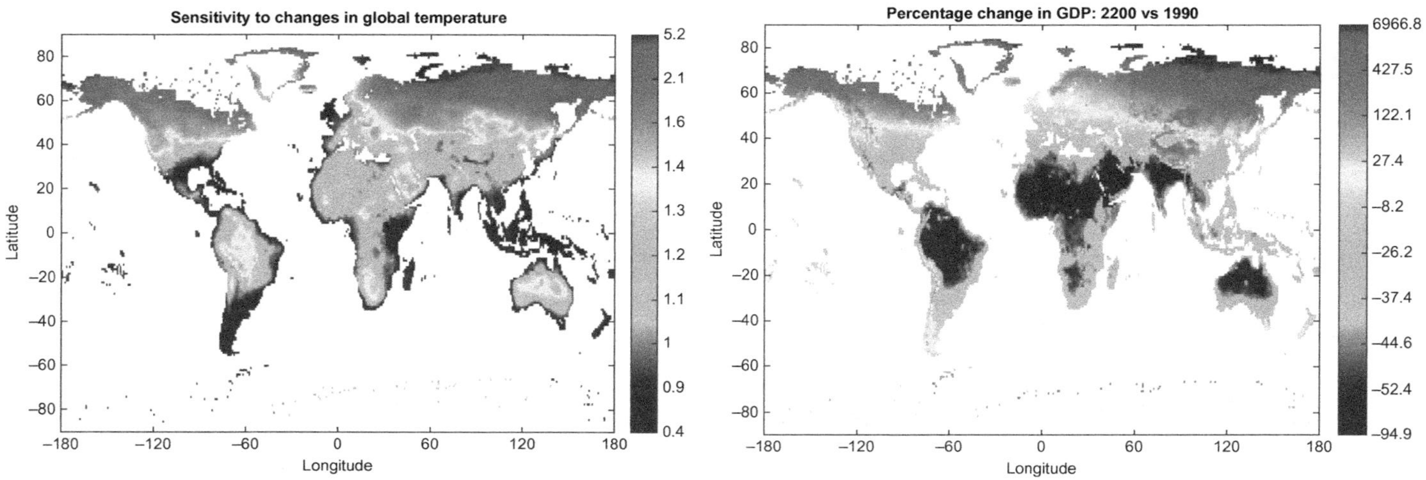

Fig. 13 *Left*: temperature increases for global warming of 1 degree. *Right*: simulation of Krusell and Smith (2015) model, future % GDP losses under laissez-faire.

structure used by Desmet and Rossi-Hansberg is particularly tractable for the analysis of migration, as it uses indifference conditions to distribute agents across space. In contrast, models where location is a state variable (in a dynamic sense) and moving is costly are much more difficult to characterize, as moving then is a highly multidimensional and nonlinear problem both with regard to state and control variables. Stylized two-region models like those studied herein and in Hémous's work can perhaps be solved for endogenous migration outcomes but full dynamics are probably very challenging to solve for.

5. DYNAMIC IAMS

Even though the static IAM setting analyzed in the previous section is useful in many ways, its value in quantitative evaluations is limited: climate change plays out very slowly over time—the dynamics of the carbon cycle especially—and the intertemporal economics aspects involving the comparison between consumption today and consumption far out in the future are therefore of essence. Thus, a quantitatively oriented integrated assessment model of economics and climate change needs to incorporate dynamics. In addition, there are some conceptual issues that cannot be properly discussed without a dynamic setting, such as time preferences.

To our knowledge, the first steps toward modern integrated assessment model appear in Nordhaus (1977). A little over a decade later, Nordhaus developed a sequence of dynamic models, all in the spirit of the simple model above, but formulated in sufficient complexity that numerical model solution is required. The core, one-region version of Nordhaus's model is DIce: a Dynamic Integrated Climate-Economy model, described in detail in Nordhaus and Boyer (2000). In one respect, almost all the dynamic IAMs, including Nordhaus's, are more restrictive than the setting in our previous section: they focus on a planning problem, ie, on characterizing optimal allocations. That is, decentralized equilibria without carbon policy, or with suboptimal carbon policy, are rarely analyzed, let alone explicitly discussed in dynamic models.[cq] In our present treatment, we insist on analyzing both optima and suboptimal equilibria, in large part because the quantitative assessments of the "cost of inaction" cannot be computed otherwise.

In what follows we will discuss a general structure for which we define the social cost of carbon and, under some additional assumptions, can derive a simple and directly interpretable formula for the tax. It is a straightforward extension of the results from the static model above. This material is contained in Section 5.1. In Section 5.2 we then make further assumptions, relying also on the finite-resource modeling from Section 2, and simplify the general structure so as to arrive at an easily solved, and yet quantitatively reasonable, model that can be used for positive as well as normative analysis. Throughout, the discussion follows Golosov et al. (2014) rather closely.

[cq] For an exception, see, eg, Leach (2007).

5.1 The Social Cost of Carbon in a General Dynamic Model

We now focus on how the SCC is determined in a dynamic setting that is reasonably general. For this, we use a typical macroeconomic model with a representative (for the global economy, at this point) agent, as in Nordhaus's DICE model, a production structure, and a specification of the climate system as well as the carbon cycle.

The representative agent has utility function

$$\mathbb{E}_0 \sum_{t=0}^{\infty} \beta^t U(C_t),$$

where U is a standard, strictly concave utility function of (the one and only) consumption good C and where $\beta \in [0,1)$ is the discount factor. The resource constraint for the consumption good is more broadly a constraint for the final good, because like in most of the macroeconomic literature we treat consumption and investment as perfect substitutes. The constraint thus reads

$$C_t + K_{t+1} = Y_t + (1-\delta)K_t,$$

which involves a typical capital accumulation specification with geometric depreciation at rate δ and where Y denotes global output. Global output, in turn, is generated from

$$Y_t = F_{0,t}(K_{0,t}, N_{0,t}, \mathbf{E}_{0,t}, S_t).$$

Here, "0" represents the sector producing the final good. The function F_0 is assumed to display constant returns to scale in the first three inputs. $N_{0,\,t}$ is labor used in this sector and $\mathbf{E}_{0,t} = (E_{0,1,t}, \ldots, E_{0,I,t})$ denotes a vector of different energy inputs. We use a subindex t on the production function to indicate that there can be technical change over time (of various sorts and deterministic as well as stochastic). S, finally, is atmospheric carbon concentration, and it appears in the production function because it causes damages—through the effect of S on the climate (in particular through the temperature).

In our formulation here, as discussed earlier, we adopt the common assumption that damages only appear in the production function. Moreover, they only appear in the time-t production function through atmospheric carbon concentration at t, thus subsuming the mapping from S to temperature and that from temperature to output loss in one mapping. As we already argued, these assumptions are convenient in that they map neatly into Nordhaus's DICE model. We should remind the reader that the inclusion of only S_t in the damages at t captures a lack of dynamics; as we pointed out, this should still be a reasonable approximation to a more complex setting where, conceptually, one would include past values of S in the production function at t as a way of capturing the full dynamics. An extension to include such lagged variables is straightforward but would not greatly change the results as the temperature dynamics are rather quick.

Turning to energy production, we assume that there are $I_g - 1$ "dirty" energy sources (involving fossil fuel), $i = 1, \ldots, I_g - 1$, and a set of green sources, $i = I_g, \ldots, I$. Each component of $\mathbf{E}_{0,\,t}$, $E_{0,\,i,\,t}$ for $i = 1, \ldots, I$, is then produced using a technology $F_{i,\,t}$, which uses the three inputs capital, labor, and the energy input vector. Some energy sources, such as oil, may be in finite supply. For those i in finite supply, $R_{i,\,t}$ denotes the beginning-of-period stock at t and $E_{i,\,t}$ the total amount extracted (produced) at t. Thus, the exhaustible stock i evolves as

$$R_{i,t+1} = R_{i,t} - E_{i,t} \geq 0. \tag{20}$$

Production for energy source i, whether it is exhaustible or not, is then assumed to obey

$$E_{i,t} = F_{i,t}(K_{i,t}, N_{i,t}, \mathbf{E}_{i,t}, R_{i,t}) \geq 0. \tag{21}$$

The resource stock appears in the production function because the production costs may depend on the remaining resource stock. Notice, also, that S_t does not appear in these production functions: we assume that climate change does not cause damages to energy production. This, again, is a simplification we make mainly to adhere to the TFP damage specification that is common in the literature, but it also simplified formulas and improves tractability somewhat. Given that the energy sector is not so large, this simplification should not be a major problem for our quantitative analysis.

To close the macroeconomic part of the model, we assume that inputs are allocated across sectors without costs, again a simplifying assumption but one that appears reasonable if the period of analysis is as long as, say, 10 years. Thus we have

$$\sum_{i=0}^{I} K_{i,t} = K_t, \quad \sum_{i=0}^{I} N_{i,t} = N_t, \text{ and } E_{j,t} = \sum_{i=0}^{I} E_{i,j,t}. \tag{22}$$

We assume that the sequence/process for N_t is exogenous.

Finally, we let the carbon cycle generally be represented by a function $\tilde{S}_t$ as follows:

$$S_t = \tilde{S}_t\left(E^f_{i,-T}, E^f_{-T+1}, \ldots, E^f_t\right). \tag{23}$$

Here, T periods back represents the end of the preindustrial era and $E^f_s \equiv \sum_{i=1}^{I_g-1} E_{i,s}$ is fossil emission at s and we recall that $E_{i,\,s}$ is measured in carbon emission units for all i. When we specialize the model, we will adopt a very simple structure for $\tilde{S}_t$ that is in line with the discussion in the section earlier on the carbon cycle.

We are now ready to state an expression for the SCC. Using somewhat abstract (but obvious) notation, and denoting the social cost of carbon at time t, in consumption units at this point in time, by SCC_t, we have

$$\text{SCC}_t = \mathbb{E}_t \sum_{j=0}^{\infty} \beta^j \frac{U'(C_{t+j})}{U'(C_t)} \frac{\partial F_{0,t+j}}{\partial S_{t+j}} \frac{\partial S_{t+j}}{\partial E^f_t}. \tag{24}$$

Before we discuss this equation, let us emphasize—as we pointed out in the context of the static model—that this expression amounts to keeping decisions fixed as emissions are increased incrementally. Ie, this concept of the social cost of carbon does not correspond to a policy experiment (where presumably induced changes in decisions would add indirect damage effects, positive or negative). Golosov et al. (2014) derive this equation as part of an optimal allocation but then the interpretation really is that the right-hand side equals the $OSCC_t$.

Eq. (24) is easily interpreted. First, $\frac{\partial S_{t+j}}{\partial E_t^f}$ captures the carbon cycle dynamics: it tells us how much the atmospheric carbon content j periods ahead is increased by a unit emission at t. That amount of increase in S_{t+j} then changes final output in period $t+1$ by $\frac{\partial F_{0,t+j}}{\partial S_{t+j}}$ per unit. The total effect (the multiplication of these two factors), which is presumably negative, is the marginal damage in that period in terms of the final output good arising from a unit of emission at t. To translate this amount into utils at $t+j$ one multiplies by $U'(C_{t+j})$, and to bring the utils at $t+j$ back to time-t utils one multiplies by β^j: utility discounting. The division by $U'(C_t)$ then translates the amount back into consumption units at t. Finally, since one needs to take into account the effect of emissions at all points in time $t, t+1, \ldots$, one needs the infinite sum.

Conceptually, thus, Eq. (24) really is straightforward. However, in its general form it is perhaps not so enlightening. A key result in Golosov et al. (2014) is that with some assumptions that the authors argue are weak, one can simplify the formula considerably and even arrive at a closed-form expression in terms of primitive parameters. We present the assumptions one by one.

Assumption 1. $U(C) = \log C$.

Logarithmic utility, both used and relaxed in our static model, is very often used in macroeconomic models and seems appropriate as a benchmark. It embodies an assumption about the intertemporal elasticity of consumption but obviously also about risk aversion.

Assumption 2.

$$F_{0,t}(K_{0,t}, N_{0,t}, \mathbf{E}_{0,t}, S_t) = \exp(-\gamma_t S_t)\widetilde{F}_{0,t}(K_{0,t}, N_{0,t}, \mathbf{E}_{0,t}),$$

where we have normalized so that S is the atmospheric CO_2 concentration in excess of that prevailing in preindustrial times, as in the earlier section, and where γ can be time- and state-dependent.

This assumption was discussed in detail in Section 3.3: we argue that it allows a good reduced-form approximation to the most commonly used assumptions on the S-to-temperature and the temperature-to-damage formulations in this literature.

Assumption 3.

$$S_t = \sum_{s=0}^{t+T} (1 - d_s) E_{t-s}^f \qquad (25)$$

where $d_s \in [0, 1]$ for all s.

A linear carbon cycle was also discussed Section 3.2.4 on carbon circulation above and argued to be a good approximation. The linear structure was also simplified further there, and we will use that simplification below.

Assumption 4.
C_t/Y_t does not depend on time.

This assumption, which is tantamount to that used in the textbook Solow model, is not an assumption on primitives as we usually define them. However, it is an assumption that can be shown to hold exactly for some assumptions on primitives—as those that will be entertained below—or that holds approximately in a range of extensions; see Barrage (2014). Major changes in saving behavior away from this assumption are needed to drastically alter the quantitative conclusions coming out of our SCC formula.

Now given these four assumptions only a minor amount of algebra suffices to arrive at a formula for the SCC, as well as for the optimal tax on carbon. It is

$$\text{SCC}_t = Y_t \left[\mathbb{E}_t \sum_{j=0}^{\infty} \beta^j \gamma_{t+j} (1 - d_j) \right]. \qquad (26)$$

As can be seen, this formula is a straightforward extension of that arrived at for the static economy. As in the static economy, the formula for the tax as a fraction of output is a primitive: there, simply γ; here, a present value of sorts of future γs. Note, of course, here as well as for the static model, that if one needs to assign a specific value to the optimal tax, one would strictly speaking need to evaluate output at its optimal level, and the optimal level of output is not expressed in closed form here (and may be cumbersome to compute). However, given our quantitative analysis later, we note that the optimal tax rate does not alter current output so much. Hence, a good approximation to the optimal tax rate is that given by the expression in brackets in Eq. (26) times current output.[cr]

In the static economy, we assumed a Cobb–Douglas form for output, as we will in the next section as well for our positive analysis. However, Cobb–Douglas production

[cr] In the dynamic model, this approximation would overstate the exact value of the tax since optimal output in the short run will be lower than laissez-faire output. In the static model with TFP damages, the reverse inequality will hold.

is apparently not necessary for the result earlier. What is true is that Cobb–Douglas production, along with logarithmic utility and 100% depreciation for capital, are very helpful assumptions for arriving at a constant C/Y ratio (Assumption 4), but we also know that an approximately constant C/Y ratio emerges out of a much broader set of economies.

We note that, aside from the damage parameter γ, utility discounting and carbon depreciation now matter very explicitly as well. This is quite intuitive: it matters how long a unit of emitted carbon stays in the atmosphere and it also matters how much we care about the future. As for how γ appears, note that the formula is an expectation over future values—as in the static model, a certainty equivalence of sorts applies—but that one could also imagine γ as evolving over time, or incorporating different amounts of uncertainty at different points in time.[cs] Of course, suppose more information is revealed about γ as time evolves, the optimal tax will evolve accordingly (as, eg, in a specification where γ is assumed to follow a unit-root process).

A final expression of our SCC is obtained by (i) assuming that $\mathbb{E}_t\left[\gamma_{t+j}\right]=\overline{\gamma}_t$ for all j (as for example for a unit root process) and (ii) letting the $1-d_j$s be defined by Eq. (13) (which we argued gives a good account of the depreciation patterns). Then we obtain

$$\mathrm{SCC}_t/Y_t=\overline{\gamma}_t\left(\frac{\varphi_L}{1-\beta}+\frac{(1-\varphi_L)\varphi_0}{1-(1-\varphi)\beta}\right). \tag{27}$$

Here, the expression inside the parenthesis on the right-hand side can be thought of as the *discount-weighted duration of emissions*, an object that is stationary by assumption here.

A remarkable feature of the formula for the SCC as a fraction of output as derived here is that it depends on very few parameters. In particular, no production parameters appear, nor do assumptions about technology or the sources of energy. In contrast, we will see in the positive analysis below that such assumptions matter greatly for the paths of output, the climate, energy use, and the total costs of suboptimal climate policy. These are obviously important as well, so we need to proceed to this analysis. However, for computing what optimal policy is, straightforward application of the formula above works very well, and in some sense is all that is needed to optimally deal with climate change. To compute the optimal quantity restrictions is much more demanding, because then precisely all these additional assumptions are made, and to predict the future of technology (especially that regarding energy supply) is extremely difficult, to say the least. Section 5.2.3 calibrates the key parameters behind the formula above and Section 5.2.4 then displays the numerical results for the social cost of carbon.

[cs] Learning (about γ or the natural-science parameters) could also be introduced formally, as in the planning problem studied by Kelly and Kolstad (1999).

5.2 A Positive Dynamic Model

The positive dynamic model will be a straightforward extension of the static model in Section 4 in combination with the basic model from Section 2.3.2 (without endogenous technical change).

Thus we assume a production function that is Cobb–Douglas in capital, labor, and an energy input, along with TFP damages from climate:

$$Y_t = e^{-\gamma_t S_t} A_t K_t^{\alpha} N_{0t}^{1-\alpha-\nu} E_t^{\nu}. \tag{28}$$

Here, we maintain the possibility that γ changes over time/is random.

There are three energy-producing sectors, as in one of the extensions of the static model. Sector 1 thus produces "oil," which is in finite supply and is extracted at zero cost. The accounting equation $E_{ot} = R_t - R_{t+1}$ thus holds for oil stocks at all times. The second and third sectors are the "coal" and the "green" sectors, respectively. They deliver energy using

$$E_{i,t} = \chi_{it} N_{it} \text{ for } i = c, g. \tag{29}$$

Here, $N_t = N_{0t} + N_{ct} + N_{gt}$. We will focus on parameters such that coal, though in finite supply, will not be used up; hence, its Hotelling premium will be zero and there will be no need to keep track of the evolution of the coal stock.[ct] This specification captures the key stylized features of the different energy sectors while maintaining tractability. In practice, oil (as well as natural gas) can be transformed into useable energy quite easily but these resources are in very limited supply compared to coal. Coal is also more expensive to produce, as is green energy.

Here, energy used in production of the final good, E_t, then obeys

$$E_t = \left(\kappa_o E_{ot}^{\rho} + \kappa_c E_{ct}^{\rho} + \kappa_g E_{gt}^{\rho}\right)^{1/\rho} \tag{30}$$

with $\sum_{i=o,c,g} \kappa_i = 1$. As before, $\rho < 1$ regulates the elasticity of substitution between different energy sources; the κs are share parameters and also influence the efficiency with with the different energy sources are used in production. In addition, coal is "dirtier" than oil in that it gives rise to higher carbon emissions per energy unit produced. With E_{ot} and E_{ct} in the same units (of carbon emitted), the calibration therefore demands $\kappa_o > \kappa_c$.

The variables A_t, χ_{it}, and N_t are assumed to be exogenous and deterministic. Population growth is possible within our analytically tractable framework but we abstract from considering it explicitly in our quantitative exercises below, since A and N play the same

[ct] This will, under some specifications, require that a *back-stop technology* emerge at a point in the future, ie, a technology that simply replaces coal perfectly at lower cost.

role.[cu] Our final assumption, which is key for tractability, is that capital depreciates fully between periods ($\delta = 1$). This is an inappropriate assumption in business-cycle analysis but much less so when a model focusing on long-run issues; a model period will be calibrated to be 10 years.

5.2.1 Solving the Planner's Problem

For brevity, we do not state the planner's problem; it is implicit from the description earlier. The first-order conditions for C_t and K_t yield

$$\frac{1}{C_t} = \beta \mathbb{E}_t \frac{\alpha}{C_{t+1}} \frac{Y_{t+1}}{K_{t+1}}.$$

Together with the resource constraint

$$C_t + K_{t+1} = Y_t$$

we then obtain an analytical solution for saving as $K_{t+1} = \alpha\beta Y_t$ for all t. It follows that C_t / Y_t is equal to $1 - \alpha\beta$ at all times, and we have therefore demonstrated that Assumption 4 is verified for this economy. A byproduct of our assumptions here, then, are that the formula for the optimal carbon tax, Eq. (26), holds exactly.

What is the planner's choice for the energy inputs, and what is the resulting effect on atmospheric carbon concentration and, hence, the climate? First, we assume that $\rho < 1$, and from this Inada property we then conclude that the energy choices will be interior at all times. Looking at the first-order conditions for E_t and E_{ot}, we obtain

$$\frac{\nu\kappa_o}{E_{ot}^{1-\rho} E_t^{\rho}} - \frac{\mathrm{SSC}_t}{Y_t} = \beta \mathbb{E}_t \left(\frac{\nu\kappa_o}{E_{o,t+1}^{1-\rho} E_{t+1}^{\rho}} - \frac{\mathrm{SSC}_{t+1}}{Y_{t+1}} \right), \tag{31}$$

where SSC_t / Y_t is, again, defined Eq. (26). This equation expresses Hotelling's formula in the case where there is a cost of using carbon: the damage externality (thus, playing a similar role to an extraction cost).

Looking at the other two energy source, by choosing $N_{i,\ t}$ optimally we obtain

$$\chi_{ct} \left(\frac{\nu\kappa_c}{E_{ct}^{1-\rho} E_t^{\rho}} - \frac{\mathrm{SCC}_t}{Y_t} \right) = \frac{1 - \alpha - \nu}{N_t - \dfrac{E_{ct}}{\chi_{ct}} - \dfrac{E_{gt}}{\chi_{gt}}} \tag{32}$$

and

[cu] We formulate the utility function in terms of total consumption, and we do not adjust discounting for population growth. One might want to consider an alternative here, but we suspect that nothing substantial will change with this alternative.

$$\chi_{gt}\frac{\nu\kappa_g}{E_{gt}^{1-\rho}E_t^{\rho}}=\frac{1-\alpha-\nu}{N_t-\frac{E_{ct}}{\chi_{ct}}-\frac{E_{gt}}{\chi_{gt}}}. \tag{33}$$

From the perspective of solving the model conveniently, it is important to note now that SSC_t/Y_t is available in closed form as a function of primitives: the remaining system of equations to be solved is a vector difference equation but only in the energy choices. Ie, the model can be solved for energy inputs first, by solving this difference equation, and then the rest of the variables (output, consumption, etc.) are available in the simple closed forms given above.

To solve the vector difference equation—to the extent there is no uncertainty—is also simple, though in general a small amount of numerical work is needed.[cv] A robust numerical method goes as follows. With any given value for E_{ot}, the Eqs. (32) and (33) can be used to solve for E_{ct} and E_{gt}, and thus E_t. The solution is nonlinear but well defined. For any given initial stock of oil R_0, one can now use a simple shooting algorithm. The "shooting" part is accomplished by (i) guessing on a number for E_{o0}; (ii) deriving the all the other energy inputs at time 0; (iii) using the Hotelling Eq. (31), which is stated in terms of E_{o1} and E_1, to obtain E_{o1} as a function of E_1; (iv) combining this relation between E_{o1} and E_1 with Eqs. (32) and (33) evaluated for period 1 to obtain all the energy choices in period 1; and (v) going back to step (iii) to repeat for the next period. The so-obtained path for all energy inputs in particular delivers a path for oil extraction. To check whether the fired shot hits the target involves simply checking that the cumulated oil use exactly exhausts the initial stock asymptotically. If too much or too little is used up, adjust E_{o0} appropriately and run through the algorithm again.

If there is uncertainty about γ that is nontrivial and does not go away over time, one needs to use recursive methods, given the nonlinearity of the vector difference equation. It is still straightforward to solve, however, with standard versions of such methods.

5.2.2 Competitive Equilibrium

It is straightforward to define a dynamic (stochastic) general equilibrium for this economy as for the static model. All markets feature perfect competition. Firms in the final-goods sector make zero profits, as do firms in the coal and green-energy sectors. In the oil sector, there is a Hotelling rent, and hence profits. These profits are delivered to the representative consumer, who otherwise receive labor and capital income and, to the extent there is a tax on fossil fuel, lump-sum transfers so that the government budget balances. When taxes are used, we assume that they are levied on the energy-producing firms (oil and coal). The consumer's Euler equation and the return to capital satisfying the first-order condition for capital from the firm's problem deliver the constant saving rate $\alpha\beta$. The energy supplies (or, equivalently, the labor allocation) is then given by a set of

[cv] Solving the model with only coal or only green energy is possible in closed form.

conditions similar to those from the planning problem. Assuming that the carbon tax in period t is set as an exogenous fraction of output in period t, we then obtain from the energy producers' problems

$$\frac{\nu\kappa_o}{E_{ot}^{1-\rho}E_t^{\rho}} - \tau_t = \beta\mathbb{E}_t\left(\frac{\nu\kappa_o}{E_{o,t+1}^{1-\rho}E_{t+1}^{\rho}} - \tau_{t+1}\right), \tag{34}$$

$$\chi_{ct}\left(\frac{\nu\kappa_c}{E_{ct}^{1-\rho}E_t^{\rho}} - \tau\right) = \frac{1-\alpha-\nu}{N_t - \frac{E_{ct}}{\chi_{ct}} - \frac{E_{gt}}{\chi_{gt}}}, \tag{35}$$

and

$$\chi_{gt}\frac{\nu\kappa_g}{E_{gt}^{1-\rho}E_t^{\rho}} = \frac{1-\alpha-\nu}{N_t - \frac{E_{ct}}{\chi_{ct}} - \frac{E_{gt}}{\chi_{gt}}}. \tag{36}$$

Since this vector difference equation is very similar to the planner's vector difference equation, it can be solved straightforwardly with the same kind of algorithm. The laissez-faire allocation is particularly simple to solve.

5.2.3 Calibration and Results

In the spirit of quantitative macroeconomic modeling, the calibration of our model parameters is critical. Also in this part, we follow Golosov et al. (2014) in selecting parameter values. The calibration is important to review in some detail here, as calibration of this class of models is not standard in the macroeconomic literature. Given our assumptions, two parameters are easy to select: we assume that α and ν are 0.3 and 0.04, respectively; the value for the capital share is standard in the macroeconomic literature and the energy share is taken from the calibration in Hassler et al. (2015).

5.2.3.1 Discounting

As will be clear from our results, the discount factor matters greatly for what optimal tax to recommend. We do not take stand here but rather report our results for a range of values for β. Nordhaus's calibrations start from interest-rate data; interest rates should mirror the interest rate, if markets work, so to set $1/\beta - 1 = 0.015$ is then reasonable. Stern, in his review on climate change, takes a very different view and uses what is essentially a zero rate: $1/\beta - 1 = 0.001$. A view that sharply differs from the market view can be motivated on purely normative grounds, though then there may be auxiliary implications of this normative view: perhaps capital accumulation should then be encouraged more broadly, eg, using broad investment/saving subsidies. Sterner and Persson (2008), however, argue informally that it is possible to discount consumption and climate services—to the extent the latter enter separately in utility—at different rates.

A third and, we think, interesting argument for using a lower discount rate is that it is reasonable to assume that discounting is time-inconsistent: people care about themselves and the next generation or so with rates in line with observed market rates but thereafter, they use virtually no discounting. The idea would be that I treat the consumption of my grand-grand-grand children and that of my grand-grand-grand-grand children identically in my own utility weighting. If this is a correct description of people's preferences, and if people have commitment tools for dealing with time inconsistency, we would see it in market rates, but there are not enough market observations for such long-horizon assets to guide a choice of discount rates. Hence, it is not easy to reject a rate such as 0.1% (but, by the same token, there is no market evidence in favor of it either). If people have no commitment tools for dealing with time inconsistency, observed market rates today would be a mix of the short- and long-run rates (and very heavily weighted toward present-bias), thus making it hard to use market observations to back out the longer-run rates. These arguments can be formalized: it turns out that the present model—if solved with a simplified energy sector (say, coal only)—can be solved analytically also with time-inconsistent preferences (see Karp, 2005, Gerlagh and Liski, 2012, and Iverson, 2014).

5.2.3.2 The carbon cycle

We calibrate the carbon cycle, as indicated, with a linear system implying that the carbon depreciation rates are given by Eq. (13). Thus with the depreciation rate at horizon j given by $1-d_j=\varphi_L+(1-\varphi_L)\varphi_0(1-\varphi)^j$, we have to select three parameter: φ_L, φ_0, and φ. Recall the interpretation that φ_L is the share of of carbon emitted into the atmosphere that stays there forever, $1-\varphi_0$ the share that disappears into the biosphere and the surface oceans within a decade, and the remaining part, $(1-\varphi_L)\varphi_0$, decays (slowly) at a geometric rate φ. We set φ_L to 0.2, given the estimate in the 2007 IPCC report that about 20% any emission pulse remains in the atmosphere for several thousand years.[cw] Archer (2005), furthermore, argues that the excess carbon that does depreciate has a mean lifetime of about 300 years. Thus, we set $(1-\varphi)^{30}=0.5$, implying $\varphi=0.0228$. Third, the 2007 IPCC report asserts that about 50% of any CO_2 emission pulse into the atmosphere has left the atmosphere after about 30 years. This means that $d_2=0.5$ so that $1-\frac{1}{2}=0.2+0.8\varphi_0(1-0.0228)^2$, and hence $\varphi_0=0.393$. Finally, to set the initial condition for carbon concentration we showed above that the assumed depreciation structure is consistent with the existence of two "virtual carbon stocks" S_1 (the part that remains in the atmosphere forever) and S_2 (the part that depreciates at rate φ), with $S_{1,t}=S_{1,t-1}+\varphi_L E_t^f$ and $S_{2,t}=\varphi S_{2,t-1}+\varphi_0(1-\varphi_L)E_t^f$, and $S_t=S_{1,t}+S_{2,t}$. We choose starting values so that time-0 (ie, year-2000) carbon equals 802, with the division

[cw] Archer (2005) argues for a slightly higher number: 0.25.

$S_1 = 684$ and $S_2 = 118$; the value of S_1 comes from taking the preindustrial stock of 581 and adding 20% of accumulation emissions.[cx]

5.2.3.3 Damages

Turning to the calibration of damages, recall that we argued that for a reasonable range of carbon concentration levels the exponential TFP expression $e^{-\gamma S}$ is a good approximation to the composed S-to-temperature and temperature-to-TFP mappings in the literature. It remains choose γ, deterministic or stochastic. Here, in our illustrations, we will focus on a deterministic γ and only comment on uncertainty later. Following the discussion in the damage section earlier and Golosov et al. (2014), with S measured in GtC (billions of tons of carbon), an exponential function with parameter $\gamma_t = 5.3 \times 10^{-5}$ fits the data well.

5.2.3.4 Energy

Turning, finally, to the energy sector, we first need to select a value for ρ, which guides the elasticity of substitution between the energy sources. Stern (2012) is a metastudy of 47 studies of interfuel substitution and reports the unweighted mean of the oil–coal, oil–electricity, and coal–electricity elasticities to be 0.95. Stern's account of estimates of "long-run dynamic elasticities" is 0.72. In terms of our ρ, the implied numbers are -0.058 and -0.390, respectively, and the former will constitute our benchmark.

As for the different energy sources, for oil we need to pin down the size of the oil reserve. According to BP (2010), the proven global reserves of oil are 181.7 gigaton. However, these figures only refer to reserves that are economically profitable to extract at current conditions. Rogner (1997), on the other hand, estimates the global reserves of potentially extractable oil, natural gas, and coal taken together to be over 5000 Gt, measured as oil equivalents.[cy] Of this amount, Rogner reports around 16% to be oil, ie, 800 Gt. We use a benchmark that is in between these two numbers: 300 Gt. To express fossil fuel in units of carbon content, we set the carbon content in crude oil to be 846 KgC/t oil. For coal, we set it to the carbon content of anthracite, which is 716 KgC/t coal.[cz] As for coal, as implied by Rogner's (1997) estimates, the coal supply is enough for several hundreds of years of consumption at current levels, and hence we have assumed the scarcity rent to be zero.

[cx] These number include the preindustrial stock and, hence, do not strictly follow the notation above, where S_t denotes the concentration in excess of preindustrial levels.

[cy] The difference in energy content between natural gas, oil, and various grades of coal is accounted for by expressing quantities in oil equivalents.

[cz] IPCC (2006, table 1.2–1.3).

To calibrate κ_o and κ_c we use relative prices of oil to coal and oil to renewable energy, given by

$$\frac{\kappa_o}{\kappa_c}\left(\frac{E_{ot}}{E_{ct}}\right)^{\rho-1} \quad \text{and} \quad \frac{\kappa_o}{1-\kappa_o-\kappa_c}\left(\frac{E_{ot}}{E_{gt}}\right)^{\rho-1},$$

respectively. The average price of Brent oil was \$70 per barrel over the period 2005–09 (BP, 2010); with a barrel measuring 7.33 metric tons and a carbon content of 84.6%, the oil price per ton of carbon is then \$606.5. As for coal, its average price over the same period is \$74 per ton. With coal's carbon content of 71.6%, this implies a price of \$103.35 per ton of carbon.[da] The implied relative price of oil and coal in units of carbon content is 5.87.

As for renewables/green energy, there is substantial heterogeneity between different such sources. With unity as a reasonable value of the current relative price between green energy and oil, we employ data on global energy consumption to finally pin down the κs. Primary global energy use in 2008 was 3.315 Gtoe (gigaton of oil equivalents) of coal, 4.059 of oil, 2.596 of gas, and $0.712+0.276+1.314=2.302$ of nuclear, hydro, and biomass/waste/other renewables. Based on the IPCC tables quoted earlier, the ratio of energy per ton between oil and anthracite is then $\frac{42.3}{26.7}=1.58$, implying that 1 t of oil equivalents is 1.58 t of coal.[db] With these numbers and the value for ρ of -0.058, we can finally use the equations above to back out $\kappa_o=0.5008$ and $\kappa_c=0.08916$.

The parameters χ_{ct}, which determines the cost of extracting coal over time, are set based on an average extraction cost of \$43 per ton of coal (see IEA, 2010, page 212). Thus, a ton of carbon in the form of coal costs \$43/0.716. The model specifies the cost of extracting a ton of carbon as $\frac{w_t}{\chi_{ct}}$, where w_t is the wage. The current shares of world labor used in coal extraction and green energy production is very close to zero, so with total labor supply normalized to unity we can approximate the wage to be $w_t=(1-\alpha-\nu)Y_t$. With world GDP at \$700 trillion per decade and a gigaton of carbon (our model unit) costing $w_t/\chi_{ct}=(1-\alpha-\nu)Y_t/\chi_{ct}$ to produce delivers $43\cdot 10^9/0.716=0.66\cdot 700\cdot 10^{12}/\chi_{c0}$ and hence $\chi_{c0}=7693$. This means, in other words, that a share $\frac{1}{7693}$ of the world's labor supply during a decade is needed to extract one gigaton of carbon in the form of coal. The calibration of χ_{g0} comes from using the fact that χ_{g0}/χ_{c0} equals the relative price between coal and green energy, thus delivering $\chi_{g0}=7693/5.87=1311$ since the prices

[da] BP (2010) gives these estimates for US Central Appalachian coal.

[db] The amounts of oil and coal in carbon units is obtained by multiplying by the carbon contents 84.6 and 71.6%, respectively.

of oil and green are assumed to be equal and the relative price of oil in terms of coal is 5.87. Lastly, we posit growth in both χ_{ct} and χ_{gt} at 2% per year.[dc]

5.2.4 Results

We begin by reporting what our model implies for the optimal tax on carbon. Given our calibration, and expressed as a function of the discount rate, we plot the tax per ton of emitted carbon in Fig. 14, given annual global output of 70 trillion dollars.[dd]

Fig. 14 displays our benchmark as a solid line along with two additional lines representing two alternative values for γ, the higher one of which represents a "catastrophe scenario" with losses amounting to about 30% of GDP and the lower one representing an opposite extreme case with very low losses. The numbers in the figure can be compared to the well-known proposals in Nordhaus and Boyer (2000) and in the Stern review (Stern, 2007), who suggest a tax of $30 and $250 dollar per ton of carbon, respectively. As already pointed out, these proposals are based on very different discount rates, with Nordhaus using 1.5% per year and Stern 0.1%. For these two discount-rate values, the optimal taxes using our analysis are $56.9 per ton and $496 per ton, respectively, thus showing larger damages than in these studies. There are a number of differences in assumptions between the model here and those maintained in, say, Nordhaus's work; perhaps the most important one quantitatively is that we calibrate the duration of carbon in the atmosphere to be significantly higher.

The figure reveals that, to the extent the catastrophe scenario—which comes from a hypothesis Nordhaus entertained in a survey study—might actually materialize, there will

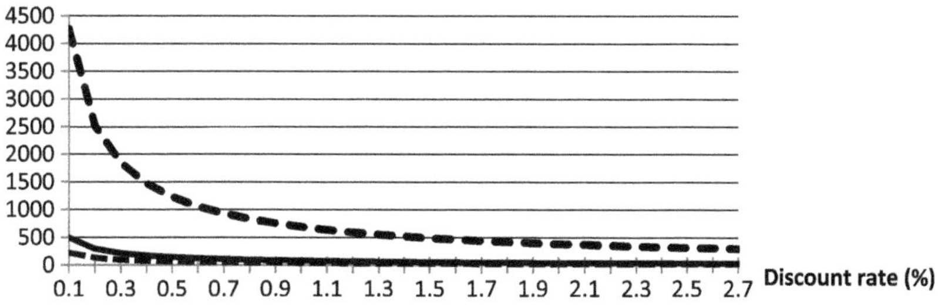

Fig. 14 Optimal tax rates in current dollars per ton of emitted fossil carbon vs yearly subjective discount rate.

[dc] Under our calibration, coal use does not go to zero, which contradicts it being a finite resource. Strictly speaking, one should instead, then, solve the model under this assumption and the implication that coal would have scarcity value. But we consider it quite likely that a competitive close and renewable substitute for coal is invented over the next couple of hundred years, in which case our solution would work well as an approximation.

[dd] The graphs are taken from Golosov et al. (2014).

be dramatic consequences on the level of the optimal tax: we see that the tax is roughly multiplied by a factor 20.

5.2.5 Positive Implications

Fossil fuel use in the optimal allocation and in the *laissez-faire* allocation are shown in Fig. 15. We base our results in this section on the discount rate 1.5%.

Looking at the comparison between the optimum and laissez faire, we see a markedly lower use of fossil fuel in the optimum.[de] In the laissez-faire scenario, there would be a continuous increase in fossil fuel use, but in the optimum the consumption of fossil fuel is virtually flat.

It is important to realize that the difference between the fossil-fuel use in the optimum and in laissez faire is almost entirely coming from a lower coal use in the former. In Figs. 16 and 17, we look separately at coal use and oil use in the optimal vs the laissez-faire allocations. Although the tax on carbon is identical for oil and coal in the optimal allocation, its effects are very different: coal use is simply curbed significantly—the whole path is shifted down radically—but oil use is simply moved forward slightly in time. With optimal taxes,

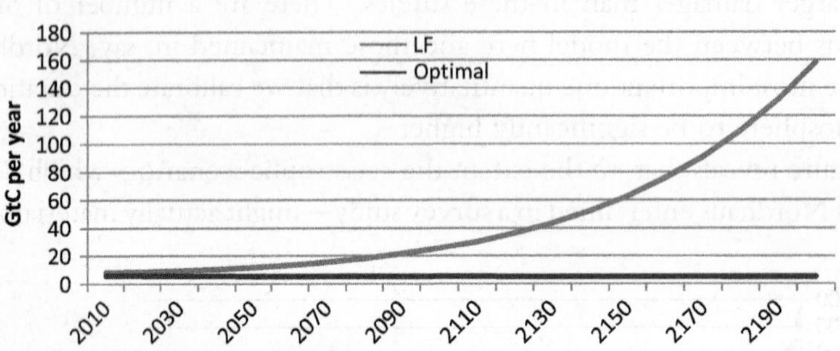

Fig. 15 Fossil fuel use: optimum vs laissez faire.

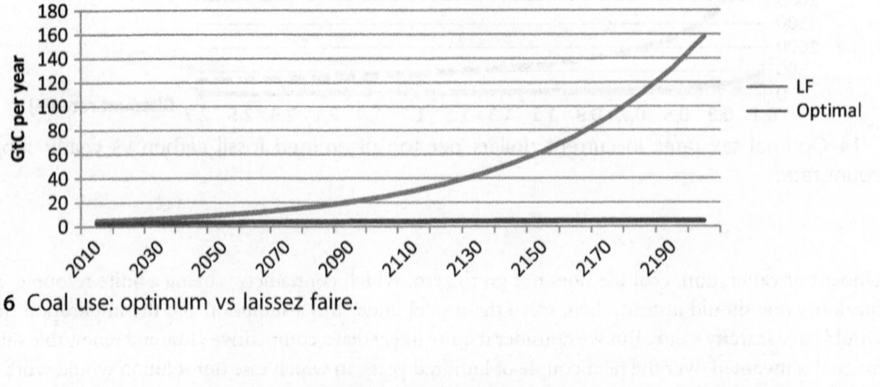

Fig. 16 Coal use: optimum vs laissez faire.

[de] The model predicts coal use in laissez faire of 4.5 GtC during the coming decade; it is currently roughly 3.8 GtC. It predicts oil use of 3.6 GtC, which is also close to the actual value for 2008 or 3.4 GtC.

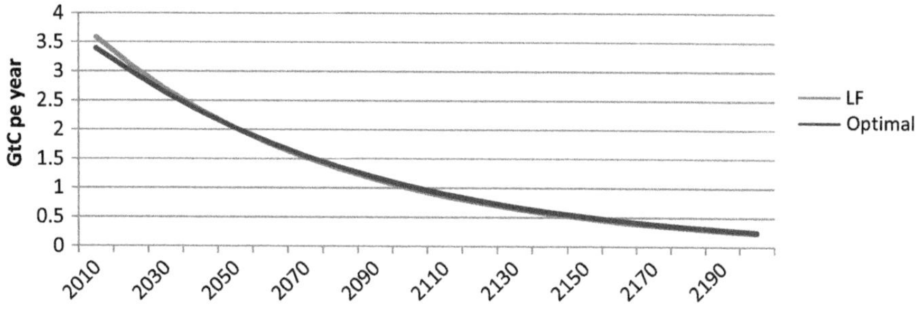

Fig. 17 Oil use: optimum vs laissez faire.

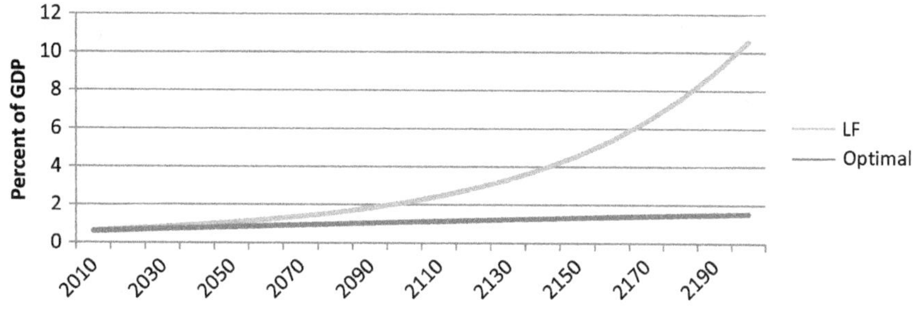

Fig. 18 Total damages as a percent of global GDP: optimum vs laissez faire.

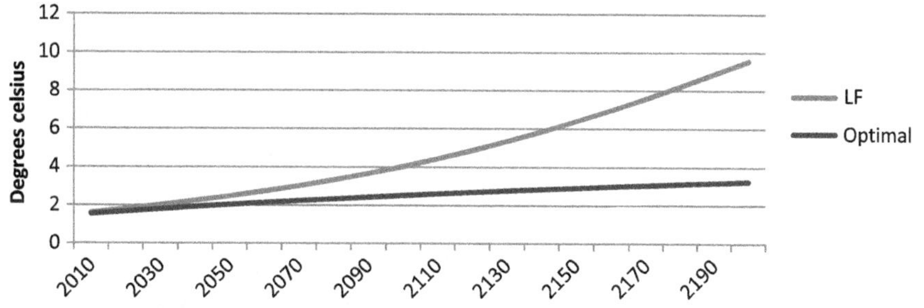

Fig. 19 Increases in global temperature: optimum vs laissez faire.

coal use would fall right now to almost half; a hundred years from now, laissez-faire coal use would be 7 × higher than optimally. Green energy use is very similar across the optimum and laissez-faire allocations.

Total damages are shown in Fig. 18. We note large, though not gigantic, gains from moving from laissez faire to the optimum allocation. The gains grow over time, with damages at a couple of percent of GDP in the laissez-faire allocation, thus about double its optimal value at that time. In 2200, the difference is a factor of six.

We can also back out the path for global temperature in the two scenarios, using the known mapping from S to temperature. Fig. 19 illustrates that laissez faire is associated

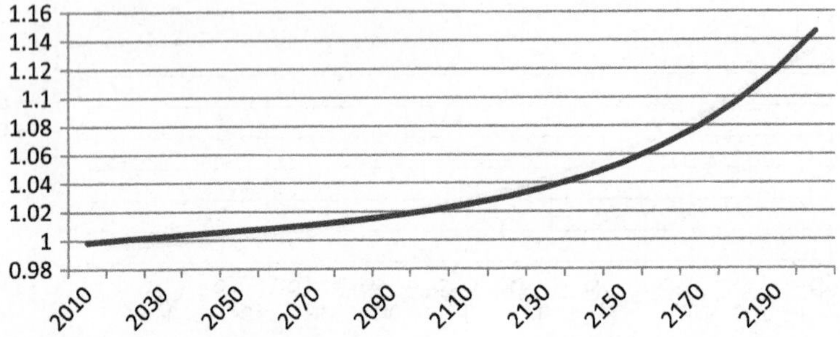

Fig. 20 Net output: optimum vs laissez faire.

with a temperature rise of 4.4°C a hundred years from now; in the optimum, heating is only 2.6 degrees. Toward the end of the simulation period, however, due to massive coal use, laissez faire predicts increased heating by almost 10°C; the optimum dictates about 3 degrees.

Finally, Fig. 20 displays the evolution of the (net-of-damage) production of final-good output (GDP). The intertemporal trade-off is clear here, but not as striking as one might have guessed: the optimal allocation involves rather limited short-run losses in GDP, with optimal output exceeding that of laissez faire as early as 2020. 100 years later, GDP net of damages is 2.5% higher in the optimum and in year 2200, it is higher by almost 15%.

5.2.6 *Discussion*

How robust are the quantitative results in Section 5.2.4? First, the tax formula appears remarkably robust. The point that only three kinds of parameters show up in the formula is a robustness measure in itself; eg, no details of the fossil-fuel stocks, production technologies, or population matter. Strictly speaking, these features begin mattering once one or more of the main assumptions behind the formula are not met, but they will only matter indirectly, eg, insofar as they influence the consumption-output path, and if their impact here is minor, the formula will be robust. In a technical appendix to the Golosov et al. (2014) paper, Barrage (2014) considers a version of the model where not all of the assumptions are met. In particular, this version of the model has more standard transitional dynamics (with a calibration in line with the macroeconomic literature). For example, the assumption that the consumption-output ratio is constant will not hold exactly along a transition path, but the departures almost do not change the results at all. Also, at least US data show very minor fluctuations in this ratio so to the extent a model delivers more drastic movements in the consumption-output ratio it will have trouble matching the data. Higher curvature in utility also delivers very minor changes in the tax rate, with the correction that discounting now involves not just β but also the consumption growth rate raised to $1-\sigma$, where $\sigma=1$ gives logarithmic curvature and $\sigma>1$ higher curvature.

Second, when it comes to the positive analysis—eg, the implications for temperature and damages under different policy scenarios—the message is quite different: many of the assumptions can matter greatly for the quantitative results. Perhaps the best example of nonrobustness is the example considered in Golosov et al. (2014): the elasticity of substitution between energy sources was raised by setting $\rho=0.5$, ie, assuming an elasticity of 2 instead of one slightly below one. If the different energy sources are highly substitutable, coal can easily be used instead of oil, making the laissez-faire allocation deliver very high coal use. On the other hand, taxes are now more powerful in affecting the use of different energy sources. This means, in particular, that the difference in outcomes between an optimal tax and laissez-faire is very large compared to the benchmark, where the different energy sources are less substitutable. Hence, the substitutability across energy sources is an example of an area where more work is needed. Relatedly, we expect that the modeling of technical change in this area—energy saving, as in Section 2.3.3 or making new energy resources available—will prove very important.

A number of straightforward extensions to the setting are also possible and, in part, they have been pursued by other researchers.[df] One is the inclusion of damages that involve growth effects; Dell et al. argue that such effects may be present.[dg] It is easy to introduce such damages to the present setting by letting the TFP term read $e^{-\gamma_l S+\gamma_g St}$, where γ_l regulates level effect of carbon concentration S, and γ_g the damages to the growth rate of output; the baseline model admits closed-form solution. As already pointed out, the baseline model can also accommodate time-inconsistent preferences rather easily.[dh]

Finally, the discussion of dynamic integrated assessment models here is based entirely on the simple baseline model in Golosov et al. (2014) not because it is the only model of this sort, or even the most satisfactory one in some overall sense; rather, this model has been chosen, first, because it is the model with the closest links to standard macroeconomic settings (with forward-looking consumers, dynamic competitive equilibrium with taxes, and so on). Second, the baseline model in Golosov et al. admits highly tractable analysis (with closed-form solutions) and hence is very well suited for illustrations; moreover, for the optimal carbon tax it gives a very robust formula that is also quantitatively adequate. The model is also useful for positive analysis but here it is important to point out that many other approaches can offer more realistic settings and, at least from some

[df] For example, Rezai and van der Ploeg (2014).

[dg] See Moyer et al. (2013).

[dh] Such cases have been discussed by Karp (2005) and, in settings closely related to the model here, Gerlagh and Liski (2012) and Iverson (2014) show that it is possible to analyze the case without commitment relatively straightforwardly; lack of commitment and Markov-perfect equilibria are otherwise quite difficult to characterize.

perspectives, do a better job at prediction. It would require a long survey to review the literature and such an endeavor is best left for another paper; perhaps the closest relative among ambitious, quantitative settings is the WITCH model, which also builds on forward-looking and, among other things, has a much more ambitiously specified energy sector.[di]

REFERENCES

Acemoglu, D., 2009. Introduction to Modern Economic Growth. Princeton University Press.

Acemoglu, D., Aghion, P., Bursztyn, L., Hémous, D., 2012. The environment and directed technical change. Am. Econ. Rev. 102 (1), 131–166.

Acemoglu, D., Aghion, P., Hémous, D., 2014. The environment and directed technical change in a north-south model. Oxf. Rev. Econ. Policy 30 (3), 513–530.

Aghion, P., Dechezlepretre, A., Hémous, D., Martin, R., Van Reenen, J., 2014. Carbon taxes, path dependency and directed technical change: evidence from the auto industry. J. Polit. Econ. (forthcoming).

Aghion, P., Howitt, P., 1992. A model of growth through creative destruction. Econometrica 60 (2), 323–351.

Aghion, P., Howitt, P., 2008. The Economics of Growth. MIT Press.

Aiyagari, R., 1994. Uninsured idiosyncratic risk and aggregate saving. Q. J. Econ. 109 (3), 659–684.

Amador, M., 2003. A political model of sovereign debt repayment. Mimeo.

Archer, D., 2005. The fate of fossil fuel CO_2 in geologic time. J. Geophys. Res. 110.

Archer, D., Eby, M., Brovkin, V., Ridgwell, A., Cao, L., Mikolajewicz, U., Tokos, K., 2009. Atmospheric lifetime of fossil fuel carbon dioxide. Annu. Rev. Earth Planet. Sci. 37, 117–134.

Arrhenius, S., 1896. On the influence of carbonic acid in the air upon the temperature of the ground. Philos. Mag. J. Sci. 41 (5), 237–276.

Azzimonti, M., 2011. Barriers to investment in polarized societies. Am. Econ. Rev. 101 (5), 2182–2204.

Bansal, R., Ochoa, M., 2011. Welfare costs of long-run temperature shifts. NBER Working Paper 17574.

Barrage, L., 2014. Sensitivity analysis for Golosov, Hassler, Krusell, and Tsyvinski (2014): 'optimal taxes on fossil fuel in general equilibrium'. Econometrica. 82. http://www.econometricsociety.org/ecta/supmat/10217_extensions.pdf.

Barrage, L., 2015. Optimal dynamic carbon taxes in a climate-economy model with distortionary fiscal policy. Mimeo.

Barro, R.J., 2013. Environmental protection, rare disasters, and discount rates. NBER Working Paper 19258.

Berndt, E.R., Christensen, L.R., 1973. The translog function and the substitution of equipment, structures, and labor in U.S. manufacturing 1929-68. J. Econom. 1 (1), 81–113.

Bosetti, V., Carraro, C., Galeotti, M., Massetti, E., Tavoni, M., 2006. Witch–a world induced technical change hybrid model. Energy J. 27, 13–37.

Bovenberg, L., Smulders, S., 1995. Environmental quality and pollution-augmenting technological change in a two-sector endogenous growth model. J. Public Econ 57 (3), 369–391.

BP, 2010, 2015. BP statistical review of world energy. http://bp.com/statisticalreview.

Brock, W., Engström, G., Xepapadeas, A., 2014. Spatial climate-economic models in the design of optimal climate policies across locations. Eur. Econ. Rev. 69, 78–103.

Burke, M., Miguel, E., Satyanath, S., Dykema, J.A., Lobell, D.B., 2009. Warming increases the risk of civil war in Africa. Proc. Natl. Acad. Sci. 106 (49), 20670–20674.

Burke, M., Hsiang, S.M., Miguel, E., 2015. Climate and conflict. Ann. Rev. Econ. 7, 577–617.

Chris, H., Anderson, J., Wenman, P., 1993. Policy analysis of the greenhouse effect: an application of the PAGE model. Energy Pol. 21, 327–338.

[di] See Bosetti et al. (2006).

Ciscar, J.C., Iglesias, A., Feyen, L., Szabó, L., Van Regemorter, D., Amelung, B., Nicholls, R., Watkiss, P., Christensen, O.B., Dankers, R., Garrote, L., Goodess, C.M., Hunt, A., Moreno, A., Richards, J., Soria, A., 2011. Physical and economic consequences of climate change in Europe. Proc. Natl. Acad. Sci. 108 (7), 2678–2683.

Cline, W.R., 1992. Economics of Global Warming. Institute for International Economics.

Crost, B., Traeger, C.P., 2014. Optimal CO_2 mitigation under damage risk valuation. Nat. Clim. Change 4, 631–636.

Cuddington, J., Nülle, G., 2014. Variable long-term trends in mineral prices: the ongoing tug-of-war between exploration, depletion, and technological change. J. Int. Money Fin. 42 (C), 224–252.

Dasgupta, P., Heal, G., 1974. The optimal depletion of exhaustable resources. Rev. Econ. Stud 41, 3–28.

Dell, M., Jones, B.F., Olken, B.A., 2012. Temperature shocks and economic growth: evidence from the last half century. Am. Econ. J.: Macroecon. 4 (3), 66–95.

Dell, M., Jones, B., Olken, B., 2014. What do we learn from the weather? The new climate-economy literature. J. Econ. Lit. 52 (3), 740–798.

Desmet, K., Rossi-Hansberg, E., 2015. On the spatial economic impact of global warming. J. Urban Econ. 88, 16–37.

Drijfhouta, S., Bathiany, S., Beaulieu, C., Brovkin, V., Claussen, M., Huntingford, C., Scheffer, M., Sgubin, G., Swingedouw, D., 2015. Catalogue of abrupt shifts in Intergovernmental Panel on Climate Change climate models. Proc. Natl. Acad. Sci. USA. 112(43).

Ellerman, A.D., Buchner, B.K., 2007. The European Union emissions trading scheme: origins, allocation, and early results. Rev. Environ. Econ. Policy 1 (1), 66–87.

Erten, B., Ocampo, J.A., 2012. Super-cycles of commodity prices since the mid-nineteenth century. DESA Working Paper No. 110.

Fankhauser, S., 1994. The economic costs of global warming damage: a survey. Glob. Environ. Chang. 4, 301–309.

Feng, S., Krueger, A.B., Oppenheimer, M., 2010. Linkages among climate change, crop yields and Mexico-US cross-border migration. Proc. Natl. Acad. Sci. USA 107 (32), 14257–14262.

Gars, J., 2012. Essays on the macroeconomics of climate change. Ph.D. thesis. IIES Monograph series No. 74, Institute for International Economic Studies, Stockholm University.

Gerlagh, R., Liski, M., 2012. Carbon prices for the next thousand years. CESifo Working Paper Series No. 3855.

Geweke, J., 2001. A note on some limitations of CRRA utility. Econ. Lett. 71, 341–345.

Gollier, C., 2013. Evaluation of long-dated investments under uncertain growth trend, volatility and catastrophes. Toulouse School of Economics, TSE, Working Papers 12-361.

Golosov, M., Hassler, J., Krusell, P., Tsyvinski, A., 2014. Optimal taxes on fossil fuel in equilibrium. Econometrica 82 (1), 41–88.

Grossman, G., Krueger, A., 1991. Environmental impacts of a North American free trade agreement. NBER Working Paper 3914.

Harari, M., La Ferrara, E, 2014. Conflict, climate and cells: a disaggregated analysis. IGIER Working Paper.

Hart, R., 2013. Directed technical change and factor shares. Econ. Lett. 119 (1), 77–80.

Harvey, D., Kellard, N., Madsen, J., Wohar, M., 2010. The Prebisch-Singer hypothesis: four centuries of evidence. Rev. Econ. Stat. 92 (2), 367–377.

Hassler, J., Krusell, P., 2012. Economics and climate change: integrated assessment in a multi-region world. J. Eur. Econ. Assoc. 10 (5), 974–1000.

Hassler, J., Krusell, P., 2014. The climate and the economy. Mistra-SWECIA Nr. 5.

Hassler, J., Krusell, P., Olovsson, C., 2015. Will we need another mad max? Or will energy-saving technical change save us? Working Paper.

Hassler, J., Krusell, P., Nycander, J., 2016. Climate policy. Econ. Policy. (forthcoming).

Hémous, D., 2013. Environmental policy and directed technical change in a global economy: the dynamic impact of unilateral environmental policies? Working Paper.

Hillebrand, E., Hillebrand, M., 2016. Optimal climate policies in a dynamic multi-country equilibrium model. Working Paper.

Hotelling, H., 1931. Economics of exhaustible resources. J. Polit. Econ. 39 (2), 137–175.

IEA (International Energy Agency), 2010. World Energy Outlook. OECD/IEA.

IPCC, 2006. 2006 IPCC guidelines for national greenhouse gas inventories. Vol. 2 energy. In: Eggleston, S., Buendia, L., Miwa, K., Ngara, T., Tanabe, K., (Eds.), IPCC National Greenhouse Inventories Programme.
IPCC, 2007a. Climate change 2007 the physical science basis. In: Solomon, S., Qin, D., Manning, M., Marquis, M., Averyt, K., Tignor, M.M.B., Miller Jr., H.L.R., Chen, Z. (Eds.), Contribution of Working Group I to the Fourth Assessment Report of the Intergovernmental Panel on Climate Change. Cambridge University Press.
IPCC, 2007b. Climate change 2007 impacts, adaptation and vulnerability. In: Parry, M., Canziani, O., Palutikof, J., van der Linden, P., Hanson, C. (Eds.), Contribution of Working Group II to the Fourth Assessment Report of the Intergovernmental Panel on Climate Change. Cambridge University Press.
IPCC, 2013. Climate change 2013 the physical science basis. In: Stocker, T.F., Qin, D., Plattner, G.-K., Tignor, M.M.B., Allen, S.K., Boschung, J., Nauels, A., Xia, Y., Bex, V., Midgley, P.M., (Eds.), Working Group I Contribution to the Fifth Assessment Report of the Intergovernmental Panel on Climate Change. Cambridge University Press.
Iverson, T., 2014. Optimal carbon taxes with non-constant time preference. Working Paper.
Jia, R., 2014. Weather shocks, sweet potatoes and peasant revolts in historical China. Econ. J. 124 (575), 92–118.
Jones, C.I., 2001. Introduction to Economic Growth. W.W. Norton.
Jorgenson, D.W., Cao, J., Ho, M.S., 2013a. The economics of environmental policies in China. In: Clearer Skies Over China. MIT Press.
Jorgenson, D.W., Goettle, R.J., Ho, M.S., Wilcoxen, P.J., 2013b. Double Dividend. MIT Press.
Kam, K., et al., 2011. Partial radiogenic heat model for earth revealed by geoneutrino measurements. Nat. Geosci. 4 (9), 647–651.
Karp, L., 2005. Global warming and hyperbolic discounting. J. Public Econ. 89 (2), 261–282.
Kelly, D., Kolstad, C., 1999. Bayesian learning, growth, and pollution. J. Econ. Dyn. Control 23 (4), 491–518.
Krautkraemer, J.A., 1998. Nonrenewable resource scarcity. J. Econ. Lit. 36 (4), 2065–2107.
Krusell, P., Smith, A., 1998. Income and wealth heterogeneity in the macroeconomy. J. Polit. Econ. 106, 867–896.
Krusell, P., Smith, A., 2014. A global economy-climate model with high regional resolution. Working Paper.
Krusell, P., Smith, A., 2015. Climate change around the world. Working Paper.
Leach, A., 2007. The welfare implications of climate change policy. J. Econ. Dyn. Control. 57.
Lemoine, D., 2015. The climate risk premium: how uncertainty affects the social cost of carbon. Working Paper.
Lenton, T.M., Held, H., Kriegler, E., Hall, J.W., Lucht, W., Rahmstorf, S., Schnellnhuber, H.J., 2008. Tipping elements in the earth's climate system. Proc. Natl. Acad. Sci. USA 105 (6), 1786–1793.
Levitan, D., 2013. Quick-change planet: do global climate tipping points exist? Sci. Am. 25.
Lucas Jr., R.E., 1988. On the mechanics of economic development. J. Monet. Econ. 22, 3–42.
Manne, A., Mendelsohn, R., Richels, R., 1995. MERGE: a model for evaluating regional and global effects of GHG reduction policies. Energy Policy 23 (1), 17–34.
Matthews, H.D., Gillet, N.P., Stott, P.A., Zickfeld, K., 2009. The proportionality of global warming to cumulative carbon emissions. Nature 459, 829–833.
Matthews, H.D., Solomon, S., Pierrehumbert, R., 2012. Cumulative carbon as a policy framework for achieving climate stabilization. Philos. Trans. A Math. Phys. Eng. Sci. 370, 4365–4379.
McGlade, C., Ekins, P., 2015. The geographical distribution of fossil fuel unused when limiting global warming to 2°C. Am. Econ. Rev. 517, 187–190.
Mendelsohn, R., Nordhaus, W., Shaw, D.G., 1994. The impact of global warming on agriculture: a Ricardian approach. Am. Econ. Rev. 84 (4), 753–771.
Miguel, E., Satyanath, S., Sergenti, E., 2004. Economic shocks and civil conflict: an instrumental variables approach. J. Polit. Econ. 112 (4), 725–753.
Moyer, E.J., Woolley, M.D., Glotter, M.J., Weisbach, D.A., 2013. Climate impacts on economic growth as drivers of uncertainty in the social cost of carbon. Working Paper.
Nordhaus, W.D., 1973. World dynamics: measurement without data. Econ. J. 83(332).

Nordhaus, W.D., 1974. Resources as a constraint on growth. Am. Econ. Rev. 64(2).
Nordhaus, W.D., 1977. Economic growth and climate: the carbon dioxide problem. Am. Econ. Rev. Pap. Proc. 67 (1), 341–346.
Nordhaus, W.D., 1991. Economic approaches to greenhouse warming. In: Dornbush, R.D., Poterba, J.M. (Eds.), Global warming: Economic policy approaches. MIT Press, Cambridge, MA, pp. 33–68.
Nordhaus, W.D., 1992. An optimal transition path for controlling greenhouse gases. Science 258, 1315–1319.
Nordhaus, W.D., 1993. Rolling the 'DICE': an optimal transition path for controlling greenhouse gases. Resour. Energy Econ. 15, 27–50.
Nordhaus, W.D., 2006. Geography and macroeconomics: new data and new findings. Proc. Natl. Acad. Sci. USA 103 (10), 3510–3517.
Nordhaus, W.D., 2007. To tax or not to tax: the case for a carbon tax. Rev. Environ. Econ. Policy 1 (1), 26–44.
Nordhaus, W.D., 2009. An analysis of the dismal theorem. Working Paper.
Nordhaus, W.D., Boyer, J., 2000. Warming the World: Economic Modeling of Global Warming. MIT Press.
Nordhaus, W.D., Sztorc, P., 2013. DICE 2013R: introduction and user's manual. Mimeo, Yale University.
Otto, A., Otto, F.E.L., Allen, M.R., Boucher, O., Church, J., Hegerl, G., Forster, P.M., Gillett, N.P., Gregory, J., Johnson, G.C., Knutti, R., Lohmann, U., Lewis, N., Marotzke, J., Stevens, B., Myhre, G., Shindell, D., 2013. Energy budget constraints on climate response. Nat. Geosci. 6 (6), 415–416.
Pigou, A., 1920. Economics of Welfare. MacMillan.
Pindyck, R.S., 1978. The optimal exploration and production of nonrenewable resources. J. Polit. Econ. 86 (5), 841–861.
Poole, W., 1970. Optimal choice of policy instruments in a simple stochastic macro model. Q. J. Econ. 84 (2), 197–216.
Prather, M.J., Holmes, C.D., Hsu, J., 2012. Reactive greenhouse gas scenarios: systematic exploration of uncertainties and the role of atmospheric chemistry. Geophys. Res. Lett. 39, 9.
Prebisch, R., 1962. The economic development of Latin America and its possible problems. Econ. Bull. Latin Am. 7 (1), 1–22. Reprinted from: United Nations Department of Economic Affairs, Lake Success, NY (1950).
Revelle, R., Suess, H., 1957. Carbon dioxide exchange between atmosphere and ocean and the question of an increase of atmospheric CO_2 during past decades. Tellus 9, 18–27.
Rezai, A., van der Ploeg, F., 2014. Robustness of a simple rule for the social cost of carbon. Econ. Lett. 132, 48–55.
Rockström, J., Steffen, W., Noone, K., Persson, A., Chapin, F.S., Lambin, E.F., Lenton, T.M., Scheffer, M., Folke, C., Schellnhuber, H.J., Nykvist, B., de Wit, C.A., Hughes, T., van der Leeuw, S., Rodhe, H., Sörlin, S., Snyder, P.K., Costanza, R., Svedin, U., Falkenmark, M., Karlberg, L., Corell, R.W., Fabry, V.J., Hansen, J., Walker, B., Liverman, D., Richardson, K., Crutzen, P., Foley, J.A., 2009. A safe operating space for humanity. Nature 461, 472–475.
Roe, G.H., Baker, M.B., 2007. Why is climate sensitivity so unpredictable. Science 318 (5850), 629–632.
Rogner, H.H., 1997. An assessment of world hydrocarbon resources. Ann. Rev. Energy Environ. 22, 217–262.
Romer, P.M., 1990. Endogenous technological change. J. Polit. Econ. 98 (5), S71–S102.
Schmitt, A., 2014. Beyond pigou: climate change mitigation, policy making and distortions. Ph.D. thesis, IIES Monograph series No. 85, Stockholm University.
Schwartz, S.E., Charlson, R.J., Kahn, R., Ogren, J., Rodhe, H., 2010. Why hasn't earth warmed as much as expected? J. Clim. 23.
Schwartz, S.E., Charlson, R.J., Kahn, R., Rodhe, H., 2014. Earth's climate sensitivity: apparent inconsistencies in recent assessments. Earth's Fut. 2.
Singer, H.W., 1950. U.S. foreign investment in underdeveloped areas: the distribution of gains between investing and borrowing countries. Am. Econ. Rev. Pap. Proc. 40, 473–485.
Sinn, H.W., 2008. Public policies against global warming: a supply side approach. Int. Tax Public Finance 15 (4), 360–394.

Solow, R., 1974. Intergenerational equity and exhaustible resources. Rev. Econ. Stud. 41, 29–45.
Spiro, D., 2014. Resource prices and planning horizons. J. Econ. Dyn. Control 48, 159–175.
Stern, D.I., 2012. Interfuel substitution: a meta-analysis. J. Econ. Surv. 26, 307–331.
Stern, N., 2007. The Economics of Climate Change: The Stern Review. Cambridge University Press.
Sterner, T., Persson, M., 2008. An even sterner review: introducing relative prices into the discounting debate. Rev. Env. Econ. Pol. 2 (1), 61–76.
Stiglitz, J., 1974. Growth with exhaustible natural resources: efficient and optimal growth paths. Rev. Econ. Stud. 41, 123–137.
Stokey, N., 1998. Are there limits to growth? Int. Econ. Rev. 39, 1–31.
Titus, J.G., 1992. The costs of climate change to the United States. In: Global Climate Change: Implications, Challenges and Mitigation Measures. Pennsylvania Academy of Science, pp. 384–409.
Tol, R.S.J., 1995. The damage costs of climate change toward more comprehensive calculations. Environ. Resour. Econ. 5, 353–374.
Tol, R.S.J., 2009. The economic effects of climate change. J. Econ. Perspect. 23 (2), 29–51.
Weitzman, M.L., 1974. Prices vs quantities. Rev. Econ. Stud. 41 (4), 477–491.
Weitzman, M.L., 1998. Why the far-distant future should be discounted at its lowest possible rate. J. Environ. Econ. Manage. 36 (3), 201–208.
Weitzman, M.L., 2009. On modeling and interpreting the economics of catastrophic climate change. Rev. Econ. Stat. 91, 1–19.
Weitzman, M.L., 2011. Fat-tailed uncertainty in the economics of catastrophic climate change. Rev. Environ. Econ. Policy 5 (2), 275–292.

CHAPTER 25

The Staying Power of Staggered Wage and Price Setting Models in Macroeconomics

J.B. Taylor
Stanford University, Stanford, CA, United States

Contents

Abstract

After many years, many critiques, and many variations, the staggered wage and price setting model is still the most common method of incorporating nominal rigidities into empirical macroeconomic models used for policy analysis. The aim of this chapter is to examine and reassess the staggered

Handbook of Macroeconomics, Volume 2B
ISSN 1574-0048, http://dx.doi.org/10.1016/bs.hesmac.2016.04.008

wage and price setting model. The chapter updates and expands on my chapter in the 1999 *Handbook of Macroeconomics* which reviewed key papers that had already spawned a vast literature. It is meant to be both a survey and user-friendly exposition organized around a simple "canonical" model. It provides a guide to the recent explosion of microeconomic empirical research on wage and price setting, examines central controversies, and reassesses from a longer perspective the advantages and disadvantages of the model as it has been applied in practice. An important question for future research is whether staggered price and wage setting will continue to be the model of choice or whether it needs to be replaced by a new paradigm.

Keywords

Staggered contracts, Time-dependent pricing, State-dependent pricing, Contract multiplier, Calvo contracts, Taylor contracts, Hazard rate, Pass-through, Wage Dynamics Network, Nominal rigidities, New Keynesian economics

JEL Classification Codes

E3, E4, E5

1. INTRODUCTION

The staggered wage and price setting model has had remarkable staying power. Originating in the 1970s before the advent of real business cycle models, it has been the theory of choice in generation after generation of monetary business cycle models. In their review of over 60 macroeconomic models in their chapter for this Handbook, Wieland et al. (2016) define three such generations each with representative models that are based on staggered price or wage setting theories.[a]

This chapter examines the role of staggered wage and price setting as a method of incorporating nominal rigidities in empirical macroeconomic models used for policy analysis. It is both an exposition and a survey. It builds on my earlier *Handbook of Macroeconomics* chapter (Taylor, 1999) which reviewed original research papers that had already spawned a vast literature. It focuses on new research since that *Handbook* chapter, and, though it is largely self-contained, a more complete history of thought in this area requires looking at that chapter too. This chapter considers the explosion of microeconomic empirical research on wage and price setting behavior, the main critiques of the model, such as by Chari et al. (2000), and the complementary work on state-dependent pricing by Dotsey et al. (1999) and Golosov and Lucas (2007). Finally, the chapter reassesses from a longer vantage point the advantages and disadvantages of the model as it has been applied in practice, and it considers possible directions for future research.

[a] See Wieland et al. (2016), table 5.

2. AN UPDATED EMPIRICAL GUIDE TO WAGE AND PRICE SETTING IN MARKET ECONOMIES

I started off my 1999 *Handbook of Macroeconomics* chapter with "an empirical guide to wage and price setting in market economies" noting that "one of the great accomplishments of research on wage and price rigidities in the 1980s and 1990s is the bolstering of case studies and casual impression with the evidence from thousands of observations of price and wage setting collected at the firm, worker, or union level." The same could be said of the new research on microeconomic data during the past two decades except that there is much more of it—a virtual explosion of "Big Data" microeconomic studies, especially in the United States and European countries. These studies have confirmed much of the earlier work, but they have also uncovered new important facts about the timing, frequency, and determinants of price and wage change which are relevant for future research and model building. Accordingly, in this section I give an "*updated* empirical guide to wage and price setting in market economies."

As a starting point, recall that informal observation informed the original theoretical research on staggered wage and price setting models in the 1970s since there was virtually no microeconomic empirical research to guide it.[b] For many firms and organizations, whether in a formal employment contract or not, wages—including fringe benefits—appeared to be adjusted about once per year after a performance review and after consideration of prevailing wages in the market. A large fraction of the wage payment appeared to be a fixed amount, though overtime pay, bonuses, profit sharing, and piece rates were not uncommon, with as many similarities as differences between union and nonunion workers. Indexing of wages was seen to be rare in wage setting arrangements of 1 year or less. And wage adjustments looked to be unsynchronized—occurring at different times for different firms throughout the year—though there were exceptions such as the Shunto (spring wage offensive) in Japan.

Regarding prices, research work by Stigler and Kindahl (1970) had begun to document the extent of price rigidity for a wide variety of products and led people to distinguish informally between "auction markets" where prices changed continuously and "customer markets" where they changed infrequently, a terminology coined by Okun (1981). Though online purchasing has begun to blur this distinction, price changes, like wage changes, appeared to be unsynchronized and firms appeared to take the prevailing price of competing sellers into account.

Fortunately, a huge number of microeconomic studies of wage and price setting over the past few decades have given modelers much more to go on than informal observation. I first consider microeconomic empirical research on wage setting and then on price setting.

[b] I will describe the 1970s modeling research in the next section. Informal observation, of course, guided earlier models of price and wage adjustment, going way back to the time of Hume's (1742) classic essay "On Money" in which he wrote "by degrees the price rises, first of one commodity, then of another."

2.1 Microeconomic Evidence on Wage Setting

To my knowledge, the first empirical study to use actual microeconomic wage data to validate or calibrate the staggered wage setting models of the 1970s was my (1983) study using union wage contracting data in the United States. At the time, the Bureau of Labor Statistics had been calculating detailed data on major collective bargaining agreements for about 10 million workers in the United States and publishing the results in *Current Wage Developments*. The "major" contracts included agreements affecting 1000 or more workers. Although that sector represented only 10% of US employment, it was where the data were, and it was a place to begin.

The data indicated that wage setting was highly nonsynchronized, with agreements spread throughout the year though with relatively more settlements in the second and third quarters. Of these 10 million workers only about 15% had contract adjustments each quarter and only 40% each year. I used these micro data to calibrate a staggered wage setting model with heterogeneous contract lengths and simulated various monetary policies, and in a companion study (Taylor, 1982), I assumed that the remaining workers had shorter contracts. Looking at the union data over a period of time, Cecchetti (1984) found that the average period between wage changes declined with higher inflation, but was still more than 1 year during the high inflation period of the 1970s. There were few international comparisons at that time, though Fregert and Jonung (1986) found that wage setting in Sweden was unsynchronized and that contract length decreased with higher inflation, but it never dropped below 1 year on average.

There was then a lull in research on microeconomic wage setting practices, perhaps due to the increased interest in real business cycles and a corresponding "dark age" of research on wage and price rigidities, as I described in Taylor (2007). In any case, a gap was left between macroeconomic models of wage setting and the microeconomic evidence.

An explosion of research since the early 2000s (just after the completion of the *Handbook of Macroeconomics, Volume 1*!) has gone a long way to filling that gap. An important example, which has contributed greatly to our knowledge of micro wage setting, is the research enabled by the data collected from firms in a survey by the Wage Dynamics Network (WDN). The WDN was created after the founding of the European Central Bank; it consists of researchers at the central banks in the Eurosystem. The WDN surveyed wage and price setting practices at 17,000 European firms. The sample was designed to reflect firm employment size and sector distribution in each country. The survey covered both firms with employees in and out of unions. The percentage of employees in unions varies greatly across countries, ranging from over 70% in Scandinavian countries to less than 10% in Central and Eastern European countries, France, Spain, a percentage similar to the United States.

The report by Lamo and Smets (2009) summarizes the research on this survey referring to 81 different WDN papers and publications. They report that about 60% of the 17,000 firms surveyed change wages once a year, while 26% change wages less frequently.

The average duration of wages is about 15 months and is longer than the average duration of prices, which is about 9.5 months according to a parallel price setting survey in European countries.

Lamo and Smets (2009) also report "strong evidence of time dependence in wage-setting" with 55% of firms reporting that their wage changes occur in a particular month.[c] The timing of wage changes is characterized by a mix of staggering and synchronization. Indeed, there is a lot of heterogeneity across countries; the percentage of firms that change wages "more frequently than once a year ranges from 2.6% in Hungary and 4.2% in Italy to 33.9% in Greece, and 42.1% in Lithuania" according to Lamo and Smets.

There is also related time series work for specific European countries. Lünnemann and Wintr (2009), for example, examined monthly micro data from the Luxembourg social security authority. The data are reported by employers about their employees and pertain to the period from January 2001 to December 2006. They report that measurement error biases upwards the frequency of wage change, but adjusting for this measurement error they find a frequency of wage change of 9–14% per month, which is lower than for consumer prices at 17%. They also find a great deal of heterogeneity across forms. There is clear time dependence with many wages set around the month of January.

Le Bihan et al. (2012) examine a time series of French wage data. They use a quarterly panel of 38,000 French establishments with 6.8 million employees. They examine the base wage for 12 employee categories over 1998–2005. They argue that the base wage is a relevant indicator of wages in France because the base wage represents 77.9% of gross earnings. Furthermore, most bonuses (like "13th month" payments or holidays bonuses) constitute a fixed part of the earnings (5.2%) and are linked to the base wage. The frequency of quarterly wage change is around 38%, and in the case of France, there is not much cross-sectoral heterogeneity in wage stickiness.

They estimate a hazard function—the probability of a change in the wage conditional on an unchanged wage spell of a given duration. Their estimates of the hazard function are shown in Fig. 1. The authors state that the hazard function has a "noticeable spike at four quarters but is rather flat otherwise" and note that "such a pattern is consistent with the prevalence of Taylor-like, 1-year contracts."

Le Bihan et al. (2012) also estimate and report the frequency of wage change each quarter and the variation of that frequency over time. Their estimates are shown in Fig. 2 for all wages as well as for wages near the minimum wage. As they argue "there is evidence of a large degree of staggering since the frequency of wage changes is in no quarter lower than 20%." Note that there is some synchronization in the first quarter for all wages and in the third quarter for minimum wages, the later corresponding

[c] Some of the terminology used in this section—such as time dependence, state dependence, Taylor fixed-length contracts, Calvo model—is defined later in the chapter.

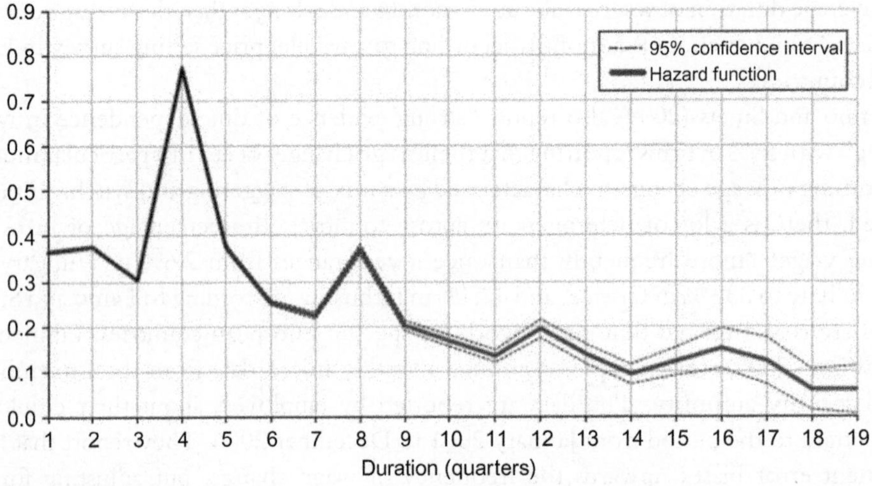

Fig. 1 Estimate of the hazard function of wage change in France. Source: *Le Bihan, H., Montornès, J., Heckel, T., 2012. Sticky wages: evidence from quarterly microeconomic data. Am. Econ. J. Macroecon. 4 (3), 1–32.*

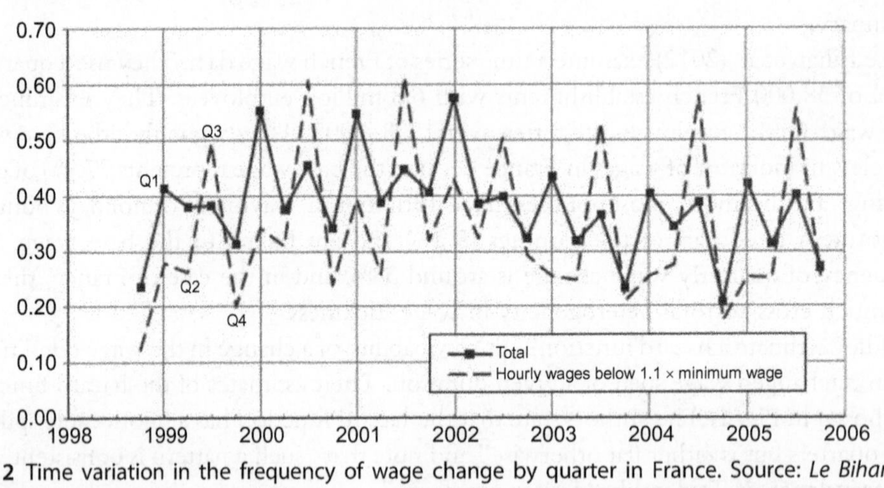

Fig. 2 Time variation in the frequency of wage change by quarter in France. Source: *Le Bihan, H., Montornès, J., Heckel, T., 2012. Sticky wages: evidence from quarterly microeconomic data. Am. Econ. J. Macroecon. 4 (3), 1–32.*

to the national minimum wage update in France each summer. They also report that their "micro-econometric evidence … suggests wage adjustment is mainly time dependent in France." And while wage changes are largely staggered across establishments, the authors report that there is a large degree of synchronization of wage changes within establishments.

Avouyi-Dovi et al. (2013) also examine the wage setting process in France. In contrast to Le Bihan et al. (2012), they collect and examine data on wage bargaining agreements, as Taylor (1983) did for the United States, but with much more detail. Their data pertain to both firms and industries. They find a sharp peak in the distribution of wage contract durations at 12 months. They also find that the "hazard rate shows a peak above 40% at twelve months and remains flat below 10% elsewhere." Indeed, their plots of the hazard function look like much like those in Figure 1 in this chapter with even more pronounced peaks. Finally, they find that the "wage change decisions are staggered over the year" with some evidence of seasonality that also shows up in the aggregate data. In many respects the findings Avouyi-Dovi et al. (2013) and those of Le Bihan et al. (2012) are very similar even though they use completely different data sets.

Another time series study is the paper by Sigurdsson and Sigurdardottir (2011) which examines wage setting behavior in Iceland. They use a micro wage dataset with a monthly frequency for the years 1998–2010. They find that average frequency of wage change is 10.8% per month. They find that "wage setting displays strong features of time dependence: half of all wage changes are synchronized in January, but other adjustments are staggered through the year" though later work by Sigurdsson and Sigurdardottir (2016), which focuses more on the global financial crisis, finds more evidence of state-dependent wage setting. The authors also estimate a hazard function and find that it has a large spike at 12 months. These facts indicate that, as the authors put it, "wage setting is consistent with the Taylor (1980) fixed duration contract model, but there exist contracts with both shorter and longer duration than precisely 1 year."

Recent work by Barattieri et al. (2014) has added important time series information about wage setting in the United States. They use high frequency panel data from the Survey of Income and Program Participation which follows people for a period of from 24 to 48 months with interviews every 4 months. The authors focus on hourly wage data (rather than salaries) which leaves them with a panel of 17,148 people from March 1996 to February 2000. The panel consisted of 49.4% women; ages ranged from 16 to 64 years and the average wage is $10.03 per hour. As with individual data reported by Lünnemann and Wintr (2009), the authors found a great deal of measurement error which adds noise to the wage series and effectively reduces the reported time that a wage is fixed. They corrected for this measurement error using structural break tests commonly used in time series analysis to look for big and persistent changes by filtering out smaller and more temporary changes.

They find that the quarterly frequency of wage adjustment, after correcting for measurement error, ranges from 12% to 27%, which is much lower than the 56% without correction for measurement error. They note that this corrected range is comparable to that found in the European studies reviewed earlier when reported on a common quarterly frequency:

Lünnemann and Wintr (2009)	19–36%
Le Bihan et al. (2012)	35%
Sigurdsson and Sigurdardottir (2011)	13–28%

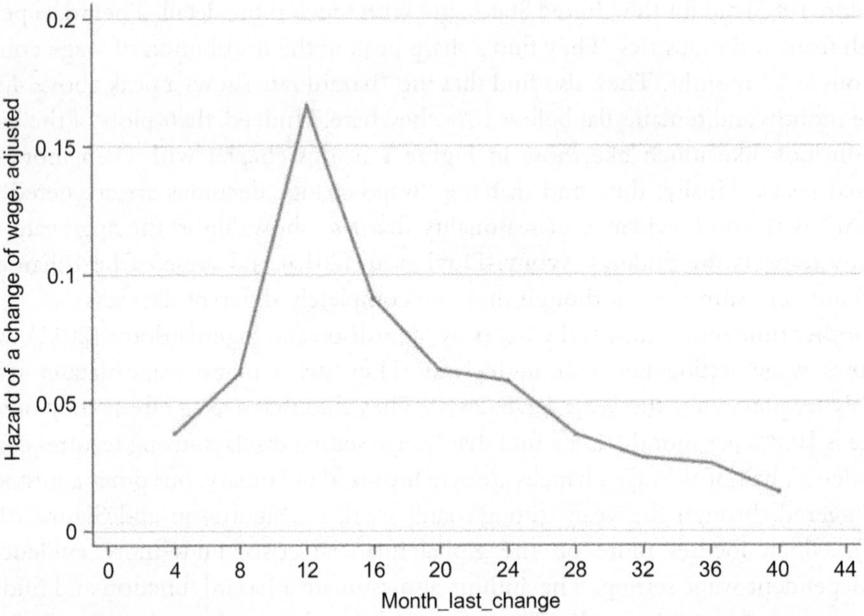

Fig. 3 Estimated hazard function for a within job wage change in the United States. Source: *Barattieri, A., Basu, S., Gottschalk, P., 2014. Some evidence on the importance of sticky wages. Am. Econ. J. Macroecon. 6 (1), 70–101.*

Finally, Barattieri et al. (2014) estimate a hazard function for the United States with their data corrected for measurement error. Their estimates are shown in Fig. 3. There is a sharp peak at 12 months leading the authors to conclude that "Taylor-type fixed-length contracts have stronger empirical support than Calvo-type constant-hazard models." This corresponds with the time series studies on wage setting in France and Iceland reported earlier.

If some structural assumptions about the general form of wage setting are made, it is also possible to extract information about individual wage setting mechanisms indirectly from the autocorrelation functions of aggregate time series data, as I explained in my chapter in the first *Handbook of Macroeconomics* with examples of these indirect methods including Backus (1984), Benabou and Bismut (1987), Levin (1991), and Taylor (1993). In a more recent example, Olivei and Tenreyro (2010) show that the impact of monetary policy shocks depends on the timing of wage changes, suggesting that time-dependent wage setting has important macroeconomic implications. They compare the effect of Japan's Shunto with different wage change timing in the United States and Germany, and they show that the impact of an aggregate monetary shock is larger when it occurs at a time when only a few wages are being adjusted. Estimates of time-varying distributions are also reported in Taylor (1993a) to accommodate the Shunto mechanism in Japan.

2.2 Microeconomic Evidence on Price Setting

Until the recent explosion of microeconomic research on price setting, the evidence on the prices of particular products showed remarkably long periods of set prices. Carlton (1989) found that the time between adjustment of prices ranged from 14 years for steel, cement, and chemicals to 4 years for plywood and nonferrous metals. Cecchetti (1986) found that the average length of time between price changes for magazines was 7 years in the 1950s and about 3 years in the 1970s. Kashyap (1995) found that mail order catalog prices were fixed for as long as 2 years. Blinder et al. (1998) found that about 40% of firms change their prices once per year, 10% change prices more frequently than once per year; and 50% leave their prices unchanged for more than a year. Dutta et al. (2002) found evidence of more frequent price changes for several types of frozen and refrigerated orange juice.

In contrast more recent detailed research by Bils and Klenow (2004), Klenow and Kryvtsov (2008), Nakamura and Steinsson (2008), and the ECB surveys in Europe shows more frequent changes in prices. A very useful review of this research is provided in a chapter in the *Handbook of Monetary Economics* by Klenow and Malin (2011), so there is no need to summarize it again here. They report that the average time between price changes is every 4 months for items in the consumer price index (CPI) and every 6–8 months for items in the producer price index. However, there is a great deal of heterogeneity across items with service prices changing less rapidly than good prices. They also report that price setting is unsynchronized, a finding that also goes back to Lach and Tsiddon (1996) who also noted within-store synchronization. Finally, Klenow and Malin (2011) emphasize that reference prices tend to be changed less frequently than regular prices.

As with wage setting, useful information about price setting in Europe comes from surveys of firms conducted by central banks. Fabiani et al. (2006) investigated the pricing behavior of more than 11,000 firms based on a survey conducted by the Eurosystem of national central banks. They found that "price reviews happen with a low frequency, of about one to three times per year in most countries, but prices are actually changed even less." They also found that "one-third of firms follow mainly time-dependent pricing rules, while two-thirds allow for elements of state dependence." The majority of the firms take into account both past and expected economic developments in their pricing decisions.

2.3 Pertinent Facts About Microeconomic Data on Wage and Price Setting

Though it is difficult to glean key facts from so many empirical studies, I would emphasize the following general features of price and wage setting as relevant to theoretical research on models of staggered wages and prices which I will review in the following sections:

(1) Both wage setting and price setting are staggered or unsynchronized over time. Even in unusual situations when there is a specific time of year for changing wages—such as in the spring in Japan and in January in some European counties, there are many other months where wages are changed. An example of evidence for staggered wage setting is that there was not one quarter where the frequency of wage change fell below 20% in France during the years from 1998 to 2006. Similarly, price changes are also typically not synchronized, as Klenow and Malin (2011) emphasize in their review.

(2) There is considerable evidence that most wages are set for a fixed length of time rather than changed at random intervals. The most common interval for wage changes is four quarters or 12 months. In Europe, the WDN survey shows that 60% of firms adjust wages once per year. Moreover, when it has been estimated, such as in France and the United States, the hazard function has a sharp peak at four quarters or 12 months.

(3) Wages and prices are set at a constant level during the length of time that they are set, rather than predetermined in advance to increase by certain amounts. Although originally clear from informal observation, this fact was confirmed for prices in empirical work by Klenow and Kryvtsov (2008) and Nakamura and Steinsson (2008). An exception in the case of wages occurs in the case of multiyear union contracts where deferred increases in later years are often agreed to in advance.

(4) There is strong evidence of time dependence in wage-setting and slightly less in price setting. Regarding wage setting, 55% of European firms report that wage changes occur in a particular month. In contrast, one-third of European firms follow mainly time-dependent pricing practices and two-thirds allow for elements of state dependence.

(5) Wage adjustment is less frequent than price adjustment, according to the most recent microeconomic empirical research, a finding which reverses the order reported in my 1999 *Handbook of Macroeconomics* chapter. In the European survey, the average duration of wages is greater than the average duration of prices. According to Barattieri et al. (2014), the quarterly frequency of wage adjustment in the United States, when correcting for measurement error, is much less than the CPI data as summarized by Klenow and Malin (2011). Price and wage rigidities are temporary, but prices and wages do not all change instantaneously and simultaneously, as if determined on a spot market with full information. There is no empirical reason—aside from the need for a simplifying assumption or the desire to illustrate a key point—to build an empirical model in which wages are perfectly flexible (determined on a spot market with full information) while prices are temporarily rigid, or vice versa.

(6) The frequency of wage and price changes depends on the average rate of inflation. While this is a robust finding, it should be emphasized that for the range of inflation rates observed in recent years in the developed economies, the average duration of wages and prices remains high. For a given target inflation rate, constant frequency of price adjustment is a good assumption to make in an empirical or policy model.

(7) There is a great deal of heterogeneity in wage and price setting practices across countries, across firms, across products, and across types of workers. Though the data reveal certain tendencies, as describe in the six points above, there is no practice that applies 100%. Wages in some industries change once per year on average, while in others wages change once per quarter or once every 2 years. There is a mixture of state dependence and time dependence in most countries. The price of services changes less frequently than goods. Wages of unskilled workers change more frequently than for skilled workers. One might hope that a model with homogeneous "representative" price or wage setting would be a good approximation to this more complex world, but models with some degree of heterogeneity are needed to describe reality accurately.

3. ORIGINS OF THE STAGGERED WAGE AND PRICE SETTING MODEL

When you look through graduate level textbooks in monetary theory and policy you find that the chapters on modern macro models with nominal rigidities begin with the idea of staggered contracts or staggered wage and price setting that had its origin in the 1970s at about the same time that the idea of rational expectations was being introduced to macroeconomics. Carl Walsh's treatment in his third edition (Walsh, 2010) of "early models of intertemporal nominal adjustment" starts with Taylor's (1979b, 1980) model of staggered nominal adjustment and then goes on to examine the version due to Calvo (1983). David Romer's chapter in his fourth edition (Romer, 2012) starts off with three modeling frameworks from this period: Phelps and Taylor (1977), Taylor (1979b), and Calvo (1983). Likewise, Woodford's (2003) chapter on nominal rigidities is mainly about staggered price or wage setting models that emanate from those days.

It is no coincidence that staggered contract models arose at about the same time as rational expectations were introduced to macroeconomics. Rational expectations meant that one could not rely on slow adjustment of expectations—so-called adaptive expectations—or on ad hoc partial adjustment models as the reason why prices and wages moved sluggishly over time. One had to think more about the economics in modeling the adjustment of prices and wages and the impact of monetary policy.

The earliest work by Fischer (1977), Gray (1976), and Phelps and Taylor (1977) assumed that the price or wage was set in advance of the period it would apply and at a value such that markets would be expected to clear.[d] In other words, prices would be set to bring expected demand into equality with expected supply. In the case of Phelps and Taylor (1977), the price was set one period in advance, and the price could change every period—no matter how short the period—much like in perfectly flexible

[d] These researchers were working largely independently of each other even though the papers were eventually published at the same time (and two in the same issue of the *Journal of Political Economy*). One possible exception was a conversation I had at the time with Stan Fischer who asked me what I was working on. I replied by describing a paper I was working with Phelps on sticky prices and rational expectations. Stan replied that he thought that it was a good topic, but I do not recall that he mentioned that he was working on the topic.

price models. In the case of Fischer (1977) and Gray (1976), the wage could be set more than one period in advance but at a different level each period, so that expected supply could equal expected demand in every period, again not much different empirically from flexible price models.

In all these models the price or the wage would change continuously, period by period. If the model was quarterly, then the price or wage could change every quarter; if the model was monthly, the price or wage could change every month. However, in the real world prices are set at the same level for more than one period; they usually remain at the level for several weeks, months, or even quarters; and the same is true for wages with the representative period of constancy being about 12 months.

In addition to being inconsistent with the microeconomic data (as later confirmed in formal microeconomic empirical research referred to in the previous section), this type of model was completely inconsistent with the aggregate dynamics of wages, prices, or output. I realized this as soon as I tried to bring models along the lines of Phelps and Taylor (1977) to the data. Such models could not come close to generating the time series persistence or autocorrelation that was in real world data. In effect, the price or wage setting assumption in these models was only slightly different from the assumption that prices and wages were market clearing. I proposed the staggered contract model and its key property—the contract multiplier—as a way to generate needed persistence and solve this problem. The model was explicitly designed to capture the key characteristics of the micro data and at the same time to match the aggregate dynamics.

4. A CANONICAL STAGGERED PRICE AND WAGE SETTING MODEL

The simplest way to see this is to consider the canonical staggered price setting model illustrated in Fig. 4 using a degree of abstraction and simplification similar to expositions of the overlapping generations model. Later in this chapter, I will discuss a range of

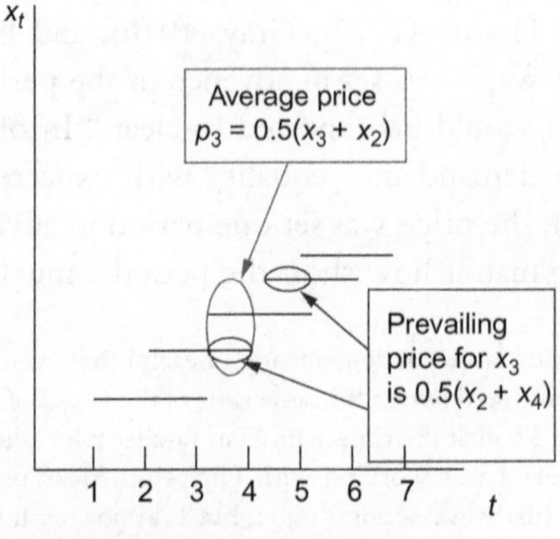

Fig. 4 Illustration of a canonical staggered contract model.

variations and extensions of this simple form. The basic idea of staggered price setting is that firms do not change their prices instantaneously from period to period. Instead there is a period of time during which the firm's price is fixed, and the pricing decisions of other firms are made the same way but at different times. Price setting is thus staggered and unsynchronized.

This "contract" or "set" price x_t is shown in Fig. 4. Note that it is fixed at the same level for two periods. Half the firms set their price each period in the canonical model. In the case where x is a wage rather than a price, it would also be set for two periods. There is no reason for either the price or the wage to be a formal contract or even an implicit contract; rather the price or wage set by the firm could apply to any particular good purchased or any worker of a certain type hired.

4.1 Canonical Assumptions

Two essential assumptions of staggered price setting are clear in Fig. 4. First, the set price lasts for more than an instant, or in this discrete time setup for more than one period. Second, the price setting is unsynchronized or overlapping. When you think about how a market might work in these circumstances, you realize two more important things not in the classic supply and demand framework. First, you realize that some firms' prices will be outstanding when another firm is deciding on a price to set. So firms need to look back at the price decisions of other firms. Second, you realize that the firm's price will be around for a while, so the firm will have to think ahead and forecast the price decisions of other firms.

Fig. 4 also illustrates two important concepts: the average price $p_t = (x_t + x_{t-1})$ and the prevailing price. For period t, the prevailing price is the average of the price in effect in period $t-1$ and the price expected to be in effect in period $t+1$, that is $0.5(x_{t-1} + E_{t-1}x_{t+1})$. This is what is relevant for the price decision of the firm in period t.

Given this setup, a decision rule for the firm setting the price x_t at time t can be written down directly, as I originally did in Taylor (1979a,b,c), as a function of the prevailing price (set by other firms in the market) and a measure of demand pressure in the market during the period the price will be in effect. The intuitive idea is simply that firms increase their price above the prevailing price if they see that demand conditions in the market are strong, and vice versa if demand conditions are weak. There can also be a random shock reflecting mistakes or other factors affecting the pricing decision. The result is shown in Eq. (1). As we will see later in this chapter, this equation can be derived explicitly from a specific profit maximization problem of a firm in monopolistic competition.[e]

[e] Note that (ignoring the expectations operator) the first term on the right-hand side of Eq. (1) can be written as $\frac{1}{2}(p_t + p_{t+1})$ because this equals $\frac{1}{2}\left[\frac{1}{2}(x_t + x_{t-1}) + \frac{1}{2}(x_{t+1} + x_t)\right]$ and thus $x_t = \frac{1}{2}(x_{t-1} + x_{t+1}) + \cdots$.

The term E_{t-1} represents the conditional expectations operator, the term y_t is a measure of demand (which for simplicity I will take to be the percentage deviation of real output from potential output), and ε_t is a serially uncorrelated, zero mean random shock.

$$x_t = \frac{1}{2}(x_{t-1} + E_{t-1}x_{t+1}) + \frac{\gamma}{2}(E_{t-1}y_t + E_{t-1}y_{t+1}) + \varepsilon_t \tag{1}$$

As I explain later, the "demand" variable on the right-hand side of Eq. (1) can also be interpreted as marginal cost in the case of a price decision (Woodford, 2003) or marginal revenue product in the case of a wage decision (Erceg et al., 2000) rather than the output gap.

4.2 Two More Equations and a Dynamic Stochastic General Equilibrium Model

To derive the implications of the staggered contracts assumption for aggregate dynamics and the persistence of shocks, we need to embed the staggered price setting equation into a model of the economy. For this purpose, consider two additional simple equations: An aggregate demand equation based on a money demand function (which could be derived from a money-in-the-utility or cash-in-advance framework) and an equation describing a monetary policy rule in which the money supply is adjusted by the central bank in response to movements in the price level. The two equations are thus:

$$y_t = \alpha(m_t - p_t) + v_t \tag{2}$$

$$m_t = gp_t \quad (g < 1) \tag{3}$$

which can be combined to get

$$y_t = -\beta p_t + v_t \tag{4}$$

where $\beta = \alpha(1 - g)$ is the key policy parameter.

Here we define y to be the log of real output (detrended) as in Eq. (1) and m to be the log of the money supply. In the case where $\alpha = 1$, ν is simply the log of velocity, which can be a random variable with zero mean. The policy rule is effectively a price rule with a price level target of 0 for the log of the price level. Now if we insert the staggered contract Eq. (1) into the model we get the following difference equation with lags and leads

$$x_t = \frac{1}{2}(x_{t-1} + E_{t-1}x_{t+1}) + \frac{\gamma}{2}\left[-\beta\left(\frac{E_{t-1}x_t + x_{t-1}}{2}\right) - \beta\left(\frac{E_{t-1}x_{t+1} + E_{t-1}x_t}{2}\right)\right] + \varepsilon_t$$

$$= \frac{1}{2}(x_{t-1} + E_{t-1}x_{t+1}) - \frac{\gamma\beta}{4}[E_{t-1}x_{t+1} + 2E_{t-1}x_t + x_{t-1}] + \varepsilon_t$$

The solution is

$$x_t = ax_{t-1} + \varepsilon_t \tag{5}$$

where $a = c \pm \sqrt{c^2 - 1}$ and where $c = (1 + \beta\gamma/2)/(1 - \beta\gamma/2)$. Clearly $c > 1$, and we can chose stable root for uniqueness. In terms of the aggregate price level, this implies that

$$p_t = ap_{t-1} + 0.5(\varepsilon_t + \varepsilon_{t-1}) \tag{6}$$

an ARMA(1,1) from which steady-state variances can easily be found

$$\sigma_p^2 = 0.5\sigma_\varepsilon^2/(1-a)$$
$$\sigma_y^2 = \beta^2\sigma_p^2$$

Note that the three equation macro model consists of a staggered price setting Eq. (1), a policy transmission Eq. (2), and a policy rule (3). The model is a combination of sticky prices and rational expectations which is the hallmark of *New Keynesian* models, a term which distinguishes them from *Old Keynesian* models in which expectations are not rational and prices are either fixed or determined in a purely backward-looking manner, unlike Eq. (1). To be sure, the term New Keynesian is used in different ways by different researchers and can be misleading. For example, in some usages the term refers only to models in which the monetary transmission equation is an IS curve—perhaps derived from a Euler equation—relating the policy interest rate to aggregate demand and the policy rule is an interest rate rule like the Taylor rule.

Observe that the persistence of the aggregate price level, which is determined by the parameter a in Eq. (6), and aggregate output depends on the structure of the staggered pricing γ but also on the policy rule g. In other words, persistence is a general equilibrium phenomenon depending on both the price setting mechanism and on policy. This idea that one needs a whole model rather than a single price setting equation to assess the degree of aggregate persistence will come up again in this chapter.

Also note that in this simple model the money supply is stationary so the persistence is in the price level rather than the inflation rate. In a more realistic model, the growth rate of the money rather than the money supply would be stationary.

4.3 The Policy Problem and the Output and Price Stability Tradeoff Curve

An objective function or loss function for monetary policy in this model can be written in terms the variances of y_t and p_t. For example, if the loss function is $\lambda\text{var}(p_t) + (1-\lambda)\text{var}(y_t)$, then the monetary policy problem is to choose a value of g (which determines β and thus a) to minimize this loss function. As the policy parameter is changed, the variances of p and y move in opposite directions tracing out a variance tradeoff curve. The lower panel of Fig. 5 illustrates this variance tradeoff curve. Inefficient monetary policies would be outside the curve. Points inside the curve are not feasible. Performance could be improved by moving toward the curve.

The upper panel of Fig. 5 is an aggregate demand–aggregate supply diagram which illustrates how the choice of g, and thus β, affects the variance of p and y. Suppose that there is a shock ε to the price setting equation. Then a steep aggregate demand

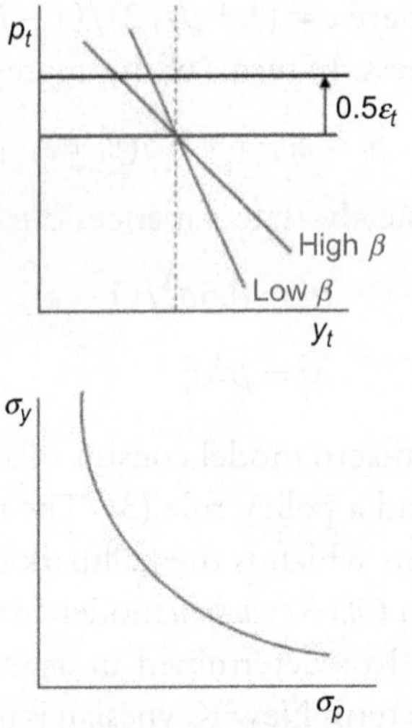

Fig. 5 Output and price stability tradeoff curve with graphical explanation.

curve (a monetary policy choice) makes for smaller fluctuations in y, but also means that a given shock to the price level takes a long time to diminish and thus a larger average fluctuation in p.

4.4 Key Implications

A number of important implications of staggered contracts can be illustrated with the canonical model, and they also hold in more complex models. I summarize these implications here.

(1) The theory centers around a simple equation that can be used and tested. I list this result first because if the theory had not yielded an equation, such as Eq. (1), it would have been difficult to achieve the progress I report in this chapter—including the empirical validation exercises reported in the previous section and the theoretical derivation of the equation using a profit maximization with monopolistic competition framework reported later. A key variable in this equation is the prevailing price (or wage) set by other firms. The prevailing price itself is an average of prices set in the past and prices to be set in the future. In this case the coefficients on past and the future are equal.

(2) Expectations of future prices matter for pricing decisions today. This is shown clearly in Eq. (1). The reason is that with the current price decision expected to last into the future, some prices set in the future will be relevant for today's decision. This is an important result because expectations of *future* inflation now come into play in the theory of inflation. It gives a rationale for central bank credibility and for having an inflation target.

(3) There is inertia or persistence in the price setting process; past prices matter because they are relevant for present price decisions. The coefficients on past prices can be calculated from the staggered price setting assumptions. This implication can be most readily seen in Eq. (5). The contract price is serially correlated. It is persistent and it can be described by an autoregressive process.

(4) The inertia or persistence is longer than the length of the period during which prices are fixed. Price shocks take a long time to run through the market because last period's price decisions depend on price decisions in the period before that and so on into the distant past. I originally called this phenomenon the "*contract multiplier*" because it was analogous to the Keynesian multiplier where a shock to consumption builds up and persists over time as it works its way through the economy from income to consumption to income back again and so on. This is most easily seen in Eq. (5) or the ARMA model in Eq. (6). The first-order autoregression implies an infinite autocorrelation function or an infinite impulse response function. The larger the autoregressive coefficient (that is, a) is, the larger will be the contract multiplier.

This is one of the most important properties of the staggered contract model because it means that very small rigidities at the micro level can generate large persistent effects for the aggregates. Klenow and Malin (2011) explain it well: "Real effects of nominal shocks … last three to five times longer than individual prices. Nominal stickiness appears insufficient to explain why aggregate prices respond so sluggishly to monetary policy shocks. For this reason, nominal price stickiness is usually combined with a 'contract multiplier' (in Taylor's, 1980 phrase)."

(5) The degree of inertia or persistence depends on monetary policy. That is, the autoregressive coefficient a depends on the policy parameter g. The more accommodative the central bank is to price level movements (higher g), the more inertia there will be (higher a).

(6) The theory implies a tradeoff curve between price stability and output stability. This tradeoff curve has provided a framework for discussion and debate about the role of policy in economic performance for many years. Originally put forth in Taylor (1979a) it is referred to as the Taylor curve in various contexts (King, 1999; Bernanke, 2004; Friedman, 2010). Bernanke (2004) used such a tradeoff curve to explain the role of monetary policy during the Great Moderation. His explanation was that monetary policy improved and this brought performance from the upper right-hand part of the diagram down and to the left closer to or even on the curve.

King (1999) made similar arguments. However, when the Great Recession and the slow recovery moved the performance in the direction of higher output instability—the end of the Great Moderation—King (2012) argued that the tradeoff curve itself shifted. As he put it, "A failure to take financial instability into account creates an unduly optimistic view of where the Taylor frontier lies …Relative to a Taylor frontier that reflects only aggregate demand and cost shocks, the addition of financial instability shocks generates what I call the Minsky-Taylor frontier."

Note that the tradeoff implies that there is no "*divine coincidence*" as put forth by Blanchard and Gali (2007). Divine coincidence means that there is no such tradeoff between output stability and price stability, completely contrary to the existence of the tradeoff in Fig. 5. Divine coincidence could occur if there were no shocks to the contract price or wage equation, but that is not the basic assumption of the staggered contract model. Broadbent (2014) suggested that the Great Moderation was due to the sudden appearance of divine coincidence, rather than to an improved monetary policy performance that brought the economy closer to the tradeoff curve as Bernanke (2004) and others argued.

(7) The costs of reducing inflation are less than in a backward-looking expectations augmented Phillips curve. In the staggered contract model, disinflation could be less costly if expectations of inflation were lower because of the forward-looking component of the model, as explained in Taylor (1982) though with reservations from others such as Gordon (1982). The disinflation costs would not normally be zero as in the case of rational expectations models with perfectly flexible prices, but they would be surprisingly small. This prediction proved accurate when people later examined the disinflation of the early 1980s.

5. GENERALIZATIONS AND EXTENSIONS

These results remain robust to variations in the model. An important variant is to allow for a greater variety of time intervals during which prices are fixed. Of course one could have longer contracts as in Taylor (1980) where contracts were of a general length N. However, a model with all price and wage setting being the same length is a simplifying assumption, not something that could be used in empirical work. The high degree of heterogeneity described in the microeconomic research reviewed earlier makes this very clear. Not all contracts are N periods in length; some are shorter and some are longer. Indeed, there is a whole distribution of contracts and this is what I assumed in early empirical work with these models. For example, a generalized distribution of price–wage setting intervals was used by Taylor (1979c) in an estimated model of the United States.

Eq. (1) was thus modified as follows:

$$x_t = \sum_{i=0}^{N-1} \theta_{it} E_t(p_{t+i} + \gamma y_{t+i} + \varepsilon_{t+i}) \tag{7}$$

$$p_t = \sum_{i=0}^{N-1} \delta_{it} x_{t-i} \tag{8}$$

The weights θ_{it} and δ_{it} were estimated using aggregate wage data in the United States. The estimation of the lag and lead coefficients was only mildly restricted, allowing for a peak somewhere between one and eight quarters. The estimated distribution from Taylor (1979c, table 4) is plotted in Fig. 6. It has a peak at three quarters with 24% of workers; only 7% had one quarter contracts and only 2% had eight quarter contracts.

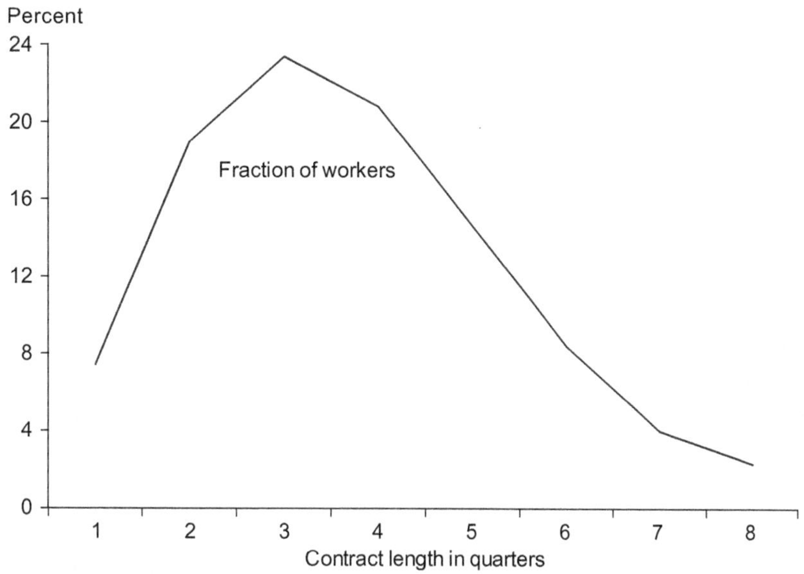

Fig. 6 The estimated distribution of workers by contract length.

The interpretation was that the economy consisted of a whole variety of price and wage setting practices.

Observing this empirical distribution of wage setting intervals in Taylor (1979c) gave my then colleague at Columbia University, Guillermo Calvo, the idea of an important simplification. Why not assume a geometric distribution, which would be considerably simpler? Moreover, such a distribution could be interpreted as being generated probabilistically rather than deterministically if each wage contract expired randomly rather than deterministically. The resulting model came to be called the Calvo model and the random selection process came to be called the Calvo fairy. The equation for the price change is a specific version of Eqs. (7) and (8) and can be written as follows:

$$x_t = (1-\beta\omega)\sum_{i=0}^{\infty}(\beta\omega)^i E_t(p_{t+i} + \gamma y_{t+i} + \varepsilon_t) \tag{9}$$

$$p_t = (1-\omega)\sum_{i=0}^{\infty}\omega^i x_{t-i} \tag{10}$$

After some manipulation, these two equations can be rewritten as

$$x_t = \beta\omega E_t x_{t+1} + (1-\beta\omega)(p_t + \gamma y_t + \varepsilon_t)$$

$$p_t = \omega p_{t-i} + (1-\omega)x_t$$

Once a model for y and the impact of monetary policy is added, you have a well-defined rational expectations model as before.

The two equations can also be rewritten in an interesting form:

$$\pi_t = \beta E_t \pi_{t+1} + \delta \gamma y_t + \delta \varepsilon_t \tag{11}$$

where

$$\delta = \left[\frac{(1-\omega)(1-\beta\omega)}{\omega}\right]$$

Which is very simple and reminiscent of an old expectations augmented Philips curve except that the expected inflation rate next period rather than this period is on the right-hand side. Calvo's modifications helped the staggered contract model grow in use and popularity.

Indeed, the form of the staggered price setting model in Eq. (1) came to be popularly known as the New Keynesian Phillips curve.

6. DERIVATION OF STAGGERED PRICE SETTING WHEN FIRMS HAVE MARKET POWER

Another important development regarding the staggered contract model was its derivation from an optimization problem in which firms face a downward sloping demand curve and decide on an optimal price subject to the staggered contract restriction that they cannot change prices every period. The idea of using market power to derive a price setting equation goes back to Svensson (1986), Blanchard and Kiyotaki (1987), and Akerlof and Yellen (1991) as I reviewed in Taylor (1999). As described below, Chari et al. (2000) used the approach as part of a critique of staggered price setting. For expository purposes here, I focus on a simple derivation used in Taylor (2000) in which firms maximize profits taking the downward sloping demand curve for their products as given.

Consider a firm selling a product that is differentiated from the other goods. The demand curve facing each firm is linear in the difference between the firm's own price for its product and the average price for the other differentiated products. Such a linear demand curve can be derived from models of consumer utility maximization. Suppose that this linear demand curve is written as

$$y_t = \varepsilon_t - \beta(x_t - p_t) \tag{12}$$

where y_t is production, x_t is the price of the good, and p_t is the average price of other (differentiated) goods. The term ε_t is a random shift to demand.

Suppose that the firm sets its price to last for two periods, and that it sets its price every second period. Other firms set their price for two periods, but at different points in time. These timing assumptions correspond to the canonical model in Fig. 1, and the average price is just as in the canonical model $p_t = 0.5(x_t + x_{t-1})$.

Let c_t be the marginal cost of producing the good. Under these assumptions, the firm's expected profit for the two periods to which the price set in period t applies is given by

$$\sum_{i=0}^{1} E_t(x_t y_{t+i} - c_{t+i} y_{t+i}) \tag{13}$$

where x_t applies in period t and period $t+1$. (I have assumed for simplicity that the discount factor is 1.) Firms maximize profits taking marginal cost and average price at other firms as given.

Differentiating with respect to x_t results in the solution for the optimal price

$$x_t = 0.25 \sum_{i=0}^{1} (E_t c_{t+i} + E_t p_{t+i} + E_t \varepsilon_{t+i}/\beta) \tag{14}$$

which is analogous to the canonical staggered contracting equation in Eq. (1) (see also Footnote a). Note however that it is marginal cost that enters the equation rather than the output gap, an issue I will come back to later in this chapter. Note that the coefficient of 0.25 implies that an increase in the price and marginal cost at other firms results in the same increase in the firm's price.

6.1 Pass-Through Implications

Though the derivation generates the same basic staggered price setting equation as assumed in the canonical model, it reveals another important implication of the theory—an "eighth" implication: a more price stability focused monetary policy—say due to inflation targeting—implies a smaller pass-through of price shocks (commodities or exchange rates) to inflation. That this implication might be borne out by reality was noted in Taylor (2000), but has now been documented in empirical studies in many countries. The reason originally given for the empirically observed decline in pass-through was that there was a reduction in the "pricing power" of firms. But another view is that the decline in pass-through is due to the low inflation rate achieved by a change in monetary policy.

To see this note that, according to Eq. (14), the amount by which a firm matches an increase in marginal cost with an increase in its own price depends on how permanent that marginal cost increase is. Similarly, the extent to which an increase in the price at other firms will lead to an increase in the firm's own price will depend on how permanent that increase in other firms' prices is expected to be. However, in neither case does the extent of this pass-through depend on the slope of the demand curve.

To see how the pass-through of an increase in marginal costs depends on the persistence of the increase, suppose that marginal cost follows a simple first-order autoregression:

$$c_t = \rho c_{t-1} + u_t$$

In this case, the pass-through coefficient will be proportional to $(1+\rho)$. Thus, less persistent marginal costs (lower ρ) reduce the pass-through coefficient, even though it might seem like a reduction in pricing power. The general point is that if an increase in costs is expected to last, then the increase will be passed-through to a greater extent. A more stable price level will reduce the persistence.

For firms that import inputs to production, marginal cost will depend on the exchange rate. Currency depreciation will raise the cost of the imports in domestic currency units. According to this model, if the depreciation is viewed as temporary, the firm will pass-through less of the depreciation in the form of a higher price. Hence, less persistent exchange rate fluctuations will lead to smaller exchange rate pass-through coefficients.

6.2 Marginal Cost vs the Output Gap

Note that Eq. (14) has marginal cost driving price movements rather than output as assumed in Eq. (1). To make the connection between Eqs. (14) and (1) (again keeping Footnote a in mind) we need to think of marginal cost as moving proportionately to the movements in the output gap. Gali and Gertler (1999) or Gali et al. (2005) argue that there are plenty of reasons why marginal cost and the output gap might diverge from time to time. So they look at a version of Eq. (11) in which marginal costs appear rather than the gap (they use the geometric distribution assumption of Calvo rather than the canonical form used here). Though the empirical accuracy of this equation was questioned by Mankiw (2001), the paper by Gali et al. (2005) finds that marginal cost is significant and quantitatively important. However, they introduce a modification in that model. They assume that a fraction of firms changes price with a backward looking "rule of thumb" which simply depends on past inflation. They thereby create a hybrid model with the lagged inflation rate on the right-hand side. The modification is ad hoc—especially compared with the theory that goes into deriving the staggered price setting equation.

Another issue noted by Nekarda and Ramey (2013) is that the markup of price over marginal cost needs to move in a countercyclical way if the equation is to explain empirically the effects of a change in demand on prices. They report, however, that markups are either "procyclical or acyclical conditional on demand shocks" and thereby conclude that the "New Keynesian explanation for the effects of government spending or monetary policy is not supported by the behavior of the markup."

Fuhrer (2006) raised further questions about the New Keynesian Phillips curve. He shows that in the New Keynesian Phillips curve inflation it is persistence of the shock rather than the equation itself that is the dominant source of persistence.

6.3 Debate Over the Contract Multiplier

Yet another issue is whether the contract multiplier is capable of explaining the persistence of prices or output. In the canonical model, including its derivation from profit maximization, the contract multiplier can be represented by the size of the autoregressive coefficient in the aggregate price equation. Chari et al. (2000) argued that for the parameters derived from the maximization problem, this coefficient is not large enough to be capable of explaining persistence, at least for contract lengths of one quarter in length and their particular measure of aggregate persistence. Woodford (2003, pp. 193–194) argues that their conclusion "depends on an exaggeration of the size of the contract multiplier that would be needed and an underestimate of the empirically plausible degree of strategic complementarities." He also argues that Chari et al. (2000) setup too high a persistence hurdle for the contract multiplier, in effect asking it to explain persistence that is more reasonably due to other serially correlated variables in the model.

Christiano et al. (2005) argue that assuming that the representative length of contracts is only one quarter is too small. If one uses somewhat longer contracts, say close to the survey summarized by Klenow and Malin (2011), the contract multiplier seems to work fine. Christiano et al. (2005) also question the persistence measure used by Chari et al. (2000).

7. PRICE AND WAGE SETTING TOGETHER

Much of this review has focused thus far on staggered *price* setting, but the original work on staggered contracts was about wages, where the time between wage changes is quite a bit longer according to the recent microeconomic empirical research summarized in this chapter. In Taylor (1980), the staggering of wages was the key part of the model, and this created a persistence of prices through a simple fixed markup of prices over wages. The micro finding summarized by Klenow and Malin (2011) that "price changes are linked to wage changes" supports this idea. Of course the markup need not be literally fixed. In the empirical multicountry model in Taylor (1993), the staggered wage contracting equations were estimated for seven countries and markups of prices over wages were influenced by the price of imports.

Erceg, Henderson, and Levin (2000) brought the focus back on wages, but with an important innovation. Rather than simply marking up prices over wages, they built a model which combined staggered price and wage setting, and, moreover, they derived both equations from profit or utility maximization considerations as in Section 5. Their work in turn helped enable the development of more empirically accurate estimated policy models, such as those due to Christiano et al. (2005), Smets and Wouters (2003), and many others that have become part of Volker Wieland's model database described in Wieland et al. (2012).

The model of Christiano et al. (2005) assumes staggered contracts for prices and wages with Calvo contracts. It was the first medium-sized, estimated example of a New Keynesian model explicitly derived from optimizing behavior of representative households and firms. It stimulated the development of similar optimization-based models for many other countries and has been dubbed the second-generation New Keynesian model along with Smets and Wouters (2003) by Wieland et al (2016).

Smets and Wouters (2003, 2007) also showed how to use Bayesian techniques (Geweke, 1999; Schorfheide, 2000) in estimating such models.

An important question for research is how the overall properties of the models changed as a result of the innovations. The eight implications mentioned earlier still hold in my view but the quantitative sizes of the impacts are important to pin down. Taylor and Wieland (2012) investigated this question using Wieland's database of models designed for this purpose. They considered a first-generation model—the Taylor (1993) multi-country model mentioned in the previous section with staggered contracts. And they compared this with two second-generation models—the Christiano et al. (2005) model and the Smets and Wouters (2007) model. Although the models differ in structure and sample period for estimation, the impacts of unanticipated changes in the federal funds rate are surprisingly similar. In the chapter prepared for this handbook, Wieland et al. (2016) show that these surprising results continue to hold if one adds a third-generation of models in which credit market frictions play a role in the monetary transmission mechanism.

There is a difference between the models in the evaluation of monetary policy rules, however. Model-specific policy rules that include the lagged interest rate, inflation, and current and lagged output gaps are not robust. Policy rules without interest-rate smoothing or with GDP-growth replacing the GDP gap are more robust, but performance in each model is worse with the more robust rule.

8. PERSISTENCE OF INFLATION AND INDEXING

Prior to the work of Chari et al. (2000), Fuhrer and Moore (1995) raised questions about the ability of the staggered contract model to explain the persistence of inflation rather than the persistence of the price level. They proposed a modification of the model to deal with this problem. As I reviewed in Taylor (1999), they transformed the model from price levels into the inflation rate, noting that it was *relative* wages rather than absolute wages that would go into the staggering equations. But the rationale for focusing on relative wages was weak and questions about this issue continued into the 2000s.

In recent years many have argued that the degree of persistence implied by the basic staggered contract model is just fine and consistent with the data. Guerrieri (2006), for example, argued that when the staggered contract model is viewed within the context of a fully specified macro model, inflation persistence and its changes over time could be explained with the regular staggered contract setup. I illustrated this idea with the canonical model I presented earlier in this chapter in which persistence is a general equilibrium phenomenon.

Guerrieri (2006) used a vector autoregression with inflation, the interest rate, and output to represent the facts that a staggered contract model should explain. He found that the basic staggered contract model did as well as the Fuhrer and Moore (1995) relative contract model in generating the actual inflation persistence in the United States through the 1990s. The impulse response functions reported in his paper show the degree to which both specifications can explain the inflation process. The staggered contract models are well within the 95% confidence bands with the exception of the cross-impulse response functions for output and inflation.

Nevertheless, both Christiano et al. (2005) and Smets and Wouters (2003) felt the need to modify the staggered price and wage setting equations in order to get the proper persistence and better match the other cross correlations. They assumed backward-looking indexation in those periods when prices and wages were not allowed to adjust. The Christiano et al. (2005) model assumes wages and prices are indexed to last period's inflation rate during periods between changes. The Smets–Wouters model assumes firms index to a weighted average of lagged and steady-state inflation.

None of these modifications are part of the optimization process; they are akin to simply assuming that wage and price inflation is autoregressive in an ad hoc way rather than deriving the equations: Why bother with a microfounded staggered wage and price setting model if you are just going to add ad hoc lag structure anyway?

According to recent research it appears that the persistence problem is not due the staggered contract model but rather to the special Calvo form it takes in these models.

9. TAYLOR CONTRACTS AND CALVO CONTRACTS

Much has been written comparing "Calvo contracts" described in Section 5 and "Taylor contracts" which appear in the canonical model in the case of two period contracts in Section 4. Walsh (2010, p. 243) notes some of the similarities between equations (his eqs. 6.17 and 6.36) derived from the two staggered price setting models, but others, including Kiley (2002), have emphasized the differences. For example, the persistence of inflation and output appears to be greater in the Calvo contracts for the same average frequency of price change.

There is no question that there is a much longer tail in the Calvo model than for any fixed-length contract, but Dixon and Kara (2006) argue that Kiley's comparison is flawed because it compares "the average age of Calvo contracts with the completed length of Taylor contracts." When Dixon and Kara (2006) compare average age Taylor contracts with the same average age Calvo contracts, the differences become much smaller. They also show that output can be more autocorrelated with Taylor contracts with "age-equivalent" Calvo contracts.

Carvalho and Schwartzman (2015) examine the differences in monetary neutrality in the two types of models by distinguishing between Taylor contracts and Calvo contracts in terms of their "selection effect." At any point in time after a monetary shock, some firms have a lot of old prices and some do not. "Positive" selection is defined as a situation where old prices are overrepresented among adjusting prices. In Taylor contracts, selection favors old prices; in Calvo contracts there is no selection, since prices change completely at random. This selection effect characterizes pricing frictions. Taylor contracts imply smaller nonneutralities of money on output than Calvo contracts because of differences in selection.

Of course there is no reason to focus—as these studies do—on the special case of "Taylor contracts" in which all contracts are the same length as in the simple exposition in the canonical model. The microeconomic evidence and casual observation suggest rather that there is a great deal of heterogeneity of lengths of both wage contracts and price contracts. In a series of papers, Dixon and Kara (2005, 2006, 2011) and Kara (2010) develop models which are built on this heterogeneity. They call these models a generalized Taylor economy (GTE) in which many sectors have staggered contracts with different lengths. When two such economies have the same average length contracts, monetary shocks are more persistent with longer contracts. They also show that when two GTE's have the same distribution of completed contract lengths, the economies behave in a similar manner. See also Huw Dixon's comprehensive web page http://huwdixon.org/GTE.html on the GTE and his paper with Dixon and Le Bihan (2012).

In a more recent paper, Kara (2015) shows that adding the heterogeneity in price stickiness to the Smets and Wouters model deals with criticisms of the staggered contract model including the Chari et al. (2009) criticism that the Smets and Wouters model relies on unrealistically large price mark-up shocks to explain the data on inflation and the Bils et al. (2012) criticism that reset price inflation in the model is more volatile than the data show. Kara (2015) shows that adding heterogeneity in the length of contracts to correspond with the data implies smaller price mark-up shocks and less volatile reset price inflation.

In yet another study comparing the two approaches, Knell (2010) examined survey data on wage setting in 15 European countries from the WDN discussed in Section 2. It is informative to quote from his paper: "There are at least four dimensions along which the data contradict the basic model with Calvo contracts. First, the majority of wage agreements seems to follow a predetermined pattern with given contract lengths. Second, while for most contracts this predetermined length is 1 year (on average 60% in the WDN survey) there exists also some heterogeneity in this context and a nonnegligible share of contracts has longer (26%) or shorter (12%) durations. Third, 54% of the firms asked in the WDN survey have indicated that they carry out wage changes in a particular month (most of them—30%—in January). Fourth, 15% of all firms report to use automatic indexation of wages to the rate of inflation. In order to be able to take these real-world characteristics of wage setting into account one has to move beyond the convenient but restrictive framework of Calvo wage contracts." Knell then presents a model along the lines of Taylor (1980) that allows one to incorporate all of these institutional details.

Musy (2006) and Ben Aissa and Musy (2010) have investigated the differences between the Calvo contracts model and the Taylor contracts model and others. Their analysis shows that criticism of a lack of persistence or an under estimate of the costs of disinflation are due to very special features of the Calvo assumptions. Recall that the "Calvo fairy" is a mechanism for randomly choosing a price to change each period. That probability is a constant, so in effect Calvo contracts are neither time dependent nor state dependent. The work of Musy and Ben Aissa shows that a change in money growth will not be accomplished in a costless manner in the Taylor model even though it is in the Calvo model, and that persistence is greater.

10. STATE-DEPENDENT MODELS AND TIME-DEPENDENT MODELS

Another development has been to relax the simplifying assumption that prices are set for an exogenous interval and allow the firm's price decision to depend on the state of the market, which gave rise to name "state dependent" pricing models and created the need to give the original canonical model a new name, "time dependent" (see Dotsey et al., 1999; Golosov and Lucas, 2007; Gertler and Leahy, 2008). There are some benefits from these improvements as Klenow and Kryvtsov (2008) have shown using new microeconomic data. Many of the key policy implication mentioned earlier hold, but the impact of monetary shocks can be smaller.

Alvarez and Lippi (2014) consider a state-dependent model with multiproduct firms, which is otherwise similar to the state-dependent model of Golosov and Lucas (2007). They find that as they alter the model from one product firm to a multiproduct firm, the impact of monetary shocks becomes larger and more persistent. For a large number of products they show that the economy works as in the staggered contract model: it has the same aggregation and impulse response to a monetary shock. In this sense, the menu cost models with multiproduct firms gives another basis to the staggered contract model.

Woodford (2003, p. 142) questions whether the state-dependent models are really any better than the staggered contract models. Not only are they more complex, he argues, but they may be less realistic and have inferior microfoundations. The idea that firms are constantly evaluating the price misses the point that firms set their prices for a while to reduce "the costs associated with information collection and decision making." Kehoe and Midrigan (2010) have developed a model in which formal considerations of such management costs do indeed increase the impact and persistence of shocks.

Bonomo and Carvalho (2004) develop a model of the microfoundations of the time-dependent model in which the length of time that prices are fixed is endogenous. In their model firms face a joint lump-sum adjustment and information cost rather than a pure adjustment cost, and for this reason optimal pricing is not state dependent. Their model is thus a way to deal with the observation that contract length depends on the rate of inflation and the variability of inflation and other shocks. They not only show that time-dependent models are optimal, they derive the optimal contract length.

They examine the effect of different policies such as a disinflation and examine the difference with invariant time-dependent arrangements. In a subsequent paper, Bonomo and Carvalho (2010) estimate the macroeconomic costs of a lack of credibility of monetary policy. They find that the costs are greater for the endogenous time-dependence model than for an exogenous time-dependent model.

11. WAGE-EMPLOYMENT BARGAINING AND STAGGERED CONTRACTS

In recent years, there has been an increased interest in explaining fluctuations in unemployment as well as output. As explained by Hall (2005), the standard wage-employment bargaining model needs to assume some form of sticky wages if it is to be consistent with the data, and for this reason the idea of nominal rigidities is common to this research. It is not surprising therefore that many of the models built to examine this question have combined staggered contracts with a formal treatment of the wage-employment bargaining. Ravenna and Walsh (2008), Gertler et al. (2008), and Christiano et al. (2013) are examples.

There are some by-products of this research too. The Christiano et al. (2013) model is able to drop the arbitrary indexing assumption in Christiano, Eichenbaum, and Evans and still get the requisite persistence. This works because when a monetary shock increases the demand for output which sticky price firms produce, the firms also purchase more wholesale goods. With this model, the authors argue that "alternating offer bargaining mutes the increase in real wages, thus allowing for a large rise in employment, a substantial decline in unemployment, and a small rise in inflation."

12. STAGGERED CONTRACTS VS INATTENTION MODELS

Mankiw and Reis (2001) have argued that the staggered wage and price setting should be replaced by a model with inattention. They argue in favor of sticky information rather than sticky prices, mainly because such a model would solve the persistence problem alluded to earlier. Recall that the concern is that there may be too little persistence of inflation following monetary shocks in staggered price setting models. Though some would argue that the persistence is fine, the lack of persistence may be more related to the specific form of the Calvo model rather than to the staggered contracts per se.

Why do Mankiw and Reis (2001) find that there is more persistence with inattention than with staggered contracts? Upon examination of their model, it appears that in the sticky information model, the price could be set to increase during the period where it is fixed in the regular model. For example in a staggered contract model of four periods the price would be 1.015, 1.015, 1.015, and 1.015 while in the sticky information it could be set as 1.0, 1.01, 1.02, and 1.03 and not change from that path. In effect, some inflation persistence is built in. Fig. 7 illustrates this and can be compared with Fig. 4.

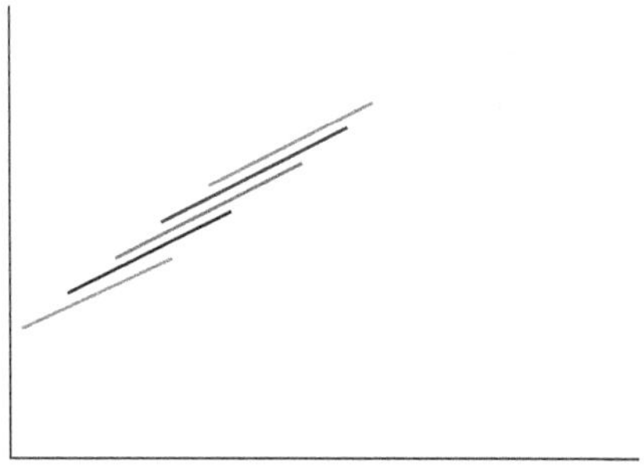

Fig. 7 Price setting with sticky information (for comparison with Fig. 4).

If prices or wages are set in this way, it is clear that there will be more persistence of inflation. It is very rare, however, for prices or wages to be set in this manner except in multiyear union contracts as explained in Taylor (1983) and Avouyi-Dovi (2013).

13. CRITICAL ASSESSMENT AND OUTLOOK

From its origins nearly four decades ago to its applications today, the staggered wage and price setting model continues to be a focus of attention in empirical and theoretical research in macroeconomics, especially in monetary business cycle models and monetary models used for policy analysis. In recent years, "Big Data" style research projects have radically expanded our knowledge of the microeconomics of wage and price setting behavior from a few salient facts about magazine prices or personal salary experiences into complex datasets with thousands or millions of observations. These datasets require new methods of analysis, but they also permit researchers to test and discriminate much more thoroughly between one type of model and another. Criticisms—whether about inadequate microfoundations, inability to explain certain facts, or questionable policy implications—have led to constructive improvements, clarifications, variations, new research lines, and, in some cases, less than fully satisfactory fixes.

In assessing the outlook for future research and applications of these models, one cannot help but be struck by a certain tension in current research. The large-scale surveys and empirical research show a great deal of heterogeneity in wage and price setting behavior, yet most models still employ simplified models clearly at odds with this heterogeneity. Yes, there is evidence that prices are set at a fixed level for 6 months or more, especially if sales and reference prices are accounted for properly. Yes, there is evidence that wages are set a fixed level for longer periods and that there is a peak in the estimated hazard function at 1 year that precludes certain simplifications such as the Calvo model. Yes, there is evidence that both wage and price decisions are staggered or unsynchronized over time, and that this staggering creates a contract multiplier which converts short spells of rigidity at the micro level into longer persistence at the macro level. Yes, there is more evidence of time dependence than state dependence. But in each of these dimensions—length, degree of staggering, shape of the hazard function, degree of state dependence—there is a great deal of heterogeneity across countries, types of product, types of employment, and types of industry structure.

This heterogeneity is not simply a nuisance; it has major implications for aggregate dynamics, and it has been offered as a response to criticism of staggered wage and price setting models. Often that criticism applies to a particular simple staggered contract model that does not capture either the regularities mentioned earlier or the heterogeneity, and that criticism disappears when heterogeneity is taken into account as Kara (2010) and Knell (2010) have emphasized. Rather than "jury-rig" simple staggered contract models with ad hoc add-ons, such as indexing in the models by Christiano et al. (2005) or Smets and Wouters (2003), this research suggests that building the heterogeneity into the model would both better fit the micro data and provide a straight forward explanation of macro persistence.

In other words, future research would likely yield large benefits if it moved on from "representative" staggered wage and price setting models to "heterogeneous" staggered wage and price setting models. The suggestion is similar to the idea of moving from "representative agent models" to "heterogeneous agent models," though the gains from such a move could be much greater.

The challenge is that building in this heterogeneity would complicate existing macro models which are already quite complicated, as I found when I began to build in such heterogeneity in my early research (Taylor, 1979c) including in a multicountry model (Taylor, 1993) with different degrees of staggered wage setting in different countries. Indeed, their complexity is the main object of criticism of the existing models as expressed by Chari et al. (2009) and others.

At the least future research could go beyond continued comparisons of simplest textbook style models—such as the random-length-contract Calvo model and the N-period-length-contract Taylor model—and look at heterogeneous or generalized models with a mix of contract types. But more fundamentally the challenge for future work is to take account of the rich variety of wage and price setting procedures in a way that is tractable and understandable for policy analysis. Indeed, that has been the challenge for all areas of macroeconomic research from the very beginning.

ACKNOWLEDGMENT

I wish to thank Susanto Basu, John Cochrane, Huw Dixon, Robert Hall, Jim Hamilton, Engin Kara, Pete Klenow, Olivier Musy, Carlos Viana de Carvalho, Harald Uhlig, and Carl Walsh for helpful comments.

REFERENCES

Akerlof, G.A., Yellen, J.L., 1991. How large are the losses from rules of thumb behavior in models of the business cycle. In: Brainard, W., Nordhaus, W., Watts, H. (Eds.), Money, Macroeconomics, and Economic Policy: Essays in Honor of James Tobin. MIT Press, Cambridge, MA.
Alvarez, F., Lippi, F., 2014. Price setting with menu cost for multiproduct firms. Econometrica 82 (1), 89–135.
Avouyi-Dovi, S., Fougère, D., Gautier, E., 2013. Wage rigidity, collective bargaining and the minimum wage: evidence from French agreement data. Rev. Econ. Stat. 95 (4), 1337–1351.
Backus, D., 1984. Exchange rate dynamics in a model with staggered wage contracts. Discussion Paper No. 561 (Queen's University).
Barattieri, A., Basu, S., Gottschalk, P., 2014. Some evidence on the importance of sticky wages. Am. Econ. J. Macroecon. 6 (1), 70–101.
Ben Aissa, M.S., Musy, O., 2010. The dynamic properties of alternative assumptions on price adjustment in New Keynesian models. Bull. Econ. Res. 63 (4), 353–384.
Benabou, R., Bismut, C., 1987. Wage bargaining and staggered contracts: theory and estimation. Discussion Paper No. 8810, CEPREMAP, Paris, France.
Bernanke, B.S., 2004. The Great Moderation. Eastern Economic Association, Washington, DC.
Bils, M., Klenow, P.J., 2004. Some evidence on the importance of sticky prices. J. Polit. Econ. 112 (5), 947–985.
Bils, M., Klenow, P.J., Malin, B.A., 2012. Reset price inflation and the impact of monetary policy shocks. Am. Econ. Rev. 102 (6), 2798–2825.
Blanchard, O., Gali, J., 2007. Real wage rigidities and the New Keynesian model. J. Money Credit Bank. 39 (Suppl. 1), 35–64.
Blanchard, O.J., Kiyotaki, N., 1987. Monopolistic competition and the effects of aggregate demand. Am. Econ. Rev. 77, 647–666.
Blinder, A.S., Canetti, E.D., Lebow, D.E., Rudd, J.B., 1998. Asking About Prices: A New Approach to Understanding Price Stickiness. Russell Sage Foundation, New York, NY.
Bonomo, M., Carvalho, C., 2004. Endogenous time-dependent rules and inflation inertia. J. Money Credit Bank. 36 (6), 1015–1041.
Bonomo, M., Carvalho, C., 2010. Imperfectly credible disinflation under endogenous time-dependent pricing. J. Money Credit Bank. 42 (5), 799–831.
Broadbent, B., 2014. Unemployment and the conduct of monetary policy in the UK. In: Federal Reserve Bank of Kansas City Economic Symposium, Jackson Hole, Wyoming, August.
Calvo, G.A., 1983. Staggered contracts in a utility-maximizing framework. J. Monet. Econ. 12, 383–398.
Carlton, D.W., 1989. The theory and the facts of how markets clear: is industrial organization valuable for understanding macroeconomics? In: Schmalensee, R., Willig, R.D. (Eds.), Handbook of Industrial Organization, vol. 1. North-Holland, Amsterdam, pp. 909–946.
Carvalho, C., Schwartzman, F., 2015. Selection and monetary non-neutrality in time-dependent pricing models. J. Monet. Econ. 76 (C), 141–156.
Cecchetti, S.G., 1986. The frequency of price adjustment: a study of newsstand prices of magazines. Econ. J. 31, 255–274.
Cecchetti, S.G., 1984. Indexation and incomes policy: a study of wage adjustment in unionized manufacturing. J. Labor Econ. 5, 391–412.
Chari, V.V., Kehoe, P., McGrattan, E., 2000. Sticky price models of the business cycle: can the contract multiplier solve the persistence problem? Econometrica 68 (5), 1151–1180.
Chari, V.V., Kehoe, P.J., McGrattan, E.R., 2009. New Keynesian models: not yet useful for policy analysis. Am. Econ. J. Macroecon. 1 (1), 242–266.
Christiano, L., Eichenbaum, M., Evans, C., 2005. Nominal rigidities and the dynamic effects of a shock to monetary policy. J. Polit. Econ. 113 (1), 1–45.
Christiano, L.J., Eichenbaum, M.S., Trabandt, M., 2013. Unemployment and Business Cycles. Unpublished working paper, Northwestern University.

Dixon, H., Kara, E., 2005. Persistence and nominal inertia in a generalized Taylor economy: how longer contracts dominate shorter contracts. Working Paper No. 489, European Central Bank.
Dixon, H., Kara, E., 2006. How to compare Taylor and Calvo contracts: a comment on Michael Kiley. J. Money Credit Bank. 38 (4), 1119–1126.
Dixon, H., Kara, E., 2011. Contract length heterogeneity and the persistence of monetary shocks in a dynamic generalized Taylor economy. Eur. Econ. Rev. 55, 280–292.
Dixon, H., le Bihan, H., 2012. Generalised Taylor and generalised Calvo price and wage setting; micro-evidence with macro implications. Econ. J. 122 (May), 532–554.
Dotsey, M., King, R.G., Wolman, A.L., 1999. State-dependent pricing and the general equilibrium dynamics of money and output. Q. J. Econ. 114 (2), 655–690.
Dutta, S., Levy, D., Bergen, M., 2002. Price flexibility in channels of distribution: evidence from scanner data. J. Econ. Dyn. Control. 26, 1845–1900.
Erceg, C., Henderson, D., Levin, A., 2000. Optimal monetary policy with staggered wage and price contracts. J. Monet. Econ. 46 (2), 281–313.
Fabiani, S., Druant, M., Hernando, I., Kwapil, C., Landau, B., Loupias, C., Martins, F., Mathä, T., Sabbatini, R., Stahl, H., Stokman, A., 2006. What firms' surveys tell us about price-setting behavior in the euro area. Int. J. Cent. Bank. 5 (3), 3–47. Special Issue on Staggered Pricing Models Face the Facts.
Fischer, S., 1977. Long-term contracts, rational expectations, and the optimal money supply rule. J. Polit. Econ. 85 (1), 191–205.
Fregert, K., Jonung, L., 1986. Monetary regimes and the length of wage contracts: Sweden 1908-1995. Working Paper 1998-3, University of Lund.
Friedman, M., 2010. Trade-offs in monetary policy. In: David Laidler's Contributions to Economics. Palgrave MacMillan, London.
Fuhrer, J.C., 2006. Intrinsic and inherited inflation persistence. Int. J. Cent. Bank. 5 (3), 49–86. Special Issue on Staggered Pricing Models Face the Facts.
Fuhrer, J.C., Moore, G.R., 1995. Inflation persistence. Q. J. Econ. 110 (1), 127–159.
Gali, J., Gertler, M., 1999. Inflation dynamics: a structural econometric analysis. J. Monet. Econ. 44, 195–222.
Gali, J., Gertler, M., Lopez-Salido, J.D., 2005. Robustness of the estimates of the hybrid New Keynesian Phillips curve. J. Monet. Econ. 52, 1107–1118.
Gertler, M., Leahy, J., 2008. A Phillips curve with an Ss foundation. J. Polit. Econ. 116, 3.
Gertler, M., Sala, L., Trigari, A., 2008. An estimated monetary DSGE model with unemployment and staggered nominal wage bargaining. J. Money Credit Bank. 40 (8), 1713–1764.
Geweke, J., 1999. Using simulation methods for Bayesian econometric models: inference, development and communication. Econ. Rev. 18, 1–126.
Golosov, M., Lucas Jr., R.E., 2007. Menu costs and Phillips curves. J. Polit. Econ. 115 (2), 199–271.
Gordon, R.J., 1982. Discussion. In: Monetary Policy Issues for the 1980s. Federal Reserve Bank of Kansas City, Symposium, Jackson Hole Wyoming.
Gray, J.A., 1976. Wage indexation: a macroeconomic approach. J. Monet. Econ. 2 (2), 221–235.
Guerrieri, L., 2006. Inflation persistence of staggered contracts. J. Money Credit Bank. 38 (2), 483–494.
Hall, R., 2005. Employment fluctuations with equilibrium wage stickiness. Am. Econ. Rev. 95 (1), 50–65.
Hume, D., 1742. On money. Part II, Essay III, paragraph 7 of his In: Essays, Moral, Political, and Literary. Liberty Fund Books. http://www.econlib.org/library/LFBooks/Hume/hmMPL.html.
Kara, E., 2010. Optimal monetary policy in the generalized Taylor economy. J. Econ. Dyn. Control. 34, 2023–2037.
Kara, E., 2015. The reset inflation puzzle and the heterogeneity in price stickiness. J. Monet. Econ. 76, 29–37.
Kashyap, A.K., 1995. Sticky prices: new evidence from retail catalogues. Q. J. Econ. 110, 245–274.
Kehoe, P., Midrigan, V., 2010. Prices are sticky after all. NBER Working Paper No. 16364.
Kiley, M., 2002. Price adjustment and staggered price-setting. J. Money Credit Bank. 34, 283–298.
King, M., 1999. Challenges for monetary policy: new and old. In: New Challenges for Monetary Policy. Federal Reserve Bank of Kansas City, Jackson Hole.

King, M., 2012. Twenty years of inflation targeting. Stamp Memorial Lecture. London School of Economics, London. October 9.

Klenow, P., Kryvtsov, O., 2008. State dependent versus time dependent pricing. Q. J. Econ. 72 (2), 863–904.

Klenow, P., Malin, B., 2011. Microeconomic evidence on price setting. In: Friedman, B., Woodford, M. (Eds.), Handbook of Monetary Economics, vol. 3. Elsevier, Amsterdam.

Knell, M., 2010. Nominal and real wage rigidities in theory and in Europe. Working Paper Series, European Central Bank.

Lach, S., Tsiddon, D., 1996. Staggering and synchronization in price-setting: evidence from multiproduct firms. Am. Econ. Rev. 86, 1175–1196.

Lamo, A., Smets, F., 2009. Wage Dynamics in Europe: Final Report of the Wage Dynamics Network (WDN). https://www.ecb.europa.eu/home/pdf/wdn_finalreport_dec2009.pdf?68e28b96d494632f27900b1c453586c4. December 4.

Le Bihan, H., Montornès, J., Heckel, T., 2012. Sticky wages: evidence from quarterly microeconomic data. Am. Econ. J. Macroecon. 4 (3), 1–32.

Levin, A., 1991. The macroeconomic significance of nominal wage contract duration. Working Paper No. 91-08, February. University of California at San Diego.

Lünnemann, P., Wintr, L., 2009. Wages are flexible, aren't they? Evidence from monthly micro wage data. Working Paper Series, No. 1074, July, Wage Dynamic Network.

Mankiw, N.G., 2001. The inexorable and mysterious tradeoff between inflation and unemployment. Econ. J. 117, 1295–1328.

Mankiw, N.G., Reis, R., 2001. Sticky information versus sticky prices: a proposal to replace the New Keynesian Phillips curve. NBER Working Paper No. 8290.

Musy, O., 2006. Inflation persistence and the real costs of disinflation in staggered prices and partial adjustment models. Econ. Lett. 91, 50–55.

Nakamura, E., Steinsson, J., 2008. Five facts about prices: a reevaluation of menu cost models. Q. J. Econ. 123 (4), 1415–1464.

Nekarda, C.J., Ramey, V.A., 2013. The Cyclical Behavior of the Price–Cost Markup. University of California, San Diego, CA.

Okun, A.M., 1981. Prices and Quantities: A Macroeconomic Analysis. Brookings Institution, Washington, DC.

Olivei, G., Tenreyro, S., 2010. Wage setting patterns and monetary policy: international evidence. J. Monet. Econ. 57, 785–802.

Phelps, E., Taylor, J.B., 1977. Stabilizing powers of monetary policy under rational expectations. J. Polit. Econ. 85 (1), 163–190.

Ravenna, F., Walsh, C., 2008. Vacancies, unemployment, and the Phillips curve. Eur. Econ. Rev. 52, 1494–1521.

Romer, D., 2012. Advanced Macroeconomics, fourth ed. McGraw-Hill, New York, NY.

Schorfheide, F., 2000. Loss function based evaluation of DSGE models. J. Appl. Econ. 15 (6), 645–670.

Sigurdsson, J., Sigurdardottir, R., 2011. Evidence of nominal wage rigidity and wage setting from Icelandic microdata. Working Paper No. 55, Central Bank of Iceland.

Sigurdsson, J., Sigurdardottir, R., 2016. Time-dependent or state-dependent wage-setting? Evidence from periods of macroeconomic instability. J. Monet. Econ. 78, 50–66.

Smets, F., Wouters, R., 2003. An estimated dynamic stochastic general equilibrium model of the euro area. J. Eur. Econ. Assoc. 1 (5), 1123–1175.

Smets, F., Wouters, R., 2007. Shocks and frictions in U.S. Business cycles: Bayesian DSGE approach. Am. Econ. Rev. 97 (3), 506–606.

Stigler, G., Kindahl, J., 1970. The Behavior of Industrial Prices. NBER General Series, No. 90, Columbia University Press, New York, NY.

Svensson, L.E.O., 1986. Sticky goods prices, flexible asset prices, monopolistic competition, and monetary policy. Rev. Econ. Stud. 52, 385–405.

Taylor, J.B., 1979a. Estimation and control of a macroeconomic model with rational expectations. Econometrica 47 (5), 1267–1286. September. Reprinted in Lucas, R.E., Sargent, T.J. (Eds.), 1981. Rational Expectations and Econometric Practice, University of Minnesota Press.

Taylor, J.B., 1979b. Staggered wage setting in a macro model. Am. Econ. Rev. 69 (2), 108–113. May. Reprinted in Gregory Mankiw, N., Romer, D. (Eds.), 1991. New Keynesian Economics. MIT Press, Cambridge.

Taylor, J.B., 1979c. An econometric business cycle model with rational expectations: some estimation results. Working Paper, June, Columbia University. http://web.stanford.edu/~johntayl/Onlinepaperscombinedbyyear/1979/An_Econometric_Business_Cycle_Model_with_Rational_Expectations-Some_Estimations_Results-1979.pdf.

Taylor, J.B., 1980. Aggregate dynamics and staggered contracts. J. Polit. Econ. 88 (1), 1–23.

Taylor, J.B., 1982. The role of expectations in the choice of monetary policy. In: Monetary Policy Issues for the 1980s. Federal Reserve Bank of Kansas City Economic Symposium, Jackson Hole, Wyoming, August.

Taylor, J.B., 1983. Union wage settlements during a disinflation. Am. Econ. Rev. 73 (5), 981–993.

Taylor, J.B., 1993. Macroeconomic Policy in a World Economy: from Econometric Design to Practical Operation. W.W. Norton, New York, NY.

Taylor, J.B., 1999. Staggered price and wage setting in macroeconomics. In: Taylor, J.B., Woodford, M. (Eds.), Handbook of Macroeconomics. first ed., part 1 Elsevier, North-Holland, pp. 1009–1050.

Taylor, J.B., 2000. Low inflation, pass-through, and the pricing power of firms. Eur. Econ. Rev. 44 (7), 1389–1408.

Taylor, J.B., 2007. Thirty-five years of model building for monetary policy evaluation: breakthroughs, dark ages, and a renaissance. J. Money Credit Bank. 39 (Suppl. 1), 193–201.

Taylor, J.B., Wieland, V., 2012. Surprising comparative properties of monetary models: results from a new model data base. Rev. Econ. Stat. 94 (3), 800–816.

Walsh, C.E., 2010. Monetary Theory and Policy, third ed. The MIT Press, Cambridge, MA.

Wieland, V., Cwik, T., Müller, G.J., Schmidt, S., Wolters, M., 2012. A new comparative approach to macroeconomic modeling and policy analysis. J. Econ. Behav. Organ. 83, 523–541.

Wieland, V., Afanasyeva, E., Kuete, M., Yoo, J., 2016. New methods for macro-financial model comparison and policy analysis. In: Handbook of Macroeconomics, vol. 2A. Elsevier, Amsterdam, Netherlands, pp. 1241–1319.

Woodford, M., 2003. Interest and Prices. Princeton University Press, Princeton, NJ.

CHAPTER 26

Neoclassical Models in Macroeconomics

G.D. Hansen[*,†], **L.E. Ohanian**[*,†,‡]
[*]UCLA, Los Angeles, CA, United States
[†]NBER, Cambridge, MA, United States
[‡]Hoover Institution, Stanford University, Stanford, CA, United States

Contents

Handbook of Macroeconomics, Volume 2B
ISSN 1574-0048, http://dx.doi.org/10.1016/bs.hesmac.2016.04.010

Abstract

This chapter develops a toolkit of neoclassical macroeconomic models, and applies these models to the US economy from 1929 to 2014. We first filter macroeconomic time series into business cycle and long-run components, and show that the long-run component is typically much larger than the business cycle component. We argue that this empirical feature is naturally addressed within neoclassical models with long-run changes in technologies and government policies. We construct two classes of models that we compare to raw data, and also to the filtered data: *simple neoclassical models*, which feature standard preferences and technologies, rational expectations, and a unique, Pareto optimal equilibrium, and *extended neoclassical models*, which build in government policies and market imperfections. We focus on models with multiple sources of technological change, and models with distortions arising from regulatory, labor, and fiscal policies. The models account for much of the relatively stable postwar US economy, and also for the Great Depression and World War II. The models presented in this chapter can be extended and applied more broadly to other settings. We close by identifying several avenues for future research in neoclassical macroeconomics.

Keywords

Neoclassical models, Dynamic general equilibrium, Great Depression World War II, Band pass filter, Productivity shocks, Low frequency fluctuations, Business cycles, Economic growth, Great moderation, Great recession

JEL Classification Codes

E13, E2, E6

1. INTRODUCTION

This chapter analyzes the role of *neoclassical models* in the study of economic growth and fluctuations. Our goal is to provide macroeconomists with a toolkit of models that are of interest in their own right, and that easily can be modified to study a broad variety of macroeconomic phenomena, including the impact of economic policies on aggregate economic activity.

Since there is no generally recognized definition of neoclassical macroeconomics within the profession, we organize the development of these models around two principles. One is based on the exogenous factors driving changes in aggregate time series, and the other is based on the classes of model economies that we consider.

The primary sources of changes in macroeconomic variables that we study are long-run changes in technologies and government policies. We focus on these factors because of the observed large changes in productivity and in policies that affect the incentives and opportunities to produce and trade. Policy factors that we consider include changes affecting competition and business regulatory policies, labor policies, and fiscal policies.

We study two classes of intertemporal models that we call *neoclassical macroeconomic models*. The first has standard preferences and technologies, competitive markets, rational expectations, and there is a unique equilibrium that is Pareto optimal. We call these *Simple Neoclassical Models*. This class of models is the foundation of neoclassical macroeconomics, and provides the most transparent description of how competitive market forces operate within a dynamic, general equilibrium environment.

In contrast to common perceptions about neoclassical macroeconomics, we acknowledge that economies are affected by policy distortions and other market imperfections that go beyond the scope of simple models. The second class of models modifies simple models as needed to incorporate changes that require departing from the model assumptions described above. We call the second class of models *Extended Neoclassical Models*, which are constructed by building explicit specifications of government policies or market imperfections and distortions into simple models.

This method nests simple models as special cases of the extended models. Developing complex models in this fashion provides a clear description of how market imperfections and economic policies affect what otherwise would be a *laissez-faire* market economy. We modify the models in very specific ways that are tailored to study episodes in US economic history, and which provide researchers with frameworks that can be applied more broadly. All of the models presented in this chapter explicitly treat fluctuations and growth within the same framework.

Neoclassical frameworks are a powerful tool for analyzing market economies. An important reason is because the US economy has displayed persistent and reasonably stable growth over much its history while undergoing enormous resource reallocation through the competitive market process in response to changes in technologies and government policies. These large reallocations include the shift out of agriculture into manufacturing and services, the shift of economic activity out of the Northern and Mideastern sections of the United States to the Southern and Western states, and large changes in government's share of output, including changes in tax, social insurance, and regulatory labor policies. This also includes the reallocation of women's time from home production to market production, and the increased intensity of employment of highly-skilled labor. Most recently, this has included the reallocation of resources out of the development of mature, mechanical technologies to the development of information processing and communication technologies, including the integrated circuit, fiber optics, microwave technology, laptop computers and tablets, software applications, cellular technology, and the internet.

Our focus on technologies and policies connects with considerable previous research. This ranges from Schumpeter (1927) and Stock and Watson (1988), who argued that changes in entrepreneurship and the development of new ideas are the primary drivers of a market economy, to Kydland and Prescott (1982) and Long Jr and Plosser (1983), who focused on technology shocks and fluctuations. This also includes Lilien (1982), who argued that sectoral shifts significantly affect fluctuations and resource reallocation, Davis and Haltiwanger (1992), who established that resource reallocation across US manufacturing establishments is very large and is continuously evolving, and Greenwood and Yorokoglu (1997) and Manuelli and Seshadri (2014), who analyze the diffusion of new technologies and their long-run economic effects. The analysis also connects with studies of the long-run consequences of government policies, including research by Ljungqvist and Sargent (1998), Prescott (2004), and Rogerson (2008), who analyze how public policies such as tax rate changes, and changes in social insurance programs, have affected long-run labor market outcomes.

Our principle of focusing on long-run movements in data requires a quantitative approach that differs from standard practice in macroeconomics that involves both the selection of the data frequencies that are analyzed, and how the model is compared to data. The standard approach removes a trend from the data that is constructed using the Hodrick–Prescott (HP) filter (1997), hereafter referred to as HP filter, with a smoothing parameter of 1600, and then typically compares either model moments to moments from the HP-filtered data, or compares model impulse response functions to those from an empirical vector autoregression (VAR).This analysis uses a band pass filter to quantify movements not only at the HP-business cycle frequency, but also at the lower frequencies. Our quantitative-theoretic analysis evaluates model economies by conducting equilibrium path analyses, in which model-generated variables that are driven by identified shocks are compared to actual raw data and to filtered data at different frequencies.

We report two sets of findings. We first document the empirical importance of very long-run movements in aggregate variables relative to traditional business cycle fluctuations using post-Korean War quarterly US data, long-run annual US data, and postwar European data. We find that low frequency movements in aggregate time series are quantitatively large, and that in some periods, they are much larger than the traditional business cycle component. Specifically, we analyze movements in periodicities ranging from 2 to 50 years, and we find that as much as 80% of the fluctuations in economic activity at these frequencies is due to the lower frequency component from 8 to 50 years.

The dominant low frequency nature of these data indicates that the business cycle literature has missed quantitatively important movements in aggregate activity. Moreover, the fact that much of the movement in aggregate data is occurring at low frequencies suggests that models that generate fluctuations from transient impediments to trade, such as temporarily inflexible prices and/or wages, may be of limited interest in understanding US time series.

The importance of low frequency movements also has significant implications for the two dominant episodes of the last 35 years, the *Great Moderation* and the *Great Recession*.

The Great Moderation, the period of stable economic activity that occurred between 1984 and 2008, features a sharp decline in volatility at the traditional business cycle frequency, but little volatility change at low frequencies. Similarly, the Great Recession and its aftermath feature a large, low frequency component. These data suggest that the Great Recession was not just a recession per se. Instead, much of this event appears to be a persistent decline in aggregate economic activity.

Following the decomposition of data into low and high frequency components, we report the results of quantitative-theoretic analyses that evaluate how well neoclassical models account for the US historical macroeconomic record from 1929 to 2014.

Our main finding is that neoclassical models can account for much of the movement in aggregate economic activity in the US economic historical record. Neoclassical models plausibly account for major economic episodes that previously were considered to be far beyond their reach, including the Great Depression and World War II. We also find that neoclassical models account for much of the post-Korean War history of the United States.

The chapter is organized as follows. Section 2 presents the United States and European data that we use in this study, and provides a decomposition of the data into low frequency and business cycle frequency components. Section 3 introduces the basic neoclassical macroeconomic model that serves as the foundation for all other models developed in the chapter. Section 4 presents one-, two-, and three-sector *simple neoclassical model* analyses of the post-Korean War US economy. Section 5 presents *extended neoclassical models* to study Depressions. Section 6 presents *extended neoclassical models* with fiscal policies with a focus on the US economy during World War II. Given the importance of productivity shocks in neoclassical models, Section 7 discusses different frameworks for understanding and interpreting TFP changes. Given the recent interest in economic inequality, Section 8 discusses neoclassical models of wage inequality. Section 9 presents a critical assessment of neoclassical models, and suggests future research avenues for neoclassical macroeconomic analysis. Section 10 presents our conclusions.

2. THE IMPORTANCE OF LOW FREQUENCY COMPONENTS IN MACROECONOMIC DATA

It is common practice in applied macroeconomics to decompose time series data into specific components that economists often refer to as *cyclical components, trend components*, and *seasonal components*, with the latter component being relevant in the event that data are not seasonally adjusted. These decompositions are performed to highlight particular features of data for analysis. The most common decomposition is to extract the cyclical component from data for the purpose of business cycle analysis, and the HP filter is the most common filtering method that is used.

Band-pass filters, which feature a number of desirable properties, and which resolve some challenges involved with applying the HP filter, are increasingly being used to filter data.[a] Band-pass filtering allows researchers to choose components that correspond to periodicities over a specific data frequency. An exact band pass filter requires an infinite length of data, so Baxter and King (1999) and Christiano and Fitzgerald (2003) have constructed approximate band pass filters. These two approaches are fairly similar. The main difference is that the Baxter–King filter is symmetric, and the Christiano–Fitzgerald filter is asymmetric.

This section presents decompositions of aggregate data into different frequency components for (i) US post-Korean War quarterly data, (ii) US annual data that extends back to 1890, and (iii) post-World War II annual European data. We use the Baxter–King filter, given its wide use in the literature. The band pass filter isolates cyclical components in data by smoothing the data using long moving averages of the data. Baxter and King develop an approximate band pass filter that produces stationary data when applied to typical economic time series.[b] Since the exact band pass filter is an infinite order process, Baxter and King construct a symmetric approximate band pass filter. They show that the optimal approximating filter for a given maximum lag length truncates the filter weight at lag K as follows:

$$y_t^* = \sum_{k=-K}^{K} a_k y_{t-k} \tag{1}$$

In (1), y^* is the filtered data, y is the unfiltered data, and the a_k denote coefficients that produce the smoothed time series. The values of the a_k coefficients depend on the filtering frequency (see Baxter and King, 1999).

Following early work on business cycles by Burns and Mitchell (1946), Baxter and King study business cycles, which they define as corresponding to periodicities associated with 6–32 quarters. In contrast, we use the band-pass filter to consider a much broader range of frequencies up to 200 quarters. Our choice to extend the frequency of analysis to 200 quarters is motivated by Comin and Gertler (2006), who studied these lower frequencies in a model with research and development spending.

We consider much lower frequencies than in the business cycle literature since changes in technologies and government policies may have a quantitatively important effect on low frequency movements in aggregate data. Relatively little is known about the nature and size of these low frequency fluctuations, however, or how these low frequency fluctuations compare to business cycle fluctuations. We therefore band-pass filter data between 2 and 200 quarters, and we split these filtered data into two components:

[a] In terms of the challenges with the HP filter, it is not clear how to adjust the HP smoothing parameter to assess data outside of the cyclical window originally studied by Hodrick and Prescott (1997). Moreover, HP-filtered data may be difficult to interpret at data endpoints.

[b] The Baxter–King filter yields stationary time series for a variable that is integrated of up to order two. We are unaware of any macroeconomic time series that is integrated of order three or higher.

a 2–32 quarters component, which approximates the business cycle results from the standard parameterization of the HP filter ($\lambda = 1600$), and a 32–200 quarters component. This allows us to assess the relative size and characteristics of these fluctuations. To our knowledge, these comparative decompositions have not been constructed in the literature.

2.1 Band-Pass Filtered Quarterly US Data

This section analyzes US quarterly post-Korean war data from 1954 to 2014, which facilitates comparison with much of the business cycle literature. We then analyze annual US data extending back to 1890, followed by an analysis of postwar European data.[c]

Figs. 1–6 show filtered real GDP, consumption of nondurables and services, gross private domestic investment, hours worked, total factor productivity (TFP), and the relative price of capital equipment. Real GDP, consumption, and investment are from the NIPA.

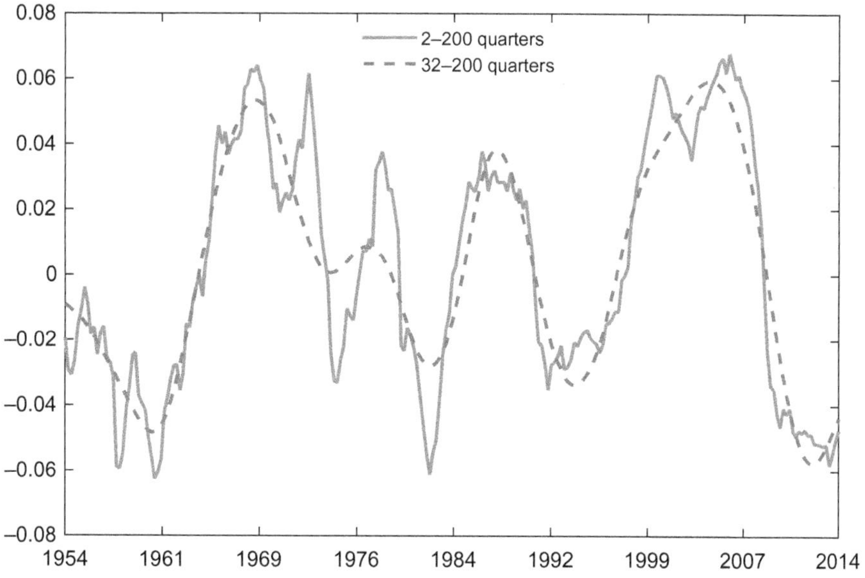

Fig. 1 Log of real GDP.

[c] The Baxter–King filter loses data at the beginning and the end of a dataset. We therefore padded all the data series at both the starting and ending dates by simulating data from ARMA models fit to each series. These simulated data extend the series before the starting date and after the end date, which allows us to construct filtered data for the entire period length. We conducted a Monte Carlo analysis of this padding procedure by generating extremely long artificial time series, and comparing band-pass filtered series using the padded data, to filtered data that doesn't use padding. The length of the data padding is equal to the number of moving average coefficients, k. We use $k = 50$ for the quarterly data, and $k = 12$ for the annual data. The results were insensitive to choosing higher values of k.

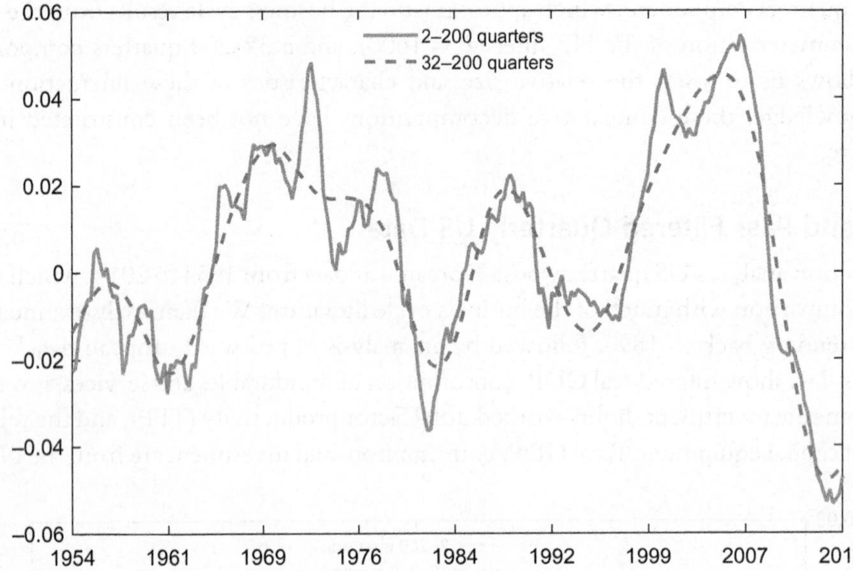

Fig. 2 Log of consumption of nondurables and services.

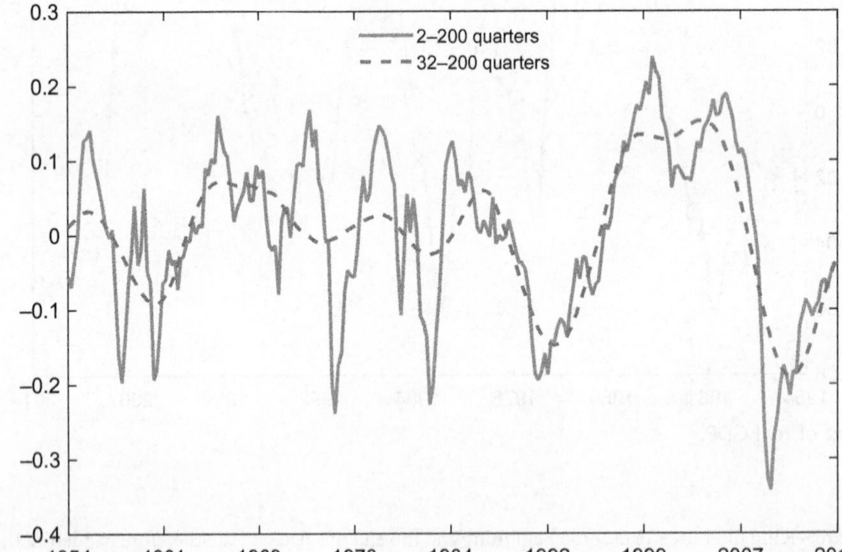

Fig. 3 Log of fixed investment.

Hours worked is constructed by updating the hours worked data of Cociuba et al. (2012), who use hours from the Current Population Survey. TFP is constructed by dividing real GDP by a Cobb–Douglas aggregate of capital, which is the sum of private and public capital stocks, and which has a share of 0.4, and hours worked, which has a share of 0.6.

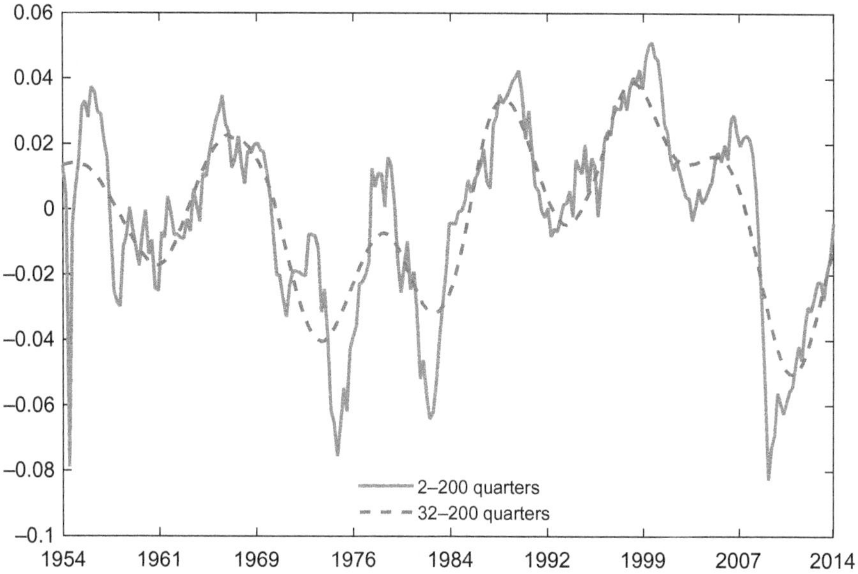

Fig. 4 Log of total hours worked.

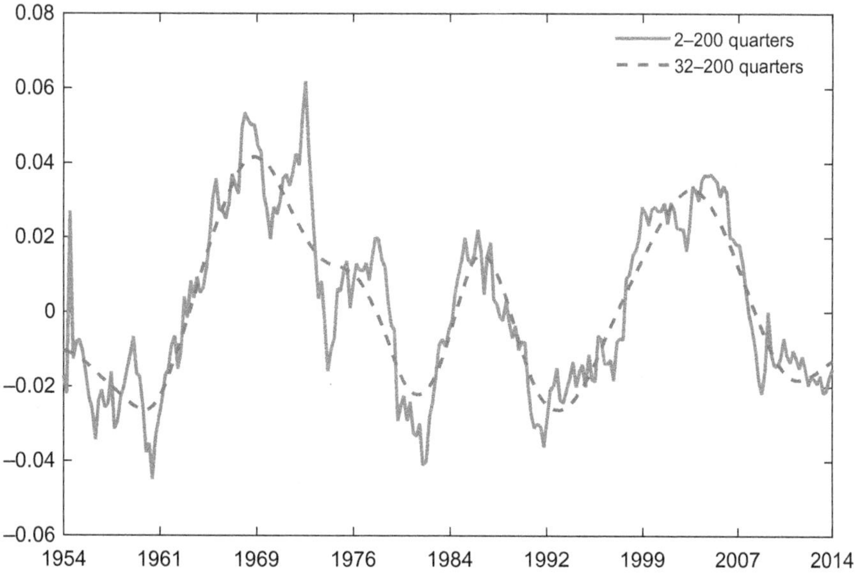

Fig. 5 Log of total factor productivity.

We include the relative price of capital equipment in this analysis because there is a large change in this relative price over time, and because the inverse of this relative price is a measure of equipment-specific technological change in some classes of models, including Greenwood et al. (1997) and Krusell et al. (2000). We construct the relative price of

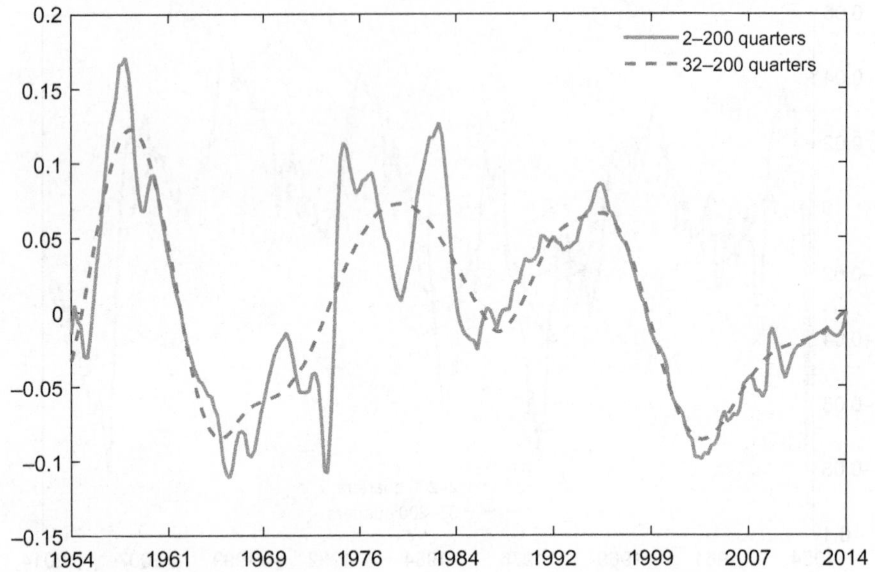

Fig. 6 Log of relative price of equipment.

equipment as the ratio of the quality-adjusted deflator for producer durable equipment, to the NIPA nondurable consumption deflator. Gordon (1990) initially constructed the quality-adjusted equipment deflator, and this time series has been continued in Cummins and Violante (2002) and in DiCecio (2009).[d]

The figures show the 2–200 component and the 32–200 component. Since the band pass filter is a linear filter, the difference between these two lines is the 2–32 component. The most striking feature of all of these filtered data is that much of the movement in the 2–200 component is due to the 32–200 component. These filtered data indicate that business cycle variability, as typically measured, accounts for a relatively small fraction of the overall post-Korean war history of US economic variability. The graphs do show that there are some periods in which the traditional business cycle component is sizeable. This occurs during part of the 1950s, which could be interpreted as the economy readjusting to peacetime policies following World War II and the Korean War. There is also a significant 2–32 component from the 1970s until the early 1980s.

[d] We do not use the NIPA equipment deflator because of Gordon's (1990) argument that the NIPA equipment price deflator does not adequately capture quality improvements in capital equipment. We use DiCecio's (2009) updating of the Gordon–Cummins–Violante data. This data is updated by DiCecio on a real time basis in the Federal Reserve Bank of St. Louis's FRED database (https://research.stlouisfed.org/fred2/series/PERIC). The mnemonic for this series is PERIC.

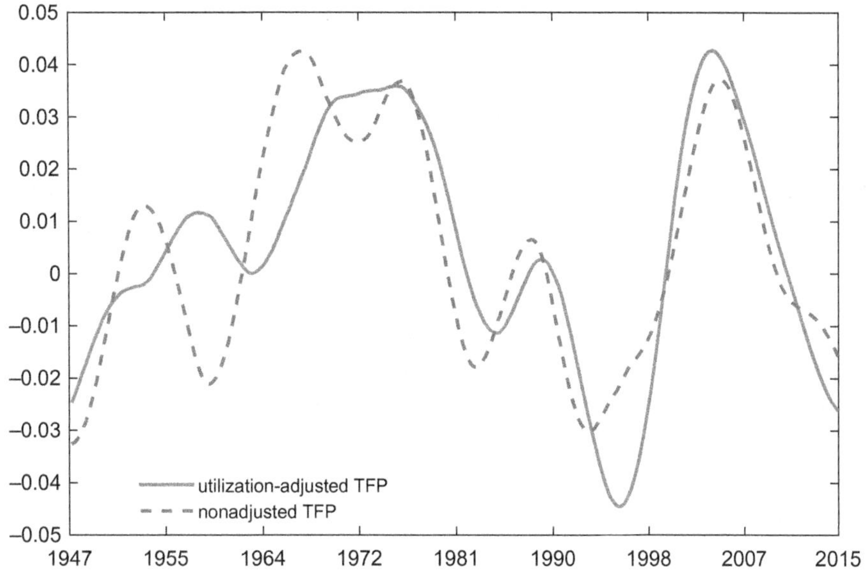

Fig. 7 Fernald TFP (filtered 32–200 quarters).

The 32–200 component of TFP has important implications for the common critique that TFP fluctuations at the standard HP frequency are affected by unmeasured cyclical factor utilization. Fernald's (2014) TFP series is a widely used measure of TFP that is adjusted for unmeasured factor utilization. Fig. 7 shows the 32–200 component of Fernald's adjusted and unadjusted measures of business sector TFP. The long-run components of the adjusted and unadjusted series are very similar, particularly over the last 40 years. This indicates that unmeasured factor utilization is not an issue for measuring TFP at these lower frequencies.

To quantify the relative contribution of the 32–200 component for these variables, we construct the following ratio, which we denote as z_i, in which x_i is the 32–200 filtered component of variable i, and y_i is the 2–200 filtered component of variable i :

$$z_i = \sum_t \frac{(x_{it})^2}{(y_{it})^2} \tag{2}$$

On average, the 32–200 component accounts for about 80% of the fluctuations in output, consumption, TFP, and the relative price of equipment and about 64% of hours. It accounts for about 56% of fluctuations in gross private domestic investment, which includes the highly volatile category of inventory change.

The 32–200 component is also large during the Great Moderation. Specifically, the well-known volatility decline of the Great Moderation, which is typically dated from

1984 to 2007, is primarily due to lower volatility of the 2–32 component. The figures show that the volatility of the 32–200 component remains quantitatively large during the Great Moderation. This latter finding may reflect the large and persistent technological advances in information processing and communications that occurred throughout this period.

This finding regarding the nature of these frequency components in the Great Moderation is consistent with the conclusions of Arias et al. (2007) and Stock and Watson (2003), who report that the traditional business cycles frequency shocks that affected the economy during this period were smaller than before the Great Moderation. This finding about the Great Moderation may also reflect more stable government policies that reduced short-run variability. Taylor (2010) has argued that more stable monetary policy is important for understanding the Great Moderation.

The 32–200 component is also important for the Great Recession and its aftermath. This largely reflects the fact that there has been limited economic recovery relative to long-run trend since the Great Recession.

2.2 Band-Pass Filtered Annual US and European Data

This section presents band-pass filtered annual long-run US data and annual European data. The output data were constructed by splicing the annual Kuznets–Kendrick data (Kendrick, 1961) beginning in 1890, with the annual NIPA data that begins in 1929. The annual Kendrick hours data, which also begins in 1890, is spliced with our update of the hours worked data from Cociuba et al. (2012). These constructions provide long annual time series that are particularly useful in measuring the low frequency components.

Figs. 8 and 9 show the filtered annual US data. The low frequency component, which is measured using the band pass filter from 8 to 50 years for these annual data, is also very large. Extending the data back to 1890 allows us to assess the importance of these different components around several major events, including the Panic of 1907 and World War I. The data show that both the Depression and World War II were dominated by lower frequency components, while the traditional business cycle component was significant during World War I and the Panic of 1907.

The large low frequency component of World War II stands in contrast to World War I, and also stands in contrast to standard theoretical models of wartime economies. These models typically specify wars as a highly transient shock to government purchases. The low frequency component is also large for the Great Depression. Sections 5 and 6 develop neoclassical models of Depressions and of wartime economies, in which both of these events are driven by persistent changes in government policies.

The decomposition ratio presented in (2), and that was used to construct the share of variation in the 2–200 quarter component due to the 32–200 quarter component, is used in a similar way to construct the share of variation in the 2–50 year component due to the

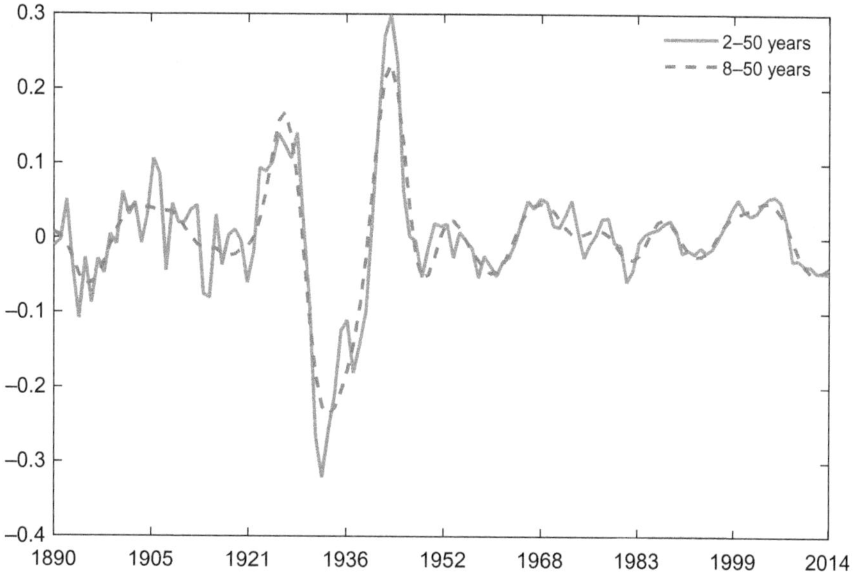

Fig. 8 Annual log of real GDP.

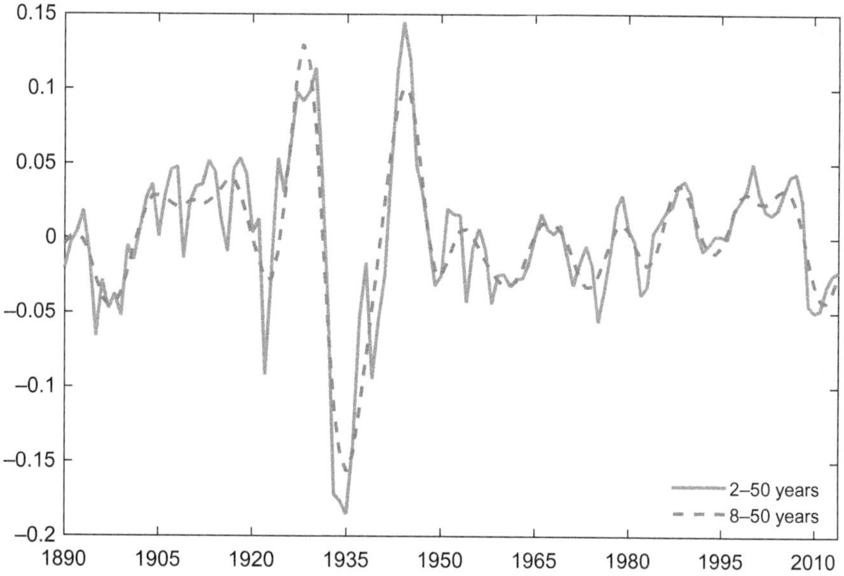

Fig. 9 Annual log of hours worked.

8–50 year component. This low frequency component share is also large in the annual data, ranging between 80% and 85% for real GNP and hours worked.

We also construct the decomposition using annual postwar logged real output data from several European economies: Germany, France, Italy, Spain, and Sweden.

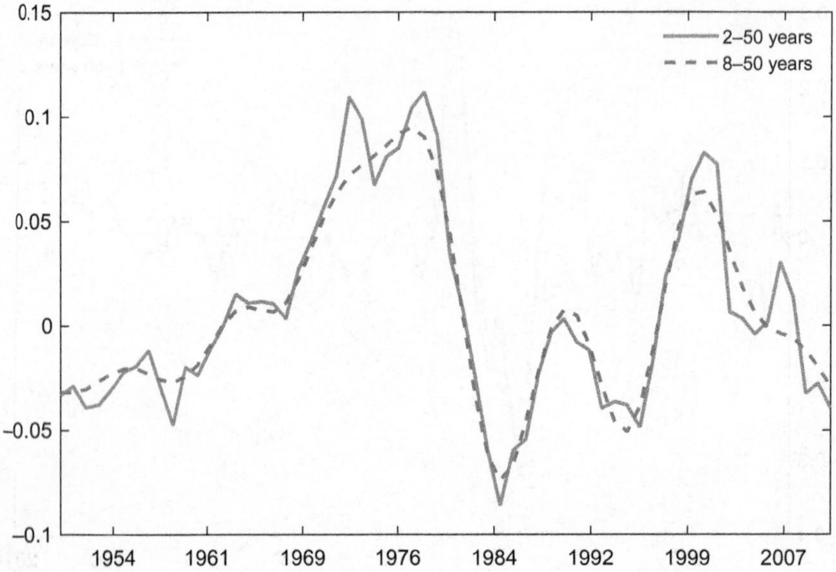

Fig. 10 Log of real GDP—France.

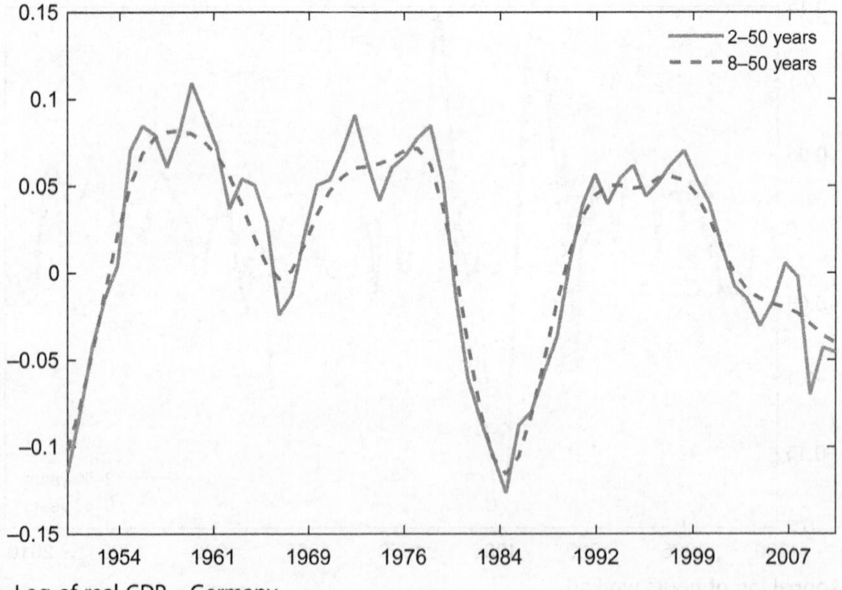

Fig. 11 Log of real GDP—Germany.

These data are from the Penn World Tables (Feenstra et al., 2015). Figs. 10–14 present the filtered data. Most of the variation in the European output data in the 2–50 year component also is accounted for by the low frequency (8–50) component. The long-run European components reflect clear patterns in these data. All of the European economies

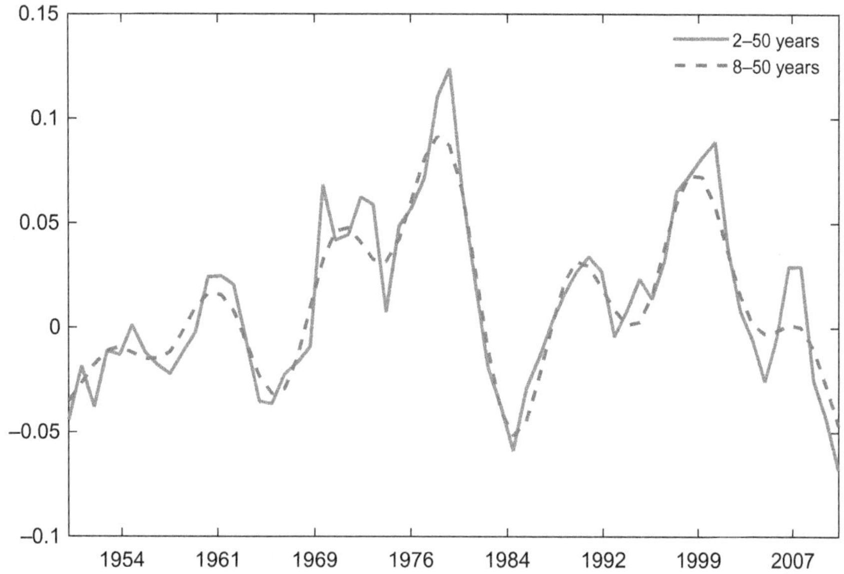

Fig. 12 Log of real GDP—Italy.

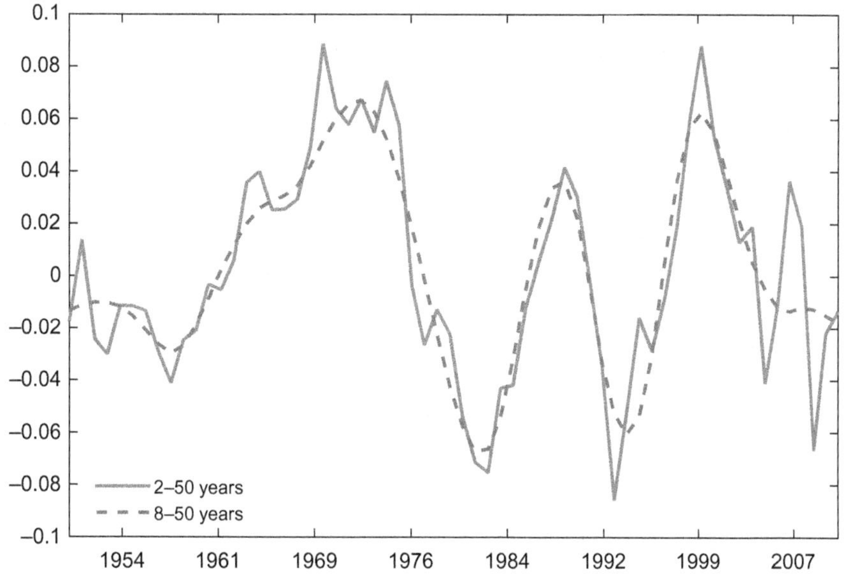

Fig. 13 Log of real GDP—Spain.

grow more rapidly than the US during the 1950s and 1960s. All of these economies then experience large declines relative to trend that begin in the early 1970s and continue to the mid-1980s. The share of the 2–50 component that is accounted for by the 8–50 component is about 80% for Germany, France, Spain, and Sweden, and is about 71% for Italy.

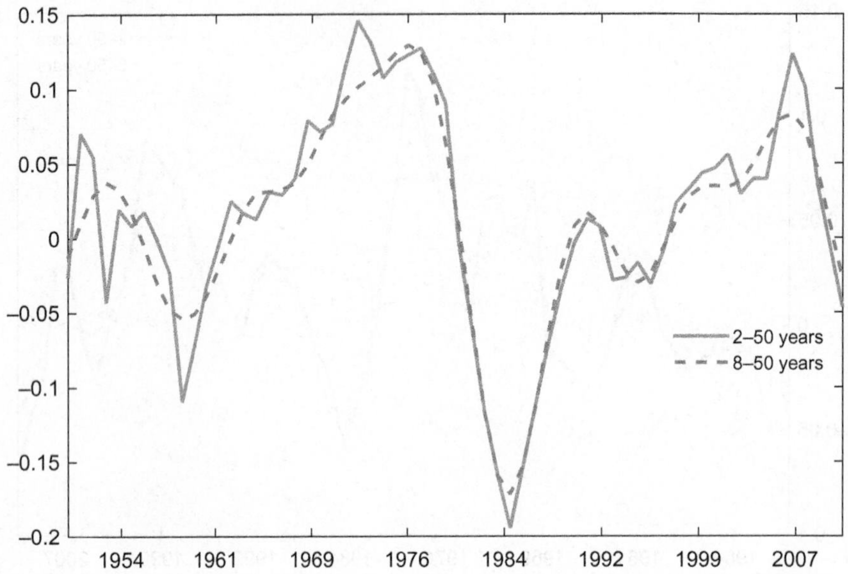

Fig. 14 Log of real GDP—Sweden.

2.3 Alternative to Band-Pass Filtering: Stochastic Trend Decomposition

This section presents an alternative decomposition method, known as stochastic trend decomposition, for assessing the relative importance of low frequency components. One approach to stochastic trend decompositions was developed by Beveridge and Nelson (1981), and is known as the Beveridge–Nelson decomposition. Watson (1986) describes an alternative approach, which is known as unobserved components model decomposition. In both frameworks, a time series is decomposed into two latent objects, a stochastic trend component, and a stationary component, which is often called the cyclical component.

Decomposing the time series into these latent components requires an identifying restriction. The Beveridge–Nelson identifying restriction is that the two components are perfectly correlated. This identifying assumption is thematically consistent with our view that permanent changes in technologies and policies generate both stationary and permanent responses in macroeconomic variables.[e]

[e] The unobserved components models have traditionally achieved identification of the two latent components by imposing that the trend and stationary components are orthogonal. More recently, Morley et al. (2003) show how to achieve identification in unobserved components models with a nonzero correlation between the two components. Morley et al. find that the decomposition for real GDP for their unobserved components model is very similar to the Beveridge–Nelson decomposition. They also present evidence that the zero correlation identifying restriction that traditionally has been used in unobserved components models is empirically rejected.

The Beveridge–Nelson decomposition, which is simple and widely used, is applied in this chapter. The Beveridge–Nelson statistical model begins with a variable that is assumed to have a stochastic trend component. The variable may also have a drift term, which drives secular growth in the variable. The Beveridge–Nelson decomposition removes the drift term, and then decomposes the variable, which we denote as y_t, into a stochastic trend component, x_t and a stationary stochastic component, s_t. The stochastic trend is a random walk, and the innovation term, which is denoted as ε_t, is a white noise process:

$$y_t = x_t + s_t \tag{3}$$

$$x_t = x_{t-1} + \varepsilon_t, E(\varepsilon) = 0, E(\varepsilon^2) = \sigma_\varepsilon^2 \tag{4}$$

This decomposition is applied to the log of US real GDP. The decomposition first requires specifying an ARIMA model for the data. We selected an ARIMA (0,1,1) model for the log of real GDP, given that the first three autocorrelations of the first difference of the logged data are 0.34, 0.19, and 0.06. Stock and Watson (1988) also use this ARIMA specification for the log of real output. The estimated statistical model for the log of real GDP using quarterly data between 1954:1 and 2013:4 is given by:

$$\Delta \ln(GDP_t) = 0.0077 + \varepsilon_t + 0.40\varepsilon_{t-1}. \tag{5}$$

These estimated coefficients are similar to the Stock and Watson estimates that were based on a shorter dataset. Stock and Watson estimated a slightly higher drift term of about 0.008, and a somewhat smaller moving average coefficient of 0.30 rather than 0.40.

Using the Wold decomposition, Beveridge and Nelson show that the permanent component for this estimated statistical model is given by:

$$1.4 * \sum_{j=1}^{t} \varepsilon_j \tag{6}$$

Fig. 15 plots the detrended log of real GDP, which is constructed as the log of real GDP less its accumulated drift component, and the Beveridge–Nelson permanent component of these detrended data. The figure shows that almost all of the movement in detrended real GDP is due to the permanent component, rather than the transitory component. This finding is consistent with the band-pass filtered results regarding the large size of the long-run component.

The results presented in this section show that the bulk of observed fluctuations in aggregate time series are from longer-run changes than those associated with traditional business cycle frequencies. This finding motivates our focus on neoclassical models that are driven by long-run changes in technologies and policies, as opposed to models that are driven by very transient shocks, such as monetary shocks that operate in models with temporarily inflexible prices and/or wages.

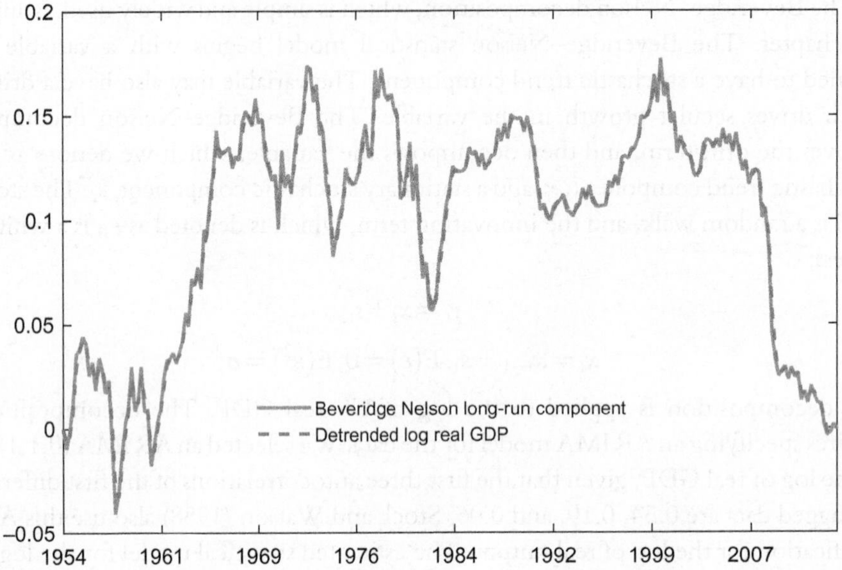

Fig. 15 Beveridge–Nelson decomposition of real GDP.

3. CASS-KOOPMANS: THE FOUNDATION OF SIMPLE MODELS

This section summarizes the one-sector Cass-Koopmans optimal growth model with elastically supplied leisure, as it serves as the foundation for the other models that are developed in this chapter. This model features (1) standard utility maximization problems for households, and standard profit maximization problems for firms, both of whom behave competitively and who have rational expectations, (2) complete markets, (3) a unique and Pareto optimal equilibrium, and (4) constant returns to scale technology.

Since the welfare theorems hold in this economy, we express this model as a social planning problem. For heuristic purposes, we assume perfect foresight. The planner's maximization problem is given by:

$$\max \beta^t \sum_{t=0}^{\infty} u(c_t, l_t). \tag{7}$$

Maximization is subject to the economy's resource constraint, a household time constraint, a transition equation for the capital stock, and nonnegativity constraints on consumption, hours, and capital:

$$f(k_t, h_t) \geq c_t + i_t \tag{8}$$

$$1 \geq h_t + l_t \tag{9}$$

$$k_{t+1} = (1-\delta)k_t + i_t \tag{10}$$

$$c_t \geq 0, h_t \geq 0, k_t \geq 0, k_0 \text{ given.} \tag{11}$$

It is also necessary to impose the transversality condition to rule out explosive paths for the capital stock:

$$\lim_{t \to \infty} \beta^t u_1(c_t, l_t) f_1(k_t, h_t) k_t = 0 \tag{12}$$

The utility function satisfies the usual restrictions: it is concave in its arguments and twice continuously differentiable. The technology, f, is constant returns to scale in the two inputs capital, k, and labor, h, and is also twice continuously differentiable.

We will tailor the construction of different neoclassical models to focus on policies and technological change that we highlight for specific historical episodes. This should not be confused with the idea that fundamentally different models are needed to address different time periods in the history of the US economy. Rather this means that the relative importance of different policies and different types of technological change has varied over time. Specifically, this includes the importance of biased technological change for understanding the post-Korean War US history, cartelization and unionization government policies for understanding the 1930s, and changes in government fiscal policies for understanding the 1940s.

4. NEOCLASSICAL MODELS OF THE US POST-KOREAN WAR ECONOMY

In this section we present a series of neoclassical models, driven by permanent changes in technologies to study the post-Korean War US economy. Our approach, which we describe in detail below, compares the equilibrium paths of the model economies in response to identified shocks, to the actual time series data. We will compare model results to unfiltered data, and also to the three different filtering frequencies described in Section 2. In addition to evaluating the fit of the model for the raw data, this will allow us to assess how well the model matches data at the traditional business cycle frequencies (2–32 quarters), and also at low frequencies (32–200) quarters.

4.1 Quantitative Methodology

Neutral technological change that affects all sectors identically is the standard specification of technology in neoclassical macroeconomic models. However, there is a growing body of evidence that technological change is advancing much more quickly in the information processing sectors of the economy, particularly in capital equipment. This includes the areas of computer hardware, computer peripherals, photocopying equipment and telecommunications equipment, among others.

As described earlier in this chapter, Gordon (1990), Cummins and Violante (2002), and DiCecio (2009) construct capital equipment price data that they argue captures much more of the quality change that has occurred in these goods than is present in the NIPA equipment price data. Fig. 16 shows the relationship between real GDP

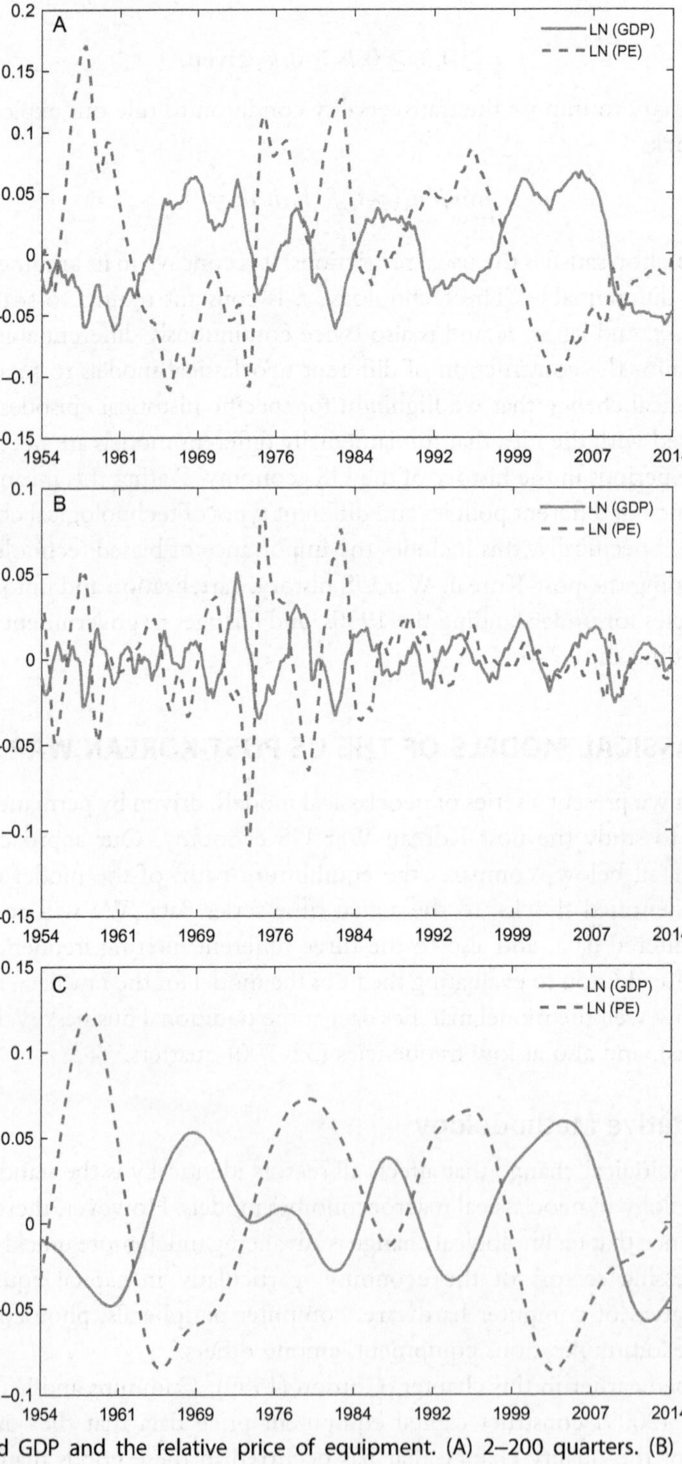

Fig. 16 Filtered GDP and the relative price of equipment. (A) 2–200 quarters. (B) 2–32 quarters. (C) 32–200 quarters.

and the relative price of equipment at the three sets of frequencies that we consider. These figures show that the relative price of equipment is strongly countercyclical at all frequencies.

These strong countercyclical patterns are interesting as a growing number of neoclassical studies are using these data to identify capital-equipment specific technological change. The following sections develop multisector growth models that include both neutral and equipment-specific technological change to study the evolution of the post-Korean War US economy. This is a particularly interesting period for applying multisector models with biased technological change since this period features a number of major advances in information processing and telecommunications technologies, including the integrated circuit, personal computers and tablet technologies, fiber optics, software applications, cellular technologies, and the internet.

Focusing on this period also allows us to connect this analysis with the large business cycle literature, including Kydland and Prescott (1982), Hansen (1985), and the studies in Cooley (1995), which have analyzed the post-Korean War US economy. Note that the post-Korean War period also includes a number of interesting subperiods: the Vietnam War (1957–71), the oil shock years (1974–81), the Great Moderation (1984–2007), and the Great Recession and its aftermath (2008–present).

Our quantitative approach differs from the standard approach used in the real business cycle literature. The real business cycle approach specifies a dynamic stochastic general equilibrium model, which includes a specification of the stochastic process for the exogenous shocks that generate fluctuations in the model economy. The equilibrium decision rules and laws of motion are computed using numerical methods, and these equations plus a random number generator are used to simulate time series for the artificial economy. Summary statistics are then computed and compared with the same summary statistics computed from actual US time series.

The approach we follow is similar to that employed in Hansen and Prescott (1993). We begin with a two-sector growth model in which movements in aggregate time series are the result of two factors we identify from US data that we take to be the exogenous forcing processes in the model. These include technology shocks that are identified with total factor productivity and equipment specific technological change, which we identify from the relative price of equipment. We then calibrate and solve the model in a manner consistent with the real business cycle literature. But, rather than drawing random realizations of the exogenous shock processes, we identify time paths for our two technology shocks from US time series data. We then compute the equilibrium time paths for the endogenous variables (output, consumption, investment and hours worked) using the actual time path of the exogenous shocks. As noted above, we compare model variables to quarterly real variables for the unfiltered data over 1954–2014, as well as for frequency bands corresponding to 2–200, 2–32, and 32–200 quarters.

After comparing the time paths from the two-sector model with the corresponding time paths from US data, we then compare these time paths with those of a standard one-sector neoclassical model in which neutral technology shocks are the only exogenous process hitting the economy. We then consider a three-sector model that adds a nonmarket home production sector to our baseline two-sector model. This extension allows us to study how equipment biased technological change may have induced movements in labor from the home production sector to the market sector.

We omit the details of numerically solving these models. Instead, we focus on the specifics of the model economies, the construction of US data counterparts to the model variables, and the calibration that we use in our computational analyses.

In terms of assessing model fit, our approach differs considerably from the recent approach that is used in the New Keynesian literature. In New Keynesian models, such as Smets and Wouters (2007), as many shocks are added to the model as needed so that the model fits all of the data very closely. While this approach delivers a very good model fit, some of the shocks in the model are often difficult to interpret. Our approach to model fit follows from our theme that permanent changes in technologies are key drivers of the economy. The models analyzed in the following sections have very few shocks, which allows us to transparently evaluate the models' successes and deviations.

4.2 A Two-Sector Model with Aggregate and Investment-Biased Technological Change

This section develops a model with investment-specific technological change, as well as aggregate technological change that impacts all sectors equally. This approach was first developed in Greenwood et al. (1997), who document and discuss investment-specific technological change and its impact on long-run growth. Biased technological change has also been used to study wage inequality (Krusell et al., 2000) and business cycles (Fisher, 2006; Justiniano et al., 2010).

The two-sector stochastic growth model we study consists of a primary sector, $i = 1$, producing C_{Mt}, which is the sum of consumer services, nondurable consumption and government consumption, and I_{st}, which is investment in structures.[f] The second sector, $i = 2$, produces equipment I_{et} and consumer durables I_{dt}. The technologies associated with each sector are as follows:

$$C_{Mt} + I_{st} = Y_{1t} = z_t A K_{e1t}^{\theta_1} K_{s1t}^{\theta_2} H_{1t}^{1-\theta_1-\theta_2} \tag{13}$$

$$I_{dt} + I_{et} = Y_{2t} = q_t z_t A K_{e2t}^{\theta_1} K_{s2t}^{\theta_2} H_{2t}^{1-\theta_1-\theta_2} \tag{14}$$

All variables are measured in per capita terms with a population growth factor η. Here, K_{eit}, K_{sit} and H_{it} are equipment, structures and hours worked, each in sector i.

[f] We will also lump investment in intellectual property with investment in structures.

The variables z_t and q_t are technology shocks that impact these sectors. The laws of motion for the stocks of equipment, structures, and durables is given by the following, where $K_{e,t} = K_{e1t} + K_{e2t}$ and $K_{s,t} = K_{s1t} + K_{s2t}$:

$$\eta K_{e,t+1} = (1-\delta_e)K_{et} + I_{et} \tag{15}$$

$$\eta D_{t+1} = (1-\delta_d)D_t + I_{dt} \tag{16}$$

$$\eta K_{s,t+1} = (1-\delta_s)K_{st} + I_{st} \tag{17}$$

The logarithms of the two shocks, z and q, follow random walks with drift.

$$\log z_{t+1} = \log z_t + \varepsilon_{1,t+1}\ ,\ \varepsilon_1 \sim N(\mu_1, \sigma_1^2) \tag{18}$$

$$\log q_{t+1} = \log q_t + \varepsilon_{2,t+1}\ ,\ \ \varepsilon_2 \sim N(\mu_2, \sigma_2^2) \tag{19}$$

The random variables ε_1 and ε_2 are i.i.d. across time and are contemporaneously uncorrelated.

There is a stand-in household who maximizes the expected discounted sum of utility defined over consumption of nondurables and services, the stock of durables, and leisure:

$$\max E_0 \left\{ \sum_{t=0}^{\infty} (\beta\eta)^t [\alpha \log C_{Mt} + (1-\alpha)\log D_t + \phi \log(1 - H_{1t} - H_{2t})] \right\} \tag{20}$$

Optimality implies that the value marginal product of each input will be equalized across sectors. Given that identical Cobb–Douglas production functions are assumed, this implies the fraction of the total quantity of each input assigned to each sector is the same across inputs. Letting $H_{Mt} = H_{1t} + H_{2t}$, this implies that $\frac{K_{eit}}{K_{et}} = \frac{K_{sit}}{K_{st}} = \frac{H_{it}}{H_{Mt}}$ for $i = 1,2$. Given this result, and the fact that the technology is constant returns to scale, it is possible to aggregate over sectors to obtain the aggregate resource constraint:

$$C_{Mt} + I_{st} + \frac{1}{q_t}(I_{dt} + I_{et}) = z_t A K_{et}^{\theta_1} K_{st}^{\theta_2} H_{Mt}^{1-\theta_1-\theta_2} \equiv Y_t \tag{21}$$

Note that in this aggregate resource constraint, the outputs I_d and I_e are divided by q. In the decentralized version of this economy, $\frac{1}{q}$ is the price of equipment goods relative to output from sector 1. This result shows that data on the relative price of equipment can be used to measure equipment-specific technological change.

Given values for K_{e0}, K_{s0} and D_0, the equilibrium stochastic process for this economy can be found by solving the planner's problem maximizing (20) subject to (15)–(19) and (21).

4.2.1 Balanced Growth Path

Due to the positive drift in the random walks (18) and (19), this model exhibits stochastic growth. In a certainty version of the model in which $\sigma_1 = \sigma_2 = 0$, there is a balanced growth path where the asymptotic growth factors are given by $g_c = \frac{Y_{t+1}}{Y_t} = \frac{C_{M,t+1}}{C_{Mt}} = \frac{I_{s,t+1}}{I_{st}} = \frac{K_{s,t+1}}{Kst} = e^{\frac{\mu_1+\theta_1\mu_2}{1-\theta_1-\theta_2}}$ and $g_e = \frac{I_{e,t+1}}{I_{et}} = \frac{I_{d,t+1}}{I_{dt}} = \frac{K_{e,t+1}}{Ket} = \frac{D_{t+1}}{D_t} = g_c e^{\mu_2}$. Given these growth factors, the asymptotic growth path can be written $Y_t = g_c^t \bar{Y}$, $H_{Mt} = \bar{H}_M$, $C_{Mt} = g_c^t \bar{C}_M$, $I_{st} = g_c^t \bar{I}_s$, $K_{st} = g_c^t \bar{K}_s$, $I_{et} = g_e^t \bar{I}_e$. $I_{dt} = g_e^t \bar{I}_d$, $K_{et} = g_e^t \bar{K}_e$ and $D_t = g_e^t \bar{D}$, where the steady state values are the solutions to the following equations (given $\bar{q}$ and $\bar{z}$):

$$\frac{g_c}{\beta} = \theta_2 \frac{\bar{Y}}{\bar{K}_s} + 1 - \delta_s \tag{22}$$

$$\frac{g_e}{\beta} = \theta_1 \frac{\bar{Y}}{\bar{K}_e} \frac{\bar{q}}{} + 1 - \delta_e \tag{23}$$

$$\frac{g_e}{\beta} = \frac{(1-\alpha)\bar{C}_M}{\alpha \bar{D}} \frac{\bar{q}}{} + 1 - \delta_d \tag{24}$$

$$\frac{\phi}{1-\bar{H}_M} = \alpha(1-\theta_1-\theta_2)\frac{\bar{Y}}{\bar{H}_M \bar{C}_M} \tag{25}$$

$$\bar{Y} = A\bar{K}_e^{\theta_1}\bar{K}_s^{\theta_2}\bar{H}_M^{1-\theta_1-\theta_2} \tag{26}$$

$$\bar{C}_M = \bar{Y} - \bar{I}_s - \frac{1}{\bar{q}}[\bar{I}_e + \bar{I}_d] \tag{27}$$

$$\bar{I}_s = (\delta_s + \eta g_c - 1)\bar{K}_s \tag{28}$$

$$\bar{I}_e = (\delta_e + \eta g_e - 1)\bar{K}_e \tag{29}$$

$$\bar{I}_d = (\delta_d + \eta g_e - 1)\bar{D} \tag{30}$$

We use this nonstochastic asymptotic growth path to help us calibrate the model and to construct capital stock series that are consistent with the model's balanced growth properties.

4.2.2 Calibrating the Model with US Data

We proceed by connecting each endogenous variable of this model with a counterpart taken from the US National Income and Product Accounts. The data we use runs from

1954Q1 to 2014Q4. On the product side, the model has one nondurable consumption good (C_{Mt}) which we take to be the sum of nondurable consumption, services and government consumption. There are three forms of investment: I_e is the sum of private and government investment in equipment; I_s is the sum of private investment in structures, intellectual property, residential structures, and government investment in structures and intellectual property; and I_d is purchases of consumer durables. Given that we have not allocated every component of Gross Domestic Product to one of these expenditure categories, we take total output to be $Y_t = C_M + I_s + \frac{1}{q}(I_d + I_e)$. The relative price of equipment in our model is equal to $\frac{1}{q_t}$, so we identify q_t from the relative price of equipment calculated by Riccardo DiCecio (see DiCecio, 2009).[g]

The capital stocks, which are the sum of both private and government fixed assets, are computed from annual quantity indexes of fixed assets obtained from the Bureau of Economic Analysis and is the stock associated with each investment series. In particular, K_s is nonresidential and residential structures along with intellectual property, K_e is the stock of equipment, and D is the stock of consumer durables. To obtain quarterly real stocks of capital, the annual quantity indexes are multiplied by the corresponding 2009 nominal value and quarterly series are obtained by iterating on the laws of motion (15)–(17) using the corresponding quarterly investment series.[h] Per capita capital stocks and output are obtained by dividing by the civilian population (16–64) plus military personnel. Finally, the hours series we use is average weekly hours per person (including military hours) based on data from the Current Population Survey. In particular, we have updated the series created by Cociuba et al. (2012).

Given these empirical counterparts, the growth factor for population is $\eta = 1.003$ and the growth factor for per capita output is $g_c = 1.0036$. The parameter $\mu_2 = 0.0104$, which is the average of $\log q_{t+1} - \log q_t$. This implies that $g_e = g_c e^{\mu_2} = 1.014$.

[g] This data series is available on the FRED database maintained by the Federal Reserve Bank of St. Louis.

[h] Given that the model assumes constant depreciation rates, which does not hold in our data sample, we allow the depreciation rate to vary across 10 year periods when constructing the quarterly capital stock series. That is, an initial value for the annual series in year t and a terminal value in year $t + 10$, we find the depreciation rate such that iterations on the law of motion of the capital stock hits the terminal value in 40 quarters using the corresponding quarterly investment series.

In particular, we find the depreciation rate δ_i for decade i such that $K_{i+10} = (1-\delta_i)^{40} K_i + \sum_{j=1}^{40} (1-\delta_i)^{40-j} I_j$, where K_i is the capital stock at the beginning of year i, K_{i+10} is capital at the beginning of year $i + 10$, and $\{I_j\}_{j=1}^{40}$ is investment for each quarter between those dates. Once we know δ_i for each subperiod in our sample, it is straightforward to construct quarterly capital stocks for each quarter of year i.

The capital stock obtained, however, is inconsistent with the trend introduced by our empirical measure of q, which is based on different price deflators than those used in producing the NIPA capital stocks. As a result, we also adjust the trend growth of the capital stocks so that these stocks are consistent with long-run growth properties of the model. That is, a trend is added to our quarterly series for K_s so that it has an average growth rate equal to g_c and D and K_e are similarly adjusted to have an average growth factor g_e.

We calibrate the model by setting $\beta = 0.99$, labor's share, $1 - \theta_1 - \theta_2$, equal to 0.6 and the depreciation rates equal to the average of the depreciation rates obtained when forming the quarterly capital stock series. This gives us $\delta_e = 0.021$, $\delta_s = 0.008$, and $\delta_d = 0.05$. The individual capital shares are based on estimates in Valentinyi and Herrendorf (2008) renormalized so they sum to 0.4. In particular, we set $\theta_1 = 0.21$ and $\theta_2 = 0.19$. The parameter α is computed from a version of equation (24) where the term $\frac{\bar{C}_M\ \bar{q}}{\bar{D}}$ is replaced with the average value of $\frac{C_{M,t}\ q_t}{D_t}$ from the empirical counterparts to these variables. This gives $\alpha = 0.817$.

Next, we set $\bar{Y}$, $\bar{H}_M$, and $\bar{q}$ equal to the initial observation in the time series for each of these variables. The seven remaining steady states ($\bar{K}_s$, $\bar{K}_e$, $\bar{D}$, $\bar{I}_s$, $\bar{I}_e$, $\bar{I}_d$, and $\bar{C}_M$) are obtained by solving seven equations (22)–(24) and (27)–(30). So that the steady state capital stocks are equal to the first observations for these variables, we multiply all observations of K_s by $\frac{\bar{K}_s}{K_{s,0}}$, all observations of K_e by $\frac{\bar{K}_e}{K_{e,0}}$ and all observations of D by $\frac{\bar{D}}{D_0}$. These are the capital stocks used to construct the empirical counterpart to z_t.

We construct a quarterly time series for the exogenous shock, z_t, from 1954Q1 to 2014Q4 by setting $z_t = \frac{Y_t}{AK_{et}^{\theta_1} K_{st}^{\theta_2} H_{Mt}^{1-\theta_1-\theta_2}}$ where the parameter A is chosen so that the first observation of z is equal to one. This implies $A = 6.21$. Somewhat surprisingly, the growth rate of z_t when computed in this way turns out to be zero ($\mu_1 = 0$). That is, when measured through the lens of this model, the average rate of growth in per capita income during the postwar period is accounted for entirely by equipment specific technological improvement.

We summarize the calibration of the model in Table 1 in the column labeled "Two sector." This table reports the calibrated parameter values for all models considered, so we will refer back to this table as we discuss these alternatives.

4.2.3 Comparison of Model with Data

Given our time series for z_t and q_t, times series for the endogenous variables of the model are computed for the sample period 1954Q1–2014Q4. This is done using log-linear approximations of the decision rules that solve the planner's problem obtained using standard numerical methods (see, for example, Uhlig, 1999). Fig. 17 shows our measures of output and hours from US data along with the time series for these variables implied by our model.

Output from the data and model are quite close to each other until the mid-1980s when model output becomes lower than in the data. By 2002, however, model output has recovered. Model hours tend to be higher than in the data during the 1960s and 1970s, and lower from the mid-1980s until the Great Recession. Following the Great Recession, the data shows some recovery in hours worked that the model does not.

Table 1 Calibrated parameter values

Parameter description		Two sector	One sector	Three sector (1)	Three sector (2)
Equipment share	θ_1	0.21		0.21	0.21
Structures share	θ_2	0.19		0.19	0.19
Capital share	θ		0.4		
Depreciation rate—Equipment	δ_E	0.021		0.021	0.021
Depreciation rate—Structures	δ_S	0.008		0.008	0.008
Depreciation rate—Durables	δ_D	0.05		0.05	0.05
Depreciation rate—Capital	δ		0.013		
Growth rate—z	μ_1	0		0	0
Growth rate—q	μ_2	0.0104		0.0104	0.0104
Growth rate—z	μ		0.0021		
Population growth factor	η	1.003	1.003	1.003	1.003
Discount factor	β	0.99	0.99	0.99	0.99
Utility share for mkt. consumption	α	0.82		0.33	0.53
Utility parameter for leisure	ϕ	2.37	2.37	1.19	1.19
Scale parameter—Market production	A	6.21	2.7	6.21	6.21
Elasticity parameter—Home production	σ			0	0.4
Elasticity parameter—Mkt./non-mkt. cons.	ω			0.6	0
Durable share—Home production	φ			0.25	0.13
Scale parameter—Home production	A_N			4.19	4.87

Three sector (1)—Standard home production
Three sector (2)—Calibration inspired by Greenwood et al. (2005)

Fig. 18 consists of four panels showing output, hours, consumption and investment—from both the model and the data—that has been filtered to show only fluctuations between 2 and 32 quarters. The real business cycle literature has demonstrated that neoclassical models of this sort generate fluctuations similar to those in postwar US data at this frequency. As the figure illustrates, this is particularly true for output and investment.

Less studied, however, are the low frequency fluctuations exhibited by models of this sort. Fig. 19 is a plot of model and US data for the same four variables that has been filtered to show fluctuations between 32 and 200 quarters. The model seems to do a pretty good job in tracking fluctuations in output, consumption and investment in this frequency band. For hours worked, the model captures some of the low frequency movements, but not others. In the late 1950s, the model shows hours falling sooner than it does in the data, while the model and data track pretty closely during the 1960s and early 1970s. In the late 1970s, the data shows an increase in hours worked that the model does not capture, but the model and data follow each other throughout the 1980s and 1990s. At the time of the Great Recession, the decline in hours—as well as other macro aggregates—is less in the model than in the data.

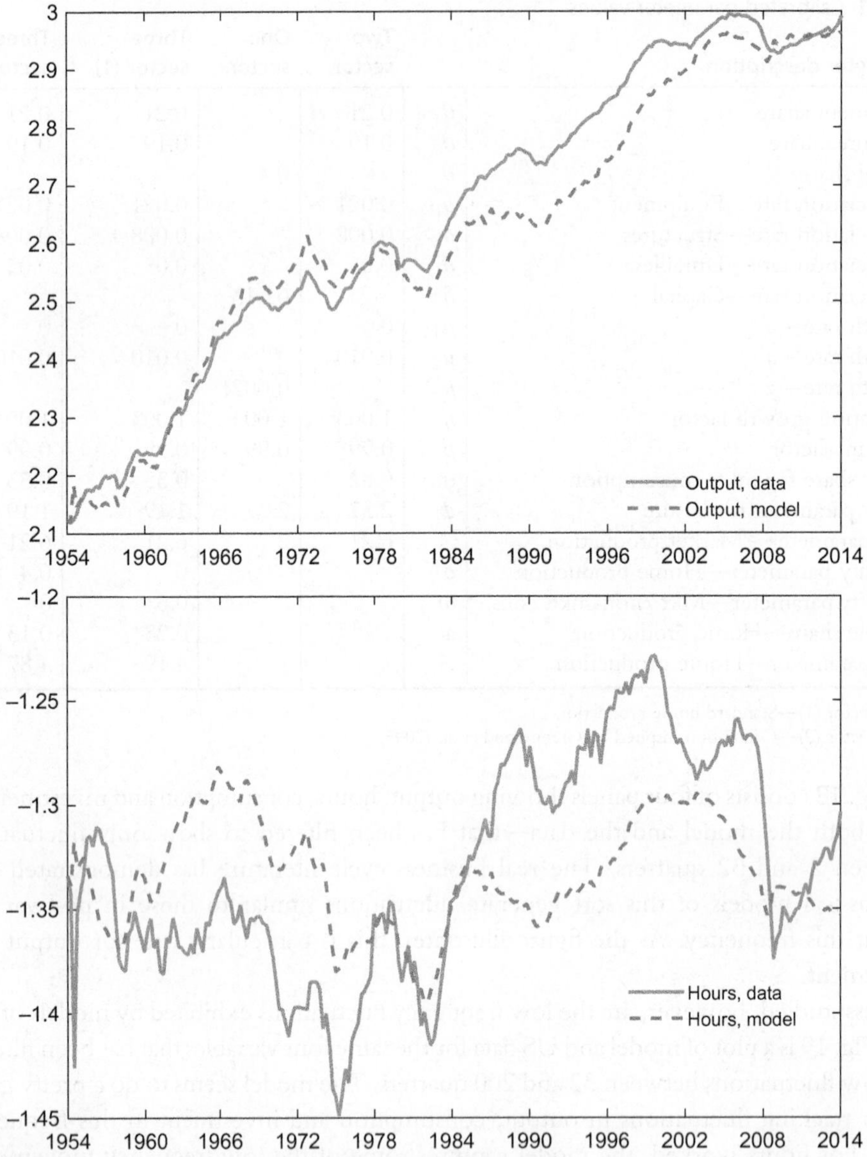

Fig. 17 Output and hours worked, data and two-sector model.

Fig. 20 plots the same data as the previous figure for filtered output and hours for both the 2–32 quarter frequency and the 32–200 quarter frequency. The difference is that we have included a third time series in each plot that shows simulated data under the assumption that there were no fluctuations in z_t and only fluctuations in q_t. That is, when

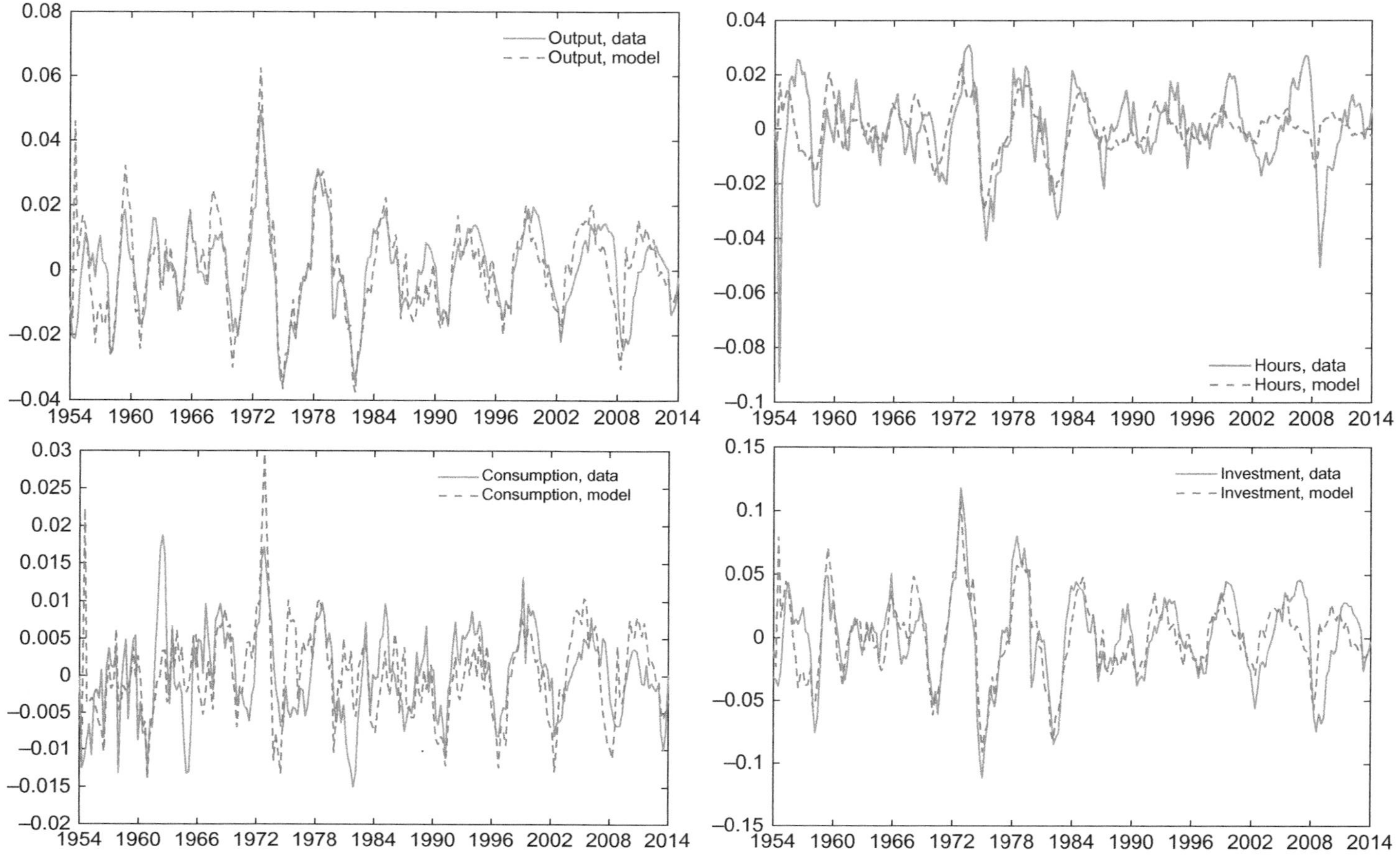

Fig. 18 Filtered actual and two-sector model data (2–32 quarters).

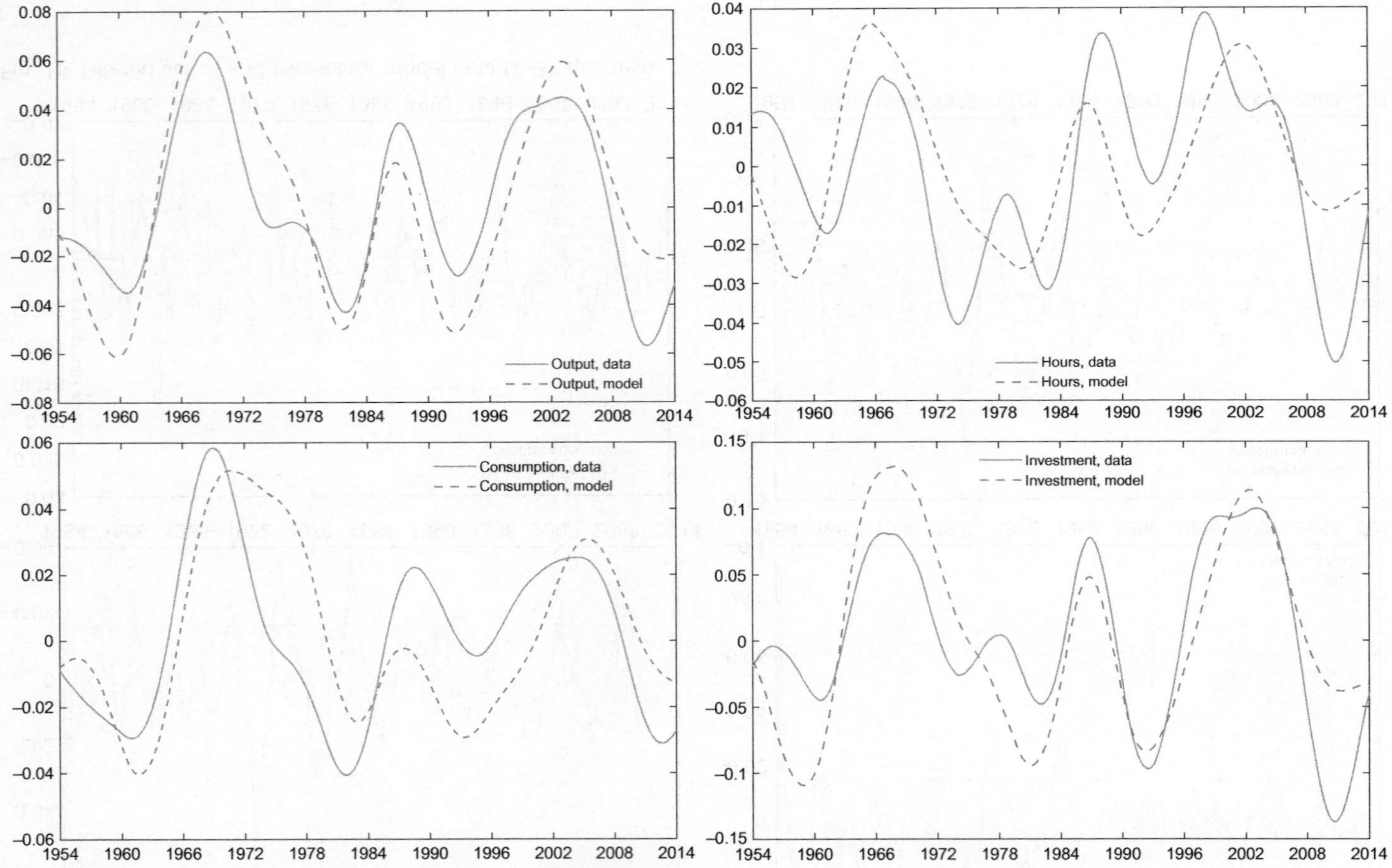

Fig. 19 Filtered actual and two-sector model data (32–200 quarters).

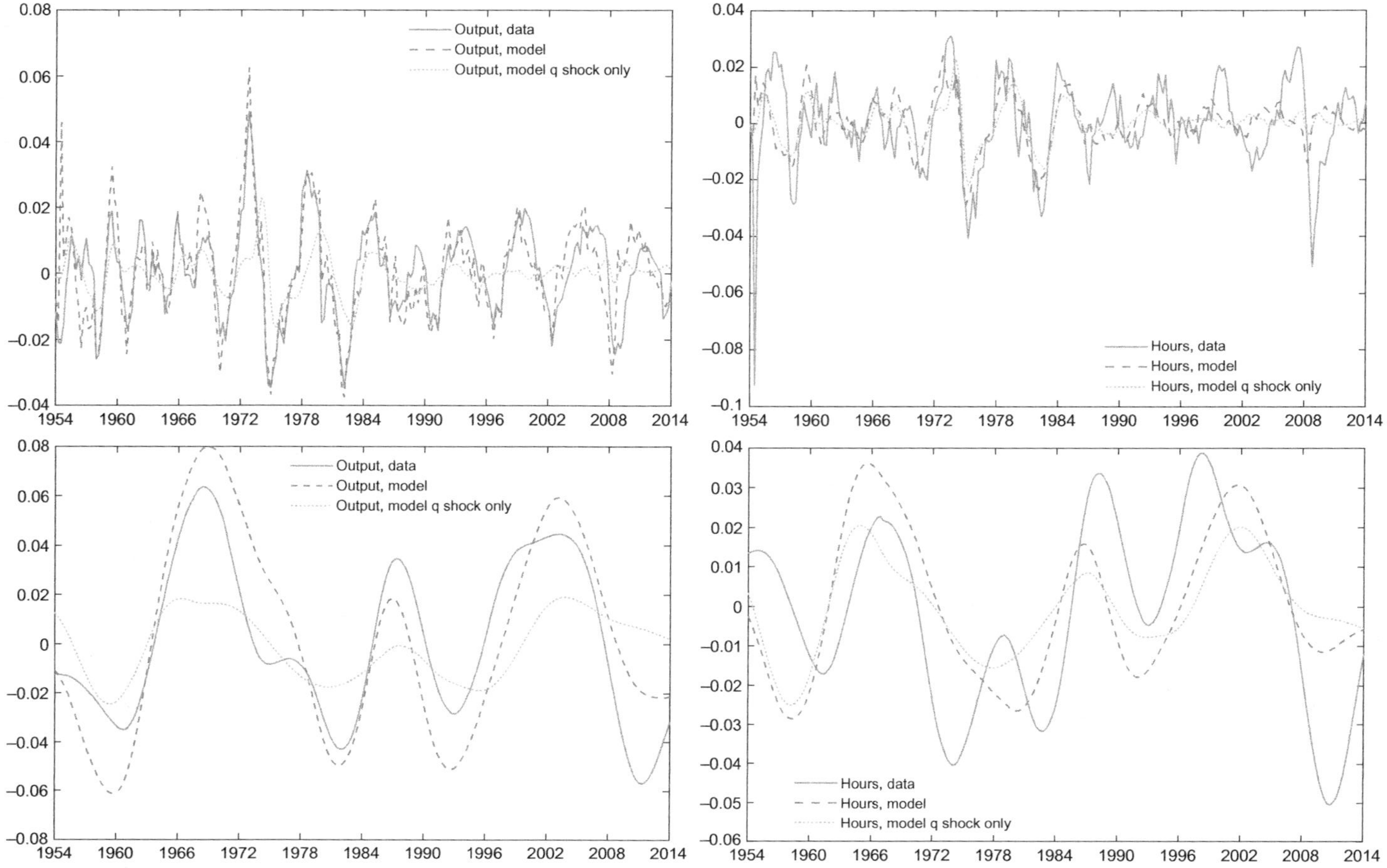

Fig. 20 Contribution of equipment specific technology fluctuations.

computing the simulation, the time series for z_t is replaced by the nonstochastic growth path for z. That is, $z_t = e^{t\mu_1}$ for all t.

This figure shows that much of the high and low frequency fluctuations in hours worked are due to movements in q_t, but this is not as true for fluctuations in output. It is also less true for business cycle fluctuations in hours worked in more recent decades.

4.3 One-Sector Model

We now proceed to compare the fluctuations exhibited by the two-sector model with a standard one-sector neoclassical stochastic growth model. This one-sector economy consists of a single production sector that produces output from capital and labor that can be consumed or invested. It differs from the two-sector model in that there is only one type of capital stock, no separate role for consumer durables, and one type of technology shock. In particular, the resource constraint, which replaces equation (21), is

$$C_t + I_t = Y_t = z_t A K_t^{\theta} H_t^{1-\theta}. \tag{31}$$

The law of motion for capital next period is given by

$$\eta K_{t+1} = (1-\delta)K_t + I_t \tag{32}$$

where the depreciation rate is $0 < \delta \leq 1$ and $1 \leq \eta \leq \frac{1}{\beta}$ is the population growth factor. The logarithm of the technology shock, z_t, is assumed to follow a random walk with drift ($\mu \geq 0$). We assume that the period t realization of z is observed at the beginning of the period.

$$\log z_{t+1} = \log z_t + \varepsilon_{t+1}\ , \ \varepsilon \sim N(\mu, \sigma^2) \tag{33}$$

The preferences of the representative infinitely-lived household are given by

$$E\sum_{t=0}^{\infty}(\beta\eta)^t[\log C_t + \phi \log L_t] \tag{34}$$

where $0 < \beta < 1$ and $\phi > 0$. The variable L_t is leisure, where

$$L_t + H_t = 1. \tag{35}$$

Given K_0, we compute an equilibrium sequence for $\{C_t, I_t, Y_t, H_t, L_t, K_{t+1}\}$ by maximizing (34) subject to (31)–(33) and (35).

4.3.1 Calibrating the One-Sector Model with US Data

For comparison purposes, we begin by keeping the definition of output the same as in the two-sector model, $Y = C + I_s + \frac{1}{q}(I_d + I_e)$. Given that there is no separate role for consumer durables in this model, we define investment in the one-sector model to be

$I = I_s + \frac{I_e}{q}$ and consumption to be the sum of nondurable consumption plus services and $\frac{I_d}{q}$. That is, $C_t = C_{Mt} + \frac{I_d}{q}$, where C_M is consumption from the two-sector model. The capital stock is the sum $K = K_e + K_s$. The quarterly capital stock series for this sum is formed using the same method as for the two-sector model and the quarterly depreciation rate turns out to be $\delta = 0.013$. As in the two-sector model, $\beta = 0.99$ and labor's share is taken to be 0.6, so $\theta = 0.4$. Given this, a quarterly time series for the exogenous shock z_t, from 1954Q1 to 2014Q4, is constructed by setting $z_t = \frac{Y_t}{AK_t^{\theta} H_t^{1-\theta}}$, where the parameter A is set so that $z_0 = 1$. This implies that $A = 2.7$. In addition, the drift parameter, μ, turns out to be 0.0021.

As in the two-sector model, we set the steady state values for K, H and Y equal to the first observation in our data sample (for 1954Q1). Steady state consumption is then obtained from the steady state version of the resource constraint (31). We can then calibrate the parameter ϕ from the steady state condition for hours worked. That is, $\phi = \frac{(1-\theta)\bar{Y}(1-\bar{H})}{\bar{C}\ \bar{H}} = 2.37$.

To facilitate comparison across models, the parameter values are also reported in Table 1.

4.3.2 Comparing the One- and Two-Sector Models with US Data

Table 2 provides two metrics for comparing the closeness of the one- and two-sector model simulations with filtered data. These measures include the ratio of the standard deviations of the model series with the standard deviation of the data series. This provides a measure of how well the model is capturing the volatility in the data. The second measure is the correlation between the model simulations and the data. We report these measures for data filtered to extract fluctuations of 2–32 quarters, 32–200 quarters and 2–200 quarters. In all cases, a number closer to one implies a better fit.[i]

The table shows that the correlation between model and data for business cycle fluctuations is higher for the two-sector model, with the exception of consumption. For low frequency fluctuations, the one-sector model does slightly better, although the correlation between hours worked from the model and data is slightly higher for the two-sector model. The volatility of the various series is generally better accounted for by the two-sector model. Hence, the main conclusion we draw from this table is that the two-sector model fits the data better than the one-sector model, with the exception of consumption fluctuations. We find it interesting that the two-sector model is able to account for

[i] In this table and subsequent tables, we only use data starting from 1955Q1. The reason is that there is an unusual hours observation in 1954 that can be seen in Fig. 17, and we don't want that observation distorting the statistics reported in these tables.

Table 2 Comparing models with data (1955Q1–2014Q4)

	One-sector model		Two-sector model	
	Standard deviation model/data	**Correlation model and data**	**Standard deviation model/data**	**Correlation model and data**
2–32 Quarters				
Y	0.86	0.80	1.09	0.84
C	0.73	0.82	1.00	0.56
I	0.71	0.64	0.86	0.79
H	0.30	0.18	0.63	0.48
32–200 Quarters				
Y	0.85	0.88	1.21	0.86
C	0.70	0.78	1.07	0.64
I	0.81	0.82	1.08	0.81
H	0.35	0.51	0.81	0.53
2–200 Quarters				
Y	0.86	0.86	1.21	0.84
C	0.72	0.77	1.09	0.62
I	0.80	0.77	1.05	0.79
H	0.33	0.40	0.74	0.50

volatility in spite of the fact that we have assumed random walk technology shocks and divisible labor. These are both assumptions that tend to reduce the size of fluctuations.[j]

Fig. 21 provides the same information as Fig. 20 except that the comparison is now with the one-sector simulation for output and hours rather the "q-shock" only simulation. The figure illustrates that much of the low frequency movements in output can be accounted for by the one-sector model almost as well as the two sector. The low frequency volatility of hours, however, is better explained by the two-sector model than the one sector.

4.4 A Three-Sector Model

This section studies a model constructed by adding a nonmarket home production sector to the two-sector model. We develop the three-sector model with two alternative home production specifications. One is the standard home production specification of Benhabib et al. (1991) and much of the literature that follows from this. This formulation

[j] See Hansen (1985) concerning the impact of divisible labor on fluctuations and Hansen (1997) for the impact of random walk technology shocks.

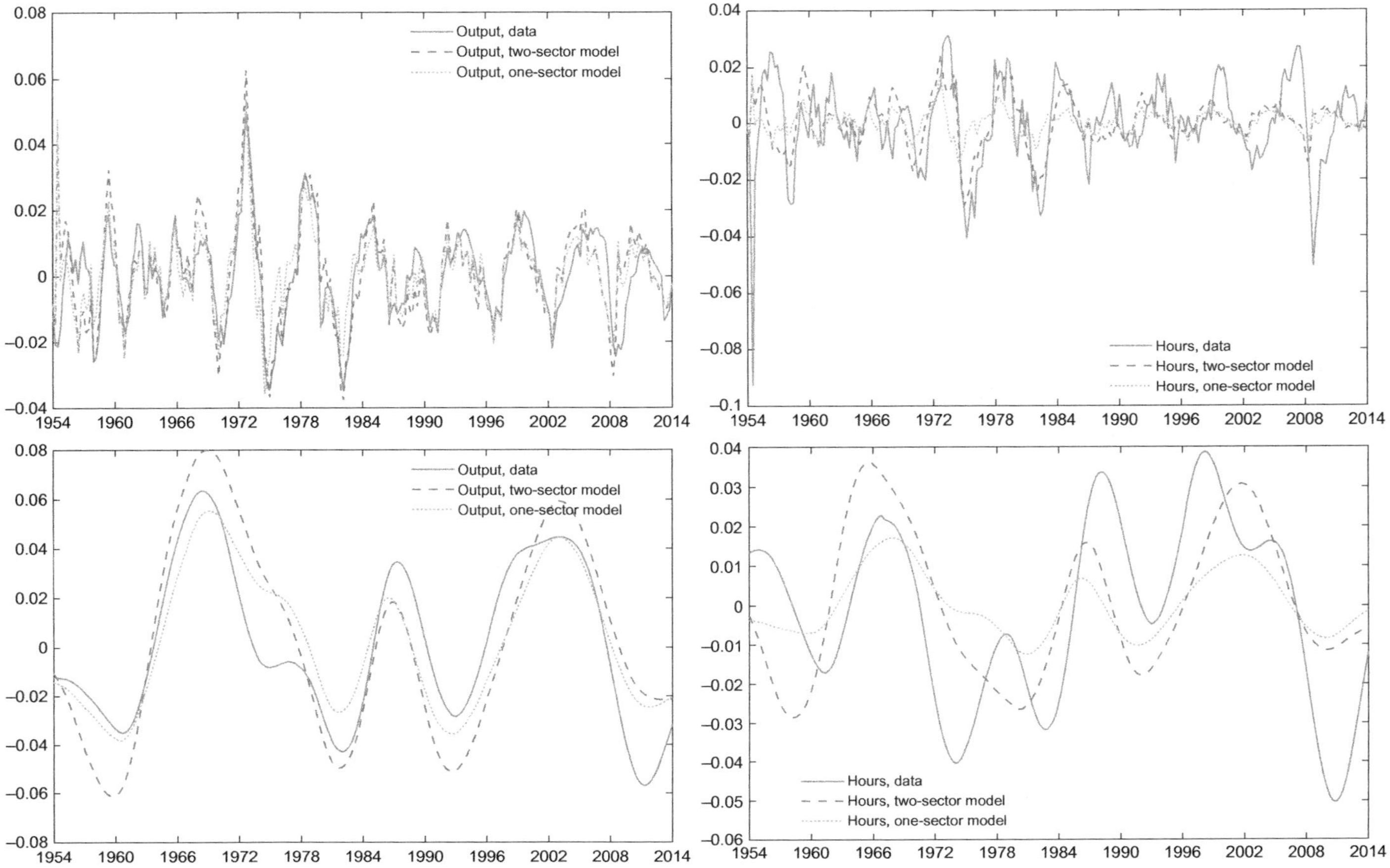

Fig. 21 Comparison of two-sector and one-sector models.

provides an additional margin of substitution for the household in which time can be allocated to market production, home production, or leisure. In the Benhabib, Rogerson and Wright model, there is a relatively high substitution elasticity between home-produced goods and market-produced goods, and this high elasticity generates significant movement of labor between the home sector and market sector in response to shocks. Home goods are produced using a Cobb–Douglas technology with labor and consumer durables.

The alternative home production formulation is motivated by Greenwood et al. (2005), which argues that rapid technological change in labor-saving consumer durables has secularly reallocated time from home production to market production, mainly by women moving into the labor force. In this specification, consumer durables are more substitutable with labor than in the Benhabib et al. (1991) specification that assumes a Cobb–Douglas technology for the home sector.

The model presented here nests both of these specifications. In particular, we assume that a nonmarket consumption good, C_{Nt}, is produced using labor (H_{Nt}) and the stock of consumer durables. As in Greenwood et al. (2005), we allow for the possibility that durables and labor are more substitutable than implied by the standard Cobb–Douglas production function. In particular, we assume the following functional form for the home production function with $\sigma > 0$:

$$C_{Nt} = A_N \left[\varphi \left(\frac{D_t}{e^{\mu_2 t}} \right)^{\sigma} + (1-\varphi)(g_c^t H_{Nt})^{\sigma} \right]^{\frac{1}{\sigma}} \tag{36}$$

The standard version of the model can be recovered by making σ close to zero. Note that the terms $e^{\mu_2 t}$ and g_c^t are included here to guarantee that C_{Nt} grows at the same rate as total output along the balanced growth path.

The second modification relative to the two-sector model is to replace the objective function (20) with the following:

$$\max E_0 \left\{ \sum_{t=0}^{\infty} (\beta\eta)^t [\log C_t + \phi \log(1 - H_{Mt} - H_{Nt})] \right\}, \tag{37}$$

where consumption, C_t, is a composite consumption good, standard in the home production literature, derived from market and nonmarket consumption goods

$$C_t = \left[\alpha C_{Mt}^{\omega} + (1-\alpha) C_{Nt}^{\omega} \right]^{\frac{1}{\omega}} \tag{38}$$

Given values for K_{e0}, K_{s0} and D_0, the equilibrium stochastic process for this economy can be found by solving the planner's problem maximizing (37) subject to (15)–(19), (21), (36), and (38).

4.4.1 Calibrating the Three-Sector Model to US Data

The calibration strategy is exactly the same as for the two-sector case, although the model introduces four new parameters (A_N, φ, ω, and σ) and two other parameters (α and ϕ) have different interpretations in this model. In addition, two new variables are introduced that are not directly observable in the US data. These are nonmarket consumption (C_N) and nonmarket hours worked (H_N). In the absence of measured counterparts to these variables, we assume that in steady state $\frac{\bar{C}_N}{\bar{C}_M}=0.25$ and $\bar{H}_N=\frac{1}{6}$, which are values consistent with the home production literature. The mapping between all other model variables and US time series is the same as in the two-sector model.

The steady state values for $\bar{K}_s$, $\bar{K}_e$, $\bar{Y}$, $\bar{C}_M$, $\bar{I}_s$, $\bar{I}_e$, $\bar{I}_d$, $\bar{D}$, $\bar{H}_M$, $\bar{H}_N$, $\bar{C}_N$, and $\bar{C}$ are determined by Eqs. (22), (23), (26)–(30), and the following five equations:

$$\frac{g_E}{\beta}=\frac{(1-\alpha)A_N^{\sigma}\varphi\bar{q}\bar{C}_M^{1-\omega}}{\alpha\bar{C}_N^{\sigma-\omega}\bar{D}^{1-\sigma}}+1-\delta_D \tag{39}$$

$$\frac{\phi}{1-\bar{H}_M-\bar{H}_N}=\alpha(1-\theta_1-\theta_2)\frac{\bar{Y}}{\bar{H}_M\bar{C}^{\omega}\bar{C}_M^{1-\omega}} \tag{40}$$

$$\frac{\phi}{1-\bar{H}_M-\bar{H}_N}=\frac{(1-\alpha)A_N^{\sigma}(1-\varphi)}{\bar{H}_N^{1-\sigma}\bar{C}^{\omega}\bar{C}_N^{\sigma-\omega}} \tag{41}$$

$$\bar{C}_N=A_N\left[\varphi\bar{D}^{\sigma}+(1-\varphi)\bar{H}_N^{\sigma}\right]^{\frac{1}{\sigma}} \tag{42}$$

$$\bar{C}=\left[\alpha\bar{C}_M^{\omega}+(1-\alpha)\bar{C}_N^{\omega}\right]^{\frac{1}{\omega}}. \tag{43}$$

We experiment with two different sets of values for the parameters σ and ω to differentiate between our two home production specifications. Given values for these parameters, values for α, ϕ, φ and A_N can be obtained from equations (39) to (42) subject to $\frac{\bar{C}_N}{\bar{C}_M}=0.25$, $\bar{H}_N=\frac{1}{6}$ and $\bar{C}$ is given by equation (43).[k]

The first calibration we consider is referred to as the "standard home production" model. In this case, $\omega=0.6$ and $\sigma=0$, which corresponds to values common in the home production literature (see Chang and Schorfheide, 2003). In this case, the utility function (38) allows for more substitutability between home consumption and market consumption than implied by a Cobb–Douglas specification while the home production

[k] We also use the fact that, as in the two-sector case, we choose parameters so that $\bar{q}$, $\bar{H}_M$ and $\bar{Y}$ are the first observation in our data sample.

function (36) is assumed to be Cobb–Douglas. The second calibration, which we refer to as the "alternative home production" model, is motivated by Greenwood et al. (2005) and sets $\omega = 0$ and $\sigma = 0.4$. Here, (38) is assumed to be Cobb–Douglas and we allow for an elasticity of substitution between durables and hours that is greater than 1 in the home production function (36). The parameter values associated with both calibrations are given in Table 1.

4.4.2 Fluctuations in the Three-Sector Model

We begin by comparing the simulations produced by the two versions of the three-sector model that we consider. Fig. 22 shows unfiltered output and hours from the two models as well as from the US time series. Both models account for output movements quite well, although the alternative calibration does a somewhat better job in the 1960s and 1970s while the standard home production calibration fits the data better in the 1980s and 1990s. Both models imply similar paths during the Great Recession period. The same is also true for hours worked—the alternative calibration does better during the early periods and less well during the 1980s and 1990s. Both calibrations give essentially identical results during the 2000s.

An interesting difference between hours worked from the two models can be seen from examining the period from about 1982 to 2000. The rise in hours worked predicted by the alternative calibration during this period is significantly larger than that predicted by the standard home production model. In the spirit of Greenwood et al. (2005), this calibration does a better job of capturing the secular increase in hours worked that occurs over this period, mainly due to women entering the labor force. As one can see from Fig. 23, this difference does not appear in the low frequency fluctuations that we report.

The two calibrations, however, give essentially the same results once the data is filtered. Fig. 23 illustrates this by plotting filtered data for output and hours from the two versions of the model. The data for both business cycle fluctuations as well as low frequency fluctuations essentially lay on top of each other. In particular, the alternative home production model does not exhibit the significantly larger increase in hours worked relative to the standard home production model during the 1980s and 1990s as was observed in Fig. 22.

The closeness of the filtered data from these models with filtered data from US time series is illustrated in Fig. 24 and Table 3. Fig. 24 shows filtered data from the standard home production calibration and the US economy for output and hours. When one compares the panels in Fig. 24 with the corresponding panels in Figs. 18 and 19, the results from the home production model appear very similar to the two-sector model with slightly more volatility in hours worked at both sets of frequencies.

The same sorts of conclusions that can be drawn from Fig. 24 are also apparent in Table 3. This table provides the same set of statistics as in Table 2 for comparing model data with actual data. Here, we compare both calibrations of our three-sector model with the US time series.

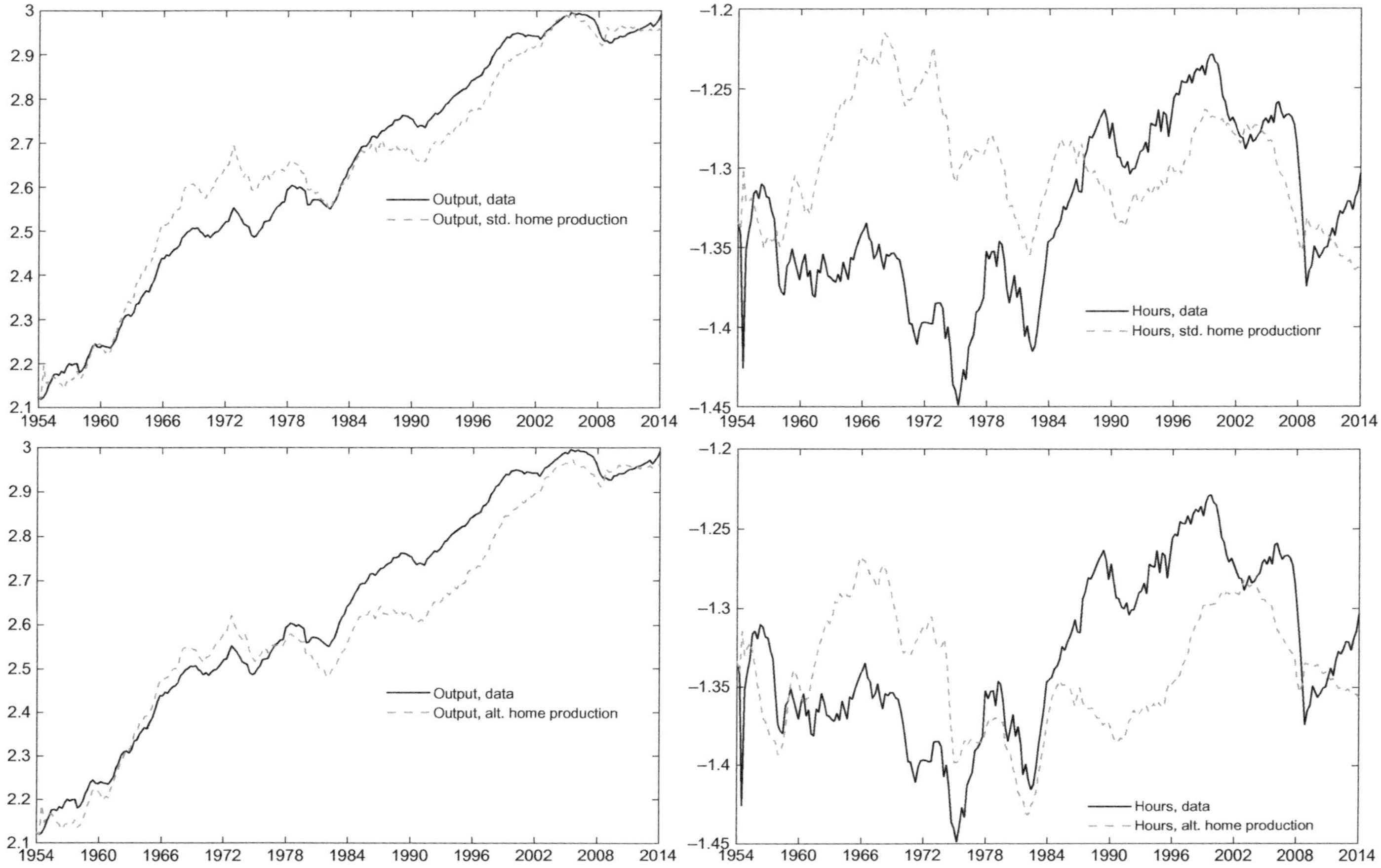

Fig. 22 Standard home production and alternative—output and hours.

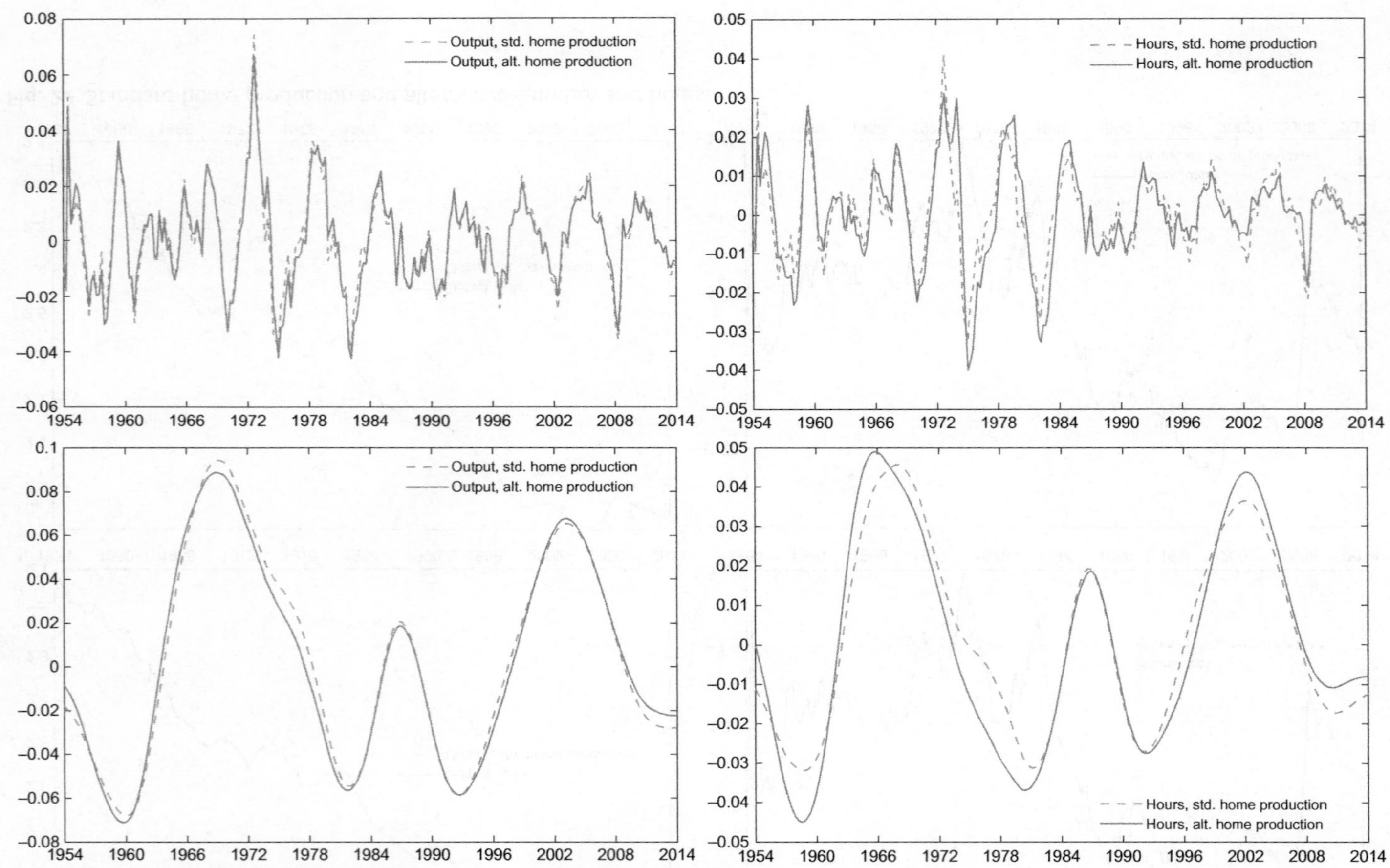

Fig. 23 Standard home production and alternative—filtered output and hours.

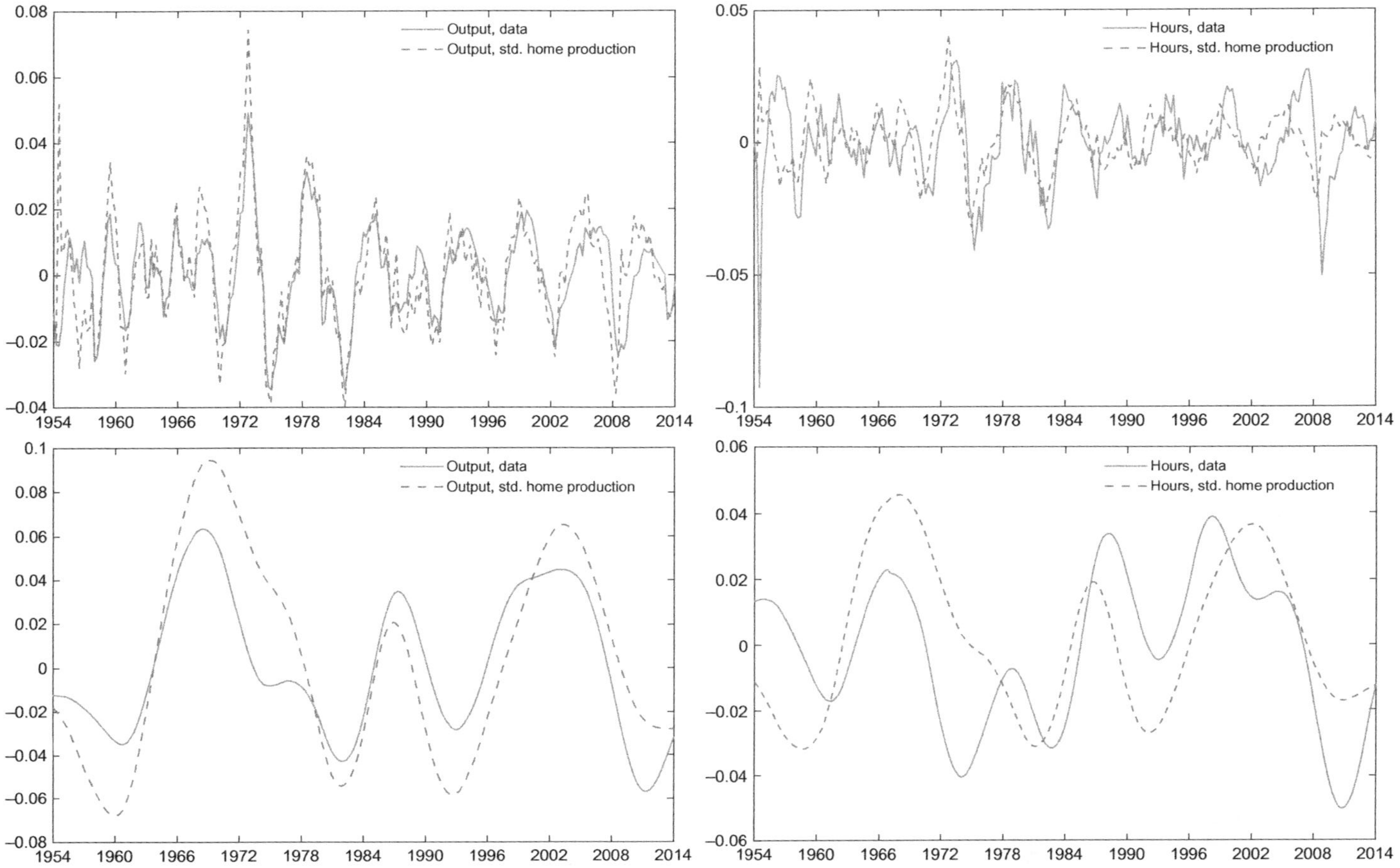

Fig. 24 Standard home production and data—filtered output and hours.

Table 3 Comparing models with data (1955Q1–2014Q4)

	Standard home production ($\omega = 0.6$ and $\sigma = 0$)		Alternative ($\omega = 0$ and $\sigma = 0.4$)	
	Standard deviation model/data	**Correlation model and data**	**Standard deviation model/data**	**Correlation model and data**
2–32 Quarters				
Y	1.23	0.84	1.23	0.84
C	1.52	0.50	1.02	0.39
I	0.95	0.80	1.09	0.78
H	0.76	0.39	0.89	0.50
32–200 Quarters				
Y	1.43	0.84	1.41	0.84
C	1.42	0.58	1.03	0.51
I	1.20	0.80	1.38	0.77
H	1.02	0.50	1.16	0.48
2–200 Quarters				
Y	1.43	0.86	1.41	0.83
C	1.45	0.56	1.05	0.49
I	1.15	0.78	1.32	0.75
H	0.95	0.44	1.07	0.45

The final set of tables we present in this section report the statistics for comparing model simulation and actual data for three subperiods of the postwar period. Table 4 looks only at the early postwar period from 1955Q1 to 1983Q4 and Table 5 reports statistics for the Great Moderation period from 1984Q1 to 2007Q3. Finally, statistics for the Great Recession and after are reported in Table 6.

Which model best explains postwar fluctuations in output, consumption, investment and hours worked? These tables show that it depends on the sample period and the frequency band of interest.

In the early postwar period (Table 4), all three models do a similar job fitting the data, but different models are better at accounting for fluctuations in different frequency bands. Hours is explained the least well by all of the models, but the correlation between model and data hours is highest for the two-sector model at business cycle frequencies and the home production model for lower frequencies. Output fluctuations are best explained by the two-sector model in all frequency bands considered. Consumption fluctuations are best explained by the one-sector model and investment fluctuations are almost equally well explained by the two- and three-sector models.

A feature seen in all three of these tables is that the volatility of model data relative to actual data rises as the number of sectors is increased. This is due to the increased substitution opportunities offered by multisector economies.

Table 4 Comparing Models with data (1955Q1–1983Q4)

	One-sector model		Two-sector model		Standard home production	
	Standard deviation model/data	Correlation model and data	Standard deviation model/data	Correlation model and data	Standard deviation model/data	Correlation model and data
2–32 Quarters						
Y	0.88	0.83	1.13	0.91	1.25	0.90
C	0.74	0.84	0.92	0.55	1.46	0.45
I	0.73	0.68	0.93	0.87	1.02	0.88
H	0.33	0.24	0.74	0.66	0.86	0.53
32–200 Quarters						
Y	0.97	0.91	1.47	0.95	1.69	0.92
C	0.70	0.80	1.10	0.74	1.44	0.67
I	1.24	0.76	1.87	0.92	2.14	0.90
H	0.46	0.41	1.09	0.44	1.45	0.45
2–200 Quarters						
Y	0.96	0.89	1.42	0.94	1.63	0.91
C	0.72	0.79	1.10	0.72	1.45	0.66
I	1.09	0.72	1.52	0.87	1.66	0.84
H	0.41	0.33	0.93	0.49	1.22	0.44

Table 5 Comparing models with data (1984Q1–2007Q3)

	One-sector model		Two-sector model		Standard home production	
	Standard deviation model/data	Correlation model and data	Standard deviation model/data	Correlation model and data	Standard deviation model/data	Correlation model and data
2–32 Quarters						
Y	0.88	0.84	1.06	0.79	1.23	0.81
C	0.71	0.81	1.10	0.70	1.55	0.68
I	0.74	0.76	0.80	0.71	0.88	0.73
H	0.33	0.24	0.53	0.20	0.73	0.26
32–200 Quarters						
Y	1.02	0.92	1.43	0.93	1.60	0.94
C	0.98	0.81	1.41	0.74	1.73	0.73
I	0.77	0.95	0.96	0.95	1.04	0.96
H	0.46	0.43	0.97	0.47	1.29	0.49
2–200 Quarters						
Y	1.09	0.91	1.52	0.91	1.71	0.92
C	1.05	0.79	1.55	0.74	1.94	0.73
I	0.79	0.91	0.98	0.91	1.06	0.92
H	0.49	0.26	0.98	0.22	1.33	0.28

Table 6 Comparing models with data (2007Q4–2014Q4)

	One-sector model		Two-sector model		Standard home production	
	Standard deviation model/data	Correlation model and data	Standard deviation model/data	Correlation model and data	Standard deviation model/data	Correlation model and data
2–32 Quarters						
Y	0.77	0.42	0.99	0.43	1.20	0.40
C	0.77	0.64	1.42	0.43	2.03	0.40
I	0.52	0.14	0.57	0.30	0.63	0.26
H	0.17	−0.34	0.26	−0.21	0.41	−0.24
32–200 Quarters						
Y	0.63	0.97	0.72	0.95	0.89	0.91
C	0.73	0.99	0.79	0.99	1.11	0.99
I	0.40	0.95	0.52	0.80	0.47	0.80
H	0.14	0.82	0.22	0.90	0.36	0.87
2–200 Quarters						
Y	0.55	0.75	0.66	0.66	0.76	0.55
C	0.67	0.93	0.68	0.91	0.94	0.88
I	0.28	0.33	0.42	0.28	0.37	0.22
H	0.10	0.02	0.16	0.10	0.23	−0.01

During the Great Moderation (Table 5), the one-sector model provides the highest correlations between model and actual data for output, consumption and investment, which is different from what is observed in the earlier period. Hours, however, are slightly better explained by the three-sector model. At lower frequencies, the three-sector model shows the highest correlation for all variables except consumption.

In the most recent period (Table 6), which covers the Great Recession and aftermath, a striking finding emerges regarding hours fluctuations. All three models show negative correlations between model and data hours worked at business cycle frequencies. However, this correlation is quite high, especially for the two- and three-sector models, at lower frequencies. At business cycle frequencies, all three models do a similarly poor job in accounting for fluctuations in output and investment. Again, the one-sector model does best in explaining consumption. But, at lower frequencies, all three neoclassical models show high correlations between model and data for these three variables as well as hours worked.

It is interesting and important that the fit of the two- and three-sector models for the 32–200 component is no different during the Great Moderation than during the 1955–1983 period. This is important because some economists have argued that neoclassical models cannot fit data from this specific period because the business cycle correlation between labor productivity and hours worked becomes negative during the Great Moderation (see Gali and van Rens, 2014). We find that the change in this higher frequency statistic has no bearing on the ability of these models to fit the large, longer-run component in the data. We also note that these models also fit the 32–200 component of the data well during the Great Recession and its aftermath. However, it should be noted that this is a short data interval for measuring the long-run component.

5. NEOCLASSICAL MODELS OF DEPRESSIONS

This section describes neoclassical models of *depressions*, which are prolonged periods in which aggregate economic activity is far below trend. Kehoe and Prescott (2007) define a Great Depression as an event in which per capita real output is at least 20% below trend, in which trend is constructed using a 2% annual growth rate. They also require that real output is at least 15% below this trend within a decade, and that real output always grows at less than 2% per year during the episode.

Neoclassical modeling of depressions has become a very active research field in the last 15 years and is providing new insights into several episodes that have long been considered economic pathologies.[1] Some of the models presented here are tailored to capture features of specific episodes, but all of these models can be modified to study other episodes of depressed economic activity.

This section focuses on the US Great Depression, which is the most widely-studied depression in the literature, and is perhaps the most striking and anomalous period of macroeconomic activity in the economic history of the US. The Great Depression began in the Fall of 1929, and the economy did not recover to its predepression trend until the early 1940s.

Lucas and Rapping (1969) developed the first modern model of the US Great Depression. This model represented a breakthrough by analyzing the Depression within an equilibrium framework. Previous studies of the Depression noted the coincidence of deflation and depression in the early 1930s, and viewed deflation as causing the Depression. The Lucas–Rapping model provided a very different interpretation of this relationship. In the Lucas–Rapping model, deflation depresses output through imperfect information about nominal price changes. Specifically, workers misinterpret falling

[1] Recent models of the Great Depression analyze a number of policies and mechanisms in order to understand this episode. This includes the wage fixing and work-sharing policies of Herbert Hoover (Ohanian, 2009; Ebell and Ritschl, 2008; and Amaral and MacGee, 2015), the worker-industry cartels of the National Industrial Recovery Act and the National Labor Relations Act (Cole and Ohanian, 1999, 2004), changes in capital income tax rates (McGrattan, 2012), the cartel policies of Mussolini in Italy, and Hitler in Germany (Cole and Ohanian, 2016), the impact of tariffs on resource allocation and productivity (Bond et al., 2013), the impact of financial market imperfections and misallocation in the Depression (Ziebarth, 2014), and the impact of contractionary monetary policy on labor markets (Bordo et al., 2000).

nominal wages as reflecting a lower relative price for their labor services. This mistaken perception of the real wage leads to lower employment and lower output. This change in employment and production reflects intertemporal substitution, in which employment and output expand during periods in which workers perceive high real wages and contract during periods of perceived low real wages. The mechanism of imperfect information and nominal price changes was developed further in Lucas's 1972 seminal contribution that rationalized Phillips Curve type relationships within an optimizing model.

Lucas and Rapping's study spawned a large neoclassical literature on fluctuations that focused on intertemporal substitution as the principal channel for understanding business cycle fluctuations. This literature includes contributions by Barro (1981), Barro and King (1984), Lucas (1973a), Sargent (1973), Sargent and Wallace (1975), among others.

But many economists were skeptical of these early neoclassical interpretations of fluctuations, particularly for deep and prolonged crises such as the US Great Depression. Modigliani (1977) argued that neoclassical models of the Depression implausibly portrayed individuals as exhibiting a "a severe attack of contagious laziness" (p. 24). Modigliani, Rees (1970) and many other economists interpreted the substantial job loss of the Depression as involuntary unemployment, which stands in sharp contrast to the market-clearing equilibrium interpretation of Lucas and Rapping. The Modigliani quip has been repeated frequently over time, and is viewed widely as a fundamental critique of neoclassical macroeconomic modeling. This section presents neoclassical models of the Depression that directly confront Modigliani's criticism. The analysis shows how simple neoclassical models can be extended to assess economies with market distortions that create substantial and persistent involuntary job loss.

5.1 The Depth, Duration, and Sectoral Differences of the US Great Depression

The depth, duration, and sectoral differences in severity of the Depression represent a significant challenge for neoclassical models, or for any quantitative theoretic model. Tables 7–9 summarize these features by presenting data on output, consumption, investment, hours worked, and productivity. The data in these tables are divided by the population. In addition, all of the data except for hours worked are detrended at 2% per year. Thus, the value of 100 means that a variable is equal to its steady state growth path value.

Table 7 shows that real GDP declines by more than 35% between 1929 and the Depression's trough in 1933, and remains far below trend after that. Consumption also falls considerably, and remains near its trough level after 1933. Investment declines by about 75%, and remains at 50% below trend by the late 1930s. Hours worked decline about 27% between 1929 and 1933, and remain more than 20% below trend after that.

Total factor productivity (TFP) declines by about 14% below trend by 1933. Such a large drop in productivity raises questions about measurement, and whether this decline reflects factors other than changes in efficiency. Ohanian (2001) found that this TFP

Table 7 US Great Depression levels of real output and its components (index, 1929 = 100)

		Consumption				Foreign trade	
Year	Real output	Nondurables and services	Consumer durables	Business investment	Government purchases	Exports	Imports
1930	87.4	90.9	76.2	79.2	105.1	85.3	84.9
1931	78.1	85.4	63.4	49.4	105.4	70.6	72.4
1932	65.2	76.0	46.7	27.9	97.3	54.5	58.1
1933	61.9	72.2	44.4	24.6	91.7	52.8	60.8
1934	64.6	72.1	49.0	28.4	101.1	52.8	58.3
1935	68.1	73.1	58.9	34.4	100.1	53.8	69.3
1936	74.9	77.0	70.8	45.9	113.9	55.1	71.9
1937	76.0	77.2	72.2	53.6	106.3	64.3	78.3
1938	70.6	74.3	56.3	37.8	112.0	62.8	58.6
1939	73.5	75.0	64.3	40.5	112.9	61.7	61.6

Data are measured in per capita terms and detrended.

Table 8 Five measures of labor input during US Great Depression (index, 1929 = 100)

	Aggregate measures			Sectoral measures	
Year	Total employment	Total hours	Private hours	Farm hours	Manufacturing hours
1930	93.8	92.0	91.5	99.0	83.5
1931	86.7	83.6	82.8	101.6	67.2
1932	78.9	73.5	72.4	98.6	53.0
1933	78.6	72.7	70.8	98.8	56.1
1934	83.7	71.8	68.7	89.1	58.4
1935	85.4	74.8	71.4	93.1	64.8
1936	89.8	80.7	75.8	90.9	74.2
1937	90.8	83.1	79.5	98.8	79.3
1938	86.1	76.4	71.7	92.4	62.3
1939	87.5	78.8	74.4	93.2	71.2

Data are measured in per capita terms.

decline was not easily reconciled with capacity utilization, labor hoarding, or compositional shifts in inputs, which suggests significant efficiency loss during this period. TFP recovers quickly and ultimately rises above trend by the late 1930s. This rapid productivity growth after 1932 led Field (2003) to describe the 1930s as "the most technologically progressive decade of the 20th century."

The severity of the Depression differed considerably across sectors. Table 8 shows that manufacturing hours declined enormously, but agricultural hours remained close to trend through the mid-1930s. These two sectors account for roughly 50% of employment at that time.

Table 9 Productivity and real wage rates during US Great Depression (index, 1929 = 100)

		Total factor productivity		Real wage rates		
Year	**Labor productivity**[a]	**Private domestic**	**Private nonfarm**	**Total**	**Manufacturing**	**Nonmanufacturing**
1930	95.3	94.8	94.8	99.3	101.9	98.2
1931	95.2	93.4	92.0	98.9	106.0	96.1
1932	89.4	87.6	85.8	95.8	105.3	92.3
1933	84.8	85.7	82.7	91.3	102.5	87.2
1934	90.3	93.1	92.7	95.7	108.8	91.1
1935	94.8	96.3	95.3	95.1	108.3	90.4
1936	93.7	99.5	99.5	97.6	107.2	94.1
1937	95.1	100.1	99.3	97.8	113.0	92.5
1938	94.6	99.9	98.1	99.1	117.4	92.8
1939	95.2	102.6	100.1	100.1	116.4	94.3

Data are detrended.
[a]Labor productivity is defined as output per hour.

The data summarized here challenge long-standing views of the Depression. Traditional studies omit productivity, and focus instead on monetary contraction and banking crises as the key determinants of the Depression (see Friedman and Schwartz, 1963 and Bernanke, 1983).

However, these factors cannot account for the early stages of the Depression, nor can they account for the post-1933 continuation of the Depression. In terms of the early stages of the Depression, industrial production declined by about 35% between the Fall of 1929 through November of 1930, but there were neither banking crises nor significant monetary contraction during this time.[m]

After 1933, the money stock expanded rapidly and banking crises were quickly eliminated by the introduction of bank deposit insurance. The Lucas–Rapping model and New Keynesian models, such as Eggertsson (2012), counterfactually predict a very rapid recovery to trend as a consequence of rapid monetary expansion and the end of banking crises. In the Lucas–Rapping model, monetary expansion stops deflation, and employment expands as workers perceive that the relative price of their labor services has recovered. In New Keynesian models, such as Eggertsson (2012), inflation moves the economy away from the zero lower interest rate bound, and hours worked increase substantially. These models cannot account for the failure of hours to remain significantly depressed after 1933. Rees (1970) and Lucas and Rapping (1972) discuss the failure of the Lucas and Rapping model to account for hours worked after 1933, and Ohanian (2011) discusses the failure of the Eggertsson model to account for hours worked after 1933.

[m] Ohanian (2010) discusses the immediate severity of the Great Depression that occurred before monetary contraction and before banking crises.

Moreover, the traditional view of the Depression counterfactually implies that the agricultural sector and the manufacturing sector were identically depressed. The large differences between these two sectors mean that any successful model of the Depression must account for the enormous manufacturing depression, but only a modest agricultural decline.

5.2 Diagnosing Depressions with Simple Neoclassical Models

Cole and Ohanian (1999) advocate using simple neoclassical models to *diagnose depressions*. Their idea is that both the successes and the deviations between model and data are informative for developing theories of specific episodes. Cole and Ohanian (1999) focused on the contribution of TFP for the Depression within a standard one-sector stochastic growth model for the 1930s.[n] They fed TFP shocks from 1930 to 1939 into the model and found that the TFP drop accounts for about 60% of the drop in output between 1929 and 1933, and about half of the drop in labor. However, the model generates a completely counterfactual path for the economy after 1933. The rapid recovery of TFP generates a rapid recovery in the model, with labor input recovering to trend by the mid-1930s. In contrast, the actual economy appears to have shifted onto a lower steady state growth path after 1933, with consumption and hours worked remaining near their 1932 trend-adjusted levels.

The post-1933 deviation between model and data provide valuable information about this episode. The results indicate that understanding the post-1933 data requires a large and persistent change in a state variable that substantially depressed and/or restricted the opportunities to produce and trade. The impact of the missing factor must be sufficiently large, such that it prevents recovery in hours worked, despite rapid productivity recovery and despite the low capital stock.

Business cycle accounting (BCA) is another neoclassical diagnostic tool, and its application provides insight regarding this state variable. Cole and Ohanian (1999, 2002), Mulligan (2005), Brinca et al. (2016), and Chari et al. (2007) use a standard one-sector neoclassical model to measure which of the decision margins in that model deviate from theory when actual data is substituted into the first order conditions of the model. For the Great Depression, the condition that equates the marginal rate of substitution between consumption and leisure to the marginal product of labor is significantly distorted. Specifically, the marginal product of labor is higher than the marginal rate of substitution throughout the decade. The deviation in this condition, which is typically called a labor wedge, grows further after 1933, and suggests a major factor that distorted the opportunities and/or the incentives to trade labor services.

[n] The idea of large productivity declines during depressions was initially met with skepticism by some economists. This skepticism is based on the narrow interpretation that lower TFP implies that society lost substantial knowledge over a short period of time. More recently, however, economists are interpreting aggregate productivity changes from alternative perspectives. Section 7 discusses this in detail.

Ohanian (2009) identified economic policies that significantly distorted the opportunities to trade labor services by depressing labor market competition and by preventing wages from adjusting. Simon (2001) analyzed "situation wanted" advertisements from the late 1920s and the early 1930s. These situation wanted advertisements are analogous to help wanted advertisements, but from the supply side of the labor market. In these ads, workers would describe their experience and qualifications, and the wage that they were seeking. Simon shows that the supply price of labor—the desired wage posted in the situation wanted ads—was much lower than the wages that were actually paid in the 1930s. This large gap between the supply price of labor and the wage was not present in the late 1920s, however, when the supply price and actual wages paid were very similar. This evidence suggests that wages were above their market–clearing level, which in turn created an excess supply of labor.

Table 9 provides further evidence of a significantly distorted labor market. The table presents wages from manufacturing and from the farm sector. These data are measured relative to trend, which is the average growth rate of productivity in these sectors (see Cole and Ohanian, 1999). These data show that wages in manufacturing are well above trend, which suggests that they are also above their market–clearing level. In contrast, real wages in the farm sector are well below trend.

Given this backdrop, a new neoclassical literature on the Depression has emerged that studies how government policy changes distorted labor markets. Ohanian (2009) studied the downturn phase of the US Great Depression, and Cole and Ohanian (2004) studied the delayed recovery from the Depression. Both papers use neoclassical frameworks that build on the facts described above. Given the large differences in hours worked and wages in the manufacturing and agricultural sectors, these models begin by modifying the standard one-sector growth model to incorporate multiple sectors, and then build in government policies.

5.3 A Neoclassical Model with Wage Fixing and Work-Sharing Policies

There were large shifts in government policies throughout the 1930s that distorted labor and product markets by significantly restricting competition in industrial labor and product markets, but not in agricultural markets. Ohanian (2009) describes how these policies began in November 1929, following the October stock market decline. President Herbert Hoover met with the leaders of the largest industrial firms, including General Motors, Ford, General Electric, US Steel, and Dupont. Hoover lobbied these firms to either raise wages, or at a minimum, to keep wages at their current levels. He also asked industry to share work among employees, rather than follow the typical practice of laying off workers and keeping retained workers on a full-time shift.

In return for maintaining nominal wages and sharing work, organized labor pledged to maintain industrial peace by not striking or engaging in any efforts that would disrupt production. The Hoover bargain was perceived by firms to be in their interest. Specifically, it is widely acknowledged that the major manufacturing firms had substantial market power at this time, with considerable industry rents. Kovacic and Shapiro (2000) note that this period represents the zenith of collusion and cartels among major industry, and capital's share of income was at an all-time high. Industry agreed to keep wages fixed, and Ford Motor in fact raised wages following the meeting with Hoover. However, as the price level declined, and as productivity declined, these fixed nominal industrial wages led to rising real wages and rising unit labor costs. Ohanian (2010) documents that industry asked Hoover several times for permission to reduce nominal wages, but Hoover declined these requests. Nominal wages among the biggest employers did not begin to fall until late 1931, after hours worked in industry had declined by almost 50%.

Ohanian (2009) develops a neoclassical model with a policy of nominal wage fixing and work-sharing that affected the industrial sector. This requires a model with multiple sectors, and also requires a distinction between hours per worker and employment in order to model work-sharing.

There is a representative family, and family members work in many industries. The population grows at rate n. Preferences over consumption and leisure, and the disutility of joining the workforce, are given by:

$$\max\sum_{t=0}^{\infty}\beta^t\{\ln(c_t)+e_{at}\mu\ln(1-h_{at})+e_{mt}\mu\ln(1-h_{mt})-v(e_{at}+e_{mt})\}(1+n)^t. \quad (44)$$

Preferences are scaled by the population, which grows at rate n. Consumption is denoted as c, e_a denotes the number of workers in the agricultural sector, e_m denotes the number of workers in the manufacturing sector, and h_a and h_m denote the length of the workweek in agriculture and manufacturing, respectively. The function $v(e_a + e_m)$ is increasing and weakly convex, and specifies the utility cost of sending different household members to work in the market. Rank-ordering family members by their position in the distribution of this utility cost, and assuming that these costs rise linearly across family members, yields:

$$-v(e_{at}+e_{mt})=-\int_{i=0}^{e_t}(\xi_0+2\xi_1x)dx=\xi_0e_t+\xi_1e_t^2. \quad (45)$$

Note that there will be an optimal number of family members working, as well as an optimal number of hours per worker.

There are two production sectors, agriculture and manufacturing, and there is a continuum of industries within each sector. Industry output is given by:

$$y_i=h_ie_s(i)^\gamma k_s(i)^{1-\gamma}, \quad (46)$$

in which the length of the workweek is given by h, employment is given by e, and capital is given by k. Kydland and Prescott (1988), Cole and Ohanian (2002), Hayashi and

Prescott (2002), Osuna and Rios-Rull (2003), and McGrattan and Ohanian (2010) use similar production technologies to study problems that require differentiating between employment and hours per worker.

The industry-level outputs are aggregated to produce sectoral output:

$$Y_s = \left(\int_0^1 y_s(i)^\theta di\right)^{\frac{1}{\theta}} \tag{47}$$

Final output, which is divided between consumption and investment, is a CES aggregate over the two sectoral outputs:

$$Y = [\alpha Y_m^\phi + (1-\alpha) Y_a^\phi]^{\frac{1}{\phi}} \tag{48}$$

The production of final goods is competitive, and the maximization problem is given by:

$$\max\{Y - \int p_m y_m(i) di - \int p_a y_a(i) di\} \tag{49}$$

subject to:

$$Y = \left[\alpha\left(\int_0^1 y_m(i)^\theta di\right)^{\frac{\phi}{\theta}} + (1-\alpha)\left(\int_0^1 y_a(i)^\theta di\right)^{\frac{\phi}{\theta}}\right]^{\frac{1}{\phi}} \tag{50}$$

The solution to the final good producer's profit maximization problem is standard, and is characterized by equating the marginal product of each intermediate input to the input price.

The parameter values for the household discount factor, the depreciation rate, and the capital and labor production share parameters are standard, with $\beta = 0.95$, $\delta = 0.06$, and $\gamma = 0.67$. The values for the three parameters that govern the disutility of hours per worker (the length of the workweek), and the utility cost of employment, are jointly set to target (i) an average employment to population ratio of 0.7, (ii) the average workweek length at that time, which was about 45 hours per week, and (iii) that employment change accounts for about 80% of cyclical fluctuations in hours worked.

Ohanian (2009) discusses the fraction of the economy affected by the Hoover program, and sets the production share parameter α so that about 40% of employment was produced in industries impacted by this program. The parameter ϕ governs the substitution elasticity between agriculture and manufacturing. This elasticity is set to 1/2, which is consistent with the fact that both the manufacturing share of value added and its relative price have declined over time.

To analyze the impact of the Hoover nominal wage-fixing and work-sharing policy, the observed real manufacturing wage sequence is exogenously fed into the model. This sequence of wages is interpreted as the result of Hoover's fixed nominal wage program in conjunction with exogenous deflation. Note that the analysis is simplified considerably by abstracting from an explicit role of money in the model, such as a cash-in-advance constraint. It is unlikely that the inclusion of explicit monetary exchange in the model would change the results in any significant way, provided that a more complicated model with monetary exchange generated the same real wage path for manufacturing.

We now discuss modeling the workweek for analyzing the Hoover program. First, recall that almost all of the cyclical change in labor input prior to the Depression was due to employment, rather than changes in hours per worker. However, about 40% of the decline in labor input between 1929 and 1931 was due to a shorter workweek. This suggests that the large decline in the workweek length was due to the Hoover work-sharing policy, rather than reflecting an optimizing choice.

The Hoover workweek is also exogenously fed into the model. The evidence that indicates that the workweek was not optimally chosen suggests that the Hoover work-sharing policy was inefficient. In this model, the inefficiency of forced work-sharing results in lower productivity, since reducing the length of the workweek operates just like a negative productivity shock. To see this, note that the Cobb–Douglas composite of employment and the capital stock in the production function is scaled by the length of the workweek.

The analysis is conducted between 1929:4 and 1931:4. The wage-fixing and work-sharing policies significantly depress economic activity by raising the cost of labor, which reflects both a rising real wage and declining labor productivity. The inflexible manufacturing wage means that the manufacturing labor market does not clear, and that the amount of labor hired is solely determined by labor demand. Table 10 shows the perfect foresight model predictions and data.[o] The model generates about a 16% output decline, which accounts for over 60% of the actual decline.[p] The model also is consistent with the fact that there is a much larger decline in manufacturing than in agriculture. Manufacturing hours fall by about 30% in the model and by about 44% in the data, and agricultural hours fall by about 12% in the model and by about 4% in the data.

The agricultural sector declines much less because it is not subject to the Hoover wage and work-sharing policies. However, the agricultural sector declines because of the general equilibrium effects of the Hoover policy. This reflects the fact that manufacturing

[o] The annual NIPA data are linearly interpolated to a quarterly frequency.

[p] The deterministic path solution is the reason for the immediate increase in economic activity. This reflects the fact that producers see higher future labor costs, and thus produce before these costs rise. Future research should assess the impact of these policies in a stochastic environment.

Table 10 US Great Depression—data and model with wage fixing and work sharing policies (index, 1929:3 = 100)

	Output		Manufacturing hours		Agricultural hours	
	Data	**Model**	**Data**	**Model**	**Data**	**Model**
1929:4	97	101	91	96	99	104
1930:1	93	98	84	92	98	102
1930:2	90	96	76	89	99	99
1930:3	87	94	69	85	99	97
1930:4	84	91	67	80	99	94
1931:1	82	87	65	76	98	92
1931:2	78	86	59	71	97	90
1931:3	75	84	56	69	96	88

output is a complement to agricultural output in final goods production. Thus, depressed manufacturing output depresses the agricultural wage, which in turn depresses agricultural hours.

Note that the model is consistent with Simon's (2001) finding of excess labor supply in manufacturing, and that job seekers in manufacturing were willing to work for much less than the manufacturing wage. The model also provides a theory for why deflation was particularly depressing in the 1930s compared to the early 1920s, when a very similar deflation coincided with a much milder downturn.

While this model was tailored to study the US Great Depression, it can be used more broadly to study nominal wage maintenance policies and/or work-sharing policies.

5.4 A Neoclassical Model with Cartels and Insider–Outsider Unions

The model economy with nominal wage-fixing, deflation, and work sharing accounts for a considerable fraction of the early years of the Depression. After 1933, however, deflation ended. Moreover, productivity grew rapidly, and real interest rates declined. These factors should have promoted a strong recovery, but the economy remained far below trend for the balance of the decade. The failure of the economy to return to trend is puzzling from a neoclassical perspective, given productivity growth, and it is puzzling from a Keynesian perspective, given the end of deflation and banking crises, and given much lower real interest rates.

The empirical key to understanding the post-1933 Depression is a growing labor wedge, as the marginal product of labor was far above the marginal rate of substitution between consumption and leisure. Cole and Ohanian (2004) develop a theory of the labor wedge that is based on changes in government competition and labor market policies. One policy was the 1933 National Industrial Recovery Act, which allowed a number of nonagricultural industries to explicitly cartelize by limiting production and raising prices. The government typically approved these cartels provided that industry raised the wages of their workers. Another policy was the 1935 National Labor Relations Act (NLRA), which provided for unionization and collective bargaining. The use of the "sit-down" strike under the NLRA, in which striking workers forcibly prevented production by taking over factories, gave workers considerable bargaining power. Cole and Ohanian describe how both of these policies created an insider–outsider friction, in which insiders received higher wages than workers in sectors that were not covered by these policies.

Cole and Ohanian present industrial wage and relative price data from individual industries covered by these policies. Industry relative prices and wages jumped around the time that the industry codes were passed, and continued to rise after that. Table 9 shows that real wages rise and ultimately are about 17% above trend by the late 1930s.

Cole and Ohanian (2004) develop a multisector growth model in which the industries in the manufacturing sectors are able to cartelize provided that they reach a wage agreement with their workers. They begin with a simple neoclassical environment, and then add in cartelization policies and a dynamic, insider–outsider model of a union, in which incumbent workers (insiders) choose the size of the insider group, and bargain over the wage. The objective of the insiders is to maximize the per-worker expected, present discounted value of the union wage premium.

While this model was developed to capture specific features of US policy, it easily can be modified to analyze a variety of dynamic bargaining games in which a firm and a union repeatedly negotiate over wages, and in which the insiders choose their size by maximizing the expected, discounted payoff to union membership. The choice of the size of the union is central in any insider–outsider environment, but is typically missing from earlier insider–outsider models.

We begin with a neoclassical, multisector growth model, and then build in these policies. Preferences are given by:

$$\max \sum_{t=0}^{\infty} \beta^t \{\ln(c_t) + \mu \ln(1-n_t)\}. \tag{51}$$

Consumption is denoted as c, and the size of the household is normalized to 1. The model is simplified by assuming that work is full-time. The term $1-n$ is the number of household members who are engaged in nonmarket activities (leisure). The household faces a present value budget constraint:

$$\sum_{t=0}^{\infty} Q_t \left[w_{ft} n_{ft} + w_{mt} n_{mt} + \Pi_0 - c_t - \sum_s r_{st} k_{st} - x_{st} \right] \geq 0, \tag{52}$$

in which Q_t is the date-t price of output, w_f is the competitive (noncartel) wage, n_f is the number of workers in the competitive sector, w_m is the cartel wage, n_m is the number of workers in the cartel sector, Π_0 are date zero profits, r_s is the rental price of sector s capital, which in turn is denoted as k_s, and x_s is investment in sector s capital. Time allocated to market activities is given by:

$$n_t = n_{ft} + n_{mt} + n_{ut}. \tag{53}$$

This indicates that total nonmarket time, n, is the sum of household time spent working in the agricultural (noncartel) sector, n_f, the time spent working in the manufacturing (cartel) sector, n_m, and the time spent searching for a job in the manufacturing sector, n_u.

There is also a law of motion for the number of workers in the cartel sector. This transition equation is given by:

$$n_{mt} \leq \pi n_{mt-1} + v_{t-1} n_{ut-1} \tag{54}$$

The transition equation for the number of workers in the manufacturing sector indicates that the number of these manufacturing workers at date t consists of two components. One is the number who worked last period, less exogenous worker attrition, in which $(1 - \pi)$ is the probability of a manufacturing worker exogenously losing their manufacturing job. The other component is $v_{t-1} n_{ut-1}$, and this is the number of new workers hired into manufacturing jobs. This is equal to the number of family members who searched for a manufacturing job in the previous period, n_{ut-1}, multiplied by the probability of finding a manufacturing job, which is denoted as v_{t-1}.

Note that job search is required for an outsider to be newly hired into manufacturing. This search process captures competition by the outsiders in the model for the scarce insider jobs. The insider attrition probability, $1 - \pi$, captures features that generate job loss, but that are not explicitly modeled, such as retirement, disability, and relocation. Note that if $\pi = 1$, then there is no insider attrition, and there will be no hiring (or job loss) in the cartel sector in the steady state of the model.

The law of motion for industry capital stocks is standard, and is given by:

$$k_{st+1} = (1 - \delta) k_{st} + x_{st} \tag{55}$$

Industry output in sector i is given by:

$$y(i)_t = z_t k_t^{\gamma}(i) n_t^{1-\gamma}(i) \tag{56}$$

Sector output is given by:

$$Y_s = \left[\int_{\varphi_{s-1}}^{\varphi_s} y(i)^{\theta} di \right]^{\frac{1}{\theta}}, s = \{f, m\} \tag{57}$$

Final output is given as a CES aggregate of the two sectoral outputs:

$$Y = [\alpha Y_f^\phi + (1-\alpha) Y_m^\phi]^{\frac{1}{\phi}} \tag{58}$$

Producers in the cartel sector have a profit maximization problem that features their market power, and which depends on the elasticity parameters ϕ and θ. Using the fact that industry price is given by $p = Y^{1-\phi} Y_m^{\phi-\theta}$, the industry profit function is given by:

$$\Pi = \max_{n,k} \{ Y^{1-\phi} Y_m^{\phi-\theta} ((z_t n_t)^{1-\gamma} k_t^\gamma)^\theta - wn - rk \} \tag{59}$$

In the insider–outsider union model, the objective for an incumbent worker (insider) is to maximize the expected present discounted value of industry wage premia. The value of being an insider, in which there are currently n insiders, is given by:

$$V_t(n) = \max_{\bar{w}_t, \bar{n}_t} \{ \min \left[1, \frac{\bar{n}}{n}\right] ([\bar{w}_t - w_{ft}) + \pi \left(\frac{Q_{t+1}}{Q_t}\right) V_{t+1}(\pi \bar{n})] \} \tag{60}$$

The insiders propose to the firm to hire $\bar{n}$ number of workers at the wage rate $\bar{w}_t$. If the offer is accepted, the current period payoff to each insider is the wage premium, which is the cartel wage less the competitive wage: $(\bar{w}_t - w_f)$. The insider's continuation value is the expected discounted value of being an insider next period, which is $\pi \left(\frac{Q_{t+1}}{Q_t}\right) V_{t+1}(\pi \bar{n})$. Note that the number of insiders at the start of period $t + 1$ is given by $\pi \bar{n}$. Note that the attrition probability, π, affects the continuation value of union membership in two different ways. First, the probability that any individual insider at date t will remain in the cartel at date $t + 1$ is π, which scales the date $t + 1$ value function. Second, the total number of date t insiders who will remain in the cartel at date $t + 1$ is $\pi \bar{n}$.

The insiders bargain with the firm at the start of each period. If a wage agreement is reached, then the firm hires $\bar{n}$ number of workers at wage $\bar{w}$. Note that the union's offer is efficient in the sense that given the wage offer, the number of workers hired, $\bar{n}$, is consistent with the firm's labor demand schedule. The bargaining protocol is that the union makes a take-it-or-leave-it offer to the firm.

In equilibrium, the union makes an offer that the firm weakly prefers to its outside option of declining the offer. The firm's outside option is given as follows. If the offer is declined, then the firm can hire labor at the competitive wage, w_f. With probability ω the firm will be able to continue to act as a monopolist. With probability $1 - \omega$, the government will discover that the firm did not bargain in good faith with the union, and the government will force the firm to behave competitively and thus the firm earns no monopoly profits.

This feature of the model empirically captures the fact that some firms did fail to reach wage agreements, or violated wage agreements, and that the government did enforce the wage bargaining provisions of the policy. The firm's outside option therefore is the expected level of monopoly profits earned by declining the insider's offer, and the firm will only accept the insider's offer of $(\bar{n}, \bar{w})$ if it delivers at least that level of profit. It is therefore optimal for the union to make an offer that does provide the firm with its outside option.

A key parameter in this model is the share of employment in the cartelized sector. While the cartel policy was intended to cover about 80% of the nonfarm economy, there is debate regarding how much of the economy was effectively cartelized. Therefore, the model conservatively specifies that only manufacturing and mining were cartelized, which is about 1/3 of the economy. Another key parameter is ω, which governs the probability that the government will identify a firm that breaks their wage agreement. This value was chosen so that the steady state cartel wage premium is about 20% above trend. This implies that ω is around 0.10. The attrition parameter, π, is set to 0.95, which yields an average job tenure in the cartel of 20 years.

Other parameters include the substitution elasticity across industries and across sectors. For these parameters, the industry substitution elasticity is picked so that the industry markup would be 10% in the absence of wage bargaining. The sectoral substitution elasticity, which refers to the substitution possibility between manufacturing and the farm sector, is picked to be 1/2. Other parameter values, including the household discount factor, the household leisure parameter, the income shares of capital and labor, and depreciation rates, are standard, and are described in Cole and Ohanian (2004).

The quantitative analysis begins in 1934. To generate model variables, the 1933 capital stocks from the manufacturing and farm sectors from this are specified, and the sequence of TFP from 1934 to 1939 is fed into the model. The model variables then transit to their steady state values. For comparative purposes, we show the results from the cartel model to those from the perfectly competitive version of this model. Table 11, which is taken from Cole and Ohanian (2004), shows the response of the competitive version of this model. Note that the rapid return of productivity to trend fosters a rapid recovery under competition, with hours worked rising above trend to rebuild the capital stock to its steady state level. Moreover, the wage is well below trend in 1933, and then recovers quickly after that, as both productivity and the capital stocks rise.

Table 11 Equilibrium path of recovery from depression in competitive model

	Output	Consumption	Investment	Employment	Wage
1934	0.87	0.90	0.73	0.98	0.89
1935	0.92	0.91	0.97	1.01	0.91
1936	0.97	0.93	1.18	1.03	0.94
1937	0.98	0.94	1.14	1.03	0.95
1938	0.98	0.95	1.12	1.02	0.96
1939	0.99	0.96	1.09	1.02	0.97

Table 12 shows the transition of the cartel model. This transition stands in sharp contrast to the transition in the competitive economy from Table 11. The cartel economy transits to a steady state that is well below the competitive economy. Despite rising productivity, the cartel economy remains depressed through the 1930s, as cartel policies create rents that raise wage rates far above trend, despite the fact that both consumption and time allocated to market activities are below trend. These results indicate that the cartel policy accounts for about 60% of the post-1933 Depression in output, consumption, and hours worked.

5.5 Neoclassical Models of Taxes and Depressions

This section describes how tax rate changes contributed to the US Great Depression and also for more recent episodes of depressed economic activity.

Tax rates rose in the United States during the Great Depression. McGrattan (2012) studies how changes in tax rates on dividends and corporate profits affected economic activity after 1933. Specifically, a new tax rate was applied to undistributed corporate profits in 1936. The goal of this new tax was to increase corporate payments to shareholders, which in turn was expected to stimulate spending.

McGrattan analyzes a representative household economy with log preferences over consumption and leisure, and with a standard constant returns to scale Cobb–Douglas production function with capital and labor inputs. She considers two formulations for taxes. In the traditional formulation, tax rates are applied to labor income (τ_h) and to capital income net of depreciation (τ_k). Tax revenue is the sum of labor income tax revenue and capital income tax revenue:

$$\tau_h wh + \tau_k(r-\delta)k \tag{61}$$

The alternative formulation includes a finer decomposition of taxes across revenue sources, and distinguishes between business and nonbusiness capital. Tax revenue in this alternative formulation is given by:

$$\begin{aligned}\tau_h wh &+\tau_p(r-\tau_k-\delta)k_b+\tau_c c+\tau_k k_b+\tau_u(k_b'-k_b)\\ &+\tau_d\{(rk_r-x_b)-\tau_p(r-\tau_k-\delta)k_b-\tau_k k_b-\tau_u(k_b'-k_b)\}\end{aligned} \tag{62}$$

In (64), τ_p is the tax rate on profits, τ_k is now the tax rate on business property, τ_c is the consumption tax rate, τ_u is the tax rate on undistributed profits, τ_d is the dividend tax rate, and primed variables refer to period $t+1$ values.

The intertemporal first order condition that governs efficient investment shows how changes in expected taxation affect investment:

$$\frac{(1+\tau_{ut})(1-\tau_{dt})}{(1+\tau_{ct})c_t}=\beta E_t\left[\frac{(1-\tau_{dt+1})}{(1+\tau_{ct+1})c_{t+1}}\{(1-\tau_{pt+1})(r_{t+1}-\tau_{kt+1}-\delta)+(1+\tau_{ut+1})\}\right] \tag{63}$$

Table 12 Equilibrium path of recovery from depression in cartel policy model

	Output	Consumption	Investment	Employment	Searchers	Employment		Wage	
						Cartel sector	Competitive sector	Cartel sector	Competitive sector
1934	0.77	0.85	0.40	0.82	0.07	0.68	0.89	1.16	0.81
1935	0.81	0.85	0.62	0.84	0.11	0.69	0.92	1.19	0.83
1936	0.86	0.85	0.87	0.89	0.06	0.72	0.97	1.20	0.83
1937	0.87	0.86	0.90	0.90	0.04	0.73	0.98	1.20	0.83
1938	0.86	0.86	0.86	0.89	0.06	0.72	0.97	1.20	0.84
1939	0.87	0.86	0.88	0.89	0.04	0.73	0.97	1.20	0.84

Note that dividend taxes and consumption taxes in (65) do not distort investment incentives at the margin in the deterministic version of this model when these tax rates are constant over time. However, expected changes in tax rates will affect investment decisions. An expected increase in these tax rates reduces the expected returns to investment, and leads firms to increase current distributions. Tax rates rose considerably in the mid-1930s, with the dividend tax rate rising from about 14% to about 25%, the corporate profit tax rate rising from about 14% to about 19%, and the newly implemented undistributed tax rate of 5%. McGrattan shows that plausible expectations of these tax rate changes can help account for the fact that business investment remained at 50% or more below trend after 1933.

McGrattan's analysis of the US Great Depression focused on changes in capital income tax rates. Prescott (2004) and Ohanian, Raffo, and Rogerson (2008) analyze how long-run changes in labor income tax rates have affected hours worked more recently. Ohanian et al. (2008) document that hours worked per adult in the OECD vary enormously over time and across countries. Hours worked in many Northern and Western European countries declined by about 1/3 between the 1950s and 2000, including a nearly 40% decline in Germany.

Ohanian et al. use a standard neoclassical growth model with log preferences over consumption, log preferences over leisure, a flat rate labor income tax, and a flat rate consumption tax rate. The economy's technology is a constant returns to scale Cobb–Douglas production function that uses capital and labor, which is given by $Y_t = A_t K_t^{\theta} H_t^{1-\theta}$. Preferences for the representative family are given by:

$$\max \sum \beta^t \{\alpha \ln(c_t - \bar{c} + \lambda g_t) + (1-\alpha)\ln(\bar{h} - h_t)\}. \tag{64}$$

Households value private consumption, c, and public consumption, g. The term $\bar{c}$ is a subsistence consumption term to account for possible nonhomotheticities in preferences that may affect trend changes in hours worked. The parameter $\lambda, 0 < \lambda \leq 1$, governs the relative value that households place on public spending. The specification that government consumption (scaled by the parameter λ) is a perfect substitute for private consumption follows from the fact that much government spending (net of military spending) is on close substitutes for private spending, such as health care.

The first order condition governing time allocation in this economy is standard, and equates the marginal rate of substitution between consumption and leisure to the wage rate, adjusted for consumption and labor income taxes. This first order condition is presented below. Note that the marginal product of labor, $(1-\theta)\frac{Y_t}{H_t}$ is substituted into the equation for the wage rate in (67):

$$\frac{(1-\alpha)}{\bar{h} - h_t} = \frac{(1-\tau_{ht})}{(1+\tau_{ct})} \frac{\alpha}{(c_t + \lambda g_t)} (1-\theta) \frac{Y_t}{H_t}. \tag{65}$$

In the first order condition, τ_h is the labor income tax rate, and τ_c is the consumption tax rate. Ohanian et al. feed McDaniel's (2011) panel data construction of consumption and income tax rates into this first order condition, along with actual labor productivity and consumption data. They choose the value of α by country so that model hours in the first year of the dataset are equal to actual hours for each country. They set $\lambda = 1$, and labor's share of income is set to 0.67. The subsistence consumption term is set to 5% of US consumption in 1956, which represents a small departure from the standard model of homothetic preferences. Ohanian et al. describe the sensitivity of results to alternative values for these parameters.

With these parameter values and data, Ohanian et al. use this equation to construct a predicted measure of hours worked from the model economy, and compare it to actual hours worked by country and over time. Fig. 25 shows actual hours worked and

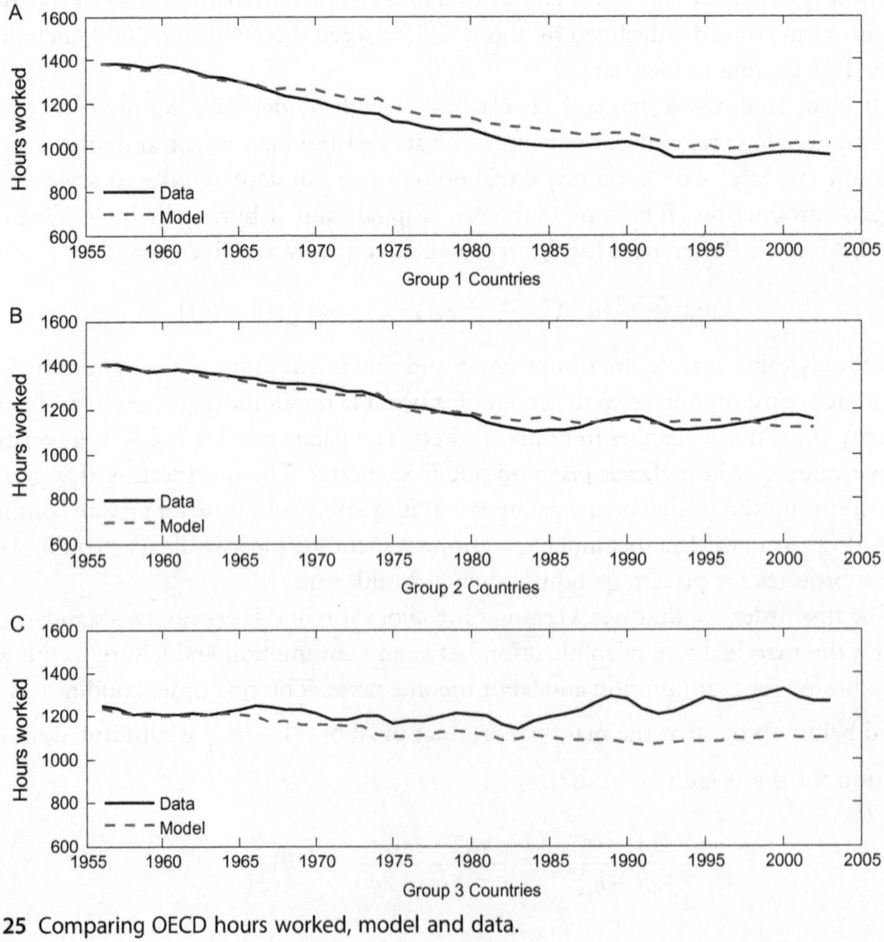

Fig. 25 Comparing OECD hours worked, model and data.

predicted hours worked from the model for 21 OECD countries.[q] Panel (A) of the graph shows results for countries which experienced at least a 25% decline in hours worked per capita. Panel (B) shows results for countries which experienced a decline in hours per capita that range between 10% and 25%. Panel (C) shows results for countries that experienced a decline in hours per capita of less than 10%, or alternatively experienced higher hours.

The figures show that the model economy accounts for much of the secular decline in hours worked, particularly for the countries which experienced the largest hours declines. Ohanian et al. also report that the contribution of tax rate changes to changes in hours worked is not sensitive to other labor market factors that may have affected hours, such as changes in employment protection policies, changes in union density, and changes in unemployment benefits.

These findings indicate that the observed increases in labor and consumption tax rates can account for the large observed declines in hours worked per adult across these countries. These neoclassical findings regarding the impact of tax rates on hours worked stand in contrast to other explanations of the decline in European hours. Other explanations include a preference shift for more leisure, or a preference shift in conjunction with policies that restrict work, and that may have been chosen in order for society to coordinate on a low-work equilibrium (see Blanchard, 2004 and Alesina et al., 2006).[r]

5.6 Summary

Depressions, which are protracted periods of substantial economic decline relative to trend, have been difficult to understand and are often presumed to extend beyond the scope of neoclassical economics. The models developed here show that government policies that depress competition can account for a considerable amount of the Great Depression, and can also account for much of the failure of economic activity to return to trend. More broadly, these models of the US Great Depression successfully confront the frequently cited view of Modigliani (1977) that neoclassical models cannot plausibly account for the behavior of labor markets during Depressions.

Modigliani interpreted the Great Depression as the failure of the market economy to right itself. This view, and associated Keynesian views of the Depression, are based on the idea that business organizations did not expand investment in the 1930s, which in turn kept employment low. The studies discussed here turn that interpretation on its head. Specifically, these new neoclassical studies indicate that the depth and persistence of the Depression was the consequence of government policies that depressed the steady

[q] Ohanian et al. (2008) describe the data sources and data construction in detail. The Group 1 countries are Austria, Belgium, Denmark, France, Finland, Germany, Italy, and Ireland. The Group 2 countries are Japan, the Netherlands, Norway, Portugal, Spain, Sweden, Switzerland, and the United Kingdom. The Group 3 countries are Australia, Canada, Greece, New Zealand, and the United States.

[r] Other neoclassical studies of taxes and labor supply include Erosa, Fuster, and Kambourov (2012) Rogerson (2009), Ragan (2013), Meza (2008), Samaniego (2008), Dalton (2015), and Davis and Henrekson (2005).

state allocation of time to market work. A lower steady state level of market hours reduced the return to capital, which in turn depressed capital accumulation.

Neoclassical models can also account for more recent periods of depressed economic activity. This includes not only the secular decline in market hours worked in much of Northern and Western Europe through higher tax rates, but also the Finish Depression of the early 1990s that reflects the trade impact of the breakup of the USSR. (Gorodnichenko et al., 2012), and tax changes and productivity changes (Conesa et al., 2007). Other studies of recent Depressions include the Korean Crisis of 1998 (Otsu, 2008), and several case studies in Kehoe and Prescott (2007).

The Depression methodology presented in this section has also been used to study the flip side of Depressions, which are Growth Miracles. This includes studies of Ireland's Growth Miracle (see Ahearne et al., 2006, who analyze a standard growth model with TFP, and Klein and Ventura (2015), who study a small open economy model with taxes, labor wedges, and TFP), and Lu (2012), who analyzes the development of some East Asian countries in a neoclassical framework.

6. NEOCLASSICAL MODELING OF LARGE FISCAL SHOCKS: THE US WORLD WAR II ECONOMY

Wartime economies are interesting and important macroeconomic episodes because they feature very large, exogenous changes in government policies, particular fiscal policies, as well as large changes in macroeconomic activity. The World War II economy in the United States represents perhaps the largest fiscal policy shift of any advanced economy. This includes a nearly 400% increase in federal government spending, large increases in income tax rates, and a large increase in the number of men drafted into military service. Moreover, there was a very large resource reallocation from private use to military use that occurred in a very short period of time.

This striking period of policy changes provides information on how large aggregate and sectoral disruptions quantitatively affect a market economy, which provides a powerful test of neoclassical theory. These episodes are also informative about what a number of economists call the *government spending multiplier*, which refers to the change in output as a consequence of a change in government spending. This research area has received considerable attention since the Great Recession, when the United States and other countries increased government spending to expand economic activity (see Barro and Redlick, 2011; Mountford and Uhlig, 2009; Ramey, 2011; and Taylor, 2011).

Neoclassical analysis of fiscal policies and wars has become an active research area.[s] These studies analyze a range of issues, including the welfare costs of different wartime fiscal policies (Ohanian, 1997), the impact of the draft on economic activity

[s] Studies include Ohanian (1993, 1997), Braun and McGrattan (1993), Siu (2008), Mulligan (2005), McGrattan and Ohanian (2010), Burnside, Eichenbaum, and Fisher (2004), Baxter and King (1993), Christiano and Eichenbaum (1992), Doepke et al. (2015), and Monacelli and Perotti (2008).

(Siu, 2008), the behavior of labor productivity and investment (Braun and McGrattan, 1993), and the extent that a neoclassical model can account for aggregate time series, particularly the impact of wars on the incentives to work (Mulligan, 2005 and McGrattan and Ohanian, 2010).

This section develops a neoclassical model of the World War II US economy to study how well a neoclassical model can fit the wartime US data. The model easily can be applied to other episodes with changes in government spending, transfers, and tax rates. The model is from McGrattan and Ohanian (2010), which in turn draws on Braun and McGrattan (1993), Ohanian (1997), and Siu (2008).

There is a representative family, with two types of family members, civilians and draftees. The size of the family is denoted as N. Both types of family members have identical preferences. At date t, a_t is the number of family members in the military, and $(1 - a_t)$ is the number who are civilians. The family optimally chooses consumption of both types, which is denoted as c_{ct} for civilians, and c_{dt}, for draftees. The family also optimally chooses investment in physical capital, i_{pt}, civilian labor input, l_{ct}, and the accumulation of government bonds, b_{t+1}. The inclusion of public debt follows from the fact that there was considerable debt issue during the war. The labor input of draftees is not a choice variable for the family, but rather is set exogenously by the government, and is denoted by $\bar{l}_d$.

The maximization problem for the representative family is:

$$\max E_0 \sum_{t=0}^{\infty} \{(1-a_t)U(c_{ct}, l_{ct}) + a_t U(c_{dt}, \bar{l}_d)\} N_t \tag{66}$$

Maximization is subject to the following constraints:

$$E_t = (1-\tau_{kt})(r_{pt}-\delta)k_{pt} + (1-\tau_{lt})w_t(1-a_t)l_{ct} + R_t b_t + (1-\tau_{lt})w_t a_t \bar{l}_d + T_t \tag{67}$$

$$E_t = (1-a_t)c_{ct} + a_t c_{dt} + i_{pt} + b_{t+1} \tag{68}$$

$$k_{pt+1} = [(1-\delta)k_{pt} + i_{pt}]/(1+\gamma_n) \tag{69}$$

$$N_t = (1+\gamma_n)^t \tag{70}$$

$$c_c, c_d, i_p \geq 0 \tag{71}$$

Note that k_p is the beginning-of-period capital stock, r_p is the rental price of capital, w is the wage rate, τ_k and τ_l are flat rate tax rates on capital income and labor income, respectively, Rb is the value of matured government debt, and T is government transfers. The depreciation rate is δ. The population grows at the constant rate γ_n.

The production technology is given by:

$$Y_t = F(K_{pt}, K_{gt}, Z_t L_t). \tag{72}$$

The production inputs include private capital, labor, and public capital, K_g. Labor-augmenting productivity is denoted as Z, and is given by:

$$Z_t = z_t(1+\gamma_z)^t. \tag{73}$$

Note that z_t is a transient productivity term and γ_z is the long-run growth rate of technology.

Government purchases consist of 3 components. This is a richer specification of government spending than is typically modeled in fiscal policy studies. Government consumption, C_g is the first component, and this is the standard approach to modeling government purchases. It is common to assume that these wartime purchases of goods do not affect marginal utility or private production possibilities. The second component is government investment, I_g which enhances production possibilities by expanding the capital stock that can be used to produce output. This is typically not modeled in the fiscal policy literature, but is modeled here because of the very large government-funded investments in plant and equipment that occurred in World War II. The government made large investments in the aircraft, automotive, and aluminum industries that raised the manufacturing capital stock by 30% between 1940 and 1945. The third component of government purchases is wage payments to military personnel. Government spending is therefore given by:

$$G_t = C_{gt} + I_{gt} + N_t w_t a_t \bar{l} \tag{74}$$

The evolution of the stock of government capital, which is assumed to have the same depreciation rate as physical capital, is given by:

$$K_{gt+1} = (1-\delta)K_{gt} + I_{gt} \tag{75}$$

The period government budget constraint is given by:

$$B_{t+1} = G_t + R_t B_t - \tau_{lt} N_t w_t((1-a_t)l_{ct} + a_t \bar{l}_d) - \tau_{kt}(r_{pt}-\delta)K_{pt} - r_{gt}K_{gt} + T_t, \tag{76}$$

in which T is a residual lump-sum tax.

A competitive firm maximizes profits, which implies that the rental prices for the factors of production are equal to their marginal productivities. Government debt that is accumulated during the war is retired gradually after the war. The exogenous variables are the tax rates on factor incomes, government consumption and government investment, and the productivity shock. The equilibrium definition of this perfectly competitive economy is standard.

The functional form for preferences is given by:

$$\ln(c) + \frac{\psi}{\xi}(1-l)^{\xi} \tag{77}$$

This specification yields a compensated labor supply elasticity of $\frac{1-l}{(l(1-\xi))}$. McGrattan and Ohanian choose $\xi = 0$ (log preferences) as the benchmark specification. The parameter ψ governs the steady state allocation of time for the household, and is chosen so that model steady state hours is equal to the average time devoted to market work between 1946 and 1960. For military time allocation, they choose $\bar{l}$ such that it matches 50 h per week, which is the average hours for soldiers in basic training (see Siu, 2008). Population growth is 1.5% per year, and the growth-rate of technological progress is 2% per year.

Government capital and private capital are modeled as perfect substitutes. This reflects the fact that much of government investment at this time was in the area of manufacturing plant and equipment:

$$Y_t = F(K_{pt}, K_{gt}, Z_t L_t) = (K_{pt} + K_{gt})^{\theta}(Z_t L_t)^{1-\theta} \tag{78}$$

It is straightforward, however, to modify the aggregator between government and private capital to accommodate government capital that is not a perfect substitute for private capital.

There are six exogenous variables in the model: conscription (the draft) (a_t), the tax rate on capital income (τ_{kt}), the tax rate on labor income (τ_{lt}), government consumption (C_{gt}), government investment(I_{gt}), and productivity (z_t). The evolution of the six exogenous variables is governed by a state vector, S_t, which specifies a particular set of values for these exogenous variables. For 1939–46, these exogenous variables are equal to their data counterparts. The model is solved under different assumptions regarding household expectations about the post-1946 evolution of the exogenous variables. The discussion here focuses on the perfect foresight solution to the model that begins in 1939, and McGrattan and Ohanian discuss the other cases in detail.

While the model described here is based on the World War II US economy, it can be tailored to study other episodes, as it includes a number of features that are relevant for wartime economies, including changes in tax rates on factor incomes, changes in conscripted labor, changes in productivity, government debt issue to help pay for the war, government payments to military personnel, and government investment.

Fig. 26 shows the model's exogenous variables. Government consumption, which includes state and local spending, as well as federal spending, rises from about 14% of steady state output in 1940 to 50% of steady state output by 1944. Government investment rises from about 4% of steady state output in 1940 to about 9% by 1942. The tax rates on labor and capital income, which are average marginal tax rates taken from Joines (1981), also rise considerably, with the labor income tax rates rising from about 8% to about 20%, and with the capital income tax rates rising from about 43% to about 63%. The draft reduces potential labor supply significantly, as almost 12% of the working age population is in the military by 1944.

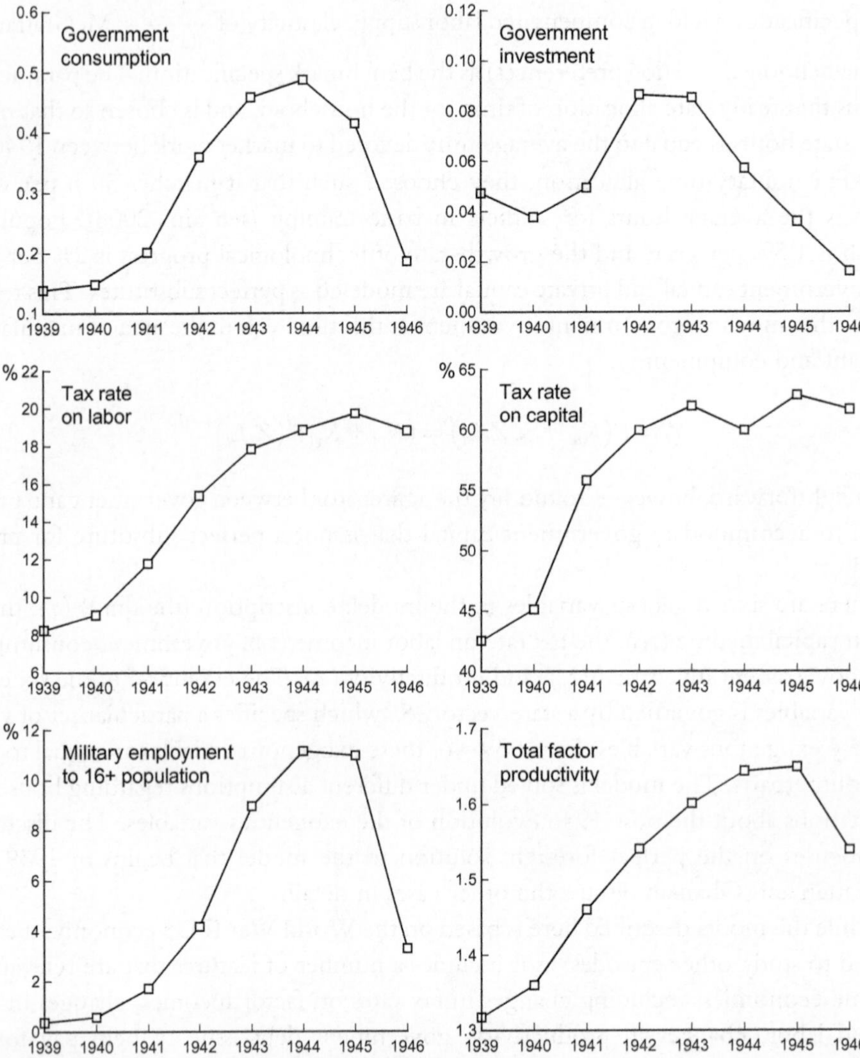

Fig. 26 US government spending, tax rates, draft, and TFP, 1939–46. *Notes*: (1) Government spending series are real and detrended by dividing by the population over 16 and by the growth trend in technology (scaled so the 1946 real detrended level of GNP less military compensation equals 1). (2) Total factor productivity is defined to be $Y/(K^{\theta}L_p^{1-\theta})$, where Y is real, detrended GNP less military compensation, K is real detrended nonmilitary capital stock, L_p is nonmilitary hours worked, and $\theta = 0.38$.

There is a considerable increase in TFP, and there are a number of good reasons why this change actually reflects higher efficiency. This includes the development of federally-funded scientific teams, the development of management science and operations research practices, and a number of technological advances during the 1940s including innovations directly or indirectly fostered by federal R & D expenditures. These include the development of modern airframes, radar, microwave technology, fertilizer, oxygen steel, synthetic rubber, nylon, sulfa drugs and chemotherapy, insecticides, and Teflon and related industrial coatings. Moreover, Herman (2012) describes how business leaders worked together in World War II to mobilize resources and to raise military output through significantly higher efficiency.

The size and diversity of these changes will affect economic activity in a variety of ways. Higher TFP will promote high labor input and output, as will public investment. In contrast, since public investment substitutes for private investment, higher public investment in plant and equipment will tend to reduce private investment. Moreover, rising tax rates and conscription of labor will tend to reduce the incentive to work.

Fig. 27 shows real GNP, real consumption, and real investment, all measured as a percent of trend output. The model output series is very close to actual output, as both increase by more than 50% over the course of the war, and then decline after the war, back to near trend. Model consumption is very flat during the war, and is close to actual consumption. Model investment has a very similar pattern as actual investment. The model investment is somewhat higher than actual investment through 1942, which reflects the perfect foresight solution. Specifically, investment rises considerably in order to build the capital stock by the time that government consumption is high. By 1944, the high level of government investment in plant and equipment, coupled with the enormous resource drain of the war, leads to investment declining significantly. Fig. 28 shows the behavior of total hours worked, and nonmilitary hours, which is the choice variable

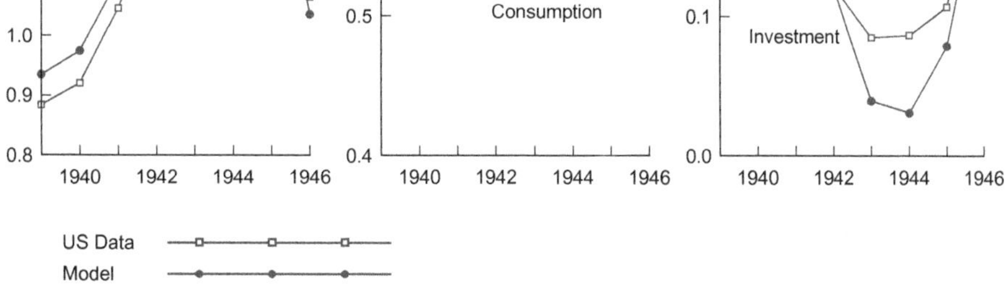

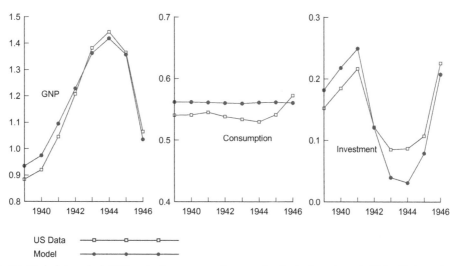

Fig. 27 Real detrended GNP, private consumption, and private investment. *Note*: Data series are divided by the 1946 real detrended level of GNP less military compensation.

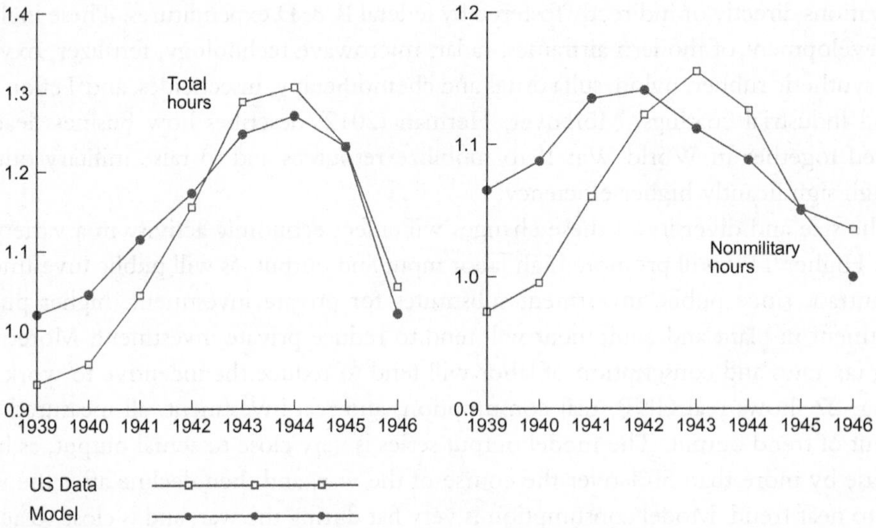

Fig. 28 Per capita total and nonmilitary hours of work, 1939–46. *Note*: Hours series are divided by the 1946–60 US averages.

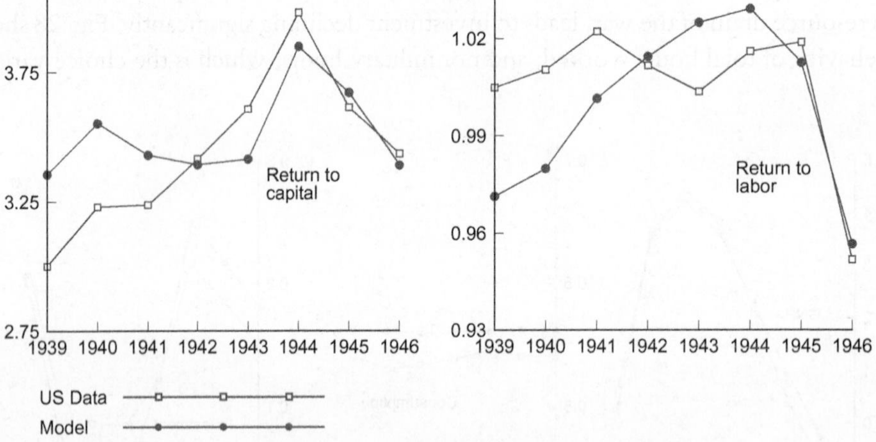

Fig. 29 After-tax returns to capital and nonmilitary labor, 1939–46. *Note*: Return to capital is equal to $100(1-\tau_k)(\theta Y/K-\delta)$. Return to labor is after-tax nonmilitary labor productivity normalized by the 1946–60 US averages.

for the family. Both hours series rise significantly in the data and in the model. The nonmilitary hours in the model rises earlier than in the data, and this again partially reflects the perfect foresight assumption. Fig. 29 shows the after-tax returns to private capital and labor. These are also quite similar to the data.

The dominant factor driving these results is the enormous expansion of government consumption that occurred during the war. This resource drain of wartime government consumption creates a sizeable wealth affect within the model that leads to higher labor input and output, and this effect is much larger than that of any of the other shocks. McGrattan and Ohanian (2010) analyzed the impact of each of the six shocks in the model on hours worked. The impact of just government consumption in the absence of any other shocks raises nonmilitary labor input by about 27% on average between 1943–45. Adding productivity shocks raises this to about a 29% increase. Adding in the draft to these two preceding shocks results in about a 25% increase. Adding in the labor and capital income tax increases has a sizeable depressing effect, and results in an increase in nonmilitary hours of about 10%. Overall, the negative wealth effect arising from government consumption is the dominant factor, followed by the impact of tax increases.

These results shed light on a number of issues that are analyzed in the literature on the macroeconomics of fiscal policy. One issue is regarding the government spending multiplier. A difficulty facing many studies of government spending multipliers is that they are primarily based on peacetime episodes, and episodes even with relatively large peacetime shifts in fiscal policy still involve small changes in fiscal policy compared to policy changes during wartime episodes. Moreover, many of these studies require exogenous changes in fiscal policy, and this can be problematic during peacetime. Consequently, it is challenging to draw sharp conclusions about the size of the multiplier based on peacetime policy changes.

The results from this World War II analysis indicate a multiplier that is considerably less than one. This is informative, not only because the wartime fiscal policy shock is so large, but also because the model explicitly distinguishes between different types of government spending. The analysis conducted here makes it possible to isolate the impacts of different types of spending and taxes on economic activity.

To see that the multiplier from this episode is fairly small, consider the following case in which we account for the impact of all government expenditures, but omit the negative impact of the tax increases and the draft. By omitting these latter two items, we construct the maximum possible effect of fiscal policy, even though tax increases, which depress labor supply, are certainly part of fiscal policy. In this experiment, the World War II episode shows that the multiplier would be about 0.6, reflecting a hypothetical 30% increase in output resulting from government purchases of goods. This multiplier is very similar to Barro and Redlick's (2011) estimates and Mountford and Uhlig's (2009) short-run estimates and is in the lower end of the range of estimates discussed in Ramey (2011).

The results have broader implications regarding neoclassical analyses of large shocks. They indicate that the US economy responded to the enormous wartime economic dislocations, as well as the peacetime reversal of these dislocations, very much along the lines of a simple neoclassical growth model augmented with several large policy changes.

These policy shifts include the massive reallocation of economic activity from peacetime to wartime production, the enormous drain of resources resulting from government purchases, the reduction of the labor endowment through the draft, higher taxes, and government-funded investment. This also includes the rapid unwinding of these unique factors after the war. While this represents just a single episode, this analysis provides a strong test of the neoclassical model in response to large fiscal policy changes.

7. NEOCLASSICAL MODELS OF PRODUCTIVITY SHOCKS

Productivity change is an important feature of the models and the data that we have used to analyze the US historical macroeconomic record in this chapter. This includes a large TFP decline in the Great Depression, a large TFP increase in World War II, and large TFP and equipment-specific productivity fluctuations in the post-Korean War US economy.

There are long-standing questions about the nature and sources of these productivity changes. Much of the profession has viewed TFP declines during downturns, and particularly during depressions, with skepticism, and naturally so. But economists are now analyzing TFP deviations during short-run and longer-run episodes from alternative perspectives than the narrow interpretation that TFP declines reflect a loss of technological know-how and knowledge.

7.1 Resource Misallocation and TFP

Restuccia and Rogerson (2008) analyze the impact of *resource misallocation* on TFP in a competitive economy. The idea is to assess how the misallocation of production inputs across locations affects measured TFP. Their model is related to Hopenhayn and Rogerson (1993), in which there is a representative family and there are different producers, or alternatively, different production locations, each with a decreasing returns to scale technology with potentially different TFP levels, and which are indexed by i. The simplest case of production heterogeneity is the case of a single final good produced at multiple locations, y_i, that is produced with a single production input, labor (h_i). The production relationship at location i is given by:

$$y_i = z_i f(h_i) \tag{79}$$

In this economy, the technology f is twice continuously differentiable, with $f' > 0, f'' < 0$. The term z_i denotes exogenous productivity. Assume that z_i is drawn from the set $\{z_1, z_2, \ldots z_I\}$, and let $\mu(i)$ be the distribution of productivity across these locations.

The efficient allocation of labor requires equating the marginal product of labor across production locations. For the isoelastic technology, $z_i h_i^{\theta}, 0 < \theta < 1$, the efficient allocation of labor between any two locations depends on the differences in productivities at those locations, and the amount of curvature in the production technology:

$$\frac{h_i}{h_j} = \left(\frac{z_i}{z_j}\right)^{\frac{1}{1-\theta}}. \tag{80}$$

We construct an economy-wide measure of TFP by aggregating TFP across all locations. Aggregate TFP in this economy is given by:

$$z = \sum_i z_i^{\frac{1}{1-\theta}} \mu(i)^{1-\theta}. \tag{81}$$

The efficient allocation of labor at any specific location depends on the location's productivity relative to aggregate productivity, as well as the amount of curvature in the technology, and is given by:

$$h_i = \left(\frac{z_i}{z}\right)^{\frac{1}{1-\theta}}. \tag{82}$$

Note that as $\theta \to 1$, even small differences in productivity generate very large differences in the efficient allocation of production inputs across locations.

Atkeson et al. (1996) use data on differences in worker firing costs and job reallocation rates between the United States and Europe to argue that θ is around 0.85. Restuccia and Rogerson use this value for specifying the level of decreasing returns in their economy, and they study how misallocation of production inputs across locations affects aggregate productivity, z. Resource misallocation means that the marginal product of labor is not equated across production locations, which implies that (82) and (84) are not satisfied.

Restuccia and Rogerson (2008) analyze various government policies that tax the output of some producers, and that subsidize the output of other producers, and they calculate the aggregate productivity and welfare losses from these policies. There is a large literature that has built on Restuccia and Rogerson along many dimensions. This includes the application of misallocation to specific Depressions and Crises (see Oberfield, 2013 and Chen and Irarrazabal, 2013 on the Chilean Depression of the early 1980s, and Sandleris and Wright, 2014 on the Argentinian Depression of 2001), the connection between financial market imperfections and misallocation (see Moll, 2014; Buera and Moll, 2015; and Midrigan and Xu, 2014) and the connection between trade barriers and productivity during the US Great Depression (see Bond et al., 2013). Other studies of misallocation focus on longer-run issues, including studies of the role of misallocation in the development experiences of China and India (Hsieh and Klenow, 2009), entry regulation and productivity (Poschke, 2010), size-dependent policies and productivity (Guner et al., 2008), imperfect information and productivity (David et al., forthcoming), the misallocation of managerial talent and productivity (Alder, 2016), and the magnification of misallocation on productivity in economies with production chains (Jones, 2013).

7.2 Intangible Investments and TFP

Neoclassical models with intangible capital are being developed to construct new measures of TFP. These studies focus on intangible investments that traditionally have not been counted as part of national product. Prior to 2013, the Bureau of Economic Analysis (BEA) counted only software as investment among the intangible categories. In 2013, the BEA implemented a comprehensive revision of the National Income and Product Accounts to include other business purchases that previously were counted as business expenses as investment, including research and development, artistic products, mineral exploration, and intellectual property. The shift of these purchases from an expensed item to business investment increases output. This BEA revision improves the measurement of real output, but the BEA does not currently count other intangible investments in the national accounts, such as marketing, advertising, and organization capital investments. These investment omissions indicate that output is mismeasured, which implies that productivity is also mismeasured.

McGrattan and Prescott (2012, 2014), and McGrattan (2016), go beyond the new NIPA measures of GDP by constructing real output measures that include other expensed items, including advertising, marketing, computer design, management consulting, public relations, and engineering expenses as intangible investment. McGrattan (2016) develops a model of the US economy that includes both tangible and intangible production, with a focus on intersectoral linkages.

McGrattan develops a model with tangible output and intangible output. Intangibles are a nonrival good. There are s sectors that use both tangibles and intangibles. There is a Cobb–Douglas aggregate over consumption goods from the S sectors. The technologies differ in terms of a sector-specific technology shock, and technology share parameters. The outputs for tangibles and intangibles is given by:

$$Y_{st} = (K^1_{Tst})^{\theta_S}(K_{Ist})^{\phi_S}(\Pi_l(M^1_{lst})^{\gamma_{ls}})(Z_t Z^1_{st} H^1_{st})^{1-\theta_S-\phi_S-\gamma_S} \tag{83}$$

$$I_{st} = (K^2_{Tst})^{\theta_S}(K_{Ist})^{\phi_S}(\Pi_l(M^2_{lst})^{\gamma_{ls}})(Z_t Z^1_{st} H^1_{st})^{1-\theta_S-\phi_S-\gamma_S} \tag{84}$$

Y_s denotes the output of the tangible sector, K^1_{Ts} is tangible capital that is used to produce tangible output in sector S, K^2_{Ts} is tangible capital used to produce intangible output in sector S, K_{Ist} is intangible capital, which is assumed to be nonrival, M^1_{ls} and M^2_{ls} are intermediate inputs used to produce tangibles in sector S, and intangibles in sector S, respectively. Z is the aggregate productivity shock and Z_s is a sector-specific productivity shock. H^1_s and H^2_s are labor input for tangibles in sector S, and intangibles in sector S, respectively.

McGrattan (2016) uses maximum likelihood to estimate the parameters of the stochastic processes for Z_t and for Z_{st}, and compares two economies, one with intangibles, and another without intangibles. The mismeasurement of productivity in the economy without intangibles generates a large labor wedge, and McGrattan argues that this may account for the empirical labor wedge measured from NIPA data. McGrattan also shows that the economy with intangibles closely accounts for the 2008–14 US economy, despite the fact that the standard measure of TFP based on NIPA data is not highly correlated with hours worked during this period.

Another literature that relates intangible investments to productivity is in the area of organization capital. As noted above, these investments are not counted in the NIPA. Atkeson and Kehoe (2005) study a neoclassical model in which an organization stochastically accumulates intangible knowledge over time. They find that the payments from these intangibles are about one-third as large as the payment from tangible capital, which suggests that organization capital is very large.

7.3 Neoclassical Models of Network Linkages and TFP

The impact of industry and/or sectoral shocks on the aggregate economy motivates a significant component of the real business cycle literature, including the seminal contribution of Long Jr and Plosser (1983), and subsequent research by Dupor (1999) and Horvath (2000). One theme of this research is to provide a theory for aggregate productivity shocks that hit the economy.

This idea is now being developed further in network models, which focus on the idea that production is organized through networks of supply chains, and that small disruptions in networks can have significant aggregate consequences, particularly if there are only a small number of suppliers of a particular input, and if there are no particularly close substitutes for that input. Carvalho (2014) describes much of the recent literature on networks and macroeconomics.

Carvalho describes a simple model of production networks in which individual sectors produce a specialized output. This output is produced using homogeneous labor and intermediate inputs from other sectors. The output of sector i is given by:

$$y_i = (z_i h_i)^{1-\theta}\left(\prod_{i=1}^{n} y_{ij}^{\omega_{ij}}\right)^{\theta}. \tag{85}$$

In this technology, y_i denotes sectoral output, z_i is a sectoral productivity shock, h_i is labor employed in sector i, and the exponents ω_{ij} denote the share of intermediate input j used in producing good i. Note that labor is supplied inelastically by a representative household, so aggregate labor is in fixed supply. For simplicity, preferences are symmetric over the i goods in the household utility function.

The empirical importance of network linkages can be identified from a standard input–output matrix. Since aggregate labor is in fixed supply, aggregate output is a weighted average of the sectoral productivity shocks:

$$\ln(y) = \sum_{i=1}^{n} \nu_i \ln(z_i). \quad (86)$$

In this expression, y is aggregate output and the ν_i are weights that are constructed from the input–output table. Note that measured aggregate productivity in this economy, which is $\frac{y}{h}$, will fluctuate even though there is no aggregate productivity shock. This simple model shows how a single shock to an important sector can have significant aggregate affects that will be observationally equivalent to a one-sector model with an aggregate productivity shock.

8. NEOCLASSICAL MODELS OF INEQUALITY

Neoclassical modeling is also making considerable progress in characterizing and quantifying how technological change has affected income distribution and wage inequality. Neoclassical studies of inequality analyze how biased technological change differentially affects the demand for different types of workers.

Early empirical studies by Katz and Murphy (1992), among others, concluded that skill-biased technological change was responsible for the widening wage gap between highly-educated workers and workers with less education. This conclusion reflects the fact that the relative supply of highly-skilled workers rose considerably, and the relative wage of these workers also rose.

Krusell et al. (2000) develop a neoclassical model to analyze how technological change has affected the relative wage of skilled to less-skilled workers. This relative wage is often called the *skill premium*. Krusell et al. provide an explicit theory of skill-biased technological change, show how to measure this change, and develop a neoclassical model to quantify its effect on inequality through observable variables.

The model features two different types of labor: high-skilled labor, who are workers with 16 or more years of education, and unskilled labor, who have fewer than 16 years of education.[t] Skill-biased technological change in this model is the combination of capital equipment-specific technological change, coupled with different substitution elasticities between the two types of labor. Krusell et al. construct a four factor production function

[t] Note that the term *unskilled* is used here not as a literal description of worker skill, but rather to clearly differentiate the two types of labor from each other.

that allows for different types of labor, and for different types of capital goods. The technology is given by:

$$y_t = A_t k_{st}^{\alpha}[\mu u_t^{\sigma} + (1-\mu)(\lambda k_{et}^{\rho} + (1-\lambda)s_t^{\rho})^{\frac{\sigma}{\rho}}]^{\frac{1-\alpha}{\sigma}} \tag{87}$$

The term A_t is a neutral technology parameter. The inputs are capital structures (k_{st}), unskilled labor input (u_t), which is the product of unskilled hours and unskilled labor efficiency ($\psi_{ut}h_{ut}$), capital equipment (k_{et}), and skilled labor input (s_t), which is the product of skilled labor hours and skilled labor efficiency ($\psi_{st}h_{st}$). These inputs are specified within a nested CES technology in which the curvature parameters σ and ρ govern the substitution elasticities among the inputs. In this technology, rapid growth of capital equipment raises the wage of skilled workers relative to the wage of unskilled workers only if capital equipment is more complementary with skilled labor than with unskilled labor. This requires that $\sigma > \rho$, which Krusell et al. call *capital-skill complementarity.*

It is straightforward to see this requirement of $\sigma > \rho$ by assuming that ψ_{st} and ψ_{ut} are constant, log-linearizing the ratio of the marginal productivities of the two types of labor, and expressing variables in terms of growth rates between periods t and $t+1$:

$$g_{\pi t} \simeq (1-\sigma)(g_{h_{ut}} - g_{h_{st}}) + (\sigma-\rho)\lambda\left(\frac{k_{et}}{s_t}\right)^{\rho}(g_{k_{et}} - g_{h_{st}}) \tag{88}$$

In (90), g_{π} is the growth rate of the skill premium, g_{h_u} and g_{h_s} are the growth rates of unskilled and skilled hours, and g_{k_e} is the growth rate of capital equipment. Since the parameter σ is less than one, the first term on the right hand side of (90) shows that the skill premium declines if the growth rate of skilled hours exceeds the growth rate of unskilled hours. Krusell et al. call this first term the *relative quantity effect.* The second term is called the *capital-skill complementarity effect.* This second term shows that the skill premium rises if the growth rate of capital equipment exceeds the growth rate of skilled hours, and if there is relatively more complementarity between skilled labor and equipment ($\sigma > \rho$).

Krusell et al. construct a dataset of skilled and unskilled labor input using data from the Current Population Survey. They use Gordon's (1990) data on equipment prices to construct a measure of the stock of capital equipment, and they use the NIPA measure of capital structures.

They estimate the parameters of the nonlinear production function with data from 1963 to 1992 using two-step simulated pseudo-maximum likelihood. They fit the model using the equations that measure the deviation between model and data for total labor's share of income, and the ratio of skilled labor income to unskilled labor income. The third equation in the criterion function measures the deviation between the rate of return to investment in structures to equipment. They estimate substitution elasticities of about 1.67 between unskilled labor and equipment, and of about 0.67 between skilled labor and

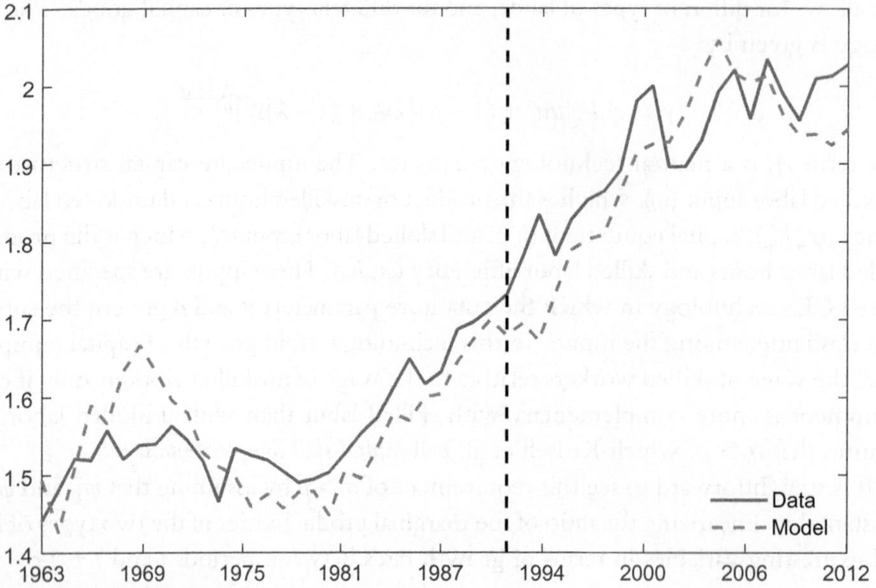

Fig. 30 Comparing college skill premium, model and data.

equipment, which provides strong support for capital-skill complementarity. They find that the model accounts for much of the movements in the skill premium over the 1963–92 period.

Given that the Krusell et al. data end in 1992, Ohanian and Orak (2016) analyze this same model, but extend the dataset through 2013 to assess the contribution of capital-skill complementarity to wage inequality for the last 20 years. Fig. 30 shows the skill premium in the model and in the data from 1963 to 2013. To compare the analysis to Krusell et al., Ohanian and Orak also estimate the model from 1963 to 1992. The dashed line in Fig. 30 corresponds to the end of the estimation period for the parameters (1992). Although Ohanian and Orak use the same sample period to estimate the parameters, they use revised data in the estimation. They find very similar elasticities to those in Krusell et al. Ohanian and Orak estimate an elasticity of about 1.78 between unskilled labor and equipment, and about 0.69 between skilled labor and equipment. The figure shows that the model accounts for the major changes in the skill premium, including the very large rise that has occurred in the last 30 years.[u]

The Krusell et al. model also fits aggregate labor share very well up until the mid-2000s. After that, the model overpredicts labor's share. This finding led Orak (2016) to analyze the same type of production function with different substitution possibilities

[u] Krusell et al. normalize the skill premium to 1 in 1963, and report fluctuations relative to the normalized value. To show the actual level of the skill premium, Ohanian and Orak estimate the model with normalized data as in Krusell et al. and then reconstruct the levels data. See Ohanian and Orak for details.

between capital equipment and different types of skills, but with three types of labor, as opposed to two types of labor. The labor types in Orak are classified based on occupational tasks, as in Autor et al. (2003), rather than on education levels, as in Krusell et al.

Orak specifies the three types of labor based on whether an occupation primarily performs cognitive tasks, manual tasks, or routine tasks. He estimates a relatively high elasticity of substitution between capital equipment and workers who perform routine tasks, and he estimates lower substitution elasticities between equipment and cognitive workers, and between equipment and manual workers. He finds that this augmented neoclassical model can account for much of the recent and significant decline in labor's share of income.

9. NEOCLASSICAL MACROECONOMICS: CRITICAL ASSESSMENTS AND FUTURE DIRECTIONS

This section discusses the open questions in the area of neoclassical macroeconomics, and presents our views on interesting future avenues for research that will address these questions. Perhaps the major open question for neoclassical models—and which is also a major question for other classes of macroeconomic models—is accounting for fluctuations in hours worked. The multisector models developed in this chapter account for considerably more of the fluctuations in hours worked than the standard one-sector neoclassical model, but there are also changes in hours that these models do not capture. Below, we describe the research areas that we view as important and promising in addressing this issue and others.

9.1 Biased Technological Change and the Labor Market

Analysis of biased technological change, and its impact on both aggregate variables and on labor market outcomes of workers with different skill levels, is an interesting avenue for future research. The home production results from the model motivated by Greenwood et al. (2005) indicate interesting trend changes in hours worked from the early 1980s through the 1990s, which coincide with the increase in women's hours worked. Important future research will further connect this demographic increase in hours worked with general equilibrium models of home production.

More broadly, it will be important to further develop models in the area of directed technological change and the shape of the production function, as in Acemoglu (2002) and Jones (2005), the relationship between technologies and secular sectoral shifts, as in Lee and Wolpin (2006), human capital accumulation and technological change, as in Heckman et al. (1998), and demographic shifts, technological change, and wage shifts as in Jeong et al. (2015). A related area is studying movements in factor income shares, as in Karabarbounis and Neiman (2014) and Orak (2016), and the impact of factor endowments on how societies choose among biased technologies, as in Caselli and Coleman (2006).

All of these research areas are in relatively early stages of development, and merit additional analysis. Research in this area can also be combined with broader empirical studies of time allocation, including the analysis and documentation of home and market time allocation, as in Aguiar and Hurst (1997) and Aguiar et al. (2013), and studies of the allocation of time across rich and poor countries, as in Bick et al. (2016).

9.2 Neoclassical Analyses of the Great Recession and Its Aftermath

Several open questions remain about the Great Recession and its aftermath. This includes accounting for macroeconomic aggregates from 2008 and onwards, particularly for hours worked. The results presented in this chapter indicate that neoclassical models with standard measures of equipment-specific productivity shocks, and TFP shocks, and without any policy components, miss some features of the Great Recession. McGrattan (2016) argues that output mismeasurement resulting from the omission of intangible investments in GDP has important implications for measured TFP and labor wedge measures during the Great Recession. Further research in this important area is needed.

There are also interesting aspects of economic policies during this period that merit additional analysis. Mulligan (2012, 2013) argues that changes in social insurance programs and the Affordable Care Act depressed labor by implicitly raising tax rates on labor. Kydland and Zarazaga (2016) study how expectations of different types of tax policies may have contributed to the weak recovery from the Great Recession. Baker et al. (2015) measure the evolution of economic policy uncertainty during the Great Recession. These uncertainty measures can be used in models in which uncertainty can depress an economy, as in Bloom (2009) and Fernández-Villaverde et al. (2015). These factors may have implications for understanding changes in hours worked in recent years.

9.3 The Effect of Policy Changes and Institutions on Macroeconomic Performance

An important area for future research is quantifying the impact of observed departures from competitive markets on economies. Cole and Ohanian (2004) developed and applied a particular methodology in their study of cartelization and unionization in the US Great Depression. This approach was also applied by Lahiri and Yi (2009) in evaluating the affect of noncompetitive policies in West Bengal Indian development. A similar approach has been used by Cheremukhin et al. (2013, 2015) to study the impact of Lenin's policies and institutions on economic development in the USSR at that time, and to study the impact of Mao's policies and institutions on Chinese development in the 1940s and 1950s. Alder (2016) uses a related approach to analyze the contribution of labor union hold-up and imperfect competition on the decline of America's Rust Belt region in the postwar United States. Similar methods also can be used to study the recent evolution of the post-Soviet Union economies, to study recent Indian and Chinese development patterns (see Dekle and Vandenbroucke (2012) for a neoclassical study of recent trends in China's economy), and to study long-run Latin American development (see Cole et al., 2005 for a long-run analysis of Latin America). As better data becomes available, these methods can also be used to study how policies and institutions have affected the stagnation and development of very poor countries. Future research along these lines will allow us to understanding the relative importance of various noncompetitive policies across countries, and will be an important input in developing growth-enhancing policies in poor countries.

9.4 Analyses of TFP

Since productivity is central in neoclassical growth models, advancing our understanding of changes in TFP is another important area for future research. In the last 10 years, progress in evaluating TFP has been made along three different research lines: resource misallocation, intangible investments, and network economies. Advancements in misallocation analysis of TFP will be facilitated by the assessment of how actual economic policies have affected resource allocation and productivity loss. Continued advances in computing power will facilitate the analysis of network economies and intersectoral linkages in the study of TFP. The continued expansion of intangible investments into NIPA data will advance our understanding of intangibles investment and TFP.

An area that to our knowledge has not been studied in detail is to link changes in what Decker et al. (2014) call "business dynamism" to aggregate measures of TFP. Specifically, Decker et al. document lower rates of resource reallocation in the United States, and also a lower rate of successful start-ups that have occurred over time. This decline has coincided with a secular decline in productivity growth. Analyzing theoretical and empirical connections between these observations has the potential to advance our understanding of secular movements in productivity.

9.5 Taxes and Macroeconomic Activity

The impact of tax and fiscal policies on economic activity in neoclassical models is another interesting area for future work, and may advance our understanding of changes in hours worked. Research in this area has been constrained by the availability of data on tax rates and hours worked. Constructing tax rates along the lines of McDaniel's (2011) tax measurements for the OECD can in principle be extended to other countries. In terms of hours worked, Ohanian and Raffo (2011) construct panel data on hours in the OECD, and similar data constructions can be made for other countries.

10. CONCLUSIONS

This chapter presented aggregate data and a series of neoclassical models to show how the historical evolution of the US economy reflects much longer-run changes in economic activity than previously recognized, and that much of this evolution is plausibly interpreted as the consequences of long-run shifts in technologies and government policies.

This chapter shows that neoclassical models can shed light on relatively stable periods of aggregate economic activity, such as the post-Korean War US economy, but also on very turbulent periods that are typically considered to be far beyond the purview of neoclassical economics, including the Great Depression and World War II. Moreover, neoclassical analysis not only provides insights into purely aggregate issues, but also sheds light on how technological change has affected individual labor market outcomes.

Future macroeconomic analyses of fluctuations should shift from the standard practice of narrowly studying business cycle frequencies, and to include the quantitatively important lower frequency component of fluctuations that dominates much of the US historical economic record. We anticipate that neoclassical research along these lines will continue to advance the profession's knowledge in a number of areas reflecting both longer-run events and business cycle fluctuations. This includes Depressions, Growth Miracles, the macroeconomic effects of various types of government regulatory and fiscal policies, the sources and nature of productivity shocks, the effects of biased technological change on the macroeconomy and on individual labor market outcomes, and understanding cyclical and longer-run fluctuations in hours worked.

ACKNOWLEDGMENTS

We thank John Cochrane, Jesus Fernández-Villaverde, Kyle Herkenhoff, Per Krusell, Ed Prescott, Valerie Ramey, John Taylor, Harald Uhlig, seminar participants at the Handbook of Macroeconomics Conference, and at the 2015 Federal Reserve Bank of Saint Louis Policy Conference for comments. Adrien D'Avernas Des Enffans, Eric Bai, Andreas Gulyas, Jinwook Hur, and Musa Orak provided excellent research assistance.

REFERENCES

Acemoglu, D., 2002. Directed technical change. Rev. Econ. Stud. 69 (4), 781–809.

Aguiar, M., Hurst, E., 1997. Life-cycle prices and production. Am. Econ. Rev. 5 (3), 1533–1599.

Aguiar, M., Hurst, E., Karabarbounis, L., 2013. Time use during the Great Recession. Am. Econ. Rev. 103 (5), 1664–1696.

Ahearne, A., Kydland, F., Wynne, M.A., 2006. Ireland's Great Depression. Econ. Soc. Rev. 37 (2), 215–243.

Alder, S., 2016. In the wrong hands: complementarities, resource allocation, and TFP. Am. Econ. J.: Macroecon. 8 (1), 199–241.

Alesina, A.F., Glaeser, E.L., Sacerdote, B., 2006. Work and leisure in the US and Europe: why so different?. In: Gertler, M., Rogoff, K. (Eds.), NBER Macroeconomics Annual 2005, vol. 20. MIT Press, Cambridge, MA, pp. 1–100.

Amaral, P.S., MacGee, J.C., 2015. Re-examining the role of sticky wages in the U.S. Great Depression: a multi-sector approach, University of Western Ontario.
Arias, A., Hansen, G., Ohanian, L.E., 2007. Why have business cycle fluctuations become less volatile? Econ. Theory 32 (1), 43–58.
Atkeson, A., Kehoe, P.J., 2005. Modeling and measuring organization capital. J. Polit. Econ. 113 (5), 1026–1053.
Atkeson, A., Khan, A., Ohanian, L.E., 1996. Are data on industry evolution and gross job turnover relevant for macroeconomics? Carn. Roch. Conf. Ser. Public Policy 44 (2), 215–250.
Autor, D.H., Levy, F., Murnane, R.J., 2003. The skill content of recent technological change: an empirical exploration. Q. J. Econ. 118 (4), 1279–1333.
Baker, S.R., Bloom, N., Davis, S.J., 2015. Measuring economic policy uncertainty. National Bureau of Economic Research. Working Paper No. 21633.
Barro, R.J., 1981. Intertemporal substitution and the business cycle. Carn. Roch. Conf. Ser. Public Policy 14 (1), 237–268.
Barro, R.J., King, R.G., 1984. Time-separable preferences and intertemporal-substitution models of business cycles. Q. J. Econ. 99 (4), 817–839.
Barro, R.J., Redlick, C.J., 2011. Macroeconomic effects from government purchases and taxes. Q. J. Econ. 126 (1), 51–102.
Braun, R.A., McGrattan, E.R., 1993. The macroeconomics of war and peace. In: Blanchard, O., Fischer, S. (Eds.), NBER Macroeconomics Annual 1993. In: MIT Press 8, Cambridge, MA, pp. 197–258.
Baxter, M., King, R.G., 1993. Fiscal policy in general equilibrium. Am. Econ. Rev. 83 (3), 315–334.
Baxter, M., King, R.G., 1999. Measuring business cycles: approximate band-pass filters for economic time series. Rev. Econ. Stat. 81 (4), 575–593.
Benhabib, J., Rogerson, R., Wright, R., 1991. Homework in macroeconomics: household production and aggregate fluctuations. J. Polit. Econ. 99 (6), 1166–1187.
Bernanke, B.S., 1983. Nonmonetary effects of the financial crisis in the propagation of the Great Depression. Am. Econ. Rev. 73 (3), 257–276.
Beveridge, S., Nelson, C.R., 1981. A new approach to decomposition of economic time series into permanent and transitory components with particular attention to measurement of the 'business cycle'. J. Monet. Econ. 7 (2), 151–174.
Bick, A., Lagakos, D., Fuchs-Schundeln, N., 2016. How do average hours worked vary with development: cross-country evidence and implications. Unpublished paper.
Blanchard, O., 2004. The economic future of Europe. J. Econ. Perspect. 18 (4), 3–26.
Bloom, N., 2009. The impact of uncertainty shocks. Econometrica 77 (3), 623–685.
Bond, E.W., Crucini, M.J., Potter, T., Rodrigue, J., 2013. Misallocation and productivity effects of the Smoot-Hawley tariff. Rev. Econ. Dyn. 16 (1), 120–134.
Bordo, M.D., Erceg, C.J., Evans, C.L., 2000. Money, sticky wages, and the Great Depression. Am. Econ. Rev. 90 (5), 1447–1463.
Brinca, P., Chari, V.V., Kehoe, P.J., McGrattan, E.R., 2016. Accounting for business cycles. In: Taylor, J., Uhlig, H. (Eds.), Handbook of Macroeconomics, vol. 2A. Elsevier, Amsterdam, Netherlands, pp. 1013–1063.
Buera, F.J., Moll, B., 2015. Aggregate implications of a credit crunch: the importance of heterogeneity. Am. Econ. J. Macroecon. 7 (3), 1–42.
Burns, A.F., Mitchell, W.C., 1946. Measuring Business Cycles. National Bureau of Economic Research, New York.
Burnside, C., Eichenbaum, M., Fisher, J.D.M., 2004. Fiscal shocks and their consequences. J. Econ. Theory 115 (1), 89–117.
Carvalho, V.M., 2014. From micro to macro via production networks. J. Econ. Perspect. 28 (4), 23–47.
Caselli, F., Coleman II, J.W., 2006. The world technology frontier. Am. Econ. Rev. 96 (3), 499–522.
Chang, Y., Schorfheide, F., 2003. Labor-supply shifts and economic fluctuations. J. Monet. Econ. 50 (8), 1751–1768.
Chari, V.V., Kehoe, P.J., McGrattan, E.R., 2007. Business cycle accounting. Econometrica 75 (3), 781–836.
Chen, K., Irarrazabal, A., 2013. Misallocation and the recovery of manufacturing TFP after a financial crisis. Norges Bank. Working Paper 2013-01.

Cheremukhin, A., Golosov, M., Guriev, S., Tsyvinski, A., 2013. Was Stalin necessary for Russia's economic development? National Bureau of Economic Research. Working Paper No. 19425.
Cheremukhin, A., Golosov, M., Guriev, S., Tsyvinski, A., 2015. The economy of People's Republic of China from 1953. National Bureau of Economic Research. Working Paper No. 21397.
Christiano, L.J., Eichenbaum, M., 1992. Current real-business-cycle theories and aggregate labor-market fluctuations. Am. Econ. Rev. 82 (3), 430–450.
Christiano, L.J., Fitzgerald, T.J., 2003. The band pass filter. Int. Econ. Rev. 44 (2), 435–465.
Cociuba, S., Prescott, E., Ueberfeldt, A., 2012. U.S. hours and productivity behavior using CPS hours worked data: 1947-III to 2011-IV. Discussion paper.
Cole, H.L., Ohanian, L.E., 1999. The Great Depression in the United States from a neoclassical perspective. Fed. Reserve Bank Minneapolis Q. Rev. 23 (1), 2–24.
Cole, H.L., Ohanian, L.E., 2002. The Great UK Depression: a puzzle and possible resolution. Rev. Econ. Dyn. 5 (1), 19–44.
Cole, H.L., Ohanian, L.E., 2004. New Deal policies and the persistence of the Great Depression. J. Polit. Econ. 112 (4), 779–816.
Cole, H.L., Ohanian, L.E., 2016. The impact of cartelization, money, and productivity shocks on the international Great Depression. Unpublished.
Cole, H.L., Ohanian, L.E., Riascos, A., Schmitz, J.A., 2005. Latin America in the rearview mirror. J. Monet. Econ. 52 (1), 69–107.
Comin, D., Gertler, M., 2006. Medium-term business cycles. Am. Econ. Rev. 96 (3), 523–551.
Conesa, J.C., Kehoe, T.J., Ruhl, K.J., 2007. Modeling great depressions: the depression in Finland in the 1990s. In: Kehoe, T.J., Prescott, E.C. (Eds.), Great Depressions of the 20th Century. Federal Reserve Bank of Minneapolis, Minneapolis, MN.
Cooley, T.F. (Ed.), 1995. Frontiers of Business Cycle Research. Princeton University Press, Princeton, NJ.
Cummins, J.G., Violante, G.L., 2002. Investment-specific technical change in the United States (1947-2000): measurement and macroeconomic consequences. Rev. Econ. Dyn. 5 (2), 243–284.
Dalton, J.T., 2015. The evolution of taxes and hours worked in Austria, 1970-2005. Macroecon. Dyn. 19 (8), 1800–1815.
David, J.M., Hopenhayn, H.A., Venkateswaran, V., forthcoming. Information, misallocation and aggregate productivity. Q. J. Econ.
Davis, S.J., Haltiwanger, J., 1992. Gross job creation, gross job destruction, and employment reallocation. Q. J. Econ. 107 (3), 819–863.
Davis, S.J., Henrekson, M., et al., 2005. Tax effects on work activity, industry mix, and shadow economy size: evidence from rich country comparisons. In: Gómez-Salvador, R. (Ed.), Labour Supply and Incentives to Work in Europe. Edward Elgar, Cheltenham, UK.
Decker, R., Haltiwanger, J., Jarmin, R., Miranda, J., 2014. The role of entrepreneurship in US job creation and economic dynamism. J. Econ. Perspect. 28 (3), 3–24.
Dekle, R., Vandenbroucke, G., 2012. A quantitative analysis of China's structural transformation. J. Econ. Dyn. Control 36 (1), 119–135.
DiCecio, R., 2009. Sticky wages and sectoral labor comovement. J. Econ. Dyn. Control. 33 (3), 538–553.
Doepke, M., Hazan, M., Maoz, Y.D., 2015. The baby boom and World War II: a macroeconomic analysis. Rev. Econ. Stud. 82 (3), 1031–1073.
Dupor, B., 1999. Aggregation and irrelevance in multi-sector models. J. Monet. Econ. 43 (2), 391–409.
Ebell, M., Ritschl, A., 2008. Real origins of the Great Depression: monopoly power, unions and the American business cycle in the 1920s. CEP Discussion Paper No. 876.
Eggertsson, G.B., 2012. Was the New Deal contractionary? Am. Econ. Rev. 102 (1), 524–555.
Erosa, A., Fuster, L., Kambourov, G., 2012. Labor supply and government programs: a cross-country analysis. J. Monet. Econ. 59 (1), 84–107.
Feenstra, R.C., Inklaar, R., Timmer, M.P., 2015. The next generation of the Penn World Table. Am. Econ. Rev. 105 (10), 3150–3182.
Fernald, J., 2014. A quarterly, utilization-adjusted series on total factor productivity. Federal Reserve Bank of San Francisco. Working Paper 2012-19.

Fernández-Villaverde, J., Guerrón-Quintana, P., Kuester, K., Rubio-Ramírez, J., 2015. Fiscal volatility shocks and economic activity. Am. Econ. Rev. 105 (11), 3352–3384.
Field, A.J., 2003. The most technologically progressive decade of the century. Am. Econ. Rev. 93 (4), 1399–1413.
Fisher, J.D.M., 2006. The dynamic effects of neutral and investment-specific technology shocks. J. Polit. Econ. 114 (3), 413–451.
Friedman, M., Schwartz, A.J., 1963. Monetary History of the United States, 1867-1960. Princeton University Press, Princeton, NJ.
Gali, J., van Rens, T., 2014. The vanishing procyclicality of labor productivity. Unpublished paper.
Gordon, R.J., 1990. The Measurement of Durable Goods Prices. University of Chicago Press, Chicago, IL.
Gorodnichenko, Y., Mendoza, E.G., Tesar, L.L., 2012. The Finnish Great Depression: from Russia with love. Am. Econ. Rev. 102 (4), 1619–1643.
Greenwood, J., Hercowitz, Z., Krusell, P., 1997. Long-run implications of investment-specific technological change. Am. Econ. Rev. 87 (3), 342–362.
Greenwood, J., Seshadri, A., Yorukoglu, M., 2005. Engines of liberation. Rev. Econ. Stud. 72 (1), 109–133.
Greenwood, J., Yorukoglu, M., 1997. Carn. Roch. Conf. Ser. Public Policy 46 (1), 49–95.
Guner, N., Ventura, G., Yi, X., 2008. Macroeconomic implications of size-dependent policies. Rev. Econ. Dyn. 11 (4), 721–744.
Hansen, G.D., 1985. Indivisible labor and the business cycle. J. Monet. Econ. 16 (3), 309–327.
Hansen, G.D., 1997. Technical progress and aggregate fluctuations. J. Econ. Dyn. Control 21 (6), 1005–1023.
Hansen, G.D., Prescott, E.C., 1993. Did technology shocks cause the 1990-1991 recession? Am. Econ. Rev. 83 (2), 280–286.
Hayashi, F., Prescott, E.C., 2002. The 1990s in Japan: a lost decade. Rev. Econ. Dyn. 5 (1), 206–235.
Heckman, J.J., Lochner, L., Taber, C., 1998. Explaining rising wage inequality: explorations with a dynamic general equilibrium model of labor earnings with heterogeneous agents. Rev. Econ. Dyn. 1 (1), 1–58.
Herman, A., 2012. Freedom's Forge: How American Business Produced Victory in World War II. Random House, New York City, NY.
Hodrick, R., Prescott, E.C., 1997. Postwar U.S. business cycles: an empirical investigation. J. Money Credit Bank. 29 (1), 1–16.
Hopenhayn, H., Rogerson, R., 1993. Job turnover and policy evaluation: a general equilibrium analysis. J. Polit. Econ. 101 (5), 915–938.
Horvath, M., 2000. Sectoral shocks and aggregate fluctuations. J. Monet. Econ. 45 (1), 69–106.
Hsieh, C.T., Klenow, P.J., 2009. Misallocation and manufacturing TFP in China and India. Q. J. Econ. 124 (4), 1403–1448.
Jeong, H., Kim, Y., Manovskii, I., 2015. The price of experience. Am. Econ. Rev. 105 (2), 784–815.
Joines, D.H., 1981. Estimates of effective marginal tax rates on factor incomes. J. Bus. 54 (2), 191–226.
Jones, C.I., 2005. The shape of production functions and the direction of technical change. Q. J. Econ. 120 (2), 517–549.
Jones, C.I., 2013. Misallocation, economic growth, and input-output economics. In: Acemoglu, D., Arellano, M., Dekel, E. (Eds.), Advances in Economics and Econometrics, Tenth World Congress. vol. II. Cambridge University Press, Cambridge.
Justiniano, A., Primiceri, G.E., Tambalotti, A., 2010. Investment shocks and business cycles. J. Monet. Econ. 57 (2), 132–145.
Karabarbounis, L., Neiman, B., 2014. The global decline of the labor share. Q. J. Econ. 129 (1), 61–103.
Katz, L.F., Murphy, K.M., 1992. Changes in relative wages, 1963-1987: supply and demand factors. Q. J. Econ. 107 (1), 35–78.
Kehoe, T.J., Prescott, E.C., 2007. Great Depressions of the Twentieth Century. Federal Reserve Bank of Minneapolis, Minneapolis, MN.
Kendrick, J., 1961. Productivity Trends in the United States. Princeton University Press, Princeton, NJ.
Klein, P., Ventura, G., 2015. Making a miracle: Ireland 1980-2005. Unpublished paper.
Kovacic, W.E., Shapiro, C., 2000. Antitrust policy: a century of economic and legal thinking. J. Econ. Perspect. 14 (1), 43–60.

Krusell, P., Ohanian, L.E., Ríos-Rull, J.V., Violante, G.L., 2000. Capital-skill complementarity and inequality: a macroeconomic analysis. Econometrica 68 (5), 1029–1053.
Kydland, F.E., Prescott, E.C., 1982. Time to build and aggregate fluctuations. Econometrica 50 (6), 1345–1370.
Kydland, F.E., Prescott, E.C., 1988. The workweek of capital and its cyclical implications. J. Monet. Econ. 21 (2), 343–360.
Kydland, F.E., Zarazaga, C.E.J.M., 2016. Fiscal sentiment and the weak recovery from the Great Recession: a quantitative exploration. J. Monet. Econ. 79, 109–125.
Lahiri, A., Yi, K.-M., 2009. A tale of two states: Maharashtra and West Bengal. Rev. Econ. Dyn. 12 (3), 523–542.
Lee, D., Wolpin, K.I., 2006. Intersectoral labor mobility and the growth of the service sector. Econometrica 74 (1), 1–46.
Lilien, D.M., 1982. Sectoral shifts and cyclical unemployment. J. Polit. Econ. 90 (4), 777–793.
Ljungqvist, L., Sargent, T.J., 1998. The European unemployment dilemma. J. Polit. Econ. 106 (3), 514–550.
Long Jr., J.B., Plosser, C.I., 1983. Real business cycles. J. Polit. Econ. 91 (1), 39–69.
Lu, S.S., 2012. East Asian growth experience revisited from the perspective of a neoclassical model. Rev. Econ. Dyn. 15 (3), 359–376.
Lucas, R.E., 1973. Expectations and the neutrality of money. J. Econ. Theory 4 (2), 103–124.
Lucas, R.E., Rapping, L.A., 1969. Real wages, employment, and inflation. J. Polit. Econ. 77 (5), 721–754.
Lucas, R.E., Rapping, L.A., 1972. Unemployment in the Great Depression: is there a full explanation? J. Polit. Econ. 80 (1), 186–191.
Manuelli, R.E., Seshadri, A., 2014. Frictionless Technology Diffusion: The Case of Tractors. Am. Econ. Rev. 104 (4), 1368–1391.
McDaniel, C., 2011. Forces shaping hours worked in the OECD, 1960-2004. Am. Econ. J.: Macroecon. 3 (4), 27–52.
McGrattan, E.R., 2012. Capital taxation during the US Great Depression. Q. J. Econ. 127 (3), 1515–1550.
McGrattan, E.R., 2016. Intangible Capital and Measured Productivity. Working Paper, University of Minnesota, Minneapolis, MN.
McGrattan, E.R., Prescott, E.C., 2014. A reassessment of real business cycle theory. Am. Econ. Rev. Papers and Proceedings 104 (5), 177–187.
McGrattan, E.R., Ohanian, L.E., 2010. Does neoclassical theory account for the effects of big fiscal shocks? Evidence from World War II. Int. Econ. Rev. 51 (2), 509–532.
McGrattan, E.R., Prescott, E.C., 2012. The Great Recession and delayed economic recovery: a labor productivity puzzle? In: Ohanian, L.E., Taylor, J.B., Wright, I. (Eds.), Government Policies and the Delayed Economic Recovery. Hoover Press, Stanford, CA.
Meza, F., 2008. Financial crisis, fiscal policy, and the 1995 GDP contraction in Mexico. J. Money Credit Bank. 40 (6), 1239–1261.
Midrigan, V., Xu, D.Y., 2014. Finance and misallocation: evidence from plant-level data. Am. Econ. Rev. 104 (2), 422–458.
Modigliani, F., 1977. The monetarist controversy or, should we forsake stabilization policies? Am. Econ. Rev. 67 (2), 1–19.
Moll, B., 2014. Productivity losses from financial frictions: can self-financing undo capital misallocation? Am. Econ. Rev. 104 (10), 3186–3221.
Monacelli, T., Perotti, R., 2008. Fiscal policy, wealth effects, and markups. National Bureau of Economic Research. Working Paper No. 14584.
Morley, J., Nelson, C.R., Zivot, E., 2003. Why are unobserved component and Beveridge-Nelson trend-cycle decompositions of GDP so different? Rev. Econ. Stat. 85 (2), 235–243.
Mountford, A., Uhlig, H., 2009. What are the effects of fiscal policy shocks? J. Appl. Econ. 24 (6), 960–992.
Mulligan, C., 2012. The Redistribution Recession: How Labor Market Distortions Contracted the Economy. Oxford University Press, Oxford.
Mulligan, C., 2013. Average marginal labor income tax rates under the Affordable Care Act. National Bureau of Economic Research. Working Paper No. 19365.
Mulligan, C.B., 2005. Public policies as specification errors. Rev. Econ. Dyn. 8 (4), 902–926.

Oberfield, E., 2013. Productivity and misallocation during a crisis: evidence from the Chilean crisis of 1982. Rev. Econ. Dyn. 16 (1), 100–119.
Ohanian, L.E., 1997. The macroeconomic effects of war finance in the United States: World War II and the Korean War. Am. Econ. Rev. 87 (1), 23–40.
Ohanian, L.E., 2001. Why did productivity fall so much during the Great Depression? Am. Econ. Rev. 91 (2), 34–38.
Ohanian, L.E., 2009. What - or - who started the Great Depression? J. Econ. Theory 144 (6), 2310–2335.
Ohanian, L.E., 2010. The economic crisis from a neoclassical perspective. J. Econ. Perspect. 24 (4), 45–66.
Ohanian, L.E., 2011. Comment on 'what fiscal policy is effective at zero interest rates'? In: Acemoglu, D., Woodford, M. (Eds.), NBER Macroeconomics Annual 2010, vol. 25. University of Chicago Press, Chicago, IL, pp. 125–137.
Ohanian, L.E., Orak, M., 2016. Capital-skill complementarity, inequality, and labor's share of income, 1963-2013. Discussion paper.
Ohanian, L.E., Raffo, A., 2011. Aggregate hours worked in OECD countries: new measurement and implications for business cycles. National Bureau of Economic Research. Working Paper 17420.
Ohanian, L., Raffo, A., Rogerson, R., 2008. Long-term changes in labor supply and taxes: evidence from OECD countries, 1956–2004. J. Monet. Econ. 55 (8), 1353–1362.
Orak, M., 2016. Capital-Task Complementarity and the Decline of the US Labor Share of Income. Working Paper, UCLA, Los Angeles, CA.
Osuna, V., Rios-Rull, J.-V., 2003. Implementing the 35 hour workweek by means of overtime taxation. Rev. Econ. Dyn. 6 (1), 179–206.
Otsu, K., 2008. A neoclassical analysis of the Korean crisis. Rev. Econ. Dyn. 11 (2), 449–471.
Poschke, M., 2010. The regulation of entry and aggregate productivity. Econ. J. 120 (549), 1175–1200.
Prescott, E.C., 2004. Why do Americans work so much more than Europeans? Federal Reserve Bank of Minneapolis. Q. Rev.Vol. 28, 2–13. No. 1, July 2004.
Ragan, K.S., 2013. Taxes and time use: fiscal policy in a household production model. Am. Econ. J.: Macroecon. 5 (1), 168–192.
Ramey, V.A., 2011. Can government purchases stimulate the economy? J. Econ. Lit. 49 (3), 673–685.
Rees, A., 1970. On equilibrium in labor markets. J. Polit. Econ. 78 (2), 306–310.
Restuccia, D., Rogerson, R., 2008. Policy distortions and aggregate productivity with heterogeneous establishments. Rev. Econ. Dyn. 11 (4), 707–720.
Rogerson, R., 2008. Structural transformation and the deterioration of European labor market outcomes. J. Polit. Econ. 116 (2), 235–259.
Rogerson, R., 2009. Market work, home work, and taxes: a cross-country analysis. Rev. Int. Econ. 17 (3), 588–601.
Samaniego, R.M., 2008. Can technical change exacerbate the effects of labor market sclerosis? J. Econ. Dyn. Control. 32 (2), 497–528.
Sandleris, G., Wright, M.L.J., 2014. The costs of financial crises: resource misallocation, productivity, and welfare in the 2001 Argentine crisis. Scand. J. Econ. 116 (1), 87–127.
Sargent, T.J., 1973. Rational expectations, the real rate of interest, and the natural rate of unemployment. Brook. Pap. Econ. Act. 2, 429–480.
Sargent, T.J., Wallace, N., 1975. 'Rational' expectations, the optimal monetary instrument, and the optimal money supply rule. J. Polit. Econ. 83 (2), 241–254.
Schumpeter, J., 1927. The explanation of the business cycle. Economica 21, 286–311.
Simon, C.J., 2001. The supply price of labor during the Great Depression. J. Econ. Hist. 61 (4), 877–903.
Siu, H.E., 2008. The fiscal role of conscription in the US World War II effort. J. Monet. Econ. 55 (6), 1094–1112.
Smets, F., Wouters, R., 2007. Shocks and frictions in US business cycles: a Bayesian DSGE approach. Am. Econ. Rev. 97 (3), 586–606.
Stock, J.H., Watson, M.W., 1988. Variable trends in economic time series. J. Econ. Perspect. 2 (3), 147–174.
Stock, J.H., Watson, M.W., 2003. Has the business cycle changed and why? NBER Macroeconomics Annual 2002, vol. 17. MIT Press, Cambridge, MA, pp. 159–230.

Taylor, J.B., 2010. Getting back on track: macroeconomic policy lessons from the financial crisis. Fed. Reserve Bank St. Louis Rev 92 (3), 165–176.

Taylor, J.B., 2011. An empirical analysis of the revival of fiscal activism in the 2000s. J. Econ. Lit. 49 (3), 686–702.

Uhlig, H., 1999. A toolkit for analysing nonlinear dynamic stochastic models easily. Ramon marimon and andrew scott: computational methods for the study of dynamic economies. Oxford University Press, Oxford and New York, pp. 30–61.

Valentinyi, A., Herrendorf, B., 2008. Measuring factor income shares at the sector level. Rev. Econ. Dyn. 11 (4), 820–835.

Watson, M.W., 1986. Univariate detrending methods with stochastic trends. J. Monet. Econ. 18 (1), 49–75.

Ziebarth, N.L., 2014. Misallocation and productivity in the Great Depression. Unpublished.

CHAPTER 27

Macroeconomics of Persistent Slumps

R.E. Hall
Hoover Institution, Stanford University, CA; National Bureau of Economic Research, Cambridge, MA, United States

Contents

Handbook of Macroeconomics, Volume 2B
ISSN 1574-0048, http://dx.doi.org/10.1016/bs.hesmac.2016.03.010

Abstract

In modern economies, sharp increases in unemployment from major adverse shocks result in long periods of abnormal unemployment and low output. This chapter investigates the processes that account for these persistent slumps. The data are from the economy of the United States, and the discussion emphasizes the financial crisis of 2008 and the ensuing slump. The framework starts by discerning driving forces set in motion by the initial shock. These are higher discounts applied by decision makers (possibly related to a loss of confidence), withdrawal of potential workers from the labor market, diminished productivity growth, higher markups in product markets, and spending declines resulting from tighter lending standards at financial institutions. The next step is to study how driving forces influence general equilibrium, both at the time of the initial shock and later as its effects, persist. Some of the effects propagate the effects of the shock—they contribute to poor performance even after the driving force itself has subsided. Depletion of the capital stock is the most important of these propagation mechanisms. I use a medium-frequency dynamic equilibrium model to gain some notions of the magnitudes of responses and propagation.

Keywords

Financial crisis, Great recession, Slump, Unemployment, Labor-force participation, Stagnation, Sources of economic fluctuations, Economic driving forces, Economic shocks, Confidence, Propagation

JEL Classification Codes

E24, E32, G12

Beginning in 2008, output and employment in the United States dropped well below its previous growth path. Eight years later, unemployment is back to normal, but output remains below the growth path. Japan has been in a persistent slump for two decades. And many of the advanced economies of Europe are in slumps, several quite deep. This chapter reviews the macroeconomics of slumps taking the American experience as a leading example.

The adverse shock that launches a slump generally triggers a rapid contraction of output and employment, with a substantial jump in unemployment. This phase—the recession—is usually brief. It ended in mid-2009 in the recent case. The recovery from the trough often lasts many years. The slump is the entire period of substandard output and employment and excess unemployment. In the recent U.S. case, the slump lasted

Table 1 Unemployment in the four serious slumps since 1948

		Ratio of later unemployment rate to peak rate, by number of years later			
Peak year	**Peak rate**	**1**	**2**	**3**	**4**
1975	8.5	0.91	0.84	0.72	0.69
1982	9.7	0.99	0.77	0.74	0.72
1992	7.5	0.92	0.81	0.75	0.72
2010	9.6	0.93	0.84	0.77	0.65

from late 2008 until around the end of 2014. Dating the end of a slump is challenging because some of the state variables accounting for depressed output, notably the capital stock, take many years to return to normal. Output in 2014 was well below its earlier trend path.

Persistent slumps did not begin with the one that originated from the financial crisis of 2008. The Great Depression remains much the deepest and longest slump in the American record since the beginning of national income accounting. Table 1 shows that the persistence of unemployment was about equally high in the four major slumps that occurred after the introduction of the household unemployment survey in 1948. Normal unemployment in the United States, measured as its average over the period starting in 1948, is 6.0%. In all four slumps, unemployment remained above normal 3 years following the peak of unemployment, and in only one slump, the milder one associated with the recession of 1990–91, did unemployment drop below normal 4 years after the peak of unemployment.

Other accounts of persistent shortfalls in output and employment, focusing on the financial crisis and its aftermath, include Kocherlakota (2013), Christiano et al. (2016), Christiano et al. (2010), Benigno and Fornaro (2015), Petrosky-Nadeau and Wasmer (2015), Gertler et al. (2008), Mian and Sufi (2010), Reifschneider et al. (2013), Hall (2013, 2014).

1. THE SLUMP FOLLOWING THE 2008 FINANCIAL CRISIS

This section provides the factual foundation for the chapter by describing events in the U.S. economy around the time of the 2008 crisis, through to 2014. I provide plots of key macroeconomic variables with brief discussions. The rest of the chapter considers the ideas and models that seem most relevant to understanding those events.

Fig. 1 shows that real GDP fell dramatically right after the crisis and remained below its prior growth path even 6 years after the crisis. Plainly the crisis had a persistent effect on the total output of goods and services. Fig. 2 shows that real consumption expenditures behaved similar to real GDP, with no sign of regaining its earlier growth path over the

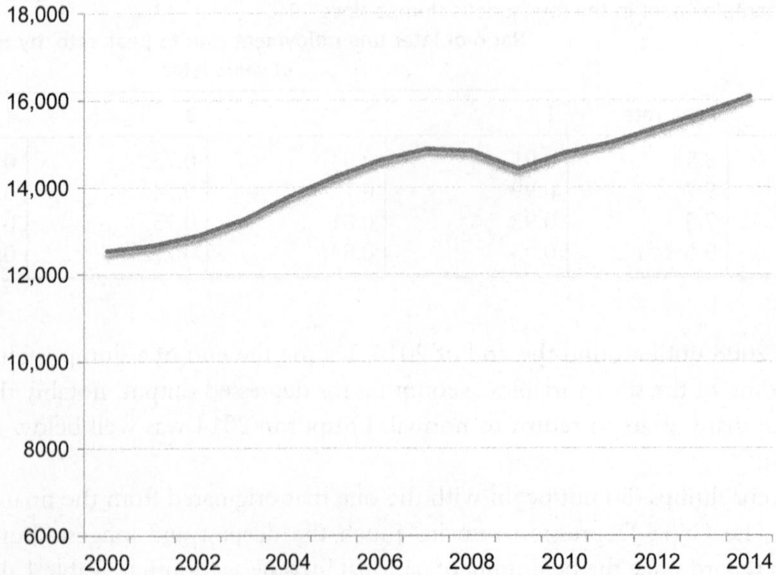

Fig. 1 Real GDP, 2000–14, billions of 2009 dollars.

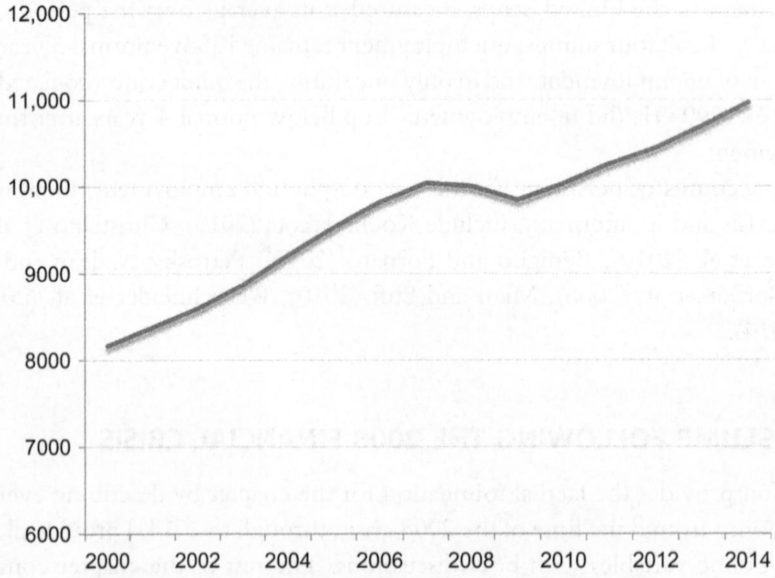

Fig. 2 Real consumption expenditure, 2000–14, billions of 2009 dollars.

period following the 2008 crisis. Fig. 3 shows persistent shortfalls from the growth path of employment. Fig. 4 shows that unemployment rose to a high level and returned to its long-run average of 5.8% at the end of 2014, 6 years after the crisis. The unemployment rate is the only major macroeconomic indicator that returned to normal within the 6-year

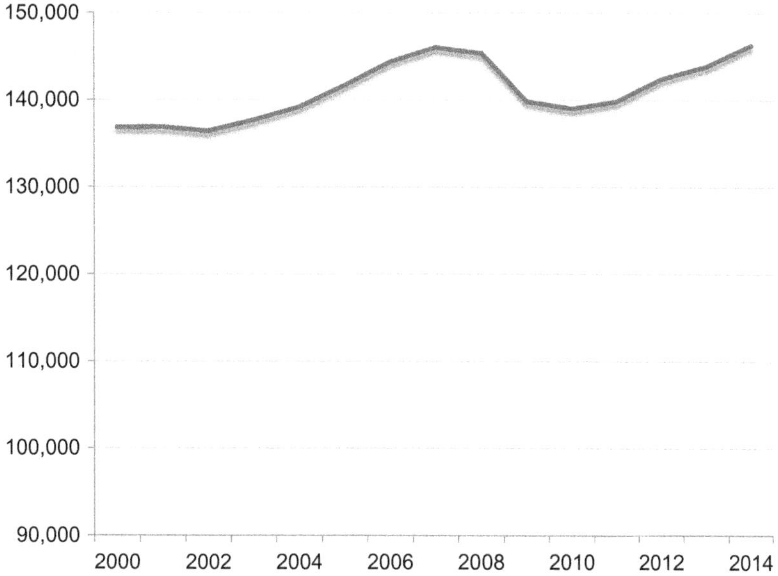

Fig. 3 Employment, 2000–14, thousands of workers.

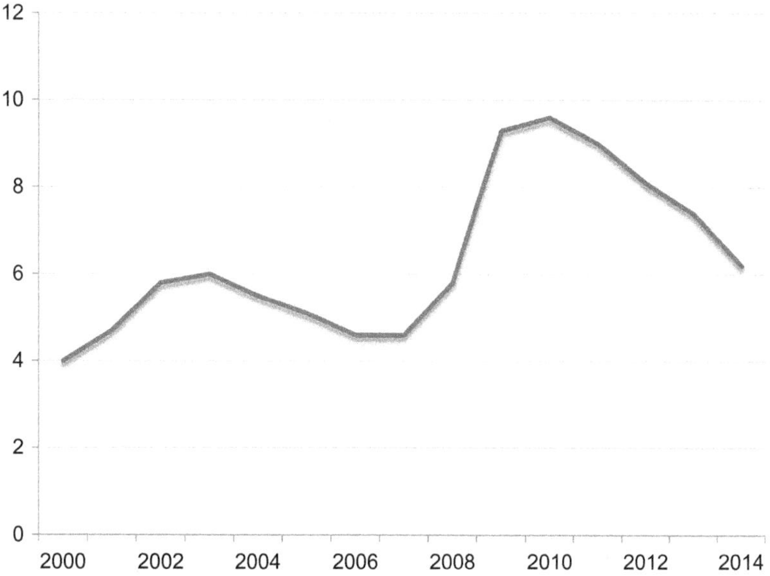

Fig. 4 Unemployment, 2000–14, percent of labor force.

period considered here. Fig. 5 shows that the labor force shrank after the crisis, relative to the working-age population, and that no recovery of the labor force occurred during the recovery. Fig. 6 shows that average real compensation per household, which had grown briskly through 2000, flattened before the crisis, fell sharply just after the crisis, and only

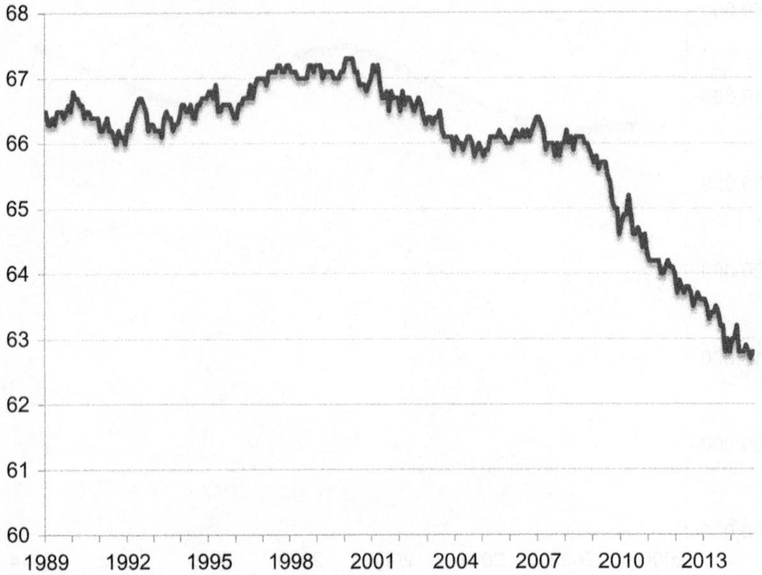

Fig. 5 Percent of working-age population in the labor force, 2000–14.

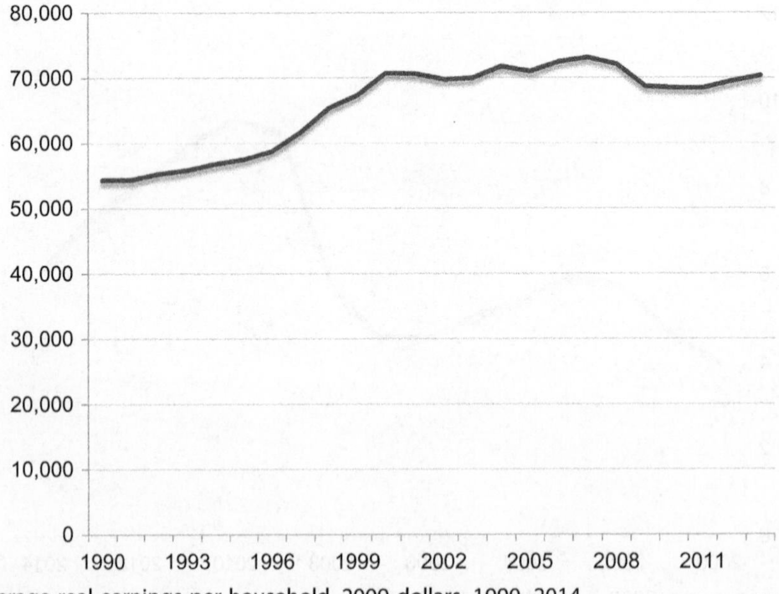

Fig. 6 Average real earnings per household, 2009 dollars, 1990–2014.

regained its previous level in 2014. Fig. 7 shows that the business capital stock—in the sense of an index of capital services available to private businesses—grew much less rapidly than normal immediately after the crisis. Its growth rate returned closer to normal, but left a considerable shortfall in capital relative to trend, as of 2014. Fig. 8 shows that

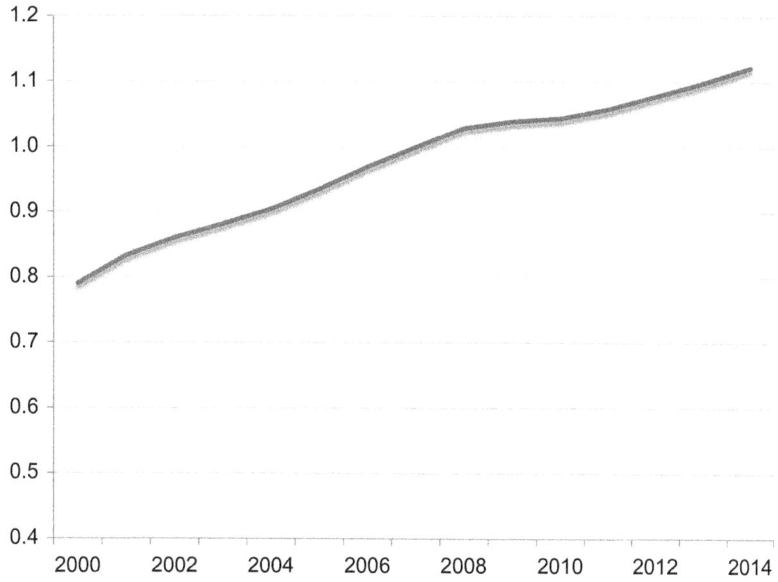

Fig. 7 Index of capital services, 2007 = 1, 2000–14.

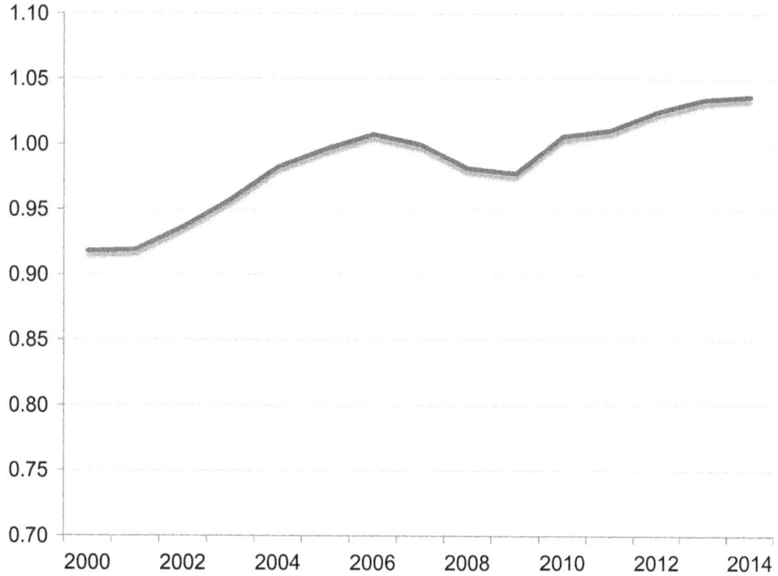

Fig. 8 Index of total factor productivity, 2007 = 1, 2000–14.

private business total factor productivity grew rapidly from 1989 through 2006. A dip in productivity began in 2007. Though productivity grew at normal rates during the recovery, it did not make up for the cumulative decline just after the crisis. Fig. 9 shows the index of the share of the total income generated in the U.S. economy that accrues to

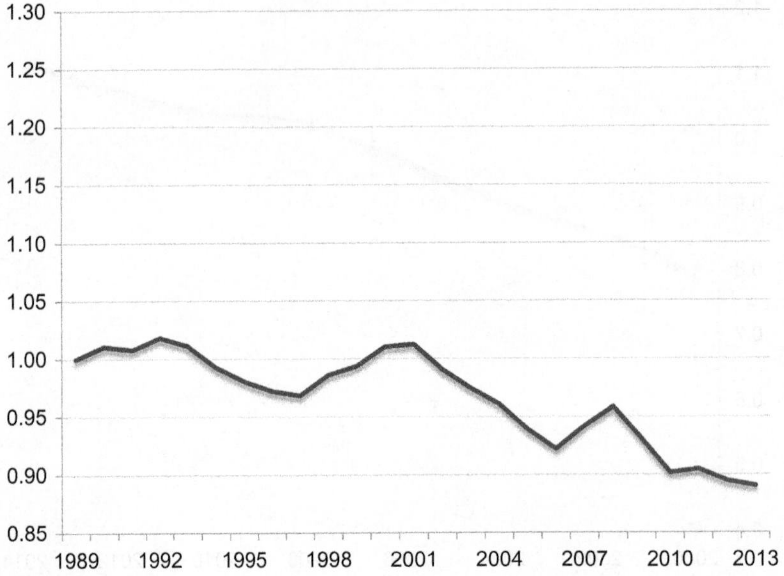

Fig. 9 Labor share.

workers, including fringe benefits. It tends to have a high level in recession years, to fall during the first half of the ensuing expansion, then to rise back to a high level at the next recession. But superimposed on that pattern is a general decline that cumulates to about 10% over the period. Like the general declining trend in earnings, the decline in the share seems to have started around 2000.

2. DRIVING FORCES

I use the term *driving force* to mean either an exogenous variable or an endogenous variable that is taken as an input to a macro model. An example of the latter case is a rise in the discount rate for investment and job creation, triggered by a financial crisis. There is no claim that the discount increase is exogenous. Rather, the hypothesis is that a process outside the model—say a collapse of house prices—influences the model through a higher discount rate. The same process outside the model may enter the model through more than one driving force. For example, the collapse of housing prices may also affect consumption demand by lowering borrowing opportunities of constrained households.

Here I provide an informal review of the driving forces that macroeconomics has identified to account for persistent slumps.

2.1 Labor-Force Participation

A discovery in recent U.S. experience has been the importance of a major decline in labor-force participation. In past slumps, participation remained close to unchanged—the economy has not had a consistent tendency for the labor force to shrink when job finding became more difficult. As of 2015, the U.S. labor market had returned to normal tightness, as measured by job-finding and job-filling rates, yet a large decline in participation starting around 2000 has not reversed. The decline in participation is an important contributor to the divergent behavior of output and employment, on the one hand, and labor-market tightness, on the other hand. Judged by the latter, the slump triggered by the financial crisis of 2008 is over, yet output and employment are far below the paths expected just prior to the crisis.

Movements in participation not directly tied to labor-market tightness need to be added to the list of phenomena associated with episodic slumps. Even if a major shock did not cause a subsequent decline in participation, if a decline happens to occur during a slump, the shortfall in employment and output will be negatively affected.

Elsby et al. (2013) is a recent investigation of the decline in participation. Autor (2011) describes the disability benefits that may be a contributor to that decline.

2.2 The Capital Wedge

A key fact in understanding the slump following the financial crisis is the stability of business earnings. Fig. 10 shows the earnings of private business (the operating surplus from the NIPAs, revenue less noncapital costs) as a ratio to the value of capital (plant, equipment, software, and other intangibles, from the Fixed Assets account of the NIPAs). Earnings fell in 2007 from their normal level of just over 20%, but recovered most of the way by 2010, when output and employment remained at seriously depressed levels.

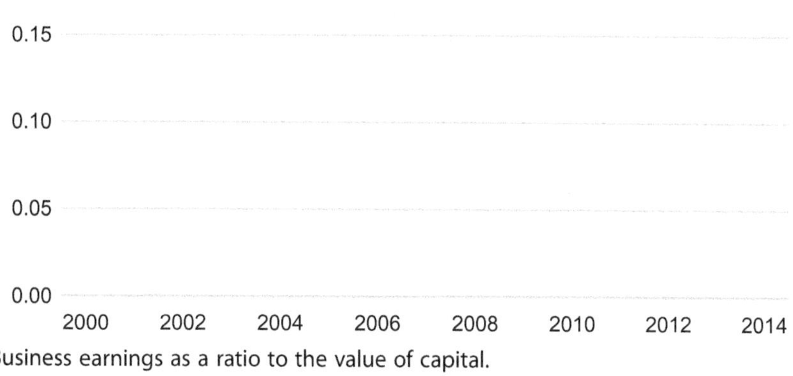

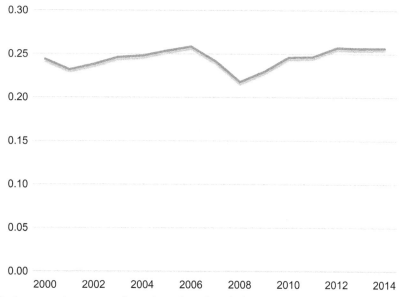

Fig. 10 Business earnings as a ratio to the value of capital.

A basic question is why investment fell so much despite the continuing profitability of business activities. Macroeconomics has gravitated toward an analysis of wedges as ways of describing what seem to be failures of incentives. The capital wedge is the difference between the measured return to investment and the financial cost of investment. I take the latter to be the risk-free real interest rate. The risk premium is one component of the wedge between the return to business capital and the risk-free interest rate. Other components are taxes, financial frictions, and liquidity premiums. To measure the total wedge, I calculate the annual return to capital and subtract the 1-year safe interest rate from it. Later, I decompose the total wedge into one component, interpreted as an extra discount on risky capital earnings not explained by finance theory, and a second, interpreted as an extra premium on safe returns not explained by finance theory.

The calculation of the return to capital uses the following thought experiment: A firm purchases one extra unit of investment. It incurs a marginal adjustment cost to install the investment as capital. During the year, the firm earns incremental gross profit from the extra unit. At the end of the year, the firm owns the depreciated remainder of the one extra unit of installed capital. Installed capital has a shadow value measured by Tobin's q.

Installation incurs a marginal cost at the beginning of the period of $\kappa(k_t/k_{t-1} - 1)$. Thus the shadow value of a unit of installed capital at the beginning of the year is

$$q_t = \kappa\left(\frac{k_t}{k_{t-1}} - 1\right) + 1 \tag{1}$$

units of capital. From its investment of a unit of capital at the beginning of year t together with the marginal installation cost—with a total cost of $q_t p_{k,t}$—the firm's nominal return ratio is the gross profit per unit of capital π_t/k_t plus the depreciated value of the capital in year $t+1$, all divided by its original investment:

$$1 + r_{k,t} = \frac{1}{q_t p_{k,t}}\left[\frac{\pi_t}{k_t} + (1-\delta_t)q_{t+1}p_{k,t+1}\right]. \tag{2}$$

Gross profit includes pretax accounting profit, interest payments, and accounting depreciation. In principle, some of proprietors' income is also a return to capital—noncorporate business owns significant amounts of capital—but attempts to impute capital income to the sector result in an obvious shortfall in labor compensation measured as a residual. The reported revenue of the noncorporate business sector is insufficient to justify its observed use of human and other capital. Note that business capital as measured in the NIPAs now includes a wide variety of intangible components in addition to plant and equipment.

The implied wedge between the return to capital and the risk-free real interest rate $r_{f,t}$ is the difference between the nominal rate of return to capital and the 1-year safe nominal interest rate:

$$r_{k,t} - r_{f,t}. \tag{3}$$

This calculation is on the same conceptual footing as the investment wedge in Chari et al. (2007), stated as an interest spread. Note that the wedge is in real units—the rate of inflation drops out in the subtraction.

Fig. 11 shows the values of the business capital wedge for two values of the adjustment cost parameter κ, calculated from Eq. (3), combining plant, equipment, and intellectual property. On the left, κ is taken as 0 and on the right, as 2. The former value accords with the evidence in Hall (2004) and the latter with the consensus of other research on capital adjustment costs. The value $\kappa = 2$ corresponds to a quarterly parameter of 8.

The two versions agree about the qualitative movements of the wedge since 1990, but differ substantially in volatility. The wedge was roughly steady or falling somewhat during the slow recovery from the recession of 1990, rose to a high level in the recession of 2001, declined in the recovery, and then rose to its highest level after the crisis. The two calculations agree that the wedge remained at a high level of about 18% per year through 2013.

Hall (2011a) discusses the surprising power of the financial wedge over general economic activity. The adverse effect of the wedge on capital formation cuts market activity in much the same way as taxes on consumption or work effort.

One branch of the recent literature on the propagation of financial collapse into a corresponding collapse of output and employment emphasizes agency frictions in businesses and financial intermediaries. The simplest model in the case of an intermediary—completely dominant in this literature though not obviously descriptive of the actual U.S. economy—grants the intermediary the opportunity to abscond with the investors' assets. Absconding takes place if the intermediary's continuation value falls short of the value of absconding, taken to be some fraction of the amount stolen from the investors. If the intermediary's equity falls on account of a crisis—for example, if mortgage-backed securities suffer a large capital loss—the investors need to restore the intermediary's incentive to perform by granting a larger spread between the lending rate the intermediary earns and the funding rate it pays to the investors. Hence spreads rise after a financial crisis. This view is consistent with the actual behavior of the spread between the return to capital and the risk-free rate.

The same type of agency friction can occur between a nonfinancial business and its outside investors. Depletion of the equity in the business will threaten the investors' capital. They need to raise the rents earned by the business to increase the continuation values of the insiders, and again spreads will rise.

Gertler and Kiyotaki (2011) cover this topic thoroughly in a recent volume of the *Handbook of Monetary Economics*. Brunnermeier et al. (2012) is another recent survey. Key contributions to the literature include Bernanke et al. (1999), Kiyotaki and Moore (2012), Gertler and Karadi (2011), Brunnermeier and Sannikov (2014), and Gertler and Kiyotaki (2011). See also Krishnamurthy and Vissing-Jorgensen (2013), He and Krishnamurthy (2015), Adrian et al. (2012), and Korinek and Simsek (2014).

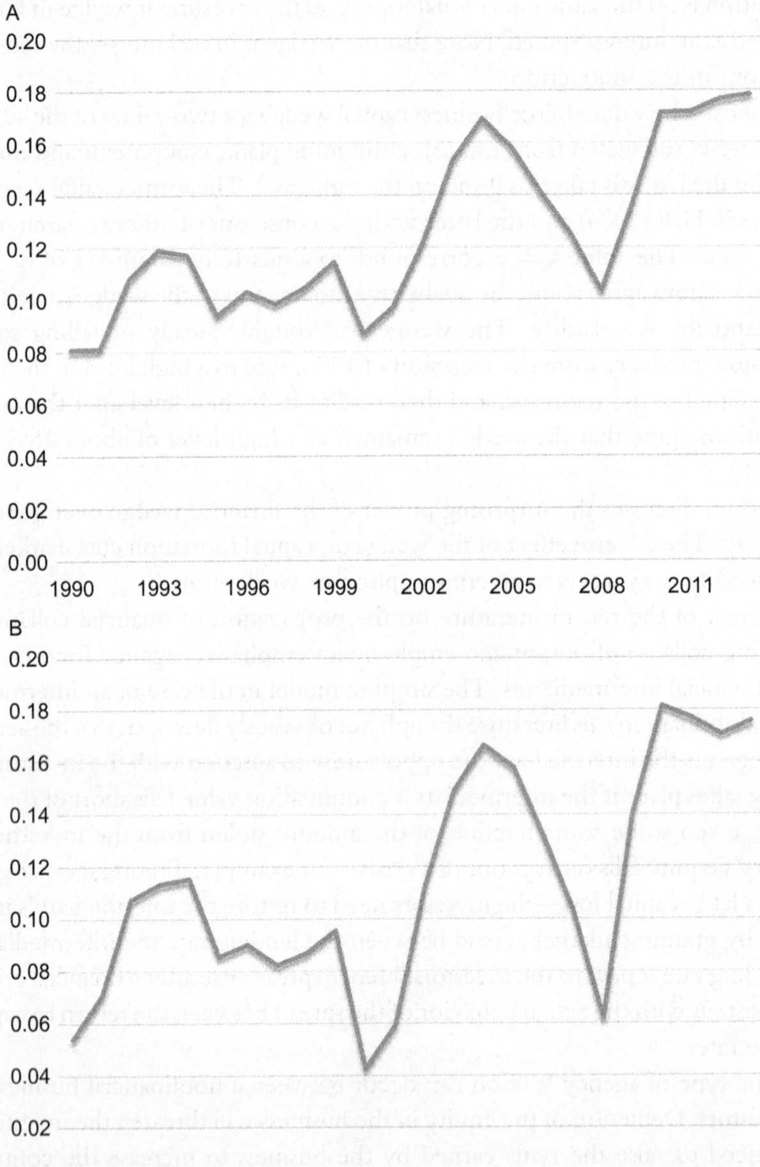

Fig. 11 The capital wedge for two values of the adjustment cost κ. (A) $\kappa = 0$ and (B) $\kappa = 2$.

2.3 Discounts and Confidence

A second branch of the literature linking financial collapse to rising spreads considers widening risk premiums in crises and ensuing slumps. Cochrane (2011) discusses the high volatility of the risk premium in the stock market, measured as the discount rate less

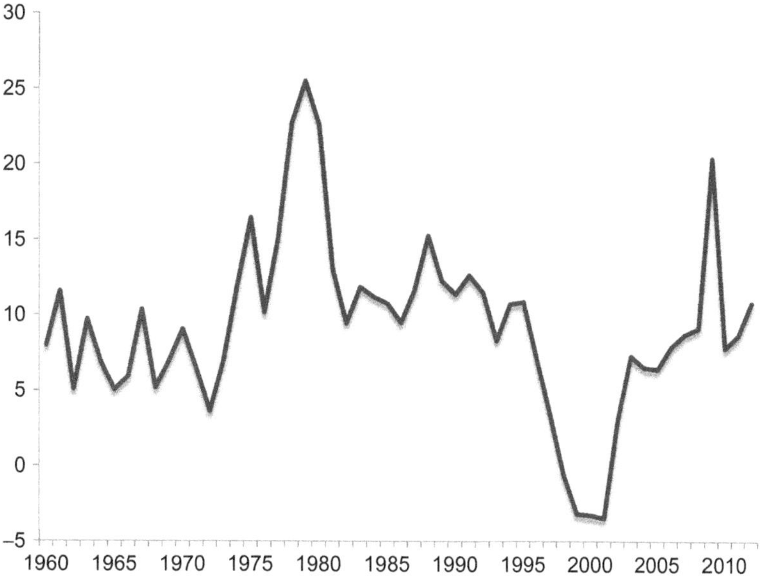

Fig. 12 The S&P Risk Premium, 1960 through 2012.

the risk-free rate. Lustig and Verdelhan (2012) document the tendency for discounts to rise in slumps.

A basic property of the stock market is that, when the level of the stock market is low, relative to a benchmark such as dividends, discounts are higher—see Campbell and Shiller (1988). Normalized consumption is another reliable predictor of returns. Fig. 12 shows the equity premium for the S&P stock-price index from a regression of annual returns on those two variables (see Hall, 2015 for further discussion and details of its construction). The risk premium spiked in 2009. Notice that it is not nearly as persistent as the slump itself—the premium was back to normal well before unemployment fell back to normal and long before investment recovered.

Macroeconomics and finance are currently debating the explanation for the high volatility of discounts. In principle, high discounts arise when the marginal utility of future consumption is high. Generating this outcome in a model is a challenge. Marginal utility would need to be highly sensitive to consumption to generate observed large movements in discounts from the modest expected declines in consumption that occur even in severe contractions. Contractions in consumption appear to be almost completely surprises. If a model implied that occasional drops in consumption occurred as surprises, and consumption then grew faster than normal to regain its previous growth path, the discount rate would *fall* after a crisis because marginal utility would be lower in the future.

Fig. 13 shows the history of the growth of real consumption of nondurable goods per person from 2001 through 2014. The largest decline was in 2009, at 2.5%, about 3.5% below its normal growth. With a coefficient of marginal utility with respect to

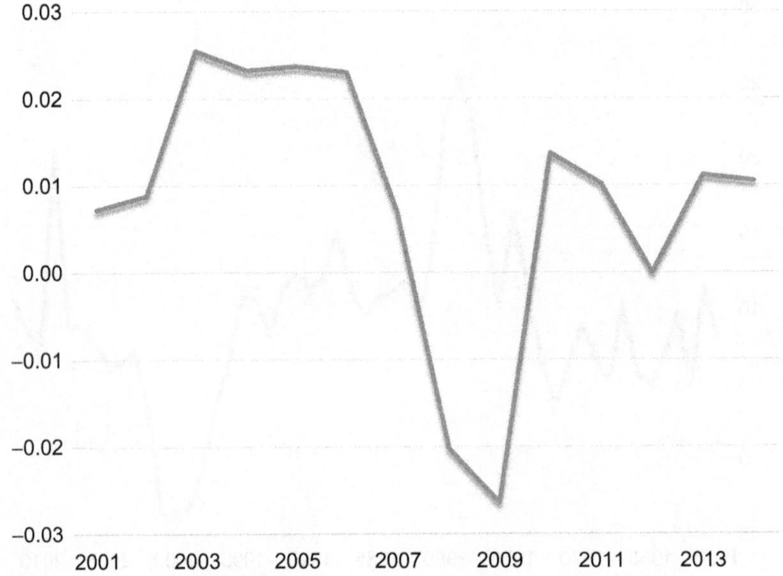

Fig. 13 Growth rate of real consumption of nondurable goods per person.

consumption of 2 (elasticity of intertemporal substitution of 0.5), the effect on marginal utility would be a substantial 7%. But this applies to a fully foreseen decline. The process for consumption change is close to white noise, so the hypothesis of a large negative expected change seems untenable.

Bianchi et al. (2012) propose a mechanism to overcome the problem that expected increases in marginal utility are inconsistent with the observed behavior of consumption. They disconnect discounts from rational expectations of changes in marginal utility by invoking ambiguity aversion. Investors form discounts based on their perceptions of a bad-case realization of marginal utility. During periods when investors have unusually pessimistic views, discounts are high.

Angeletos et al. (2014) overcome the problem in a related way. Investors form expectations about the future state of the economy based on biased beliefs about beliefs of other decision makers. When these second-order beliefs are unusually pessimistic, investors believe that their own future consumption will be lower and their future marginal utility higher, and thus apply higher discounts. The authors use the term *confidence* to refer to optimism in second-order beliefs.

In general, if a financial crisis or other salient event causes investors to shift their beliefs toward higher future marginal utility, discounts will rise. To the extent that the mean of future marginal utility rises, the safe real rate will increase along with the discounts applied to risky returns. To harness the mechanism to explain the decline in the safe rate in the Great Slump along with the rise in the risky discount, the change in the distribution of future marginal utility needs to lower the mean but raise the expected product of marginal utility and the payoffs that govern the levels of employment and output.

The spreads between yields on risky and safe bonds of the same maturity are informative about variations in discounts. Philippon (2009) argues that the bond spread may be more informative. Because the difference in the values of a risky bond and a safe bond is sensitive only to shocks that alter payoffs conditional on default, and default is relatively rare for bonds, the bond spread encodes information about the rare, serious events that could account for high discounts on business income and low discounts on safe payoffs. Fig. 14 shows the option-adjusted spread between BBB-rated bonds and Treasurys of the same maturity.

The spread widened dramatically in 2009, supporting the hypothesis that the perceived probability of a collapse of business cash flow had increased substantially. But the widening was transitory. The spread returned to historically normal levels in 2010 and remained there subsequently. It would take a powerful propagation mechanism for the change in perceptions to account for the persistent slump after 2010.

Gilchrist et al. (2014b), figs. 2 and 3, show IRFs for a spread shock, derived from a vector autoregression. These show relatively little persistence in the shock, but substantial persistence in investment and GDP responses. See also Cúrdia and Woodford (2015).

Other contributions relating to discounts and confidence include Kozlowski et al. (2015), Farmer (2012), He and Krishnamurthy (2013), Gourio (2012), Bianchi et al.

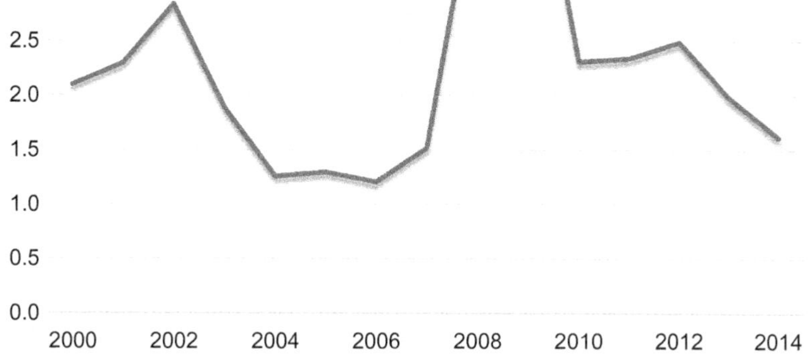

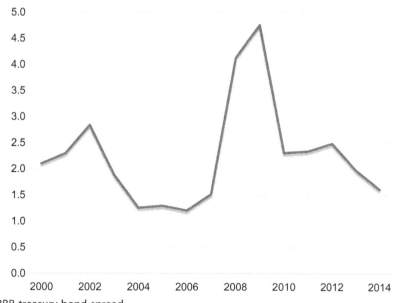

Fig. 14 BBB-treasury bond spread.

(2012), Lustig et al. (2013), and Eckstein et al. (2015). A related topic is the role of fluctuations in uncertainty as a driving force—see Ludvigson et al. (2015) for cites and discussion.

2.4 Productivity

A decline in TFP growth was an important factor in the shortfall of output during the post-crisis U.S. slump. Fernald (2014) makes the case that the productivity slowdown was unrelated to the crisis. Rather, he argues, it was a slowdown only relative to rapid TFP growth in the late 1990s and the early 2000s, associated with adoption of modern information technology. The episode illustrates the importance of TFP growth as a driving force of medium-term fluctuations, even though TFP is not a consistent driver of sharp contractions.

2.5 Product-Market Wedge

Market power in product markets creates a wedge that has been discussed extensively as a driving force of fluctuations, mainly in the context of the new Keynesian model. Rotemberg and Woodford (1999) discuss how sticky product prices result in cyclical fluctuations in markups—in a slump, prices fall less than costs, so market power rises. In almost any modern macro model, the market-power wedge has a negative effect on employment and output. Nekarda and Ramey (2013) question the evidence supporting this view, with respect to shocks apart from productivity. Bils et al. (2014) defend the view, using new evidence.

Gilchrist et al. (2014a) show that firms facing higher financial stress after the crisis raised prices (and thus the wedge) relative to other firms, a finding that supports the idea that the product-market wedge rose in general when overall financial stress worsened. The likely mechanism is different from the one in Rotemberg and Woodford (1999)—it is an idea launched in Phelps and Winter (1970). Financially constrained firms borrow, in effect, by raising prices relative to cost and shedding some of their customer bases.

Chari et al. (2007) provide a comprehensive discussion of wedges in general. See also Gourio and Rudanko (2014).

2.6 Household Deleveraging

Survey data also show a belief that lending standards to households tightened, for mortgages, loans against home equity, and unsecured borrowing (mostly credit cards). Mian and Sufi (2010) use detailed geographic data to argue that household credit restrictions caused declines in consumption. Mian and Sufi (2012), Mian et al. (2013), and Dynan (2012) document the relation between economic activity and household debt. Bhutta (2012) uses household data to show that families did not repay debt more quickly than usual during the slump. Rather, they took on less debt as it became more difficult to qualify for loans, thanks to rising lending standards and declining equity for existing homeowners who prior to 2008 were using cash-out refinancing and home-equity loans. See also Blundell et al. (2008), Petev et al. (2012), and De Nardi et al. (2011).

3. PROPAGATION MECHANISMS

3.1 Capital

The capital stock is an important source of propagation in slumps, a point that has escaped analysis in the cycle-around-trend view of fluctuations. Investment falls sharply in slumps, leaving a depleted capital stock in a slump that lasts several years. Capital depletion also helps account for the divergent behavior of output and labor-market tightness. See Gilchrist et al. (2014b) and Gomme et al. (2011).

3.2 Unemployment Dynamics

In the standard search-and-matching model, calibrated as in Shimer (2005), the unemployment rate is a fast-moving state variable. With job-finding rates around 50% per month even during slumps, unemployment converges to the stationary level dictated by tightness and the job-finding rate within a few months. Unemployment dynamics have essentially nothing to do with the persistence of slumps.

Some facts about the U.S. labor market call this view into question. Hall (1995) observed that research on the experiences of workers who lost jobs after gaining substantial tenure gave a quite different view of unemployment. Davis and von Wachter (2011) summarize more recent results with the same conclusion and emphasize the discord between the quick recovery from job loss implicit in the basic search-and-matching model and the actual experience of workers with three or more years of tenure following job loss. That experience involves an extended period of low employment—much greater loss than a 50% per month reemployment rate—and years of loss of hourly earnings. Jarosch (2014) confirms this view. The aggregate implications are that a wave of layoffs from a major shock, such as the financial crisis, results in an extended period of unemployment and a much longer period of lower productivity of the higher-tenure workers who lose jobs from the shock. Ravn and Sterk (2012) develop a model with two kinds of unemployment to capture this type of heterogeneity among the unemployed.

Some progress has been made in reconciling high monthly job-finding rates with the low recovery from high unemployment following a shock. Hyatt and Spletzer (2013) show that short jobs are remarkably frequent—the distribution of job durations is utterly unlike the exponential distribution with a constant separation hazard usually assumed in search-and-matching models. This finding explains the high job-finding rates found in the CPS—there is a huge amount of churn in the U.S. labor market. Hall and Schulhofer-Wohl (2015) show that job-finding rates over year-long periods are well below what would be expected from monthly job-finding rates. The obvious explanation of this finding is that job-seekers often take interim jobs during much longer spells of mixed unemployment and brief employment.

Shimer (2008) discusses the labor-market wedge as a convenient summary of the effects of labor-market frictions.

Other contributions relating to propagation through unemployment dynamics include Valletta and Kuang (2010b), Cole and Rogerson (1999), Chodorow-Reich and Karabarbounis (2015), Davis and von Wachter (2011), Davis et al. (2012), Petrosky-Nadeau and Wasmer (2013), Fujita and Moscarini (2013), Jarosch (2014), Rothstein (2011), Petrosky-Nadeau and Zhang (2013), Mortensen (2011), Valletta and Kuang (2010a), Sahin et al. (2012), Daly et al. (2011a,b, 2012), Kuehn et al. (2013), Mulligan (2012a), Barnichon and Figura (2012), Estevão and Tsounta (2011), Krueger et al. (2014), Herz and van Rens (2011), Sahin et al. (2012), Farber and Valletta (2013), Kaplan and Menzio (2016), Elsby et al. (2011), Krueger and Mueller (2011), Davis and Haltiwanger (2014), Hall (2012), Fujita (2011), Hagedorn et al. (2013), Mulligan (2012b), Restrepo (2015), Farber (2015), and Ravn and Sterk (2012).

3.3 The Zero Lower Bound

The policy of every modern central bank is to issue two types of debt: reserves and currency. The bank pays interest or collects negative interest on reserves. No direct force constrains the rate on reserves. It is impractical to pay or collect interest on currency. Central banks keep currency and reserves at par with each other by standing ready to exchange currency for reserves or reserves for currency in unlimited amounts. If the bank sets a reserve rate below the negative of the storage cost of currency, owners of reserves will convert them to higher-yielding currency. A number of European central banks have experimented recently with increasingly negative reserve rates.

The lower bound on the real interest rate is the bound on the nominal rate less the expected rate of inflation. Fig. 15 shows three time series relevant for measuring expected inflation. The top line is the median expected rate of inflation over the coming year for the Michigan Survey of Consumers. The line starting in 2007 is the median forecast of the average annual rate of change of the PCE price index over the coming 5 years, in the Survey of Professional Forecasters of the Philadelphia Federal Reserve Bank. The bottom line is the breakeven inflation rate in the 5-year TIPSs and nominal 5-year note—the rate of inflation that equates the nominal yields of the two instruments. See also Fleckenstein et al. (2013) on extracting expected inflation from inflation swaps.

The three measures agree that essentially nothing happened to expected inflation over the period of the post-crisis slump. All recorded a drop around the time of the crisis, but

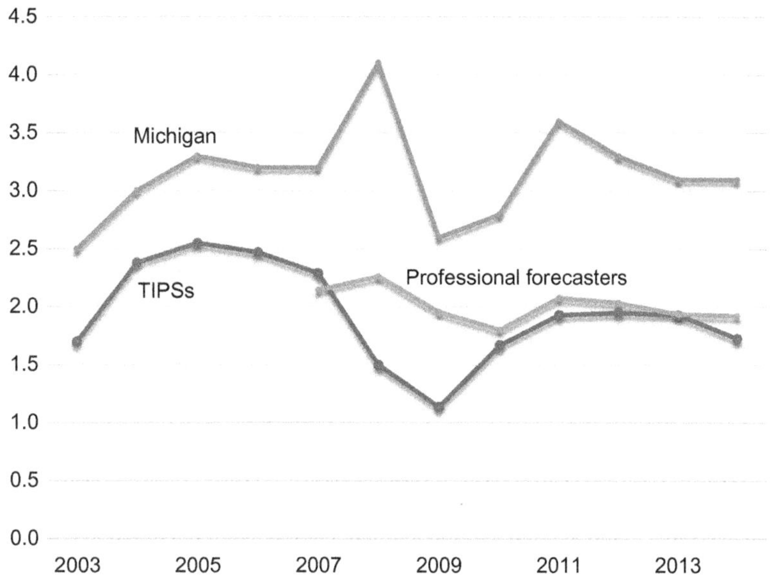

Fig. 15 Inflation expectations and forecasts.

then returned to close to precrisis levels despite high unemployment. This finding pretty much eliminates an idea that permeated macroeconomics over the past 50 years, that slack more or less automatically results in lower inflation. Some combination of factors in 2008 prevented the collapse of the price level that occurred, for example, in the much deeper slump following the contraction of 1929–33.

Had expected inflation declined by the amounts that occurred in the earlier slumps of the past 50 years, the influence of the zero lower bound on the real interest rate would have been more severe. And if deflation at the rate experienced in 1929–33 had occurred, a catastrophe similar to the Great Depression would probably have occurred. Good fortune kept expected inflation at normal levels and avoided high real interest rates and their likely adverse effects on output and employment.

In view of the importance of the inflation rate in determining the real interest rate corresponding to a zero nominal rate, the complete absence of a model of inflation is a considerable shortcoming of current macroeconomic thinking. About the best that macro modeling can do is to take expected inflation as an exogenous constant, currently around 2%. It is common for macroeconomists to say that "inflation is firmly anchored at the Fed's target of two percent" as if that amounted to a model. But it is not—at best it is an observation that expected inflation has remained at about that level despite large changes in output, employment, and other macro variables.

With exogenous, constant inflation, the bound on the nominal interest rate places a bound on the safe real rate at the nominal bound minus the rate of inflation—minus

2% in the recent slump if the nominal bound is zero; minus 3% if the nominal bound is minus 1%.

Stock and Watson (2010) study the joint behavior of inflation and unemployment with conclusions similar to those stated here. Ball and Mazumder (2011) argue in favor of the conventional view that inflation has a stable relation to slack.

3.3.1 Incorporating the Zero Lower Bound in Macro Models

Hall (2011b) discusses the issues in modeling an economy with a safe real rate fixed above the value that would clear the output market under normal conditions. In brief, the high real rate creates the illusion of an opportunity to defer consumption spending when deferral is actually infeasible. Because of the mispricing of the benefit of saving, consumers create congestion as they try to save and defer spending. Congestion arises from the same force that slows traffic on a highway that is underpriced, so more drivers try to use it than its capacity. As a practical matter, the congestion appears to take the form of low job-finding rates and abnormally high unemployment.

Modeling of the congestion resulting from the mispricing of saving is still at a formative stage. To frame the issue, consider a simple frictionless general-equilibrium macro model with a unique equilibrium. The model will describe an equilibrium value of the short-term safe real interest rate. Now implant a central bank in the model with a policy of setting that rate at a value above the equilibrium value. In particular, suppose that the bank's interest rate is elevated by the zero lower bound. What happens in the model? It cannot have an equilibrium—its only equilibrium is ruled out by assumption. One solution in macro theory is to disable one equation. Then the model has one less endogenous variable, the interest rate (made exogenous by the zero lower bound), and one less equation. One example is to drop a clearing condition for the labor market and to interpret the gap between labor supply and labor demand as unemployment. When the central bank sets a rate above equilibrium, labor demand will fall short of labor supply and unemployment will be above its normal level. This approach has some practical appeal and often gives reasonable answers.

A closely related approach is to place the demand gap in the product market. Krugman (1998) and Korinek and Simsek (2014) are examples of that approach. Farhi and Werning (2013) present a general analysis of demand gaps, where any set of prices and wages can be jointly restricted and gaps can occur in any market.

The new Keynesian tradition takes a different and more subtle approach to this issue by adding the price level as another endogenous variable without any corresponding equation. The model has demand gaps in the product market associated with temporarily sticky prices that adjust over time to close the gaps. Eggertsson and Krugman (2012) and Christiano et al. (2011) apply the NK model to the zero lower bound issue. One branch of the NK literature—notably Walsh (2003), Gertler et al. (2008), and, most recently,

Christiano et al. (2016)—uses the Diamond–Mortensen–Pissarides framework to describe the labor market, so the only role of demand gaps is in the product market.

Hall (2016) tackles the congestion issue directly, in the DMP setup. Both the output and labor markets suffer from congestion when the central bank elevates the real rate above the market-clearing level. The central bank's acceptance of deposits at the elevated real rate creates an outside option in the product-price bargain that creates slack according to standard DMP principles.

In general, a model that combines the DMP view of unemployment with a real interest rate held above its market-clearing level will incorporate an additional variable, analogous to congestion in the highway case, that changes the DMP unemployment rate and the demand-gap rate until they are equal. To be concrete about that variable, suppose it is matching efficiency. A decline in efficiency increases hiring cost, raises the cost of labor, lowers the demand for labor, and raises demand-gap unemployment. The decline in efficiency lowers the job-finding rate and raises the DMP unemployment rate. The second effect is robust in the DMP model and presumably exceeds the effect on demand-gap unemployment. In equilibrium, unemployment is less than demand-gap unemployment would be at normal matching efficiency but higher than DMP unemployment would be at normal efficiency. The model would need to tie matching efficiency to the spread between the bank's interest rate and the rate that cleared the output and labor markets. Though this mechanism is attractive because matching efficiency did fall after the 2008 crisis, I do not have a model embodying variations in matching efficiency. The model in Hall (2016) is rather more complicated and invokes DMP principles in both product and labor markets.

If the effect of congestion in the labor market on labor demand is small enough to be neglected, the gap between labor supply and labor demand controls unemployment. In this case, the traditional view that ignores DMP-type considerations applies. In that case, the general-equilibrium model simply omits the DMP-based equations. In the background, labor-market congestion fluctuates to bring unemployment into line with the level dictated by product demand. In the model later in this chapter, I take this approach as an interim solution pending development of fully articulated models of congestion induced by above-equilibrium real interest rates.

Michaillat and Saez (2014) build a model of labor- market congestion that differs from the DMP model in one crucial respect—it lacks a resource decision to control the tightness of the market. In the DMP model, recruiting effort determines the tightness of the labor market. Employers expand recruiting effort until the payoff to creating an incremental vacancy equals the expected recruiting cost. In a simple real business-style macro model with a DMP labor market, equilibrium is determinate. By contrast, in the model of Michaillat and Saez, the corresponding basic model is indeterminate. It has a continuum of equilibria indexed by the real interest rate, with tightness depending on that rate. A monetary intervention that sets the real interest rate picks out one of those equilibria.

Adding that monetary intervention to the DMP-based model would make it over-determined.

This discussion presupposes that the central bank can set any path it chooses for the real interest rate. Friedman (1968) reached the opposite conclusion. In his view, a bank that tried to keep the real rate below the market-clearing level would cause exploding inflation (the case that concerned him in 1967), and a policy aiming to keep the real rate above the market-clearing level presumably would cause exploding deflation. Recent experience does not bear his prediction out—the lower bound froze the safe real rate at around minus 2% because expected inflation remained unchanged at around 2% per year. Our lack of understanding of inflation stands in the way of fully satisfactory modeling of central bank policies that control the real interest rate.

See also Attanasio and Weber (1995), Correia et al. (2010), Eggertsson and Krugman (2012), Cochrane (2014), Hall (2016), and Eggertsson and Mehrotra (2014).

3.3.2 The Zero Lower Bound and Product Demand

The zero lower bound, together with low expected inflation, has prevented central banks from lowering interest rates as much as would seem appropriate. Lower rates should stimulate output and employment. The Federal Reserve and the Bank of Japan have kept rates slightly positive since the crisis, while the European Central Bank did the same until recently, when it pushed the rate just slightly negative. All three economies had combinations of high unemployment and substandard inflation that unambiguously called for lower rates, according to standard principles of modern monetary economics. Under normal conditions, fluctuations in product demand are not a source of important fluctuations in output and employment, because interest rates change as needed to clear those markets. Under almost any view of purposeful monetary policy, the central bank adjusts its policy rate in response to those demand fluctuations. But the zero lower bound is an exception to that principle. Economies with low inflation rates and low equilibrium real interest rates run the danger of episodic slumps when the lower bound is binding.

In the slump that began in 2008, three driving forces for product demand appeared to be important: rising discounts, tightening lending standards to businesses, and tightening lending standards to households. All three of these declines may also reflect the rising importance of another driving force, financial frictions. Other sources could be declining government purchases and transfers and declining export demand. In the recent slump, government purchases fell slightly relative to trend, transfers rose dramatically, and exports fell.

3.3.3 Discounts

As documented elsewhere in this section, discounts applied to future risky cash flows appeared to rise dramatically during and immediately after the financial crisis. Basic principles of investment theory hold that purchases of new capital goods decline when discounts rise. In fact, all three major categories of investment fell sharply: (1) business purchases of new plant, equipment, and intellectual property, (2) residential construction, and (3) autos and other consumer durables. Eggertsson and Krugman (2012) describe how a rise in discounts pushes the economy into a regime where the zero lower bound binds.

3.3.4 Lending Standards to Businesses

Survey data show unambiguously that bank officials believe that they tightened lending standards after the crisis. It remains controversial whether the tightening is an independent driving force or just a symptom of other adverse forces. Chodorow-Reich (2014), using data on individual bank–borrower relationships, argues for a separate role for tightening standards. Tighter standards may also be a driving force for the sharp decline in residential construction, given the dependence of major house-builders on bank lending.

3.3.5 Lending Standards to Households

I noted earlier that rising lending standards and declining equity resulted in cutbacks in consumption because families who had previously financed high consumption levels in part by taking on more and more debt could no longer qualify for those loans.

4. FISCAL DRIVING FORCE AND MULTIPLIER

The multiplier is the derivative of total GDP or a component, such as consumption, with respect to an exogenous shift in product demand. The obvious source of such a shift is government purchases, but the same multiplier describes the propagation of other shifts in product demand, notably those induced by changes in household access to credit.

Ramey (2011a) is a recent survey of the literature on the multiplier, and her chapter in this volume also treats the subject in detail. See also Coenen et al. (2012), Shapiro and Slemrod (2009), Spilimbergo et al. (2009), Hall (2009), Barro and Redlick (2011), Parker et al. (2011), Kaplan and Violante (2014), and Ramey (2011b).

5. OTHER ISSUES

5.1 Decline in the Labor Share

Economists have pursued multiple explanations of the decline, but no consensus has formed. Rognlie (2015) provides a comprehensive discussion of this topic. See also Karabarbounis and Neiman (2014).

5.2 Time Use

Some indication about the changing balance between work and other uses of time comes from the American Time Use Survey, which began in 2003. Table 2 shows the change in

Table 2 Changes in weekly hours of time use, between 2003 and 2013, people 15 and older

	Personal care	Household work	Market work	Education	Leisure	Other
Men	1.3	0.1	−2.5	0.2	1.3	−0.4
Women	1.6	−0.7	−0.8	−0.1	0.8	−0.8

weekly hours between 2003 and 2013 in a variety of activities. For men, the biggest change by far is the decline of 2.5 h per week at work, a big drop relative to a normal 40-h work week. A small part of the decline is attributable to higher unemployment—the unemployment rate was 6.0% in 2003 and 7.4% in 2013. The decline for women is much smaller, at 0.8 h per week. For both sexes, the big increases were in personal care (including sleep) and leisure (mainly video-related activities). Essentially no change occurred in time spent in education. Women cut time spent on housework. See also Aguiar et al. (2013).

6. A MODEL

Many macro-fluctuations models omit slower-moving driving forces and are correspondingly estimated or calibrated to data filtered to remove slower movements. Growth models generally omit cyclical and medium-frequency driving forces. A small literature—notably including Comin and Gertler (2006)—deals explicitly with medium-frequency driving forces and corresponding movements of key macro variables. That paper focuses on technology and productivity. The model developed here considers other medium-frequency driving forces, such as labor-force participation and discounts. Hall (2005) discusses evidence of the importance of medium-frequency movements and argues against the suitability of superimposing a high-frequency business-cycle model on an underlying growth model. Instead, a unified model appears to be a better approach.

The model is inherently nonstationary—its labor force grows randomly and so does productivity. Solution methods widely used for stochastic macro models, either near-exact solutions using projection methods or approximate solutions based on log-linearization, require that models be restated in stationary form. I take a different approach. The model has random driving forces that are functions of a Markov discrete state. Over a finite horizon the model has an event space with a large but finite set of nodes. Models with this structure are widely used in finance and banking. I find essentially exact solutions for the contingent values of continuous state variables and other key macro variables at each node. Finance models, such as the binary option-pricing model, have backward-recursive solutions, but macro models require solving the entire model as a system of simultaneous equations. Recursive models are highly sparse, and solution methods that fully exploit the sparsity are fast.

6.1 Specification

The equations of the model are the familiar first-order conditions for optimization by the decision makers in the model and laws of motion of the state variables, together with initial and terminal conditions. The framework does not require that the model be recursive, though the model here is actually recursive—it can be expressed in equations that consider only three dates: *Now* (for example, k), *Soon* (for example, k'), and *Later* (for example, k''). Each value *Now* branches stochastically into N_t values in the *Soon* period and N_t^2 values in the *Later* period. Here N_t is the number of states in the discrete Markov process in period t. The economy operates for T periods.

The driving forces of the model are:

a: increment to total factor productivity

l: increment to the labor force

d_k: discount or confidence with respect to capital

d_n: discount or confidence with respect to job creation

d_f: discount or flight to safety factor with respect to safe 1-year returns (found to be negative, implying a safety premium)

z: product-market wedge arising from market power

g: government purchases of goods and services, serving as a proxy for shifts in product demand arising from forces not considered explicitly in the model

The continuous state variables are:

k: physical capital stock (endogenous)

A: total factor productivity (exogenous)

L: labor force (exogenous)

Endogenous variables that are functions of the state variables are:

y: output

n: employment

c: consumption

q: Tobin's q, the value of installed capital

r': the realized return to holding installed capital from now to later

r_f: the safe real interest rate from now to later, known now

m: the stochastic discounter, not including d_k, d_n, and d_f

x: the marginal revenue product of labor

6.2 States

An integer-valued state s governs the outcomes of random influences on the economy. It follows a Markov process:

$$\text{Prob}[s'|s] = \pi_{s,s'}. \tag{4}$$

6.3 Technology

Output at the beginning of a period combines labor and capital services according to a Cobb–Douglas technology:

$$y' = A' n^{1-\alpha} k^{\alpha}. \tag{5}$$

Installation of capital incurs quadratic adjustment costs. The marginal cost of adjustment, q, is

$$q' = \kappa\left(\frac{k'}{k} - 1\right) + 1. \tag{6}$$

Total factor productivity evolves as

$$A' = \exp(a_{s'})A. \tag{7}$$

Here $a_{s'}$ is a state-dependent log-increment to TFP. The law of motion of the capital stock is

$$k' = (1-\delta)k + y' - c' - g'. \tag{8}$$

Here δ is the rate of depreciation of capital.

6.4 Financial Markets

The realized rate of return to holding capital is

$$r'_k = \frac{\alpha \dfrac{y'}{z'k} + (1-\delta)q'}{q} - 1. \tag{9}$$

Here z is a product-marked wedge. The economy's normal stochastic discount factor is

$$m' = \beta\left(\frac{c'}{c}\right)^{-1/\sigma}. \tag{10}$$

The pricing condition for the return to capital is

$$\mathbb{E}[(1 + r'_k)m'] - d_k = 1. \tag{11}$$

Here d_k is a distortion of the discounter for the return to capital, interpreted as loss of confidence or increased pessimism, that lowers the perceived present value of the future payoff to capital.

The pricing condition for the risk-free rate is

$$\mathbb{E}\ [(1 + r_f)m'] - d_f = 1. \tag{12}$$

Here d_f is a distortion of the discounter for the safe real return, whose negative value is interpreted as a liquidity premium or flight to safety premium.

6.5 The Zero Lower Bound

The model does not embody a bound on the short safe interest rate. Rather, it identifies conditions when the rate is low—generally negative. Times of negative rates are times when the lower bound would be binding, and the model's equilibrium would not actually hold. As noted earlier, macroeconomics has yet to provide a coherent account of equilibrium with a binding lower bound. All the literature simply assumes that a demand gap implies output and employment gaps, without further explanation of why economic behavior results in gaps. The predictions of the demand-gap model may well be correct—the point is that models do not meet normal standards of explanation imposed on modeling other economic phenomena. See Hall (2016) for further discussion of this point.

6.6 Initial and Terminal Values of the Capital Stock

The capital stock grows stochastically along with growth in TFP, A, and the labor force, L. I calculate the initial capital stock and the stock at each terminal node as

$$k^* = (1-u^*)L\left(\frac{\alpha A}{r^*+\delta}\right)^{1/(1-\alpha)}. \tag{13}$$

Here u^* is the normal unemployment rate. The quantity r^* is the constant discount rate equivalent to actual stochastic discounting, including the extra discount d_k. I pick the value of r^* that generates roughly constant growth of capital. If r^* is below that level, the capital stock grows more rapidly at first until it reaches the stochastic turnpike path, then shrinks back to the terminal condition toward the end. The stock sags below its initial level and grows extra-rapidly at the end of the period if r^* is too high.

6.7 The Labor Market

The model incorporates the idea that hiring is a form of investment, as in the Diamond–Mortensen–Pissarides model of the labor market. As with other forms of investment, the discount rate influences hiring, as discussed with citations in Hall (2015). The equation also takes the marginal revenue product of labor as the measure of the benefit of a hire—subject to variation through changes in market power as in Rotemberg and Woodford (1999), stated in DMP terms in Walsh (2003).

DMP employment depends on the present value of the ratio, $x'/\bar{x}'$ of the actual future marginal revenue product of labor to the normal level based on future technology A' and current capital k. The numerator is

$$x' = (1-\alpha)A'\left(\frac{k}{z'n}\right)^{\alpha} \tag{14}$$

and the denominator is

$$\bar{x}' = (1-\alpha)A'\left(\frac{k}{\bar{n}}\right)^{\alpha}. \tag{15}$$

There is a downward distortion, d_n, in the discounted value of the ratio. Employment is

$$\begin{aligned} n &= \bar{n}\left[\frac{\mathbb{E}(m'x')}{\mathbb{E}(m'\bar{x}')}\exp(-d_n)\right]^{\omega} \\ &= \bar{n}\left[\left(\frac{\bar{n}}{zn}\right)^{\alpha}\exp(-d_n)\right]^{\omega}. \end{aligned} \tag{16}$$

The value of d_n implied by the data is

$$d_n = -\left(\alpha + \frac{1}{\omega}\right)\log\frac{n}{\bar{n}} - \alpha\log z. \tag{17}$$

Given d_n, the resulting solution is

$$\log\frac{n}{\bar{n}} = -\left(\frac{\omega}{1+\alpha\omega}\right)(\alpha\log z + d_n). \tag{18}$$

The labor force evolves as

$$L' = \exp(l_s)L. \tag{19}$$

Unemployment is

$$n = (1-u)L. \tag{20}$$

6.8 Timing

Timing is easiest to understand in the nonstochastic case, where $N_t = 1$ for all periods t. In period 1, capital is at its specified initial value k_I. No consumption occurs in period 1. In period T, capital is at its specified terminal value, k_T. No employment occurs. Consumption c_T is an unknown to be determined. Thus there are $T-2$ values of capital to be determined, k_2 through k_{T-1}, and $T-1$ values of consumption, c_2 through c_T. Given candidate values for these, and the exogenous variables A_t and L_t, one can calculate corresponding candidate values of the other variables, y_t, q_t, $r_{k,t}$, $m_{t,t+1}$, x_t, n_t, and u_t. The $T-1$ residuals of the material balance condition

$$\epsilon_{M,t} = k' - [y' + (1-\delta)k - c' - g'], t = 1 : T-1 \tag{21}$$

and the $T-2$ residuals of the Euler equation

$$\epsilon_{E,t} = \mathbb{E}_t(1 + r_{k,t+1})(m_{t,t+1} - d_t) - 1, t = 2 : T-1 \tag{22}$$

define a system of equations

$$\epsilon(x) = 0. \tag{23}$$

Here $\epsilon(x)$ is the combined vector of the $2T - 3$ residuals and x is a vector of the $2T - 3$ unknown values of k_t and c_t. A standard nonlinear equation solver finds a solution, which is the dynamic stochastic contingent equilibrium of the model.

6.9 Summary

Equations with a zero on the right-hand side enter the solution with discrepancies ϵ which are driven to zero by Newton's method:

$$\text{Prob}[s'|s] = \pi_{s,s'}, \tag{24}$$

$$k' - (1-\delta)k - y' + c' + g' = 0, \tag{25}$$

$$A' = \exp(a)A, \tag{26}$$

$$L' = \exp(l)L, \tag{27}$$

$$y' = A' n^{1-\alpha} k^{\alpha}, \tag{28}$$

$$q' = \kappa\left(\frac{k'}{k} - 1\right) + 1, \tag{29}$$

$$r_k' = \frac{\alpha \dfrac{y'}{zk} + (1-\delta)q'}{q} - f' - 1, \tag{30}$$

$$m' = \beta\left(\frac{c'}{c}\right)^{-1/\sigma}, \tag{31}$$

$$x' = (1-\alpha)\frac{y'}{zn}, \tag{32}$$

$$\mathbb{E}[(1 + r_k')(m' - d)] - 1 = 0, \tag{33}$$

$$r_f = \frac{1}{\mathbb{E}m'} - 1, \tag{34}$$

$$n = (1-u)L, \tag{35}$$

$$\log\frac{n}{\bar{n}} = \left(\frac{\omega}{1+\alpha\omega}\right)\left(\alpha\log\frac{k}{z\bar{k}} - d_n\right). \tag{36}$$

7. APPLICATION TO THE U.S. ECONOMY

7.1 States of the Economy

The model operates at an annual frequency. I constructed its states by the *k*-cluster method with six clusters, based on the following variables measured over the period from 1953 through 2014:

- TFP growth, from Fernald (2012), without utilization adjustment
- The discount implicit in the S&P stock-market index, measured as the expected real return based on the Livingston survey
- The annual growth rate of the civilian labor force
- The unemployment rate

Table 3 shows the discrete states of the model, in terms of the values of the four variables. It also shows the classification of years by state. Each of the four variables defining the states has six state-dependent values. In a row in the table, *Low* refers to the two lowest values of a variable across the states, *Med* to the middle two values, and *High* to the upper two values. Table 4 shows the state-contingent values of the variables that define the states. The states are:

1. Strong economy with low discount, low unemployment, high growth of labor force, and high productivity growth
2. Strong economy with medium TFP growth
3. Mediocre economy with low TFP growth
4. Mediocre economy with high discount and low TFP growth
5. Slump with average TFP growth
6. Slump with high TFP growth

Table 3 The states of the model

State	TFP growth	Discount	Labor-force growth	Unemployment	Years in state
1	Low	Low	High	High	1955, 1957, 1959, 1960, 1964, 1966, 1968, 1969, 1972, 1995, 1996, 1997, 1999, 2000, 2006
2	Low	Low	High	Med	1953, 1956, 1962, 1965, 1973, 1978, 1988, 1989, 1998
3	Med	Med	Med	Low	1954, 1958, 1963, 1967, 1971, 1977, 1979, 1980, 1985, 1986, 1987, 1990, 1991, 1993, 1994, 2007, 2013, 2014
4	High	Med	Med	Low	1961, 1970, 1974, 1975, 1981, 1982, 1983, 2001, 2002, 2004, 2005, 2008
5	High	High	Low	Med	2003, 2009
6	Med	High	Low	High	1976, 1984, 1992, 2010, 2011, 2012

Table 4 State-contingent values of the variables defining the states

State	State-contingent value (%) Discount	Unemployment	Labor-force growth	TFP growth
1	2.79	4.67	1.68	2.00
2	−1.84	4.81	1.79	1.80
3	5.40	6.22	1.48	0.43
4	10.73	6.63	1.40	0.27
5	20.74	7.63	0.52	0.92
6	3.94	8.22	1.03	2.42

Table 5 Transition matrix and ergodic distribution

		To state 1	2	3	4	5	6	Ergodic probability
From state	1	0.33	0.27	0.20	0.20	0.00	0.00	0.25
	2	0.33	0.11	0.44	0.11	0.00	0.00	0.13
	3	0.35	0.12	0.35	0.12	0.00	0.06	0.30
	4	0.08	0.08	0.08	0.42	0.17	0.17	0.20
	5	0.00	0.00	0.00	0.50	0.00	0.50	0.03
	6	0.00	0.00	0.67	0.00	0.00	0.33	0.10

Table 5 shows the annual transition matrix among the four states together with the ergodic probabilities of the states. Fig. 16 illustrates the persistence of the six states. It shows the expected value of the unemployment rate starting in each of the six states and evolving toward the ergodic distribution over a 10-year period. For example, the curve labeled 6 shows unemployment starting at the state-contingent level for state 6, which is over 8%. The rate falls quickly, dropping slightly below its ergodic value before converging back to that value. In the first few years, the dynamics of these impulse response functions differ, corresponding to the differences in the rows of the transition matrix. In later years, the paths are similar, because they are all controlled by the largest eigenvalue of the transition matrix.

The model starts in period 1 with initial values of TFP and the labor force both equal to one. In the base case, the distribution of the state in period 2 is the ergodic distribution. For 4 years, the transition matrix governs the succeeding states. In year 5, the economy has $6^4 = 1296$ possible configurations. For the next 10 years, the economy continues to evolve, but no further random events occur. The exogenous variables—TFP and the labor force—grow at constant rates equal to the average of the state-contingent rates, weighted by the ergodic distribution. The model has $1+6+36+216+1296+10\times 1296=14{,}515$ nodes, each with distinct values of all the variables of the model.

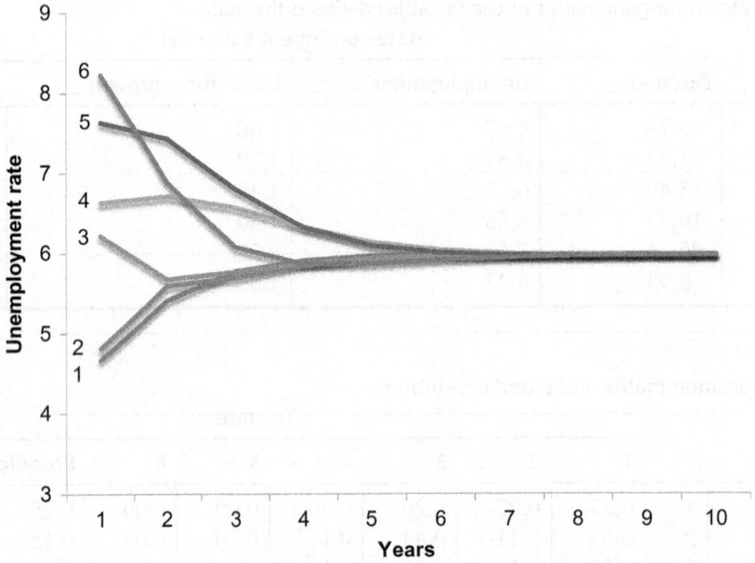

Fig. 16 Persistence of the states.

7.2 State-Based Driving Forces

Two of the variables used to define the states are also treated as driving forces in the model. These are the increments to TFP and the labor force. Another two driving forces are calculated from the data. These are the discount shock for capital, calculated as the residual in the pricing condition for capital,

$$d_k = \mathbb{E}[(1 + r_k')m'] - 1, \tag{37}$$

averaged over states to measure the expectation, and the discount shock for job creation, calculated as

$$d_n = -\left(\alpha + \frac{1}{\omega}\right) \log \frac{n}{\bar{n}}. \tag{38}$$

I also calculate the values of the discount shock for the safe 1-year interest rate, as

$$d_f = \mathbb{E}[(1 + r_f)m'] - 1, \tag{39}$$

but this value does not feed back into the rest of the model, so it is not a driving force, provided no bound on the rate is binding. Table 6 shows the state-contingent values of the driving forces.

TFP growth varies substantially across the economy's states. It is generally higher in the better, lower-numbered, states, but is highest in state 6. The reason is that most of the

Table 6 Values of the driving forces

	State-contingent value (%)				
State	**TFP growth**	**Labor-force growth**	**Capital discount**	**Liquidity discount**	**Labor discount**
1	2.00	1.68	15.01	−1.09	−0.81
2	1.80	1.79	14.93	−1.23	−0.72
3	0.43	1.48	13.39	−2.25	0.17
4	0.27	1.40	12.14	−0.90	0.44
5	0.92	0.52	12.98	−4.87	1.08
6	2.42	1.03	14.25	−3.05	1.46

years classified into state 6 are in the later years of slumps, when the economy is recovering. Historically, recoveries enjoyed high measured TFP growth because of improving utilization (recall that the model uses Fernald's TFP measure without his utilization adjustment). Labor-force growth, a driving force omitted from most models of fluctuations, also shows substantial variability across states, in a pattern similar to TFP. The capital discount is high, definitely in excess of almost all measures of the equity premium. The reason is that it includes factors that cause the return to capital to exceed the payout to owners that are not normally included in the equity premium. These include corporate taxes and agency frictions. The capital discount is higher in the favorable, lower-numbered states, again with the exception of state 6, so it is not much of a contributor to the business cycle. The table shows the calculated values of the liquidity discount, though it is not actually a driving force. The negative of the discount is a safety premium, associated with liquidity services and, in the bad states, a flight to safety. The most negative value of the discount is in the rare state 5 when the economy is in an unusually bad condition. That fact is important for the model's message about the conditions when the zero lower bound on the safe rate will matter. Finally, the labor discount, calculated from the unemployment rate, naturally tracks unemployment perfectly, because the other determinant of unemployment in the model, the product-market wedge, is taken to be the same in all states, for want of a reliable basis for computing it.

Two additional driving forces are present in the model, but do not have empirical counterparts. These are the product-market wedge, z, and the variable g, interpreted as a shift in product demand. The product-market wedge plays a central role in the new Keynesian model, but the measurement has proven controversial. Shifts in product demand resulting from tightening financial constraints on consumption have played a big role in understanding the financial crisis of 2008 and its aftermath, but again measurement of the shifts has proven controversial. The model tracks the effects of z and g, but its base case does not include their actual movements as driving forces in the economy. They both play important roles in the application of the model to the crisis of 2008 and the ensuing slump.

7.3 Parameters

Table 7 shows the parameter values used in the model. All are standard except for r_k^*, which is special to this framework, to ensure that the model's initial and terminal capital are close to its turnpike level of capital in relation to TFP and the size of the labor force.

7.4 Equilibrium

An equilibrium of the model is a complete set of values of the variables at every node. Fig. 17 provides some basic information about the equilibrium—it shows the means and standard deviations of the two exogenous variables, TFP and the size of the labor force, and two key endogenous variables, consumption and the unemployment rate, in each year. The distributions are conditional on the state of the economy in the first year. The standard deviations are calculated across the nodes for each year. Each should be interpreted as the standard deviation of the corresponding variable, conditional on the state of the economy in year 1, defined by the initial values of TFP, the labor force, and the capital stock. Because the capital stock is chosen to start the economy on its (stochastic) turnpike path, the subsequent values of the variables are distributed symmetrically around the path as time passes. Some of the variables grow and some have stable distributions around constant means. The upper left graph shows the distribution of TFP, A, which is close to a random walk. Its mean grows smoothly and its standard deviation fans out, rising approximately as the square root of the year number. The size of the labor force, L, shown in the upper right, behaves similarly, but its growth rate is somewhat higher and its conditional standard deviation is smaller. The variables in the lower part of Fig. 17 are not defined in period 1, but, again, the figures show the distributions conditional on the state of the economy in period 1. The conditional standard deviation of consumption, shown in the lower left, evolves by the same square-root principle as the ones for TFP and the labor force. The unemployment rate, shown in the lower right, has a stationary distribution along the turnpike path.

Table 7 Parameter values

Parameter	Interpretation	Value
α	Elasticity of output with respect to capital	0.35
δ	Depreciation rate of capital	0.1
β	Household discount ratio	0.95
σ	Intertemporal elasticity of substitution	0.5
κ	Capital adjustment parameter	2
u^*	Normal unemployment rate	0.0596
ω	Elasticity of employment function with respect to present value of a worker's contribution	4
rk^*	Effective discount rate for initial and terminal capital	0.3

Table 8 compares the volatility of some of the model's variables to the volatility of the corresponding data. In the case of variables that share the random-walk character of TFP and the labor force, the table describes rates of growth. The left column shows the standard deviations of the variables in the original annual data. The middle column shows the standard deviation, calculated using the model's ergodic distribution, of the state-contingent averages calculated from the original annual data. The right column shows

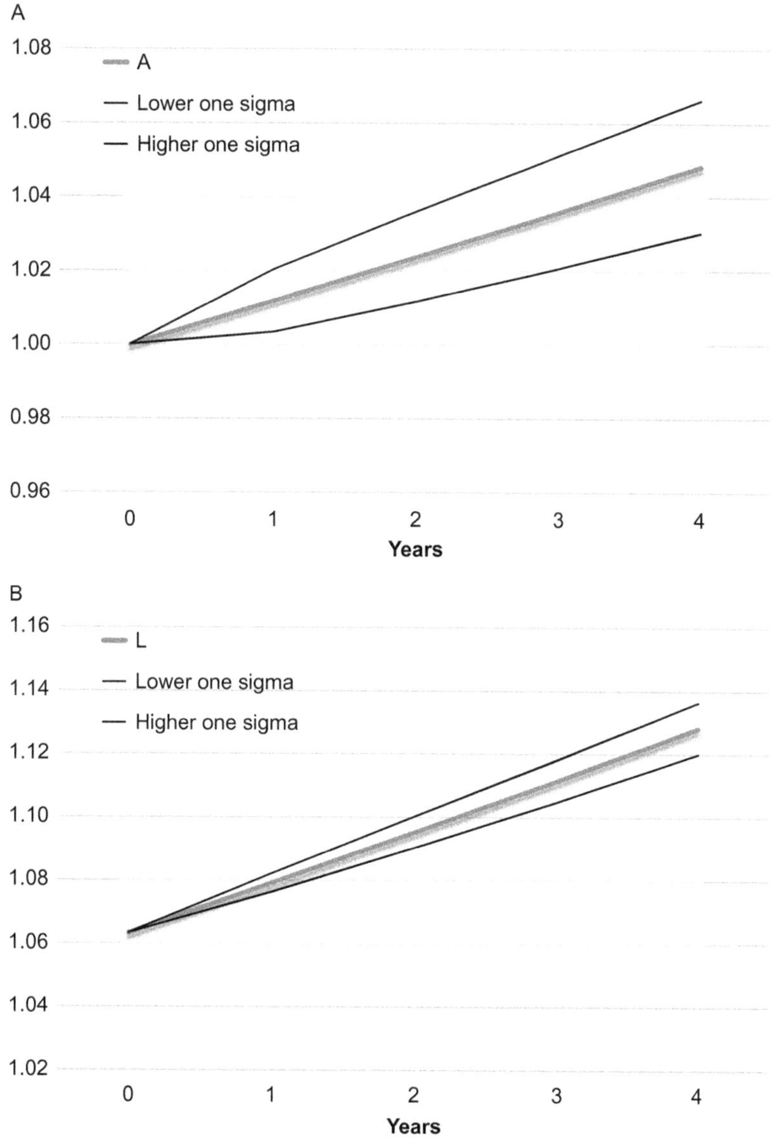

Fig. 17 Distributions of four variables in equilibrium. (A) TFP, (B) labor force,

(Continued)

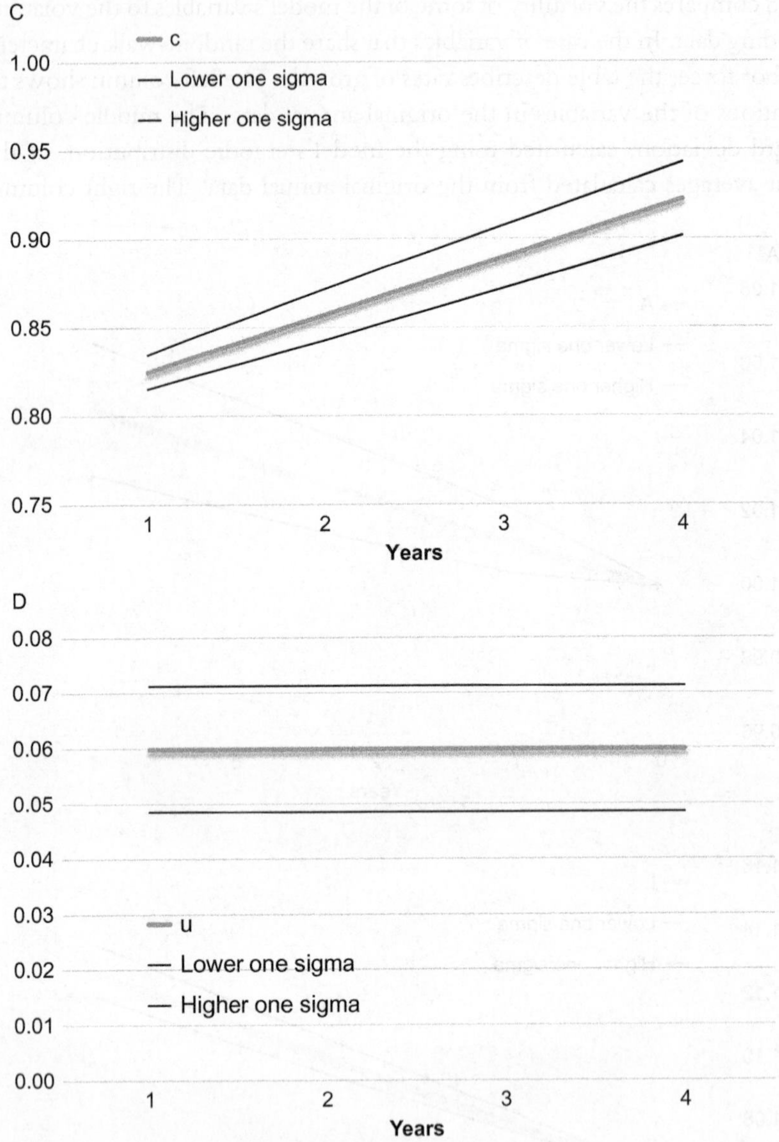

Fig. 17—Cont'd (C) consumption, and (D) unemployment rate.

the standard deviations in year 5 of the equilibrium. Comparison of the middle to the left column shows the success of the state setup in capturing the volatility of the corresponding variable. By necessity, the state setup falls short of full success. In most cases, the standard deviation across the states, weighted by the ergodic distribution, is around half of the actual standard deviation. Employment, unemployment, output, consumption,

Table 8 Standard deviations of selected variables in the data and in the model's equilibrium

Variable	Standard deviation		
	Data	**State-based data**	**Model**
TFP growth	1.65	0.83	0.84
Labor-force growth	0.81	0.27	0.27
Capital wedge	NA	1.42	1.42
Employment wedge	1.02	0.73	0.73
Output growth	2.19	1.34	1.18
Consumption growth	1.81	1.04	1.17
Investment growth	8.88	5.32	4.63
Return to capital	3.81	1.05	1.63
Unemployment	1.59	1.13	1.14

and investment do better than half, while labor-force growth and the return to capital fall short. Comparison of the right column to the middle column of Table 8 shows the success of the model in matching its target, the state-contingent values in the middle. For TFP growth, labor-force growth, the capital wedge, and the employment wedge, the match is perfect by construction. The match is reasonably good for the other variables.

7.5 Effects of the Driving Forces

The popular vector autoregression framework emphasizes *shocks* as the starting point for dynamic macro models. Shocks are uncorrelated with each other contemporaneously and uncorrelated with all lagged variables. See Ramey's chapter "Macroeconomic shocks and their propagation" in this handbook for a discussion of these assumptions. The framework of this chapter is different. Each year, a new value of the underlying state, s, occurs. Its probability distribution is known from the transition probabilities of the Markov process, but the realization from that distribution is a shock. The realization determines the new values of the driving forces. These movements are mutually correlated. Because the model incorporates the hypothesis of rational expectations, adjusted by the known state-dependent distortions, the model incorporates the notion that rational actors respond to the surprise elements of current realizations.

In this framework, it is interesting but challenging to answer questions about the separate effects of the driving forces. Because those forces are correlated, the variance decomposition often presented along with a VAR model is not available—potentially large components of the variance of a given endogenous variable arise from the covariance of a pair of driving forces, so their distinct contributions are not defined. The position of the VAR modeler, as Ramey explains, is that shocks must be uncorrelated, because otherwise they would not have distinct contributions. The approach in this chapter is that driving forces are fundamental and that their correlation is a matter of measurement, not assumption.

One way to understand the roles of the driving forces is to consider a set of counterfactual economies, each with only one driving force. Table 9 shows the results of that exercise. The top row shows the standard deviations of annual output growth for the base case, with all four driving forces in action, and for the four counterfactuals, with single driving forces. Table 10 shows the correlation matrix of the driving forces, based on the state-contingent values, using the ergodic probabilities (the one-period-ahead correlation matrix is state dependent). Two correlations stand in the way of even an approximate allocation of explanatory role: The capital wedge is correlated 0.83 with TFP growth and the labor wedge is correlated −0.89 with the labor-force growth.

Table 9 suggests that all four driving forces have important roles in economic fluctuations. An economy with only TFP fluctuations has substantial fluctuations in all of the variables except unemployment. An economy with only labor-force fluctuations has moderate volatility of investment growth—but recall that this driving force is not well captured by the states of the model, so this finding probably understates the importance of labor-force fluctuations. An economy with only a capital wedge has some volatility of consumption, quite a bit of volatility of the return to capital, and a lot of volatility of investment. An economy with only a labor wedge has substantial volatility of all the variables.

In addition to the ambiguities associated with the correlation among the four observed driving forces, the results in Table 9 need to be interpreted in the light of

Table 9 Standard deviations of selected variables in counterfactual economies with single driving forces

	All driving forces	TFP growth only	Labor-force growth only	Capital wedge only	Labor wedge only
Output growth	1.18	0.84	0.15	0.09	0.73
Consumption growth	1.17	0.80	0.12	0.44	0.41
Investment growth	4.63	1.18	0.71	2.64	3.26
Return to capital	1.63	0.62	0.26	0.84	1.03
Unemployment	1.14	0.00	0.00	0.00	1.14

Table 10 Correlations of driving forces

	TFP growth	Labor-force growth	Capital wedge	Labor wedge
TFP growth	1.00			
Labor-force growth	0.15	1.00		
Capital wedge	0.83	−0.03	1.00	
Labor wedge	−0.28	−0.89	−0.18	1.00

the inability to measure other driving forces, notably fluctuations in product demand. The large role of the labor wedge in the table may actually reflect effects operating through shifts of consumption and investment from forces not included in the model. A later section of this chapter on the forces unleashed by the 2008 crisis shows the potential importance of the product demand and product-market-wedge driving forces.

The model takes a simplified view of the role of confidence, ambiguity aversion, and other factors that may discourage economic activity in ways not included in traditional macro models. Both the capital wedge and the labor wedge are modeled as extra discounts that have adverse effects, but the labor wedge appears to be much the more important of the two. In the model, a decline in confidence and the corresponding increase in the labor discount d_n have a direct effect on job creation through the mechanisms associated with the DMP model. Lower job creation results in lower job-finding rates and higher unemployment. The result enters the rest of the economy as an adverse shift in net labor supply resulting in declines in output, shared between consumption and investment. As Table 9 shows, in the base model, there is no effect on unemployment from other driving forces—the rise in unemployment in bad times is entirely assigned to a decline in confidence among businesses that cuts back their job-creation flows. Obviously this property is an oversimplification, but the macro-labor research community has made more progress recently in demonstrating the near-irrelevance of driving forces of unemployment such as productivity than in finding driving forces to account for fluctuations in unemployment as responses to other forces. The later section on the crisis shows how the product-market wedge influences unemployment.

8. CRISIS AND SLUMP

This section explores the model's properties when the driving forces are tuned to data from the years 2009 through 2012, the years of the maximum effects of the crisis of late 2008 and its aftermath. This exercise assigns those 4 years to an altered state 5 with more negative effects, including values of the two driving forces not measured for the base model covering all the years starting in 1953. Table 11 shows the values for the six driving

Table 11 Values of driving forces hypothesized for crisis slump

Driving force	Value in state 5
TFP growth	0.92
Labor-force growth	0.10
Capital discount	16.70
Liquidity discount	−6.00
Labor discount	1.96
Product-market wedge	3.00
Product demand	−5.00

forces. TFP growth retains its value from the base case, which was close to actual growth over 4 years. Labor-force growth is much lower than normal, just above zero. The capital discount is well above its actual value in any state in the base case, reflecting the belief that agency frictions and a loss of confidence occurred during the immediate post-crisis years. The liquidity discount for the safe 1-year interest rate is lower than in any state in the base case, reflecting an unusual flight to safety after the crisis. The labor discount is 0.4 percentage points higher than in state 5 in the base case, corresponding to an unemployment rate (with no product-market wedge) around 9%, that actually occurred after the crisis. The product-market wedge is taken at the hypothetical value of 3% and the product demand shift at minus 5%.

Table 12 shows the average effects of the driving forces over 4 years of adverse shocks, in comparison to an economy that stayed all 4 years in a different version of state 5 in which the driving forces all had the average of their values from the base case. Thus the figures in the table are the effects of the crisis in the sense of the differences in the outcomes between an economy with the special crisis driving forces and one with driving forces typical of the U.S. economy historically in normal times. The left column shows the average with all the crisis-specific driving forces in action. The rise of 4.54 percentage points of unemployment resembles the actual behavior of the economy. The decline in output is substantial but falls short of the actual decline of about 10%. But the *positive* numbers for consumption and investment are dramatically the opposite of the actual sharp decline in consumption and collapse of investment. This result is not a failure of the model, but rather a consequence of the model's implication of a huge decline in the safe interest rate. This decline could not have occurred, because of the zero lower bound. The story of the table is that the decline in the interest rate unhindered by the lower bound would have brought about an increase in interest-sensitive consumption and investment that would more than offset the direct decline in the spending shift g and the adverse effects of other driving forces.

Table 12 Effects of crisis shocks on key variables, averaged over 4 years

	Driving force						
Variable	**All**	**Capital discount**	**Labor discount**	**Safe rate discount**	**Labor force**	**Product-market wedge**	**Spending shift**
Unemployment, percentage points	4.54	0.00	2.98	0.00	0.00	1.61	0.00
Consumption, %	0.23	0.32	−1.33	0.00	−1.72	−0.71	2.51
Output, %	−3.30	−0.26	−1.84	0.00	−1.30	−1.00	0.53
Investment, %	1.47	−0.57	−0.51	0.00	0.43	−0.28	1.77
Safe interest rate, percentage points	−11.37	−1.48	−0.33	−4.48	−0.88	−0.17	−3.20

The right panel of Table 12 breaks down the effects by the driving forces. Because the model is nonlinear, the sum of the effects on the right side is slightly different from the combined effect on the left. The increase in the capital discount had no effect on unemployment, moved a small amount of spending from investment to consumption, lowered output modestly, and depressed the safe interest rate. The rise in the labor discount raised unemployment substantially and cut output by 1.84%, 1.33% of output from consumption and 0.51% from investment. The rise in the liquidity-safety premium for the short rate had an effect only on that rate, as there is no direct feedback from changes in that rate induced by changes in the premium in the model. The adverse effect of the crisis on the labor force cut output by 1.30%. Consumption fell by 1.72% of normal output, while investment rose by 0.43%. The rise in the product-market wedge accounted for 1.61 percentage points of the rise in unemployment, by raising market power and lowering the marginal revenue product of labor and thus cutting the incentive to create jobs. The spending shift, modeled as a decline in government purchases, resulted in increases of 2.51% of output in consumption and 1.77% in investment, thanks to the income effect of lower implied taxes and the induced decline in the safe short rate of 3.20 percentage points.

8.1 The Zero Lower Bound

Obviously the main lesson of Table 12 is the central importance of the zero lower bound for the severity of the post-crisis slump in the U.S. economy. Although the model does not implement a lower bound on the safe real rate, the results are informative about the incidence of the bound and, to some extent, about the magnitude of adverse effects that would have resulted from the bound. During the slump following the 2008 crisis, the short safe nominal rate was essentially zero, at its bound as perceived by the Federal Reserve, and the expected inflation rate was around two percent—see Fig. 15—so the corresponding bound on the real rate is around minus 2%.

In the model, the normal value of the safe real rate during the years after 2008 is about 3%. According to the lower left figure in Table 12, with all driving forces active at the levels in Table 11, the rate would have been about 11% lower, or minus 8%. Most macroeconomists would probably agree that the effects of a monetary force that raised the safe real rate 8 percentage points above its equilibrium would be severely contractionary. More than half of that is the direct result of the depression of the safe rate on account of the flight to safety hypothesized in the crisis-slump scenario. The other big negative force is the downward shift in product demand, shown in the lower right corner of Table 12. The model supports the idea that the collapse of house prices and tightening of bank lending battered the economy by discouraging consumption and investment. The third-biggest contributor to the decline in the safe rate was the capital discount, good for about 1.5 percentage points of decline. The labor discount, on the other hand, had only a small effect—it is a supply effect. Whereas demand effects are more than fully offset by the decline in the safe rate, reductions in supply cannot be offset that way.

9. PERSISTENCE

Effects lasting longer than the driving forces themselves operate through the model's state variables. It has two exogenous state variables, TFP and the labor force, and one endogenous state variable, the capital stock.

9.1 Exogenous Persistence

In the model, each shock to the labor force has permanent effects. Where the shocks operate through births and immigration, this property is a reasonable approximation. Whether the substantial decline in the labor-force participation of existing individuals that occurred during the slump will ultimately reverse itself is an open question. As of early 2016, there was no sign that the return to essentially normal conditions in the labor market would result in a restoration of any of the large decline that accompanied the slump. Fig. 18 shows the path of the labor force as a percent of its initial normal value in the hypothetical crisis slump studied in the previous section. With four consecutive large incremental shortfalls in the labor force during years 1–4, the cumulative shortfall in the labor force in year 4 is about 6%. Though the labor-force growth rate returns to normal in year 5, the cumulative shortfall continues to become larger, because the growth process is multiplicative and is always at a lower base, post-crisis.

9.2 Endogenous Persistence

Endogenous persistence occurs through the capital stock. The effect of the capital discount is concentrated on investment, as shown in Table 12. An increase in that discount

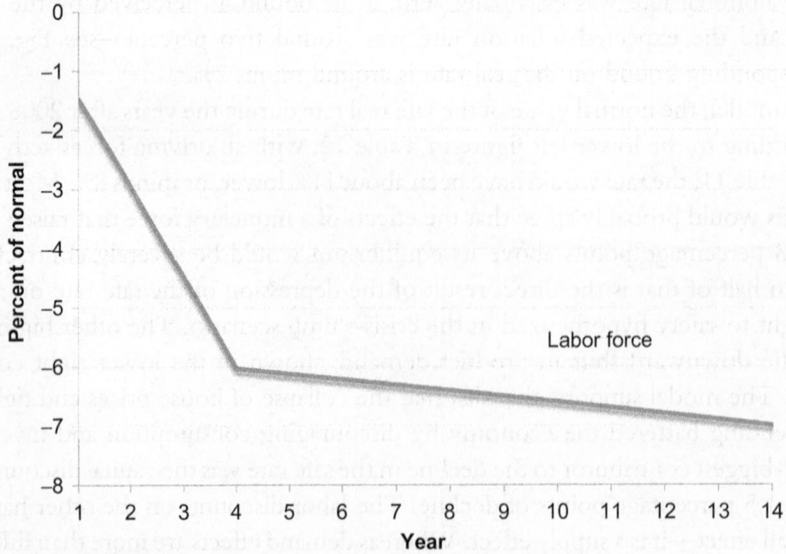

Fig. 18 Persistence of a labor-force shock.

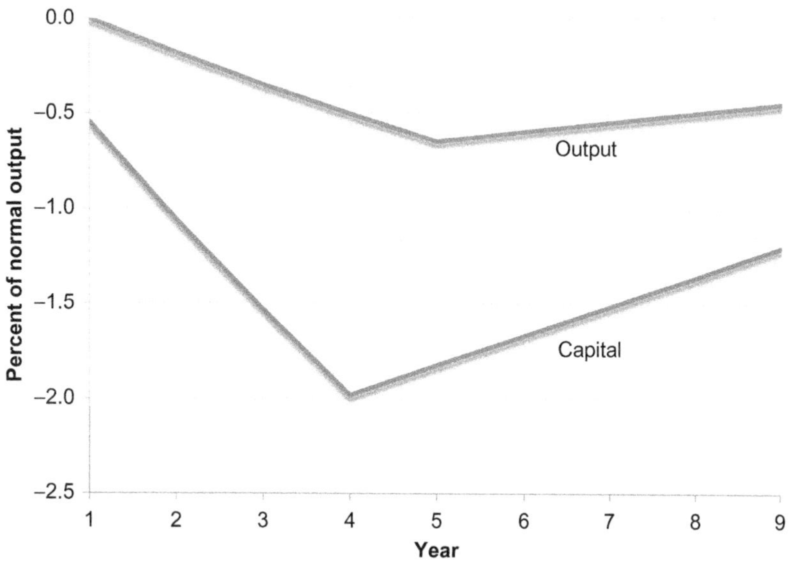

Fig. 19 Persistent effects of an elevation of the capital discount.

causes businesses to place a lower value on the future payoff to capital formation, so capital falls further and further below its normal growth path during a period of higher discount. The effects on output and other variables persist beyond the time when the discount declines back to normal. The capital stock returns only gradually to its normal growth path. Fig. 19 shows the effects of the 4-year period of increased capital discount described in Table 11 on the capital stock and on output. The figure shows the difference between the expected values of those variables conditional on the crisis values of the capital discount and the expected values with normal, noncrisis values of the discount. The effects on both variables cumulate during the 4 years with the higher crisis discount and then begin to return toward zero. Five years after the end of the crisis values, the effects remain strong.

Similar results apply to the other driving forces that have negative effects on investment in Table 11. These are the labor discount, which cuts investment by reducing the effective supply of labor, and the product-market wedge, which lowers the marginal revenue product of capital.

10. CONCLUDING REMARKS

This chapter is complementary to Ramey's chapter in this volume. Most of her discussion relates to empirical evidence from VARs and other econometric specifications, or to the properties of new Keynesian structural models, though she does also consider structural models more closely affiliated with the tradition of the real business-cycle model. She focuses extensively on monetary shocks—departures of monetary policy from its usual relation to current developments in the economy. No monetary shocks occur in the economy considered in this chapter. The central bank never pushes the short rate away from its equilibrium value to restore inflation to its target rate. In the context of the literature that includes monetary policy and monetary nonneutrality, the model here reveals the values of the interest rate and other variables that would prevail in the absence of sticky prices and wages. Both chapters consider government purchases as a driving force. In the empirical work Ramey considers, the focus is on the purchases multiplier, as revealed by the empirical relation between output and purchases. She finds that the multiplier is around one but with considerable dispersion across studies. In this chapter, Table 12 shows a multiplier of 0.53, the value in the row for output and the column for the spending shift. The lower value may be the result of the model's assumption of full monetary response to government purchases, letting the interest rate track the change in its equilibrium value. The sample period for the model includes times when, for example, monetary policy kept the interest rate constant in the face of an increase in purchases, which would considerably amplify the response of output. On the tax side of fiscal policy, Ramey considers taxes as explicit driving forces. Taxes have a role in this chapter because they are one of the sources of historical shifts in the capital discount. But I do not consider tax changes as special driving forces of the post-crisis slump. Ramey's chapter includes a detailed treatment of the measurement of technology shifts and their effects, as measured in empirical work. To measure TFP growth, she concludes in favor of measures with utilization adjustments. This chapter uses Fernald's measure without that adjustment. She also discusses, in detail, measures of technological change apart from TFP, relating to investment. She briefly mentions oil-price changes, credit conditions, policy uncertainty, fluctuations in the labor force, and the labor wedge as additional driving forces. She does not mention the product-market wedge as a driving force.

The importance of total factor productivity as a determinant of medium-term growth and economic performance is widely agreed among macroeconomists today, and is confirmed in the results of this chapter—Table 9 shows that, historically, movements of TFP by themselves would account for a standard deviation of output around 75% of the total of all driving forces. A decline in productivity growth occurred during the slump that began in 2008 and contributed to the shortfall in output, consumption, and capital formation during the slump. Whether the crisis of 2008 contributed to the decline in productivity growth is unresolved.

On the other hand, fluctuations in the size of the work force relative to the working-age population—the labor-force participation rate—are about as big as fluctuations in productivity and have similar effects. Research on medium-run fluctuations has neglected this driving force, even though research on participation itself has been extensive. The continuation during the recent slump of a major decline in participation that began in 2000—and is not the result of demographic shifts—worsened the slump. The evidence seems to point in the direction that the decline in participation was not the result of the crisis and resulting explosion of unemployment.

Evidence from financial markets appears to confirm the proposition that discounts applied to risky investments rose as a result of the crisis even as the safe rate fell to zero. In normal times, without the zero lower bound, higher discounts result in lower output and employment. There is an interesting unresolved question about the role of discount increases when the real rate is held fixed by the zero lower bound on the nominal interest rate and the immovability of inflation.

Models that attribute some of the depth and persistence of the response of the economy to financial shocks hold that the shocks cause increases in agency frictions within financial intermediaries or nonfinancial businesses. Financial wedges develop to ensure that managers deprived of equity still have continuation values sufficient to prevent misconduct. The evidence of widening wedges between the return to capital and the safe short rate is convincing, as is the sharp but transitory rise in the spreads between risky private bonds and Treasurys of the same maturity. The model in this chapter assigns a moderate but important role to financial frictions, as part of the driving force called the capital discount.

The new Keynesian model has called attention to the product-market wedge—the markup of price over cost—as the transmission mechanism of shocks to economic activity. With sticky prices, an increase in demand raises cost but not price, so the markup declines. The economy expands because the product-market wedge functions like a tax wedge in depressing activity and the decline in markups relieves that adverse effect. An interesting debate has yet to resolve the issue of the importance of the product-market wedge in the depth and persistence of slumps.

Finally, the model confirms earlier findings about the multiplier effects of shifts in product demand. As an important cause of declining consumption demand, household deleveraging has been assigned a major role in the recent slump and is an obvious candidate for explaining the persistence of the slump. In the model, an exogenous decline in product demand results in a large decrease in the interest rate, which stimulates consumption and investment. Rather than collapsing, the economy undergoes a large reallocation of resources. But with the zero lower bound in effect, the reallocation fails to occur. Instead, output and employment fall. As yet, the profession has not come forth with a well-founded model of that failure.

ACKNOWLEDGMENTS

Chapter prepared for the *Handbook of Macroeconomics*, John Taylor and Harald Uhlig, eds. The Hoover Institution supported this research. The research is also part of the National Bureau of Economic Research's Economic Fluctuations and Growth Program. I thank Gauti Eggertsson, Wouter den Haan, and Cosmin Ilut for illuminating conference discussions, and Valerie Ramey and the editors for comments. Complete backup for all of the calculations is available from my website, stanford.edu/~rehall

REFERENCES

Adrian, T., Colla, P., Shin, H.S., 2012. Which financial frictions? Parsing the evidence from the financial crisis of 2007–9. Working Paper 18335. National Bureau of Economic Research. http://www.nber.org/papers/w18335.

Aguiar, M., Hurst, E., Karabarbounis, L., 2013. Time use during the great recession. Am. Econ. Rev. 103, 1664–1696.

Angeletos, G.-M., Collard, F., Dellas, H., 2014. Quantifying confidence. Working Paper 20807. National Bureau of Economic Research. http://www.nber.org/papers/w20807.

Attanasio, O.P., Weber, G., 1995. Is consumption growth consistent with intertemporal optimization? Evidence from the consumer expenditure survey. J. Polit. Econ. 103 (6), 1121–1157.

Autor, D.H., 2011. The unsustainable rise of the disability rolls in the united states: causes, consequences, and policy options. Working Paper 17697, National Bureau of Economic Research. http://www.nber.org/papers/w17697.

Ball, L., Mazumder, S., 2011. The evolution of inflation dynamics and the great recession. Brookings Papers Econ. Act. (1), 337–405.

Barnichon, R., Figura, A., 2012. The determinants of the cycles and trends in U.S. Unemployment. Federal Reserve Board.

Barro, R.J., Redlick, C.J., 2011. Macroeconomic effects from government purchases and taxes. Q. J. Econ. 126 (1), 51–102. http://dx.doi.org/10.1093/qje/qjq002. http://qje.oxfordjournals.org/content/126/1/51.full.pdf+html, http://qje.oxfordjournals.org/content/126/1/51.abstract.

Benigno, G., Fornaro, L., 2015. Stagnation Traps. London School of Economics, London.

Bernanke, B.S., Gertler, M., Gilchrist, S., 1999. The financial accelerator in a quantitative business cycle framework. In: Taylor, J.B., Woodford, M. (Eds.), Handbook of Macroeconomics. Elsevier, North Holland, pp. 1341–1393 (Chapter 21).

Bhutta, N., 2012. Mortgage debt and household deleveraging: accounting for the decline in mortgage debt using consumer credit record data. Finance and Economics Discussion Series, Divisions of Research & Statistics and Monetary Affairs, Federal Reserve Board, Washington, DC.

Bianchi, F., Ilut, C., Schneider, M., 2012. Uncertainty Shocks, Asset Supply and Pricing over the Business Cycle. Duke University, Department of Economics, Durham, NC.

Bils, M., Klenow, P.J., Malin, B.A., 2014. Resurrecting the role of the product market wedge in recessions. Working Paper 20555, National Bureau of Economic Research. http://www.nber.org/papers/w20555.

Blundell, R., Pistaferri, L., Preston, I., 2008. Consumption inequality and partial insurance. Am. Econ. Rev. 98 (5), 1887–1921.

Brunnermeier, M.K., Sannikov, Y., 2014. A macroeconomic model with a financial sector. Am. Econ. Rev. 104 (2), 379–421. http://dx.doi.org/10.1257/aer.104.2.379.

Brunnermeier, M.K., Eisenbach, T.M., Sannikov, Y., 2012. Macroeconomics with financial frictions: a survey. Working Paper 18102, National Bureau of Economic Research. http://www.nber.org/papers/w18102.

Campbell, J.Y., Shiller, R.J., 1988. The dividend-price ratio and expectations of future dividends and discount factors. Rev. Finan. Stud. 1 (3), 195–228. ISSN 0893-9454. http://search.ebscohost.com/login.aspx?direct=true&db=eoh&AN=EP4233837&site=ehost-live&scope=site.

Chari, V.V., Kehoe, P.J., McGrattan, E.R., 2007. Business cycle accounting. Econometrica 75 (3), 781–836. http://ideas.repec.org/a/ecm/emetrp/v75y2007i3p781-836.html.

Chodorow-Reich, G., 2014. The employment effects of credit market disruptions: firm-level evidence from the 2008–9 financial crisis. Q. J. Econ. 129 (1), 1–59. http://dx.doi.org/10.1093/qje/qjt031. http://qje.oxfordjournals.org/content/129/1/1.full.pdf+html. http://qje.oxfordjournals.org/content/129/1/1.abstract.

Chodorow-Reich, G., Karabarbounis, L., 2015. The cyclicality of the opportunity cost of employment. J. Polit. Econ. Working Paper 19678, forthcoming. http://www.nber.org/papers/w19678.

Christiano, L.J., Trabandt, M., Walentin, K., 2010. DSGE models for monetary policy analysis. Working Paper 16074. National Bureau of Economic Research. http://www.nber.org/papers/w16074.

Christiano, L.J., Eichenbaum, M., Rebelo, S., 2011. When is the government spending multiplier large? J. Polit. Econ. 119 (1), 78–121.

Christiano, L.J., Eichenbaum, M.S., Trabandt, M., 2016. Unemployment and business cycles. Econometrica, forthcoming.

Cochrane, J.H., 2011. Presidential address: discount rates. J. Finan. 66 (4), 1047–1108. ISSN 0022-1082. http://search.ebscohost.com/login.aspx?direct=true&db=eoh&AN=1254835&site=ehost-live&scope=site.

Cochrane, J.H., 2014. The New-Keynesian Liquidity Trap. Booth School of Business, University of Chicago, Chicago.

Coenen, G., Erceg, C.J., Freedman, C., Furceri, D., Kumhof, M., Lalonde, R., Laxton, D., Lind, J., Mourougane, A., Muir, D., Mursula, S., de Resende, C., Roberts, J., Roeger, W., Snudden, S., Trabandt, M., in't Veld, J., 2012. Effects of fiscal stimulus in structural models. Am. Econ. J. Macroecon. 4 (1), 22–68. http://dx.doi.org/10.1257/mac.4.1.22.

Cole, H., Rogerson, R., 1999. Can the Mortensen-Pissarides matching model match the business cycle facts? Int. Econ. Rev. 40 (4), 933–960.

Comin, D., Gertler, M., 2006. Medium-term business cycles. Am. Econ. Rev. 96 (3), 523–551. http://dx.doi.org/10.1257/aer.96.3.523.

Correia, I., Farhi, E., Nicolini, J.P., Teles, P., 2010. Policy at the Zero Bound. Banco de Portugal.

Cúrdia, V., Woodford, M., 2015. Credit frictions and optimal monetary policy. Working Paper 21820, National Bureau of Economic Research. http://www.nber.org/papers/w21820.

Daly, M., Hobijn, B., Şahin, A., Valletta, R., 2011a. A rising natural rate of unemployment: transitory or permanent? Working Paper 2011-05, Federal Reserve Bank of San Francisco.

Daly, M.C., Hobijn, B., Valletta, R.G., 2011b. The recent evolution of the natural rate of unemployment. IZA Discussion Paper No. 5832.

Daly, M.C., Hobijn, B., Şahin, A., Valletta, R.G., 2012. A search and matching approach to labor markets: did the natural rate of unemployment rise. J. Econ. Perspect. 26 (3), 3–26.

Davis, S.J., Haltiwanger, J., 2014. Labor market fluidity and economic performance. Proceedings of the Jackson Hole Symposium, Federal Reserve Bank of Kansas, pp. 17–107.

Davis, S.J., von Wachter, T., 2011. Recessions and the costs of job loss. Brookings Papers Econ. Act. (2), 1–55.

Davis, S.J., Faberman, R.J., Haltiwanger, J.C., 2012. Recruiting intensity during and after the great recession: national and industry evidence. Am. Econ. Rev. Papers Proc. 102 (3), 584–588. http://dx.doi.org/10.1257/aer.102.3.584.

De Nardi, M., French, E., Benson, D., 2011. Consumption and the great recession. Working Paper, National Bureau of Economic Research. http://www.nber.org/papers/w17688.

Dynan, K., 2012. Is a household debt overhang holding back consumption? Brookings Papers Econ. Act. Spring, 299–362. ISSN 0007-2303. http://www.jstor.org/stable/23287219.

Eckstein, Z., Setty, O., Weiss, D., 2015. Financial Risk and Unemployment. Tel Aviv University, Tel Aviv, Israel.

Eggertsson, G.B., Krugman, P., 2012. Debt, deleveraging, and the liquidity trap: a Fisher-Minsky-Koo approach. Q. J. Econ. 127 (3), 1469–1513. ISSN 0033-5533. http://search.ebscohost.com/login.aspx?direct=true&db=eoh&AN=1323598&site=ehost-live&scope=site.

Eggertsson, G.B., Mehrotra, N.R., 2014. A model of secular stagnation. Working Paper 20574, National Bureau of Economic Research. http://www.nber.org/papers/w20574.

Elsby, M.W., Hobijn, B., Şahin, A., Valletta, R.G., 2011. The labor market in the great recession: an update to September 2011. Brookings Papers Econ. Act. Fall, 353–384. ISSN 0007-2303. http://www.jstor.org/stable/41473602.

Elsby, M.W., Hobijn, B., Şahin, A., 2013. On the importance of the participation margin for market fluctuations. Working Paper 2013-05, Federal Reserve Bank of San Francisco.

Estevão, M., Tsounta, E., 2011. Has the Great Recession Raised U.S. Structural Unemployment? International Monetary Fund.

Farber, H.S., 2015. Job loss in the great recession and its aftermath: U.S. evidence from the displaced workers survey. Working Paper 21216, National Bureau of Economic Research. http://www.nber.org/papers/w21216.

Farber, H.S., Valletta, R.G., 2013. Do extended unemployment benefits lengthen unemployment spells? Evidence from recent cycles in the U.S. labor market. Working Paper 19048, National Bureau of Economic Research.

Farhi, E., Werning, I., 2013. A Theory of Macroprudential Policies in the Presence of Nominal Rigidities. Department of Economics, Harvard University, Cambridge, MA.

Farmer, R.E., 2012. The stock market crash of 2008 caused the great recession: theory and evidence. J. Econ. Dyn. Control 36 (5), 693–707. ISSN 0165-1889, http://dx.doi.org/10.1016/j.jedc.2012.02.003. http://www.sciencedirect.com/science/article/pii/S0165188912000401.

Fernald, J.G., 2012. A quarterly, utilization-adjusted series on total factor productivity. 2012–19, Federal Reserve Bank of San Francisco. Updated regularly on Fernald's FRBSF website.

Fernald, J., 2014. Productivity and potential output before, during, and after the great recession. NBER Macroecon. Annu. 29, 1–51.

Fleckenstein, M., Longstaff, F.A., Lustig, H., 2013. Deflation Risk. Anderson School, UCLA, Los Angeles.

Friedman, M., 1968. Presidential address. Am. Econ. Rev. 58 (1), 1–15.

Fujita, S., 2011. Effects of extended unemployment insurance benefits: evidence from the monthly CPS. Federal Reserve Bank of Philadelphia.

Fujita, S., Moscarini, G., 2013. Recall and unemployment. Working Paper 19640, National Bureau of Economic Research. http://www.nber.org/papers/w19640.

Gertler, M., Karadi, P., 2011. A model of unconventional monetary policy. J. Monetary Econ. 58 (1), 17–34. ISSN 0304-3932. http://dx.doi.org/10.1016/j.jmoneco.2010.10.004. Carnegie-Rochester Conference Series on Public Policy: The Future of Central Banking April 16–17, 2010. http://www.sciencedirect.com/science/article/pii/S0304393210001261.

Gertler, M., Kiyotaki, N., 2011. Financial intermediation and credit policy in business cycle analysis. In: Friedman, B., Woodford, M. (Eds.), Handbook of Monetary Economics. Elsevier, North Holland, pp. 547–599.

Gertler, M., Sala, L., Trigari, A., 2008. An estimated monetary DSGE model with unemployment and staggered nominal wage bargaining. J. Money Credit Bank. 40 (8), 1713–1764. ISSN 1538-4616. http://dx.doi.org/10.1111/j.1538-4616.2008.00180.x.

Gilchrist, S., Schoenle, R., Sim, J.W., Zakrašek, E., 2014a. Inflation Dynamics During the Financial Crisis. Department of Economics, Boston University, Boston.

Gilchrist, S., Sim, J.W., Zakrajek, E., 2014b. Uncertainty, financial frictions, and investment dynamics. National Bureau of Economic Research. Working Paper 20038, http://www.nber.org/papers/w20038.

Gomme, P., Ravikumar, B., Rupert, P., 2011. The return to capital and the business cycle. Rev. Econ. Dyn. 14 (2), 262–278. ISSN 1094-2025. http://dx.doi.org/10.1016/j.red.2010.11.004. http://www.sciencedirect.com/science/article/pii/S1094202510000591.

Gourio, F., 2012. Disaster risk and business cycles. Am. Econ. Rev. 102 (6), 2734–2766. http://dx.doi.org/10.1257/aer.102.6.2734.

Gourio, F., Rudanko, L., 2014. Customer capital. Rev. Econ. Stud. 81 (3), 1102–1136. http://dx.doi.org/10.1093/restud/rdu007. http://restud.oxfordjournals.org/content/81/3/1102.abstract.

Hagedorn, M., Karahan, F., Manovskii, I., Mitman, K., 2013. Unemployment benefits and unemployment in the great recession: the role of macro effects. Working Paper 19499. National Bureau of Economic Research. http://www.nber.org/papers/w19499.

Hall, R.E., 1995. Lost jobs. Brookings Papers Econ. Act. (1), 221–273.

Hall, R.E., 2004. Measuring factor adjustment costs. Q. J. Econ. 119 (3), 899–927.

Hall, R.E., 2005. Separating the business cycle from other economic fluctuations. The Greenspan era: lessons for the Future, Proceedings of the Federal Reserve Bank of Kansas City, 133–179.

Hall, R.E., 2009. By how much does GDP rise if the government buys more output? Brookings Papers Econ. Act. (2), 183–231.

Hall, R.E., 2011a. The high sensitivity of economic activity to financial frictions. Econ. J. 121, 351–378.

Hall, R.E., 2011b. The long slump. Am. Econ. Rev. 101 (2), 431–469. http://dx.doi.org/10.1257/aer.101.2.431. 2011 AEA Presidential Address.

Hall, R.E., 2012. How the financial crisis caused persistent unemployment. In: Wright, I.J., Ohanian, L.E., Taylor, J.B. (Eds.), Government Policies and the Delayed Economic Recovery. Hoover Institution Press, Stanford, pp. 57–83.

Hall, R.E., 2013. The routes into and out of the zero lower bound. Proceedings of the Jackson Hole Symposium, Federal Reserve Bank of Kansas City, pp. 1–35.
Hall, R.E., 2014. Quantifying the lasting harm to the U.S. economy from the financial crisis. NBER Macroecon. Annu. 29 (1), 71–128.
Hall, R.E., 2015. High Discounts and High Unemployment. Hoover Institution, Stanford University, Stanford.
Hall, R.E., 2016. Search-and-matching analysis of high unemployment caused by the zero lower bound. Rev. Econ. Dyn. 19, 210–217.
Hall, R.E., Schulhofer-Wohl, S., 2015. Measuring job-finding rates and matching efficiency with heterogeneous jobseekers. Working Paper 20939, National Bureau of Economic Research. http://www.nber.org/papers/w20939.
He, Z., Krishnamurthy, A., 2013. Intermediary asset pricing. Am. Econ. Rev. 103 (2), 732–770. http://dx.doi.org/10.1257/aer.103.2.732.
He, Z., Krishnamurthy, A., 2015. A Macroeconomic Framework for Quantifying Systemic Risk. Graduate School of Business, Stanford University, Stanford.
Herz, B., van Rens, T., 2011. Structural Unemployment. Universitat Pompeu Fabra, Barcelona.
Hyatt, H.R., Spletzer, J.R., 2013. The Recent Decline in Employment Dynamics. Center for Economic Studies, US Census Bureau, Washington, DC.
Jarosch, G., 2014. Searching for Job Security and the Consequences of Job Loss. Department of Economics, University of Chicago, Chicago.
Kaplan, G., Menzio, G., 2016. Shopping externalities and self-fulfilling unemployment fluctuations. J. Polit. Econ. forthcoming.
Kaplan, G., Violante, G.L., 2014. A model of the consumption response to fiscal stimulus payments. Econometrica 82 (4), 1199–1239. ISSN 1468-0262. http://dx.doi.org/10.3982/ECTA10528.
Karabarbounis, L., Neiman, B., 2014. The global decline of the labor share. Q. J. Econ. 129 (1), 61–103. http://dx.doi.org/10.1093/qje/qjt032. http://qje.oxfordjournals.org/content/129/1/61.abstract.
Kiyotaki, N., Moore, J., 2012. Liquidity, business cycles, and monetary policy. Working Paper 17934, National Bureau of Economic Research. http://www.nber.org/papers/w17934.
Kocherlakota, N.R., 2013. Impact of a land price fall when labor markets are incomplete. Federal Reserve Bank of Minneapolis.
Korinek, A., Simsek, A., 2014. Liquidity trap and excessive leverage. Working Paper 19970, National Bureau of Economic Research. http://www.nber.org/papers/w19970.
Kozlowski, J., Veldkamp, L., Venkateswaran, V., 2015. The tail that wags the economy: belief-driven business cycles and persistent stagnation. Working Paper 21719, National Bureau of Economic Research. http://www.nber.org/papers/w21719.
Krishnamurthy, A., Vissing-Jorgensen, A., 2013. Short-Term Debt and Financial Crises: What We Can Learn from U.S. Treasury Supply. Kellogg School, Northwestern University, Chicago.
Krueger, A.B., Mueller, A.I., 2011. Job search, emotional well-being, and job finding in a period of mass unemployment: evidence from high-frequency longitudinal data. Brookings Papers Econ. Act. (1), 1–70.
Krueger, A.B., Cramer, J., Cho, D., 2014. Are the long-term unemployed on the margins of the labor market? Brookings Papers Econ. Act. Spring, 229–299.
Krugman, P.R., 1998. It's Baaack: Japan's slump and the return of the liquidity trap. Brookings Papers Econ. Act. (2), 137–205.
Kuehn, L.A., Petrosky-Nadeau, N., Zhang, L., 2013. An Equilibrium Asset Pricing Model with Labor Market Search. Carnegie Mellon University, Tepper School of Business, Pittsburgh.
Ludvigson, S.C., Ma, S., Ng, S., 2015. Uncertainty and business cycles: exogenous impulse or endogenous response? Working Paper 21803, National Bureau of Economic Research. http://www.nber.org/papers/w21803.
Lustig, H., Verdelhan, A., 2012. Business cycle variation in the risk-return trade-off. J. Monetary Econ. 0304-3932. 59, S35–S49. http://dx.doi.org/10.1016/j.jmoneco.2012.11.003. http://www.sciencedirect.com/science/article/pii/S0304393212001511.
Lustig, H., Van Nieuwerburgh, S., Verdelhan, A., 2013. The wealth-consumption ratio. Rev. Asset Pricing Stud. 3 (1), 38–94. http://dx.doi.org/10.1093/rapstu/rat002. http://raps.oxfordjournals.org/content/3/1/38.abstract.

Mian, A., Sufi, A., 2010. The great recession: lessons from microeconomic data. Am. Econ. Rev. 100 (2), 51–56. ISSN 0002-8282. http://www.jstor.org/stable/27804962.

Mian, A.R., Sufi, A., 2012. What explains high unemployment? The aggregate demand channel. Working Paper 17830, National Bureau of Economic Research. http://www.nber.org/papers/w17830.

Mian, A., Rao, K., Sufi, A., 2013. Household balance sheets, consumption, and the economic slump. Q. J. Econ. 128 (4), 1687–1726. http://dx.doi.org/10.1093/qje/qjt020. http://qje.oxfordjournals.org/content/128/4/1687.abstract.

Michaillat, P., Saez, E., 2014. An economical business-cycle model. Working Paper 19777, National Bureau of Economic Research. http://www.nber.org/papers/w19777.

Mortensen, D.T., 2011. Comments on Hall's Clashing Theories of Unemployment. Department of Economics, Northwestern University, Chicago.

Mulligan, C.B., 2012. Do welfare policies matter for labor market aggregates? Quantifying safety net work incentives since 2007. Working Paper 18088. National Bureau of Economic Research. http://www.nber.org/papers/w18088.

Mulligan, C.B., 2012. The Redistribution Recession: How Labor Market Distortions Contracted the Economy. Oxford University Press, New York.

Nekarda, C.J., Ramey, V.A., 2013. The cyclical behavior of the price-cost markup. Working Paper 19099, National Bureau of Economic Research. http://www.nber.org/papers/w19099.

Parker, J.A., Souleles, N.S., Johnson, D.S., McClelland, R., 2011. Consumer spending and the economic stimulus payments of 2008. Working Paper 16684, National Bureau of Economic Research. http://www.nber.org/papers/w16684.

Petev, I., Pistaferri, L., Eksten, I.S., 2012. Consumption and the great recession: an analysis of trends, perceptions, and distributional effects. In: Grusky, D.B., Western, B., Wimer, C. (Eds.), The Great Recession. Russell Sage Foundation, New York.

Petrosky-Nadeau, N., Wasmer, E., 2013. The cyclical volatility of labor markets under frictional financial markets. Am. Econ. J. Macroecon. 5 (1), 193–221. http://dx.doi.org/10.1257/mac.5.1.193. http://www.ingentaconnect.com/content/aea/aejma/2013/00000005/00000001/art00007.

Petrosky-Nadeau, N., Wasmer, E., 2015. Macroeconomic dynamics in a model of goods, labor, and credit market frictions. J. Monetary Econ. 72 May, 97–113. ISSN 0304-3932. http://dx.doi.org/10.1016/j.jmoneco.2015.01.006. http://www.sciencedirect.com/science/article/pii/S0304393215000161.

Petrosky-Nadeau, N., Zhang, L., 2013. Unemployment crises. Working Paper 19207, National Bureau of Economic Research. http://www.nber.org/papers/w19207.

Phelps, E.S., Winter, S.G., 1970. Optimal price policy under atomistic competition. In: Phelps, E.S. et al. (Eds.), Microeconomic Foundations of Employment and Inflation Theory. Norton, New York, pp. 309–337.

Philippon, T., 2009. The bond market's q. Q. J. Econ. 124 (3), 1011–1056. http://ideas.repec.org/a/tpr/qjecon/v124y2009i3p1011-1056.html.

Ramey, V.A., 2011a. Can government purchases stimulate the economy? J. Econ. Liter. 49 (3), 673–685. http://dx.doi.org/10.1257/jel.49.3.673.

Ramey, V.A., 2011b. Identifying government spending shocks: it's all in the timing. Q. J. Econ. 126 Feb., 1–50. http://dx.doi.org/10.1093/qje/qjq008.. http://qje.oxfordjournals.org/content/early/2011/03/21/qje.qjq008.abstract

Ravn, M.O., Sterk, V., 2012. Job Uncertainty and Deep Recessions. University College London, London.

Reifschneider, D., Wascher, W., Wilcox, D., 2013. Aggregate supply in the United States: recent developments and implications for the conduct of monetary policy. Technical Report, Finance and Economics Discussion Series Divisions of Research & Statistics and Monetary Affairs Federal Reserve Board, Washington, DC.

Restrepo, P., 2015. Skill Mismatch and Structural Unemployment. Massachusetts Institute of Technology, Cambridge, MA.

Rognlie, M., 2015. Deciphering the fall and rise in the net capital share. Broookings Papers Econ. Act. 50 (1 (Spring)), 1–69.

Rotemberg, J.J., Woodford, M., 1999. The cyclical behavior of prices and costs. In: Taylor, Woodford, (Eds.), Handbook of Macroeconomics. Elsevier, North Holland, pp. 1051–1135 (Chapter 16).

Rothstein, J., 2011. Unemployment insurance and job search in the great recession. Brookings Papers Econ. Act. 43 (2 (Fall)), 143–213.
Sahin, A., Song, J., Topa, G., Violante, G.L., 2012. Mismatch unemployment. Working Paper 18265, National Bureau of Economic Research. http://www.nber.org/papers/w18265.
Shapiro, M.D., Slemrod, J., 2009. Did the 2008 tax rebates stimulate spending? Am. Econ. Rev. Papers Proc. 99 (2), 374–379.
Shimer, R., 2005. The cyclical behavior of equilibrium unemployment and vacancies. Am. Econ. Rev. 95 (1), 24–49.
Shimer, R., 2008. Convergence in macroeconomics: the labor wedge. Am. Econ. J. Macroecon. 1 (1), 280–297.
Spilimbergo, A., Symansky, S., Schindler, M., 2009. Fiscal multipliers, IMF Staff Position Note 2009.
Stock, J.H., Watson, M.W., 2010. Modeling inflation after the crisis. Proceedings of the Economic Policy Symposium, Federal Reserve Bank of Kansas City Working Paper. pp. 172–220. http://www.nber.org/papers/w16488.
Valletta, R., Kuang, K., 2010a. Extended unemployment and UI benefits. Federal Reserve Bank of San Francisco Economic Letter, pp. 1–4.
Valletta, R., Kuang, K., 2010b. Is structural unemployment on the rise? Federal Reserve Bank of San Francisco Economic Letter, pp. 1–5.
Walsh, C.E., 2003. Labor market search and monetary shocks. In: Altug, S., Chadha, J., Nolan, C. (Eds.), Elements of Dynamic Macroeconomic Analysis, Cambridge University Press, Cambridge, UK, pp. 451–486.

SECTION 5

Macroeconomic Policy

CHAPTER 28

Challenges for Central Banks' Macro Models

J. Lindé[*,†,‡], **F. Smets**[§,¶,‡], **R. Wouters**[||,‡]
[*]Sveriges Riksbank, Stockholm, Sweden
[†]Stockholm School of Economics, Stockholm, Sweden
[‡]CEPR, London, United Kingdom
[§]ECB, Frankfurt, Germany
[¶]KU Leuven, Leuven, Belgium
[||]National Bank of Belgium, Brussels, Belgium

Contents

Handbook of Macroeconomics, Volume 2B
ISSN 1574-0048, http://dx.doi.org/10.1016/bs.hesmac.2016.04.009

Abstract

In this chapter, we discuss a number of challenges for structural macroeconomic models in the light of the Great Recession and its aftermath. It shows that a benchmark DSGE model that shares many features with models currently used by central banks and large international institutions has difficulty explaining both the depth and the slow recovery of the Great Recession. In order to better account for these observations, the chapter analyses three extensions of the benchmark model. First, we estimate the model allowing explicitly for the zero lower bound constraint on nominal interest rates. Second, we introduce time variation in the volatility of the exogenous disturbances to account for the non-Gaussian nature of some of the shocks. Third and finally, we extend the model with a financial accelerator and allow for time variation in the endogenous propagation of financial shocks. All three extensions require that we go beyond the linear Gaussian assumptions that are standard in most policy models. We conclude that these extensions go some way in accounting for features of the Great Recession and its aftermath, but they do not suffice to address some of the major policy challenges associated with the use of nonstandard monetary policy and macroprudential policies.

Keywords

Monetary policy, DSGE, and VAR models, Regime switching, Zero lower bound, Financial frictions, Great recession, Macroprudential policy, Open economy

JEL Classification Codes

E52, E58

1. INTRODUCTION

In this chapter, we discuss new challenges for structural macroeconomic models used at central banks in light of the Great Recession in United States and other advanced economies. This recession has had widespread implications for economic policy and economic performance, with historically low nominal interest rates and elevated unemployment levels in its aftermath. The fact that the intensification of the crisis in the fall of 2008 was largely unexpected and much deeper than central banks predicted and that the subsequent recovery was much slower, has raised many questions about the design of macroeconomic models at use in these institutions. Specifically, the models have been criticized for omitting key financial mechanisms and shocks stemming from the financial sector.

We start by analyzing the performance of a benchmark macroeconomic model during the Great Recession. The model we use—the well-known Smets and Wouters (2007)

model—shares many features with the models currently used by central banks. When we analyze this model estimated over the precrisis period we find, confirming previous results in Del Negro and Schorfheide (2013), that actual GDP growth was outside the predictive density of the model during the most acute phase of the recession. To account for the depth of the recession, the model needs a cocktail of extremely unlikely shocks that mainly affect the intertemporal decision of households and firms to consume or invest such as risk-premium and investment-specific technology shocks. We then proceed to document that these shocks are non-Gaussian, and strongly related to observable financial variables such as the Baa-Aaa and term spread, suggesting the importance of including financial shocks and frictions to account for large recessions. Moreover, in order to account for the slow recovery, restrictive monetary policy shocks reflecting a binding lower bound on the nominal interest rate, negative investment shocks, and positive price mark-up shocks are needed. This configuration of shocks explains the slow recovery and the missing disinflation following the great recession.

To try to better account for these observations, we proceed to amend the benchmark model along three dimensions. First, we take the zero lower bound (ZLB henceforth) explicitly into account when estimating the model over the full sample. We do this using two alternative approaches. First, we implement the ZLB as a binding constraint on the policy rule with an expected duration that is determined endogenously by the model in each period. Second, we impose the expected duration of the ZLB spells during the recession to be consistent with external information derived from overnight index swap rates. Importantly, we find that the variants of the model estimated subject to the ZLB constraint typically feature a substantially higher degree of nominal stickiness in both prices and wages which helps to understand the inflation dynamics during the recession period and the subsequent slow recovery. In addition, an important characteristic of these variants of the model is a substantially higher response coefficient on the output gap in the policy rule. Incorporating the ZLB in the estimation and simulation of the model does not materially affect the median forecast of output and inflation in 2008Q3 as the probability of hitting the lower bound is estimated to be low before the crisis. It does, however, tilt the balance of risks towards the downside in the subsequent periods as the likelihood of monetary policy being constrained increases.

Second, in order to account for the non-Gaussian nature of the shocks driving most recessions, we allow for time-varying volatility in some of the shocks. In line with the previous literature, we find that the empirical performance of the model improves a lot when two regime change processes are allowed in the variance of the shocks. One of those regime switches captures the great moderation period from the mid-1980s to the mid-2000s, when overall macroeconomic volatility was much lower than both before and after this period. The other regime switching process captures the higher volatility of the risk-premium, the monetary policy, and the investment-specific technology shocks in recession periods. This regime switching process can account for the non-Gaussian nature of those shocks and also helps widening the predictive density of output growth at the end of 2008 as the probability of a financial recession increases.

Finally, we proceed to examine how the performance and properties of the basic model can be improved by introducing a financial accelerator mechanism and explicit shocks stemming from the financial sector. This exercise is initiated by embedding a variant of the Bernanke et al. (1999) financial accelerator into the workhorse model and estimating it under the standard assumption that the financial sector excerpts a time-invariant influence on business cycles: that is, we follow, eg, Christiano et al. (2003a), De Graeve (2008) and Queijo von Heideken (2009), and assume that the parameters characterizing the financial frictions are constant and that shocks stemming from the financial bloc are Gaussian. In this specification, we do not find that the financial accelerator adds much propagation of other macroeconomic shocks, and that movements in the Baa-Aaa spread we add as observable is mostly explained by the exogenous shock stemming from the financial sector. Driven by this result, and because of the non-Gaussian features of the smoothed shocks in the benchmark model, we examine if the performance of this augmented model can be improved by allowing for regime switching in the sensitivity of the external finance premium to the leverage ratio, which one may think of as risk-on/risk-off behavior in the financial sector. We find that allowing for regime switching in the sensitivity of external finance premium to the leverage ratio introduces a high degree of skewness in the predictive density of the spread and makes the model put nonzero probability in the predictive density on the observed 2008Q4 output growth outcome. Moreover, when we follow Del Negro and Schorfheide (2013) and condition on the actual spread outcome during the fourth quarter of 2008—which is reasonable since the spread reached its quarterly mean in the beginning of October—the model's ability to account for the severe growth outcome further improves. This result indicates that if we appropriately could integrate the nonlinear accelerator dynamics from financial frictions in our models, we may obtain a more realistic predictive density in line with reduced form time-varying volatility models.

The three extensions discussed in this chapter go some way to address some of the challenges faced by the benchmark DSGE model in accounting for the Great Recession and its aftermath. They all involve going beyond the linear Gaussian-modeling framework. However, they do not suffice to fully address some of the major empirical policy challenges. These new challenges stem from the fact that, following the crisis and hitting the zero lower bound, central banks have implemented a panoply of nonstandard monetary policy measures such a Large-Scale-Asset-Purchases and other credit easing policies. Basic extensions of the benchmark model with financial frictions (such as a financial accelerator) are not sufficient to be able to fully analyze the effectiveness of those policies and their interaction with the standard interest rate policy. Similarly, the financial crisis has given rise to the new macroprudential policy domain that aims at containing systemic risk and preserving financial stability. Current extensions of the benchmark model are often not rich enough to analyze the interaction between monetary and macroprudential policy. Being able to do so will require incorporating of a richer description of both solvency (default) and liquidity (bank runs) dynamics with greater complexity in terms of both nonlinearities and heterogeneity.

The rest of the chapter is structured as follows. Section 2 provides an incomplete survey of the macroeconomic models used by central banks and other international organizations. Following this survey, Section 3 presents the prototype model—the estimated model of Smets and Wouters (2003). This model shares many features of models in use by central banks. The section also discusses the data and the estimation of this model on precrisis data. In Section 4, we use this model estimated on precrisis data to analyze the crisis episode, which gives us valuable insights into the workings of the model. We also compare the performance of our structural model to a reduced-form benchmark VAR, which is estimated with Bayesian priors. As this analysis points to some important shortcomings of the benchmark model, we augment the baseline model in Section 5 along the three dimensions discussed earlier.

Finally, Section 6 sums up by discussing some other new and old challenges for structural macro models used in policy analysis and presents some conclusions. Appendices contain some technical details on the model, methods, and the data used in the analysis.

2. COMMON FEATURES OF CENTRAL BANK MODELS

In this section, we provide an incomplete survey of the key policy models currently in use at central banks and other key policy institutions like the IMF, European Commission, and the OECD. We aim at determining the similarity between models, and assess if—and how—they have been changed in response to the recession and developments since then.

A good starting point for the discussion is the paper by Coenen et al. (2012). Wieland et al. (2012) provides a complementary and very useful overview of policy models in use at central banks. An additional advantage with the paper by Wieland et al. is that they have pulled together an archive with well-know estimated macroeconomic models (both policy and academic) that can conveniently be used to run and compare various diagnostic shocks using a Matlab graphical user interface.[a] We nevertheless base our discussion on Coenen et al., as they focus exclusively on models in use at policy institutions. Coenen et al. studies the effects of monetary and fiscal shocks in the key policy models in use at the Bank of Canada (BoC-GEM), the Board of Governors of the Federal Reserve System (with two models, FRB-US and SIGMA), the European Central Bank (NAWM), the European Commission (QUEST), the International Monetary Fund (GIMF), and the OECD (OECD Fiscal). Out of the seven models, six are dynamic

[a] Taylor and Wieland (2012) use the database to compare the responses to monetary policy shocks. Wieland and Wolters (2013) study the forecasting behavior for a large set of models in the database.

stochastic general equilibrium (DSGE) models, while one–the FRB-US—is based on the polynomial adjustment cost (PAC) framework. Hence, an overwhelming majority of key policy institutions today use DSGE models as the core policy tool.[b] The switch from traditional backward-looking macroeconometric models (see, eg, Rudebusch and Svensson, 1999) to DSGEs occurred amid the forceful critique by Lucas (1976) and Sims (1980) of such models, and was made feasible due to the progress in the solution and estimation of such models (see, eg, Blanchard and Kahn, 1980 and Fair and Taylor, 1983) as well as the contribution of Christiano et al. (2005) who showed that such models, carefully specified, could feature a realistic monetary policy transmission mechanism. As pointed out by Clarida et al. (1999), Woodford (2003) and Galí (2008), these models assigns an important role to expectations for macroeconomic stabilization, and this view was embraced by policy makers at central banks. However, although macroeconomic models have been used in scenario analysis and affected policy making more generally, it is probably fair to say that the models impact on the short- and medium-term economic projections have been limited, see, eg, Iversen et al. (2016).

As outlined in detail in tables 1 and 2 by Coenen et al. (2012), the DSGE models share many similarities to the seminal models of Christiano et al. (2005) (CEE henceforth) and Smets and Wouters (2003, 2007). They typically feature imperfect competition in product and labor markets as vehicles to introduce sticky prices and wages. They also include important real rigidities like habit formation, costs of adjusting investment and variable capital utilization. Monetary policy is generally determined by a simple Taylor-type policy rule which allows for interest rate smoothing, but although they share many similarities with the academic benchmark models of CEE and Smets and Wouters (2007) (SW07 henceforth), policy models often embed some additional features. One such important feature is that they have a significant share of financially constrained households, ranging between 20% and 50%. In some models these are hand-to-mouth households, who take their labor income as given and determine consumption residually from a period-by-period budget constraint. In other models these are liquidity-constrained households, who face the same period-by-period budget constraint but solve an intertemporal decision problem between consumption and work effort. An additional difference between the policy models and the academic style ones is that the former generally has a much more detailed fiscal sector with many distortionary taxes, types of government spending and various transfers from the government to the households.[c]

[b] Other prominent institutions that have adopted estimated DSGE model as their core policy tool include Bank of England (COMPASS, see Burgess et al., 2013), Norges Bank (NEMO, see Brubakk et al., 2006), Sveriges Riksbank (RAMSES, see Adolfson et al., 2013), Federal Reserve Bank of New York (Del Negro et al., 2013), and the Federal Reserve Bank of Chicago (Brave et al., 2012).

[c] These results are broadly in line with the findings of Wieland et al. (2012).

Another interesting observation is that neither CEE nor SW07 include frictions in financial markets or a detailed banking sector in their models.[d] Four of the seven policy models included financial frictions prior to the crisis. By asking the policy institutions that were part of this study about their development efforts since then, it is clear that efforts have been made towards better integration of financial markets, with a focus on the interaction between banks and the firms in the economy. For instance, following the crisis, financial frictions following the approach of Bernanke et al. (1999) have been introduced in (at least) two of the three models that did not feature them before.[e]

The key lesson we draw from this is that while the crisis has had some impact on improving the modeling of the financial sector in DSGE models, it has not so far had a material impact on the type of models used at key policy institutions, which still share many features of the basic model developed by CEE.

3. A BENCHMARK MODEL

In this section, we show the benchmark model environment, which is the model of Smets and Wouters (2007). The SW07-model builds on the workhorse model by CEE, but allows for a richer set of stochastic shocks. In Section 3.4, we describe how we estimate it using aggregate times series for the United States.

3.1 Firms and Price Setting

3.1.1 Final Goods Production

The single final output good Y_t is produced using a continuum of differentiated intermediate goods $Y_t(f)$. Following Kimball (1995), the technology for transforming these intermediate goods into the final output good is

$$\int_0^1 G_Y\left(\frac{Y_t(f)}{Y_t}\right) df = 1. \tag{1}$$

As in Dotsey and King (2005), we assume that $G_Y(\cdot)$ is given by a strictly concave and increasing function:

[d] The CEE, but not the SW07-model, includes a working capital—or cost channel—of monetary policy whereby firms have to borrow at the policy rate to finance the wage bill. This channel allows the CEE model to account for the "Price-puzzle" (ie, that inflation rises on impact following a hike in the policy rate) that often emerges for monetary policy shocks in identified VAR models.

[e] We are grateful to Günter Coenen (ECB) and John Roberts (Federal Reserve Board) for providing very helpful responses to our questionnaire.

$$G_Y\left(\frac{Y_t(f)}{Y_t}\right)=\frac{\phi_t^p}{1-(\phi_t^p-1)\epsilon_p}\left[\left(\frac{\phi_t^p+(1-\phi_t^p)\epsilon_p}{\phi_t^p}\right)\frac{Y_t(f)}{Y_t}+\frac{(\phi_t^p-1)\epsilon_p}{\phi_t^p}\right]^{\frac{1-(\phi_t^p-1)\epsilon_p}{\phi_t^p-(\phi_t^p-1)\epsilon_p}} \\ +\left[1-\frac{\phi_t^p}{1-(\phi_t^p-1)\epsilon_p}\right], \tag{2}$$

where $\phi_t^p \geq 1$ denotes the gross markup of the intermediate firms. The parameter ϵ_p governs the degree of curvature of the intermediate firm's demand curve. When $\epsilon_p = 0$, the demand curve exhibits constant elasticity as with the standard Dixit–Stiglitz aggregator. When ϵ_p is positive the firms instead face a quasi-kinked demand curve, implying that a drop in the good's relative price only stimulates a small increase in demand. On the other hand, a rise in its relative price generates a large fall in demand. Relative to the standard Dixit–Stiglitz aggregator, this introduces more strategic complementary in price setting which causes intermediate firms to adjust prices less to a given change in marginal cost. Finally, notice that $G_Y(1) = 1$, implying constant returns to scale when all intermediate firms produce the same amount of the good.

Firms that produce the final output good are perfectly competitive in both product and factor markets. Thus, final goods producers minimize the cost of producing a given quantity of the output index Y_t, taking the price $P_t(f)$ of each intermediate good $Y_t(f)$ as given. Moreover, final goods producers sell the final output good at a price P_t, and hence solve the following problem:

$$\max_{\{Y_t, Y_t(f)\}} P_t Y_t - \int_0^1 P_t(f) Y_t(f) df, \tag{3}$$

subject to the constraint in (1). The first order conditions (FOCs) for this problem can be written

$$\frac{Y_t(f)}{Y_t}=\frac{\phi_t^p}{\phi_t^p-(\phi_t^p-1)\epsilon_p}\left(\left[\frac{P_t(f)}{P_t}\frac{1}{\Lambda_t^p}\right]^{-\frac{\phi_t^p-(\phi_p-1)\epsilon_p}{\phi_t^p-1}}+\frac{(1-\phi_t^p)\epsilon_p}{\phi_t^p}\right)$$

$$P_t\Lambda_t^p=\left[\int P_t(f)^{-\frac{1-(\phi_t^p-1)\epsilon_p}{\phi_t^p-1}}df\right]^{-\frac{\phi_t^p-1}{1-(\phi_t^p-1)\epsilon_p}} \tag{4}$$

$$\Lambda_t^p=1+\frac{(1-\phi_t^p)\epsilon_p}{\phi_p}-\frac{(1-\phi_t^p)\epsilon_p}{\phi_t^p}\int\frac{P_t(f)}{P_t}df,$$

where Λ_t^p denotes the Lagrange multiplier on the aggregator constraint in (1). Note that when $\epsilon_p = 0$, it follows from the last of these conditions that $\Lambda_t^p = 1$ in each period t, and the demand and pricing equations collapse to the usual Dixit–Stiglitz expressions, ie,

$$\frac{Y_t(f)}{Y_t} = \left[\frac{P_t(f)}{P_t}\right]^{-\frac{\phi_t^p}{\phi_t^p - 1}}, P_t = \left[\int P_t(f)^{\frac{1}{1-\phi_t^p}} df\right]^{1-\phi_t^p}.$$

3.1.2 Intermediate Goods Production

A continuum of intermediate goods $Y_t(f)$ for $f \in [0, 1]$ is produced by monopolistic competitive firms, each of which produces a single differentiated good. Each intermediate goods producer faces the demand schedule in Eq. (4) from the final goods firms through the solution to the problem in (3), which varies inversely with its output price $P_t(f)$ and directly with aggregate demand Y_t.

Each intermediate goods producer utilizes capital services $K_t(f)$ and a labor index $L_t(f)$ (defined later) to produce its respective output good. The form of the production function is Cobb–Douglas:

$$Y_t(f) = \varepsilon_t^a K_t(f)^\alpha [\gamma^t L_t(f)]^{1-\alpha} - \gamma^t \Phi,$$

where γ^t represents the labor-augmenting deterministic growth rate in the economy, Φ denotes the fixed cost (which is related to the gross markup ϕ_t^p so that profits are zero in the steady state), and ε_t^a is a total productivity factor which follows a Kydland and Prescott (1982) style process:

$$\ln \varepsilon_t^a = \rho_a \ln \varepsilon_{t-1}^a + \eta_t^a, \eta_t^a \sim N(0, \sigma_a). \tag{5}$$

Firms face perfectly competitive factor markets for renting capital and hiring labor. Thus, each firm chooses $K_t(f)$ and $L_t(f)$, taking as given both the rental price of capital R_{Kt} and the aggregate wage index W_t (defined later). Firms can without costs adjust either factor of production, thus, the standard static first-order conditions for cost minimization implies that all firms have identical marginal costs per unit of output.

The prices of the intermediate goods are determined by nominal contracts in Calvo (1983) and Yun (1996) staggered style nominal contracts. In each period, each firm f faces a constant probability, $1 - \xi_p$, of being able to reoptimize the price $P_t(f)$ of the good. The probability that any firm receives a signal to reoptimize the price is assumed to be independent of the time that it last reset its price. If a firm is not allowed to optimize its price in a given period, this is adjusted by a weighted combination of the lagged and steady state rate of inflation, ie, $P_t(f) = (1 + \pi_{t-1})^{\iota_p}(1 + \pi)^{1-\iota_p} P_{t-1}(f)$ where $0 \leq \iota_p \leq 1$ and π_{t-1} denotes net inflation in period $t - 1$, and π the steady state net inflation rate. A positive value of the indexation parameter ι_p introduces structural inertia into the inflation process. All told, this leads to the following optimization problem for the intermediate firms

$$\max_{\tilde{P}_t(f)} \mathrm{E}_t \sum_{j=0}^{\infty} (\beta \xi_p)^j \frac{\Xi_{t+j} P_t}{\Xi_t P_{t+j}} \left[\tilde{P}_t(f) \left(\Pi_{s=1}^{j} (1 + \pi_{t+s-1})^{\iota_p} (1 + \pi)^{1-\iota_p}\right) - MC_{t+j}\right] Y_{t+j}(f),$$

where $\widetilde{P}_t(f)$ is the newly set price and $\beta^j \frac{\Xi_{t+j} P_t}{\Xi_t P_{t+j}}$ the stochastic discount factor. Notice that given our assumptions, all firms that reoptimize their prices actually set the same price.

As noted previously, we assume that the gross price-markup is time varying and given by $\phi_t^p = \phi^p \varepsilon_t^p$, for which the exogenous component ε_t^p is given by an exogenous ARMA (1,1) process:

$$\ln \varepsilon_t^p = \rho_p \ln \varepsilon_{t-1}^p + \eta_t^p - \vartheta_p \eta_{t-1}^p, \eta_t^p \sim N(0, \sigma_p). \tag{6}$$

3.2 Households and Wage Setting

Following Erceg et al. (2000), we assume a continuum of monopolistic competitive households (indexed on the unit interval), each of which supplies a differentiated labor service to the production sector; that is, goods-producing firms regard each household's labor services $L_t(h)$, $h \in [0, 1]$, as imperfect substitutes for the labor services of other households. It is convenient to assume that a representative labor aggregator combines households' labor hours in the same proportions as firms would choose. Thus, the aggregator's demand for each household's labor is equal to the sum of firms' demands. The aggregated labor index L_t has the Kimball (1995) form:

$$L_t = \int_0^1 G_L\left(\frac{L_t(h)}{L_t}\right) dh = 1, \tag{7}$$

where the function $G_L(\cdot)$ has the same functional form as does (2), but is characterized by the corresponding parameters ϵ_w (governing convexity of labor demand by the aggregator) and a time-varying gross wage markup ϕ_t^w. The aggregator minimizes the cost of producing a given amount of the aggregate labor index L_t, taking each household's wage rate $W_t(h)$ as given, and then sells units of the labor index to the intermediate goods sector at unit cost W_t, which can naturally be interpreted as the aggregate wage rate. From the FOCs, the aggregator's demand for the labor hours of household h—or equivalently, the total demand for this household's labor by all goods-producing firms—is given by

$$\frac{L_t(h)}{L_t} = G_L^{\prime -1}\left[\frac{W_t(h)}{W_t} \int_0^1 G_L^{\prime}\left(\frac{L_t(h)}{L_t}\right) \frac{L_t(h)}{L_t} dh\right], \tag{8}$$

where $G_L^{\prime}(\cdot)$ denotes the derivative of the $G_L(\cdot)$ function in Eq. (7).

The utility function of a typical member of household h is

$$\mathrm{E}_t \sum_{j=0}^{\infty} \beta^j \left[\frac{1}{1-\sigma_c}\left(C_{t+j}(h) - \varkappa C_{t+j-1}\right)\right]^{1-\sigma_c} \exp\left(\frac{\sigma_c - 1}{1+\sigma_l} L_{t+j}(h)^{1+\sigma_l}\right), \tag{9}$$

where the discount factor β satisfies $0 < \beta < 1$. The period utility function depends on household h's current consumption $C_t(h)$, as well as lagged aggregate consumption per capita, to allow for external habit persistence (captured by the parameter $\varkappa$). The period utility function also depends inversely on hours worked $L_t(h)$.

Household h's budget constraint in period t states that expenditure on goods and net purchases of financial assets must equal to the disposable income:

$$\begin{aligned} & P_t C_t(h) + P_t I_t(h) + \frac{B_{t+1}(h)}{\varepsilon_t^b R_t} + \int_s \xi_{t,t+1} B_{D,t+1}(h) - B_{D,t}(h) \\ & = B_t(h) + W_t(h) L_t(h) + R_t^k Z_t(h) K_t^p(h) - a(Z_t(h)) K_t^p(h) + \Gamma_t(h) - T_t(h). \end{aligned} \tag{10}$$

Thus, the household purchases part of the final output good (at a price of P_t), which is chosen to be consumed $C_t(h)$ or invest $I_t(h)$ in physical capital. Following Christiano et al. (2005), investment augments the household's (end-of-period) physical capital stock $K_{t+1}^p(h)$ according to

$$K_{t+1}^p(h) = (1-\delta) K_t^p(h) + \varepsilon_t^i \left[1 - S\left(\frac{I_t(h)}{I_{t-1}(h)} \right) \right] I_t(h). \tag{11}$$

The extent to which investment by each household turns into physical capital is assumed to depend on an exogenous shock ε_t^i and how rapidly the household changes its rate of investment according to the function $S\left(\frac{I_t(h)}{I_{t-1}(h)} \right)$, which we assume satisfies $S(\gamma) = 0, S'(\gamma) = 0$ and $S''(\gamma) = \varphi$ where γ is the steady state gross growth rate of the economy. The stationary investment-specific shock ε_t^i follows the process:

$$\ln \varepsilon_t^i = \rho_i \ln \varepsilon_{t-1}^i + \eta_t^i, \eta_t^i \sim N(0, \sigma_i).$$

In addition to accumulating physical capital, households may augment their financial assets through increasing their nominal bond holdings (B_{t+1}), from which they earn an interest rate of R_t. The return on these bonds is also subject to a risk-shock, ε_t^b, which follows

$$\ln \varepsilon_t^b = \rho_b \ln \varepsilon_{t-1}^b + \eta_t^b, \eta_t^b \sim N(0, \sigma_b). \tag{12}$$

Fisher (2015) shows that this shock can be given a structural interpretation.

We assume that agents can engage in friction-less trading of a complete set of contingent claims to diversify away idiosyncratic risk. The term $\int_s \xi_{t,t+1} B_{D,t+1}(h) - B_{D,t}(h)$ represents net purchases of these state-contingent domestic bonds, with $\xi_{t,t+1}$ denoting the state-dependent price, and $B_{D,t+1}(h)$ the quantity of such claims purchased at time t.

On the income side, each member of household h earns labor income $W_t(h)L_t(h)$, capital rental income of $R_t^k Z_t(h) K_t^p(h)$, and pays a utilization cost of the physical capital equal to $a(Z_t(h))K_t^p(h)$ where $Z_t(h)$ is the capital utilization rate. The capital services provided by household h, $K_t(h)$ thereby equals $Z_t(h)K_t^p(h)$. The capital utilization adjustment function $a(Z_t(h))$ is assumed to satisfy $a(1) = 0$, $a'(1) = r^k$, and $a''(1) = \psi/(1-\psi) > 0$, where $\psi \in [0, 1)$ and a higher value of ψ implies a higher cost of changing the utilization rate. Finally, each member also receives an aliquot share $\Gamma_t(h)$ of the profits of all firms, and pays a lump-sum tax of $T_t(h)$ (regarded as taxes net of any transfers).

In every period t, each member of household h maximizes the utility function in (9) with respect to consumption, investment, (end-of-period) physical capital stock, capital utilization rate, bond holdings, and holdings of contingent claims, subject to the labor demand function (8), budget constraint (10), and transition equation for capital (11).

Households also set nominal wages in Calvo-style staggered contracts that are generally similar to the price contracts described previously. Thus, the probability that a household receives a signal to reoptimize its wage contract in a given period is denoted by $1 - \xi_w$. In addition, SW07 specify the following dynamic indexation scheme for the adjustment of wages for those households that do not get a signal to reoptimize: $W_t(h) = \gamma(1+\pi_{t-1})^{\iota_w}(1+\pi)^{1-\iota_w} W_{t-1}(h)$. All told, this leads to the following optimization problem for the households

$$\max_{\tilde{W}_t(h)} E_t \sum_{j=0}^{\infty} (\beta\xi_w)^j \frac{\Xi_{t+j}P_t}{\Xi_t P_{t+j}} \left[\tilde{W}_t(h) \left(\Pi_{s=1}^{j} \gamma (1+\pi_{t+s-1})^{\iota_w} (1+\pi)^{1-\iota_w} \right) - W_{t+j} \right] L_{t+j}(h),$$

where $\tilde{W}_t(h)$ is the newly set wage and $L_{t+j}(h)$ is determined by Eq. (7). Notice that with our assumptions all households that reoptimize their wages will actually set the same wage.

Following the same approach as with the intermediate-goods firms, we introduce a shock ε_t^w to the time-varying gross markup, $\phi_t^w = \phi^w \varepsilon_t^w$, where ε_t^w is assumed being given by an exogenous ARMA(1,1) process:

$$\ln \varepsilon_t^w = \rho_w \ln \varepsilon_{t-1}^w + \eta_t^w - \vartheta_w \eta_{t-1}^w, \eta_t^w \sim N(0, \sigma_w). \qquad (13)$$

3.3 Market Clearing Conditions and Monetary Policy

Government purchases G_t are exogenous, and the process for government spending relative to trend output in natural logs, ie, $g_t = G_t/(\gamma^t Y)$, is given by the following exogenous AR(1) process:

$$\ln g_t = \left(1-\rho_g\right) \ln g + \rho_g \left(\ln g_{t-1} - \rho_{ga} \ln \varepsilon_{t-1}^a \right) + \eta_t^g, \eta_t^g \sim N(0, \sigma_g).$$

Government purchases neither have any effects on the marginal utility of private consumption, nor do they serve as an input into goods production. The consolidated government sector budget constraint is

$$\frac{B_{t+1}}{R_t} = G_t - T_t + B_t,$$

where T_t are lump-sum taxes. By comparing the debt terms in the household budget constraint in Eq. (10) with the equation earlier, one can see that receipts from the risk shock are subject to iceberg costs, and hence do not add any income to the government.[f] We acknowledge that this is an extremely simplistic modeling of the fiscal behavior of the government relative to typical policy models, and there might be important feedback effects between fiscal and monetary policies that our model does not allow for.[g] As discussed by Benigno and Nisticó (2015) and Del Negro and Sims (2014), the fiscal links between governments and central banks may be especially important today when central banks have employed unconventional tools in monetary policy. Nevertheless, we maintain our simplistic modeling of fiscal policy throughout the chapter, as it allows us to examine the partial implications of amending the benchmark model with more elaborate financial markets modeling and the zero lower bound constraint more directly.

The conduct of monetary policy is assumed to be approximated by a Taylor-type policy rule (here stated in nonlinearized form)

$$R_t = \max\left(0, R^{1-\rho_R} R_{t-1}^{\rho_R} \left(\frac{\Pi_t}{\Pi}\right)^{r_\pi(1-\rho_R)} \left(\frac{Y_t}{Y_t^{pot}}\right)^{r_y(1-\rho_R)} \left(\frac{Y_t}{Y_t^{pot}} \Big/ \frac{Y_{t-1}}{Y_{t-1}^{pot}}\right)^{r_{\Delta y}(1-\rho_R)} \varepsilon_t^r\right), \tag{14}$$

where Π_t denotes the is gross inflation rate, Y_t^{pot} is the level of output that would prevail if prices and wages were flexible, and variables without subscripts denote steady state values. The policy shock ε_t^r is supposed to follow an AR(1) process in natural logs:

$$\ln \varepsilon_t^r = \rho_r \ln \varepsilon_{t-1}^r + \eta_t^r, \eta_t^r \sim N(0, \sigma_r). \tag{15}$$

Total output of the final goods sector is used as follows:

$$Y_t = C_t + I_t + G_t + a(Z_t) - K_t,$$

where $a(Z_t) - K_t$ is the capital utilization adjustment cost.

3.4 Estimation on Precrisis Data

We now proceed to discuss how the model is estimated. To begin with, we limit the sample to the period 1965Q1–2007Q4 to see how a model estimated on precrisis data fares during the recession. Subsequently, we will estimate the model on data spanning the crisis.

[f] But even if they did, it would not matter as the government is assumed to balance its expenditures each period through lump-sum taxes, $T_t = G_t + B_t - B_{t+1}/R_t$, so that government debt $B_t = 0$ in equilibrium. Furthermore, as Ricardian equivalence (see Barro, 1974) holds in the model, it does not matter for equilibrium allocations whether the government balances its debt or not in each period.

[g] See, eg, Leeper and Leith (2016) and Leeper et al. (2015).

3.4.1 Solving the Model

Before estimating the model, we log-linearize all the equations of the model. The log-linearized representation is provided in Appendix A. To solve the system of log-linearized equations, we use the code packages Dynare (see Adjemian et al. (2011) and RISE (see Maih (2015)) which provides an efficient and reliable implementation of the method proposed by Blanchard and Kahn (1980).

3.4.2 Data

We use seven key macroeconomic quarterly US time series as observable variables: the log difference of real GDP, real consumption, real investment and the real wage, log hours worked, the log difference of the GDP deflator and the federal funds rate. A full description of the data used is given in Appendix C. The solid blue line in Fig. 1 shows the data for the full sample, which spans 1965Q1–2014Q2.[h] From the figure, we see the extraordinary large fall in private consumption, which exceeded the fall during the recession in the early 1980s. The strains in the labor market are also evident, with hours worked per capita falling to a postwar bottom low in early 2010. Finally, we see that the Federal reserve cut the federal funds rate to near zero in 2009Q1 (the FFR is measured as an average of daily observations in each quarter). Evidently, the zero bound was perceived as an effective lower bound by the FOMC committee, and they kept it as this level during the crisis and adopted alternative tools to make monetary policy more accommodating (see, eg, Bernanke, 2013). Meanwhile, inflation fell to record lows and into deflationary territory by late 2009. Since then, inflation has rebounded close to the new target of 2% announced by the Federal Reserve in January 2012.

The measurement equation, relating the variables in the model to the various variables we match in the data, is given by:

$$Y_t^{obs} = \begin{bmatrix} \Delta \ln GDP_t \\ \Delta \ln CONS_t \\ \Delta \ln INVE_t \\ \Delta \ln W_t^{real} \\ \ln HOURS_t \\ \Delta \ln PGDP_t \\ FFR_t \end{bmatrix} = \begin{bmatrix} \ln Y_t - \ln Y_{t-1} \\ \ln C_t - \ln C_{t-1} \\ \ln I_t - \ln I_{t-1} \\ \ln (W/P)_t - \ln (W/P)_{t-1} \\ \ln L_t \\ \ln \Pi_t \\ \ln R_t \end{bmatrix} \approx \begin{bmatrix} \overline{\gamma} \\ \overline{\gamma} \\ \overline{\gamma} \\ \overline{\gamma} \\ \overline{l} \\ \overline{\pi} \\ \overline{r} \end{bmatrix} + \begin{bmatrix} \widehat{y}_t - \widehat{y}_{t-1} \\ \widehat{c}_t - \widehat{c}_{t-1} \\ \widehat{\imath}_t - \widehat{\imath}_{t-1} \\ \widehat{w}_t^{real} - \widehat{w}_{t-1}^{real} \\ \widehat{l}_t \\ \widehat{\pi}_t \\ \widehat{R}_t \end{bmatrix} \tag{16}$$

where ln and Δ ln stand for log and log-difference, respectively, $\overline{\gamma} = 100(\gamma - 1)$ is the common quarterly trend growth rate to real GDP, consumption, investment and wages, $\overline{\pi} = 100\pi$ is the quarterly steady state inflation rate and $r = 100\left(\beta^{-1}\gamma^{\sigma_c}(1+\pi) - 1\right)$ is the

[h] The figure also includes a red-dashed line, whose interpretation will be discussed in further detail within Section 4.

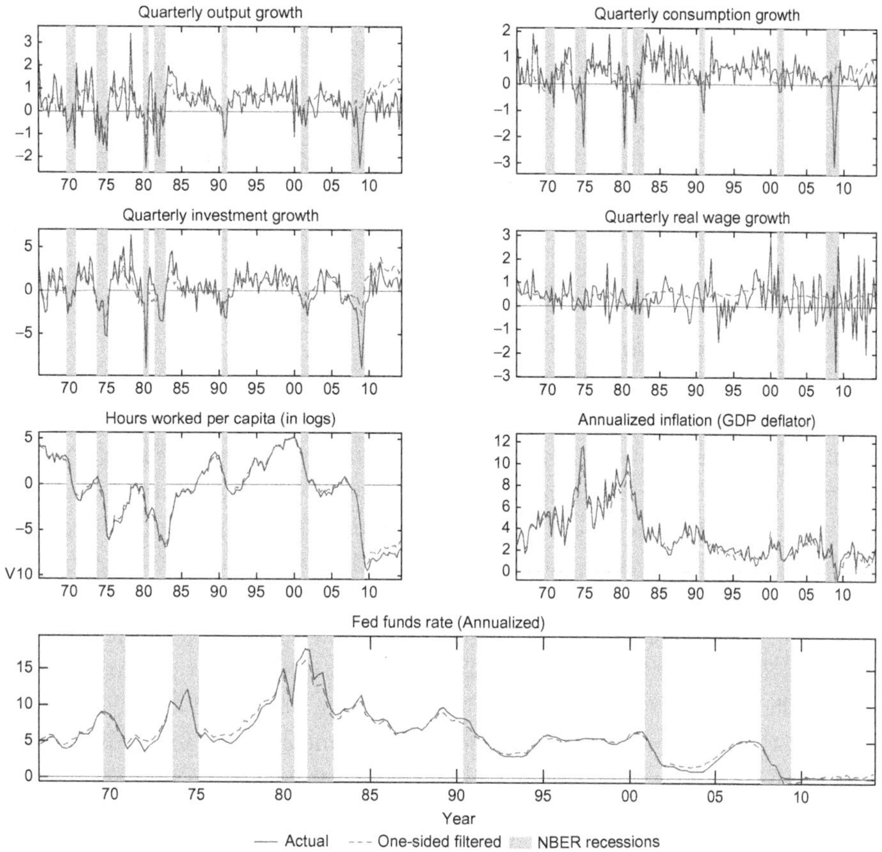

Fig. 1 Actual and filtered data in model estimated on precrisis data.

steady state nominal interest rate. Given the estimates of the trend growth rate and the steady state inflation rate, the latter will be determined by the estimated discount rate. Finally, $\bar{l}$ is steady state hours worked, which is normalized to be equal to zero.

Structural models impose important restrictions on the dynamic cross-correlation between the variables but also on the long run ratios between the macroaggregates. Our transformations in (16) impose a common deterministic growth component for all quantities and the real wage, whereas hours worked per capita, the real interest rate and the inflation rate are assumed to have a constant mean. These assumptions are not necessarily in line with the properties of the data and may have important implications for the estimation results. Some prominent papers in the literature assume real quantities to follow a stochastic trend, see, eg, Altig et al. (2011). Fisher (2006) argues that there is a stochastic trend in the relative price of investment and examines to what extent shocks that can explain this trend matter for business cycles. There is also an ongoing debate on whether hours worked per capita should be treated as stationary or not, see, eg, Christiano et al. (2003b), Galí and Pau (2004), and Boppart and Krusell (2015). Within the context of policy models, it is probably fair to say that less attention and resources have been spent to mitigate possible gaps in the low frequency properties of models and data, presumably partly because the jury is still out on the deficiencies of the benchmark specification, but also partly because the focus is on the near-term behavior of the models (ie, monetary transmission mechanism, forecasting performance, and historical decomposition) and these shortcomings do not seriously impair the model's behavior in this dimension.

3.4.3 Estimation Methodology

Following SW07, Bayesian techniques are adopted to estimate the parameters using the seven US macroeconomic variables in Eq. (16) during the period 1965Q1–2007Q4. Bayesian inference starts out from a prior distribution that describes the available information prior to observing the data used in the estimation. The observed data is subsequently used to update the prior, via Bayes' theorem, to the posterior distribution of the model's parameters which can be summarized in the usual measures of location (eg, mode or mean) and spread (eg, standard deviation and probability intervals).[i]

Some of the parameters in the model are kept fixed throughout the estimation procedure (ie, having infinitely strict priors). We choose to calibrate the parameters we think are weakly identified by the variables included in $\widetilde{Y}_t$ in (16). In Table 1, we report the parameters we have chosen to calibrate. These parameters are calibrated to the same values as had SW07.

The remaining 36 parameters, which mostly pertain to the nominal and real frictions in the model as well as the exogenous shock processes, are estimated. The first three columns in Table 2 shows the assumptions for the prior distribution of the estimated parameters. The location of the prior distribution is identical to that of SW07. We use the beta distribution for all parameters bounded between 0 and 1. For parameters assumed to be positive, we use the inverse gamma distribution, and for the unbounded parameters,

Table 1 Calibrated parameters

Parameter	Description	Calibrated value
δ	Depreciation rate	0.025
ϕ_w	Gross wage markup	1.50
g_y	Government G/Y ss-ratio	0.18
ϵ_p	Kimball curvature GM	10
ϵ_w	Kimball curvature LM	10

Note: The calibrated parameters are adapted from SW07.

[i] We refer the reader to Smets and Wouters (2003) for a more detailed description of the estimation procedure.

Table 2 Prior and posterior distributions: 1966Q1–2007Q4

Parameter		Prior distribution			Posterior distribution					SW07 results
					Optimization		Metropolis chain			
		Type	Mean	Std.dev. /df	Mode	Std.dev. Hess.	Mean	5%	95%	Posterior mode
Calvo prob. wages	ξ_w	Beta	0.50	0.10	0.79	0.055	0.75	0.61	0.82	0.73
Calvo prob. prices	ξ_p	Beta	0.50	0.10	0.69	0.051	0.69	0.60	0.76	0.65
Indexation wages	ι_w	Beta	0.50	0.15	0.63	0.136	0.58	0.36	0.79	0.59
Indexation prices	ι_p	Beta	0.50	0.15	0.23	0.093	0.26	0.13	0.44	0.22
Gross price markup	ϕ_p	Normal	1.25	0.12	1.64	0.076	1.64	1.52	1.77	1.61
Capital production share	α	Normal	0.30	0.05	0.21	0.018	0.20	0.18	0.24	0.19
Capital utilization cost	ψ	Beta	0.50	0.15	0.60	0.100	0.59	0.43	0.75	0.54
Investment adj. cost	φ	Normal	4.00	1.50	5.50	1.019	5.69	4.23	7.65	5.48
Habit formation	$\varkappa$	Beta	0.70	0.10	0.67	0.042	0.69	0.62	0.76	0.71
Inv subs. elast. of cons.	σ_c	Normal	1.50	0.37	1.53	0.138	1.44	1.23	1.69	1.59
Labor supply elast.	σ_l	Normal	2.00	0.75	2.15	0.584	2.03	1.13	2.99	1.92
Log hours worked in S.S.	$\bar{l}$	Normal	0.00	2.00	1.56	0.985	1.15	−0.56	2.72	−0.10
Discount factor	$100(\beta^{-1}-1)$	Gamma	0.25	0.10	0.13	0.052	0.16	0.08	0.25	0.16
Quarterly growth in S.S.	$\bar{\gamma}$	Normal	0.40	0.10	0.43	0.014	0.43	0.41	0.45	0.43
Stationary tech. shock	ρ_a	Beta	0.50	0.20	0.96	0.008	0.96	0.93	0.97	0.95
Risk premium shock	ρ_b	Beta	0.50	0.20	0.18	0.081	0.22	0.10	0.38	0.18
Invest. spec. tech. shock	ρ_i	Beta	0.50	0.20	0.71	0.053	0.71	0.61	0.80	0.71
Gov't cons. shock	ρ_g	Beta	0.50	0.20	0.97	0.008	0.97	0.96	0.98	0.97
Price markup shock	ρ_p	Beta	0.50	0.20	0.90	0.038	0.89	0.80	0.95	0.90
Wage markup shock	ρ_w	Beta	0.50	0.20	0.98	0.010	0.97	0.94	0.98	0.97
Response of g_t to ε_t^a	ρ_{ga}	Beta	0.50	0.20	0.52	0.086	0.49	0.38	0.67	0.52

Continued

Table 2 Prior and posterior distributions: 1966Q1–2007Q4—cont'd

Parameter		Prior distribution			Posterior distribution					SW07 results
					Optimization		Metropolis chain			
		Type	Mean	Std.dev. /df	Mode	Std.dev. Hess.	Mean	5%	95%	Posterior mode
Stationary tech. shock	σ_a	Invgamma	0.10	2.00	0.44	0.026	0.45	0.40	0.49	0.45
Risk premium shock	σ_b	Invgamma	0.10	2.00	0.24	0.022	0.24	0.19	0.27	0.24
Invest. spec. tech. shock	σ_i	Invgamma	0.10	2.00	0.41	0.041	0.41	0.34	0.48	0.45
Gov't cons. shock	σ_g	Invgamma	0.10	2.00	0.50	0.028	0.51	0.46	0.57	0.52
Price markup shock	σ_p	Invgamma	0.10	2.00	0.12	0.015	0.13	0.10	0.15	0.14
MA(1) price markup shock	ϑ_p	Beta	0.50	0.20	0.74	0.080	0.72	0.46	0.83	0.74
Wage markup shock	σ_w	Invgamma	0.10	2.00	0.31	0.025	0.30	0.25	0.34	0.24
MA(1) wage markup shock	ϑ_w	Beta	0.50	0.20	0.95	0.030	0.92	0.77	0.95	0.88
Quarterly infl. rate. in S.S.	$\overline{\pi}$	Gamma	0.62	0.10	0.79	0.114	0.82	0.65	1.01	0.81
Inflation response	r_π	Normal	1.50	0.25	2.01	0.174	2.07	1.75	2.33	2.03
Output gap response	r_y	Normal	0.12	0.05	0.10	0.023	0.10	0.05	0.13	0.08
Diff. output gap response	$r_{\Delta y}$	Normal	0.12	0.05	0.23	0.026	0.23	0.18	0.27	0.22
Mon. pol. shock std	σ_r	Invgamma	0.10	2.00	0.23	0.014	0.24	0.21	0.26	0.24
Mon. pol. shock pers.	ρ_r	Beta	0.50	0.20	0.12	0.062	0.15			0.12
Interest rate smoothing	ρ_R	Beta	0.75	0.10	0.82	0.022	0.82			0.81
Log marginal likelihood					Laplace	−961.81	MCMC	−960.72		

Note: Data for 1965Q1–1965Q4 are used as presample to form a prior for 1966Q1, and the log-likelihood is evaluated for the period 1966Q1–2007Q4. A posterior sample of 250, 000 postburn-in draws was generated in the Metropolis-Hastings chain. Convergence was checked using standard diagnostics such as CUSUM plots and the potential scale reduction factor on parallel simulation sequences. The MCMC marginal likelihood was numerically computed from the posterior draws using the modified harmonic estimator of Geweke (1999).

we use the normal distribution. The exact location and uncertainty of the prior can be seen in Table 2, but for a more comprehensive discussion of our choices regarding the prior distributions we refer the reader to SW07.

3.4.4 Posterior Distributions of the Estimated Parameters

Given these calibrated parameters in Table 1, we obtain the joint posterior distribution mode for the estimated parameters in Table 2 on precrisis data in two steps. First, the posterior mode and an approximate covariance matrix, based on the inverse Hessian matrix evaluated at the mode, is obtained by numerical optimization on the log posterior density. Second, the posterior distribution is subsequently explored by generating draws using the Metropolis-Hastings algorithm. The proposal distribution is taken to be the multivariate normal density centered at the previous draw with a covariance matrix proportional to the inverse Hessian at the posterior mode; see Schorfheide (2000) and Smets and Wouters (2003) for further details. The results in Table 2 shows the posterior mode of all the parameters along with the approximate posterior standard deviation obtained from the inverse Hessian at the posterior mode. In addition, it shows the mean along with the 5th and 95th percentiles of the posterior distribution, and finally, the last column reports the posterior mode in the SW07 paper.

There two important features to notice with regards to the posterior parameters in Table 2. First, the policy- and deep-parameters are generally very similar to those estimated by SW07, reflecting a largely overlapping estimation sample (SW07 used data for the 1965Q1–2004Q4 period to estimate the model). The only noticeable difference relative to SW07 is that the estimated degree of wage and price stickiness is somewhat more pronounced (posterior mode for ξ_w is 0.79 instead of 0.73 in SW07, and the mode for ξ_p has increased from 0.65 (SW07) to 0.69). The tendency of an increased degree of price and wage stickiness in the extended sample is supported by Del Negro et al. (2015b), who argue that a New Keynesian model similar to ours augmented with financial frictions points towards a high degree of price and wage stickiness to fit the behavior of inflation during the Great Recession. Second, the estimated variances of the shocks are somewhat lower (apart from the wage markup shock). Given that SW07 ended their estimation in 2004, and the so-called "Great Moderation" was still in effect from 2005 into the first half of 2007, the finding of reduced shock variances is not surprising.

4. EMPIRICAL PERFORMANCE OF BENCHMARK MODELS DURING THE GREAT RECESSION

We will now assess the performance of our benchmark DSGE model during the great recession in a number of dimensions. First and foremost, we study the forecasting performance of the model during the most intense phase of the recession, ie, the third and fourth quarters of 2008. In addition, we look into what the model has to say about the speed of recovery in the economy during the postcrisis period. In this exercise, we benchmark the performance of the DSGE model against a standard Bayesian VAR, which includes the same set of variables.

Second, we examine how the model interprets the "Great Recession", and assess the plausibility of the shocks the model needs to explain it. We do this from both a statistical and economic viewpoint.

4.1 Forecasting Performance of Benchmark Models During the Recession

We now use the DSGE model estimated on data up to 2007Q4 to forecast for the out-of-sample data. We start to make forecasts for 1, 2, ..., 12 quarters ahead in the third and fourth quarter of 2008, conditional on observing data up to and including 2008Q3 and 2008Q4, respectively. Forecasts starting in these quarters are of particular interest as output plummeted in 2008Q4 (about −9.75% at an annualized quarterly rate) and in 2009Q1 (roughly −5.75% at an annualized rate). To provide a benchmark for the DSGE forecasts, we also report the forecasts of a Bayesian vector autoregressive (BVAR) model estimated on the same sample. While both models have been estimated for the same time series stated in Equation (16), we only show results for a subset of variables; the federal funds rate, output growth and price inflation (where inflation and output growth have been transformed into yearly rates by taking four-quarter averages). Warne et al. (2015) study how the predictive likelihood can be estimated, by means of marginalization, for any subset of the observables in linear Gaussian state-space models. Our exposition later is less formal and focuses on the univariate densities.[j]

The BVAR uses the standard Doan–Litterman–Sims (Doan et al., 1984) prior on the dynamics and an informative prior on the steady state following the procedure outlined in Villani (2009). We select the priors on the steady state in the BVAR to be consistent with those used in the DSGE model, which facilitates comparison between the two models. In both the DSGE and the BVAR, the median projections and 50%, 90%, and 95% uncertainty bands are based on 10, 000 simulations of respective model in which we allow for both shock and parameter uncertainty.[k]

In Fig. 2, the left column shows the forecasts in the DSGE conditional on observing data up to 2008Q3. As can be seen in the upper left panel, the endogenous DSGE model forecast predicted yearly GDP growth (four quarter change of log-output) to be about unchanged, whereas actual economic activity fell dramatically in the fourth quarter. Moreover, the 95% uncertainty band suggests that the large drop in output was

[j] We perform these forecasts on *ex post* data, collected on September 25th 2014 (see Appendix C).

[k] For an extensive comparison of the forecasting performance of the Smets and Wouters model along with a comparison to a BVAR and Greenbook forecasts on real-time data, see Edge and Gürkaynak (2010) and Wieland and Wolters (2013). Adolfson et al. (2007a, d) examine the forecasting properties of an open economy DSGE model on Swedish data.

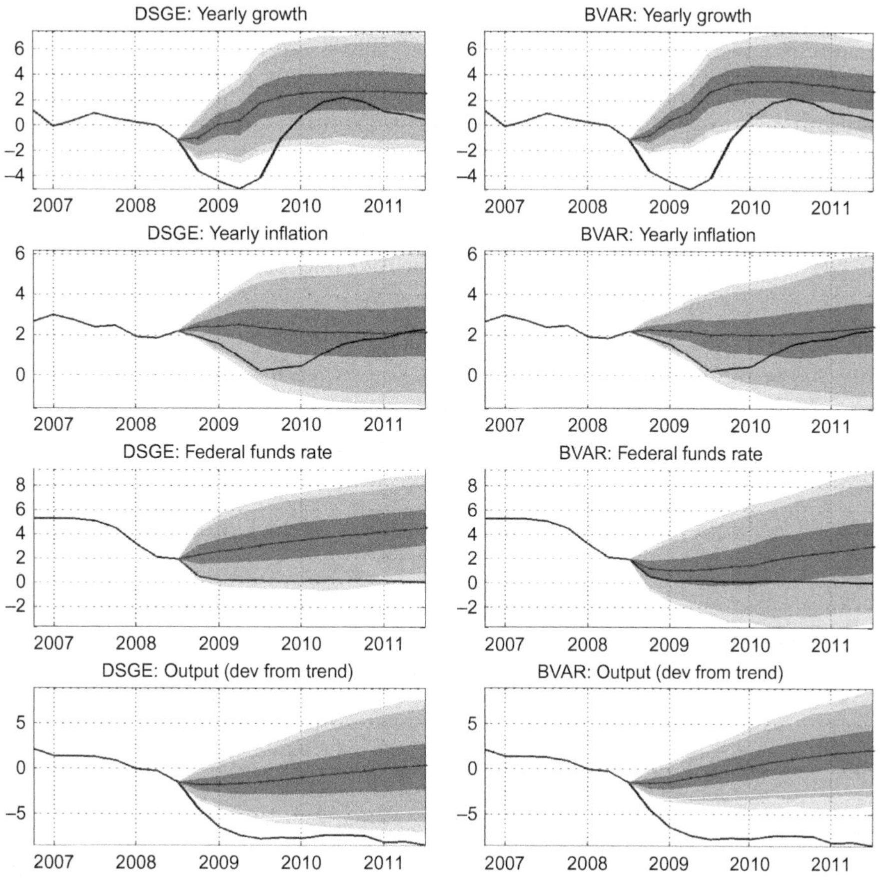

Fig. 2 Forecast 2008Q4–2011Q3 conditional on state in 2008Q3.

completely unexpected from the point of the view of the DSGE model. Thus, in line with Del Negro and Schorfheide (2013), our estimated model carries the implication that the "Great Recession" as late as of observing the outcome in 2008Q3 was a highly unlikely tail event. Turning to yearly inflation and the federal funds rate in the middle and bottom left panels, we also see that they fell considerably more than predicted by the model, but their decline are within or close to the 95% uncertainty bands of the linearized DSGE model and hence, cannot be considered as tail events to the same extent as the Great Recession.

Turning to the results for the BVAR, which are reported in the right column in Fig. 2, we see that the forecast distribution in the BVAR for yearly GDP growth is both quantitatively and qualitatively very similar to that in the DSGE model. Hence, the Great Recession was also a highly unlikely tail event according to the BVAR model. Given that the BVAR and the DSGE are both linearized models, the relatively high degree of similarity of the two model forecasts is not completely surprising. We also see that the uncertainty bands for the output roughly are equally sized in the DSGE as those in the BVAR model. This finding is neither obvious nor trivial as the DSGE model does not have a short-lag BVAR representation. The BVAR, on the other hand, does not impose nearly as many cross-restrictions on the parameter space as the DSGE model. Hence, allowing for parameter uncertainty will tend to increase the uncertainty bands considerably more in the BVAR relative to the DSGE model (the BVAR has around 190 free parameters, while the DSGE has 36). On net, these two forces appear to cancel each other out.

Moreover, as is clear from Fig. 3, the high degree of coherence between the DSGE and BVAR output growth forecasts also holds up when conditioning on the state in 2008Q4 and using the estimated models to make predictions for 2009Q1, 2009Q2, …, 2011Q4. For yearly inflation and the federal funds rate, the forecasts conditional on the state in 2008Q3 are very similar, as can be seen in the middle rows in Fig. 2.

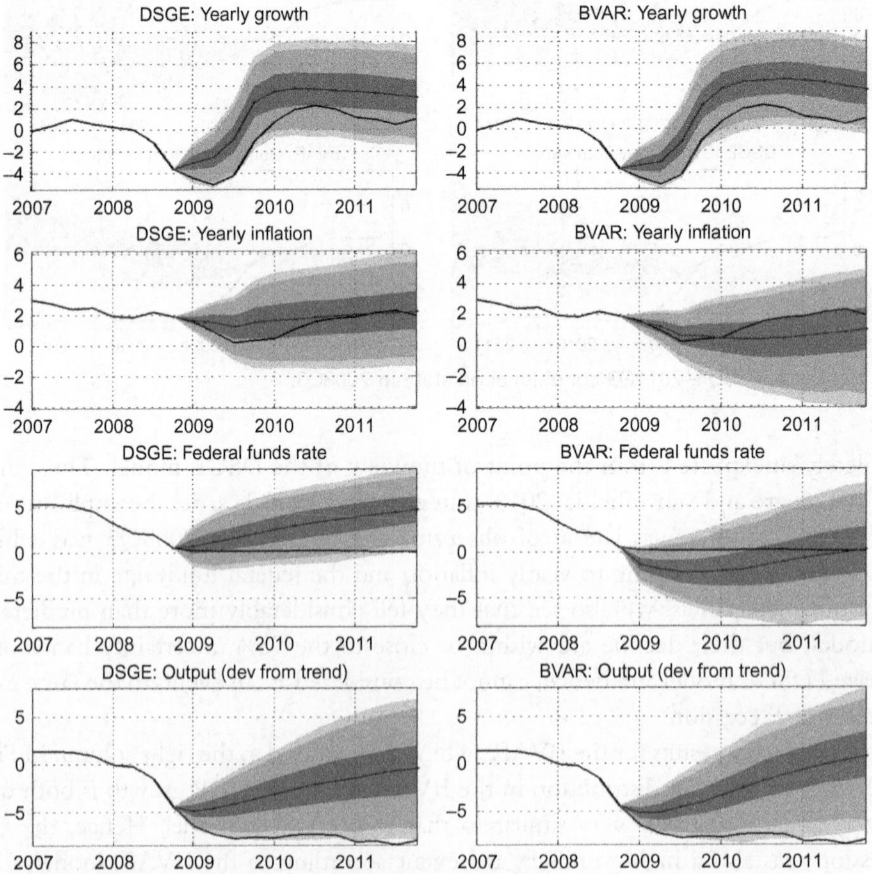

Fig. 3 Forecast 2009Q1–2011Q4 conditional on state in 2008Q4.

However, for the forecast made conditional on the state in 2008Q4 (Fig. 3), the DSGE and BVAR forecasts differ substantially, at least qualitatively. In this period, the BVAR predicts a prolonged period with near-zero inflation and a federal funds rate well below zero for 2 years, whereas the modal outlook in the DSGE model is that inflation would quickly return to near 2% and that the federal funds rate should therefore be increased steadily throughout the forecast horizon. The zero lower bound is not much of a concern in the DSGE model, while the BVAR suggests that it should be a binding constraint longer than 2 years.

Apart from failing to predict the crisis in the first place, both the BVAR and the DSGE model also have a clear tendency to forecast a quick recovery. For the benchmark DSGE model, this feature is evident already from Fig. 1. In this figure, the red-dotted line shows the one-sided filtered Kalman projections of the observed variables; that is, the projection for period t given all available information in period $t-1$. By comparing the one-sided filtered Kalman projections against the outcome (the blue-solid line) it is evident that the benchmark DSGE model predicts that growth in output, consumption and investment would pick up much quicker than they did following the recession. Hence, consistent with the findings in Chung et al. (2012), the benchmark DSGE model consistently suggests a V-shaped recovery and that better times were just around the corner, whereas the outcome is consistent with a much more slower recovery out of the recession as is evident from Figs. 2 and 3. Fig. 4 shows sequential BVAR forecasts 1, 2, ..., 12 quarters ahead for the period 2008Q3–2014Q1 conditional on observing the state up to the date in which the forecasts start. In line with the results for the DSGE model, the results in this figure indicate that the BVAR also tends to predict a quick recovery of economic activity. Consistent with this reasoning, the forecasts for the level of output (as deviation from the deterministic trend), shown in the bottom row in Figs. 2 and 3, display that both the DSGE and the BVAR models overestimate the speed of recovery out of the recession.[l]

The slow recovery following the recession is consistent with the work by Reinhart and Rogoff (2009) and Jordà et al. (2012), who suggest that recoveries from financial crises are slower than recoveries from other recessions. The empirical observation by Reinhart and Rogoff has also been corroborated in subsequent theoretical work by Queralto (2013) and Anzoategui et al. (2015).[m] As our benchmark equilibrium model does not include the mechanisms of Queralto, it has a hard time accounting for the slow recovery following the recession, both in terms of the level and the growth rate of GDP. Our benchmark models—both the DSGE and the BVAR—rely on significant influence of adverse

[l] For both the BVAR and the DSGE model, the series for detrended output is the smoothed estimate from the DSGE model. When we construct the forecast of detrended output in the BVAR, we accumulate the projected quarterly growth rate of output after subtracting the estimated steady state growth rate in each period.

[m] Notwithstanding these results, Howard et al. (2011) argue out that the finding pertains to the level of economic activity, and not the growth rate (which is what we focused on in Fig. 1).

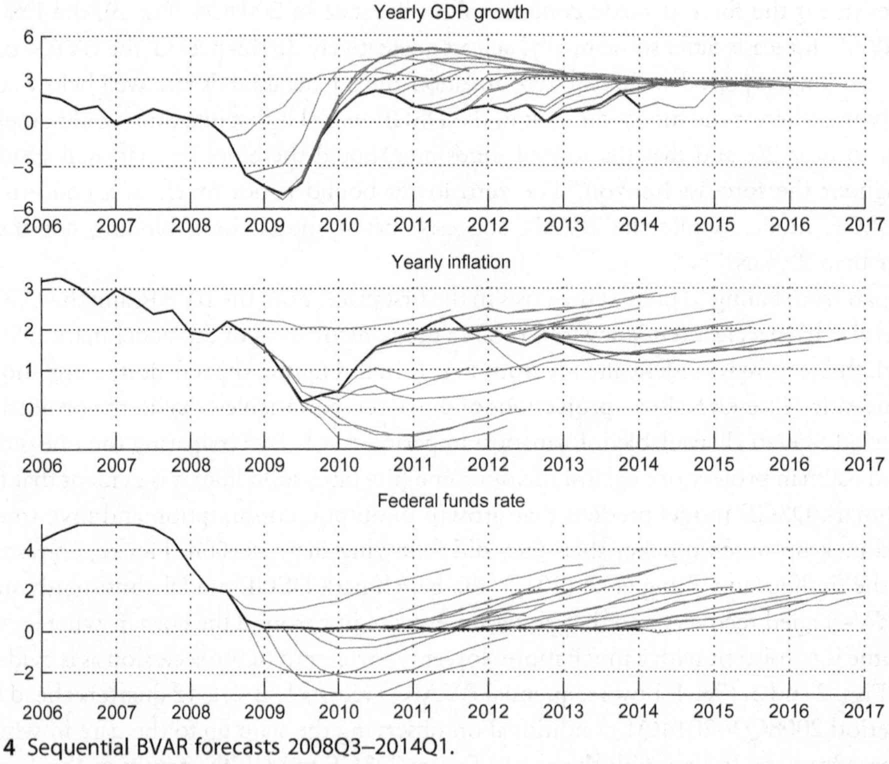

Fig. 4 Sequential BVAR forecasts 2008Q3–2014Q1.

exogenous shocks which weighs on economic activity during the recovery. While this might be deemed to be a significant weakness of these models, it should be noted that some major negative events may have contributed to hold back the recovery; eg, the European debt crisis which intensified in May 2010, and the showdown between the Republicans and democrats in the congress which created significant uncertainty in the US economy according to estimates by Fernández-Villaverde et al. (2011). With these events in mind, it is not entirely implausible that the models need some adverse shocks to account for the slow recovery.

4.2 Economic Interpretation of the Recession

As indicated in the previous section, both the DSGE and BVAR models are dependent on major adverse shocks to account for the recession. In this section, we examine what shocks are filtered out as the drivers of the recession and its aftermath. We will focus entirely on the benchmark DSGE, as it would be hard to identify all the shocks in the BVAR model. We extract the smoothed shocks through the Kalman filter by using the model estimated on the precrisis period for the full sample (without reestimating the parameters).

In Fig. 5, the left column shows the two-sided smoothed Kalman filtered innovations—eg, η_t^a for the technology shock in Eq. (5)—for the seven shock processes in

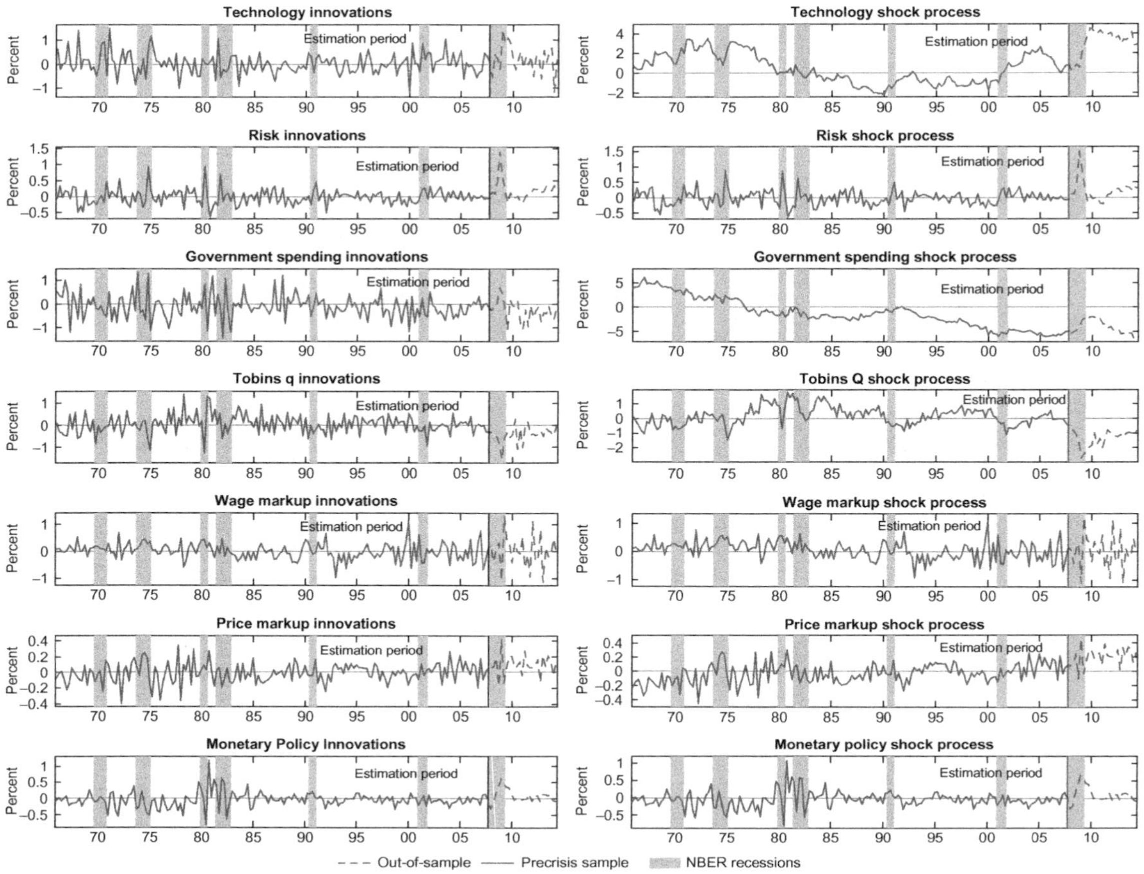

Fig. 5 Smoothed innovations and shocks in model estimated on precrisis data.

the model using the posterior mode parameters. In the right column, we show the two-sided smoothed shock processes in levels—eg, ε_t^a for the technology shock in Eq. (5). The blue solid-line indicates the in-sample period, and the blue-dotted line the out-of-sample period. The grey bars are NBER dated recessions.

Before analyzing the role various shocks played during the crisis and its aftermath, it is insightful to discuss if there are any signs in the precrisis shocks about what events might have been causal for the crisis itself. As is clear from the left column in the figure, there is nothing that stands out in the innovations between 2000 and the burst of the crisis. There were a string of positive innovations to technology during 2003–2005, which led to a run-up in technology (right upper panel) during this period. To the extent that households and firms expected this positive development to continue and were taken off-guard by the adverse outcomes 2006 and onward, this could have been a contributing factor to the crisis. Christiano et al. (2010b) argue that over-optimistic expectations of future technology have been associated with credit cycles that have contributed to boom-bust cycles in the real US economy in a model with a more elaborate financial sector.[n] Our benchmark model does not include a financial sector and thus, cannot be used to assess this possibility explicitly. Loose monetary policy have also been argued as a possible driver for the crisis, see, eg, Taylor (2007). Our estimated model lend some, but limited, support to this view; although the estimated policy rule suggest that monetary policy was on average expansionary between 2002 and 2006, the magnitude of the deviations are not very large though, as seen from the lower panels in Fig. 5. Based on the shock decomposition, it is therefore hard to argue that the Fed's conduct of monetary policy was causal for the crisis.[o]

With this discussion in mind, we now turn to the crisis and its aftermath. As is clear from Fig. 5, the key innovations happened to technology, investment specific technology (the Tobin's Q-shock), and the risk-premium shock during the most intense phase of the recession. More specifically, the model filters out a very large positive shock to technology (about 1.5% as shown in the upper left panel, which corresponds to a 3.4 standard error shock) in 2009Q1. In 2008Q4 and 2009Q1, the model also filters out two negative investment specific technology shocks (about −1 and −1.5%—or 2.0 and 3.7 standard errors—respectively). The model moreover filters out a large positive risk shocks in

[n] The focus of Christiano et al. is what monetary policy should do to mitigate the inefficient boom-bust cycle. They do not consider the role macroprudential regulation could play to mitigate the cycle.

[o] The main reason why our policy shocks are much smaller in magnitude than those computed by Taylor is that we consider a more elaborate policy rule with considerable interest rate smoothing ($\rho_R = 0.82$, see Table 2). One could argue about whether one should allow for interest rate smoothing or whether this persistence should be attributed to the exogenous monetary policy shock (ie, a higher ρ_r in the process for ε_t^r in Eq. (15). In our estimated model, however, the log marginal likelihood strongly favors a high degree of interest rate smoothing and low persistence of the exogenous policy shocks (ie, a combination of high ρ_R and low ρ_r).

2008Q3–Q4, and in 2009Q1 (0.5%, 1.5%, and 0.5%, respectively, equivalent to 1.9, 6.0, and 2.8 standard errors). These smoothed shocks account for the bulk of the sharp decline in output, consumption and investment during the acute phase of the crisis at the end of 2008 and the beginning of 2009. Our finding of a large positive technology shock in the first quarter of 2009 may at first glance be puzzling, but can be understood from Figs. 1 and 3. In these, we see that output (as deviation from trend) fell less during the recession than did hours worked per capita. Hence, labor productivity rose sharply during the most acute phase of the recession. The model replicates this feature of the data by filtering out a sequence of positive technology shocks. These technology shocks will stimulate for output, consumption and investment. The model thus needs some really adverse shocks that depresses these quantities even more and causes hours worked per capita to fall, and this is where the positive risk premium and investment specific technology shocks come into play. These shocks cause consumption (risk premium) and investment (investment specific)—and thereby GDP—to fall. Lower consumption and investment also causes firms to hire less labor, resulting in hours worked per capita to fall.

Another shock that helps account for the collapse in activity at the end of 2008 is the smoothed monetary policy shock shown in the bottom left panel (expressed at a quarterly rate). This shock becomes quite positive in 2008Q4 and 2009Q1; in annualized terms it equals roughly 150 (1.6 standard errors) and 250 (2.8 standard errors) basis points in each of these quarters, respectively. As the actual observations for the annualized federal funds rate is about 50 and 20 basis points, these sizable policy shocks suggests that the zero lower bound is likely to have been a binding constraint, at least in these quarters. This finding is somewhat different from those of Del Negro and Schorfheide (2013) and Del Negro et al. (2015b), who argued that the zero lower bound was not a binding constraint in their estimated models.

The large smoothed innovations translate into very persistent movements in some of the smoothed shock processes, reported in the right column in Fig. 5. For the simple AR(1) shock processes, the degree of persistence is governed by the posterior for ρ. As can be seen from Table 2, the posterior for $\rho_a(\rho_b)$ is very high (low), whereas the posterior for ρ_i is somewhere in between. It is therefore not surprising that the technology process is almost permanently higher following the crisis, whereas the risk shock process quickly recedes towards steady state. Our finding of a very persistent rise in the exogenous component of total factor productivity (TFP) is seemingly at odds with Christiano et al. (2015), who reports that TFP fell in the aftermath of the recession. Christiano et al. (2015) and Gust et al. (2012) also report negative innovations to technology in 2008 (see fig. 5 in their paper). While a closer examination behind the differences in the results would take us too far, we note that our findings aligns very well with Fernald (2012). Specifically, our smoothed innovations to technology are highly correlated with the two TFP measures computed by Fernald (2012), as can be seen from Table 3. The table shows the correlations between our technology innovations η_t^a, shown in the left column

Table 3 Correlations between smoothed and actual TFP shocks

TFP measure	**Sample period** Precrisis: 66Q1–07Q4	Full: 66Q1–14Q2
$\mathrm{Corr}(\Delta\mathrm{Raw}, \eta_t^a)$	0.483	0.522
$\mathrm{Corr}(\Delta\mathrm{Corrected}, \eta_t^a)$	0.602	0.608

Note: "ΔRaw" denotes the first difference of the quarterly unadjusted measure in Fernald (2012), while "ΔCorrected" is the first difference Fernald's capacity utilization adjusted TFP measure. In the model, the smoothed estimates of the innovations η_t^a (see Eq. (5)) are used. This series is depicted in the upper left column of Fig. 5.

in Fig. 5, and the period-by-period change in the raw and utilization-corrected measure of TFP by Fernald. From the first column in the table, we learn that the correlation between our innovations and his raw measure is almost 0.5 for the estimation sample period. As we are studying first differences and innovations, this correlation must be considered quite high. Even more reassuring for our model is that the correlation between our smoothed innovation series and Fernald's utilization adjusted series is as high as 0.6. When extending the sample to include the crisis and postcrisis period, we see that these correlations remain high; if anything, they become slightly higher. We believe this lends support for our basic result that weak TFP growth was not a key contributing factor to the crisis.

For the two markup shocks, we notice that they are not nearly as highly correlated as the technology shock although the estimated AR(1) coefficients for these processes are quite high (0.89 for the price markup shock, and 0.97 for the wage markup shock, see Table 2). The reason why their correlation is so low is the estimated MA(1) coefficients, ϑ_p and ϑ_w in Eqs. (6) and (13) are rather high, ie, 0.72 and 0.92, respectively. Despite the generally low correlation of the price shock process during the precrisis period, we see that its outcome is driven by a sequence of positive innovations during the crisis period. This finding is in line with Fratto and Uhlig (2014), who found that price markup shocks played an important role to avoid an even larger fall in inflation during the crisis, and contributed to the slow decline in employment during the postcrisis recovery.[p] The wage markup shock process does not display any clear pattern after the precrisis period, but it is clear that its variance has increased since the end of the 1990s suggesting that the model provides a less accurate description of wage-setting behavior in the US labor market since

[p] The prominent role of the price and wage markup for explaining inflation and behavior of real wages in the SW07-model have been criticized by Chari et al. (2009) as implausibly large. Galí et al. (2011), however, shows that the size of the markup shocks can be reduced substantially by allowing for preference shocks to household preferences.

then. However, it should be kept in mind that this finding may not necessarily remain if alternative wage series are used.[q]

The historical decompositions in Fig. 6 summarizes the impact of the various shocks on the output growth, inflation, federal funds rate and output as deviation from a trend during 2007Q1–2014Q2 in the benchmark model estimated on data up to 2007Q4 (see Table 2). Notice that the scale on the left- and right-axes are not the same (except for the two-sided-smoothed output as deviation from trend): the left axis shows the

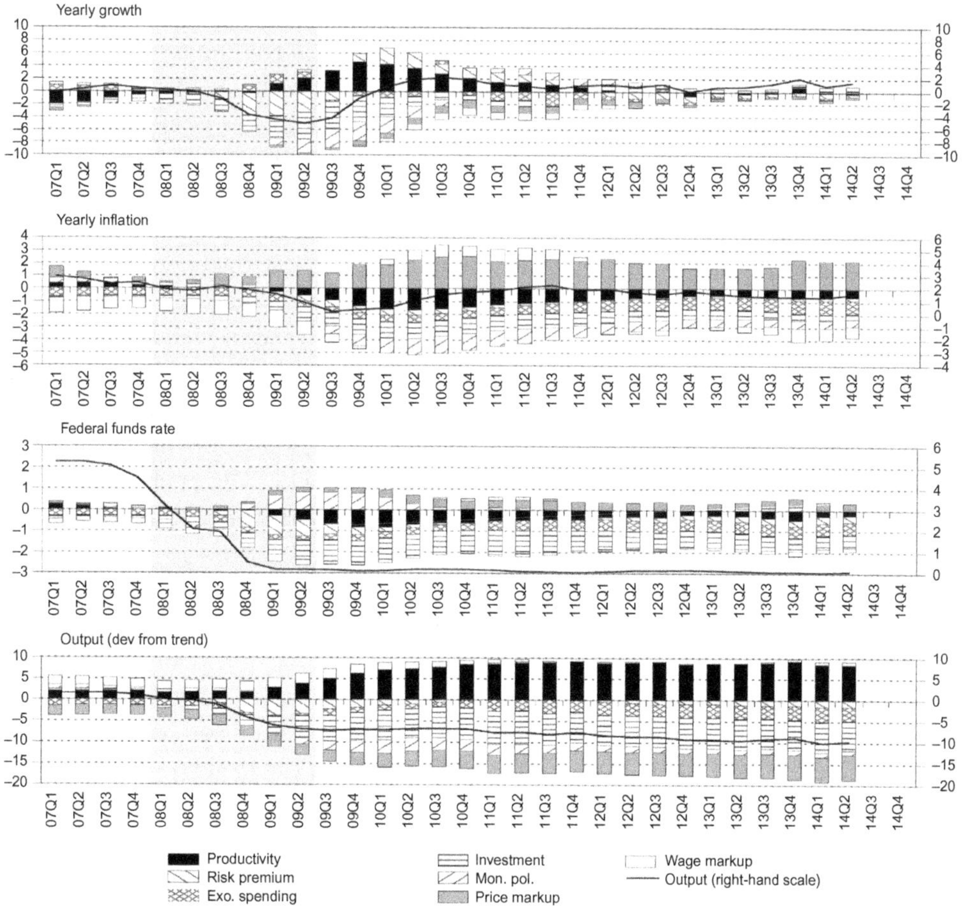

Fig. 6 Historical decompositions of yearly output growth (four-quarter change), yearly inflation (four-quarter change), fed funds rate, and output (deviation from trend). Left axis shows the contributions of the shocks (bars) to fluctuations around the steady state and right axis shows actual outcomes (in levels).

[q] Because of potential measurement problems pertaining to Galí et al. (2011) and Justiniano et al. (2013b) use two series for real wage growth when estimating their DSGE model.

contributions of the various shocks to fluctuations around the steady state, whereas the right axis shows evolution of each variable in levels. Thus, for each period the sum of the bars on the left axis plus the steady state value for each variable (not shown) equals the actual outcome (thin line). For output as deviation from trend, the steady state value is nil, why the sum of the bars directly equals the smoothed values.

As seen from the figure, the risk premium, the investment specific technology and the monetary policy shocks are the key drivers behind the decline in output during the recession period, whereas TFP as discussed earlier had some offsetting impact on output. However, all four shocks contributed to the gradual decline in inflation. The nominal interest rate would clearly have dropped below zero in absence of the zero bound constraint. The slow recovery is attributed to the persistence of the shocks that were responsible for the recession, but also captures new unexpected headwinds along with positive innovations to markups in prices and wages. Interestingly, the negative impact of the risk premium shock is relatively short lived. To a large extent this of course reflects that the model is not rich enough to propagate financial shocks sufficiently, but it is also conceivable that this partly captures the stimulus coming from the nonconventional monetary policy actions. The continuously low interest rate is consistent with the weak state of the economy during this period; output (as deviation from trend) is well below its precrisis trend and inflation persistently below its targeted rate, and sustained subpar growth (slow or nonexistent recovery in output as deviation from trend). As the precrisis model features a moderate degree of price and wage stickiness, inflation would have fallen persistently into negative territory in the absence of other shocks. This is counter-factual relative to the data, and the missing deflation in the model estimated on precrisis data is accounted for by inflationary markup shocks.

While the smoothed shocks—that the model needs to explain the crisis period—are not too surprising given the model's specification, it is nevertheless clear that the benchmark model needs a highly unlikely combination of adverse shocks in 2008Q4 and 2009Q1 to account for the most intense phase of the recession. Therefore, we now discuss the statistical properties of the shocks and examine if they correlate with some key observable financial variables not included in our set of observables.

4.3 Statistical Properties of the Innovations and Their Relation to Financial Indicators

Table 4 provides an overview of the statistical properties of the estimated structural shocks and of the forecast errors for the seven observed macro variables. Most of the forecast errors display a significant amount of kurtosis, a feature that they inherit from the underlying macro variables. For the structural shocks, the problems are mostly concentrated in two shocks—the monetary policy and the risk premium shock—that display highly significant deviations from the underlying Gaussian assumption. The structural innovations in the policy rate and the risk premium are characterized by a highly skewed

Table 4 Statistical distribution of innovations

	Sample period							
	Precrisis: 66Q1–07Q4				Full Sample: 66Q1–14Q2			
Innovations in	**Mean**	**Std**	**Skew**	**Kurt**	**Mean**	**Std**	**Skew**	**Kurt**
Technology	0.04	0.44	0.43*	4.09*	0.04	0.46	0.32	3.76
Risk premium	0.00	0.24	0.74**	5.12**	0.00	0.19	1.03**	7.08**
Inv. spec. techn.	0.02	0.42	0.09	3.95*	0.02	0.37	0.09	3.73
Exog. spending	−0.07	0.50	0.30	3.66	−0.07	0.49	0.25	3.65
Price markup	0.00	0.12	−0.14	3.49	0.00	0.12	0.01	3.62
Wage markup	0.01	0.31	0.10	3.89	0.01	0.37	0.03	4.48**
Monetary policy	−0.03	0.23	0.76**	8.09**	−0.04	0.23	0.80**	8.45**
Forecast errors in								
Output growth	−0.04	0.66	0.38*	5.05**	0.01	0.69	0.12	5.10**
Consumption growth	0.01	0.56	−0.42*	4.50**	0.08	0.62	−0.89**	6.77**
Investment growth	0.25	1.62	0.14	5.24**	0.25	1.73	−0.02	5.43**
Hours per capita	−0.04	0.53	0.03	4.25**	−0.02	0.55	−0.03	3.96*
Inflation	0.05	0.26	0.22	4.05*	0.04	0.25	0.30	4.14**
Real wage growth	−0.05	0.63	0.14	3.89	−0.04	0.73	−0.03	4.72**
Short rate	−0.01	0.24	1.29**	12.25**	−0.02	0.22	1.80**	15.31**

Note: *, ** indicate a significance at 5% and 1%, respectively.

and fat-tailed distribution.[r] We identified the large disturbances in these shocks already in the previous section as crucial drivers of the recent recession, but Table 4 illustrates that both processes were already affected by non-Gaussian innovations in the precrisis model as well. As observed in Fig. 5, these negative outliers occur mostly during the recession periods.

This feature implies that the predictive density of linear Gaussian DSGE models underestimates systematically the probability of these large recession events. This observation is important because it means that the model considers the strong economic downturns that we typically observe during recession periods as extremely unlikely tail events.[s] Linear Gaussian models may therefore be inappropriate instruments for analyzing policy questions related to risk scenario's or stress test exercises.

[r] The innovations in the structural shocks are also characterized by a significant ARCH effect illustrating the systematic time-varying volatility structures.

[s] This observation is consistent with the findings presented by Chung et al. (2012).

It is also interesting to note that the two structural shocks that generate most of the extreme events are directly related to the intertemporal decisions and to the developments in the monetary and the financial sector of the economy. The non-Gaussian nature of financial returns, spreads and risk premiums is widely documented in the financial literature. Therefore, it appears like a natural hypothesis to assume that the non-Gaussian shocks that are identified in our macro model reflect the influence—or the feedback—from financial disruptions to the rest of the economy. To support this argument, we calculate the correlations between our estimated structural innovations and a set of popular financial returns and spreads. We selected seven measures related to the different segments of the financial sector and for which long time series are available: the Baa-Aaa spread, the term spread, the Ted spread, the return on the S&P index, the return on the Fama-French financial sector portfolio, the change in the Shiller house price index and the VOX index. Table 5 summarizes the correlation between these seven financial indicators and our seven structural innovations. The strongest correlations in this table—exceeding 0.3 in absolute terms—are observed between our identified risk premium innovation and the Baa-Aaa and Term spreads, and between the monetary policy innovation and the Term and Ted spreads.

To see the strong linkages between some of the smoothed shocks and the financial variables in an alternative way, we regress the structural innovations on this set of financial

Table 5 Correlation between innovations and financial indicators

Innovations in		Innovations						
		σ_a	σ_b	σ_i	σ_g	σ_p	σ_w	σ_r
Technology	σ_a	1.00						
Risk premium	σ_b	−0.11	1.00					
Inv. spec. techn.	σ_i	−0.19	−0.08	1.00				
Exog. spending	σ_g	0.01	0.27	−0.06	1.00			
Price markup	σ_p	−0.03	0.18	0.05	0.13	1.00		
Wage markup	σ_w	0.00	−0.01	−0.07	−0.21	−0.09	1.00	
Monetary policy	σ_m	0.09	−0.17	−0.05	0.17	−0.05	−0.04	1.00

Financial Indicator	Innovations						
	σ_a	σ_b	σ_i	σ_g	σ_p	σ_w	σ_r
Baa-Aaa	−0.10	0.39	−0.21	0.28	0.04	−0.02	0.04
Term spread	0.11	0.33	−0.11	−0.04	−0.07	0.10	−0.46
Ted spread	−0.20	−0.13	0.13	0.18	0.14	−0.02	0.34
Return S&P	0.14	−0.24	0.18	−0.20	−0.13	0.02	−0.13
Return Fin	0.02	0.03	0.01	−0.05	−0.14	0.02	−0.10
Return HP	−0.07	−0.07	0.25	−0.06	0.00	0.02	−0.14
VOX	−0.12	0.10	0.03	0.13	0.09	0.01	−0.05

Note: The data sources are provided in Appendix C.

Table 6 Regression analysis of innovations and financial indicators

	Precrisis sample			Full sample		
Innovations in	σ_b	σ_i	σ_r	σ_b	σ_i	σ_r
Contemporaneous impact from financial indicator on innovations						
Baa-Aaa	0.29*	−0.57*	0.09	0.28*	−0.26*	−0.02
Term spread	0.10*	−0.05	−0.18*	0.09*	−0.02	−0.18*
Ted spread	−0.09*	0.16*	0.15*	−0.08*	0.12*	0.14*
Return S&P	−0.64	1.51*	−0.27	−0.70*	1.37*	−0.45
Return Fin	0.46*	−0.24	−0.05	0.33*	−0.22	−0.01
Return HP	1.35	5.41*	−3.52	0.10	4.67*	−2.63
VOX	0.38	0.00	−0.44	0.34	0.67	−0.61
F/p-value	7.00/0.00	4.45/0.00	15.80/0.00	11.79/0.00	4.86/0.00	14.31/0.00
Skew/kurt resid	0.04/2.97	0.17/3.22	0.60/4.39	0.15/3.11	0.14/3.15	0.57/4.08
Granger Causality regressions						
F/p-value	1.73/0.06	1.53/0.11	2.11/0.01	1.67/0.06	2.05/0.02	1.62/0.07

Note: * indicates significance at 5%. The financial indicators do not have a significant effect on the other nonreported innovations.

observables. The results of these multivariate regressions are shown in Table 6. In contemporaneous regressions, the significant coefficients are again only apparent in the risk premium, monetary policy and—at a slightly weaker significance level—for the investment specific technology innovation. The most interesting feature of the regression results is that the remaining unexplained variation (ie, the regression residuals) are basically normally distributed. Thus, shock outliers seem to coincide with periods of clear financial stress as measured by our observed financial indicators. Also noteworthy is that in Granger causality regression tests, none of the financial indicators carry significant predictive power for the structural innovations. Because financial variables can essentially be observed in real time; however, they can still provide timely indications of big structural innovations. Including these variables in our list of observables can therefore be very useful to improve the model now-cast and the conditional forecast performance.[t] Even so, this strategy will probably not improve the out-of-sample prediction performance of our linearized models *ex ante* to the observation of financial stress signals. It might also require non-Gaussian and nonlinear models to exploit this information from financial variables more efficiently in our macro models.

[t] See Del Negro and Schorfheide (2013) for strong evidence in this direction.

5. AUGMENTING THE BENCHMARK MODEL

As the analysis in Section 4 suggested that the benchmark model suffers from some important shortcomings, we study in this section to which extent its performance can be improved by allowing for zero lower bound on policy rates, time-varying volatility of the shocks, and by introducing financial frictions and a cost-channel into the model. The modeling of financial frictions follows the basic approach in the seminal work of Bernanke et al. (1999). In contrast to the analysis in Section 3.4, we estimate the different perturbations of the model on data including the crisis period in this section.

5.1 Assessing the Impact of the Zero Lower Bound

We assess the impact of imposing the zero lower bound (ZLB) in the estimation in two alternative ways. These procedures differ in the way the duration of the ZLB spells is determined. In our first approach, the incidence and duration of the ZLB spells are endogenous and consistent with the model expectations. In the second approach, we model them as "exogenous" and require the model to match information from the market-based overnight index swap rates following Del Negro et al. (2015b). In both approaches, we make use of the same linearized model equations (stated in Appendix A), except that we impose the nonnegativity constraint on the federal funds rate. To do this, we adopt the following policy rule for the federal funds rate

$$\begin{aligned} \widehat{R}_t^* &= \rho_R \widehat{R}_{t-1} + (1-\rho_R)\left(r_\pi \widehat{\pi}_t + r_y(\widehat{ygap}_t)\right) + r_{\Delta y}\Delta(\widehat{ygap}_t) \ , \\ \widehat{R}_t &= \max\left(-\bar{r}, \widehat{R}_t^* + \widehat{\varepsilon}_t^r\right). \end{aligned} \tag{17}$$

The policy rule in (17) assumes that the interest rate set by the bank, $\widehat{R}_t$, equals $\widehat{R}_t^* + \widehat{\varepsilon}_t^r$ if unconstrained by the ZLB. $\widehat{R}_t^*$, in turn, is a shadow interest rate that is not subject to the policy shock $\widehat{\varepsilon}_t^r$. Note that $\widehat{R}_t$ in the policy rule (17) is measured as percentage point deviation of the federal funds rate from its quarterly steady state level $(\bar{r})$, so restricting $\widehat{R}_t$ not to fall below $-\bar{r}$ is equivalent to imposing the ZLB on the nominal policy rate.[u] In its setting of the shadow or notional rate we assume that the Fed is smoothing over the lagged actual interest rate, as opposed to the lagged notional rate $\widehat{R}_{t-1}^*$. We made this assumption to preserve the property that $\widehat{\varepsilon}_t^r$ is close to white noise. Smoothing over the notional rate in (17) would cause the policy shock to become highly persistent, with an AR(1) coefficient roughly equal to ρ_R.[v]

[u] See (16) for the definition of $\bar{r}$. If writing the policy rule in levels, the first part of (17) bee replaced by (14) (omitting the policy shock), and the ZLB part would bee $R_t = \max\left(1, R_t^* \varepsilon_t^r\right)$.

[v] To see this, replace $\hat{R}_{t-1}$ with $\hat{R}_{t-1}^*$ in the first equation in (17) and then substitute $\hat{R}_t = \hat{R}_t^* + \hat{\varepsilon}_t^r$ from the second equation to write the unconstrained policy rule with the actual policy rate $\hat{R}_t$. Then, the residual will be $\hat{u}_t^r \equiv \hat{\varepsilon}_t^r - \rho_R \hat{\varepsilon}_{t-1}^r$. Hence, the residual $\hat{u}_t^r$ will be roughly white noise in this case when $\hat{\varepsilon}_t^r$ has an AR (1)-root ρ_R.

To impose the policy rule (17) when we estimate the model, we use the method outlined in Hebden et al. (2010). This method is convenient because it is quick even when the model contains many state variables, and we provide further details about the algorithm in Appendix A.[w] In a nutshell, the algorithm imposes the nonlinear policy rule in Eq. (17) through current and anticipated shocks (add factors) to the policy rule. More specifically, if the projection of $\widehat{R}_{t+h}$ in (17) given the filtered state in period t in any of the periods $h = 0, 1, \ldots, T$ for some sufficiently large nonnegative integer T is below $-\bar{r}$, the algorithm adds a sequence of anticipated policy shocks $\widehat{\varepsilon}^{r}_{t+h|t}$ such that $\mathrm{E}_t\widehat{R}_{t+h} \geq 0$ for all $h = \tau_1, \tau_1 + 1, \ldots, \tau_2$. If the added policy shocks put enough downward pressure on the economic activity and inflation, the duration of the ZLB spell will be extended both backwards (τ_1 shrinks) and forwards (τ_2 increases) in time. Moreover, as we think about the ZLB as a constraint on monetary policy, we further require all current and anticipated policy shocks to be *positive* whenever $\widehat{R}^{*}_{t} < -\bar{r}$. Imposing that all policy shocks are strictly positive whenever the ZLB binds, amounts to think about these shocks as Lagrangian multipliers on the nonnegativity constraint on the interest rate, and implies that we should not necessarily be bothered by the fact that these shocks may not be normally distributed even when the ZLB binds for several consecutive periods $t, t+1, \ldots, t+T$ with long expected spells each period (h large).

We will subsequently refer to this method as "Endogenous ZLB duration", as it implies that both the incidence and the duration of the ZLB is endogenous determined by the model subject to the criterion to maximize the log marginal likelihood. In this context, it is important to understand that the nonnegativity requirement on the current and anticipated policy shocks for each possible state and draw from the posterior, forces the posterior itself to move into a part of the parameter space where the model can account for long ZLB spells which are contractionary to the economy. Without this requirement, DSGE models with endogenous lagged state variables may experience sign switches for the policy shocks, so that the ZLB has a stimulative rather than contractionary impact on the economy even for fairly short ZLB spells as documented by Carlstrom et al. (2012).[x] As discussed in further detail in Hebden et al., the nonnegativity assumption for all states and draws from the posterior also mitigates the possibility of multiple equilibria (indeterminacy). Finally, it is important to point our that when the ZLB is not a binding constraint, we assume the contemporaneous policy shock $\widehat{\varepsilon}^{r}_{t}$ in Eq. (17) can be either negative or positive; in this case we do not use any anticipated policy shocks as monetary policy is unconstrained.

[w] Iacoviello and Guerrieri (2015) have subsequently shown how this method can be applied to solve DSGE models with other types of asymmetry constraints.

[x] This can be beneficial if we think that policy makers choose to let the policy rate remain at the ZLB although the policy rule dictated that the interest rate should be raised ($\hat{R}^{*}_{t}$ is above $-\bar{r}$). In the case of the United States, this possibility might be relevant in the aftermath of the crisis and we therefore subsequently use an alternative method which allows for this.

However, a potentially serious shortcoming of the method we adapt to assess the implications of the ZLB is that it relies on perfect foresight and hence does not explicitly account for the role of future shock uncertainty as in the work of Adam and Billi (2006) and Gust et al. (2012). Even so, we implicitly allow for parameter and shock uncertainty by requiring that the filtered current and anticipated policy shocks in each time point are positive for all parameter and shock draws from the posterior whenever the ZLB binds. More specifically, when we evaluate the likelihood function and find that $E_t\widehat{R}_{t+h} < 0$ in the modal outlook for some period t and horizon h conditional on the parameter draw and associated filtered state, we draw a large number of sequences of fundamental shocks for $h = 0, 1, \ldots, 12$ and verify that the policy rule (17) can be implemented for all possible shock realizations through positive shocks only. For those parameter draws this is not feasible, we add a smooth penalty to the likelihood which is set large enough to ensure that the posterior will satisfy the constraint.[y] As we document below, the nonnegativity constraint on the anticipated policy shocks in the face of parameter and fundamental shock uncertainty has considerable implications for the estimation of the model, and shock and parameter uncertainty is therefore partly accounted for in our estimation procedure.[z]

To provide a reference point for the ZLB estimations we start out by estimating the model for the full sample period, but disregarding the existence of the ZLB. The posterior mode and standard deviation in this case are shown in the first two columns in Table 7, and labeled "No ZLB model". The only difference between these results and those reported in Table 2 is that the sample period has been extended from 2007Q4 to 2014Q2. By comparing the results, a noteworthy difference is that the estimated degree of wage and price stickiness has increased even further relative to the precrisis sample. The posterior mode for the sticky wage parameter (ξ_w) has increased from 0.79 to 0.83, and the sticky price parameter (ξ_p) from 0.69 to 0.75. Relative to the SW07 posterior mode, ξ_w has increased from 0.73 to 0.83 and ξ_p from 0.65 to 0.75. These increases are substantial, considering that the sample has been expanded with less than 10 years and that these parameters affect the slope of the wage and price pricing curves in a nonlinear fashion, implying an even sharper reduction in the slope coefficients for the forcing variables

[y] For example, it turns out that the model in 2008Q4 implies that the ZLB would be a binding constraint in 2009Q1 through 2009Q3 in the modal outlook. For this period we generated 1000 shock realizations for 2009Q1,2009Q2, ..., 2011Q4 and verified that we could implement the policy rule (17) for all forecast simulations of the model through nonnegative current and anticipated policy shocks. For the draws with adverse shocks, the duration of the ZLB was prolonged substantially during the forecast horizon, with expected ZLB spells close to 4 years occurring. We provide further details in Appendix B how the likelihood function is constructed when we impose the ZLB in the estimations.

[z] Alternatively, we could implement this type of restriction by using a stochastic filter in which the prediction is calculated by integrating over a simulated forecast distribution. Parameter values that generate explosive paths and positive outliers typical for sign reversal realizations would be punished automatically in the likelihood evaluation.

Table 7 Posterior distributions in SW07-Model 1966Q1–2014Q2

Parameter		No ZLB model		Endogenous ZLB duration		OIS-based ZLB duration	
		Posterior		Posterior		Posterior	
		Mode	Std.dev. Hess.	Mode	Std.dev. Hess.	Mode	Std.dev. Hess.
Calvo prob. wages	ξ_w	0.83	0.040	0.85	0.026	0.86	0.035
Calvo prob. prices	ξ_p	0.75	0.039	0.83	0.032	0.89	0.023
Indexation wages	ι_w	0.69	0.122	0.57	0.120	0.56	0.122
Indexation prices	ι_p	0.22	0.081	0.25	0.085	0.38	0.106
Gross price markup	ϕ_p	1.60	0.073	1.46	0.073	1.39	0.072
Capital production share	α	0.19	0.015	0.16	0.018	0.14	0.016
Capital utilization cost	ψ	0.80	0.075	0.73	0.094	0.60	0.120
Investment adj. cost	φ	4.58	0.941	4.61	0.61	5.84	1.095
Habit formation	$\varkappa$	0.62	0.054	0.62	0.031	0.68	0.041
Inv subs. elast. of cons.	σ_c	1.49	0.138	1.02	0.105	0.80	0.080
Labor supply elast.	σ_l	1.81	0.555	2.03	0.465	2.06	0.576
Hours worked in S.S.	$\bar{l}$	−0.40	1.178	−0.18	1.024	0.25	0.844
Discount factor	$100(\beta^{-1}-1)$	0.10	0.042	0.13	0.056	0.12	0.054
Quarterly growth in S.S.	$\bar{\gamma}$	0.41	0.014	0.42	0.026	0.43	0.016
Stationary tech. shock	ρ_a	0.96	0.008	0.97	0.014	0.97	0.018
Risk premium shock	ρ_b	0.40	0.104	0.85	0.055	0.97	0.008
Invest. spec. tech. shock	ρ_i	0.84	0.039	0.85	0.057	0.78	0.075
Gov't cons. shock	ρ_g	0.97	0.007	0.98	0.010	0.97	0.009
Price markup shock	ρ_p	0.92	0.030	0.88	0.046	0.86	0.048
Wage markup shock	ρ_w	0.97	0.010	0.98	0.024	0.99	0.005
Response of g_t to ε_t^a	ρ_{ga}	0.51	0.077	0.52	0.063	0.52	0.069
Stationary tech. shock	σ_a	0.46	0.025	0.48	0.032	0.50	0.029
Risk premium shock	σ_b	0.19	0.026	0.10	0.015	0.08	0.007
Invest. spec. tech. shock	σ_i	0.36	0.032	0.31	0.028	0.30	0.044
Gov't cons. shock	σ_g	0.49	0.025	0.48	0.026	0.48	0.025

Continued

Table 7 Posterior distributions in SW07-Model 1966Q1–2014Q2—cont'd

Parameter		No ZLB model		Endogenous ZLB duration		OIS-based ZLB duration	
		Posterior		Posterior		Posterior	
		Mode	Std.dev. Hess.	Mode	Std.dev. Hess.	Mode	Std.dev. Hess.
Price markup shock	σ_p	0.12	0.013	0.13	0.011	0.14	0.012
MA(1) price markup shock	ϑ_p	0.80	0.058	0.79	0.070	0.80	0.071
Wage markup shock	σ_w	0.37	0.022	0.36	0.020	0.36	0.021
MA(1) wage markup shock	ϑ_w	0.96	0.013	0.96	0.025	0.98	0.007
Quarterly infl. rate. in S.S..	$\overline{\pi}$	0.81	0.102	0.76	0.106	0.70	0.103
Inflation response	r_π	1.69	0.153	1.86	0.159	2.15	0.165
Output gap response	r_y	0.05	0.016	0.10	0.013	0.16	0.027
Diff. output gap response	$r_{\Delta y}$	0.24	0.027	0.24	0.020	0.23	0.024
Mon. pol. shock std	σ_r	0.23	0.013	0.22	0.012	0.21	0.011
Mon. pol. shock pers.	ρ_r	0.21	0.070	0.10	0.058	0.06	0.041
Interest rate smoothing	ρ_R	0.80	0.028	0.83	0.016	0.85	0.018
Log marginal likelihood		Laplace	−1146.69	Laplace	−1151.99	Laplace	−1175.24

Note: See notes to Table 2. The "No ZLB model" neglects the presence of the zero lower bound in the estimations, whereas the "Endogenous ZLB duration" allows the duration of the ZLB to be endogenous as described in the main text. Finally, the "OIS-based ZLB duration" imposes the duration of the ZLB in each point in time according to OIS rates for the federal funds rate between 2008Q4 and 2011Q2.

(wage markup and marginal costs, respectively) in the linearized price and wage equations. Evidently, the much higher degree of price and wage stickiness is only partly driven by the fact that prices and real wages fell modestly relative to output during the Great Recession (as can be seen in Fig. 1); even before the recession materialized there was already a strong trend in the data towards higher stickiness parameters, consistent with the findings by Del Negro et al. (2015b).[aa] Even so, we note that our estimated full sample model without the ZLB still features a much lower degree of price and wage stickiness than the policy model recently estimated by Brave et al. (2012).[ab]

In Fig. 7, we plot conditional forecast distributions for selected variables for the "No ZLB model" posterior in Table 7. In the left column, the forecast is conditional on the state in 2008Q3, whereas in the other two columns it is conditional on the filtered state in 2008Q4. Similarly to the results for the precrisis models in Fig. 2, the results in the left column shows that the severe drop in economic activity in 2008Q4 was outside the 95th percent uncertainty bands, even though the model is estimated on the full sample. This thus should be considered as an in-sample exercise. However, the median forecast conditional on the state in 2008Q4 is very accurate for yearly output growth and output (as deviation from trend) and the actual outcome is well within the uncertain bands for these variables, even disregarding the ZLB. For the federal funds rate, we see that the median forecast for the federal funds rate falls only slightly below nil for three quarters (2009Q1–2009Q3). This seemingly suggest that the ZLB was not much of a binding constraint during the Great Recession, consistent with the finding and interpretation in Del Negro et al. (2015b). This interpretation, however, ignores the fact that the forecast distribution for the federal funds rate has considerable mass below nil. Shifting this part of the distribution to 0 and above may therefore change the median outlook considerably.

To examine this possibility, the third column in Fig. 7 reports the forecast distribution when sampling parameters and shocks from the posterior distribution for the "No ZLB model" in Table 7, but with the unconstrained policy rule replaced by the policy rule in (17). This means that the actual and expected federal funds rate will respect the ZLB during the forecast horizon. Importantly, the 1000 different shock realizations used to construct the forecast distribution in the ZLB case are identical to those used to construct the unconstrained forecast distribution. Given the state in 2008Q4 the only difference between the results in the second and third column is that the federal funds rate is

[aa] This finding implies that the lower slope does not seem to be related to aggregate volatility, consistent with the findings by Vavra (2013).

[ab] As different models make alternative assumptions about strategic complements in price and wage setting, we have the reduced form coefficient for the wage and price markups in mind when comparing the degree of price and wage stickiness. In our benchmark model this coefficient equals 0.012 at the posterior mode for the New Keynesian Phillips curve which is similar to the estimate of Del Negro et al. (2013) (0.016). The estimate of Brave et al. (2012); however, the mode is as low as 0.002.

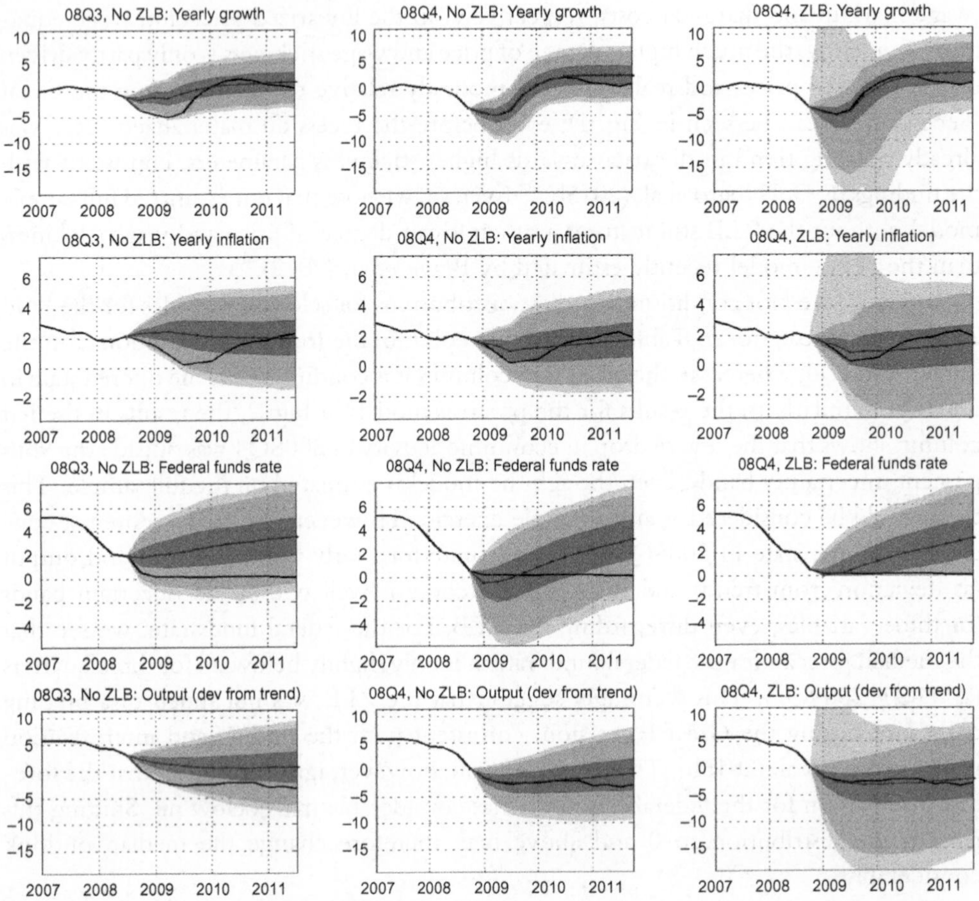

Fig. 7 Forecast 2009Q1–2011Q4 conditional on state in 2008Q4 for model estimated through 2014Q2 without imposing the ZLB.

constrained from falling below zero. As can be seen from the panels for output growth and output as deviation from trend, imposing the ZLB on the federal funds rate widens their uncertainty bands downwards quite notably. For output as deviation from trend, the lower 95th percentile shifts down from roughly −10% to nearly −20% in 2010. Hence, in the absence of unconventional monetary policies and coordination between monetary and fiscal policy (ie, fiscal stimulus when the economy enters a long-lived liquidity trap), the baseline model suggests that the ZLB may be associated with large economic costs.

On the other hand, the upper-95th percent bands for these variables are also much higher when the federal funds rate is constrained to fall below zero conditional on the given state in 2008Q4. For detrended output, the upper 95th percentile is above 10% in 2009. For yearly inflation, the upper 95th percentile is above 6%. Despite these elevated upper uncertainty bands for output growth, detrended output and inflation, the upper 95th percentile for the federal funds rate is lower than the corresponding percentile in the unconstrained policy rate distribution. This seemingly goes against the specification of the policy rule in (17) as the systematic part of the policy rule governing $\widehat{R}_t^*$ calls for a high policy rate whenever inflation, output growth and the output gap is high. The reason why this does not happen in the conditional ZLB distribution in Fig. 7 is that the model estimated without the imposed ZLB constraint needs large *negative* current and anticipated policy shocks $\widehat{\varepsilon}^r_{t+h|t}$ to satisfy $E_t\widehat{R}_{t+h} \geq 0$. In essence, when the economy is hit by some really adverse shocks in these simulations and the policy rate is constrained to respond to these shocks for a sufficiently long period, inflation expectations and economic activity fall to such a large extent that a sequence of *negative* instead of *positive* policy shocks $\widehat{\varepsilon}^r_{t+h|t}$ for $h = 0, 1, \ldots, \tau_2$ are needed to prevent the federal funds rate to fall below nil. As discussed in Hebden et al. (2010) and Carlstrom et al. (2012), the switch in signs of the policy shocks only happens in the relatively few draws for which the policy rate is expected to be constrained by the lower bound for a very prolonged period of time (ie, τ_2 is large). This also explains why the upper 95th percentiles for inflation and output shifts up so much while the 90th percentile is roughly unchanged relative to the unconstrained distribution. The 90th percentile is associated with simulations of favorable fundamental shocks and parameter draws for which no large negative policy shocks are needed to prevent the policy rate to fall below nil.

We believe this result—that the ZLB can trigger adverse shocks to have sharply expansionary effects on the economy—is an unpalatable feature of the model. Therefore when we reestimate the model subject to the ZLB constraint on the federal funds rate, we believe it is crucial to impose the additional constraint—discussed in the beginning of this section—that the parameters of the economy have to be such that all current and expected policy shocks used to impose the policy rule in (17) are positive whenever the ZLB binds. By imposing this constraint, we ensure that the reestimated model does not feature any sign reversals of the policy shocks even for the most long-lived liquidity traps in our forecast distributions.

The estimation results for this variant of the model are reported in Table 7 and labeled "Endogenous ZLB duration". We use this label because both the incidence and duration of the ZLB spells are endogenous estimation outcomes in the model, and do not necessarily conform with other commonly used measures of the expected future path of the federal funds rate such as overnight index swap (OIS, henceforth) rates. By comparing the results with the "No ZLB model", we see that imposing the ZLB in the estimations have quite important implications for the posterior distribution. First of all the degree of price and wage stickiness is elevated even further, and the estimated parameters imply a slope of the New Keynesian Phillips curve of 0.006. This is somewhat lower than the median estimates of literature which cluster in the range of about 0.009–0.014, but well within standard confidence intervals provided by empirical studies (see, eg, Adolfson et al., 2005;

Altig et al., 2011; Galí and Gertler, 1999; Galí et al., 2001; and Lindé, 2005). In addition, the higher degree of nominal wage stickiness makes marginal costs even more sticky in the ZLB model. Together these features makes inflation and inflation expectations more slow to react to various shocks and therefore allow the model to cope with long spells at the ZLB without triggering indeterminacy problems (ie, switches in signs for the policy shocks). This finding is consistent with Erceg and Lindé (2010), who argue that a low slope of the Phillips curve is consistent with the development during the recent crisis where inflation and inflation expectations have fallen very moderately despite large contractions in output. It is also consistent with many recent papers which have estimated similar DSGE models, see, eg, Brave et al. (2012) and Del Negro et al. (2015b).

In addition to the higher degree of wage and price stickiness, there are two other important differences. Firstly, the coefficient on the output gap in the policy rule (Eq. (17)), r_y, is about twice as high as in the "No ZLB model". To the extent the output gap becomes significantly negative during the Great Recession, this will tend to push down the path of the federal funds rate and extend the duration of the ZLB. Secondly, the persistence coefficient in the risk premium shock process, ρ_b, increases sharply from 0.40 to 0.85. However, since the posterior mode for σ_b is reduced from 0.19 to 0.10, the unconditional variance for the risk-premium shock nevertheless falls slightly (from 0.044 to 0.039) in the ZLB model. Therefore the higher persistence does not imply a significantly larger role for the risk-premium shocks (apart from expectational effects). Even so, the likelihood prefers naturally more persistence in the shock process of the risk premium above a repeated set of positive innovations to explain the duration of the crisis and the slow pace of the recovery, but this shift in the posterior distribution of the parameters goes with a cost during the tranquil periods. This time variation in the role of the financial wedge over periods with more or less financial stress will be further discussed in Section 5.3.

Fig. 8 shows the forecast distribution (given the state in 2008Q4) in the "Endogenous ZLB duration" variant of the model. The left column gives the results when the ZLB is counterfactually neglected, whereas the right column shows the results when the ZLB is imposed. As expected, we see that the forecast distribution in the variant of the model which counterfactually neglects the ZLB features symmetric uncertainty bands around the modal outlook, and is a little bit too optimistic about the outlook for output relative to the model which imposes the ZLB (right column). More surprisingly is that the modal outlook for 2008Q4 in the model estimated and imposing ZLB constraint (right column in Fig. 8) differs very little to the modal outlook in the "No ZLB model" which completely neglects the ZLB (the middle column in Fig. 7). Obviously, a key difference is that the median path of the federal funds rate is constrained by the lower bound in 2009, but below nil in the unconstrained version of the model. Still, the quantitative difference for the median projection is small. The most noticeable difference between the No ZLB model and the model estimated under

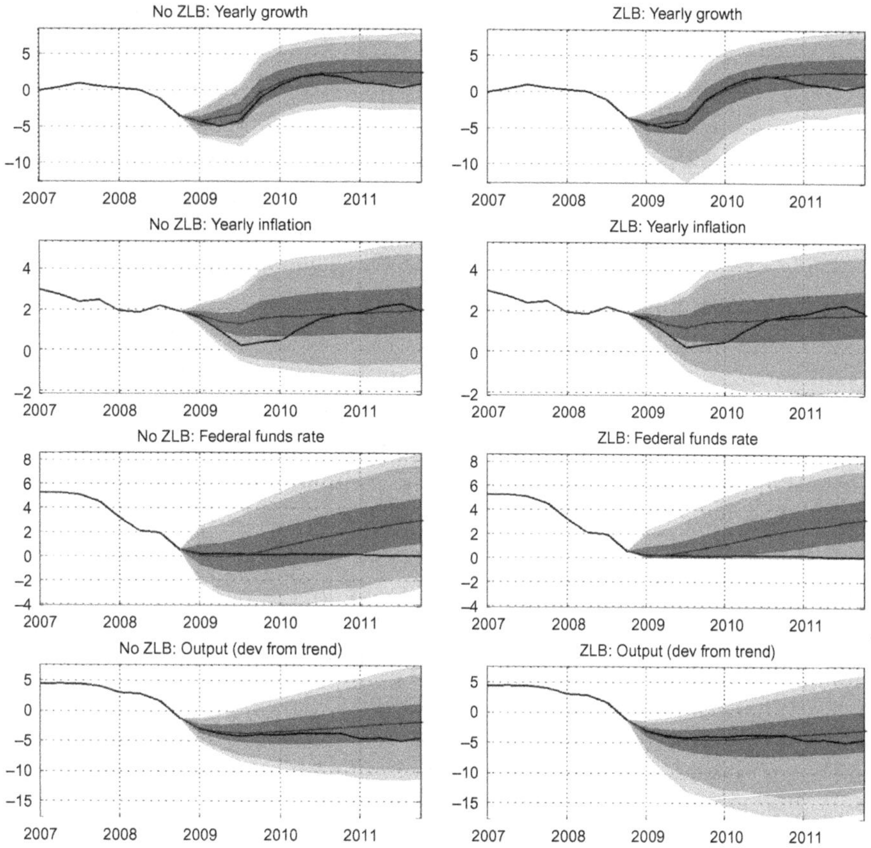

Fig. 8 Forecast 2009Q1–2011Q4 conditional on state in 2008Q4 for model estimated through 2014Q2 when imposing the ZLB.

the ZLB is the uncertainty bands: they are wider and downward skewed in the model that imposes the ZLB constraint (the right column of Fig. 8) compared to the No ZLB model that neglects the presence of the ZLB constraint.

However, the forecast distributions in the "No ZLB model"(the right column in Fig. 7)—which enforces the ZLB *ex post*—differs dramatically to the forecast distributions in the model estimated under the ZLB constraint (the right column in Fig. 8). The higher degree of wage and price stickiness in the model estimated under the ZLB constraint insulate the economy from the disaster scenarios and the indeterminate equilibria, and therefore shrink the uncertainty bands considerably. Overall this suggests that taking the ZLB into account in the estimation stage may be of key importance in assessing its economic consequences, and that it is not evident that models estimated on precrisis data can be useful for policy analysis when the economy enters into a long-lived liquidity trap. In such situations, the precrisis policy models may feature too much flexibility in price and wage setting, and, eg, yield implausibly large fiscal multipliers as noted by, eg, Erceg and Lindé (2010).

Another interesting feature of the model which neglects the ZLB and the variant of the model which is constrained to imposing Equation (17) through positive current and anticipated policy shocks is that the former has a higher log-marginal likelihood (−1146.7 vs −1152). This implies that imposing the ZLB on the model is somewhat costly in terms of data coherence. However, as suggested by the small differences in the conditional forecast distributions in Figs. 7 (middle column) and 8 (right column), it is not evident if this difference in log marginal likelihood is important from an economic viewpoint, although it is large enough to be sizable in terms of a Bayesian posterior odds ratio.

As the model is endogenously determining the incidence and duration of the ZLB spell, it is interesting to note that according to the model, the ZLB is expected in 2008Q4 to be a binding constraint from 2009Q1 to 2009Q3 in the modal outlook. The expected positive policy shocks we use to impose the ZLB partially substitute for the exceptionally huge risk premium shocks that drive the economy to the ZLB in the first place.[ac] The constraint is then expected to be binding during 2009 with a maximum duration of five quarters given the state in 2009Q1, and from 2010Q2 and onward, the model expects the interest rate to lift off already in the next quarter. The short duration of the ZLB spells is consistent with the findings of Chung et al. (2012). The fact that the federal funds rate has remained at the ZLB since then is by the model explained either as a result of expansionary monetary policy actions—forward guidance—or as standard policy reactions to unexpected headwinds. The filtered shocks suggest a dominant role for the second interpretation.

As noted previously, an alternative to letting the DSGE model determine the expected duration of the ZLB in each time period is to use OIS data for the federal funds rate as observables when estimating the model. By doing so, we follow Del Negro et al. (2015b) and require that the expected federal funds rate in the model matches the OIS data in each point in time when the ZLB is binding, ie, from 2008Q4 and onward. We use OIS data (acquired from the Federal Reserve Board) for 1, 2, …, 12 quarters' expected federal funds rates, and require the model to match those rates exactly through anticipated policy shocks following the general idea outlined by Maih (2010). The appealing feature of Maih's algorithm is that it does not require us to include standard

[ac] This high substitutability between anticipated monetary shocks that capture the effect of the ZLB on the one hand and the risk premium shock on the other hand, implies that it is very difficult to quantify accurately the precise impact of the ZLB on growth during the crisis. For instance, when a lagged shadow rate is used in the monetary policy rule instead of the lagged actual rate, the anticipated monetary policy shocks needed to impose the ZLB becomes much larger and more of the recession would then be attributed to the ZLB constraint while the contribution of the exogenous risk premium shock would decline significantly in the decomposition.

deviations for each of the anticipated policy shocks we use to fit the OIS data, and that the log-marginal likelihood can be compared to the models which does not condition on OIS data.

Before we turn to the results in Table 7, there are two additional important pieces of information. First, as we interpret the OIS data as expected means of future federal funds rates, we set them equal to nil in each point in time whenever they are lower than 50 basis points. We do this as our OIS estimation procedure does not explicitly account for future shock uncertainty, and the projected path of the interest rate from the model should therefore be viewed as a modal outlook (which will be lower than the mean of the forecast distribution when the ZLB binds). Second, because the Federal Reserve did not use explicit time-dependent forward guidance until August 2011, we restrict all anticipated policy shocks to be positive prior to this date. After this date we do not impose any signs on the anticipated policy shocks, because credible forward guidance—or a "lower for longer policy"—in the spirit of Reifschneider and Williams (2000) and Eggertsson and Woodford (2003), which extends the duration of the ZLB, is better viewed as expansionary than contractionary policy. Specifically, we allow the model to explain the sharp flattening of the OIS curve between the second and third quarter in 2011 with negative policy shocks, and do not impose this flattening to be associated with a noticeable deterioration in the economic outlook. According to the data, however, the magnitude of these expansionary "forward guidance" shocks are modest: interpreting the long ZLB spells as a deliberate "lower for longer" decision by the policy makers would further boost the predicted recovery by the model which goes against the observed slow and disappointing recovery in growth following the crisis.[ad]

The results when imposing the incidence and duration of the ZLB to adhere with OIS rates are shown in the left panel in Table 7, labeled "OIS-based ZLB duration." Relative to the posterior "Endogenous ZLB duration," for which the incidence and duration of the ZLB is determined endogenously in the model, we see that the degree of price stickiness is elevated further (from 0.83 to 0.89), and now implies a slope of the Phillips curve (ie, direct sensitivity of current inflation to marginal cost) of 0.003. This is substantially lower than, eg, the estimate in Altig et al. (2011), but still higher than Brave et al. (2012). To square this estimate with the microliterature is a challenge, and probably requires a combination of firm-specific capital (as in Altig et al., 2011),

[ad] There is a growing literature on the effectiveness of forward guidance. While Andrade et al. (2015) argue mainly on theoretical grounds that forward guidance may not be effective when agents have heterogeneous beliefs, Campbell et al. (2012), Williams (2014), and Del Negro et al. (2015a) argue on empirical grounds that forward guidance have had some positive impact. Even so, Del Negro, Giannoni and Patterson recognize that forward guidance may be too potent in a standard New Keynesian model relative to what the empirical evidence supports, and therefore integrate perpetual youth structure into the model to reduce its effectiveness. By and large, our estimated model produces results that are in line with their findings and suggests that forward guidance have had some, but limited, impact on the economy.

firm-specific labor (as in Woodford, 2003), and a higher sensitivity of demand to relative prices (ie, higher Kimball parameter ε_p). Apart from the higher stickiness we also see an elevated role for the risk-premium shock in this model (ρ_b rises sharply from 0.85 to 0.97, whereas the std of the innovations only falls moderately from 0.10 to 0.08), and that the degree of habit formation consumption ($\varkappa$) and investment adjustment costs (φ) rises somewhat. Finally, the response coefficient for the output gap in the policy rule is increased further, and is now 3× higher than in the model which neglects the presence of the ZLB.

The reason why these parameters are further changed relative to the "No ZLB model" is that the OIS data generally imposes longer-lived ZLB episodes than the model endogenously produces. In order to be able to explain those episodes with *positive* anticipated policy shocks through 2011Q2 the model needs to make dynamics more sluggish and explain the rebound in inflation during 2010 with temporary shocks. However, enforcing this sluggish dynamics on the model is rather costly in terms of log-marginal likelihood, which falls from −1152 in the model with endogenous ZLB duration to −1175.2 for the OIS-based ZLB duration. This is a sizable drop and a possible interpretation is that the SW07-model despite imposing the ZLB constraint, was more optimistic about the recovery than market participants during this episode.

There are of course other possibilities as to why the ZLB episodes in the model are short-lived relative to what OIS data suggest. They include that; (i) the model miss-measures the size and persistence of the relevant output gap, (ii) the model-consistent or rational expectation hypothesis fails to capture the stickiness and persistence in expectations that might be caused by learning dynamics or information filtering issues, (iii) the steady state natural real rate has fallen (eg, due to lower trend growth) and this has caused the (gross) steady state nominal interest rate R in Eq. (14) to fall; *ceteris paribus* this calls for an extended ZLB duration, and (iv), the Federal Reserve decided to respond more vigorously to the negative output gap (ie, r_y in Eq. (14) increased) from the outset of the Great Recession and thereafter.[ae] Yet other possibilities is that our model above misses out on time-varying volatility of the shocks and omits financial frictions and the cost channel of monetary policy. We explore these latter possibilities below.

5.2 Allowing for Time-Varying Volatility

As documented earlier, the prototype linear Gaussian model with constant volatility does not provide a realistic predictive density for the forecast, in particular around severe recession periods or periods of high financial and monetary stress. A large share

[ae] To the extent that these mechanisms are at work, they should be picked up in our estimated model as expansionary monetary policy shocks due to the presumption in our analysis that the Fed before and after the crisis (ie, upon exit from the ZLB) adheres to the same Taylor-type policy rule (Eq. (17)), and that agents form their expectations accordingly.

of the research effort on DSGE models since the financial crisis and the Great recession has tried to overcome these weaknesses of the basic DSGE setup. By now, most models used in academia and in policy institutions contain financial frictions and financial shocks in an effort to introduce stronger amplification mechanisms in the model. As we will discuss in the next section, however, to the extent that even the modified models adopt a Gaussian linear framework, they still depend on extremely large shocks to predict important recessions. The explicit modeling of the nonlinear macrofinance interactions is complex and ambitious and the research in that direction has not yet been integrated in empirical macro models. A technically feasible avenue to improve the predictive densities of the linear DSGE model is to allow for a more complicated stochastic structure. Here we illustrate this approach by considering a Markov Switching (MS) stochastic structure following Liu et al. (2013).[af] By allowing for such a shock structure, the hope is that the estimated model can capture the phenomena that the economic outlook is sometimes very uncertain (ie, the economy is filtered to be in the high volatility regime), without necessarily destroying its ability to provide reasonably narrow forecast uncertainty bands in normal times (ie, in the low volatility regime).

Low frequency changes in the shock variances have been analyzed by Fernández-Villaverde and Rubio-Ramírez (2007) and Justiniano and Primiceri (2008) via stochastic volatility processes. Chib and Ramamurthy (2014) and Curdia et al. (2014) show that a Student's *t*-distribution for the innovations is also strongly favored by the data as it allows for rare large shocks. The latter authors makes the point that the time variation in shock variances should contain both a low and a high frequency component.

To capture these insights, we consider a version of the benchmark model in which we allow for two independent Markov Switching processes in the shock variances. Each Markov process can switch between a low and a high volatility regime. One process affects the volatility of all the structural innovations with exception of the wage markup shock, based on the observation that the wage markup and the observed real wage variable has a completely different volatility profile compared to the other shocks and variables as shown in Figs. 1 and 5. The second Markov process is restricted to the non-Gaussian structural shocks as identified in Table 6 in Section 4.3: this process affects the volatility in the monetary policy, the risk premium and the investment specific innovations. The volatility in these three shocks is scaled by both the common (σ_c) and the monetary/financial volatility factor (σ_{mf}). The typical process for these three shocks is now written as follows:

$$\widehat{\varepsilon}_t = \rho\widehat{\varepsilon}_{t-1} + \sigma_{mf}\left(s_{mf}\right)\cdot\sigma_c(s_c)\cdot\sigma\cdot\eta_t,\ \eta_t \sim N(0,1).$$

[af] We use the RISE toolbox to implement this exercise, see Maih (2015).

The estimated transition probabilities are summarized by the following matrices:

$$Q_c\begin{pmatrix} low \\ high \end{pmatrix} = \begin{bmatrix} 0.95 & 0.07 \\ 0.05 & 0.93 \end{bmatrix} \quad Q_{mf}\begin{pmatrix} low \\ high \end{pmatrix} = \begin{bmatrix} 0.92 & 0.46 \\ 0.08 & 0.54 \end{bmatrix}.$$

The relative volatility of the two regimes are estimated as:

$$\sigma_c\begin{pmatrix} low \\ high \end{pmatrix} = \begin{bmatrix} 1 \\ 1.74 \end{bmatrix} \text{ and } \sigma_{mf}\begin{pmatrix} low \\ high \end{pmatrix} = \begin{bmatrix} 1 \\ 2.33 \end{bmatrix}.$$

In Fig. 9, we plot the smoothed regime probabilities for the model estimated over the complete sample. A filtered probability near unity (zero) implies that the economy is filtered to be in the high (low) volatility regime.

The common volatility process captures the great moderation phenomena. The high volatility regime is typically preferred during most of the 1970s and the first half of the 1980s, while the low volatility regime is active during the great moderation and is interrupted by the financial crisis and the resulting Great Recession. Both regimes are estimated to be persistent and the relative volatility during the high volatility regime is almost twice as high as in the low volatility regime. The monetary/financial volatility process captures the increase in the volatility during most of the recession periods and in the late 1970s- and early 1980s-episode of increased monetary policy uncertainty. The expected duration of this high volatility/financial stress regime is relatively short lived with a quarterly transition probability of 0.46%. The estimated parameters that describe the regimes and the regime probabilities are very stable when estimating the model for the precrisis period or for the complete sample (not shown).

Table 8 shows that the estimated log marginal likelihood of our model with switching volatility outperforms the log marginal likelihood of the homoscedastic Gaussian models by far. In this sense, our results confirm the results in the literature based on stochastic

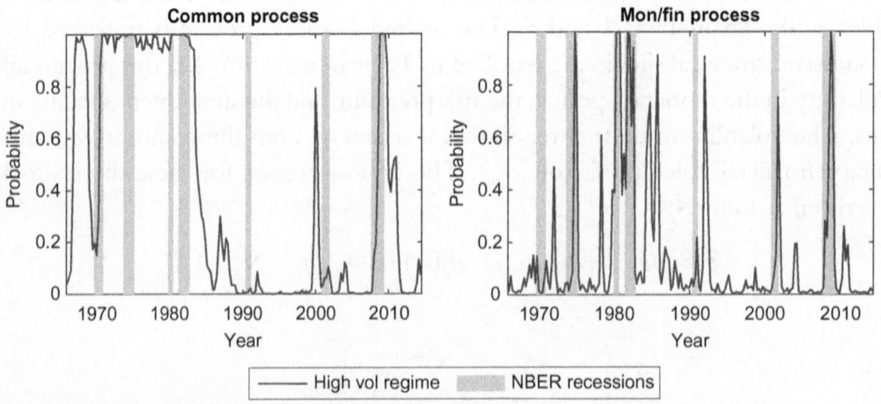

Fig. 9 Smoothed probabilities of the two volatility Markov processes.

Table 8 Log marginal likelihood of alternative regime switching specifications

	Sample period	
	Precrisis: 66Q1–07Q4	**Full sample: 66Q1–14Q2**
No regime switching (RS)	−961.8	−1146.7
RS in common process	−894.6	−1060.9
RS in mon/fin process	−911.8	−1082.1
RS in common and mon/fin process	−881.7	−1046.0

Note: None of the models in this table are estimated subject to the ZLB on policy rates.

volatility or *t*-distributed shocks. In contrast with Liu et al. (2013) and in support of the results of Curdia et al. (2014), we find strong evidence in favor of a setup that allows for multiple sources of volatility changes. The time-varying volatility structure requires sufficient flexibility to account for a common low frequency trend on the one hand, and a more cyclical high frequency process that controls mainly the monetary and financial shocks on the other hand.[ag]

Accounting for the non-Gaussian stochastic structure drastically improves the log marginal likelihood of our models, but leaves the estimated parameters, ie, the central forecasts and identified innovations, relatively unaffected. Most of the gains are realized because the predictive densities attribute appropriate probabilities to the extreme tail events: the large downturns in recessions and the corresponding sharp responses in policy rates. To illustrate this property, we consider the predictive forecast distribution with the precrisis model conditional on data up to 2008Q3, and we calculated the percentile interval that contains the 2008Q4 realized output growth observation (see Fig. 10). For our baseline precrisis model, the realized 2008Q4 growth rate falls completely outside of the simulated predictive densities based on 10,000 draws with parameter and shock volatility, as is clear from the left panel in the figure (see also Fig. 2). In contrast, in the model with Markov Switching volatility, almost 1% of the simulated forecasts fall below the 2008Q4 realization, as shown in the figure's right panel.[ah] The Markov

[ag] Our restrictive setup of two processes improve the log marginal likelihood by 115 for the complete sample. More flexible structures could easily improve this result but this goes with a cost because these setups are less robust, are computational much more intensive and lack an intuitive interpretation of the regimes. Curdia et al. report a gain of 154 in the log marginal likelihood for a setup that contains a combination of shock specific stochastic volatility and *t*-distributed innovations.

[ah] We want to emphasize that it is not the case that we are more content with this model just because it gives a positive probability that the great recession could indeed happen. As pointed out earlier, our rationale for going in this direction is that the models with regime switching in shock variances and the propagation of financial frictions (see analysis in the next section) improves the statistical properties of the model (as suggested by the strong improvement in log marginal likelihood) and makes sense from an economic viewpoint (supporting the widely held belief that financial frictions are key to understand the crisis).

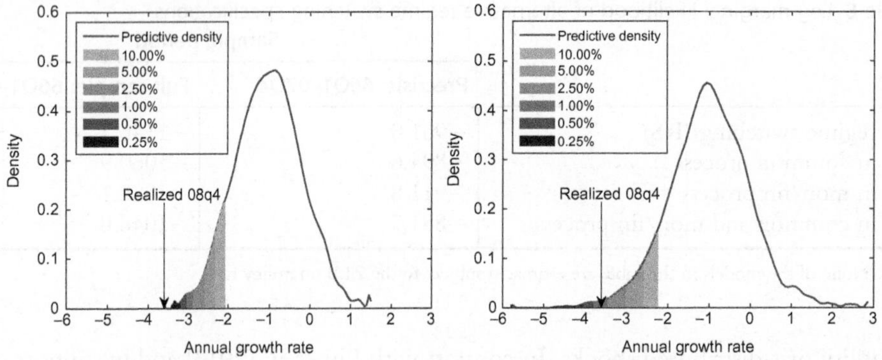

Fig. 10 Distributions for output growth (four-quarter change) in 2008Q4 given state in 2008Q3 in models with constant volatility (left panel) and time-varying volatility (right panel).

Switching volatility structure, by allowing for a mixture of normal distributions, gives more probability to the tails in general. In addition, the probability of the high volatility regimes in both the high and the low frequency Markov processes increased already by 2008Q3 because the magnitude of the realized shocks preceding the fourth quarter observation were relatively large.

5.3 Augmenting the Model with Financial Frictions and a Cost Channel

We incorporate a financial accelerator mechanism into the benchmark model in Section 3 following the basic approach of Bernanke et al. (1999). Thus, the intermediate goods producers rent capital services from entrepreneurs rather than directly from households. Entrepreneurs purchase physical capital from competitive capital goods producers (at price $\widehat{Q}_t^k$, and resell it back at the end of each period), with the latter employing the same technology to transform investment goods into finished capital goods as described by Eq. (11). To finance the acquisition of physical capital ($\widehat{\bar{k}}_t$), each entrepreneur combines his net worth ($\widehat{NW}_t^e$) with a loan from a bank, for which the entrepreneur must pay an external finance premium due to an agency problem. We follow Christiano et al. (2008) by assuming that the debt contract between entrepreneurs and banks is written in nominal terms (rather than real terms as in Bernanke et al., 1999). Banks, in turn, obtain funds to lend to the entrepreneurs by receiving deposits from households, with households bearing no credit risk (reflecting assumptions about free competition in banking and the ability of banks to diversify their portfolios). In equilibrium, shocks that affect entrepreneurial net worth—ie, the leverage of the corporate sector—induce fluctuations in the corporate finance premium.[ai]

[ai] For further details about the setup, see Bernanke, Gertler and Gilchrist, and Christiano, Motto and Rostagno. Excellent expositions are also provided by Christiano et al. (2007) and Gilchrist et al. (2009).

When estimating the model with the financial friction mechanism embedded, we add one more observable variable, the widely-used Baa-Aaa corporate credit spread (see Appendix C for exact definition and data sources). This spread plays a key role in the Bernanke–Gertler–Gilchrist framework. Since we also want to learn about the importance of shocks originating in the financial sector, and because we need as many shocks as observables to avoid stochastic singularity, we also add a "net worth" shock to the set of estimated shocks. We derive this shock by allowing the survival probability of the entrepreneurs to vary over time. Hence, this shock will enter in the accumulation equation for the entrepreneurs net worth. An alternative would have been to allow for a shock directly in the equation which relates the spread (or equivalently, the external finance premium) to the entrepreneurs leverage ratio following, eg, Del Negro and Schorfheide (2013) or Christiano et al. (2008). We preferred, however, not to add a shock directly in the spread equation in an attempt to elevate the endogenous propagation of the financial accelerator mechanism.[aj] Even so, the equation for the external finance premium,

$$\mathrm{E}_t\widehat{R}^e_{t+1} - \widehat{R}^b_t = \chi\left(\widehat{Q}^k_t + \widehat{\bar{k}}_t - \widehat{NW}^e_t\right), \tag{18}$$

still contains a shock because we assume that the financing rate of the banks, $\widehat{R}^b_t$, is not the risk-free rate set by the central bank, but rather the sum of the policy rate $\widehat{R}_t$ and the risk-premium shock $\widehat{\varepsilon}^b_t$.

As recent research by Christiano et al. (2015) and Gilchrist et al. (2015) emphasize the importance of firms financing conditions for their price setting behavior, we also embed a cost channel into the model. Specifically, we assume that firms have to borrow short to finance their wage bill following Christiano et al. (2005). As shown in the CEE paper, the working capital channel can cause inflation to rise following a tightening of monetary policy if firms financing costs rise sufficiently. To allow for sharp increases in firms financing costs, we assume that the relevant financing rate is the expected nominal return on capital for the entrepreneurs as opposed to the risk-free policy rate. However, instead of imposing that all firms borrow to finance their entire wage bills as in CEE, we estimate a parameter, ν, which determines the share of firms that are subject to working capital, so that the expression for log-linearized marginal costs becomes

$$\widehat{mc}_t = (1-\alpha)\ \left(\widehat{w}_t + \widehat{R}^f_t\right) + \alpha\ \widehat{r}^k_t - \widehat{\varepsilon}^a_t,$$

[aj] Christiano et al. (2008) embed a complete banking sector into their model and estimate it using 17× series and an equal number of shocks. A benefit, however, of our more modest perturbation of the model size and number of observables matched is that it allows for a straightforward comparison with the findings in the benchmark SW07-model.

where $\widehat{R}_t^f$ is the effective working capital interest rate given by

$$\widehat{R}_t^f = \frac{\nu R}{\nu R + 1 - \nu} \mathrm{E}_t \widehat{R}_{t+1}^e, \tag{19}$$

in which $\mathrm{E}_t \widehat{R}_{t+1}^e$ is the nominal expected return on capital for the entrepreneurs. From Eq. (19), we notice that $\widehat{R}_t^f = \mathrm{E}_t \widehat{R}_{t+1}^e$ when $\nu = 1$.

The SW07-model embedded with the financial friction mechanism and the cost-channel thus include five additional estimated parameters; ν, the two parameters for the AR(1) process for net worth (ρ_{nw} and σ_{nw}), the monitoring cost parameter μ which indirectly determines the sensitivity of the external finance premium to the entrepreneurs leverage ratio (χ in Eq. (18), and a constant ($\bar{c}_{sp}$) which captures the mean of the credit spread. Estimation results for three specifications of the model are provided in Table 9; first we have the "Precrisis sample" (sample 1966Q1–2007Q4 without the ZLB), second, the full sample (66Q1–14Q2) when imposing the ZLB constraint with endogenous duration, and third we study a variant of the model with the ZLB which allows the key parameter μ to switch stochastically between a high and low value. The adopted priors for the five new parameters are provided in the notes to the table. The priors for the other parameters are the same as before (and already stated in Table 2).

In the precrisis model, the external finance premium delivers only a very modest amplification of the standard shocks. The estimated elasticity of the spread to the net worth ratio is small (with $\mu = 0.033$ and χ in Eq. (18) equals 0.012, implying an annualized spread sensitivity of 0.048), a result that is in line with the estimates reported in Gilchrist et al. (2009). The exogenous risk-premium shock and—to a lower degree—the monetary policy shock are most impacted by the introduction of the FA mechanism because they have the biggest impact on the price of capital and net worth. The net worth channel tends to support the persistence in the response of investment to these shocks. The low sensitivity of the spread to the traditional shocks also implies that most of the fluctuations in the external finance premium are generated by the new exogenous shock that is assumed to hit directly the net worth of the entrepreneurs. This highly volatile shock explains up to 70% of the variance in the spread and one-third of the variance in investment. As such, the net worth shock substitutes for the exogenous risk premium and for the investment-specific technology shock. The latter also captures financial frictions as suggested by Justiniano et al. (2013a). Overall, the impact of the net worth shock on the macrodynamics remains modest and one important reason for this is that the net worth shock typically crowds out private consumption and this clashes with the observed strong comovement between consumption, and investment over the business cycle.[ak]

[ak] This crowding out problem is not present for our reduced form risk-premium shock ε_t^b in Eq. (12), see Fisher (2015) for a structural interpretation of this risk-premium shock.

Table 9 Posterior distributions in SW model with financial frictions

Parameter		Precrisis sample		Endogenous ZLB duration		Endog. ZLB dur. with regime switch	
		Mode	Std.dev.Hess.	Mode	Std.dev.Hess.	Mode	Std.dev.Hess.
Calvo prob. wages	ξ_w	0.72	0.082	0.83	0.009	0.86	0.017
Calvo prob. prices	ξ_p	0.68	0.045	0.84	0.024	0.83	0.029
Indexation wages	ι_w	0.67	0.129	0.63	0.125	0.60	0.130
Indexation prices	ι_p	0.21	0.084	0.23	0.081	0.23	0.085
Gross price markup	ϕ_p	1.61	0.077	1.45	0.062	1.43	0.063
Capital production share	α	0.21	0.018	0.17	0.016	0.17	0.016
Capital utilization cost	ψ	0.44	0.114	0.50	0.100	0.64	0.096
Investment adj. cost	φ	4.71	0.845	4.61	0.564	4.00	0.560
Habit formation	$\varkappa$	0.77	0.037	0.67	0.018	0.63	0.025
Inv subs. elast. of cons.	σ_c	1.27	0.110	0.97	0.100	1.04	0.084
Labor supply elast.	σ_l	1.50	0.565	1.58	0.437	1.85	0.459
Hours worked in S.S.	$\bar{l}$	0.85	1.082	−0.48	0.804	−0.23	0.768
Discount factor	$100(\beta^{-1}-1)$	0.13	0.051	0.12	0.049	0.12	0.049
Quarterly growth in S.S.	$\bar{\gamma}$	0.43	0.015	0.42	0.015	0.42	0.017
Stationary tech. shock	ρ_a	0.96	0.011	0.96	0.012	0.97	0.012
Risk premium shock	ρ_b	0.26	0.083	0.83	0.022	0.85	0.029
Invest. spec. tech. shock	ρ_i	0.80	0.055	0.84	0.040	0.88	0.035
Gov't cons. shock	ρ_g	0.96	0.010	0.97	0.009	0.97	0.009
Price markup shock	ρ_p	0.92	0.034	0.89	0.039	0.89	0.040
Wage markup shock	ρ_w	0.98	0.013	0.98	0.007	0.97	0.001
Response of g_t to ε_t^a	ρ_{ga}	0.49	0.076	0.53	0.068	0.53	0.068
Stationary tech. shock	σ_a	0.47	0.029	0.49	0.027	0.49	0.027
Risk premium shock	σ_b	0.21	0.021	0.11	0.010	0.10	0.010
Invest. spec. tech. shock	σ_i	0.35	0.036	0.31	0.020	0.32	0.013
Gov't cons. shock	σ_g	0.47	0.029	0.47	0.024	0.47	0.024
Price markup shock	σ_p	0.12	0.015	0.12	0.013	0.13	0.013
MA(1) price markup shock	ϑ_p	0.75	0.079	0.79	0.070	0.79	0.071
Wage markup shock	σ_w	0.31	0.025	0.37	0.020	0.37	0.021
MA(1) wage markup shock	ϑ_w	0.92	0.049	0.96	0.008	0.96	0.001

Continued

Table 9 Posterior distributions in SW model with financial frictions—cont'd

Parameter		Precrisis sample		Endogenous ZLB duration		Endog. ZLB dur. with regime switch	
		Mode	**Std.dev.Hess.**	**Mode**	**Std.dev.Hess.**	**Mode**	**Std.dev.Hess.**
Quarterly infl. rate. in S.S.	$\overline{\pi}$	0.78	0.105	0.73	0.097	0.76	0.093
Inflation response	r_π	1.91	0.170	1.78	0.119	1.83	0.133
Output gap response	r_y	0.07	0.022	0.10	0.008	0.11	0.012
Diff. output gap response	$r_{\Delta y}$	0.24	0.028	0.24	0.014	0.24	0.015
Mon. pol. shock std	σ_r	0.23	0.014	0.22	0.012	0.22	0.011
Mon. pol. shock pers.	ρ_r	0.14	0.068	0.10	0.047	0.09	0.047
Interest rate smoothing	ρ_R	0.81	0.026	0.84	0.006	0.84	0.009
Net worth shock pers.	ρ_{nw}	0.25	0.080	0.30	0.088	0.30	0.084
Net worth shock std	σ_{nw}	0.27	0.031	0.19	0.024	0.23	0.032
Working capital share	ν	0.34	0.120	0.64	0.228	0.60	0.251
Credit spread in S.S.	$\bar{c}_{sp}$	1.51	0.292	1.28	0.285	0.97	0.059
Monitoring cost	μ	0.03	0.004	0.06	0.007		
Monitoring cost—Regime 1	μ_1					0.03	0.004
Monitoring cost—Regime 2	μ_2					0.08	0.011
Trans. Prob.—R1 to R2	p_{12}					0.04	0.015
Trans. Prob.—R2 to R1	p_{21}					0.16	0.055
Log marginal likelihood		Laplace	−897.80	Laplace	−1112.00	Laplace	−1063.00

Note: For the financial friction parameters, we use the same prior as for the other exogenous shocks (stated in Table 2). For μ and $\bar{c}_{sp}$, we use a normal distribution with means 0.25 and 1.00 and standard deviations 0.10 and 0.50, respectively. Finally, for ν we use a beta distribution with mean 0.50 and standard deviation 0.20. The "Precrisis sample" neglects the presence of the ZLB and is estimated on data up to 2007Q4, whereas the "Endogenous ZLB duration" imposes the ZLB as described in Section 5.1, and is estimated up to 2014Q2. "Endog. ZLB dur. with regime switch" also imposes the ZLB, but allows μ to vary stochastically between a low (μ_1) and high (μ_2) value. For μ_1 and μ_2, we use a normal distribution with means 0.025 and 0.25, and standard deviations 0.01 and 0.10, respectively. For the transition probabilities p_{12} and p_{21}, we use a beta distribution with means 0.10 and 0.30 and standard deviations 0.05 and 0.10, respectively.

The direct comparison of the marginal likelihood with the baseline model is complicated because the financial frictions model (FF model henceforth) has an additional observable in the form of the Baa-Aaa spread. When we estimate the FF-model without this additional observable, the log marginal likelihood improves by a factor of 10 when no additional shock is considered and by a factor of 20 when the net worth shock is retained. With a posterior mode for $\mu = 0.2$ in this variant of the model, the estimated sensitivity of the spread to the net worth ratio in this model is much higher, ie, 0.08, or 0.32 in annualized terms. This result is more supportive for an important endogenous amplification effect of the standard shocks through the net worth channel (see also De Graeve (2008) for a similar result). This observation suggests that the use of the Baa-Aaa spread as an observable for the external finance premium in the model can be too restrictive. Baa-Aaa spread is only one specific measure for default risk, and the cost of credit for firms is determined by various risks and constraints in the financial sector.[al]

Not surprisingly, when we evaluate the performance of the FF-model for the complete sample including the 2008Q4–2009Q1 crisis period, the monitoring cost parameter μ and the implied elasticity of the spread to the net-worth ratio doubles. Perhaps surprisingly, the standard error of the exogenous net-worth shock is substantially lower, 0.19 vs 0.27 in the model estimated on precrisis data. We interpret this finding to imply that the endogenous amplification becomes more important when including the crisis period in the estimation sample. As we also impose the ZLB constraint in the estimation of this model, the estimated nominal wage and price stickiness is again very high (0.83 and 0.84, respectively) so that all the expected policy shocks that are required for the model to respect the ZLB constraint are positive. It is also striking that in this full-sample model, the estimated fraction of the wage bill that requires external financing is substantially higher than in the precrisis version, supporting the argument in Christiano et al. (2015) that this channel was important during crisis. The magnitude of this cost channel increases from 0.33 to 0.64, but in both models the uncertainty in the posterior distribution for this parameter is very high. These two observations, the time variation in the role of financial frictions and the potential role of the cost channel for the inflation dynamics, are discussed in more detail below.

5.3.1 A Regime Switching Model with Occasionally More Severe Financial Frictions

Precrisis DSGE models typically neglected the role of financial frictions. This additional transmission mechanism was considered nonvital for forecasting output and inflation during the great moderation period, and by Occam's razor arguments this mechanism was typically left out. However, as our discussion of the in-sample innovations illustrated, there was already strong evidence in our estimated precrisis model for occasionally big

[al] Gilchrist et al. (2009) and Gilchrist and Zakrajsek (2012) present alternative indicators of the default spread that have a stronger predictive power for economic activity than the Baa-Aaa spread.

disturbances that seemed to be highly correlated with financial spreads and return indicators. When looking at these results from a broader perspective that also gives appropriate attention to the potential risks around the central banks forecast, these outliers should not be disregarded. A linear Gaussian approach is not the most efficient framework for handling these issues. The instability in the estimated parameters of our FF-model depending on the estimation sample clearly illustrates these limitations. To more efficiently capture the time-varying relevance of the financial frictions in our model, we therefore consider here a Markov switching setup in which the constraints from the financial frictions can become much more binding occasionally.

In our Regime Switching Financial Friction model (RS-FF), we allow for two possible regimes: one regime (high-FF) with a high monitoring costs—implying a high sensitivity of the spread to the net worth position—and another regime (low-FF) with a low monitoring costs and low sensitivity of spread to leverage.[am] The estimation results for this model is reported last in Table 9, and the data prefer this RS-FF setting compared to the linear FF-model as shown by the gain in the log marginal likelihood of more than 30 in the precrisis context (not shown) and around 50 in the sample with the recent crisis.[an] The transition probabilities and the regime-specific μ parameter are given by:

$$Q_{FF}\begin{pmatrix}\text{low}\\ \text{high}\end{pmatrix} = \begin{bmatrix}0.96 & 0.16\\ 0.04 & 0.84\end{bmatrix} \quad \mu_{FF}\begin{pmatrix}\text{low}\\ \text{high}\end{pmatrix} = \begin{bmatrix}0.029\\ 0.084\end{bmatrix}.$$

The estimation results indicate that the elasticity of the spread to the leverage ratio varies between the two regimes by a factor of 2.7. As shown in Fig. 11, the high-FF regime is active mainly around the two recession periods in the 1970s, and its probability increases slightly during all recessions. When evaluated over the more recent period the probability of the high-FF regime starts to rise early in 2008 and remains active during the financial crisis in 2009, but quickly returns to the low-FF regime after 2009. The higher marginal likelihood is due to the time-varying volatility in the spread: in the high-FF regime, the financial friction is strongly binding and the spread reacts more than twice as strong to the leverage ratio. The impact of shocks on investment is also higher but the magnitude of the amplification is moderate up to a factor of 1.5 maximum. The expected period-by-period persistence of the high-FF regime is limited (0.84) and this reduces the impact of spread increases on the discounted value of future expected returns on investment.

As evidenced in Fig. 12, the central forecast of the single-regime precrisis FF-model, conditional on data up to 2008Q3 is completely missing the magnitude of the 2008Q4

[am] Christiano et al. (2014) focus instead on the distribution of the idiosyncratic productivity risk as the source for time-varying financial frictions. Levin et al. (2004) identify the time variation in the bankruptcy cost parameter, the equivalent of our monitoring cost, as the source for the counter-cyclical external premium behavior.

[an] Suh and Walker (2016) also finds support for time-variation in parameters governing financial frictions.

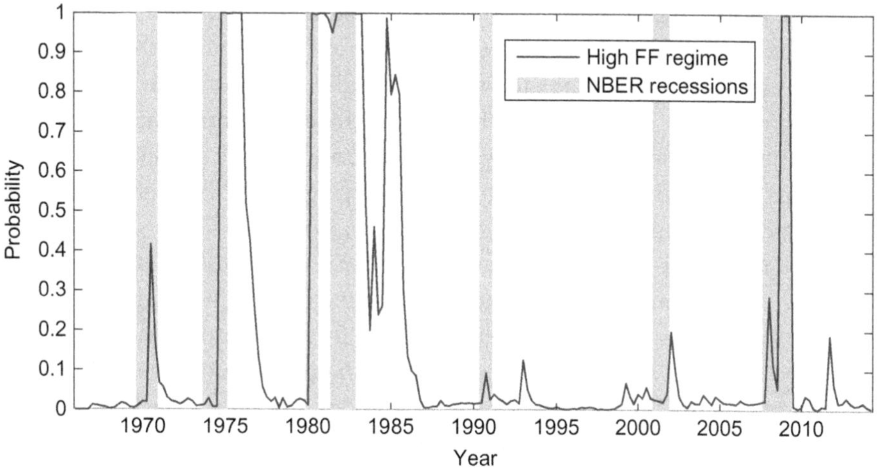

Fig. 11 Markov process in the financial frictions model.

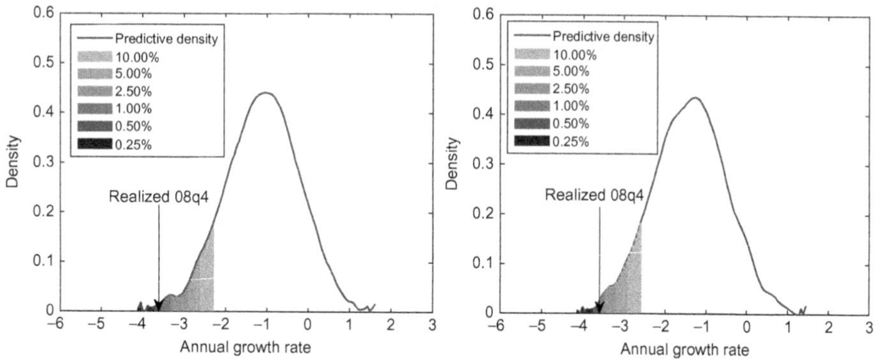

Fig. 12 Distributions for output growth (four-quarter change) in 2008Q4 given state in 2008Q3 in financial friction models with constant parameters (left panel) vs regime switching (right panel).

downturn just as the benchmark SW07-model without financial frictions. By comparing the no-financial friction model—left panel in Fig. 10—with the constant parameter FF-model—left panel in Fig. 12, we see that the distribution around the FF-forecast is more disperse due to the extra volatility that is generated by the spread and the additional net worth shock. As a result, the extreme negative output growth realization of 2008Q4 now falls within the 0.25% interval of the predictive density, which is some improvement relative to the baseline model. The precrisis RS-FF model, shown in the right panel in Fig. 12, further improves on this result because the probability of being in the high friction regime increased in 2008Q3 (56% against an unconditional probability of 20%) and this introduces a high degree of skewness in the predictive density of the spread. While the precrisis FF-model predicts a 1% upper tail for the expected spread above 2.3 percentage points in 2008Q4, this becomes as high as 3 percentage points in the RS-FF model. The probability of the observed 2008Q4 output growth outcome now lies around the 0.5% tail interval, which is still small but at least the *ex post* realized event obtains some nonzero probability in the predictive density. This result indicates that if we appropriately could integrate the nonlinear accelerator dynamics from financial frictions in our DSGE models we may obtain a more realistic predictive density that resembles these from the reduced form time-varying volatility models such as our RS-volatility example in Section 5.2.

Given the important role of the spread in the short run forecast, it is also informative to show how a conditional forecast, conditional on the timely observation of the spread, performs in the crisis period. Therefore, we make a forecast conditional on the 2008Q3 state of the economy as filtered by the precrisis FF-model but now we also provide the model with the information that the spread increased to the exceptionally high observed level of 3.02 percentage points in 2008Q4 (from 1.55 percentage points in 2008Q3). This conditioning is plausible in real time as the spread already in the beginning of the fourth quarter in 2008 (mid-October) had reached 3 percentage points. Fig. 13 shows the unconditional (left panel) and conditional (right panel) forecast distributions for GDP growth in 2008Q4. As seen from the figure, the forecast conditional on the timely information from the spread display a median prediction for annual GDP growth of −2.11% in 2008Q4 and −1.92% in 2009Q1 (not shown), which should to be compared to the observed −3.61% and −4.42% in the actual data and unconditional forecast of −1.05% (left panel in the figure) and 0.06% (not shown).

In the RS-FF model, the result depends very much on the regime in which the economy is finding itself in 2008Q3: the impact of conditioning on the spread is most disturbing when the economy is in the low friction regime. Extreme high spreads are very difficult to reconcile with the low friction regime, with its low elasticity of spread to leverage, and therefore the spreads are translated in huge negative shocks in net worth

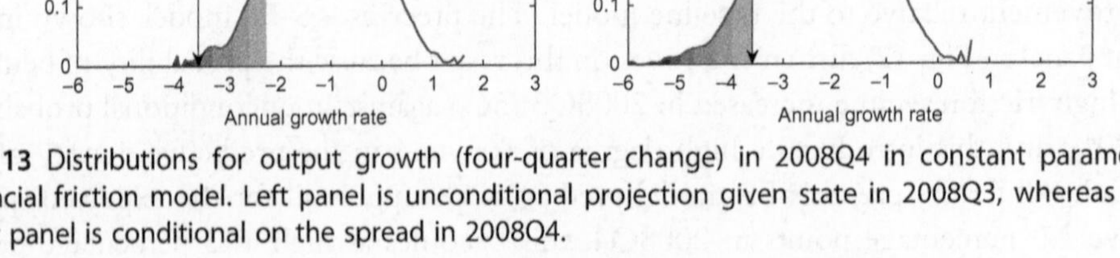

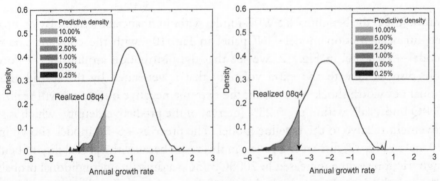

Fig. 13 Distributions for output growth (four-quarter change) in 2008Q4 in constant parameter financial friction model. Left panel is unconditional projection given state in 2008Q3, whereas the right panel is conditional on the spread in 2008Q4.

and/or risk premiums which then also result in worse output growth predictions of −2.53% and −3.01% in 2008Q4 and 2009Q1.[ao] The real-time information on the spread and the presence of the additional transmission mechanism allow the FF-model to considerably improve the accuracy of the central forecast in the crisis period. Our results confirm the findings of Del Negro and Schorfheide (2013), who also compare the predictive performance of a standard SW setup with an augmented SW-FF model. They observe that the relative performance of the two models changes over time. On average the model without financial frictions generates more accurate forecasts, but during the recent financial crisis a SW-FF model—that also exploits the timely information on spread and interest rate—produces better forecasts for output and inflation. Del Negro et al. (2014) built on these results and develop a new method for combining predictive densities from recursively estimated models using time-varying weights. As in our RS-approach, this dynamic linear prediction pooling relies on weights that follow an exogenous process. The next step in this research agenda would be to endogenize the occurrence of financial stress periods during which constraints are reinforced and additional feedback mechanisms are activated.[ap]

5.3.2 The Cost Channel of Financial Spreads and Inflation Dynamics

In Section 4.2, when we discussed the economic interpretation of the great recession through the lense of the baseline SW07-model, we observed that the model requires a series of positive mark up shocks to explain the maintained inflation rate during the period of slow recovery and persistent negative output gap. These positive mark up shocks are necessary despite the high estimate of nominal stickiness in price and wage setting. This trend towards more nominal stickiness was already present in the subsample estimates presented by SW07. The high nominal stickiness also plays a crucial role in the explanation of the recent inflation dynamics by Del Negro et al. (2015b) and Fratto and Uhlig (2014). These positive markup shocks disappear completely in our version of the SW07-model, in which we implement the ZLB, and that features an even higher degree of nominal stickiness. The question arises whether this estimated stickiness parameter should be interpreted effectively as a sign of pure nominal stickiness in the price setting practice or whether it reflects some other mechanism that lowered the responsiveness of inflation to the slack in production capacity.

[ao] This somewhat counter-intuitive result of the RS-FF model is related to the nature of the conditional forecast exercise: conditioning on a given spread observation has larger effects when that observation deviates more from the baseline unconditional forecast. The gain from the RS-FF model is precisely that the unconditional forecast will show larger dispersion in the high-FF regime and lower dispersion in the low-FF regime.

[ap] Various approaches have been developed in this context: Guerrieri and Iacoviello (2013) with occasionally binding constraints, Dewachter and Wouters (2014) with third order nonlinear approximations and Bocola (2013) with a combination of occasionally binding constraints and nonlinear risk premiums.

As noted by Christiano et al. (2015), one mechanism that might contribute to this inflation resilience, in particular during periods of increased financial constraints and high financing costs, is the cost channel. Firms that are financially constrained and that must finance their operations with expensive external capital can experience an increase in their marginal production costs if these financing costs dominate the influence of the other cost components. Related to this cost channel, firms can have other arguments to keep their prices high during periods of financial constraints: high markups can be necessary for firms to generate sufficient cash flow or firms might be forced by their financing constraints to give up on market share (see Gilchrist et al., 2015). Note that this cost channel also plays a crucial role in the explanation of the inflation inertia following a monetary policy shock in Christiano et al. (2005).

Our FF-model contains a parameter that controls the strength of the cost channel. This parameter reflects the fraction of the wage bill that firms have to finance with credit. In this setup, we assume that the external finance premium is also affecting the cost for these intertemporal loans of the firms. In the precrisis model, this fraction of the wage bill on which the financial cost applies is estimated to be quite low (0.33) and the posterior distribution has a large uncertainty margin around this mode. This parameter increases to 0.63 in the complete sample estimation, still with a large uncertainty, but at least there is some indication that the cost channel was more relevant during the recent crisis. To examine the potency of this channel in our model, Fig. 14 plots the impulse response functions of the three shocks that directly affect the external financing costs—the monetary policy shock, the exogenous risk premium shock, and the wealth shock—on the marginal cost and inflation for the two extreme values (zero and one) of the cost channel parameter. Given the large estimation uncertainty around the magnitude of the cost channel parameter, these two extreme values are not completely unlikely and their relevance can probably change depending on the nature of the financial shocks and the constraints. We plot the results for both the precrisis model, with a moderate degree of nominal stickiness, and the full sample ZLB model with a high degree of stickiness.

In both model versions and for all three shocks, it is obvious that marginal cost behaves quite different if the cost channel is fully active compared to a situation in which the cost channel is completely absent. The presence of the cost channel implies that the marginal cost increases at least during the first quarters following each of these shocks. The persistence of this positive effect depends on the type of shock and tends to be shorter for the risk-premium shock and most persistent for the net-worth shock.

The impact on inflation can differ substantially depending on the volatility of the cost shock and on the persistence of the shock relative to the degree of nominal stickiness which determines the degree of forward-lookingness in price setting. In the precrisis model, the exogenous risk-premium shock is highly volatile, but short lived. Combined with the moderate degree of stickiness the cost channel drastically changes the response of inflation to this shock. Inflation rises on impact due to the high risk-premium component

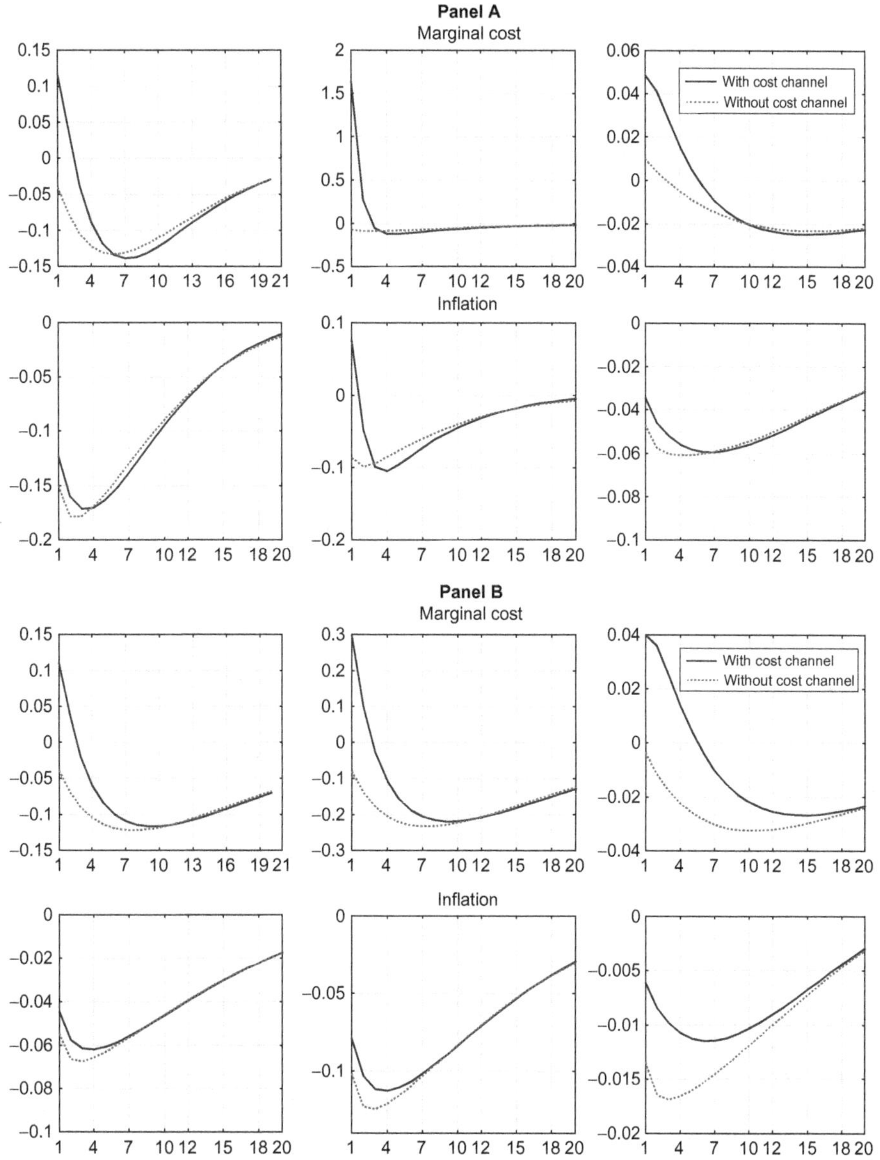

Fig. 14 The transmission of financial shocks: monetary policy (left column); risk premium (middle column) and net-worth (right column) shock. Panel A: Precrisis model. Panel B: Endogenous ZLB model.

in the financing costs, but the effect is very short lived. In the model with ZLB constraint—with more stickiness—the price setting is more forward looking and the persistence of the shock is crucial. In such a context, the smooth inflation process is dependent on the long-run expected marginal cost. In this case, only the net worth shock has a sufficiently persistent effect on the financing cost to exert a positive impact on inflation; the temporarily high risk free rate and risk premium shock are missing sufficient persistence to have a substantial impact on the inflation dynamics.

From this impulse response analysis, it follows that the cost channel can contribute to the slow response of inflation in a financial crisis context. When the external finance shock for firms are sufficiently high and/or sufficiently persistent, as it is the case for a net worth shock that is expected to have long lasting effects on the financing costs, this inflationary pressure from the cost channel can be quantitatively important. These results illustrate that the financial crisis should not necessarily be viewed as a purely negative aggregate demand shock without an impact on the supply side of the economy. With both aggregate demand and aggregate supply shifting inward by the financial shock, inflation should not necessarily be expected to react that much in a financial crisis situation.

6. STATE OF MACROECONOMIC MODELING: CRITICAL ASSESSMENT AND OUTLOOK

In this section, we conclude by discussing both "new" and "old" challenges for macroeconomic models. As evidenced earlier, the financial crisis has generated new challenges for macroeconomic models used at central banks. When the Great Recession and the financial crisis are included in the estimation sample, we must adjust the specification and empirical estimation strategy of our policy models. Our chapter provides some avenues for moving in that direction, and suggests that the gains of doing so may be considerable. Our suggested modifications have in common of moving away from the standard linear Gaussian setup by including time variation in exogenous and endogenous disturbances. An important short-cut, however, in our adopted Markow Switching framework is that the regime changes are modeled as exogenous events and hence, unrelated to the conduct of policy. At this stage we therefore consider our extensions as a shortcut for truly endogenous nonlinear and state dependent propagation mechanisms. Further progress on the specification of nonlinear methods, solution and filtering techniques, as well as computational techniques, are ongoing for analyzing nonlinear integrated macrofinance models. Together with a broader set of observable variables, these models should allow us to more efficiently identify the nature of shocks, their transmission, and their implications for policy. At this stage, it is important that different theoretical frameworks should be exploited to formulate and validate alternative model specifications.

There were also well-known challenges for central bank models prior to the financial crisis, and they have not been mitigated by the evidence brought forward by the crisis.[aq]

[aq] For instance, the influential work of Del Negro et al. (2007) suggested that workhorse closed economy DSGE models suffered from misspecification problems. Adolfson et al. (2008) confirmed this finding for a standard open economy model.

The balanced growth and the stationarity assumptions provide discipline to the model forecasts, but these long term restrictions often conflict with the observed stochastic trends in many important macro ratios. This mismatch between the theoretical assumptions and the empirical properties can result in overestimation of the persistence in the endogenous frictions and exogenous shocks. It may also be necessary to reevaluate the forecast implications of full information and rational expectations in the models with alternative assumptions about information and expectations formation building on the seminal work of Evans and Honkapohja (2001), Sims (2003, 2010), and Woodford (2014).

Macro models necessarily abstract of many sector details. Recently, a lot of effort have been devoted to model the financial sector. In the standard Smets and Wouters (2007) model analyzed in this chapter, the risk premium shock combines the impact of credit supply conditions, risk aversion, anticipations about future policy actions and the effect of quantitative easing (QE) policies targeting yield curve or risk spreads. Integrating the analysis of financial markets explicitly into general equilibrium is hence of first-order importance, both for firms (the focus of our chapter) and households, eg, along the lines suggested by Iacoviello (2005) and Liu et al. (2013). Other models incorporate an active role for financial institutions in the credit supply process or the asset pricing functions: Christiano et al. (2003a, 2008, 2014), Gerali et al. (2010), and Gertler and Kiyotaki (2010) are inspiring examples. Innovative new macrofinance models, as in, eg, Brunnermeier and Sannikov (2014), He and Krishnamurthy (2012), and Mendoza (2010) suggest that strong endogenous risk and feedback channels between the real and the financial sectors can go a long way in explaining the change in volatility and correlations between tranquil and stress periods. A more explicit recognition of default in both the financial and nonfinancial private sectors as in Clerc et al. (2015) is also an important avenue.

However, other sectors of the economy also have very similar problems in that the exogenous shocks represent a large range of influences that might call for different policy responses depending on the specific underlying distortion or inefficiency. One obvious example is the labor market with very diverging underlying trends in labor participation at intensive and extensive margins, and with shocks and distortions affecting both the labor supply and demand conditions. More work is needed to examine in which dimensions the labor market implications of the standard New Keynesian sticky wage model analyzed by Galí et al. (2011) fall short relative to the data, and if recent work with a more elaborate labor market modeling (see, eg, Gertler et al., 2008; Christiano et al., 2010a; and Christiano et al., 2016) can remedy those shortcomings. Some prominent economists, like Kocherlakota (2009), have recently reiterated that incomplete insurance and heterogeneity in labor and product markets is key for understanding the propagation and welfare costs of business cycles. Thus, the representative agents framework preserved by Gertler et al. and Christiano et al. may not be sufficient in the end, although it represents a clear step forward relative to current generation of policy models.

In a world increasingly integrated through trade of goods and services and more globalized financial markets, policy models also need to be able to account for the impact of foreign shocks. Two old challenges for open economy models is to account for the high degree of observed comovement between real quantities (see, eg, Backus et al., 1992 and Justiniano and Preston, 2010), and the relationship between interest rate differentials and exchange rate movements (ie, the uncovered interest rate parity condition, see, eg, Eichenbaum and Evans, 1995 and Chaboud and Wright, 2005). A voluminous literature deals with these issues, but there is yet no consensus on the "solutions" to these challenges.[ar]

Another key challenge posed for macro models at use in central banks following the crisis is that they have to provide a framework where topical questions can be addressed. First, they have to provide a framework where the central bank can use both conventional monetary policy (manipulating short rates) and unconventional policies (large scale asset purchases (LSAPs) and QE) to affect the economy. A serious treatment of unconventional monetary policy in policy models seems to imply that we have to tackle one old key challenge in macro modeling, namely the failure of the expectations hypothesis (see, eg, Campbell and Shiller, 1991), in favor of environments where the expectations hypothesis does not necessarily hold. One theoretical framework consistent with the idea that large scale asset purchases can reduce term premiums for different maturities and put downward pressure on long-term yields is the theory of preferred habit, see, eg, Andrés et al. (2004) and Vayanos and Vila (2009). Extensions in this direction appear crucial for evaluating the unconventional monetary policy measures during the crisis. Second, apart from analyzing unconventional policies during the crisis, the aftermath of the crisis have brought a renewed focus on financial stability issues, which implies that we need to be able to integrate financial stability considerations into macro models traditionally used for monetary policy analysis only. This involves stress testing exercises and the creation of an environment with an effective role for various macroprudential tools. This requires a more realistic modeling of the interbank market as the one by Boissay et al. (2015). The "3D model" developed by Clerc et al. (2015) and IMF's GIMF model with banks (see Andrle et al., 2015) represent important steps in this direction. Unconventional monetary policy and macroprudential instruments have important distributional effects and this calls for sufficient heterogeneity among agents that are affected by these measures. As mentioned before, the actual and potential budgetary implications of these measures require an explicit modeling of the systematic fiscal reaction function.

[ar] The estimated open economy DSGE model developed by Adolfson et al. (2007b, 2008, 2011) which early on was integrated into operational use at the Riksbank (see Adolfson et al., 2007c) attempted to account for this by modifying the UIP condition following the insights in Duarte and Stockman (2005) and allowing for a common unitroot technology shock.

We believe the benchmark model analyzed in this chapter can serve as the starting point to analyze various extensions for topical questions and policy purposes. Specific model extensions combined with broader set of observed data should help us to better identify the various blocks. This applies equally for the financial, fiscal, labor market and the open economy blocks of the models. Bayesian methodology provides the tools to evaluate and combine these model predictions. In this endeavor, a challenge will be to keep the model size manageable by finding the most parsimonious ways to capture the necessary frictions and shocks, and to understand its implications as the models become increasingly complicated. To keep the models tractable, a critical decision point will be which frictions and shocks that are really needed in the core model, and which features that can be abstracted from in the core model and instead meaningfully analyzed in satellite models. Developing and maintaining empirically validated models with strong theoretical foundations is a daunting task ahead for policy making institutions, even the ones with the most resources.

APPENDICES

A. Linearized Model Representation

In this appendix, we summarize the log-linear equations of the basic SW07-model stated in Section 3. The complete model also includes the seven exogenous shocks $\varepsilon_t^a, \varepsilon_t^b, \varepsilon_t^i, \varepsilon_t^p, \varepsilon_t^w, \varepsilon_t^r$ and g_t, but their processes are not stated here as they were already shown in the main text. Consistent with the notation of the log-linearized *endogenous* variables $\widehat{x}_t = dx_t/x$, the exogenous shocks are denoted with a 'hat', ie, $\widehat{\varepsilon}_t = \ln \varepsilon_t$.

First, we have the consumption Euler equation:

$$\widehat{c}_t = \frac{1}{(1+\varkappa/\gamma)}\mathrm{E}_t\widehat{c}_{t+1} + \frac{\varkappa/\gamma}{(1+\varkappa/\gamma)}\widehat{c}_{t-1} - \frac{1-\varkappa/\gamma}{\sigma_c(1+\varkappa/\gamma)} (\widehat{R}_t - \mathrm{E}_t\widehat{\pi}_{t+1}) - \frac{(\sigma_c - 1)(w_*^h L/c_*)}{\sigma_c(1+\varkappa/\gamma)}(\mathrm{E}_t\widehat{L}_{t+1} - \widehat{L}_t) + \widehat{\varepsilon}_t^b, \tag{A.1}$$

where $\varkappa$ is the external habit parameter, σ_c the reciprocal of the intertemporal substitution elasticity, $w_*^h L/c_*$ the steady state nominal labor earnings to consumption ratio, and the exogenous risk premium shock $\widehat{\varepsilon}_t^b$ is rescaled so that it enters additive with a unit coefficient.

Next, we have the investment Euler equation:

$$\hat{i}_t = \frac{1}{(1+\overline{\beta}\gamma)}\left(\hat{i}_{t-1} + \overline{\beta}\gamma \mathrm{E}_t\hat{i}_{t+1} + \frac{1}{\gamma^2\varphi}\widehat{Q}_t^k\right) + \widehat{\varepsilon}_t^q, \tag{A.2}$$

where $\overline{\beta} = \beta\gamma^{-\sigma_c}$, φ is the investment adjustment cost, and the investment specific technology shock $\widehat{\varepsilon}_t^q$ has been rescaled so that it enters linearly with a unit coefficient.

Additionally $i_1 = 1/(1+\beta)$ and $i_2 = i_1/\psi$, where β is the discount factor and ψ is the elasticity of the capital adjustment cost function.

The price of capital is determined by:

$$\widehat{Q}_t^k = -(\widehat{R}_t - E_t\widehat{\pi}_{t+1}) + q_1 E_t r_{t+1}^k + (1-q_1)E_t Q_{t+1}^k + \frac{\sigma_c(1+\varkappa/\gamma)}{1-\varkappa/\gamma}\widehat{\varepsilon}_t^b, \tag{A.3}$$

where $q_1 \equiv r_*^k/(r_*^k + (1-\delta))$ in which r_*^k is the steady state rental rate to capital, δ the depreciation rate, and $\widehat{\varepsilon}_t^b$ is multiplied by $\frac{\sigma_c(1+\varkappa/\gamma)}{1-\varkappa/\gamma}$ reflecting the rescaling of this shock in the consumption Euler equation (A.1).

Fourth, we have the optimal condition for the capital utilization rate $\hat{u}_t$:

$$\hat{u}_t = (1-\psi)/\psi \widehat{r}_t^k, \tag{A.4}$$

where ψ is the elasticity of the capital utilization cost function and capital services used in production $(\widehat{k}_t)$ is defined as:

$$\widehat{k}_t = \hat{u}_t + \widehat{\bar{k}}_{t-1}, \tag{A.5}$$

where $\widehat{\bar{k}}_{t-1}$ is the physical capital stock which evolves according to the capital accumulation equation:

$$\widehat{\bar{k}}_t = \kappa_1 \ \widehat{\bar{k}}_{t-1} + (1-\kappa_1)\hat{i}_t + \kappa_2 \widehat{\varepsilon}_t^q \tag{A.6}$$

with $\kappa_1 = (1-(i_*/\bar{k}_*)$ and $\kappa_2 = (i_*/\bar{k}_*)\gamma^2\varphi$.

The following optimal capital/labor input condition also holds:

$$\widehat{k}_t = \widehat{w}_t - \ \widehat{r}_t^k + \widehat{L}_t, \tag{A.7}$$

where $\widehat{w}_t$ is the real wage.

The log-linearized production function is given by:

$$\widehat{y}_t = \phi_p \ (\alpha\widehat{k}_t + (1-\alpha)\widehat{L}_t + \widehat{\varepsilon}_t^a), \tag{A.8}$$

in which ϕ_p is the fixed costs of production corresponding to the gross price markup in the steady state, and $\widehat{\varepsilon}_t^a$ is the exogenous TFP process.

Aggregate demand must equal aggregate supply:

$$\widehat{y}_t = \frac{c_*}{y_*}\widehat{c}_t + \frac{i_*}{y_*}\hat{i}_t + g_t + \frac{r_*^k k_*}{y_*}\hat{u}_t, \tag{A.9}$$

where g_t represents the exogenous demand component.

Next, we have the following log-linearized price-setting equation with dynamic indexation ι_p:

$$\widehat{\pi}_t - \iota_p\widehat{\pi}_{t-1} = \pi_1\left(E_t\widehat{\pi}_{t+1} - \iota_p\widehat{\pi}_t\right) - \pi_2\widehat{\mu}_t^p + \widehat{\varepsilon}_t^p, \tag{A.10}$$

where $\pi_1 = \beta$, $\pi_2 = (1 - \xi_p\beta)(1 - \xi_p)/[\xi_p(1 + (\phi_p - 1)\epsilon_p)]$, $1 - \xi_p$ is the probability of each firm being able to reoptimize the price each period, ϵ_p is the curvature of the aggregator function Eq. (2), and the markup shock $\widehat{\varepsilon}_t^p$ has been rescaled to enter with a unit coefficient. The price markup $\widehat{\mu}_t^p$ equals the inverse of the real marginal cost, $\widehat{\mu}_t^p = -\widehat{mc}_t$, which in turn is given by:

$$\widehat{mc}_t = (1-\alpha)\ \widehat{w}_t^{real} + \alpha\ \widehat{r}_t^k - \widehat{\varepsilon}_t^a. \tag{A.11}$$

We also have the following wage-setting equation allowing for dynamic indexation of wages for nonoptimizing households:

$$\begin{aligned}(1+\overline{\beta}\gamma)\widehat{w}_t^{real} - \widehat{w}_{t-1}^{real} - \overline{\beta}\gamma \mathrm{E}_t\widehat{w}_{t+1}^{real} = {} & \frac{(1-\xi_w\overline{\beta}\gamma)(1-\xi_w)}{[\xi_w(1+(\phi_w-1)\epsilon_w)]} \\ & \left(\frac{1}{1-\varkappa/\gamma}\widehat{c}_t - \frac{\varkappa/\gamma}{1-\varkappa/\gamma}\widehat{c}_{t-1} + \sigma_l\widehat{L}_t - \widehat{w}_t\right) \\ & -(1+\overline{\beta}\gamma\iota_w)\widehat{\pi}_t + \iota_w\widehat{\pi}_{t-1} + \overline{\beta}\gamma \mathrm{E}_t\widehat{\pi}_{t+1} + \widehat{\varepsilon}_t^w,\end{aligned} \tag{A.12}$$

where ϕ_w the gross wage markup, $1 - \xi_p$ is the probability of each household being able to reoptimize its wage each period, ϵ_w is the curvature of the aggregator function (eq. 7), and σ_l determines the elasticity of labor supply given σ_c (see Eq. (9)). The exogenous wage markup shock $\widehat{\varepsilon}_t^w$ has been rescaled to enter linearly with a unit coefficient.

Finally, we have the monetary policy rule:

$$\widehat{R}_t = \rho_R\widehat{R}_{t-1} + (1-\rho_R)\left(r_\pi\widehat{\pi}_t + r_y\widehat{y}_t^{gap} + r_{\Delta y}\Delta\widehat{y}_t^{gap}\right) + \widehat{\varepsilon}_t^r, \tag{A.13}$$

where $\widehat{y}_t^{gap} = \widehat{y}_t - \widehat{y}_t^{pot}$, or in words: the difference between actual output and the output prevailing in the flexible price and wage economy in absence of the inefficient price and wage markup shocks. We solve for $\widehat{y}_t^{pot}$ by setting $\xi_p = \xi_w = 0$ (or arbitrary close to nil) and removing $\widehat{\varepsilon}_t^w$ and $\widehat{\varepsilon}_t^p$ from the system of equations given by (A.1)–(A.13). Note that when we impose the ZLB on the model, Eq. (A.13) is replaced by Eq. (17).

B. The ZLB Algorithm and the Likelihood Function

This appendix provides some details on the ZLB algorithm we use and how the likelihood function takes the ZLB into account. For more details on the ZLB algorithm we refer to Hebden et al. (2010), whereas more details on the computation of the likelihood is provided by Jesper et al. (2016).

B.1 The ZLB Algorithm

The DSGE model can be written in the following practical state-space form,

$$\begin{bmatrix} X_{t+1} \\ Hx_{t+1|t} \end{bmatrix} = A\begin{bmatrix} X_t \\ x_t \end{bmatrix} + Bi_t + \begin{bmatrix} C \\ 0 \end{bmatrix}\varepsilon_{t+1}. \quad \text{(B.1)}$$

Here, X_t is an n_X-vector of *predetermined* variables in period t (where the period is a quarter) and x_t is a n_x-vector of *forward-looking* variables. The i_t is generally a n_i-vector of (policy) *instruments* but in the cases examined here it is a scalar—the central bank's policy rate—giving $n_i = 1$. The ε_t is an n_ε-vector of independent and identically distributed shocks with mean zero and covariance matrix I_{n_ε}, while A, B, C, and H are matrices of the appropriate dimension. Lastly $x_{t+\tau|t}$ denotes $\mathrm{E}_t x_{t+\tau}$, ie, the rational expectation of $x_{t+\tau}$ conditional on information available in period t. The forward-looking variables and the instruments are the *nonpredetermined* variables.[as]

The variables are measured as differences from steady state values, in which case their unconditional means are zero. In addition, the elements of the matrices A, B, C, and H are considered fixed and known.

We let i_t^* denote the policy rate when we disregard the ZLB. We call it the *unrestricted* policy rate. We let i_t denote the actual or *restricted* policy rate that satisfies the ZLB,

$$i_t + \bar{\imath} \geq 0,$$

where $\bar{\imath} > 0$ denotes the steady state level of the policy rate and we use the convention that i_t and i_t^* are expressed as deviations from the steady state level. The ZLB can therefore be written as

$$i_t + \bar{\imath} = \max\{i_t^* + \bar{\imath}, 0\}. \quad \text{(B.2)}$$

We assume the unrestricted policy rate follows the (possibly reduced form) unrestricted linear policy rule,

$$i_t^* = f_X X_t + f_x x_t, \quad \text{(B.3)}$$

where f_X and f_x are row vectors of dimension n_X and n_x, respectively. From (B.2) it then follows that the restricted policy rate is given by:

$$i_t + \bar{\imath} = \max\{f_X X_t + f_x x_t + \bar{\imath}, 0\}. \quad \text{(B.4)}$$

Consider now a situation in period $t \geq 0$ where the ZLB may be binding in the current or the next finite number T periods but not beyond period $t + T$. That is, the ZLB constraint

$$i_{t+\tau} + \bar{\imath} \geq 0, \quad \tau = 0, 1, \ldots, T \quad \text{(B.5)}$$

may be binding for some $\tau \leq T$, but we assume that it is not binding for $\tau > T$,

[as] A variable is predetermined if its one-period-ahead prediction error is an exogenous stochastic process (Klein, 2000). For (B.1), the one-period-ahead prediction error of the predetermined variables is the stochastic vector $C\varepsilon_{t+1}$.

$$i_{t+\tau} + \bar{i} > 0, \qquad \tau > T.$$

We will implement the ZLB with anticipated shocks to the unrestricted policy rule, using the techniques of Laséen and Svensson (2011). Thus, we let the restricted and unrestricted policy rate in each period t satisfy

$$i_{t+\tau,t} = i^{*}_{t+\tau,t} + z_{t+\tau,t}, \tag{B.6}$$

for $\tau \geq 0$. The ZLB policy rule in (B.4)—as we explain in further detail later—implies that all current and future anticipated shocks $z_{t+\tau,t}$ in (B.6) must be nonnegative, and that $z_{t,t}$ is strictly positive in periods when the ZLB is binding.

Disregarding for the moment when z_t are nonnegative, we follow Laséen and Svensson (2011) and call the stochastic variable z_t the deviation and let the $(T+1)$-vector $z^t \equiv (z_{t,t}, z_{t+1,t}, \ldots, z_{t+T,t})'$ denote a projection in period t of future realizations $z_{t+\tau}$, $\tau = 0, 1, \ldots, T$, of the deviation. Furthermore, we assume that the deviation satisfies

$$z_t = \eta_{t,t} + \sum_{s=1}^{T} \eta_{t,t-s}$$

for $T \geq 0$, where $\eta^t \equiv (\eta_{t,t}, \eta_{t+1,t}, \ldots, \eta_{t+T,t})'$ is a $(T+1)$-vector realized in the beginning of period t. For $T = 0$, the deviation is given by $z_t = \eta_t$. For $T > 0$, the deviation is given by the moving-average process

$$z_{t+\tau,t+1} = z_{t+\tau,t} + \eta_{t+\tau,t+1}$$
$$z_{t+\tau+T+1,t+1} = \eta_{t+T+1,t+1},$$

where $\tau = 1, \ldots, T$. It follows that the dynamics of the projection of the deviation can be written more compactly as

$$z^{t+1} = A_z z^t + \eta^{t+1}, \tag{B.7}$$

where the $(T+1) \times (T+1)$ matrix A_z is defined as

$$A_z \equiv \begin{bmatrix} 0_{T\times 1} & I_T \\ 0 & 0_{1\times T} \end{bmatrix}.$$

Hence, z^t is the projection in period t of current and future deviations, and the innovation η^t can be interpreted as the new information received in the beginning of period t about those deviations.

Let us now combine the model, (B.1), the dynamics of the deviation, (B.7), the unrestricted policy rule, (B.3), and the relation (B.6). Taking the starting period to be $t = 0$, we can then write the combined model as

$$\begin{bmatrix} \widetilde{X}_{t+1} \\ \widetilde{H}\widetilde{x}_{t+1|t} \end{bmatrix} = \tilde{A} \begin{bmatrix} \widetilde{X}_t \\ \widetilde{x}_t \end{bmatrix} + \begin{bmatrix} C & 0_{n_X\times(T+1)} \\ 0_{(T+1)\times n_\varepsilon} & I_{T+1} \\ 0_{(n_x+2)\times n_\varepsilon} & 0_{(n_x+2)\times(T+1)} \end{bmatrix} \begin{bmatrix} \varepsilon_{t+1} \\ \eta^{t+1} \end{bmatrix} \tag{B.8}$$

for $t \geq 0$, where

$$\tilde{X}_t \equiv \begin{bmatrix} X_t \\ z^t \end{bmatrix}, \quad \tilde{x}_t \equiv \begin{bmatrix} x_t \\ i_t^* \\ i_t \end{bmatrix}, \quad \tilde{H} \equiv \begin{bmatrix} H & 0_{n_x \times 1} & 0_{n_x \times 1} \\ 0_{1 \times n_x} & 0 & 0 \\ 0_{1 \times n_x} & 0 & 0 \end{bmatrix}.$$

Under the standard assumption of the saddle-point property (that the number of eigenvalues of $\tilde{A}$ with modulus larger than unity equals the number of nonpredetermined variables, here $n_x + 2$), the system of difference equations (B.8) has a unique solution and there exist unique matrices M and F returned by the Klein (2000) algorithm such that the solution can be written:

$$\tilde{x}_t = F\tilde{X}_t \equiv \begin{bmatrix} F_x \\ F_{i^*} \\ F_i \end{bmatrix} \tilde{X}_t, \tilde{X}_{t+1} = M\tilde{X}_t + \begin{bmatrix} C\varepsilon_{t+1} \\ \eta^{t+1} \end{bmatrix} \equiv \begin{bmatrix} M_{XX} & M_{Xz} \\ 0_{(T+1)\times nx} & A_z \end{bmatrix} \begin{bmatrix} X_t \\ z^t \end{bmatrix} + \begin{bmatrix} C\varepsilon_{t+1} \\ \eta^{t+1} \end{bmatrix},$$

for $t \geq 0$, and where X_0 in $\tilde{X}_0 \equiv (X_0', z^{0\prime})'$ is given but the projections of the deviation z^0 and the innovations η^t for $t \geq 1$ (and thereby z^t for $t \geq 1$) remain to be determined. They will be determined such that the ZLB is satisfied, ie, Eq. (B.4) holds. Thus, the *policy-rate projection* is given by

$$i_{t+\tau,t} = F_i M^\tau \begin{bmatrix} X_t \\ z^t \end{bmatrix} \tag{B.9}$$

for $\tau \geq 0$ and for given X_t and z^t.

We will now show how to determine the $(T+1)$-vector $z^t \equiv (z_t, z_{t+1,t}, \ldots, z_{t+T,t})'$, ie, the projection of the deviation, such that policy-rate projection satisfies the ZLB restriction (B.5) and the policy rule (B.4).

When the ZLB restriction (B.5) is disregarded or not binding, the policy-rate projection in period t is given by

$$i_{t+\tau,t} = F_i M^\tau \begin{bmatrix} X_t \\ 0_{(T+1)\times 1} \end{bmatrix}, \quad \tau \geq 0. \tag{B.10}$$

The policy-rate projection disregarding the ZLB hence depends on the initial state of the economy in period t, represented by the vector of predetermined variables X_t. If the ZLB is disregarded, or not binding for any $\tau \geq 0$, the projections of the restricted and unrestricted policy rates will be the same,

$$i_{t+\tau,t} = i_{t+\tau,t}^* = f_X X_{t+\tau,t} + f_x x_{t+\tau,t}, \quad \tau \geq 0.$$

Assume now that the policy-rate projection according to (B.10) violates the ZLB for one or several periods, that is,

$$i_{t+\tau,t} + \bar{\imath} < 0, \quad \text{for some } \tau \text{ in the interval } 0 \leq \tau \leq T. \tag{B.11}$$

In order to satisfy the ZLB, we then want to find a projection of the deviation z^t such that the policy-rate projection satisfies (B.5) and

$$i_{t+\tau,t} + \bar{\imath} = \max\{i^*_{t+\tau,t} + \bar{\imath}, 0\} = \max\{f_X X_{t+\tau,t} + f_x x_{t+\tau,t} + \bar{\imath}, 0\} \tag{B.12}$$

for $\tau \geq 0$. This requires that the projection of the deviation satisfies a nonnegativity constraint

$$z_{t+\tau,t} \geq 0, \quad \tau \geq 0, \tag{B.13}$$

and that the policy-rate projection and the projection of the deviation satisfies the complementary-slackness condition

$$(i_{t+\tau,t} + \bar{\imath}) z_{t+\tau,t} = 0, \quad \tau \geq 0. \tag{B.14}$$

Notice that the complementary-slackness condition implies that $z_{t+\tau,t} = 0$ if $i_{t+\tau,t} + \bar{\imath} > 0$.

For given X_t, we now proceed under the presumption that there exists a unique projection of the deviation z^t that satisfies (B.9) and (B.12)–(B.14).[at] We call this projection of the deviation and the corresponding policy-rate projection the *equilibrium*projection. This projection of the deviation either has all elements equal to zero (in which case the ZLB is not binding for any period) or has some elements positive and other elements zero. Let

$$\mathcal{T}_t \equiv \{0 \leq \tau \leq T \mid z_{t+\tau,t} > 0\}$$

denote the set of periods for which the projection of the deviation are positive in equilibrium.

For each $\tau \in \mathcal{T}_t$, the solution will satisfy

$$i_{t+\tau,t} + \bar{\imath} = F_i M^\tau \begin{bmatrix} X_t \\ z^t \end{bmatrix} + \bar{\imath} = 0 \quad \text{for} \quad \tau \in \mathcal{T}_t. \tag{B.15}$$

Let $n_{\mathcal{T}_t}$ denote the number of elements of $\mathcal{T}_t$, that is, the number of periods that the ZLB binds. The equation system (B.15) then has $n_{\mathcal{T}}$ equations to determine the $n_{\mathcal{T}}$ elements of z^t that are positive. From the system (B.15), it is clear that the solution for z^t and the set $\mathcal{T}_t$ will depend on X_t as well as the initial situation, and thereby also on the initial innovation ε_t. For other periods (that is $\tau \notin \mathcal{T}_t$), the ZLB will not be binding and the elements in z^t will be zero. The equation system (B.15) and the periods in the set $\mathcal{T}_t$ hence refer to the periods where the ZLB is *strictly* binding, that is, when $z_{t+\tau,t}$ is positive. Furthermore, it is important to notice that the set of periods τ in (B.11), for which the policy-rate projection (B.10) violates the ZLB, is not necessarily the same as the set of periods $\mathcal{T}_t$ for which the ZLB is strictly binding *in equilibrium*. That is because the projections of

[at] This assumption is discussed in further detail in Hebden et al. (2010).

the predetermined and forward-looking variables $X_{t+\tau,t}$ and $x_{t+\tau,t}$, that determine the unrestricted policy rate differ, depending on whether z^t is zero or not. This means that the whole policy-rate path is affected when the ZLB is imposed.

The difficulty in imposing the ZLB is to find the set $\mathcal{T}_t$ for which the ZLB is strictly binding in equilibrium, that is, to find the periods for which the equation system (B.15) applies. Once this is done, solving the equation system (B.15) is trivial. Hebden et al. (2010) outline a simple shooting algorithm to find the set $\mathcal{T}_t$.

B.2 Computation of the Likelihood Function

To compute the likelihood function, we follow the general idea outlined by Maih (2010). Maih's algorithm allows us to add anticipated policy shocks (using the algorithm outlined earlier) to the state space formulation of the model and filter those shocks with the Kalman filter to impose the zero lower bound on policy rates in the estimation. The appealing feature of Maih's algorithm is that it does not require us to include standard deviations for each of the anticipated policy shocks. Thus, the log-marginal likelihood can be directly compared to the models which does not impose the ZLB. For further details on the computation of the likelihood function in the face of the ZLB constraint, we refer to Lindé et al. (2016).

C. Data

In this appendix, we provide the sources on the data we use in the analysis.

C.1 Benchmark Model

The benchmark model is estimated using seven key macroeconomic time series: real GDP, consumption, investment, hours worked, real wages, prices, and a short-term interest rate. The Bayesian estimation methodology is extensively discussed by Smets and Wouters (2003). GDP, consumption and investment were taken from the US Department of Commerce—Bureau of Economic Analysis data-bank—on September 25, 2014. Real gross domestic product is expressed in billions of chained 2009 dollars. Nominal personal consumption expenditures and fixed private domestic investment are deflated with the GDP-deflator. Inflation is the first difference of the log of the implicit price deflator of GDP. Hours and wages come from the BLS (hours and hourly compensation for the nonfarm business, NFB, sector for all persons). Hourly compensation is divided by the GDP price deflator in order to get the real wage variable. Hours are adjusted to take into account the limited coverage of the NFB sector compared to GDP (the index of average hours for the NFB sector is multiplied with the Civilian Employment (16 years and over). The aggregate real variables are expressed per capita by dividing with the population size aged 16 or older. All series are seasonally adjusted. The interest rate is the Federal Funds Rate. Consumption, investment, GDP, wages, and hours are expressed in $100\times$ log. The interest rate and inflation rate are expressed on a quarterly basis during the estimation (corresponding with their appearance in the model), but in the figures the series are reported on an annualized (400× first log difference) or yearly (100× the four-quarter log difference) basis.

C.2 Model with Financial Frictions

The first seven variables are exactly those used to estimate the benchmark model, which are described in Appendix C.1. In addition to those series, this model features an interest rate spread. Following Bernanke et al. (1999), this spread is measured as the difference between the BAA corporate interest rate and the US 10-year government yield.

ACKNOWLEDGMENTS

We thank the editors John B. Taylor and Harald Uhlig, as well as our discussant Jonas Fisher, for very helpful suggestions that significantly improved the chapter. Comments by participants in the Handbook conference at the Becker-Friedman institute in Chicago, the 18th Central Bank Macro Modeling Workshop (hosted by the Reserve Bank of New Zealand in Wellington), and seminars at the ECB and Sveriges Riksbank were also useful. We are heavily indebted to Junior Maih for developing code in RISE which allowed us to estimate models subject to the zero lower bound. A special thank you is also due to Mattias Villani, who allowed us to use his BVAR-code in which we could set steady state priors. Leonard Voltaire and Jessica Radeschnig provided excellent research assistance, but all remaining errors are ours. Frank Smets and Raf Wouters acknowledge financial support from the EU FP7-Project MACFINROBODS, grant 612796. The views, analysis, and conclusions in this chapter are solely the responsibility of the authors and do not necessarily agree with ECB, National Bank of Belgium, or the Sveriges Riksbank, or those of any other person associated with these institutions.

REFERENCES

Adam, K., Billi, R., 2006. Optimal monetary policy under commitment with a zero bound on nominal interest rates. J. Money Credit Bank. 38 (7), 1877–1906.

Adjemian, S., Bastani, H., Juillard, M., Karamé, F., Mihoubi, F., Perendia, G., Pfeifer, J., Ratto, M., Villemot, S., 2011. Dynare: Reference Manual, Version 4. Dynare Working Papers 1, CEPREMAP.

Adolfson, M., Laséen, S., Lindé, J., Villani, M., 2005. The role of sticky prices in an open economy DSGE model: a bayesian investigation. J. Eur. Econ. Assoc. Pap. Proc. 3 (2-3), 444–457.

Adolfson, M., Andersson, M.K., Lindé, J., Villani, M., Vredin, A., 2007a. Modern forecasting models in action: improving macroeconomic analyses at central banks. Int. J. Cent. Bank. 3 (4), 111–144.

Adolfson, M., Laséen, S., Lindé, J., Villani, M., 2007b. Bayesian estimation of an open economy DSGE model with incomplete pass-through. J. Int. Econ. 72, 481–511.

Adolfson, M., Laséen, S., Lindé, J., Villani, M., 2007c. RAMSES–a new general equilibrium model for monetary policy analysis. Sveriges Riksbank Econ. Rev. 2, 5–40.

Adolfson, M., Lindé, J., Villani, M., 2007d. Forecasting performance of an open economy DSGE model. Econ. Rev. 26, 289–328.

Adolfson, M., Laséen, S., Lindé, J., Villani, M., 2008. Evaluating an estimated new Keynesian small open economy model. J. Econ. Dyn. Control. 32 (8), 2690–2721.

Adolfson, M., Laséen, S., Lindé, J., Svensson, L.E., 2011. Optimal monetary policy in an operational medium-sized model. J. Money Credit Bank. 43 (7), 1287–1330.

Adolfson, M., Laséen, S., Christiano, L.J., Trabandt, M., Walentin, K., 2013. Ramses II–model description. Sveriges Riksbank Occasional Paper Series No. 12.

Altig, D., Christiano, L., Eichenbaum, M., Lindé, J., 2011. Firm-specific capital, nominal rigidities and the business cycle. Rev. Econ. Dyn. 14 (2), 225–247.
Andrade, P., Gaballoy, G., Mengusz, E., Mojon, B., 2015. Forward guidance and heterogeneous beliefs. Banque de France Working Paper Series No. 573.
Andrés, J., López-Salido, J.D., Nelson, E., 2004. Tobin's imperfect asset substitution in optimizing general equilibrium. J. Money Credit Bank. 36 (4), 666–690.
Andrle, M., Kumhof, M., Laxton, D., Muir, D., 2015. Banks in the global integrated monetary and fiscal model. IMF Working Paper No. 15-150.
Anzoategui, D., Comin, D., Gertler, M., Martinez, J., 2015. Endogenous technology adoption and R&D as sources of business cycle persistence. University Working Paper, New York.
Backus, D.K., Kehoe, P.J., Kydland, F.E., 1992. International real business cycles. J. Polit. Econ. 100, 745–773.
Barro, R.J., 1974. Are government bonds net wealth? J. Polit. Econ. 82 (6), 1095–1117.
Benigno, P., Nisticó, S., 2015. Non-neutrality of open-market operations. CEPR Working Paper No. 10594.
Bernanke, B.S., 2013. Communication and monetary policy. In: Herbert Stein Memorial Lecture at the National Economists Club Annual Dinner, November 19, Washington, DC.
Bernanke, B., Gertler, M., Gilchrist, S., 1999. The financial accelerator in a quantitative business cycle framework. In: Taylor, J.B., Woodford, M. (Eds.), Handbook of Macroeconomics. North-Holland/Elsevier Science, New York.
Blanchard, O., Kahn, C.M., 1980. The solution of linear difference models under rational expectations. Econometrica 48, 1305–1313.
Bocola, L., 2013. The pass-through of sovereign risk. University of Pennsylvania, manuscript.
Boissay, F., Collard, F., Smets, F., 2015. Booms and banking crises. J. Polit. Econ. 124 (2), 489–538.
Boppart, T., Krusell, P., 2015. Labor supply in the past, present, and future: a balanced-growth perspective. Stockholm University, manuscript.
Brave, S.A., Campbell, J.R., Fisher, J.D., Justiniano, A., 2012. The Chicago fed DSGE model. Federal Reserve Bank of Chicago Working Paper No. 2012-02.
Brubakk, L., Husebø, T., Maih, J., Olsen, K., Østnor, M., 2006. Finding NEMO: documentation of the Norwegian economy model. Staff Memo 2006/6, Norges Bank.
Brunnermeier, M.K., Sannikov, Y., 2014. A macroeconomic model with a financial sector. Am. Econ. Rev. 104 (2), 379–421.
Burgess, S., Fernandez-Corugedo, E., Groth, C., Harrison, R., Monti, F., Theodoridis, K., Waldron, M., 2013. The Bank of England's forecasting platform: COMPASS, MAPS, EASE and the suite of models. Bank of England Working Paper No. 471.
Calvo, G., 1983. Staggered prices in a utility maximizing framework. J. Monet. Econ. 12, 383–398.
Campbell, J.Y., Shiller, R.J., 1991. Yield spreads and interest rate movements: a bird's eye view. Rev. Econ. Stud. 58, 495–514.
Campbell, J.R., Evans, C.L., Fisher, J.D.M., Justiniano, A., 2012. Macroeconomic effects of federal reserve forward guidance. Brook. Pap. Econ. Act. 1–80 (Spring issue).
Carlstrom, C., Fuerst, T., Paustian, M., 2012. Inflation and output in new Keynesian models with a transient interest rate peg. Bank of England Working Paper No. 459.
Chaboud, A.P., Wright, J.H., 2005. Uncovered interest parity: it works, but not for long. J. Int. Econ. 66 (2), 349–362.
Chari, V., Kehoe, P.J., McGrattan, E.R., 2009. New Keynesian models: not yet useful for policy analysis. Am. Econ. J. Macroecon. 1 (1), 242–266.
Chib, S., Ramamurthy, S., 2014. DSGE models with Student-t errors. Econ. Rev. 33 (1-4), 152–171.
Christiano, L., Motto, R., Rostagno, M., 2003a. The great depression and the Friedman-Schwartz hypothesis. J. Money Credit Bank. 35 (6), 1119–1197.
Christiano, L.J., Eichenbaum, M., Vigfusson, R.J., 2003b. What happens after a technology shock? NBER Working Paper Series No. 9819.
Christiano, L.J., Eichenbaum, M., Evans, C., 2005. Nominal rigidities and the dynamic effects of a shock to monetary policy. J. Polit. Econ. 113 (1), 1–45.

Christiano, L., Trabandt, M., Walentin, K., 2007. Introducing financial frictions and unemployment into a small open economy model. Sveriges Riksbank Working Paper Series No. 214.

Christiano, L., Motto, R., Rostagno, M., 2008. Shocks, structures or monetary policies? The Euro area and the US after 2001. J. Econ. Dyn. Control. 32 (8), 2476–2506.

Christiano, L., Trabandt, M., Walentin, K., 2010a. Involuntary unemployment and the business cycle. Sveriges Riksbank Working Paper Series No. 238.

Christiano, L.J., Ilut, C., Motto, R., Rostagno, M., 2010b. Monetary policy and stock market booms. In: Proceedings–Economic Policy Symposium–Jackson Hole, Federal Reserve Bank of Kansas City, pp. 85–145.

Christiano, L.J., Motto, R., Rostagno, M., 2014. Risk shocks. Am. Econ. Rev. 104 (1), 27–65.

Christiano, L.J., Eichenbaum, M., Trabandt, M., 2015. Understanding the great recession. Am. Econ. J. Macroecon. 7 (1), 110–167.

Christiano, L.J., Eichenbaum, M., Trabandt, M., 2016. Unemployment and business cycles. Econometrica. (forthcoming in Vol. 84, No.3, 1289).

Chung, H., Laforte, J.P., Reifschneider, D., 2012. Have we underestimated the likelihood and severity of zero lower bound events? J. Money Credit Bank. 44 (2012), 47–82.

Clarida, R., Galí, J., Gertler, M., 1999. The science of monetary policy: a new Keynesian perspective. J. Econ. Lit. 37 (4), 1661–1707.

Clerc, L., Derviz, A., Mendicino, C., Moyen, S., Nikolov, K., Stracca, L., Suarez, J., Vardoulakis, A.P., 2015. Capital regulation in a macroeconomic model with three layers of default. Int. J. Cent. Bank. 15 (3), 9–63.

Coenen, G., Erceg, C., Freedman, C., Furceri, D., Kumhof, M., Lalonde, R., Laxton, D., Lindé, J., Mourougane, A., Muir, D., Mursula, S., de Resende, C., Roberts, J., Roeger, W., Snudden, S., Trabandt, M., in't Veld, J., 2012. Effects of fiscal stimulus in structural models. Am. Econ. J. Macroecon. 4 (1), 22–68.

Curdia, V., Del Negro, M., Greenwald, D.L., 2014. Rare shocks, great recessions. J. Econ. 29 (7), 1031–1052.

De Graeve, F., 2008. The external finance premium and the macroeconomy: US post-WWII evidence. J. Econ. Dyn. Control. 32 (11), 3415–3440.

Del Negro, M., Schorfheide, F., 2013. DSGE model-based forecasting. In: Elliott, G., Timmermann, A. (Eds.), Handbook of Economic Forecasting, vol. 2. Elseiver, Amsterdam, pp. 57–140.

Del Negro, M., Sims, C.A., 2014. When does a central bank's balance sheet require fiscal support? FRB of New York Staff Report No. 701.

Del Negro, M., Schorfheide, F., Smets, F., Wouters, R., 2007. On the fit of new Keynesian models. J. Bus. Econ. Stat. 25 (2), 123–162.

Del Negro, M., Eusepi, S., Giannoni, M., Sbordone, A., Tambalotti, A., Cocci, M., Hasegawa, R., Henry Linder, M., 2013. The FRBNY DSGE model. Federal Reserve Bank of New York Staff Report No. 647.

Del Negro, M., Hasegawa, R., Schorfheide, F., 2014. Dynamic prediction pools: an investigation of financial frictions and forecasting performance. NBER Working Paper 20575.

Del Negro, M., Giannoni, M.P., Patterson, C., 2015a. The forward guidance puzzle. Federal Reserve Bank of New York Staff Reports No. 574.

Del Negro, M., Giannoni, M.P., Schorfheide, F., 2015b. Inflation in the great recession and new Keynesian models. Am. Econ. J. Macroecon. 7 (1), 168–196.

Dewachter, H., Wouters, R., 2014. Endogenous risk in a DSGE model with capital-constrained financial intermediaries. J. Econ. Dyn. Control. 43 (C), 241–268.

Doan, T., Litterman, R., Sims, C.A., 1984. Forecasting and conditional projection using realistic prior distributions. Econ. Rev. 3 (1), 1–100.

Dotsey, M., King, R.G., 2005. Implications of state dependent pricing for dynamic macroeconomic models. J. Monet. Econ. 52, 213–242.

Duarte, M., Stockman, A., 2005. Rational speculation and exchange rates. J. Monet. Econ. 52, 3–29.

Edge, R.M., Gürkaynak, R., 2010. How useful are estimated DSGE model forecasts for central bankers? Brook. Pap. Econ. Act. 2, 209–244.

Eggertsson, G., Woodford, M., 2003. The zero bound on interest rates and optimal monetary policy. Brook. Pap. Econ. Act. 1, 139–211.
Eichenbaum, M., Evans, C.L., 1995. Some empirical evidence on the effects of shocks to monetary policy on exchange rates. Q. J. Econ. 110 (4), 975–1009.
Erceg, C.J., Lindé, J., 2010. Is there a fiscal free lunch in a liquidity trap? CEPR Discussion Paper Series No. 7624.
Erceg, C.J., Henderson, D.W., Levin, A.T., 2000. Optimal monetary policy with staggered wage and price contracts. J. Monet. Econ. 46, 281–313.
Evans, G.E., Honkapohja, S., 2001. Learning and Expectations in Macroeconomics. Princeton University Press, Princeton.
Fair, R.C., Taylor, J.B., 1983. Solution and maximum likelihood estimation of dynamic nonlinear a rational expecations models. Econometrica 51 (4), 1169–1185.
Fernald, J., 2012. A quarterly, utilization-adjusted series on total factor productivity. Federal Reserve Bank of San Francisco Working Paper 2012-19.
Fernández-Villaverde, J., Rubio-Ramírez, J., 2007. Estimating macroeconomic models: a likelihood approach. Rev. Econ. Stud. 74, 1059–1087.
Fernández-Villaverde, J., Guerrón-Quintana, P.A., Kuester, K., Rubio-Ramírez, J., 2011. Fiscal volatility shocks and economic activity. NBER Working Paper 17317.
Fisher, J.D., 2006. The dynamic effects of neutral and investment-specific technology shocks. J. Polit. Econ. 114 (3), 413–451.
Fisher, J.D., 2015. On the structural interpretation of the Smets–Wouters "risk premium" shock. J. Money Credit Bank. 47 (2-3), 511–516.
Fratto, C., Uhlig, H., 2014. Accounting for post-crisis inflation and employment: a retro analysis. NBER Working Paper No. 20707.
Galí, J., 2008. Monetary Policy, Inflation and the Business Cycle: An Introduction to the New Keynesian Framework. Princeton University Press, Princeton.
Galí, J., Gertler, M., 1999. Inflation dynamics: a structural econometric analysis. J. Monet. Econ. 44, 195–220.
Galí, J., Pau, R., 2004. Technology shocks and aggregate fluctuations: how well does the RBC model fit postwar U.S. data? NBER Macroeconomics Annual.
Galí, J., Gertler, M., López-Salido, D., 2001. European inflation dynamics. Eur. Econ. Rev. 45, 1237–1270.
Galí, J., Smets, F., Wouters, R., 2011. Unemployment in an estimated new Keynesian model. NBER Macroeconomics Annual.
Gerali, A., Neri, S., Sessa, L., Signoretti, F.M., 2010. Credit and banking in a DSGE model of the Euro area. J. Money Credit Bank. 42, 107–141.
Gertler, M., Kiyotaki, N., 2010. Financial intermediation and credit policy in business cycle analysis. In: Friedman, B.M., Woodford, M. (Eds.), Handbook of Monetary Economics, vol. III. North-Holland Elsevier Science, New York (Chapter 11).
Gertler, M., Sala, L., Trigari, A., 2008. An estimated monetary DSGE model with unemployment and staggered nominal wage bargaining. J. Money Credit Bank. 40 (8), 1713–1764.
Geweke, J., 1999. Using simulation methods for bayesian econometrics models: inference, development and communication. Econ. Rev. 18 (1), 1–73.
Gilchrist, S., Zakrajsek, E., 2012. Credit spreads and business cycle fluctuations. Am. Econ. Rev. 102 (4), 1692–1720.
Gilchrist, S., Ortiz, A., Zakrasej, E., 2009. Credit risk and the macroeconomy: evidence from an estimated DSGE model. Manuscript.
Gilchrist, S., Sim, J.W., Schoenle, R., Zakrajsek, E., 2015. Inflation dynamics during the financial crisis. Finance and Economics Discussion Series 2015-012, Board of Governors of the Federal Reserve System.
Guerrieri, L., Iacoviello, M., 2013. Collateral constraints and macroeconomic asymmetries. International Finance Discussion Papers 1082, Board of Governors of the Federal Reserve System.
Gust, C., López-Salido, D., Smith, M.E., 2012. The empirical implications of the interest-rate lower bound. Finance and Economics Discussion Series 2012-83, Board of Governors of the Federal Reserve System.

He, Z., Krishnamurthy, A., 2012. A model of capital and crises. Rev. Econ. Stud. 79 (2), 735–777.
Hebden, J.S., Lindé, J., Svensson, L.E., 2010. Optimal monetary policy in the hybrid new-Keynesian model under the zero lower bound. Federal Reserve Board, manuscript.
Howard, G., Martin, R., Wilson, B.A., 2011. Are recoveries from banking and financial crises really so different? International Finance Discussion Papers No. 1037, Board of Governors of the Federal Reserve System.
Iacoviello, M., 2005. House prices, borrowing constraints, and monetary policy in the business cycle. Am. Econ. Rev. 95 (3), 739–764.
Iacoviello, M., Guerrieri, L., 2015. OccBin: a toolkit for solving dynamic models with occasionally binding constraints easily. J. Monet. Econ. 70, 22–38.
Iversen, J., Laséen, S., Lundvall, H., Söderström, U., 2016. Real-time forecasting for monetary policy analysis: the case of Sveriges riksbank. Sveriges Riksbank, manuscript.
Jordà, O., Moritz, H.P.S., Alan, M.T., 2012. When credit bites back: leverage, business cycles, and crises. Federal Reserve Bank of San Francisco Working Paper 2011-27.
Justiniano, A., Preston, B., 2010. Can structural small open-economy models account for the influence of foreign disturbances? J. Int. Econ. 81 (1), 61–74.
Justiniano, A., Primiceri, G.E., 2008. The time varying volatility of macroeconomic fluctuations. Am. Econ. Rev. 98 (3), 604–641.
Justiniano, A., Primiceri, G.E., Tambalotti, A., 2013a. Investment shocks and the relative price of investment. Rev. Econ. Dyn. 14 (1), 101–121.
Justiniano, A., Primiceri, G.E., Tambalotti, A., 2013b. Is there a trade-off between inflation and output stabilization. Am. Econ. J. Macroecon. 5 (2), 1–31.
Kimball, M.S., 1995. The quantitative analytics of the basic neomonetarist model. J. Money Credit Bank. 27 (4), 1241–1277.
Klein, P., 2000. Using the generalized schur form to solve a multivariate linear rational expectations model. J. Econ. Dyn. Control. 24, 1405–1423.
Kocherlakota, N., 2009. Modern macroeconomic models as tools for economic policy. 2009 Annual Report Essay, Federal Reserve Bank of Minneapolis.
Kydland, F., Prescott, E., 1982. Time to build and aggregate fluctuations. Econometrica 50, 1345–1371.
Laséen, S., Svensson, L.E., 2011. Anticipated alternative instrument-rate paths in policy simulations. Int. J. Cent. Bank. 7 (3), 1–36.
Leeper, E.M., Leith, C., 2016. Understanding inflation as a joint monetary—fiscal phenomenon. In: Taylor, J., Uhlig, H. (Eds.), Handbook of Macroeconomics, vol. 2B. Elsevier, Amsterdam, Netherlands, pp. 2305–2415.
Leeper, E.M., Traum, N., Walker, T.B., 2015. Clearing up the fiscal multiplier morass. NBER Working Paper No. 21433.
Levin, A.T., Natalucci, F.M., Zakrajsek, E., 2004. The magnitude and cyclical behavior of financial market frictions. Finance and Economics Discussion Series 2004-70, Board of Governors of the Federal Reserve System.
Lindé, J., 2005. Estimating new Keynesian Phillips curves: a full information maximum likelihood approach. J. Monet. Econ. 52 (6), 1135–1149.
Lindé, J., Maih, J., Wouters, R., 2016. Alternative approaches to incorporate the ZLB in the estimation of DSGE models. National Bank of Belgium, manuscript.
Liu, Z., Wang, P., Zha, T., 2013. Land-price dynamics and macroeconomic fluctuations. Econometrica 81 (3), 1147–1184.
Lucas, R.E., 1976. Econometric policy evaluation: a critique. Carn. Roch. Conf. Ser. Public Policy 1, 19–46.
Maih, J., 2010. Conditional forecasts in DSGE models. Norges Bank Working Paper No. 2010/7.
Maih, J., 2015. Efficient perturbation methods for solving regime-switching DSGE models. Norges Bank Working Paper No. 2015/1.
Mendoza, E.G., 2010. Sudden stops, financial crises, and leverage. Am. Econ. Rev. 100, 1941–1966.
Queijo von Heideken, V., 2009. How important are financial frictions in the United States and the Euro area? Scand. J. Econ. 111 (3), 567–596.

Queralto, A., 2013. A model of slow recoveries from financial crises. International Finance Discussion Papers No. 1097, Board of Governors of the Federal Reserve System.
Reifschneider, D., Williams, J.C., 2000. Three lessons for monetary policy in a low inflation era. J. Money Credit Bank. 32 (4), 936–966.
Reinhart, C.M., Rogoff, K.S., 2009. The aftermath of financial crises. Am. Econ. Rev. 99 (2), 466–472.
Rudebusch, G.D., Svensson, L.E., 1999. Policy rules for inflation targeting. In: Taylor, J.B. (Ed.), Monetary Policy Rules. University of Chicago Press, Chicago, pp. 203–246.
Schorfheide, F., 2000. Loss function-based evaluation of DSGE models. J. Appl. Econ. 15 (6), 645–670.
Sims, C.A., 1980. Macroeconomics and reality. Econometrica 48 (1), 1–48.
Sims, C.A., 2003. Implications of rational inattention. J. Monet. Econ. 50 (3), 665–690.
Sims, C.A., 2010. Rational inattention and monetary economics. In: Friedman, B.M., Woodford, M. (Eds.), Handbook of Monetary Economics, vol. 3A. Elsevier, Amsterdam, pp. 155–181.
Smets, F., Wouters, R., 2003. An estimated stochastic dynamic general equilibrium model of the Euro area. J. Eur. Econ. Assoc. 1 (5), 1123–1175.
Smets, F., Wouters, R., 2007. Shocks and frictions in US business cycles: a bayesian DSGE approach. Am. Econ. Rev. 97 (3), 586–606.
Suh, H., Walker, T.B., 2016. Taking financial frictions to the data. J. Econ. Dyn. Control. 64, 39–65.
Taylor, J.B., 2007. Housing and monetary policy, in housing, housing finance, and monetary policy. In: Proceedings–Economic Policy Symposium–Jackson Hole, Federal Reserve Bank of Kansas City, vols. 463-476.
Taylor, J.B., Wieland, V., 2012. Surprising comparative properties of monetary models: results from a new monetary model base. Rev. Econ. Stat. 94 (3), 800–816.
Vavra, J., 2013. Time-varying phillips curves. University of Chicago, manuscript.
Vayanos, D., Vila, J.L., 2009. A preferred-habitat model of the term structure of interest rates. London School of Economics, manuscript.
Villani, M., 2009. Steady state priors for vector autoregressions. J. Appl. Econ. 24, 630–650.
Warne, A., Coenen, G., Christoffel, K., 2015. Marginalized predictive likelihood comparisons of linear Gaussian state-space models with applications to DSGE, DSGE-VAR, and VAR models. J. Appl. Econ. (forthcoming). http://dx.doi.org/10.1002/jae.2514.
Wieland, V., Wolters, M., 2013. Forecasting and policy making. In: Elliott, G., Timmermann, A. (Eds.), Handbook of Economic Forecasting, vol. 2, Elseiver, Amsterdam, pp. 239–325 (Chapter 5).
Wieland, V., Cwik, T., Müller, G.J., Schmidt, S., Wolters, M., 2012. A new comparative approach to macroeconomic modeling and policy analysis. J. Econ. Behav. Organ. 83, 523–541.
Williams, J.C., 2014. Monetary policy at the zero lower bound: putting theory into practice. Hutchins Center Working Paper No. 2, Brookings Institution, Washington, DC.
Woodford, M., 2003. Interest Rates and Prices. Princeton University Press, Princeton.
Woodford, M., 2014. Stochastic choice: an optimizing neuroeconomic model. Am. Econ. Rev. 104 (5), 495–500.
Yun, T., 1996. Nominal price rigidity, money supply endogeneity, and business cycles. J. Monet. Econ. 37, 345–370.

CHAPTER 29

Liquidity Requirements, Liquidity Choice, and Financial Stability

D.W. Diamond*,†, A.K. Kashyap*,†
*University of Chicago Booth School of Business, Chicago, IL, United States
†National Bureau of Economic Research, Cambridge, MA, United States

Contents

Abstract

We study a modification of the Diamond and Dybvig (1983) model in which the bank may hold a liquid asset, some depositors see sunspots that could lead them to run, and all depositors have incomplete information about the bank's ability to survive a run. The incomplete information means that the bank is not automatically incentivized to always hold enough liquid assets to survive runs. Regulation similar to the liquidity coverage ratio and the net stable funding ratio (that are soon be implemented) can change the bank's incentives so that runs are less likely. Optimal regulation would not mimic these rules.

Handbook of Macroeconomics, Volume 2B
ISSN 1574-0048, http://dx.doi.org/10.1016/bs.hesmac.2016.03.011

Keywords

Bank runs, Bank regulation, Liquidity regulation, Net stable funding ratio, Liquidity coverage ratio

1. INTRODUCTION

In September 2009, the leaders of 20 major economies created the Financial Stability Board (FSB) whose purpose is to "coordinate at the international level the work of national financial authorities and international standard setting bodies (SSBs) in order to develop and promote the implementation of effective regulatory, supervisory, and other financial sector policies." Since that time the financial system has undergone a regulatory overhaul.

The term "macroprudential" regulation has become synonymous with much of this effort. As we explain in the next section, what that means in practice remains somewhat elusive. But, there are two tangible changes that are on track to occur over the remainder of this decade. One widely studied set of reforms pertain to the rules regarding capital requirements for banks. Less well-understood is that, through their cooperation via the Basel Committee on Bank Supervision, the major economies have also agreed also to implement by 2019 new rules governing banks' debt structures and requirements to hold certain types of liquid assets.

To date there is a remarkable asymmetry in the economic analysis of the capital and liquidity regulations. The pioneering work of Modigliani and Miller (1958) provides a solid theoretical framework for analyzing capital regulation. Any student taking a first course in corporate finance will encounter this theory, and there is a massive empirical literature that explores the theory's predictions. International regulations governing bank capital were introduced in 1988 and there many empirical examinations of the impact of these regulations. A recent book directed toward the general public, Admati and Hellwig (2013), makes a case for substantially increased capital requirements for commercial banks.

The discussion about regulating liquidity is much less advanced. For example, there is no benchmark theory regarding liquidity provision by intermediaries. Indeed, financial economists even have competing concepts that they have in mind when discussing liquidity, so that there is no generally accepted empirical measure of liquidity economists study. Allen (2014), in his survey of the nascent literature on liquidity regulation, concludes by writing "much more research is required in this area. With capital regulation there is a huge literature but little agreement on the optimal level of requirements. With liquidity regulation, we do not even know what to argue about."

Nonetheless, the global regulatory community has agreed on certain liquidity requirements (Basel Committee on Bank Supervision, 2013a, 2014). Two new concepts, the liquidity coverage ratio (LCR) and the net stable funding ratio (NSFR), have been proposed and banks by 2019 will be compelled to meet requirements for these ratios. Thus, it seems fair to say we are in a situation where practice is ahead of both theory and measurement.

In this chapter, we survey the existing work on liquidity regulation and develop a framework for discussing the regulation. The theory that we propose suggests, in certain parameterizations, regulations bearing some resemblance to the LCR and NSFR can emerge as ones which will improve outcomes relative to an unregulated benchmark. However, the regulations that arise in our model would naturally differ across banks, depending on certain bank characteristics, so they do not mimic exactly the ones that are on track to be implemented.

The critical ingredients in our model are the following. First, we consider banks which are spatially separated and hence do not compete aggressively for deposits. Treating the bank as monopolist simplifies the analysis by allowing us to side-step some complications that arise from having to model the deposit market equilibrium. The model can also be interpreted as a description of the aggregate banking system, which for many financial stability and regulatory discussions, is the object of primary concern, and under this interpretation ignoring the deposit competition is perhaps more natural.

Second, we assume that intermediaries provide liquidity insurance for customers who have uncertain withdrawal needs (or consumption desires). We build on the Diamond and Dybvig (1983), henceforth DD, model of banking in which banks provide this insurance by relying on the law of large numbers to eliminate idiosyncratic customer liquidity needs.

For those familiar with DD, we make two modifications. The first is allowing the bank to invest in a liquid asset that has a rate of return exceeding the return from liquidating illiquid assets and thus is the efficient way to arrange to pay customers that need liquidity. This introduces a trade-off between lending and holding liquidity as in Bhattacharya and Gale (1987), several papers of Allen and Gale (1997), and others.

The other modification to DD is the form of run risk that the banks face. Banks are assumed to have a good assessment of the aggregate needs of their customers for fundamental reasons. But, they also know that some customers will receive a signal about the bank which could lead to a run. The sunspots that we consider are a metaphor for people being concerned with the health of the bank, but not having a fully formed set of beliefs about the bank's solvency status. In making their decisions, we assume that customers are unable to fully evaluate the ability of the bank to honor deposits. Given the complexity of modern banks it seems realistic to presume that most customers cannot precisely determine their bank's maturity mismatch and hence its vulnerability to a run. The imperfect information creates a challenge for the banks because their customers will not necessarily know if the bank is prudently holding liquidity or not, which reduces the incentive to hold liquidity.

In the event that a run does occur, we depart from DD and Ennis and Keister (2006) to allow for the possibility that not all customers seek to withdraw their funds. We believe it is useful to analyze partial runs for two separate reasons. One is that in practice there do seem to be some sticky deposits that do not flee even in times of considerable banking stress. In addition, even before troubles occur it is usually clear which types of deposits are prone to running. So this allows us to talk about policies for different types of withdrawal risk.

Within this environment we can assess the vulnerability of the financial system to runs under different regulatory arrangements. In the baseline case, we assume that banks simply maximize their profits and see which types of equilibria arise. As usual in DD style models, the outcomes depend critically on how depositors form beliefs. It is possible, under certain parameter configurations, that the pure self-interest motives of the banks will sufficient to insure that the system will be run proof even if depositors had no detailed information about a bank's liquidity holdings. In these situations, added liquidity could not influence whether a given depositor would choose to join a run if one was feared.

We describe several reasons why depositors may not be able to use some types of disclosure of a bank's liquidity holdings to determine if the holding is sufficient to allow it to survive a run. To fix ideas, one can consider whether a bank would choose to hold this sufficient amount of liquidity even if its choice between liquid assets and illiquid loans was completely unobservable. In circumstances where depositors cannot be sure about how changes in liquidity holdings impact the robustness of banks to runs, the banks will typically face a tension in deciding how much to fortify themselves against the risk of a run. They can always choose to be sufficiently conservative to be able to withstand a worst case of fundamental withdrawals as well as a panic. But in order to do that, they will engage in very little lending, and the forgone profits from deterring the run will be high. The additional liquidity to survive a run will turn out to be excessive whenever a run is avoided. Hence, it is possible they will make more profits from added lending which would leave them unable to always be able to sustain a run.

We next allow regulatory interventions that place restrictions on present and possibly on future bank portfolio choices. In the baseline setup, the banks have perfectly aligned incentives to prepare to service fundamental aggregate withdrawal needs. So the regulatory challenge is to determine whether a requirement that distorts their private incentives toward being more robust to a run will improve outcomes. We allow for regulation that is inspired by the two impending Basel rules.

One variant requires an initial liquidity position that must be established before depositors make their intentions clear. This can function like the "NSFR" that is proposed as part of the Basel reforms. A second option is a mandate to always hold additional liquid assets beyond those needed for the fundamental withdrawals. This imposes both present and future minimum holdings of liquid assets. This regulation looks like a traditional reserve requirement for the bank but can also be interpreted as a kind of "liquidity coverage" ratio that is part of the Basel reforms.

One point of contention regarding the LCR that has emerged is whether required liquidity can be deployed in the case of a crisis. Goodhart (2008) framed the issue nicely with a now famous analogy of "the weary traveller who arrives at the railway station late at night, and, to his delight, sees a taxi there who could take him to his distant destination. He hails the taxi, but the taxi driver replies that he cannot take him, since local bylaws require that there must always be one taxi standing ready at the station."

One way to interpret the Goodhart conundrum is to recognize that, broadly speaking, there are two ways to think about the purpose behind liquidity regulations. One motivation can be to make sure that banks can better withstand a surge in withdrawals should one occur. From this perspective, mandating that the last cab cannot depart the station seems foolish. Another possible motivation is to design regulations aimed at reducing the likelihood of a withdrawal surge in the first place. Our model helps highlight the potential incentive properties of regulation and can potentially explain why mandating the presence of some unused liquidity could be beneficial.

In studying how private and social incentives for liquidity choices diverge, our main conclusion from analyzing the two Basel-style regulations is that they may improve outcomes relative to the ones that arise from pure self-interest, but each brings potential inefficiencies. Hence, we briefly also describe the solution of the mechanism design problem for a social planner who has less information about withdrawal risk than the bank does and seeks to optimally regulate banks to avoid runs. That solution provides a natural benchmark against which to judge the Basel-style regulations.

The remainder of the chapter is divided into five parts. Section 2 contains our selective overview of previous work. We organize this into three subsections. We begin with an overview of the emerging policy proposals and research regarding macroprudential regulation. We then hone in on the enormous and rapidly growing literature on capital regulation. We provide our perspective on how to group these papers and highlight several recent excellent surveys on the pure effects of capital regulation. We close with a review of the most relevant papers for our questions that motivate us about liquidity regulation.

Section 3 introduces the benchmark model. We explain how it works under complete information. We also derive a generic proposition that holds with incomplete information that describes when the bank's preferred liquidity choice will be sufficient to deter a run. Generically, however, privately chosen levels of liquidity need not be sufficient to deter runs. So this opens the door for regulations that might do so.

In Section 4, we analyze the two types of liquidity regulation that are akin to the ones contemplated under the Basel process. We first demonstrate that a particular type of regulation that requires the bank to hold liquid assets equal to a fixed percentage of deposits at all times can potentially deter runs. This works because the liquidity mandate, combined the bank's self-interest to prepare to service predictable deposit outflows, leads the bank to hold more overall liquidity than it would otherwise. Because depositors understand this, it removes the incentive to run in some cases. We also consider alternative assumptions about depositors' knowledge and the information available to regulators and assess the vulnerability of the bank to runs in these scenarios.

In Section 5, we describe a couple of extensions of the baseline model. The first sketches a mechanism design problem where the regulator does not have all of the bank's information and seeks to implement run-free banking. We fully characterize the solution to this problem in Diamond and Kashyap (2016), here we describe the main findings from this exercise. It turns out that a regulator with sufficient tools can induce the bank to hold the proper amount of liquidity despite the private information advantage possessed by the bank.

We also briefly discuss capital regulation. We explain why, as a tool for managing liquidity problems, capital requirements can be relatively inefficient compared to the other regulations that we have reviewed. Obviously in a richer model where both credit risk and liquidity risk are present, capital, and liquidity regulations can serve different purposes. We describe some of these differences.

Section 6 presents our conclusions. Besides summarizing our findings, we also pose a few open questions that are natural next steps to consider in addressing the issues analyzed in this chapter.

2. LITERATURE REVIEW

Research on financial regulation has exploded since the global financial crisis (GFC), and the number of regulatory interventions and tools has also expanded massively. To review all of this work would require a book. To keep our review manageable, we limit our discussion to focusing on the theoretical underpinnings and rationale behind these changes.[a]

2.1 Macroprudential Regulation

Clement (2010) provides the interesting history of the origins and evolution in the meaning of the phrase "macroprudential." His best estimate is that the term appeared first in 1979 in the documents of the committee that was the fore-runner to the Basel Committee on Bank Supervision. The first public document using the term which he can identify was a report by the committee now known as the Committee on the Global Financial System. It defined macroprudential policy as promoting "the safety and soundness of the broad financial system and payments mechanism."

The phrase took on added prominence when it was the focus of a Sept. 2000 speech by Andrew Crockett (who was then the General Manager of the Bank for International Settlements (Crockett, 2000)). He defined the objective of macroprudential policy to be "limiting the costs to the economy from financial distress, including those that arise from any moral hazard induced by the policies pursued." Crockett's rational for calling for macroprudential policies was his belief that optimal choices for a single institution could create problems for the financial system as a whole. He was explicitly focused on the distinction between the supervisory challenges for monitoring an individual institution and those for protecting the aggregate financial system.

[a] For a diverse set of perspectives on the changing postcrisis regulatory landscape see Čihák et al. (2013), Financial Stability Board (2015), Claessens and Kodres (2014), Basel Committee on Bank Supervision (2013a,b), and Fisher (2015).

Crockett did not offer precise microeconomic foundations for why the private actions of individual actors would not be aligned with social welfare, but he did give a few examples where he saw the potential for divergence. One possibility he cited is that one bank seeking to limit its credit exposures could choose to cut lending to its clients, but if all banks did this a credit crunch could ensue that would trigger a recession. A second example was the possibility of what we would now dub to be a fire-sale where all agents simultaneously cut back on asset exposures due to falling prices and in the course of doing so exacerbate the price decline. A third problem arises if many lenders shorten the maturity of their funding to a particular borrower, then the risk of a run can increase so that they are all more vulnerable.

Our view is that Crockett's spotlight on the divergence between the narrow private interests of individual institutions (or supervisors monitoring a single institution) and the interests of overall society is exactly the right focus for considering macroprudential policies. Indeed, this literature would be well-served to move in the direction where all macroprudential papers start by clarifying why (and when) social and private interests diverge. The challenge for both for researchers and policymakers is the difficulty in formalizing and prioritizing the exact reasons for the divergence. To clearly see the problem, compare three prominent perspectives on macroprudential regulation that have followed Crockett.

First, various BIS documents (eg, Clement, 2010) now interpret Crockett as having identified two types of problems that are to be addressed. One relates to the buildup of risks over time that are often now referred to as the procyclicality of the financial system or the "time dimension" of the macroprudential policy problem. The other relates to the distribution of risks within the financial system, the so-called cross-sectional dimension of the problem. Many official sector documents adopt the convention of separating time-series and cross-sectional macroprudential problems. As Clement (2010) notes, while the BIS work in this area has been relatively precise in the way these issues are discussed, "the usage of the term in the public sphere has on occasion been loose. It is not uncommon for it to be employed almost interchangeably with policies designed to address systemic risk or concerns that lie at the intersection between the macroeconomy and financial stability, regardless of the specific tools used."

In contrast, Hanson et al. (2011) start with a particular view of "how modern financial crises unfold, and why both an unregulated financial system, as well as one based on capital rules that only apply to traditional banks, is likely to be fragile." Their perspective, appealing to the model in Stein (2012), presumes that banks will find it cheaper to fund themselves with short-term debt than equity, so that banks have limited incentives to build strong equity buffers in normal times. If, in a crisis, such banks suffer substantial losses, then the market value of debt claims can fall below the face value, which will deter them from raising new equity (Myers, 1977). Consequently, in this case the banks are likely to comply with capital regulations by shrinking their asset base. Hence, Hanson et al. argue that the goal of macroprudential regulation should be to "control the social costs associated with excessive balance sheet shrinkage on the part of multiple financial institutions hit with a common shock."

A recent survey by the Norges bank staff, Borchgrevink et al. (2014), argues that in fact there are six market failures that can give rise to macroprudential concerns. These are pecuniary externalities, interconnectedness externalities, strategic complementarities, aggregate demand externalities, market for lemons, and deviations from full rationality. Not surprisingly they conclude "Because of the diversity of these categories, policy lessons diverge. There is yet no 'workhorse' model for policy analysis." Though they do argue that capital and liquidity regulation should tuned to aggregate conditions, not just those of individual banks, and that borrowers should be subjected to time-varying policies that aim to force them to internalize the costs of excessive borrowing.[b]

We share the Borchgrevink et al (2014) conclusion that the macroprudential literature at this point remains in sufficient flux that it is too soon to reach firm conclusions about where it will lead. Hence, for the remainder of our analysis we focus on capital and liquidity regulation where the range of issues to be considered can be narrowed and where specific global policies are being implemented.

2.2 Capital Regulation

For an overview of the literature on capital regulation, it is useful to sort papers along two dimensions. The first regards what is assumed regarding the Modigliani–Miller (1958) (henceforth MM) capital structure propositions. As in all models of corporate finance, absent failures of one of the MM propositions any choices regarding capital structure will be inconsequential. There have been four primary MM violations that have drawn attention in the literature.

One concerns that existence of deposit insurance. If certain parts of a bank's capital structure is protected from losses by the government, that can create risk-shifting incentives for equity holders. In many models, bank managers working on behalf of the equity owners face an incentive to gamble after adverse shocks that goes unchecked because depositors are immune from losses that they would suffer if the gamble fails.

A second distortion is concerns over guarantees to protect equity holders of banks from losses. Usually this is couched as a problem of having some banks that are assumed to be "too big" or "too-interconnected" to fail. But, in the recent GFC, there were also

[b] Others have also chosen to organize their analyses around distinctions between the kinds of tools that can be deployed. For example, Aikman et al. (2013) classify tools into three groups: those that operate on financial institutions' balance sheets; those that affect the terms and conditions on financial transactions; and those that influence market structures. While Cerutti et al. (2015) present empirical analyses comparing 12 types of different regulations.

cases in some countries where equity owners of smaller, nonsystemic banks were insulated from losses due to political connections.

A third violation regards the MM assumption of complete financial markets. With incomplete markets, an institution that creates new securities could be valuable. In the banking context, deposits are a leading example of special security that banks might create.

Finally, there are many models where either asymmetric information or moral hazard problems are considered. Some of the prominent examples include the possibility that borrowers know more about their investment opportunities than lenders, or that borrowers can shift the riskiness of their investments after receiving funding.

So unlike much of the research on nonfinancial corporations, the trade-off theory of capital structure, whereby firms prefer debt for its tax advantages and balance those benefits against costs of financial distress, has not figured prominently in the banking research on capital regulation. Rather, regulation is usually justified on the grounds of addressing one of these other four problems. The type of regulation that can be welfare improving will differ depending on which of these other frictions is assumed to be present.

The second important dimension one which the literature can be organized concerns the economic services that banks are assumed to provide.[c] Broadly, there are three types of services that have been modeled. The first presumes that certain financial institutions can expand the amount of credit that borrowers can obtain (say, relative to direct lending by individual savers). The micro-founded theories typically assume that borrowers can potentially default on loans and so any lender has to be diligent in monitoring borrowers (Diamond, 1984). By concentrating the lending with specialized agents, these monitoring costs can be conserved and the amount of credit extended can be expanded.

A second widely posited role for intermediaries is helping people and businesses share risks (Allen and Gale, 1997; Benston and Smith, 1976). There are many ways to formalize how this takes place, but perhaps the simplest is to recognize that because banks offer both deposits and equity to savers, they can create two different types of claims that would be backed by bank assets. These two choices allow savers to hedge some risks associated with lending, and this hedging improves the consumption opportunities for savers. More broadly, these theories suppose that banks help pool and tranche risks.[d]

A third class of models, which complements the second, supposes that the financial system creates liquid claims that facilitate transactions. There are various motivations behind how this can be modeled. In DD style models, an intermediary can cross-insure consumers' needs for liquidity by exploiting the law of large numbers among customers. But doing so exposes banks to the possibility of a run, which can be disastrous for the bank and its borrowers and depositors. Calomiris and Kahn (1991) and Diamond and Rajan (2001)

[c] The next few paragraphs are taken from Kashyap et al. (2014).

[d] For instance, if there are transactions costs associated with buying securities, a bank that makes no loans but holds traded securities could still be valuable.

explain that the very destructive nature of a run is perhaps helpful in disciplining the bank to work hard to honor its claims. So the fragility of runs is potentially important in allowing both high amounts of lending and large amounts of liquidity creation.

Gorton and Winton (2003) give a much more complete review of these three classes of theories and one clear conclusion that emerges is that depending on which of these three services is presumed to be operative, and which of the MM failures are present, one can reach very different conclusions about the efficacy of capital regulation in improving welfare. For instance, in models where liquidity creation is not one of the services provided by banks, the costs of mandating higher amounts of equity financing are often modest. Likewise, the benefits of protecting taxpayers from having to bail out banks or depositors by forcing more equity issuance are potentially substantial.

Rather than reviewing the results from many papers on capital regulation we refer interested readers to several recent surveys including Brooke et al (2015), Martynova (2015), Rochet (2014), and the references therein. Both Brooke et al. and Rochet attempt to compare the macroeconomic costs and benefits of higher levels of required capital and use a variety of calculations to assess them. In both cases, the benefits are presumed to be a reduction in likelihood and potential severity of financial crises (and the associated reductions in output). While the costs of higher capital requirements are the possible potential reductions in lending and losses of output. One humbling observation from both of these papers is that despite drawing on many different types of evidence, empirically estimating the net effects is difficult and there is substantial uncertainty about the overall net effects.

One other important observation is that most of the papers in these reviews are not very informative regarding liquidity regulation or the potential interactions of liquidity and capital regulation because in the environment being analyzed there is no value to liquidity creation (and hence no cost to limiting it). Indeed, Bouwman (2015), in a review article, emphasizes the dearth of research on potential interactions between capital and liquidity regulation and argues that it "is critically important to develop a good understanding of how capital and liquidity requirements interact."

2.3 Liquidity Regulation

As mentioned in Section 1, there are far fewer papers that seek to investigate the purpose and effect of liquidity regulation. Allen (2014) offers a survey of this nascent literature and we share the sentiment of the concluding paragraph of his survey. He writes, "much more research is required in this area. With capital regulation there is a huge literature but little agreement on the optimal level of requirements. With liquidity regulation, we do not even know what to argue about."

It is possible to again use a similar kind of two-way to classification regarding capital regulation to describe much of the thinking on liquidity. Trivially, if the economic services offered by a bank do not include the provision of liquidity, then regulation that focuses on liquidity will not be particularly interesting to consider. It is possible that in such environments regulating liquidity could make sense to achieve other aims, such as supplementing or substituting for capital requirements. However, if maturity transformation is not one of the outputs of the financial system, assessments of the efficacy of liquidity regulation in such models will be incomplete. Put bluntly, if there are no costs to limiting liquidity provision per se, then obviously the cost of regulations that have this effect cannot be fully assessed.

It is worth noting that will most of the literature on liquidity and liquidity regulation label the institutions that undertake this activity as "banks." However, as became evident in the GFC this activity is hardly limited to banks. Fig. 1, reproduced from

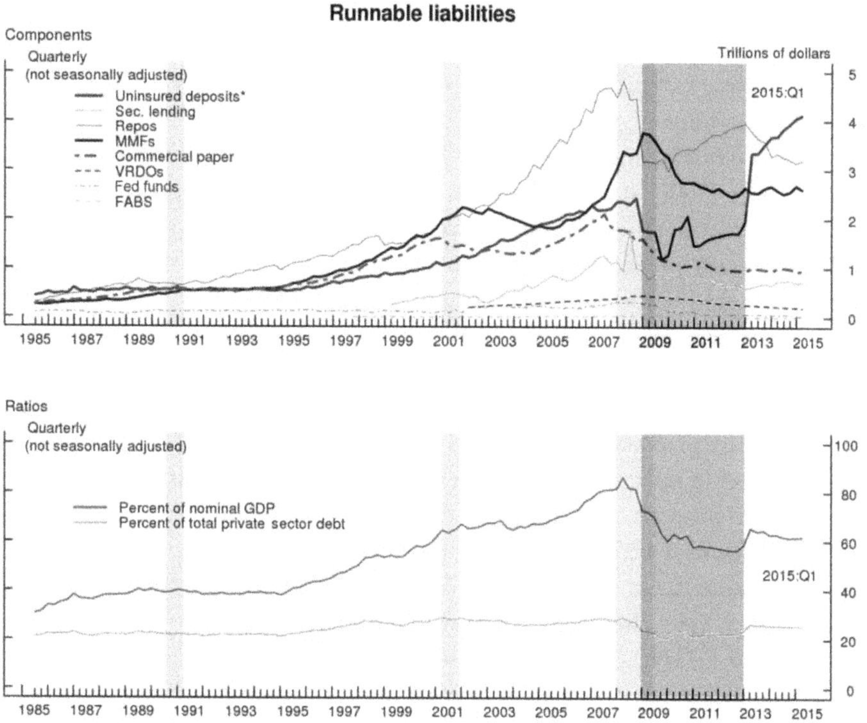

Fig. 1 Bao et al. (2015) estimates of runnable funding in the United States. *Uninsured deposits equal the difference between total deposits and insured deposits. The quarterly insured deposits series between 1985 and 1990 are obtained by interpolating the available annual data. For 2008:Q4–2012:Q4 (*red* (*light gray* in print version)) *shades*, insured deposits increased due to the Transaction Account Guarantee (TAG) program. For 2008:Q4–2009:Q2, some insured deposits were not accounted for because the FDIC did not collect data on insured amounts for those TAG accounts with balances between \$100,000 and \$250,000. *Note*: The *gray shades*, which overlap the *red* (*light gray* in print version) *shades*, indicate NBER recession dates. Source: *Staff calculations using data from RMA, DTCC, SIFMA, Call Reports, Financial Accounts, M3 monetary aggregates, and Bloomberg Finance LP.*

Bao et al. (2015), shows the total amount of runnable funding inside the US financial system over the past 30 years.

We draw three conclusions from their estimates that are worth bearing in mind throughout the rest of the discussion. First, there has been a sizable increase in the amount maturity transformation over the last 20 years. From 1995 until 2015, the scale of such activity rose by 50% as measured relative to gross domestic product (GDP). Second, as far back as 1985 as much of this activity has occurred outside the banking system as inside it. Third, the decline immediately after the GFC was sizable. The drop in repurchase agreements and money market funds were especially pronounced, but even as a percent of GDP, the level in 2015 is very similar to the level in 2005 (just before the frenzied period ahead of the GFC). Hence, maturity transformation is still happening on a substantial scale even after the GFC and all of the various regulatory reforms that have been introduced.

Given this evidence, we focus only on papers where one of the services of the financial system is to provide liquidity. Among these it is helpful to separate them into papers that model liquidity provision in the same way or similarly to DD, and those that introduce other mechanisms.

Among the DD style models, we focus on three that are closely related to our analysis. Ennis and Keister (2006) have a DD style model (related to Cooper and Ross, 1998) which determines how much liquidity banks need to hold to deter runs. They compute the amount of excess liquidity the bank must hold to buffer it against a run by all depositors, and also determine the optimal amounts to promise depositors. In their model with full information, when depositors desire safe banks, there will be private incentives to hold enough excess liquidity to deter a sunspot-based run. They do not study regulation because there is no need for any under their assumptions, but we will see that some of the same forces that are present in their model arise in ours.

Vives (2014) analyzes a question similar to that in Ennis and Keister (2006): what are the efficient combinations of equity capital and liquidity holdings to make a bank safe when it subject to runs based on private information about its solvency? He studies a global game where a bank can be insolvent or illiquid. The need for regulation is not considered explicitly, but he does examine what capital and liquidity levels would make the bank safer. He finds that capital and liquidity are differentially successful in attending to insolvency and illiquidity. In particular, if depositors are very conservative (and which makes them more inclined to run in the model), increased liquidity holdings which reduce profits by investing more in liquid assets can enhance stability.

Farhi et al. (2009) investigate a DD model where consumers need banks to invest and where the consumers can trade bank deposits. Absent a minimum liquidity regulation, it is profitable to free ride on the liquidity held by other banks, because banks offer rates which subsidize those who need to withdraw their deposit early (which is the spirit of Jacklin, 1987). A floor on liquidity holdings removes the incentive for this free riding.

Among the non-DD models, one that is related is Calomiris et al. (2014). They have a six period model where banks can potentially engage in risk-shifting so that when banks suffer loan losses they may not be able to honor their deposit contracts. Cash is observable and mandating that banks must have minimum levels of cash reserves can limit the risk-shifting.

Santos and Suarez (2015) examine another role for liquidity when runs occur slowly; it allows time to decide if the bank's assets are sufficient to imply solvency absent a run. This channel is foreclosed in our setup with assets which are free of risk.

More generally, our approach is closely related to the mechanism design approach to regulation of monopolists in Baron and Myerson (1982). They also were interested in investigating how regulation could be structured to induce the party being regulated to efficiently use information that is private.

3. BASELINE MODEL

We begin by describing a baseline setup in which the timing and preferences are as in DD. We then modify certain informational assumptions to bound the possible outcomes. Throughout we maintain that there are three dates: $T=0$, 1, and 2. The interest rates that bank must offer are taken as given, motivated by a monopoly bank which must meet the outside option of depositors to attract deposits. Equivalently, the single bank can be thought of as representing the overall banking system.

For a unit investment at date 0, the bank offers a demand deposit which pays either r_1 at date 1 or r_2 at date 2. This effectively offers a gross rate of return r_2/r_1 between dates 1 and 2 which is equal to the exogenous outside option (such as government bonds) for depositors between these dates. Essentially, the bank offers one period deposits which equal the interest rate on the outside option. We will assume that depositors are sufficiently risk averse that they would like the banking system to supply one period deposits that are riskless. Hence, when we consider interventions they will be designed to deliver as this as the only possible equilibrium.

The residual claim after deposits are paid is limited liability equity retained by the banker. All equity payments are made at date 2.[e]

The bank can invest in two assets with constant returns to scale. One is a liquid asset (which we will interchangeably refer to as the safe asset) that returns $R_1 > 0$ per unit invested in the previous period. The other is an illiquid asset for which a unit investment at date 0 returns at date 2 an amount that exceeds the return from rolling over liquid assets ($R_2 > R_1{*}R_1$). The illiquid asset (which we will interchangeably refer to a loan)

[e] We could introduce another incentive problem for the banker to motive a minimum value of equity at all dates and states, but for now the bank will operate efficiently as long as equity remains positive in equilibrium.

can be liquidated for θR_2 date 1, where $\theta R_2 < R_1$ and $\theta \geq 0$. These restrictions imply that when the bank knows it must make a payment at date 1, it is always more efficient to do that by investing in the safe asset rather than planning to liquidate the loan.

We also assume that banking is profitable even if the bank invests exclusively in the liquid asset, so that $r_1 \leq R_1$ and $r_2 \leq R_1^2$. This is a sufficient condition to guarantee that requiring excess liquidity will not make the bank insolvent (though it still will reduce the efficiency of investment). In addition, we assume that bank profits from investing in illiquid assets when depositors hold their deposits for two periods (borrowing short-term repeatedly to fund long-term illiquid investment) is greater than from investing in liquid assets when depositors hold their deposits for only one period (or $\frac{r_2}{R_2} < \frac{r_1}{R_1}$). This implies that a bank is most profitable when in can finance loans returning R_2 with deposits for two periods at cost r_2 (as compared with financing liquid assets for one period). This second assumption is used only to obtain some results on optimal liquidity holdings.

There are many possible reasons to presume that the illiquid asset can be liquidated for only θR_2. For instance, in DD liquidation can be thought of as a nontradable production technology. Alternatively it could reflect the bank's lending skills, implying that it would be worth less to a buyer than to the bank because (compared to the bank) the buyer would be able to collect less from a borrower, as in Diamond and Rajan (2001). Nothing in our analysis hinges on why this discount exists, though we do insist that it is operative for everyone in the economy including a potential lender of last resort (LOLR). Also, our assumption that θ is a constant implies that we are not modeling a situation where the sale price depends only on the amount of remaining liquidity held by potential buyers (as in Bhattacharya and Gale, 1987; Allen and Gale, 1997; and Diamond, 1997).

For fundamental reasons, a fraction t_s of depositors want to withdraw at date 1 and $1 - t_s$ want to withdraw at date 2 in state s. The realizations of t_s are bounded below by $\underline{t} \geq 0$ and above by $\bar{t} \leq 1$. The banker will know the realization of t_s when the asset composition choice is made. This assumption is meant to capture the fact that banks have superior information about their customers. Indeed, some early theories of banking supposed that the advantage of tying lending and deposit making was that by watching a customer's checking account activities a bank could gauge that customer's creditworthiness (Black, 1975).

Mester et al. (2007) provide direct evidence supporting the assumption that banks can learn about customer credit needs by monitoring transactions accounts. Drawing on a unique data set from a Canadian bank, they demonstrate the bank is able to infer changes in the value of borrowers' collateral that is posted against commercial loans by tracking flows into and out of the borrowers' transaction accounts. At this bank, they document that the number of prior borrowings in excess of collateral is an important predictor of credit downgrades and loan write-downs. Most importantly, the bank uses this information in making credit decisions. Loan reviews become longer and more frequent for borrowers with deteriorating collateral.[f] In what follows, we make the simplifying assumption t_s is always known exactly by the bank, but the analysis also goes through so long as the bank is simply better informed than the depositors and the regulator.

To understand agents' incentives, note that if the ex-post state is s and there is not a run, a fraction $f_1 = t_s$ will withdraw r_1 each, requiring $r_1 t_s$ in date 1 resources, and this will leave a fraction $1 - t_s$ depositors at date 2 who are collectively owed $r_2(1 - t_s)$ (in date 2 resources). If we let α_s be the fraction of the bank's portfolio that is invested in the liquid asset and $(1 - \alpha_s)$ be the portion invested in the illiquid one, then the bank's profits, and hence its value of equity in general will be

$$\text{Value of equity} = \left\{ \begin{array}{ll} (1-\alpha_s)R_2 + (\alpha_s R_1 - f_1 r_1)R_1 - (1-f_1)r_2 & \text{if } f_1 r_1 \leq \alpha_s R_1 \\ \text{Max}\left\{0, \left(1 - \alpha_s - \dfrac{(f_1 r_1 - \alpha_s R_1)}{\theta R_2}\right) R_2 - (1-f_1)r_2\right\} & \text{if } f_1 r > \alpha_s R \end{array} \right\} \tag{1}$$

Because we are assuming that the bank knows t_s, its own self-interest will lead it to make sure to always have enough invested in the liquid asset to cover these withdrawals. So absent a run, the profits are very intuitive and easy to understand. The first term in Eq. (1) when $f_1 r_1 \leq \alpha_s R_1$ represents the returns from the illiquid investment, the second reflects the spread on the safe asset relative to deposits (recognizing that any leftover funds are rolled over), and the third term reflects the funding costs of the remaining two period deposits. When $f_1 r_1 > \alpha_s R_1$, the bank needs to pay out more than its liquid assets are worth at date 1. To honor its promises, the bank must liquidate illiquid assets worth θR_2 each, implying that each unit of withdrawn in excess of $\alpha_s R_1$ removes $(1/\theta R_2)$ loans from the bank's balance sheet. These loans would each be worth R_2 at date 2. For a bank in this situation that can honor all early and late withdrawals the residual profits go to the banker (otherwise the bank is insolvent). Given our assumptions about interest rates and liquidation discounts, if actual withdraws, f_1, were known, the bank would choose to hold enough liquid assets to avoid needing to liquidate any loans. We know that at all times, even absent a run in state s, $f_1 \geq t_s$. As a result, the bank will always have an incentive to choose $\alpha_s \geq \frac{t_s r_1}{R_1} \equiv \alpha_s^{AIC}$. As a result, we refer to α_s^{AIC} as the *automatically incentive compatible* liquidity holding of the bank.

It is interesting to consider what happens when a run is possible. We suppose that a fixed number Δ of the patient depositors are highly likely to see a sunspot. All depositors (and the bank) know Δ and upon seeing the sunspot they must decide whether they believe that the others who see it will decide withdraw their funds early. As mentioned

[f] Norden and Weber (2010) also find that credit line usage, credit limit violations, and cash inflows into checking accounts are unusual in the periods preceding defaults by small businesses and individuals in Germany.

earlier, the sunspot is intended to stand in for general fears about the solvency of the bank, so the inference problem relates to their conjecture about whether others investors might panic. In that case, they have to decide whether to join the run.[g] So in general $f_1 > t_s$ is possible.

If the bank will be insolvent with a fraction of withdrawals of any amount less than $t_s + \Delta$, then we assume each depositor who sees then sunspot will withdraw and $f_1 = t_s + \Delta$. This will give zero to all who do not withdraw, and the goal of bank or its regulator is to prevent this outcome from ever being a Nash equilibrium. We will refer to a bank as unstable if its asset holdings admit the possibility of a run. Alternatively, we refer to a bank as stable if its asset holding eliminate the possibility of a run.

In addition, we will assume that if the bank is exactly solvent at $f_1 = t_s + \Delta$, no depositor who does not need to withdraw (and only sees the sunspot) will withdraw. This condition establishes exactly how much liquidity is needed to deter a run (as opposed to providing a floor which must be exceeded). We define the *minimum stable amount of liquidity holdings*, α_s^{Stable} as the minimum fraction of liquid assets in state s which eliminate the possibility of a run. This implies that a bank with $\alpha_s \geq \alpha_s^{\text{Stable}}$ will be run-free.

3.1 Complete Information

We presume that depositors desire run-free bank deposits. As a first benchmark, suppose that depositors know all of the choices and information which banks know, and thus observe α_s, Δ, and t_s. In this case, the need to attract deposits will force the bank to make itself run-free. If, given depositor knowledge of α_s, Δ, and t_s, the bank would remain solvent in a run, then it never is individually rational to react to the sunspot, and there will be no runs. Proposition 1 shows that it is possible that the bank will not need to distort its holding of liquidity to implement run-free banking.

Proposition 1

If the bank chooses $\alpha_s^{\text{AIC}} = \frac{t_s r_1}{R_1}$, and if

$$t_s + \Delta_s < \frac{t_s r_1 + \left(1 - \frac{t_s r_1}{R_1}\right)\theta R_2 - r_2\theta}{r_1 - r_2\theta} \left(\text{equivalently } \theta \geq \frac{\Delta r_1 R_1}{R_2(R_1 - r_1 t_s) - r_2 R_1(1 - t_s - \Delta)}\right),$$

investors will not run and the bank is stable with $\alpha_s^{\text{AIC}} = \frac{t_s r_1}{R_1}$.

[g] Uhlig (2010) shows that partial bank runs in a DD style model can arise if there other types of dispersion in agents' beliefs. For instance, if depositors are highly uncertainty averse and differ in their estimates of θ that heterogeneity can lead to a partial bank run in his setup.

Proof

If $f_1 r > \alpha R_1$, the bank's equity is positive when $\left(1-\alpha_s - \frac{(f_1 r_1 - \alpha_s R_1)}{\theta R_2}\right) R_2 - (1-f_1) r_2 \geq 0.$

So, when the automatically incentive compatible level of initial liquidity α^{AIC} is chosen $\left(\alpha_s^{\mathrm{AIC}} = \frac{t_s r_1}{R_1}\right)$, the value of equity is decreasing in f_1 and equal zero when $f_1^* = \frac{\frac{t_s r_1}{R_1} R_1 + \left(1 - \frac{t_s r_1}{R_1}\right)\theta R_2 - r_2\theta}{r_1 - r_2\theta}$. Therefore, if $t_s + \Delta$ is less than f_1^*, then the depositors always know the bank will be solvent and there is no Nash equilibrium with a run. □

The proposition simply states the condition when the bank is sufficiently profitable and liquid, so that by holding only enough of the liquid asset to service fundamental withdrawals, the bank will nonetheless be solvent in the event of a run. Under these conditions, $\alpha_s^{\mathrm{AIC}} \geq \alpha_s^{\mathrm{Stable}}$.

When the conditions for Proposition 1 fail, because loans are quite illiquid or the bank is not very profitable, then to deter runs, a bank must hold more liquidity than is needed to meet normal withdrawals. One useful case to contemplate is when loans are totally illiquid ($\theta = 0$). In this case, the bank must always hold enough liquidity to fully finance the run because there is no other way to get access to liquidity or $\alpha_s^{\mathrm{Stable}} = (t_s + \Delta)\frac{r_1}{R_1} > \alpha_s^{\mathrm{AIC}} = \frac{t_s r_1}{R_1}$. Therefore, the bank must always hold more liquidity than is needed for normal withdrawals in order to deter a run. More generally, whenever

$$t_s + \Delta > \frac{t_s r_1 + \left(1 - \frac{t_s r_1}{R_1}\right)\theta R_2 - r_2\theta}{r_1 - r_2\theta} \quad \text{or } \theta < \frac{\Delta r_1 R_1}{R_2(R_1 - r_1 t_s) - r_2 R_1(1 - t_s - \Delta)}$$

then the bank must increase α_s to $\alpha_s^{\mathrm{stable}}$ to definitely deter the run, where $\alpha_s^{\mathrm{stable}}$ is such that $t_s + \Delta = \frac{\alpha_s^{\mathrm{stable}} R_1 + \left(1 - \alpha_s^{\mathrm{stable}}\right)\theta R_2 - r_2\theta}{r_1 - r_2\theta}$. This yields

$$\alpha_s^{\mathrm{stable}} = \frac{(t_s + \Delta) r_1 + \theta((1 - t_s - \Delta) r_2 - R_2)}{R_1 - \theta R_2}.$$

So when it is sufficiently illiquid, merely preparing to service fundamental withdrawals will not always be enough to deter a run.

This threshold tells us how much liquidity is needed when there is full information such that all variables including t_s are known and all parties understand the bank's incentives. Under the conditions of Proposition 1, the bank will choose $\alpha_s = \frac{t_s r_1}{R_1}$ and no unused liquidity is held from dates 1 to 2. Because depositors might choose to run and the incentive for this must be removed, this will not be enough liquidity when the conditions for Proposition 1 do not hold. To always deter a possible run, the bank will have to hold $\alpha_s = \alpha_s^{\text{Stable}} > \alpha_s^{\text{AIC}}$. This will require that some unused liquidity, $(\alpha_s^{\text{Stable}} - \alpha_s^{\text{AIC}})R_1 \equiv U(t_s) > 0$, to be held from date 1 to 2, after the normal withdraws are met at date 1. If the bank is free to use all of this unused liquidity if a run should occur, then depositors can see that the liquidity is present and will never choose to run. Once the run is deterred, the liquidity will be in excess of what is needed. This is the simplest example of the benefits of holding unused liquidity or leaving extra taxicabs at the train station.

With full information available to all parties, market forces will produce run-free banking. Alternatively, suppose the depositors do not observe t_s or α_s, but the bank and a regulator do. Then the following arrangement is possible, but only by regulation.

Proposition 2
With full information available to the bank or regulators, a bank (or a regulator) seeking to deter runs will choose $\alpha_s^* = \max\{\alpha_s^{\text{AIC}}, \alpha_s^{\text{Stable}}\}$.

Proof
The bank is automatically stable when $\frac{r_1 t_s}{R_1} \geq \alpha_s^{\text{Stable}}$ so the regulator would always want to maximize lending and allow the bank to follow its self-interest and select that level $\left(\frac{r_1 t_s}{R_1}\right)$ of liquidity. Otherwise, the minimum amount of liquidity that is needed is α_s^{Stable}. □

More generally, for arbitrary anticipated withdrawals of t_s, α_s^{AIC} and α_s^{Stable} will differ and if liquidity, θ, is not too high or too low, and their relationship will be similar to what is shown in Fig. 2. For very low levels of anticipated withdrawals, where the condition in

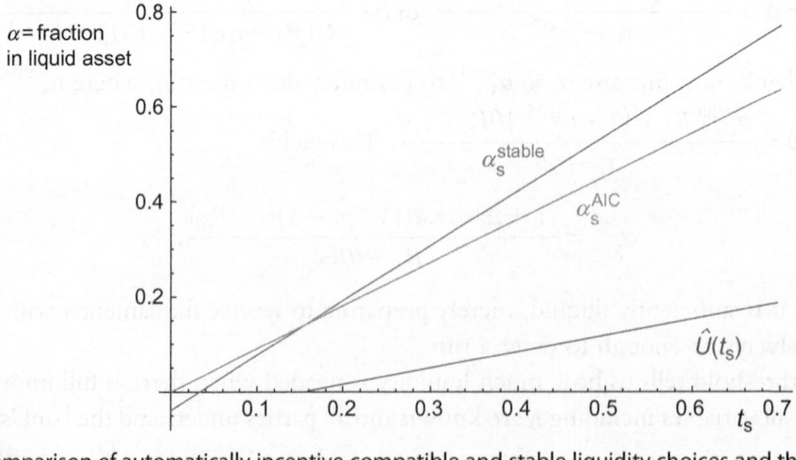

Fig. 2 Comparison of automatically incentive compatible and stable liquidity choices and the implied amount of unused liquidity held from date 1 to 2. *Note*: parameter values are $\Delta = 0.3$, $\theta = 0.5$, $R_1 = 1.1$, $R_2 = 1.33$, $r_1 = r_2 = 1$.

Proposition 1 holds, the bank is sufficiently solvent that chooses to hold more ex-ante liquidity than is need to be stable, so that runs are impossible. At some point, however, this ceases to be true and the amount needed to just be solvent in a run is higher than the bank would hold out of pure self-interest. So in this case run deterrence would require a higher level of initial liquidity. This observation will be helpful in understanding some of the regulatory trade-offs that we subsequently explore.

Note that because some liquidity must be unused, it will appear that there is an unneeded amount of liquidity. With full information, this amount will serve to deter runs and will be chosen at date 0 with all knowing the amount of normal withdrawals at date 1 t_s. If more than a fraction t_s were to withdraw at date 1, the unused liquidity could be used because all would know that a run was occurring. The bank, or regulator acting for depositors, could use liquidity holdings to deter runs in the efficient way which maximizes lending. Because depositors always desire run-free deposits, with full information, banks would be forced to hold the extra unused liquidity because otherwise no deposits would be attracted.

To summarize, with complete information, a bank will be forced to hold enough liquidity to deter runs, and its desire to maximize profits will assure that it holds no more than this amount. The next section explains why the complete information benchmark may not be very informative. Once the possibility of incomplete information is considered, we can see that arriving at run-free banking can be challenging.

3.2 Incomplete Information: Is It a Problem?

While the full-information benchmark is helpful, we think it is too extreme to be realistic. Banks disclosures may be very difficult to interpret. We describe a few compelling reasons to doubt that simply disclosing some information about liquidity holdings will make depositors (or regulators) well informed about all of these quantities. This suggests that disclosure of such information may not, by itself, force a bank to make the decisions, which they would make under complete information.

There is one important situation where incomplete information is not necessarily a problem. Even if there is no disclosure of asset holdings, depositors, who know Δ and observe a such t_s the conditions of Proposition 1 are satisfied, will know that the bank's choice will eliminate run risk in state s, because $\alpha_s^{\text{AIC}} = \frac{t_s r_1}{R_1} \geq \alpha_s^{\text{Stable}}$ (the bank is automatically stable in this case). If this was satisfied for all states, s, a bank would always choose a level of liquid asset holdings which always results in stability even if no one could verify those holdings and if no depositor knew the state s. Whenever this condition is not universally satisfied, the bank's incentives to hold liquidity will depend on the information available to depositors (or regulators) and on the incentives provided to the bank.

We believe that in most cases a bank's liquidity choice is not always automatically stable. This suggests that some forms of disclosure or regulation will influence its choice of liquidity. We describe two types of reasons that simple disclosure of liquidity is difficult to interpret. First, if disclosure (or a regulatory requirement) regarding liquidity only applies on some dates (such as the end of an accounting period), the bank can distort the disclosure. Second, even if a liquidity disclosure (or requirement) is on all dates, it is plausible that the bank knows much more about its customers liquidity needs than anyone else, which makes it very difficult to determine if a given level of liquidity is sufficient to make the bank stable and run-free.

3.2.1 Problems with the Periodic Disclosure of Liquidity

One important problem facing depositors is the difficulty in interpreting the kind of accounting data that must be parsed in order to decide whether to join a run. Disclosures that are made on liquidity positions typically occur with a delay and are periodic (such as at the end of a quarter or a fiscal year). The inference problem for depositors can be compounded by the temptation for banks to engage in window dressing of their accounting information.

One eye-opening example of the problem, analyzed in Munyan (2015), is the tendency of (mostly) European banks to disguise borrowing around quarter-end dates. As Munyan (2015) explains, many non-US banks are required to report their accounting information that forms the basis various regulatory ratios only on the last day of the quarter. In the United States, banks also have to show average daily ratios for critical balance sheet variables which caps the gains from manipulating end-of-quarter data. The non-US banks apparently sell some safe assets just before the end of the quarter and then buy them back shortly afterwards. This transaction allows them to report lower leverage across the quarter-end date.

The ingenious aspect of Munyan's analysis is using detailed data on the tri-party repo market to infer this behavior. He explains how the banks' would normally be borrowing in this market to fund these assets. Because they step back only briefly, their window dressing shows up in reduced repo volumes. Fig. 3 (reproduced from fig. 1 of Munyan) shows the raw data on repo volumes with the quarter-end dates indicated with dashed vertical lines. The pattern is so strong that it is clearly evident from inspection. Munyan's econometric estimates suggest that the non-US banks trim their end of quarter borrowing by about $170 billion, with the vast majority of the decline coming from European banks.

This problem of the potential window dressing of periodic disclosures is relevant to measuring bank liquidity, due to the complicated nature of the kind of liquidity information that needs to be inferred. Cetina and Gleason (2015) provide a series of examples about how the LCR is vulnerable to this type of manipulation. Some of the problems come because of the ability to use repurchase agreements (and reverse repurchase

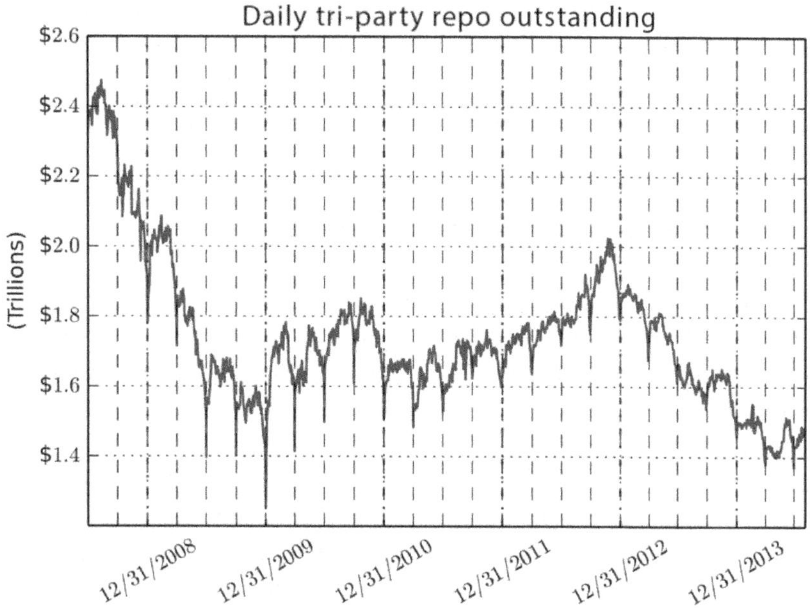

Fig. 3 Tri-party repo volumes outstanding from Munyan (2015).

agreements) to move the timing of cash flows. But the rules also distinguish between the assumed levels of liquidity of different asset class and some types of transactions can alter both the numerator and denominator of a ratio in different ways. Moreover, the computations in different jurisdictions vary which further complicates comparisons.

In summary, this possibility for window dressing implies that liquidity disclosures and regulations should hold on all dates rather than being applied periodically. In our model, this will mean that it may be difficult to credibly disclose α_s, the initial holding of liquidity, because this could be invested in illiquid loans after the disclosure. Requiring liquidity to be held on all dates (after date 1 in our model) will of course limit its use to meet withdraws of deposits. This again brings back the problem of not allowing the last taxicab to leave the station. In addition, disclosure or regulation of complicated liquidity holdings may require careful auditing (for disclosure) or supervision (for regulation).

3.2.2 Liquidity Disclosures Are Difficult to Interpret

A second challenge facing depositors and regulators in interpreting disclosed information is placing it in appropriate context. Suppose all parties are truthfully told the level of liquid asset holdings in the banking system at a given date (or even on every date). Judging whether these are adequate to service impending withdrawals requires knowledge of how far along a potential run might be on that date and how many normal withdrawals are anticipated. If a bank has a small amount of liquidity after its normal withdraws (of $t_s r_1$ in state s), this is very different than if normal withdrawals have not yet occurred. It is possible that very little additional liquidity would be needed if most potential withdrawals have already occurred. How could banks credibly communicate such information? The next section provides a model of this, based on the bank's private information about the normal level of withdrawals, t_s.

3.2.3 A Bank Has Private Information About Needed Liquidity

Before turning to the details of the model, it is helpful to provide some intuition about how private information possessed by the bank interacts with the incentives of depositors to run. Similar problems arise at both date 0 and date 1 in the model, but we will describe them in turn. One reason for separating out the discussion is because in our framework the most natural analogs to the Basel-style regulation can be thought of in terms what they imply as of different dates.

If there is no way to communicate what the bank knows, and it is not automatically stable, then disclosing a level of liquidity at date 0, α_s, which would make the bank stable only in some states of nature, t_s, will not be adequate completely eliminate runs. In these cases, depositors will have two reasons to be worried. First, in the states of nature where it would not be stable, a run would cause the bank to fail and thus would be self-fulfilling, leading to losses by depositors who did not run.

Second, because depositors do not know t_s, a depositor (whom we assume to be very risk averse) who sees a sunspot and worries about a run will always withdraw rather than face losses if the unknown state turns out to be one that makes the bank fail. As a result, a level of liquidity disclosure, which is not sufficient to makes a bank run-free for all levels of t_s, will lead to runs whenever they are feared, even for the levels of t_s where this does not cause bank failure. In the next section, we will explain why an NSFR approach to liquidity regulation (which can be mapped into restrictions on date 0 liquidity choices) can be susceptible to such concerns.

Suppose that a positive level of liquidity held at date 1, after withdrawals from a fraction f_1 of deposits, is regulated and required. It can also be very difficult to interpret this level when the normal level of withdrawals, t_s, is unknown. Any liquidity which must be held from date 1 to date 2 is not available to service withdrawals at date 1. From Proposition 2, we would like to require a level of unused liquidity $U(t_s)$ that coincides with the amount specified under full information. This amount would deter runs in state s by being available to be completely used to meet the withdrawals in a run from a fraction $t_s + \Delta$ of depositors.

When depositors must guess about the level of normal withdrawals, merely observing the actual outflows in period 1 is not necessarily enough to assure them about the safety of their deposits. To see the problem consider two levels of normal withdrawals, High and Low such that $t_{s=\text{High}} = t_{s=\text{Low}} + \Delta$. A positive level of liquidity which must be held if $f_1 = t_{s=\text{high}}$ cannot be released to meet with the same number of withdrawals during a

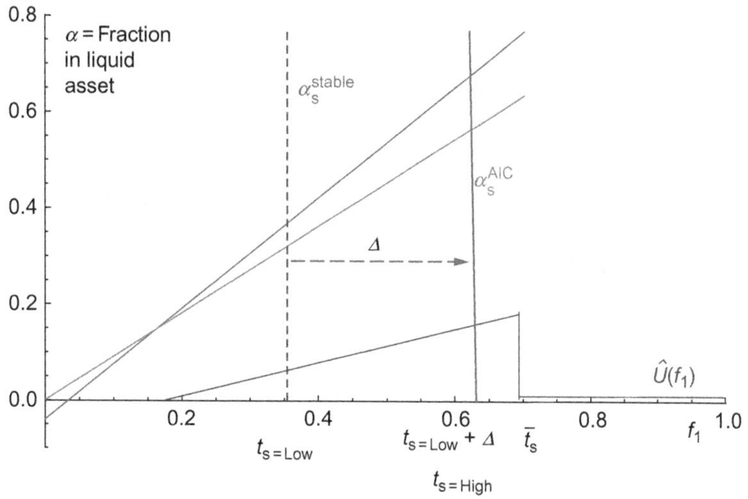

Fig. 4 Inability to distinguish between runs and large fundamental withdrawals.

run with $f_1 = t_{s=\text{low}} + \Delta$. This is shown in Fig. 4. Therefore, the full-information level of liquidity required at date 1 cannot be implemented without a way to learn the bank's information about the normal level of withdrawals, t_s. We will show how this is related to the implementation of the LCR approach to regulating liquidity in the next section.

For the balance of this chapter, we assume that liquidity on date 0 and date 1 can be measured (for example by a regulator) but that the bank has private information about the normal levels of withdrawals, t_s. This information friction alone is sufficient to study many interesting issues in the regulation of liquidity needed to make banks run-free. If the regulator cannot learn this information, it will constrain the efficiency of regulation.

4. BASEL-STYLE REGULATORY OPTIONS

Based on these observations about the efficacy of disclosure, for the remainder of our analysis we assume that liquidity on date 0 and date 1 can be measured (for example by a regulator), but we want understand the limitations that arise if the bank has private information about the normal levels of withdrawals, t_s. This information friction alone is sufficient to study many interesting issues in the regulation of liquidity needed to make banks run-free. To see how things unfold, we will begin again with a case where the regulator can also observe the state and then contrast that with what happens if the regulator cannot learn this information. Throughout we continue to assume that depositors are sufficiently risk averse so that run-free banking is social optimum which we seek to implement.

We consider two potential approaches that a regulator could pursue. These are inspired by the kinds of regulations that are proposed as part of Basel III. We suppose that she can credibly certify that the bank has some level of the liquid asset present (as a percentage of deposits). One option is to report on this ratio at the time when the liquid assets are acquired at time zero. This would amount to regulating α, and this is similar in spirit the NSFR. The NSFR requires "banks to maintain a stable funding profile in relation to the composition of their assets and off-balance sheet activities" (Basel Committee on Bank Supervision 2014). Loosely speaking, the NSFR can be thought of as forcing banks to match long-term assets with long-term funding. Our interpretation of this requirement is that the bank is free to violate the requirement temporarily in the future, so it is not always a binding restriction. As a result, it is very much like a requirement that the bank chooses a level of liquid holdings at date 0, α_s. From Proposition 2, we know that with complete information a regulation that is bank and state specific can be effective in delivering run-free banking, the question we ask now is what happens in other situations.

Alternatively, a regulator could insist that the bank will always have a certain amount of liquid assets relative to deposits at all times, including after any withdrawals. This kind of regulation is more like the LCR. The LCR requires "that banks have an adequate stock of unencumbered high-quality liquid assets that can be converted easily and immediately in private markets into cash to meet their liquidity needs for a 30 calendar day liquidity stress scenario" (Basel Committee on Bank Supervision, 2013a).

4.1 An LCR Regulation

Ultimately we are interested in understanding how the LCR works when the regulator cannot learn the bank's information about t_s. As a first step, we consider an LCR regulation where the state is known by the regulator and where the regulation says the bank must always (on both dates) hold a fraction ρ_s of deposits in liquid assets in state s. At date, 1 the bank has promised depositors $r_1(1-f_1)$. The important consequence of this is that regulation would even apply after first period withdrawals (f_1), when the bank would have to have a minimum level of safe assets equal to $\rho_s r_1(1-f_1)$.

If the bank is subject to this requirement, and it conjectures that f_1 depositors will withdraw in state s, then its optimal initial level of safe assets (α_s) will satisfy $\alpha_s R_1 = f_1 r_1 + \rho_s r_1(1-f_1)$. This choice follows trivially because it is never efficient to make loans with intention of liquidating them, and this is the minimum amount of liquid assets that will satisfy the regulation. Accordingly, the bank knows that the depositors will know this (and also understand that the bank is trying to maximize its profits). The residual value of the bank's equity will be:

$$E_2(f_1;\rho)=\begin{cases}(\alpha_s R_1-f_1 r_1)R_1+(1-\alpha_s)R_2-(1-f_1)r_2 & \text{if } f_1<\dfrac{\alpha_s R_1-r_1\rho_s}{r_1(1-\rho_s)},\\ \left((1-\alpha_s)-\dfrac{f_1 r_1-\alpha_s R_1+\rho_s(1-f_1)}{\theta R_2}\right)R_2 & \text{if } f_1\geq\dfrac{\alpha_s R_1-r_1\rho_s}{r_1(1-\rho_s)}\text{ and}\\ +(\rho_s R_1-r_2)(1-f_1) & \text{if } f_1\leq\dfrac{\alpha_s R_1+(1-\alpha_s)\theta R_2-\rho_s r_1(1-\theta R_1)-r_2\theta}{r_1-\rho_s r_1(1-\theta R_1)-r_2\theta},\\ 0 & \text{if } f_1>\dfrac{\alpha_s R_1+(1-\alpha_s)\theta R_2-\rho_s r_1(1-\theta R_1)-r_2\theta}{r_1-\rho_s r_1(1-\theta R_1)-r_2\theta}.\end{cases}$$

Each branch of the expression is intuitive. The top branch shows the profits that accrue when withdrawals are small enough that the bank can pay all depositors without liquidating any loans and still satisfy the LCR; this will be the case whenever $f_1 r_1<\alpha_s R_1+\rho_s r_1(1-f_1)$, which when rearranged is the threshold condition that is listed. In this case, the bank has two sources of revenue, one coming from rolling over the residual safe assets after paying early depositors and the other coming from the return on the loans. The date 2 depositors must be paid and the banker keeps everything that is left.

The second branch represents a case where the bank must liquidate some loans to service the early withdrawals. In this case, the bank liquidates just enough loans so that after the deposits are paid, it exactly satisfies the LCR. The same two sources of revenues and deposit cost are present, but the formula adjusts for the liquidations. Recall that each loan that is liquidated yields θR_2 at date 1. Hence rather than having the revenue from the full set of loans $(1-\alpha_s)$ that were initially granted, the bank only receives returns on the portion that remains after some loans that were liquidated in order to pay the depositors and comply with the LCR. Because the LCR is binding from date 1 until date 2, the bank has exactly $\rho_s r_1(1-f_1)$ of the safe asset that is rolled over and that money can also be used to pay the remaining patient depositors. Notice that if the loans are totally illiquid and $\theta=0$, then there is no possibility of this second branch (where free liquidity in excess of the coverage ratio is fully used but the bank remains solvent).

The third branch obtains when the level of withdrawals is sufficiently large that the bank becomes insolvent. Insolvency occurs when $f_1>\dfrac{\alpha_s R_1+(1-\alpha_s)\theta R_2-\rho_s r_1(1-\theta R_1)-r_2\theta}{r_1-\rho_s r_1(1-\theta R_1)-r_2\theta}$ because at that point the depositors can see that the liquidations do not generate enough to fully cover the promised repayments.

The bank knows that depositors consider all these possibilities in trying to infer what the bank will do. If the coverage ratio can be set such that the bank chooses to hold sufficient liquidity to remain solvent during a run, then runs will be deterred. Proposition 3 examines the outcomes if the bank faces a state-contingent LCR in state s, $\rho_s\in[0, 1]$.

Proposition 3
There is an LCR in state s, $\rho_s \in [0, 1]$ which will deter runs. When ρ_s is not zero or one it satisfies:

$$t_s + \Delta = \frac{\dfrac{t_s r_1 + \rho_s r_1 (1-t_s)}{R_1} R_1 + \left(1 - \dfrac{t_s r_1 + \rho_s r_1 (1-t_s)}{R_1}\right) \theta R_2 - \rho_s r_1 (1 - \theta R_1) - r_2 \theta}{r_1 - \rho_s r_1 (1 - \theta R_1) - r_2 \theta},$$

implying that

$$\rho_s = \frac{\theta R_1((1 - t_s - \Delta) r_2 - R_2) + r_1(\Delta R_1 + t_s \theta R_2)}{r_1(\Delta R_1 + (1 - t_s - \Delta)\theta R_1^2 - (1 - t_s)\theta R_2)}.$$

A regulator who knows t_s can choose ρ_s so as to deter runs.

Proof
If the bank is run-free in state s and $f_1 = t_s$, then it will pick α_s to satisfy:

$$\alpha_s R_1 = t_s r_1 + \rho_s r_1 (1 - t_s)$$

Because the bank will be solvent for all $f_1 \leq \bar{f}_1(\rho_s) = \dfrac{\alpha_s R_1 + (1 - \alpha_s)\theta R_2 - \rho_s r_1 (1 - \theta R_1) - r_2 \theta}{r_1 - \rho_s r_1 (1 - \theta R_1) - r_2 \theta}$, the regulator can pick ρ_s such that it delivers $t_s + \Delta \leq \bar{f}_1(\rho_s)$ and $\alpha_s = \dfrac{t_s r_1 + \rho_s r_1 (1 - t_s)}{R_1}$. If $t_s + \Delta \leq \bar{f}(\rho_s)$ at $\rho_s = 0$, then $\rho_s = 0$ suffices. If instead $t_s + \Delta > \bar{f}(\rho_s)$ at $\rho_s = 0$, then either a $\rho_s < 1$ solves (2) as an equality or if not then we will see that $\rho_s = 1$ satisfies (2):

$$t_s + \Delta \leq \frac{\dfrac{t_s r_1 + \rho_s (1-t_s)}{R_1} R_1 + \left(1 - \dfrac{t_s r_1 + \rho_s (r_1 1 - t_s)}{R_1}\right) \theta R_2 - \rho_s r_1 (1 - \theta R_1) - r_2 \theta}{r_1 - \rho_s r_1 (1 - \theta R_1) - r_2 \theta} \quad (2)$$

From our assumptions that $r_1 \leq R_1$ and $r_2 \leq R_1^2$, the bank is solvent with $\rho_s = 1$ and there will always be a value of ρ between 0 and 1 which satisfies (2). If the bank is not solvent given a run with $\rho_s = 0$, then either a $\rho_s \in (0, 1)$ exists where (2) holds with equality or no $\rho_s < 1$ keeps the bank solvent and then lowest ρ_s is given by $\rho_s = \min\left[1, \dfrac{\theta R_1((1 - t_s - \Delta) r_2 - R_2) + r_1(\Delta R_1 + t_s \theta R_2)}{r_1(\Delta R_1 + (1 - t_s - \Delta)\theta R_1^2 - (1 - t_s)\theta R_2)}\right]$. □

If the regulator chooses an appropriate level of $\rho_s \leq 1$ knowing t_s, then depositors can be sure that the bank is stable and will never want to join a run, even though they cannot observe or interpret the level of liquidity at any instant. The intuition for why the regulation (which is a combination of a rule which can be enforced and credibly auditing) is sufficient to foreclose a run, even when the bank's liquidity choice is unobservable to depositors, is straightforward. The LCR forces the bank to invest in more liquid assets than it would voluntarily prefer to hold and the depositors know that the regulator is doing this to try to prevent runs. The bank's own self-interest continues to insure that it plans to always hold enough liquid assets to cover its anticipated fundamental withdrawals, and we are assuming that it can do that perfectly. Consequently, knowing that the extra liquidity cannot be avoided removes the incentive to run.

Importantly, once the run has been prevented the liquidity still will have to remain on the bank's balance sheet. So, under these assumptions it is beneficial to force the last taxi cab to always remain at the train station.

There are several special cases where there is an interesting corner solution. If $\theta = 0$, then for all values of t_s, $\rho_s = \frac{r_1(\Delta R_1)}{r_1 \Delta R_1} = 1$ and as a result $\alpha_s = \frac{t_s r_1 + r_1(1-t_s)}{R_1} = \frac{r_1}{R_1}$. This implies that the bank must invest in a sufficient fraction of liquid assets to finance a withdrawal of 100% of deposits. This is not surprising because in this case the loans are so illiquid as to have no value during a run.

Alternatively, if the asset is not totally illiquid, $\theta > 0$, but $r_1 = R_1 = 1$, then the bank earns no spread between its deposits and its liquid asset holdings and there exists a possible value of t_s such that a complete run is possible, $t_s + \Delta = 1$, then for that value of t_s

$$\rho_s = \frac{\theta R_1((1-t_s-\Delta)r_2 - R_2) + r_1(\Delta R_1 + t_s \theta R_2)}{r_1(\Delta R_1 + (1-t_s-\Delta)\theta R_1^2 - (1-t_s)\theta R_2)} = \frac{\Delta - (1-t_s)\theta R_2}{\Delta - (1-t_s)\theta R_2} = 1.$$

In this case, if the bank experiences a complete run and holds just enough liquid assets to meet withdrawals in a complete run ($\alpha_s = \frac{r_1}{R_1} = 1$, ie, 100% liquid assets), it is just solvent (net worth is just zero), and any reduction in holdings of liquidity would make it insolvent given a run by all depositors.

To better understand how the model works, consider the following example (which is not calibrated in any particular way). Suppose the value of t_s is $t_s = ½$, and $\theta = ½$, $R_1 = 1.1$, $R_2 = 1.5$, $r_1 = r_2 = 1$, then it is possible to solve for the ρ_s needed to deter the run as a function of Δ. Fig. 5 shows this correspondence.

For these parameters, there are two interesting regions. First, up until the point when Δ reaches about 0.32, the optimal value of ρ_s is zero. In this region runs that are small enough so that the condition in Proposition 1 holds and the bank selfishly will always hold enough liquid assets so as to deter a run.

At certain point, however, the condition in Proposition 1 no longer applies and profits are no longer sufficient to prevent the run. For potential runs that are this size (or larger), ρ_s must be positive and it increases as the size of the potential run does, up until the point where a full run is a possibility.

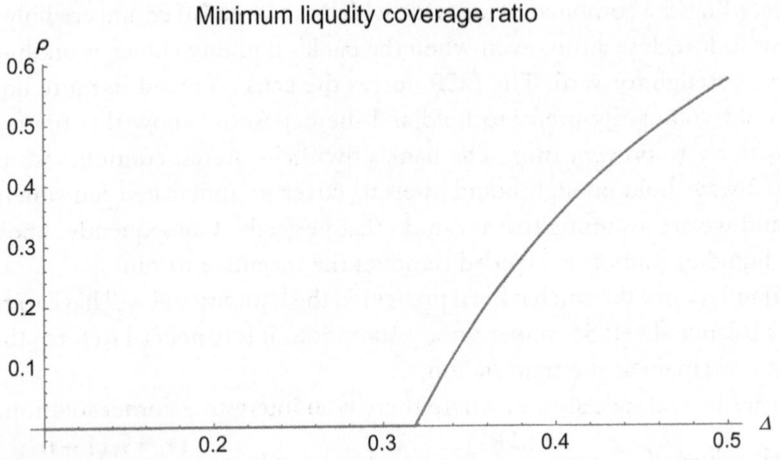

Fig. 5 Liquidity coverage ratio as a function of the potential run risk.

While a highly contingent LCR type regulation is a useful benchmark, we believe a more accurate description of this type of regulation is one where ρ is identical in all states. The constancy could arise because of limited information available to regulators and/or the desire for simplicity. Proposition 4 characterizes the optimal LCR when t_s is private information to the bank and required ratio is constant, ρ.

Proposition 4

If the regulator must specify an LCR with a constant ρ knowing only the distribution of outcomes, then a value which leads the bank to be stable for all t_s must be specified. The worst case for solvency given a run is the bank with anticipated withdrawals of $\bar{t}$ (the highest possible value of t_s). An LCR ratio which makes the bank with $\bar{t}$ anticipated withdrawals just solvent in a complete run will make all types of banks safe.

Proof

A bank of type t_s, subject to an LCR of ρ will choose $\alpha_s R_1 = t_s r_1 + \rho r_1(1-t_s)$ and given a run, the value of its equity when withdrawals exceed t_s and $f_1 = t_s + \Delta$ is

$$E(\rho, t = t_s, f_1 = t_s + \Delta)$$
$$= \left(1 - \left(\frac{t_s r_1 + r_1 \rho(1-t_s)}{R_1}\right) - \frac{t_s r_1 - \dfrac{t_s r_1 + \rho r_1(1-t_s)}{R_1} R_1 + \rho r_1(1-t_s-\Delta)}{\theta R_2}\right) R_2$$
$$+ (\rho r_1 R_1 - r_2)(1 - t_s - \Delta)$$

Define $\hat{\rho}$ to be the lowest ρ for a type $\hat{t}_s$, such that the value of equity given a run for that type will be exactly zero (so it will just be solvent). To determine the solvency of types

$t_s < \hat{t}_s$ subject to this sort of regulation, note each will choose $\alpha_s = \frac{t_s r_1 + \hat{\rho} r_1 (1 - t_s)}{R_1}$. Differentiating $E(\hat{\rho}, t = t_s, f_1 = t_s + \Delta)$ with respect to t_s yields:

$$\frac{\partial E(\hat{\rho}, t = t_s, f_1 = t_s + \Delta)}{\partial t_s} = r_2 + \frac{(r_1 \hat{\rho} - r_1) R_2}{R_1} - \hat{\rho} r_1 R_1.$$

From the assumption that it is more profitable to finance illiquid assets with deposits absent a withdrawal than to finance liquid asset with one period deposits, $\frac{r_1}{R_1} > \frac{r_2}{R_2}$, we know $r_2 < \frac{R_2 r_1}{R_1}$, which implies that:

$$r_2 + \frac{(\hat{\rho} r_1 - r_1) R_2}{R_1} - \hat{\rho} r_1 R_1 < \frac{R_2 r_1}{R_1} + \frac{(\hat{\rho} r_1 - r_1) R_2}{R_1} - \hat{\rho} r_1 R_1 = \hat{\rho} r_1 \left(\frac{R_2}{R_1} - R_1 \right) < 0.$$

The final inequality follows from the profitability of the illiquid asset (ie, $R_2 > R_1^2$). This implies that for all $t_s \leq \hat{t}$, banks are stable and no one would join an anticipated run. An LCR ratio $\rho^* = \hat{\rho}$ which makes the bank with anticipated withdrawals of $t_s = \bar{t}$ just solvent in a run of $\bar{t}_s + \Delta$ will therefore make all types of banks stable. No lower value of ρ will suffice. □

Finally, recall that we already have seen a couple of special cases where stability requires that the LCR must be set at $\rho = 1$: when either the assets are totally illiquid, $\theta = 0$, or when there is no spread earned from investing in liquidity, $r_1 = R_1 = 1$, and the worst case is a complete run, $\bar{t}_s + \Delta = 1$.

4.2 NSFR Regulation

In our interpretation of an NSFR, a bank is subject to a long-term limit on how many illiquid assets it can fund, but this is not imposed as a real time constraint at all times in the future. As a result, when a bank is subject only to an NSFR, it gets to release all of its liquidity in the event of a run. That is the initial level of liquidity is regulated but not future liquidity after withdrawals have occurred. If the regulator knows all the information as in Proposition 2, then the best NSFR is the full-information amount, $\alpha_s^* = \max\{\alpha^{AIC}, \alpha_s^{stable}\}$. This will always be better than the LCR which does not release all liquidity after a run, except in the case of a complete run where $t_s = 1 - \Delta$.

More realistically, suppose depositors or regulators can perfectly observe α_s, but do not know how many people need to withdraw for fundamental reasons (t_s) and only know its probability distribution (where we again denote the maximum value by $\bar{t}$). The bank can continue to see t_s, and all parties know Δ.

While these assumptions allow for regulations akin to the NSFR, the regulation still must be very crude. The only certain way to assure the depositors that adequate ex-ante liquidity is being held is to insist that the bank invests in enough safe assets to cover the worst case withdrawals, $\bar{t}+\Delta$. Otherwise there will be an equilibrium where there is a run under the belief that other depositors conjecture that $t_s=\bar{t}$.[h] Only covering this worst case will definitely remove the incentive to run, but whenever fewer fundamental withdrawals are required, the bank is left with many liquid assets that must be rolled over.

4.3 Comparing the LCR and NSFR

Having characterized the two types of regulation, we can now compare them. First, we contrast an NSFR which is sufficient to make stable a bank with $t_s=\bar{t}$ to an LCR which will make that same type of bank stable. Either will make stable banks of all values of t_s (and no lower values will achieve this). To illustrate the possible disadvantages of a constant NSFR, we show what happens when the worst case is $\bar{t}+\Delta=1$, and where the best possible LCR is implemented

Proposition 5
An LCR regulation can potentially support more lending than an NSFR regulation when depositors and regulators cannot condition on t_s.

Proof
The simplest way to see that this might occur is to suppose that in the worst case the run is complete, $\bar{t}+\Delta=1$. In this case, we know that $\alpha=\alpha^*=\dfrac{r_1-\theta R_2}{R_1-\theta R_2}$ is the optimal NSFR, because this is the full-information level of liquidity given by α_s^{Stable} when $t_s=1-\Delta$. But in this case, the regulator can choose $\rho=\rho^*$, where $\rho^*=\dfrac{\theta R_1((1-t_s-\Delta)r_2-R_2)+r_1(\Delta R_1+t_s\theta R_2)}{r_1(\Delta R_1+(1-t_s-\Delta)\theta R_1^2-(1-t_s)\theta R_2)}=\dfrac{\theta R_1(-R_2)+r_1(\Delta R_1+(1-\Delta)\theta R_2)}{r_1(\Delta R_1+(\Delta)\theta R_2)}$ and implement the same outcome with the same amount of liquidity when $t_s=\bar{t}=1-\Delta$ such that $\alpha^*=\dfrac{\bar{t}r_1+\rho^*r_1(1-\bar{t})}{R_1}$. Because a run on a bank with $\bar{t}+\Delta=1$ will be complete, all its liquidity can be released in a run (the LCR becomes $\rho^*(1-\bar{t}-\Delta)=0$). From Proposition 4, this LCR will make stable the other types of banks with lower $t_s<\bar{t}$, and they will be able to invest a smaller amount in liquid assets $\alpha_s=\dfrac{t_s r_1+\rho^* r_1(1-t_s)}{R_1}$. Because they are stable, there will not be runs and they will never need to liquidate illiquid assets. Each bank will choose $\alpha_s=\dfrac{t_s r_1+\rho^*(1-t_s)}{R_1}<\alpha^*$ while a bank subject to the NSFR would still have to hold α^*. □

The complete run case is some sense the most favorable environment for the LCR-style regulation because in the event of a full run, the requirement to maintain extra

[h] Because depositors are very risk averse and there is a positive probability of receiving zero if there is a run, then a signal (observed by a fraction Δ of depositors) which indicates a positive probability of a run will always lead to a run if the other depositors who see the signal believe that it will.

liquidity after the first date is irrelevant. In this case, the last taxicab is allowed to depart (because $\rho^*(1-t_s-\Delta)=0$). If the worst possible case involves only a partial run, there would then be a trade-off because the incentive effects of the LCR require that some liquid assets remain on the balance sheet and the NSFR ratio does not. Further, if there is no private information (uncertainty about t_s), then the NSFR achieves the full-information outcome, with $\alpha_s=\alpha_s^{\text{Stable}}$ (and for a partial run, the LCR cannot).

These polar cases provide some general guidance about the relative efficacy of the two types of regulations. The LCR will work well when monitoring the bank's liquidity is difficult because the regulation forces the bank to carry more safe assets than it would prefer to. Depositors understand this and in some cases this will be enough to quell any concerns about the bank having insufficient funds to withstand a run.

The main cost of the LCR is that deterring the run requires the bank to continue to have some funds invested in liquid assets, even if a run has occurred. Ex-post this liquidity is inefficient and everyone would be better off if more loans had been made instead. But, the incentive effects vanish if the depositors are not convinced that the liquidity will always be present. The only situation when this is not true in the case of a full run.

Conversely, the NSFR is an attractive run deterrent when the regulator is well informed about the fundamental deposit outflows, so that initial liquidity requirement can be varied. In this case, the bank can be forced to hold just enough to survive a run, but never have to hold more than is needed. Importantly, during a run a bank subject to an NSFR can always use all of its liquid assets to serve depositors. So this kind of regulation does not require the bank to liquidate any more loans than is necessary, and hence in the best-case it avoids the inefficiency associated with the LCR.

Once the regulator does not have good knowledge about the fundamental needs of the depositors, using the NSFR becomes less efficient. In this case, depositors cannot generally be confident that the bank will have a portfolio that guarantee solvency in all cases. The best the regulator can, therefore, accomplish is to protect against a worst case set of withdrawals. This can remove the incentive to run, but doing so will mean that all but the worst case the bank over-invests in safe assets. The LCR potentially is less distorting in this case.

This intuition suggests that the relative advantages of the two approaches to regulation will hinge on two considerations. One is the variability of potential fundamental withdrawal requirements. When t_s fluctuates considerably, then regulation that relies on a fixed value of α will only deter runs if the liquidity requirement is set high enough to cover the worst case outcome. When the worst case does not materialize, this will result in the banking holding surplus liquidity. Because the LCR regulation exploits the bank's knowledge about impending withdrawals and relies on its incentives to plan for these withdrawals, variability of t_s is not as severe a problem for this kind of regulation.

The other consideration is the size of the runs that are possible. The Achilles' heel of the LCR is that even after a run has taken place, the bank must continue to hold liquid assets. The NSFR avoids this (ex-post) inefficiency because all the liquid assets that the bank has can be used in the event of a run. So if runs are never complete, the inefficiency associated with the LCR will be at a disadvantage.

It strikes us that the information requirements that would favor the NSFR are relatively onerous. One of the most difficult challenges in a real-time crisis is gauging the extent of a run. In that case, even if it possible to verify and certify that some liquid assets are present at any given point in time, it make be difficult to forecast whether they will be adequate to meet potential subsequent withdrawals. Hence, releasing all liquidity on hand can be risky.

One can see a further disadvantage of the NSFR by introducing the possibility that the bank can secretly alter its liquidity holdings after meeting the NSFR, and this can happen at date 0. This is similar to window dressing when liquidity must be reported only at the end of a calendar year. In this case, liquidity must be disclosed at every date and there must be a future commitment to hold liquidity. The LCR is just such a commitment. It does not do as well as the full-information commitment, but it does succeed in forcing the bank to remain free of runs (while an NSFR single disclosure will not).

5. EXTENSIONS

Having characterized the properties of Basel-style regulations in this model, we now discuss the implications of extending the model in two directions. First, there is no reason to restrict regulations to only look like the NSFR and the LCR, so it makes sense to expand the range of regulatory tools considered. Diamond and Kashyap (2016) provide a complete analysis of how to optimally regulate liquidity in this kind of a model, and we begin with a review of those results.

Second, we discuss several of the issues that arise if the bank faces capital regulation. Allowing savers to have a choice between investing in deposits and equity greatly complicates the model. Part of the complication comes because our model abstracts from asset risk, and many of the benefits of capital regulation arise from creating a buffer against loan losses so that any discussion of capital without asset risk is necessarily incomplete. Nonetheless, there are a couple of interesting possible comparisons between capital and liquidity regulation that can be made even without developing a full-blown model.

5.1 Optimal Regulation of Liquidity

Stepping away from the Basel approach, how should liquidity optimally be regulated in this kind of environment? To find the most efficient set of choices which can be implemented, we describe the results from undertaking a mechanism design analysis.[i] This will achieve the best outcome by providing incentives for the bank to reveal to a regulator the

[i] The analysis here is a special case of the more general treatment in Diamond and Kashyap (2016).

information needed to implement run-free banking most efficiently. Proposition 2 already describes the full-information choices, and it turns out that these can be implemented with the optimal regulation.

To understand what happens where t_s is known only to the bank, we describe a mechanism to which accounts for this information asymmetry and still induces the bank to make efficient choices. The challenge in this situation is that a bank with private information about t_s could have an incentive to misreport t_s. The condition for efficient investment from the bank's point of view without a run remains $\alpha_s = \frac{r_1 t_s}{R_1}$. When the conditions of Proposition 1 regarding the range of possible withdrawals are satisfied, this level of liquidity automatically leads to a stable, run-free bank. This is what both the bank and its depositors desire and runs will be avoided without any regulation or even any disclosure.

When the bank is not automatically stable, to make it incentive compatible to honestly report t_s, the bank must be provided an incentive for reporting high levels of anticipated withdrawals that offsets any increased profits that could arise from underreporting. The potential gains from underreporting come from making more loans and hence having less unused liquidity which is held after normal withdrawals occur. Diamond and Kashyap (2016) prove that under our assumptions there is a way to implement the full-information choice of α_s^* (from Proposition 2) and, which is similar to, but not exactly the same as an LCR requirement.

This is possible whenever the regulator has sufficient tools to penalize the banker when actual withdrawals deviate from those that the banker reports are anticipated. These tools share the feature that they eliminate the profits that accrue from underreporting. There are various tools that can achieve this outcome. For instance, one approach is to place limits on compensation whenever reports turn out to be inaccurate (to reduce spoils from underreporting). Another strategy is to deploy fines that would be tied to the use of the supposedly required liquidity given the report. If such tools exist, then the regulator can require the bank to hold α_s^* and can punish any cases where the unused liquidity after the withdrawals departs from what would be needed when the bank is run-free (ie, when actual withdrawals, f_1, deviate from what the bank reports as anticipated withdrawals, t_s), but also allow the bank to use the extra liquidity if a run were to occur.

In other words, it is possible to implement the full-information outcomes because if the bank can be induced to be run-free, the actual withdrawals, f_1, will be exactly equal to the (state-contingent) fraction of normal withdrawals, t_s. In essence, an honestly reported value of t_s allows the regulator to determine whether the realized withdrawal f_1 is or is not due to a run and release liquidity only in a run. The critical decision by the regulator is to carefully choose how much mandated excess liquidity must be held in all circumstances to create the right incentives for the banker to truthfully report anticipated fundamental withdrawals. Diamond and Kashyap (2016) characterize these choices under various assumptions about the nature of run risk.

The formal mechanism design problem in Diamond and Kashyap (2016) solves for the optimal mechanism by looking for the one where the bank is given incentives to honestly report its private information to the regulator and the regulator uses the honestly reported information to choose a run-free level of liquidity to make the bank stable. Once the bank is run-free, any misreporting of t_s by the bank will be measured by a level of withdrawals, f_1, which differ from t_s. Assessing a sufficiently large penalty (such as driving the banker's compensation to zero without imposing losses on depositors) for such a misreport will provide incentives for accurate reporting without the need to distort liquidity holding away from the full-information level.

As in the analysis in this chapter, the full-information level of liquidity results in excess liquidity held from date 1 to date 2, but with the optimal mechanism all of this liquidity can always be used if a run should occur. While the excess liquidity is available for use, because it deters runs, it is in fact never needed. Returning to our metaphor, the last taxicab is allowed to leave the station, but in equilibrium there are enough cabs such that some always remain at the station.

5.2 Integrating Liquidity Regulation with LOLR Policy

If the regulator can also serve as an LOLR, then the efficient mechanism, that we just described earlier, can be implemented by requiring a level of liquidity holdings which depends on the quantity of deposits. This is essentially a generalized LCR. In this case, no actual report of anticipated withdrawals, t_s, is required. This is implemented by requiring the amount of unused liquidity at date 1 (to be held until date 2) equal to the full-information level from Proposition 2, α_s^{Stable}, which is given by $U(f_1 = t_s) = \text{Max}\left[0, \alpha_s^{\text{Stable}} - \alpha_s^{\text{AIC}}\right] R_1$, and allowing the bank to use this liquidity in a run, but with a penalty which drives banker compensation to zero in that case.

The goal from this policy is to induce the bank to always use its private information to choose to hold just enough liquidity to make sure that after normal withdrawals, t_s, it will meet the requirement, $U(f_1 = t_s)$. This is the equal to the investment in liquidity from the full-information level presented in Proposition 2.

To accomplish this outcome, liquidity requirements and LOLR policy should be integrated in the following way. Banks are forced to hold the specified amount of liquidity but are allowed to borrow against it for use during a run. If there is a sufficient penalty to the bank for violating its liquidity requirement, the bank will hold the specified amount of liquidity and will never use borrowing to meet normal withdrawals. As a result, the run will be deterred and the extra liquidity need not be borrowed against.

Remarkably, there is historical precedent for this sort of policy: the original United States Federal Reserve Act prohibited dividend payments for banks which were in violation of the reserve (liquidity) requirement. In that period, most banks were closely held, implying that a dividend was a significant part of management compensation. This policy is not necessarily akin to charging a high interest rate for such borrowing, because a penalty rate could be so severe that it might make the bank fail due to a run (making the bank unstable and defeating the purpose of holding extra liquidity).

Note that this type of LOLR lends against liquid assets, allowing them to be used during a crisis while providing incentives to get the bank to hold the higher level of liquidity needed to make it stable. This lending does not have moral hazard of inducing the bank to hold excessive amounts of illiquid assets (as described in Bagehot (1873), Goodfriend and King (1988), and Diamond and Rajan (2012)). It may appear pointless to lend against liquid assets, but the ability to penalize the bank for such the borrowing induces the bank to make the proper ex-ante liquidity choice. Once the liquidity is in place, its existence can deter bank runs. Finally, notice that if the LOLR acquired (or lent against) illiquid assets and could then only recover their illiquid value, θR_2, if the bank were to fail, then lending an amount in excess of this value could distort bank incentives and lead to losses by the LOLR. Lending against liquid assets has no such problem.

To summarize, the optimal mechanism induces a bank to hold excess liquidity but allows access to it during a run. The robust conclusion from this analysis is that the optimal regulation requires less unused liquidity than the simple Basel-style regulations because the excess liquidity can be released if a run should occur. If there are additional constraints on what the regulator can do, which limit the ability to release this liquidity, then a regulation like the LCR could be nearly optimal. If all liquidity cannot be released in a run, then the best regulations will have the property that as anticipated withdrawals rise, the amount of required surplus liquidity falls.

5.3 Interactions Between Capital and Liquidity Regulations

Finally, it is worth noting several observations about interactions between capital and liquidity regulation. In our baseline model, there is no credit risk associated with loans, so the usual arguments for capital requirements do not hold. Generically, however, the incentive to run is still related to depositors' assessments about the solvency of the bank so the presence of equity could still matter.

The role that capital would play in deterring a run is subtle. On the one hand, if the bank issued capital (nondemandable liabilities) and invested the proceeds in loans, this can leave the bank more solvent when a fixed number of deposits are withdrawn, moving the bank to a situation where it is solvent during a (potential) run of fixed size. This is due to the liquidation value of the additional loans made. On the other hand, added equity would be irrelevant if a (potential) run of given size given is still going to make the bank insolvent. In our framework, this is easiest to see if the liquidation value of the loans (θ) is zero. In that case, the future value of the assets that would otherwise be the basis of the equity value would be of no value in a run. So the liquidity requirements needed to deliver stability would be unchanged, and capital requirements would be completely ineffective.

Once assets become risky, the analysis becomes much more complicated. In this kind of environment, depositors will make withdrawals based both on their fundamental liquidity needs and based on beliefs about the future value a bank's assets. In addition, if the bank can fail simply because loans turn out to default, the bank's choice between loans and liquid assets can also be distorted if there is limited liability; banks in this kind of an environment can in some situations have an incentive to shift risk on depositors.

A full analysis of this kind of model is beyond the scope of our survey, especially because there are so many additional assumptions that are needed to maintain tractability. However, Kashyap et al. (2015) have solved one particular version of this kind of model, and their analysis does deliver one apparently general result about the interactions between capital and liquidity requirements in deterring runs that is worth mentioning.

They show that there is a fundamental asymmetry in the way that liquidity and capital regulations work in preventing runs. Capital requirements essentially work on the liability-side of a bank's balance sheet without directly constraining the bank's asset choices. Hence, when a bank is forced to have higher equity, it can on the margin reduce its reliance on deposit financing. The need for fewer deposits means that the bank can marginally reduce liquid asset holdings too. This frees up the bank to make marginally more loans. While this marginal adjustment is not enough to raise the overall risk of a run, it does suggest that the bank's assets will become less liquid.[j]

Conversely, liquidity regulation, either in the form of an LCR or NSFR, work very differently. The LCR, as we have seen, directly forces the bank to substitute from illiquid assets toward liquid assets. So the run deterrence automatically is accompanied by having less liquidity risk. The NSFR forces the bank to finance illiquid assets with long-term liabilities. Therefore, if the bank wants to take on additional illiquid assets, it cannot fund them with runnable deposits. Instead, short-term deposits will shrink along with liquid assets.

Kashyap et al. (2015) describe many other ways in which capital regulations and liquidity regulations can complement or substitute for each other. The asymmetry in how they marginally influence asset illiquidity is robust.

6. CONCLUSION

Our analysis provides some novel insights that can inform subsequent discussions of how to design liquidity regulation. Our starting point is the recognition that for a forward looking intermediary, anticipated withdrawals, and access to other funding influences the desired ex-ante, profit-maximizing choice of how much liquidity to hold. Absent

[j] This is not arising because of a Modigliani–Miller type fallacy whereby depositors fail to recognize that the bank's deposits are safer. Instead, this happens because the liquid assets are held only to deter runs, and when capital requirements make them less likely the bank cut back on liquid assets.

any regulation, the bank will voluntarily opt to hold more liquidity when higher exogenous deposit reductions are anticipated. Hence, it is helpful to understand whether, and when, this incentive alone will lead to banking stability even when it is not directly a goal of the bank.

In this kind of model that we have explored, stability is not guaranteed when bank assets are sufficiently illiquid and profitability is below a certain level because depositors may have doubts about whether the bank will make choices which lead it to able to withstand a panic. The lack of confidence that creates this problem can arise for various reasons. Banks are opaque and even for sophisticated counterparties assessing their balance sheet can be challenging. Information about the balance sheet is rarely available contemporaneously, so some forecasting (about the bank's condition and the decisions of other depositors) is inevitable. This will cause problems when the bank's incentives are not automatically aligned with enhancing stability.

Imperfect information also creates a problem for the bank. Cutting back on lending and holding additional liquidity is not fully rewarded when depositors cannot determine if the given amount of liquidity is sufficient to make the bank stable, so the bank's private incentive to become super-safe is limited (unless it can show depositors that it is sufficiently stable to cover all possible circumstances). Regulation that mandates some additional liquidity can potentially circumvent this problem.

Analogs to both of the two regulations contemplated as part of the Basel process, the NSFR and LCR, are among the various types of regulations that we explore. These can arise as approximations of a general type of regulation that is optimally designed to resolve the information friction. All of the ones we consider are designed to eliminate runs.

The generic form of the optimal regulation specifies that the bank must hold a level of liquid assets that is tied to anticipated withdrawals, but which often will exceed the level that it would choose on its own. If the regulator is well-informed about these withdrawals (and the risk of a run), then there are many equivalent ways to guarantee that the bank makes adequate liquidity choices. In particular, stability can be achieved either by having the bank hold the correct amount of liquid assets up-front as with an NSFR, or by imposing restrictions that require liquidity be available even after withdrawals are underway (as with an LCR). Using combinations of these kinds of policies will work too.

To achieve the efficient outcome (which in our model is the same as that which would prevail with full-information available to all), the regulator must be able to induce the bank to disclose everything it knows about the deposit risk that it faces (or have access to that information from some other way). With the ability to impose taxes on bank compensation, the regulator could elicit this from the bank. This need not even involve any direct communication of information to regulators by the bank. A liquidity regulation combined with an LOLR policy which penalizes liquidity regulation violations by limiting compensation, but allows the bank to borrow can implement this optimal arrangement.

One generic property of all of the optimally designed regulations when banks are not automatically stable is that they involve requiring the bank to hold some liquidity that goes unused. So even in the best possible case, the last taxi cab often remains at the station. Fundamentally, this occurs because the unused liquidity is needed to deter the run.

There are two separate forces that lead to this result. First, a prudent provision that forecloses a run necessarily requires that the bank has enough liquidity to be able to service depositors if they did run. This might be possible through liquidating loans. But liquidations are highly inefficient so this typically this will not be sufficient and the bank needs to have some liquid assets which could be deployed if needed. By mandating the "dry powder," the regulator preserves solvency in a run and thus removes the depositors' incentive to run.

The second consideration is that a regulator cannot count on being able to distinguish a run from a situation where fundamental withdrawal needs are simply high. The goal in preventing runs is to do so without mandating more dry powder than is needed. Unfortunately, even when exceptionally high levels of withdrawals are anticipated, some dry powder is needed.

These observations suggest are a number of other directions that would be interesting to explore. In Diamond and Kashyap (2016), we generalize the environment to allow for different types of run dynamics and investigate the implications for regulation. Let us close with three much broader issues that merit further consideration.

First, our analysis suggests a novel type of interaction between LOLR policy and liquidity regulation. Most discussions of the LOLR start with the Bagehot dictum of lending freely against good collateral but at a penalty rate. However, the reason which many loans are illiquid is because they are difficult to quickly value and their value may depend on actions or relationships of the bank. A system where all assets were illiquid and all liquidity (even for normal withdrawals) is provided by the LOLR could be highly problematic. If a private bank is to provide much of its own liquidity, our analysis shows that there is a role for integrating liquidity regulation with an LOLR which lends against required liquid holdings of a bank. This allows banks to access to liquidity without distorting their incentives to minimize the risk of a run.

Carlson et al. (2015) make one attempt to investigate the degree to which liquidity requirements and LOLR policies complement each other. More work in this vein that could probe other interactions between these tools seems promising.

Second, it would also be interesting in future research to examine other mechanisms to provide incentives for banks to hold sufficient liquidity to make them stable and run-free. We focus on liquid asset quantity requirements, but there may be interesting price-based mechanisms. One example is adjusting the interest rates paid on central bank reserves. This is especially relevant in times (like today) when the aggregate quantity of central bank reserves is large in many countries. On a related note, the large central bank balance sheets and the low interest rates in the many counties today make it difficult to use historical data to calibrate the incentive effect of liquidity requirements or the effects of changes in the interest on reserves on endogenous liquidity holdings.

Finally, there are interesting issues involving the need for and effect of liquidity regulation on interbank competition for funding and liquidity sharing between banks. When banks can raise liquidity from the customers of other banks (or from others outside the banking system) then some interactions that we have ignored come into play. As noted by Bhattacharya and Gale (1987) and Farhi et al. (2009), in these circumstances, liquidity regulation can be needed to prevent banks from free riding on others' liquidity. This becomes even more difficult if some of the participants in the market are unregulated "shadow banks." It would be interesting to examine how this interacts with our notion of providing incentives for banks to choose an efficient level of liquidity based on their private information about their own future needs for liquidity.

ACKNOWLEDGMENTS

We thank Franklin Allen, Gary Gorton, Guido Lorenzoni, Annette Vissing-Jorgenson, Nancy Stokey, Nao Sudo, John Taylor, Harald Uhlig, and seminar participants at the Asian Development Bank Institute, East Asian Economic Seminar, Imperial College, Melbourne Institute Macroeconomic Policy Meetings, National Bureau of Economic Research Monetary Economics meeting, the Bank of England, European Central Bank, Centre for Economic Policy Research and Centre for Macroeconomics Conference on Credit Dynamics and the Macroeconomy, Riksbank, and the University of Chicago for helpful comments and Adam Jorring for expert research assistance. We thank the Initiative on Global Markets at Chicago Booth, the Fama Miller Center at Chicago Booth and the National Science Foundation for grants administered through the NBER for research support. All errors are solely our responsibility.

REFERENCES

Admati, A., Hellwig, M., 2013. The Bankers' New Clothes: What's Wrong with Banking and What to Do about It. Princeton University Press.

Aikman, D., Haldane, A., Kapadia, S., 2013. Operationalising a macroprudential regime: goals, tools and open issues. Banco Espana Financ. Stability J. 24, 9–30.

Allen, F., 2014. How Should Bank Liquidity Be Regulated? Mimeo, Imperial College London.

Allen, F., Gale, D., 1997. Financial markets, intermediaries, and intertemporal smoothing. J. Polit. Econ. 105 (3), 523–546.

Bagehot, W., 1873. Lombard Street: A Description of the Money Market. H. S. King, London.

Bao, J., David, J., Han, S., 2015. The Runnables, FED Notes, Board of Governors of the Federal Reserve. https://www.federalreserve.gov/econresdata/notes/feds-notes/2015/the-runnables-20150903.html.

Baron, D.P., Myerson, R.B., 1982. Regulating a monopolist with unknown costs. Econometrica 50, 911–930.

Basel Committee on Bank Supervision, 2013a. Basel III: The Liquidity Coverage Ratio and Liquidity Risk Monitoring Tools. Bank for International Settlements, Basel, Switzerland.

Basel Committee on Bank Supervision, 2013b. Liquidity Stress Testing: A Survey of Theory, Empirics and Current Industry and Supervisory Practices. Bank for International Settlements. Basel Committee on Bank Supervision Working Paper 24.

Basel Committee on Bank Supervision, 2014. Basel III: The Net Stable Funding Ratio. Bank for International Settlements.

Benston, G.J., Smith, C.W., 1976. A transactions cost approach to the theory of financial intermediation. J. Financ. 31 (2), 215–231.
Bhattacharya, S., Gale, D., 1987. Preference shocks, liquidity and central bank policy. In: Barnett, W.A., Singleton, K.J. (Eds.), New Approaches to Monetary Economics. Cambridge University Press, Cambridge.
Black, F., 1975. Bank funds management in an efficient market. J. Financ. Econ. 2 (4), 323–339.
Borchgrevink, H., Ellingsrud, S., Hansen, F., 2014. Macroprudential Regulation: What, Why and How. Norges Bank Staff Memo Number 13, 2014.
Bouwman, C.H.S., 2015. Liquidity: how banks create it and how it should be regulated. In: Berger, Al., Molyneux, P., Wilson, J. (Eds.), The Oxford Handbook of Banking, second ed. Oxford University Press, Oxford, UK, pp. 184–218.
Brooke, M., Bush, O., Edwards, R., Ellis, J., Francis, B., Harimohan, R., Neiss, K., Siegert, C., 2015. Measuring the Macroeconomic Costs and Benefits of Higher UK Bank Capital Requirements. Bank of England Financial Stability Paper No. 35.
Calomiris, C.W., Kahn, C.M., 1991. The role of demandable debt in structuring optimal banking arrangements. Am. Econ. Rev. 81 (3), 497–513.
Calomiris, C.W., Heider, F., Hoerova, M., 2014. A Theory of Bank Liquidity Requirements. Columbia Business School Research Paper No. 14-39.
Carlson, M., Duygan-Bump, B., Nelson, W., 2015. Why Do We Need Both Liquidity Regulations and a Lender of Last Resort? A Perspective from Federal Reserve Lending during the 2007–09 U.S. Financial Crisis. Board of Governors of the Federal Reserve System, Washington. Finance and Economics Discussion Series 2015-011, http://dx.doi.org/10.17016/FEDS.2015.011.
Cerutti, E., Claessens, S., Laeven, L., 2015. The Use and Effectiveness of Macroprudential Policies: New Evidence. International Monetary Fund WP/15/61.
Cetina, J., Gleason, K., 2015. The Difficult Business of Measuring Banks' Liquidity: Understanding the Liquidity Coverage Ratio. Office of Financial Research Working Paper 15-20.
Čihák, M., Demirgüç-Kunt, A., Martínez Pería, M.S., Mohseni-Cheraghlou, A., 2013. Bank Regulation and Supervision Around the World: A Crisis Update. World Bank Policy Research Working Paper 6286.
Claessens, S., Kodres, L., 2014. The Regulatory Responses to the Global Financial Crisis: Some Uncomfortable Questions. International Monetary Fund Working Paper 14/46.
Clement, P., 2010. The term "macroprudential": origins and evolution. BIS Q. Rev. 2010, 59–67.
Cooper, R., Ross, T.W., 1998. Bank runs: liquidity costs and investment distortions. J. Monet. Econ. 41 (1), 27–38.
Crockett, A., 2000. Marrying the micro- and macro-prudential dimensions of financial stability. Remarks by Mr. Andrew Crockett, General Manager of the Bank for International Settlements and Chairman of the Financial Stability Forum, before the Eleventh International Conference of Banking Supervisors, held in Basel, 20–21 September.
Diamond, D.W., 1984. Financial intermediation and delegated monitoring. Rev. Econ. Stud. 51 (3), 393–414.
Diamond, D.W., 1997. Liquidity, banks and markets. J. Polit. Econ. 105, 928–956.
Diamond, D.W., Dybvig, P.H., 1983. Bank runs, deposit insurance and liquidity. J. Polit. Econ. 91 (3), 401–419.
Diamond, D.W., Kashyap, A.K., 2016. Optimal Regulation of Bank Liquidity. (still in preparation).
Diamond, D.W., Rajan, R.G., 2001. Liquidity risk, liquidity creation and financial fragility: a theory of banking. J. Polit. Econ. 109 (2), 287–327.
Diamond, D.W., Rajan, R.G., 2012. Illiquid banks, financial stability, and interest rate policy. J. Polit. Econ. 120 (3), 552–591.
Ennis, H., Keister, T., 2006. Bank runs and investment decisions revisited. J. Monet. Econ. 53 (2), 217–232.
Farhi, E., Golosov, M., Tsyvinski, A., 2009. A theory of liquidity and regulation of financial intermediation. Rev. Econ. Stud. 76 (3), 973–992.
Financial Stability Board, 2015. Transforming Shadow Banking into Resilient Market-based Finance: An Overview of Progress. Financial Stability Board Working Paper.

Fisher, P., 2015. The Financial Regulation Reform Agenda: What Has Been Achieved and How Much Is Left to Do? Speech at Richmond, the American International University, London 30 September 2015.
Goodfriend, M., King, R.G., 1988. Financial deregulation, monetary policy, and central banking. Fed. Reserve Bank Richmond Econ. Rev. 74 (3), 3–22.
Goodhart, C.A.E., 2008. Liquidity risk management. Banque France Financ. Stability Rev. 12, 39–44.
Gorton, G., Winton, A., 2003. Financial intermediation. In: Constantinides, G.M., Harris, M., Stulz, R. (Eds.), The Handbook of the Economics of Finance: Corporate Finance, North Holland, pp. 431–552.
Hanson, S.G., Kashyap, A.K., Stein, J.C., Winter 2011. A macroprudential approach to financial regulation. J. Econ. Perspect. 25 (1), 3–28.
Jacklin, C.J., 1987. Demand deposits, trading restrictions, and risk sharing. In: Prescott, E.C., Wallace, N. (Eds.), Contractual Arrangements for Intertemporal Trade. University of Minnesota Press, Minneapolis, MN, pp. 26–47.
Kashyap, A.K., Tsomocos, D.P., Vardoulakis, A.P., 2014. Principles for macroprudential regulation. Banque France Financ. Stability Rev. 18, 173–181.
Kashyap, A.K., Tsomocos, D.P., Vardoulakis, A.P., 2015. How Does Macroprudential Regulation Change Bank Credit Supply? Revision of National Bureau of Economic Research Working Paper 20165.
Martynova, N., 2015. Effect of bank capital requirements on economic growth: a survey. De Nederlandsche Bank Working Paper, DNB Working Paper No. 467.
Mester, L., Nakamura, L., Renualt, M., 2007. Transactions accounts and loan monitoring. Rev. Financ. Stud. 20 (3), 529–556.
Modigliani, F., Miller, M.H., 1958. The cost of capital, corporate finance and the theory of investment. Am. Econ. Rev. 48 (3), 261–297.
Munyan, B., 2015. Regulatory Arbitrage in Repo Markets. Office of Financial Research Working Paper 15-22.
Myers, S.C., 1977. Determinants of corporate borrowing. J. Financ. Econ. 5, 147–175.
Norden, L., Weber, M., 2010. Credit line usage, checking account activity, and default risk of bank borrowers. Rev. Financ. Stud. 23 (10), 3665–3699.
Rochet, J.C., 2014. The Extra Cost of Swiss Banking Regulation. Swiss Finance Institute White Paper.
Santos, J.C., Suarez, J., 2015. Liquidity Standards and the Value of an Informed Lender of Last Resort. Working paper, Federal Reserve Bank of New York, May.
Stein, J.C., 2012. Monetary policy as financial-stability regulation. Q. J. Econ. 127 (1), 57–95.
Uhlig, H., 2010. A model of a systemic bank run. J. Monet. Econ. 57, 78–96.
Vives, X., 2014. Strategic complementarity, fragility, and regulation. Rev. Financ. Stud. 27 (12), 3547–3592.

CHAPTER 30

Understanding Inflation as a Joint Monetary–Fiscal Phenomenon

E.M. Leeper*,†, C. Leith‡
*Indiana University, IN, United States
†NBER, Cambridge, MA, United States
‡University of Glasgow, Glasgow, United Kingdom

Contents

Handbook of Macroeconomics, Volume 2B
ISSN 1574-0048, http://dx.doi.org/10.1016/bs.hesmac.2016.03.012

Abstract

We develop the theory of price-level determination in a range of models using both ad hoc policy rules and jointly optimal monetary and fiscal policies and discuss empirical issues that arise when trying to identify monetary–fiscal regime. The chapter concludes with directions in which theoretical and empirical developments may go.

Keywords

Monetary policy, Fiscal policy, Price level determination, Optimal policy, Tax smoothing, Government debt

JEL Classification Codes

E4, E5, E6, H3, H6

1. INTRODUCTION

There is a long tradition in macroeconomics of modeling inflation in stable economies by focusing on monetary policy and abstracting from fiscal policy.[a] As the global financial crisis and its aftermath rocked the world economy, the tenability of that modeling approach has been strained.

This chapter introduces readers to the interactions between monetary and fiscal policies and their role in determining macroeconomic outcomes, particularly the aggregate price level. By incrementally widening the scope of those interactions and considering both simple ad hoc rules and optimal policy, we aim to make accessible the intricacies that policy interactions entail. We hope the material will entice young macroeconomists to engage a set of issues that we regard as both not fully resolved and fundamental to macroeconomic policy analysis.

1.1 Some Observations

Let us start with a few observations of economic developments since 2008:

1. Many countries reacted to the financial crisis and recession that began in 2008 with joint policy actions that sharply reduced monetary policy interest rates and implemented large fiscal stimulus packages.
2. Central banks reacted to the financial crisis by purchasing large quantities of private assets and government bonds in actions that bear a striking resemblance to fiscal policy (Brunnermeier and Sannikov, 2013; Leeper and Nason, 2014).
3. Sovereign debt crises in the Euro zone culminated in the European Central Bank's 2012 policy of "outright monetary transactions," a promise to purchase sovereign debt in secondary markets in unlimited quantities for countries that satisfied conditionality restrictions.
4. Rapid adoption of fiscal austerity measures beginning in 2010 and 2011 created challenges for central banks that were already operating at or near the lower limits for nominal interest rates.
5. Exploding central bank balance sheets also grew riskier, increasing concerns about whether the requisite fiscal backing or support for monetary policy is guaranteed (Del Negro and Sims, 2015).
6. In 2013, Japan's newly elected prime minister Shinzō Abe adopted "Abenomics," a mix of fiscal stimulus, monetary easing, and structural reforms designed to reinflate a Japanese economy that has languished since the early 1990s.

[a] Focusing on stable economies rules out hyperinflations, which are widely believed to have fiscal origins.

Table 1 Net general government debt as percentage of GDP

	2008	2015
Euro area	54.0	74.0
Japan	95.3	140.0
United Kingdom	47.5	85.0
United States	50.4	80.9

Projections for 2015.
Source: International Monetary Fund, 2014. Fiscal Monitor-Back To Work: How Fiscal Policy Can Help. IMF, Washington, DC.

7. Table 1 reports that government debt expansions during the recession were significant: net debt as a share of GDP rose between 37% and 79% across four advanced-economy country groups. As central banks begin to raise interest rates toward more normal levels, these debt expansions will carry with them dramatically higher debt service to create fresh fiscal pressures. The Congressional Budget Office (2014) projects that U.S. federal government net interest payments will rise dramatically as a share of GDP from 2014 to 2024. Evidently, there are substantial fiscal consequences from central bank exits from very low policy interest rates.
8. With an increasing number of central banks now paying interest on reserves at rates close to those on short-term government bonds, one important distinction between high-powered money and nominal government bonds has disappeared, removing a principal distinction between monetary and fiscal policy (Cochrane, 2014).
9. Sovereign debt troubles in the Euro area and political polarization in many countries remind us that every country faces a fiscal limit, which is the point at which the adjustments in primary surpluses needed to stabilize debt are not assured. Uncertainty about future fiscal adjustments can untether fiscal expectations, making it difficult or impossible for monetary policy to achieve its objectives (Davig et al., 2010, 2011).
10. Exacerbating the fiscal fallout from the crisis, aging populations worldwide create long-run fiscal stress whose resolution in most countries is uncertain. This kind of uncertainty operates at low frequencies and may conflict with the long-run objectives of monetary policy (Carvalho and Ferrero, 2014).

It is hard to think about these developments without bringing monetary and fiscal policy *jointly* into the analysis. Several of these examples also run counter to critical maintained assumptions in monetarist/Wicksellian perspectives, including:

- fiscal policies will adjust government revenues and expenditures as needed to finance and stabilize government debt; this ensures that fiscal actions are "self-correcting" and need not concern monetary policymakers;
- sufficiently creative monetary policies—which include interest rate settings, quantitative easing, credit easing, government debt management, forward guidance—can always achieve desired inflation and macroeconomic objectives;
- impacts of monetary policy on fiscal choices are small enough to be of negligible importance to monetary policy decisions, freeing central banks to focus on a narrow set of goals.

As even this handful of examples makes clear, it is unlikely to be fruitful to interpret recent macroeconomic policy issues by studying monetary or fiscal policy in isolation. This chapter takes that premise as given to explore how macro policies interact to determine aggregate prices and quantities.

1.2 Our Remit

We were invited to write a chapter on the "fiscal theory of the price level," an assignment that we gladly accepted, but chose to broaden to the theory of price-level determination. A broader perspective, like the observations earlier, brings monetary and fiscal policy jointly into the picture to produce a more general understanding of the inflation process than either the monetarist/Wicksellian or the fiscal theory alone provide. We show that only in very special circumstances can the two perspectives be treated as distinct theories. Despite this broader perspective, both to fulfill our remit and to draw attention to aspects of monetary and fiscal policy interaction that are often overlooked, the chapter will often (but not solely) focus on the mechanisms that the fiscal theory emphasizes.

1.3 What Is the Fiscal Theory?

We consider a class of dynamically efficient models with monetary policy, a maturity structure for nominal government debt, taxes—distorting or lump-sum—government expenditures—purchases or transfers—and a government budget identity. In models of this kind, four key features of equilibrium may emerge:

1. There is a prominent role for nominal government debt revaluations that stabilize debt through surprise changes in inflation and bond prices.
2. It is possible for monetary–fiscal policy mixes to permit nominal government debt expansions or increases in the monetary policy interest rate instrument to increase nominal private wealth, nominal aggregate demand, and the price level.
3. Expectations of fiscal policy are equally important to those of monetary policy in determining prices and, sometimes, quantities, as in Brunner and Meltzer (1972), Tobin (1980), and Wallace (1981).[b]
4. Debt management policies matter for equilibrium dynamics, contributing an additional instrument to the standard macroeconomic policy toolkit, as Tobin (1963) argued.

Analyses of the implications of these features in this class of models constitute what we call the "fiscal theory of the price level."[c]

[b] Brunner and Meltzer anticipate the fiscal theory by showing that a government debt expansion unaccompanied by higher base money is inflationary when the fiscal deficit is held constant. But they dismiss this result on the grounds that "Price-level changes of this kind have not been important [foonote 13]."

[c] Early contributors to the theory include Begg and Haque (1984), Auernheimer and Contreras (1990), Leeper (1991), Sims (1994), Woodford (1995), and Cochrane (1999).

The fiscal theory is a complement to, rather than a substitute for, conventional views of price-level determination. It emerges by filling in the fiscal sides of models and broadening the rules that monetary and fiscal authorities can obey. By doing so, the fiscal theory extracts what assumptions about fiscal behavior are required to deliver conventional views. More importantly, being explicit about both monetary and fiscal behavior reveals that a far richer set of equilibria can arise from the previously suppressed, but undeniable, fact that monetary and fiscal policies are intrinsically intertwined.

The chapter aims to be constructive and instructive, so it does not refight the battles that surround the fiscal theory. Accusations against the fiscal theory include: it confuses equilibrium conditions with budget constraints; it violates Walras' law; it treats private agents and the government differently; it is merely an equilibrium selection device; it is little more than a retread of Sargent and Wallace's (1981) unpleasant monetarist arithmetic.[d] Each of these arguments has been discussed at length in Sims (1999a), Cochrane (2005), and Leeper and Walker (2013). Rehashing those debates detracts from the chapter's aims.

Cochrane (2011b, 2014) and Sims (1999b, 2013), two leading proponents of the fiscal theory, explore a wide range of issues through the lens of the fiscal theory to reach conclusions that contrast sharply with conventional perspective. This chapter also reexamines some practical issues in the light of the fiscal theory.

Most of the chapter focuses on the nature of equilibrium, including price-level determination, in models with nontrivial specifications of monetary and fiscal policy behavior. In this sense, the chapter, like the fiscal theory itself, echoes Wallace's (1981) insight that the effects of central bank open-market operations hinge on the precise sense in which fiscal policy is held constant. Under some assumptions on fiscal behavior, open-market operations are neutral, but different fiscal behavior permits monetary policy actions to have different impacts. Wallace did not explore the nature of price-level determination in the presence of nominal government bonds, which the fiscal theory emphasizes, but his results nonetheless foreshadow the newer literature. We also examine interactions in the opposite direction: how monetary policy behavior can influence the impacts of fiscal actions.

1.3.1 Real vs Nominal Government Debt

Central to the fiscal theory is the distinction between real and nominal government debt. This distinction matters little in conventional views that maintain that future revenues and expenditures always adjust to stabilize government debt. But the presence—in fact, the prevalence, of nominal government debt in many countries—lies at the core of the fiscal theory.[e]

[d] These accusations appear in Kocherlakota and Phelan (1999), McCallum (2001), Bassetto (2002), Buiter (2002), and Ljungqvist and Sargent (2004).

[e] See Cochrane (2011b) and Sims (2013).

Real debt can take the form of inflation-indexed bonds or bonds denominated in units whose supply the country does not control. Real debt is a claim to real goods, which the government must acquire through taxation. This imposes a budget constraint that the government's choices must satisfy. If the government does not have the taxing capacity to acquire the goods necessary to finance outstanding debt, it has no option other than outright default. Under the gold standard with fixed parities, countries effectively issued real debt because the real value of government bonds was determined by factors outside their control—worldwide supply and demand for gold.

Nominal debt is much like government-issued money: it is merely a claim to fresh currency in the future. The government may choose to raise taxes to acquire the requisite currency or it may opt to print up new currency, if currency creation is within its purview. Because the value of nominal debt depends on the price level and bond prices, the government really does not face a budget constraint when all its debt is nominal. Some readers may object to the idea that a government does not face a budget constraint, but the logic here is exactly the logic that underlies fiat currency. By conventional quantity theory reasoning, the central bank is free to double or half the money supply without fear of violating a budget constraint because the price level will double or half to maintain the real value of money. The direct analog to this reasoning is that the government is free to issue any quantity of nominal bonds, whose real value adjusts with the price level, without reference to a budget constraint. Of course, as with a money rain, by doing so the government is giving up control of the price level.

Member nations of the European Monetary Union issue debt denominated in euros, their home currency, but because monetary policy is under the control of the ECB rather than individual nations, the debt is effectively real from the perspective of member nations. The United States issues indexed debt, but it comprises only 10% of the debt outstanding. Even in the United Kingdom, which is known for having a thick market in indexed bonds, the percentage is only about 20. Five percent or less of total debt issued is indexed in the Euro Area, Japan, Australia, and Sweden.

1.3.2 Themes of the Chapter

Several themes run through this paper. First, it is always the *joint* behavior of monetary and fiscal policies that determine inflation and stabilize debt. While this point might seem obvious—echoing, as it does, a viewpoint that dates back at least to Friedman (1948)—it is easily missed in the classes of models and descriptions of policy typically employed in modern macroeconomic policy analyses. In those models, inflation appears to be determined entirely by monetary policy behavior—specifically, by the responsiveness of monetary policy to inflation—while debt dynamics seem to be driven only by fiscal behavior—the strength of primary surplus responses to debt. Of course, *in equilibrium* the two policies must interact in particular ways to deliver a determinate equilibrium with bounded debt, but this point is often swept under the carpet in order to focus the analysis solely on monetary policy.[f]

In dynamic models, macroeconomic policies have two fundamental tasks to achieve: determine the price level and stabilize debt. Two distinct monetary–fiscal policy mixes can accomplish those tasks. A second theme is that it is useful for some purposes to categorize those policy mixes in terms of "active" or "passive" policy behavior.[g] An active authority pursues its objectives unconstrained by the state of government debt and is free to set its control variables as it sees fit. But then the other authority must behave passively to stabilize debt, constrained by the active authority's actions and private-sector behavior. A determinate bounded equilibrium requires the mix of one active and one passive policy; that mix achieves the two macroeconomic objectives of delivering unique inflation and stable debt processes.[h] The combination of active monetary and passive fiscal policies delivers the usual monetarist/new Keynesian setup in which monetary policy can target inflation and fiscal policy exhibits Ricardian equivalence. We call this policy mix regime M, but it also goes by the label "monetary dominance." An alternative combination of passive monetary and active fiscal policies gives fiscal policy important effects on inflation, while monetary policy ensures that debt is stable. The latter policy regime has been given the unfortunate label "the fiscal theory of the price level." The fiscal theory mix is called regime F or "fiscal dominance."

Third, regime F policies produce equilibria in which the maturity structure of government debt affects equilibrium dynamics, as Cochrane (2001) and Sims (2011) emphasize. In contrast, without frictions that make short and long debt imperfect substitutes and in the special case of flexible prices and lump-sum taxes, maturity structure is irrelevant in regime M. Under the fiscal theory, long debt permits both current and future inflation (bond prices) to adjust to shocks that perturb the market value of debt, which serves to make inflation and, if prices are sticky, real activity less volatile than they would be if all debt were one period.

Fourth, only in the special cases of flexible prices and lump-sum fiscal shocks/surplus adjustments can simple active monetary policy rules hit their inflation target in regime M. More generally, with sticky prices and distortionary taxation, we observe revaluation effects and pervasive interactions between monetary and fiscal policy across both the M and F regimes.

Fifth, the "active/passive" rubrics also lose their usefulness once one considers optimal policies. Jointly optimal monetary and fiscal policies generally combine elements of

[f] See, for example, Woodford (2003) and Galí (2008).

[g] Leeper (1991) develops this categorization to study bounded equilibria.

[h] There are unbounded equilibria also. Sims (2013) and Cochrane (2011a) emphasize the possibility of solutions with unbounded inflation; McCallum (1984) and Canzoneri et al. (2001b) display solutions with unbounded debt that hinge on the presence of nondistorting taxes.

both regimes M and F: when long-maturity government debt is outstanding, it is always optimal to stabilize debt partly through distorting taxes and partly through surprise changes in inflation and bond prices (Cochrane, 2001; Leeper and Zhou, 2013; Sims, 2013). How important inflation is as a debt stabilizer—or in Sims' (2013) terminology, a "fiscal cushion"—depends on model specifics: the maturity structure of debt, the costliness of inflation variability, the level of outstanding government debt, whether optimal policy is with commitment or discretion, proximity of the economy to its fiscal limit, and so forth.

The fact that key features of the fiscal theory emerge as jointly optimal monetary and fiscal policy elevates the theory from a theoretical oddity to an integral part of macroeconomic policies that deliver desirable outcomes.

1.4 Overview of the Chapter

As we progress through the chapter we gradually widen the extent of monetary and fiscal policy interactions. We start with a simple flexible-price endowment economy subject to shocks to lump-sum transfers. This environment limits the extent of monetary and fiscal interactions to the revaluation effects emphasized by the fiscal theory and supports the strong dichotomy between the M and F regimes. Even in this simple environment, though, there are important spillovers between monetary and fiscal policy under either regime when we allow for either government spending or monetary policy shocks.

We then turn to consider the same rules in a production economy subject to nominal rigidities, but where we retain the assumption that taxes are lump sum. This adds a new channel for monetary and fiscal interactions because monetary policy can affect real interest rates when prices are sticky which, in turn, influence debt dynamics through real debt service costs. We then generalize this further by adding distortionary taxation to a new Keynesian economy. Then tax policy affects inflation through its impact on marginal costs, government spending feeds into aggregate demand, and monetary policy affects real interest rates to influence the size of the tax base. In this richer specification, equilibrium outcomes are always the result of interactions between monetary and fiscal policy and a key issue is the balance between monetary and fiscal policy in the control of inflation and stabilization of debt. We show that the conventional policy assignment of delegating monetary policy to achieve an inflation target and fiscal policy to stabilize debt is not always optimal.

Most expositions of the fiscal theory posit simple ad hoc rules for monetary and fiscal behavior and characterize the nature of equilibria under alternative settings of those rules. This chapter follows that path in the next two sections to derive clean analytical results that explain how the fiscal theory operates and how it differs from alternative policy mixes. Then the paper turns to study jointly optimal monetary and fiscal policies as an alternative vehicle for describing the economic mechanisms that underlie the fiscal theory. Optimal policies make clear that the distinguishing features of the fiscal theory are generally part of a policy mix that produces desirable economic outcome. But the incentive to use surprise inflation to stabilize debt, especially when debt levels are high, can also create significant time-consistency issues when policymakers cannot credibly commit. When private agents know that policymakers may be tempted to induce inflation surprises to reduce the debt burden, economic agents raise their inflation expectations as debt levels rise until that temptation has been offset. This produces a sizeable debt stabilization bias that drives policymakers to reduce debt levels rapidly, at large cost in terms of social welfare, to avoid the high equilibrium rates of inflation associated with the temptation to inflate that debt away. We explore the sharp contrast between time-consistent and time-inconsistent optimal policy in this context in detail.

After those purely theoretical explorations, the paper turns to consider the empirical relevance of those mechanisms. We describe some subtle issues that arise in efforts to identify monetary–fiscal regime and review existing evidence both for and against fiscal interpretations of time series. The chapter then discusses three practical applications of the theory: fiscal prerequisites for successful inflation targeting, consequences of alternative fiscal reactions to a return to more normal levels of interest rates, and why the central bank needs understand the prevailing monetary–fiscal regime in order to conduct monetary policy. To wrap up, we describe outstanding issues in both theoretical and empirical analyses of monetary and fiscal policy interactions to point out directions for future research.

2. ENDOWMENT ECONOMIES WITH AD HOC POLICY RULES

This section aims to present the distinguishing features of the fiscal theory listed in Section 1.3 in the simplest possible model. A representative consumer lives forever and receives a constant endowment of goods, y, each period. The economy is cashless and financial markets are complete.

2.1 A Simple Model

The consumer optimally chooses consumption, c_t, may buy or sell nominal assets, D_t, at price $Q_{t,t+1}$, receives lump-sum transfers from the government, z_t, and pays lump-sum taxes, τ_t.[i] The representative household maximizes

$$E_0\left\{\sum_{t=0}^{\infty}\beta^t U(c_t)\right\}$$

with $0<\beta<1$, subject to the sequence of flow budget constraints

[i] D_t consists of privately issued, B_t^p, and government issued, B_t, assets. Government bonds cost $\$1/R_t$ per unit and are perfectly safe pure discount bonds.

$$P_t c_t + P_t \tau_t + E_t[Q_{t,t+1} D_t] = P_t y + P_t z_t + D_{t-1} \tag{1}$$

given D_{-1}. $Q_{t,t+1}$ is the nominal price at t of an asset that pays \$1 in period $t+1$ and P_t is the general price level in units of mature government bonds required to purchase one unit of goods. Government bonds sold at t, which are included in D_t, pay gross nominal interest R_t in period $t + 1$. Letting $m_{t,t+1}$ denote the real contingent claims price, a no-arbitrage condition implies that

$$Q_{t,t+1} = m_{t,t+1} \frac{P_t}{P_{t+1}} \tag{2}$$

The short-term nominal interest rate, R_t, which is also the central bank's policy instrument, is linked to the nominal bond price: $1/R_t = E_t[Q_{t,t+1}]$.

Setting government purchases of goods to zero,[j] the primary surplus is simply $s_t \equiv \tau_t - z_t$. The household's intertemporal budget identity comes from iterating on (1) and imposing the no-arbitrage condition, (2), and the transversality condition

$$\lim_{T \to \infty} E_t \left[m_{t,T} \frac{D_{T-1}}{P_T} \right] = 0 \tag{3}$$

to yield

$$E_t \sum_{j=0}^{\infty} m_{t,t+j} c_{t+j} = \frac{D_{t-1}}{P_t} + E_t \sum_{j=0}^{\infty} m_{t,t+j} (y - s_{t+j}) \tag{4}$$

where $m_{t,t+j} \equiv \prod_{k=0}^{j} m_{t+k,t+k+1}$ is the real discount factor, with $m_{t,t} = 1$.

After imposing equilibrium in the goods market, $c_t = y$, the real discount factor is constant, $m_{t,t+1} = \beta$, and the nominal interest rate obeys a Fisher relation

$$\frac{1}{R_t} = \beta E_t \frac{P_t}{P_{t+1}} = \beta E_t \frac{1}{\pi_{t+1}} \tag{5}$$

where $\pi_t \equiv P_t / P_{t-1}$ is the gross inflation rate. In equilibrium there will be no borrowing or lending among private agents, so the household's bond portfolio consists entirely of government bonds. Imposing both bond and goods market clearing and the constant real discount factor the household's intertemporal constraint produces the ubiquitous equilibrium condition

$$\frac{B_{t-1}}{P_t} = E_t \sum_{j=0}^{\infty} \beta^j s_{t+j} \tag{6}$$

Cochrane (2001) refers to (6) as an "equilibrium valuation equation" because it links the market value of debt outstanding at the beginning of period t, B_{t-1}/P_t, to the expected

[j] We shall relax this assumption below.

present value of the cash flows that back debt, primary surpluses. Notice that we derived this valuation equation entirely from private optimizing behavior and market clearing, without reference to government behavior or to the government's budget identity. The valuation equation imposes no restrictions on the government's choices of future surpluses, in the same way that the Fisher relation does not limit the central bank's choices of the nominal interest rate.

For each date t, equations (5) and (6) constitute two equilibrium conditions in four unknowns: $R_t, P_t, E_t(1/P_{t+1}), E_t\sum_{j=0}^{\infty}\beta^j s_{t+j}$. Private-sector behavior alone cannot uniquely determine the equilibrium. We turn now to a class of monetary and fiscal policy rules that may deliver determinate equilibria.

2.1.1 Policy Rules

The central bank obeys a simple interest rate rule, come to be called a Taylor (1993) rule, that makes deviations of the nominal interest rate from steady state proportional to deviations of inflation from steady state

$$\frac{1}{R_t} = \frac{1}{R^*} + \alpha_\pi\left(\frac{1}{\pi_t} - \frac{1}{\pi^*}\right) + \varepsilon_t^M \tag{7}$$

where ε_t^M is an exogenous shock to monetary policy. The government sets deviations of the primary surplus from steady state proportional to steady-state deviations of debt

$$s_t = s^* + \gamma\left(\frac{1}{R_{t-1}}\frac{B_{t-1}}{P_{t-1}} - \frac{b^*}{R^*}\right) + \varepsilon_t^F \tag{8}$$

where ε_t^F is an exogenous fiscal shock to the primary surplus. The inverse of the nominal interest rate is the price of nominal debt, so $\frac{1}{R_{t-1}}\frac{B_{t-1}}{P_{t-1}}$ is the real market value of debt issued at $t-1$. Policy choices must be consistent with the government's flow budget identity

$$\frac{1}{R_t}\frac{B_t}{P_t} + s_t = \frac{B_{t-1}}{P_t}$$

where the steady state of the model is

$$\frac{B}{P} = b^*, \quad s^* = (\beta^{-1} - 1)\frac{b^*}{R^*}, \quad R^* = \frac{\pi^*}{\beta}, \quad m^* = \beta$$

It is convenient to express things in terms of the inverse of inflation (ie, deflation) and real debt, so let $\nu_t \equiv \pi_t^{-1}$ and $b_t \equiv B_t/P_t$. Combining the monetary policy rule with the Fisher equation yields the difference equation in deflation

$$E_t(\nu_{t+1} - \nu^*) = \frac{\alpha_\pi}{\beta}(\nu_t - \nu^*) + \frac{1}{\beta}\varepsilon_t^M \tag{9}$$

Combining the fiscal rule and the government's flow budget identity, taking expectations, and employing the Fisher relation yield real debt dynamics

$$E_t\left(\frac{b_{t+1}}{R_{t+1}}-\frac{b^*}{R^*}\right)=(\beta^{-1}-\gamma)\left(\frac{b_t}{R_t}-\frac{b^*}{R^*}\right)-E_t\varepsilon^F_{t+1} \tag{10}$$

Equations (9) and (10) constitute a system of expectational difference equations in inflation and real debt, which is driven by the exogenous policy disturbances ε^M and ε^F. Given the consumer's discount factor, β, this system appears as though inflation dynamics depend only on the monetary policy choice of α_π, while debt dynamics hinge only on the fiscal policy choice of γ: it is not obvious that monetary and fiscal behavior *jointly* determine inflation and real debt. This apparent separation of the system is deceptive. Because the government issues *nominal* bonds, B_t, the price level appears in both equations and $1/P_t$ is the value of bonds maturing at t.

2.1.2 Solving the Model

We focus on bounded solutions.[k] Stability of inflation depends on α_π/β and stability of debt depends on $\beta^{-1}-\gamma$.[l]

2.1.2.1 Regime M

If $\alpha_\pi/\beta > 1$, then the bounded solution for inflation is

$$\nu_t=\nu^*-\frac{1}{\alpha_\pi}\sum_{j=0}^{\infty}\left(\frac{\beta}{\alpha_\pi}\right)^j E_t\varepsilon^M_{t+j} \tag{11}$$

which delivers a solution for $\{P_{t-1}/P_t\}$ for $t\geq 0$ and the equilibrium nominal interest rate is

$$\frac{1}{R_t}=\frac{1}{R^*}-\sum_{j=1}^{\infty}\left(\frac{\beta}{\alpha_\pi}\right)^j E_t\varepsilon^M_{t+j}$$

In this simple model, both actual and expected inflation depend on the monetary policy parameter and shock, but they appear not to depend in any way on fiscal behavior.

[k] Unbounded solutions for inflation also exist, as Benhabib et al. (2001) show. Sims (1999b), Cochrane (2011a), and Del Negro and Sims (2015) thoroughly explore those equilibria to argue that a determinate price level requires appropriate fiscal backing. As Del Negro and Sims (2015, p. 3) define it: "Fiscal backing requires that explosive inflationary or deflationary behavior of the price level is seen as impossible because the fiscal authority will respond to very high inflation with higher primary surpluses and to near-zero interest rates with lower, or negative, primary surpluses." Solutions with unbounded debt inevitably rely on nondistorting taxes, which permit revenues to grow forever at the same rate as interest receipts on government bond holdings. Although such paths for revenues are equilibria in the present model, because they are infeasible in economies where taxes distort, we find them to be uninteresting.

[l] We consider the implications of temporarily being in active–active or passive–passive regimes in Section 7.3.

This appearance is deceptive because (11) does not constitute a complete solution to the model; we also need to ensure that there is a bounded solution for real debt. If fiscal policy chooses $\gamma > \beta^{-1} - 1$, then when real debt rises, future surpluses rise by more than the net real interest rate with the change in debt in order to cover both debt service and a little of the principal. In this case, the debt dynamics in (10) imply that for arbitrary deviations of real debt from steady state, $\lim_{T\to\infty} E_t b_{T+1} = b^*$, so debt eventually returns to steady state.

Digging into exactly what fiscal policy does to stabilize debt reveals the underlying policy interactions. Suppose that at time t news arrives of a higher path for $\{\varepsilon^M_{t+j}\}$. This news reduces ν_t, raising the price level P_t. With fiscal rule (8), in the first instance the monetary news leaves s_t unaffected, but household holdings of outstanding bonds, B_{t-1}/P_t, decline. From the government budget identity, this implies that the market value of debt issued at t also falls, even if there is no change in the price of bonds, $1/R_t$

$$\frac{B_t}{P_t R_t} = -s_t + \frac{B_{t-1}}{P_t}$$

In the absence of future fiscal adjustments—such as those in which $\gamma > \beta^{-1} - 1$—household wealth would decline, reducing aggregate demand and counteracting the inflationary effect of the monetary expansion. But when fiscal policy reduces surpluses with debt by more than the real interest rate, surpluses are expected to fall by an amount equal in present value to the initial drop in the value of household bond holdings. This eliminates the negative wealth effect to render monetary policy expansionary.

When the news of higher $\{\varepsilon^M_{t+j}\}$ extends to affect the equilibrium beyond the current period, the nominal interest rate rises, reducing the price of new bonds at t. Lower bond prices implicitly raise interest yields on these bonds that mature in period $t+1$ to create a second channel by which monetary policy affects household wealth. As with the first channel, though, these wealth effects evaporate with the expected adjustments in surpluses.

These fiscal adjustments connect to Wallace's (1981) point that the impacts of open-market operations hinge on the sense in which fiscal policy is "held constant." In regime M, the "constancy" of fiscal policy is quite specific: it eliminates any monetary effects on balance sheets. By neutralizing the fiscal consequences of monetary policy actions, this regime leaves the impression that, in Friedman's (1970) famous aphorism, "inflation is always and everywhere a monetary phenomenon." Of course, it is the *joint* behavior of monetary and fiscal policies that delivers this impression.

Regime M also delivers the fiscal counterpart to Friedman's monetarist adage: Ricardian equivalence.[m] A fiscal shock at t that reduces the surplus by one unit is financed

[m] Tobin (1980, p. 53) made this point: "Thus the Ricardian equivalence theorem is fundamental, perhaps indispensable, to monetarism."

initially by an expansion in nominal debt of P_t units. With inflation pinned down by expression (11), real debt also increases by P_t units. Higher real debt, through the fiscal rule, triggers higher future surpluses whose present value equals the original debt expansion. Even in this completely standard Ricardian experiment, it is the joint policy behavior—monetary policy's aggressive response to inflation and fiscal policy's passive adjustment of surpluses—that produces the irrelevance result.

2.1.2.2 Regime F

Consider the case in which fiscal policy is active, with exogenous surpluses, so $\gamma = 0$ to make the fiscal rule is $s_t = s^* + \varepsilon_t^F$. The solution for real debt is[n]

$$\frac{b_t}{R_t} = \frac{b^*}{R^*} + \sum_{j=1}^{\infty} \beta^j E_t \varepsilon_{t+j}^F \tag{12}$$

which implies that the value of debt at t depends on the expected present value of surpluses from $t + 1$ onward.

We can solve for inflation by combining this solution for b_t with the government's flow budget identity, noting that $B_{t-1}/P_t = \nu_t b_{t-1}$

$$\nu_t = \frac{(1-\beta)^{-1} s^* + \sum_{j=0}^{\infty} \beta^j E_t \varepsilon_{t+j}^F}{b_{t-1}} \tag{13}$$

where at t, b_{t-1} is predetermined, which produces the solution for the price level

$$P_t = \frac{B_{t-1}}{(1-\beta)^{-1} s^* + \sum_{j=0}^{\infty} \beta^j E_t \varepsilon_{t+j}^F} \tag{14}$$

News of lower surpluses raises the price level and reduces the value of outstanding debt. In contrast to regime M equilibria, in regime F *nominal* government debt is an important state variable.[o] Higher nominal debt or higher debt service raises the price level next period. These results reflect the impacts of higher nominal household wealth. Lower future surpluses—stemming from either lower taxes or higher transfers—or higher initial nominal assets raise households' demand for goods when there is no prospect that future taxes will rise to offset the higher wealth. Unlike regime M, now equilibrium inflation, as given by (13), depends explicitly on current and expected fiscal choices—through the steady-state surplus, s^*, and fiscal disturbances, $\sum_{j=0}^{\infty} \beta^j E_t \varepsilon_{t+j}^F$.

[n] To derive (12), define $\tilde{b}_t \equiv B_t/P_t R_t$ to write the flow government budget identity as $\tilde{b}_t + s_t = R_{t-1} \nu_t \tilde{b}_{t-1}$. Take expectations at $t-1$, apply the Euler equation $\beta^{-1} = E_{t-1} R_{t-1} \nu_t$, iterate forward, and impose transversality to obtain (12).

[o] Debt is also a state variable in regime M because it contains information about future surpluses. But in M, changes in the *real* value of debt induce changes in expectations of future *real* government claims on private resources.

Expression (12) gives the real market value of debt. But in the absence of any stabilizing response of surpluses to real debt ($\gamma = 0$), debt's deviations from steady state are expected to grow over time at the real rate of interest, $1/\beta$, according to (10). Such growth in debt would violate the household's transversality condition, which is inconsistent with equilibrium. To reconcile these seemingly contradictory implications of the equilibrium, we need to understand the role that monetary policy plays in regime F.

Monetary policy ensures that actual debt, as opposed to expected debt, is stable by preventing interest payments on the debt from exploding and permitting surprise inflation to revalue government debt. In regime F, higher interest payments raise nominal wealth, increasing nominal aggregate demand, and future inflation, as both (13) and (14) indicate. To understand monetary policy behavior, substitute the solution for ν_t from (13) into the monetary policy rule, (7). To simplify the expression, assume that the policy shocks are *i.i.d.* so that

$$\frac{1}{R_t} - \frac{1}{R^*} = \frac{\alpha_\pi}{\beta}\left[\frac{\beta(1-\beta)^{-1}s^* + \beta\varepsilon_t^F}{b_{t-1}} - \frac{1}{R^*}\right] + \varepsilon_t^M \tag{15}$$

In response to a fiscal expansion—$\varepsilon_t^F < 0$—the central bank reduces $1/R_t$ by $\alpha_\pi \varepsilon_t^F$ to lean against the fiscally induced inflation. A serially uncorrelated fiscal disturbance leaves the market value of debt at its steady state, $b_{t+j}/R_{t+j} = b^*/R^*$ for $j \geq 0$. This greatly simplifies the time $t+1$ version of (15) to yield

$$\frac{1}{R_{t+1}} - \frac{1}{R^*} = \frac{\alpha_\pi}{\beta}\left(\frac{1}{R_t} - \frac{1}{R^*}\right) \tag{16}$$

If monetary policy were to respond aggressively to inflation by setting $\alpha_\pi/\beta > 1$, $1/R$ would diverge to positive or negative infinity, both situations that violate lower bound conditions on the net, $R-1$, nominal interest rate. Economically, these exploding paths stem from strong wealth effects that arise from ever-growing interest receipts to holders of government bonds. When $\alpha_\pi/\beta > 1$ the central bank raises the nominal interest rate by a factor that exceeds the real interest rate, which increases private agents' nominal wealth and inflation in the next period; this process repeats in subsequent periods. Active monetary policy essentially converts stable fiscally induced inflation into explosive paths.

Existence of equilibrium requires that the monetary reaction to inflation not be too strong—specifically, that $\alpha_\pi/\beta < 1$, what is called "passive monetary policy." A pegged nominal interest rate, $\alpha_\pi = 0$, is the easiest case to understand. By holding the nominal rate fixed at R^*, monetary policy prevents the fiscal expansion from affecting future inflation by fixing interest payments on the debt. A one-time reduction in s_t that is financed by new nominal bond sales raises P_t enough to keep B_t/P_t unchanged. But the higher price level also reduces the real value of existing nominal debt, B_{t-1}/P_t, and in doing so reduces the implicit real interest payments. In terms of the flow budget identity

$$\frac{b^*}{R^*} + s_t = \frac{B_{t-1}}{P_t}$$

where real debt remains at steady state because $\gamma = 0$ implies that expected surpluses are unchanged. The larger is the stock of outstanding debt, the less the price level must rise to keep the budget in balance.

More interesting results emerge when there is some monetary policy response to inflation—$0 < \alpha_\pi < \beta$.[p] When monetary policy tries to combat fiscal inflation by raising the nominal interest rate, inflation is both amplified and propagated. Pegging R_t forces all inflation from a fiscal shock to occur at the time of the shock. Raising R_t permits the inflation to persist and the more strongly monetary policy reacts to inflation, the longer the inflation lasts.

Difference equations (15) and (16) make the monetary policy impacts clear. When $\alpha_\pi = 0$, a shock to ε_t^F has no effect on the nominal interest rate. But the larger is α_π, though still less than β, the stronger are the effects of ε_t^F on future nominal interest rates and, through the Fisher relation, future inflation.

Even though the transitory fiscal expansion has no effect on real debt, higher nominal rates bring forth new nominal bond issuances that are proportional to the increases in the price level. Higher nominal debt coupled with higher interest on the debt increases interest payments that raise household nominal wealth in the future. Because future taxes do not rise to offset that wealth increase, aggregate demand and the price level rise in the future.

Expression (15) reveals that an exogenous monetary contraction—lower ε_t^M that raises R_t—triggers exactly the same macroeconomic effects as an exogenous fiscal expansion. Higher interest rates raise debt service and nominal wealth, which increases inflation in the future. In this simple model with a fixed real interest rate, only this perverse implication for monetary policy obtains. We shall discuss the effects of monetary policy contractions in a production economy with longer maturity debt in Section 2.2.[q]

2.2 The Role of Maturity Structure

Tobin (1963) discusses debt management in the context of the "monetary effect of the debt," contrasting this to the "direct fiscal effect" that is determined by the initial increase in the bond-financed deficit. The monetary effect stems from the maturity structure of the debt, which Tobin reasons outlasts the direct effect because it endures over the maturity horizon of the debt. Changes in the maturity composition of debt operate through

[p] Impulse responses to this case are considered in Section 2.3.

[q] The result that a monetary contraction raises future inflation is reminiscent of Sargent and Wallace's (1981) unpleasant monetarist arithmetic, but the mechanism is completely different. In Sargent and Wallace, tighter money today implies looser money in the future and the higher future inflation can feed back to reduce money demand today. Their result does not stem from wealth effects of monetary policy.

impacts on the size and composition of private wealth. Such changes can affect the macro economy, even if they do not entail changing the overall size of the debt. This section obtains closely related impacts from maturity structure in regime F.

The section introduces a full maturity structure of government debt in general form to derive the bond valuation equation and develop some intuition about the role that maturity plays in the endowment economy in regime F. It then uses a simple special case to make transparent the mechanisms at work in regime F.[r]

2.2.1 A General Maturity Structure

Let $B_t(t+j)$ denote the nominal quantity of zero-coupon bonds outstanding in period t that matures in period $t+j$ and let the dollar-price of those bonds be $Q_t(t+j)$. The government's flow budget identity at t is

$$B_{t-1}(t) - \sum_{j=1}^{\infty} Q_t(t+j)[B_t(t+j) - B_{t-1}(t+j)] = P_t s_t$$

In a constant-endowment economy, the bond-pricing equations are

$$Q_t(t+k) = \beta^k E_t \frac{P_t}{P_{t+k}} \tag{17}$$

for $k = 1, 2, \ldots$. These pricing equations imply the no-arbitrage condition that links the price of a k-period bond to the expected sequence of k 1-period bonds

$$Q_t(t+k) = E_t[Q_t(t+1)Q_{t+1}(t+2)\ldots Q_{t+k-1}(t+k)]$$

To derive the bond valuation equation with a general maturity structure, define

$$B_{t-1} \equiv B_{t-1}(t) + \sum_{j=1}^{\infty} Q_t(t+j)B_{t-1}(t+j)$$

as the portfolio of bonds outstanding at the end of period $t-1$ and rewrite the government budget identity as

$$\frac{B_{t-1}}{P_t} = Q_t(t+1)\frac{B_t}{P_t} + s_t$$

Iterating on this bond portfolio version of the constraint, taking expectations and imposing the bond-pricing relations and the consumer's transversality condition yields the valuation equation

$$\frac{B_{t-1}}{P_t} = \sum_{j=0}^{\infty} \beta^j E_t s_{t+j}$$

[r] These derivations draw on Cochrane (2001, 2014).

or, in terms of the underlying bonds

$$\frac{B_{t-1}(t)}{P_t} + \sum_{j=1}^{\infty} \beta^j E_t \frac{B_{t-1}(t+j)}{P_{t+j}} = \sum_{j=0}^{\infty} \beta^j E_t s_{t+j} \tag{18}$$

Use (18) to repeatedly substitute out future price levels to make explicit how maturity structure enters the valuation equation

$$\begin{aligned}\frac{B_{t-1}(t)}{P_t} = E_t \Bigg\{ & s_t + \beta \underbrace{\left[1 - \frac{B_{t-1}(t+1)}{B_t(t+1)}\right]}_{\text{weight on } t+1} s_{t+1} \\ & + \beta^2 \underbrace{\left\{1 - \left[\frac{B_{t-1}(t+2)}{B_{t+1}(t+2)} \frac{B_{t-1}(t+1)}{B_t(t+1)} \left(1 - \frac{B_t(t+2)}{B_{t+1}(t+2)}\right)\right]\right\}}_{\text{weight on } t+2} s_{t+2} + \dots \Bigg\}\end{aligned} \tag{19}$$

We write this valuation equation more compactly by defining

$$\Lambda_t(t+k) \equiv \frac{B_t(t+k) - B_{t-1}(t+k)}{B_{t+k-1}(t+k)}$$

as newly issued debt that matures in period $t + k$ as a share of total outstanding debt in period $t + k - 1$ that matures at $t + k$. We can now define the maturity weight on the surplus at $t + k$, $L_{t,t+k}$, as depending recursively on these ratios

$$\begin{aligned} L_{t,t} &= 1 \\ L_{t,t+1} &= \Lambda_t(t+1) \\ L_{t,t+2} &= \Lambda_{t+1}(t+2) L_{t,t+1} + \Lambda_t(t+2) \\ L_{t,t+3} &= \Lambda_{t+2}(t+3) L_{t,t+2} + \Lambda_{t+1}(t+3) L_{t,t+1} + \Lambda_t(t+3) \\ &\vdots \\ L_{t,t+k} &= \sum_{j=0}^{k-1} \Lambda_{t+j}(t+k) L_{t,t+j} \end{aligned}$$

The compact form of valuation equation (19) is now

$$\frac{B_{t-1}(t)}{P_t} = \sum_{j=0}^{\infty} \beta^j E_t [L_{t,t+j} s_{t+j}] \tag{20}$$

Given a sequence of surpluses, $\{s_t\}$, discount factors and maturity determine the expected present value of surpluses. Shortening maturity (eg, reducing $\frac{B_{t-1}(t+1)}{B_t(t+1)}$) raises the weights on s_{t+1}, s_{t+2}, s_{t+3}, raising that present value—the backing of debt—and the value of debt. Shortening maturity of bonds due at $t+k$ raises weights on all $s_{t+j}, j \geq k$. In this sense, shortening maturity can offset a decline in surpluses.

Surprise changes in future maturity structure appear as innovations in the weights, $L_{t,t+j}$, in valuation equation (20). If primary surpluses are given, an unanticipated shortening of maturity of bonds held by the public would, by raising the value of outstanding debt, reduce the current price level. Viewed through the lens of the fiscal theory, the Federal Reserve's "operation twist" in 2011 would have a contractionary effect on the economy initially.[s] As the example to which we now turn illustrates, the lower price level at t would ultimately be offset by a higher future price level.

2.2.1.1 An Illustrative Example

To cleanly illustrate the role that changes in maturity structure play in determining the timing of inflation, we examine an example from Cochrane (2014). We use the same constant-endowment economy, but it operates only in periods $t = 0, 1, 2$, and then ends; we set the real interest rate to zero, so the discount factor is $\beta = 1$. The government issues one- and two-period nominal bonds at the beginning of time, $t = 0$, denoted by $B_0(1)$ and $B_0(2)$, and uses surpluses in periods 1 and 2, s_1 and s_2, to retire the debt. At date $t = 1$ the government may choose to issue new one-period debt, $B_1(2)$, so the change in debt at $t = 1$ is $B_1(2) - B_0(2)$. The three potentially different quantities of bonds sell at nominal prices $Q_0(1), Q_0(2), Q_1(2)$ that obey (17) with $\beta = 1$.[t]

Given initial choices of debt, $B_0(1)$ and $B_0(2)$, the government's budget identities in periods 1 and 2 are

$$B_0(1) = P_1 s_1 + Q_1(2)[B_1(2) - B_0(2)] \tag{21}$$

$$B_1(2) = P_2 s_2 \tag{22}$$

When primary surpluses are given at $\{s_1, s_2\}$, expression (22) immediately yields the price level in period 2 as

$$\frac{B_1(2)}{P_2} = s_2$$

because $B_1(2)$ is predetermined in period 2.

[s] The premise of the Fed's actions was that if short and long bonds are imperfect substitutes, then increasing demand for long bonds would reduce long-term interest rates. Lower long rates, it was hoped, would stimulate business investment and the housing market.

[t] We normalize the initial price level to be $P_0 = 1$.

Now impose the asset-pricing relations on the bond prices in the period 1 government budget identity, (21), to obtain the bond valuation equation

$$\frac{B_0(1)}{P_1} = s_1 + \left[\frac{B_1(2) - B_0(2)}{B_1(2)}\right] E_1 s_2$$

P_1 depends on the choice of newly issued bonds in period 1.

Solving for expected inflation and bond prices yields

$$E_0\left(\frac{1}{P_2}\right) = Q_0(2) = E_0\left(\frac{s_2}{B_1(2)}\right) = E_0\left[\frac{1}{B_0(2) + (B_1(2) - B_0(2))}\right] s_2$$

$$E_0\left(\frac{1}{P_1}\right) = Q_0(1) = \frac{E_0[s_1]}{B_0(1)} + \frac{1}{B_0(1)} E_0\left[\frac{B_1(2) - B_0(2)}{B_1(2)}\right] s_2$$

So the term structure of interest rates also depends on choices about maturity structure.

We can derive explicit solutions for the actual or realized price level at $t = 1$ in terms of innovations

$$B_0(1)(E_1 - E_0)\left(\frac{1}{P_1}\right) = (E_1 - E_0)s_1 + (E_1 - E_0)\left(\frac{B_1(2) - B_0(2)}{B_1(2)}\right) s_2$$

Surprise increases in the price level in period 1 depend negatively on innovations in time-1 and time-2 surpluses and on unexpected lengthening of the maturity of bonds due in period 2.

These derivations show that the government can achieve any path of the nominal term structure—and in this example, expected inflation—that it wishes by adjusting maturity structure. By unexpectedly selling less time-2 debt, the government reduces the claims to time-2 surpluses, which reduces the revenues that can be used to pay off period-1 bonds. This raises inflation in period 1. That increase in inflation comes from reducing $B_1(2)$, which lowers the price level in period 2, as seen from

$$(E_1 - E_0)\left(\frac{B_1(2)}{P_2}\right) = (E_1 - E_0)s_2$$

If s_2 is given, selling less $B_1(2)$ requires P_2 to fall.

2.2.2 A Useful Special Case

Suppose that the maturity structure declines at a constant rate $0 \leq \rho \leq 1$ each period so that the pattern of bonds issued at $t - 1$ obeys

$$B_{t-1}(t+j) = \rho^j B_{t-1}^m$$

where B_{t-1}^m is the portfolio of these specialized bonds in $t - 1$. When $\rho = 0$ all bonds are one period, whereas when $\rho = 1$ all bonds are consols. The average maturity of the portfolio is $1/(1 - \beta\rho)$.

With this specialization, the government's flow constraint is

$$B_{t-1}^{m}\left[1-\sum_{j=1}^{\infty}Q_t(t+j)\rho^{j}\right]=P_t s_t+B_t^{m}\sum_{j=1}^{\infty}Q_t(t+j)\rho^{j-1}$$

If we define the price of the bond portfolio as

$$P_t^{m}\equiv\sum_{j=1}^{\infty}Q_t(t+j)\rho^{j-1}$$

then the government's budget identity becomes

$$B_{t-1}^{m}(1+\rho P_t^{m})=P_t s_t+P_t^{m}B_t^{m} \tag{23}$$

Bond portfolio prices obey the recursion

$$P_t^{m}=Q_t(t+1)[1+\rho E_t P_{t+1}^{m}]=R_t^{-1}[1+\rho E_t P_{t+1}^{m}] \tag{24}$$

This shows that a constant geometric decay rate in the maturity structure of zero-coupon bonds is equivalent to the interpretation of bonds that pay geometrically decaying coupon payments, as in Woodford (2001) and Eusepi and Preston (2013).

Let R_{t+1}^{m} denote the gross nominal return on the bond portfolio between t and $t+1$. Then $R_{t+1}^{m}=(1+\rho P_{t+1}^{m})/P_t^{m}$ and the no-arbitrage condition implies that

$$\frac{1}{R_t}=\beta E_t \nu_{t+1}=E_t\left(\frac{1}{R_{t+1}^{m}}\right) \tag{25}$$

Combining (24) and (25) and iterating forward connects bond prices to expected paths of the short-term nominal interest rate and inflation

$$P_t^{m}=\sum_{j=0}^{\infty}\rho^{j}E_t\left(\prod_{i=0}^{j}R_{t+i}^{-1}\right)=\beta\sum_{j=0}^{\infty}(\beta\rho)^{j}E_t\left(\prod_{i=0}^{j}\nu_{t+i+1}\right) \tag{26}$$

2.3 Maturity Structure in Regime F

Ricardian equivalence in regime M makes the maturity structure of debt irrelevant for inflation, so in this section we focus solely on regime F. When surpluses are exogenous ($\gamma=0$), the debt valuation equation becomes[u]

[u] To derive (27), convert the nominal budget identity in (23) into a difference equation in the real value of debt, $P^{m}B^{m}/P$, impose pricing equations (24) and (25), using the fact that $\beta^{-1}=E_{t-1}[\nu_t(1+\rho P_t^{m})/P_{t-1}^{m}]$, iterate forward, and impose the household's transversality condition for debt.

$$\frac{(1+\rho P_t^m)B_{t-1}^m}{P_t} = (1-\beta)^{-1}s^* + \sum_{j=0}^{\infty}\beta^j E_t \varepsilon_{t+j}^F \tag{27}$$

In contrast to the situation with only one-period debt ($\rho = 0$) when fiscal news appeared entirely in jumps in the price level, now there is an additional channel through which debt can be revalued: bond prices that reflect expected inflation over the entire duration of debt. News of lower future surpluses reduces the value of debt through both a higher P_t and a lower P_t^m. By (26), the lower bond price portends higher inflation and higher one-period nominal interest rates. The ultimate mix between current and future inflation is determined by the monetary policy rule. Long-term debt opens a new channel for monetary and fiscal policy to interact.

No-arbitrage condition (26) reveals a key aspect of regime F equilibria with long debt. With the simplified maturity structure, ρ determines the average maturity of the zero-coupon bond portfolio. A given future inflation rate has a larger impact on the price of bonds, the larger is ρ or the longer is the average maturity of debt. The maturity parameter serves as an additional discount factor, along with β, so more distant inflation rates have a smaller impact on bond prices than do rates in the near future. Of course, the date t expected present value of inflation influences only the price of bonds that are outstanding at the beginning of t, namely, B_{t-1}^m.

To understand monetary policy's influence on the timing of inflation, note that when monetary policy is passive, $\alpha_\pi/\beta < 1$, (9) implies that k-step-ahead expected inflation is

$$E_t \nu_{t+k} = \left(\frac{\alpha_\pi}{\beta}\right)^k (\nu_t - \nu^*) + \nu^*$$

which may be substituted into the pricing equation that links P_t^m to the term structure of inflation rates, (26), to yield[v]

$$\rho P_t^m = \sum_{j=1}^{\infty}(\beta\rho)^j \left\{\prod_{i=0}^{j-1}\left[\left(\frac{\alpha_\pi}{\beta}\right)^{i+1}(\nu_t - \nu^*) + \nu^*\right]\right\}$$

Monetary policy's reaction to inflation—through α_π—interacts with the average maturity of debt—ρ—to determine how current inflation—ν_t, which is given by (13) in regime F—affects the price of bonds. More aggressive monetary policy and longer maturity debt both serve to amplify the impact of current inflation on bond prices, suggesting that higher α_π and higher ρ permit fiscal disturbances to have a smaller impact on current inflation at the cost of a larger impact on future inflation.

[v] Here we shut down the exogenous monetary policy shock, $\varepsilon_t^M \equiv 0$.

Consider two polar cases of passive monetary policy. When $\alpha_\pi = 0$, so the central bank pegs the nominal interest rate and bond prices at $\rho P_t^m = \beta\rho\nu^*/(1-\beta\rho\nu^*)$, the valuation expression becomes

$$\left(\frac{1}{1-\beta\rho\nu^*}\right)\nu_t b_{t-1}^m = (1-\beta)^{-1}s^* + \sum_{j=0}^{\infty}\beta^j E_t \varepsilon_{t+j}^F$$

where we define $b_{t-1}^m \equiv B_{t-1}^m/P_{t-1}$. In this case, expected inflation returns to target immediately, $E_t\nu_{t+j} = \nu^*$ for $j \geq 1$.

The second case is when monetary policy reacts as strongly as possible to inflation, while still remaining passive: $\alpha_\pi = \beta$.[w] Then $\rho P_t^m = \beta\rho\nu_t/(1-\beta\rho\nu_t)$ and the valuation equation is[x]

$$\left(\frac{\nu_t}{1-\beta\rho\nu_t}\right)b_{t-1}^m = (1-\beta)^{-1}s^* + \sum_{j=0}^{\infty}\beta^j E_t \varepsilon_{t+j}^F$$

Now inflation follows a martingale with $E_t\nu_{t+j} = \nu_t$ for $j \geq 1$.

The two polar cases are starkly different. By pegging the nominal interest rate, monetary policy anchors expected inflation on the steady-state (target) inflation rate and bond prices are constant. The full impact of a lower present value of surpluses must be absorbed by higher current inflation—lower ν_t—alone. But when monetary policy raises the nominal rate with current inflation by a proportion equal to the discount factor, higher current inflation is expected to persist indefinitely. Bond prices fall by the expected present value of that higher inflation rate, discounted at the rate $\beta\rho$. With the required change in inflation spread evenly over the term to maturity of outstanding debt, when fiscal news arrives, inflation needs to rise by far less than it does when bond prices are pegged. Of course, the "total"—present value—inflation effect of the fiscal shock is identical in the two cases. Although aggressive monetary policy cannot diminish the total inflationary impact, it can influence the timing of when inflation occurs.

We can consider both these polar cases and the intermediate case where $0 < \alpha_\pi < \beta$, by solving the model numerically in the presence of transfer shocks.[y] These are calibrated following Bi et al. (2013). We assume that the steady-state ratio of transfers to GDP is 0.18, government spending is 21% of GDP and taxes amount to 41% of GDP implying an (annualized) steady-state debt–GDP ratio of 50%. Transfers fluctuate according to an autoregressive process with persistence parameter of $\rho_z = 0.9$, and variance of $(0.005z^*)$.

[w] If monetary policy were to turn active, while fiscal policy remained active, then we would have an unstable equilibrium. The implications of temporarily being in such a regime are considered in Section 7.3.

[x] This result requires that $\beta\rho\nu_t < 1$ for all realizations of ν_t, so there cannot be "too much" deflation.

[y] The solution procedure follows Leith and Liu (2014), which relies on Chebyshev collocation methods and Gauss–Hermite quadrature to evaluate the expectations terms.

In this simple model with an active fiscal policy that does not respond to debt levels, the equilibrium outcome depends on the maturity of the debt stock and the responsiveness of monetary policy to inflation.

Fig. 1 plots the response to an increase in transfers. Each column represents a different value of the response of monetary policy to inflation. Monetary policy pegs the nominal rate in the first column, so the paths of all variables are the same across maturities: the entire adjustment occurs through surprise inflation in the initial period. In the second column $\alpha_\pi = 0.5$. Now differences emerge across maturities. With one-period debt the magnitude of the initial jump in inflation is the same as under a pegged interest rate because this is the price-level jump that is required to reduce the real value of debt to be consistent with lower surpluses. But the monetary policy reaction keeps inflation high for a prolonged period even though it is only the initial jump in inflation that serves to reduce the debt burden. As average maturity increases, the initial jump in inflation becomes smaller. A sustained rise in interest rates depresses bond prices, which allow the bond valuation equation to be satisfied at lower initial inflation rates. It is the surprise change in the *path* of inflation that occurs over the life of the maturing debt stock that reduces the real value of debt. With a positive value of α_π, any jump in inflation is sustained, which unexpectedly reduces the real returns that bondholders receive before that debt is rolled over. As we increase the responsiveness of the interest rate to inflation further to $\alpha_\pi = 0.9$, the surprise inflation needed to deflate the real value of debt remains unchanged for single-period debt, but is dramatically reduced for longer period debt. When $\alpha_\pi = 0.99$, as demonstrated analytically earlier, and $\rho > 0$, the rate of inflation follows a near-random walk, jumping to the level needed to satisfy the valuation equation.

The timing of the transfer shock—whether it is *i.i.d.* or persistent, realized immediately or in the future—does not matter beyond the change in the expected discounted value of surpluses that it produces. That present value must be financed with a path of inflation that combines current inflation surprises, and through bond prices, future inflation surprises, to ensure solvency. An anticipated increase in transfers produces surprise inflation today that reduces the current value of the outstanding debt stock, but whose value increase after the increase in transfers is realized.

This result foreshadows an important aspect of optimal policy, which Sections 4 and 5 explore: monetary policy can smooth the distortionary effects of fiscally induced inflation. The above analysis uses an endowment economy subjected to transfer shocks. That environment has the feature that under regime M, monetary policy can perfectly control inflation, while under regime F, prices are determined by the needs of fiscal solvency—the dichotomy across regimes that was emphasized in the original fiscal theory. The more general case breaks the dichotomy to produce interactions between monetary and fiscal policy in both policy regimes. This situation can arise even in the endowment economy when we consider government spending shocks rather than shocks to lump-sum transfers.

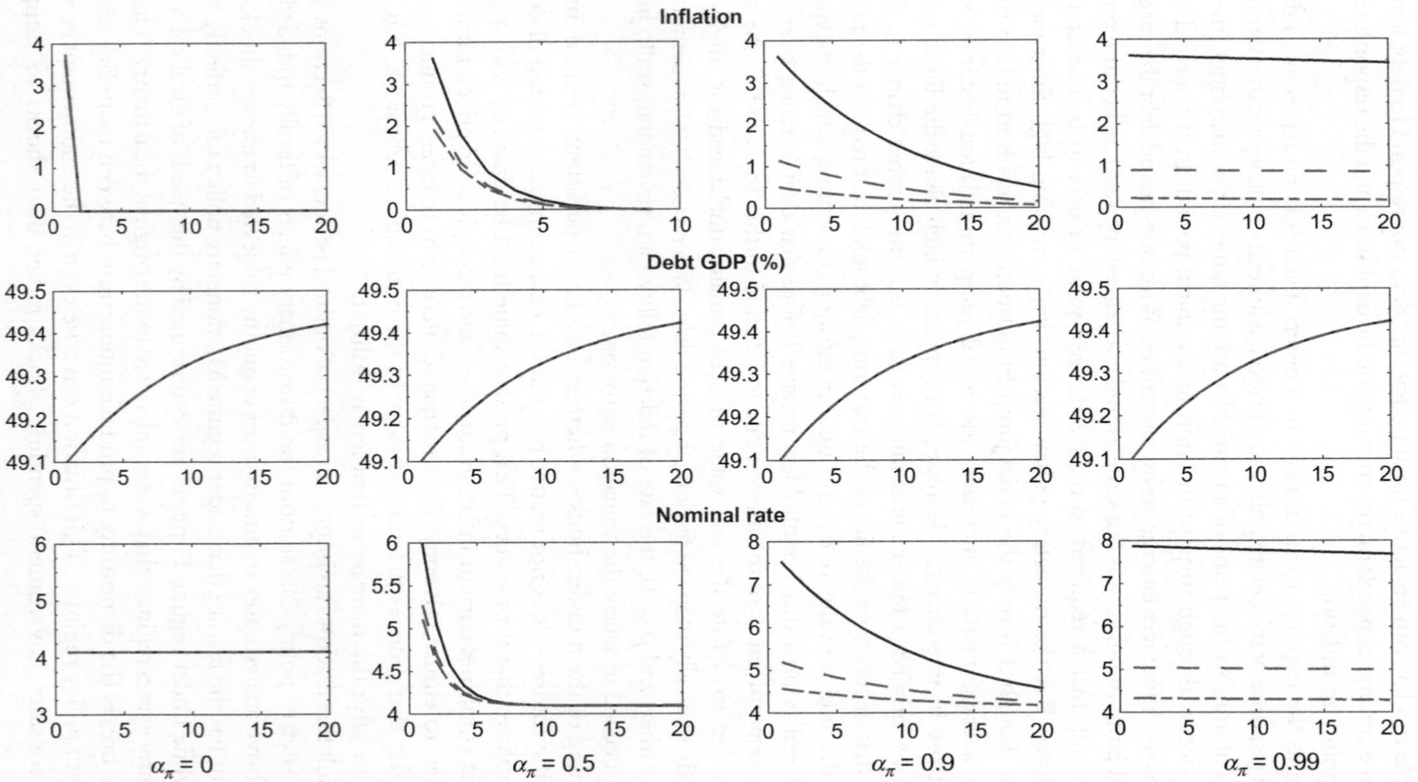

Fig. 1 Responses to an increase in transfers under alternative monetary policy rules and alternative maturity structures. 1-period debt (*solid lines*), 1-year debt (*dashed lines*), and 5-year debt (*dot-dashed lines*).

2.3.1 Increase in Government Spending

Government spending has implications for both monetary and fiscal policy. The direct impact on the government's finances is obvious. But given the resource constraint, $y = c_t + g_t$, variations in public consumption will have a one-for-one impact on private consumption which affects the stochastic discount factor. Through this channel government purchases carry additional effects on inflation and debt dynamics. Again we distinguish between the M and F regimes, although monetary and fiscal policy will interact under both.

2.3.1.1 Policy Under Regime M

When monetary policy is active and fiscal policy is passive, the analysis of the case of transfer shocks largely carries through, although with some additional monetary and fiscal interactions. Substituting the Fisher relation into the monetary policy rule yields the deflation dynamics[z]

$$v_t - v^* = \frac{\beta}{\alpha_\pi} E_t \left[\frac{u'(c_{t+1})}{u'(c_t)} v_{t+1} - v^* \right]$$

which can be solved forward as

$$v_t = \frac{\alpha_\pi - \beta}{\alpha_\pi} E_t \sum_{i=0}^{\infty} \left(\frac{\beta}{\alpha_\pi} \right)^i \frac{u'(c_{t+i})}{u'(c_t)} v^*$$

Inflation deviates from target in proportion to the deviations of the real interest rate path from steady state. Higher government spending raises the real interest rate and inflation.

Debt dynamics emerge from three distinct impacts of government spending: the direct effect on the fiscal surplus, the surprise inflation that arises in conjunction with the monetary policy rule, and movements in real interest rates. Monetary policy can insulate inflation from government spending shocks by reacting to real interest rates, as well as inflation, with the rule

$$\frac{1}{R_t} = \frac{1}{R^*} E_t \frac{u'(c_{t+1})}{u'(c_t)} + \alpha_\pi (v_t - v^*) \tag{28}$$

By this rule, the policymaker accommodates changes in the natural rate of interest caused by fluctuations in public consumption without deviating from the inflation target. To see this, combine this rule with the Fisher equation to get

[z] When the real interest rate can vary, the Fisher relation is

$$\frac{1}{R_t} = \beta E_t \frac{u'(c_{t+1})}{u'(c_t)} v_{t+1}$$

$$\nu_t - \nu^* = \frac{\beta}{\alpha_\pi} E_t \frac{u'(c_{t+1})}{u'(c_t)} (\nu_{t+1} - \nu^*)$$

Policy rule (28) implies that inflation/deflation is always equal to target, $\nu_t = \nu^*$. If the monetary policy rule does not respond to fiscal variables, inflation will be influenced by government spending shocks. Inflation can be insulated from fiscal shocks by allowing monetary policy to directly respond to the effects of fiscal policy on the natural rate of interest.

2.3.1.2 Policy Under Regime F

In regime F government spending shocks require jumps in inflation to satisfy the bond valuation equation[aa]

$$\begin{aligned}(1+\rho P_t^m)\frac{B_{t-1}^m}{P_t} &= E_t \sum_{i=0}^{\infty} \beta^i \frac{u'(c_{t+i})}{u'(c_t)} s_{t+i} \\ &= E_t \sum_{i=0}^{\infty} \beta^i \frac{u'(c_{t+i})}{u'(c_t)} s^* - E_t \sum_{i=0}^{\infty} \beta^i \frac{u'(c_{t+i})}{u'(c_t)} \varepsilon_{t+i}^G\end{aligned}$$

An increase in government spending increases the marginal utility of consumption, which increases real interest rates and requires a larger initial jump in inflation and drop in bond prices. Bond prices themselves are directly affected by the change in private consumption that arises when the government absorbs a larger share of resources, as the bond-pricing equation shows

$$P_t^m = \beta E_t (1 + \rho P_{t+1}^m) \nu_{t+1} \frac{u'(c_{t+1})}{u'(c_t)}$$

Bond prices fall initially and then gradually increase as the period of raised public consumption passes.

Adopting a specific form of utility, $u(c_t) = c_t^{1-\sigma}/(1-\sigma)$, with $\sigma = 2$, we can solve the model in the face of autocorrelated government spending shocks with $\rho_g = 0.9$, and variance of $0.005g^*$. As before, the stochastic model is solved nonlinearly using Chebyshev collocation methods (see Leith and Liu, 2014). Fig. 2 reflects the response to government spending shocks which are broadly consistent with the impacts of transfer shocks that appear in Fig. 1. The main difference is that the growth in consumption as government spending returns to steady state is equivalent to an increase in the real interest rate. But the main message that single-period debt requires an initial jump in inflation to stabilize debt and that this jump is unaffected by the description of the monetary policy parameter α_π remains. Once debt maturity extends beyond a single period, prolonging the initial

[aa] Shutting down shocks to lump-sum taxes and transfers, the surplus is defined as $s_t = \tau^* - z^* - g_t$, where $g_t = g^* \varepsilon_t^G$, and $\ln \varepsilon_t^g = \rho_g \ln \varepsilon_{t-1}^g + \xi_t$.

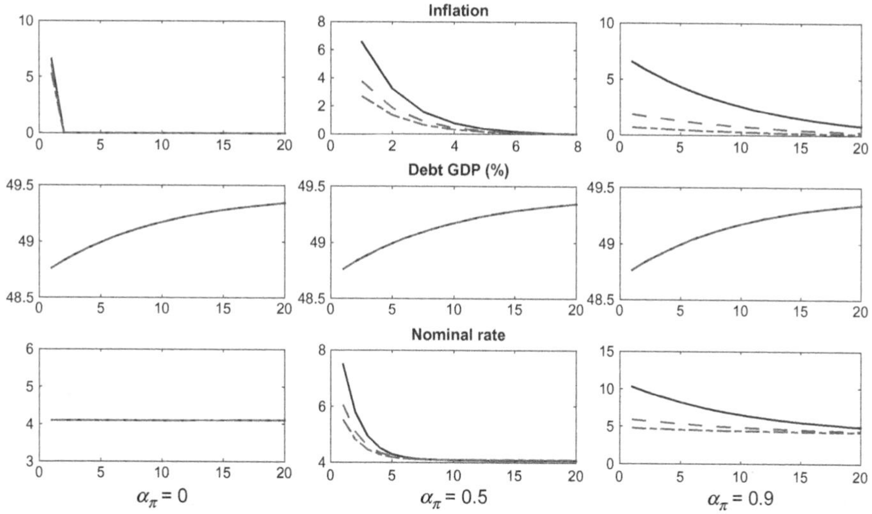

Fig. 2 Responses to an increase in government purchases under alternative monetary policy rules and alternative maturity structures. 1-period debt (*solid lines*), 1-year debt (*dashed lines*), and 5-year debt (*dot-dashed lines*).

jump in inflation can serve to reduce the magnitude of that initial jump. A sustained rise in inflation can also serve to satisfy the government's intertemporal budget identity through reducing bond prices. Essentially the inflation surprise is spread throughout the life to maturity of the outstanding debt stock.

3. PRODUCTION ECONOMIES WITH AD HOC POLICY RULES

The endowment economy is useful for understanding the mechanisms that underlie the fiscal theory. But the exogeneity of the real interest rate and the constancy of output limit a complete understanding of the theory and, in some cases, distort that understanding. We now turn to a conventional model in which inflation and output are determined jointly. In extending the analysis to the new Keynesian model we are widening the potential channels through which monetary and fiscal policy interact. To do so incrementally, we assume that taxes remain lump sum so that the effects of monetary policy on output do not affect the tax base to which a distortionary tax is applied. This means that the extra channel we are adding by introducing nominal inertia to a production economy is that monetary policy has influence over ex-ante real interest rates as well as nominal interest rates. This in turn means that the policymaker can ensure the bond valuation equation holds following fiscal shocks through a reduction in ex-ante real interest rates and not just ex-post real interest rates through inflation surprises.[ab] When we consider optimal policy in the new Keynesian model we shall allow taxes to distort behavior.

3.1 A Conventional New Keynesian Model

Endogenous output together with sticky prices allow both monetary policy and, in the case of regime F, fiscal policy to have real effects on the economy. We use a textbook version of a new Keynesian model of the kind that Woodford (2003) and Galí (2008) present. Because existing literature, including those two textbooks, thoroughly examines the nature of regime M equilibria, our exposition focuses exclusively on regime F.[ac]

The model's key features include: a representative consumer and firm; monopolistic competition in final goods; Calvo (1983) sticky prices in which a fraction $1-\phi$ of goods suppliers sets a new price each period; a cashless economy with one-period nominal bonds, B_t, that sell at price $1/R_t$, where R_t is also the monetary policy instrument; for now, government purchases are zero, so the aggregate resource constraint is $c_t = y_t$; an exogenous primary government surplus, s_t, with lump-sum taxes; and shocks only to monetary and fiscal policies.[ad] We solve a version of the model that is log-linearized around the deterministic steady state with zero inflation.

Let $\hat{x}_t \equiv \ln(x_t) - \ln(x^*)$ denote log deviations of a variable x_t from its steady-state value. Private-sector behavior reduces to a consumption-Euler equation

$$\hat{y}_t = E_t\hat{y}_{t+1} - \sigma(\hat{R}_t - E_t\hat{\pi}_{t+1}) \tag{29}$$

and a Phillips curve

$$\hat{\pi}_t = \beta E_t\hat{\pi}_{t+1} + \kappa\hat{y}_t \tag{30}$$

where $\sigma \equiv -\dfrac{u'(y^*)}{u''(y^*)y^*}$ is the intertemporal elasticity of substitution, $\omega \equiv \dfrac{w'(y^*)}{w''(y^*)y^*}$ is the elasticity of supply of goods, $\kappa \equiv \dfrac{(1-\phi)(1-\phi\beta)}{\phi}\dfrac{\omega+\sigma}{\sigma(\omega+\theta)}$ is the slope of the Phillips curve, and θ is the elasticity of substitution among differentiated goods. The parameters obey $0 < \beta < 1, \sigma > 0, \kappa > 0$.

[ab] By introducing this channel we could, in fact, turn off the revaluation effects stressed by the fiscal theory by assuming debt was solely real but still consider equilibria where monetary policy was passive and fiscal active. In this sense, as we widen the range of monetary and fiscal interactions, unconventional policy assignments do not necessarily require the revaluation mechanisms inherent in the fiscal theory to support determinate equilibria.

[ac] We draw from Woodford (1998a), but Kim (2003), Cochrane (2014), and Sims (2011) study closely related models.

[ad] Because these shocks have no effects on the natural rate of output, there is no distinction between deviations in output from steady state and the output gap.

3.1.1 Policy Rules

Monetary policy follows a conventional interest rate rule

$$\hat{R}_t = \alpha_\pi \hat{\pi}_t + \alpha_y \hat{y}_t + \varepsilon_t^M \tag{31}$$

and fiscal policy sets the surplus process, $\{\hat{s}_t\}$, exogenously, where $\hat{s}_t \equiv (s_t - s^*)/s^*$. By setting the surplus exogenously, we are implicitly assuming that taxes are lump sum so that any variations in real activity do not impact on the size of the tax base.

Policy choices must satisfy the flow budget identity, $\frac{1}{R_t}\frac{B_t}{P_t} + s_t = \frac{B_{t-1}}{P_t}$, which is linearized as

$$\hat{b}_t - \hat{R}_t + (\beta^{-1} - 1)\hat{s}_t = \beta^{-1}(\hat{b}_{t-1} - \hat{\pi}_t) \tag{32}$$

where b_t is real debt at the end of period t and π_t is the inflation rate between $t-1$ and t. Although this linearized budget identity does not appear to contain the steady-state debt-to-GDP ratio, the calibration of the surplus shock does implicitly capture the underlying steady-state level of debt.

3.1.2 Solving the Model in Regime F

The four-equation system—(29)–(32)—together with exogenous $\{\hat{s}_t\}$ yields solutions for $\{\hat{y}_t, \hat{\pi}_t, \hat{R}_t, \hat{b}_t\}$. Woodford (1998a) shows that a unique equilibrium requires that monetary policy react relatively weakly to inflation and output: α_π and α_y must satisfy

$$-1 - \frac{1+\beta}{\kappa}\alpha_y - \frac{2(1+\beta)}{\kappa\sigma} < \alpha_\pi < 1 - \frac{1-\beta}{\kappa}\alpha_y$$

For practical reasons, we restrict α_π's lower bound to 0. In this case, when monetary policy does not respond to output, this reduces to the condition that passive monetary policy requires $0 \le \alpha_\pi < 1$. In the analytical results that follow, we use this simplified policy rule; numerical results will bring the output response of monetary policy back in.

Substituting the simplified version of the monetary policy rule ($\alpha_y = 0$) into the government budget identity and iterating forward immediately yield several robust features of regime F equilibria

$$E_t \sum_{j=0}^{\infty} \beta^j \hat{\pi}_{t+j} = \left(\frac{1}{1-\alpha_\pi\beta}\right)\left[\hat{b}_{t-1} - (1-\beta)E_t \sum_{j=0}^{\infty} \beta^j \hat{s}_{t+j} + \beta E_t \sum_{j=0}^{\infty} \beta^j \varepsilon_{t+j}^M\right] \tag{33}$$

Although expression (33) is not an equilibrium solution to the model (since we still need to solve the path for inflation), it highlights several features that the solution displays. First, higher initial debt, a lower expected path of surpluses, or a higher expected path of the monetary shock all raise the present value of inflation. Second, a stronger response of monetary policy to inflation, but still consistent with existence of a bounded equilibrium, *amplifies* those inflationary effects. Dependence of inflation on the debt stock and surpluses is ubiquitous in regime F. Perversely, a higher path of the monetary shock or a higher value for α_π constitute a tightening of policy, yet they raise inflation.

In the flexible-price case, $\kappa = \infty$, so $\hat{y}_t \equiv 0$, and a solution for equilibrium inflation is immediate. This case collapses back to the endowment economy in Section 2.1.2.2 with a constant real rate and the simple Fisher relation $\hat{R}_t = E_t \hat{\pi}_{t+1}$. Combine the monetary policy rule with $\alpha_y = 0$ with the Fisher relation to solve for expected inflation

$$E_t \hat{\pi}_{t+j} = \alpha_\pi^j \hat{\pi}_t + \alpha_\pi^{j-1} \varepsilon_t^M + \alpha_\pi^{j-2} E_t \varepsilon_{t+1}^M + \cdots + \alpha_\pi E_t \varepsilon_{t+j-2}^M + E_t \varepsilon_{t+j-1}^M$$

and use this expression to replace expected inflation rates in (33). Equilibrium inflation is

$$\hat{\pi}_t = \hat{b}_{t-1} + \beta(1 - \alpha_\pi \beta) E_t \sum_{j=0}^{\infty} \beta^j \varepsilon_{t+j}^M - (1 - \beta) E_t \sum_{j=0}^{\infty} \beta^j \hat{s}_{t+j}$$

Actual inflation rises with initial debt, a higher path of the monetary policy shock, or a lower path for surpluses. The effects of surpluses on inflation are independent of the monetary policy choice of α_π, although we saw above that those fiscal effects on expected inflation are amplified by more aggressive monetary policy.

Solving the sticky-price new Keynesian model is more complicated. When $0 < \kappa < \infty$, both output and the real interest rate are endogenous. Defining the real interest rate as $\hat{r}_{t+j} \equiv \hat{R}_{t+j-1} - \hat{\pi}_{t+j}$, write the bond valuation equation as

$$\hat{\pi}_t - E_t \sum_{j=1}^{\infty} \beta^j \hat{r}_{t+j} = \hat{b}_{t-1} - (1 - \beta) E_t \sum_{j=0}^{\infty} \beta^j \hat{s}_{t+j}$$

News about lower future surpluses shows up as a mix of higher current inflation and a lower path for the real interest rate. Lower real rates, in turn, transmit into higher output. Fiscal expansions have the old-Keynesian effects—higher real activity and inflation—and monetary policy behavior determines the split between them.

Combining the Euler equation, the Phillips curve and the monetary policy rule produce a second-order difference equation in inflation

$$E_t \hat{\pi}_{t+2} - \frac{1 + \beta + \sigma\kappa}{\beta} E_t \hat{\pi}_{t+1} + \frac{1 + \alpha_\pi \sigma \kappa}{\beta} \hat{\pi}_t = -\frac{\sigma\kappa}{\beta} \varepsilon_t^M$$

One can show that, given the restrictions on the underlying model parameters, this difference equation has two real roots, one inside $|\lambda_1| < 1$ and one outside $|\lambda_2 > 1|$ the unit circle, which yields the solution for expected inflation[ae]

[ae] Letting $\gamma_1 \equiv (1 + \beta + \sigma\kappa)/\beta$ and $\gamma_0 \equiv (1 + \alpha_\pi \sigma \kappa)/\beta$, the roots are $\lambda_1 = (1/2)(\gamma_1 - \sqrt{\gamma_1^2 - 4\gamma_0})$ and $\lambda_2 = (1/2)(\gamma_1 + \sqrt{\gamma_1^2 - 4\gamma_0})$. These derivations owe much to Tan (2015) who employs the techniques that Tan and Walker (2014) develop.

$$E_t\hat{\pi}_{t+1} = \lambda_1\hat{\pi}_t + (\beta\lambda_2)^{-1}\sigma\kappa E_t\sum_{j=0}^{\infty}\lambda_2^j\varepsilon_{t+j}^M \tag{34}$$

We can now solve for the j-step-ahead expectation of inflation by defining the operator $\mathcal{B}^{-j}x_t \equiv E_t x_{t+j}$ and iterating on (34)

$$\mathcal{B}^{-j}\hat{\pi}_t = \lambda_1^j\hat{\pi}_t + \frac{\sigma\kappa}{\lambda_2\beta}\frac{1}{1-\lambda_2^{-1}\mathcal{B}^{-1}}\left(\lambda_1^{j-1} + \lambda_1^{j-2}\mathcal{B}^{-1} + \cdots + \mathcal{B}^{-j+1}\right)\varepsilon_t^M$$

This yields the solution for expected discounted inflation that appears in (33)

$$E_t\sum_{j=0}^{\infty}\beta^j\hat{\pi}_{t+j} = \frac{1}{1-\lambda_1\beta}\hat{\pi}_t + \frac{\sigma\kappa}{\lambda_2(1-\lambda_1\beta)}\frac{1}{(1-\lambda_2^{-1}\mathcal{B}^{-1})(1-\beta\mathcal{B}^{-1})}\varepsilon_t^M$$

Using this expression for discounted inflation in (33) delivers a solution for equilibrium inflation

$$\begin{aligned}\hat{\pi}_t = &\left(\frac{1-\lambda_1\beta}{1-\alpha_\pi\beta}\right)\left[\hat{b}_{t-1} - \left(\frac{1-\beta}{1-\beta\mathcal{B}^{-1}}\right)\hat{s}_t\right] \\ &+ \left[\frac{1-\lambda_1\beta}{1-\alpha_\pi\beta} - \frac{\sigma\kappa}{\lambda_2}\frac{1}{(1-\lambda_2^{-1}\mathcal{B}^{-1})}\right]\frac{1}{1-\beta\mathcal{B}^{-1}}\varepsilon_t^M\end{aligned} \tag{35}$$

It is straightforward to show how the monetary policy parameter affects inflation

$$\frac{\partial\lambda_1}{\partial\alpha_\pi} > 0, \quad \frac{\partial\lambda_2}{\partial\alpha_\pi} < 0, \quad \frac{\partial[\lambda_2(1-\lambda_1\beta)]}{\partial\alpha_\pi} < 0 \quad \frac{\partial\left(\frac{1-\lambda_1\beta}{1-\alpha_\pi\beta}\right)}{\partial\alpha_\pi} > 0$$

More aggressive monetary policy—larger α_π—affects the equilibrium in the following ways

- amplifies the impacts on inflation from outstanding debt and exogenous disturbances to monetary policy and surpluses
- makes the effects of these shocks on inflation more persistent.

Evidently, if fiscal policies set surpluses exogenously, monetary policy is impotent to offset fiscal effects on inflation. And adopting a more hawkish monetary policy stance has the perverse effect of amplifying and propagating the effects of shocks on inflation.

In this basic new Keynesian model, fiscal disturbances are transmitted to output through the path of the ex-ante real interest rate, as the consumption-Euler equation, (29), makes clear. Define the one-period real interest rate as $\hat{r}_t \equiv \hat{R}_t - E_t\hat{\pi}_{t+1}$. To simplify expressions, temporarily shut down the monetary policy shock, $\varepsilon_t^M \equiv 0$. Date the solution for inflation from (35) at $t+1$, take expectations, and substitute the monetary policy rule for the interest rate. After some tedious algebra, the equilibrium real interest rate is

$$\hat{r}_t = \frac{(\alpha_\pi - \lambda_1)(1-\lambda_1\beta)}{1-\alpha_\pi\beta}\left[\hat{b}_{t-1} - (1-\beta)\sum_{j=0}^{\infty}\hat{s}_{t+j}\right]$$

The lead coefficient, $\alpha_\pi - \lambda_1$, depends on monetary policy behavior and on all the model parameters. Because its sign can be positive or negative, lower expected surpluses may lower or raise the short-term real interest rate on impact.

Substituting the monetary policy rule into the definition of the real interest rate and suppressing the monetary policy shock yield

$$\hat{r}_t = \alpha_\pi \hat{\pi}_t - E_t \hat{\pi}_{t+1}$$

Using the Phillips curve to eliminate inflationary expectations we obtain

$$\hat{r}_t = (\alpha_\pi - \beta^{-1})\hat{\pi}_t - \beta^{-1}\kappa\hat{y}_t$$

which shows that a given level of positive inflation and output deviations from steady state will be consistent with lower real interest rates the smaller is the monetary policy response to inflation. The intuition is very similar to that in the endowment economy: a passive monetary policy that responds to inflation generates a sustained rise in inflation which does not facilitate the stabilization of single-period debt. In the new Keynesian case such a policy response mitigates the reduction in debt service costs which are an additional channel through which the passive monetary policy stabilizes debt in a sticky-price economy.

3.2 Maturity Structure in Regime F

We introduce the simplified maturity structure that Section 2.2.2 describes, in which government debt maturity decays at the constant rate ρ each period, into the new Keynesian model of Section 3.1. The no-arbitrage condition links bond prices to the one-period nominal interest rate

$$\hat{P}_t^m = -\hat{R}_t + \beta\rho E_t \hat{P}_{t+1}^m$$

which implies the term structure relation

$$\begin{aligned}\hat{P}_t^m &= -E_t\sum_{j=0}^{\infty}(\beta\rho)^j \hat{R}_{t+j} \\ &= -\frac{1}{1-\beta\rho B^{-1}}\left[\alpha_\pi\hat{\pi}_t + \varepsilon_t^M\right]\end{aligned}$$

where we have substituted the simpler monetary policy rule in for the nominal interest rate.

The government's flow budget identity is

$$\beta(1-\rho)\hat{P}_t^m + \beta\hat{b}_t^m + (1-\beta)\hat{s}_t + \hat{\pi}_t = \hat{b}_{t-1}^M \tag{36}$$

where we are defining $b_t^m \equiv B_t^m / P_t$ to be the real face value of outstanding debt.[af] Because bond prices depend on the expected infinite path of inflation and the monetary policy shock, analytical solutions along the lines of Section 3.1.2, though feasible, are cumbersome. For example, the analog to the discounted inflation expression, (33), is

$$\frac{1}{1-\beta\mathcal{B}^{-1}}\left[1-\frac{\alpha_\pi\beta(1-\rho)}{1-\beta\rho\mathcal{B}^{-1}}\right]\hat{\pi}_t=\hat{b}_{t-1}^m-\left(\frac{1-\beta}{1-\beta\mathcal{B}^{-1}}\right)\hat{s}_t+\frac{\beta(1-\rho)}{(1-\beta\mathcal{B}^{-1})(1-\beta\rho\mathcal{B}^{-1})}\varepsilon_t^M$$

which collapses to (33) when $\rho = 0$ so all debt is one period. The solution for equilibrium inflation, like that when there is only one-period debt in equation (35), depends on all the parameters of the model through the eigenvalues λ_1 and λ_2, but the analytical expression for inflation is too complex to offer useful intuition.

One-period debt makes the value of debt depend only on the current nominal interest rate and, through the monetary policy rule, current inflation. A maturity structure makes that value depend on the entire expected path of nominal interest rates. This gives monetary policy an expanded role in debt stabilization, allowing expected future monetary policy to affect the value of current debt. This additional channel operates through terms in $1/(1-\beta\rho\mathcal{B}^{-1})$ that create double infinite sums in the equilibrium solution.

3.2.1 Impacts of Fiscal Shocks

Figs. 3 and 4 illustrate the impacts of a serially correlated increase in the primary fiscal deficit financed by nominal bond sales.[ag] Fig. 3 maintains that all debt is one period to focus on how different monetary policy rules alter the impacts of a fiscal expansion.

When monetary policy pegs the nominal interest rate—$\alpha_\pi = \alpha_Y = 0$—it fixes the bond price, which front loads fiscal adjustments through current inflation and the real interest rate. Inflation rises, the real rate falls and output increases. Responses inherit the serial correlation properties of the fiscal disturbance. As monetary policy becomes progressively less passive, reacting more strongly to inflation and output, it amplifies and propagates the fiscal shock (dashed lines in Fig. 3). By reacting more strongly to inflation, monetary policy ensures that the real interest rate declines by less, tempering the short-run output increases.

The figure makes clear the role that debt plays in propagating shocks in regime F. Stronger and more persistent nominal interest rate increases transmit directly into stronger and more persistent growth in the nominal market value of debt.[ah] And persistently higher nominal debt keeps household nominal wealth and, therefore, nominal demand elevated, creating strong serial correlation in inflation and output. This internal

[af] The real market value is $P_t^m B_t^m / P_t$. To derive (36), we use the steady-state relationships $P^{m*} = 1/(\beta^{-1} - \rho)$ and $s^*/b^{m*} = (1-\beta)/(1-\beta\rho)$ in log-linearizing the government budget identity.

[ag] We calibrate the model to an annual frequency, setting $\beta = 0.95, \sigma = 1, \kappa = 0.3$. The surplus is $AR(1)$, $\hat{s}_t = \rho_{FP}\hat{s}_{t-1} + \varepsilon_t^F$, with $\rho_{FP} = 0.6$.

[ah] Growth in the nominal market value of debt is $P_t^m B_t^M / P_{t-1}^m B_{t-1}^m$.

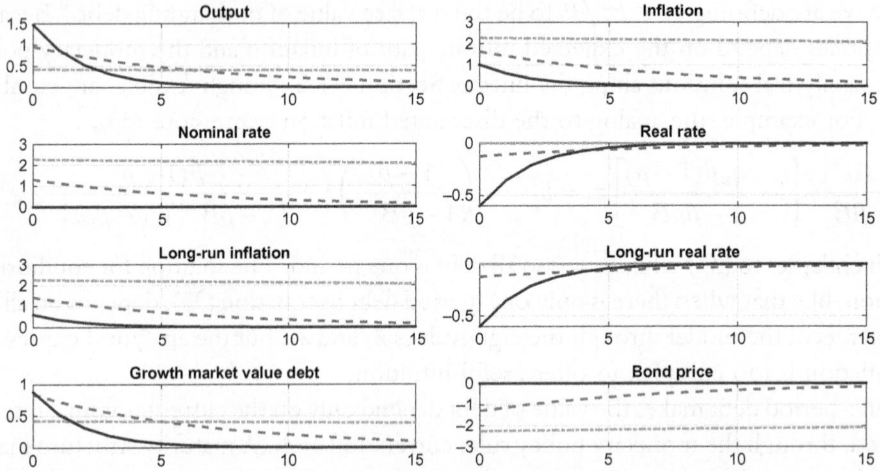

Fig. 3 Responses to a 20% increase in the initial deficit under alternative monetary policy rules when all debt is one period. Calibration reported in Footnote ag. $\alpha_\pi = \alpha_Y = 0$ (*solid lines*), $\alpha_\pi = \alpha_Y = 0.5$ (*dashed lines*), and $\alpha_\pi = 0.9$, $\alpha_Y = 0.5$ (*dot-dashed lines*).

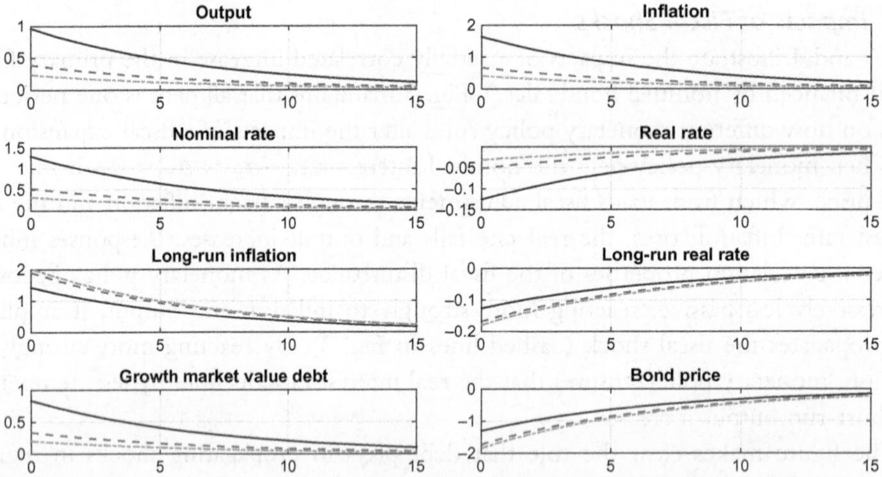

Fig. 4 Responses to a 20% increase in the initial deficit under alternative maturity structures. Calibration reported in Footnote ag with $\alpha_\pi = \alpha_Y = 0.5$. 1-year debt (*solid lines*), 5-year debt (*dashed lines*), and consol debt (*dot-dashed lines*).

propagation mechanism through government debt is absent from regime M, where higher debt carries with it the promise of higher taxes that eliminate wealth effects.

Fig. 4 holds the monetary policy rule fixed, setting $\alpha_\pi = \alpha_Y = 0.5$, to reveal how changes in maturity affect fiscal impacts. The figure contrasts one-period debt (solid lines) to an average of 5-year maturity (dashed lines) and consol debt (dot-dashed lines). Longer

Table 2 The fiscal shock initially raises the deficit by 20%

α_π	α_Y	Maturity	% due to $\hat{\pi}_t$	% due to $\hat{P}_t^m$	% due to $\hat{r}_{t+j}^m$
0	0	1 period	44	0	56
0.5	0.5	1 period	71	0	29
0.9	0.5	1 period	98	0	2
0.5	0.5	5 years	29	59	12
0.9	0.5	5 years	20.4	79.2	0.4
0.5	0.5	Consol	18	75	7
0.9	0.5	Consol	6	94	0

"% due to" are the ratios of the right-hand components of (38) to ξ_t, which is computed from the impulse response of $\hat{s}_{t+j}$, as described in the text. Calibration reported in Footnote ag.

maturities force more of the adjustment to higher deficits into lower bond prices, which push more of the impacts into low-frequency movements in long-run inflation and real interest rates.[ai]

Although short-run inflation is higher with one-period debt, in the long run inflation is lower with shorter maturity bonds. With long debt, bond prices reflect anticipated inflation rates farther into the future, in essence spreading inflationary effects over longer horizons. The cost of doing so is to raise the long-run inflation impacts of fiscal policy.

Another way to summarize the dynamic impacts of fiscal disturbances is to ask how a shock that raises primary deficits by a certain amount gets financed intertemporally, as a function of various model parameters. Underlying the calculations in Table 2 are two basic mechanisms that stabilize debt in the face of the surplus shock. First are the revaluation effects that we can summarize by examining the ex-post real return to holding government bonds in any period

$$r_t^m = \frac{(1+\rho P_t^m)}{P_{t-1}^m}\frac{1}{\pi_t}$$

or in linearized form

$$\hat{r}_t^m = \rho\beta\hat{P}_t^m - \hat{\pi}_t - \hat{P}_{t-1}^m$$

By contrasting this with the ex-ante returns the bond holders were expecting when they purchased the bonds in period $t-1$ we can identify the scale of the revaluation effects, which linearized, are

$$\hat{r}_t^m - E_{t-1}\hat{r}_t^m = -(\hat{\pi}_t - E_{t-1}\hat{\pi}_t) + \rho\beta(\hat{P}_t^m - E_{t-1}\hat{P}_t^m) \tag{37}$$

[ai] The long-term real interest rate, $\hat{r}_t^L$, comes from combining the bond-pricing equation and the Fisher relation to yield the recursion $\hat{r}_t^L = \hat{r}_t + \beta\rho E_t\hat{r}_{t+1}^L$. The long-run inflation rate, $\hat{\pi}_t^L$, which is the expected path of inflation discounted by $\beta\rho$, may be computed as $\hat{\pi}_t^L = -\hat{r}_t^L - \hat{P}_t^m$.

The first term on the right in (37) gives the losses suffered by bondholders due to surprise inflation in the initial period. The second term gives the losses suffered by holders of mature debt ($\rho > 0$) arising from jumps in bond prices caused by innovations to the expected future path of inflation. These latter revaluation effects are borne by the existing holders of government debt and arise for innovations to the path of inflation over the time to maturity of the debt stock they hold. In the sticky-price economy these effects can be complemented by reductions in the ex-ante real rates of return received by future bondholders, which reduce effective debt service costs to create an additional channel through which debt can be stabilized.[aj]

In the case of one-period debt it is only the surprise inflation in the initial period that reduces the real value of government debt. This is then combined with reductions in ex-ante real interest rates to stabilize debt. As α_π increases, there is less reliance on the latter effect and larger jumps in the initial rate of inflation are required to satisfy the bond valuation equation. When we move to longer period debt, there is an additional revaluation effect through the impact of innovations to the path of inflation on bond prices. With bond prices adjusting, we can have smaller, but more sustained, increases in inflation that reduce the real market value of debt. These continue to be combined with reductions in ex-ante real interest rates to satisfy the bond valuation equation with these debt service cost effects falling as monetary policy becomes less passive.

To see how this affects the decomposition of the adjustment required to stabilize the debt stock in the face of a surplus shock consider the evolution of the market value of government debt

$$\widetilde{b}_t = r_t^m \widetilde{b}_{t-1} - s_t$$

where $\widetilde{b}_t \equiv \dfrac{P_t^m Bt}{P_t}$. This can be linearized as

$$\beta \hat{\widetilde{b}}_t = \hat{r}_t^m + \hat{\widetilde{b}}_{t-1} - (1-\beta)\hat{s}_t$$

Using the expected value of surpluses, $\xi_t \equiv (1-\beta)E_t\sum_{j=0}^{\infty}\beta^j \hat{s}_{t+j}$ which implies $(1-\beta)\hat{s}_t = \xi_t - \beta E_t \xi_{t+1}$, this becomes

$$\beta(\hat{\widetilde{b}}_t - E_t\xi_{t+1}) - \hat{r}_t^m = \hat{\widetilde{b}}_{t-1} - \xi_t$$

Iterating forward we obtain

[aj] An equivalent interpretation comes from thinking about the value of debt in the "forward" direction, as being determined by the expected present value of surpluses. Lower real interest rates raise real discount factors to increase the present value of a given stream of surpluses.

$$\begin{aligned}\xi_t &= \hat{\tilde{b}}_{t-1} + \hat{r}_t^m + E_t \sum_{j=1}^{\infty} \beta^j \hat{r}_{t+j}^m \\ &= \hat{\tilde{b}}_{t-1} - \hat{P}_{t-1}^m + \beta\rho\hat{P}_t^m - \hat{\pi}_t + E_t \sum_{j=1}^{\infty} \beta^j \hat{r}_{t+j}^m\end{aligned} \tag{38}$$

The required adjustment to a change in expected surpluses is made up of surprise changes in the returns to existing bond holders $\hat{r}_t^m$ as well as expected future returns on bond holdings, $E_t \sum_{j=1}^{\infty} \beta^j \hat{r}_{t+j}^m$. The former is made up of jumps in the initial rate of inflation combined with changes in bond prices to the extent that bonds have a maturity greater than one period, $\rho > 0$. The latter captures the reduction in ex-ante real interest rates which can occur in our sticky-price economy.

Table 2 computes the objects in (38) from impulse responses to a deficit innovation. When debt is single period, bond prices do not contribute to financing the deficit. If monetary policy pegs the nominal interest rate, current inflation and future real interest rates play nearly equally important roles. As monetary policy reacts more aggressively to inflation and output, real interest rate responses are tempered, and an increasing fraction of the adjustment occurs through inflation at the time of the fiscal innovation. Longer maturity debt brings bond prices into the adjustment process, and their role grows with both the maturity of debt and the aggressiveness of monetary policy. As a consequence, current inflation moves much less. Consol bonds, together with aggressive monetary policy, push nearly all the adjustment into bond prices, with contemporaneous inflation playing only a minimal role, as the last row of the table reports.

3.2.2 Impacts of Monetary Shocks

Section 2.1.2.2 describes the effects of exogenous monetary policy disturbances in an endowment economy under regime F. Because future surpluses do not adjust to neutralize the wealth effects of monetary policy, contractionary policy—a higher path for the nominal interest rate—raises household interest receipts and wealth, raising nominal aggregate demand. A similar phenomenon can arise in the new Keynesian model, though the dynamics are more interesting.

Fig. 5 reports the impacts of an exogenous monetary policy action that raises the nominal interest rate. To highlight the behavior of monetary policy in regime F, we consider three different monetary policy rules. A rule that does not respond to inflation (solid lines) raises the short-term real interest rate and depresses output in the short run. Despite the drop in output, inflation rises immediately, even in a model where the Phillips curve implies a strong positive relationship between output and inflation contemporaneously ($\kappa = 0.3$).

This seemingly anomalous outcome underscores the centrality of wealth effects in regime F. Higher nominal interest rates raise households' interest receipts in the future,

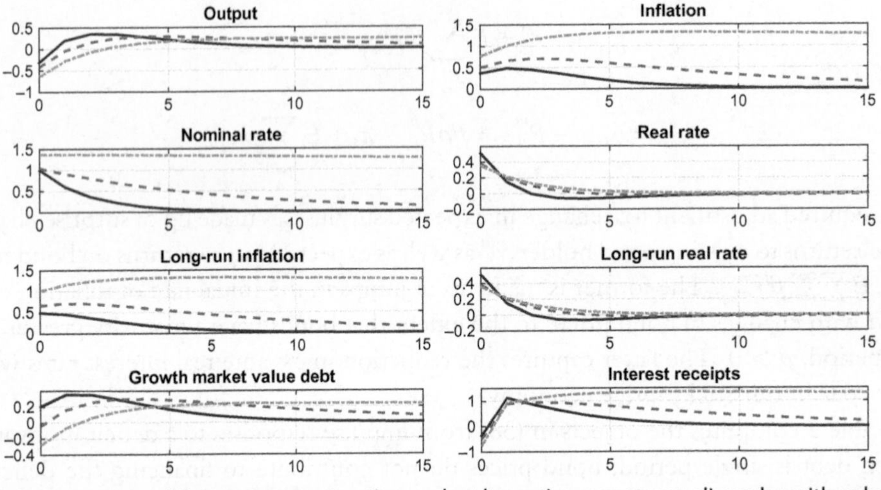

Fig. 5 Responses to a 1% monetary contraction under alternative monetary policy rules with only one-period government debt. Calibration reported in Footnote ag. The monetary policy shock follows the $AR(1)$ process $\epsilon_t^M = \rho_{MP}\epsilon_{t-1}^M + \zeta_t^M$ with $\rho_{MP} = 0.6.\alpha_\pi = \alpha_Y = 0$ (*solid lines*), $\alpha_\pi = \alpha_Y = 0.5$ (*dashed lines*), and $\alpha_\pi = 0.9$, $\alpha_Y = 0.5$ (*dot-dashed lines*).

triggering an expectation of higher future demand and inflation.[ak] Through the Phillips curve, the higher expected inflation dominates the deflationary effects of lower output to raise inflation on impact. Expectations are critical to output effects as well. After an initial decline, output always eventually rises because the real interest rate declines at longer horizons.

More aggressive monetary policy behavior (dashed lines) transforms the transitory increase in the policy rate into larger and more persistent increases. Those higher nominal interest rates raise both the growth rate of the nominal market value of debt and real interest receipts. The resulting wealth effects raise and prolong the higher inflation.

That an exogenous monetary policy "contraction," which raises the nominal interest rate, also raises inflation may seem to contradict evidence from the monetary VAR literature. This pattern, dubbed the "price puzzle" by Eichenbaum (1992), is sometimes taken to indicate that monetary policy behavior is poorly identified, perhaps by misspecifying the central bank's information set, as Sims (1992) argues. Fig. 5 makes clear that there is nothing puzzling about the pattern from the perspective of the fiscal theory.

Introducing long debt makes impulse responses accord better with VAR evidence because bond prices absorb much of the monetary shock. Fig. 6 contrasts one-period (solid lines) with 5-year (dashed lines) and consol debt (dot-dashed lines). By reducing growth in the market value of debt, longer maturities attenuate the inflationary effects and make the short-run decline in output longer lasting. Inflation does eventually rise,

[ak] Real interest receipts are defined as $[(1 + \rho P_t^m)/P_{t-1}^m](b_{t-1}^m/\pi_t)$.

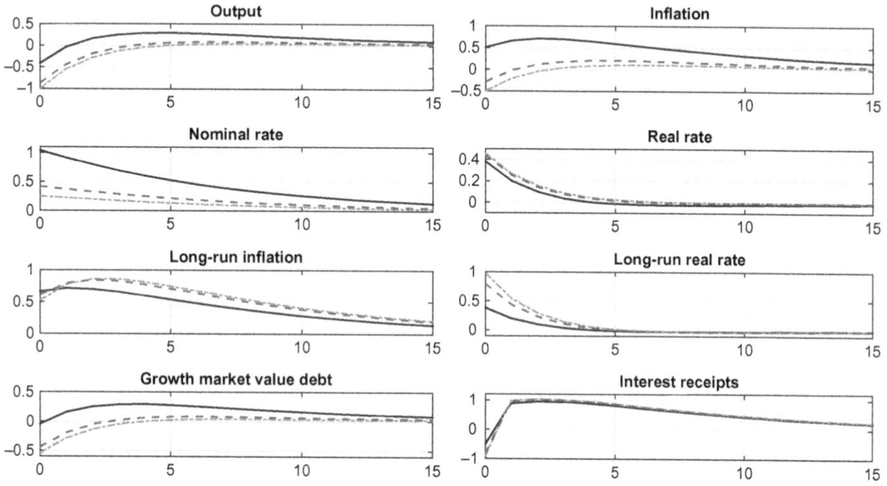

Fig. 6 Responses to a 1% monetary contraction under alternative maturity structures. Calibration reported in Footnote ag. The monetary policy shock follows the *AR*(1) process $\epsilon_t^M = \rho_{MP}\epsilon_{t-1}^M + \zeta_t^M$ with $\rho_{MP} = 0.6$ and $\alpha_\pi = \alpha_Y = 0.5$. 1-period debt (*solid lines*), 5-year debt (*dashed lines*), and consol debt (*dot-dashed lines*).

Table 3 A 1% monetary shock initially raises the short-term nominal interest rate

κ	σ	$\hat{\pi}_t$	$\hat{P}_t^m$	$\hat{r}_{t+j}^m$
0.3	1.0	−0.29	1.12	−0.83
∞	1.0	−1.54	1.54	0.0
0.1	1.0	−0.09	1.03	−0.94
0.3	5.0	−0.50	0.76	−0.26
0.3	0.5	−0.17	1.32	−1.15

"π_t" and "$\hat{P}_t^m$" are impacts of the monetary policy shock on contemporaneous inflation and bond prices; "$\hat{r}_{t+j}^m$" are the impacts on discounted real returns to bonds from expression (39). Calibration reported in Footnote ag plus $\alpha_\pi = \alpha_Y = 0.5$ and maturity set at 5 periods.

as it must if bond prices are lower. Sims (2011) calls the pattern of falling, then rising inflation following a monetary contraction "stepping on a rake."

While Fig. 6 shows how the response of short-run inflation to a monetary contraction varies with debt maturity, Table 3 reports how other model parameters affect this relationship. Following a monetary contraction, $\xi_t \equiv 0$ in expression (38), so if the monetary shock hits at time t, we have that

$$\hat{\pi}_t - \beta\rho\hat{P}_t^m - E_t\sum_{j=1}^{\infty}\beta^j\hat{r}_{t+j}^m = 0 \tag{39}$$

so the three sources of fiscal financing—higher current inflation, lower current bond prices, and lower future real bond returns—must sum to zero.

The first row of Table 3 shows that for the benchmark calibration with five-period average bond maturity, the monetary contraction initially lowers inflation along with the price of bonds, while it raises discounted real interest rates. As prices become more flexible ($\kappa \rightarrow \infty$), the impact on inflation becomes more pronounced, while that on real rates diminishes. A higher intertemporal elasticity of substitution ($\sigma \rightarrow 0$) pushes more of the adjustment into the future, reduces the effect on current inflation, and raises the impacts on bond prices and future real rates.

4. ENDOWMENT ECONOMIES WITH OPTIMAL MONETARY AND FISCAL POLICIES

In this section we turn to consider the nature of optimal policy in our simple endowment economy. In doing so we cut across various strands of the literature that addresses optimal monetary and fiscal policy issues.

4.1 Connections to the Optimal Policy Literature

We begin by considering Ramsey policies where the policymaker has an ability to make credible promises about how they will behave in the future, before turning to time-consistency issues below. We start by building on Sims' (2013) analysis. He considers a simple linearized model of tax smoothing under commitment in the face of transfer shocks and long-term debt. The policymaker can use costly inflation surprises as an alternative to distortionary taxation to ensure fiscal solvency. We extend that work in several ways. Specifically, we allow for a geometric maturity structure which nests single-period debt and consols as special cases, employ nonlinear model solution techniques, and allow for anticipated and unanticipated government spending shocks, in addition to transfer shocks. Nonlinear solutions allow us to consider the way in which the size of the debt stock, together with its maturity structure, influences the optimal combination of monetary and fiscal policy in debt stabilization. Innovations to the expected path for inflation can affect bond prices in a way which helps to satisfy the bond valuation equation even without any fiscal adjustment. These bond price movements are effective only if applied to a nonzero stock of outstanding liabilities so the optimal balance between inflation and tax financing of fiscal shocks depends on both the level of government debt and its maturity structure.

Without an ability to issue state-contingent debt or use inflation surprises to stabilize debt, Barro (1979) showed that debt and taxes should follow martingale processes to minimize the discounted value of tax distortions. While Barro did consider the impact of surprise inflation on the government's finances, these were treated as exogenous shocks rather than something that can be optimally employed to further reduce tax distortions. Lucas and Stokey (1983) is an equally influential paper that reaches quite different conclusions on the optimal response of tax rates to shocks. Lucas and Stokey consider an economy where the government can issue real state-contingent debt and show that it is optimal for a government to issue a portfolio of debt where the state-contingent returns to that debt isolate the government's finances from shocks so that there is no need for taxes to jump in the manner of Barro's tax-smoothing result. Instead, taxes are largely flat and inherit the dynamic properties of the exogenous shocks hitting the economy.

A large part of the post-Lucas and Stokey literature considers the implications of debt that is not state contingent, as well as ways of converting the payoffs from portfolios of nonstate-contingent debt into state-contingent payoffs. A key result is that when debt payoffs are not (or cannot be made) state contingent, then the optimal policy looks more like Barro's tax-smoothing result. Aiyagari et al. (2002) show this by assuming that debt is single period and noncontingent in a model otherwise identical to that of Lucas and Stokey. How might noncontingent debt instruments be made to mimic the payoffs that would be generated by state-contingent debt? Two approaches have been suggested in the literature. First, surprise inflation can render the real payoffs from risk-free nominal bonds state contingent. For example, Chari et al. (1994) use a model where surprise inflation is costless to show that the real contingencies in debt exploited by Lucas and Stokey could be created through monetary policy via surprise inflation when government debt is nominal. This underpins Sims' (2001) results in a model with costless inflation in which tax rates should be held constant to finance any fiscal shocks solely with surprise movements in inflation.

When we start to introduce a cost to surprise inflation, the optimal policy can be strikingly different. For a jointly determined optimal monetary and fiscal policy operating under commitment, Schmitt-Grohé and Uribe (2004) show that in a sticky-price stochastic production economy, even a miniscule degree of price stickiness will result, under the optimal policy, in a steady-state rate of inflation marginally less than zero, with negligible inflation volatility. In other words, although the optimal policy under flexible prices would be to follow the Friedman rule and use surprise inflation to create the desired state contingencies in the real payoffs from nominal debt, even a small amount of nominal inertia heavily tilts optimal policy toward zero inflation with little reliance on inflation surprises to insulate the government's finances from shocks. As in Benigno and Woodford (2004) and Schmitt-Grohé and Uribe (2004) we return to the tax-smoothing results of Barro (1979) thanks to the effective loss of state-contingent returns to debt when prices are sticky. Sims (2013) argues that this may be due to the fact that Schmitt-Grohé and Uribe only consider single-period debt; with longer term debt the efficacy of using innovations to the expected path of inflation to affect bond prices would be enhanced. This is the first issue to which we turn: to what extent will the optimizing policymaker rely on fiscal theory-type revaluations of debt through innovations to the expected path of prices?

While the state contingencies in real bond payoffs can be generated through the impact of surprise inflation on nominal bonds, an alternative approach when bonds are real is to exploit variations in the yield curve to achieve the same contingencies for the government's whole bond portfolio. With single-period risk-free real bonds, Ramsey policy in the Lucas and Stokey model possesses a unit root as in Barro. Angeletos (2002) and Buera and Nicolini (2004) use the maturity structure of nonstate-contingent real bonds to render the overall portfolio state contingent. With two states for government spending, for example, a portfolio of positive short-term assets funded by issuing long-term debt can insulate the government's finances from government spending shocks. More generally, with a sufficiently rich maturity structure the policymaker can match the range of the stochastic shocks hitting the economy and achieve this hedging. The second broad optimal policy question we consider is: what is the role of debt management in insulating the government's finances from shocks?

Having looked at the ability of the Ramsey policymaker to both hedge against shocks and utilize monetary policy as a debt stabilization tool when complete hedging is not possible, we turn to consider the time-inconsistency problem inherent in such policies. We find that constraining policy to be time consistent radically affects the policymaker's ability to hedge against fiscal shocks and generates serious "debt stabilization bias" problems, as in Leith and Wren-Lewis (2013), that are akin to the inflationary bias problems analyzed in the context of monetary economies.

We begin by considering the role inflation surprises play in optimal policy in our simple endowment economy with a geometrically declining maturity structure. We then generalize these results to a more general maturity structure and consider the role of debt management in hedging for fiscal shocks. We then turn to a simple example where complete hedging is feasible.

4.2 The Model

We follow Sims (2013) in defining the inverse of inflation as $\nu_t = \pi_t^{-1}$, and assuming the policymaker's objective function is given by

$$-E_0 \frac{1}{2} \sum_{t=0}^{\infty} \beta^t \left[\tau_t^2 + \theta (\nu_t - 1)^2 \right]$$

which the policymaker maximizes subject to the constraints given by the resource constraint in our endowment economy,

$$y = c_t + g_t$$

the bond valuation equation (after assuming a specific form for per-period utility, $u(c_t) = \frac{c_t^{1-\sigma}}{1-\sigma}$)

$$\beta E_t \frac{(1+\rho P^m_{t+1})}{P^m_t} \nu_{t+1} \left(\frac{c_{t+1}}{c_t}\right)^{-\sigma} = 1$$

the government's flow budget identity

$$b_t P^m_t = (1+\rho P^m_t) b_{t-1} \nu_t + g_t - \tau_t - z_t$$

and the associated transversality condition

$$\lim_{j\to\infty} E_t \left(\prod_{i=0}^{j} \frac{1}{R^m_{t+i+1} \nu_{t+i+1}} \right) \frac{P^m_{t+j} B^m_{t+j}}{P_{t+j}} \geq 0$$

where $R^m_{t+1} \equiv (1-\rho P^m_{t+1})/P^m_t$, and government spending and/or transfers follow exogenous stochastic processes. Our adopted objective function is clearly ad hoc in the context of our simple endowment economy. However, it can easily be motivated as capturing the trade-off between the costs of tax vs inflation financing in richer production economies. Indeed, many of the insights this analysis offers will reappear when considering optimal policy in a fully microfounded economy subject to distortionary taxation and nominal inertia in Section 5.

4.3 Ramsey Policy

We analyze the time-inconsistent Ramsey policy for our endowment economy given the policymaker's objective function by forming the following Lagrangian

$$\begin{aligned} L_t = E_0 \frac{1}{2} \sum_{t=0}^{\infty} \beta^t [& -\frac{1}{2}(\tau_t^2 + \theta(\nu_t - 1)^2) \\ & + \mu_t \left(\beta E_t \frac{(1+\rho P^m_{t+1})}{P^m_t} \nu_{t+1} \left(\frac{c_{t+1}}{c_t}\right)^{-\sigma} - 1 \right) \\ & + \lambda_t (b_t P^m_t - (1+\rho P^m_t) b_{t-1} \nu_t - g_t - z_t + \tau_t)] \end{aligned}$$

which yields the first-order conditions

$$\begin{aligned} & \tau_t : -\tau_t + \lambda_t = 0 \\ & \nu_t : -\theta(\nu_t - 1) + \mu_{t-1} \frac{(1+\rho P^m_t)}{P^m_{t-1}} \left(\frac{c_t}{c_{t-1}}\right)^{-\sigma} - (1+\rho P^m_t)\lambda_t b_{t-1} = 0 \\ & P^m_t : -\frac{\mu_t}{P^m_t} + \mu_{t-1} \rho \frac{\nu_t}{P^m_{t-1}} \left(\frac{c_t}{c_{t-1}}\right)^{-\sigma} + \lambda_t (b_t - \rho \nu_t b_{t-1}) = 0 \\ & b_t : \lambda_t P^m_t - \beta E_t (1+\rho P^m_{t+1}) \nu_{t+1} \lambda_{t+1} = 0 \end{aligned}$$

Defining $\tilde{\mu}_t \equiv \frac{\mu_t}{P^m_t c_t^{-\sigma}}$ the system to be solved for $\{P^m_t, \tilde{\mu}_t, \nu_t, \tau_t, b_t, c_t\}$ is given by

$$-\theta(\nu_t - 1) + \widetilde{\mu}_{t-1}(1+\rho P_t^m)c_t^{-\sigma} - (1+\rho P_t^m)\tau_t b_{t-1} = 0$$

$$\tau_t b_t - \widetilde{\mu}_t c_t^{-\sigma} - \rho\nu_t(\tau_t b_{t-1} - \widetilde{\mu}_{t-1} c_t^{-\sigma}) = 0$$

$$\tau_t P_t^m - \beta E_t(1+\rho P_{t+1}^m)\nu_{t+1}\tau_{t+1} = 0$$

$$\beta E_t \frac{(1+\rho P_{t+1}^m)}{P_t^m}\left(\frac{c_{t+1}}{c_t}\right)^{-\sigma}\nu_{t+1} - 1 = 0$$

$$b_t P_t^m - (1+\rho P_t^m) b_{t-1}\nu_t - g_t + \tau_t - z_t = 0$$

$$g_t - (1-\rho_g)g^* - \rho_g g_{t-1} - \varepsilon_t^g = 0$$

$$z_t - (1-\rho_z)z^* - \rho_z z_{t-1} - \varepsilon_t^z = 0$$

$$y - c_t - g_t = 0$$

with two exogenous shocks describing the evolution of government consumption, g_t, and transfers, z_t and two endogenous state variables, $\widetilde{\mu}_{t-1}$ and b_{t-1}, where the former captures the history dependence in policymaking under commitment.

To obtain some intuition for how policy operates under commitment, it is helpful to consider three polar cases. First, where inflation is costless, so that $\theta = 0$. Second, where inflation is so costly that the economy can be considered to be real, $\theta \to \infty$. Third, we allow inflation to be costly $\theta > 0$, but assume that taxes have reached the peak of the Laffer curve so that they are no longer available to engage in tax smoothing and instead are held constant, $\tau_t = \overline{\tau}$.

4.3.1 Costless Inflation

In the former case, where inflation is costless ($\theta = 0$), the first two first-order conditions imply

$$\widetilde{\mu}_{t-1} c_t^{-\sigma} = \tau_t b_{t-1}$$

and

$$\tau_t b_t - \widetilde{\mu}_t c_t^{-\sigma} = \rho\nu_t(\tau_t b_{t-1} - \widetilde{\mu}_{t-1} c_t^{-\sigma})$$

Substituting the first into the second, lagging one period, and comparing the first condition yield

$$\tau_t = \left(\frac{c_t}{c_{t-1}}\right)^{-\sigma}\tau_{t-1}$$

In the absence of government spending shocks (the only source of variation in private consumption in our simple endowment economy) taxes are unchanged. But taxes are higher whenever government spending is higher. In the case of transfer shocks, inflation jumps to satisfy the bond valuation equation and this is a pure case of the fiscal theory. But when bonds have a maturity beyond a single period, there are an infinite number of patterns of inflation which can satisfy this, due to the impact inflation has on bond prices. While there is a unique required discounted magnitude of surprise inflation needed to satisfy the government debt valuation condition, there are a variety of paths which can achieve that magnitude. When the fiscal shock is a shock to government consumption, this affects real interest rates so that even though inflation can costlessly stabilize debt at its initial steady-state level, there is still tilting of tax rates: during periods of high real interest rates, it is desirable to suffer the short-run costs of higher taxation to avoid the longer run costs of supporting the higher steady-state level of debt that would emerge when higher interest rates raise the rate of debt accumulation. In this case it is only because of the commitment to honor the past promises not to deflate away the government's outstanding liabilities that there are positive tax rates at all.

4.3.2 Real Economy

In the second case, inflation is so costly it would never be used under the optimal policy, $\theta \rightarrow \infty$ and $\nu_t = 1$. As a result, we rely on jumps in the tax rate to satisfy government solvency and we return to a world of pure tax smoothing, where the tax rate follows the path implied by the first-order condition

$$\tau_t P_t^m = \beta E_t (1 + \rho P_{t+1}^m) \tau_{t+1}$$

Under a perfect foresight equilibrium this reduces to

$$\frac{\tau_t}{c_t^{-\sigma}} = \frac{\tau_{t+1}}{c_{t+1}^{-\sigma}}$$

This tax rate is constant in the face of transfer shocks, but will be tilted in the presence of government spending shocks—the tax rate at t is higher (lower) when public consumption is anticipated to rise (fall). The fact that it is purely forward-looking captures the usual tax-smoothing result that the tax rate will jump to the level required to satisfy the government's budget identity, although we have tilting in the tax rate to capture changes in real interest rates induced by government spending shocks. Eventually, the tax rate will achieve a new long-run value consistent with servicing the new steady-state level of debt.

4.3.3 Intermediate Case

In the intermediate case where $0 < \theta < \infty$, the tax-smoothing condition remains as above, but is combined with a pattern of inflation described by

$$-\theta(\nu_t-1)+\frac{\mu_{t-1}}{P^m_{t-1}}(1+\rho P^m_t)-(1+\rho P^m_t)\tau_t b_{t-1}=0$$

$$\tau_t b_t-\frac{\mu_t}{P^m_t}-\rho\nu_t\left(\tau_t b_{t-1}-\frac{\mu_{t-1}}{P^m_{t-1}}\right)=0$$

$$b_t P^m_t-(1+\rho P^m_t)b_{t-1}\nu_t-g_t-z_t+\tau_t=0$$

which will deliver initial jumps in inflation, bond prices, and tax rates to ensure fiscal solvency. These first-order conditions also imply that gross inflation returns to 1 in steady state, so the optimal commitment policy makes any inflation only temporary. But there is a continuum of steady-state debt levels, each with an associated optimal tax rate, that are consistent with the steady state of the first-order conditions under commitment.

When we consider a variant on the third case where taxes are no longer available for tax smoothing, either for political reasons or because the tax rate has reached the peak of the Laffer curve, the relevant optimality conditions become

$$\lambda_t P^m_t-\beta E_t(1+\rho P^m_{t+1})\nu_{t+1}\lambda_{t+1}=0$$

$$-\theta(\nu_t-1)+\tilde{\mu}_{t-1}(1+\rho P^m_t)c_t^{-\sigma}-(1+\rho P^m_t)\lambda_t b_{t-1}=0$$

$$\lambda_t b_t-\tilde{\mu}_t c_t^{-\sigma}-\rho\nu_t(\lambda_t b_{t-1}-\tilde{\mu}_{t-1}c_t^{-\sigma})=0$$

where the tax rate is fixed at $\overline{\tau}$.

Here the unit root in government debt is no longer present because taxes cannot adjust to support a new steady-state debt level, and inflation cannot influence future surpluses. Instead, inflation must be adjusted to ensure fiscal solvency by returning debt to the steady-state level consistent with the unchanged tax rate. The pattern of inflation also depends on the maturity structure of the inherited debt stock. To see this more clearly we consider the perfect foresight solution in the face of a transfers shock in which the first-order condition for debt implies that $\lambda_t=\lambda_{t+1}$ since $g_t=g^*$. Combining the second and third conditions yields

$$\nu_t(\nu_t-1)=\left[1+(\rho P^m_t)^{-1}\right]\beta\nu_{t+1}(\nu_{t+1}-1)$$

which describes the dynamics of inflation. Inflation rises following a fiscal shock that would otherwise make debt initially higher and then decline toward its steady-state value. The rate of convergence depends on the inverse of the maturity parameter multiplied by the bond price, which initially falls, but then recovers as the period of inflation passes. When $\rho=0$ the inflation only occurs in the initial period, but becomes more protracted the longer is the maturity of government debt. Similar inflation dynamics are observed when taxes are smoothed, although the magnitude of the initial jump in inflation will be reduced to the extent that tax rates rise to stabilize debt at a higher level in the face of a given shock.

4.4 Numerical Results

The grid-based approach to solving the stochastic version of the model under the simple rules works well when the economy has a well-defined steady state to which it returns. With commitment policies the model enters a new steady state following the realization of a shock, which makes the model difficult to solve using these techniques. For this reason, when considering commitment we restrict attention to perfect foresight equilibrium paths following an initial shock. These paths are computed as follows. We guess the new steady-state value of debt and solve the steady state of the Ramsey problem conditional on that guess. This serves as a terminal condition on the model solution 800 periods in the future. The Ramsey first-order conditions are then solved for 800 periods conditional on this guess for the ultimate steady state. If the solution exhibits a discontinuity between the final period of the solution and the imposed terminal condition, the steady-state guess is revised. This process continues until the guessed new steady state is indeed the steady state to which the economy now settles.

We begin by considering the same transfers shock considered above for various degrees of maturity and different initial debt-to-GDP ratios. The autocorrelated shock to transfers reduces the discounted value of future surpluses and requires a monetary and/or fiscal adjustment. These adjustments are plotted in Fig. 7 for various initial debt-to-GDP ratios and debt maturities. The first column starts from an initial debt-to-GDP ratio of zero. When debt is initially zero and the initial tax rate of $\tau = 0.39$ can support the initial level of transfers and public consumption, under the optimal policy there is no inflation, regardless of the maturity of debt. This is due to the fact that surprise changes in inflation or bond prices only help satisfy the government's intertemporal budget identity if there is already an initial debt stock for them to act on. Even though the debt that will be issued as a result of the transfer shock is of different maturities across the experiments reported in the first column of the figure, this will not affect the optimal policy response to the transfers shock when there is initially no debt. The tax rate jumps to a permanently higher level to support a higher steady-state debt level, as under Barro's (1979) original tax-smoothing result.

The second column begins from an initial steady state with a debt-to-GDP ratio of 25% (and a supporting initial tax rate of $\tau = 0.4$). Now there is mild use of inflation to offset the effects of the transfers shock. Inflation is smaller but more sustained the longer is the average maturity of debt. As maturity lengthens, inflation surprises play an increasingly important role in stabilizing debt, with smaller adjustments in taxes. At higher debt levels, the role of inflation and maturity grows in importance as substitutes for distorting taxes. Ultimately, the increase in inflation is unwound (it serves no purpose as the initial debt stock matures) and there is a permanent increase in both the debt stock and tax rates. These examples underscore that optimal policy is highly state dependent, particularly with respect to the level and maturity of debt at the time the shock hits.

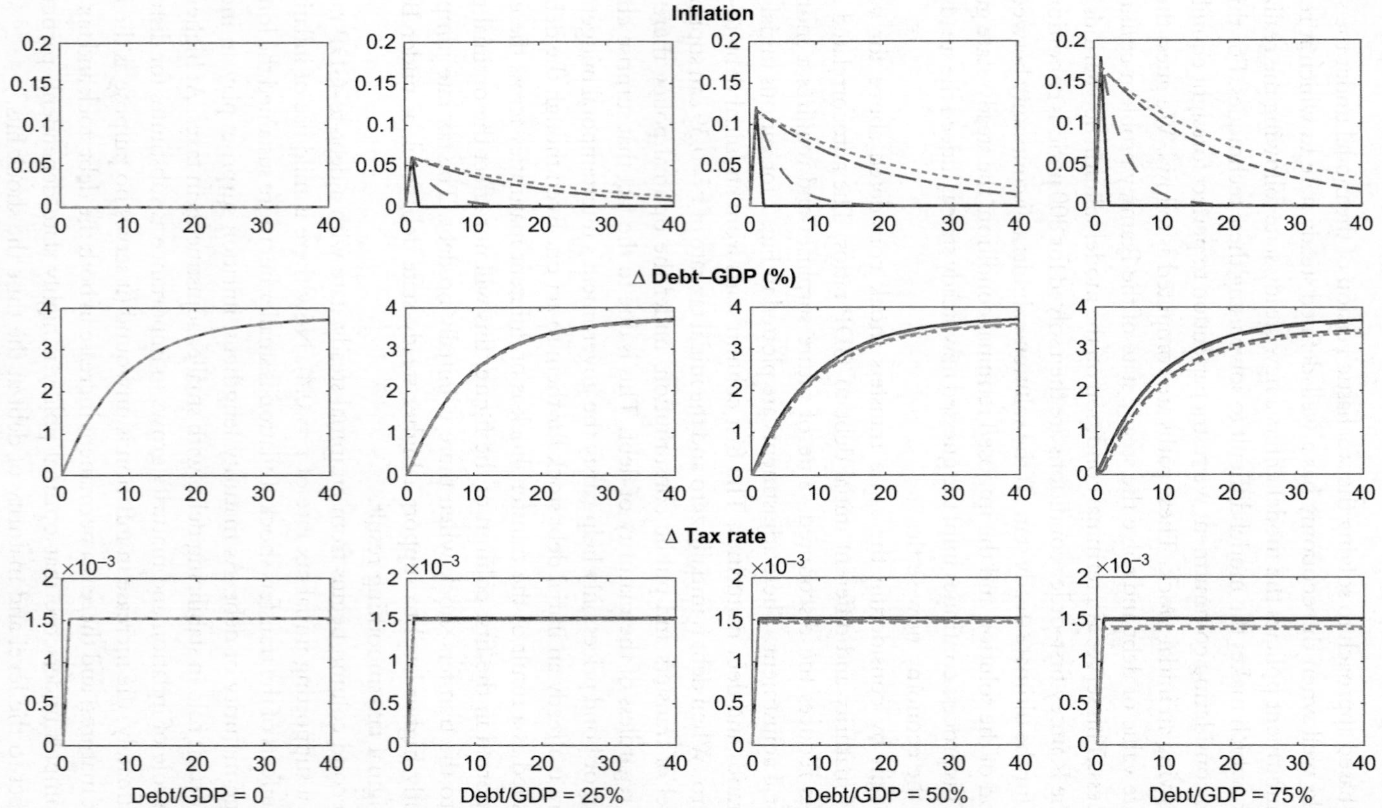

Fig. 7 Optimal policy in response to higher transfers with different debt levels and maturities. 1-period debt (*solid lines*), 1-year debt (*dashed lines*), 4-year debt (*dot-dashed lines*), and 5-year debt (*dotted lines*).

When we turn to government spending shocks in Fig. 8, the story is similar except that now, through the stochastic discount factor, public consumption tilts the optimal path of taxes and affects the magnitude of the fiscal and inflation adjustments needed to satisfy the debt valuation equation. With no initial stock of debt, the subsequent debt maturity structure is irrelevant and the optimal policy does not generate any inflation. But for a positive initial debt level, the spike in inflation for one-period debt is several orders of magnitude larger than for the portfolio of bonds with an average maturity of 8 years. With only short debt, the inflation is immediately eliminated, while the slight rise in inflation is sustained in the presence of longer term debt. Sustained inflation decreases bond prices that reduce the value of debt to for the more mature bonds, permitting the policymaker to reduce the required jump in the tax rate needed to support the higher level of steady-state debt. Interestingly, the higher tax rates during the period of raised public consumption end up reducing the new steady-state level of debt so that the new steady-state tax rate is actually lower than before the shock. This contrasts to the case of the transfer shock where debt levels were raised following the shock.

Fig. 9 reports optimal responses to news of a sustained increase in government spending 5 years in the future. Initially inflation falls and the tax rate jumps down in support of a debt level that is ultimately lower, despite the increase in government spending. This occurs because the policymaker raises the tax rate for the duration of the rise in public consumption to avoid the rapid accumulation of government debt in a period when real interest rates are relatively high. Bond prices rise as the anticipated increase in government spending approaches and then drop dramatically when the spending is realized.

In this experiment the cost of inflation is quite high, $\theta = 10$. A lower cost would lead to greater reliance on the use of monetary policy and innovations in the anticipated path of prices to stabilize debt. As we show later, even this relatively conservative weight on the costs of inflation still generates a sizeable endogenous inflation bias when we consider time-consistent policy.

4.5 Ramsey Policy with a General Maturity Structure

Although the geometrically declining maturity structure is a tractable and plausible description of the profile of government debt for many economies, it is useful to broaden the analysis with a more general description of the maturity structure. This generalization refines the description of the role of optimal inflation surprises in stabilizing debt and begins to consider the role of debt management in insulating the government's finances from fiscal shocks. We employ Cochrane's (2001) notation, allowing the bond valuation equation to be written as in (19) in Section 2.2.1. The government's optimization problem becomes

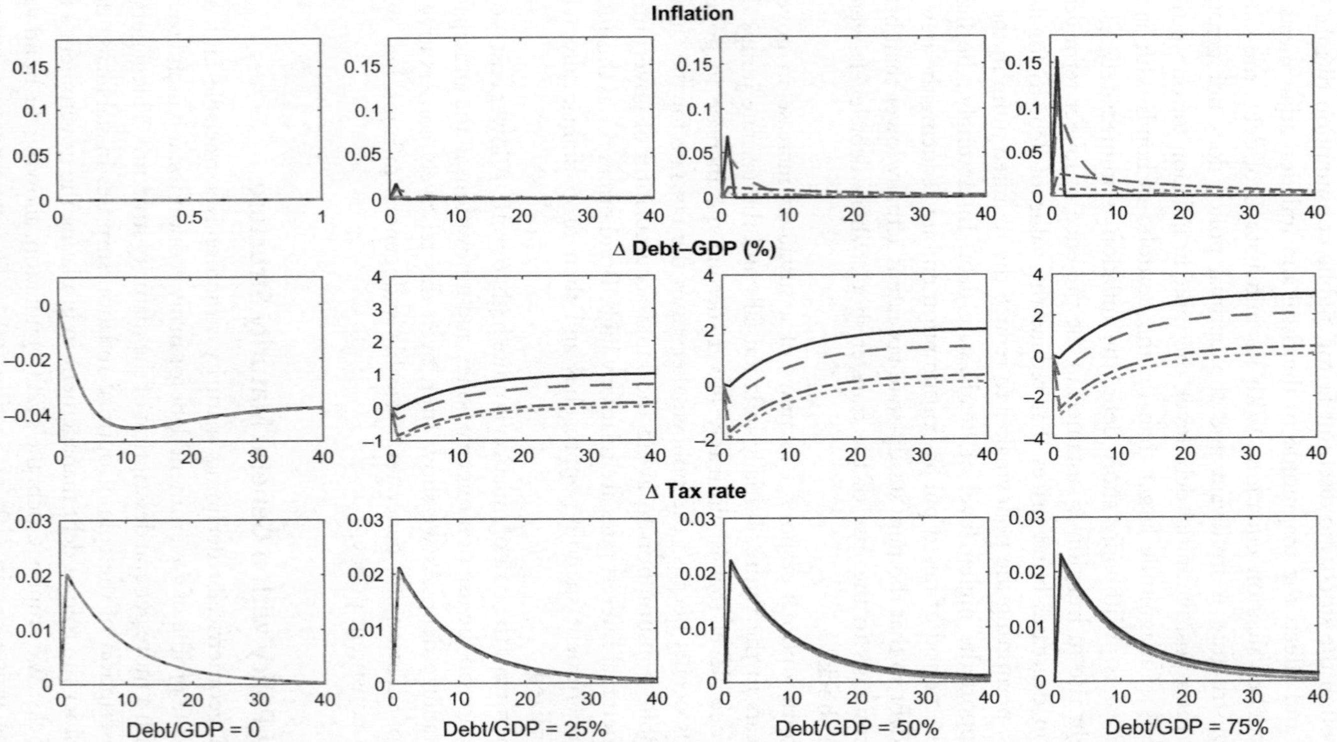

Fig. 8 Optimal policy in response to higher government spending with different debt levels and maturities. 1-period debt (*solid lines*), 1-year debt (*dashed lines*), 4-year debt (*dotted–dashed lines*), and 5-year debt (*dotted lines*).

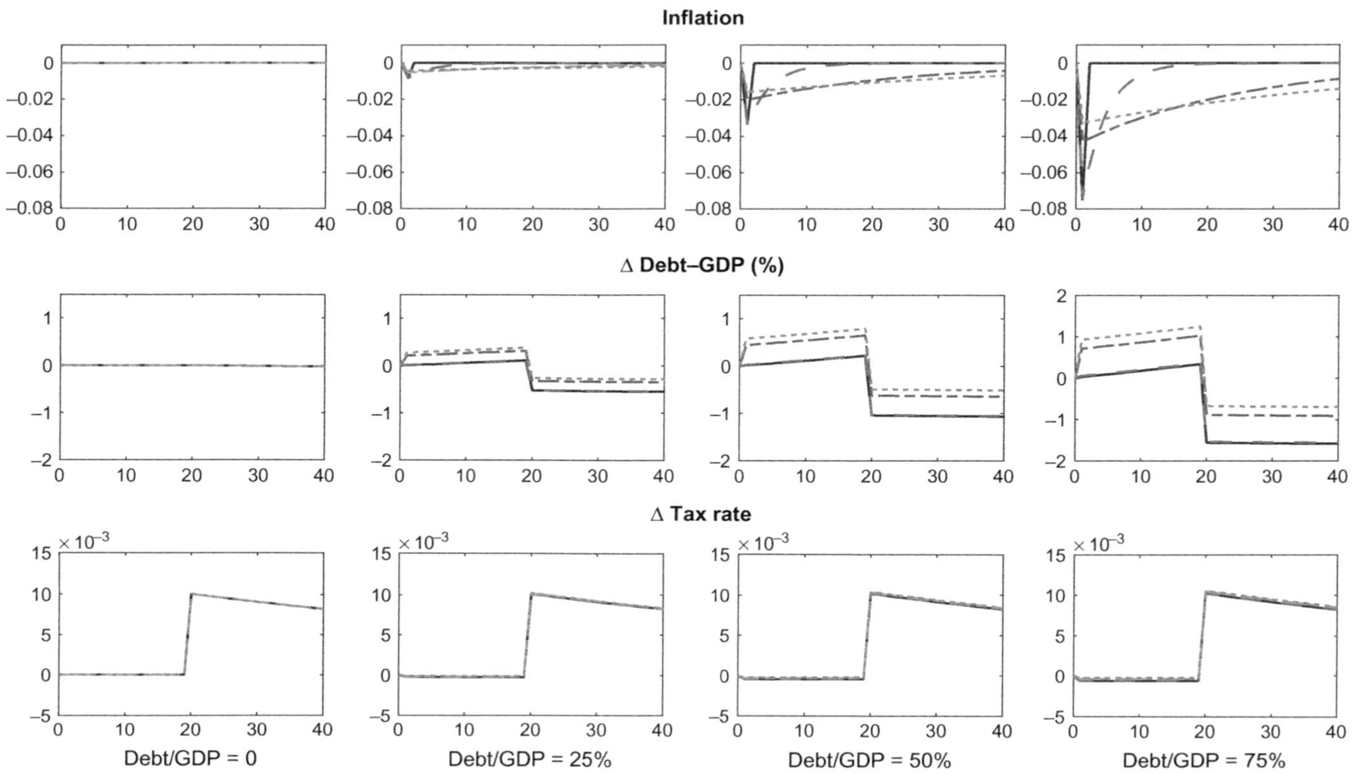

Fig. 9 Optimal policy in response to an anticipated increase in government spending with different debt levels and maturities. 1-period debt (*solid lines*), 1-year debt (*dashed lines*), 4-year debt (*dotted–dashed lines*), and 5-year debt (*dotted lines*).

$$L_0 = E_0 \sum_{t=0}^{\infty} \beta^t \left[-\frac{1}{2}(\tau_t^2 + \theta(\nu_t - 1)^2) \right.$$
$$\left. + \lambda_t \left(-\sum_{j=0}^{\infty} E_t \left[\beta^j u'(c_{t+j}) \prod_{s=0}^{j} \nu_{t+s} \right] \left[\frac{B_t(t+j)}{P_{t-1}} - \frac{B_{t-1}(t+j)}{P_{t-1}} \right] - u'(c_t)(\tau_t - g_t - z_t) \right) \right]$$

The first-order condition for taxation is

$$-\tau_t = u'(c_t)\lambda_t$$

The debt management problem optimally chooses the maturity structure of debt issued in period t which is repayable at future dates, $B_t(t + j)$, to yield the optimality condition

$$-\beta^t \lambda_t \beta^j E_t u'(c_{t+j}) \prod_{s=0}^{j} \nu_{t+s} \frac{1}{P_{t-1}} = -\beta^{t+1} E_t \lambda_{t+1} \beta^{j-1} u'(c_{t+j}) \prod_{s=0}^{j} \nu_{t+s} \frac{1}{P_{t-1}}$$

which can be simplified as

$$\frac{\tau_t}{u'(c_t)} E_t u'(c_{t+j}) \prod_{s=0}^{j} \nu_{t+s} = E_t \frac{\tau_{t+1}}{u'(c_{t+1})} u'(c_{t+j}) \prod_{s=0}^{j} \nu_{t+s}$$

which implies

$$E_t \left[\left[\frac{u'(c_t)}{u'(c_{t+1})} \tau_{t+1} - \tau_t \right] \frac{u'(c_{t+j})}{u'(c_t)} \frac{P_{t-1}}{P_{t+j}} \right] = 0$$

The covariance between the payoff of debt instrument of maturity j periods and next period's tax rate is zero (Bohn, 1990). This is the hedging across states that Angeletos (2002) and Buera and Nicolini (2004) explore. By structuring debt in this way the policymaker minimizes the fiscal and monetary adjustments required in the face of shocks; those policy adjustments then depend on the magnitude and maturity of the outstanding debt stock. To see how debt management can mitigate the need for adjusting tax rates and generating inflation in the face of fiscal shocks, we construct a simple example in the following section where the policymaker can completely insulate the government's finances from government spending shocks.

The final first-order condition is for deflation

$$-\beta^t \theta(\nu_t - 1)\nu_t + \sum_{i=0}^{t} \beta^i \lambda_i \left(-\sum_{j=0}^{\infty} \left[\beta^j u'(c_{i+j}) \prod_{s=0}^{j} \nu_{i+s} \right] \left[\frac{B_i(i+j)}{P_{i-1}} - \frac{B_{i-1}(i+j)}{P_{i-1}} \right] \right)$$

This can be combined with the condition for debt management and quasi-differenced to obtain, under perfect foresight

$$(\nu_t - 1)\nu_t = \beta(\nu_{t+1} - 1)\nu_{t+1} + \theta^{-1}\lambda_0 u'(c_t)\left[\frac{B_{-1}(t)}{P_t}\right]$$

This expression highlights more clearly the link between inflation and the maturity structure of the predetermined debt stock than does the geometrically declining maturity structure. The inflation dynamics under the optimal policy are in a very similar form to the nonlinear new Keynesian Phillips curve when price stickiness results from Rotemberg (1982) quadratic adjustment costs. The key difference is that the forcing variable is the element of the predetermined debt stock that matures in period t. Deflation/inflation anticipates the rate at which the debt stock issued at time $t = -1$ when the plan was formulated, matures. This makes current inflation reflect the discounted value of future debt as it matures. As debt matures, the effectiveness of inflation diminishes and inflation falls: the optimal rate of inflation jumps and gradually erodes until all the initial outstanding debt stock has matured. Notice that this Ramsey plan for inflation is only affected by debt dated at time $t = -1$, and the maturity structure of debt issued after this initial period is irrelevant in a perfect foresight environment. Future maturities will affect the government's ability to insure against fiscal shocks in a stochastic environment. We can see this latter point more clearly by considering a simple example.

4.6 Commitment and Hedging

Angeletos (2002) and Buera and Nicolini (2004) argue that debt maturity should be structured to insure the economy against shocks by having the government issue long-term liabilities, but hold an almost offsetting portfolio of short-term assets (the net difference being the government's overall level of indebtedness). In the face of fluctuating spending needs and interest rates, bond prices adjust to help finance debt without requiring any change in taxation. In these papers the short and long positions are constant over time, so that they do not require active management, although numerically they are extremely large positions (for example, five or six times the value of GDP in Buera and Nicolini, 2004). This approach amounts to another way to introduce the contingency in overall debt payments even though these individual assets/liabilities are not state contingent.

To construct a simple example of the use of debt management for hedging purposes we consider an environment where taxes and transfers are at their steady-state values ($\tau_{t+j} = \tau^*$ and $z_{t+j} = z^*$). Government spending can either take the value of $g^h > g^*$, with probability 1/2, or $g^l < g^*$ with complementary probability. Government debt takes the form of a single-period bond of quantity b^s issued in period t, repayable in period $t + 1$, and a portfolio of longer term bonds of geometrically declining maturity, so that the quantity of debt issued in period t maturing in period $t + j$ is $\rho^j b^m$. With a single *i.i.d.* shock all that is required for complete hedging is that the maturity structure contains both one- and two-period debt to enable us to perfectly hedge, as in Buera and Nicolini. With additional *i.i.d.* shock processes, complete hedging is not possible, as we would require some persistence in the shock process and longer term debt. Because we wish to contrast this case with a scenario where a time-consistent policymaker seeks to use debt management for the purposes of hedging and mitigating time-consistency problems, we allow for a combination of longer term bonds and short-term bonds in which varying proportions of the two types can act as a proxy for changes in average debt maturity. In this example, transfer shocks, which amount to shocks that do not directly affect bond prices and interest rates, cannot be completed hedged, although movements in inflation as part of the optimal policy response could provide some hedging opportunities.

Generalizing the Ramsey policy considered above to include a single-period nominal bond as well as the portfolio of bonds with geometrically declining maturity, the system of first-order conditions to be solved as part of the Ramsey problem is

$$-\theta(\nu_t - 1) + \tilde{\mu}_{t-1}(1+\rho P_t^m)c_t^{-\sigma} + \tilde{\gamma}_{t-1}c_t^{-\sigma} - (1+\rho P_t^m)\tau_t b_{t-1} - \tau_t b_{t-1}^s = 0$$

$$\tau_t b_t - \tilde{\mu}_t c_t^{-\sigma} - \rho\nu_t(\tau_t b_{t-1} - \tilde{\mu}_{t-1}c_t^{-\sigma}) = 0\tau_t b_t^s - \tilde{\gamma}_t c_t^{-\sigma} = 0$$

$$\tau_t P_t^m - \beta E_t(1+\rho P_{t+1}^m)\nu_{t+1}\tau_{t+1} = 0$$

$$\tau_t P_t^s - \beta E_t \nu_{t+1}\tau_{t+1} = 0$$

$$\beta E_t \frac{(1+\rho P_{t+1}^m)}{P_t^m}\left(\frac{c_{t+1}}{c_t}\right)^{-\sigma}\nu_{t+1} - 1 = 0$$

$$\beta E_t\left(\frac{c_{t+1}}{c_t}\right)^{-\sigma}\nu_{t+1} - P_t^s = 0$$

$$b_t P_t^m + b_t^s P_t^s - (1+\rho P_t^m)b_{t-1}\nu_t - b_{t-1}^s\nu_t - g_t - z^* + \tau_t = 0$$

$$g_t = g^i, \quad i = h, l \text{ with prob } 1/2$$

where $\tilde{\mu}_{t-1} = \frac{\mu_{t-1}}{P_{t-1}^m c_{t-1}^{-\sigma}}, \tilde{\gamma}_{t-1} = \frac{\gamma_{t-1}}{P_{t-1}^s c_{t-1}^{-\sigma}}$, and γ_t is the Lagrange multiplier associated with the pricing of single-period bonds, $P_t^s = \beta E_t\left(\frac{c_{t+1}}{c_t}\right)^{-\sigma}\nu_{t+1}$. There are four state variables—$\tilde{\mu}_{t-1}, \tilde{\gamma}_{t-1}, b_t, b_t^s$—the first two of which capture the history dependence in policymaking under commitment. Despite the complexity of these first-order conditions, the policymaker can fulfill this Ramsey program with a constant tax rate and no inflation by buying an appropriate quantity of single-period assets paid for by issuing longer term bonds. Shocks to public consumption then induce fluctuations in the prices of these assets/liabilities which perfectly insulate the government's finances.

With *i.i.d.* fluctuations in government spending, the current level of spending is also a state variable: we are either in the high- or in the low-government spending regime and may exit that regime with a probability of 1/2 each period.

The pricing equation for geometrically declining coupon bonds is

$$P_t^m = \beta E_t (1 + \rho P_{t+1}^m) \left(\frac{c_{t+1}}{c_t} \right)^{-\sigma} \nu_{t+1}$$

With government spending fluctuating between high and low states, bond prices will fluctuate depending on the spending state. Define $u_{ij} = \frac{u'(1-g^i)}{u'(1-g^j)} = \frac{(1-g^i)^{-\sigma}}{(1-g^j)^{-\sigma}}$, $i,j = l,h$, and $i \neq j$ bond prices in spending regime i, $i = h,l$ are given by

$$\begin{aligned} P_i^m &= \beta \frac{1}{2}(1 + \rho P_i^m) + \beta \frac{1}{2}(1 + \rho P_j^m) u_{ji} \\ &= A_i + B_i P_j^m \end{aligned}$$

where $A_i = (1 - \frac{1}{2}\beta\rho)^{-1}(\frac{1}{2}\beta + \frac{1}{2}\beta u_{ji})$ and $B_i = (1 - \frac{1}{2}\beta\rho)^{-1}\frac{1}{2}\beta\rho u_{ji}$, $i, j = l, h$, and $i \neq j$, which can be solved as

$$P_i^m = \frac{A_i + B_i A_j}{1 - B_i B_j}$$

For one-period debt this reduces to

$$P_i^s = \frac{1}{2}\beta + \frac{1}{2}\beta u_{ji}$$

Optimal hedging uses these fluctuations in bond prices to construct portfolio of government debt that negates the need to vary taxes or induce inflation surprises, despite the random movements in government consumption.

The flow budget identity conditional on the government spending regime, but with constant tax rates and no inflation, is

$$P_i^m b^m + P_i^s b^s = (1 + \rho P_i^m) b^m + b^s - (\tau^* - g^i - z^*)$$

We choose b^m and b^s to ensure this equation holds regardless of the government spending regime, so that the government does not need to issue or retire debt as it moves between low and high spending regimes. This portfolio is given by

$$\begin{bmatrix} b^m \\ b^s \end{bmatrix} = - \begin{bmatrix} P_i^m(1-\rho) - 1 & P_i^s - 1 \\ P_j^m(1-\rho) - 1 & P_j^s - 1 \end{bmatrix}^{-1} \begin{bmatrix} \tau^* - g^i - z^* \\ \tau^* - g^j - z^* \end{bmatrix}$$

We can achieve the same portfolio by considering the debt valuation equation in a given period, which is contingent on the government spending state. If government spending is currently high, that equation is

$$b^s(u'(c^h)) + b^m(u'(c^h)) + \sum_{j=1}^{\infty}(\rho\beta)^j\left[\frac{1}{2}u'(c^l) + \frac{1}{2}u'(c^h)\right]b^m$$
$$= u'(c^h)(\tau^* - g^h - z^*) + \sum_{j=1}^{\infty}\beta^j\left[\frac{1}{2}u'(c^l)(\tau^* - g^l - z^*) + \frac{1}{2}u'(c^h)(\tau^* - g^h - z^*)\right]$$

and if government spending is low it is

$$b^s(u'(c^l)) + b^m(u'(c^l)) + \sum_{j=1}^{\infty}(\rho\beta)^j\left[\frac{1}{2}u'(c^l) + \frac{1}{2}u'(c^h)\right]b^m$$
$$= u'(c^l)(\tau^* - g^l - z^*) + \sum_{j=1}^{\infty}\beta^j\left[\frac{1}{2}u'(c^l)(\tau^* - g^l - z^*) + \frac{1}{2}u'(c^h)(\tau^* - g^h - z^*)\right]$$

subtracting one from the other implies

$$[b^s + b^m](u'(c^h) - u'(c^l)) = u'(c^h)(\tau^* - g^h - z^*) - u'(c^l)(\tau^* - g^l - z^*) \tag{40}$$

Without any change in taxation or inflation, government solvency is ensured, provided that debt maturing in the current period has the value implied by this equation. Assuming a sufficiently low level of net indebtedness, the primary budget will swing between deficit and surplus as government spending moves from high to low regimes, implying that the right side of (40) is negative. Since $u'(c^h) > u'(c^l)$, this condition requires that the Ramsey policymaker buys short-term assets to such an extent that $b^s < -b^m$. The budget identity is insulated from the effects of government spending shocks, which can be absorbed by bond prices without any need to issue new debt, change taxes, or generate inflation surprises.

The size of the longer term liabilities must, equivalently, satisfy the solvency conditions conditional on the current level of government consumption. For example

$$b^s(u'(c^h)) + b^m(u'(c^h)) + \sum_{j=1}^{\infty}(\rho\beta)^j\left[\frac{1}{2}u'(c^l) + \frac{1}{2}u'(c^h)\right]b^m$$
$$= u'(c^h)(\tau^* - g^h - z^*) + \sum_{j=1}^{\infty}\beta^j\left[\frac{1}{2}u'(c^l)(\tau^* - g^l - z^*) + \frac{1}{2}u'(c^h)(\tau^* - g^h - z^*)\right]$$

which can be written as

$$\frac{\rho\beta}{1-\rho\beta}\left[\frac{1}{2}u'(c^l) + \frac{1}{2}u'(c^h)\right]b^s + b^s u'(c^h) + b^m u'(c^h)$$
$$= \frac{\beta}{1-\beta}\left[\frac{1}{2}u'(c^l)(\tau^* - g^l - z^*) + \frac{1}{2}u'(c^h)(\tau^* - g^h - z^*)\right] + u'(c^h)(\tau^* - g^h - z^*)$$

This expression can either define the steady-state level of long-term debt given the tax rate or the tax rate given the long-term debt stock. Either interpretation is consistent with a steady-state solution to the Ramsey tax-smoothing plan where the solution of the remainder of the Ramsey problem is $\tau_t = \tau^*$, $z_t = z^* = 0.18y$, $\nu_t = 1$, $\frac{\gamma_i}{P_i^s} = \tau^* b^s$, $\frac{\mu_i}{P_i^m} = \tau^* b^m$, $i = h, l$ with probability of 1/2. In other words, the steady-state tax rate can support the average level of government spending, steady-state transfers, and the steady-state net debt stock, while fluctuations in bond prices mitigate the need for further tax adjustments to compensate for fluctuations in government spending.

Fig. 10 reveals the pattern of bond returns and the underlying asset positions for a series of random draws across the two spending regimes. The figure's bottom right panel describes a particular realization of the government spending shocks. Despite these movements in spending the budget identity can be satisfied with a constant tax rate and no inflation surprises by buying short-term assets that are funded by issuing longer term debt. The portfolio that achieves this implies that the government holds short-term assets of around 22% of GDP, with longer term liabilities of around 70% of GDP and a net debt of around 48%. Although large, these positions are less than those typically found for richer stochastic processes, where positions often exceed the economy's total endowment by several factors (Buera and Nicolini, 2004). Since the ability to hedge relies on variation in the yield curve, having longer term liabilities to set against the short-term assets is most effective. Then a portfolio of single-period assets matched with 1-year liabilities requires far more short-term assets, compared to a portfolio made up of the same assets and bonds

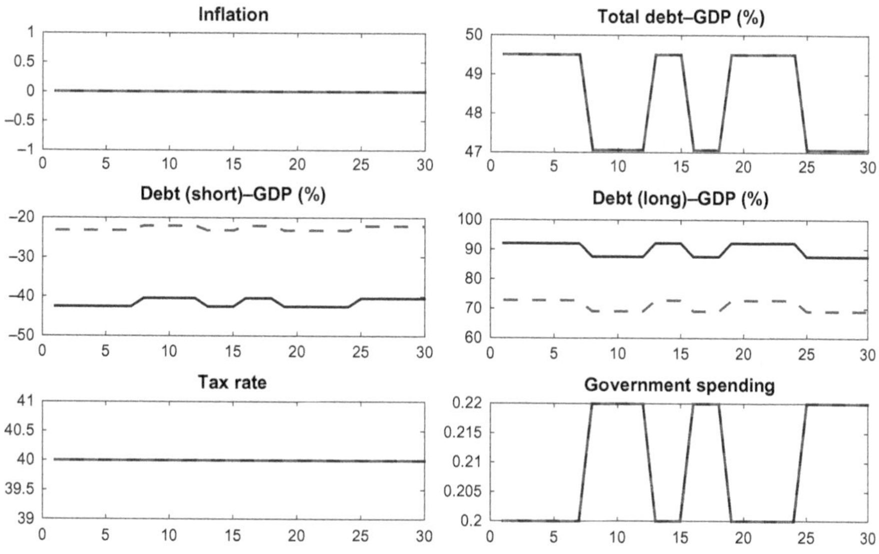

Fig. 10 Optimal hedging under commitment. 1-year debt (*solid lines*) and 5-year debt (*dashed lines*).

with an average maturity of 5 years. Hedging in this way implies that a positive shock to government spending, which raises the primary deficit, actually leads to a reduction in the value of government indebtedness, rather than to an increase. This is a general prediction of models that have achieved financial market completeness which Marcet and Scott (2009) use as the basis of an empirical test, but the data strongly reject.

Faraglia et al. (2008) extend Buera and Nicolini's analysis to move away from an endowment economy to consider a production economy with capital. This makes the size of the extreme portfolio positions even larger, and now the liability/asset positions are no longer constant, but highly volatile, possibly even reversing the issue-long-buy-short recommendation. Because yield premia are not very volatile, they are therefore not very effective as a source of insurance. They then consider what happens if the government is unsure about the specification of some element of the model. The sensitivity of results to small changes in model specification means that it is often better to run a balanced budget than run the risk of getting the portfolio composition wrong. Similarly, even modest transaction costs would make it undesirable to construct such huge portfolios.

4.7 Discretion

A large part of the literature that extends Lucas and Stokey's (1983) analysis focuses on the importance of having access to state-contingent debt either directly or by using inflation surprises and debt management to render state dependent the real payoffs from government debt. When the policymaker can replicate the Ramsey policy in Lucas and Stokey through such devices, there remains the issue of whether the underlying policy is time consistent. In the original Lucas and Stokey model, the Ramsey policy can be made time consistent by adhering to a particular debt maturity structure. Lucas and Stokey then conjecture that allowing debt to be nominal would make the policy problem trivial: positive debt would be costlessly deflated by positive surprise inflation and negative debt would be adjusted by surprise deflation to the level sufficient to support the first-best allocation (the interest on the debt paying for government consumption, consistent with any fiscal taxes/subsidies required by offset other market distortions). This reasoning suggests that the only interesting case is when the outstanding debt stock is zero.

Persson et al. (1987) initiated a debate exploring the Lucas and Stokey conjecture.[al] Alvarez et al. (2004) conclude that the Lucas and Stokey structure of state-contingent indexed debt, in combination with a condition that net nominal debt is zero so that government debt liabilities equal the stock of money, can ensure the time consistency of the original Lucas and Stokey Ramsey policy in a monetary economy that follows the Friedman rule. As Persson et al. (2006) note, these conditions essentially reduce the monetary version of the Lucas and Stokey economy to its real version.

[al] Persson et al. (2006) chart the course of this debate.

Bohn (1988) argues that in issuing nominal debt the policymaker trades off the ability to use inflation surprises as a hedging device when debt is nominal against the inflation bias that a positive stock of debt creates. In models where the problem is not constructed to mimic the Lucas and Stokey Ramsey policy, the time-consistent policy typically implies a mean reverting steady-state level of debt. Debt can be positive or negative, depending on the nature of the time-inconsistency problem. The issue of the time consistency of policy is also dependent on the cost of inflation surprises. Persson et al. (2006) use beginning- rather than end-of-period money balances in the provision of liquidity services to make unexpected inflation costly, which allows them to construct a time-consistent portfolio of indexed and nominal debt. Martin (2009) adopts the cash–credit good distinction in Lucas and Stokey to generate a cost to inflation which is then balanced against the gains from using inflation to reduce the value of single-period nominal debt. This generates a mean reverting steady-state level of debt under discretion, rather than the random walk in steady-state debt, which is a feature of the Ramsey tax-smoothing policy without state-contingent debt. Martin (2011) combines the Lagos and Wright (2005) monetary search model with fiscal policy and explores the time-consistency problem to find that the welfare costs of an inability to commit are small. This conclusion likely reflects the nature of the costs of surprise inflation; as noted earlier, when Schmitt-Grohé and Uribe (2004) introduce even a tiny degree of nominal inertia, the time-inconsistent Ramsey policy tilts very firmly in favor of price stability, away from the Friedman rule and the use of inflation surprises.

We now turn to consider the impact on the balance between monetary and fiscal policy of constraining the policymaker to be time consistent. We continue to use the endowment economy where inflation is assumed to be costly as a shortcut to introducing nominal inertia.

The policymaker cannot make credible promises about how they will behave in the future in order to improve policy trade-offs today. However, even in this simple model there is an endogenous state variable in the form of government debt, so that policy actions today will affect future expectations through the level of debt that the policy bequeaths to the future. We define the auxiliary variable

$$M(b_{t-1},g_{t-1})=(1+\rho P_t^m)\nu_t(c_t)^{-\sigma}$$

to write the Bellman equation of the associated policy problem as

$$\begin{aligned}V(b_{t-1},g_{t-1})&=-\frac{1}{2}(\tau_t^2+\theta(\nu_t-1)^2)+\beta E_t V(b_t,g_t)\\&+\mu_t(\beta\frac{c_t^{\sigma}}{P_t^m}E_t M(b_t,g_t)-1)\\&+\lambda_t(b_t P_t^m-(1+\rho P_t^m)b_{t-1}\nu_t-g_t-z_t+\tau_t)\end{aligned}$$

We have replaced the expectations in the bond-pricing equation with the auxiliary variable to indicate that the policymaker cannot influence those expectations directly by making policy commitments. But those expectations are a function of the state variables. We take government spending and transfers to be exogenous autoregressive processes.

The implies the first-order conditions

$$\tau_t : -\tau_t + \lambda_t = 0$$

$$\nu_t : -\theta(\nu_t - 1) - \lambda_t(1 + \rho P_t^m)b_{t-1} = 0$$

$$P_t^m : -\frac{\mu_t}{P_t^m} + \lambda_t(b_t - \rho b_{t-1}\nu_t) = 0$$

$$b_t : \frac{\mu_t}{P_t^m} c_t^\sigma \beta E_t \frac{\partial M(b_t, g_t)}{\partial b_t} + \lambda_t P_t^m + \beta E_t \frac{\partial V(b_t, g_t)}{\partial b_t} = 0$$

From the envelope theorem

$$\frac{\partial V(b_{t-1}, g_{t-1})}{\partial b_{t-1}} = -(1 + \rho P_t^m)\nu_t \lambda_t$$

which can be led one period and substituted into the first-order condition for government debt

$$\frac{\mu_t}{P_t^m} c_t^\sigma \beta E_t \frac{\partial M(b_t, g_t)}{\partial b_t} + \lambda_t P_t^m - \beta E_t(1 + \rho P_{t+1}^m)\nu_{t+1}\tau_{t+1} = 0$$

Combining the condition for the bond price P_t^m with the Fisher equation implies

$$\frac{\mu_t}{P_t^m} = \lambda_t(b_t - \rho \nu_t b_{t-1})$$

which can be used to eliminate $\frac{\mu_t}{P_t^m}$ from the condition for debt. The system to be solved for $\{P_t^m, \nu_t, \tau_t, b_t, g_t\}$ is

$$\nu_t : -\theta(\nu_t - 1) - \tau_t(1 + \rho P_t^m)b_{t-1} = 0$$

$$b_t : \tau_t(b_t - \rho \nu_t b_{t-1})\beta c_t^\sigma E_t \frac{\partial M(b_t, g_t)}{\partial b_t} + \tau_t P_t^m - \beta E_t(1 + \rho P_{t+1}^m)\nu_{t+1}\tau_{t+1} = 0$$

along with the bond-pricing equation and the government's budget constraint.

The first-order condition for inflation is now

$$-\theta(\nu_t - 1) = (1 + \rho P_t^m)b_{t-1}\tau_t$$

Under commitment, inflation persisted only for as long as the maturity structure of the predetermined debt stock at the time a shock hit. Under time-consistent policy, outside of the policymaker's bliss point (of zero inflation and no taxation), with a nonzero debt stock there will always be a state-dependent mix of taxation and inflation. A positive stock of debt delivers positive inflation, regardless of the maturity structure of that debt. This reflects the inflation bias inherent in the time-consistent policy in the presence of nominal debt.

We can see some more differences between discretion and commitment by contrasting the equivalent expressions describing the evolution of the tax rate. Under commitment we obtain the standard tax-smoothing result adjusted for the tilting implied by variations in the stochastic discount factor

$$\tau_t P_t^m = \beta E_t (1 + \rho P_{t+1}^m) \nu_{t+1} \tau_{t+1}$$

The equivalent condition under discretion is

$$\tau_t P_t^m = \beta E_t (1 + \rho P_{t+1}^m) \nu_{t+1} \tau_{t+1} - \tau_t (b_t - \rho \nu_t b_{t-1}) \beta c_t^\sigma E_t \frac{\partial M(b_t, g_t)}{\partial b_t}$$

The additional term captures the effects of the tax rate on expectations of inflation and bond prices through the level of debt carried into the future. Increased debt raises expected inflation and lowers expected bond prices, so $E_t \frac{\partial M(b_t, g_t)}{\partial b_t} < 0$. This captures the debt-contingent nature of the time-consistency problem facing the policymaker. As debt levels rise the policymaker faces a greater temptation to utilize surprise inflation to reduce the debt burden. Economic agents anticipate this and raise their inflationary expectations until the temptation to induce surprises is offset. However, unlike in the standard analysis of the inflationary bias problem this bias is not static since the policymaker can raise additional distortionary taxes to reduce debt and its associated inflation. Therefore the additional term in the above expression raises the tax rate above the level implied by the tax-smoothing condition observed under commitment. Where the tax rate under commitment was carefully constructed to allow debt levels to permanently rise, under discretion the tax rate prevents debt from rising permanently.[am] Moreover, the rate at which the policymaker reduces debt under discretion depends crucially on the term, $(b_t - \rho \nu_t b_{t-1})$ which in turn depends on the maturity structure of the debt stock. Effectively the lower bond prices mean the policymaker must issue more bonds to finance a given deficit, but pays less to buy back the existing debt stock. As debt maturity is increased this latter effect comes to dominate the former and the speed of debt reduction is reduced. Therefore, in contrast to the random walk in steady-state debt observed under commitment, the time-consistent policymaker returns debt to a steady-state value that is very close to zero, but slightly negative where the speed of adjustment depends crucially on average debt maturity. This cannot be seen entirely analytically, so we

[am] Calvo and Guidotti (1992) label this the "debt aversion" effect and Leith and Wren-Lewis (2013) call it the "debt stabilization bias."

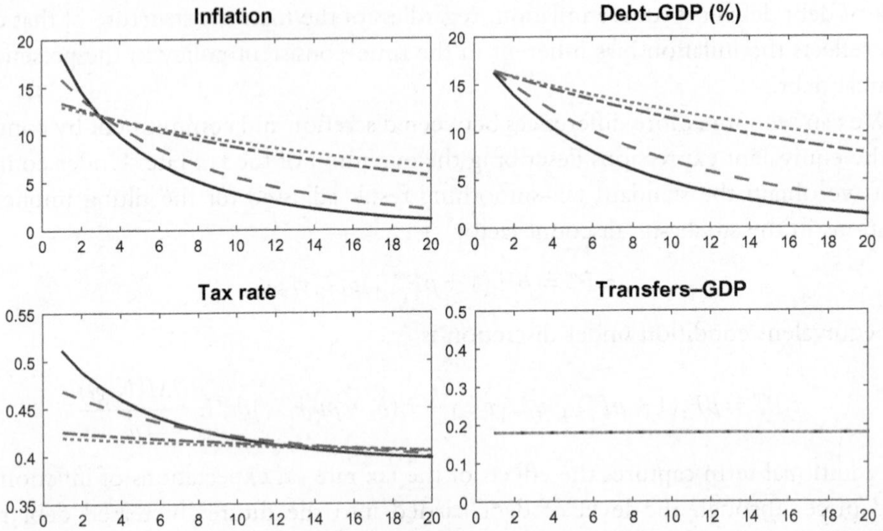

Fig. 11 Optimal time-consistent policy when debt is above its steady-state level. 1-period debt (*solid lines*), 1-year debt (*dashed lines*), 5-year debt (*dotted–dashed lines*), and 7-year debt (*dotted lines*).

need to analyze the numerical solution to the time-consistent policy problem to gain further insight.

The numerical solution under discretion is radically different from that under commitment (Fig. 11). Under commitment, policy allows the steady-state level of debt to follow a random walk and the use of inflation to offset shocks is relatively modest. Under discretion there is a unique steady state at which the policy supporting the steady-state debt level is time consistent, and this occurs at a slightly negative debt stock with a mild deflation. The negative steady-state debt stock falls far short of the negative debt levels that would be needed to support the first-best allocation—that is, the stock of government-held assets generates interest income sufficient to pay for all transfers and government spending without levying any distortionary taxes. Private-sector expectations ensure that the policymaker does not accumulate such a level of assets. Bondholders know that once the government has accumulated a positive stock of assets, it has an incentive to introduce surprise deflation to increase the real value of those assets. This knowledge reduces agents' inflation expectations until the policymaker no longer wishes to introduce such deflationary surprises. Accumulating more assets would then worsen this incentive to deflate confronting the policymaker with a trade-off between accumulating assets to reduce tax rates and the expected deflation that the accumulation of assets implies. In the steady state a balance is struck with a mild deflation and small negative debt stock, although both are extremely close to zero.

At positive debt levels there is a significant desire to reduce debt through inflation surprises. Economic agents anticipate this and raise their inflationary expectations.

Positive debt levels raise inflation in a highly nonlinear way because they introduce a state-dependent inflationary bias which can be very large. Even modest debt-to-GDP ratios can imply double-digit inflation. This is a surprising outcome since the same model and parameterization under commitment imply no inflation at all in the absence of shocks and only small inflation with shocks and positive debt levels.

As noted earlier, the policymaker's desire to mitigate this bias leads to a deviation from tax smoothing where the policymaker raises distortionary taxation above the tax-smoothing level to not only stabilize debt but reduce it toward its steady-state value. Debt maturity lessens this debt stabilization bias problem so that for a given debt-to-GDP ratio inflation is lower, the longer is debt maturity. The debt stabilization bias is heavily dependent on the magnitude of the government debt stock. When debt is high, the efficacy of surprise inflation—either current inflation or through bond prices—is also much higher and this raises the government's incentives to use this device to stabilize debt. As a result the debt stabilization bias rises dramatically with debt levels.

In the absence of innovations to the fiscal surplus, this higher inflation does not actually stabilize debt. As in the original inflation bias problem, there is a pure cost in the form of higher inflation which does not generate any reduction in debt.[an] But unlike the original inflation bias problem, in our case the magnitude of the bias is endogenous and depends on the size and maturity of the government debt. The policymaker can choose to reduce debt through taxation to gradually reduce the bias. Under discretion the reduction in debt can be a quite rapid, particularly when the debt stock is large and of short maturity. The costs of the policymaker being unable to commit in this context are not that debt is unstable, but that the policymaker too aggressively returns government debt to its steady-state level following shocks. This message resonates when thinking about actual fiscal austerity policies in many countries after the 2008 global financial crisis.

4.8 Debt Management under Discretion

The above results highlight the time-consistency issues created by nominal debt. The existing optimal policy literature also considers time-consistency issues in relation to debt management issues. Specifically, in the Lucas and Stokey model with state-contingent debt, the maturity structure is key in ensuring that the Ramsey policy described in Lucas and Stokey is time consistent. At the same time, the optimal hedging analysis shows that the maturity structure can create a portfolio of government bonds that features the right state-contingent payoffs even when the underlying bonds are not state contingent. In the context of a real model, Debortoli et al. (2014) also allow the government to hold

[an] Analogously, in Barro and Gordon (1983) this additional inflation does not reduce unemployment.

short-term assets and longer term liabilities (which are individually not state contingent), but require the policy to be time-consistent. They show that the optimal policy results in a relatively flat maturity structure that offsets the costs of not being able to commit even though this removes the tilting in maturity that is beneficial in terms of insurance effects.

To assess the trade-offs between optimal hedging and time consistency, we use the same model that delivered complete hedging of government expenditure shocks under commitment and solve that model under discretion. In introducing single-period bonds to the time-consistent policy problem we need to define an additional auxiliary variable

$$N(b_{t-1}, b^s_{t-1}, g_{t-1}) = \nu_t (c_t)^{-\sigma}$$

All expectations are now a function of three state variables, longer term bonds, b_{t-1}, single-period bonds, b^s_{t-1} and government spending, g_{t-1}, which will either equal $0.22y$ in the high spending regime, or $0.2y$ in the low spending case.

The policy problem is

$$\begin{aligned} V(b_{t-1}, b^s_{t-1}, g_{t-1}) = & -\frac{1}{2}(\tau_t^2 + \theta(\nu_t - 1)^2) + \beta E_t V(b_t, b^s_t, g_t) \\ & + \mu_t \left(\beta \frac{c_t^\sigma}{P_t^m} E_t M(b_t, b^s_t, g_t) - 1\right) \\ & + \gamma_t \left(\beta E_t \frac{c_t^\sigma}{P_t^s} E_t N(b_t, b^s_t, g_t) - 1\right) \\ & + \lambda_t (b_t P_t^m + b^s_t P^s_t - (1 + \rho P_t^m) b_{t-1} \nu_t - b^s_{t-1} \nu_t - g_t + \tau_t - z_t) \end{aligned}$$

which has an additional constraint associated with the pricing of short-term bonds, and the government's flow budget identity contains both single-period and declining coupon bonds. After applying the envelope theorem this implies the first-order conditions. For inflation

$$-\theta(\nu_t - 1) = \tau_t [(1 + \rho P_t^m) b_{t-1} + b^s_{t-1}]$$

The level of inflation depends on the total level of indebtedness across short and long bonds, so that a positive level of net indebtedness implies an inflationary bias. As before, this bias serves no purpose in terms of reducing the real debt burden, but reflects economic agents' expectations that if inflation were any lower, the policy would be tempted to introduce a surprise inflation to facilitate debt reduction.

The tax-smoothing conditions are

$$\begin{aligned} \tau_t P_t^m = & \beta E_t (1 + \rho P_{t+1}^m) \nu_{t+1} \tau_{t+1} - \tau_t (b_t - \rho \nu_t b_{t-1}) \beta c_t^\sigma E_t \frac{\partial M(b_t, b^s_t, g_t)}{\partial b_t} \\ & - \tau_t b^s_t \beta c_t^\sigma E_t \frac{\partial N(b_t, b^s_t, g_t)}{\partial b_t} \end{aligned}$$

and

$$\tau_t P_t^s = \beta E_t \nu_{t+1} \tau_{t+1} - \tau_t (b_t - \rho \nu_t b_{t-1}) \beta c_t^\sigma E_t \frac{\partial M(b_t, b_t^s, g_t)}{\partial b_t^s}$$
$$- \tau_t b_t^s \beta c_t^\sigma E_t \frac{\partial N(b_t, b_t^s, g_t)}{\partial b_t^s}$$

The first two terms of these expressions reflect the same tax-smoothing conditions found under commitment, where the choice of short-term assets and longer term bonds could satisfy these conditions while perfectly insulating the government's finances from the fluctuations in government spending. The final two terms in each condition capture the impact that another unit of short or long debt has on long- and short-term bond prices through the impact of debt on inflation expectations. These effects highlight the incentives that the policymaker has to reduce indebtedness to reduce inflation, given the inflationary bias problem created by a positive stock of government debt. The magnitude of the effect of reducing either short- or long-term debt by one bond may vary depending on the relative proportions of the two bonds. In other words, by varying the relative proportions of single period and longer term debt, the policymaker can vary the average debt maturity and thereby influence the inflationary bias problem implied by a given level of indebtedness.

Solving the model without switching in government spending generates a steady state with near-zero debt and inflation (Fig. 12). Introducing government spending switches induces fluctuations in all variables. The movements in spending are largely matched with movements in tax rates (even though these could have been eliminated by issuing an

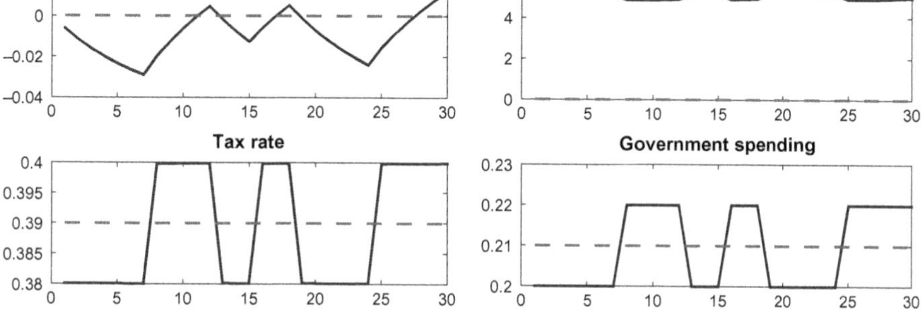

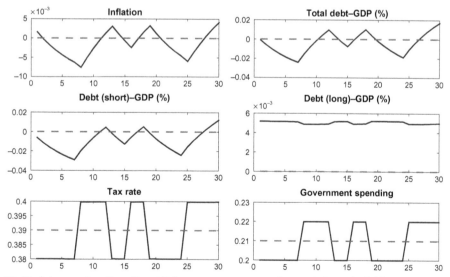

Fig. 12 Hedging under discretion. With government spending switching (*solid lines*) and without government spending switching (*dashed lines*).

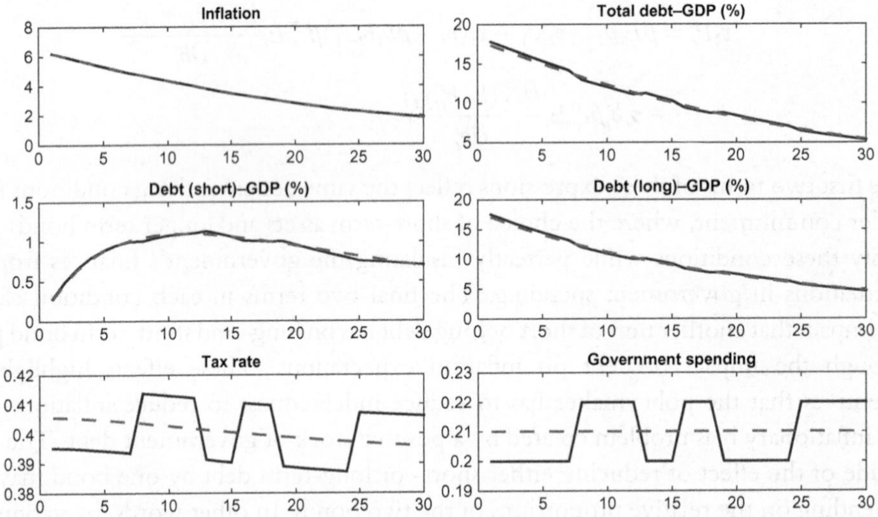

Fig. 13 Hedging and time-consistent policy. With government spending switching (*solid lines*) and without government spending switching (*dashed lines*).

appropriately constructed portfolio of short-term assets and longer term liabilities), although with some increase in the debt/deficit when we are in the high spending regime. The stochastic steady-state asset and liability positions are only slightly positive for assets, and slightly negative for liabilities, but quite distant from the magnitude of the positions required for perfect hedging. Inflation follows the level of indebtedness, giving rise to a positive (negative) inflation bias when the level of indebtedness is positive (negative).

Starting from a positive level of indebtedness, Fig. 13 plots the mix of short- and long-term debt as the economy transitions toward the stochastic steady-state. Calvo and Guidotti's (1992) debt aversion appears as the policymaker fairly rapidly reduces indebtedness in an attempt to eliminate the inflationary bias that debt induces. The fluctuations in debt induced by the changing spending regime are small relative to the general debt dynamics implied by the transition to steady state. The fact that the single-period debt does not rise dramatically when overall indebtedness increases implies that there is an effective lengthening of maturity as overall debt levels increase. This echoes the results of Calvo and Guidotti, which are also discussed in Missale (1999).

5. PRODUCTION ECONOMIES WITH OPTIMAL MONETARY AND FISCAL POLICIES

5.1 The Model

Until now our analysis of optimal policy has been based on a simple flexible price endowment economy, where we have captured the costs of inflation and distortionary taxation by adding quadratic terms in these variables to the policymaker's objective function. We now attempt to generalize these results by considering a production economy where households supply labor to imperfectly competitive firms who are subject to quadratic costs in changing prices as in Rotemberg (1982). The government levies a tax on sales to finance exogenous processes for transfers and government consumption. The policymaker aims to maximize the utility of the representative household. This section therefore endogenizes the welfare costs of both inflation and distortionary taxation. We also widen the scope for monetary and fiscal policy interactions because monetary policy not only generates revaluations of government bonds but also affects real debt service costs and the size of the tax base. Changes in distortionary taxation not only influence the government's budget identity, but they also affect production decisions and have a direct cost-push effect on inflation.

This basic setup is similar to that in Benigno and Woodford (2004) and Schmitt-Grohé and Uribe (2004) but with some differences.[ao] We model price stickiness using Rotemberg's (1996) adjustment costs rather than Calvo (1983) pricing because this reduces the number of state variables when solving the model nonlinearly. We also consider a richer maturity structure rather than single-period bonds.

5.1.1 Households

There is a continuum of households of size one. We assume complete asset markets so that through risk sharing households face the same budget constraint. The typical household seeks to maximize

$$E_0 \sum_{t=0}^{\infty} \beta^t \left(\frac{c_t^{1-\sigma}}{1-\sigma} - \frac{N_t^{1+\varphi}}{1+\varphi} \right)$$

where c and N are a consumption aggregate and labor supply, respectively. The consumption basket is made up of a continuum of differentiated products, $c_t = \left(\int_0^1 c(j)_t^{\epsilon-1/(\epsilon)} dj\right)^{\epsilon/(\epsilon-1)}$, and the basket of public consumption takes the same form.

The budget constraint at time t is given by

$$\int_0^1 P_t(j) c_t(j) dj + P_t^m B_t^m = \Pi_t + (1 + \rho P_t^m) B_{t-1}^m + W_t N_t + Z_t \tag{41}$$

where $P_t(j)$ is the price of variety j, Π is the representative household's share of profits in the imperfectly competitive firms (after tax), W are wages, and Z are lump-sum transfers and the bonds the household can invest in are the geometrically declining coupon bonds used above.

We maximize utility subject to the budget constraint (41) to obtain the optimal allocation of consumption across time and the associated pricing of declining coupon bonds

[ao] Leeper and Zhou (2013) study a linear-quadratic version of this setup.

$$\beta E_t\left[\left(\frac{c_t}{c_{t+1}}\right)^{\sigma}\left(\frac{P_t}{P_{t+1}}\right)(1+\rho P_{t+1}^m)\right]=P_t^m$$

Notice that when these reduce to single-period bonds, $\rho=0$, the price of these bonds is $P_t^m=R_t^{-1}$.

The second first-order condition relates to the labor supply decision

$$\left(\frac{W_t}{P_t}\right)=N_t^{\varphi}c_t^{\sigma}$$

5.1.2 Firms

Firms produce output using to a linear production function, $y(j)_t=AN(j)_t$, where $a_t=\ln(A_t)$ is time varying and stochastic, such that the real marginal costs of production are $mc_t=\frac{W_t}{P_tA_t}$. Household demand for their product is given by $y(j)_t=\left(\frac{P(j)_t}{P_t}\right)^{-\epsilon}y_t$ and firms are also subject to quadratic adjustment costs in changing prices

$$v_t^jP_t=\frac{\phi}{2}\left(\frac{p_t(j)}{\pi^*p_{t-1}(j)}-1\right)^2P_ty_t$$

where $\pi^*=1$ is the steady-state gross inflation rate. In a symmetric equilibrium where $p_t(j)=P_t$ the first-order condition for firms' profit maximization implies

$$(1-\theta)(1-\tau_t)+\theta mc_t-\phi\frac{\pi_t}{\pi^*}\left(\frac{\pi_t}{\pi^*}-1\right)+\phi\beta E_t\left(\frac{c_t}{c_{t+1}}\right)^{\sigma}\frac{\pi_{t+1}}{\pi^*}\frac{y_{t+1}}{y_t}\left(\frac{\pi_{t+1}}{\pi^*}-1\right)=0$$

which is the nonlinear version of the Phillips curve and includes the effects of a distortionary tax on sales revenues, τ_t.

5.1.3 Equilibrium

Goods market clearing requires, for each good j

$$y(j)_t=c(j)_t+g(j)_t+v(j)_t$$

which allows us to write

$$y_t\left[1-\frac{\phi}{2}\left(\frac{\pi_t}{\pi^*}-1\right)^2\right]=c_t+g_t$$

There is also market clearing in the bonds market where the longer term bond portfolio evolves according to the government's budget identity which we now describe.

5.1.4 Government Budget Identity

Combining the series of the representative consumer's flow budget constraints, (41), and noting the equivalence between factor incomes and national output, we obtain the government's flow budget identity

$$P_t^m b_t = (1+\rho P_t^m)\frac{b_{t-1}}{\pi_t} - y_t\tau_t + g_t - z_t$$

where real debt is defined as $b_t \equiv \frac{B_t^M}{P_t}$.

5.2 Commitment Policy in the New Keynesian Model

Setting up the Lagrangian

$$\begin{aligned} L_t &= E_0\sum_{t=0}^{\infty}\beta^t\left[\left(\frac{c_t^{1-\sigma}}{1-\sigma}-\frac{N_t^{1+\varphi}}{1+\varphi}\right)+\lambda_{1t}\left(y_t\left(1-\frac{\phi}{2}\left(\frac{\pi_t}{\pi^*}-1\right)^2\right)-c_t-g_t\right)\right.\\ &+\lambda_{2t}\left(\beta\left(\frac{c_t}{c_{t+1}}\right)^\sigma\left(\frac{P_t}{P_{t+1}}\right)(1+\rho P_{t+1}^m)-P_t^m\right)\\ &+\lambda_{3t}\left((1-\theta)(1-\tau_t)+\theta y_t^\varphi c_t^\sigma A_t^{-1-\varphi}-\phi\pi_t(\pi_t-1)+\phi\beta\left(\frac{c_t}{c_{t+1}}\right)^\sigma\pi_{t+1}\frac{y_{t+1}}{y_t}(\pi_{t+1}-1)\right)\\ &\left.+\lambda_{4t}\left(P_t^M b_t-(1+\rho P_t^M)\frac{b_{t-1}}{\pi_t}+y_t\tau_t-g_t-tr_t\right)\right] \end{aligned}$$

and differentiating with respect to $\{c_t, y_t, \tau_t, P_t^m, b_t^m, \pi_t\}$ yield the first-order conditions for the Ramsey program. Those conditions are sufficiently complex to afford little additional insight that was not already gained from the analysis of the comparable problem for our simple endowment economy. But when we solve the model numerically, several interesting results relating to the optimal monetary and fiscal policy mix emerge.

5.3 Numerical Results

The first experiment considers a transfers shock at different initial levels of debt (Fig. 14).[ap] Transfers start at 18% of GDP and then increase with an autocorrelated shock, but do not respond further to GDP. When, as in the first column, the initial debt level is zero the maturity structure of the debt issued after the shock has hit is irrelevant. There is an initial one-period burst in inflation caused by the rise in the tax rate and not fully offset by the tightening of monetary policy. Then a coordinated use of monetary and fiscal policy stabilizes debt at its new steady-state level. The tax rate does not jump immediately to its new steady state, but follows a dynamic path which captures the movement in the real interest rate in the sticky-price economy, while monetary policy ensures that inflation is zero outside of the initial period.

Moving to column 2, at a higher initial debt level radically different policy responses emerge that depend on debt levels and maturity structures. As in Leith and Wren-Lewis (2013) with single-period debt and a sufficiently high debt stock, the transfers shock

[ap] In all cases we solve the model nonlinearly under perfect foresight following an initial perturbation from the steady state.

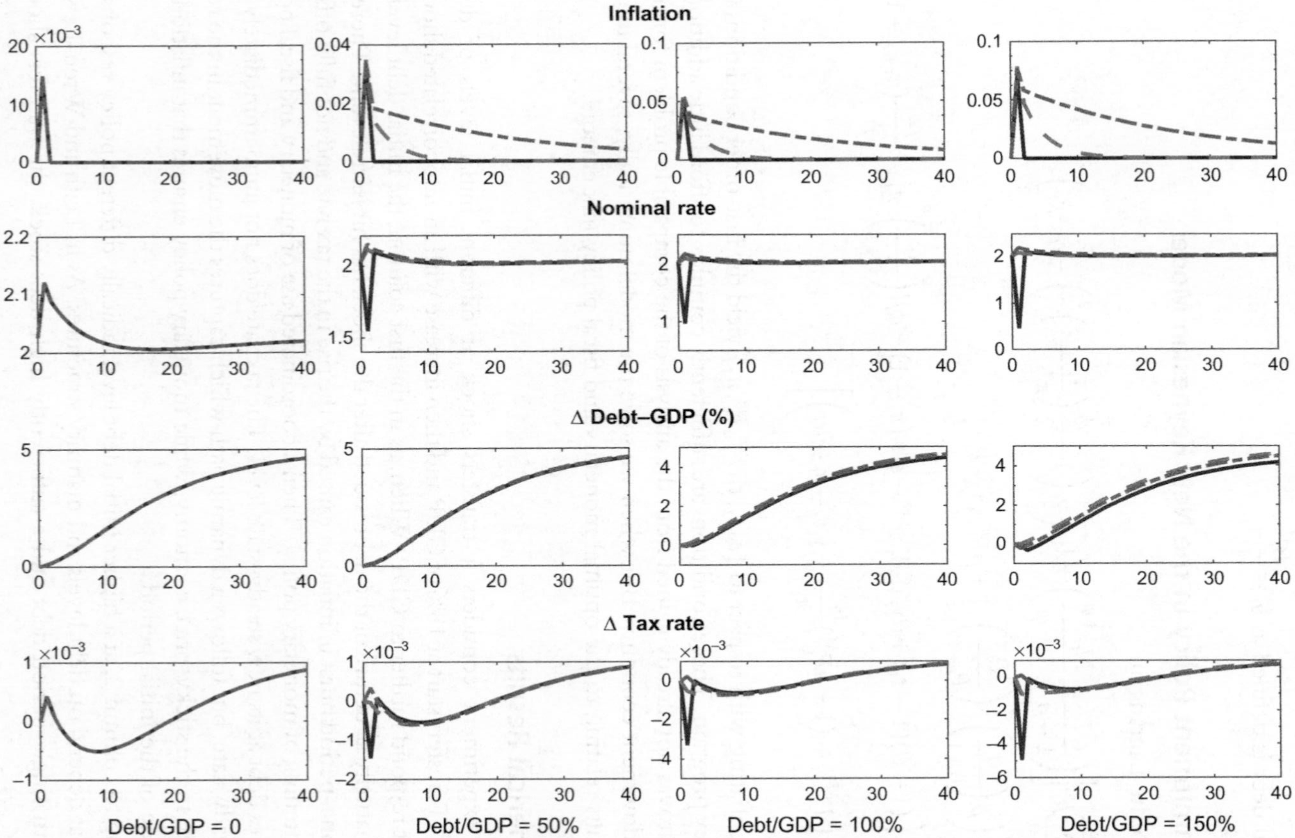

Fig. 14 Optimal policy response to higher transfers with different debt levels and maturities. 1-period debt (*solid lines*), 1-year debt (*dashed lines*), and 4-year debt (*dotted–dashed lines*).

results in the policymaker relaxing monetary policy to reduce debt service costs and fuel the initial burst in inflation. Monetary policy stabilizes the debt—just as in the fiscal theory—while tax rates fall to moderate the rise in inflation. Thereafter a combination of monetary and fiscal policy stabilizes the debt without generating any further inflation. When the debt is of longer term maturity (1 or 5 years), the initial policy response is quite different, with a tighter monetary policy and higher tax rates. The initial rise in inflation extends beyond the first period to help stabilize debt through reduced bond prices.

We now turn to the government spending shock in Fig. 15. The first column sets the initial tax rate at $\tau = 0.39$, sufficient to pay for both the initial value of transfers and public consumption, so there is no debt. In this case, as in the simple endowment economy, debt maturity does not matter and the policy response is the same regardless of the maturity of the debt. Unlike the endowment economy, there is surprise inflation, but this plays no direct role in stabilizing debt. Here the inflation reflects initial jumps in tax rates and interest rates that deliver the optimal balance between monetary and fiscal policy. There is a tax-smoothing jump in taxation that would fuel inflation, but which is offset by a tighter monetary policy that makes inflation zero after the initial period. As private consumption recovers, the tax rate rises, and ultimately there is a high tax rate to support an increased level of debt.

As we increase the initial level of debt, maturity structure generates differences in policy responses. As before, longer maturity delivers a smaller, but more sustained increase in inflation that stabilizes debt by reducing bond prices. But there are differences in the policy mix behind this result. When initial debt to GDP is just under 50%, with only single-period debt the policymaker actually cuts taxes to reduce the inflationary consequences of the government spending shock.

At higher initial debt, more radical differences in the policy mix arise across maturities. Sticky prices mean that not only surprises in the path of inflation influence debt dynamics: the policymaker can also influence real ex-ante interest rates and, through the Phillips curve, the size of the tax base. At a debt level near 100%, we observe a substantial fall in both tax rates and interest rates when debt is only single period. This amounts to a reversal of the conventional assignment of monetary and fiscal policy: monetary policy acts to stabilize debt by cutting real interest rates, while fiscal policy mitigates the inflationary consequences of this by reducing tax rates. For an average debt maturity of 5 years we retain the conventional assignment, with tax rates rising and monetary policy tightening to offset the rise in inflation that higher tax rates would generate.

5.4 An Independent Central Bank

Two key features of jointly optimal policy are worth highlighting. First, price-level control, which is typically a feature of optimal monetary policy in the new Keynesian model, is absent in the presence of fiscal policy and the associated tax-smoothing objective.

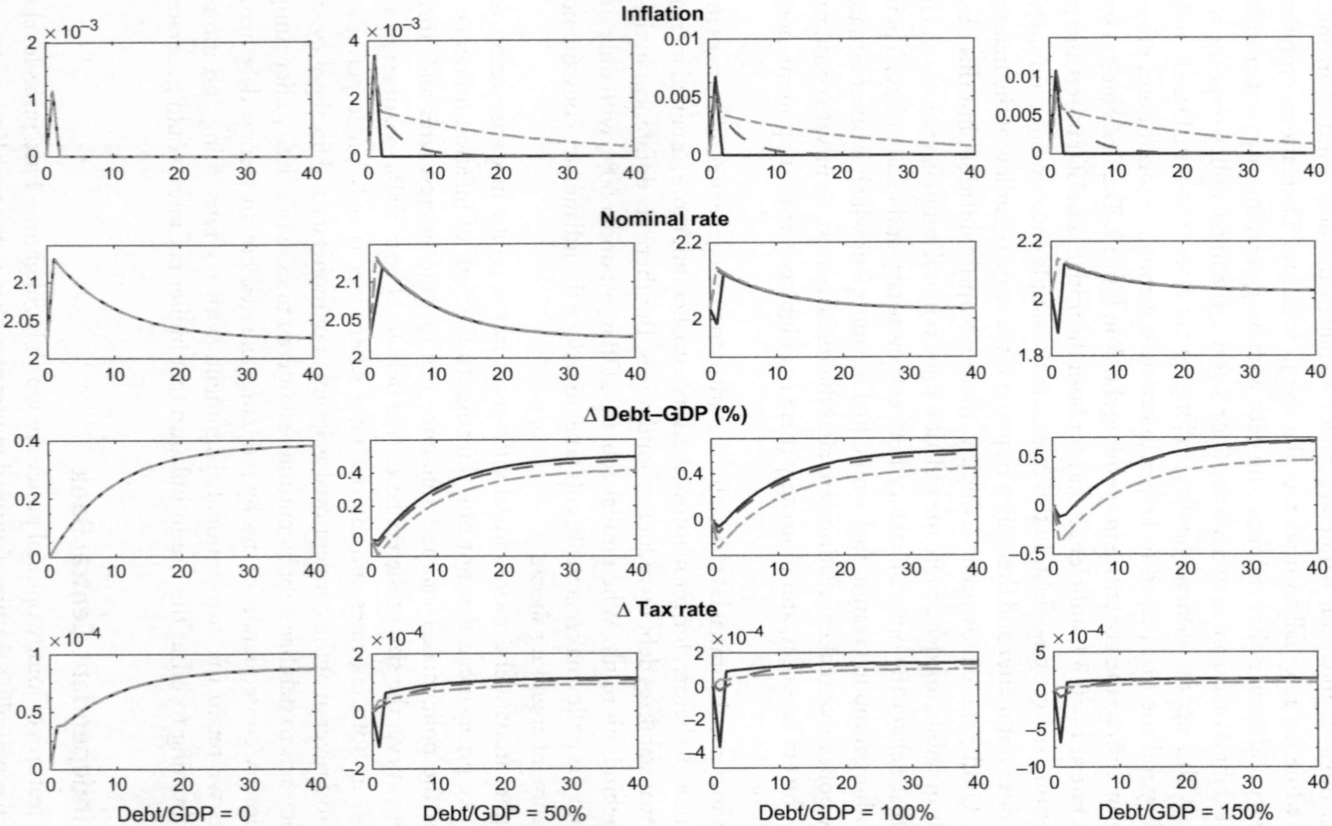

Fig. 15 Optimal policy response to an increase in government spending with different debt levels and maturities. 1-period debt (*solid lines*), 1-year debt (*dashed lines*), and 4-year debt (*dotted–dashed lines*).

Typical analyses have policymakers commit not only to return inflation to target after a shock hits but also to return the *price level* back to its preshock level. This commitment reduces inflation expectations and improves the trade-off between stabilization of inflation and the real economy. When fiscal policy enters the picture, the initial inflation becomes a desirable means of stabilizing debt through the revaluation effects that are a distinguishing feature of the fiscal theory.

Second, the policy mix depends on the size and maturity of government debt. With short maturity and high debt levels, optimal policy reverses the usual policy assignment—raising taxes and interest rates in the face of higher transfers or government consumption—and instead cuts interest rates to reduce debt interest dynamics and cuts taxes to offset the inflation that the relaxation in monetary policy would otherwise induce. Many economists would be uncomfortable with using monetary policy as a tool of fiscal stabilization in this way and would argue in favor of independent central banks to avoid this policy mix.

We assess the implications of independent monetary policy by deriving the optimal fiscal policy conditional on a given monetary policy rule. We assume that the central bank follows a simple Taylor rule with a coefficient on inflation of $\alpha_\pi = 1.5$. The fiscal authority faces the same optimization described earlier, but with the additional constraint that monetary policy follows this rule. Fig. 16 reports that the policy response to higher government spending exhibits some notable differences from the outcome when monetary and fiscal policies are jointly optimal. Inflation's increase is far more prolonged under an independent central bank. When monetary and fiscal policy operate cooperatively, even for the largest stock of debt we analyzed, inflation is less than half that observed when decoupling monetary from fiscal policy. This gives rise to the second surprising result. The active independent monetary policy results in the fiscal policymaker *cutting* rather than raising taxes in response to the government spending shock. The magnitude of the tax cut increases with the stock of debt, but does not vary much across maturities. Optimal fiscal policy counteracts the higher debt service costs that active monetary policy generates by cutting tax rates. This offsets the increase in inflation and under the policy rule mitigates the rise in real interest rates. Because this action is more important the higher the debt, the magnitude of the tax cuts increases with rising debt levels. Similar inflation paths across all debt levels imply that the value of longer maturity debt gets reduced through revaluation effects by more than the other maturities. This also has the implication that the spillovers from monetary policy shocks to the government's finances are likely to be greater at higher and longer maturity debt levels.

These results point to the ubiquity of a central feature of the fiscal theory—debt revaluation through surprise changes in inflation and bond prices. Whether policies are jointly optimal or optimal fiscal policy is constrained by an independent central bank, debt revaluation continues to characterize optimal policy behavior.

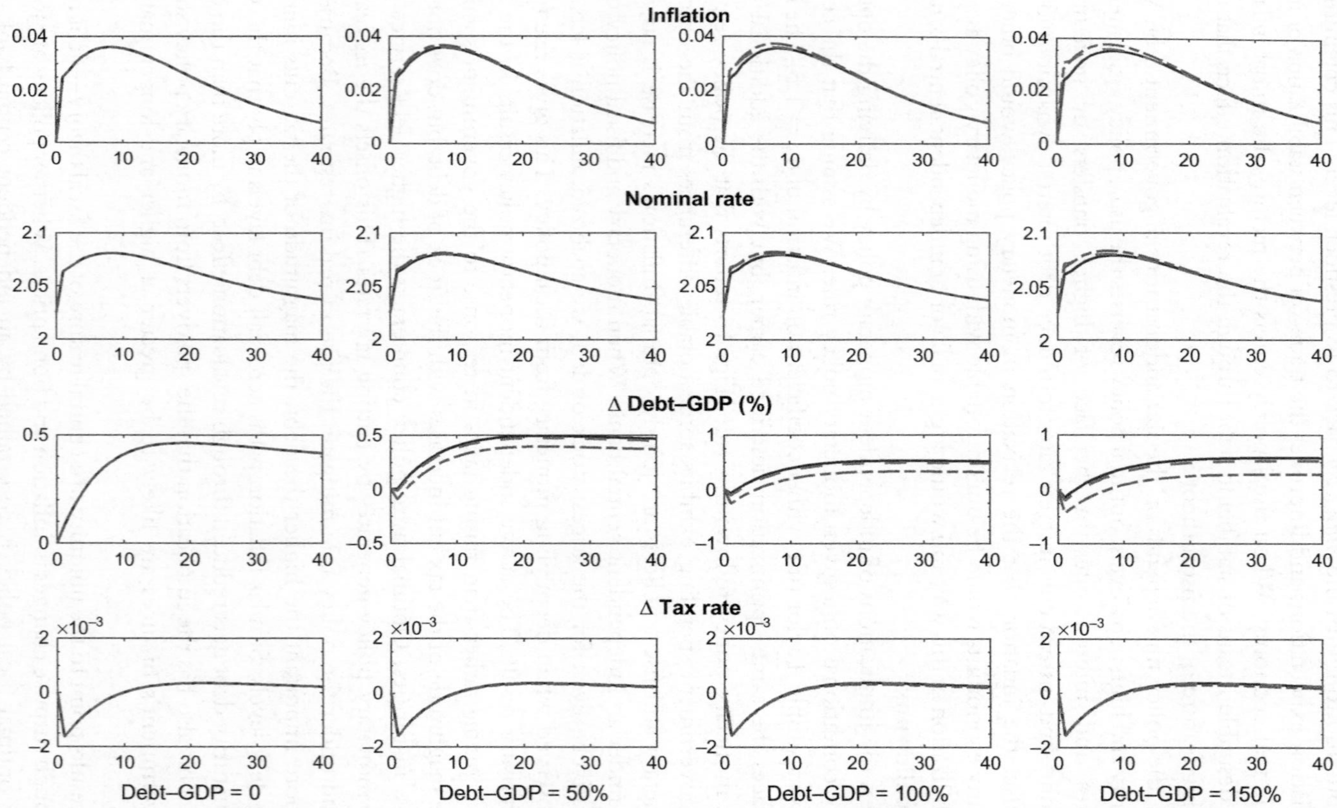

Fig. 16 Optimal fiscal policy response to an increase in government spending with an independent central bank. 1-period debt (*solid lines*), 1-year debt (*dashed lines*), and 4-year debt (*dotted–dashed lines*).

5.5 Discretion in the New Keynesian Economy

This subsection turns to optimal discretionary policy, following the setup in Leeper et al. (2015a). That setup employs a new Keynesian model in which the tax applies to labor income rather than sales revenue and government spending is treated as an endogenous policy instrument rather than an exogenous stream of purchases that need to be financed. There are no transfers. The policy under discretion is a set of decision rules for $\{c_t, y_t, \pi_t, b_t, \tau_t, g_t, P_t^M\}$ that maximize

$$V(b_{t-1}, A_t) = \max\left\{\frac{c_t^{1-\sigma}}{1-\sigma} + \chi\frac{g_t^{1-\sigma_g}}{1-\sigma_g} - \frac{(y_t/A_t)^{1+\varphi}}{1+\varphi} + \beta E_t[V(b_t, A_{t+1})]\right\}$$

subject to the resource constraint

$$y_t\left(1 - \frac{\phi}{2}\left(\frac{\pi_t}{\pi^*} - 1\right)^2\right) - c_t - g_t$$

the Phillips curve

$$(1-\epsilon) + \epsilon(1-\tau_t)^{-1} y_t^{\varphi} c_t^{\sigma} A_t^{-1-\varphi} - \phi\frac{\pi_t}{\pi^*}\left(\frac{\pi_t}{\pi^*} - 1\right) + \phi\beta c_t^{\sigma} y_t^{-1} E_t\left[c_{t+1}^{-\sigma}\frac{\pi_{t+1}}{\pi^*}\left(\frac{\pi_{t+1}}{\pi^*} - 1\right)\right] = 0$$

and the government's budget identity

$$\begin{aligned}
&\beta E_t\left[\left(\frac{c_t}{c_{t+1}}\right)^{\sigma}\left(\frac{P_t}{P_{t+1}}\right)\left(1 + \rho P_{t+1}^M\right)\right] b_t \\
&= \left\{1 + \rho\beta E_t\left[\left(\frac{c_t}{c_{t+1}}\right)^{\sigma}\left(\frac{P_t}{P_{t+1}}\right)\left(1 + \rho P_{t+1}^M\right)\right]\right\}\frac{b_{t-1}}{\pi_t} \\
&\quad - \left(\frac{\tau_t}{1-\tau_t}\right)\left(\frac{y_t}{A_t}\right)^{1+\varphi} c_t^{\sigma} + g_t
\end{aligned}$$

where we have used the bond-pricing equation to eliminate the current value of the portfolio of bonds.

Leeper et al. (2015a) solve the nonlinear system consisting of seven first-order conditions and the three constraints to yield the time-consistent optimal policy using the Chebyshev collocation method. In contrast to the case of commitment where steady-state inflation is zero, discretion implies a steady state with a mildly negative debt stock and a mild deflation. Fig. 17 shows that starting from high debt levels produces significant policy differences across differing bond maturities. These impulse responses reflect the time-consistent adjustment from a high debt level to the ultimate steady-state debt level, which is slightly negative. The most notable element in these dynamic paths is the very high levels of inflation. This inflation does not serve to reduce the real value of debt; instead, it reflects the state-dependent inflationary bias problem generated by high

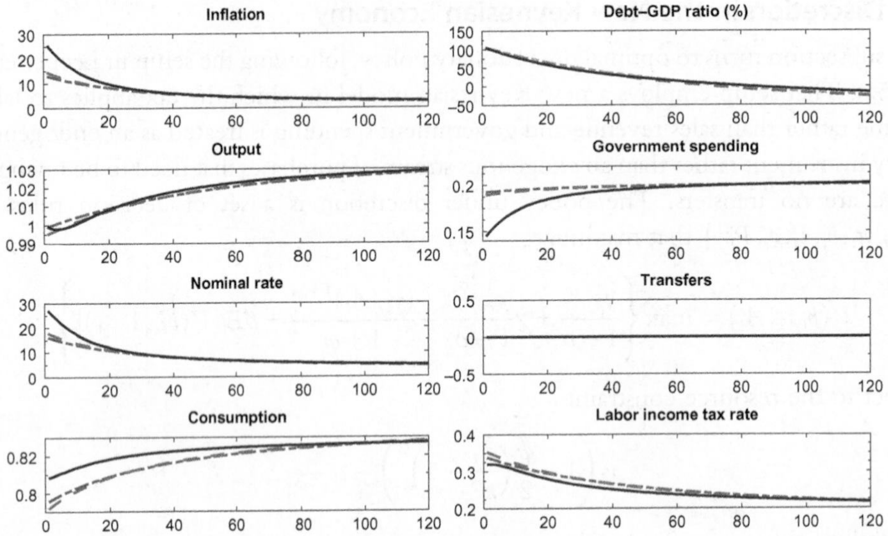

Fig. 17 New Keynesian model under discretionary policy. 1-year debt (*solid lines*), 5-year debt (*dashed lines*), and 8-year debt (*dotted–dashed lines*).

debt levels. When debt levels are raised, the policymaker faces a temptation to use surprise inflation or surprise reductions in bond prices to reduce the real value of government debt. Knowing this, economic agents raise their inflationary expectations until this temptation is no longer present. At empirically plausible debt levels, this temptation is very strong and very high rates of inflation are required to ensure the policy remains time consistent. The shorter the debt maturity, the greater the temptation to inflate and reduce debt levels quickly—what we label "the debt stabilization bias." The steady-state economy eventually achieves a small negative long-run optimal value for debt and a slight undershooting of the inflation target. This falls far short of the accumulated level of assets that would be needed to finance government consumption and eliminate tax and other distortions.

6. EMPIRICAL CONSIDERATIONS

The chapter's emphasis to this point reflects the bulk of the literature on the fiscal theory in its theoretical focus. This section discusses a set of empirical considerations that arise from work on monetary and fiscal interactions. First, we briefly explain why it is difficult to distinguish whether time series data were generated by regime M or by regime F. Then we turn to both reduced form and structural evidence about the prevailing policy regime, including work on regime-switching policies. We end the section by clarifying some common misperceptions about the nature of equilibrium under regime F.

6.1 Distinguishing Regimes M and F

It is well established that regimes M and F can generate equivalent (or nearly equivalent) equilibrium processes. Cochrane (1999) discusses this point and Woodford's (1999) comments on Cochrane's paper elaborate on the issue in some detail. Leeper and Walker (2013) display a simple theoretical example in which the two regimes are observationally equivalent.

Observational equivalence of the two regimes may be surprising. After all, Sections 2 and 3 went to great length to show that monetary and fiscal disturbances produce strikingly different dynamic responses in the two regimes. To understand the equivalence, consider the linearized new Keynesian model that Section 3.1 describes. That model's economic state in period t is the triple $X_t \equiv (\varepsilon_t^M, \varepsilon_t^F, \hat{b}_{t-1})$ and in regime M, each endogenous variable—including the policy variables $\hat{R}_t$ and $\hat{s}_t$—is a linear function of X_t in equilibrium. But those mappings from X_t to the policy variables are consistent with regime F policy behavior: the interest rate depends only on ε_t^M and the surplus depends on ε_t^F.[aq]

Some critics argue that this equivalence result renders the fiscal theory "untestable" and therefore empirically vacuous. Naturally, *equivalence* implies that the conventional view—regime M—is also "untestable." But the critics' nihilism is unwarranted. Observational equivalence merely implies that *in the absence of identifying restrictions* it is impossible to discern which regime produced observed data. But this is nearly a truism. No set of simple correlations—among debt, deficits, inflation, and interest rates—can tell us whether the underlying policy behavior comes from regime M or regime F.[ar]

Yet correlation-based "tests" of the fiscal theory abound in the literature. Canzoneri et al. (2001b) argue that if a positive shock to surpluses both raises future surpluses and lowers the real value of government debt, regime M prevails; if the positive surplus shock raises the value of debt, then regime F prevails. Cochrane (1999) succinctly explains why this is not a "test" of regime. Like any asset, government debt has both a "backward-looking" and a "forward-looking" representation. Let $b_t \equiv B_t/P_t$ denote the real market value of debt. Debt's law of motion—the budget identity—yields the backward view

$$b_{t+1} = r_{t+1}(b_t - s_t)$$

where $r_{t+1} \equiv R_t P_t / P_{t+1}$ is ex-post real return on bonds between t and $t+1$ and s_t is the primary surplus at t. Higher s_t seems to imply a lower value for debt at $t+1$. But the forward view, which determines the asset value of debt yields

[aq] If the economy starts with an initial level of debt, the $\{\hat{s}_t\}$ process must be chosen to be consistent with that level.

[ar] Much of the evidence that Friedman and Schwartz (1963a,b) compiled in favor of the quantity theory sought to show that erratic monetary policy drove nominal income movements. But that evidence came from efforts to *identify* "exogenous" or "autonomous" changes in the money stock, as Sims (1972) later showed. Friedman and Schwartz recognized that reduced form correlations alone cannot establish causality.

$$b_t = E_t \sum_{j=0}^{\infty} \left(\frac{1}{r}\right)^j s_{t+j} \tag{42}$$

to suggest that a persistent increase in surpluses raises the value of debt.[as] Evidently, manipulations of identities do not impose enough structure to distinguish between regimes.

A second branch of the correlation-based "testing" literature follows Bohn (1998) in using limited information techniques to estimate

$$s_t = \gamma b_{t-1} + \delta' Z_t + \varepsilon_t^F \tag{43}$$

where s_t is the primary surplus at t, b_{t-1} is the real value of government debt at $t-1$, Z_t is a vector of control variables, and ε_t^F is a possibly serially correlated disturbance. This line of work interprets estimates of (43) as descriptions of fiscal policy behavior.[at] When $\hat{\gamma} > 0$, researchers infer that fiscal behavior is passive, while if $\hat{\gamma} >$ net real interest rate, fiscal policy reacts sufficiently to stabilize debt. Based on such estimates, researchers conclude the economy resides in regime M, so the fiscal theory does not apply.[au]

Missing from this analysis is the bond valuation equation, which is an equilibrium condition that holds regardless of the prevailing policy regime. As condition (42) makes clear, b_{t-1} must be positively correlated with future surpluses *in any equilibrium*. When (43) is estimated without imposing this equilibrium condition, estimates of γ are subject to simultaneous equations bias.

Leeper and Li (2015) use a linearized variant on the endowment economy in Section 2 to study the nature of the simultaneity bias. If the policy disturbance is serially uncorrelated or a lagged dependent variable is added to the regression in (43), then the limited information procedure is valid only if the underlying monetary and fiscal policies are in regime M. Serious biases can arise when data are equilibria in regime F. The sign and severity of bias in $\hat{\gamma}$ depend on monetary policy behavior: the weaker is the reaction of monetary policy to inflation, the stronger is the positive bias. In periods like the aftermath of the 2008 financial crisis, when central banks pegged the nominal interest rate, estimates of γ are more likely to imply a strong response of surpluses to debt. This finding is consistent with Bohn's (1998) estimates, which rarely find evidence that the surplus response is weak.

There are two natural solutions to the simultaneous equations bias. The first is to impose the bond valuation equation on estimates of the fiscal rule, as Chung and

[as] For convenience, (42) assumes a constant real return.

[at] See, for example, Mendoza and Ostry (2008). Ghosh et al. (2012) employ such estimates to compute a country's "fiscal space." Woodford (1999) raises issues with this interpretation.

[au] Canzoneri et al. (2001b) estimate an unrestricted bivariate VAR for the primary surplus and the real value of debt, a technique that is equivalent to estimating a version of (43).

Leeper (2007) and Hur (2013) do in a structural VAR, and estimate monetary and fiscal rules jointly. The second solution is to estimate a fully specified DSGE model.

6.2 Some Suggestive Empirical Evidence

A complete account of empirical evidence about policy regime is beyond the scope of this chapter, so we will briefly recount two kinds of evidence that regime F has prevailed in some historic periods. The first is suggestive evidence that points to empirical facts that are consistent with regime F; then we turn to more formal econometric analysis.

Cochrane (1999) was the first to suggest that U.S. post-World War II inflation could be interpreted through the lens of the fiscal theory. He stresses that readily available fiscal data do not line up well with the theoretical concepts and constructs a data series for the real market value of government debt, from which he infers two different real primary surplus series. Not surprisingly, substantial differences emerge between the primary surplus and conventionally measured surplus (inclusive of debt service), particularly in periods of high debt or high interest rates. He further contrasts his computed surplus series with the Treasury's reported net-of-interest surplus, which does not account for capital gains and losses incurred from bond transactions. Cochrane's calculations make the broad methodological point that scrutiny of regime F equilibria requires careful data construction.

But Cochrane's substantive contribution lies in interpreting the data correlations. He specifies an exogenous—regime F—process for primary surpluses from which he computes the real value of debt as the present value of those artificial surpluses. Processes are chosen to match correlations in the data. Simulations produce observed gross movements in post-war U.S. inflation when the equilibrium price-level sequence emerges from the debt valuation equation.[av] As it happens, the chosen processes would pass either the Bohn (1998) or the Canzoneri et al. (2001b) "test" that those authors claim refutes the fiscal theory. Cochrane's analysis illustrates the difficulties in distinguishing between regimes M and F.[aw]

Woodford (2001) argues that Federal Reserve policy from before World War II until the Treasury-Fed Accord in March 1951 is a clear example in which monetary policy was explicitly assigned the task of maintaining the value of government debt, as it is in regime F. Beginning in April 1942, as Woodford writes

[av] Shim (1984) is an early effort to use VAR analysis to find cross-country evidence of a link between fiscal deficit innovations and inflation.

[aw] Cochrane (2011b) uses the government debt valuation condition to interpret monetary and fiscal policy actions in the wake of the 2008 global recession. He argues that recent policy developments suggest that in coming years the equilibrium condition is likely to have a stronger influence on economies than it has in the past.

> *The yield on ninety-day Treasury bills was pegged at 3/8 of a percent; this peg was maintained through June 1947, and … until that point the price of bills was completely fixed, as the Treasury offered both to buy and sell bills at that price. An intention was also announced of supporting one-year Treasury certificates at a price corresponding to a 7/8 percent annual yield; this policy continued after 1947, though at a slightly higher yield. Finally, the prices of twenty-five-year Treasury bonds were supported at a price corresponding to a 2 and 1/2 percent annual yield; this price floor was maintained up until the time of the "Accord."*
>
> **(Woodford, 2001, pp. 672–673)**

Woodford, however, seems to regard regime F as the exception, arising during wartime and in special circumstances when monetary policy is subordinated to fiscal needs.

Loyo (1999) uses Brazil in the late 1970s and the early 1980s as an example where the fiscal consequences of monetary policy led to explosive inflation. His case does not fall into either of the two regimes in which a determinate bounded equilibrium exists. Instead, Loyo argues that a combination of active fiscal policy and active monetary policy that aggressively sought to combat inflation by raising interest rates strongly in response to inflation produced exactly the phenomenon that Section 3.2.2 describes. Higher interest rates raised bondholders' interest receipts which, in the absence of commensurately higher taxes, raised wealth and aggregate demand. Higher demand increased inflation still further, to which monetary policy responded by raising interest rates, setting off an explosive cycle that produced double-digit inflation rates *per month*. Importantly, this hyperinflation arose with no appreciable change in real seigniorage revenues, as Loyo documents. Loyo's work illustrates a theme that runs through the chapter. If fiscal behavior is active, refusing to raise surpluses to stabilize government debt, more aggressive inflation fighting by the central bank exacerbates the problem: when monetary policy is passive, it amplifies shocks more as it becomes more active; if it is active, those shocks lead to ever-increasing inflation. An alternative monetary policy rule—one that merely pegged the nominal interest rate, for example—would have prevented the explosive inflation.

As of 2015, Brazil may be poised to rerun the experience that Loyo describes. Brazil's 1988 Constitution mandates that government benefits are indexed to inflation, effectively putting 90% of expenditures out of the legislature's reach. With sizeable tax adjustments apparently politically unviable, the gross-of-interest budget deficit reached over 10% of GDP in 2015. Consumer price inflation rose steadily through the year to breach double digits by year-end, despite the Banco Central do Brasil's aggressive antiinflationary efforts that raised the policy interest rate to 14.25% in the second half of 2015 (Banco Central do Brasil, 2015). As *The Economist* (2016) put it: "Fiscal dominance has left arcane discussions among economic theorists and burst onto newspaper columns." As in the period that Loyo studies, rising inflation is driven by the combination of active fiscal behavior and single-minded inflation targeting by the central bank. Coupling that fiscal behavior with passive monetary policy, as in regime F, would not generate explosive inflation rates.

Another recurring theme of the chapter's theory is that debt revaluation effects are a ubiquitous feature of both ad hoc and optimal policy rules. Sims (2013) calculates that since 1960 the surprise gains and losses on U.S. government debt as a percentage of GDP are similar in magnitude to the fluctuations in the deficit relative to GDP: debt revaluations are an important aspect of monetary–fiscal dynamics.[ax] Similarly, Akitoby et al. (2014) calculate that there would be substantial reductions in debt-to-GDP ratios for several developed economies from raising inflation targets to 6%. But Hilscher et al. (2014) argue that it is important to account for the maturity structure of the debt which is actually held by the private sector when undertaking such calculations, concluding that for the United States this may be lower than the maturity of the overall debt stock. Sections 4.4 and 5.3 found that the efficacy of using revaluation effects as a tool of optimal policy increases with both the size and the maturity of the outstanding debt stock. This suggests that the recent increase in debt-to-GDP ratios in most advanced economies raises the likelihood that such revaluation effects may become an increasingly important feature of policy. This does not establish that revaluation effects of the magnitude that Sims reports can come only from regime F-style policies. Instead, it points toward an important source of fiscal financing that formal macro models must confront.

6.3 Some Formal Empirical Evidence

Sims (1998) argues that to assess which part of the policy space—regime M or F—is empirically relevant, it is essential to embed alternative descriptions of policy within a general equilibrium model before taking them to the data. This leads to a more direct attack on the empirical problem of discerning policy regime, as well as the possibility of "testing" which regime is most consistent with observed data.

Leeper and Sims (1994) is an early attempt to estimate a DSGE model with a complete specification of monetary and fiscal policy. Real and nominal rigidities made the analogs to regimes M and F lie in a complicated geometry and the numerical search algorithm had to traverse regions of the parameter space in which either no equilibrium exists or the equilibrium is indeterminate—both cases where the likelihood function is not defined. These difficulties prevented the paper from reaching a conclusion about which policy combination yielded the best fit.[ay]

Bayesian estimation methods have permitted researchers to overcome some of the limitations of earlier work to make progress on the question of the prevailing regime. Expanding on the money-only specification of Smets and Wouters (2007), the models

[ax] See also Taylor (1995), King (1995), and Hall and Sargent (2011) for discussions of and estimates of revaluation effects.

[ay] Leeper (1989) is an even earlier effort that uses a calibrated DSGE model to ask whether impulse response functions from regime M or regime F best match empirical responses. When agents are endowed with foresight about future fiscal actions, there is weak evidence in favor of regime F.

fill in fiscal details and impose the government's budget identity to estimate monetary and fiscal behavior jointly with private behavior. Traum and Yang (2011) impose priors that are centered on either regime M or regime F for various subperiods of U.S. data from 1955 to 2007 and find that the data least prefer the parameter space associated with regime F.

Using a simpler new Keynesian model, but with a maturity structure for government bonds, Tan (2014) argues that rejection of regime F stems from a test procedure that Geweke (2010) calls the "strong interpretation." The strong interpretation takes literally all the cross-equation restrictions of a fully specified dynamic general equilibrium model, which necessarily includes any and all possible sources of misspecification. When Tan employs the methods that DeJong et al. (1996) and Del Negro and Schorfheide (2004) developed, which take the DSGE model as a prior for a VAR, he finds that data no longer strongly prefer regime M. Tan argues that tests of model fit that are robust to misspecification no longer find compelling support for one regime over the other.

Leeper et al. (2015b) estimate medium-scale models that include additional fiscal details—government consumption that may complement or substitute for private consumption, a maturity structure for government debt, explicit rules for several fiscal instruments, and steady-state distorting taxes. For U.S. data covering 1955–2014, even under the strong interpretation, marginal data densities suggest nearly equivalent fits under the two regimes for the full sample and for pre- and post-Volcker subsamples. Details of model specification are as important as policy rules for determining the relative fit of the two regimes.

That paper also reports estimated revaluation effects that arise from government spending expansions that are initially financed by selling debt (partially reproduced in Table 4). These are analogous to the first two columns in Table 2, but the estimated model also includes many other sources of financing—capital, labor and consumption

Table 4 Reports 90% credible intervals around posterior modes

	% due to $\hat{\pi}_t$	% due to $\hat{P}_t^m$
1955q1–2014q2		
Regime M	[0.3,0.6]	[8.2,13.6]
Regime F	[0.5,0.8]	[11.8,17.0]
1955q1–1979q4		
Regime M	[−0.3,0.3]	[0.7,12.7]
Regime F	[0.6,1.2]	[18.4,29.9]
1982q1–2007q4		
Regime M	[0.1,0.4]	[7.3,14.2]
Regime F	[0.1,0.9]	[13.2,22.9]

"% due to" are the ratios of the analogs to the right-hand components of (38) to ξ_t, which are computed from the impulse response to a shock to government spending.
Source: Leeper, E.M., Traum, N., Walker, T.B., 2015b. Clearing up the fiscal multiplier morass. NBER Working Paper No. 21433, July.

tax revenues, real interest rates, government transfers, and endogenous government spending. Over the full sample and the post-Volcker subsample, the 90% credible intervals display substantial overlap for both inflation and bond prices, suggesting no large differences in revaluation effects in the two regime. Intervals do not overlap in the pre-Volcker period, with larger revaluation effects in regime F for both components.

Both the theory in this chapter and the empirical evidence just cited make clear that revaluation effects that stabilize the value of government bonds are not solely the preserve of regime F. Even in the endowment economy with policy described by simple rules in Section 2, monetary policy and government spending shocks both induce revaluation effects in the two policy regimes. Optimal policy exercises show that it is desirable to use a combination of surprise inflation and tax smoothing to stabilize the economy in the face of fiscal shocks, blurring the lines between the M and F regimes. Such exercises also suggest that the balance between inflationary and fiscal financing is also highly state dependent. In richer production economies subject to nominal inertia, the range of monetary and fiscal policy interactions is far wider: monetary and fiscal policy jointly determine the extent to which there are inflation surprises, movements in real interest rates and bond prices and changes in the tax base. The relative magnitudes of these effects, though, depend on the nature of the policy regime and on the level and maturity of the debt stock.

6.4 Regime-Switching Policies

A growing body of work estimates Markov-switching policy rules and embeds them in otherwise conventional DSGE models. Davig and Leeper (2006) find recurring switches between active and passive monetary and fiscal rules, with some periods in which both policies are active or passive. In a rational expectations model in which agents are endowed with knowledge of the policy process, no single monetary–fiscal mix determines the nature of the equilibrium. Instead, expectations of future policy regimes spill-over to affect the current equilibrium. In a new Keynesian model with lump-sum taxes, Davig and Leeper show that even if regime M currently prevails, a tax cut can produce quantitatively important increases in output and the price level. The effects are still larger conditional on being in regime F.

Gonzalez-Astudillo (2013) uses limited information Bayesian methods to estimate a new Keynesian model with monetary and fiscal policy rules whose coefficients are time varying and interdependent. He finds that monetary policy switches more frequently than fiscal policy—a result that contrasts with findings from Markov-switching models—and that the policies are interdependent. But other findings align closely to models with recurring Markov switching: a monetary contraction reduces inflation in the short run, but raises it over longer horizons; lump-sum tax changes always affect output and inflation.

Kliem et al. (2016) find some provocative reduced-form support for time-varying fiscal effects. Using U.S. data from 1900 to 2011, they discovered that the low-frequency correlation between inflation and the fiscal stance—defined as the ratio of primary deficits to government debt—is significantly positive most of the time until 1980 when it becomes zero. They attribute the shift in correlation to a change in monetary policy behavior.

Those authors extend their analysis in Kliem et al. (2015) to include Germany and Italy and to interpret their findings with an estimated DSGE model. Germany never exhibits a significant low-frequency correlation between fiscal stance and inflation, while in Italy the correlation is positive until the Banca d' Italia gained its independence in the 1990s.

Bianchi (2012) and Bianchi and Ilut (2014) estimate a simple new Keynesian model with fiscal policy, habits, and inflation inertia and that also allows for switches in monetary and fiscal policy rules. Bianchi permits a circular movement across three regimes where policy can transition from the conventional assignment (active monetary policy/passive fiscal policy) through the fiscal theory assignment of passive monetary/active fiscal policy, to an unstable regime where both monetary and fiscal policy are active. He finds that the 1960s and 1970s featured a combination of passive monetary and active fiscal policy, before the Volcker disinflation resulted in a combination of active monetary and fiscal policies. Only around 1990 did fiscal policy turn passive. Bianchi and Ilut model a slightly different set of policy transitions that allows the two stable regimes (active monetary/passive fiscal and passive monetary/active fiscal) to briefly transition through the unstable, doubly active, regime. In their estimates, regime F prevails until before monetary policy turns active in 1979 and fiscal policy turns passive shortly afterward (by 1982). These papers suggest that regime M, though not always in place historically, has been the predominant regime in the United States from at least the early 1990s until the financial crisis.

Chen et al. (2015) build on this work in two ways. First, they allow additional permutations of policy in which monetary and fiscal policy may be simultaneously passive and they make the nature of transitions across regimes less restrictive. Their estimates find that the switch to regime M after the Volcker disinflation is far less certain, with both monetary and fiscal policy repeatedly falling outside regime M, even in the recent data.

Second, Chen et al. move away from ad hoc rules for policy to permit monetary and, in some exercises, fiscal policy to be chosen optimally. Monetary policy turns out to be both optimal and time-consistent, but with switches in the degree of anti-inflation conservatism. Those switches imply that monetary policy was not only less conservative in the 1970s, but also intermittently during the 1960s and briefly after the financial market turmoil from the stock market crash of 1987, the Russian default in 1998, and the dot-com crash. At the same time, fiscal policy can rarely be described as optimal (except in the early 1990s), and instead tends to move between an active and passive rule. For the bulk of the period between 1954 and the 2008 financial crisis, fiscal policy was primarily active with the only sustained periods of passive fiscal policy from the late 1950s until the late 1960s, between 1995 and 2000, and briefly between 2005 and the financial crisis. These estimates imply that regime M is the exception rather than the norm.

More subtle findings in Chen et al. emerge from examining the roles of the maturity structure and the level of debt in determining optimal policy. Sections 4.4 and 5.3 found that the Ramsey plan does resemble regime M in periods when debt levels are low and maturity is long: monetary policy was tightened to stabilize inflation in the face of a government spending shock, while tax rates were raised to stabilize debt. But as debt levels rise, especially when maturity is short, policy assignments get reversed: monetary policy responds weakly to higher inflation from increased government spending to reduce debt service costs and stabilize debt, while tax rates are cut to stabilize inflation. In contrast, under the institutional design of policy with an independent central bank that follows an active Taylor rule, the Ramsey policy actually cuts taxes in the face of the same government spending shock, reducing inflation and offsetting the increase in debt service costs that active monetary policy induces. Despite this anti-inflationary policy on the part of the fiscal policymaker, the equilibrium rate of inflation when the central bank was independent is an order of magnitude higher than when monetary and fiscal policy were jointly optimal. Evidently, the nature of the policy interactions in theory is complex and state contingent, as it appears to be in the empirical regime-switching literature.

Empirical evidence and optimal policy argue that regime M is not the only relevant monetary–fiscal policy mix. Interactions between monetary and fiscal policy are both pervasive and changeable. Understanding the nature of the policy dynamics—both the interactions between monetary and fiscal authorities and the political conflict that drives fiscal policy choices—is likely to be critical to identifying and understanding the evolution of observed policy regimes.

6.5 Common Misperceptions

Economists generally agree that historical episodes of high and volatile inflation rates inevitably have fiscal roots. Building on Sargent and Wallace's (1981) unpleasant monetarist arithmetic logic, Sargent (1986) makes a forceful historical case for hyperinflation's fiscal roots. The association between fiscal dominance—exogenous primary surpluses in Sargent and Wallace—and rampant inflation outcomes is so ingrained that many macroeconomists also believe that regime F fiscal behavior—a weak response of surpluses to debt—necessarily produces bad economic performance.[az]

That belief is unfounded. Bad economic policies can produce bad economic outcomes in any policy regime. And regime F is no more susceptible to undesirable

[az] Cochrane (2005) and Leeper and Walker (2013) give detailed descriptions of how the fiscal theory differs from unpleasant monetarist arithmetic.

equilibria than any other monetary–fiscal mix. Both the theoretical and the empirical results we have reviewed underscore this point.

Fiscal dominance can produce explosive inflation, as Loyo (1999) argues happened in Brazil. But explosiveness is the outgrowth of monetary behavior that is incompatible with fiscal dominance. When fiscal policy is active, ever-increasing inflation arises when the central bank aggressively raises the policy interest rate in a misguided effort to combat inflation. The active fiscal behavior transforms higher interest rates into more rapid growth in nominal government debt, higher aggregate demand, and higher inflation.

Perhaps ironically, Cochrane (2011a), Sims (2013), and Del Negro and Sims (2015) argue that many of the monetary anomalies in the theoretical literature arise primarily because money-only analyses trivialize the role that fiscal policy can play in delivering stable price-level behavior. Those anomalies include Obstfeld and Rogoff's (1983) speculative hyperinflations and Benhabib et al.'s (2002) deflationary traps. Fiscal policy can rule out both cases by adopting behavior that deviates in some fashion from typical regime M fiscal behavior. To eliminate hyperinflations, surpluses need to rise proportionately to excess inflation outside inflation's target range.[ba] To ensure that the economy will not get mired in a deflationary trap, fiscal policy must commit to running deficits or shrinking primary surpluses until inflation reaches its target. Both of these policy functions make fiscal choices explicitly contingent on inflation outcomes.

Monetary policy alone is powerless to eliminate these undesirable equilibria. Ruling out those equilibria requires fiscal policy to deviate from purely passive behavior that centers entirely on debt stabilization.

Skeptics who question whether the economic mechanisms in regime F have ever been observed point to instances in which government debt has grown rapidly, while inflation has been low and steady as *prima facie* evidence that inflation is solely a monetary phenomenon. But this criticism is akin to treating the income velocity of money as constant and finding cases where monetary expansions were not followed by higher nominal spending.

Consider the U.S. experience in the aftermath of the financial crisis. Nominal government debt grew from \$4.4 trillion to \$10.6 trillion from December 2007 and December 2014, a growth rate of 240% that raised the debt–GDP ratio from 30.5% to 61.0%.[bb] Despite this massive growth in debt, U.S. consumer price inflation averaged 1.9% between 2008 and 2014. With the Federal Reserve pegging the federal funds rate near zero from December 2008 onward, monetary policy behavior appears to have been

[ba] Cochrane (2011a) points out that hyperinflations do not violate any equilibrium conditions, so they are perfectly reasonable equilibria. They are also likely to be welfare reducing and undesirable.

[bb] These numbers come from the Federal Reserve Bank of Dallas's privately held gross federal debt and the U.S. Department of Commerce's annual nominal GDP data. Congressional Budget Office (2015) reports that federal debt held by the public rose from 35% to 74% over the same period.

passive, as in regime F. But the theory in this chapter predicts that if the debt expansion is not associated with higher taxes, private-sector wealth increases, raising aggregate demand and inflation. Where is the inflation that the fiscal theory predicts?

Like constant velocity, simple expositions of the fiscal theory serve pedagogical purposes, but severely constrain the theory's empirical predictions. Missing from the simple theory is that debt's value derives from the *present value* of expected surpluses and that the present value also depends on the expected path of real discount rates. Real interest rates have been decidedly negative in the United States. Kiley (2015) estimates that the real federal funds rate was negative from the onset of the recession through the middle of 2015. Even yields on 5-year Treasury inflation-indexed securities were negative or hovering around zero from September 2010 through 2015, reaching a nadir of −1.47% in October 2012. To the extent that these low rates flowed into real discount rates applied to government debt, the expected present value of surpluses was very high indeed over this period, even in the absence of any anticipated increases in primary surpluses. And along with the low real interest rates that the Federal Reserve sought to achieve, the crisis brought a flight to quality in which investors fled from nongovernment-insured asset classes to government securities, which drove down real treasury bond yields.

Any demand stimulus created by the nominal debt expansion would be offset, at least in part, by the increase in the value of debt that low real discount rates induce. It would take a careful quantitative analysis to make this case convincingly, but we see no a priori refutation of regime F from these observations.

If anything, the logic of the fiscal theory may help to explain the anomaly of why inflation did not fall *as much* as conventional money-only models predicted. The lack of persistent deflation during the recent recession caused some prominent economists to question the validity of conventional Phillips curve models where inflation is driven by measures of economic slack.[bc] Del Negro et al. (2015) argue that conventional models with a new Keynesian Phillips curve can account for the lack of deflation despite a large negative output gap provided prices are sufficiently sticky and inflation expectations remain anchored at positive levels. In their model, the anchoring comes from the anticipation that monetary policy will achieve future rates of inflation that are close to target. An alternative hypothesis is that expectations of future inflationary financing of the large increases in government debt are providing the necessary anchor.

A second canonical example thrown up by skeptics is Japan. Since 1993, Japanese government debt has risen from 75% to 230% of GDP, while inflation has averaged a mere 0.21%. For 20 years beginning in 1995, the Bank of Japan's overnight call rate has been below 0.5% and at 0.1% or lower for more than 12 of those years. Evidently, Japanese monetary policy has been passive. Once again, where is the inflation that the fiscal theory predicts?

[bc] For example, Hall (2011) and Ball and Mazumder (2011).

Japan is a complicated case. Real interest rates have been low, just as in the United States recently, but there is more to the story.[bd] Japan is the poster child for inconsistency in macroeconomic policies, as Krugman (1998), Ito (2006), Ito and Mishkin (2006), and Hausman and Wieland (2014) document. Fiscal policies have see-sawed between stimulus and austerity. Even as Prime Minister Abe appeared to announce an end to the inconsistency and Japanese economic activity and inflation were showing signs of life, Japan raised the consumption tax rate from 5% to 8% in April 2014. Consumer price inflation fell from 2.7% in 2014 to below 1% in 2015 (Leeper, 2016).

Japan has been mired in the trade-off between fiscal sustainability and economic reflation. To a fiscal theorist, Japan's obsession with government debt reduction is puzzling. Central to a regime F equilibrium is that agents' expectations are anchored on fiscal policies that do not raise surpluses when debt expands. Unsettled fiscal policies like those in Japan are unlikely to have so anchored expectations, so it is not clear that Japan resides in regime F; there may be no contradiction of the fiscal theory to explain.

7. PRACTICAL IMPLICATIONS

Viewing practical issues through the joint lenses of monetary and fiscal policies sheds fresh light on policy problems. That new light can also lead to sharply different perspectives on these problems.

7.1 Inflation Targeting

Nearly 30 countries with independent central banks have embraced numerical inflation targeting as the operating principle for monetary policy. Very few of these countries sought simultaneously to adopt fiscal policies that are compatible with the chosen inflation targets. This discussion of the policy interactions that are prerequisites for successful inflation targeting does not depend on the prevailing monetary–fiscal regime, so it applies whether policies reside in regime M or regime F.

The derivations rely on a few generic first-order conditions, a government budget identity, and the condition that optimizing households will not want to over- or under-accumulate assets. For this reason, the results have broad implications that extend well beyond the details of particular models. Consider an economy with a geometrically decaying maturity structure of zero-coupon nominal government bonds. The government's budget identity is

[bd] Imakubo et al. (2015) calculate that real yields on zero-coupon bonds at 1-, 2-, and 3-year maturities fluctuated between 0.5% and −0.5% from the middle of 1995 until 2012, when they fell to almost −2.0% in 2014.

$$\frac{P_t^m B_t^m}{P_t} = \frac{(1+\rho P_t^m)B_{t-1}^m}{P_t} - s_t$$

Letting $Q_{t,t+k} \equiv \beta^k \frac{u'(c_{t+k})}{u'(c_t)} \frac{P_t}{P_{t+k}}$, asset-pricing conditions yield

$$\frac{1}{R_t} = E_t Q_{t,t+1}$$
$$P_t^m = E_t Q_{t,t+1}(1+\rho P_{t+1}^m)$$

and the term structure relationship is

$$P_t^m = E_t \sum_{k=0}^{\infty} \rho^k \left(\prod_{j=0}^{k} \frac{1}{R_{t+j}} \right)$$

These conditions deliver the usual bond valuation equation

$$\frac{(1+\rho P_t^m)B_{t-1}^m}{P_t} = E_t \sum_{i=0}^{\infty} \beta^i \frac{u'(c_{t+i})}{u'(c_t)} s_{t+i}$$

Rewrite the valuation equation by replacing $(1+\rho P_t^m)$ using

$$1+\rho P_t^m = 1 + E_t \sum_{k=1}^{\infty} (\beta\rho)^k \frac{u'(c_{t+k})}{u'(c_t)} \frac{P_t}{P_{t+k}}$$

and, for simplicity, assume a constant-endowment economy, so $\frac{u'(c_{t+i})}{u'(c_t)} = 1$, to generate

$$\left[\sum_{k=0}^{\infty} (\beta\rho)^k \left(\prod_{j=1}^{k} \frac{1}{\pi_{t+j}} \right) \right] \frac{B_{t-1}^m}{P_t} = E_t \sum_{k=0}^{\infty} \beta^k s_{t+k} \tag{44}$$

Imagine an economy that takes as given variables dated $t-1$ and earlier, but commits to hitting an inflation target in all subsequent dates, so $\pi_{t+k} \equiv \pi^*$ for $k \geq 0$. Valuation equation (44) becomes

$$\frac{B_{t-1}^m / P_{t-1}}{EPV_t(s)} = \pi^* - \beta\rho \tag{45}$$

where $EPV_t(s) \equiv E_t \sum_{k=0}^{\infty} \beta^k s_{t+k}$.

This expression imposes stringent conditions on the expected present value of primary surpluses, though not on the surplus path, if the inflation target is to be achieved. For given initial real debt, if the economy adopts a policy of "too high" surpluses, then the inflation target that is achievable is lower than the desired target, π^*. Another way of seeing the tension between monetary and fiscal policy in this equation is to note that the condition requires the fiscal policymaker to adopt a debt target, which it passively adjusts surpluses to achieve. This means that any period of austerity that raises surpluses must induce a subsequent relaxation of policy to bring $EPV_t(s)$ in line with the outstanding debt stock and the inflation target. An austerity program that never took its foot off the gas would undermine the inflation target just as surely as would a myopic fiscal policymaker prone to runaway deficits. Are current fiscal frameworks consistent with such targets?

Both before and since the recent crisis, policymakers have been adopting fiscal rules designed to reverse increases in government debt. For example, following its banking crisis of 1992 Sweden adopted two fiscal rules: a net lending target of 1% of GDP over the economic cycle and a nominal expenditure ceiling 3 years ahead. This ceiling is consistent with ensuring that government expenditure falls as a share of GDP. Similarly, the "debt brake" in Switzerland requires that central government expenditure cannot grow faster than average revenue growth, while the German debt brake introduced in 2011 imposes a limit on federal net lending of 0.35% of GDP. In the United Kingdom, the 2015 Charter for Budget Responsibility requires the government to run a primary surplus in "normal" times. All these measures aim not only to stabilize the debt-to-GDP ratio but to ensure that it is falling over time. And to the extent that the rules are maintained, the pace of debt reduction should increase over time as less of any surplus is devoted to servicing the existing stock of debt. Because these rules fail to include provisions to target a long-run debt-to-GDP ratio, which would relax austerity measures as that target was approached, the rules run the risk of chronically undershooting the inflation target.

From a theoretical perspective, the rules do not make surpluses contingent on debt or the price level. This makes fiscal behavior active, placing it in regime F. When the fiscal policymaker adopts an active rule, as Section 2.3 shows, the monetary authority's ability to control inflation depends crucially on the maturity structure of the outstanding debt and on the nature of its policy response. With a pegged nominal interest rate, inflationary expectations remain consistent with the inflation target and surprise deviations from that target provide the revaluation effects needed to stabilize debt. But if the central bank attempts to come as close to active as possible by setting $\alpha_\pi = \beta$, the rate of inflation follows a random walk, permanently deviating from the inflation target in the face of fiscal shocks. If the policy objective is to smooth the inflationary costs of revaluation effects, then the optimal policy exercises suggest that a persistent deviation from the inflation target is desirable, so long as the persistence matches the maturity structure of the government's debt portfolio. With only single-period debt, there is no advantage in having a prolonged increase or decrease in inflation following a fiscal shock because only the initial period's inflation helps to reduce the real value of government liabilities. But when debt is of longer maturity, allowing inflation to rise and then gradually decline as the predetermined debt stock matures reduces the discounted value of inflationary costs associated with the required revaluation effects.

Successful inflation targeting requires more than a resolute central bank that follows "best practice" monetary policy behavior that includes clear objectives, transparency that leads to effective communications, and accountability. Even with all these elements in place, expression (45) implies that the central bank can achieve π^* only if fiscal policy is compatible with that target. If fiscal behavior requires a long-run inflation rate that differs from π^*, even best practice monetary policy cannot succeed in anchoring long-run inflation expectations or inflation outturns on target.

7.2 Returning to "Normal" Monetary Policy

The financial crisis has seen a substantial increase in debt-to-GDP ratios in many advanced economies, although the immediate need for fiscal adjustment may have been muted due to the reduced debt service costs as real interest rates have fallen since the financial crisis. To see this consider a small change to our policy problem in the endowment economy, in Section 4.2, where we allow the households' discount factor, $\tilde{\beta}_t$, to rise temporarily to $\tilde{\beta} > \beta$, capturing the flight to quality observed in the financial crisis. If we assume government spending is held constant, the policy problem becomes

$$L_t = E_0 \frac{1}{2} \sum_{t=0}^{\infty} \beta^t [-\frac{1}{2}(\tau_t^2 + \theta(\nu_t - 1)^2)$$
$$+ \mu_t(\tilde{\beta}_t E_t \frac{(1 + \rho P_{t+1}^m)}{P_t^m} \nu_{t+1} - 1)$$
$$+ \lambda_t(b_t P_t^m - (1 + \rho P_t^m) b_{t-1} \nu_t - g_t - z_t + \tau_t)$$

which yields the first-order conditions

$$\tau_t : -\tau_t + \lambda_t = 0$$

$$\nu_t : -\theta(\nu_t - 1) + \mu_{t-1} \frac{(1 + \rho P_t^m)}{P_{t-1}^m} \beta^{-1} \tilde{\beta}_{t-1} - (1 + \rho P_t^m) \lambda_t b_{t-1} = 0$$

$$P_t^m : -\frac{\mu_t}{P_t^m} + \mu_{t-1} \rho \frac{\nu_t}{P_{t-1}^m} \beta^{-1} \tilde{\beta}_{t-1} + \lambda_t (b_t - \rho \nu_t b_{t-1}) = 0$$

$$b_t : \lambda_t P_t^m - \beta E_t (1 + \rho P_{t+1}^m) \nu_{t+1} \lambda_{t+1} = 0$$

Under a perfect foresight equilibrium this implies the tax-smoothing result is recast as

$$\tau_t = \beta \tilde{\beta}_t^{-1} \tau_{t+1}$$

which means that the tax rate will be rising during the period in which households have an increased preference for holding government bonds over consumption. Intuitively, the original tax-smoothing result balances the short-run costs of raising taxes to reduce debt against the long-run benefit of lower debt. These costs and benefits are finely balanced with the interest rate on the debt being exactly offset by the policymaker's rate of time preference so that steady-state debt follows a random walk in the face of shocks. When the interest on debt is less than the policymaker's rate of time preference, the policymaker prefers to delay the fiscal adjustment and will allow debt to accumulate, stabilizing debt only after the period of increased household preference for debt holdings has passed.

To the extent that a return to "normal" monetary policy is associated with a rise in debt service costs, optimal policy suggests that efforts to stabilize debt are enhanced at this point. But under the Ramsey policy, inflation surprises to revalue debt are effective only if carried out before the predetermined debt stock matures. Therefore the delay in debt stabilization also reduces the efficacy of promising to raise prices in the future placing more of the burden of adjustment on taxation. At the same time, the higher debt stock that emerges at the point of normalization raises the potential time-inconsistency problems inherent in the Ramsey policy; at this point we may start to see increased pressure to inflate away the debt.

More generally, higher central bank interest rates have powerful fiscal consequences when government debt levels are elevated. In the United States, the Congressional Budget Office (2014) estimates that net interest costs will quadruple between 2014 and 2024 to reach 3.3% of GDP.[be] Those interest costs must be financed somehow—by higher taxes and lower spending now or by faster growth in debt and other adjustments in the future. In light of the political dynamics today in the United States, it is not obvious how those costs will be financed.

Central bankers are well aware of the fiscal consequences of their actions. King (1995) refers to "unpleasant fiscal arithmetic"—a process of monetary disinflation raises real interest rates and destabilizes government debt until the credibility of the disinflation is established. But, he argues, the higher debt may actually undermine that credibility and unpleasant monetarist arithmetic may re-emerge. One interpretation is that King worries about the danger that the fiscal consequences of disinflation may force the central bank to reverse a return to "normal" interest rates.

7.3 Why Central Banks Need to Know the Prevailing Regime

Davig and Leeper (2006), Bianchi (2012), Bianchi and Ilut (2014), and Chen et al. (2015) suggest that there have been switches in the conduct of fiscal policy between passive and active rules. And fiscal switches are not always associated with compensating switches in monetary policy that place the economy in either regime M or regime F. If these policy permutations were permanent, they would either result in indeterminacy (passive

[be] The CBO expects a relatively modest interest in treasury interest rates over that period, with the 10-year rate rising from 2.8 to 4.7 percentage points and the average rate on debt held by the public rising from 1.8 to 3.9 percentage points. Cochrane (2014) considers a scenario in which the Fed raises interest rates to 5% and with them, real interest rates. At a 100% debt–GDP ratio, the increased interest costs amount to $900 billion.

monetary and fiscal policy) or nonexistence of equilibrium (active monetary and fiscal policy). But if policy is expected to return to either the M or F regime sufficiently often, then these policy combinations can still deliver determinate equilibria. So there are four possible permutations of monetary and fiscal policy that may coexist, but only two, if permanent, deliver unique bounded equilibria. The prevailing policy configuration can have profound implications for the conduct of monetary policy, as we illustrate in the endowment economy with Section 2's policy rules.[bf]

Regardless of regime, inflationary dynamics are

$$E_t(\nu_{t+1} - \nu^*) = \frac{\alpha_\pi}{\beta}(\nu_t - \nu^*) \tag{46}$$

Under regime M with an active monetary policy ($\alpha_\pi > \beta$), monetary policy can target inflation in each period, $\nu_t = \nu^*$, while the passive fiscal policy stabilizes debt

$$E_t\left(\frac{b_{t+1}}{R_{t+1}} - \frac{b^*}{R^*}\right) = (\beta^{-1} - \gamma)\left(\frac{b_t}{R_t} - \frac{b^*}{R^*}\right) - E_t\varepsilon^F_{t+1}$$

provided $\gamma > \beta^{-1} - 1$.

Suppose we know the economy will enter this regime in period T, at which point inflation will be at its target $\nu_T = \nu^*$ and the fiscal rule will stabilize whatever debt is inherited at time T. In this case, it does not matter whether or not the monetary policy rule is active or passive prior to period T, since T-step-ahead expected inflation is

$$E_t\nu_{t+T} - \nu^* = \left(\frac{\alpha_\pi}{\beta}\right)^{T-t}(\nu_t - \nu^*)$$

which implies that inflation will be on target between today and period T. If fiscal policy is active, debt will be moving off target between today and period T, but the passive fiscal rule will, from that point on, stabilize debt. If fiscal policy is passive before period T, this would facilitate the debt stabilization prior to T and the targeting of inflation would be uninterrupted by any change of regime at time T.

We now assume that at time T agents anticipate the economy will enter regime F where monetary policy is passive ($\alpha_\pi < \beta$), and fiscal policy does not respond to debt ($\gamma = 0$). Now the period T price level needs to adjust to satisfy the bond valuation equation at time T given the level of inherited nominal debt B_{T-1}. When $\gamma = 0$, the fiscal rule is $s_t = s^* + \varepsilon^F_t$ and the solution for real debt is

$$E_t\frac{B_{T-1}}{R_{T-1}P_{T-1}} = \frac{b^*}{R^*} + \sum_{j=1}^{\infty}\beta^j E_t\varepsilon^F_{T-1+j}$$

[bf] See Davig et al. (2010) and Leeper (2011) for related analyses.

The price level does not jump in period T, but it does adjust in period t when the switch to regime F in period T is first anticipated. The implications for inflation beyond period T depend on how passive the monetary policy rule is. With an interest rate peg, $\alpha = 0$, inflationary expectations remain on target, $E_t\nu_{t+1} = \nu^*$, but there will be innovations to inflation to ensure the bond valuation equation holds in the face of additional fiscal shocks occurring from period T onwards. With some monetary policy response to inflation, $0 < \alpha_\pi < \beta$, the initial jump in the price level will result in a temporary, but sustained rise in inflation whose evolution obeys equation (46). As Section 4 shows, sustaining the rise in inflation enhances the revaluation effect, but the longer is debt maturity, the greater is the reduction in distortions caused by higher inflation.

How does anticipating the F regime in period T affect the conduct of policy prior to period T? With fiscal policy following a rule that may or may not be passive, the expected evolution of government debt follows

$$E_t\left(\frac{B_{t+1}}{R_{t+1}P_{t+1}} - \frac{b^*}{R^*}\right) = (\beta^{-1} - \gamma)\left(\frac{B_t}{R_tP_t} - \frac{b^*}{R^*}\right) - E_t\varepsilon^F_{t+1}$$

We can iterate this forward until period T as

$$E_t\left(\frac{B_{T-1}}{R_{T-1}P_{T-1}} - \frac{b^*}{R^*}\right) = (\beta^{-1} - \gamma)^{T-1-t}\left(\frac{B_t}{R_tP_t} - \frac{b^*}{R^*}\right) + \sum_{j=0}^{T-1-t}(\beta^{-1} - \gamma)^j E_t\varepsilon^F_{t+1+j}$$

which defines the initial debt level $\frac{B_t}{R_tP_t}$ required to ensure the economy enters regime F in period T with the appropriate level of debt $\frac{B_{T-1}}{R_{T-1}P_{T-1}}$ without any discrete jumps in the price level at that time. This depends upon the extent to which fiscal policy prior to period T acts to stabilize debt as determined by the fiscal feedback parameter, γ, and the expected value of fiscal shocks over that period. If the move to the F regime is sufficiently long in the future and fiscal policy is sufficiently aggressive in stabilizing debt, then there will be little need for surprise inflation in the initial period to ensure the appropriate debt level is bequeathed to the future. But if the switch is more imminent or the fiscal stabilization prior to period T is muted, then an initial jump in prices will be required to ensure the bond valuation equation holds. The inflationary implications of this prior to period T depend on the conduct of monetary policy. If monetary policy is active prior to period T, any initial jump in prices will be explosive until the F regime is established in period T. This happens because the period t price-level jump ensures the bond valuation equation holds, while inflation dynamics are determined by equation (46), which is explosive under an active monetary policy. This is a bounded equilibrium because the process for inflation stabilizes when the policy regime changes in period T. But before period T, the active monetary policy actually destabilizes prices. Postponing the switch to the F regime means that the period of explosive inflation dynamics remains in place for longer.

This analysis has the flavor of a game of chicken between the monetary and fiscal policymakers. The monetary authority can stick to an active monetary policy rule and achieve its inflation target, provided everyone is sure that policy will eventually be supported by a passive fiscal policy which stabilizes debt. Debt dynamics will be unstable in such a scenario until the fiscal authorities relent and adopt a passive fiscal policy. But when there is the suspicion that monetary policy will eventually turn passive to support a fiscal policy that does not stabilize debt, then conventional anti-inflation policies today may actually worsen inflation outcomes.

8. CRITICAL ASSESSMENT AND OUTLOOK

We conclude by examining the areas where further theoretical and empirical work is needed.

8.1 Further Theoretical Developments

This section highlights areas in which additional theoretical work on monetary–fiscal interactions would be fruitful.

8.1.1 Default and the Open Economy

This chapter has focused on closed-economy models, abstracting from issues of sovereign default and open-economy dimensions that have come together in the recent sovereign debt crisis in the Euro Area. In the early applications of the fiscal theory to the open economy, a key issue was whether or not individual country government budget identities were consolidated into a single global bond valuation equation.[bg] If so, with multiple passive monetary policies, each country's price level and exchange rate are indeterminate. In this equilibrium, one country accumulates the debt of another, an outcome whose political equilibrium Sims (1997) argues is unstable. If such equilibria are ruled out, then we return to having a bond valuation equation for each country and fiscal policies in one economy carry implications for outcomes in the second economy. For example, a determinate active/passive policy pair can be achieved across countries rather than within countries (Leith and Wren-Lewis, 2008).

Similar issues arise in a monetary union. With a single passive monetary policy, it is possible to ensure determinacy with only one active fiscal policy (Leith and Wren-Lewis, 2006). These analyses have the troubling feature that the tail seems to wag the dog—a small monetary union member that fails to pursue passive fiscal policy can determine the price level for the entire union. This raises questions about whether these early applications of the fiscal theory to the open economy have appropriately captured

[bg] See Sims (1997), Loyo (1997), Woodford (1998b), Dupor (2000), Canzoneri et al. (2001a), and Daniel (2001).

cross-country heterogeneity—including different price-level processes across member states—and the cross-country implications of the interactions between monetary and fiscal policy. More recent work seeks to model the gross asset/liability positions of countries to capture the kinds of revaluation effects generated by price level and exchange rate movements.[bh] That work finds that the gross asset/liability positions can be several multiples of GDP even when net positions are not, implying that the revaluation effects stressed in this chapter are likely to be both quantitatively important and more complex in open-economy settings.

Recent events highlight the need to bring sovereign default into the analysis. In a model similar to our endowment economy, but augmented with an exogenous default risk, Uribe (2006) demonstrates that default can give rise to fiscal theory-type effects, with anticipated, but delayed defaults potentially destabilizing an active inflation targeting policy in much the same way that anticipating a move to regime F can do.

While many analyses of strategic default focus on real economies—for example, D'Erasmo et al. (2016)—when default through inflation is available as an alternative financing option, it is either assumed to be equivalent to outright default, or possibly less costly if it is less damaging to the balance sheets of a country's banking sector than an outright default (Gros, 2011). Given that inflation is costly, it is not obvious that this will always be the case. A useful line of work would consider the nature of the strategic default decision in environments in which debt revaluations through surprise current inflation and bond prices are possible. Kriwoluzky et al. (2014) is an interesting paper that contrasts outright default for a country engaged in a monetary union with the redenomination of debt following exit from the union. They find that the possibility of exit significantly worsens the preexit/default debt dynamics. Similarly, Burnside et al. (2001) argue that the speculative attacks on fixed-currency regimes in the Asian crisis of 1997 sprung from expectations that large revaluations of debt were required to finance the projected deficits that ongoing bank bailouts were expected to engender. In richer models where default is state dependent and the economic costs of default arise through the impact of default on domestic banks' balance sheets the set of monetary and fiscal interactions is widened further (Bi et al., 2015; Bocola, 2016). There is plenty of scope to deepen our understanding of default vs inflation financing in a sovereign debt crisis.

8.1.2 Better Rules

Analyses of optimal monetary and fiscal policy rules in approximated economies is quite clear about the kinds of simple rules that can mimic the Ramsey policy. Fairly aggressive inflation targeting using an inertial Taylor rule, coupled with a passive fiscal policy that

[bh] See Lane and Milesi-Ferretti (2001) for the first issue of a dataset of external portfolios and Devereux and Sutherland (2011) for a numerical method to endogenously embed such positions in open-economy macro models.

very gradually stabilizes debt, comes close to achieving the welfare levels that the Ramsey policy acquires (Schmitt-Grohé and Uribe, 2007; Kirsanova and Wren-Lewis, 2012). The nonlinear solutions to the optimal policy problem that this chapter described reveal that the policy mix depends crucially on both the level of debt and its maturity. With high levels of short-maturity debt, it is optimal to use monetary policy to stabilize debt and adjust distortionary taxation to mitigate the inflationary consequences of such a policy. This suggests that there may be a family of simple implementable rules which could improve welfare by introducing a degree of state-dependence to the policy mix.

Similarly, studies often seek to assess the importance of automatic stabilizers by adding output to the fiscal rules. Kliem and Kriwoluzky (2014) argue, though, that this is not the most data-coherent specification of policy behavior and that rules conditioned on other macroeconomic variables better capture the cyclical properties of fiscal instruments. Those proposed rules also improve welfare in DSGE models. Taken together, this suggests that there is scope for extending the range of simple rules considered in the literature to find alternatives that are both empirically and normatively more appealing.

8.1.3 Strategic Interactions

Estimates of regime-switching policies find that the policy mix is not always aligned with either regime M or regime F. There are also periods in which policies are in conflict—either doubly active or doubly passive. Introducing strategic interactions between policy authorities into optimal policy analysis may help to put theory in better line with data. Literature that looks at such interactions often relies on linear-quadratic approximation or simplifying assumptions to obtain tractable results.[bi] Blake and Kirsanova (2011) consider the desirability of central bank conservatism in a standard new Keynesian economy augmented with fiscal policy and an associated independent fiscal policymaker. They consider three forms of strategic interaction: either monetary or fiscal leadership, where the leader anticipates the response of the follower, or a Nash equilibrium between the two policymakers. The striking result, which echoes Section 5.4 in which the monetary authority followed a Taylor rule while the fiscal authority optimized, is that central bank conservatism always reduces welfare. Blake and Kirsanova also find that the quantitative results depend on the level of debt around which the economy is linearized. This argues that such analyses could usefully be extended to a nonlinear framework to explore the state dependencies in the strategic monetary and fiscal policy interactions. How robust is the institutional policy design to the strategic interactions implied by independent fiscal and monetary policymakers? To what extent can such interactions explain the observed policy switches in empirical analyses based on simple ad hoc rules?

[bi] Adam and Billi (2008) and Dixit and Lambertini (2003) consider the strategic interactions between monetary and fiscal policymakers, although in abstracting from the existence of government debt they rule out the mechanisms that have been the focus of this chapter.

8.1.4 Political Economy

Theoretical work on optimal policy, particularly fiscal policy, often implies policy behavior that bears little resemblance to observed policy. Benigno and Woodford's (2004) and Schmitt-Grohé and Uribe's (2004) analyses of jointly optimal monetary and fiscal policies suggest that when the policymaker can make credible promises about future actions, the steady-state level of debt should follow a random walk—in response to shocks, debt will be allowed to rise permanently because the short-run costs of reducing debt exactly balance the long-run benefits. This policy prescription is clearly at odds with the mounting concerns over rising debt levels in several advanced economies, which have led the IMF to predict that most governments will be involved with consolidation efforts for several years. The expected pace of consolidation is particularly rapid in the economies that are subject to pressures in the financial markets from worries over fiscal sustainability (International Monetary Fund, 2011).

If instead we assume that policymakers cannot make credible promises about how they behave in the future—policy is constrained to be time-consistent—then the implied policy outcomes can be equally unconvincing: instead of implying that debt should permanently rise following negative fiscal shocks, the theory tends to imply that the policymaker will be tempted to aggressively reduce the debt stock, often at rates that far exceed those observed in practice (Leith and Wren-Lewis, 2013). In standard new Keynesian models, time-consistent policy will not only call for a rapid debt correction, but it will make the long-run equilibrium value of debt negative, as the fiscal authority seeks to accumulate a stock of assets to help offset other frictions in the economy. The analysis in this chapter and in Leeper et al. (2015a), by allowing for a realistically calibrated debt maturity structure, can plausibly slow the pace of fiscal adjustments to levels which are not obviously inconsistent with those observed. And by assuming that the fiscal policymaker discounts the future more highly than households, as a crude means of capturing the short-termism that political frictions can engender, Leeper et al. (2015a) find that the time-consistent policy can support reversion to plausible debt–GDP ratios.

Although an inability to commit can go some way toward explaining this discrepancy between actual policy and the normative prescriptions of the theoretical literature, it seems likely that the political dimensions of policymaking are also important. Political economy aspects of actual fiscal policy have recently been laid bare in the abandoning of fiscal rules in Europe during the financial crisis, the brinkmanship over the raising of the debt ceiling in the United States, and the withholding or awarding of bail-out funds to Greece and other Eurozone economies from the Troika composed of the European Commission, the ECB, and the IMF. In this vein the New Political Economy literature seeks to identify mechanisms that can explain the trends in debt–GDP levels in many developed economies in recent decades.

Alesina and Passalacqua (2016) identify several reasons why governments may pursue policies that raise government debt to suboptimally high levels: (1) fiscal illusion—voters misunderstand the budget identity and are enticed to vote for a party that supports unsustainable tax cuts or spending increases; (2) political business cycles—voters are unsure of the competence of potential governments, so fiscal policy can be used by incumbents to signal competence; (3) delayed stabilization—political factions squabble over who bears the costs of fiscal consolidations, thereby delaying debt stabilization; (4) debt as a strategic variable—political parties use debt to tie the hands of their political opponents when they are out of office; (5) bargaining over policy in heterogeneous legislatures; (6) rent seeking by politicians; and (7) intergenerational redistributions. Some of these mechanisms are more naturally located in majoritarian systems—for example, political business cycles and strategic use of debt—while others are more likely to be associated with continuous strategic interactions between political actors outside of election periods—for example, delayed stabilizations and bargaining within legislatures—which are a feature of proportional/multiparty systems or heterogeneity within parties under a two-party system.

This New Political Economy literature typically does not consider monetary and fiscal policy interactions of the type considered in this chapter, so there is a need to integrate the two literatures. Political conflict inherent in the conduct of fiscal policy may explain why it is possible to obtain a data-coherent optimal policy description of monetary policy—albeit with fluctuations in the degree of monetary policy conservatism—while a similar description for fiscal policy is less easily achieved with policy switching between active and passive rules, with only short-lived periods in which policy is optimal (Chen et al., 2015).

Despite the difficulty of allowing for strategic interactions between the monetary and fiscal policymakers, this may not be going far enough if we are to understand the evolution of the monetary–fiscal policy mix. While treating an independent central bank as a single policymaker may be an acceptable approximation, it is less obvious that fiscal policy is best described by the actions of a single benevolent policymaker. A longer term research goal is to tractably integrate the New Political Economy literature into the analysis of monetary and fiscal policy interactions. Can we explain the changing nature of those interactions?

Political frictions vary substantially across countries. For example, in the United States and the United Kingdom debt levels fell fairly consistently following World War II until the early 1980s, before expanding consistently under Republican administrations in the United States, while not having such a clear partisan pattern in the United Kingdom. The current Conservative government in the United Kingdom is promising an aggressive austerity policy which seeks to run a permanent surplus from 2017. Any use of political frictions to explain the dynamics of debt and other macro variables must also explain such cross-country differences, particularly since it is not obvious that U.S. Republicans and U.K. Conservatives have fundamentally different views on the optimal size of the state.

8.1.5 Money

By focusing on cashless economies we have side-stepped the literature that considers the role of inflation as a tool of public finance vs its impact on money as a medium of exchange (Phelps, 1973). More recent research finds that the nature of the time-consistency problem facing a policymaker who issues nominal debt can depend crucially on the effects of inflation on the transactions technology (Martin, 2009, 2011; Niemann et al., 2013). We have also ignored the central bank's balance sheet, which precludes an analysis of fiscal aspects of unconventional monetary policies which have been discussed in Sims (2013), Del Negro and Sims (2015), and Reis (2013, 2015). Analyzing such unconventional monetary policies or technological developments like virtual money within frameworks that allow for interactions between such developments and fiscal policy are obvious areas for further research.

8.2 Further Empirical Work

This section proposes several directions in which to take empirical work on monetary–fiscal interactions.

8.2.1 Data Needs

In the early days of real business cycle research, Prescott (1986) argued that "theory is ahead of measurement," and, in particular, that theory can guide the measurement of key economic time series. This rings especially true for research on how monetary and fiscal policies affect inflation. Empirical applications in which the debt valuation equation plays a central role require observations on objects that are not readily available: the market value of privately held government liabilities—explicit debt and other commitments—the maturity structure of that debt, actual and expected primary surpluses, and actual and expected real discount rates. Compiling such data across countries and across monetary–fiscal regimes is the first step in an empirical agenda on policy interactions.

8.2.2 Identifying Regime

Empirical work surveyed in Section 6 highlights the difficulties in distinguishing whether regime M, regime F, or some other regimes generated observed time series. It remains to thoroughly explore which features of private and policy behavior are critical for breaking the near observational equivalence of regimes. Surprisingly, little work experiments with alternative specifications of policy behavior, particularly in DSGE models. Instead, most researchers—including us—adopt the simple rules that have become "standard." There is ample room for such experimentation.

Closely related is Geweke's (2010) argument that models are inherently incomplete in the sense that they lack "some aspect of a joint distribution over all parameters, latent variables, and models under consideration [p. 3]." For example, central bank money-only models that follow Smets and Wouters (2007) impose a dogmatic prior that places zero probability mass on regime F parameters. This procedure rejects a priori regions of the parameter space that the work reviewed in Section 6.3 finds fit data equally well. As we have seen, monetary policy actions have very different impacts in regimes M and F, so it matters a great deal to a policymaker, who is using model output to reach decisions, whether regime F is even possible. It would be valuable to apply existing tools for confronting model uncertainty to issues of monetary–fiscal regime (Hansen and Sargent, 2007; Geweke, 2010).

A different angle on model fit pursues DeJong and Whiteman's (1991) idea to ask: what type of prior over policy parameters is needed to support the inference that regime M (or regime F) generated the data? This exercise elicits the strength of a researcher's beliefs about regime when the researcher chooses to focus solely on one possible monetary–fiscal mix.

8.2.3 Generalizing Regime Switching

Existing work that estimates DSGE models with recurring policy regime switching tends to make simplifying assumptions about the nature of both private behavior and the policy process. Those assumptions can be systematically relaxed to arrive at more general models usable for policy analysis. And the fit of the models needs to be scrutinized in the manner that, for example, Smets and Wouter's (2007) specification has been. Until the fit of switching models is carefully evaluated, fixed-regime DSGE models will continue to dominate in policy institutions.[bj]

Recent econometric innovations permit estimation of endogenous regime change (Chang et al., 2015a). That technique treats policy regime as a latent process akin to time-varying probabilities of regime change. Generalizations of those methods to multivariate settings with multiple regimes that switch nonsynchronously could be integrated with DSGE models in which agents learn about the prevailing regime. Setups like that could shed empirical light on endogenous interactions among monetary and fiscal regimes, such as those that arise from the strategic interactions and political economy dynamics that Sections 8.1.3 and 8.1.4 mention.[bk]

8.2.4 Historical Analyses

Friedman and Schwartz (1963a) set the standard for historical analyses of monetary policy. But fiscal policy plays almost no role in their narrative. Stein (1996) is an excellent account of the evolution of fiscal policy in the United States, but his goals are different,

[bj] Sims and Zha (2006) is an exception, though they consider only monetary switching.

[bk] Chang et al. (2015b) estimate single-equation models of U.S. monetary and fiscal behavior to infer how an endogenous switch in one policy's regime predicts and switch in the other policy's regime. Empirical work along these lines connects more clearly to theory than do estimates in which regimes change exogenously.

so he does not connect the fiscal actions on which he reports to macroeconomic activity. A thorough analysis of the monetary–fiscal history of a country that brings to bear modern macroeconomic theory is a bit ambitious, though sorely needed. Short of a "Monetary *and Fiscal* History" that parallels Friedman and Schwartz, there are a great many historical episodes that can be reinterpreted in light of monetary–fiscal interactions.

Across countries there have been many short- and long-lived periods in which central banks have pegged interest rates, yet inflation has remained stable, as Cochrane (2015) points out. This observation seems to contradict Friedman's (1968) warning that pegged rates produce ever-increasing inflation. Has fiscal behavior played a role in delivering stable prices during interest rate pegs?

It would be instructive to bring fiscal behavior explicitly into a reexamination of the gold standard. What are the fiscal requirements of maintaining a fixed parity under the classical gold standard? Or of resuming convertibility after a suspension? Bordo and Hautcoeur (2007) contrast the French and British experiences after they suspended during World War I. Bordo (2011) suggests that France adopted a passive monetary/active fiscal policy mix that lead to substantially larger price-level increases in France than in Britain, which pursued active monetary and passive fiscal policies.

What role has fiscal policy played in accommodating or ending deflationary episodes? These have been well documented—Temin and Wigmore (1990), Bernanke and James (1991), Bordo and Filardo (2005), and Velde (2009) for example—but in the absence of an analytical understanding of how fiscal policy behaves under a gold standard, discussions of policy interactions remain informal (Eggertsson, 2008; Jalil and Rua, 2015).

How have large runups of government debt been financed historically? Hall and Sargent (2011, 2014) have made substantial progress on this important question in recent years.[bl] Although historically most large debt expansions were associated with wars, advanced economies since the financial crisis—and quite possibly going forward—are experiencing nonwar-related debt growth. What does history teach about how policy can best respond to high levels of government debt?

8.3 A Final Word

Macroeconomists have an unfortunate history of arguing over whether monetary or fiscal policy in *the* primary force behind inflation.[bm] If a reader leaves this chapter with a single message, that message should be: the fiscal theory and the quantity theory—or its recent manifestation, the Wicksellian theory—are parts of a more general theory of price-level determination in which monetary and fiscal policies always interact with private-sector behavior to produce the equilibrium aggregate level of prices. Within a certain

[bl] But see also Bordo and White (1991) on the Napoleonic wars and Sargent and Velde (1995) on the French revolution.

[bm] See, for example, Andersen and Jordan (1968) or Friedman and Heller (1969).

parametric family of monetary and fiscal rules, the two seemingly distinct perspectives arise from different regions of the policy parameter space, but there is no sense in which one view is "right" and the other is "wrong." Ultimately, it is an empirical question whether we can discern whether and under what circumstances one view is the dominant factor in inflation dynamics.

We would also encourage macroeconomists to entertain the possibility that both views are "right" most of the time and that the process of price-level determination is more complex than benchmark theories have so far described.

ACKNOWLEDGMENTS

This chapter has benefited from collaborations and discussions with many coauthors and colleagues and we thank them. We also thank Jon Faust, Ding Liu, Jim Nason, Charles Nolan, Fei Tan, and Todd Walker for conversations and Bob Barsky, John Cochrane, John Taylor, and Harald Uhlig for comments.

REFERENCES

Adam, K., Billi, R.M., 2008. Monetary conservatism and fiscal policy. J. Monetary Econ. 55 (8), 1376–1388.
Aiyagari, S.R., Marcet, A., Sargent, T.J., Seppälä, J., 2002. Optimal taxation without state-contingent debt. J. Polit. Econ. 110 (6), 1220–1254.
Akitoby, B., Komatsuzaki, T., Binder, A., 2014. Inflation and public debt reversals in the G7 countries. IMF Working Paper No. 14/96, June.
Alesina, A., Passalacqua, A., 2016. The political economy of government debt. In: Taylor, J.B., Uhlig, H. (Eds.), Handbook of Macroeconomics, vol. 2B. Elsevier, Amsterdam, Netherlands, pp. 2605–2657.
Alvarez, F., Kehoe, P.J., Neumeyer, P.A., 2004. The time consistency of optimal monetary and fiscal policies. Econometrica 72 (2), 541–567.
Andersen, L.C., Jordan, J.L., 1968. Monetary and fiscal actions: a test of their relative importance in economic stabilization. Fed. Reserve Bank St. Louis Rev. November, 11–24.
Angeletos, G.M., 2002. Fiscal policy with non-contingent debt and the optimal maturity structure. Q. J. Econ. 117 (3), 1105–1131.
Auernheimer, L., Contreras, B., 1990, February. Control of the Interest Rate with a Government Budget Constraint: Determinacy of the Price Level and Other Results. Texas A&M University, College Station, TX.
Ball, L., Mazumder, S., 2011. Inflation dynamics and the great recession. Brookings Papers Econ. Act. Spring, 337–402.
Banco Central do Brasil, 2015. Inflation report. 17(4), December.
Barro, R.J., 1979. On the determination of the public debt. J. Polit. Econ. 87 (5), 940–971.
Barro, R.J., Gordon, D.B., 1983. A positive theory of monetary policy in a natural-rate model. J. Polit. Econ. 91 (4), 589–610.
Bassetto, M., 2002. A game-theoretic view of the fiscal theory of the price level. Econometrica 70 (6), 2167–2195.
Begg, D.K.H., Haque, B., 1984. A nominal interest rate rule and price level indeterminacy reconsidered. Greek Econ. Rev. 6 (1), 31–46.
Benhabib, J., Schmitt-Grohé, S., Uribe, M., 2001. The perils of Taylor rules. J. Econ. Theor. 96 (1–2), 40–69.
Benhabib, J., Schmitt-Grohé, S., Uribe, M., 2002. Avoiding liquidity traps. J. Polit. Econ. 110 (3), 535–563.
Benigno, P., Woodford, M., 2004. Optimal monetary and fiscal policy: a linear-quadratic approach. In: Gertler, M., Rogoff, K. (Eds.), NBER Macroeconomics Annual 2003. MIT Press, Cambridge, MA, pp. 271–333.

Bernanke, B., James, H., 1991. The gold standard, deflation, and financial crisis in the great depression: an international comparison. In: Hubbard, R.G. (Ed.), Financial Markets and Financial Crises. University of Chicago Press, Chicago, pp. 33–68.

Bi, H., Leeper, E.M., Leith, C., 2013. Uncertain fiscal consolidations. Econ. J. 123 (566), F31–F63.

Bi, H., Leeper, E.M., Leith, C., 2015. Financial Intermediation and Government Debt Default. University of Glasgow, Glasgow, Scotland.

Bianchi, F., 2012. Evolving monetary/fiscal policy mix in the United States. Am. Econ. Rev. Papers Proc. 101 (3), 167–172.

Bianchi, F., Ilut, C., 2014. Monetary/Fiscal Policy Mix and Agents' Beliefs. Duke University, Durham, NC.

Blake, A.P., Kirsanova, T., 2011. Inflation conservatism and monetary-fiscal interactions. Int. J. Central Bank. 7 (2), 41–83.

Bocola, L., 2016. The pass through of sovereign risk. J. Polit. Econ. forthcoming.

Bohn, H., 1988. Why do we have nominal government debt? J. Monetary Econ. 21 (1), 127–140.

Bohn, H., 1990. Tax smoothing with financial instruments. Am. Econ. Rev. 80, 1217–1230.

Bohn, H., 1998. The behavior of U.S. public debt and deficits. Q. J. Econ. 113 (3), 949–963.

Bordo, M., 2011. Comments on 'Perceptions and misperceptions of fiscal inflation'. Slides, Rutgers University, June.

Bordo, M., Filardo, A., 2005. Deflation and monetary policy in a historical perspective: remembering the past or being condemned to repeat it. Econ. Policy (October), 799–844.

Bordo, M.D., Hautcoeur, P.C., 2007. Why didn't France follow the British stabilisation after World War I? Eur. Rev. Econ. Hist. 11 (1), 3–37.

Bordo, M., White, E.N., 1991. A tale of two currencies: British and French finance during the napoleonic wars. J. Econ. Hist. 51 (2), 303–316.

Brunner, K., Meltzer, A.H., 1972. Money, debt, and economic activity. J. Polit. Econ. 80 (5), 951–977.

Brunnermeier, M.K., Sannikov, Y., 2013. Redistributive monetary policy. In: The Changing Policy Landscape. Federal Reserve Bank of Kansas City Economic Conference Proceedings, 2012 Jackson Hole Symposium, pp. 331–384.

Buera, F., Nicolini, J.P., 2004. Optimal maturity structure of government debt without state contingent bonds. J. Monetary Econ. 51 (3), 531–554.

Buiter, W.H., 2002. The fiscal theory of the price level: a critique. Econ. J. 112 (481), 459–480.

Burnside, C., Eichenbaum, M., Rebelo, S., 2001. Prospective deficits and the Asian currency crisis. J. Polit. Econ. 109 (6), 1155–1197.

Calvo, G.A., 1983. Staggered prices in a utility maximizing model. J. Monetary Econ. 12 (3), 383–398.

Calvo, G.A., Guidotti, P., 1992. Optimal maturity of nominal government debt. Int. Econ. Rev. 33 (4), 895–919.

Canzoneri, M.B., Cumby, R.E., Diba, B.T., 2001a. Fiscal discipline and exchange rate systems. Econ. J. 111 (474), 667–690.

Canzoneri, M.B., Cumby, R.E., Diba, B.T., 2001b. Is the price level determined by the needs of fiscal solvency? Am. Econ. Rev. 91 (5), 1221–1238.

Carvalho, C., Ferrero, A., 2014. What Explains Japan's Persistent Deflation? University of Oxford, Oxford, UK.

Chang, Y., Choi, Y., Park, J.Y., 2015a. Regime Switching Model with Endogenous Autoregressive Latent Factor. Indiana University, Bloomington, IN.

Chang, Y., Kwak, B., Leeper, E.M., 2015b. Monetary-Fiscal Interactions with Endogenous Regime Change. Indiana University, Bloomington, IN.

Chari, V.V., Christiano, L.J., Kehoe, P.J., 1994. Optimal fiscal policy in a business cycle model. J. Polit. Econ. 102 (4), 617–652.

Chen, X., Leeper, E.M., Leith, C., 2015. U.S. Monetary and Fiscal Policy: Conflict or Cooperation? University of Glasgow, Glasgow, Scotland.

Chung, H., Leeper, E.M., 2007. What has financed government debt? NBER Working Paper No. 13425, September.

Cochrane, J.H., 1999. A frictionless view of U.S. inflation. In: Bernanke, B.S., Rotemberg, J.J. (Eds.), NBER Macroeconomics Annual 1998, vol. 13. MIT Press, Cambridge, MA, pp. 323–384.

Cochrane, J.H., 2001. Long term debt and optimal policy in the fiscal theory of the price level. Econometrica 69 (1), 69–116.
Cochrane, J.H., 2005. Money as stock. J. Monetary Econ. 52 (3), 501–528.
Cochrane, J.H., 2011a. Determinacy and identification with Taylor rules. J. Polit. Econ. 119 (3), 565–615.
Cochrane, J.H., 2011b. Understanding policy in the great recession: some unpleasant fiscal arithmetic. Eur. Econ. Rev. 55 (1), 2–30.
Cochrane, J.H., 2014. Monetary policy with interest on reserves. J. Econ. Dyn. Control 49 (December), 74–108.
Cochrane, J.H., 2015. Do Higher Interest Rates Raise or Lower Inflation? Hoover Institution, Stanford, CA.
Congressional Budget Office, 2014. CBO's projection of federal interest payments. http://www.cbo.gov/publication/45684. September 3.
Congressional Budget Office, 2015. The Long-Term Budget Outlook. U.S. Congress, Washington, DC.
Daniel, B.C., 2001. The fiscal theory of the price level in an open economy. J. Monetary Econ. 48 (2), 293–308.
Davig, T., Leeper, E.M., 2006. Fluctuating macro policies and the fiscal theory. In: Acemoglu, D., Rogoff, K., Woodford, M. (Eds.), NBER Macroeconomics Annual, vol. 21. MIT Press, Cambridge, pp. 247–298.
Davig, T., Leeper, E.M., Walker, T.B., 2010. 'Unfunded liabilities' and uncertain fiscal financing. J. Monetary Econ. 57 (5), 600–619.
Davig, T., Leeper, E.M., Walker, T.B., 2011. Inflation and the fiscal limit. Eur. Econ. Rev. 55 (1), 31–47.
Debortoli, D., Nunes, R.C., Yared, P., 2014. Optimal Government Debt Maturity. Columbia University, New York, NY.
DeJong, D.N., Whiteman, C.H., 1991. Reconsidering 'trends and random walks in macroeconomic time series'. J. Monetary Econ. 28 (2), 221–254.
DeJong, D.N., Ingram, B.F., Whiteman, C.H., 1996. A Bayesian approach to calibration. J. Business Econ. Stat. 14 (1), 1–9.
Del Negro, M., Schorfheide, F., 2004. Priors from general equilibrium models for VARs. Int. Econ. Rev. 45 (2), 643–673.
Del Negro, M., Sims, C.A., 2015. When does a central bank's balance sheet require fiscal support? In: Goodfriend, M., Zin, S.E. (Eds.), Monetary Policy: An Unprecedented Predicament, Carnegie-Rochester-NYU Conference Series on Public Policy, vol. 73. Amsterdam, pp. 1–19.
Del Negro, M., Giannoni, M.P., Schorfheide, F., 2015. Inflation in the great recession and new Keynesian models. Am. Econ. J. Macroecon. 7 (1), 168–196.
D'Erasmo, P., Mendoza, E.G., Zhang, J., 2016. What is a sustainable public debt? In: Taylor, J.B., Uhlig, H. (Eds.), Handbook of Macroeconomics, vol. 2B. Elsevier, Amsterdam, Netherlands, pp. 2499–2603.
Devereux, M.B., Sutherland, A., 2011. Country portfolios in open economy macro models. J. Eur. Econ. Assoc. 9 (2), 337–369.
Dixit, A., Lambertini, L., 2003. Interactions of commitment and discretion in monetary and fiscal policies. Am. Econ. Rev. 93 (5), 1522–1542.
Dupor, B., 2000. Exchange rates and the fiscal theory of the price level. J. Monetary Econ. 45 (3), 613–630.
Eggertsson, G.B., 2008. Great expectations and the end of the depression. Am. Econ. Rev. 98 (4), 1476–1516.
Eichenbaum, M., 1992. Comment on 'interpreting the macroeconomic time series facts: the effects of monetary policy'. Eur. Econ. Rev. 36, 1001–1011.
Eusepi, S., Preston, B., 2013. Fiscal Foundations of Inflation: Imperfect Knowledge. Monash University, Melbourne, Australia.
Faraglia, E., Marcet, A., Scott, A., 2008. Fiscal insurance and debt management in OECD economies. Econ. J. 118 (527), 363–386.
Friedman, M., 1948. A monetary and fiscal framework for economic stability. Am. Econ. Rev. 38 (2), 245–264.
Friedman, M., 1968. The role of monetary policy. Am. Econ. Rev. 58 (1), 1–17.
Friedman, M., 1970. The Counter-Revolution in Monetary Theory. Institute of Economic Affairs, London.

Friedman, M., Heller, W.W., 1969. Monetary vs. Fiscal Policy—A Dialogue. W.W. Norton & Company, New York.
Friedman, M., Schwartz, A.J., 1963a. A Monetary History of the United States, 1867–1960. Princeton University Press, Princeton, NJ.
Friedman, M., Schwartz, A.J., 1963b. Money and business cycles. Rev. Econ. Stat. 45 (1 Pt. 2, Suppl.), 32–64.
Galí, J., 2008. Monetary Policy, Inflation, and the Business Cycle. Princeton University Press, Princeton, NJ.
Geweke, J., 2010. Complete and Incomplete Econometric Models. Princeton University Press, Princeton, NJ.
Ghosh, A., Kim, J.I., Mendoza, E.G., Ostry, J.D., Qureshi, M.S., 2012. Fiscal fatigue, fiscal space and debt sustainability in advanced economies. Econ. J. 123 (566), F4–F30.
Gonzalez-Astudillo, M., 2013. Monetary-fiscal policy interaction: interdependent policy rule coefficients. Finance and Economics Discussion Series No. 2013-58, Federal Reserve Board, July.
Gros, D., 2011. Speculative attacks within or outside a monetary union: default versus inflation. CEPS Policy Briefs, No. 257, November.
Hall, G.J., Sargent, T.J., 2011. Interest rate risk and other determinants of post-WWII U.S. government debt/GDP dynamics. Am. Econ. J. Macroecon. 3 (3), 1–27.
Hall, G.J., Sargent, T.J., 2014. Fiscal discriminations in three wars. In: Goodfriend, M., Zin, S.E. (Eds.), Fiscal Policy in the Presence of Debt Crises. Carnegie-Rochester-NYU Conference Series on Public Policy. J. Mon. Econ., vol. 61. Amsterdam, pp. 148–166.
Hall, R.E., 2011. The long slump. Am. Econ. Rev. 101 (2), 431–469.
Hansen, L.P., Sargent, T.J., 2007. Robustness. Princeton University Press, Princeton.
Hausman, J.K., Wieland, J.F., 2014. Abenomics: preliminary analysis and outlook. Brookings Papers Econ. Act. Spring, 1–63.
Hilscher, J., Raviv, A., Reis, R., 2014. Inflating away the debt? An empirical assessment. NBER Working Paper No. 20339, July.
Hur, J., 2013. Fiscal Financing and the Effects of Government Spending: A VAR Approach. California State University, Northridge.
Imakubo, K., Kojima, H., Nakajima, J., 2015. The natural yield curve: its concept and measurement. Bank of Japan Working Paper Series No. 15-E-5, June.
International Monetary Fund, 2011. Fiscal Monitor–Shifting Gears: Tacking Challenges on the Road to Fiscal Adjustment. IMF, Washington, DC.
Ito, T., 2006. Japanese monetary policy: 1998–2005 and beyond. In: Monetary Policy in Asia: Approaches and Implementation. Bank for International Settlements, pp. 105–132.
Ito, T., Mishkin, F.S., 2006. Two decades of Japanese monetary policy and the deflation problem. In: Rose, A.K., Ito, T. (Eds.), Monetary Policy Under Very Low Inflation in the Pacific Rim, NBER-EASE, vol. 15. University of Chicago Press, Chicago, pp. 131–193.
Jalil, A., Rua, G., 2015. Inflation Expectations and Recovery from the Depression in 1933: Evidence from the Narrative Record. Occidental College, Los Angeles, CA.
Kiley, M.T., 2015. What can the data tell us about the equilibrium real interest rate? Finance and Economics Discussion Series No. 2015-077, Federal Reserve Board, August.
Kim, S., 2003. Structural shocks and the fiscal theory of the price level in the sticky price model. Macroecon. Dyn. 7 (5), 759–782.
King, M., 1995. Commentary: monetary policy implications of greater fiscal discipline. In: Budget Deficits and Debt: Issues and OptionsFederal Reserve Bank of Kansas City Economic Conference Proceedings, 1995 Jackson Hole Symposium, pp. 171–183.
Kirsanova, T., Wren-Lewis, S., 2012. Optimal feedback on debt in an economy with nominal rigidities. Econ. J. 122 (559), 238–264.
Kliem, M., Kriwoluzky, A., 2014. Toward a Taylor rule for fiscal policy. Rev. Econ. Dyn. 17 (2), 294–302.
Kliem, M., Kriwoluzky, A., Sarferaz, S., 2015. Monetary-fiscal policy interaction and fiscal inflation: a tale of three countries. Eur. Econ. Rev. forthcoming.
Kliem, M., Kriwoluzky, A., Sarferaz, S., 2016. On the low-frequency relationship between public deficits and inflation. J. Appl. Econ. 31 (3), 566–583.

Kocherlakota, N., Phelan, C., 1999. Explaining the fiscal theory of the price level. Fed. Reserve Bank Minneapolis Q. Rev. 23, 14–23.

Kriwoluzky, A., Müller, G.J., Wolf, M., 2014. Exit Expectations in Currency Unions. University of Bonn, Bonn, Germany.

Krugman, P.R., 1998. It's Baaack: Japan's slump and the return of the liquidity trap. Brookings Papers Econ. Act. 2, 137–187.

Lagos, R., Wright, R., 2005. A unified framework for monetary theory and policy analysis. J. Polit. Econ. 113 (3), 463–484.

Lane, P.R., Milesi-Ferretti, G.M., 2001. The external wealth of nations: measures of foreign assets and liabilities for industrial and developing countries. J. Int. Econ. 55 (2), 263–294.

Leeper, E.M., 1989. Policy rules, information, and fiscal effects in a 'Ricardian' model. Federal Reserve Board, International Finance Discussion Paper No. 360, August.

Leeper, E.M., 1991. Equilibria under 'active' and 'passive' monetary and fiscal policies. J. Monetary Econ. 27 (1), 129–147.

Leeper, E.M., 2011. Anchors aweigh: how fiscal policy can undermine 'good' monetary policy. In: Céspedes, L.F., Chang, R., Saravia, D. (Eds.), Monetary Policy Under Financial Turbulence. Banco Central de Chile, Santiago, pp. 411–453.

Leeper, E.M., 2016. Fiscal analysis is darned hard. In: Ódor, ´L. (Ed.), Rethinking Fiscal Policy After the Crisis. Cambridge University Press, Cambridge, UK.

Leeper, E.M., Li, B., 2015. On the Bias in Estimates of Fiscal Policy Behavior. Indiana University, Bloomington, IN.

Leeper, E.M., Nason, J.M., 2014. Bringing financial stability into monetary policy. Center for Applied Economics and Policy Research Working Paper No. 2014-003, Indiana University, November.

Leeper, E.M., Sims, C.A., 1994. Toward a modern macroeconomic model usable for policy analysis. In: Fischer, S., Rotemberg, J.J. (Eds.), NBER Macroeconomics Annual. MIT Press, Cambridge, MA, pp. 81–118.

Leeper, E.M., Walker, T.B., 2013. Perceptions and misperceptions of fiscal inflation. In: Alesina, A., Giavazzi, F. (Eds.), Fiscal Policy After the Financial Crisis. University of Chicago Press, Chicago, pp. 255–299.

Leeper, E.M., Zhou, X., 2013. Inflation's role in optimal monetary-fiscal policy. NBER Working Paper No. 19686, November.

Leeper, E.M., Leith, C., Liu, D., 2015a. Optimal Time-Consistent Monetary, Fiscal and Debt Maturity Policy. University of Glasgow, Glasgow, Scotland.

Leeper, E.M., Traum, N., Walker, T.B., 2015b. Clearing up the fiscal multiplier morass. NBER Working Paper No. 21433, July.

Leith, C., Liu, D., 2014. The inflation bias under Calvo and Rotemberg pricing. University of Glasgow Working Paper No. 2014-6.

Leith, C., Wren-Lewis, S., 2006. Compatibility between monetary and fiscal policy under emu. Eur. Econ. Rev. 50 (6), 1529–1556.

Leith, C., Wren-Lewis, S., 2008. Interactions between monetary and fiscal policy under flexible exchange rates. J. Econ. Dyn. Control 32 (9), 2854–2882.

Leith, C., Wren-Lewis, S., 2013. Fiscal sustainability in a new Keynesian model. J Money Credit Bank. 45 (8), 1477–1516.

Ljungqvist, L., Sargent, T.J., 2004. Recursive Macroeconomic Theory, second ed. MIT Press, Cambridge, MA.

Loyo, E., 1997. Going International with the Fiscal Theory of the Price Level. Princeton University, Princeton, NJ.

Loyo, E., 1999. Tight Money Paradox on the Loose: A Fiscalist Hyperinflation. Harvard University, Cambridge, MA.

Lucas Jr., R.E., Stokey, N.L., 1983. Optimal fiscal and monetary policy in an economy without capital. J. Monetary Econ. 12 (1), 55–93.

Marcet, A., Scott, A., 2009. Debt and deficit fluctuations and the structure of bond markets. J. Econ. Theory 21 (1), 473–501.

Martin, F.M., 2009. A positive theory of government debt. Rev. Econ. Dyn. 12 (4), 608–631.

Martin, F.M., 2011. On the joint determination of fiscal and monetary policy. J. Monetary Econ. 58 (2), 132–145.
McCallum, B.T., 1984. Are bond-financed deficits inflationary? J. Polit. Econ. 92 (February), 123–135.
McCallum, B.T., 2001. Indeterminacy, bubbles, and the fiscal theory of price level determination. J. Monetary Econ. 47 (1), 19–30.
Mendoza, E.G., Ostry, J.D., 2008. International evidence on fiscal solvency: is fiscal policy 'responsible'? J. Monetary Econ. 55 (6), 1081–1093.
Missale, A., 1999. Public Debt Management. Oxford University Press, Oxford.
Niemann, S., Pichler, P., Sorger, G., 2013. Public debt, discretionary policy, and inflation persistence. J. Econ. Dyn. Control 37 (6), 1097–1109.
Obstfeld, M., Rogoff, K., 1983. Speculative hyperinflations in maximizing models: can we rule them out? J. Polit. Econ. 91 (4), 675–687.
Persson, M., Persson, T., Svensson, L.E.O., 1987. Time consistency of fiscal and monetary policy. Econometrica 55 (6), 1419–1431.
Persson, M., Persson, T., Svensson, L.E.O., 2006. Time consistency of fiscal and monetary policy: a solution. Econometrica 74 (1), 193–212.
Phelps, E.S., 1973. Inflation in the theory of public finance. Swedish J. Econ. 75 (1), 67–82.
Prescott, E.C., 1986. Theory ahead of business cycle measurement. Carnegie-Rochester Conference Series on Public Policy, North-Holland, pp. 11–44.
Reis, R., 2013. The mystique surrounding the central bank's balance sheet, applied to the European crisis. Am. Econ. Rev. Papers Proc. 103 (3), 135–140.
Reis, R., 2015. QE in the Future: The Central Bank's Balance Sheet in a Fiscal Crisis. Columbia University, New York, NY.
Rotemberg, J.J., 1982. Sticky prices in the United States. J. Polit. Econ. 90 (December), 1187–1211.
Rotemberg, J.J., 1996. Prices, output, and hours: an empirical analysis based on a sticky price model. J. Monetary Econ. 37 (June), 505–533.
Sargent, T.J., 1986. The ends of four big inflations. In: Sargent, T.J. (Ed.), Rational Expectations and Inflation. Harper & Row, New York.
Sargent, T.J., Velde, F.R., 1995. Macroeconomic features of the French revolution. J. Polit. Econ. 103 (3), 474–518.
Sargent, T.J., Wallace, N., 1981. Some unpleasant monetarist arithmetic. Fed. Reserve Bank Minneapolis Q. Rev. 5 (Fall), 1–17.
Schmitt-Grohé, S., Uribe, M., 2004. Optimal fiscal and monetary policy under sticky prices. J. Econ. Theor. 114 (2), 198–230.
Schmitt-Grohé, S., Uribe, M., 2007. Optimal simple and implementable monetary and fiscal rules. J. Monetary Econ. 54 (6), 1702–1725.
Shim, S.D., 1984. Inflation and the Government Budget Constraint: International Evidence. Department of Economics, University of Minnesota. Unpublished Ph.D. Dissertation, August.
Sims, C.A., 1972. Money, income, and causality. Am. Econ. Rev. 62 (4), 540–552.
Sims, C.A., 1992. Interpreting the macroeconomic time series facts: the effects of monetary policy. Eur. Econ. Rev. 36, 975–1000.
Sims, C.A., 1994. A simple model for study of the determination of the price level and the interaction of monetary and fiscal policy. Econ. Theor. 4 (3), 381–399.
Sims, C.A., 1997, September. Fiscal Foundations of Price Stability in Open Economies. Yale University, New Haven, CT.
Sims, C.A., 1998. Econometric implications of the government budget constraint. J. Econ. 83 (1–2), 9–19.
Sims, C.A., 1999a. Domestic currency denominated government debt as equity in the primary surplus. Presented at the August 1999 Meetings of the Latin American region of the Econometric Society.
Sims, C.A., 1999b. The precarious fiscal foundations of EMU. De Economist 147 (4), 415–436.
Sims, C.A., 2001. Fiscal consequences for mexico of adopting the dollar. Journal of Money, Credit and Banking 33 (2, Part 2), 597–616.
Sims, C.A., 2011. Stepping on a rake: the role of fiscal policy in the inflation of the 1970s. Eur. Econ. Rev. 55 (1), 48–56.

Sims, C.A., 2013. Paper money. Am. Econ. Rev. 103 (2), 563–584.
Sims, C.A., Zha, T., 2006. Were there regime switches in US monetary policy? Am. Econ. Rev. 96 (1), 54–81.
Smets, F., Wouters, R., 2007. Shocks and frictions in US business cycles: a Bayesian DSGE approach. Am. Econ. Rev. 97 (3), 586–606.
Stein, H., 1996. The Fiscal Revolution in America, second ed. revised AEI Press, Washington, DC.
Tan, F., 2014. Two Econometric Interpretations of U.S. Fiscal and Monetary Policy Interactions. Indiana University, Bloomington, IN.
Tan, F., 2015. An Analytical Approach to New Keynesian Models Under the Fiscal Theory. Indiana University, Bloomington, IN.
Tan, F., Walker, T.B., 2014. Solving Generalized Multivariate Linear Rational Expectations Models. Indiana University, Bloomington, IN.
Taylor, J.B., 1993. Discretion versus policy rules in practice. Carnegie-Rochester Conf. Series Publ. Policy 39, 195–214.
Taylor, J.B., 1995. Monetary policy implications of greater fiscal discipline. In: Budget Deficits and Debt: Issues and Options. Federal Reserve Bank of Kansas City Economic Conference Proceedings, 1995 Jackson Hole Symposium, pp. 151–170.
Temin, P., Wigmore, B.A., 1990. The end of one big deflation. Explorations Econ. Hist. 27 (4), 483–502.
The Economist, 2016. Irredeemable? A former star of the emerging world faces a lost decade. http://www.economist.com/news/briefing/21684778-formerstar-emerging-world-faces-lost-decade-irredeemable, January 2.
Tobin, J., 1963. An essay on the principles of debt management. In: Commission on Money and Credit (Ed.), Fiscal and Debt Management Policies. Prentice-Hall, Englewood Cliffs, NJ, pp. 143–218.
Tobin, J., 1980. Asset Accumulation and Economic Activity. University of Chicago Press, Chicago.
Traum, N., Yang, S.C.S., 2011. Monetary and fiscal policy interactions in the post-war U.S. Eur. Econ. Rev. 55 (1), 140–164.
Uribe, M., 2006. A fiscal theory of sovereign risk. J. Monetary Econ. 53 (8), 1857–1875.
Velde, F.R., 2009. Chronicle of a deflation unforetold. J. Polit. Econ. 117 (4), 591–634.
Wallace, N., 1981. A Modigliani-Miller theorem for open-market operations. Am. Econ. Rev. 71 (3), 267–274.
Woodford, M., 1995. Price-level determinacy without control of a monetary aggregate. Carnegie-Rochester Conf. Series Publ. Policy 43, 1–46.
Woodford, M., 1998a. Control of the public debt: a requirement for price stability? In: Calvo, G., King, M. (Eds.), The Debt Burden and Its Consequences for Monetary Policy. St. Martin's Press, New York, pp. 117–154.
Woodford, M., 1998b. Public Debt and the Price Level. Princeton University, Princeton, NJ.
Woodford, M., 1999. Comment on Cochrane's 'a frictionless view of U.S. inflation'. In: Bernanke, B.S., Rotemberg, J.J. (Eds.), NBER Macroeconomics Annual 1998, vol. 13. MIT Press, Cambridge, MA, pp. 390–419.
Woodford, M., 2001. Fiscal requirements for price stability. J. Money Credit Bank. 33 (3), 669–728.
Woodford, M., 2003. Interest and Prices: Foundations of a Theory of Monetary Policy. Princeton University Press, Princeton, NJ.

CHAPTER 31

Fiscal Multipliers: Liquidity Traps and Currency Unions☆

E. Farhi*, I. Werning†
*Harvard University, Cambridge, MA, United States
†MIT, Cambridge, MA, United States

Contents

☆ We thank the editors John Taylor and Harald Uhlig for detailed comments, as well as suggestions and comments by Gabriel Chodorow-Reich, Jon Steinsson, and Michael Weber.

Handbook of Macroeconomics, Volume 2B
ISSN 1574-0048, http://dx.doi.org/10.1016/bs.hesmac.2016.06.006

Abstract

We provide explicit solutions for government spending multipliers during a liquidity trap and within a fixed exchange regime using standard closed and open-economy New Keynesian models. We confirm the potential for large multipliers during liquidity traps. For a currency union, we show that self-financed multipliers are small, always below unity, unless the accompanying tax adjustments involve substantial static redistribution from low to high marginal propensity to consume agents, or dynamic redistribution from future to present non-Ricardian agents. But outside-financed multipliers which require no domestic tax adjustment can be large, especially when the average marginal propensity to consume on domestic goods is high or when government spending shocks are very persistent. Our solutions are relevant for local and national multipliers, providing insight into the economic mechanisms at work as well as the testable implications of these models.

Keywords

Currency unions, Non-Ricardian effects, Open economy model, Liquidity traps, New Keynesian effects

JEL Classification Code

E62

1. INTRODUCTION

Economists generally agree that macroeconomic stabilization should be handled first and foremost by monetary policy. Yet monetary policy can run into constraints that impair its effectiveness. For example, the economy may find itself in a liquidity trap, where interest rates hit zero, preventing further reductions in the interest rate. Similarly, countries that belong to currency unions, or states within a country, do not have the option of an independent monetary policy. Some economists advocate for fiscal policy to fill this void, increasing government spending to stimulate the economy. Others disagree, and the issue remains deeply controversial, as evidenced by vigorous debates on the magnitude of fiscal multipliers. No doubt, this situation stems partly from the lack of definitive empirical evidence, but, in our view, the absence of clear theoretical benchmarks also plays an important role. Although various recent contributions have substantially furthered our understanding, to date, the implications of standard macroeconomic models have not been fully worked out. This is the goal of this chapter. By clarifying the theoretical mechanisms in a unified way, we hope that it will help stimulate more research to validate or invalidate different aspects of the models.

We solve for the response of the economy to changes in the path for government spending during liquidity traps or within currency unions using standard New Keynesian closed and open-economy monetary models. A number of features distinguish our approach and contribution. First, our approach departs from the existing literature by focusing on *fiscal multipliers* that encapsulate the effects of spending for any path for government spending, instead of solving for a particular multiplier associated with the expansion of a single benchmark path for spending (eg, an autoregressive shock process to spending). Second, we obtain simple closed-form solutions for these multipliers. The more explicit and detailed expressions help us uncover the precise mechanisms underlying the effects of fiscal policy and allow us to deliver several new results.

Third, our analysis confirms that constraints on monetary policy are crucial, but also highlights that the nature of the constraint is also important. In particular, we draw a sharp contrast between a liquidity trap, with a binding zero-lower bound, and a currency union, with a fixed exchange rate.

Finally, in addition to nominal rigidities and constraints on monetary policy, we stress the importance of incorporating financial frictions for the analysis of fiscal policy. We do so by extending the benchmark models to include both incomplete markets and non-Ricardian borrowing constrained consumers, allowing for high and heterogeneous marginal propensities to consume out of current income. These financial market imperfections may be especially relevant in the aftermath of a financial crisis, situations where fiscal stimulus is often considered.

Our analysis has obvious implications for the interpretation of recent empirical studies on national and local multipliers. The empirical literature adopts different definitions of summary fiscal multipliers. For example, one popular notion used in many empirical studies consists in computing the ratio of some (discounted or not) average of the impulse responses of output and government spending in response to an innovation in government spending, up to some horizon (in practice 2 or 3 years). We show how our results can be used to compute such numbers analytically, and also discuss alternative definitions of summary fiscal multipliers.

Our results confirm that, in these standard models, fiscal policy can be especially potent during a liquidity trap. In the standard Ricardian model, the multiplier for output is always greater than one. We explicit the way in which the mechanism works through inflation. Higher government spending during a liquidity trap stimulates inflation. With fixed nominal interest rates, this reduces real interest rates which increases current private consumption. The increase in consumption in turn leads to more inflation, creating a feedback loop. The fiscal multiplier is increasing in the degree of price flexibility, which is intuitive given that the mechanism relies on the response of inflation. We show that in the model, backloading spending leads to larger effects; the rationale is that inflation then has more time to affect spending decisions.

For a country or region in a currency union, by contrast, government spending is less effective at increasing output. In particular, in the standard Ricardian model, we show that private consumption is crowded out by government spending, so that the multiplier is less than one. Moreover, price flexibility diminishes the effectiveness of spending, instead of increasing it. We explain this result using a simple argument that illustrates its robustness. Government spending leads to inflation in domestically produced goods and this loss in competitiveness depresses private spending.

It may seem surprising that fiscal multipliers are less than one when the exchange rate is fixed, contrasting with multipliers above one in liquidity traps. We show that even though in both cases the nominal interest rate is fixed, there is a crucial difference: a fixed exchange rate implies a fixed nominal interest rate, but the reverse is not true. Indeed, we prove that the liquidity trap analysis implicitly combines a shock to government spending with a one-off devaluation. The positive response of consumption relies entirely on this devaluation. A currency union rules out such a devaluation, explaining the difference in the response of consumption.

In the context of a country in a currency union, our results uncover the importance of transfers from outside—from other countries or regions. In the short run, when prices have not fully adjusted, positive transfers from outside increase the demand for home goods, stimulating output. We compute "transfer multipliers" that capture the response of the economy to such transfers. We show that these multipliers may be large when there is a high degree of home bias (ie, low degree of openness).

Note that the analysis of outside transfers requires some form of market incompleteness. Otherwise, with complete financial markets, any outside transfer would be completely undone by private insurance arrangements with outsiders. Such an extreme offset is unlikely to be realistic. Thus, we modify the standard open-economy model, which assumes complete markets, to consider the case with incomplete markets.

Understanding the effect of outside transfers is important because such transfers are often tied to government spending. This is relevant for the literature estimating local multipliers, which exploits cross-sectional variation, examining the effects of government spending across regions, states, or municipalities, within a country. In the US federal military spending allocated to a particular state is financed by the country as a whole. The same is true for exogenous differences, due to idiosyncratic provisions in the law, in the distribution of a federal stimulus package. Likewise, idiosyncratic portfolio returns accruing to a particular state's coffers represent a windfall for this state against the rest.

When changes in spending are financed by such outside transfers, the associated multipliers are a combination of self-financed multipliers and transfer multipliers. As a result, multipliers may be substantially larger than one even in a currency union. This difference is more significant when the degree of home bias is large, since this increases the marginal propensity to spend on home produced goods.

The degree of persistence in government spending is also important. Because agents seek to smooth consumption over time, the more temporary the government spending shock, the more the per-period transfer that accompanies the increase in spending is saved in anticipation of lower per-period transfers in the future. As a result, the difference in the effects on current output between outside-financed and self-financed government spending can be large for relatively persistent shocks, but may be small if shocks are relatively temporary. However, as we shall see, this distinction is blurred in the presence of liquidity constraints.

We explore non-Ricardian effects from fiscal policy by introducing hand-to-mouth consumers in addition to permanent income consumers. We think of this as a tractable way of modeling liquidity constraints. Both in a liquidity trap and in a currency union, government spending now has additional effects because of the differences in marginal propensities to consume of both groups of agents.

First, the incidence of taxes across these two groups matters, and redistribution from low marginal propensity to consume permanent-income agents to high marginal propensity to consume hand-to-mouth agents increases output. Second, since the model is non-Ricardian, the timing of taxes matters.

Both these effects can play a role independently of government spending. Indeed, one may consider tax changes without any change in government spending. However, changes in government spending must be accompanied by changes in taxes. As a result, whether government spending is, at the margin, debt-financed or tax-financed matters. Likewise, the distributional makeup of tax changes, across marginal propensities to consume, also matters. These effects can potentially substantially increase fiscal multipliers, both in liquidity traps and for countries or regions in a currency union. In particular, they may raise the multipliers above one for a region within a currency union.

Most importantly, liquidity constraints significantly magnify the difference between self-financed and outside-financed fiscal multipliers for temporary government spending shocks. Intuitively, a higher marginal propensity to consume implies that a greater part of the outside transfer is spent in the short run, contributing towards an increase in fiscal multipliers.

Overall, this discussion brings back the old Keynesian emphasis on the marginal propensity to consume. In particular, for temporary government spending shocks, the difference between self-financed and outside-financed fiscal multipliers is large when the average marginal propensity to consume on domestic goods is large—either due to a large number of liquidity constrained agents or due to a high degree of home bias in spending.

Finally, we show how to bridge our results for small open economies in a currency union and closed economies in a liquidity trap by simultaneously considering the effects government spending in all the countries within a currency union, depending on whether the currency union is in a liquidity trap or whether the central bank of the union can target inflation by adjusting interest rates.

Related Literature

Our chapter is related to several strands of theoretical and empirical literatures. We will discuss those that are most closely related.

We contribute to the literature that studies fiscal policy in the New Keynesian model in liquidity traps. Eggertsson (2011), Woodford (2011), and Christiano et al. (2011) show that fiscal multipliers can be large at the zero lower bound, while Werning (2012) studies optimal government spending with and without commitment to monetary policy. Gali and Monacelli (2008) study optimal fiscal policy in a currency union, but they conduct an exclusively normative analysis and do not compute fiscal multipliers. The results and simulations reported in Corsetti et al. (2011), Nakamura and Steinsson (2011), and Erceg and Linde (2012) show that fiscal multipliers are generally below one under fixed exchange rates yet higher than under flexible exchange rates (away from the zero bound), somewhat validating the conventional Mundell–Flemming view that fiscal policy is more effective with fixed exchange rates (see, eg, Dornbusch, 1980). Our solutions extend these results and help sharpen the intuition for them, by discussing the role of implicit devaluations and transfers. Gali et al. (2007) introduce hand-to-mouth consumers and study the effects of government spending under a Taylor rule in a closed economy. Our setup extends such an analysis to liquidity traps and currency unions in an open economy. Cook and Devereux (2011) study the spillover effects of fiscal policy in open economy models of the liquidity trap. We also examine this question but focus on a different context, that of a currency union, depending on whether it is or not in a liquidity trap.

Our chapter is also related to a large empirical literature on fiscal multipliers. Estimating national fiscal multipliers poses serious empirical challenges. The main difficulties arise from the endogeneity of government spending, the formation of expectations about future tax and spending policies, and the reaction of monetary policy. Most of the literature tries to resolve these difficulties by resorting to Structural VARs. Some papers use military spending as an instrument for government spending. The relevant empirical literature is very large, so we refer the reader to Ramey (2011) for a recent survey. Estimating fiscal multipliers in liquidity traps is nearly impossible because liquidity traps are rare. The closest substitute is provided by estimates that condition of the level of economic activity. Some authors (see, eg, Gordon and Krenn, 2010; Auerbach and Gorodnichenko, 2012) estimate substantially larger national multipliers during deep recessions, but the magnitude of these differential effects remains debated (see, eg, Barro and Redlick, 2009).

States or regions within a country offer an attractive alternative with plausible exogenous variations in spending. Indeed the literature on local multipliers has recently been very active, with contributions by Clemens and Miran (2010), Cohen et al. (2010), Serrato and Wingender (2010), Shoag (2010), Acconcia et al. (2011), Chodorow-Reich et al. (2011), Fishback and Kachanovskaya (2010), and Nakamura and Steinsson (2011). These papers tend to find large multipliers. Our chapter helps interpret these findings. Government spending at the local level in these experiments is generally tied to transfers from outside. It follows that these estimates may be interpreted as combining spending and transfer multipliers, as we define them here.

2. MULTIPLIERS AND SUMMARY MULTIPLIERS

We first set the stage by taking a purely statistical perspective and use it discuss the connection between theory and empirical work.

Suppose one has isolated a relationship between output and government spending encoded in the dynamic response of both variables to a particular structural shock of interest. One may then summarize this relationship into a single "fiscal multiplier" number in a number of ways. Of course, the entire impulse response contains strictly more information, but the multiplier may be a convenient way to summarize it. In the rest of this chapter, we derive the response of output to *any* spending shock for a set of standard macroeconomic models. The implications of each model are encoded in a set of coefficients or loadings, which can be mapped into dynamic responses to output for any impulse from spending.

2.1 Responses and Shocks

2.1.1 Impulse Responses

Suppose we have two time series $\{\hat{g}_t, \hat{y}_t\}$ for government spending and output respectively and that these series (after detrending) are stationary. Assume we can write these two series as a linear function of current and past shocks

$$\hat{g}_t = \hat{A}^g(L)\hat{\varepsilon}_t = \sum_{j=1}^{J} A^{gj}(L)\varepsilon_t^j = \sum_{j=1}^{J}\sum_{k=0}^{\infty} \psi_k^{gj}\varepsilon_{t-k}^j$$

$$\hat{y}_t = \hat{A}^y(L)\hat{\varepsilon}_t = \sum_{j=1}^{J} A^{yj}(L)\varepsilon_t^j = \sum_{j=1}^{J}\sum_{k=0}^{\infty} \psi_k^{yj}\varepsilon_{t-k}^j$$

where the vector of shocks $\hat{\varepsilon}_t = (\varepsilon_t^1, \varepsilon_t^2, \ldots, \varepsilon_t^J)'$ have zero mean and are uncorrelated over time, $\mathbb{E}[\varepsilon_t] = 0$ and $\mathbb{E}[\hat{\varepsilon}_t \hat{\varepsilon}_s'] = 0$ for $t \neq s$. Let us next isolate the effect of one particular shock $j \in J$ and define the components $\{g_t, y_t\}$ explained by this shock. Dropping the j subscript we write this as

$$g_t = A^g(L)\varepsilon_t = \sum_{k=0}^{\infty} \psi_k^g \varepsilon_{t-k} \tag{1a}$$

$$y_t = A^y(L)\varepsilon_t = \sum_{k=0}^{\infty} \psi_k^y \varepsilon_{t-k} \tag{1b}$$

where ε_t is a scalar shock with zero mean and is uncorrelated over time, $\mathbb{E}[\varepsilon_t] = 0$ and $\mathbb{E}[\varepsilon_t \varepsilon_s] = 0$ for $t \neq s$. The natural interpretation is that this particular shock, ε_t, is an exogenous structural shock to government spending. The coefficients $\{\psi_k^i\}$ are the impulse response functions (IRFs) to this shock. The responses can then be interpreted as encompassing a causal relationship. Strictly speaking, however, most of the discussion below does not require this interpretation.

2.1.2 VARs and Instruments

One way to obtain the decomposition of the series described above is using a structural VAR approach. To see this, suppose the original variables $\hat{g}_t$ and $\hat{y}_t$ are part of a VAR, which may include $J-2$ other variables (eg, inflation and interest rates). Suppose ε_t is one of the shocks. By definition, this shock is white noise and is orthogonal to the remaining $J-1$ shocks in the VAR at all leads and lags. In practice, the shock ε_t may be identified using structural assumptions, such as short-run or long-run restrictions. Under appropriate conditions, the shock may then acquire the economic interpretation of a fiscal shock and the response to output can be interpreted as an estimate of the causal relationship between spending and output.

Alternatively, the decomposition may result from an external instrumental variable. Suppose we have a scalar time series $\{z_t\}$ and let the Wold representation of z_t be[a]

$$z_t = A^z(L)\varepsilon_t = \sum_{k=0}^{\infty} \psi_k^z \varepsilon_{t-k}.$$

Thus, the shock ε_t is defined and identified as the innovation from the Wold representation of the instrument z_t. Now project $(\hat{g}_t, \hat{y}_t)$ linearly onto contemporaneous and lagged values of z_t, obtaining the predictors g_t and y_t (with residuals $\tilde{g}_t$ and $\tilde{y}_t$). These can then be represented as in (1). Once again, if the instrument is deemed exogenous to other economic fundamental shocks, then this shock may acquire economic interpretation as a fiscal shock and the response of output and spending can be interpreted as an estimate of the causal relationship between these variables.

2.2 Summary Multipliers

The sequences $\{\psi_k^g, \psi_k^y\}$ provide a full characterization of the joint behavior of $\{y_t\}$ and $\{g_t\}$, with respect to the shock $\{\varepsilon_t\}$. Suppose one insists on summarizing this

[a] Abstracting from the deterministic component.

relationship by a single number, called a "fiscal multiplier." First define the contemporaneous multiplier

$$m_k = \frac{\psi_k^y}{\psi_k^g}$$

indexed by $k=0,1,\ldots$ A general summary multiplier may take a ratio of the form

$$M^y = \frac{\sum_{k=0}^{\infty} \lambda_k^y \psi_k^y}{\sum_{k=0}^{\infty} \lambda_k^g \psi_k^g} = \frac{\sum_{k=0}^{\infty} \lambda_k^y \psi_k^g}{\sum_{k=0}^{\infty} \lambda_k^g \psi_k^g} \sum_{k=0}^{\infty} m_k \omega_k$$

where $\omega_k = \lambda_k^y \psi_k^g / \sum_{k=0}^{\infty} \lambda_k^y \psi_k^g$ is a weight that adds up to unity. A simple case is to add up the unweighted the reaction over the first N periods,

$$M^y = \frac{\sum_{k=0}^{N} \psi_k^y}{\sum_{k=0}^{N} \psi_k^g} = \sum_{k=0}^{N} m_k \omega_k,$$

where $\omega_k = \psi_k^g / \sum_{k=0}^{N} \psi_k^g$.

2.2.1 Regression Based Summary Multipliers: OLS and IV

Another popular way to proceed in obtaining a summary fiscal multiplier is regress output on spending and to take the coefficient on spending as a summary multiplier. Consider the relationship

$$\hat{y}_t = \beta^{OLS} \hat{g}_t + u_t^{OLS},$$

where $\mathbb{E}[\hat{g}_t u_t^{OLS}] = 0$ and

$$\beta^{OLS} \equiv \frac{\mathbb{E}[\hat{g}_t \hat{y}_t]}{\mathbb{E}[\hat{g}_t^2]} = \frac{\sum_{j=1}^{J} \sum_{k=0}^{\infty} \psi_k^{yj} \psi_k^{gj}}{\sum_{j=1}^{J} \sum_{k=0}^{\infty} \left(\psi_k^{gj}\right)^2} = \sum_{j=1}^{J} \sum_{k=0}^{\infty} m_k^j \omega_k^j.$$

where

$$m_k^j = \frac{\psi_k^{yj}}{\psi_k^{gj}}, \qquad \omega_k^j \equiv \frac{(\psi_k^{gj})^2}{\sum_{l=0}^{\infty} (\psi_l^{gj})^2}.$$

Thus, the population regression recovers a weighted average of the k-multipliers associated with each shock j.

Consider next an instrumental variable regression

$$\hat{y}_t = \beta^{IV} \hat{g}_t + u_t^{IV}$$

where $\mathbb{E}[z_t u_t^{IV}] = 0$ and

$$\beta^{IV} \equiv \beta^{OLS} \equiv \frac{\mathbb{E}[y_t z_t]}{\mathbb{E}[g_t z_t]} = \frac{\sum_{k=0}^{\infty} \psi_k^y \psi_k^z}{\sum_{k=0}^{\infty} \psi_k^g \psi_k^z} = \sum_{k=0}^{\infty} m_k \omega_k,$$

with weights

$$\omega_k \equiv \frac{\psi_k^g \psi_k^z}{\sum_{l=0}^{\infty} \psi_l^g \psi_k^z}.$$

These weights are positive if ψ_k^g and ψ_k^z take the same sign.[b]

2.3 Connection to Models

As we will show, the implications of a model for fiscal spending can be encoded in a sequence of theoretical multipliers $\{\alpha_{t,k}\}$, where the element $\alpha_{t,k}$ represents the predicted response of output in period t to government spending in period k. This response is calculated as the first-order effect by linearizing the model.

What is the connection between $\{\alpha_{t,k}\}$ and the impulse responses $\{\psi_k^g\}$ and $\{\psi_k^g\}$ discussed above? Suppose we can interpret ε_t as an exogenous shock to the path for spending as summarized by $\{\psi_k^g\}$ and we can interpret the change in spending as a having causal endogenous response in output summarized by $\{\psi_t^y\}$. In the model both responses would be related by

$$\psi_k^y = \sum_{k'=0}^{\infty} \psi_{k'}^g \alpha_{k,k'},$$

for all $t = 0, 1, \ldots$ Given the theoretical multipliers, this relationship give us the output response $\{\psi_k^y\}$ for any given government spending response $\{\psi_t^g\}$.

Under what conditions can we invert this relationship and identify the theoretical multipliers $\{\alpha_{t,k}\}$ from the responses $\{\psi_k^g\}$ and $\{\psi_k^y\}$? For a single pair of $\{\psi_k^g\}$ and $\{\psi_k^y\}$ the answer is generally negative. For any given k the $\alpha_{k,\cdot}$ sequence is not identified: we can only identify the value of the sum $\sum_{k'=0}^{\infty} \psi_{k'}^g \{\alpha_{k,k'}\}$.

[b] In some cases, for example, Nakamura and Steinsson (2011), the IV regressions are run in differences. It is straightforward to adjust the calculations above in this case.

Without further information identification would only be possible if we had multiple responses, $\{\psi_k^g\}$ restrictions, $\{\psi_k^y\}$, that is, multiple spending shocks.

A special case obtains if the response is purely forward looking, as is the case in some of the simplest macroeconomic models. To see this, assume that $\alpha_{t,k} = \alpha_{0,k-t}$ for $k = t, t+1, \ldots$ and $\alpha_{t,k} = 0$ for $k = 1, 2, \ldots, t-1$. Then we have

$$\psi_t^y = \sum_{k=t}^{\infty} \psi_k^g \alpha_{0,k-t}.$$

Then we can identify the entire sequence $\{\alpha_{0,k-t}\}$ from the pair of sequences $\{\psi_k^g\}$ and $\{\psi_k^y\}$, provided we satisfy a standard rank condition (so that the set of sequences $\{\psi_{k-t}^g\}$ for $t \in \{0, 1, \ldots\}$ are linearly independent).

3. A CLOSED ECONOMY

We consider a one-time shock to the current and future path of spending that is realized at the beginning of time $t = 0$ that upsets the steady state. To simplify and focus on the impulse response to this shock, we abstract from ongoing uncertainty at other dates.[c] We adopt a continuous time framework. This is convenient for some calculations but is completely inessential to any of our results.

The remainder of this section specifies a standard New Keynesian model environment; readers familiar with this setting may wish to skip directly to Section 4.

Households

There is a representative household with preferences represented by the utility function

$$\int_0^\infty e^{-\rho t} \left[\frac{C_t^{1-\sigma}}{1-\sigma} + \chi \frac{G_t^{1-\sigma}}{1-\sigma} - \frac{N_t^{1+\phi}}{1+\phi} \right] dt,$$

where N_t is labor, and C_t is a consumption index defined by

$$C_t = \left(\int_0^1 C_t(j)^{\frac{\epsilon-1}{\epsilon}} dj \right)^{\frac{\epsilon}{\epsilon-1}},$$

where $j \in [0, 1]$ denotes an individual good variety. Thus, ϵ is the elasticity between varieties produced within a given country. We denote by $P_t(j)$ is the price of variety j, and by

$$P_t = \left(\int_0^1 P_t(j)^{1-\epsilon} dj \right)^{\frac{1}{1-\epsilon}}$$

the corresponding price index.

[c] Since we are interested in a first order approximation of the equilibrium response to shocks, which can be solved by studying the log-linearized model, the presence of ongoing uncertainty would not affect any of our calculation or conclusions (we have certainty equivalence).

Households seek to maximize their utility subject to the budget constraints

$$\dot{D}_t = i_t D_t - \int_0^1 P_t(j) C_t(j) dj + W_t N_t + \Pi_t + T_t$$

for $t \geq 0$ together with a no-Ponzi condition. In this equation, W_t is the nominal wage, Π_t represents nominal profits and T_t is a nominal lump sum transfer. The bond holdings of home agents are denoted by D_t and the nominal interest rate for the currency union is denoted by i_t.

Government

Government consumption G_t is an aggregate of varieties just as private consumption,

$$G_t = \left(\int_0^1 G_t(j)^{\frac{\epsilon-1}{\epsilon}} dj \right)^{\frac{\epsilon}{\epsilon-1}}.$$

For any level of expenditure $\int_0^1 P_t(j) G_t(j) dj$, the government splits its expenditure across these varieties to maximize G_t. Spending is financed by lump-sum taxes. Ricardian equivalence holds, so that the timing of these taxes is irrelevant.

Firms

A typical firm produces a differentiated good with a linear technology

$$Y_t(j) = A_t N_t(j),$$

where A_t is productivity in the home country.

We allow for a constant employment tax $1 + \tau^L$, so that real marginal cost is given by $\frac{1+\tau^L}{A_t}\frac{W_t}{P_t}$. We take this employment tax to be constant in our model, as in standard in the literature. The tax rate is set to offset the monopoly distortion so that $\tau^L = -\frac{1}{\varepsilon}$. However, none of our results hinge on this particular value.

We adopt the standard Calvo price-setting framework. In every moment a randomly flow ρ_δ of firms can reset their prices. Those firms that reset choose a reset price P_t^r to solve

$$\max_{P_t^r} \int_0^\infty e^{-\rho_\delta s - \int_0^s i_{t+z} dz} \left(P_t^r Y_{t+s|t} - (1+\tau^L) W_t \frac{Y_{t+s|t}}{A_t} \right),$$

where $Y_{t+k|t} = \left(\frac{P_t^r}{P_{t+k}} \right)^{-\epsilon} Y_{t+k}$, taking the sequences for W_t, Y_t and P_t as given.

3.1 Equilibrium Conditions

We now summarize equilibrium conditions for the home country. Market clearing in the goods and labor market requires that:

$$Y_t = C_t + G_t,$$

$$N_t = \frac{Y_t}{A_t}\Delta_t,$$

where Δ_t is an index of price dispersion $\Delta_t = \int_0^1 \left(\frac{P_{H,t}(j)}{P_{H,t}}\right)^{-\epsilon}$. The Euler equation

$$\sigma\frac{\dot{C}_t}{C_t} = i_t - \pi_t - \rho$$

ensures the agents' intertemporal optimization, where $\pi_t = \dot{P}_t/P_t$ is inflation.

The natural allocation is a reference allocation that prevails if prices are flexible and government consumption is held constant at its steady state value G. We denote the natural allocation with a bar over variables.

We omit the first-order conditions for the price-setting problem faced by firms here. We shall only analyze a log-linearized version of the model which collapses these equilibrium conditions into the New Keynesian Phillips curve presented below.

4. NATIONAL MULTIPLIERS IN A LIQUIDITY TRAP

To obtain multipliers, we study the log-linearized equilibrium conditions around the natural allocation with constant government spending. Define

$$c_t = (1-\mathcal{G})(\log(C_t) - \log(\bar{C}_t)) \approx \frac{C_t - \bar{C}_t}{Y},$$

$$y_t = \log Y_t - \log \bar{Y}_t \approx \frac{Y_t - \bar{Y}_t}{Y} \qquad g_t = \mathcal{G}(\log G_t - \log G) \approx \frac{G_t - G}{Y},$$

where $\mathcal{G} = \frac{G}{Y}$. So that we have, up to a first order approximation,

$$y_t = c_t + g_t.$$

The log linearized system is then

$$\dot{c}_t = \hat{\sigma}^{-1}(i_t - \pi_t - \bar{r}_t), \tag{2}$$

$$\dot{\pi}_t = \rho\pi_t - \kappa(c_t + (1-\xi)g_t), \tag{3}$$

where $\hat{\sigma} = \frac{\sigma}{1-\mathcal{G}}$, $\lambda = \rho_\delta(\rho + \rho_\delta)$, $\kappa = \lambda(\hat{\sigma} + \phi)$ and $\xi = \frac{\hat{\sigma}}{\hat{\sigma} + \phi}$. Eq. (2) is the Euler equation and Eq. (3) is the New Keynesian Philips curve. Here, $\bar{r}_t$ is the natural rate of interest, defined as the real interest rate that prevail at the natural allocation, ie, Eq. (2) with $c_t = 0$ for all $t \geq 0$ implies $i_t - \pi_t = \bar{r}_t$ for all $t \geq 0$.

It will prove useful to define the following two numbers ν and $\bar{\nu}$ (the eigenvalues of the system):

$$\nu = \frac{\rho - \sqrt{\rho^2 + 4\kappa\hat{\sigma}^{-1}}}{2} \qquad \bar{\nu} = \frac{\rho + \sqrt{\rho^2 + 4\kappa\hat{\sigma}^{-1}}}{2}.$$

If prices were completely flexible, then consumption and labor are determined in every period by two static conditions: the labor consumption condition and the resource constraint. Spending affects the solution and gives rise to the neoclassical multiplier $1 - \xi$, which is positive but less than 1 and entirely due to a wealth effect on labor supply.

From now on, we take as given a path for the interest rate $\{i_t\}$ summarizing monetary policy. To resolve or sidestep issues of multiplicity one can assume that there is a date T such that $c_t = g_t = \pi_t = 0$ and $i_t = \bar{r}_t$ for $t \geq T$.[d] A leading example is a liquidity trap scenario where $i_t = 0$ and $\bar{r}_t < 0$ for $t < T$. However, although this is a useful interpretation but is not required for the analysis below.

Remark 1 Suppose $c_T = 0$ for some date T, then

$$c_t = \int_t^T (i_{t+s} - \pi_{t+s} - \bar{r}_{t+s})ds,$$

so that given the inflation path $\{\pi_t\}$ the consumption path $\{c_t\}$ is independent of the spending path $\{g_t\}$.

This remark highlights that the mechanism by which government spending affects consumption, in the New Keynesian model, is inflation which affects the real interest rate. One can draw two implications from this. First, other policy instruments that affect inflation, such as taxes, may have similarly policy effects. Second, empirical work on fiscal multipliers has not focused on the role inflation plays and it may be interesting to test the predicted connection between output and inflation present in New Keynesian models.

4.1 Fiscal Multipliers Solved

Since the system is linear it admits a closed form solution. We can express any solution with government spending as

$$c_t = \tilde{c}_t + \int_0^\infty \alpha_s^c g_{t+s} ds, \tag{4a}$$

[d] Note that T may be arbitrarily large and will have no impact on the solution provided below. Indeed, the characterization of the equilibrium is valid even without selecting an equilibrium this way: one just interprets c^* and π^* below any equilibrium in the set of equilibrium attained when $g_t = 0$ for all t. The solution then describes the entire set of equilibria for other spending paths $\{g_t\}$.

$$\pi_t = \tilde{\pi}_t + \int_0^\infty \alpha_s^\pi g_{t+s} ds, \tag{4b}$$

where $\{\tilde{c}_t, \tilde{\pi}_t\}$ are equilibria with $g_t = 0$ for all t. We focus on the integral term $\int_0^\infty \alpha_s^i g_{t+s} ds$ for $i = c$, π as a measure of the effects of fiscal policy $g \neq 0$. We assume the integrals are well defined, although we allow and discuss the case where it is $+\infty$ or $-\infty$ below.

Focusing on consumption, we call the sequence of coefficients $\{\alpha_s^c\}$ *fiscal multipliers.* It is crucial to note that these are *total private consumption multipliers* and not *output multipliers*. Indeed, output is given by

$$y_t = \tilde{y}_t + g_t + \int_0^\infty \alpha_s^c g_{t+s} ds.$$

Whereas the natural benchmark for consumption multipliers is 0, that for output multipliers is 1.

The coefficients α_s^c do not depend on calendar time t, nor do they depend on the interest rate paths $\{i_t\}$ and $\{r_t\}$. Thus, the impact on consumption or output, given by the term $\int_0^\infty \alpha_s^c g_{t+s} ds$, depends only on the future path for spending summarized weighted by $\{\alpha_s^c\}$.

There are two motivations for adopting $\int_0^\infty \alpha_s^c g_{t+s} ds$ as a measure of the impact of fiscal policy, one more practical, the other more conceptual.

1. The more practical motivation applies if the economy finds itself in a liquidity trap with nominal interest rates immobilized at zero, at least for some time. Fiscal multipliers $\{\alpha_s^c\}$ can then be used to predict the effects of fiscal policy. To see this, suppose the zero lower bound is binding until T so that $i_t = 0$ for $t < T$; suppose that after T monetary policy delivers an equilibrium with zero inflation, so that $\pi_t = 0$ for $t \geq T$. As is well known, the resulting equilibrium without government spending ($g_t = 0$ for all t) features a negative consumption gap and deflation: $\tilde{c}_t$, $\tilde{\pi}_t < 0$ for $t < T$ (see, eg, Werning, 2012).

   Now, consider a stimulus plan that attempts to improve this outcome by setting $g_t > 0$ for $t < T$ and $g_t = 0$ for $t \geq T$. Then $\int_0^\infty \alpha_s^c g_{t+s} ds = \int_0^{T-t} \alpha_s^c g_{t+s} ds$ is precisely the effect of the fiscal expansion on consumption c_t, relative to the outcome without the stimulus plan $\tilde{c}_t$.

   More generally, suppose that after the trap spending may be nonzero and that monetary may or may not be described as securing zero inflation. Even in this case, we may still use fiscal multipliers to measure the impact of fiscal policy during the liquidity trap: one can write $c_t = c_T + \int_0^{T-t} \alpha_s^c g_{t+s} ds$ for $t < T$, where the c_T encapsulates the combined effects of fiscal and monetary policy after the trap $t \geq T$.
2. More conceptually, our fiscal multipliers provide a natural decomposition of the effects of the fiscal policy, over what is attainable by monetary policy alone.

   Eqs. (4a) and (4b) characterize the entire set of equilibria for $g \neq 0$ by providing a one-to-one mapping between equilibria with $g = 0$. Both $\tilde{c}_t$ and $\tilde{\pi}_t$ are equilibria with

$g = 0$ and are affected by monetary policy, as summarized, among other things, by the interest rate path $\{i_t\}$.

We can represent these facts as a relationship between the set of equilibria with and without government spending,

$$\mathcal{E}_g = \mathcal{E}_0 + \alpha \cdot g,$$

where $\mathcal{E}_0$ represents the set of equilibria when $g_t = 0$ for all t, while $\mathcal{E}_g$ is the set of equilibria for a given path for spending $g = \{g_t\}$. Here $\alpha = \{\alpha_s^c, \alpha_s^\pi\}$ collects the fiscal multipliers and the cross product $\alpha \cdot g$ represents the integrals $\int_0^\infty \alpha_s^i g_{t+s} ds$ for $i = c, \pi$. The set $\mathcal{E}_g$ is a displaced version of $\mathcal{E}_0$ in the direction $\alpha \cdot g$. Each equilibrium point in $\mathcal{E}_0$ is shifted in parallel by $\alpha \cdot g$ to another equilibrium point in $\mathcal{E}_g$ and it shares the same nominal interest rate path $\{i_t\}$. This last fact is unimportant for this second conceptual motivation, since the focus is on comparing the two sets, not equilibrium points. Instead, the important issue is that $\alpha \cdot g$ measures the influence of government spending on the set of equilibria. This provides a conceptual motivation for studying the multipliers α, since they summarize this influence. In other words, without spending one can view monetary policy as selecting from the set $\mathcal{E}_0$, while with government spending monetary policy can choose from $\mathcal{E}_g$. The effects of fiscal policy on the new options is then precisely determined by the shift $\alpha \cdot g$. Fig. 1 represents this idea pictorially.[e]

Our first result delivers a closed-form solution for fiscal multipliers. Using this closed form one can characterize the multiplier quite tightly.

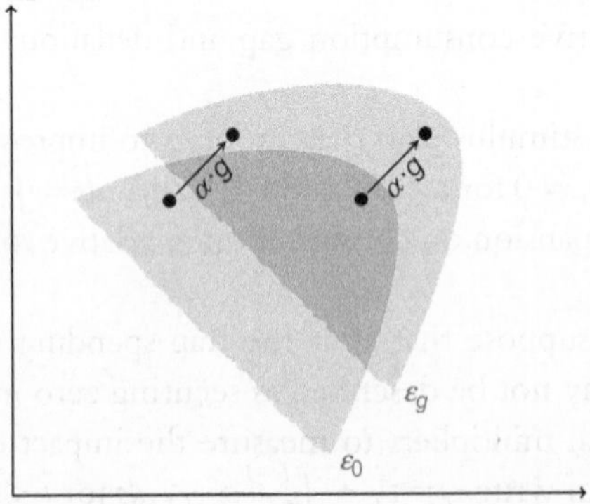

Fig. 1 A schematic depiction of the set of equilibria without government spending and the set of equilibria for a given spending path $\{g_t\}$.

[e] The figure is purposefully abstract and meant to convey the notion of a parallel shift only, so we have not labeled either axis and the shape of the sets is purely for illustrative purposes.

Proposition 1 (Closed Economy Multipliers) *The fiscal multipliers are given by*

$$\alpha_s^c = \hat{\sigma}^{-1}\kappa(1-\xi)e^{-\bar{\nu}s}\left(\frac{e^{(\bar{\nu}-\nu)s}-1}{\bar{\nu}-\nu}\right).$$

The instantaneous fiscal multiplier is zero $\alpha_0^c = 0$, *but the fiscal multipliers are positive, increasing and convex for large* s *so that* $\lim_{s\to\infty}\alpha_s^c = \infty$.

The left panel of Fig. 2 displays these consumption multipliers α_s^c as a function of s for a standard calibration. The proposition states that current spending has no effect on consumption: $\alpha_0^c = 0$. By implication, changes in spending that are very temporary are expected to have negligible effects on consumption and have an output multiplier that is near unity. As stated earlier, the effects of government spending on consumption work through inflation. Current spending does affect the current inflation rate and thus affects the growth rate of consumption. However, since this higher inflation is so short lived the lower growth rate for consumption has no significant stretch of time to impact the level of consumption.

In contrast, spending that takes place in the far future can have a very large impact. The further out into the future, the larger the impact, since α_s^c is increasing in s. Indeed, in the limit the effect becomes unbounded, since $\lim_{s\to\infty}\alpha_s^c = \infty$. The logic behind these results is that spending at $s > 0$ increases inflation over the entire interval of time $[0, s]$. This then lowers the real interest over this same time interval and lowers the growth rate of consumption. Since the long-run consumption level is fixed, the lower growth rate raises the level of consumption. This rise in consumption in turn leads to higher inflation, creating a feedback cycle. The larger the interval $[0, s]$ over which these effect have time to act, the larger is the effect on consumption.

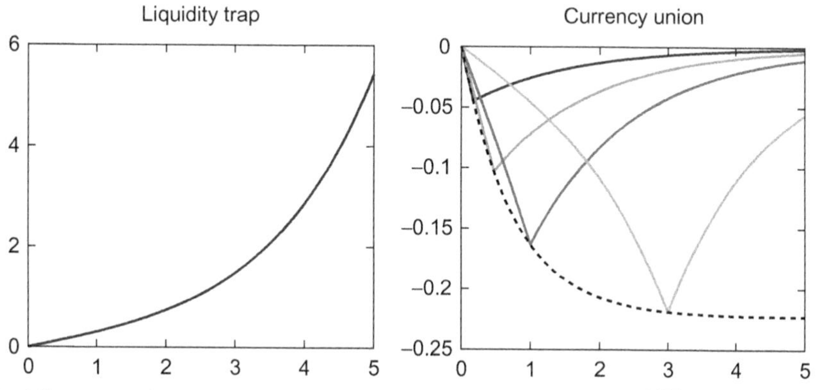

Fig. 2 Liquidity trap and currency union consumption multipliers α_s^c and $\alpha_{s-t}^{c,t,CM}$ as a function of s. Each curve for $\alpha_{s-t}^{c,t,CM}$ is plotted for different values of $t \in \{0.25, 0.5, 1, 3\}$. The black dashed line shows the lower envelope. Parameters are $\sigma = 1$, $\eta = \gamma = 1$, $\varepsilon = 6$, $\phi = 3$, $\lambda = 0.14$, and $\alpha = 0.4$.

The fact that fiscal multipliers are unbounded as $s \to \infty$ stands in strong contrast to the zero multiplier at $s = 0$. It also has important implications. For example, a positive path for spending $\{g_t\}$ that is very backloaded can create a very large response for consumption. This is the case if the shock to spending is very persistent.

Example 1 (AR(1) Spending) Suppose $g_t = ge^{-\rho_g t}$, then if $\rho_g > -\nu > 0$ the response of consumption c_t is finite and given by

$$\int \alpha_s^c g e^{-\rho_g(t+s)} ds = \frac{\hat{\sigma}^{-1}\kappa(1-\xi)}{(\rho_g+\nu)(\rho_g+\bar{\nu})} g e^{-\rho_g t}.$$

The condition $\rho_g > -\nu > 0$ requires spending to revert to zero fast enough to prevent the integral from being infinite.

Some paths for spending imply an infinite value for $\int_0^\infty \alpha_s^c g_s ds$. For instance, this is the case in the example above when $\rho_g < -\nu$. How should one interpret such cases? Technically, this may invalidate our approximation. However, we think the correct economic conclusion to draw is that spending will have an explosive positive effect on consumption. One way to see this is to truncate the path of spending $\{g_t\}$, by setting $g_t = 0$ for all $t \geq T$ for some large T. This ensures that $\int_0^T \alpha_s^c g_s ds$ is finite but the response is guaranteed to be very large if the cutoff is large.

Next, we ask how fiscal multipliers are affected by the degree of price stickiness. Departures from the neoclassical benchmark, where the consumption multiplier is negative, require some stickiness in prices. Perhaps surprisingly, the resulting Keynesian effects turn out to be decreasing in the degree of price stickiness.

Proposition 2 (Price Stickiness) *The fiscal multipliers* $\{\alpha_s^c\}$

1. *are zero when prices are rigid* $\kappa = 0$;
2. *are increasing in price flexibility* κ;
3. *converge to infinity,* $\alpha_s^c \to \infty$, *in the limit as prices become fully flexible so that* $\kappa \to \infty$.

The logic for these results relies on the fact that spending acts on consumption through inflation. At one extreme, if prices were perfectly rigid then inflation would be fixed at zero and spending has no effect on consumption. As prices become more flexible spending has a greater impact on inflation and, hence, on consumption. Indeed, in the limit as prices become perfectly flexible, inflation becomes so responsive that the effects on consumption explode.

Recall that our fiscal multipliers are calculated under the assumption that the path for interest rates remains unchanged when spending rises. These results seem less counterintuitive when one realizes that such a monetary policy, insisting on keeping interest rates unchanged, may be deemed to be looser when prices are more flexible and inflation reacts more. Of course, this is precisely the relevant calculation when the economy finds itself in a liquidity trap, so that interest rates are up against the zero lower bound.

We capture backloading by a first order dominant shift in the cumulative distribution of spending for a given net present value of output. Backloading leads to a higher path of consumption at every point in time. This is simply because backloading gives more time to the feedback loop between output and inflation to play out.

When applied in a liquidity trap setting it is important to keep in mind the correct interpretation of this result. Our calculations compare spending paths at constant interest rates. In a liquidity trap, this translates to changes in spending before the end of the liquidity trap. If spending is delayed past the liquidity trap this affects consumption differently. For example, if after the end of the trap T monetary policy targets zero inflation, then government spending lowers consumption at T. This feeds back to consumption at $t = 0$, according to $c_t = c_T + \int_0^{T-t} \alpha_s^c g_{t+s} ds$ for $t < T$, lowering the impact on consumption and potentially reversing it. We conclude that backloading spending within the trap increases summary multipliers, but delaying spending past the trap reduce it.

4.2 Summary Fiscal Multipliers Again

Up to now we have discussed properties of fiscal multipliers $\{\alpha_s^c\}$. Usually, fiscal multipliers are portrayed as a single number that summarizes the impact of some change in spending on output or consumption, perhaps conditional on the state of the economy or monetary policy. This requires collapsing the entire sequence of fiscal multipliers $\{\alpha_s^c\}$ into a single number $\bar{\alpha}$, which we shall call a *summary fiscal multiplier,* such as

$$M^c = \frac{\int_0^\infty \lambda_t^c \int_0^\infty \alpha_s^c g_{t+s} ds\, dt}{\int_0^\infty \lambda_t^g g_t dt},$$

where $\{\lambda_t^c\}$ and $\{\lambda_t^g\}$ are weights. It is most natural to consider symmetric weights, with $\lambda_t^g = \lambda_t^c = \lambda_t$, which assume from now on. The simplest weight sets $\lambda_t = 1$ for $t \leq \tau$ and $\lambda_t = 0$ for $t > \tau$, which then computes the ratio of the total responses over the interval $[0, \tau]$. Another possibility is to set $\lambda_t = e^{-\rho t}$, to compute the ratio of the present value responses over the entire horizon.[f]

Note that since $y_t = c_t + g_t$ we have that the output multiplier (defined analogously to the consumption multiplier) is simply[g]

$$M^y = M^c + 1.$$

As this discussion makes clear there are many possibilities for summary multipliers and no universal criteria to select them. Instead, one can adapt the summary multiplier to the

[f] The empirical counterpart of such an infinite-horizon calculation is, however, impractical.

[g] That is, we define

$$M^y = \frac{\int_0^\infty \lambda_t \left(\int_0^\infty \alpha_s^c g_{t+s} ds + g_t\right) dt}{\int_0^\infty \lambda_t g_t dt}.$$

application and relevant policy at hand. The characterizations provided in the previous section have implications for any of these measures. Namely,

i if spending $\{g_t\}$ converges to being concentrated at $t = 0$ then $M^c \to 0$;

ii the more backloaded is government spending for a given net present value, the higher is M^c;

iii the multiplier M^c is increasing in flexibility, it is zero with rigid prices $\kappa = 0$ and goes to infinity in the limit of flexible prices $\kappa \to \infty$.

Example 2 Suppose we have an autoregressive spending path $g_t = ge^{-\rho_g t}$ for $\rho_g > 0$. The summary multiplier is independent of g_0 and given by

$$M^c = \frac{\int_0^\infty \lambda_t \int_0^\infty \alpha_s^c g_{t+s} ds\, dt}{\int_0^\infty \lambda_t g_t dt} = \frac{\int_0^\infty \lambda_t \int_0^\infty \alpha_s^c e^{-\rho_g (t+s)} ds\, dt}{\int_0^\infty \lambda_t e^{-\rho_g t} dt} = \int_0^\infty \alpha_s^c e^{-\rho_g s} ds.$$

Higher values of ρ_g shift weight towards the future. More persistence leads to higher summary multipliers.

4.3 Endogenous Spending: Policy Shocks vs Policy Rules

Up to now we have considered exogenous changes in government spending and their impact on output—a fiscal policy shock. Many stimulus policies, however, are best thought of as responding endogenously to the state of the economy—a fiscal policy rule.

Since the state of the economy depends on the model parameters, this implies that model parameters may play a double role when evaluating fiscal policy rules, as opposed to evaluating fiscal policy shocks.

In this short section we briefly touch on this issue using two examples. Formally, a change in parameters may affect both the structural fiscal multipliers $\{\alpha_t^c\}$, as we have discussed, and the path for government spending $\{g_t\}$. Both may have effects on output and summary fiscal multipliers.

Example 3 Christiano et al. (2011) compute summary fiscal multipliers in a liquidity trap. They assume a policy for government spending that increases spending by a constant amount as long the economy remains in the liquidity trap. They vary the degree of price flexibility and the duration of the liquidity trap and compute the fiscal multiplier (see Fig. 2).

Their summary multiplier is equivalent to computing the initial output response divided by the initial spending increase. Their results suggest that parameter values that make the recession worse also lead to larger multipliers. In some cases, this follows because the parameters affect the fiscal multipliers $\{\alpha_s^c\}$ directly. For example, this is the case for the degree of price flexibility κ. Higher price flexibility makes the recession worse and leads to higher fiscal multipliers, as shown in Proposition 2.

However, in other cases their conclusion rely on the indirect effects that these parameters have on the policy experiment $\{g_t\}$ itself. Indeed, this may affect summary multipliers even when our multipliers $\{\alpha_s^c\}$ are unchanged. Their setup features Poisson uncertainty regarding the length of the trap, but the same logic applies in a deterministic setting, when the liquidity trap has a known duration T.[h]

Suppose the economy is in a liquidity trap with zero interest rates for $t \le T$ and returns to the natural allocation $c_t = g_t = 0$ for $t \ge T$. Consider fiscal policy interventions that increase spending during the trap, $g_t = g$ for $t \le T$ and $g_t = 0$ for $t > T$. Higher T then leads to a deeper recession (see Werning, 2012) but has no effect on fiscal multipliers $\{\alpha_t^c\}$. However, the summary impact multiplier computed as

$$\frac{\int_0^T \alpha_s^c g \, ds}{g} = \int_0^T \alpha_s^c \, ds,$$

is increasing and convex in T. A longer liquidity trap increases this summary multiplier even though spending at any point in time is equally effective (α_s^c unchanged). It would be wrong to conclude that a stimulus plan with a fixed duration $\tau \le T$ (a policy *shock*), such as a year or two, becomes more powerful when T increases. Rather, if $g_t = g$ for all $t \le T$ (a policy rule) when T increases, then the effect on output is larger simply because the increase in T extends the time frame over which a fixed increase in spending g takes place, leading to an increase in the cumulative change in spending, Tg. Since cumulative spending increases, the impact effect would be larger even if, counter to the model, α_s^c were constant. Moreover, this effect is amplified because the extension backloads spending, and Proposition 1 shows that this is particularly effective since α_s^c is increasing in s.

Example 4 Another perspective is provided when g_t is set as a linear function of current consumption

$$g_t = -\Psi c_t,$$

for some $\Psi > 0$. Then the Phillips curve becomes

$$\dot{\pi}_t = \rho \pi_t - \kappa(c_t + (1-\xi)g_t) = \rho \pi_t - \kappa(1-(1-\xi)\Psi)c_t.$$

Suppose further that $\Psi = (1-\xi)^{-1}$, so that spending "fills the gap" and $c_t + (1-\xi)g_t = 0$. We maintain the assumption that $c_t = g_t = 0$ for $t \ge T$. Inflation is then zero for all $t \ge 0$ and the outcome for consumption is *as if* prices were completely rigid. Now, with this fiscal policy in place, consider different values for price flexibility κ. Neither the outcome for consumption $\{c_t\}$ nor the spending path $\{g_t\}$ depend on κ. Thus, in this special case, for given T, the fiscal rule can be interpreted as a fiscal shock, since it is independent of κ.

[h] Their parameter p, which represents the probability of remaining in the trap, has an effect similar to T in our deterministic setting.

However, the benchmark equilibrium outcome without spending, ie, $g_t = 0$, is decreasing in price flexibility κ (see Werning, 2012). Thus, fiscal policy has a greater effect on consumption when prices are more flexible. This is consistent with Proposition 2 regarding the effects of price flexibility on $\{\alpha_s^c\}$.

5. AN OPEN ECONOMY MODEL OF A CURRENCY UNION

We now turn to open economy models similar to Farhi and Werning (2012a,b) which in turn build on Gali and Monacelli (2005, 2008).

The model focuses on a continuum of regions or countries that share a common currency. One interpretation is that these regions are states or provinces within a country. Our analysis is then directly relevant to the literature estimating "local" multipliers, exploiting cross-sectional variation in spending behavior across states in the United States to estimate the effects on income and employment. Another interpretation is to member countries within a currency union, such as the European Monetary Union (EMU). Our analysis then sheds light on the debates over fiscal policy, stimulus vs austerity, for periphery countries.

For concreteness, from now on we will refer to these economic units (regions or countries) simply as countries. We focus on the effects around a symmetric steady state after a fiscal policy is realized in every country. A crucial ingredient is how private agents share risk internationally. We consider the two polar cases: (i) incomplete markets, where agents can only trade a risk-free bond; and (ii) complete markets with perfect risk sharing. These two market structures have different implications for fiscal multipliers.

5.1 Households

There is a continuum measure one of countries $i \in [0, 1]$. We focus attention on a single country, which we call "home" and can be thought of as a particular value $H \in [0, 1]$. We will focus on a one time shock, so that all uncertainty is realized at $t = 0$. Thus, we can describe the economy after the realization of the shock as a deterministic function of time.

In every country, there is a representative household with preferences represented by the utility function

$$\int_0^\infty e^{-\rho t}\left[\frac{C_t^{1-\sigma}}{1-\sigma}+\chi\frac{G_t^{1-\sigma}}{1-\sigma}-\frac{N_t^{1+\phi}}{1+\phi}\right]dt,$$

where N_t is labor, and C_t is a consumption index defined by

$$C_t=\left[(1-\alpha)^{\frac{1}{\eta}}C_{H,t}^{\frac{\eta-1}{\eta}}+\alpha^{\frac{1}{\eta}}C_{F,t}^{\frac{\eta-1}{\eta}}\right]^{\frac{\eta}{\eta-1}},$$

where $C_{H,t}$ is an index of consumption of domestic goods given by

$$C_{H,t} = \left(\int_0^1 C_{H,t}(j)^{\frac{\epsilon-1}{\epsilon}} dj \right)^{\frac{\epsilon}{\epsilon-1}},$$

where $j \in [0, 1]$ denotes an individual good variety. Similarly, $C_{F,t}$ is a consumption index of imported goods given by

$$C_{F,t} = \left(\int_0^1 C_{i,t}^{\frac{\gamma-1}{\gamma}} di \right)^{\frac{\gamma}{\gamma-1}},$$

where $C_{i,t}$ is, in turn, an index of the consumption of varieties of goods imported from country i, given by

$$C_{i,t} = \left(\int_0^1 C_{i,t}(j)^{\frac{\epsilon-1}{\epsilon}} dj \right)^{\frac{\epsilon}{\epsilon-1}}.$$

Thus, ϵ is the elasticity between varieties produced within a given country, η the elasticity between domestic and foreign goods, and γ the elasticity between goods produced in different foreign countries. An important special case obtains when $\sigma = \eta = \gamma = 1$. We call this the Cole–Obstfeld case, in reference to Cole and Obstfeld (1991).

The parameter α indexes the degree of home bias, and can be interpreted as a measure of openness. Consider both extremes: as $\alpha \to 0$ the share of foreign goods vanishes; as $\alpha \to 1$ the share of home goods vanishes. Since the country is infinitesimal, the latter captures a very open economy without home bias; the former a closed economy barely trading with the outside world.

Households seek to maximize their utility subject to the budget constraints

$$\dot{D}_t = i_t D_t - \int_0^1 P_{H,t}(j) C_{H,t}(j) dj - \int_0^1 \int_0^1 P_{i,t}(j) C_{i,t}(j) dj di + W_t N_t + \Pi_t + T_t$$

for $t \geq 0$. In this equation, $P_{H,t}(j)$ is the price of domestic variety j, $P_{i,t}$ is the price of variety j imported from country i, W_t is the nominal wage, Π_t represents nominal profits and T_t is a nominal lump-sum transfer. All these variables are expressed in the common currency. The bond holdings of home agents is denoted by D_t and the common nominal interest rate within the union is denoted by i_t.

We sometimes allow for transfers across countries that are contingent on shocks. These transfers may be due to private arrangements in complete financial markets. or due to government arrangements. These transfers can accrue to the government or directly to the agents. This is irrelevant since lump-sum taxes are available. For example, we sometimes consider the assumption of complete markets where agents in different countries can perfectly share risks in a complete set of financial markets. Agents form international portfolios, the returns of which result in international transfers that are contingent on the realization of the shock. A different example is in

Section 8 where we consider government spending in the home country paid for by a transfer from the rest of the world. In this case, we have in mind a direct transfer to the government of the home country, or simply spending paid for and made by the rest of the world.

5.2 Government

Government consumption G_t is an aggregate of different varieties. Importantly, we assume that government spending is concentrated exclusively on domestic varieties

$$G_t = \left(\int_0^1 G_t(j)^{\frac{\epsilon-1}{\epsilon}} dj \right)^{\frac{\epsilon}{\epsilon-1}}.$$

For any level of expenditure $\int_0^1 P_{H,t}(j) G_t(j) dj$, the government splits its expenditure across varieties to maximize government consumption G_t. Spending is financed by lump-sum taxes. The timing of these taxes is irrelevant since Ricardian equivalence holds in our basic model. We only examine a potentially non-Ricardian setting in Section 7 where we introduce hand-to-mouth consumers into the model.

5.3 Firms

5.3.1 Technology

A typical firm in the home economy produces a differentiated good using a linear technology

$$Y_t(j) = A_{H,t} N_t(j),$$

where $A_{H,t}$ is productivity in the home country. We denote productivity in country i by $A_{i,t}$.

We allow for a constant employment tax $1 + \tau^L$, so that real marginal cost deflated by Home PPI is $\frac{1+\tau^L}{A_{H,t}} \frac{W_t}{P_{H,t}}$. We take this employment tax to be constant and set to offset the monopoly distortion so that $\tau^L = -\frac{1}{\varepsilon}$, as is standard in the literature. However, none of our results hinge on this particular value.

5.3.2 Price-Setting Assumptions

We assume that the Law of One Price holds so that at all times, the price of a given variety in different countries is identical once expressed in the same currency.

We adopt the Calvo price setting framework, where in every period, a randomly flow ρ_δ of firms can reset their prices. Those firms that get to reset their price choose a reset price P_t^r to solve

$$\max_{P_t^r} \int_0^\infty e^{-\rho_\delta s - \int_0^s i_{t+z} dz} \left(P_t^r Y_{t+s|t} - (1+\tau^L) W_t \frac{Y_{t+s|t}}{A_{H,t}} \right),$$

where $Y_{t+k|t} = \left(\frac{P_t^r}{P_{H,t+k}} \right)^{-\epsilon} Y_{t+k}$, taking the sequences for W_t, Y_t, and $P_{H,t}$ as given.

5.4 Terms of Trade and Real Exchange Rate

It is useful to define the following price indices: the home Consumer Price Index (CPI) is

$$P_t = [(1-\alpha) P_{H,t}^{1-\eta} + \alpha P_t^{*1-\eta}]^{\frac{1}{1-\eta}},$$

the home Producer Price Index (PPI)

$$P_{H,t} = \left[\int_0^1 P_{H,t}(j)^{1-\epsilon} dj \right]^{\frac{1}{1-\epsilon}},$$

and P_t^* is the price index for imported goods. The terms of trade are defined by

$$S_t = \frac{P_t^*}{P_{H,t}}.$$

Similarly let the real exchange rate be

$$Q_t = \frac{P_t^*}{P_t}.$$

5.5 Equilibrium Conditions

We now summarize the equilibrium conditions. For simplicity of exposition, we focus on the case where all foreign countries are identical. Because agents face the same sequence of interest rates optimal consumption satisfies

$$C_t = \Theta C_t^* Q_t^{\frac{1}{\sigma}},$$

where Θ is a relative Pareto weight which might depend on the realization of the shocks, and C_t^* is union-wide consumption. The goods market clearing condition is

$$Y_t = (1-\alpha) C_t \left(\frac{Q_t}{S_t} \right)^{-\eta} + \alpha S_t^\gamma C_t^* + G_t.$$

We also have the labor market clearing condition

$$N_t = \frac{Y_t}{A_{H,t}} \Delta_t,$$

where Δ_t is an index of price dispersion $\Delta_t = \int_0^1 \left(\frac{P_{H,t}(j)}{P_{H,t}} \right)^{-\epsilon}$ and the Euler equation

$$\sigma\frac{\dot{C}_t}{C_t} = i_t - \pi_t - \rho,$$

where $\pi_t = \dot{P}_t/P_t$ is CPI inflation. Finally, we must include the country-wide budget constraint

$$N\dot{F}A_t = (P_{H,t}Y_t - P_tC_t) + i_tNFA_t,$$

where NFA_t is the country's net foreign assets at t, which for convenience, we measure in home numeraire. We impose a standard no-Ponzi condition, $e^{-\int_0^t i_s ds}NFA_t \to 0$ as $t \to \infty$.

Absent transfers or insurance across countries NFA_0 must be equal to zero. Instead, when markets are complete we require that $\Theta = 1$. We then solve for the initial value of NFA_0 that is needed, for each shock realization. This value can be interpreted as an insurance transfer from the rest of the world.

Finally with Calvo price setting we have the equations summarizing the first-order condition for optimal price setting. We omit these conditions since we will only analyze a log-linearized version of the model.

6. NATIONAL AND LOCAL FISCAL MULTIPLIERS IN CURRENCY UNIONS

To compute local multipliers, we study the log-linearized equilibrium conditions around a symmetric steady state with zero inflation. We denote the deviations of total private consumption (by domestic and foreigners), output, and public consumption on domestic goods relative to steady state output by

$$c_t = (1-\mathcal{G})(\log(Y_t - G_t) - \log(Y - G)) \approx \frac{Y_t - G_t - (Y-G)}{Y},$$

$$y_t = \log(Y_t) - \log(Y) \approx \frac{Y_t - Y}{Y} \qquad g_t = \mathcal{G}(\log G_t - \log G) \approx \frac{G_t - G}{Y},$$

where $\mathcal{G} = \frac{G}{Y}$ denotes the steady state share of government spending in output. Then we have, up to a first order approximation,

$$y_t = c_t + g_t,$$

Note that c_t does not represent private domestic total consumption (of home and foreign goods); instead it is private consumption (domestic and foreign) of domestic goods. In a closed economy the two coincide, but in an open economy, for our purposes, the latter is more relevant and convenient.

The log linearized system can then be written as a set of differential equations

$$\dot{\pi}_{H,t} = \rho\pi_{H,t} - \kappa(c_t + (1-\xi)g_t) - \lambda\hat{\sigma}\alpha(\omega - 1)c_t^* - (1-\mathcal{G})\lambda\hat{\sigma}\alpha\omega\theta, \tag{5}$$

$$\dot{c}_t = \hat{\sigma}^{-1}(i_t^* - \pi_{H,t} - \rho) - \alpha(\omega - 1)\dot{c}_t^*, \tag{6}$$

with an initial condition and the definition of the variable θ,

$$c_0 = (1 - \mathcal{G})(1 - \alpha)\theta + c_0^*, \tag{7}$$

$$\theta = (1 - \mathcal{G})\int_0^{+\infty} e^{-\rho s}\rho\frac{(\omega - \sigma)}{\omega + (1 - \alpha)(1 - \sigma)}c_s ds + (1 - \mathcal{G})\frac{1 - \alpha + \alpha\omega}{\omega + (1 - \alpha)(1 - \sigma)}\frac{\rho}{\alpha}\mathrm{nfa}_0, \tag{8}$$

and either

$$\mathrm{nfa}_0 = 0 \tag{9}$$

if markets are incomplete or

$$\theta = 0 \tag{10}$$

if markets are complete, where $\mathrm{nfa}_0 = \frac{NFA_0}{Y}$ is the normalized deviation of the initial net foreign asset position from ($\mathrm{nfa}_0 = 0$ at the symmetric steady state) and $\theta = \log\Theta$ is the wedge in the log-linearized Backus–Smith equation ($\theta = 0$ at the symmetric steady state). In these equations, we have used the following definitions: $\lambda = \rho_\delta(\rho + \rho_\delta)$, $\kappa = \lambda(\hat{\sigma} + \phi)$, $\xi = \frac{\hat{\sigma}}{\hat{\sigma} + \phi}$,

$$\omega = \sigma\gamma + (1 - \alpha)(\sigma\eta - 1),$$

$$\hat{\sigma} = \frac{\sigma}{1 - \alpha + \alpha\omega}\frac{1}{1 - \mathcal{G}}.$$

Eq. (5) is the New Keynesian Philips Curve. Eq. (6) is the Euler equation. Eq. (7) is derived from the requirement that the terms of trade are predetermined at $t = 0$ because prices are sticky and the exchange rate is fixed. Finally Eq. (8) together with either (9) or (10) depending on whether markets are incomplete or complete, represents the country budget constraint. In the Cole–Obstfeld case $\sigma = \eta = \gamma = \Omega = 1$, so that the complete and incomplete markets solutions coincide. Away from the Cole–Obstfeld case, the complete and incomplete markets solutions differ. The incomplete markets solution imposes that the country budget constraint (8) with $\mathrm{nfa}_0 = 0$, while the complete markets solution solves for the endogenous value of nfa_0 that ensures that the country budget constraint (8) holds with $\theta = 0$. This can be interpreted as an insurance payment from the rest of the world.

These equations form a linear differential system with forcing variables $\{g_t, g_t^*, i_t^*\}$. It will prove useful to define the following two numbers ν and $\bar{\nu}$ (the eigenvalues of the system):

$$\nu = \frac{\rho - \sqrt{\rho^2 + 4\kappa\hat{\sigma}^{-1}}}{2} \qquad \bar{\nu} = \frac{\rho + \sqrt{\rho^2 + 4\kappa\hat{\sigma}^{-1}}}{2}.$$

6.1 Domestic Government Spending

We first consider the experiment where the only shock is domestic government spending, so that $i_t^* = \rho$, $g_t^* = y_t^* = c_t^* = 0$. Note that if $g_t = 0$ throughout then $\theta = 0$ and $y_t = c_t = 0$. We shall compute the deviations from this steady state when $g_t \neq 0$.

The assumptions one makes about financial markets can affect the results. We consider, in turn, both the cases of complete markets and incomplete markets.

6.1.1 *Complete Markets*

We start by studying the case where markets are complete. This assumption is representative of most of the literature, and is often adopted as a benchmark due to its tractability. The key implication is that consumption is insured against spending shocks. In equilibrium, private agents make arrangements with the rest of the world to receive transfers when spending shoots up and, conversely, to make transfers when spending shoots down. As a result, government sending shocks to not affect consumption on impact. Formally, we have $\theta = 0$, so the system becomes

$$\dot{\pi}_{H,t} = \rho\pi_{H,t} - \kappa(c_t + (1-\xi)g_t),$$
$$\dot{c}_t = -\hat{\sigma}^{-1}\pi_{H,t},$$

with initial condition

$$c_0 = 0.$$

Because the system is linear, we can write

$$c_t = \int_{-t}^{\infty} \alpha_s^{c,t,CM} g_{t+s} ds,$$
$$\pi_{H,t} = \int_{-t}^{\infty} \alpha_s^{\pi,t,CM} g_{t+s} ds,$$

where the superscript *CM* stands for complete markets. Note two important differences with the closed economy case. First, there are both forward- and backward-looking effects from government spending; the lower bound in these integrals is now given by $-t$ instead of 0. At every point in time, consumption is pinned down by the terms of trade which depend on past inflation. Second, the multipliers depend on calendar time t.

It is important to remind the reader that the sequence of coefficients $\{\alpha_s^{c,t,CM}\}$ represents a notion of fiscal multiplier for total private consumption of domestic goods (by domestic and foreigners) and not for domestic output, which is given by

$$y_t = g_t + \int_{-t}^{\infty} \alpha_s^{c,t,CM} g_{t+s} ds.$$

Whereas the natural benchmark for consumption multipliers is 0, that for output multipliers is 1.

Proposition 3 (Open Economy Multipliers, Complete Markets) *Suppose that markets are complete, then the fiscal multipliers are given by*

$$\alpha_s^{c,t,CM} = \begin{cases} -\hat{\sigma}^{-1}\kappa(1-\xi)e^{-\nu s}\dfrac{1-e^{(\nu-\bar{\nu})(t+s)}}{\bar{\nu}-\nu} & s<0, \\ -\hat{\sigma}^{-1}\kappa(1-\xi)e^{-\bar{\nu}s}\dfrac{1-e^{-(\bar{\nu}-\nu)t}}{\bar{\nu}-\nu} & s\geq 0. \end{cases}$$

It follows that

1. *for $t=0$ we have $\alpha_s^{c,t,CM}=0$ for all s;*
2. *for $t>0$ we have $\alpha_s^{c,t,CM}<0$ for all s;*
3. *for $t\to\infty$ we have $\alpha_{s-t}^{c,t,CM}\to 0$ for all s;*
4. *spending at zero and infinity have no impact: $\alpha_{-t}^{c,t,CM}=\lim_{s\to\infty}\alpha_s^{c,t,CM}=0$.*

The right panel of Fig. 2 displays consumption multipliers for a standard calibration. Consumption multipliers are very different in an open economy with a fixed exchange rate. For starters, part (1) says that the initial response of consumption is always zero, simply restating the initial condition above that $c_0=0$. This follows from the fact that the terms of trade are predetermined and complete markets insure consumption.

Part (2) proves that the consumption response at any other date is actually negative. Note that the Euler equation and the initial condition together imply that

$$c_t = -\hat{\sigma}^{-1}\log\frac{P_{H,t}}{P_H}.$$

Government spending increases demand, leading to inflation, a rise in $P_{H,t}$. In other words, it leads to an appreciation in the terms of trade and this loss in competitiveness depresses private demand, from both domestic and foreign consumers. Although we have derived this result in a specific setting, we expect it to be robust. The key ingredients are that consumption depends negatively on the terms of trade and that government spending creates inflation.

It may seem surprising that the output multiplier is necessarily less than one whenever the exchange rate is fixed, because this contrasts sharply with our conclusions in a closed economy with a fixed interest rate. They key here is that a fixed exchange rate implies a fixed interest rate, but the reverse is not true. We expand on this idea in the next section.

Part (3) says that the impact of government spending at any date on private consumption vanishes in the long run. This exact long run neutrality relies on the assumption of complete markets; otherwise, there are potential long-run neoclassical wealth effects from accumulation of foreign assets.

Part (4) says that spending near zero and spending in the very far future have negligible impacts on consumption at any date. Spending near zero affects inflation for a trivial amount of time and thus have has insignificant effects on the level of home prices. Similarly, spending in the far future has vanishing effects on inflation at any date.

Example 5 (AR(1) Spending) Suppose that $g_t = ge^{-\rho_g t}$ and that markets are complete. Then

$$c_t = -ge^{\nu t}\frac{1-e^{-(\nu+\rho_g)t}}{\nu+\rho_g}\frac{\hat{\sigma}^{-1}\kappa(1-\xi)}{\bar{\nu}+\rho_g}.$$

For $g > 0$, this example shows that c_t is always negative. In other words, in the open economy model with complete markets, output always expands less than the increase in government spending. The intuition is simple. Because the terms of trade are predetermined, private spending on home goods is also predetermined so that $c_0 = 0$. Government spending initially leads to inflation because the total (public and private) demand for home goods is increased in the short run. With fixed nominal interest rates, inflation depresses real interest rates, leading to a decreasing path of private consumption of domestic goods, so that c_t becomes negative. The inflationary pressures are greatest at $t = 0$ and they then recede over time as public and private demand decrease. Indeed at some point in time, inflation becomes negative and in the long run, the terms of trade return to their steady state value. At that point, private consumption of domestic goods $\hat{c}_t$ reaches its minimum and starts increasing, returning to 0 in the long run. The crucial role of inflation in generating $c_t < 0$ is most powerfully illustrated in the rigid price case. When prices are entirely rigid, we have $\kappa = 0$ so that $c_t = 0$ throughout.[i]

An interesting observation is that the openness parameter α enters Proposition 3 or Example 5 only through its effect on $\hat{\sigma}$.[j] As a result, in the Cole–Obstfeld case $\sigma = \eta = \gamma = 1$ and the private consumption multipliers $\alpha_s^{c,t,CM}$ are completely independent of openness α. Away from the Cole–Obstfeld case, $\alpha_s^{c,t,CM}$ depends on α, but its dependence can be positive or negative depending on the parameters.[k]

Next, we ask how fiscal multipliers are affected by the degree of price stickiness.

Proposition 4 (Price Stickiness) *The fiscal multipliers $\{\alpha_s^{c,t,CM}\}$ depend on price flexibility as follows:*

1. *when prices are rigid so that $\kappa = 0$, we have $\alpha_s^{c,t,CM} = 0$ for all s and t;*

[i] Note that the above calculation is valid even if $\rho_g < 0$, as long as $\bar{\nu} + \rho_g > 0$. If this condition is violated, then c_t is $-\infty$ for $g > 0$ and $+\infty$ for $g < 0$.

[j] Recall that $\hat{\sigma} = \frac{\sigma}{1+\alpha[(\sigma\gamma-1)+(\sigma\eta-1)-\alpha(\sigma\eta-1)]}\frac{1}{1-\mathcal{G}}$.

[k] For example, when $\sigma\eta > 1$ and $\sigma\gamma > 1$, $\alpha_s^{c,t,CM}$ is increasing in α for $\alpha \in [0, \min\{\frac{(\sigma\gamma-1)+(\sigma\eta-1)}{2(\sigma\eta-1)}, 1\}]$ and decreasing in α for $\alpha \in [\min\{\frac{(\sigma\gamma-1)+(\sigma\eta-1)}{2(\sigma\eta-1)}, 1\}, 1]$.

2. *when prices become perfectly flexible $\kappa \to \infty$, then for all t, the function $s \to \alpha_s^{c,t,CM}$ converges in distributions to $-(1-\xi)$ times a Dirac distribution concentrated at $s=0$, implying that $\int_{-t}^{\infty} \alpha_s^{c,t,CM} g_{t+s} ds = -(1-\xi)g_t$ for all (continuous and bounded) paths of government spending $\{g_t\}$.*

Unlike in the liquidity trap, fiscal multipliers do not explode when prices become more flexible. In a liquidity trap, government spending sets into motion a feedback loop between consumption and inflation: government spending increases inflation, which lower real interest rates, increases private consumption, further increasing inflation, etc. ad infinitum. This feedback loop is nonexistent in a currency union: government spending increases inflation, appreciates the terms of trade, reduces private consumption, reducing the inflationary pressure. Instead, the allocation converges to the flexible price allocation $c_t = -(1-\xi)g_t$ when prices become very flexible. At the flexible price allocation, private consumption is entirely determined by contemporaneous government spending. Hence the function $\alpha_s^{c,t,CM}$ of s converges in distributions to $-(1-\xi)$ times a Dirac function at $s=0$. This implies that fact that for $s=0$, $\lim_{\kappa\to\infty}\alpha_s^{c,t,CM} = -\infty$ and for $s \neq 0$, $\lim_{\kappa\to\infty}\alpha_s^{c,t,CM} = 0$.

One can reinterpret the neoclassical outcome with flexible prices as applying to the case with rigid prices and a flexible exchange rate that is adjusted to replicate the flexible price allocation. The output multiplier is then less than one. The first result says that with rigid prices but fixed exchange rates, output multipliers are equal to one. In this sense, the comparison between fixed with flexible exchange rates confirms the conventional view from the Mundell–Flemming model that fiscal policy is more effective with fixed exchange rates (see, eg, Dornbusch, 1980). This is consistent with the simulation findings in Corsetti et al. (2011).

6.1.2 Incomplete Markets

We now turn our attention to the case where markets are incomplete. Although the complete market assumption is often adopted for tractability, we believe incomplete markets may be a better approximation to reality in most cases of interest.

A shock to spending may create income effects that affect consumption and labor responses. The complete markets solution secures transfers from the rest of the world that effectively cancel these income effects. As a result, the incomplete markets solution is in general different from the complete market case. One exception is the Cole–Obstfeld case, where $\sigma = \eta = \gamma = 1$.

With incomplete markets, the system becomes

$$\dot{\pi}_{H,t} = \rho\pi_{H,t} - \kappa(c_t + (1-\xi)g_t) - (1-\mathcal{G})\lambda\hat{\sigma}\alpha\omega\theta,$$
$$\dot{c}_t = -\hat{\sigma}^{-1}\pi_{H,t},$$

with initial condition

$$c_0 = (1-\mathcal{G})(1-\alpha)\theta,$$
$$\theta = (1-\mathcal{G})\int_0^{+\infty} e^{-\rho s}\rho\frac{(\omega-\sigma)}{\omega+(1-\alpha)(1-\sigma)}c_s ds.$$

We denote the consumption multipliers with a superscript *IM*, which stands for incomplete markets. We denote by $\hat{t}$ the time such that

$$\frac{e^{\nu\hat{t}}}{1-e^{\nu\hat{t}}} = \omega\frac{\hat{\sigma}}{\hat{\sigma}+\phi}\frac{\alpha}{1-\alpha}.$$

We also define

$$\hat{\Sigma} = (1-\mathcal{G})(1-\alpha)\frac{1}{\bar{\nu}} + (1-\mathcal{G})\frac{\hat{\sigma}}{\hat{\sigma}+\phi}\alpha\omega\frac{1}{\rho}\frac{\nu}{\bar{\nu}}.$$

Note that $\bar{\Omega} = 0$ in the Cole–Obstfeld case.

Proposition 5 (Open Economy Multipliers, Incomplete Markets) *Suppose that markets are incomplete, then fiscal multipliers are given by*

$$\alpha_s^{c,t,IM} = \alpha_s^{c,t,CM} + \delta_s^{c,t,IM},$$

where $\alpha_s^{c,t,CM}$ is the complete markets consumption multiplier characterized in Proposition 3 and

$$\delta_s^{c,t,IM} = \rho\left[\frac{1-\alpha}{\alpha}e^{\nu t} - \lambda\hat{\sigma}\omega\kappa^{-1}(1-e^{\nu t})\right] \times \frac{\alpha\frac{\omega-\sigma}{\omega+(1-\alpha)(1-\sigma)}}{1-\hat{\Sigma}\frac{1}{1-\mathcal{G}}\rho\frac{\omega-\sigma}{\omega+(1-\alpha)(1-\sigma)}}(1-\xi)e^{-\rho(t+s)}(1-e^{\nu(t+s)}).$$

The difference $\delta_s^{c,t,IM}$ is 0 in the Cole–Obstfeld case $\sigma=\eta=\gamma=1$. Away from the Cole–Obstfeld case, the sign of $\delta_s^{c,t,IM}$ is the same as the sign of $\left(\frac{\omega}{\sigma}-1\right)(t-\hat{t})$; moreover, $\delta_{-t}^{c,t,IM}=0$ and $\lim_{s\to\infty}\delta_s^{c,t,IM}=0$.

The difference between the complete and incomplete market solution vanishes in the Cole–Obstfeld case. Although, away from the this case $\delta_s^{c,t,IM}$ is generally nonzero, it necessarily changes signs (both as a function of s for a given t, and as a function of t, for a given s). In this sense, incomplete markets cannot robustly overturn the conclusion of Proposition 3 and guarantee positive multipliers for consumption.

With complete markets

$$\theta = 0,$$

while with incomplete markets

$$\theta = \int_0^{+\infty} e^{-\rho s}(1-\mathcal{G})\rho\frac{\omega-\sigma}{\omega+(1-\alpha)(1-\sigma)}c_t ds.$$

This means that with complete markets, home receives an endogenous transfer nfa_0 from the rest of the world following a government spending shock. In the Cole–Obstfeld case, this transfer is zero, but away from this case, this transfer is nonzero. The difference between these two solutions can then be obtained as the effect of this endogenous transfer.

6.2 Understanding Closed vs Open Economy Multipliers

Fig. 2 provides a sharp illustration of the difference between a liquidity trap and a currency union. In a liquidity trap, consumption multipliers are positive, increase with the date of spending, and become arbitrarily large for long-dated spending. By contrast, in a currency union, consumption multipliers are negative, V-shaped and bounded as a function of the date of spending, and asymptote to zero for long-dated spending.

Before continuing it is useful to pause to develop a deeper understanding of the key difference between the closed and open economy results. The two models are somewhat different—the open economy features trade in goods and the closed economy does not—yet they are quite comparable. Indeed, we will highlight that the crucial difference lies in monetary policy, not model primitives. Although a fixed exchange rate implies a fixed nominal interest rate, the converse is not true.

To make the closed and open economies more comparable, we consider the limit of the latter as $\alpha \to 0$. This limit represents a closed economy in the sense that preferences display an extreme home bias and trade is zero. To simplify, we focus on the case of complete markets so that $\theta = 0$. Even in this limit case, the closed and open economy multipliers differ. This might seems surprising since, after all, both experiments consider the effects of government spending for a fixed nominal interest rate. To understand the difference, we allow for an initial devaluation.

Consider then the open economy model in the closed-economy limit $\alpha \to 0$ and let e_0 denote the new value for the exchange rate after the shock in log deviations relative to its steady-state value (so that $e_0 = 0$ represents no devaluation). The only difference introduced in the system by such one-time devaluation is a change the initial condition to[1]

$$c_0 = \hat{\sigma}^{-1} e_0.$$

[1] The full system allowing for a flexible exchange rate and an independent monetary policy i_t is (with $\theta = 0$ and $c_t^* = 0$)

$$\dot{\pi}_{H,t} = \rho \pi_{H,t} - \kappa(c_t + (1-\xi) g_t),$$
$$\dot{c}_t = \hat{\sigma}^{-1}(i_t - \pi_{H,t} - \rho),$$
$$\dot{e}_t = i_t - i_t^*,$$

with initial condition

$$c_0 = \hat{\sigma}^{-1} e_0.$$

If we set $i_t = i_t^*$ then $\dot{e}_t = 0$ so that $e_t = e_0$, which amounts to a one-time devaluation.

The exchange rate devaluation e_0 depreciates the initial terms of trade one for one and increases the demand for home goods through an expenditure switching effect. Of course, this stimulative effect is present in the short run, but vanishes in the long run once prices have adjusted. A similar intuition for the effect of fiscal policy on the exchange rate in a liquidity trap is also discussed in Cook and Devereux (2011).

Now if in the closed economy limit of the open economy model, we set the devaluation e_0 so that $\hat{\sigma}^{-1}e_0$ exactly equals the initial consumption response $\int_0^\infty \alpha_s^c g_{t+s} ds$ of the closed economy model, ie,

$$e_0 = \int_0^\infty \kappa(1-\xi)e^{-\bar{\nu}s}\left(\frac{e^{(\bar{\nu}-\nu)s}-1}{\bar{\nu}-\nu}\right)g_s ds, \tag{11}$$

then we find exactly the same response for consumption and inflation as in the closed economy model. This means that if we combined the government spending shock with an initial devaluation given by (11), then the multipliers of the closed economy limit of the open economy model would coincide with those of the closed economy model.[m]

This analysis shows that the policy analysis conducted for our closed economy model implicitly combines a shock to government spending with a devaluation.[n] In contrast, our open economy analysis assumes fixed exchange rates, ruling out such devaluations. The positive response of consumption in the closed economy model relies entirely on this one-time devaluation. Thus, the key difference between the two models is in monetary policy, not whether the economy is modeled as open or closed. Indeed, we have taken the closed-economy limit $\alpha \to 0$, but the results hold more generally: the degree of openness α matters only indirectly through its impact on $\hat{\sigma}$, ν and $\bar{\nu}$ and in the Cole–Obstfeld case, α actually does not even affect these parameters.

7. LIQUIDITY CONSTRAINTS AND NON-RICARDIAN EFFECTS

In this section, we explore non-Ricardian effects of fiscal policy in a closed and open economy setting. To do so, we follow Campbell and Mankiw (1989), Mankiw (2000), and Gali et al. (2007) and introduce hand-to-mouth consumers, a tractable

[m] Note that the size of this devaluation is endogenous and grows without bound as prices become more flexible, ie, as κ increases. This explains why large multipliers are possible with high values of κ in the closed economy model: they are associated with large devaluations.

[n] To see what this implies, suppose the spending shock has a finite life so that $g_t = 0$ for $t \geq T$ for some T and that monetary policy targets inflation for $t \geq T$. In the closed economy model, inflation is always positive and the price level does not return to its previous level. In contrast, in the open economy model with a fixed exchange rate (no devaluation) inflation is initially positive but eventually negative and the price level returns to its initial steady state value. Indeed, if $g_t > 0$ for $t < T$ and $g_t = 0$ for $t \geq T$ for some T, then inflation is strictly negative for $t \geq T$ and the price level falls towards its long run value asymptotically.

way of modeling liquidity constraints. The latter paper studied the effects of government spending under a Taylor rule in a closed economy. Instead, our focus here is on liquidity traps and currency unions.

7.1 Hand-to-Mouth in a Liquidity Trap

The model is modified as follows. A fraction $1-\chi$ of agents are optimizers, and a fraction χ are hand-to-mouth. Optimizers are exactly as before. Hand-to-mouth agents cannot save or borrow, and instead simply consume their labor income in every period, net of lump-sum taxes. These lump-sum taxes are allowed to differ between optimizers (T_t^o) and hand-to-mouth agents (T_t^r). We define

$$t_t^o = \frac{T_t^o - T^o}{Y} \qquad t_t^r = \frac{T_t^r - T^r}{Y},$$

where T^o and T^r are the per-capita steady state values of T_t^o and T_t^r.

We log-linearize around a steady state where optimizers and hand-to-mouth consumers have the same consumption and supply the same labor. In the appendix, we show that the model can be summarized by the following two equations

$$\dot{c}_t = \tilde{\sigma}^{-1}(i_t - \bar{r}_t - \pi_t) + \tilde{\Theta}_n \dot{g}_t - \tilde{\Theta}_\tau \dot{t}_t^r,$$
$$\dot{\pi}_t = \rho\pi_t - \kappa[c_t + (1-\xi)g_t],$$

where $\tilde{\sigma}$, $\tilde{\Theta}_n$ and $\tilde{\Theta}_\tau$ are positive constants defined in the appendix, which are increasing in χ and satisfy $\tilde{\Theta}_n = \tilde{\Theta}_\tau = 0$ and $\tilde{\sigma} = \hat{\sigma}$ when $\chi = 0$. The presence of hand-to-mouth consumers introduces two new terms in the Euler equation, one involving government spending and the other one involving taxes—both direct determinants of the consumption of hand-to-mouth agents. These terms drop out without hand-to-mouth consumers, since $\chi = 0$ implies $\tilde{\Theta}_n = \tilde{\Theta}_\tau = 0$ and $\tilde{\sigma} = \hat{\sigma}$.

As before we define

$$\tilde{\nu} = \frac{\rho - \sqrt{\rho^2 + 4\kappa\tilde{\sigma}^{-1}}}{2} \qquad \tilde{\bar{\nu}} = \frac{\rho + \sqrt{\rho^2 + 4\kappa\tilde{\sigma}^{-1}}}{2}.$$

We write the corresponding multipliers with a HM superscript to denote "hand-to-mouth."

Proposition 6 (Closed Economy Multipliers, Hand-to-Mouth) *With hand-to-mouth consumers, we have*

$$c_t = \tilde{c}_t + \tilde{\Theta}_n g_t - \tilde{\Theta}_\tau t_t^r + \int_0^\infty \alpha_s^{c,HM} g_{t+s} ds - \int_0^\infty \gamma_s^{c,HM} t_{t+s}^r ds,$$

where

$$\alpha_s^{c,HM} = \left(1 + \frac{\widetilde{\Theta}_n}{1-\xi}\right)\widetilde{\alpha}_s^{c,HM} \qquad \gamma_s^{c,HM} = \frac{\widetilde{\Theta}_\tau}{1-\xi}\widetilde{\alpha}_s^{c,HM}.$$

$$\widetilde{\alpha}_s^{c,HM} = \widetilde{\sigma}^{-1}\kappa(1-\xi)e^{-\widetilde{\nu}s}\left(\frac{e^{(\widetilde{\overline{\nu}}-\widetilde{\nu})s}-1}{\widetilde{\overline{\nu}}-\widetilde{\nu}}\right).$$

In these expressions, g_t and t_t^r can be set independently of each other because the government can always raise the necessary taxes on optimizing agents by adjusting t_t^o, so that total taxes $t_t = \chi t_t^r + (1-\chi)t_t^o$ are sufficient to balance the government budget over time

$$0 = \int_0^\infty (t_t - g_t)e^{-\rho t}dt.$$

If there are additional constraints on the tax system, then g_t and t_t^r become linked. For example, imagine that tax changes on optimizing and hand-to-mouth have to be identical so that $t_t^o = t_t^r = t_t$. In this case, taxes on hand-to-mouth agents satisfy

$$0 = \int_0^\infty (t_t^r - g_t)e^{-\rho t}dt.$$

Imagine in addition that the government must run a balanced budget, then we must have $t_t^o = t_t^r = t_t = g_t$. In this case, taxes on hand-to-mouth agents satisfy

$$t_t^r = g_t.$$

The presence of hand-to-mouth consumers affects the closed-form solution by modifying the coefficients on spending and adding new terms. The terms fall under two categories: the terms $\widetilde{\Theta}_n g_t - \widetilde{\Theta}_\tau t_t^r$ capturing the concurrent effects of spending and the integral terms $\int_0^\infty \alpha_s^{c,HM} g_{t+s}ds - \int_0^\infty \gamma_s^{c,HM} t_{t+s}^r ds$ capturing the effects of future government spending and future taxes.

The concurrent terms appear because, with hand-to-mouth consumers, current fiscal policy has a direct and contemporaneous impact on spending. They represent traditional Keynesian effects, which are independent of the degree of price flexibility κ. The integral terms capture the effects of future fiscal policy through inflation. They represent New Keynesian terms, which scale with the degree of price flexibility κ, and disappear when prices are perfectly rigid $\kappa = 0$.

Let us start by discussing the concurrent terms $\widetilde{\Theta}_n g_t - \widetilde{\Theta}_\tau t_t^r$. First, the term $-\widetilde{\Theta}_\tau t_t^r$ captures the fact that a reduction in current taxes on hand-to-mouth consumers increases their total consumption directly by redistributing income towards them, away from either unconstrained consumers, who have a lower marginal propensity to consume, or from future hand-to-mouth consumers. Second, the term $\Theta_n g_t$ captures the fact that higher current government spending increases labor income and hence consumption of hand-to-mouth consumers, who have a higher marginal propensity to consume than optimizers. Even when government spending is balanced so that $g_t = \chi t_t^o + (1-\chi)t_t^r$ and taxes are levied equally on optimizers and hand-to-mouth agents so that $t_t^r = g_t$, the sum of the concurrent terms is not exactly zero because of the different effects of government spending and taxes on real wages.

In this case, since $\widetilde{\Theta}_\tau = \widetilde{\Theta}_n \frac{\mu}{1+\phi}$, the sum of the concurrent terms $\widetilde{\Theta}_n g_t - \widetilde{\Theta}_\tau t_t^r = \left(1 - \frac{\mu}{1+\phi}\right)\widetilde{\Theta}_n g_t$ is likely to be positive in typical calibrations where steady state markups $\mu - 1$ are small compared to ϕ. This is because with sticky prices and flexible wages, real wages increase following increases in government spending, which reduces profit. With heterogeneous marginal propensities to consume, the incidence of this loss across agents matters for private spending, and hence for multipliers, and as we shall see below, these effects can be very large. We refer the reader to the appendix for a complete characterization of fiscal multipliers when these profit effects are taken out (profit offset).

We now turn to the integral terms $\int_0^\infty \alpha_s^{c,HM} g_{t+s} ds - \int_0^\infty \gamma_s^{c,HM} t_{t+s}^r ds$, lower taxes on hand-to-mouth consumers in the future, or higher government spending in the future, stimulates total future consumption.[o] This increases inflation, reducing the real interest rate which increases the current consumption of optimizing agents. This, in turn, stimulates spending by hand-to-mouth consumers. These indirect effects all work through inflation.

Going back to the example where tax changes on hand-to-mouth agents and optimizers discussed above $t_t^o = t_t^r = t_t$, our formulas reveal that the timing of deficits matters. Front-loading fiscal surpluses reduces multipliers through the New Keynesian effects, but increases multipliers early on (and lowers them eventually) through the Keynesian effects.

It is important to understand how these results depend on fixed interest rates, due, say, to a binding zero lower bound. Away from this bound, monetary policy could be chosen

[o] Note that there are conflicting effects of the fraction of hand-to-mouth consumers χ on $\alpha_s^{c,HM} = \left(1 + \frac{\widetilde{\Theta}_n}{1-\xi}\right)\widetilde{\alpha}_s^{c,HM}$ with $\widetilde{\alpha}_s^{c,HM} = \widetilde{\sigma}^{-1}\kappa(1-\xi)e^{-\widetilde{\bar{\nu}}s}\left(\frac{e^{(\widetilde{\bar{\nu}}-\widetilde{\nu})s}-1}{\widetilde{\bar{\nu}}-\widetilde{\nu}}\right)$. On the one hand, future spending increases future output and hence current inflation more when χ is higher, as captured by the multiplicative term $1 + \frac{\widetilde{\Theta}_n}{1-\xi}$ which increases with χ. On the other hand, a given amount of inflation leads to less intertemporal substitution when χ is higher, because hand-to-mouth consumers do not substitute intertemporally, as captured by the term $\widetilde{\sigma}^{-1}$ which decreases with χ. Overall, for plausible simulations, we find that the former effect tends to be stronger, and potentially much stronger, than the latter. Similar comments apply to the term $\gamma_s^{c,HM}$, which is always positive for $\chi > 0$ but is zero for $\chi = 0$.

to replicate the flexible price allocation with zero inflation. The required nominal interest rate is impacted by the presence of hand-to-mouth consumer

$$i_t = \tilde{\sigma}\left[(1-\xi) + \tilde{\Theta}_n\right]\dot{g}_t + \tilde{\sigma}\,\tilde{\Theta}_\tau \dot{t}_t^r,$$

but consumption is not

$$c_t = -(1-\xi)g_t.$$

Hence away from the zero bound, we get the neoclassical multiplier, which is determined completely statically and does not depend on the presence of hand-to-mouth consumers.[p] In contrast, whenever monetary policy does not or cannot replicate the flexible price allocation, then hand-to-mouth consumers do make a difference for fiscal multipliers. Gali et al. (2007) consider a Taylor rule which falls short of replicating the flexible price allocation. Here, we have focused on fixed interest rates, motivated by liquidity traps.

7.2 Hand-to-Mouth in a Currency Union

We now turn to the open economy version with hand-to-mouth agents.

7.2.1 Complete Markets

We start with the case of complete markets for optimizers. In the appendix, we show that the system becomes

$$\dot{\pi}_{H,t} = \rho\pi_{H,t} - \tilde{\kappa}(c_t + (1-\tilde{\xi})g_t) - (1-\mathcal{G})\lambda\tilde{\sigma}\tilde{\alpha}\tilde{\omega}\theta - \tilde{\kappa}\tilde{\tilde{\Theta}}_\tau t_t^r,$$
$$\dot{c}_t = -\tilde{\sigma}^{-1}\pi_{H,t} + \tilde{\Theta}_n\dot{g}_t - \tilde{\Theta}_\tau \dot{t}_t^r,$$

with initial condition

$$c_0 = \tilde{\tilde{\Theta}}_n g_0 - \tilde{\tilde{\Theta}}_\tau t_0^r,$$

for some constants $\tilde{\kappa}, \tilde{\alpha}, \tilde{\omega}, \tilde{\sigma}, \tilde{\Theta}_n, \tilde{\Theta}_\tau$ and $\tilde{\tilde{\Theta}}_\tau$ defined in the appendix. Importantly $\tilde{\sigma}, \tilde{\Theta}_n, \tilde{\Theta}_\tau$ are increasing in χ and $\tilde{\Theta}_n$ and $\tilde{\Theta}_\tau$ are decreasing in α. When $\chi = 0$ we have $\tilde{\kappa} = \kappa$, $\tilde{\alpha} = \alpha$, $\tilde{\omega} = \omega$, $\tilde{\sigma} = \hat{\sigma}$, $\tilde{\Theta}_n = 0$, $\tilde{\Theta}_\tau = 0$ and $\tilde{\tilde{\Theta}}_\tau = 0$. As usual, we define

$$\tilde{\nu} = \frac{\rho - \sqrt{\rho^2 + 4\tilde{\kappa}\tilde{\sigma}^{-1}}}{2} \qquad \tilde{\bar{\nu}} = \frac{\rho + \sqrt{\rho^2 + 4\tilde{\kappa}\tilde{\sigma}^{-1}}}{2}.$$

[p] Note, however, that hand-to-mouth agents might change the associated allocation of optimizers. They just don't matter for the aggregate allocation.

Proposition 7 (Open Economy Multipliers, Hand-to-Mouth, Complete Markets) *With hand-to-mouth agents and complete markets for optimizers, we have*

$$c_t = \tilde{\Theta}_n g_t - \tilde{\Theta}_\tau t_t^r + \int_{-t}^{\infty} \alpha_s^{c,t,HM,CM} g_{t+s} ds - \int_{-t}^{\infty} \gamma_s^{c,t,HM,CM} t_{t+s}^r ds,$$

where

$$\alpha_s^{c,t,HM,CM} = \left(1 + \frac{\tilde{\Theta}_n}{1-\tilde{\xi}}\right)\tilde{\alpha}_s^{c,t,HM,CM}, \qquad \gamma_s^{c,t,HM,CM} = \frac{\tilde{\Theta}_\tau - \tilde{\tilde{\Theta}}_\tau}{1-\tilde{\xi}}\tilde{\alpha}_s^{c,t,HM,CM},$$

$$\tilde{\alpha}_s^{c,t,HM,CM} = \begin{cases} -\tilde{\sigma}^{-1}\tilde{\kappa}(1-\tilde{\xi})e^{-\tilde{\nu}s}\dfrac{1-e^{(\tilde{\nu}-\tilde{\tilde{\nu}})(t+s)}}{\tilde{\tilde{\nu}}-\tilde{\nu}} & s<0, \\ -\tilde{\sigma}^{-1}\tilde{\kappa}(1-\tilde{\xi})e^{-\tilde{\tilde{\nu}}s}\dfrac{1-e^{-(\tilde{\tilde{\nu}}-\tilde{\nu})t}}{\tilde{\tilde{\nu}}-\tilde{\nu}} & s\geq 0. \end{cases}$$

Just as in the closed economy case, hand-to-mouth consumers introduce additional Keynesian effects and New Keynesian effects through cumulated inflation, where the former are independent of price flexibility κ while the latter scale with price flexibility κ and disappear when prices are perfectly rigid so that $\kappa = 0$. Just as in the closed economy case, the Keynesian effects increase consumption in response to contemporaneous positive government spending shocks and decrease consumption in response to contemporaneous increases in taxes on hand-to-mouth agents. The difference with the closed economy case is that the New Keynesian effects tend to depress consumption in response to positive government spending shocks. A pure illustration of the Keynesian effect is initial consumption c_0 (for which New Keynesian effects are 0), which is not 0 anymore, but instead $c_0 = \tilde{\Theta}_n g_0 - \tilde{\Theta}_\tau t_0^r$. Importantly $\tilde{\Theta}_n$ and $\tilde{\Theta}_\tau$ are decreasing with the degree of openness α, simply because higher values of α reduce the marginal propensity to consume on domestic goods of hand-to-mouth agents, capturing the "leakage abroad" of fiscal policy.

7.2.2 Incomplete Markets

We now treat the case of incomplete markets for optimizers. We refer the reader to the appendix for the definitions of the constants $\tilde{\Omega}_n$, $\tilde{\Omega}_c$, Σ.

Proposition 8 (Open Economy Multipliers, Hand-to-Mouth, Incomplete Markets) *With hand-to-mouth agents and incomplete markets for optimizers, we have*

$$c_t = \tilde{\Theta}_n g_t - \tilde{\Theta}_\tau t_t^r + \int_{-t}^{\infty} \alpha_s^{c,t,HM,IM} g_{t+s} ds - \int_{-t}^{\infty} \gamma_s^{c,t,HM,IM} t_{t+s}^r ds,$$

where

$$\alpha_s^{c,t,HM,IM} = \alpha_s^{c,t,HM,CM} + \delta_s^{c,t,HM,IM},$$

$$\gamma_s^{c,t,HM,IM} = \gamma_s^{c,t,HM,CM} + \epsilon_s^{c,t,HM,IM},$$

with

$$\begin{aligned}\delta_s^{c,t,HM,IM} = {} & \rho\left[\frac{1-\tilde{\alpha}}{\tilde{\alpha}}e^{\tilde{\nu}t} - (1-\mathcal{G})\lambda\widetilde{\sigma\kappa}^{-1}\tilde{\omega}(1-e^{\tilde{\nu}t})\right] \\ & \times \frac{\tilde{\alpha}}{1-\Sigma\tilde{\Omega}_c}\left[e^{-\rho(t+s)}\frac{(1-\mathcal{G})\tilde{\Omega}_n}{\rho} + e^{-\rho(t+s)}\frac{(1-\mathcal{G})\tilde{\Omega}_c}{\rho}\tilde{\Theta}_n\right. \\ & \left. + \frac{(1-\mathcal{G})\tilde{\Omega}_c}{\rho}\left(1-\tilde{\xi}\right)\left(1+\frac{\tilde{\Theta}_n}{1-\tilde{\xi}}\right)e^{-\rho(t+s)}\left(1-e^{\tilde{\nu}(t+s)}\right)\right],\end{aligned}$$

$$\begin{aligned}\epsilon_s^{c,t,HM,IM} = {} & -\rho\left[\frac{1-\tilde{\alpha}}{\tilde{\alpha}}e^{\tilde{\nu}t} - \lambda\widetilde{\sigma\kappa}^{-1}\tilde{\omega}(1-e^{\tilde{\nu}t})\right] \\ & \times \frac{\tilde{\alpha}}{1-\Sigma\tilde{\Omega}_c}\left[e^{-\rho(t+s)}\frac{(1-\mathcal{G})\tilde{\Omega}_\tau}{\rho} - e^{-\rho(t+s)}\frac{(1-\mathcal{G})\tilde{\Omega}_c}{\rho}\tilde{\Theta}_\tau\right. \\ & \left. + \frac{(1-\mathcal{G})\tilde{\Omega}_c}{\rho}\left(1-\tilde{\xi}\right)\frac{\tilde{\tilde{\Theta}}_\tau - \tilde{\Theta}_\tau}{1-\tilde{\xi}}e^{-\rho(t+s)}\left(1-e^{\tilde{\nu}(t+s)}\right)\right].\end{aligned}$$

The difference between the complete and incomplete market solution $\delta_s^{c,t,HM,IM}$ and $\epsilon_s^{c,t,HM,IM}$ are generally nonzero, can be understood along the same lines as in Section 6 in the absence of hand-to-mouth agents, generally switch signs with t and s, but do not substantively overturn the forces identified in the case of complete markets.

8. OUTSIDE-FINANCED FISCAL MULTIPLIERS

Up to this point, in our open economy analysis of currency unions, we have assumed that each country pays for its own government spending. Actually, with complete markets it does not matter who is described as paying for the government spending, since regions will insure against this expense. In effect, any transfers across regions arranged by governments are undone by the market. With incomplete markets, however, who pays matters. Transfers between regions cannot be undone and affect the equilibrium. Thus, for the rest of this section we assume incomplete markets.

We first examine what happens when the domestic country doesn't pay for the increase in domestic government spending. We show that this can make an important difference and lead to larger multipliers. This is likely to be important in practice: indeed, a large part of the "local multiplier" literature considers experiments where government spending is not paid by the economic region under consideration.

8.1 Outside-Financed Fiscal Multipliers with No Hand-to-Mouth

We first start with the case where there are no hand-to-mouth agents. The only difference with the results with incomplete markets from Section 6.1 is that we now have

$$\theta = (1-\mathcal{G})\int_0^{+\infty} e^{-\rho s}\rho\frac{(\omega-\sigma)}{\omega+(1-\alpha)(1-\sigma)}c_s ds + (1-\mathcal{G})\frac{1-\alpha+\alpha\omega}{\omega+(1-\alpha)(1-\sigma)}\frac{\rho}{\alpha}\mathrm{nfa}_0,$$

where

$$\mathrm{nfa}_0 = \int_0^{\infty} e^{-\rho t} g_t dt$$

is the transfer from foreign to home that pays for the increase in government spending. In the Cole–Obstfeld case $\sigma = \eta = \gamma = \Omega = 1$.

We denote the consumption multipliers with a superscript *PF*, which stands for "paid for" by foreigners.

Proposition 9 (Outside-Financed Open Economy Multipliers) *When domestic government spending is outside-financed, the fiscal multipliers are given by the same expressions as in Proposition 5 with the difference that*

$$\alpha_s^{c,t,PF} = \alpha_s^{c,t,IM} + \delta_s^{c,t,PF},$$

where $\alpha_s^{c,t,IM}$ is the incomplete markets consumption multiplier characterized in Proposition 5 and

$$\delta_s^{c,t,PF} = \rho\left[\frac{1-\alpha}{\alpha}e^{\nu t} - \lambda\hat{\sigma}\omega\kappa^{-1}(1-e^{\nu t})\right] \times \frac{1}{1-\hat{\Sigma}\frac{1}{1-\mathcal{G}}\rho\frac{\omega-\sigma}{\omega+(1-\alpha)(1-\sigma)}}\frac{1-\alpha+\alpha\omega}{\omega+(1-\alpha)(1-\sigma)}e^{-\rho(t+s)}.$$

The sign of $\delta_s^{c,t,PF}$ is the same as that of $(\hat{t}-t)$ and $\lim_{s\to\infty}\delta_s^{c,t,PF} = 0$.

In the Cole–Obstfeld case $\sigma = \eta = \gamma = 1$, the expression simplifies to

$$\delta_s^{c,t,PF} = \left[e^{\nu t}\frac{1-\alpha}{\alpha} - (1-e^{\nu t})\frac{1}{1-\mathcal{G}}\frac{1}{\frac{1}{1-\mathcal{G}}+\phi}\right]\rho e^{-\rho(t+s)}.$$

The intuition is most easily grasped by considering the Cole–Obstfeld case, which we focus on for now. When government spending is outside-financed, there is an associated transfer to domestic agents. Because agents are permanent-income consumers, only the net present value of the per-period transfer matters, which in turn depends on the persistence of the shock to government spending. The effects of this transfer is captured by the term $\delta_s^{c,t,PF}$, which is higher, the higher the degree of home bias (the lower α). Indeed, more generally, we can compute net-present-value transfer multipliers for pure transfers nfa_0 unrelated to government spending[q]:

$$c_t = \beta^{c,t}\mathrm{nfa}_0$$

with

$$\beta^{c,t} = \left[e^{\nu t}\frac{1-\alpha}{\alpha} - (1-e^{\nu t})\frac{1}{1-\mathcal{G}}\frac{1}{\frac{1}{1-\mathcal{G}}+\phi}\right]\rho.$$

We can also compute the effects of net-present-value transfers on inflation $\beta^{\pi,t} = -\nu e^{\nu t}\left[\rho\frac{1-\alpha}{\alpha} + \rho\frac{1}{\frac{1}{1-\mathcal{G}}+\phi}\right]$ and on the terms of trade $\beta^{s,t} = -[1-e^{\nu t}]\left[\rho\frac{1-\alpha}{\alpha} + \rho\frac{1}{\frac{1}{1-\mathcal{G}}+\phi}\right]$ (note that the terms of trade gap equals accumulated inflation $s_t = -\int_0^t \pi_{H,s}ds$). The presence of the discount factor ρ in all these expressions is natural because what matters is the annuity value $\rho\mathrm{nfa}_0$ of the transfer.

Net-present-value transfers have opposite effects on output in the short and long run. In the short run, when prices are rigid, there is a Keynesian effect due to the fact that transfers stimulate the demand for home goods: $\beta^{c,0} = \rho\frac{1-\alpha}{\alpha}$. In the long run, when prices adjust, the neoclassical wealth effect on labor supply lowers output: $\lim_{t\to\infty}\beta^{c,t} = -\rho\frac{1}{\frac{1}{1-\mathcal{G}}+\phi}$. In the medium run, the speed of adjustment, from the Keynesian short-run response to the neoclassical long-run response, is controlled by the degree of price flexibility κ, which affects ν.[r]

Note that the determinants of the Keynesian and neoclassical wealth effects are very different. The strength of the Keynesian effect hinges on the relative expenditure share of home goods $\frac{1-\alpha}{\alpha}$: the more closed the economy, the larger the Keynesian effect. The strength of the neoclassical wealth effect depends on the elasticity of labor supply $\frac{1}{\phi}$: the more elastic labor supply, the larger the neoclassical wealth effect.

Positive net-present-value transfers also increase home inflation. The long-run cumulated response in the price of home produced goods equals $\rho\frac{1-\alpha}{\alpha} + \rho\frac{1}{\frac{1}{1-\mathcal{G}}+\phi}$.

[q] In the particular case that we study here, transfers occur concurrently with an increase in government spending and exactly pay for the increase in government spending $\mathrm{nfa}_0 = \int_0^\infty e^{-\rho t}g_t dt$.

[r] Note that ν is decreasing in κ, with $\nu = 0$ when prices are rigid ($\kappa = 0$), and $\nu = -\infty$ when prices are flexible ($\kappa = \infty$).

The first term $\rho\frac{1-\alpha}{\alpha}$ comes from the fact that transfers increase the demand for home goods, due to home bias. The second term $\rho\frac{1}{\frac{1}{1-\mathcal{G}}+\phi}$ is due to a neoclassical wealth effect that reduces labor supply, raising the wage. How fast this increase in the price of home goods occurs depends positively on the flexibility of prices through its effect on ν.[s]

These effects echo the celebrated Transfer Problem controversy of Keynes (1929) and Ohlin (1929). With home bias, a transfer generates a boom when prices are sticky, and a real appreciation of the terms of trade when prices are flexible. The neoclassical wealth effect associated with a transfer comes into play when prices are flexible, and generates an output contraction and a further real appreciation.

In the closed economy limit we have $\lim_{\alpha\to 0}\beta^{c,t}=\infty$. In the fully open economy limit we have $\lim_{\alpha\to 0}\beta^{c,t}=0$. The intuition is that the Keynesian effect of transfers is commensurate with the relative expenditure share on home goods $\frac{1-\alpha}{\alpha}$. This proposition underscores that transfers are much more stimulative than government spending, the more so, the more closed the economy. This robust negative dependence of transfer multipliers $\beta^{c,t}$ on openness α should be contrasted with the lack of clear dependence on openness of government spending multipliers $\alpha_s^{c,t,CM}$ noted above (indeed in the Cole–Obstfeld case, $\alpha_s^{c,t,CM}$ is independent of α).

Example 6 (Outside-Financed Spending, Cole–Obstfeld, AR(1)) Suppose that $g_t = ge^{-\rho_g t}$ and that domestic government spending is outside-financed. In the Cole–Obstfeld case $\sigma=\eta=\gamma=1$, we have

$$c_t = g\left[e^{\nu t}\frac{1-\alpha}{\alpha}-(1-e^{\nu t})\frac{1}{1-\mathcal{G}}\frac{1}{\frac{1}{1-\mathcal{G}}+\phi}\right]\frac{\rho}{\rho+\rho_g}$$
$$-ge^{\nu t}\left(\frac{1-e^{-(\nu+\rho_g)t}}{\nu+\rho_g}\right)\kappa(1-\xi)\frac{1-\mathcal{G}}{\bar{\nu}+\rho_g}.$$

Moreover we have $c_0 = g\frac{1-\alpha}{\alpha}\frac{\rho}{\rho+\rho_g}$ and $\lim_{t\to\infty}c_t = -g\frac{1}{1-\mathcal{G}}\frac{1}{\frac{1}{1-\mathcal{G}}+\phi}\frac{\rho}{\rho+\rho_g}$.

Note that the second term on the right-hand side of the expression for c_t in Example 6 is simply the term identified in Example 5 in the complete markets case. The first term arises precisely because government spending is now paid for by foreign.

It is particularly useful to look at the predictions of this proposition for $t=0$ and $t\to\infty$. In the case of a stimulus $g>0$, we have $c_0>0>\lim_{t\to\infty}c_t$. Following a positive stimulus shock, we can get $c_0>0$ and actually $c_t>0$ for some time (because $\theta>0$) and eventually $c_t<0$. The conclusion would be that an unpaid for fiscal stimulus at

[s] Recall that ν is decreasing in the degree of price flexibility κ.

home has a larger consumption multiplier in the short run and smaller in the long run. This is true as long as there is home bias $\alpha < 1$. The reason is that the associated transfer redistributes wealth from foreign to home consumers. This increases the demand for home goods because of home bias. In the neoclassical model with flexible prices, there would be an appreciation of the terms of trade and a reduction in the output of home goods because of a neoclassical wealth effect. With sticky prices, prices cannot adjust in the short term, and so this appreciation cannot take place right away, and so the output of home goods increases. In the long run, prices adjust and we get the neoclassical effect.

The lesson of this section is that we can partly overturn the conclusion of Proposition 3 when government spending is outside-financed. When the degree of home bias $1-\alpha$, is high, or when increases in government spending are very persistent, then local multipliers estimates that involve increases in government spending that are not self-financed are potentially substantially inflated compared to the counterfactual of self-financed increases in government spending.

8.2 Outside-Financed Fiscal Multipliers with Hand-to-Mouth

We now turn to the case where there are hand-to-mouth agents.

Proposition 10 (Outside-Financed Open Economy Multipliers, Incomplete Markets, Hand-to-Mouth) *With hand-to-mouth agents, when domestic government spending is outside-financed, the fiscal multipliers are given by the same expressions as in Proposition 8 with the difference that*

$$\alpha_s^{c,t,HM,PF} = \alpha_s^{c,t,HM,IM} + \delta_s^{c,t,PF},$$

where

$$\delta_s^{c,t,HM,PF} = \rho\left[\frac{1-\tilde{\alpha}}{\tilde{\alpha}}e^{\tilde{\nu}t} - \lambda\tilde{\sigma}\tilde{\kappa}^{-1}\tilde{\omega}\left(1-e^{\tilde{\nu}t}\right)\right]\frac{1}{1-\Sigma\tilde{\Omega}_c}\frac{\tilde{\alpha}(1-\mathcal{G})\tilde{\Omega}_f}{\rho}e^{-\rho(t+s)}.$$

When domestic government spending is outside-financed, the question of the incidence of the accompanying transfer across domestic optimizers and hand-to-mouth agents naturally arises. These distributive effects are entirely captured by the adjustment in the taxes t_t^r paid by hand-to-mouth agents.

From now on, we focus on the benchmark case where taxes and the accompanying per-period transfer are distributed equally on optimizers and hand-to-mouth agents and where the domestic government runs a balanced budget, because this case is the most relevant to think about most of the estimates in the local multipliers literature where regions correspond to states with limited de jure or de facto ability to borrow.

When domestic government spending is self-financed, we have $t_t^o = t_t^r = g_t$, and instead when government spending is outside-financed, we have $t_t^o = t_t^r = 0$. Comparing fiscal multipliers when government spending is self-financed vs outside-financed, the effect of reduced taxes on optimizers in the latter case is captured by the corrective term

$\delta_s^{c,t,PF}$, while the effect of reduced taxes on hand-to-mouth agents is captured by the reduction in t_t^r from g_t to zero. In particular, in the short run before prices can fully adjust, both effects increase fiscal multipliers, the first effect for reasons already discussed in the case without hand-to-mouth agents in Section 8.1, the second effect because hand-to-mouth agents have a higher marginal propensity to consume than optimizers.

The presence of hand-to-mouth agents magnifies the difference between self-financed and outside-financed fiscal multipliers for temporary government spending shocks, simply because hand-to-mouth agents spend more of the temporary implicit transfer from foreigners that separate these two experiments in the short run, the more so, the more temporary the government spending shock.

Overall, this analysis shows that when the average marginal propensity to consume on domestic goods, as captured by the fraction of hand-to-mouth agents χ and by the degree of home bias $1 - \alpha$, is high, or when increases in government spending are very persistent, then local multipliers estimates that involve increases in government spending that are not self-financed are potentially substantially inflated compared to the counterfactual of self-financed increases in government spending.

9. TAKING STOCK: SOME SUMMARY MULTIPLIER NUMBERS

In this section, we provide numerical illustrations for the forces that we have identified in the chapter. We report summary multipliers $M^Y = 1 + M^c$ in liquidity traps and currency unions, computed as the ratio of the average response of output over the 2 years following the increase in spending to the average increase in government spending over the same period. Our baseline calibration features $\chi = 0$, $\sigma = 1$, $\epsilon = 6$, $\phi = 3$, and $\mathcal{G} = 0.3$ for liquidity traps and $\chi = 0$, $\sigma = 1$, $\eta = \gamma = 1$, $\epsilon = 6$, $\phi = 3$, $\mathcal{G} = 0.3$, and $\alpha = 0.4$ for currency unions. We take the government spending shock to be constant for $\tau_g = 1.25$ years (5 quarters) and zero afterwards.[t] We then explore variations with higher values of χ. In all these experiments, we maintain the assumption that taxes fall equally on hand-to-mouth agents and on optimizers, and that markets are incomplete. In the deficit financed experiments, taxes are increased (discretely) only after three years, and are then constant for 1.25 years before reverting to zero. The first part of Table 1 corresponds to the case of perfectly rigid prices $\lambda = 0$ (infinite price duration), the second part to $\lambda = 0.12$ (price duration of 2.9 years), and $\lambda = 1.37$ (price duration of 0.9 year).

We start with the case of perfectly rigid prices in the first part of Table 1. This table presents summary multipliers in liquidity traps and currency unions, depending on whether

[t] This shock has the same duration $\frac{\tau_g}{2} = \frac{1}{\rho_g}$ as an AR(1) with a coefficient with $\rho_g = 1.6$ (corresponding to a quarterly mean-reversion coefficient of 0.7), but dies off completely in finite time (after 1.6 years), leading to more reasonable values for liquidity trap multipliers when prices are somewhat flexible (the tail of the shock matters a great deal in this case because α_s^c and $\tilde{\alpha}_s^{c,HM}$ increase exponentially with the horizon s).

Table 1 Summary output multipliers

	Liquidity trap						Currency union								
	Tax-financed			Deficit-financed			Tax-financed			Deficit-financed			Foreign-financed		
Rigid prices ($\lambda=0$)	$o=0$	$o=0.5$	$o=1$	$o=0$	$o=0.5$	$o=1$	$o=0$	$o=0.5$	$o=1$	$o=0$	$o=0.5$	$o=1$	$o=0$	$o=0.5$	$o=1$
$\chi=0$	1.0000	1.0000	1.0000	1.0000	1.0000	1.0000	1.0000	1.0000	1.0000	1.0000	1.0000	1.0000	1.1160	1.1160	1.1160
$\chi=0.25$	4.5000	1.4804	1.0000	6.0000	1.8922	1.2386	1.6459	1.1956	1.0000	1.9474	1.3786	1.1314	2.0387	1.4823	1.2446
$\chi=0.5$	*	*	1.0000	*	*	1.7159	*	2.2835	1.0000	*	3.4861	1.3361	*	3.5041	1.4514
$\chi=0.75$	*	*	1.0000	*	*	3.1477	*	*	1.0000	*	*	1.7385	*	*	2.4971
Sticky prices ($\lambda=0.12$)	$o=0$	$o=0.5$	$o=1$	$o=0$	$o=0.5$	$o=1$	$o=0$	$o=0.5$	$o=1$	$o=0$	$o=0.5$	$o=1$	$o=0$	$o=0.5$	$o=1$
$\chi=0$	1.0542	1.0542	1.0542	1.0542	1.0542	1.0542	0.8968	0.8968	0.8968	0.8968	0.8968	0.8968	0.9550	0.9550	0.9550
$\chi=0.25$	6.9420	1.6437	1.0542	−191.4702	−1.0069	0.5347	1.2856	1.0321	0.8984	1.5476	1.2020	1.0241	1.5819	1.2410	1.0611
$\chi=0.5$	*	*	1.0542	−*	−*	−0.5044	*	1.5451	0.9009	*	2.5252	1.2233	*	2.3385	1.2302
$\chi=0.75$	*	*	1.0542	−*	−*	−3.6218	*	*	0.9083	*	*	1.5770	*	*	1.6241
Sticky prices ($\lambda\simeq1.37$)	$o=0$	$o=0.5$	$o=1$	$o=0$	$o=0.5$	$o=1$	$o=0$	$o=0.5$	$o=1$	$o=0$	$o=0.5$	$o=1$	$o=0$	$o=0.5$	$o=1$
$\chi=0$	1.8315	1.8315	1.8315	1.8315	1.8315	1.8315	0.6529	0.6529	0.6529	0.6529	0.6529	0.6529	0.6638	0.6638	0.6638
$\chi=0.25$	168.2368	4.5741	1.8315	−3.4965e8	−5153.3064	−242.9734	0.8142	0.7101	0.6542	0.9127	0.7795	0.7096	0.9266	0.7883	0.7141
$\chi=0.5$	*	*	1.8315	−*	−*	−732.5833	*	0.9238	0.6563	*	1.2767	0.7999	*	1.2515	0.7941
$\chi=0.75$	*	*	1.8315	−*	−*	−2201.4125	*	*	0.6612	*	*	0.9670	*	*	0.9559

or not they are tax-financed (taxes equal to government spending in every period), deficit-financed (taxes are raised only 3 years after the increase in spending, and then mean-revert at the same rate as spending), or outside-financed (no change in taxes). For all these cases, we also report multipliers for different values of the profit-offset coefficient o: 0, 0.5, and 1. This profit-offset coefficient is equal to the share of marginal profits per agent which is transferred to each hand-to-mouth agent: when it is equal to 0, hand-to-mouth agents are completely shielded from the impact of government spending on profits, and when it is equal to 1, they are impacted exactly like optimizers. This is important because with sticky prices and flexible wages, real wages increase following increases in government spending, so that profits increase less than proportionately with output, while labor income increases more than proportionately. With heterogeneous marginal propensities to consume, the incidence of this loss across agents matters for private spending, and hence for multipliers, and as we shall see below, these effects can be very large. While our analysis in the main text of the paper is confined to the case $o = 0$, the appendix gives a full treatment of the arbitrary o case. We also vary the fraction of hand-to-mouth agents χ between 0 and 0.75.

The results are as follows. We start with our baseline calibration. The multiplier is always 1 in a liquidity trap, independently of whether government spending is tax- or debt-financed. In a currency union, the multiplier is 1 independently of whether government spending is tax- or debt-financed, but it increases to 1.1 when it is outside-financed.

We then depart from the baseline increasing the fraction of hand-to-mouth agents χ from 0 to 0.25, 0.5, and 0.75. We start with the case of full profit offset $o = 1$ and explain the role of profit offset later. In a liquidity trap, the tax-financed multiplier remains at 1 irrespective of χ. The deficit-financed multiplier increases with χ to 1.2 ($\chi = 0.25$), 1.7 ($\chi = 0.5$), or 3.1 ($\chi = 0.75$). Turning to currency unions, the tax-financed multiplier is 1 irrespective of χ. The deficit-financed multiplier increases with χ to 1.1 ($\chi = 0.25$), 1.3 ($\chi = 0.5$), or 1.8 ($\chi = 0.75$). Finally the outside-financed multiplier increases with χ to 1.3 ($\chi = 0.25$), 1.5 ($\chi = 0.5$), or 2.7 ($\chi = 0.75$). Importantly, the difference between outside- and self-financed multipliers is now larger than in our baseline, and the deficit-financed multiplier is in between these two multipliers.

In general, lower values of the profit offset coefficient o lead to higher multipliers. This is because with no profit offset, the contemporaneous reduction in profits resulting from the increase in government spending acts like a redistribution from low marginal propensity to consume optimizers toward high marginal propensity to consume hand-to-mouth agents, which increases output (and vice versa for the increase in taxes). This effect, which can be very large, disappears with full profit offset. The * in Table 1 indicates that the feedback loop between output and the distributive effects of profits on agents with different marginal propensities to consume is so powerful that it "blows up". When it occurs, our formulas cease to apply and the correct interpretation is that multipliers are positive infinite.

We continue with the case of sticky but not perfectly rigid prices in the second and third parts of Table 1, where we run through the exact same experiments as in the first part of Table 1. The key differences are as follows. First, in the case of liquidity traps, tax-financed multipliers are a lot higher than with rigid prices, illustrating the power of the positive feedback loop between inflation and output. Deficit-financed multipliers can be a lot lower than with rigid prices and can actually be negative when there are enough hand-to-mouth agents because the positive feedback loop for front-loaded government spending is weaker than the more back-loaded negative one for taxes (in this case, lower profit offset reduces multipliers, potentially leading to negative infinite values indicated by −*). Second, in the case of currency unions, multipliers are lower than with rigid prices, but the difference is not as large as in the case of liquidity traps. This is because in this case, there is no feedback loop between output and inflation since inflation lowers spending instead of increasing it, because of its accumulated effect appreciates the terms of trade and rebalances spending away from home goods toward foreign goods.

Although this is not illustrated in the table, we briefly comment on the role of the persistence of shocks and of the openness of the economy. In liquidity traps, more persistent government spending shocks tend to increase tax-financed multipliers because of the feedback loop between output and inflation (in fact tax-financed multipliers can become infinite when prices are not entirely rigid, even without hand-to-mouth agents). They increase deficit-financed multipliers with no hand-to-mouth agents but can decrease them with enough hand-to-mouth agents and somewhat flexible prices because the feedback loop between output and inflation is more potent for back-loaded taxes than for front-loaded government spending. In currency unions, more persistent government spending shocks tend to decrease tax-financed and deficit-financed multipliers, but to increase outside-financed multipliers when prices are rigid enough. In currency unions, multipliers tend to increase when the economy is more closed (α is lower) when government spending is outside-financed and prices are not too flexible or when it is deficit-financed and larger than one (less leakage abroad).

Our simulations are illustrative and do not attempt to explore a wide range of possible parameters. For example, we have kept the fraction of hand-to-mouth agents at a modest level. Likewise, we only explore a relatively open economy. Overall, even within this limited range, our results show that fiscal multipliers are somewhat sensitive to various primitive parameters, as well as the nature of the fiscal experiment. Differences were found comparing completely rigid prices to standard degrees of price stickiness, especially for the liquidity trap case. The presence of hand-to-mouth agents also affects the responses significantly. Perhaps most surprisingly, distributional impacts appear to be crucial. First, there is the difference between tax-financed, deficit-financed, and outside-financed spending. Second, there is the difference in the responses obtained depending on the way profits are redistributed. As explained earlier, this effect relies on the model prediction that profits relative to labor earnings are countercyclical. Thus, this effect could be mitigated if wages, which are flexible in our standard New Keynesian model, were also assumed to be sticky.

Theoretically, in currency unions, outside-financed multipliers can be much larger than deficit-financed multipliers, especially when the economy is relatively closed and government spending shocks are relatively persistent. However, in our simulations with relatively open economies and relatively transitory government spending shocks (which capture the characteristics of many local multiplier studies), these differences are not very large. Since deficit-financed multipliers tend to be larger in liquidity traps than in currency unions (because there is less "leakage" abroad) with rigid enough prices, it would appear that outside-financed multipliers in currency unions (as estimated in the local multipliers literature) may provide a rough lower bound for national multipliers deficit-financed in liquidity traps with rigid enough prices. When prices are more flexible, the comparison is more delicate and the rough lower bound need not apply.

10. COUNTRY SIZE, AGGREGATION, AND FOREIGN GOVERNMENT SPENDING

So far, we have focused on the case where the country undertaking the fiscal stimulus is a small (infinitesimal) part of the currency union—this is implied by our modeling of countries as a continuum. Here, we relax this assumption. To capture country size, we interpret i as indexing regions and we imagine that countries $i \in [0, x]$ are part of a single country. They undertake the same fiscal stimulus g_t^i. We denote with a $-i \in (x, 1]$ the index of a typical region that is not undertaking fiscal stimulus so that $g_t^{-i} = 0$. We consider two situations: (1) monetary policy i_t^* at the union level achieves perfect inflation targeting (2) monetary policy at the union level is passive because the union is in a liquidity trap where interest rates i_t^* are at the zero lower bound. For simplicity, we focus on the Cole–Obstfeld case throughout.

10.1 Inflation Targeting at the Union Level

The aggregates variables satisfy

$$g_t^* = \int_0^1 g_t^i di = x g_t^i,$$

$$c_t^* = \int_0^1 c_t^i di = x c_t^i + (1 - x) c_t^{-i},$$

$$\pi_t^* = \int_0^1 \pi_t^i di = x \pi_t^i + (1 - x)] \pi_t^{-i}.$$

As long as the zero lower bound is not binding, monetary policy at the union level can be set to target zero inflation $\pi_t^* = 0$. The required interest rate i_t^* is

$$i_t^* - \rho = -\hat{\sigma}(1-\xi)x\dot{g}_t^i,$$

and the corresponding value of c_t^* is

$$c_t^* = -(1-\xi)xg_t^i.$$

The allocation for regions in the country undertaking the stimulus solves

$$\dot{\pi}_t^i = \rho\pi_t^i - \kappa(c_t^i + (1-\xi)g_t^i),$$
$$\dot{c}_t^i = (1-\xi)x\dot{g}_t^i - \hat{\sigma}^{-1}\pi_t^i,$$
$$c_0^i = -(1-\xi)xg_0^i.$$

Similarly the allocation for regions not undertaking the stimulus solves

$$\dot{\pi}_t^{-i} = \rho\pi_t^{-i} - \kappa c_t^{-i},$$
$$\dot{c}_t^{-i} = -(1-\xi)x\dot{g}_t^i - \hat{\sigma}^{-1}\pi_t^{-i},$$
$$c_0^{-i} = -(1-\xi)xg_0^i.$$

In the Cole–Obstfeld case, we define

$$\alpha_s^{c,t,CM*} = \begin{cases} \hat{\sigma}^{-1}\kappa(1-\xi)e^{-\nu s}\dfrac{1-e^{(\nu-\bar{\nu})(t+s)}}{\bar{\nu}-\nu} & s<0, \\ \hat{\sigma}^{-1}\kappa(1-\xi)e^{-\bar{\nu}s}\dfrac{1-e^{(\nu-\bar{\nu})t}}{\bar{\nu}-\nu} & s\geq 0. \end{cases}$$

Proposition 11 (Large Countries, Union-Wide Inflation Targeting) *Suppose that the zero bound is not binding at the union level and that monetary policy targets union-wide inflation $\pi_t^* = 0$. Then in the Cole–Obstfeld case, we have*

$$c_t^i = -x(1-\xi)g_t^i + (1-x)\int_{-t}^{\infty} \alpha_s^{c,t,CM} g_{t+s}^i ds,$$

$$c_t^{-i} = -(1-\xi)xg_t^i + x\int_{-t}^{\infty} \alpha_s^{c,t,CM*} g_t^i ds.$$

Let us first focus on the regions in the country undertaking the spending. This proposition shows that for regions in the country undertaking the stimulus, the effects on private spending on domestic goods are simply a weighted average of the effect $-(1-\xi)g_t^i$ that would arise if the country undertaking the stimulus could set monetary policy to target their own domestic inflation $\pi_t^i = 0$, and the effect that arises if the country is a small (infinitesimal) part of a currency union, with weights given by x and $1 - x$, where x is the relative size of the country undertaking the stimulus.

Let us now turn to the regions in countries not undertaking the spending. There are both direct effects and indirect effects. The indirect effects work through inflation, which affect the terms of trade and, hence, the demand for the goods produced by these regions. To isolate the direct effects set $\kappa = 0$, so that there is no inflation and $\alpha_s^{c,t,CM*} = 0$. The demand for home goods is then equal to $c_t^{-i} = -(1-\xi)g_t^* = -(1-\xi)xg_t^i$. When spending rises in regions $i \in [0, x]$, it depresses private spending by agents of these regions, lowering the demand for output in regions $-i \in (x, 1]$. When $\kappa > 0$, the indirect effect works through inflation. The lower demand for goods in regions $-i \in (x, 1]$ creates deflation in these regions, which makes these economies more competitive. The lower prices then increase the demand for the goods produced by these regions.

Example 7 (Union-Wide Inflation Targeting, AR(1)) Suppose that $g_t^i = g^i e^{-\rho_g t}$, then we have

$$c_t^{-i} = -e^{\nu t}(1-\xi)xg^i\left[1 - \frac{1-e^{-(\nu+\rho_g)t}}{\rho_g+\nu}\frac{\rho_g(\rho+\rho_g)}{\rho_g+\bar{\nu}}\right].$$

This implies that c_0^{-i} is negative if g^i is positive. If $\rho_g + \nu < 0$ then c_t^{-i} will remain negative. If instead $\rho_g + \nu > 0$ then c_t^{-i} starts out negative, but eventually switches signs.

This results suggests that a temporary increase in government spending abroad accompanied by monetary tightening to ensure no union-wide inflation induces a recession at home. This fits a common narrative regarding the post German reunification in the early 90s. The fiscal expansion was combined with a monetary contraction in Germany, so as to avoid inflation. The quasi-fixed exchange rate arrangements of the EMS forced other countries to follow suit and tighten monetary policy, negatively affecting their economic performance.

10.2 Zero Bound at the Union Level

If the zero bound binds at the union level, then c_t^* is given by

$$c_t^* = x\int_0^\infty \alpha_s^c g_{t+s}^i ds.$$

The allocation for regions in the country undertaking the stimulus solves

$$\dot{\pi}_t^i = \rho\pi_t^i - \kappa(c_t^i + (1-\xi)g_t^i),$$
$$\dot{c}_t^i = -\hat{\sigma}^{-1}\pi_t^i,$$
$$c_0^i = x\int_0^\infty \alpha_s^c g_{t+s}^i ds.$$

Similarly the allocation for regions not undertaking the stimulus solves

$$\dot{\pi}_t^{-i} = \rho\pi_t^{-i} - \kappa c_t^{-i},$$
$$\dot{c}_t^{-i} = -\hat{\sigma}^{-1}\pi_t^{-i},$$

$$c_0^{-i} = x \int_0^\infty \alpha_s^c g_{t+s}^i ds.$$

Proposition 12 (Large Countries, Union-Wide Zero Bound) *Suppose that the zero bound is binding at the union level, then in the Cole–Obstfeld case, we have*

$$c_t^i = x \int_0^\infty \alpha_s^c g_{t+s}^i ds + (1-x) \int_{-t}^\infty \alpha_s^{c,t,CM} g_{t+s}^i ds,$$

$$c_t^{-i} = x e^{\nu t} \int_0^\infty \alpha_s^c g_s^i ds.$$

Similarly to Proposition 11, this proposition shows that for the country undertaking the stimulus, the effects on private spending on domestic goods are simply a weighted average of the effect $\int_0^\infty \alpha_s^c g_{t+s}^i ds$ that would arise if the country undertaking the stimulus were a closed economy at the zero lower bound, and the effect that arises if the country were a small (infinitesimal) part of a currency union, with weights given by x and $1-x$, where x is the relative size of the country undertaking the stimulus.

In contrast to the inflation targeting case, when the zero lower bound binds, an increase in government spending by regions $i \in [0, x]$ increases the demand for the goods of regions $-i \in (x, 1]$. This is natural since we now have a general expansion in private demand because inflation reduces real interest rates.[u]

11. CONCLUSION

We have explored the economic response to changes in government spending in a few benchmark models. Relative to the existing literature, our contribution is to characterize the dynamics of these responses analytically in some detail, rather than summarizing the effects in a single "summary multiplier." We have done so by defining the multipliers to be the partial derivative of private spending at any point in time, to public spending at any other date. We have also attempted to be relatively exhaustive in incorporating various elements that are important, but sometimes missing in standard analyses. In particular, we considered both closed and open economies and incorporated hand-to-mouth agents in both these frameworks. Most importantly, our analysis is the first to emphasize different forms of financing for the government spending shock, including tax-financed, deficit-financed, and outside-financed. It is our hope that our approach and analysis will prove useful in interpreting and unifying the large theoretical and empirical research on fiscal multipliers.

[u] These findings on the spillover effects of fiscal policy complement the results in Cook and Devereux (2011) who focus on different configurations than us: they show that the spillover effects of fiscal policy at home on foreign when home is in a liquidity trap are negative with flexible exchange rates, but positive with fixed exchange rates. In this section, we focus on fixed exchange rates in a currency union and show how these spillover effects switch signs depending on whether the union is in a liquidity trap or targets inflation.

APPENDICES

Appendix A

This appendix derives the linear systems of equations to be solved for in order to derive fiscal multipliers in the following cases: liquidity trap; currency union with either complete markets (CM), incomplete markets (IM), and outside-financed government spending (PF). Appendix B then solves these systems equations to derive fiscal multipliers.

In both appendices, the general case with an arbitrary fraction χ of hand-to-mouth agents and with arbitrary profit offset o is derived first, followed by two special cases: no hand-to-mouth agents $\chi = 0$ (as in Sections 1–6) and no profit offset $o = 0$ (as in Sections 1–8).

Compared to the main text, the environment is generalized by allowing hand-to-mouth agents to receive a profit offset which redistributes a share of profits $o \in [0, 1]$ to hand-to-mouth agents:

$$P_t C_t^r = W_t N_t^r + \frac{o}{\chi}\Pi_t - P_t \underline{T}_t^r,$$

with

$$P_t \underline{T}_t^r = P_t T_t^r - \frac{o}{\chi}\Pi_t,$$
$$\Pi_t = P_{H,t} Y_t - w_t N_t.$$

A.1 Liquidity Trap

Assume that $c_t^* = 0, i_t^* = \bar{r}_t$ for all $t \geq 0$. The log-linearized equations are

$$\dot{c}_t^o = (1-\mathcal{G})\sigma^{-1}(i_t - \bar{r}_t - \pi_t),$$
$$c_t^r = \frac{WN^r}{Y}\left(w_t + n_t^r\right) - \underline{t}_t^r,$$
$$w_t = \frac{\sigma}{1-\mathcal{G}} c_t^r + \phi n_t^r,$$
$$w_t = \frac{\sigma}{1-\mathcal{G}} c_t + \phi n_t,$$
$$c_t = \chi c_t^r + (1-\chi) c_t^o,$$
$$n_t = \chi n_t^r + (1-\chi) n_t^o,$$
$$\dot{\pi}_t = \rho \pi_t - \kappa[c_t + (1-\xi) g_t],$$
$$\underline{t}_t^r = t_t^r - o\left[\left(1 - \frac{1}{\mu}\right) n_t - \frac{1}{\mu} w_t\right],$$

where w_t denotes real wages and μ is the steady state markup, with $\lambda = \rho_\delta(\rho + \rho_\delta), \kappa = \lambda(\hat{\sigma} + \phi), \xi = \frac{\hat{\sigma}}{\hat{\sigma} + \phi}$.

Combining and rearranging, we get

$$n_t^r = \phi^{-1}\left(w_t - \frac{\sigma}{1-\mathcal{G}}c_t^r\right),$$

$$c_t^r = \frac{WN^r}{Y}\left[(1+\phi^{-1})\left(\frac{\sigma}{1-\mathcal{G}}c_t + \phi n_t\right) - \phi^{-1}\frac{\sigma}{1-\mathcal{G}}c_t^r\right] - \underline{t}_t^r,$$

$$c_t^r = \frac{\frac{WN^r}{Y}(1+\phi^{-1})\left(\frac{\sigma}{1-\mathcal{G}}c_t + \phi n_t\right) - \underline{t}_t^r}{1+\phi^{-1}\frac{\sigma}{1-\mathcal{G}}\frac{WN^r}{Y}},$$

$$c_t\left[\frac{1-\chi\frac{WN^r}{Y}\frac{\sigma}{1-\mathcal{G}} + (1-\chi)\phi^{-1}\frac{\sigma}{1-\mathcal{G}}\frac{WN^r}{Y}}{1+\phi^{-1}\frac{\sigma}{1-\mathcal{G}}\frac{WN^r}{Y}}\right] = \chi\frac{\frac{WN^r}{Y}(1+\phi^{-1})\phi n_t - \underline{t}_t^r}{1+\phi^{-1}\frac{\sigma}{1-\mathcal{G}}\frac{WN^r}{Y}} + (1-\chi)c_t^o,$$

$$c_t = \chi\frac{\frac{WN^r}{Y}(1+\phi^{-1})\phi n_t - \underline{t}_t^r}{1-\chi\frac{WN^r}{Y}\frac{\sigma}{1-\mathcal{G}} + (1-\chi)\phi^{-1}\frac{\sigma}{1-\mathcal{G}}\frac{WN^r}{Y}} + (1-\chi)\frac{1+\phi^{-1}\frac{\sigma}{1-\mathcal{G}}\frac{WN^r}{Y}}{1-\chi\frac{WN^r}{Y}\frac{\sigma}{1-\mathcal{G}} + (1-\chi)\phi^{-1}\frac{\sigma}{1-\mathcal{G}}\frac{WN^r}{Y}}c_t^o,$$

$$c_t = \chi\frac{\phi(1+\phi)n_t - \frac{Y}{WN^r}\phi\underline{t}_t^r}{\frac{Y}{WN^r}\phi - \chi\frac{\sigma}{1-\mathcal{G}}\phi + (1-\chi)\frac{\sigma}{1-\mathcal{G}}} + (1-\chi)\frac{\frac{Y}{WN^r}\phi + \frac{\sigma}{1-\mathcal{G}}}{\frac{Y}{WN^r}\phi - \chi\frac{\sigma}{1-\mathcal{G}}\phi + (1-\chi)\frac{\sigma}{1-\mathcal{G}}}c_t^o,$$

$$c_t = \chi(1-\mathcal{G})\frac{\phi(1+\phi)n_t - \mu\phi\underline{t}_t^r}{(1-\mathcal{G})\mu\phi + \sigma - \chi\sigma(1+\phi)} + (1-\chi)\frac{(1-\mathcal{G})\mu\phi + \sigma}{(1-\mathcal{G})\mu\phi + \sigma - \chi\sigma(1+\phi)}c_t^o,$$

and finally

$$c_t = \Theta_n n_t - \Theta_\tau \underline{t}_t^r + \bar{\sigma}^{-1}\sigma\frac{1}{1-\mathcal{G}}c_t^o,$$

where

$$\bar{\sigma}^{-1} = \sigma^{-1}(1-\chi)(1-\mathcal{G})\frac{(1-\mathcal{G})\mu\phi + \sigma}{\phi(1-\mathcal{G})\mu + \sigma - \chi\sigma(1+\phi)},$$

$$\Theta_n = \chi(1-\mathcal{G})\frac{(1+\phi)\phi}{\phi(1-\mathcal{G})\mu + \sigma - \chi\sigma(1+\phi)},$$

$$\Theta_\tau = \chi(1-\mathcal{G})\frac{\mu\phi}{\phi(1-\mathcal{G})\mu + \sigma - \chi\sigma(1+\phi)},$$

Differentiating, we get

$$\dot{c}_t = \Theta_n \dot{n}_t - \Theta_\tau \dot{\underline{t}}_t^r + \bar{\sigma}^{-1}(i_t - \bar{r}_t - \pi_t),$$

and using $\dot{n}_t = \dot{c}_t + \dot{g}_t$, we find the Euler equation

$$\dot{c}_t = \widetilde{\sigma}^{-1}(i_t - \overline{r}_t - \pi_t) + \widetilde{\Theta}_n \dot{g}_t - \widetilde{\Theta}_\tau \underline{t}_t^r,$$

where

$$\widetilde{\sigma}^{-1} = \frac{\overline{\sigma}^{-1}}{1 - \Theta_n},$$
$$\widetilde{\Theta}_n = \frac{\Theta_n}{1 - \Theta_n},$$
$$\widetilde{\Theta}_\tau = \frac{\Theta_\tau}{1 - \Theta_n}.$$

By definition of t_t^r and using the expression for the wage,

$$\underline{t}_t^r = t_t^r - \frac{o}{\chi}\left[\left(1 - \frac{1}{\mu}\right)(c_t + g_t) - \frac{1}{\mu}\left[\frac{\sigma}{1 - \mathcal{G}} c_t + \phi(c_t + g_t)\right]\right].$$

Thus,

$$\underline{t}_t^r = t_t^r + \psi_c c_t + \psi_n g_t,$$

where

$$\psi_c = -\frac{o}{\chi}\left[1 - \frac{1}{\mu}\left(\frac{\sigma}{1 - \mathcal{G}} + (1 + \phi)\right)\right],$$
$$\psi_n = -\frac{o}{\chi}\left[1 - \frac{1}{\mu}(1 + \phi)\right].$$

Using the Euler equation and the expression for t_t^r, we get

$$[1 - \Theta_n + \Theta_\tau \psi_c]\dot{c}_t = -\overline{\sigma}^{-1}\pi_t + [\Theta_n - \Theta_\tau \psi_n]\dot{g}_t - \Theta_\tau \dot{t}_t^r.$$

Thus,

$$\dot{c}_t = -\underline{\widetilde{\sigma}}^{-1}\pi_t + \underline{\widetilde{\Theta}}_n \dot{g}_t - \underline{\widetilde{\Theta}}_\tau \dot{t}_t^r,$$

where

$$\underline{\widetilde{\sigma}}^{-1} = \frac{1}{\underline{\widetilde{\Theta}}_c}\overline{\sigma}^{-1},$$
$$\underline{\widetilde{\Theta}}_n = \frac{1}{\underline{\widetilde{\Theta}}_c}[\Theta_n - \Theta_\tau \psi_n],$$
$$\underline{\widetilde{\Theta}}_\tau = \frac{1}{\underline{\widetilde{\Theta}}_c}\Theta_\tau,$$
$$\underline{\widetilde{\Theta}}_c = 1 - \Theta_n + \Theta_\tau \psi_c.$$

Special case: no hand-to-mouth agents $\chi = 0$

The log-linear system is

$$\dot{c}_t = -\hat{\sigma}^{-1}\pi_t,$$
$$\dot{\pi}_t = \rho\pi_t - \kappa[c_t + (1-\xi)g_t],$$

for all $t \geq 0$.

Special case: no profit offset $o = 0$

The log-linear system is

$$\dot{c}_t = -\widetilde{\sigma}^{-1}\pi_t + \widetilde{\Theta}_n\dot{g}_t - \widetilde{\Theta}_\tau\dot{t}^r_t,$$
$$\dot{\pi}_t = \rho\pi_t - \kappa[c_t + (1-\xi)g_t].$$

for all $t \geq 0$.

A.2 Currency Union

Assume that $c^*_t = 0, i^*_t = \bar{r}_t$ for all $t \geq 0$. The log-linearized equations are

$$c^o_t = (1-\mathcal{G})\theta + \frac{(1-\alpha)(1-\mathcal{G})}{\sigma}s_t,$$

$$y_t = (1-\alpha)\hat{c}_t + (1-\mathcal{G})\alpha\left[\frac{\omega}{\sigma} + \frac{1-\alpha}{\sigma}\right]s_t + g_t,$$

$$y_t = n_t,$$
$$\dot{c}^o_t = -(1-\mathcal{G})\sigma^{-1}(\pi_{H,t} + \alpha\dot{s}_t),$$
$$c^r_t = \frac{1}{\mu}(w_t + n^r_t) - \underline{t}^r_t,$$

$$w_t = \frac{\sigma}{1-\mathcal{G}}c^r_t + \phi n^r_t,$$
$$w_t = \frac{\sigma}{1-\mathcal{G}}\hat{c}_t + \phi n_t,$$

$$\hat{c}_t = \chi c^r_t + (1-\chi)c^o_t,$$
$$n_t = \chi n^r_t + (1-\chi)n^o_t,$$
$$\dot{\pi}_{H,t} = \rho\pi_{H,t} - \lambda(w_t + \alpha s_t),$$

$$\int_0^{+\infty} e^{-\rho t} nx_t dt = -\mathrm{nfa}_0,$$

$$\underline{t}^r_t = t^r_t - \frac{o}{\chi}\left[\left(1 - \frac{1}{\mu}\right)n_t + \alpha p_{H,t} - \frac{1}{\mu}w_t\right],$$

with $\mathrm{nfa}_0 = 0$ in the IM case and $\mathrm{nfa}_0 = \int_0^{+\infty} e^{-\rho t} g_t dt$ in the PF case, where $\omega = \sigma\gamma + (1-\alpha)(\sigma\eta - 1)$. Note that we have denoted total consumption of home agents by $\hat{c}_t$ to avoid a confusion with c_t, the total consumption of home goods by private agents (both home and foreign).

Using the expressions for the wage, aggregate consumption, and labor,

$$\hat{c}_t = \Theta_n n_t - \Theta_\tau \underline{t}_t^r + \bar{\sigma}^{-1}\sigma \frac{1}{1-\mathcal{G}} c_t^o,$$

where Θ_n, Θ_τ, and $\bar{\sigma}$ have been defined above. Differentiating the Backus–Smith condition, we get (we could have gotten this equation directly from the definition of s_t)

$$\dot{s}_t = -\pi_{H,t}.$$

Now we can get to an equation involving total (home + foreign) consumption of the domestic good $c_t = y_t - g_t$ which yields

$$c_t = (1-\alpha)\hat{c}_t + (1-\mathcal{G})\alpha\left[\frac{\omega}{\sigma} + \frac{1-\alpha}{\sigma}\right] s_t.$$

Differentiating, we get

$$\dot{c}_t = (1-\alpha)\dot{\hat{c}}_t + (1-\mathcal{G})\alpha\left[\frac{\omega}{\sigma} + \frac{1-\alpha}{\sigma}\right] \dot{s}_t,$$

then combining with the equation for $\hat{c}_t$,

$$\dot{c}_t = (1-\alpha)\left[\Theta_n \dot{n}_t - \Theta_\tau \dot{\underline{t}}_t^r + \bar{\sigma}^{-1}\sigma \frac{1}{1-\mathcal{G}} \dot{c}_t^o\right] + (1-\mathcal{G})\alpha\left[\frac{\omega}{\sigma} + \frac{1-\alpha}{\sigma}\right] \dot{s}_t,$$

and replacing $n_t = c_t + g_t$,

$$\dot{c}_t = (1-\alpha)\left[\Theta_n(\dot{c}_t + \dot{g}_t) - \Theta_\tau \dot{\underline{t}}_t^r + \bar{\sigma}^{-1}\sigma \frac{1}{1-\mathcal{G}} \dot{c}_t^o\right] + (1-\mathcal{G})\alpha\left[\frac{\omega}{\sigma} + \frac{1-\alpha}{\sigma}\right] \dot{s}_t,$$

and rearranging

$$\dot{c}_t = \widetilde{\Theta}_n \dot{g}_t - \widetilde{\Theta}_\tau \dot{\underline{t}}_t^r + \frac{(1-\alpha)\bar{\sigma}^{-1}}{1-(1-\alpha)\Theta_n}\sigma\frac{1}{1-\mathcal{G}}\dot{c}_t^o + \frac{1}{1-(1-\alpha)\Theta_n}\frac{\alpha(1-\mathcal{G})(\omega+1-\alpha)}{\sigma}\dot{s}_t,$$

where

$$\widetilde{\Theta}_n = \frac{(1-\alpha)\Theta_n}{1-(1-\alpha)\Theta_n},$$

$$\widetilde{\Theta}_\tau = \frac{(1-\alpha)\Theta_\tau}{1-(1-\alpha)\Theta_n},$$

then using the Euler equation for optimizers

$$\dot{c}_t = \widetilde{\Theta}_n \dot{g}_t - \widetilde{\Theta}_\tau \dot{\underline{t}}_t^r - \frac{(1-\alpha)\bar{\sigma}^{-1}}{1-(1-\alpha)\Theta_n}\left[\pi_{H,t} + \alpha\dot{s}_t\right] + \frac{1}{1-(1-\alpha)\Theta_n}\frac{\alpha(1-\mathcal{G})(\omega+1-\alpha)}{\sigma}\dot{s}_t,$$

and finally combining with the expression for $\dot{s}_t = -\pi_{H,t}$

$$\dot{c}_t = \widetilde{\Theta}_n \dot{g}_t - \widetilde{\Theta}_\tau \dot{\underline{t}}_t^r - \frac{(1-\alpha)\bar{\sigma}^{-1}}{1-(1-\alpha)\Theta_n}[(1-\alpha)\pi_{H,t}]$$

$$-\frac{1}{1-(1-\alpha)\Theta_n}\frac{\alpha(1-\mathcal{G})(\omega+1-\alpha)}{\sigma}\dot{\pi}_{H,t},$$

which we can rewrite as

$$\dot{c}_t = \widetilde{\Theta}_n \dot{g}_t - \widetilde{\Theta}_\tau \dot{\underline{t}}_t^r - \frac{\bar{\sigma}^{-1}}{1-(1-\alpha)\Theta_n}\left[(1-\alpha)^2 + \alpha\frac{\bar{\sigma}}{\sigma}(1-\mathcal{G})(\omega+1-\alpha)\right]\dot{\pi}_{H,t},$$

$$\dot{c}_t = \widetilde{\Theta}_n \dot{g}_t - \widetilde{\Theta}_\tau \dot{\underline{t}}_t^r - \widetilde{\sigma}^{-1}\pi_{H,t},$$

where

$$\widetilde{\sigma}^{-1} = \frac{\bar{\sigma}^{-1}}{1-(1-\alpha)\Theta_n}\left[(1-\alpha)^2 + \alpha\frac{\bar{\sigma}}{\sigma}(1-\mathcal{G})(\omega+1-\alpha)\right].$$

This is our Euler equation.[v]

To derive an initial condition, we use

$$c_t = (1-\alpha)\hat{c}_t + (1-\mathcal{G})\alpha\left[\frac{\omega}{\sigma} + \frac{1-\alpha}{\sigma}\right]s_t,$$

$$\hat{c}_t = \Theta_n n_t - \Theta_\tau \underline{t}_t^r + \bar{\sigma}^{-1}\sigma\frac{1}{1-\mathcal{G}}c_t^o,$$

$$c_t^o = (1-\mathcal{G})\theta + \frac{(1-\alpha)(1-\mathcal{G})}{\sigma}s_t,$$

and

$$n_t = c_t + g_t,$$

to get

$$c_t = \widetilde{\Theta}_n g_t - \widetilde{\Theta}_\tau \underline{t}_t^r + \frac{(1-\alpha)\bar{\sigma}^{-1}}{1-(1-\alpha)\Theta_n}\sigma\frac{1}{1-\mathcal{G}}\left((1-\mathcal{G})\theta + \frac{(1-\alpha)(1-\mathcal{G})}{\sigma}s_t\right)$$

$$+\frac{(1-\mathcal{G})\alpha\left[\frac{\omega}{\sigma}+\frac{1-\alpha}{\sigma}\right]}{1-(1-\alpha)\Theta_n}s_t,$$

and apply it at $t=0$ with $s_0=0$ to get

[v] We can check that when there are no hand-to-mouth consumers, this boils down to

$$\dot{c}_t = -\sigma^{-1}(1-\mathcal{G})[1+\alpha(\omega-1)]\pi_t,$$

which is exactly the expression that we found.

$$c_0 = \widetilde{\Theta}_n g_0 - \widetilde{\Theta}_\tau \underline{t}_0^r + \frac{(1-\alpha)\bar{\sigma}^{-1}}{1-(1-\alpha)\Theta_n} \sigma \frac{1}{1-\mathcal{G}} (1-\mathcal{G})\theta.$$

Hence with complete markets, this boils down to the simple condition

$$c_0 = \widetilde{\Theta}_n g_0 - \widetilde{\Theta}_\tau \underline{t}_0^r.$$

Finally we need to compute

$$mc_t = w_t + p_t - p_{H,t} = w_t + \alpha s_t,$$

We have

$$w_t = \frac{\sigma}{1-\mathcal{G}} \hat{c}_t + \phi n_t,$$
$$w_t = \frac{\sigma}{1-\mathcal{G}} \hat{c}_t + \phi (c_t + g_t),$$

which using

$$\hat{c}_t = \Theta_n n_t - \Theta_\tau \underline{t}_t^r + \bar{\sigma}^{-1} \sigma \frac{1}{1-\mathcal{G}} c_t^o,$$

we can rewrite as

$$w_t = \frac{\sigma}{1-\mathcal{G}} \left(\Theta_n (c_t + g_t) - \Theta_\tau \underline{t}_t^r + \bar{\sigma}^{-1} \sigma \frac{1}{1-\mathcal{G}} c_t^o \right) + \phi (c_t + g_t),$$
$$w_t = \frac{\sigma}{1-\mathcal{G}} \left[\Theta_n (c_t + g_t) - \Theta_\tau \underline{t}_t^r + \bar{\sigma}^{-1} \sigma \frac{1}{1-\mathcal{G}} \left((1-\mathcal{G})\theta + \frac{(1-\alpha)(1-\mathcal{G})}{\sigma} s_t \right) \right] + \phi (c_t + g_t),$$

so that

$$w_t + \alpha s_t = \left(\frac{\sigma \Theta_n}{1-\mathcal{G}} + \phi \right) (c_t + g_t) - \frac{\sigma}{1-\mathcal{G}} \Theta_\tau \underline{t}_t^r + \left(\frac{\sigma}{1-\mathcal{G}} \right)^2 \bar{\sigma}^{-1} (1-\mathcal{G})\theta$$
$$+ \left[\alpha + \left(\frac{\sigma}{1-\mathcal{G}} \right)^2 \bar{\sigma}^{-1} \frac{(1-\alpha)(1-\mathcal{G})}{\sigma} \right] s_t,$$

which using

$$c_t = \widetilde{\Theta}_n g_t - \widetilde{\Theta}_\tau \underline{t}_t^r + \frac{(1-\alpha)\bar{\sigma}^{-1}}{1-(1-\alpha)\Theta_n} \sigma \frac{1}{1-\mathcal{G}} (1-\mathcal{G})\theta$$
$$+ \left[\frac{(1-\alpha)\bar{\sigma}^{-1}}{1-(1-\alpha)\Theta_n} \sigma \frac{1}{1-\mathcal{G}} \frac{(1-\alpha)(1-\mathcal{G})}{\sigma} + \frac{(1-\mathcal{G})\alpha \left[\frac{\omega}{\sigma} + \frac{1-\alpha}{\sigma} \right]}{1-(1-\alpha)\Theta_n} \right] s_t,$$

i.e.

$$s_t = \frac{c_t - \widetilde{\Theta}_n g_t + \widetilde{\Theta}_\tau \underline{t}_t^r - \dfrac{(1-\alpha)\bar{\sigma}^{-1}}{1-(1-\alpha)\Theta_n}\sigma\dfrac{1}{1-\mathcal{G}}(1-\mathcal{G})\theta}{\dfrac{(1-\alpha)\bar{\sigma}^{-1}}{1-(1-\alpha)\Theta_n}\sigma\dfrac{1}{1-\mathcal{G}}\dfrac{(1-\alpha)(1-\mathcal{G})}{\sigma} + \dfrac{(1-\mathcal{G})\alpha\left[\dfrac{\omega}{\sigma}+\dfrac{1-\alpha}{\sigma}\right]}{1-(1-\alpha)\Theta_n}},$$

we can rewrite as

$$\begin{aligned}
w_t + \alpha s_t = {} & \left(\frac{\sigma\Theta_n}{1-\mathcal{G}} + \phi\right)(c_t + g_t) - \frac{\sigma}{1-\mathcal{G}}\Theta_\tau \underline{t}_t^r + \left(\frac{\sigma}{1-\mathcal{G}}\right)^2 \bar{\sigma}^{-1}(1-\mathcal{G})\theta \\
& + \frac{\alpha + \dfrac{\sigma}{1-\mathcal{G}}\bar{\sigma}^{-1}(1-\alpha)}{\dfrac{(1-\alpha)\bar{\sigma}^{-1}}{1-(1-\alpha)\Theta_n}(1-\alpha) + \dfrac{(1-\mathcal{G})\alpha\left[\dfrac{\omega}{\sigma}+\dfrac{1-\alpha}{\sigma}\right]}{1-(1-\alpha)\Theta_n}} \\
& \times \left[c_t - \widetilde{\Theta}_n g_t + \widetilde{\Theta}_\tau \underline{t}_t^r - \frac{(1-\alpha)\bar{\sigma}^{-1}}{1-(1-\alpha)\Theta_n}\sigma\frac{1}{1-\mathcal{G}}(1-\mathcal{G})\theta\right],
\end{aligned}$$

$$\begin{aligned}
w_t + \alpha s_t = {} & \left(\frac{\sigma\Theta_n}{1-\mathcal{G}} + \phi\right)(c_t + g_t) - \frac{\sigma}{1-\mathcal{G}}\Theta_\tau \underline{t}_t^r + \left(\frac{\sigma}{1-\mathcal{G}}\right)^2 \bar{\sigma}^{-1}(1-\mathcal{G})\theta \\
& + \frac{\alpha + \dfrac{\sigma}{1-\mathcal{G}}\bar{\sigma}^{-1}(1-\alpha)}{\dfrac{(1-\alpha)\bar{\sigma}^{-1}}{1-(1-\alpha)\Theta_n}(1-\alpha) + \dfrac{(1-\mathcal{G})\alpha\left[\dfrac{\omega}{\sigma}+\dfrac{1-\alpha}{\sigma}\right]}{1-(1-\alpha)\Theta_n}} \\
& \times \left[c_t - \widetilde{\Theta}_n g_t + \widetilde{\Theta}_\tau \underline{t}_t^r - \frac{(1-\alpha)\bar{\sigma}^{-1}}{1-(1-\alpha)\Theta_n}\sigma\frac{1}{1-\mathcal{G}}(1-\mathcal{G})\theta\right].
\end{aligned}$$

We can then replace this expression in to get the New Keynesian Phillips Curve

$$\dot{\pi}_{H,t} = \rho\pi_{H,t} - \lambda(w_t + \alpha s_t).$$

The system is summarized by

$$\begin{aligned}
\dot{c}_t &= \widetilde{\Theta}_n \dot{g}_t - \widetilde{\Theta}_\tau \underline{t}_t^r - \widetilde{\sigma}^{-1}\pi_{H,t}, \\
\dot{\pi}_{H,t} &= \rho\pi_{H,t} - \lambda(w_t + \alpha s_t), \\
c_0 &= \widetilde{\Theta}_n g_0 - \widetilde{\Theta}_\tau \underline{t}_0^r + \frac{(1-\alpha)\bar{\sigma}^{-1}}{1-(1-\alpha)\Theta_n}\sigma\frac{1}{1-\mathcal{G}}(1-\mathcal{G})\theta,
\end{aligned}$$

and the nfa condition, where

$$w_t + \alpha s_t = \left(\frac{\sigma\Theta_n}{1-\mathcal{G}} + \phi\right)(c_t + g_t) - \frac{\sigma}{1-\mathcal{G}}\Theta_\tau \underline{t}_t^r + \left(\frac{\sigma}{1-\mathcal{G}}\right)^2 \bar{\sigma}^{-1}(1-\mathcal{G})\theta$$

$$+ \frac{\alpha + \frac{\sigma}{1-\mathcal{G}}\bar{\sigma}^{-1}(1-\alpha)}{\frac{(1-\alpha)\bar{\sigma}^{-1}}{1-(1-\alpha)\Theta_n}(1-\alpha) + \frac{(1-\mathcal{G})\alpha\left[\frac{\omega}{\sigma} + \frac{1-\alpha}{\sigma}\right]}{1-(1-\alpha)\Theta_n}}$$

$$\times \left[c_t - \widetilde{\Theta}_n g_t + \widetilde{\Theta}_\tau \underline{t}_t^r - \frac{(1-\alpha)\bar{\sigma}^{-1}}{1-(1-\alpha)\Theta_n}\sigma\frac{1}{1-\mathcal{G}}(1-\mathcal{G})\theta\right].$$

Define $\widetilde{\kappa}$ by

$$\widetilde{\kappa} = \lambda\left[\frac{\sigma\Theta_n}{1-\mathcal{G}} + \phi + \frac{\alpha + \frac{\sigma}{1-\mathcal{G}}\bar{\sigma}^{-1}(1-\alpha)}{\frac{(1-\alpha)\bar{\sigma}^{-1}}{1-(1-\alpha)\Theta_n}(1-\alpha) + \frac{(1-\mathcal{G})\alpha\left[\frac{\omega}{\sigma} + \frac{1-\alpha}{\sigma}\right]}{1-(1-\alpha)\Theta_n}}\right].$$

Define $\widetilde{\xi}$ by

$$\widetilde{\kappa}\left(1-\widetilde{\xi}\right) = \lambda\left[\frac{\sigma\Theta_n}{1-\mathcal{G}} + \phi - \frac{\alpha + \frac{\sigma}{1-\mathcal{G}}\bar{\sigma}^{-1}(1-\alpha)}{\frac{(1-\alpha)\bar{\sigma}^{-1}}{1-(1-\alpha)\Theta_n}(1-\alpha) + \frac{(1-\mathcal{G})\alpha\left[\frac{\omega}{\sigma} + \frac{1-\alpha}{\sigma}\right]}{1-(1-\alpha)\Theta_n}}\widetilde{\Theta}_n\right].$$

Define $\widetilde{\alpha}$ by

$$\widetilde{\alpha} = 1 - \frac{(1-\alpha)\bar{\sigma}^{-1}}{1-(1-\alpha)\Theta_n}\sigma\frac{1}{1-\mathcal{G}}.$$

Define $\widetilde{\omega}$ by

$$\widetilde{\omega} = \frac{1}{(1-\mathcal{G})\widetilde{\sigma}\widetilde{\alpha}} \times \left[\left(\frac{\sigma}{1-\mathcal{G}}\right)^2 \bar{\sigma}^{-1}(1-\mathcal{G}) - \frac{\alpha + \frac{\sigma}{1-\mathcal{G}}\bar{\sigma}^{-1}(1-\alpha)}{\frac{(1-\alpha)\bar{\sigma}^{-1}}{1-(1-\alpha)\Theta_n}(1-\alpha) + \frac{(1-\mathcal{G})\alpha\left(\frac{\omega}{\sigma} + \frac{1-\alpha}{\sigma}\right)}{1-(1-\alpha)\Theta_n}}\frac{(1-\alpha)\bar{\sigma}^{-1}\sigma}{1-(1-\alpha)\Theta_n}\right].$$

Define $\widetilde{\widetilde{\Theta}}_\tau$ by

$$\widetilde{\widetilde{\Theta}}_\tau = \frac{\lambda}{\widetilde{\widetilde{\kappa}}}\left[-\frac{\sigma}{1-\mathcal{G}}\Theta_\tau + \frac{\alpha + \frac{\sigma}{1-\mathcal{G}}\bar{\sigma}^{-1}(1-\alpha)}{\frac{(1-\alpha)\bar{\sigma}^{-1}}{1-(1-\alpha)\Theta_n}(1-\alpha) + \frac{(1-\mathcal{G})\alpha\left[\frac{\omega}{\sigma}+\frac{1-\alpha}{\sigma}\right]}{1-(1-\alpha)\Theta_n}}\widetilde{\Theta}_\tau\right].$$

Define Γ_1 by

$$\Gamma_1 = (1-\alpha)^2\bar{\sigma}^{-1} + (1-\mathcal{G})\alpha\left(\frac{\omega}{\sigma}+\frac{1-\alpha}{\sigma}\right),$$

Then we can rewrite the system as

$$\dot{\pi}_{H,t} = \rho\pi_{H,t} - \widetilde{\kappa}\left(c_t + \left(1-\widetilde{\xi}\right)g_t\right) - (1-\mathcal{G})\lambda\widetilde{\sigma}\widetilde{\alpha}\widetilde{\omega}\theta - \widetilde{\kappa}\widetilde{\widetilde{\Theta}}_\tau \underline{t}_t^r,$$

$$\dot{c}_t = -\widetilde{\sigma}^{-1}\pi_{H,t} + \widetilde{\Theta}_n\dot{g}_t - \widetilde{\Theta}_\tau\dot{\underline{t}}_t^r,$$

with an initial condition

$$c_0 = (1-\mathcal{G})(1-\widetilde{\alpha})\theta + \widetilde{\Theta}_n g_0 - \widetilde{\Theta}_\tau \underline{t}_0^r,$$

and the nfa condition.

For net exports we get

$$nx_t = -(1-\mathcal{G})\alpha s_t + y_t - \hat{c}_t - g_t,$$

$$nx_t = (1-\mathcal{G})\left[\alpha\frac{\omega}{\sigma} + \alpha\frac{1-\alpha}{\sigma} - \alpha\right]s_t - \alpha\hat{c}_t,$$

$$nx_t = (1-\mathcal{G})\left[\alpha\frac{\omega}{\sigma} + \alpha\frac{1-\alpha}{\sigma} - \alpha\right]s_t - \alpha\left[\Theta_n(c_t+g_t) - \Theta_\tau\underline{t}_t^r + \bar{\sigma}^{-1}\sigma\frac{1}{1-\mathcal{G}}c_t^o\right],$$

and finally

$$nx_t = (1-\mathcal{G})\left[\alpha\frac{\omega}{\sigma} + \alpha\frac{1-\alpha}{\sigma} - \alpha\right]s_t - \alpha\left[\Theta_n(c_t+g_t) - \Theta_\tau\underline{t}_t^r + \bar{\sigma}^{-1}\sigma\frac{1}{1-\mathcal{G}}\left((1-\mathcal{G})\theta + \frac{(1-\alpha)(1-\mathcal{G})}{\sigma}s_t\right)\right],$$

where

$$s_t = \frac{c_t - \widetilde{\Theta}_n g_t + \widetilde{\Theta}_\tau \underline{t}_t^r - \frac{(1-\alpha)\bar{\sigma}^{-1}}{1-(1-\alpha)\Theta_n}\sigma\frac{1}{1-\mathcal{G}}(1-\mathcal{G})\theta}{\frac{(1-\alpha)\bar{\sigma}^{-1}}{1-(1-\alpha)\Theta_n}\sigma\frac{1}{1-\mathcal{G}}\frac{(1-\alpha)(1-\mathcal{G})}{\sigma} + \frac{(1-\mathcal{G})\alpha\left[\frac{\omega}{\sigma}+\frac{1-\alpha}{\sigma}\right]}{1-(1-\alpha)\Theta_n}}.$$

Using the Euler equation,

$$p_{H,t} = -s_0 - \frac{1}{\Gamma_1}[1-(1-\alpha)\Theta_n](c_t - c_0) + \frac{1}{\Gamma_1}(1-\alpha)\Theta_n(g_t - g_0) - (1-\alpha)\frac{1}{\Gamma_1}\Theta_\tau(\underline{t}_t^r - \underline{t}_0^r).$$

Using the initial condition for consumption,

$$p_{H,t} = -\frac{1}{\Gamma_1}[1-(1-\alpha)\Theta_n]c_t + \frac{1}{\Gamma_1}(1-\alpha)\Theta_n g_t - (1-\alpha)\frac{1}{\Gamma_1}\Theta_\tau \underline{t}_t^r + (1-\alpha)\frac{1}{\Gamma_1}\bar{\sigma}^{-1}\sigma\theta,$$

since $s_0 = 0$.

By definition of $\underline{t}_t^r$ and using the expressions for output, for prices and for the real wage,

$$\begin{aligned}
\underline{t}_t^r = t_t^r - \frac{o}{\chi}\Bigg[&\left(1-\frac{1}{\mu}\right)(c_t + g_t)\\
&+\alpha\left[-\frac{1}{\Gamma_1}[1-(1-\alpha)\Theta_n]c_t + \frac{1}{\Gamma_1}(1-\alpha)\Theta_n g_t - (1-\alpha)\frac{1}{\Gamma_1}\Theta_\tau \underline{t}_t^r + (1-\alpha)\frac{1}{\Gamma_1}\bar{\sigma}^{-1}\sigma\theta\right]\\
&-\frac{1}{\mu}\left[\frac{\sigma}{1-\mathcal{G}}\frac{1}{1-\alpha}\left[c_t - (1-\mathcal{G})\alpha\left(\frac{\omega}{\sigma}+\frac{1-\alpha}{\sigma}\right)s_t\right] + \phi n_t\right]\Bigg].
\end{aligned}$$

Using the expression for the terms-of-trade,

$$\begin{aligned}
\underline{t}_t^r = t_t^r - \frac{o}{\chi}\Bigg[&\left(1-\frac{1}{\mu}\right)(c_t + g_t)\\
&+\alpha\left[-\frac{1}{\Gamma_1}[1-(1-\alpha)\Theta_n]c_t + \frac{1}{\Gamma_1}(1-\alpha)\Theta_n g_t - (1-\alpha)\frac{1}{\Gamma_1}\Theta_\tau \underline{t}_t^r + (1-\alpha)\bar{\sigma}^{-1}\sigma\theta\right]\\
&-\frac{1}{\mu}\frac{\sigma}{1-\mathcal{G}}\frac{1}{1-\alpha}c_t\\
&+\frac{1}{\mu}\sigma\frac{\alpha}{1-\alpha}\left(\frac{\omega}{\sigma}-\frac{1-\alpha}{\sigma}\right)\frac{1}{\Gamma_1}\left[[1-(1-\alpha)\Theta_n]c_t - (1-\alpha)\Theta_n g_t + (1-\alpha)\Theta_\tau \underline{t}_t^r - (1-\alpha)\bar{\sigma}^{-1}\sigma\theta\right]\\
&-\frac{1}{\mu}\phi n_t\Bigg].
\end{aligned}$$

Thus,

$$\underline{t}_t^r = \psi_\tau t_t^r + \psi_c c_t + \psi_n g_t + \psi_\theta \theta,$$

where

$$\psi_c = -\frac{o}{\chi}\frac{1}{\hat{\psi}_\tau}\left[\left(1-\frac{1}{\mu}\right) - \alpha\frac{1}{\Gamma_1}[1-(1-\alpha)\Theta_n] - \frac{1}{\mu}\left[\frac{\sigma}{1-\alpha}\left[\frac{1}{1-\mathcal{G}} - \alpha\left(\frac{\omega}{\sigma}+\frac{1-\alpha}{\sigma}\right)\frac{1}{\Gamma_1}[1-(1-\alpha)\Theta_n]\right] + \phi\right]\right],$$

$$\psi_n = -\frac{o}{\chi}\frac{1}{\hat{\psi}_\tau}\left[\left(1-\frac{1}{\mu}\right) + \alpha\frac{1}{\Gamma_1}(1-\alpha)\Theta_n - \frac{1}{\mu}\left[\sigma\alpha\left(\frac{\omega}{\sigma}+\frac{1-\alpha}{\sigma}\right)\frac{1}{\Gamma_1}\Theta_n + \phi\right]\right],$$

$$\psi_\theta = -\frac{o}{\chi}\frac{1}{\hat{\psi}_\tau}\left[\alpha\frac{1}{\Gamma_1}(1-\alpha)\bar{\sigma}^{-1}\sigma - \frac{1}{\mu}\sigma\alpha\left(\frac{\omega}{\sigma}+\frac{1-\alpha}{\sigma}\right)\frac{1}{\Gamma_1}\bar{\sigma}^{-1}\sigma\right],$$

$$\psi_\tau = \frac{1}{\hat{\psi}_\tau},$$

$$\hat{\psi}_\tau = 1 - \frac{o}{\chi}\left[\alpha\frac{1}{\Gamma_1}(1-\alpha)\Theta_\tau - \frac{1}{\mu}\sigma\alpha\left(\frac{\omega}{\sigma}+\frac{1-\alpha}{\sigma}\right)\frac{1}{\Gamma_1}\Theta_\tau\right].$$

Using the Euler equation and the expression for $\underline{t}_t^r$,

$$[1-(1-\alpha)\Theta_n + (1-\alpha)\Theta_\tau\psi_c]\dot{c}_t = \Gamma_1\pi_{H,t} + (1-\alpha)[\Theta_n - \Theta_\tau\psi_n]\dot{g}_t - (1-\alpha)\Theta_\tau\psi_\tau t_t^r.$$

Thus,

$$\dot{c}_t = -\underline{\tilde{\sigma}}^{-1}\pi_{H,t} + \underline{\tilde{\Theta}}_n\dot{g}_t - \underline{\tilde{\Theta}}_\tau t_t^r,$$

where

$$\underline{\tilde{\sigma}}^{-1} = \frac{1}{\underline{\tilde{\Theta}}_c}\Gamma_1,$$

$$\underline{\tilde{\Theta}}_n = (1-\alpha)\frac{1}{\underline{\tilde{\Theta}}_c}[\Theta_n - \Theta_\tau\psi_n],$$

$$\underline{\tilde{\Theta}}_\tau = (1-\alpha)\frac{1}{\underline{\tilde{\Theta}}_c}\Theta_\tau\psi_\tau,$$

$$\underline{\tilde{\Theta}}_c = 1-(1-\alpha)\Theta_n + (1-\alpha)\Theta_\tau\psi_c.$$

Using the New Keynesian Phillips Curve and the expression for $\underline{t}_t^r$,

$$\dot{\pi}_{H,t} = \rho\pi_{H,t} - \tilde{\kappa}\left[c_t + \left(1-\tilde{\xi}\right)g_t\right] - (1-\mathcal{G})\lambda\tilde{\sigma}\tilde{\alpha}\tilde{\omega}\theta - \tilde{\kappa}\tilde{\tilde{\Theta}}_\tau\left[\psi_\tau t_t^r + \psi_c c_t + \psi_n g_t + \psi_\theta\theta\right].$$

Thus,

$$\dot{\pi}_{H,t} = \rho\pi_{H,t} - \underline{\tilde{\kappa}}_c c_t - \underline{\tilde{\kappa}}_n g_t - \underline{\tilde{\kappa}}_\theta\theta - \underline{\tilde{\kappa}}_\tau t_t^r,$$

where

$$\underline{\tilde{\kappa}}_c = \tilde{\kappa}\left(1 + \underline{\tilde{\tilde{\Theta}}}_\tau \psi_c\right),$$

$$\underline{\tilde{\kappa}}_n = \tilde{\kappa}\left(1 - \tilde{\xi} + \underline{\tilde{\tilde{\Theta}}}_\tau \psi_n\right),$$

$$\underline{\tilde{\kappa}}_\theta = (1-\mathcal{G})\lambda\tilde{\sigma}\tilde{\alpha}\tilde{\omega} + \tilde{\kappa}\underline{\tilde{\tilde{\Theta}}}_\tau \psi_\theta,$$

$$\underline{\tilde{\kappa}}_\tau = \tilde{\kappa}\underline{\tilde{\tilde{\Theta}}}_\tau \psi_\tau.$$

Using the initial condition for consumption and the expression for $\underline{t}_t^r$,

$$c_0 = \Upsilon\theta + \underline{\tilde{\Theta}}_n g_0 - \underline{\tilde{\Theta}}_\tau t_0^r,$$

where

$$\Upsilon = \frac{1}{\underline{\tilde{\tilde{\Theta}}}_c}\left[(1-\mathcal{G})(1-\tilde{\alpha})[1-(1-\alpha)\Theta_n] - (1-\alpha)\Theta_\tau \psi_\theta\right].$$

Using the expressions for net exports and for $\underline{t}_t^r$,

$$nx_t = \alpha(1-\mathcal{G})\left[\frac{1}{1-\alpha}\left(\frac{\omega}{\sigma} + \frac{1-\alpha}{\sigma}\right) - 1\right]s_t - \frac{\alpha}{1-\alpha}c_t.$$

Using the expression for the terms-of-trade,

$$\begin{aligned} nx_t = {} & \alpha(1-\mathcal{G})\left[\frac{1}{1-\alpha}\left(\frac{\omega}{\sigma} + \frac{1-\alpha}{\sigma}\right) - 1\right] \\ & \times \frac{1}{\Gamma_1}\left[[1-(1-\alpha)\Theta_n]c_t - (1-\alpha)\Theta_n g_t + (1-\alpha)\Theta_\tau \underline{t}_t^r - (1-\alpha)\bar{\sigma}^{-1}\sigma\theta\right] \\ & - \frac{\alpha}{1-\alpha}c_t. \end{aligned}$$

Thus,

$$\begin{aligned} nx_t = {} & \Omega_c c_t - (1-\mathcal{G})\frac{\Gamma_2}{\Gamma_1} \\ & \times \left[[(1-\alpha)\Theta_n - (1-\alpha)\Theta_\tau \psi_n]g_t - (1-\alpha)\Theta_\tau \psi_\tau t_t^r + \left[(1-\alpha)\bar{\sigma}^{-1}\sigma - (1-\alpha)\Theta_\tau \psi_\theta\right]\theta\right], \end{aligned}$$

where

$$\Omega_c = (1-\mathcal{G})\frac{\Gamma_2}{\Gamma_1}[1-(1-\alpha)\Theta_n + (1-\alpha)\Theta_\tau \psi_c] - \frac{\alpha}{1-\alpha},$$

$$\Gamma_2 = \alpha\left[\frac{1}{1-\alpha}\left(\frac{\omega}{\sigma} + \frac{1-\alpha}{\sigma}\right) - 1\right].$$

Using the expressions for the Pareto weight and for net exports,

$$\theta = \int_0^{+\infty} e^{-\rho s}\left[\widetilde{\Omega}_c c_s + \widetilde{\Omega}_n g_s + \widetilde{\Omega}_\tau t_s^r\right] ds + \widetilde{\Omega}_f \mathrm{nfa}_0,$$

where

$$\widetilde{\Omega}_c = \rho \frac{\Gamma_1}{\Gamma_2} \frac{\Omega_c}{1-\mathcal{G}} \frac{1}{(1-\alpha)\bar{\sigma}^{-1}\sigma - \Theta_\tau \Psi_\theta},$$

$$\widetilde{\Omega}_n = -\rho \frac{(1-\alpha)\Theta_n - (1-\alpha)\Theta_\tau \Psi_n}{(1-\alpha)\bar{\sigma}^{-1}\sigma - \Theta_\tau \Psi_\theta},$$

$$\widetilde{\Omega}_\tau = \rho \frac{(1-\alpha)\Theta_\tau \Psi_\tau}{(1-\alpha)\bar{\sigma}^{-1}\sigma - \Theta_\tau \Psi_\theta},$$

$$\widetilde{\Omega}_f = \rho \frac{\Gamma_1}{\Gamma_2} \frac{1}{1-\mathcal{G}} \frac{1}{(1-\alpha)\bar{\sigma}^{-1}\sigma - \Theta_\tau \Psi_\theta}.$$

Special case: no hand-to-mouth agents $\chi = 0$

The log-linear system is

$$\dot{c}_t = -\hat{\sigma}^{-1}\pi_{H,t},$$

$$\dot{\pi}_{H,t} = \rho \pi_{H,t} - \kappa[c_t + (1-\xi)g_t] - (1-\mathcal{G})\lambda\hat{\sigma}\alpha\omega\theta,$$

for all $t \geq 0$, with

$$c_0 = (1-\mathcal{G})(1-\alpha)\theta$$

And

$$\theta = \int_0^{+\infty} e^{-\rho s}\rho(1-\mathcal{G})\frac{\omega-\sigma}{\omega+(1-\alpha)(1-\sigma)} c_s ds + \rho \frac{1}{\alpha\omega+(1-\alpha)(1-\sigma)} \frac{\alpha\omega+1-\alpha}{1-\mathcal{G}} \frac{1}{} \mathrm{nfa}_0,$$

where $\kappa = \lambda[\phi + \hat{\sigma}]$, $\xi = \frac{\hat{\sigma}}{\phi + \hat{\sigma}}$, $\hat{\sigma} = \frac{\sigma}{1-\mathcal{G}} \frac{1}{(1-\alpha)+\alpha\omega}$.

Special case: no profit offset $o = 0$

The log-linear system is

$$\dot{c}_t = -\widetilde{\sigma}^{-1}\pi_{H,t} + \widetilde{\Theta}_n \dot{g}_t - \widetilde{\Theta}_\tau \dot{t}_t^r,$$

$$\dot{\pi}_{H,t} = \rho \pi_{H,t} - \widetilde{\kappa}\left[c_t + \left(1-\widetilde{\xi}\right)g_t\right] - (1-\mathcal{G})\lambda\widetilde{\sigma}\widetilde{\alpha}\widetilde{\omega}\theta - \widetilde{\kappa}\widetilde{\widetilde{\Theta}}_\tau t_t^r,$$

for all $t \geq 0$, with

$$c_0 = \frac{1}{1-\Theta_n}[(1-\mathcal{G})(1-\widetilde{\alpha})[1-(1-\alpha)\Theta_n]]\theta + \widetilde{\Theta}_n g_0 - \widetilde{\Theta}_\tau t_0^r$$

and

$$\theta = \int_0^{+\infty} e^{-\rho s}\left[\rho\frac{\Gamma_1}{\Gamma_2}\frac{(1-\mathcal{G})\frac{\Gamma_2}{\Gamma_1}[1-(1-\alpha)\Theta_n] - \frac{\alpha}{1-\alpha}}{1-\mathcal{G}}\frac{1}{(1-\alpha)\bar{\sigma}^{-1}\sigma}c_s - \rho\frac{\Theta_n}{\bar{\sigma}^{-1}\sigma}g_s + \rho\frac{\Theta_\tau}{\bar{\sigma}^{-1}\sigma}t_s^r\right]ds$$
$$+\rho\frac{\Gamma_1}{\Gamma_2}\frac{1}{1-\mathcal{G}}\frac{1}{(1-\alpha)\bar{\sigma}^{-1}\sigma}\mathrm{nfa}_0.$$

Appendix B

This appendix derives the solutions to the linear systems obtained in Appendix A. The same special cases are considered.

B.1 Liquidity Trap

Define

$$\widetilde{\nu} = \frac{\rho - \sqrt{\rho^2 + 4\kappa\widetilde{\underline{\sigma}}^{-1}}}{2}, \quad \widetilde{\bar{\nu}} = \frac{\rho + \sqrt{\rho^2 + 4\kappa\widetilde{\underline{\sigma}}^{-1}}}{2}.$$

The equilibrium is completely characterized by the following:

$$\dot{X}_t = AX_t + B_t,$$

where

$$X_t = [\pi_t, c_t]^t, \quad A = \begin{bmatrix} \rho & -\kappa \\ -\widetilde{\underline{\sigma}}^{-1} & 0 \end{bmatrix}, \quad B_t = -\kappa(1-\xi)g_t E_1 + \left[\widetilde{\underline{\Theta}}_n \dot{g}_t - \widetilde{\underline{\Theta}}_\tau \dot{t}_t^r\right] E_2,$$

for all $t \geq 0$.

The (unique) solution that satisfies saddle-path stability writes:

$$X_t = \int_t^{+\infty} \kappa(1-\xi)g_s e^{-A(s-t)} E_1\, ds - \int_t^{+\infty}\left(\widetilde{\underline{\Theta}}_n \dot{g}_s - \widetilde{\underline{\Theta}}_\tau \dot{t}_s^r\right) e^{-A(s-t)} E_2\, ds.$$

Equivalently, integrating the relevant objects by part,

$$\begin{aligned} X_t = & \int_t^{+\infty} \kappa(1-\xi)g_s e^{-A(s-t)} E_1\, ds + \left(\widetilde{\underline{\Theta}}_n g_t - \widetilde{\underline{\Theta}}_\tau t_t^r\right) E_2 \\ & - \int_t^{+\infty}\left(\widetilde{\underline{\Theta}}_n g_s - \widetilde{\underline{\Theta}}_\tau t_s^r\right) A e^{-A(s-t)} E_2\, ds \end{aligned}.$$

Thus,

$$c_t = \int_t^{+\infty} \kappa(1-\xi)E_2^t e^{-A(s-t)} E_1\, ds + \left(\widetilde{\underline{\Theta}}_n g_t - \widetilde{\underline{\Theta}}_\tau t_t^r\right) - \int_t^{+\infty}\left(\widetilde{\underline{\Theta}}_n g_s - \widetilde{\underline{\Theta}}_\tau t_s^r\right) E_2^t A e^{-A(s-t)} E_2\, ds.$$

Note that

$$E_2^t e^{-At} E_1 = \underline{\widetilde{\sigma}}^{-1} \frac{e^{-\widetilde{\nu}t} - e^{-\bar{\widetilde{\nu}}t}}{\bar{\widetilde{\nu}} - \widetilde{\nu}}, \quad E_2^t A e^{-At} E_2 = -\kappa(1-\xi)\underline{\widetilde{\sigma}}^{-1} \frac{e^{-\widetilde{\nu}t} - e^{-\bar{\widetilde{\nu}}t}}{\bar{\widetilde{\nu}} - \widetilde{\nu}},$$

for all $t \geq 0$.

Thus,

$$\begin{aligned} c_t = {} & \underline{\widetilde{\Theta}}_n g_t - \underline{\widetilde{\Theta}}_\tau t_t^r \\ & + \kappa \underline{\widetilde{\sigma}}^{-1}\left(1 - \xi + \underline{\widetilde{\Theta}}_n\right) \int_t^{+\infty} \frac{e^{-\widetilde{\nu}(s-t)} - e^{-\bar{\widetilde{\nu}}(s-t)}}{\bar{\widetilde{\nu}} - \widetilde{\nu}} g_s ds \\ & - \kappa(1-\xi)\underline{\widetilde{\sigma}}^{-1} \underline{\widetilde{\Theta}}_\tau \int_t^{+\infty} \frac{e^{-\widetilde{\nu}(s-t)} - e^{-\bar{\widetilde{\nu}}(s-t)}}{\bar{\widetilde{\nu}} - \widetilde{\nu}} t_s^r ds. \end{aligned}$$

Therefore,

$$c_t = \underline{\widetilde{\Theta}}_n g_t - \underline{\widetilde{\Theta}}_\tau t_t^r + \int_0^{+\infty} \alpha_s^{c,HM} g_{t+s} ds - \int_0^{+\infty} \gamma_s^{c,HM} t_{t+s}^r ds,$$

where

$$\alpha_s^{c,HM} = \left(1 + \frac{\underline{\widetilde{\Theta}}_n}{1-\xi}\right) \widetilde{\alpha}_s^{c,HM}, \quad \gamma_s^{c,HM} = \frac{\underline{\widetilde{\Theta}}_\tau}{1-\xi} \widetilde{\alpha}_s^{c,HM},$$

$$\widetilde{\alpha}_s^{c,HM} = \kappa \underline{\widetilde{\sigma}}^{-1}(1-\xi) e^{-\bar{\widetilde{\nu}}s} \frac{e^{(\bar{\widetilde{\nu}} - \widetilde{\nu})s} - 1}{\bar{\widetilde{\nu}} - \widetilde{\nu}}.$$

Special case: no hand-to-mouth agents $\chi = 0$

Define

$$\nu = \frac{\rho - \sqrt{\rho^2 + 4\kappa\hat{\sigma}^{-1}}}{2}, \quad \bar{\nu} = \frac{\rho + \sqrt{\rho^2 + 4\kappa\hat{\sigma}^{-1}}}{2}.$$

We have

$$c_t = \int_0^{+\infty} \alpha_s^{c,HM} g_{t+s} ds,$$

where

$$\alpha_s^{c,HM} = \kappa\hat{\sigma}^{-1}(1-\xi) e^{-\bar{\nu}s} \frac{e^{(\bar{\nu}-\nu)s} - 1}{\bar{\nu} - \nu}.$$

Special case: no profit offset $o=0$

We have

$$c_t=\widetilde{\Theta}_n g_t-\widetilde{\Theta}_\tau t_t^r+\int_0^{+\infty}\alpha_s^{c,HM}g_{t+s}ds-\int_0^{+\infty}\gamma_s^{c,HM}t_{t+s}^r ds,$$

where

$$\alpha_s^{c,HM}=\left(1+\frac{\widetilde{\Theta}_n}{1-\xi}\right)\widetilde{\alpha}_s^{c,HM}\ ,\ \gamma_s^{c,HM}=\frac{\widetilde{\Theta}_\tau}{1-\xi}\widetilde{\alpha}_s^{c,HM},$$
$$\widetilde{\alpha}_s^{c,HM}=\kappa\widetilde{\sigma}^{-1}(1-\xi)e^{-\tilde{\tilde{\nu}}s}\frac{e^{(\tilde{\tilde{\nu}}-\tilde{\nu})s}-1}{\tilde{\tilde{\nu}}-\tilde{\nu}}.$$

B.2 Currency Union

The IM and PF cases are considered here. The results for the CM case are obtained by direct analogy.

Define

$$\widetilde{\nu}=\frac{\rho-\sqrt{\rho^2+4\widetilde{\kappa}_c\underline{\widetilde{\sigma}}^{-1}}}{2}\ ,\ \widetilde{\widetilde{\nu}}=\frac{\rho+\sqrt{\rho^2+4\widetilde{\kappa}_c\underline{\widetilde{\sigma}}^{-1}}}{2}.$$

The equilibrium is completely characterized by the following:

$$\dot{X}_t=AX_t+B_t,$$

With

$$E_2^t X_0=\Upsilon\theta+\underline{\widetilde{\Theta}}_n g_0-\underline{\widetilde{\Theta}}_\tau t_0^r,$$
$$\theta=\int_0^{+\infty}e^{-\rho s}\left[\widetilde{\Omega}_c c_t+\widetilde{\Omega}_n g_t+\widetilde{\Omega}_\tau t_t^r\right]ds+\widetilde{\Omega}_f\mathrm{nfa}_0,$$

where

$$X_t=[\pi_t,c_t]^t\ ,\ A=\begin{bmatrix}\rho & -\widetilde{\kappa}_c\\ -\underline{\widetilde{\sigma}}^{-1} & 0\end{bmatrix}\ ,\ B_t=-\left(\underline{\widetilde{\kappa}}_n g_t+\underline{\widetilde{\kappa}}_\theta\theta+\underline{\widetilde{\kappa}}_\tau t_t^r\right)E_1+\left[\underline{\widetilde{\Theta}}_n\dot{g}_t-\underline{\widetilde{\Theta}}_\tau\dot{t}_t^r\right]E_2,$$

for all $t\geq 0$.

The (unique) solution that satisfies saddle-path stability writes:

$$X_t=\alpha_{\tilde{\nu}}e^{\tilde{\nu}t}X_{\tilde{\nu}}+\int_t^{+\infty}\left(\underline{\widetilde{\kappa}}_n g_s+\underline{\widetilde{\kappa}}_\theta\theta+\underline{\widetilde{\kappa}}_\tau t_s^r\right)e^{-A(s-t)}E_1 ds-\int_t^{+\infty}\left(\underline{\widetilde{\Theta}}_n\dot{g}_s-\underline{\widetilde{\Theta}}_\tau\dot{t}_s^r\right)e^{-A(s-t)}E_2 ds,$$

with

$$E_2^t X_0 = \Upsilon\theta + \underline{\widetilde{\Theta}}_n g_0 - \underline{\widetilde{\Theta}}_\tau t_0^r,$$
$$\theta = \int_0^{+\infty} e^{-\rho s}\left[\widetilde{\Omega}_c c_t + \widetilde{\Omega}_n g_t + \widetilde{\Omega}_\tau t_t^r\right] ds + \widetilde{\Omega}_f \mathrm{nfa}_0,$$

where $\alpha_{\tilde{\nu}} \in \mathbb{R}$.

Equivalently, integrating the relevant objects by part,

$$X_t = \alpha_{\tilde{\nu}} e^{\tilde{\nu} t} X_{\tilde{\nu}} + \int_t^{+\infty} \left(\underline{\widetilde{\kappa}}_n g_s + \underline{\widetilde{\kappa}}_\theta \theta + \underline{\widetilde{\kappa}}_\tau t_s^r\right) e^{-A(s-t)} E_1 ds + \left(\underline{\widetilde{\Theta}}_n g_t - \underline{\widetilde{\Theta}}_\tau t_t^r\right) E_2$$
$$- \int_t^{+\infty} \left(\underline{\widetilde{\Theta}}_n g_s - \underline{\widetilde{\Theta}}_\tau t_s^r\right) A e^{-A(s-t)} E_2 ds,$$

with

$$E_2^t X_0 = \Upsilon\theta + \underline{\widetilde{\Theta}}_n g_0 - \underline{\widetilde{\Theta}}_\tau t_0^r,$$
$$\theta = \int_0^{+\infty} e^{-\rho s}\left[\widetilde{\Omega}_c c_t + \widetilde{\Omega}_n g_t + \widetilde{\Omega}_\tau t_t^r\right] ds + \widetilde{\Omega}_f \mathrm{nfa}_0.$$

Thus,

$$\Upsilon\theta - \int_0^{+\infty} \left(\underline{\widetilde{\kappa}}_n g_s + \underline{\widetilde{\kappa}}_\theta \theta + \underline{\widetilde{\kappa}}_\tau t_s^r\right) E_2^t e^{-As} E_1 ds$$
$$+ \int_0^{+\infty} \left(\underline{\widetilde{\Theta}}_n g_s - \underline{\widetilde{\Theta}}_\tau t_s^r\right) A E_2^t e^{-As} E_2 ds = \alpha_{\tilde{\nu}}.$$

Therefore,

$$c_t = \left[\Upsilon\theta - \int_0^{+\infty} \left(\underline{\widetilde{\kappa}}_n g_s + \underline{\widetilde{\kappa}}_\theta \theta + \underline{\widetilde{\kappa}}_\tau t_s^r\right) E_2^t e^{-As} E_1 ds + \int_0^{+\infty} \left(\underline{\widetilde{\Theta}}_n g_s - \underline{\widetilde{\Theta}}_\tau t_s^r\right) E_2^t A e^{-As} E_2 ds\right] e^{\tilde{\nu} t}$$
$$+ \int_t^{+\infty} \left(\underline{\widetilde{\kappa}}_n g_s + \underline{\widetilde{\kappa}}_\theta \theta + \underline{\widetilde{\kappa}}_\tau t_s^r\right) E_2^t e^{-A(s-t)} E_1 ds + \left(\underline{\widetilde{\Theta}}_n g_t - \underline{\widetilde{\Theta}}_\tau t_t^r\right)$$
$$- \int_t^{+\infty} \left(\underline{\widetilde{\Theta}}_n g_s - \underline{\widetilde{\Theta}}_\tau t_s^r\right) E_2^t A e^{-A(s-t)} E_2 ds.$$

Equivalently,

$$c_t = \left[\Upsilon e^{\tilde{\nu} t} - \underline{\widetilde{\kappa}}_\theta \left[e^{\tilde{\nu} t} \int_0^{+\infty} E_2^t e^{-As} E_1 ds - \int_t^{+\infty} E_2^t e^{-A(s-t)} E_1 ds\right]\right] \theta + \underline{\widetilde{\Theta}}_n g_t - \underline{\widetilde{\Theta}}_\tau t_t^r$$
$$- \underline{\widetilde{\kappa}}_n \left[e^{\tilde{\nu} t} \int_0^{+\infty} E_2^t e^{-As} E_1 g_s ds - \int_t^{+\infty} E_2^t e^{-A(s-t)} E_1 g_s ds\right]$$
$$+ \underline{\widetilde{\Theta}}_n \left[e^{\tilde{\nu} t} \int_0^{+\infty} E_2^t A e^{-As} E_2 g_s ds - \int_t^{+\infty} E_2^t A e^{-A(s-t)} E_2 g_s ds\right]$$
$$- \underline{\widetilde{\kappa}}_\tau \left[e^{\tilde{\nu} t} \int_0^{+\infty} E_2^t e^{-As} E_1 t_s^r ds - \int_t^{+\infty} E_2^t e^{-A(s-t)} E_1 t_s^r ds\right]$$
$$- \underline{\widetilde{\Theta}}_\tau \left[e^{\tilde{\nu} t} \int_0^{+\infty} E_2^t e^{-As} A E_2 t_s^r ds - \int_t^{+\infty} E_2^t A e^{-A(s-t)} E_2 t_s^r ds\right].$$

Note that

$$E_2^t e^{-At} E_1 = \underline{\widetilde{\sigma}}^{-1} \frac{e^{-\widetilde{\nu}t} - e^{-\bar{\widetilde{\nu}}t}}{\bar{\widetilde{\nu}} - \widetilde{\nu}}, \quad E_2^t A e^{-At} E_2 = -\widetilde{\kappa}_c \underline{\widetilde{\sigma}}^{-1} \frac{e^{-\widetilde{\nu}t} - e^{-\bar{\widetilde{\nu}}t}}{\bar{\widetilde{\nu}} - \widetilde{\nu}},$$

for all $t \geq 0$.

Thus,

$$c_t = \left[\frac{\Upsilon e^{\widetilde{\nu}t} - \underline{\widetilde{\kappa}_\theta} \underline{\widetilde{\sigma}}^{-1} \left(e^{\widetilde{\nu}t} - 1 \right) \int_0^{+\infty} e^{-\widetilde{\nu}s} - e^{-\bar{\widetilde{\nu}}} s}{\bar{\widetilde{\nu}} - \widetilde{\nu} ds} \right] \theta + \underline{\widetilde{\Theta}}_n g_t - \underline{\widetilde{\Theta}}_\tau t_t^r$$

$$- \left(\underline{\widetilde{\kappa}}_n + \underline{\widetilde{\kappa}}_c \underline{\widetilde{\Theta}}_n \right) \underline{\widetilde{\sigma}}^{-1} \left[e^{\widetilde{\nu}t} \int_0^{+\infty} \frac{e^{-\widetilde{\nu}s} - e^{-\bar{\widetilde{\nu}}s}}{\bar{\widetilde{\nu}} - \widetilde{\nu}} g_s ds - \int_t^{+\infty} \frac{e^{-\widetilde{\nu}(s-t)} - e^{-\bar{\widetilde{\nu}}(s-t)}}{\bar{\widetilde{\nu}} - \widetilde{\nu}} g_s ds \right]$$

$$- \left(\underline{\widetilde{\kappa}}_\tau - \underline{\widetilde{\kappa}}_c \underline{\widetilde{\Theta}}_\tau \right) \underline{\widetilde{\sigma}}^{-1} \left[e^{\widetilde{\nu}t} \int_0^{+\infty} \frac{e^{-\widetilde{\nu}s} - e^{-\bar{\widetilde{\nu}}s}}{\bar{\widetilde{\nu}} - \widetilde{\nu}} t_s^r ds - \int_t^{+\infty} \frac{e^{-\widetilde{\nu}(s-t)} - e^{-\bar{\widetilde{\nu}}(s-t)}}{\bar{\widetilde{\nu}} - \widetilde{\nu}} t_s^r ds \right].$$

Using the expression for the Pareto weight θ,

$$c_t = \left[\Upsilon e^{\widetilde{\nu}t} - \underline{\widetilde{\kappa}_\theta} \underline{\widetilde{\sigma}}^{-1} \left(e^{\widetilde{\nu}t} - 1 \right) \frac{\widetilde{\nu}^{-1} - \bar{\widetilde{\nu}}^{-1}}{\bar{\widetilde{\nu}} - \widetilde{\nu}} \right] \left(\int_0^{+\infty} e^{-\rho s} \left[\widetilde{\Omega}_c c_s + \widetilde{\Omega}_n g_s + \widetilde{\Omega}_\tau t_s^r \right] ds + \widetilde{\Omega}_f \mathrm{nfa}_0 \right)$$

$$+ \underline{\widetilde{\Theta}}_n g_t - \underline{\widetilde{\Theta}}_\tau t_t^r$$

$$- \left(\underline{\widetilde{\kappa}}_n + \underline{\widetilde{\kappa}}_c \underline{\widetilde{\Theta}}_n \right) \underline{\widetilde{\sigma}}^{-1} \left[e^{\widetilde{\nu}t} \int_0^{+\infty} \frac{e^{-\widetilde{\nu}s} - e^{-\bar{\widetilde{\nu}}s}}{\bar{\widetilde{\nu}} - \widetilde{\nu}} g_s ds - \int_t^{+\infty} \frac{e^{-\widetilde{\nu}(s-t)} - e^{-\bar{\widetilde{\nu}}(s-t)}}{\bar{\widetilde{\nu}} - \widetilde{\nu}} g_s ds \right]$$

$$- \left(\underline{\widetilde{\kappa}}_\tau - \underline{\widetilde{\kappa}}_c \underline{\widetilde{\Theta}}_\tau \right) \underline{\widetilde{\sigma}}^{-1} \left[e^{\widetilde{\nu}t} \int_0^{+\infty} \frac{e^{-\widetilde{\nu}s} - e^{-\bar{\widetilde{\nu}}s}}{\bar{\widetilde{\nu}} - \widetilde{\nu}} t_s^r ds - \int_t^{+\infty} \frac{e^{-\widetilde{\nu}(s-t)} - e^{-\bar{\widetilde{\nu}}(s-t)}}{\bar{\widetilde{\nu}} - \widetilde{\nu}} t_s^r ds \right].$$

From Fubini's Theorem, assuming that the integrals are finite,

$$\int_0^{+\infty} e^{-\rho t} \int_t^{+\infty} \frac{e^{-\widetilde{\nu}(s-t)} - e^{-\bar{\widetilde{\nu}}(s-t)}}{\bar{\widetilde{\nu}} - \widetilde{\nu}} x_s ds dt = \int_0^{+\infty} e^{-\rho s} \int_0^s \frac{e^{(\rho - \widetilde{\nu})(s-t)} - e^{(\rho - \bar{\widetilde{\nu}})(s-t)}}{\bar{\widetilde{\nu}} - \widetilde{\nu}} dt x_s ds$$

$$= -\frac{1}{\bar{\widetilde{\nu}}} - \widetilde{\nu} \int_0^{+\infty} e^{-\rho s} \left[(\rho - \widetilde{\nu})^{-1} \left(1 - e^{(\rho - \widetilde{\nu})s} \right) - \left(\rho - \bar{\widetilde{\nu}} \right)^{-1} \left(1 - e^{(\rho - \widetilde{\nu})s} \right) \right] x_s ds,$$

for each $x \in \{g, t^r\}$.

Note that $\frac{\widetilde{\nu}^{-1} - \bar{\widetilde{\nu}}^{-1}}{\bar{\widetilde{\nu}} - \widetilde{\nu}} = -\underline{\widetilde{\kappa}}_c^{-1} \underline{\widetilde{\sigma}}$ by definition of $\widetilde{\nu}, \bar{\widetilde{\nu}}$. Thus,

$$\int_0^{+\infty} e^{-\rho t} c_t dt = \frac{1}{1 - \Sigma \widetilde{\Omega}_c} \left(\int_0^{+\infty} \varsigma_n^t g_s ds + \int_0^{+\infty} \varsigma_\tau^t t_s^r ds + \varsigma_f \mathrm{nfa}_0 \right),$$

where

$$
\begin{aligned}
\varsigma_n^t &= \Sigma e^{-\rho t}\widetilde{\Omega}_n + e^{-\rho t}\underline{\widetilde{\Theta}}_n - \left(\underline{\widetilde{\kappa}}_n + \underline{\widetilde{\kappa}}_c \underline{\widetilde{\Theta}}_n\right)\underline{\widetilde{\sigma}}^{-1}\left[\frac{1}{\rho-\widetilde{\nu}}\frac{e^{-\tilde{\nu}t}-e^{-\bar{\tilde{\nu}}t}}{\bar{\tilde{\nu}}-\widetilde{\nu}}\right. \\
&\qquad \left. + \frac{1}{\bar{\tilde{\nu}}-\widetilde{\nu}}e^{-\rho t}\left[(\rho-\widetilde{\nu})^{-1}\left(1-e^{(\rho-\tilde{\nu})t}\right) - (\rho-\bar{\tilde{\nu}})^{-1}\left(1-e^{(\rho-\bar{\tilde{\nu}})t}\right)\right]\right], \\
\varsigma_\tau^t &= \Sigma e^{-\rho t}\widetilde{\Omega}_\tau - e^{-\rho t}\underline{\widetilde{\Theta}}_\tau - \left(\underline{\widetilde{\kappa}}_\tau - \underline{\widetilde{\kappa}}_c \underline{\widetilde{\Theta}}_\tau\right)\underline{\widetilde{\sigma}}^{-1}\left[\frac{1}{\rho-\widetilde{\nu}}\frac{e^{-\tilde{\nu}t}-e^{-\bar{\tilde{\nu}}t}}{\bar{\tilde{\nu}}-\widetilde{\nu}}\right. \\
&\qquad \left. + \frac{1}{\bar{\tilde{\nu}}-\widetilde{\nu}}e^{-\rho t}\left[(\rho-\widetilde{\nu})^{-1}\left(1-e^{-(\rho-\tilde{\nu})t}\right) - (\rho-\bar{\tilde{\nu}})^{-1}\left(1-e^{(\rho-\bar{\tilde{\nu}})t}\right)\right]\right], \\
\varsigma_f &= \Sigma\widetilde{\Omega}_f, \\
\Sigma &= \Upsilon\frac{1}{\rho-\widetilde{\nu}} - \underline{\widetilde{\kappa}}_\theta \underline{\widetilde{\kappa}}_c^{-1}\left(\frac{1}{\rho} - \frac{1}{\rho-\widetilde{\nu}}\right).
\end{aligned}
$$

Therefore,

$$
c_t = \underline{\widetilde{\Theta}}_n g_t - \underline{\widetilde{\Theta}}_\tau t_t^r + \int_{-t}^{+\infty} \alpha_s^{c,t,HM,IM} g_{t+s}\,ds - \int_{-t}^{+\infty} \gamma_s^{c,t,HM,IM} t_{t+s}^r\,ds,
$$

where

$$
\begin{aligned}
\alpha_s^{c,t,HM,IM} &= \alpha_s^{c,t,HM,CM} + \delta_s^{c,t,HM,IM} + \delta_s^{c,t,HM,PF}, \\
\gamma_s^{c,t,HM,IM} &= \gamma_{s0}^{c,t,HM,CM} + \epsilon_s^{c,t,HM,IM},
\end{aligned}
$$

with

$$
\begin{aligned}
\alpha_s^{c,t,HM,CM} &= -\left(\underline{\widetilde{\kappa}}_n + \underline{\widetilde{\kappa}}_c \underline{\widetilde{\Theta}}_n\right)\underline{\widetilde{\sigma}}^{-1}\left[e^{\tilde{\nu}t}\frac{e^{-\tilde{\nu}(t+s)}-e^{-\bar{\tilde{\nu}}(t+s)}}{\bar{\tilde{\nu}}-\widetilde{\nu}} - \mathbb{1}_{s\geq 0}\frac{e^{-\tilde{\nu}s}-e^{-\bar{\tilde{\nu}}s}}{\bar{\tilde{\nu}}-\widetilde{\nu}}\right], \\
\gamma_s^{c,t,HM,CM} &= \left(\underline{\widetilde{\kappa}}_\tau - \underline{\widetilde{\kappa}}_c \underline{\widetilde{\Theta}}_\tau\right)\underline{\widetilde{\sigma}}^{-1}\left[e^{\tilde{\nu}t}\frac{e^{-\tilde{\nu}(t+s)}-e^{-\bar{\tilde{\nu}}(t+s)}}{\bar{\tilde{\nu}}-\widetilde{\nu}} - \mathbb{1}_{s\geq 0}\frac{e^{-\tilde{\nu}s}-e^{-\bar{\tilde{\nu}}s}}{\bar{\tilde{\nu}}-\widetilde{\nu}}\right], \\
\delta_s^{c,t,HM,IM} &= \left(\frac{1}{1-\Sigma\widetilde{\Omega}_c}\widetilde{\Omega}_c\varsigma_n^{t+s} + e^{-\rho(t+s)}\widetilde{\Omega}_n\right)\left[\Upsilon e^{\tilde{\nu}t} - \underline{\widetilde{\kappa}}_\theta \underline{\widetilde{\kappa}}_c^{-1}\left(1-e^{\tilde{\nu}t}\right)\right], \\
\epsilon_s^{c,t,HM,IM} &= -\left(\frac{1}{1-\Sigma\widetilde{\Omega}_c}\widetilde{\Omega}_c\varsigma_\tau^{t+s} + e^{-\rho(t+s)}\widetilde{\Omega}_\tau\right)\left[\Upsilon e^{\tilde{\nu}t} - \underline{\widetilde{\kappa}}_\theta \underline{\widetilde{\kappa}}_c^{-1}\left(1-e^{\tilde{\nu}t}\right)\right],
\end{aligned}
$$

and $\delta_s^{c,t,HM,PF} = 0$ in IM case, and

$$
\delta_s^{c,t,HM,PF} = \left(\frac{1}{1-\Sigma\widetilde{\Omega}_c}\widetilde{\Omega}_c\varsigma_f + \widetilde{\Omega}_f\right)\left[\Upsilon e^{\tilde{\nu}t} - \underline{\widetilde{\kappa}}_\theta \underline{\widetilde{\kappa}}_c^{-1}\left(1-e^{\tilde{\nu}t}\right)\right]e^{-\rho(t+s)}
$$

in PF case.

We can reexpress these as

$$\alpha_s^{c,t,HM,CM} = -\left(\underline{\widetilde{\kappa}}_n + \underline{\widetilde{\kappa}}_c \underline{\widetilde{\Theta}}_n\right) \underline{\widetilde{\sigma}}^{-1} \left[e^{\widetilde{\nu} t} \frac{e^{-\widetilde{\nu}(t+s)} - e^{-\bar{\widetilde{\nu}}(t+s)}}{\bar{\widetilde{\nu}} - \widetilde{\nu}} - \mathbb{1}_{s \geq 0} \frac{e^{-\widetilde{\nu} s} - e^{-\bar{\widetilde{\nu}} s}}{\bar{\widetilde{\nu}} - \widetilde{\nu}} \right],$$

$$\gamma_s^{c,t,HM,CM} = \left(\underline{\widetilde{\kappa}}_\tau - \underline{\widetilde{\kappa}}_c \underline{\widetilde{\Theta}}_\tau\right) \underline{\widetilde{\sigma}}^{-1} \left[e^{\widetilde{\nu} t} \frac{e^{-\widetilde{\nu}(t+s)} - e^{-\bar{\widetilde{\nu}}(t+s)}}{\bar{\widetilde{\nu}} - \widetilde{\nu}} - \mathbb{1}_{s \geq 0} \frac{e^{-\widetilde{\nu} s} - e^{-\bar{\widetilde{\nu}} s}}{\bar{\widetilde{\nu}} - \widetilde{\nu}} \right],$$

$$\begin{aligned}\delta_s^{c,t,HM,IM} = {} & \left[\Upsilon e^{\widetilde{\nu} t} - \underline{\widetilde{\kappa}}_\theta \underline{\widetilde{\kappa}}_c^{-1}\left(1 - e^{\widetilde{\nu} t}\right)\right] \times \\ & \frac{1}{1 - \Sigma \widetilde{\Omega}_c} \left[e^{-\rho(t+s)} \widetilde{\Omega}_n + e^{-\rho(t+s)} \widetilde{\Omega}_c \underline{\widetilde{\Theta}}_n \right. \\ & \left. + \widetilde{\Omega}_c \left(\underline{\widetilde{\kappa}}_n + \underline{\widetilde{\kappa}}_c \underline{\widetilde{\Theta}}_n\right) \underline{\widetilde{\sigma}}^{-1} \frac{1}{\widetilde{\kappa}_c \underline{\widetilde{\sigma}}^{-1}} e^{-\rho(t+s)} \left(1 - e^{\widetilde{\nu}(t+s)}\right) \right],\end{aligned}$$

$$\begin{aligned}\epsilon_s^{c,t,HM,IM} = {} & -\left[\Upsilon e^{\widetilde{\nu} t} - \underline{\widetilde{\kappa}}_\theta \underline{\widetilde{\kappa}}_c^{-1}\left(1 - e^{\widetilde{\nu} t}\right)\right] \times \\ & \frac{1}{1 - \Sigma \widetilde{\Omega}_c} \left[e^{-\rho(t+s)} \widetilde{\Omega}_\tau - e^{-\rho(t+s)} \widetilde{\Omega}_c \underline{\widetilde{\Theta}}_\tau \right. \\ & \left. + \widetilde{\Omega}_c \left(\underline{\widetilde{\kappa}}_\tau - \underline{\widetilde{\kappa}}_c \underline{\widetilde{\Theta}}_\tau\right) \underline{\widetilde{\sigma}}^{-1} \frac{1}{\widetilde{\kappa}_c \underline{\widetilde{\sigma}}^{-1}} e^{-\rho(t+s)} \left(1 - e^{\widetilde{\nu}(t+s)}\right) \right],\end{aligned}$$

and $\delta_s^{c,t,HM,PF} = 0$ in the IM case, and

$$\delta_s^{c,t,HM,PF} = \left[\Upsilon e^{\widetilde{\nu} t} - \underline{\widetilde{\kappa}}_\theta \underline{\widetilde{\kappa}}_c^{-1}\left(1 - e^{\widetilde{\nu} t}\right)\right] \frac{1}{1 - \Sigma \widetilde{\Omega}_c} \widetilde{\Omega}_f e^{-\rho(t+s)}$$

in the PF case.

By direct analogy,

$$c_t = \underline{\widetilde{\Theta}}_n g_t - \underline{\widetilde{\Theta}}_\tau t_t^r + \int_{-t}^{+\infty} \alpha_s^{c,t,HM,CM} g_{t+s} ds - \int_0^{+\infty} \gamma_s^{c,t,HM,CM} t_{t+s}^r ds$$

in CM case.

Special case: no hand-to-mouth agents $\chi = 0$

Define

$$\nu = \frac{\rho - \sqrt{\rho^2 + 4\kappa \hat{\sigma}^{-1}}}{2}, \quad \bar{\nu} = \frac{\rho + \sqrt{\rho^2 + 4\kappa \hat{\sigma}^{-1}}}{2},$$

and

$$\hat{\Sigma} = (1 - \mathcal{G})(1 - \alpha)\frac{1}{\bar{\bar{\nu}}} + (1 - \mathcal{G})\frac{\hat{\sigma}}{\phi + \hat{\sigma}} \alpha \omega \frac{1}{\bar{\bar{\nu}}} \frac{\widetilde{\nu}}{\rho}.$$

Define

$$\alpha_s^{c,t,HM,CM} = -\kappa(1-\xi)\hat{\sigma}^{-1}\left[e^{\nu t}\frac{e^{-\nu(t+s)} - e^{-\bar{\nu}(t+s)}}{\bar{\nu}-\nu} - \mathbb{1}_{s\geq 0}\frac{e^{-\nu s} - e^{-\bar{\nu}s}}{\bar{\nu}-\nu}\right].$$

We have

$$c_t = \int_{-t}^{+\infty} \alpha_s^{c,t,HM,IM} g_{t+s} ds,$$

where

$$\alpha_s^{c,t,HM,IM} = \alpha_s^{c,t,HM,CM} + \delta_s^{c,t,HM,IM} + \delta_s^{c,t,HM,PF},$$

with

$$\delta_s^{c,t,HM,IM} = \rho\left[\frac{1-\alpha}{\alpha}e^{\tilde{\nu}t} - \frac{\hat{\sigma}}{\phi+\hat{\sigma}}\omega\left(1-e^{\tilde{\nu}t}\right)\right] \times \frac{\alpha\frac{\omega-\sigma}{\omega+(1-\alpha)(1-\sigma)}}{1-\hat{\Sigma}\rho\frac{\omega-\sigma}{\omega+(1-\alpha)(1-\sigma)}\frac{1}{1-\mathcal{G}}}(1-\xi)e^{-\rho(t+s)}\left(1-e^{\tilde{\nu}(t+s)}\right),$$

and $\delta_s^{c,t,HM,PF} = 0$ in the IM case, and

$$\delta_s^{c,t,HM,PF} = \rho\left[\frac{1-\alpha}{\alpha}e^{\tilde{\nu}t} - \frac{\hat{\sigma}}{\phi+\hat{\sigma}}\omega\left(1-e^{\tilde{\nu}t}\right)\right]\frac{\frac{\alpha\omega+1-\alpha}{\omega+(1-\alpha)(1-\sigma)}}{1-\hat{\Sigma}\rho\frac{\omega-\sigma}{\omega+(1-\alpha)(1-\sigma)}\frac{1}{1-\mathcal{G}}}e^{-\rho(t+s)}$$

in the PF case.

Special case: no profit offset $o = 0$

In that case we have

$$\Sigma = (1-\mathcal{G})(1-\widetilde{\alpha})\frac{1}{\bar{\bar{\nu}}} + (1-\mathcal{G})\lambda\widetilde{\sigma}\widetilde{\alpha}\widetilde{\omega}\widetilde{\kappa}^{-1}\frac{1}{\rho}\frac{\widetilde{\nu}}{\bar{\bar{\nu}}}.$$

Define

$$\widetilde{\alpha}_s^{c,t,HM,CM} = -\widetilde{\kappa}\left(1-\widetilde{\xi}\right)\widetilde{\sigma}^{-1}\left[e^{\widetilde{\nu}t}\frac{e^{-\widetilde{\nu}(t+s)} - e^{-\bar{\widetilde{\nu}}(t+s)}}{\bar{\widetilde{\nu}}-\widetilde{\nu}} - \mathbb{1}_{s\geq 0}\frac{e^{-\widetilde{\nu}s} - e^{-\bar{\widetilde{\nu}}s}}{\bar{\widetilde{\nu}}-\widetilde{\nu}}\right].$$

We have

$$c_t = \widetilde{\Theta}_n g_t - \widetilde{\Theta}_\tau t_t^r + \int_{-t}^{+\infty} \alpha_s^{c,t,HM,IM} g_{t+s} ds - \int_{-t}^{+\infty} \gamma_s^{c,t,HM,IM} t_{t+s}^r ds,$$

where

$$\alpha_s^{c,t,HM,IM} = \alpha_s^{c,t,HM,CM} + \delta_s^{c,t,HM,IM} + \delta_s^{c,t,HM,PF},$$
$$\gamma_s^{c,t,HM,IM} = \gamma_s^{c,t,HM,CM} + \epsilon_s^{c,t,HM,IM},$$

with

$$\alpha_s^{c,t,HM,CM} = -\left(1 + \frac{\widetilde{\Theta}_n}{1-\widetilde{\xi}}\right)\widetilde{\kappa}\left(1-\widetilde{\xi}\right)\widetilde{\sigma}^{-1}\left[e^{\widetilde{\nu}t}\frac{e^{-\widetilde{\nu}(t+s)} - e^{-\bar{\widetilde{\nu}}(t+s)}}{\bar{\widetilde{\nu}}-\widetilde{\nu}} - \mathbb{1}_{s\geq 0}\frac{e^{-\widetilde{\nu}s} - e^{-\bar{\widetilde{\nu}}s}}{\bar{\widetilde{\nu}}-\widetilde{\nu}}\right],$$

$$\gamma_s^{c,t,HM,CM} = -\frac{\widetilde{\Theta}_\tau - \widetilde{\widetilde{\Theta}}_\tau}{1-\widetilde{\xi}}\widetilde{\kappa}\left(1-\widetilde{\xi}\right)\widetilde{\sigma}^{-1}\left[e^{\widetilde{\nu}t}\frac{e^{-\widetilde{\nu}(t+s)} - e^{-\bar{\widetilde{\nu}}(t+s)}}{\bar{\widetilde{\nu}}-\widetilde{\nu}} - \mathbb{1}_{s\geq 0}\frac{e^{-\widetilde{\nu}s} - e^{-\bar{\widetilde{\nu}}s}}{\bar{\widetilde{\nu}}-\widetilde{\nu}}\right],$$

$$\delta_s^{c,t,HM,IM} = \rho\left[\frac{1-\widetilde{\alpha}}{\widetilde{\alpha}}e^{\widetilde{\nu}t} - \lambda\widetilde{\sigma}\widetilde{\kappa}^{-1}\widetilde{\omega}\left(1-e^{\widetilde{\nu}t}\right)\right]$$
$$\times\frac{\widetilde{\alpha}}{1-\Sigma\widetilde{\Omega}_c}\left[e^{-\rho(t+s)}\frac{(1-\mathcal{G})\widetilde{\Omega}_n}{\rho} + e^{-\rho(t+s)}\frac{(1-\mathcal{G})\widetilde{\Omega}_c}{\rho}\widetilde{\Theta}_n.\right.$$
$$\left.+\frac{(1-\mathcal{G})\widetilde{\Omega}_c}{\rho}\left(1-\widetilde{\xi}\right)\left(1+\frac{\widetilde{\Theta}_n}{1-\widetilde{\xi}}\right)e^{-\rho(t+s)}\left(1-e^{\widetilde{\nu}(t+s)}\right)\right],$$

$$\epsilon_s^{c,t,HM,IM} = -\rho\left[\frac{1-\widetilde{\alpha}}{\widetilde{\alpha}}e^{\widetilde{\nu}t} - \lambda\widetilde{\sigma}\widetilde{\kappa}^{-1}\widetilde{\omega}\left(1-e^{\widetilde{\nu}t}\right)\right]$$
$$\times\frac{\widetilde{\alpha}}{1-\Sigma\widetilde{\Omega}_c}\left[e^{-\rho(t+s)}\frac{(1-\mathcal{G})\widetilde{\Omega}_\tau}{\rho} - e^{-\rho(t+s)}\frac{(1-\mathcal{G})\widetilde{\Omega}_c}{\rho}\widetilde{\Theta}_\tau.\right.$$
$$\left.+\widetilde{\Omega}_c\left(1-\widetilde{\xi}\right)\frac{\widetilde{\widetilde{\Theta}}_\tau - \widetilde{\Theta}_\tau}{1-\widetilde{\xi}}e^{-\rho(t+s)}\left(1-e^{\widetilde{\nu}(t+s)}\right)\right],$$

and $\delta_s^{c,t,HM,PF} = 0$ in the IM case, and

$$\delta_s^{c,t,HM,PF} = \rho\left[\frac{1-\widetilde{\alpha}}{\widetilde{\alpha}}e^{\widetilde{\nu}t} - \lambda\widetilde{\sigma}\widetilde{\kappa}^{-1}\widetilde{\omega}\left(1-e^{\widetilde{\nu}t}\right)\right]\frac{1}{1-\Sigma\widetilde{\Omega}_c}\frac{\widetilde{\alpha}(1-\mathcal{G})\widetilde{\Omega}_f}{\rho}e^{-\rho(t+s)}$$

in the PF case.

REFERENCES

Acconcia, A., Corsetti, G., Simonelli, S., 2011. Mafia and public spending: evidence on the fiscal multiplier from a quasi-experiment. CEPR Discussion Papers.

Auerbach, A., Gorodnichenko, Y., 2012. Fiscal multipliers in recession and expansion. In: Fiscal Policy After the Financial Crisis, NBER Chapters. National Bureau of Economic Research, Inc. NBER working paper #17447.

Barro, R.J., Redlick, C.J., 2009. Macroeconomic effects from government purchases and taxes. NBER Working Papers No. 15369, National Bureau of Economic Research, Inc.
Campbell, J.Y., Mankiw, N.G., 1989. Consumption, income and interest rates: reinterpreting the time series evidence. In: Blanchard, O., Fischer, S. (Eds.), NBER Macroeconomics Annual 1989, NBER Chapters, vol. 4. National Bureau of Economic Research, Inc, pp. 185–246.
Chodorow-Reich, G., Feiveson, L., Liscow, Z., Woolston, W., 2011. Does state fiscal relief during recessions increase employment? Evidence from the American Recovery and Reinvestment Act. Working Paper, University of California at Berkeley.
Christiano, L., Eichenbaum, M., Rebelo, S., 2011. When is the government spending multiplier large? J. Polit. Econ. 119 (1), 78–121.
Clemens, J., Miran, S., 2010. The effects of state budget cuts on employment and income. Working Paper, Harvard University.
Cohen, L., Coval, J.D., Malloy, C., 2010. Do powerful politicians cause corporate downsizing? NBER Working Papers, National Bureau of Economic Research, Inc.
Cole, H.L., Obstfeld, M., 1991. Commodity trade and international risk sharing: how much do financial markets matter? J. Monet. Econ. 28 (1), 3–24.
Cook, D., Devereux, M.B., 2011. Optimal fiscal policy in a world liquidity trap. Eur. Econ. Rev. 55 (4), 443–462.
Corsetti, G., Kuester, K., Muller, G.J., 2011. Floats, pegs and the transmission of fiscal policy. J. Econ. (Chin.) 14 (2), 5–38.
Dornbusch, R., 1980. Exchange rate economics: where do we stand? Brook. Pap. Econ. Act. 11 (1), 143–206.
Eggertsson, G.B., 2011. What fiscal policy is effective at zero interest rates? In: Acemoglu, D., Woodford, M. (Eds.), NBER Macroeconomics Annual 2010, NBER Chapters, vol. 25. National Bureau of Economic Research, Inc, pp. 59–112.
Erceg, C.J., Linde, J., 2012. Fiscal consolidation in an open economy. Am. Econ. Rev. 102 (3), 186–191.
Farhi, E., Werning, I., 2012a. Dealing with the trilemma: optimal capital controls with fixed exchange rates. NBER Working Papers No.18199, National Bureau of Economic Research, Inc.
Farhi, E., Werning, I., 2012b. Fiscal unions. NBER Working Papers No.18280, National Bureau of Economic Research, Inc.
Fishback, P.V., Kachanovskaya, V., 2010. In search of the multiplier for federal spending in the states during the great depression. NBER Working Papers, National Bureau of Economic Research, Inc.
Gali, J., Monacelli, T., 2005. Monetary policy and exchange rate volatility in a small open economy. Rev. Econ. Stud. 72 (3), 707–734.
Gali, J., Monacelli, T., 2008. Optimal monetary and fiscal policy in a currency union. J. Int. Econ. 76 (1), 116–132.
Gali, J., Lopez-Salido, J.D., Valles, J., 2007. Understanding the effects of government spending on consumption. J. Eur. Econ. Assoc. 5 (1), 227–270.
Gordon, R.J., Krenn, R., 2010. The end of the great depression 1939-41: policy contributions and fiscal multipliers. NBER Working Papers No. 16380, National Bureau of Economic Research, Inc.
Keynes, J., 1929. The german transfer problem. Econ. J. 39 (153), 1–7.
Mankiw, G.N., 2000. The savers-spenders theory of fiscal policy. Am. Econ. Rev. 90 (2), 120–125.
Nakamura, E., Steinsson, J., 2011. Fiscal stimulus in a monetary union: evidence from U.S. regions. NBER Working Papers No.17391, National Bureau of Economic Research, Inc.
Ohlin, B., 1929. The reparation problem: a discussion. Econ. J. 39 (154), 172–182.
Ramey, V.A., 2011. Can government purchases stimulate the economy? J. Econ. Lit. 49 (3), 673–685.
Serrato, J.C.S., Wingender, P., 2010. Estimating local multipliers. Working Paper, University of California at Berkeley.
Shoag, D., 2010. The impact of government spending shocks: evidence on the multiplier from state pension plan returns. Working Paper, Harvard University.
Werning, I., 2012. Managing a liquidity trap: monetary and fiscal policy. NBER Working Papers, National Bureau of Economic Research, Inc.
Woodford, M., 2011. Monetary policy and financial stability. Working Paper, Columbia University.

CHAPTER 32

What is a Sustainable Public Debt?

P. D'Erasmo*, E.G. Mendoza[†,‡], J. Zhang[§]
*Federal Reserve Bank of Philadelphia, Philadelphia, PA, United States
†PIER, University of Pennsylvania, Philadelphia, PA, United States
‡NBER, Cambridge, MA, United States
§Federal Reserve Bank of Chicago, Chicago, IL, United States

Contents

Handbook of Macroeconomics, Volume 2B
ISSN 1574-0048, http://dx.doi.org/10.1016/bs.hesmac.2016.03.013

Abstract

The question of what is a sustainable public debt is paramount in the macroeconomic analysis of fiscal policy. This question is usually formulated as asking whether the outstanding public debt and its projected path are consistent with those of the government's revenues and expenditures (ie, whether fiscal solvency conditions hold). We identify critical flaws in the traditional approach to evaluate debt sustainability, and examine three alternative approaches that provide useful econometric and model-simulation tools to analyze debt sustainability. The first approach is Bohn's nonstructural empirical framework based on a fiscal reaction function that characterizes the dynamics of sustainable debt and primary balances. The second is a structural approach based on a calibrated dynamic general equilibrium framework with a fully specified fiscal sector, which we use to quantify the positive and normative effects of fiscal policies aimed at restoring fiscal solvency in response to changes in debt. The third approach deviates from the others in assuming that governments cannot commit to repay their domestic debt and can thus optimally decide to default even if debt is sustainable in terms of fiscal solvency. We use these three approaches to analyze debt sustainability in the United States and Europe after the sharp increases in public debt following the 2008 crisis, and find that all three raise serious questions about the prospects of fiscal adjustment and its consequences.

Keywords

Debt sustainability, Fiscal reaction function, Fiscal austerity, Tax policy, Sovereign default

JEL Classification Codes:

E62, F34, F42, H21, H6, H87

1. INTRODUCTION

The question of what is a sustainable public debt has always been paramount in the macroeconomic analysis of fiscal policy, and the recent surge in the debt of many advanced and emerging economies has made it particularly critical. This question is often understood as equivalent to asking whether the government is solvent. That is, whether the outstanding stock of public debt matches the projected present discounted value of the primary fiscal balance, measuring both at the general government level and including all forms of fiscal revenue as well as all current expenditures, transfers and entitlement payments. This chapter revisits the question of public debt sustainability, identifies critical flaws in traditional ways to approach it, and discusses three alternative approaches that provide useful econometric and model-simulation tools to evaluate debt sustainability.

The first approach is an empirical approach proposed in Bohn's seminal work on fiscal solvency. The advantage of this approach is that it provides a straightforward and powerful method to conduct nonstructural empirical tests. These tests require only data on the primary balance, outstanding debt, and a few control variables. The data are then used to estimate linear and nonlinear *fiscal reaction functions* (FRFs), which map the response of the primary balance to changes in outstanding debt, conditional on the control variables. A positive, statistically significant response coefficient is a sufficient condition for the debt to be sustainable. A key lesson from Bohn's work, however, is that using this or other time-series econometric tools just to test for fiscal solvency is futile, because the intertemporal government budget constraint holds under very weak time-series assumptions that are generally satisfied in the data. In particular, Bohn (2007) showed that the constraint holds if either the debt or revenues and expenditures (including debt service) are integrated of *any* finite order. In light of this result, he proposed shifting the focus to analyzing the characteristics of the FRFs in order to study the dynamics of fiscal adjustment that have maintained solvency.

We provide new FRF estimation results for historical data spanning the 1791–2014 period for the United States, and for a cross-country panel of advanced and emerging economies for the period 1951–2013. The results are largely in line with previous findings showing that the response coefficient of the primary balance to outstanding debt is positive and statistically significant in most countries (ie, the sufficiency condition for debt sustainability is supported by the data).[a] On the other hand, the results provide clear evidence of a large structural shift in the response coefficients since the 2008 crisis, which is reflected in large negative residuals in the FRFs since 2009. The primary balances predicted by the FRF of the United States for the period 2008–14 are much larger than the observed ones, and the debt and primary balance dynamics that FRFs predict after 2014 for both the United States and European economies yield higher primary surpluses and lower debt ratios than what official projections show. Moreover, in the case of the United States, the pattern of consistent primary deficits since 2009 and continuing until at least 2020 in official projections, is unprecedented. In all previous episodes of large increases in public debt of comparable magnitudes (the Civil War, the two World Wars, and the Great Depression), the primary balance was in surplus 5 years after the debt peaked.

Using the estimated FRFs, we illustrate that there are multiple parameterizations of a FRF that support the same expected present discounted value of primary balances, and thus all of them make the same initial public debt position sustainable. However, these multiple reaction functions yield different short- and long-run dynamics of debt and primary balances, and therefore differ in terms of social welfare and their macro effects. At this point, this nonstructural approach reaches its limits. The standard Lucas-critique argument implies that estimated FRFs cannot be used to study the implications of fiscal policy changes. Hence, comparing different patterns of fiscal adjustment requires a structural framework that models explicitly the mechanisms and distortions by which tax and expenditure policies affect the economy, the structure of financial markets the government can access, and the implications of the government's inability to commit to repay its obligations.

The second approach to study debt sustainability that we examine picks up at this point. We use a calibrated two-country dynamic general equilibrium framework with

[a] Formally, the null hypothesis that the response coefficient is nonpositive is rejected at the standard confidence level.

a fully specified fiscal sector to study the effects of alternative fiscal strategies to restore fiscal solvency in the aftermath of large increases in debt, assuming that the government is committed to repay. The model is calibrated to data from the United States and Europe and used to quantify the positive and normative effects of fiscal policies that governments may use seeking to increase the present value of the primary fiscal balance by enough to match the increases in debt observed since 2008 (ie, by enough to restore fiscal solvency). This framework has many of the standard elements of the workhorse open-economy Neoclassical model with exogenous long-run balanced growth, but it includes modifications designed to make the model consistent with the observed elasticity of tax bases. As a result, the model captures more accurately the relevant tradeoffs between revenue-generating capacity and distortionary effects in the choice of fiscal instruments.

The results show that indeed alternative fiscal policy strategies that are equivalent in that they restore fiscal solvency, have very different effects on welfare and macro aggregates. Moreover, some fiscal policy setups fall short from producing the changes in the equilibrium present discounted value of primary balances that are necessary to match the observed increases in debt. This is particularly true for taxes on capital in the United States and labor taxes in Europe. The dynamic Laffer curves for these taxes (ie, Laffer curves in terms of the present discounted value of the primary fiscal balance) peak below the level required to make the higher post-2008 debts sustainable.

We also find that, in line with findings in the international macroeconomics literature, the fact that the United States and Europe are financially integrated economies implies that the revenue-generating capacity of taxation on capital income is adversely affected by international externalities.[b] At the prevailing tax structures, increases in US capital income taxes (assuming European taxes are constant) generate significantly smaller increases in the present value of US primary balances than if the United States implemented the same taxes under financial autarky. The model also predicts that at its current capital tax rate, Europe is in the inefficient side of its dynamic Laffer curve for the capital income tax. Hence, lowering its tax, assuming the United States keeps its capital tax constant, induces externalities that enlarge European fiscal revenues, and thus the present value of European primary balances rises significantly more than if Europe implemented the same taxes under financial autarky. This does not imply that debt is easier to sustain in Europe but that the incentives for tax competition are strong, and hence that the assumption that US taxes would remain invariant is unlikely to hold.

The results from the empirical and structural approach suggest that public debt sustainability analysis needs to be extended to consider the implications of the government's lack of commitment to repay domestic obligations. In particular, the evidence of

[b] There is a large empirical and theoretical literature on international taxation and tax competition examining the effects of these externalities. See for example, Frenkel et al. (1991), Huizinga et al. (2012), Klein et al. (2007), Mendoza and Tesar (1998, 2005), Persson and Tabellini (1995), and Sorensen (2003).

structural changes weakening the response of primary balances to debt post-2008, and the findings that tax increases may not be able to generate enough revenue to restore fiscal solvency and are hampered by international externalities, indicate that the risk of default on domestic public debt should be considered. In addition, the ongoing European debt crisis and the recurrent turmoil around federal debt ceiling debates in the United States demonstrate that domestic public debt is not in fact the risk-free asset that is generally taken to be. The first two approaches to study debt sustainability covered in this chapter are not useful for addressing this issue, because they are built on the premise that the government is committed to repay. Note also that the risk here is not that of external sovereign default, which is the subject of a different chapter in this Handbook and has been widely studied in the literature. Instead, the risk here is the one that Reinhart and Rogoff (2011) referred to as "the forgotten history of domestic debt:" Historically, there have been episodes in which governments have defaulted outright on their domestic public debt, and until very recently the macro literature had paid little attention to these episodes. Hence, the third approach we examine assumes that governments cannot commit to repay domestic debt, and decide optimally to default even if standard solvency conditions hold, and even when domestic debt holders enter in the payoff function of the sovereign making the default decision. Sustainable debt in this setup is the debt that can be supported as a market equilibrium with positive quantity and price, exposed with positive probability to a government default, and with actual episodes in which default is the equilibrium outcome.

In this framework, the government maximizes a social welfare function that assigns positive weight to the welfare of all domestic agents in the economy, including those who are holders of government debt. Defaulting on public debt is useful as a tool for redistributing resources across agents, but is also costly because debt effectively provides liquidity to credit-constrained agents and serves as a vehicle for tax-smoothing and self-insurance.[c] If default is costless, debt is unsustainable for a utilitarian government because default is always optimal. Debt can be sustainable if default carries a cost or if the government's social welfare function has a bias in favor of bond holders. In addition, this second assumption can be an equilibrium outcome under majority voting if the fraction of agents that do not own debt is sufficiently large, because these agents benefit from the consumption-smoothing ability that public debt issuance provides for them, and may thus choose a government biased in favor of bond holders over a utilitarian government. A quantitative application of this setup calibrated to data from Europe shows how the

[c] This view of default costs is motivated by the findings of Aiyagari and McGrattan (1998) on the social value of domestic public debt as the vehicle for self insurance in a model of heterogeneous agents assuming the government is committed to repay. Birkeland and Prescott (2006) show that public debt also has social value as a mechanism for tax smoothing when population growth declines, taxes distort labor, and intergenerational transfers fund retirement. Welfare when public debt is used to save for retirement is larger than in a tax-and-transfer system.

tradeoff between these costs and benefits of default determines sustainable debt. Domestic default occurs with low probability and returns on government debt carry default premia, and in the setup with a government biased in favor of bondholders the sustainable debt is large and rises with the concentration of debt ownership.

The rest of this chapter is organized as follows: Section 2 discusses the classic and empirical approaches to evaluate debt sustainability, including the new FRF estimation results. Section 3 focuses on the structural approach. It examines the quantitative predictions of the two-country dynamic general equilibrium model for the positive and normative effects of fiscal policies aimed at restoring fiscal solvency in response to large increases in debt, including the application to the case of the United States and Europe. Section 4 covers the domestic default approach, with the quantitative example based on European data. Section 5 provides a critical assessment of all three approaches and an outlook with directions for future research. Section 6 summarizes the main conclusions.

2. EMPIRICAL APPROACH

Several articles and conference volumes survey the large literature on indicators of public debt sustainability and empirical tests of fiscal solvency (eg, Buiter, 1985; Blanchard, 1990; Blanchard et al., 1990; Chalk and Hemming, 2000; IMF, International Monetary Fund, 2003; Afonso, 2005; Bohn, 2008; Neck and Sturm, 2008, and Escolano, 2010). These surveys generally start by formulating standard concepts of government accounting, and then build around them the arguments to construct indicators of debt sustainability or tests of fiscal solvency. We proceed here in a similar way, but adopting a general formulation following the analysis of government debt in the textbook by Ljungqvist and Sargent (2012). The advantage of this formulation is that it is explicit about the structure of asset markets, which as we show below turns out to be critical for the design of empirical tests of fiscal solvency.

Consider a simple economy in which output and total government outlays (ie, current expenditures and transfer payments) are exogenous functions of a vector of random variables s denoted $y(s_t)$ and $g(s_t)$, respectively. The exogenous state vector follows a standard discrete Markov process with transition probability matrix $\pi(s_{t+1},s_t)$. Taxes at date t depend on s_t and on the outstanding public debt, but since the latter is the result of the history of values of s up to and including date t, denoted s^t, taxes can be expressed as $\tau_t(s^t)$. In terms of asset markets, this economy has a full set of state-contingent Arrow securities with a j-step ahead equilibrium pricing kernel given by $Q_j(s_{t+j}|s_t) = MRS(c_{t+j},c_t)\pi^j(s_{t+j},s_t)$.[d]

[d] $MRS(c_{t+j},c_t) \equiv \beta^j u'(c(s_{t+j}))/u'(c(s_t))$ is the marginal rate of substitution in consumption between date $t+j$ and date t. Note also that in this simple economy the resource constraint implies that consumption is exogenous and given by $c(s_{t+j}) = y(s_{t+j}) - g(s_{t+j})$.

Public debt outstanding at the beginning of date t is denoted as $b_{t-1}(s_t|s^{t-1})$, which is the amount of date-t goods that the government promised at $t-1$ to deliver if the economy is in state s_t at date t with history s^{t-1}. The government's budget constraint can then be written as follows:

$$\sum_{s_{t+1}} Q_1(s_{t+1}|s_t)b_t(s_{t+1}|s^t)\pi(s_{t+1},s_t) - b_{t-1}(s_t|s^{t-1}) = g(s_t) - \tau_t(s^t).$$

Notice that there are no restrictions on what type of financial instruments the government uses to borrow. In particular, the typical case in which the government issues only risk-free debt is not ruled out. In this case, the above budget constraint reduces to the familiar form: $[b_t(s^t)/R_1(s_t)] - b_{t-1}(s^{t-1}) = g(s_t) - \tau_t(s^t)$, where $R_1(s_t)$ is the one-step-ahead risk-free real interest rate (which at equilibrium satisfies $R_1(s_t)^{-1} = E_t[MRS(c_{t+1}, c_t)]$).

Imposing the no-Ponzi game condition $\lim\inf_{j\to\infty} E_t[MRS(c_{t+j}, c_t)b_{t+j}] = 0$ on the above budget constraint, and using the equilibrium asset pricing conditions, yields the following intertemporal government budget constraint (IGBC):

$$b_{t-1} = pb_t + \sum_{j=1}^{\infty} E_t[MRS(c_{t+j}, c_t)pb_{t+j}], \tag{1}$$

where $pb_t \equiv \tau_t - g_t$ is the primary fiscal balance. This IGBC condition is the familiar fiscal solvency condition that anchors the standard concept of debt sustainability: b_{t-1} is said to be sustainable if it matches the expected present discounted value of the stream of future primary fiscal balances. Hence, the two main goals of most of the empirical literature on public debt sustainability have been: (a) to construct simple indicators that can be used to assess debt sustainability, and (b) to develop formal econometric tests that can determine whether the hypothesis that IGBC holds can be rejected by the data.

2.1 Classic Debt Sustainability Analysis

Classic public debt sustainability analysis focuses on the long-run implications of a deterministic version of the IGBC. This approach uses the government budget constraint evaluated at steady state as a condition that relates the long-run primary fiscal balance as a share of GDP and the debt-output ratio, and defines the latter as the sustainable debt (see Buiter, 1985, Blanchard, 1990, and Blanchard et al., 1990). To derive this condition from the setup described earlier, first remove uncertainty from the government budget constraint with nonstate contingent debt to obtain: $[b_t/(1+r_t)] - b_{t-1} = -pb_t$. Then rewrite the equation with government bonds at face value instead of discount bonds: $b_t - (1+r_t)b_{t-1} = -pb_t$. Finally, apply a change of variables so that debt and primary balances are measured as GDP ratios, which implies that the effective interest rate becomes $r_t \equiv (1+i_t^r)/(1+\gamma_t) - 1$, where i_t^r is the real interest rate and γ_t is the growth rate of GDP (or alternatively use the nominal interest rate and the growth rate of nominal GDP). Solving for the steady-state debt ratio yields:

$$b^{ss} = \frac{pb^{ss}}{r} \approx \frac{pb^{ss}}{i^r - \gamma}. \tag{2}$$

Thus, the steady-state debt ratio $b^{ss}$is the annuity value of the steady state primary balance pb^{ss}, discounted at the long-run, growth-adjusted interest rate. In policy applications, this condition is used either as an indicator of the primary balance-output ratio needed to stabilize a given debt-output ratio (the so-called "debt stabilizing" primary balance), or as an indicator of the sustainable target debt-output ratio that a given primary balance-output ratio can support. There are also variations of this approach that use the constraint $b_t - (1 + r_t)b_{t-1} = -pb_t$ to construct estimates of primary balance targets needed to produce desired changes in debt at shorter horizons than the steady state. For instance, imposing the condition that the debt must decline $(b_t - b_{t-1} < 0)$, implies that the primary balance must yield a surplus that is at least as large as the growth-adjusted debt service: $pb_t \geq r_t b_{t-1}$.

The Classic Approach was developed in the 1980s but remains a tool widely used in policy assessments of sustainable debt. In particular, Annex VI of IMF (2013) instructs IMF economists to use a variation of the Blanchard ratio, called the Exceptional Fiscal Performance Approach, as one of three methodologies for estimating maximum sustainable public debt ranges (the other two methodologies introduce uncertainty and are discussed later in this section). This variation determines a country's maximum sustainable primary balance and "appropriate" levels of i^r and γ, and then applies them to the Blanchard ratio to estimate the maximum level of debt that the country can sustain.

The main flaw of the Classic Approach is that it only *defines* what long-run debt is for a given long-run primary balance (or vice versa) if stationarity holds, or *defines* lower bounds on the short-run dynamics of the primary balance. It does not actually connect the outstanding initial debt of a particular period b_{t-1} with b^{ss}, where the latter should be $\lim_{j\to\infty} b_{t+j}$ starting from b_{t-1}, and thus it cannot actually guarantee that b_{t-1} is sustainable in the sense of satisfying the IGBC. In fact, as we show below, for a given b_{t-1} there are multiple dynamic paths of the primary balance that satisfy IGBC. A subset of these paths converges to stationary debt positions, with different values of b^{ss} that vary widely depending on the primary balance dynamics, and there is even a subset of these paths for which the debt diverges to infinity but is still consistent with IGBC!

A second important flaw of the Classic approach is the absence of uncertainty and considerations about the asset market structure. Policy institutions have developed several methodologies that introduce uncertainty into debt sustainability analysis. For example, Barnhill and Kopits (2003) proposed incorporating uncertainty by adapting the value-at-risk (VaR) methodology of the financial industry to debt instruments issued by governments. Their methodology aims to quantify the probability of a negative net worth position for the government. Other methodologies described in IMF (2013) use stochastic time-series simulation tools to examine debt dynamics, estimating models for the individual components of the primary balance or nonstructural vector-autoregression models that include these variables jointly with key macroeconomic aggregates (eg, output growth, inflation) and a set of exogenous variables. The goal is to compute probability density functions of possible debt-output ratios based on forward simulations of the time-series models. The distributions are then used to make assessments of sustainable debt in terms of the probability that the simulated debt ratios are greater or equal than a critical value, or to construct "fan charts" summarizing the confidence intervals of the future evolution of debt. More recently, Ostry et al. (2015) use the fiscal reaction functions estimated by Ghosh et al. (2013) and discussed later in this section to construct measures of "fiscal space," which are intended to show the space a country has for increasing its debt ratio while still satisfying the IGBC.

IMF (2013) proposes two other stochastic tools as part of the framework for quantifying maximum sustainable debt (complementing the deterministic Exceptional Fiscal Performance estimates discussed earlier). The first is labeled the Early Warning Approach. This method computes a threshold debt ratio above which a country is likely to experience a debt crisis. The threshold is optimized with respect to the type-1 (false alarms of crises) and type-2 (missed warnings of crises) errors it produces, by minimizing the sum of the ratio of missed crises to total crises periods and false alarms to total noncrises periods. The second tool, labeled the Uncertainty Approach, is actually the same as the method proposed by Mendoza and Oviedo (2009), to which we turn next.[e]

The stochastic methods reviewed above have the significant shortcoming that, as with the Blanchard ratio, they cannot guarantee that their sustainable debt estimates satisfy the IGBC. Moreover, they introduce uncertainty without taking into account the fact that typically government debt is in the form of non-state-contingent instruments. The setup proposed by Mendoza and Oviedo (2006, 2009) addresses these two shortcomings. In this setup, the government issues non-state-contingent debt facing stochastic Markov processes for government revenues and outlays (ie, asset markets are incomplete). The key assumption is that the government is committed to repay, which imposes a constraint on public debt akin to Ayagari's Natural Debt Limit for private debt in Bewley models of heterogeneous agents with incomplete markets.

Following the simple version of this framework presented in Mendoza and Oviedo (2009), assume that output follows a deterministic trend, with an exogenous growth rate given by γ, and that the real interest rate is constant. Assume also that the government

[e] IMF (2013) refers to this approach as "a derivative of the exceptional fiscal performance approach and relies on the same underlying concepts and equations." As we explain, however, Blanchard ratios and their variations differ significantly from the debt limits and debt dynamics characterized by Mendoza and Oviedo (2009).

keeps its outlays smooth, unless it finds itself unable to borrow more, and when this happens it cuts its outlays to minimum tolerable levels.[f] Since the government cannot have its outlays fall below this minimum level, it does not hold more debt than the amount it could service after a long history in which $pb(s^t)$ remains at its worst possible realization (ie, the primary balance obtained with the worst realization of revenues, $\tau^{\min}$, and public outlays cut to their tolerable minimum $g^{\min}$), which can happen with positive probability. This situation is defined as a state of fiscal crisis and it sets and upper bound on debt denoted the "Natural Public Debt Limit" (NPDL), which is given by the growth-adjusted annuity value of the primary balance in the state of fiscal crisis:

$$b_t \leq NPDL \equiv \frac{\tau^{\min} - g^{\min}}{i^r - \gamma}. \quad (3)$$

This result together with the government budget constraint yields a law of motion for debt that follows this simple rule: $b_t = \min[NPDL, (1 + r_t)b_{t-1} - pb_t] \geq \bar{b}$, where $\bar{b}$ is an assumed lower bound for debt that can be set to zero for simplicity (ie, the government cannot become a net creditor).[g]

Notice that NPDL is lower for governments that have (a) higher variability in public revenues (ie, lower $\tau^{\min}$ in the support of the Markov process of revenues), (b) less flexibility to adjust public outlays (higher $g^{\min}$), or (c) lower growth rates and/or higher real interest rates. The stark differences between NPDL and b^{ss} from the classic debt sustainability analysis are also important to note. The expressions are similar, but the two methods yield sharply different implications for debt sustainability: The classic approach will always identify as sustainable debt ratios that are unsustainable according to the NPDL, because in practice b^{ss} uses the average primary fiscal balance, instead of its worst realization, and as a result it yields a long-run debt ratio that violates the NPDL. Moreover, while b^{ss} cannot be related to the IGBC, the debt rule $b_t = \max[NPDL, (1 + r_t)b_{t-1} - pb_t] \geq \bar{b}$ always satisfies the IGBC, because debt is bounded above at the NPDL, which guarantees that the no-Ponzi game condition cannot be violated. Note also, however, that the NPDL is a measure of the largest debt that a government can maintain, and not an estimate of the long-run average debt ratio or of the stationary debt ratio.

[f] This is a useful assumption to keep the setup simple, but is not critical. Mendoza and Oviedo (2006) model government expenditures entering a CRRA utility function as an optimal decision of the government, and here the curvature of the utility function imposes the debt limit in the same way as in Bewley models.

[g] This debt rule has an equivalent representation as a lower bound on the primary balance: $pb_t \geq (1 + r_t)b_{t-1} - NPDL$. On the date of a fiscal crisis, b_t hits NPDL. The next period, if the lowest realization of revenues is drawn again, pb_{t+1} hits $\tau^{\min} - g^{\min}$. Debt and the primary balance remain unchanged until higher revenue realizations are drawn, and the larger surpluses reduce the debt. See section III.3 of Mendoza and Oviedo (2009) for stochastic simulations of a numerical example.

The NPDL can be turned into a policy indicator by characterizing the probabilistic processes of the components of the primary balance together with some simplifying assumptions. On the revenue side, the probabilistic process of tax revenues reflects the uncertainty affecting tax rates and tax bases. This uncertainty includes domestic tax policy variability, the endogenous response of the economy to that variability, and other factors that can be largely exogenous to the domestic economy (eg, the effects of fluctuations in commodity prices and commodity exports on government revenues). On the expenditure side, government expenditures adjust partly in response to policy decisions, but the manner in which they respond varies widely across countries, as the literature on procyclical fiscal policy in emerging economies has shown (eg, see Alesina and Tabellini, 2005; Kaminsky et al., 2005; Talvi and Vegh, 2005).

The quantitative analysis in Mendoza and Oviedo (2009) treats the revenue and expenditures processes as exogenous, and calibrates them to 1990–2005 data from four Latin American economies.[h] Since the value of the expenditure cuts that each country can commit to is unobservable, they calculate instead the implied cuts in government outlays, relative to each country's average (ie, $g^{\min} - E[g]$), that would be needed so that each country's NPDL is consistent with the largest debt ratio observed in the sample. The largest debt ratios are around 55% for all four countries (Brazil, Colombia, Costa Rica, and Mexico), but the cuts in outlays that make these debt ratios consistent with the NPDL range from 3.8 percentage points of GDP for Costa Rica to 6.2 percentage points for Brazil. This is the case largely because revenues in Brazil have a coefficient of variation of 12.8%, vs 7% in Costa Rica, and hence to support a similar NPDL at a much higher revenue volatility requires higher $g^{\min}$. Mendoza and Oviedo also showed that the time-series dynamics of debt follow a random walk with boundaries at NPDL and $\bar{b}$.

2.2 Bohn's Debt Sustainability Framework

In a series of influential articles published between 1995 and 2011, Henning Bohn made four major contributions to the empirical literature on debt sustainability tests:

1. *IGBC tests that discount future primary balances at the risk-free rates are misspecified, because the correct discount factors are determined by the state-contingent equilibrium pricing kernel (Bohn, 1995).*[i] Tests affected by this problem include those reported in several well-known empirical studies (eg, Hamilton and Flavin, 1986, Hansen et al., 1991, and Gali, 1991). Following Ljungqvist and Sargent (2012), this mispecification

[h] Mendoza and Oviedo (2006) endogenize the choice of government outlays and decentralize the private and public borrowing decisions in a small open economy model with nonstate-contingent assets.

[i] Lucas (2012) raised a similar point in a different context. She argued that the relevant discount rate for government flows should not be the risk-free rate but a cost of capital that incorporates the market risk associated with government activities.

error is easy to illustrate by using the equilibrium risk-free rates $(R_{t+j}^{-1} = E_t[MRS(c_{t+j}, c_t)])$ to rewrite the IGBC as follows:

$$b_{t-1} = pb_t + \sum_{j=1}^{\infty}\left[\frac{E_t[pb_{t+j}]}{R_{t+j}} + cov_t\left(MRS(c_{t+j}, c_t), pb_{t+j}\right)\right]. \tag{4}$$

Hence, discounting the primary balances at the risk-free rates is only correct if

$$\sum_{j=1}^{\infty} cov_t\left(MRS(c_{t+j}, c_t), pb_{t+j}\right) = 0.$$

This would be true under one of the following assumptions: (a) perfect foresight, (b) risk-neutral private agents, or (c) primary fiscal balances that are uncorrelated with future marginal utilities of consumption. All of these assumptions are unrealistic, and (c) in particular runs contrary to the strong empirical evidence showing that primary balances are not only correlated with macro fluctuations, but show a strikingly distinct pattern across industrial and developing countries: primary balances are procyclical in industrial countries, and acyclical or countercyclical in developing countries. Moreover, Bohn (1995) also showed examples in which this misspecification error leads to incorrect inferences that reject fiscal solvency when it actually does hold. For instance, a rule that maintains g/y and b/y constant in a balanced-growth economy with i.i.d. output growth violates the mispeficied IGBC if mean output growth is greater or equal than the interest rate, but it does satisfy condition (1).

2. *Testing for debt sustainability is futile, because the IGBC holds under very weak assumptions about the time-series processes of fiscal data that are generally satisfied. The IGBC holds if either debt or revenue and spending inclusive of debt service are integrated of finite but arbitrarily high order (Bohn, 2007).* This invalidates several fiscal solvency tests based on specific stationarity and cointegration conditions (eg, Hamilton and Flavin, 1986; Trehan and Walsh, 1988; Quintos, 1995), because neither a particular order of integration of the debt data, nor the cointegration of revenues and government outlays is necessary for debt sustainability. As Bohn explains in the proof of this result, the reason is intuitive: In the forward conditional expectation that forms the no-Ponzi game condition, the jth power of the discount factor asymptotically dominates the expectation $E_t(b_{t+j})$ as $j \to \infty$ if the debt is integrated of any finite order. This occurs because $E_t(b_{t+j})$ is *at most* a polynomial of order n if b is integrated of order n, while the discount factor is exponential in j, and exponential growth dominates polynomial growth. But perhaps of even more significance is the implication that, since integration of finite order is indeed a very weak condition, testing for fiscal solvency or debt sustainability per se is not useful: The data are all but certain to reject the hypotheses that debt or revenue and spending inclusive of debt service are nonstationary after differencing the

data a finite number of times (usually only once!). Bohn (2007) concluded that, in light of this result, using econometric tools to try and identify in the data fiscal reaction functions that support fiscal solvency and studying their dynamics is "more promising for understanding deficit problems."

3. *A linear fiscal reaction function (FRF) with a statistically significant, positive (conditional) response of the primary balance to outstanding debt is sufficient for the IGBC to hold (Bohn, 1998, 2008).* Proposition 1 in Bohn (2008) demonstrates that this linear FRF is sufficient to satisfy the IGBC:

$$pb_t = \mu_t + \rho b_{t-1} + \varepsilon_t,$$

for all t, where $\rho > 0$, μ_t is a set of additional determinants of the primary balance, which typically include an intercept and proxies for temporary fluctuations in output and government expenditures, and ε_t is i.i.d. The proof only requires that μ_t be bounded and that the present value of GDP be finite. Intuitively, the argument of the proof is that with pb changing by the positive factor ρ when debt rises, the growth of the debt j periods ahead is lowered by $(1-\rho)^j$. Formally, for any small $\rho > 0$, the following holds as $j \to \infty$: $E_t[MRS(c_{t+j}, c_t) b_{t+j}] \approx (1-\rho)^j b_t \to 0$, which in turn implies that the NPG condition and thus the IGBC hold. Note also that while debt sustainability holds for any $\rho > 0$, the long-run behavior of the debt ratio differs sharply depending on the relative values of the mean r and ρ. To see why, combine the FRF and the government budget constraint to obtain the law of motion of the debt ratio $b_t = -\mu_t + (1 + r_t - \rho) b_{t-1} + \varepsilon_t$. Hence, debt is stationary only if $\rho > r$, otherwise it explodes, but as long as $\rho > 0$ it does so at a slow enough pace to still satisfy IGBC.[j] In addition, the IGBC holds for the same value of initial debt for any $\rho > 0$, but, if $\rho > r$, debt converges to a higher long-run average as ρ falls.

The above results also show why the steady-state debt b^{ss} of the classic debt sustainability analysis is not useful for assessing debt sustainability: With the linear FRF, multiple well-defined long-run averages of debt are consistent with debt sustainability, each determined by the particular value of the response coefficient in the range $\rho > r$, and even exploding debt is consistent with debt sustainability if $0 < \rho < r$. Moreover, in the limit as $r \to 0$, the Blanchard ratio of the classic analysis predicts that debt diverges to infinity ($b^{ss} \to \infty$ if pb^{ss} is finite), while the linear FRF predicts that both b and pb are mean-reverting to well-defined long-run averages given by $-\mu/\rho$ and 0. Similarly, notions of a "maximal sustainable interest rate" are meaningless from

[j] Bohn (2007) shows that this result holds for any of the following three assumptions about the interest rate process: (i) $r_t = r$ for all t, (ii) r_t is a stochastic process that is serially uncorrelated with $E_t[r_{t+1}] = r$, or (iii) r_t is any stochastic process with mean r subject only to implicit restrictions such that $b_t = \frac{1}{1+r} E_t[pb_{t+1} + b_{t+1} - (r_{t+1} - r) b_t]$.

the perspective of assessing whether the debt satisfies the IGBC, because $\rho > 0$ is sufficient for IGBC to hold regardless of the value of r.[k]

4. *Empirical tests of the linear FRF based on historical U.S. data and various subsamples reject the hypothesis that $\rho \leq 0$, so IGBC holds (Bohn, 1998, 2008).* In his 2008 article, Bohn constructed a dataset going back to 1791, the start of US public debt after the Funding Act of 1790, and found that the response coefficient estimated with 1793–2003 data is positive and significant, ranging from 0.1 to 0.12. Moreover, looking deeper into the fiscal dynamics he found that economic growth has been sufficient to cover the entire servicing costs of US public debt, but there are structural breaks in the response coefficient. The 1793–2003 estimates are about twice as large as those obtained in Bohn (1998) using data for 1916–2005, which is a period that emphasizes the cold-war era of declining debt but high military spending.

Bohn's framework has been applied to cross-country datasets by Mendoza and Ostry (2008) and extended to include a nonlinear specification allowing for default risk by Ghosh et al. (2013).[1] Mendoza and Ostry found estimates of response coefficients for a panel of industrial countries that are similar to those Bohn (1998) obtained for the United States. In addition, they found that the solvency condition holds for a panel that includes both industrial and developing countries, as well as in a subpanel that includes only the latter. They also found, however, that cross-sectional breaks are present in the data at particular debt thresholds. In the combined panel and the subpanels with only advanced or only developing economies, there are high-debt country groups for which the response coefficient is not statistically significantly different from zero. Ghosh et al. found that the response coefficients fall sharply at high debt levels, and obtained estimates of fiscal space that measure the distance between observed debt ratios and the largest debt ratios that can be supported given debt limits implied by the presence of default risk.

2.3 Estimated Fiscal Reaction Functions and Their Implications

We provide below new estimation results for linear FRFs for the United States using historical data from 1791 to 2014, and for a cross-country panel using data for the 1951–2013 period. Some of the results are in line with the findings of previous studies, but the key difference is that there is a significant break in the response of the primary

[k] This is not the case if the government cannot commit to repay its debt. In external sovereign default models in the vein of Eaton and Gersovitz (1981), for example, the interest rate is an increasing, convex function of the debt stock, and there exists a debt level at which rationing occurs because future default on newly issued debt becomes a certain event.

[1] The same approach has also been used to test for external solvency (ie, whether the present discounted value of the balance of trade matches the observed net foreign asset position). Durdu et al. (2013) conducted cross-country empirical tests using data for 50 countries over the 1970–2006 period and found that the data cannot reject the hypothesis of external solvency, which in this case is measured as a negative response of net exports to net foreign assets.

balance to debt after 2008. We then use the estimation results and the historical data to put in perspective the current fiscal situation of the United States and Europe. In particular, we show that: (a) primary balance adjustment in the United States is lagging significantly behind what has been observed in the aftermath of previous episodes of large increases in debt, (b) observed primary deficits have been much larger than what the FRFs predict, and (c) hypothetical scenarios with alternative response coefficients produce sharply different patterns of transitional dynamics and long-run debt ratios, but they are all consistent with the same observed initial debt ratios (ie, IGBC holds for all of them).

2.3.1 FRF Estimation Results

Table 1 shows estimation results for the FRF of the United States using historical data for the 1791–2014 period. The table shows results for five regression models similar to those estimated in Bohn (1998, 2008). Column (1) shows the base model, which uses as regressors the initial debt ratio, the cyclical component of output, and temporary military expenditures as a measure of transitory fluctuations in government expenditures.[m] Column (2) introduces a nonlinear spline coefficient when the debt is higher than the mean. Column (3) introduces an AR(1) error term. Column (4) adds the squared mean deviation of the debt ratio. Column (5) includes a time trend. Columns (6) and (7) provide modifications that are important for showing the structural instability of the FRF post-2008: Column (6) reruns the base model truncating the sample in last year of the sample used in Bohn (2008) and Column (7) uses a sample that ends in 2008. The signs of the debt, output gap and military expenditures coefficients are the same as in Bohn's regressions, and in particular the response coefficient estimates are generally positive, which satisfies the sufficiency condition for debt sustainability.

In Columns (1)–(5), the point estimates of ρ range between 0.077 and 0.105, which are lower than Bohn's 2008 estimates based on 1793–2003 data, but higher than his (1998) estimates based on 1916–95 data. The ρ estimates are always statistically significant, although only at the 90% confidence level in the base and squared-debt models.

Column (6) shows that if we run the linear FRF over the same sample period as in Bohn (2008), the results are very similar to his (see in particular Column 1 of table 7 in his paper).[n] The point estimate of ρ is 0.105, compared with 0.121 in Bohn's study (both statistically significant at the 99% confidence level). But in our base model of Column (1) we found that using the full sample that runs through 2014 the point estimate of ρ falls to 0.078. Moreover, excluding the post-2008-crisis data in Column (7), the results

[m] We follow Bohn in measuring this temporary component as the residual of an AR(2) process for military expenditures.

[n] They only differ because we defined military expenditures as the sum of expenditures by the Department of Defense and the Veterans Administration for the full sample, excluding international relations, while Bohn includes Veterans starting in 1940 and adds international relations.

Table 1 Fiscal reaction function of the United States: 1792–2014

Model:	Base model	Asymmetric response	AR(1) term	Debt squared	Time trend	Bohn's sample (1793–2003)	Prerecession (1793–2008)
Coefficient	**(1)**	**(2)**	**(3)**	**(4)**	**(5)**	**(6)**	**(7)**
Constant	0.00648	0.00540	0.00974	0.00653	0.00601	0.00485	0.00470
	(0.004)	(0.003)*	(0.008)	(0.004)	(0.006)	(0.003)*	(0.003)
Initial debt d_t^*	0.07779	0.08689	0.10477	0.07715	0.07674	0.10498	0.10188
	(0.040)*	(0.030)***	(0.032)***	(0.038)*	(0.035)**	(0.023)***	(0.022)***
GDP gap	0.07404	0.07300	0.15330	0.07390	0.07490	0.07987	0.07407
	(0.078)	(0.079)	(0.043)***	(0.079)	(0.077)	(0.086)	(0.086)
Military expenditure	−0.72302	−0.72001	−0.98955	−0.72320	−0.72462	−0.77835	−0.76857
	(0.133)***	(0.136)***	(0.110)***	(0.133)***	(0.135)***	(0.135)***	(0.135)***
$\max(0, d_t^* - \bar{d})$		−0.14487					
		(0.061)					
AR(1)			0.89154				
			(0.029)***				
$(d_t^* - \bar{d})^2$				0.00261			
				(0.044)			
Time trend					6.89×10^{-06}		
					(5.9×10^{-05})		
s.e.	0.0239	0.0240	0.198	0.0120	0.0240	0.0210	0.0209
Adj. R-squared:	0.606	0.605	0.901	0.614	0.605	0.695	0688
Observations:	223	223	222	223	223	213	217

Note: HAC standard errors shown in parenthesis, 2-lag window prewhitening. "*," "**," and "***" denote that the corresponding coefficient is statistically significant at the 90%, 95%, and 99% confidence levels. Output gap is percent deviation from Hodrick–Prescott trend. Military expenditure includes all Department of Defense and Department of Veterans Affairs outlays.

are very similar to those obtained with the same sample period as Bohn's. Hence, these results suggest that the addition of the post-2008 data, a tumultous period in the fiscal stance of the United States, produces a structural shift in the FRF.[o] Testing formally for this hypothesis, we found that Chow's forecast test rejects strongly the null hypothesis of no structural change in the value of ρ when the post-2008 data are added. Hence, the decline in the estimate of ρ from 0.102 to 0.078 is statistically significant. This change in the response of the primary balance to higher debt ratios may seem small, but it implies that the primary balance adjustment is about 25% smaller, and as we show later this results in large changes in the short- and long-run dynamics of debt.

The regressions with nonlinear features (Column (2) with the debt spline at the mean debt ratio, and Column (4) with the squared deviation from the mean debt ratio) are very different from Bohn's estimates. In Bohn (1998), the FRF with the same spline term has a negative point estimate $\rho = -0.015$ and a large, positive spline coefficient of 0.105 when debt is above its mean, so that for above-average debt ratios the response of the primary balance is stronger than for below-average debt ratios, and becomes positive with a net effect of 0.09, which is consistent with debt sustainability. In contrast, Table 1 shows a ρ estimate of 0.09 with a spline coefficient of -0.14. Hence, these results suggest that the response of the primary balance is weaker for above-average debt ratios, and the net effect is negative at -0.05, which violates the linear FRF's sufficiency condition for debt sustainability. The spline coefficient is not, however, statistically significant. For the squared-debt regressions, Bohn (2008) estimated a positive coefficient of 0.02, while the coefficient shown in Table 1 is only 0.003 (both not statistically significant). Thus, both the debt-spline and debt-squared regressions are also consistent with the possibility of a structural change in the FRF. In particular, the stronger primary balance response at higher debt ratios that Bohn identified in his 1998 and 2008 studies changed to a much weaker response once the data up to 2014 are introduced. The rationale for this is that the large debt increases since 2008 have been accompanied by adjustments in the primary balance that differ sharply from what has been observed in previous episodes of large debt increases, as we illustrate below.

Tables 2–4 show the results of cross-country panel regressions similar to those reported by Mendoza and Ostry (2008) and Ghosh et al. (2013), but expanded to include data for the 1951–2013 period for 25 advanced and 33 emerging economies. The first six columns of results in these tables show three pairs of regression models. Each pair uses a different measure of government expenditures, since the measure based on military expenditures used in the US regressions is unavailable and/or less relevant as a measure of the temporary component of government expenditures in the international dataset.

[o] Bohn (2008) also found evidence of structural shifts when contrasting his results for 1784–2003 with his 1916–95 results, with sharply lower response coefficients for the shorter sample, which he attributed to the larger weight of the cold-war era (in which debt declined while military spending remained high).

Table 2 Fiscal reaction functions of advanced economies (1951–2013)

	All advanced economies					
Model	**(1)**	**(2)**	**(3)**	**(4)**	**(5)**	**(6)**
Constant	11.23917	1.76019	−1.02696	−0.07294	−1.42979	0.02521
	(3.134)***	(0.037)***	(0.472)**	(0.195)	(2.651)	(0.222)
Previous debt	0.06916	0.01461	0.01983	0.00295	0.02750	−0.00076
d_{t-1}	(0.013)***	(0.001)***	(0.010)**	(0.005)	(0.010)***	(0.005)
GDP gap	0.17053	0.28046	0.31501	0.34696	0.34939	0.40503
	(0.050)***	(0.058)***	(0.065)***	(0.060)***	(0.073)***	(0.073)***
Government	−0.35654	−0.06305				
Expenditure	(0.078)***	(0.013)***				
Government			−0.10449	−0.12511		
Expenditure gap			(0.031)***	(0.031)***		
Govt consumption					−0.20579	−0.33638
Gap (Nat. Acc.)					(0.064)***	(0.070)***
Country AR(1)	Yes	No	Yes	No	Yes	No
s.e.	1.603	2.814	1.709	2.813	1.796	2.884
Adj. R-squared:	0.766	0.277	0.755	0.306	0.733	0.304
Observations:	1285	1346	1218	1273	1139	1186
Countries:	25	25	25	25	25	25

Note: All regressions include country fixed effect and White cross-section corrected standard errors and covariances. Standard errors shown in parenthesis. "*,""**," and "***" denote that the corresponding coefficient is statistically significant at the 90%, 95%, and 99% confidence levels. Output, government expenditure, and government consumption gaps are percent deviation from Hodrick–Prescott trend.

Table 3 Fiscal reaction functions of emerging economies (1951–2013)

Model	(1)	(2)	(3)	(4)	(5)	(6)
Constant	9.99549	1.32486	−2.38214	−1.88325	−2.33727	−1.70461
	(1.473)***	(0.409)***	(0.462)***	(0.284)***	(0.544)***	(0.322)***
Previous debt	0.03806	0.05657	0.05452	0.04519	0.05280	0.04376
d_{t-1}	(0.009)***	(0.006)***	(0.006)***	(0.005)***	(0.008)***	(0.006)***
GDP gap	0.03698	0.07352	0.15962	0.15509	0.07568	0.06831
	(0.029)	(0.027)***	(0.034)***	(0.027)***	(0.042)*	(0.030)**
Government Expenditure	−0.44322	−0.15638				
	(0.049)***	(0.020)***				
Government Expenditure gap			−0.11986	−0.12420		
			(0.012)***	(0.012)***		
Govt Consumption Gap (Nat. Acc.)					−0.01302	−0.02662
					(0.018)	(0.014)*
Country AR(1)	Yes	No	Yes	No	Yes	No
s.e.	1.854	2.630	1.772	2.450	2.072	2.795
Adj. R-squared:	0.666	0.346	0.698	0.437	0.589	0.321
Observations:	1071	1144	977	1035	967	1022
Countries:	33	33	33	33	33	33

Note: All regressions include country fixed effect and White cross-section corrected standard errors and covariances. Standard errors shown in parenthesis. "*,""**," and "***" denote that the corresponding coefficient is statistically significant at the 90%, 95%, and 99% confidence levels. Output, government expenditure, and government consumption gaps are percent deviation from Hodrick–Prescott trend.

Table 4 Fiscal reaction functions for advanced and emerging economies (1951–2013)

Model	**(1)**	**(2)**	**(3)**	**(4)**	**(5)**	**(6)**
Constant	10.53960	1.50777	−2.23188	−0.65482	−2.29040	−0.57649
	(1.528)***	(0.357)***	(0.400)***	(0.160)***	(0.466)***	(0.172)***
Previous debt	0.05138	0.02962	0.04576	0.01634	0.04661	0.01500
d_{t-1}	(0.007)***	(0.004)***	(0.006)***	(0.004)***	(0.006)***	(0.004)***
GDP gap	0.07864	0.12611	0.20956	0.20590	0.16205	0.15198
	(0.031)**	(0.030)***	(0.043)***	(0.032)***	(0.051)***	(0.036)***
Government Expenditure	−0.40043 (0.047)***	−0.08823 (0.015)***				
Government Expenditure Gap			−0.11558 (0.014)***	−0.12788 (0.016)***		
Govt consumption Gap (Nat. Acc.)					−0.03764 (0.021)*	−0.07534 (0.020)***
Country AR(1)	Yes	No	Yes	No	Yes	No
s.e.	1.729	2.796	1.756	2.727	1.970	2.915
Adj R-squared:	0.720	0.275	0.718	0.328	0.656	0.254
Observations:	2356	2490	2195	2308	2106	2208
Countries:	58	58	58	58	58	58

Note: All regressions include country fixed effect and White cross-section corrected standard errors and covariances. Standard errors shown in parenthesis. "*,""**," and "***" denote that the corresponding coefficient is statistically significant at the 90%, 95%, and 99% confidence levels. Output, government expenditure, and government consumption gaps are percent deviation from Hodrick–Prescott trend.

Models (1) and (2) use total real government outlays (ie, current expenditures plus all other noninterest expenditures, including transfer payments), models (3) and (4) use the cyclical component of total real outlays, and models (5) and (6) follow Mendoza and Ostry (2008) and use the cyclical component of real government absorption from the national accounts (ie, real current government expenditures). Models (1), (3) and (5) include country-specific AR(1) terms, which Mendoza and Ostry also found important to consider, while model (2), (4), and (6) do not.

Two caveats about the measures of government expenditures used in these regressions. First, they are less representative of unexpected increases in government expenditures, particularly the HP cyclical component because of the double-sided nature of the HP filter. Second, since the primary balance is the difference between total revenues and expenditures, adding the latter as a regressor implies that revenues are the only endogenous component of the dependent variable that can respond to changes in debt. This is less true when we use only the cyclical component of expenditures and/or use only current expenditures instead of total outlays, but it remains a potential limitation. Interestingly, the coefficients on government expenditures do have the same sign as in the US regressions with temporary military expenditures (although they are about half the size), and they are statistically significant at the 99% confidence level. These caveats do imply, however, that the coefficients on government expenditures cannot be interpreted as measuring only the response of the primary balance to unexpected increases in government expenditures, but can reflect also differences in the cyclical stance of fiscal policies and in the degree of access to debt markets (see Mendoza and Ostry, 2008 for a discussion of these issues).

Table 2 shows that, as in Mendoza and Ostry, considering the country-specific AR(1) terms in the cross-country panel is important. The advanced economies' response coefficients are higher and with significantly smaller standard errors when the autocorrelation of error terms is corrected. Hence, we focus the rest of the discussion of the panel results on the results with AR(1) terms.

The advanced economies' response coefficients of the primary balance on debt in the AR(1) models are positive and statistically significant in general. The coefficients are smaller in the regressions that use cyclical components of either total outlays or current expenditures (models (3) and (5)) than in the one that uses the level of government outlays (model (1)), but across the first two the ρ coefficients are similar (0.02 vs 0.028). Following again Mendoza and Ostry, we focus on the regressions that use the cyclical components of current government expenditures.

Comparing the FRFs with country AR(1) terms and using the cyclical component of current government expenditures across the three panel datasets, Tables 2–4 show that the estimates of ρ are 0.028 for advanced economies, 0.053 for emerging economies, and 0.047 for the combined panel. Mendoza and Ostry obtained estimates of 0.02 for advanced economies and 0.036 for both emerging economies and the combined panel.

The results are somewhat different, but the two are consistent in producing larger values of ρ for emerging economies and the combined panel than for advanced economies.

The difference in the response coefficients across advanced and emerging economies highlights important features of their debt dynamics. Condition (4) suggests that countries with procyclical fiscal policy (ie, acyclical or countercyclical primary balances) can sustain higher debt ratios than countries with countercyclical fiscal policy (ie, procyclical primary balances). Yet we observe the opposite in the data: Advanced economies conduct countercyclical fiscal policy and show higher average debt ratios than emerging economies, which display procyclical or acyclical fiscal policy (ie, significantly lower primary balance-output gap correlations). Indeed, the higher ρ of the emerging economies implies that these countries converge to lower mean debt ratios in the long run. As Mendoza and Ostry (2008) concluded, this higher ρ is not an indicator of "more sustainable" fiscal policies in emerging economies, but evidence of the fact that past increases in debt of a given magnitude in these countries require a stronger conditional response of the primary balance, and hence less reliance on debt markets, than in advanced economies.

2.3.2 Implications for Europe and the United States

Public debt and fiscal deficits rose sharply in several advanced economies after the 2008 global financial crisis, in response to both expansionary fiscal policies and policies aimed at stabilizing financial systems. To put in perspective the magnitude of this recent surge in debt, it is useful to examine Bohn's historical dataset of public debt and primary balances for the United States. Defining a public debt crisis as a year-on-year increase in the public debt ratio larger than twice the historical standard deviation, which is equivalent to more than 8.15 percentage points in Bohn's dataset, we identify five debt crisis events (see Fig. 1): The two world wars (World War I with an increase of 28.7 percentage points of GDP over 1918–19 and World War II with 59.3 percentage points over 1943–45), the Civil War (19.7 percentage points over 1862–63), the Great Depression (18.5 percentage points over 1932–33), and the Great Recession (22.3 percentage points over 2009–10). The Great Recession episode is the third largest, ahead of the Civil War and the Great Depression episodes.

Fig. 2 illustrates the short-run dynamics of the US primary fiscal balance after each of the five debt crises. Each crisis started with large deficits, ranging from 4% of GDP for the Great Depression to nearly 20% of GDP for World War II, but the Great Recession episode is unique in that the primary balance remains in deficit 4 years after the crisis. In the three war-related crises, a large primary deficit turned into a small surplus within 3 years. By contrast, the latest baseline scenario from the Congressional Budget Office (*Updated Budget and Economic Outlook: 2015–2025*, January 2015), projects that the US primary balance will continue in deficit for the next 10 years. The primary deficit is projected to shrink to 0.6% of GDP in 2018 and then hover near 1% through 2025. In addition,

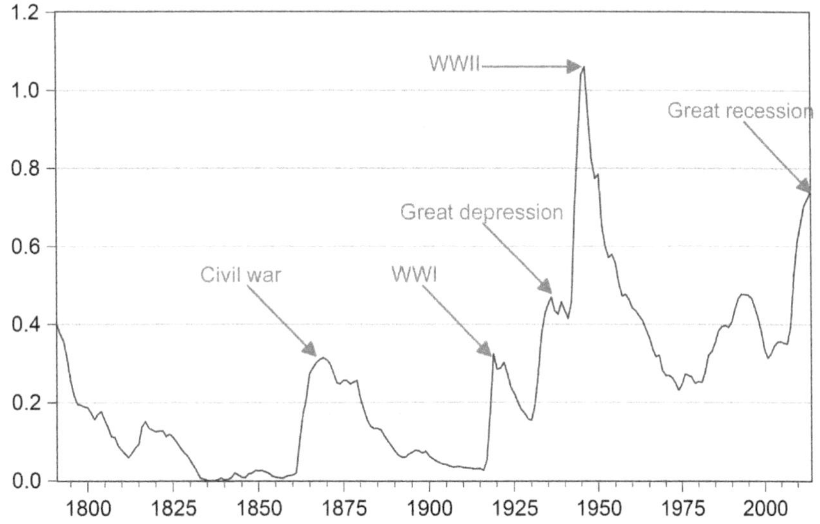

Fig. 1 US government debt as percentage of GDP.

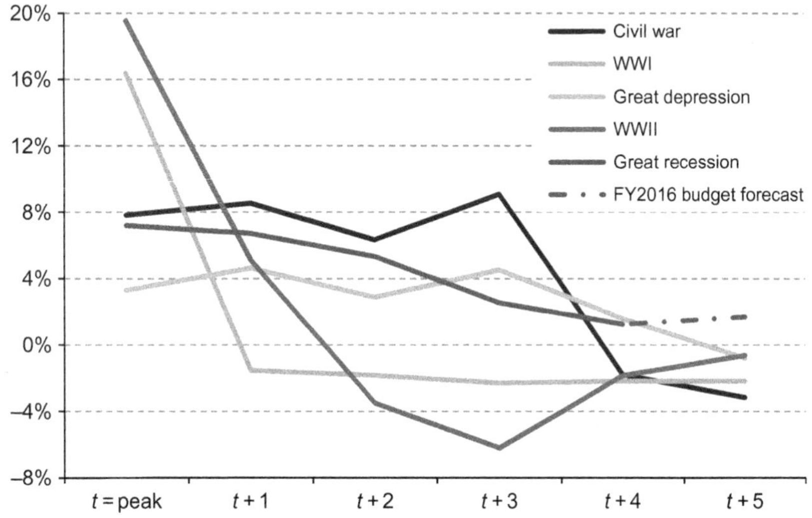

Fig. 2 US government deficits after debt crises.

relative to the Great Depression, the first three deficits of the Great Recession were nearly twice as large, and by 5 years after the debt crisis of the Great Depression the United States had a primary surplus of nearly 1% of GDP. In summary, the post-2008 increase in public debt has been of historic proportions, and the absence of primary surpluses in both the 4 years after the surge in debt and the projections for 2015–25 is *unprecedented* in US history.

Many advanced European economies have not fared much better. Weighted by GDP, the average public debt ratio of the 15 largest European economies rose from 38% to 58% between 2007 and 2011. The increase was particularly large in the five countries at the center of the European debt crisis (Greece, Ireland, Italy, Portugal and Spain), where the debt ratio weighted by GDP rose from 75% to 105%, but even in some of the largest European economies public debt rose sharply (by 33 and 27 percentage points in the United Kingdom and France, respectively).

The estimated FRFs can be used to examine the implications of these rapid increases in public debt ratios for debt sustainability and for the short- and long-run dynamics of debt and deficits. Consider first the regression residuals. Fig. 3 shows the residuals of the US fiscal reaction function estimated in the base model (1) of Table 1, and Fig. 4 shows rolling residuals from the same regression. These two plots show that the residuals for 2008–14 are significantly negative, and much larger in absolute value than the residuals in the rest of the sample period. In fact, the residuals for 2009–11 are twice as large as the corresponding minus-two-standard-error bound. Thus, the primary deficits observed during the post-2008 years have been much larger than what the FRFs predicted, even after accounting for the larger deficits that the FRFs allow on account of the depth of the recession and expansionary government expenditures. These large residuals are of course consistent with the results documented earlier showing evidence of structural change in the FRF when the post-2008 data are added.

The structural change in the FRF can also be illustrated by comparing the actual primary balances from 2009 to 2014 and the government-projected primary balances for

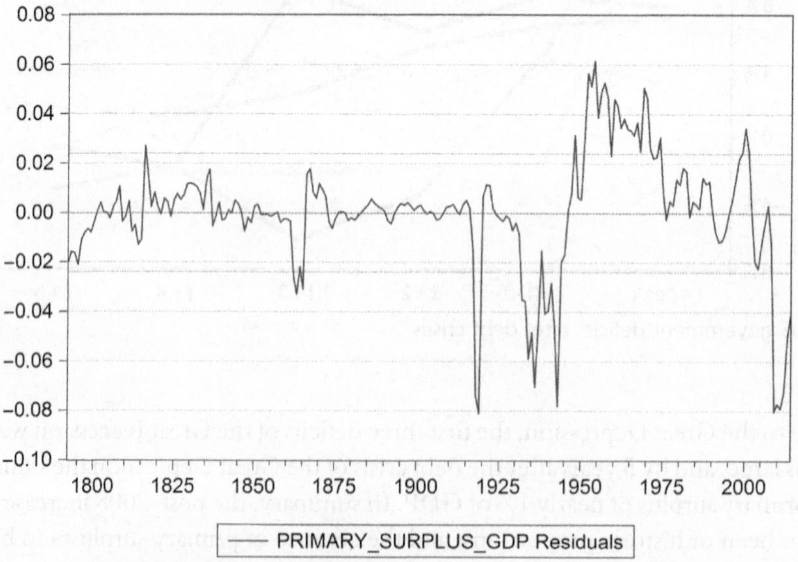

Fig. 3 Residuals for the US fiscal reaction function. *Note*: This residuals correspond to the Base Model (1) in Table 1. The dotted lines are at two s.d. above and below zero.

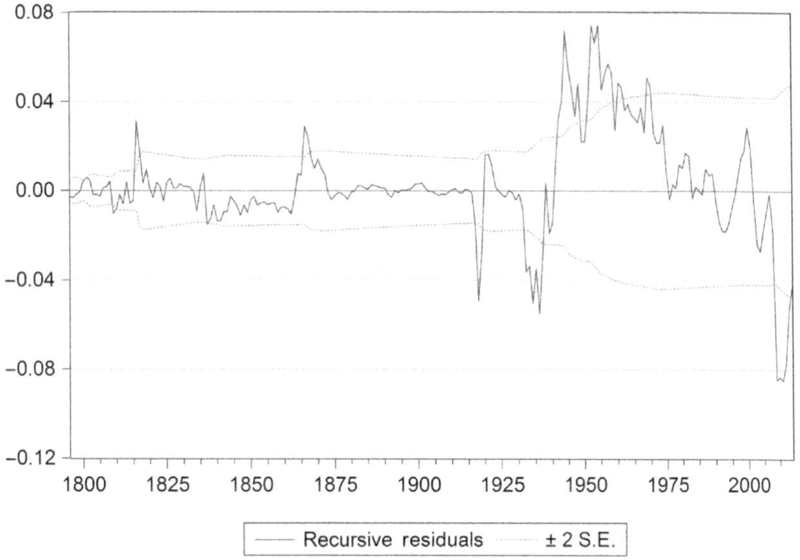

Fig. 4 Rolling residuals for the US fiscal reaction function. *Note*: For each sample 1791-*t*, the baseline specification, model (1) in Table 1, is estimated and the residual at time *t* is reported together with the 2 standard deviation band for the errors in that sample.

2015 to 2020 in the *President's Budget for Fiscal Year 2016* with the out-of-sample forecast that the FRF estimated with data up to 2008 in Column (7) of Table 1 produces (see Fig. 5). To construct this forecast, we use the observed realizations of the cyclical components of output and government expenditures from 2009 to 2014, and for 2015 to 2020 we use again data from the projections in the *President's Budget.*

As Fig. 5 shows, for the period 2009–14, the primary balance showed deficits significantly larger than what the FRF predicted, and also much larger than the deficit at the minus-two-standard-error bound of the forecast band. The mean forecast of the FRF predicted a rising primary surplus from zero to about 4% of GDP between 2009 and 2014, while the data showed deficits narrowing from 8% to about 2% of GDP. In addition, the primary deficits projected in the *President's Budget* are also much larger than predicted by the mean forecast of the FRF, with the projections at or below the minus-two-standard error band. Bohn (2011) warned that already by 2011 there were signs of a likely structural break, because his estimated FRFs called for primary surpluses when the debt ratio surpassed 55–60%, while the 2012 *Budget* projected large and persistent primary deficits at debt ratios much higher than those.

The estimated FRF results can also be used to study projected time-series paths for public debt and the primary balance as of the latest actual observations (2014). To simulate the debt dynamics, we use the law of motion for public debt that results from combining the government budget constraint and the FRF mentioned earlier: $b_t = -\mu_t + (1 + r_t - \rho)b_{t-1} + \varepsilon_t$. We consider baseline scenarios in which we use estimated

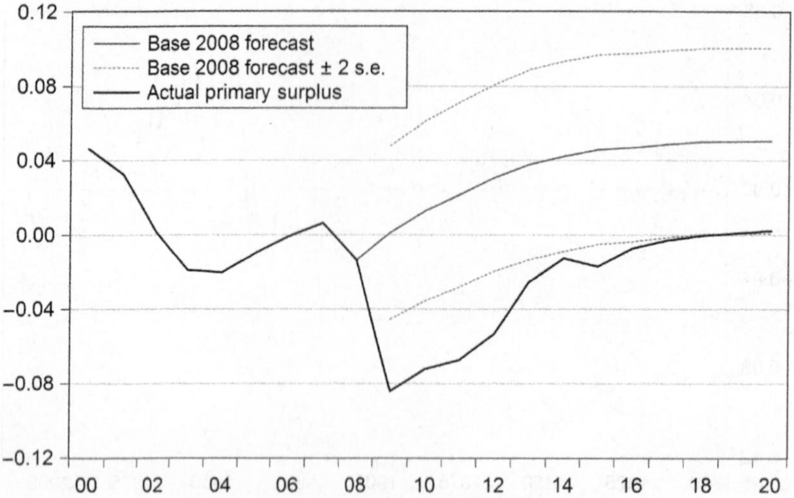

Fig. 5 US primary surplus actual value and 2008 based forecast. *Note*: The forecast is based on model (7) in Table 1 which has the sample restricted to 1791–2008. Given actual values of debt-to-GDP ratio, GDP gap, and military expenditure a forecast of the primary surplus to GDP ratio is generated for the sample 2009–20. Actual variables from 2015 onward correspond to estimates included in The president's budget for fiscal year 2016. Chow's forecast test rejects the null hypothesis of no structural change starting in 2009 with 99.9% confidence.

ρ coefficients for Europe and the United States, and simulate forward starting from the 2014 observations. For the United States, we used model (3) in Table 1. For Europe, we use model (5) from Table 2 and take a simple cross-section average among European industrialized countries. Projections of the future values of the fluctuations in output and government expenditures are generated with simple univariate AR models. In addition, we compare these baseline projection scenarios with scenarios in which we lower the response coefficient to half of the regression estimates or lower the intercept of the FRFs. Recall from the earlier discussion that changing these parameters, as long as $\rho > 0$, generates the same present discounted value of the primary balance as the baseline scenarios, but as we show below the transitional dynamics and long-run debt ratios they produce are very different. These simulations also require assumptions about the values of the real interest rate and the growth rate that determine $1 + r$. For simplicity, we assume that $r = 0$, which rules out the range in which debt can grown infinitely large but still be consistent with the IGBC (ie, the range $0 < \rho < r$), and it also implies that primary balances converge to zero in the long run.[p]

[p] Real interest rates on government debt and rates of output growth in large industrial countries are low but with expectations of an eventual increase. Rather than taking a stance on the difference between the two, we just assumed here that they are equal.

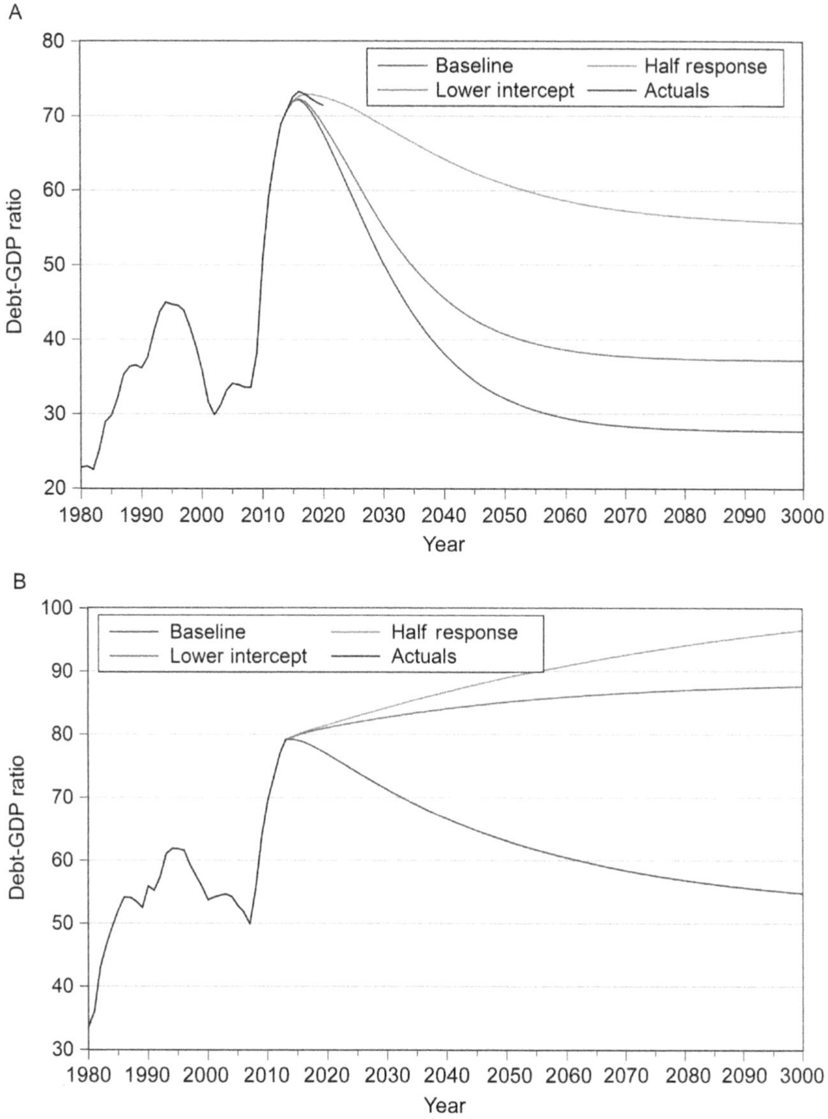

Fig. 6 Debt-to-GDP actuals and simulations since 2014. (A) US debt to GDP. (B) Europe debt to GDP. *Note*: For the United States: Model (3) in Table 1 is used in conjunction with estimated AR(2) processes for the output gap and military expenditure, plus the government budget constraint. For Europe: Model (5) in Table 2 is used in conjunction with estimated AR(1) processes for the output gap and government consumption gap in each country, and a simple average among advanced European countries is taken.

Fig. 6 and 7 show the projected paths of debt ratios and primary balances for the baseline and the alternative scenarios, for both the United States and Europe. These plots show that under the baseline scenario the countries should be reporting primary surpluses that will decline monotonically over time, and should therefore display a monotonically

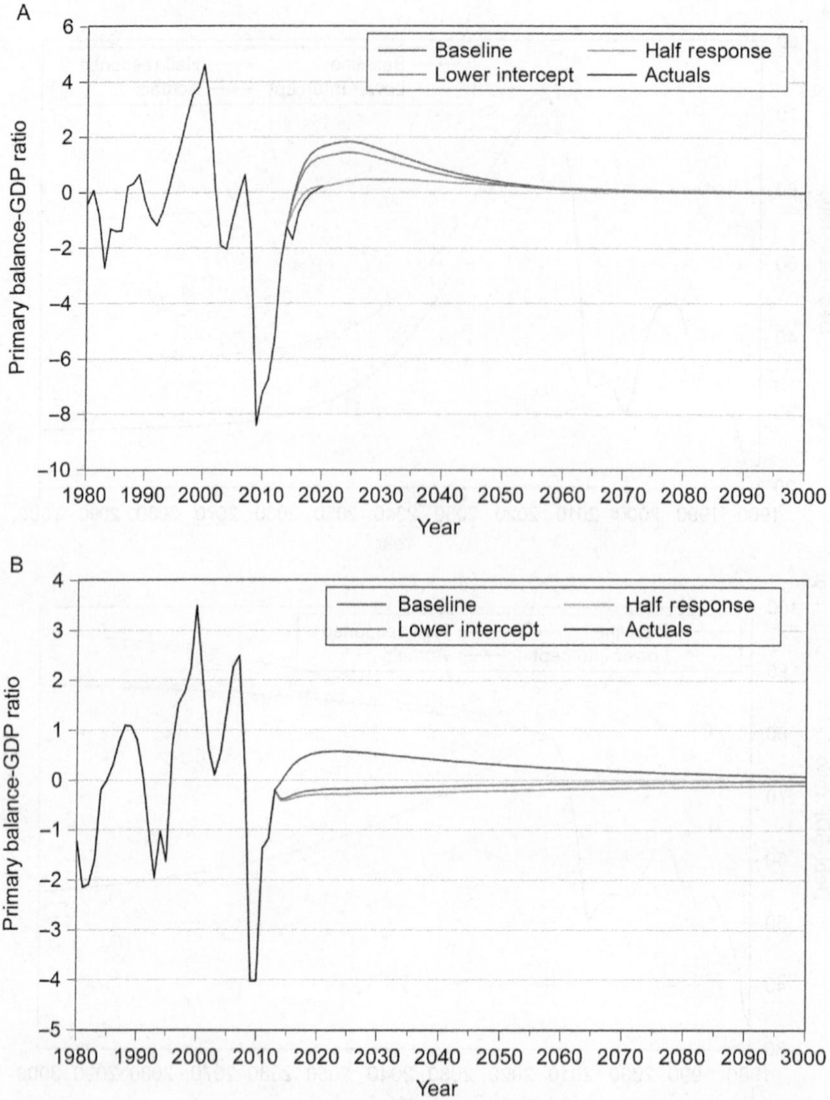

Fig. 7 Primary balance to GDP actuals and simulations since 2014. (A) US primary balance to GDP. (B) Europe primary balance to GDP. *Note*: For details on the construction of this simulations see note on Fig. 6.

declining path for the debt ratio converging back to the average observed in the sample period of the FRF estimates. With lower ρ or lower intercept, the initial surpluses can be significantly smaller or even turned into deficits, but the long-run mean debt ratio would increase significantly. In the case of the United Sates, for example, the long-run average of the debt ratio would rise from 29% in the baseline case to around 57% in the scenario with lower ρ.

All the debt and primary balance paths shown in Figs. 6 and 7 satisfy the same IGBC, and therefore make the same initial debt ratio sustainable, but clearly their macroeconomic implications cannot be the same. Unfortunately, at this point the FRF approach reaches its limits. To evaluate the positive and normative implications of alternative paths of fiscal adjustment, we need a structural framework that can be used to quantify the implications of particular revenue and expenditure policies for equilibrium allocations and prices and for social welfare.

3. STRUCTURAL APPROACH

This section presents a two-country dynamic general equilibrium framework of fiscal adjustment, and uses it to quantify the positive and normative effects of alternative fiscal policy strategies to restore fiscal solvency (ie, maintain debt sustainability) in the United States and Europe after the recent surge in public debt ratios. The structure of the model is similar to the Neoclassical models widely studied in the large quantitative literature on optimal taxation, the effects of tax reforms, and international tax competition (see, for example, Lucas, 1990, Chari et al., 1994, Cooley and Hansen, 1992, Mendoza and Tesar, 1998, 2005, Prescott, 2004, Trabandt and Uhlig, 2011, etc.). In particular, we use the two-country model proposed by Mendoza et al. (2014), which introduces modifications to the Neoclassical model that allow it to match empirical estimates of the elasticity of tax bases to change in tax rates. This is done by introducing endogenous capacity utilization and by limiting the tax allowance for depreciation of physical capital to approximate the allowance reflected in the data.[q]

3.1 Dynamic Equilibrium Model

Consider a world economy that consists of two countries or regions: home (H) and foreign (F). Each country is inhabited by an infinitely-lived representative household, and has a representative firm that produces a single tradable good using as inputs labor, l, and units of utilized capital, $\tilde{k} = mk$ (where k is installed physical capital and m is the utilization rate). Capital and labor are immobile across countries, but the countries are perfectly integrated in goods and asset markets. Trade in assets is limited to one-period discount bonds denoted by b and sold at a price q. Assuming this simple asset-market structure is without loss of generality, because the model is deterministic.

Following King et al. (1988), growth is exogenous and driven by labor-augmenting technological change that occurs at a rate γ. Accordingly, stationarity of all variables (except labor and leisure) is induced by dividing them by the level

[q] Dynamic models of taxation that consider endogenous capacity utilization include the theoretical analysis of optimal capital income taxes by Ferraro (2010) and the quantitative analysis of the effects of taxes in an RBC model by Greenwood and Huffman (1991).

of this technological factor.[r] The stationarity-inducing transformation of the model also requires discounting utility flows at the rate $\widetilde{\beta}=\beta(1+\gamma)^{1-\sigma}$, where β is the standard subjective discount factor and σ is the coefficient of relative risk aversion of CRRA preferences, and adjusting the laws of motion of k and b so that the date $t+1$ stocks grow by the balanced-growth factor $1+\gamma$.

We describe below the structure of preferences, technology and the government sector of the home country. The same structure applies to the foreign country, and when needed foreign country variables are identified by an asterisk.

3.1.1 Households, Firms, and Government

3.1.1.1 Households

The preferences of the representative home household are standard:

$$\sum_{t=0}^{\infty}\widetilde{\beta}^{t}\frac{\left(c_t(1-l_t)^{a}\right)^{1-\sigma}}{1-\sigma}, \sigma>1, a>0, \text{ and } 0<\widetilde{\beta}<1. \tag{5}$$

The period utility function is CRRA in terms of a CES composite good made of consumption, c_t, and leisure, $1-l_t$ (assuming a unit time endowment). $\frac{1}{\sigma}$ is the intertemporal elasticity of substitution in consumption, and a governs both the Frisch and intertemporal elasticities of labor supply for a given value of σ.[s]

The household takes as given proportional tax rates on consumption, labor income and capital income, denoted τ_C, τ_L, and τ_K, respectively, lump-sum government transfers or entitlement payments, denoted by e_t, the rental rates of labor w_t and capital services r_t, and the prices of domestic government bonds and international-traded bonds, q_t^g and q_t.[t]

The household rents $\widetilde{k}$ and l to firms, and makes the investment and capacity utilization decisions. As is common in models with endogenous utilization, the rate of depreciation of the capital stock increases with the utilization rate, according to a convex function $\delta(m)=\chi_0 m^{\chi_1}/\chi_1$, with $\chi_1>1$and $\chi_0>0$ so that $0\le\delta(m)\le 1$.

Investment incurs quadratic adjustment costs:

$$\phi(k_{t+1},k_t,m_t)=\frac{\eta}{2}\left(\frac{(1+\gamma)k_{t+1}-(1-\delta(m_t))k_t}{k_t}-z\right)^2 k_t,$$

[r] The assumption that growth is exogenous implies that tax policies do not affect long-run growth, in line with the empirical findings of Mendoza et al. (1997).

[s] We are using the standard functional form of the utility function from the canonical exogenous balanced growth model as in King et al. (1988) and many RBC applications. This function implies a constant Frisch elasticity for $\sigma=1$. See Trabandt and Uhlig (2011) for a generalized formulation of the utility function that maintains the constant Frisch elasticity when $\sigma>1$, and a discussion of the role of the Frisch elasticity in the use of Neoclassical models to quantify the macroeconomic effects of tax changes.

[t] The gross yields in these bonds are simply the reciprocal of these prices.

where the coefficient η determines the speed of adjustment of the capital stock, while z is a constant set equal to the long-run investment-capital ratio, so that at steady state the capital adjustment cost is zero.

The household chooses intertemporal sequences of consumption, leisure, investment inclusive of adjustment costs x, international bonds, domestic government bonds d, and utilization to maximize (5) subject to a sequence of period budget constraints given by:

$$\begin{aligned}(1+\tau_c)c_t + x_t + (1+\gamma)(q_t b_{t+1} + q_t^g d_{t+1}) =& (1-\tau_L)w_t l_t + (1-\tau_K)r_t m_t k_t \\ &+\theta\tau_K\bar{\delta}k_t + b_t + d_t + e_t,\end{aligned} \tag{6}$$

and the following law of motion for the capital stock:

$$x_t = (1+\gamma)k_{t+1} - (1-\delta(m_t))k_t + \phi(k_{t+1}, k_t, m_t),$$

for $t = 0, \ldots, \infty$, given the initial conditions $k_0 > 0$, b_0, and d_0.

The left-hand-side of equation (6) includes all the uses of household income, and the right-hand-side includes all the sources of income net of income taxes. We impose a standard no-Ponzi-game condition on households, and hence the present value of total household expenditures equals the present value of after-tax income plus initial asset holdings.

Notice that in calculating post-tax income in the above budget constraints, we consider a capital tax allowance $\theta\tau_K\bar{\delta}k_t$ for a fraction θ of depreciation costs. This formulation of the depreciation allowance reflects two assumptions about how the allowance works in actual tax codes: First, depreciation allowances are usually set in terms of fixed depreciation rates applied to the book or tax value of capital, instead of the true physical depreciation rate that varies with utilization. Hence, we set the depreciation rate for the capital tax allowance at a constant rate $\bar{\delta}$ that differs from the actual physical depreciation rate $\delta(m)$. The second assumption is that the depreciation allowance only applies to a fraction θ of the capital stock, because in practice it generally applies only to the capital income of businesses and self-employed, and not to residential capital.[u]

We assume that capital income is taxed according to the residence principle, in line with features of the tax systems in the United States and Europe, but countries are allowed to tax capital income at different rates.[v] This also implies, however, that in order

[u] Using the standard 100% depreciation allowance also has two unrealistic implications. First, it renders m independent of τ_K in the long-run. Second, in the short-run τ_K affects the utilization decision margin only to the extent that it reduces the marginal benefit of utilization when traded off against the marginal cost due to changes in the marginal cost of investment.

[v] In principle, the choice of residence vs source based taxation can be viewed as part of the choices made along with the values of tax rates. Indeed, Huizinga (1995) shows that generally optimal taxation would call for a mix of source- and residence-based taxation. In practice, however, most tax systems are effectively residence-based, because widespread bilateral tax treaties provide for source-based-determined tax payments of residents of one country to claim credits for taxes paid to foreign governments.

to support a competitive equilibrium with different capital taxes across countries we must assume that physical capital is owned entirely by domestic residents. Without this assumption, cross-country arbitrage of returns across capital and bonds at common world prices implies equalization of pre- and post-tax returns on capital, which therefore requires identical capital income taxes across countries. For the same reason, we must assume that international bond payments are taxed at a common world rate, which we set to zero for simplicity. For more details, see Mendoza and Tesar (1998). Other forms of financial-market segmentation, such as trading costs or short-selling constraints, could be introduced for the same purpose, but make the model less tractable.

3.1.1.2 Firms

Firms hire labor and effective capital services to maximize profits, given by $y_t - w_t l_t - r_t \tilde{k}_t$, taking factor rental rates as given. The production function is assumed to be Cobb–Douglas:

$$y_t = F(\tilde{k}_t, l_t) = \tilde{k}_t^{1-\alpha} l_t^{\alpha}$$

where α is labor's share of income and $0 < \alpha < 1$. Firms behave competitively and thus choose $\tilde{k}_t$ and l_t according to standard conditions:

$$(1-\alpha)\tilde{k}_t^{-\alpha} l_t^{\alpha} = r_t,$$

$$\alpha \tilde{k}_t l_t^{\alpha-1} = w_t.$$

Because of the linear homogeneity of the production technology, these factor demand conditions imply that at equilibrium $y_t = w_t l_t + r_t \tilde{k}_t$.

3.1.1.3 Government

Fiscal policy has three components. First, government outlays, which include predetermined sequences of government purchases of goods, g_t, and transfer/entitlement payments, e_t, for $t = 0, \ldots, \infty$. In our baseline results, we assume that $g_t = \bar{g}$ and $e_t = \bar{e}$ where $\bar{g}$ and $\bar{e}$ are the steady state levels of government purchases and transfers before the post-2008 surge in public debt. Because entitlements are lump-sum transfer payments, they are always nondistortionary in this representative agent setup, but still a calibrated value of $\bar{e}$ creates the need for the government to raise distortionary tax revenue, since we do not allow for lump-sum taxation. Government purchases do not enter in household utility or the production function, and hence it would follow trivially that a strategy to restore fiscal solvency after an increase in debt should include setting $g_t = 0$. We rule out this possibility because it is unrealistic, and also because if the model is modified to allow government purchases to provide utility or production benefits, cuts in these purchases would be distortionary in a way analogous to raising taxes.

The second component of fiscal policy is the tax structure. This includes time invariant tax rates on consumption τ_C, labor income τ_L, capital income τ_K, and the depreciation allowance limited to a fraction θ of depreciation expenses.

The third component is government debt, d_t. We assume the government is committed to repay its debt, and thus it must satisfy the following sequence of budget constraints for $t=0,\ldots,\infty$:

$$d_t-(1+\gamma)q_t^g d_{t+1}=\tau_C c_t+\tau_L w_t l_t+\tau_K(r_t m_t-\theta\overline{\delta})k_t-(g_t+e_t).$$

The right-hand-side of this equation is the primary fiscal balance, which is financed with the change in debt net of debt service in the left-hand-side of the constraint.

Public debt is sustainable in this setup in the same sense as we defined it in Section 2. The IGBC must hold (or equivalently, the government must also satisfy a no-Ponzi-game condition): The present value of the primary fiscal balance equals the initial public debt d_0. Since we calibrate the model using shares of GDP, it is useful to re-write the IGBC also in shares of GDP. Defining the primary balance as $pb_t\equiv\tau_C c_t+\tau_L w_t l_t+\tau_K(r_t m_t-\theta-\delta)k_t-(g_t+e_t)$, the IGBC in shares of GDP is:

$$\frac{d_0}{y_{-1}}=\psi_0\left[\frac{pb_0}{y_0}+\sum_{t=1}^{\infty}\left(\left[\prod_{i=0}^{t-1}v_i\right]\frac{pb_t}{y_t}\right)\right], \tag{7}$$

where $v_i\equiv(1+\gamma)\psi_i q_i^g$ and $\psi_i\equiv y_{i+1}/y_i$. In this expression, primary balances are discounted to account for long-run growth at rate γ, transitional growth ψ_i as the economy converges to the long-run, and the equilibrium price of public debt q_i^g. Since y_0 is endogenous (ie, it responds to increases in d_0 and the fiscal policy adjustments needed to offset them), we write the debt ratio in the left-hand-side as a share of pre-debt-shock output y_{-1}, which is predetermined.

Combining the budget constraints of the household and the government, and the firm's zero-profit condition, we obtain the home resource constraint:

$$F(m_t k_t,l_t)-c_t-g_t-x_t=(1+\gamma)q_t b_{t+1}-b_t.$$

3.1.2 Equilibrium, Tax Distortions, and International Externalities

A competitive equilibrium for the model is a sequence of prices $\{r_t,\ r_t^*,\ q_t,\ q_t^g,\ q_t^{g*},\ w_t,\ w_t^*\}$ and allocations $\{k_{t+1},\ k_{t+1}^*,\ m_{t+1},\ m_{t+1}^*,\ b_{t+1},\ b_{t+1}^*,\ x_t,\ x_t^*,\ l_t,\ l_t^*,\ c_t,\ c_t^*,\ d_{t+1},\ d_{t+1}^*\}$ for $t=0,\ldots,\infty$ such that: (a) households in each region maximize utility subject to their corresponding budget constraints and no-Ponzi game constraints, taking as given all fiscal policy variables, pretax prices, and factor rental rates; (b) firms maximize profits subject to the Cobb–Douglas technology taking as given pretax factor rental rates; (c) the government budget constraints hold for given tax rates and exogenous sequences of government purchases and entitlements; and (d) the following market-clearing conditions hold in the global markets of goods and bonds:

$$\omega(y_t - c_t - x_t - g_t) + (1-\omega)\left(y_t^* - c_t^* - x_t^* - g_t^*\right) = 0,$$
$$\omega b_t + (1-\omega) b_t^* = 0,$$

where ω denotes the initial relative size of the two regions.

The model's optimality conditions are useful for characterizing the model's tax distortions and their international externalities. Consider first the Euler equations for capital (excluding adjustment costs for simplicity), international bonds and domestic government bonds. These equations yield the following arbitrage conditions:

$$\frac{(1+\gamma)u_1(c_t, 1-l_t)}{\tilde{\beta}\, u_1(c_{t+1}, 1-l_{t+1})} = (1-\tau_K)F_1(m_{t+1}k_{t+1}, l_{t+1})m_{t+1} + 1 - \delta(m_{t+1}) + \tau_K \theta \bar{\delta} = \frac{1}{q_t} = \frac{1}{q_t^g},$$
$$\frac{(1+\gamma)u_1(c_t^*, 1-l_t^*)}{\tilde{\beta}\, u_1(c_{t+1}^*, 1-l_{t+1}^*)} = (1-\tau_K^*)F_1(m_{t+1}^* k_{t+1}^*, l_{t+1}^*)m_{t+1}^* + 1 - \delta(m_{t+1}^*) + \tau_K^* \theta \bar{\delta} = \frac{1}{q_t} = \frac{1}{q_t^{g*}}. \tag{8}$$

Fully integrated financial markets imply that intertemporal marginal rates of substitution in consumption are equalized across regions, and are also equal to the rate of return on international bonds. Since physical capital is immobile across countries, and capital income taxes are residence-based, households in each region face their own region's tax on capital income. Arbitrage equalizes the after-tax returns on capital across regions, but pre-tax returns differ, and hence differences in tax rates are reflected in differences in capital stocks and output across regions. Arbitrage in asset markets also implies that bond prices are equalized. Hence, at equilibrium: $q_t = q_t^g = q_t^{g*}$.

As shown in Mendoza and Tesar (1998), unilateral changes in the capital income tax result in a permanent reallocation of physical capital, and ultimately a permanent shift in wealth, from a high-tax to a low-tax region. Thus, even though physical capital is immobile across countries, perfect mobility of financial capital and arbitrage of asset returns induces movements akin to international mobility of physical capital. In the stationary state with balanced growth, however, the global interest rate R (the inverse of the bond price, $R \equiv 1/q$) is a function of β, γ and σ:

$$R = \frac{(1+\gamma)^{\sigma}}{\beta},$$

and thus is independent of tax rates. The interest rate does change along the transition path and alters the paths of consumption, output and international asset holdings. In particular, as is standard in the international tax competition literature, each country would have an incentive to behave strategically by tilting the path of the world interest rate in its favor to attract more capital. When both countries attempt this, the outcome is lower capital taxes but also lower welfare for both (which is the well-known race-to-the-bottom result of the tax competition literature).

Consider next the optimality condition for labor:

$$\frac{u_2(c_t, 1-l_t)}{u_1(c_t, 1-l_t)} = \frac{1-\tau_L}{1+\tau_C} F_2(k_t, l_t).$$

Labor and consumption taxes drive the standard wedge $(1 - \tau_W) \equiv (1 - \tau_L)/(1 + \tau_C)$ between the leisure-consumption marginal rate of substitution and the pre-tax real wage (which is equal to the marginal product of labor). Since government outlays are kept constant and the consumption tax is constant, consumption taxation does not distort saving plans, and hence any (τ_C, τ_L) pair consistent with the same τ_W yields identical allocations, prices, and welfare.

Many Neoclassical and Neokeynesian dynamic equilibrium models feature tax distortions like the ones discussed above, but they also tend to underestimate the elasticity of the capital tax base to changes in capital taxes, because k is predetermined at the beginning of each period, and changes gradually as it converges to steady state. In the model we described, the elasticity of the capital tax base can be adjusted to match the data because capital income taxes have an additional distortion absent from the other models: They distort capacity utilization decisions. In particular, the optimality condition for the choice of m_t is:

$$F_1(m_t k_t, l_t) = \frac{1+\Phi_t}{1-\tau_K} \delta'(m_t), \tag{9}$$

where $\Phi_t = \eta\left(\frac{(1+\gamma)k_{t+1} - (1-\delta(m_t))k_t}{k_t} - z\right)$ is the marginal adjustment cost of investment. The capital tax creates a wedge between the marginal benefit of utilization on the left-hand-side of this condition and the marginal cost of utilization on the right-hand-side. An increase in τ_K, everything else constant, reduces the utilization rate.[w] Intuitively, a higher capital tax reduces the after-tax marginal benefit of utilization, and thus reduces the rate of utilization. Note also that the magnitude of this distortion depends on where the capital stock is relative to its steady state, because the sign of Φ_t depends on Tobin's Q, which is given by $Q_t = 1 + \Phi_t$. If $Q_t > 1$ ($\Phi_t > 0$), the desired investment rate is higher than the steady-state investment rate. In this case, $Q_t > 1$ increases the marginal cost of utilization (because higher utilization means faster depreciation, which makes it harder to attain the higher target capital stock). The opposite happens if $Q_t < 1$ ($\Phi_t < 0$). In this case, the faster depreciation at higher utilization rates makes it easier to

[w] This follows from the concavity of the production function and the fact that $\delta(m_t)$ is increasing and convex.

run down the capital stock to reach its lower target level. Thus, an increase in τ_K induces a larger decline in the utilization rate when the desired investment rate is higher than its long-run target (ie, $\Phi_t > 0$).

The interaction of endogenous utilization and the limited depreciation allowance plays an important role in this setup. Endogenous utilization means that the government cannot treat the existing (predetermined) k as an inelastic source of taxation, because effective capital services decline with the capital tax rate even when the capital stock is already installed. This weakens the revenue-generating capacity of capital taxation, and it also makes capital taxes more distorting, since it gives agents an additional margin of adjustment in response to capital tax hikes (ie, capital taxes increase the post-tax marginal cost of utilization, as shown in eq. 9). The limited depreciation allowance widens the base of the capital tax, but it also strengthens the distortionary effect of τ_K by reducing the post-tax marginal return on capital (see eq. 8). As we show in the quantitative results, the two mechanisms result in a dynamic Laffer curve with a standard bell shape and consistent with empirical estimates of the capital tax base elasticity, while removing them results in a Laffer curve that is nearly-linearly increasing for a wide range of capital taxes.

The cross-country externalities from tax changes work through three distinct transmission channels that result from the tax distortions discussed in the previous paragraphs. First, relative prices, because national tax changes alter the prices of financial assets (including internationally traded assets and public debt instruments) as well as the rental prices of effective capital units and labor. Second, the distribution of wealth across the regions, because efficiency effects of tax changes by one region affect the allocations of capital and net foreign assets across regions (even when physical capital is not directly mobile). Third, the erosion of tax revenues, because via the first two channels the tax policies of one region affect the ability of the other region to raise tax revenue. When one region responds to a debt shock by altering its tax rates, it generates external effects on the other region via these three channels. Given the high degree of financial and trade integration in the world economy today, abstracting from these considerations in quantitative estimates of the effects of fiscal policy is a significant shortcoming.

3.2 Calibration to Europe and the United States

We use data from the United States and the 15 largest European countries to calibrate the model at a quarterly frequency.[x] We calibrate the home region (US) to the United States, and the foreign region (EU15) to the aggregate of the 15 European countries. The EU15 aggregates are GDP-weighted averages. Table 5 presents key macroeconomic statistics and fiscal variables for the all the countries and the two region aggregates in 2008.

[x] The European countries include Austria, Belgium, Denmark, Finland, Greece, France, Germany, Ireland, Italy, the Netherlands, Poland, Portugal, Spain, Sweden, and the United Kingdom. These countries account for over 94% of the European Union's GDP.

Table 5 Macroeconomic stance as of 2008

	EU15											GDP-weighted ave.		
	AUT	BEL	DEU	ESP	FRA	GBR	ITA	NLD	POL	SWE	Other	EU15	US	All
(a) Macro aggregates														
τ_C	0.19	0.17	0.17	0.12	0.17	0.14	0.13	0.20	0.21	0.26	0.23	0.17	0.04	0.11
τ_L	0.51	0.47	0.41	0.35	0.45	0.30	0.48	0.47	0.38	0.55	0.39	0.41	0.27	0.35
τ_K	0.25	0.45	0.24	0.25	0.38	0.40	0.38	0.26	0.16	0.37	0.31	0.32	0.37	0.34
c/y	0.53	0.52	0.56	0.57	0.57	0.64	0.59	0.45	0.62	0.47	0.58	0.57	0.68	0.62
x/y	0.22	0.24	0.19	0.29	0.22	0.17	0.21	0.20	0.24	0.20	0.23	0.21	0.21	0.21
g/y	0.19	0.23	0.18	0.19	0.23	0.22	0.20	0.26	0.19	0.26	0.21	0.21	0.16	0.19
tb/y	0.06	0.01	0.06	−0.06	−0.02	−0.02	−0.01	0.08	−0.04	0.07	−0.02	0.00	−0.05	−0.02
Rev/y	0.48	0.49	0.44	0.37	0.50	0.42	0.46	0.47	0.40	0.54	0.45	0.45	0.32	0.39
$\text{Total Exp}/y$	0.49	0.50	0.44	0.41	0.53	0.47	0.49	0.46	0.43	0.52	0.48	0.47	0.39	0.43
(b) Debt shocks														
d_{2007}/y_{2007}	0.31	0.73	0.43	0.18	0.36	0.28	0.87	0.28	0.17	−0.23	0.13	0.38	0.43	0.40
d_{2011}/y_{2011}	0.45	0.80	0.51	0.46	0.63	0.62	1.00	0.38	0.32	−0.25	0.45	0.58	0.74	0.65
$\Delta d/y$	0.14	0.07	0.09	0.28	0.27	0.33	0.14	0.10	0.15	−0.02	0.32	0.20	0.31	0.25

Other is a GDP-weighted average of Denmark, Finland, Greece, Ireland, and Portugal.
Source: OECD Revenue Statistics, OECD National income Accounts, and EuroStat. Tax rates are author's calculations based on Mendoza, E.G., Razin, A., Tesar, L.L. 1994. Effective tax rates in macroeconomics: cross-country estimates of tax rates on factor incomes and consumption. J. Monet. Econ. 34 (3), 297323. "Total Exp" is total noninterest government outlays.

The first three rows of Table 5 show estimates of effective tax rates on consumption, labor, and capital calculated from revenue and national income accounts statistics using the methodology originally introduced by Mendoza et al. (1994) (MRT). The United States and EU15 have significantly different tax structures. Consumption and labor tax rates are much higher in EU15 than in the United States (0.17 vs 0.04 for τ_C and 0.41 vs 0.27 for τ_L), while capital taxes are higher in the United States (0.37 vs 0.32). The labor and consumption tax rates imply a consumption-leisure tax wedge τ_W of 0.298 for the United States vs 0.496 in EU15. Thus, EU15 has much higher effective tax distortion on labor supply. Notice also that inside of EU15 there is also some tax heterogeneity, particularly with respect to Great Britain, which has higher capital tax and lower labor tax than most of the other EU15 countries.

With regard to aggregate expenditure–GDP ratios, the United States has a much higher consumption share than EU15, by 11 percentage points. EU15 has a larger government expenditure share (current purchases of goods and services, excluding transfers) than the United States by 5 percentage points. Their investment shares are about the same, at 0.21. For net exports, the United States has a deficit of 5% while EU15 has a balanced trade (with the caveat that the latter includes all trade the individual EU15 countries conduct with each other and with the rest of the world). In light of this, we set the trade balance to zero in both countries for simplicity. In terms of fiscal flows, both total tax revenues and government outlays (including expenditures and transfer payments) as shares of GDP are higher in EU15 than in the United States, by 13 and 8 percentage points, respectively. Thus, the two regions differ sharply in all three fiscal instruments (taxes, current government expenditures, and transfer payments).

The bottom panel of Table 5 reports government debt to GDP ratios and their change between end–2007 (beginning of 2008) and end–2011. These changes are our estimate of the increases in debt (or "debt shocks") that each country and region experienced, and hence they are the key exogenous impulse used in the quantitative experiments. These debt ratios correspond to general government net financial liabilities as a share of GDP as reported in *Eurostat*. As the table shows, debt ratios between end–2007 and 2011 rose sharply for all countries except Sweden, where the general government actually has a net asset position (ie, negative net liabilities) that changed very little. The size of the debt shocks differs substantially across the two regions. The United States entered the Great Recession with a higher government debt to output ratio than EU15 (0.43 vs 0.38) and experienced a larger increase in the debt ratio (0.31 vs 0.20).

Table 6 lists the calibrated parameter values and the main source for each value. The calibration is set so as to represent the balanced-growth steady state that prevailed before the debt shocks occurred using 2008 empirical observations for the corresponding allocations. The value of ω is set at 0.46 so as to match the observation that the United States accounts for about 46% of the combined GDP of the United States and EU15 in 2008. Tax rates, government expenditure shares and debt ratios are calibrated to the values in the United States and EU15 columns of Table 5, respectively. The limit on the

Table 6 Parameter values

Preferences:		**US**	**EU15**	**Sources**
β	Discount factor	0.998		Steady state Euler equation for capital
σ	Risk aversion	2.000		Standard DSGE value
a	Labor supply elasticity	2.675		$\bar{l}=0.18$ (Prescott, 2004)
Technology:				
α	Labor income share	0.61		Trabandt and Uhlig (2011)
γ	Growth rate	0.0038		Real GDP p.c. growth of sample countries (Eurostat 1995–2011)
η	Capital adjustment cost	2		Elasticity of capital tax base (Gruber and Rauh, 2007; Dwenger and Steiner, 2012)
$\bar{m}$	Capacity utilization	1		Steady state normalization
$\delta(\bar{m})$	Depreciation rate	0.0163		Capital law of motion, $x/y = 0.19$, $k/y = 2.62$ (OECD, AMECO)
χ_0	$\delta(m)$ coefficient	0.023	0.024	Optimality condition for utilization given $\delta(\bar{m})$, $\bar{m}$
χ_1	$\delta(m)$ exponent	1.44	1.45	Set to yield $\delta(\bar{m})=0.0164$
ω	Country size	0.46	0.54	GDP share in all sample countries
Fiscal policy:				
g/y	Gov't exp share in GDP	0.16	0.21	OECD National Income Accounts
τ_C	Consumption tax	0.04	0.17	MRT modified
τ_L	Labor income tax	0.27	0.41	MRT modified
τ_K	Capital income tax	0.37	0.32	MRT modified
θ	Depreciation allowance limitation	0.20		$(REV_K^{corp}/REV_K)(K^{NR}/K)$, OECD Revenue Statistics and EU KLEMS

Note: The implied growth adjusted discount factor $\tilde{\beta}$ is 0.995, and the implied precrisis annual interest rate is 3.8%. REV_K^{corp}/REV_K is the ratio of corporate tax revenue to total capital tax revenue. K^{NR}/K is the ratio of nonresidential fixed capital to total fixed capital.

depreciation allowance, θ, is set to capture the facts that tax allowances for depreciation costs apply only to capital income taxation levied on businesses and self-employed, and do not apply to residential capital (which *is* included in k). Hence, the value of θ is set as $\theta=(REV_K^{corp}/REV_K)(K^{NR}/K)$, where (REV_K^{corp}/REV_K) is the ratio of revenue from corporate capital income taxes to total capital income tax revenue, and (K^{NR}/K) is the ratio of nonresidential fixed capital to total fixed capital. Using 2007 data from OECD *Revenue Statistics* for revenues, and from the European Union's *EU KLEMS* database for capital stocks for the ten countries with sufficient data coverage,[y] these ratios range from 0.32% to 0.5% for (REV_K^{corp}/REV_K) and from 27% to 52% for (K^{NR}/K). Weighting by

[y] These countries are Austria, Denmark, Finland, Germany, Italy, Netherlands, Spain, Sweden, the United Kingdom, and the United States.

GDP, the aggregate value of θ is 0.20. Also the value for the United States is close to the weighted value for the European countries.

The technology and preference parameters are set the same across the United States and EU15, except the parameters χ_0 and χ_1 in the depreciation function. The common parameters are calibrated to target the weighted average statistics for all sample countries. The labor share of income, α, is set to 0.61, following Trabandt and Uhlig (2011). The quarterly rate of labor-augmenting technological change, γ, is 0.0038, which corresponds to the 1.51% weighted average annual growth rate in real GDP per capita of all the countries in our sample between 1995 and 2011, based on Eurostat data. We normalize the long-run capacity utilization rate to $\bar{m}=1$. Given γ at 0.0038, x/y at 0.19 and k/y at 2.62 from the data, we solve for the long-run depreciation rate from the steady-state law of motion of the capital stock, $x/y=(\gamma+\delta(\bar{m}))k/y$.[z] This yields $\delta(\bar{m})=0.0163$ per quarter. The constant depreciation rate for claiming the depreciation tax allowance, $\bar{\delta}$, is set equal to the steady state depreciation rate of 0.0163.

The value of χ_0 follows then from the optimality condition for utilization at steady state, which yields $\chi_0=\delta(\bar{m})+\dfrac{1+\gamma-\beta}{\beta}-\tau_K\bar{\delta}$. Given this, the value of χ_1 follows from evaluating the depreciation rate function at steady state, which implies $\chi_0\bar{m}^{\chi_1}/\chi_1=\delta(\bar{m})$. Given the different capital tax rates in the United States and EU15, the implied values for χ_0 and χ_1 are slightly different across countries: χ_0 is 0.0233 in the United States and 0.0235 in EU15, and χ_1 is 1.435 in the United States and 1.445 in EU15.

The preference parameter, σ, is set at a commonly used value of 2. The exponent of leisure in utility is set at $a=2.675$, which is taken from Mendoza and Tesar (1998). This value supports a labor allocation of 18.2 h, which is in the range of the 1993–96 averages of hours worked per person aged 15–64 reported by Prescott (2004). The value of β follows from the steady-state Euler equation for capital accumulation, using the values set above for the other parameters that appear in this equation:

$$\frac{\gamma}{\tilde{\beta}}=1+(1-\tau_K)(1-\alpha)\frac{y}{k}-\delta(\bar{m})+\tau_K\theta\bar{\delta}.$$

This yields $\tilde{\beta}=0.995$, and then since $\tilde{\beta}=\beta(1+\gamma)^{1-\sigma}$ it follows that $\beta=0.998$. The values of β, γ and σ pin down the steady-state gross real interest rate, $R=\beta^{-1}(1+\gamma)^{\sigma}=1.0093$. This is equivalent to a net annual real interest rate of about 3.8%.

Once R is determined, the steady-state ratio of net foreign assets to GDP is pinned down by the net exports-GDP ratio. Since we set $tb/y=0$, $b/y=(tb/y)/\left[(1+\gamma)R^{-1}-1\right]=0$. In addition, the steady-state government budget constraint yields

[z] Investment rates are from the OECD National Income Accounts and capital-output ratios are from the AMECO database of the European Commission.

an implied ratio of government entitlement payments to GDP $e/y = Rev/y - g/y - (d/y)\left[1-(1+\gamma)R^{-1}\right] = 0.196$. Under this calibration approach, both b/y and e/y are obtained as residuals, given that the values of all the terms in the right-hand-side of the equations that determine them have already been set. Hence, they generally will not match their empirical counterparts. In particular, for entitlement payments the model underestimates the 2008 observed ratio of entitlement payments to GDP (0.196 in the model vs 0.26 in the data for All EU). Notice, however, that when the model is used to evaluate tax policies to restore fiscal solvency, the fact that entitlement payments are lower than in the data strengthens our results, because lower entitlements means a lower required amount of revenue than what would be needed to support observed transfer payments, thus making it easier to restore solvency. We show below that restoring fiscal solvency is difficult and implies nontrivial tax adjustments with sizable welfare costs and cross-country spillovers, all of which would be larger with higher government revenue requirements due to higher entitlement payments.

The value of the investment-adjustment-cost parameter, η, cannot be set using steady-state conditions, because adjustment costs wash out at steady state. Hence, we set the value of η so that the model is consistent with the mid-point of the empirical estimates of the short-run elasticity of the capital tax base to changes in capital tax rates. The range of empirical estimates is 0.1–0.5, so the target midpoint is 0.3.[aa] Under the baseline symmetric calibration, the model matches this short-run elasticity with $\eta = 2.0$. This is also in line with estimates in House and Shapiro (2008) of the response of investment in long-lived capital goods to relatively temporary changes in the cost of capital goods.[ab]

Table 7 reports the 2008 GDP ratios of key macro-aggregates in the data and the model's corresponding steady-state allocations for the US–EU15 calibration. As noted earlier, this calibration captures the observed differences in the size of the regions, their fiscal policy parameters, and their public debt-GDP ratios. Notice in particular that the consumption-output ratios and the fiscal revenue-output ratios from the data were not directly targeted in the calibration, but the two are closely matched by the model. Hence, the model's initial stationary equilibrium before the increases in public debt is a reasonably good match to the observed initial conditions in the data.

[aa] The main estimate of the elasticity of the *corporate* tax base relative to corporate taxes in the United States obtained by Gruber and Rauh (2007) is 0.2. Dwenger and Steiner (2012) obtained around 0.5 for Germany. Grubler and Rauh also reviewed the large literature estimating the elasticity of *individual* tax bases (which include both labor and capital income taxes collected from individuals) to individual tax rates and noted this: "The broad consensus…is that the elasticity of taxable income with respect to the tax rate is roughly 0.4. Moreover, the elasticity of actual income generation through labor supply/savings, as opposed to reported income, is much lower. And most of the response of taxable income to taxation appears to arise from higher income groups."

[ab] They estimated an elasticity of substitution between capital and consumption goods in the 6–14 range. In the variant of our model without utilization choice, this elasticity is equal to $1/(\eta\delta)$. Hence, for $\delta(\bar{m}) = 0.0164$, elasticities in that range imply values of η in the 1–2.5 range.

Table 7 Balanced growth allocations (GDP ratios) of 2008

	United States		EU15	
	Data	**Model**	**Data**	**Model**
c/y	0.68	0.63	0.57	0.56
i/y	0.21	0.21	0.21	0.23
g/y^*	0.16	0.16	0.21	0.21
tb/y	− 0.05	0.00	0.00	0.00
Rev/y	0.32	0.32	0.45	0.46
d/y^*	0.76	0.76	0.60	0.60

3.3 Quantitative Results

The goal of the quantitative experiments is to use the numerical solutions of the model to study whether alternative fiscal policies can restore fiscal solvency, which requires increasing the present discounted value of the primary balance in the right-hand-side of (7) by as much as the observed increases in debt.[ac] Notice that the change in this present value reflects changes in the endogenous equilibrium dynamics of the primary balance-GDP ratio in response to the changes in fiscal policy variables. In turn, the changes in primary balance dynamics reflect the effects of these policy changes on equilibrium allocations and prices that determine tax bases, and the computation of the present value reflects also the response of the equilibrium interest rates (ie, debt prices).

We conduct a set of experiments in which we assume that the United States or EU15 implement unilateral increases in either capital or labor tax rates, so we can quantify the effects on equilibrium allocations and prices, sustainable debt (ie, primary balance dynamics), and social welfare in both regions. We also compare these results with those obtained if the same tax changes are implemented assuming the countries are closed economies, so we can highlight the cross-country externalities of unilateral tax changes.

The model is solved numerically using a modified version of the algorithm developed by Mendoza and Tesar (1998, 2005), which is based on a first-order approximation to the equilibrium conditions around the steady state. Standard perturbation methods cannot be applied directly, because trade in bonds implies that, when the model's pre-debt-crisis steady state is perturbed, the equilibrium transition paths of allocations and prices, and the new steady-state equilibrium need to be solved for simultaneously.[ad] This is because

[ac] The observed increases in debt between end–2007 (beginning of 2008) and end–2011 can be viewed as exogenous increases in d_0/y_{-1} in the left-hand-side of the IGBC (7). As reported in Table 5, the US debt ratio rose by 31 percentage points from 41%, and that of the EU15 rose by 20 percentage points from 38%.

[ad] Alternative solution methods that make the interest rate or the discount factor ad-hoc functions of net foreign assets (NFA), or that assume that holding these assets is costly, are also not useful, because they impose calibrated NFA positions that cannot be affected by tax changes, whereas the "true" model without these modifications can yield substantial world redistribution of wealth as a result of tax policy changes.

in models of this class stationary equilibria depend on initial conditions, and thus cannot be determined separately from the models' dynamics. Mendoza and Tesar dealt with this problem by developing a solution method that nests a perturbation routine for solving transitional dynamics within a shooting algorithm. This method iterates on candidate values of the new long-run net foreign asset positions to which the model converges after being perturbed by debt and tax changes, until the candidate values match the positions the model converges to when simulated forward to its new steady state starting from the calibrated pre-debt-crisis initial conditions.

3.3.1 Dynamic Laffer Curves

We start the analysis of the quantitative results by constructing "Dynamic Laffer Curves" (DLC) that show how unilateral changes in capital or labor taxes in one region affect that region's sustainable public debt. These curves map values of τ_K or τ_L into the equilibrium present discounted value of the primary fiscal balance. For each value that a given tax rate in the horizontal axis takes, we solve the model to compute the intertemporal sequence of total tax revenue, which varies as equilibrium allocations and prices vary, while government purchases and entitlement payments are kept constant. Then we compute the present value of the primary balance, which therefore captures the effect of changes in the equilibrium sequence of interest rates. We take the ratio of this present value to the initial output y_{-1} (ie, GDP in the steady state calibrated to pre-2008 data) so that it corresponds to the term in the right-hand-side of the IGBC (7), and plot the result as a *change* relative to the 2007 public debt ratio. Hence, the values along the vertical axis of the DLCs show the change in d_0/y_{-1} that particular values of τ_K or τ_L can support as sustainable debt at equilibrium (ie, debt that satisfies the IGBC with equality). By construction, the curves cross the zero line at the calibrated tax rates of the initial stationary equilibrium, because those tax rates yield exactly the same present discounted value of the primary balance as the initial calibration. To make the observed debt increases sustainable, there needs to be a value of the tax rate in the horizontal axis such that the DLC returns a value in the vertical axis that matches the observed change in debt.

Since the "passive" region whose taxes are not being changed unilaterally is affected by spillovers of the other region's tax changes, there needs be an adjustment in the passive region so that its IGBC is unchanged (ie, it maintains the same present discounted value of primary fiscal balances). We refer to this adjustment as maintaining "revenue neutrality" in the passive region. In principle this can be done by changing transfers, taxes or government purchases. However, since we have assumed already that government purchases are kept constant in both regions, reducing distortionary tax rates in response to favorable tax spillovers would be more desirable than increasing transfer payments, which are nondistortionary. Hence, we maintain revenue neutrality in the passive region by adjusting the labor tax rate.

3.3.1.1 Dynamic Laffer Curves for Capital Taxes

The DLCs for capital taxes are plotted in Fig. 8. The panel (A) is for the US region, and the panel (B) is for EU15. The solid lines show the open-economy curves and the dotted lines are for when the countries are in autarky. As explained above, the DLCs intersect the zero line at the initial tax rates of $\tau_K = 0.37$ and $\tau_K^* = 0.32$ by construction. We also show in the plots the increases in debt observed in each region, as shown in Table 5: The

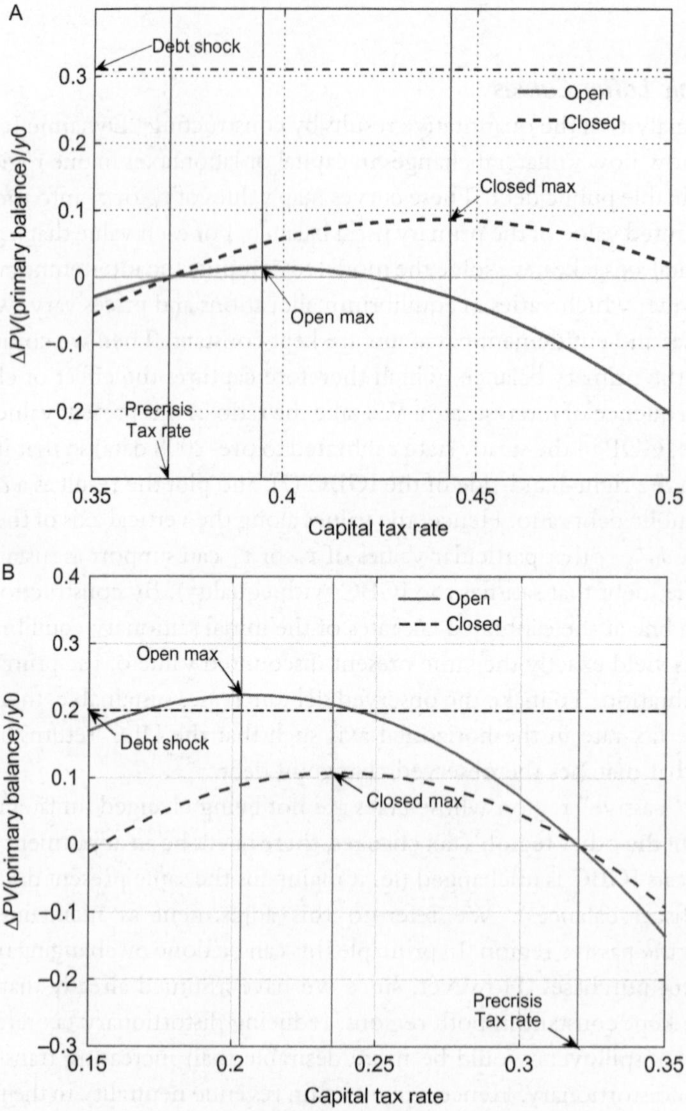

Fig. 8 Dynamic Laffer curves of capital tax rates. (A) United States. (B) EU15.

US net public debt ratio rose 31 percentage points and that of EU15 rose 20 percentage points. These increases are marked with the "Debt Shock" line in Fig. 8.

Fig. 8 shows that the DLCs of the United States and EU15 are very different, with those for EU15 seating higher, shifted to the left, and showing more curvature than those for the United States. Hence, unilateral changes in capital tax rates show a capacity to sustain larger debt increases in EU15 than in the United States, and can do so at lower tax rates. These marked differences are the result of the heterogeneity in fiscal policies present in the data and captured in the calibration, and in the open-economy scenario they are also partly explained by the international externalities of the unilateral tax changes assumed in constructing the DLCs. EU15 has higher revenue-generating capacity because of higher labor and consumption taxes at identical labor income shares and similar consumption shares, although in terms of primary balance the higher revenue is partly offset by higher government purchases. On the other hand, the United States has a lower capital tax rate and by enough to make a significant difference in the inefficiencies created by capital taxes across the two regions, as we illustrate in more detail below. Moreover, the magnitude of heterogeneity in the capital tax DLCs that results from a given magnitude of heterogeneity in fiscal variables depends on the model's modifications made to match the observed elasticity of the capital base. We illustrate below that DLCs are very different if we remove capacity utilization and the limited depreciation allowance.

Beyond the difference in position and shape of the capital tax DLCs across the United States and EU15, these DLCs deliver three striking results: First, unilateral changes in the US capital tax cannot restore fiscal solvency and make the observed increase in debt unsustainable (the peaks of the DLCs of the US region either as a closed or an open economy are significantly below the debt shock line). The maximum point of the open-economy DLC is attained at $\tau_K = 0.402$, which produces an increase in the present value of the primary balance of only 2 percentage points of GDP, far short of the required 31. In contrast, the maximum point of the open-economy DLC for EU15 is attained around $\tau_K^* = 0.21$, which rises the present value of the primary balance by 22 percentage points of GDP, slightly more than the required 20. Under autarky, however, the EU15 DLC also peaks below the required level, and hence capital taxes also cannot restore fiscal solvency for EU15 as a closed economy. This result also reflects the strong cross-country externalities that we discuss in more detail below (ie, unilateral capital tax *cuts* yield significantly more sustainable debt for EU15 as an open economy than under autarky).

Second, capital income taxes in EU15 are highly inefficient. The current capital tax rate is on the increasing segment of the DLC for the United States but on the decreasing segment for EU15. This has two important implications. One is that EU15 could have sustained the calibrated initial debt ratio of 38% at capital taxes below 15%, instead of the 32% tax rate obtained from the data. The second is that to make the observed 20 percentage points increase in debt sustainable, EU15 can *reduce* its capital tax almost in half to about 17% in the open-economy DLC. In both cases, the sharply lower capital taxes would be much less distortionary and thus would increase efficiency significantly.

Third, cross-country externalities of capital income taxes are very strong, and under our baseline calibration, they hurt (favor) the capacity to sustain debt of the United States (EU15). For the United States, the DLC under autarky is steeper than in the open-economy case, and it peaks at a higher tax rate of 43% and with a higher increase in the present value of the primary balance of about 10 percentage points. Thus, the United States can always sustain more debt, or support higher debt increases relative to the calibrated baseline, for a given increase in τ_K under autarky than as an open economy. This occurs because by increasing its capital tax *unilaterally* as an open economy the United States not only suffers the efficiency losses in capital accumulation and utilization, but it also triggers reallocation of physical capital from the United States to EU15, which results in reductions (increases) in the United States (EU15) factor payments and consumption, and thus lower (higher) tax bases in the United States (EU15). The same mechanism explains why reducing the capital tax in EU15 unilaterally generates much less revenue under autarky than in the open-economy case. In the latter, cutting the EU15 capital tax unilaterally triggers the same forces as a unilateral increase in the US capital tax.

This quantitative evidence of strong externalities of capital taxes across financially integrated economies demonstrates that evaluating "fiscal space," or the capacity to sustain debt, using closed-economy models leads to seriously flawed estimates of the effectiveness of capital taxes as a tool to restore debt sustainability. The results also suggest that incentives for strategic interaction leading to capital income tax competition are strong, and get stronger as higher debts need to be reconciled with fiscal solvency (as evidenced by the history of corporate tax competition inside the EU since the 1980s). Mendoza et al. (2014) study this issue using a calibration that splits the European Union into two regions, one including the countries most affected by the European debt crisis (Greece, Ireland, Italy, Portugal, and Spain) and the second including the rest of the Eurozone members.

3.3.1.2 Dynamic Laffer Curves of Labor Tax Rates

Fig. 9 shows the DLCs for the labor tax rate. Notice that the open-economy and autarky DLCs are similar within each region (although more similar for EU15 than for the United States), which indicates that international externalities are much weaker in this case. This is natural, because labor is an immobile factor, and although it can still trigger cross-country spillovers via general-equilibrium effects, these are much weaker than the first-order effects created by unilateral changes of capital taxes via the condition that arbitrages after-tax returns on all assets across countries.

The main result of the DLCs for labor taxes is that the DLCs for the United States are much higher than those for EU15. Since the international externalities are weak for the

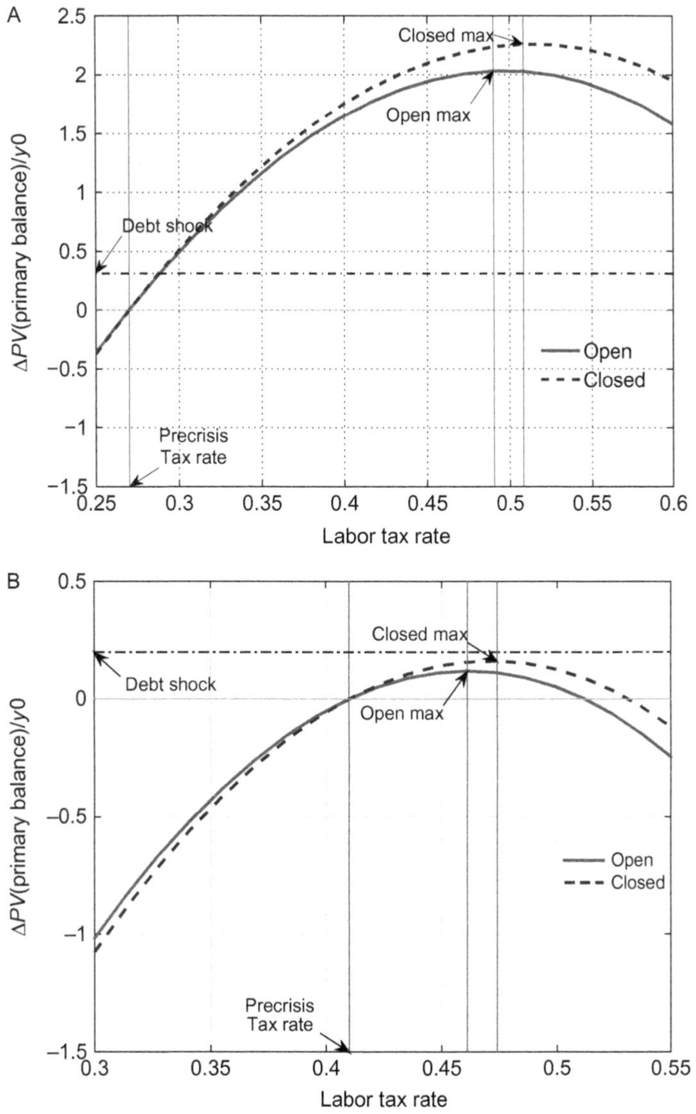

Fig. 9 Dynamic Laffer curves of labor tax rates. (A) United States. (B) EU15.

labor tax, this result is only due to the different initial conditions resulting from the fiscal heterogeneity captured in our calibration, and in particular to the large differences in initial labor and consumption taxes (41 vs 27% for labor and 17 vs 4% for consumption in EU15 vs the United States, respectively). Increasing the calibrated τ_L for the US region to the EU15 rate of 41%, keeping all other US parameters unchanged, shifts down its labor tax DLC almost uniformly by about 200 percentage points in the 0.25–0.55 interval of labor tax rates. This happens because, for an increase in the labor tax of a given size, the difference in initial conditions implies that the US region generates a larger increase in the present value of total tax revenue than EU15, and since the present value of government outlays is nearly unchanged in both, the larger present value of revenue is amplified into a significantly larger increase in the present value of the primary balance.[ae]

The US open-economy DLC for τ_L is considerably steeper than for τ_K, and it peaks at a tax rate of 0.48, which would make sustainable an initial debt ratio larger than in the initial baseline by 200 percentage points of GDP, much more than the 31 percentage points required by the data. The labor tax rate that the United States as an open or closed economy needs to make the observed debt increase sustainable is about 29%, which is just a two-percentage-point increase relative to the initial tax rate. Hence, these results show that, from the perspective of macroeconomic efficiency that representative-agent models of financially integrated economies like the one we are using emphasize, labor taxes are a significantly more effective tool for restoring fiscal solvency in the United States than capital taxes.

The DLC of EU15 yields much less positive results. Since the initial consumption-labor wedge is already much higher in this region than in the United States, the fiscal space of the labor tax rate is very limited. In either the closed- or open-economy cases, the DLC peaks at a labor tax rate of 46% and yields an increase of only about 10 percentage points in the present value of the primary balance, which is half of the 20-percentage-points increase EU15 needs make the observed debt increase sustainable.

It is interesting to note that the debt increase in the United States was about 10 percentage points larger than in Europe, yet the model predicts that given the initial conditions in tax rates and government outlays before the increases in debt, unilateral tax adjustments in Europe cannot generate a sufficient increase in the present value of the primary balance to make their higher debt sustainable. The exception is the capital tax in the open-economy scenario, in which this is possible only because EU15 would benefit significantly from a negative externality on the US region. In contrast, the results show that a modest increase in labor taxes (or consumption taxes since they are equivalent in this model) can restore fiscal solvency in the United States.

It is useful to compare the results we reported here with those of similar exercises in other existing studies based on Neoclassical models, particularly those by Trabandt and

[ae] The percent change in the present value of the primary balance after a tax change of a given magnitude relative to before (assuming that the present value of government outlays does not change) can be expressed as $z[1 + PDV(g + e)/PDV(pb)]$, where $z$is the percent change in the present value of tax revenues after the tax change relative to before, and $PDV(g + e)$ and $PDV(pb)$ are the pretax-change present values of total government outlays and the primary balance, respectively. Hence, for $z > 0$ and since total outlays are much larger than the primary balance $[PDV(g + e)/PDV(pb)] >> 1$, a given difference in z across the United States and EU15 translates into a much larger percent difference in the present value of the primary balance.

Uhlig (2011, 2012) and Auray et al. (2013). Trabandt and Uhlig (2011, 2012) used a closed-economy model without endogenous capacity utilization and focused mainly on steady-state Laffer curves (ie, Laffer curves that map tax rates into steady state tax revenues), while the DLCs studied here are for present values taking into account both transitional dynamics and steady-state changes caused by tax changes relative to the calibrated tax rates. Qualitatively, the results in Trabandt and Uhlig (2011) are similar to the ones in this chapter because they find that capital tax hikes generate much smaller increases in revenue than labor taxes. They find that the maximum increases in steady-state tax revenue obtained with capital (labor) taxes are 6 (30)% for the United States and 1 (8)% for Europe. Quantitatively; however, the results reported here differ not only because both transitional dynamics and steady-states are included, but also because the two-country model with capacity utilization captures the cross-country externalities of tax policy and the observed elasticity of the capital tax base, and these two features undermine the revenue-generating capacity of tax hikes.

Trabandt and Uhlig (2012) extend their analysis to gauge the sustainability of observed debt levels in response to hypothetical permanent increases in interest rates. Keeping government transfers, total outlays and debt constant at observed levels, they calculate the maximum real interest rate at which the revenue generated at the peak of steady-state Laffer curves would satisfy the steady-state government budget constraint. That is, effectively they compute the interest rate at which the Blanchard ratio of the previous section holds with debt and spending set at observed levels and tax revenue set at the maxima of steady-state Laffer curves. They find that the maximum real interest rate for the United States is larger than for European countries if labor taxes are moved to the peak of the Laffer curves. These calculations, however, inherit the limitations of the Blanchard ratios as measures of sustainable debt discussed in the previous section, and imply unusually large primary fiscal surpluses. For instance, depending on the debt measure used, Trabandt and Uhlig estimate the maximum interest rate for the United States in the 12–15.5% range. With a 92% debt ratio, a 1.5% annualized output growth rate and the 12% interest rate, the US economy requires a 9.6% steady-state primary surplus. The largest primary surplus observed in US history using Bohn's historical dataset starting in 1790 was 6.3%, and the average was just 0.4%. Moreover, moving the labor tax to the peak of the Laffer curve reduces steady-state output by 27%, which suggests that the welfare cost of the tax hike is quite large.

Auray et al. (2013) use a Neoclassical model of a small open economy to conduct a quantitative comparison of tax policies aimed at lowering European debt ratios. They introduce a FRF in the class of the ones examined in the previous section: Increases of the debt ratio at date t above its date-t target induce increases in the date-t primary surplus above its date-t target. The primary balance adjustment is obtained by adjusting one of the tax rates as needed to satisfy the FRF. In this environment, lowering the debt ratio requires higher tax rates in the short term in exchange for lower rates in the long term as steady-state debt service falls. They find that a cut of 10 percentage points in the debt ratio can be attained with an increase in welfare using the capital income tax, roughly no change in welfare using the consumption tax, and a welfare loss using the labor income tax. Qualitatively, the model studied here would produce similar results if applied to a similar debt-reduction experiment. Since the capital income tax is highly distorting, using the benefit of the lower debt service burden to cut the capital income tax would be best for welfare and efficiency. Their setup, however, is not calibrated to match the capital tax base elasticity and abstracts from cross-country externalities because of the small-open-economy assumption.

3.3.2 Macroeconomic Effects of Tax Rate Changes

We analyze next the macroeconomic effects of unilateral changes in capital and labor tax rates. In the first experiment, the United States increases its capital tax rate from the initial value of 0.37 to 0.402, which is the maximum point of the open-economy DLC for the United States. Table 8 shows the effects of this change on both regions in the open-economy model and on the US region as a closed economy. EU15 reduces its labor tax rate from 0.41 to 0.40 to maintain revenue neutrality, which is the result of favorable externalities from the tax hike in the United States.

The capital tax hike in the United States as an open economy leads to an overall welfare cost of 2.19% vs 2.22% as a closed economy, while EU15 obtains a welfare gain of 0.74%.[af] Comparing the US outcomes as an open economy relative to the closed economy under the same 40.2% capital tax rate, we find that the sustainable debt (ie, the present value of the primary balance) rises by a factor of 4.5 (from 1.37% to 6.16%). The welfare loss is nearly the same (2.2%), but normalizing by the amount of revenue generated, the United States is much better off in autarky. Thus, seen from this perspective, the United States would have strong incentives for either engaging in strategic interaction (ie, tax competition) or for considering measures to limit international capital mobility.

The 0.74% welfare gain that EU15 obtains from the US unilateral capital tax hike is a measure of the normative effect of the cross-country externalities of capital tax changes. The United States can raise more revenue by increasing τ_K along the upward-sloping region of its DLC, but its ability to do so is significantly hampered by the adverse externality it faces due to the erosion of its tax bases. In EU15, the same externality indirectly improves government finances, or reduces the distortions associated with tax collection, and provides it with an unintended welfare gain.

[af] Welfare effects are computed as in Lucas (1987), in terms of a percent change in consumption constant across all periods that equates lifetime utility under a given tax rate change with that attained in the initial steady state. The overall effect includes transitional dynamics across the pre- and post-tax-change steady states, as well as changes across steady states. The steady-state effect only includes the latter.

Table 8 Macroeconomic effects of an increase in US capital tax rate (the EU15 maintains revenue neutrality with labor tax)

	Open economy				Closed economy	
	United States		EU15		United States	
Tax rates	**Old**	**New**	**Old**	**New**	**Old**	**New**
τ_K	0.37	0.40	0.32	0.32	0.37	0.40
τ_C	0.04	0.04	0.17	0.17	0.04	0.04
τ_L	0.27	0.27	0.41	0.40	0.27	0.27
PV of fiscal deficit over precrisis GDP as percentage point change from original ss		1.37		0.00		6.16
Welfare effects (percent)						
Steady-state gain		−2.27		0.59		−2.55
Overall gain		−2.19		0.74		−2.22
Percentage changes	**Impact effect**	**Long-run effect**	**Impact effect**	**Long-run effect**	**Impact effect**	**Long-run effect**
y	−1.23	−3.87	−0.15	1.25	−2.35	−3.57
c	−1.87	−2.83	1.44	1.28	−1.53	−2.91
k	0.00	−7.61	0.00	1.25	0.00	−7.32
Percentage point changes						
tb/y	3.21	−0.30	−2.70	0.24		
i/y	−3.01	−1.02	1.77	0.00	−0.91	−1.02
r	−0.00	−0.00	−0.00	−0.00	−0.00	−0.00
l	0.11	−0.17	−0.01	0.21	−0.13	−0.11
m	−4.23	−0.866	−0.315	−0.000	−5.277	−0.866

The impact and long-run effects on key macro-aggregates in both regions are shown in the bottom half of Table 8. The corresponding transition paths of macroeconomic variables as the economies move from the precrisis steady state to the new steady state are illustrated in Fig. 10. The increase in τ_K causes US capital to fall over time to a level 7.6% below the precrisis level, while EU15's capital rises to a level 1.25% above the pre-tax-change level. Capacity utilization falls at home in both the short run and the long run, which is a key component of the model capturing the reduced revenue-generating capacity of capital tax hikes when the endogeneity of capacity utilization is considered. We show later in this section that this mechanism indeed drives the elasticity of the capital tax base in the model, which matches that of the data and is higher than what standard representative-agent models of taxation show.

On impact when the United States increases its capital tax, labor increases in the United States and falls slightly in EU15, but this pattern reverses during the transition

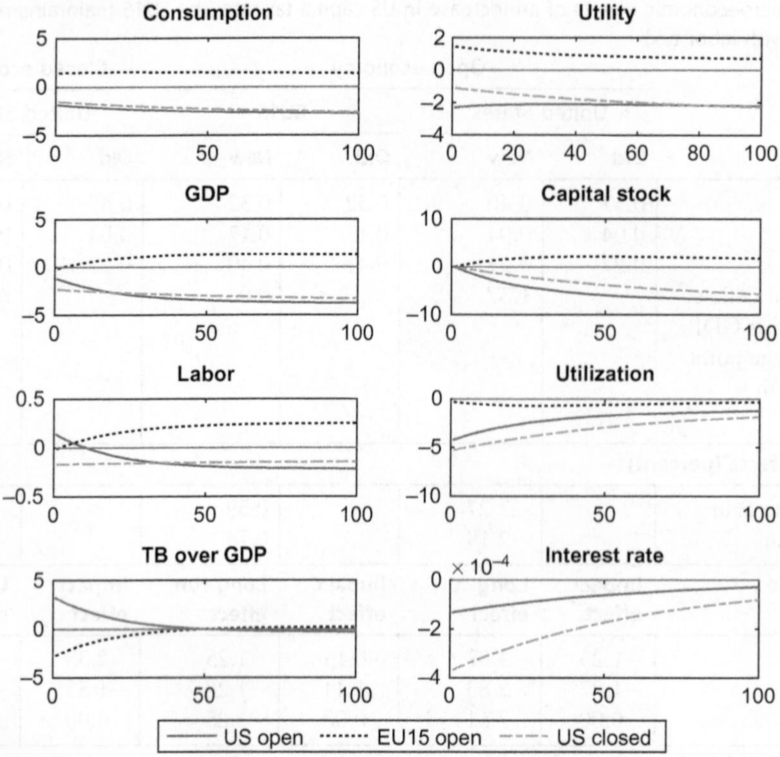

Fig. 10 Responses of macro variables to a US capital tax rate increase.

to steady state because of the lower (higher) capital stock in US (EU15) region in the new steady state. Consequently, US output contracts by almost 4% in the long-run, underscoring efficiency losses due to the capital tax increase and the costs of the fiscal adjustment. The United States increases its net foreign asset position (NFA) by running trade surpluses (tb/y) in the early stages of transition, while EU15 decreases its NFA position by running trade deficits. The US trade surpluses reflect saving to smooth out the cost of the efficiency losses, as output follows a monotonically decreasing path. Still, utility levels are lower than when the United States implements the same capital tax under autarky, because of the negative cross-country spillovers.

We next look at the responses of fiscal variables when the United States increases its capital tax, plotted in Fig. 11. In the United States, tax revenue from capital income increases almost immediately to a higher constant level when τ_K rises, while the revenues from labor and consumption taxes decline both on impact and in the long run. Labor and consumption tax rates are not changing, but both tax bases fall on impact and then decline monotonically to their new, lower steady states. The primary fiscal balance and total revenue both rise initially but then converge to about the same levels as in the precrisis stationary equilibrium. For the primary balance, this pattern is implied by the pattern of the

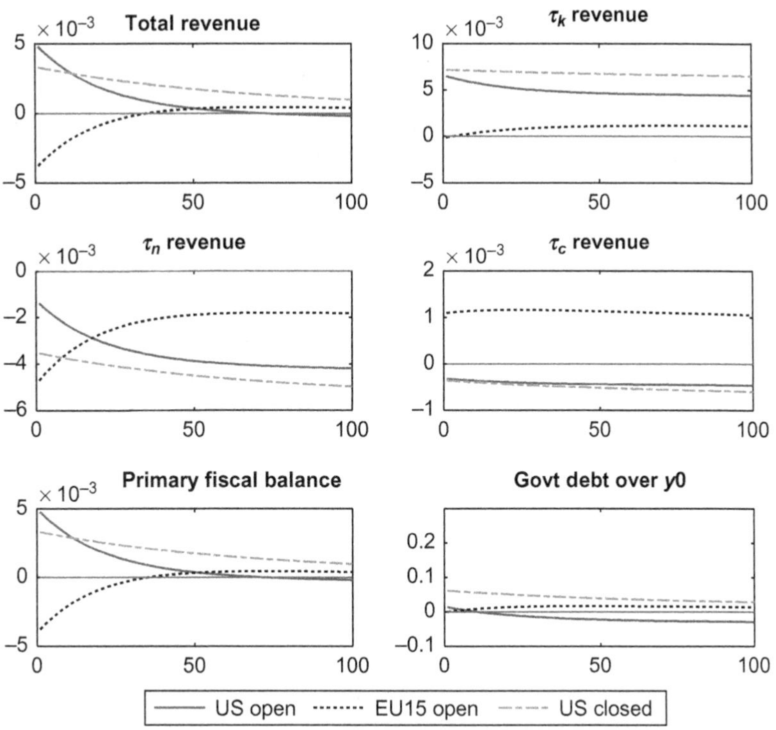

Fig. 11 Responses of fiscal variables to a US capital tax rate increase.

total revenue, since government expenditures and entitlements are held constant. For total revenue, the transitional increase indicates that the rise in capital tax revenue more than offsets the decline in the revenue from the other taxes in the transition, while in the long-run they almost offset each other exactly. This is possible because the change in τ_K to 0.4 is on the increasing side of the Laffer curve, and in fact it is the maximum point of the curve. Hence, this capital tax hike does not reduce capital tax revenues.

The public debt dynamics in the bottom-right panel of Fig. 11 shows that on impact, government debt in the United States responds to the 40% tax rate by increasing 5 percentage points, reflecting the extra initial debt that can be supported at the higher capital tax rate. Since the primary fiscal balance rises on impact and then declines monotonically, the debt ratio also falls monotonically during the transition, and converges to a ratio that is actually about 4 percentage points below the precrisis level. Hence, the initial debt increase allowed by the capital tax hike is followed by a protracted decline in debt converging to a debt ratio even lower that in the precrisis steady state. If the United States implements the same tax hike under autarky, it generates significantly larger revenues and primary balances, and hence the debt ratio increases more initially and converges to a higher steady state of 1 percentage points above the precrisis level. This is again a reflection of the cross-country externalities faced by the United States as an open economy, since equally sized tax hikes produce significantly higher revenues under autarky.

The cross-country externalities are also reflected in the fiscal dynamics of EU15 shown in Fig. 11. Maintaining revenue neutrality (in present value) still allows both its revenue and primary balance to fall initially, while in the long run both converge to very similar levels as in the precrisis steady state. Removing the labor tax adjustment in EU15 that maintains revenue neutrality, the present value of its primary balance as a share of GDP would increase by 10.1 percentage points relative to the precrisis ratio, and both its revenue and primary balances would be higher than in the plots shown in Fig. 11. The welfare gain, however, would be negligible instead of 0.74% in lifetime consumption.

The next experiment examines the effects of lowering the EU15 capital tax rate so as to move it out of the decreasing segment of the DLC. To make this change analogous to the one in the previous experiment, we change the EU15 capital tax to the value at the maximum point of the DLC for EU15, which is about 21%. Table 9 summarizes the results. The cut in the EU15 capital tax rate generates an increase of about 22 percentage points in sustainable debt (just a notch above what is required to make the observed debt increase sustainable), and a large welfare gain of 6.9% for this region. Its capital stock rises over time to a level 26% higher than in the pre-tax-change steady state. Output, consumption, labor supply, and utilization all rise in both the short-run and the long-run in EU15, while the trade balance moves initially into a large trade deficit and then converges to a small surplus. The same tax cut in EU15 as a closed economy yields a much smaller rise in sustainable debt, of just under 10 percentage points, though the welfare gain is about the same as in the open economy. This result indicates that in this case the welfare gain largely reflects the reduction of the large inefficiencies due to the initial capital tax being in the decreasing side of the DLC. In the US region, the tax cut in EU15 causes a welfare loss of 0.2%, with capital declining 1.5 percent from the pre-tax-change level.

The next two experiments focus on changes in labor tax rates. The DLCs for the labor tax rate (Fig. 9) show that the US region has substantial capacity to raise tax revenues and sustain higher debt ratios by raising labor taxes. We examine in particular an increase of the labor tax rate that completely offsets the observed debt increase, which as we noted earlier is only about 2 percentage points higher than in the initial calibration (ie, the labor tax in the United States rises from 27% to 29%). The results are reported in Table 10. The declines in US output, consumption, capital, and welfare are much smaller than with the capital tax hike. Since the international spillovers are small, this tax change produces a welfare gain of just 0.18% in EU15. For the same reason, comparing the United States results as a closed vs open economy, the change in the present value of the primary balance is almost the same, in contrast with the large difference obtained for the capital tax. Also, keep in mind that the capital tax hike, even though it was set at the maximum point of the capital tax DLC of the United States as open economy, cannot generate enough revenue to offset the observed debt increase, whereas the labor tax hike does.

Table 9 Macroeconomic effects of a decrease in EU15 capital tax rate (the United States maintains revenue neutrality with labor tax)

	Open economy				Closed economy	
	United States		EU15		EU15	
Tax rates	**Old**	**New**	**Old**	**New**	**Old**	**New**
τ_K	0.37	0.37	0.32	0.20	0.37	0.37
τ_C	0.04	0.04	0.17	0.17	0.04	0.17
τ_L	0.27	0.28	0.41	0.41	0.27	0.41
PV of fiscal deficit over precrisis GDP as percentage point change from original ss		−0.00		22.34		9.62
Welfare effects (percent)						
Steady-state gain		0.36		7.35		7.93
Overall gain		−0.23		6.86		6.99
Percentage changes	**Impact effect**	**Long-run effect**	**Impact effect**	**Long-run effect**	**Impact effect**	**Long-run effect**
y	2.30	−1.40	6.05	12.77	8.38	11.99
c	−1.59	−0.64	5.82	9.03	5.14	9.19
k	0.00	−1.50	0.00	26.10	0.00	25.23
Percentage point changes						
tb/y	8.92	−0.75	−6.57	0.56		
i/y	−5.64	0.00	8.18	3.66	3.31	3.66
r	0.00	−0.00	0.00	−0.00	0.00	−0.00
l	0.47	−0.31	0.05	0.48	0.43	0.36
m	2.34	0.00	12.93	3.31	14.94	3.31

Now consider the case of increasing the EU15 labor tax. As explained earlier in discussing the labor DLCs, the EU15 initial consumption/labor wedge is already high, so the capacity for raising tax revenues using labor taxes is limited. In this experiment, we increase the labor tax in EU15 to the rate at the maximum point of the labor tax DLC of EU15 as an open economy, which implies a labor tax rate of 0.465. The results are summarized in Table 11. The higher EU15 labor tax increases the present value of the primary balance-GDP ratio by only 0.118, falling well short of the observed debt increase of 0.2. The welfare loss is large, at nearly 5%, with output, consumption, capital, and labor falling. EU15 can produce a higher present value of the primary balance (0.16) in the closed economy at a similar welfare loss. Again the international spillover for the labor tax rate is small, so the US region makes a negligible welfare gain.

Taken together these findings are consistent with two familiar results from tax analysis in representative-agent models, which emphasize the efficiency costs of tax distortions. First, the capital tax rate is the most distorting tax. Second, in open-economy models,

Table 10 Macroeconomic effects of an increase in the US labor tax rate (the EU15 maintains revenue neutrality with labor tax)

	United States		EU15		United States	
Tax rates	**Old**	**New**	**Old**	**New**	**Old**	**New**
τ_K	0.37	0.37	0.32	0.32	0.37	0.37
τ_C	0.04	0.04	0.17	0.17	0.04	0.04
τ_L	0.27	0.29	0.41	0.41	0.27	0.29
PV of fiscal deficit over precrisis GDP as percentage point change from original ss		31.00		0.00		31.95
Welfare effects (percent)						
Steady-state gain		−0.92		0.15		−0.98
Overall gain		−0.90		0.18		−0.91
Percentage changes	**Impact effect**	**Long-run effect**	**Impact effect**	**Long-run effect**	**Impact effect**	**Long-run effect**
y	−1.16	−1.75	−0.02	0.30	−1.41	−1.68
c	−1.88	−2.09	0.34	0.31	−1.80	−2.10
k	0.00	−1.75	0.00	0.30	0.00	−1.68
Percentage point changes						
tb/y	0.72	−0.07	−0.61	0.06		
i/y	−0.46	0.00	0.40	0.00	0.02	−0.00
r	−0.00	−0.00	−0.00	−0.00	−0.00	−0.00
l	−0.29	−0.35	0.00	0.05	−0.35	−0.34
m	−0.73	0.00	−0.06	−0.00	−0.96	0.00

taxation of a mobile factor (ie, capital) yields less revenue at greater welfare loss than taxation of the immobile factor (ie, labor). This is in line with our results showing that the cross-country tax externalities are strong for capital taxes but weak for labor taxes.

The sharp differences we found between the United States and EU15 also have important policy implications in terms of debates about debt-sustainability and the effects of fiscal adjustment via capital and labor taxes in Europe and the United States. With capital taxes, the model suggests that the United States is on the increasing side of the Laffer curve, though it cannot restore fiscal solvency for the observed debt shock of 31 percentage points (neither as an open economy nor as a closed economy). In contrast, the model suggests that Europe is on the decreasing side of the Laffer curve, and can make its observed debt increase of 20 percentage point sustainable by reducing its capital taxes and moving away from the decreasing side of the Laffer curve, and in the process make a substantial welfare gain. This is only possible, however, because the United States is assumed to maintain its capital tax rate unchanged as Europe's drops, which results in

Table 11 Macroeconomic effects of an increase in the EU15 labor tax rate (the United States maintains revenue neutrality with labor tax)

	United States		EU15		EU15	
Tax rates	**Old**	**New**	**Old**	**New**	**Old**	**New**
τ_K	0.37	0.37	0.32	0.32	0.37	0.37
τ_C	0.04	0.04	0.17	0.17	0.04	0.17
τ_L	0.27	0.27	0.41	0.47	0.27	0.47
PV of fiscal deficit over precrisis GDP as percentage point change from original ss		0.00		11.75		16.02
Welfare effects (percent)						
Steady-state gain		−0.12		−5.04		−5.19
Overall gain		0.07		−4.91		−4.92
Percentage changes	**Impact effect**	**Long-run effect**	**Impact effect**	**Long-run effect**	**Impact effect**	**Long-run effect**
y	−0.68	0.41	−4.28	−6.20	−5.06	−5.99
c	0.45	0.16	−7.35	−8.18	−7.13	−8.22
k	0.00	0.41	0.00	−6.20	0.00	−5.99
Percentage point changes						
tb/y	−2.47	0.22	2.16	−0.20		
i/y	1.64	−0.00	−1.29	−0.00	0.11	−0.00
r	−0.00	−0.00	−0.00	−0.00	−0.00	−0.00
l	−0.14	0.08	−0.90	−1.05	−1.04	−1.01
m	−0.67	−0.00	−2.87	0.00	−3.59	−0.00

large externalities that benefit Europe at the expense of the United States. Capital tax hikes under autarky cannot restore fiscal solvency for Europe either.

With labor taxes, although the model indicates that both the United States and Europe are on the increasing side of their DLCs, the US pre-2008 started with a much smaller consumption/labor distortion than Europe. As a result, the United States has substantial fiscal space to easily offset the debt increase with a small labor tax hike and a small welfare cost of 0.9%. In contrast, the model suggests that Europe cannot restore fiscal solvency after the observed increase in debt using labor taxes.

3.3.3 Why Are Utilization and Limited Depreciation Allowance Important?

As explained earlier, we borrowed from Mendoza et al. (2014) the idea of using endogenous capacity utilization and a limited tax allowance for depreciation expenses to build into the model a mechanism that produces capital tax base elasticities in line with empirical estimates. In contrast, standard dynamic equilibrium models without these features tend to have unrealistically low responses of the capital base to increases in capital taxes. To illustrate this point, we follow again Mendoza et al. in comparing DLCs for capital taxes in three scenarios (see Fig. 12): (i) a standard Neoclassical model with exogenous utilization and a full depreciation allowance ($\theta = 1$), shown as a dashed-dotted line; (ii) the same model but with a limited depreciation allowance ($\theta = 0.2$), shown as a dotted line; and (iii) the baseline calibration of our model with both endogenous utilization and a limited depreciation allowance (using again $\theta = 0.2$), shown as a solid line. All other

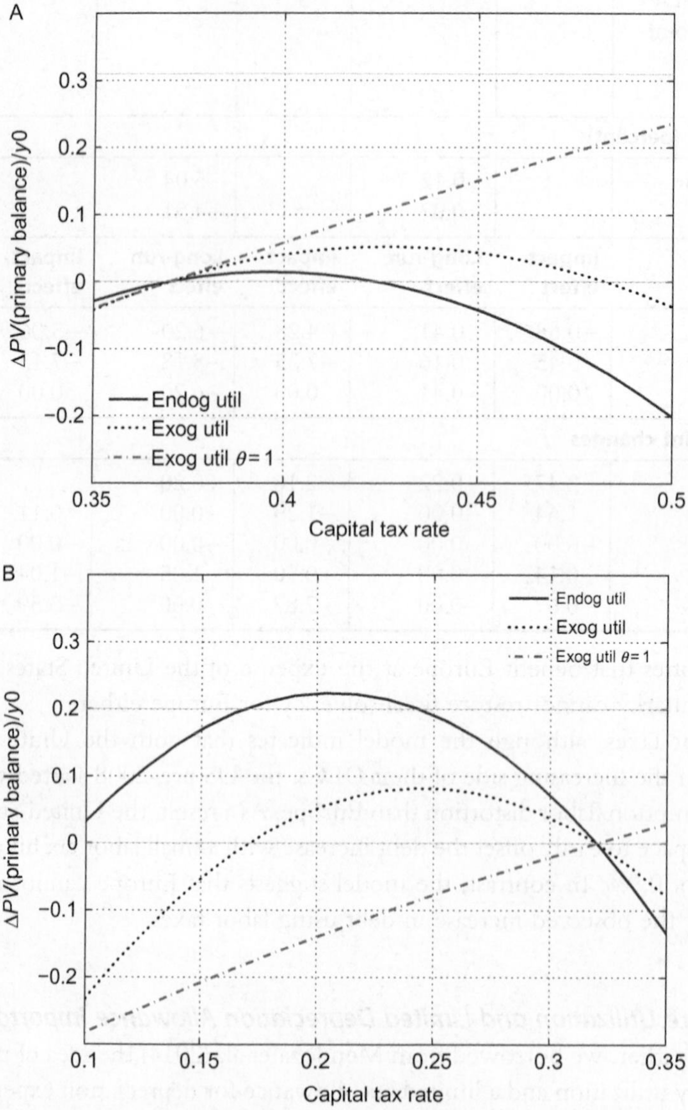

Fig. 12 Comparing dynamic Laffer curves for the capital tax rate. (A) United States. (B) EU15.

parameter values are kept the same. We show the three cases for the United States and EU15 region in panels (A) and (B) of the figure, respectively.

The DLCs for the three cases intersect at the initial calibrated tax rates of 0.37 and 0.32 for the United States and EU15 by construction. To the right of this point, the curves for case (i) are always above the other two, and the ones for case (ii) are always above the ones for case (iii). The opposite occurs to the left of the intersection points.

Consider the US plots. In case (i), the DLC has a positive, approximately linear slope in the 0.35–0.5 domain of capital tax rates. This curve continues to be increasing even when we extend the capital tax rate to 0.9, which is in line with the results obtained by Trabandt and Uhlig (2011).[ag] This behavior of the DLC for the capital tax follows from the fact that at any given date the capital stock is predetermined and has a low short-run elasticity. As a result, the government can raise substantial revenue over the transition period because the capital stock declines only gradually. The increased tax revenue during the transition dominates the fall in the steady-state, resulting in a nondecreasing DLC (recall the DLC is based on present value calculations).

Introducing limited depreciation allowance without endogenizing the utilization choice (case (ii)) has two effects that induce concavity in the DLC. First, it increases the effective rate of taxation on capital income, and thus weakens the incentive to accumulate capital and lowers the steady-state capital-output ratio and tax bases. On the other hand, it has a positive impact on revenue by widening the capital tax base. The first effect dominates the latter when the capital tax rate rises relative to the initial tax of 0.37, resulting in sharply lower DLC curve values than in case (i).

In case (iii) the tax allowance is again limited but now capacity utilization is endogenous. This introduces additional effects that operate via the distortions on efficiency and the ability to raise revenue discussed earlier: On the side of tax distortions, equation (9) implies that endogenous utilization adds to the efficiency costs of capital income taxation by introducing a wedge between the marginal cost and benefits of capital utilization. On the revenue side, endogenous utilization allows agents to make adjustments in effective capital (reducing it when taxes rise and increasing it when it falls), and thus alters the amount of taxable capital income. Hence, when utilization falls in response to increases in capital tax rates, it also weakens the government's ability to raise capital tax revenue. These effects lead to a bell-shaped DLC that has more curvature and is significantly below those in cases (i) and (ii). Thus, endogenous utilization makes capital taxes more distorting and weakens significantly the revenue-generating capacity of capital taxes.[ah]

[ag] They find that present-value Laffer curves of capital tax revenue peak at very high tax rates (discounting with the constant steady state interest rate) or have a positive slope over the full range (discounting with equilibrium interest rates).

[ah] Mendoza et al. also found that removing the limited depreciation allowance from case (iii) still results in a DLC below those of cases (i) and (ii), but it is also flatter and increasing for a wider range of capital taxes than case (iii).

Panel (B) of Fig. 12 shows DLCs for the three cases in the EU15 region. The results are analogous to Panel (A) but emphasizing now the region to the left of the intersection point, which is at the initial tax of 32%. In case (i), again the DLC has an increasing positive slope over a large range of the capital tax rate. Case (ii) shows that limiting the depreciation allowance again induces concavity in the DLC, with the EU15 initial capital tax already in the decreasing segment of the curve. Comparing with case (iii), the exogenous utilization case generates much less revenue. As in the US results, this occurs because with endogenous utilization, reductions in capital taxes lead to higher utilization rates that result in higher levels of capital income and higher wages, thus widening the two income tax bases.

The effects of endogenous utilization and limited depreciation have significant implications for the elasticity of the capital income tax base with respect to the capital tax. In particular, as Mendoza et al. (2014) showed, the model can be calibrated to match a short-run elasticity consistent with empirical estimates because of the combined effects of those two features. As documented earlier, the empirical literature finds estimates of the short-run elasticity of the capital tax base in the 0.1–0.5 range. Table 12 reports the model's comparable elasticity estimates and the effects on output, labor, and utilization 1 year after a 1% increase in the capital tax (relative to the calibrated baseline values), again for cases (i), (ii), and (iii) and in both the United States and EU15 regions.

The United States and EU15 results differ somewhat quantitatively, but qualitatively they make identical points: The neoclassical model with or without limited depreciation allowance (cases (i) and (ii)) yields short-run elasticities with the wrong sign (ie, the capital tax base *rises* in the short run in response to capital tax rate increases). The reason is that capital does not change much, since capital is predetermined in the period of the tax hike and changes little in the first period after because of investment adjustment costs, and

Table 12 Short-run elasticity of US capital tax base

	Elasticity	y_1	l_1	m_1
Empirical estimates	[0.1, 0.5]			
Model implications for the United States				
Exog. utilization and $\theta = 1$	−0.09	0.04%	0.011	
Exog. utilization and $\theta = 0.2$	−0.09	0.08%	0.028	
Endog. utilization and $\theta = 0.2$	0.29	−0.15%	0.010	−0.471
Model implications for the EU15				
Exog. utilization and $\theta = 1$	−0.04	0.01%	0.004	
Exog. utilization and $\theta = 0.2$	−0.02	0.03%	0.008	
Endog. utilization and $\theta = 0.2$	0.32	−0.14%	0.004	−0.393

Note: Elasticity is measured as the percentage decrease of capital tax base in the first year after a 1% increase in the capital tax rate is introduced. For empirical estimates, see Gruber and Rauh (2007) and Dwenger and Steiner (2012). y_1 and m_1 provides the percent deviation from the initial steady state in the impact year. l_1 denotes the percentage points change from the initial steady state.

labor supply rises due to a negative income shock from the tax hike. Since capital does not fall much and labor rises, output rises on impact, and thus taxable labor and capital income both rise, producing an elasticity of the opposite sign than that found in the data. In contrast, the model with endogenous utilization (case (iii)), generates a decline in output on impact due to a substantial drop in the utilization rate, despite the rise in labor supply. With the calibrated values of η, the model generates short-run elasticities of 0.29 and 0.32 for the United States and EU15, respectively, which are both well inside the range of empirical estimates.

It is also worth noting that with exogenous utilization, the model can produce a capital tax base elasticity in line with empirical evidence only if we set η to an unrealistically low value. The short-run elasticity of the capital tax base is negative for any $\eta > 1$, and it becomes positive and higher than 0.1 only for $\eta < 0.1$.[ai] This is significantly below the empirically relevant range of 1–2.5 documented in the calibration section. Moreover, at the value of $\eta = 2$ determined in our baseline calibration, the model without utilization choice yields a capital tax base elasticity of -0.09.

3.3.4 Further Considerations

We close this section with some important considerations and caveats of the structural analysis. In particular, we discuss the predictions of the structural framework for the case of Japan, which is challenging because of its high debt ratio, and the implications of considering the possibility of taxes on wealth or the capital stock.

Japan had a very high public debt to GDP ratio already before the global financial crisis, at about 82% by the end of 2007. By the end of 2011, its debt ratio had increased 46 percentage points to 128%. Hence the level and the change of Japan's debt ratio are both larger than what we saw in the United States and Europe.

What does the structural approach to debt sustainability tell us about the Japanese case? To answer this question, we reset the model so that the foreign region is now a proxy for Japan instead of EU15 and recompute the DLCs. In particular, we calibrate the foreign tax rates to match Japan's precrisis tax structure, using the same Mendoza-Razin-Tesar method we used for the United States and Europe. In 2007, Japan's capital tax rate was 39%, the labor tax rate was 31% and the consumption tax was 6%. This tax structure is similar to that of the United States. In fact, Japan's consumption-leisure tax wedge τ_W is 0.35, which is much closer to the 0.3 estimate for the United States than 0.5 for Europe. We also reset the relative country size to match the fact that Japan's GDP per capita is about 78% that of the United States. The rest of the structural parameters are kept the same as in our baseline analysis. The DLCs for Japan are shown in Fig. 13. The panel (A) is the DLC for the capital tax and the panel (B) is for the labor tax.

[ai] The intuition is simple. As η approaches zero the marginal adjustment cost of investment approaches zero, and hence the capital stock 1 year after the tax hike can respond with large declines.

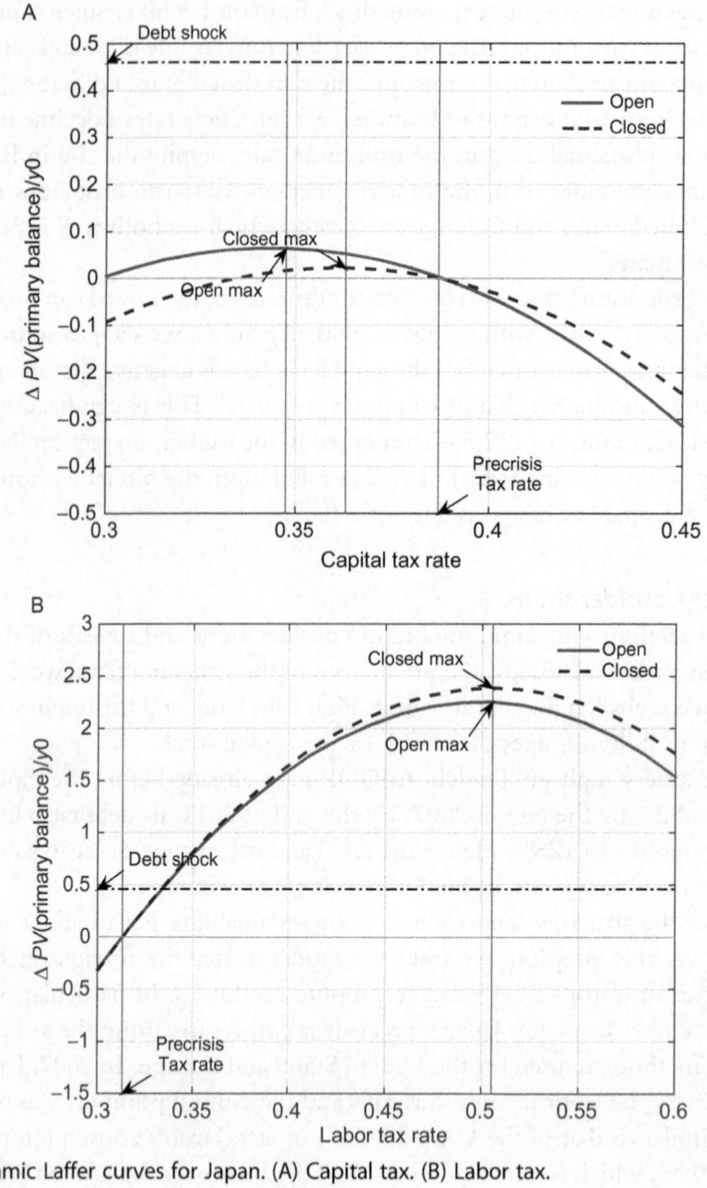

Fig. 13 Dynamic Laffer curves for Japan. (A) Capital tax. (B) Labor tax.

In general, the DLC results for Japan are a more extreme version of those for the United States: The capital tax cannot restore fiscal solvency because Japan's DLC for this tax peaks well below the required increase, while there is a lot of room for labor (or consumption) taxes to do it. One important difference is that the precrisis high capital tax rate in Japan is inefficient (ie, in the decreasing segment of the DLC). Because of this, the tax externalities work in the opposite direction to those observed for the US DLC, and so cutting the capital tax in Japan relative to the precrisis rate as a closed economy yields a smaller increase in the present value of the primary balance than as an open economy. One important caveat to the above results is that Japan has been stuck with slow growth and deflation for about two decades. Although raising consumption and labor taxes helps balance government budgets, higher taxes still cause efficiency and welfare losses. Japan did increase its consumption tax from 5% to 8% in April 2014, but after that the economy tipped back into recession and a further hike of the consumption tax to 10% was postponed. Moreover, if we reduce the long-run growth rate in the model to the 0.8% per-capita GDP growth rate observed on average in Japan between 2001 and 2014, the two DLCs shift downward sharply. The capital tax becomes effectively useless as it yields negligible amounts of extra revenue. The labor tax needed to make the debt sustainable is significantly higher, and thus the associated efficiency and welfare losses are larger as well.

Another caveat is that our analysis abstracts from Japan's aging demographics, rising pressures on government finance from public pensions and medical expenses, etc. These considerations place heavy burdens on the sustainability of public debt. Imrohoroglu and Sudo (2011) and Hansen and Imrohoroglu (2013) use a Neoclassical growth model to quantify the implications of the projected low population growth rate and permanent increase in total government outlays on fiscal sustainability. Imrohoroglu and Sudo find that even an increase in the consumption tax to 15% and an annual GDP growth of 3% over the next 20 years is not sufficient to restore fiscal balance unless expenditures are also contained. Hansen and Imrohoroglu find that fiscal sustainability requires the consumption tax rate be set to unprecedentedly high levels of 40–60%. Moreover, Imrohoroglu et al. (2016) and Braun and Joines (2015) use overlapping generation models and also find that current fiscal policies are not sustainable and large fiscal adjustments are needed.[aj]

Another important consideration in assessing the results of the structural analysis is that we abstracted from the possibility of taxing wealth, in particular taxing the initial capital stock. The optimal taxation literature has made the well-known argument that from an efficiency standpoint taxing the initial, predetermined capital stock is optimal. However, the argument hinges on the assumption of government commitment, which sets aside key issues of time consistency and the implications of lack of commitment.

In our model, a wealth tax would be equivalent to confiscation of a fraction of k_0 unexpectedly. Since utilization is endogenous, this tax would also affect utilization as of date 0: The marginal product of utilization declines with lower capital, utilization falls, and thus capital income and capital income tax revenue fall. But more importantly, three arguments raise serious questions about the possibility of taxing wealth in this way.

[aj] In the next section we discuss the implications of unfunded pension and entitlement liabilities for debt sustainability when the government is not committed to repay and responds to distributional incentives to default.

First, the government would have to sell confiscated capital to raise revenue (in the realistic scenario in which confiscated capital and government outlays involve different goods and services), which would lower the price at which capital goods can be sold. Second, the expectation of future confiscation of capital would not be zero, and to the extent that is positive it would act as a tax on future capital accumulation and capital income. Third, as an implication of the first two arguments, the wealth tax actually looks more like a government default that would seem to necessitate modeling government behavior without commitment (in fact, in a setup without utilization and capital as the only productive factor, the government confiscating some of k_0 is equivalent to defaulting on a fraction of the date-0 debt repayment).

Perhaps because of the above arguments, the history of wealth taxes has not been a happy one. Wealth taxes were discarded by Austria, Denmark, and Germany in 1997, by Finland, Iceland, and Luxembourg in 2006 and by Sweden in 2007. Interestingly, these countries claimed to ditch the wealth tax in efforts to get more revenue, not less. Moreover, implementing wealth taxation faces serious hurdles, particularly for the valuation of assets and for preventing tax evasion. Global financial integration also makes taxing wealth more difficult, because the expectation of potential future confiscation via wealth taxes mentioned above discourages investment and encourages capital flight (see the discussion in Eichengreen, 1989 and the recent experience with "tax inversions" in the United States).

To summarize where the chapter is at this point, we first explored the question of public debt sustainability from the viewpoint of an empirical approach based on the estimation and analysis of fiscal reaction functions. We found that the sufficiency condition for public debt to be sustainable (ie, for IGBC to hold), reflected in a positive conditional response of the primary balance to public debt, cannot be rejected by the data. At the same time, however, there is clear evidence that the fiscal dynamics observed in the aftermath of the recent surge in debt in advanced economies represent a significant structural break in the reaction functions. In plain terms, primary deficits have been too large, and are projected to remain too large, to be in line with the path projected by the reaction functions, and also relative to the fiscal adjustment process observed in previous episodes of large surges in debt.

The main limitation of the empirical approach is that it cannot say much about the macroeconomic effects of multiple fiscal adjustment paths that can restore debt sustainability. To address this issue, this section explored a structural approach that takes a variation of the workhorse two-country Neoclassical dynamic equilibrium model with an explicit fiscal sector. Capacity utilization and a limited tax allowance for depreciation expenses were used to match the observed elasticity of the capital tax base to capital tax changes. Then we calibrated this model to the United States and European data and used it to quantify the effects of unilateral changes in capital and labor taxes aimed at altering the ability of countries to sustain debt. The results suggest striking differences across Europe and the United States. For the United States, the results suggest that changes in capital taxes cannot make the observed increase in debt sustainable, while small increases in labor taxes could. For Europe, the model predicts that the ability of the tax system to make higher debt ratios sustainable is nearly fully exhausted. Capital taxation is highly inefficient and in the decreasing segment of DLCs, so cuts in capital taxes would be needed to restore fiscal solvency. Labor taxes are near the peak of the DLC, and even if increased to the maximum point they fail to increase the present value of the primary balance to make the observed surge in debt sustainable. Moreover, international externalities of capital income taxes are quantitatively large, suggesting that incentives for strategic interaction, and the classic race-to-the-bottom in capital income taxation are nontrivial.

In short, the results from the empirical and the structural approaches to evaluate debt sustainability cast doubt on the presumption that the high debt ratios reached by many advanced economies in the years since 2008 will be fully repaid. To examine debt sustainability allowing for the possibility of nonrepayment, however, we must consider a third approach that relaxes the assumption that the government is committed to repay domestic debt, which is central to the two approaches we have covered. In the next section of this chapter we turn our attention to this issue.

4. DOMESTIC DEFAULT APPROACH

We now examine debt sustainability from the perspective of a framework that abandons the assumption of a government committed to repay domestic debt. The emphasis is on the risk of de-jure, or outright, default on domestic public debt, not the far more studied issues of external sovereign default, which is the subject of another chapter in this Handbook, or de-facto default on domestic debt via inflation. Interest on domestic sovereign default is motivated by the seminal empirical study of Reinhart and Rogoff (2011), which documents episodes of outright default on domestic public debt in a cross-country historical dataset going back to 1750.[ak] Hall and Sargent (2014) describe in detail a similar episode in the process by which the US government handled the management of its debt in the aftermath of the Revolutionary War.

Reinhart and Rogoff noted that the literature has paid little attention to domestic sovereign default, and thus chose to title their paper *The Forgotten History of Domestic Debt*. As we document below, the situation has changed somewhat recently, but relatively speaking the study of domestic government defaults remains largely uncharted territory.

[ak] Reinhart and Rogoff identified 68 outright domestic default episodes, which occurred via mechanisms such as forcible conversions, lower coupon rates, unilateral reductions of principal, and suspensions of payments.

The ongoing European debt crisis also highlights the importance of studying domestic sovereign default, because four features of the crisis (thinking of Europe as a whole) make it resemble more a domestic default than an external default. First, countries in the Eurozone are highly integrated, with the majority of their public debt denominated in their common currency and held by European residents. Hence, a default means, to a large extent, a suspension of payments to "domestic" (ie, European) agents instead of external creditors. Second, domestic public-debt-GDP ratios are high in the Eurozone in general, and very large in the countries at the epicenter of the crisis (Greece, Ireland, Italy, Spain, and Portugal). Third, the Eurozones common currency and common central bank rule out the possibility of individual governments resorting to inflation as a means to lighten their debt burden without an outright default. Fourth, and perhaps most important from the standpoint of the theory proposed in this section, European-wide institutions such as the European Central Bank (ECB) and the European Commission are weighting the interests of both creditors and debtors in assessing the pros and cons of sovereign defaults by individual countries, and creditors and debtors are aware of these institutions concern and of their key role in influencing expectations and default risk.

Table 13 shows that the Eurozone's fiscal crisis has been characterized by rapid increases in public debt ratios and sovereign spreads that coincided with rising government expenditure ratios. The table also shows that debt ownership, as proxied by Gini coefficients of wealth distributions, is unevenly distributed in the seven countries listed, with mean and median Gini coefficients of around two-thirds. The degree of concentration in the ownership of public debt plays a key role in the framework of optimal

Table 13 Euro area: Key fiscal statistics and wealth inequality

	Gov. debt		Gov. exp.		Spreads		
Moment (%)	**Avg.**	**2011**	**Avg.**	**"Crisis peak"**	**Avg.**	**"Crisis peak"**	**Gini Wealth**
France	34.87	62.72	23.40	24.90	0.08	1.04	0.73
Germany	33.34	52.16	18.80	20.00	–	–	0.67
Greece	84.25	133.09	18.40	23.60	0.37	21.00	0.65
Ireland	14.07	64.97	16.10	20.50	0.11	6.99	0.58
Italy	95.46	100.22	19.40	21.40	0.27	3.99	0.61
Portugal	35.21	75.83	20.00	22.10	0.20	9.05	0.67
Spain	39.97	45.60	17.60	21.40	0.13	4.35	0.57
Avg.	48.17	76.37	19.10	21.99	0.22	7.74	0.64
Median	35.21	64.97	18.80	21.40	0.17	5.67	0.65

Note: Author's calculations are based on OECD Statistics, Eurostat, ECSB, and Davies et al. (2009). "Gov. debt" refers to total general government net financial liabilities (avg 1990–2007); "Gov. Exp." corresponds to government purchases in national accounts (avg 2000–07); "Sov spreads" correspond to the difference between interest rates of the given country and Germany for bonds of similar maturity (avg 2000–07). For a given country i, they are computed as $(1 + r^i)/(1 + r^{Ger}) - 1$. "Crisis Peak" refers to the maximum value observed during 2008–12 using data from Eurostat. "Gini wealth" are Gini wealth coefficients for 2000 from Davies, J., Sandstr´om, S., Shorrocks, A., Wolff, E. 2009. The level and distribution of global household wealth. NBER Working Paper 15508, appendix V.

domestic default examined in this section. The framework also predicts that spreads and the probability of default at higher when government outlays are higher.

The model on which this section is based follows the work of D'Erasmo and Mendoza (2013) and D'Erasmo and Mendoza (2014). The goal is to analyze the optimal default and borrowing decisions of a government unable to commit to repay debt placed with domestic creditors in an environment with incomplete markets. The key difference with standard external default models is in that the payoff of the government includes the utility of agents who are government bondholders, as well as nonbondholders. As a result, the main incentive to default is to redistribute resources across these two groups of agents.[al] Default is assumed to be nondiscriminatory (ie, the government cannot discriminate across any of its creditors when it defaults). There is explicit aggregate risk in the form of shocks to government outlays, and also implicit in the form of default risk.

Government bondholders and nonbondholders are modeled with identical CRRA preferences. Default is useful as a vehicle for redistribution across the two, but it also has costs. We explore the case in which there is an exogenous cost in terms of disposable income, similar to the exogenous income costs typical of the external default literature. But there can also be endogenous costs related to the reduced ability to smooth taxation and provide liquidity, and, in long-horizon environments, to the loss of access to government bonds as the asset used for self-insurance.

In this framework, public debt is sustainable when it is supported as part of the equilibrium without commitment. This implies that a particular price and stock of defaultable government bonds are sustainable only if they are consistent with the optimal debt-issuance and default plans of the government, the optimal savings plans of private agents, and the bond market-clearing condition. Sustainable debt thus factors in the risk of default, which implies paying positive risk premia on current debt issuance when future default is possible. Debt becomes unsustainable when default becomes the optimal choice ex post, or is unsustainable ex ante for debt levels that cannot be issued at a positive price (ie, when a given debt issued at t entails a 100% probability of default at t+1).

This model is not necessarily limited to a situation in which private agents hold directly government debt. It is also applicable to situations in which pension funds hold government bonds and retirement accounts are structured as individual accounts, or where the financial sector holds domestic sovereign debt and households hold claims

[al] The model should not be viewed as focusing necessarily on redistribution across the poor and rich, but across agents that hold public debt and those who do not. The two are correlated but need not be the same. For instance, Hall and Sargent (2014) describe how the domestic default after the US Revolutionary War implied redistribution from bondholders in the South to nonbondholders in the North, with both groups generally wealthy. Similarly, in the European debt crisis, a Greek default can be viewed as redistributing from German tax payers to Greek households and not according to their overall wealth.

on the financial sector. Moreover, the general principle that domestic default is driven by government's distributional incentives traded off against exogenous or endogenous default costs applies to more complex environments that include implicit (or contingent) government liabilities due, for example, to expected funding shortfalls in entitlement programs. Default in these cases can take the form of reforms like increasing retirement eligibility ages or imposing income ceilings in eligibility for programs like medicare. For simplicity, however, the quantitative analysis conducted later in this section is calibrated to data that includes only explicit government debt (total general government net financial liabilities as defined in Eurostat).

We develop the argument using the two-period model proposed by D'Erasmo and Mendoza (2013), which highlights the importance of the distributional incentives of default at the expense of setting aside endogenous default costs due to the loss of access to self-insurance assets. D'Erasmo and Mendoza (2014) and Dovis et al. (2014) study the role of distributional incentives to default on domestic debt, and the use of public debt in infinite horizon models with domestic agent heterogeneity. The two differ in that Dovis et al. (2014) assume complete domestic asset markets, which removes the role of public debt as providing social insurance for domestic agents. In addition, they focus on the solution to the Ramsey problem, in which default is not observed along the equilibrium path. D'Erasmo and Mendoza study an economy with incomplete markets, which turns the loss of the vehicle for self-insurance, and the severity of the associated liquidity constraints, into an endogenous cost of default that plays a central role in their results. They also solve for Markov-perfect equilibria in which default is possible as an equilibrium outcome.

The model discussed here is also related to the literature that analyzes the role of public debt as a self-insurance mechanism and a tool for altering consumption dispersion in heterogeneous-agents models without default (eg, Aiyagari and McGrattan (1998), Golosov and Sargent (2012), Azzimonti et al. (2014), Floden (2001) , Heathcote (2005), and Aiyagari et al. (2002)). A recent article by Pouzo and Presno (2014) introduces the possibility of default into models in this class. They study optimal taxation and public debt dynamics in a representative-agent setup similar to Aiyagari et al. (2002) but allowing for default and renegotiation.

The recent interest in domestic sovereign default also includes a strand of literature focusing on the consequences of default on domestic agents, its relation with secondary markets, discriminatory vs nondiscriminatory default, and the role of domestic debt in providing liquidity to the corporate sector (see Guembel and Sussman, 2009, Broner et al., 2010, Broner and Ventura, 2011, Gennaioli et al., 2014, Basu, 2009, Brutti, 2011, Mengus, 2014, and Di Casola and Sichlimiris, 2014). There are also some recent studies motivated by the 2008 financial crisis that focus on the interaction between sovereign debt and domestic financial institutions such as Sosa-Padilla (2012), Bocola (2014), Boz et al. (2014), and Perez (2015).

4.1 Model Structure

Consider a two-period economy $t=0, 1$ inhabited by a continuum of agents with aggregate unit measure. All agents have the same preferences, which are given by:

$$u(c_0)+\beta E[u(c_1)],\ u(c)=\frac{c^{1-\sigma}}{1-\sigma}$$

where $\beta \in (0, 1)$ is the discount factor and c_t for $t=0, 1$ is individual consumption. The utility function $u(\cdot)$ takes the standard CRRA form.

All agents receive a nonstochastic endowment y each period and pay lump-sum taxes τ_t, which are uniform across agents. Taxes and newly issued government debt are used to pay for government consumption g_t and repayment of outstanding government debt. The (exogenous) initial supply of outstanding government bonds at $t=0$ is denoted B_0. Agents differ in their initial wealth position, which is characterized by their holdings of government debt at the beginning of the first period.[am] Given B_0, the initial wealth distribution is defined by a fraction γ of households who are the L-type individuals with initial bond holdings b_0^L, and a fraction $(1-\gamma)$ who are the H-types and hold b_0^H, where $b_0^H=\frac{B_0-\gamma b_0^L}{1-\gamma}\geq b_0^L\geq 0$. This value of b_0^H is the amount consistent with market-clearing in the government bond market at $t=0$, since we are assuming that the debt is entirely held by domestic agents. The initial distribution of wealth is exogenous, but the distribution at the beginning of the second period is endogenously determined by the agents' savings choices of the first period.

The budget constraints of the two types of households in the first period are given by:

$$c_0^i+q_0b_1^i=y+b_0^i-\tau_0 \quad \text{for } i=L,H. \tag{10}$$

Agents collect the payout on their initial holdings of government debt (b_0^i), receive endowment income y, and pay lump-sum taxes τ_0. These net-of-tax resources are used to pay for consumption and purchases of new government bonds b_1^i. Agents are not allowed to take short positions in government bonds, which is equivalent to assuming that bond purchases must satisfy the familiar no-borrowing condition often used in heterogeneous-agents models: $b_1^i\geq 0$.

The budget constraints in the second period differ depending on whether the government defaults or not. If the government repays, the budget constraints take the standard form:

$$c_1^i=y+b_1^i-\tau_1 \quad \text{for } i=L,H. \tag{11}$$

[am] Andreasen et al. (2011), Ferriere (2014), and Jeon and Kabukcuoglu (2014) study environments in which domestic income heterogeneity plays a central role in the determination of external defaults.

If the government defaults, there is no repayment on the outstanding debt, and the agents' budget constraints are:

$$c_1^i = (1-\phi(g_1))y - \tau_1 \quad \text{for } i = L, H. \tag{12}$$

As is standard in the external sovereign default literature, we allow for default to impose an exogenous cost that reduces income by a fraction ϕ. This cost is often modeled as a function of the realization of a stochastic endowment income, but since income is constant in this setup, we model it as a function of the realization of government expenditures in the second period g_1. In particular, the cost is a nonincreasing, step-wise function: $\phi(g_1) \geq 0$, with $\phi'(g_1) \leq 0$ for $g_1 \leq \bar{g}_1$, $\phi'(g_1) = 0$ otherwise, and $\phi''(g_1) = 0$. Hence, $\bar{g}_1$ is a threshold high value of g_1 above which the marginal cost of default is zero. This formulation is analogous to the step-wise default cost as a function of income proposed by Arellano (2008) and now widely used in the external default literature, and it also captures the idea of asymmetric costs of tax collection (see Barro, 1979 and Calvo, 1988). Note, however, that for the model to support equilibria with debt under a utilitarian government all we need is $\phi(g_1) > 0$. The additional structure is useful for the quantitative analysis and for making it easier to compare the model with the standard external default models.[an]

At the beginning of $t=0$, the government has outstanding debt B_0 and can issue one-period, nonstate contingent discount bonds $B_1 \in \mathcal{B} \equiv [0, \infty)$ at the price $q_0 \geq 0$. Each period it collects lump-sum revenues τ_t and pays for outlays g_t. Since g_0 is known at the beginning of the first period, the relevant uncertainty with respect to government expenditures is for g_1, which follows a log-normal distribution $N\left((1-\rho_g)\mu_g + \rho_g \ln(g_0), \frac{\sigma_g^2}{(1-\rho_g^2)}\right)$.[ao] We do not restrict the sign of τ_t, so $\tau_t < 0$ represents lump-sum transfers.[ap]

[an] In external default models, the nonlinear cost makes default more costly in "good" states, which alters default incentives to make default more frequent in "bad" states, and it also contributes to support higher debt levels.

[ao] This is similar to an AR(1) process and allows us to control the correlation between g_0 and g_1 via ρ_g, the mean of the shock via μ_g and the variance of the unpredicted portion via σ_g^2. Note that if $\ln(g_0) = \mu_g$, $g_1 \sim N\left(\mu_g, \frac{\sigma_g^2}{(1-\rho_g^2)}\right)$.

[ap] Some studies in the sovereign debt literature have examined models that include tax and expenditure policies, as well as settings with foreign and domestic lenders, but always maintaining the representative agent assumption (eg, Cuadra et al., 2010; Vasishtha, 2010). More recently Dias et al. (2012) examined the benefits of debt relief from the perspective of a *global* social planner with utilitarian preferences. Also in this literature, Aguiar and Amador (2013) analyze the interaction between public debt, taxes and default risk and Lorenzoni and Werning (2013) study the dynamics of debt and interest rates in a model where default is driven by insolvency and debt issuance driven by a fiscal reaction function.

At equilibrium, the price of debt issued in the first period must be such that the government bond market clears:

$$B_t = \gamma b_t^L + (1-\gamma) b_t^H \quad \text{for } t = 0, 1. \tag{13}$$

This condition is satisfied by construction in period 0. In period 1, however, the price moves endogenously to clear the market.

The government has the option to default at $t = 1$. The default decision is denoted by $d_1 \in \{0, 1\}$ where $d_1 = 0$ implies repayment. The government evaluates the values of repayment and default using welfare weight ω for L −type agents and $1 - \omega$ for H −type agents. This specification encompasses cases in which, for political reasons for example, the welfare weights are biased toward a particular type so $\omega \neq \gamma$ or the case in which the government acts as a utilitarian social planner in which $\omega = \gamma$.[aq] At the moment of default, the government evaluates welfare using the following function:

$$\omega u(c_1^L) + (1-\omega) u(c_1^H).$$

At $t = 0$, the government budget constraint is

$$\tau_0 = g_0 + B_0 - q_0 B_1. \tag{14}$$

The level of taxes in period 1 is determined after the default decision. If the government repays, taxes are set to satisfy the following government budget constraint:

$$\tau_1^{d_1=0} = g_1 + B_1. \tag{15}$$

Notice that, since this is a two-period model, equilibrium requires that there are no outstanding assets at the end of period 1 (ie, $b_2^i = B_2 = 0$ and $q_1 = 0$). If the government defaults, taxes are simply set to pay for government purchases:

$$\tau_1^{d_1=1} = g_1. \tag{16}$$

The analysis of the model's equilibrium proceeds in three stages. First, characterize the households' optimal savings problem and determine their payoff (or value) functions, taking as given the government debt, taxes and default decision. Second, study how optimal government taxes and the default decision are determined. Third, examine the optimal choice of debt issuance that internalizes the outcomes of the first two stages. We characterize these problems as functions of B_1, g_1, γ and ω, keeping the initial conditions (g_0, B_0, b_0^L) as exogenous parameters. Hence, for given γ and ω, we can index the value

[aq] This relates to the literature on political economy and sovereign default, which largely focuses on external default (eg, Amador, 2003, Dixit and Londregan, 2000, D'Erasmo, 2011, Guembel and Sussman, 2009, Hatchondo et al., 2009, and Tabellini, 1991), but includes studies like those of Alesina and Tabellini (1990) and Aghion and Bolton (1990) that focus on political economy aspects of government debt in a closed economy, and the work of Aguiar et al. (2013) on optimal policy in a monetary union subject to self-fulfilling debt crises.

of a household as of $t = 0$, before g_1 is realized, as a function of $\{B_1\}$. Given this, the level of taxes τ_0 is determined by the government budget constraint once the equilibrium bond price q_0 is set. Bond prices are forward looking and depend on the default decision of the government in period 1, which will be given by the decision rule $d(B_1, g_1, \gamma, \omega)$.

4.2 Optimization Problems and Equilibrium

Given B_1, γ, and ω a household with initial debt holdings b_0^i for $i = L, H$ chooses b_1^i by solving this maximization problem:

$$v^i(B_1,\gamma,\omega) = \max_{b_1^i} \left\{u(y + b_0^i - q_0 b_1^i - \tau_0) + \beta E_{g_1}\left[(1-d_1)u(y + b_1^i - \tau_1^{d_1=0}) + d_1 u(y(1-\phi(g_1)) - \tau_1^{d_1=1})\right]\right\}, \tag{17}$$

subject to $b_1^i \geq 0$. The term $E_{g_1}[.]$ represents the expected payoff across the repayment and default states in period 1. Notice in particular that the payoff in case of default does not depend on the level of individual debt holdings (b_1^i), reflecting the fact that the government cannot discriminate across households when it defaults.

A key feature of the above problem is that agents take into account the possibility of default in choosing their optimal bond holdings. The first-order condition, evaluated at the equilibrium level of taxes, yields this Euler equation:

$$u'(c_0^i) \geq \beta(1/q_0)E_{g_1}\left[u'(y - g_1 + b_1^i - B_1)(1 - d_1(B_1,g_1,\gamma))\right], = \text{ if } b_1^i > 0 \tag{18}$$

In states in which, given (B_1, γ, ω), the value of g_1 is such that the government chooses to default ($d_1(B_1, g_1, \gamma, \omega) = 1$), the marginal benefit of an extra unit of debt is zero.[ar] Thus, conditional on B_1, a larger default set (ie, a larger set of values of g_1 such that the government defaults), implies that the expected marginal benefit of an extra unit of savings decreases. As a result, everything else equal, a higher default probability results in a lower demand for government bonds, a lower equilibrium bond price, and higher taxes. This has important redistributive implications, because when choosing the optimal debt issuance, the government will internalize how, by altering the bond supply, it affects the expected probability of default and the equilibrium bond prices. Note also that from the agents' perspective, the default choice $d_1(B_1, g_1, \gamma, \omega)$ is independent of b_1^i.

The above Euler equation is useful for highlighting some important properties of the equilibrium pricing function of bonds:

1. The premium over a world risk-free rate (defined as q_0/β, where $1/\beta$ can be viewed as a hypothetical opportunity cost of funds for an investor, analogous to the role played by the world interest rate in the standard external default model) generally differs from the default probability for two reasons: (a) agents are risk averse, and (b) in the repayment state, agents face higher taxes, whereas in the standard model investors are not

[ar] Utility in the case of default equals $u(y(1 - \phi(g_1)) - g_1)$, which is independent of b_1^i.

taxed to repay the debt. For agents with positive bond holdings, the above optimality condition implies that the premium over the risk-free rate is $E_{g_1}\left[u'(y-g_1+b_1^i-B_1)(1-d_1)/u'(c_0^i)\right]$.

2. If the Euler equation for H –type agents holds with equality (ie, $b_1^H>0$) and L –type agents are *credit constrained* (ie, $b_1^L=0$), the H –type agents are the marginal investor and their Euler equation can be used to derive the equilibrium price.
3. For sufficiently high values of B_1, γ or $1-\omega$ the government chooses $d_1(B_1, g_1, \gamma, \omega)=1$ for all g_1. In these cases, the expected marginal benefit of purchasing government bonds vanishes from the agents' Euler equation, and hence the equilibrium for that B_1 does not exist, since agents would not be willing to buy debt at any finite price.[as] These values of B_1 are therefore unsustainable ex ante (ie, these debt levels cannot be sold at a positive price).

The equilibrium bond pricing functions $q_0(B_1, \gamma, \omega)$, which returns bond prices for which, as long as consumption for all agents is nonnegative and the default probability of the government is less than 1, the following market-clearing condition holds:

$$B_1=\gamma b_1^L(B_1, \gamma, \omega)+(1-\gamma)b_1^H(B_1, \gamma, \omega), \tag{19}$$

where B_1 in the left-hand-side of this expression represents the public bonds supply, and the right-hand-side is the aggregate government bond demand.

As explained earlier, we analyze the government's problem following a backward induction strategy by studying first the default decision problem in the final period $t=1$, followed by the optimal debt issuance choice at $t=0$.

4.2.1 Government Default Decision at t = 1

At $t=1$, the government chooses to default or not by solving this optimization problem:

$$\max_{d\in\{0,1\}}\left\{W_1^{d=0}(B_1, g_1, \gamma, \omega), W_1^{d=1}(g_1, \gamma, \omega)\right\}, \tag{20}$$

where $W_1^{d=0}(B_1, g_1, \gamma, \omega)$ and $W_1^{d=1}(B_1, g_1, \gamma, \omega)$ denote the values of the social welfare function at the beginning of period 1 in the case of repayment and default, respectively. Using the government budget constraint to substitute for $\tau_1^{d=0}$ and $\tau_1^{d=1}$, the government's payoffs can be expressed as:

$$W_1^{d=0}(B_1, g_1, \gamma, \omega)=\omega u(y-g_1+b_1^L-B_1)+(1-\omega)u(y-g_1+b_1^H-B_1) \tag{21}$$

and

$$W_1^{d=1}(g_1, \gamma, \omega)=u(y(1-\phi(g_1))-g_1). \tag{22}$$

[as] This result is similar to the result in standard models of external default showing that rationing emerges at t for debt levels so high that the government would choose default at all possible income realizations in $t+1$.

Combining these payoff functions, if follows that the government defaults if this condition holds:

$$\omega\left[u(y-g_1+\overbrace{(b_1^L-B_1)}^{\leq 0})-u(y(1-\phi(g_1))-g_1)\right]$$
$$+(1-\omega)\left[u(y-g_1+\overbrace{(b_1^H-B_1)}^{\geq 0})-u(y(1-\phi(g_1))-g_1)\right]\leq 0 \tag{23}$$

Notice that all agents forego g_1 of their income to government absorption regardless of the default choice. Moreover, debt repayment reduces consumption and welfare of L types and rises them for H types, whereas default implies the same consumption and utility for both types of agents.

The distributional effects of a default are implicit in condition (23). Given that debt repayment affects the cash-in-hand for consumption of L and H types according to $(b_1^L - B_1) \leq 0$ and $(b_1^H - B_1) \geq 0$, respectively, it follows that, for a given B_1, the payoff under repayment allocates (weakly) lower welfare to L agents and higher to H agents, and that the gap between the two is larger the larger is B_1. Moreover, since the default payoffs are the same for both types of agents, this is also true of the *difference* in welfare under repayment vs default: It is higher for H agents than for L agents and it gets larger as B_1 rises. To induce default, however, it is necessary not only that L agents have a smaller difference in the payoffs of repayment vs default, but that the difference is negative (ie, they must attain lower welfare under repayment than under default), which requires $B_1 > b_1^L + y\phi(g_1)$. This also implies that taxes under repayment need to be necessarily larger than under default, since $\tau_1^{d=0} - \tau_1^{d=1} = B_1$.

We can illustrate the distributional mechanism driving the default decision by comparing the utility levels associated with the consumption allocations of the default and repayment states with those that would be socially efficient. To this end, it is helpful to express the values of hypothetical optimal private debt holdings in period 1 as $b_1^L = B_1 - \epsilon$ and $b_1^H(\gamma) = B_1 + \frac{\gamma}{1-\gamma}\epsilon$, for some $\epsilon \in [0, B_1]$. That is, ϵ represents a given hypothetical decentralized allocation of debt holdings across agents.[at] Consumption allocations under repayment would therefore be $c_1^L(\epsilon) = y - g_1 - \epsilon$ and $c_1^H(\gamma,\epsilon) = y - g_1 + \frac{\gamma}{1-\gamma}\epsilon$, so ϵ also determines the decentralized consumption dispersion.

[at] We take ϵ as given at this point because it helps us explain the intuition behind the distributional default incentives of the government, but ϵ is an equilibrium outcome solved for later on. Also, ϵ must be nonnegative, otherwise H types would be the nonbondholders.

The government payoff under repayment can be rewritten as:

$$W^{d=0}(\epsilon, g_1, \gamma, \omega) = \omega u(y - g_1 + \epsilon) + (1-\omega) u\left(y - g_1 + \frac{\gamma}{1-\gamma}\epsilon\right).$$

The efficient dispersion of consumption that the social planner would choose is characterized by the value of ϵ^{SP} that maximizes social welfare under repayment. In the particular case of $\omega = \gamma$ (ie, when the government is utilitarian and uses welfare weights that match the wealth distribution), ϵ^{SP} satisfies this first-order condition:

$$u'\left(y - g_1 + \frac{\gamma}{1-\gamma}\epsilon^{SP}\right) = u'\left(y - g_1 - \epsilon^{SP}\right). \tag{24}$$

Hence, the efficient allocations are characterized by zero consumption dispersion, because equal marginal utilities imply $c^{L,SP} = c^{H,SP} = y - g_1$, which is attained with $\epsilon^{SP} = 0$.

Continuing under the utilitarian government assumption ($\omega = \gamma$), consider now the government's default decision when default is costless ($\phi(g_1) = 0$). Given that the only policy instruments the government can use, other than the default decision, are nonstate contingent debt and lump-sum taxes, it is straightforward to show that default will always be optimal. This is because default supports the socially efficient allocations in the decentralized equilibrium (ie, it yields zero consumption dispersion with consumption levels $c^L = c^H = y - g_1$). This outcome is invariant to the values of B_1, g_1, γ and ϵ (over their relevant ranges). This result also implies, however, that in this model a utilitarian government without default costs can never sustain debt.

The above scenario is depicted in Fig. 14, which plots the social welfare function under repayment as a function of ϵ as the bell-shaped curve, and the social welfare under default (which is independent of ϵ), as the black dashed line. Clearly, the maximum welfare under repayment is attained when $\epsilon = 0$ which is also the efficient amount of consumption dispersion ϵ^{SP}. Moreover, since the relevant range of consumption dispersion is $\epsilon > 0$, welfare under repayment is decreasing in ϵ over the relevant range.

These results can be summarized as follows:

Result 1. *If $\phi(g_1) = 0$ for all g_1 and $\omega = \gamma$, then for any $\gamma \in (0, 1)$ and any (B_1, g_1), the social value of repayment $W^{d=0}(B_1, g_1, \gamma)$ is decreasing in ϵ and attains its maximum at the socially efficient point $\epsilon^{SP} = 0$ (ie, when welfare equals $u(y - g_1)$). Hence, default is always optimal for any given decentralized consumption dispersion $\epsilon > 0$.*

The outcome is very different when default is costly. With $\phi(g_1) > 0$, default still yields zero consumption dispersion, but at lower levels of consumption and therefore utility,

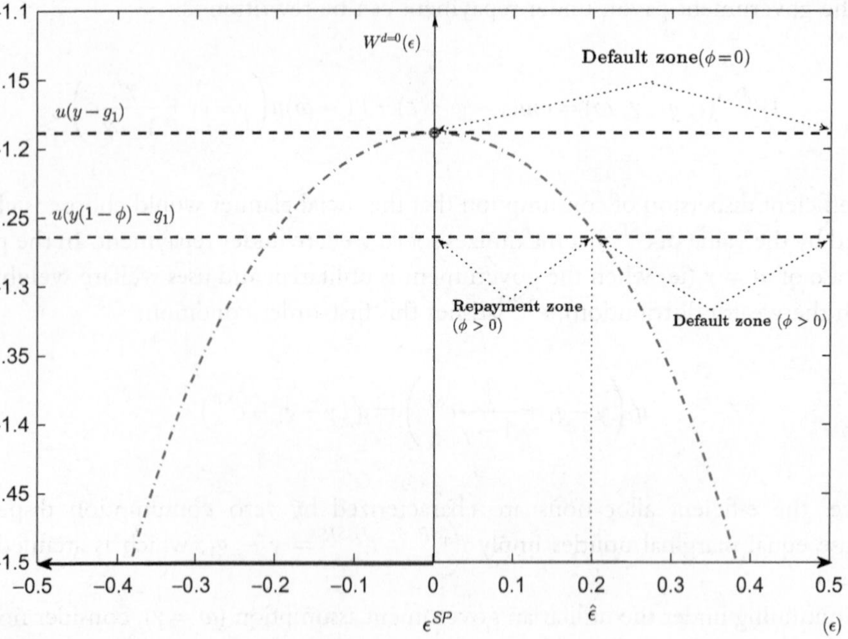

Fig. 14 Default decision and consumption dispersion.

since consumption allocations under default are $c^L = c^H = (1 - \phi(g_1))y - g_1$. This does not alter the result that the social optimum is $\epsilon^{SP} = 0$, but what changes is that default can no longer support the socially efficient consumption allocations. Instead, there is now a threshold amount of consumption dispersion in the decentralized equilibrium, $\hat{\epsilon}(\gamma)$, which varies with γ and such that for $\epsilon \geq \hat{\epsilon}(\gamma)$ default is again optimal, but for lower ϵ repayment is now optimal. This is because when ϵ is below the threshold, repayment produces a level of social welfare higher than under default.

Fig. 14 also illustrates this scenario. The default cost lowers the common level of utility of both types of agents, and hence of social welfare, in the default state (shown in the figure as the blue dashed line), and $\hat{\epsilon}(\gamma)$ is determined where social welfare under repayment and under default intersect. If the decentralized consumption dispersion with the debt market functioning (ϵ) is between 0 and less than $\hat{\epsilon}(\gamma)$ then it is optimal for the government to repay. Intuitively, if consumption dispersion is not too large, the government prefers to repay because the income cost imposed on agents to remove consumption dispersion under default is too large. Moreover, as γ rises the domain of $W_1^{d=0}$ narrows, and thus $\hat{\epsilon}(\gamma)$ falls and the interval of decentralized consumption dispersions that supports repayment narrows. This is natural because a higher γ causes the planner to weight more L-types in the social welfare function, which are agents with weakly lower utility in the repayment state.

These results can be summarized as follows:

Result 2. *If $\phi(g_1) > 0$, then for any $\gamma \in (0, 1)$ and any (B_1, g_1), there is a threshold value of consumption dispersion $\hat{\epsilon}(\gamma)$ such that the payoffs of repayment and default are equal: $W^{d=0}(B_1, g_1, \gamma) = u(y(1-\phi(g_1)) - g_1)$. The government repays if $\epsilon < \hat{\epsilon}(\gamma)$ and defaults otherwise. Moreover, $\hat{\epsilon}(\gamma)$ is decreasing in γ.*

Introducing a bias in the welfare function of the government (relative to utilitarian social welfare) can result in repayment being optimal even without default costs, which provides for an alternative way to sustain debt subject to default risk. Assuming $\phi(g_1) = 0$, there are two possible scenarios depending on the relative size of γ and ω. First, if $\omega > \gamma$, the planner again always chooses default as in the setup with $\omega = \gamma$. This is because for any $\epsilon > 0$, the decentralized consumption allocations feature $c^H > c^L$, while the planner's optimal consumption dispersion requires $c^H \leq c^L$, and hence ϵ^{SP} cannot be implemented. Default brings the planner the closest it can get to the payoff associated with ϵ^{SP} and hence it is always chosen.

In the second scenario $\omega < \gamma$, which means that the government's bias assigns more (less) weight to H (L) types than the fraction of each type of agents that actually exists. In this case, the model can support equilibria with debt even without default costs. In particular, there is a threshold consumption dispersion $\hat{\epsilon}$ such that default is optimal for $\epsilon \geq \hat{\epsilon}$, where $\hat{\epsilon}$ is the value of ϵ at which $W_1^{d=0}(\epsilon, g_1, \gamma, \omega)$ and $W_1^{d=1}(g_1)$ intersect. For $\epsilon < \hat{\epsilon}$, repayment is preferable because $W_1^{d=0}(\epsilon, g_1, \gamma, \omega) > W_1^{d=0}(g_1)$. Thus, without default costs, equilibria for which repayment is optimal require two conditions: (a) that the government's bias favors bond holders ($\omega < \gamma$), *and* (b) that the debt holdings chosen by private agents do not produce consumption dispersion in excess of $\hat{\epsilon}$.

Fig. 15 illustrates the outcomes just described. This figure plots $W_1^{d=0}(\epsilon, g_1, \gamma, \omega)$ for $\omega \gtrless \gamma$. The planner's default payoff and the values of ϵ^{SP} for $\omega \gtrless \gamma$ are also identified in the plot. The vertical intercept of $W_1^{d=0}(\epsilon, g_1, \gamma, \omega)$ is always $W^{d=1}(g_1)$ for any values of ω and γ, because when $\epsilon = 0$ there is zero consumption dispersion and that is also the outcome under default. In addition, the bell-shaped form of $W_1^{d=0}(\epsilon, g_1, \gamma, \omega)$ follows from $u'(.) > 0, u''(.) < 0$.[au]

Take first the case with $\omega > \gamma$. In this case, the planner's payoff under repayment is the dotted bell curve. Here, $\epsilon^{SP} < 0$, because the optimality condition implies that the planner's optimal choice features $c^L > c^H$. Since default is the only instrument available to the government, however, these consumption allocations are not feasible, and by choosing

[au] Note in particular that $\frac{\partial W_1^{d=0}(\epsilon, g_1, \gamma, \omega)}{\partial \epsilon} \gtrless 0 \Leftrightarrow \frac{u'(c^H(\epsilon))}{u'(c^L(\epsilon)}) \gtrless \left(\frac{\omega}{\gamma}\right)\left(\frac{1-\gamma}{1-\omega}\right)$. Hence, the planner's payoff is increasing (decreasing) at values of ϵ that support sufficiently low (high) consumption dispersion so that $\frac{u'(c^H(\epsilon))}{u'(c^L(\epsilon))}$ is above (below) $\left(\frac{\omega}{\gamma}\right)\left(\frac{1-\gamma}{1-\omega}\right)$.

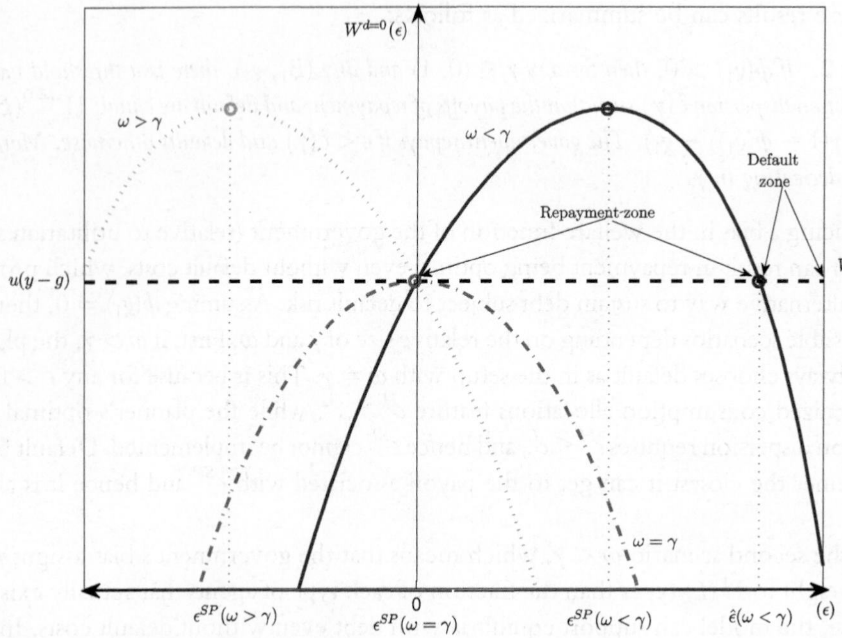

Fig. 15 Default decision with nonutilitarian planner ($\phi = 0$).

default the government attains $W^{d=1}$, which is the highest feasible government payoff for any $\epsilon \geq 0$. In contrast, in the case with $\omega = \gamma$, for which the planner's payoff function is the dashed bell curve, the planner chooses $\epsilon^{SP} = 0$, and default attains exactly the same payoff, so default is chosen. In short, if $\omega \geq \gamma$, the government always defaults for any decentralized distribution of debt holdings represented by $\epsilon > 0$, and thus equilibria with debt cannot be supported.

When $\omega < \gamma$, the planner's payoff is the continuous curve. The intersection of the downward-sloping segment of $W_1^{d=0}(\epsilon, g_1, \gamma, \omega)$ with $W^{d=1}$ determines the default threshold $\hat{\epsilon}$ such that default is optimal only in the *default zone* where $\epsilon \geq \hat{\epsilon}$. Default is still a second-best policy for the planner, because with it the planner cannot attain $W^{d=0}(\epsilon^{SP})$, it just gets the closest it can get. In contrast, the choice of repayment is preferable in the *repayment zone* where $\epsilon < \hat{\epsilon}$,, because in this zone $W_1^{d=0}(\epsilon, g_1, \gamma, \omega) > W^{d=1}(g_1)$.

Adding default costs to this political bias setup ($\phi(g_1) > 0$) makes it possible to support repayment equilibria even when $\omega \geq \gamma$. As Fig. 16 shows, with default costs there are threshold values of consumption dispersion, $\hat{\epsilon}$, separating repayment from default zones for $\omega \lesseqgtr \gamma$.

It is also evident in Fig. 16 that the range of values of ϵ for which repayment is chosen widens asγ rises relative to ω. Thus, when default is costly, equilibria with repayment require only the condition that the debt holdings chosen by private agents, which are implicit in ϵ, do not produce consumption dispersion larger than the value of $\hat{\epsilon}$ associated

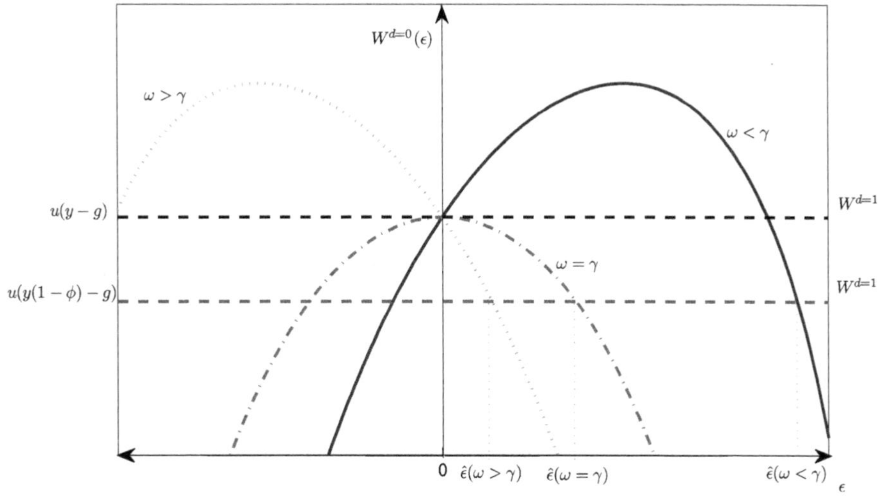

Fig. 16 Default decision with nonutilitarian planner when $\phi(g_1) > 0$.

with a given (ω, γ) pair. Intuitively, the consumption of H-type agents must not exceed that of L-type agents by more than what $\hat{\epsilon}$ allows, because otherwise default is optimal.

The fact that a government biased in favor of bond holders can find it optimally to repay may seem unsurprising. As we argue later, however, in fact governments with this bias can be an endogenous outcome of majority voting if the fraction of agents that are nonbondholders is sufficiently large. This occurs when these agents are liquidity constrained (ie, hitting the no-borrowing constraint), because in this case they prefer that the government favors bondholders so that it can sustain higher debt levels because public debt provides them with liquidity.

4.2.2 Government Debt Issuance Decision at t = 0

We are now in a position to study how the government chooses the optimal amount of debt to issue in the initial period. These are the model's predicted sustainable debt levels ex ante, some of which will be optimally defaulted on ex post, depending on the realization of g_1 in the second period. Both the government and the private sector are aware of this, so the debt levels that can be issued at equilibrium in the first period are traded at prices that can carry a default risk premium, which will be the case if for a given debt stock there are some values of g_1 for which default is the optimal choice in the second period.

The government's optimization problem is easier to understand if we first illustrate how public debt serves as a tool for altering consumption dispersion across agents both within a period and across periods. In particular, consumption dispersion in each period and repayment state is given by these conditions:

$$c_0^H - c_0^L = \frac{1}{1-\gamma}[B_0 - q_0(B_1,\gamma,\omega)B_1],$$

$$c_1^{H,d=0} - c_1^{L,d=0} = \frac{1}{1-\gamma}B_1,$$

$$c_1^{H,d=1} - c_1^{L,d=1} = 0.$$

These expressions make it clear that, given B_0, issuing at least some debt ($B_1 > 0$) reduces consumption dispersion at $t = 0$ compared with no debt ($B_1 = 0$), but increases it at $t = 1$ if the government repays (ie, $d = 0$). Moreover, the use of debt as tool for redistribution of consumption at $t = 0$ is hampered by a Laffer curve relationship just like the distortionary taxes of the previous section. In this case, it takes the form of the debt Laffer curve familiar from the external default literature, which is defined by the mapping from an amount of debt issued B_1 to the resources the government acquires with that amount of borrowing, $q_0(B_1, \gamma, \omega)B_1$. This mapping behaves like a Laffer curve because higher debt issuance carries a higher default risk, which reduces the price of the debt. Near zero debt the default risk is also zero so higher debt increases resources for the government, at very high debt near the region at which debt is unsustainable ex ante, higher debt reduces resources because the price falls proportionally much more than the debt rises, and in between we obtain the bell-shaped Laffer curve relationship. It follows then from this Laffer curve that, starting from $B_1 = 0$, consumption dispersion at $t = 0$ first falls as B_1 increases, but there is a critical positive value of B_1 beyond which it becomes an increasing function of debt.

At $t = 0$, the government chooses its debt policy internalizing the above consumption dispersion effects, including the debt Laffer curve affecting date-0 dispersion, and their implications for social welfare. Formally, the government chooses B_1 so as to maximize the "indirect" social welfare function:

$$W_0(\gamma,\omega) = \max_{B_1} \left\{\omega v^L(B_1,\gamma,\omega) + (1-\omega)v^H(B_1,\gamma,\omega)\right\}. \tag{25}$$

where v^L and v^H are the private agents' value functions obtained from solving the problems defined in the Bellman equation (17) taking into account the government budget constraints and the equilibrium pricing function of bonds.

Focusing on the case with utilitarian government ($\omega = \gamma$), we can gain some intuition about the solution of this maximization problem from its first-order condition (assuming that the relevant functions are differentiable):

$$u'(c_0^H) = u'(c_0^L) + \frac{\eta}{q_0(B_1,\gamma,\omega)\gamma}\{\beta E_{g_1}[\Delta d \Delta W_1] + \gamma\mu^L\}$$

where

$$\eta \equiv q_0(B_1, \gamma, \omega)/\left(q_0'(B_1, \gamma, \omega)B_1\right) < 0,$$

$$\Delta d \equiv d(B_1 + \delta, g_1, \gamma) - d(B_1, g_1, \gamma) \geq 0, \quad \text{for } \delta > 0 \text{ small},$$

$$\Delta W_1 \equiv W_1^{d=1}(g_1, \gamma) - W_1^{d=0}(B_1, g_1, \gamma) \geq 0,$$

$$\mu^L \equiv q_0(B_1, \gamma, \omega)u'(c_0^L) - \beta E_{g_1}\left[(1-d^1)u'(c_1^L)\right] > 0.$$

In these expressions, η is the price elasticity of the demand for government bonds, $\Delta d \Delta W_1$ represents the marginal distributional benefit of a default, and μ^L is the shadow value of the borrowing constraint when it binds for L-type agents.

If both types of agents could be unconstrained in their savings decisions, so that $\mu_L = 0$, and if there is no change in the risk of default (or assuming commitment to remove default risk entirely), so that $E_{g_1}[\Delta d \Delta W_1] = 0$, then the optimality condition simplifies to:

$$u'(c_0^H) = u'(c_0^L).$$

Hence, in this case the social planner would want to issue debt so as to equalize marginal utilities of consumption across agents at date 0, which requires simply setting B_1 to satisfy $q_0(B_1, \gamma, \omega)B_1 = B_0$. If it is the case that L-types are constrained (ie, $\mu_L > 0$), and still assuming no change in default risk or a government committed to repay, the optimality condition becomes:

$$u'(c_0^H) = u'(c_0^L) + \frac{\eta \mu^L}{q_0(B_1, \gamma, \omega)}.$$

Since $\eta < 0$, this result implies $c_0^L < c_0^H$, because $u'(c_0^L) > u'(c_0^H)$. Thus, even with unchanged default risk or no default risk at all, the government's debt choice sets B_1 as needed to maintain an optimal, positive level of consumption dispersion, which is the one that supports an excess in marginal utility of L-type agents relative to H-type agents equal to $\frac{\eta \mu^L}{q_0(B_1, \gamma, \omega)}$. Moreover, since optimal consumption dispersion is positive, we can also ascertain that $B_0 > q_0(B_1, \gamma, \omega)B_1$, which using the government budget constraint implies that the government runs a primary surplus at $t = 0$. The government borrows resources, but less than it would need in order to eliminate all consumption dispersion (which requires zero primary balance).

The intuition for the optimality of issuing debt can be presented in terms of tax smoothing and savings: Date-0 consumption dispersion without debt issuance would be $B_0/(1 - \gamma)$, but this is more dispersion than what the government finds optimal, because by choosing $B_1 > 0$ the government provides tax smoothing (ie, reduces date-0 taxes) for everyone, which in particular eases the L-type agents credit constraint, and provides also a desired vehicle of savings for H types. Thus, positive debt increases consumption of L types (since $c_0^L = y - g_0 - B_0 + q_0(B_1,\gamma,\omega)B_1$), and reduces consumption of H types (since $c_0^H = y - g_0 + \left(\frac{\gamma}{1-\gamma}\right)(B_0 - q_0(B_1,\gamma,\omega)B_1)$). But issuing debt (assuming repayment) also increases consumption dispersion a $t = 1$, since debt is then paid with higher taxes on all agents, while H agents collect also the debt repayment. Thus, the debt is being chosen optimally to trade off the social costs and benefits of reducing (increasing) date-0 consumption and increasing (reducing) date-1 consumption for agents who are bondholders (nonbondholders). In doing so, the government internalizes the debt Laffer curve and the fact that additional debt lowers the price of bonds and helps reduce μ^L, which in turn reduces the government's optimal consumption dispersion.[av]

In the presence of default risk and if default risk changes near the optimal debt choice, the term $E_{g_1}[\Delta d \Delta W_1]$ enters in the government's optimality condition with a positive sign, which means the optimal gap in the date-0 marginal utilities across agents widens even more. Hence, the government's optimal choice of consumption dispersion for $t = 0$ is greater than without default risk, and the expected dispersion for $t = 1$ is lower, because in some states of the world the government will choose to default and consumption dispersion would then drop to zero. This also suggests that the government chooses a lower value of B_1 than in the absence of default risk, since date-0 consumptions are further apart. Moreover, the debt Laffer curve now plays a central role in the government's weakened incentives to borrow, because as default risk rises the price of bonds drops to zero faster and the resources available to reduce date-0 consumption dispersion peak at lower debt levels. In short, default risk reduces the government's ability to use nonstate-contingent debt in order to reduce consumption dispersion.

In summary, the more constrained the L −types agents are (higher μ^L) or the higher the expected distributional benefit of a default (higher $E_{g_1}[\Delta d \Delta W_1]$), the larger the level of debt the government finds optimal to issue. Both of these mechanisms operate as pecuniary externalities: They matter only because the government debt choice can alter the equilibrium price of bonds which is taken as given by private agents.

For given values of γ and ω, a *Competitive Equilibrium with Optimal Debt and Default Policies* is a pair of value functions $v^i(B_1, \gamma, \omega)$ and decision rules $b^i(B_1, \gamma, \omega)$ for $i = L,H$, a government bond pricing function $q_0(B_1, \gamma, \omega)$ and a set of government policy functions $\tau_0(B_1, \gamma, \omega)$, $\tau_1^{d\in\{0,1\}}(B_1, g_1, \gamma, \omega)$, $d(B_1, g_1, \gamma, \omega)$, $B_1(\gamma, \omega)$ such that:

1. Given the pricing function and government policy functions, $v^i(B_1, \gamma, \omega)$ and $b_1^i(B_1, \gamma, \omega)$ solve the households' problem.
2. $q_0(B_1, \gamma, \omega)$ satisfies the market-clearing condition of the bond market (equation (19)).
3. The government default decision $d(B_1, g_1, \gamma, \omega)$ solves problem (20).

[av] Note, however, that without default risk the Laffer curve has less curvature than with default risk, because $q_0^{ND}(B_1,\gamma) \geqq q_0(B_1,\gamma)$.

4. Taxes $\tau_0(B_1, \gamma, \omega)$ and $\tau_1^d(B_1, g_1, \gamma, \omega)$ are consistent with the government budget constraints.
5. The government debt policy $B_1(\gamma, \omega)$ solves problem (25).

4.3 Quantitative Analysis

We study the quantitative predictions of the model using a calibration based on European data. Since the model is simple, the goal is not to match closely the observed dynamics of debt and risk premia in Europe, but to show that a reasonable set of parameter values can support an equilibrium in which sustainable debt subject to default risk exists.[aw] We also use this numerical analysis to study show the dispersion of initial wealth and the bias in government welfare affect sustainable debt.

4.3.1 Calibration

The model is calibrated to annual frequency, and most of the parameter values are set to match moments computed using European data. The parameter values that need to be set are the subjective discount factor β, the coefficient of relative risk aversion σ, the moments of the stochastic process of government expenditures $\{\mu_g, \rho_g, \sigma_g\}$, the initial levels of government debt and expenditures (B_0, g_0), the level of income y, the initial wealth of $L-$type agents b_0^L and the default cost function $\phi(g_1)$. The calibrated parameter values are summarized in Table 14. We evaluate equilibrium outcomes for values of γ and ω in the [0,1] interval. Data for the United States and Europe documented in D'Erasmo and Mendoza (2013) suggest that the empirically relevant range for γ is [0.55,0.85]. Hence, when taking a stance on a particular value of γ is useful we use $\gamma = 0.7$, which is the mid point of the plausible range.

The preference parameters are set to standard values: $\beta = 0.96$, $\sigma = 1$. We also assume for simplicity that $L-$types start with zero wealth, $b_0^L = 0$.[ax] This and the other calibration parameters result in savings plans such that L-type agents are credit constrained, and hence $b_1^L = 0$.

We estimate an AR(1) process for government expenditures-GDP ratio (in logs) for France, Germany, Greece, Ireland, Italy, Spain and Portugal and set $\{\mu_g, \rho_g, \sigma_g\}$ to the cross-country averages of the corresponding estimates. This results in the following

[aw] We solve the model following a backward-recursive strategy analogous to the one used in the theoretical analysis. First, for each pair $\{\gamma, \omega\}$ and taking as given B_1, we solve for the equilibrium price and default functions by iterating on $\{d_1, q_0, b_1^i\}$. Then, in the second stage we complete the solution of the equilibrium by finding the optimal choice of B_1 that solves the government's date-0 optimization problem (25). As explained earlier, for given values of B_1, γ and ω an equilibrium with debt will not exist if either the government finds it optimal to default on B_1 for all realizations of g_1 or if at the given B_1 the consumption of L types is nonpositive.

[ax] $\sigma = 1$ and $b_0^L = 0$ are also useful because under these assumptions we can obtain closed-form solutions and establish some results analytically.

Table 14 Model parameters

Parameter		Value
Discount factor	β	0.96
Risk aversion	σ	1.00
Avg. Income	γ	0.79
Low household wealth	b_0^L	0.00
Avg. gov. consumption	μ_g	0.18
Autocorrel. G	ρ_g	0.88
Std. dev. error	σ_g	0.017
Initial gov. debt	B_0	0.79
Output cost default	ϕ_0	0.02

Note: Government expenditures, income, and debt values are derived using Eurostat data for France, Germany, Greece, Ireland, Italy, Spain, and Portugal.

values $\mu_g = 0.1812$, $\rho_g = 0.8802$ and $\sigma_e = 0.017$. We set $g_0 = \mu_g$ and use the quadrature method proposed by Tauchen (1986) with 45 nodes in $G_1 \equiv \{\underline{g}_1, \ldots, \bar{g}_1\}$ to generate the realizations and transition probabilities of g_1.

Average income y is calibrated such that the model's aggregate resource constraint is consistent with the data when GDP is normalized to one. This implies that the value of the agents' aggregate endowment must equal GDP net of fixed capital investment and net exports, since the latter two are not modeled. The average for the period 1970–2012 for the same set of countries used to estimate the g_1 process implies $y = 0.7883$.[ay]

We set the initial debt level $B_0 = 0.79$ so that at the maximum observed level of inequality in the data, $\gamma = 0.85$, there is at least one feasible level of B_1 when $\omega = \gamma$. We assume that the default cost takes the following form: $\phi(g_1) = \phi_0 + (\bar{g} - g_1)/y$, where $\bar{g}$ is calibrated to represent an "unusually large" realization of g_1 set equal to the largest realization in the Markov process of government expenditures, which is in turn set equal to 3 standard deviations from the mean (in logs).[az]

We calibrate ϕ_0 to match an estimate of the observed frequency of *domestic* defaults. According to Reinhart and Rogoff (2011), historically, domestic defaults are about 1/4 as frequent as external defaults (68 domestic vs 250 external in their data since 1750). Since the probability of an external default has been estimated in the range of 3–5% (see, for example, Arellano, 2008), the probability of a domestic default is about 1%. The model is close to this default frequency on average when solved over the empirically relevant

[ay] Note also that under this calibration of y and the Markov process of g_1, the gap $y - g_1$ is always positive, even for $g_1 = \bar{g}_1$, which in turn guarantees $c_1^H > 0$ in all repayment states.

[az] This cost function shares a key feature of the default cost functions widely used in the external default literature to align default incentives so as to support higher debt ratios and trigger default during recessions (see Arellano, 2008 and Mendoza and Yue, 2012): The default cost is an *increasing* function of disposable income $(y - g_1)$. In addition, this formulation ensures that the agents' consumption during a default never goes above a given threshold.

range of γ's ($\gamma \in [0.55,0.85]$) if we set $\phi_0 = 0.02$. Note, however, that the calibration of ϕ_0 and B_0 to match their corresponding targets needs to be done jointly by repeatedly solving the model until both targets are well approximated.

4.3.2 Utilitarian Government ($\omega=\gamma$)

We study first a set of results obtained under the assumption $\omega = \gamma$, because the utilitarian government is a natural benchmark. Since the default decision of the government derives from the agents' utility under the repayment and default alternatives at $t = 1$, it is useful to map the ordinal utility measures into cardinal measures by computing "individual welfare gains of default," which are standard consumption-equivalent values that equalize utility under default and repayment. Given the CRRA functional form, the individual welfare gains of default reduce simply to the percent changes in consumption across the default and no-default states of each agent at $t = 1$:

$$\alpha^i(B_1, g_1, \gamma) = \frac{c_1^{i,d=1}(B_1, g_1, \gamma)}{c_1^{i,d=0}(B_1, g_1, \gamma)} - 1 = \frac{(1-\phi(g_1))y - g_1}{y - g_1 + b_1^i - B_1} - 1$$

A positive (negative) value of $\alpha^i(B_1, g_1, \gamma)$ implies that agent i prefers government default (repayment) by an amount equivalent to an increase (cut) of $\alpha^i(\cdot)$ percent in consumption. The individual welfare gains of default are aggregated using γ to obtain the utilitarian representation of the social welfare gain of default:

$$\overline{\alpha}(B_1, g_1, \gamma) = \gamma \alpha^L(B_1, g_1, \gamma) + (1-\gamma)\alpha^H(B_1, g_1, \gamma).$$

A positive value indicates that default induces a social welfare gain and a negative value a loss.

Fig. 17 shows two intensity plots of the social welfare gain of default for the ranges of values of B_1 and γ in the vertical and horizontal axes, respectively. Panel (A) is for a low value of government purchases, $\underline{g}_1$, set 3 standard deviations below μ_g, and panel (B) is for a high value $\bar{g}_1$ set 3 standard deviations above μ_g. "No Equilibrium Zone", represent values of (B_1,γ) for which the debt market collapses and no equilibrium exists.[ba]

The area in which the social welfare gains of default are well defined in these intensity plots illustrates two of the key mechanisms driving the government's distributional incentives to default: First, fixing γ, the welfare gain of default is higher at higher levels of debt, or conversely the gain of repayment is lower. Second, keeping B_1 constant, the welfare gain of default is also increasing in γ (ie, higher wealth concentration increases

[ba] Note that to determine if $c_0^L \leq 0$ at some (B_1, γ) we also need $q_0(B_1, \gamma)$, since combining the budget constraints of the L types and the government yields $c_0^L = y - g_0 - B_0 + q_0 B_1$. Hence, to evaluate this condition we take the given B_1 and use the H-types Euler equation and the market clearing condition to solve for $q_0(B_1, \gamma, \omega)$, and then determine if $y - g_0 - B_0 + q_0 B_1 \leq 0$, if this is true, then (B_1, γ) is in the lower no-equilibrium zone.

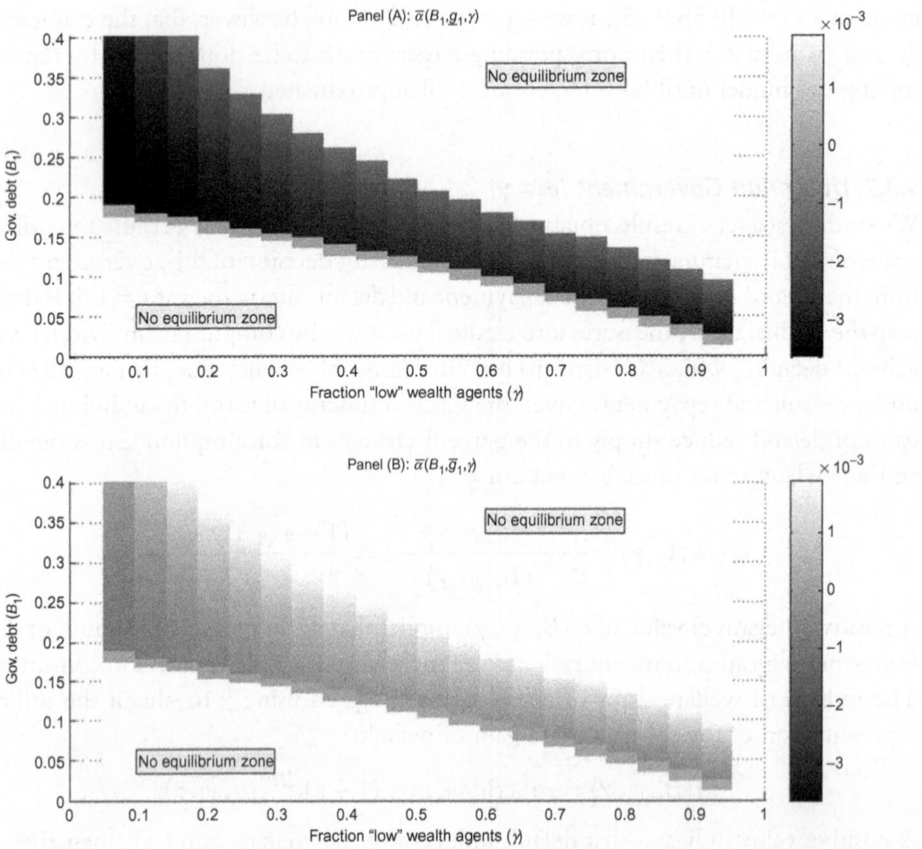

Fig. 17 Social welfare gains of default $\overline{\alpha}(B_1, g_1, \gamma)$. *Note:* The intensity of the color or shading in these plots indicates the magnitude of the welfare gain according to the legend shown to the right of the plots. The regions shown in white and marked as "no equilibrium zone," represent values of (B_1, γ) for which the debt market collapses and no equilibrium exists.

the welfare gain of default). This implies that lower levels of wealth dispersion are sufficient to trigger default at higher levels of debt.[bb] For example, for a debt ratio of 20% of GDP ($B_1 = 0.20$) and $g_1 = \overline{g}_1$, social welfare is higher under repayment if $0 \leq \gamma \leq 0.25$ but it becomes higher under default if $0.25 < \gamma \leq 0.6$, and for higher γ there is no equilibrium because the government prefers default not only for $g_1 = \overline{g}_1$ but for all possible g_1. If instead the debt is 40% of GDP, then social welfare is higher under default for all the values of γ for which an equilibrium exists.

[bb] Note that the cross-sectional variance of initial debt holdings is given by $Var(b) = B^2 \frac{\gamma}{1-\gamma}$ when $b_0^L = 0$. This implies that the cross-sectional coefficient of variation is equal to $CV(b) = \frac{\gamma}{1-\gamma}$, which is increasing in γ for $\gamma \leq 1/2$.

The two panels in Fig. 17 differ in that panel (B) displays a well-defined transition from a region in which repayment is socially optimal ($\overline{\alpha}(B_1,g_1,\gamma) < 0$) to one where default is optimal ($\overline{\alpha}(B_1,g_1,\gamma) > 0$) but in panel (A) the social welfare gain of default is never positive, so repayment is always optimal. This reflects the fact that higher g_1 also weakens the incentives to repay. In the "No Equilibrium Zone" in the upper right, there is no equilibrium because at the given γ the government chooses to default on the given B_1 for all values of g_1. In the "No Equilibrium Zone" in the lower left, there is no equilibrium because the given (B_1, γ) would yield $c_0^L \leq 0$, and so the government would not supply that particular B_1.

Consider next the government's default decision choice, which is driven by the sign of the social welfare gains of default. It is evident from Fig. 17 that the government defaults the higher g_1 for given B_1 and γ, the higher B_1 for a given γ and g_1, or at higher γ at given B_1 and g_1. It follows then that we can compute a threshold value of γ such that the government is indifferent between defaulting and repaying in period $t = 1$ for a given (B_1,g_1). These indifference thresholds ($\hat{\gamma}(B_1, g_1)$) are plotted in Fig. 18 against debt levels ranging from 0 to 0.4 for three values of government expenditures $\{\underline{g}_1, \mu_g, \overline{g}_1\}$. For any given (B_1, g_1), the government chooses to default if $\gamma \geq \hat{\gamma}$.

Fig. 18 shows that the default threshold is decreasing in B_1. Hence, the government tolerates higher debt ratios without defaulting only if wealth concentration is sufficiently low. Also, default thresholds are decreasing in g_1, because the government has stronger

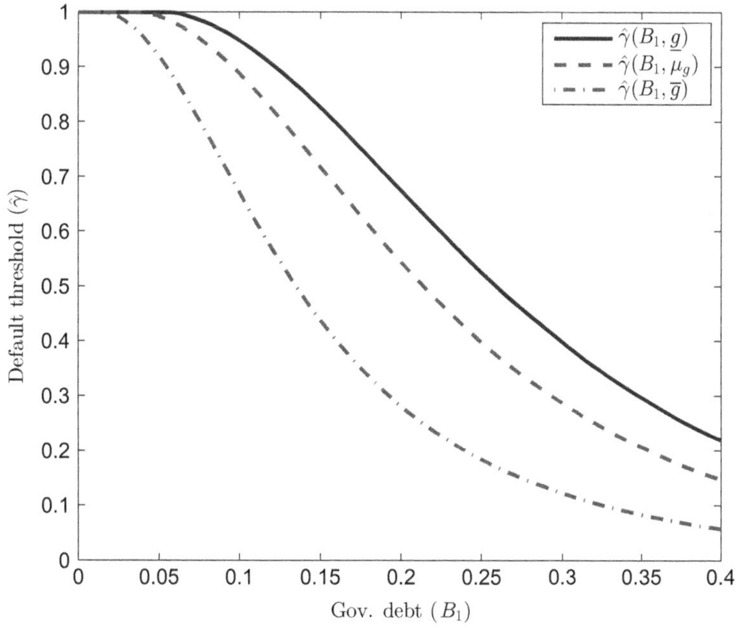

Fig. 18 Default threshold $\hat{\gamma}(B_1, g_1)$.

incentives to default when government expenditures are higher (ie, the threshold curves shift inward).[bc] This last feature of $\hat{\gamma}$ is very important to determine equilibria with sustainable debt subject to default risk. If, for a given value of B_1, γ is higher than the curve representing $\hat{\gamma}$ for the lowest realization in the Markov process of g_1 (which is also the value of $\underline{g}_1$), the government defaults for sure and, as explained earlier, there is no sustainable debt at equilibrium. Alternatively, if for a given value of B_1, γ is lower than the curve representing $\hat{\gamma}$ for the highest realization of g_1 (which is the value of $\bar{g}_1$), the government repays for sure and debt would be issued effectively without default risk. Thus, for the model to support equilibria with sustainable debt subject to default risk, the optimal debt chosen by the government in the first period for a given γ must lie between these two extreme threshold curves. We show below that this is the case in this quantitative experiment.

Before showing those results, it is important to highlight three key properties of the bond pricing function. The quantitative results for this function, the details of which we omit to save space, reflect the properties discussed in the model analysis:

1. *The equilibrium price is decreasing in B_1 for given γ* (the pricing functions shift downward as B_1 rises). This follows from a standard demand-and-supply argument: For a given γ, as the government borrows more, the price at which the H types are willing to demand the additional debt falls and the interest rate rises.
2. *Default risk reduces the price of bonds below the risk-free price and thus induces a risk premium.* Intuitively, when there is no default risk (ie, for combinations of B_1 and γ such that the probability of default is zero) both prices are identical. However, as the probability of default rises, agents demand a premium in order to clear the bond market.
3. *Bond prices are a nonmonotonic function of wealth dispersion*: When default risk is sufficiently low, bond prices are increasing in γ, but eventually they become a steep decreasing function of γ. Higher γ implies a more dispersed wealth distribution, so that H-type agents become a smaller fraction of the population, and hence they must demand a larger amount of debt per capita in order to clear the bond market (ie, b_1^H increases with γ), which pushes bond prices up. While default risk is low this "demand composition effect" dominates and thus bond prices rise with γ, but as γ increases and default risk rises (since higher wealth dispersion strengthens default incentives), the growing risk premium becomes the dominating force (at about $\gamma > 0.5$) and produces bond prices that fall sharply as γ increases.

Finally we examine the numerical solutions of the model's full equilibrium with optimal debt and default policies. The key element of the solution is the sustainable debt, which is also the government's optimal choice of debt issuance in the first period at the equilibrium price (ie, the optimal B_1 that solves problem (25)). We show this sustainable debt as an equilibrium manifold (ie, as a plot of the sustainable debt obtained by

[bc] $\hat{\gamma}$ approaches zero for B_1 sufficiently large, but in Fig. 18 B_1 reaches 0.40 only for exposition purposes.

solving the model's equilibrium over a range of values of γ). Given this sustainable debt, we can then use the functions that describe optimal debt demand plans of private agents in both periods, the government's default choice in period 1, bond prices, and default risk for *any* value of B_1 to determine the corresponding *equilibrium* manifold values of all of the model's endogenous variables.

Fig. 19 shows the four main components of the equilibrium manifolds: Panel (A) plots the manifold of sustainable first-period debt issuance of the model with default risk, $B_1^*(\gamma)$, and also, for comparison, the debt in the case when the government is committed to repay so that debt is risk free, $B_1^{RF}(\gamma)$. Panel (B) shows equilibrium debt prices that correspond to the sustainable debt of the same two economies. Panel (C) shows the default spread (the difference in the inverses of the bond prices). Panel (D) shows the probability of default. Since in principle the government that has the option to default can still choose a debt level for which it could prefer to repay in all realizations of g_1,

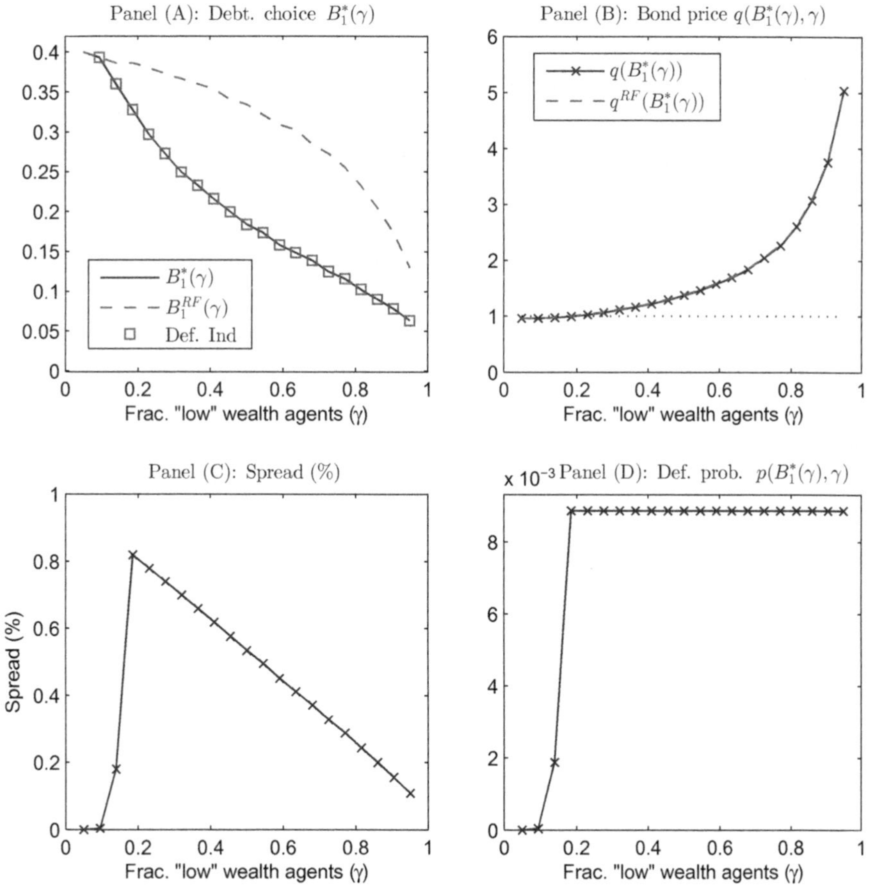

Fig. 19 Equilibrium manifolds.

we identify with a square in Panel (A) the equilibria in which $B_1^*(\gamma)$ has a positive default probability. This is the case for all but the smallest value of gamma considered ($\gamma = 0.05$), in which the government sets $B_1^*(\gamma)$ at 40% of GDP with zero default probability.

Panel (A) shows that sustainable debt falls as γ increases in both the economy with default risk and the economy with a government committed to repay. This occurs because in both cases the government seeks to reallocate consumption across agents and across periods by altering the product $q(B_1)B_1$ optimally, and in doing this it internalizes the response of bond prices to its debt choice. As γ rises, this response is influenced by stronger default incentives and a stronger demand composition effect. The latter dominates in this quantitative experiment, because panel (B) shows that the equilibrium bond prices always rise with γ. Hence, the government internalizes that as γ rises the demand composition effect strengthens demand for bonds, pushing bond prices higher, and as a result it can actually attain a higher $q(B_1)B_1$ by choosing lower B_1. This is a standard Laffer curve argument: In the upward sloping segment of this curve, increasing debt increases the amount of resources the government acquires by borrowing in the first period.

In the range of empirically relevant values of γ, sustainable debt ratios range from 20% to 32% of GDP without default risk and from 8% to 15% with default risk. Since the median in the European data is 35%, these ratios are relatively low, but still they are notable given the simplicity of the two-period setup. In particular, the model lacks the stronger income- and tax-smoothing effects and the self-insurance incentives of a longer life horizon (see Aiyagari and McGrattan, 1998), and it has an upper bound on the optimal debt choice for $\gamma = [0,1]$ lower than $B_0/(1+\beta)$ (which is the upper bound as $\gamma \to 0$ in the absence of default risk).

Panel (B) shows that bond prices of sustainable debt range from very low to very high as γ rises, including prices sharply above 1 that imply large negative real interest rates on public debt. In fact, as D'Erasmo and Mendoza (2013) explain, equilibrium bond prices are similar and increasing in γ with or without default risk, because at equilibrium the government chooses debt positions for which default risk is low (see panel (D)), and thus the demand composition effect that strengthens as γ rises dominates and yields bond prices increasing in γ and similar with or without default risk.[bd]

[bd] Everything else equal, our model predicts that higher income dispersion (either due to less progressive tax systems or underlying households' income or bond positions) results in higher spreads. In D'Erasmo and Mendoza (2013), we show that an economy with more progressive tax system results in lower spreads. The intuition is simple. The more the government can redistribute via means of taxation the lower the incentives to redistribute through a domestic default on the debt. The results in that paper show that incentives to default do not disappear but spreads decrease considerably. Also in D'Erasmo and Mendoza (2013), we present evidence of the nonlinear relationship between debt to income ratios and wealth inequality. Data limitations prevents us from extending this analysis to the relationship between spreads and income dispersion or the progressivity of the tax system.

Panels (C) and (D) show that, in contrast with standard models of external default, in this model the default spread is neither similar to the probability of default nor does it have a monotonic relationship with it.[be] Both the spread and the default probability start at zero for $\gamma = 0.05$ because $B_1^*(0.05)$ has zero default probability. As γ increases up to 0.2, both the spread and the default probability of the sustainable debt are similar in magnitude and increase together, but for $\gamma > 0.2$ the spread falls with γ while the default probability remains unchanged around 0.9%. For $\gamma = 0.95$ the probability of default is 9 times larger than the spread (0.9 vs 0.1%).

The role of the government's incentives to reallocate consumption across agents and across periods internalizing the response of bond prices when choosing debt can be illustrated further by examining the debt Laffer curve. Fig. 20 shows debt Laffer curves for five values of γ in the [0.05,0.95] range.

In all but one case, the sustainable debt $B_1^*(\gamma)$ (ie, the equilibrium debt chosen optimally by the government at the equilibrium price) is located at the maximum of the corresponding Laffer curve. In these cases, setting debt higher than at the maximum is

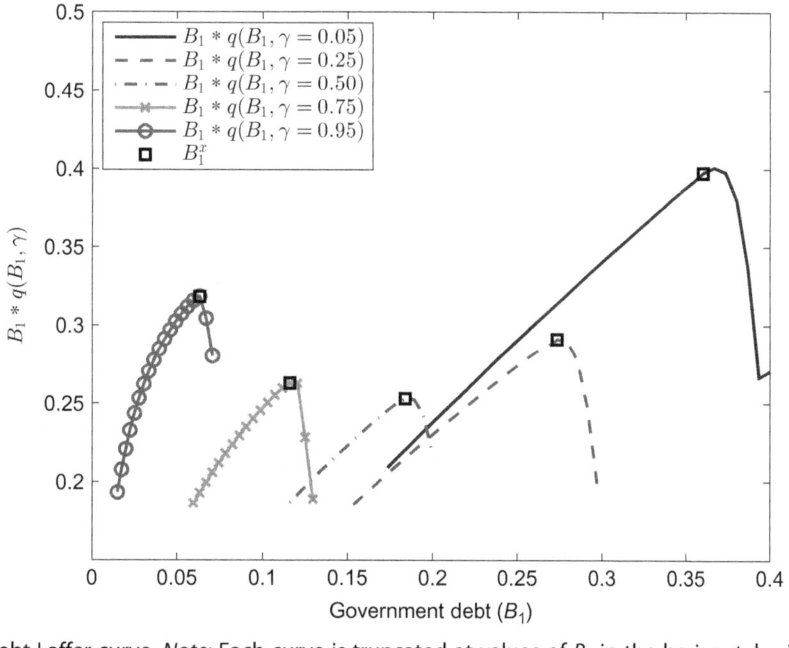

Fig. 20 Debt Laffer curve. *Note*: Each curve is truncated at values of B_1 in the horizontal axis that are either low enough for $c_0^L \leq 0$ or high enough for default to be chosen for all realizations of g_1, because as noted before in these cases there is no equilibrium.

[be] In the standard models, the two are similar and a monotonic function of each other because of the arbitrage condition of a representative risk-neutral investor.

suboptimal because default risk reduces bond prices sharply, moving the government to the downward-sloping segment of the Laffer curve. Setting debt lower than the maximum is also suboptimal, because then default risk is low and extra borrowing generates more resources since bond prices change little, leaving the government in the upward-sloping segment region of the Laffer curve. Thus, if the optimal debt has a nontrivial probability of default, the government's debt choice exhausts its ability to raise resources by borrowing. The exception is the case with $\gamma = 0.05$, in which $B_1^*(\gamma)$ has zero default probability. In this case, the government's optimal debt is to the left of the maximum of the Laffer curve, and thus the debt choice does not exhaust the government's ability to raise resources by borrowing. This also happens when the default probability is positive but negligible. For example, when $\gamma = 0.15$ the default probability is close to zero and the optimal debt choice is again slightly to the left of the maximum of the corresponding Laffer curve.

4.3.3 Biased Welfare Weights ($\omega \neq \gamma$)

The final experiment we conduct examines how the results change if we allow the weights of the government's payoff function to display a bias in favor of bondholders. Fig. 21 shows how the planner's welfare gain of default varies with ω and γ for two different levels of government debt ($B_{1,L} = 0.143$ and $B_{1,H} = 0.185$). The no-equilibrium region, which exists for the same reasons as before, is shown in white.

In line with the previous discussion, within the region where the equilibrium is well-defined, the planner's value of default increases monotonically as ω increases, keeping γ constant, and falls as actual wealth concentration (γ) rises, keeping ω constant. Because of this, the north-west and south-east corners in each of the panels present cases that are at very different positions on the preference-for-default spectrum. When ω is low, even for very high values of γ, the government prefers to repay (north-west corner), because the government puts relatively small weight on L-type agents. On the contrary, when ω is high, even for low levels of γ, a default is preferred. It is also interesting to note that as we move from Panel (A) to Panel (B), so that government debt raises, the set of γ's and ω's such that the equilibrium exists or repayment is preferred (ie, a negative $\overline{\alpha}(B_1, g_1, \gamma, \omega)$) expands. This is because as we increase the level of debt B_1, as long as the government does not choose to default for all g_1, the higher level of debt allows L-type agents to attain positive levels of consumption (since initial taxes are lower).

Panels (A)–(D) in Fig. 22 display the model's equilibrium outcomes for the sustainable debt chosen by the government in the first period and the associated equilibrium bond prices, spreads and default probabilities under three possible values of ω, all plotted as functions of γ. It is important to note that along the blue curve of the utilitarian case both ω and γ effectively vary together because they are always equal to each other, while in the other two plots ω is fixed and γ varies. For this reason, the line corresponding to the ω_L

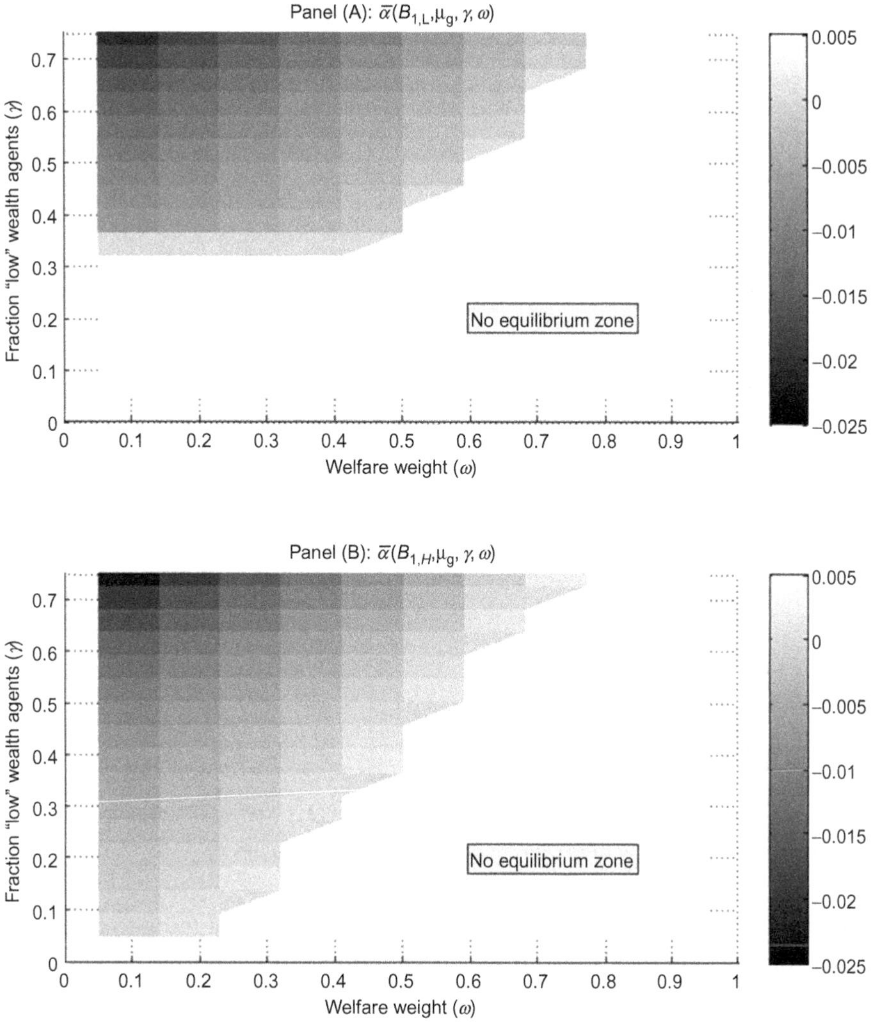

Fig. 21 Planner's welfare gain of default $\overline{\alpha}(B_1, g_1, \gamma, \omega)$.

case intersects the benchmark solution when $\gamma = 0.32$, and the one for ω_H intersects the benchmark when $\gamma = 0.50$.

Fig. 22 shows that the optimal debt level is increasing in γ. This is because the incentives to default grow weaker and the repayment zone widens as γ increases for a fixed value of ω. It is also interesting to note that in the ω_L and ω_H cases the equilibrium exists only for a small range of values of γ that are lower than ω. Without default costs each curve would be truncated exactly where γ equals either ω_H or ω_H, but since these simulations retain the default costs used in the utilitarian case, there can still be equilibria with debt for some lower values of γ (as explained earlier).

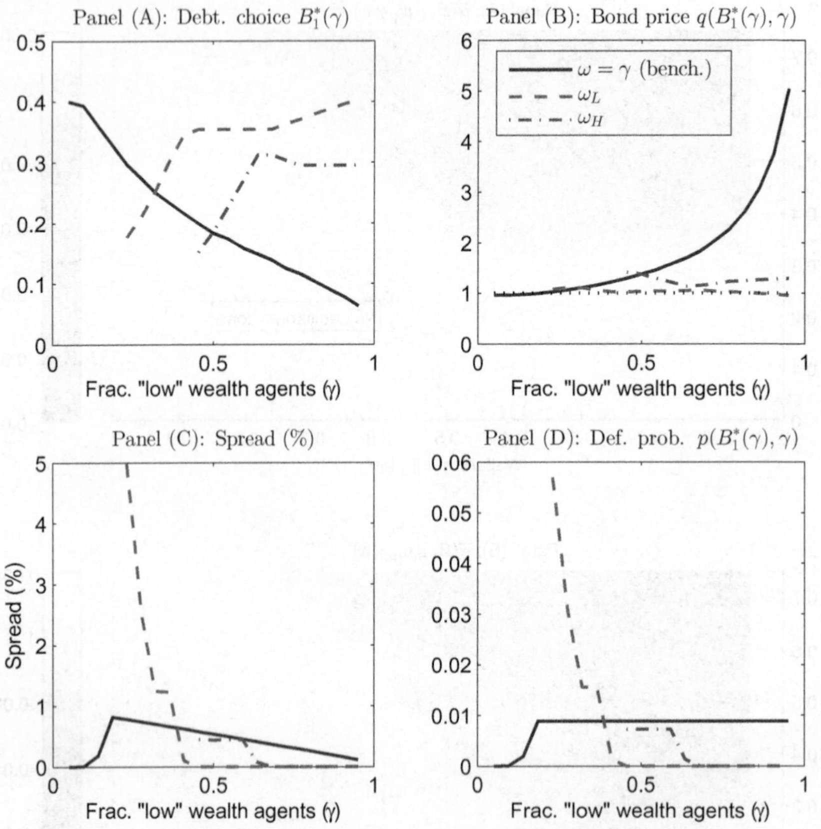

Fig. 22 Equilibrium manifolds with government bias at different values of ω.

With the bias in favor of bondholders, the government is still aiming to optimize debt by focusing on the resources it can reallocate across periods and agents, which are still determined by the debt Laffer curve $q_0(.)B_1$, and internalizing the response of bond prices to debt choices.[bf] This relationship, however, behaves very differently than in the benchmark model, because now *higher* sustainable debt is carried at increasing equilibrium bond prices, which leads the planner internalizing the price response to choose higher debt, whereas in the benchmark model *lower* debt was sustained at increasing equilibrium bond prices, which led the planner internalizing the price response to choose lower debt.[bg]

[bf] When choosing B_1, the government takes into account that higher debt increases disposable income for L-type agents in the initial period but it also implies higher taxes in the second period (as long as default is not optimal). Thus, the government is willing to take on more debt when ω is lower.

[bg] Fig. 22 makes clear that with the government bias, the level of sustainable debt changes with the preferences of the government. Even though we do not model how these preferences arise, it is evident that two countries with the same fundamentals (ie, distribution of wealth and income) could end up with very different levels of sustainable debt depending on how household preferences are aggregated by the government in power.

The behavior of equilibrium bond prices (panel (B)) with either $\omega_L = 0.32$ or $\omega_H = 0.50$ differs markedly from the utilitarian case. In particular, the prices no longer display an increasing, convex shape, instead they are a relatively flat and nonmonotonic function of γ. This occurs because the higher supply of bonds that the government finds optimal to provide offsets the demand composition effect that increases individual demand for bonds as γ rises.

The domestic default approach to study sustainable debt adds important insights to those obtained from the empirical and structural approaches, both of which assumed repayment commitment. In particular, panel (A) of Fig. 19 shows that sustainable debt falls sharply once risk of default is present, even when it is very small, and that (if the government is utilitarian) sustainable debt falls sharply with the concentration of bond ownership, because of the strengthened incentive to use default as a tool for redistribution. Hence, estimates of sustainable debt based on models in which the government is assumed to be committed to repay are likely to be too optimistic. Intuitively, one can infer that in the structural model, a given increase in the initial debt would be harder to offset with higher primary balances if the interest rate at which those primary balances are discounted rises with higher debt because of default risk. Moreover, the representative-agent assumption is also likely to lead to optimistic estimates of sustainable debt, because representative-agents models abstract from the strong incentives to use debt default as a tool for redistribution across heterogeneous agents. These incentives are likely to be weaker than in the model in practice, because tax and transfer policies that we did not include in the model can be used for redistribution as well. But when these other instruments have been exhausted, and if inequality in bond holdings is sufficiently concentrated, the incentives to default as vehicle for redistribution are likely to be very strong.

A second important insight from this analysis is that sustainable debt is higher if the government's payoff function is biased in favor of bondholders, and can even exceed debt that is sustainable without default risk when the government has a utilitarian social welfare function. Furthermore, D'Erasmo and Mendoza (2013) show that nonbondholders may prefer equilibria where the government favors bondholders, instead of being utilitarian, because higher sustainable debt help relax their liquidity constraints. Hence, at sufficiently high levels of concentration of bond ownership, a biased government can sustain high debt and the biased government can be elected as a majority government.

The main caveat of this analysis is that, because it was based on a two-period model, it misses important endogenous costs of default that would be added to the model by introducing a longer life horizon. In this case, default costs due to the reduced ability to smooth taxation and consumption when the debt market closes, and due to the loss of access to the self-insurance vehicle and the associated tightening of liquidity constraints, can take up the role of the exogenous default costs and/or government bias for bondholders, enabling the model to improve its ability to account for key features of the data and sustain higher debt levels at nontrivial default premia. D'Erasmo and Mendoza (2014) examine a model with these features and study its quantitative implications.

5. CRITICAL ASSESSMENT AND OUTLOOK

We started this chapter by noting that the question of what is a sustainable public debt has always been paramount in the macroeconomics of fiscal policy. The question will remain paramount for years to come, as the precarious public debt and deficit positions of many advanced and emerging economies today will make it a central focus of both policy analysis and academic research. This chapter aimed to demonstrate the flaws that affect the classic, but still widely used, approach to analyze public debt sustainability, and to show how three approaches based on recent research can provide powerful alternative ways to tackle the question. Two of these approaches, the empirical approach and the structural approach, assume that the government is committed to repay its debt, and the third approach, the domestic default approach, assumes that the government cannot commit to repay. In this section, we reflect further on the limitations of each of these approaches and suggest directions for further research.

The empirical approach has been widely studied and is by now very well established. Its strengths are in that it can easily determine whether debt has been consistent with fiscal solvency in available time-series data via straightforward estimation of a fiscal reaction function, and in that analyzing the characteristics of this FRF it can shed light on the dynamics of adjustment of debt and the primary balance. Unfortunately, as we explained earlier, it is not helpful for comparing alternative fiscal policy strategies to maintain debt sustainability and/or cope with public debt crises in the future.

The structural approach showed how an explicit dynamic general equilibrium model can be used to compare alternative fiscal policy strategies aimed at maintaining fiscals solvency at different levels of observed outstanding debt. We used a variation of the workhorse two-country Neoclassical framework with exogenous, balanced growth in which endogenous capacity utilization and a limited tax allowance for capital depreciation allow the model to match a key feature of the data for fiscal sustainability analysis: The observed elasticity of the capital tax revenue. Yet, the model is also very limited inasmuch as it abstracts from other important features of the data. In particular, the model is purely "real," and hence abstracts from the fact that public debt is largely nominal debt denominated in domestic currencies, and also abstracts from linkages between potentially important nominal rigidities, relative prices, and the evolution of government revenues and outlays.

The model used in the structural approach also has the drawbacks that it abstracts from heterogeneity in households and firms and assumes that agents are infinitely lived. Hence, while it takes into account important efficiency effects resulting from alternative fiscal policies, it cannot capture their distributional implications across agents and/or generations. The fiscal policy research on heterogeneous-agents and overlapping-generations models has shown that these distributional effects can be quite significant, and hence it is important to develop models of debt sustainability that incorporate them. For instance, Aiyagari (1995) showed that reductions in capital taxes have adverse distributional consequences that can offset the efficiency gains emphasized in representative agent models. Aiyagari and McGrattan (1998) showed that public debt has social value because it acts as vehicle to provide liquidity (ie, relax borrowing constraints) of the agents at the low end of the wealth distribution, and Birkeland and Prescott (2006) provide a setup in which using debt to save for retirement dominates a tax-and-transfer system. Imrohoroglu et al. (2016) and Braun and Joines (2015) also show how sophisticated overlapping-generations models can be applied to study debt-sustainability issues, with a particular focus on the implications of the adverse demographics dynamics facing Japan.

Of the approaches to debt sustainability analysis reviewed here, the domestic default approach is the one that has been studied the least. We provided a very simple canonical model in which default on domestic debt can emerge as an optimal outcome for a government with incentives to redistribute across debt holders and nonholders, but clearly significant further research in this area is needed (in addition to the recent work by D'Erasmo and Mendoza (2014) and Dovis et al. (2014) that we cited).

There are also two other directions in which research on debt sustainability should go. First, to model the role of public debt in financial intermediation in general and in financial stabilization policies in particular. In terms of the former, domestic banking systems are often large holders of domestic public debt, so a domestic default of the kind the third approach we examined seeks to explain tends to materialize in terms of a redistribution that hurts the balance sheets of banks. A deeper question in a similar vein is why public debt is such a high-demand asset, or liquidity vehicle, in modern financial systems. Macro/finance research is looking into this questions, but introducing these considerations into debt sustainability analysis is still a pending task. Regarding crisis-management policies, the aftermath of the global financial crisis has been characterized by strong demand for public debt instruments driven by quantitative easing policies and by the new regulatory environment. This may account for the apparent paradox between the pessimistic fiscal prospects that the analysis of this chapter presents and the observation that we currently observe near-zero and even negative yields on the public debt of some advanced economies (ie, demand for public debt remains very strong despite the highly questionable capacity of governments to repay it through standard improvements of the primary fiscal balance). But to be certain we need a richer model of debt sustainability that incorporates both the long-term forces that drive the government's capacity to repay and short-term debt dynamics around a financial crisis in which demand for risk-free asset surges.

The second direction in which debt sustainability analysis needs to branch out is to develop tools to incorporate considerations of potential multiplicity of equilibria in public debt markets. The seminal work of Calvo (1988) showed how debt can move between two equilibria supported by self-fulfilling expectations. In one the debt is repaid because agents expect that the government will be able to access the debt market, and thus maintain the efficiency losses of taxation small enough to indeed generate enough revenue to repay. In the other, the government defaults because agents expect that it will not be able to access the debt market and will be forced into highly distorting levels of taxation that indeed result in revenues that are insufficient to repay. The external default literature has explored models with this kind of equilibrium multiplicity extensively, as documented in the corresponding chapter of this handbook, and theoretical work applying these ideas to domestic debt crises is also available, but research to incorporate this mechanism into quantitative models of domestic debt sustainability is still needed.

6. CONCLUSIONS

What is a sustainable public debt? Assuming that the government is committed to repay, the answer is a debt that satisfies the intertemporal government budget constraint (ie, a debt that is equal to the present discounted value of the primary fiscal balance). In this chapter we showed that the traditional approach to debt sustainability analysis is flawed. This approach uses the steady-state government budget constraint to define sustainable debt as the annuity value of the primary balance, but it cannot establish if current or projected debt and primary balance dynamics are consistent with that debt level. We then discussed two approaches to study public debt sustainability under commitment to repay: First, an empirical approach, based on a linear fiscal reaction function, according to which a positive, conditional response of the primary balance to debt is sufficient to establish debt sustainability. Second, a structural approach based on a two-country variant of the workhorse Neoclassical dynamic general equilibrium model with an explicit fiscal sector. The model differs from the standard Neoclassical setup in that it introduces endogenous capacity utilization and a limited tax allowance for depreciation expenses in order to match the observed elasticity of the capital tax base to changes in capital taxes. In this setup, the initial debt that is sustainable is the one determined by the present value of primary balances evaluated using equilibrium allocations and prices.

Applications of these first two approaches to cross-country data produced key insights. With the empirical approach, we found in tests based on historical US data and cross-country panels that the sufficiency condition for public debt to be sustainable (the positive, conditional response of the primary balance to debt), cannot be rejected. We also found, however, clear evidence showing that the fiscal dynamics observed in the aftermath of the recent surge in debt in advanced economies represent a significant structural break in the estimated reaction functions. Primary deficits have been too large, and are projected to remain too large, relative to what the fiscal reaction functions predict, and they are also large compared with those observed in the aftermath previous episodes of large surges in debt.

The structural approach differs from the empirical approach in that it can be used to evaluate the positive and normative effects of alternative paths of fiscal adjustment to attain debt sustainability, whereas the empirical approach is silent about these effects. We calibrated the model to the United States and European data and used it to quantify the effects of unilateral changes in capital and labor taxes, particularly their effects on sustainable debt. The results suggest key differences across Europe and the United States. For the United States, the results suggest that changes in capital taxes cannot make the observed increase in debt sustainable, while small increases in labor taxes could. For Europe, the model predicts that the capacity to use taxes to make higher debt ratios sustainable is nearly fully exhausted. Capital taxation is highly inefficient (in the decreasing segment of dynamic Laffer curves), so cuts in capital taxes would be needed to restore fiscal solvency. Labor taxes are near the peak of the dynamic Laffer curve, and even if increased to the maximum point they do not generate enough revenue to make the present value of the primary balance match the observed surge in debt. In addition, international externalities of capital income taxes were quantitatively large, which suggest that incentives for strategic interaction are nontrivial and could lead to a classic race-to-the-bottom in capital income taxation.

The results of the applications of the empirical and structural approaches paint a bleak picture of the prospects for fiscal adjustment in advanced economies to restore fiscal solvency and make the post-2008 surge in public debt ratios sustainable. In light of these findings, and with the ongoing turbulence in European sovereign debt markets and recurrent debt ceiling debates in the United States, we examined a third approach to debt sustainability that relaxes the assumption of a government committed to repay and allows for the risk of default on domestic public debt. In this environment, debt is sustainable when it is part of the equilibrium that includes the optimal debt issuance and default choices of the government. The government has incentives to default as a vehicle for redistribution across agents who are heterogeneous in wealth. Public debt is not sustainable in the absence of default costs or a political bias to weigh the welfare of bond holders by more than their share of the wealth distribution. This is the case because without these assumptions default is always the optimal choice that maximizes the social welfare function of a government who values the utility of all agents, and this is the case regardless of the present value of primary balances used to characterize sustainable debt under the other two approaches.

Quantitatively, this domestic default approach adds valuable insights to those obtained from the empirical and structural approaches without default risk. In particular, sustainable debt falls sharply once risk of default is present, even when it is very small, and it also falls sharply with wealth inequality, because of the strengthened incentive to use default as a tool for redistribution. Hence, estimates of sustainable debt based on models in which the government is assumed to be committed to repay are too optimistic. Moreover, the representative-agent assumption is also likely to lead to optimistic estimates of sustainable debt, because models in this class abstract from the strong incentives to use debt default as a tool for redistribution across heterogeneous agents. A second important insight from the domestic default approach is that sustainable debt is higher if the government's payoff function weighs the welfare of bond holders more heavily than their share of the wealth distribution. In addition, it is possible that low-wealth agents may also prefer that the government weights high-wealth agents more heavily, instead of acting as a utilitarian government, because higher debt stocks help relax their liquidity constraints.

The three approaches reviewed in this chapter provide useful tools for conducting debt sustainability analysis. When applied to the current fiscal situation of advanced economies, all three suggest that substantial fiscal adjustment is still needed, is likely to entail substantial welfare costs, and is likely to continue to be challenged by potential default risk in domestic sovereign debt markets.

APPENDIX: DETAILS ON MEASUREMENT OF EFFECTIVE TAX RATES

Effective tax rates have been widely used in a number of studies including Carey and Tchilinguirian (2000), Sorensen (2001), and recently by Trabandt and Uhlig (2011, 2012). The MRT methodology uses the wedge between reported pretax and post-tax macro estimates of consumption, labor income and capital income to estimate the effective tax rate levied on each of the three tax bases. This methodology has two main advantages. First, it provides a fairly simple approach to estimating effective tax rates at the macro level using readily available data, despite the complexity of the various credits and deductions of national tax codes. Second, these tax rates correspond directly to the tax rates in a wide class of representative-agent models with taxes on consumption and factor incomes, including the model proposed here. The main drawback of the MRT tax rates is that they are average, not marginal, tax rates, but because they are intended for use in representative-agent models, this disadvantage is less severe than it would be in a model with heterogeneous agents. Moreover Mendoza et al. (1994) show that existing estimates of aggregate marginal tax rates have a high time-series correlation with the MRT effective tax rates, and that both have similar cross-country rankings.

Following Trabandt and Uhlig (2011), we modify the MRT estimates of labor and capital taxes by adding supplemental wages (ie, employers' contributions to social security and private pension plans) to the tax base for personal income taxes. These data were not available at the time of the MRT 1994 calculations and, because this adjustment affects the calculation of the personal income tax rate, which is an initial step for the calculation of labor and capital income tax rates, it alters the estimates of both. In general, this adjustment makes the labor tax base bigger and therefore the labor tax rate smaller than the MRT original estimates.[bh]

[bh] Trabandt and Uhlig make a further adjustment to the MRT formulae by attributing some of the operating surplus of corporations and nonincorporated private enterprises to labor, with the argument that this represents a return to entrepreneurs rather than to capital. We do not make this modification because the data do not provide enough information to determine what fraction of the operating surplus should be allocated to labor.

ACKNOWLEDGMENTS

We are grateful to Juan Hernandez, Christian Probsting and Valentina Piamiotti for their valuable research assistance. We are also grateful to our discussant, Kinda Hachem, the Handbook editors, John Taylor and Harald Uhlig, and Henning Bohn for their valuable suggestions and comments. We also acknowledge comments by Jonathan Heathcote, Andy Neumeyer, Juan Pablo Nicolini, Martin Uribe, and Vivian Yue, and by participants attending presentations at the Bank for International Settlements, Emory University, the third RIDGE seminar on International Macroeconomics, and the April 2015 Handbook conference at the University of Chicago. The views expressed in this paper are those of the authors and do not necessarily reflect those of the Federal Reserve Bank of Chicago, the Federal Reserve Bank of Philadelphia, or the Federal Reserve System.

REFERENCES

Afonso, A., 2005. Fiscal Sustainability: the Unpleasant European Case. FinanzArchiv 61 (1), 19–44. http://ideas.repec.org/a/mhr/finarc/urnsici0015-2218(200503)611_19fstuec_2.0.tx_2-r.html.
Aghion, P., Bolton, P., 1990. Government domestic debt and the risk of default: a political-economic model of the strategic role of debt. In: Dornbusch, R., Draghi, M. (Eds.), Public Debt Management: Theory and History. Cambridge University Press, Cambridge, pp. 315–344.
Aguiar, M., Amador, M., 2013. Fiscal policy in debt constrained economies. NBER Working Papers 17457.
Aguiar, M., Amador, M., Farhi, E., Gopinath, G., 2013. Crisis and commitment: inflation credibility and the vulnerability to sovereign debt crises. NBER Working Papers 19516.
Aiyagari, S.R., 1995. Optimal capital income taxation with incomplete markets, borrowing constraints, and constant discounting. J. Polit. Econ. 103 (6), 1158–1175.
Aiyagari, R., McGrattan, E., 1998. The optimum quantity of debt. J. Monet. Econ. 42, 447–469.
Aiyagari, R., Marcet, A., Sargent, T., Seppala, J., 2002. Optimal taxation without state-contingent debt. J. Polit. Econ. 110 (6), 1220–1254.
Alesina, A., Tabellini, G., 1990. A positive theory of fiscal deficits and government debt. Rev. Econ. Stud. 57, 403–414.
Alesina, A., Tabellini, G., 2005. Why is fiscal policy often procyclical? National Bureau of Economic Research, Working Paper 11600. doi: 10.3386/w11600, http://www.nber.org/papers/w11600.
Amador, M., 2003. A political economy model of sovereign debt repayment. Mimeo, Stanford University.
Andreasen, E., Sandleris, G., der Ghote, A.V., 2011. The political economy of sovereign defaults. Universidad Torcuato Di Tella, Business School Working Paper.
Arellano, C., 2008. Default risk and income fluctuations in emerging economies. Am. Econ. Rev. 98 (3), 690–712.
Auray, S., Eyquem, A., Gomme, P., 2013. A tale of tax policies in open economies. Mimeo, Department of Economics, Concordia University.
Azzimonti, M., de Francisco, E., Quadrini, V., 2014. Financial globalization, inequality, and the rising public debt. Am. Econ. Rev. 104 (8), 2267–2302.
Barnhill Jr., M.T., Kopits, G., 2003. Assessing fiscal sustainability under uncertainty. IMF Working Paper, WP 03-79.
Barro, R., 1979. On the determination of the public debt. J. Polit. Econ. 87 (5), 940–971.
Basu, S., 2009. Sovereign debt and domestic economic fragility. Manuscript, Massachusetts Institute of Technology.
Birkeland, K., Prescott, E.C., 2006. On the needed quantity of government debt. Research Department, Federal Reserve Bank of Minneapolis, Working Paper 648.
Blanchard, O.J., 1990. Suggestions for a new set of fiscal indicators. OECD Economics Department Working Papers 79, OECD Publishing, http://ideas.repec.org/p/oec/ecoaaa/79-en.html.
Blanchard, O.J., Chouraqui, J.C., Hagemann, R.P., Sartor, N., 1990. The sustainability of fiscal policy: new answers to an old question. OECD Econ. Stud. 15 (2), 7–36.
Bocola, L., 2014. The pass-through of sovereign risk. Manuscript, University of Pennsylvania.

Bohn, H., 1995. The sustainability of budget deficits in a stochastic economy. J. Money Credit Bank. 27 (1), 257–271. http://ideas.repec.org/a/mcb/jmoncb/v27y1995i1p257-71.html.
Bohn, H., 1998. The behavior of U.S. public debt and deficits. Q. J. Econ. 113 (3), 949–963. http://ideas.repec.org/a/tpr/qjecon/v113y1998i3p949-963.html.
Bohn, H., 2007. Are stationarity and cointegration restrictions really necessary for the intertemporal budget constraint? J. Monet. Econ. 54 (7), 1837–1847. http://ideas.repec.org/a/eee/moneco/v54y2007i7p1837-1847.html.
Bohn, H., 2008. The sustainability of fiscal policy in the United States. In: Neck, R., Sturm, J.E. (Eds.), Sustainability of public debt. MIT Press, Cambridge, MA.
Bohn, H., 2011. The economic consequences of rising U.S. government debt: privileges at risk. Finanzarchiv 67 (3), 282–302.
Boz, E., D'Erasmo, P., Durdu, B., 2014. Sovereign risk and bank balance sheets: the role of macroprudential policies. Manuscript.
Braun, R.A., Joines, D.H., 2015. The implications of a graying Japan for government policy. J. Econ. Dyn. Control 57, 1–23.
Broner, F., Martin, A., Ventura, J., 2010. Sovereign risk and secondary markets. Am. Econ. Rev. 100 (4), 1523–1555.
Broner, F., Ventura, J., 2011. Globalization and risk sharing. Rev. Econ. Stud. 78 (1), 49–82.
Brutti, F., 2011. Sovereign defaults and liquidity crises. J. Int. Econ. 84 (1), 65–72.
Buiter, W.H., 1985. A guide to public sector debt and deficits. Econ. Policy 1 (1), 13–61.
Calvo, G., 1988. Servicing the public debt: the role of expectations. Am. Econ. Rev. 78 (4), 647–661.
Carey, D., Tchilinguirian, H., 2000. Average effective tax rates on capital, labour and consumption. OECD Economics Department Working Papers: 258.
Chalk, N.A., Hemming, R., 2000. Assessing fiscal sustainability in theory and practice. International Monetary Fund.
Chari, V.V., Christiano, L.J., Kehoe, P.J., 1994. Optimal fiscal policy in a business cycle model. J. Polit. Econ. 102 (4), 617–652.
Cooley, T.F., Hansen, G.D., 1992. Tax distortions in a neoclassical monetary economy. J. Econ. Theory 58 (2), 290–316. ISSN 0022-0531. doi:10.1016/0022-0531(92)90056-N. http://www.sciencedirect.com/science/article/pii/002205319290056N.
Cuadra, G., Sanchez, J., Sapriza, H., 2010. Fiscal policy and default risk in emerging markets. Rev. Econ. Dyn. 13 (2), 452–469.
Davies, J., Sandström, S., Shorrocks, A., Wolff, E., 2009. The level and distribution of global household wealth. NBER Working Paper 15508.
D'Erasmo, P., 2011. Government reputation and debt repayment in emerging economies. Mimeo.
D'Erasmo, P., Mendoza, E., 2013. Distributional incentives in an equilibrium model of domestic sovereign default. National Bureau of Economic Research, No. w19477.
D'Erasmo, P., Mendoza, E., 2014. Optimal domestic sovereign default. Manuscript, University of Pennsylvania.
Di Casola, P., Sichlimiris, S., 2014. Domestic and external sovereign debt. Stockholm School of Economics, Working Paper.
Dias, D., Richmond, C., Wright, M., 2012. In for a penny, in for a 100 billion pounds: quantifying the welfare benefits from debt relief. Mimeo.
Dixit, A., Londregan, J., 2000. Political power and the credibility of government debt. J. Econ. Theory 94, 80–105.
Dovis, A., Golosov, M., Shourideh, A., 2014. Sovereign debt vs redistributive taxes: financing recoveries in unequal and uncommitted economies. Mimeo.
Durdu, B.C., Mendoza, E.G., Terrones, M.E., 2013. On the solvency of nations: cross-country evidence on the dynamics of external adjustment. J. Monet. Econ. 32, 762–780.
Dwenger, N., Steiner, V., 2012. Profit taxation and the elasticity of the corporate income tax base: evidence from German corporate tax return data. Natl. Tax J. 65 (1), 117–150.
Eaton, J., Gersovitz, M., 1981. Debt with potential repudiation: theoretical and empirical analysis. Rev. Econ. Stud. 48 (2), 289–309.

Eichengreen, B., 1989. The capital Levy in theory and practice. National Bureau of Economic Research, Working Paper Series 3096.
Escolano, J., 2010. A practical guide to public debt dynamics, fiscal sustainability, and cyclical adjustment of budgetary aggregates. International Monetary Fund.
Ferraro, D., 2010. Optimal capital income taxation with endogenous capital utilization. Mimeo, Department of Economics, Duke University.
Ferriere, A., 2014. Sovereign default, inequality, and progressive taxation. Mimeo.
Floden, M., 2001. The effectiveness of government debt and transfers as insurance. J. Monet. Econ. 48, 81–108.
Frenkel, J., Razin, A., Sadka, E., 1991. The sustainability of fiscal policy in the United States. In: International Taxation in an Integrated World. MIT Press, Cambridge, MA.
Gali, J., 1991. Budget constraints and time-series evidence on consumption. Am. Econ. Rev. 81 (5), 1238–1253. http://ideas.repec.org/a/aea/aecrev/v81y1991i5p1238-53.html.
Gennaioli, N., Martin, A., Rossi, S., 2014. Sovereign default, domestic banks, and financial institutions. The Journal of Finance 69 (2), 819–866.
Ghosh, A.R., Kim, J.I., Mendoza, E.G., Ostry, J.D., Qureshi, M.S., 2013. Fiscal fatigue, fiscal space and debt sustainability in advanced economies. Econ. J. 123, F4–F30.
Golosov, M., Sargent, T., 2012. Taxation, redistribution, and debt with aggregate shocks. Princeton University, Working Paper.
Greenwood, J., Huffman, G.W., 1991. Tax analysis in a real-business-cycle model. J. Monet. Econ. 22 (2), 167–190.
Gruber, J., Rauh, J., 2007. How elastic is the corporate income tax base? In: Taxing Corporate Income in the 21st Century. Cambridge University Press, New York.
Guembel, A., Sussman, O., 2009. Sovereign debt without default penalties. Rev. Econ. Stud. 76, 1297–1320.
Hall, G., Sargent, T., 2014. Fiscal discrimination in three wars. J. Monet. Econ. 61, 148–166.
Hamilton, J.D., Flavin, M.A., 1986. On the Limitations of Government Borrowing: a Framework for Empirical Testing. Am. Econ. Rev. 76 (4), 808–819. http://ideas.repec.org/a/aea/aecrev/v76y1986i4p808-19.html.
Hansen, G., Imrohoroglu, S., 2013. Fiscal reform and government debt in Japan: a neoclassical perspective. National Bureau of Economic Research, No. w19477.
Hansen, L.P., Roberds, W., Sargent, T.J., 1991. Time series implications of present value budget balance and of martingale models of consumption and taxes. In: Hansen, L.P., Sargent, T.J., Heaton, J., Marcet, A., Roberds, W. (Eds.), Rational xpectations econometrics. Westview Press, Boulder, CO, pp. 121–161.
Hatchondo, J.C., Martinez, L., Sapriza, H., 2009. Heterogeneous borrowers in quantitative models of sovereign default. Int. Econ. Rev. 50, 129–151.
Heathcote, J., 2005. Fiscal policy with heterogeneous agents. Rev. Econ. Stud. 72, 161–188.
House, C.L., Shapiro, M.D., 2008. Temporary investment tax incentives: theory with evidence from bonus depreciation. Am. Econ. Rev. 98 (3), 737–768. doi: 10.1257/acr.98.3.737.
Huizinga, H., 1995. The optimal taxation of savings and investment in an open economy. Econ. Lett. 47 (1), 59–62.
Huizinga, H., Voget, J., Wagner, W., 2012. Who bears the burden of international taxation? Evidence from cross-border m&as. J. Int. Econ. 88, 186–197.
IMF, International Monetary Fund, 2003. World economic outlook. IMF Occasional Papers 21, International Monetary Fund.
IMF, 2013. Staff guidance note for public debt sustainability in market access countries. http://www.imf.org/external/np/pp/eng/2013/050913.pdf.
Imrohoroglu, S., Sudo, N., 2011. Productivity and fiscal policy in Japan: short-term forecasts from the standard growth model. Monetary Econ. Stud. 29, 73–106.
Imrohoroglu, S., Kirao, S., Yamada, T., 2016. Achieving fiscal balance in Japan. Int. Econ. Rev. 57 (1), 117–154.
Jeon, K., Kabukcuoglu, Z., 2014. Income inequality and sovereign default. University of Pittsburgh, Working Paper.

Kaminsky, G.L., Reinhart, C.M., Vegh, C.A., 2005. When it rains, it pours: procyclical capital flows and macroeconomic policies. In: NBER Macroeconomics Annual 2004, NBER Chapters, National Bureau of Economic Research, Inc., pp. 11–82. vol.19. http://ideas.repec.org/h/nbr/nberch/6668.html

King, R.G., Plosser, C.I., Rebelo, S.T., 1988. Production, growth and business cycles: I. the basic neoclassical model. J. Monet. Econ. 21 (2), 195–232.

Klein, P., Quadrini, V., Rios-Rull, J.V., 2007. Optimal time-consistent taxation with international mobility of capital. B.E. J. Macroecon. 5.1, 186–197.

Ljungqvist, L., Sargent, T.J., 2012. Recursive Macroeconomic Theory, third ed. The MIT Press, Cambridge, Massachusetts.

Lorenzoni, G., Werning, I., 2013. Slow moving debt crises. NBER Working Paper No. w19228.

Lucas, R.E., 1987. Models of Business Cycles. Basil Blackwell, Oxford.

Lucas, R.E., 1990. Why doesn't capital flow from rich to poor countries? In: Papers and Proceedings of the Hundred and Second Annual Meeting of the American Economic Association, Am. Econ. Rev. vol. 80, pp. 92–96.

Lucas, D., 2012. Valuation of government policies and projects. Ann. Rev. Financ. Econ. 4, 39–58.

Mendoza, E.G., Ostry, J.D., 2008. International evidence on fiscal solvency: is fiscal policy responsible. J. Monet. Econ. 55, 1081–1093.

Mendoza, E.G., Oviedo, P.M., 2006. Fiscal policy and macroeconomic uncertainty in emerging markets: the tale of the tormented insurer. 2006 Meeting Papers 377, Society for Economic Dynamics, http://ideas.repec.org/p/red/sed006/377.html, 2006 Meeting Papers.

Mendoza, E.G., Oviedo, P.M., 2009. Public debt, fiscal solvency and macroeconomic uncertainty in Latin America the cases of Brazil, Colombia, Costa Rica and Mexico. Econ. Mex. NUEVA POCA XVIII (2), 133–173. http://ideas.repec.org/a/emc/ecomex/v18y2009i2p133-173.html.

Mendoza, E.G., Tesar, L.L., 1998. The international ramifications of tax reforms: supply-side economics in a global economy. Am. Econ. Rev. 88 (1), 226–245.

Mendoza, E.G., Tesar, L.L., 2005. Why hasn't tax competition triggered a race to the bottom? Some quantitative lessons from the EU. J. Monet. Econ. 52 (1), 163–204.

Mendoza, E.G., Yue, V.Z., 2012. A general equilibrium model of sovereign default and business cycles. Q. J. Econ. 127 (2), 889–946.

Mendoza, E.G., Razin, A., Tesar, L.L., 1994. Effective tax rates in macroeconomics: cross-country estimates of tax rates on factor incomes and consumption. J. Monet. Econ. 34 (3), 297–323.

Mendoza, E.G., Milesi-Ferretti, G.M., Asea, P., 1997. On the ineffectiveness of tax policy in altering long-run growth: Harberger's superneutrality conjecture. J. Public Econ. 66 (2), 99–126.

Mendoza, E.G., Tesar, L.L., Zhang, J., 2014. Saving Europe? the unpleasant arithmetic of fiscal austerity in integrated economies. University of Michigan Working Paper.

Mengus, E., 2014. Honoring sovereign debt or bailing out domestic residents? A theory of internal cost of default. WP Banque de France 480.

Neck, R., Sturm, J.E., 2008. Sustainability of Public Debt. MIT Press, Cambridge.

Ostry, J.D., David, J., Ghosh, A., Espinoza, R., 2015. When should public debt be reduced? International Monetary Fund, Staff Discussion Notes No. 15/10.

Perez, D., 2015. Sovereign debt, domestic banks and the provision of public liquidity. Manuscript.

Persson, T., Tabellini, G., 1995. Double-edged incentives: institutions and policy coordination. In: Grossman, G., Rogoff, K. (Eds.), Handbook of International Economics, vol. III. North-Holland, Amsterdam.

Pouzo, D., Presno, I., 2014. Optimal taxation with endogenous default under incomplete markets. U.C. Berkeley, Mimeo.

Prescott, E.C., 2004. Why Do Americans Work So Much More Than Europeans? Federal Reserve Bank of Minneapolis Quarterly Review 28 (1), 2–13.

Quintos, C.E., 1995. Sustainability of the Deficit Process with Structural Shifts. J. Bus. Econ. Stat. 13 (4), 409–417. http://ideas.repec.org/a/bes/jnlbes/v13y1995i4p409-17.html.

Reinhart, C.M., Rogoff, K.S., 2011. The forgotten history of domestic debt. Econ. J. 121 (552), 319–350. ISSN 1468-0297. doi:10.1111/j.1468-0297.2011.02426.x.

Sorensen, P., 2003. International tax coordination: regionalism versus globalism. J. Public Econ. 88, 1187–1214.

Sorensen, P.B., 2001. Tax coordination and the European Union: what are the issues? University of Copenhagen, Working Paper.

Sosa-Padilla, C., 2012. Sovereign defaults and banking crises. Manuscript.

Tabellini, G., 1991. The politics of intergenerational redistribution. J. Polit. Econ. 99, 335–357.

Talvi, E., Vegh, C.A., 2005. Tax base variability and procyclical fiscal policy in developing countries. J. Dev. Econ. 78 (1), 156–190. http://ideas.repec.org/a/eee/deveco/v78y2005i1p156-190.html.

Tauchen, G., 1986. Finite state Markov-chain approximation to univariate and vector autoregressions. Econ. Lett. 20, 177–181.

Trabandt, M., Uhlig, H., 2011. The Laffer curve revisited. J. Monet. Econ. 58 (4), 305–327.

Trabandt, M., Uhlig, H., 2012. How do laffer curves differ across countries? BFI Paper no. 2012-001.

Trehan, B., Walsh, C., 1988. Common trends, the government's budget constraint, and revenue smoothing. J. Econ. Dyn. Control 12 (2-3), 425–444. http://EconPapers.repec.org/RePEc:eee:dyncon:v:12:y:1988:i:2-3:p:425-444.

Vasishtha, G., 2010. Domestic versus external borrowing and fiscal policy in emerging markets. Rev. Int. Econ. 18 (5), 1058–1074.

CHAPTER 33

The Political Economy of Government Debt

A. Alesina*^,†^, A. Passalacqua*
*Harvard University, Cambridge, MA, United States
†IGIER, Bocconi University, Milan, Italy

Contents

Handbook of Macroeconomics, Volume 2B
ISSN 1574-0048, http://dx.doi.org/10.1016/bs.hesmac.2016.03.014

Abstract

This chapter critically reviews the literature which explains why and under which circumstances governments accumulate more debt than it would be consistent with optimal fiscal policy. We also discuss numerical rules or institutional designs which might lead to a moderation of these distortions.

Keywords

Political economy, Optimal taxation, Budget rules, Government debt

JEL Classification Codes

E62, H63, H21

1. INTRODUCTION

Fiscal policy is deeply intertwined with politics since it is mostly about redistribution across individuals, regions, and generations: the core of political conflict. The redistributive role of governments has been increasing over time starting with the welfare programs introduced during the Great Depression and then with the additional jumps in the sixties and seventies of last century. But even recently the size of social spending (as defined by the OECD[a]) in 18 OECD countries jumped from 18% of GDP in 1980 to 26% in 2014.[b] In addition, the provision of public goods, which is therefore not classified as directly redistributive, has a redistributive component to the extent that public goods are used more or less intensively by individuals in different income brackets. The structure of taxation, such as the progressivity of the income tax brackets, also implies redistributions.[c] Politics matter for other macro policy areas, such as monetary policy and financial regulation. The recent financial crisis, for example, has reopened issues regarding the desirable conduct of monetary policy and the connection between

[a] OECD defines Social Expenditure as the provision by public (and private) institutions of benefits to, and financial contributions targeted at, households and individuals in order to provide support during circumstances which adversely affect their welfare, provided that the provision of the benefits and financial contributions constitutes neither a direct payment for a particular good or service nor an individual contract or transfer. Such benefits can be cash transfers, or can be the direct (in-kind) provision of goods and services.

[b] OECD (2014). The list of countries is: Australia, Austria, Belgium, Canada, Denmark, Finland, France, Germany, Ireland, Italy, Japan, Netherlands, Norway, Portugal, Spain, Sweden, United Kingdom, United States.

[c] Alesina and Giuliano (2012) review the vast literature which has investigated the political and social determinants for the demand of redistribution.

monetary and fiscal policy. The ECB is at the center stage of the political discussion about institutional building in the Euro area. In the present chapter we focus exclusively on fiscal policy.[d]

The politics of fiscal policy could cover issues as diverse as the level of centralization vs decentralization, the structure of taxation, pension systems, the design of insurance programs like health care and unemployment subsidies, the optimal taxation of capital, international coordination of tax systems, just to name a few topics. In this chapter we focus on debt. Many countries have been struggling with large debt over GDP ratios even before the financial crisis: countries which faced the Great Recession starting with large debt risked (or experienced) debt crises, like Greece, Italy, and Portugal putting at risk even the survival of the Monetary Union. Japan has a public debt held by the private sector of at least 140% of GDP.[e] The political debate on how and at what speed to reduce the public debt after the Great Recession is at the center stage of the political debate.[f] When adding expected future liabilities of entitlements and pensions the public budget of most OECD countries, including the Unites States, look bleak. Debt problems in developing countries, especially in Latin America have been common. Any attempt to explain all of these phenomena leaving politics out is completely pointless.

In particular we ask two broad questions. First, is there a tendency in democracies to pursue suboptimal fiscal policies which lead to the accumulation of excessive debt, where "excessive" is in reference of what a benevolent social planner would do? In other words, how far are the observed pattern of debt accumulation and fluctuations in line with normative prescription of the literature on debt management like, in particular, Barro (1979), Lucas and Stokey (1983), and Aiyagari et al. (2002)? What explains substantial departure from optimality?[g] Second, are fiscal rules (and which ones) a possible solution to limit the extent of the problem of excessive deficits? The balanced budget rule is the most famous one, but may other have been proposed, especially in the Euro area. Two are the key issues in this debate. The trade off between the rigidity of a rule and the lack of flexibility which these rules create. More flexible rules may be superior but harder to enforce because they have too many escape clauses. Finally, assuming that a rule would work, would a country adopt it? Or would political distortions prevent it?[h]

We shall begin with a brief sketch of the prescriptions of the optimal debt management in order to identify the normative implication against which to confront actual

[d] Alesina and Stella (2010) address old and new issues regarding the politics of monetary policy.

[e] The gross figure is well above 200% but it includes debt held by various public institutions.

[f] Reinhart and Rogoff (2010) and Rogoff (1990) have emphasized the cost of debt burden for long run growth.

[g] For a review of an early literature on this point see Alesina and Perotti (1995). For more recent surveys see Persson and Tabellini (2000) and Drazen (2000).

[h] An issue which we do not consider in this chapter is the question of procyclicality of budget deficits and the political distortions which may lead to this problem. See Gavin and Perotti (1997) and Alesina et al. (2008).

policies. The goal of this chapter is not to review in detail the optimal debt literature. We will exclusively focus on models with distortionary taxation and we will not enter the discussion of the Ricardian equivalence. We will not discuss issues regarding governments' defaults on their liabilities, a topic which would deserve an entire chapter on its own. After having described which are the implications of the optimal taxation theory regarding debt management, we show that even a cursory look at the empirical evidence suggest substantial deviations from these prescriptions even amongst OECD countries. In fact, in terms of empirical evidence we will focus almost exclusively on OECD economies. Then, we discuss several different approaches which have tried to explain these deviations from optimality, by introducing political variables in debt management models. Finally, we return to a normative question. Given the presence of all of the potential political distortions examined above, which rules, institutions, procedures or a combination of them is more likely to bring actual fiscal policy closer to the social planner ideal policy? In addition, are these rule and procedures likely to be chosen? Have they worked in the past?.

This chapter is organized as follows. In Section 2, we briefly review the theories of optimal deficit management and the related empirical evidence. In Section 3 to 7, we address the first question, namely whether or not there is a deficit bias in modern economies, and what explains it. In Sections 7 to 10, we cover the question of fiscal rules and of which institutional arrangement would be more suitable to limit suboptimal conduct of fiscal policy. The last section discusses open issues for future research.

2. OPTIMAL DEBT POLICIES: A BRIEF REVIEW

2.1 Tax Smoothing

The theory of tax smoothing is due to Barro (1979) in a model where debt is not contingent and risk free, spending needs are exogenously given and known, taxes have convex costs. The public debt takes the form of one-period, single-coupon bond and the rate of return on public and private debt is constant over time. The government raises in each period tax revenues τ_t. Government spending is indicated with G_t and debt with b_t and the interest rate on debt with r. Thus the government budget constraint in each period is given by:

$$G_t + rb_{t-1} = \tau_t + (b_t - b_{t-1}) \tag{1}$$

The lifetime government budget constraint is given by:

$$\sum_{t=1}^{\infty}\left[\frac{G_t}{(1+r)^t}\right] + b_0 = \sum_{t=1}^{\infty}\left[\frac{\tau_t}{(1+r)^t}\right] \tag{2}$$

Raising taxes generates some extra costs which can be interpreted as collection costs, or more in general deadweight losses or excess burden of taxes and the timing in which taxes are collected. Let Z_t be this cost which depends on the taxes of that period τ_t and negatively on the pool of taxable income/resources Y_t. In particular, let Z_t be defined as:

$$Z_t = F(\tau_t, Y_t) = \tau_t f\left(\frac{\tau_t}{Y_t}\right) \tag{3}$$

with $f'(\cdot) > 0$ and $f''(\cdot) > 0$. The present discounted value of these costs is:

$$Z = \sum_{t=1}^{\infty} \tau_t \frac{f\left(\frac{\tau_t}{Y_t}\right)}{(1+r)^t} \tag{4}$$

The social planner chooses τ_t in order to minimize (4) subject to the budget constraint (2). From the first order conditions, one can find that the tax–income ratio $\frac{\tau}{Y}$ is equal in all periods. Given that, the level of taxes in each period is determined from the values of income $(Y_1, Y_2, \ldots)$, government expenditure $(G_1, G_2, \ldots)$, interest rate r and the initial debt stock b_0. The properties of the solution are considered under different assumptions about the time paths of income Y and government expenditure G. With constant income and government expenditure (ie, $Y_t = Y_{t+1} = \ldots = Y$ and $G_t = G_{t+1} = \ldots = G$) since the tax–income ratio is constant, this implies that τ is also constant and the government budget is always balanced. With transitory income and government expenditure (eg, transitory expenditure during wartime or during recessions) deficits are larger the longer and the larger is the transitory shock. The debt–income ratio would be expected to be constant on average, but would rise in periods of abnormally high government spending or abnormally low aggregate income.

2.2 Keynesian Stabilization

This is not the place to discuss the potential benefits of discretionary countercyclical fiscal policy actions, namely increases in discretionary spending during recessions and reductions during booms. According to Keynesian theories, higher government spending or lower taxes during a recession may help economic recovery. The reason is that under high unemployment and low capacity utilization, higher government spending, and lower tax rates may increase aggregate demand. Note that Keynesian models would prescribe that deficits should be countercyclical (ie, increase in recessions), but should not lead to a secular increase in debt over GDP. The reason being that spending increases during recessions should be compensated by discretionary spending cuts during booms.

We only note that the "long and variable lags" argument raised by Milton Friedman regarding monetary stabilization policy applies even more to fiscal policy where the lags are even longer and less predictable than for monetary policy. Friedman's original argument was applied to monetary policy. He argued that the lags in between the uncovering of the need of, say, a stimulus, the discussion of it, the implementation and the realization of its effects were "long and variable." Therefore, by the time the expansionary policy came into action it was too late and it was counterproductive. This argument applies even more strongly to fiscal policy since the latter requires also an explicit political process, debate, and approval in parliaments. The recent Great Recession and the lower bound issue for monetary policy has made popular the view that in this scenario, aggressive discretionary fiscal policies are necessary since automatic stabilizers are not enough. We do not enter in the zero lower bound debate in the present chapter.

2.3 Contingent Debt

Lucas and Stokey (1983) build on Ramsey (1927) and show that Barro's intuition does not generally apply. The main difference with Barro (1979) is in the set of instruments available to the government to smooth the distortionary cost of taxation. While Barro (1979) focuses in only one instrument, namely noncontingent one-period bonds, Lucas and Stokey (1983) consider a model with complete markets, no capital, exogenous Markov government expenditures, state-contingent taxes, and government debt. In this, environment optimal tax rates and government debt are not random walks, and the serial correlations of optimal taxes are tied closely to those for government expenditures. Moreover, they find that taxes should be smooth, not by being random walks, but in having a smaller variance than a balanced budget would imply. Thus, to some extent, the idea of tax smoothing holds but not in the extreme version as in Barro (1979).[i]

2.4 Accumulation of Government Assets

Aiyagari et al. (2002) reconsider the optimal taxation problem in an incomplete markets setting. They begin with the same economy as in Lucas and Stokey (1983), but allow only risk-free government debt. Under some restrictions on preferences and the quantities of risk-free claims that the government can issue and own, it is possible to obtain back Barro's random walk characterization of optimal taxation. However, by dropping the restriction on government asset holdings (or modifying preferences) generates different results.

More specifically, under the special case of utility linear in consumption and concave in leisure, the authors show that as long as the government can use lump-sum transfers and spending shocks are bounded, then distortionary labor taxes converge to zero in the long run. The optimal solution prescribes reducing debt in good times, so that eventually the government has accumulated enough assets to finance the highest possible

[i] Interestingly, Klein et al. (2008) address the same issue raised in Lucas and Stokey (1983) but find different and strikingly results. In particular, they find that the time series of debt in the economy without commitment is extremely similar to that with commitment. Welfare is very similar as well. This result is surprising: under commitment, there is always an incentive for a once-and-for-all tax cut/debt hike, thus suggesting ever-increasing debt under lack of commitment. However, they show that the incentives that naturally arise in the dynamic game between successive governments actually help limit the time-consistency problem: they lead to very limited debt accumulation, and long-run debt levels can even be lower than under commitment. This incentive mechanism is a result of forward looking and strategic use of debt.

expenditure shock with the interest earned on its stock of assets. This is the so-called "war chest of the government." Instead, if one set a binding upper bound on the government asset level (Ad Hoc Asset Limit) the Ramsey solution for taxes and government debt will resemble the results stated in Barro (1979).[j]

2.5 Evidence on Optimal Policy

The very basic principles of optimal debt policies, namely the debt–income ratio would be expected to be constant on average, but would rise in periods of abnormally high government spending or abnormally low aggregate income, are generally not satisfied by the data.

Government debts do go up during wars and major recessions, but beyond that, deviations from optimal policy are widespread. Figs. 1 and 2 clearly show that government debts do go up in wars and recessions in the United Kingdom and United States.

The major role played by wars is evident in these graphs. However, even the United States shows anomalous features, like the accumulation of debt in the eighties, which is a

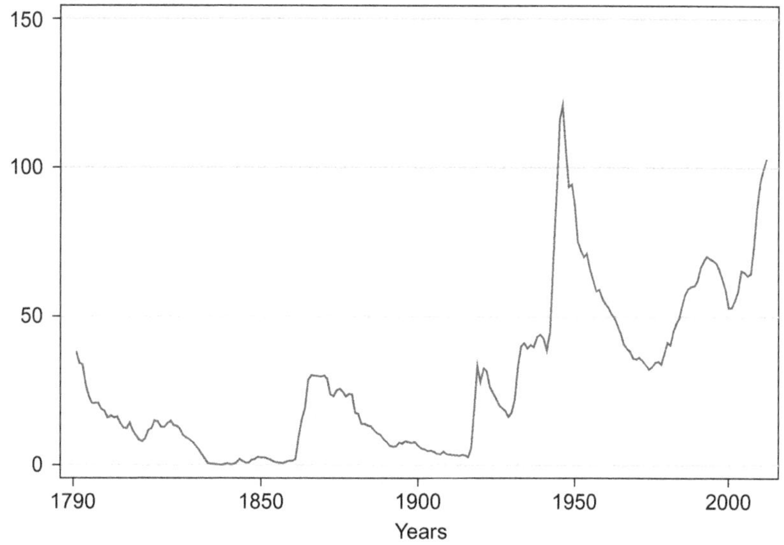

Fig. 1 Ratio of public debt to trend real GDP, the United States, 1790–2012. *Source: Abbas, S.A., Belhocine, N., Elganainy, A., Horton, M. 2010. A historical public debt database. Working Papers 245, International Monetary Fund.*

[j] By imposing a time invariant ad hoc limit on debt, the distribution of government debt will have a non-trivial distribution with randomness that does not disappear even in the limit. In particular, rather than converging surely to a unique distribution, it may continue to fluctuate randomly if randomness on government expenditures persists sufficiently.

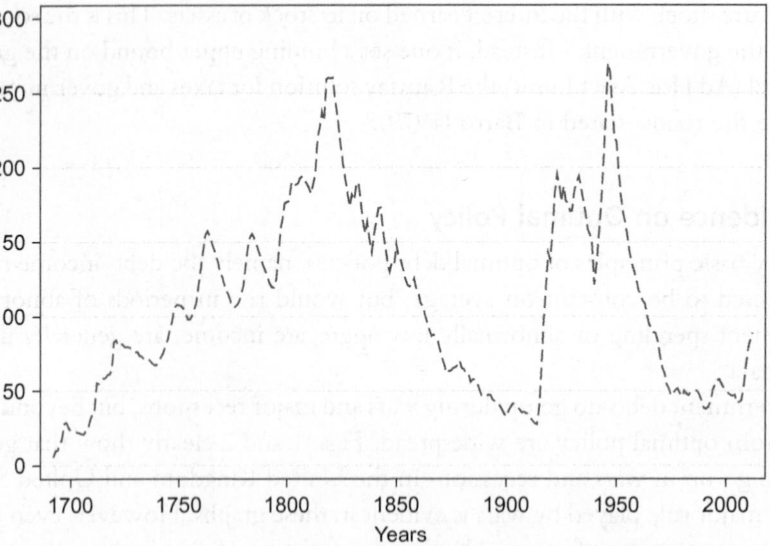

Fig. 2 Ratio of public debt to trend real GDP, United Kingdom, 1692–2012. *Source: Abbas, S.A., Belhocine, N., Elganainy, A., Horton, M. 2010. A historical public debt database. Working Papers 245, International Monetary Fund.*

period of peace. This episode (the so-called "Reagan deficits") in fact inspired a few papers reviewed later and, at the time, generated a major policy debate about the political forces which led to these deficits. Other OECD countries show remarkable deviation from optimality.

We show in Figs. 3 and 4 two graphs for a group of relatively high and low debt countries.

Several observations are in order. First, the decline in the debt ratios after the Second World War in both groups of countries stopped in the seventies. In both groups of countries it increased for several decades in peace time, obviously much more in the high debt group. For instance, in Italy and Greece the debt to GDP ratio skyrocketed in the eighties and nineties in a period of relatively rapid growth for these countries. Belgium and Ireland as well entered the nineties with debt level normally typical of postwar periods well above 100% of GDP. Second, several countries (ie, Ireland, Belgium, Denmark) had massive variations up and down of their debt ratios in peace time. Third, very few countries when they adopted the Euro satisfied the requirement of a less than 60% debt over GDP ratio. In addition, in the first decade of the Euro, up to the financial crisis, there was not much of an effort to converge to the prescribed target of 60%. Fourth, no country comes even close to a policy as prescribed by Aiyagari et al. (2002) which would imply the accumulation of assets to build a "war chest." Fifth, the Great Recession has led to very large accumulation of government debts and this is, at least in large part, consistent

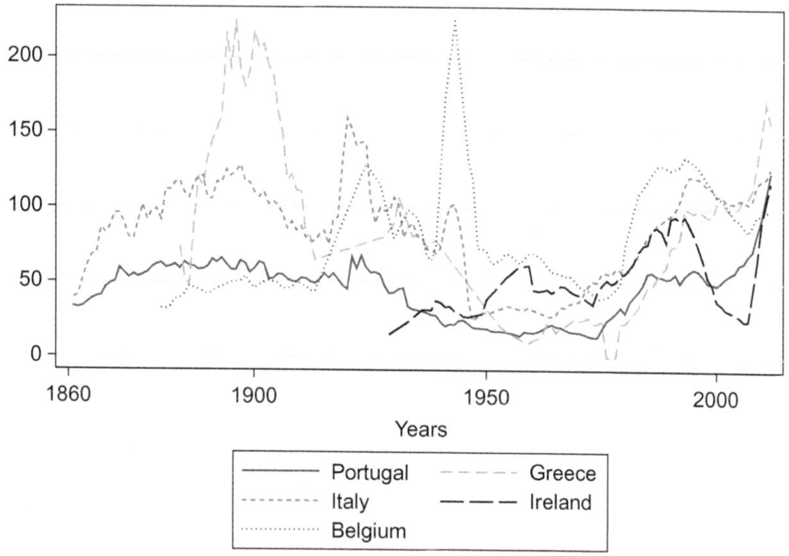

Fig. 3 High debt countries, ratio of public debt to trend real GDP. *Source: Abbas, S.A., Belhocine, N., Elganainy, A., Horton, M. 2010. A historical public debt database. Working Papers 245, International Monetary Fund.*

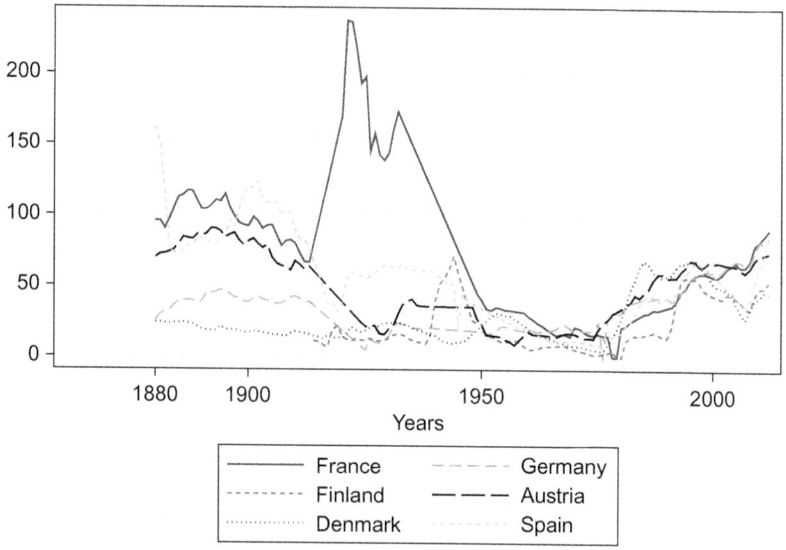

Fig. 4 Low debt countries, ratio of public debt to trend real GDP. *Source: Abbas, S.A., Belhocine, N., Elganainy, A., Horton, M. 2010. A historical public debt database. Working Papers 245, International Monetary Fund.*

with the tax smoothing hypothesis. However, countries which had already accumulated large debts for no obvious reasons before the crisis were constrained in how much they could accumulate more. Some additional accumulation created market panics; Greece had a partial default; Italy in 2011 was on the brink of a major crisis. Fifth, a few countries like Ireland and Spain entered the Great Recession with relatively low debt/GDP ratio but their fiscal position looked better than they really were due to extraordinarily and temporary tax revenues, namely the housing boom. When this became apparent these countries also faced debt panics. In fact, public debt problem in Europe almost degenerated to the point of a collapse of the Euro.

Table 1 shows that out of 20 OECD countries only 4 had a deficit for less than 50% of the time since 1960, and 11 countries had a deficit for more than 80% of the years. Italy and Portugal achieved a "perfect" 100%! These data do not distinguish between primary and total deficit, do not account for the cycle but nevertheless raise a significant flag about government profligacy. After the first oil shock of 1973–74, surpluses close to disappear. Easterly (1993) suggests that at that time (early seventies) many countries did not internalize a secular downturn of their growth process which would have required a reduction in the growth of government spending to keep the size of government constant. This lead to an accumulation of debt. Whether this misperception was an "honest mistake" or it was due to political distortions is a topic of discussion. In fact, it is pretty common for governments to justify large spending programs with very optimistic growth forecasts.

When considering the future liabilities of government, the picture regarding debt levels, appears substantially worse. The aging of the population (and the retirement of the baby boomers) will induce substantial strains over the social security budgets.

Table 1 Percent years of deficit over 1960–2011

	Australia	Austria	Belgium	Canada	Germany
Percent	80	82	96	76	78
Last surplus	2008	1974	2006	2007	2008
	Denmark	**Spain**	**Finland**	**France**	**United Kingdom**
Percent	48	78	20	90	84
Last surplus	2008	2007	2008	1974	2001
	Greece	**Ireland**	**Italy**	**Japan**	**Netherlands**
Percent	80	80	100	68	88
Last surplus	1972	2007		1992	2008
	Norway	**New Zealand**	**Portugal**	**Sweden**	**United States**
Percent	4	46	100	42	92
Last surplus	2011	2008		2008	2000

Source: Wyplosz (2014). Fiscal rules: theoretical issues and historical experiences. In: Alesina, A., Giavazzi, F. (Eds.), Fiscal Policy After the Financial Crisis, Volume Fiscal Rules: Theoretical Issues and Historical Experiences. University of Chicago Press and National Bureau of Economic Research, pages 495–529.

In different degrees, in various countries health expenses (also related to the aging of the population) are rising at phenomenal rates. The US Congressional budget office (CBO (2014)) predicts that with unchanged legislature, the debt over GDP ratio in the United States will never fall in the most optimistic scenarios in the next couple of decades. With "middle range" assumptions, the (net) debt over GDP ratio may be well above 100%. The forecasts of the social security administration have been called into question for being too optimistic and not transparent (Kashin et al., 2015). Similar considerations apply to Japan and European countries. There is a large difference between United States vs European countries, and also within European countries. Specifically, in the United States these entitlement programs are about 18.5% of the GDP, while in the European countries between 20% and 30% of GDP. Within the European countries, Norway is the leading country which spent about 30% of the GDP in Entitlement programs. Regarding the type of entitlement programs, pension expenditures account for more than half of the entitlements in Italy and Greece, while they are less than 20% in Ireland and Denmark.[k] In countries like Italy, we are reaching paradoxes in which youngsters do not find jobs because of high labor taxes and high labor cost for firms to collect tax revenues needed to pay pensions for the parents who then support the unemployed children.

The intergenerational accounting procedure for evaluating liabilities of the government offers an alternative measure to federal budget deficit to gauge intergenerational policy. It was developed by Auerbach et al. (1991) and it computes the net amount in present value that current and future generations are projected to pay to the government now and in the future. If one thinks that the government has an intertemporal budget constraint, then this constraint would require that the sum of generational accounts of all current and future generations plus existing government net wealth be sufficient to finance the present value of current and future government consumption. The generational accounts can be viewed simply as a tabulation of the net effect of future taxes paid and transfers received by various generations, assuming that current policy remains unchanged into the indefinite future. Auerbach et al. (1991) compute the "lifetime net tax rate," which measures the burden of taxes minus transfer payment on a generation over its lifetime. The Generational accounting criteria presumes that fiscal policies should be generational balanced. This would imply that the net tax rate for current and future generations should be the same. If the net tax rate for future generations exceeds the net tax rate for newborns, then according to this criteria, fiscal policy is not in generational balance. Haveman (1994) provides an excellent discussions of the pros and cons of generational accounting methods.

[k] Specifically, in 2011 pensions account for 51.9% of total Entitlement programs in Italy, 51.1% in Greece, 19.6% in Denmark, and 16.8% in Ireland. *Source*: OECD (2015).

3. DEFICITS AND ELECTIONS

3.1 Fiscal Illusion

The idea of "fiscal illusion" is due to the public choice school (see in particular Buchanan and Wagner, 1977). According to this argument voters do not understand the notion of intertemporal budget constraint for the government, therefore when (especially close to elections) voters see pending hikes or tax cuts (the public choice schools was especially concerned with the former) they reward the incumbent, and remain unaware of the consequences of such policies on public debt and the future costs of taxation needed to service it. The problem, according to the Public Choice school, is aggravated by the "Keynesian" policy stand. Politicians are eager to follow the Keynesian rule of increasing discretionary spending during recessions, but then they do not counterbalance it with cuts during booms. Thus, the result of keynesianism and fiscal illusion leads to persistent deficits and explosive debt levels.

In general, the view that the best way to please the voters is to spend more and tax less is so pervasive that it is assumed to be an obvious fact. As we show later, the evidence is much more nuanced than it would appear. In addition, given the extensive discussion of the deficits, the pros and cons of austerity policies in the United States and Europe, it is hard to believe that today's voters are unaware of the potential cost of deficits because of fiscal illusion, even though there may be disagreement on what policies to follow to respond to deficits. The fiscal illusion argument is overly simplistic although it does raise important warning bells on the conduct of fiscal policies in democracies.

3.2 Political Budget Cycles: Theory

The traditional fiscal illusion argument rely on some form of irrationality or ignorance on the part of the voters. However, political budget cycles can be derived also in models where voters are fully rational but imperfectly informed as in Rogoff (1990) and Rogoff and Sibert (1988). What leads to these cycles is a combination of delays in the acquisition of information on the part of the voters regarding the realization of certain policy variables and different degrees of "competence" of policymakers.[1]

In Rogoff and Sibert (1988) more competent governments can tax less to provide public goods, because they introduce less wastage in the fiscal process. However, the full combination of income taxes, spending, seigniorage, and government wastage (ie, negative competence) is learned with one period delay by the voters. A higher level of competence implies that the government can provide public goods with lower taxes (or seigniorage). Suppose that before an election voters see a tax cut. They cannot distinguish whether the cut is due to a high realization of competence (which is unobservable by them immediately) or transitory deficit which they do not fully observe.

[1] For a review of political business cycles in general see Alesina et al. (1993) and Drazen (2000).

After the election, a less competent government would have to increase seigniorage generating also an inflation cycle. With a finite time horizon the only equilibrium that exists is a separating equilibrium, ie, the one in which voters are able to infer exactly the incumbent's level of competency from the tax she selects in order to signal her competence. The competent policymaker cut taxes before election to a level that cannot be matched by the less competent one. A somewhat unpleasant feature of these models is that the more competent policymakers engages in budget cycles by cutting taxes before elections to signal their competence and distinguish themselves from the less competent ones who cannot afford such a large tax cut. Rogoff (1990) adds a distinction between two types of public goods, those that are clearly visible before an election, say fixing the holes in the street, and those less immediately visible, like increasing the quality of the training of teachers. In this model politicians have an interest in overspending in more visible but not necessarily the most productive public goods close to election time.

While, in principle, the implication of rationally based modern theories of political business cycles may be similar to the traditional one, they differ in two ways. First, the rationality of voters output a limit on the extent of these policies. Second, and this will be revealed by the empirical evidence, the more the voters are informed and understand the incentive of policymakers, the less they reward them for their behavior; thus for instance more freedom of the press in established democracies would be a constraint on this behavior.[m]

Drazen and Eslava (2010b) present models of political budget cycles in which the incumbent favors with certain spending projects specific and critical to constituencies and/or localities. By varying the composition of government spending the incumbent can target swing voters before elections. Incidentally, this imply that a political budget cycles may imply distribution of spending from one district to another, holding constant the total amount of government spending.[n]

3.3 Political Budget Cycles: Evidence

Are political budget cycles common? Persson and Tabellini (2000) argue that the answer depends upon the nature of the political institutions of the country. In particular, they argue that political budget cycles are less likely to occur in majoritarian systems rather than proportional representation systems. Brender and Drazen (2005), however, challenge these results. They find that the existence of political budget cycles do not depend on voting rules. Political budget cycles exist only in "new democracies," where fiscal

[m] For instance, Besley and Prat (2006) develop a model in which more press freedom reduces the space for policymakers to extract rents. For a review of the political economy of mass media refer to Prat and Stromberg (2013).

[n] Hassler et al. (2005) show an interesting result, namely that the introduction of political distortions would reduce, instead of exacerbate, oscillations in tax rates. This is contrast with the predictions of the literature on political business cycles.

manipulation may work because voters are inexperienced with electoral politics or may simply lack information, which may be one of the main factors generating the political budget cycle, as implied by the models reviewed earlier.

The role of information is tested by Brender (2003) for local elections in Israel. Peltzman (1992) and Drazen and Eslava (2010a) perform an analogous analysis in the United States and Colombia, respectively.[o] Gonzalez (2002) and Shi and Svensson (2006) test the importance of transparency, which ultimately means the probability that voters at no costs learn the incumbent's characteristics. They find that the higher the degree of transparency, the smaller the political budget cycle. Moreover, while the proportion of uninformed voters may be initially large, it is likely to decrease over time, thus decreasing the magnitude of the budget cycle. Akhmedov and Zhuravskaya (2003) find that measures of the freedom of the regional media and the transparency of the regional governments are important predictors of the magnitude of the cycle. Alt and Lassen (2006) find that, in the sample of OECD countries, higher fiscal transparency eliminates the electoral cycle.[p]

The other important aspect is whether or not governments which generated political budget cycles are more easily reelected. Brender and Drazen (2008) consider the effect of deficits on the probability of reelection and show that voters are (weakly) likely to punish rather than reward budget deficits over the leader's term in office. Their results are robust by considering different subsamples: (i) developed countries and less developed countries; (ii) new and old democracies; (iii) countries with presidential or parliamentary government systems; (iv) countries with proportional or majoritarian electoral systems; (v) countries with different levels of democracy.

A related literature directly tests the political consequences of large fiscal adjustments, ie, whether large reductions of budget deficit have important negative political consequences. Alesina et al. (1998) consider a sample of OECD countries and they find that fiscal austerity has a weakly positive, rather than negative, electoral effect. However, they focus on cabinet changes and opinion pools, rather than on election results. Alesina et al. (2012) fill this gap, by looking directly at the election results. They find no evidence of a negative effect on the election results due to a fiscal adjustment. Buti et al. (2010) find that the probability of reelection for the incumbent politicians are not affected by their efforts in implementing pro-market reforms. This literature, however, suffers from a potential sort of reverse causality problem, namely governments which are especially popular for whatever reasons, manage to get reelected despite their deficit reduction policies, not

[o] Schuknecht (2000) presents evidence of cycles in 35 developing countries and Buti and Van Den Noord (2004) some evidence on European Union countries.

[p] Alesina and Paradisi (2014) show evidence of political budget cycles in Italian cities. Foremny et al. (2015) provide evidence on political budget cycles using data on two German regions. Arvate et al. (2009) find evidence on localities in Brazil.

because of them. While the authors are aware of this issues and try to asses it, measuring the "popularity" of a government is not always straightforward.

The bottom line is that political budget cycles may explain relative small departures from optimal policy around election times, especially in new democracies. However, they cannot be the main explanation for large and long lasting accumulation of public debt, as we documented earlier. Also, the cross country empirical evidence seems to have been exhausted. Perhaps natural experiments at the local level might be interesting.

4. SOCIAL CONFLICT: WAR OF ATTRITION AND RIOTS

4.1 War of Attrition: Theory

War of attrition models do not explain "why" a deficit occurs, but they explain why deficit reduction policies are postponed. Alesina and Drazen (1991) focus on the case of a country that for whatever reason, due a permanent shock on revenues (or on expenditures), is on a "nonsustainable" path of government debt growth. The debt is held by foreigners and the interest rate is constant and exogenously given and there is no default. The longer the country waits to raise tax rates to stop the growth of debt, the more the interest burden accumulates and the more expensive the stabilization will be. The latter implies a reduction to zero of total deficits.

There are two equally sized groups of equal (exogenous) income which cannot agree on how to share the costs of the stabilization. The social planner would choose an equal division of costs for each group since the groups have the same income and size. In this case, stabilization would occur immediately since delays only create inefficient costs, namely higher interests on the accumulated foreign debt. The critical feature of the model is that without a social planner political polarization leads to an uneven distribution of the costs of the stabilization. In particular, one group has to pay more than 1/2 of the taxes needed for the stabilization and in every period after that. When both groups perceive the possibility of shifting this burden elsewhere, each group attempts to wait the other out. In order for this to happen there has to be some uncertainty about the costs of each group to wait the other out, namely how long a group can bear the costs of delaying the stabilization. These costs are modeled as the economic costs of living in the distorted prestabilization economy (for instance with inflation) or the political cost of "blocking" attempts of the opponent to impose an undesired stabilization plan. This war of attrition ends, and a stabilization is enacted, when a group concedes and allows its political opponents to be the winner. The loser then pays more than half of the costs of the stabilization, allowing the winner to pay less. The condition which determines the concession time is the one which equals the marginal cost living an extra moment in the unstable economy to the probability that in the next moment the opponent group will concede, multiplied by the differences the costs of being the winner rather than the loser. This is why uncertainty about the strength of the groups is critical. If one group knew from the beginning that its cost of living in an unstable economy were larger than those of the other group, it would know that it may end up losing the war of attrition and therefore it would concede immediately; this would be cheaper than postponing the inevitable loss. The passage of time reveals the type of the groups, namely which one is stronger. The more unequal are the divisions of the cost of the stabilization, which can be interpreted as a degree of polarization of a society, the longer the war of attrition and the higher the level of debt accumulated since the relative benefit of winning increase.

The war of attrition implies that individually (group level) rational strategies lead to a suboptimal accumulation of debt. The group which will end up being the loser is the one with the highest cost of prolonging the war of attrition. This is why uncertainty about these cost are critical. If it was common knowledge which was the weaker groups, the latter would capitulate immediately, since waiting adds to the costs and this group would lose anyway. Therefore anything that eliminates this uncertainty ends the war of attrition.

4.2 War of Attrition: Empirical Evidence

The model has several empirical implications. The first one is that the passage of time may lead a country to stabilize even if nothing observable happens, simply because one group has reached the condition of "conceding," namely has learned its relative strength to that of the opponent. Second, an electoral or legislative victory of one of the groups may signal its superior political strength and may lead the opponent to concede. Third, longer delays and higher debt should occur in polarized societies which cannot reach a "fair" and acceptable distribution of costs. In addition, delays are longer when many groups have a "veto power" to block policy decisions which they do not like. Fourth, a worsening of the economic crisis may lead to a resolution of the war of attrition. When the costs of delay increase for one of the groups the latter may concede sooner. Drazen and Grilli (1993) show that in their case a "crisis" can be beneficial, since it worsens the utility level of one of the groups in the short run, but it may be welfare improving for all in the long run since the war of attrition ends sooner. Fourth, for the opposite reason foreign aid can be counterproductive (Casella and Eichengreen, 1996). If foreign aid makes life easier before the stabilization, delays are longer and in the long run welfare is lower. The result, however, depends on how aid is disbursed; for instance foreign aid that implicitly "picks" a winner would end the war of attrition sooner. Finally, an external commitment, say an IMF conditionality agreement, may accelerate the resolution of the war of attrition making it more costly to "fight it." Several authors have suggested empirical observations consistent with the implications of the war of attrition model. Alesina and Drazen (1991) discuss a few historical examples of cases in which the same government first fails to stabilize because it encounters political opposition then it succeeds because the opposition is defeated. The idea that multiple veto players delay the elimination of deficits is consistent with the evidence by Grilli et al. (1991) and Kontopoulos and Perotti (1999).

The former argue that in the eighties, debt accumulated more in parliamentary democracies with multiparty systems. The latter argue that the number of spending ministers is associated with looser fiscal controls, an issue upon which we return later. Volkerink and De Haan (2001) and Elgie and McMenamin (2008) provide evidence on a sample of 22 advanced economies showing that more fragmented governments with smaller majorities in parliaments have larger deficits. Persson and Tabellini (2000) review and add to this line of research with additional evidence. These authors and Milesi-Ferretti et al. (2002) show also that coalition governments spend more on welfare, a point analyzed also by Alesina and Glaeser (2005) in a comparison of United States vs Europe. As we discussed earlier, Easterly (1993) noted that countries accumulated debt because they did not adjust their spending programs to the secular reduction of growth which started in the late seventies. These delays in adjusting to a permanent shock is consistent with the general message of the war of attrition. Various constituencies objected to reducing the growth of their favorite spending programs.

A second line of inquiry has focused on the idea that "crisis generates reforms," as in Drazen and Easterly (2001). Needless to say, the evidence suffers from problems of reverse causality: why would you need a reform if you did not have a problem to begin with?[q] Alesina et al. (2010) combine these institutional hypothesis with the crisis hypothesis, making a step closer toward testing the war of attrition model. In particular, they test whether certain institutions are more likely and rapid to resolve crisis, a result consistent with the model by Spolaore (2004). Alesina et al. (2010) define a country as being in a "crisis" if at time *t* the country is in the "worst" 25% of the countries in the (large) sample in terms of budget deficits.[r] They find support for the view that "stronger governments" stabilize more in time of crisis, ie, when a crisis comes, strong governments adjust more and exit more quickly from the state of "crisis." Strong governments are presidential systems and amongst parliamentary systems those in which the majority has a greater share advantage over the minority. They also find that stabilization (ie, exit from crisis) are more likely to occur at the beginning of a term of office of a new government. These results are consistent with the war of attrition model in the sense that in an unstable situation (ie, a crisis), a stabilization occurs sooner with fewer veto players or with a clear political winner. Results on the effect of IMF programs are inconclusive but, as discussed earlier, causality problems are especially serious in this case.

4.3 War of Attrition: Summing up

The war of attrition model has proven to be successful as an explanation of observed characteristics of run away debts and the timing of stabilization. One issue with this model is that it has been proven difficult to extend it. In particular, the division of costs of the

[q] Similar issues arise on the huge literature on foreign aid, which we can not even begin to survey here.

[r] In their paper these authors also consider inflation crisis, not only deficit crisis.

stabilization is taken as exogenous and not bargained amongst groups. Moving in that direction would lead to bargaining models where institutional details on how the game occurs are critical. Perhaps one may think about connecting this approach with the one discussed later on voting in legislatures. Also the extensions to n rather than 2 groups implies results which are not clear cut and the formation of coalitions amongst n groups are intractable (thus far) problems. Finally, in the model, a stabilization is a zero-one event. Partial or failed attempts are not explicitly modeled even though in reality are quite common.

4.4 Riots

Passarelli and Tabellini (2013) provide a model of political competition which has some connection to the war of attrition although with substantial differences and a "behavioral" bend. In their model several social groups have views about what is a "fair" allocation of resources. The sum of those views about what is fair for each group may be larger than the available resources. In addition groups are willing to engage in costly political actions (riots) when they feel that they have not obtain their fair allocation. When a group perceives that fairness (according to this group's view) has been violated, individuals are willing to engage in costly political actions, like riots, because of this emotional reaction to a perceived unfair behavior. The groups which are more homogeneous are also more likely to be more successful in organizing riots. This feeling of "anger" when perceived fairness has been violated solves the free rider problem of political actions. In a dynamic setting the threats of riots pose constraints to the government. In particular, even a benevolent government may be forced to accumulate excessive debt (above the optimal level) to reduce the threats of riots. Empirically, Woo (2003) shows that public debt accumulation is associated with the occurrence of riots. Ponticelli and Voth (2011) and Passarelli and Tabellini (2013) show how budget cuts are sometimes followed by riots.

It is interesting to compare this evidence on riots and the one reviewed earlier by Brender and Drazen (2008) and Alesina et al. (2012) which suggest that, at least in democracies fiscal adjustments are not associated with consistent electoral losses for the incumbent. Perhaps homogeneous and organized groups organize riots while the less organized median voter is much more prone to accept fiscal retrenchments when necessary. In other words, a government may face strikes and riots organized by specific homogeneous constituencies and those actions may block fiscal adjustment policies and increase public debt. However, the unorganized voters (which may be the majority) may not approve those policies.

It would be interesting to expand Passarelli and Tabellini (2013) framework to incorporate these features in which part of the electorate is organized and has this behavioral bend about fairness, and another part of the electoral is unorganized and does not have self serving feelings of fairness.

5. DEBT AS A STRATEGIC VARIABLE

Government debt is a state variable which "links" several successive governments. Different governments may have different preferences over fiscal policy, say the level and/or composition of public spending. If the current government is not sure of its reappointment, it may want to choose a level of deficit while in office (thus a level of debt) in order to influence the fiscal choices of future governments. In these models, deficits do not affect the probability of reelection since the voters are fully rational, fully informed, and forward looking, but deficits serve the purpose of insuring that future governments follow policies closer to the preference of the current government by constraining future governments' actions. The asymmetry of information that would lead to political business cycles, as we discussed earlier, are assumed away here, and the strategic manipulation of the debt by the current government or majority in office is fully in the interest of those who supported the current government. Another way to put this is the following. Given the inability of current government to control future public spending, it may prefer to take a \$1 of tax revenue away from the future government by borrowing because it may not be in power and be able to decide how that \$1 is spent in future, but it can decide how it can be spent today. Clearly, this logic applies only if there is political turnover and heterogeneity of preferences over fiscal policy amongst the different potential governments.

In Alesina and Tabellini (1990) two parties, with exogenously given preferences, stochastically alternate in office. They care about the level of income of the representative individual and care about two different public goods, say military spending vs domestic spending (more generally they place different weights on these two public goods). In the model there is a representative voter/citizen in terms of his/her choices of labor and leisure but with a distribution of preferences about the type of public goods that they prefer, so they would vote for different parties depending on the parties' choice of public goods. Private and public goods enter separately in the utility function. If a party is unsure of being reappointed, it will issue debt. By doing so it "forces" the following government (possibly of a different party) to spend less on the public good the current government does not care as much. In other words, the current government chooses to distort the path of income taxation in order to spend more on the public goods that it prefers leaving future governments with the task of reducing the debt since default is ruled out by assumption. The future government will do so, at least in part, by cutting spending on the public good the current government does not care much about.[5] The lower is the probability of reappointment of the current government the higher the level of

[5] When both parties care (with different weights) about the two public goods the result about excessive deficit require a weak condition on the third derivative of the utility function on the public goods.

debt chosen. Only a government sure of reappointment would issue no debt. The social planner would issue no debt since there is no reason to do so and would choose a stable combination of the two public goods in order to satisfy, say, utilitarian social preferences. Tabellini and Alesina (1990) provide analogous results in a model in which fiscal decisions are taken by the median voter. The current median voter is uncertain about the preferences of future median voters, because of shocks to the distribution of preferences. Today's median voter choose to issue debt for the political incentives of creating "facts" for future majorities. Alesina and Tabellini (1989) extend this type of model to a small open economy and show a connection between excessive public debts and private capital flights.

Persson and Svensson (1989) provide a related model which, however, does not imply a deficit bias but nonobvious implications about which government would lead a deficit and which would run a surplus. In their model, there are two parties, one of the left who likes a large amount of public goods even at the cost of high taxes, and a party of the right which, on the contrary dislikes public spending and taxation. The public debts links the two alternating parties in office. When the left is in office it chooses to leave a surplus by taxing more in order to generate an incentive for the right when in office to spend more on public goods. The right, when in office, will cut taxes creating a deficit in order to prevent easy spending when the left comes in to office.[t]

In a similar vein Aghion and Bolton (1990) consider the commitment effect of debt in two ways. First, by limiting future expenditure on public goods. Second, in forcing to raise higher tax revenues to repay the debt. Lizzeri (1999) uses similar insights, linking excessive debt accumulation and redistributive policies. In his model, two candidates, motivated purely by the desire of winning elections, can redistribute to some citizens and cannot make promises on future redistribution. In the first period, by running deficits they can target with "excessive" redistribution of transfer skewed in favor of a majority and against a minority.

6. THE COMMON POOL PROBLEM

In these types of models agents do not fully internalize the tax burden of spending decisions leading to "excessive" spending. The most widely studied "common pool problem" is the one of legislators (like the United States Congress) which would like to approve spending programs for their districts without fully internalizing the cost of taxation; in fact, the latter are spread on all (or many other) districts. As we discuss later, similar political distortions arise in different institutional settings.

[t] Pettersson-Lidbom (2001) presents supporting evidence for this model using Swedish data on localities.

6.1 Bargaining in Legislatures

Weingast et al. (1981) provide a model of excessive spending on pork barrel projects which was later extended to various voting rules and applied to study debt accumulation. These authors show how representatives with a geographically based constituency overestimate the benefits of public projects in their districts relative to their financing costs, which are distributed nationwide. The voters of district i receive benefits equal to B_i for a project, but have to pay $1/N$ of the total costs if taxes are equally distributed among districts. Thus, a geographically based representative does not internalize the effect of his proposals on the tax burden of the nation. The aggregate effect of rational representatives facing these incentives is an oversupply of geographically based public projects. Specifically, the size of the budget is larger with N legislators elected in N districts than with a single legislator elected nationwide, and the budget size is increasing in N, the number of districts.

Baron and Ferejohn (1989) substantially improve upon this model by considering voting on the distribution of taxes rather than assuming that every district pays $1/N$ of the cost of every project. They study decisions with majority rule with various alternative procedural rules. In their model there are n members (they can be interpreted as people, districts, or States) in the legislature. The task of the legislature is to choose the distribution of one unit of benefits among the n districts, with no side payments outside the legislature. A "recognition rule" defines who, at each session is going to be the agenda setter with the task of making a proposal. In each session, member i is chosen with probability p_i. Member i then puts forward a bargaining proposal of the form $x^i = (x_1^i, x_2^i, \ldots, x_n^i)$ such that $\sum_j^n x_j^i \leq 1$. If no proposal is approved, each member of the legislature gets zero benefits, the status quo. Members of the legislature have a common discount factor δ.

These authors distinguish between a "close amendment rule" and an "open amendment rule." In the first case, the proposal on the floor is voted upon against the status quo, with no amendments. If the proposal is approved, then the benefits are distributed and the legislature adjourns. If the proposition is rejected the benefits are not distributed and the legislature moves to the next turn. In this case the process starts over, but the benefits are discounted by the factor δ. With an "open amendment rule," after the member is randomly chosen to make the proposal, another member can be recognized at random and may either offer an amendment (ie, an alternative allocation) or move to vote. If the proposal is seconded, the legislature votes as previously. If the proposal is amended, a runoff election is held to determine which proposal will be on the floor. The process is repeated until a recognized member moves the previous question and a yes vote is reached.

In the case of closed amendment Rule, the subgame perfect equilibrium has the following characteristics: (i) the equilibrium distributions of benefits is majoritarian, ie, only a minimum majority gets something; (ii) the agenda setter can get a strictly greater allocation; and (iii) the legislature completes its task in the first session. In the case of open amendment rule, the agenda-setting power of the first proposer is diminished. Indeed, each member must consider the fact that her proposal may be pitted against an amendment. Thus, she has to take this into account when making the proposal. In particular, the proposing member must make a proposal acceptable for at least m out of $n - 1$ other members in the legislature. By choosing m, the original proposer determines the likelihood of acceptance. The higher is m, the higher the probability that the section rule will choose one of the m legislators and the proposal is accepted, but also the lower the benefits that the agenda setter can keep for himself.

6.2 Bargaining in Legislatures and Government Debt

In Velasco (1999, 2000) several interest groups benefit from a particular kind of government spending. Each group can influence the central fiscal authorities to set net transfers on the group's target item at some desired level. The equilibrium implies a debt level at the maximum feasible level. In fact each group demands transfers large enough to cause fiscal deficits and a sustained increase in government debt. Eventually, the government hits its credit ceiling and is locked forever in a position of paying sufficient taxes to service the associated maximal debt level. The intuition for this result is simple. Property rights are not defined over each group's share of overall revenue or assets. A portion of any government asset, which is not spent by one group, will be spent by the other group. Hence, there are incentives to raise net transfers above the collectively efficient rate. Groups do not fully internalize the costs of public spending, namely each of them uses the whole stock of resources instead of a fraction, as the basis for consumption of spending decisions. Krogstrup and Wyplosz (2010) provide a related common pool model of deficit bias in an open economy.

Battaglini and Coate (2008) adopt the Baron and Ferejohn (1989) framework described earlier and study how such bargaining leads to deviations from the optimal path of debt. They focus on the case in which a social planner would implement the solution by Aiyagari et al. (2002). Battaglini and Coate (2008) link the Baron and Ferejohn (1989) model of bargaining in a legislature with the insight of the literature on strategic debt which we have reviewed earlier, in particular the model by Tabellini and Alesina (1990). Current majorities in the legislature will bargain over spending with uncertainty about the nature of future majorities and the debt becomes, as earlier, a strategic tool to control future fiscal decisions.[u] While in Tabellini and Alesina (1990) the will of the majority is simply represented by the optimal policy of the median voter, Battaglini

[u] In a related work Barseghyan et al. (2013) consider, as a driver of fiscal policy persistent tax revenue shocks, which come from business cycle impacts on the private sector. Battaglini and Coate (2015) consider an economic model with unemployment and the distinction between private and public sector jobs. They explore the relationship between debt, unemployment, and the relative size of the public and private sector.

and Coate (2008) provide a much richer institutional setting to characterize decision making.

Battaglini and Coate (2008) model a continuum of infinitely lived citizens located in n identical districts. A single (nonstorable) consumption good z and a public good g are produced using labor. Citizens maximize their lifetime utility which depend on consumption, labor supply, and a parameter A_t, which is the realization at time t of a random variable, which represents the value of the public good for citizens at time t. If, for instance, the public good is defense spending, we value it a lot higher during a war. The legislature provides the public good g and it can finance targeted-district specific transfers s_i, ie, "pork barrel" spending. To finance its activities, the legislature can either set a proportional tax on labor τ or issue one-period risk free bonds x. The legislature faces three different constraints. A feasibility constraint, which imposes that the government revenues have to be high enough to cover expenditures. The "District Transfer Constraint," which imposes that the district-specific transfers must be nonnegative. This constraint excludes lump negative transfers (lump sum taxes) to finance government spending. Finally, the government has to satisfy the Borrowing Constraint, which implies setting an upper and lower bound on the amount of bonds that can be issued or bought back each period. The lower bound is set without loss of generality. Indeed, the government would never need more than the assets the lower bound implies so the constraint never binds. An upper bound is necessary to avoid the government to issue an amount of debt which is unable to pay back the next period. A lower bound is defined by the level according to which it is possible to finance the optimal level of public good just with the interests on the assets the government has accumulated.[v] The legislature, consisting of a representative from each of the n districts, make decisions with closed rules. The legislature meets at the beginning of each period knowing both b_t and A_t. One representative is randomly selected to make the government policy proposal, which consists of the tax rate on labor r_t, the level of public good g_t, the level of bonds x_t, and the district-specific transfers $(s_1,\ldots,s_n)$. The proposal requires consensus of a minimum winning coalition of $q < n$ legislators to be accepted and implemented. If the proposal is rejected another legislator is randomly chosen to make a new proposal. If, after τ rounds, all the proposals are rejected, then the government implements the "Default Policy," which has to satisfy the feasibility constraint and has to treat all the districts equally, ie, $s_1 = \ldots = s_n$.

In this model a social planner would choose the optimal debt path as in Aiyagari et al. (2002). More specifically, the social planner takes as given (b,A) and chooses a policy $\{r,g,x,s_1,\ldots,s_n\}$ which maximizes the utility of citizens in all district. Given (b,A) there

[v] The optimal level of public good is the one which satisfies the Samuelson Rule, ie, the level at which the sum of marginal benefits is equal to the sum of marginal costs.

are two possible cases, namely with or without transfers to the districts. In the first case, with positive pork barrel transfers, the optimal tax rate on labor is set to zero and the optimal level of public good is set to $g_S(A)$, ie, the level that satisfies the Samuelson's Rule. The reason is straightforward. Suppose that the tax rate is positive. Then, the Social planner finds strictly dominant to reduce the pork barrel transfers and to reduce the (distortionary) tax. If the Social Planner does not make any pork barrel transfer, it must be the case that the tax rate is positive, the level of public good provided is less than $g_S(A)$ and the level of public debt exceeds the one with transfers. Thus, pork barrel transfers depend upon the realization of the value for the public good, A. In particular, for high enough values of A, the optimal policy has no transfers: g is high and no room is left for pork barrel. Instead, if the government has resources left to provide pork barrel transfers, then the level of debt must be the lowest possible, ie, the lower bound $\underline{x}$. (Remember that the lower bound implies accumulation of assets). Intuitively, if the planner is willing to give revenues back to citizens through district transfers $(s_1,\ldots,s_n)$, then it must expect not to be imposing taxes in the next period; otherwise, he would be better off reducing transfers and acquiring more bonds. This suggests that the steady state debt level must be such that future taxes are equal to zero, implying it to be equal to $\underline{x}$.

Consider now bargaining in the legislature. The agenda setter has to find $q-1$ supporters for his proposal to pass. The equilibrium policies are driven by the realization of the value of the public good, A, and the value of the public debt left from the previous period. For high enough values of A and/or b, the marginal value of the public good is so high that the proposer does not find it optimal to make positive pork barrel transfers. Thus, the equilibrium policy consists of the outcome as the proposer maximize the utility of all representatives. In other words, we are back to the Social Planner solution with no transfer. For low levels of b and/or A, there may be resources left that can be transferred to the q districts. This implies there exists a cutoff value A^* which divides the space into two different regimes. For $A > A^*$ the economy is in the "responsible policy making" regime (RPM). In this case, the optimal level of the tax rate, the public good and the debt to issue are defined by the Social Planner's optimal conditions with no pork barrel. For $A < A^*$ the economy is in the "business-as-usual" regime (BAU). In this case the proposer defines $(r^*, g^*(A), x^*)$ by maximizing the utility for the q districts included in the "Minimum Winning Coalition." This equilibrium includes also transfers $(s_1,\ldots,s_q)$ high enough to induce the member of the coalition to accept the proposal.

The same optimal conditions can be defined in terms of the public debt. In particular, the equilibrium debt distribution converges to a unique invariant distribution whose support is a subset $[x^*, -x]$. When the debt level is x^*, then the optimal conditions for the tax rate and the public good are those defined by the BAU, with the proposer who makes pork barrel transfers to the q districts. If instead the debt level exceeds x^*, then the economy is in the RPM regime where the tax rate is higher than the one defined in BAU, the provision of public good is lower, and no districts receive transfers.

In the long run, the economy oscillates between BAU and RPM regimes, depending on the realization of the value of the public good A. For instance, pork barrel would disappear during a war when A is large.[w]

In summary, the political distortions which make the social planner solution differs from the political equilibrium arises for two specific reasons. The first one, which can be related to the "Common Pool problem" discussed in the previous section. The minimum winning coalition does not fully internalize the costs of raising taxes or reducing the public good but it fully enjoys the benefit of receiving the pork barrel transfers. The other distortion comes from the uncertainty suffered by the legislators. They do not know ex-ante whether they are going to be included in the minimum winning coalition next period. Thus, they do not fully internalize costs and benefits across periods. In particular, they compare $\$\frac{1}{q}$ benefit today by belonging to the coalition, vs $\$\frac{1}{n}$ expected costs tomorrow. This intuition is similar to the strategic model of debt of Tabellini and Alesina (1990) reviewed earlier. In conclusion, this section makes two important contributions. First, it merges the results found in Tabellini and Alesina (1990) by using Baron and Ferejohn (1989) type of model. Second, it shows that taxation smoothing "a la Barro" is still an important factor in a political economy model, but distortion smoothing through debt is inefficient, and therefore not only this results in excessive accumulation of debt, but also in excessive volatility of the policies in the steady state. From an empirical standpoint, Baqir (2002) shows results consistent with the common pool problem using data from US cities. He shows that larger city council, where the common pool problems may be larger, are associated with more public spending, holding other determinants of the latter constant.

There is also a potential connection with the war of attrition model discussed earlier. In these bargaining models the passage of time is not considered. With a closed rule agreement is immediate but even with an open rule to the extent that proposals and amendments can be made instantaneously time does not matter. In reality, bargaining in legislatures takes time, and the passage of time is critical in the war of attrition models to allow the game to be resolved. At the same time the passage of time leads to the accumulation of debt. Allowing for a realistic consideration of time in these bargaining model could be an interesting avenue for theoretical and empirical research.

6.3 The Common Pool Problems in Other Institutional Settings

The general idea of the common pool problem with strategic debt is relevant for other institutional settings beyond the US Congress.

[w] Battaglini (2014) illustrates an extension of that model, which includes two-party competition in a legislature modeled as earlier.

In particular, in many democracies the budget is crafted by a government (possibly formed by more than one party), it is presented in the legislature and approved, if the parties of the government have a majority, with or without amendments. In this case, we may have a common pool problem with the spending ministers in the government even before the budget reaches the legislature. Each spending minister would generally like to obtain more spending for its own ministry, often pushed by the bureaucracy of the latter. A winning coalition of spending ministers may lead to the approval of a budget which, like in the BAU regime of Battaglini and Coate lead to a sort of "pork barrel" transfers to a minimum winning coalition of spending ministers. These pork barrel spending may be geographically or functionally defined and the bargaining may get especially complicated when different spending ministers belong to different competing parties. In this institutional setting normally the Treasury Minister has the task of preventing spending ministers to overspend but he or she may be overruled by a minimum winning coalition of spending ministers. In fact, as we shall discuss later, different institutional settings attribute different levels of prerogatives to spending ministers vs the Treasury, making the problem arising in the BAU regime more or less serious. In addition, even in parliamentary democracies, legislatures have the ability of proposing and voting upon amendments on the budget presented by the government.[x]

Often budget deficits at the national levels originate at subnational levels of governments. Some famous examples are both from Latin America (ie, Argentina) and European countries (Italy and Spain, for instance). This is related to suboptimal allocation of spending and taxing prerogatives amongst various level of governments. Suppose that spending is decided by local governments and revenues are collected by the national government and allocated to localities on the basis of their spending decisions. Obviously, in this case localities do not internalize the full cost of taxation of their spending decisions since taxes are levied nationally. Most countries have arrangements which attempt to put a limit on these incentives, such as having some local taxes required to finance some type of spending, or having budget rules on local governments (as we will discuss later). In many cases, however, these arrangements are imperfect and a common pool problem remains. The relationship between local governments and the Central Government may also imply a case of soft budget constraint (see Kornai et al., 2003). Localities expect Central Government to bail them out and overspend. Pettersson-Lidbom (2010) provides a test using Swedish data.

[x] Tornell and Lane (1999) develop a model of a sort of common pool problem applicable more directly to developing countries with poorly developed institutions and large informal sectors. They develop a dynamic model of the economic growth process that contains two common characteristics of those developing countries that have grown slowly in the last decades, namely (i) the absence of strong legal and political institutions and (ii) the presence of multiple powerful groups in society. The focus is on the fiscal process as it is the mechanism through which powerful groups interact with the society (which is characterized by weak legal and political institutions) and where they can enforce discretionary fiscal redistribution—a kind of pork barrel transfer—as a way to appropriate national resources for themselves.

This discussion is of course related to the fundamental issues of fiscal federalism.[y] The trade off is well known. On the one hand, one wants to allow to federal countries some freedom of choice on their localities. On the other hand, such freedom should not imply a deficit bias at the national level.

7. INTERGENERATIONAL REDISTRIBUTION

Current generations, by means of government debt, redistribute from future generations to themselves. The argument is very appealing. However, it needs to take into account the fact that private bequest are positive, thus one needs to account for negative "public" bequest (government debt) and private positive bequests. In this respect Cukierman and Meltzer (1986) consider the standard framework with overlapping generation model, lump sum taxes and intergenerational transfers from parent to child, and no uncertainty. Individuals differ in their abilities, (and therefore in wage earnings) and in their nonhuman wealth. Some of them desire to leave positive bequests, and others would prefer to borrow resources from future generations. Individuals who would choose to leave negative bequests are "bequest-constrained" individuals. These individuals favor any fiscal policy that increases their lifetime income at the expense of future generations. Individuals who are not bequest constrained are indifferent to an intergenerational reallocation of taxes. In fact they can adjust up or down their private bequest when public bequests (government debt or assets) move up or down. By majority rule, if the decisive voter is bequest constrained, he will choose lower current taxes financed by additional debt, which cannot be defaulted. If instead the decisive voter is not bequest constrained, he is indifferent to a reallocation of taxes and social security over time that maintains present value. Thus, in this model by majority rule we will easily have an accumulation of debt. The likelihood to have deficits increases with an extension of the franchise to low wealth individuals who are likely to be bequest constrained. This is a simple but very powerful idea which strikes us as just right.

Tabellini (1991) explores a different argument, that is the redistribution consequences of debt repudiation in an overlapping generation framework implying both intra and intergenerational redistributions. The main idea is that issuing debt creates a constituency in support of repaying it. Thus, issuing debt makes a coalition of voters favorable to repaying it in order to avoid intragenerational redistributive consequences of the debt repudiation. In particular, parents have a first-mover advantage since they can vote on how much debt they want to be issued (ie, how much resources they want to extract from future, yet-unborn generation), without the future generation to have a word. Issuing government debt results in intergenerational redistribution to be tight to intragenerational consequences of choosing how much debt to repay. In particular, debt reputation harms the old, but it harms the wealthy more than the poor.

[y] See Oates (2011) for the classic work.

Young voters (specifically the children of the wealthiest debt holder parents) want to avoid intragenerational redistribution (ie, repudiation would result in redistributing wealth from rich to poor families) and for this reason they are willing to accept to repay some debt (ie, transferring resources to the parents), an action that would have been opposed by them ex-ante.[z] Therefore, there is a coalition that includes both old and young voters (the wealthiest) who vote in favor of debt repayment. The most interesting and valuable aspect of this chapter is the joint consideration of intra and intergenerational redistribution, a topic which is surprisingly understudied both theoretically and empirically. In many countries pension systems redistribute both across and within generations, to the extent that poor citizen get proportionally more than rich ones from pensions. This is an excellent topic for further theoretical and empirical research.

Song et al. (2012) develop a dynamic general equilibrium model of small open economies where voters in each period choose domestic public goods and the financing via taxes and debt. Within each country, old agents support high spending on public goods, high labor taxes and large debt. Instead, the young dislike debt, since it crowds out public good provision when they will be old. Specifically, the model consists of a set of small open economies populated by overlapping generations of two-period-lived agents who work in the first period and live off savings in the second period. In each country j there two types of goods: a private good c and a domestic public good g provided by each economy's government. There are two types of agents, the young and the old, each with a different preference towards the public good, which are represented, respectively, by the parameters θ_j and $\lambda\theta_j$. λ represents a preference weight that old put on the public good. Intuitively, this parameter can take value 0—individuals do not value the public good—or positive values—not necessarily bounded to 1. There are cross-country differences in θ which may reflect cultural diversity or differences in the efficiency and quality of public good provision, related to the technology and organization of the public sector. Capital is perfectly mobile across countries and it fully depreciates after one period. The private good is produced by using both capital and labor as inputs in the production function. The domestic fiscal policy is determined through repeated elections and government debt is traded on worldwide markets. Given an inherited debt b_j, the elected government chooses the labor tax rate τ_j, public expenditure g_j and debt accumulation b_j', subject to a standard dynamic government budget constraint. A probabilistic voting model delivers an equilibrium in which fiscal policy maximizes a weighted sum of young and old voters' utility. The weights assigned to each group represent the relative political influence of

[z] This is because, ex-ante issuing debt has only intergenerational, but not intragenerational effect. Given that agents would prefer not to redistribute resources, they would vote against this policy ex-ante. However, ex-post the policy has also intragenerational effect and the young generation would prefer to transfer resources to their parents rather than to the fraction of poor people in the same cohort.

each group. The model yields a trade-off between the marginal costs of taxation, due to the reduction in private consumption c suffered by the young, and the marginal benefit of public good provision. Such a trade-off reveals a conflict of interest between young and old voters. The old want higher taxes and current spending on public goods. Thus, the more power held by the old, the greater the reduction in private consumption. The preference for public good provision affects this trade-off: a higher θ or a higher λ reduces private consumption c. Moreover, there exists a sort of "disciplining effect" exercised by the young voters. In particular, they anticipate that increasing debt will prompt a fiscal adjustment reducing their future public good consumption. A key result is that the model provides a politico-economic theory of the determination of the debt level. In particular, in spite of the complete lack of intergenerational altruism (assumed through finite lives) debt converges to a finite level, strictly below the natural borrowing constraint. This results from the combination of forward-looking repeated voting and distortionary taxation. Higher debt can be financed by increasing taxes or cutting public good provision. As debt grows larger, the convexity of tax distorsions (a Laffer curve effect) implies that most of the adjustment will be in the form of less future public goods. The concern for avoiding a future situation of private affluence and public poverty makes young voters oppose debt increases. Given the prediction of a determined debt level, the model yields mean-reverting debt dynamics. Suppose that the economy is hit by a one-time fiscal shock (eg, a surprise war) requiring an exogenous spending. The government reacts by increasing taxes and decreasing nonwar expenditure in wartime. After the war, debt, taxes, and expenditure revert slowly to the original steady state. These predictions accord well with the empirical evidence of Bohn (1998), who finds the US debt-to-output ratio to be highly persistent, but mean reverting and Müller et al. (2016) which provide similar evidence for the period 1950–2010 for a panel of OECD countries.

Müller et al. (2016) extend their model by assuming that there are two types of voters, left wing (l-type) and right wing (r-type), who differ in their trade-off between private consumption and public good consumption: l-type voters like government expenditure and public good provision more than do r-type voters. Voters choose sequentially a fiscal policy which includes labor taxation, government expenditure on public goods, and debt policy, subject to the government's dynamic budget constraint. The novelty of this model compared to Song et al. (2012) is that, here there are political shocks which can be interpreted as shocks over time to the preference for public goods. In particular, during a left-wing wave the government increases taxation and public expenditure while reducing debt. Instead, during a right-wing wave the opposite occurs. In fact the driver of fiscal discipline of the young is based on their preferences for public good when old—that is how much the young expect that they will appreciate public good provision as they become old. During left-wing governments, the demand for fiscal discipline is stronger because the young left-wing voters—who are more concerned for future public good provision than right-wing voters of the same age—detain more political influence.

This is because r-type voters have less appeal to public good and more for private consumption. Thus, when the right-wing party is in power is less concerned to the provision of public good in the future and instead it would push up current debt today in order to use the resources as subsidies for private consumption. Left-wing voters are instead concerned with future public good provision, and would oppose such fiscal policy. The key predictions of the model are that, on the one hand, right-leaning governments are more prone to issue debt in normal times, while on the other hand left-leaning government engage in more proactive countercyclical fiscal policy—including issuing more debt during recessions. In other words, during normal times left-leaning governments do more public savings but use the debt to smooth income shortfalls associated with recessions.[aa] This result is reminiscent of the model by Persson and Svensson (1989) reviewed earlier, in a nonoverlapping generation framework.[ab]

It should be mentioned that all the models discussed earlier imply voting. Mulligan and Sala-i Martin (1999) argue that indeed spending on pensions is high in nondemocracies as well as democracies, namely variables like the aging of population and the relative size of young and old matter in both regimes. In fact the relative "strength" (ie, political influence) of the constituencies of young and old may be relevant in both democracies and nondemocracies even though the nature of the way in which this relative strength manifests itself is of course different. These differences in the intergenerational games in perfect and imperfect democracies and in dictatorships is an excellent topic for additional research.[ac]

8. RENT SEEKING

Acemoglu et al. (2008, 2010, 2011) study the dynamic taxation in a standard neoclassical model under the assumption that taxes and public good provision are decided by a self-interested politician who cannot commit to policies. Citizens can discipline politicians by means of election as in Barro (1973) and Ferejohn (1986) in a dynamic game. The self-interested politician creates distortions, namely he wants to extract rents from being

[aa] They show that these theoretical predictions are consistent with US postwar data on debt, and also with a panel of OECD countries.

[ab] However, the key difference between the two papers is that in Persson and Svensson (1989) a conservative government expecting to be replaced in the future strategically issues more debt. In contrast, the results in Müller et al. (2016) are unrelated to persistence or reelection probabilities. The robust prediction of their theory is that a left-leaning government issues less debt, irrespective of the probability of being replaced.

[ac] Azzimonti et al. (2014) make the case that the secular increase in debt to output ratios can be due to the liberalization of financial markets that took place in the mid eighties. While the political-economy comes from probabilistic voting, the paper provides an alternative theory of debt (to that of tax smoothing) and an explanation of why we could observe inefficiently higher debt to GDP ratios in the recent years. Specifically, they propose a multicountry political economy model with incomplete markets and endogenous government borrowing and show that governments choose higher levels of public debt when financial markets become internationally integrated and inequality increases.

in office. This adds an additional constraint in the economy, the political economy constraint. This constraint implies that politicians in power compare the lifetime utility from extracting rents in each period vs the one-time shot deviation of extracting all the resources available in the economy in one period and being voted out of office. Distortions are generated by the fact that citizens have to provide incentives to politicians to stay in office. These distortions may or may not disappear in the long run. In particular, if politicians are as patient or more patient than citizens, they value more staying in office and thus they set a tax rate equal to zero. If politicians are less patient than citizens, it may be optimal to set positive taxation. The idea is that, starting from a situation with no distortions as before, an increase in taxation has a second-order effect on the welfare of the citizens holding politician rents constant, but reduces the resources available in the economy and, thus, the rents that should be provided to politicians by a first-order amount.[ad] Thus, it is less costly to reduce the potential output in the economy, than to provide a higher rents to politicians to stay in office. These types of models therefore focus on the role of taxation as a tool to govern the interaction between citizens and self-interested politicians. There is no role for government deficit.

Yared (2010) develops a rent seeking model with implications on the accumulation of public debt using a Lucas and Stokey (1983) model. Yared considers a closed economy with no capital, with shocks to the productivity of public spending, and with complete markets. The self-interested politician has a utility function which is increasing in rents (namely tax revenues not used for productive public goods, ie, spending with no social value). A politician cannot commit to policies once in office and citizens cannot commit to keeping the incumbent in power in the future. Thus, in an infinitely repeated game, reputation sustains equilibrium policies. The focus is on "Efficient Sustainable Equilibria" in which a politician who pursues rent seeking extractive policies is voted out of office, and a politician who purses the policies expected by citizens is rewarded with future office.[ae] Therefore, the incumbent politician follows equilibrium policies as long as rents are sufficiently high, since this raises the value of cooperation, and as long as government debt is sufficiently high, since this limits what he can acquire through maximally extractive policies prior to removal from office. There is no default. Citizens reward a

[ad] Specifically, the marginal cost of additional savings for the citizens is higher in equilibrium than in the undistorted allocation, because a greater level of the resources in the economy increases the politician's temptation to deviate and thus necessitates greater rents to the politician to satisfy the political sustainability constraint.

[ae] The equilibrium refinement used is the sustainable equilibrium as in Chari and Kehoe (1993). In particular, individual households are anonymous and nonstrategic in their private market behavior (ie, buying government debt), while the representative citizen is strategic in the replacement decision. The politician in office is strategic in his decision regarding the policies, which have to satisfy the government dynamic budget constraint. The set of sustainable equilibrium are those in which citizens solve their optimal decision with respect to consumption, labor supply and bonds' decision given their individual budget constraints. Within the set of sustainable equilibrium, the focus is on the efficient ones, ie, the ones that maximize citizens' utility.

well-behaved incumbent by not replacing him as long as equilibrium taxes are sufficiently low and productive public spending is sufficiently high. Note that given the fact that citizens are all identical, there is no conflict in the political decision. Efficient sustainable policies thus solve the standard program of the benevolent government subject to incentive compatibility constraints for the politician and the representative citizen.

Consider now the rent seeking politicians. Given the lack of commitment, there are two set of incentives that have to be satisfied, the politician's and the citizens' incentives. The incumbent politician knows that citizens will remove him from office at the beginning of the following period if he misbehaves. In particular, a politician who is removed after period t receives period t rents and a punishment which is a function of χ^p, ie, an exogenous parameter representing the strength of political institutions, namely the institutional constraints on politicians. The optimal policy for the citizens has to satisfy the constraint that the politician does not want to extract maximal rents and be removed from office. Maximal rents implies getting as much revenues as possible today, take out as much debt as possible today, delivering zero public goods, and repaying current debt. Therefore, the incumbent politician is less likely to deviate from the equilibrium policies if: (i) he is receiving a high level of equilibrium rents today and in the future because in this case the value of cooperation is high; (ii) if government debt is high because there is little space for him to expropriate resources through increasing his rents. Satisfaction of this incentive compatibility constraint implies a lower bound on taxes and an upper bound on public spending which both bind whenever the incentive compatibility constraint binds. This is because there has to be a limit on the size of resources owed to the government in each period. Indeed, if the size of these resources is too large, there is a high incentive for the politician to deviate and appropriate them as rents. This implies that resources going into a given period cannot be too large, and government activity must be financed mostly with current and future taxes, instead of past taxes.

The second set of incentives to take into account are those for the citizens. In this model, citizens may have an incentive to replace an incumbent politician even if he is well behaving. In this sense, citizens cannot commit to a plan where they keep an incumbent in power no matter what. Therefore, the incumbent politician has to set fiscal policies such that they define a sufficiently low level of taxation and/or a sufficiently high level of public expenditure in order to have some chances to stay in office the subsequent period. In this framework, replacing an incumbent politician provides a benefit for the citizens which is a function of the exogenous parameter χ^c. Here, χ^c represents the lack of popularity of the incumbent.[af] These conditions provide upper bounds on revenues and lower bounds on public spending.

[af] Another interpretation may be the gains for the citizens from having a new incumbent, reflected in the policies that are promoted during the electoral campaign. The author interprets it as a general "social benefit of political turnover."

Summing up, satisfying the incentives of politicians requires sufficiently high revenues and sufficiently low levels of public spending. In contrast, satisfying the incentives of citizens requires sufficiently low level of taxes and sufficiently high level of public spending. The best policy is therefore found to be the one that maximizes citizens' lifetime utility subject to the two set of incentive compatible constraints. This political distortion leads to several departures from the social planner policies. In particular, taxes are not constant but *volatile*. This is because the constant revenue policy characterizing the benevolent government is associated with too much rent seeking by politicians. Second, the increase in debt reduces the potential rents that the politician can appropriate and thus make it easier for citizens to provide the incentives to politicians. This approach is elegant, although contingent debt as in Lucas and Stokey (1983) is not issued by real world governments.

9. BUDGET RULES

Given that for so many reasons there are incentives for the government to run excessive deficits, is it feasible to devise rules and institutions that limit or eliminate those problems? By rules we mean numerical targets like a balanced budget rules, or a limit on the level of deficit, perhaps adjusted by the cycles, or excluding certain items such as public investment.[ag]

9.1 Balanced Budget Rule for National Governments

The pros and cons of national balanced budget rules, namely rules which imply zero or negative deficits (surpluses) are clear. A balanced budget rule does not allow to smooth out spending shocks (ie, to run deficits when the need for spending are especially large) or fluctuations of tax revenues over the cycle for given tax rates. However, to the extent that political distortions are so large that governments may be far from the optimal policy, then a balanced budget rule might be a second best solution to massive political distortions.

The political debate on balanced budget rules is extensive, since the pros and cons are, in principle, straightforward but there are strong prior views about which costs or benefits are bigger and those views are not likely to be changed by the available, relatively scant, evidence.[ah] An additional set of issues relates to the enforceability of balanced budget rules, namely whether governments restricted by these rules would engage in "creative accounting" to circumvent them or simply *de facto* ignore them.

[ag] For a review see Fatás and Mihov (2003b).

[ah] See Sabato (2008) for a presentation of the policy debate. Fatás and Mihov (2003a) present evidence on a cross section of countries consistent with the view that the presence of budget rules limits the volatility of fiscal policy.

Azzimonti et al. (2015) present a quantitative evaluation of the net benefits of a balanced budget rule (BBR) for the US economy using the political economy model developed by Battaglini and Coate (2008).[ai] As reviewed earlier, political economy frictions lead to inefficiently high levels of government debt in the long run. A constitutional requirement that imposes that tax revenues must be sufficient to cover spending and the interest on debt (eg, permitting surpluses but not deficits) may improve welfare by restraining policymakers from excessive debt creation. The authors show that the BBR leads to a gradual reduction of debt in equilibrium. Intuitively, the reduction in flexibility to smooth taxes imposed by the rule increases the expected costs of taxation. Therefore, savings become more valuable as a buffer against adverse shocks. By lowering the stock of debt in good times, legislators reduce interest payments, which decreases pressure on the budget in bad times. In the long run, this results in lower taxes and higher spending in equilibrium than in the unconstrained case, "pushing" the model on the direction of optimal fiscal policy. The impact of a BBR on welfare is theoretically ambiguous: in the short run, citizens experience a loss in utility since the government has to cut spending and raise taxes to reduce debt above what might be optimal. In the long run, citizens benefit from lower debt levels but, due to the inability to borrow in bad times, suffer from higher volatility. Because the net effect depends on parameters, the authors calibrate the model to the US economy using data between 1940 and 2013, and show that it can fit the path of US fiscal policy reasonably well. One immediately wonders whether including the Second World War years in this exercise is appropriate given that during a major war probably the balanced budget rule could be easily abandoned. By including a major war period they, in a sense, may set the stage for a framework with high costs for balanced budget rules. The authors find that the short run costs are too large to compensate for the steady state benefits of a lower stock of debt. However, quite apart from the parametrization (which, as always, could be debatable) the model makes an interesting point: the balanced budget rule could be costly in the short run and beneficial in the long run. This result leads to interesting and immediate consequences on the political economy implications on voting upon a balanced budget rule in say, an overlapping generations model.

Halac and Yared (2015) discuss the optimal design of centralized supranational fiscal rules like those for Euro area countries, and how they compare to decentralized (national) fiscal rules in an environment in which there is a trade-off between allowing flexibility while also reducing a government's deficit bias. They consider a two-period model in which a continuum of identical governments choose deficit-financed public spending. At the beginning of the first period, each government suffers an idiosyncratic shock to the social value of spending in that period. Governments are benevolent ex-ante, prior to the realization of the shock, but present-biased ex-post, when it is time to choose

[ai] See also Stockman (2001) for calibrations of balanced budget rules in RBC models.

spending—which can be interpreted as the results of the potential political turnover (ie, the political business cycle). The results of the chapter compare optimal rules—which maximize the social welfare of all countries—when it is set by a central authority or an individual government. The results can be summarized as follows: when governments are not too impatient when choosing public spending, then the optimal centralized fiscal rule is tighter than the decentralized one, and hence interest rates are lower under centralization. The idea is that, in choosing decentralized rules, an individual country does not internalize the fact that by allowing itself more flexibility, a country pushes the global interest rate up, and thus redistributing resources away from governments that borrow more towards governments that borrow less. Instead, committing ex-ante to tighter rules is good as this pushes down the global interest rate and therefore allows countries with higher marginal value of spending to borrow more cheaply. If governments' present bias is large, the optimal centralized fiscal rule is slacker than the decentralized one, and hence interest rates are higher under centralization. The idea is that governments choosing rules independently do not internalize the fact that by reducing their own discretion—ie, by choosing very tight borrowing limits—they lower interest rates, thus increasing governments' desire to borrow more and worsening fiscal discipline for all. Instead, committing ex-ante to more flexibility is socially beneficial: the cost of increasing discretion for over borrowing countries is mitigated by the rising interest rate, which induces everyone to borrow less. The interest rate has a disciplining effect in the sense that it reduces the incentives for over borrowing countries to borrow more.

Aguiar et al. (2015) investigate the conditions under which the imposition of debt ceilings is welfare improving. Specifically, they study the interaction between fiscal and monetary policy in a monetary union with the potential for rollover crises in sovereign debt markets. Each member-country chooses how much to consume and borrow by issuing nominal bonds. A common monetary authority chooses inflation for the union, taking as given the fiscal policy of its member countries. Both types of policies are implemented without commitment. The lack of commitment on fiscal policy is especially critical because it may lead to the possibility of default. They show the existence of a "fiscal externality" in this type of environment. This externality leads countries to over borrow and thus, higher inflation and lower welfare. This gives credit to the imposition of debt ceiling in a monetary union which overcome the problem of lack of commitment on fiscal policy. Aguiar et al. (2015) go further and investigate the impact of the composition of debt in a monetary union, that is the fraction of high-debt vs low-debt members, on the occurrence of self-fulfilling debt crisis. Specifically, they show that a high-debt country may be less vulnerable to crises and have a higher welfare when it belongs to a union with an intermediate mix of high- and low-debt members, than one where all other members are low debt.

One could also think of balanced budget rule with escape clauses. An obvious one, mentioned earlier already would be a major world war. This (fortunately) rare event may be used as a relatively easy contingency to verify, but if the contingencies become too frequent then not only the stringency of the rule but even its enforceability is called into question. For instance, how does one define a "major" war? Clearly the Second World War was major, but would the Iraq war be a major one? Also one might think of cyclically adjusted balanced budget rules to overcome some of the rigidity of the latter, but then debates about how to measure the cyclical adjustment might lead to strategic manipulation of the rule itself. With specific reference to the United States, Primo (2007) discusses the pitfalls of balanced budget rules with complicated escape clauses.

An additional argument against formal budget rules is that financial markets might impose increasing borrowing costs on government which move far away from the optimal policy and accumulate large debts. Increasing borrowing costs would lead to more discipline even without rules. The recent experience of the Euro area and its fiscal crisis, casts doubts on this argument. Until 2008 the interest rate spread on, say German government bonds and even Greek ones was virtually nil. In fact, as a result of this low spreads several countries accumulated large debts in the first decade of the monetary union even when these countries were growing at respectable rates, including Greece whose economy was booming and debt skyrocketing. The reason of this is that probably investors did not believe the no bail out case of European treaties and assumed (largely correctly) that in case of a debt crisis they would be protected. In fact, probably because market discipline was not considered sufficient the funding fathers of the monetary union introduced contingent budget rules, like the stability and growth pact. These rules have been changed repeatedly and generally implied a maximum level of deficit (3% of GDP) with various escape clauses in case of major recessions. The discussion about the optimality of such rules in the Euro area is immense and we do not review it here (see the excellent discussion in Wyplosz, 2014).[aj] However, we want to make three points here. One is that the enforceability of these rules has been questionable. Even as early as 2002 Germany itself broke the rule and then many countries followed this example. The complexity and contingency of these rules did not help. The second is that probably now some European countries are feeling the bite of such rules, binding during a prolonged recession. The third is that especially at the time of the introduction of the Euro much creative accounting was widely used to satisfy "on paper" the 3% rule. These procedures introduced confusion and decreased trust amongst members of the Euro area.[ak]

How can balanced budget rules for a sovereign national government can be enforced? One possibility is to have the law in the constitution so that it would take a Constitutional revision to change it. An alternative would be to require a qualified majority. Such rules need to be stable, namely they should not imply that the rule itself can be changed, as in Barbera and Jackson (2004). For some discussion of this issue, see Primo (2007) which

[aj] For some empirical evidence on the stability and growth pact see von Hagen and Wolff (2006).

[ak] Von Hagen (2006) compare the effectiveness of budget rules in the EU vs Japan.

elaborates over the Baron and Ferejohn (1989) approach with specific reference to the US institutional setting. This is an excellent topic for future research not only within the specific American institutions.

9.2 Balanced Budget Rules for Local Governments

The pros and cons of balanced budget rules discussed earlier for national government apply also to subnational ones. However, there are reasons to believe that balanced budget rules for local governments may be more attractive than for national governments. First, as we discussed earlier, local governments add an additional political distortion: a common pool problem given by the fact that their local spending is at least in part financed by national transfers and therefore local governments do not fully internalize the taxation costs of their spending decisions. Second, some (or most) of the countercyclical fiscal stabilizers may be national not local. In fact, balanced budget rules for local governments should be accompanied by nationally based automatic stabilizers, to avoid procyclical fiscal policy, unless, as were discussed earlier, a balanced budget rule is chosen also for the national government. Third, enforcement of local balanced budget rule may be easier since it may be done by the national governments. Fourth, a balanced budged rule for local governments would avoid accumulation of unsustainable debts with the related uncertainty, disruption and costs associated with bail outs of excessively indebted localities. In summary, balanced budget rules for local government may be a tool of an optimal allocation of fiscal responsibilities between national and local governments.[al]

Indeed, work by Alt and Lowry (1994), Poterba (1995), Bayoumi and Eichengreen (1994), Bohn and Inman (1996), and Alesina and Bayoumi (1996) show that more strength budget rules in the United States, namely tight fiscal controls which impose restrictions on government deficit, have been more effective at creating incentives to states more quickly responding to spending or revenue shocks.[am]

9.3 Other Types of Budget Rules

The policy discussion over balanced budget rules has also dealt with other types of budget restrictions. One is the so-called "golden rule," namely a rule which allows budget deficits only to finance public investments but not current expenditures. Bassetto and Sargent (2006) discuss the optimality of such rules. In principle, this may be a "good" rule especially for developing countries in need of investment in infrastructures. The problem, however, is that this rule may lead to creative accounting, namely simply reporting as spending in infrastructures what is really current spending. For developed countries one may wonder whether the political incentives to spend in physical

[al] See Inman (1997) and Poterba (1996) for a review of this literature.

[am] Canova and Pappa (2006), however, present results suggesting that in some cases US states managed to circumvent the rules.

infrastructures which would be induced by this rule is really necessary. In Western Europe, in particular, the emphasis on physical infrastructures seem overplayed already, relative to other fiscal problems in this continent, and a budget rule of this type may add to this misperception and lead to overinvestment in physical infrastructures.

Another possible budget rule would impose limits on spending. The issue here is that while we have a theory of optimal deficit management, reasonable people can disagree on the optimal size of government spending because of different views about the role of the state and the size of welfare policies, for instance. Thus, while pork barrel inefficient programs (like bridges to nowhere) might be constrained by spending limits, the latter may interfere with programs desired by the majority.

10. BUDGET INSTITUTIONS

10.1 Theory

The definition and approval of a budget in an advanced democracy is often a complex process, possibly kept strategically complex to achieve behind the scene deals or to be able to introduce them in some corner of the budget provisions in a sufficiently obscure manner to escape detection of the voters. One can identify three phases in the budget process: (1) the formulation of a budget proposal within the executive; (2) the presentation and approval of the budget in the legislature; and (3) the implementation of the budget by the bureaucracy. Two issues are crucial: the voting procedures leading to the formulation and approval of the budget, and the degree of transparency of the budget. We begin with the former.

We focus upon a key trade-off between two types of institutions. One type, which we label "hierarchical," limits the democratic accountability of the budget process with a high degree of delegation. The second type, we label "collegial," has the opposite features. Hierarchical institutions are those that, for instance, attribute strong prerogatives to the prime minister (or the Finance or Treasury minister) to overrule spending ministers within intergovernmental negotiations on the formulation of the budget. Hierarchical institutions also limit in a variety of ways the capacity of the legislature to amend the budget proposed by the government. Collegial institutions emphasize the democratic rule in every stage, like the prerogatives of spending ministers within the government, the prerogatives of the legislature vis-a-vis the government, and the rights of the minority opposition in the legislature. There is a trade-off between these two types of institutions: hierarchical institutions are more likely to enforce fiscal restraints, avoid large and persistent deficits, and implement fiscal adjustments more promptly. On the other hand, they are less respectful of the rights of the minority, and more likely to generate budgets heavily tilted in favor of the interests of the majority. Collegial institutions have the opposite features.

Let's begin with the definition of the budget within the government where we have a division of responsibilities between spending ministers and the Treasury minister. The latter has the role of aggregating the spending proposals of other ministers and produce a budget document. Spending ministers prefer a larger fraction of the budget devoted to their department: more money means more favors to constituencies. Thus, more hierarchical institutions are those which attribute stronger prerogatives to the Treasury. In the legislature, as we discussed earlier, different amendment rules may aggravate or reduce the common pool problem. Much of this research is based, directly or indirectly, upon a view of the budget as the result of conflicting interests of representatives with geographically based constituencies. The literature on procedures has addressed three related questions: what procedural rules mitigate or aggravate the problem of oversupply of pork barrel projects? What procedural rules make the choice of projects, given a certain total budget, more or less efficient? How do different procedural rules influence the final allocation of net benefits among districts? Two issues are particularly interesting for our purposes: (a) the sequence of voting on the budget, and (b) the type of admissible amendments on the proposed budget. Intuitively, one may argue that by voting first on the maximum size of the budget (and eventually of the deficit) one would limit the excessive multiplication of budget proposal. Ferejohn and Krehbiel (1987) study theoretically the determination of the size of the budget under the two alternative voting procedures. They assume that the budget can be allocated to two projects and different legislators have different preferences for the relative benefits of these two projects. It is not always the case that the size of the budget is smaller when the legislatures vote first on the size and then on the composition, relative to the case in which the overall budget size is determined as a residual. While the size of the budget is in general not independent on the order of votes, the relative size of the budget with different orders of votes depends on the distribution of legislatures' preferences for budget composition.[an]

In parliamentary democracies, the agenda setter in the budget process is the government. Thus, closed rules attribute more power to the government and less to the floor of the legislature. The result is that closed rules are more hierarchical as we discussed earlier. They give more influence to the government and lead to an immediate approval of the budget than the government poses. Open rules require more time for voting and with those rules the government gets a lower surplus relative to the nongovernmental minority. With a closed rule you achieve quick approval of a proposal, at the cost of implementing "unfair" budgets. Budgets are unfair in the sense that they are tilted in favor of those who make the first proposal, and always distribute benefits to the smallest possible majority. Hierarchical procedures are obviously preferable when the key problem is the control of the size of the budget and the implied deficit.

[an] The same issue has been revisited by Hallerberg and Von Hagen (1999).

Finally, the issue of transparency. The budgets of modern economies are very complex, sometimes unnecessarily so. This complexity, partly unavoidable, partly artificially created, helps in various practices to "hide" the real balance (current and future) of costs and benefits for the taxpayers. Politicians have incentives to hide taxes, overemphasize the benefits of spending, and hide government liabilities (the equivalent of future taxes). At least two theoretical arguments support this claim. The first is the theory of "fiscal illusion" reviewed earlier. By taking advantage of voters' irrational confusion, politicians can engage in strategic fiscal policy choices for reelection. The second argument does not rely on voters' irrationality and confusion. Several papers, although in different contexts (eg, Cukierman and Meltzer, 1986 and Alesina and Cukierman, 1990), highlight the benefit for policymakers of a certain amount of ambiguity even when they face a rational electorate. The idea is that, by creating confusion and, in particular, by making it less clear how policies translate into outcomes, policymakers can retain a strategic advantage vs rational, but not fully informed, voters. This advantage would disappear with "transparent" procedures; therefore, policymakers would often choose to adopt ambiguous procedures. Milesi-Ferretti (2004) shows that politicians who want to run excessive deficits would choose nontransparent procedures, and the latter would help them to achieve their (distorted) goals. As we discussed earlier, Rogoff and Sibert (1988) and Rogoff (1990) make a similar point in the context of political business cycle models. They show that if voters cannot easily observe the composition of the budget (on the spending or on the financing side), then policymakers can follow loose fiscal policies before elections and increase their chances of reappointment. Gavazza and Lizzeri (2009) develop a model in which the lack of voters' information about the complexity of the budget lead to transfers to voters even when taxation is distortionary and voters are homogeneous. Transfers are financed with debt and the latter is higher the less transparent the system is, that is the less likely it is that voters can fully observe fiscal variables.[ao]

How, in reality, do policymakers obfuscate the budget? and what to do about it? In practice, a variety of tricks can serve the purpose of strategically influencing the beliefs and information of taxpayers/voters. For instance: (1) Overestimate the expected growth of the economy, so as to overestimate tax revenues, and underestimate the level of interest rates, so as to underestimate outlays. At the end of the fiscal year, the "unexpected" deficit can be attributed to unforeseen macroeconomic developments, for which the government can claim no responsibility; (2) Project overly optimistic forecasts of the effect on the budget of various policies, so that, for instance, a small new tax is forecast to have major revenue effects, thus postponing to the following budget the problem of a real adjustment; (3) Keep various items off budget; (4) Use budget projections strategically. For example, in all the discussions about future budgets, a key element is the

[ao] The same authors (Gavazza and Lizzeri, 2011) investigate how lack of transparency may lead to the choice of inefficient fiscal tolls for redistribution.

"baseline." By inflating the baseline, politicians can claim to be fiscally conservative without having to create real costs for the constituencies. In this way, they create an illusion: they appear conservative in the eyes of the taxpayers, worried about the size of the budget, but they do not really hurt key constituencies with spending cuts. Clearly, this illusion cannot last forever, since adjustment, rigorous only relative to inflated baseline, in the end will not stop the growth of the debt. However, this procedure creates confusion and, at the very least, delays the electorate's realistic perception of the actual state of public finance; (5) Strategic use of multiyear budgeting. By announcing a, say, 3-year adjustment plan in which all the hard policies occur in years 2 and 3, politicians can look responsible and can buy time; then, they can revise the next 3-year budget policies to further postpone the hard choices.[ap]

We can think of three possibilities for increasing transparency. The first and most commonly followed is a "legalistic" approach. That is, more and more rules and regulations are imposed on how the budget should be prepared, organized, and executed. This approach is unlikely to be successful: complicated rules and regulations provide fertile ground for nontransparent budget procedures. A second alternative is to create legislative bodies in charge of evaluating the transparency, accuracy, and projections of the government budget. This approach is superior to the legalistic one, but it relies heavily on the political independence of this public body. This independence may be problematic, particularly in a parliamentary system where the government parties control a majority in the legislature. A third alternative, the most radical but the most effective, is to delegate to a respected private institution the task of verifying the accuracy and transparency of the budget process. In addition, the government budget should be based on an average of the economic forecasts of and projections derived by international organizations or private institutions.

10.2 Empirical Evidence

The empirical evidence on the relationship between rules and deficit is, generally speaking, supportive of the idea that hierarchical institutions are associated with lower deficits. Hallerberg et al. (2009), in a book which also summarizes and consolidate previous works by the same authors, classify budget institutions for the EU countries in terms of delegation of prerogatives to the Treasury minister versus a contracting approach within ministers, the presence of targets, voting rules in parliament, relationship between central and local governments. They argue that institutions matter and delegations and targets (ie, hierarchical institutions) are effective at containing deficits and debts. Alesina et al. (1998) and Stein et al. (1999) consider Latin America countries and construct an index of their budget institutions based upon surveys of local officials. In doing so they can distinguish up to a point between *de iure* and *de facto* procedures. These authors correlated

[ap] See Alesina et al. (2015) for a detailed study of multiyear fiscal adjustment plans.

positively an index of hierarchical of budget institutions and of transparency to lower levels of debt. Fabrizio and Mody (2006) obtain similar results for Center and Eastern European countries. Dabla-Norris et al. (2010) on a vast sample of developing countries. These results should be taken very cautiously since they are based upon a handful of countries and often the classification of procedures is open to question. For instance, *de iure* and *de facto* procedures may differ substantially. Also comparing along those lines very different countries might be challenging, for instance think of a comparison of United States vs parliamentary democracies budget institutions. Debrun et al. (2008) compile a detailed data set for European Union countries for the period 1990–2005. They consider numerical fiscal rules on any fiscal aggregate, their legal status (normal law, constitutional law, supranational rules, accepted norms) and consider both national and subnational governments. Based upon this vast data set they build an index of stringency of the rules and they find that it strongly correlates with fiscal performance. More stringent rules reduce a deficit bias and improves upon the countercyclical stance of fiscal policy in EU countries. Miano (2015) has shown that national rules have the effect of reducing deficits. A recent work at IMF (Budina et al., 2012) provide extensive data on budget institutions for many countries and examine how the recent financial and fiscal crisis in many countries have led to reforms in budget institutions. These data have not been used yet for extensive empirical analysis.

11. QUESTIONS FOR FUTURE RESEARCH

In this final section, we elaborate on some issues which in our view are left open in this literature.

11.1 Endogenous Institutions

The literature which we have reviewed thus far uses certain political institutions (eg, type of government, electoral rules, presidential vs parliamentary systems) as exogenous or at least predetermined in explaining economic variables. In the present chapter we focus on debt and deficits but a vast literature also considers other related variables like the size of government and the level of redistribution for instance.

The assumption of exogeneity of predetermined institutions as "cause" of deficits can, however, be called into question. The same historical, sociological, cultural variables which may have led to the choice of certain institutions may also be correlated with fiscal policies.[aq] For instance, suppose that a parliamentary proportional system (generating a multiparty system with many veto players) was adopted because it was the only way to guarantee representation to very polarized and divided societies (across income, ideological, religious or ethnic lines). Those same characteristics of society might lead to

[aq] See Alesina and Giuliano (2015) for a discussion of the relationship between culture and institutions.

certain choices of fiscal policies (spending, deficits, debt). Thus, proportional representation and deficits would correlate but causality is called into question. Along those lines, Alesina and Glaeser (2005) review the literature showing that in many European countries proportional representation was introduced after the First or Second World War under pressure from Socialist and Communist parties. The presence of the latter clearly is not exogenous to fiscal policy decisions. Aghion et al. (2004) discuss how certain types of voting rules would be chosen optimally or not (ie, with or without a veil of ignorance) in divided societies.[ar] Empirically, they show how ethnic fractionalization is correlated with various institutional variables. Galor and Klemp (2015) present results along similar lines using different measures of diversity. On the other hand a vast literature on ethnic fractionalization (see the survey by Alesina and La Ferrara, 2005) show how the latter variable is correlated with several economic variables which may be directly or indirectly correlated with deficits and debt. Thus, diversity of populations may "cause" both institutions and fiscal outcomes. The correlation between the latter two does not imply causality, strictly speaking. Persson and Tabellini (2000) in their work on institutional determinants of fiscal policies are aware of this limitation and make some progress in addressing causality, but this remains an open question. The literature on fiscal policy which appeals to institutional variables as causal explanation for deviations from optimality (especially when thinking of long run horizons) needs to make the extra step. At this point, the correlations seem clear, identification of causality is not.

These arguments apply even more strongly when focusing specifically to budget institutions. The latter may work very differently in different countries depending upon their interaction with other features of the country itself. Hallerberg et al. (2009) argue that delegations to the Treasury minister does not work well in countries with sharp differences in the preferences of different parties for fiscal policy, a result which is consistent also with the model of political delegation by Trebbi et al. (2008). With a deep political conflict delegation to one decision maker is hard, undesirable by the minority and possibly counterproductive. Budget institutions are clearly endogenous. Why do countries choose different budget institutions and therefore to what extent the latter can be used as right hand side variables in a regression with debt and deficits on the left hand side? Countries with lower polarization and more homogeneous governments may be more likely to choose more hierarchical fiscal institutions, since delegation is easier, as argued earlier. But then it may be that the lower political conflict leads to more restrained fiscal policies; in this case, institutions are just an "intermediate" variable. In other words, paradoxically countries which needs stringent budget rules the least, since they have a lower tendency to run deficits, may be those which adopt more stringent budget rules. As noted by Hallerberg et al. (2009), some institutional reforms in the direction of making them more hierarchical have followed deep crisis, like the case of Sweden in the nineties. But again,

[ar] See also Trebbi et al. (2008) for an application to US cities.

causality is an issue: perhaps changes in attitudes due to the crisis might have led to a political equilibrium with more fiscal restraints regardless of the institutions. It is virtually impossible to establish causality from budget institutions to fiscal outcomes, although the correlations are interesting. Debrun et al. (2008) are fully aware of this problem and attempt to instrument their index of stringency of rules with some institutional variables but the exclusionary restriction is highly questionable. Miano (2015) shows how the adopting of various budget institutions are endogenous to a host of sociopolitical variables and are affected by the timing of elections. Overall, the argument that budget institutions "cause" fiscal discipline is virtually impossible to make empirically given the endogeneity of these institutions. Countries with a culture of fiscal profligacy will not adopt them (or will not enforce them) while countries with a culture of rigor will adopt and enforce them. The evidence presented earlier is consistent with a weaker argument namely that countries which, for whatever reason, cultural or otherwise, prefer budget discipline will be helped in their goal by choosing certain institutions rather than others. We think that we need more research on this point: to what extent institutions "cause" fiscal policies? Perhaps more natural experiment-based research may help address this question.

A second line of argument relates to the time consistency of institutional rules. To what extent institutional choices would be time consistent and not reversed as a result of various shocks? Halac and Yared (2014) address precisely this issue in a model where a government has an incentive to overspend. The government chooses a fiscal rule to trade off its desire to commit to not overspend against its desire to have the flexibility to react to shocks. These authors show that in the case of persistent shocks the ex-ante optimal rule is not sequentially optimal. The optimal rule in fact is time dependent with large fiscal shocks leading to an erosion of future fiscal discipline. It would be very useful to investigate the choice of budget rules under a Rawlsian veil of ignorance at the constitutional table or in a situation in which the veil of ignorance has holes, as in related work by Trebbi et al. (2008) on voting rules.

11.2 Culture

A rapidly growing literature has recently explored how various cultural traits affect economic decisions in a variety of dimensions including, savings, investment, trade, labor markets and the private or public provisions of safety networks and, more generally, growth and development.[as] Cultural traits like trust, relationship between family members (including intergenerational generosity), individualism, respect of the rules of laws, propensity to save and in which form, have been widely studied and their relevance for economic behavior is well established. Many of these attitudes are relevant for a society's acceptance of government deficits, including their intergenerational redistributive effects. Also the acceptability of policies geared towards reducing excessive deficits

[as] Guiso et al. (2006) and Alesina and Giuliano (2015) provide surveys of this literature.

may be different in different cultural settings. For instance, Guiso et al. (2015) investigate how cultural differences among Euro area countries may have led to the aggravation of conflict over debt policies and delayed resolutions of the latter. Cultural values certainly affect decisions about tax evasion,[at] another variables which clearly determines the accumulation of debt. While a relatively vast literature studies tax evasion, we are not aware of much work linking it to the accumulation of debt.[au]

The connection between institutions and culture is important (Alesina and Giuliano, 2015; Bisin and Verdier, 2015). The adoption of certain budget institutions may be endogenous to certain cultural traits. Countries more prone to thriftiness (say Germany) may be more likely to adopt certain budget rules and institutions, others may do the opposite. In addition, the rigorous application of certain budget rules (say a balanced budget amendments) may be endogenous to certain cultural traits having to do, for instance with the social acceptability towards "bending the rules," which may vary greatly across countries.[av] Both cross-country and within-country evidence would be useful. The latter could hold constant national institutions and examine the effect of difference cultural attitudes within the same national institutions.

The control of politicians is also a "public good" which may be under supplied in certain cultures, as shown by Nannicini et al. (2012) who develop an intuition by Banfield (1958). When "social capital" is low, people do not feel compelled to participate in political activities, control politicians and punish the latter when they misbehave. In fact, with low social capital individuals may expect private favors rather than public goods. Politicians then feel more free to exert less effort, be self-motivated or corrupt. Less control by voters may also allow powerful lobbies to have easier access to politicians. For instance, Campante and Do (2014) show that more isolated capital cities show more levels of corruption and are associated with a greater role for money in state-level elections. In particular, firms and individuals contribute disproportionately more compared to nonisolated capital cities. Thus, lower social capital may be associated with more political distortions and rent seeking of policymakers which may aggravate the deficit bias problem.

11.3 Delegation

In the case of monetary policy, the benefit of delegation to an independent (up to a point) agency is widely accepted. For fiscal policy this kind of delegation is virtually nonexistent. The question is why and whether some delegation in fiscal policy (and how and to whom) might be useful.

[at] See Richardson (2008).

[au] An exception on Italy is Alesina and Maré (1996) on Italy.

[av] On this point see for instance Guiso et al. (2011), Tabellini (2010), and Guiso et al. (2015).

The fundamental reason why delegation of an independent agency in monetary policy is more acceptable than fiscal policy goes back to where we started in this chapter. Fiscal policy is perceived as much more closely linked to redistributions of various type than monetary policy. In the case of the latter, instead a policy based upon some form of Taylor rule is (at least in normal times) considered as beneficial for society as a whole and redistribution issues may eventually be corrected by fiscal policy (say unemployment benefits during a recession). Alesina and Tabellini (2007) and Alesina et al. (2008) discuss issues of delegation and show results consistent with this argument: delegation is much less agreed upon when it involves redistribution while it is easier to achieve for more technical questions (say the conduct of monetary policy) with less direct distributional consequences.[aw] Blinder (1997) argues that even aspects of fiscal policies may benefit from some delegation. He notes that the benefits of Central Bank independence derived from the technical nature of the task, the long term effects of certain decisions, the desire to delegate to bureaucrats through choices when needed (say creating unemployment to fight inflation and diffuse the blame away from politicians) and the tendency of policymakers to inflate too much, possibly close to elections. This author correctly notes how many of these features apply also to certain fiscal policy decisions, especially in the case of tax policy. During the financial crisis, the close connections between monetary and fiscal policy (immortalized by the dramatic joint appearance of Henry Paulson and Ben Bernanke in front of Congress at the outset of the crisis) also made the sharp distinction between independent central banks and totally "political" governments even more striking and possibly artificial.

An intermediate step which does not imply delegation can be to create an independent fiscal council which examines the fiscal policy of the government and expresses an evaluation in terms of its short and long run effects and its technical problems. In the United States, the Congressional Budget Office with a reputation of skills and independence has this role. In Sweden a highly respected fiscal council issues an influential document every year to review the policy of the Swedish government. In the matter of delegation, even to a Council, probably cultural variables examined above play a role. In countries with high level of trust, delegation is easier and the independence of, say, a fiscal council would be (correctly) believed. This might be precisely the case of Sweden. In countries with low levels of trust (say Italy, Spain, or France), the independence of the council would not be believed, and this skepticism might not be unreasonable. Thus, the status of the council would be compromised and it would be viewed as politically influenced and would lose its legitimacy and its potentially useful role. This is another example of the interaction between institutions and culture discussed earlier. What and how to delegate in the area of fiscal policy remains an excellent topic of research.

[aw] Pettersson-Lidbom (2012) discuss evidence on legislature and bureaucratic relationship as a determinant of the size of government using two natural experiments.

11.4 Lobbyist and Bureaucrats

The role of the bureaucracy in the implementation of the budget is hardly studied by economists.[ax] Highly ranked bureaucrats may have an influence which goes well beyond the implementation of executive decisions. Thus, even without any formal delegation (discussed earlier) highly ranked bureaucrats when applying the fiscal provisions of the budget may have sufficient discretion to favor this or that pressure groups. Up to a point this may be a sort of "unwanted" delegation, that is a delegation which *de facto* but not *de iure* has the bureaucracy gains. This may increase the difficulty in implementing reforms because of a status quo preferences of existing bureaucratic bodies.

Finally, virtually all of the models we have considered model the polity by means of voting. A different view about the political process sees voting in legislatures simply as a result of lobbying pressure and therefore modeling lobbies' behavior is the fundamental step. While a rich literature on lobbies exists (see Grossman and Helpman, 2008), especially with regard to trade issues, we are not aware of lobbying models related to optimal debt management. Lobbyist and bureaucrats may be connected because the former may have access to the latter and may obtain favors in the implementation of various fiscal measures. This is especially the case when budget procedures and prescriptions are sufficiently opaque so as to guarantee a *de facto* discretion of bureaucrats. In turn, this lack of transparency may be strategically preserved precisely to allow for such pressures from lobbyist, with the related gains for policymakers. Linking the lobbying literature to government debt is an excellent topic of research.

11.5 Empirical Work

Much of the politico-economic literature reviewed earlier is theoretical. We think that there are high payoff in empirical research. Probably cross-country regressions have exhausted what they can teach us in most (but necessarily all) cases. Other tools are available. One is of course dynamic general equilibrium models where one could introduce political constraints or distortions and quantify their effects. A good example of this type of empirical work is the paper by Azzimonti et al. (2015) on the balanced budget rule reviewed earlier. At the opposite extreme of methodology one can think of historical case studies which would be especially helped by "natural experiment." For instance, imagine natural experiments which imply institutional changes (or other kind of changes) which can be considered relatively exogenous to fiscal policy. These studies may help address the question of endogeneity emphasized earlier. The use of historical evidence with time period spanning over institutional changes can be especially useful.

Within-country studies can also be helpful. Imagine a situation in which different localities within a country display very different policy stance regarding deficits. These

[ax] See Bertrand et al. (2015) and Gratton et al. (2015) for some recent work on the bureaucracy in India and Italy, respectively.

studies may shed some light on determinants of deficits, holding institutions constant. Evidence on localities is useful for two reasons. One because local public finance is important and interesting per se. Second, because, holding constant national institutions, we can investigate variations in other determinants of deficits. Much of this type of research is on US localities. Thus, there is room for work on other countries.

Another dimension in which progresses could be made is in the disaggregation of fiscal variables. Most of the literature refers to government spending, taxes and debt, without distinguishing within these broad categories. This is true (with few exceptions) both for the macro literature on fiscal policy and for the political economy literature. There is much unexplored territory here.

ACKNOWLEDGMENTS

We thank Marina Azzimonti, Marco Battaglini, Stephen Coate, Casey Mulligan, Per Pettersson-Lindbom, Guido Tabellini, Pierre Yared, Fabrizio Zilibotti. and the editors for very useful conversations and comments on earlier drafts.

REFERENCES

Acemoglu, D., Golosov, M., Tsyvinski, A., 2008. Markets versus governments. J. Monet. Econ. 55 (1), 159–189.

Acemoglu, D., Golosov, M., Tsyvinski, A., 2010. Dynamic mirrlees taxation under political economy constraints. Rev. Econ. Stud. 77 (3), 841–881.

Acemoglu, D., Golosov, M., Tsyvinski, A., 2011. Political economy of Ramsey taxation. J. Public Econ. 95 (7-8), 467–475.

Aghion, P., Bolton, P., 1990. Government domestic debt and the risk of default: a political-economic model of the strategic role of debt. In: Dornbusch, R., Draghi, M. (Eds.), Public Debt Management: Theory and History. Cambridge University Press, Cambridge, MA.

Aghion, P., Alesina, A., Trebbi, F., 2004. Endogenous political institutions. Q. J. Econ. 119 (2), 565–611.

Aguiar, M., Amador, M., Farhi, E., Gopinath, G., 2015. Coordination and crisis in monetary unions. Q. J. Econ. 130 (4), 1–50.

Aiyagari, S.R., Marcet, A., Sargent, T.J., Seppälä, J., 2002. Optimal taxation without state-contingent debt. J. Polit. Econ. 110 (6), 1220–1254.

Akhmedov, A., Zhuravskaya, E., 2003. Opportunistic political cycles: test in a young democracy setting. Q. J. Econ. 119 (4), 1301–1338.

Alesina, A., Bayoumi, T., 1996. The costs and benefits of fiscal rules: evidence from U.S. states. NBER Working Paper Series, http://www.nber.org/papers/w5614.pdf.

Alesina, A., Cukierman, A., 1990. The politics of ambiguity. Q. J. Econ. 105 (4), 829–850.

Alesina, A., Drazen, A., 1991. Why are stabilizations delayed? Am. Econ. Rev. 81 (5), 1170–1177.

Alesina, A., Giuliano, P., 2012. Preferences for redistribution. In: Bisin, A., Jackson, M.O. (Eds.), Handbook of Social Economics, vol. 1. North Holland, The Netherlands, pp. 93–131.

Alesina, A., Giuliano, P., 2015. Culture and Institutions. J. Econ. Lit., Am. Econ. Assoc. 53 (4), 898–944.

Alesina, A., Glaeser, E.L., 2005. Fighting Poverty in the US and Europe: A World of Difference. Oxford University Press, Oxford, UK.

Alesina, A., La Ferrara, E., 2005. Ethnic diversity and economic performance. J. Econ. Lit. 43, 762–800.

Alesina, A., Maré, M., 1996. Evasione e Debito. In: Monorchio, A. (Ed.), La Finanza Italiana Dopo la Svolta del 1992.
Alesina, A., Paradisi, M., 2014. Political budget cycles: evidence from Italian cities. NBER Working Paper 20570.
Alesina, A., Perotti, R., 1995. The political economy of budget deficits. NBER Working Paper Series 4637.
Alesina, A., Stella, A., 2010. The politics of monetary policy. In: Friedman, B.M., Woodford, M. (Eds.), Handbook of Monetary Economics, vol. 3. Elsevier Inc., pp. 1001–1054
Alesina, A., Tabellini, G., 1989. External debt, capital flight and political risk. J. Int. Econ. 27, 199–220.
Alesina, A., Tabellini, G., 1990. A positive theory of fiscal deficits and government debt. Rev. Econ. Stud. 57 (3), 403–414.
Alesina, A., Tabellini, G., 2007. Bureaucrats or politicians? Part I: A single policy task. Am. Econ. Rev. 97 (1), 169–179.
Alesina, A., Cohen, G.D., Roubini, N., 1993. Electoral business cycle in industrial democracies. Eur. J. Polit. Econ. 9 (1), 1–23.
Alesina, A., Perotti, R., Tavares, J., 1998. The political economy of fiscal adjustments. Brook. Pap. Econ. Act. 1 (1), 197–266.
Alesina, A., Tabellini, G., Campante, F.R., 2008. Why is fiscal policy often procyclical? J. Eur. Econ. Assoc. 6 (5), 1006–1036.
Alesina, A., Ardagna, S., Galasso, V., 2010. The Euro and structural reforms. In: Review of Economics and Institutions, vol. 2. National Bureau of Economic Research, Inc., University of Chicago Press and NBER, Chicago, pp. 1–37.
Alesina, A.F., Carloni, D., Lecce, G., 2012. The electoral consequences of large fiscal adjustments. In: Alesina, A., Giavazzi, F. (Eds.), Fiscal Policy after the Financial Crisis. National Bureau of Economic Research, Inc., The University of Chicago Press, Chicago and London, pp. 531–570.
Alesina, A., Favero, C., Giavazzi, F., 2015. The output effect of fiscal consolidation plans. J. Int. Econ. 96, 19–42.
Alt, J.E., Lassen, D.D., 2006. Fiscal transparency, political parties, and debt in OECD countries. Eur. Econ. Rev. 50 (6), 1403–1439.
Alt, J.E., Lowry, R.C., 1994. Divided government, fiscal institutions, and budget deficits: evidence from the states. Am. Polit. Sci. Rev. 88 (4), 811–828.
Arvate, P.R., Avelino, G., Tavares, J., 2009. Fiscal conservatism in a new democracy: "sophisticated" versus "naïve" voters. Econ. Lett. 102 (2), 125–127.
Auerbach, A.J., Gorkhale, J., Kotlikoff, L.J., 1991. Generational accounts: a meaningful alternative to deficit accounting. Tax Policy Econ. 5, 55–110.
Azzimonti, M., Francisco, E.D., Quadrini, V., 2014. Financial globalization, inequality, and the raising of public debt. Am. Econ. Rev. 104 (8), 2267–2302.
Azzimonti, M., Battaglini, M., Coate, S., 2015. Costs and benefits of balanced budget rules: Lessons from a political economy model of fiscal policy. MPRA Paper 25935.
Banfield, E., 1958. The Moral Basis of a Backward Society. The Free Press, Glencoe, Illinois.
Baqir, R., 2002. Districting and government overspending. J. Polit. Econ. 110, 1318–1354.
Barbera, S., Jackson, M.O., 2004. Choosing how to choose: Self-stable majority rules and constitutions. Q. J. Econ. 119 (3), 1011–1048.
Baron, D.P., Ferejohn, J.A., 1989. Bargaining in legislatures. Am. Polit. Sci. Rev. 83 (4), 1181–1206.
Barro, R.J., 1973. The control of politicians: an economic model. Public Choice 14-14 (1), 19–42.
Barro, R.J., 1979. On the determination of the public debt. J. Polit. Econ. 87 (5), 940.
Barseghyan, L., Battaglini, M., Coate, S., 2013. Fiscal policy over the real business cycle: a positive theory. J. Econ. Theory 148 (6), 2223–2265.
Bassetto, M., Sargent, T.J., 2006. Politics and efficiency of separating capital and ordinary government budgets. Q. J. Econ. 121 (4), 1167–1210.
Battaglini, M., 2014. A dynamic theory of electoral competition. Theor. Econ. 9 (2), 515–554.
Battaglini, M., Coate, S., 2008. A dynamic theory of public spending, taxation, and debt. Am. Econ. Rev. 98 (1), 201–236.

Battaglini, M., Coate, S., 2015. A political economy theory of fiscal policy and unemployment. J. Eur. Econ. Assoc. (forthcoming).
Bayoumi, T., Eichengreen, B., 1994. Restraining yourself: fiscal rules and stabilization. CEPR Discussion Papers 1029.
Bertrand, M., Burgess, R., Chawla, A., Xu, G., 2015. Determinants and consequences of bureaucrat effectiveness: evidence from the Indian administrative service. Unpublished.
Besley, T., Prat, A., 2006. Handcuffs for the grabbing hand? Media capture and government accountability. Am. Econ. Rev. 96 (3), 720–736.
Bisin, A., Verdier, T., 2015. On the joint evolution of culture and institutions. Unpublished.
Blinder, Alan S., 1997. Is Government Too Political? Foreign Affairs November/December 1997, 115–126.
Bohn, H., 1998. The behavior of U.S. public debt and deficits. Q. J. Econ. 113 (3), 949–963.
Bohn, H., Inman, R.P., 1996. Balanced budget rules and public deficits: Evidence from the U.S. states. Carn.-Roch. Conf. Ser. Public Policy 45 (1), 13–76.
Brender, A., 2003. The effect of fiscal performance on local government election results in israel: 1989-1998. J. Public Econ. 87 (9-10), 2187–2205.
Brender, A., Drazen, A., 2005. Political budget cycles in new versus established democracies. J. Monet. Econ. 52 (7), 1271–1295.
Brender, A., Drazen, A., 2008. How do budget deficits and economic growth affect reelection prospects? Evidence from a large panel of countries. Am. Econ. Rev. 98 (5), 2203–2220.
Buchanan, M.J., Wagner, E.R., 1977. Democracy in Deficit: The Political Legacy of Lord Keynes. Academic Press, Ney York, NY.
Budina, N., Schaechter, A., Weber, A., Kinda, T., 2012. Fiscal rules in response to the crisis: Toward the "next-generation" rules: A new dataset. International Monetary Fund, Working Papers 12/187.
Buti, M., Van Den Noord, P., 2004. Fiscal discretion and elections in the early years of EMU. J. Common Mark. Stud. 42 (4), 737–756.
Buti, M., Turrini, A., Van den Noord, P., Biroli, P., 2010. Reforms and re-elections in OECD countries. Econ. Policy 25, 61–116.
Campante, F.R., Do, Q.A., 2014. Isolated capital cities, accountability, and corruption: evidence from US states. Am. Econ. Rev. 104 (8), 2456–2481.
Canova, F., Pappa, E., 2006. The elusive costs and the immaterial gains of fiscal constraints. J. Public Econ. 90 (8-9), 1391–1414.
Casella, A., Eichengreen, B., 1996. Can foreign aid accelerate stabilisation. Econ. J. 106, 605–619.
Chari, V.V., Kehoe, P.J., 1993. Sustainable plans and debt. J. Econ. Theory 61 (2), 230–261.
Cukierman, A., Meltzer, A.H., 1986. A positive theory of discretionary policy, the cost of democratic government and the benefits of a constitution. Econ. Inq. 24 (3), 367–388.
Dabla-Norris, E., Allen, R., Zanna, L.F., Prakash, T., Kvintradze, E., Lledo, V.D., Yackovlev, I., Gollwitzer, S., 2010. Budget Institutions and Fiscal Performance in Low-Income Countries. p. 57.
Debrun, X., Moulin, L., Turrini, A., Ayuso-i Casals, J., Kumar, M.S., 2008. Tied to the mast? National fiscal rules in the European Union. Econ. Policy 23, 297–362.
Drazen, A., 2000. Political Economy in Macroeconomics. Princeton University Press, Princeton, NJ.
Drazen, A., Easterly, W., 2001. Do crises induce reform? Simple empirical tests of conventional wisdom. Econ. Polit. 13 (2), 129–157.
Drazen, A., Eslava, M., 2010a. Electoral manipulation via voter-friendly spending: theory and evidence. J. Dev. Econ. 92 (1), 39–52.
Drazen, A., Eslava, M., 2010b. Pork barrel cycles. NBER Working Paper Series 12190.
Drazen, A., Grilli, V., 1993. The benefits of crises for economic reforms. Am. Econ. Rev. 83, 598–607.
Easterly, W., 1993. How much do distortions affect growth? J. Monet. Econ. 32 (2), 187–212.
Elgie, R., McMenamin, I., 2008. Political fragmentation, fiscal deficits and political institutionalisation. Public Choice 136 (3-4), 255–267.
Fabrizio, S., Mody, A., 2006. Can budget institutions counteract political indiscipline? Econ. Policy 21 (48), 689–739.
Fatás, A., Mihov, I., 2003a. The case for restricting fiscal policy discretion. Q. J. Econ. 118 (4), 1419–1447.

Fatás, A., Mihov, I., 2003b. On constraining fiscal policy discretion in EMU. Oxford Rev. Econ. Policy 19 (1), 112–131.
Ferejohn, J., 1986. Incumbent performance and electoral control. Public Choice 50, 5–25.
Ferejohn, J.A., Krehbiel, K., 1987. The budget process and the size of the budget. Am. J. Polit. Sci. 31 (2), 296–320.
Foremny, D., Freier, M.D.M., Yeter, M., 2015. Overlapping political budget cycles. IEB Working Paper 02.
Galor, O., Klemp, M., 2015. Roots of autocracy. Unpublished.
Gavazza, A., Lizzeri, A., 2009. Transparency and economic policy. Rev. Econ. Stud. 76 (3), 1023–1048.
Gavazza, A., Lizzeri, A., 2011. Transparency and manipulation of public accounts. J. Public Econ. Theory 13 (3), 327–349.
Gavin, M., Perotti, R., 1997. Fiscal policy in Latin America. In: Bernanke, B., Rotemberg, J. (Eds.), NBER Macroeconomics Annual, vol. 12. MIT Press, Cambridge, USA, pp. 11–72.
Gonzalez, M.D.L.A., 2002. Do changes in democracy affect the political budget cycle? Evidence from Mexico. Rev. Dev. Econ. 6 (2), 204–224.
Gratton, G., Guiso, L., Michelacci, C., Morelli, M., 2015. From Weber to Kafka: political activism and the emergence of an inefficient bureaucracy. Unpublished.
Grilli, V., Masciandaro, D., Tabellini, G., Malinvaud, E., Pagano, M., 1991. Political and monetary institutions and public financial policies in the industrial countries. Econ. Policy 6 (13), 342–392.
Grossman, G.M., Helpman, E., 2008. Separation of powers and the budget process. J. Public Econ. 92 (3-4), 407–425.
Guiso, L., Sapienza, P., Zingales, L., 2006. Does culture affect economic outcomes? J. Econ. Perspect. 20 (2), 23–48.
Guiso, L., Sapienza, P., Zingales, L., 2011. Civic capital as the missing link. In: Benhabib, J., Bisin, A., Jackson, M.O. (Eds.), Handbook of Social Economics. In: vol. 1. North Holland, The Netherlands, pp. 417–480.
Guiso, L., Herrera, H., Morelli, M., 2015. A cultural clash view of the EU crisis. CEPR Discussion Papers 9679 (unpublished).
Halac, M., Yared, P., 2014. Fiscal rules and discretion under persistent shocks. Econometrica 82 (5), 1557–1614.
Halac, M., Yared, P., 2015. Fiscal rules and discretion in a world economy. NBER Working Paper 21492.
Hallerberg, M., Von Hagen, J., 1999. Electoral institutions, cabinet negotiations, and budget deficits in the European Union. In: Fiscal Institutions and Fiscal Performance. National Bureau of Economic Research, Inc., pp. 209–232.
Hallerberg, M., Strauch, R., Von Hagen, J., 2009. Fiscal Governance: Evidence from Europe. Cambridge University Press, Cambridge, UK.
Hassler, J., Krusell, P., Storesletten, K., Zilibotti, F., 2005. The dynamics of government. J. Monet. Econ. 52 (7), 1331–1358.
Haveman, R., 1994. Should generational accounts replace public budgets and deficits? J. Econ. Perspect. 8 (1), 95–111.
Inman, R.P., 1997. Rethinking federalism. J. Econ. Perspect. 11 (4), 43–64.
Kashin, K., King, G., Soneji, S., 2015. Systematic bias and nontransparency in US Social Security Administration forecasts. J. Econ. Perspect. 29, 239–258.
Klein, P., Krusell, P., Ríos-Rull, J.V., 2008. Time-consistent public policy. Rev. Econ. Stud. 75 (3), 789–808.
Kontopoulos, Y., Perotti, R., 1999. Government fragmentation and fiscal policy outcomes: evidence from OECD countries. In: Fiscal Institutions and Fiscal Performance. National Bureau of Economic Research, Inc., pp. 81–102.
Kornai, J., Maskin, E., Roland, G., 2003. Understanding the soft budget constraint. J. Econ. Lit. 41 (4), 1095–1136.
Krogstrup, S., Wyplosz, C., 2010. A common pool theory of supranational deficit ceilings. Eur. Econ. Rev. 54 (2), 269–278.
Lizzeri, A., 1999. Budget deficits and redistributive politics. Rev. Econ. Stud. 66 (4), 909–928.

Lucas, R.E.J., Stokey, N.L., 1983. Optimal fiscal and monetary policy in an economy without capital. J. Monet. Econ. 12 (1), 55–93.
Miano, A., 2015. Determinants and Consequences of Fiscal Rules: Evidence form the World Economy. Bocconi University.
Milesi-Ferretti, G.M., 2004. Good, bad or ugly? On the effects of fiscal rules with creative accounting. J. Public Econ. 88 (1-2), 377–394.
Milesi-Ferretti, G.M., Perotti, R., Rostagno, M., 2002. Electoral systems and public spending. Q. J. Econ. 117 (2), 609–657.
Müller, A., Storesletten, K., Zilibotti, F., 2016. The political color of fiscal responsibility. J. Eur. Econ. Assoc. 14 (1), 252–302.
Mulligan, C., Sala-i Martin, X., 1999. Gerontocracy, retirement, and social security. NBER Working Paper 7117.
Nannicini, T., Stella, A., Tabellini, G., Troiano, U., 2012. Social capital and political accountability. Am. Econ. J.: Econ. Policy 5 (230088), 222–250.
Oates, W.E., 2011. Fiscal Federalism. Edward Elgar Pub, Northampton, MA, USA.
OECD, 2014. Social spending–StatExtracs. http://stats.oecd.org/Index.aspx?DataSetCode=SOCX_AGG.
OECD, 2015. Social expenditure. www.oecd.org/els/social/expenditure.
Passarelli, F., Tabellini, G., 2013. Emotions and political unrest. CESifo Working Paper Series.
Peltzman, S., 1992. Voters as fiscal conservatives. Q. J. Econ. 107 (2), 327–361.
Persson, T., Svensson, L.E.O., 1989. Why a stubborn conservative would run a deficit: policy with time-inconsistent preferences. Q. J. Econ. 104 (2), 325–345.
Persson, T., Tabellini, G., 2000. Political Economics: Explaining Economic Policy. MIT Press, Cambridge.
Pettersson-Lidbom, P., 2001. An empirical investigation of the strategic use of debt. J. Polit. Econ. 109 (3), 570–583.
Pettersson-Lidbom, P., 2010. Dynamic commitment and the soft budget constraint: an empirical test. Am. Econ. J.: Econ. Policy 2, 154–179.
Pettersson-Lidbom, P., 2012. Does the size of the legislature affect the size of government? Evidence from two natural experiments. J. Public Econ. 96 (3-4), 269–278.
Ponticelli, J., Voth, H.J., 2011. Austerity and anarchy: budget cuts and social unrest in Europe, 1919-2008. CEPR Discussion Papers 8513, C.E.P.R. Discussion Papers.
Poterba, J.M., 1995. Capital budgets, borrowing rules, and state capital spending. J. Public Econ. 56, 165–187.
Poterba, J.M., 1996. Budget institutions and fiscal policy in the U.S. states. Am. Econ. Rev. 86 (2), 395–400.
Prat, A., Stromberg, D., 2013. The Political Economy of Mass Media. Cambridge University Press, Cambridge, UK.
Primo, D., 2007. Rules and Restraint: Government Spending and the Design of Institutions. University of Chicago Press, Chicago, IL.
Ramsey, F.P., 1927. A contribution to the theory of taxation. Econ. J. 37 (145), 47–61.
Reinhart, C.M., Rogoff, K.S., 2010. Growth in a time of debt. Am. Econ. Rev. 100 (2), 573–578.
Richardson, G., 2008. The relationship between culture and tax evasion across countries: additional evidence and extensions. J. Int. Account. Audit. Tax. 17 (2), 67–78.
Rogoff, K., 1990. Equlibrium political budget cycles. Am. Econ. Rev. 80 (1), 21–36.
Rogoff, K., Sibert, A., 1988. Elections and macroeconomic policy cycles. Rev. Econ. Stud. 55 (1), 1–16.
Sabato, L.J., 2008. A More Perfect Constitution: Why the Constitution Must Be Revised: Ideas to Inspire a New Generation. Walker Publishing Company, New York, NY.
Schuknecht, L., 2000. Fiscal policy cycles and public expenditure in developing countries. Public Choice 102 (1/2), 115–130.
Shi, M., Svensson, J., 2006. Political budget cycles: do they differ across countries and why? J. Public Econ. 90 (8-9), 1367–1389.
Song, Z., Storesletten, K., Zilibotti, F., 2012. Rotten parents and disciplined children: a politico-economic theory of public expenditure and debt. Econometrica 80 (6), 2785–2803.
Spolaore, E., 2004. Adjustments in different government systems. Econ. Polit. 16 (2), 117–146.

Stein, E., Talvi, E., Grisanti, A., 1999. Institutional arrangements and fiscal performance: the Latin American experience. In: Poterba, J.M., Von Hagen, J. (Eds.), Fiscal Institutions and Fiscal Performance. University of Chicago Press, Chicago, IL, pp. 103–134.
Stockman, D.R., 2001. Balanced-budget rules: welfare loss and optimal policies. Rev. Econ. Dyn. 4 (2), 438–459.
Tabellini, G., 1991. The politics of intergenerational redistribution. J. Polit. Econ. 99, 335.
Tabellini, G., 2010. Culture and institutions: economic development in the regions of Europe. J. Eur. Econ. Assoc. 8 (4), 677–716.
Tabellini, G., Alesina, A., 1990. Voting on the budget deficit. Am. Econ. Rev. 80 (1), 37–43.
Tornell, A., Lane, P.R., 1999. The voracity effect. Am. Econ. Rev. 89 (1), 22–46.
Trebbi, F., Aghion, P., Alesina, A., 2008. Electoral rules and minority representation in U.S. cities. Q. J. Econ. 123 (1), 325–357.
Velasco, A., 1999. A model of endogenous fiscal deficits and delayed fiscal reforms. In: Poterba, J.M., Von Hagen, J. (Eds.), Fiscal Institutions and Fiscal Performance. University of Chicago Press, Chicago, pp. 37–58.
Velasco, A., 2000. Debts and deficits with fragmented fiscal policymaking. J. Public Econ. 76 (1), 105–125.
Volkerink, B., De Haan, J., 2001. Fragmented government effects on fiscal policy: new evidence. Public choice 109 (3-4), 221–242.
Von Hagen, J., 2006. Fiscal rules and fiscal performance in the EU and Japan. Discussion Paper Series of SFB/TR 15 Governance and the Efficiency of Economic Systems 147.
von Hagen, J., Wolff, G.B., 2006. What do deficits tell us about debt? Empirical evidence on creative accounting with fiscal rules in the EU. J. Bank. Finance 30 (12), 3259–3279.
Weingast, B., Shepsle, K., Johnsen, C., 1981. The political economy of benefits and costs: a neoclassical approach to distributive politics. J. Polit. Econ. 84 (4), 642–664.
Woo, J., 2003. Economic, political, and institutional determinants of public deficits. J. Public Econ. 87 (3-4), 387–426.
Wyplosz, C., 2014. Fiscal rules: theoretical issues and historical experiences. In: Alesina, A., Giavazzi, F. (Eds.), Fiscal Policy After the Financial Crisis. University of Chicago Press and National Bureau of Economic Research, Chicago and London, pp. 495–529.
Yared, P., 2010. Politicians, taxes and debt. Rev. Econ. Stud. 77 (2), 806–840.

INDEX

Note: Page numbers followed by "*f*" indicate figures, "*t*" indicate tables, "*b*" indicate boxes, and "*np*" indicate footnotes.

C

E

H

M

V

W

Z